For the professor

◎ **Teaching Resources** provide material contributed by professors including teaching tips, techniques, academic papers, and sample syllabi–and **Talk to the Team**, a moderated faculty chat room.

◎ **Online Faculty** Support includes downloadable supplements, additional cases, articles, links, and suggested answers to Current Events Activities.

◎ **What's New** gives you one-click access to all newly posted PHLIP resources.

For the student

◎ **Talk to the Tutor** schedules virtual office hours that allow students to post questions from any supported discipline and receive responses from the dedicated PHLIP/CW faculty team.

◎ **Writing Resource Center** provides an online writing center that supplies links to online directories, thesauruses, writing tutors, style and grammar guides, and additional tools.

◎ **Career Center** helps students access career information, view sample résumés, even apply for jobs online.

◎ **Study Tips** provides an area where students can learn to develop better study skills.

ONLINE LEARNING SOLUTIONS IN BLACKBOARD, WEBCT, AND PEARSON COURSECOMPASS

NOW AVAILABLE IN **TWO** LEVELS OF CONTENT!

STANDARD COURSES

(Free with New Text Purchase) Standard courses include traditional online course features:

- Online Testing
- Course Management and Page Tracking
- Gradebook
- Course Information
- Multiple-Section Chat Rooms
- Bulletin Board Conferencing
- Syllabus and Calendar Functions
- E-mail Capability

PREMIUM COURSES

(Available at a nominal charge with New Text Purchase)
The Premium course for Accounting, 5th ed., provides these additional enhancements:

- **Rich, Prentice Hall Custom-Created** course and lecture materials ready for immediate use.

- **Custom-Created PowerPoint slides with audio** (by an accounting faculty member) to assist students in understanding key concepts.

- **Unique video "wraps"** for each text chapter feature an accounting faculty member experienced in conducting on-line courses. The insights he or she shares with students help them (1) better prepare to read the chapter and (2) review the key concepts and takeaway lessons prior to taking an exam.

ACCOUNTING

ACCOUNTING

FIFTH EDITION

Charles T. Horngren
Stanford University

Walter T. Harrison Jr.
Baylor University

Linda Smith Bamber
University of Georgia

 Upper Saddle River, New Jersey 07458

To Betsy Willis and Becky Jones for their wisdom on learning and teaching over a 10-year period and to Michael Bamber for his insight on business practices and ethical issues in management accounting.

Library of Congress Cataloging-in-Publication Data

Horngren, Charles T.
    Accounting / Charles T. Horngren, Walter T. Harrison, Linda Smith Bamber; annotations by Betsy Willis, Becky Jones. — 5th ed.

        p. cm.
    Includes index.
    ISBN 0-13-090699-9
    1. Accounting.   I. Harrison, Walter T.   II. Bamber, Linda S. (Linda Smith),   III. Willis, Betsy.   IV. Jones, Becky.   V. Title.

HF5635.H8 2001
657—dc21   2001016424

Executive Editor:	Deborah Hoffman
Developmental Editor:	Jeannine Ciliotta
Assistant Editor:	Kasey Sheehan
Director of Development:	Steve Deitmer
Editor-in-Chief:	P.J. Boardman
Senior Editorial Assistant:	Jane Avery
Media Project Manager:	Nancy Welcher
Executive Marketing Manager:	Beth Toland
Senior Production Editor:	Anne Graydon
Managing Editor (Production):	Sondra Greenfield
Production Manager:	Arnold Vila
Associate Director, Manufacturing:	Vincent Scelta
Text Permissions Coordinator:	Suzanne Grappi
Design Manager:	Pat Smythe
Interior Design:	Blair Brown, Christine Cantera
Cover Design and Illustration:	Blair Brown
Infographic Illustrations:	Kenneth Batelman
Manager, Multimedia Production:	Christy Mahon
Photo Researcher:	Abby Reip
Photo Permissions Coordinator:	Michelina Viscusi
Composition:	Progressive Information Technologies
Full-Service Project Management:	Progressive Publishing Alternatives
Printer/Binder:	R.R. Donnelley, Willard

Credits and acknowledgments of images borrowed from other sources and reproduced, with permission: **page 4** Harry Cabluck/AP/Wide World Photos; **page 8** Todd Cross/Washington Post © 1999; **pages 38 & 50** Hisham F. Ibrahim/PhotoDisc, Inc.; **page 82** It's Just Lunch! Inc.; **page 98** The Image Bank; **page 126** NetGenesis; **page 143** Corbis; **page 166** Target; **page 187** PhotoDisc, Inc. **page 226** Price & Associates, PLLC; **page 231** TADOnline; **page 266** Stone; **page 269** Corbis; **page 310** AP/Wide World Photos; **page 320** Index Stock Imagery, Inc.; **page 346** Corbis; **page 352** Richard Neville/Check Six/George Hall Photography LLC; **page 386** PhotoEdit; **page 407** Corbis; **page 424** AP/Wide World Photos; **page 429** PhotoEdit; **page 464** Stone; **page 469** Ed Kashi/Corbis; **page 500** The Image Works; **page 509** Photo-Edit; **page 540** AP/Wide World Photos; **page 548** Corbis; **page 576** AP/Wide World Photos; **page 582** AP/ Wide World Photos; **page 622** Corbis; **page 638** Avon Products, Inc.; **page 719** Photo courtesy of Fourth Shift Corporation; **page 754** Archive Photos; **page 758** The Image Works; **page 796** AP Wide World Photos; **page 807** Intermec Technologies Corporation; **page 840** Reagan Bradshaw-Bradshaw Studio; **page 886** Al Richmond/Grand Canyon Railway; **page 900** AP/Wide World Photos; **page 926** AP/Wide World Photos; **page 941** Maple Communications, Inc.; **page 972** Roberto Brosnan/Time Life Syndication; **page 983** Corbis; **page 1016** Bob Daemmrich/Photo, Inc.; **page 1028** Courtesy of General Motors Media Archives; **page 1062** The Image Bank; **page 1072** Motorola, Inc.

Microsoft Excel, Solver, and Windows are registered trademarks of Microsoft Corporation in the U.S.A. and other countries. Screen shots and icons reprinted with permission from the Microsoft Corporation. This book is not sponsored or endorsed by or affiliated with Microsoft Corporation.

10 9 8 7 6 5 4 3 2

ISBN 0-13-090699-9

About the Authors

Charles T. Horngren is the Edmund W. Littlefield Professor of Accounting, Emeritus, at Stanford University. A graduate of Marquette University, he received his MBA from Harvard University and his Ph.D. from the University of Chicago. He is also the recipient of honorary doctorates from Marquette University and DePaul University.

A Certified Public Accountant, Horngren served on the Accounting Principles Board for six years, the Financial Accounting Standards Board Advisory Council for five years, and the Council of the American Institute of Certified Public Accountants for three years. For six years, he served as a trustee of the Financial Accounting Foundation, which oversees the Financial Accounting Standards Board and the Government Accounting Standards Board.

Horngren is a member of the Accounting Hall of Fame.

A member of the American Accounting Association, Horngren has been its President and its Director of Research. He received its first annual Outstanding Accounting Educator Award.

The California Certified Public Accountants Foundation gave Horngren its Faculty Excellence Award and its Distinguished Professor Award. He is the first person to have received both awards.

The American Institute of Certified Public Accountants presented its first Outstanding Educator Award to Horngren.

Horngren was named Accountant of the Year, Education, by the national professional accounting fraternity, Beta Alpha Psi.

Professor Horngren is also a member of the Institute of Management Accountants, where he has received its Distinguished Service Award. He was a member of the Institute's Board of Regents, which administers the Certified Management Accountant examinations.

Horngren is the author of other accounting books published by Prentice-Hall: *Cost Accounting: A Managerial Emphasis*, Tenth Edition, 2000 (with George Foster and Srikant Datar); *Introduction to Management Accounting*, Twelfth Edition (with Gary L. Sundem and William Stratton); *Introduction to Financial Accounting*, Eighth Edition, 2002 (with Gary L. Sundem and John A. Elliott); and *Financial Accounting*, Fourth Edition, 2001 (with Walter T. Harrison, Jr.).

Horngren is the Consulting Editor for the Charles T. Horngren Series in Accounting.

Walter T. Harrison, Jr. is Professor of Accounting at the Hankamer School of Business, Baylor University. He received his B.B.A. degree from Baylor University, his M.S. from Oklahoma State University, and his Ph.D. from Michigan State University.

Professor Harrison, recipient of numerous teaching awards from student groups as well as from university administrators, has also taught at Cleveland State Community College, Michigan State University, the University of Texas, and Stanford University.

A member of the American Accounting Association and the American Institute of Certified Public Accountants, Professor Harrison has served as Chairman of the Financial Accounting Standards Committee of the American Accounting Association, on the Teaching/Curriculum Development Award Committee, on the Program Advisory Committee for Accounting Education and Teaching, and on the Notable Contributions to Accounting Literature Committee.

Professor Harrison has lectured in several foreign countries and published articles in numerous journals, including *The Accounting Review*, *Journal of Accounting Research*, *Journal of Accountancy*, *Journal of Accounting and Public Policy*, *Economic Consequences of*

Financial Accounting Standards, Accounting Horizons, Issues in Accounting Education, and *Journal of Law and Commerce.* He is coauthor of *Financial Accounting,* Fourth Edition, 2001 (with Charles T. Horngren and *Accounting, Fifth Edition,* 2002 (with Charles T. Horngren and Linda S. Bamber) published by Prentice Hall. Professor Harrison has received scholarships, fellowships, research grants or awards from PriceWaterhouseCoopers, Deloitte & Touche, the Ernst & Young Foundation, and the KPMG Foundation.

Linda Smith Bamber is Professor of Accounting at the J.M. Tull School of Accounting at the University of Georgia. She graduated summa cum laude from Wake Forest University, where she was a member of Phi Beta Kappa. She is a certified public accountant. For her performance on the CPA examination, Professor Bamber received the Elijah Watt Sells Award in addition to the North Carolina Bronze Medal. Before returning to graduate school, she worked in cost accounting at RJR Foods. She then earned an MBA from Arizona State University, and a Ph.D. from The Ohio State University.

Professor Bamber has received numerous teaching awards from The Ohio State University, the University of Florida, and the University of Georgia, including selection as Teacher of the Year at the University of Florida's Fisher School of Accounting.

She has lectured in Canada and Australia in addition to the U.S., and her research has appeared in numerous journals, including *The Accounting Review, Journal of Accounting Research, Journal of Accounting and Economics, Journal of Finance, Contemporary Accounting Research, Auditing: A Journal of Practice and Theory, Accounting Horizons, Issues in Accounting Education,* and *CPA Journal.* She provided the annotations for the *Annotated Instructor's Edition* of Horngren, Foster, and Datar's *Cost Accounting: A Managerial Emphasis,* Seventh, Eighth, and Ninth Editions.

A member of the Institute of Management Accounting, the American Accounting Association (AAA), and the AAA's Management Accounting Section and Financial Accounting and Reporting Section, Professor Bamber has chaired the AAA New Faculty Consortium Committee, served on the AAA Council, the AAA Research Advisory Committee, the AAA Corporate Accounting Policy Seminar Committee, the AAA Wildman Medal Award Committee, the AAA Nominations Committee, and has chaired the Management Accounting Section's Membership Outreach Committee. She served as Associate Editor of *Accounting Horizons,* and is serving as editor of *The Accounting Review* from 1999 to 2002.

This is what I especially like about this textbook. There are always ways of checking yourself to make sure you are understanding what you are reading. I am really impressed with the book. It is so well put together that all the subjects seem to flow together and offer a complete knowledge of the accounting world.

—*Lisa Cronauer, student, Saint Leo University*

[This textbook is] easy to understand and made me feel that accounting could possibly be my major. . . . This textbook [is] a valuable learning tool that will aid me in the future.

—*Carrie Hupp, student, Middle Tennessee State University*

Teaching accounting today means helping students navigate a changing business world. It means helping them succeed in the classroom and in their careers. Whether this is the first or only accounting course students take, learning the fundamentals of accounting can help them make better decisions, evaluate real-world situations, and understand the value of "crunching the numbers."

In *Accounting, fifth ed.*, publisher, authors, faculty, and students target a common goal: improving student success and understanding of accounting concepts. This edition provides:

- The most motivational text and writing style
- The best assessment and reinforcement tools
- The widest assortment of technology resources
- The best free student resources
- The best service and support for faculty

We believe *Accounting, fifth ed.*, offers the best possible system for student success, and we invite you to learn more about it. We welcome your comments and suggestions.

CHARLES T. HORNGREN ◎ WALTER T. HARRISON, JR. ◎ LINDA SMITH BAMBER
STANFORD UNIVERSITY   BAYLOR UNIVERSITY   UNIVERSITY OF GEORGIA

Chapter Opening Vignettes and On Location! Videos

The chapter-opening vignettes thrust students into the real world of accounting—where business decisions affect the future of actual organizations. Vignettes provide the real business context for chapter topics. Companies include Target, NetGenesis, Lucent and MCI WorldCom, McDonald's, AOL Time Warner, and more.

Many of the chapter-opening vignettes are linked to our unique, custom-created **On Location! Videos**. Each 5- to 10-minute video provides a "plant tour" introducing students to the business professionals who are using accounting information to enhance the success of their organizations. **NEW segments** include Cisco, Nantucket Nectars, Teva Sandals, Oracle, and others.

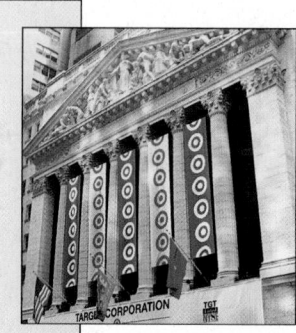

You probably recognize the bulls'-eye logo. You may even do your shopping at a **Target, Mervyn, Marshall Field, Dayton,** or **Hudson** store. All these companies are part of the retail empire known as **Target Corporation**. It is a pacesetter in retailing: Target stores are currently the place to find the latest fashions at the best prices. Target is also a pacesetter in philanthropy and community relations. Through its Five Percent Club, the company donates 5% of its taxable income to support charities in the communities where it operates. In 2000, Target gave more than $1 million every week to local communities. The company, which employs about 189,000 people nationwide, is considered a good employer. *Working Mother* magazine has recognized Target as a "Top Work Place for Women." Target sells its merchandise through nearly 900 stores in 44 states, and through its Web site on the Internet. It is one of the largest mass-merchandise retailers in the United States, ringing up sales of over $33 billion in the year ended January 31, 2000.

NEW Featured Company: Target

The fifth edition includes the **Target Annual Report** both as an appendix within the text and as a separate booklet shrinkwrapped with each copy. We also highlight Target in Chapter 5 and in financial statement cases throughout the book.

e-Accounting

Varsitybooks.com: A Textbook Case on the Fulfillment Cost Conundrum

Order the fifth edition of *Accounting* from Varsitybooks.com and the company arranges for Baker & Taylor—book distributors—to ship it to you immediately. Varsitybooks doesn't have a warehouse or any inventory, but it does have to pay Baker & Taylor for this convenient arrangement. How does the fledgling dot.com account for these costs?

As you know from personal experience, e-commerce has revolutionized business. It has bent certain accounting rules in the process. One such rule is that the cost of goods sold to customers is usually considered the "cost of goods sold." Yet, on-line powerhouses like Amazon.com and eToys, Inc. count some of this cost as "sales and marketing expenses because they never own the inventory." By listing these "fulfillment costs" as marketing expense, new-age companies don't have to subtract the costs from their gross profit. This seemed like a good idea to Varsitybooks, and its managers announced to their auditor, KPMG, that they wanted to do the same.

After all, Varsitybooks argued, mail-order companies have always done this. And the practice would allow the new agers to keep from reporting razor-thin profit margins. For instance, if the SEC tightens the rules and makes Amazon.com account for fulfillment cost as "cost of sales," gross profit margins for the last quarter of 1999 would go from 15% to −3%. The company's sales and net profit or net loss amounts would remain the same, but analysts looked at the gross profit figure to see how well a company can make money from basic business operations.

Small wonder that this approach is controversial! Varsitybooks.com fired KPMG when the auditors objected to it. They hired PricewaterhouseCoopers instead, but in the end Varsitybooks had to follow the traditional accounting procedures anyway. The auditors knew best after all.

Source: Based on Shannon Henry, "An E-Tail Identity Crisis," *The Washington Post*, May 4, 2000, p. E01. Anonymous, "Web Retailers' 'Gross Profit' Questioned; E-commerce; The SEC may make some firms account f distribution costs, possibly turning their profits into losses," *The Los Angeles Times*, February 19, 2000, p. 2.

Exhibits 5-10 and 5-11 tell an interesting at a low gr

NEW e-Accounting Boxes

Nothing has changed business more in recent years than the Internet. Horngren/Harrison/Bamber's new e-Accounting boxes focus on the accounting issues affecting companies doing business on the World Wide Web, such as CDNow, Priceline.com, and DHL.

Work It Out Boxes

These exercises allow students to work out problems related to text concepts. Answers are provided for immediate reinforcement.

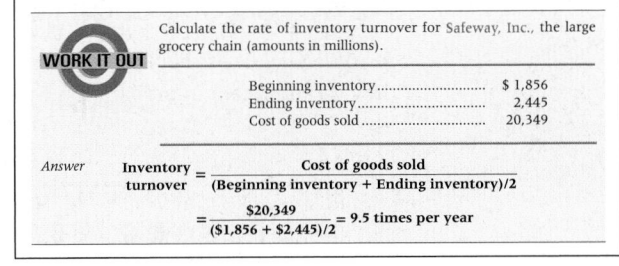

WORK IT OUT

Calculate the rate of inventory turnover for Safeway, Inc., the large grocery chain (amounts in millions).

Beginning inventory	$ 1,856
Ending inventory	2,445
Cost of goods sold	20,349

Answer

$$\text{Inventory turnover} = \frac{\text{Cost of goods sold}}{(\text{Beginning inventory} + \text{Ending inventory})/2}$$

$$= \frac{\$20,349}{(\$1,856 + \$2,445)/2} = 9.5 \text{ times per year}$$

Think It Over Boxes

THINK IT OVER

How much did Proctor & Gamble (P&G) borrow from the bank? $98,000 or $100,000? How much will they pay back?

Answers

P&G borrowed $98,000, the amount of cash the company received. They will pay back $100,000 at maturity.

These exercises ask students to reflect on and apply concepts they've just learned. Again, answers are provided for immediate reinforcement.

Decision Guidelines with *NEW* Excel Application Problems

Why should English or engineering majors care about accounting? Easy! **Decision Guidelines** are designed to show *when, why, and how* all managers—not just accountants—use accounting information to make good business decisions. Many of the Decision Guidelines now include **optional Excel Application Problems** for a hands-on approach. Excel is the single piece of applications software every business professional must master. These problems give students a step-by-step guide to creating Excel templates to solve accounting and financial dilemmas.

DECISION GUIDELINES

Merchandising Operations and the Accounting Cycle

DECISION

How do merchandising operations differ from service operations?

How do a merchandiser's financial statements differ from the financial statements of a service business?

Income Statement:

Merchandiser

Sales revenue	$ XXX
− Cost of goods sold	(X)
= Gross profit	XX
− Operating expenses	(X)
= Net income	$ X

Statements of Owner's Equity:

Which type of inventory system to use?

How do the adjusting and closing processes of merchandisers and service entities differ?

GUIDELINES

- Merchandisers buy and sell *merchandise inventory*
- Service entities perform a *service*.

Balance sheet:

- Merchandiser has *inventory*, an asset.
- Service business has no inventory.

Service Business

Service revenue	$XX
− Operating expenses	(X)
= Net income	$ X

No difference

- *Perpetual system* shows the amount of *inventory* on hand (the asset) and the cost of goods sold (the expense) at all times.
- *Periodic system* shows the correct balances of inventory and cost of goods sold only after a physical count of the inventory, which occurs at least once each year.

Very little. The merchandiser may have to adjust Inventory account for spoilage a

NEW "Lessons Learned"

At the end of each chapter, this feature gives students the key "takeaway" lessons from the chapter that they should retain in preparation for testing.

LESSONS LEARNED

1. *Use sales and gross profit to evaluate a company.* The major revenue of a merchandising business is *sales revenue*, or *sales*. The major expense is *cost of goods sold*. Net sales minus cost of goods sold is *gross profit*, or *gross margin*. This amount measures the business's success or failure in selling its products at a higher price than it paid for them.

2. *Account for the purchase and sale of inventory.* The merchandiser's major asset is inventory. In a merchandising entity, the accounting cycle is from cash to inventory as the inventory is purchased for resale, and back to cash as the inventory is sold. The *invoice* is the business document generated by a purchase or sale transaction. Most merchandising entities allow customers to *return* unsuitable ~~merchandise and also offer dis~~

4. *Prepare a merchandise* income statement may ap *step format.* A single-step i sections—one for revenue and a single income amou income statement has s income from operations. F

5. *Use the gross profit percen ratio to evaluate a busine* merchandiser are the *gross* sales revenue) and the *r* goods sold/average inver sures usual

UNIQUE Concept Links

To keep previously covered material fresh in students' minds, concept links appear in the margins of the text. They explain how earlier topics are relevant to the new material being introduced. For students who need to go back and review, the margin links include a page cross reference.

Running Glossary

Is terminology important to student success? You bet! All key terms are boldface within the text at introduction, with a definition in the margin.

MORE Internet Exercises

Internet Exercises now appear in every chapter, and include such companies as eBay, Intuit Inc., Southwest Airlines, General Motors, FedEx, and Amazon.com. To do these exercises, students go first to the book Web site, and then use hotlinks to the company sites to complete the work.

NEW CyberCoach

www.prenhall.com/horngren

At three points in each chapter, the CyberCoach icon directs the student to exercises on the text Web site at *www.prenhall.com/horngren*

- At the beginning of each chapter, to see if they have mastered concepts covered in the previous chapter. (*Readiness Assessment*)

- At mid-chapter, to see if they have learned chapter topics up to this point. (*Mid-Chapter Assessment*)

- At the end of each chapter, to see if they have mastered the chapter as a whole. (*End-of-Chapter Assessment*)

With CyberCoach, students can check their answers and monitor their progress as they learn. Now they're better prepared for class, for homework assignments, and for examinations.

TARGET STUDENT SUCCESS: REINFORCEMENT

In addition to CyberCoach, the fifth edition offers other unique, targeted student self-evaluation materials, plus a full program of assignment exercises, problems, and cases for each chapter.

Daily Exercises

These unique, single-concept exercises appear in the end-of-chapter assignment material. Daily Exercises serve as warm-ups or confidence builders. Each is linked to the text material so that students may refer back for additional assistance. Each is also cited in the margin at the appropriate point in the text.

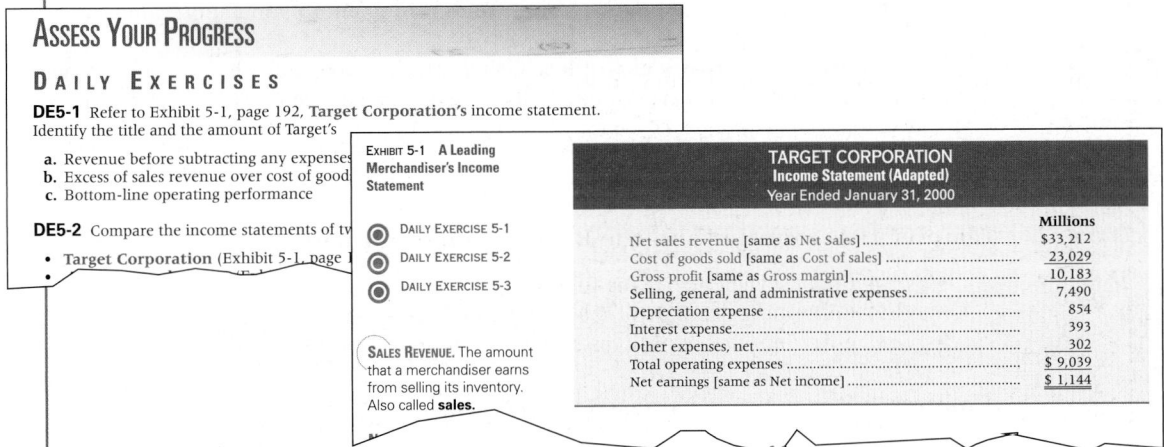

ASSESS YOUR PROGRESS

DAILY EXERCISES

DE5-1 Refer to Exhibit 5-1, page 192, **Target Corporation's** income statement. Identify the title and the amount of Target's

a. Revenue before subtracting any expenses
b. Excess of sales revenue over cost of goods
c. Bottom-line operating performance

DE5-2 Compare the income statements of tw

• **Target Corporation** (Exhibit 5-1, page

EXHIBIT 5-1 A Leading Merchandiser's Income Statement

DAILY EXERCISE 5-1
DAILY EXERCISE 5-2
DAILY EXERCISE 5-3

SALES REVENUE. The amount that a merchandiser earns from selling its inventory. Also called **sales.**

TARGET CORPORATION Income Statement (Adapted) Year Ended January 31, 2000	
	Millions
Net sales revenue [same as Net Sales]	$33,212
Cost of goods sold [same as Cost of sales]	23,029
Gross profit [same as Gross margin]	10,183
Selling, general, and administrative expenses	7,490
Depreciation expense	854
Interest expense	393
Other expenses, net	302
Total operating expenses	$ 9,039
Net earnings [same as Net income]	$ 1,144

Enhanced PH ReEnforcer Tutorial Software*

This Windows-based tutorial software enables students to test their understanding of key concepts through a variety of exercises, with immediate feedback. A "Quick Tour" tutorial provides an overview of the program. New and enhanced exercise types include:

- *Multiple Choice Questions*
- *Financial Statement Analysis Questions* (Students manipulate a financial statement by entering transactions.)
- *T-account Problems* (Students complete journal entries, then select the T-accounts, and then enter numbers.)
- *General Problems* (Students integrate accounting terms into their vocabulary by writing journal entries, using terms from the text.)

Enhanced PHAS General Ledger Tutorial*

This Windows-based software reinforces accounting procedures through hands-on activity. Problem templates allow students to enter their own problems and complete the entire accounting cycle: journalize, post, print multiple reports, and close. A "Quick Tour" overviews the program and offers online help.

*The software is free to students when downloaded from the text Web site. Students may also purchase a CD-ROM containing the software packaged to their book.

TARGET STUDENT SUCCESS: WHAT'S NEW IN THIS EDITION

Every topic, every sentence, every word in every chapter has been carefully reviewed to

- **Streamline the exposition** to make text clearer and more direct.
- **Enhance readability** to make the text as accessible as possible to students taking accounting for the first time.
- **Place exhibits** as close to the introductory text reference as possible to make them easier for students to use and learn from.
- **Integrate e-commerce, Internet, and technology** information and examples wherever possible.
- **Add new real-company examples,** including hi-tech companies like Lucent Technologies and Cisco Systems, MCI WorldCom, Dell Computer, and dot.coms like Priceline.com, and Amazon.com.

Here are the major chapter changes:

Chapter 1: Accounting and the Business Environment

- *NEW* Chapter vignette: Texas Tobacco Lawyers
- *NEW* Continuing example of sole proprietorship: Gay Gillen eTravel
- *NEW* e-Accounting box: Microstrategy: A Cautionary Tale for the New Economy

Chapter 2: Recording Business Transactions

- *NEW* Chapter vignette: e-Retailers
- *NEW* e-Accounting box: The Seven Trillion Dollar Mistake (the Pentagon's accounting problems)

Chapter 3: Measuring Business Income: The Adjusting Process

- *NEW* e-Accounting box: Grossing up the Revenue: Priceline.com and Ventro
- *NEW* Decision Guidelines Excel exercise

Chapter 4: Completing the Accounting Cycle

- *NEW* Vignette: NetGenesis
- *NEW* e-Accounting box: A Forced Debt Ratio for South Korea's Companies
- *NEW* Decision Guidelines Excel exercise

Chapter 5: Merchandising Operations and the Accounting Cycle

- *NEW* Vignette: Target (annual report company), also used throughout chapter
- *NEW* e-Accounting box: Varsitybooks.com: A Textbook Case on the Fulfillment Cost Conundrum
- *NEW* Comparison of service entities vs. merchandisers for ease of understanding

Chapter 6: Accounting Information Systems

- *NEW* e-Accounting box: Accounting Pioneers on the Virtual Frontier (virtual/online accountants)

Chapter 7: Internal Control, Managing Cash, and Making Ethical Judgments

- *NEW* e-Accounting box: The Barings Bank Debacle
- *NEW* section on Internal Controls for e-Commerce

Chapter 8: Accounts and Notes Receivable

- *NEW* Vignette: NYJets/Oracle
- *NEW* e-Accounting box: Merchant Beware: Credit Cards Boom with Online Sales . . . But So Does Fraud

Chapter 9: Merchandise Inventory

- *NEW* Vignette: Deckers Outdoor (Teva)
- *NEW* e-Accounting box: It's a Bird . . . It's a Plane . . . It's a Warehouse! DHL Worldwide Express
- *NEW* Decision Guidelines Excel exercise

Chapter 10: Plant Assets and Intangible Assets

- *NEW* e-Accounting box: Singapore International Airlines: Ratcheting Up the Value of Tangibles and Intangibles
- Intangibles: expanded and updated section to reflect fact that intangibles are sometimes now more important than tangibles.

Chapter 11: Current Liabilities and Payroll

- *NEW* e-Accounting box: A Taxing Dilemma: Sales Tax Liability and the Internet
- Simplified and revised section on Contingent Liabilities with new and current example of Sun Microsystems and Microsoft lawsuit

Chapter 12: Partnerships

- *NEW* Vignette: Arthur Andersen
- *NEW* e-Accounting box: The Limited But Lively Life of a Dot.Com Partnership
- Updated and expanded section on S Corporations

Chapter 13: Corporations: Paid-in Capital and the Balance Sheet

- *NEW* e-Accounting box: UPS Delivers the Dough at Record-breaking IPO
- *NEW* Work It Out boxes using IHOP

Chapter 14: Retained Earnings, Treasury Stock, and the Income Statement

- *NEW* Vignette: America OnLine and TimeWarner
- *NEW* e-Accounting box: Stock Buybacks Catch On in Europe
- Streamlined and revised: Recording Stock Dividends, Stock Splits, Treasury Stock

Chapter 15: Long-Term Liabilities

- *NEW* Vignette on Internet startups and online information
- *NEW* e-Accounting box: Borrowers OnLine: Click Here to Lend Us $6 Billion
- Extensive example material using Amazon.com and eBay throughout chapter
- Internet startups like Vista.com

Chapter 16: Investments and International Operations

- *NEW* Vignette: McDonald's
- *NEW* e-Accounting box: Avon Products Inc.: Staying Up When the Currency Goes Down
- Streamlined coverage of Accounting for International Operations, with new examples such as Infosys and Nokia

Chapter 17: The Statement of Cash Flows

- *NEW* Vignette: drkoop.com's and MotherNature.com's cash flow problems
- *NEW* e-Accounting box: Cash Crunch Turns CDNow into CDThen

Chapter 18: Financial Statement Analysis

- *NEW* Vignette: Lucent and MCI WorldCom
- *NEW* e-Accounting box: Peer Performance: Benchmarking on the Web
- *NEW* Decision Guidelines Excel exercise

Chapter 19: Introduction to Management Accounting

- *NEW* e-Accounting box: Refining Dining with Data Mining
- *NEW* section on Time-Based Competition including updated e-commerce and JIT discussion
- *NEW* Decision Guidelines Excel exercise

Chapter 20: Job Costing

- *NEW* e-Accounting box: Radio-frequency Identification System: Smart Tags for Tracking Parts and Products
- *NEW* Think It Over exercises on how managers can use job costing information
- *NEW* section: "How Technology Has Affected Job Costing"

Chapter 21: Process Costing

- *NEW* e-Accounting box: Using Overseas Labor to Cut Process Costs
- Step-by-step explanation of conversion costs and equivalent units in "Building Blocks of Process Costing," with detailed example

Chapter 22: Cost-Volume-Profit Analysis

- *NEW* e-Accounting box: Kozmo.com and Urbanfetch.com: Can They Continue to Deliver the Goods for Free?
- *NEW* continuing CVP example: e-retailer
- *NEW* discussion of ERP and CVP analysis
- *NEW* Financial Statement Case, using Target
- *NEW* Decision Guidelines Excel exercise

Chapter 23: The Master Budget and Responsibility Accounting

- *NEW* Vignette: Habitat for Humanity
- *NEW* section: Budgeting, Sensitivity Analysis, and Information Technology
- Responsibility Accounting revised to highlight role of budget in performance evaluation
- *NEW* Financial Statement case linked to Target annual report

Chapter 24: Flexible Budgets and Standard Costs

- Setting Standards: Completely revised, with new discussion of effects of e-commerce on price standards
- *NEW* Think It Over with user emphasis
- *NEW* examples of how real companies use variance information

Chapter 25: Activity-Based Costing and Other Cost Management Tools

- *NEW* e-Accounting box: Point, Click, Buy, Sell: Businesses Cut Costs by Buying and Selling Online
- Heavily revised to provide more and better coverage of ABC, including numerical examples and more user focus, plus more and better coverage of JIT
- More real-world examples and survey evidence
- *NEW* Discussion of supply chain management and JIT

Chapter 26: Special Business Decisions and Capital Budgeting

- *NEW* e-Accounting box: We Brand It, You Make It: The Outsourcing Trend
- Expanded discussion of outsourcing, including Web's role in outsourcing decisions
- *NEW* Decision Guidelines Excel exercise

TARGET STUDENT SUCCESS: THE TEACHING AND LEARNING PACKAGE

ACCOUNTING, FIFTH ED., OFFERS A COMPLETE TEACHING AND LEARNING PACKAGE TO PROVIDE STUDENTS AND INSTRUCTORS WITH THE BEST AIDS TO SUCCESS. AND DEPENDING ON HOW YOU TEACH YOUR COURSE, WE OFFER ACCOUNTING, FIFTH ED., IN SEVERAL VERSIONS: HARD COVER CHAPTERS 1–26; PAPERBACKS CHAPTERS 1–13 AND CHAPTERS 12–26; AND A NEW! HARDCOVER CHAPTERS 1–18, THE FINANCIAL ACCOUNTING CHAPTERS.

Instructor Resources

- Annotated Instructor's Edition
- Instructor's Manual and Video Guide
- Solutions Manual with Transparencies
- Four-Color Teaching Transparencies
- Test Item File
- Prentice Hall Test Manager
- *NEW Free* Instructor's CD-ROM (contains all print and technology resources on CD-ROM)
- Accounting and Taxation Services Hotline (call your PH representative for hotline number and e-mail address)
- Prentice Hall Accounting Faculty Directory (call your PH representative for information)

Student Resources

- *NEW Free* Target Annual Report
- *NEW* Student CD-ROM (contains all PowerPoint slides, tutorial, and general ledger software)
- *NEW Free e-BIZ: The Prentice Hall Guide to e-Business and e-Commerce in Accounting*
- *Free How to Study Accounting* Guidebook
- *NEW The Wall Street Journal* discount subscription offer
- *NEW* MoviesDoorToDoor.com by Mark Beasley and Frank Buckless
- Working Papers
- Study Guides
- Practice Sets

Technology Resources

- *NEW Free* Standard Online Distance Learning Course (WebCT, Blackboard, Pearson CourseCompass)
- *NEW* Premium Online Distance Learning Course (WebCT, Blackboard, Pearson CourseCompass)
- *NEW Free* myPHLIP companion Web site available at www.prenhall.com/horngren
- *Enhanced Free* ReEnforcer Tutorial Software*
- *Free* General Ledger Software*
- *Enhanced Free* Excel Spreadsheet Templates with Excel Tutorial
- *Free* Powerpoint Slides/Ready Notes*
- *NEW Free* "Getting Started with Peachtree" Guidebook
- *NEW Free* "Getting Started with QuickBooks" Guidebook
- *NEW Free* "Getting Started with Simply Accounting" Guidebook
- *NEW* Peachtree Software
- *NEW* Mastering Accounting CD-ROM
- *On Location!* Videos with *NEW segments on* Cisco, Nantucket Nectars (The Juice Guys!), Teva Sandals, Oracle, Amy's Ice Cream, and more
- PHACTS Tutorial Videos
- Accounting Made Easy CD-ROM (available in two CDs)

All may be downloaded at no charge from the text Web site by adopters. These items are also available on our Student CD-ROM, at a nominal price, with text purchase.

TARGET STUDENT SUCCESS: ONLINE AND INTEGRATED COURSE SOLUTIONS

Online Courses

Are you interested in offering a complete and fully functional online course? Would you like to take advantage of existing technology to better communicate with your students, post supplementary course materials, or conduct online testing and grading?

As the leading college textbook publisher, Prentice Hall has formed close alliances with each of the leading online platform providers—Blackboard, WebCT, and our own Pearson CourseCompass.

TWO LEVELS OF CONTENT

We offer two levels of content for most of our online principles of accounting courses:

Standard Courses

(Free with New Text Purchase)
Standard Courses include traditional online course features: online testing, course management and page tracking, communication (i.e., bulletin board, chat rooms, and e-mail), course information, calendar, Powerpoints, Gradebook, etc. Test questions for faculty use, along with sample quizzes and tests for students, are **pre-loaded** for ease of use. Both may be edited by an instructor.

Premium Courses

(Available at a Nominal Price with New Text Purchase)
Prentice Hall offers many distinctive features for our textbook adopters—**including the highest possible service** from our platform partners. For several of our online courses, including Horngren/Harrison/Bamber *Accounting*, fifth ed., the Premium course provides:

- **Rich, Prentice Hall custom-created** course and lecture materials
- **Custom-created PowerPoint slides with audio** to assist students in understanding key concepts
- **Unique video segments** for each text chapter feature an accounting faculty member experienced in conducting online courses, who shares insights with students that help them (1) better prepare to read the chapter and then (2) review the key concepts and takeaway lessons prior to taking an exam.

Each of these features is designed to personalize the course and enhance student understanding of the material.

myPHLIP

Welcome to myPHLIP— your personal guide to the FREE online resources for your book.

Featuring one-click access to all the new materials created by our award-winning team of educators, myPHLIP provides a personalized view of the great new resources available:

- **myPHLIP pages**—your personal access page unites all your myPHLIP texts.
- **Notes**—add personal notes to our resources.
- **Messages**—send messages to individual students, or all students linked to your course.
- **Student Resources**—such as our PowerPoints, videos, and spreadsheets
- **Business Headlines**—provide links to articles in today's business news!
- **Search**—search all PHLIP resources for relevant articles and exercises.
- **Instructor Manual**—tips and suggestions for integrating PHLIP resources into your course.

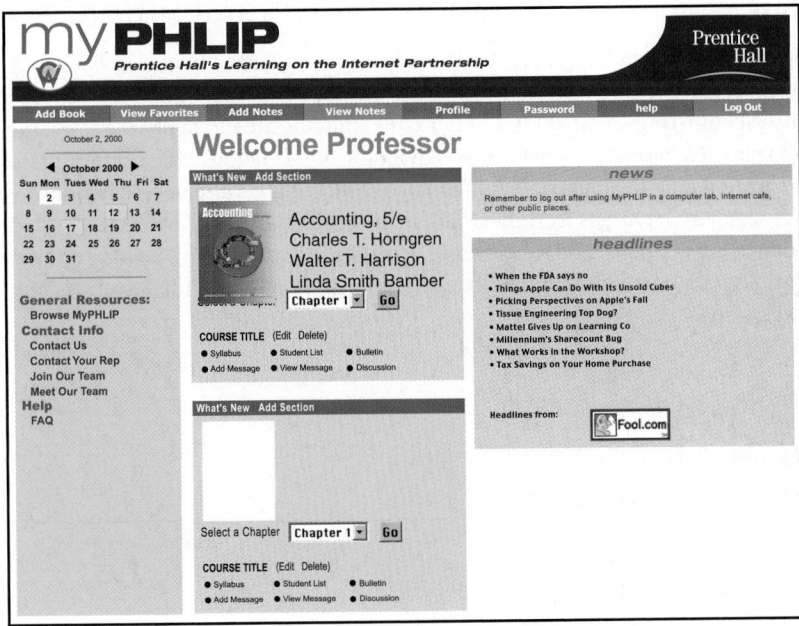

And of course you and your students will still have access to the original PHLIP resources you have trusted throughout the years to provide the best business education support available:

For Instructors

- In the News current events articles
- Teaching Resources
- Online faculty support
- Research Area
- Internet Resources
- What's New on your myPHLIP Web site

For the Student

1. In the News current events articles
2. Research Area
3. Internet Resources
4. Online Study Guide
5. Talk to the Tutor virtual office hours
6. Writing Resource Center
7. Career Center

MoviesDoorToDoor.com: How Accounting Helped Make the Difference

Mark Beasley and Frank Buckless, both of North Carolina State University

MoviesDoorToDoor.com is the fictional story of three college friends who sense a unique business opportunity. Although none of them majored in accounting, the book shows how accounting information is a key component of the major business decisions they make for their start-up business—one that enables customers to select and order videotape rentals via the Internet, which are then delivered direct to the customer's home. The book can be a supplementary reading assignment or a team project.

 The Mastering Business Series

Mastering Business is a multisegment, multimedia CD-ROM series that uses video and interactive exercises. The series covers all the core business disciplines. Through dramatic situations and rigorous exercises, the **Mastering Accounting** CD-ROM will teach your students how to apply the fundamental concepts of accounting to practical problems facing today's dynamic organizations. The Mastering Business series has been developed around an e-business startup, CanGo. By seeing the same people handle a variety of situations in each of the segments, students learn how all the areas of a business are affected by decisions such as making a new product, going public, and starting a new marketing campaign. The Mastering Accounting CD-ROM may be shrinkwrapped to this text for a nominal fee. Go to <u>www.prenhall.com/accountingconnection</u> for more details.

ACKNOWLEDGMENTS

Special thanks to

Student reviewers who provided us with quotable assessments of the book:
Patricia Colarusso, Luzerne County Community College
Lisa Cronauer, Saint Leo University
Carla Hillhouse, Middle Tennessee State University
Carrie Hupp, Middle Tennessee State University
JoAnne Jones, Macomb Community College
Pam Walsh, Oakland Community College

Professor Michael Bamber of the University of Georgia for help and support in preparing text and assignments

Professor Lynn Mazzola of Nassau Community College for her help in checking assignment material and reading the text of Chapters 19–26

Students Chaundolyn Johnson and Grant Rumsey, at the University of Georgia, for their help in checking assignments for Chapters 19–26

Professor Jean Hawkes of William Jewell College for revising the instructor's edition annotations

Writer Nancy Brandwein for the new e-Accounting boxes

Reviewers of ACCOUNTING, Fifth Ed.

Hicks E. Anderson Jr., Montreat College
Thomas Badley, Baker College
David S. Baglia, Grove City College
Robert C. Brush, Cecil Community College
David T. Collins, Bellarmine College
Joan E. Cook, Milwaukee Area Technical College
Kenneth P. Couvillion, San Joaquin Delta College
Ann S. DeCapite, Coastal Carolina College
Anthony J. Dellarte, Luzerne Community College
Joan Demko, Wor-Wic Community College
Mari Suzanne duToit, Okaloosa-Walton Community College
James J. Formosa, Nashville State Technical College
Sally W. Gilfillan, Longwood College
Shirley Glass, Macomb Community College
Janet L. Grange, Chicago State University
Susan S. Hamlen, State University of New York at Buffalo
Ken Harmon, Middle Tennessee State University
Steven Jackson, University of Southern Maine
Fred R. Jex, Macomb Community College
Peg Johnson, Metropolitan Community College

Thomas K. Y. Kam, Hawaii Pacific University
John E. Karayan, California State Polytechnic University, Pomona
Lynn R. Krausse, Bakersfield College
Steven P. Landry, University of Hawaii at Hilo
Suzanne Lowensohn, Barry University
Angelo Luciano, Columbia College-Chicago
Susan Murphy, Monroe Community College
Michael Palma, Gwinnett Technical Institute
William D. Parrish, Delgado Community College
James E. Racic, Lakeland Community College
Rodney R. Ridenour, Montana State University-Bozeman
E. Thomas Robinson, University of Alaska-Fairbanks
Barbara E. Roper, Chicago State University
Gerald W. Rosson, Lynchburg College
Robin D. Turner, Dabney S. Lancaster Community College
Scott Wallace, Blue Mountain Community College
Idalene Williams, Metropolitan Community College
Kitty Williams, Georgia Southern University
Lori S. Zulauf, Slippery Rock University

Focus Group Participants

Richard Ahrens, Los Angeles Pierce College
Charles Alvis, Winthrop University
Juanita Ardevany, Los Angeles Valley College
Patricia Ayres, Arapahoe Community College
David S. Baglia, Grove City College
Carl Ballard, Central Piedmont Community College
Maria Barillas, Phoenix College
James F. Benedum, Milwaukee Area Technical College
Dorcus Berg, Wingate College
Angela Blackwood, Belmont Abbey College
Gary R. Bower, Community College of Rhode Island
Jack Brown, Los Angeles Valley College
Virginia Brunell, Diablo Valley College
James Carriger, Ventura College
Stan Carroll, New York City Technical College
Janet Cassagio, Nassau Community College
Lester Chadwick, University of Delaware
Stanley Chu, Borough of Manhattan Community College
Kerry Colton, Aims Community College
Shaun Crayton, New York City Technical College
Susan Crosson, Santa Fe Community College
Donald Daggett, Mankato State University
Joneal W. Daw, Los Angeles Valley College
Lyle E. Dehning, Metropolitan State College
Wanda DeLeo, Winthrop University
Jim Donnelly, Bergen Community College
Bruce England, Massasoit Community College
Dave Fellows, Red Rocks Community College
Mike Foland, Southwestern Illinois College
Roger Gee, San Diego Mesa College
Martin Ginsberg, Rockland Community College
Earl Godfrey, Gardner Webb University
Edward S. Goodhart, Shippensburg University
Janet L. Grange, Chicago State University
Jean Gutmann, University of Southern Maine
Ralph W. Hernandez, New York City Technical College
Carl High, New York City Technical College
Mary Hill, University of North Carolina - Charlotte
Jean Insinga, Middlesex Community College
Fred R. Jex, Macomb Community College
Bernard Johnson, Santa Monica College
Diane G. Kanis, Bergen Community College

John Keelan, Massachusetts Bay Community College
Mary Thomas Keim, California State University - Bakersfield
Shirly A. Kleiner, Johnson County Community College
Cynthia Kreisner, Austin Community College
Raymond L. Larson, Appalachian State University
Cathy Larson, Middlesex Community College
Linda Lessing, SUNY College of Technology - Farmingdale
Angela Letourneau, Winthrop University
Frank Lordi, Widener University
Audra Lowray, New York City Technical College
Grace Lyons, Bergen Community College
Edward Malmgren, University of North Carolina - Charlotte
Paola Marocchi, New York City Technical College
Larry McCarthy, Slippery Rock University
Linda Spotts Michael, Maple Woods Community College
Greg Mostyn, Mission College
Kitty Nessmith, Georgia Southern University
Lee Nicholas, University of Northern Iowa
Terry Nunnelly, University of North Carolina - Charlotte
Alfonso R. Oddo, Niagara University
Margie Sinclair-Parish, Lewis & Clark Community College
Al Partington, Los Angeles Pierce College
Lynn Mazzola Paluska, Nassau Community College
Juan Perez, New York City Technical College
Ronald Pierno, University of Missouri
Geraldine Powers, Northern Essex Community College
Harry Purcell, Ulster County Community College
John Ribezzo, Community College of Rhode Island
Rosemarie Ruiz, York University
Stephen Schaefer, Contra Costa College
Parmar Sejal, Bergen Community College
Lynn Shoaf, Belmont Abbey College
Walter J. Silva, Roxbury Community College
Leon Singleton, Santa Monica College
David Skougstad, Metropolitan State College
Donna Sum, Prairie State College
Paul Sunko, Olive-Harvey College
Mary Ann Swindlehurst, Carroll Community College
Chandra Taylor, New York City Technical College
Phillip Thornton, Metropolitan State College
John L. Vaccaro, Bunker Hill Community College

Supplement Authors/Reviewers

Instructor's Manual and Video Guides

Betsy Willis, Baylor University
Becky Jones, Baylor University

Video Guides by Beverly Amer, Northern Arizona University

Study Guide

Stephen C. Schaefer, Contra Costa Community College

Allan D. Campbell, Saint Leo University

Mastering Accounting CD

Active Learning Technologies

Working Papers

Ellen Sweatt, Georgia Perimeter College

Anthony Dellarte, Luzerne County Community College

Solutions Manual and Solutions Transparencies

Charles T. Horngren, Stanford University
Walter T. Harrison, Baylor University

Linda Smith Bamber, University of Georgia

Technical Reviewers:

Robert Bauman, Allan Hancock College
Becky Jones, Baylor University
Betsy Willis, Baylor University
Thomas Hoar, Houston Community College

Lynn Mazzola, Nassau Community College
Blake Willis
Chaundolyn Johnson
Grant Rumsey

Test Item File

Alice B. Sineath, Forsyth Technical Community College

Sharie L. Dow, Saint Leo University Center for Online Learning

WIN PH Custom Test Manager

Alice B. Sineath and Engineering Software Associates

Student Resource CD-ROM

Instructor's Resource CD-ROM

PowerPoint Presentations by Olga Quintana, University of Miami
PHAS General Ledger by Lanny Nelms and Jean Insinga

PH ReEnforcer by Albert Oddo, Niagra Univeristy
Spreadsheet Templates by Albert Fisher, Community College of Southern Nevada

On Location Videos

Beverly Amer, Northern Arizona University

Companion Website PHLIP/COMPANION WEBSITE

Randy Kidd, Penn Valley Community College

OnLine Courses (WebCT, Blackboard, Pearson Course Compass)

Michele Bevan, Anthony Fortini, and Maryann Pionegro Carol, with special thanks to Nancy Welcher at Prentice Hall Business Publishing for her technical assistance.

Brief Contents

Contents

xxiii

Chapter 7
Internal Control, Managing Cash, and Making Ethical Judgments 266

Chapter 8
Accounts and Notes Receivable 310

Chapter 9
Merchandise Inventory 346

xxviii

ACCOUNTING

Prologue: Careers in Accounting

Every organization uses accounting. The corner store keeps accounting records to measure its success selling groceries. The largest corporations need accounting to keep track of their locations, employees, and transactions. And all the dot.coms must account for their transactions. Why is accounting so important? Because it helps an organization the same way a model helps an architect construct a building. Accounting helps the manager understand the organization without drowning in its details.

Accounting offers exciting career opportunities. Accounting careers are usually divided into two areas: private accounting and public accounting.

PRIVATE ACCOUNTING

Private accountants work for a single business, such as a local department store, the **McDonald's** restaurant chain, or **Eastman Kodak Company.** Charitable organizations, educational institutions, and government agencies also employ private accountants. The chief accounting officer usually carries the title of controller, treasurer, or chief financial officer (CFO). This person often has the status of a vice president. Accountants who have met certain professional requirements in the area of management accounting are designated as *certified management accountants (CMAs).*

Private accountants perform a wide variety of services:

- *Budgeting* sets sales and profit goals and develops detailed plans (called *budgets*) for achieving those goals. Some of the most successful companies in the United States have been pioneers in the field of budgeting—**Procter & Gamble** and **General Electric,** for example.
- *Information systems design* identifies the organization's information needs, both internal and external. Systems designers develop and implement information systems to meet those needs.
- *Cost accounting* analyzes a business's costs to help managers control expenses. Cost accounting records guide managers in pricing their products and services to achieve greater profits. Also, cost accounting information shows when a product is not profitable and should be dropped.
- *Internal auditing* is performed by a business's own accountants. Large organizations—**Motorola, Bank of America,** and **3M** among them—maintain a staff of internal auditors. These accountants evaluate the firm's accounting and management systems to improve operating efficiency and to ensure that employees follow company policies.

PUBLIC ACCOUNTING

Public accountants serve the general public and collect professional fees for their work, much as doctors and lawyers do. Public accountants are a small fraction (about 10%) of all accountants. Accountants who have met certain professional requirements in law, auditing, and accounting are designated as *certified public accountants (CPAs).*

Like private accountants, public accountants provide valuable services:

- *Consulting* describes the wide scope of advice CPAs provide to help managers run a business. As accountants look deep into an organization, they find many ways to improve the business's operations. Accountants help their clients recruit executives, reorganize the business, and plan mergers with other companies.
- *Assurance* is the service of providing a professional statement that certain information is accurate. CPAs *audit,* or examine, the financial statements of companies and attest to the accuracy and completeness of the data in the statements. Auditors also examine companies' Web sites and provide statements that the information is accurate.
- *Tax accounting* has two aims: complying with the tax laws and minimizing the company's tax bill. Reducing the company's tax bill is an important management consideration. CPAs advise companies and individuals on what type of investments to make and how to structure transactions.

Some public accountants pool their talents and work together within a single firm. Most of their professional employees are CPAs. CPA firms vary greatly in size. Most are small businesses, but many are large partnerships. Exhibit P-1 gives data on the largest U.S. accounting firms.

Exhibit P-2 shows the accounting positions within public accounting firms and other organizations. Note the upward movement of accounting personnel, as indicated by the arrows. In particular, note how accountants may move from positions in public accounting firms to similar or higher positions in industry and government. This is a frequently traveled career path. Because accounting deals with all facets of an organization—such as purchasing, manufacturing, marketing, and distribution—it provides an excellent opportunity for gaining broad business experience.

During this term, you will learn how to use accounting to make business decisions. Consider a career in accounting as you work through this first course.

Rank (2000)	Firm Location	Net Revenue (in millions)	Partners	Number of Offices	Revenue per Partner (in millions)
1	Andersen Worldwide* New York	$7,824	2,117	92	$3.7
2	PricewaterhouseCoopers New York	$6,750	2,938	189	$2.3
3	Ernst & Young New York	$6,375	2,546	87	$2.5
4	Deloitte & Touche Wilton, Connecticut	$5,300	1,913	101	$2.8
5	KPMG New York	$4,656	1,800	136	$2.6
6	H&R Block Tax Services Kansas City, Missouri	$1,267	3,361	8,923	$0.4
7	Century Business Services** Cleveland, Ohio	$460	N/A	798	N/A
8	RSM McGladrey Bloomington, Minnesota	$381	369	65	$1.1
9	Grant Thornton Chicago	$375	274	48	$1.5
10	BDO Seidman Chicago	$298	335	42	$0.9

* During 2000, Andersen Worldwide separated into two firms: Arthur Andersen and Accenture.
** Unlike the other firms, Century Business Services is not a partnership.
Source: Adapted from *Accounting Today* (March 13–April 2, 2000), Special Supplement.

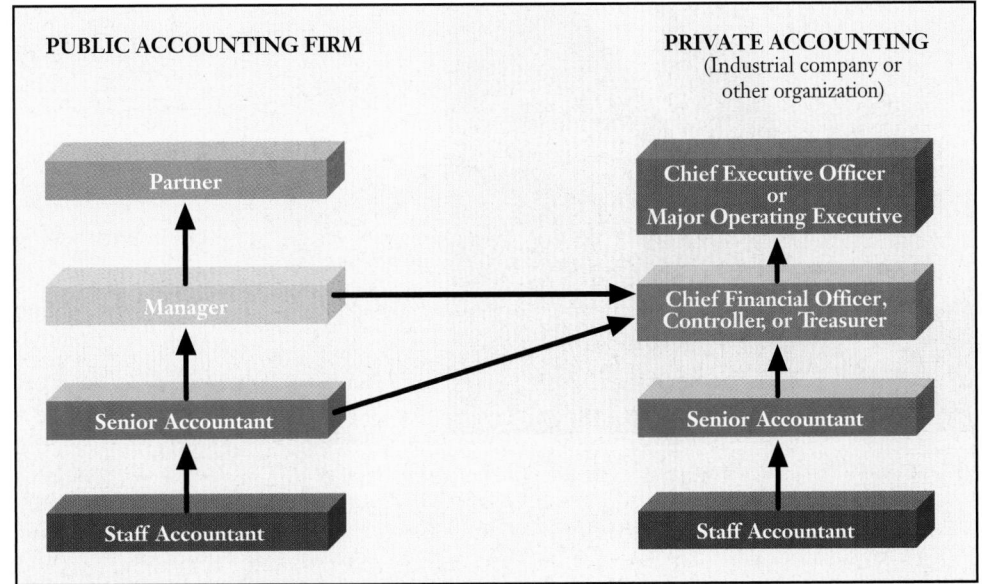

1

Accounting and the Business Environment

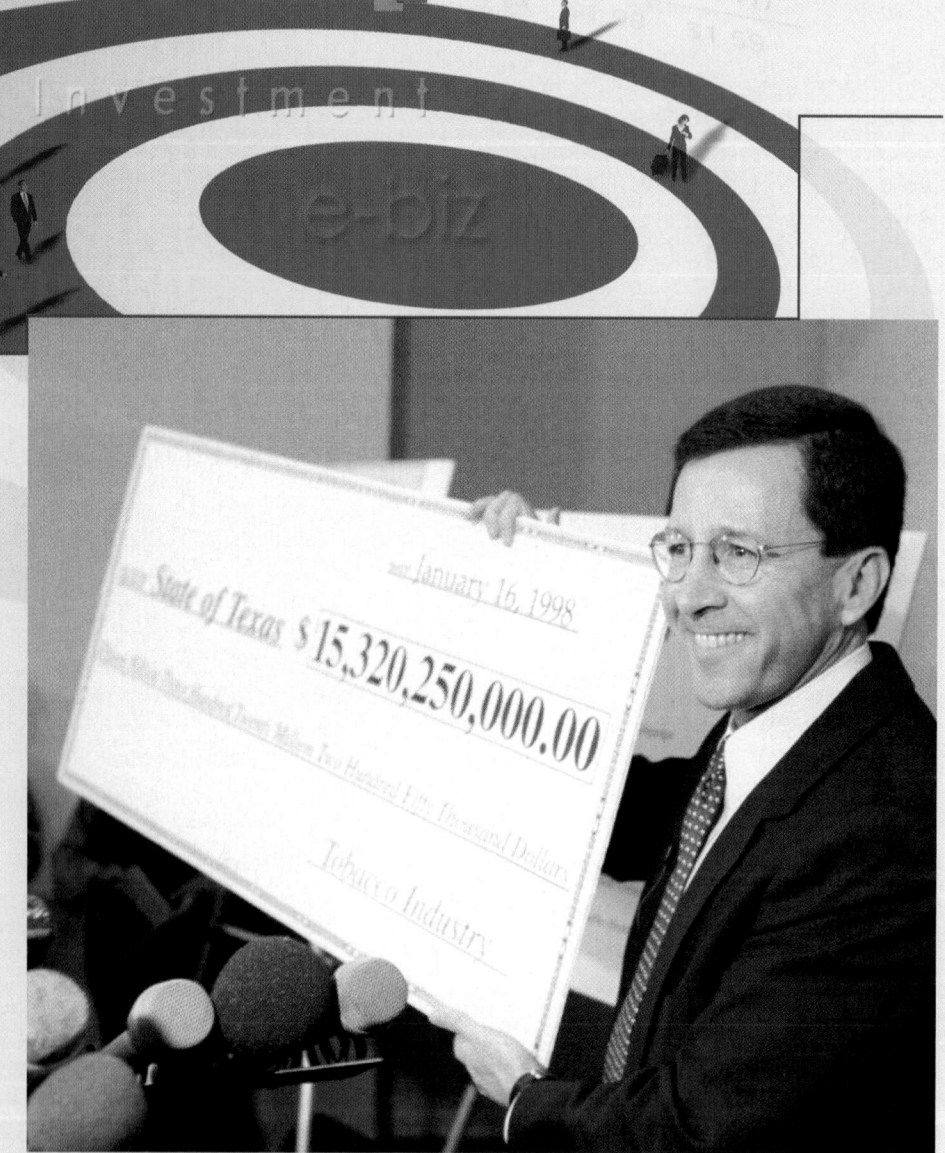

LEARNING OBJECTIVES

After studying this chapter, you should be able to

1. Use accounting vocabulary
2. Apply accounting concepts and principles to business situations
3. Use the accounting equation to describe an organization's financial position
4. Use the accounting equation to analyze business transactions
5. Prepare and use the financial statements
6. Evaluate the performance of a business

Every three months, five Texas lawyers receive $25 million for their work in a lawsuit against the large tobacco companies. These attorneys proved in court that the tobacco companies withheld information that could have helped people make better decisions about whether to smoke. So far the attorneys have collected more than $400 million from the cigarette makers. With this new-found income, they are helping build a new law center for Baylor University, their college alma mater. How do the attorneys account for this legal income? How do they account for the donations to Baylor? The legal agreements require the tobacco companies to pay billions to the states and to their attorneys. How do the cigarette makers, such as **Philip Morris** and **American Brands,** account for these payments?

As you work through this book, you will learn how to account for the attorneys' earnings and for the tobacco companies' expenses. In this chapter, you'll see how one of the attorneys, Harold Nix, uses accounting to manage his practice. We begin the study of accounting with a small single-person business, known as a proprietorship. Many attorneys practice law alone as a proprietorship. Others, such as the "Texas tobacco lawyers," work in partnerships with other attorneys. The large tobacco companies are corporations, the most complex form of business organization. As you study accounting principles, you will also learn to account for the affairs of partnerships and corporations.

Let's begin our study by learning exactly what accounting is.

ACCOUNTING: THE BASIS FOR BUSINESS DECISIONS

Objective 1
Use accounting vocabulary

Accounting is the information system that measures business activities, processes that information into reports, and communicates the results to decision makers. Accounting is not the same as bookkeeping. *Bookkeeping* is a procedure in accounting, just as arithmetic is a procedure in mathematics. Accounting is often called "the language of business." The better you understand this language, the better your business decisions will be, and the better you can manage the financial aspects of living. Personal financial planning, education expenses, loans, car payments, income taxes, and investments are based on the information system that we call accounting.

ACCOUNTING. The information system that measures business activities, processes that information into reports, and communicates the results to decision makers.

A key product of an accounting system is a set of financial statements. **Financial statements** report on a business in monetary terms. Is my business making a profit? Should I hire assistants? Am I earning enough money to pay my rent? Answers to business questions like these are based on accounting information.

FINANCIAL STATEMENTS. Documents that report on a business in monetary amounts, providing information to help people make informed business decisions.

Today people use computers to do detailed bookkeeping—in households, businesses, and organizations of all types. Exhibit 1-1 illustrates the role of accounting in business. The process starts and ends with people making decisions.

Decision Makers: The Users of Accounting Information

Decision makers need information. The more important the decision, the greater the need for information. Virtually all businesses and most individuals keep accounting records to aid in making decisions.

INDIVIDUALS   People such as you use accounting information to manage bank accounts, evaluate job prospects, make investments, and decide whether to rent or buy a house. Harold Nix, one of the Texas tobacco lawyers, uses accounting information to manage his law office.

BUSINESSES   Business managers use accounting information to set goals for their organizations, to evaluate progress toward those goals, and to take corrective action if necessary. Decisions based on accounting information may include which building to purchase, how much merchandise to keep on hand, and how much cash to borrow.

Exhibit 1-1   The Accounting System: The Flow of Information

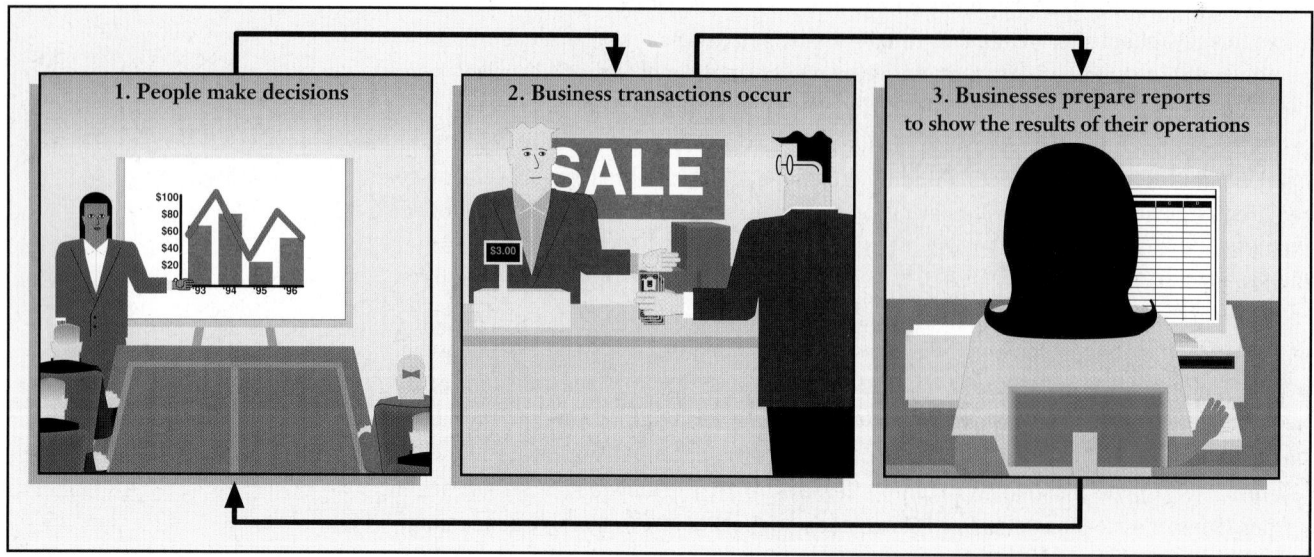

INVESTORS   Investors provide the money a business needs to begin operations. To decide whether to invest in a company, potential investors evaluate what income they can expect from their investment. This means analyzing the financial statements of the business and keeping up with developments in the business press—for example, *The Wall Street Journal* and *Business Week*.

CREDITORS   Before making a loan, creditors (lenders) such as banks determine the borrower's ability to meet scheduled payments. This evaluation includes a report on the borrower's financial position and a prediction of future operations, both of which are based on accounting information. To borrow from a bank before striking it rich, Harold Nix probably had to document his income and financial position.

GOVERNMENT REGULATORY AGENCIES   Most organizations face government regulation. For example, the *Securities and Exchange Commission (SEC),* a federal agency, requires businesses to disclose certain financial information to the investing public.

TAXING AUTHORITIES   Local, state, and federal governments levy taxes on individuals and businesses. Income tax is figured using accounting information. Businesses determine the sales tax they owe from accounting records that show how much they have sold.

NONPROFIT ORGANIZATIONS   Nonprofit organizations—such as churches, hospitals, government agencies, and colleges—use accounting information in much the same way that profit-oriented businesses do.

OTHER USERS   Employees and labor unions make wage demands based on employers' reported income. Consumer groups and the general public are also interested in the amount of income businesses earn. Newspapers report "improved profit pictures" for companies as the nation emerges from economic downturns. Such news, based on accounting information, has an effect on our standard of living.

Financial Accounting and Management Accounting

Users of accounting information may be categorized as *external users or internal users.* This distinction allows us to classify accounting into two fields—financial accounting and management accounting.

FINANCIAL ACCOUNTING. The branch of accounting that focuses on information for people outside the firm.

    Financial accounting focuses on information for people outside the firm. Creditors and outside investors, for example, are not part of the day-to-day management of the company. Government agencies and the general public are external users of a firm's accounting information. Chapters 2–18 of this book deal primarily with financial accounting.

Management accounting focuses on information for internal decision makers, such as top executives, department heads, college deans, and hospital administrators. Chapters 19–26 cover management accounting.

THE AUTHORITY UNDERLYING ACCOUNTING

In the United States, a private organization called the **Financial Accounting Standards Board (FASB)** determines how accounting is practiced. The FASB works with a governmental agency, the Securities and Exchange Commission (SEC), the American Institute of Certified Public Accountants (AICPA), and the Institute of Management Accountants (IMA), two large professional organizations of accountants. **Certified public accountants,** or **CPAs,** are accountants who are licensed to serve the general public rather than one particular company. **Certified management accountants,** or **CMAs,** are licensed accountants who work for a single company. The rules that govern public accounting information are called generally accepted accounting principles (GAAP). Exhibit 1-2 diagrams the relationships among the various accounting organizations.

MANAGEMENT ACCOUNTING. The branch of accounting that focuses on information for internal decision makers of a business.

FINANCIAL ACCOUNTING STANDARDS BOARD (FASB). The private organization that determines how accounting is practiced in the United States.

CERTIFIED PUBLIC ACCOUNTANT (CPA). A licensed accountant who serves the general public rather than one particular company.

CERTIFIED MANAGEMENT ACCOUNTANT (CMA). A licensed accountant who works for a single company.

EXHIBIT 1-2   Key Accounting Organizations

PUBLIC SECTOR
The Securities and Exchange Commission (SEC), a government agency, regulates securities markets in the United States.

PRIVATE SECTOR
Accountants apply generally accepted accounting principles.

PRIVATE SECTOR
The Financial Accounting Standards Board (FASB) determines generally accepted accounting principles.

Generally accepted accounting principles (GAAP)

Ethics in Accounting and Business

Ethical considerations pervade all areas of accounting and business. Consider a current situation: Tobacco companies are defendants in a large number of lawsuits. The managers of **Philip Morris, RJR Nabisco,** and **American Brands** have reason to downplay these lawsuits for fear investors will stop buying their stock and banks will stop lending them money. Should Philip Morris, RJR Nabisco, and American Brands disclose this sensitive information? Accounting guidelines require companies to describe such lawsuits in their financial statements. And each company's auditor is required to state whether the information each company reports to the public is adequate.

By what criteria do accountants address such ethical questions? The AICPA, other professional accounting organizations, and most large companies have codes of ethics that bind members and employees to high standards of ethical conduct.

Standards of Professional Conduct

The AICPA's Code of Professional Conduct for Accountants was adopted by its members to provide guidance to CPAs in their work. Ethical standards in accounting are designed to produce accurate information for decision making. The preamble to the Code states: "[A] certified public accountant assumes an obligation of self-discipline above and beyond the requirements of laws and regulations . . . [and] an unswerving commitment to honorable behavior. . . ."

The opening paragraph of the Standards of Ethical Conduct of the Institute of Management Accountants (IMA) states: "Management accountants have an

e-Accounting

MicroStrategy: A Cautionary Tale for the New Economy

MicroStrategy illustrates both the tremendous rise of e-commerce and the accounting temptations that go with it. MicroStrategy was founded ten years ago as a data-mining software company, and the Internet helped its revenues soar. The company became a darling of Wall Street. In 12 months, the stock rose from $7.34 to $333 and turned its CEO, 35-year-old Michael Saylor, into one of the nation's youngest billionaires. Then boom: On March 20, 2000, MicroStrategy announced a change in accounting practices and the stock lost 60% of its value in one day. Suddenly 1999's profit of $12.6 million turned into a loss of around $40 million. Seems that MicroStrategy had been booking revenue for software contracts even though the revenue would be earned over a multi-year period.

In the frenzy accompanying the rise of e-commerce—estimated to reach $4 trillion by 2003—there is tremendous pressure to project optimism and push up stock prices. Fledgling companies are spending tremendous amounts of investors' money to launch, promote, and maintain their Web sites, and many are losing money. Hence, the new wizards of e-commerce face the temptation to make the financials look better than the actual results. The SEC has formed a new team to investigate and get tough on issues such as the overstatement of revenues. "Think about a bottle of fine wine," says SEC chairman Arthur Levitt: "You wouldn't pop the cork on that bottle before it was ready. But some companies are doing this—recognizing revenues before a sale is complete, before the product is delivered, or [while] the customer still [can] void . . . the sale." MicroStrategy popped the cork prematurely, and in so doing, alerted its dot.com cousins to some real-world consequences.

Sources: Based on Adam Zagorin, "The E-numbers game," *Time,* April 3, 2000, p. 66. Sandra Sugawara, "SEC Unit Targets Accounting Tricks; New Team to Focus on Cooked Books," *The Washington Post,* May 26, 2000, p. E5. James Lardner, "A tech highflier's day of reckoning: How Michael Saylor went from 'boy visionary' to poster boy for dot-com shenanigans," *U.S. News & World Report,* April 10, 2000, pp. 42–43. Robert J. Samuelson, "A high-tech accounting?" *Newsweek,* April 3, 2000, p. 37.

obligation to the organizations they serve, their profession, the public, and themselves to maintain the highest standards of ethical conduct." The requirements are similar to those in the AICPA code.

Most corporations also set standards of ethical conduct for their employees. For example, **The Boeing Company,** a leading manufacturer of aircraft, has a highly developed set of business conduct guidelines. In the introduction to those guidelines, the chairperson of the board and the chief executive officer state: "We owe our success as much to our reputation for integrity as we do to the quality and dependability of our products and services. This reputation is fragile and can easily be lost."

TYPES OF BUSINESS ORGANIZATIONS

A business takes one of three forms of organization. In some cases, accounting procedures depend on which form the organization takes. You should understand the differences among the three: proprietorships, partnerships, and corporations.

PROPRIETORSHIP. A business with a single owner.

PROPRIETORSHIPS A **proprietorship** has a single owner, called the proprietor, who is generally also the manager. Suppose the law office of Harold Nix started out as a proprietorship. Proprietorships tend to be small retail establishments or individual professional businesses, such as those of physicians, attorneys, and accountants. From the accounting viewpoint, each proprietorship is distinct from its proprietor: The accounting records of the proprietorship do *not* include the proprietor's personal financial records.

PARTNERSHIPS A **partnership** joins two or more individuals together as co-owners. Each owner is a partner. Mr. Nix's law firm will become a partnership if Nix takes on a partner. Many retail establishments, as well as some professional organizations of physicians, attorneys, and accountants, are partnerships. Most partnerships are small or medium-sized, but some are gigantic, exceeding 2,000 partners. Accounting treats the partnership as a separate organization, distinct from the personal affairs of each partner.

PARTNERSHIP. A business with two or more owners.

CORPORATIONS A **corporation** is a business owned by **stockholders,** or shareholders, people who own stock (shares of ownership) in the business. A business becomes a corporation when the state approves its articles of incorporation. A corporation is a legal entity, an "artificial person" that conducts its business in its own name. Like the proprietorship and the partnership, the corporation is an organization with an existence separate from its owners.

CORPORATION. A business owned by stockholders; it begins when the state approves its articles of incorporation. A corporation is a legal entity, an "artificial person," in the eyes of the law.

Corporations differ significantly from proprietorships and partnerships in one very important way. If a proprietorship or a partnership cannot pay its debts, lenders can take the owners' personal assets—cash and belongings—to satisfy the business's obligations. But if a corporation goes bankrupt, lenders cannot take the personal assets of the stockholders. This *limited personal liability* of stockholders for corporate debts partly explains why corporations are the dominant form of business organization: People can invest in corporations with limited personal risk.

STOCKHOLDER. A person who owns stock in a corporation. Also called a **shareholder.**

Another factor in corporate growth is the division of ownership into individual shares. **The Coca-Cola Company,** for example, has 3.5 billion shares of stock owned by many stockholders. An investor with no personal relationship either to the corporation or to any other stockholder can become a co-owner by buying 30, 100, 5,000, or any number of shares of its stock.

Exhibit 1-3 summarizes the differences among the three types of business organization.

EXHIBIT 1-3 **Comparison of the Three Forms of Business Organization**

	Proprietorship	Partnership	Corporation
1. Owner(s)	Proprietor—there is only one owner	Partners—there are two or more owners	Stockholders—there are generally many owners
2. Life of the organization	Limited by the owner's choice, or death	Limited by the owners' choices, or death	Indefinite
3. Personal liability of the owner(s) for the business's debts	Proprietor is personally liable	Partners are personally liable	Stockholders are not personally liable
4. Accounting status of the organization	The proprietorship is separate from the proprietor	The partnership is separate from the partners	The corporation is separate from the stockholders

ACCOUNTING CONCEPTS AND PRINCIPLES

Objective 2
Apply accounting concepts and principles to business situations

Accounting follows certain guidelines. The rules that govern how accountants measure, process, and communicate financial information fall under the heading **GAAP,** which stands for **generally accepted accounting principles.** GAAP is the "law" of accounting—rules for conducting behavior in a way acceptable to the majority of people.

GAAP rests on a conceptual framework written by the FASB: *The primary objective of financial reporting is to provide information useful for making investment and lending decisions.* To be useful, information must be relevant, reliable, and comparable. We begin the discussion of GAAP by introducing basic accounting concepts and principles.

GENERALLY ACCEPTED ACCOUNTING PRINCIPLES (GAAP). Accounting guidelines, formulated by the Financial Accounting Standards Board, that govern how accountants measure, process, and communicate financial information.

The Entity Concept

The most basic concept in accounting is that of the **entity.** An accounting entity is an organization or a section of an organization that stands apart as a separate economic unit. In accounting, boundaries are drawn around each entity so as not to confuse its affairs with those of other entities.

Consider Harold Nix, one of the Texas lawyers. Think back to when Nix was starting out as a young lawyer, fresh out of law school. Suppose he began his law practice with $5,000 obtained from a bank loan. Following the entity concept, Nix would account for the $5,000 separately from his personal assets, such as his clothing, house, and automobile. To mix the $5,000 of business cash with his personal assets would make it difficult to measure the financial position of Nix's business.

Consider **Toyota,** a huge organization with several divisions. Toyota management evaluates each division as a separate accounting entity. If sales in the Lexus division are dropping, Toyota can find out why. If sales figures from all divisions of the company are combined, management will not know that Lexus sales are going down. Thus, the entity concept also applies to the parts of a large organization—in fact, *to any economic unit that needs to be evaluated separately.*

The Reliability (Objectivity) Principle

Accounting records and statements are based on the most reliable data available so that they will be accurate and useful. This guideline is the *reliability principle,* also called the *objectivity principle.* Reliable data are verifiable. They may be confirmed by any independent observer. For example, Harold Nix's $5,000 bank loan is supported by a promissory note. This is objective evidence of the loan. Ideally, accounting records are based on information that flows from activities documented by objective evidence. Without the reliability principle, accounting data might be based on whims and opinions.

Suppose you want to open a stereo shop. For a store location, you transfer a small building to the business. You believe the building is worth $155,000. To confirm its cost to the business, you hire two real estate appraisers, who value the building at $147,000. Which is the more reliable estimate of the building's value, your estimate of $155,000 or the $147,000 professional appraisal? The appraisal of $147,000 is more reliable because it is supported by an independent, objective observation. The business should record the building cost as $147,000.

The Cost Principle

The *cost principle* states that acquired assets and services should be recorded at their actual cost (also called *historical cost*). Even though the purchaser may believe the price is a bargain, the item is recorded at the price paid in the transaction and not at the "expected" cost. Suppose your stereo shop purchases equipment from a supplier who is going out of business. Assume that you get a good deal and pay only $2,000 for equipment that would have cost you $3,000 elsewhere. The cost principle requires you to record the equipment at its actual cost of $2,000, not the $3,000 that you believe the equipment is worth.

The cost principle also holds that the accounting records should maintain the historical cost of an asset for as long as the business holds the asset. Why? Because cost is a reliable measure. Suppose your store holds the stereo equipment for six months. During that time, stereo prices rise, and the equipment can be sold for $3,500. Should its accounting value—the figure "on the books"—be the actual cost of $2,000 or the current market value of $3,500? According to the cost principle, the accounting value of the equipment remains at actual cost, $2,000.

The Going-Concern Concept

Another reason for measuring assets at historical cost is the *going-concern concept,* which holds that the entity will remain in operation for the foreseeable future. Most firm resources—such as supplies, land, buildings, and equipment—are acquired to use rather than to sell. Under the going-concern concept, accountants assume that the business will remain in operation long enough to use existing resources for their intended purpose.

To understand the going-concern concept better, consider the alternative, which is to go out of business. A store that is holding a Going-Out-of-Business Sale is trying to sell all its holdings. In that case, instead of historical cost, the relevant measure is current market value. Going out of business, however, is the exception rather than the rule.

The Stable-Monetary-Unit Concept

In the United States, we record transactions in dollars because the dollar is the medium of exchange. British accountants record transactions in pounds sterling, and the Japanese record transactions in yen. The value of a dollar or a Mexican peso changes over time. A rise in the price level is called *inflation*. During inflation, a dollar will purchase less milk, less toothpaste, and less of other goods. When prices are stable—when there is little inflation—a dollar's purchasing power is also stable.

Accountants assume that the dollar's purchasing power is stable. The *stable-monetary-unit concept* is the basis for ignoring the effect of inflation in accounting. It allows us to add and subtract dollar amounts as though each dollar has the same purchasing power as any other dollar at any other time.

 DAILY EXERCISE 1-1

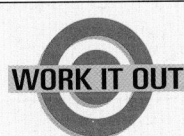 **WORK IT OUT**

You are considering the purchase of land for future expansion. The seller is asking $50,000 for land that cost her $35,000. An appraisal shows a value of $47,000. You first offer $44,000. The seller counter-offers with $48,000, and you agree on a price of $46,000. What dollar value for this land is reported on your financial statements? Which accounting concept or principle guides your answer?

Answer: According to the *cost principle*, assets and services should be recorded at their actual cost. You paid $46,000 for the land. Therefore, $46,000 is the cost to report on your financial statements.

THE ACCOUNTING EQUATION

Financial statements tell how a business is performing and where it stands. They are the final product of the accounting process. But how do we produce the financial statements? The basic tool of accounting is the **accounting equation.** It presents the resources of the business and the claims to those resources.

Assets and Liabilities

Assets are the economic resources of a business that are expected to be of benefit in the future. Cash, office supplies, merchandise, furniture, land, and buildings are assets.

Claims to those assets come from two sources. **Liabilities** are *outsider* claims, which are economic obligations—debts—payable to outsiders. These outside parties are called *creditors*. For example, a creditor who has loaned money to a business has a claim—a legal right—to a part of the assets until the business pays the debt. *Insider* claims to the business's assets are called **owner's equity,** or **capital.** These are the claims held by the owners of the business. Owners have a claim to the entity's assets because they have invested in the business.

The accounting equation shows the relationship among assets, liabilities, and owner's equity. Assets appear on the left-hand side of the equation. The legal and economic claims against the assets—the liabilities and owner's equity—appear on the right-hand side of the equation. As Exhibit 1-4 shows, the two sides must be equal:

(Economic Resources)   *(Claims to Economic Resources)*

ASSETS = **LIABILITIES + OWNER'S EQUITY**

Let's take a closer look at the elements that make up the accounting equation. Suppose you run Top Cut Meats, which supplies beef to **McDonald's** and other restaurants. Some customers pay you in cash when you deliver the meat. Cash is an asset. Other customers buy on credit and promise to pay you within a certain time after delivery. This promise is also an asset because it is an economic resource that will benefit you in the future, when you receive the cash. To Top Cut Meats, this

Objective 3
Use the accounting equation to describe an organization's financial position

ACCOUNTING EQUATION. The basic tool of accounting, presenting the resources of the business and the claims to those resources: Assets = Liabilities + Owner's Equity.

ASSET. An economic resource that is expected to be of benefit in the future.

LIABILITY. An economic obligation (a debt) payable to an individual or an organization outside the business.

OWNER'S EQUITY. The claim of a business owner to the assets of the business. Also called **capital.**

EXHIBIT 1-4
The Accounting Equation

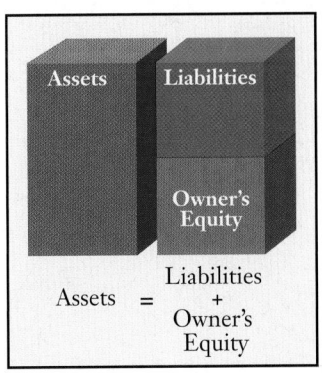

ACCOUNT RECEIVABLE. A promise to receive cash from customers to whom the business has sold goods or for whom the business has performed services.

NOTE RECEIVABLE. A written promise for future collection of cash.

ACCOUNT PAYABLE. A liability backed by the general reputation and credit standing of the debtor.

NOTE PAYABLE. A written promise of future payment.

REVENUE. Amounts earned by delivering goods or services to customers. Revenues increase owner's equity.

promise is an **account receivable.** A *written* promise for future collection is called a **note receivable.** McDonald's promise to pay you for the meat it purchases on credit creates a debt for McDonald's. This liability is an **account payable** of McDonald's—the debt is not written. Instead, it is backed by the reputation and the credit standing of McDonald's. A written promise of future payment is called a **note payable.** All receivables are assets. All payables are liabilities.

Owner's Equity

Owner's equity is the amount of an entity's assets that remain after the liabilities are subtracted.

ASSETS – LIABILITIES = OWNER'S EQUITY

The purpose of business is to increase owner's equity through **revenues,** which are increases in owner's equity earned by delivering goods or services to customers. Revenues increase owner's equity because they increase the business's assets or decrease its liabilities. As a result, the owner's share of business assets increases. Exhibit 1-5 shows that owner investments and revenues increase the owner's equity of the business.

EXHIBIT 1-5

Transactions That Increase or Decrease Owner's Equity

⊙ **DAILY EXERCISE 1-2**

OWNER WITHDRAWALS. Amounts removed from the business by an owner.

EXPENSE. Decrease in owner's equity that occurs from using assets or increasing liabilities in the course of delivering goods or services to customers.

Exhibit 1-5 also indicates the types of transactions that decrease owner's equity. **Owner withdrawals** are amounts removed from the business by the owner. Withdrawals are the opposite of owner investments. **Expenses** are decreases in owner's equity that occur from using assets or increasing liabilities in the course of delivering goods and services to customers. Expenses are the cost of doing business and are the opposite of revenues. Expenses include

- office rent
- salaries of employees
- newspaper advertisements
- utility payments
- interest on loans
- insurance
- property taxes

⊙ **DAILY EXERCISE 1-3**

⊙ **DAILY EXERCISE 1-4**

WORK IT OUT

1. If the assets of a business are $174,300 and the liabilities total $82,000, how much is the owner's equity?
2. If the owner's equity in a business is $22,000 and the liabilities are $36,000, how much are the assets?

Answers: To answer both questions, use the accounting equation:

1.

ASSETS	–	LIABILITIES	=	OWNER'S EQUITY
$174,300	–	$82,000	=	$92,300

2.

ASSETS	=	LIABILITIES	+	OWNER'S EQUITY
$58,000	=	$36,000	+	$22,000

ACCOUNTING FOR BUSINESS TRANSACTIONS

In accounting terms, a **transaction** is any event that *both* affects the financial position of the business entity *and* can be recorded reliably. Many events can affect a company, including (1) elections, (2) economic booms and downturns, (3) purchases and sales of merchandise inventory, (4) payment of rent, and (5) collection of cash from customers. But an accountant records only those events with effects that can be measured reliably. Which of these events would an accountant record? The answer is events (3), (4), and (5), because their dollar amounts can be measured reliably. The accountant would not record events (1) and (2) because the dollar effects of elections and economic trends cannot be measured reliably.

> **TRANSACTION.** An event that affects the financial position of a particular entity and can be recorded reliably.

To illustrate accounting for a business, let's use Gay Gillen eTravel. Gillen operates a travel agency that offers service in two ways. Some customers phone or e-mail Gay Gillen eTravel. Other customers do business with the travel agency strictly on-line. On-line customers plan and pay for their trips through the Gillen Web site. The Web site is linked to airlines, hotels, and cruise lines, so clients can obtain the latest information 24 hours a day, 7 days a week. Gillen's Web site allows the agency to transact more business than would be possible through phone calls, fax, or e-mail. As a result, Gillen is able to operate with fewer employees, and this saves on operating expenses. She passes along the cost savings to clients by charging them lower commissions. It is a win/win situation for both parties. Gillen provides more service and generates a nice profit. Customers save on travel costs.

Now let's analyze Gillen eTravel's transactions.

TRANSACTION 1: STARTING THE BUSINESS   Gay Gillen invests $30,000 of her own money to begin the business. Specifically, she deposits $30,000 in a bank account entitled Gay Gillen eTravel. The effect of this transaction on the accounting equation of the Gay Gillen eTravel business entity is

> **Objective 4**
> Use the accounting equation to analyze business transactions

Assets		Liabilities		Owner's Equity	Type of Owner's Equity Transaction
Cash	=		+	Gay Gillen, Capital	
(1) +30,000				+30,000	*Owner investment*

For every transaction, the amount on the left side of the equation must equal the amount on the right side. The first transaction increases both the assets (in this case, Cash) and the owner's equity of the business (Gay Gillen, Capital). To the right of the transaction, we write "Owner investment" to keep track of the reason for the effect on the owner's equity.

TRANSACTION 2: PURCHASE OF LAND   Gillen purchases land for an office location, paying cash of $20,000. The effect of this transaction on the accounting equation is

Assets			Liabilities		Owner's Equity	Type of Owner's Equity Transaction
Cash	+	Land	=	+	Gay Gillen, Capital	
(1) 30,000					30,000	*Owner investment*
(2) −20,000	+	20,000				
Bal. 10,000		20,000			30,000	
30,000					30,000	

 DAILY EXERCISE 1-5

 DAILY EXERCISE 1-6

The cash purchase of land increases one asset, Land, and decreases another asset, Cash, by the same amount. After the transaction is completed, Gillen's business has cash of $10,000, land of $20,000, no liabilities, and owner's equity of $30,000. Note that the sums of the balances (abbreviated Bal.) on both sides of the equation must always be equal.

TRANSACTION 3: PURCHASE OF OFFICE SUPPLIES Gillen buys stationery and other office supplies, agreeing to pay $500 within 30 days. This transaction increases both the assets and the liabilities of the business. Its effect on the accounting equation is

		Assets				Liabilities	+	Owner's Equity
	Cash	+	Office Supplies	+	Land	Accounts Payable	+	Gay Gillen, Capital
Bal.	10,000				20,000			30,000
(3)			+500			+500		
Bal.	10,000		500		20,000	500		30,000
			30,500				30,500	

Office Supplies is an asset, not an expense, because the supplies can be used in the future. The liability created by this transaction is an account payable. Recall that a *payable* is a liability.

TRANSACTION 4: EARNING OF SERVICE REVENUE Gay Gillen eTravel earns service revenue by providing travel services for clients. She earns $5,500 revenue and collects this amount in cash. The effect on the accounting equation is an increase in the asset Cash and an increase in Gay Gillen, Capital, as follows:

		Assets			Liabilities +	Owner's Equity	Type of Owner's Equity Transaction
	Cash	+ Office Supplies	+ Land		Accounts Payable	+ Gay Gillen, Capital	
Bal.	10,000	500	20,000		500	30,000	
(4)	+5,500					+5,500	*Service revenue*
Bal.	15,500	500	20,000		500	35,500	
		36,000				36,000	

⊙ DAILY EXERCISE 1-7

This revenue transaction caused the business to grow, as shown by the increases in total assets and in the sum of total liabilities plus owner's equity. A company that sells goods to customers is a merchandising business. Its revenue is called *sales revenue*. By contrast, Gay Gillen and Harold Nix, the attorney, perform services for clients; their revenue is called *service revenue*.

WORK IT OUT

Gillen's travel business has now completed four business transactions. Answer these questions about the business:

1. How much in total assets does Gillen's business have to work with?
2. How much of the total assets of the business does Gillen actually own? How much does the business owe outsiders?

Answers

1. Look at the balances under the Assets heading for transaction 4. Gillen's business owns three assets: Cash ($15,500), Office Supplies ($500), and Land ($20,000). By adding these amounts, we see that the business has $36,000 in total assets.
2. Recall that *owner's equity* represents the owner's claim to the assets of the business. Gillen's owner's equity is $35,500.
   Liabilities are the amounts that a business owes to outsiders. After transaction 4, the company owes $500 in liabilities.

TRANSACTION 5: EARNING OF SERVICE REVENUE ON ACCOUNT Gillen performs services for clients who do not pay immediately. In return for her travel services, Gillen receives clients' promises to pay $3,000 within one month. This promise is an asset to Gillen, an account receivable because she expects to collect the cash in the future. In accounting, we say that Gillen performed this service *on account*. When the business performs service for a client, the business earns revenue whether it receives cash now or expects to collect the cash later. This $3,000 of service revenue increases the wealth of Gillen's business just like the $5,500 of revenue that she collected immediately in transaction 4. Gillen records an increase in the asset Accounts Receivable and an increase in owner's equity as follows:

		Assets						Liabilities +	Owner's Equity		Type of Owner's Equity Transaction
	Cash	+	Accounts Receivable	+	Office Supplies	+	Land	Accounts Payable	+	Gay Gillen, Capital	
Bal.	15,500				500		20,000	500		35,500	
(5)			+3,000							+3,000	Service revenue
Bal.	15,500		3,000		500		20,000	500		38,500	
			39,000							39,000	

TRANSACTION 6: PAYMENT OF EXPENSES During the month, Gillen pays $3,100 in cash expenses: lease expense on a computer, $400; office rent, $1,100; employee salary, $1,200 (part-time assistant); and utilities, $400. The effects on the accounting equation are:

		Assets						Liabilities +	Owner's Equity		Type of Owner's Equity Transaction
	Cash	+	Accounts Receivable	+	Office Supplies	+	Land	Accounts Payable	+	Gay Gillen, Capital	
Bal.	15,500		3,000		500		20,000	500		38,500	
	− 400									− 400	Lease expense, computer
(6)	− 1,100									− 1,100	Rent expense, office
	− 1,200									− 1,200	Salary expense
	− 400									− 400	Utilities expense
Bal.	12,400		3,000		500		20,000	500		35,400	
			35,900							35,900	

Because expenses have the opposite effect of revenues, they cause the business to shrink, as shown by the smaller balances of total assets and owner's equity.

Each expense should be recorded in a separate transaction. They are listed together here for simplicity. We could record the cash payment in a single amount for the sum of the four expenses, $3,100 ($400 + $1,100 + $1,200 + $400). In all cases, the "balance" of the equation holds, as we know it must.

Businesspeople, Gay Gillen included, run their businesses to have more revenues than expenses. An excess of total revenues over total expenses is called **net income, net earnings,** or **net profit.** If total expenses exceed total revenues, the result is a **net loss.**

TRANSACTION 7: PAYMENT ON ACCOUNT Gillen pays $300 to the store from which she purchased $500 worth of office supplies in transaction 3. In accounting, we say that she pays $300 *on account*. The effect on the accounting equation is a decrease in the asset Cash and a decrease in the liability Accounts Payable as shown at the top of page16.

NET INCOME. Excess of total revenues over total expenses. Also called **net earnings** or **net profit.**

NET LOSS. Excess of total expenses over total revenues.

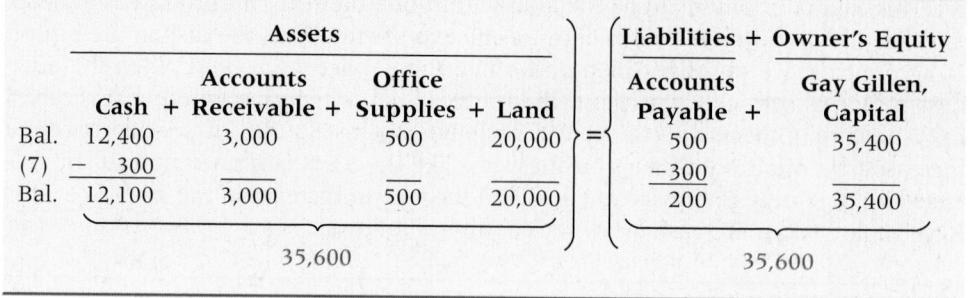

	Assets						Liabilities + Owner's Equity	
	Cash +	Accounts Receivable +	Office Supplies +	Land			Accounts Payable +	Gay Gillen, Capital
Bal.	12,400	3,000	500	20,000	} = {		500	35,400
(7)	− 300						−300	
Bal.	12,100	3,000	500	20,000			200	35,400
		35,600					35,600	

The payment of cash on account has no effect on the asset Office Supplies because the payment does not increase or decrease the supplies available to the business.

TRANSACTION 8: PERSONAL TRANSACTION Gillen remodels her home at a cost of $15,000, paying cash from personal funds. This event is *not* a transaction of Gay Gillen eTravel. It has no effect on the travel agency and therefore is not recorded by the business. It is a transaction of the Gay Gillen *personal* entity, not Gay Gillen eTravel. This transaction illustrates the *entity concept*.

TRANSACTION 9: COLLECTION ON ACCOUNT In transaction 5, Gillen performed services for a client on account. The business now collects $1,000 from the client. We say that Gillen collects the cash *on account*. Gillen will record an increase in the asset Cash. Should she also record an increase in service revenue? No, because she already recorded the revenue when she earned it in transaction 5. The phrase "collect cash on account" means to record an increase in Cash and a decrease in the asset Accounts Receivable. The effect on the accounting equation of Gay Gillen eTravel is:

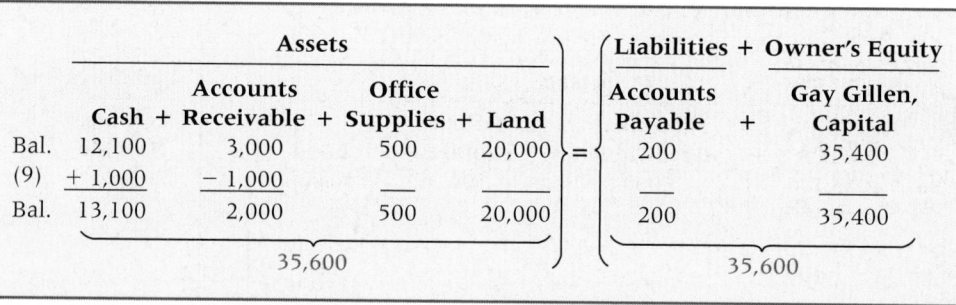

	Assets						Liabilities + Owner's Equity	
	Cash +	Accounts Receivable +	Office Supplies +	Land			Accounts Payable +	Gay Gillen, Capital
Bal.	12,100	3,000	500	20,000	} = {		200	35,400
(9)	+ 1,000	− 1,000						
Bal.	13,100	2,000	500	20,000			200	35,400
		35,600					35,600	

● **DAILY EXERCISE 1-8**

Total assets are unchanged from the preceding transaction's total. Why? Because Gillen merely exchanged one asset for another. Also, total liabilities and owner's equity are unchanged.

TRANSACTION 10: SALE OF LAND An individual approaches Gillen about selling land owned by the travel agency. Gillen and the other person agree to a sale price of $9,000, which is equal to Gillen's cost of the land. Gillen's business sells the land and receives $9,000 cash. The effect on the accounting equation of the travel agency is as follows:

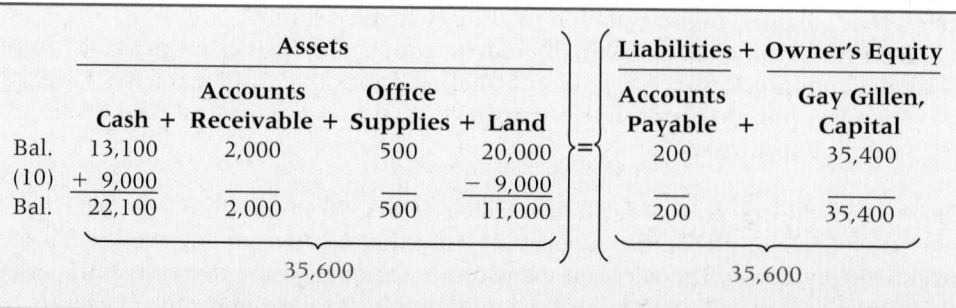

	Assets						Liabilities + Owner's Equity	
	Cash +	Accounts Receivable +	Office Supplies +	Land			Accounts Payable +	Gay Gillen, Capital
Bal.	13,100	2,000	500	20,000	} = {		200	35,400
(10)	+ 9,000			− 9,000				
Bal.	22,100	2,000	500	11,000			200	35,400
		35,600					35,600	

Transaction 11: Withdrawing of Cash Gillen withdraws $2,100 cash from the business for personal use. The effect on the accounting equation is

		Assets						Liabilities	+	Owner's Equity	Type of Owner's Equity Transaction
	Cash	+	Accounts Receivable	+	Office Supplies	+	Land	=	Accounts Payable	+	Gay Gillen, Capital	
Bal.	22,100		2,000		500		11,000		200		35,400	
(11)	− 2,100										− 2,100	Owner withdrawal
Bal.	20,000		2,000		500		11,000		200		33,300	
			33,500							33,500		

Gillen's withdrawal of $2,100 cash decreases the asset Cash and also the owner's equity of the business. *The withdrawal does not represent a business expense because the cash is used for personal affairs.* We record this decrease in owner's equity as Withdrawals or as Drawings. The double underlines below each column indicate a final total.

Evaluating Business Transactions

Exhibit 1-6 on page 18 summarizes the 11 preceding transactions. Panel A lists the details of the transactions, and Panel B presents the analysis. As you study the exhibit, note that every transaction maintains the equality

$$ \text{ASSETS} = \text{LIABILITIES} + \text{OWNER'S EQUITY} $$

The Financial Statements

After analyzing transactions, we need a way to present the results. We look now at the *financial statements,* the formal reports of an entity's financial information. The primary financial statements are the

- income statement
- statement of owner's equity
- balance sheet
- statement of cash flows

Objective 5
Prepare and use the financial statements

Income Statement The **income statement** presents a summary of an entity's revenues and expenses for a specific period of time, such as a month or a year. The income statement, also called the **statement of earnings** or **statement of operations,** is like a video—it presents a moving financial picture of business operations during the period. The income statement holds one of the most important pieces of information about a business—its *net income,* or revenues minus expenses. If expenses exceed revenues, there is a net loss for the period.

Statement of Owner's Equity The **statement of owner's equity** presents a summary of the changes that occurred in the entity's *owner's equity* during a specific time period, such as a month or a year. Increases in owner's equity arise from investments by the owner and from net income earned during the period. Decreases result from owner withdrawals and from a net loss for the period. Net income or net loss come directly from the income statement. Owner investments and withdrawals are capital transactions between the business and its owner, so they do not affect the income statement.

Balance Sheet The **balance sheet** lists all the entity's assets, liabilities, and owner's equity as of a specific date, usually the end of a month or a year. The balance sheet is like a snapshot of the entity. For this reason, it is also called the **statement of financial position.**

Statement of Cash Flows The **statement of cash flows** reports the amount of cash coming in (cash receipts) and the amount of cash going out (*cash payments* or

INCOME STATEMENT. Summary of an entity's revenues, expenses, and net income or net loss for a specific period. Also called the **statement of earnings** or the **statement of operations.**

STATEMENT OF OWNER'S EQUITY. Summary of the changes in an entity's owner's equity during a specific period.

BALANCE SHEET. List of an entity's assets, liabilities, and owner's equity as of a specific date. Also called the **statement of financial position.**

STATEMENT OF CASH FLOWS. Reports cash receipts and cash payments during a period.

EXHIBIT 1-6   Analysis of Transactions, Gay Gillen eTravel

PANEL A—Details of Transactions

(1) Gillen invested $30,000 cash in the business.
(2) Paid $20,000 cash for land.
(3) Bought $500 of office supplies on account.
(4) Received $5,500 cash from clients for service revenue earned.
(5) Performed travel service for clients on account, $3,000.
(6) Paid cash expenses: computer lease, $400; office rent, $1,100; employee salary, $1,200; utilities, $400.
(7) Paid $300 on the account payable created in transaction 3.
(8) Remodeled Gillen's personal residence. This is *not* a transaction of the business.
(9) Collected $1,000 on the account receivable created in transaction 5.
(10) Sold land for cash at its cost of $9,000.
(11) Withdrew $2,100 cash for personal expenses.

PANEL B—Analysis of Transactions

	Cash	+ Accounts Receivable	+ Office Supplies	+ Land	=	Accounts Payable	+ Gay Gillen, Capital	Type of Owner's Equity Transaction
(1)	+30,000						+30,000	Owner investment
Bal.	30,000						30,000	
(2)	−20,000			+20,000				
Bal.	10,000			20,000			30,000	
(3)			+500			+500		
Bal.	10,000		500	20,000		500	30,000	
(4)	+ 5,500						+ 5,500	Service revenue
Bal.	15,500		500	20,000		500	35,500	
(5)		+3,000					+ 3,000	Service revenue
Bal.	15,500	3,000	500	20,000		500	38,500	
	− 400						− 400	Lease expense, computer
(6)	− 1,100						− 1,100	Rent expense, office
	− 1,200						− 1,200	Salary expense
	− 400						− 400	Utilities expense
Bal.	12,400	3,000	500	20,000		500	35,400	
(7)	− 300					−300		
Bal.	12,100	3,000	500	20,000		200	35,400	
(8)	Not a transaction of the business							
(9)	+ 1,000	−1,000						
Bal.	13,100	2,000	500	20,000		200	35,400	
(10)	+ 9,000			− 9,000				
Bal.	22,100	2,000	500	11,000		200	35,400	
(11)	− 2,100						− 2,100	Owner withdrawal
Bal.	20,000	2,000	500	11,000		200	33,300	

33,500   =   33,500

disbursements) during a period. Business activities result in a net cash inflow (receipts greater than payments) or a net cash outflow (payments greater than receipts). The statement of cash flows shows the net increase or net decrease in cash during the period and the cash balance at the end of the period. (We cover the statement of cash flows in greater depth in Chapter 17.)

Financial Statement Headings

Each financial statement has a heading giving the name of the business (in our discussion, Gay Gillen eTravel), the name of the particular statement, and the date or time period covered by the statement. A balance sheet taken at the end of year 20X1 would be dated December 31, 20X1. A balance sheet prepared at the end of March 20X3 is dated March 31, 20X3.

An income statement or a statement of owner's equity that covers an annual period ended in December 20X5 is dated "Year Ended December 31, 20X5." A monthly income statement or statement of owner's equity for September 20X4 has in its heading "Month Ended September 30, 20X4," "For the Month Ended September 30, 20X4," or "For the Month of September 20X4." Income is meaningless unless identified with a particular time period.

Software programs such as Quick Books and Peachtree have streamlined the preparation of the financial statements. These statements can now be produced instantaneously after the financial records are entered into the computer. Of course, any errors in the financial records will show up in the financial statements. So the person who analyzes the data controls the accuracy of the financial statements.

Relationships Among the Financial Statements

Objective 6
Evaluate the performance of a business

Exhibit 1-7 illustrates all four financial statements. Their data come from the transaction analysis in Exhibit 1-6, which covers the month of April 20X1. Study the exhibit carefully. Specifically, observe the following in Exhibit 1-7:

1. The *income statement* for the month ended April 30, 20X1
   a. Reports all revenues and all expenses during the period. Expenses are listed in decreasing order of amount, with the largest expense first.
   b. Reports *net income* of the period if total revenues exceed total expenses, as in the case of Gay Gillen eTravel's operations for April. If total expenses exceed total revenues, a *net loss* is reported instead.
2. The *statement of owner's equity* for the month ended April 30, 20X1
   a. Opens with the owner's capital balance at the beginning of the period.
   b. Adds *investments by the owner* and adds net income (or subtracts net loss, as the case may be). Net income or net loss come directly from the income statement (see arrow ① in Exhibit 1–7).
   c. Subtracts withdrawals by the owner. Parentheses indicate a subtraction.
   d. Ends with the owner's capital balance at the end of the period.
3. The *balance sheet* at April 30, 20X1
   a. Reports all assets, all liabilities, and owner's equity at the end of the period.
   b. Reports that total assets equal the sum of total liabilities plus total owner's equity.
   c. Reports the owner's ending capital balance, taken directly from the statement of owner's equity (see arrow ②).
4. The *statement of cash flows* for the month ended April 30, 20X1
   a. Reports cash flows from three types of business activities (*operating, investing,* and *financing activities*) during the month.
      • *Operating activities* are cash receipts from revenues and cash payments of expenses.
      • *Investing activities* are the results of purchasing and selling the long-term assets that the business uses for operations.
      • *Financing activities* are the cash receipts from people who finance the organization (the owner and the lenders), and also payments back to those people.
      Each category of cash-flow activities includes both cash receipts, which are positive amounts, and cash payments, which are negative amounts (denoted by parentheses). Each category results in a net cash inflow or a net cash outflow for the period. We discuss these categories in detail in later chapters.
   b. Reports a net increase in cash during the month and ends with the cash balance at April 30, 20X1. This is the amount of cash to report on the balance sheet (see arrow ③).

EXHIBIT 1-7
Financial Statements of
Gay Gillen eTravel

GAY GILLEN ETRAVEL
Income Statement
Month Ended April 30, 20X1

Revenue		
Service revenue		$8,500
Expenses:		
Salary expense	$1,200	
Rent expense, office	1,100	
Lease expense, computer	400	
Utilities expense	400	
Total expenses		3,100
Net income		$5,400

①

GAY GILLEN ETRAVEL
Statement of Owner's Equity
Month Ended April 30, 20X1

Gay Gillen, capital, April 1, 20X1	$	0
Add: Investments by owner		30,000
Net income for the month		5,400
		35,400
Less: Withdrawals by owner		(2,100)
Gay Gillen, capital, April 30, 20X1		$33,300

②

GAY GILLEN ETRAVEL
Balance Sheet
April 30, 20X1

Assets		Liabilities		
Cash	$20,000	Accounts payable	$	200
Accounts receivable	2,000			
Office supplies	500	**Owner's Equity**		
Land	11,000	Gay Gillen, capital		33,300
		Total liabilities and		
Total assets	$33,500	owner's equity		$33,500

③

GAY GILLEN ETRAVEL
Statement of Cash Flows*
Month Ended April 30, 20X1

Cash flows from **operating** activities:		
Receipts:		
Collections from customers ($5,500 + $1,000)		$ 6,500
Payments:		
To suppliers ($1,100 + $400 + $400 + $300)	$ (2,200)	
To employees	(1,200)	(3,400)
Net cash inflow from operating activities		3,100
Cash flows from **investing** activities:		
Acquisition of land	$(20,000)	
Sale of land	9,000	
Net cash outflow from investing activities		(11,000)
Cash flows from **financing** activities:		
Investment by owner	$ 30,000	
Withdrawal by owner	(2,100)	
Net cash inflow from financing activities		27,900
Net increase in cash		20,000
Cash balance, April 1, 20X1		0
Cash balance, April 30, 20X1		$20,000

*Chapter 17 explains how to prepare this statement.

The Decision Guidelines feature summarizes the chapter in terms of decisions businesspeople must make. Decision Guidelines appear in each chapter of this book. They serve as useful summaries of the decision-making process in business.

DECISION GUIDELINES

Major Business Decisions

DECISION	GUIDELINES
How to organize the business?	If a single owner—a *proprietorship*.
	If two or more owners, but not incorporated—a *partnership*.
	If the business issues stock to stockholders—a *corporation*.
What to account for?	Account for the business, a separate entity apart from its owner *(entity concept)*.
	Account for transactions and events that affect the business and can be measured objectively *(reliability principle)*.
How much to record for assets and liabilities?	Actual historical amount *(cost principle)*.
How to organize the various effects of a transaction?	The accounting equation: Assets = Liabilities + Owner's Equity
How to measure profits and losses?	Income statement: Revenues − Expenses = Net Income (or Net Loss)
Did owner's equity increase or decrease?	Statement of owner's equity: Beginning capital + Owner investments + Net income (or − Net loss) − Owner withdrawals = Ending capital
Where does the business stand financially?	Balance sheet (accounting equation): Assets = Liabilities + Owner's Equity
Where did the business's cash come from? Where did cash go?	Statement of cash flows *Operating activities* Net cash inflow (or outflow) + *Investing activities* Net cash inflow (or outflow) + *Financing activities* Net cash inflow (or outflow) = Net increase (decrease) in cash

REVIEW ACCOUNTING AND THE BUSINESS ENVIRONMENT

SUMMARY PROBLEM

Jill Smith opens an apartment-location business near a college campus. She is the sole owner of the proprietorship, which she names Campus Apartment Locators. During the first month of operations, July 20X1, she engages in the following transactions:

a. Smith invests $35,000 of personal funds to start the business.
b. She purchases on account office supplies costing $350.
c. Smith pays cash of $30,000 to acquire a lot next to the campus. She intends to use the land as a future building site for her business office.
d. Smith locates apartments for clients and receives cash of $1,900.
e. She pays $100 on the account payable she created in transaction (b).
f. She pays $2,000 of personal funds for a vacation.
g. She pays cash expenses for office rent, $400, and utilities, $100.
h. The business sells office supplies to another business for its cost of $150.
i. Smith withdraws cash of $1,200 for personal use.

www.prenhall.com/horngren
End-of-Chapter Assessment

21

Required

1. Analyze the preceding transactions in terms of their effects on the accounting equation of Campus Apartment Locators. Use Exhibit 1-6 as a guide, but show balances only after the last transaction.
2. Prepare the income statement, statement of owner's equity, and balance sheet of the business after recording the transactions. Use Exhibit 1-7 as a guide.

Solution

Requirement 1

PANEL A—Details of transactions

(a) Smith invested $35,000 cash to start the business.
(b) Purchased $350 of office supplies on account.
(c) Paid $30,000 to acquire land as a future building site.
(d) Earned service revenue and received cash of $1,900.
(e) Paid $100 on account.
(f) Paid for a personal vacation, which is not a transaction of the business.
(g) Paid cash expenses for rent, $400, and utilities, $100.
(h) Sold office supplies for cost of $150.
(i) Withdrew $1,200 cash for personal use.

PANEL B—Analysis of transactions:

	Cash	+	Office Supplies	+	Land	=	Accounts Payable	+	Jill Smith, Capital	Type of Owner's Equity Transaction
(a)	+35,000								+35,000	*Owner investment*
(b)			+350				+350			
(c)	−30,000				+30,000					
(d)	+ 1,900								+ 1,900	*Service revenue*
(e)	− 100						−100			
(f)	Not a transaction of the business									
(g)	− 400								− 400	*Rent expense*
	− 100								− 100	*Utilities expense*
(h)	+ 150		−150							
(i)	− 1,200								− 1,200	*Owner withdrawal*
Bal.	5,250		200		30,000		250		35,200	

Assets = 35,450

Liabilities + Owner's Equity = 35,450

Requirement 2   **Financial Statements of Campus Apartment Locators**

CAMPUS APARTMENT LOCATORS
Income Statement
Month Ended July 31, 20X1

Revenue:		
Service revenue...............		$1,900
Expenses:		
Rent expense...................	$400	
Utilities expense	100	
Total expenses		500
Net income.........................		$1,400

CAMPUS APARTMENT LOCATORS
Statement of Owner's Equity
Month Ended July 31, 20X1

Jill Smith, capital, July 1, 20X1	$	0
Add: Investment by owner		35,000
Net income for the month		1,400
		36,400
Less: Withdrawals by owner		(1,200)
Jill Smith, capital, July 31, 20X1		$35,200

CAMPUS APARTMENT LOCATORS
Balance Sheet
July 31, 20X1

Assets		Liabilities	
Cash	$ 5,250	Accounts payable	$ 250
Office supplies	200	**Owner's Equity**	
Land	30,000	Jill Smith, capital	35,200
		Total liabilities and	
Total assets	$35,450	owner's equity	$35,450

LESSONS LEARNED

1. *Use accounting vocabulary.* Accounting is an information system for measuring, processing, and communicating financial information. As the "language of business," accounting helps a wide range of decision makers.

2. *Apply accounting concepts and principles to analyze business situations.* Generally accepted accounting principles (GAAP) guide accountants in their work. Accountants use the entity concept to keep the business's records separate from other economic units. Other important guidelines are the *reliability principle,* the *cost principle,* the *going-concern concept,* and the *stable-monetary-unit concept.*

3. *Use the accounting equation to describe an organization's financial position.* In its most common form, the accounting equation is

   Assets = Liabilities + Owner's Equity

4. *Use the accounting equation to analyze business transactions.* A transaction is any event that both affects the financial position of a business entity and can be reliably recorded. Transactions affect a business's assets, liabilities, and owner's equity.

5. *Prepare and use the financial statements.* The *financial statements* communicate information for decision making by an entity's managers, owners, and creditors and by government agencies. The *income statement* summarizes the entity's operations in terms of revenues earned and expenses incurred during a specific period. The *statement of owner's equity* reports the changes in owner's equity during the period. The *balance sheet* lists the entity's assets, liabilities, and owner's equity at a specific time. The *statement of cash flows* reports the cash receipts and the cash payments during the period.

6. *Evaluate the performance of a business.* High net income indicates success in business; net loss indicates a bad business year.

ACCOUNTING VOCABULARY

Accounting has a special vocabulary and it is important that you understand the following terms. They are explained in the chapter and also in the glossary at the end of the book.

account payable (p. 12)
account receivable (p. 12)
accounting (p. 5)
accounting equation (p. 11)
asset (p. 11)
balance sheet (p. 17)
capital (p. 11)
certified management accountant (CMA) (p. 7)
certified public accountant (CPA) (p. 7)
corporation (p. 9)

entity (p. 10)
expense (p. 12)
financial accounting (p. 6)
Financial Accounting Standards Board (FASB) (p. 7)
financial statements (p. 5)
generally accepted accounting principles (GAAP) (p. 9)
income statement (p. 17)
liability (p. 11)
management accounting (p. 7)
net earnings (p. 15)

net income (p. 15)
net loss (p. 15)
net profit (p. 15)
note payable (p. 12)
note receivable (p. 12)
owner's equity (p. 11)
owner withdrawals (p. 12)
partnership (p. 9)
proprietorship (p. 8)
revenue (p. 12)
shareholder (p. 9)
statement of cash flows (p. 17)

QUESTIONS

1. Distinguish between accounting and bookkeeping.
2. Identify five users of accounting information, and explain how they use it.
3. What organization formulates generally accepted accounting principles? Is this organization a government agency?
4. Why are ethical standards important in accounting? Which organization directs its standards toward independent auditors? Which organization directs its standards more toward management accountants?
5. Why is the entity concept so important to accounting?
6. Briefly describe the reliability principle.
7. What role does the cost principle play in accounting?
8. If *assets = liabilities + owner's equity,* then how can liabilities be expressed?
9. Explain the difference between an account receivable and an account payable.

10. Give a more descriptive title for the balance sheet. What feature of the balance sheet gives this financial statement its name?
11. Give another title for the income statement. Which financial statement is like a snapshot of the entity at a specific time? Which financial statement is like a video of the entity's operations during a period of time?
12. What information does the statement of owner's equity report?
13. Give a synonym for the owner's equity of a proprietorship.
14. What piece of information flows from the income statement to the statement of owner's equity? What information flows from the statement of owner's equity to the balance sheet? What balance sheet item is explained by the statement of cash flows?

ASSESS YOUR PROGRESS

DAILY EXERCISES

Applying accounting concepts and principles
(Obj. 2)

DE1-1 Suppose you are starting a business, Montvale Delivery Service, that will provide delivery services for law firms in your city. In organizing the business and setting up its accounting records, consider the following:

1. In keeping the books of the business, you must decide the amount to record for assets purchased and liabilities incurred. At what amount should you record assets and liabilities? Which accounting concept or principle provides guidance?
2. Should you account for your personal assets and personal liabilities along with the assets and the liabilities of the business, or should you keep the two sets of records separate? Why? Which accounting concept or principle provides guidance?

Explaining assets, liabilities, owner's equity
(Obj. 1)

DE1-2 Shortly after starting Gifts for You, you realize the need for a bank loan in order to purchase office equipment. In evaluating your loan request, the banker asks about the assets and liabilities of your business. In particular, he wants to know the amount of your owner's equity. In your own words, explain the differences among *assets, liabilities,* and *owner's equity.* Give the mathematical relationship among assets, liabilities, and owner's equity.

Explaining revenues, expenses
(Obj. 1)

DE1-3 Gay Gillen eTravel has been open for one year, and Gillen wants to know the amount of the business's profit (net income) or net loss for the year. First, she must identify the revenues earned and the expenses incurred during the year. What are *revenues* and *expenses?* How do revenues and expenses enter into the determination of net income or net loss? Review the definitions on page 12 and Exhibit 1-7 on page 20.

Using the accounting equation
(Obj. 3)

DE1-4 You begin Montvale Delivery Service by investing $2,000 of your own money in a business bank account. Before starting operations, you borrow $8,000 cash by signing a note payable to Summit Bank. Write the business's accounting equation (page 12) after completing these transactions.

Using the accounting equation
(Obj. 3)

DE1-5 Brenda Trujillo owns Town East Travel, near the campus of Birmingham College. The business has cash of $5,000 and furniture that cost $12,000. Debts include accounts payable of $1,000 and a $6,000 note payable. How much equity does Trujillo have in the business? Using Trujillo's figures, write the accounting equation (page 11) of the travel agency.

Analyzing transactions
(Obj. 4)

DE1-6 Review transaction 2 of Gay Gillen eTravel, on page 13. In that transaction, Gillen's business purchased land for $20,000. To buy the land, Gillen was obligated to pay for it. Why, then, did she record no liability in this transaction?

Analyzing transactions
(Obj. 4)

DE1-7 Study Gay Gillen's transaction 4 on page 14. Gillen recorded revenues she earned from providing travel planning services for clients. Suppose the amount of revenue earned in transaction 4 was $3,500 instead of $5,500. How much are the business's cash and total assets after the transaction? How much is Gay Gillen, Capital?

DE1-8 Review transaction 9 of Gay Gillen eTravel, on page 16. Gillen collected cash from a client for whom she had provided travel services earlier. Why did the travel agency not record any revenue in transaction 9?

Analyzing transactions (Obj. 4)

DE1-9 Return to Gay Gillen's first business transaction on page 13. Gillen deposited $30,000 in a business bank account to start her company (assume Gillen started on April 2, 20X1). Prepare the travel agency's balance sheet on April 2, 20X1, immediately after the first transaction. The figures are given on page 13, and Exhibit 1-7 (page 20), shows the format of the balance sheet.

Preparing a balance sheet (Obj. 5)

Note: This exercise shows that financial statements can be prepared at any time. Usually, however, they are prepared at the end of the accounting period.

DE1-10 Examine Exhibit 1-6 on page 18. The exhibit summarizes the transactions of Gay Gillen eTravel for the month of April 20X1. Suppose Gillen has completed only the first seven transactions and needs a bank loan on April 21, 20X1. The vice president of the bank requires financial statements to support all loan requests.

Preparing the financial statements (Obj. 5)

Prepare the income statement, statement of owner's equity, and balance sheet that Gay Gillen would present to the banker after completing the first seven transactions on April 21, 20X1. Exhibit 1-7, page 20, shows the format of these financial statements.

DE1-11 Gay Gillen wishes to know how well her business performed during April. The income statement in Exhibit 1-7, page 20, helps answer this question. Write the formula for the income statement as an equation: $X - Y = Z$. What are X, Y, and Z?

Format of the income statement (Obj. 5)

DE1-12 Examine Exhibit 1-7 on page 20. The exhibit gives the financial statements of Gay Gillen eTravel at the end of the company's first month of operations. Focus on the arrows that show the flow of information from statement to statement, and then answer these questions:

Using the financial statements (Obj. 5)

1. Which statement measures net income or net loss? Into which other statement does net income flow? That is, where is net income's final resting place in the financial statements?
2. Which statement lists the assets, liabilities, and owner's equity of the business? Which of these elements is most directly affected by net income?

DE1-13 Return to Exhibit 1-7 on page 20, which gives the financial statements of Gay Gillen eTravel, at April 30, 20X1. Suppose Gay Gillen's travel agency paid Salary Expense of $2,500 for April instead of the actual amount of $1,200.

Evaluating performance (Obj. 6)

1. What would be the amount of the business's net income or net loss for April?
2. What would be the amount of Gay Gillen's capital at April 30?
3. What would be the ending amount of cash at April 30?

DE1-14 Exhibit 1-7, page 20, gives the statement of cash flows of Gay Gillen eTravel for the month of April. Study the exhibit and answer these questions to solidify your understanding of the accounting process and the financial statements:

Using the statement of cash flows (Obj. 5)

1. The statement of cash flows is organized in terms of three categories of *activities*. What are the three main categories of cash-flow activities?
2. Why do you think collections from customers is an operating activity? Why is the acquisition of land an investing activity? Why is the business's receipt of cash from the investment by the owner a financing activity? Answer in your own words.
3. How does the statement of cash flows relate to the balance sheet?

DE1-15 Montvale Delivery Service has just completed operations for the year ended December 31, 20X3. This is the third year of operations for the company. As the proprietor, you want to know how well the business performed during the year. You also wonder where the business stands financially at the end of the year. To address these questions, you have assembled the following data:

Preparing the income statement (Obj. 5)

Salary expense	$32,000	Insurance expense	$ 4,000
Accounts payable	8,000	Service revenue	101,000
Owner, capital,		Accounts receivable	17,000
December 31, 20X2	13,000	Supplies expense	1,000
Supplies	2,000	Cash	16,000
Withdrawals by owner	36,000	Fuel expense	6,000
Rent expense	8,000		

Prepare the income statement of Montvale Delivery Service for the year ended December 31, 20X3. Follow the format shown in Exhibit 1-7, page 20.

DE1-16 Use the data in Daily Exercise 1-15 to prepare the statement of owner's equity of Montvale Delivery Service for the year ended December 31, 20X3. Follow the format in Exhibit 1-7. Compute net income from the data in Daily Exercise 1-15.

Preparing the statement of owner's equity (Obj. 5)

DE1-17 Use the data in Daily Exercise 1-15 to prepare the balance sheet of Montvale Delivery Service at December 31, 20X3. The year-end balance sheet will show where the business stands financially at the end of the year. Follow the format in Exhibit 1-7. Owner's equity (Owner, capital) at December 31, 20X3, is $27,000.

Preparing the balance sheet (Obj. 5)

Note: Daily Exercise 1-18 should be used in conjunction with Daily Exercises 1-15, 1-16, and 1-17.

Evaluating performance
(Obj. 6)

DE1-18 Review the Montvale Delivery Service financial statements that you prepared for Daily Exercises 1-15, 1-16, and 1-17. Use the statements to evaluate the business's performance by answering these questions:

1. The income statement gives the results of operations. Did the business earn a profit or suffer a loss? The owner had hoped to earn at least $40,000. Will he be pleased or disappointed?
2. The statement of owner's equity reveals whether the owner's capital increased or decreased during the year—and why. Did Montvale Delivery Service's equity increase or decrease? Is this a good sign or a bad sign about the company? State your reason.
3. The balance sheet reports the financial position of the business. Which are greater, total assets or total liabilities? By how much? What is the name of the difference between assets and liabilities? Is the financial position of Montvale Delivery Service strong or weak? Give your reason.

EXERCISES

Explaining the income statement and the balance sheet
(Obj. 1)

E1-1 Lisa Malesovas publishes a travel magazine. In need of cash, she asks Community Bank & Trust for a loan. The bank's procedures require borrowers to submit financial statements to show likely results of operations for the first year and likely financial position at the end of the first year. With little knowledge of accounting, Malesovas doesn't know how to proceed. Explain to her the information provided by the balance sheet and the income statement. Indicate why a lender would require this information.

Business transactions
(Obj. 2)

E1-2 For each of the following items, give an example of a business transaction that has the described effect on the accounting equation:

a. Increase an asset and increase a liability.
b. Increase one asset and decrease another asset.
c. Decrease an asset and decrease owner's equity.
d. Decrease an asset and decrease a liability.
e. Increase an asset and increase owner's equity.

Transaction analysis
(Obj. 2)

E1-3 Sterling Design, a proprietorship (Eric Sterling, owner), experienced the following events. State whether each event (1) increased, (2) decreased, or (3) had no effect on the total assets of the business. Identify any specific asset affected.

a. Sterling Design received a cash investment from the owner.
b. Cash purchase of land for a building site.
c. Paid cash on accounts payable.
d. Purchased machinery and equipment for a manufacturing plant; signed a promissory note in payment.
e. Performed service for a customer on account.
f. Sterling withdrew cash from the business for personal use.
g. Received cash from a customer on account receivable.
h. Sterling used personal funds to purchase a swimming pool for his home.
i. Sold land for a price equal to the cost of the land; received cash.
j. Borrowed money from the bank.

Accounting equation
(Obj. 3)

E1-4 Compute the missing amount in the accounting equation for each entity:

	Assets	Liabilities	Owner's Equity
Company A	$?	$61,800	$34,400
Company B	65,900	?	34,000
Company C	81,700	79,800	?

Accounting equation
(Obj. 4, 5)

E1-5 Oracle Corporation started 19X9 with total assets of $5,819 million and total liabilities of $2,861 million. At the end of 19X9, Oracle's total assets stood at $7,260 million, and total liabilities were $3,565 million.

Required

1. Did the owners' equity of Oracle Corporation increase or decrease during 19X9? By how much?
2. Identify two possible reasons for the change in owners' equity of Oracle during the year.

E1-6 Telemarketing Associates' balance sheet data at May 31, 20X2, and June 30, 20X2, follow:

Accounting equation (Obj. 4, 5)

	May 31, 20X2	June 30, 20X2
Total assets	$150,000	$195,000
Total liabilities	109,000	131,000

Required

Following are three assumptions about investments and withdrawals by the owner of the business during June. For each assumption, compute the amount of net income or net loss of the business during June 20X2.

1. The owner invested $5,000 in the business and made no withdrawals.
2. The owner made no additional investments in the business but withdrew $11,000 for personal use.
3. The owner invested $41,000 in the business and withdrew $6,000 for personal use.

E1-7 Indicate the effects of the following business transactions on the accounting equation. Transaction (a) is answered as a guide.

Transaction analysis (Obj. 4)

a. Received cash of $18,000 from the owner, who was investing in the business.
   Answer: Increase asset (Cash)
              Increase owner's equity (Capital)
b. Paid $700 cash to purchase office supplies.
c. Performed legal service for a client on account, $3,000.
d. Purchased on account office furniture at a cost of $500.
e. Received cash on account, $900.
f. Paid cash on account, $250.
g. Sold land for $12,000, which was our cost of the land.
h. Performed legal service for a client and received cash of $680.
i. Paid monthly office rent of $500.

E1-8 Lance Huber opens a medical practice. During the first month of operation, May, the business, entitled Lance Huber, M.D., experienced the following events.

Transaction analysis; accounting equation (Obj. 2, 4)

May 6	Huber invested $90,000 in the business by opening a bank account in the name of Lance Huber, M.D.
9	Huber paid $55,000 cash for land. He plans to build an office building on the land.
12	He purchased medical supplies for $2,000 on account.
15	Huber officially opened for business.
15–31	During the rest of the month, he treated patients and earned service revenue of $7,000, receiving cash.
15–31	He paid cash expenses: employees' salaries, $1,400; office rent, $1,000; utilities, $300.
28	He sold supplies to another physician for the cost of those supplies, $500.
31	He paid $1,500 on account.

Required

Analyze the effects of these events on the accounting equation of the medical practice of Lance Huber, M.D. Use a format similar to that of Exhibit 1-6, with headings for Cash; Medical Supplies; Land; Accounts Payable; and Lance Huber, Capital.

E1-9 The analysis of the transactions that Sinclair Leasing completed during its first month of operations follows. The company buys equipment that it leases out to earn revenue. The owner of the business made only one investment to start the business and no withdrawals.

Business organization, transactions, and net income (Obj. 1, 2, 3, 4)

	Cash	+	Accounts Receivable	+	Lease Equipment	=	Accounts Payable	+	Owner Capital
(a)	+50,000								+50,000
(b)	− 750				+ 750				
(c)					+100,000		+100,000		
(d)			+800						+ 800
(e)	− 2,000								− 2,000
(f)	+ 6,600								+ 6,600
(g)	−10,000						− 10,000		
(h)	+ 150		−150						

Required

1. Describe each transaction of Sinclair Leasing.
2. If these transactions fully describe the operations of Sinclair Leasing during the month, what was the amount of net income or net loss?

Business organization, balance sheet
(Obj. 1, 2, 5)

E1-10 The balances of the assets and liabilities of TELETAX as of September 30, 20X2, follow. Also included are the revenue and expense figures of this tax-preparation business for September.

Delivery service revenue	$9,100	Office equipment	$15,500
Accounts receivable	6,900	Supplies	600
Accounts payable	1,750	Note payable	8,000
M. Dalton, capital	?	Rent expense	500
Salary expense	2,000	Cash	950

Required

1. What type of business organization is TELETAX? How can you tell?
2. Prepare the balance sheet of TELETAX as of September 30, 20X2.
3. What does the balance sheet report—financial position or operating results? Which financial statement reports the other information?

Income statement
(Obj. 2, 5)

E1-11 The assets, liabilities, owner's equity, revenues, and expenses of Venecor Import Service at December 31, 20X3, the end of its first year of business, have the following balances. During the year, T. Venecor, the owner, invested $15,000 in the business.

Office furniture	$ 45,000	Note payable	$30,000
Utilities expense	6,800	Rent expense	24,000
Accounts payable	3,300	Cash	3,600
T. Venecor, capital	27,100	Office supplies	4,800
Service revenue	161,200	Salary expense	49,000
Accounts receivable	9,000	Salaries payable	2,000
Supplies expense	4,000	Property tax expense	1,200

Required

1. Prepare the income statement of Venecor Import Service for the year ended December 31, 20X3. What is the result of Venecor's operations for 20X3?
2. What was the amount of the proprietor's withdrawals during the year?

Evaluating the performance of a real company
(Obj. 6)

E1-12 In this exercise you will practice using the actual data of a well-known company. The 19X9 annual report of **Toys "Я" Us** reported net sales revenue of $11,170 million. Total expenses for the year were $11,302 million. Toys "Я" Us ended the year with total assets of $7,899 million, and the company owed debts totaling $4,275 million at year end.

During the preceding year, 19X8, Toys "Я" Us earned net income of $490 million. At year-end 19X8, Toys "Я" Us reported total assets of $7,963 million and total liabilities of $3,535 million.

Required

1. Compute Toys "Я" Us's net income for 19X9. Did net income increase or decrease from 19X8 to 19X9, and by how much?
2. Did Toys "Я" Us's owners' equity increase or decrease during 19X9? By how much?
3. Toys "Я" Us management strives for a steady increase in net income and owners' equity. How would you rate Toys "Я" Us's performance for 19X9—excellent, fair, or poor? Give your reason.

Preparing a statement of cash flows
(Obj. 5)

E1-13 During 19X8, **Lands' End, Inc.**, the catalog merchant located in Dodgeville, Wisconsin, experienced the following cash flows (adapted):

	Millions
Collections from customers	$1,257
Payments to suppliers and employees	1,284
Purchases of assets	35
Dividend payments to owners (same as withdrawals by owner)	10
Cash balance, beginning of year	93

Required

Prepare the statement of cash flows of Lands' End, Inc., for the year. Follow the format of the statement of cash flows in Exhibit 1-7, page 20.

CHALLENGE EXERCISE

E1-14 Compute the missing amounts for each of the following companies. For each company, you will need to prepare a statement of owner's equity.

Using the financial statements (Obj. 5)

	Circle Co.	Triangle Co.	Square Co.
Beginning:			
Assets	$105,000	$ 50,000	$110,000
Liabilities	50,000	20,000	60,000
Ending:			
Assets	$160,000	$ 70,000	$?
Liabilities	70,000	35,000	80,000
Owner's Equity:			
Investments by owner	$?	$ 0	$ 10,000
Withdrawals by owner	100,000	40,000	70,000
Income Statement:			
Revenues	$430,000	$230,000	$400,000
Expenses	320,000	?	300,000

PROBLEMS

(Group A)

P1-1A Blake Dubis practiced law with a partnership for five years after graduating from law school. Recently he resigned his position to open his own law office, which he operates as a proprietorship. The name of the new entity is Blake Dubis, Attorney. Dubis experienced the following events during the organizing phase of his new business and its first month of operations. Some of the events were personal and did not affect his law practice. Others were business transactions and should be accounted for by the business.

Entity concept, transaction analysis, accounting equation (Obj. 2, 4)

Feb. 4	Dubis received $90,000 cash from his former law-firm partners.
5	Dubis deposited $80,000 cash in a new business bank account entitled Blake Dubis, Attorney.
6	Dubis paid $300 cash for letterhead stationery for his new law office.
7	Dubis purchased office furniture for his law office. He agreed to pay the account payable, $7,000, within six months.
10	Dubis sold 500 shares of IBM stock, which he and his wife had owned for several years, receiving $75,000 cash from his stockbroker.
11	Dubis deposited the $75,000 cash from sale of the IBM stock in his personal bank account.
12	A representative of a large company telephoned Dubis and told him of the company's intention to transfer its legal business to the new entity of Blake Dubis, Attorney.
18	Dubis finished court hearings on behalf of a client and submitted his bill for legal services, $5,000. Dubis expected to collect from this client within two weeks.
25	Dubis paid office rent, $1,000.
28	Dubis withdrew $1,000 cash from the business for personal living expenses.

Required

1. Classify each of these events as one of the following:
   a. A business transaction to be accounted for by the proprietorship of Blake Dubis, Attorney.
   b. A business-related event but not a transaction to be accounted for by the proprietorship of Blake Dubis, Attorney.
   c. A personal transaction not to be accounted for by the proprietorship of Blake Dubis, Attorney.
2. Analyze the effects of the above events on the accounting equation of the proprietorship of Blake Dubis, Attorney. Use a format similar to that in Exhibit 1-6.

P1-2A The bookkeeper of Trésoro Publishing Co. prepared the company's balance sheet while the accountant was ill. The balance sheet contains numerous errors. In particular, the bookkeeper knew that the balance sheet should balance, so he plugged in the owner's equity amount needed to achieve this balance. The owner's equity amount, however, is not correct. All other amounts are accurate, but some are out of place.

Balance sheet (Obj. 2, 5)

TRÉSORO PUBLISHING CO.
Balance Sheet
Month Ended July 31, 20X3

Assets		Liabilities	
Cash.................................	$12,000	Accounts receivable	$ 3,000
Office supplies	1,000	Service revenue	68,000
Land	44,000	Property tax expense	800
Salary expense................	2,500	Accounts payable	9,000
Office furniture..............	8,000		
Note payable..................	16,000	**Owner's Equity**	
Rent expense..................	4,000	Owner's equity.........................	6,700
Total assets.....................	$87,500	Total liabilities	$87,500

Required

1. Prepare the correct balance sheet, and date it correctly. Compute total assets, total liabilities, and owner's equity.
2. Identify the accounts that should *not* be presented on the balance sheet and state why you excluded them from the correct balance sheet you prepared for requirement 1.

Balance sheet, entity concept (Obj. 2, 3, 5)

P1-3A Olivia Casinelli is a realtor. She buys and sells properties on her own, and she also earns commissions as a real estate agent for buyers and sellers. She organized her business as a proprietorship on November 24, 20X4. Consider the following facts as of November 30, 20X4.

a. Casinelli owed $55,000 on a note payable for some undeveloped land that had been acquired by her business for a total price of $100,000.
b. Casinelli's business had spent $20,000 for a Century 21 real estate franchise, which entitled her to represent herself as a Century 21 agent. Century 21 is a national affiliation of independent real estate agents. This franchise is a business asset.
c. Casinelli owed $60,000 on a personal mortgage on her personal residence, which she acquired in 20X1 for a total price of $150,000.
d. Casinelli had $8,000 in her personal bank account and $22,000 in her business bank account.
e. Casinelli owed $1,800 on a personal charge account with the Neiman-Marcus store.
f. Casinelli acquired business furniture for $17,000 on November 25. Of this amount, her business owed $6,000 on open account at November 30.
g. Office supplies on hand at the real estate office totaled $1,000.
   (1) Prepare the balance sheet of the real estate business of Olivia Casinelli, Realtor, at November 30, 20X4.
   (2) Identify the personal items that would not be reported on the balance sheet of the business.

Business transactions and analysis (Obj. 4)

P1-4A Mandarin Enterprises was recently formed. The balance of each item in the company's accounting equation is shown for October 10 and for each of the nine following business days.

	Cash	Accounts Receivable	Supplies	Land	Accounts Payable	Owner's Equity
Oct. 10	$ 4,000	$4,000	$1,000	$ 8,000	$4,000	$13,000
11	13,000	4,000	1,000	8,000	4,000	22,000
12	6,000	4,000	1,000	15,000	4,000	22,000
15	6,000	4,000	3,000	15,000	6,000	22,000
16	5,000	4,000	3,000	15,000	5,000	22,000
17	7,000	2,000	3,000	15,000	5,000	22,000
18	15,000	2,000	3,000	15,000	5,000	30,000
19	12,000	2,000	3,000	15,000	2,000	30,000
22	11,000	2,000	4,000	15,000	2,000	30,000
23	3,000	2,000	4,000	15,000	2,000	22,000

Required

Assuming that a single transaction took place on each day, briefly describe the transaction that most likely occurred on each day, beginning with October 11. Indicate which accounts were increased or decreased and by what amount. No revenue or expense transactions occurred on these dates.

Income statement, statement of owner's equity, balance sheet (Obj. 5)

P1-5A Presented below are (a) the assets and liabilities of Starmate Talent Search as of December 31, and (b) the revenues and expenses of the company for the year ended on that date. The items are listed in alphabetical order.

Accounts payable	$ 19,000	Land	$ 60,000
Accounts receivable	12,000	Note payable	85,000
Advertising expense	13,000	Property tax expense	4,000
Building	170,000	Rent expense	23,000
Cash	14,000	Salary expense	63,000
Equipment	20,000	Salary payable	1,000
Insurance expense	2,000	Service revenue	178,000
Interest expense	9,000	Supplies	3,000

The owner's beginning balance, Brian Sartor, Capital, was $150,000, and during the year Sartor withdrew $40,000 for personal use.

Required

1. Prepare Starmate's income statement for the year ended December 31 of the current year.
2. Prepare the company's statement of owner's equity for the year ended December 31.
3. Prepare the company's balance sheet at December 31.
4. Answer these questions about the company:
   a. Was the result of operations for the year a profit or a loss? How much?
   b. Did Sartor drain off all the earnings for the year, or did he build the company's capital during the period? How will his actions affect the company's ability to borrow in the future?
   c. How much in total economic resources does the company have as it moves into the new year? How much does the company owe? What is the dollar amount of Sartor's equity interest in the business at the end of the year?

Transaction analysis, accounting equation, financial statements (Obj. 4, 5)

P1-6A Helen Ingersoll owns and operates an interior design studio called Ingersoll Interiors. The following amounts summarize the financial position of her business on August 31, 20X2:

	Assets				=	Liabilities	+	Owner's Equity
	Cash +	Accounts Receivable +	Supplies +	Land	=	Accounts Payable	+	Helen Ingersoll, Capital
Bal.	2,250	1,500		12,000		8,000		7,750

During September 20X2, the following events occurred.

a. Ingersoll inherited $20,000 and deposited the cash in the business bank account.
b. Performed services for a client and received cash of $700.
c. Paid off the beginning balance of accounts payable.
d. Purchased supplies on account, $1,000.
e. Collected cash from a customer on account, $1,000.
f. Invested personal cash of $1,000 in the business.
g. Consulted on the interior design of a major office building and billed the client for services rendered, $2,400.
h. Recorded the following business expenses for the month:
   (1) Paid office rent, $900.
   (2) Paid advertising, $100.
i. Sold supplies to another business for $150 cash, which was the cost of the supplies.
j. Withdrew cash of $1,100 for personal use.

Required

1. Analyze the effects of the preceding transactions on the accounting equation of Ingersoll Interiors. Adapt the format of Exhibit 1-6.
2. Prepare the income statement of Ingersoll Interiors for the month ended September 30, 20X2. List expenses in decreasing order by amount.
3. Prepare the entity's statement of owner's equity for the month ended September 30, 20X2.
4. Prepare the balance sheet of Ingersoll Interiors at September 30, 20X2.

Entity concept, transaction
analysis, accounting equation
(Obj. 2, 4)

P1-1B Sharon Marsh practiced law with a partnership for ten years after graduating from law school. Recently she resigned her position to open her own law office, which she operates as a proprietorship. The name of the new entity is Sharon Marsh, Attorney. Marsh experienced the following events during the organizing phase of her new business and its first month of operation. Some of the events were personal and did not affect the law practice. Others were business transactions and should be accounted for by the business.

July 1	Marsh sold 1,000 shares of Eastman Kodak stock, which she had owned for several years, receiving $68,000 cash from her stockbroker.
2	Marsh deposited the $68,000 cash from sale of the Eastman Kodak stock in her personal bank account.
3	Marsh received $170,000 cash from her former law-firm partners.
5	Marsh deposited $100,000 cash in a new business bank account entitled Sharon Marsh, Attorney.
6	A representative of a large company telephoned Marsh and told her of the company's intention to transfer its legal business to the new entity of Sharon Marsh, Attorney.
7	Marsh paid $450 cash for letterhead stationery for her new law office.
9	Marsh purchased office furniture for the law office, agreeing to pay the account payable, $9,500, within three months.
23	Marsh finished court hearings on behalf of a client and submitted her bill for legal services, $3,000. She expected to collect from this client within one month.
30	Marsh paid office rent, $1,900.
31	Marsh withdrew $5,500 cash from the business for personal living expenses.

Required

1. Classify each of these events as one of the following:
   a. A business transaction to be accounted for by the proprietorship of Sharon Marsh, Attorney.
   b. A business-related event but not a transaction to be accounted for by the proprietorship of Sharon Marsh, Attorney.
   c. A personal transaction not to be accounted for by the proprietorship of Sharon Marsh, Attorney.

2. Analyze the effects of the preceding events on the accounting equation of the proprietorship of Sharon Marsh, Attorney. Use a format similar to Exhibit 1-6.

P1-2B The bookkeeper of Haynes Editorial Service prepared the balance sheet of the company while the accountant was ill. The balance sheet contains numerous errors. In particular, the bookkeeper knew that the balance sheet should balance, so he plugged in the owner's equity amount to achieve this balance. The owner's equity amount, however, is not correct. All other amounts are accurate, but some are out of place.

HAYNES EDITORIAL SERVICE
Balance Sheet
Month Ended October 31, 20X7

Assets		Liabilities	
Cash	$ 5,400	Notes receivable	$14,000
Insurance expense	300	Interest expense	2,000
Land	31,500	Office supplies	800
Salary expense	3,300	Accounts receivable	2,600
Office furniture	6,700	Note payable	21,000
Accounts payable	3,000		
Utilities expense	2,100	**Owner's Equity**	
		Owner's equity	11,900
Total assets	$52,300	Total liabilities	$52,300

Required

1. Prepare the correct balance sheet, and date it correctly. Compute total assets, total liabilities, and owner's equity.
2. Identify the accounts that should *not* be presented on the balance sheet and state why you excluded them from the correct balance sheet you prepared for requirement 1.

P1-3B Nik Tahari is a realtor. He buys and sells properties on his own, and he also earns commission as a real estate agent for buyers and sellers. He organized his business as a proprietorship on March 10, 20X2. Consider the following facts as of March 31, 20X2:

a. Tahari had $15,000 in his personal bank account and $7,000 in his business bank account.

b. Office supplies on hand at the real estate office totaled $1,000.

c. Tahari's business had spent $15,000 for an Electronic Realty Associates (ERA) franchise, which entitled Tahari to represent himself as an ERA agent. ERA is a national affiliation of independent real estate agents. This franchise is a business asset.

d. Tahari owed $34,000 on a note payable for some undeveloped land that had been acquired by his business for a total price of $60,000.

e. Tahari owed $65,000 on a personal mortgage on his personal residence, which he acquired in 20X1 for a total price of $90,000.

f. Tahari owed $950 on a personal charge account with Sears.

g. Tahari had acquired business furniture for $12,000 on March 26. Of this amount, Tahari's business owed $6,000 on open account at March 31.

Required

1. Prepare the balance sheet of the real estate business of Nik Tahari, Realtor, at March 31, 20X2.

2. Identify the personal items that would not be reported on the balance sheet of the business.

P1-4B Royal Gulf Oil Company was recently formed. The balance of each item in the company's accounting equation follows for April 4 and for each of the nine business days given:

Business transactions and analysis (Obj. 4)

	Cash	Accounts Receivable	Supplies	Land	Accounts Payable	Owner's Equity
Apr. 4	$2,000	$7,000	$ 800	$11,000	$3,800	$17,000
9	6,000	3,000	800	11,000	3,800	17,000
14	4,000	3,000	800	11,000	1,800	17,000
17	4,000	3,000	1,100	11,000	2,100	17,000
19	5,000	3,000	1,100	11,000	2,100	18,000
20	3,900	3,000	1,100	11,000	1,000	18,000
22	9,900	3,000	1,100	5,000	1,000	18,000
25	9,900	3,700	400	5,000	1,000	18,000
26	9,300	3,700	1,000	5,000	1,000	18,000
28	4,200	3,700	1,000	5,000	1,000	12,900

Required

Assuming that a single transaction took place on each day, describe briefly the transaction that most likely occurred on each day, beginning with April 9. Indicate which accounts were increased or decreased and by what amount. No revenue or expense transactions occurred on these dates.

P1-5B The amounts of (a) the assets and liabilities of Aspen Supply Co. as of December 31, 20X4, and (b) the revenues and expenses of the company for the year ended on that date follow. The items are listed in alphabetical order.

Income statement, statement of owner's equity, balance sheet (Obj. 5)

Accounts payable....................	$12,000	Note payable...........................	$ 31,000
Accounts receivable................	3,000	Property tax expense..............	2,000
Building.................................	56,000	Rent expense.........................	14,000
Cash......................................	7,000	Salary expense.......................	38,000
Equipment..............................	21,000	Service revenue.....................	108,000
Interest expense......................	4,000	Supplies.................................	7,000
Interest payable	1,000	Utilities expense	3,000
Land.......................................	8,000		

The owner's beginning balance, Linda Elkins, Capital, was $43,000, and during the year Elkins withdrew $32,000 for personal use.

Required

1. Prepare the income statement of Aspen Supply Co. for the year ended December 31, 20X4.

2. Prepare the company's statement of owner's equity for the year ended December 31, 20X4.

3. Prepare the company's balance sheet at December 31, 20X4.

4. Answer these questions about the company.
   a. Was the result of operations for the year a profit or a loss? How much?
   b. Did Elkins drain off all the earnings for the year, or did she build the company's capital during the period? How would her actions affect the company's ability to borrow in the future?

c. How much in total economic resources does the company have as it moves into the new year? How much does the company owe? What is the dollar amount of Elkins's equity interest in the business at the end of the year?

Transaction analysis, accounting equation, financial statements (Obj. 4, 5)

P1-6B Joel Clark owns and operates an interior design studio called Clark Design Studio. The following amounts summarize the financial position of his business on April 30, 20X5:

	Assets				= Liabilities +	Owner's Equity
	Cash +	Accounts Receivable +	Supplies +	Land =	Accounts Payable +	Joel Clark, Capital
Bal.	1,720	3,240		24,100	5,400	23,660

During May 20X5, the following events occurred.

a. Clark received $12,000 as a gift and deposited the cash in the business bank account.
b. Paid off the beginning balance of accounts payable.
c. Performed services for a client and received cash of $1,100.
d. Collected cash from a customer on account, $750.
e. Purchased supplies on account, $720.
f. Consulted on the interior design of a major office building and billed the client for services rendered, $5,000.
g. Invested personal cash of $1,700 in the business.
h. Recorded the following business expenses for the month:
  (1) Paid office rent, $1,200.
  (2) Paid advertising, $660.
i. Sold supplies to another interior designer for $80 cash, which was the cost of the supplies.
j. Withdrew cash of $1,400 for personal use.

Required

1. Analyze the effects of the preceding transactions on the accounting equation of Clark Design Studio. Adapt the format of Exhibit 1-6.
2. Prepare the income statement of Clark Design Studio for the month ended May 31, 20X5. List expenses in decreasing order by amount.
3. Prepare the statement of owner's equity of Clark Design Studio for the month ended May 31, 20X5.
4. Prepare the balance sheet of Clark Design Studio at May 31, 20X5.

APPLY YOUR KNOWLEDGE

DECISION CASES

Using financial statements to evaluate a request for a loan (Obj. 1, 2, 6)

Case 1. The proprietors of two businesses, L. L. Sams Company and Melinda Garcia Career Services, have sought business loans from you. To decide whether to make the loans, you have requested their balance sheets.

L. L. SAMS COMPANY
Balance Sheet
August 31, 20X4

Assets			Liabilities		
Cash	$	9,000	Accounts payable	$	12,000
Accounts receivable		14,000	Note payable		18,000
Merchandise inventory		85,000	Total liabilities		30,000
Store supplies		500			
Furniture and fixtures		9,000	**Owner's Equity**		
Building		80,000	L. L. Sams, capital		181,500
Land		14,000	Total liabilities		
Total assets		$211,500	and owner's equity		$211,500

```
                MELINDA GARCIA CAREER SERVICES
                         Balance Sheet
                        August 31, 20X4
```

Assets		Liabilities	
Cash...............................	$ 11,000	Accounts payable	$ 6,000
Accounts receivable...............	7,000	Note payable...........................	168,000
Office supplies	1,000	Total liabilities........................	174,000
Office furniture......................	56,000		
Land	169,000	**Owner's Equity**	
		Melinda Garcia, capital...........	70,000
		Total liabilities and	
Total assets............................	$244,000	owner's equity	$244,000

Required

1. Solely on the basis of these balance sheets, to which entity would you be more comfortable lending money? Explain fully, citing specific items and amounts from the balance sheets.
2. In addition to the balance sheet data, what other information would you require? Be specific.

Case 2. Camp Trinity conducts summer camps for children with disabilities. Samuel and Margaret Shields operate the camp near Leander, Texas. Because of the nature of its business, the camp experiences many unusual transactions. Evaluate each of the following transactions in terms of its effect on Camp Trinity's income statement and balance sheet.

Transaction analysis, effects on the financial statements (Obj. 4)

1. A camper suffered an injury that was not covered by insurance. Camp Trinity paid $900 for the child's medical care. How does this transaction affect the camp's income statement and balance sheet?
2. Camp Trinity sold land adjacent to the camp for $190,000, receiving cash of $70,000 and a note receivable for $120,000. When purchased five years earlier, the land cost Camp Trinity $100,000. How should the camp account for the sale of the land?
3. One camper's father is a physician. Camp Trinity allows this child to attend camp in return for the father's serving part-time in the camp infirmary for the two-week term. The standard fee for a camp term is $1,000. The physician's salary for this part-time work would be $1,000. How should Camp Trinity account for this arrangement?
4. A tornado damaged the camp dining hall. The cost to repair the damage will be $12,000 over and above what the insurance company will pay.

ETHICAL ISSUES

Ethical Issue 1. The chapter-opening story relates to the billions of dollars the tobacco companies have paid because of smoking-related illnesses. In particular, **Philip Morris,** a leading cigarette manufacturer, paid over $3 billion in 1998.

Required

1. Suppose you are the chief financial officer (CFO) responsible for the financial statements of Philip Morris. What ethical issue would you face as you consider what to report in your company's annual report about the cash payments? What is the ethical course of action for you to take in this situation?
2. What are some of the negative consequences to Philip Morris for not telling the truth? What are some of the negative consequences to Philip Morris for telling the truth?

Ethical Issue 2. The board of directors of Silvertron Corporation is meeting to discuss the past year's results before releasing financial statements to the public. The discussion includes this exchange: Amanda Blume, company president: "Well, this has not been a good year! Revenue is down and expenses are up—way up. If we don't do some fancy stepping, we'll report a loss for the third year in a row. I can temporarily transfer some land that I own into the company's name, and that will beef up our balance sheet. Kent, can you shave $500,000 from expenses? Then we can probably get the bank loan that we need."

Kent Kohler, company chief accountant: "Amanda, you are asking too much. Generally accepted accounting principles are designed to keep this sort of thing from happening."

Required

1. What is the fundamental ethical issue in this situation?
2. Discuss how Amanda Blume's proposals violate generally accepted accounting principles. Identify the specific concept or principle involved.

FINANCIAL STATEMENT CASE

Identifying items from a company's financial statements (Obj. 4)

This and similar cases in later chapters focus on the financial statements of a real company—**Target Corporation,** the upscale discount chain. As you work each problem, you will build your confidence in understanding and using the financial statements of real companies.

Refer to Target Corporation's financial statements in Appendix A at the end of the book.

Required

1. How much in cash (including cash equivalents) did Target Corporation have on January 29, 2000?
2. What were the company's total assets at January 29, 2000? At January 30, 1999?
3. Write the company's accounting equation at January 29, 2000, by filling in the dollar amounts:

ASSETS = LIABILITIES + STOCKHOLDERS' EQUITY

4. Identify total revenue for the year ended January 29, 2000 (fiscal year 1999). How much did total revenue increase or decrease in fiscal year 1999?
5. How much net income or net loss did Target experience for fiscal year 1999 and for fiscal year 1998? Was fiscal year 1999 a good year or a bad year compared to 1998? State your reasons.

TEAM PROJECTS

Project 1. You are opening a pet kennel. Your purpose is to earn a profit, so you will need to establish the business. Assume you organize as a proprietorship.

1. Make a detailed list of ten factors you must consider to establish the business.
2. Identify ten or more transactions that your business will undertake to open and operate the kennel.
3. Prepare the kennel's income statement, statement of owner's equity, and balance sheet at the end of the first month of operations before you have had time to pay all the business's bills. Use made-up figures and include a complete heading for each financial statement. Date the balance sheet as of August 31, 20XX.
4. Discuss how you will evaluate the success of your business and how you will decide whether to continue its operation.

Project 2. You are promoting a rock concert in your area. Your purpose is to earn a profit, so you will need to establish the business. Assume you organize as a proprietorship.

Required

1. Make a detailed list of ten factors you must consider to establish the business.
2. Describe ten of the items your business must arrange in order to promote and stage the rock concert.
3. Prepare your business's income statement, statement of owner's equity, and balance sheet on August 31, 20XX, immediately after the rock concert and before you have had time to pay all the business's bills and to collect all receivables. Use made-up amounts, and include a complete heading for each financial statement. For the income statement and the statement of owner's equity, assume the period is the three months ended August 31, 20XX.
4. Assume that you will continue to promote rock concerts if the venture is successful. If it is unsuccessful, you will terminate the business within three months after the concert. Discuss how you will evaluate the success of your venture and how you will decide whether to continue in business.

INTERNET EXERCISE

Hoover's Online, The Business Network offers information about companies, industries, people, and products. For researching a company, this site is a good place to start gathering basic information.

1. Go to **http://www.hoovers.com** and then use the "Search" scroll bar to select *Company*. In the next box type eBay and then click on *Go*. For **eBay Inc.** click on *Capsule*.
   a. Read the written description of the company and briefly summarize its contents.
   b. Review the other site information and comment on one item of interest.
2. Go to the top of the page and click on the *Financials* tab. Under "Free Financial Information" click on *Annual Financials*.

a. For the three most recent years, list the amounts reported for "Revenue" and "Total Net Income." Is eBay growing and expanding? Is eBay a profitable company?

b. For the most recent year, list amounts reported for "Total Assets," "Total Liabilities," and "Total (Owner's) Equity." Does the accounting equation hold true? Are assets primarily financed by debt or owner's equity?

3. Go to the top of the page and click on the *Company Capsule* tab. Click on the URL for eBay (www.ebay.com) and then click on *Browse* to explore the world's largest online marketplace. Comment on one item you found of interest.

Recording Business
Transactions

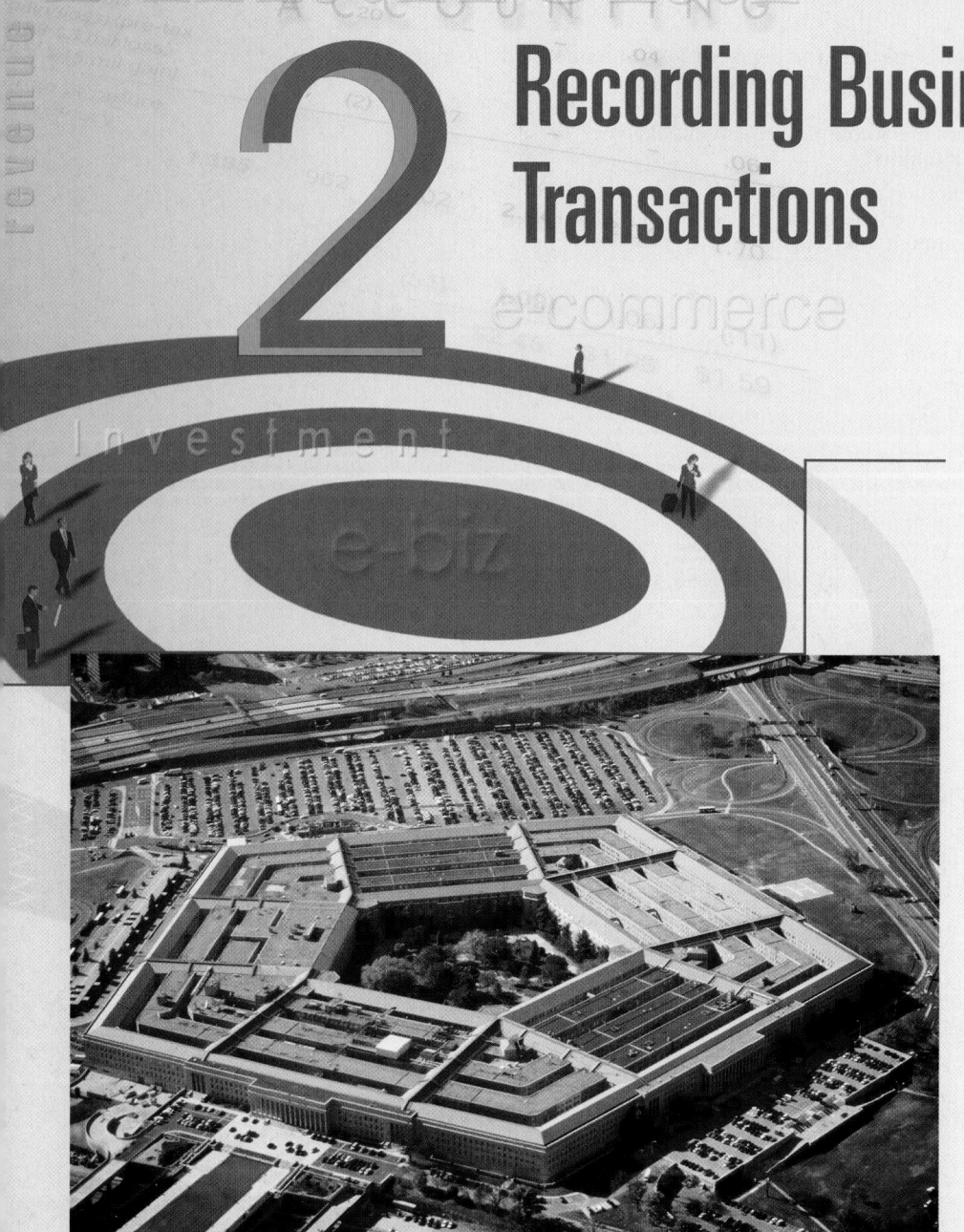

LEARNING OBJECTIVES

*After studying this chapter,
you should be able to*

1. Define and use key accounting terms

2. Apply the rules of debit and credit

3. Record transactions in the journal

4. Post from the journal to the ledger

5. Prepare and use a trial balance

6. Set up a chart of accounts for a business

7. Analyze transactions without a journal

www.prenhall.com/horngren
Readiness Assessment

Forget about e-retailers putting **Wal-Mart** out of business. Their task now is simply to stay alive. Time is running out because many e-retailers have yet to turn a profit. They are spending so much on advertising they may soon run out of cash. In fact, during the fourth quarter of 1999, only four e-retailers—**priceline.com, Drugstore.com, Value America,** and **eBay**—increased their gross profit margins.

How do these companies monitor their financial progress, or lack of it? Managers don't roll dice to decide whether to launch a new product or whether the business is profitable. They keep accounting records like those we illustrate in this chapter. Accounting helps to measure profits and losses.

Chapter 1 introduced transaction analysis and the financial statements but did not show how the financial statements are prepared. Chapters 2, 3, and 4 cover the accounting process that results in the financial statements.

Chapter 2 discusses the processing of accounting information as it is done in practice. Throughout this and the next two chapters, we continue to illustrate accounting procedures with service businesses, such as Gay Gillen eTravel, a CPA, a law practice, or a sports franchise like the **Atlanta Braves.** In Chapter 5, we move into merchandising businesses such as **Macy's** and **Wal-Mart.** All these businesses use the basic accounting system we illustrate in this book.

THE ACCOUNT

Objective 1
Define and use key accounting terms

The basic summary device of accounting is the **account,** the detailed record of the changes that have occurred in a particular asset, liability, or owner's equity during a period of time. For convenient access to the information, accounts are grouped in a record called the **ledger.** This is what we mean when we say "keeping the books" and "auditing the books." A ledger usually takes the form of a computer listing.

Accounts are grouped in three broad categories, according to the accounting equation ➡ :

ACCOUNT. The detailed record of the changes that have occurred in a particular asset, liability, or owner's equity during a period. The basic summary device of accounting.

LEDGER. The book of accounts.

← In Chapter 1, p. 11, we learned that the accounting equation is the basic tool in all of accounting. It measures the assets of the business and the claims to those assets.

$$\text{ASSETS} = \text{LIABILITIES} + \text{OWNER'S EQUITY}$$

WORK IT OUT

Suppose you bought a $20,000 Pontiac Grand Am and had to borrow $12,000 to pay for it. Can you write your personal accounting equation for this transaction?

Answer

Assets	= Liabilities	+ Owner's Equity
$20,000 =	$12,000	+ $8,000

Assets

Assets are economic resources that benefit the business and will continue to do so in the future. Most firms use the following asset accounts.

CASH The Cash account is a record of the cash effects of a business's transactions. Cash includes money and any medium of exchange that a bank accepts at face value, such as bank account balances, paper currency, coins, certificates of deposit, and checks. Successful companies such as **Wal-Mart** have plenty of cash. Many e-retailers may go bankrupt due to a shortage of cash.

NOTES RECEIVABLE A business may sell its goods or services in exchange for a *promissory note,* which is a written pledge that the customer will pay a fixed amount of money by a certain date. The Notes Receivable account is a record of the promissory notes the business expects to collect in cash. A note receivable offers more security for collection than an account receivable.

ACCOUNTS RECEIVABLE A business may sell its goods or services in exchange for an oral or implied promise of future cash receipt. Such sales are made on credit ("on account"). The Accounts Receivable account contains these amounts. Most sales in the United States and in other developed countries are made on account receivable.

PREPAID EXPENSES A business often pays certain expenses, such as rent and insurance, in advance. A *prepaid expense* is an asset because the prepayment provides a future benefit for the business. The ledger has a separate asset account for each prepaid expense. Prepaid Rent, Prepaid Insurance, and Office Supplies are prepaid expense accounts.

LAND The Land account is a record of the cost of land a business owns and uses in its operations. Land held for sale is accounted for separately—in an investment account.

BUILDING The cost of a business's buildings—office, warehouse, store, and the like—appear in the Buildings account. The e-retailers need little in the way of buildings because of the electronic nature of their business. Wal-Mart, on the other hand, owns buildings in many locations. Buildings held for sale are separate assets accounted for as investments.

EQUIPMENT, FURNITURE, AND FIXTURES A business has a separate asset account for each type of equipment—Computer Equipment, Office Equipment, and Store Equipment, for example. The Furniture and Fixtures account shows the cost of this asset. Computers and the related software are the most important assets of e-retailers.

Liabilities

Recall that a *liability* is a debt. A business generally has fewer liability accounts than asset accounts because a business's liabilities are summarized in a few accounts.

NOTES PAYABLE The Notes Payable account is the opposite of the Notes Receivable account. Notes Payable represents amounts the business must pay because it signed promissory notes to borrow money or to purchase goods or services.

ACCOUNTS PAYABLE The Accounts Payable account is the opposite of Accounts Receivable. The oral or implied promise to pay off debts arising from credit purchases appears in the Accounts Payable account. Such a purchase is said to be made on account. All companies, including **CBS, Coca-Cola,** and **eBay** have accounts payable.

ACCRUED LIABILITIES An *accrued liability* is a liability for an expense that has not been paid. Accrued liability accounts are added as needed. Taxes Payable, Interest Payable, and Salary Payable are liability accounts of most companies.

Owner's Equity

The owner's claim to the assets of the business is called *owner's equity*. In a proprietorship or a partnership, owner's equity is split into separate accounts for the owner's capital balance and the owner's withdrawals.

CAPITAL The Capital account shows the owner's claim to the assets of the business. Consider Gay Gillen eTravel. After the travel agency's total liabilities are subtracted from its total assets, the remainder is the owner's capital. The Capital balance equals the owner's investments in the business plus the business's net income and minus any net losses and owner withdrawals. ◄

➤ See the statement of owner's equity in Chapter 1, Exhibit 1-7.

WITHDRAWALS When Gay Gillen withdraws cash or other assets from the business for her personal use, the travel agency's assets and owner's equity decrease. The amounts taken out of the business appear in a separate account entitled Gay Gillen, Withdrawals, or Gay Gillen, Drawing. If withdrawals were recorded directly in the Capital account, the amount of owner withdrawals would not be highlighted and decision making would be more difficult. The Withdrawals account *decreases* owner's equity.

REVENUES   The increase in owner's equity created by delivering goods or services to customers or clients is called *revenue*. The ledger contains as many revenue accounts as needed. Gay Gillen eTravel needs a Service Revenue account for amounts earned by providing travel services for clients. If a business lends money to an outsider, it needs an Interest Revenue account for the interest earned on the loan. If the business rents a building to a tenant, it needs a Rent Revenue account.

EXPENSES   Expenses use up assets or create liabilities in the course of operating a business. Expenses have the opposite effect of revenues; they *decrease* owner's equity. A business needs a separate account for each type of expense, such as Salary Expense, Rent Expense, Advertising Expense, and Utilities Expense. Businesses of all sizes strive to minimize their expenses in order to maximize net income — whether it's **General Electric** or Gay Gillen eTravel.

Exhibit 2-1 shows how asset, liability, and owner's equity accounts can be grouped in the ledger.

⊙ DAILY EXERCISE 2-1

EXHIBIT 2-1
The Ledger (Asset, Liability, and Owner's Equity Accounts)

DOUBLE-ENTRY ACCOUNTING

Accounting is based on a *double-entry system,* which means that we record the *dual effects* of a business transaction. *Each transaction affects at least two accounts.* For example, Gay Gillen's $30,000 cash investment in her travel agency increased both the Cash account and the Capital account of the business. It would be incomplete to record only the increase in the entity's cash without recording the increase in its owner's equity.

Consider a cash purchase of supplies. What are the dual effects of this transaction? The purchase (1) decreases cash and (2) increases supplies. A purchase of supplies on credit (1) increases supplies and (2) increases accounts payable. All transactions have at least two effects on the entity.

The T-Account

The most widely used account format is called the *T-account* because it takes the form of the capital letter "T." The vertical line in the T-account divides the account into its left and right sides. The account title rests on the horizontal line. For example, the Cash account of a business appears in the following T-account format:

CASH

(Left side)	(Right side)
Debit	*Credit*

DEBIT. The left side of an account.

CREDIT. The right side of an account.

The left side of the account is called the **debit** side, and the right side is called the **credit** side. The words *debit* and *credit* can be confusing because they are new. To become comfortable using them, remember that

$$\text{Debit = Left side} \qquad \text{Credit = Right side}$$

Even though *left side* and *right side* are more descriptive, the terms *debit* and *credit* are deeply entrenched in business.[1] Debit and credit are abbreviated as follows:

- **Dr = Debit**   • **Cr = Credit**

Increases and Decreases in the Accounts

The account category determines how increases and decreases in it are recorded. For any given account, all increases are recorded on one side, and all decreases are recorded on the other side.

Objective 2
Apply the rules of debit and credit

- Increases in *assets* are recorded on the left (*debit*) side of the account.
- Decreases in assets are recorded on the right (credit) side.

Conversely,

- Increases in *liabilities* and *owner's equity* are recorded by *credits.*
- Decreases in liabilities and owner's equity are recorded by debits.

These are the *rules of debit and credit.*

In your study of accounting, forget the general usage of credit and debit. Remember that *debit means left side* and *credit means right side.* Whether an account is increased or decreased by a debit or a credit depends on the type of account. In a computerized accounting system, the computer interprets debits and credits as increases or decreases by account category. For example, a computer reads a debit to Cash as an increase to that account and an increase to Accounts Payable as a credit.

DAILY EXERCISE 2-2

This pattern of recording debits and credits is based on the accounting equation:

$$\text{Assets = Liabilities + Owner's Equity}$$
$$\text{Debits = Credits}$$

Assets are on the opposite side of the equation from liabilities and owner's equity. Therefore, increases and decreases in assets are recorded in the opposite manner from those in liabilities and owner's equity. And liabilities and owner's equity, which are on the same side of the equal sign, are treated in the same way. Exhibit 2-2 shows the relationship between the accounting equation and the rules of debit and credit.

EXHIBIT 2-2
The Accounting Equation and the Rules of Debit and Credit

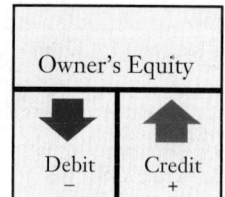

Accounting Equation:	Assets	=	Liabilities	+	Owner's Equity
Rules of Debit and Credit:	Debit + / Credit −		Debit − / Credit +		Debit − / Credit +

To illustrate the ideas diagrammed in Exhibit 2-2, reconsider the first transaction from Chapter 1. Gay Gillen invested $30,000 in cash to begin her travel agency. The business received $30,000 cash from Gillen and gave her the owner's equity in the business. We are accounting for the business entity, Gay Gillen eTravel. Which accounts of the business are affected? By what amounts? On what side (debit or credit)? The answer: The business's Assets and Capital would increase by $30,000, as the following T-accounts show.

ASSETS	=	LIABILITIES	+	OWNER'S EQUITY
CASH				GAY GILLEN, CAPITAL
Debit for Increase, 30,000				Credit for Increase, 30,000

---

[1]The words *debit* and *credit* have a Latin origin (*debitum* and *creditum*). Luca Pacioli, the Italian monk who wrote about accounting in the 15th century, popularized these terms.

The amount remaining in an account is called its *balance*. The first transaction gives Cash a $30,000 debit balance and Gay Gillen, Capital a $30,000 credit balance.

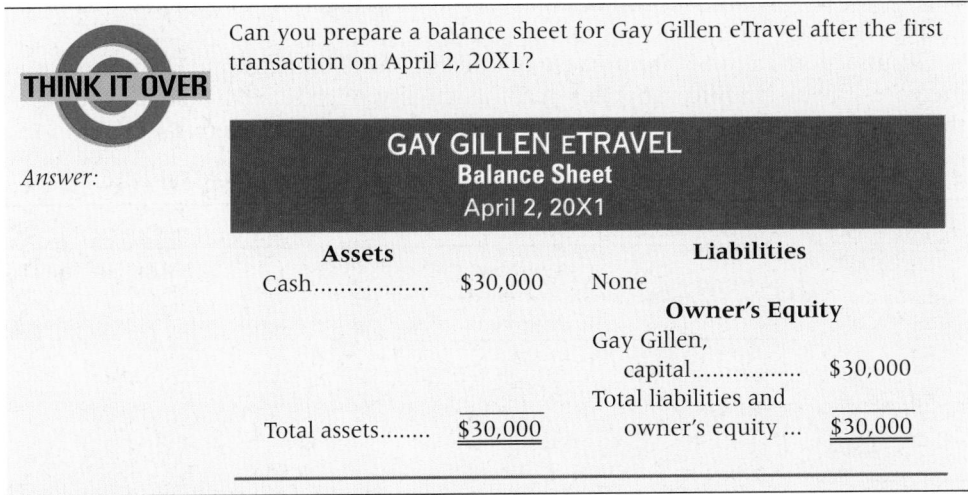

THINK IT OVER

Can you prepare a balance sheet for Gay Gillen eTravel after the first transaction on April 2, 20X1?

Answer:

GAY GILLEN ETRAVEL
Balance Sheet
April 2, 20X1

Assets		Liabilities	
Cash.................	$30,000	None	
		Owner's Equity	
		Gay Gillen,	
		capital.................	$30,000
		Total liabilities and	
Total assets........	$30,000	owner's equity ...	$30,000

Notice that Assets = Liabilities + Owner's Equity *and* that total debit amounts = total credit amounts. Exhibit 2-3 illustrates the accounting equation and Gay Gillen eTravel's first three transactions.

EXHIBIT 2-3 **The Accounting Equation and the First Three Transactions of the Business Entity, Gay Gillen eTravel**

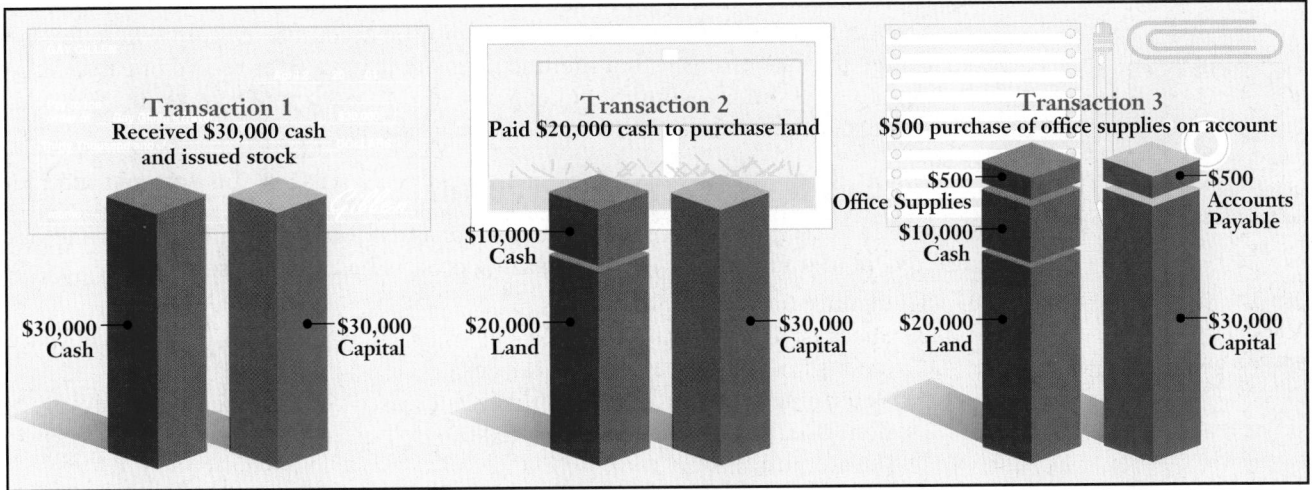

The second transaction is a $20,000 cash purchase of land. This transaction affects two assets: Cash and Land. It decreases (credits) Cash and increases (debits) Land, as shown in the T-accounts:

ASSETS	=	LIABILITIES	+	OWNER'S EQUITY

CASH		
Balance 30,000	**Credit for**	
	Decrease,	
	20,000	
Balance 10,000		

GAY GILLEN, CAPITAL	
	Balance 30,000

LAND	
Debit for	
Increase,	
20,000	
Balance 20,000	

After this transaction, Cash has a $10,000 debit balance ($30,000 debit amount minus $20,000 credit amount), Land has a debit balance of $20,000, and Gay Gillen, Capital has a $30,000 credit balance, as shown here and in the middle section of Exhibit 2-3 (labeled transaction 2).

Transaction 3 is a $500 purchase of office supplies on account. This transaction increases the asset Office Supplies and the liability Accounts Payable, as shown in the following accounts and in the right side of Exhibit 2-3 (labeled transaction 3):

We create accounts as needed. The process of creating a new T-account in preparation for recording a transaction is called *opening the account*. For transaction 1, we opened the Cash account and the Gay Gillen, Capital account. For transaction 2, we opened the Land account and for transaction 3, Office Supplies and Accounts Payable. For each transaction, total debits must equal total credits.

We could record all transactions directly in the accounts, as shown here for the first three transactions. But that method does not leave a clear record of each transaction. To save time, accountants keep a record of each transaction in a journal. They transfer the information from the journal into the accounts.

Recording Transactions in the Journal

Objective 3
Record transactions in the journal

JOURNAL. The chronological accounting record of an entity's transactions.

In practice, accountants record transactions first in a **journal,** which is a chronological record of transactions. The journalizing process has four steps:

1. Identify the transaction and its data.
2. Specify each account affected by the transaction and classify each account by type (asset, liability, or owner's equity).
3. Determine whether each account is increased or decreased by the transaction. Use the rules of debit and credit to determine whether to debit or credit the account.
4. Enter the transaction in the journal, including a brief explanation for the journal entry. The debit side of the entry is entered first and the credit side last.

Step 4, "Enter the transaction in the journal," means to record the transaction in the journal. This step is also called "making the journal entry" or "journalizing the transaction."

These four steps are the same in a computerized accounting system or in a manual system. In step 4, however, the journal entry is generally entered into the computer by account number, and the account name is then listed automatically.

Let's apply the four steps to journalize the first transaction of Gay Gillen eTravel–the receipt of Gillen's $30,000 cash investment in the business.

Step 1. The data appear on Gillen's bank deposit slip and on her $30,000 check, which she deposits in the business bank account. See Exhibit 2-3.

Step 2. The accounts affected by the transaction are *Cash* and *Gay Gillen, Capital.* Cash is an asset account. Gay Gillen, Capital is an owner's equity account.

Step 3. Both accounts increase by $30,000. Therefore, we debit Cash, the asset account, and we credit Gay Gillen, Capital, the owner's equity account.

Step 4. The journal entry is

Journal			Page 1	
Date	Accounts and Explanation	Debit	Credit	
Apr. 2[a]	Cash[b]	30,000[d]		
	Gay Gillen, Capital[c].................................		30,000[e]	
	Received initial investment from owner.[f]			

The journal entry includes (a) the date of the transaction; (b) the title of the account debited (placed flush left); (c) the title of the account credited (indented); the dollar amounts of the (d) debit (left) and (e) credit (right), and (f) a short explanation of the transaction. Note that dollar signs are omitted in the money columns. It is understood that the debit and credit amounts are in dollars.

To journalize a transaction, first pinpoint the obvious effects on the accounts. For example, cash effects are easy to identify. Did cash increase or decrease? Then find the transaction's effects on other accounts.

The journal holds information that the ledger accounts do not provide. Each journal entry shows the complete effect of a business transaction. Consider Gay Gillen's initial investment. The Cash account shows a single figure, the $30,000 debit. We know that every transaction must also have a credit, so in what account will we find the corresponding $30,000 credit? In this illustration, we know that the Capital account holds this figure. But imagine the difficulty of linking debits and credits for hundreds of transactions without a separate record of each transaction. The journal solves this problem and presents the full story for each transaction. Exhibit 2-4 shows how Journal page 1 looks after Gillen has recorded the first transaction.

EXHIBIT 2-4 The Journal

Journal			Page 1	
Date	Accounts and Explanation	Debit	Credit	
Apr. 2	Cash	30,000		
	Gay Gillen, Capital.................................		30,000	
	Received initial investment from owner.			

WORK IT OUT

Prepare the journal entry to record a $1,600 payment on account.

1. Identify the accounts.
2. Are these accounts increased or decreased? Should they be debited or credited?
3. Make the journal entry, with an explanation.

Answers

1. The company paid $1,600 on account. The accounts affected are Cash and Accounts Payable.
2. Cash (an asset) decreases by $1,600. Accounts Payable (a liability) decreases by $1,600. To account for a decrease in an asset, we record a credit. For a decrease in a liability, we use a debit. Review Exhibit 2-2.
3. The journal entry is   Accounts Payable 1,600
                                          Cash..   1,600
                          Made payment on account.

Objective 4
Post from the journal to the ledger

Copying Information (Posting) from the Journal to the Ledger

Posting means copying the amounts from the journal to the accounts in the ledger. Debits in the journal are posted as debits in the ledger, and credits in the journal are credits in the ledger. The initial investment transaction of Gay Gillen eTravel is posted to the ledger in Exhibit 2-5. Here we ignore the date of the transaction to focus on the accounts and their dollar amounts.

POSTING. Copying amounts from the journal to the ledger.

EXHIBIT 2-5
Journal Entry and Posting to
the Ledger

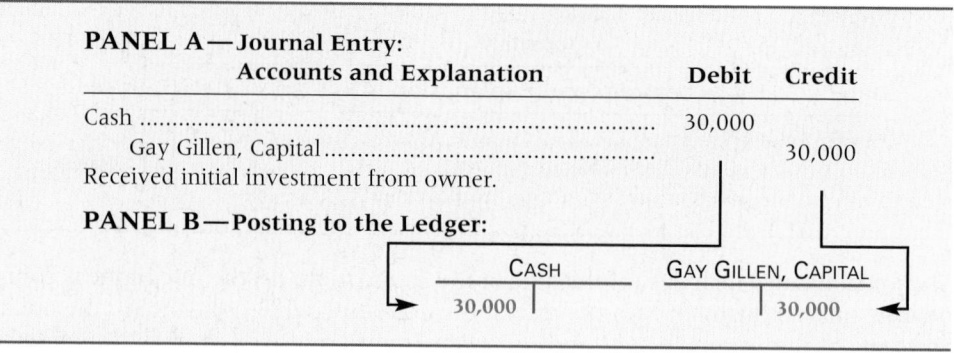

PANEL A—Journal Entry:

Accounts and Explanation	Debit	Credit
Cash	30,000	
Gay Gillen, Capital...		30,000
Received initial investment from owner.		

PANEL B—Posting to the Ledger:

CASH	GAY GILLEN, CAPITAL
30,000	30,000

THE FLOW OF ACCOUNTING DATA

Exhibit 2-6 summarizes the flow of accounting data from a business transaction through the accounting system to the ledger. In the pages that follow, we account for six of Gay Gillen eTravel's early transactions. Keep in mind that we are accounting for the travel agency. We are *not* accounting for Gay Gillen's *personal* transactions.

EXHIBIT 2-6 Flow of Accounting Data from the Journal to the Ledger

Transaction Analysis, Journalizing, and Posting to the Accounts

1. *Transaction Analysis*   The business received $30,000 cash that Gay Gillen invested to begin her travel agency. The business increased its asset cash, so we debit Cash. The business also increased its owner's equity; to record this increase, credit Gay Gillen, Capital.

Accounting Equation

ASSETS	=	LIABILITIES	+	OWNER'S EQUITY
Cash				Gay Gillen, Capital
+50,000	=	0	+	+30,000

Journal Entry

	Debit	Credit
Cash	30,000	
Gay Gillen, Capital		30,000
Received investment from owner.		

The journal entry records the same information that you learned by using the accounting equation in Chapter 1. Both accounts—Cash and Gay Gillen, Capital—increased because the business received $30,000 cash and gave Gillen $30,000 of capital (owner's equity) in the business.

Ledger Accounts

CASH	GAY GILLEN, CAPITAL
(1) 30,000	(1) 30,000

2. *Transaction Analysis*   Gillen paid $20,000 cash for land to be used as an office location. The purchase decreased the business's cash; therefore, credit Cash. The entity's asset, land, increased, so we debit the Land account.

Accounting Equation

ASSETS		=	LIABILITIES	+	OWNER'S EQUITY
Cash	Land				
−20,000	+20,000 =		0	+	0

Journal Entry

Land 20,000
    Cash 20,000
Paid cash for land.

This transaction increased one asset, land, and decreased another asset, cash. The *net* effect on total assets was zero, and there was no effect on liabilities or owner's equity. (The term *net* in business means an amount after a subtraction.)

Ledger Accounts

CASH			LAND	
(1) 30,000	(2) 20,000	(2) 20,000		

⦿ DAILY EXERCISE 2-3

3. *Transaction Analysis*   Gillen purchased $500 in office supplies on account payable. The asset office supplies increased, so we debit Office Supplies. The purchase also increased the liability accounts payable; to record this increase, credit Accounts Payable.

Accounting Equation

ASSETS	=	LIABILITIES	+	OWNER'S EQUITY
Office Supplies		Accounts Payable		
+500	=	+500	+	0

Journal Entry

Office Supplies... 500
    Accounts Payable 500
Purchased office supplies on account.

Ledger Accounts

OFFICE SUPPLIES	ACCOUNTS PAYABLE	
(3) 500		(3) 500

4. *Transaction Analysis*   Gillen paid $300 on the account payable created in transaction 3. The payment decreased the asset cash; therefore, credit Cash. The payment also decreased the liability accounts payable, so we debit Accounts Payable.

Accounting Equation

ASSETS	=	LIABILITIES	+	OWNER'S EQUITY
Cash		Accounts Payable		
−300	=	−300	+	0

Journal Entry

Accounts Payable... 300
    Cash 300
Paid cash on account.

Ledger Accounts

CASH		ACCOUNTS PAYABLE		
(1) 30,000	(2) 20,000	(4) 300	(3) 500	
	(4) 300			

5. *Transaction Analysis*   Gay Gillen remodeled her home with personal funds and a loan from Nations Bank. This is not a transaction of the travel agency, so we make no journal entry on its books.

6. *Transaction Analysis*   Gillen withdrew $2,100 cash for personal living expenses. The withdrawal decreased the entity's cash; therefore, credit Cash. The transaction also decreased owner's equity. Decreases in a proprietorship's owner's equity that result from owner withdrawals are debited to a separate account, Withdrawals. Therefore, debit Gay Gillen, Withdrawals.

Accounting Equation	ASSETS	=	LIABILITIES	+	OWNER'S EQUITY
	Cash				Gay Gillen, Withdrawals
	−2,100	=	0		−2,100

Journal Entry

Gay Gillen, Withdrawals 2,100
      Cash 2,100
Withdrawal of cash by owner.

Ledger Accounts

CASH			GAY GILLEN, WITHDRAWALS	
(1) 30,000	(2) 20,000		(6) 2,100	
	(4) 300			
	(6) 2,100			

Each journal entry posted to the ledger is keyed by date or by transaction number. In this way, any transaction can be traced from the journal to the ledger and back to the journal. This linking allows you to locate any information you may need for decision making.

Accounts After Posting

We next show how the accounts look when the preceding transactions have been posted. The accounts are grouped under their headings.

Each account has a balance, denoted *Bal.* An account balance is the difference between the account's total debits and its total credits. For example, the balance in the Cash account is the difference between the total debits, $30,000, and the total amount of the credits, $22,400 ($20,000 + $300 + $2,100). Thus, the cash balance is $7,600. The balances are residual amounts left over after the journal entries have been posted to the accounts. We set an account balance apart from the transaction amounts by a horizontal line. The final figure in an account, below the horizontal line, is the balance after the transactions have been posted.

ASSETS = LIABILITIES + OWNER'S EQUITY

CASH			ACCOUNTS PAYABLE			GAY GILLEN, CAPITAL	
(1) 30,000	(2) 20,000		(4) 300	(3) 500			(1) 30,000
	(4) 300			Bal. 200			Bal. 30,000
	(6) 2,100						
Bal. 7,600							

OFFICE SUPPLIES			GAY GILLEN, WITHDRAWALS	
(3) 500			(6) 2,100	
Bal. 500			Bal. 2,100	

LAND	
(2) 20,000	
Bal. 20,000	

If the sum of an account's debits is greater than the sum of its credits, that account has a debit balance, as the Cash account does. If the sum of its credits is greater, that account has a credit balance, as for Accounts Payable.

Objective 5
Prepare and use a trial balance

TRIAL BALANCE. A list of all the accounts with their balances.

The Trial Balance

A **trial balance** is a list of all the accounts with their balances—assets first, followed by liabilities and then owner's equity—taken from the ledger. Before computers, the trial balance provided a check on accuracy by showing whether total debits equal total credits. The trial balance is now a useful summary of all the accounts and their balances. A trial balance may be taken whenever the postings are up to date. The most common time is at the end of the accounting period. Exhibit 2-7 is the trial balance of Gay Gillen eTravel after the first six transactions.

EXHIBIT 2-7
Trial Balance

 DAILY EXERCISE 2-4

GAY GILLEN ETRAVEL Trial Balance April 30, 20X1		
	Balance	
Account Title	**Debit**	**Credit**
Cash	$ 7,600	
Office supplies	500	
Land	20,000	
Accounts payable		$ 200
Gay Gillen, capital		30,000
Gay Gillen, withdrawals	2,100	
Total	$30,200	$30,200

Correcting Trial Balance Errors

In a trial balance, total debits and total credits should be equal. If they are not, there must be an accounting error. Computerized accounting systems eliminate most errors because the journal amounts are posted precisely as they have been journalized. But computers cannot *eliminate* all errors because humans sometimes input the wrong data.

Out-of-balance conditions are detected by computing the difference between total debits and total credits on the trial balance. Then perform one or more of the following actions:

1. Search the trial balance for a missing account. For example, suppose the accountant omitted Gay Gillen, Withdrawals, from the trial balance in Exhibit 2-7. The total amount of the debits would be $28,100 ($30,200 − $2,100). Trace each account from the ledger to the trial balance, and you will locate the missing account.

2. Divide the difference between total debits and total credits by 2. A debit treated as a credit, or vice versa, doubles the amount of error. Suppose Gay Gillen's accountant posted a $300 credit as a debit. Total debits contain the $300, and total credits omit the $300. The out-of-balance amount is $600. Dividing the difference by 2 identifies the $300 amount of the transaction. Then search the journal for a $300 transaction and trace to the account affected.

3. Divide the out-of-balance amount by 9. If the result is evenly divisible by 9, the error may be a *slide* (example: writing $300 as $30) or a *transposition* (example: treating $61 as $16). Suppose Gillen printed her $2,100 Withdrawal as $21,000 on the trial balance—a slide-type error. Total debits would differ from total credits by $18,900 ($21,000 − $2,100 = $18,900). Dividing $18,900 by 9 yields $2,100, the correct amount of withdrawals. Trace this amount through the ledger until you reach the Gay Gillen, Withdrawals account with a balance of $2,100. Computer-based systems avoid such errors.

A warning: Do not confuse the trial balance with the balance sheet. A trial balance is an internal document seen only by the company's owners, managers, and accountants. The company reports its balance sheet, a formal financial statement, to the public.

The Seven Trillion Dollar Mistake

"If we can send missiles to a bull's-eye at a . . . training camp in Afghanistan, we ought to be able to set up an accounting system at the Defense Department. . . ." This is what Senator Charles Grassley (R-Iowa) said in 1998 after embezzlements at U.S. military installations were allowed to occur because of weaknesses in the Pentagon's accounting system.

A year later, precision was still lacking at the Department of Defense. Pentagon money managers required almost $7 trillion of accounting adjustments to make their books balance. Each adjustment represents an accountant's correction of a discrepancy. The lesson of the $7 trillion mistake is this: Computers don't keep books; people do.

These bookkeeping errors affect all our pocketbooks. Without sound costing data, military managers simply can't make good decisions—like whether to close a base or keep it open. The public never knows the real cost of defense programs such as the missile defense shield or the cost of health care for military retirees. With more reliable accounting data, we would know how to vote on these issues.

Sources: Based on: Julia Malone, "Auditors cite failings in 11 of 24 agencies," *The Atlanta Constitution,* March 31, 2000, p. A; 20. John M. Donnelly, "Pentagon's Finances Just Don't Add Up; Audit: Hundreds of computer systems fail to keep running totals of income and outgo. Last year, the Defense Department's bookkeeping errors totaled more than the entire federal budget," *The Los Angeles Times,* March 5, 2000, p. 8. Ralph Vartabedian, "Thefts Reveal Flawed Pentagon Contract System," *The Los Angeles Times,* September 28, 1998, p. 1.

MID-CHAPTER

SUMMARY PROBLEM

On August 1, 20X5, Liz Shea opens Shea's Research Service. She is the owner of the proprietorship. During the entity's first ten days of operations, the business completes these transactions:
a. To begin operations, Shea deposits $40,000 of personal funds in a bank account entitled Shea's Research Service. The business receives the cash and gives Shea capital (owner's equity).
b. Shea pays $30,000 cash for a small building to be used as an office for the business.
c. Shea purchases office supplies for $500 on account.
d. Shea pays cash of $6,000 for office furniture.
e. Shea pays $150 on the account payable she created in transaction (c).
f. Shea withdraws $1,000 cash for personal use.

Required

1. Give the accounting equation for each transaction. Then journalize these transactions and post to the accounts. Key the journal entries by letter.
2. Show all the T-accounts after posting.
3. Prepare the trial balance of Shea's Research Service at August 10, 20X5.

Solution

Requirement 1

a. *Accounting Equation*

ASSETS	=	LIABILITIES	+	OWNER'S EQUITY
Cash				Liz Shea, Capital
+40,000	=	0	+	$40,000

Journal Entry

Cash 40,000
    Liz Shea, Capital 40,000
Received investment from owner.

Ledger Accounts

CASH		LIZ SHEA, CAPITAL	
(a) 40,000			(a) 40,000

b. *Accounting Equation*

ASSETS		=	LIABILITIES	+	OWNER'S EQUITY
Cash	Building				
−30,000	+30,000	=	0	+	0

Journal Entry

Building 30,000
    Cash 30,000
Purchased building.

Ledger Accounts

CASH			BUILDING	
(a) 40,000	(b) 30,000		(b) 30,000	

c. *Accounting Equation*

ASSETS	=	LIABILITIES	+	OWNER'S EQUITY
Office Supplies		Accounts Payable		
+500	=	+500	+	0

Journal Entry

Office Supplies 500
    Accounts Payable 500
Purchased office supplies on account.

Ledger Accounts

OFFICE SUPPLIES		ACCOUNTS PAYABLE	
(c) 500			(c) 500

d. *Accounting Equation*

ASSETS		=	LIABILITIES	+	OWNER'S EQUITY
	Office				
Cash	Furniture				
−6,000	+6,000	=	0	+	0

Journal Entry

Office Furniture 6,000
    Cash 6,000
Purchased office furniture.

Ledger Accounts

CASH		OFFICE FURNITURE	
(a) 40,000	(b) 30,000	(d) 6,000	
	(d) 6,000		

e. *Accounting Equation*

ASSETS	=	LIABILITIES	+	OWNER'S EQUITY
Cash		Accounts Payable		
−150	=	−150	+	0

Journal Entry

Accounts Payable 150
    Cash 150
Paid cash on account.

Ledger Accounts

CASH		ACCOUNTS PAYABLE	
(a) 40,000	(b) 30,000	(e) 150	(c) 500
	(d) 6,000		
	(e) 150		

f. *Accounting Equation*

ASSETS	=	LIABILITIES	+	OWNER'S EQUITY
Cash				Liz Shea, Withdrawals
−1,000	=	0		−1,000

Journal Entry

Liz Shea, Withdrawals	1,000	
Cash		1,000

Ledger Accounts

CASH					LIZ SHEA, WITHDRAWALS	
(a)	40,000	(b)	30,000		(f)	1,000
		(d)	6,000			
		(e)	150			
		(f)	1,000			

Requirement 2

ASSETS

CASH			
(a)	40,000	(b)	30,000
		(d)	6,000
		(e)	150
		(f)	1,000
Bal.	2,850		

OFFICE FURNITURE		
(d)	6,000	
Bal.	6,000	

OFFICE SUPPLIES		
(c)	500	
Bal.	500	

BUILDING		
(b)	30,000	
Bal.	30,000	

LIABILITIES

ACCOUNTS PAYABLE			
(e)	150	(c)	500
		Bal.	350

OWNER'S EQUITY

LIZ SHEA, CAPITAL			
		(a)	40,000
		Bal.	40,000

LIZ SHEA, WITHDRAWALS		
(f)	1,000	
Bal.	1,000	

Requirement 3

SHEA'S RESEARCH SERVICE
Trial Balance
August 10, 20X5

	Balance	
Account Title	Debit	Credit
Cash..	$ 2,850	
Office supplies	500	
Office furniture	6,000	
Building......................................	30,000	
Accounts payable		$ 350
Liz Shea, capital.........................		40,000
Liz Shea, withdrawals	1,000	
Total..	$40,350	$40,350

DETAILS OF JOURNALS AND LEDGERS

To focus on the main points of journalizing and posting, we purposely omitted certain essential data. In practice, the journal and the ledger provide additional details that create a "trail" through the accounting records. For example, a supplier may bill us twice for the same item that we purchased on account. To prove we paid the bill, we would search the accounts payable records to find our payment. To see how this process works, let's take a closer look at the journal and the ledger.

DETAILS IN THE JOURNAL Exhibit 2-8, Panel B, presents the journal. The journal page number appears in the upper right corner, and the journal displays the following information:

1. The *date* when the transaction occurred, April 2, 20X1, for the first transaction.
2. The *account title* and explanation of the transaction.

Exhibit 2-8   Journalizing and Posting

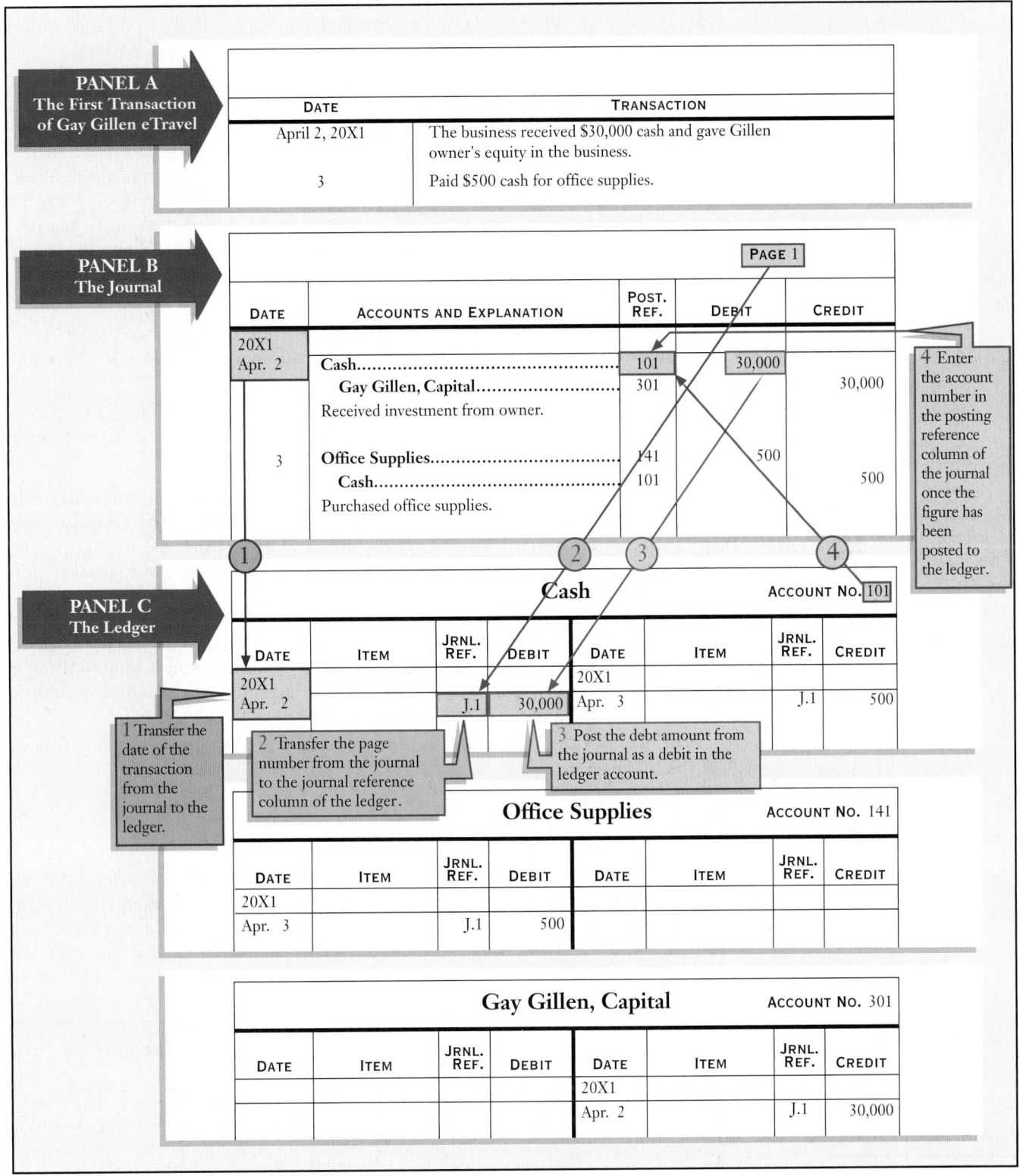

PANEL A
The First Transaction
of Gay Gillen eTravel

DATE	TRANSACTION
April 2, 20X1	The business received $30,000 cash and gave Gillen owner's equity in the business.
3	Paid $500 cash for office supplies.

PANEL B
The Journal

PAGE 1

DATE	ACCOUNTS AND EXPLANATION	POST. REF.	DEBIT	CREDIT
20X1 Apr. 2	Cash...	101	30,000	
	Gay Gillen, Capital............................	301		30,000
	Received investment from owner.			
3	Office Supplies...................................	141	500	
	Cash...	101		500
	Purchased office supplies.			

① ② ③ ④

4 Enter the account number in the posting reference column of the journal once the figure has been posted to the ledger.

PANEL C
The Ledger

Cash   ACCOUNT NO. 101

DATE	ITEM	JRNL. REF.	DEBIT	DATE	ITEM	JRNL. REF.	CREDIT
20X1 Apr. 2		J.1	30,000	20X1 Apr. 3		J.1	500

1 Transfer the date of the transaction from the journal to the ledger.

2 Transfer the page number from the journal to the journal reference column of the ledger.

3 Post the debt amount from the journal as a debit in the ledger account.

Office Supplies   ACCOUNT NO. 141

DATE	ITEM	JRNL. REF.	DEBIT	DATE	ITEM	JRNL. REF.	CREDIT
20X1 Apr. 3		J.1	500				

Gay Gillen, Capital   ACCOUNT NO. 301

DATE	ITEM	JRNL. REF.	DEBIT	DATE	ITEM	JRNL. REF.	CREDIT
				20X1 Apr. 2		J.1	30,000

3. The *posting reference,* abbreviated Post. Ref. Use of this column will become clear when we discuss the details of posting.
4. The *debit* column, which shows the dollar amount debited.
5. The *credit* column, which shows the dollar amount credited.

DETAILS IN THE LEDGER   Exhibit 2-8, Panel C, presents the T-accounts affected by the first transaction: Cash and Gay Gillen's Capital account. The account number appears at the upper right corner of each account. Each account has a separate column for

1. The date.
2. The item column, which can be used for any special notation.
3. The journal reference column, abbreviated Jrnl. Ref. The importance of this column will become clear when we discuss the mechanics of posting.
4. The debit column, with the amount debited.
5. The credit column, with the amount credited.

Posting from the Journal to the Ledger

We know that posting means copying information from the journal to the ledger accounts. But how do we handle the additional details that we have just seen? Exhibit 2-8 illustrates the steps in full detail. Panel A lists the first transaction of the business entity, Gay Gillen eTravel; Panel B presents the journal; and Panel C shows the ledger.

The posting process includes four steps. After recording the transaction in the journal:

> *Arrow* ① — Copy (post) the transaction **date** from the journal to the ledger.
> *Arrow* ② — Copy (post) the journal page number from the journal to the ledger. We use several abbreviations:
>
> > **Jrnl. Ref.** means Journal Reference. **J.1** refers to Journal page 1.
> > This step indicates where the information in the ledger came from: Journal page 1.
>
> *Arrow* ③ — Copy (post) the dollar amount of the debit (**$30,000**) from the journal as a debit to the same account (Cash) in the ledger. Likewise, post the dollar amount of the credit (also **$30,000**) from the journal to the appropriate account in the ledger. Now the ledger accounts have their correct amounts.
> *Arrow* ④ — Copy (post) the account number (**101**) from the ledger back to the journal. This step indicates that the $30,000 debit to Cash has been posted to the Cash account in the ledger. Also, copy the account number (**301**) for Gay Gillen, Capital, back to the journal to show that the $30,000 amount of the credit has been posted to the ledger.

Post. Ref. is the abbreviation for Posting Reference. After posting, you can prepare the trial balance.

The Four-Column Account Format: An Alternative to the T-Account Format

The ledger accounts illustrated in Exhibit 2-8 appear in the T-account format, with the debit on the left and the credit on the right. The T-account clearly separates debits from credits and is used for teaching purposes in situations that do not have much detail. Another standard format has four amount columns, as illustrated for the Cash account in Exhibit 2-9.

EXHIBIT 2-9
Account in Four-Column Format

Account Cash   **Account No. 101**

Date	Item	Jrnl. Ref.	Debit	Credit	Balance Debit	Balance Credit
20X1						
Apr. 2		J.1	30,000		30,000	
3		J.1		500	29,500	

The first pair of amount columns are for the debit and credit amounts posted from individual entries, as just discussed. The second pair of amount columns are for the account balance. This four-column format keeps a running balance in the account. For this reason, it is used more often in practice than the two-column format. In Exhibit 2-9, Cash has a debit balance of $30,000 after the first transaction and a debit balance of $29,500 after the second transaction.

Chart of Accounts in the Ledger

Objective 6
Set up a chart of accounts for a business

As you know, the ledger contains the business's accounts grouped under these headings:

- Balance sheet accounts: Assets, Liabilities, and Owner's Equity
- Income statement accounts: Revenues and Expenses

Organizations use a **chart of accounts** to list all the accounts they use along with their account numbers. These account numbers are used as posting references, illustrated by arrow 4 in Exhibit 2-8.

CHART OF ACCOUNTS. List of all the accounts and their account numbers in the ledger.

Accounts are identified by account numbers with two or more digits. Assets are often numbered beginning with 1, liabilities with 2, owner's equity with 3, revenues with 4, and expenses with 5. The second, third, and higher digits in an account number indicate the position of each account within the category. For example, Cash may be account number 101, which is the first asset account. Accounts Receivable may be account number 111, the second asset account. Accounts Payable may be number 201, the first liability account. All accounts are numbered by this system. Organizations with many accounts use lengthy account numbers.

The chart of accounts for Gay Gillen eTravel, appears in Exhibit 2-10. Notice the gap in account numbers between 111 and 141. Gillen realizes that at some later dates she may need to add another category of receivables—for example, Notes Receivable, which she might number 121.

EXHIBIT 2-10
Chart of Accounts—Gay Gillen eTravel

BALANCE SHEET ACCOUNTS:

Assets	Liabilities	Owner's Equity
101 Cash	201 Accounts Payable	301 Gay Gillen, Capital
111 Accounts Receivable	231 Notes Payable	311 Gay Gillen, Withdrawals
141 Office Supplies		
151 Office Furniture		
191 Land		

**INCOME STATEMENT ACCOUNTS
(PART OF OWNER'S EQUITY):**

Revenues	Expenses
401 Service Revenue	501 Rent Expense
	502 Salary Expense
	503 Utilities Expense

Appendix B gives two expanded charts of accounts that you will find helpful as you work through this course. The first chart lists the typical accounts of a large *service* proprietorship, such as Gay Gillen eTravel after a period of growth. The second chart is for a *merchandising* corporation, one that sells a product rather than a service. The third chart gives some accounts that a *manufacturing* company uses. You will use these accounts in Chapters 19–26. Study the service proprietorship now, and refer to the other charts of accounts as needed later.

The Normal Balance of an Account

 DAILY EXERCISE 2-5

An account's **normal balance** appears on the side of the account—debit or credit—where we record *increases*. That is, the normal balance is on the side that is positive. For example, Cash and other assets usually have a debit balance (the debit side is positive and the credit side negative), so the normal balance of assets is on the debit side. Assets are called *debit-balance accounts*. Conversely, liabilities and owner's equity usually have a credit balance, so their normal balances are on the credit side. They are called *credit-balance accounts*. Exhibit 2-11 illustrates the normal balances of assets, liabilities, and owner's equity.

NORMAL BALANCE. The account balance that appears on the side of the account—debit or credit—where we record increases.

An account that normally has a debit balance may occasionally have a credit balance. That indicates a negative amount of the item. For example, Cash will have a temporary credit balance if the entity overdraws its bank account. Similarly, the

EXHIBIT 2-11
Normal Balances of the Balance Sheet Accounts

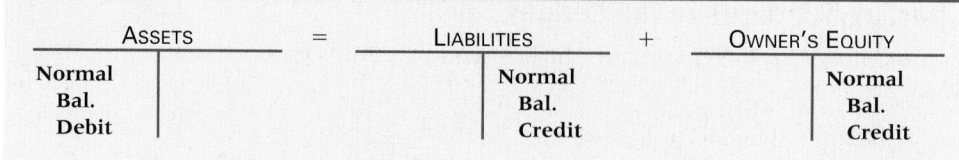

liability Accounts Payable—normally a credit-balance account—will have a debit balance if the entity overpays its account. In other instances, an odd balance may indicate an accounting error. For example, a credit balance in Office Supplies, Office Furniture, or Buildings indicates an error because negative amounts of these assets cannot exist.

As we saw earlier, owner's equity contains the Capital account and the Withdrawals account. In total, these accounts show a normal credit balance. An individual owner's equity account with a normal credit balance, such as Gay Gillen, Capital, represents an *increase* in owner's equity. An owner's equity account that has a normal debit balance, such as Gay Gillen, Withdrawals, represents a *decrease* in owner's equity.

DAILY EXERCISE 2-15

EXPANDING THE ACCOUNTING EQUATION TO ACCOUNT FOR REVENUES AND EXPENSES

Owner's equity also includes Revenues and Expenses because revenues and expenses make up net income or net loss, which flows into owner's equity. As we have noted, *revenues* are increases in owner's equity that result from delivering goods or services to customers in the course of operating the business. *Expenses* are decreases in owner's equity that occur from using assets or increasing liabilities in the course of operations. Therefore, the accounting equation may be expanded as shown in Exhibit 2-12. Revenues and expenses appear in parentheses to highlight the fact that their net effect—revenues minus expenses—equals net income, which increases owner's equity. If expenses are greater than revenues, the net effect of operations is a net loss, which decreases owner's equity.

We can now express the rules of debit and credit in final form, as shown in Exhibit 2-13, Panel A. Panel B shows the *normal* balances of the five types of accounts: *Assets; Liabilities;* and *Owner's Equity* and its subparts, *Revenues and Expenses*. All of accounting is based on these five types of accounts.

You should not proceed until you have learned the rules of debit and credit and the normal balances of the five types of accounts.

PANEL A—Rules of Debit and Credit:

ASSETS			LIABILITIES			CAPITAL	
Debit for Increase	**Credit for Decrease**	**=**	**Debit for Decrease**	**Credit for Increase**	**+**	**Debit for Decrease**	**Credit for Increase**

PANEL B—Normal Balances:

Assets	Debit
Liabilities	Credit
Owner's equity—overall	Credit
Capital	Credit
Withdrawals	Debit
Revenues..	Credit
Expenses	Debit

WITHDRAWALS

Debit for Increase	**Credit for Decrease**

REVENUES

Debit for Decrease	**Credit for Increase**

EXPENSES

Debit for Increase	**Credit for Decrease**

 DAILY EXERCISE 2-6

WORK IT OUT

Compute the missing amounts in each of the following T-accounts.

1. CASH			2. ACCOUNTS RECEIVABLE			3. ANNIE TODD, CAPITAL	
Bal. 10,000			Bal. 12,800				Bal. ?
20,000	13,000		45,600	?		22,000	56,000
							15,000
Bal. ?			Bal. 23,500				Bal. 73,000

Answers

1. The ending balance (X) for Cash is:

$$X = \$10,000 + \$20,000 - \$13,000$$
$$X = \$17,000$$

2. We are given the beginning and ending balances. We can compute the credit entry (X) as follows for Accounts Receivable:

$$\$12,800 + \$45,600 - X = \$23,500$$
$$\$58,400 - \$23,500 = X$$
$$X = \$34,900$$

3. The Capital account has an ending credit balance of $73,000. We can figure the beginning credit balance (X), as follows:

$$X + \$56,000 + \$15,000 - \$22,000 = \$73,000$$
$$X = \$73,000 - \$56,000 - \$15,000 + \$22,000$$
$$X = \$24,000$$

EXPANDED PROBLEM INCLUDING REVENUES AND EXPENSES

Let's account for the revenues and expenses of the law practice of Jeff Hatton, Attorney, for the month of July 20X1. We follow the same steps illustrated earlier in this chapter: Analyze the transaction, journalize, post to the ledger, and prepare the trial balance.

Transaction Analysis, Journalizing, and Posting

1. *Transaction Analysis*   Jeff Hatton invested $10,000 cash in a business bank account to open his law practice. The business received the cash and gave Hatton owner's equity. The business's asset cash is increased; therefore, debit Cash. The owner's equity of the business increased, so credit Jeff Hatton, Capital.

Accounting Equation

ASSETS	=	LIABILITIES	+	OWNER'S EQUITY
Cash				Jeff Hatton,
+10,000	=	0	+	Capital 10,000

Journal Entry

Cash 10,000
    Jeff Hatton, Capital   10,000
Received investment from owner.

Ledger Accounts

	CASH		JEFF HATTON, CAPITAL	
(1)	10,000		(1)	10,000

2. *Transaction Analysis*

Hatton performed service for a client and collected $3,000 cash. The asset cash is increased, so debit Cash. The revenue account Service Revenue is increased; credit Service Revenue.

Accounting Equation

ASSETS	=	LIABILITIES	+	OWNER'S EQUITY	+	REVENUES
						Service
Cash						Revenue
+3,000	=	0			+	3,000

Journal Entry

Cash 3,000
    Service Revenue   3,000
Performed service and received cash.

Ledger Accounts

	CASH		SERVICE REVENUE	
(1)	10,000		(2)	3,000
(2)	3,000			

3. *Transaction Analysis*

Hatton performed service for a client and billed the client for $500 on account receivable. This means the client owes the business $500, and Hatton expects to collect the $500 later. The asset accounts receivable is increased; therefore, debit Accounts Receivable. Service revenue is increased; credit Service Revenue. Remember that revenues are credit-balance accounts.

Accounting Equation

ASSETS	=	LIABILITIES	+	OWNER'S EQUITY	+	REVENUES
Accounts						Service
Receivable						Revenue
+500	=	0			+	500

Journal Entry

Accounts Receivable 500
    Service Revenue   500
Performed service on account.

Ledger Accounts

	ACCOUNTS RECEIVABLE		SERVICE REVENUE	
(3)	500		(2)	3,000
			(3)	500

4. *Transaction Analysis*

Hatton earned $700 service revenue by performing legal service for a client. The client paid Hatton $300 cash immediately. Hatton billed the remaining $400 to the client on account receivable. The assets cash and accounts receivable are increased; therefore, debit both of these asset accounts. Service revenue is increased; credit Service Revenue for the sum of the two debit amounts.

Accounting Equation

ASSETS		=	LIABILITIES	+	OWNER'S EQUITY	+	REVENUES
	Accounts						Service
Cash	Receivable						Revenue
+300	+400	=	0			+	700

Journal *Entry*	Cash..	300	
	Accounts Receivable..	400	
	Service Revenue		700
	Performed service for cash and on account.		

● DAILY EXERCISE 2-7

Note: Because this transaction affects more than two accounts at the same time, the entry is called a *compound entry*. **No matter how many accounts a compound entry affects—there may be any number—total debits must equal total credits.**

Ledger
Accounts

CASH			ACCOUNTS RECEIVABLE			SERVICE REVENUE	
(1)	**10,000**		**(3)**	**500**		**(2)**	**3,000**
(2)	**3,000**		**(4)**	**400**		**(3)**	**500**
(4)	**300**					**(4)**	**700**

5. *Transaction*
Analysis

Hatton paid the following cash expenses: office rent, $900; employee salary, $1,500; and utilities, $500. The asset cash is decreased; therefore, credit Cash for the sum of the three expense amounts. The following expenses are increased: Rent Expense, Salary Expense, and Utilities Expense. Each expense account should be debited separately. Remember that expenses are debit-balance accounts, the opposite of revenues.

Accounting
Equation

ASSETS	=	LIABILITIES	+	OWNER'S EQUITY	–		EXPENSES	
						Rent Expense	Salary Expense	Utilities Expense
Cash −2,900	=	0				−900	−1,500	−500

Journal
Entry

Rent Expense		900	
Salary Expense		1,500	
Utilities Expense		500	
Cash			2,900
Paid cash expenses.			

Note: In practice, the business would record these three transactions separately. To save space, we can record them together in a compound journal entry.

Ledger
Accounts

CASH				RENT EXPENSE	
(1)	**10,000**	**(5)**	**2,900**	**(5)**	**900**
(2)	**3,000**				
(4)	**300**				

SALARY EXPENSE			UTILITIES EXPENSE	
(5)	**1,500**		**(5)**	**500**

6. *Transaction*
Analysis

Hatton received a telephone bill for $120 and will pay this expense next week. There is no cash payment now. Utilities expense is increased, so debit this expense. The liability accounts payable is increased, so credit Accounts Payable.

Accounting
Equation

ASSETS	=	LIABILITIES	+	OWNER'S EQUITY	–	EXPENSES
		Accounts Payable				Utilities Expense
0	=	+120			–	120

Journal
Entry

Utilities Expense...	120	
Accounts Payable		120
Received utility bill.		

Ledger
Accounts

ACCOUNTS PAYABLE			UTILITIES EXPENSE	
	(6)	**120**	**(5)**	**500**
			(6)	**120**

7. *Transaction Analysis* Hatton collected $200 cash from the client established in transaction 3. The asset cash is increased, so debit Cash. The asset accounts receivable is decreased; credit Accounts Receivable.

Accounting Equation

ASSETS		=	LIABILITIES	+	OWNER'S EQUITY
Cash	Accounts Receivable				
+200	−200	=	0	+	0

Journal Entry

Cash 200
    Accounts Receivable 200
Received cash on account.

Note: This transaction has no effect on revenue; the related revenue was accounted for in transaction 3.

Ledger Accounts

	CASH				ACCOUNTS RECEIVABLE			
(1)	10,000	(5)	2,900	(3)	500	(7)	200
(2)	3,000			(4)	400		
(4)	300						
(7)	200						

8. *Transaction Analysis* Hatton paid the telephone bill that was received and recorded in transaction 6. The asset cash is decreased; credit Cash. The liability accounts payable is decreased; therefore, debit Accounts Payable.

Accounting Equation

ASSETS	=	LIABILITIES	+	OWNER'S EQUITY
Cash		Accounts Payable		
−120	=	−120	+	0

Journal Entry

Accounts Payable 120
    Cash 120
Paid cash on account.

Note: This transaction has no effect on expense because the related expense was recorded in transaction 6.

Ledger Accounts

	CASH				ACCOUNTS PAYABLE			
(1)	10,000	(5)	2,900	(8)	120	(6)	120
(2)	3,000	(8)	120				
(4)	300						
(7)	200						

9. *Transaction Analysis* Hatton withdrew $1,100 cash for personal use. The asset cash decreased; credit Cash. The withdrawal decreased owner's equity; therefore, debit Jeff Hatton, Withdrawals.

◉ DAILY EXERCISE 2-8

◉ DAILY EXERCISE 2-9

◉ DAILY EXERCISE 2-10

◉ DAILY EXERCISE 2-11

Accounting Equation

ASSETS	=	LIABILITIES	+	OWNER'S EQUITY
Cash				Jeff Hatton, Withdrawals
−1,100	=	0		−1,100

Journal Entry

Jeff Hatton, Withdrawals 1,100
    Cash 1,100
Withdrew cash for personal use.

Ledger Accounts

	CASH				JEFF HATTON, WITHDRAWALS	
(1)	10,000	(5)	2,900	(9)	1,100	
(2)	3,000	(8)	120			
(4)	300	(9)	1,100			
(7)	200					

Ledger Accounts After Posting

	ASSETS				LIABILITIES				OWNER'S EQUITY			REVENUE			EXPENSES	

ASSETS

CASH

(1)	10,000	(5)	2,900
(2)	3,000	(8)	120
(4)	300	(9)	1,100
(7)	200		
Bal.	9,380		

ACCOUNTS RECEIVABLE

(3)	500	(7)	200
(4)	400		
Bal.	700		

LIABILITIES

ACCOUNTS PAYABLE

(8)	120	(6)	120
		Bal.	0

OWNER'S EQUITY

JEFF HATTON, CAPITAL

		(1)	10,000
		Bal.	10,000

JEFF HATTON, WITHDRAWALS

(9)	1,100	
Bal.	1,100	

REVENUE

SERVICE REVENUE

		(2)	3,000
		(3)	500
		(4)	700
		Bal.	4,200

EXPENSES

RENT EXPENSE

(5)	900	
Bal.	900	

SALARY EXPENSE

(5)	1,500	
Bal.	1,500	

UTILITIES EXPENSE

(5)	500	
(6)	120	
Bal.	620	

Trial Balance

The trial balance lists the balance of each account.

DAILY EXERCISE 2-12

DAILY EXERCISE 2-13

DAILY EXERCISE 2-14

JEFF HATTON, ATTORNEY
Trial Balance
July 31, 20X1

	Balance	
Account Title	Debit	Credit
Cash	$ 9,380	
Accounts receivable	700	
Accounts payable		$ 0
Jeff Hatton, capital		10,000
Jeff Hatton, withdrawals..............	1,100	
Service revenue		4,200
Rent expense	900	
Salary expense	1,500	
Utilities expense	620	
Total	$14,200	$14,200

Now you have seen how to record business transactions, post to the ledger accounts, and prepare a trial balance. Solidify your understanding of the accounting process by reviewing the Decision Guidelines below.

DECISION GUIDELINES

Analyzing and Recording Transactions

DECISION	GUIDELINES
• Has a transaction occurred?	If the event affects the entity's financial position and can be reliably recorded—*Yes* If either condition is absent—*No*
• Where to record the transaction?	In the *journal*, the chronological record of transactions
• What to record for each transaction?	Increases and/or decreases in all the accounts affected by the transaction
• How to record an increase/decrease in a (an)	Rules of debit and credit:

	Increase	Decrease
Asset	Debit	Credit
Liability	Credit	Debit
Owner's Equity...............................	Credit	Debit
Revenue	Credit	Debit
Expense	Debit	Credit

DECISION GUIDELINES (CONT.)

DECISION	GUIDELINES
• Where to store all the information for each account?	In the *ledger*, the book of accounts and their balances
• Where to list all the accounts and their balances?	In the *trial balance*
• Where to report the results of operations?	In the income statement (Revenues − Expenses = Net income or Net loss)
• Where to report financial position?	In the balance sheet (Assets = Liabilities + Owner's equity)

USING ACCOUNTING INFORMATION FOR QUICK DECISION MAKING

Objective 7
Analyze transactions without a journal

⊙ DAILY EXERCISE 2-16

Often businesspeople make decisions without taking the time to follow all the steps in an accounting system. For example, suppose Drugstore.com needs more warehouse space to meet customer demand. The company can purchase a warehouse building for $700,000, or it can rent a building at an overall cost of $100,000. Whether to buy or rent the building will depend on the decision's financial and other effects on the company.

The Drugstore.com vice president does not need to record in the journal all the transactions that would be affected by his decision. After all, the company has not completed a transaction yet. But the vice president does need to know how the decision will affect Drugstore.com. If he knows accounting, he can visualize how the ledger accounts would be affected. The following accounts summarize the immediate effects of renting or purchasing the warehouse building.

RENT THE BUILDING		BUY THE BUILDING	
CASH	RENT EXPENSE	CASH	BUILDING
100,000	100,000	700,000	700,000

Immediately the Drugstore.com vice president can see that buying the building will require more cash. But he can also see that he will obtain the building as an asset. This may motivate him to borrow cash and buy the building. A low cash balance may lead to renting.

Companies do not actually keep their records in this short-cut fashion. But a decision maker who needs information immediately can quickly analyze the effect of a set of transactions on the company's financial statements.

REVIEW THE RECORDING OF BUSINESS TRANSACTIONS

SUMMARY PROBLEM

www.prenhall.com/horngren
End-of-Chapter Assessment

The trial balance of Tomassini Computer Service Center on March 1, 20X2, lists the entity's assets, liabilities, and owner's equity on that date.

Account Title	Balance Debit	Balance Credit
Cash	$26,000	
Accounts receivable	4,500	
Accounts payable		$ 2,000
Larry Tomassini, capital..............		28,500
Total..	$30,500	$30,500

During March, the business engaged in the following transactions:

a. Borrowed $45,000 from the bank and signed a note payable in the name of the business.
b. Paid cash of $40,000 to a real estate company to acquire land.
c. Performed service for a customer and received cash of $5,000.
d. Purchased supplies on credit, $300.
e. Performed customer service and earned revenue on account, $2,600.
f. Paid $1,200 on account.
g. Paid the following cash expenses: salaries, $3,000; rent, $1,500; and interest, $400.
h. Received $3,100 on account.
i. Received a $200 utility bill that will be paid next week.
j. Withdrew $1,800 for personal use.

Required

1. Open the following accounts, with the balances indicated, in the ledger of Tomassini Computer Service Center. Use the T-account format.
  - Assets—Cash, $26,000; Accounts Receivable, $4,500; Supplies, no balance; Land, no balance
  - Liabilities—Accounts Payable, $2,000; Note Payable, no balance
  - Owner's Equity—Larry Tomassini, Capital, $28,500; Larry Tomassini, Withdrawals, no balance
  - Revenues—Service Revenue, no balance
  - Expenses—(none have balances) Salary Expense, Rent Expense, Utilities Expense, Interest Expense
2. For each transaction, give the accounting equation. Then journalize the transaction. Key journal entries by transaction letter.
3. Post to the ledger.
4. Prepare the trial balance of Tomassini Computer Service Center at March 31, 20X2.

Solution

Requirement 1

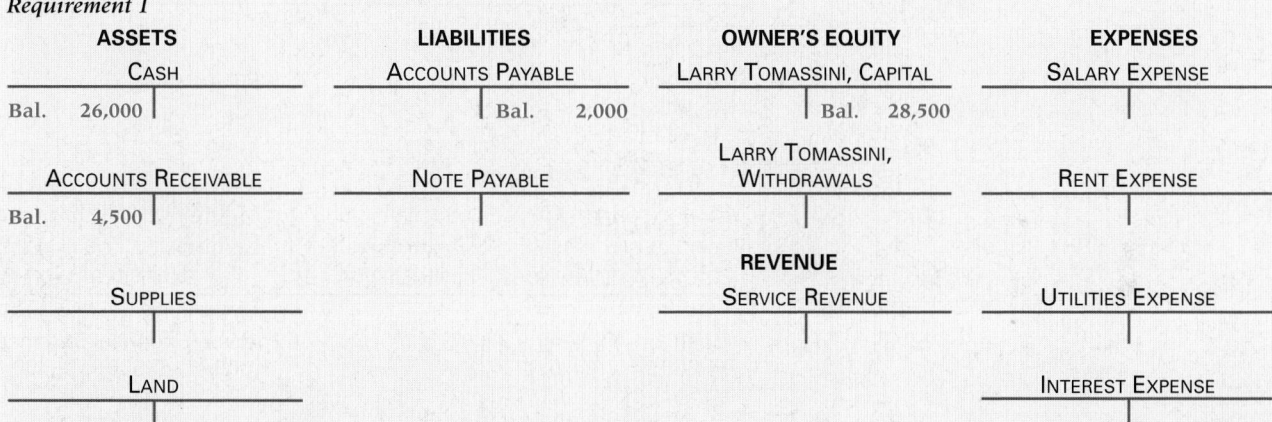

Requirement 2

a. *Accounting Equation*

ASSETS	=	LIABILITIES	+	OWNER'S EQUITY
Cash		Note Payable		
+45,000	=	+45,000	+	0

Journal Entry

Cash 45,000
    Note Payable.................................   45,000
Borrowed cash on note payable.

b. *Accounting Equation*

ASSETS		=	LIABILITIES	+	OWNER'S EQUITY
Cash	Land				
−40,000	+40,000	=	0	+	0

Journal Entry

Land 40,000
    Cash   40,000
Purchased land.

c. *Accounting Equation*

ASSETS	=	LIABILITIES	+	OWNER'S EQUITY	+	REVENUES
Cash						Service Revenue
+5,000	=	0			+	5,000

Journal Entry

Cash	5,000	
Service Revenue		5,000
Performed service and received cash.		

d. *Accounting Equation*

ASSETS	=	LIABILITIES	+	OWNER'S EQUITY
Supplies		Accounts Payable		
+300	=	+300	+	0

Journal Entry

Supplies	300	
Accounts Payable..................................		300
Purchased supplies on account.		

e. *Accounting Equation*

ASSETS	=	LIABILITIES	+	OWNER'S EQUITY	+	REVENUES
Accounts Receivable						Service Revenue
+2,600	=	0			+	2,600

Journal Entry

Accounts Receivable	2,600	
Service Revenue		2,600
Performed service on account.		

f. *Accounting Equation*

ASSETS	=	LIABILITIES	+	OWNER'S EQUITY
Cash		Accounts Payable		
−1,200	=	−1,200	+	0

Journal Entry

Accounts Payable..	1,200	
Cash		1,200
Paid on account.		

g. *Accounting Equation*

ASSETS	=	LIABILITIES	+	OWNER'S EQUITY	−	EXPENSES		
						Salary Expense	Rent Expense	Interest Expense
Cash								
−4,900	=	0				−3,000	−1,500	−400

Journal Entry

Salary Expense	3,000	
Rent Expense...	1,500	
Interest Expense	400	
Cash..		4,900
Paid expenses.		

h. *Accounting Equation*

ASSETS		=	LIABILITIES	+	OWNER'S EQUITY
Cash	Accounts Receivable				
+3,100	−3,100	=	0	+	0

Journal Entry

Cash	3,100	
Accounts Receivable		3,100
Received cash on account.		

i. *Accounting Equation*

ASSETS	=	LIABILITIES	+	OWNER'S EQUITY	−	EXPENSES
		Accounts Payable				Utilities Expense
0	=	+200			−	200

Journal Entry	Utilities Expense......................................	200	
	Accounts Payable		200
	Received utility bill.		

j. *Accounting Equation*

ASSETS	=	LIABILITIES	+	OWNER'S EQUITY
				Larry Tomassini, Withdrawals
Cash −1,800	=	0		−1,800

Journal Entry	Larry Tomassini, Withdrawals................	1,800	
	Cash		1,800
	Owner withdrawal.		

Requirement 3

ASSETS			
CASH			
Bal.	26,000	(b)	40,000
(a)	45,000	(f)	1,200
(c)	5,000	(g)	4,900
(h)	3,100	(j)	1,800
Bal.	31,200		

ACCOUNTS RECEIVABLE			
Bal.	4,500	(h)	3,100
(e)	2,600		
Bal.	4,000		

SUPPLIES		
(d)	300	
Bal.	300	

LAND		
(b)	40,000	
Bal.	40,000	

LIABILITIES			
ACCOUNTS PAYABLE			
(f)	1,200	Bal.	2,000
		(d)	300
		(i)	200
		Bal.	1,300

NOTE PAYABLE			
		(a)	45,000
		Bal.	45,000

OWNER'S EQUITY			
LARRY TOMASSINI, CAPITAL			
		Bal.	28,500

LARRY TOMASSINI, WITHDRAWALS		
(j)	1,800	
Bal.	1,800	

REVENUE			
SERVICE REVENUE			
		(c)	5,000
		(e)	2,600
		Bal.	7,600

EXPENSES		
SALARY EXPENSE		
(g)	3,000	
Bal.	3,000	

RENT EXPENSE		
(g)	1,500	
Bal.	1,500	

INTEREST EXPENSE		
(g)	400	
Bal.	400	

UTILITIES EXPENSE		
(i)	200	
Bal.	200	

Requirement 4

TOMASSINI COMPUTER SERVICE CENTER
Trial Balance
March 31, 20X2

Account Title	Balance	
	Debit	Credit
Cash..	$31,200	
Accounts receivable.............................	4,000	
Supplies	300	
Land..	40,000	
Accounts payable		$ 1,300
Note payable...		45,000
Larry Tomassini, capital........................		28,500
Larry Tomassini, withdrawals...............	1,800	
Service revenue.....................................		7,600
Salary expense......................................	3,000	
Rent expense	1,500	
Interest expense	400	
Utilities expense	200	
Total..	$82,400	$82,400

LESSONS LEARNED

1. **Define and use key accounting terms.** Accounts can be viewed in the form of the letter "T." The left side of each T-account is its *debit* side. The right side is its *credit* side. The *ledger,* which contains a record for each account, groups and numbers accounts by category in the following order: assets, liabilities, and owner's equity (and its subparts, revenues and expenses).

2. **Apply the rules of debit and credit.** *Assets* and *expenses* are increased by debits and decreased by credits. *Liabilities, owner's equity,* and *revenues* are increased by credits and decreased by debits. An account's *normal balance* is the side of the account—debit or credit—in which increases are recorded. Thus, the normal balance of assets and expenses is a debit, and the normal balance of liabilities, owner's equity, and revenues is a credit. The Withdrawals account, which decreases owner's equity, normally has a debit balance. Revenues, which are increases in owner's equity, have a normal credit balance. Expenses, which are decreases in owner's equity, have a normal debit balance.

3. **Record transactions in the journal.** The recording process begins by entering each transaction in the *journal,* a chronological list of all the entity's transactions.

4. **Post from the journal to the ledger.** *Posting* means copying the amounts from the journal to the *ledger* accounts. Posting references are used to trace amounts back and forth between journal and ledger.

5. **Prepare and use a trial balance.** *The trial balance* is a summary of all the account balances in the ledger. When *double-entry accounting* is done correctly, the total debits and the total credits in the trial balance are equal.

6. **Set up a chart of accounts for a business.** A chart of accounts lists all the accounts in the ledger and their account numbers.

7. **Analyze transactions without a journal.** Decision makers must often make decisions without a complete accounting system. They can analyze the transactions without a journal.

ACCOUNTING VOCABULARY

account   (p. 39)
chart of accounts   (p. 55)
credit   (p. 42)

debit   (p. 42)
journal   (p. 44)
ledger   (p. 39)

normal balance   (p. 55)
posting   (p. 45)
trial balance   (p. 48)

QUESTIONS

1. Name the basic summary device of accounting. What letter of the alphabet does it resemble? Name its two sides.
2. Is the following statement true or false? Debit means decrease and credit means increase. Explain your answer.
3. What are the three *basic* types of accounts? Name two additional types of accounts. Which of the three basic types are these two additional types of accounts most closely related to?
4. Briefly describe the flow of accounting information.
5. Indicate the normal balance of the five types of accounts.

Account Type	Normal Balance
Assets	
Liabilities	
Capital	
Revenues	
Expenses	

6. What does posting accomplish? Why is it important? Does it come before or after journalizing?
7. Label each of the following transactions as increasing owner's equity (+), decreasing owner's equity (−), or as having no effect on owner's equity (0). Write the appropriate symbol in the space provided.

_____**a.** Investment by owner
_____**b.** Revenue transaction
_____ **c.** Purchase of supplies on credit
_____**d.** Expense transaction
_____**e.** Cash payment on account
_____ **f.** Withdrawal by owner
_____**g.** Borrowing money on a note payable
_____**h.** Sale of service on account

8. Rearrange the following accounts in their logical sequence in the ledger:

Notes Payable   Cash
Accounts Receivable   Jane East, Capital
Sales Revenue   Salary Expense

9. What is the meaning of this statement? Accounts Payable has a credit balance of $1,700.
10. Why do accountants prepare a trial balance?
11. What is a compound journal entry?
12. The accountant for Bower Construction Company mistakenly recorded a $500 purchase of supplies on account as a $5,000 purchase. He debited Supplies and credited Accounts Payable for $5,000. Does this error cause the trial balance to be out of balance? Explain your answer.
13. What is the effect on total assets of collecting cash on account from customers?
14. What is the advantage of analyzing transactions without the use of a journal? Describe how this analysis works.

Assess Your Progress

Daily Exercises

DE2-1 There are three broad categories of accounts: assets, liabilities, and owner's equity.

Using key terms (Obj. 1)

1. Owner's equity is more complex than assets and liabilities. What is the definition of *owner's equity*? Suppose your assets total $8,000 and your liabilities are $5,000. How much is your owner's equity?
2. Identify two categories of transactions that *increase* owner's equity. Name two categories of transactions that *decrease* owner's equity. This concept is discussed beginning on page 40.
3. Give a short (one- or two-word) synonym for an *asset* and a *liability*. Then list several individual assets and several specific liabilities.

DE2-2 Review basic accounting definitions by completing the following crossword puzzle.

Using key terms (Obj. 1)

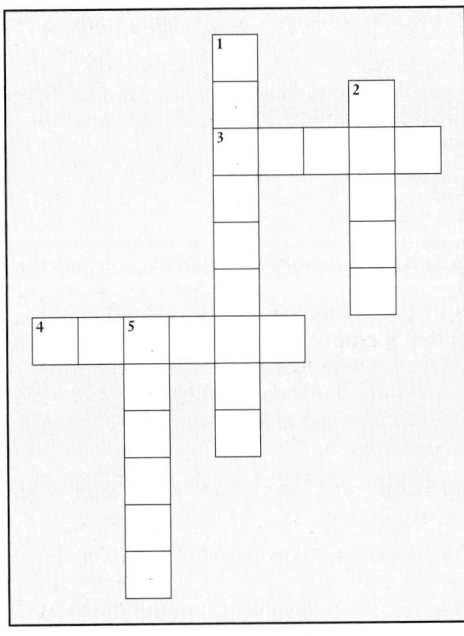

Across:
3. Economic resource of an entity.
4. Records an increase in a liability or owner's equity.

Down:
1. A debt.
2. Records an increase in an asset or an expense.
5. Assets − Liabilities = Owner's _____.

DE2-3 Rolfe Schmidt opened an architectural firm and immediately paid $60,000 for equipment to be used in the business. Was Schmidt's payment an expense of the business? If not, what did he acquire? Explain your reasoning after reviewing the definitions of *assets* on page 39 and *expenses* on page 41.

Explaining an asset versus an expense (Obj. 1)

DE2-4 Understanding basic concepts is essential for success in accounting. Tighten your grip on the accounting process by filling in the blanks to review the definitions of key terms.

Using key terms (Obj. 1)

Erika Darby, an introductory accounting student, is describing the accounting process for a friend who is a philosophy major. Erika states, "The basic summary device in accounting is the **account,** which can be represented by the letter _____. The left side of an account is called the _____ side, and the right side is called the _____ side.

"We record transactions first in a _____. Then we post (copy the data) to the accounts in the _____. It is helpful to list all the accounts with their balances on a _____ _____."

DE2-5 Accounting has its own vocabulary and basic relationships. Match the accounting terms at left with the corresponding definition at right.

Using accounting terms (Obj. 1)

____ 1. Ledger	A. Record of transactions
____ 2. Posting	B. Always an asset
____ 3. Normal balance	C. Left side of an account
____ 4. Payable	D. Side of an account where increases are recorded
____ 5. Journal	E. Copying data from the journal to the ledger
____ 6. Receivable	F. Using up assets in the course of operating a business
____ 7. Capital	G. Always a liability
____ 8. Debit	H. Revenues − Expenses
____ 9. Expense	I. Grouping of accounts
____ 10. Net income	J. Owner's equity in the business

Explaining the rules of debit and credit
(Obj. 2)

DE2-6 Josh Birbary, a recent graduate, is tutoring Trevor Grant, who is taking introductory accounting. Josh explains to Trevor that *debits* are used to record increases in accounts and *credits* record decreases. Trevor is confused and seeks your advice.

- When are credits increases? When are credits decreases?
- When are debits increases? When are debits decreases?

Exhibit 2-13, page 57, gives the rules of debit and credit.

Recording transactions
(Obj. 3)

DE2-7 Lee Jackson opened a medical practice in Cincinnati, Ohio. Record the following transactions in the journal of Lee Jackson, M.D. Include an explanation with each journal entry.

June 1   Jackson invested $25,000 cash in a business bank account to start his medical practice. The business received the cash and gave Jackson owner's equity in the business.

     2   Purchased medical supplies on account, $10,000.

     2   Paid monthly office rent of $4,000.

     3   Recorded $5,000 revenue for service rendered to patients. Received cash of $1,000 and sent bills to patients for the remainder.

Recording transactions
(Obj. 3)

DE2-8 After operating for a month, Lee Jackson, M.D., completed the following transactions during the latter part of July:

July 15   Borrowed $20,000 from the bank, signing a note payable.

     22   Performed service for patients on account, $2,800.

     30   Received cash on account from patients, $1,000.

     31   Received a utility bill, $200, which will be paid during August.

     31   Paid monthly salary to nurse, $3,000.

     31   Paid interest expense of $200 on the bank loan.

Journalize the transactions of Lee Jackson, M.D. Include an explanation with each journal entry.

Normal account balances
(Obj. 2)

DE2-9 The accounting records of all businesses include three basic categories of accounts: assets, liabilities, and owner's equity. In turn, owner's equity is divided into the following categories: capital, withdrawals, revenues, and expenses. Identify which categories of accounts—including the subparts of owner's equity—have a normal debit balance and which categories of accounts have a normal credit balance. Exhibit 2-13, Panel B, on page 57, gives the normal balance in each category of account.

Journalizing transactions; posting
(Obj. 3, 4)

DE2-10 Marianne Vogel purchased supplies on account for $3,000. Two weeks later, Vogel paid half on account.

1. Journalize the two transactions on the books of Marianne Vogel. Include an explanation for each transaction.
2. Open the Accounts Payable account and post to Accounts Payable. Compute the balance, and denote it as *Bal.*
3. How much does Vogel owe after both transactions? In which account does this amount appear?

Journalizing transactions; posting
(Obj. 3, 4)

DE2-11 Peter Nguyen performed legal service for a client who could not pay immediately. Nguyen expected to collect the $5,000 the following month. Later, Nguyen received $2,700 cash from the client.

1. Record the two transactions on the books of Peter Nguyen, Attorney. Include an explanation for each transaction.
2. Open these accounts: Cash; Accounts Receivable; Service Revenue. Post to all three accounts. Compute each account's balance, and denote as *Bal.*
3. Answer these questions based on your analysis:
   a. How much did Nguyen earn? Which account shows this amount?
   b. How much in total assets did Nguyen acquire as a result of the two transactions? Show the amount of each asset.

Note: Daily Exercise 2-12 should be used in connection with Daily Exercise 2-7.

Posting; preparing a trial balance
(Obj. 4, 5)

DE2-12 Use the June transaction data for Lee Jackson, M.D., given in Daily Exercise 2-7.

1. Open the following T-accounts of Lee Jackson, M.D.: Cash; Accounts Receivable; Medical Supplies; Accounts Payable; Lee Jackson, Capital; Service Revenue; Rent Expense.
2. After making the journal entries in Daily Exercise 2-7, post from the journal to the ledger. No dates or posting references are required. Compute the balance of each account, and denote it as *Bal.*
3. Prepare the trial balance, complete with a proper heading, at June 3, 20X8. Use the trial balance on page 52 as a guide.

Preparing a trial balance
(Obj. 5)

DE2-13 **Intel Corporation,** famous for the Pentium© processor, reported the following summarized data at December 31, 19X9. Accounts appear in no particular order; dollar amounts are in billions.

Revenues............................	$29	Other liabilities................	$11
Other assets........................	40	Cash.................................	4
Accounts payable	1	Expenses..........................	22
Capital.................................	25		

Prepare the trial balance of Intel Corporation at December 31, 19X9. List the accounts in their proper order, as on page 52.

Correcting a trial balance
(Obj. 5)

DE2-14 Jeff Hatton, Attorney, prepared the business's trial balance on page 61. Suppose Hatton made two errors in preparing the trial balance, as follows:

Error 1—Hatton erroneously listed his capital balance of $10,000 as a debit rather than as a credit.

Error 2—Hatton erroneously listed Service Revenue as a credit balance of $42,000 rather than the correct amount of $4,200.

Consider each error separately.

1. For each error, compute the incorrect trial balance totals for total debits and total credits.
2. Refer to the discussion of correcting trial balance errors on page 49 and show how to correct each error.

Setting up a chart of accounts
(Obj. 6)

DE2-15 Metrolink Apartment Finder Service helps college students locate apartments because Dundalk Community College has no student housing on campus. Wayne Gibbs, the owner of Metrolink, is setting up the business's chart of accounts after making an initial investment of cash in the business.

Gibbs will perform apartment locator services for clients on account. His office will need some supplies, a computer (equipment), and furniture. Gibbs has borrowed money by signing a note payable to the bank. The business will also purchase on account some of the things it needs.

Expenses of the business will include rent, utilities, and advertising.

Prepare the chart of accounts for Metrolink Apartment Finder Service, including three-digit account numbers. Use Exhibit 2-10, page 55, as a guide.

Analyzing transactions without a journal
(Obj. 7)

DE2-16 Marta Fraser established Bodyfit, a health club, with an initial cash investment of $100,000. The business immediately purchased equipment on account for $45,000. Marta needs to know her account balances immediately and doesn't have time to journalize the transactions.

1. Open the following T-accounts on the books of Bodyfit. Cash; Equipment; Accounts Payable; Marta Fraser, Capital.
2. Record the first two transactions of Bodyfit directly in the T-accounts without using a journal.
3. Compute the balance in each account and show that total debits equal total credits.

EXERCISES

Using accounting vocabulary
(Obj. 1)

E2-1 Your employer, Digitech Enterprises, has just hired an office manager who does not understand accounting. Digitech's trial balance lists Cash of $43,000. Write a short memo to the office manager, explaining the accounting process that produced this listing on the trial balance. Mention *debits, credits, journal, ledger, posting,* and *trial balance.*

Using debits and credits with the accounting equation
(Obj. 1, 2)

E2-2 ←← *Link Back to Chapter 1 (Accounting Equation).* **The Coca-Cola Company** is famous worldwide for its soft drinks. At the end of 1999, Coca-Cola had total assets of $22 billion and liabilities totaling $12 billion.

Required

1. Write the company's accounting equation, and label each element as a debit amount or a credit amount.
2. Coca-Cola's total revenues for 1999 were $20 billion, and total expenses for the year were $18 billion. How much was Coca-Cola's net income (or net loss) for 1999? Write the equation to compute Coca-Cola's net income, and indicate which element is a debit amount and which element is a credit amount. Does net income represent a net debit or a net credit? Does net loss represent a net debit or a net credit? Review Exhibit 1-7, page 20, if needed.
3. During 1999, the owners of Coca-Cola withdrew $1 billion in the form of dividends (same as owner Withdrawals). Did the dividends represent a debit amount or a credit amount?

4. Considering both Coca-Cola's net income (or net loss) and dividends for 1999, by how much did the company's owners' equity increase or decrease during 1999? Was the increase in owners' equity a debit amount or a credit amount?

Analyzing and journalizing transactions
(Obj. 2, 3)

E2-3 Analyze the following transactions in the manner shown for the December 1 transaction of Miramar Electronics. Also record each transaction in the journal. Explanations are not required.

Dec. 1   Paid utilities expense of $700. (*Analysis:* The expense, Utilities Expense, is increased; therefore, debit Utilities Expense. The asset, Cash, is decreased; therefore, credit Cash.)

     1   Utilities Expense   700

             Cash..........................   700

   5   Purchased office furniture on account, $800.
  10   Performed service on account for a customer, $1,600.
  12   Borrowed $7,000 cash, signing a note payable.
  19   Sold for $29,000 land that had cost this same amount.
  24   Purchased building for $140,000; signed a note payable.
  27   Paid the liability created on December 5.

Applying the rules of debit and credit
(Obj. 2)

E2-4 Refer to Exercise 2-3 for the transactions of Miramar Electronics.

Required

1. Open the following T-accounts with their December 1 balances: Cash, debit balance $6,000; Land, debit balance $29,000; Martha Cross, Capital, credit balance $35,000.
2. Record the transactions of Exercise 2-3 directly in the T-accounts affected. Use the dates as posting references. Journal entries are not required.
3. Compute the December 31 balance for each account, and prove that total debits equal total credits.

Journalizing transactions
(Obj. 3)

E2-5 New Balance Spa engaged in the following transactions during March 20X3, its first month of operations:

Mar. 1   Joy Liebermann invested $55,000 of cash to start the business.
    2   Purchased office supplies of $200 on account.
    4   Paid $40,000 cash for a building to use as an office in the very near future.
    6   Performed service for customers and received cash, $3,000.
    9   Paid $100 on accounts payable.
  17   Performed service for customers on account, $1,600.
  23   Received $1,200 cash from a customer on account.
  31   Paid the following expenses: salary, $1,200; rent, $500.

Required

Record the preceding transactions in the journal of New Balance Spa. Key transactions by date and include an explanation for each entry, as illustrated in the chapter. Use the following accounts: Cash; Accounts Receivable; Office Supplies; Building; Accounts Payable; Joy Liebermann, Capital; Service Revenue; Salary Expense; Rent Expense.

Posting to the ledger and preparing a trial balance
(Obj. 4, 5)

E2-6 Refer to Exercise 2-5 for the transactions of New Balance Spa.

Required

1. After journalizing the transactions of Exercise 2-5, post the entries to the ledger, using T-account format. Key transactions by date. Date the ending balance of each account Mar. 31.
2. Prepare the trial balance of New Balance Spa at March 31, 20X3.

Describing transactions and posting
(Obj. 2, 3)

E2-7 The journal of Freebin & Associates includes the following transaction entries for May 20X6.

Required

1. Describe each transaction.
2. Post the transactions to the ledger using the following account numbers: Cash, 110; Accounts Receivable, 120; Supplies, 130; Accounts Payable, 210; Note Payable, 230; Leonard Freebin, Capital, 310; Service Revenue, 410; Rent Expense, 510; Advertising Expense, 520; Utilities Expense, 530. Use dates, journal references, and posting references as illustrated in Exhibit 2-8. You may write the account numbers as posting references directly in your book unless directed otherwise by your instructor.
3. Compute the balance in each account after posting. Prepare Freebin & Associates' trial balance at May 31, 20X6.

Journal				Page 5
Date	Accounts and Explanation	Post. Ref.	Debit	Credit
May 2	Cash		20,000	
	Leonard Freebin, Capital................			20,000
5	Cash...		15,000	
	Note Payable			15,000
9	Supplies		270	
	Accounts Payable			270
11	Accounts Receivable.........................		2,630	
	Service Revenue			2,630
14	Rent Expense.....................................		3,200	
	Cash			3,200
22	Accounts Payable..............................		270	
	Cash			270
25	Advertising Expense		350	
	Cash			350
27	Cash...		1,400	
	Accounts Receivable			1,400
31	Utilities Expense		220	
	Accounts Payable..............................			220

E2-8 The first five transactions of Flores Security Company have been posted to the company's accounts as follows:

Journalizing transactions
(Obj. 3)

	CASH			
(1)	62,000	(3)	56,000
(4)	7,000	(5)	6,000

	SUPPLIES	
(2)	400	

	EQUIPMENT	
(5)	6,000	

	LAND	
(3)	56,000	

	ACCOUNTS PAYABLE	
	(2)	400

	NOTE PAYABLE	
	(4)	7,000

	TONY FLORES, CAPITAL	
	(1)	62,000

Required

Prepare the journal entries that served as the sources for the five transactions. Include an explanation for each entry as illustrated in the chapter.

E2-9 Prepare the trial balance of Flores Security Company at April 30, 20X4, using the account data from Exercise 2-8.

Preparing a trial balance
(Obj. 5)

E2-10 The accounts of Beaulieu Company follow with their normal balances at December 31, 20X4. The accounts are listed in no particular order.

Preparing a trial balance
(Obj. 5)

Account	Balance
Pierre Beaulieu, capital........................	$48,800
Advertising expense............................	650
Accounts payable................................	4,300
Sales commission revenue..................	26,000
Land..	29,000
Supplies expense	300
Cash...	5,000
Salary expense	6,000
Building	65,000
Rent expense	2,000
Pierre Beaulieu, withdrawals...............	6,000
Utilities expense..................................	400
Accounts receivable	9,500
Note payable	45,000
Supplies	250

Required

Prepare the company's trial balance at December 31, 20X4, listing accounts in proper sequence, as illustrated in the chapter. For example, Supplies comes before Building and Land. List the expense with the largest balance first, the expense with the next largest balance second, and so on.

E2-11 The trial balance of Atlantis Enterprises at March 31, 20X9, does not balance:

Cash	$ 4,500	
Accounts receivable	2,000	
Supplies....................................	600	
Land	66,000	
Accounts payable		$23,000
Paige Dylan, capital................		41,600
Service revenue		9,700
Salary expense	1,700	
Rent expense	800	
Utilities expense	300	
Total..	$75,900	$74,300

Investigation of the accounting records reveals that the bookkeeper

a. Recorded a $400 cash revenue transaction by debiting Accounts Receivable. The credit entry was correct.
b. Posted a $1,000 credit to Accounts Payable as $100.
c. Did not record utilities expense or the related account payable in the amount of $200.
d. Understated Paige Dylan, Capital, by $700.

Required

Prepare the correct trial balance at March 31, complete with a heading; journal entries are not required.

E2-12 Open the following T-accounts of Cole Gates, CPA: Cash; Accounts Receivable; Office Supplies; Office Furniture; Accounts Payable; Cole Gates, Capital; Cole Gates, Withdrawals; Service Revenue; Salary Expense; Rent Expense.

Record the following transactions directly in the T-accounts without using a journal. Use the letters to identify the transactions. Compute the balance of each account.

a. Gates opened an accounting firm by investing $12,400 cash and office furniture valued at $5,400.
b. Paid monthly rent of $1,500.
c. Purchased office supplies on account, $700.
d. Paid employee's salary, $1,800.
e. Paid $400 of the account payable created in transaction (c).
f. Performed accounting service on account, $1,600.
g. Withdrew $7,000 for personal use.

E2-13 After recording the transactions in Exercise 2-12, prepare the trial balance of Cole Gates, CPA, at May 31, 20X7.

E2-14 Moseley Supply began when Lynette Moseley invested $75,000 cash in a business bank account. During the first week, the business purchased supplies on credit for $8,000 and paid $12,000 cash for equipment. Moseley later paid $5,000 on account.

Required

1. Open the following T-accounts: Cash; Supplies; Equipment; Accounts Payable; Lynette Moseley, Capital.
2. Record the four transactions described above directly in the T-accounts without using a journal.
3. Compute the balance in each account, and show that total debit balances equal total credit balances after you have recorded all the transactions. The T-accounts on page 48 provide a guide for your answer.

Continuing Exercise Exercise 2-15 is the first exercise in a sequence that begins an accounting cycle. The cycle is completed in Chapter 5.

Recording transactions and
preparing a trial balance
(Obj. 2, 3, 4, 5)

E2-15 Amos Faraday completed these transactions during the first half of December:

Dec.	2	Invested $14,000 to start a consulting practice, Amos Faraday, Consultant.
	2	Paid monthly office rent, $500.
	3	Paid cash for a Dell computer, $2,000. The computer is expected to remain in service for five years.
	4	Purchased office furniture on account, $3,600. The furniture should last for five years.
	5	Purchased supplies on account, $300.
	9	Performed consulting service for a client on account, $1,700.
	12	Paid utility expenses, $200.
	18	Performed service for a client and received cash for the full amount of $800.

Required

1. Open T-accounts in the ledger: Cash; Accounts Receivable; Supplies; Equipment; Furniture; Accounts Payable; Amos Faraday, Capital; Amos Faraday, Withdrawals; Service Revenue; Rent Expense; Utilities Expense; and Salary Expense.
2. Journalize the transactions. Explanations are not required.
3. Post to the T-accounts. Key all items by date, and denote an account balance as *Bal.* Formal posting references are not required.
4. Prepare a trial balance at December 18. In the Continuing Exercise of Chapter 3, we will add transactions for the remainder of December and prepare a trial balance at December 31.

Challenge Exercises

E2-16 The owner of Midwest Catering Services needs to compute the following summary information from the accounting records:

Computing financial statement amounts without a journal (Obj. 7)

a. Net income for the month of March.
b. Total cash paid during March.
c. Cash collections from customers during March.
d. Cash paid on a note payable during March.

The quickest way to compute these amounts is to analyze the following accounts:

Account	Balance Feb. 28	Mar. 31	Additional Information for the Month of March
a. Owner, Capital........................	$ 9,000	$15,000	Withdrawals, $7,000
b. Cash	7,000	2,000	Cash receipts, $61,000
c. Accounts Receivable	24,000	26,000	Revenues on account, $76,000
d. Note Payable	11,000	16,000	New borrowing on a note payable, $7,500

The net income for March can be computed as follows:

OWNER, CAPITAL

		Feb. 28 Bal.	9,000	
March Withdrawals	7,000	March Net Income	X = $13,000	
		March 31 Bal.	15,000	

Use a similar approach to compute the other three items.

E2-17 Tara Hale has trouble keeping her debits and credits equal. During a recent month, she made the following errors:

Analyzing accounting errors (Obj. 2, 3, 4, 5)

a. In journalizing a receipt of cash for service revenue, Hale debited Cash for $1,800 instead of the correct amount of $800. Hale credited Service Revenue for $1,800, the incorrect amount.
b. Hale recorded a $120 purchase of supplies on account by debiting Supplies and crediting Accounts Payable for $210.
c. In preparing the trial balance, Hale omitted a $40,000 note payable.
d. Hale posted a $700 utility expense as $70. The credit posting to Cash was correct.
e. In recording a $400 payment on account, Hale debited Supplies and credited Accounts Payable.

Required

1. For each of these errors, state whether the total debits equal total credits on the trial balance.
2. Identify any accounts with misstated balances, and indicate the amount and direction of the error (such as account balance too high or too low).

PROBLEMS

(Group A)

P2-1A ◄ *Link Back to Chapter 1 (Balance Sheet, Income Statement).* The owner of Cantor Polling Service is selling the business. She offers the trial balance shown here to prospective buyers. Your best friend is considering buying Cantor Polling Service. He seeks your advice in interpreting this information. Specifically, he asks whether this trial balance is the same as a balance sheet and an income statement. He also wonders whether Cantor is a sound business. After all, the company's accounts are in balance.

Analyzing a trial balance (Obj. 1)

```
                    CANTOR POLLING SERVICE
                           Trial Balance
                         December 31, 20X8

       Cash ..................................................  $ 12,000
       Accounts receivable ..........................    27,000
       Prepaid expenses...............................      4,000
       Land...................................................    63,000
       Accounts payable ..............................                    $ 35,000
       Note payable .....................................                      32,000
       Kendra Cantor, capital .......................                      30,000
       Kendra Cantor, withdrawals..............    48,000
       Service revenue ................................                     116,000
       Rent expense .....................................    26,000
       Advertising expense...........................      3,000
       Wage expense ....................................    23,000
       Supplies expense................................      7,000
       Total ..................................................  $213,000     $213,000
```

Required

Write a short note to answer your friend's questions. To aid his decision, state how he can use the information on the trial balance to compute Cantor's net income or net loss for the current period. State the amount of net income or net loss in your note. Refer to Exhibit 1-7, page 20, if needed.

Analyzing and journalizing transactions
(Obj. 2, 3)

P2-2A Silverstar Cinemas owns movie theaters in the shopping centers of a major metropolitan area. Its owner, Joseph Reese, engaged in the following business transactions:

April 1   Reese invested $500,000 personal cash in the business by depositing that amount in a bank account entitled Silverstar Cinemas. The business gave Reese owner's equity in the company.
       2   Paid $400,000 cash to purchase a theater building.
       5   Borrowed $220,000 from the bank. Reese signed a note payable to the bank in the name of Silverstar Cinemas.
     10   Purchased theater supplies on account, $1,700.
     15   Paid $800 on account.
     15   Paid property tax expense on theater building, $1,200.
     16   Paid employee salaries, $2,800, and rent on equipment, $1,800.
     17   Withdrew $6,000 from the business for personal use.
     30   Received $20,000 cash from ticket sales and deposited that amount in the bank. (Label the revenue as Sales Revenue.)

Silverstar uses the following accounts: Cash; Supplies; Building; Accounts Payable; Notes Payable; Joseph Reese, Capital; Joseph Reese, Withdrawals; Sales Revenue; Salary Expense; Rent Expense; Property Tax Expense.

Required

1. Analyze each business transaction of Silverstar Cinemas, as shown for the April 1 transaction:

Apr. 1   The asset Cash is increased. Increases in assets are recorded by debits; therefore, debit Cash. The owner's equity of the entity is increased. Increases in owner's equity are recorded by credits; therefore, credit Joseph Reese, Capital.

2. Journalize each transaction. Explanations are not required.

Journalizing transactions, posting to T-accounts, and preparing a trial balance
(Obj. 2, 3, 4, 5)

P2-3A Terence Larkin opened a law office on September 3 of the current year. During the first month of operations, the business completed the following transactions:

Sep. 3   Larkin transferred $43,000 cash from his personal bank account to a business account entitled Terence Larkin, Attorney. The business gave Larkin owner's equity in the business.
     4   Purchased supplies, $200, and furniture, $1,800, on account.
     6   Performed legal services for a client and received $4,000 cash.
     7   Paid $15,000 cash to acquire land for a future office site.
    10   Defended a client in court, billed the client, and received her promise to pay the $800 within one week.
    14   Paid for the furniture purchased September 4 on account.
    15   Paid secretary's salary, $600.
    17   Received partial collection from client on account, $500.

Sep. 20   Prepared legal documents for a client on account, $800.
28   Received $1,500 cash for helping a client sell real estate.
30   Paid secretary's salary, $600.
30   Paid rent expense, $500.
30   Withdrew $2,900 for personal use.

Required

Open the following T-accounts: Cash; Accounts Receivable; Supplies; Furniture; Land; Accounts Payable; Terence Larkin, Capital; Terence Larkin, Withdrawals; Service Revenue; Salary Expense; Rent Expense.

1. Record each transaction in the journal, using the account titles given. Key each transaction by date. Explanations are not required.
2. Post the transactions to the ledger, using transaction dates as posting references in the ledger. Label the balance of each account *Bal.*, as shown in the chapter.
3. Prepare the trial balance of Terence Larkin, Attorney, at September 30 of the current year.

P2-4A The trial balance of the accounting practice of Jill Case, CPA, is dated February 14, 20X3:

Journalizing transactions, posting to accounts in four-column format, and preparing a trial balance (Obj. 2, 3, 4, 5)

JILL CASE, CPA
Trial Balance
February 14, 20X3

Account Number	Account	Debit	Credit
11	Cash...	$ 2,000	
12	Accounts receivable................	9,500	
13	Supplies	800	
14	Land..	18,600	
21	Accounts payable.....................		$ 3,000
31	Jill Case, capital		26,500
32	Jill Case, withdrawals..............	1,200	
41	Service revenue........................		7,200
51	Salary expense..........................	3,600	
52	Rent expense.............................	1,000	
	Total...	$36,700	$36,700

During the remainder of February, Case completed the following transactions:

Feb. 15   Case collected $3,500 cash from a client on account.
16   Performed tax services for a client on account, $700.
20   Paid on account, $1,000.
21   Purchased supplies on account, $100.
21   Withdrew $1,200 for personal use.
21   Paid for a wooden deck for private residence, using personal funds, $9,000.
22   Received cash of $5,100 for consulting work just completed.
28   Paid rent, $800.
28   Paid employees' salaries, $1,800.

Required

1. Record the transactions that occurred during February 15–28 in page 3 of the journal. Include an explanation for each entry.
2. Open the ledger accounts listed in the trial balance, together with their balances at February 14. Use the four-column account format illustrated in the chapter (Exhibit 2-9). Enter *Bal.* (for previous balance) in the Item column, and place a check mark (✓) in the journal reference column for the February 14 balance in each account. Post the transactions to the ledger using dates, account numbers, journal references, and posting references.
3. Prepare the trial balance of Jill Case, CPA, at February 28, 20X3.

P2-5A ◄ *Link Back to Chapter 1 (Income Statement).* The trial balance for Chapel Lawn Service at the top of the next page does not balance.
    The following errors were detected:

Correcting errors in a trial balance (Obj. 2, 5)

a. The cash balance is understated by $700.
b. The cost of the land was $43,000, not $46,000.
c. A $200 purchase of supplies on account was neither journalized nor posted.
d. The balance of Utilities Expense is overstated by $70.
e. Rent expense of $200 was erroneously posted as a credit rather than a debit.

CHAPEL LAWN SERVICE
Trial Balance
June 30, 20X2

Cash...	$ 3,000	
Accounts receivable..........................	10,000	
Supplies...	900	
Equipment...	5,100	
Land	46,000	
Accounts payable		$ 5,000
Note payable		22,000
Rob Rylander, capital		31,600
Rob Rylander, withdrawals	2,000	
Service revenue................................		6,500
Salary expense	2,100	
Rent expense....................................	1,000	
Advertising expense	500	
Utilities expense	400	
Total...	$71,000	$65,100

f. The balance of Advertising Expense is $600, but it was listed as $500 on the trial balance.
g. A $300 debit to Accounts Receivable was posted as $30.
h. A $4,300 credit to Service Revenue was not posted.
i. A $900 debit to the Withdrawals account was posted as a debit to Rob Rylander, Capital.

Required

1. Prepare the correct trial balance at June 30. Journal entries are not required.
2. Prepare the company's income statement for the month ended June 30, 20X2, in order to determine Chapel Lawn Service's net income or net loss for the month. Refer to Exhibit 1-7, page 20, if needed.

Recording transactions directly in T-accounts; preparing a trial balance
(Obj. 2, 5, 7)

P2-6A Allen Musser started a consulting service and during the first month of operations (June 20X3) completed the following selected transactions:

a. Musser began the business with an investment of $5,000 cash and a building valued at $60,000. The business gave Musser owner's equity in the business.
b. Borrowed $30,000 from the bank; signed a note payable.
c. Purchased office supplies on account, $2,100.
d. Paid $18,000 for office furniture.
e. Paid employee's salary, $2,200.
f. Performed consulting service on account for client, $5,100.
g. Paid $800 of the account payable created in transaction (c).
h. Received a $600 bill for advertising expense that will be paid in the near future.
i. Performed consulting service for customers and received cash, $1,600.
j. Received cash on account, $1,200.
k. Paid the following cash expenses:
    (1) Rent on land, $700.   (2) Utilities, $400.
l. Withdrew $7,500 for personal use.

Required

1. Open the following T-accounts: Cash; Accounts Receivable; Office Supplies; Office Furniture; Building; Accounts Payable; Note Payable; Allen Musser, Capital; Allen Musser, Withdrawals; Service Revenue; Salary Expense; Advertising Expense; Rent Expense; Utilities Expense.
2. Record each transaction directly in the T-accounts without using a journal. Use the letters to identify the transactions.
3. Prepare the trial balance of Musser Consulting Service at June 30, 20X3.

Note: Problem 2-7A should be used in conjunction with Problem 2-6A.

Preparing the financial statements
(Obj. 5)

P2-7A ◄ *Link Back to Chapter 1 (Income Statement, Statement of Owner's Equity, Balance Sheet).* Refer to Problem 2-6A. After completing the trial balance in Problem 2-6A, prepare the following financial statements for Musser Consulting Service:

1. Income statement for the month ended June 30, 20X3.
2. Statement of owner's equity for the month ended June 30, 20X3.
3. Balance sheet at June 30, 20X3.

Draw arrows to link the statements. If needed, use Exhibit 1-7, page 20, as a guide for preparing the financial statements.

PROBLEMS

P2-1B ◄ *Link Back to Chapter 1 (Balance Sheet, Income Statement).* The owner of Biokinetic Engineering is selling the business. He offers the following trial balance to prospective buyers. Your best friend is considering buying Biokinetic. She seeks your advice in interpreting this information. Specifically, she asks whether this trial balance is the same as a balance sheet and an income statement. She also wonders whether Biokinetic is a sound business. After all, the company's accounts are in balance.

Analyzing a trial balance (Obj. 1)

BIOKINETIC ENGINEERING Trial Balance December 31, 20X4		
Cash	$ 7,000	
Accounts receivable	6,000	
Prepaid expenses.............................	4,000	
Land	51,000	
Accounts payable		$ 31,000
Note payable		20,000
Avery Patella, capital......................		33,000
Avery Patella, withdrawals..............	21,000	
Service revenue...............................		72,000
Wage expense	28,000	
Rent expense...................................	14,000	
Advertising expense........................	18,000	
Supplies expense.............................	7,000	
Total	$156,000	$156,000

Required

Write a short note to answer your friend's questions. To aid her decision, state how she can use the information on the trial balance to compute Biokinetic's net income or net loss for the current period. State the amount of net income or net loss in your note. Refer to Exhibit 1-7, page 20, if needed.

P2-2B Deborah Fedro practices medicine under the business title Deborah Fedro, M.D. During June, her medical practice engaged in the following transactions:

Analyzing and journalizing transactions (Obj. 2, 3)

June 1	Fedro deposited $55,000 cash in the business bank account. The business gave Fedro owner's equity in the business.
5	Paid monthly rent on medical equipment, $700.
9	Paid $22,000 cash to purchase land for an office site.
10	Purchased supplies on account, $1,200.
19	Borrowed $20,000 from the bank for business use. Fedro signed a note payable to the bank in the name of the business.
22	Paid $1,000 on account.
30	Revenues earned during the month included $6,000 cash and $5,000 on account.
30	Paid employees' salaries ($2,400), office rent ($1,500), and utilities ($400).
30	Withdrew $10,000 from the business for personal use.

Fedro's business uses the following accounts: Cash; Accounts Receivable; Supplies; Land; Accounts Payable; Notes Payable; Deborah Fedro, Capital; Deborah Fedro, Withdrawals; Service Revenue; Salary Expense; Rent Expense; Utilities Expense.

Required

1. Analyze each transaction of Deborah Fedro, M.D., as shown for the June 1 transaction:

June 1	The asset Cash is increased. Increases in assets are recorded by debits; therefore, debit Cash. The owner's equity is increased. Increases in owner's equity are recorded by credits; therefore, credit Deborah Fedro, Capital.

2. Journalize each transaction. Explanations are not required.

P2-3B Rodney Troon opened a law office on December 2 of the current year. During the first month of operations, the business completed the following transactions:

Dec.	2	Troon deposited $50,000 cash in the business bank account Rodney Troon, Attorney.
	3	Purchased supplies, $500, and furniture, $2,600, on account.
	4	Performed legal service for a client and received cash, $1,500.
	7	Paid cash to acquire land for a future office site, $22,000.
	11	Prepared legal documents for a client on account, $900.
	15	Paid secretary's salary, $570.
	16	Paid for the furniture purchased December 3 on account.
	18	Received $1,800 cash for helping a client sell real estate.
	19	Defended a client in court and billed the client for $800.
	29	Received partial collection from client on account, $400.
	31	Paid secretary's salary, $570.
	31	Paid rent expense, $700.
	31	Withdrew $2,200 for personal use.

Required

Open the following T-accounts: Cash; Accounts Receivable; Supplies; Furniture; Land; Accounts Payable; Rodney Troon, Capital; Rodney Troon, Withdrawals; Service Revenue; Salary Expense; Rent Expense.

1. Record each transaction in the journal, using the account titles given. Key each transaction by date. Explanations are not required.
2. Post the transactions to the ledger, using transaction dates as posting references in the ledger. Label the balance of each account *Bal.,* as shown in the chapter.
3. Prepare the trial balance of Rodney Troon, Attorney, at December 31 of the current year.

P2-4B The trial balance of the law practice of Brent Busch, Attorney, at November 15, 20X3, follows.

BRENT BUSCH, ATTORNEY
Trial Balance
November 15, 20X3

Account Number	Account	Debit	Credit
11	Cash	$ 3,000	
12	Accounts receivable	8,000	
13	Supplies..	600	
14	Land	35,000	
21	Accounts payable		$ 4,600
31	Brent Busch, capital		40,000
32	Brent Busch, withdrawals..............	2,300	
41	Service revenue..............................		7,100
51	Salary expense	1,800	
52	Rent expense..................................	1,000	
	Total...	$51,700	$51,700

During the remainder of November, Busch completed the following transactions:

Nov.	16	Collected $6,000 cash from a client on account.
	17	Performed tax service for a client on account, $1,700.
	21	Used personal funds to pay for the renovation of private residence, $55,000.
	22	Purchased supplies on account, $800.
	23	Withdrew $2,100 for personal use.
	23	Paid on account, $2,600.
	24	Received $1,900 cash for legal work just completed.
	30	Paid rent, $700.
	30	Paid employees' salaries, $2,100.

Required

1. Record the transactions that occurred during November 16–30 on page 6 of the journal. Include an explanation for each entry.
2. Post the transactions to the ledger, using dates, account numbers, journal references, and posting references. Open the ledger accounts listed in the trial balance together with their balances at November 15. Use the four-column account format illustrated in the chapter

(Exhibit 2-9). Enter *Bal.* (for previous balance) in the Item column, and place a check mark (✓) in the journal reference column for the November 15 balance of each account.

3. Prepare the trial balance of Brent Busch, Attorney, at November 30, 20X3.

P2-5B ← *Link Back to Chapter 1 (Income Statement).* The trial balance for Ballard Financial Services does not balance. The following errors were detected:

Correcting errors in a trial balance (Obj. 2, 5)

a. The cash balance is understated by $400.
b. Rent expense of $350 was erroneously posted as a credit rather than a debit.
c. An $8,300 credit to Service Revenue was not posted.
d. A $600 debit to Accounts Receivable was posted as $60.
e. The balance of Utilities Expense is understated by $60.
f. A $1,300 debit to the Withdrawal account was posted as a debit to Meredith Ballard, Capital.
g. A $100 purchase of supplies on account was neither journalized nor posted.
h. The balance of Advertising Expense is $300, but it is listed as $400 on the trial balance.
i. Office furniture should be listed in the amount of $1,300.

BALLARD FINANCIAL SERVICES
Trial Balance
March 31, 20X1

Cash	$ 6,200	
Accounts receivable	2,000	
Supplies	500	
Office furniture	2,300	
Land	46,000	
Accounts payable		$ 2,700
Note payable		18,300
Meredith Ballard, capital		29,500
Meredith Ballard, withdrawals	3,700	
Service revenue		4,900
Salary expense	1,300	
Rent expense	500	
Advertising expense	400	
Utilities expense	200	
Total	$63,100	$55,400

Required

1. Prepare the correct trial balance at March 31. Journal entries are not required.
2. Prepare Ballard Financial Services' income statement for the month ended March 31, 20X1, to determine whether the business had a net income or a net loss for the month. Refer to Exhibit 1-7, page 20, if needed.

P2-6B Vince Serrano started Serrano Catering Service, and during the first month of operations (January 20X7), he completed the following selected transactions:

Recording transactions directly in T-accounts; preparing a trial balance (Obj. 2, 5, 7)

a. Serrano began the business with an investment of $23,000 cash and a van (automobile) valued at $13,000. The business gave Serrano owner's equity in the business.
b. Borrowed $25,000 from the bank; signed a note payable.
c. Paid $32,000 for food-service equipment.
d. Purchased supplies on account, $400.
e. Paid employee's salary, $1,300.
f. Received $800 for a catering job performed for customers.
g. Received an $800 bill for advertising expense that will be paid in the near future.
h. Paid $100 of the account payable created in transaction (d).
i. Performed service at a wedding on account, $3,300.
j. Received cash on account, $1,100.
k. Paid the following cash expenses:
    (1) Rent, $1,000.   (2) Insurance, $600.
l. Withdrew $2,600 for personal use.

Required

1. Open the following T-accounts: Cash; Accounts Receivable; Supplies; Food-Service Equipment; Automobile; Accounts Payable; Note Payable; Vince Serrano, Capital; Vince Serrano, Withdrawals; Service Revenue; Salary Expense; Rent Expense; Advertising Expense; Insurance Expense.
2. Record the transactions directly in the T-accounts without using a journal. Use the letters to identify the transactions.
3. Prepare the trial balance of Serrano Catering Service at January 31, 20X7.

Note: Problem 2-7B should be used in conjunction with Problem 2-6B.

P2-7B ◄ *Link Back to Chapter 1 (Income Statement, Statement of Owner's Equity, Balance Sheet).* Refer to Problem 2-6B. After completing the trial balance in Problem 2-6B, prepare the following financial statements for Serrano Catering Service:

1. Income statement for the month ended January 31, 20X7.
2. Statement of owner's equity for the month ended January 31, 20X7.
3. Balance sheet at January 31, 20X7.

Draw arrows to link the statements. If needed, use Exhibit 1-7, page 20, as a guide for preparing the financial statements.

APPLY YOUR KNOWLEDGE

DECISION CASES

Case 1. Answer the following questions. Consider each question separately.

1. Explain the advantages of double-entry bookkeeping over single-entry bookkeeping to a friend who is opening a used book store.
2. When you deposit money in your bank account, the bank credits your account. Is the bank misusing the word *credit* in this context? Why does the bank use the term *credit* to refer to your deposit, and not *debit*?
3. Your friend asks, "When revenues increase assets and expenses decrease assets, why are revenues credits and expenses debits and not the other way around?" Explain to your friend why revenues are credits and expenses are debits.

Case 2. You have been requested by a friend named Belinda Nathews to give advice on the effects that certain transactions will have on her business. Time is short, so you cannot journalize the transactions. Instead, you must analyze the transactions without the use of a journal. Nathews will continue the business only if she can expect to earn monthly net income of $5,000. The following transactions have occurred during March:

a. Nathews deposited $8,000 cash in a business bank account to start the company.
b. Borrowed $6,000 cash from the bank and signed a note payable due within one year.
c. Paid $300 cash for supplies.
d. Paid cash for advertising in the local newspaper, $700.
e. Paid the following cash expenses for one month: secretary's salary, $1,400; office rent, $800; utilities, $300; interest, $50.
f. Earned service revenue on account, $5,300.
g. Earned service revenue and received $3,500 cash.
h. Collected cash from customers on account, $1,200.

Required

1. Open the following T-accounts: Cash; Accounts Receivable; Supplies; Notes Payable; Belinda Nathews, Capital; Service Revenue; Salary Expense; Rent Expense; Advertising Expense; Utilities Expense; Interest Expense.
2. Record the transactions directly in the accounts without using a journal. Key each transaction by letter.
3. Prepare a trial balance at March 31, 20X9. List expenses with the largest amount first, the next largest amount second, and so on. The business name is Nathews Apartment Locators.
4. Compute the amount of net income or net loss for this first month of operations. Would you recommend that Nathews continue in business?

ETHICAL ISSUE

Brave Hearts, a charitable organization in Panama City, Florida, has a standing agreement with De Leon State Bank. The agreement allows Brave Hearts to overdraw its cash balance at the bank when donations are running low. In the past, Brave Hearts managed funds wisely and rarely used this privilege. Jacob Henson has recently become the president of Brave Hearts. To expand operations, Henson acquired office equipment and spent large amounts on fundraising. During Henson's presidency, Brave Hearts has maintained a negative bank balance of approximately $6,000.

Required

What is the ethical issue in this situation? State why you approve or disapprove of Henson's management of Brave Hearts' funds.

FINANCIAL STATEMENT CASE

Journalizing transactions for a company
(Obj. 2, 3)

This problem helps you develop skill in recording transactions by using a company's actual account titles. Refer to the **Target Corporation** financial statements in Appendix A. Assume that Target completed the following selected transactions during October 2001:

Oct. 5 Earned sales revenue on account, $110,000.
9 Borrowed $500,000 by signing a note payable (long-term debt).
12 Purchased equipment and paid cash, $50,000.
17 Paid $100,000, a current maturity of a long-term debt, plus interest expense of $8,000.
19 Earned sales revenue and immediately received cash of $86,000.
22 Collected half the cash on account that was earned on October 5.
28 Received a home-office electricity bill for $3,000, which will be paid in November (this is an administrative expense).

Required

Journalize these transactions, using the following account titles taken from the Target financial statements: Cash; Retained Securitized Receivables (same as Accounts Receivable), Equipment; Accounts Payable; Current Portion of Long-Term Debt; Long-Term Debt; Sales (Revenue), Selling, General and Administrative Expense; Interest Expense. Explanations are not required.

TEAM PROJECT

Contact a local business and arrange with the owner to learn what accounts the business uses.

Required

1. Obtain a copy of the business's chart of accounts.
2. Prepare the company's financial statements for the most recent month, quarter, or year. You may use either made-up account balances or balances supplied by the owner.

If the business has a large number of accounts within a category, combine related accounts and report a single amount on the financial statements. For example, the company may have several cash accounts. Combine all cash amounts and report a single Cash amount on the balance sheet.

You will probably encounter numerous accounts that you have not yet learned. Deal with these as best you can. The chart of accounts given in Appendix B at the end of the book will be helpful.

Keep in mind that the financial statements report the balances of the accounts listed in the company's chart of accounts. Therefore, the financial statements must be consistent with the chart of accounts.

INTERNET EXERCISE

The accounting process illustrated in this chapter may be simplified with the aid of financial software. **Intuit Inc.** is a leader in e-finance and develops and supports Quicken®, the leading personal finance software; Turbo Tax®, the best-selling tax preparation software; and QuickBooks®, the most popular small business accounting software.

Intuit Inc.

1. Go to **http://www.quicken.com** and read the "Top News" headlines. In the "Get Quotes & Research" section type <u>INTU</u>, the stock symbol of Intuit Inc., and then click on *Go*. Review the information provided and comment on one item of interest.
2. In the left-hand column, click on *Financial Statements*. Amounts are reported in thousands.
   a. For the three most recent fiscal years, list the amounts reported for "Total Revenues" and "Net Incomes." For each of these amounts, comment on the results from 1997 to 1999. Is the trend favorable or unfavorable? In 1999, Intuit started to promote its Internet financial support services. Has this marketing strategy been profitable for Intuit?
   b. For the three most recent years, list the amounts reported for "Property and Equipment, Net" and "Total Assets." What percentage of total assets does property and equipment comprise? Would you expect this for an e-finance company?
   c. For property and equipment, what is the normal balance? Is the amount reported from before or after posting to the ledger?
3. It is important to understand the accounting process even though financial software is available. Explain why this is true.
4. Select one other feature of this Web site to explore. Comment on what you found and whether you consider this feature useful.

3

Measuring Business Income: The Adjusting Process

LEARNING OBJECTIVES

After studying this chapter, you should be able to

1. Distinguish accrual-basis accounting from cash-basis accounting

2. Apply the revenue and matching principles

3. Make adjusting entries at the end of the accounting period

4. Prepare an adjusted trial balance

5. Prepare the financial statements from the adjusted trial balance

www.prenhall.com/horngren

Readiness Assessment

Disappointed by blind dates and personal ads, Andrea McGinty started her own dating service. She also found a lucrative career. When McGinty's fiancé walked out on her five weeks before the wedding, it was back to the singles scene. Wouldn't it be nice if a dating service could arrange prescreened lunch dates for busy professionals like herself? "Lunch is over in an hour, and you don't have to kiss goodnight," she dreamed.

McGinty made her dream a reality. Her company, **It's Just Lunch,** now has thousands of customers. McGinty charges $1,000 to arrange 12 dates. "These are people who work long hours in fast-track careers. They need help with their social lives," says McGinty.

The business is a money-making machine, netting over $2 million of profit in a recent year.

Source: Adapted from Suzanne Oliver, "Yuppie Yenta," *Forbes* (March 25, 1996), pp. 102–103.

What do we mean when we say that **It's Just Lunch** *nets* over $2 million per year? The business earns net income, or profit, of more than $2 million, as reported on its income statement. The business's revenues consist of service-revenue fees earned by arranging lunch dates for clients. What are its expenses? Advertising, computer data searches, mailings to clients, and office expenses (such as employee salaries, rent, and supplies). It's Just Lunch operates in much the same way as **Gay Gillen eTravel,** the business studied in Chapters 1 and 2.

Whether the business is **It's Just Lunch,** Gillen's travel agency, or **IBM,** the profit motive increases the owner's drive to carry on the business. In this chapter, we'll consider how important net income is to a business.

FINANCIAL STATEMENTS AND ADJUSTING ENTRIES

How does a business know whether it is profitable? At the end of each accounting period, the entity prepares its financial statements. The period may be a month, three months, or a full year. **It's Just Lunch** is typical. The company reports on a quarterly basis every three months—with annual financial statements at the end of each year.

Whatever the length of the period, the main product of the accounting system is the financial statements. And the most important single amount in these statements is net income or net loss—the profit or loss—for the period. Net income captures much information: total revenues minus total expenses for the period.

An important step in financial statement preparation is the trial balance that we covered in Chapter 2. To measure its income, a business must bring the records up to date at the end of the period. This process is called *adjusting the books,* and it consists of making special journal entries called *adjusting entries.* This chapter focuses on these adjusting entries to show how to measure business income.

The accounting profession has concepts and principles to guide the measurement of business income. Chief among these are accrual-basis accounting, the accounting period, the revenue principle, and the matching principle. In this chapter, we apply these (and other) concepts and principles to measure income and prepare the financial statements of Gay Gillen eTravel for the month of April.

Accrual-Basis Accounting Versus Cash-Basis Accounting

There are two ways to do accounting:

- **Accrual-basis accounting** records the effect of every business transaction as it occurs. Most businesses use the accrual basis, and that is the method covered in this book.
- **Cash-basis accounting** records only cash receipts and cash payments. It ignores receivables, payables, and depreciation. Only very small businesses use cash-basis accounting.

Suppose **Drugstore.com** purchased $2,000 of supplies on account from **Johnson & Johnson,** the health-care products company. On the accrual basis, Drugstore.com records the asset Supplies and the liability Accounts Payable as follows:

Supplies	2,000	
Accounts Payable		2,000
Purchased supplies on account.		

Under the accrual basis, Drugstore.com's balance sheet reports the asset Supplies and the liability Accounts Payable.

In contrast, cash-basis accounting ignores this transaction because Drugstore.com paid no cash. The cash basis records only cash receipts and cash payments. *Cash receipts are treated as revenues, and cash payments are handled as expenses.* Therefore, under the cash basis, Drugstore.com would record a $2,000 cash payment as an expense rather than as an asset. This is faulty accounting: Drugstore.com acquired supplies, which are assets because they provide future benefit to the company.

Now let's see how differently the accrual basis and the cash basis account for a revenue. Suppose Drugstore.com sold goods on account. Under the accrual basis, Drugstore.com records a $10,000 sale as follows:

Accounts Receivable	10,000	
Sales Revenue		10,000
Sold goods on account.		

The balance sheet then reports the asset Accounts Receivable, and the income statement reports Sales Revenue. We have a complete picture of the transaction.

Under the cash basis, Drugstore.com would not even bother to record a sale *on account* because there is no cash receipt. Instead, it would wait until cash is received and then record the cash as revenue. As a result, cash-basis accounting never reports accounts receivable from customers. It shows the revenue in the wrong accounting period, when cash is received. Revenue should be recorded when it is earned, and that is how the accrual basis operates.

Exhibit 3-1 illustrates the difference between the accrual basis and the cash basis. Keep in mind that the accrual basis is the correct way to do accounting. Panel A of the exhibit illustrates a revenue, and Panel B covers an expense.

EXHIBIT 3-1
Accrual-Basis Accounting Versus Cash-Basis Accounting

DAILY EXERCISE 3-1

DAILY EXERCISE 3-2

PANEL A (a revenue)—Collect $3,000 cash on January 1. The $3,000 of revenue is to be earned evenly during January, February, and March.

		Jan.	Feb.	Mar.
Accrual-basis accounting:	Service revenue....................	$1,000	$1,000	$1,000
Cash-basis accounting:	Service revenue....................	$3,000		

PANEL B (an expense)—Prepay $6,000 for TV advertising to be run during October, November, and December.

		Oct.	Nov.	Dec.
Accrual-basis accounting:	Advertising expense.............	$2,000	$2,000	$2,000
Cash-basis accounting:	Advertising expense.............	$6,000		

The Accounting Period

The only way to know for certain how successfully a business has operated is to close its doors, sell all its assets, pay the liabilities, and return any leftover cash to the owners. This process, called *liquidation,* is the same as going out of business. It is not practical to measure business income in this manner. Instead, businesses need periodic reports on their situation. Accountants slice time into small segments and prepare financial statements for specific periods.

The basic accounting period is one year, and virtually all businesses prepare annual financial statements. For about 60% of large companies in a recent survey, the annual accounting period runs the calendar year from January 1 through December 31. Other companies use a *fiscal year*, which can end on any date other than December 31. The year-end date is usually the low point in business activity for the year. Retailers are a notable example. For instance, **J.C. Penney Company** uses a fiscal year ending on January 31 because the low point in Penney's business activity falls after the Christmas sales. J.C. Penney does more than 30% of its yearly sales during November and December, but only 5% in January.

Managers and investors cannot wait until the end of the year to gauge a company's progress. Companies therefore prepare financial statements for *interim* periods. Managers want financial information often, so monthly statements are common. A series of monthly statements can be combined for quarterly and semiannual periods. Most of the discussions in this book are based on an annual accounting period, but the procedures and statements can be applied to interim periods as well.

The Revenue Principle

The **revenue principle** tells accountants (1) *when* to record revenue by making a journal entry, and (2) the *amount* of revenue to record. ➻ When we speak of "recording" something in accounting, we mean "make an entry in the journal." That is where the accounting process starts.

The general principle guiding *when* to record revenue says to record revenue once it has been earned—but not before. In most cases, revenue is earned when the business has delivered a completed good or service to the customer. The business has done everything required by the sale agreement, including transferring the item to the customer. Exhibit 3-2 shows two situations that provide guidance on when to record revenue. The first situation illustrates when *not* to record revenue—because the client merely states her plans. Situation 2 illustrates when revenue should be recorded—after Gay Gillen has performed a service for the client.

Objective 2
Apply the revenue and matching principles

REVENUE PRINCIPLE. The basis for recording revenues; tells accountants when to record revenue and the amount of revenue to record.

◄ Revenue, defined in Chapter 1, p. 12, is the increase in owner's equity from delivering goods and services to customers in the course of operating a business.

EXHIBIT 3-2   **Recording Revenue: The Revenue Principle**

DAILY EXERCISE 3-3

The general principle guiding the *amount* of revenue says to record revenue equal to the cash value of the goods or the service transferred to the customer. Suppose that in order to obtain a new client, Gillen Travel performs accounting service for the price of $500. Ordinarily, Gillen would have charged $600 for this service. How much revenue should Gillen record? The answer is $500, because that was the cash value of the transaction. Gillen will not receive the full value of $600, so that is not the amount of revenue to record. She will receive only $500 cash, so that is the amount of revenue she has earned.

The Matching Principle

MATCHING PRINCIPLE. The basis for recording expenses. Directs accountants to identify all expenses incurred during the period, to measure the expenses, and to match them against the revenues earned during that same span of time.

The **matching principle** is the basis for recording expenses. ◂ Recall that expenses—such as rent, utilities, and advertising—are the costs of operating a business. Expenses are the costs of assets that are used up and liabilities that are increased in the earning of revenue. The matching principle directs accountants to (1) identify all expenses incurred during the accounting period, (2) measure the expenses, and (3) match the expenses against the revenues earned during that same span of time. To match expenses against revenues means to subtract expenses from revenues in order to compute net income or net loss. Exhibit 3-3 illustrates the matching principle.

EXHIBIT 3-3
Recording Expenses:
The Matching Principle

➥ An expense, defined in Chapter 1, p. 12, is a decrease in owner's equity that occurs from using assets or increasing liabilities in the course of operating a business.

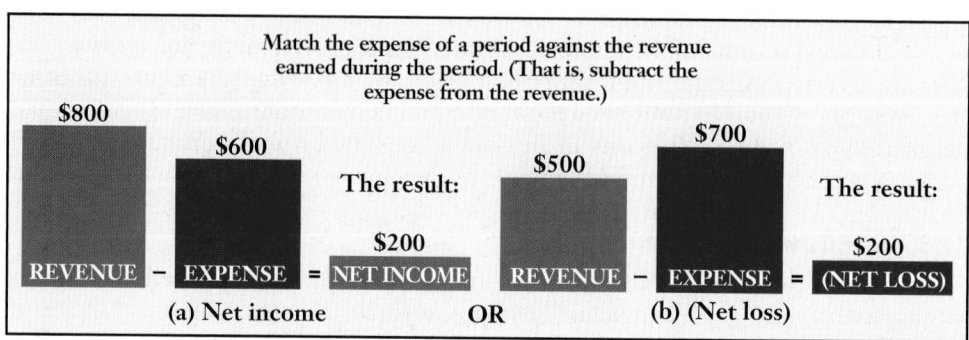

There is a natural link between revenues and some types of expenses. Accountants first identify a period's revenues and the expenses that can be linked to particular revenues. For example, a business that pays sales commissions to its sales personnel will have commission expense only if the employees make sales. *Cost of goods sold* is another example. If there are no sales of Ford automobiles, **Ford Motor Company** has no cost of goods sold.

Other expenses are not so easy to link with particular sales. For example, monthly rent expense occurs regardless of the revenues earned during the period. The matching principle directs accountants to identify those expenses with a particular time period, such as a month or a year. If Gay Gillen eTravel employs a secretary at a monthly salary of $1,900, the business will record salary expense of $1,900 for each month.

How does Gay Gillen account for a transaction that begins in April but ends in May? How does she bring the accounts up to date for preparing the financial statements? To answer these questions, accountants use the time-period concept.

The Time-Period Concept

TIME-PERIOD CONCEPT. Ensures that accounting information is reported at regular intervals.

Managers, investors, and creditors make decisions daily and need periodic readings on the state of the business. The **time-period concept** ensures that accounting information is reported at regular intervals. It interacts with the revenue principle and the matching principle. To measure income accurately, companies update the revenue and expense accounts immediately before the end of the period. **US Airways** provides an example of an expense accrual. At December 31, 1999, US Airways recorded employee compensation of $341 million that the company owed its workers for unpaid services performed before year end. The company's accrual entry, adapted and in millions of dollars, was

1999			
Dec. 31	Salary Expense............................	341	
	Salary Payable		341
	Accrued salary expense.		

This entry serves two purposes. First, it assigns the expense to the proper period. Without the accrual entry at December 31, total expenses of 1999 would be understated, and as a result, net income would be overstated. The expense would incorrectly fall in 2000 when US Airways pays the next payroll. Second, the accrual entry

DAILY EXERCISE 3-4

DAILY EXERCISE 3-5

DAILY EXERCISE 3-6

records the liability for the balance sheet at December 31, 1999. Without the accrual entry, total liabilities would be understated.

At the end of an accounting period, companies also accrue revenues that have been earned but not collected. The remainder of the chapter discusses how to make the adjusting entries to show these transactions and bring the accounts up to date.

ADJUSTING THE ACCOUNTS

At the end of the period, the accountant prepares the financial statements. The end-of-period process begins with the trial balance, which lists the accounts and their balances after the period's transactions have been recorded in the journal and posted to the accounts. We saw how to prepare the trial balance in Chapter 2.

Objective 3
Make adjusting entries at the end of the accounting period

Exhibit 3-4 is the trial balance of Gay Gillen eTravel at April 30, 20X1. This *unadjusted trial balance* includes some new accounts that we will explain in this section. It lists most of the revenues and expenses of the travel agency for the month of April. These trial balance amounts are incomplete because they omit certain revenue and expense transactions that affect more than one accounting period. That is why the trial balance is *unadjusted*. In most cases, however, we refer to it simply as the trial balance, without the label "unadjusted."

EXHIBIT 3-4
Unadjusted Trial Balance

GAY GILLEN eTRAVEL
Unadjusted Trial Balance
April 30, 20X1

Cash	$24,800	
Accounts receivable	2,250	
Supplies	700	
Prepaid rent	3,000	
Furniture	16,500	
Accounts payable		$13,100
Unearned service revenue		450
Gay Gillen, capital		31,250
Gay Gillen, withdrawals	3,200	
Service revenue		7,000
Salary expense	950	
Utilities expense	400	
Total	$51,800	$51,800

Under cash-basis accounting, there is no need for adjustments to the accounts because all April cash transactions have already been recorded. However, the accrual basis requires adjusting entries at the end of the period in order to produce correct balances for the financial statements. To see why, consider the Supplies account in Exhibit 3-4.

Gay Gillen eTravel uses supplies in providing travel services for clients during the month. This reduces the quantity of supplies on hand and thus constitutes an expense, just like salary or rent. It is not worth the effort to record supplies expense more than once a month. It takes time to make daily or weekly journal entries. So how does Gillen account for supplies expense?

By the end of the month, the Supplies balance of $700 on the unadjusted trial balance (Exhibit 3-4) is not correct. The unadjusted balance represents the amount of supplies on hand at the start of the month plus any supplies purchased during the month. This balance fails to take into account the supplies used (*supplies expense*) during the accounting period. It is necessary, then, to subtract the month's expenses from the amount of supplies listed on the trial balance. The resulting new adjusted balance will measure the cost of supplies that are still on hand at April 30, say $400. This is the correct amount of Supplies to report on the balance sheet—$400. The adjusting entry will bring the supplies account up to date.

Adjusting entries assign revenues to the period in which they are earned and expenses to the period in which they are incurred. Adjusting entries also update the asset and liability accounts. They are needed to (1) properly measure the period's

ADJUSTING ENTRY. Entry made at the end of the period to assign revenues to the period in which they are earned and expenses to the period in which they are incurred. Adjusting entries help measure the period's income and bring the related asset and liability accounts to correct balances for the financial statements.

income on the income statement, and (2) bring related asset and liability accounts to correct balances for the balance sheet. Adjusting entries, which are the key to accrual-basis accounting, are made before the financial statements are prepared. The end-of-period process of updating the accounts is called *adjusting the accounts, making the adjusting entries,* or *adjusting the books.*

A large company uses accounting software to print out a trial balance. For example, **Occidental Petroleum (OXY),** a large oil company, has accounting software that prints a monthly trial balance. The accountants then analyze the amounts on the trial balance. This analysis results in the adjusting entries that OXY makes. The trial balance has now become the *adjusted* trial balance. This chapter shows the adjusting process as it moves from the trial balance to the adjusted trial balance. Two basic types of adjustments are *prepaids* and *accruals.*

PREPAIDS (DEFERRALS) AND ACCRUALS

In a *prepaid* adjustment, the cash transaction occurs before the related expense or revenue is recorded. Prepaids are also called *deferrals* because the recording of the expense or the revenue is deferred until after cash is paid or received. *Accrual*-type adjustments are the opposite of prepaids. For accruals, we record the expense or revenue before the related cash settlement.

Adjusting entries can be further divided into five categories:

1. Prepaid expenses
2. Depreciation of plant assets
3. Accrued expenses
4. Accrued revenues
5. Unearned revenues

The core of this chapter is the discussion of these five types of adjusting entries on pages 88–96. Study this material carefully because it is the most challenging topic in all of introductory accounting.

Prepaid Expenses

Prepaid expenses are advance payments of expenses. The category includes prepayments that typically expire or that will be used up in the near future. Prepaid rent and prepaid insurance are examples. They are called "prepaid" expenses because they are paid in advance. Salary expense and utilities expense, among others, are typically *not* prepaid because they are not paid in advance. All companies, large and small, must make adjustments regarding prepaid expenses. For example, **McDonald's Corporation,** the restaurant chain, must contend with such prepayments as rents, packaging supplies, and insurance. Keep in mind that prepaid expenses are assets, not expenses.

PREPAID EXPENSE. Advance payments of expenses. A category of current assets that typically expire or are used up in the near future. Examples include prepaid rent, prepaid insurance, and supplies.

PREPAID RENT   Landlords usually require tenants to pay rent in advance. This prepayment creates an asset for the renter, who has purchased the future benefit of using the rented item. Suppose Gay Gillen eTravel prepays three months' office rent on April 1, 20X1. If the lease specifies monthly rental amounts of $1,000, the entry to record the payment for three months is a debit to the asset account, Prepaid Rent, as follows:

Apr. 1	Prepaid Rent ($1,000 × 3)	3,000	
	Cash		3,000
	Paid three months' rent in advance.		

After posting, Prepaid Rent appears as follows:

ASSETS

PREPAID RENT

Apr. 1	3,000	

The trial balance at April 30, 20X1, lists Prepaid Rent as an asset with a debit balance of $3,000. Throughout April, the Prepaid Rent account maintains this beginning balance, as shown in Exhibit 3-4. But $3,000 is *not* the amount to report for Prepaid Rent on the travel agency's balance sheet at April 30. Why?

At April 30, Prepaid Rent should be adjusted to remove from its balance the amount of the asset that has been used up, which is one month's worth of the prepayment. By definition, the amount of an asset that has expired is *expense*. The adjusting entry transfers one-third, or $1,000 ($3,000 × 1/3), of the debit balance from Prepaid Rent to Rent Expense. The debit side of the entry records an increase in Rent Expense, and the credit records a decrease in the asset Prepaid Rent:

Apr. 30	Rent Expense ($3,000 × 1/3)	1,000	
	Prepaid Rent		1,000
	To record rent expense.		

After posting, Prepaid Rent and Rent Expense appear as follows:

ASSETS		EXPENSES	
PREPAID RENT		RENT EXPENSE	
Apr. 1 3,000	Apr. 30 1,000	Apr. 30 1,000	
Bal. 2,000		Bal. 1,000	

Correct asset	→	Total accounted	←	Correct expense
amount: $2,000		for: $3,000		amount: $1,000

The full $3,000 has been accounted for: Two-thirds measures the asset, and one-third measures the expense. Recording this expense illustrates the matching principle.

The same analysis applies to prepayment of three months of insurance premiums. The only difference is in the account titles, which would be Prepaid Insurance and Insurance Expense instead of Prepaid Rent and Rent Expense. In a computerized system, the adjusting entry crediting the prepaid account and debiting the expense account could be established to recur automatically in each accounting period until the prepaid account has a zero balance.

The chapter appendix shows an alternative treatment of prepaid expenses. The end result on the financial statements is the same as illustrated here.

SUPPLIES Supplies are accounted for in the same way as prepaid expenses. On April 2, Gay Gillen paid cash of $700 for office supplies:

Apr. 2	Supplies	700	
	Cash		700
	Paid cash for supplies.		

Assume that Gillen purchased no additional supplies during April. The April 30 trial balance, therefore, lists Supplies with a $700 debit balance, as shown in Exhibit 3-4. But Gillen's April 30 balance sheet should *not* report supplies of $700. Why?

During April, Gillen used supplies in performing services for clients. The cost of the supplies used is the measure of *supplies expense* for the month. To measure supplies expense during April, Gillen counts the supplies on hand at the end of the month. This is the amount of the asset (the economic resource) still available to the business. Assume the count at April 30 indicates that supplies costing $400 remain. Subtracting the $400 of supplies on hand at the end of April from the cost of supplies available during April ($700) measures supplies expense during the month ($300).

Cost of asset available during the period	−	Cost of asset on hand at the end of the period	=	Cost of asset used (expense) during the period
$700	−	$400	=	$300

The April 30 adjusting entry to update the Supplies account and to record the supplies expense for the month debits the expense and credits the asset, as follows:

Apr. 30	Supplies Expense ($700 − $400)	300	
	Supplies		300
	To record supplies expense.		

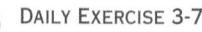

After posting, the Supplies and Supplies Expense accounts appear as follows:

ASSETS				EXPENSES		
SUPPLIES				SUPPLIES EXPENSE		
Apr. 2	700	Apr. 30	300	Apr. 30	300	
Bal.	400			Bal.	300	

Correct asset amount: $400	→	Total accounted for: $700	←	Correct expense amount: $300

The Supplies account then enters the month of May with a $400 balance, and the adjustment process is repeated at the end of May.

 WORK IT OUT

At the beginning of the month, Supplies were $5,000. During the month, the company purchased $7,800 of supplies. At month's end, $3,600 of supplies were still on hand.

1. What was the cost of supplies used during the month?
2. What is the ending balance of Supplies? Where is this item reported?
3. Make the adjusting entry to update the Supplies account at the end of the month.

Answers

1.

Beginning balance	$ 5,000
+Purchases	7,800
=Supplies available	12,800
−Ending balance	(3,600)
=Expense (supplies used during the period)	$ 9,200

2. The ending balance of Supplies is $3,600. This is the amount that should be reported on the *balance sheet*.

3.

Supplies Expense	9,200	
Supplies		9,200

Depreciation of Plant Assets

The logic of the accrual basis is probably best illustrated by how businesses account for plant assets. **Plant assets** are long-lived tangible assets—such as land, buildings, furniture, machinery, and equipment—used in the operations of the business. As one accountant said, "All assets but land are on a march to the junkyard." That is, all plant assets except land decline in usefulness as they age. This decline is an expense to the business. Accountants systematically spread the cost of each plant asset, except land, over the years of its useful life. This allocation of a plant asset's cost to expense over its useful life is called **depreciation.**

PLANT ASSET. Long-lived tangible assets—such as land, buildings, and equipment—used in the operations of a business.

DEPRECIATION. The allocation of a plant asset's cost to expense over its useful life.

SIMILARITY TO PREPAID EXPENSES   The concept underlying accounting for plant assets is the same as for prepaid expenses. In a sense, plant assets are merely prepaid expenses that expire over a number of periods. With both prepaid expenses and plant assets, the business purchases an asset that wears out. As the asset is used, its cost is transferred from the asset account to the expense account. The major difference between prepaid expenses and plant assets is the length of time it takes for the asset to expire. Prepaid expenses usually expire within a year, while most plant assets remain useful for a number of years.

Consider Gay Gillen eTravel. Suppose that on April 3 Gillen purchased furniture on account for $16,500 and made this journal entry:

Apr. 3	Furniture	16,500	
	Accounts Payable		16,500
	Purchased office furniture on account.		

After posting, the Furniture account appears as follows:

ASSETS

FURNITURE

Apr. 3 16,500	

Gillen believes the furniture will remain useful for five years and will be worthless at the end of its life. One way to compute the amount of depreciation for each year is to divide the cost of the asset ($16,500 in our example) by its expected useful life (five years). This procedure—called the straight-line method—computes annual depreciation of $3,300 ($16,500/5 years = $3,300 per year). Depreciation for the month of April is $275 ($3,300/12 months = $275 per month).

THE ACCUMULATED DEPRECIATION ACCOUNT Depreciation expense for April is recorded by the following entry:

Apr. 30	Depreciation Expense—Furniture.............................	275	
	Accumulated Depreciation—Furniture		275
	To record depreciation on furniture.		

Accumulated Depreciation is credited instead of Furniture because the original cost of a plant asset (the furniture) should remain in the asset account as long as the business uses the asset. Accountants and managers can then refer to the Furniture account to see how much the asset cost. This information may be useful in a decision about whether to replace the furniture and how much to pay.

The amount of depreciation is an estimate. The Accumulated Depreciation account holds the cumulative sum of all depreciation expense recorded for the asset. The balance of the Accumulated Depreciation account increases over the life of the asset.

Accumulated Depreciation is a contra asset account, which means an asset account with a normal credit balance. A **contra account** has two distinguishing characteristics:

- A contra account has a companion account.
- A contra account's normal balance (debit or credit) is opposite that of the companion account.

In this case, Accumulated Depreciation is the contra account that accompanies Furniture. It appears in the ledger directly after Furniture. Furniture has a debit balance, and therefore Accumulated Depreciation, a contra asset, has a credit balance. *All contra asset accounts have credit balances.*

A business carries an accumulated depreciation account for each depreciable asset. If a business has a building and a machine, for example, it will carry the accounts Accumulated Depreciation—Building and Accumulated Depreciation—Machine.

After the depreciation entry has been posted, the Furniture, Accumulated Depreciation, and Depreciation Expense accounts of Gay Gillen eTravel, appear as follows:

ASSETS		**CONTRA ASSET**		**EXPENSES**	
FURNITURE		ACCUMULATED DEPRECIATION—FURNITURE		DEPRECIATION EXPENSE—FURNITURE	
Apr. 3 16,500			Apr. 30 275	Apr. 30 275	
Bal. 16,500			Bal. 275	Bal. 275	

BOOK VALUE   The balance sheet shows the relationship between Furniture and Accumulated Depreciation. The balance of Accumulated Depreciation is subtracted from the balance of Furniture. The resulting net amount of a plant asset (cost minus accumulated depreciation) is called its **book value,** or *net book value,* as shown at top of next page for Furniture:

ACCUMULATED DEPRECIATION. The cumulative sum of all depreciation expense recorded for an asset.

CONTRA ACCOUNT. An account that always has a companion account and whose normal balance is opposite that of the companion account.

BOOK VALUE (OF A PLANT ASSET). The asset's cost minus accumulated depreciation.

Plant Assets:	
Furniture..	$16,500
Less: Accumulated depreciation..............	(275)
Book value..	$16,225

Suppose Gillen eTravel also owns a building that cost $48,000 and on which annual depreciation is $2,400 ($48,000/20 years). The amount of depreciation for one month would be $200 ($2,400/12), and the following entry records depreciation for April:

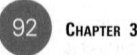DAILY EXERCISE 3-8

Apr. 30	Depreciation Expense—Building.............................	200	
	Accumulated Depreciation—Building............		200
	To record depreciation on building.		

The balance sheet at April 30 reports Gillen's plant assets as shown in Exhibit 3-5.

EXHIBIT 3-5
Plant Assets on the Balance Sheet of Gay Gillen eTravel (April 30)

Plant Assets:		
Furniture..	$16,500	
Less: Accumulated depreciation..............	(275)	$16,225
Building	48,000	
Less: Accumulated depreciation..............	(200)	47,800
Book value of plant assets...........................		$64,025

Exhibit 3-6 shows how **Johnson & Johnson**—maker of Band-Aids, Tylenol, and other health-care products—displayed Property, Plant, and Equipment in its annual report. Johnson & Johnson has real-estate holdings around the world; they are reported in line 1 of Exhibit 3-6. Line 2 includes the cost of buildings and the related equipment (air conditioners and elevators) in those buildings. The company's manufacturing machinery, office equipment, and furniture are given in line 3, and line 4 reports the cost of assets that are under construction.

EXHIBIT 3-6
Johnson & Johnson's Reporting of Property, Plant, and Equipment

	Millions
(1) Land and land improvements	$ 344
(2) Buildings and building equipment..............	2,611
(3) Machinery and equipment..........................	4,217
(4) Construction in progress	1,003
	8,175
Less: Accumulated depreciation........................	(2,979)
	$5,196

Johnson & Johnson's cost of plant assets was $8,175 million (cost principle). Of the total cost, Johnson & Johnson has depreciated a total of $2,979 million (matching principle). The book value of J&J's plant assets is therefore $8,175 − $2,979 = $5,196 million.

Now let's return to Gay Gillen eTravel.

Accrued Expenses

ACCRUED EXPENSE. An expense that the business has incurred but not yet paid.

Businesses often incur expenses before they pay for them. Consider an employee's salary. The employer's salary expense and salary payable grow as the employee works, so the liability is said to *accrue*. Another example is interest expense on a note payable. Interest accrues as the clock ticks. The term **accrued expense** refers to an expense the business has incurred but has not yet paid. Accrued expenses can be viewed as the opposite of prepaid expenses.

It is time-consuming to make weekly journal entries to accrue expenses. Consequently, the accountant waits until the end of the period. Then an adjusting entry brings each expense (and related liability) up to date just before the financial statements are prepared.

Remember the key difference between a prepaid expense and an accrued expense: A prepaid expense is paid first and expensed later. An accrued expense is expensed first and paid later. Prepaids and accruals are opposites.

SALARY EXPENSE Most companies pay their employees at set times. Suppose Gay Gillen pays her employee a monthly salary of $1,900, half on the 15th and half on the last day of the month. Here is a calendar for April with the two paydays circled:

APRIL						
S	M	T	W	T	F	S
					1	2
3	4	5	6	7	8	9
10	11	12	13	14	(15)	16
17	18	19	20	21	22	23
24	25	26	27	28	29	(30)

Assume that if either payday falls on the weekend, Gillen pays the employee on the following Monday. During April, Gillen paid her employee's first half-month salary of $950 on Friday, April 15, and recorded the following entry:

Apr. 15   Salary Expense   950
                    Cash   950
            To pay salary.

After posting, the Salary Expense account is

EXPENSES
SALARY EXPENSE

| Apr. 15 | 950 | |

The trial balance at April 30 (Exhibit 3-4) includes Salary Expense, with its debit balance of $950. This unadjusted balance of $950 is Gillen's salary expense for only the first half of April. Because April 30, the second payday of the month, falls on a Saturday, the second half-month amount of $950 will be paid on Monday, May 2. However, Gillen must record salary expense for the second half of April. Because of the need to accrue salary expense at April 30, Gillen makes an adjusting entry for additional Salary Expense and Salary Payable of $950 as follows:

Apr. 30   Salary Expense   950
                    Salary Payable   950
            To accrue salary expense.

This is the accrual basis of accounting in action. After posting, the Salary Expense and Salary Payable accounts are updated to April 30:

EXPENSES   **LIABILITIES**
SALARY EXPENSE   SALARY PAYABLE

Apr. 15	950				Apr. 30	950
Apr. 30	950				Bal.	950
Bal.	1,900	

○ DAILY EXERCISE 3-9

The accounts at April 30 now contain complete salary information for the month of April. The expense account has a full month's salary, and the liability account shows the portion that the business still owes at April 30. Gillen will record the payment of this liability on Monday, May 2.

 WORK IT OUT

Weekly salaries for a five-day workweek total $3,500, payable on a Friday. This month, November 30 falls on a Tuesday.
1. Which accounts require adjustment at November 30?
2. Make the adjusting entry.

Answers
1. Salary Expense and Salary Payable.
2.

	Salary Expense ($3,500 × 2/5)	1,400	
	Salary Payable		1,400
	To accrue salary expense.		

Accrued Revenues

ACCRUED REVENUE. A revenue that has been earned but not yet collected in cash.

Some expenses occur before the cash payment, and we must record an accrued expense. Likewise, businesses may also earn revenue before they receive the cash. This calls for an **accrued revenue,** which is a revenue that has been earned but not yet collected in cash.

 DAILY EXERCISE 3-10

Assume that Gay Gillen eTravel is hired on April 15 by **Procter & Gamble** to perform travel services on a continuing basis. Under this agreement, Gillen will receive $500 monthly, with the first cash receipt on May 15. During April, she will earn half a month's fee, $250, for work performed April 15 through April 30. On April 30, she makes the following adjusting entry to accrue the revenue earned during April 15–30:

Apr. 30	Accounts Receivable ($500 × 1/2)	250	
	Service Revenue		250
	To accrue service revenue		

We see from the unadjusted trial balance in Exhibit 3-4 that Accounts Receivable has an unadjusted balance of $2,250. Service Revenue's unadjusted balance is $7,000. Posting the April 30 adjusting entry has the following effects on these two accounts:

ASSETS		REVENUES	
ACCOUNTS RECEIVABLE		SERVICE REVENUE	
2,250			7,000
Apr. 30 250			Apr. 30 250
Bal. 2,500			Bal. 7,250

This adjusting entry illustrates the revenue principle. Without the adjustment, Gillen's financial statements would be incomplete and misleading—they would understate Accounts Receivable and Service Revenue by $250 each. All accrued revenues are accounted for similarly—by debiting a receivable and crediting a revenue.

Now we turn to a different category of adjusting entries.

Unearned Revenues

UNEARNED REVENUE. A liability created when a business collects cash from customers in advance of doing work. The obligation is to provide a product or a service in the future. Also called **deferred revenue.**

Some businesses collect cash from customers in advance of doing work for them. Receiving cash in advance creates a liability called **unearned revenue** or **deferred revenue.** This liability arises from receiving cash in advance of providing a product or a service. Only when the job is completed will the business have *earned* the revenue.

Suppose **Baldwin Piano Company** engages Gillen to provide travel services, agreeing to pay her $450 monthly, beginning immediately. Baldwin makes the first payment on April 20. Gillen records the cash receipt and the related increase in liabilities as follows:

Apr. 20	Cash	450	
	Unearned Service Revenue		450
	Collected revenue in advance.		

After posting, the liability account Unearned Service Revenue appears as follows:

LIABILITIES

UNEARNED SERVICE REVENUE

	Apr. 20	450

Unearned Service Revenue is a liability account because it represents Gillen's obligation to perform service for the client. The April 30 unadjusted trial balance (Exhibit 3-4) lists Unearned Service Revenue with a $450 credit balance prior to the adjusting entries. During the last ten days of the month—April 21 through April 30—Gillen will have *earned* one-third (10 days divided by April's total 30 days) of the $450, or $150. Therefore, Gillen makes the following adjustment to decrease the liability, Unearned Service Revenue, and to record an increase in Service Revenue, as follows:

Apr. 30	Unearned Service Revenue ($450 × 1/3)	150	
	Service Revenue		150
	To record service revenue that was collected in advance.		

This adjusting entry shifts $150 of the total amount of unearned service revenue from the liability account to the revenue account. After posting, the balance of Service Revenue is increased by $150, and the balance of Unearned Service Revenue is reduced by $150, to $300. Now, both accounts have the correct balances at April 30:

LIABILITIES

UNEARNED SERVICE REVENUE

Apr. 30	150	Apr. 20	450
		Bal.	300

REVENUES

SERVICE REVENUE

			7,000
		Apr. 30	250
		Apr. 30	150
		Bal.	7,400

Correct liability amount: $300	→	Total accounted for: $450	←	Correct revenue amount: $150

All types of revenues collected in advance are accounted for in the same way.

An unearned revenue to one company is a prepaid expense to the company that made the payment. For example, suppose that **Xerox Corporation** paid **American Airlines** $1,800 two months in advance for the air travel expenses of Xerox executives. To Xerox, the payment is Prepaid Travel Expense. To American Airlines, the receipt of cash creates Unearned Service Revenue. After the executives take the trip, American Airlines records the revenue and Xerox records travel expense.

Remember: An unearned revenue is a liability, not a revenue.

DAILY EXERCISE 3-11

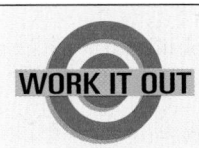

WORK IT OUT

Consider the tuition you pay your college or university. Assume that one semester's tuition costs $500 and that you make a single payment at the start of the term. Can you make the journal entries to record the tuition transactions on your own books and on the books of your college or university?

Answer

	Your Books			**Your College's Books**		
Start of Semester	Prepaid Tuition	500		Cash...........................	500	
	Cash		500	Unearned Tuition Revenue...............		500
	Paid semester tuition.			Collected revenue in advance.		
End of Semester	Tuition Expense	500		Unearned Tuition Revenue	500	
	Prepaid Tuition		500	Tuition Revenue ...		500
	To record tuition expense.			To record tuition revenue that was collected in advance.		

Exhibit 3-7 summarizes the timing of prepaid- and accrual-type adjusting entries. The chapter appendix shows an alternative treatment for unearned revenues.

EXHIBIT 3-7 *Prepaid- and Accrual-Type Adjustments*

PREPAIDS—The cash transaction occurs initially.

	Initially		Later	
Prepaid Expenses	Pay cash and record an asset: Prepaid Expense .... XXX Cash	 XXX	Record an expense and decrease the asset: Expense...................................... XXX Prepaid Expense	 XXX
Unearned Revenues	Receive cash and record unearned revenue: Cash... XXX Unearned Revenue	 XXX	Record a revenue and decrease unearned revenue: Unearned Revenue .... XXX Revenue	 XXX

ACCRUALS—The cash transaction occurs later.

	Initially		Later	
Accrued Expenses	Accrue an expense and the related payable: Expense .... XXX Payable...............................	 XXX	Pay cash and decrease the payable: Payable.................................... XXX Cash......................................	 XXX
Accrued Revenues	Accrue a revenue and the related receivable: Receivable.................................. XXX Revenue	 XXX	Receive cash and decrease the receivable: Cash .... XXX Receivable	 XXX

Source: The authors thank Darrel Davis and Alfonso Oddo for suggesting this exhibit.

---

www.prenhall.com/horngren
Mid-Chapter Assessment

Summary of the Adjusting Process

The adjusting process has two purposes:

1. Measure net income or net loss on the *income statement*. Every adjusting entry affects either a *Revenue* or an *Expense*.
2. Update the *balance sheet*. Every adjusting entry affects either an *Asset* or a *Liability*.

No adjusting entry debits or credits Cash because the cash transactions are recorded before the end of the period. Exhibit 3-8 summarizes the adjusting entries.

EXHIBIT 3-8
Summary of Adjusting Entries

	Type of Account	
Category of Adjusting Entry	**Debited**	**Credited**
Prepaid expense	Expense	Asset
Depreciation	Expense	Contra asset
Accrued expense	Expense	Liability
Accrued revenue	Asset	Revenue
Unearned revenue	Liability	Revenue

Source: Adapted from material provided by Beverly Terry.

Exhibit 3-9 summarizes the adjusting entries of Gay Gillen eTravel at April 30. Panel A briefly describes the data for each adjustment, Panel B gives the adjusting entries, and Panel C shows the accounts after they have been posted. The adjustments are keyed by letter.

Objective 4
Prepare an adjusted trial balance

THE ADJUSTED TRIAL BALANCE

This chapter began with the trial balance before any adjusting entries—the unadjusted trial balance (Exhibit 3-4). After the adjustments are journalized and posted, the accounts appear as shown in Exhibit 3-9, Panel C. A useful step in preparing the

PANEL A—Information for Adjustments at April 30, 20X1

(a) Prepaid rent expired, $1,000.
(b) Supplies on hand, $400.
(c) Depreciation on furniture, $275.
(d) Accrued salary expense, $950.

(e) Accrued service revenue, $250
(f) Service revenue earned that was collected in advance, $150.

PANEL B—Adjusting Entries

(a)	Rent Expense	1,000	
	Prepaid Rent		1,000
	To record rent expense.		
(b)	Supplies Expense	300	
	Supplies...		300
	To record supplies used.		
(c)	Depreciation Expense—Furniture	275	
	Accumulated Depreciation—Furniture..............		275
	To record depreciation on furniture.		
(d)	Salary Expense..	950	
	Salary Payable		950
	To accrue salary expense.		
(e)	Accounts Receivable	250	
	Service Revenue		250
	To accrue service revenue.		
(f)	Unearned Service Revenue..	150	
	Service Revenue		150
	To record revenue that was collected in advance.		

PANEL C—Ledger Accounts

ASSETS

CASH
| Bal. 24,800 | |

PREPAID RENT
| | 3,000 | (a) | 1,000 |
| Bal. | 2,000 | | |

ACCOUNTS RECEIVABLE
	2,250	
(e)	250	
Bal.	2,500	

FURNITURE
| Bal. 16,500 | |

SUPPLIES
| | 700 | (b) | 300 |
| Bal. | 400 | | |

ACCUMULATED DEPRECIATION—FURNITURE
| | (c) | 275 |
| | Bal. | 275 |

LIABILITIES

ACCOUNTS PAYABLE
| | Bal. 13,100 |

SALARY PAYABLE
| | (d) | 950 |
| | Bal. | 950 |

UNEARNED SERVICE REVENUE
| (f) | 150 | | 450 |
| | | Bal. | 300 |

OWNER'S EQUITY

GAY GILLEN, CAPITAL
| | Bal. 31,250 |

GAY GILLEN, WITHDRAWALS
| Bal. 3,200 | |

REVENUE

SERVICE REVENUE
			7,000
		(e)	250
		(f)	150
		Bal.	7,400

EXPENSES

RENT EXPENSE
| (a) | 1,000 | |
| Bal. | 1,000 | |

SALARY EXPENSE
	950	
(d)	950	
Bal.	1,000	

SUPPLIES EXPENSE
| (b) | 300 | |
| Bal. | 300 | |

DEPRECIATION EXPENSE—FURNITURE
| (c) | 275 | |
| Bal. | 275 | |

UTILITIES EXPENSE
| Bal. | 400 | |

financial statements is to list the accounts, along with their adjusted balances, on an **adjusted trial balance.** This document has the advantage of listing all the accounts and their adjusted balances in a single place. Exhibit 3-10 shows the preparation of the adjusted trial balance.

Exhibit 3-10 is a *work sheet.* We will discuss the work sheet in detail in Chapter 4. For now, simply note how clearly this format presents the data. The information in

ADJUSTED TRIAL BALANCE. A list of all the accounts with their adjusted balances.

Grossing up the Revenue: Priceline.com and Ventro

Suppose you're going to Australia. You want a cheap air ticket, and **Priceline.com** lets you "name your price" for airline tickets and hotel rooms. Your bid of $975 is accepted, and Priceline pockets the spread between your price and the amount that Priceline pays the airline company. What should Priceline claim as revenue—the fee Priceline earns or the full price of your ticket?

Priceline.com and other Internet service companies are claiming the entire value of the products sold through their sites. The SEC and the FASB call this practice "grossing up" revenue. Dot.com companies do it to show a profit when they're actually operating at a loss. The practice draws investors and pushes up stock prices. Grossing up may be legal, but the SEC and the FASB are considering placing restrictions on it.

Ventro, which handles the sale of specialty medical products over the Internet, is one company that would be adversely affected by such a restriction. Ventro's $29 million in grossed-up revenue for 1999 was expected to more than quadruple to $140 million in 2000. The company argues that its accounting method is sound since the company assumes various revenue risks: shelling out money if a product is returned, bearing credit risk if the customer won't pay, and taking title to the products sold. Yet Ventro never takes actual products into its own inventory and only takes title to the products during the time it takes to ship them. Ventro's suppliers are happy to absorb refund costs and Ventro's blue-chip customers rarely pose credit problems. If the accounting rulemakers decide that grossing up is okay, expect to see the value of business-to-business sites like Ventro soar.

Sources: Based on: Elizabeth McDonald, "Plump from Web Sales, Some Dot.Coms Face Crash Diet of Restriction on Booking Revenue," *Wall Street Journal,* February 28, 2000, p. C4. Jeremy Kahn, "Presto chango! Sales are huge!" *Fortune,* March 20, 2000, pp. 90–96.

---

the Account Title column and in the Trial Balance columns is copied directly from the trial balance. The two Adjustments columns list the debit and credit adjustments directly across from the appropriate account title. Each adjusting debit is identified by a letter that refers to the adjusting entry. For example, the debit labeled (a) on the work sheet refers to the debit adjusting entry of $1,000 to Rent Expense in Panel B of Exhibit 3-9. For adjusting credits, the corresponding credit—labeled (a)—refers to the $1,000 credit to Prepaid Rent.

The Adjusted Trial Balance columns give the adjusted account balances. Each amount in these columns is computed by combining the amounts from the unadjusted trial balance plus or minus the adjustments. For example, Accounts Receivable starts with a debit balance of $2,250. Adding the $250 debit amount from adjusting entry (e) gives Accounts Receivable an adjusted debit balance of $2,500. Supplies begins with a debit balance of $700. After the $300 credit adjustment, its adjusted balance is $400. More than one entry may affect a single account, as is the case for Service Revenue. If an account is unaffected by the adjustments, it will show the same amount on both the unadjusted and the adjusted trial balances. In this example, the balances of Cash, Furniture, Accounts Payable, Capital, and Withdrawals do not change.

⊙ DAILY EXERCISE 3-12

⊙ DAILY EXERCISE 3-13

⊙ DAILY EXERCISE 3-14

⊙ DAILY EXERCISE 3-15

⊙ DAILY EXERCISE 3-16

EXHIBIT 3-10   Preparation of Adjusted Trial Balance

GAY GILLEN ETRAVEL
Preparation of Adjusted Trial Balance
April 30, 20X1

Account Title	Trial Balance Debit	Trial Balance Credit	Adjustments Debit		Adjustments Credit		Adjusted Trial Balance Debit	Adjusted Trial Balance Credit
Cash	24,800						24,800	
Accounts receivable	2,250		(e)	250			2,500	
Supplies	700				(b)	300	400	
Prepaid rent	3,000				(a)	1,000	2,000	
Furniture	16,500						16,500	
Accumulated depreciation					(c)	275		275
Accounts payable		13,100						13,100
Salary payable					(d)	950		950
Unearned service revenue		450	(f)	150				300
Gay Gillen, capital		31,250						31,250
Gay Gillen, withdrawals	3,200						3,200	
Service revenue		7,000			(e)	250		7,400
					(f)	150		
Rent expense			(a)	1,000			1,000	
Salary expense	950		(d)	950			1,900	
Supplies expense			(b)	300			300	
Depreciation expense			(c)	275			275	
Utilities expense	400						400	
	51,800	51,800		2,925		2,925	53,275	53,275

Account Title	Adjusted Trial Balance Debit	Adjusted Trial Balance Credit	
Cash	24,800		
Accounts receivable	2,500		
Supplies	400		
Prepaid rent	2,000		
Furniture	16,500		**Balance Sheet** (Exhibit 3-14)
Accumulated depreciation		275	
Accounts payable		13,100	
Salary payable		950	
Unearned service revenue		300	
Gay Gillen, capital		31,250	**Statement of Owner's Equity** (Exhibit 3-13)
Gay Gillen, withdrawals	3,200		
Service revenue		7,400	
Rent expense	1,000		**Income Statement** (Exhibit 3-12)
Salary expense	1,900		
Supplies expense	300		
Depreciation expense	275		
Utilities expense	400		
	53,275	53,275	

PREPARING THE FINANCIAL STATEMENTS

The April financial statements of Gay Gillen eTravel can be prepared from the adjusted trial balance. Exhibit 3-11 shows how the accounts are distributed from the adjusted trial balance to three of the four main financial statements. As we have seen in Chapters 1–3, the income statement (Exhibit 3-12) comes from the revenue and expense accounts. The statement of owner's equity (Exhibit 3-13) shows why the owner's capital changed during the period. The balance sheet (Exhibit 3-14) reports the assets, liabilities, and owner's equity.

The financial statements are best prepared in the order shown: the income statement first, followed by the statement of owner's equity, and then the balance sheet.

EXHIBIT 3-12
Income Statement

GAY GILLEN eTRAVEL
Income Statement
Month Ended April 30, 20X1

Revenue:		
Service revenue		$7,400
Expenses:		
Salary expense	$1,900	
Rent expense......................	1,000	
Utilities expense	400	
Supplies expense...............	300	
Depreciation expense.........	275	
Total expenses...................		3,875
Net income		$3,525

EXHIBIT 3-13
Statement of Owner's Equity

GAY GILLEN eTRAVEL
Statement of Owner's Equity
Month Ended April 30, 20X1

Gay Gillen, capital, April 1, 20X1................	$31,250
Add: Net income	3,525
	34,775
Less: Withdrawals.......................................	(3,200)
Gay Gillen, capital, April 30, 20X1..............	$31,575

EXHIBIT 3-14
Balance Sheet

GAY GILLEN eTRAVEL
Balance Sheet
April 30, 20X1

Assets			Liabilities		
Cash		$24,800	Accounts payable		$13,100
Accounts			Salary payable....................		950
receivable		2,500	Unearned service		
Supplies		400	revenue		300
Prepaid rent		2,000	Total liabilities		14,350
Furniture	$16,500				
Less:					
Accumulated					
depreciation	(275)	16,225	**Owner's Equity**		
			Gay Gillen, capital...............		31,575
			Total liabilities and		
Total assets		$45,925	owner's equity.................		$45,925

The essential features of all financial statements are these:

> Heading
>
> - Name of the entity
> - Title of the statement
> - Date, or period, covered by the statement
>
> Body of the statement

It is customary to list expenses in descending order by amount on the income statement, as shown in Exhibit 3-12. However, Miscellaneous Expense, a catchall account for expenses that do not fit another category, is usually reported last.

RELATIONSHIPS AMONG THE THREE FINANCIAL STATEMENTS

The arrows in Exhibits 3-12, 3-13, and 3-14 illustrate the relationships among the income statement, the statement of owner's equity, and the balance sheet. ➡ Consider why the income statement is prepared first and the balance sheet last.

◄ The relationships among the financial statements were introduced in Chapter 1, p. 20.

1. The income statement reports net income or net loss (revenues minus expenses). Because revenues and expenses are owner's equity accounts, their net amount is transferred to the statement of owner's equity. Note that net income in Exhibit 3-12, $3,525, increases owner's equity in Exhibit 3-13. A net loss would decrease owner's equity.
2. Capital is a balance sheet account, so the ending balance in the statement of owner's equity is transferred to the balance sheet. This amount is the final balancing element of the balance sheet. To solidify your understanding of this relationship, trace the $31,575 figure from Exhibit 3-13 to Exhibit 3-14.

You may be wondering why the total assets on the balance sheet ($45,925 in Exhibit 3-14) do not equal the total debits on the adjusted trial balance ($53,275 in Exhibit 3-11). Likewise, the total liabilities and owner's equity ($45,925 in Exhibit 3-14) do not equal the total credits on the adjusted trial balance ($53,275 in Exhibit 3-11). The reason for these differences is that Accumulated Depreciation and Owner's Withdrawals are contra accounts. Recall that contra accounts are *subtracted* from their companion accounts on the balance sheet. But on the adjusted trial balance, contra accounts are *added* as a debit or a credit in their respective columns.

WORK IT OUT

Examine Gillen eTravel's adjusted trial balance in Exhibit 3-10. Suppose Gillen forgot to record the $950 accrual of salary expense at April 30. What net income would the travel agency then report for April? What total assets, total liabilities, and total owner's equity would the balance sheet report at April 30?

Answer: Omitting the salary accrual would produce these effects:

1. Net income (Exhibit 3-12) would have been $4,475 ($3,525 + $950).
2. Total assets would have been unaffected by the error—$45,925 (Exhibit 3-14).
3. Total liabilities (Exhibit 3-14) would have been $13,400 ($14,350 − $950).
4. Owner's equity (Gay Gillen, capital) would have been $32,525 ($31,575 + $950) (Exhibit 3-14).

ETHICAL ISSUES IN ACCRUAL ACCOUNTING

Like other aspects of business, accounting poses ethical challenges. At the most fundamental level, accountants must be honest in their work. Only with honest and complete information, including accounting data, can people expect to make wise decisions. An example will illustrate.

It's Just Lunch has done well as a business. Andrea McGinty is an excellent businesswoman. The company has opened offices in most major cities in the United States. Suppose It's Just Lunch wishes to open an office in Nashville, Tennessee, and needs to borrow $100,000 for prepaid rent, office equipment, and so on. Assume It's Just Lunch understated expenses in order to inflate net income as reported on the company's income statement. A banker could be tricked into lending the company money. Then if It's Just Lunch could not repay the loan, the bank would lose money—all because the banker relied on incorrect accounting information.

Accrual accounting provides several opportunities for unethical accounting. It would be easy for a dishonest businessperson to overlook an accrued expense or depreciation expense at the end of the period. Failing to make these adjustments would overstate net income and paint an overly favorable picture of the company's financial situation.

The cash basis of accounting poses fewer ethical challenges because either the company has the cash, or it does not. Therefore, the amount of cash a company reports is rarely disputed. By contrast, adjusting entries for accrued expenses, accrued revenues, and depreciation often must be estimated. Whenever there is an estimate, the accountant must deal with the temptation to make the company look different from its true condition. Fortunately, accounting has a good reputation for honesty.

The Decision Guidelines feature provides a map of the adjusting process that leads to the financial statements.

DECISION GUIDELINES

Measuring Business Income: The Adjusting Process

DECISION	GUIDELINES
Which basis of accounting better measures business income (revenues − expenses)?	*Accrual basis*, because it provides more complete reports of operating performance and financial position
How to measure revenues?	Revenue principle
How to measure expenses?	Matching principle
Where to start with the measurement of income at the end of the period?	Unadjusted trial balance, usually referred to simply as the *trial balance*
How to update the accounts for preparation of the financial statements?	*Adjusting entries* at the end of the accounting period
What are the categories of adjusting entries?	Prepaid expenses Accrued revenues Depreciation of plant assets Unearned revenues Accrued expenses
How do the adjusting entries differ from other journal entries?	1. Adjusting entries are usually made only at the end of the accounting period. 2. Adjusting entries never affect cash. 3. All adjusting entries debit or credit. • At least one *income statement* account (a revenue or an expense), and • At least one *balance sheet* account (an asset or a liability)
Where are the accounts with their adjusted balances summarized?	*Adjusted trial balance*, which becomes the basis for preparing the financial statements

EXCEL APPLICATION PROBLEM

Goal: Create an Excel spreadsheet that contains an income statement, statement of owner's equity, and balance sheet, complete with the formula relationships among all three statements.

Scenario: The three financial statements are related. The relationships show up when net income changes. Using Exhibits 3-12, 3-13, and 3-14, replicate the Income Statement, Statement of Owner's Equity, and Balance sheet for Gay Gillen eTravel. When you are finished, you will change just two related variables, but see the effect ripple through all the statements you have created.

1. Change service revenue from $7,400 to $10,900 and cash from $24,800 to $28,300. (Remember, every transaction requires at least one debit entry and one credit entry.) What is the new net income figure?
2. What is the new balance for Gay Gillen, Capital, April 30, 20X1?
3. Did any other amounts change? If so, which ones?

Step-by-step:

1. Open a new Excel spreadsheet.
2. Create a boldfaced heading for your spreadsheet that contains the following:

   a. Chapter 3 Decision Guidelines
   b. Gay Gillen eTravel
3. Refer to Exhibit 3-12. Prepare the Income Statement as it appears in the text near the top of your spreadsheet, formatting and using formulas as appropriate. When finished, put a border around the Income Statement.
4. Refer to Exhibit 3-13. In your spreadsheet, prepare the Statement of Owner's Equity as it appears in the text to the right of the Income Statement. Be sure "Net Income" is a cell reference to your Income Statement's Net Income. Format and use formulas as appropriate. When finished, put a border around the Statement of Owner's Equity.
5. Refer to Exhibit 3-14. Prepare the Balance Sheet as it appears in the text below the income statement in your spreadsheet. Be sure "Gay Gillen, Capital" is a cell reference to the ending capital balance in your Statement of Owner's Equity. When finished, put a border around the Balance Sheet.
6. Make the two changes in scenario question 1. Save your file to disk and print a copy for comparison against Exhibits 3-12, 3-13, and 3-14 in the textbook.

REVIEW THE ADJUSTING PROCESS

SUMMARY PROBLEM

The trial balance of State Service Company pertains to December 31, 20X3, which is the end of its year-long accounting period. Data needed for the adjusting entries include

a. Supplies on hand at year end, $2,000.
b. Depreciation on furniture and fixtures, $20,000.
c. Depreciation on building, $10,000.
d. Salaries owed but not yet paid, $5,000.
e. Accrued service revenue, $12,000.
f. Of the $45,000 balance of unearned service revenue, $32,000 was earned during the year.

www.prenhall.com/horngren

End-of-Chapter Assessment

Required

1. Open the ledger accounts with their unadjusted balances. Show dollar amounts in thousands as done for Accounts Receivable:

ACCOUNTS RECEIVABLE	
370	

2. Journalize State Service Company's adjusting entries at December 31, 20X3. Key entries by letter, as in Exhibit 3-9.
3. Post the adjusting entries.
4. Write the trial balance on a work sheet, enter the adjusting entries, and prepare an adjusted trial balance, as shown in Exhibit 3-10.
5. Prepare the income statement, the statement of owner's equity, and the balance sheet. Draw arrows linking these three financial statements.

STATE SERVICE COMPANY
Trial Balance
December 31, 20X3

Cash	$ 198,000	
Accounts receivable	370,000	
Supplies	6,000	
Furniture and fixtures	100,000	
Accumulated depreciation—furniture and fixtures		$ 40,000
Building	250,000	
Accumulated depreciation—building		130,000
Accounts payable		380,000
Salary payable		
Unearned service revenue		45,000
Owner's capital		293,000
Owner's withdrawals	65,000	
Service revenue		286,000
Salary expense	172,000	
Supplies expense		
Depreciation expense—furniture and fixtures		
Depreciation expense—building		
Miscellaneous expense	13,000	
Total	$1,174,000	$1,174,000

Solution

Requirements 2 and 3 (amounts in thousands)

ASSETS

CASH

Bal. 198	

ACCOUNTS RECEIVABLE

370	
(e) 12	
Bal. 382	

SUPPLIES

6	(a) 4
Bal. 2	

FURNITURE AND FIXTURES

Bal. 100	

ACCUMULATED DEPRECIATION—FURNITURE AND FIXTURES

	40
	(b) 20
	Bal. 60

BUILDING

Bal. 250	

ACCUMULATED DEPRECIATION—BUILDING

	130
	(c) 10
	Bal. 140

LIABILITIES

ACCOUNTS PAYABLE

	Bal. 380

SALARY PAYABLE

	(d) 5
	Bal. 5

UNEARNED SERVICE REVENUE

(f) 32	45
	Bal. 13

OWNER'S EQUITY

OWNER'S CAPITAL

	Bal. 293

OWNER'S WITHDRAWALS

Bal. 65	

REVENUE

SERVICE REVENUE

	286
(e)	12
(f)	32
	Bal. 330

EXPENSES

SALARY EXPENSE

172	
(d) 5	
Bal. 177	

SUPPLIES EXPENSE

(a) 4	
Bal. 4	

DEPRECIATION EXPENSE—FURNITURE AND FIXTURES

(b) 20	
Bal. 20	

DEPRECIATION EXPENSE—BUILDING

(c) 10	
Bal. 10	

MISCELLANEOUS EXPENSE

Bal. 13	

Requirement 2

20X3

a. Dec. 31   Supplies Expense ($6,000 − $2,000) 4,000

            Supplies...   4,000

         To record supplies used.

b.   31   Depreciation Expense—Furniture and Fixtures................. 20,000

            Accumulated Depreciation—Furniture and Fixtures   20,000

         To record depreciation expense on furniture and fixtures.

c.   31   Depreciation Expense—Building 10,000

            Accumulated Depreciation—Building   10,000

         To record depreciation expense on building.

d.   31   Salary Expense... 5,000

            Salary Payable..   5,000

         To accrue salary expense.

e.   31   Accounts Receivable 12,000

            Service Revenue   12,000

         To accrue service revenue.

f.   31   Unearned Service Revenue.. 32,000

            Service Revenue   32,000

         To record service revenue that was collected in advance.

Requirement 4

STATE SERVICE COMPANY
Preparation of Adjusted Trial Balance
December 31, 20X3
(amounts in thousands)

Account Title	Trial Balance Debit	Trial Balance Credit	Adjustments Debit	Adjustments Credit	Adjusted Trial Balance Debit	Adjusted Trial Balance Credit
Cash...	198				198	
Accounts receivable	370		(e) 12		382	
Supplies...	6			(a) 4	2	
Furniture and fixtures................................	100				100	
Accumulated depreciation— furniture and fixtures		40		(b) 20		60
Building..	250				250	
Accumulated depreciation—building......		130		(c) 10		140
Accounts payable		380				380
Salary payable				(d) 5		5
Unearned service revenue		45	(f) 32			13
Owner's capital..		293				293
Owner's withdrawals	65				65	
Service revenue......................................		286		(e) 12		330
				(f) 32		
Salary expense	172		(d) 5		177	
Supplies expense.....................................			(a) 4		4	
Depreciation expense— furniture and fixtures			(b) 20		20	
Depreciation expense—building			(c) 10		10	
Miscellaneous expense............................	13				13	
	1,174	1,174	83	83	1,221	1,221

STATE SERVICE COMPANY
Income Statement
Year Ended December 31, 20X3
(amounts in thousands)

Revenue:		
Service revenue		$330
Expenses:		
Salary expense...	$177	
Depreciation expense—furniture and fixtures	20	
Depreciation expense—building...............................	10	
Supplies expense	4	
Miscellaneous expense	13	
Total expenses...		224
Net income		$106

STATE SERVICE COMPANY
Statement of Owner's Equity
Year Ended December 31, 20X3
(amounts in thousands)

Capital, January 1, 20X3............................	$293
Add: Net income	106
	399
Less: Withdrawals	(65)
Capital, December 31, 20X3	$334

STATE SERVICE COMPANY
Balance Sheet
December 31, 20X3
(amounts in thousands)

Assets			Liabilities		
Cash.................................		$198	Accounts payable		$380
Accounts receivable.........		382	Salary payable		5
Supplies		2	Unearned service revenue ..		13
Furniture and fixtures	$100		Total liabilities		398
Less: Accumulated					
depreciation..............	(60)	40			
Building	$250		**Owner's Equity**		
Less: Accumulated					
depreciation..............	(140)	110	Owner's capital...................		334
Total assets......................		$732	Total liabilities and		
			owner's equity................		$732

LESSONS LEARNED

1. *Distinguish accrual-basis accounting from cash-basis accounting.* In *accrual-basis accounting,* business events are recorded as they occur. In *cash-basis accounting,* only those events that affect cash are recorded. Some small organizations use cash-basis accounting, but the generally accepted method is the accrual basis.

2. *Apply the revenue and matching principles.* Businesses divide time into definite periods—such as a month, a quarter, or a year—to report the entity's financial statements. The year is the basic *accounting period,* but companies prepare financial statements as often as they need the information. The *revenue principle* helps accountants determine when to record revenue and the amount of revenue to record. Revenue is recorded after it has been earned, and not before. The *matching principle* directs accountants to match expenses against revenues earned during a particular period of time.

3. *Make adjusting entries at the end of the accounting period.* Adjusting entries are a result of the accrual basis of accounting. Made at the end of the period, these entries update the accounts for preparation of the financial statements. Adjusting entries are divided into five categories: *prepaid expenses, depreciation, accrued expenses, accrued revenues,* and *unearned revenues.*

4. *Prepare an adjusted trial balance.* To prepare the *adjusted trial balance,* accountants enter the adjusting entries next to the *unadjusted trial balance* and compute each account's balance.

5. *Prepare the financial statements from the adjusted trial balance.* The adjusted trial balance can be used to prepare the financial statements. Income, shown on the *income statement,* increases the owner's capital, which also appears on the *statement of owner's equity.* The ending balance of capital is the last amount reported on the *balance sheet.*

ACCOUNTING VOCABULARY

accrual-basis accounting (p. 83)
accrued expense (p. 92)
accrued revenue (p. 94)
Accumulated Depreciation (p. 91)
adjusted trial balance (p. 97)
adjusting entry (p. 87)

book value (of a plant asset) (p. 91)
cash-basis accounting (p. 83)
contra account (p. 91)
deferred revenue (p. 94)
depreciation (p. 90)
matching principle (p. 86)

plant asset (p. 90)
prepaid expense (p. 88)
revenue principle (p. 85)
time-period concept (p. 86)
unearned revenue (p. 94)

QUESTIONS

1. Distinguish accrual-basis accounting from cash-basis accounting.
2. How long is the basic accounting period? What is a fiscal year? What is an interim period?
3. What two questions does the revenue principle help answer?
4. Briefly explain the matching principle.
5. What is the purpose of making adjusting entries?
6. Why are adjusting entries made at the end of the accounting period?
7. Name five categories of adjusting entries, and give an example of each.
8. Do all adjusting entries affect the net income or net loss of the period? Include the definition of an adjusting entry.
9. Why must the balance of Supplies be adjusted at the end of the period?
10. On January 1, ABC Company pays $1,800 for an insurance policy that covers three years. At the end of the first year, the balance of its Prepaid Insurance account contains two elements. What are the two elements, and what is the correct amount of each?
11. The title Prepaid Expense suggests that this account is an expense. If it is, explain why. If it is not, what type of account is it?
12. What is a contra account? Identify the contra account introduced in this chapter, along with the account's normal balance.
13. The balance sheet reports plant assets at book value of $135,000 and accumulated depreciation of $65,000. What does *book value* of a plant asset mean? What was the cost of the plant assets?
14. Why is an unearned revenue a liability? Give an example.
15. What purposes does the adjusted trial balance serve?
16. Explain the relationship among the income statement, the statement of owner's equity, and the balance sheet.

ASSESS YOUR PROGRESS

DAILY EXERCISES

DE3-1 Study Exhibit 3-1, and the related discussion on pages 83 and 84. Suppose Drugstore.com is preparing its income statement. Identify the amount of revenue Drugstore.com would report on its January income statement under (a) cash-basis accounting and (b) accrual-basis accounting. How much advertising expense would Drugstore.com report for December under the (a) cash basis and (b) accrual basis?

Accrual accounting versus cash-basis accounting for revenues (Obj. 1)

DE3-2 **It's Just Lunch,** the business featured at the beginning of this chapter, uses computer databases to help its clients meet each other. Suppose It's Just Lunch paid $2,900 for a Dell computer. Review pages 00 and 00, and then describe how It's Just Lunch would account for the $2,900 expenditure under (a) the cash basis and (b) the accrual basis. State in your own words why the accrual basis is more realistic for this situation.

DE3-3 **Intel Corporation** produces the Pentium© processor that is featured in many computers. Demand for Pentium© processors is very strong. Suppose Intel has completed production of 2,000 processor units that it expects to sell to IBM. Assume that Intel's cost to manufacture each processor is $140 and that Intel sells each processor for $375.

Apply the revenue principle to determine (1) when Intel should record revenue for this situation, and (2) the amount of revenue Intel should record for the sale of 2,000 Pentium© processors.

DE3-4 Return to the **Intel Corporation** situation described in Daily Exercise 3-3. Suppose that Intel has sold 2,000 Pentium© processors to IBM. What will Intel record in order to apply the matching principle? Give the name of the expense that Intel will record, and specify its amount.

DE3-5 **Storage USA** operates approximately 475 miniwarehouses across the United States. The company's headquarters are in Memphis, Tennessee. During 1998, Storage USA earned rental revenue of $217 million and collected cash of $223 million from customers. Total expenses for 1998 were $162 million, of which Storage USA paid $153 million.

1. Using the data supplied here, apply the revenue principle and the matching principle to compute Storage USA's net income for 1998.
2. Identify the information that you did not use to compute Storage USA's net income. Give the reason for not using the information.

DE3-6 At December 31, 1999, **US Airways** recorded Salary Expense and Salary Payable of $341 million, as shown on page 86. Suppose US Airways paid $350 million to its employees on January 3, 2000, the company's next payday after the end of the 1999 year.

1. Consider the salary expense that US Airways accrued at December 31, 1999, and the related payment on January 3, 2000. Assuming no other expenses in this category, how much Salary Expense would US Airways report on its 1999 income statement? How much Salary Expense would the company report on its year 2000 income statement?
2. Journalize US Airways' entry for payment of the payroll on January 3, 2000. Include the date and an explanation for the entry.

DE3-7 Answer the following questions.

1. Prepaid expenses are discussed beginning on page 88. Focus on the accounting for prepaid rent. Assume that Gay Gillen's initial $3,000 prepayment of rent on April 1 (page 88) was for 12 months rather than three. Give Gay Gillen's adjusting entry to record rent expense at April 30. Include the date of the entry and an explanation. Then post to the two accounts involved, and show their balances at April 30.
2. Refer to the supplies example on pages 88–90. Assume that Gillen's travel agency has $200 of supplies on hand (rather than $400) at April 30. Give the adjusting entry, complete with date and explanation, at April 30. Post to the accounts and show their balances at April 30.

DE3-8 ◄═ *Link Back to Chapters 1 and 2 (Income Statement and Balance Sheet).* **It's Just Lunch** uses computers for data searches. Suppose that on May 1 the company paid cash of $36,000 for Gateway computers that are expected to remain useful for two years. At the end of two years, the value of the computers is expected to be zero.

1. Make journal entries to record (a) purchase of the computers on May 1 and (b) depreciation on May 31. Include dates and explanations, and use the following accounts: Computer Equipment; Accumulated Depreciation—Computer Equipment; and Depreciation Expense—Computer Equipment.
2. Post to the accounts listed in requirement 1, and show their balances at May 31.
3. What is the equipment's book value at May 31?
4. Which account(s) listed in requirement 1 will It's Just Lunch report on the income statement for the month of May? Which account(s) will appear on the balance sheet at May 31? Show the amount to report for each account.

DE3-9 Suppose Gay Gillen borrowed $20,000 on October 1 by signing a note payable to Community One Bank. Gillen's interest expense for each month is $100. The loan agreement requires Gillen to pay October interest at the end of December, along with the interest that will accrue for November and December.

1. Make the same adjusting entry to record interest expense and interest payable at October 31, at November 30, and at December 31. Date each entry and include its explanation.
2. Post all three entries to the Interest Payable account. You need not take the balance of the account at the end of each month.

3. On which financial statement and under what category will Gillen report the interest payable? How much interest payable will Gillen report at October 31 and at November 30?

DE3-10 Return to the situation of Daily Exercise 3-9. Suppose you are accounting for the same transactions on the books of Community One Bank, which lent the money to Gay Gillen eTravel. Perform all three requirements of Daily Exercise 3-9 for Community One Bank using its own accounts: Interest Receivable and Interest Revenue. (For requirements 2 and 3, use the Interest Receivable account.)

Accruing and receiving cash from interest revenue
(Obj. 3)

DE3-11 Write a paragraph to explain why unearned revenues are liabilities rather than revenues. In your explanation, use the following actual example: **Southern Living Magazine** collects cash from subscribers in advance and later mails the magazines to subscribers over a one-year period. Explain what happens to the unearned subscription revenue over the course of a year as Southern Living mails the magazines to subscribers. Where (into what account) does the unearned subscription revenue go as Southern Living mails magazines to subscribers? Give the adjusting entry that Southern Living makes to record the earning of $20,000 of Subscription Revenue. Include an explanation for the entry, as illustrated in the chapter.

Explaining unearned revenues
(Obj. 3)

DE3-12 Study the T-accounts in Exhibit 3-9, Panel C, on page 97. Focus on the Prepaid Rent account. Which amount in the Prepaid Rent account appeared on the *unadjusted* trial balance (Exhibit 3-10, page 99)? Which amount in the Prepaid Rent account will appear on the *adjusted* trial balance? Which amount will be reported on the balance sheet at April 30? Why will the balance sheet report this amount? Under what balance sheet category will Prepaid Rent appear?

Contrasting the unadjusted and the adjusted trial balances
(Obj. 4)

DE3-13 In the Adjustments columns of Exhibit 3-10, page 99, two adjustments affected Service Revenue.

Using the adjusted trial balance
(Obj. 4)

1. Make journal entries for the two adjustments. Date each entry and include an explanation.
2. The journal entries you just made affected three accounts: Accounts Receivable; Unearned Service Revenue; and Service Revenue. Show how Gay Gillen eTravel will report all three accounts in its financial statements at April 30. For each account, identify its (a) financial statement, (b) category on the financial statement, and (c) balance.

DE3-14 Write a business memorandum to your supervisor explaining the difference between the unadjusted amounts and the adjusted amounts in Exhibit 3-10, page 99. Use Accounts Receivable in your explanation. If necessary, refer to the discussion of Accrued Revenues that begins on page 94.

Business memos are formatted as follows:

Explaining the adjusted trial balance
(Obj. 4)

Date:	_____
To:	_____
From:	_____
Subject:	Difference between the *unadjusted* and the *adjusted* amounts on an adjusted trial balance

DE3-15 Refer to the adjusted trial balance in Exhibit 3-10, page 99.

Preparing the balance sheet
(Obj. 5)

1. Focus first on the *unadjusted* amounts. Compute the amount of **total assets** that Gay Gillen would have reported on the balance sheet at April 30 if she had *not* made the adjusting entries at the end of the period. Also compute unadjusted **total liabilities.**
2. Now focus on the *adjusted* figures. Compute Gillen's total assets and total liabilities at April 30. Compare your totals to the balance sheet in Exhibit 3-14, page 100. Are they the same?
3. Why does a business need to make adjusting entries at the end of the period?

DE3-16 Refer to the adjusted trial balance in Exhibit 3-10 page 99.

Preparing the income statement
(Obj. 5)

1. Focus first on the *unadjusted* amounts. Compute the amount of **total revenues** that Gay Gillen eTravel would have reported on the income statement for the month of April if she had *not* made the adjusting entries at the end of the period. Also compute unadjusted **total expenses.** Finally, determine the amount of **net income** Gillen would have reported if she had not adjusted the accounts.
2. Now focus on the *adjusted* figures. Compute Gillen's total revenues, total expenses, and net income for April. Compare your totals to the income statement in Exhibit 3-12, page 100. Are they the same?
3. Why does a business need to make adjusting entries at the end of the period?

Cash basis versus accrual basis
(Obj. 1)

E3-1 Homewood Suites had the following selected transactions during January:

Jan. 1   Prepaid rent for three months, $2,700.
    5   Paid electricity expenses, $400.
    9   Received cash for the day's room rentals, $1,400.
  14   Paid cash for six television sets, $3,000.
  23   Served a banquet, receiving a note receivable, $1,600.
  31   Made the adjusting entry for rent (from Jan. 1).
  31   Accrued salary expense, $900.

Show how each transaction would be handled using the accrual basis. Give the amount of revenue or expense for January. Journal entries are not required. Use the following format for your answer, and show your computations:

Amount of Revenue (Expense) for January		
Date	Revenue or (Expense)	Accrual-Basis Amount

Applying accounting concepts and principles
(Obj. 2)

E3-2 Identify the accounting concept or principle (there may be more than one) that gives the most direction on how to account for each of the following situations:

a. The owner of a business desires monthly financial statements to measure the progress of the entity on an ongoing basis.
b. Expenses of the period total $6,700. This amount should be subtracted from revenue to compute the period's income.
c. Expenses of $1,200 must be accrued at the end of the period to measure income properly.
d. A customer states her intention to switch health clubs. Should the new health club record revenue based on this intention? Give the reason for your answer.

Applying accounting concepts
(Obj. 2)

E3-3 Write a memo to your supervisor explaining in your own words the need for adjusting entries at the end of the period. Cite two accounts that need to be adjusted. Adapt the format for a business memo that is given with Daily Exercise 3-14.

Allocating prepaid expense to the asset and the expense
(Obj. 2, 3)

E3-4 Compute the amounts indicated by question marks for each of the following situations for Prepaid Insurance. For situations A and B, journalize the needed entry. Consider each situation separately.

	Situation			
	A	B	C	D
Beginning Prepaid Insurance.........	$ 450	$500	$ 900	$ 600
Payments for Prepaid Insurance during the year	1,400	?	1,100	?
Total amount to account for..........	?	?	2,000	1,500
Ending Prepaid Insurance..............	250	400	?	700
Insurance Expense.......................	?	$900	$1,200	$ 800

Journalizing adjusting entries
(Obj. 3)

E3-5 Journalize the entries for the following adjustments at January 31, the end of the accounting period.

a. Employee salaries owed for Monday and Tuesday of a five-day workweek; weekly payroll, $15,000.
b. Unearned service revenue earned, $800.
c. Depreciation, $3,200.
d. Prepaid insurance expired, $300.
e. Interest revenue accrued, $4,400.

Analyzing the effects of adjustments on net income
(Obj. 3)

E3-6 Suppose the adjustments required in Exercise 3-5 were not made. Compute the overall overstatement or understatement of net income as a result of the omission of these adjustments.

Journalizing adjusting entries
(Obj. 3)

E3-7 Journalize the adjusting entry needed at December 31 for each of the following independent situations.

a. On July 1, when we collected $10,000 rent in advance, we debited Cash and credited Unearned Rent Revenue. The tenant was paying for one year's rent in advance.

b. The business owes interest expense of $400, which it will pay early in the next period.

c. Interest revenue of $700 has been earned but not yet received. The business holds a $20,000 note receivable.

d. Salary expense is $1,500 per day—Monday through Friday—and the business pays employees each Friday. This year December 31 falls on a Wednesday.

e. The unadjusted balance of the Supplies account is $3,100. The cost of supplies on hand is $1,200.

f. Equipment was purchased last year at a cost of $10,000. The equipment's useful life is four years. Record the year's depreciation.

g. On September 1, when we prepaid $1,200 for a two-year insurance policy, we debited Prepaid Insurance and credited Cash.

Recording adjustments in T-accounts (Obj. 3)

E3-8 The accounting records of Lane Ginsburg, Architect, include the following unadjusted balances at March 31: Accounts Receivable, $1,000; Supplies, $600; Salary Payable, $0; Unearned Service Revenue, $400; Service Revenue, $4,700; Salary Expense, $1,200; Supplies Expense, $0. Ginsburg's accountant develops the following data for the March 31 adjusting entries:

a. Service revenue accrued, $650.

b. Unearned service revenue that has been earned, $200.

c. Supplies on hand, $100.

d. Salary owed to employee, $600.

Open T-accounts for each and record the adjustments directly in the accounts, keying each adjustment amount by letter. Show each account's adjusted balance. Journal entries are not required.

Adjusting the accounts (Obj. 3, 4)

E3-9 The adjusted trial balance of Signet Repair Company is incomplete. Enter the adjustment amounts directly in the adjustment columns of the text. Service Revenue is the only account affected by more than one adjustment.

SIGNET REPAIR COMPANY
Preparation of Adjusted Trial Balance
May 31, 20X2

Account Title	Trial Balance Debit	Trial Balance Credit	Adjustments Debit	Adjustments Credit	Adjusted Trial Balance Debit	Adjusted Trial Balance Credit
Cash	3,000				3,000	
Accounts receivable	4,500				7,400	
Supplies	1,040				800	
Office furniture	32,300				32,300	
Accumulated depreciation		14,040				14,400
Salary payable						900
Unearned service revenue		900				690
Capital		26,360				26,360
Owner's withdrawals	6,000				6,000	
Service revenue		9,630				12,740
Salary expense	2,690				3,590	
Rent expense	1,400				1,400	
Depreciation expense					360	
Supplies expense					240	
	50,930	50,930			55,090	55,090

Journalizing adjustments (Obj. 3, 4)

E3-10 Make journal entries for the adjustments that would complete the preparation of the adjusted trial balance in Exercise 3-9. Date the entries and include explanations.

Preparing the financial statements (Obj. 5)

E3-11 Refer to the adjusted trial balance in Exercise 3-9. Prepare Signet Repair Company's income statement and statement of owner's equity for the month ended May 31, 20X2, and its balance sheet on that date. Draw arrows linking the three statements.

Preparing the financial statements (Obj. 5)

E3-12 The accountant for Kay Fuston, Publisher, has posted adjusting entries (a)–(e) to the accounts at December 31, 20X2. Selected balance sheet accounts and all the revenues and expenses of the entity follow in T-account form.

ACCOUNTS RECEIVABLE		SUPPLIES		ACCUMULATED DEPRECIATION— EQUIPMENT		ACCUMULATED DEPRECIATION—BUILDING	
23,000		4,000	(a) 1,000		5,000		33,000
(e) 7,000					(b) 2,000		(c) 5,000

SALARY PAYABLE						SERVICE REVENUE	
	(d) 1,500						105,000
							(e) 7,000

SALARY EXPENSE		SUPPLIES EXPENSE		DEPRECIATION EXPENSE— EQUIPMENT		DEPRECIATION EXPENSE— BUILDING	
28,000		(a) 1,000		(b) 2,000		(c) 5,000	
(d) 1,500							

Required

1. Prepare the income statement of Kay Fuston, Publisher, for the year ended December 31, 20X2. List expenses in order from the largest to the smallest.
2. Were 20X2 operations successful? Give the reason for your answer.

Preparing the statement of owner's equity (Obj. 5)

E3-13 Quikwash Laundromat began the year with capital of $155,000. On July 12, Kent Carmichael (the owner) invested $12,000 cash in the business. On September 26, he transferred to the company land valued at $70,000. The income statement for the year ended December 31, 20X5, reported a net loss of $28,000. During this fiscal year, Carmichael withdrew $1,500 monthly for personal use.

Required

1. Prepare the laundromat's statement of owner's equity for the year ended December 31, 20X5.
2. Did the owner's equity of the business increase or decrease during the year? What caused this change?

Continuing Exercise. *Exercise 3-14 continues the Amos Faraday, Consultant, situation begun in Exercise 2-15 of Chapter 2.*

Adjusting the accounts, preparing an adjusted trial balance, and preparing the financial statements (Obj. 3, 4, 5)

E3-14 Refer to Exercise 2-15 of Chapter 2. Start from the trial balance and the posted T-accounts that Amos Faraday, Consultant, prepared for his business at December 18, as follows:

AMOS FARADAY, CONSULTANT
Trial Balance
December 18, 20XX

Account	Debit	Credit
Cash	$12,100	
Accounts receivable	1,700	
Supplies	300	
Equipment	2,000	
Furniture	3,600	
Accounts payable		$ 3,900
Amos Faraday, capital		14,000
Amos Faraday, withdrawals	—	
Service revenue		2,500
Rent expense	500	
Utilities expense	200	
Salary expense		
Total	$20,400	$20,400

Later in December, the business completed these transactions, as follows:

Dec. 21   Received $900 in advance for client service to be performed evenly over the next 30 days.

21   Hired a secretary to be paid $1,500 on the 20th day of each month. The secretary begins work immediately.

26   Paid $300 on account.

28   Collected $600 on account.

30   Withdrew $1,600 for personal use.

Required

1. Open these additional T-accounts: Accumulated Depreciation—Equipment; Accumulated Depreciation—Furniture; Salary Payable; Unearned Service Revenue; Depreciation Expense—Equipment; Depreciation Expense—Furniture; Supplies Expense.
2. Journalize the transactions of December 21–30.
3. Post to the T-accounts, keying all items by date.
4. Prepare a trial balance at December 31. Also set up columns for the adjustments and for the adjusted trial balance, as illustrated in Exhibit 3-10.
5. At December 31, Faraday gathers the following information for the adjusting entries:
   a. Accrued service revenue, $400.
   b. Earned a portion of the service revenue collected in advance on December 21.
   c. Supplies on hand, $100.
   d. Depreciation expense—equipment, $50; furniture, $60.
   e. Accrued expense for secretary's salary—10 days worked.

   Make these adjustments directly in the adjustments columns, and complete the adjusted trial balance at December 31. Throughout the book, to avoid rounding errors, we base adjusting entries on 30-day months and 360-day years.

6. Journalize and post the adjusting entries. Denote each adjusting amount as *Adj.* and an account balance as *Bal.*
7. Prepare the income statement and the statement of owner's equity of Amos Faraday, Consultant, for the month ended December 31, and prepare the balance sheet at that date.

Challenge Exercises

E3-15 Morris Chang Enterprises aids Chinese students upon their arrival in the United States. Paid by the Chinese government, Morris Chang collects some service revenue in advance. In other cases, he receives cash after performing relocation services. At the end of August—a particularly busy period—Morris Chang's books show the following:

Computing the amount of revenue (Obj. 3)

	July 31	August 31
Accounts receivable........................	$1,900	$2,500
Unearned service revenue..............	1,200	300

During August, Morris Chang Enterprises received cash of $7,000 from the Chinese government. How much service revenue did the business earn during August? Show your work.

E3-16 For the situation of Exercise 3-15, assume the service revenue of Morris Chang Enterprises was $5,900 during August. How much cash did the business collect from the Chinese government that month? Show your work.

Computing cash amounts (Obj. 3)

PROBLEMS

(Group A)

P3-1A Normandy Psychiatric Group had the following selected transactions during January:

Cash basis versus accrual basis (Obj. 1, 2)

Jan.	1	Prepaid insurance for January through March, $600.
	4	Performed medical service on account, $1,000.
	5	Purchased office furniture on account, $150.
	8	Paid advertising expense, $450.
	11	Purchased office equipment for cash, $800.
	19	Performed medical service and received cash, $700.
	24	Collected $400 on account for January 4 service.
	26	Paid account payable from January 5.
	29	Paid salary expense, $900.
	31	Recorded adjusting entry for January insurance expense (see Jan. 1).
	31	Debited unearned revenue and credited revenue to adjust the accounts, $600.

Required

1. Show how each transaction would be handled using the accrual basis of accounting. Give the amount of revenue or expense for January. Journal entries are not required. Use the following format for your answer, and show your computations:

Amount of Revenue (Expense) for January

Date   Revenue (Expense)   Accrual-Basis Amount

---

2. Compute January net income or net loss under the accrual basis of accounting.
3. State why the accrual basis of accounting is preferable to the cash basis.

Applying accounting principles
(Obj. 1, 2)

P3-2A As the controller of Lake Cypress Lumber Company, you have hired a new bookkeeper, whom you must train. He objects to making an adjusting entry for accrued salaries at the end of the period. He reasons, "We will pay the salaries soon. Why not wait until payment to record the expense? In the end, the result will be the same." Write a business memo to explain to the bookkeeper why the adjusting entry for accrued salary expense is needed. The format of a business memo follows.

Date:	_____
To:	New Bookkeeper
From:	(Student Name)
Subject:	Why the adjusting entry for salary expense is needed

Journalizing adjusting entries
(Obj. 3)

P3-3A Journalize the adjusting entry needed on December 31, end of the current accounting period, for each of the following independent cases affecting Arvin Marketing Associates.

a. Each Friday, Arvin pays its employees for the current week's work. The amount of the payroll is $6,000 for a five-day workweek. The current accounting period ends on Thursday.
b. Arvin has received notes receivable from some clients for professional services. During the current year, Arvin has earned accrued interest revenue of $170, which will be collected next year.
c. The beginning balance of Supplies was $3,800. During the year, the entity purchased supplies costing $5,530, and at December 31, the inventory of supplies on hand is $2,970.
d. Arvin designed a marketing campaign, and the client paid Arvin $36,000 at the start of the project. Arvin recorded this amount as Unearned Service Revenue. The campaign will run for several months. Arvin estimates that the company has earned three-fourths of the total fee during the current year.
e. Depreciation for the current year includes: Office Furniture, $5,500; Building, $3,790. Make a compound entry, as illustrated in Chapter 2.
f. Details of Prepaid Insurance are shown in the account:

PREPAID INSURANCE		
Jan. 1	Bal.	900
April 30		2,700

Arvin pays insurance each year on April 30. At December 31, part of the last payment is still in force.

Analyzing and journalizing
adjustments
(Obj. 3)

P3-4A Platt Investment Brokers' unadjusted and adjusted trial balances at December 31, 20X7, follow at the top of page 115.

Required

Journalize the adjusting entries that account for the differences between the two trial balances.

*Journalizing and posting adjustments to T-accounts; preparing
the adjusted trial balance
(Obj. 3, 4)*

P3-5A The trial balance of Liberty Duplicating Services at August 31, 20X6, year and the data needed for the month-end adjustments follow at the bottom of page 115.

Adjustment data:

a. Unearned service revenue still unearned at August 31, $1,670.
b. Prepaid rent still in force at August 31, $620.
c. Supplies used during the month, $700.
d. Depreciation for the month, $400.
e. Accrued advertising expense at August 31, $610. (Credit Accounts Payable.)
f. Accrued salary expense at August 31, $550.

Required

1. Open T-accounts for the accounts listed in the trial balance, inserting their August 31 unadjusted balances.
2. Journalize the adjusting entries and post them to the T-accounts. Key the journal entries and the posted amounts by letter.
3. Prepare the adjusted trial balance.
4. How will the company use the adjusted trial balance?

PLATT INVESTMENT BROKERS
Adjusted Trial Balance
December 31, 20X7

Account Title	Trial Balance		Adjusted Trial Balance	
	Debit	Credit	Debit	Credit
Cash.....................................	4,120		4,120	
Accounts receivable...........	5,260		14,090	
Supplies	1,200		280	
Prepaid insurance	2,600		2,330	
Office furniture..................	21,630		21,630	
Accumulated depreciation		8,220		10,500
Accounts payable..............		6,420		6,420
Salary payable				960
Interest payable				480
Note payable.....................		12,000		12,000
Unearned commission revenue		1,840		1,160
Claire Platt, capital............		13,510		13,510
Claire Platt, withdrawals ...	29,370		29,370	
Commission revenue.........		66,890		76,400
Depreciation expense			2,280	
Supplies expense			920	
Utilities expense	4,960		4,960	
Salary expense...................	26,660		27,620	
Rent expense	12,200		12,200	
Interest expense.................	880		1,360	
Insurance expense.............			270	
	108,880	108,880	121,430	121,430

LIBERTY DUPLICATING SERVICES
Trial Balance
August 31, 20X6

	Debit	Credit
Cash	$ 7,100	
Accounts receivable	19,780	
Prepaid rent	2,420	
Supplies	1,180	
Furniture	19,740	
Accumulated depreciation..............		$ 3,630
Accounts payable............................		3,310
Salary payable.................................		
Unearned service revenue		2,790
Milton Hupp, capital.......................		35,510
Milton Hupp, withdrawals..............	5,350	
Service revenue		15,700
Salary expense.................................	3,800	
Rent expense		
Depreciation expense		
Advertising expense	1,570	
Supplies expense		
Total	$60,940	$60,940

P3-6A The adjusted trial balance of Mastercraft Marble Cutters at December 31, 20X8, follows.

MASTERCRAFT MARBLE CUTTERS
Adjusted Trial Balance
December 31, 20X8

Cash	$ 2,340	
Accounts receivable	50,490	
Prepaid rent	1,350	
Supplies	970	
Equipment	75,690	
Accumulated depreciation—equipment		$ 22,240
Office furniture	24,100	
Accumulated depreciation—office furniture		3,670
Accounts payable		13,600
Unearned service revenue		4,520
Interest payable		2,130
Salary payable		930
Note payable		45,000
B. Masters, capital		32,380
B. Masters, withdrawals	48,000	
Service revenue		204,790
Depreciation expense—equipment	11,300	
Depreciation expense—office furniture	2,410	
Salary expense	87,800	
Rent expense	12,000	
Interest expense	4,200	
Utilities expense	3,770	
Insurance expense	3,150	
Supplies expense	1,690	
Total	$329,260	$329,260

Required

1. Prepare Mastercraft's 20X8 income statement and statement of owner's equity and year-end balance sheet. List expenses in decreasing order on the income statement and show total liabilities on the balance sheet. Draw arrows linking the three financial statements.
2. **a.** Which financial statement reports Mastercraft's results of operations? Were 20X8 operations successful? Cite specifics from the financial statements to support your evaluation.
   b. Which statement reports the company's financial position? Does Mastercraft's financial position look strong or weak? Give the reason for your evaluation.

P3-7A Consider the unadjusted trial balance of ReliaMark Insurers at October 31, 20X2, and the related month-end adjustment data.

RELIAMARK INSURERS
Trial Balance
October 31, 20X2

Cash	$ 6,300	
Accounts receivable	8,000	
Prepaid rent	6,000	
Supplies	600	
Equipment	27,000	
Accumulated depreciation		$ 3,000
Accounts payable		2,800
Salary payable		
Karen Cabot, capital		38,000
Karen Cabot, withdrawals	3,600	
Service revenue		9,400
Salary expense	1,400	
Rent expense		
Utilities expense	300	
Depreciation expense		
Supplies expense		
Total	$53,200	$53,200

Adjustment data:

a. Accrued service revenue at October 31, $2,000.
b. Prepaid rent expired during the month. The unadjusted prepaid balance of $6,000 relates to the period October 20X2 through January 20X3.
c. Supplies on hand October 31, $200.
d. Depreciation on equipment for the month. The equipment's expected useful life is five years.
e. Accrued salary expense at October 31 for one day only. The five-day weekly payroll is $2,000.

Required

1. Write the trial balance on a work sheet, using Exhibit 3-10 as an example, and prepare the adjusted trial balance of ReliaMark Insurers at October 31, 20X2. Key each adjusting entry by letter.
2. Prepare the income statement and the statement of owner's equity for the month ended October 31, 20X2, and the balance sheet at that date. Draw arrows linking the three financial statements.

PROBLEMS

(Group B)

P3-1B Valleydale Bone and Joint Clinic completed the following selected transactions during May:

Cash basis versus accrual basis (Obj. 1, 2)

May	2	Prepaid insurance for May through July, $800.
	4	Paid gas bill, $550.
	5	Performed services on account, $1,000.
	9	Purchased office equipment for cash, $1,400.
	12	Received cash for services performed, $900.
	14	Purchased office equipment on account, $300.
	28	Collected $500 on account from May 5.
	29	Paid salary expense, $1,100.
	30	Paid account payable from May 14.
	31	Recorded adjusting entry for May insurance expense (see May 2).
	31	Debited unearned revenue and credited revenue in an adjusting entry, $700.

Required

1. Show how each transaction would be handled using the accrual basis of accounting. Give the amount of revenue or expense for May. Journal entries are not required. Use the following format for your answer, and show your computations:

Amount of Revenue (Expense) for May

Date	Revenue (Expense)	Accrual-Basis Amount

---

2. Compute May net income or net loss under the accrual basis of accounting.
3. Why is the accrual basis of accounting preferable to the cash basis?

P3-2B Write a business memo to a new bookkeeper to explain the difference between the cash basis of accounting and the accrual basis. Mention the roles of the revenue principle and the matching principle in accrual-basis accounting. The format of a business memo follows.

Applying accounting principles (Obj. 1, 2)

Date:	_____
To:	New Bookkeeper
From:	(Student Name)
Subject:	Difference between the cash basis and the accrual basis

P3-3B Journalize the adjusting entry needed on December 31, end of the current accounting period, for each of the following independent cases affecting Coronado Heating and Cooling.

Journalizing adjusting entries (Obj. 3)

a. Details of Prepaid Rent are shown in the account:

PREPAID RENT

| Jan. 1 | Bal. | 600 | |
| Mar. 31 | | 2,400 | |

Coronado pays office rent annually on March 31. At December 31, part of the last payment is still an asset.

b. Coronado pays its employees each Friday. The amount of the weekly payroll is $2,000 for a five-day workweek, and the daily salary amounts are equal. The current accounting period ends on Monday.

c. Coronado has loaned out money, receiving notes receivable. During the current year, the entity has earned accrued interest revenue of $737, which it will collect next year.

d. The beginning balance of Supplies was $2,680. During the year, the entity purchased supplies costing $6,180, and at December 31, the cost of supplies on hand is $2,150.

e. Coronado is servicing the air-conditioning system in a large building, and the owner of the building paid Coronado $12,900 as the annual service fee. Coronado recorded this amount as Unearned Service Revenue. Enrique Coronado, the owner, estimates that the company has earned one-fourth the total fee during the current year.

f. Depreciation for the current year includes Equipment, $3,850; Trucks, $10,320. Make a compound entry, as illustrated in Chapter 2.

Analyzing and journalizing adjustments
(Obj. 3)

P3-4B Olen Chemical Servicing's unadjusted and adjusted trial balances at April 30, 20X1, follow.

	OLEN CHEMICAL SERVICING			
	Adjusted Trial Balance			
	April 30, 20X1			
	Trial Balance		**Adjusted Trial Balance**	
Account Title	**Debit**	**Credit**	**Debit**	**Credit**
Cash	6,180		6,180	
Accounts receivable	5,990		6,700	
Interest receivable........................			300	
Note receivable	4,100		4,100	
Supplies..	980		290	
Prepaid rent	2,480		720	
Building	66,450		66,450	
Accumulated depreciation		16,010		17,290
Accounts payable........................		6,920		6,920
Wages payable				320
Unearned service revenue		670		110
Paul Olen, capital........................		58,790		58,790
Paul Olen, withdrawals..............	3,600		3,600	
Service revenue		9,570		10,840
Interest revenue..........................				300
Wage expense	1,600		1,920	
Rent expense			1,760	
Depreciation expense.................			1,280	
Insurance expense	370		370	
Supplies expense.........................			690	
Utilities expense..........................	210		210	
	91,960	91,960	94,570	94,570

Required

Journalize the adjusting entries that account for the differences between the two trial balances.

Journalizing and posting adjustments to T-accounts; preparing the adjusted trial balance
(Obj. 3, 4)

P3-5B The trial balance of Great Lakes Investments at December 31, 20X2, and the data needed for the month-end adjustments follow at the top of the next page.

Adjustment data:

a. Prepaid rent still in force at December 31, $600.
b. Supplies used during the month, $640.
c. Depreciation for the month, $900.
d. Accrued advertising expense at December 31, $320. (Credit Accounts Payable.)
e. Accrued salary expense at December 31, $180.
f. Unearned commission revenue still unearned at December 31, $1,150.

GREAT LAKES INVESTMENTS
Trial Balance
December 31, 20X2

Cash	$ 2,200	
Accounts receivable	14,100	
Prepaid rent	3,100	
Supplies	780	
Furniture	22,710	
Accumulated depreciation		$11,640
Account payable		1,940
Salary payable		
Unearned commission revenue		2,290
Gina Pulver, capital		25,060
Gina Pulver, withdrawals	2,900	
Commission revenue		7,750
Salary expense	2,160	
Rent expense		
Depreciation expense		
Advertising expense	730	
Supplies expense		
Total	$48,680	$48,680

Required

1. Open T-accounts for the accounts listed in the trial balance, inserting their December 31 unadjusted balances.
2. Journalize the adjusting entries and post them to the T-accounts. Key the journal entries and the posted amounts by letter.
3. Prepare the adjusted trial balance.
4. How will the company use the adjusted trial balance?

P3-6B The adjusted trial balance of Marineland Travel Designers at December 31, 20X6, follows.

Preparing the financial statements from an adjusted trial balance (Obj. 5)

MARINELAND TRAVEL DESIGNERS
Adjusted Trial Balance
December 31, 20X6

Cash	$ 1,320	
Accounts receivable	4,920	
Supplies	2,300	
Prepaid rent	1,600	
Office equipment	20,180	
Accumulated depreciation—office equipment		$ 4,350
Office furniture	37,710	
Accumulated depreciation—office furniture		4,870
Accounts payable		4,740
Interest payable		830
Unearned service revenue		620
Note payable		13,500
Ken Sorley, capital		26,090
Ken Sorley, withdrawals	29,000	
Service revenue		120,910
Depreciation expense—office equipment	6,680	
Depreciation expense—office furniture	2,370	
Salary expense	39,900	
Rent expense	17,400	
Interest expense	3,100	
Utilities expense	2,670	
Insurance expense	3,810	
Supplies expense	2,950	
Total	$175,910	$175,910

Required

1. Prepare Marineland's 20X6 income statement and statement of owner's equity and year-end balance sheet. List expenses in decreasing order on the income statement and show total liabilities on the balance sheet. Draw arrows linking the three financial statements.
2. **a.** Which financial statement reports Marineland's results of operations? Were operations successful during 20X6? Cite specifics from the financial statements to support your evaluation.
   b. Which statement reports the company's financial position? Does Marineland's financial position look strong or weak? Give the reason for your evaluation.

Preparing an adjusted trial balance and the financial statements

(Obj. 3, 4, 5)

P3-7B The unadjusted trial balance of Christine Salomon, at July 31, 20X2, and the related month-end adjustment data follow.

CHRISTINE SALOMON, CPA
Trial Balance
July 31, 20X2

Cash	$ 5,600	
Accounts receivable	11,600	
Prepaid rent	4,000	
Supplies	800	
Furniture	28,800	
Accumulated depreciation		$ 3,500
Accounts payable		3,450
Salary payable		
Christine Salomon, capital		39,050
Christine Salomon, withdrawals	4,000	
Accounting service revenue		11,750
Salary expense	2,400	
Rent expense		
Utilities expense	550	
Depreciation expense		
Supplies expense		
Total	$57,750	$57,750

Adjustment data:

a. Accrued accounting service revenue at July 31, $900.
b. Prepaid rent expired during the month. The unadjusted prepaid balance of $4,000 relates to the period July through October.
c. Supplies on hand at July 31, $400.
d. Depreciation on furniture for the month. The estimated useful life of the furniture is four years.
e. Accrued salary expense at July 31 for one day only. The five-day weekly payroll is $1,000.

Required

1. Using Exhibit 3-10 as an example, write the trial balance on a work sheet and prepare the adjusted trial balance of Christine Salomon, CPA, at July 31, 20X2. Key each adjusting entry by letter.
2. Prepare the income statement and the statement of owner's equity for the month ended July 31, 20X2, and the balance sheet at that date. Draw arrows linking the three financial statements.

APPLY YOUR KNOWLEDGE

DECISION CASES

Valuing a business on the basis of its net income

(Obj. 4, 5)

Case 1. Benjamin O'Henry has owned and operated O'Henry's Data Services since its beginning ten years ago. From all appearances, the business has prospered. In the past few years, you have become friends with O'Henry and his wife through your church. Recently, O'Henry mentioned that he has lost his zest for the business and would consider selling it for the right price. You are interested in buying this business and obtain its most recent monthly unadjusted trial balance, which follows.

O'HENRY'S DATA SERVICES
Unadjusted Trial Balance
November 30, 20XX

Cash	$ 9,700	
Accounts receivable	7,900	
Prepaid expenses	2,600	
Furniture, fixtures, and equipment	151,300	
Accumulated depreciation		$ 15,600
Accounts payable		3,800
Salary payable		
Unearned service revenue		6,700
Benjamin O'Henry, capital		137,400
Benjamin O'Henry, withdrawals	2,000	
Service revenue		14,300
Rent expense		
Salary expense	3,400	
Utilities expense	900	
Depreciation expense		
Supplies expense		
Total	$177,800	$177,800

Revenues and expenses vary little from month to month, and November is a typical month. Your investigation reveals that the unadjusted trial balance does not include the effects of monthly revenues of $2,100 and monthly expenses totaling $2,750. If you were to buy O'Henry's Data Services, you would hire a manager who would require a monthly salary of $3,000.

Required

1. The most you would pay for the business is 20 times the monthly net income *you could expect to earn* from it. Compute this possible price.
2. The least O'Henry will take for the business is his ending capital. Compute this amount.
3. Under these conditions, how much should you offer O'Henry? Give your reason.

Case 2. Suppose a new management team is in charge of Sunpool, Inc., an appliance manufacturer. Assume Sunpool's new top managers rose through the ranks in the sales and marketing departments and have little appreciation for the details of accounting. Consider the following conversation between these two managers:

Explaining why adjusting entries are needed
(Obj. 3)

Morgan Gummelt, President:	"I want to avoid the hassle of adjusting the books every time we need financial statements. Sooner or later we receive cash for all our revenues, and we pay cash for all our expenses. I can understand cash transactions, but all these accruals confuse me. If I cannot understand *our own accounting,* I'm fairly certain the average person who invests in our company cannot understand it either. Let's start recording only our cash transactions. I bet it won't make any difference to anyone."
Sarah Mead, Chief Financial Officer:	"Sounds good to me. This will save me lots of headaches. I'll implement the new policy immediately."

Write a business memo to the company president giving your response to the new policy. Identify at least five individual items (such as specific accounts) in the financial statements that will be reported incorrectly. Will outside investors care? Adapt the format of a business memo given with Daily Exercise 3-14.

ETHICAL ISSUE

The net income of Simon & Hobbs, a department store, decreased sharply during 2000. Carol Simon, owner of the store, anticipates the need for a bank loan in 2001. Late in 2000, Simon instructs the store's accountant to record a $10,000 sale of furniture to the Simon family, even though the goods will not be shipped from the manufacturer until January 2001. Simon also tells the accountant *not* to make the following December 31, 2000, adjusting entries:

Salaries owed to employees.......................... $900
Prepaid insurance that has expired............... 400

Required

1. Compute the overall effects of these transactions on the store's reported income for 2000.
2. Why is Simon taking this action? Is her action ethical? Give your reason, identifying the parties helped and the parties harmed by Simon's action.
3. As a personal friend, what advice would you give the accountant?

FINANCIAL STATEMENT CASE

Journalizing and posting transactions and tracing account balances to the financial statements (Obj. 3, 5)

Target Corporation—like all other businesses—makes adjusting entries prior to year end in order to measure assets, liabilities, revenues, and expenses properly. Examine Target's balance sheet, and pay particular attention to Other Current Assets (which includes Prepaid Expenses) and Accrued Liabilities (which includes Salary Payable and Interest Payable).

1. Open T-accounts for Other Current Assets (Prepaid Expenses), Accrued Liabilities, and Accumulated Depreciation. Insert Target's balances (in millions) at January 30, 1999. (Example: Other Current Assets (Prepaid Expenses), $619)
2. Journalize the following transactions for the current year, ended January 29, 2000. Key entries by letter. Explanations are not required.
   Cash transactions (amounts in millions):
   a. Paid prepaid expenses, $2,113.
   b. Paid the January 30, 1999, accrued liabilities.
   Adjustments at January 29, 2000 (amounts in millions):
   c. Prepaid expenses expired, $2,104. (Debit Administrative Expense)
   d. Accrued liabilities, $1,520. (Debit Selling Expense.)
   e. Depreciation expense, $157.
3. Post to the Other Current Assets (Prepaid Expenses) account the Accrued Liabilities account and the Accumulated Depreciation account. Then these accounts should agree with the corresponding amounts reported in the January 29, 2000, balance sheet. Check to make sure they do agree with Target's actual balances.

TEAM PROJECT

Return to the chapter-opening story, which describes Andrea McGinty's business, **It's Just Lunch.** Suppose your group is opening an It's Just Lunch office in your area. You must make some important decisions—where to locate, how to advertise, and so on—and you must also make some accounting decisions. For example, what will be the end of your business's accounting year? How often will you need financial statements to evaluate operating performance and financial position? Will you use the cash basis or the accrual basis? When will you account for the revenue that the business earns? How will you account for the expenses?

Required

Write a report (or prepare an oral presentation, as directed by your professor) to address the following considerations:

1. Will you use the cash basis or the accrual basis of accounting? Give a complete explanation of your reasoning.
2. How often do you want financial statements? Why? Discuss how you will use each financial statement.
3. What kind of revenue will you earn? When will you record it as revenue? How will you decide when to record the revenue?
4. Prepare a made-up income statement for It's Just Lunch for the Year ended December 31, 1998. List all the business's expenses, starting with the most important (largest dollar amount) and working through the least important (smallest dollar amount). Try to come as close as you can to the actual figures, as follows: Net revenues, $20,175,920; Net income, $2,018,516.
5. Using made-up dollar amounts, prepare all the adjusting entries your business will need at the end of the year. Identify the date of your adjustments.

INTERNET EXERCISE

1. **It's Just Lunch** customers may meet their dates at one of the many **Darden** restaurants. Go to **http://www.darden.com** and list at least three of the Darden restaurant chains.
2. In the left-hand column click on *The Numbers* followed by *Annual Report and Financials.* Select the HTML version of the *most recent annual report.* Click on *next* to reach the table of contents. Use the Consolidated Balance Sheets to answer the following questions.
   a. Does the Darden Restaurants company use cash-basis or accrual-basis accounting? How can you tell?
   b. For the two most recent years list the amounts reported for "Cash and cash equivalents" and for "Land, Buildings and Equipment." For each of these accounts, identify whether it requires an adjustment at the end of the accounting period.
3. Use the Consolidated Statements of Earnings to answer the following questions.
   a. For the three most recent fiscal years list the amounts reported for "Sales." Comment on whether the three-year trend of sales is favorable or unfavorable. Sales is what type of an account? Which principle of accounting is relevant for recording these amounts?
   b. For the three most recent fiscal years list the amounts reported for "Total Cost of Sales." Total Cost of Sales is what type of account? Were all of these amounts paid in cash? Which principle of accounting is relevant for recording these amounts?
   c. For the three most recent fiscal years list the amounts reported for "Net Earnings (Loss)." Is the three-year trend of net income favorable or unfavorable? What title does the text use to refer to net earnings?

Darden Corporation

Go to the "Deferrals (Unearned Revenues and Prepaid Expenses)" episode on the *Mastering Accounting* CD-ROM for an interactive, video-enhanced exercise explaining the principles of income statements and timing of recorded transactions to CanGo managers to help them interpret financial reports.

APPENDIX TO CHAPTER 3

ALTERNATIVE TREATMENT OF PREPAID EXPENSES AND UNEARNED REVENUES

Chapters 1–3 illustrate the most popular way to account for prepaid expenses and unearned revenues. This appendix illustrates an alternative—and equally appropriate—approach.

Prepaid Expenses

Prepaid expenses are advance payments of expenses. Prepaid Insurance, Prepaid Rent, Prepaid Advertising, and Prepaid Legal Cost are prepaid expenses. Supplies that will be used up in the current period or within one year are also accounted for as prepaid expenses.

When a business prepays an expense—rent, for example—it can debit an *asset* account (Prepaid Rent), as illustrated on page 88:

Aug. 1	Prepaid Rent	XXX	
	Cash		XXX

Alternatively, it can debit an *expense* account to record this cash payment:

Aug. 1	Rent Expense	XXX	
	Cash		XXX

Regardless of the account debited at the time of the prepayment, the business must adjust the accounts at the end of the period to report the correct amounts of the expense and the asset.

Prepaid Expense Recorded Initially as an Expense

Prepaying an expense creates an asset, as explained on page 88. However, the asset may be so short-lived that it will expire in the current accounting period—within one year or less. Thus, the accountant may decide to debit the prepayment to an expense account at the time of payment. A $6,000 cash payment for rent (one year, in advance) on August 1 may be debited to Rent Expense:

20X6			
Aug. 1	Rent Expense	6,000	
	Cash		6,000

At December 31, only five months' prepayment has expired (for August through December), leaving seven months' rent still prepaid. In this case, the accountant must transfer 7/12 of the original prepayment of $6,000, or $3,500, to the asset account Prepaid Rent. At December 31, 20X6, the business still has the benefit of the prepayment for January through July of 20X7. The adjusting entry at December 31 is

Adjusting Entries		
20X6		
Dec. 31 Prepaid Rent ($6,000 × 7/12)	3,500	
Rent Expense		3,500

After posting, the two accounts appear as follows (where CP = cash payment entry; Adj = adjusting entry):

PREPAID RENT				RENT EXPENSE			
20X6				20X6		20X6	
Dec. 31 Adj. 3,500				Aug. 1 CP 6,000		Dec. 31 Adj. 3,500	
Dec. 31 Bal. 3,500				Dec. 31 Bal. 2,500			

The balance sheet at the end of 20X6 reports Prepaid Rent of $3,500, and the income statement for 20X6 reports Rent Expense of $2,500, regardless of whether the business initially debits the prepayment to an asset account or to an expense account.

Unearned (Deferred) Revenues

Unearned (deferred) revenues arise when a business collects cash before earning the revenue. Unearned revenues are liabilities because the business that receives cash owes the other party goods or services to be delivered later.

Unearned (Deferred) Revenue Recorded Initially as a Revenue

Receipt of cash in advance creates a liability, as recorded on page 000. Another way to account for the receipt of cash is to credit a *revenue account*. If the business has earned all the revenue within the same period, no adjusting entry is needed at the end of the period. However, if the business earns only part of the revenue at the end of the period, it must make an adjusting entry.

Suppose on October 1, 20X2, a law firm records as revenue the receipt of cash for a nine-month fee of $7,200 received in advance. The cash receipt entry is

20X2		
Oct. 1 Cash	7,200	
Legal Revenue		7,200

At December 31, the attorney has earned only 3/9 of the $7,200, or $2,400, for the months of October, November, and December. Accordingly, the firm makes an adjusting entry to transfer the unearned portion (6/9 of $7,200, or $4,800) from the revenue account to a liability account, as follows:

Adjusting Entries		
20X2		
Dec. 31 Legal Revenue ($7,200 × 6/9)	4,800	
Unearned Legal Revenue		4,800

The adjusting entry transfers the unearned portion (6/9, or $4,800) of the original amount to the liability account because the law firm still owes legal service to the client during January through June of 20X3. After posting, the total amount ($7,200) is properly divided between the liability account ($4,800) and the revenue account ($2,400), as follows (where CR = Cash receipt entry and Adj. = Adjusting entry).

UNEARNED LEGAL REVENUE		LEGAL REVENUE		
	20X2	**20X2**	**20X2**	
	Dec. 31 Adj. 4,800	Dec. 31 Adj 4,800	Oct. 1 CR 7,200	
	Dec. 31 Bal. 4,800		Dec. 31 Bal. 2,400	

The attorney's 20X2 income statement reports legal revenue of $2,400, and the balance sheet at December 31, 20X2, reports the unearned legal revenue of $4,800 as a liability, regardless of whether the business initially credits a liability account or a revenue account.

ASSESS YOUR PROGRESS

APPENDIX EXERCISES

E3A-1 At the beginning of the year, supplies of $1,190 were on hand. During the year, Laser Printing Company paid $5,400 cash for supplies. At the end of the year, the count of supplies indicates the ending balance is $860.

Recording supplies transactions two ways
(Obj. A1)

Required

1. Assume that Laser Printing records supplies by initially debiting an *asset* account. Therefore, place the beginning balance in the Supplies T-account, and record the preceding entries directly in the accounts without using a journal.
2. Assume that Laser Printing records supplies by initially debiting an *expense* account. Therefore, place the beginning balance in the Supplies Expense T-account, and record the preceding entries directly in the accounts without using a journal.
3. Compare the ending account balances under both approaches. Are they the same?

E3A-2 At the beginning of the year, Laser Printing Company owed customers $2,750 for unearned service collected in advance. During the year, Laser Printing received advance cash receipts of $7,000. At year end, the liability for unearned revenue is $3,700.

Recording unearned revenues two ways
(Obj. A2)

Required

1. Assume that Laser Printing records unearned revenues by initially crediting a *liability* account. Open T-accounts for Unearned Service Revenue and Service Revenue, and place the beginning balance in Unearned Service Revenue. Journalize the cash collection and adjusting entries, and post their dollar amounts. As references in the T-accounts, denote a balance by *Bal.,* a cash receipt by *CR,* and an adjustment by *Adj.*
2. Assume that Laser Printing records unearned revenues by initially crediting a *revenue* account. Open T-accounts for Unearned Service Revenue and Service Revenue, and place the beginning balance in Service Revenue. Journalize the cash collection and adjusting entries, and post their dollar amounts. As references in the T-accounts, denote a balance by *Bal.,* a cash receipt by *CR,* and an adjustment by *Adj.*
3. Compare the ending balances in the two accounts.

APPENDIX PROBLEM

P3A-1 Diebolt Sales and Service completed the following transactions during 20X4:

Recording prepaid rent and rent revenue collected in advance two ways
(Obj. A1, A2)

Oct. 1 Paid $4,500 store rent covering the six-month period ending March 31, 20X5.
Dec. 1 Collected $3,200 cash in advance from customers. The service revenue will be earned $800 monthly over the period ending March 31, 20X5.

Required

1. Journalize these entries by debiting an asset account for Prepaid Rent and by crediting a liability account for Unearned Service Revenue. Explanations are unnecessary.
2. Journalize the related adjustments at December 31, 20X4.
3. Post the entries to the ledger accounts, and show their balances at December 31, 20X4. Posting references are unnecessary.
4. Repeat requirements 1–3. This time, debit Rent Expense for the rent payment and credit Service Revenue for the collection of revenue in advance.
5. Compare the account balances in requirements 3 and 4. They should be equal.

Completing the Accounting Cycle

4

LEARNING OBJECTIVES

After studying this chapter, you should be able to

1. Prepare an accounting work sheet
2. Use the work sheet to complete the accounting cycle
3. Close the revenue, expense, and withdrawal accounts
4. Classify assets and liabilities as current or long-term
5. Use the current and debt ratios to evaluate a business's ability to pay its debts

---

NetGenesis, The Ultimate E-Metrics Solution - Microsoft Internet Explorer

File Edit View Go Favorites Help

Links

Back Forward Stop Refresh Home Search Favorites History Channels Fullscreen Mail Print Edit

Address http://www.netgenesis.com/

NetGenesis

NETGENESIS IS REDEFINING eCRM BY EMPOWERING e-BUSINESSES TO ANALYZE, PREDICT, AND TAKE ACTION ON CUSTOMER DATA.

The Ultimate E-Metrics Solution

"NetGenesis 5 goes beyond count-the-clicks to offer count-the-money capabilities. Given the increasing emphasis on profitability in the online world, this is a bottom-line orientation that is sorely needed."

Guy Creese, Senior Analyst at the Aberdeen Group

ABOUT NETGENESIS PRODUCTS SERVICES GLOBAL PARTNERS CUSTOMERS SUPPORT

OFFERINGS AND SOLUTIONS   NEWS AND MEDIA

NetGenesis 5

NetGenesis, the leader in e-customer intelligence, announces the arrival of NetGenesis 5, the ultimate e-metrics solutions suite.

October 30, 2000

NetGenesis and TechnoInteractive Form Strategic Alliance To Manage Customer Relationships More Effectively and Profitably

SEARCH

GO

Done   Internet zone

Start   Inbox - Outlook Express   NetGenesis, The Ultim...   9:57 PM

---

www.prenhall.com/horngren

Readiness Assessment

Matt Cutler is 27 years old and the co-founder of **NetGenesis,** which sells software to help other companies understand their customers better. He started NetGenesis in 1994 and in February 2000 he took the company public. That means Cutler and his co-founder sold some shares of NetGenesis stock (the ownership in the company) to the public. By May 2000, NetGenesis was worth about $350 million. When asked how a business downturn would affect NetGenesis, Matt replied: "Any organization successful in dealing with rapid change in an upswing will be able to deal with a downswing." The key is to be able to deal with rapid change.

The way for Matt to convince people that NetGenesis is a sound company is the same way that **Procter and Gamble, Xerox Corporation,** and **Sony** do it. Earn a profit year after year, and build up more assets than liabilities. In this chapter, we complete the accounting cycle that produces the financial statements investors use for their decision making.

Source: *Wall Street Journal,* May 22, 2000, p. R18.

In Chapter 3, we prepared the financial statements of Gay Gillen eTravel from an adjusted trial balance. That approach works well for quick decision making, but organizations of all sizes take the accounting process a step further. At the end of each period, after making the adjusting entries, they close their books. Whether the company is **NetGenesis, Xerox,** or Gay Gillen eTravel, the closing process follows the same basic pattern. Closing the books marks the end of the *accounting cycle* for a given period.

Accountants often use a document known as the *work sheet.* There are many different types of work sheets in business—as many, in fact, as there are needs for summary data. Work sheets are valuable because they summarize lots of data.

THE ACCOUNTING CYCLE

The **accounting cycle** is the process by which companies produce their financial statements for a specific period of time. For a new business, the cycle begins with setting up (opening) the ledger accounts. **NetGenesis** opened its doors in January 1994, and the first step in the accounting cycle was to open the accounts. After a business has operated for one period, the account balances carry over from period to period. Therefore, the accounting cycle starts with the beginning account balances. Exhibit 4-1 outlines the complete accounting cycle of NetGenesis, Gillen eTravel, and every other business. The boldface items in Panel A indicate the new concepts we introduce in this chapter.

The accounting cycle includes work performed at two different times:

- During the period—Journalizing transactions
    Posting to the ledger
- End of the period—Adjusting the accounts, including journalizing and posting the adjusting entries
    Closing the accounts, including journalizing and posting the closing entries
    Preparing the financial statements (income statement, statement of owner's equity, and balance sheet)

The end-of-period work also readies the accounts for the next period. In Chapters 3 and 4, we cover the end-of-period accounting for a service business such as Gay Gillen eTravel. Chapter 5 shows how a merchandising entity adjusts and closes its books.

Companies prepare financial statements on a monthly or a quarterly basis. Steps 1–6a in Exhibit 4-1 are adequate for statement preparation. Steps 6b–7 can be performed monthly or quarterly, but are necessary only at the end of the year.

> **Accounting Cycle.** Process by which companies produce an entity's financial statements for a specific period.

Exhibit 4-1   The Accounting Cycle

PANEL A

During the Period	End of the Period

1. Start with the account balances in the ledger at the beginning of the period.
 2. Analyze and journalize transactions as they occur.
 3. Post journal entries to the ledger accounts.
	4. Compute the unadjusted balance in each account at the end of the period.
	 5. Enter the trial balance on the work sheet, and complete the work sheet (optional).
	 6. Using the adjusted trial balance or the full work sheet as a guide,
	   a. Prepare the financial statements.
	   b. Journalize and post the adjusting entries.
	   c. Journalize and post the closing entries.
	 7. Prepare the **postclosing trial balance.** This trial balance becomes step 1 for the next period.

PANEL B

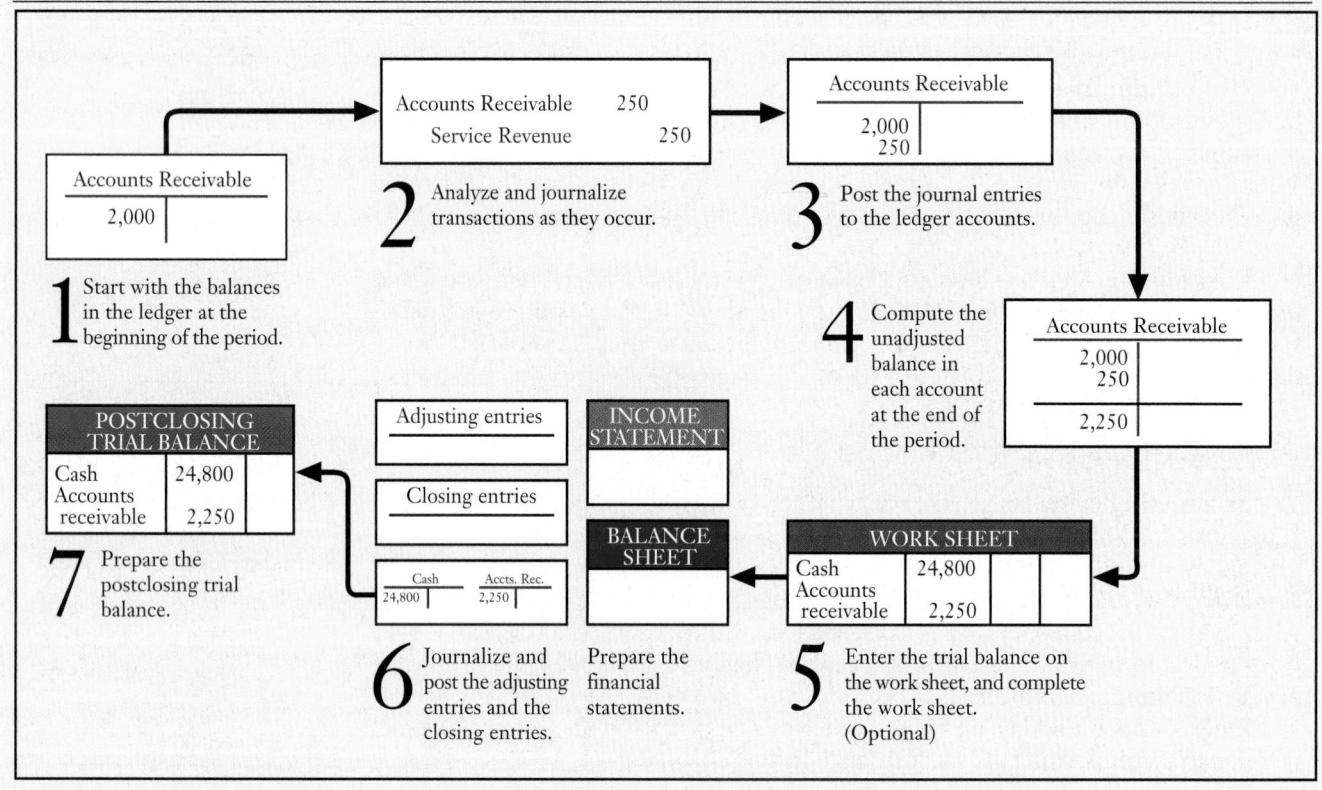

THE WORK SHEET

Objective 1
Prepare an accounting work sheet.

WORK SHEET. A columnar document designed to help move data from the trial balance to the financial statements.

Accountants often use a **work sheet**—a document with several columns—to help summarize and move data from the trial balance to the financial statements. The work sheet is not part of the ledger or the journal, and it is not a financial statement. It is merely a summary device that aids the accounting process. Listing all the accounts and their unadjusted balances helps identify accounts that need adjustment.

Exhibits 4-2 through 4-6 illustrate the development of a typical work sheet for the business of Gay Gillen eTravel. The heading at the top names the business, identifies the document, and states the accounting period.

A step-by-step description of its preparation follows.

Steps introduced in Chapter 3 to prepare the adjusted trial balance:

1. Enter the account titles and their unadjusted ending balances in the Trial Balance columns of the work sheet, and total the amounts (Exhibit 4-2).

2. Enter the adjustments in the Adjustments columns, and total the amounts (Exhibit 4-3). Total debits must equal total credits.

3. Compute each account's adjusted balance by combining the trial balance and adjustment figures. Enter the adjusted amounts in the Adjusted Trial Balance columns (Exhibit 4-4). Then compute the total for each column. Total debits should equal total credits.

Steps introduced in this chapter:

4. Extend the asset, liability, and owner's equity amounts from the Adjusted Trial Balance to the Balance Sheet columns. Extend the revenue and expense amounts to the Income Statement columns. Total the statement columns (Exhibit 4-5). For a change, total debits will not equal total credits.

5. Compute net income or net loss as the difference between total revenues and total expenses on the income statement. Enter net income or net loss as a balancing amount on the income statement and on the balance sheet, and compute the final column totals (Exhibit 4-6). Now all pairs of debit and credit columns should hold equal totals.

Let's examine these steps in greater detail.

1. *Enter the account titles and their unadjusted balances in the Trial Balance columns of the work sheet, and total the amounts.* Total debits must equal total credits, as shown in Exhibit 4-2. The account titles and unadjusted balances come directly from the ledger accounts before the adjusting entries are prepared. Accounts are grouped on the work sheet by category (assets, liabilities, owner's equity, revenues, and expenses) and are usually listed in the order they appear in the ledger (Cash first, Accounts Receivable second, and so on).

Accounts may have zero balances (for example, Depreciation Expense). All accounts are listed on the trial balance because they appear in the ledger.

2. *Enter the adjusting entries in the Adjustments columns, and total the amounts.* Exhibit 4-3 includes the April adjusting entries. These are the same adjustments that we used in Chapter 3 to prepare the adjusted trial balance.

 DAILY EXERCISE 4-1

We can identify the accounts that need to be adjusted by scanning the trial balance. Cash needs no adjustment because all cash transactions are recorded as they occur during the period. Consequently, Cash's balance is up to date.

Accounts Receivable is listed next. Has Gay Gillen earned revenue she has not yet recorded? The answer is yes. At April 30, Gillen has earned $250 that she has not yet recorded because the cash will be received during May. Gillen debits Accounts Receivable and credits Service Revenue on the work sheet in Exhibit 4-3. A letter is used to link the debit and the credit of each adjusting entry.

By moving down the trial balance, Gillen identifies the remaining accounts that need adjustment. Supplies is next. The business has used supplies during April, so Gillen debits Supplies Expense and credits Supplies. The other adjustments are analyzed and entered on the work sheet as in Chapter 3.

Listing the accounts in proper sequence aids the process of identifying accounts that need to be adjusted. But suppose some accounts are omitted from the trial balance. An account title can always be written below the first column totals—51,800. Assume that Supplies Expense was accidentally omitted and thus did not appear on the trial balance. The accountant can write Supplies Expense beneath the amount totals and enter the debit adjustment—$300—on the Supplies Expense line. After the adjustments are entered on the work sheet, the amount columns are totaled.

3. *Compute each account's adjusted balance by combining the trial balance and adjustment figures. Enter the adjusted amounts in the Adjusted Trial Balance columns.* Exhibit 4-4 shows the work sheet with the adjusted trial balance columns completed. For example, the Cash balance is up to date, so it receives no adjustment. Accounts Receivable's adjusted balance of $2,500 is computed by adding the trial balance amount of $2,250 to the $250 debit adjustment. Supplies' adjusted balance is determined by subtracting the $300 credit adjustment from the unadjusted debit balance of $700. An account may receive more than one adjustment, as Service Revenue does. The column totals must maintain the equality of debits and credits.

 DAILY EXERCISE 4-2

EXHIBIT 4-2 Trial Balance

GAY GILLEN ETRAVEL
Accounting Work Sheet
For the Month Ended April 30, 20X1

Account Title	Trial Balance		Adjustments		Adjusted Trial Balance		Income Statement		Balance Sheet	
	Dr.	Cr.	Dr.	Cr.	Dr.	Cr.	Dr.	Cr.	Dr.	Cr.
Cash	24,800									
Accounts receivable	2,250									
Supplies	700									
Prepaid rent	3,000									
Furniture	16,500									
Accumulated depreciation										
Accounts payable		13,100								
Salary payable										
Unearned service revenue		450								
Gay Gillen, capital		31,250								
Gay Gillen, withdrawals	3,200									
Service revenue		7,000								
Rent expense										
Salary expense	950									
Supplies expense										
Depreciation expense										
Utilities expense	400									
	51,800	51,800								
Net income										

Write the account titles and their unadjusted ending balances in the Trial Balance columns of the work sheet, and total the amounts.

4. *Extend (that is, copy) the asset, liability, and owner's equity amounts from the Adjusted Trial Balance to the Balance Sheet columns. Copy the revenue and expense amounts to the Income Statement columns. Total the statement columns.* Every account is either a balance sheet account or an income statement account. The asset, liability, and owner's equity accounts go to the balance sheet, and the revenues and expenses go to the income statement. Debits on the adjusted trial balance remain debits in the statement columns, and credits remain credits. Each account's balance should appear in only one statement column, as shown in Exhibit 4-5.

First, total the *income statement columns,* as follows:

INCOME STATEMENT

- Debits (Dr.) Total expenses = $3,875 } Difference = $3,525, a net income
- Credits (Cr.) Total revenues = $7,400 } because revenues exceed expenses

Then total the *balance sheet* columns:

BALANCE SHEET

- Debits (Dr.) Total assets and withdrawals = $49,400 } Difference = $3,525,
- Credits (Cr.) Total liabilities, owner's equity, = $45,875 } a net income because
  and accumulated depreciation } total assets are greater

5. *Compute net income or net loss as the difference between total revenues and total expenses on the income statement. Enter net income as the balancing amount on the income statement and as the balancing amount on the balance sheet. Then compute the adjusted column totals.* Exhibit 4-6 presents the completed accounting work sheet, which shows net income of $3,525, computed as follows:

Revenue (total credits on the income statement)......................	$7,400
Less: Expenses (total debits on the income statement)..............	(3,875)
Net income...	$3,525

Net income of $3,525 is entered in the debit column of the income statement to balance with the credit column of the income statement, which totals $7,400. The net income amount is then extended to the credit column of the balance sheet, because an excess of revenues over expenses increases capital, and increases in capital are recorded by a credit. In the closing process, net income will find its way into the Capital account.

If expenses exceed revenues, the result is a net loss. In that event, Net Loss is printed on the work sheet. The loss amount should be entered in the *credit* column of the income statement (to balance out) and in the *debit* column of the balance sheet (to balance out). After completion, total debits equal total credits in the Income Statement columns and in the Balance Sheet columns. The balance sheet columns are totaled at $49,400.

SUMMARY PROBLEM

The trial balance of State Service Company at December 31, 20X1, the end of its fiscal year, is as follows.

STATE SERVICE COMPANY Trial Balance December 31, 20X1		
Cash	$ 198,000	
Accounts receivable	370,000	
Supplies	6,000	
Furniture and fixtures	100,000	
Accumulated depreciation—furniture and fixtures		$ 40,000
Building	250,000	
Accumulated depreciation—building		130,000
Accounts payable		380,000
Salary payable		
Unearned service revenue		45,000
Capital		293,000
Withdrawals	65,000	
Service revenues		286,000
Salary expense	172,000	
Supplies expense		
Depreciation expense—furniture and fixtures		
Depreciation expense—building		
Miscellaneous expense	13,000	
Total	$1,174,000	$1,174,000

Data needed for the adjusting entries include:
a. Supplies on hand at year end, $2,000.
b. Depreciation on furniture and fixtures, $20,000.
c. Depreciation on building, $10,000.
d. Salaries owed but not yet paid, $5,000.
e. Accrued service revenue, $12,000.
f. Of the $45,000 balance of Unearned Service Revenue, $32,000 was earned during 20X1.

Required

Prepare the accounting work sheet of State Service Company for the year ended December 31, 20X1. Key each adjusting entry by the letter corresponding to the data given.

Solution

STATE SERVICE COMPANY
Work Sheet
Year Ended December 31, 20X1

Account Title	Trial Balance Dr.	Trial Balance Cr.	Adjustments Dr.	Adjustments Cr.	Adjusted Trial Balance Dr.	Adjusted Trial Balance Cr.	Income Statement Dr.	Income Statement Cr.	Balance Sheet Dr.	Balance Sheet Cr.
Cash..............................	198,000				198,000				198,000	
Accounts receivable........	370,000		(e) 12,000		382,000				382,000	
Supplies.........................	6,000			(a) 4,000	2,000				2,000	
Furniture and fixtures....	100,000				100,000				100,000	
Accumulated depreciation— furniture and fixtures.......................		40,000		(b) 20,000		60,000				60,000
Building..........................	250,000				250,000				250,000	
Accumulated depreciation— building......................		130,000		(c) 10,000		140,000				140,000
Accounts payable............		380,000				380,000				380,000
Salary payable				(d) 5,000		5,000				5,000
Unearned service revenue......................		45,000	(f) 32,000			13,000				13,000
Capital		293,000				293,000				293,000
Withdrawals	65,000				65,000				65,000	
Service revenue.............		286,000		(e) 12,000 (f) 32,000		330,000		330,000		
Salary expense................	172,000		(d) 5,000		177,000		177,000			
Supplies expense			(a) 4,000		4,000		4,000			
Depreciation expense— furniture and fixtures.......................			(b) 20,000		20,000		20,000			
Depreciation expense— building......................			(c) 10,000		10,000		10,000			
Miscellaneous expense...	13,000				13,000		13,000			
	1,174,000	1,174,000	83,000	83,000	1,221,000	1,221,000	224,000	330,000	997,000	891,000
Net income							106,000			106,000
							330,000	330,000	997,000	997,000

COMPLETING THE ACCOUNTING CYCLE

Objective 2
Use the work sheet to complete the accounting cycle

The work sheet helps organize the data for the computation of the net income or net loss for the period. The work sheet aids in preparing the financial statements, recording the adjusting entries, and closing the accounts.

Preparing the Financial Statements

The work sheet shows the amount of net income or net loss for the period, but we still must prepare the financial statements. ➡ The sorting of accounts to the balance sheet and the income statement eases the preparation of the statements. The work sheet also provides the data for the statement of owner's equity. Exhibit 4-7 presents the April financial statements for Gay Gillen eTravel (based on data from the work sheet in Exhibit 4-6). Most accountants prepare the financial statements immediately after completing the work sheet.

⬅ The financial statements can be prepared directly from the adjusted trial balance; see p. 99. This is why completion of the work sheet is optional.

Recording the Adjusting Entries

The actual adjustment of the accounts requires journal entries and posting to the ledger accounts. Panel A of Exhibit 4-8 gives the adjusting entries of Gay Gillen eTravel at April 30. Panel B shows the postings to the accounts; *Adj.* denotes an amount posted from an adjusting entry. The adjusting entries can be recorded in the journal when they are entered on the work sheet. Only the revenue and expense accounts are presented in the exhibit in order to focus on the closing process.

EXHIBIT 4-7
April Financial Statements of Gay Gillen eTravel

GAY GILLEN eTRAVEL
Income Statement
Month Ended April 30, 20X1

Revenue:		
Service revenue		$7,400
Expenses:		
Salary expense	$1,900	
Rent expense	1,000	
Utilities expense	400	
Supplies expense	300	
Depreciation expense—furniture	275	
Total expenses		3,875
Net income		$3,525

GAY GILLEN eTRAVEL
Statement of Owner's Equity
Month Ended April 30, 20X1

Gay Gillen, capital, April 1, 20X1	$31,250
Add: Net income	3,525
	34,775
Less: Withdrawals	(3,200)
Gay Gillen, capital, April 30, 20X1	$31,575

GAY GILLEN eTRAVEL
Balance Sheet
April 30, 20X1

Assets			Liabilities		
Cash		$24,800	Accounts payable		$13,100
Accounts receivable		2,500	Salary payable		950
Supplies		400	Unearned service		
Prepaid rent		2,000	revenue		300
Furniture	$16,500		Total liabilities		14,350
Less:					
Accumulated			**Owner's Equity**		
depreciation	(275)	16,225	Gay Gillen, capital		31,575
			Total liabilities and		
Total assets		$45,925	owner's equity		$45,925

CLOSING THE ACCOUNTS. Step in the accounting cycle at the end of the period. Closing the accounts consists of journalizing and posting the closing entries to set the balances of the revenue, expense, and withdrawal accounts to zero for the next period.

Many companies journalize and post the adjusting entries (as in Exhibit 4-8) only once annually—at the end of the year. Accountants can use the work sheet to prepare monthly or quarterly statements without journalizing and posting the adjusting entries.

Closing the Accounts

Closing the accounts is the end-of-period process that prepares the accounts for the next period. Closing the accounts consists of journalizing and posting the closing entries. Closing zeroes out the balances of the revenue and expense accounts in order to clearly measure the net income of each period separately from all other periods.

Recall that the income statement reports only one period's net income. For example, net income for **NetGenesis Corp.** for 2001 relates exclusively to 2001. At December 31, 2001, the NetGenesis accountants close the company's revenue and expense accounts for that year. Because the revenue and expense account balances

EXHIBIT 4-8 Journalizing and Posting the Adjusting Entries

PANEL A — Journalizing: Page 4

Adjusting Entries

Apr. 30	Accounts Receivable....................................	250	
	Service Revenue		250
30	Supplies Expense...	300	
	Supplies..		300
30	Rent Expense..	1,000	
	Prepaid Rent		1,000
30	Depreciation Expense................................	275	
	Accumulated Depreciation		275
30	Salary Expense	950	
	Salary Payable...................................		950
30	Unearned Service Revenue	150	
	Service Revenue		150

PANEL B — Posting the Adjustments to the Revenue and Expense Accounts:

REVENUE

SERVICE REVENUE
		7,000
Adj.		250
Adj.		150
	Bal.	7,400

EXPENSES

RENT EXPENSE
Adj.	1,000	
Bal.	1,000	

SALARY EXPENSE
	950	
Adj.	950	
Bal.	1,900	

SUPPLIES EXPENSE
Adj.	300	
Bal.	300	

DEPRECIATION EXPENSE
Adj.	275	
Bal.	275	

UTILITIES EXPENSE
	400	
Bal.	400	

Adj. = Amount posted from an adjusting entry   Bal. = Balance

relate to a particular accounting period and are therefore closed at the end of the period (December 31, 2001), the revenue and expense accounts are called **temporary (nominal) accounts.** For example, Gay Gillen's balance of Service Revenue at April 30, 20X1, is $7,400. This balance relates exclusively to the month of April and must be zeroed out before Gillen records revenue for May.

The owner's Withdrawal account—although not a revenue or an expense—is also a temporary account because it measures withdrawals for only one period. The Withdrawals account is also closed.

To better understand the closing process, contrast the nature of the temporary accounts with the nature of the **permanent (real) accounts**—the asset, liability, and capital accounts. The asset, liability, and owner's capital accounts are *not* closed at the end of the period because their balances are not used to measure income. Consider Cash, Accounts Receivable, Accounts Payable, and Gay Gillen, Capital. These accounts do not represent business *activity* for a single period and thus are not closed at the end of the period. Their balances carry over to become the beginning balances of the next period. For example, the Cash balance at December 31, 20X1, becomes the beginning balance for 20X2.

Closing entries transfer the revenue, expense, and owner withdrawal balances from their respective accounts to the capital account. As you know,

TEMPORARY ACCOUNTS. The revenue and expense accounts that relate to a particular accounting period and are closed at the end of the period. For a proprietorship, the owner withdrawal account is also temporary. Also called **nominal accounts.**

PERMANENT ACCOUNTS. Accounts that are *not* closed at the end of the period— asset, liability, and capital accounts. Also called **real accounts.**

CLOSING ENTRIES. Entries that transfer the revenue, expense, and owner withdrawal balances from these respective accounts to the capital account.

Posting the closing entries causes the Capital account to absorb the balances in all temporary accounts.

Exhibit 4-9 Journalizing and Posting the Closing Entries

PANEL A—Journalizing   Page 5

Closing Entries

①	Apr. 30	Service Revenue...	7,400	
②		Income Summary		7,400
	30	Income Summary..	3,875	
		Rent Expense....................................		1,000
		Salary Expense		1,900
		Supplies Expense..............................		300
		Depreciation Expense........................		275
		Utilities Expense...............................		400
③	30	Income Summary ($7,400 − $3,875).............	3,525	
		Gay Gillen, Capital.............................		3,525
④	30	Gay Gillen, Capital	3,200	
		Gay Gillen, Withdrawals.....................		3,200

PANEL B—Posting

Adj. = Amount posted from an adjusting entry   Clo. = Amount posted from a closing entry   Bal. = Balance

INCOME SUMMARY. A temporary "holding tank" account into which revenues and expenses are transferred prior to their final transfer to the capital account.

As an intermediate step, the revenues and the expenses are transferred first to an account entitled **Income Summary,** which collects the total debit for the sum of all expenses and the total credit for the sum of all revenues of the period. The Income Summary account is like a "holding tank." The balance of Income Summary is then transferred to capital.

The steps in closing the accounts of a proprietorship such as Gay Gillen eTravel are as follows (the circled numbers are keyed to Exhibit 4-9).

① Debit each *revenue* account for the amount of its credit balance. Credit Income Summary for the total of the revenues. This entry transfers total revenues to the *credit* side of Income Summary.

② Credit each *expense* account for the amount of its debit balance. Debit Income Summary for the total of the expenses. This entry transfers total expenses to the *debit* side of Income Summary. It is not necessary to make a separate closing entry for each expense. In one closing entry, record one debit to Income Summary and a separate credit to each expense account.

③ To close net income, debit Income Summary for the amount of its *credit balance* (if there is a *net income*), and credit the Capital account. If there is a *net loss,* Income Summary has a *debit balance.* In that case, credit Income Summary for the amount of the loss, and debit Capital. This closing entry transfers net income or net loss from Income Summary to the Capital account.

④ Credit the *Withdrawals* account for the amount of its debit balance. Debit the Capital account of the proprietor. This entry transfers the amount of owner withdrawals during the period to the *debit* side of the Capital account. *Withdrawals do not affect net income or net loss because withdrawals are not an expense.*

 DAILY EXERCISE 4-5

These steps are best illustrated with an example. Suppose Gay Gillen closes the books at the end of April. Exhibit 4-9 presents the complete closing process for Gillen's travel agency. Panel A gives the closing journal entries, and Panel B shows the accounts after the closing entries have been posted.

Each expense account holds its adjusted balance. For example, Rent Expense has a $1,000 debit balance. Service Revenue has a credit balance of $7,400 before closing. These amounts come directly from the adjusted balances in Exhibit 4-8, Panel B.

- Closing entry ① in Exhibit 4-9 transfers Service Revenue's balance to the Income Summary account. This entry zeroes out Service Revenue for April and transfers total revenue to the credit side of Income Summary.
- Closing entry ② zeroes out the expenses and moves their total ($3,875) to the debit side of Income Summary. At this point, Income Summary contains all of April's revenues and expenses. Income Summary's credit balance shows the month's net income ($3,525).
- Closing entry ③ closes the Income Summary account by transferring net income ($3,525) to the credit side of Gay Gillen, Capital.[1]
- The last closing entry, entry ④, moves the owner withdrawals to the debit side of Gay Gillen, Capital, leaving a zero balance in Withdrawals.

The closing entries set all the revenues, the expenses, and the Withdrawals account back to zero. Now the owner's Capital account includes the full effects of April's revenues, expenses, and withdrawals, plus the beginning Capital balance. The Gay Gillen, Capital account has an ending balance of $31,575. Trace this ending Capital balance to the statement of owner's equity and also to the balance sheet in Exhibit 4-7.

DAILY EXERCISE 4-6

DAILY EXERCISE 4-7

DAILY EXERCISE 4-8

DAILY EXERCISE 4-9

CLOSING A NET LOSS   What would the closing entries be if Gillen's travel agency had suffered a net *loss* during April? Suppose expenses totaled $7,700 and all other factors were unchanged (revenues were $7,400, so Gillen's business suffered a net loss of $300 for April). Only closing entries ② and ③ would change. Closing entry ② would transfer expenses of $7,700 to the debit side of Income Summary, as follows:

INCOME SUMMARY			
Clo.	7,700	Clo.	7,400
Bal.	300		

Closing entry ③ would then credit Income Summary to close this account and to transfer the net loss to Gay Gillen, Capital:

③ Apr. 30   Gay Gillen, Capital 300
                  Income Summary............. 300

After posting, these two accounts would appear as follows:

INCOME SUMMARY				GAY GILLEN, CAPITAL		
Clo.	7,700	Clo.	7,400	Clo.	300	31,250
Bal.	300	Clo.	300			

---

[1]The Income Summary account is a convenience for combining the effects of the revenues and expenses before transferring their income effect to Capital. It is not necessary to use the Income Summary account in the closing process. In an alternative procedure, revenues and expenses are closed directly to Capital.

Finally, the Withdrawals balance would be closed to Capital, as before. The double underline in an account means that the account has a zero balance; nothing more will be posted to it in the current period.

The closing process is fundamentally mechanical and is completely automated in a computerized system. Accounts are identified as either temporary or permanent. The temporary accounts are closed automatically by selecting that option from the software menu. Posting also occurs automatically.

Postclosing Trial Balance

The accounting cycle ends with the **postclosing trial balance** (Exhibit 4-10). It lists the accounts and their adjusted balances after closing. This step shows where the business stands as it moves into the next accounting period. The postclosing trial balance is dated as of the end of the period.

GAY GILLEN eTRAVEL Postclosing Trial Balance April 30, 20X1		
Cash	$24,800	
Accounts receivable	2,500	
Supplies	400	
Prepaid Rent	2,000	
Furniture	16,500	
Accumulated depreciation		$ 275
Accounts payable		13,100
Salary Payable		950
Unearned service revenue		300
Gay Gillen, capital		31,575
Total	$46,200	$46,200

The postclosing trial balance resembles the balance sheet. It contains the ending balances of the permanent accounts—the balance sheet accounts: the assets, liabilities, and capital. No temporary accounts—revenues, expenses, or withdrawal accounts—are included because their balances have been closed. The ledger is up to date and ready for the next period's transactions.

Reversing entries are special journal entries that ease the burden of accounting for transactions that key off the adjustments at the end of the period. Reversing entries are optional, and for that reason, we cover them in the appendix at the end of this chapter.

CLASSIFYING ASSETS AND LIABILITIES

Assets and liabilities are classified as either *current* or *long-term* to indicate their relative liquidity. **Liquidity** measures how quickly an item can be converted to cash. Cash is the most liquid asset. Accounts receivable is relatively liquid because the business expects to collect the money in the near future. Supplies are less liquid than receivables, and furniture and buildings are even less liquid.

Managers and owners are interested in liquidity because business difficulties often arise from a shortage of cash. How quickly can the business convert an asset to cash and pay a debt? How soon must a liability be paid? These are questions of liquidity. A classified balance sheet helps to answer questions such as these.

Assets

CURRENT ASSETS **Current assets** are assets that are expected to be converted to cash, sold, or consumed during the next 12 months or within the business's normal operating cycle. The **operating cycle** is the time span during which (1) cash is used to acquire goods and services, (2) these goods and services are sold to customers, and (3) the business collects cash. For most businesses, the operating cycle is a few

POSTCLOSING TRIAL BALANCE. List of the accounts and their balances at the end of the period after journalizing and posting the closing entries. The last step of the accounting cycle, the postclosing trial balance ensures that the ledger is in balance to start the next accounting period.

EXHIBIT 4-10
Postclosing Trial Balance

 DAILY EXERCISE 4-10

REVERSING ENTRIES. Special journal entries that ease the burden of accounting for transactions that key off adjustments at the end of the period.

Objective 4
Classify assets and liabilities as current or long-term

LIQUIDITY. Measure of how quickly an item can be converted to cash.

CURRENT ASSET. An asset that is expected to be converted to cash, sold, or consumed during the next 12 months, or within the business's normal operating cycle.

months. A few types of businesses have operating cycles longer than a year. Cash, Accounts Receivable, Notes Receivable due within a year or less, and Prepaid Expenses are current assets. Merchandising entities such as **Intel, Sears,** and **IBM** have an additional current asset, Inventory. This account shows the cost of the goods the business is holding for sale to customers.

OPERATING CYCLE. Time span during which cash is paid for goods and services, which are then sold to customers from whom the business collects cash.

LONG-TERM ASSETS   **Long-term assets** are all assets other than current assets. One category of long-term assets is **plant** (or **fixed**) **assets,** another name for Property, Plant, and Equipment. Land, Buildings, Furniture and Fixtures, and Equipment are fixed assets. Of these, Gay Gillen eTravel has only Furniture.

Other categories of long-term assets include Long-Term Investments in Stock, and Other Assets (a catchall category). We discuss these categories in later chapters.

LONG-TERM ASSET. An asset other than a current asset.

PLANT OR FIXED ASSET. Another name for property, plant, and equipment.

Liabilities

Managers and owners are interested in the due dates of an entity's liabilities. Liabilities that must be paid the quickest create the greatest strain on cash. Therefore, the balance sheet lists liabilities in the order in which they are due to be paid. Knowing how much of a business's liabilities is current and how much is long-term helps creditors assess the likelihood of collecting cash from the entity. Balance sheets have two liability classifications, *current liabilities* and *long-term liabilities.*

CURRENT LIABILITIES   **Current liabilities** are debts that must be paid with cash or with goods and services within one year or within the entity's operating cycle if the cycle is longer than a year. Accounts Payable, Notes Payable due within one year, Salary Payable, Unearned Revenue, and Interest Payable owed on notes payable are current liabilities.

CURRENT LIABILITY. A debt due to be paid with cash or with goods and services within one year or within the entity's operating cycle if the cycle is longer than a year.

LONG-TERM LIABILITIES   All liabilities that are not current are classified as **long-term liabilities.** Many notes payable are long-term—payable after one year or the entity's operating cycle. Some notes payable are paid in installments, with the first installment due within one year, the second installment due the second year, and so on. In that case, the first installment is a current liability, and the remaining installments long-term liabilities. For example, a $100,000 note payable to be paid $10,000 per year over ten years would include a current liability of $10,000 for next year's payment and a long-term liability of $90,000.

Thus far we have presented the *unclassified* balance sheet of Gay Gillen eTravel. Our purpose was to focus on the main points of assets, liabilities, and owner's equity without the details of *current* assets, *current* liabilities, and so on. Exhibit 4-11 presents Gillen's classified balance sheet.

LONG-TERM LIABILITY. A liability other than a current liability.

 DAILY EXERCISE 4-11

EXHIBIT 4-11 Classified Balance Sheet of Gay Gillen eTravel

<table>
<tr><td colspan="6" align="center">GAY GILLEN ETRAVEL
Balance Sheet
April 30, 20X1</td></tr>
<tr><td colspan="3" align="center">**Assets**</td><td colspan="3" align="center">**Liabilities**</td></tr>
<tr><td>Current assets:</td><td></td><td></td><td>Current liabilities:</td><td></td><td></td></tr>
<tr><td>Cash</td><td></td><td>$24,800</td><td>Accounts payable</td><td></td><td>$13,100</td></tr>
<tr><td>Accounts receivable</td><td></td><td>2,500</td><td>Salary payable</td><td></td><td>950</td></tr>
<tr><td>Supplies</td><td></td><td>400</td><td>Unearned service revenue</td><td></td><td>300</td></tr>
<tr><td>Prepaid rent</td><td></td><td>2,000</td><td>Total current liabilities</td><td></td><td>14,350</td></tr>
<tr><td>Total current assets</td><td></td><td>29,700</td><td>Long-term liabilities (None)</td><td></td><td>0</td></tr>
<tr><td>Fixed assets:</td><td></td><td></td><td>Total liabilities</td><td></td><td>14,350</td></tr>
<tr><td>Furniture</td><td>$16,500</td><td></td><td></td><td></td><td></td></tr>
<tr><td>Less: Accumulated</td><td></td><td></td><td colspan="3" align="center">**Owner's Equity**</td></tr>
<tr><td>depreciation</td><td>(275)</td><td>16,225</td><td>Gay Gillen, capital</td><td></td><td>31,575</td></tr>
<tr><td></td><td></td><td></td><td>Total liabilities and</td><td></td><td></td></tr>
<tr><td>Total assets</td><td></td><td>$45,925</td><td>owner's equity</td><td></td><td>$45,925</td></tr>
</table>

Gillen classifies each asset and each liability as current or long-term. She could have labeled fixed assets as *long-term assets.*

Compare Gillen's *classified* balance sheet in Exhibit 4-11 with the *unclassified* balance sheet in Exhibit 4-7. The classified balance sheet reports more information—totals for current assets and current liabilities, which do not appear on the unclassified balance sheet. Gillen has no long-term liabilities, so there are none to report on either balance sheet.

 THINK IT OVER Why is the classified balance sheet in Exhibit 4-11 more useful than an unclassified balance sheet (Exhibit 4-7) to (a) Gay Gillen and (b) a banker considering whether to lend $10,000 to Gillen?

Answer: A classified balance sheet indicates to (a) Gillen and (b) a banker

• Which of Gillen's liabilities, and the dollar amounts, Gillen must pay within the next year
• Which of Gillen's assets are the most liquid and thus available to pay the liabilities
• Which assets and liabilities (and amounts) are long-term

A Real Classified Balance Sheet

Exhibit 4-12 is an actual classified balance sheet of **PepsiCo, Inc.** Dollar amounts are reported in millions to avoid clutter. You should be familiar with all but a few of PepsiCo's account titles. Among the Current Assets are Short-term investments, which are investments that PepsiCo expects to sell within one year. These assets are very liquid, which explains why they are reported before the receivables.

EXHIBIT 4-12
PepsiCo's Classified Balance Sheet

PEPSICO, INC. Balance Sheet (Adapted) December 31,1999	
ASSETS	*(In millions)*
Current Assets	
Cash and cash equivalents...	$ 964
Short-term investments, at cost	92
	1,056
Accounts and notes receivable, net..............................	1,704
Inventories..	899
Prepaid expenses and other current assets...................	514
Total Current Assets..	4,173
Property, plant and equipment, net of	
Accumulated depreciation of $3,550.........................	5,266
Intangible assets, net	4,735
Investments in other companies	2,846
Other assets	531
Total Assets..	$17,551
LIABILITIES AND SHAREHOLDERS' EQUITY	
Current Liabilities	
Short-term borrowings..	$ 233
Accounts payable and other current liabilities..............	3,399
Income taxes payable	156
Total Current Liabilities..	3,788
Long-term debt..	2,812
Other liabilities	4,070
Shareholders' equity..	6,881
Total Liabilities and Shareholders' Equity..................	$17,551

 DAILY EXERCISE 4-12

PepsiCo reports Property, Plant, and Equipment, *net,* of $5,266 million. *Net* means the amount of the assets after subtracting Accumulated Depreciation. At

December 31, 1999, Accumulated Depreciation of PepsiCo's property, plant, and equipment totaled $3,550 million. Another way for PepsiCo to report property, plant, and equipment would be (in millions)

Property, Plant, and Equipment, at cost..............	$8,816
Less: Accumulated Depreciation.........................	(3,550)
Property, Plant and Equipment, net....................	$5,266

INTANGIBLE ASSETS. Assets, such as patents, trademarks, and goodwill, which have no physical form.

PepsiCo also reports **Intangible Assets.** Intangibles are assets, such as patents, trademarks, and goodwill, which have no physical form. Intangibles are valuable because of the rights they provide the owner. PepsiCo's trademarks (Pepsi and Tropicana drinks, Lay's chips, and Aquafina) are worth a lot.

All of PepsiCo's liabilities should be familiar to you. We can compute total liabilities two ways, as follows (in millions):

- Add: Total Current liabilities, Long-Term Debt, and Other Liabilities ($3,788 + $2,812 + $4,070) $10,670
- Total Liabilities = Total Assets − Shareholders' (Owners') Equity ($17,551 − $6,881) $10,670

Both computations are valid. When all the liability amounts are available, as on PepsiCo's balance sheet, you can add them up. When some data are missing, you can still compute total liabilities by using the accounting equation: Assets = Liabilities + Shareholders' Equity (same as Owners' Equity).

BALANCE SHEET FORMATS

The balance sheet of PepsiCo in Exhibit 4-12 lists the assets at the top and the liabilities and owners' equity below. This arrangement is known as the *report format*. The balance sheet of Gay Gillen eTravel presented in Exhibit 4-7 lists the assets at the left and the liabilities and the owner's equity at the right. That arrangement is known as the *account format*.

Either format is acceptable. A recent survey of 600 companies indicated that 73% (436 companies) use the report format and only 27% (164 companies) use the account format.

ACCOUNTING RATIOS

Objective 5
Use the current and debt ratios to evaluate a business's ability to pay its debts

The purpose of accounting is to provide information for decision making. Chief users of accounting information are managers, business owners, and creditors. A creditor considering lending money must predict whether the borrower can repay the loan. If the borrower already has a lot of debt, the probability of repayment is lower than if the borrower doesn't owe much money. To assess a company's financial position, decision makers use ratios computed from the company's financial statements.

Current Ratio

CURRENT RATIO. Current assets divided by current liabilities. Measures the company's ability to pay current liabilities from current assets.

One of the most widely used financial ratios is the **current ratio,** which compares an entity's current assets to its current liabilities:

$$\text{Current ratio} = \frac{\textbf{Total current assets}}{\textbf{Total current liabilities}}$$

The current ratio measures the ability to pay current liabilities with current assets. A company prefers to have a high current ratio, which means that the business has plenty of current assets to pay current liabilities. An increasing current ratio from period to period indicates improvement in the ability to pay current debts.

A rule of thumb: A very strong current ratio is 2.00, which indicates that the company has $2.00 in current assets for every $1.00 in current liabilities. A company with a current ratio of 2.00 would probably have little trouble paying its current liabilities. Most successful businesses operate with current ratios between 1.50 and 2.00. A current ratio of 1.00 is considered low.

WORK IT OUT

Compute PepsiCo's current ratio at December 31, 1999. Use the company's balance sheet in Exhibit 4-12 and show dollar amounts in millions.

Answer: $$\textbf{Current} = \frac{\textbf{Total current assets}}{\textbf{Total current liabilities}} = \frac{\$4{,}173}{\$3{,}788} = \textbf{1.10}$$

How much in current assets does PepsiCo have for every dollar the company owes in current liabilities?

Answer: $1.10

Is PepsiCo's current ratio high or low? Is this ratio value risky?

Answer: PepsiCo's current ratio is low, which makes it look risky. However, PepsiCo operates successfully with a low current ratio because the company sells food products that people buy in both good times and hard times. Thus far, PepsiCo has had no trouble paying its debts.

Debt Ratio

DEBT RATIO. Ratio of total liabilities to total assets. Tells the proportion of a company's assets that it has financed with debt.

A second aid to decision making is the **debt ratio,** which is the ratio of total liabilities to total assets:

$$\textbf{Debt ratio} = \frac{\textbf{Total liabilities}}{\textbf{Total assets}}$$

The debt ratio indicates the proportion of a company's assets that are financed with debt. This ratio measures a business's overall ability to pay both current and long-term debts—total liabilities. The debt ratio measures debt-paying ability differently than the current ratio.

A low debt ratio is safer than a high debt ratio. Why? Because a company with a small amount of liabilities has low required payments. Such a company is unlikely to get into financial difficulty. By contrast, a business with a high debt ratio may have trouble paying its liabilities, especially when sales are low and cash is scarce. When a company fails to pay its debts, the creditors can take the business away from its owner. The largest retail bankruptcy in history, **Federated Department Stores,** the parent company of Bloomingdale's, was due largely to high debt during an economic recession in the retail industry. Federated was unable to weather the downturn and had to declare bankruptcy.

A rule of thumb: A debt ratio below 0.60, or 60%, is considered safe for most businesses. A debt ratio above 0.80, or 80%, borders on high risk. Most companies have debt ratios in the range of 0.60–0.80.

THINK IT OVER

We saw that PepsiCo has a low current ratio, but PepsiCo nevertheless operates successfully (profits are high, cash is plentiful, and the company grows steadily). Now compute PepsiCo's debt ratio from the company's balance sheet in Exhibit 4-12. Show dollar amounts in millions.

Answer: $$\textbf{Debt ratio} = \frac{\textbf{Total liabilities}}{\textbf{Total assets}} = \frac{\$10{,}670^*}{\$17{,}551} = \textbf{0.61, or 61\%}$$

For each dollar of its total assets, how much does PepsiCo owe in total liabilities?

Answer: $0.61

What percentage of PepsiCo's total assets is financial with debt?

Answer: 0.61, or 61%

If you owed $0.61 for every dollar of your total assets, would you worry about your ability to pay your debts?

Answer: You would probably be worried if your cash flow (excess of cash receipts over cash payments) was weak. But if your cash flow is strong—as PepsiCo's cash flow is—you shouldn't worry about a debt ratio of 0.61, or 61%. Many companies operate successfully with higher (more risky) debt ratios.

---

*\$3,788 + \$2,812 + \$4,070 = \$10,670

Managing Both the Current Ratio and the Debt Ratio

 DAILY EXERCISE 4-13

 DAILY EXERCISE 4-14

In general, a *high* current ratio is preferable to a low current ratio. *Increases* in the current ratio indicate improving financial position. By contrast, a low debt ratio is preferable to a high debt ratio. Improvement is indicated by a *decrease* in the debt ratio.

Financial ratios aid decision making. It is unwise, however, to place too much confidence in a single ratio. A company may have a high current ratio, which indicates financial strength. It may also have a high debt ratio, which suggests weakness. Which ratio gives the more reliable signal? Experienced lenders and investors examine a large number of ratios over several years to spot trends and turning points. They also consider other factors, such as the company's cash flow and its trend of net income.

As you progress through your study of accounting, we will introduce key ratios used for decision making. Chapter 18 summarizes all the ratios discussed in this book and provides an overview of the more common ratios used in decision making.

e-Accounting

A Forced Debt Ratio for South Korea's Companies

Samsung. Daewoo. Hyundai. Just five years ago these companies were the economic engines driving South Korea's economy. Now they are mired in debt. When the Asian currency crisis hit South Korea in 1997, investors fled and companies had to borrow money. The bigger the company, the more debt they had to take on. According to the **Bank of Korea,** the average debt ratio of Korea's manufacturing companies was 71% in 1999.

According to the government of President Kim Dae Jung, the only way for the giant family-run companies to move toward financial stability is to meet a hard and fast debt ratio target of 67%. Carmaking giant Daewoo was struggling to meet payments on \$47 billion in debt—equivalent to the entire national debt of Poland or Malaysia. The Korean government strong-armed Daewoo into selling off the pieces of the company. President Kim's reform plan may save some companies from going bust, but it may hurt others.

Source: Based on Howard W. French, "Dismantling of yesterday's economic engines," *New York Times,* September 3, 1999, p. C1. Jane L. Lee, "Korea moves anew to reform top 5 chaebols; this time, control by families could diminish," *Wall Street Journal,* August 26, 1999, p. A13. Anonymous, "Government under fire for strict debt ratio target," *Business Korea,* December 1999, pp. 18–19.

Now study the Decision Guidelines feature, which summarizes what you have learned in this chapter.

DECISION GUIDELINES

Completing the Accounting Cycle

DECISION	GUIDELINES
How (where) to summarize the effects of all the entity's transactions and adjustments throughout the period?	Accountant's *work sheet* with columns for • Trial balance • Income statement • Adjustments • Balance sheet • Adjusted trial balance
What is the last *major* step in the accounting cycle?	*Closing entries* for the *temporary accounts:* • Revenues $\Big\}$ Income statement accounts • Expenses • Owner's withdrawals
Why close out revenues, expenses, and owner withdrawals?	Because these *temporary accounts* have balances that relate only to one accounting period and do *not* carry over to the next period.
Which accounts do not get closed out?	*Permanent (balance sheet) accounts:* • Assets • Owner's capital • Liabilities The balances of these accounts *do* carry over to the next period.
How do businesses classify their assets and liabilities for reporting on the balance sheet?	*Current* (within one year or the entity's operating cycle if longer than a year) *Long-term* (not current)
How do decision makers evaluate a company?	There are many ways, such as the company's net income or net loss on the income statement. Another way to evaluate a company is based on the company's *financial ratios.* Two key ratios: $$\text{Current ratio} = \frac{\text{Total current assets}}{\text{Total current liabilities}}$$ The *current ratio* measures the entity's ability to pay its current liabilities with its current assets. $$\text{Debt ratio} = \frac{\text{Total liabilities}}{\text{Total assets}}$$ The *debt ratio* shows the proportion of the entity's assets that are financed with debt. The debt ratio measures the entity's overall ability to pay its liabilities.

EXCEL APPLICATION PROBLEM

Goal: Create an Excel spreadsheet to calculate the current ratio and debt ratio for Target and use the results to answer questions about the company.

Scenario: You are deciding whether to buy the stock in **Target.** You know that the current ratio and the debt ratio measure whether a company has the assets to cover its liabilities.

Your task is to create a simple spreadsheet to calculate the current ratio and the debt ratio for the company. Data may be found in Target's annual report (Web site: www.target-corp.com). When done, answer these questions:
1. Does the company have an acceptable current ratio? How can you tell?
2. Does the company have an acceptable debt ratio? How can you tell?

3. What is the trend (up or down) for the ratios? Is the trend positive or negative? Why?

Step-by-step:
1. Locate the following current and prior years' information for Target (found on the "Consolidated Statements of Financial Position"):
   a. Current Assets
   b. Total Assets
   c. Current Liabilities
   d. Long-Term Liabilities (computed on the spreadsheet)
   e. Total Liabilities (computed on the spreadsheet)
   f. Total Shareholders' Investment (Owners' Equity)
   g. Total Liabilities and Shareholders' Investment
2. Open a new Excel spreadsheet.

EXCEL APPLICATION PROBLEM (CONT.)

Step-by-step *(cont.)*

3. Create a boldfaced heading for your spreadsheet that contains the following:
   a. Chapter 4 Decision Guideline
   b. The Current Ratio and the Debt ratio
   c. Target
   d. Today's date
4. Two rows down from your worksheet heading, create a column heading titled "TARGET (in millions)." Make it bold and underline the heading.
5. One row down from Target's column heading, create a row with the following bold, underlined column titles:
   a. Account
   b. FYxx (xx = the most recent fiscal year, for example, 00)
   c. FYyy (yy = the prior fiscal year, for example, 99)

6. Starting with the "Account" column heading, enter the data found in 1, above. You should have seven rows of data, with row descriptions (for example, "Current Assets"). Format the columns as necessary.
7. Skip a row at the end of your data, and then create a row titled "Current Ratio" and another row titled "Debt Ratio."
8. Enter the formula for each ratio in the "Fyxx" and "FYyy" columns. You should have four formulas. Make both rows bold.
9. Save your work to disk, and print a copy for your files.

REVIEW THE ACCOUNTING CYCLE

SUMMARY PROBLEM

Refer to the data in the Mid-Chapter Summary Problem (State Service Company, page 132–133).

www.prenhall.com/horngren

End-of-Chapter Assessment

Required

1. Journalize and post the adjusting entries. (Before posting to the accounts, enter into each account its balance as shown in the trial balance. For example, enter the $370,000 balance in the Accounts Receivable account before posting its adjusting entry.) Key adjusting entries by *letter*, as shown in the work sheet solution to the Mid-Chapter Summary Problem. You can take the adjusting entries straight from the work sheet on page 133.
2. Journalize and post the closing entries. (Each account should carry its balance as shown in the adjusted trial balance.) To distinguish closing entries from adjusting entries, key the closing entries by *number*. Draw arrows to illustrate the flow of data, as shown in Exhibit 4-9. Indicate the balance of the Capital account after the closing entries are posted.
3. Prepare the income statement for the year ended December 31, 20X1. List Miscellaneous Expense last among the expenses, a common practice.
4. Prepare the statement of owner's equity for the year ended December 31, 20X1. Draw an arrow linking the income statement to the statement of owner's equity.
5. Prepare the classified balance sheet at December 31, 20X1. Use the report form. All liabilities are current. Draw an arrow linking the statement of owner's equity to the balance sheet.

Solution

Requirement 1

Adjusting Entries

a. Dec. 31	Supplies Expense	4,000	
	Supplies		4,000
b. 31	Depreciation Expense—Furniture and Fixtures	20,000	
	Accumulated Depreciation—Furniture and Fixtures		20,000
c. 31	Depreciation Expense—Building	10,000	
	Accumulated Depreciation—Building		10,000
d. 31	Salary Expense	5,000	
	Salary Payable		5,000
e. 31	Accounts Receivable	12,000	
	Service Revenue		12,000
f. 31	Unearned Service Revenue	32,000	
	Service Revenue		32,000

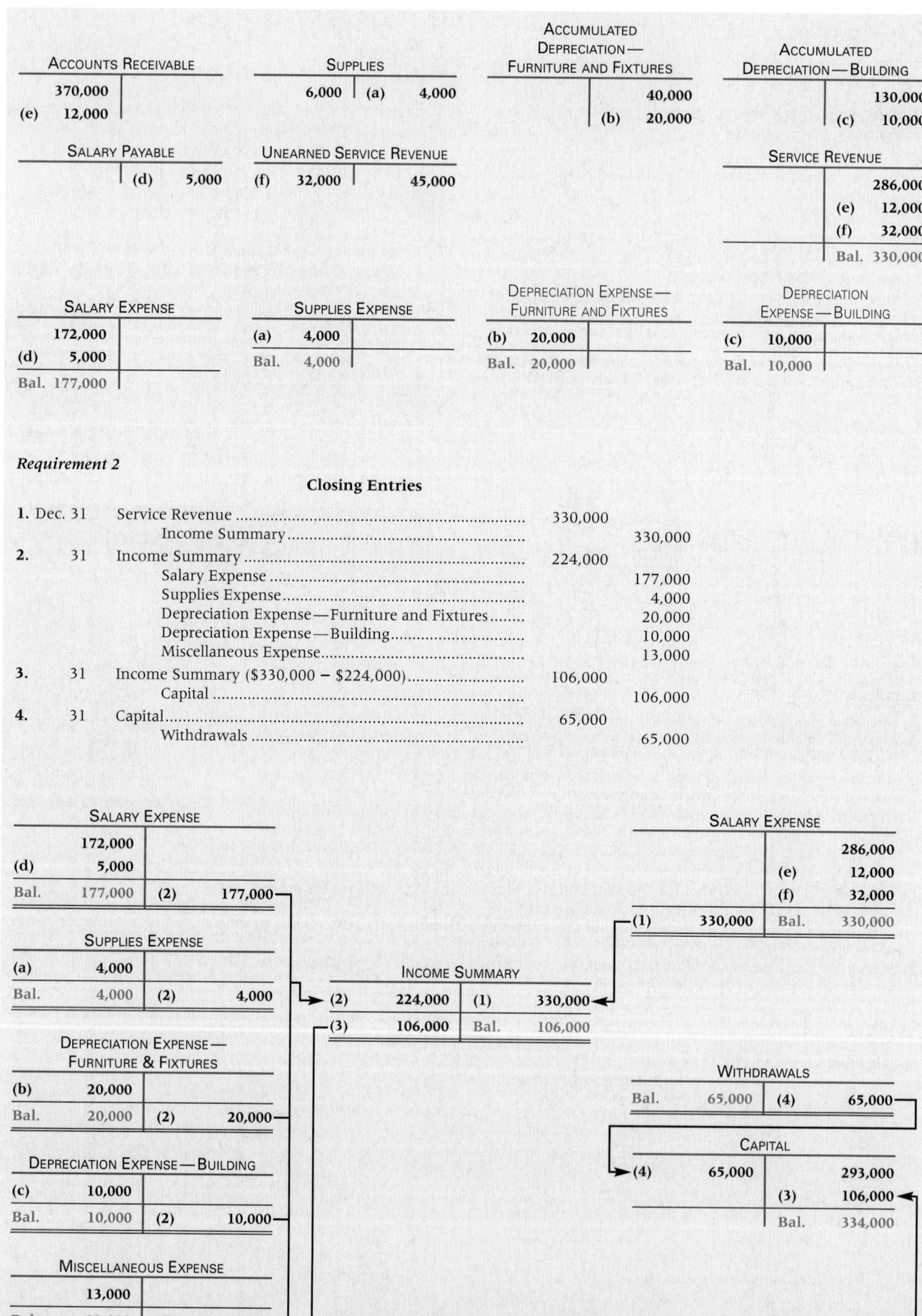

ACCOUNTS RECEIVABLE			SUPPLIES			ACCUMULATED DEPRECIATION— FURNITURE AND FIXTURES			ACCUMULATED DEPRECIATION—BUILDING	
370,000		6,000	(a) 4,000			40,000			130,000
(e) 12,000					(b) 20,000			(c) 10,000

SALARY PAYABLE		UNEARNED SERVICE REVENUE			SERVICE REVENUE	
	(d) 5,000	(f) 32,000	45,000			286,000
					(e) 12,000
					(f) 32,000
					Bal. 330,000

SALARY EXPENSE		SUPPLIES EXPENSE		DEPRECIATION EXPENSE— FURNITURE AND FIXTURES		DEPRECIATION EXPENSE—BUILDING	
172,000		(a) 4,000		(b) 20,000		(c) 10,000	
(d) 5,000		Bal. 4,000		Bal. 20,000		Bal. 10,000	
Bal. 177,000							

Requirement 2

Closing Entries

1. Dec. 31	Service Revenue	330,000	
	Income Summary...		330,000
2. 31	Income Summary	224,000	
	Salary Expense		177,000
	Supplies Expense...		4,000
	Depreciation Expense—Furniture and Fixtures........		20,000
	Depreciation Expense—Building............................		10,000
	Miscellaneous Expense..		13,000
3. 31	Income Summary ($330,000 − $224,000)..........................	106,000	
	Capital		106,000
4. 31	Capital..	65,000	
	Withdrawals		65,000

SALARY EXPENSE						SALARY EXPENSE			
172,000									286,000
(d) 5,000								(e)	12,000
Bal. 177,000	(2)	177,000						(f)	32,000
						(1) 330,000	Bal.	330,000

SUPPLIES EXPENSE			
(a) 4,000			
Bal. 4,000	(2)	4,000	

INCOME SUMMARY			
(2) 224,000	(1)	330,000
(3) 106,000	Bal.	106,000

DEPRECIATION EXPENSE— FURNITURE & FIXTURES			
(b) 20,000			
Bal. 20,000	(2)	20,000	

WITHDRAWALS			
Bal. 65,000	(4)	65,000	

DEPRECIATION EXPENSE—BUILDING			
(c) 10,000			
Bal. 10,000	(2)	10,000	

CAPITAL			
(4) 65,000		293,000
	(3)	106,000
	Bal.	334,000

MISCELLANEOUS EXPENSE			
13,000			
Bal. 13,000	(2)	13,000	

Requirement 3

STATE SERVICE COMPANY
Income Statement
Year Ended December 31, 20X1

Revenue:		
Service revenue		$330,000
Expenses:		
Salary expense	$177,000	
Depreciation expense—furniture and fixtures		20,000
Depreciation expense—building....................	10,000	
Supplies expense..	4,000	
Miscellaneous expense	13,000	
Total expenses...		224,000
Net income		$106,000

Requirement 4

STATE SERVICE COMPANY
Statement of Owner's Equity
Year Ended December 31, 20X1

Capital, January 1, 20X1	$293,000
Add: Net income	106,000
	399,000
Less: Withdrawals	(65,000)
Capital, December 31, 20X1	$334,000

Requirement 5

STATE SERVICE COMPANY
Balance Sheet
December 31, 20X1

Assets		
Current assets:		
Cash		$198,000
Accounts receivable.......................		382,000
Supplies		2,000
Total current assets		582,000
Long-term assets:		
Furniture and fixtures	$100,000	
Less: Accumulated depreciation.	(60,000)	40,000
Building	$250,000	
Less: Accumulated depreciation.	(140,000)	110,000
Total assets		$732,000
Liabilities		
Current liabilities:		
Accounts payable...........................		$380,000
Salary payable................................		5,000
Unearned service revenue.............		13,000
Total current liabilities		398,000
Owner's Equity		
Capital		334,000
Total liabilities and owner's equity....		$732,000

LESSONS LEARNED

1. **Prepare an accounting work sheet.** The *accounting cycle* is the process by which accountants produce the financial statements for a specific period of time. The cycle starts with the beginning account balances. During the period, the business journalizes transactions and posts them to the ledger accounts. At the end of the period, the trial balance is prepared, and the accounts are adjusted in order to measure the period's net income or net loss. A *work sheet* summarizes the effects of all the period's activity.

2. Use the work sheet to complete the accounting cycle. The work sheet is a convenient device for completing the accounting cycle. It has columns for the trial balance, the adjustments, the adjusted trial balance, the income statement, and the balance sheet. It aids the adjusting process, and it is the place where the period's net income or net loss is first computed. The work sheet also provides the data for the financial statements and the *closing entries*. However, the accounting cycle can also be completed from the less elaborate adjusted trial balance.

3. Close the revenue, expense, and withdrawal accounts. Revenues, expenses, and withdrawals represent increases and decreases in owner's equity for a specific period. At the end of the period, their balances are closed out to zero. For this reason, they are called *temporary accounts*. Assets, liabil-

ities, and capital are not closed because they are the *permanent accounts*. Their balances at the end of one period become the beginning balances of the next period. The final accuracy check of the period is the *postclosing trial balance*.

4. Classify assets and liabilities as current or long-term. The balance sheet reports *current* and *long-term assets* and *current* and *long-term liabilities*. It can be presented in *report format* or *account format*.

5. Use the current and debt ratios to evaluate a business's ability to pay its debts. Two decision-making aids are the *current ratio* (total current assets divided by total current liabilities) and the *debt ratio* (total liabilities divided by total assets).

ACCOUNTING VOCABULARY

accounting cycle (p. 127)	Income Summary (p. 136)	permanent account (p. 135)
closing the accounts (p. 134)	intangible assets (p. 141)	plant asset (p. 139)
closing entries (p. 135)	liquidity (p. 138)	postclosing trial balance (p. 138)
current asset (p. 138)	long-term asset (p. 139)	real account (p. 135)
current liability (p. 139)	long-term liability (p. 139)	reversing entry (p. 138)
current ratio (p. 141)	nominal account (p. 135)	temporary account (p. 135)
debt ratio (p. 142)	operating cycle (p. 139)	work sheet (p. 128)
fixed asset (p. 139)		

QUESTIONS

1. Identify the steps in the accounting cycle. Distinguish those that occur during the period from those that are performed at the end.
2. Why is the work sheet a valuable accounting tool?
3. Why must the adjusting entries be journalized and posted if they have already been entered on the work sheet?
4. Which types of accounts are closed?
5. What purpose is served by closing the accounts?
6. Distinguish between permanent accounts and temporary accounts; indicate which type is closed at the end of the period. Give five examples of each type of account.
7. Is Income Summary a permanent account or a temporary account? When and how is it used?
8. Give the closing entries for the following accounts (balances in parentheses): Service Revenue ($5,900); Salary Expense ($1,100); Income Summary (credit balance of $2,000); Asa Warner, Withdrawals ($2,300).
9. Why are assets classified as current or long-term? On what basis are they classified? Where do the classified amounts appear?

10. Indicate which of the following accounts are current assets and which are long-term assets: Prepaid Rent, Building, Furniture, Accounts Receivable, Merchandise Inventory, Cash, Note Receivable (due within one year), Note Receivable (due after one year).
11. In what order are assets and liabilities listed on the balance sheet?
12. Identify an outside party that would be interested in whether a liability is current or long-term. Why would this party be interested in this information?
13. A friend tells you that the difference between a current liability and a long-term liability is that the two types are payable to different types of creditors. Is your friend correct? Define these two categories of liabilities.
14. Show how to compute the current ratio and the debt ratio. Indicate what ability each ratio measures, and state whether a high value or a low value is safer for each.

ASSESS YOUR PROGRESS

DAILY EXERCISES

Explaining items on the work sheet
(Obj. 1)

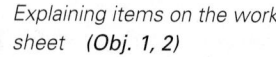

DE4-1 ← *Link Back to Chapter 3 (Adjusting Entries).* Return to the trial balance in Exhibit 4-2, on the acetate between pages 130 and 131. In your own words, explain why at April 30 the following accounts must be adjusted:

a. Supplies
b. Prepaid rent
c. Accumulated depreciation

d. Salary payable
e. Unearned service revenue

Explain why these accounts do *not* need to be adjusted at April 30:

f. Cash

g. Furniture

Explaining items on the work sheet (Obj. 1, 2)

DE4-2 ← *Link Back to Chapters 1, 2, and 3 (Definitions of Accounts).* Examine the Adjusted Trial Balance columns of Exhibit 4-4, on the acetate between pages 130 and 131. Explain what the following items mean at April 30:

a. Accounts receivable
b. Supplies
c. Prepaid rent
d. Furniture
e. Accumulated depreciation

f. Accounts payable
g. Unearned service revenue
h. Service revenue
i. Rent expense

DE4-3 Study the completed work sheet (Exhibit 4-6) on the acetates between pages 130 and 131. How is the work sheet in Exhibit 4-2 similar to the adjusted trial balance in Chapter 3? How does the work sheet differ from the adjusted trial balance of Chapter 3 (Exhibit 3-10, page 99)?

Comparing the work sheet and the adjusted trial balance (Obj. 1, 2) ▭▭▷

DE4-4 Consider the Income Statement columns and the Balance Sheet columns of the work sheet in Exhibit 4-6, on the acetates between pages 130 and 131. Answer the following questions:

Using the work sheet and closing entries (Obj. 2, 3)

1. What balance does the Owner's Capital account have—debit or credit?
2. Which Income Statement account has the same type of balance as the Capital account?
3. Which Income Statement accounts have the opposite type of balance?
4. What do we call the difference between the total dollar amounts in the debit and credit columns of the Income Statement? Into what account is the difference figure closed?

DE4-5 Examine Exhibits 4-2 and 4-4 on the acetates between pages 130 and 131. Answer this question about closing entries:

Identifying accounts that need to be closed (Obj. 3)

Exhibit 4-2, the (unadjusted) Trial Balance, lists all the accounts of the business entity Gay Gillen eTravel. Draw a horizontal line to separate the accounts that do *not* get closed out at the end of the period from those accounts that *do* get closed out. Identify the categories of accounts that *do* and do *not* get closed (assets, liabilities, and so on).

DE4-6 Study Exhibit 4-5 on the acetates between pages 130 and 131.

Making closing entries (Obj. 3)

1. Journalize the closing entries for
   a. Owner's withdrawals
   b. Service revenue
   c. All the expenses (make a single closing entry for all the expenses)
   d. Income Summary
2. Set up all the T-accounts affected by requirement 1 and insert their adjusted balances (denote as *Bal.*) at April 30. Also set up a T-account for Income Summary. Post the closing entries to the accounts, denoting posted amounts as *Clo.*
3. What is the ending balance of
   a. Gay Gillen, Capital?
   b. All the other accounts for which you set up T-accounts?

DE4-7 This exercise should be used in conjunction with Daily Exercise 4-6.

Analyzing the overall effect of the closing entries on the owner's capital account (Obj. 3)

1. Return to Exhibit 4-5 on the acetates between pages 130 and 131. Without making any closing entries or using any T-accounts, compute the ending balance of Gay Gillen, Capital.
2. Trace Gay Gillen's ending capital balance to its two appropriate places in Exhibit 4-7 (page 134). In which financial statements do you find Gay Gillen, Capital? Where on each statement?

DE4-8 **Oracle Corporation,** the world's second largest software company, reported the following items adapted from its financial statements at May 31, 1999 (amounts in millions):

Making closing entries (Obj. 3)

Cash	$1,786	Sales and marketing expense	$2,622
Service revenue	5,139	Other assets	477
Accounts payable	284	Interest expense	21
Accounts receivable	2,238	Long-term liabilities	382

Make Oracle's closing entries, as needed, for these accounts.

DE4-9 This exercise should be used in conjunction with Daily Exercise 4-8. Use the data in Daily Exercise 4-8 to set up T-accounts for those accounts that **Oracle Corporation** closed out at May 31, 1999. Insert these account balances prior to closing, post the closing entries to these accounts, and show each account's final balance after closing. Denote a balance as *Bal.* and a closing entry amount as *Clo.* For posting to the T-accounts, you may ignore the Income Summary account.

Posting closing entries (Obj. 3)

DE4-10 After closing its accounts at May 31, 1999, **Oracle Corporation** had the following account balances (adapted) with amounts given in millions:

Preparing a postclosing trial balance (Obj. 3)

Property......................................	$ 988	Long-term liabilities..................	$ 518
Cash...	1,786	Other assets...............................	825
Service revenue.........................	0	Accounts receivable	2,479
Owners' equity..........................	3,695	Total expenses	0
Other current assets	1,182	Accounts payable	284
Short-term notes payable........	4	Other current liabilities.............	2,759

Prepare Oracle's postclosing trial balance at May 31, 1999. List accounts in proper order, as shown in Exhibit 4-10, page 138.

Classifying assets and liabilities as current or long-term (Obj. 4)

DE4-11 **Lands' End** had sales of $1,320 million during the year ended January 31, 2000, and total assets of $456 million at January 31, 2000, the end of the company's fiscal year. The financial statements of Lands' End reported the following (amounts in millions):

Land and buildings..................	$ 103	Sales revenue	$1,320
Accounts payable	75	Inventory	162
Total expenses	1,073	Receivables................................	18
Accumulated depreciation.......	117	Interest expense	2
Accrued liabilities (such as		Equipment	176
Salary payable)	44	Prepaid expenses.......................	22

1. Identify the assets (including contra assets) and liabilities.
2. Classify each asset and each liability as current or long-term.

Classifying assets and liabilities as current or long-term (Obj. 4)

DE4-12 ↜ *Link Back to Chapter 3 (Book Value).* Examine **PepsiCo's** balance sheet in Exhibit 4-12 on page 140. Identify or compute the following amounts for PepsiCo at December 31, 1999.

    a. Total current assets   **d.** Total long-term assets
    b. Total current liabilities   **e.** Total long-term liabilities
    c. Book value of Property, Plant, and Equipment

Computing and using the current ratio and the debt ratio (Obj. 5)

DE4-13 This exercise should be used in conjunction with Daily Exercise 4-10. Use the postclosing trial balance that you prepared for Daily Exercise 4-10 to compute **Oracle Corporation's** current ratio and debt ratio.

1. How much in *current* assets does Oracle have for every dollar of *current* liabilities that it owes?
2. What percentage of Oracle's total assets are financed with debt?
3. What percentage of Oracle's total assets do the owners of the company actually own free and clear of debt?

Computing and evaluating the current ratio and the debt ratio (Obj. 5)

DE4-14 Use Gay Gillen eTravel's classified balance sheet in Exhibit 4-11, page 139, to compute the current ratio and the debt ratio of Gillen's business at April 30.

1. How do Gillen's ratios compare to those of **PepsiCo,** which are presented in the Work It Out feature on page 142 and the Think It Over feature on pages 142–143? Based solely on these ratios, which business looks stronger? Why?
2. Do these two ratios tell the complete story of a company's financial position? What other factors should a lender consider in evaluating a business's ability to pay its debts?

E X E R C I S E S

Preparing a work sheet (Obj. 1)

E4-1 The trial balance of Pfeiffer Pack-n-Mail Service follows at the top of the next page.

Additional information at September 30, 20X6:

    a. Accrued service revenue, $600.   **d.** Prepaid rent expired, $800.
    b. Depreciation, $40.   **e.** Supplies used, $1,650
    c. Accrued salary expense, $500.

Journalizing adjusting and closing entries (Obj. 2, 3)

Required

Complete Pfeiffer's work sheet for September 20X6. How much was net income for September?

E4-2 Journalize the adjusting and closing entries in Exercise 4-1.

Posting adjusting and closing entries (Obj. 2, 3)

E4-3 Set up T-accounts for those accounts affected by the adjusting and closing entries in Exercise 4-1. Post the adjusting and closing entries to the accounts; denote adjustment amounts by *Adj.,* closing amounts by *Clo.,* and balances by *Bal.* Double underline the accounts with zero balances after you close them, and show the ending balance in each account.

PFEIFFER PACK-N-MAIL SERVICE
Trial Balance
September 30, 20X6

Cash	$ 3,560	
Accounts receivable	3,440	
Prepaid rent	1,200	
Supplies	3,390	
Equipment	32,600	
Accumulated depreciation		$ 1,840
Accounts payable		3,600
Salary payable		
Gail Pfeiffer, capital		36,030
Gail Pfeiffer, withdrawals	2,000	
Service revenue		7,300
Depreciation expense		
Salary expense	1,800	
Rent expense		
Utilities expense	780	
Supplies expense		
Total	$48,770	$48,770

Preparing a postclosing trial balance (Obj. 2, 3)

E4-4 After completing Exercises 4-1, 4-2, and 4-3, prepare the postclosing trial balance in Exercise 4-1.

Adjusting and closing the accounts (Obj. 2, 3)

E4-5 ↞ *Link Back to Chapter 2 (Adjusting Entries).* TelSurf accounting records include the following account balances:

	December 31,	
	20X1	**20X2**
Prepaid insurance	$1,400	$1,600
Unearned service revenue	4,100	3,700

During 20X2, TelSurf recorded these transactions and adjusting entries:

a. Collected $17,000 cash in advance for service revenue to be earned later.
b. Made the year-end adjustment to record the earning of $17,400 service revenue that had been collected in advance.
c. Paid the annual insurance premium of $4,400.
d. Made the year-end adjustment to record insurance expense for the year. You must compute this amount.

Required

1. Set up T-accounts for Prepaid Insurance, Insurance Expense, Unearned Service Revenue, and Service Revenue. Insert beginning and ending balances for Prepaid Insurance and Unearned Service Revenue.
2. Journalize entries a–d above, and post to the T-accounts. Explanations are not required. Ensure that the ending balances for Prepaid Insurance and Unearned Service Revenue agree with the December 31, 20X2, balances given here for those accounts.
3. Make the closing entries for the above accounts, as needed. Post to the accounts to bring their balances to zero. You need not post to the Income Summary account.

Identifying and journalizing entries (Obj. 3)

E4-6 From the following selected accounts of Hyundai Energy at June 30, 20X4, prepare the entity's closing entries:

Liu Hyundai, capital	$ 21,600	Interest expense	$ 2,200
Service revenue	101,100	Accounts receivable	14,000
Unearned revenues	1,350	Salary payable	850
Salary expense	12,500	Depreciation expense	10,200
Accumulated depreciation	35,000	Rent expense	5,900
Supplies expense	1,700	Liu Hyundai, withdrawals	40,000
Interest revenue	700	Supplies	1,400

What is Hyundai's ending capital balance at June 30, 20X4?

E4-7 The accountant for MissouriOne.com has posted adjusting entries (a) through (e) to the following selected accounts at December 31, 20X8. All the revenue, expense, and owner's equity accounts—plus a few of the assets and liabilities—of the entity are listed here in T-account form.

ACCOUNTS RECEIVABLE		SUPPLIES		ACCUMULATED DEPRECIATION—FURNITURE		ACCUMULATED DEPRECIATION—BUILDING	
126,000		4,000	(b) 2,000		5,000		33,000
(a) 9,500					(c) 1,100		(d) 6,000

SALARY PAYABLE		FELIX ROHR, CAPITAL		FELIX ROHR, WITHDRAWALS		SERVICE REVENUE	
	(e) 700		52,400	61,400			211,000
							(a) 9,500

SALARY EXPENSE		SUPPLIES EXPENSE		DEPRECIATION EXPENSE—FURNITURE		DEPRECIATION EXPENSE—BUILDING	
26,000		(b) 2,000		(c) 1,100		(d) 6,000	
(e) 700							

Required

1. Journalize MissouriOne.com's closing entries at December 31, 20X8.
2. Determine Felix Rohr's ending capital balance at December 31, 20X8.

E4-8 From the following accounts of Lubricon Chemical Company, prepare the entity's statement of owner's equity for the year ended December 31, 20X2.

MATTHEW KNOWLES, CAPITAL		MATTHEW KNOWLES, WITHDRAWALS		INCOME SUMMARY	
Dec. 31 142,000	Jan. 1 436,000	Mar. 31 39,000	Dec. 31 142,000	Dec. 31 285,000	Dec. 31 428,000
	Mar. 9 28,000	Jun. 30 27,000		Dec. 31 143,000	
	Dec. 31 143,000	Sep. 30 39,000			
		Dec. 31 37,000			

E4-9 The trial balance and income statement amounts from the April work sheet of H.B. Fuller Polling Company follow:

Account Title	Unadjusted Trial Balance		Income Statement	
Cash	$ 5,200			
Supplies	2,400			
Prepaid rent	1,100			
Computer equipment	51,100			
Accumulated depreciation		$ 6,200		
Accounts payable		4,600		
Salary payable				
Unearned service revenue		4,400		
Long-term note payable		10,000		
H.B. Fuller, capital		25,800		
H.B. Fuller, withdrawals	1,000			
Service revenue		14,800		$19,100
Salary expense	3,000		$ 3,800	
Rent expense	1,200		1,400	
Depreciation expense			300	
Supplies expense			400	
Utilities expense	800		800	
	$65,800	$65,800	6,700	19,100
Net income or net loss			?	
			$19,100	$19,100

Required

1. Journalize the adjusting and closing entries of H.B. Fuller Polling Company at April 30.
2. How much net income or net loss did Fuller have for April? How can you tell?

E4-10 Refer to Exercise 4-9.

Preparing a classified balance sheet
(Obj. 4, 5)

Required

1. After solving Exercise 4-9, use the data in that exercise to prepare the classified balance sheet of H.B. Fuller Polling Company at April 30 of the current year. Use the report format.
2. Compute Fuller Polling's current ratio and debt ratio at April 30. One year ago, the current ratio was 1.20 and the debt ratio was 0.30. Indicate whether Fuller's ability to pay its debts has improved or deteriorated or hasn't changed much during the current year.

Continuing Exercise. *This exercise continues the Amos Faraday, Consultant, situation begun in Exercise 2-15 of Chapter 2 and continued in Exercise 3-14 of Chapter 3.*

E4-11 Refer to Exercise 3-14 of Chapter 3. Start from the posted T-accounts and the adjusted trial balance that Amos Faraday, Consultant, prepared for his business at December 31:

Closing the books, preparing a classified balance sheet, and evaluating a business
(Obj. 3, 4, 5)

AMOS FARADAY, CONSULTANT
Adjusted Trial Balance
December 31, 20XX

	Adjusted Trial Balance	
Account	**Debit**	**Credit**
Cash	$11,700	
Accounts receivable	1,500	
Supplies	100	
Equipment	2,000	
Accumulated depr.—equipment		$ 50
Furniture	3,600	
Accumulated depr.—furniture		60
Accounts payable		3,600
Salary payable		500
Unearned service revenue		600
Amos Faraday, capital		14,000
Amos Faraday, withdrawals	1,600	
Service revenue		3,200
Rent expense	500	
Utilities expense	200	
Salary expense	500	
Depreciation expense—equipment	50	
Depreciation expense—furniture	60	
Supplies expense	200	
Total	$22,010	$22,010

Required

1. Journalize and post the closing entries at December 31. Denote each closing amount as *Clo.* and an account balance as *Bal.*
2. Prepare a classified balance sheet at December 31.
3. If your instructor assigns it, complete the accounting work sheet at December 31.

Challenge Exercise

E4-12 Data for the unadjusted trial balance of Links Resorts at December 31, 20X2, follow:

Computing financial statement amounts
(Obj. 2, 4)

Cash	$ 3,000	Horst Schulz, capital	$49,100
Other current assets	9,400	Horst Schulz, withdrawals	51,800
Property, plant,		Service revenue	93,600
and equipment	66,200	Salary expense	42,700
Accumulated depreciation	21,800	Depreciation expense	
Accounts payable	6,100	Supplies expense	
Salary payable		Insurance expense	
Unearned service revenue	5,300	Utilities expense	2,800

Adjusting data at the end of the year include the following:

a. Unearned service revenue that has been earned, $3,600.

b. Accrued service revenue, $8,100

c. Supplies used in operations, $600.

d. Accrued salary expense, $1,400.

e. Insurance expense, $1,800.

f. Depreciation expense, $2,900.

Horst Schulz, the owner, has received an offer to sell the company. He needs to know the following information within one hour: Net income for the year covered by these data.

Required

Without opening any accounts, making any journal entries, or using a work sheet, provide Schulz with the requested information. Prepare an income statement, and show all computations.

(Group A) PROBLEMS

Preparing a work sheet (Obj. 1)

P4-1A The trial balance of Cohen Construction Co. at June 30, 20X3, follows.

COHEN CONSTRUCTION CO.
Trial Balance
June 30, 20X3

Cash	$ 21,200	
Accounts receivable	37,820	
Supplies	17,660	
Prepaid insurance	2,300	
Equipment	32,690	
Accumulated depreciation—equipment		$ 26,240
Building	42,890	
Accumulated depreciation—building		10,500
Land	28,300	
Accounts payable		22,690
Interest payable		
Wages payable		
Unearned service revenue		10,560
Note payable, long-term		22,400
Lynn Cohen, capital		79,130
Lynn Cohen, withdrawals	4,200	
Service revenue		20,190
Depreciation expense—equipment		
Depreciation expense—building		
Wage expense	3,200	
Insurance expense		
Interest expense		
Utilities expense	1,110	
Advertising expense	340	
Supplies expense		
Total	$191,710	$191,710

Additional data at June 30, 20X3:

a. Depreciation: equipment, $630; building, $370.

b. Accrued wage expense, $240.

c. Supplies on hand, $14,370

d. Prepaid insurance expired during June, $500.

e. Accrued interest expense, $180.

f. Unearned service revenue earned during June, $4,970.

g. Accrued advertising expense, $100 (credit Accounts Payable).

h. Accrued service revenue, $1,100.

Required

Complete Cohen Construction's work sheet for June. Key adjusting entries by letter.

P4-2A The *adjusted* trial balance of Gallo Shipping & Handling at June 30, 20X9, after all adjustments, follows.

Preparing financial statements
from an adjusted trial balance;
journalizing the adjusting and
closing entries
(Obj. 2, 3, 5)

GALLO SHIPPING & HANDLING
Adjusted Trial Balance
June 30, 20X9

Cash	$ 12,350	
Accounts receivable	26,470	
Supplies	31,290	
Prepaid insurance	3,200	
Equipment	135,800	
Accumulated depreciation—equipment		$ 16,480
Building	34,900	
Accumulated depreciation—building		16,850
Land	30,000	
Accounts payable		38,400
Interest payable		1,490
Wages payable		770
Unearned service revenue		2,300
Note payable, long-term		97,000
Linda Gallo, capital		58,390
Linda Gallo, withdrawals	45,300	
Service revenue		139,860
Depreciation expense—equipment	7,300	
Depreciation expense—building	3,970	
Wage expense	21,470	
Insurance expense	3,100	
Interest expense	8,510	
Utilities expense	4,300	
Supplies expense	3,580	
Total	$371,540	$371,540

Adjusting data at June 30, 20X9, which have all been incorporated into the *adjusted* trial balance figures:

a. Prepaid insurance expired during the year, $2,200.
b. Accrued interest expense, $540.
c. Accrued service revenue, $940.
d. Unearned service revenue earned during the year, $7,790.
e. Accrued wage expense, $770.
f. Depreciation for the year: equipment, $7,300; building, $3,970.
g. Supplies used during the year, $3,580.

Required

1. Journalize the adjusting entries that would lead to the adjusted trial balance shown here. Also journalize the closing entries.
2. Prepare Gallo's income statement and statement of owner's equity for the year ended June 30, 20X9, and the classified balance sheet on that date. Use the account format for the balance sheet.
3. Compute Gallo's current ratio and debt ratio at June 30, 20X9. One year ago, the current ratio stood at 1.41 and the debt ratio was 0.71. Did Gallo's ability to pay debts improve or deteriorate during fiscal year 20X9?

P4-3A The unadjusted T-accounts of Fidelity Sound Studio, at December 31, 20X2, and the related year-end adjustment data follow at the top of the next page.

Taking the accounting cycle
through the closing entries
(Obj. 2, 3)

Adjustment data at December 31, 20X2:

a. Unearned service revenue earned during the year, $5,000.
b. Supplies on hand, $1,000.
c. Depreciation for the year, $9,000.
d. Accrued salary expense, $1,000.
e. Accrued service revenue, $2,000.

Required

1. Enter the trial balance on a work sheet, and complete the work sheet. Key each adjusting entry by the letter corresponding to the data given. List all the accounts, including those with zero balances. Leave a blank line under Service Revenue.
2. Prepare the income statement, the statement of owner's equity, and the classified balance sheet in account format.
3. Journalize the adjusting and closing entries.
4. Did Fidelity Sound Studio have a good or a bad year during 20X2? Give the reason for your answer.

CASH		ACCOUNTS RECEIVABLE		SUPPLIES		EQUIPMENT	
Bal. 15,000		Bal. 36,000		Bal. 9,000		Bal. 99,000	

ACCUMULATED DEPRECIATION		ACCOUNTS PAYABLE		SALARY PAYABLE		UNEARNED SERVICE REVENUE	
	Bal. 13,000		Bal. 6,000				Bal. 5,000

NOTE PAYABLE, LONG-TERM				BETSY WILLIS, CAPITAL		BETSY WILLIS, WITHDRAWALS	
	Bal. 60,000				Bal. 36,000	Bal. 62,000	

SERVICE REVENUE				SALARY EXPENSE		SUPPLIES EXPENSE	
	Bal. 182,000			Bal. 53,000			

DEPRECIATION EXPENSE		INTEREST EXPENSE		RENT EXPENSE		INSURANCE EXPENSE	
		Bal. 6,000		Bal. 15,000		Bal. 7,000	

Completing the accounting cycle (Obj. 2, 3)

P4-4A This problem should be used in conjunction with Problem 4-3A. It completes the accounting cycle by posting to T-accounts and preparing the postclosing trial balance.

Required

1. Using the Problem 4-3A data, post the adjusting and closing entries to the T-accounts, denoting adjusting amounts by *Adj.,* closing amounts by *Clo.,* and account balances by *Bal.,* as shown in Exhibit 4-9. You must set up a T-account for Income Summary. Double underline all accounts with a zero ending balance.
2. Prepare the postclosing trial balance.

Completing the accounting cycle (Obj. 2, 3, 4)

P4-5A The trial balance of Allianz Publishing at August 31, 20X9, and the data needed for the month-end adjustments follow:

ALLIANZ PUBLISHING
Trial Balance
August 31, 20X9

Account Number	Account Title	Debit	Credit
11	Cash	$ 23,800	
12	Accounts receivable	15,560	
13	Prepaid rent	1,290	
14	Supplies	900	
15	Equipment	15,350	
16	Accumulated depreciation—equipment		$ 12,800
17	Building	89,900	
18	Accumulated depreciation—building		28,600
21	Accounts payable		4,240
22	Salary payable		
23	Unearned service revenue		8,900
31	Lou Kraft, capital		71,920
32	Lou Kraft, withdrawals	4,800	
41	Service revenue		27,300
51	Salary expense	1,100	
52	Rent expense		
53	Utilities expense	410	
54	Depreciation expense—equipment		
55	Depreciation expense—building		
56	Advertising expense	650	
57	Supplies expense		
	Total	$153,760	$153,760

Adjustment data:

a. Unearned commission revenue still unearned at August 31, $6,500.
b. Prepaid rent still in force at August 31, $1,050.
c. Supplies used during the month, $340.
d. Depreciation on equipment for the month, $370.
e. Depreciation on building for the month, $130.
f. Accrued salary expense at August 31, $460.

Required

1. Open the accounts listed in the trial balance and insert their August 31 unadjusted balances. Also open the Income Summary account, number 33. Use four-column accounts. Date the balances of the following accounts as of August 1: Prepaid Rent, Supplies, Equipment, Accumulated Depreciation—Equipment, Building, Accumulated Depreciation—Building, Unearned Service Revenue, and Lou Kraft, Capital.
2. Enter the trial balance on a work sheet and complete the work sheet of Allianz Publishing for the month ended August 31, 20X9. See the trial balance on page 156.
3. Prepare the income statement, the statement of owner's equity, and the classified balance sheet in report format.
4. Using the work sheet data that you prepare, journalize and post the adjusting and closing entries. Use dates and posting references. Use 7 as the number of the journal page.
5. Prepare a postclosing trial balance.

P4-6A The accounts of Martinez Political Consulting at December 31, 20X6, follow:

Preparing a classified balance sheet in report format (Obj. 4, 5)

Accounts payable	$ 5,100	Angel Martinez, capital,	
Accounts receivable	6,600	December 31, 20X5	$59,800
Accumulated depreciation—		Angel Martinez, withdrawals	50,400
building	37,800	Note payable, long-term	27,800
Accumulated depreciation—		Other assets	3,600
computers	11,600	Other current liabilities	4,700
Advertising expense	2,200	Prepaid insurance	1,100
Building	104,400	Prepaid rent	6,600
Cash	16,500	Salary expense	24,600
Service revenue	93,500	Salary payable	3,900
Computers	22,700	Supplies	2,500
Depreciation expense	1,300	Supplies expense	5,700
Insurance expense	800	Unearned service	
Interest payable	600	revenue	5,400
Interest expense	1,200		

Required

1. All adjustments have been journalized and posted, but the closing entries have not yet been made. Prepare the company's classified balance sheet in report format at December 31, 20X6. Show totals for total assets, total liabilities, and total liabilities and owner's equity.
2. Compute Martinez's current ratio and debt ratio at December 31, 20X6. At December 31, 20X5, the current ratio was 1.52 and the debt ratio was 0.39. Did Martinez's ability to pay debts improve or deteriorate during 20X6?

P4-7A ◄ *Link Back to Chapter 2 (Accounting Errors).* The accountant for Liberty Landscaping encountered the following situations while adjusting and closing the books at December 31. Consider each situation independently.

Analyzing errors and journalizing adjusting and closing entries (Obj. 3)

a. A $500 credit to Accounts Receivable was posted as a debit.
   (1) At what stage of the accounting cycle will this error be detected?
   (2) Describe the technique for identifying the amount of the error.

b. The $16,000 balance of Equipment was entered as $1,600 on the trial balance.
   (1) What is the name of this type of error?
   (2) Assume that this is the only error in the trial balance. Which will be greater, the total debits or the total credits, and by how much?
   (3) How can this type of error be identified?

c. The accountant failed to make the following adjusting entries at December 31:
   (1) Accrued property tax expense, $200.
   (2) Supplies expense, $1,090.
   (3) Accrued interest revenue on a $50,000 note receivable, $1,650.
   (4) Depreciation of equipment, $400.
   (5) Earned service revenue that had been collected in advance, $1,100.
   Compute the overall net income effect of these omissions.

d. Record each of the adjusting entries identified in item c.

PROBLEMS

(Group B)

P4-1B The trial balance of Reneé Greenspan Productions at May 31, 20X2, follows at the top of the next page.

Preparing a work sheet (Obj. 1)

RENEÉ GREENSPAN PRODUCTIONS
Trial Balance
May 31, 20X2

Cash	$ 4,370	
Notes receivable	10,340	
Interest receivable		
Supplies	560	
Prepaid insurance	1,790	
Furniture	27,410	
Accumulated depreciation—furniture		$ 1,480
Building	53,900	
Accumulated depreciation—building		34,560
Land	18,700	
Accounts payable		14,730
Interest payable		
Salary payable		
Unearned service revenue		8,800
Note payable, long-term		18,700
Reneé Greenspan, capital		29,990
Reneé Greenspan, withdrawals	3,800	
Service revenue		16,970
Interest revenue		
Depreciation expense—furniture		
Depreciation expense—building		
Salary expense	2,170	
Insurance expense		
Interest expense		
Utilities expense	1,130	
Advertising expense	1,060	
Supplies expense		
Total	$125,230	$125,230

Additional data at May 31, 20X2:

a. Depreciation: furniture, $480; building, $460.
b. Accrued salary expense, $420.
c. Supplies on hand, $410.
d. Prepaid insurance expired during May, $390.
e. Accrued interest expense, $220.

f. Unearned service revenue earned during May, $4,400.
g. Accrued advertising expense, $60 (credit Accounts Payable).
h. Accrued interest revenue, $170.

Required

Complete Greenspan's work sheet for May. Key adjusting entries by letter.

Preparing financial statements from an adjusted trial balance; journalizing the adjusting and closing entries
(Obj. 2, 3, 5)

P4-2B The *adjusted* trial balance of Chase Webmaster Service at April 30, 20X2, after all adjustments, follows at the top of the next page. Adjusting data at April 30, 20X2, which have all been incorporated into the *adjusted* trial balance figures above, consist of

a. Accrued service revenue, $2,200.
b. Depreciation for the year: equipment, $6,900; building, $3,710.
c. Accrued wage expense, $830.
d. Unearned service revenue earned during the year, $4,180.

e. Supplies used during the year, $5,880.
f. Prepaid insurance expired during the year, $5,110.
g. Accrued interest expense, $1,280.

Required

1. Journalize the adjusting entries that would lead to the adjusted trial balance shown here. Also journalize the closing entries.
2. Prepare Chase's income statement and statement of owner's equity for the year ended April 30, 20X2, and the classified balance sheet on that date. Use the account format for the balance sheet.
3. Compute Chase's current ratio and debt ratio at April 30, 20X2. One year ago, the current ratio stood at 1.61 and the debt ratio was 0.72. Did Chase's ability to pay debts improve or deteriorate during fiscal year 20X2?

CHASE WEBMASTER SERVICE
Adjusted Trial Balance
April 30, 20X2

Cash	$ 14,570	
Accounts receivable	43,740	
Supplies	3,690	
Prepaid insurance	2,290	
Equipment	63,930	
Accumulated depreciation—equipment		$ 28,430
Building	74,330	
Accumulated depreciation—building		18,260
Land	20,000	
Accounts payable		19,550
Interest payable		2,280
Wages payable		830
Unearned service revenue		3,660
Note payable, long-term		69,900
Monica Chase, capital		77,140
Monica Chase, withdrawals	27,500	
Service revenue		98,550
Depreciation expense—equipment	6,900	
Depreciation expense—building	3,710	
Wage expense	32,810	
Insurance expense	5,110	
Interest expense	8,170	
Utilities expense	4,970	
Supplies expense	6,880	
Total	$318,600	$318,600

Taking the accounting cycle through the closing entries (Obj. 2, 3)

P4-3B The unadjusted T-accounts of Lisa Tenney, M.D., at December 31, 20X2, and the related year-end adjustment data follow.

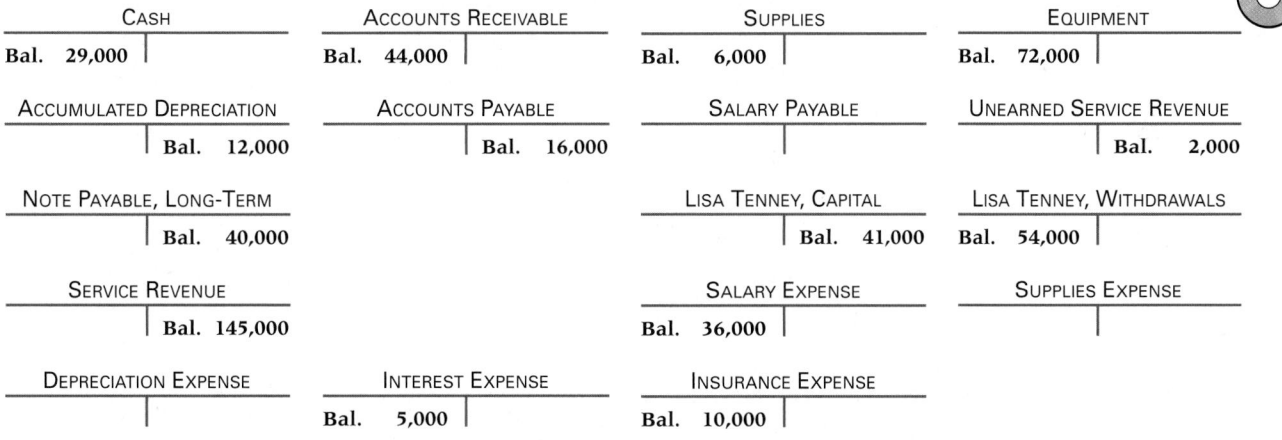

CASH	ACCOUNTS RECEIVABLE	SUPPLIES	EQUIPMENT
Bal. 29,000	Bal. 44,000	Bal. 6,000	Bal. 72,000

ACCUMULATED DEPRECIATION	ACCOUNTS PAYABLE	SALARY PAYABLE	UNEARNED SERVICE REVENUE
Bal. 12,000	Bal. 16,000		Bal. 2,000

NOTE PAYABLE, LONG-TERM		LISA TENNEY, CAPITAL	LISA TENNEY, WITHDRAWALS
Bal. 40,000		Bal. 41,000	Bal. 54,000

SERVICE REVENUE		SALARY EXPENSE	SUPPLIES EXPENSE
Bal. 145,000		Bal. 36,000	

DEPRECIATION EXPENSE	INTEREST EXPENSE	INSURANCE EXPENSE
	Bal. 5,000	Bal. 10,000

Adjustment data at December 31, 20X2:

a. Depreciation for the year, $5,000.
b. Supplies on hand, $2,000.
c. Accrued service revenue, $4,000.
d. Unearned service revenue earned during the year, $2,000.
e. Accrued salary expense, $4,000.

Required

1. Enter the trial balance on a work sheet, and complete the work sheet. Key each adjusting entry by the letter corresponding to the data given. List all the accounts, including those with zero balances. Leave a blank line under Service Revenue.
2. Prepare the income statement, the statement of owner's equity, and the classified balance sheet in account format.
3. Journalize the adjusting and closing entries.
4. Did Tenney have a good or a bad year during 20X2? Give the reason for your answer.

Completing the accounting cycle (Obj. 2, 3)

P4-4B This problem should be used in conjunction with Problem 4-3B. It completes the accounting cycle by posting to T-accounts and preparing the postclosing trial balance.

1. Using the Problem 4-3B data, post the adjusting and closing entries to the T-accounts, denoting adjusting amounts by *Adj.*, closing amounts by *Clo.*, and account balances by *Bal.*, as shown in Exhibit 4-9. You must set up a T-account for Income Summary. Double underline all accounts with a zero ending balance.
2. Prepare the postclosing trial balance.

Completing the accounting cycle (Obj. 2, 3, 4)

P4-5B The trial balance of Uniworld Language Services at October 31, 20X0, follows. The data needed for the month-end adjustments also follow.

UNIWORLD LANGUAGE SERVICES			
Trial Balance			
October 31, 20X0			
Account Number	Account Title	Debit	Credit
11	Cash	$ 4,900	
12	Accounts receivable	15,310	
13	Prepaid rent	2,200	
14	Supplies	840	
15	Equipment	26,830	
16	Accumulated depreciation—equipment..		$ 3,400
17	Building	68,300	
18	Accumulated depreciation—building		12,100
21	Accounts payable		7,290
22	Salary payable		
23	Unearned service revenue		5,300
31	Chris Stott, capital		84,490
32	Chris Stott, withdrawals	3,900	
41	Service revenue		12,560
51	Salary expense	1,840	
52	Rent expense		
53	Utilities expense	1,020	
54	Depreciation expense—equipment		
55	Depreciation expense—building		
56	Supplies expense		
	Total	$125,140	$125,140

Adjusting data:

a. Unearned service revenue still unearned at October 31, $800.
b. Prepaid rent still in force at October 31, $2,000.
c. Supplies used during the month, $770.
d. Depreciation on equipment for the month, $250.
e. Depreciation on building for the month, $580.
f. Accrued salary expense at October 31, $310.

Required

1. Open the accounts listed in the trial balance, inserting their October 31 unadjusted balances. Also open the Income Summary account, number 33. Use four-column accounts. Date the balances of the following accounts October 1: Prepaid Rent, Supplies, Equipment, Accumulated Depreciation—Equipment, Building, Accumulated Depreciation—Building, Unearned Service Revenue, and Chris Stott, Capital.
2. Enter the trial balance on a work sheet and complete the work sheet of Uniworld Language Services for the month ended October 31, 20X0.
3. Prepare the income statement, the statement of owner's equity, and the classified balance sheet in report format.
4. Using the work sheet data that you prepare, journalize and post the adjusting and closing entries. Use dates and posting references. Use 12 as the number of the journal page.
5. Prepare a postclosing trial balance.

Preparing a classified balance sheet in report format (Obj. 4, 5)

P4-6B The accounts of Justin Leonard, Architect, at December 31, 20X3, are listed on the following page:

Required

1. All adjustments have been journalized and posted, but the closing entries have not yet been made. Prepare the company's classified balance sheet in report format at December 31, 20X3. Show totals for total assets, total liabilities, and total liabilities and owner's equity.

Accounts payable.....................	$34,700	Insurance expense....................	$ 600
Accounts receivable................	41,500	Interest payable	300
Accumulated depreciation—		Interest receivable	900
building.................................	47,300	Note payable, long-term............	3,200
Accumulated depreciation—		Note receivable, long-term........	6,900
equipment............................	7,700	Other assets	2,300
Advertising expense	900	Other current liabilities	1,100
Building...................................	55,900	Prepaid insurance.....................	600
Cash..	3,400	Prepaid rent..............................	4,700
Depreciation expense	1,900	Salary expense..........................	17,800
Justin Leonard, capital,		Salary payable	2,400
December 31, 20X2..............	50,700	Service revenue........................	71,100
Justin Leonard,		Supplies	3,800
withdrawals	31,200	Supplies expense	4,600
Equipment...............................	43,200	Unearned service revenue........	1,700

2. Compute Leonard's current ratio and debt ratio at December 31, 20X3. At December 31, 20X2, the current ratio was 1.28 and debt ratio was 0.42. Did Leonard's ability to pay debts improve, deteriorate, or change very little during 20X3?

P4-7B ← *Link Back to Chapter 2 (Accounting Errors).* The accountant of Iowa Packing Company encountered the following situations while adjusting and closing the books at February 28. Consider each situation independently.

Analyzing errors and journalizing adjusting and closing entries (Obj. 3)

a. A $1,400 debit to Supplies was posted as $4,100.
   (1) At what stage of the accounting cycle will this error be detected?
   (2) What is the name of this type of error? Explain how to identify the error.

b. The $1,300 balance of Computer Software was entered as $13,000 on the trial balance.
   (1) What is the name of this type of error?
   (2) Assume that this is the only error in the trial balance. Which will be greater, the total debits or the total credits, and by how much?
   (3) How can this type of error be identified?
c. The accountant failed to make the following adjusting entries at February 28:
   (1) Depreciation of equipment, $700.
   (2) Earned service revenue that had been collected in advance, $2,700.
   (3) Accrued service revenue, $1,400.
   (4) Insurance expense, $360.
   (5) Accrued interest expense on a note payable, $520.
   Compute the overall net income effect of these omissions.
d. Record each of the adjusting entries identified in item c.

APPLY YOUR KNOWLEDGE

DECISION CASES

Case 1. One year ago, Alex Fleming founded Jack-of-All-Trades Job Search, and the business has prospered. Fleming comes to you for advice. He wishes to know how much net income his business earned during the past year. He also wants to know what the entity's total assets, liabilities, and capital are. The accounting records consist of the T-accounts in the ledger, which were prepared by an accountant who has moved. The ledger at December 31 appears at the top of the next page.

Completing the accounting cycle to develop the information for a bank loan (Obj. 3, 4)

Fleming indicates that at year end customers owe him $1,600 accrued service revenue, which he expects to collect early next year. These revenues have not been recorded. During the year, he collected $4,130 service revenue in advance from customers, but the business has earned only $2,500 of that amount. Rent expense for the year was $2,400, and he used up $2,100 of the supplies. Fleming estimates that depreciation on equipment was $5,900 for the year. At December 31, he owes his employee $1,200 accrued salary.

Fleming expresses concern that his withdrawals during the year might have exceeded the business's net income. To get a loan to expand the business, Fleming must show the bank that his capital account has grown from its original $25,000 balance. Has it? You and Fleming agree that you will meet again in one week.

Required

Prepare the work sheet and the financial statements to answer Fleming's questions.

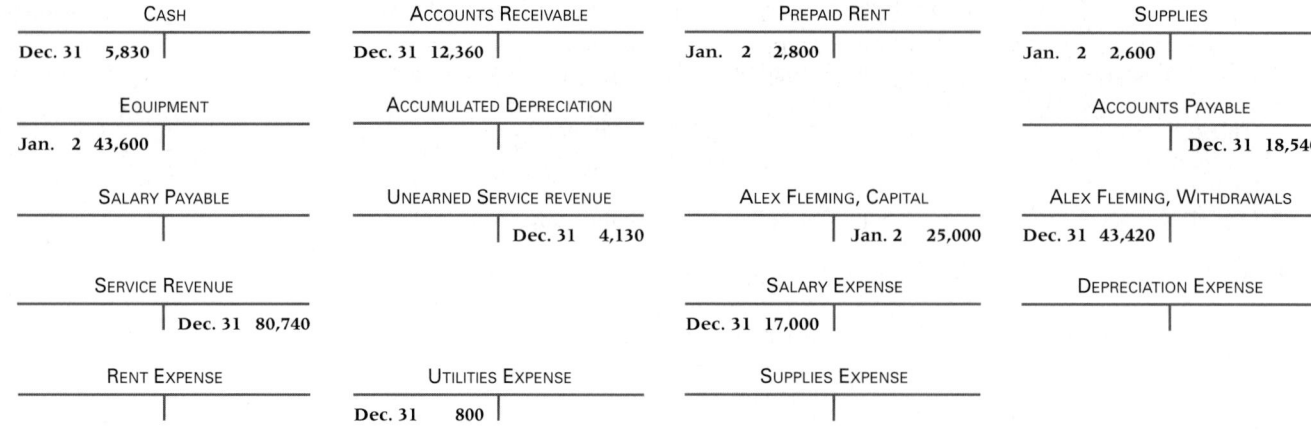

CASH	ACCOUNTS RECEIVABLE	PREPAID RENT	SUPPLIES
Dec. 31 5,830	Dec. 31 12,360	Jan. 2 2,800	Jan. 2 2,600

EQUIPMENT	ACCUMULATED DEPRECIATION		ACCOUNTS PAYABLE
Jan. 2 43,600			Dec. 31 18,540

SALARY PAYABLE	UNEARNED SERVICE REVENUE	ALEX FLEMING, CAPITAL	ALEX FLEMING, WITHDRAWALS
	Dec. 31 4,130	Jan. 2 25,000	Dec. 31 43,420

SERVICE REVENUE		SALARY EXPENSE	DEPRECIATION EXPENSE
Dec. 31 80,740		Dec. 31 17,000	

RENT EXPENSE	UTILITIES EXPENSE	SUPPLIES EXPENSE	
	Dec. 31 800		

Finding an error in the work sheet
(Obj. 1)

Case 2. You are preparing the financial statements for the year ended October 31, 20X5, for Zadell Software Company.

- You began with the trial balance of the ledger, which balanced, and then made the required adjusting entries.
- To save time, you omitted preparing an adjusted trial balance.
- After making the adjustments on the work sheet, you extended the balances from the trial balance, adjusted for the adjusting entries, and computed amounts for the income statement and the balance sheet columns.

Required

a. When you added the total debits and the total credits on the income statement, you found that the credits exceeded the debits by $45,000. Did the business have a profit or a loss?
b. You took the balancing amount from the income statement columns to the debit column of the balance sheet and found that the total debits exceeded the total credits in the balance sheet. The difference between the total debits and the total credits on the balance sheet is $90,000. What is the cause of this difference? (Except for these errors, everything else is correct.)

ETHICAL ISSUE

↞ *Link Back to Chapter 3 (Revenue Principle).* Forbes Painting Company wishes to expand and has borrowed $2 million. As a condition for making this loan, the bank requires that Forbes maintain a current ratio of at least 1.50.

Business has been good but not great. Expansion costs have brought the current ratio down to 1.40 at December 15. Jacob Forbes, owner of the company, is considering what might happen if the business reports a current ratio of 1.40 to the bank. One course of action for Forbes is to record in December some revenue that the business will earn in January of next year. The contract for this job has been signed.

Required

1. Journalize the revenue transaction, and indicate how recording this revenue in December would affect the current ratio.
2. State whether it is ethical to record the revenue transaction in December. Identify the accounting principle relevant to this situation.
3. Propose a course of action that is ethical for Forbes.

FINANCIAL STATEMENT CASE

Using a balance sheet
(Obj. 4, 5)

This problem, based on the balance sheet of **Target Corporation** in Appendix A, will familiarize you with some of the assets and liabilities of that company. Use the Target balance sheet to answer the following questions.

Required

1. Which balance sheet format does Target Corporation use?
2. Name the company's largest current asset and largest current liability at January 29, 2000.
3. Compute Target's current ratios and debt ratios at January 30, 1999, and at January 29, 2000. Target treats Convertible Preferred Stock as a liability. Did the ratio values improve, worsen, or hold steady during the fiscal year ended January 29, 2000? Refer to the income statement to explain your evaluation of the ratio values.
4. Under what category does Target report land, buildings, fixtures, and equipment?
5. What was the cost of the company's plant assets at January 29, 2000? What was the amount of accumulated depreciation? What was the book value of the plant assets?

TEAM PROJECT

Doug Maltbee formed a lawn service business as a summer job. To start the business on May 1, he deposited $1,000 in a new bank account in the name of the proprietorship. The $1,000 consisted of a $600 loan from his father and $400 of his own money. Doug rented lawn equipment, purchased supplies, and hired fellow students to mow and trim his customer's lawns.

At the end of each month, Doug mailed bills to his customers. On August 31, he was ready to dissolve the business and return to Louisiana State University for the fall semester. Because he was so busy, he kept few records other than his checkbook and a list of amounts owed to him by customers.

At August 31, Doug's checkbook shows a balance of $690, and his customers still owe him $500. During the summer, he collected $4,250 from customers. His checkbook lists payments for supplies totaling $400, and he still has gasoline, weedeater cord, and other supplies that cost a total of $50. He paid his employees $1,900, and he still owes them $200 for the final week of the summer.

Doug rented some equipment from Scholes Machine Shop. On May 1, he signed a six-month lease on mowers and paid $600 for the full lease period. Scholes will refund the unused portion of the prepayment if the equipment is in good shape. In order to get the refund, Doug has kept the mowers in excellent condition. In fact, he had to pay $300 to repair a mower.

To transport employees and equipment to jobs, Doug used a trailer that he bought for $300. He figures that the summer's work used up one-third of the trailer's service potential. The business checkbook lists a payment of $460 for cash withdrawals by Doug during the summer. Doug paid his father back during August.

Required

1. Prepare the income statement of Maltbee Lawn Service for the four months May through August.
2. Prepare the classified balance sheet of Maltbee Lawn Service at August 31.
3. Was Maltbee's summer work successful? Give the reason for your answer.

INTERNET EXERCISE

Southwest Airlines Company started in 1971 with three planes and now has more than 300 planes that fly into 55 different cities. In years when many other airlines reported net losses, Southwest Airlines' low-cost, no-frills flights resulted in profits.

Southwest Airlines

1. Go to **http://www.Southwest.com,** click on *About SWA,* and read "A Brief History of Southwest Airlines." Who is the CEO of Southwest Airlines? Why can Southwest Airlines offer lower fares than other airlines?
2. In the left-hand column click on *History* and read the information provided. What is the Triple Crown? How often has Southwest Airlines won this award? Comment on one other item that you found of interest.
3. Go to **http://www.Forbes.com** to get the latest financial information. In the "Stock" section type <u>LUV</u>, the stock symbol of Southwest Airlines Co., and then click on *Go.* In the left-hand column, click on "Company Info" and read the information provided. Comment on one item that makes Southwest Airlines different from other airlines.
4. In the left-hand column, click on "Financials." Menu selections are presented in the left-hand column.
   a. For the most recent year, list the amount reported for "Passenger revenue." Is this account closed at the end of the accounting period?
   b. For the two most recent years, list the amounts reported for "Cash/Equivalents," "Total current assets," "Total assets," "Total current liabilities," and "Total liabilities."
   c. Is the balance sheet presented in a classified format? How can you tell?
   d. Is Cash/Equivalents closed at the end of the accounting period? Why or why not?
   e. For the two most recent years, calculate Southwest's current ratio and debt ratio. Do these values look strong or weak?

APPENDIX TO CHAPTER 4

REVERSING ENTRIES: AN OPTIONAL STEP

Reversing entries are special types of entries that ease the burden of accounting for transactions that key off the adjustments at the end of the period. Reversing entries are used most often in conjunction with accrual-type adjustments such as accrued salary expense and accrued service revenue. *Generally accepted accounting principles do not require reversing entries. They are used only for convenience and to save time.*

Accounting for Accrued Expenses

To see how reversing entries work, return to Gay Gillen's unadjusted trial balance at April 30 (Exhibit 4-2, page 130). Salary Expense has a debit balance of $950 for salaries paid during April. At April 30, the business still owes its employee an additional $950 for the last half of the month, so Gillen makes this adjusting entry:

Adjusting Entries

Apr. 30	Salary Expense	950	
	Salary Payable		950

After posting, the accounts are updated at April 30.[2]

SALARY PAYABLE			SALARY EXPENSE		
	Apr. 30 Adj. 950		Paid during April CP	950	
	Apr. 30 Bal. 950		Apr. 30 Adj.	950	
			Apr. 30 Bal.	1,900	

After the adjusting entry,

- The April income statement reports salary expense of $1,900.
- The April 30 balance sheet reports salary payable of $950.

The $1,900 debit balance of Salary Expense is closed at April 30, 20X1, with this closing entry:

Closing Entries

Apr. 30	Income Summary	1,900	
	Salary Expense		1,900

After posting, Salary Expense has a zero balance as follows:

SALARY EXPENSE			
Paid during April CP	950		
Apr. 30 Adj.	950		
Apr. 30 Bal.	1,900	Apr. 30 Clo.	1,900

Zero balance

Assume for this illustration that on May 5, the next payday, Gillen will pay the $950 of accrued salary left over from April 30 plus $100 of salary for the first few days of May. Gillen's next payroll payment will be $1,050 ($950 + $100).

Accounting Without a Reversing Entry

On May 5, the next payday, Gillen pays the payroll of $1,050 and makes this journal entry:

May 5	Salary Payable	950	
	Salary Expense	100	
	Cash		1,050

This method of recording the cash payment is correct. However, it wastes time because Gillen must refer to the adjusting entries of April 30. Otherwise, she does not know the amount of the debit to Salary Payable (in this example, $950). Searching the preceding period's adjusting entries takes time and, in business, time is money. To save time, accountants use reversing entries.

---

[2]Entry explanations used throughout this discussion are

Adj. = entry	CP = Cash payment entry—a credit to Cash
Bal. = Balance	CR = Cash receipt entry—a debit to Cash
Clo. = Closing entry	Rev. = Reversing entry

MAKING A REVERSING ENTRY

A **reversing entry** switches the debit and the credit of a previous adjusting entry. *A reversing entry, then, is the exact opposite of a prior adjusting entry.* The reversing entry is dated the first day of the period that follows the adjusting entry.

To illustrate reversing entries, recall that on April 30, Gillen made the following adjusting entry to accrue Salary Payable:

Adjusting Entries

Apr. 30	Salary Expense	950	
	Salary Payable.....................		950

The reversing entry simply reverses the debit and the credit of the adjustment:

Reversing Entries

May 1	Salary Payable	950	
	Salary Expense....................		950

Observe that the reversing entry is dated the first day of the new period. It is the exact opposite of the April 30 adjusting entry. Ordinarily, the accountant who makes the adjusting entry also prepares the reversing entry at the same time. Gillen dates the reversing entry as of the first day of the next period, however, so that it affects only the new period. Note how the accounts appear after Gillen posts the reversing entry:

SALARY PAYABLE					SALARY EXPENSE			
May 1 Rev. 950	Apr. 30 Bal. 950				Apr. 30 Bal. 1,900	Apr. 30 Clo. 1,900		
Zero balance					Zero balance			
						May 1 Rev. 950		

The arrow shows the transfer of the $950 credit balance from Salary Payable to Salary Expense. This credit balance in Salary Expense does not mean that the entity has negative salary expense, as you might think. Instead, the odd credit balance in the Salary Expense account is merely a temporary result of the reversing entry. The credit balance is eliminated on May 5, when Gillen pays the payroll and debits Salary Expense in the customary manner:

May 5	Salary Expense	1,050	
	Cash		1,050

Then this cash payment entry is posted as follows:

SALARY EXPENSE	
May 5 CP 1,050	May 1 Rev. 950
May 5 Bal. 100	

Now Salary Expense has its correct debit balance of $100, which is the amount of salary expense incurred thus far in May. The $1,050 cash disbursement also pays the liability for Salary Payable so that Salary Payable has a zero balance, which is correct.

ASSESS YOUR PROGRESS

APPENDIX PROBLEM

P4A-1 Refer to the data in Problem 4-5A, page 156.

Using reversing entries

Required

1. Open accounts for Salary Payable and Salary Expense. Insert their unadjusted balances at August 31, 20X9.
2. Journalize adjusting entry (f) and the closing entry for Salary Expense at August 31. Post to the accounts.
3. On September 5, Allianz Publishing paid the next payroll amount of $580. Journalize this cash payment, and post to the accounts. Show the balance in each account.
4. Using a reversing entry, repeat requirements 1–3. Compare the balances of Salary Payable and Salary Expense computed using a reversing entry with those balances computed without the reversing entry (as they appear in your answer to requirement 3).

5

Merchandising Operations and the Accounting Cycle

LEARNING OBJECTIVES

After studying this chapter, you should be able to

1. Use sales and gross profit to evaluate a company

2. Account for the purchase and sale of inventory

3. Adjust and close the accounts of a merchandising business

4. Prepare a merchandiser's financial statements

5. Use the gross profit percentage and the inventory turnover ratio to evaluate a business

6. Compute cost of goods sold

You probably recognize the bulls'-eye logo. You may even do your shopping at a **Target, Mervyn, Marshall Field, Dayton,** or **Hudson** store. All these companies are part of the retail empire known as **Target Corporation.** It is a pacesetter in retailing: Target stores are currently the place to find the latest fashions at the best prices. Target is also a pacesetter in philanthropy and community relations. Through its Five Percent Club, the company donates 5% of its taxable income to support charities in the communities where it operates. In 2000, Target gave more than $1 million every week to local communities. The company, which employs about 189,000 people nationwide, is considered a good employer. *Working Mother* magazine has recognized Target as a "Top Work Place for Women." Target sells its merchandise through nearly 900 stores in 44 states, and through its Web site on the Internet. It is one of the largest mass-merchandise retailers in the United States, ringing up sales of over $33 billion in the year ended January 31, 2000.

Chapter 5 marks a new direction for this book. In Chapters 1–4, we studied accounting through the lens of Gay Gillen eTravel, which earns revenue by providing travel services for clients. **Yahoo!, Sprint,** physicians, and lawyers are other examples of service entities.

We now shift gears and focus on merchandising operations like **Target** stores, **Drugstore.com,** and **Best Buy** electronics centers. They earn their revenues by selling products rather than services. These companies are identified by the goods they sell—their *merchandise inventory,* or simply *inventory.*

This chapter demonstrates the central role of inventory in a business that sells merchandise. **Inventory** includes all goods that the company owns and expects to sell in the normal course of operations. We illustrate accounting for the purchase and sale of inventory, and we also illustrate how to adjust and close the books of a merchandiser. The chapter covers two ratios investors and creditors use to evaluate companies. Before launching into merchandising, let's compare service entities, with which you are familiar, to merchandising companies.

Chapters 1–4 have used both service entities and merchandisers to illustrate key accounting concepts. Chapter 5 jumps into the world of merchandising with both feet. As you make this transition, the following summarized financial statements will show how the two types of companies are similar and different. Observe that Merchandising Co.'s income statement reports Sales Revenue, Cost of Goods Sold, and Gross Profit. Merchandising Co.'s balance sheet reports Inventory. Service Co. reports none of these items. All the new merchandising items are italicized for easy reference.

INVENTORY. All the goods that the company owns and expects to sell in the normal course of operations.

SERVICE CO.*			**MERCHANDISING CO.****	
Income Statement			**Income Statement**	
Year Ended June 30, 20XX			Year Ended June 30, 20XX	

SERVICE CO.* Income Statement Year Ended June 30, 20XX		MERCHANDISING CO.** Income Statement Year Ended June 30, 20XX	
Service revenue	$XXX →	*Sales* revenue.....................	$XXX
Expenses: ————————————→		*Cost of goods sold*	X
Salary expense	X	*Gross profit*	XX
Depreciation expense....	X	→ Operating *expenses:*	
Income tax expense	X	Salary expense	X
Net income........................	$ X	Depreciation expense...	X
		Income tax expense	$ X
		Net income.......................	$ X
*Such as Gay Gillen eTravel		**Such as Target Corporation	

SERVICE CO. Balance Sheet June 30, 20XX		MERCHANDISING CO. Balance Sheet June 30, 20XX	
Assets		**Assets**	
Current assets:		Current assets:	
Cash..................................	$X	Cash	$X
Short-term investments	X	Short-term investments	X
Accounts receivable, net	X	Accounts receivable, net	X
Prepaid expenses................	X	*Inventory*	X
		Prepaid expenses................	X

WHAT ARE MERCHANDISING OPERATIONS?

Objective 1
Use sales and gross profit to evaluate a company

EXHIBIT 5-1
A Leading Merchandiser's Income Statement

◉ DAILY EXERCISE 5-1

◉ DAILY EXERCISE 5-2

◉ DAILY EXERCISE 5-3

Exhibit 5-1 shows the income statement of **Target Corporation.** The six highlighted items are unique to merchandisers.

TARGET CORPORATION Income Statement (Adapted) Year Ended January 31, 2000	
	Millions
Net sales revenue [same as Net sales]	$33,212
Cost of goods sold [same as Cost of sales]	23,029
Gross profit [same as Gross margin]...	10,183
Selling, general, and administrative expenses............................	7,490
Depreciation expense	854
Interest expense..	393
Other expenses, net...	302
Total operating expenses	$ 9,039
Net earnings [same as Net income]	$ 1,144

SALES REVENUE. The amount that a merchandiser earns from selling its inventory. Also called **sales.**

NET SALES. Sales revenue less sales discounts and sales returns and allowances.

COST OF GOODS SOLD. The cost of the inventory that the business has sold to customers. Also called cost of sales.

Sales Revenue, Cost of Goods Sold, and Gross Profit

The amount that a business earns from selling merchandise inventory is called **sales revenue,** often abbreviated as **sales.** (**Net sales** equals sales revenue minus any returns and discounts.) The major revenue of a merchandising entity is sales revenue, which results from delivering inventory to customers. The major expense of a merchandiser is **cost of goods sold,** also called **cost of sales.** It represents the entity's cost of the goods (the inventory) sold to customers.

While the inventory is held by a business, the inventory is an asset. When the inventory is sold, the inventory's cost becomes an expense to the seller. When Target sells you a shirt, the shirt's cost is expensed as cost of goods sold on Target's books.

Net sales revenue minus cost of goods sold is called **gross profit** or **gross margin.**

Net sales revenue (abbreviated as Sales)	−	Cost of goods sold (same as Cost of sales)	=	Gross profit (same as Gross margin)

GROSS PROFIT. Excess of net sales revenue over cost of goods sold. Also called **gross margin.**

or, more simply,

Sales − Cost of sales = Gross profit

Gross profit is a measure of business success. A sufficiently high gross profit is vital to a merchandiser. Target's operations were quite successful during the year ended January 31, 2000. Target's gross profit was over $10 billion.

The following example will clarify the nature of gross profit. Suppose Target's cost to purchase a man's shirt is $30 and Target sells the shirt for $50. Target's gross profit per shirt is $20, computed as follows:

Sales revenue earned by selling one shirt........	$50
Less: Cost of goods sold for the shirt	
(what the shirt cost Target)	(30)
Gross profit on the sale of one shirt................	$20

The gross profit reported on Target Corporation's income statement, $10,183 million, is the sum of the gross profits on all the shirts and other products the company sold during its fiscal year.

The Operating Cycle of a Merchandising Business

A merchandising entity buys inventory, sells the goods to customers, and uses the cash to purchase more inventory and repeat the cycle. Exhibit 5-2 diagrams the operating cycle for *cash sales* and for *sales on account.*

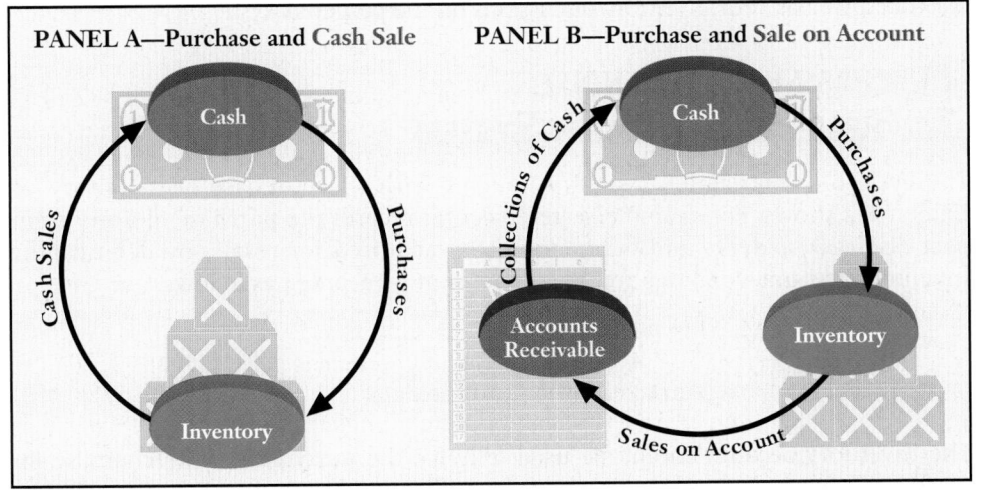

EXHIBIT 5-2
Operating Cycle of a Merchandiser

For a cash sale—Panel A—the cycle is from cash to inventory, and back to cash. For a sale on account—Panel B—the cycle is from cash to inventory to accounts receivabfle and back to cash. In all lines of business, managers try to shorten the cycle in order to keep assets active. The faster the sale of inventory and the collection of cash, the higher the profits.

Inventory Systems: Perpetual and Periodic

There are two main types of inventory accounting systems:

- the periodic system
- the perpetual system

The **periodic inventory system** is used by businesses that sell relatively inexpensive goods. A grocery store without optical-scanning cash registers does not keep a

PERIODIC INVENTORY SYSTEM. An inventory accounting system in which the business does not keep a continuous record of the inventory on hand. Instead, at the end of the period the business makes a physical count of the on-hand inventory and uses this information to prepare the financial statements.

daily running record of every loaf of bread and every can of pineapple that it sells. The cost of recordkeeping would be overwhelming. Instead, grocers count their inventory periodically—at least once a year—to determine the quantities on hand. The inventory amounts are used to prepare the annual financial statements. Businesses such as restaurants and small retail stores also use the periodic inventory system. The end-of-chapter appendix covers this system, which is becoming less popular as more businesses keep their inventory records by computer.

Under the **perpetual inventory system,** the business maintains a running record of inventory and cost of goods sold. This system achieves control over expensive goods such as automobiles, jewelry, and furniture. The loss of one item would be significant, and this justifies the cost of a perpetual system. Computers increase a company's ability to control its merchandise. But even under a perpetual system, the business counts inventory on hand at least once a year. The physical count establishes the correct amount of ending inventory and serves as a check on the perpetual records.

The following chart compares the periodic and perpetual systems:

PERPETUAL INVENTORY SYSTEM
- Keeps a running record of all goods bought and sold.
- Inventory counted at least once a year.
- Used for all types of goods.

PERIODIC INVENTORY SYSTEM
- Does *not* keep a running record of all goods bought and sold.
- Inventory counted at least once a year.
- Used for *inexpensive* goods.

Computerized Inventory Systems

A computerized inventory system can keep accurate, up-to-date records of the number of units purchased, the number of units sold, and the quantities on hand. Inventory systems are often integrated with accounts receivable and sales. For example, Target's computers keep up-to-the-minute records, so managers can call up current inventory information at any time. In a perpetual system, the "cash register" at a Target store is a computer terminal that records the sale and also updates inventory records. Bar codes are scanned by a laser as part of the perpetual inventory system. The lines of the bar coding represent coded data that keep track of each item. Because most businesses use bar codes, we base our inventory discussions on the perpetual system.[1]

PURCHASING MERCHANDISE: THE PERPETUAL INVENTORY SYSTEM

The cycle of a merchandising entity begins with the purchase of inventory, as Exhibit 5-2 shows. For example, a stereo center records the purchase of **Sony** compact disc (CD) players and other inventory acquired for resale, by debiting the Inventory account. A $500 purchase on account is recorded as follows:

June 14	Inventory...	500	
	Accounts Payable		500
	Purchased inventory on account.		

The Inventory account should be used only for the purchases of merchandise for resale. Purchases of other assets are recorded in other accounts. For example, the purchase of supplies is debited to Supplies, not to Inventory.

The Purchase Invoice: A Basic Business Document

Business documents give tangible evidence of transactions. In this section, we trace the steps that **Austin Sound Center,** in Austin, Texas, takes to order, receive, and pay for inventory. Many companies buy and sell their goods electronically—with no invoices, no checks, and so on. Here we use actual documents to illustrate what takes place behind the scenes.

---

[1]For instructors who prefer to concentrate on the periodic inventory system, an overview starts on page 188 and a comprehensive treatment of that system begins on page 211. Follow Appendix Objectives A2–A5 instead of Chapter Objectives 2 through 4.

1. Suppose Austin Sound wants to stock **JVC** brand CD players and speakers. Austin Sound prepares a *purchase order* and faxes it to JVC.

2. On receipt of the purchase order, JVC's computer scans its warehouse for the inventory that Austin Sound ordered. JVC ships the equipment and sends the invoice to Austin the same day. The **invoice** is the seller's request for cash from the purchaser. It is also called the *bill*.

3. Often the purchaser receives the invoice before the inventory arrives. Austin Sound does not pay immediately. Instead, Austin waits until the inventory arrives in order to ensure that it is the correct type and quantity ordered, and in good condition. After the inventory is inspected and approved, Austin Sound pays JVC the invoice amount.

> **INVOICE.** A seller's request for cash from the purchaser.

Exhibit 5-3 is an updated copy of an actual invoice from JVC to Austin Sound Center.

- From Austin Sound's perspective, this document is a *purchase invoice*.
- To JVC, it is a *sales invoice*.

EXHIBIT **5-3   An Invoice**

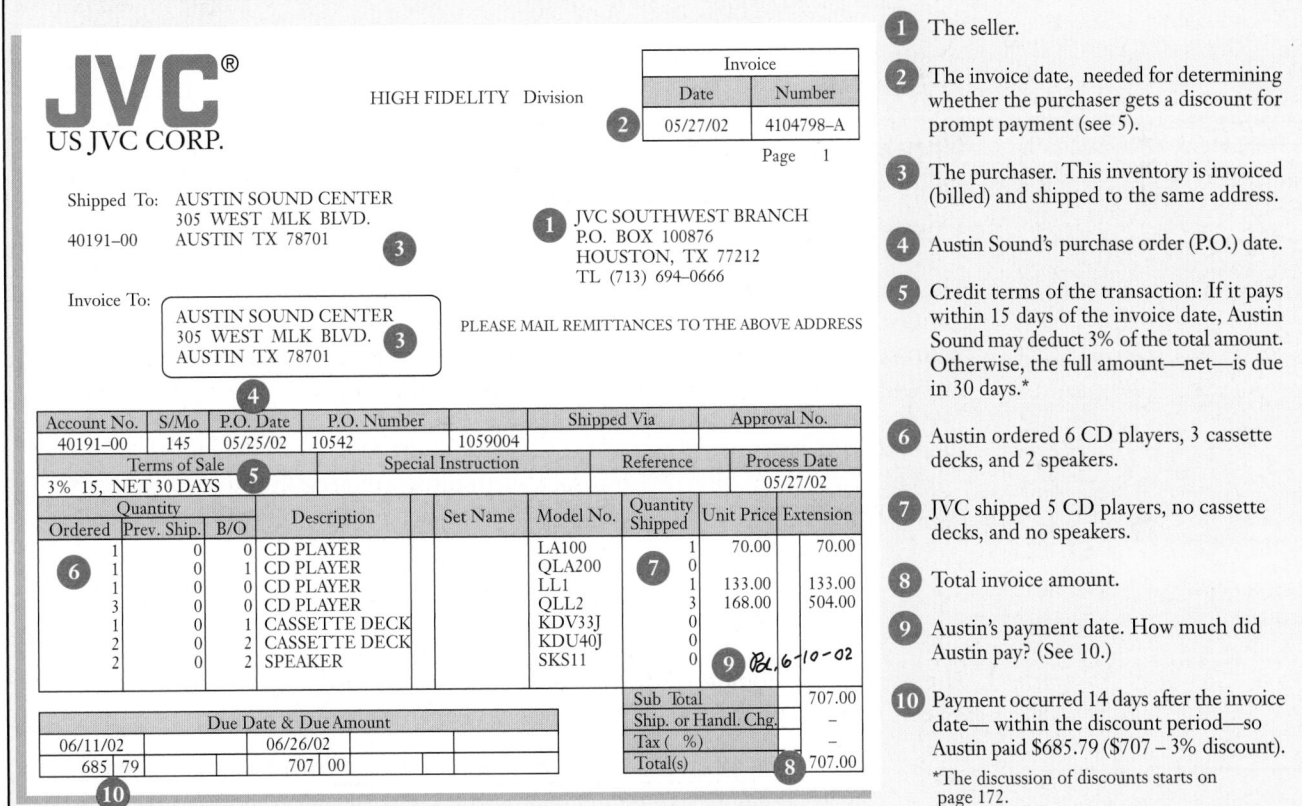

Purchase Returns and Allowances

Most businesses allow their customers to *return* merchandise that is defective, damaged in shipment, or otherwise unsuitable. But if the buyer chooses to keep the damaged goods, the seller may deduct an *allowance* from the amount the buyer owes. Both purchase returns and purchase allowances decrease the amount that the buyer must pay the seller.

Suppose the $70 CD player purchased by Austin Sound (top line of section 6 in Exhibit 5-3) was not the CD player Austin ordered. Austin returns the merchandise to the seller and records the purchase return as follows:

June 3	Accounts Payable	70.00	
	Inventory		70.00
	Returned inventory to seller.		

Now assume that one of the CD players was damaged in shipment to Austin Sound. The damage is minor, and Austin decides to keep the CD player in exchange for a $10 allowance from JVC. To record this purchase allowance, Austin Sound makes this entry:

June	4	Accounts Payable............................	10.00	
		Inventory		10.00
		Received a purchase allowance.		

The return and the allowance have two effects:

1. They decrease Austin Sound's liability, which is why we debit Accounts Payable.
2. They decrease Austin Sound's net cost of the goods, so we credit Inventory.

Assume that Austin Sound has not yet paid its debt to JVC. After the return ($70) and the allowance ($10) transactions are posted, Austin Sound's accounts will show these balances:

<table>
<tr><td>⊙ DAILY EXERCISE 5-4</td></tr>
<tr><td>⊙ DAILY EXERCISE 5-5</td></tr>
<tr><td>⊙ DAILY EXERCISE 5-6</td></tr>
</table>

INVENTORY				ACCOUNTS PAYABLE			
May 27	707.00	June 3	70.00	June 3	70.00	May 27	707.00
		June 4	10.00	June 4	10.00		
Bal.	627.00					Bal.	627.00

Austin Sound's cost of the *inventory* is $627, and Austin Sound owes JVC $627 on *account payable*.

Purchase Discounts

Many businesses also offer their customers purchase discounts. A purchase discount reduces the cost of inventory.

JVC's credit terms of 3% 15, NET 30 DAYS can also be expressed as 3/15 n/30. This means that Austin Sound may deduct 3% of the total debt if Austin pays within 15 days of the invoice date. Otherwise, the full amount—NET—is due in 30 days. Terms of simply n/30 mean that no discount is offered and that payment is due 30 days after the invoice date. Terms of *eom* mean that payment is due at the end of the current month. But a purchase after the 25th of the month can be paid at the end of the following month.

Let's use the Exhibit 5-3 transaction to illustrate accounting for a purchase discount. Austin Sound records this purchase on account as follows:

May 27	Inventory..	707.00	
	Accounts Payable		707.00
	Purchased inventory on account.		

The accounting equation shows that a credit purchase of inventory increases both assets (Inventory) and liabilities (Accounts Payable), as follows:

ASSETS	=	LIABILITIES	+	OWNER'S EQUITY
Inventory	=	Accounts Payable		
$707	=	$707	+	0

Austin Sound paid within the discount period, so its cash payment entry is

⊙ DAILY EXERCISE 5-7

June 10	Accounts Payable............................	707.00	
	Cash ($707.00 × 0.97)..........		685.79
	Inventory ($707.00 × 0.03)..		21.21
	Paid within discount period.		

After paying the account, Austin Sound's assets and liabilities both decrease, as follows:

ASSETS			=	LIABILITIES	+	OWNER'S EQUITY
Cash	+	Inventory	=	Accounts Payable		
−$685.29		−$21.21	=	−$707	+	0
	−$707					

Note the credit to Inventory. After Austin Sound has taken its discount, this inventory costs Austin Sound $685.79 ($707.00 – Purchase discount of $21.21), as shown in the Inventory account:

INVENTORY			
May 27	707.00	June 10	21.21
Bal.	685.79		

But if Austin Sound pays this invoice after the discount period, it must pay the full amount of $707. In that case, the payment entry is

					INVENTORY	
June 29	Accounts Payable	707.00				
	Cash		707.00	May 27	707.00	
	Paid after discount period.					

WORK IT OUT

On September 15, Austin Sound purchases $1,000 of merchandise on account, with terms 2/10, n/30. Austin returns $100 of merchandise for credit on September 20, then makes payment in full on September 25. Journalize these transactions.

Answer: Three separate journal entries are needed here. The initial purchase entry is

Purchase:	Sep. 15	Inventory.....................................	1,000	
		Accounts Payable		1,000

The second entry records the return of inventory, as follows:

Return:	Sep. 20	Accounts Payable........................	100	
		Inventory		100

The third entry records the payment of $882, as follows: Original amount, $1,000, minus the $100 return equals the net payable of $900. Now subtract the 2% discount ($900 × 0.02 = $18) to arrive at the final payment of $882.

Payment:	Sep. 25	Accounts Payable........................	900	
		Cash		882
		Inventory		18

Transportation Cost: Who Pays?

The transportation cost of moving inventory from seller to buyer can be significant. The purchase agreement specifies FOB terms to indicate who pays the shipping charges. *FOB* means *free on board*. FOB governs (1) when legal title to the goods passes from seller to buyer, and (2) who pays the freight.

- Under FOB *shipping point* terms, title passes when the inventory leaves the seller's place of businesss—the shipping point. The buyer owns the goods while they are in transit and therefore the buyer pays the transportation cost.
- Under FOB *destination* terms, title passes when the goods reach the destination, so the seller pays the transportation cost.

Exhibit 5-4 summarizes FOB terms.

Factors to Consider	FOB Shipping Point	FOB Destination
When does the title to the goods pass to the buyer?	At the shipping point	At the destination
Who pays the transportation cost?	Buyer	Seller

EXHIBIT 5-4
FOB Terms

FREIGHT IN FOB shipping point terms are most common, so the buyer generally pays the freight. A freight cost that the buyer pays on an inventory purchase is called *freight in*. In accounting, the cost of an asset includes all costs incurred to bring the asset to its intended use. For inventory, cost therefore includes the

- *Net cost* after all discounts and returns have been subtracted, plus
- *Freight* (transportation, or shipping) costs to be paid

To record the payment for freight in, the buyer debits Inventory and credits Cash or Accounts Payable for the amount. Suppose Austin Sound receives a $60 shipping bill directly from the freight company. Austin Sound's entry to record payment of the freight charge is

June 1	Inventory...................................	60	
	Cash		60
	Paid a freight bill.		

The freight charge increases the final cost of the inventory to $687, as follows:

		INVENTORY				
May 27	Purchase	707.00	June 3	Return	70.00
June 1	Freight	60.00	June 4	Allowance	10.00
Bal.	Net cost	687.00			

Any discounts would be computed only on the account payable to the seller, not on the transportation costs, because the freight company offers no discount.

Under FOB shipping point terms, the seller sometimes prepays the transportation cost as a convenience and lists this cost on the invoice. The buyer debits Inventory for the combined cost of the inventory and the shipping cost because both costs apply to the merchandise. A $5,000 purchase of goods, coupled with a related freight charge of $400, would be recorded as follows:

March 12	Inventory.......................................	5,400	
	Accounts Payable		5,400
	Purchased on account including freight.		

If the buyer pays within the discount period, the discount will be computed on the $5,000 merchandise cost, not on the $5,400. For example, a 2% discount would be $100 ($5,000 × 0.02).

FREIGHT OUT The cost of freight charges paid to ship goods sold to customers is called *freight out*. Freight out is delivery expense paid by the seller. Delivery expense is an operating expense for the seller. It is debited to the Delivery Expense account.

WORK IT OUT

This Work It Out example is exactly like the preceding one, but with freight in added to illustrate the accounting for shipping cost. On September 15, Austin Sound purchased $1,000 of merchandise, with *$80 freight added*, for an invoice total of $1,080. Austin returns $100 of the goods for credit on September 20 and pays the account payable in full on September 25. Journalize these transactions.

Answer

Purchase:	Sept. 15	Inventory ($1,000 + $80)...................................	1,080	
		Accounts Payable		1,080
Return:	Sept. 20	Accounts Payable	100	
		Inventory		100
Payment:	Sept. 25	Accounts Payable ($1,080 − $100).....................	980	
		Inventory [($1,000 − $100) × 0.02]..........		18
		Cash ($1,000 + $80 − $100 − $18)..........		962

The buyer does *not* get a discount on the cost of freight in.

Detailed Accounting for Purchase Returns and Allowances, Discounts, and Transportation Costs

Some businesses keep detailed records of purchase returns and allowances, discounts, and transportation costs. For example, Austin Sound receives defective CD players from an off-brand manufacturer. In recording purchase returns, Austin Sound can credit a special account, Purchase Returns and Allowances, which serves as a running record of defective merchandise.

The Purchase Returns and Allowances account carries a credit balance and is a contra account to Inventory. Freight In can be debited for transportation costs. Then, for reporting on the financial statements, these accounts can be combined with the Inventory account to determine the total cost of inventory (amounts assumed):

Inventory		$35,000
Less: Purchase discounts	$(700)	
Purchase returns and allowances	(800)	(1,500)
Net purchases of inventory		33,500
Freight in		2,100
Total cost of inventory		$35,600

SELLING INVENTORY AND RECORDING COST OF GOODS SOLD

After a company buys inventory, the next step in the operating cycle is to sell the goods. We shift now to the selling side and follow **Austin Sound Center** through a sequence of selling transactions. A sale earns a reward, Sales Revenue. A sale also requires a sacrifice in the form of an expense, Cost of Goods Sold, as the seller gives up the asset Inventory.

After making a sale on account, Austin Sound may experience any of the following:

- A sales return: The customer may return goods to Austin Sound.
- A sales allowance: Austin Sound may grant a sales allowance to reduce the amount of cash collected from the customer.
- A sales discount: If the customer pays within the discount period—under terms such as 2/10 n/30—Austin Sound collects the discounted amount.
- Freight out: Austin Sound may have to pay delivery expense to transport the goods to the buyer's location.

Let's begin with a cash sale.

Cash Sale

Sales of retailers, such as grocery stores and restaurants, are often for cash. Cash sales of $3,000 would be recorded by debiting Cash and crediting Sales Revenue as follows:

Jan. 9	Cash	3,000	
	Sales Revenue		3,000
	Cash sale.		

To update the inventory records, the business also must decrease the Inventory balance. Suppose these goods cost the seller $1,900. An accompanying entry is needed to transfer the $1,900 cost of the goods—not their selling price of $3,000—from the Inventory account to Cost of Goods Sold as follows:

Jan. 9	Cost of Goods Sold	1,900	
	Inventory		1,900
	Recorded the cost of goods sold.		

Cost of goods sold (also called cost of sales) is the largest single expense of most merchandisers. ➡ The Cost of Goods Sold account keeps a current balance throughout the period as transactions are journalized and posted.

> ← The recording of cost of goods sold along with sales revenue is an example of the matching principle (Chapter 3, p. 86).

After posting, the Cost of Goods Sold account holds the cost of the merchandise sold ($1,900 in this case):

INVENTORY				COST OF GOODS SOLD	
Purchases 50,000	Jan. 9	1,900	⟷	Jan. 9	1,900
(amount					
assumed)					

The computer automatically records the cost of goods sold entry when the cashier keys in the code number of the inventory that is sold. Optical scanners perform this task in most stores.

Sale on Account

Most sales in the United States are made on account (on credit). A $5,000 sale on account is recorded by a debit to Accounts Receivable and a credit to Sales Revenue, as follows:

Jan. 11	Accounts Receivable............................	5,000	
	Sales Revenue		5,000
	Sale on account.		

If we assume that these goods cost the seller $2,900, the accompanying cost of goods sold entry is

Jan. 11	Cost of Goods Sold..............................	2,900	
	Inventory		2,900
	Recorded the cost of goods sold.		

When the cash comes in, the seller records the related cash receipt on account as follows:

Jan. 19	Cash..	5,000	
	Accounts Receivable		5,000
	Collection on account.		

Offering Sales Discounts and Sales Returns and Allowances

SALES RETURNS AND ALLOWANCES. Decreases in the seller's receivable from a customer's return of merchandise or from granting the customer an allowance from the amount owed to the seller. A contra account to Sales Revenue.

We just saw that purchase purchase returns and allowances and purchase discounts decrease the cost of inventory purchases. In the same way, **sales returns and allowances** and **sales discounts,** which are contra accounts to Sales Revenue, decrease the net amount of revenue earned on sales.

Credit-balance account		Debit-balance accounts					Credit subtotal (*not* a separate account)
Sales Revenue	−	Sales Returns and Allowances	−	Sales Discounts	=		Net sales revenue[2]

This equation calculates net sales. Note that sales discounts can be given on both goods and services.

SALES DISCOUNT. Reduction in the amount receivable from a customer, offered by the seller as an incentive for the customer to pay promptly. A contra account to Sales Revenue.

Companies keep close watch on their customers' paying habits and on their own sales of defective and unsuitable merchandise. They maintain separate accounts for Sales Discounts and Sales Returns and Allowances. Now let's examine a sequence of JVC sale transactions. Assume **JVC** is selling to Austin Sound.

On July 7, JVC sells stereo components for $7,200 on credit terms of 2/10 n/30. These goods cost JVC $4,700. JVC's entries to record this credit sale and the related cost of the goods sold are

July 7	Accounts Receivable................................	7,200	
	Sales Revenue....................................		7,200
	Sale on account.		
July 7	Cost of Goods Sold	4,700	
	Inventory......................................		4,700
	Recorded the cost of goods sold.		

[2]Often abbreviated as Net sales.

Assume that the buyer returns goods that sold for $600. JVC records the sales return and the related decrease in Accounts Receivable as follows:

July 12	Sales Returns and Allowances	600	
	Accounts Receivable		600
	Received returned goods.		

JVC receives the returned merchandise and updates the inventory records. JVC must also decrease Cost of Goods Sold as follows (these goods cost JVC $400):

July 12	Inventory	400	
	Cost of Goods Sold..............................		400
	Placed goods back in inventory.		

Suppose JVC grants a $100 sales allowance for damaged goods. Austin Sound then subtracts $100 from the amount it will pay JVC. JVC journalizes this transaction by debiting Sales Returns and Allowances and crediting Accounts Receivable as follows:

July 15	Sales Returns and Allowances	100	
	Accounts Receivable		100
	Granted a sales allowance for damaged goods.		

No inventory entry is needed for a sales allowance transaction because the seller receives no returned goods from the customer. Instead, JVC will simply receive less cash from the customer.

After the preceding entries are posted, all the accounts have up-to-date balances. Accounts Receivable has a $6,500 debit balance, as follows:

ACCOUNTS RECEIVABLE					
July 7	Sale	7,200	July 12	Return	600
			15	Allowance	100
Bal.		6,500			

On July 17, the last day of the discount period, JVC collects $4,000 of this receivable. Assume JVC allows customers to take discounts on all amounts JVC receives within the discount period. JVC's cash receipt is $3,920 [$4,000 − ($4,000 × 0.02)], and the collection entry is

July 17	Cash	3,920	
	Sales Discounts ($4,000 × 0.02)	80	
	Accounts Receivable		4,000
	Cash collection within the discount period.		

⊙ DAILY EXERCISE 5-8

⊙ DAILY EXERCISE 5-9

⊙ DAILY EXERCISE 5-10

Suppose that JVC collects the remainder, $2,500, on July 28. That date falls after the discount period, so there is no sales discount. To record this collection on account, JVC makes this entry:

July 28	Cash ($6,500 − $4,000)..............................	2,500	
	Accounts Receivable		2,500
	Cash collection within the discount period.		

Now, JVC's Accounts Receivable balance is zero, as follows:

ACCOUNTS RECEIVABLE					
July 7	Sale	7,200	July 12	Return	600
			15	Allowance	100
			17	Collection	4,000
			28	Collection	2,500
Bal.		−0−			

SUMMARY PROBLEM

Brun Sales Company engaged in the following transactions during June of the current year:

www.prenhall.com/horngren

Mid-Chapter Assessment

June 3 Purchased inventory on credit terms of 1/10 net eom (end of month), $1,610.
  9 Returned 40% of the inventory purchased on June 3. It was defective.
  12 Sold goods for cash, $920 (cost, $550).
  15 Purchased goods of $5,000. Credit terms were 3/15 net 30.
  16 Paid a $260 freight bill on goods purchased.
  18 Sold inventory on credit terms of 2/10 n/30, $2,000 (cost, $1,180).
  22 Received damaged goods from the customer of the June 18 sale, $800 (cost, $480).
  24 Borrowed money from the bank to take advantage of the discount offered on the June 15 purchase. Signed a note payable to the bank for the net amount.
  24 Paid supplier for goods purchased on June 15, less the discount.
  28 Received cash in full settlement of the account from the customer who purchased inventory on June 18, less the return on June 22.
  29 Paid the amount owed on account from the purchase of June 3, less the June 9 return.

Required

1. Journalize the preceding transactions. Explanations are not required.
2. Set up T-accounts and post the journal entries to show the ending balances in the Inventory and the Cost of Goods Sold accounts.
3. Assume that the note payable signed on June 24 requires the payment of $95 interest expense. Was borrowing funds to take the cash discount a wise or unwise decision?

Solution   *Requirement 1*

June 3	Inventory	1,610	
	Accounts Payable		1,610
9	Accounts Payable ($1,610 × 0.40)	644	
	Inventory		644
12	Cash	920	
	Sales Revenue		920
12	Cost of Goods Sold	550	
	Inventory		550
15	Inventory	5,000	
	Accounts Payable		5,000
16	Inventory	260	
	Cash		260
18	Accounts Receivable	2,000	
	Sales Revenue		2,000
18	Cost of Goods Sold	1,180	
	Inventory		1,180
22	Sales Returns and Allowances	800	
	Accounts Receivable		800
22	Inventory	480	
	Cost of Goods Sold		480
24	Cash [$5,000 − 0.03($5,000)]	4,850	
	Note Payable		4,850
24	Accounts Payable	5,000	
	Inventory ($5,000 × 0.03)		150
	Cash ($5,000 × 0.97)		4,850
28	Cash [($2,000 − $800) × 0.98]	1,176	
	Sales Discounts [($2,000 − $800) × 0.02]	24	
	Accounts Receivable ($2,000 − $800)		1,200
29	Accounts Payable ($1,610 − $644)	966	
	Cash		966

Requirement 2

INVENTORY					COST OF GOODS SOLD			
June 3	1,610	June 9	644		June 12	550	June 22	480
15	5,000	12	550		18	1,180		
16	260	18	1,180		Bal.	1,250		
22	480	24	150					
Bal.	4,826							

Requirement 3

The decision to borrow funds was wise because the discount ($150) exceeded the interest paid ($95). Thus the entity was $55 better off as a result of its decision.

ADJUSTING AND CLOSING THE ACCOUNTS OF A MERCHANDISER

Objective 3
Adjust and close the accounts of a merchandising business

A merchandising business adjusts and closes the accounts the same way a service entity does. If a work sheet is used, the trial balance is entered, and the work sheet is completed to determine net income or net loss. The work sheet aids the adjusting and closing processes and helps the accountant prepare the financial statements.

Adjusting Inventory Based on a Physical Count

In theory, the Inventory account stays current at all times. However, the actual amount of inventory on hand may differ from what the books show. Theft losses and damage occur. Accounting errors can require adjustments. For this reason, virtually all businesses, like the bookstore chain **Barnes & Noble,** take a physical count of inventory at least once a year. The most common time for a business to count its inventory is at the end of the fiscal year, before the financial statements are prepared. The business then adjusts the Inventory account on the basis of the physical count.

Exhibit 5-5, **Austin Sound's** trial balance at December 31, 20X2, lists a $40,500 balance for inventory. With no shrinkage—due to theft or error—the business should have on hand inventory costing $40,500. But on December 31, when Charles Ernest, the owner of Austin Sound, counts the merchandise in the store, the total cost of the goods on hand comes to only $40,200. Austin Sound then records the $300 of inventory shrinkage with this adjusting entry:

Dec. 31	Cost of Goods Sold	300	
	Inventory ($40,500 − $40,200)		300

This entry brings Inventory and Cost of Goods Sold to their correct balances. Austin Sound's December 31, 20X2, adjustment data, including the correct inventory information [item (b)], are given at the bottom of Exhibit 5-5 on page 180.

The physical count can indicate that more inventory is present than the books show. Austin Sound may have made a purchase it did not record. This would be entered the standard way: Debit Inventory and credit Cash or Accounts Payable.

If the reason for the excess inventory cannot be identified, the business adjusts the accounts by debiting Inventory and crediting Cost of Goods Sold. To illustrate a merchandiser's adjusting and closing process, let's use Austin Sound's December 31, 20X2, trial balance in Exhibit 5-5. All the new accounts—Inventory, Cost of Goods Sold, and the contra accounts—are highlighted for emphasis.

Additional data at December 31, 20X2.
  a. Interest revenue earned but not yet collected, $400.
  b. Inventory on hand, $40,200.
  c. Supplies on hand, $100.
  d. Prepaid insurance expired during the year, $1,000.
  e. Depreciation, $600.
  f. Unearned sales revenue earned during the year, $1,300.
  g. Accrued wage expense, $400.
  h. Accrued interest expense, $200.

EXHIBIT 5-5   Trial Balance

AUSTIN SOUND CENTER
Trial Balance
December 31, 20X2

Cash	$ 2,850	
Accounts receivable	4,600	
Note receivable, current	8,000	
Interest receivable		
Inventory	40,500	
Supplies	650	
Prepaid insurance	1,200	
Furniture and fixtures	33,200	
Accumulated depreciation		$ 2,400
Accounts payable		47,000
Unearned sales revenue		2,000
Wages payable		
Interest payable		
Note payable, long-term		12,600
C. Ernest, capital		25,900
C. Ernest, withdrawals	54,100	
Sales revenue		168,000
Sales discounts	1,400	
Sales returns and allowances	2,000	
Interest revenue		600
Cost of goods sold	90,500	
Wage expense	9,800	
Rent expense	8,400	
Depreciation expense		
Insurance expense		
Supplies expense		
Interest expense	1,300	
Total	$258,500	$258,500

Preparing and Using the Work Sheet

The Exhibit 5-6 work sheet is similar to the work sheets we have seen so far, but there are a few differences. This work sheet does not include adjusted trial balance columns. ◄◄ In most accounting systems, a single operation combines trial balance amounts with the adjustments and extends the adjusted balances directly to the income statement and balance sheet columns. Therefore, to reduce clutter, the adjusted trial balance columns are omitted here.

➤➤ This work sheet is slightly different from the one introduced in the Chapter 4 acetates following p. 130—it contains four pairs of columns, not five.

ACCOUNT TITLE COLUMNS   The trial balance lists a number of accounts without balances. Ordinarily, these accounts are affected by the adjusting process. Examples include Interest Receivable, Wages Payable, and Depreciation Expense. The accounts are listed in the order they appear in the ledger. If additional accounts are needed, they can be entered at the bottom of the work sheet, above net income.

TRIAL BALANCE COLUMNS   Examine the Inventory account in the trial balance. Inventory has a balance of $40,500 before the physical count at the end of the year. Cost of Goods Sold's balance is $90,500 before any adjustment. Any difference between the Inventory amount on the trial balance ($40,500) and the correct amount based on the physical count ($40,200) is unexplained and should be debited or credited to Cost of Goods Sold.

Exhibit **5-6** Accounting Work Sheet

AUSTIN SOUND CENTER
Accounting Work Sheet
Year Ended December 31, 20X2

Account Title	Trial Balance Debit	Credit	Adjustments Debit	Credit	Income Statement Debit	Credit	Balance Sheet Debit	Credit
Cash	2,850						2,850	
Accounts receivable	4,600						4,600	
Note receivable, current ..	8,000						8,000	
Interest receivable			(a) 400				400	
Inventory	40,500			(b) 300			40,200	
Supplies	650			(c) 550			100	
Prepaid insurance	1,200			(d) 1,000			200	
Furniture and fixtures	33,200						33,200	
Accumulated depreciation		2,400		(e) 600				3,000
Accounts payable		47,000						47,000
Unearned sales revenue ..		2,000	(f) 1,300					700
Wages payable				(g) 400				400
Interest payable				(h) 200				200
Note payable, long-term..		12,600						12,600
C. Ernest, capital		25,900						25,900
C. Ernest, withdrawals.....	54,100						54,100	
Sales revenue		168,000		(f) 1,300		169,300		
Sales discounts	1,400				1,400			
Sales returns and allowances	2,000				2,000			
Interest revenue		600		(a) 400		1,000		
Cost of goods sold	90,500		(b) 300		90,800			
Wage expense	9,800		(g) 400		10,200			
Rent expense	8,400				8,400			
Depreciation expense			(e) 600		600			
Insurance expense			(d) 1,000		1,000			
Supplies expense			(c) 550		550			
Interest expense...............	1,300		(h) 200		1,500			
	258,500	258,500	4,750	4,750	116,450	170,300	143,650	89,800
Net income					53,850			53,850
					170,300	170,300	143,650	143,650

⊙ Daily Exercise 5-11

ADJUSTMENTS COLUMNS The adjustments are similar to those discussed in Chapters 3 and 4. The adjustments may be entered in any order desired. The debit amount of each entry should equal the credit amount, and total debits should equal total credits. You should review the adjusting data in Exhibit 5-5 to reassure yourself that the adjustments are correct.

INCOME STATEMENT COLUMNS The income statement columns on the work sheet in Exhibit 5-6 contain adjusted amounts for the revenues and the expenses. Sales Revenue, for example, has an adjusted balance of $169,300.

The income statement column subtotals indicate whether the business had a net income or a net loss.

- Net income: Total credits > Total debits
- Net loss: Total debits > Total credits

Austin Sound's total credits of $170,300 exceed the total debits of $116,450, so the company earned a net income.

Insert the *net income* amount in the debit column to bring total debits into agreement with total credits. Insert a *net loss* amount in the credit column to equalize total debits and total credits. Net income or net loss is then extended to the opposite column of the balance sheet.

BALANCE-SHEET COLUMNS The only new item in the balance sheet columns is Inventory. The balance listed in Exhibit 5-6 is the ending amount of $40,200, as determined by the physical count of goods on hand at the end of the period.

PREPARING THE FINANCIAL STATEMENTS OF A MERCHANDISER

Objective 4
Prepare a merchandiser's financial statements

Exhibit 5-7 presents **Austin Sound's** financial statements.

EXHIBIT 5-7
Financial Statements of Austin Sound Center

DAILY EXERCISE 5-12

DAILY EXERCISE 5-13

DAILY EXERCISE 5-14

AUSTIN SOUND CENTER
Income Statement
Year Ended December 31, 20X2

Sales revenue		$169,300	
Less: Sales discounts	$(1,400)		
Sales returns and allowances	(2,000)	(3,400)	
Net sales revenue			$165,900
Cost of goods sold			90,800
Gross profit			75,100
Operating expenses:			
Wage expense		$ 10,200	
Rent expense		8,400	
Insurance expense		1,000	
Depreciation expense		600	
Supplies expense		550	20,750
Operating income			54,350
Other revenue and (expense):			
Interest revenue		$ 1,000	
Interest expense		(1,500)	(500)
Net income			$ 53,850

AUSTIN SOUND CENTER
Statement of Owner's Equity
Year Ended December 31, 20X2

C. Ernest, capital, December 31, 20X1	$25,900
Add: Net income	53,850
	79,750
Less: Withdrawals	(54,100)
C. Ernest, capital, December 31, 20X2	$25,650

AUSTIN SOUND CENTER
Balance Sheet
December 31, 20X2

Assets			**Liabilities**		
Current:			Current:		
Cash		$ 2,850	Accounts payable		$47,000
Accounts receivable		4,600	Unearned sales		
Note receivable		8,000	revenue		700
Interest receivable		400	Wages payable		400
Inventory		40,200	Interest payable		200
Prepaid insurance		200	Total current		
Supplies		100	liabilities		48,300
Total current assets		56,350	Long-term:		
Plant:			Note payable		12,600
Furniture and fixtures	$33,200		Total liabilities		60,900
Less: Accumulated					
depreciation	(3,000)	30,200	**Owner's Equity**		
			C. Ernest, capital		25,650
			Total liabilities and		
Total assets		$86,550	owner's equity		$86,550

To solidify your understanding of how the financial statements are prepared, you should trace the amounts in the work sheet (Exhibit 5-6) to the statements in Exhibit 5-7.

INCOME STATEMENT   The income statement reports **operating expenses,** which are those expenses other than cost of goods sold that are incurred in the entity's major line of business. Austin Sound's operating expenses include wage expense, rent, depreciation, insurance, and supplies expense.

Many companies report their operating expenses in two categories:

- *Selling expenses* are expenses related to marketing the company's products— sales salaries; sales commissions; advertising; depreciation, rent, and utilities on store buildings; and delivery expense.
- *General expenses* include office expenses, such as the salaries of the company president and office employees; depreciation, rent, utilities, and property taxes on the home office building.

Target Corporation (Exhibit 5-1) groups selling, general, and administrative expenses together for reporting on the income statement.

Gross profit minus operating expenses plus any other operating revenues equals **operating income,** or **income from operations.** Many people view operating income as an important indicator of performance because it measures the results of the entity's major ongoing activities.

The last section of Austin Sound's income statement is **other revenue and expense.** This category reports revenues and expenses that are outside the main operations of the business. Examples include gains and losses on the sale of plant assets (not inventory) and gains and losses on lawsuits. Accountants have traditionally viewed Interest Revenue and Interest Expense as "other" items because they arise from loaning and borrowing money. These financing activities are outside the operating scope of selling merchandise. Target (Exhibit 5-1) lists Interest expense among the operating expenses, also a common practice.

The bottom line of the income statement is net income:

Net income = Total revenues and gains − Total expenses and losses

We often hear the term *bottom line* used to refer to a final result. *Bottom line* originated from the position of net income on the income statement.

STATEMENT OF OWNER'S EQUITY   A merchandiser's statement of owner's equity looks exactly like that of a service business. In fact, you cannot determine whether the entity sells merchandise or services from looking at the statement of owner's equity.

BALANCE SHEET   If the business is a merchandiser, the balance sheet shows inventory as a major current asset. Service businesses usually have no inventory at all or minor amounts of inventory.

Journalizing the Adjusting and Closing Entries

Exhibit 5-8 presents Austin Sound's adjusting entries, which are similar to those you have seen previously, except for the inventory adjustment [entry (b)]. ➡ The closing entries in the exhibit also follow the pattern illustrated in Chapter 4.

The *first closing entry* debits the revenue accounts for their ending balances. The offsetting credit of $170,300 transfers the sum of total revenues to Income Summary. This amount comes directly from the credit column of the income statement on the work sheet (Exhibit 5-6).

The *second closing entry* includes credits to Cost of Goods Sold, to the contra revenue accounts (Sales Discounts and Sales Returns and Allowances), and to all the expense accounts. The offsetting $116,450 debit to Income Summary represents the amount of total expenses plus the contra revenues, which come from the debit column of the income statement on the work sheet.

The *last two closing entries* close net income from Income Summary to the Capital account and also close the owner Withdrawals into the Capital account.

OPERATING EXPENSES. Expenses, other than cost of goods sold, that are incurred in the entity's major line of business. Examples include rent, depreciation, salaries, wages, utilities, and supplies expense.

OPERATING INCOME. Gross profit minus operating expenses plus any other operating revenues. Also called **income from operations.**

OTHER REVENUE. Revenue that is outside the main operations of a business, such as a gain on the sale of plant assets.

OTHER EXPENSE. Expense that is outside the main operations of a business, such as a loss on the sale of plant assets.

◄◄ The closing entries also close the Cost of Goods Sold expense account. See Chapter 4, pp. 135, 136.

EXHIBIT 5-8
Adjusting and Closing Entries for a Merchandiser

Journal

Adjusting Entries

a.	Dec. 31	Interest Receivable......................................	400	
		Interest Revenue		400
b.	31	Cost of Goods Sold	300	
		Inventory...		300
c.	31	Supplies Expense ($650 – $100)..................	550	
		Supplies		550
d.	31	Insurance Expense......................................	1,000	
		Prepaid Insurance.............................		1,000
e.	31	Depreciation Expense	600	
		Accumulated Depreciation		600
f.	31	Unearned Sales Revenue	1,300	
		Sales Revenue		1,300
g.	31	Wage Expense...	400	
		Wages Payable		400
h.	31	Interest Expense...	200	
		Interest Payable		200

Closing Entries

1.	Dec. 31	Sales Revenue...	169,300	
		Interest Revenue...............................	1,000	
		Income Summary...............................		170,300
2.	31	Income Summary	116,450	
		Sales Discounts.................................		1,400
		Sales Returns and Allowances............		2,000
		Cost of Goods Sold		90,800
		Wage Expense....................................		10,200
		Rent Expense.....................................		8,400
		Depreciation Expense........................		600
		Insurance Expense		1,000
		Supplies Expense...............................		550
		Interest Expense		1,500
3.	31	Income Summary ($170,300 – $116,450)....	53,850	
		C. Ernest, Capital..............................		53,850
4.	31	C. Ernest, Capital	54,100	
		C. Ernest, Withdrawals.......................		54,100

Study Exhibits 5-6, 5-7, and 5-8 carefully because they illustrate the entire end-of-period process that leads to the financial statements.

Here is an easy way to remember the closing process. First, look at the work sheet. Then:

1. Debit all income statement accounts with a credit balance. Credit Income Summary for the total.
2. Credit all income statement accounts with a debit balance. Debit Income Summary for the total.
3. Take the balance in the Income Summary account. A debit balance indicates a net loss; credit Income Summary for that amount, and debit Capital. If Income Summary has a credit balance, there is a net income; debit Income Summary for that amount, and credit Capital.
4. Withdrawals has a debit balance. Credit Withdrawals to close its balance, and debit Capital for the same amount.

Income Statement Formats: Multi-Step and Single-Step

We have seen that the balance sheet appears in two formats:

- the report format (assets on top, . . . , owner's equity at bottom)
- the account format (assets at left, liabilities and owner's equity at right)

➤ There are also two basic formats for the income statement:

- the multi-step format
- the single-step format

The multi-step format is by far the more popular.

◀ For a review of balance sheet formats, see Chapter 4, p. 141.

Multi-Step Income Statement

The **multi-step format** shows subtotals to highlight significant relationships. In addition to net income, it also presents gross profit and income from operations. This format communicates a merchandiser's results of operations especially well because gross profit and income from operations are important to investors. Exhibit 5-1 shows the multi-step format. The income statements presented thus far in this chapter have also been multi-step. Austin Sound's multi-step income statement for the year ended December 31, 20X2, appears in Exhibit 5-7.

Single-Step Income Statement

The **single-step format** groups all revenues together and then lists and deducts all expenses together without drawing any subtotals. **IBM** and **Wal-Mart** use this format. The single-step format clearly distinguishes revenues from expenses as Exhibit 5-9 shows. This format works well for service entities because they have no gross profit to report.

AUSTIN SOUND CENTER
Income Statement
Year Ended December 31, 20X2

Revenues:	
Net sales (net of sales discounts, $1,400, and returns and allowances, $2,000)	$165,900
Interest revenue	1,000
Total revenues	166,900
Expenses:	
Cost of goods sold	90,800
Wage expense	10,200
Rent expense	8,400
Interest expense	1,500
Insurance expense	1,000
Depreciation expense	600
Supplies expense	550
Total expenses	113,050
Net Income	$ 53,850

Most published financial statements are highly condensed. Appendix A at the end of the book gives the income statement of Target Corporation. Of course, condensed statements can be supplemented with desired details.

TWO KEY RATIOS FOR DECISION MAKING

Merchandise inventory is the most important asset for a merchandising business. To manage the firm, owners and managers focus on the best way to sell the inventory. They use several ratios to evaluate operations, among them gross profit percentage and rate of inventory turnover.

The Gross Profit Percentage

A key decision-making tool for a merchandiser is related to gross profit, which is net sales minus cost of goods sold. Merchandisers strive to increase the **gross profit percentage,** which is computed as follows:

$$\text{Gross profit percentage} = \frac{\text{Gross profit}}{\text{Net sales revenue}} = \frac{\$75,100}{\$165,900} = 0.453 = 45.3\%$$

The gross profit percentage (also called the *gross margin percentage*) is one of the most carefully watched measures of profitability. A 45% gross margin means that each dollar of sales generates 45 cents of gross profit. On average, the goods cost the seller 55 cents. For most firms, the gross profit percentage changes little from year to year. A small increase may signal an important rise in income, and vice versa for a decrease.

Exhibit 5-10 compares **Austin Sound's** gross margin to that of both **Target** and **Wal-Mart.**

EXHIBIT 5-10
**Gross Profit on $1 of Sales
for Three Merchandisers**

The Rate of Inventory Turnover

INVENTORY TURNOVER. Ratio of cost of goods sold to average inventory. Measures the number of times a company sells its average level of inventory during a year.

Owners and managers strive to sell inventory as quickly as possible because it generates no profit until it is sold. The faster the sales occur, the higher the income. The slower the sales, the lower the income. Ideally, a business could operate with zero inventory. Most businesses, however, including retailers such as Target and Austin Sound, must keep goods on hand. **Inventory turnover,** the ratio of cost of goods sold to average inventory, indicates how rapidly inventory is sold. It is computed as follows:

$$\frac{\text{Inventory}}{\text{turnover}} = \frac{\text{Cost of goods sold}}{\text{Average inventory}} = \frac{\text{Cost of goods sold}}{(\text{Beginning inventory} + \text{Ending inventory})/2}$$

$$= \frac{\$90,800}{(\$38,600^* + \$40,200)/2} = \frac{2.3 \text{ times per year}}{(\text{every } 159 \text{ days})}$$

*Taken from balance sheet at the end of the preceding period.

DAILY EXERCISE 5-17

DAILY EXERCISE 5-18

Inventory turnover is usually computed for an annual period, and the relevant cost-of-goods sold figure is the amount for the entire year. Average inventory is computed from the beginning and ending balances. Austin Sound's beginning inventory would be taken from the business's balance sheet at the end of the preceding year. A high turnover rate is preferable, and an increase in the turnover rate usually means higher profits.

Inventory turnover varies from industry to industry. Grocery stores, for example, turn their goods over much faster than automobile dealers do. Drug stores have a higher turnover rate than furniture stores. Retailers of electronic products, such as Austin Sound, have an average turnover of 3.6 times per year. A turnover rate of 2.3 times per year suggests that Austin Sound is not very successful. Exhibit 5-11 compares the inventory turnover rate of Austin Sound, Target, and Wal-Mart Stores.

Varsitybooks.com: A Textbook Case on the Fulfillment Cost Conundrum

Order the fifth edition of *Accounting* from **Varsitybooks.com** and the company arranges for **Baker & Taylor**—book distributors—to ship it to you immediately.

Varsitybooks doesn't have a warehouse or any inventory, but it does have to pay Baker & Taylor for this convenient arrangement. How does the fledgling dot.com account for these costs?

As you know from personal experience, e-commerce has revolutionized business. It has bent certain accounting rules in the process. One such rule is that the cost of goods sold to customers is usually considered the "cost of goods sold." Yet, on-line powerhouses like Amazon.com and eToys, Inc. count some of this cost as "sales and marketing expenses because they never own the inventory." By listing these "fulfillment costs" as marketing expense, new-age companies don't have to subtract the costs from their gross profit. This seemed like a good idea to Varsitybooks, and its managers announced to their auditor, **KPMG**, that they wanted to do the same.

After all, Varsitybooks argued, mail-order companies have always done this. And the practice would allow the new agers to keep from reporting razor-thin profit margins. For instance, if the SEC tightens the rules and makes Amazon.com account for fulfillment cost as "cost of sales," gross profit margins for the last quarter of 1999 would go from 15% to −3%.

Small wonder that this approach is controversial! Varsitybooks.com fired KPMG when the auditors objected to it. They hired **PricewaterhouseCoopers** instead, but in the end Varsitybooks had to follow the traditional accounting procedures anyway. The auditors knew best after all.

Source: Based on Shannon Henry, "An E-Tail Identity Crisis," *The Washington Post,* May 4, 2000, p. E01. Anonymous, "Web Retailers' "Gross Profit" Questioned; E-commerce; The SEC may make some firms account for distribution costs, possibly turning their profits into losses," *The Los Angeles Times,* February 19, 2000, p. 2.

Exhibits 5-10 and 5-11 tell an interesting story. Wal-Mart sells a lot of inventory at a low gross profit percentage. Wal-Mart earns its profits by turning its inventory over rapidly—7.0 times during the year. Target sells slightly more upscale merchandise and therefore turns its inventory over only 6.3 times per year.

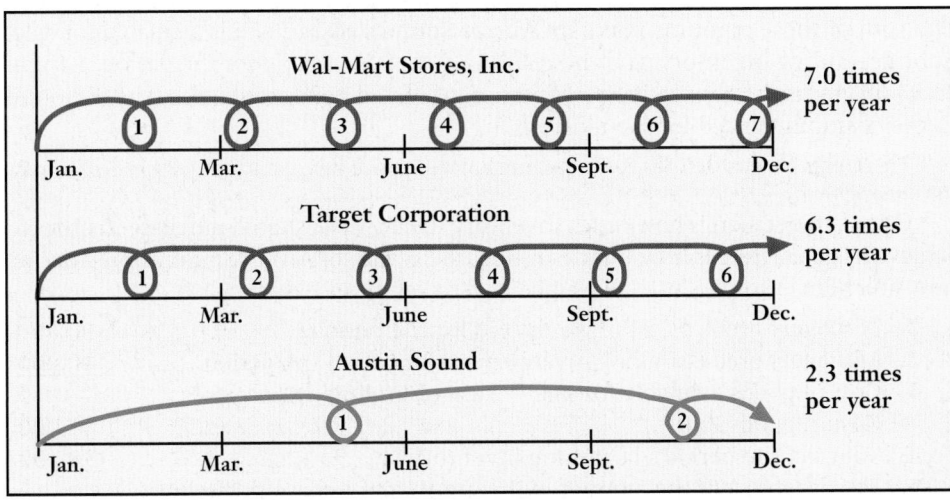

EXHIBIT 5-11
Rate of Inventory Turnover for Three Merchandisers

Calculate the rate of inventory turnover for **Safeway, Inc.,** the large grocery chain (amounts in millions).

Beginning inventory..............	$ 1,856
Ending inventory..................	2,445
Cost of goods sold................	20,349

Answer

$$\text{Inventory turnover} = \frac{\text{Cost of goods sold}}{\text{(Beginning inventory + Ending inventory)/2}}$$

$$= \frac{\$20,349}{(\$1,856 + \$2,445)/2} = 9.5 \text{ times per year}$$

THE PERIODIC SYSTEM: MEASURING COST OF GOODS SOLD AND INVENTORY PURCHASES

Objective 6
Compute cost of goods sold

The perpetual inventory accounting system we have illustrated provides up-to-date records of inventory and cost of goods sold. That system aids both day-to-day decisions and the preparation of the financial statements. However, managers have other information needs that the perpetual system does not meet. For example, buyers for **Target** and **Austin Sound** must know how much inventory to purchase in order to reach their sales goals.

Computation of cost of goods sold from the periodic inventory system helps managers determine how much inventory to purchase. This alternative computation is used so often in accounting that your education would be incomplete without it. (The appendix at the end of the chapter covers the periodic inventory system in more detail.)

EXHIBIT 5-12
Measuring Austin Sound's Cost of Goods Sold in the Periodic Inventory System

Beginning inventory....................................	$ 38,600
+ **Net purchases**.......................................	87,200*
+ Freight in	5,200
= Cost of goods available for sale..................	131,000
− Ending inventory......................................	(40,200)
= Cost of goods sold	$ 90,800
*Computation of **Net purchases:**	
Purchases...	$ 91,400
− Purchase discounts	(3,000)
− Purchase returns and allowances	(1,200)
= Net purchases	$ 87,200

DAILY EXERCISE 5-19

DAILY EXERCISE 5-20

DAILY EXERCISE 5-21

NET PURCHASES. Purchases less purchase discounts and purchase returns and allowances.

Exhibit 5–12 gives the alternative computation of Austin Sound's cost of goods sold for 20X2. Austin Sound began the year with inventory of $38,600. During the year, it purchased more goods, also paying freight charges. Note that **net purchases** equals purchases minus purchase discounts and purchase returns and allowances. The sum of these amounts make up Austin Sound's cost of goods available for sale. Subtract ending inventory, and the result is cost of goods sold for the period. Exhibit 5–13 diagrams the alternative computation of cost of goods sold, with Austin Sound Center's amounts used for the illustration.

The Decision Guidelines feature summarizes some key decisions of a merchandising business.

One such decision is how much inventory the business should purchase in order to achieve its goals. Here is how Charles Ernest, the owner of Austin Sound, would decide how much inventory to buy (all numbers are taken from Exhibit 5-12):

1. Managers predict Cost of goods sold for the period...................... $ 90,800
2. Managers predict Ending inventory at the end of the period........ 40,200
3. Cost of goods available for sale = Sum of Ending inventory + Cost of goods sold 131,000
4. Subtract the period's beginning inventory .... (38,200)
5. The difference is the amount of inventory to purchase (including Freight in) during the coming year .... $ 92,000

EXHIBIT 5-13 Relationship Between the Inventory Account and Cost of Goods Sold in the Periodic Inventory System (Amounts for Austin Sound)

INVENTORY			
Beginning balance	38,600		
Net purchases	87,200		
Freight in	5,200	Cost of goods sold	90,800
Ending balance	40,200		

This T-account shows that the *perpetual* and the *periodic* inventory systems compute the same amounts for ending inventory and for cost of goods sold:

- The *perpetual* system accumulates the balances of Inventory and Cost of Goods Sold throughout the period.
- The *periodic* system determines the correct amounts for Inventory and Cost of Goods Sold only at the end of the period.

Source: The authors thank Betsy Willis for suggesting this exhibit.

DECISION GUIDELINES

Merchandising Operations and the Accounting Cycle

DECISION	GUIDELINES
How do merchandising operations differ from service operations?	• Merchandisers buy and sell *merchandise inventory* • Service entities perform a *service*.

Balance sheet:

How do a merchandiser's financial statements differ from the financial statements of a service business?	• Merchandiser has *inventory,* an asset. • Service business has no inventory.

Income Statement:

Merchandiser

Sales revenue	$ XXX
– Cost of goods sold	(X)
= Gross profit	XX
– Operating expenses.............	(X)
= Net income	$ X

Service Business

Service revenue......................	$XX
– Operating expenses	(X)
= Net income.........................	$ X

Statements of Owner's Equity:

No difference

Which type of inventory system to use?

- *Perpetual system* shows the amount of *inventory* on hand (the asset) and the cost of goods sold (the expense) at all times.
- *Periodic system* shows the correct balances of inventory and cost of goods sold only after a physical count of the inventory, which occurs at least once each year.

How do the adjusting and closing processes of merchandisers and service entities differ?

Very little. The merchandiser may have to *adjust* the Inventory account for spoilage and theft. The merchandiser must *close* the Cost of Goods Sold account. Service entities have no inventory to adjust or cost of goods sold to close.

DECISION GUIDELINES (CONT.)

How to format the merchandiser's income statement?

Multi-step Format

Sales revenue	$ XXX
− Cost of goods sold	(X)
= Gross profit	$ XX
− Operating expenses	(X)
+ Other revenues	X
= Net income	$ XX

Single-step Format

Revenues:	
Sales revenue	$ XXX
Other revenues	X
Total revenues	XXXX
Expenses:	
Cost of goods sold	(X)
Operating expenses	(X)
Total expenses	XX
Net income	$ XX

How to evaluate inventory operations?

Two key ratios: Gross profit percentage* $= \dfrac{\text{Gross profit}}{\text{Net sales revenue}}$

Inventory turnover* $= \dfrac{\text{Cost of goods sold}}{\text{Average inventory}}$

*In most cases—the higher, the better

How to determine the amount of cost of goods sold?

Can use the *cost of goods sold* model (assumed amounts):

Beginning inventory	$100
+ Net purchases and freight in	800
= Cost of goods available	900
− Ending inventory	(200)
= Cost of goods sold	$700

REVIEW MERCHANDISING OPERATIONS

SUMMARY PROBLEM

www.prenhall.com/horngren

End-of-Chapter Assessment

The following trial balance and additional data are related to Jan King Distributing Company.

JAN KING DISTRIBUTING COMPANY
Trial Balance
December 31, 20X3

Cash	$ 5,670	
Accounts receivable	37,100	
Inventory	60,500	
Supplies	3,930	
Prepaid rent	6,000	
Furniture and fixtures	26,500	
Accumulated depreciation		$ 21,200
Accounts payable		46,340
Salary payable		
Interest payable		
Unearned sales revenue		3,500
Note payable, long-term		35,000
Jan King, capital		23,680
Jan King, withdrawals	48,000	
Sales revenue		346,700
Sales discounts	10,300	
Sales returns and allowances	8,200	
Cost of goods sold	171,770	
Salary expense	82,750	
Rent expense	7,000	
Depreciation expense		
Utilities expense	5,800	
Supplies expense		
Interest expense	2,900	
Total	$476,420	$476,420

Additional data at December 31, 20X3:

a. Supplies used during the year, $2,580.

b. Prepaid rent in force, $1,000.

c. Unearned sales revenue still not earned, $2,400.

d. Depreciation. The furniture and fixtures' estimated useful life is 10 years, and they are expected to be worthless when they are retired from service.

e. Accrued salaries, $1,300.

f. Accrued interest expense, $600.

g. Inventory on hand, $65,800.

Required

1. Enter the trial balance on a work sheet and complete the work sheet.

2. Journalize the adjusting and closing entries at December 31. Post to the Income Summary account as an accuracy check on the entries affecting that account. The credit balance closed out of Income Summary should equal net income computed on the work sheet.

3. Prepare the company's multi-step income statement, statement of owner's equity, and balance sheet in account format. Draw arrows linking the statements.

4. Compute the inventory turnover for 20X3. Inventory at December 31, 20X2, was $61,000. Turnover for 20X2 was 2.1 times. Would you expect Jan King Distributing Company to be more profitable or less profitable in 20X3 than in 20X2? Give your reason.

Solution

Requirement 1

JAN KING DISTRIBUTING COMPANY
Accounting Work Sheet (Perpetual Inventory System)
Year Ended December 31, 20X3

Account Title	Trial Balance Debit	Trial Balance Credit	Adjustments Debit	Adjustments Credit	Income Statement Debit	Income Statement Credit	Balance Sheet Debit	Balance Sheet Credit
Cash............................	5,670						5,670	
Accounts receivable	37,100						37,100	
Inventory	60,500		(g) 5,300				65,800	
Supplies.......................	3,930			(a) 2,580			1,350	
Prepaid rent.................	6,000			(b) 5,000			1,000	
Furniture and fixtures....................	26,500						26,500	
Accumulated depreciation.............		21,200		(d) 2,650				23,850
Accounts payable		46,340						46,340
Salary payable				(e) 1,300				1,300
Interest payable...........				(f) 600				600
Unearned sales revenue....................		3,500	(c) 1,100					2,400
Note payable, long-term.................		35,000						35,000
Jan King, capital..........		23,680						23,680
Jan King, withdrawals	48,000						48,000	
Sales revenue		346,700		(c) 1,100		347,800		
Sales discounts	10,300				10,300			
Sales returns and allowances	8,200				8,200			
Cost of goods sold........	171,770			(g) 5,300	166,470			
Salary expense	82,750		(e) 1,300		84,050			
Rent expense...............	7,000		(b) 5,000		12,000			
Depreciation expense....................			(d) 2,650		2,650			
Utilities expense	5,800				5,800			
Supplies expense.........			(a) 2,580		2,580			
Interest expense	2,900		(f) 600		3,500			
	476,420	476,420	18,530	18,530	295,550	347,800	185,420	133,170
Net income..................					52,250			52,250
					347,800	347,800	185,420	185,420

Requirement 2

Adjusting Entries

20X3

Dec. 31	Supplies Expense		2,580	
	Supplies			2,580
31	Rent Expense		5,000	
	Prepaid Rent			5,000
31	Unearned Sales Revenue ($3,500 − $2,400)		1,100	
	Sales Revenue			1,100
31	Depreciation Expense ($26,500/10)		2,650	
	Accumulated Depreciation			2,650
31	Salary Expense		1,300	
	Salary Payable			1,300
31	Interest Expense		600	
	Interest Payable			600
31	Inventory ($65,800 − $60,500)		5,300*	
	Cost of Goods Sold			5,300

*Excess of inventory on hand over the balance in the Inventory account. This adjustment brings Inventory to its correct balance.

Closing Entries

20X3

Dec. 31	Sales Revenue		347,800	
	Income Summary			347,800
31	Income Summary		295,550	
	Sales Discounts			10,300
	Sales Returns and Allowances			8,200
	Cost of Goods Sold			166,470
	Salary Expense			84,050
	Rent Expense			12,000
	Depreciation Expense			2,650
	Utilities Expense			5,800
	Supplies Expense			2,580
	Interest Expense			3,500
31	Income Summary ($347,800 − $295,550)		52,250	
	Jan King, Capital			52,250
31	Jan King, Capital		48,000	
	Jan King, Withdrawals			48,000

INCOME SUMMARY			
Clo.	295,550	Clo.	347,800
Clo.	52,250	Bal.	52,250

Requirement 3

JAN KING DISTRIBUTING COMPANY
Income Statement
Year Ended December 31, 20X3

Sales revenue..		$347,800	
Less: Sales discounts....................................	$(10,300)		
Sales returns and allowances	(8,200)	(18,500)	
Net sales revenue......................................			329,300
Cost of goods sold...			166,470
Gross profit			162,830
Operating expenses:			
Salary expense	$ 84,050		
Rent expense..	12,000		
Utilities expense.......................................	5,800		
Depreciation expense...............................	2,650		
Supplies expense......................................	2,580	107,080	
Income from operations			55,750
Other expense:			
Interest expense...			3,500
Net income			$ 52,250

JAN KING DISTRIBUTING COMPANY
Statement of Owner's Equity
Year Ended December 31, 20X3

Jan King, capital, December 31, 20X2...............	$23,680
Add: Net income	52,250
	75,930
Less: Withdrawals	(48,000)
Jan King, capital, December 31, 20X3	$27,930

JAN KING DISTRIBUTING COMPANY
Balance Sheet
December 31, 20X3

Assets			Liabilities		
Current:			Current:		
Cash		$ 5,670	Accounts payable		$ 46,340
Accounts receivable		37,100	Salary payable....................		1,300
Inventory		65,800	Interest payable		600
Supplies..............................		1,350	Unearned sales revenue.....		2,400
Prepaid rent........................		1,000	Total current liabilities		50,640
Total current assets		110,920	Long-term:		
Plant:			Note payable		35,000
Furniture and					
fixtures............	$26,500		Total liabilities........................		85,640
Less:					
Accumulated					
depreciation...	(23,850)	2,650	**Owner's Equity**		
			Jan King, capital....................		27,930
			Total liabilities and owner's		
Total assets		$113,570	equity................................		$113,570

Requirement 4

$$\text{Inventory turnover} = \frac{\text{Cost of goods sold}}{\text{Average inventory}} = \frac{\$166,470}{(\$61,000 + \$65,800)/2} = \textbf{2.6 times}$$

The increase in the rate of inventory turnover from 2.1 to 2.6 suggests higher profits in 20X3 than in 20X2.

LESSONS LEARNED

1. *Use sales and gross profit to evaluate a company.* The major revenue of a merchandising business is *sales revenue,* or *sales.* The major expense is *cost of goods sold.* Net sales minus cost of goods sold is *gross profit,* or *gross margin.* This amount measures the business's success or failure in selling its products at a higher price than it paid for them.

2. *Account for the purchase and sale of inventory.* The merchandiser's major asset is inventory. In a merchandising entity, the accounting cycle is from cash to inventory as the inventory is purchased for resale, and back to cash as the inventory is sold. The *invoice* is the business document generated by a purchase or sale transaction. Most merchandising entities allow customers to *return* unsuitable merchandise and also offer *discounts* for early payment. They grant *allowances* for damaged goods that the buyer chooses to keep. Returns and Allowances and Discounts are contra accounts to Sales Revenue.

3. *Adjust and close the accounts of a merchandising business.* The end-of-period adjusting and closing process of a merchandising business is similar to that of a service business. In addition, a merchandiser adjusts inventory for theft losses, damage, and accounting errors.

4. *Prepare a merchandiser's financial statements.* The income statement may appear in *single-step format* or *multi-step format.* A single-step income statement has only two sections—one for revenues and the other for expenses—and a single income amount for net income. A multi-step income statement has subtotals for gross profit and income from operations. Both formats are widely used.

5. *Use the gross profit percentage and the inventory turnover ratio to evaluate a business:* Two key decision aids for a merchandiser are the *gross profit percentage* (gross profit/net sales revenue) and the *rate of inventory turnover* (cost of goods sold/average inventory). Increases in these measures usually signal an increase in profits.

6. *Compute cost of goods sold.* Cost of goods sold is the cost of the inventory that the business has sold. It is the largest single expense of most merchandising businesses. Cost of goods sold is the sum of the cost of goods sold amounts recorded during the period. In a periodic inventory system, Cost of goods sold = Beginning inventory + Purchases + Freight in − Ending inventory.

ACCOUNTING VOCABULARY

cost of goods sold (p 168)
cost of sales (p. 168)
gross margin (p. 169)
gross margin percentage (p. 185)
gross profit (p. 169)
gross profit percentage (p. 185)
income from operations (p. 183)
inventory (p. 167)
inventory turnover (p. 186)
invoice (p. 171)

multi-step income statement (p. 185)
net purchases (p. 188)
net sales (p. 168)
operating expenses (p. 183)
operating income (p. 183)
other expense (p. 183)
other revenue (p. 183)
periodic inventory system (p. 169)

perpetual inventory system (p. 170)
sales (p. 168)
sales discount (p. 176)
sales returns and allowances (p. 176)
sales revenue (p. 168)
single-step income statement (p. 185)

QUESTIONS

1. Gross profit is often mentioned in the business press as an important measure of success. What does gross profit measure, and why is it important?

2. Describe the operating cycle for (a) the purchase and cash sale of inventory, and (b) the purchase and sale of inventory on account.

3. Identify ten items of information on an invoice.

4. Indicate which accounts are debited and credited for (a) a credit purchase of inventory and the subsequent cash payment, and (b) a credit sale of inventory and the subsequent cash collection. Assume no discounts, returns, allowances, or freight.

5. Inventory costing $1,000 is purchased and invoiced on July 28 under terms of 3/10 n/30. Compute the payment amount on August 6. How much would the payment be on August 9? What explains the difference? What is the latest acceptable payment date under the terms of sale?

6. Name the new contra accounts introduced in this chapter.

7. Why is the title Cost of Goods Sold especially descriptive? What type of account is Cost of Goods Sold?

8. Beginning inventory is $5,000, net purchases total $30,000, and freight in is $1,000. If ending inventory is $8,000, what is the cost of goods sold?

9. You are beginning the adjusting and closing process at the end of your company's fiscal year. Does the trial balance carry the final ending amount of inventory? Why or why not?

10. Give the adjusting entry for inventory if shrinkage is $9,100.

11. Name and describe two formats for the income statement, and identify the type of business to which each format best applies.

12. Which financial statement reports sales discounts and sales returns and allowances? Show how they are reported, using any reasonable amounts in your illustration.

13. Does a merchandiser prefer a high or a low rate of inventory turnover? Explain.

14. In general, what does a decreasing gross profit percentage, coupled with an increasing rate of inventory turnover, suggest about a business's pricing strategy?

DAILY EXERCISES

DE5-1 Refer to Exhibit 5-1, page 168, **Target Corporation's** income statement. Identify the title and the amount of Target's

  a. Revenue before subtracting any expenses
  b. Excess of sales revenue over cost of goods sold
  c. Bottom-line operating performance

Using sales, gross profit, and net income to evaluate a company (Obj. 1)

DE5-2 Compare the income statements of two merchandisers:

  • **Target Corporation** (Exhibit 5-1, page 168)
  • **Austin Sound Center** (Exhibit 5-7, page 182)

For every item on the Target income statement, give the title and the amount of the same item on Austin Sound's income statement. You can ignore Target's four individual *expenses* and the related total of $9,039 million.

Using sales, cost of goods sold, gross profit, and net income (Obj. 1)

DE5-3 Refer to Target's income statement in Exhibit 5-1. Give some alternative titles for the following items:

  • Net sales revenue   • Gross profit
  • Cost of goods sold   • Net earnings

Using merchandising terminology (Obj. 1)

DE5-4 You may have shopped at a **Gap** store. Suppose Gap purchases 2,000 pairs of slacks on account for $45,000. Credit terms are 2/10 n/30. As part of this shipment, the supplier, Miralu Products of Hong Kong, shipped $8,000 worth of defective merchandise, which Gap rejected and sent back. Gap then paid the balance within the discount period.
Journalize the following transactions for Gap:

  a. Purchase of inventory.   **c.** Payment within the discount period.
  b. Return of defective goods.

Recording purchase, purchase return, and cash payment transactions (Obj. 2)

DE5-5 **Toys "Я" Us** purchases inventory from a variety of suppliers, including **Mattel, Hasbro,** and **Tonka.** Suppose Toys "Я" Us buys $150,000 worth of **Lego** toys on credit terms of 3/15 n/45. Unfortunately, the goods are damaged in shipment, so Toys "Я" Us returns $20,000 (original amount, before any discounts) of the merchandise to Lego.
    How much must Toys "Я" Us pay Lego

  a. After the discount period?   **b.** Within the discount period?

Accounting for the purchase of inventory—quantity discount (Obj. 2)

DE5-6 Refer to the **Toys " Я " Us** situation in Daily Exercise 5-5 and journalize the following transactions on the books of Toys "Я"Us. Explanations are not required.

  a. Original purchase of the goods on May 6, 20X1.
  b. Return of the damaged goods on May 13.
  c. Payment on May 15. Before journalizing this transaction, it is helpful to post the first two transactions to the Accounts Payable T-account.

Recording purchase, purchase return, and cash payment transactions (Obj. 2)

DE5-7 Suppose a **Lord & Taylor** store purchases $140,000 of women's sportswear on account from **Liz Claiborne, Inc.** Credit terms are 2/10 net 30. Lord & Taylor pays electronically, and Liz Claiborne receives the money on the tenth day.
    Journalize Lord & Taylor's (a) purchase and (b) payment transactions. What was Lord & Taylor's net cost of this inventory?

Note: Daily Exercise 5-8 covers this same situation for the seller.

Recording purchase transactions (Obj. 2)

DE5-8 **Liz Claiborne, Inc.,** sells $140,000 of women's sportswear to a **Lord & Taylor** store under credit terms of 2/10 net 30. Liz Claiborne's cost of the goods is $82,000, and Claiborne receives the appropriate amount of cash from Lord & Taylor on the tenth day.
    Journalize Liz Claiborne's (a) sale, (b) cost of goods sold, and (c) cash receipt. How much gross profit did Liz Claiborne earn on this sale?

Note: Daily Exercise 5-7 covers the same situation for the buyer.

Recording sales, cost of goods sold, and cash collections (Obj. 2)

Recording sale, sales return, and cash collection entries
(Obj. 2)

DE5-9 Refer to the **Gap/Miralu Products** situation in Daily Exercise 5-4. Record the three transactions on the books of the seller, Miralu Products. Assume Miralu keeps its records in U.S. dollars and that the goods cost Miralu $22,500. Miralu's transactions are

a. Sale of inventory and the related cost of goods sold.
b. The $8,000 sales return and the related receipt of defective goods (cost, $4,000) from the purchaser.
c. Collection of cash within the discount period.

Computing net sales and gross profit
(Obj. 2)

DE5-10 **Intel Corporation,** famous for the Pentium© processor that powers many personal computers, offers sales discounts to the computer companies to which Intel sells its products. Intel also allows its customers to return defective processors. Suppose that during a recent period, Intel made sales of $600,000 on credit terms of 2/10 net 30. Assume that Intel received sales returns of $12,000. Later, Intel collected cash within the discount period. Cost of goods sold for the period was $255,000 after all sales returns.

For this particular period, compute Intel's

a. Net sales revenue   b. Gross profit

Adjusting the accounts of a merchandiser
(Obj. 3)

DE5-11 Examine the work sheet of **Austin Sound Center** in Exhibit 5-6, page 181. Focus on adjusting entries (a) and (b). Which entry is exactly the same as for a service company? Which entry relates to a merchandiser only? Explain the reason for the merchandiser's adjusting entry.

Using a merchandiser's financial statements
(Obj. 4)

DE5-12 Examine the financial statements of **Austin Sound Center** in Exhibit 5-7, page 182. Identify every item, including subtotals and totals, that relates exclusively to a merchandiser and will not appear in the financial statements of a service entity.

Note: An early-payment discount, similar to a sales discount, can relate to a service entity because a service business can allow its customers to take a discount for early payment.

Preparing a merchandiser's income statement
(Obj. 4)

DE5-13 **Dell Computer Corporation** reported these figures in its January 31, 2000, financial statements (adapted, and in millions):

Cash	$ 3,809	Other assets (long-term)	$ 3,025
Total operating expenses	3,552	Other current liabilities	1,654
Accounts payable	3,538	Property and equipment, net	765
Owners' equity	5,308	Net sales revenue	25,265
Long-term liabilities	971	Other current assets	873
Inventory	391	Accounts receivable	2,608
Cost of goods sold	20,047		

Prepare Dell's multi-step income statement for the year ended January 31, 2000.

Preparing a merchandiser's balance sheet
(Obj. 4)

DE5-14 Use the data in Daily Exercise 5-13 to prepare **Dell Computer's** classified balance sheet at January 31, 2000. Use the report format with all headings, and list accounts in proper order.

Making closing entries
(Obj. 3)

DE5-15 Refer to the work sheet of **Austin Sound Center** in Exhibit 5-6, page 181. Based solely on the Income Statement columns of the work sheet, make two closing entries, as follows:

• Journalize the closing entry for the *first account* listed that must be closed at the end of the period.
• Journalize the closing entry for the *last account* listed on the work sheet (not net income, which is not an account).

All closing entries for revenues and expenses follow the pattern of the closing entries you just made. Now make the final two closing entries of Austin Sound Center:

• Journalize the closing entry for the Owner's Withdrawals account.
• Journalize the closing entry for net income.

Set up a T-account for the Owner's Capital account, and insert the balance from the work sheet. Then post your closing entries to the Capital account. Its ending balance should be the same as the amount reported on Austin Sound's balance sheet in Exhibit 5-7 on page 182. Is it?

DE5-16 Refer to the income statement of **Target Corporation** in Exhibit 5-1, page 168.

Closing the accounts
(Obj. 3)

1. Identify every account on Target's income statement that the company will close out at the end of the year. Make two closing entries for these accounts at January 31, 2000:

   • Close the revenue   • Close the expenses

2. Target's balance sheet reports the following selected accounts:

   • Inventory   • Long-term debt
   • Accounts payable   • Other assets
   • Land   • Owners' equity

Which of these accounts does Target close, if any? Give your reason.

DE5-17 Refer to the **Dell Computer** situation in Daily Exercise 5-13. Compute Dell's gross profit percentage and rate of inventory turnover for 2000. One year earlier, at January 31, 1999, Dell's inventory balance was $320 million.

Computing the gross profit percentage and the rate of inventory turnover (Obj. 5)

DE5-18 Lands' End, the catalog merchant, reported the following for the year ended January 31, 2000 (as adapted, with amounts in millions):

Contrasting accounting income and cash flows
(Obj. 4)

Cash collections from		Cash payments to suppliers	$ 682
customers	$1,323	Net sales revenue......................	1,320
Selling, general, and		Cost of sales	727
administrative expenses.........	529		

As an investor, you wonder which was greater, Lands' End's (a) gross profit, or (b) the company's excess of cash collections from customers over cash payments to suppliers? Compute both amounts to answer this question.

DE5-19 At January 31, 1999, **Target Corporation** had merchandise inventory of $3,475 million. During the following year, Target purchased inventory costing $23,352 million, including freight in. At January 31, 2000, Target's inventory stood at $3,798 million.

Computing cost of goods sold in a periodic inventory system (Obj. 6)

1. Compute Target's cost of goods sold as in the periodic inventory system.
2. Compare your cost-of-goods-sold figure to Exhibit 5-1, page 000. The two amounts should be equal. Are they?

DE5-20 Les Fleurs, a boutique in Paris, France, had the following accounts in its accounting records at December 31, 20X2 (amounts in French francs, denoted as "F"):

Computing net sales, cost of goods sold and gross profit in a periodic inventory system (Obj. 6)

Purchases.............................	F250,000	Freight in................................	F 8,000
Sales discounts......................	4,000	Purchase returns	7,000
Inventory:.............................		Sales	400,000
December 31, 20X1...........	20,000	Purchase discounts................	3,000
December 31, 20X2...........	30,000	Sales returns..........................	8,000

Compute the following for Les Fleurs during 20X2:

1. Net sales revenue   2. Cost of goods sold   3. Gross profit

DE5-21 Gap Inc., reported Cost of Goods Sold totaling $6,775 million. Ending inventory was $1,462 million, and beginning inventory was $1,056 million. How much inventory did Gap purchase during the year?

Computing inventory purchases (Obj. 6)

E5-1 Toys "Я" Us reported the following:

TOYS "Я" US, INC.
Statements of Earnings (adapted)

(In millions)	January 31, 2000	January 31, 1999
	Fiscal Years Ended	
Net sales..	$11,862	$11,170
Costs and expenses:		
Cost of sales	8,321	8,191
Other expenses..	3,262	3,111
Net earnings (net loss)..	$ 279	$ (132)

TOYS "Я" US, INC.
Balance Sheets (partial, adapted)

Assets (In millions)	January 31, 2000	January 31, 1999
Current Assets:		
Cash and cash equivalents...	$ 584	$ 410
Accounts and other receivables....................................	182	204
Merchandise inventories	2,027	1,902
Prepaid expenses and other current assets....................	80	81
Total Current Assets..	$2,873	$2,597

Required

1. Is Toys "Я" Us a merchandising entity, a service business, or both? How can you tell? List the items in the Toys "Я" Us financial statements that influence your answer.
2. Compute Toys "Я" Us's gross profit for fiscal years 2000 and 1999. Did the gross profit increase or decrease in 2000? Is this a good sign or a bad sign about the company?
3. Write a brief memo to investors advising them of Toys "Я" Us's trend of sales, gross profit, and net income. Indicate whether the outlook for Toys "Я" Us is favorable or unfavorable, based on this trend. Use the following memo format:

Date:	_____
To:	Investors
From:	Student Name
Subject:	Trend of sales, gross profit and net income for Toys " Я " Us

E5-2 Journalize, without explanations, the following transactions of Lane's Fine Gifts during the month of September:

Sept. 3   Purchased $1,900 of inventory on account under terms of 2/10 n/eom (end of month) and FOB shipping point.

7   Returned $300 of defective merchandise purchased on September 3.

9   Paid freight bill of $30 on September 3 purchase.

10   Sold inventory on account for $3,100. Payment terms on the remainder were 2/15 n/30. These goods cost Lane's Fine Gifts $1,700.

12   Paid amount owed on credit purchase of September 3, less the discount and the return.

16   Granted a sales allowance of $800 on the September 10 sale.

23   Received cash from September 10 customer in full settlement of her debt, less the allowance and the discount.

E5-3 As the proprietor of Stevens Goodyear Tire Co., you receive the following invoice from a supplier:

BELTLINE TIRE WHOLESALE DISTRIBUTORS, INC.
2600 Commonwealth Avenue
Boston, Massachusetts 02215

Invoice date: May 14, 20X3

Payment terms: 2/10 n/30

Sold to: Stevens Goodyear Tire Co.
4219 Crestwood Parkway
Lexington, Mass. 02173

Quantity Ordered	Description	Quantity Shipped	Price	Amount
4	P135–X4 Radials	4	$37.14	$ 148.56
8	L912 Belted-bias	8	41.32	330.56
14	R39 Truck tires	10	50.02	500.20
	Total			$979.32

Due date:	Amount:
May 24, 20X3	$959.73
May 25 through June 13, 20X3	$979.32

Paid:

Required

1. Stevens received the invoice on May 15. Record the May 15 purchase on account. Carry to the nearest cent throughout.
2. The R39 truck tires were ordered by mistake and were therefore returned to Beltline. Journalize the return on May 19.
3. Record the May 22 payment of the amount owed.

E5-4 On April 30, De Boulle Jewelers purchased inventory of $8,000 on account from Intergem Jewels, a jewelry importer. Terms were 3/15 net 45. On receiving the goods, De Boulle checked the order and found $800 of unsuitable merchandise. De Boulle returned $800 of the merchandise to Intergem on May 4.

Journalizing purchase transactions (Obj. 2)

To pay the remaining amount owed, De Boulle borrowed the net amount of the invoice from the bank. On May 14, De Boulle signed a short-term note payable to the bank and immediately paid the borrowed funds to Intergem. On June 14, De Boulle paid the bank the net amount of the invoice, which De Boulle had borrowed plus 1% monthly interest (round to the nearest dollar).

Required

Record the indicated transactions in the journal of De Boulle Jewelers. Explanations are not required.

E5-5 Refer to the business situation in Exercise 5-4. Journalize the transactions of Intergem Jewels. Intergem's gross profit is 40%, so cost of goods sold is 60% of sales. Explanations are not required.

Journalizing sales transactions (Obj. 2)

E5-6 The Home Depot is one of the largest retailers in the United States. For a recent year, The Home Depot's accounting records carried the following accounts (adapted, with amounts in millions) at January 31, 2000:

Making closing entries (Obj. 3)

Receivables	$ 587	Selling expense	$ 6,832
Interest revenue	37	Sales revenue	38,434
Accounts payable	1,993	Interest expense	28
Cost of goods sold	27,023	Merchandise inventories	5,489
Other expense	1,597	General and administrative	
Owner withdrawals	255	expense	671

Required

1. Journalize all of The Home Depot's closing entries at January 31, 2000. Use an Owner Capital account.

2. Set up T-accounts for the Income Summary account and the Owner Capital account. Post to these accounts and take their ending balances. One year earlier, at January 31, 1999, the Owner Capital balance was $8,740 million.

Using work sheet data to make the closing entries (Obj. 3)

E5-7 The trial balance and adjustments columns of the work sheet of Northstar Auto Supply at March 31, 20X2 follow.

Account Title	Trial Balance		Adjustments	
	Debit	Credit	Debit	Credit
Cash..	2,000			
Accounts receivable............................	8,500		(a) 6,100	
Inventory...	36,100			(b) 4,290
Supplies	13,000			(c) 8,600
Equipment...	42,470			
Accumulated depreciation..................		11,250		(d) 2,250
Accounts payable..................................		9,300		
Salary payable				(e) 1,200
Note payable, long-term......................		7,500		
Jack Potter, capital..............................		33,920		
Jack Potter, withdrawals......................	45,000			
Sales revenue..		233,000		(a) 6,100
Sales discounts.....................................	2,000			
Cost of goods sold...............................	111,600		(b) 4,290	
Selling expense.....................................	21,050		(c) 5,200	
			(e) 1,200	
General expense	10,500		(c) 3,400	
			(d) 2,250	
Interest expense...................................	2,750			
Total...	294,970	294,970	22,440	22,440

Compute the adjusted balance for each account that must be closed. Then journalize Northstar's closing entries at March 31, 20X2. How much was Northstar's net income or net loss?

Preparing a multi-step income statement (Obj. 4)

E5-8 Use the data in Exercise 5-7 to prepare the multi-step income statement of Northstar Auto Supply for the year ended March 31, 20X2.

Using the gross profit percentage and the rate of inventory turnover to evaluate profitability (Obj. 5)

E5-9 Refer to Exercise 5-8. After completing Northstar's income statement for the year ended March 31, 20X2, compute these ratios to evaluate Northstar's performance:

- Gross profit percentage
- Inventory turnover (Ending inventory one year earlier, at March 31, 20X1, was $30,500.)

Compare your figures with the 20X1 gross profit percentage of 48% and the inventory turnover rate of 3.16 for 20X1. Does the two-year trend suggest that Northstar's profits are increasing or decreasing?

Preparing a merchandiser's multi-step income statement to evaluate the business (Obj. 4, 5)

E5-10 Selected amounts from the accounting records of Barringer Boats, Ltd., are listed in alphabetical order.

Accounts payable	$16,200	Owner's equity,	
Accumulated depreciation	18,700	December 31, 20X0	$126,070
Cost of goods sold	99,300	Sales discounts.................	9,000
General expenses	23,500	Sales returns	4,600
Interest revenue............................	1,500	Sales revenue	204,000
Inventory, December 31, 19X9....	21,000	Selling expenses	37,800
Inventory, December 31, 20X0....	19,400	Unearned sales revenue....	6,500

Required

1. Prepare the business's multi-step income statement for the year ended December 31, 20X0.
2. Compute the rate of inventory turnover for the year. Last year the turnover rate was 3.8 times. Does this two-year trend suggest improvement or deterioration in inventory turnover?

E5-11 Prepare Barringer Boats, Ltd.'s single-step income statement for 20X0, using the data from Exercise 5-10. Compute the gross profit percentage, and compare it with last year's gross profit percentage of 50%. Does this two-year trend in the gross profit percentage suggest better or worse profitability during the current year?

Preparing a single-step income statement to evaluate the business
(Obj. 4, 5)

E5-12 **General Motors (GM)** is a business empire, with both automotive operations and financial services. During 1999, GM's automotive operations made sales of $153 billion and had cost of goods sold totaling $127 billion. GM's automotive assets totaled $126 billion at December 31, 1999. Total automotive liabilities were $115 billion. During 1999, GM's automotive operations paid $123 billion for inventory and collected $152 billion from customers.

Comparing gross profit and cash flows
(Obj. 4)

Required

As an investor, you wonder which was greater, (a) GM's gross profit on automotive sales or (b) GM's excess of cash collections from customers over cash payments to suppliers. Compute both amounts to answer this question.

E5-13 The periodic inventory records of Barringer Boats, Ltd. include these accounts at December 31, 20X0:

Computing cost of goods sold in a periodic inventory system
(Obj. 6)

Purchases of inventory	$98,600
Purchase discounts	3,000
Purchase returns and allowances	2,000
Freight in	4,100
Inventory	19,400

One year ago, at December 31, 19X9, Barringer's inventory balance stood at $21,000.

Required

Compute Barringer's cost of goods sold for 20X0 as in the periodic inventory system.

E5-14 Supply the missing income statement amounts in each of the following situations:

Computing inventory and cost of goods sold amounts in a periodic inventory system *(Obj. 6)*

Sales	Sales Discounts	Net Sales	Beginning Inventory	Net Purchases	Ending Inventory	Cost of Goods Sold	Gross Profit
$98,300	(a)	$92,800	$32,500	$66,700	$39,400	(b)	$33,000
62,400	$2,100	(c)	27,450	43,000	(d)	$44,100	(e)
91,500	1,800	89,700	(f)	44,900	22,900	59,400	(g)
(h)	3,000	(i)	40,700	(j)	48,230	72,500	39,600

E5-15 For the year ended December 31, 20X1, Lighthouse Designs, a retailer of home-related products, reported net sales of $338 million and cost of goods sold of $154 million. The company's balance sheet at December 31, 20X0 and 20X1, reported inventories of $103 million and $129 million, respectively. How much were Lighthouse Designs' net purchases during 20X1?

Computing an actual company's net purchases
(Obj. 6)

Continuing Exercise. *This exercise completes the Amos Faraday, Consultant, situation from Exercise 2-15 of Chapter 2, Exercise 3-14 of Chapter 3, and Exercise 4-11 of Chapter 4.*

E5-16 Amos Faraday's consulting practice includes a great deal of systems consulting business. Faraday has begun selling accounting software. During January, the business completed these transactions:

Jan.	2	Completed a consulting engagement and received cash of $7,200.
	2	Prepaid three months' office rent, $1,500.
	7	Purchased accounting software inventory on account, $4,000.
	16	Paid employee salary, $1,400.
	18	Sold accounting software on account, $1,100 (cost $700).
	19	Consulted with a client for a fee of $900 on account.
	21	Paid on account, $2,000.
	24	Paid utilities, $300.
	28	Sold accounting software for cash, $600 (cost $400).
	31	Recorded these adjusting entries:
		Accrued salary expense, $1,400.
		Accounted for expiration of prepaid rent.
		Depreciation of office furniture, $200.

Required

1. Open the following selected T-accounts in the ledger: Cash; Accounts Receivable; Accounting Software Inventory; Prepaid Rent; Accumulated Depreciation; Accounts Payable; Salary Payable; Amos Faraday, Capital; Income Summary; Service Revenue; Sales Revenue; Cost of Goods Sold; Salary Expense; Rent Expense; Utilities Expense; and Depreciation Expense.
2. Journalize and post the January transactions. Key all items by date. Compute each account balance, and denote the balance as *Bal*. Journalize and post the closing entries. Denote each closing amount as Clo. After posting all closing entries, prove the equality of debits and credits in the ledger.
3. Prepare the January income statement of Amos Faraday, Consultant. Use the single-step format.

(Group A) PROBLEMS

P5-1A **Wal-Mart Stores, Inc.,** is the largest retailer in the world, with almost 4,000 stores. A key Wal-Mart advantage is its sophisticated perpetual inventory accounting system.

Required

You are the manager of a Wal-Mart store in Nashville, Tennessee. Write a one-paragraph business memo to a new employee explaining how the company accounts for the purchase and sale of merchandise inventory. Use the following heading for your memo:

Date:	_____
To:	New Employee
From:	Store Manager
Subject:	Wal-Mart's accounting system for inventories

P5-2A Assume the following transactions occurred between **Johnson & Johnson (J&J),** the healthcare products company, and **CVS Drugstores,** during February of the current year:

Feb.	6	Johnson & Johnson sold $8,000 worth of merchandise to CVS on terms of 2/10 n/30, FOB shipping point. J&J prepaid freight charges of $500 and included this amount in the invoice total. (J&J's entry to record the freight payment debits Accounts Receivable and credits Cash.) These goods cost J&J $6,100.
	10	CVS returned $900 of the merchandise purchased on February 6. J&J accounted for the $900 sales return and placed the goods back in inventory (cost, $590).
	15	CVS paid $3,000 of the invoice amount owed to J&J for the February 6 purchase, less the discount. This payment included none of the freight charge.
	27	CVS paid the remaining amount owed to J&J for the February 6 purchase.

Required

Journalize these transactions, first on the books of CVS and second on the books of Johnson & Johnson.

P5-3A Preakness Wholesale Grocery engaged in the following transactions during May:

Journalizing purchase and sale transactions
(Obj. 2)

May 3 Purchased office supplies for cash, $300.
   7 Purchased inventory on credit terms of 3/10 net eom, $2,000.
   8 Returned half the inventory purchased on May 7. It was not the inventory ordered.
  10 Sold goods for cash, $450 (cost, $250).
  13 Sold inventory on credit terms of 2/15 n/45, $3,900 (cost, $1,800).
  16 Paid the amount owed on account from the purchase of May 7, less the discount and the return.
  17 Receive defective inventory as a sales return from May 13 sale, $900. Preakness's cost of the inventory received was $600.
  18 Purchased inventory of $4,000 on account. Payment terms were 2/10 net 30.
  26 Borrowed $3,920 from the bank to take advantage of the discount offered on the May 18 purchase. Signed a note payable to the bank for this amount.
  28 Received cash in full settlement of the account from the customer who purchased inventory on May 13, less the discount and the return.
  29 Purchased inventory for cash, $2,000, plus freight charges of $160.

Required

1. Journalize the preceding transactions on the books of Preakness Wholesale Grocery.
2. The note payable signed on May 26 requires Preakness to pay $30 interest expense. Was the decision to borrow funds in order to take advantage of the cash discount wise or unwise? Support your answer by comparing the discount to the interest paid.

P5-4A House of India Restaurant's trial balance pertains to December 31, 20X9.

Preparing a merchandiser's work sheet
(Obj. 3)

HOUSE OF INDIA RESTAURANT		
Trial Balance		
December 31, 20X9		
Cash	$ 1,270	
Accounts receivable	4,430	
Inventory	73,900	
Prepaid rent	4,400	
Fixtures	22,100	
Accumulated depreciation		$ 8,380
Accounts payable		6,290
Salary payable		
Interest payable		
Note payable, long-term		18,000
Reshma Desai, capital		55,920
Reshma Desai, withdrawals	39,550	
Sales revenue		170,150
Cost of goods sold	67,870	
Salary expense	24,700	
Rent expense	7,700	
Advertising expense	4,510	
Utilities expense	3,880	
Depreciation expense		
Insurance expense	2,770	
Interest expense	1,660	
Total	$258,740	$258,740

Additional data at December 31, 20X9:

a. Total rent expense for the year, $10,200.
b. Store fixtures have an estimated useful life of ten years and are expected to be worthless when they are retired from service.
c. Accrued salaries at December 31, $900.
d. Accrued interest expense at December 31, $360.
e. Inventory on hand at December 31, $72,700.

Required

Complete House of India's accounting work sheet for the year ended December 31, 20X9. Key adjusting entries by letter.

P5-5A Refer to the data in Problem 5-4A.

1. Journalize the adjusting and closing entries.
2. Determine the December 31 balance of Reshma Desai, Capital.

P5-6A ← *Link Back to Chapter 4 (Classified Balance Sheet).* Selected accounts of Mother Earth Organic Products are listed along with their balances before closing at May 31, 20X9.

Accounts payable..................	$ 16,900	Interest expense	$ 400
Accounts receivable.............	33,700	Interest payable	1,100
Accumulated depreciation—		Inventory: May 31	45,500
equipment........................	38,000	Note payable, long-term...........	45,000
P. Debruge, capital,		Salary payable	2,800
April 30	73,900	Sales discounts	10,400
P. Debruge, withdrawals.......	9,000	Sales returns and allowances ...	18,000
Cash....................................	7,800	Sales revenue	701,000
Cost of goods sold................	362,000	Selling expenses	137,900
Equipment...........................	146,000	Supplies	5,100
General expenses	116,700	Unearned sales revenue	13,800

Required

1. Prepare the business's *multi-step* income statement for the month ended May 31, 20X9.
2. Prepare Mother Earth's classified balance sheet in *report format* at May 31, 20X9. Show your computation of the May 31 balance of P. Debruge, Capital.

P5-7A ← *Link Back to Chapter 4 (Classified Balance Sheet).*

Required

1. Use the data of Problem 5-6A to prepare a *single-step* income statement for the month ended May 31, 20X9.
2. Prepare Mother Earth's classified balance sheet in *report format* at May 31, 20X9. Show your computation of the May 31 balance of P. Debruge, Capital.

P5-8A The trial balance and adjustments columns of the work sheet of Purcell Music Company include the following accounts and balances at November 30, 20X4:

Account Title	Trial Balance Debit	Trial Balance Credit	Adjustments Debit	Adjustments Credit
Cash	24,000			
Accounts receivable	14,500		(a) 4,000	
Inventory	36,330		(b) 1,010	
Supplies................................	2,800			(c) 2,400
Furniture..............................	39,600			
Accumulated depreciation		4,900		(d) 2,450
Accounts payable		12,600		(f) 1,000
Salary payable				
Unearned sales revenue........		13,570	(e) 6,700	
Note payable, long-term		15,000		
H. Purcell, capital		60,310		
H. Purcell, drawing...............	42,000			
Sales revenue		174,000		(a) 4,000
				(e) 6,700
Sales returns.........................	6,300			
Cost of goods sold................	72,170			(b) 1,010
Selling expense	28,080		(f) 1,000	
General expense....................	13,100		(c) 2,400	
			(d) 2,450	
Interest expense	1,500			
Total......................................	280,380	280,380	17,560	17,560

Required

1. Inventory on hand one year ago, at November 30, 20X3, was $32,650. Without entering the preceding data on a formal work sheet, prepare the company's multi-step income statement for the year ended November 30, 20X4.
2. Compute the gross profit percentage and the rate of inventory turnover for 20X4. For 20X3, Purcell's gross profit percentage was 55%, and inventory turnover was 1.91 times during the year. Does the two-year trend in these ratios suggest improvement or deterioration in profitability?

P5-9A The accounting records of Copeland Appliance list the following at November 30, 20X1:

(Computing cost of goods sold and gross profit in a periodic inventory system; evaluating the business (Obj. 5, 6)

Purchases of inventory	$132,000	Inventory: November 30, 20X0	$41,700
Selling expenses	8,800	November 30, 20X1	41,500
Furniture	37,200	Cash	3,700
Purchase returns and allowances	900	Freight in	1,600
Salary payable	300	Accumulated depreciation	
Jim Copeland, capital	52,800	—furniture	13,600
Sales revenue	199,600	Purchase discounts	600
Sales returns and allowances	3,200	Sales discounts	2,100
Accounts payable	9,500	General expenses	19,300

Required

1. Show the computation of Copeland's net sales, cost of goods sold, and gross profit for the year ended November 30, 20X1. Compute cost of goods sold as in the periodic inventory system.
2. Jim Copeland, owner of the company, strives to earn a gross profit percentage of 30%. Did he achieve this goal?
3. Did the rate of inventory turnover reach the industry average of 3.5 times per year?

PROBLEMS

(Group B)

P5-1B **Optic Nerve** is a regional chain of optical shops in the southwestern United States. The company offers a large selection of eyeglass frames, and Optic Nerve stores provide while-you-wait service. The company has launched a vigorous advertising campaign to promote two-for-the-price-of-one frame sales.

Explaining the perpetual inventory system (Obj. 2)

Required

Optic Nerve expects to grow rapidly and to increase its level of inventory. As the chief accountant of this company, you wish to install a perpetual inventory system. Write a one-paragraph business memo to the company president to explain how that system would work. Use the following heading for your memo:

Date:	_____
To:	Company President
From:	Chief Accountant
Subject:	How a perpetual inventory system works

P5-2B Assume the following transactions occurred between **Eckerd Drug Stores** and **Johnson & Johnson (J&J)**, the healthcare products company, during June of the current year:

Accounting for the purchase and sale of inventory (Obj. 2)

June 8   Johnson & Johnson sold $6,000 worth of merchandise to Eckerd Drug Stores on terms of 2/10 n/30, FOB shipping point. J&J prepaid freight charges of $200 and included this amount in the invoice total. (J&J's entry to record the freight payment debits Accounts Receivable and credits Cash.) These goods cost J&J $2,100.

11   Eckerd returned $600 of the merchandise purchased on June 8. J&J accounted for the $600 sales return and placed the goods back in inventory (J&J's cost, $250).

17   Eckerd paid $2,000 of the invoice amount owed to J&J for the June 8 purchase, less the discount. This payment included none of the freight charge.

26   Eckerd paid the remaining amount owed to J&J for the June 8 purchase.

Required

Journalize these transactions, first on the books of Eckerd Drug Stores and second on the books of Johnson & Johnson.

P5-3B Larkspur Lighting Company engaged in the following transactions during July:

July 2   Purchased inventory for cash, $800.
5   Purchased store supplies on credit terms of net eom, $450.
8   Purchased inventory of $3,000, plus freight charges of $230. Credit terms are 3/15 n/30.
9   Sold goods for cash, $1,200. Larkspur's cost of these goods was $700.
11   Returned $200 of the inventory purchased on July 8. It was damaged.
12   Purchased inventory on credit terms of 3/10 n/30, $3,330.
14   Sold inventory on credit terms of 2/10 n/30, $9,600 (cost $5,000).
16   Paid utilities expense, $275.
20   Received returned inventory from the July 14 sale, $400. Larkspur shipped the wrong goods by mistake. Larkspur's cost of the inventory received was $250.
21   Borrowed the amount owed on the July 8 purchase. Signed a note payable to the bank for $2,946, which takes into account the return of inventory on July 11.
21   Paid supplier for goods purchased on July 8 less the discount and the return.
23   Received $6,860 cash in partial settlement of his account from the customer who purchased inventory on July 14. Granted the customer a 2% discount and credited his account receivable for $7,000.
30   Paid for the store supplies purchased on July 5.

Required

1. Journalize the preceding transactions on the books of Larkspur Lighting Company.
2. Compute the amount of the receivable at July 31 from the customer to whom Larkspur sold inventory on July 14. What amount of cash discount applies to this receivable at July 31?

P5-4B Fresh Market Grocery's trial balance pertains to December 31, 20X1.

FRESH MARKET GROCERY Trial Balance December 31, 20X1		
Cash..	$ 2,910	
Accounts receivable.........................	6,560	
Inventory..	101,760	
Store supplies	1,990	
Prepaid insurance.............................	3,200	
Store fixtures....................................	63,900	
Accumulated depreciation................		$ 37,640
Accounts payable		29,770
Salary payable		
Interest payable		
Note payable, long-term...................		37,200
Elaine Lorens, capital		63,120
Elaine Lorens, withdrawals..............	36,300	
Sales revenue		286,370
Cost of goods sold............................	161,090	
Salary expense..................................	46,580	
Rent expense.....................................	14,630	
Utilities expense	6,780	
Depreciation expense		
Insurance expense............................	5,300	
Store supplies expense		
Interest expense	3,100	
Total...	$454,100	$454,100

Additional data at December 31, 20X1:

a. Insurance expense for the year, $6,090.
b. Store fixtures have an estimated useful life of ten years and are expected to be worthless when they are retired from service.
c. Accrued salaries at December 31, $1,260.
d. Accrued interest expense at December 31, $870.
e. Store supplies on hand at December 31, $760.
f. Inventory on hand at December 31, $94,780.

Required

Complete Fresh Market's accounting work sheet for the year ended December 31, 20X1. Key adjusting entries by letter.

P5-5B Refer to the data in Problem 5-4B at the bottom of the facing page.

Journalizing the adjusting and closing entries of a merchandising business (Obj. 3)

Required

1. Journalize the adjusting and closing entries of Fresh Market Grocery.
2. Determine the December 31 balance of Elaine Lorens, Capital.

P5-6B ← *Link Back to Chapter 4 (Classified Balance Sheet).* Selected accounts of Genesis Electronics are listed along with their balances before closing at July 31, 20X2.

Preparing a multi-step income statement and a classified balance sheet (Obj. 3, 4)

Accounts payable...................	$127,300	Interest payable.......................	$ 3,000
Accounts receivable...............	46,200	Inventory: July 31...................	187,300
Accumulated depreciation—		Note payable, long-term	160,000
store equipment.................	16,400	Salary payable	6,100
A. L. Genesis, capital,		Sales discounts	8,300
June 30	69,100	Sales returns and allowances ..	17,900
A. L. Genesis, withdrawals	11,000	Sales revenue	556,600
Cash......................................	24,300	Selling expense	84,600
Cost of goods sold..................	360,900	Store equipment	126,000
General expense	75,800	Supplies...................................	4,300
Interest expense.....................	1,200	Unearned sales revenue..........	9,300

Required

1. Prepare the entity's *multi-step* income statement for the month ended July 31, 20X2.
2. Prepare Genesis's classified balance sheet in *report format* at July 31, 20X2. Show your computation of the July 31 balance of A.L. Genesis, Capital.

P5-7B ← *Link Back to Chapter 4 (Classified Balance Sheet).*

Preparing a single-step income statement and a classified balance sheet (Obj. 4)

Required

1. Use the data of Problem 5-6B to prepare Genesis Electronics' *single-step* income statement for July 31, 20X2.
2. Prepare Genesis's classified balance sheet in *report format* at July 31, 20X2. Show your computation of the July 31 balance of A. L. Genesis, Capital.

P5-8B The trial balance and adjustments columns of the work sheet of **Carolina Crystal Company** follow.

Using work sheet data to prepare financial statements and evaluate the business; multi-step income statement (Obj. 4, 5)

Account Title	Trial Balance		Adjustments	
	Debit	**Credit**	**Debit**	**Credit**
Cash......................................	7,300			
Accounts receivable.............	4,360		(a) 1,400	
Inventory.............................	9,630		(b) 2,100	
Supplies	10,700			(c) 7,940
Equipment............................	99,450			
Accumulated depreciation...		29,800		(d) 9,900
Accounts payable		13,800		
Salary payable				(f) 200
Unearned sales revenue		3,780	(e) 2,600	
Note payable, long-term......		10,000		
Claire Burke, capital............		58,360		
Claire Burke, drawing	35,000			
Sales revenue		212,000		(a) 1,400
				(e) 2,600
Sales returns........................	3,100			
Cost of goods sold...............	95,600			(b) 2,100
Selling expense....................	40,600		(c) 7,940	
			(f) 200	
General expense..................	21,000		(d) 9,900	
Interest expense	1,000			
Total......................................	327,740	327,740	24,140	24,140

Required

1. Inventory on hand at September 30, 20X2, was $9,250. Without completing a formal accounting work sheet, prepare the company's multi-step income statement for the year ended September 30, 20X3.
2. Compute the gross profit percentage and the inventory turnover for 20X3. For 20X2, Carolina's gross profit percentage was 50% and the inventory turnover rate was 7.8 times. Does the two-year trend in these ratios suggest improvement or deterioration in profitability?

Computing cost of goods sold and gross profit in a periodic inventory system; evaluating the business
(Obj. 5, 6)

P5-9B The accounting records of Vanguard Security Systems at June 30, 20X2 list the following:

Cash	$ 13,600	Inventory: June 30, 20X1	$23,800
Purchases of inventory	98,100	June 30, 20X2	28,500
Freight in	4,300	Equipment	44,700
Sales revenue	199,100	Purchase discounts	1,300
Purchase returns		Accumulated depreciation—	
and allowances	1,400	equipment	6,900
Salary payable	1,800	Sales discounts	3,400
Luke Stover, capital	36,000	General expenses	16,300
Sales returns and allowances	12,100	Accounts payable	23,800
Selling expenses	29,800		

Required

1. Show the computation of Vanguard Security Systems' net sales, cost of goods sold, and gross profit for the year ended June 30, 20X2. Compute cost of goods sold as in the periodic inventory system.
2. Luke Stover, owner of the business, strives to earn a gross profit percentage of 44%. Did he achieve this goal?
3. Did the rate of inventory turnover reach the industry average of 4.0 times per year?

APPLY YOUR KNOWLEDGE

DECISION CASES

Using the financial statements to decide on a business expansion
(Obj. 4, 5)

Case 1. ◄ *Link Back to Chapter 4 (Classified Balance Sheet, Current Ratio, Debt Ratio).* David Wheelis owns Heights Pharmacy, which has prospered during its second year of operation. In deciding whether to open another pharmacy in the area, Wheelis has prepared the current financial statements of the business (on page 209). Wheelis read in an industry trade journal that a successful pharmacy meets all of these criteria:

a. Gross profit percentage is at least 60%.
b. Current ratio is at least 2.0.
c. Debt ratio is no higher than 0.50.
d. Inventory turnover rate is at least 3.40. (Heights Pharmacy's inventory one year ago, at December 31, 20X0, was $19,200.)

Basing his opinion on the entity's financial statement data, Wheelis believes the business meets all four criteria. He intends to go ahead with the expansion plan and asks your advice on preparing the pharmacy's financial statements in accordance with generally accepted accounting principles. When you point out that the statements are not properly prepared, he assures you that all amounts are correct. However, he admits that some items may be listed in the wrong place.

Required

1. Compute the four ratios based on the Heights Pharmacy financial statements prepared by Wheelis. Does the business appear to be ready for expansion?
2. Prepare a correct multi-step income statement, a correct statement of owner's equity, and a correct classified balance sheet in report format.
3. On the basis of the corrected financial statements, compute correct measures of the four ratios listed in the trade journal.
4. Make a recommendation about whether Wheelis should undertake the expansion.

HEIGHTS PHARMACY
Income Statement
Year Ended December 31, 20X1

Sales revenue		$195,000
Gain on sale of land		24,600
Total revenue		219,600
Cost of goods sold		85,200
Gross profit		134,400
Operating expenses:		
Salary expense	$18,690	
Rent expense	12,000	
Interest expense	6,000	
Depreciation expense	4,900	
Utilities expense	2,330	
Supplies expense	1,400	
Total operating expense		45,320
Income from operations		89,080
Other expense:		
Sales discounts ($3,600)		
and returns ($7,100)		10,700
Net income		$78,380

HEIGHTS PHARMACY
Statement of Owner's Equity
Year Ended December 31, 20X1

D. Wheelis, capital, December 31, 20X0	$ 30,000
Add increases in owner's equity:	
Net income	78,380
D. Wheelis, capital, December 31, 20X1	$108,380

HEIGHTS PHARMACY
Balance Sheet
December 31, 20X1

Assets

Current:	
Cash	$ 5,320
Accounts receivable	9,710
Inventory	30,100
Supplies	2,760
Store fixtures	63,000
Total current assets	110,890
Other:	
Withdrawals	65,000
Total assets	$175,890

Liabilities

Current:	
Accumulated depreciation—store fixtures	$ 6,300
Accounts payable	10,310
Salary payable	900
Total current liabilities	17,510
Other:	
Note payable due in 90 days	50,000
Total liabilities	67,510

Owner's Equity

D. Wheelis, capital	108,380
Total liabilities and owner's equity	$175,890

Case 2. The employees of Ewald Systems made an error when they performed the inventory count at year end, October 31, 20X8. Part of one warehouse was not counted, and therefore its inventory was not included in the company's total ending inventory.

Required

1. Indicate the effect of the inventory error on ending inventory, cost of goods sold, gross profit, and net income for the year ended October 31, 20X8.
2. Will the error affect cost of goods sold, gross profit, and net income in 20X9? If so, what will the effects be?

ETHICAL ISSUE

Greg Ogden Belting Company makes all sales of industrial conveyor belts under terms of FOB shipping point. The company usually receives orders for sales approximately one week before shipping inventory to customers. For orders received late in December, Greg Ogden, the owner, decides when to ship the goods. If profits are already at an acceptable level, Ogden delays shipment until January. If profits for the current year are lagging behind expectations, Ogden ships the goods during December.

Required

1. Under Ogden's FOB policy, when should the company record a sale?
2. Do you approve or disapprove of Ogden's manner of deciding when to ship goods to customers and record the sales revenue? If you approve, give your reason. If you disapprove, identify a better way to decide when to ship goods. (There is no accounting rule against Ogden's practice.)

FINANCIAL STATEMENT CASE

This case uses both the income statement (statement of income) and the balance sheet of **Target Corporation,** in Appendix A. It will help you understand the closing process of a business with inventories.

Required

1. Journalize Target's closing entries for fiscal year 1999. You may be unfamiliar with certain revenues and expenses, but treat them as either revenues or expenses. *Net credit revenue* is interest revenue. *Provision for income taxes* is another name for income tax expense and the *extraordinary charge* is like an expense. Close the Income Summary account to the Retained Earnings account. For this purpose, Retained Earnings is similar to the Owner's Capital account.
2. What amount was closed to Retained Earnings? How is this amount labeled on the income statement?
3. Compute Target's gross profit percentage and inventory turnover rate for fiscal year 1999.

TEAM PROJECT

With a small team of classmates, visit one or more actual merchandising businesses in your area. Interview a responsible official of the company to learn about its inventory policies and accounting system. Obtain answers to the following questions, write a report, and be prepared to make a presentation to the class if your instructor so directs:

Required

1. What merchandise inventory does the business sell?
2. From whom does the business buy its inventory? Is the relationship with the supplier new or longstanding?
3. What are the FOB terms on inventory purchases? Who pays the freight, the buyer or the seller? Is freight a significant amount or is freight cost low? What percentage of total inventory cost is the freight?
4. What are the credit terms on inventory purchases—2/10 n/30, or other? Does the business pay early to get purchase discounts? If so, why? If not, why not?
5. How does the business actually pay its suppliers? Does it mail a check or pay electronically? What is the actual payment procedure?
6. Which type of inventory accounting system does the business use—perpetual or periodic? Is this system computerized?
7. How often does the business take a physical count of its inventory? When during the year is the count taken? Describe the count procedures followed by the company.
8. Does the owner or manager use the gross profit percentage and the rate of inventory turnover to evaluate the business? If not, show the manager how to use these ratios in decision making.
9. Ask any other questions your group considers appropriate.

INTERNET EXERCISE

You can now compare prices for consumer electronics, personal computers, and entertainment software online by visiting the **Best Buy** and **Circuit City** Web sites. You can also compare their financial information online. Let's see how these companies compare.

Required

1. Go to **http://www.hoovers.com** and then use the "Search" scroll bar to select *Company*. In the next box type *BBY*, the stock symbol for Best Buy, and click on *Go*. For Best Buy Co., Inc., click on *capsule* and read the written description of the company. In what parts of the country are Best Buy stores located?
2. Go to the top of the page and click on the *Financials* tab. Under "Free Financial Information," click on *Annual Financials*.
   a. For the two most recent fiscal years, list the amounts reported for "Revenue," "Cost of Goods Sold," "Gross Profit Margin" percentage, "Total Net Income," and "Inventories."
   b. For the most recent year, calculate the rate of inventory turnover. Explain what this ratio indicates for Best Buy.
3. In the "Search for" box at the top of page, type *CC*, the stock symbol for Circuit City, and click on *Go*. For Circuit City Stores, Inc., click on *capsule* and read the written description of the company. What is Circuit City's rank among major appliance and electronics chains? Which company is the leader?
4. Gather the same information requested in (2a) and (2b) above for Circuit City.
5. Which company is more profitable? Why?

Best Buy and Circuit City

Go to the "Alternative Income Statement Formats and Extraordinary Items" episode on the *Mastering Accounting* CD-ROM for an interactive, video-enhanced exercise on CanGo managers' need to consider the different income statement formats and their effect on investors.

APPENDIX TO CHAPTER 5

ACCOUNTING FOR MERCHANDISE IN A PERIODIC INVENTORY SYSTEM

After studying this appendix to Chapter 5, you should be able to:

A2. Account for purchase and sale of inventory
A3. Compute cost of goods sold
A4. Adjust and close the accounts of a merchandising business
A5. Prepare a merchandiser's financial statement

PURCHASING MERCHANDISE

Some businesses find it uneconomical to invest in a computerized (perpetual) inventory system. These types of business use a periodic system.

Recording Purchases of Inventory

Objective A2
Account for the purchase and sale of inventory

All inventory systems use the Inventory account. But in a periodic system, purchases, purchase discounts, purchase returns and allowances, and transportation costs are recorded in separate accounts. Let's account for **Austin Sound Center's** purchase of the **JVC** goods in Exhibit 5A-1. The following entries record the purchase and payment on account within the discount period:

May 27	Purchases	707.00	
	Accounts Payable		707.00
	Purchased inventory on account.		
June 10	Accounts Payable	707.00	
	Cash ($707.00 × 0.97)		685.79
	Purchase Discounts ($707.00 × 0.03)		21.21
	Paid on account.		

Recording Purchase Returns and Allowances

Suppose that, prior to payment, **Austin Sound** returned to **JVC** goods costing $70 and also received from JVC a purchase allowance of $10. Austin Sound would record these transactions as follows:

June 3	Accounts Payable	70.00	
	Purchase Returns and Allowances		70.00
	Returned inventory to seller.		

MERCHANDISING OPERATIONS
AND THE ACCOUNTING CYCLE

211

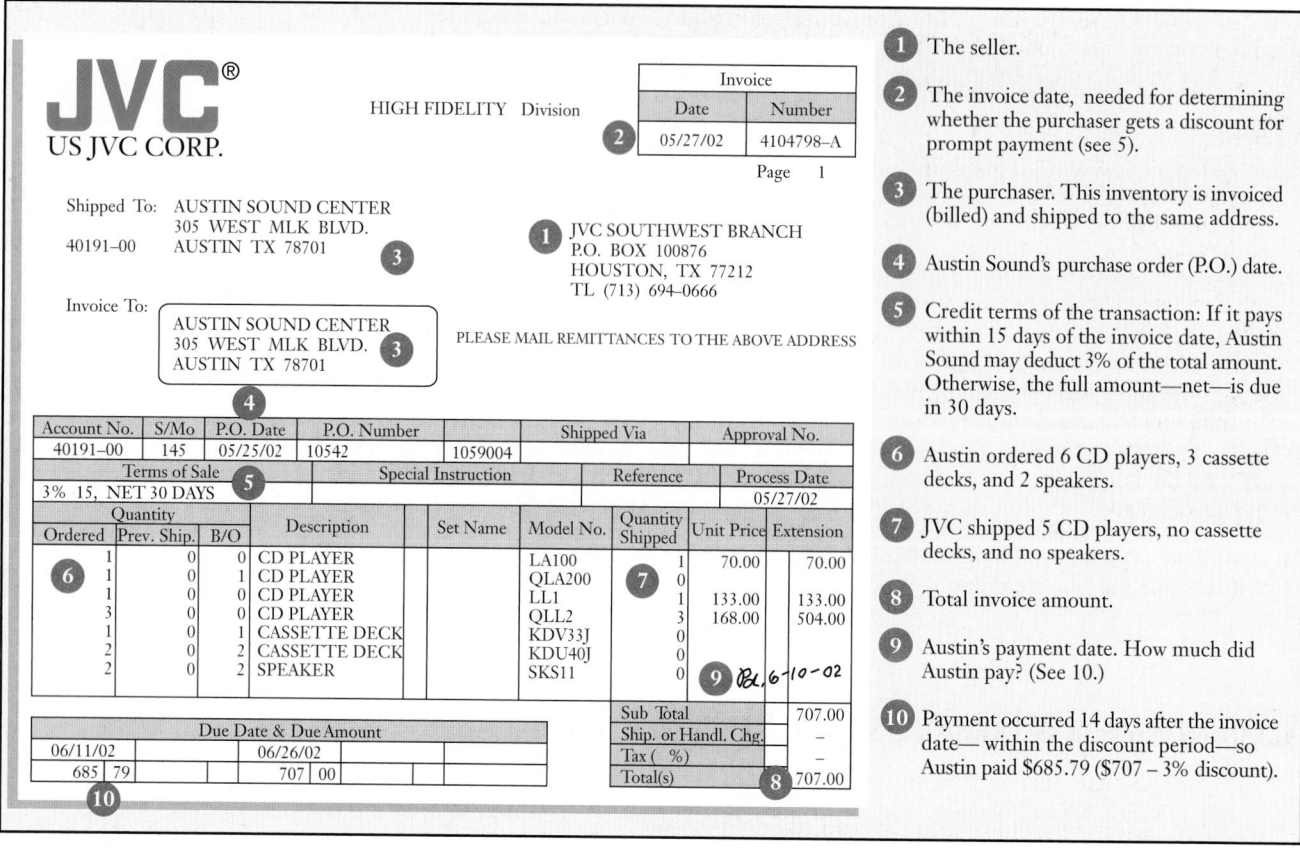

The numbered callouts on the invoice:

1. The seller.

2. The invoice date, needed for determining whether the purchaser gets a discount for prompt payment (see 5).

3. The purchaser. This inventory is invoiced (billed) and shipped to the same address.

4. Austin Sound's purchase order (P.O.) date.

5. Credit terms of the transaction: If it pays within 15 days of the invoice date, Austin Sound may deduct 3% of the total amount. Otherwise, the full amount—net—is due in 30 days.

6. Austin ordered 6 CD players, 3 cassette decks, and 2 speakers.

7. JVC shipped 5 CD players, no cassette decks, and no speakers.

8. Total invoice amount.

9. Austin's payment date. How much did Austin pay? (See 10.)

10. Payment occurred 14 days after the invoice date— within the discount period—so Austin paid $685.79 ($707 – 3% discount).

June 4	Accounts Payable	10.00	
	Purchase Returns and Allowances		10.00
	Received a purchase allowance.		

During the period, the business records the cost of all inventory bought in the Purchases account. The balance of Purchases is a *gross* amount because it does not include subtractions for discounts, returns, or allowances. **Net purchases** is the remainder computed by subtracting the contra accounts from Purchases:

> **Net Purchases.** Purchases less purchase discounts and purchase returns and allowances.

	Purchases (*debit* balance account)
−	**Purchase Discounts** (*credit* balance account)
−	**Purchase Returns and Allowances** (*credit* balance account)
=	**Net purchases (a *debit* subtotal, not a separate account)**

Recording Transportation Costs

Under the periodic system, costs to transport purchased inventory from seller to buyer are debited to the freight in account, as shown for a $60 freight bill:

June 1	Freight In	60.00	
	Cash		60.00
	Paid a freight bill.		

RECORDING THE SALE OF INVENTORY

Recording sales is streamlined in the periodic system. With no running record of inventory to maintain, we can record a $3,000 sale as follows:

June 5	Accounts Receivable	3,000	
	Sales Revenue		3,000
	Sale on account.		

No accompanying entry to Inventory and Cost of Goods Sold is required. Also, discounts and returns and allowances are recorded as shown for the perpetual system on pages 176–177, but with no entry to Inventory and Cost of Goods Sold.

Cost of goods sold (also called **cost of sales**) is the largest single expense of most businesses that sell merchandise, such as **Gap Inc.**, and **Austin Sound**. It is the cost of the inventory the business has sold to customers. In a periodic system, cost of goods sold must be computed as in Exhibit 5A-2.

Objective A3
Compute cost of goods sold

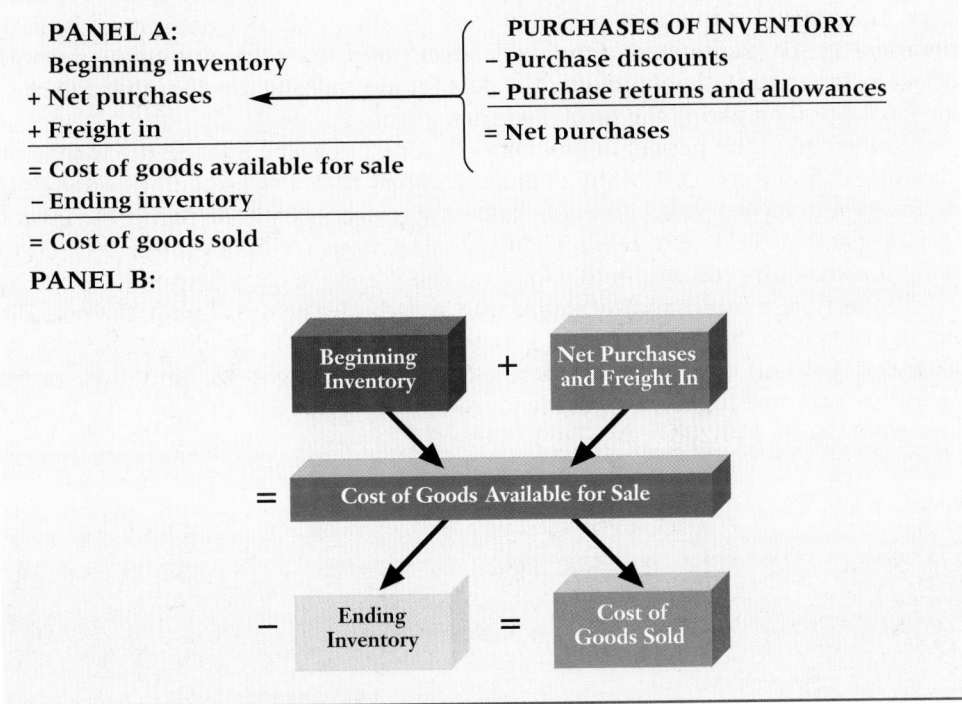

EXHIBIT **5A-2**
Measuring Cost of Goods Sold in the Periodic Inventory System

EXHIBIT **5A-3**
Partial Income Statement

AUSTIN SOUND CENTER
Income Statement
Year Ended December 31, 20X2

PANEL A—Detailed Gross Profit Section

Sales revenue...		$169,300	
Less: Sales discounts	$ (1,400)		
Sales returns and allowances...	(2,000)	(3,400)	
Net sales			$165,900
Cost of goods sold:			
Beginning inventory........................		$38,600	
Purchases	$91,400		
Less: Purchase discounts..................	$(3,000)		
Purchase returns and			
allowances..........................	(1,200)	(4,200)	
Net purchases..................................		87,200	
Freight in		5,200	
Cost of goods available for sale............		131,000	
Less: Ending inventory		(40,200)	
Cost of goods sold...............................			90,800
Gross profit			$ 75,100

**PANEL B—Gross Profit Section
(Streamlined in Annual Reports to Outsiders)**

Net sales.......................................	$165,900
Cost of goods sold	90,800
Gross profit	$ 75,100

Exhibit 5A-3 on page 213 summarizes the first half of this appendix by showing Austin Sound's net sales revenue, cost of goods sold—including net purchases and freight in—and gross profit on the income statement for the periodic system. (All amounts are assumed.)

ADJUSTING AND CLOSING THE ACCOUNTS

A merchandising business adjusts and closes the accounts much as a service entity does. The steps of this end-of-period process are the same: If a work sheet is used, the trial balance is entered and the work sheet completed to determine net income or net loss. The work sheet provides the data for journalizing the adjusting and closing entries and preparing the financial statements.

At the end of the period, before any adjusting or closing entries, the Inventory account still holds the cost of the ending inventory from the preceding period. It is necessary to remove this beginning balance and replace it with the cost of the inventory on hand at the end of the current period. Various techniques may be used to bring the inventory records up to date.

To illustrate a merchandiser's adjusting and closing process under the periodic inventory system, let's use **Austin Sound's** December 31, 20X2, trial balance in Exhibit 5A-4. All the new accounts—Inventory, Freight In, and the contra accounts—are highlighted for emphasis. Additional data item (h) gives the ending inventory figure, $40,200.

EXHIBIT 5A-4
Trial Balance

AUSTIN SOUND CENTER
Trial Balance
December 31, 20X2

Cash	$ 2,850	
Accounts receivable	4,600	
Note receivable, current	8,000	
Interest receivable		
Inventory	38,600	
Supplies	650	
Prepaid insurance	1,200	
Furniture and fixtures	33,200	
Accumulated depreciation		$ 2,400
Accounts payable		47,000
Unearned sales revenue		2,000
Wages payable		
Interest payable		
Note payable, long-term		12,600
C. Ernest, capital		25,900
C. Ernest, withdrawals	54,100	
Sales revenue		168,000
Sales discounts	1,400	
Sales returns and allowances	2,000	
Interest revenue		600
Purchases	91,400	
Purchase discounts		3,000
Purchase returns and allowances		1,200
Freight in	5,200	
Wage expense	9,800	
Rent expense	8,400	
Depreciation expense		
Insurance expense		
Supplies expense		
Interest expense	1,300	
Total	$262,700	$262,700

Additional data at December 31, 20X2

a. Interest revenue earned but not yet collected, $400.
b. Supplies on hand, $100.
c. Prepaid insurance expired during the year, $1,000.
d. Depreciation, $600.
e. Unearned sales revenue earned during the year, $1,300.
f. Accrued wage expense, $400.
g. Accrued interest expense, $200.
h. Inventory on hand, $40,200.

Preparing and Using the Work Sheet in a Periodic System

The Exhibit 5A-5 work sheet is similar to the work sheets we have seen so far, with a few differences. ➡ In most accounting systems, a single operation combines trial balance amounts with the adjustments and extends the adjusted balances directly to the income statement and balance sheet columns. Therefore, to reduce clutter, the adjusted trial balance columns are omitted.

◀ This work sheet is slightly different from the one introduced in the Chapter 4 acetates following page 128— it contains four pairs of columns, not five.

EXHIBIT 5A-5   Accounting Work Sheet

AUSTIN SOUND CENTER Accounting Work Sheet (Periodic Inventory System) Year Ended December 31, 20X2								
	Trial Balance		Adjustments		Income Statement		Balance Sheet	
Account Title	**Debit**	**Credit**	**Debit**	**Credit**	**Debit**	**Credit**	**Debit**	**Credit**
Cash..............................	2,850						2,850	
Accounts receivable...........	4,600						4,600	
Note receivable, current....	8,000						8,000	
Interest receivable			(a) 400				400	
Inventory...........................	38,600				38,600	40,200	40,200	
Supplies.............................	650			(b) 550			100	
Prepaid insurance..............	1,200			(c) 1,000			200	
Furniture and fixtures.......	33,200						33,200	
Accumulated depreciation		2,400		(d) 600				3,000
Accounts payable		47,000						47,000
Unearned sales revenue....		2,000	(e) 1,300					700
Wages payable				(f) 400				400
Interest payable.................				(g) 200				200
Note payable, long-term....		12,600						12,600
C. Ernest, capital		25,900						25,900
C. Ernest, withdrawals	54,100						54,100	
Sales revenue		168,000		(e) 1,300		169,300		
Sales discounts	1,400				1,400			
Sales returns and allowances	2,000				2,000			
Interest revenue		600		(a) 400		1,000		
Purchases...........................	91,400				91,400			
Purchase discounts...........		3,000				3,000		
Purchase returns and allowances		1,200				1,200		
Freight in...........................	5,200				5,200			
Wage expense.....................	9,800		(f) 400		10,200			
Rent expense.....................	8,400				8,400			
Depreciation expense			(d) 600		600			
Insurance expense.............			(c) 1,000		1,000			
Supplies expense			(b) 550		550			
Interest expense	1,300		(g) 200		1,500			
	262,700	262,700	4,450	4,450	160,850	214,700	143,650	89,800
Net income					53,850			53,850
					214,700	214,700	143,650	143,650

ACCOUNT TITLE COLUMNS The trial balance lists a number of accounts without balances. Ordinarily, these accounts are affected by the adjusting process. Examples include Interest Receivable, Interest Payable, and Depreciation Expense. The accounts are listed in the order they appear in the ledger. If additional accounts are needed, they are written in at the bottom, above net income.

TRIAL BALANCE COLUMNS Examine the Inventory account, $38,600 in the trial balance. This $38,600 is the cost of the beginning inventory. The work sheet is designed to replace this outdated amount with the new ending balance, which in our example is $40,200 [additional data item (h) in Exhibit 5A-4].

ADJUSTMENTS COLUMNS The adjustments are similar to those discussed in Chapters 3 and 4. They may be entered in any order desired. The debit amount of each entry should equal the credit amount, and total debits should equal total credits. You should review the adjusting data in Exhibit 5A-5 to reassure yourself that the adjustments are correct.

INCOME STATEMENT COLUMNS The income statement columns contain adjusted amounts for the revenues and the expenses. Sales Revenue, for example, is $169,300, which includes the $1,300 adjustment.

You may be wondering why the two inventory amounts appear in the income statement columns. The reason is that both beginning inventory and ending inventory enter the computation of cost of goods sold. *Placement of beginning inventory ($38,600) in the work sheet's income statement Debit column has the effect of adding beginning inventory in computing cost of goods sold. Placing ending inventory ($40,200) in the Credit column decreases cost of goods sold.*

Purchases and Freight In appear in the Debit column because they are added in computing cost of goods sold. Purchase Discounts and Purchase Returns and Allowances appear as Credits because they are subtracted in computing cost of good sold—$90,800 on the income statement in Exhibit 5A-6.

The income statement column subtotals on the work sheet indicate whether the business earned net income or incurred a net loss. If total credits are greater, the result is net income, as shown in Exhibit 5A-5. If total debits are greater, a net loss has occurred.

BALANCE SHEET COLUMNS The only new item on the balance sheet is inventory. The balance listed is the ending amount of $40,200, which is determined by a physical count of inventory on hand at the end of the period.

Objective A5
Prepare a merchandiser's financial statements

Preparing the Financial Statements of a Merchandiser

Exhibit 5A-6 presents Austin Sound's financial statements. The *income statement* through gross profit repeats Exhibit 5A-3. This information is followed by the **operating expenses,** expenses other than cost of goods sold that are incurred in the entity's major line of business. Wage expense is Austin Sound's cost of employing workers. Rent is the cost of obtaining store space. Insurance helps to protect the inventory. Store furniture and fixtures wear out; the expense is depreciation. Supplies expense is the cost of stationery, mailing, and the like, used in operations. Many companies report their operating expenses in two categories.

- *Selling expenses* are those expenses related to marketing the company's products—sales salaries, sales commissions, advertising, depreciation, rent, and utilities, delivery expense, and so on.
- *General expenses* include office expenses, such as the salaries of office employees, and depreciation, rent, utilities, and property taxes on the home office building.

Gross profit minus operating expenses and plus any other operating revenues equals **operating income,** or **income from operations.** Many businesspeople view operating income as the most reliable indicator of a business's success because it measures the results of the entity's major ongoing activities.

The last section of Austin Sound's income statement is **other revenue and expenses,** which is handled the same way in both inventory systems. This category reports revenues and expenses that are outside the company's main line of business.

AUSTIN SOUND CENTER
Income Statement
Year Ended December 31, 20X2

Sales revenue			$169,300
Less: Sales discounts		$ (1,400)	
Sales returns and allowances		(2,000)	(3,400)
Net sales revenue			$165,900
Cost of goods sold:			
Beginning inventory		$ 38,600	
Purchases	$91,400		
Less: Purchases discounts	$(3,000)		
Purchase returns and allowances	(1,200)	(4,200)	
Net purchases		87,200	
Freight in		5,200	
Cost of goods available for sale		131,000	
Less: Ending inventory		(40,200)	
Cost of goods sold			90,800
Gross profit			75,100
Operating expenses:			
Wage expense		10,200	
Rent expense		8,400	
Insurance expense		1,000	
Depreciation expense		600	
Supplies expense		550	20,750
Income from operations			54,350
Other revenue and (expense):			
Interest revenue		1,000	
Interest expense		(3,400)	(500)
Net income			$53,850

AUSTIN SOUND CENTER
Statement of Owner's Equity
Year Ended December 31, 20X2

C. Ernest, capital, December 31, 20X1	$25,900
Add: Net income	53,850
	79,750
Less: Withdrawals	(54,100)
C. Ernest, capital, December 31, 20X2	$25,650

AUSTIN SOUND CENTER
Balance Sheet
December 31, 20X2

Assets		Liabilities	
Current:		Current:	
Cash	$ 2,850	Accounts payable	$47,000
Accounts receivable	4,600	Unearned sales revenue	700
Note receivable	8,000	Wages payable	400
Interest receivable	400	Interest payable	200
Inventory	40,200	Total current liabilities	48,300
Prepaid insurance	200	Long-term:	
Supplies	100	Note payable	12,600
Total current assets	56,350	Total liabilities	60,900
Plant:			
Furniture and fixtures	$33,200	**Owner's Equity**	
Less: Accumulated		C. Ernest, capital	25,650
depreciation	(3,000) 30,200	Total liabilities and	
Total assets	$86,550	owner's equity	$86,550

Journalizing Adjusting and Closing Entries

Exhibit 5A-7 presents Austin Sound's adjusting entries. These entries follow the same pattern illustrated in Chapter 4 for a service entity.

EXHIBIT 5A-7
Adjusting and Closing Entries

Journal

Adjusting Entries

a.	Dec. 31	Interest Receivable		400	
		Interest Revenue			400
b.	31	Supplies Expense ($650 − $100)		550	
		Supplies			550
c.	31	Insurance Expense		1,000	
		Prepaid Insurance			1,000
d.	31	Depreciation Expense..		600	
		Accumulated Depreciation			600
e.	31	Unearned Sales Revenue		1,300	
		Sales Revenue...			1,300
f.	31	Wage Expense		400	
		Wages Payable			400
g.	31	Interest Expense		200	
		Interest Payable			200

Closing Entries

1.	Dec. 31	Sales Revenue...		169,300	
		Interest Revenue		1,000	
		Income Summary			170,300
2.	31	Cost of Goods Sold..		135,200	
		Inventory (beginning balance)			38,600
		Purchases			91,400
		Freight In			5,200
3.	31	Inventory (ending balance).....................................		40,200	
		Purchase Discounts.......................................		3,000	
		Purchase Returns and Allowances		1,200	
		Cost of Goods Sold			44,400
4.	31	Income Summary		116,450	
		Sales Discounts			1,400
		Sales Returns and Allowances			2,000
		Cost of Goods Sold ($135,200 − $44,400)			90,800
		Wage Expense..			10,200
		Rent Expense			8,400
		Depreciation Expense			600
		Insurance Expense..			1,000
		Supplies Expense			550
		Interest Expense			1,500
5.	31	Income Summary ($170,300 − $116,450)		53,850	
		C. Ernest, Capital			53,850
6.	31	C. Ernest, Capital...		54,100	
		C. Ernest, Withdrawals			54,100

The exhibit also gives Austin Sound's closing entries. The first closing entry closes the revenue accounts. Closing entries 2 and 3 are new. Entry 2 closes the beginning balance of the Inventory account ($38,600), along with Purchases and Freight In, into the Cost of Goods Sold account. Entry 3 sets up the ending balance of Inventory ($40,200) with a debit and also closes the Purchases contra accounts to Cost of Goods Sold.[1] Now Inventory and Cost of Goods Sold have their correct ending balances as follows:

INVENTORY						
Jan. 1	Bal.	38,600	Dec. 31	Clo.	38,600
Dec. 31	Clo.	40,200			

COST OF GOODS SOLD			
Beg. Inventory	38,600	Pur. discounts	3,000
Purchases	91,400	Pur. returns and	
Freight in	5,200	allowances	1,200
		End. inventory	40,200
Bal.	90,800		

[1]Some accountants make the inventory entries as adjustments rather than as part of the closing process. The adjusting-entry approach adds these adjustments (shifted out of the closing entries):

The entries to the Inventory account deserve additional explanation. Recall that before the closing process, Inventory still had the period's beginning balance. At the end of the period, this balance is one year old and must be replaced with the ending balance in order to prepare the financial statements at December 31, 20X2. Closing entries 2 and 3 give Inventory its correct ending balance of $40,200.

Closing entry 4 then closes the Sales contra accounts and Cost of Goods Sold along with the other expense accounts into Income Summary. Closing entries 5 and 6 complete the closing process. All data for the closing entries are taken from the income statement columns of the work sheet.

Study Exhibits 5A-5, 5A-6, and 5A-7 carefully because they illustrate the entire end-of-period process that leads to the financial statements. As you progress through this book, you may want to refer to these exhibits to refresh your understanding of the adjusting and closing process for a merchandising business.

Net sales, cost of goods sold, operating income, and net income are unaffected by the choice of inventory system. You can prove this by comparing Austin Sound's financial statements given in Exhibit 5A-6 with the corresponding statements in Exhibit 5-7. The only differences appear in the cost-of-goods-sold section of the income statement, and those differences are unimportant. In fact, virtually all companies report cost of goods sold in streamlined fashion, as shown for **Target Corporation** in Exhibit 5-1 and for **Austin Sound** in Exhibit 5-7.

REVIEW PERIODIC INVENTORY SYSTEM

APPENDIX SUMMARY PROBLEM

The following trial balance pertains to Jan King Distributing Company:

JAN KING DISTRIBUTING COMPANY
Trial Balance (Periodic Inventory System)
December 31, 20X3

Cash	$ 5,670	
Accounts receivable	37,100	
Inventory	60,500	
Supplies	3,930	
Prepaid rent	6,000	
Furniture and fixtures	26,500	
Accumulated depreciation		$ 21,200
Accounts payable		46,340
Salary payable		
Interest payable		
Unearned sales revenue		3,500
Note payable, long-term		35,000
Jan King, capital		23,680
Jan King, withdrawals	48,000	
Sales revenue		346,700
Sales discounts	10,300	
Sales returns and allowances	8,200	
Purchases	175,900	
Purchase discounts		6,000
Purchase returns and allowances		7,430
Freight in	9,300	
Salary expense	82,750	
Rent expense	7,000	
Depreciation expense		
Utilities expense	5,800	
Supplies expense		
Interest expense	2,900	
Total	$489,850	$489,850

Additional data at December 31, 20X3:

    a. Supplies used during the year, $2,580.

    b. Prepaid rent in force, $1,000.

    c. Unearned sales revenue still not earned, $2,400. The company expects to earn this amount during the next few months.

    d. Depreciation. The furniture and fixtures' estimated useful life is ten years, and they are expected to be worthless when they are retired from service.

    e. Accrued salaries, $1,300.

    f. Accrued interest expense, $600.

    g. Inventory on hand, $65,800.

Required

1. Enter the trial balance on an accounting work sheet and complete the work sheet.
2. Journalize the adjusting and closing entries at December 31. Post to the Income Summary account as an accuracy check on the entries affecting that account. The credit balance closed out of Income Summary should equal net income computed on the work sheet.
3. Prepare the company's multi-step income statement, statement of owner's equity, and balance sheet in account format. Draw arrows linking the statements.

Solution

Requirement 1

JAN KING DISTRIBUTING COMPANY
Accounting Work Sheet (Periodic Inventory System)
Year Ended December 31, 20X3

Account Title	Trial Balance Debit	Trial Balance Credit	Adjustments Debit	Adjustments Credit	Income Statement Debit	Income Statement Credit	Balance Sheet Debit	Balance Sheet Credit
Cash	5,670						5,670	
Accounts receivable	37,100						37,100	
Inventory	60,500				60,500	65,800	65,800	
Supplies	3,930			(a) 2,580			1,350	
Prepaid rent	6,000			(b) 5,000			1,000	
Furniture and fixtures	26,500						26,500	
Accumulated depreciation		21,200		(d) 2,650				23,850
Accounts payable		46,340						46,340
Salary payable				(e) 1,300				1,300
Interest payable				(f) 600				600
Unearned sales revenue		3,500	(c) 1,100					2,400
Note payable, long-term		35,000						35,000
Jan King, capital		23,680						23,680
Jan King, withdrawals	48,000						48,000	
Sales revenue		346,700		(c) 1,100		347,800		
Sales discounts	10,300				10,300			
Sales returns and allowances	8,200				8,200			
Purchases	175,900				175,900			
Purchase discounts		6,000				6,000		
Purchase returns and allowances		7,430				7,430		
Freight in	9,300				9,300			
Salary expense	82,750		(e) 1,300		84,050			
Rent expense	7,000		(b) 5,000		12,000			
Depreciation expense			(d) 2,650		2,650			
Utilities expense	5,800				5,800			
Supplies expense			(a) 2,580		2,580			
Interest expense	2,900		(f) 600		3,500			
	489,850	489,850	13,230	13,230	374,780	427,030	185,420	133,170
Net income					52,250			52,250
					427,030	427,030	185,420	185,420

Requirement 2

Adjusting Entries

20X3

Dec. 31	Supplies Expense	2,580	
	Supplies		2,580
31	Rent Expense	5,000	
	Prepaid Rent		5,000
31	Unearned Sales Revenue ($3,500 − $2,400)	1,100	
	Sales Revenue		1,100
31	Depreciation Expense ($26,500/10)	2,650	
	Accumulated Depreciation		2,650
31	Salary Expense	1,300	
	Salary Payable		1,300
31	Interest Expense	600	
	Interest Payable		600

Closing Entries

20X3

Dec. 31	Sales Revenue	347,800	
	Income Summary		347,800
31	Cost of Goods Sold	245,700	
	Inventory (beginning balance)		60,500
	Purchases		175,900
	Freight In		9,300
31	Inventory	65,800	
	Purchase Discounts	6,000	
	Purchase Returns and Allowances	7,430	
	Cost of Goods Sold		79,230
31	Income Summary	295,550	
	Sales Discounts		10,300
	Sales Returns and Allowances		8,200
	Cost of Goods Sold ($245,700 − $79,230)		166,470
	Salary Expense		84,050
	Rent Expense		12,000
	Depreciation Expense		2,650
	Utilities Expense		5,800
	Supplies Expense		2,580
	Interest Expense		3,500
31	Income Summary ($347,800 − $295,550)	52,250	
	Jan King, Capital		52,250
31	Jan King, Capital	48,000	
	Jan King, Withdrawals		48,000

INCOME SUMMARY

Clo.	295,550	Clo.	347,800
Clo.	52,250	Bal.	52,250

Requirement 3

JAN KING DISTRIBUTING COMPANY
Income Statement
Year Ended December 31, 20X3

Sales revenue			$347,800
Less: Sales discounts............................		$(10,300)	
Sales returns and allowances		(8,230)	(18,500)
Net sales revenue			$329,300
Cost of goods sold:			
Beginning inventory		$ 60,500	
Purchases...	$175,900		
Less: Purchase discounts...............	$(6,000)		
Purchase returns and			
allowances..........................	(7,430)	(13,430)	
Net purchases....................................		162,470	
Freight in..		9,300	
Cost of goods available for sale		232,270	
Less: Ending inventory.....................		(65,800)	
Cost of goods sold.............................			166,470
Gross profit			162,830
Operating expenses:			
Salary expense		84,050	
Rent expense.....................................		12,000	
Utilities expense		5,800	
Depreciation expense		2,650	
Supplies expense		2,580	107,080
Income from operations			55,750
Other expense:			
Interest expense			3,500
Net income...			$ 52,250

JAN KING DISTRIBUTING COMPANY
Statement of Owner's Equity
Year Ended December 31, 20X3

Jan King, capital, December 31, 20X2	$23,680
Add: Net income	52,250
	75,930
Less: Withdrawals	(48,000)
Jan King, capital, December 31, 20X3	$27,930

JAN KING DISTRIBUTING COMPANY
Balance Sheet
December 31, 20X3

Assets			Liabilities		
Current:			**Current:**		
Cash	$ 5,670		Accounts payable...............	$ 46,340	
Accounts receivable	37,100		Salary payable....................	1,300	
Inventory	65,800		Interest payable	600	
Supplies...............................	1,350		Unearned sales revenue.....	2,400	
Prepaid rent........................	1,000		Total current liabilities	50,640	
Total current assets	110,920		**Long-term:**		
Plant:			Note payable	35,000	
Furniture and					
fixtures............ $26,500			Total liabilities.........................	85,640	
Less:					
Accumulated					
depreciation... (23,850)	2,650		**Owner's Equity**		
			Jan King, capital....................	27,930	
			Total liabilities and owner's		
Total assets	$113,570		equity.................................	$113,570	

Assess Your Progress

Appendix Exercises

E5A-1 Journalize, without explanations, the following transactions of Lane's Fine Gifts during June:

Journalizing purchase and sale transactions
(Obj. A2)

June 3 Purchased $700 of inventory under terms of 2/10 n/eom (end of month) and FOB shipping point.
    7 Returned $300 of defective merchandise purchased on June 3.
    9 Paid freight bill of $30 on June 3 purchase.
  10 Sold inventory for $3,200. Payment terms were 2/15 n/30.
  12 Paid amount owed on credit purchase of June 3, less the discount and the return.
  16 Granted a sales allowance of $800 on the June 10 sale.
  23 Received cash from June 10 customer in full settlement of her debt, less the allowance and the discount.

E5A-2 As the proprietor of Stevens Goodyear Tire Company you receive the following invoice from a supplier:

Journalizing transactions from a purchase invoice
(Obj. A2)

BELTLINE TIRE WHOLESALE DISTRIBUTORS, INC.
2600 Commonwealth Avenue
Boston, Massachusetts 02215

Invoice date: May 14, 20X3   **Payment terms:** 2/10 n/30

Sold to: Stevens Goodyear Tire Co.
4219 Crestwood Parkway
Lexington, Mass. 02173

Quantity Ordered	Description	Quantity Shipped	Price	Amount
4	P135–X4 Radials	4	$37.14	$ 148.56
8	L912 Belted-bias	8	41.32	330.56
14	R39 Truck tires	10	50.02	500.20
	Total			$979.32

Due date: **Amount:**
May 24, 20X3 $959.73
May 25 through June 13, 20X3 $979.32

Paid:

Required

1. Stevens received the invoice on May 15. Record the May 15 purchase on account. Carry to the nearest cent throughout.
2. The R39 truck tires were ordered by mistake and were therefore returned to Beltline. Journalize the return on May 19.
3. Record the May 22 payment of the amount owed.

E5A-3 On April 30, De Boulle Jewelers purchased inventory of $8,000 on account from Intergem Jewels, a jewelry importer. Terms were 3/15 net 45. On receiving the goods, De Boulle checked the order and found $800 of unsuitable merchandise. Therefore, De Boulle returned $800 of merchandise to Intergem on May 4.

Journalizing purchase transactions
(Obj. A2)

    To pay the remaining amount owed, De Boulle borrowed the net amount of the invoice from the bank. On May 14, De Boulle signed a short-term note payable to the bank and immediately paid the borrowed funds to Intergem. On June 14, De Boulle paid the bank the net amount of the invoice, which De Boulle had borrowed, plus 1% monthly interest (round to the nearest dollar).

Required

Record the indicated transactions in the journal of De Boulle Jewelers. Explanations are not required.

E5A-4 Refer to the business situation in Exercise 5A-3. Journalize the transactions of Intergem Jewels. Explanations are not required.

Note: Exercises 5-13 (page 201), 5-14 (page 201), and 5-15 (page 201) also pertain to the periodic inventory system.

APPENDIX PROBLEMS

Accounting for the purchase and sale of inventory
(Obj. A2)

P5A-1 The following transactions occurred between Abba Medical Supply and a Hillcrest Drug store during November of the current year:

Nov. 6 Abba Medical Supply sold $6,200 worth of merchandise to Hillcrest on terms of 2/10 n/30, FOB shipping point. Abba prepaid freight charges of $300 and included this amount in the invoice total. (Abba's entry to record the freight payment debits Accounts Receivable and credits Cash.)

10 Hillcrest returned $900 of the merchandise purchased on November 6. Abba issued a credit memo for this amount.

15 Hillcrest paid $3,000 of the invoice amount owed to Abba for the November 6 purchase, less the discount. This payment included none of the freight charge.

27 Hillcrest paid the remaining amount owed to Abba for the November 6 purchase.

Required

Journalize these transactions, first on the books of the Hillcrest Drug store and second on the books of Abba Medical Supply.

Journalizing purchase and sales transactions
(Obj. A2)

P5A-2 Preakness Wholesale Grocery engaged in the following transactions during May of the current year:

May 3 Purchased office supplies for cash, $300.

7 Purchased inventory on credit terms of 3/10 net eom, $2,000.

8 Returned half the inventory purchased on May 7. It was not the inventory ordered.

10 Sold goods for cash, $450.

13 Sold inventory on credit terms of 2/15 n/45, $3,900.

16 Paid the amount owed on account from the purchase of May 7, less the discount and the return.

17 Received defective inventory returned from May 13 sale, $900.

18 Purchased inventory of $4,000 on account. Payment terms were 2/10 net 30.

26 Borrowed $3,920 from the bank to take advantage of the discount offered on May 18 purchase. Signed a note payable to the bank for this amount.

26 Paid supplier for goods purchased on May 18, less the discount.

28 Received cash in full settlement of the account from the customer who purchased inventory on May 13, less the discount and the return.

29 Purchased inventory for cash, $2,000, plus freight charges of $160.

Required

1. Journalize the preceding transactions. Explanations are not required.
2. The note payable signed on May 26 requires the payment of $30 interest expense. Was the decision to borrow funds in order to take advantage of the cash discount wise or unwise? Support your answer by comparing the discount to the interest paid.

Journalizing purchase and sale transactions
(Obj. A2)

P5A-3 Larkspur Lighting Company engaged in the following transactions during July of the current year:

July 2 Purchased inventory for cash, $800.

5 Purchased store supplies on credit terms of net eom, $450.

8 Purchased inventory of $3,000, plus freight charges of $230. Credit terms are 3/15 n/30.

9 Sold goods for cash, $1,200.

11 Returned $200 of the inventory purchased on July 8. It was damaged.

12 Purchased inventory on credit terms of 3/10 n/30, $3,330.

14 Sold inventory on credit terms of 2/10 n/30, $9,600.

16 Paid utilities expense, $275

20 Received a sales return from July 14 sale, $400. Larkspur shipped the wrong goods by mistake.

21 Borrowed the amount owed on the July 8 purchase. Signed a note payable to the bank for $2,946, which takes into account the return of inventory on July 11.

21 Paid supplier for goods purchased on July 8 less the discount and the return.

23 Received $6,860 cash in partial settlement of the account from the customer who purchased inventory on July 14. Granted the customer a 2% discount and credited this account receivable for $7,000.

30 Paid for the store supplies purchased on July 5.

Required

1. Journalize the preceding transactions. Explanations are not required.
2. Compute the amount of the receivable at July 31 from the customer to whom Larkspur sold inventory on July 14. What amount of cash discount applies to this receivable at July 31?

P5A-4 The year-end trial balance of Latham Sales Company pertains to March 31, 20X4.

Preparing a merchandiser's accounting work sheet, financial statements, and adjusting and closing entries
(Obj. A3, A4, A5)

LATHAM SALES COMPANY
Trial Balance
March 31, 20X4

Cash..	$ 7,880	
Note receivable, current............................	12,400	
Interest receivable		
Inventory...	130,050	
Prepaid insurance......................................	3,600	
Notes receivable, long-term	62,000	
Furniture	6,000	
Accumulated depreciation		$ 4,000
Accounts payable		12,220
Sales commission payable		
Sales payable		
Unearned sales revenue		9,610
Ben Latham, capital		172,780
Ben Latham, withdrawals	66,040	
Sales revenue		440,000
Sales discounts	4,800	
Sales returns and allowances	11,300	
Interest revenue		8,600
Purchases..	233,000	
Purchase discounts		3,100
Purchase returns and allowances..............		7,600
Freight in..	10,000	
Sales commission expense	78,300	
Salary expense	24,700	
Rent expense...	6,000	
Utilities expense	1,840	
Depreciation expense................................		
Insurance expense.....................................		
Total..	$657,910	$657,910

Additional data at March 31, 20X4:

a. Accrued interest revenue, $1,030.
b. Insurance expense for the year, $3,000.
c. Furniture has an estimated useful life of six years. Its value is expected to be zero when it is retired from service.
d. Unearned sales revenue still unearned, $7,400.
e. Accrued salaries, $1,200.
f. Accrued sales commission expense, $1,700.
g. Inventory on hand, $133,200.

Required

1. Enter the trial balance on an accounting work sheet, and complete the work sheet for the year ended March 31, 20X4.
2. Prepare the company's multi-step income statement and statement of owner's equity for the year ended March 31, 20X4. Also prepare its classified balance sheet at that date. Long-term notes receivable should be reported on the balance sheet between current assets and plant assets in a separate section labeled Investments.
3. Journalize the adjusting and closing entries at March 31, 20X4.
4. Post to the Ben Latham, Capital account and to the Income Summary account as an accuracy check on the adjusting and closing process.

Note: Problems 5-9A (page 205) and 5-9B (page 208) also pertain to the periodic inventory system.

MERCHANDISING OPERATIONS
AND THE ACCOUNTING CYCLE
225

6
Accounting Information Systems

Price & Associates - Certified Public Accountants - Microsoft Internet Explorer

File   Edit   View   Go   Favorites   Help   Links

Back   Forward   Stop   Refresh   Home   Search   Favorites   History   Channels   Fullscreen   Mail   Print   Edit

Address http://www.price-assoc.com/

Price & Associates, PLLC
Certified Public Accountants

**2711 LBJ Freeway, Suite 150
Dallas, TX 75234
Phone: (972) 888-0950
Fax: (972) 888-0956
brian@price-assoc.com**

*Do you want an accounting firm that can really make a difference in you
bottom line results?*

Letting Price & Associates work as a true partner in your business will pay dividends you can't imagine.

800x600x16M

Start   In...   M...   E...   M...   Pr...   I...   S...   2:54 PM

LEARNING OBJECTIVES

*After studying this chapter,
you should be able to*

1. Describe the features of an effective accounting information system

2. Understand how both computerized and manual accounting systems work

3. Understand how spreadsheets are used in accounting

4. Use the sales journal, the cash receipts journal, and the accounts receivable subsidiary ledger

5. Use the purchases journal, the cash payments journal, and the accounts payable subsidiary ledger

With QuickBooks and Peachtree taking over, you'd think accountants would be worried about the future. After all, why does a business need an accountant when there's a virtual one on a disk? But the reverse is true. The new developments in software and Web applications are creating lots of new career opportunities in accounting.

Many entrepreneurs don't know how to do more than boot up their software, and they don't have time to learn how to use it. Many won't pay a full-time accountant to do their books. Enter the Accounting Software Consultant. Brian Price of **Price and Associates** has built a $400,000 business by consulting on small business accounting software. Price's clients range from mom-and-pop businesses that bring in $100,000–$200,000 a year to a $2 million services firm. The typical engagement for his firm brings in $1,100 of revenue. For a flat fee, Price installs QuickBooks or other software and provides five hours of training. Of course, five hours is never enough, so clients end up buying additional training time for $65 to $100 an hour.

The best part for Price is that clients then can do the bookkeeping. This frees Price to do the more creative work: analyzing financial information and helping clients make decisions based on the information.

Source: Adapted from Jeff Stimpson, "The new consultant," *The Practical Accountant,* September 1999, pp. 325–42.

Every organization needs an accounting system. An **accounting information system** is the combination of personnel, records, and procedures that a business uses to provide financial data. We have already been using an accounting information system in this text. It consists of two basic components: a general journal and a general ledger.

Every accounting system has these components, but this simple system can efficiently handle only a few transactions per period. Businesses cope with heavy transaction loads in two ways: computerization and specialization. We *computerize* to do the accounting faster and more reliably. *Specialization* comes when we group similar transactions to speed the process. We explore special journals in the second half of this chapter.

EFFECTIVE ACCOUNTING INFORMATION SYSTEMS

Good personnel are critical to the success of any operation. Employees must be both competent and honest. And several design features can make the accounting system run more efficiently. A good system—whether computerized or manual—includes control, compatibility, flexibility, and a favorable cost/benefit relationship.

Objective 1
Describe the features of an effective accounting information system

Features of Effective Systems

Managers need *control* over operations. *Internal controls* are the methods and procedures used to authorize transactions and safeguard assets. For example, in companies such as **Coca-Cola, America Online,** and **Kinko's,** managers control cash disbursements to avoid theft through unauthorized payments. **VISA, MasterCard,** and **Discover** keep records of their accounts receivable to ensure that they receive collections on time.

A *compatible* system is one that works smoothly with the business's operations, personnel, and organizational structure. An example is **Bank of America,** which is organized as a network of branch offices. Bank of America's top managers want to know revenues in each region where the bank does business. They also want to analyze loans in different geographic regions. If revenues in California are lagging, managers can concentrate their efforts in that state. They may relocate some branch offices or hire new personnel.

Organizations evolve. They develop new products, sell off unprofitable operations and acquire new ones, and adjust employee pay scales. Changes in the business often call for changes in the accounting system. A well-designed system is *flexible* if it accommodates changes without a complete overhaul. Consider **Monsanto Company's** acquisition of the pharmaceuticals firm **Searle** including Searle's Nutrasweet division. Monsanto's accounting system was flexible enough to fold Searle/Nutrasweet financial statements into those of Monsanto.

Achieving control, compatibility, and flexibility costs money. Managers strive for a system that offers maximum benefits at a minimum cost—that is, a favorable *cost/benefit relationship.* Most small companies use off-the-shelf computerized accounting packages, and the very smallest businesses might not computerize at all. But large companies, such as the brokerage firm **Edward Jones,** have specialized needs for information. For them, custom programming is a must. The benefits—in terms of information tailored to the company's needs—far outweigh the costs. The result? Better decisions.

Components of a Computerized System

Three components form the heart of a computerized accounting system: hardware, software, and company personnel. Each component is critical to the system's success.

Hardware is the electronic equipment: It includes computers, disk drives, monitors, printers, and the network that connects them. Most modern accounting systems require a **network,** the system of electronic linkages that allows different computers to share the same information. In a networked system, many computers can be connected to the main computer, or **server,** which stores the program and the data. With the right network, a **PricewaterhouseCoopers** auditor in London can access the data of a client located in Sydney, Australia. The result is a speedier audit for the client.

Software is the set of programs that drive the computer to perform the work desired. Accounting software accepts, edits (alters), and stores transaction data and generates the reports managers use to run the business. Many software packages operate independently from the other computing activities of the system. For example, a company that is only partly computerized may use software programs to account for employee payrolls and sales and accounts receivable. Other parts of the accounting system may not be automated.

For large enterprises, like **Hershey Foods** and **Caterpillar Tractor,** the accounting software is integrated within the overall company **database,** or computerized storehouse of information. Many business databases include accounting and nonaccounting data. In negotiating a union contract, the **Union Pacific Railroad** often needs to examine the relationship between the employment history and salary levels of company employees. Union Pacific's database provides the data managers need to negotiate effectively. During negotiations, both parties carry laptop computers to analyze the effects of decisions on the spot.

HOW COMPUTERIZED AND MANUAL ACCOUNTING SYSTEMS WORK

Computerized accounting systems have replaced manual systems in many organizations—even in small businesses such as your neighborhood pharmacy. As we discuss the stages of data processing, observe the differences between a computerized system and a manual system. The three stages of data processing (inputs, processing, outputs) are shown in Exhibit 6-1.

⊙ DAILY EXERCISE 6-1

HARDWARE. Electronic equipment that includes computers, disk drives, monitors, printers, and the network that connects them.

NETWORK. The system of electronic linkages that allows different computers to share the same information.

SERVER. The main computer in a network, where the program and data are stored.

⊙ DAILY EXERCISE 6-2

⊙ DAILY EXERCISE 6-3

SOFTWARE. Set of programs or instructions that drive the computer to perform the work desired.

DATABASE. A computerized storehouse of information.

Objective 2
Understand how both computerized and manual accounting systems work

EXHIBIT 6-1
The Three Stages of Data Processing

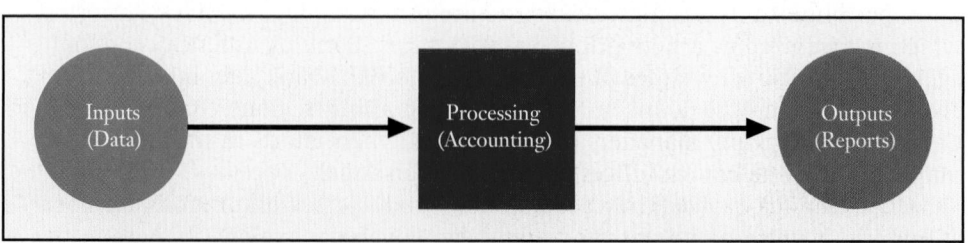

Inputs represent data from source documents, such as sales receipts, bank deposit slips, fax orders, and other telecommunications. Inputs are usually grouped by type. For example, a firm would enter cash-sale transactions separately from credit sales and purchase transactions.

In a manual system, *processing* includes journalizing transactions, posting to the accounts, and preparing the financial statements. A computerized system also processes, but without the intermediate steps (journal, ledger, and trial balance).

Outputs are the reports used for decision making, including the financial statements (income statement, balance sheet). Business owners are making better decisions—and prospering—because of the reports produced by their accounting system. Exhibit 6-2 is an overview of a computerized system. Start with data inputs in the lower left corner.

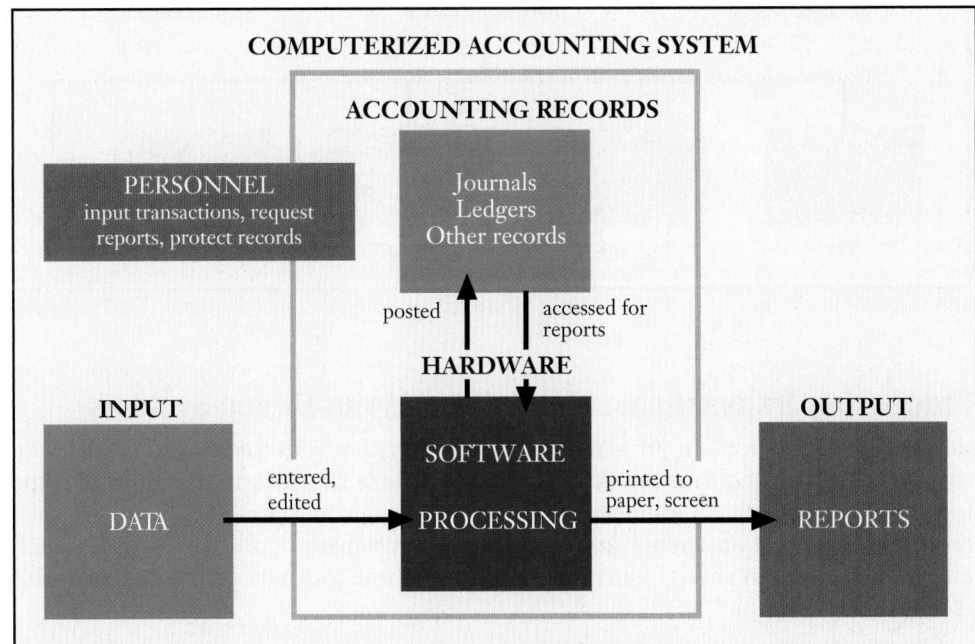

EXHIBIT 6-2
Overview of a Computerized Accounting System

Designing a System: The Chart of Accounts

Design of the accounting system begins with the chart of accounts. ➡➡ In the accounting system of a large, complex company such as **Eastman Kodak,** account numbers take on added importance. It is efficient to represent a complex account title, such as Accumulated Depreciation—Photographic Equipment, with a concise account number (for example, 12570).

Recall that asset accounts generally begin with the digit 1, liabilities with the digit 2, owner's equity accounts with the digit 3, revenues with 4, and expenses with 5. Exhibit 6-3 diagrams one structure for computerized accounts. Assets are divided into current assets, fixed assets (property, plant, and equipment), and other assets. Among the current assets, we illustrate only three general ledger accounts: Cash in Bank (Account No. 111), Accounts Receivable (No. 112), and Prepaid Insurance (No. 115).

The account numbers in Exhibit 6-3 get longer and more detailed as you move from top to bottom. For example, Customer A's account number is 1120001: 112 represents Accounts Receivable, and 0001 refers to Customer A.

Computerized accounting systems rely on account *number ranges* to translate accounts and their balances into properly organized financial statements and other reports. For example, accounts numbered 101–399 (assets, liabilities, and owner's equity) are sorted to the balance sheet, while accounts numbered 401–599 (revenues and expenses) go to the income statement.

◄◄ Recall from Chapter 2 that the chart of accounts lists all the accounts and their account numbers.

DAILY EXERCISE 6-4

EXHIBIT 6-3
Structure for Computerized Accounts

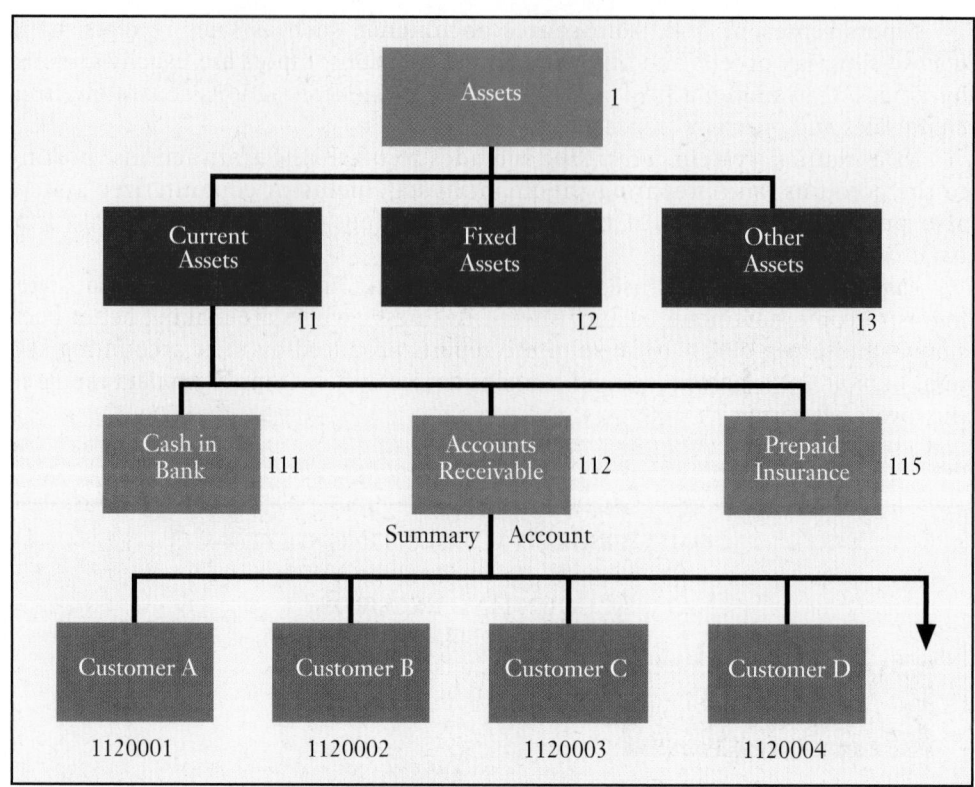

Processing Transactions: Manual and Menu-Driven Systems

Recording transactions in an actual accounting system requires an additional step that we have skipped thus far. A business of any size classifies transactions by type for efficient handling. In a manual system, credit sales, purchases on account, cash receipts, and cash payments are treated as four separate categories, with each entered into its own special journal. (We discuss these journals in detail later in this chapter.) For example:

- Credit sales are recorded in a special journal called a *sales journal.*
- Cash receipts are entered into a *cash receipts journal.*
- Credit purchases of inventory and other assets are recorded in a *purchases journal.*
- Cash payments are entered in a *cash payments journal.*
- Transactions that do not fit any of the special journals, such as the adjusting entries at the end of the period, are recorded in the *general journal,* which serves as the "journal of last resort."

MENU. A list of options for choosing computer functions.

ON-LINE PROCESSING. Computerized processing of related functions, such as the recording and posting of transactions, on a continuous basis.

BATCH PROCESSING. Computerized accounting for similar transactions in a group or batch.

Computerized systems are organized by function, or task. Access to functions is arranged in terms of menus. A **menu** is a list of options for choosing computer functions. In a *menu-driven* system, you first access the most general group of functions, called the *main menu.* You then choose from one or more submenus until you finally reach the function you want.

Exhibit 6-4 illustrates one type of menu structure. The row at the top of the exhibit shows the main menu. The computer operator (or accountant) has chosen the General option (short for General Ledger), highlighted by the cursor. This action opened a submenu of four items—Transactions, Posting, Account Maintenance, and Closing. The Transactions option was then chosen (highlighted).

Posting in a computerized system can be performed continuously as transactions are being recorded (**on-line processing**) or later for a group or batch of similar transactions (**batch processing**). In either case, posting is automatic. Batch processing of accounting data allows accountants to check the entries for accuracy before posting them. In effect, data are "parked" in the computer to await posting, which simply updates the account balances.

e-Accounting

Accounting Pioneers on the Virtual Frontier

As you saw in the chapter-opening story, computer and Internet technology are remaking the bookkeeping and tax aspects of accounting. There are "virtual" software consultants, and now there are "virtual" or "on-line" accountants. Slogans like "Real Accounting in a Virtual World" and "Outsourced Accounting Services for a Wired World" are advertising

- basic bookkeeping
- full-service outsourcing
- real-time accounting
- 24-hour access to accounting data

TADOnline, founded by Lance and Deanna Gildea in San Diego, is one such service. TAD starts clients out scanning their invoices, bank statements, and other documents into the computer. Scanned documents are transmitted to TAD, and within minutes, TAD updates the client's accounts. Customers then use a Web browser to sign in to a home page prepared by TAD, where they can view, print, and download reports, checks, and other information. Soon clients will be able to get real-time access to their accounting data through a new Web-based service.

For clients—typically small- to mid-sized businesses—the key benefits of TADOnline are price and reliability. In some cases, TAD's monthly fees are half what it would cost to hire a bookkeeper—and TAD doesn't call in sick or take vacations. A big plus for the "virtual accountants" is being able to live wherever they please, regardless of where clients are located. For TAD's Lance and Deanna Gildea, that means San Diego half the year and scenic Vashon Island, Washington, for the other half.

Source: Adapted from Antoinette Alexander, "Pioneers on the virtual frontier," *Accounting Technology,* Jan./Feb. 2000, pp. 18–24.

EXHIBIT 6-4   Main Menu of a Computerized Accounting System

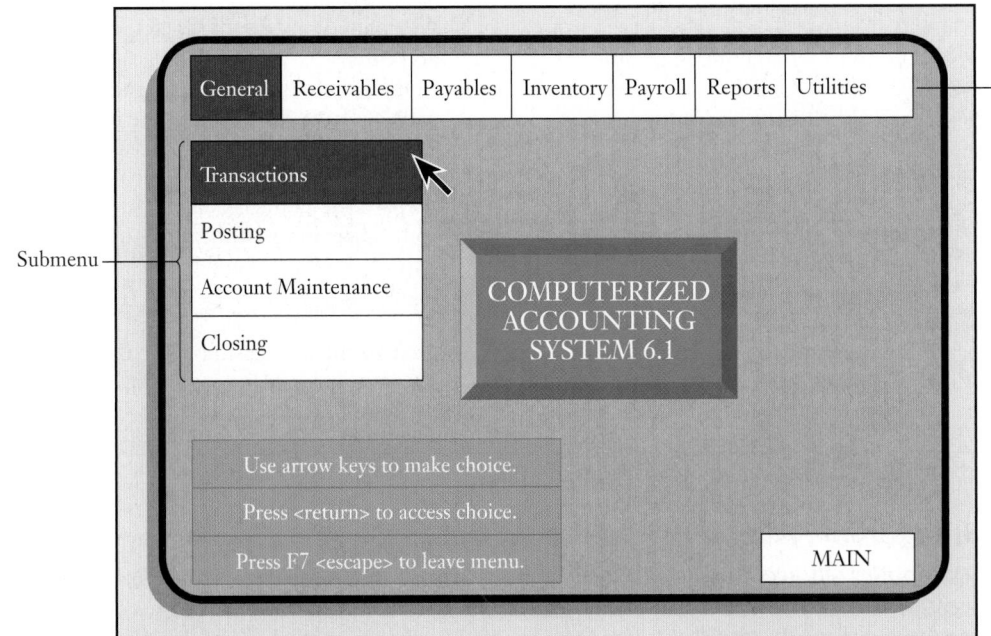

Outputs—accounting reports—are the final stage of data processing. In a computerized system, financial statements can be printed automatically. For example, the Reports option in the main menu gives the operator various report choices, which are expanded in the Reports submenu of Exhibit 6-5. In the exhibit, the operator is working with the financial statements, and specifically the balance sheet, as shown by the highlighting.

EXHIBIT 6-5
Reports Submenu of a
Computerized Accounting
System

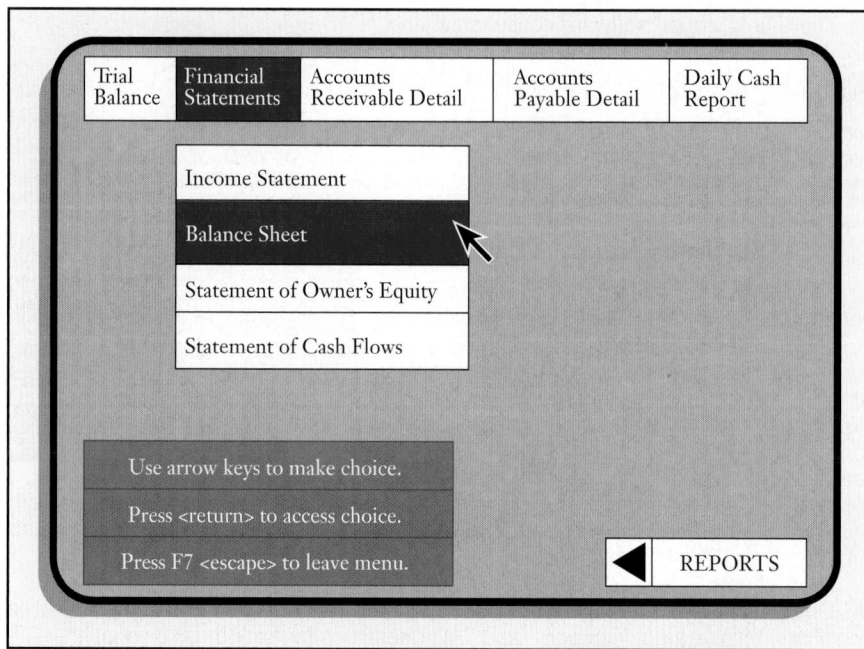

| Trial Balance | Financial Statements | Accounts Receivable Detail | Accounts Payable Detail | Daily Cash Report |

Income Statement

Balance Sheet

Statement of Owner's Equity

Statement of Cash Flows

Use arrow keys to make choice.

Press <return> to access choice.

Press F7 <escape> to leave menu.

◀ REPORTS

Exhibit 6-6 summarizes the accounting cycle in a computerized system and in a manual system. Compare and contrast the two types of systems.

EXHIBIT 6-6
Comparison of the Accounting
Cycle in a Computerized and a
Manual System

Computerized System	Manual System
1. Start with the account balances in the ledger at the beginning of the period.	1. Same.
2. Classify transactions by type. Access appropriate menus for data entry.	2. Analyze and journalize transactions as they occur.
3. Automatic posting of transactions as a batch or when entered on-line.	3. Post journal entries to the ledger accounts.
4. Unadjusted balances available immediately after each posting.	4. Compute the unadjusted balance in each account at the end of the period.
5. The trial balance, if needed, can be accessed as a report.	5. Enter the trial balance on the work sheet, and complete the work sheet.
6. Enter and post the adjusting entries. Print the financial statements. Run automatic closing procedure after backing up the period's accounting records.	6. Prepare the financial statements. Journalize and post the adjusting entries. Journalize and post the closing entries.
7. The next period's opening balances are created automatically as a result of closing.	7. Prepare the postclosing trial balance. This trial balance becomes step 1 for the next period.

MODULE. Separate compatible units of an accounting package that are integrated to function together.

Integrated Accounting Software: Spreadsheets

Computerized accounting packages are organized by **modules,** separate but integrated units that are compatible and that function together. Changes affecting one module will affect others. For example, entering and posting a credit-sale

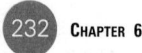

transaction will update two modules: Accounts Receivable/Sales and Inventory/Cost of Goods Sold. Accounting packages, such as QuickBooks and Peachtree, come as an integrated system.

You may be preparing your homework assignments manually. Imagine preparing a work sheet for **General Motors** (GM). Each adjustment changes the company's financial statement totals. Consider computing GM's revenue amounts by hand. The task would be overwhelming. For even a small business with only a few departments, the computations are tedious, time-consuming, and therefore expensive. Also, errors are likely.

Spreadsheets are computer programs that link data by means of formulas and functions. These electronic work sheets were invented to update budgets. Spreadsheets are organized as a rectangular grid composed of *cells,* each defined by a row number and a column number. A cell can contain words (called labels), numbers, or formulas (relationships among cells). The *cursor,* or electronic highlighter, indicates which cell is active. When the cursor is placed over any cell, information can be entered there for processing.

Exhibit 6-7 shows a simple income statement on a spreadsheet screen. The labels were entered in cells A1 through A4. The dollar amount of revenues was entered in cell B2 and expenses in cell B3. A formula was placed in cell B4 as follows: =B2−B3. This formula subtracts expenses from revenues to compute net income in cell B4. If revenues in cell B2 increase to $170,000, net income in B4 automatically increases to $80,000. No other cells will change.

Objective 3
Understand how spreadsheets are used in accounting

SPREADSHEET. A computer program that links data by means of formulas and functions; an electronic work sheet.

EXHIBIT 6-7
A Spreadsheet Screen

Formula for B4:   =B2−B3

Column:	A	B	C
Row: 1	Income Statement:		
2	Revenues	150,000	
3	Expenses	90,000	
4	Net Income	60,000	
5			

Cursor is on cell B4.

Spreadsheets are ideally suited to preparing a budget, which summarizes the financial goals of a business. Consider **Procter & Gamble,** whose Health-Care Sector has an annual advertising budget of several hundred million dollars. Suppose Procter & Gamble allocates $50 million for its Crest Complete toothbrush. Procter & Gamble's advertising expenses will increase. The company will also forecast an increase in sales revenue, cost of goods sold, and other expenses. A spreadsheet computes all these changes in response to the advertising. It lets Procter & Gamble's managers track the profitability of each product. Armed with current data, the managers can make informed decisions. The result is higher profits.

We can add or delete whole rows and columns of data and move blocks of numbers and words on a spreadsheet. The power of a spreadsheet is apparent when enormous amounts of data must be analyzed. Change only one number, and you save hours of manual recalculation. Exhibit 6-8 shows the basic arithmetic operations in popular spreadsheet programs such as Excel.

EXHIBIT 6-8
Basic Arithmetic Operations in Excel Spreadsheets

Operation	Symbol
Addition	+
Subtraction..	−
Multiplication...	*
Division	/
Addition of a range of cells	=SUM(beginning cell:ending cell)
Examples:	
Add the contents of cells A2 through A9	=SUM(A2:A9)
Divide the contents of cell C2 by the	
contents of cell D1	=C2/D1

DAILY EXERCISE 6-5

www.prenhall.com/horngren
Mid-Chapter Assessment

SPECIAL JOURNALS

Exhibit 6-9 diagrams a typical accounting system for a merchandising business. The remainder of this chapter describes some of the more important aspects of that system.

EXHIBIT 6-9 Overview of an Accounting System with Special Journals for a Merchandising Business

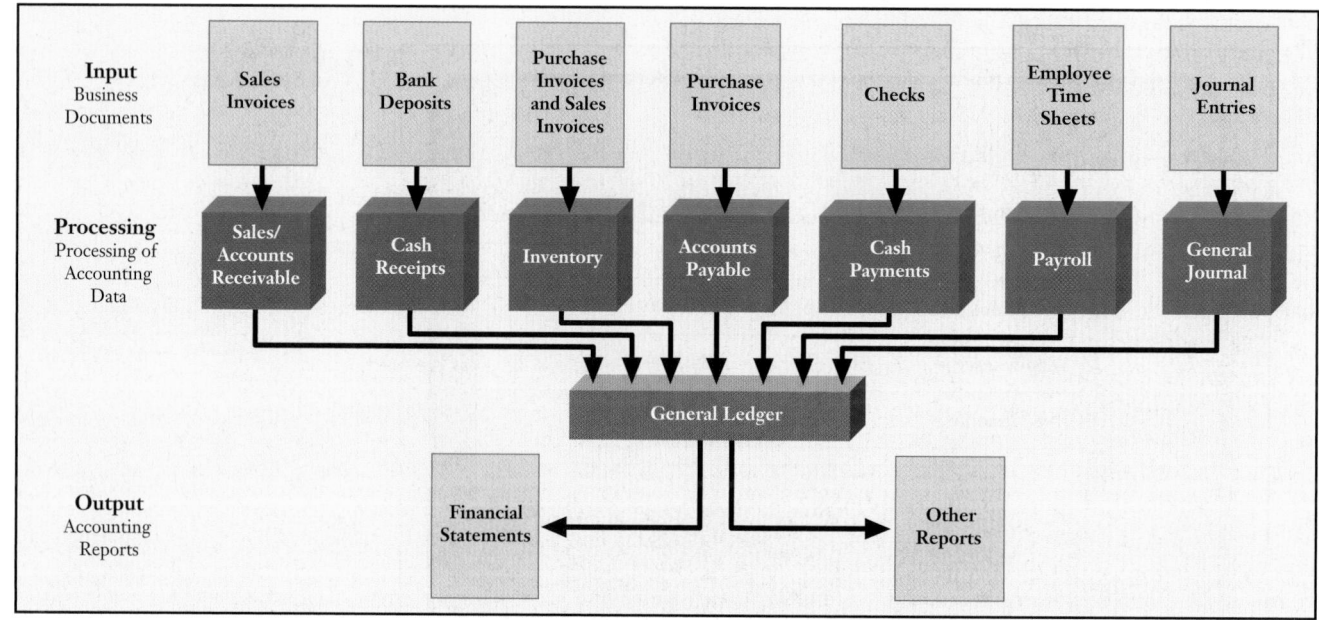

Special Accounting Journals

GENERAL JOURNAL. Journal used to record all transactions that do not fit one of the special journals.

SPECIAL JOURNAL. An accounting journal designed to record one specific type of transaction.

The journal entries illustrated so far in this book have been made in the **general journal.** This journal is used to record all transactions that do not fit one of the special journals. In practice, it is not efficient to record all transactions in the general journal, so we use special journals. A **special journal** is an accounting journal designed to record one specific type of transaction.

Both manual and computerized systems organize transaction entries by type using special journals and accounting modules. In a computerized system, accountants input data through various modules, such as the Accounts Receivable module for credit sales. In a manual system, they enter transaction data in special journals. But the underlying accounting principles are the same in both manual and computerized systems.

In all likelihood, you will be working with a computerized system. We would rather you *not* view the process as a black box. To help you understand the basic accounting, over the next several pages we take you through the steps in a manual system.

Most of a business's transactions fall into one of five categories, so accountants use five different journals to record these transactions. This system reduces the time and cost otherwise spent journalizing. The five categories of transactions, the related journal, and the posting abbreviations are as follows:

Transaction	Special Journal	Posting Abbreviation
1. Sale on account	Sales journal	S
2. Cash receipt	Cash receipts journal	CR
3. Purchase on account	Purchases journal	P
4. Cash payment	Cash payments journal	CP
5. All others	General journal	J

● DAILY EXERCISE 6-6

Adjusting and closing entries are entered in the general journal. Transactions are recorded in either the general journal or a special journal, but not in both.

Using the Sales Journal

Objective 4
Use the sales journal, the cash receipts journal, and the accounts receivable subsidiary ledger

Most merchandisers sell at least some of their inventory on account. These credit sales are entered in the **sales journal.** Credit sales of assets other than inventory— for example, buildings—occur infrequently and are recorded in the general journal.

SALES JOURNAL. Special journal used to record credit sales.

Exhibit 6-10 illustrates a sales journal (Panel A) and the related posting to the ledgers (Panel B) of **Austin Sound Center,** introduced in Chapter 5. Each entry in the Accounts Receivable/Sales Revenue column of the sales journal in Exhibit 6-10 is a debit (Dr.) to Accounts Receivable and a credit (Cr.) to Sales Revenue, as the heading above this column indicates. For each transaction, the accountant enters the date, invoice number, customer account, and transaction amount. This streamlined way of recording sales on account saves a vast amount of time that, in a manual system, would be spent entering account titles and dollar amounts in the general journal.

In recording credit sales in previous chapters, we did not keep a record of the names of credit-sale customers. In practice, the business must know the amount receivable from each customer. How else can the company keep track of who owes it money, when collection is due, and how much?

Consider the first transaction in Panel A. On November 2, Austin Sound sold stereo equipment on account to Maria Galvez for $935. The invoice number is 422. All this information appears on a single line in the sales journal. No explanation is necessary. The transaction's presence in the sales journal means it is a credit sale, debited to Accounts Receivable—Maria Galvez and credited to Sales Revenue. To gain additional information about the transaction, we would look up the actual invoice.

● DAILY EXERCISE 6-7

● DAILY EXERCISE 6-8

Recall from Chapter 5 that Austin Sound uses a *perpetual* inventory system. At the time of recording the sale, Austin Sound also records the cost of the goods sold and the decrease in inventory. Many computerized accounting systems are programmed to read both the sales amount (from the bar code on the package of the item sold) and the cost of goods sold. A separate column of the sales journal holds the cost of goods sold and inventory amount—$505 for the sale to Maria Galvez. If Austin Sound used a *periodic* inventory system, it would not record cost of goods sold and the decrease in inventory at the time of sale. The sales journal would need only one column to debit Accounts Receivable and to credit Sales Revenue for the amount of the sale.

POSTING TO THE GENERAL LEDGER   The ledger we have used so far is the **general ledger,** which holds the accounts reported in the financial statements. We will soon introduce other ledgers.

GENERAL LEDGER. Ledger of accounts that are reported in the financial statements.

Posting from the sales journal to the general ledger can be done only once each month. In Exhibit 6-10 (Panel A), November's credit sales total $4,319. This column has two headings, Accounts Receivable and Sales Revenue. When the $4,319 is posted to these accounts in the general ledger, their account numbers are written beneath the total in the sales journal. In Panel B of Exhibit 6-10, the account number for Accounts Receivable is 112 and the account number for Sales Revenue is

Exhibit 6-10   Sales Journal (Panel A) and Posting to the Ledgers (Panel B)

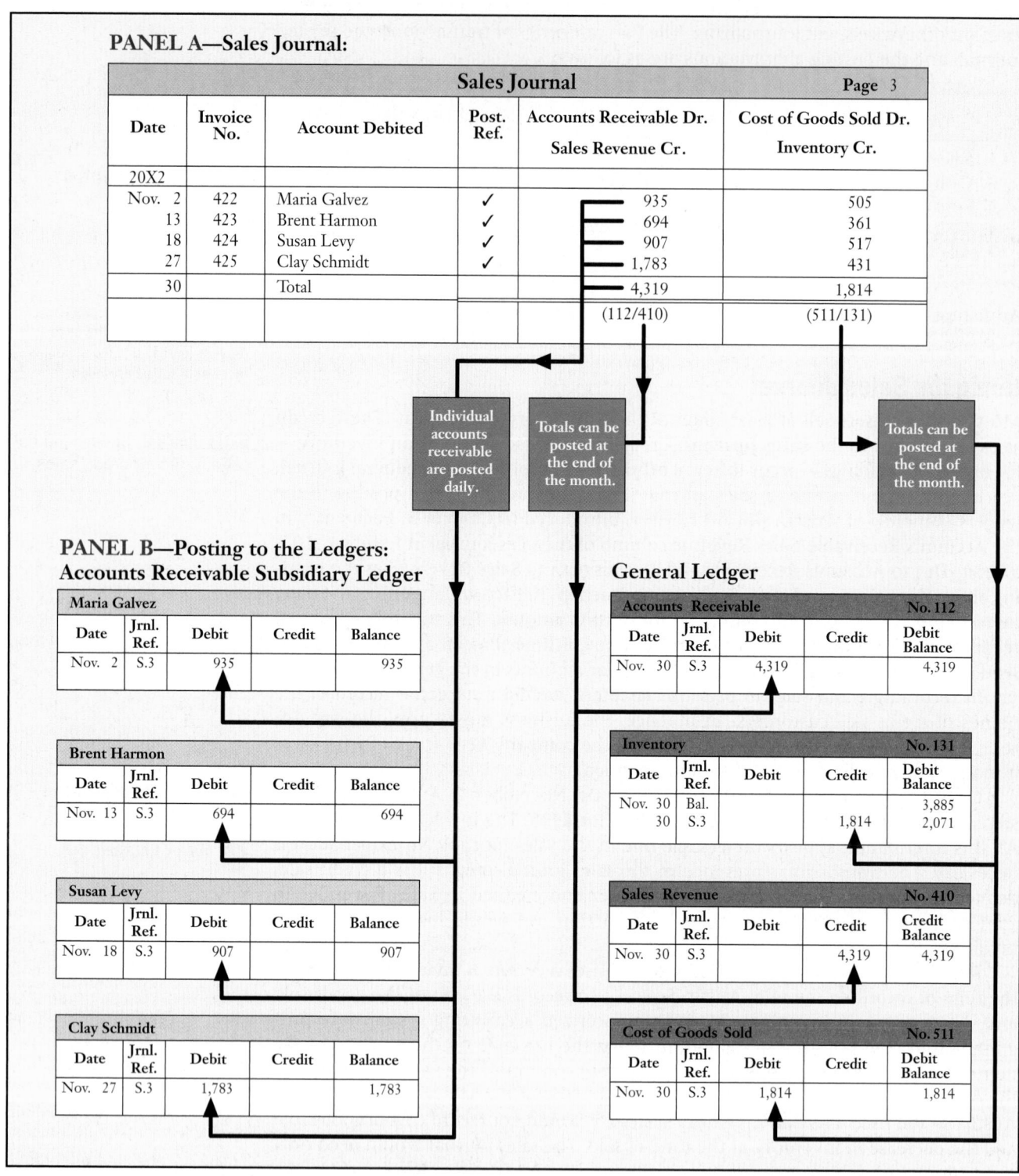

410. Printing these account numbers beneath the credit-sales total in the sales journal signifies that the $4,319 has been posted to the two accounts.

The debit to Cost of Goods Sold and the credit to Inventory for the monthly total of $1,814 can also be posted at the end of the month. After posting, these accounts' numbers are entered beneath the total to show that Cost of Goods Sold and Inventory have been updated.

POSTING TO THE ACCOUNTS RECEIVABLE SUBSIDIARY LEDGER The $4,319 sum of the November debits to Accounts Receivable does not identify the amount receivable from any specific customer. A business may have thousands of customers. For example, the **Consumers Digest Company,** a Chicago-based firm that publishes the bimonthly magazine *Consumers Digest,* has 1.2 million customer accounts—one for each subscriber.

To streamline operations, businesses place the accounts of their individual credit customers in a subsidiary ledger, called the Accounts Receivable ledger. A **subsidiary ledger** is a record of accounts that provides supporting details on individual balances, the total of which appears in a general ledger account. The customer accounts are arranged in alphabetical order.

Amounts in the sales journal are posted to the subsidiary ledger *daily* to keep a current record of the amount receivable from each customer. Daily posting allows the business to answer customer inquiries promptly. Suppose Maria Galvez telephones Austin Sound on November 3 to ask how much money she owes. The subsidiary ledger readily provides that information, $935 in Exhibit 6-10, Panel B.

When each transaction amount is posted to the subsidiary ledger, a check mark or some other notation is entered in the posting reference column of the sales journal (see Exhibit 6-10, Panel A).

JOURNAL REFERENCES IN THE LEDGERS When amounts are posted to the ledgers, the journal page number is printed in the account to identify the source of the data. All transaction data in Exhibit 6-10 originated on page 3 of the sales journal, so all journal references in the ledger accounts are S.3. The "S." indicates sales journal.

Trace all the postings in Exhibit 6-10. The most effective way to learn about accounting systems and special journals is to study the flow of data. The arrows indicate the direction of the information. The arrows also show the links between the individual customer accounts in the subsidiary ledger and the Accounts Receivable account. The Accounts Receivable debit balance in the general ledger should equal the sum of the individual customer balances in the subsidiary ledger, as follows:

General Ledger

Accounts Receivable debit balance............... $4,319 ◄

Subsidiary Ledger: Customer Accounts Receivable

Customer	Balance
Maria Galvez	$ 935
Brent Harmon	694
Susan Levy	907
Clay Schmidt	1,783
Total accounts receivable.............................	$4,319 ◄

Accounts Receivable in the general ledger is a **control account.** Its balance equals the sum of the balances of a group of related accounts in a subsidiary ledger. The individual customer accounts are subsidiary accounts. They are said to be "controlled" by the Accounts Receivable account in the general ledger.

Additional data can be recorded in the sales journal. For example, a company may add a column to record sales terms, such as 2/10 n/30. The design of the journal depends on managers' needs for information.

SUBSIDIARY LEDGER. Record of accounts that provides supporting details on individual balances, the total of which appears in a general ledger account.

CONTROL ACCOUNT. An account whose balance equals the sum of the balances in a group of related accounts in a subsidiary ledger.

THINK IT OVER Suppose Austin Sound had 400 credit sales for the month. How many postings to the general ledger would be made from the sales journal? (Ignore Cost of Goods Sold and Inventory.) How many would there be if all sales transactions were routed through the general journal?

Answer: There are only two postings from the sales journal to the general ledger: one to Accounts Receivable and one to Sales Revenue. There would be 800 postings from the general journal: 400 to Accounts Receivable and 400 to Sales Revenue. This difference clearly shows the benefit of using a sales journal.

Using Documents as Journals

Many small businesses streamline their accounting systems by using their business documents as the journals. This practice avoids the need for special journals and saves money. For example, Austin Sound could keep sales invoices in a loose-leaf binder and let the invoices serve as the sales journal. At the end of the period, the accountant simply totals the sales on account and posts the total as a debit to Accounts Receivable and a credit to Sales Revenue. The accountant can also post directly from the invoices to customer accounts in the accounts receivable ledger.

Using the Cash Receipts Journal

CASH RECEIPTS JOURNAL. Special journal used to record cash receipts.

Cash transactions are common in most businesses. To record repetitive cash receipt transactions, accountants use the **cash receipts journal.**

Exhibit 6-11, Panel A, illustrates the cash receipts journal. The related posting to ledgers is shown in Panel B. The exhibit illustrates November transactions for Austin Sound Center.

Every transaction recorded in this journal is a cash receipt, so the second column (after the date) is for debits to the Cash account. The next column is for debits to Sales Discounts on collections from customers. In a typical merchandising business, the main sources of cash are collections on account and cash sales.

The cash receipts journal has credit columns for Accounts Receivable and Sales Revenue. The journal also has a credit column for Other Accounts, which lists sources of cash other than cash sales and collections on account. This Other Accounts column is also used to record the names of customers from whom cash is received on account.

In Exhibit 6-11, cash sales occurred on November 6, 19, and 28. Observe the debits to Cash and the credits to Sales Revenue ($517, $853, and $1,802). Each sale entry is accompanied by a separate entry that debits Cost of Goods Sold and credits Inventory for the cost of the merchandise sold. The column for this entry is at the far right side of the cash receipts journal.

On November 11, Austin Sound borrowed $1,000 from First Bank. Cash is debited, and Note Payable to First Bank is credited in the Other Accounts column because no specific credit column is set up to account for borrowings. For this transaction, we print the account title, Note Payable to First Bank, in the Other Accounts/Account Title column. This entry records the source of cash.

On November 25, Austin Sound collected $762 of interest revenue. The account credited, Interest Revenue, is printed in the Other Accounts column. The November 11 and 25 transactions illustrate a key fact about business. Different entities have different types of transactions; they design their special journals to meet their particular needs for information. In this case, the Other Accounts credit column is the catchall used to record all nonroutine cash receipt transactions.

 DAILY EXERCISE 6-9

On November 14, Austin Sound collected $900 from Maria Galvez. Referring to Exhibit 6-10, we see that on November 2, Austin Sound sold merchandise for $935 to Galvez. The terms of sale allowed a $35 discount for prompt payment, and she paid within the discount period. Austin's cash receipt is recorded by debiting Cash for $900 and Sales Discounts for $35, and by crediting Accounts Receivable for $935. The customer's name appears in the Other Accounts/Account Title column.

Total debits should equal total credits in the cash receipts journal. This equality holds for each transaction and for the monthly totals. For the month, total debits ($6,134 + $35 = $6,169) equal total credits ($1,235 + $3,172 + $1,762 = $6,169). The debit to Cost of Goods Sold and the credit to Inventory are separate.

POSTING TO THE GENERAL LEDGER   Column totals can be posted monthly. To indicate their posting, the account number is written below the column total in the cash receipts journal. Note the account number for Cash (101) below the column total $6,134, and trace the posting to Cash in the general ledger. Likewise, the other column totals also are posted to the general ledger.

The column total for *Other Accounts* is *not* posted. Instead, these credits are posted individually. In Exhibit 6-11, the November 11 transaction reads "Note Payable to

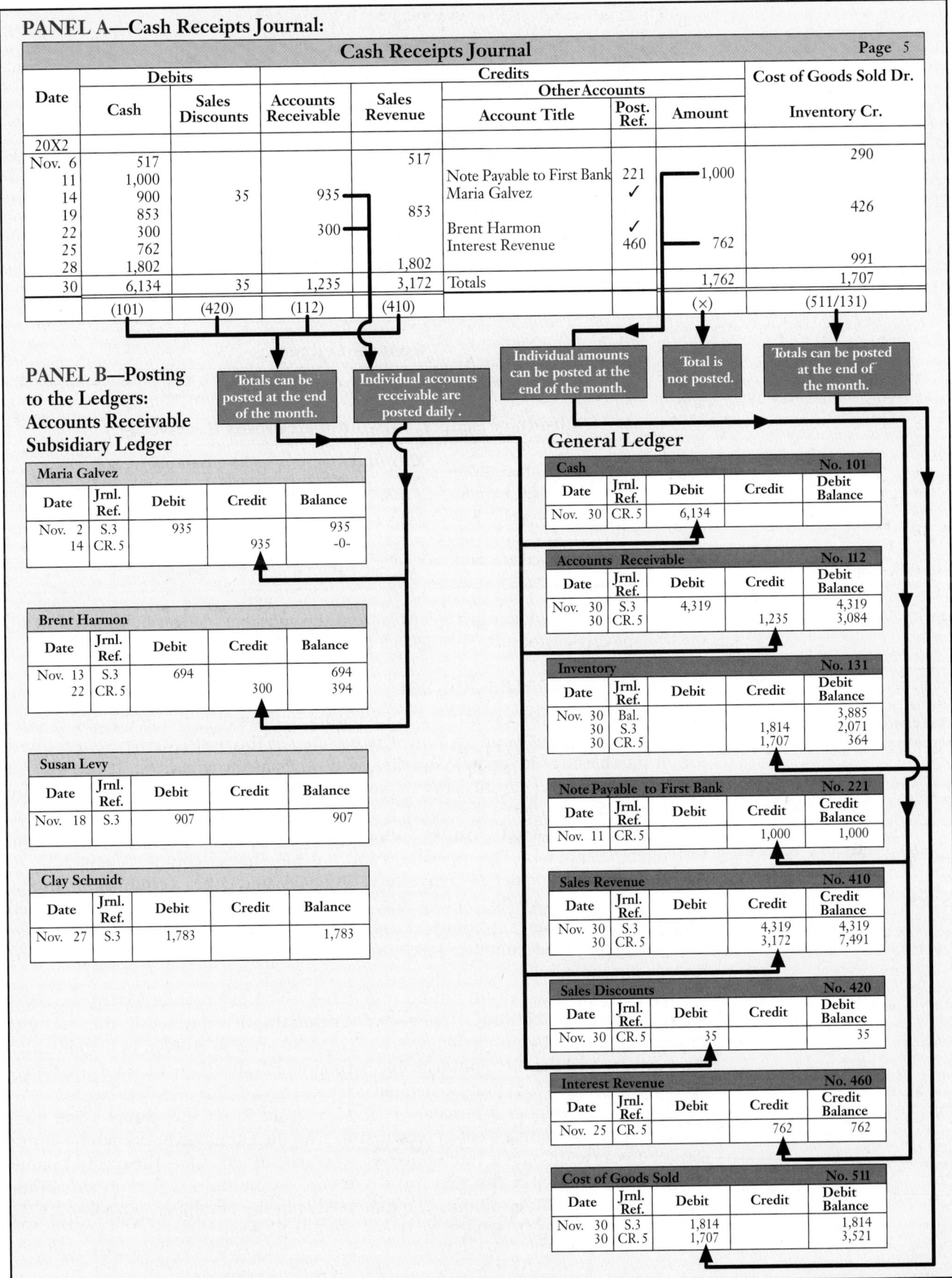

PANEL A—Cash Receipts Journal:

Cash Receipts Journal   Page 5

| Date | Debits | | | Credits | | | | Cost of Goods Sold Dr. |
| | Cash | Sales Discounts | Accounts Receivable | Sales Revenue | Other Accounts | | | |
					Account Title	Post. Ref.	Amount	Inventory Cr.
20X2								
Nov. 6	517			517				290
11	1,000				Note Payable to First Bank	221	1,000	
14	900	35	935		Maria Galvez	✓		
19	853			853				426
22	300		300		Brent Harmon	✓		
25	762				Interest Revenue	460	762	
28	1,802			1,802				991
30	6,134	35	1,235	3,172	Totals		1,762	1,707
	(101)	(420)	(112)	(410)			(×)	(511/131)

PANEL B—Posting to the Ledgers: Accounts Receivable Subsidiary Ledger

Totals can be posted at the end of the month.	Individual accounts receivable are posted daily .	Individual amounts can be posted at the end of the month.	Total is not posted.	Totals can be posted at the end of the month.

Maria Galvez

Date	Jrnl. Ref.	Debit	Credit	Balance
Nov. 2	S.3	935		935
14	CR.5		935	-0-

Brent Harmon

Date	Jrnl. Ref.	Debit	Credit	Balance
Nov. 13	S.3	694		694
22	CR.5		300	394

Susan Levy

Date	Jrnl. Ref.	Debit	Credit	Balance
Nov. 18	S.3	907		907

Clay Schmidt

Date	Jrnl. Ref.	Debit	Credit	Balance
Nov. 27	S.3	1,783		1,783

General Ledger

Cash   No. 101

Date	Jrnl. Ref.	Debit	Credit	Debit Balance
Nov. 30	CR.5	6,134		

Accounts Receivable   No. 112

Date	Jrnl. Ref.	Debit	Credit	Debit Balance
Nov. 30	S.3	4,319		4,319
30	CR.5		1,235	3,084

Inventory   No. 131

Date	Jrnl. Ref.	Debit	Credit	Debit Balance
Nov. 30	Bal.			3,885
30	S.3		1,814	2,071
30	CR.5		1,707	364

Note Payable to First Bank   No. 221

Date	Jrnl. Ref.	Debit	Credit	Credit Balance
Nov. 11	CR.5		1,000	1,000

Sales Revenue   No. 410

Date	Jrnl. Ref.	Debit	Credit	Credit Balance
Nov. 30	S.3		4,319	4,319
30	CR.5		3,172	7,491

Sales Discounts   No. 420

Date	Jrnl. Ref.	Debit	Credit	Debit Balance
Nov. 30	CR.5	35		35

Interest Revenue   No. 460

Date	Jrnl. Ref.	Debit	Credit	Credit Balance
Nov. 25	CR.5		762	762

Cost of Goods Sold   No. 511

Date	Jrnl. Ref.	Debit	Credit	Debit Balance
Nov. 30	S.3	1,814		1,814
30	CR.5	1,707		3,521

First Bank." This account's number (221) in the Post. Ref. column indicates that the transaction amount was posted individually. The letter x below the column indicates the column total was *not* posted. Individual amounts can be posted to the general ledger at the end of the month. But their date in the ledger accounts should be their actual date in the journal, to make it easier to trace each amount back to the journal.

POSTING TO THE SUBSIDIARY LEDGER   Amounts from the cash receipts journal are posted to the subsidiary accounts receivable ledger daily to keep the individual balances up to date. The postings to the accounts receivable ledger are credits. Trace the $935 posting to Maria Galvez's account. It reduces her balance to zero. The $300 receipt from Brent Harmon reduces his accounts receivable balance to $394.

After posting, the sum of the individual balances in the accounts receivable ledger equals the general ledger balance in Accounts Receivable.

General Ledger

Accounts Receivable debit balance.............. $3,084 ◄

Subsidiary Ledger: Customer Accounts Receivable

Customer	Balance
Brent Harmon	$ 394
Susan Levy	907
Clay Schmidt	1,783
Total accounts receivable............................	$3,084 ◄

Austin Sound's list of account balances from the subsidiary ledger helps it follow up on slow-paying customers. This helps a business manage cash.

Using the Purchases Journal

A merchandising business purchases inventory and supplies frequently. Such purchases are usually made on account. The **purchases journal** is designed to account for all purchases of inventory, supplies, and other assets *on account*. It can also be used to record expenses incurred on account. Cash purchases are recorded in the cash payments journal.

Exhibit 6-12 illustrates Austin Sound's purchases journal (Panel A) and posting to ledgers (Panel B).[1] This purchases journal has special columns for credits to Accounts Payable and debits to Inventory, Supplies, and Other Accounts. A periodic inventory system would replace the Inventory column with a column titled "Purchases." The Other Accounts columns accommodate purchases of items other than inventory and supplies. Accounts Payable is credited for all transactions recorded in the purchases journal.

On November 2, Austin Sound purchased inventory costing $700 from **JVC Corporation.** The creditor's name (JVC Corporation) is entered in the Account Credited column. The purchase terms of 3/15 n/30 are also entered to help identify the due date and the discount available. Accounts Payable is credited for the transaction amount, and Inventory is debited.

Note the November 9 purchase of fixtures from City Office Supply. The purchases journal contains no column for fixtures, so the Other Accounts debit column is used. Because this was a credit purchase, the accountant enters the creditor name (City Office Supply) in the Account Credited column and Fixtures in the Other Accounts/Account Title column. The total credits in the purchases journal ($2,876) equal the total debits ($1,706 + $103 + $1,067 = $2,876).

Objective 5 box:

Objective 5
Use the purchases journal, the cash payments journal, and the accounts payable subsidiary ledger

PURCHASES JOURNAL. Special journal used to record all purchases of inventory, supplies, and other assets on account.

---

[1]This is the only special journal that we illustrate with the credit column placed to the left and the debit columns to the right. This arrangement of columns focuses on Accounts Payable (which is credited for each entry to this journal).

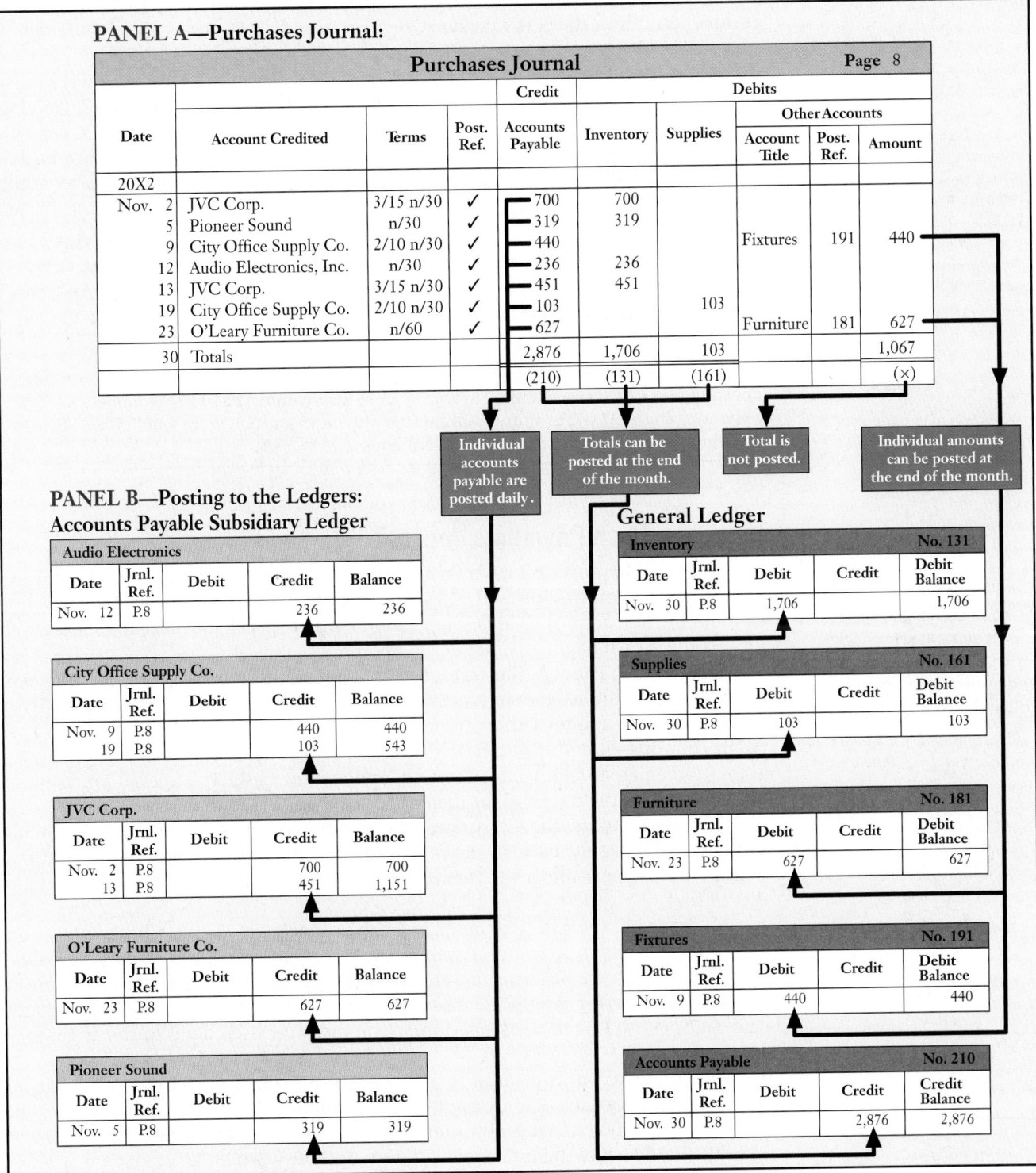

PANEL A—Purchases Journal:

				Credit	Debits				

Purchases Journal — Page 8

Table (full structure):

Date	Account Credited	Terms	Post. Ref.	Accounts Payable (Credit)	Inventory (Debit)	Supplies (Debit)	Other Accounts — Account Title	Other Accounts — Post. Ref.	Other Accounts — Amount
20X2									
Nov. 2	JVC Corp.	3/15 n/30	✓	700	700				
5	Pioneer Sound	n/30	✓	319	319				
9	City Office Supply Co.	2/10 n/30	✓	440			Fixtures	191	440
12	Audio Electronics, Inc.	n/30	✓	236	236				
13	JVC Corp.	3/15 n/30	✓	451	451				
19	City Office Supply Co.	2/10 n/30	✓	103		103			
23	O'Leary Furniture Co.	n/60	✓	627			Furniture	181	627
30	Totals			2,876	1,706	103			1,067
				(210)	(131)	(161)			(×)

Callout boxes:
- Individual accounts payable are posted daily.
- Totals can be posted at the end of the month.
- Total is not posted.
- Individual amounts can be posted at the end of the month.

PANEL B—Posting to the Ledgers:
Accounts Payable Subsidiary Ledger

Audio Electronics

Date	Jrnl. Ref.	Debit	Credit	Balance
Nov. 12	P.8		236	236

City Office Supply Co.

Date	Jrnl. Ref.	Debit	Credit	Balance
Nov. 9	P.8		440	440
19	P.8		103	543

JVC Corp.

Date	Jrnl. Ref.	Debit	Credit	Balance
Nov. 2	P.8		700	700
13	P.8		451	1,151

O'Leary Furniture Co.

Date	Jrnl. Ref.	Debit	Credit	Balance
Nov. 23	P.8		627	627

Pioneer Sound

Date	Jrnl. Ref.	Debit	Credit	Balance
Nov. 5	P.8		319	319

General Ledger

Inventory — No. 131

Date	Jrnl. Ref.	Debit	Credit	Debit Balance
Nov. 30	P.8	1,706		1,706

Supplies — No. 161

Date	Jrnl. Ref.	Debit	Credit	Debit Balance
Nov. 30	P.8	103		103

Furniture — No. 181

Date	Jrnl. Ref.	Debit	Credit	Debit Balance
Nov. 23	P.8	627		627

Fixtures — No. 191

Date	Jrnl. Ref.	Debit	Credit	Debit Balance
Nov. 9	P.8	440		440

Accounts Payable — No. 210

Date	Jrnl. Ref.	Debit	Credit	Credit Balance
Nov. 30	P.8		2,876	2,876

ACCOUNTS PAYABLE SUBSIDIARY LEDGER   To pay debts efficiently, a company must know how much it owes particular creditors. The Accounts Payable account in the general ledger shows only a single total for the amount owed on account. It does not indicate the amount owed to each creditor. Companies keep an accounts payable subsidiary ledger that is similar to the accounts receivable subsidiary ledger used in conjunction with credit sales.

The accounts payable subsidiary ledger lists the creditors in alphabetical order, along with the amounts owed to them. Exhibit 6-12, Panel B, shows Austin Sound's accounts payable subsidiary ledger, which includes accounts for Audio Electronics,

City Office Supply, and others. After the daily posting is done, the total of the individual balances in the subsidiary ledger equals the balance in the Accounts Payable control account in the general ledger.

POSTING FROM THE PURCHASES JOURNAL   Posting from the purchases journal is similar to posting from the sales journal and the cash receipts journal. Exhibit 6-12, Panel B, illustrates the posting process.

Individual accounts payable in the *accounts payable subsidiary ledger* are posted daily, and column totals and other amounts can be posted to the *general ledger* at the end of the month. In the ledger accounts, P.8 indicates the source of the posted amounts—that is, purchases journal page 8.

THINK IT OVER   Contrast the number of *general ledger* postings from the purchases journal in Exhibit 6-12 with the number that would be required if the general journal were used to record the same seven transactions.

Answer: Use of the purchases journal requires only five *general ledger* postings—$2,876 to Accounts Payable, $1,706 to Inventory, $103 to Supplies, $440 to Fixtures, and $627 to Furniture. Without the purchases journal, there would have been 14 postings, two for each of the seven transactions.

Using the Cash Payments Journal

CASH PAYMENTS JOURNAL.
Special journal used to record cash payments by check. Also called the **check register** or **cash disbursements journal.**

Businesses make most cash payments by check. All payments by check are recorded in the **cash payments journal.** Other titles of this special journal are the *check register* and the *cash disbursements journal.* Like the other special journals, it has columns for recording cash payments that occur frequently.

Exhibit 6-13, Panel A, illustrates the cash payments journal, and Panel B shows the postings to the ledgers of Austin Sound. This cash payments journal has two debit columns—one for Other Accounts and one for Accounts Payable. It has two credit columns—one for purchase discounts, which are credited to the Inventory account in a perpetual inventory system, and one for Cash. This special journal also has columns for the date and for the check number of each cash payment.

Suppose a business makes numerous cash purchases of inventory. What additional column would its cash payments journal need? A column for Inventory, which would appear under the Debits heading, would streamline the information in the journal.

All entries in the cash payments journal include a credit to Cash. Payments on account are debits to Accounts Payable. On November 15, Austin Sound paid JVC on account, with credit terms of 3/15 n/30 (for details, see the first transaction in Exhibit 6-12). Paying within the discount period, Austin took the 3% discount and paid $679 ($700 less the $21 discount). The discount is credited to the Inventory account.

The Other Accounts column is used to record debits to accounts for which no special column exists. For example, on November 3, Austin Sound paid rent expense of $1,200. As with all other journals, the total debits ($3,461 + $819 = $4,280) should equal the total credits ($21 + $4,259 = $4,280).

DAILY EXERCISE 6-10

DAILY EXERCISE 6-11

DAILY EXERCISE 6-12

POSTING FROM THE CASH PAYMENTS JOURNAL   Posting from the cash payments journal is similar to posting from the cash receipts journal. Individual creditor amounts are posted daily, and column totals and Other Accounts can be posted at the end of the month. Exhibit 6-13, Panel B, illustrates the posting process.

Observe the effect of posting to the Accounts Payable account in the general ledger. The first posted amount in the Accounts Payable account (credit $2,876) originated in the purchases journal, page 8 (P.8). The second posted amount (debit $819) came from the cash payments journal, page 6 (CP.6). The resulting credit balance in Accounts Payable is $2,057. Also, see the Cash account; after posting, its debit balance is $1,875.

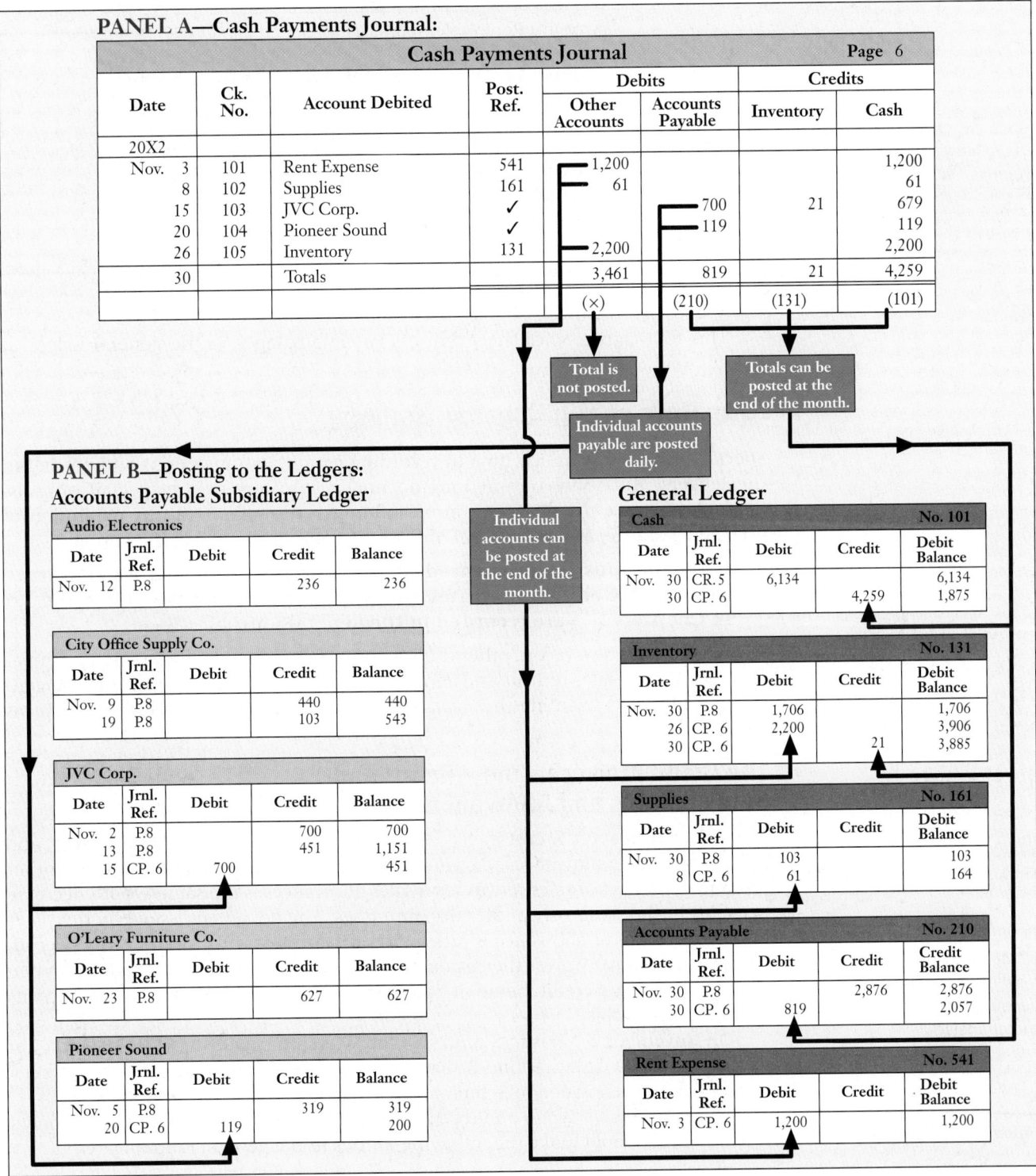

Amounts in the Other Accounts column are posted individually (for example, Rent Expense—debit $1,200). When each amount in the Other Accounts column is posted to the general ledger, the account number is entered in the Post. Ref. column of the journal. The letter x below the column signifies that the total is *not* posted.

To review their accounts payable, companies list the individual creditor balances in the accounts payable subsidiary ledger, as follows:

General Ledger

Accounts Receivable credit balance..............	<u>$2,057</u> ←

Subsidiary Ledger: Customer Accounts Receivable

Creditor	Balance
Audio Electronics	$ 326
City Office Supply	543
JVC Corp	451
O'Leary Furniture	627
Pioneer Sound..	<u>200</u>
Total accounts payable	<u>$2,057</u> ←

This total agrees with the Accounts Payable balance in the general ledger in Exhibit 6-13.

THE ROLE OF THE GENERAL JOURNAL

Special journals save much time in recording repetitive transactions and posting to the ledgers. But some transactions do not fit into any of the special journals. Examples include the depreciation of buildings and equipment, the expiration of prepaid insurance, and the accrual of salary payable at the end of the period.

Even the most sophisticated accounting system needs a general journal. The adjusting entries and the closing entries we illustrated in Chapters 3–5 are recorded in the general journal.

Accountants also record other transactions in the general journal. Many companies record their sales returns and allowances and their purchase returns in the general journal. Let's examine the *credit memorandum,* the document for sales returns and allowances.

The Credit Memorandum—Recording Sales Returns and Allowances

As we saw in Chapter 5, customers sometimes return merchandise to the seller, and sellers grant sales allowances to customers because of product defects and for other reasons. The effect of sales returns and sales allowances is the same—both decrease net sales in the same way a sales discount does. The document issued by the seller for a sales return or allowance is called a **credit memorandum,** or **credit memo,** because the company gives the customer credit for the returned merchandise. When a company issues a credit memo, it debits Sales Returns and Allowances and credits Accounts Receivable.

On November 27, Austin Sound sold four stereo speakers for $1,783 on account to Clay Schmidt. Later, Schmidt discovered a defect and returned the speakers. Austin Sound then issued to Schmidt a credit memo like the one in Exhibit 6-14.

To record the *sale return* and receipt of the defective speakers from the customer, Austin Sound would make the following entries in the general journal:

CREDIT MEMORANDUM OR CREDIT MEMO. A document issued by a seller to credit a customer account for returned merchandise.

	General Journal			Page 9
Date	**Accounts**	**Post Ref.**	**Debit**	**Credit**
Dec. 1	Sales Returns and Allowances	430	1,783	
	Accounts Receivable—Clay Schmidt............	112/✓		1,783
	Credit memo no. 27.			
Dec. 1	Inventory	131	431	
	Cost of Goods Sold	511		431
	Received defective goods from customer.			

EXHIBIT 6-14
Credit Memorandum Issued by
Austin Sound Center

```
                Credit Memorandum                    No. 27

Austin Sound Center                    Date   December 1, 20X2
305 West Martin Luther King Blvd.
Austin, Texas 78701

Customer Name      Clay Schmidt

                   538 Rio Grande, Apt.236

                   Austin, Texas 78703

Reason for Credit  Defective merchandise returned


        Description                          Amount

4 Trailblazer JU170456 Speakers              $1,783
```

Focus on the first entry. The debit side of the entry is posted to Sales Returns and Allowances. Its account number (430) is written in the posting reference column. The credit side of the entry requires two $1,783 postings, one to Accounts Receivable, the control account in the general ledger (account number 112), and the other to Clay Schmidt's account in the accounts receivable subsidiary ledger. These credit postings explain why the document is called a *credit memo*. The account number (112) denotes the posting to Accounts Receivable in the general ledger. The check mark (✓) denotes the posting to Schmidt's account in the subsidiary ledger. A business with a high volume of sales returns, such as a department store chain, may use a special journal for sales returns and allowances.

The second entry records Austin Sound's receipt of the defective inventory from the customer. The speakers cost Austin Sound $431, and Austin Sound, like all other merchandisers, records its inventory at cost. Now let's see how Austin Sound records the return of the defective speakers to JVC, from which Austin Sound purchased them.

The Debit Memorandum—Recording Purchase Returns and Allowances

Purchase returns occur when a business returns goods to the seller. The procedures for handling purchase returns are similar to those for handling sales returns. The purchaser gives the merchandise back to the seller and receives either a cash refund or replacement goods.

When a business returns merchandise to the seller, it may also send a business document known as a **debit memorandum,** or **debit memo.** This document states that the buyer no longer owes the seller for the goods. The buyer debits Accounts Payable and credits Inventory for the cost of the goods returned to the seller.

DEBIT MEMORANDUM OR DEBIT MEMO. A document issued by a buyer when returning merchandise. The memo informs the seller that the buyer no longer owes the seller for the amount of the returned purchases.

Many businesses record their purchase returns in the general journal. Austin Sound would record its return of defective speakers to JVC as follows:

	General Journal			Page 9
Date	**Accounts**	**Post Ref.**	**Debit**	**Credit**
Dec. 2	Accounts Payable—JVC Corp.	210/✓	431	
	Inventory...	131		431
	Debit memo no. 16.			

Balancing the Ledgers

At the end of the period, after all postings, equality should exist between

1. *General ledger:*

Total debits = Total credits of all account balances

2. *General ledger and Accounts receivable subsidiary ledger:*

$$\begin{array}{c}\textbf{Balance} \\ \textbf{Accounts Receivable} \\ \textbf{control account}\end{array} = \begin{array}{c}\textbf{Sum of individual customer account} \\ \textbf{balances in the Accounts receivable} \\ \textbf{subsidiary ledger}\end{array}$$

3. *General ledger and Accounts payable subsidiary ledger:*

$$\begin{array}{c}\textbf{Balance of Accounts} \\ \textbf{Payable control account}\end{array} = \begin{array}{c}\textbf{Sum of individual creditor account} \\ \textbf{balances in the Accounts payable} \\ \textbf{subsidiary ledger}\end{array}$$

The process of ensuring that these equalities exist is called *balancing the ledgers,* or *proving the ledgers.* It is an important control procedure because it helps ensure the accuracy of the accounting records.

Blending Computers and Special Journals in an Accounting Information System

Computerizing special journals requires no drastic change in system design. Systems designers create a special screen for each accounting application (module)—credit sales, cash receipts, credit purchases, and cash payments. The special screen for credit sales would ask the computer operator to enter the following information: date, customer number, customer name, invoice number, and the dollar amount of the sale. These data can generate debits to the subsidiary accounts receivable and files from which the monthly customer statements that show account activity and ending balance are generated. For purchases on account, additional computer files keep the subsidiary ledger information on individual vendors.

The Decision Guidelines feature provides guidelines for some of the major decisions accountants must make as they use an information system.

DECISION GUIDELINES

Using Special Journals and Control Accounts

DECISION	GUIDELINES

What are the main components of an accounting system?

Journals
- General journal
- Special journals

Ledgers
- General ledger
- Subsidiary ledgers
  - Accounts receivable
  - Accounts payable

Where to record
- Sales on account?
- Cash receipts?
- Purchases on account?
- Cash payments?
- All other transactions?

Journals
- Sales journal
- Cash receipts journal
- Purchases journal
- Cash payments journal
- General journal

How does the general ledger relate to the subsidiary ledgers?

GENERAL LEDGER

ACCOUNTS RECEIVABLE	ACCOUNTS PAYABLE
X,XXX		XX

SUBSIDIARY LEDGERS

ACCOUNTS RECEIVABLE FROM:

ARNOLD	BARNES
XX		XX	

ACCOUNTS PAYABLE TO:

AGNEW	BLACK
X		X

Using Special Journals and Control Accounts

DECISION	GUIDELINES
When to post from the journals to • General ledger? • Subsidiary ledgers?	—Monthly (or more often, if needed) —Daily
How to achieve control over • Accounts receivable? • Accounts payable?	Balance the ledgers, as follows:

General Ledger		Subsidiary Ledger
Accounts receivable	=	Sum of individual *customer* account balances
Accounts payable	=	Sum of individual *creditor* account balances

REVIEW ACCOUNTING INFORMATION SYSTEMS

SUMMARY PROBLEM

Riggs Company completed the following selected transactions during March:

Mar. 4   Received $500 from a cash sale to a customer (cost, $319).

    6   Received $60 on account from Brady Lee. The full invoice amount was $65, but Lee paid within the discount period to gain the $5 discount.

    9   Received $1,080 on a note receivable from Beverly Mann. This amount includes the $1,000 note receivable plus interest revenue.

  15   Received $800 from a cash sale to a customer (cost, $522).

  24   Borrowed $2,200 by signing a note payable to Interstate Bank.

  27   Received $1,200 on account from Lance Albert. Collection was received after the discount period lapsed.

www.prenhall.com/horngren

End-of-Chapter Assessment

Required

The general ledger showed the following balances at February 28: Cash, $1,117; Accounts Receivable, $2,790; Note Receivable—Beverly Mann, $1,000; and Inventory, $1,819. The accounts receivable subsidiary ledger at February 28 contained debit balances as follows: Lance Albert, $1,840; Melinda Fultz, $885; Brady Lee, $65.

1. Record the transactions in the cash receipts journal, page 7.
2. Compute column totals at March 31. Show that total debits equal total credits in the cash receipts journal.
3. Post to the general ledger and the accounts receivable subsidiary ledger. Use complete posting references, including the following account numbers: Cash, 11; Accounts Receivable, 12; Note Receivable—Beverly Mann, 13; Inventory, 14; Note Payable—Interstate Bank, 22; Sales Revenue, 41; Sales Discounts, 42; Interest Revenue, 46; and Cost of Goods Sold, 51. Insert a check mark (✓) in the posting reference column for each February 28 account balance.
4. Show that the total of the customer balances in the subsidiary ledger equals the general ledger balance in Accounts Receivable.

Solution

Requirements 1 and 2

Cash Receipts Journal

Page 7

Date	Cash	Sales Discounts	Accounts Receivable	Sales Revenue	Account Title	Post. Ref.	Amount	Cost of Goods Sold Debit Inventory Credit
		Debits			**Credits**			
					Other Accounts			
Mar. 4	500			500				319
6	60	5	65		Brady Lee	✓		
9	1,080				Note Receivable—			
					Beverly Mann	13	1,000	
					Interest Revenue	46	80	
15	800			800				522
24	2,200				Note Payable—			
					Interstate Bank	22	2,200	
27	1,200		1,200		Lance Albert	✓		
31	5,840	5	1,265	1,300	Total		3,280	841
	(11)	(42)	(12)	(41)			(✓)	(51/14)

Total Dr. = 5,845   Total Cr. = 5,845

Requirement 3

Accounts Receivable Ledger

Lance Albert

Date	Jrnl. Ref.	Debit	Credit	Balance
Feb. 28	✓			1,840
Mar. 27	CR.7		1,200	640

Melinda Fultz

Date	Jrnl. Ref.	Debit	Credit	Balance
Feb. 28	✓			885

Brady Lee

Date	Jrnl. Ref.	Debit	Credit	Balance
Feb. 28	✓			65
Mar. 6	CR.7		65	—

General Ledger

Cash   **No. 11**

Date	Jrnl. Ref.	Debit	Credit	Balance
Feb. 28	✓			1,117
Mar. 31	CR.7	5,840		6,957

Sales Revenue   **No. 41**

Date	Jrnl. Ref.	Debit	Credit	Balance
Mar. 31	CR.7		1,300	1,300

Accounts Receivable   **No. 12**

Date	Jrnl. Ref.	Debit	Credit	Balance
Feb. 28	✓			2,790
Mar. 31	CR.7		1,265	1,525

Sales Discounts   **No. 42**

Date	Jrnl. Ref.	Debit	Credit	Balance
Mar. 31	CR.7	5		5

Note Receivable—Beverly Mann   **No. 13**

Date	Jrnl. Ref.	Debit	Credit	Balance
Feb. 28	✓			1,000
Mar. 9	CR.7		1,000	—

Interest Revenue   **No. 46**

Date	Jrnl. Ref.	Debit	Credit	Balance
Mar. 9	CR.7		80	80

Inventory   **No. 14**

Date	Jrnl. Ref.	Debit	Credit	Balance
Feb. 28	✓			1,819
Mar. 31	CR.7		841	978

Cost of Goods Sold   **No. 51**

Date	Jrnl. Ref.	Debit	Credit	Balance
Mar. 31	CR.7	841		841

Note Payable—Interstate Bank   **No. 22**

Date	Jrnl. Ref.	Debit	Credit	Balance
Mar. 24	CR.7		2,200	2,200

Requirement 4

General Ledger

Accounts Receivable debit balance .... $1,525 ◄

Accounts Receivable Subsidiary Ledger: Customer Accounts Receivable

Customer	Balance
Lance Albert	$ 640
Melinda Fultz	885
Total accounts receivable	$1,525 ◄

LESSONS LEARNED

1. **Describe the features of an effective accounting information system.** An effective *accounting information system* has (1) control over operations; (2) compatibility with the particular features of the business; (3) flexibility in response to changes in the business; and (4) a favorable cost/benefit relationship.

2. **Understand how both computerized and manual accounting systems work.** Computerized accounting systems process inputs faster than manual systems. The key components of a system are *hardware, software,* and company personnel. Both computerized and manual accounting systems require transactions to be classified by type.

   Computerized accounting systems use a *menu* structure to organize accounting functions. Computerized systems are integrated so that the different modules are updated together. Manual systems use special journals for sales, cash receipts, purchases, and cash payments.

3. **Understand how spreadsheets are used in accounting.** *Spreadsheets* are electronic work sheets whose grid points, or cells, are linked by formulas. Numerical relationships remain whenever changes are made to the spreadsheet. Spreadsheets aid in detailed computations, such as budgeting.

4. **Use the sales journal, the cash receipts journal, and the accounts receivable subsidiary ledger.** Many accounting systems use special journals to record transactions by category. Credit sales are recorded in a *sales journal,* and cash receipts in a *cash receipts journal.* The accounts receivable *subsidiary ledger* lists each customer and the amount receivable from that customer. It is the main device for ensuring that the company collects from customers.

5. **Use the purchases journal, the cash payments journal, and the accounts payable subsidiary ledger.** Credit purchases in a manual system are recorded in a *purchases journal,* and cash payments in a *cash payments journal.* The accounts payable subsidiary ledger helps the company stay current in its payments to suppliers.

ACCOUNTING VOCABULARY

accounting information system (p. 227)
batch processing (p. 230)
cash disbursements journal (p. 242)
cash payments journal (p. 242)
cash receipts journal (p. 238)
check register (p. 242)
control account (p. 237)

credit memorandum or credit memo (p. 244)
database (p. 228)
debit memorandum or debit memo (p. 245)
general journal (p. 234)
general ledger (p. 235)
hardware (p. 228)
menu (p. 230)
module (p. 232)

network (p. 228)
on-line processing (p. 230)
purchases journal (p. 240)
sales journal (p. 235)
server (p. 228)
software (p. 228)
special journal (p. 234)
spreadsheet (p. 233)
subsidiary ledger (p. 237)

QUESTIONS

1. Describe the four criteria for an effective accounting system.
2. Distinguish batch computer processing from on-line computer processing.
3. What accounting categories correspond to the account numbers 1, 2, 3, 4, and 5 in a typical computerized accounting system?
4. Why might the number 112 be assigned to Accounts Receivable and the number 1120708 to Bill Thomas, a customer?
5. Describe the function of menus in a computerized accounting system.
6. How do formulas in spreadsheets speed the process of budget preparation and revision?
7. Name four special journals used in accounting systems. For what type of transaction is each designed?
8. Describe the two advantages that special journals have over recording all transactions in the general journal.
9. What is a control account, and how is it related to a subsidiary ledger? Name two common control accounts.

10. DeLay Company's sales journal has one amount column headed Accounts Receivable Dr. and Sales Revenue Cr. In this journal, 86 transactions are recorded. How many posting references appear in the journal? What does each posting reference represent?
11. The accountant for T-Questa Company posted all amounts correctly from the cash receipts journal to the general ledger. However, he failed to post three credits to customer accounts in the accounts receivable subsidiary ledger. How would this error be detected?
12. At what two times is posting done from a special journal? What items are posted at each time?
13. What is the purpose of balancing the ledgers?
14. Posting from the journals of Lexite Sales is complete. But the total of the individual balances in the accounts payable subsidiary ledger does not equal the balance in the Accounts Payable control account in the general ledger. Does this discrepancy necessarily indicate that the trial balance is out of balance? Explain.

ASSESS YOUR PROGRESS

DAILY EXERCISES

DE6-1 Suppose you have just invested your life savings in a **Baskin Robbins** franchise. The business is growing fast, and you need a better accounting information system. Consider the features of an effective system, as discussed on pages 227–228. Which do you regard as most important? Why? Which feature must you consider if your financial resources are limited?

Features of an effective information system (Obj. 1)

DE6-2 Match each component of a computerized accounting system with its meaning.

Components of a computerized accounting system (Obj. 1)

Component		Meaning
A. Server	_____	Electronic linkages that allow different computers to share the same information
B. Hardware	_____	Electronic equipment
C. Software	_____	Programs that drive a computer
D. Network	_____	Main computer in a networked system

DE6-3 Complete the crossword puzzle that follows.

Accounting system vocabulary (Obj. 1)

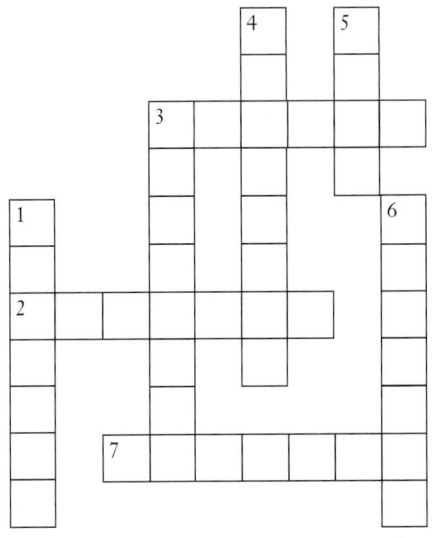

Down:

1. Managers need _____ over operations in order to authorize transactions and safeguard assets
3. Programs that drive a computer
4. Electronic computer equipment
5. A _____ible information system accommodates changes as the organization evolves
6. The opposite of debits

Across:

2. Electronic linkage that allows different computers to share the same information
3. Main computer in a networked system
7. Cost-_____ relationship must be favorable

DE6-4 Use account numbers 11–16, 21, 22, 31, 32, 41, 51, and 52 to correspond to the following selected accounts from the general ledger of Entreé Home Furnishings. List the accounts and their account numbers in proper order, starting with the most liquid current asset.

Setting up a chart of accounts (Obj. 2)

Depreciation expense
Cash
Madeline Jacobs, withdrawals
Prepaid insurance
Accumulated depreciation

Madeline Jacobs, capital
Cost of goods sold
Accounts payable
Inventory
Sales revenue

Accounts receivable
Note payable, long-term
Store fixtures

DE6-5 Refer to the spreadsheet screen in Exhibit 6-7, page 233. Suppose cells B1 through B4 are your business's actual income statement for the current year. You wish to develop your financial plan for the coming year. Assume that you expect revenues to increase by 15% and expenses to increase by 10%. Write the formulas in cells C2 through C4 to compute the amounts of expected revenues, expenses, and net income for the coming year.

Using a spreadsheet (Obj. 3)

DE6-6 Use the following abbreviations to indicate the journal in which you would record transactions a–n.

Using the journals (Obj. 4, 5)

J = General journal
S = Sales journal
CR = Cash receipts journal

P = Purchases journal
CP = Cash payments journal

Transactions:

_____ a. Cash purchase of inventory.

_____ b. Collection of dividend revenue earned on an investment.

_____ c. Prepayment of insurance.

_____ d. Borrowing money on a long-term note payable.

_____ e. Purchase of equipment on account.

_____ f. Cost of goods sold along with a credit sale.

_____ g. Cash sale of inventory.

_____ h. Payment of rent.

_____ i. Depreciation of computer equipment.

_____ j. Purchases of inventory on account.

_____ k. Collection of accounts receivable.

_____ l. Expiration of prepaid insurance.

_____ m. Sale on account.

_____ n. Payment on account.

Using the sales journal and the related ledgers (Obj. 4)

DE6-7 ◄ *Link Back to Chapter 5 (Gross Profit).* Use the sales journal and the related ledger accounts in Exhibit 6-10, page 236, to answer these questions about **Austin Sound Center.**

1. How much gross profit did Austin Sound earn on credit sales during November? For this answer, ignore sales discounts and sales returns and allowances.
2. What amount did Austin Sound post to the Sales Revenue account? When did Austin Sound post to the Sales Revenue account? Assume a manual accounting system.
3. After these transactions, how much does Susan Levy owe Austin Sound? Where do you obtain this information? Be specific.
4. If there were no discounts, how much would Austin Sound hope to collect from all its customers? Where is this amount stored in a single figure?

Using accounts receivable records (Obj. 4)

DE6-8

1. Where does the total amount receivable from all the customers appear? Be specific.
2. A key control feature of **Austin Sound Center's** accounting system lies in the agreement between the detailed customer receivable records and the summary total in the general ledger. Use the data in Exhibit 6-10, page 236, to prove that Austin Sound's accounts receivable records are accurate.
3. A business that sells on account must have good accounts receivable records to ensure collection from customers. What is the name of the detailed record of amounts collectible from individual customers?

Using cash receipts data (Obj. 4)

DE6-9 The cash receipts journal of **Austin Sound Center** appears in Exhibit 6-11, page 239, along with the company's various ledger accounts. Use the data in Exhibit 6-11 to answer the following questions that Charles Ernest, owner of the business, might face.

1. How much were cash sales during November?
2. How much did Austin Sound borrow during November? Where else could you look to determine whether Austin Sound has paid off part of the loan?
3. How much were total cash receipts during November?
4. How much cash did Austin Sound collect on account from customers? How much in total discounts did customers earn by paying quickly? How much did Austin Sound's accounts receivable decrease because of collections from customers during November?

Using the purchases journal and the cash payments journal (Obj. 5)

DE6-10 Refer to **Austin Sound Center's** purchases journal (Exhibit 6-12, page 241) and cash payments journal (Exhibit 6-13, page 243). Charles Ernest, the owner, has raised the following questions about the business.

1. At November 30, after all purchases and all cash payments, how much does Austin Sound owe **JVC Corporation?** How much in total does Austin Sound owe on account?
2. How much did total credit purchases of inventory, supplies, fixtures, and furniture increase Austin Sound's accounts payable during November?
3. How much of the accounts payable did Austin Sound pay off during November? What amount of cash did Austin Sound pay on account? Explain the difference.

Using the purchases journal and the cash payments journal (Obj. 5)

DE6-11 ◄ *Link Back to Chapters 1 and 2 (Recording transactions).* Use **Austin Sound's** purchases journal (Exhibit 6-12, page 241) and cash payments journal (Exhibit 6-13, page 243) to address these real-world questions faced by Charles Ernest, owner of the business.

1. Why did Austin Sound debit Rent Expense for the rent payment on November 3?
2. How much were Austin Sound's total purchases of inventory during November? How much were net purchases of inventory? What explains the difference between total purchases and net purchases? Which account holds these amounts?
3. Suppose it is December 1 and Ernest wishes to pay the full amount that Austin Sound owes on account. Examine the purchases journal (page 241) to determine whether Ernest can take any purchase discounts, and also consider the cash payments journal. Then make a general journal entry to record payment of the correct amount on December 1. Include an explanation.

DE6-12 Answer the following questions about the November transactions of Austin Sound Center. You will need to refer to Exhibits 6-10 through 6-13, which begin on page 236.

Using all the journals (Obj. 4, 5)

1. How did Austin Sound purchase furniture—for cash or on account? Indicate the basis for your answer.
2. From whom did Austin Sound purchase supplies on account? How much in total does Austin Sound owe this company on November 30? Can Austin Sound take a discount when Austin Sound pays? Why or why not?
3. How much cash does Austin Sound have on hand at November 30? How much inventory does Austin Sound have after all transactions are recorded, including the cash receipts journal (Exhibit 6-11, page 239)? Indicate which exhibit provides each answer.
4. Determine Austin Sound's gross sales revenue and net sales revenue for November. Indicate which ledger provides the data for your answer.
5. Did Austin Sound's interest revenue for November result from a cash receipt or from an accrual of interest? How can you tell?

EXERCISES

E6-1 Assign account numbers (from the list that follows) to the accounts of AudioBasket. Identify the headings, which are *not* accounts and would not be assigned an account number.

Assigning account numbers (Obj. 2)

Assets	Mark Lancaster, Capital
Current Assets	Mark Lancaster, Withdrawals
Accounts Receivable	Revenues
Note Payable, Long-Term	Depreciation Expense

Numbers from which to choose:

100	111	281
200	121	311
300	161	321
400	171	331
500	211	531

E6-2 The following accounts of Kim Fisher Company show some of the company's adjusted balances before closing:

Using a trial balance (Obj. 2)

Total assets	$?	Long-term liabilities	$?
Current assets	31,600	Kim Fisher, capital...................	8,600
Plant assets.............................	63,400	Kim Fisher, withdrawals	2,000
Total liabilities	?	Total revenues	28,000
Current liabilities	41,100	Total expenses	21,000

Compute the missing amounts. You must also compute ending owner's equity.

E6-3 Equipment listed on a spreadsheet has a cost of $400,000; this amount is located in cell B9. The number of years of the asset's useful life is found in cell C3. Write the spreadsheet formula to express annual depreciation expense for the equipment.

Using a spreadsheet to compute depreciation (Obj. 3)

E6-4 The values of the following items are stored in the cells of a Kovar Associates spreadsheet:

Computing financial statement amounts with a spreadsheet (Obj. 3)

Item	Cell
Total assets	B14
Current assets	B6
Fixed assets	B9
Total liabilities	C13
Current liabilities	C8
Long-term liabilities	C10

Write the spreadsheet formula to calculate the company's

a. Current ratio   b. Total owner's equity   c. Debt ratio

E6-5 The sales and cash receipts journals of Keester.com include the following entries:

Sales Journal

Date	Account Debited	Post. Ref.	Accounts Receivable Dr. Sales Revenue Cr.	Cost of Goods Sold Dr. Inventory Cr.
May 7	L. Ewald	✓	930	550
10	T. Ross	✓	4,100	1,970
10	E. Lovell	✓	690	410
12	B. Goebel	✓	5,470	3,340
31	Total		11,190	6,270

Cash Receipts Journal

	Debits			Credits				
					Other Accounts			**Cost of Goods Sold Dr.**
Date	Cash	Sales Discounts	Accounts Receivable	Sales Revenue	Account Title	Post. Ref.	Amount	Inventory Cr.
May 16					L. Ewald	✓		
19					E. Lovell	✓		
24	300			300				190
30					T. Ross	✓		

Keester.com makes all credit sales on terms of 2/10 n/30. Complete the cash receipts journal for those transactions indicated. Also, total the journal and show that total debits equal total credits. Each cash receipt was for the appropriate amount of the receivable.

E6-6 The cash receipts journal of EnvisioNet follows.

Cash Receipts Journal   Page 7

	Debits			Credits			
					Other Accounts		
Date	Cash	Sales Discounts	Accounts Receivable	Sales Revenue	Account Title	Post. Ref.	Amount
Jan. 2	794	16	810		Annan Corp.	(e)	
9	491		491		Kamm, Inc.	(f)	
19	4,480				Note Receivable	(g)	4,000
					Interest Revenue	(h)	480
30	314	7	321		J. T. Franz	(i)	
31	4,235			4,235			
31	10,314	23	1,622	4,235	Totals		4,480
	(a)	(b)	(c)	(d)			(j)

EnvisioNet's general ledger includes the following selected accounts, along with their account numbers:

Number	Account	Number	Account
111	Cash	511	Sales revenue
112	Accounts receivable	512	Sales discounts
113	Note receivable	513	Sales returns
119	Land	521	Interest revenue

Required

Indicate whether each posting reference (a) through (j) should be a

- Check mark (✓) for a posting to a customer account in the accounts receivable subsidiary ledger.
- Account number for a posting to an account in the general ledger. If so, give the account number.
- Letter (x) for an amount not posted.

E6-7 A customer account in the accounts receivable ledger of Vitria Paint Company follows.

Identifying transactions from postings to the accounts receivable subsidiary ledger (Obj. 4)

Jo Mei Chang

Date		Jrnl. Ref.	Dr.	Cr.	Balance Dr.	Balance Cr.
Nov. 3	....				403	
6	....	S.5	1,180		1,583	
14	....	J.8		191	1,392	
27	....	CR.9		703	689	

Required

Describe the three posted transactions.

E6-8 During April, Nike/Time completed the following *credit purchase* transactions:

April 5 Purchased supplies, $1,106, from Disch Corporation
11 Purchased inventory, $3,600, from Conn Corp. Nike/Time uses a perpetual inventory system.
19 Purchased equipment, $14,300, from Saturn Co.
22 Purchased inventory, $2,210, from Milan, Inc.

Recording purchase transactions in the general journal and in the purchases journal (Obj. 5)

Record these transactions first in the general journal—with explanations—and then in the purchases journal. Omit credit terms and posting references. Which procedure for recording transactions is quicker? Why?

Posting from the purchases journal; balancing the ledgers (Obj. 5)

E6-9 The purchases journal of Hans Bauman Company follows.

							Other Accounts Dr.		
Date	Account Credited	Terms	Post. Ref.	Account Payable Cr.	Inventory Dr.	Supplies Dr.	Acct. Title	Post. Ref.	Amt. Dr.
Sep. 2	Lancer Technologies	n/30		800	800				
5	Saturn Office Supply	n/30		175		175			
13	Lancer Technologies	2/10 n/30		1,151	1,151				
26	Faver Equipment Company	n/30		916			Equipment		916
30	Totals			3,042	1,951	175			916

Purchases Journal — Page 7

Required

1. Open ledger accounts for Inventory, Supplies, Equipment, and Accounts Payable. Post to these accounts from the purchases journal. Use dates and posting references in the accounts.
2. Open accounts in the accounts payable subsidiary ledger for Faver Equipment Company, Lancer Technologies, and Saturn Office Supply. Post from the purchases journal. Use dates and journal references in the ledger accounts.
3. Balance the Accounts Payable control account in the general ledger with the total of the balances in the accounts payable subsidiary ledger.

ACCOUNTING INFORMATION SYSTEMS 255

E6-10 During August, Silicon Valley Sporting Goods had the following transactions:

Aug. 1 Paid $490 on account to Rabin Associates, net of a $10 discount for an earlier purchase of inventory.
5 Purchased inventory for cash, $4,300.
9 Paid $375 for supplies.
15 Purchased inventory on credit from Monroe Corporation, $774.
16 Paid $4,062 on account to LaGrange Company; there was no discount.
21 Purchased furniture for cash, $960.
26 Paid $3,910 on account to VisioNet Software for an earlier purchase of inventory. The discount was $90.
30 Made a semiannual interest payment of $800 on a long-term note payable. The entire payment was for interest.

Required

1. Prepare a cash payments journal similar to the one illustrated in this chapter. Omit the check number (Ck. No.) and posting reference (Post. Ref.) columns.
2. Record the transactions in the journal. Which transaction should not be recorded in the cash payments journal? In what journal does it belong?
3. Total the amount columns of the journal. Determine that total debits equal total credits.

E6-11 *Link Back to Chapter 5 (Recording Purchases, Sales, and Returns).* The following documents describe two business transactions.

Invoice		
Date:	May 14, 20X0	
Sold to:	BiWheel Bicycle Shop	
Sold by:	Schwinn Company	
Terms:	2/10 n/30	

Items Purchased   Bicycles

Quantity	Price	Total
8	$95	$760
1	70	70
5	60	300
Total		$1,130

Debit Memo		
Date:	May 20, 20X0	
Issued to:	Schwinn Company	
Issued by:	BiWheel Bicycle Shop	

Items Returned   Bicycles

Quantity	Price	Total
1	$95	$ 95
1	70	70
Total		$165

Reason: Damaged in shipment

Required

Use the general journal to record these transactions and BiWheel's cash payment on May 21. Record the transactions first on the books of BiWheel Bicycle Shop and, second, on the books of **Schwinn Company,** which makes and sells bicycles. Both BiWheel and Schwinn use a perpetual inventory system as illustrated in Chapter 5. Schwinn's cost of the bicycles sold to BiWheel was $690. Schwinn's cost of the returned merchandise was $80. Round to the nearest dollar. Explanations are not required. Set up your answer in the following format:

Date	BiWheel Journal Entries	Schwinn Journal Entries

Challenge Exercise

E6-12 *Link Back to Chapter 5 (Cost of Goods Sold, Gross Profit).*

1. **Austin Sound Center's** special journals in Exhibits 6-10 through 6-13 (pages 236–243) provide the owner with much of the data needed for preparation of the financial statements. Austin Sound uses the *perpetual* inventory system, so the amount of cost of goods sold is simply the ending balance in that account. Charles Ernest, the owner, needs to know the business's gross profit for November. Compute the gross profit.
2. Suppose Austin Sound uses the *periodic* inventory system. In that case, the business must compute cost of goods sold by the following formula:

Cost of goods sold:

Beginning inventory	$	X*
+ Net purchases....................................		XXX
= Cost of goods available for sale		X,XXX
− Ending inventory		(XX)
= Cost of goods sold..............................	$	XX

*$0 for Austin Sound at November 1.

Perform this calculation of cost of goods sold for Austin Sound. Does this computation of cost of goods sold agree with your answer to requirement 1?

PROBLEMS

(Group A)

P6-1A The following spreadsheet shows the income statement of Tradex Technologies:

Using a spreadsheet to prepare an income statement and evaluate operations (Obj. 3)

	Column	
Row Number	**A**	**B**
7	Revenues:	
8	Service revenue ⟶	
9	Rent revenue ⟶	
10		_____
11	Total revenue ⟶	
12		
13	Expenses:	
14	Salary expense ⟶	
15	Supplies expense ⟶	
16	Rent expense ⟶	
17	Depreciation expense ⟶	
18		_____
19	Total expenses ⟶	
20		_____
21	Net income ⟶	
22		=====

Required

1. Write the word *number* in the cells (indicated by arrows) where numbers will be entered.
2. Write the appropriate formula in each cell that will need a formula. Choose from these symbols.

+	add	*	multiply
−	subtract	/	divide
= SUM(beginning cell:ending cell)			

3. Last year, Tradex used this spreadsheet to prepare the company's budgeted income statement—which shows the company's net income goal—for the current year. It is now one year later, and Tradex has prepared its actual income statement for the year. State how the owner of the company can use this income statement in decision making.

P6-2A The general ledger of Ariba Genetics includes the following selected accounts:

Using the sales, cash receipts, and general journals (Obj. 4)

Cash	11	Sales Revenue..................................	41
Accounts Receivable	12	Sales Discounts	42
Inventory	13	Sales Returns and Allowances........	43
Notes Receivable	15	Interest Revenue	47
Supplies..	16	Cost of Goods Sold..........................	51
Land	18		

All credit sales are on the company's standard terms of 2/10 n/30. Transactions in July that affected sales and cash receipts were as follows:

July 2 Sold inventory on credit to Intelysis, Inc., $2,400. Ariba's cost of these goods was $1,400.

3 As an accommodation to a competitor, sold supplies at cost, $85, receiving cash.

7 Cash sales for the week totaled $1,890 (cost, $1,640).

9 Sold merchandise on account to A. L. Prince, $7,320 (cost, $5,110).

10 Sold land that cost $10,000 for cash of $10,000.

11 Sold goods on account to Sloan Electric, $5,104 (cost, $3,520).

12 Received cash from Intelysis in full settlement of its account receivable from July 2.

14 Cash sales for the week were $2,106 (cost, $1,530).

15 Sold inventory on credit to the partnership of Wilkie & Blinn, $3,650 (cost, $2,260).

18 Received inventory sold on July 9 to A. L. Prince for $600. The goods shipped were unsatisfactory. These goods cost Ariba $440.

20 Sold merchandise on account to Sloan Electric, $629 (cost, $450).

21 Cash sales for the week were $990 (cost, $690).

22 Received $4,000 cash from A. L. Prince in partial settlement of his account receivable.

25 Received cash from Wilkie & Blinn for its account receivable from July 15.

25 Sold goods on account to Olsen Co., $1,520 (cost, $1,050).

27 Collected $5,125 on a note receivable, of which $125 was interest.

28 Cash sales for the week totaled $3,774 (cost, $2,460).

29 Sold inventory on account to R. O. Bankston, $242 (cost, $170).

30 Received goods sold on July 25 to Olsen Co. for $40. The inventory was damaged in shipment. The salvage value of these goods was $10. Record the inventory at its salvage value.

31 Received $2,720 cash on account from A. L. Prince.

Required

1. Ariba records sales returns and allowances in the general journal. Use the appropriate journal to record the preceding transactions in a sales journal (omit the Invoice No. column), a cash receipts journal, and a general journal.
2. Total each column of the cash receipts journal. Show that total debits equal total credits.
3. Show how postings would be made from the journals by writing the account numbers and check marks in the appropriate places in the journals.

Correcting errors in the cash receipts journal (Obj. 4)

P6-3A The following cash receipts journal of Trilogy Buying Cooperative contains five entries. All five entries are for legitimate cash receipt transactions, but the journal contains some errors in recording the transactions. In fact, only one entry is correct, and each of the other four entries contains one error.

Cash Receipts Journal — Page 22

| | Debits | | Credits | | | | | Cost of Goods Sold Debit Inventory Credit |
| | | | | | Other Accounts | | | |
Date	Cash	Sales Discounts	Accounts Receivable	Sales Revenue	Account Title	Post. Ref.	Amount	
2/6		7,200		7,200				2,900
7	429	22			Paul Dalton	✓	451	
14	8,200				Note Receivable	15	7,700	
					Interest Revenue	45	500	
18				330				150
24	1,100		770					
28	9,729	7,222	770	7,530	Totals		8,651	3,050
	(11)	(42)	(12)	(41)			(x)	(51/13)

Total Dr. = $16,951   Total Cr. = $16,951

Required

1. Identify the correct entry.
2. Identify the error in each of the other four entries.
3. Using the following format, prepare a corrected cash receipts journal.

	Debits		Credits					Cost of Goods
					Other Accounts			Sold Debit
Date	Cash	Sales Discounts	Accounts Receivable	Sales Revenue	Account Title	Post. Ref.	Amount	Inventory Credit
2/6 7 14 18 24					Paul Dalton Note Receivable Interest Revenue	✓ 15 45		
28	16,929	22	1,221	7,530	Totals		8,200	3,050
	(11)	(42)	(12)	(41)			(x)	(51/13)

Total Dr. = $16,951   Total Cr. = $16,951

P6-4A The general ledger of Sun Network.com includes the following accounts:

Using the purchases, cash payments, and general journals (Obj. 5)

Cash	111	Furniture	187
Inventory	131	Accounts Payable	211
Prepaid Insurance	161	Rent Expense	564
Supplies	171	Utilities Expense	583

Transactions in December that affected purchases and cash payments were as follows:

Dec. 2 Purchased inventory on credit from **Microsoft,** $4,000. Terms were 2/10 n/30.
3 Paid monthly rent, debiting Rent Expense for $2,000.
5 Purchased supplies on credit terms of 2/10 n/30 from Ross Supply, $450.
8 Paid electricity utility bill, $588.
9 Purchased furniture on account from A-1 Office Supply, $4,100. Payment terms were net 30.
10 Returned the furniture to A-1 Office Supply. It was the wrong color.
11 Paid Microsoft the amount owed on the purchase of December 2.
12 Purchased inventory on account from Wynne, Inc., $4,400. Terms were 3/10 n/30.
13 Purchased inventory for cash, $655.
14 Paid a semiannual insurance premium, debiting Prepaid Insurance, $1,200.
16 Paid our account payable to Ross Supply, from December 5.
18 Paid gas and water utility bills, $196.
21 Purchased inventory on credit terms of 1/10 n/45 from Software, Inc., $5,200.
21 Paid account payable to Wynne, Inc., from December 12.
22 Purchased supplies on account from Office Sales, Inc., $274. Terms were net 30.
26 Returned to Software, Inc., $1,200 of the inventory purchased on December 21.
31 Paid Software, Inc., the net amount owed from December 21 less the return on December 26.

Required

1. Sun Network.com records purchase returns in the general journal. Use the appropriate journal to record the preceding transactions in a purchases journal, a cash payments journal (omit the Check No. column), and a general journal.
2. Total each column of the special journals. Show that total debits equal total credits in each special journal.
3. Show how postings would be made from the journals by writing the account numbers and check marks in the appropriate places in the journals.

P6-5A Fairchild Fidelity Co., which uses the perpetual inventory system and makes all credit sales on terms of 2/10 n/30, completed the following transactions during May:

Using all the journals, posting, and balancing the ledgers (Obj. 4, 5)

May 2 Issued invoice no. 913 for sale on account to K. D. Forbes, $2,000. Fairchild's cost of this inventory was $900.
3 Purchased inventory on credit terms of 3/10 n/60 from Chicosky Co., $2,467.
5 Sold inventory for cash, $1,077 (cost, $480).
5 Issued check no. 532 to purchase furniture for cash, $2,185.

May 8 Collected interest revenue of $1,775.
   9 Issued invoice no. 914 for sale on account to Bell Co., $5,550 (cost, $2,310).
   10 Purchased inventory for cash, $1,143, issuing check no. 533.
   12 Received cash from K. D. Forbes in full settlement of her account receivable from the sale on May 2.
   13 Issued check no. 534 to pay Chicosky Co. the net amount owed from May 3. Round to the nearest dollar.
   13 Purchased supplies on account from Manley, Inc., $441. Terms were net end-of-month.
   15 Sold inventory on account to M. O. Brown, issuing invoice no. 915 for $665 (cost, $240).
   17 Issued credit memo to M. O. Brown for $665 for defective merchandise returned to us by Brown. Also accounted for receipt of the inventory.
   18 Issued invoice no. 916 for credit sale to K. D. Forbes, $357 (cost, $127).
   19 Received $5,439 from Bell Co. in full settlement of its account receivable from May 9. Bell earned a discount by paying early.
   20 Purchased inventory on credit terms of net 30 from Sims Distributing, $2,047.
   22 Purchased furniture on credit terms of 3/10 n/60 from Chicosky Co., $645.
   22 Issued check no. 535 to pay for insurance coverage, debiting Prepaid Insurance for $1,000.
   24 Sold supplies to an employee for cash of $54, which was Fairchild's cost.
   25 Issued check no. 536 to pay utilities, $453.
   28 Purchased inventory on credit terms of 2/10 n/30 from Manley, Inc., $675.
   29 Returned damaged inventory to Manley, Inc., issuing a debit memo for $675.
   29 Sold goods on account to Bell Co., issuing invoice no. 917 for $496 (cost, $220).
   30 Issued check no. 537 to pay Manley, Inc., in full on account from May 13.
   31 Received cash in full on account from K. D. Forbes on credit sale of May 18. There was no discount.
   31 Issued check no. 538 to pay monthly salaries of $2,347.

Required

1. For Fairchild Fidelity, open the following general ledger accounts using the account numbers given:

Cash	111	Sales Revenue	411
Accounts Receivable	112	Sales Discounts	412
Supplies	116	Sales Returns and Allowances	413
Prepaid Insurance	117	Interest Revenue	419
Inventory	118	Cost of Goods Sold	511
Furniture	151	Salary Expense	531
Accounts Payable	211	Utilities Expense	541

2. Open these accounts in the subsidiary ledgers: Accounts receivable subsidiary ledger—Bell Co., M. O. Brown, and K. D. Forbes; accounts payable subsidiary ledger—Chicosky Co., Manley, Inc., and Sims Distributing.
3. Enter the transactions in a sales journal (page 7), a cash receipts journal (page 5), a purchases journal (page 10), a cash payments journal (page 8), and a general journal (page 6), as appropriate.
4. Post daily to the accounts receivable subsidiary ledger and to the accounts payable subsidiary ledger. On May 31, post to the general ledger.
5. Total each column of the special journals. Show that total debits equal total credits in each special journal.
6. Balance the total of the customer account balances in the accounts receivable subsidiary ledger against Accounts Receivable in the general ledger. Do the same for the accounts payable subsidiary ledger and Accounts Payable in the general ledger.

(Group B) PROBLEMS

Using a spreadsheet to prepare a partial balance sheet and evaluate financial positions (Obj. 3)

P6-1B The following spreadsheet on page 261 shows the assets of the Clarus Consulting balance sheet:

Required

1. Write the word *number* in the cells (indicated by arrows) where numbers will be entered.
2. Write the appropriate formula in each cell that will need a formula. Choose from these symbols:

Row Number	Column		
	A		B
2	Assets:		
3	Current assets:		
4	Cash ⟶		
5	Receivables ⟶		
6	Inventory ⟶		_____
7			
8	Total current assets ⟶		
9			
10	Equipment ⟶		
11	Accumulated depreciation ⟶		
12			_____
13	Equipment, net ⟶		
14			_____
15	Total assets ⟶		
16			═══════

3. Last year Clarus used this spreadsheet to prepare the company's budgeted balance sheet for the current year. The budgeted balance sheet shows the company's goal for total current assets at the end of the year. It is now one year later, and Clarus has prepared its actual year-end balance sheet. State how the owner of the company can use this balance sheet in decision making.

P6-2B The general ledger of Remedy Corporation includes the following selected accounts:

Using the sales, cash receipts, and general journals
(Obj. 4)

Cash	111		Sales Revenue	411
Accounts Receivable	112		Sales Discounts	412
Notes Receivable	115		Sales Returns and Allowances	413
Inventory	131		Interest Revenue	417
Equipment	141		Gain on Sale of Land	418
Land	142		Cost of Goods Sold	511

All credit sales are on the company's standard terms of 2/10 n/30. Transactions in November that affected sales and cash receipts were as follows:

Nov.	2	Sold inventory on credit to Grant Thornton $800. Remedy's cost of these goods was $314.
	6	As an accommodation to another company, sold new equipment for its cost of $770, receiving cash in this amount.
	7	Cash sales for the week totaled $2,107 (cost, $1,362).
	8	Sold merchandise on account to McNair Co., $2,830 (cost, $1,789).
	9	Sold land that cost $22,000 for cash of $40,000. The difference is a gain.
	11	Sold goods on account to Nickerson Builders, $6,099 (cost, $3,853).
	11	Received cash from Grant Thornton in full settlement of his account receivable from November 2.
	13	Cash sales for the week were $1,995 (cost, $1,286).
	15	Sold inventory on credit to Montez and Montez, a partnership, $800 (cost, $517).
	18	Received inventory sold on November 8 to McNair Co. for $120. The goods we shipped were unsatisfactory. These goods cost Remedy $73.
	19	Sold merchandise on account to Nickerson Builders, $3,900 (cost, $2,618).
	20	Cash sales for the week were $2,330 (cost, $1,574).
	21	Received $1,200 cash from McNair Co. in partial settlement of its account receivable. There was no discount.
	22	Received cash from Montez and Montez for its account receivable from November 15.
	22	Sold goods on account to Diamond Co., $2,022 (cost, $1,325).
	25	Collected $4,200 on a note receivable, of which $200 was interest.

Nov. 27 Cash sales for the week totaled $2,970 (cost, $1,936).
27 Sold inventory on account to Littleton Corporation, $2,290 (cost, $1,434).
28 Received goods sold on November 22 to Diamond Co. for $680. The goods were damaged in shipment. The salvage value of these goods was $96. Record the inventory at its salvage value.
30 Received $1,510 cash on account from McNair Co. There was no discount.

Required

1. Use the appropriate journal to record the preceding transactions in a sales journal (omit the Invoice No. column), a cash receipts journal, and a general journal. Remedy Corporation records sales returns and allowances in the general journal.
2. Total each column of the cash receipts journal. Determine that total debits equal total credits.
3. Show how postings would be made from the journals by writing the account numbers and check marks in the appropriate places in the journals.

Correcting errors in the cash receipts journal
(Obj. 4)

P6-3B The following cash receipts journal contains five entries. All five entries are for legitimate cash receipt transactions, but the journal contains some errors in recording the transactions. In fact, only one entry is correct, and each of the other four entries contains one error.

Cash Receipts Journal — Page 16

	Debits			Credits					Cost of Goods
						Other Accounts			Sold Debit
Date	Cash	Sales Discounts	Accounts Receivable	Sales Revenue	Account Title	Post. Ref.	Amount	Inventory Credit	
7/3	582	18	600		Alliance Chemicals	✓			
9			346	346	Carl Ryther	✓			
10	22,000			22,000	Land	19			
19	73							44	
30	1,060			1,133				631	
31	23,715	18	946	23,479	Totals			675	
	(11)	(42)	(12)	(41)			(x)	(51/13)	

Total Dr. = $23,733   Total Cr. = $24,425

Required

1. Identify the correct entry.
2. Identify the error in each of the other four entries.
3. Using the following format, prepare a corrected cash receipts journal.

Cash Receipts Journal — Page 16

	Debits			Credits					Cost of Goods
						Other Accounts			Sold Debit
Date	Cash	Sales Discounts	Accounts Receivable	Sales Revenue	Account Title	Post. Ref.	Amount	Inventory Credit	
7/3					Alliance Chemicals	✓			
9					Carl Ryther	✓			
10					Land	19			
19									
30									
31	24,061	18	946	1,133	Totals		22,000	675	
	(11)	(42)	(12)	(41)			(x)	(51/13)	

Total Dr. = $24,079   Total Cr. = $24,079

P6-4B The general ledger of Commerce One includes the following accounts:

Using the purchases, cash payments, and general journals
(Obj. 5)

Cash	111	Equipment	189
Inventory	131	Accounts Payable	211
Prepaid Insurance	161	Rent Expense	562
Supplies	171	Utilities Expense	565

Transactions in January that affected purchases and cash payments were as follows:

Jan. 4 Paid monthly rent, debiting Rent Expense for $1,350.
   5 Purchased inventory on credit from Sylvania Co., $5,000. Terms were 2/15 n/45.
   6 Purchased supplies on credit terms of 2/10 n/30 from Harmon Sales, $800.
   7 Paid gas and water utility bills, $406.
   10 Purchased equipment on account from Lancer Co., $1,050. Payment terms were 2/10 n/30.
   11 Returned the equipment to Lancer Co. It was defective.
   12 Paid Sylvania Co. the amount owed on the purchase of January 5.
   12 Purchased inventory on account from Lancer Co., $1,100. Terms were 2/10 n/30.
   14 Purchased inventory for cash, $1,585.
   15 Paid an insurance premium, debiting Prepaid Insurance, $2,416.
   17 Paid electricity utility bill, $165.
   19 Paid our account payable to Harmon Sales, from January 6.
   20 Paid account payable to Lancer Co., from January 12.
   21 Purchased supplies on account from Master Supply, $754. Terms were net 30.
   22 Purchased inventory on credit terms of 1/10 n/30 from Linz Brothers, $3,400.
   26 Returned inventory purchased for $500 on January 22, to Linz Brothers.
   31 Paid Linz Brothers the net amount owed from January 22, less the return on January 26.

Required

1. Use the appropriate journal to record the preceding transactions in a purchases journal, a cash payments journal (omit the Check No. column), and a general journal. Commerce One records purchase returns in the general journal.
2. Total each column of the special journals. Show that total debits equal total credits in each special journal.
3. Show how postings would be made from the journals by writing the account numbers and check marks in the appropriate places in the journals.

P6-5B Contour Publishing, which uses the perpetual inventory system and makes all credit sales of 2/10 n/30, had these transactions during March:

Using all the journals, posting, and balancing the ledgers
(Obj. 4, 5)

Mar. 2 Issued invoice no. 191 for sale on account to L. E. Wooten, $2,350. Contour's cost of this inventory was $1,390.
   3 Purchased inventory on credit terms of 3/10 n/60 from Delwood Plaza, $5,900.
   4 Sold inventory for cash, $1,413 (cost, $820).
   5 Issued check no. 473 to purchase furniture for cash, $1,087.
   8 Collected interest revenue of $2,440.
   9 Issued invoice no. 192 for sale on account to Cortez Co., $6,250 (cost, $3,300).
   10 Purchased inventory for cash, $776, issuing check no. 474.
   12 Received $2,303 cash from L. E. Wooten in full settlement of her account receivable, net of the discount, from the sale of March 2.
   13 Issued check no. 475 to pay Delwood Plaza net amount owed from March 3.
   13 Purchased supplies on account from Havrilla Corp., $689. Terms were net end-of-month.
   15 Sold inventory on account to J. R. Wakeland, issuing invoice no. 193 for $743 (cost, $410).
   17 Issued credit memo to J. R. Wakeland for $743 for defective merchandise returned to us by Wakeland. Also accounted for receipt of the inventory.
   18 Issued invoice no. 194 for credit sale to L. E. Wooten, $1,825 (cost, $970).
   19 Received $6,125 from Cortez Co. in full settlement of its account receivable from March 9.
   20 Purchased inventory on credit terms of net 30 from Jasper Sales, $2,150.
   22 Purchased furniture on credit terms of 3/10 n/60 from Delwood Plaza, $775.
   22 Issued check no. 476 to pay for insurance coverage, debiting Prepaid Insurance for $1,345.
   24 Sold supplies to an employee for cash of $86, which was Contour's cost.
   25 Issued check no. 477 to pay utilities, $388.
   28 Purchased inventory on credit terms of 2/10 n/30 from Havrilla Corp., $421.
   29 Returned damaged inventory to Havrilla Corp., issuing a debit memo for $421.
   29 Sold goods on account to Cortez Co., issuing invoice no. 195 for $567 (cost, $314).
   30 Issued check no. 478 to pay Havrilla Corp. on account from March 13.

Mar. 31   Received cash in full on account from L. E. Wooten on credit sale of March 18. There was no discount.

31   Issued check no. 479 to pay monthly salaries of $2,600.

Required

1. For Contour Publishing, open the following general ledger accounts using the account numbers given:

Cash	111	Sales Revenue	411
Accounts Receivable	112	Sales Discounts	412
Supplies	116	Sales Returns and Allowances	413
Prepaid Insurance	117	Interest Revenue	419
Inventory	118	Cost of Goods Sold	511
Furniture	151	Salary Expense	531
Accounts Payable	211	Utilities Expense	541

2. Open these accounts in the subsidiary ledgers. Accounts receivable subsidiary ledger: Cortez Co., J. R. Wakeland, and L. E. Wooten. Accounts payable subsidiary ledger: Delwood Plaza, Havrilla Corp., and Jasper Sales.

3. Enter the transactions in a sales journal (page 8), a cash receipts journal (page 3), a purchases journal (page 6), a cash payments journal (page 9), and a general journal (page 4), as appropriate.

4. Post daily to the accounts receivable subsidiary ledger and to the accounts payable subsidiary ledger. On March 31, post to the general ledger.

5. Total each column of the special journals. Show that total debits equal total credits in each special journal.

6. Balance the total of the customer account balances in the accounts receivable subsidiary ledger against Accounts Receivable in the general ledger. Do the same for the accounts payable subsidiary ledger and Accounts Payable in the general ledger.

APPLY YOUR KNOWLEDGE

DECISION CASES

Designing a special journal (Obj. 4, 5)

Case 1. AccuTrac Software creates and sells cutting-edge networking software. AccuTrac's quality control officer estimates that 20% of the company's sales and purchases of inventory are returned for additional debugging. AccuTrac needs special journals for

- Sales returns and allowances
- Purchase returns and allowances

Required

1. Design the two special journals. For each journal, include a column for the appropriate business document.

2. Enter one transaction in each journal, using the **Austin Sound** transaction data illustrated on pages 236–243. Show all posting references, including those for column totals.

Reconstructing transactions from amounts posted to the accounts receivable subsidiary ledger (Obj. 4)

Case 2. A fire destroyed certain accounting records of DuPont Science Corp. The owner, François DuPont, asks for your help in reconstructing the records. *He needs to know the beginning and ending balances of Accounts Receivable and the credit sales and cash receipts on account from customers during March.* All of DuPont's sales are on credit, with payment terms of 2/10 n/30. All cash receipts on account reached DuPont within the 10-day discount period, except as noted. Round all amounts to the nearest dollar. The only accounting record preserved from the fire is the accounts receivable subsidiary ledger, which appears on page 265.

ETHICAL ISSUE

On a recent trip to Ireland, Ian O'Shea, sales manager of Elán, Inc., took his wife along at company expense. Martha Gibney, vice president of sales and O'Shea's boss, thought his travel and entertainment expenses seemed excessive. Gibney approved the reimbursement, however, because she owed O'Shea a favor. Gibney, well aware that the company president reviews all expenses recorded in the cash payments journal, had the accountant record O'Shea's wife's expenses in the *general* journal as follows:

Sales Promotion Expense	3,500	
Cash		3,500

Garcia Sales

Date		Item	Jrnl. Ref.	Debit	Credit	Balance
Apr.	1	Balance				440
	3		CR.8		440	-0-
	25		S.6	3,655		3,655
	29		S.6	1,123		4,778

Leewright, Inc.

Date		Item	Jrnl. Ref.	Debit	Credit	Balance
Apr.	1	Balance				2,378
	15		S.6	2,635		5,518
	29		CR.8		2,883*	2,635

*Cash receipt did not occur within the discount period.

Sally Jones

Date		Item	Jrnl. Ref.	Debit	Credit	Balance
Apr.	1	Balance				1,096
	5		CR.8		1,096	-0-
	11		S.6	396		396
	21		CR.8		396	-0-
	24		S.6			5,108

Jacques LeHavre

Date		Item	Jrnl. Ref.	Debit	Credit	Balance
Apr.	8	Balance	S.6	2,378		2,378
	16		S.6	903		3,281
	18		CR.8		2,378	903
	19		J.5		221	682
	27		CR.8		682	-0-

Ethical Issue (continued)

Required

1. Does recording the transaction in the *general* journal rather than in the cash payments journal affect the amounts of cash and total expenses reported in the financial statements?
2. Why did O'Shea want this transaction recorded in the *general* journal?
3. What is the ethical issue in this situation? What role does accounting play in this issue?

TEAM PROJECTS

Project 1: Preparing a Business Plan for a Merchandising Entity. As you work through Part 2 of this book (Chapters 7–12), you will be examining in detail the current assets, current liabilities, and plant assets of a business. Most of the organizations that form the context for business activity in the remainder of the book are merchandising entities. Therefore, in a group or individually—as directed by your instructor—develop a plan for beginning and operating an audio/video store or other type of business. Develop your plan in as much detail as you can. Remember that the business manager who attends to the most details delivers the best product at the lowest price for customers!

Project 2: Preparing a Business Plan for a Service Entity. List what you have learned thus far in the course. On the basis of what you have learned, refine your plan for promoting a rock concert (from Team Project 2 in Chapter 1) to include everything you believe you must do to succeed in this business venture.

INTERNET EXERCISE

The Internet has opened new consulting opportunities for the accounting profession. The government has regulations and forms available on-line. Individual accountants have Web sites explaining the services they offer. Accounting organizations provide information to members at low cost through the Internet.

1. Go to **http://www.AICPA.org** and read the information displayed. (Note: Make certain the URL uses the .org suffix for organizations rather than the .com suffix for companies.) What is the AICPA? How many accountants belong to this organization? What do the initials AICPA stand for?
2. In the left-hand column are links to a variety of accounting information. Click on *Students* and then *becoming a CPA*. List two characteristics of what earnings the CPA certification indicates.
3. In the left-hand column, click on *Pubs* and then the *current issue* of the "Journal of Accountancy." Scan one of the articles. List the title and author of the article and comment on one item of interest.
4. In the left-hand column, click on *CPA Links.*
   a. Click on *Accounting Associations.* Many of these associations offer scholarships and student memberships. What is Beta Alpha Psi?
   b. Go back to the CPA Links menu and click on *State Boards of Accountancy.* This board grants certificates and licenses to practice public accounting in that state. Click on the link to your state board of accountancy and comment on one item of interest.

7 Internal Control, Managing Cash, and Making Ethical Judgments

LEARNING OBJECTIVES

After studying this chapter, you should be able to

1. Define internal control

2. Identify the characteristics of an effective system of internal control

3. Prepare a bank reconciliation and the related journal entries

4. Apply internal controls to cash receipts

5. Apply internal controls to cash payments

6. Use a budget to manage cash

7. Make ethical judgments in business

Darlyne Lopez was a cashier at the Waco, Texas, office of the brokerage firm **Merrill Lynch.** Only after Lopez had an auto accident that landed her in the hospital did the Merrill Lynch office manager receive complaints from customers who had not received credit for their deposits. The result: Merrill Lynch uncovered a five-year-old embezzlement scheme.

The court found that Lopez stole over $600,000 in a "rob-Peter-to-pay-Paul" scheme. She transferred customer deposits into her own account and then concealed the missing amounts with deposits from other customers. Thus, customer accounts appeared to be in balance as long as Lopez manipulated the computerized records. But her replacement was unable to explain the missing deposits. All the evidence pointed in the direction of the absent employee. Lopez was sentenced to jail, and the Merrill Lynch office manager belatedly understood why his dedicated cashier never took a vacation.

What went wrong at **Merrill Lynch?** Darlyne Lopez controlled not only the cash received from customers, but also part of her company's computerized accounting records. By manipulating the records, she hid her theft for several years. Evidently, no one checked her work. Several procedures we discuss in this chapter will explain how Merrill Lynch could have prevented the embezzlement.

To protect people's money and avoid situations like the one at Merrill Lynch, the Foreign Corrupt Practices Act requires companies under SEC jurisdiction to maintain a system of internal control, whether or not they have foreign operations. This chapter discusses *internal control*—the organizational plan managers use to protect company assets. The chapter applies control techniques mainly to cash (the most liquid asset) and provides a framework for making ethical judgments in business. Later chapters discuss how managers control other assets.

INTERNAL CONTROL

Objective 1
Define internal control

A key responsibility of managers is to control operations. Owners and top managers set a company's goals, managers lead the way, and employees carry out the plan. **Internal control** is the organizational plan and all the related measures that an entity adopts to

1. Safeguard the assets the business uses in its operations,
2. Encourage adherence to company policies,
3. Promote operational efficiency (obtain the best outcome at the lowest cost), and
4. Ensure accurate and reliable accounting records.

Internal controls are most effective when employees at all levels adopt the organization's goals and ethical standards. Top managers need to communicate these goals and standards to workers. Lee Iacocca, former president of **Chrysler Corporation,** instilled goals in Chrysler employees by spending time with assembly-line workers. (Japanese firms pioneered this style of participative management.) The result? Defects decreased, and Chrysler products became more competitive.

Exhibit 7-1 presents an excerpt from **Target Corporation's** Report of Management. The company's top managers take responsibility for the financial statements and for the related system of internal control. Let's examine in more detail how companies create an effective system of internal control.

INTERNAL CONTROL. Organizational plan and all the related measures adopted by an entity to safeguard assets, encourage adherence to company policies, promote operational efficiency, and ensure accurate and reliable accounting records.

 DAILY EXERCISE 7-1

An Effective Internal Control System

Objective 2
Identify the characteristics of an effective system of internal control

Whether the business is **First Fidelity, Target Corporation,** or a local department store, an effective system of internal controls has the following characteristics.

Report of Management

Management is responsible for the consistency, integrity and presentation of the information in the Annual Report.

To fulfill our responsibility, we maintain comprehensive systems of internal control designed to provide reasonable assurance that assets are safeguarded and transactions are executed in accordance with established procedures.

Robert J. Ulrich

Robert J. Ulrich
Chairman of the Board and
Chief Executive Officer
February 28, 2000

Douglas A. Scovanner

Douglas A. Scovanner
Executive Vice President and
Chief Financial Officer

COMPETENT, RELIABLE, AND ETHICAL PERSONNEL Employees should be *competent, reliable, and ethical.* Paying top salaries to attract top-quality employees, training them to do their job well, and supervising their work all help a company build a competent staff.

ASSIGNMENT OF RESPONSIBILITIES In a business with a good internal control system, no important duty is overlooked. Each employee is assigned certain responsibilities. A model of this *assignment of responsibilities* appears in the corporate organizational chart in Exhibit 7-2. Notice that the company has a vice president of finance and accounting. Two other officers, the treasurer and the controller, report to that vice president. The treasurer is responsible for cash management. The **controller** is the chief accounting officer.

Within this organization, the controller may be responsible for approving invoices (bills) for payment, and the treasurer may actually sign the checks. Working under the controller, one accountant may be responsible for payroll,

CONTROLLER. The chief accounting officer of a company.

EXHIBIT 7-2 A Corporate Organization Chart

The Barings Bank Debacle: What Your Internal Auditor Tells You Might Save Your Company

On February 26, 1995, one fresh-faced 28-year-old trader brought a venerable 233-year-old British bank to its knees. Nick Leeson, a trader for **Barings Bank,** had bought $27

billion worth of securities on Japan's Nikkei stock market. When the Nikkei plunged, Barings lost $27 billion and collapsed. All fingers pointed to Leeson. How could a conservative bank allow this to happen? It soon became clear that nobody was supervising Leeson's trades.

Leeson worked in Barings' Singapore office from 1992 to the time of the collapse. Barings fell because it lacked internal controls. Leeson was allowed to execute *cross trades,* transactions in which he acted as both buyer and seller. Leeson's transactions were not at "arms' length," where the seller tries to get the highest price, and the buyer tries to pay the lowest price. Without arms' length trading, the amount of the transaction could be anything Leeson entered into the system. Amazingly, the bank did not require Leeson to give up his job as head of selling when he became head of buying.

From the start, Leeson lost money in Singapore, but he hid the losses—$296 million in 1994 alone. What did Leeson's bosses think of his performance that year? They thought he made a $46 million profit for the bank, and proposed paying him a bonus of $720,000.

Months before the collapse, Barings knew of Leeson's dual role. Internal auditors warned of "significant general risk" because Leeson controlled both the buying and the selling sides of transactions. But Barings' higher-ups viewed Leeson as a golden boy, and they ignored the audit report—with disastrous consequences.

Source: Based on Lillian Chew, "Not just one man," *http://www.risk.ifci.ch/137560.htm.* Robert D. Allen, "Managing internal audit conflicts," *Internal Auditor,* August 1996, p. 58. Anonymous, "The collapse of Barings: A fallen star," *Economist,* March 4, 1995, p. 19.

another accountant for depreciation. All duties should be clearly defined and assigned to individuals who bear responsibility for carrying them out.

 DAILY EXERCISE 7-2

PROPER AUTHORIZATION   An organization generally has written rules to outline its procedures. Any deviation from policy requires *proper authorization.* For example, an assistant manager of a retail store must approve customer checks for amounts above a certain limit. Likewise, a dean or department chair of a college and university must authorize a junior to enroll in courses restricted to seniors.

SEPARATION OF DUTIES   Smart management divides responsibility for transactions between two or more people or departments. *Separation of duties* limits the chances for fraud and promotes the accuracy of the accounting records. This crucial component of the internal control system can be divided into four parts:

1. *Separation of operations from accounting.* Accounting should be completely separate from the operating departments, such as manufacturing and sales. This

allows reliable records to be kept. What would happen if the sales personnel controlled the company's revenue records? Sales figures would probably be inflated, and top managers wouldn't know how much the company actually sold. Notice how accounting and marketing (sales) are separate in Exhibit 7-2.

2. *Separation of the custody of assets from accounting.* Temptation and fraud are reduced if accountants do not handle cash and if cashiers do not have access to the accounting records. If one employee has both cash-handling and accounting duties, that person can steal cash and conceal the theft by making a bogus entry on the books. We see this component of internal control in Exhibit 7-2. The treasurer has custody of the cash, and the controller accounts for the cash. Neither person has both responsibilities. Darlyne Lopez was able to apply one customer's cash deposit to another customer's account at **Merrill Lynch.** Apparently, Lopez, a cashier, controlled some data that went into the accounting system.

3. *Separation of authorization of transactions from custody of related assets.* Persons who authorize transactions should not handle the related asset. For example, the same person should not authorize a payment and also sign the check to pay the bill. Otherwise the person can authorize payments to him- or herself and then sign the checks. When these duties are separated, only legitimate bills get paid.

4. *Separation of duties within the accounting function.* Different people should perform the various accounting duties to minimize errors and the opportunities for fraud. For example, different accountants should be responsible for recording cash receipts and cash payments. The employee who processes cash payments should have nothing to do with the approval process.

◉ DAILY EXERCISE 7-3

◉ DAILY EXERCISE 7-6

 THINK IT OVER

Ralph works at the Galaxy Theater. Occasionally, he must both sell tickets and take them as customers enter the theater. Standard procedure requires that Ralph tear the tickets, give half to the customer, and keep the other half. To control cash receipts, the theater manager compares each night's cash receipts with the number of ticket stubs on hand.

1. How could Ralph steal cash receipts and hide the theft? What additional steps should the manager take to strengthen the control over cash receipts?
2. What is the internal control weakness in this situation? Explain the weakness.

Answers

1. Ralph could
   • Issue no ticket and keep the customer's cash.

   Management could
   • Physically count the number of people watching a movie and compare that number to the number of ticket stubs retained.

   • Destroy some tickets and keep the customers' cash.
   • Account for all ticket stubs by serial number. Missing serial numbers raise questions.

2. The internal control weakness is the lack of separation of duties. Ralph receives cash and also controls the tickets.

INTERNAL AND EXTERNAL AUDITS   To guarantee the accuracy of their accounting records, most companies undergo periodic audits. An **audit** is an examination of the company's financial statements and the accounting system.

AUDIT. An examination of a company's financial statements and the accounting system.

It is not economically feasible for auditors to examine all transactions, so they must rely on the accounting system to produce accurate records. To evaluate the company's accounting system, auditors examine its system of internal controls. Auditors often spot weaknesses in the system because they are objective in their outlook. The company's managers, on the other hand, are immersed in day-to-day operations and may overlook their own weaknesses.

Audits can be internal or external. Exhibit 7-2 shows *internal auditors* as employees of the business. Throughout the year, the internal auditors examine various segments of the organization to ensure that employees are following company policies and that operations are running efficiently.

DAILY EXERCISE 7-4

DAILY EXERCISE 7-5

External auditors are entirely independent of the business. They are hired to determine that the company's financial statements are prepared in accordance with generally accepted accounting principles. Both internal and external auditors are independent of the operations they examine, and both suggest improvements that help the business run efficiently.

DOCUMENTS AND RECORDS Business *documents and records* vary from invoices and purchase orders to special journals and subsidiary ledgers. Documents should be prenumbered. A gap in the numbered sequence draws attention.

Prenumbering sale receipts discourages theft by cashiers because the copies retained by the cashiers list the amount of the sale. These figures can be checked against the actual amount of cash received. If the receipts are not prenumbered, a cashier can destroy the sale receipt and pocket the cash received.

In a bowling alley a key document is the score sheet. The manager can compare the number of games scored with the amount of cash received. By multiplying the number of games by the price per game and comparing the result with each day's cash receipts, the manager can see whether the business is collecting all the revenue.

ELECTRONIC DEVICES AND COMPUTER CONTROLS Accounting systems are relying less and less on documents and more and more on digital storage devices. Computers shift the internal controls to the people who write the programs. Programmers then become the focus of internal controls because they can write programs that transfer company assets to themselves.

Businesses use electronic devices to protect assets and control operations. Retailers such as **Target Stores, Macy's,** and **Dillard's** control inventory by attaching an electronic sensor to merchandise. The cashier removes the sensor when a sale is made. If a customer tries to remove an item from the store with the sensor attached, an alarm is activated. According to **Checkpoint Systems,** which manufactures the sensors, these devices reduce theft by as much as 50%.

OTHER CONTROLS Businesses keep cash and important business documents (such as contracts and titles to property) in *fireproof vaults. Burglar alarms* protect buildings and other property.

Retailers receive most of their cash from customers on the spot. To safeguard cash, they use *point-of-sale terminals* that serve as a cash register and also record each transaction entered into the machine. Several times each day, a supervisor removes the cash for deposit in the bank.

Employees who handle cash are in an especially tempting position. Many businesses purchase *fidelity bonds* on cashiers. The bond is an insurance policy that reimburses the company for any losses due to employee theft. Before issuing a fidelity bond, the insurance company investigates the employee's past record.

Mandatory vacations and *job rotation* require that employees be trained to do a variety of jobs. **General Electric, Eastman Kodak,** and other large companies move employees from job to job—often at six-month intervals. This improves morale by giving employees a broad view of the business and helps them decide where they want to specialize. Knowing that someone else will be doing their job next month also keeps employees honest. Had Merrill Lynch moved Darlyne Lopez from job to job and required her to take a vacation, her embezzlement would probably have been detected much earlier.

Internal Controls for e-Commerce

e-Commerce creates some new risks. Buying and selling over the Internet can give hackers access to confidential information unavailable in face-to-face transactions. Confidentiality is a significant challenge for dotcoms. Pitfalls include

1. Stolen credit-card numbers
2. Computer viruses and Trojan horses
3. Impersonation of companies

To convince people to buy on-line, companies must ensure security of data.

COMPUTER VIRUS. A malicious program that (a) reproduces itself, (b) gets included in program code without consent, and (c) performs actions that can be destructive.

TROJAN HORSE. A malicious program that works like a virus but does not reproduce.

Stolen credit-card numbers. Suppose you buy several CDs from **EMusic.com**. To make the purchase, your credit-card number must travel through cyberspace. Amateur hacker Carlos Salgado, Jr., used his home computer to steal 100,000 credit-card numbers with a combined limit exceeding $1 billion from an Internet service provider. Salgado was caught when he tried to sell the credit-card numbers to an undercover FBI agent.

Computer viruses and Trojan horses. A **computer virus** is a malicious program that (a) reproduces itself, (b) gets included into program code without consent, and (c) performs actions that can be destructive. A **Trojan horse** works like a virus, but it does not reproduce. Viruses can destroy or alter data, make bogus calculations, and infect word-processing and spreadsheet files. The International Computer Security Association reports that 99.3% of firms it surveyed found a virus somewhere in their system.

Suppose the U.S. Department of Defense solicits bids for the design of a missile defense system. **Raytheon, Lockheed-Martin,** and **General Dynamics** bid on the contract. A hacker infects Raytheon's system and alters two small details of Raytheon's design. In evaluating the three bids, Pentagon engineers label the Raytheon design as flawed even though Raytheon has designed the best system for the lowest price. The American public winds up paying too much—all because of a trickster's prank.

Impersonation. Hackers sometimes create bogus Web sites, such as AOL4Free.com. The neat-sounding Web site attracts lots of visitors, and the hackers are able to solicit confidential data from unsuspecting people. The hackers then use the data for a variety of illicit purposes.

FIREWALLS AND ENCRYPTION   Information traveling the Internet is secure, but the server holding the information may be insecure. A server is a computer that performs a particular function (for example, data storage or printing) in a network. Two standard techniques companies use to secure e-commerce data are encryption and firewalls.

Encryption is the primary method of achieving confidentiality in e-commerce. Plain-text messages are rearranged by some mathematical process. The encrypted message cannot be read by anyone who does not know the process. A simple accounting example is the use of check-sum digits for customer account numbers. Each account number is set up so that the last digit is the sum of the previous digits, for example Customer Number 2237, where $2 + 2 + 3 = 7$. Any account number that fails this test triggers an error message.

Firewalls limit access to a local network. The intent is to keep intruders out. Often firewalls work between two networks, such as between a local network and the Internet. Firewalls enable members of the local network to access the Internet but keep nonmembers out of the network. Usually several firewalls are built into the local network so that hackers must work their way around more than one. Think of a fortress with multiple walls protecting the king's chamber in the center. At the point of entry, passwords, PINs (personal identification numbers), fingerprints, and signatures are used. More sophisticated firewalls are used deeper in the network.

The Limitations of Internal Control

Unfortunately, most internal control measures can be overcome. Two or more employees working as a team—*colluding*—can beat an internal control system and defraud the firm. Consider Galaxy Theater. Ralph and another employee could put together a scheme in which the ticket seller pockets the cash from ten customers and the ticket taker admits ten customers without tickets. To prevent this situation, the manager must take additional control measures, such as matching the number of people in the theater against the number of ticket stubs retained. But that would take time away from other duties. The stricter the internal control system, the more expensive and time-consuming it becomes.

A system of internal control that is too complex can strangle the business with red tape. How tight should controls be? Managers must make sensible judgments. Investments in internal control must be judged in light of the costs and benefits.

THE BANK ACCOUNT AS A CONTROL DEVICE

Cash is the most liquid asset because it is the medium of exchange. Cash often consists of electronic impulses in a bank's accounting system with no accompanying paper checks or deposit slips. Cash is easy to conceal, easy to move, and relatively easy to steal. As a result, most businesses create specific controls to safeguard cash.

Keeping cash in a *bank account* is important because banks have established practices for safeguarding cash. Banks also provide depositors with detailed records of their transactions. To take full advantage of these control features, the business should deposit all cash receipts in the bank account and make all cash payments through it (except petty cash transactions, which we examine later in this chapter).

The documents used to control a bank account include the

- signature card
- deposit ticket
- check
- bank statement
- bank reconciliation

SIGNATURE CARD Banks require each person authorized to transact business through an account to sign a *signature card.* The bank compares the signatures on documents against the signature card to protect against forgery.

DEPOSIT TICKET Banks supply standard forms such as *deposit tickets.* The customer fills in the dollar amount and the date of deposit. As proof of the transaction, the customer retains either (1) a duplicate copy of the deposit ticket, or (2) a deposit receipt, depending on the bank's practice.

CHECK To draw money from an account, the depositor writes a **check,** which is a document instructing the bank to pay the designated person or business a specified amount of money. There are three parties to a check: the *maker,* who signs the check; the *payee,* to whom the check is paid; and the *bank* on which the check is drawn. Most checks are serially numbered and preprinted with the name of the maker and the bank.

Exhibit 7-3 shows a check drawn on the bank account of Business Research, Inc. The check has two parts, the check itself and the *remittance advice,* an optional attachment that tells the payee the reason for the payment. The maker (Business Research) retains a duplicate copy of the check for its cash payments journal.

> **CHECK.** Document that instructs a bank to pay the designated person or business a specified amount of money.

EXHIBIT 7-3 **Check with Remittance Advice**

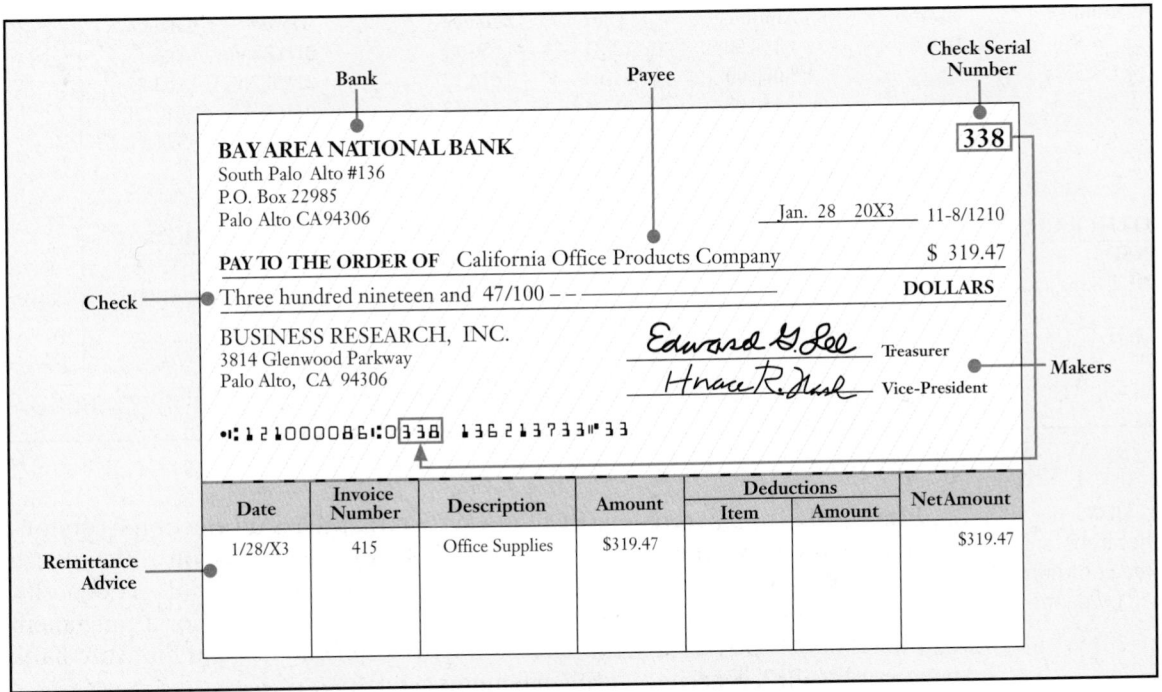

BANK STATEMENT Banks send monthly bank statements to depositors. A **bank statement** is the document the bank uses to report what it did with the depositor's cash. The statement shows the bank account's beginning and ending cash balances for the period and lists the month's cash transactions conducted through the bank. Included with the statement are the maker's *canceled checks,* those checks the bank has paid on behalf of the depositor. The bank statement also lists any deposits and other changes in the account. Deposits appear in chronological order and checks in a logical order (usually by check serial number), along with the date each check cleared the bank. Exhibit 7-4 is the bank statement of Business Research, Inc., for the month ended January 31, 20X3.

EXHIBIT 7-4 Bank Statement

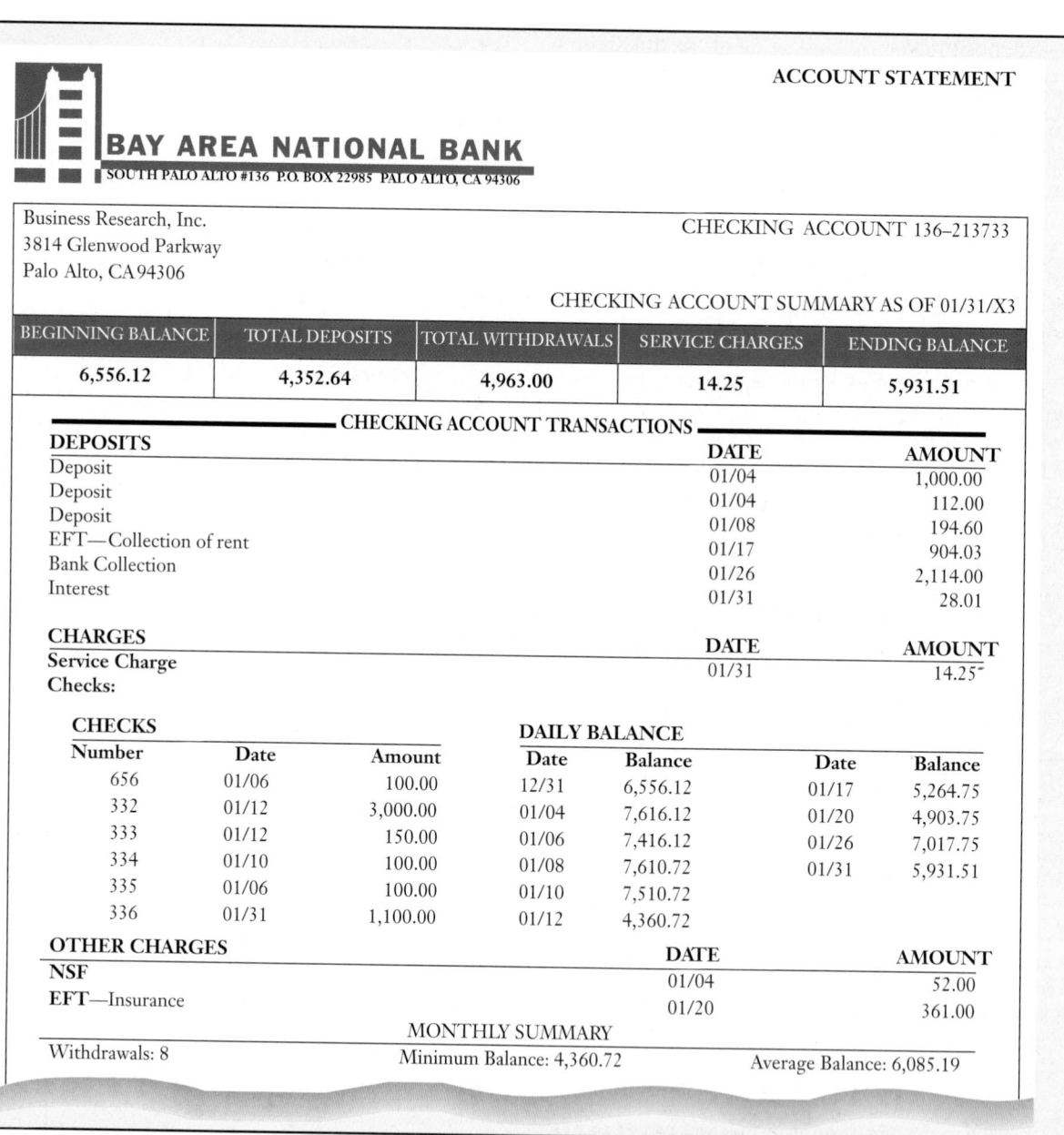

ACCOUNT STATEMENT

BAY AREA NATIONAL BANK
SOUTH PALO ALTO #136 P.O. BOX 22985 PALO ALTO, CA 94306

Business Research, Inc.
3814 Glenwood Parkway
Palo Alto, CA 94306

CHECKING ACCOUNT 136–213733

CHECKING ACCOUNT SUMMARY AS OF 01/31/X3

BEGINNING BALANCE	TOTAL DEPOSITS	TOTAL WITHDRAWALS	SERVICE CHARGES	ENDING BALANCE
6,556.12	4,352.64	4,963.00	14.25	5,931.51

———— CHECKING ACCOUNT TRANSACTIONS ————

DEPOSITS

	DATE	AMOUNT
Deposit	01/04	1,000.00
Deposit	01/04	112.00
Deposit	01/08	194.60
EFT—Collection of rent	01/17	904.03
Bank Collection	01/26	2,114.00
Interest	01/31	28.01

CHARGES

	DATE	AMOUNT
Service Charge	01/31	14.25⁻

Checks:

CHECKS				DAILY BALANCE			
Number	Date	Amount		Date	Balance	Date	Balance
656	01/06	100.00		12/31	6,556.12	01/17	5,264.75
332	01/12	3,000.00		01/04	7,616.12	01/20	4,903.75
333	01/12	150.00		01/06	7,416.12	01/26	7,017.75
334	01/10	100.00		01/08	7,610.72	01/31	5,931.51
335	01/06	100.00		01/10	7,510.72		
336	01/31	1,100.00		01/12	4,360.72		

OTHER CHARGES

	DATE	AMOUNT
NSF	01/04	52.00
EFT—Insurance	01/20	361.00

MONTHLY SUMMARY

Withdrawals: 8	Minimum Balance: 4,360.72	Average Balance: 6,085.19

Electronic funds transfer (EFT) is a system that relies on electronic communications to transfer cash. More and more businesses today rely on EFT for cash transactions. It is cheaper for a company to pay employees by EFT (direct deposit). Many people make mortgage, rent, and insurance payments by prior arrangement with their bank and never write checks for those payments. The monthly bank statement lists EFT deposits and EFT payments.

The Bank Reconciliation

There are two records of a business's cash: (1) its Cash account in its own general ledger (Exhibit 7-5), and (2) the bank statement, which shows the actual amount of cash the business has in the bank.

EXHIBIT **7-5**
Cash Records of Business Research, Inc.

General Ledger:

ACCOUNT Cash   No. 111

Date	Item	Jrnl. Ref.	Debit	Credit	Balance
20X3					
Jan. 1	Balance	✓			6,556.12
2	Cash receipt	CR. 9	1,112.00		7,668.12
7	Cash receipt	CR. 9	194.60		7,862.72
31	Cash payments	CP. 17		6,160.14	1,702.58
31	Cash receipt	CR. 10	1,591.63		3,294.21

 DAILY EXERCISE 7-9

Cash Payments:

Check No.	Amount	Check No.	Amount
332	$3,000.00	338............	$ 319.47
333	510.00	339............	83.00
334	100.00	340............	203.14
335	100.00	341............	458.53
336	1,100.00		
337	286.00	Total...........	$6,160.14

The books and the bank statement can show different amounts, yet both be correct. The difference arises because of a time lag in recording certain transactions. When a firm writes a check, it immediately credits its Cash account. The bank, however, does not subtract the amount of the check from the business's balance until the bank receives the check and pays it. This step may take days, even weeks, if the payee waits to cash the check. Likewise, the business immediately debits Cash for all cash receipts, but it may take a day or so for the bank to add these amounts to the business's bank balance.

To ensure accuracy of the financial records, the firm's accountant must explain all differences between the firm's own cash records and the bank statement figures on a certain date. The result of this process is a document called the **bank reconciliation,** which is prepared by the company (not by the bank). Properly done, the bank reconciliation ensures that all cash transactions have been accounted for and that the bank and book records of cash are correct. Knowing where cash comes from, how it is spent, and the balance of cash available is vital to success in business.

Here are some common items that cause differences between the bank balance and the book balance:

1. Items recorded by the company but not yet recorded by the bank
   a. **Deposits in transit** (outstanding deposits). The company has recorded these deposits, but the bank has not.
   b. **Outstanding checks.** The company has issued these checks and recorded them on its books, but the bank has not yet paid them.
2. Items recorded by the bank but not yet recorded by the company
   a. **Bank collections.** Banks sometimes collect money for their depositors. Many businesses have customers pay directly to the company bank account. This practice, called a *lock-box system,* reduces theft and places the business's cash in circulation faster than if the cash is collected and deposited by company personnel. An example is a bank's collecting cash and interest on a note receivable for the depositor.
   b. *Electronic funds transfers.* The bank may receive or pay cash on behalf of the depositor. The bank statement will list the EFTs.

BANK RECONCILIATION. Document explaining the reasons for the difference between a depositor's cash records and the depositor's cash balance in its bank account.

DEPOSIT IN TRANSIT. A deposit recorded by the company but not yet by its bank.

OUTSTANDING CHECK. A check issued by the company and recorded on its books but not yet paid by its bank.

BANK COLLECTION. Collection of money by the bank on behalf of a depositor.

c. *Service charge.* This is the bank's fee for processing the depositor's transactions. Banks base the service charge on the account balance or on the number of transactions. The depositor learns the amount of the service charge from the bank statement.

d. *Interest revenue on checking account.* Depositors earn interest if they keep enough cash in their account. The bank notifies depositors of this interest on the bank statement.

e. Nonsufficient funds (NSF) checks are worthless checks received from customers. To understand how NSF checks (sometimes called *hot checks*) are handled, consider the route a check takes. Exhibit 7-6 diagrams the paths that two checks take in the bank clearing process. The first diagram tracks the path of a good check. The second diagram shows what happens to an NSF (hot) check.

NSF checks are cash *receipts* that turn out to be worthless. The payee may learn of NSF checks through the bank statement, which lists the NSF check as a charge (subtraction). See the $52 item near the bottom of Exhibit 7-4. Because an NSF check is worthless, the customer still owes Business Research $52 in Exhibit 7-4. As a result, Business Research has a receivable from the customer who wrote the NSF check.

> **NONSUFFICIENT FUNDS (NSF) CHECK.** A "hot" check, one for which the maker's bank account has insufficient money to pay the check.

EXHIBIT 7-6   The Paths That Two Checks Take

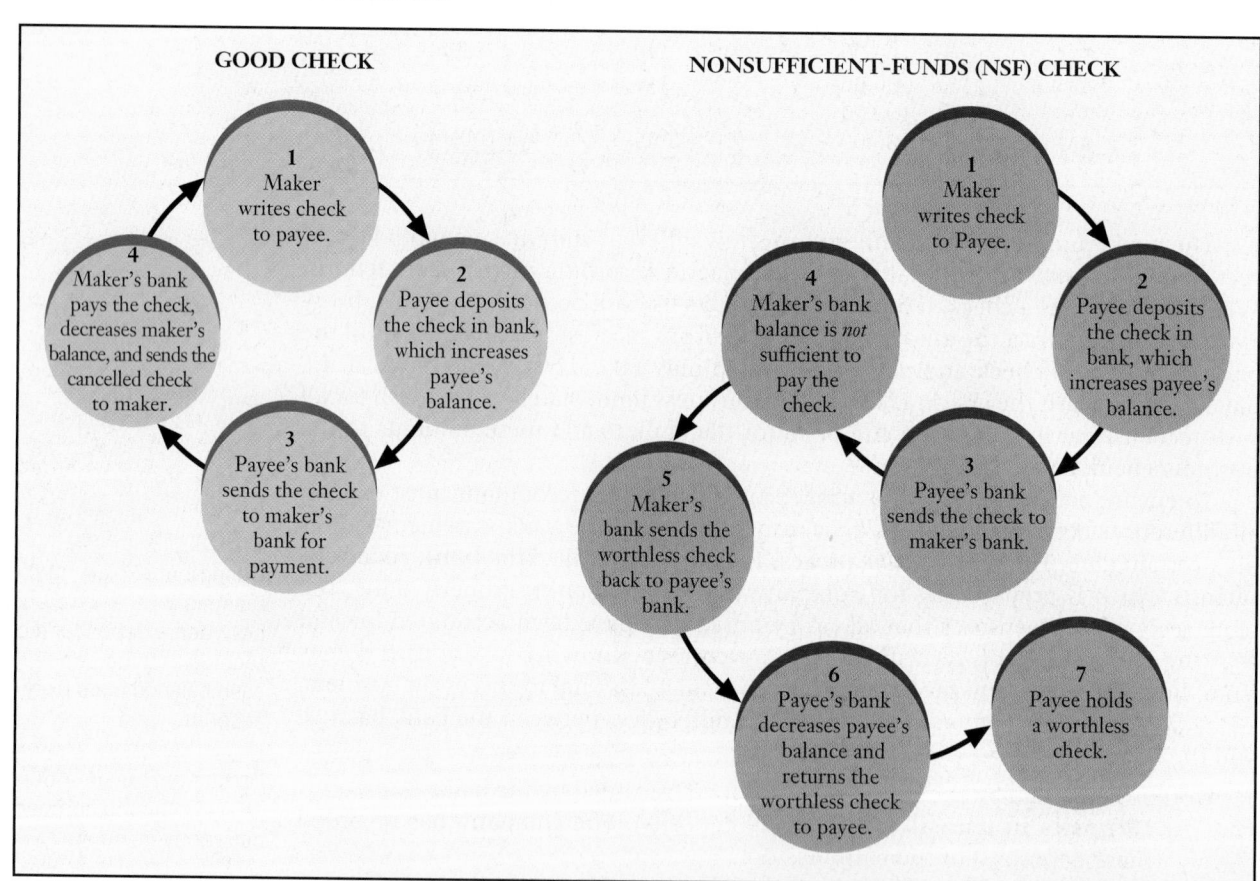

f. *Checks collected, deposited, and returned to payee by the bank for reasons other than NSF.* Banks return checks to the payee if (1) the maker's account has closed, (2) the date is "stale" (some checks state "void after 30 days"), (3) the signature is not authorized, (4) the check has been altered, or (5) the check form is improper (for example, a counterfeit). Accounting for all returned checks is the same as for NSF checks.

g. *The cost of printed checks.* This charge is handled like a service charge.

3. Errors by the company or the bank. For example, a bank may improperly charge (decrease) the bank balance of Business Research, Inc., for a check drawn by another company, perhaps Business Research Associates. Or a company may miscompute its bank balance on its own books. Error correction will be part of the bank reconciliation.

PREPARING THE BANK RECONCILIATION The steps in preparing the bank reconciliation are as follows:

Objective 3
Prepare a bank reconciliation and the related journal entries

1. Start with two figures, the balance shown on the bank statement (*balance per bank*) and the balance in the company's Cash account (*balance per books*). These two amounts will probably disagree because of the differences discussed earlier.
2. Add to, or subtract from, the *bank* balance those items that appear on the books but not on the bank statement:
   a. Add *deposits in transit* to the bank balance. Deposits in transit show up as cash receipts on the books but not as deposits on the bank statement.
   b. Subtract *outstanding checks* from the bank balance. Outstanding checks show up as cash payments on the books but not as paid checks on the bank statement. Outstanding checks are usually the most numerous items on a bank reconciliation.
3. Add to, or subtract from, the *book* balance those items that appear on the bank statement but not on the company books:
   a. Add to the book balance (1) *bank collections,* (2) *EFT cash receipts,* and (3) *interest revenue* earned on money in the bank. These items show up as cash receipts on the bank statement but not on the books.
   b. Subtract from the book balance (1) *EFT cash payments,* (2) *service charges,* (3) *cost of printed checks,* and (4) *NSF checks received, and other bank charges* (for example, stale-date checks). These items show up as subtractions on the bank statement but not as cash payments on the books.
4. Compute the *adjusted bank balance* and the *adjusted book balance.* The two adjusted balances should be equal.
5. Journalize each item in step 3—those items listed on the *Book* portion of the bank reconciliation. These transactions must be recorded on the company books because they affect cash.
6. Correct all book errors and notify the bank of any errors it has made.

BANK RECONCILIATION ILLUSTRATED The bank statement in Exhibit 7-4 indicates that the January 31 bank balance of Business Research, Inc., is $5,931.51. However, the company's Cash account has a balance of $3,294.21, as shown in Exhibit 7-5. The following reconciling items explain why the bank balance and the book balance differ:

1. The January 31 deposit of $1,591.63 (deposit in transit) does not appear on the bank statement. See the last item in the Company's Cash Account (Exhibit 7-5).
2. The bank erroneously charged to the Business Research, Inc., account a $100 check—number 656—written by Business Research Associates (a bank error).
3. Five company checks issued late in January and recorded in the cash payments journal have not been paid by the bank. The following checks are outstanding:

Check No.	Date	Amount
337	Jan. 17	$286.00
338	26	319.47
339	27	83.00
340	28	203.14
341	30	458.53

These checks are listed under cash payments in Exhibit 7-5.

4. The bank received $904.03 by EFT on behalf of Business Research, Inc. (an EFT receipt).
5. The bank collected on behalf of the company a note receivable, $2,114 (including interest revenue of $214). Business Research has not recorded this cash receipt (a bank collection).

The bank statement shows interest revenue of $28.01, which the company has earned on its cash balance (interest revenue).

7. Check number 333 for $150 paid to Brown Company on account was recorded as a cash payment of $510, creating a $360 understatement of the Cash balance in the books (a book error).

DAILY EXERCISE 7-7

8. The bank service charge for the month was $14.25 (service charge).

9. The bank statement shows an NSF check for $52, which was received from customer L. Ross (NSF check).

DAILY EXERCISE 7-10

10. Business Research pays insurance expense monthly by EFT. The company has not yet recorded this $361 payment (an EFT payment).

Exhibit 7-7 is the bank reconciliation based on the preceding data. Panel A lists the reconciling items, which are keyed by number to the reconciliation in Panel B.

EXHIBIT 7-7 Bank Reconciliation

PANEL A—Reconciling Items

1. Deposit in transit, $1,591.63.
2. Bank error, add $100 to bank balance.
3. Outstanding checks; no. 337, $286; no. 338, $319.47; no. 339, $83; no. 340, $203.14; no. 341, $458.53.
4. EFT receipt of rent revenue, $904.03.
5. Bank collection, $2,114, including interest revenue of $214.

6. Interest earned on bank balance, $28.01.
7. Book error, add $360 to book balance.
8. Bank service charge, $14.25.
9. NSF check from L. Ross, $52.
10. EFT payment of insurance expense, $361.

PANEL B—Bank Reconciliation

BUSINESS RESEARCH, INC.
Bank Reconciliation
January 31, 20X3

Bank			Books		
Balance, January 31		$5,931.51	Balance, January 31		$3,294.21
Add:			Add:		
1. Deposit of January 31 in transit		1,591.63	4. EFT receipt of rent revenue		904.03
2. Correction of bank error— Business Research Associates check 656 erroneously charged against company account		100.00	5. Bank collection of note receivable, including interest revenue of $214		2,114.00
		7,623.14	6. Interest revenue earned on bank balance		28.01
			7. Correction of book error— overstated amount of check no. 333		360.00
					6,700.25
Less:					
3. Outstanding checks					
No. 337	$286.00		Less:		
No. 338	319.47		8. Service charge	$ 14.25	
No. 339	83.00		9. NSF check	52.00	
No. 340	203.14		10. EFT payment of		
No. 341	458.53	(1,350.14)	insurance expense	361.00	(427.25)
Adjusted bank balance		$6,273.00	Adjusted book balance		$6,273.00

↑ **Amounts agree.** ↑

Each reconciling item is treated in the same way in every situation. Here is a summary of how to treat the various reconciling items:

BANK BALANCE—ALWAYS
- *Add* deposits in transit.
- *Subtract* outstanding checks.
- *Add* or *subtract* corrections of bank errors.

BOOK BALANCE—ALWAYS
- *Add* bank collections, interest revenue, and EFT receipts.
- *Subtract* service charges, NSF checks, and EFT payments.
- *Add* or *subtract* corrections of book errors.

JOURNALIZING TRANSACTIONS FROM THE RECONCILIATION   The bank reconciliation does not place entries in the journals or the ledgers. The reconciliation is an accountant's tool, separate from the company's books.

The bank reconciliation acts as a control device. It signals the company to record transactions for all the reconciling items listed in the Books section of the reconciliation. The company has not yet recorded these items. For example, the bank collected the note receivable for the company, but the company has not yet recorded this cash receipt. In fact, the company learned of the cash receipt only when it received the bank statement.

THINK IT OVER   Why doesn't the company need to record the reconciling items on the Bank side of the reconciliation?

Answer: Those items have already been recorded on the company books.

On the basis of the reconciliation in Exhibit 7-7, Business Research, Inc., makes the following journal entries. They are dated January 31 to bring the Cash account to the correct balance on that date. Numbers in parentheses correspond to the reconciling items listed in Exhibit 7-7, Panel A.

DAILY EXERCISE 7-8

(4) Jan. 31	Cash	904.03	
	Rent Revenue.........		904.03
	Receipt of monthly rent.		
(5) 31	Cash	2,114.00	
	Notes Receivable.....		1,900.00
	Interest Revenue		214.00
	Note receivable collected by bank.		
(6) 31	Cash	28.01	
	Interest Revenue		28.01
	Interest earned on bank balance.		
(7) 31	Cash	360.00	
	Accounts Payable		
	—Brown Co.........		360.00
	Correction of check no. 333.		

(8) 31	Miscellaneous Expense[1]	14.25	
	Cash..............................		14.25
	Bank service charge.		
(9) 31	Accounts Receivable		
	—L. Ross.........................	52.00	
	Cash..............................		52.00
	NSF check returned by bank.		
(10) 31	Insurance Expense...........	361.00	
	Cash..............................		361.00
	Payment of monthly insurance.		

These entries bring the company's books up to date.

The entry for the NSF check (entry 9) needs explanation. Upon learning that L. Ross's $52 check was not good, Business Research credits Cash to bring the Cash account up to date. Business Research still has a receivable from Ross, so the company debits Accounts Receivable—L. Ross and pursues collection from him.

DAILY EXERCISE 7-11

WORK IT OUT   The bank statement balance is $4,500 and shows a service charge of $15, interest earned of $5, and an NSF check for $300. Deposits in transit total $1,200; outstanding checks are $575. The bookkeeper recorded as $152 a check of $125 in payment of an account payable.

1. What is the adjusted bank balance?

2. Prepare the journal entries needed to update the company's (not the bank's) books.

Answers

1. $5,125 ($4,500 + $1,200 − $575)

2. Journal entries on the books:

Miscellaneous Expense	15	Accounts Receivable	300
Cash	15	Cash..............................	300
Cash	5	Cash ($152 − $125)............	27
Interest Revenue................	5	Accounts Payable...........	27

---
[1]Note: Miscellaneous Expense is debited for the bank service charge because the service charge pertains to no particular expense category.

INTERNAL CONTROL, MANAGING
CASH, AND MAKING
ETHICAL JUDGMENTS

How Owners and Managers Use the Bank Reconciliation

The bank reconciliation is a powerful control device in the hands of a business owner or manager, as the following example illustrates.

Randy Vaughn is a CPA in Houston, Texas. He owns several apartment complexes that his aunt manages. His accounting practice leaves little time to devote to his apartments. Vaughn's aunt signs up tenants, collects the monthly rent, arranges custodial work, hires and fires employees, writes the checks, and performs the bank reconciliation. In short, she does it all. This concentration of duties in one person is terrible from an internal control standpoint. Vaughn's aunt could be stealing from him, and as a CPA he is aware of this possibility.

Vaughn trusts his aunt because she is a member of the family. Nevertheless, he exercises some loose controls over her management of his apartments. Vaughn periodically drops by his properties to see whether the custodial staff is keeping them in good condition.

To control cash, Vaughn uses the bank statement and the bank reconciliation. On an irregular basis, he examines the bank reconciliations. He matches every paid check to the journal entry on the books. Vaughn would know immediately if his aunt is writing checks to herself. Vaughn sometimes prepares his own bank reconciliation to see whether he agrees with his aunt's work. To keep his aunt on her toes, Vaughn lets her know that he periodically audits her work.

Vaughn has a simple method for controlling cash receipts. He knows the occupancy level of his apartments. He also knows the monthly rent he charges. He multiplies the number of apartments—say 20—by the monthly rent (which averages $500 per unit) to arrive at expected monthly rent revenue of $10,000. By tracing the $10,000 revenue to the bank statement, Vaughn can tell that his rent money went into his bank account.

Control activities such as these are critical in small businesses. With only a few employees, a separation of duties may not be feasible. The owner must oversee the operations of the business, or the assets will slip away, as they did for Merrill Lynch in the chapter opening story.

⊙ DAILY EXERCISE 7-12

⊙ DAILY EXERCISE 7-13

MID-CHAPTER

SUMMARY PROBLEM

www.prenhall.com/horngren

Mid-Chapter Assessment

The Cash account of Zuboff Associates at February 28, 20X3, is as follows:

	CASH			
Feb. 1	Bal. 3,995	Feb. 3	400
6	800	12	3,100
15	1,800	19	1,100
23	1,100	25	500
28	2,400	27	900
Feb. 28	Bal. 4,095		

Zuboff Associates received the bank statement—shown on facing page—on February 28, 20X3 (as always, negative amounts are in parentheses):

Beginning balance		$3,995
Deposits:		
Feb. 7	$ 800	
15	1,800	
24	1,100	3,700
Checks (total per day):		
Feb. 8	$ 400	
16	3,100	
23	1,100	(4,600)
Other items:		
Service charge		(10)
NSF check from M. E. Crown		(700)
Bank collection of note receivable for the company........		1,000*
EFT—monthly rent expense		(330)
Interest on account balance		15
Ending balance		$3,070

*Includes interest of $119.

Additional data: Zuboff deposits all cash receipts in the bank and makes all payments by check.

Required

1. Prepare the bank reconciliation of Zuboff Associates at February 28, 20X3.
2. Record the entries based on the bank reconciliation.

Solution

Requirement 1

ZUBOFF ASSOCIATES
Bank Reconciliation
February 28, 20X3

Bank:		
Balance, February 28, 20X3		$3,070
Add: Deposit of February 28 in transit		2,400
		5,470
Less: Outstanding checks issued on Feb. 25 ($500)		
and Feb. 27 ($900)		(1,400)
Adjusted bank balance, February 28, 20X3		$4,070
Books:		
Balance, February 28, 20X3		$4,095
Add: Bank collection of note receivable, including		
interest of $119		1,000
Interest earned on bank balance......................................		15
		5,110
Less: Service charge	$ 10	
NSF check	700	
EFT—Rent expense..	330	(1,040)
Adjusted book balance, February 28, 20X3		$4,070

Requirement 2

Feb. 28	Cash	1,000		Feb. 28	Accounts Receivable—		
	Note Receivable				M. E. Crown.....................	700	
	($1,000 − $119)...		881		Cash		700
	Interest Revenue......		119		NSF check returned by bank.		
	Note receivable collected by bank.			28	Rent Expense	330	
28	Cash	15			Cash		330
	Interest Revenue......		15		Monthly rent expense.		
	Interest earned on bank balance.						
28	Miscellaneous Expense.......	10					
	Cash		10				
	Bank service charge.						

INTERNAL CONTROL OVER CASH RECEIPTS

Internal control over cash receipts ensures that all cash receipts are deposited in the bank and that the company's accounting record is correct. Many businesses receive cash over the counter and through the mail. Each source of cash receipts calls for its own security measures.

Objective 4
Apply internal controls to cash receipts

 DAILY EXERCISE 7-14
 DAILY EXERCISE 7-15

CASH RECEIPTS OVER THE COUNTER   The point-of-sale terminal (cash register) offers management control over the cash received in a store. Consider a **Macy's** store. First, the terminal should be positioned so that customers can see the amounts the cashier enters into the computer. Company policy should require issuance of a receipt to make sure each sale is recorded by the cash register.

Second, the cash drawer opens only when the sales clerk enters an amount on the keypad, and the machine records each sale and cash transaction. At the end of the day, a manager proves the cash by comparing the total amount in the cash drawer against the machine's record of the day's sales. This step helps prevent outright theft by the clerk.

Third, pricing merchandise at "uneven" amounts—say, $3.95 instead of $4.00—means that the clerk generally must make change, which in turn means having to get into the cash drawer. This requires entering the amount of the sale on the keypad and so onto the register tape—another way to prevent fraud.

At the end of the day, the cashier or other employee with cash-handling duties deposits the cash in the bank. The tape then goes to the accounting department as the basis for an entry in the accounting records. These security measures, coupled with periodic on-site inspection by a manager, discourage theft.

CASH RECEIPTS BY MAIL   All incoming mail should be opened by a mailroom employee. This person should compare the amount of the check received with the attached remittance advice (the slip of paper that lists the amount of the check). If no advice was sent, the mailroom employee should prepare one and enter the amount of each receipt on a control tape. At the end of the day, this control tape is given to a responsible official, such as the controller, for verification. Cash receipts should be given to the cashier, who combines them with any cash received over the counter and prepares the bank deposit.

Having a mailroom employee handle postal cash receipts is another application of a good separation of duties. If the accountants were to open postal cash receipts, they could easily hide a theft.

The mailroom employee forwards the remittance advices to the accounting department. These provide the data for entries in the cash books and postings to customers' accounts in the accounts receivable ledger. As a final step, the controller compares the three records of the day's cash receipts:

1. The control tape total from the mailroom
2. The bank deposit amount from the cashier
3. The debit to Cash from the accounting department

DAILY EXERCISE 7-16

Many companies use a lock-box system to separate cash duties and establish control over cash receipts. Customers send their checks directly to an address that is essentially a bank account. Internal control over the cash is enhanced because company personnel do not handle incoming cash. The lock-box system improves efficiency because the cash goes to work for the company immediately.

THINK IT OVER   The bookkeeper in your company has stolen cash received from customers. The bookkeeper prepared fake documents that indicate the customers returned the merchandise. What internal control feature could have prevented this theft?

Answer: The bookkeeper should not have access to cash.

CASH SHORT AND OVER   Differences sometimes exist between actual cash receipts and the day's record of cash received. Usually, these differences are small and result from honest errors. When the recorded cash balance exceeds cash on hand, a *cash short* situation exists. When actual cash exceeds the recorded cash balance, there is a *cash over* situation. Suppose the cash register tapes of Macy's indicated sales revenue of $25,000, but the cash received was $24,980. To record the day's sales, the store would make this entry:

Cash	24,980	
Cash Short and Over............	20	
Sales Revenue		25,000
Daily cash sales.		

As the entry shows, Cash Short and Over is debited when cash receipts are less than sales revenue. This account is credited when cash receipts exceed sales. A debit balance in Cash Short and Over appears on the income statement as Miscellaneous Expense, a credit balance as Other Revenue.

Exhibit 7-8 summarizes the controls over cash receipts.

EXHIBIT 7-8   Internal Controls over Cash Receipts

Elements of Internal Control	Internal Controls over Cash Receipts
Competent, reliable, ethical personnel	Companies carefully screen employees for undesirable traits. They commit time and effort to training programs.
Assignment of responsibilities	Specific employees are designated as cashiers, supervisors, or accountants.
Proper authorization	Only designated employees, such as department managers, can approve check receipts above a certain amount.
Separation of duties	Cashiers and mailroom employees who handle cash do not have access to the accounting records. Accountants have no opportunity to handle cash.
Internal and external audits	Internal auditors examine company transactions for agreement with management policies. External auditors examine the internal controls to determine whether the accounting system produces accurate amounts for revenues and receivables.
Documents and records	Customers receive receipts as transaction records. Bank statements list cash receipts for deposits.
Electronic devices and computer controls	Cash registers serve as transaction records. Each day's receipts are matched with customer remittance advices and with the day's deposit ticket from the bank.
Other controls	Cashiers are bonded. Cash is stored in vaults and banks. Employees are rotated among jobs and are required to take vacations.

INTERNAL CONTROL OVER CASH PAYMENTS (DISBURSEMENTS)

Objective 5
Apply internal controls to cash payments

Exercising control over cash payments is as important as controlling cash receipts.

Controls over Payment by Check

Payment by check is an important control over cash payments. First, the check provides a record of the payment. Second, to be valid, the check must be signed by an authorized official. Before signing the check, the manager should study the evidence supporting the payment. To illustrate the internal control over cash payments, let's suppose the business is buying merchandise inventory.

CONTROLS OVER PURCHASING   The purchasing process—outlined in Exhibit 7-9—starts when the sales department prepares a *purchase request* (or *requisition*). A separate purchasing department locates the goods and mails a *purchase order* to the supplier. When the supplier ships the merchandise, the supplier also mails the *invoice,* or bill. � The goods arrive, and the receiving department checks the goods for damage and lists the merchandise received on a document called the *receiving report.* The accounting department combines all the foregoing documents and forwards this *payment packet* to officers for payment. The packet includes the purchase request, purchase order, invoice, and receiving report, as shown in Exhibit 7-10.

◄ We introduced purchase orders and invoices in Chapter 5.

283

EXHIBIT 7-9
Purchasing Process

Business Document	Prepared by	Send to
Purchase request (requisition)	Sales department	Purchasing department
Purchase order	Purchasing department	Outside company that sells the needed merchandise (supplier or vendor)
Invoice (bill)	Outside company that sells the needed merchandise (supplier or vendor)	Accounting department
Receiving report	Receiving department	Accounting department
Payment packet	Accounting department	Officer who signs the check

EXHIBIT 7-10
Payment Packet

CONTROLS OVER APPROVAL OF PAYMENTS Before approving the payment, the controller or the treasurer should examine the packet to ascertain that the accounting department has performed the following control steps:

1. The invoice is compared with a copy of the purchase order and purchase request to ensure that the business pays only for the goods that it ordered.
2. The invoice is compared with the receiving report to ensure that cash is paid only for the goods actually received.
3. The mathematical accuracy of the invoice is proved.

 DAILY EXERCISE 7-17

To avoid document alteration, some firms use machines that stamp the amount on the check in indelible ink. After payment, the check signer punches a hole through the payment packet. This hole makes it hard to run the documents through for a duplicate payment.

Technology is streamlining cash payment procedures. Evaluated Receipts Settlement (ERS) compresses the approval process into a single step: compare the receiving report to the purchase order. If the two documents match, that proves **Kinko's** received the paper it ordered, and then Kinko's pays **Hammermill Paper,** the supplier. ERS requires fewer employees and saves on accounting expense.

An even more streamlined process bypasses people and documents altogether. In Electronic Data Interchange (EDI), **Wal-Mart's** computers communicate directly with the computers of suppliers like **Goodyear Tire, Rubbermaid,** and **Procter & Gamble.** When Wal-Mart's inventory of auto tires reaches a low level, the computer sends a purchase order to Goodyear. Goodyear ships the tires and invoices Wal-Mart electronically. Then an electronic fund transfer (EFT) sends the cash from Wal-Mart to Goodyear.

These streamlined procedures depend on the mutual trust of the companies involved. They know each other well and operate ethically. They cannot afford to do otherwise. Exhibit 7-11 summarizes the internal controls over cash payments.

EXHIBIT 7-11   Internal Controls over Cash Payments

Element of Internal Control	Internal Controls over Cash Payments
Competent, reliable, ethical personnel	Cash payments are entrusted to high-level employees.
Assignment of responsibilities	Specific employees approve purchase documents for payment. Executives examine approvals, then sign checks.
Proper authorization	Large expenditures must be authorized by the company owner or board of directors.
Separation of duties	Computer operators and other employees who handle checks have no access to the accounting records. Accountants have no opportunity to handle cash.
Internal and external audits	Internal auditors examine company transactions for agreement with management policies. External auditors examine the internal controls over cash payments and the accounting records.
Documents and records	Suppliers issue invoices. Bank statements list cash payments. Checks are renumbered in sequence to account for payments.
Electronic devices, computer controls, and other controls	Blank checks are stored in a vault and controlled by a responsible official. Machines stamp the amount on a check in indelible ink. Paid invoices are punched to avoid duplicate payment.

THINK IT OVER   Talon Computer Concepts processes payroll checks for small businesses. Clients give their employee time cards to Talon, and Talon programmers write the software to meet the clients' payrolls. Talon computer operators deliver the checks to clients for distribution to employees. Identify two employee functions of Talon's cash payment system that should be separated. Give your reason.

Answer: The *programmers* should not also be computer *operators*. Persons who both program and operate computers can write the program to process checks to themselves and then pocket the printed checks.

Controlling Petty Cash Payments

It is uneconomical for a business to write a separate check for an executive's taxi fare, floppy disks needed right away, or the delivery of a package across town. To meet these needs, companies keep a small amount of cash on hand to pay for such minor amounts. This fund is called **petty cash.**

Even though amounts paid through the petty cash fund are small, the business needs to set up controls such as the following:

1. Designate an employee to administer the fund as its custodian.
2. Keep a specific amount of cash on hand.
3. Support all fund payments with a petty cash ticket.
4. Replenish the fund through normal cash payment procedures.

The petty cash fund is opened when a payment is approved for a predetermined amount and a check for that amount is issued to Petty Cash. Assume that on February 28, the business decides to establish a petty cash fund of $200. The custodian cashes the check and places the currency and coin in the fund, which may be a cash box, safe, or other device. The petty cash custodian is responsible for controlling the fund. Starting the fund is recorded as follows:

Feb. 28	Petty Cash..	200	
	Cash in Bank		200
	To open the petty cash fund.		

PETTY CASH. Fund containing a small amount of cash that is used to pay for minor expenditures.

For each petty cash payment, the custodian prepares a *petty cash ticket* like the one illustrated in Exhibit 7-12.

EXHIBIT 7-12
Petty Cash Ticket

```
                        PETTY CASH TICKET
    Date    Mar. 25, 20X6                          No.   47
    Amount    $23.00
    For    Box of floppy diskettes
    Debit    Office Supplies, Acct. No. 145
    Received by  Lewis Wright      Fund Custodian   MAR
```

IMPREST SYSTEM. A way to account for petty cash by maintaining a constant balance in the petty cash account, supported by the fund (cash plus payment tickets) totaling the same amount.

Observe that signatures (or initials) identify the recipient of petty cash and the fund custodian. Requiring both signatures reduces unauthorized payments. The custodian keeps all the petty cash tickets in the fund. The sum of the cash plus the total of the ticket amounts should equal the opening balance at all times—in this case, $200. Also, the Petty Cash account keeps its prescribed $200 balance at all times. Maintaining the Petty Cash account at this balance, supported by the fund (cash plus tickets totaling the same amount), is a characteristic of an **imprest system.** In an imprest system, the amount of cash for which the custodian is responsible is clearly identified. This is the system's main internal control feature.

Payments reduce the amount of cash in the fund, so periodically the fund must be replenished. Suppose that on March 31, the fund has $118 in cash and $82 in tickets. A check for $82 is issued, made payable to Petty Cash. The fund custodian cashes this check and puts the money in the fund to return its actual cash to $200. The petty cash tickets identify the accounts to be debited, as shown in the entry to record replenishment of the fund:

Mar. 31	Office Supplies..	23	
	Delivery Expense	17	
	Miscellaneous Selling Expense..................	42	
	Cash in Bank...................................		82
	To replenish the petty cash fund.		

DAILY EXERCISE 7-18

If this cash payment exceeds the sum of the tickets—that is, if the fund comes up short, Cash Short and Over is debited for the missing amount. If the sum of the tickets exceeds the payment, Cash Short and Over is credited. Replenishing the fund does *not* affect the Petty Cash account. Petty Cash keeps its $200 balance at all times.

Petty Cash is debited only when the fund is started (see the February 28 entry) or when its amount is changed. Suppose the business decides to raise the fund amount from $200 to $250. This step would require a $50 debit to Petty Cash.

Objective 6
Use a budget to manage cash

USING A BUDGET TO MANAGE CASH

BUDGET. A quantitative expression of a plan that helps managers coordinate the entity's activities.

Owners and managers control their organizations with the help of budgets. A **budget** is a quantitative expression of a plan that helps managers coordinate the entity's activities. Cash receives the most attention in the budgeting process because all transactions ultimately affect cash.

How does **MCI WorldCom** decide when to invest in new telecommunications equipment? How will the company decide how much to spend? Similarly, by what process do you decide how much to spend on your education? On an automobile? All these decisions depend to some degree on the information that a cash budget provides. A cash budget helps a business manage its cash by expressing the plan for the receipt and payment of cash during a future period.

To prepare for the future, a company must determine how much cash it will need and then figure out how to obtain the needed cash. Preparation of a cash budget includes four steps:

1. Start with the entity's cash balance at the beginning of the period. This is the amount of cash left over from the preceding period.
2. Add the budgeted cash receipts and subtract the budgeted cash payments, including

a. Revenue and expense transactions

b. Asset acquisition and sale transactions

c. Liability and stockholders' equity transactions

3. The beginning balance plus the expected receipts minus the expected payments equals the expected cash balance at the end of the period.

4. Compare the expected cash balance to the desired, or *budgeted,* cash balance at the end of the period. Owners and managers know the minimum amount of cash they need (the budgeted balance) to keep the entity running. If there is excess cash, they can invest more than originally planned. If the expected cash balance falls below the budgeted amount, the company must raise more money to reach the desired cash balance.

Exhibit 7-13 shows a hypothetical cash budget for **Gap Inc.,** for the year ended January 31, 20X2. Study it carefully, because at some point in your career or personal affairs you will use a cash budget.

GAP INC. Cash Budget (Hypothetical) Year Ended January 31, 20X2		
		(In millions)
(1) Cash balance, February 1, 20X1		$ 203
Estimated cash receipts:		
(2) Collections from customers.....................................	$ 2,858	
(3) Interest and dividends on investments	6	
(4) Sale of store fixtures..	5	2,869
		3,072
Estimated cash payments:		
(5) Purchases of inventory...	$(1,906)	
(6) Operating expenses	(561)	
(7) Expansions of existing stores....................................	(206)	
(8) Opening of new stores	(349)	
(9) Payment of long-term debt	(145)	
(10) Payment to owners of the business............................	(219)	(3,386)
(11) Cash available (needed) before new financing...............		(314)
(12) Budgeted cash balance, January 31, 20X2		(200)
(13) Cash available for additional investments, or (New financing needed)..		$ (514)

EXHIBIT 7-13
Cash Budget (Hypothetical)

DAILY EXERCISE 7-19

The cash budget has sections for cash receipts and cash payments. The budget is prepared *before* the period's transactions and can take any form that helps people make decisions. The cash budget is an internal document, so it is not bound by generally accepted accounting principles.

Gap Inc.'s hypothetical cash budget in Exhibit 7-13 begins with the company's actual cash balance at the beginning of the period. At February 1, 20X1, Gap had cash of $203 million (line 1). The budgeted cash receipts and payments are expected to create a need for additional financing during the year (line 13).

Assume that managers of Gap wish to maintain a cash balance of at least $200 million (line 12). Because the year's activity is expected to leave the company with a *negative* cash balance of $314 million (line 11), Gap's managers must arrange $514 million of financing (line 13). *Add* lines 11 and 12 to arrive at the amount of new financing needed.

DAILY EXERCISE 7-20

WORK IT OUT

Suppose line 11 of Exhibit 7-13 showed cash available of $250 million. What would Gap Inc. do, borrow additional money, or have an excess to invest?

Answer: Gap would have an additional $50 million to invest ($250 million available − $200 million needed = excess of $50 million).

INTERNAL CONTROL, MANAGING
CASH, AND MAKING
ETHICAL JUDGMENTS

International transactions add to the complexity of managing cash. When a U.S. company buys goods internationally, it may pay cash in a foreign currency, such as Canadian dollars or Mexican pesos. Foreign currencies change in value from day to day. In settling up, a company may have a gain or a loss on the foreign currency. We show how to account for foreign currency transactions in Chapter 16.

REPORTING CASH ON THE BALANCE SHEET

Cash is the first current asset listed on the balance sheet. Businesses often have many bank accounts and petty cash funds, but they usually combine all cash amounts into a single total called "Cash and Cash Equivalents."

Cash equivalents include liquid assets such as time deposits and certificates of deposit, which are interest-bearing accounts that can be withdrawn with no penalty. Although they are slightly less liquid than cash, these assets are sufficiently similar to be reported along with cash. The balance sheet of **Intel Corporation** recently reported the following:

INTEL CORPORATION Balance Sheet (Adapted) December 31, 1999	
	(In millions)
Assets	
Current assets:	
Cash and cash equivalents	$ 3,695
Short-term investments	8,093
Accounts receivable........................	3,700
Inventories	1,478
Other current assets	853
Total current assets............................	$17,819

Source: Intel Corporation. *Annual Report 1999,* p. 19.

Intel's cash balance means that $3,695 million is available for use as needed. Cash that is restricted should not be reported as a current asset. For example, banks require customers to keep a *compensating balance* on deposit in order to borrow from the bank. The compensating balance is restricted and therefore is not included in the cash amount on the balance sheet.

ETHICS AND ACCOUNTING

A *Wall Street Journal* article described a Russian entrepreneur who claimed he was getting ahead in business by breaking laws. "Older people have an ethics problem," he said. "By that I mean they *have* ethics." Conversely, Roger Smith, former chairman of **General Motors,** said, "Ethical practice is, quite simply, good business." Smith has been around long enough to see the danger in unethical behavior. Sooner or later unethical conduct comes to light. Moreover, ethical behavior wins out in the end because it is the right thing to do.

Corporate and Professional Codes of Ethics

Most large companies have a code of ethics to encourage employees to behave ethically and responsibly. But codes of ethics are not enough by themselves. Senior management must set a high ethical tone. They must make it clear that the company will not tolerate unethical conduct by employees.

As professionals, accountants are expected to maintain higher standards than society in general. Their ability to do business depends entirely on their reputation. Most independent accountants are members of the American Institute of Certified Public Accountants and must abide by the *AICPA Code of Professional Conduct.* Accountants who are members of the Institute of Management Accountants are bound by the *Standards of Ethical Conduct for Management Accountants.*

 See Chapter 19, p. 776.

Ethical Issues in Accounting

Objective 7
Make ethical judgments in business

In many situations, the ethical choice is easy. For example, stealing cash is both unethical and illegal. In our chapter opening story, the cashier's actions landed her in jail. In other cases, the choices are more difficult. But in every instance, ethical judgments boil down to a personal decision: What should I do in a given situation? Let's consider three ethical issues in accounting. The first two are easy to resolve. The third is more difficult.

SITUATION 1 Sonja Kleberg is preparing the income tax return of a client who has had a particularly good year—higher income than expected. On January 2, the client pays for newspaper advertising and asks Sonja to backdate the expense to the preceding year. The tax deduction would help the client more in the year just ended than in the current year. Backdating would decrease taxable income of the earlier year and lower the client's tax payments. After all, there is a difference of only two days between January 2 and December 31. This client is important to Kleberg. What should she do?

She should refuse the request because the transaction took place in January of the new year.

What control device could prove that Kleberg behaved unethically if she backdated the transaction in the accounting records? An IRS audit and documents and records—the date of the cash payment could prove that the expense occurred in January rather than in December.

SITUATION 2 Jack Mellichamp's software company owes $40,000 to Bank of America. The loan agreement requires Mellichamp's company to maintain a current ratio (current assets divided by current liabilities) of 1.50 or higher. ➡ It is late in the year, and the bank will review Mellichamp's situation early next year. At present, the company's current ratio is 1.40. At this level, Mellichamp is in violation of his loan agreement. He can increase the current ratio to 1.53 by paying off some current liabilities right before year end. Is it ethical to do so?

◄ For a review of the current ratio, see Chapter 4.

Yes, because the action is a real business transaction.

However, paying off the liabilities is only a delaying tactic. It will hold off the creditors for now, but the business still must improve its underlying operations.

SITUATION 3 Emilia Gomez, an accountant for the Democratic Party, discovers that her supervisor, Myles Packer, made several errors last year. Campaign contributions received from foreign citizens, which are illegal, were recorded as normal. It is not clear whether the errors were deliberate or accidental. Gomez knows that Packer evaluates her job performance. What should Gomez do? She is uncertain.

 DAILY EXERCISE 7-21

To make her decision, Gomez could follow the framework outlined in the Decision Guidelines feature on the next page.

DECISION GUIDELINES

Framework for Making Ethical Judgments

Weighing tough ethical judgments requires a decision framework. Answering these six questions will guide you through tough decisions. Apply them to Emilia Gomez's situation.

QUESTION	DECISION GUIDELINE
1. What are the facts?	**1.** *Determine the facts.* They are given on page 289.
2. What is the ethical issue, if any?	**2.** *Identify the ethical issues.* The root work of ethical is *ethics*, which Webster's dictionary defines as the "the discipline dealing with what is good and bad and with moral duty and obligation." Gomez's ethical dilemma is to decide what she should do with the information she has uncovered.
3. What are the options?	**3.** *Specify the alternatives.* For Emilia Gomez, three reasonable alternatives include (a) reporting the errors to Packer, (b) reporting the errors to Packer's boss, and (c) doing nothing.
4. Who is involved in the situation?	**4.** *Identify the people involved.* Individuals who could be affected include Gomez, Packer, the Democratic Party, and Gomez's co-workers who observe her behavior.
5. What are the possible consequences?	**5.** *Assess the possible outcomes.*
	a. If Gomez reports the errors to Packer, he may penalize her, or he may reward her for careful work. Reporting the errors preserves her integrity and will probably lead to returning the money to the donors. But the Democratic Party could suffer embarrassment if this situation is made public.
	b. If Gomez reports to Packer's boss, her integrity is preserved. Her relationship with Packer will be strained. If Packer's boss has colluded with Packer in recording the campaign contribution, Gomez could be penalized. If the error is corrected and outsiders notified, the Democratic Party will be embarrassed. Others observing this situation would be affected by the outcome.
	c. If Gomez does nothing, she avoids a confrontation with Packer or his boss. They may or may not discover the error. If they discover it, they may or may not correct it. They may criticize Gomez for not bringing the error to their attention. Colleagues might learn of the situation.
6. What shall I do?	**6.** *Make the decision.* The choice is difficult. Gomez must balance the likely effects on the various people against the dictates of her own conscience. Gomez should report the errors. Ordinarily, Packer should be the first person contacted. If Packer fails to act in an honest way, then Gomez should inform Packer's boss. Senior management should always protect the messenger of accurate news, whether good or bad.

Ethics and External Controls

There is another dimension to most ethical issues: *external controls,* the discipline placed on business conduct by outsiders who interact with the company.

- In situation 1, for example, Sonja Kleberg could give in to the client's request to backdate the advertising expense. But this action would be both dishonest and illegal. These external controls arise from the business's interaction with the taxing authorities. An IRS audit of Kleberg's client could uncover her action.

- In situation 2, the external controls arise from Jack Mellichamp's relationship with the bank that lent money to his software company. As long as the loan agreement is in effect, the company must maintain a current ratio of 1.50 or higher. Paying off current liabilities to improve the current ratio would be a short-term solution to Mellichamp's problem. Over the long run, his business must generate more current assets through operations.

- The primary external control in situation 3 results from U.S. laws and their enforcement through the legal system. Campaign contributions are public information, and sooner or later the public will learn that the Democratic Party received illegal campaign contributions. It would be in the party's best interest to admit its mistake and correct the errors as quickly as possible—by returning the illegal contributions to the donors.

REVIEW INTERNAL CONTROL AND CASH

SUMMARY PROBLEM

Grudnitski Company established a $300 petty cash fund. James C. Brown is the fund custodian. At the end of the first week, the petty cash fund contains the following:

a. Cash: $171   **b.** Petty cash tickets:

www.prenhall.com/horngren
End-of-Chapter Assessment

No.	Amount	Issued to	Signed by	Account Debited
44	$14	B. Jarvis	B. Jarvis and JCB	Office Supplies
45	9	S. Bell	S. Bell	Miscellaneous Expense
47	43	R. Tate	R. Tate and JCB	—
48	33	L. Blair	L. Blair and JCB	Travel Expense

Required

1. Identify the four internal control weaknesses revealed in the given data.
2. Prepare the general journal entries to record:
   a. Establishment of the petty cash fund.
   b. Replenishment of the fund. Assume that petty cash ticket no. 47 was issued for the purchase of office supplies.
3. What is the balance in the Petty Cash account immediately before replenishment? Immediately after replenishment?

Solution

Requirement 1

The four internal control weaknesses are

a. Petty cash ticket no. 46 is missing. Coupled with weakness (b), this omission raises questions about the administration of the petty cash fund and about how the petty cash funds were used.

b. The $171 cash balance means that $129 has been disbursed ($300 − $171 = $129). However, the total amount of the petty cash tickets is only $99 ($14 + $9 + $43 + $33). The fund, then, is $30 short of cash ($129 − $99 = $30). Was petty cash ticket no. 46 issued for $30? The data in the problem offer no hint that helps answer this question. In practice, management would investigate the problem.

c. The petty cash custodian (JCB) did not sign petty cash ticket no. 45. This omission may have been an oversight on his part. However, it raises the question of whether he authorized the payment. Both the fund custodian and the recipient of cash should sign the ticket.

d. Petty cash ticket no. 47 does not indicate which account to debit. What did Tate do with the money, and what account should be debited? With no better choice available, debit Miscellaneous Expense.

Requirement 2

Petty cash journal entries:
a. Entry to establish the petty cash fund: **b.** Entry to replenish the fund:

Petty Cash............................	300		Office Supplies ($14 + $43).............	57
Cash in Bank............		300	Miscellaneous Expense	9
			Travel Expense	33
			Cash Short and Over........................	30
			Cash in Bank	129

Requirement 3

The balance in Petty Cash is *always* its specified balance, in this case $300.

LESSONS LEARNED

1. **Define internal control.** *Internal control* is the organizational plan and all the related measures an entity uses to safeguard assets, encourage adherence to company policies, promote operational efficiency, and ensure accurate and reliable accounting records.

2. **Identify the characteristics of an effective system of internal control.** An effective internal control system includes these features: competent, reliable, and ethical personnel; clear-cut assignment of responsibilities; proper authorization; separation of duties; internal and external audits; documents and records; and electronic devices and computer controls.

3. **Prepare a bank reconciliation and the related journal entries.** The *bank account* helps control and safeguard cash. Businesses use the *bank statement* and the *bank reconciliation* to account for banking transactions.

4. **Apply internal controls to cash receipts.** To control cash receipts over the counter, companies use point-of-sale terminals that customers can see, and require that cashiers provide customers with receipts. The machine records each sale and cash transaction.

   To control cash receipts by mail, a mailroom employee should be charged with opening the mail, comparing the enclosed amount with the remittance advice, and preparing a control tape. This is an essential separation of duties—the accounting department should not open the mail. At the end of the day, the controller compares the three records of the day's cash receipts: the control tape total from the mailroom, the bank deposit amount from the cashier, and the debit to Cash from the accounting department.

5. **Apply internal controls to cash payments.** To control payments by check, checks should be issued and signed only when a *payment packet* including the purchase request, purchase order, invoice (bill), and receiving report (with all appropriate signatures) has been prepared. To control petty cash payments, the custodian of the fund should require a completed petty cash ticket for all disbursements.

6. **Use a budget to manage cash.** A budget is a quantitative expression of a plan to help managers coordinate the entity's activities. First, a company must determine how much cash it will need. Then it budgets cash receipts and payments for the upcoming period. By comparing the ending budgeted cash balance to the amount needed, managers can determine whether they need to borrow or will have extra cash to invest.

7. **Make ethical judgments in business.** To make ethical decisions, people should follow six steps: (1) Determine the facts. (2) Identify the ethical issues. (3) Specify the alternatives. (4) Identify the people involved. (5) Assess the possible outcomes. (6) Make the decision.

ACCOUNTING VOCABULARY

audit (p. 270)
bank collection (p. 275)
bank reconciliation (p. 275)
bank statement (p. 274)
budget (p. 286)
check (p. 273)
computer virus (p. 272)

controller (p. 268)
deposit in transit (p. 275)
electronic funds transfer (EFT) (p. 274)
encryption (p. 272)
firewalls (p. 272)
imprest system (p. 286)

internal control (p. 267)
nonsufficient funds (NSF) check (p. 276)
outstanding check (p. 275)
petty cash (p. 285)
Trojan horse (p. 272)

QUESTIONS

1. Which feature of effective internal control is the most fundamental? Why?
2. Identify seven features of an effective system of internal control.
3. Separation of duties may be divided into four parts. What are they?
4. Are internal control systems designed to be foolproof and perfect? What is a fundamental constraint in planning and maintaining systems?
5. Briefly state how each of the following serves as an internal control measure over cash: bank account, signature card, deposit ticket, and bank statement.
6. Each of the following items affects the bank reconciliation. Next to each item, enter the appropriate letter from the following possible treatments: (a) bank side of reconciliation—add the item; (b) bank side of reconciliation—subtract the item; (c) book side of reconciliation—add the item; (d) book side of reconciliation—subtract the item.
   _____ Deposit in transit
   _____ Bank collection
   _____ Customer check returned because of un-authorized signature
   _____ Book error that increased balance of Cash account
   _____ Outstanding check
   _____ NSF check
   _____ Bank service charge
   _____ Cost of printed checks
   _____ Bank error that decreased bank balance
7. What purpose does a bank reconciliation serve?
8. A company has six bank accounts, two petty cash funds, and three certificates of deposit that can be withdrawn on demand. How many cash amounts would this company likely report on its balance sheet?
9. What role does a cash register play in an internal control system?
10. Describe internal control procedures for cash received by mail.
11. What documents make up the payment packet? Describe three procedures that use the payment packet to ensure that each payment is appropriate.
12. What balance does the Petty Cash account have at all times? Does this balance always equal the amount of cash in the fund? When are the two amounts equal? When are they unequal?
13. Describe how a budget helps a company manage its cash.
14. Why should accountants adhere to a higher standard of ethical conduct than many other members of society?

ASSESS YOUR PROGRESS

DAILY EXERCISES

DE7-1 Give the title of the chief finance officer and the title of the chief accounting officer in an organization. What are the responsibilities of each person? How does separating their duties provide good internal control?

Aspects of internal control (Obj. 1)

DE7-2 Internal controls are designed to safeguard assets, encourage employees to follow company policies, promote operational efficiency, and ensure accurate records. Which goal is most important? Which goal must the internal controls accomplish for the business to survive? Give your reason.

Definition of internal control (Obj. 1)

DE7-3 Explain in your own words why separation of duties is often described as the cornerstone of internal control for safeguarding assets. Describe what can happen if the same person has custody of an asset and also accounts for the asset.

Characteristics of an effective system of internal control (Obj. 2)

DE7-4 Examine the organization chart in Exhibit 7-2, page 268. What is the main duty of the internal auditors? To whom do the internal auditors report? Why don't the internal auditors report directly to the treasurer?

Characteristics of an effective system of internal control (Obj. 2)

DE7-5 How do external auditors differ from internal auditors? How does an external audit differ from an internal audit? How are the two types of audits similar?

Characteristics of an effective system of internal control (Obj. 2)

DE7-6 Review the characteristics of an effective system of internal control that begin on page 267. Then identify two things that **Merrill Lynch** in the chapter-opening story could have done to make it harder for Darlyne Lopez, the cashier, to steal from the company and hide the theft. Explain how each new measure taken by Merrill Lynch would have accomplished its goal.

Characteristics of an effective system of internal control (Obj. 2)

DE7-7 Make a simple diagram with three boxes and two arrows to show the relationships among (a) the bank statement, (b) the bank reconciliation, and (c) the accounting records. Use the arrows to show the flow of data.

Bank reconciliation (Obj. 3)

DE7-8 Answer the following questions about the bank reconciliation:

Aspects of a bank reconciliation (Obj. 3)

1. What is the difference between a bank statement and a bank reconciliation?
2. Is the bank reconciliation a journal, a ledger, an account, or a financial statement? If none of these, what is it?
3. Which side of the bank reconciliation generates data for new journal entries in the company's accounting records?

DE7-9 Compare Business Research, Inc.'s Cash account in Exhibit 7-5, page 275, with the bank statement that the company received in Exhibit 7-4, page 274.

Identifying reconciling items from bank documents (Obj. 3)

1. Trace each cash receipt from the Cash account (Exhibit 7-5) to a deposit on the bank statement (Exhibit 7-4). Which deposit is in transit on January 31? Give its date and dollar amount.
2. Trace each Business Research check from the cash payments record in Exhibit 7-5 to the bank statement in Exhibit 7-4. List all outstanding checks by check number and dollar amount.
3. On which side of the bank reconciliation do deposits in transit and outstanding checks appear—the bank side or the book side? Are they added or subtracted on the bank reconciliation?

DE7-10 The Cash account of Theraband Equipment reported a balance of $2,280 at May 31. Included were outstanding checks totaling $900 and a May 31 deposit of $200 that did not appear on the bank statement. The bank statement, which came from Park Cities Bank, listed a May 31 balance of $3,270. Included in the bank balance was a May 30 collection of $300 on account from Kelly Brooks, a Theraband customer who pays the bank directly. The bank statement also shows a $20 service charge and $10 of interest revenue that Theraband earned on its bank balance. *Prepare Theraband's bank reconciliation at May 31.*

Preparing a bank reconciliation (Obj. 3)

DE7-11 After preparing Theraband Equipment's bank reconciliation in Daily Exercise 7-10, make Theraband's general journal entries for transactions that arise from the bank reconciliation. Include an explanation with each entry.

Recording transactions from a bank reconciliation (Obj. 3)

DE7-12 Who in an organization should prepare the bank reconciliation? Should it be someone with cash-handling duties, someone with accounting duties, or someone with both duties? Does it matter? Give your reason.

Internal controls and the bank reconciliation (Obj. 2, 3)

DE7-13 Barry Cruise owns Cruise Vacation Planners. He fears that a trusted employee has been stealing from the company. This employee receives cash from customers and also prepares the monthly bank reconciliation. To check up on the employee, Cruise prepares his own bank reconciliation, as follows:

CRUISE VACATION PLANNERS
Bank Reconciliation
August 31, 20X7

Bank			Books		
Balance, August 31		$3,000	Balance, August 31		$2,500
Add: Deposit in transit		400	Add: Bank collection		800
			Interest revenue		10
Less: Outstanding checks		(1,100)	Less: Service charge		(30)
Adjusted bank balance		$2,300	Adjusted book balance		$3,280

Does it appear that the employee has stolen from the company? If so, how much? Explain your answer. Which side of the bank reconciliation shows the company's true cash balance?

DE7-14 Consider the men's sportswear department of a **Macy's** department store. What could a dishonest salesperson do if he had access to the record of transactions conducted through his cash register? How does Macy's keep employees from behaving in this manner?

DE7-15 Ted Carter sells furniture at Dupree Home & Garden in Huntsville, Alabama. Company procedure requires Carter to write a customer receipt for all sales. The receipt forms are prenumbered. Carter is having personal financial problems and takes $500 that he received from a customer. To hide his theft, Carter simply destroys the company copy of the sales receipt he gave the customer. What will alert Gerald Dupree, the owner, that something is wrong? What will this knowledge lead Dupree to do?

DE7-16 Review the internal controls over cash receipts by mail, discussed on page 282. Briefly describe how the final step in the process, performed by the controller, establishes that **(1)** the cash receipts went into the bank; and **(2)** the business's customers received credit for their payments.

How does a lock-box system protect cash from theft?

DE7-17 Answer the following questions about internal control over cash payments.

1. Payment of cash payments by check carries two basic controls over cash. What are they?
2. Suppose a purchasing agent receives the goods that he purchases and also approves payment for the goods. How could a dishonest purchasing agent cheat his company? How do companies avoid this internal control weakness?

DE7-18

1. Describe how an *imprest* petty cash system works. What is the main control feature of an imprest system?
2. Atlantic Press Publishers maintains an imprest $400 petty cash fund, which is under the control of Brenda Chavez. At November 30, the fund holds $220 cash and petty cash tickets for travel expense, $80; office supplies, $60; and delivery expense, $40.

    Journalize (a) establishment of the petty cash fund on November 1, and (b) replenishment of the fund on November 30.
3. Draw a T-account for Petty Cash, and post to the account. What is Petty Cash's account balance at all times?

DE7-19

1. Return to **Gap Inc.'s** hypothetical cash budget in Exhibit 7-13, page 287. Suppose Gap postpones the opening of new stores until 20X3. In that case, how much additional financing will Gap need for the year ended January 31, 20X2?
2. Now suppose Gap postpones both existing-store expansions and new-store openings until 20X3. How much new financing will Gap need, or how much cash would Gap have available for additional investment during the year ended January 31, 20X2?

DE7-20 Florida Progreso Growers is a major food cooperative. The company begins 2002 with cash of $6 million. Florida Progreso estimates cash receipts during 2002 will total $147 million. Planned disbursements for the year will require cash of $158 million. To meet daily cash needs, Florida Progreso must maintain a cash balance of at least $5 million.

Prepare Florida Progreso's cash budget for 2002.

DE7-21 Peter Larson, an accountant for BSI Consulting, discovers that his supervisor, Rose Kwan, made several errors last year. Overall, the errors overstated BSI's net income by 20%. It is not clear whether the errors were deliberate or accidental. What should Larson do?

Making an ethical judgment
(Obj. 7)

EXERCISES

E7-1 Consider this adaptation of a *Wall Street Journal* article:

Correcting an internal control weakness
(Obj. 2)

TOKYO—Toshima Corp., a Japanese trading company, said unauthorized trades by its former head of copper trading caused losses that may total $1.8 billion. Toshima learned of the damage when Yuji Takeda confessed to making unauthorized trades that led to losses over a 10-year period. Mr. Takeda concealed the losses by falsifying Toshima's books and records.

What internal control weakness at Toshima allowed this loss to grow so large? How could the company have avoided and/or limited the size of the loss?

E7-2 The following situations describe two cash receipts situations and two equipment purchase situations. In each pair, one situation's internal controls are significantly better than the other's. Evaluate the internal controls in each situation as strong or weak, and give the reason for your answers.

Identifying internal control strengths and weaknesses
(Obj. 1)

Cash Receipts:

a. Cash received by mail goes straight to the accountant, who debits Cash and credits Accounts Receivable to record collections from customers. The accountant then deposits the cash in the bank.
b. Cash received by mail goes to the mail room, where a mail clerk opens envelopes and totals the cash receipts for the day. The mail clerk forwards customer checks to the cashier for deposit in the bank and forwards the remittance slips to the accounting department for posting credits to customer accounts.

Equipment Purchases:

a. Centennial Homes policy calls for construction supervisors to request the equipment needed for construction jobs. The home office then purchases the equipment and has it shipped to the construction site.
b. Wayside Construction Company policy calls for project supervisors to purchase the equipment needed for construction jobs. The supervisors then submit the paid receipts to the home office for reimbursement. This policy enables supervisors to get the equipment they need quickly and keep construction jobs moving along.

E7-3 The following situations suggest a strength or a weakness in internal control. Identify each as *strength* or *weakness*, and give the reason for your answer.

Identifying internal control strengths and weaknesses.
(Obj. 2)

a. Cash received over the counter is controlled by the sales clerk, who rings up the sale and places the cash in the register. The sales clerk matches the total recorded on the control tape stored in the register to each day's cash sales.
b. The vice president who signs checks does not examine the payment packet because the accounting department has matched the invoice with other supporting documents.
c. Top managers delegate all internal control measures to the accounting department.
d. The accounting department orders merchandise and approves invoices for payment.
e. The operator of a computer has no other accounting or cash-handling duties.

E7-4 Identify the missing internal control characteristic in the following situations:

Identifying internal controls
(Obj. 2)

a. When business is brisk, Stop-n-Go and many other retail stores deposit cash in the bank several times during the day. The manager at one store wants to reduce the time employees spend delivering cash to the bank, so he starts a new policy. Cash will build up over Saturdays and Sundays, and the total two-day amount will be deposited on Sunday evening.
b. While reviewing the records of Discount Pharmacy, you find that the same employee orders merchandise and approves invoices for payment.
c. Business is slow at Fun City Amusement Park on Tuesday, Wednesday, and Thursday nights. To reduce expenses, the owner decides not to use a ticket taker on those nights. The ticket seller (cashier) is told to keep the tickets as a record of the number sold.
d. The manager of a discount store wants to speed the flow of customers through check-out. She decides to reduce the time cashiers spend making change, so she prices merchandise at round dollar amounts—such as $8.00 and $15.00—instead of the customary amounts—$7.95 and $14.95.
e. Grocery stores such as **Safeway** and **Meier's** purchase large quantities of merchandise from a few suppliers. At another grocery store, the manager decides to reduce paperwork. He eliminates the requirement that a receiving department employee prepare a receiving report, which lists the quantities of items actually received from the supplier.

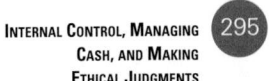

E7-5 The following questions pertain to internal control. Consider each situation separately.

a. Many managers think that safeguarding assets is the most important objective of internal control systems, while auditors emphasize internal control's role in ensuring reliable accounting data. Explain why managers are more concerned about safeguarding assets and auditors are more concerned about the quality of the accounting records.

b. Separation of duties is an important consideration if a system of internal control is to be effective. Why is this so?

c. Cash can be a relatively small item on the financial statements. Nevertheless, internal control over cash is very important. Why is this true?

d. Ling Ltd. requires that all documents supporting a check be canceled (stamped Paid) by the person who signs the check. Why do you think this practice is required? What might happen if it were not?

E7-6 The following items could appear on a bank reconciliation:

a. Book error: We debited Cash for $200. The correct debit was $2,000.
b. Outstanding checks.
c. Bank error: The bank charged our account for a check written by another customer.
d. Service charge.
e. Deposits in transit.
f. NSF check.
g. Bank collection of a note receivable on our behalf.

Required

Classify each item as (1) an addition to the book balance, (2) a subtraction from the book balance, (3) an addition to the bank balance, or (4) a subtraction from the bank balance.

E7-7 Bill Westphal's checkbook lists the following:

Date	Check No.	Item	Check	Deposit	Balance
9/1					$ 525
4	622	JD's Art Café	$ 19		506
9		Dividends received		$ 116	622
13	623	General Tire Co.	43		579
14	624	Exxon Oil Co.	58		521
18	625	Cash	50		471
26	626	Redeemer Presbyterian Church	75		396
28	627	Bent Tree Apartments	275		121
30		Paycheck		1,800	1,921

Westphal's September bank statement shows the following:

Balance			$525
Add: Deposits			116
Debit checks:	No.	Amount	
	622	$19	
	623	43	
	624	68*	
	625	50	(180)
Other charges:			
Printed checks		$ 8	
Service charge		12	(20)
Balance			$441

*This is the correct amount for check number 624.

Required

Prepare Westphal's bank reconciliation at September 30.

E7-8 Mario Bocelli operates four Quik Pak convenience stores. He has just received the monthly bank statement at October 31 from City National Bank, and the statement shows an ending balance of $2,750. Listed on the statement are an EFT rent collection of $400, a service charge of $12, two NSF checks totaling $74, and a $9 charge for printed checks. In reviewing his cash records, Bocelli identifies outstanding checks totaling $467 and an October 31 deposit in transit of $1,788. During October, he recorded a $290 check for the salary of a part-time employee by debiting Salary Expense and crediting Cash for $29. Bocelli's Cash account shows an October 31 cash balance of $4,027. *Prepare the bank reconciliation at October 31.*

Preparing a bank reconciliation (Obj. 3)

E7-9 Using the data from Exercise 7-8, make the journal entries Bocelli should record on October 31. Include an explanation for each entry.

Making journal entries from a bank reconciliation (Obj. 3)

E7-10 A grand jury indicted the manager of a Hickory Stick restaurant for stealing cash from the company. Over a 3-year period, the manager allegedly took almost $100,000 and attempted to cover the theft by manipulating the bank reconciliation.

Applying internal controls to the bank reconciliation (Obj. 2, 3)

What is the most likely way that a person would manipulate a bank reconciliation to cover a theft? Be specific. What internal control arrangement could have avoided this theft?

E7-11 At the check-out of **Best Buy** stores, cash registers display the amount of each sale, the cash received from the customer, and any change returned to the customer. The registers also produce a customer receipt but keep no internal record of transactions. At the end of the day, clerks count the cash in the register and give it to the cashier for deposit in the company bank account.

Evaluating internal control over cash receipts (Obj. 4)

Write a memo to convince the store manager that there is an internal control weakness over cash receipts. Identify the weakness that gives an employee the best opportunity to steal cash, and state how to prevent such a theft.

E7-12 Record the following selected transactions of Rosetree Florist in general journal format (explanations are not required):

Petty cash, cash short and over (Obj. 5)

April 1 Established a petty cash fund with a $300 balance.
  2 Journalized the day's cash sales. Cash register tapes show a $2,869 total, but the cash in the register is $2,873.
  10 The petty cash fund has $119 in cash and $161 in petty cash tickets that were issued to pay for Office Supplies ($111), Delivery Expense ($13), and Entertainment Expense ($37). Replenished the fund and recorded the expenses.

E7-13 Operation Recycle in Seattle created a $500 imprest petty cash fund. During the first month of use, the fund custodian authorized and signed petty cash tickets as follows:

Accounting for petty cash (Obj. 5)

Petty Cash Ticket No.	Item	Account Debited	Amount
1	Delivery of pledge cards to donors	Delivery Expense	$22.19
2	Mail package	Postage Expense	52.80
3	Newsletter	Supplies Expense	34.14
4	Key to closet	Miscellaneous Expense	2.85
5	Wastebasket	Miscellaneous Expense	13.78
6	Computer diskettes	Supplies Expense	85.37

Required

1. Make the general journal entries that **(a)** first create the petty cash fund and **(b)** show its replenishment. Include explanations.
2. Describe the items in the fund immediately before replenishment.
3. Describe the items in the fund immediately after replenishment.

E7-14 Suppose **Sprint Corporation,** the long-distance telephone company, is preparing its cash budget for 20X4. The company ended 20X3 with $135 million, and top management foresees the need for a cash balance of at least $137 million to pay all bills as they come due in 20X4.

Preparing a cash budget (Obj. 6)

Collections from customers are expected to total $11,813 million during 20X4, and payments for the cost of services and products should reach $6,166 million. Operating expense payments are budgeted at $2,744 million.

During 20X4, Sprint expects to invest $1,826 million in new equipment, $275 million in the company's cellular division, and to sell older assets for $116 million. Debt payments scheduled for 20X4 will total $597 million. The company forecasts net income of $890 million for 20X4 and plans to pay $338 million to its owners.

Required

Prepare Sprint's cash budget for 20X4. Will the budgeted level of cash receipts leave Sprint with the desired ending cash balance of $137 million, or will the company need additional financing?

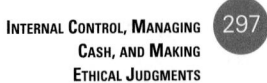

<table>
<tr><td>*Evaluating the ethics of conduct by government legislators*
(Obj. 7)</td></tr>
</table>

Evaluating the ethics of conduct
by government legislators
(Obj. 7)

E7-15 Approximately 300 current and former members of the U.S. House of Representatives—on a regular basis—wrote a quarter million dollars of checks on the House bank without having the cash in their accounts. In effect, the delinquent check writers were borrowing money from each other on an interest-free, no-service-charge basis. The House closed its bank after the events became public.

Required

Suppose you are a new congressional representative from your state. Apply the ethical judgment framework outlined in the Decision Guidelines feature on page 290 to decide whether you would write NSF checks on a regular basis through the House bank.

Challenge Exercise.

Preparing and using a cash
budget
(Obj. 6)

E7-16 ◄ *Link Back to Chapter 4 (Current Ratio and Debt Ratio).* Among its many products, Continental Paper Company makes paper for shopping bags, canned-food labels, and magazines. Ruth Majer, the Chief Budget Officer, is responsible for Continental's cash budget for 20X5. The budget helps Majer determine the amount of long-term borrowing needed to end the year with a cash balance of $300 million. Majer has assembled budget data for 20X5. Not all of the following items are used in preparing the cash budget. Receipts are positive amounts; payments are in parentheses.

	(In millions)
Acquisition of other companies	$ (1,168)
Actual cash balance, December 31, 20X4	340
Borrowing	?
Budgeted total assets before borrowing	23,977
Budgeted total current assets before borrowing	5,873
Budgeted total current liabilities before borrowing	4,863
Budgeted total liabilities before borrowing	16,180
Budgeted total stockholder's equity before borrowing	7,797
Collections from customers	19,467
Payments to owners	(237)
Investments by owners	516
Net income	1,153
Other cash receipts	111
Payment of long-term and short-term debt	(950)
Payment of operating expenses	(2,349)
Purchases of inventory	(14,345)
Purchase of property and equipment	(1,518)

Required

1. Prepare the cash budget to determine the amount of borrowing Continental Paper needs during 20X5.
2. Compute Continental Paper's expected current ratio and debt ratio at December 31, 20X5, both before and after borrowing on long-term debt. Assume you are the chief loan officer at a bank. Based on these figures, and on the budgeted levels of assets and liabilities, would you lend the requested amount to Continental Paper? Give the reason for your decision.

(Group A) PROBLEMS

Identifying the characteristics
of an effective internal control
system (Obj. 1, 2)

P7-1A An employee of Suntech Oil Company recently stole thousands of dollars of the company's cash. The company has installed a new system of internal controls. As a consultant for Suntech Oil Company, write a memo to the president explaining how a separation of duties helps to safeguard assets.

Correcting internal control
weaknesses
(Obj. 2, 4, 5)

P7-2A The following situations have an internal control weakness.

a. Roberson Computer Programs is a software company that specializes in programs with accounting applications. The company's most popular program prepares the journal, accounts receivable subsidiary ledger, and general ledger. In the company's early days, the owner and eight employees wrote the computer programs, sold the products to stores such as ComputerWorld, and performed general management and accounting. As the company has grown, the number of employees has increased dramatically. Recently, the development of a new software program stopped while the programmers redesigned Roberson's accounting system. Roberson's accountants could have performed this task.

b. Emma Blue, a widow with no known sources of outside income, has been a trusted employee of Stone Products Company for 15 years. She performs all cash-handling and accounting duties, including opening the mail, preparing the bank deposit, accounting for all aspects of cash and accounts receivable, and preparing the bank reconciliation. She has just purchased a new Mercedes and a new home in an expensive suburb. Juan Perez, owner of the company, wonders how she can afford these luxuries.

c. Harriet Laman employs three professional interior designers in her design studio. She is located in an area with a lot of new construction, and her business is booming. Ordinarily, Laman does all the purchasing of draperies, fabrics, and labor needed to complete jobs. During the summer she takes a long vacation, and in her absence she allows each designer to purchase materials and labor. On her return, Laman observes that expenses are much higher and net income much lower than in the past.

d. Discount stores such as **Target** and **Sam's** receive a large portion of their sales revenue in cash, with the remainder in credit-card sales. To reduce expenses, one store manager ceases purchasing fidelity bonds on the cashiers.

e. The office supply company from which Champs Sporting Goods purchases cash receipt forms recently notified Champs that the last shipped receipts were not prenumbered. Alex Champ, the owner, replied that he never uses the receipt numbers.

Required

1. Identify the missing internal control characteristics in each situation.
2. Identify the business's possible problem.
3. Propose a solution to the internal control problem.

P7-3A The cash receipts and the payments of Veralux Interiors for March 20X5 follow:

Using the bank reconciliation as a control device
(Obj. 3)

Cash Receipts (Posting reference is CR)		Cash Payments (Posting reference is CP)	
Date	Cash Debit	Check No.	Cash Credit
Mar. 4	$2,716	1413	$1,465
9	544	1414	1,004
11	1,655	1415	450
14	896	1416	8
17	367	1417	775
25	890	1418	88
31	2,038	1419	4,126
Total	$9,106	1420	970
		1421	200
		1422	2,267
		Total	$11,353

The Cash account of Veralux Interiors shows the following on March 31, 20X5:

		Cash			
Date	Item	Jrnl. Ref.	Debit	Credit	Balance
Mar. 1	Balance				12,188
31		CR. 10	9,106		21,294
31		CP. 16		11,353	9,941

On March 31, 20X5, Veralux Interiors received the bank statement at the top of the next page.

Additional data for the bank reconciliation:

a. The EFT deposit was a receipt of rent. The EFT debit was payment of insurance.
b. The NSF check was received late in February from Mark Anthony.
c. The $1,000 bank collection of a note receivable on March 31 included $122 interest revenue.
d. The correct amount of check number 1419, a payment on account, is $4,216. (The Veralux Interiors accountant mistakenly recorded the check for $4,126.)

Bank Statement for March 20X5		

Beginning balance		$12,188
Deposits and other Credits:		
Mar. 1..	$ 625 EFT	
5..	2,716	
10..	544	
11..	1,655	
15..	896	
18..	367	
25..	890	
31..	1,000 BC	8,693
Checks and other Debits:		
Mar. 8..	$ 441 NSF	
9..	1,465	
13..	1,004	
14..	450	
15..	8	
19..	340 EFT	
22..	775	
29..	88	
31..	4,216	
31..	25 SC	(8,812)
Ending balance		$12,069

Explanations: BC—bank collection, EFT—electronic funds transfer,
NSF—nonsufficient funds check, SC—service charge.

Required

1. Prepare the bank reconciliation of Veralux Interiors at March 31, 20X5.
2. Describe how a bank account and the bank reconciliation help Veralux managers control the business's cash.

Preparing a bank reconciliation and the related journal entries (Obj. 3)

P7-4A The May 31 bank statement of Payne Stationers has just arrived from First State Bank. To prepare the Payne bank reconciliation, you gather the following data.

a. The May 31 bank balance is $21,110.82.
b. The bank statement includes two charges for returned checks from customers. One is an NSF check in the amount of $67.50 received from Sarah Batten, a student, recorded on the books by a debit to Cash, and deposited on May 19. The other is a $195.03 check received from Lena Masters and deposited on May 21. It was returned by Masters' bank with the imprint "Unauthorized Signature."
c. The following Payne checks are outstanding at May 31:

Check No.	Amount
616	$403.00
802	74.25
806	36.60
809	161.38
810	229.05
811	48.91

d. Payne Stationers collects from a few customers by EFT. The May bank statement lists a $200 deposit for a collection on account from customer Jack Oates.
e. The bank statement includes two special deposits: $899.14, which is the amount of dividend revenue the bank collected from General Electric Company on behalf of Payne, and $16.86, the interest revenue Payne earned on its bank balance during May.
f. The bank statement lists a $6.25 subtraction for the bank service charge.
g. On May 31, the Payne treasurer deposited $381.14, but this deposit does not appear on the bank statement.
h. The bank statement includes a $410.00 deduction for a check drawn by Marimont Freight Company. Payne promptly notified the bank of its error.
i. Payne's Cash account shows a balance of $20,101.55 on May 31.

Required

1. Prepare the bank reconciliation for Payne Stationers at May 31.
2. Record the entries necessary to bring the book balance of Cash into agreement with the adjusted book balance on the reconciliation. Include an explanation for each entry.

P7-5A East Coast Heating makes all sales on credit. Cash receipts arrive by mail. Kenneth Sartain opens envelopes and separates the checks from the accompanying remittance advices. Sartain forwards the checks to another employee, who makes the daily bank deposit but has no access to the accounting records. Sartain sends the remittance advices, which show cash received, to the accounting department for entry in the accounts. Sartain's only other duty is to grant sales allowances to customers. (Recall that a *sales allowance* decreases the amount receivable.) When Sartain receives a customer check for less than the full amount of the invoice, he records the sales allowance and forwards the document to the accounting department.

Identifying internal control weakness in cash receipts
(Obj. 4)

Required

You are a new employee of East Coast Heating. Write a memo to the company president identifying the internal control weakness in this situation. State how to correct the weakness.

P7-6A On April 1, Sealy Electronics creates a petty cash fund with an imprest balance of $400. During April, Elise Nelson, the fund custodian, signs the petty cash tickets:

Accounting for petty cash transactions
(Obj. 5)

Petty Cash Ticket Number	Item	Amount
101	Office supplies	$86.89
102	Cab fare for executive	25.00
103	Delivery of package across town	37.75
104	Dinner money for sales manager entertaining a customer	80.00
105	Inventory	85.70
106	Decorations for office party	19.22
107	Six boxes of floppy disks	44.37

On April 30, prior to replenishment, the fund contains these tickets plus $17.36. The accounts affected by petty cash payments are Office Supplies Expense, Travel Expense, Delivery Expense, Entertainment Expense, and Freight In.

Required

1. Explain the characteristics and the internal control features of an imprest fund.
2. Make the general journal entries to (a) create the fund and (b) replenish it. Include explanations. Also, briefly describe what the custodian does on April 1 and April 30.
3. Make the May 1 entry to increase the fund balance to $500. Include an explanation, and briefly describe what the custodian does.

P7-7A Suppose you are preparing your personal cash budget for the year 20X2. During 20X2, assume you expect to earn $3,600 from your summer job and $1,500 for work in the college cafeteria. Also, your family always gives you gifts totaling around $800 during the year. A scholarship from your home church adds $1,000 each year while you are in college.

Preparing a personal cash budget
(Obj. 6)

Your family pays your college costs except for room and board. Planned expenditures for 20X2 include apartment rent of $150 per month for 12 months and annual food costs of $4,800. Gas and other auto expenses usually run about $50 per month. You need to have a little fun, so entertainment will eat up $100 per month.

You need to keep a little cash in reserve for auto repairs and other emergencies, so you maintain a cash reserve of $300 at all times. To start 20X2, you have this cash reserve plus $200.

Will you need a loan during 20X2? To answer this question, prepare your personal cash budget for the year based on the data given.

P7-8A Lesa Krause, Chief Financial Officer of Datek Enterprises, is responsible for the company's budgeting process. Suppose Krause's staff is preparing the Datek cash budget for 20X9. A key input to the budgeting process is last year's statement of cash flows, which provides the data at the top of the next page for 20X8 (in millions). Cash receipts appear as positive amounts; cash payments are negative amounts, denoted within parentheses.

Preparing a cash budget
(Obj. 6)

DATEK ENTERPRISES			
Cash-Flow Data for 20X8			

Cash and Cash Equivalents			
Beginning of year 20X8	$ 764	Purchases of plant assets	$ (614)
End of year 20X8	792	Borrowings	160
Collections from customers	8,089	Long-term debt repayments	(1)
Interest revenue collected	24	Cash received for	
Purchases of inventory	(5,597)	investments by owners	30
Operating expenses paid	(1,859)	Payments to owners	(183)

Required

1. Prepare the Datek cash budget for 20X9. Date the budget "20X9" and denote the beginning and ending cash balances as "beginning" and "ending." Round to the nearest million dollars. Assume the company expects 20X9 to be similar to 20X8, but with the following changes:
   a. In 20X9, the company expects a 7% increase in collections from customers and a 5% increase in purchases of inventory.
   b. Krause plans for Datek to end the year with a cash balance of $400 million.
2. Based on the cash budget you prepared, how much additional cash does it appear that Datek will have available for other investments during 20X9?

Making an ethical judgment (Obj. 7)

P7-9A Tri State Bank in Cairo, Illinois, has a loan receivable from Cortez Manufacturing Company. Cortez is six months late in making payments to the bank, and Milton Reed, a Tri State vice president, is helping Cortez restructure its debt. Reed learns that Cortez is depending on landing a manufacturing contract from Peters & Sons, another Tri State client. Reed also serves as Peters' loan officer at the bank. In this capacity, he is aware that Peters is considering declaring bankruptcy. No one outside Peters & Sons knows this. Reed has been a great help to Cortez Manufacturing, and Cortez's owner is counting on him to carry the company through this difficult restructuring. To help the bank collect on this large loan, Reed has a strong motivation to help Cortez survive.

Apply the ethical judgment framework from the chapter to help Reed plan his next action.

(Group B) PROBLEMS

Identifying the characteristics of an effective internal control system (Obj. 1, 2)

P7-1B Caldwell-Bailey Development Company prospered during the lengthy economic expansion of the 1990s. Business was so good that the company used very few internal controls. A recent decline in the local real estate market caused Caldwell-Bailey to experience a shortage of cash. Dave Matthews, the company owner, is looking for ways to save money.

As a consultant for the company, write a memo to convince Matthews of the company's need for a system of internal control. Be specific in explaining how an internal control system could save the company money. Include the definition of internal control, and briefly discuss each characteristic of an effective internal control system, beginning with competent, reliable, and ethical personnel.

Correcting internal control weaknesses (Obj. 2, 4, 5)

P7-2B Each of the following situations has an internal control weakness.

a. Aimee Atkins has been an employee of Mary V's Bridal Salon for many years. Because the business is relatively small, Atkins performs all accounting duties, including opening the mail, preparing the bank deposit, and preparing the bank reconciliation.
b. Most large companies have internal audit staffs that continuously evaluate the business's internal control. Part of the auditor's job is to evaluate how efficiently the company is running. For example, does the company purchase inventory from the least expensive wholesaler? After a particularly bad year, Design Company eliminates its internal audit department to reduce expenses.
c. CPA firms, law firms, and other professional organizations use paraprofessional employees to perform routine tasks. For example, an accounting paraprofessional might examine documents to assist a CPA in conducting an audit. In the CPA firm of Lee & Dunham, Joseph Lee, the senior partner, turns over a significant portion of his own audit work to his paraprofessional staff.
d. In evaluating the internal control over cash payments, an auditor learns that the purchasing agent is responsible for purchasing diamonds for use in the company's manufacturing process, approving the invoices for payment, and signing the checks.
e. Blake Lemmon owns an engineering firm. His staff consists of 12 engineers, and he manages the office. Often, his work requires him to travel. He notes that when he returns from business trips, the engineering jobs in the office have not pro-

gressed much. When he is away, his senior employees take over office management and neglect their engineering duties. One employee could manage the office.

Required

1. Identify the missing internal control characteristic in each situation.
2. Identify the business's possible problem.
3. Propose a solution to the internal control problem.

P7-3B The cash receipts and the cash payments of Good Eats Café for April 20X4 are as follows:

Using the bank reconciliation as a control device
(Obj. 3)

Cash Receipts (Posting reference is CR)		Cash Payments (Posting reference is CP)	
Date	**Cash Debit**	**Check No.**	**Cash Credit**
Apr. 2	$ 4,174	3113	$ 891
8	407	3114	147
10	559	3115	1,930
16	2,187	3116	664
22	1,854	3117	1,472
29	1,060	3118	1,000
30	337	3119	632
Total	$10,578	3120	1,675
		3121	100
		3122	2,413
		Total	$10,924

The Cash account of Good Eats Café shows the following at April 30, 20X4:

Cash					
Date	**Item**	**Jrnl. Ref.**	**Debit**	**Credit**	**Balance**
Apr. 1	Balance				5,911
30		CR. 6	10,578		16,489
30		CP. 11		10,924	5,565

On April 30, 20X4, Good Eats received the bank statement shown on the top of page 304. Additional data for the bank reconciliation:

a. The EFT deposit was a receipt of rent. The EFT debit was an insurance payment.
b. The unauthorized-signature check was received from S. M. Holt.
c. The $1,368 bank collection of a note receivable included $185 interest revenue.
d. The correct amount of check number 3115, a payment on account, is $1,390. (Good Eats' accountant mistakenly recorded the check for $1,930.)

Required

1. Prepare the Good Eats Café bank reconciliation at April 30, 20X4.
2. Describe how a bank account and the bank reconciliation help Good Eats managers control the business's cash. See the bank statement at the top of page 304.

P7-4B The August 31 bank statement of Beeson Nursery has just arrived from United Bank. To prepare the Beeson bank reconciliation, you gather the following data:

Preparing a bank reconciliation and the related journal entries
(Obj. 3)

a. Beeson's Cash account shows a balance of $3,998.14 on August 31.
b. The bank statement includes two charges for returned checks from customers. One is a $395.00 check received from Lakeland Express and deposited on August 20, returned by Lakeland's bank with the imprint "Unauthorized Signature." The other is an NSF check for $146.67 received from Veracruz, Inc. This check was deposited on August 17.
c. Beeson pays rent expense ($750) and insurance expense ($290) each month by EFT.

(continued near the middle of page 304)

Bank Statement for April 20X4		
Beginning balance..........................		$ 5,911
Deposits and other Credits:		
Apr. 1...	$ 326 EFT	
4...	4,174	
9...	407	
12...	559	
17...	2,187	
22...	1,368 BC	
23...	1,854	10,875
Checks and other Debits:		
Apr. 7...	$ 891	
13...	1,390	
14...	903 US	
15...	147	
18...	664	
21...	219 EFT	
26...	1,472	
30...	1,000	
30...	20 SC	(6,706)
Ending balance..........................		$10,080

Explanations: EFT—electronic funds transfer, BC—bank collection, US—unauthorized signature, SC—service charge.

d. The Beeson checks below are outstanding at August 31.

Check No.	Amount
237	$ 46.10
288	141.00
291	578.05
293	11.87
294	609.51
295	8.88
296	101.63

e. The bank statement includes a deposit of $1,191.17, collected by the bank on behalf of Beeson Nursery. Of the total, $1,011.81 is collection of a note receivable, and the remainder is interest revenue.

f. The bank statement shows that Beeson earned $38.19 of interest on its bank balance during August. This amount was added to Beeson's account by the bank.

g. The bank statement lists a $10.50 subtraction for the bank service charge.

h. On August 31, the Beeson treasurer deposited $316.15, but this deposit does not appear on the bank statement.

i. The bank statement includes a $300.00 deposit that Beeson did not make. The bank erroneously credited the Beeson account for another bank customer's deposit.

j. The August 31 bank balance is $5,116.22.

Required

1. Prepare the bank reconciliation for Beeson Nursery at August 31.
2. Record the journal entries necessary to bring the book balance of Cash into agreement with the adjusted book balance on the reconciliation. Include an explanation for each entry.

Identifying internal control weakness in cash receipts
(Obj. 4)

P7-5B SpreadMax, Inc., makes all sales of its spreadsheet software on credit. Cash receipts arrive by mail. Nick Vaughn opens envelopes and separates the checks from the accompanying remittance advices. Vaughn forwards the checks to another employee, who makes the daily bank deposit but has no access to the accounting records. Vaughn sends the remittance advices, which show the cash received, to the accounting department for entry in the accounts. Vaughn's only other duty is to grant sales allowances to customers. (Recall that a *sales allowance* decreases the amount receivable.) When he receives a customer check for less than the full amount of the invoice, he records the sales allowance and forwards the document to the accounting department.

Required

You are a new employee of SpreadMax, Inc. Write a memo to the company president identifying the internal control weakness in this situation. State how to correct the weakness.

P7-6B Suppose that on June 1, Alpha Audio-Video opens a district office in Omaha and creates a petty cash fund with an imprest balance of $350. During June, Carol McColgin, fund custodian, signs the following petty cash tickets:

Accounting for petty cash transactions
(Obj. 5)

Petty Cash Ticket Number	Item	Amount
1	Postage for package received	$ 18.40
2	Decorations and refreshments for office party	13.19
3	Two boxes of floppy disks	20.82
4	Printer cartridges	27.13
5	Dinner money for sales manager entertaining a customer	50.00
6	Plane ticket for executive business trip to Memphis	169.00
7	Delivery of package across town	6.30

On June 30, prior to replenishment, the fund contains these tickets plus cash of $42.37. The accounts affected by petty cash payments are Office Supplies Expense, Travel Expense, Delivery Expense, Entertainment Expense, and Postage Expense.

Required

1. Explain the characteristics and the internal control features of an imprest fund.
2. Make the general journal entries to (a) create the fund and (b) replenish it. Include explanations. Also, briefly describe what the custodian does on these dates.
3. Make the entry on July 1 to increase the fund balance to $500. Include an explanation, and briefly describe what the custodian does.

P7-7B Suppose you are preparing your personal cash budget for 20X2. During 20X2, assume that you can expect to earn $3,000 from your summer job and $2,000 for work in the college cafeteria. Also, your family always gives you gifts totaling around $300 during the year. A scholarship from your home church adds $500 each year while you are in college.

Preparing a personal cash budget
(Obj. 6)

Assume your family pays your college costs except for room and board. Planned expenditures for 20X2 include apartment rent of $175 per month for 12 months and annual food costs of $5,000. Gas and other auto expenses usually run about $50 per month. You need to have a little fun, so entertainment will eat up $125 per month.

You need some cash in reserve for auto repairs and other emergencies, so you maintain a cash reserve of $500 at all times. To start 20X2, you have this cash reserve plus $100.

Will you need a loan during 20X2? To answer this question, prepare your personal cash budget for the year based on the data given.

P7-8B Len Filer, Chief Financial Officer of Toys.com, is responsible for the company's budgeting process. Filer's staff is preparing the company's cash budget for 20X1. A key input to the budgeting process is last year's statement of cash flows, which provides the data in the table (in millions) for 20X0. Cash receipts appear as positive amounts; cash payments are negative amounts, denoted within parentheses.

Preparing a cash budget
(Obj. 6)

TOYS.COM			
Cash-Flow Data for 20X0			
Cash and Cash Equivalents			
Beginning of year 20X0.............	$ 370	Purchases of plant assets.............	$(535)
End of year 20X0.......................	203	Borrowings	292
Collections from customers	9,414	Long-term debt repayments	(9)
Interest revenue collected..........	17	Cash received for	
Purchases of inventory	(6,750)	investments by owners	16
Operating expenses paid............	(2,431)	Payments to owners	(200)

Required

1. Prepare the Toys.com cash budget for 20X1. Date the budget "20X1" and denote the beginning and ending cash balances as "beginning" and "ending." Round to the nearest million dollars. Assume the company expects 20X1 to be the same as 20X0, but with the following changes:
    a. In 20X1, the company expects a 9% increase in collections from customers and an 8% increase in purchases of inventory.
    b. Filer plans for the company to end the year with a cash balance of $400 million.

2. Based on the cash budget you prepared, how much additional financing will Toys.com need beyond the borrowings already scheduled for 20X1?

Making an ethical judgment
(Obj. 7)

P7-9B Beth Youngdale is vice president of Stateline Loan Associates in Yellowstone, Wyoming. Active in community affairs, Youngdale serves on the board of directors of Baker Publishing Company. Baker is expanding and relocating its plant. At a recent meeting, board members decided to buy 15 acres of land on the edge of town. The owner of the property, Jack Fletcher, is a customer of Stateline Loan. Fletcher is completing a divorce, and Youngdale knows that Fletcher is eager to sell his property. In view of Fletcher's difficult situation, Youngdale believes he would accept almost any offer for the land. Realtors have appraised the property at $5 million.

Apply the ethical judgment framework from the Decision Guidelines feature (page 290) to help Youngdale decide what her role should be in Baker's attempt to buy the land from Fletcher.

APPLY YOUR KNOWLEDGE

DECISION CASES

Using the bank reconciliation to detect a theft
(Obj. 3)

Case 1. Flexall Plastics Company has poor internal control over its cash transactions. Genevieve Gilbreath, the owner, suspects Sam Knicks, the cashier, of stealing. Here are some details of the business's cash position at September 30.

a. The Cash account shows a balance of $17,502. This amount includes a September 30 deposit of $3,794 that does not appear on the September 30 bank statement.

b. The September 30 bank statement shows a balance of $14,124. The bank statement lists a $200 credit for a bank collection, an $8 debit for the service charge, and a $36 debit for an NSF check. The Flexall accountant has not recorded any of these items on the books.

c. At September 30, the following checks are outstanding:

Check No.	Amount
154	$116
256	150
278	353
291	190
292	206
293	145

d. The cashier handles all incoming cash and makes bank deposits. He also reconciles the monthly bank statement. Here is his September 30 reconciliation:

Balance per books, September 30..............			$17,502
Add: Outstanding checks.........................			260
Bank collection			200
			17,962
Less: Deposits in transit		$3,794	
Service charge.................................		8	
NSF check		36	3,838
Balance per bank, September 30..............			$14,124

Gilbreath asks you to determine whether the cashier has stolen cash from the business and, if so, how much. She also asks how the cashier concealed the theft. Perform your own bank reconciliation using the format illustrated in the chapter. There are no bank or book errors. Gilbreath also wants your input on changes that will improve Flexall's internal controls.

Correcting an internal control weakness
(Obj. 1, 5)

Case 2. This case is based on an actual situation. A-1 Construction Company, headquartered in Terre Haute, Indiana, built a Rest Easy Motel 35 miles east of Terre Haute. The construction foreman, whose name was Monty, hired the 40 workers needed to complete the project. Monty had the construction workers fill out the necessary tax forms, and sent the employment documents to the home office, which opened a payroll file for each employee.

Work on the motel began on April 1 and ended September 1. Each week, Monty filled out a time card of the hours worked by each employee during the week. Monty faxed the time sheets to the home office, which prepared the payroll checks on Friday morning. Monty drove to the home office after lunch on Friday, picked up the payroll checks, and returned to the construction site. At 5 P.M. on Friday, Monty distributed the payroll checks to the workers.

a. Describe in detail the main internal control weakness in this situation. Specify what negative result(s) could occur because of the internal control weakness.

b. Describe what you would do to correct the internal control weakness.

ETHICAL ISSUE

Internal control over cash payments; ethical considerations (Obj. 5, 7)

Jill Hudson owns apartment buildings in Oklahoma. Each property has a manager who collects rent, arranges for repairs, and runs advertisements in the local newspaper. The property managers transfer cash to Hudson monthly and prepare their own bank reconciliations. The manager in Tulsa has been stealing large sums of money. To cover the theft, he understates the amount of the outstanding checks on the monthly bank reconciliation. As a result, each monthly bank reconciliation appears to balance. However, the balance sheet reports more cash than Hudson actually has in the bank. In negotiating the sale of the Tulsa property, Hudson is showing the balance sheet to prospective investors.

Required

1. Identify two parties other than Hudson who can be harmed by this theft. In what ways can they be harmed?
2. Discuss the role accounting plays in this situation.

FINANCIAL STATEMENT CASE

Internal controls and cash (Obj. 1, 3)

Study the responsibility statement (labeled Report of Management) and the audit opinion (labeled Report of Independent Auditors) of **Target Corporation,** financial statements given at the end of Appendix A. Answer the following questions about the company's internal controls and cash position.

Required

1. What is the name of Target's outside auditing firm (independent auditors)? What office of this firm signed the audit report? How long after the Target year end did the auditors issue their opinion?
2. Who bears primary responsibility for the financial statements? How can you tell?
3. Does it appear that the Target internal controls are adequate? How can you tell?
4. What standard of auditing did the outside auditors use in examining the Target financial statements? By what accounting standards were the statements evaluated?
5. By how much did Target's cash balance (including cash equivalent) change during the year ended January 29, 2000? What were the beginning and ending cash balances?

TEAM PROJECT

You are promoting a rock concert in your area. Each member of your team will invest $10,000 of their hard-earned money in this venture. It is April 1, and the concert is on June 30. Your promotional activities begin immediately, and ticket sales start on May 1. You expect to sell all the business's assets, pay all the liabilities, and distribute all remaining cash to the group members by July 31.

Required

Write an internal control manual that will help safeguard the assets of the business. The starting point of the manual is to assign responsibilities among the group members. Authorize individuals, including group members and any outsiders that you need to hire, to perform specific jobs. Separate duties among the group and any employees.

INTERNET EXERCISE

Telemate.Net Software, Inc.

Corporate managers face internal control and ethical challenges with Internet access at the fingertips of many employees. Is it okay for an employee to log on to make a quick personal stock trade? What about sending personal e-mail, checking sports team scores, playing games, visiting chat rooms, or shopping online? These dilemmas face corporate America every day.

1. Discuss several internal control issues that may concern management regarding personal use of the Internet by employees during working hours.
2. Do any special issues arise for company e-mail?
3. Many web sites can trace and identify the company making visits. Do any special issues arise as to which Web sites are accessed by company employees?
4. Expanded Internet use has created a new industry to monitor Web site visits and the duration of employee time online. Go to **http://www.telemate.net/** and read the information displayed. What services does this company provide?
5. Go to **http://www.Forbes.com.** Under "Stocks" type *TMNT*, the stock symbol for **Telemate.Net Software, Inc.,** and then click on *Go.* In the left-hand column, click on *Financials.* Use the latest financial information to answer the following questions:
   a. Is the demand for the services and products of Telemate.Net Software, Inc., increasing? How can you tell?
   b. For the most recent year was Telemate.Net Software, Inc., profitable?
   c. How much did Cash/Equivalents increase (decrease) during the current year? Compute Telemate's current ratio at the most recent financial statement date.

APPENDIX TO CHAPTER 7

THE VOUCHER SYSTEM

The voucher system for recording cash payments improves internal control over cash payments by formalizing the process of approving and recording invoices for payment. The voucher system uses (1) vouchers, (2) a voucher register (similar to a purchases journal), (3) an unpaid voucher file, (4) a check register (similar to a cash payments journal), and (5) a paid voucher file. The improvement in internal control comes from recording all payments through the voucher register. In a voucher system, all expenditures must be approved before payment can be made. This approval takes the form of a voucher. The larger the business, the more likely it is to need strict control over payments. The voucher system helps supply this control.

VOUCHER. Instrument authorizing a cash payment.

A **voucher** is a document authorizing a cash payment. The accounting department prepares vouchers. Exhibit 7A-1 illustrates the voucher of Bliss Wholesale Company. In addition to places for writing in the *payee, due date, terms, description,* and *invoice amount,* the voucher includes a section for designated officers to sign their approval for payment. The back of the voucher has places for recording the *account debited, date paid,* and *check number.* You should locate these eight items in Exhibit 7A-1.

EXHIBIT 7A-1   **Voucher**

Front of Voucher / Back of Voucher

Voucher No. 326
BLISS WHOLESALE COMPANY
Payee Address: Van Heusen, Inc. / 4619 Shotwell Avenue / Brooklyn, NY 10564
Due Date: March 7
Terms: 2/10, n/30

Date	Invoice No.	Description	Amount
Mar. 1	6380	144 men's shirts stock no. X14	$1,764

Approved *Jane Trent* Controller   Approved *Bob Kraft* Treasurer

Voucher No. 326
Payee Van Heusen, Inc.
Invoice Amount $1,800
Discount 36
Net Amount $1,764
Due Date Mar. 7
Date Paid Mar. 6
Check No. 694

Account Distribution		
Account Debited	**Acct. No.**	**Amount**
Inventory	105	1,800
Store Supplies	145	
Salary Expense	538	
Advertising Expense	542	
Utilities Expense	548	
Delivery Expense	544	
Total		$1,800

Exhibit 7A-2 lists the various business documents used to ensure that the company receives the goods it ordered and pays only for the goods it receives. Exhibit 7A-3 shows how a voucher added to the other documents can provide the evidence for a cash payment. The amounts on all these documents should agree.

Business Document	Prepared by	Sent to
Purchase request	Sales department	Purchasing department
Purchase order	Purchasing department	Outside company that sells the needed merchandise (supplier or vendor)
Invoice	Outside company that sells the needed merchandise (supplier or vendor)	Accounting department
Receiving report	Receiving department	Accounting department
Voucher	Accounting department	Officer who signs the check

8 Accounts and Notes Receivable

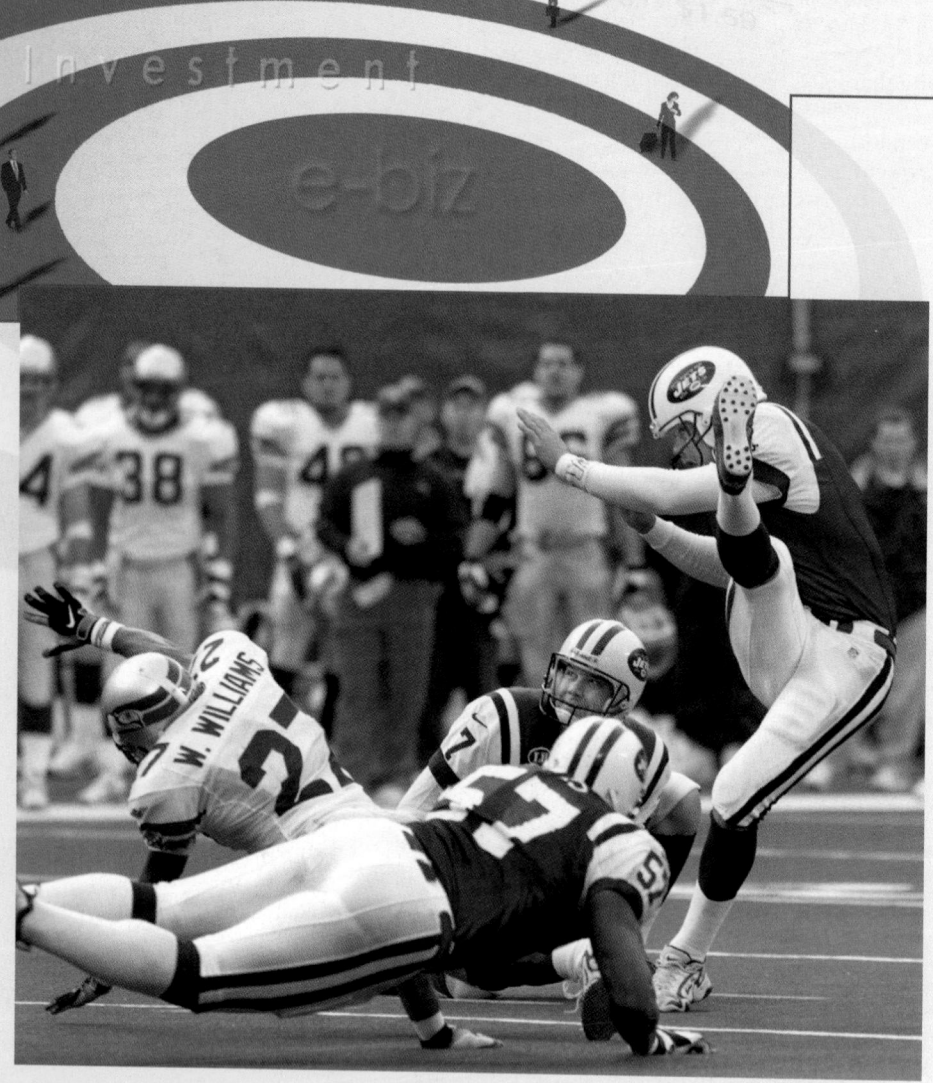

LEARNING OBJECTIVES

After studying this chapter, you should be able to

1. Design internal controls for receivables

2. Use the allowance method to account for uncollectibles by the percent-of-sales and aging-of-accounts methods

3. Use the direct write-off method to account for uncollectibles

4. Account for notes receivable

5. Report receivables on the balance sheet

6. Use the acid-test ratio and days' sales in receivables to evaluate a company's financial position

www.prenhall.com/horngren

Readiness Assessment

In the **New York Jets** locker room, pregame reviews have taken on a whole new look. Gone are the old-style playbooks with *X-and-O* diagrams of opponents' alignments. In their place is an exciting world of multimedia.

Desktop computers turn football formations into live animation. With help from **Oracle Corporation**, Carl Banks, the Jets' director of player development, has turned passive training into an interactive success. Using Developer/2000 and multimedia software, Banks has developed a state-of-the-art teaching model that gives the Jets a competitive edge. Banks states: "By the time [the players] hit the practice field, [they] lose the ability to visualize *X's* and *O's* as actual plays. Oracle [helps] create a learning environment that increases [players'] retention by as much as 250%."

Oracle is the word's second largest software company. With annual revenues exceeding $8.0 billion, the company offers its products and services in more than 145 countries around the world.

Source: Adapted from Oracle Corporation's Web site.

With exciting new products and services like Developer/2000, **Oracle** is growing rapidly. Revenues are increasing, and so are the company's receivables. Accounts receivable (also called trade receivables) are the company's largest asset. Receivables present an accounting challenge: How much of its receivables will the company be able to collect in cash? This chapter shows how to answer this and other questions about receivables. It also covers notes receivable, a more formal type of receivable supported by a written promise.

Like most other assets, accounts receivable can represent good news or bad news: Good news because receivables represent a claim to the customer's cash; bad news when the business fails to collect the cash.

A *receivable* arises when a business (or person) sells goods or services to a second business (or person) on credit. The receivable is the seller's claim against the buyer for the amount of the transaction. Each credit transaction involves at least two parties:

- The **creditor** sells goods or a service and obtains a receivable, which is an asset.
- The **debtor** makes the purchase and has a payable, which is a liability.

This chapter focuses on accounting for receivables by the seller (the creditor).

RECEIVABLES: AN INTRODUCTION

The Types of Receivables

Receivables are monetary claims against businesses and individuals. The two major types of receivables are accounts receivable and notes receivable. A business's *accounts receivable* are the amounts to be collected from customers. Accounts receivable, which are *current assets,* are also called *trade receivables.*

The Accounts Receivable account in the general ledger serves as a *control account.* It summarizes the total amounts receivable from all customers. Companies also keep a *subsidiary ledger* of accounts receivable with a separate account for each customer, illustrated at the top of the next page. *Notes receivable* are more formal than accounts receivable. The debtor for a note receivable promises in writing to pay the creditor a definite sum at a future date—the *maturity* date. A written document known as a *promissory note* serves as evidence of the receivable. The note may require the debtor to pledge *security* for the loan: This means the borrower promises that the lender can claim certain assets if the borrower fails to pay the amount due at maturity.

Notes receivable due within one year or less are current assets. Notes due beyond one year are *long-term receivables.* Some notes receivable are collected in periodic installments. The portion due within one year is a current asset, and the

CREDITOR. The party to a credit transaction who sells goods or a service and obtains a receivable.

DEBTOR. The party to a credit transaction who makes a purchase and has a payable.

RECEIVABLES. Monetary claims against a business or individual.

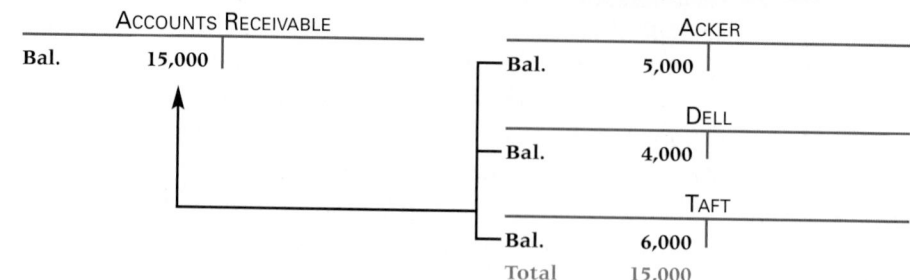

GENERAL LEDGER

ACCOUNTS RECEIVABLE

Bal. | 15,000 |

ACCOUNTS RECEIVABLE SUBSIDIARY LEDGER

ACKER

Bal. | 5,000 |

DELL

Bal. | 4,000 |

TAFT

Bal. | 6,000 |

Total | 15,000

remaining amount is a long-term asset. **General Motors** may hold a $6,000 note receivable from you, but only the $2,000 you owe this year is a current asset to GM. The remaining $4,000 is a long-term receivable.

Other receivables is a miscellaneous category that includes loans to employees and subsidiary companies. Usually, these are long-term receivables, but they are current assets if due within one year or less. Long-term notes receivable and other receivables are often reported on the balance sheet, as illustrated in Exhibit 8-1. Receivables are highlighted for emphasis.

EXHIBIT 8-1   Balance Sheet with Receivables Highlighted for Emphasis

EXAMPLE COMPANY
Balance Sheet
Date

Assets			Liabilities		
Current:			Current:		
Cash...		$X,XXX	Accounts payable		$X,XXX
Accounts receivable..........................	$X,XXX		Notes payable, short-term..................		X,XXX
Less: Allowance for			Accrued current liabilities		X,XXX
uncollectible accounts	(XXX)	X,XXX	Total current liabilities........................		X,XXX
Notes receivable, short-term		X,XXX			
Inventories		X,XXX			
Prepaid expenses.............................		X,XXX			
Total...		X,XXX	Long-term:		
Investments and long-term receivables:			Notes payable, long-term....................		X,XXX
Investments in other companies		X,XXX	Total liabilities		X,XXX
Notes receivable, long-term		X,XXX			
Other receivables.............................		X,XXX			
Total...		X,XXX			
Plant assets:			**Owner Equity**		
Property, plant, and equipment		X,XXX	Capital..		X,XXX
Total assets		$X,XXX	Total liabilities and owner equity...........		$X,XXX

Establishing Internal Control over Collection of Receivables

Businesses that sell on credit receive most cash receipts by mail. Internal control over collections of cash on account is an important part of the overall internal control system (see Chapter 7). A critical element of internal control is the separation of cash-handling and cash-accounting duties. Consider the following case.

Butler Supply Co. is a family-owned office supply business that takes pride in the loyalty of its workers. Most company employees have been with the Butlers for years. The company makes 90% of its sales on account.

The office staff consists of a bookkeeper and a supervisor. The bookkeeper maintains the accounts receivable subsidiary ledger. He also makes the daily bank deposit. The supervisor prepares monthly financial statements and special reports.

Can you identify the internal control weakness here? The bookkeeper has access to the accounts receivable subsidiary ledger, and also has custody of the cash. The bookkeeper could steal a customer check and write off the customer's account as uncollectible.[1] Unless the supervisor or some other manager reviews the bookkeeper's work, the theft may go undetected. In a small business like Butler Supply Co., such a review may never be performed.

How can this control weakness be corrected? The supervisor could open incoming mail and make the daily bank deposit. *The bookkeeper should not be allowed to handle cash.* Only the remittance advices would go to the bookkeeper to indicate which customer accounts to credit. By removing cash-handling duties from the bookkeeper, the company strengthens internal control.

 DAILY EXERCISE 8-2

Using a bank lock box achieves the same result. Customers send payments directly to Butler Supply's bank, which deposits the cash into the company's bank account. ➤→

◄◄ We examined the lock-box system in detail in Chapter 7, p. 275.

Managing the Collection of Receivables: The Credit Department

Most companies have a department to evaluate customers who apply for credit. The extension of credit requires a balancing act. The company doesn't want to lose sales to good customers who need time to pay. It also wants to avoid selling to deadbeats.

 DAILY EXERCISE 8-3

For good internal control over the collections of receivables, it is critical that the credit department have no access to cash. For example, if a credit employee handles cash, he can pocket money received from a customer. He can then label the customer's account as uncollectible, and the accounting department will write off the account receivable, as discussed in the next section. The company stops billing the customer, and the credit employee has covered up the embezzlement. For this reason, a sharp separation of duties is important indeed.

The Decision Guidelines feature identifies the main issues in controlling, managing, and accounting for receivables. These guidelines serve as a framework for the remainder of the chapter.

DECISION GUIDELINES

Controlling, Managing, and Accounting for Receivables

The main issues in *controlling* and *managing* the collection of receivables, plus a plan of action, are as follows:

ISSUE	ACTION
Extend credit only to customers most likely to pay.	Run a credit check on prospective customers.
Separate cash-handling, credit, and accounting duties to keep employees from stealing the cash collected from customers.	Design the internal control system to separate duties.
Pursue collection from customers to maximize cash flow.	Keep a close eye on collections from customers.

The main issues in *accounting* for receivables, and the related plan of action, are as follows:

ISSUE	ACTION
Measure and report receivables on the balance sheet at their *net realizable value,* the amount we expect to collect. This is necessary to report assets accurately.	Estimate the amount of uncollectible receivables.
Measure and report the expense associated with failure to collect receivables, which we call *uncollectible-account expense,* on the income statement. This helps to report net income at a reasonable amount.	Report receivables at their net realizable value (accounts receivable minus the allowance for uncollectibles). Measure the expense of failing to collect from customers.

---

[1]The bookkeeper would need to forge the endorsements on the checks and deposit them in a bank account he controls.

ACCOUNTING FOR UNCOLLECTIBLE ACCOUNTS (BAD DEBTS)

Selling on credit creates both a benefit and a cost.

- *The benefit:* The business increases revenues and profits by making sales to good customers who cannot pay cash immediately.
- *The cost:* The company will be unable to collect from some customers, and that creates an expense, which is called **uncollectible-account expense, doubtful-account expense,** or **bad-debt expense.**

Uncollectible-account expense varies from company to company. In certain businesses, a six-month-old receivable of $1 is worth only 67 cents, and a five-year-old receivable of $1 is worth only 4 cents. The older the receivable, the less valuable it is because of the increasing likehood that the customer will not pay. For **Oracle Corporation,** featured in the chapter opening story, each $1 of accounts receivable is worth 91 cents.

For a firm that sells on credit, uncollectible-account expense is as much a part of doing business as salary expense and utilities expense. Uncollectible-Account Expense—an operating expense—must be measured, recorded, and reported. To do so, accountants use the allowance method or, in certain limited cases, the direct write-off method (which we discuss on page 318).

The Allowance Method

Accountants in firms with large credit sales use the **allowance method** to measure bad debts. This method does not wait to see which customers the business will not collect from. Instead, it records collection losses on the basis of estimates. In this sense, the allowance method can be viewed as an *indirect* approach.

Rather than try to guess which accounts will go bad, managers estimate the total bad-debt expense for the period on the basis of the company's experience. The business records Uncollectible-Account Expense for the estimated amount and sets up **Allowance for Uncollectible Accounts** (or **Allowance for Doubtful Accounts**), a contra account to Accounts Receivable. This allowance account shows the amount of receivables the business expects *not* to collect.

Subtracting the uncollectible allowance amount from Accounts Receivable yields the net amount the company does expect to collect, as shown here (using Oracle Corporation's actual figures, in millions):

Balance sheet (partial):

Accounts receivable	$2,455
Less: Allowance for uncollectible accounts	(217)
Accounts receivable, net	$2,238

Customers owe Oracle $2,455 million, of which Oracle expects to collect $2,238 million. Oracle estimates it will not collect $217 million of these accounts receivable.

Another way to report receivables follows the pattern actually used by Oracle and other companies, as adapted from the Oracle balance sheet (in millions):

Accounts receivable, net of allowance for uncollectible accounts of $217	$2,238

The income statement can report Uncollectible-Account Expense (Doubtful-Account Expense) among the operating expenses, as follows (assumed figures):

Income statement (partial):

Expenses:	
Uncollectible-account expense	$4,000

UNCOLLECTIBLE-ACCOUNT EXPENSE. Cost to the seller of extending credit. Arises from the failure to collect from credit customers. Also called **doubtful-account expense,** or **bad-debt expense.**

ALLOWANCE METHOD. A method of recording collection losses on the basis of estimates, instead of waiting to see which customers the company will not collect from.

ALLOWANCE FOR UNCOLLECTIBLE ACCOUNTS. A contra account, related to accounts receivable, that holds the estimated amount of collection losses. Also called **Allowance for Doubtful Accounts.**

DAILY EXERCISE 8-4

Estimating Uncollectibles

The more accurate the estimate of uncollectibles, the more reliable the financial statements. How are bad-debt estimates made? Companies examine their past records. There are two basic ways to estimate uncollectibles:

- Percentage-of-sales method
- Aging-of-accounts method

Both approaches work with the allowance method.

Objective 2
Use the allowance method to account for uncollectibles by the percent-of-sales and aging methods

PERCENT-OF-SALES METHOD The **percent-of-sales method** computes uncollectible-account expense as a percentage of net credit sales. This method is also called the **income statement approach** because it focuses on the amount of expense to be reported on the income statement. Uncollectible-account expense is recorded as an adjusting entry at the end of the period. Assume it is December 31, 20X3, and the accounts have these balances *before the year-end adjustments:*

ACCOUNTS RECEIVABLE	ALLOWANCE FOR UNCOLLECTIBLE ACCOUNTS
120,000	500

PERCENT-OF-SALES METHOD. A method of estimating uncollectible receivables that calculates uncollectible-account expense. Also called the **income statement approach.**

Customers owe the business $120,000, and the Allowance for Uncollectible Accounts is only $500. The $500 balance is left over from the preceding period. Prior to any adjustments, the net receivable amount is $119,500 ($120,000 − $500), which is more than the business expects to collect from customers.

Based on prior experience, the credit department estimates that uncollectible-account expense is 1.5% of net credit sales, which were $500,000 for 20X3. The adjusting entry to record uncollectible-account expense for the year and to update the allowance is

```
20X3
    Dec. 31     Uncollectible-Account Expense
                ($500,000 × 0.015) ........................................   7,500
                    Allowance for Uncollectible Accounts.......              7,500
                Recorded expense for the year.
```

The accounting equation shows that the transaction to record the expense decreases the business's assets by the amount of the expense:

	ASSETS	=	LIABILITIES	+	OWNER'S EQUITY	−	EXPENSES
	−7,500	=	0			−	7,500

Now the accounts are ready for reporting in the 20X3 financial statements.

ACCOUNTS RECEIVABLE	ALLOWANCE FOR UNCOLLECTIBLE ACCOUNTS
120,000	500
	7,500
	8,000

DAILY EXERCISE 8-5

Customers still owe the business $120,000, but now the allowance for uncollectible accounts is realistic. The balance sheet will report accounts receivable at the net amount of $112,000 ($120,000 − $8,000). The income statement will report the period's uncollectible-account expense of $7,500, along with the other operating expenses for the period.

AGING-OF-ACCOUNTS The second popular approach for estimating uncollectibles is the **aging-of-accounts method.** This method is also called the **balance sheet approach** because it focuses on accounts receivable. Individual accounts receivable from specific customers are analyzed according to the length of time they have been receivable from the customer.

Computerized accounting packages now routinely age the accounts receivable. The computer sorts customer accounts by number and date of invoice. For example,

AGING-OF-ACCOUNTS METHOD. A way to estimate bad debts by analyzing individual accounts receivable according to the length of time they have been receivable from the customer. Also called the **balance-sheet approach.**

EXHIBIT 8-2 Aging the Accounts Receivable of Schmidt Builders Supply

Customer Name	Age of Account				
	1–30 Days	31–60 Days	61–90 Days	Over 90 Days	Total Balance
T-Bar-M Co.	$20,000				$ 20,000
Chicago Pneumatic Parts..	10,000				10,000
Sarasota Pipe Corp.		$13,000	$10,000		23,000
Oneida, Inc.			3,000	$1,000	4,000
Other accounts*	39,000	12,000	2,000	2,000	55,000
Totals..	$69,000	$25,000	$15,000	$3,000	112,000
Estimated percent uncollectible.............................	× 0.1%	× 1%	× 5%	× 90%	
Allowance for Uncollectible Accounts balance.......	$ 69 +	$ 250 +	$ 750 +	$2,700 +	$ 3,769

*Each of the "Other accounts" would appear individually.

the credit department of Schmidt Builders Supply groups its accounts receivable into 30-day periods, as Exhibit 8-2 shows.

Schmidt's accounts receivable total $112,000. Of this amount, the aging schedule estimates that Schmidt will *not* collect $3,769. The allowance for uncollectible accounts is not up-to-date *before the year-end adjustment,* as follows (note the $1,100 balance in the allowance):

ACCOUNTS RECEIVABLE	ALLOWANCE FOR UNCOLLECTIBLE ACCOUNTS
112,000	1,100

The aging method is designed to bring the balance of the allowance account to the needed amount as determined by the aging schedule in Exhibit 8-2 (see the lower-right corner for the final result—a needed credit balance of $3,769.)

To update the allowance, Schmidt makes this adjusting entry:

20X3
Dec. 31   Uncollectible-Account Expense.............................   2,669
                  Allowance for Uncollectible Accounts
                  ($3,769 − $1,100)...   2,669
              Recorded expense for the year.

Again, the recording of the expense decreases the business's assets by the amount of the expenses. The accounting equation for the expense transaction is

ASSETS	=	LIABILITIES	+	OWNER'S EQUITY	−	EXPENSES
−2,669	=	0			−	2,669

Now the balance sheet can report receivables at the amount that Schmidt expects to collect from customers, $108,231 ($112,000 − $3,769), as follows:

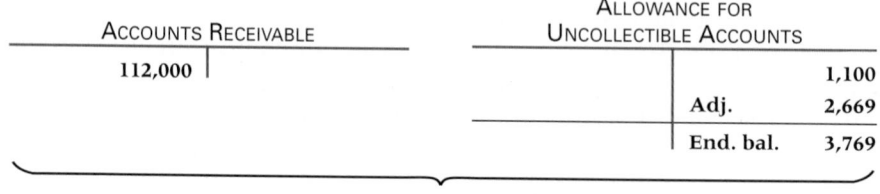

ACCOUNTS RECEIVABLE		ALLOWANCE FOR UNCOLLECTIBLE ACCOUNTS	
112,000			1,100
		Adj.	2,669
		End. bal.	3,769

Net accounts receivable, 108,231

The *net* amount of accounts receivable—$108,231 in this case—is called *net realizable value* because it is the amount Schmidt expects to realize (collect in cash) from the receivables.

USING THE PERCENT-OF-SALES AND AGING METHODS TOGETHER   In practice, companies use the percent-of-sales and the aging-of-accounts methods together.

- For *interim statements* (monthly or quarterly), companies use the percent-of-sales method because it is easier. This method focuses on the amount of uncollectible-account *expense*. But that is not enough.
- At the end of the year, these companies use the aging method to ensure that Accounts Receivable is reported at *expected realizable value*. The aging method focuses on the amount of the receivables—the *asset*—that is uncollectible.
- Using the two methods together provides good measures of both the expense and the asset. Exhibit 8-3 summarizes and compares the two methods.

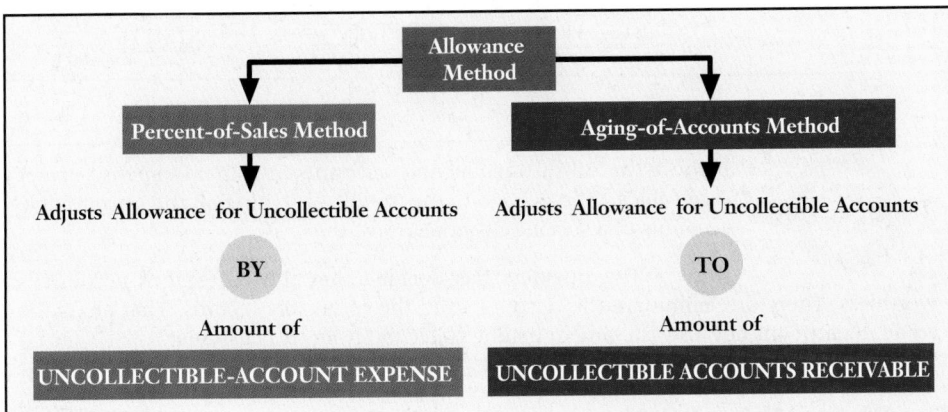

EXHIBIT **8-3**
Comparing the Percent-of-Sales and Aging Methods

◉ DAILY EXERCISE 8-6

◉ DAILY EXERCISE 8-7

Writing Off Uncollectible Accounts

Early in 20X4, Schmidt Builders Supply collects on most of its $112,000 accounts receivable and records the cash receipts as follows:

```
20X4
Jan.–Mar.   Cash...........................................................  92,000
                 Accounts Receivable ............................         92,000
            Collected on account.
```

Cash increases, and Accounts Receivable decrease by the same amount. Total assets are unchanged.

ASSETS	=	LIABILITIES	+	OWNER'S EQUITY
+92,000				
−92,000	=	0	+	0

Suppose that, after repeated attempts to collect from customers, Schmidt's credit department determines that Schmidt cannot collect a total of $1,200 from customers Abbott ($900) and Smith ($300). Schmidt's accountant then writes off Schmidt's receivables from the two delinquent customers with this entry:

```
20X4
Mar. 31     Allowance for Uncollectible Accounts............  1,200
                 Accounts Receivable—Abbott..............          900
                 Accounts Receivable—Smith...............          300
            Wrote off uncollectible accounts.
```

The accounting equation shows that the write-off of the uncollectible receivables has no impact on total assets or liabilities or equity.

ASSETS	=	LIABILITIES	+	OWNER'S EQUITY
+1,200				
−1,200	=	0	+	0

DAILY EXERCISE 8-8

DAILY EXERCISE 8-9

Study the write-off entry carefully. It affects no expense account, so it *does not affect net income.* The write-off has no effect on net receivables either, as shown for Schmidt Builders Supply in Exhibit 8-4.

EXHIBIT 8-4 Net Receivables Are the Same Before and After the Write-Off of Uncollectible Accounts

	Before Write-Off	After Write-Off	
Accounts Receivable ($112,000 − $92,000) ..	$20,000	($20,000 − $1,200)	$18,800
Less: Allowance for uncollectible accounts ...	(3,769)	(3,769 − $1,200)	(2,569)
Accounts receivable, net	$16,231 ◄——— same ———►		$16,231

THINK IT OVER

If the write off of uncollectible accounts affects no expense or net receivables, then why go to the trouble of writing off the uncollectible accounts of a specific customer?

Answer: The business has decided that the customer's account is worthless. Therefore, eliminate this account from the receivable records. That alerts the credit department not to waste time pursuing collection from this customer.

Objective 3
Use the direct write-off method to account for uncollectibles

DIRECT WRITE-OFF METHOD. A method of accounting for uncollectible receivables, in which the company waits until the credit department decides that a customer's account receivable is uncollectible, and then debits Uncollectible-Account Expense and credits the customer's Account Receivable.

DAILY EXERCISE 8-10

DAILY EXERCISE 8-11

The Direct Write-Off Method

There is another way to account for uncollectible receivables. Under the **direct write-off method,** the company waits until it decides that it will never collect from the customer. Then the accountant writes off the customer's account receivable by debiting Uncollectible-Account Expense and crediting the customer's Account Receivable, as follows (using assumed data):

```
20X7
Jan. 2      Uncollectible-Account Expense ...................    2,000
                 Accounts Receivable—Jones ...............             2,000
            Wrote off a bad account.
```

This method is defective for two reasons:

1. It does not set up an allowance for uncollectibles. As a result, it always reports the receivables at their full amount, which is more than the business expects to collect. Assets are therefore overstated on the balance sheet.
2. It may not match the uncollectible-account expense of each period against the revenue of the period. In this example, the company made the sale to Jones in 20X6 and should have recorded the uncollectible-account expense during 20X6 to measure net income properly. By recording the expense in 20X7, the company overstates net income in 20X6 and understates net income in 20X7.

Don't confuse the direct write-off method with the allowance method. The two methods of accounting for uncollectible receivables are totally different, and a company adopts one method or the other. The direct write-off method is acceptable only when the amount of uncollectible receivables is very low. It works well for retailers such as **Wal-Mart, Lands' End,** and **Gap,** which carry almost no receivables.

Recovery of Accounts Previously Written Off

When an account receivable is written off as uncollectible, the receivable does not die: The customer still has an obligation to pay. However, the company stops pursuing collection and writes off the account as uncollectible.

Some companies turn delinquent receivables over to an attorney and recover some of the cash. This is called the recovery of a bad account. Let's see how to record the recovery of an account that we wrote off earlier. Recall that on March 31, 20X4, Schmidt Builders Supply wrote off the $900 receivable from customer Lou Abbott (see page 317). It is now January 4, 20X5, and Schmidt unexpectedly receives $900 from Abbott. To account for this recovery. Schmidt makes two journal entries to (1) reverse the earlier write-off and (2) record the cash collection, as follows:

(1) Accounts Receivable—Abbott	900	
Allowance for Uncollectible Accounts		900
Reinstated Abbott's account receivable.		
(2) Cash	900	
Accounts Receivable—Abbott		900
Collected on account.		

CREDIT-CARD, BANKCARD, AND DEBIT-CARD SALES

Credit-Card Sales

Credit-card sales are common in retailing. Customers present credit cards like **American Express** and **Discover** to pay for purchases. The credit-card company then pays the seller the transaction amount and bills the customer, who then pays the credit-card company.

Credit cards offer customers the convenience of buying without having to pay cash immediately. An American Express customer receives a monthly statement from American Express, detailing each of his or her transactions. The customer can write one check to cover the entire month's credit-card purchases.

Retailers also benefit from credit-card sales. They do not have to check a customer's credit rating. The company that issued the card has already done so. Retailers do not have to keep accounts receivable records, and they do not have to collect cash from customers.

These benefits do not come free. The seller receives less than 100% of the face value of the sale. The credit-card company takes a fee of 1–5% on the sale. Suppose you have lunch at the Russian Tea Room, and pay the bill—$100—with a Discover card. The Russian Tea Room's entry to record the $100 sale, subject to the credit-card company's 3% discount, is

Accounts Receivable—Discover	97	
Credit-Card Discount Expense	3	
Sales Revenue		100
Recorded credit-card sales.		

On collection of the discounted value, the Russian Tea Room records the following:

Cash	97	
Accounts Receivable—Discover		97
Collected from Discover.		

Bankcard Sales

Most banks issue their own cards, known as *bankcards*, which operate much like credit cards. **VISA** and **MasterCard** are the two main bankcards. When an **Exxon** station makes a sale and takes a VISA card, the station receives cash at the point of the sale. The cash received is less than the full amount of the sale because the bank deducts its fee. Suppose the Exxon station sells $150 of fuel to a family vacationing in its motor home. The station takes a VISA card, and the bank that issued the card charges a 2% fee. The Exxon station records the bankcard sale as follows:

Cash	147	
Bankcard Discount Expense ($150 × 0.02)	3	
Sales Revenue		150
Recorded a bankcard sale.		

⊙ DAILY EXERCISE 8-12

Debit-Card Sales

Debit cards are fundamentally different from credit cards and bankcards. Using a debit card to buy groceries is like paying with cash, except that the customer doesn't have to carry cash or write a check.

At **Safeway** (or **Kroger** or **Wal-Mart**), the buyer "swipes" the card through a special terminal, and the buyer's bank balance is automatically decreased. Safeway's Cash account is increased immediately—without having to deposit a check and wonder if it will clear the bank. With a debit card there is no third party, such as VISA or MasterCard, so there is no Credit-Card Discount Expense.

e-Accounting

Merchant Beware: Credit Cards Boom with Online Sales . . . But So Does Fraud

The TV ad blends e-commerce and credit cards: A cloistered nun is shown with all the comforts of the outside world, compliments of **Amazon.com** and **VISA**. Currently 97% of all Web payments are made via credit cards. At the end of every month, e-tailers send up to 2.5% of their revenues to credit-card companies. **VISA, MasterCard, American Express,** and their cousins earn millions in transaction fees.

Who takes the hit when customers deny credit-card charges they actually made (chargebacks) or when criminals commit "identity theft" and make purchases with stolen card numbers? It's the online merchants.

Lack of face-to-face transactions has led to an increase in chargebacks for online sales. The online merchant never touches the card, and the online consumer never signs a ticket. The result: There is no paper trail to prove that the cardholder actually okayed the charge. Anonymity also paves the way for identity theft. Online travel company **Expedia, Inc.,** was recently victimized by criminals who used stolen credit-card numbers to buy airplane tickets. The Bellevue, Washington, company lost $6 million on the fraud.

Source: Based on Marcia Savage, "Online fraud: New twist on old issue," *Computer Reseller News,* March 27, 2000, p. 28. Leslie Beyer, "The Internet revolution," *Credit Card Management,* November 1999, Mercedes M. Cardona, "Visa teams up with e-tailers to acquire online dominance," *Advertising Age,* December 6, 1999, p. 4. Patricia A. Murphy, "The murky world of 'Net chargebacks," *Credit Card Management,* February 2000, pp. 54–60.

MID-CHAPTER

www.prenhall.com/horngren

Mid-Chapter Assessment

SUMMARY PROBLEM

CPC International, Inc., produces Skippy peanut butter, Hellmann's mayonnaise, and Mazola corn oil. Suppose CPC's balance sheet at December 31, 20X2, reported the following:

	Millions
Notes and accounts receivable [total]	$549.9
Allowance for uncollectible accounts	(12.5)

Required

1. How much of the December 31, 20X2, balance of the receivable did CPC expect to collect? Stated differently, what was the expected realizable value of these receivables?

2. Journalize, without explanations, 20X3 entries for CPC International, assuming
   a. Total estimated Uncollectible-Account Expense was $19.2 million for the first three quarters of the year, based on the percent-of-sales method.
   b. Write-offs of accounts receivable totaled $23.6 million.
   c. December 31, 20X3, aging of receivables, which indicates that $15.3 million of the total receivables of $582.7 million is uncollectible. Post all three entries to Allowance for Uncollectible Accounts.
3. Show how CPC International's receivables and related allowance will appear on the December 31, 20X3, balance sheet.

   What is the expected realizable value of receivables at December 31, 20X3? How much is uncollectible-account expense for 20X3?

Solution

Requirement 1

	(In millions)
Expected realizable value of receivables ($549.9 − $12.5)	$537.4

Requirement 2

	(In millions)	
(a) Uncollectible-Account Expense.......................................	19.2	
Allowance for Uncollectible Accounts.......................		19.2
(b) Allowance for Uncollectible Accounts	23.6	
Accounts Receivable..		23.6
(c) Uncollectible-Account Expense ($15.3 − $8.1)..............	7.2	
Allowance for Uncollectible Accounts.......................		7.2

ALLOWANCE FOR UNCOLLECTIBLE ACCOUNTS

20X3 Write-offs	23.6	Dec. 31, 20X2 Bal.	12.5
		20X3 Expense	19.2
		Bal. before adj.	8.1
		Dec. 31, 20X3 Adj.	7.2
		Dec. 31, 20X3 Bal.	15.3

Requirement 3

	(In millions)
Notes and accounts receivable...	$582.7
Less: Allowance for uncollectible accounts	(15.3)
Notes and accounts receivable, net..	$567.4
Uncollectible-account expense for 20X3 ($19.2 + $7.2).......	$26.4

NOTES RECEIVABLE: AN OVERVIEW

As we pointed out earlier in this chapter, notes receivable are more formal arrangements than accounts receivable. The debtor signs a promissory note, which serves as evidence of the debt. Before launching into the accounting for notes receivable, let's define the special terms used for them.

- **Promissory note:** A written promise to pay a specified amount of money at a particular future date.
- **Maker of the note (debtor):** The person or business that signs the note and promises to pay the amount required by the note agreement; the maker of the note is the *debtor*.

- **Payee of the note (creditor):** The person or business to whom the maker promises future payment; the payee of the note is the *creditor*.
- **Principal amount,** or **principal:** The amount loaned out by the payee and borrowed by the maker of the note.
- **Interest:** The revenue to the payee for loaning money, and the expense of borrowing for the maker.
- **Interest period:** The period of time during which interest is to be computed. It extends from the original date of the note to the maturity date. Also called the **note period, note term,** or simply **time.**
- **Interest rate:** The percentage rate that is multiplied by the principal amount to compute the amount of interest on the note. Interest rates are almost always stated for a period of one year. A 9% note means that the amount of interest for *one year* is 9% of the principal amount of the note.
- **Maturity date:** The date when final payment of the note is due. Also called the **due date.**
- **Maturity value:** The sum of the principal plus interest due at the maturity date.

Exhibit 8-5 illustrates a promissory note. Study it carefully.

EXHIBIT 8-5   A Promissory Note

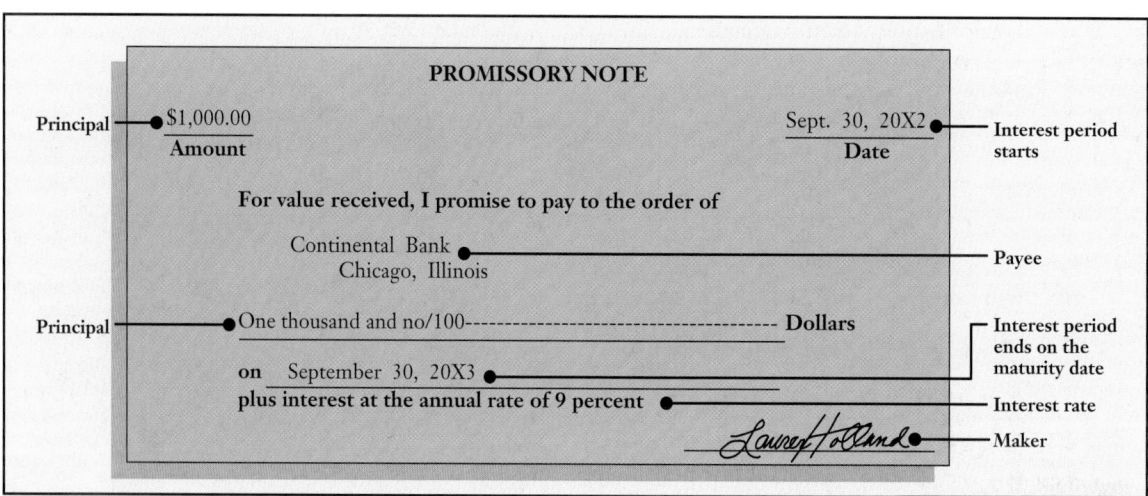

Identifying a Note's Maturity Date

Some notes specify the maturity date, as shown in Exhibit 8-5. Other notes state the period of the note in days or months. When the period is given in months, the note's maturity date falls on the same day of the month as the date the note was issued. For example, a six-month note dated February 16 matures on August 16.

When the period is given in days, the maturity date is determined by counting the days from the date of issue. A 120-day note dated September 14, 20X2, matures on January 12, 20X3, as shown here:

Month	Number of Days	Cumulative Total
Sep. 20X2	30 − 14 = 16	16
Oct. 20X2	31	47
Nov. 20X2	30	77
Dec. 20X2	31	108
Jan. 20X3	12	120

In counting the days remaining for a note, remember to count the maturity date and to omit the date the note was issued.

Computing Interest on a Note

The formula for computing the dollar amount of interest on a note is

$$\text{Principal} \times \frac{\text{Interest rate}}{} \times \text{Time} = \text{Amount of interest}$$

 DAILY EXERCISE 8-13

Using the data in Exhibit 8-5, Continental Bank computes its interest revenue for one year on its note receivable as

Principal ×	Interest rate	× Time =	Amount of interest
$1,000	0.09	1 yr.	$90

The maturity value of the note is $1,090 ($1,000 principal + $90 interest). The time element is 1 because interest is computed over a one-year period.

When the interest period of a note is stated in months, we compute the interest based on the 12-month year. Interest on a $2,000 note at 15% for three months is computed as

Principal ×	Interest rate	× Time =	Amount of interest
$2,000	0.15	3/12	$75

When the interest period is stated in days, we sometimes compute interest based on a 360-day year rather than on a 365-day year.[2] The interest on a $5,000 note at 12% for 60 days can be computed as

Principal ×	Interest rate	× Time =	Amount of interest
$5,000	0.12	60/360	$100

Keep in mind that interest rates are stated as an annual rate. Therefore, the time in the formula for computing interest should also be expressed in terms of a year.

WORK IT OUT

Practice calculating interest on
1. A $30,000, 12 1/2%, 180-day note
2. An $8,000, 9%, 6-month note

Answers
1. ($30,000 × 0.125 × 180/360) = $1,875   2. ($8,000 × 0.09 × 6/12) = $360

ACCOUNTING FOR NOTES RECEIVABLE

Recording Notes Receivable

Objective 4
Account for notes receivable

Consider the loan agreement shown in Exhibit 8-5. After Lauren Holland signs the note, Continental Bank gives her $1,000 cash. At maturity, Holland pays the bank $1,090 ($1,000 principal plus $90 interest). The bank's entries are

 DAILY EXERCISE 8-14

Sep. 30, 20X2	Note Receivable—L. Holland..................................	1,000	
	Cash..		1,000
	Loaned out money.		
Sep. 30, 20X3	Cash	1,090	
	Note Receivable—L. Holland.........................		1,000
	Interest Revenue ($1,000 × 0.09 × 1)...........		90
	Collected note receivable.		

---

[2]A 360-day year eliminates some rounding, which is consistent with our use of whole-dollar amounts throughout this book.

Some companies sell merchandise in exchange for notes receivable. Suppose that on October 20, 20X3, **General Electric** sells household appliances for $15,000 to Dorman Builders. Dorman signs a 90-day promissory note at 10% annual interest. General Electric's entries to record the sale and collection from Dorman are

Oct. 20, 20X3	Note Receivable—Dorman Builders	15,000	
	Sales Revenue		15,000
	Made a sale.		
Jan. 18, 20X4	Cash	15,375	
	Note Receivable—Dorman Builders...................		15,000
	Interest Revenue ($15,000 × 0.10 × 90/360)		375
	Collected note receivable.		

 DAILY EXERCISE 8-15

A company may accept a note receivable from a trade customer who fails to pay an account receivable within the customary 30–60 days. The customer signs a promissory note—that is, becomes the **maker of the note**—and gives it to the creditor, who becomes the **payee.** Suppose Interlogic, Inc., cannot pay Hoffman Supply. Hoffman may accept a one-year, $2,400 note receivable, with 9% interest, from Interlogic on October 1, 20X1. Hoffman's entry is

> **MAKER OF A NOTE.** The person or business that signs the note and promises to pay the amount required by the note agreement; the debtor.

> **PAYEE OF A NOTE.** The person or business to whom the maker of a note promises future payment; the creditor.

Oct. 1, 20X1	Note Receivable—Interlogic, Inc................................	2,400	
	Accounts Receivable—Interlogic, Inc.................		2,400
	Received a note on account.		

Accruing Interest Revenue

Notes receivable may be outstanding at the end of an accounting period. The interest revenue earned on the note during the year is part of that year's earnings. Recall that interest revenue is earned over time, not just when cash is received. ◄

> ➤ We saw in Chapter 3 on p. 94 that accrued revenue creates an asset because the revenue has been earned but not received.

Let's continue with the Hoffman Supply note receivable from Interlogic, Inc. Hoffman Supply's accounting period ends December 31. How much of the total interest revenue does Hoffman earn in 20X1? How much does it earn in 20X2?

Hoffman will earn three months' interest in 20X1—for October, November, and December. In 20X2, Hoffman will earn nine months' interest—for January through September. At December 31, 20X1, Hoffman Supply will make the following adjusting entry to accrue interest revenue:

Dec. 31, 20X1	Interest Receivable ($2,400 × 0.09 × 3/12).................	54	
	Interest Revenue		54
	Accrued interest revenue.		

Then, on the maturity date, Hoffman Supply records collection of principal and interest as follows:

Sep. 30, 20X2	Cash [$2,400 + ($2,400 × 0.09)].................................	2,616	
	Note Receivable—Interlogic, Inc........................		2,400
	Interest Receivable ($2,400 × 0.09 × 3/12)		54
	Interest Revenue ($2,400 × 0.09 × 9/12)		162
	Collected note receivable on which interest has been accrued previously.		

 DAILY EXERCISE 8-16

 DAILY EXERCISE 8-17

The entries for interest earned in 20X1 and for collection in 20X2 assign the correct amount of interest to each year. This follows the revenue principle.

A company holding a note receivable may need the cash before the note matures. There is a procedure for selling the note, called discounting a note receivable. The chapter appendix covers this topic.

Dishonored Notes Receivable

> **DISHONOR OF A NOTE.** Failure of a note's maker to pay a note receivable at maturity. Also called **default on a note.**

If the maker of a note does not pay at maturity, the maker is said to **dishonor,** or **default on,** the note. Because the term of the note has expired, the note agreement is no longer in force. However, the payee still has a claim against the debtor and usually transfers the note receivable amount to Accounts Receivable. The payee records the amount of interest revenue the payee has earned on the note and debits Accounts Receivable for the maturity value of the note.

Rubinstein Jewelers has a six-month, 10% note receivable for $1,200 from Mario Adair, and on the February 3 maturity date, Adair defaulted. Rubinstein Jewelers will record the default as follows:

Feb. 3	Accounts Receivable—M. Adair	
	[$1,200 + ($1,200 × 0.10 × 6/12)] 1,260	
	Note Receivable—M. Adair	1,200
	Interest Revenue ($1,200 × 0.10 × 6/12)	60
	Recorded a dishonored note receivable.	

Rubinstein will pursue collection from Adair as an account receivable. If the account receivable later proves uncollectible, Rubinstein will then write off the account as previously discussed. Note that all notes receivable bear interest until they are proved dead.

Reporting Receivables on the Balance Sheet

Objective 5
Report receivables on the balance sheet

Let's look at how some well-known companies report their receivables and related allowances for uncollectibles on the balance sheet. All receivables and the related allowance accounts appear on the balance sheet, but terminology may vary. **Intel Corporation,** maker of the Pentium® processor, reports accounts receivable under Current Assets (in millions):

Accounts receivable, net of allowance for doubtful accounts of $67.... $3,700

The net realizable value of Intel's accounts receivable is $3,700 million. To compute Intel's total amount receivable, add the allowance to the net receivable: $67 + $3,700 = $3,767. Customers actually owe Intel $3,767 million, of which the company expects to collect $3,700 million.

General Electric Company reports a single amount—net realizable value—for receivables in the balance sheet and uses a note to give the details (adapted with amounts in millions):

Current receivables (note 10)	$8,743
Note 10: Current Receivables:	
Aircraft Engines.............................	$ 1,541
Appliances	285
Power Systems................................	3,350
Other	3,887
	9,063
Less: Allowance for losses..............	(320)
	$8,743

DAILY EXERCISE 8-18

DAILY EXERCISE 8-19

WORK IT OUT

1. How much did customers owe General Electric (GE)?
2. How much did GE expect to collect?
3. How much did GE expect *not* to collect?

Answers

1. $9,063 million   **2.** $8,743 million   **3.** $320 million

Computers and Accounts Receivable

Accounting for receivables by a large company like **M&M Mars** requires tens of thousands of postings to customer accounts each month for credit sales and cash collections. Manual accounting methods cannot keep up.

ACCOUNTS AND NOTES RECEIVABLE 325

As we saw in Chapter 6, Accounts Receivable can be set up on a computerized system. The order entry and shipping systems interface with the billing system, which credits Sales Revenue and debits Accounts Receivable. The computer then creates a sale invoice for each customer. At the same time, the computer prints out the sales for the period. Finally, computerized posting to the general ledger and accounts receivable subsidiary ledger occurs.

Objective 6
Use the acid-test ratio and days' sales in receivables to evaluate a company's financial position

USING ACCOUNTING INFORMATION FOR DECISION MAKING

The balance sheet lists assets in order of liquidity (closeness to cash):

- Cash comes first because it is the medium of exchange.
- Short-term investments (covered in a later chapter) come next because they can be sold for cash whenever the owner wishes.
- Current receivables are less liquid than short-term investments because the receivables must be collected.
- Merchandise inventory is less liquid than receivables because the goods must be sold.

The balance sheet of **Oracle Corporation,** as adapted, provides an example in Exhibit 8-6. Focus on the current assets at May 31, 1999. Oracle reports no inventory because the company earns revenue by providing services, not by selling products.

EXHIBIT 8-6
Oracle Corporation Balance Sheet

Oracle Corporation Balance Sheet (partial, adapted) May 31, 1999 and May 31, 1998	(In millions)	
Assets	**May 31, 1999**	**1998**
Current assets:		
Cash and cash equivalents	$1,786	$1,274
Short-term investments	777	645
Trade receivables net of allowance for doubtful accounts of $217 in 1999 and $196 in 1998	2,238	1,857
Prepaid expenses	405	339
Other current assets	241	208
Total current assets	$5,447	$4,323
Liabilities		
Current liabilities:		
Total current liabilities	$3,046	$2,484

Acid-Test (or Quick) Ratio

ACID-TEST RATIO. Ratio of the sum of cash plus short-term investments plus net current receivables, to total current liabilities. Tells whether the entity could pay all its current liabilities if they came due immediately. Also called the quick ratio.

Owners and managers use ratios for decision making. In Chapter 4, we discussed the current ratio, which measures the ability to pay current liabilities with current assets. A more stringent measure of ability to pay current liabilities is the **acid-test (or quick) ratio.** The acid-test ratio reveals whether the entity can pay all its current liabilities if they come due immediately:

For Oracle Corporation (Exhibit 8-6)
(Dollar amounts in millions)

$$\text{Acid-test ratio} = \frac{\text{Cash} + \text{Short-term investments} + \text{Net current receivables}}{\text{Total current liabilities}} \qquad \frac{\$1,786 + \$777 + \$2,238}{\$3,046} = 1.58$$

The higher the acid-test ratio, the more able the business is to pay its current liabilities. Oracle's acid-test ratio of 1.58 means that Oracle has $1.58 of quick assets to pay each $1 of current liabilities—an extremely strong position.

What is an acceptable acid-test ratio? The answer depends on the industry. **Wal-Mart** operates smoothly with an acid-test ratio of 0.18. Several things make this possible: Wal-Mart has almost no current receivables. The acid-test ratios for most department stores cluster about 0.80, while travel agencies average 1.10. In general, an acid-test ratio of 1.00 is considered safe.

WORK IT OUT

Use the data in Exhibit 8-6 to compute Oracle Corporation's current ratio at May 31, 1999. Then compare Oracle's current ratio and acid-test ratio. Why is the current ratio higher?

Answer:

$$\text{Current ratio} = \frac{\text{Total current assets}}{\text{Total current liabilities}} = \frac{\$5,447}{\$3,046} = 1.79$$

$$\text{Acid-test ratio} = \qquad\qquad 1.58$$

The current ratio is higher because it includes all current assets and not just cash, short-term investments, and receivables.

Days' Sales in Receivables

After making a credit sale, the next step is to collect the receivable. **Days' sales in receivables,** also called the **collection period,** indicates how many days it takes to collect the average level of receivables. The shorter the collection period, the more quickly the organization can use cash for operations. The longer the collection period, the less cash is available to pay bills and expand. Days' sales in receivables can be computed in two steps, as follows:[3]

DAYS' SALES IN RECEIVABLES.
Ratio of average net accounts receivable to one day's sales. Tells how many days' sales it takes to collect the average level of receivables. Also called the **collection period.**

For Oracle Corporation (Exhibit 8-6)
(Dollar amounts in millions)

1.
$$\text{One day's sales} = \frac{\substack{\text{Net sales} \\ \text{(or Total revenues)}}}{365 \text{ days}} =$$

$$\frac{\$8,827^*}{365} = \$24.2 \text{ per day}$$

2.
$$\text{Days' sales in average accounts receivable} = \frac{\text{Average net accounts receivable}}{\text{One day's sales}} = \frac{\left(\substack{\text{Beginning net} \\ \text{receivables}} + \substack{\text{Ending net} \\ \text{receivables}}\right) \div 2}{\text{One day's sales}}$$

$$= \frac{(\$1,857 + \$2,238)/2}{\$24.2} = 85 \text{ days}$$

*Taken from Oracle Corporation's 1999 income statement, which is not reproduced here.

The length of the collection period depends on the credit terms of the company's revenues. For example, sales on net 30 terms should be collected within approximately 30 days. When there is a discount, such as 2/10 net 30, the collection period may be shorter. Terms of net 45 or net 60 result in longer collection periods. ➤

Investors and creditors do not evaluate a company on the basis of one or two ratios. Instead, they perform a thorough analysis of all the information available. Then they stand back from the data and ask, "What is our overall impression of this company?"

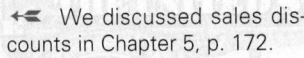
◄ We discussed sales discounts in Chapter 5, p. 172.

DAILY EXERCISE 8-20

DAILY EXERCISE 8-21

THINK IT OVER

AMR Corporation, the parent company of American Airlines, had a collection period of only 24 days during 1999. Why was it so short?

Answer: Generally, people pay for airline tickets before they travel. This causes the airlines' days' sales in receivables to be very low.

The **Decision Guidelines** feature summarizes some key decisions people must make in order to manage and evaluate receivables.

[3]Days' sales in average receivables can also be computed in this one step:

$$\text{Days' sales in average receivables} = \frac{\text{Average net receivables}}{\text{Net sales}} \times 365$$

DECISION GUIDELINES

Accounting for Receivables Transactions

DECISION	GUIDELINES
Accounts Receivable	
How much of our receivables will we collect?	Less than the full amount of the receivables because we will be unable to collect from some customers.

How to report receivables at their net realizable value?	1. Use the *allowance method* to account for uncollectible receivables. Set up the allowance for Uncollectible Accounts.
	2. Estimate uncollectibles by the
	  a. *Percent-of-sales method* (income statement approach)
	  b. *Aging-of-accounts method* (balance sheet approach)
	3. Write off uncollectible receivables as they are deemed uncollectible.
	4. $\dfrac{\text{Net accounts}}{\text{receivable}} = \dfrac{\text{Accounts}}{\text{Receivable}} - \dfrac{\text{Allowance for}}{\text{Uncollectible Accounts}}$

Is there another way to account for uncollectible receivables?	The *direct write-off method* uses no Allowance for Uncollectibles Accounts. It simply debits Uncollectible-Account Expense and credits a customer's Account Receivable to write it off when uncollectible. This method is acceptable only when uncollectibles are insignificant.
Notes Receivable	
What two other accounts are related to notes receivable?	Notes receivable are related as follows: • Notes receivable earn *Interest Revenue.* • Interest revenue that has not been collected is debited to *Interest Receivable.*
How to compute the interest on a note receivable?	Amount of interest = Principal × Interest rate × Time
Receivables in General	
What two key decision aids use receivables to evaluate a company's financial position?	• Acid-test ratio $= \dfrac{\text{Cash} + \overset{\text{Short-term}}{\text{investments}} + \overset{\text{Net current}}{\text{receivables}}}{\text{Total current liabilities}}$ • $\dfrac{\text{Day's sales in}}{\text{average receivables}} = \dfrac{\overset{\text{Average net}}{\text{accounts receivable}}}{\text{One day's sales}}$
How to report receivables on the balance sheet?	Accounts (or Notes) Receivable .... \$XXX Less: Allowance for uncollectible accounts .... (X) Accounts (or notes) receivable, net .... \$ XX

REVIEW ACCOUNTS AND NOTES RECEIVABLE

SUMMARY PROBLEM

www.prenhall.com/horngren

End-of-Chapter Assessment

Suppose First Fidelity, Inc., engaged in the following transactions:

20X4

Apr.	1	Loaned \$8,000 to Bland Co. Received a six-month, 10% note.
Oct.	1	Collected the Bland note at maturity.
Dec.	1	Loaned \$6,000 to Flores, Inc., on a 180-day, 12% note.
Dec.	31	Accrued interest revenue on the Flores note.

20X5

May	30	Collected the Flores note at maturity.

First Fidelity's accounting period ends on December 31.

Required

Explanations are not needed.

1. Record the 20X4 transactions on April 1 through December 1 on First Fidelity's books.
2. Make the adjusting entry needed on December 31, 20X4.
3. Record the May 30, 20X5, collection of the Flores note.

Solution

Requirement 1

20X4

Apr. 1	Note Receivable—Bland Co.	8,000	
	Cash..		8,000
Oct. 1	Cash ($8,000 + $400)	8,400	
	Note Receivable—Bland Co.		8,000
	Interest Revenue ($8,000 × 0.10 × 6/12)		400

Requirement 2

20X4

Dec. 1	Note Receivable—Flores, Inc.	6,000	
	Cash..		6,000
31	Interest Receivable	60	
	Interest Revenue ($6,000 × 0.12 × 30/360)		60

Requirement 3

20X5

May 30	Cash ($6,000 + $360)	6,360	
	Note Receivable—Flores, Inc.		6,000
	Interest Receivable		60
	Interest Revenue ($6,000 × 0.12 × 150/360)		300

LESSONS LEARNED

1. Design internal controls for receivables. Companies that sell on credit receive most customer collections in the mail. Good *internal control* over mailed-in cash receipts means separating cash-handling duties from cash-accounting duties.

2. Use the allowance method to account for uncollectibles by the percent-of-sales and aging-of-accounts methods. Uncollectible receivables are accounted for by the allowance method or the direct write-off method. The *allowance method* matches expenses against revenue and also results in a more realistic measure of net accounts receivable. The *percent-of-sales method* and the *aging-of-accounts method* are the two main approaches to estimating bad debts under the allowance method.

3. Use the direct write-off method to account for uncollectibles. The *direct write-off method* is easy to apply, but it fails to match bad debt expense to the corresponding rev-enue. Also, Accounts Receivable are reported at their full amount, which is misleading because it suggests that the company expects to collect all its accounts receivable.

4. Account for notes receivable. *Notes receivable* are formal credit agreements. Interest earned by the creditor is computed by multiplying the note's principal amount by the interest rate times the length of the interest period.

5. Report receivables on the balance sheet. All accounts receivable, notes receivable, and allowance accounts appear in the balance sheet. Companies use various formats to report these assets at net realizable value.

6. Use the acid-test ratio and days' sales in receivables to evaluate a company's financial position. The *acid-test ratio* measures the company's ability to pay current liabilities from the most liquid current assets. *Days' sales in receivables* indicates how long it takes to collect the average level of receivables.

ACCOUNTING VOCABULARY

acid-test ratio (p. 326)
aging-of-accounts method (p. 315)
Allowance for Doubtful Accounts (p. 314)
Allowance for Uncollectible Accounts (p. 314)
allowance method (p. 314)
bad-debt expense (p. 314)
balance sheet approach (p. 315)
collection period (p. 327)

contingent liability (p. 344)
creditor (p. 311)
days' sales in receivables (p. 327)
debtor (p. 311)
default on a note (p. 324)
direct write-off method (p. 318)
discounting a note receivable (p. 343)
dishonor of a note (p. 324)
doubtful-account expense (p. 314)

due date (p. 322)
income statement approach (p. 315)
interest (p. 322)
interest period (p. 322)
interest rate (p. 322)
maker of a note (p. 324)
maturity date (p. 322)
maturity value (p. 322)
note period (p. 322)
note term (p. 322)

payee of a note (p. 324)
percent-of-sales method (p. 315)
principal (p. 322)
principal amount (p. 322)

promissory note (p. 321)
quick ratio (p. 326)
receivables (p. 311)
time (p. 322)

uncollectible-account expense
(p. 314)

QUESTIONS

1. Name the two parties to a receivable/payable transaction. Which party has the receivable? Which has the payable? Which has the asset? The liability?
2. List the two main categories of receivables. State how receivables are classified for reporting on the balance sheet.
3. Name the two methods of accounting for uncollectible receivables. Which method is easier to apply? Which method is consistent with generally accepted accounting principles?
4. Identify the accounts debited and credited to account for uncollectibles under (a) the allowance method, and (b) the direct write-off method.
5. What is another term for Allowance for Uncollectible Accounts? What are two other terms for Uncollectible-Account Expense?
6. Identify and briefly describe the two ways to estimate bad-debt expense and uncollectible accounts, using the allowance method.

7. Use the terms *maker, payee, principal amount, maturity date, promissory note,* and *interest* in an appropriate sentence or two describing a note receivable.
8. Name three situations in which a company might receive a note receivable. For each situation, show the account debited and the account credited to record receipt of the note.
9. When the maker of a note dishonors the note at maturity, what accounts does the payee debit and credit?
10. Why does the payee of a note receivable usually need to make adjusting entries for interest at the end of the accounting period?
11. Show three ways to report Accounts Receivable of $100,000 and Allowance for Uncollectible Accounts of $2,800 on the balance sheet or in the related notes.
12. Why is the acid-test ratio a more stringent measure of the ability to pay current liabilities than the current ratio?
13. Which measure of days' sales in receivables is preferable, 30 or 40? Give your reason.

ASSESS YOUR PROGRESS

DAILY EXERCISES

Accounts receivable records (Obj. 1)

DE8-1 Examine the Accounts Receivable T-accounts on page 312, and answer these questions:

1. Which account (and which amount) will appear on the company's balance sheet? Suppose the company has cash of $2,000. Show how the balance sheet will report cash and the other item on page 312.
2. Who are Acker, Dell, and Taft? What do their accounts indicate that these three persons are obligated to do?

Internal control over the collection of receivables (Obj. 1)

DE8-2 Return to the Accounts Receivable T-accounts on page 312. Suppose Nathan Forester is the accountant responsible for these records. What duty will a good internal control system withhold from Forester? Why?

Internal control over the credit department (Obj. 1)

DE8-3 What duty must be withheld from a company's credit department in order to safeguard its cash? If this duty is granted to the credit department, what can a dishonest credit department employee do to hurt the company?

Applying the allowance method to account for uncollectibles (Obj. 2)

DE8-4 The allowance method of accounting for uncollectible receivables uses two accounts in addition to Accounts Receivable. Identify the two accounts and indicate which financial statement reports each account. Which of these is a contra account? Make up reasonable amounts to show how to report the contra account under its companion account on the balance sheet.

Applying the allowance method (percent-of-sales) to account for uncollectibles (Obj. 2)

DE8-5 During its first year of operations, SBC Communications had net sales of $600,000, all on account. Industry experience suggests that SBC's bad debts will amount to 2% of net sales. At December 31, 20X3, SBC's accounts receivable total $90,000. The company uses the allowance method to account for uncollectibles.

1. Journalize SBC's uncollectible-account expense using the percent-of-sales method.
2. Show how SBC should report accounts receivable on its balance sheet at December 31, 20X3. Follow the reporting format illustrated in the middle of page 314.

Applying the allowance method (percent-of-sales) to account for uncollectibles (Obj. 2)

DE8-6 ◄ *Link Back to Chapter 5 (Recording Sales Transactions).* This exercise continues the situation of Daily Exercise 8-5, in which SBC Communications ended the year 20X3 with accounts receivable of $90,000 and an allowance for uncollectible accounts of $12,000.

During 20X4, SBC Communications completed the following transactions:

1. Net credit sales, $800,000 (ignore cost of goods sold).
2. Collections on account, $690,000.
3. Write-offs of uncollectibles, $15,000.
4. Uncollectible-account expense, 1.8% of net credit sales.

Journalize the foregoing 20X4 transactions for SBC Communications.

DE8-7 Use the solution to Daily Exercise 8-6 to answer these questions about SBC Communications.

Applying the allowance method (percent-of-sales) to account for uncollectibles
(Obj. 2)

1. Start with Accounts Receivable's beginning balance ($90,000), and then post to the Accounts Receivable T-account. How much do SBC's customers owe the company at December 31, 20X4?
2. Start with the Allowance account's beginning balance ($12,000), and then post to the Allowance for Uncollectible Accounts T-account. How much of the receivables at December 31, 20X4, does SBC expect *not* to collect?
3. At December 31, 20X4, how much cash does SBC expect to collect on its accounts receivable?

DE8-8 ← *Link Back to Chapter 5 (Recording Sales Transactions).* Guardian Medical Group started 20X0 with accounts receivable of $120,000 and an allowance for uncollectible accounts of $6,000. The 20X0 credit sales were $800,000, and cash collections on account totaled $720,000. During 20X0, Guardian wrote off uncollectible accounts receivable of $12,000. At December 31, 20X0, the aging of accounts receivable indicated that Guardian will *not* collect $4,000 of its accounts receivable.

Applying the allowance method (aging-of-accounts) to account for uncollectibles
(Obj. 2)

Journalize Guardian's (a) credit sales (ignore cost of goods sold), (b) cash collections on account, (c) write-offs of uncollectible receivables, and (d) uncollectible-account expense for the year. Prepare a T-account for Allowance for Uncollectible Accounts to show your computation of uncollectible-account expense for the year.

DE8-9 Hot Button.com accounts include the following balances at December 31, 20X1, before the year-end adjustments:

Applying the allowance method (aging-of-accounts) to account for uncollectibles
(Obj. 2)

ACCOUNTS RECEIVABLE	ALLOWANCE FOR UNCOLLECTIBLE ACCOUNTS
104,000		1,300	

The aging of accounts receivable yields these data:

	Age of Accounts Receivable				
	0–30 Days	31–60 Days	61–90 Days	Over 90 Days	Total Receivables
Amount receivable	$70,000	$20,000	$10,000	$4,000	$104,000
Percent uncollectible	× 1%	× 2%	× 5%	× 50%	

Journalize Hot Button's entry to adjust the allowance account to its correct balance at December 31, 20X1.

DE8-10 Buchwald, Inc.'s experience indicates that Buchwald will fail to collect 3% of net credit sales, which totaled $100,000 during the three-month period January through March of 20X3. During this period Buchwald wrote off $4,000 of accounts receivable as uncollectible. Record Buchwald's uncollectible-account expense for January through March under

Contrasting the allowance method and the direct write-off method of accounting for uncollectibles
(Obj. 2, 3)

a. The allowance method.
b. The direct write-off method. You need not identify individual customer accounts.

Which method of accounting for uncollectibles is preferred? What makes this method better?

DE 8-11 Masahiro Oguchi is an attorney in San Francisco. Oguchi uses the direct write-off method to account for his uncollectible receivables.

Applying the direct write-off method to account for uncollectibles
(Obj. 3)

At May 31, Oguchi's accounts receivable were $8,000. During June, he earned service revenue of $60,000 and collected $62,000 from clients on account. He also wrote off uncollectible receivables of $500. What is Oguchi's balance of Accounts Receivable at June 30? Does he expect to collect all of this amount? Why or why not?

DE 8-12 Gas stations do a large volume of business by customer credit cards and bankcards. Suppose the **Shell** station near Lenox Square in Atlanta, Georgia, had these transactions on a busy Saturday in July:

Recording credit-card sales
(Obj. 3)

American Express credit-card sales	$6,000
VISA bankcard sales	8,000

Suppose **American Express** charges merchants 4% and **VISA** charges 2%. Record these sale transactions for the Shell station.

Identifying key items for a note receivable
(Obj. 4)

DE 8-13 Examine the promissory note in Exhibit 8-5, page 322. Answer these questions:

1. When does interest on the note start running? When does the interest stop running?
2. Who is the debtor? Who is the creditor?
3. Which party to the note has a note receivable? Which party has a note payable? Which party has interest revenue? Which party has interest expense?
4. When must Lauren Holland pay off the note?
5. How much interest must Holland pay on the maturity date of the note? How much cash must Holland pay in total at maturity?

Computing interest amounts on notes receivable
(Obj. 4)

DE 8-14 For each of the following notes receivable, compute the amount of interest revenue earned during 20X5. Use a 360-day year.

	Principal	Interest Rate	Interest Period	Maturity Date
Note 1	$ 10,000	9%	60 days	11/30/20X5
Note 2	50,000	10%	3 months	9/30/20X5
Note 3	100,000	8%	$1\frac{1}{2}$ years	12/31/20X6
Note 4	15,000	12%	90 days	1/15/20X6

Accounting for a note receivable
(Obj. 4)

DE 8-15 Deutsche Bank lent $400,000 to Jean Nowlin on a 90-day, 8% note. Record the following transactions for Deutsche Bank (explanations are not required):

a. Lending the money on June 12.
b. Collecting the principal and interest at maturity. Specify the date. For the computation of interest, use a 360-day year.

Accruing interest receivable and collecting a note receivable
(Obj. 4)

DE 8-16 Return to the promissory note in Exhibit 8-5, page 322. The accounting year of Continental Bank ends on December 31, 20X2. Journalize Continental Bank's (a) lending money on the note receivable at September 30, 20X2, (b) accrual of interest at December 31, 20X2, and (c) collection of principal and interest at September 30, 20X3, the maturity date of the note. Carry amounts to the nearest cent.

Reporting receivables amounts
(Obj. 5)

DE 8-17 Using your answers to Daily Exercise 8–16 for Continental Bank, and carrying amounts to the nearest cent, show how the bank will report

a. Note receivable and interest receivable on the bank's classified balance sheet at December 31, 20X2.
b. Whatever needs to be reported on the bank's income statement for the year ended December 31, 20X2.
c. Whatever needs to be reported for the note and related interest on the bank's classified balance sheet at December 31, 20X3. You may ignore Cash.
d. Whatever needs to be reported on the bank's income statement for the year ended December 31, 20X3.

Reporting receivables
(Obj. 5)

DE 8-18 Examine the receivables for **Intel, General Electric,** and **Oracle** shown on page 325 and in Exhibit 8-6, page 326. Complete the table below to show the amounts (in millions of dollars) that each company will report on its balance sheet:

Company	Total Current Receivables	–	Allowance for Uncollectibles =	Net Realizable Value
Intel Corporation......................	$		$( )	$
General Electric........................				
Oracle Corporation(1999 only).				

At May 31, 1999, how much does Oracle expect to collect from its customers?

Reporting receivables and other accounts in the financial statements
(Obj. 5)

DE 8-19 ← *Link Back to Chapters 1–3 (Debit/Credit Balances; Income Statement).* **Sprint Corporation,** the telecommunications company, included the following items in its financial statements (adapted, in millions):

Unearned revenues...................	$ 200	Service revenue	$14,045
Allowance for doubtful		Other assets...........................	355
accounts................................	117	Cost of services sold and	
Cash	1,151	other expenses	12,861
Accounts receivable	2,581	Notes payable........................	3,281
Accounts payable	1,027		

1. How much net income did Sprint earn for the year?
2. Show how Sprint reported receivables on its classified balance sheet. Follow the reporting format shown in the middle of page 314.

DE 8-20 Vision Maker, a cable TV company, reported the following items at February 28, 20X0 (amounts in millions, with last-year's 19X9 amounts also given as needed):

Using the acid-test ratio and days' sales in receivables to evaluate an actual company (Obj. 6)

Accounts payable.........................	$369	Accounts receivable:	
Cash..	215	February 28, 20X0	$ 235
Allowance for uncollectible		February 29, 19X9	160
accounts:		Cost of goods sold	575
February 28, 20X0	15	Short-term investments.............	165
February 29, 19X9	7	Other current assets..................	93
Inventories:		Other current liabilities.............	145
February 28, 20X0	198	Net sales revenue......................	1,406
February 29, 19X9	161	Long-term assets.......................	416
Long-term liabilities.....................	11		

Compute Vision Maker's (a) acid-test ratio and (b) days' sales in average receivables for 20X0. Evaluate each ratio value as strong or weak. Assume Vision Maker sells on terms of net 45.

DE 8-21 ↞ *Link Back to Chapter 4 (Current Ratio and Debt Ratio) and Chapter 5 (Gross Profit Percentage and Inventory Turnover).* Using the data in Daily Exercise 8-20, compute for Vision Maker the following ratios for 20X0:

Computing key ratios for an actual company (Obj. 6)

   a. Current ratio   **c.** Gross profit percentage
   b. Debt ratio   **d.** Rate of inventory turnove

EXERCISES

E8-1 As a recent college graduate, you land your first job in the customer collections department of Sun Systems. Karla Bates, one of the owners, has asked you to propose a system to ensure that cash received by mail from customers is handled properly. Draft a short memorandum identifying the essential element in your plan, and state why it is important.

Controlling cash receipts from customers (Obj. 1)

Refer to Chapter 7 if necessary. Use this format for your memo:

Date:	_____
To:	Karla Bates
From:	Your Name
RE:	Essential element of internal control over customer collections

E8-2 ↞ *Link Back to Chapter 7 (Internal Control Over Cash Receipts).* Suppose **Carnation,** the instant breakfast company, is opening an office in Chicago. Timothy Mayborne, the office manager, is designing the internal control system. Mayborne proposes the following procedures for credit checks on new customers, sales on account, cash collections, and write-offs of uncollectible receivables:

Identifying and correcting an internal control weakness (Obj. 1)

- The credit department will run a credit check on all customers who apply for credit.
- Sales on account are the responsibility of the Carnation salespersons. Credit sales above a reasonable limit require the approval of the credit manager.
- Cash receipts come into the credit department, which separates the cash received from the customer remittance slips. The credit department lists all cash receipts by customer name and amount of cash received. The cash goes to the treasurer for deposit in the bank. The remittance slips go to the accounting department for posting to customer accounts. Each day's listing of cash receipts goes to the controller for comparison with the daily deposit slip and the day's listing of the total dollar amount posted to customer accounts. The three amounts must agree.

Identify the internal control weakness in this situation, and propose a way to correct it.

E8-3 On September 30, Ageless Technology had a $28,000 debit balance in Accounts Receivable. During October, the company had sales of $187,000, which included $120,000 in credit sales. October collections were $91,000. Other data include

Using the allowance method for bad debts (Obj. 2, 5)

- September 30 credit balance in Allowance for Uncollectible Accounts, $1,600.
- Uncollectible-account expense, estimated as 2% of credit sales.
- Write-offs of uncollectible receivables totaled $1,070.

Required

1. Prepare journal entries to record sales, collections, uncollectible-account expense by the allowance method (percent-of-sales method), and write-offs of uncollectibles during October.
2. Show the ending balances in Accounts Receivable, Allowance for Uncollectible Accounts, and *net* accounts receivable at October 31. How much does Ageless expect to collect?
3. Show how Ageless will report Accounts Receivable on its October 31 balance sheet. Use the format illustrated for Intel on page 325.

Using the direct write-off method for bad debts
(Obj. 3)

E8-4 Refer to Exercise 8-3.

Required

1. Record uncollectible-account expense for October using the direct write-off method.
2. What amount of accounts receivable would Ageless report on its October 31 balance sheet under the direct write-off method? Does Ageless expect to collect the full amount?

Using the aging method to estimate bad debts
(Obj. 2, 5)

E8-5 At December 31, 20X4, the accounts receivable balance of Quest Corp. is $300,000. The Allowance for Doubtful Accounts has a $3,910 credit balance. Accountants for Quest prepare the following aging schedule for its accounts receivable:

	Total Balance	Age of Accounts			
		1–30 Days	31–60 Days	61–90 Days	Over 90 Days
$300,000.............................		$140,000	$78,000	$69,000	$13,000
Estimated percent uncollectible...................		0.3%	1.2%	6.0%	50%

Required

1. Journalize the adjusting entry for doubtful accounts on the basis of the aging schedule. Show the T-account for the Allowance.
2. Show how Quest Corp. will report Accounts Receivable on its December 31 balance sheet.

Reporting bad debts by the allowance method
(Obj. 2, 5)

E8-6 At December 31, 20X2, Circuit Software has an accounts receivable balance of $137,000. Sales revenue for 20X2 is $950,000, including credit sales of $450,000. For each of the following situations, prepare the year-end adjusting entry to record uncollectible-account expense. Show how the accounts receivable and the allowance for uncollectible accounts are reported on the balance sheet. Use the reporting format illustrated for Intel on page 325.

a. Allowance for Uncollectible Accounts has a credit balance of $1,600 before adjustment. Circuit estimates that uncollectible-account expense for the year is 1/2 of 1% of credit sales.
b. Allowance for Uncollectible Accounts has a debit balance of $1,700 before adjustment. Circuit estimates that $2,600 of the accounts receivable will prove uncollectible.

Computing notes receivable amounts
(Obj. 4)

E8-7 On April 30, 20X7, First National Bank of Kansas City lent $1,000,000 to Marjorie Redwine on a two-year, 9% note.

Required

1. Compute the interest during 20X7, 20X8, and 20X9 for the Redwine note receivable.
2. Which party has a
   a. Note receivable?   c. Interest revenue?
   b. Note payable?   d. Interest expense?
3. How much in total would Redwine pay First National Bank if she paid off the note early—say, on November 30, 20X7?

Recording notes receivable and accruing interest revenue
(Obj. 4)

E8-8 Record the following transactions in the journal of Glacial Enterprises, Inc.:

Nov. 1 Loaned $50,000 cash to Victor Rashad on a one-year, 8% note.
Dec. 3 Sold goods to Lendox Corp., receiving a 90-day, 11% note for $3,750.
     16 Received a $4,000, six-month, 12% note on account from CFO Co.
     31 Accrued interest revenue on all notes receivable. Use a 360-day year for interest computations.

Recording bankcard sales and a note receivable, and accruing interest revenue
(Obj. 4)

E8-9 Record the following transactions in Wachovia Company's journal:

20X3
Feb. 12 Recorded VISA bankcard sales of $55,000, less a 2% discount.
Apr. 1 Loaned $8,000 to Peter Liu on a one-year, 12% note.
Dec. 31 Accrued interest revenue on the Liu note.

20X4
Apr. 1 Collected the maturity value of the note from Liu.

E8-10 Horizon Energy Corp. sells on account. When a customer account becomes two months old, Horizon converts the account to a note receivable. During 20X2, Horizon completed these transactions:

Aug. 29 Sold goods on account to M. Tallus, $5,400.
Nov. 1 Received a $5,400, 60-day, 10% note from M. Tallus in satisfaction of his past-due account receivable.
Dec. 31 Collected the Tallus note at maturity.

Required

Record the transactions in Horizon Energy's journal.

E8-11 Bernstein Bros., a clothing store, reported the following amounts in its 20X3 financial statements. The 20X2 figures are given for comparison.

		20X3		20X2
Current assets:				
Cash		$ 3,000		$ 10,000
Short-term investments		23,000		11,000
Accounts receivable	$80,000		$74,000	
Less: Allowance for uncollectibles	(7,000)	73,000	(6,000)	68,000
Inventory		192,000		189,000
Prepaid insurance		2,000		2,000
Total current assets		293,000		280,000
Total current liabilities		$124,000		$127,000
Net sales		$703,000		$732,000

Required

1. Determine whether Bernstein's acid-test ratio improved or deteriorated from 20X2 to 20X3. How does Bernstein's acid-test ratio compare with the industry average of 0.80?
2. Compare the days' sales in receivables for 20X3 with Bernstein's credit terms of net 30.

E8-12 **Wal-Mart Stores, Inc.,** is the largest retailer in the United States. Recently, Wal-Mart reported these figures (in billions of dollars):

	1999	1998
Net sales	$165	$138
Receivables at end of year	1	1

The Wal-Mart financial statements include no uncollectible-account expense or allowance.

Required

1. Compute Wal-Mart's average collection period on receivables during 1999.
2. Why are Wal-Mart's receivables so low? How can Wal-Mart have $1 billion of receivables at January 31, 1999, and no significant allowance for uncollectibles?

Challenge Exercise

E8-13 Slazenger Sporting Equipment sells on store credit and manages its own receivables. Average experience each year for the past three years has been as follows:

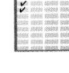

	Total
Sales	$350,000
Cost of goods sold	210,000
Uncollectible-account expense	4,000
Other expenses	61,000

Bruce Slazenger, the owner, is considering whether to accept bankcards (**VISA, MasterCard**). Typically, accepting bankcards increases total sales and cost of goods sold by 12%. But VISA and MasterCard charge approximately 2% of bankcard sales. If Slazenger switches to bankcards, he can save $2,000 on accounting and other expenses. After the switchover to bankcards, Slazenger expects cash sales of $200,000.

Required

Should Slazenger start accepting bankcards? Show the computations of net income under the present plan and under the bankcard plan.

Controlling cash receipts from customers
(Obj. 1)

P8-1A Newcastle Sporting Goods distributes merchandise to sporting goods stores. All sales are on credit, so virtually all cash receipts arrive in the mail. William Borrows, the company president, has just returned from a meeting with new ideas for the business. Among other things, Borrows plans to institute stronger internal controls over cash receipts from customers.

Required

Assume you are William Borrows. Write a memo to employees outlining a set of procedures to ensure that all cash receipts are deposited in the bank and that the total amounts of each day's cash receipts are posted as credits to customer accounts receivable. Use the memorandum format given in Exercise 8-1, page 333.

Accounting for uncollectibles by the direct write-off and allowance methods
(Obj. 2, 3, 5)

P8-2A On February 28, Signa, Inc., had a $75,000 debit balance in Accounts Receivable. During March, Signa made sales of $445,000, all on credit. Other data for March include

- Collections on account, $422,600.
- Write-offs of uncollectible receivables, $3,500.

Required

1. Record sales and collections on account. Then record uncollectible-account expense for March using the *direct write-off* method. Post to Accounts Receivable and Uncollectible-Account Expense and show their balances at March 31.
2. Record sales and collections on account. Then record uncollectible-account expense and write-offs of customer accounts for March using the *allowance* method. Show all March activity in Accounts Receivable, Allowance for Uncollectible Accounts, and Uncollectible-Account Expense (post to these T-accounts). The February 28 unadjusted balance in Allowance for Uncollectible Accounts was $800 (debit). Uncollectible-account expense was estimated at 2% of credit sales.
3. What amount of uncollectible-account expense would Signa, Inc., report on its March income statement under the two methods? Which amount better matches expense with revenue? Give your reason.
4. What amount of *net* accounts receivable would Signa, Inc., report on its March 31 balance sheet under the two methods? Which amount is more realistic? Give your reason.

Using the percent-of-sales and aging methods for uncollectibles
(Obj. 2, 5)

P8-3A The June 30, 20X4, balance sheet of Delforce Associates, Inc., reports the following:

Accounts Receivable	$265,000
Allowance for Uncollectible Accounts (credit balance)	7,100

At the end of each quarter, Delforce estimates uncollectible-account expense to be 2% of credit sales. At the end of the year, the company ages its accounts receivable and adjusts the balance in Allowance for Uncollectible Accounts to correspond to the aging schedule. During the second half of 20X4, Delforce completed the following transactions:

July	14	Made a compound entry to write off the following uncollectible accounts: T. J. Dooley, $766; Design Works, Inc., $2,413; and S. DeWitt, $134.
Sep.	30	Recorded uncollectible-account expense equal to 2% of credit sales of $141,400.
Nov.	22	Wrote off the following accounts receivable as uncollectible: Transnet Corp., $1,345; Webvan, Inc., $2,109; and The Avenue Group, $755.
Dec.	31	Recorded uncollectible-account expense based on the aging of accounts receivable.

		Age of Accounts			
	Total Balance	1–30 Days	31–60 Days	61–90 Days	Over 90 Days
	$256,600	$121,500	$86,000	$34,000	$15,100
Estimated percent uncollectible		0.2%	0.5%	4.0%	50.0%

Required

1. Record the transactions in the journal.
2. Open the Allowance for Uncollectible Accounts, and post entries affecting that account. Keep a running balance.
3. Most companies report two-year comparative financial statements. If Delforce's Accounts Receivable balance was $271,400 and the Allowance for Uncollectible Accounts stood at

$8,240 at December 31, 20X3, show how the company will report its accounts receivable in a comparative balance sheet for 20X4 and 20X3.

P8-4A ← *Link Back to Chapter 4 (Closing Entries).* Minnetonk Enterprises completed the following selected transactions during 20X1 and 20X2:

Using the percent-of-sales method for uncollectibles (Obj. 2, 5)

20X1
Dec. 31   Estimated that uncollectible-account expense for the year was 2/3 of 1% on credit sales of $450,000, and recorded that amount as expense.
     31   Made the closing entry for uncollectible-account expense.

20X2
Feb. 4   Sold inventory to Sam Vesper, $1,521, on credit terms of 2/10 n/30. Ignore cost of goods sold.
July 1   Wrote off Sam Vesper's account as uncollectible after repeated efforts to collect from him.
Oct. 19   Received $521 from Sam Vesper, along with a letter stating his intention to pay his debt in full within 30 days. Reinstated his account in full.
Nov. 15   Received the balance due from Sam Vesper.
Dec. 31   Made a compound entry to write off the following accounts as uncollectible: Kaycee Britt, $899; Tim Sands, $530; and Anna Chin, $1,272.
     31   Estimated that uncollectible-account expense for the year was 2/3 of 1% on credit sales of $585,000 and recorded the expense.
     31   Made the closing entry for uncollectible-account expense.

Required
1. Open general ledger accounts for Allowance for Uncollectible Accounts and Uncollectible-Account Expense. Keep running balances.
2. Record the transactions in the general journal, and post to the two ledger accounts.
3. The December 31, 20X2, balance of Accounts Receivable is $164,500. Show how Accounts Receivable would be reported on the balance sheet at that date.

P8-5A Windows Company received the following notes during 20X3.

Accounting for notes receivable, including accruing interest revenue (Obj. 4)

Note	Date	Principal Amount	Interest Rate	Term
(1)	Oct. 31	$11,000	12%	3 months
(2)	Nov. 19	15,000	10%	60 days
(3)	Dec. 1	12,000	9%	1 year

Required
Identify each note by number, compute interest using a 360-day year for those notes with terms specified in days or years, round all interest amounts to the nearest dollar, and present entries in general journal form. Explanations are not required.

1. Determine the due date and maturity value of each note.
2. Journalize a single adjusting entry at December 31, 20X3, to record accrued interest revenue on all three notes.
3. Journalize the collection of principal and interest on note (1).

P8-6A ← *Link Back to Chapter 4 (Closing Entries).* Record the following selected transactions in the general journal of Recognition Systems. Explanations are not required.

Accounting for notes receivable, dishonored notes, and accrued interest revenue (Obj. 4)

20X2
Dec. 21   Received a $2,800, 30-day, 10% note on account from Lindsey Fitzhugh.
     31   Made an adjusting entry to accrue interest on the Fitzhugh note.
     31   Made a closing entry for interest revenue.

20X3
Jan. 20   Collected the maturity value of the Fitzhugh note.
Sept. 14 Loaned $4,000 cash to Bullseye Investors, receiving a three-month, 13% note.
      30 Received a $1,675, 60-day, 16% note from Chuck Powers on his past-due account receivable.
Nov. 29   Chuck Powers dishonored his note at maturity; wrote off the note as uncollectible, debiting Allowance for Uncollectible Accounts.
Dec. 14   Collected the maturity value of the Bullseye Investors note.

P8-7A Assume that **Sherwin Williams,** the paint manufacturer, completed the following selected transactions:

Journalizing uncollectibles, notes receivable, and accrued interest revenue (Obj. 4)

20X1

Dec. 1 Sold goods to Kelly Paint Supply, receiving a $13,500, three-month, 10% note. Ignore cost of goods sold.

31 Made an adjusting entry to accrue interest on the Kelly note. Round the interest amount to the nearest dollar.

31 Made an adjusting entry to record uncollectible-account expense based on an aging of accounts receivable. The aging analysis indicates that $355,800 of accounts receivable will not be collected. Prior to this adjustment, the credit balance in Allowance for Uncollectible Accounts is $346,100.

20X2

Mar. 1 Collected the maturity value of the Kelly Paint Supply note.

July 21 Sold merchandise to Mellon Co., receiving a 60-day, 9% note for $4,000. Ignore cost of goods sold.

Sep. 19 Mellon Co. dishonored its note (failed to pay) at maturity; we converted the maturity value of the note to an account receivable.

Nov. 11 Loaned $40,000 cash to Thermo Control, Inc., receiving a 90-day, 9% note.

Dec. 2 Collected in full from Mellon Co.

31 Accrued the interest on the Thermo Control note.

Required

Record the transactions in the journal of Sherwin Williams. Explanations are not required.

Using ratio data to evaluate a company's financial position (Obj. 6)

P8-8A *Link Back to Chapter 4 (Current Ratio).* The comparative financial statements of Grapevine Securities for 20X3, 20X2, and 20X1 include the data shown here:

	(In millions)		
	20X3	**20X2**	**20X1**
Balance sheet			
Current assets:			
Cash	$ 27	$ 26	$ 22
Short-term investments...	93	101	69
Receivables, net of allowance for doubtful			
accounts of $7, $6, and $4, respectively	146	154	127
Inventories...	454	383	341
Prepaid expenses	32	31	25
Total current assets...	752	695	584
Total current liabilities	$ 440	$ 446	$ 388
Income statement			
Sales revenue	$2,671	$2,505	$1,944
Cost of sales..	1,380	1,360	963

Required

1. Compute these ratios for 20X3 and 20X2:
   a. Current ratio   **b.** Acid-test ratio   **c.** Days' sales in receivables
2. Write a memo explaining to top management which ratios improved from 20X2 to 20X3 and which ratios deteriorated. Which item in the financial statements caused some ratios to improve and others to deteriorate? Discuss whether this factor conveys a favorable or an unfavorable sign about the company.

(Group B) PROBLEMS

Controlling cash receipts from customers (Obj. 1)

P8-1B Molson Appliance Co., prepares crowns, dentures, and other dental appliances. All work is performed on account, with regular monthly billing to participating dentists. Eve Nations, accountant for Molson, opens the mail. Company procedure requires her to separate customer checks from the remittance slips, which list the amounts she posts as credits to customer accounts receivable. Nations deposits the checks in the bank. She computes each day's total amount posted to customer accounts and matches this total to the bank deposit slip. This procedure is intended to ensure that all receipts are deposited in the bank.

Required

As a consultant hired by Molson Appliance Co., write a memo to management evaluating the company's internal controls over cash receipts from customers. If the system is effective, identify its strong features. If the system has flaws, propose a way to strengthen the controls. Use the memorandum format given in Exercise 8-1, page 333.

P8-2B On May 31, Nortell Networks, had a $210,000 debit balance in Accounts Receivable. During June, Nortell made sales of $640,000, all on credit. Other data for June include

Accounting for uncollectibles by the direct write-off and allowance methods
(Obj. 2, 3, 5)

- Collections on account, $567,400.
- Write-offs of uncollectible receivables, $8,900.

Required

1. Record sales and collections on account. Then record uncollectible-account expense for June using the *direct write-off* method. Post to Accounts Receivable and Uncollectible-Account Expense and show their balances at June 30.
2. Record sales and collections on account. Then record uncollectible-account expense and write-offs of customer accounts for June using the *allowance* method. Show all June activity in Accounts Receivable, Allowance for Uncollectible Accounts, and Uncollectible-Account Expense (post to these T-accounts). The May 31 unadjusted balance in Allowance for Uncollectible Accounts was $2,800 (credit). Uncollectible-account expense was estimated at 2% of credit sales.
3. What amount of uncollectible-account expense would Nortell report on its June income statement under the two methods? Which amount better matches expense with revenue? Give your reason.
4. What amount of *net* accounts receivable would Nortell report on its June 30 balance sheet under the two methods? Which amount is more realistic? Give your reason.

P8-3B The June 30, 20X1, balance sheet of Clarus Consultants, Inc., reports the following:

Using the percent-of-sales and aging methods for uncollectibles
(Obj. 2, 5)

Accounts Receivable	$143,000
Allowance for Uncollectible Accounts (credit balance)	3,200

At the end of each quarter, Clarus estimates uncollectible-account expense to be 1 1/2% of credit sales. At the end of the year, the company ages its accounts receivable and adjusts the balance in Allowance for Uncollectible Accounts to correspond to the aging schedule. During the second half of 20X1, Clarus completed the following selected transactions:

Aug.	9	Made a compound entry to write off the following uncollectible accounts: Aguilar, Inc., $235; Seaton Co., $188; and T. Taylor, $706.
Sep.	30	Recorded uncollectible-account expense equal to $1\frac{1}{2}$% of credit sales of $140,000.
Oct.	18	Wrote off as uncollectible the $767 account receivable from Lintz Co. and the $430 account receivable from Navisor Corp.
Dec.	31	Recorded uncollectible-account expense based on the aging of accounts receivable.

	Age of Accounts			
Total Balance	1–30 Days	31–60 Days	61–90 Days	Over 90 Days
$136,500	$81,700	$31,100	$14,000	$9,700
Estimated percent uncollectible	0.1%	0.4%	5.0%	30.0%

Required

1. Record the transactions in the journal. Round all amounts to the nearest dollar.
2. Open the Allowance for Uncollectible Accounts, and post entries affecting that account. Keep a running balance.
3. Most companies report two-year comparative financial statements. If Clarus's Accounts Receivable balance was $118,000 and the Allowance for Uncollectible Accounts stood at $2,700 at December 31, 20X0 show how the company will report its accounts receivable on a comparative balance sheet for 20X1 and 20X0.

P8-4B ← *Link Back to Chapter 4 (Closing Entries)*. Interbiz Interactive completed the following transactions during 20X1 and 20X2:

Using the percent-of-sales method for uncollectibles
(Obj. 2, 5)

20X1

Dec.	31	Estimated that uncollectible-account expense for the year was 3/4 of 1% on credit sales of $290,000, and recorded that amount as expense.
	31	Made the closing entry for uncollectible-account expense.

20X2

Jan. 17 Sold inventory to Mitch Vanez, $652, on credit terms of 2/10 n/30. Ignore cost of goods sold.

June 29 Wrote off the Mitch Vanez account as uncollectible after repeated efforts to collect from him.

Aug. 6 Received $250 from Mitch Vanez, along with a letter stating his intention to pay his debt in full within 30 days. Reinstated his account in full.

Sept. 4 Received the balance due from Mitch Vanez.

Dec. 31 Made a compound entry to write off the following accounts as uncollectible: Bernard Klaus, $737; Marie Monet, $348; and Terry Fuhrman, $622.

31 Estimated that uncollectible-account expense for the year was 2/3 of 1% on credit sales of $400,000, and recorded that amount as expense. Round to the nearest dollar.

31 Made the closing entry for uncollectible-account expense.

Required

1. Open general ledger accounts for Allowance for Uncollectible Accounts and Uncollectible-Account Expense. Keep running balances.
2. Record the transactions in the general journal, and post to the two ledger accounts.
3. The December 31, 20X2, balance of Accounts Receivable is $139,000. Show how Accounts Receivable would be reported on the balance sheet at that date.

Accounting for notes receivable, including accruing interest revenue (Obj. 4)

P8-5B Mindgames Company received the following notes during 20X3.

Note	Date	Principal Amount	Interest Rate	Term
(1)	Nov. 30	$12,000	12%	6 months
(2)	Dec. 7	9,000	10%	30 days
(3)	Dec. 23	13,000	9%	1 year

Required

Identify each note by number, compute interest using a 360-day year for those notes with terms specified in days or years, round all interest amounts to the nearest dollar, and present entries in general journal form. Explanations are not required.

1. Determine the due date and maturity value of each note.
2. Journalize a single adjusting entry at December 31, 20X3, to record accrued interest revenue on all three notes.
3. Journalize the collection of principal and interest on note (2).

Accounting for notes receivable, dishonored notes, and accrued interest revenue (Obj. 4)

P8-6B ◄ *Link Back to Chapter 4 (Closing Entries).* Record the following selected transactions in the general journal of SAS Services. Explanations are not required.

20X4

Dec. 19 Received a $3,000, 60-day, 12% note on account from Arnold Cohen.
31 Made an adjusting entry to accrue interest on the Cohen note.
31 Made a closing entry for interest revenue.

20X5

Feb. 17 Collected the maturity value of the Cohen note.

June 1 Loaned $8,000 cash to Blues Brothers, receiving a 6-month, 11% note.

Oct. 31 Received a $1,500, 60-day, 12% note from Juan Juarez on his past-due account receivable.

Dec. 1 Collected the maturity value of the Blues Brothers note.
30 Juan Juarez dishonored his note at maturity; wrote off the note receivable as uncollectible, debiting Allowance for Uncollectible Accounts.

Journalizing uncollectibles, notes receivable, and accrued interest revenue (Obj. 4)

P8-7B Assume that **Del Monte Foods,** famous for fruits and vegetables, completed the following selected transactions:

20X1

Nov. 1 Sold goods to **Kroger,** receiving a $20,000, three-month, 8% note. Ignore cost of goods sold.

Dec. 31 Made an adjusting entry to accrue interest on the Kroger note. Round to the nearest dollar.

31 Made an adjusting entry to record uncollectible-account expense based on an aging of accounts receivable. The aging analysis indicates that $197,400 of accounts receivable will not be collected. Prior to this adjustment, the credit balance in Allowance for Uncollectible Accounts is $189,900.

20X2

Feb. 1	Collected the maturity value of the Kroger note.
June 23	Sold merchandise to Artesian Corp., receiving a 60-day, 10% note for $9,000. Ignore cost of goods sold.
Aug. 22	Artesian Corp. dishonored (failed to pay) its note at maturity; we converted the maturity value of the note to an account receivable.
Nov. 16	Loaned $6,800 cash to Crane, Inc., receiving a 90-day, 12% note.
Dec. 5	Collected in full from Artesian Corp.
31	Accrued the interest on the Crane, Inc., note.

Required

Record the transactions in the journal of Del Monte Foods. Explanations are not required.

P8-8B ←⊆ *Link Back to Chapter 4 (Current Ratio).* The comparative financial statements of American Dataset, for 20X3, 20X2, and 20X1 include the following selected data:

Using ratio data to evaluate a company's financial position (Obj. 6)

	(In millions)		
	20X3	**20X2**	**20X1**
Balance sheet			
Current assets:			
Cash	$ 82	$ 80	$ 60
Short-term investments	140	174	122
Receivables, net of allowance for doubtful accounts of $6, $6, and $5, respectively	257	265	218
Inventories	429	341	302
Prepaid expenses	21	27	46
Total current assets	929	887	748
Total current liabilities	$ 503	$ 528	$ 413
Income statement			
Sales revenue	$5,189	$4,995	$4,206
Cost of sales	2,734	2,636	2,418

Required

1. Compute these ratios for 20X3 and 20X2:
   a. Current ratio   **b.** Acid-test ratio   **c.** Days' sales in receivables
2. Write a memo explaining to top management which ratios improved from 20X2 to 20X3 and which ratios deteriorated. Which item in the financial statements caused some ratios to improve and others to deteriorate? Discuss whether this factor conveys a favorable or an unfavorable impression about American Dataset.

APPLY YOUR KNOWLEDGE

DECISION CASES

Case 1. Deutschetek Corporation performs service either for cash or on notes receivable. The business uses the direct write-off method to account for bad debts. Hilda Lyth, the owner, has prepared the company's financial statements. The most recent comparative income statements, for 20X3 and 20X2, are as follows:

Uncollectible accounts and evaluating a business (Obj. 2, 3)

	20X3	20X2
Total revenue	$220,000	$195,000
Total expenses	107,000	103,000
Net income	$113,000	$ 92,000

On the basis of the increase in net income, Lyth wants to expand operations. She asks you to invest $50,000 in the business. You and Lyth have several meetings, at which you learn that notes receivable from customers were $200,000 at the end of 20X1 and $400,000 at the end of 20X2. Also, total revenues for 20X3 and 20X2 include interest at 13% on the year's beginning notes receivable balance. Total expenses include uncollectible-account expense of $2,000 each year, based on the direct write-off method. Lyth estimates that uncollectible-account expense would be 5% of sales revenue if the allowance method were used.

Required

1. Prepare for Deutschetek a comparative single-step income statement that identifies service revenue, interest revenue, uncollectible-account expense, and other expenses, all computed in accordance with generally accepted accounting principles.
2. Is Deutschetek's future as promising as Lyth's income statement makes it appear? Give the reason for your answer.

Computing receivables amounts to report on the balance sheet (Obj. 5)

Case 2. This case takes the statement of cash flows a step beyond the chapter's coverage of this topic. However, you should be able to apply the principles learned thus far to solve it. Treasure Point Jewelry's statement of cash flows reported the following for the year ended June 30, 20X1.

TREASURE POINT JEWELRY	
Statement of Cash Flows	
Year Ended June 30, 20X1	
Cash flows from operating activities:	
Collections from customers on account	$260,000
Cash flows from investing activities:	
Loaned out money on notes receivable	$ (45,000)
Collected on notes receivable............................	60,000

Treasure Point's balance sheet one year earlier—at June 30, 20X0—reported Accounts Receivable of $40,000 and Notes Receivable of $20,000. Credit sales for the year ended June 30, 20X1, totaled $310,000, and the company collects all of its accounts receivable because uncollectibles rarely occur.

Treasure Point Jewelry needs a loan and the owner is preparing Treasure Point's balance sheet at June 30, 20X1. To complete the balance sheet, the owner needs to know the balances of Accounts Receivable and Notes Receivable at June 30, 20X1. Supply the needed information; T-accounts are helpful.

ETHICAL ISSUE

QuiKash Finance Company is in the consumer loan business. It borrows from banks and loans out the money at higher interest rates. QuiKash's bank requires QuiKash to submit quarterly financial statements in order to keep its line of credit. QuiKash's main asset is Notes Receivable. Therefore, Uncollectible-Account Expense and Allowance for Uncollectible Accounts are important accounts.

Cameron Karr, the company's owner, wants net income to increase in a smooth pattern, rather than increase in some periods and decrease in others. To report smoothly increasing net income, Karr underestimates Uncollectible-Account Expense in some periods. In other periods, Karr overestimates the expense. He reasons that over time the income overstatements roughly offset the income understatements.

Required

Is QuiKash's practice of smoothing income ethical? Why or why not?

FINANCIAL STATEMENT CASE

Analyzing accounts receivable and uncollectibles (Obj. 2, 6)

Use the balance sheet and income statement of **Target Corporation,** in Appendix A.

1. How much did customers owe Target at January 29, 2000? Of this amount, how much did Target expect to collect? How much did Target expect *not* to collect? To answer these questions, refer to (a) Target's balance sheet (statement of financial position) and (b) the note entitled "Allowance for Doubtful Accounts" on page 22 of the Target Annual Report. *Retained securitized receivables* is Target's name for its accounts receivable.

2. During the year ended January 29, 2000, Target recorded doubtful-account expense of $147 million. The company also wrote off uncollectible receivables of $147 million. Prepare a T-account for Allowance for Doubtful Accounts. Insert the current year's beginning and ending balances as reported in the note. Then post the doubtful-account expense for the year and the write-offs for the year into the T-account. After your postings, the Allowance account should show all of Target's bad-debt activity for the current year.

3. Compute Target's acid-test ratio at January 29, 2000. If all the current liabilities came due immediately, could Target pay them?

TEAM PROJECT

Bob Opper and Denise Shapp worked for several years as sales representatives for **Xerox Corporation.** During this time, they became close friends as they acquired expertise with the company's full range of copier equipment. Now they see an opportunity to put their experience to work and fulfill lifelong desires to establish their own business. Lakeside College, located in their city, is expanding, and there is no copy center within five miles of the campus. Business in the area is booming—office buildings and apartments are springing up, and the population in this section of the city is growing.

Opper and Shapp want to open a copy center, similar to a **Kinko's,** near the campus. A small shopping center across the street from the college has a vacancy that would fit their needs. Opper and Shapp each have $20,000 to invest in the business, and they forecast the need for $30,000 to renovate the store. **Xerox Corporation** will lease two large copiers to them at a total monthly rental of $4,000. With enough cash to see them through the first six months of operation, they are confident they can make the business succeed. The two work very well together, and both have excellent credit ratings. Opper and Shapp must borrow $80,000 to start the business, advertise its opening, and keep it running for its first six months.

Assume the roles of Opper and Shapp, the partners who will own Lakeside Copy Center.

1. As a group, visit a copy center to familiarize yourselves with its operations. If possible, interview the manager or another employee. Then write a loan request that Opper and Shapp will submit to a bank with the intent of borrowing $80,000 to be paid back over three years. The loan will be a personal loan to the partnership of Opper and Shapp, not to Lakeside Copy Center. The request should specify all the details of Opper's and Shapp's plan that will motivate the bank to grant the loan. Include a budgeted income statement for the first six months of the copy center's operation.

2. As a group, interview a loan officer in a bank. Have the loan officer evaluate your loan request. Write a report, or make a presentation to your class—as directed by your instructor—to reveal the loan officer's decision.

INTERNET EXERCISE

As the baby boomers age, the demand for pharmaceuticals has increased. Over the past several years **Pfizer Inc.** helped introduce three record-breaking products: Lipitor, Viagra, and Celebrex. As a result, in 1999 Pfizer became the world's number one pharmaceutical company in prescription sales.

1. Go to **http://www.Pfizer.com.** Click on *Investing in Pfizer* and select the *most recent annual report.* Use the pull-down menu to select *Our Global Presence.* In how many countries does Pfizer sell its products?

2. Use the pull-down menu to select the *Consolidated Balance Sheet.*
   a. To account for the uncollectible receivables, does Pfizer use the allowance method or the direct write-off method? How can you tell?
   b. For the most recent year, how much do customers owe Pfizer? How much does Pfizer expect to collect? How much does Pfizer expect not to collect?

3. Use the pull-down menu to select the *Consolidated Statement of Income.*
   a. Which expense listed includes the amount for uncollectible-account expense? How do you think Pfizer estimates its uncollectible-account expense? Do you think Pfizer wrote off any uncollectible accounts this past year?
   b. For the most recent year, research and development (R&D) expenses are what percentage of total revenues? R&D costs are a major expense for pharmaceutical companies. Explain why this is true.

4. For the two most recent years calculate the acid-test ratio. Show your work for the ratio calculations. For the most recent year comment on what the ratio indicates. Is the trend increasing or decreasing? Favorable or unfavorable? Explain why.

5. For the two most recent years calculate one day's sales using the amount reported for net sales in the numerator. For the two most recent years calculate days' sales in receivables. Please show your work for the ratio calculations. For the most recent year comment on what the days' sales in receivables ratio indicates. Is the trend increasing or decreasing? Favorable or unfavorable? Explain why.

APPENDIX TO CHAPTER 8

DISCOUNTING A NOTE RECEIVABLE

A payee of a note receivable may need the cash before the maturity date of the note. When this occurs, the payee may sell the note, a practice called **discounting a note receivable.** The price to be received for the note is determined by present-value

DISCOUNTING NOTE RECEIVABLE.
Selling a note receivable
before its maturity date.

➤➤ We discuss these concepts in Chapter 15.

concepts. ◂◂ But the transaction between the seller and the buyer of the note can take any form agreeable to the two parties. Here we illustrate one procedure used for discounting short-term notes receivable. To receive cash immediately, the seller accepts a lower price than the note's maturity value.

To illustrate discounting a note receivable, suppose **General Electric** loaned $15,000 to Dorman Builders on October 20, 20X3. GE took a note receivable from Dorman. The maturity date of the 90-day 10% Dorman note is January 18, 20X4. Suppose GE discounts the Dorman note at First City Bank on December 9, 20X3, when the note is 50 days old. The bank applies a 12% annual interest rate to determine the discounted value of the note. The bank will use a discount rate that is higher than the note's interest rate in order to earn some interest on the transaction. The discounted value, called the *proceeds,* is the amount GE receives from the bank. The proceeds can be computed in five steps, as shown in Exhibit 8A-1. GE's entry to record discounting (selling) the note on December 9, 20X3, is:

Dec. 9, 20X3	Cash.. 15,170	
	Note Receivable—Dorman Builders	15,000
	Interest Revenue ($15,170 − $15,000)....	170
	Discounted a note receivable.	

EXHIBIT 8A-1
Discounting (Selling) a Note Receivable: GE Discounts the Dorman Builders Note

Step	Computation	
1. Compute the original amount of interest on the note receivable.	$15,000 × 0.10 × 90/360	= $375
2. Maturity value of the note = Principal + Interest	$15,000 + $375	= $15,375
3. Determine the period (number of days, months, or years) the *bank* will hold the note (the discount period).	Dec. 9, 19X3 to Jan. 18, 19X4	= 40 days
4. Compute the bank's discount on the note. This is the bank's interest revenue from holding the note.	$15,375 × 0.12 × 40/360	= $205
5. Seller's proceeds from discounting the note receivable = Maturity value of the note − Bank's discount on the note.	$15,375 − $205	= $15,170

The authors thank Doug Hamilton for suggesting this exhibit.

DAILY EXERCISE 8-1A

When the proceeds from discounting a note receivable are less than the principal amount of the note, the payee records a debit to Interest Expense for the amount of the difference. For example, GE could discount the note receivable for cash proceeds of $14,980. The entry to record this discounting transaction is

Dec. 9, 20X3	Cash 14,980	
	Interest Expense 20	
	Note Receivable—Dorman Builders	15,000
	Discounted a note receivable.	

CONTINGENT LIABILITIES ON DISCOUNTED NOTES RECEIVABLE

CONTINGENT LIABILITY. A potential liability that will become an actual liability only if a particular event does occur.

A **contingent liability** is a potential liability that will become an actual liability only if a particular event occurs. Discounting a note receivable creates a contingent liability for the endorser. If the maker of the note (Dorman, in our example) fails to pay at maturity, then the original payee (GE) must pay the bank the amount due.[1] If Dorman pays the bank, then GE can forget the note.

DAILY EXERCISE

Discounting notes receivable (Obj. 4)

DE 8A-1 General Telecom installs telephone systems and receives its pay in the form of notes receivable. General Telecom installed a system for the city of Durango, Colorado, receiv-

[1]The discounting agreement can be "without recourse." That means the seller of the note has no liability if the note is dishonored at maturity. In that case, there is no contingent liability.

ing a nine-month, 8%, $500,000 note receivable on May 31, 20X1. To obtain cash quickly, General Telecom discounted the note with Rocky Mountain Bank on June 30, 20X1. The bank charged a discount rate of 9%.

Compute General Telecom's cash proceeds from discounting the note. Follow the five-step procedure outlined in Exhibit 8A-1.

EXERCISES

E8A-1A ⤎ *Link Back to Chapter 5 (Recording a Sale).* Use your answers to Daily Exercise 8A-1 to journalize General Telecom's transactions as follows:

Accounting for a discounted note receivable
(Obj. 4)

May 31 Sold a telecommunications system, receiving a 9-month, 8%, $500,000 note from the city of Durango. General Telecom's cost of the system was $450,000.

June 30 Received cash for interest revenue for one month. Round to the nearest dollar.

30 Discounted the note to Rocky Mountain Bank at a discount rate of 9%.

E8A-2A Rider Systems, Inc., sells on account. When a customer account becomes three months old, Rider converts the account to a note receivable and immediately discounts the note to a bank. During 20X4, Rider completed these transactions:

Recording notes receivable, discounting a note, and reporting the contingent liability in a note
(Obj. 4)

Aug. 29 Sold goods on account to V. Moyer, $3,900.

Dec. 1 Received a $3,900, 60-day, 10% note from V. Moyer in satisfaction of his past-due account receivable.

1 Sold the Moyer note by discounting it to a bank for $3,600.

Required

Record the transactions in Rider Systems' journal.

PROBLEMS

P8A-1 A company received the following notes during 20X3. Notes (1), (2), and (3) were discounted on the dates and at the rates indicated.

Discounting notes receivable
(Obj. 4)

Note	Date	Principal Amount	Interest Rate	Term	Date Discounted	Discount Rate
(1)	July 12	$10,000	10%	3 months	Aug. 12	15%
(2)	Aug. 4	6,000	11%	90 days	Aug. 30	13%
(3)	Oct. 21	8,000	15%	60 days	Nov. 3	18%

Required

Identify each note by number, compute interest using a 360-day year for those notes with terms specified in days, round all interest amounts to the nearest dollar, and present entries in general journal form. Explanations are not required.

1. Determine the due date and maturity value of each note.
2. Determine the discount and proceeds from the sale (discounting) of each note.
3. Journalize the discounting of notes (1) and (2).

P8A-2 A company received the following notes during 20X5. Notes (1), (2), and (3) were discounted on the dates and at the rates indicated.

Discounting notes receivable
(Obj. 4)

Note	Date	Principal Amount	Interest Rate	Term	Date Discounted	Discount Rate
(1)	July 15	$6,000	10%	6 months	Oct. 15	12%
(2)	Aug. 19	9,000	12%	90 days	Aug. 30	15%
(3)	Sept. 1	8,000	15%	120 days	Nov. 2	20%

Required

Identify each note by number, compute interest using a 360-day year for those notes with terms specified in days, round all interest amounts to the nearest dollar, and present entries in general journal form. Explanations are not required.

1. Determine the due date and maturity value of each note.
2. Determine the discount and proceeds from the sale (discounting) of each note.
3. Journalize the discounting of notes (1) and (2).

Merchandise Inventory

9

LEARNING OBJECTIVES

After studying this chapter, you should be able to

1. Account for inventory by the perpetual and periodic systems

2. Apply inventory costing methods: specific unit cost, weighted-average cost, FIFO, and LIFO

3. Identify the income effects and the tax effects of the inventory costing methods

4. Apply the lower-of-cost-or-market rule to inventory

5. Determine the effects of inventory errors on cost of goods sold and net income

6. Estimate ending inventory by the gross profit method

Deckers Outdoor Corporation began when University of California at Santa Barbara student Doug Otto started making sandals. From a fledgling operation, Deckers has grown into an international company, with footwear brands Teva and Simple. The company also sells clothing lines Teva and Picante. (Teva is a play off the Hebrew word *Teh-vah* for *nature*.) Teva sandals were initially designed by a Grand Canyon river guide for river rafting. Their quality and stability touched off a small revolution in footwear.

Deckers Outdoor had sales of almost $110 million in 1999, and the company's assets totaled $73 million. As the company has grown, Doug Otto and Deckers have faced a number of accounting decisions. Which method should Deckers use to account for its inventory of sandals and clothing? How much inventory should the company purchase from suppliers? This chapter discusses how to account for and manage inventory—the asset that defines a merchandising business.

D eckers Outdoor is a **merchandising company.** This means that Deckers sells a product rather than a service. To a merchandiser, inventory is the lifeblood of the organization. Deckers' balance sheet in Exhibit 9-1 lists inventory of $18.1 million among its current assets.

A merchandiser's major expense is *cost of goods sold,* also called *cost of sales*. This is Deckers' cost of the sandals and clothing it sold. For Deckers and other merchandisers, cost of goods sold is greater than the sum of all the other expenses combined. Exhibit 9-1 shows that Deckers had cost of sales of $64.5 million during 1999.

MERCHANDISING COMPANY. A company that resells products bought from suppliers.

DECKERS OUTDOOR CORPORATION
Income Statement (partial, adapted)
Year Ended December 31, 1999

	Millions
Net sales	$109.6
Cost of goods sold	64.5
Gross profit	45.1
Total operating expenses (can be detailed)	42.2
Net income	$ 2.9

EXHIBIT 9-1
Financial Statements of
Deckers Outdoor Corporation,
Maker of Teva Sandals

DECKERS OUTDOOR CORPORATION
Balance Sheet (Current assets only)
December 31, 1999

Assets	Millions
Current assets:	
Cash	$ 1.6
Trade accounts receivable,	
Less Allowance of $1.8	24.4
Inventories	18.1
Prepaid expenses	4.9
Total current assets	$49.0

We begin this chapter with the basic concept of accounting for inventories. Then we examine different inventory systems (perpetual and periodic), the different inventory methods (FIFO, LIFO, and average), and several related topics.

ACCOUNTING FOR INVENTORY AND INVENTORY SYSTEMS

Basic Concepts

The basic concept of accounting for inventory is straightforward. Suppose **Deckers Outdoor Corporation** buys three pairs of sandals for $30 each, marks them up by $20, and sells two of the pairs for $50 each. Deckers' balance sheet reports the inventory that the company still holds, and the income statement reports cost of goods sold for the units sold, as follows (focus on the highlights):

Balance Sheet (partial)		Income Statement (partial)	
Current assets:	$XXX	Sales revenue	
Cash	XXX	(2 pairs @ $50)........................	$100
Accounts receivable	XXX	Cost of goods sold	
Inventory (1 pair @ $30)	30	(2 pairs @ $30)........................	60
Prepaid expenses	XXX	Gross profit	$ 40

GROSS PROFIT OR GROSS MARGIN.
Excess of sales revenue over cost of goods sold.

 DAILY EXERCISE 9-1

Objective 1
Account for inventory by the perpetual and periodic systems

➤ We described these methods in Chapter 5.

PERIODIC INVENTORY SYSTEM. An inventory accounting system in which the business does not keep a continuous record of the inventory on hand. Instead, at the end of the period, the business counts the inventory on hand and uses this information to prepare the financial statements.

PERPETUAL INVENTORY SYSTEM. An inventory accounting system in which the business keeps a running record to show the inventory on hand at all times.

As we saw in Chapter 5, **gross profit,** also called **gross margin,** is the excess of sales revenue over cost of goods sold. It is called *gross* profit because operating expenses have not yet been subtracted. Gross profit minus all the operating expenses then equals *net* income. In practice, accounting for inventory is more complex than our simple example.

There are two main types of inventory accounting systems: the periodic system and the perpetual system. ◄ The **periodic inventory system** is used by businesses that sell relatively inexpensive goods. Many small businesses use the periodic system. Stores without optical-scanning cash registers do not keep a running record of every loaf of bread and every six-pack of drinks they sell. Instead, these stores count their inventory periodically—at least once a year—to determine the quantities on hand and prepare the financial statements.

Under the **perpetual inventory system,** the business maintains a running record of inventory on hand, usually on computer. This system achieves control over goods such as automobiles, jewelry, and furniture. The loss of one item would be significant and this justifies the cost of a perpetual system. Because computers are costing less and less, many small businesses now use perpetual inventory systems.

Under both systems, the business still counts its inventory annually. The physical count establishes the amount of ending inventory and serves as a check on the records. The following chart compares the periodic and perpetual systems:

Periodic Inventory System	Perpetual Inventory System
• Does not keep a running record of inventory	• Keeps a running record of all goods
• Used for inexpensive goods	• Used for all types of goods
• Inventory counted at least once a year	• Inventory counted at least once a year

Perpetual Inventory System

Perpetual inventory records can be a computer printout like the Deckers' record shown for a line of Teva sandals in Exhibit 9-2. The quantities of goods on hand are updated daily, as inventory transactions occur. Many companies keep their perpetual records in terms of quantities only, as shown in the exhibit. When a customer orders 10 pairs of sandals, Deckers can refer to its perpetual inventory record.

In the perpetual system, the business records purchases of inventory by debiting the Inventory account. When the business makes a sale, two entries are needed: one to record the sale and the other to record the decrease in inventory on hand.

Exhibit 9-3 illustrates the accounting in a perpetual system for a single line of Teva sandals at Deckers Outdoor. Panel A gives the journal entries and the

Item: Teva Sandals			
Date	Quantity Received	Quantity Sold	Quantity on Hand
Nov. 1			10
5		6	4
7	25		29
12		13	16
26	25		41
30		21	20
Totals	50	40	20

T-accounts, and Panel B shows the resulting income statement and balance sheet. All amounts are assumed.

 DAILY EXERCISE 9-2

DAILY EXERCISE 9-3

EXHIBIT 9-3   Recording and Reporting Inventory Transactions of Deckers Outdoor—Perpetual System (amounts assumed)

PANEL A—Recording in the Journal and Posting to the T-accounts—Perpetual System

INVENTORY AND COST OF GOODS SOLD ACCOUNTS

1. Credit purchases of $560,000:
   Inventory 560,000
      Accounts Payable............. 560,000
2. Credit sales of $900,000 (cost $540,000):
   Accounts Receivable 900,000
      Sales Revenue................... 900,000

   Cost of Goods Sold 540,000
      Inventory......................... 540,000
3. End-of-period entries:
   None required. Both Inventory and Cost of Goods Sold are up to date.

INVENTORY		COST OF GOODS SOLD
100,000*	540,000	540,000
560,000		
120,000		

* Beginning inventory was $100,000.

PANEL B—Reporting in the Financial Statements

Income Statement (partial)

Sales revenue	$ 900,000
Cost of goods sold...........................	540,000
Gross profit.....................................	$ 360,000

Balance Sheet (partial)

Current assets:		
Cash	$	XXX
Short-term investments		XXX
Accounts receivable		XXX
Inventories...................................		120,000
Prepaid expenses.........................		XXX

In Exhibit 9-3, Panel A, the first entry to Inventory summarizes a lot of detail. The cost of the inventory, $560,000, is the *net* amount of the purchases, determined as follows (using assumed amounts):

Net Purchases	
Purchase price of the inventory (including freight in)	$600,000
− Purchase returns for unsuitable goods returned to the seller	(25,000)
− Purchase allowances granted by the seller	(5,000)
− Purchase discounts taken for early payment.............	(10,000)
= Net purchases of inventory.......................................	$560,000

Throughout the remainder of the book, we often refer to Net Purchases simply as Purchases, as in Exhibit 9-3.

The cost of the goods purchased by Deckers Outdoor during the year was $560,000. This is based on a general principle:

$$\text{The cost of an asset} = \begin{array}{c} \textbf{The sum of all the costs} \\ \textbf{incurred to bring the} \\ \textbf{asset to its intended purpose,} \\ \textbf{after subtracting all discounts} \end{array}$$

The buyer's cost of transporting goods from the supplier (called freight in) is part of the purchase cost of the inventory. Freight in is *not* recorded as an expense.

At the end of the period, no adjusting entries are required. Both Inventory and Cost of Goods Sold are up to date.[1]

Cost of Goods Sold (Cost of Sales) and Gross Profit

Exhibit 9-3 illustrates the measurement of cost of goods sold (cost of sales) in the perpetual inventory system. Cost of sales is simply the sum of all the amounts posted to the Cost of Goods Sold account throughout the period (see Exhibit 9-3, Panel A). There is another way to compute cost of goods sold, and it comes from the periodic inventory system. Using the periodic system, the cost-of-goods-sold computation is as follows, using the data from Exhibit 9-3:

Cost of Goods Sold	
Beginning inventory.....................................	$100,000
+ Purchases (including freight in)..............	560,000
= Cost of goods available for sale	660,000
− Ending inventory.....................................	(120,000)
= Cost of goods sold	$540,000

COST OF GOODS AVAILABLE FOR SALE Beginning inventory plus purchases.

The business began the period with $100,000 of inventory. During the period, purchases totaled $560,000. The sum of the beginning inventory plus purchases equals the **cost of goods available for sale,** $660,000. Goods available are either in ending inventory, $120,000, or were sold. Cost of goods sold was therefore $660,000 − $120,000 = $540,000.

This computation of cost of goods sold is so important that all companies use it to bring together all the inventory data of an accounting period. Even companies that use the perpetual system summarize their inventory data this way.

How Owners and Managers Use the Cost-of-Goods-Sold Model

Suppose you are in charge of a line of Teva Sandals at Deckers Outdoor. You are planning your buying of inventory for the next period, and you must decide how much inventory to purchase from your supplier in Taiwan. How will you make the decision? The amount of inventory to purchase depends on three factors:

- budgeted cost of goods sold
- budgeted ending inventory
- the beginning inventory with which you started the period

A rearrangement of the cost-of-goods-sold formula helps you decide how much to purchase for the coming year (all budgeted amounts for the next period are assumed):

---

[1]An adjusting entry is needed only if the Inventory account does not agree with the physical count of goods on hand.

Computation of Budgeted Purchases	
Cost of goods sold (budgeted for the next period)	$600,000
+ Ending inventory (budgeted for the next period)	150,000
= Cost of goods available for sale, as budgeted	750,000
− Beginning inventory (actual amount left over from the prior period)	(120,000)
= Purchases (the inventory you need to buy to reach your goal)	$630,000

Business owners and managers use this formula to determine how much to spend on inventory, regardless of the inventory system used. The power of the cost-of-goods-sold model lies in the information it captures: beginning and ending inventory levels, purchases, and cost of goods sold.

Computing the Cost of Inventory

The Deckers Outdoor inventory record in Exhibit 9-2 follows the common practice of recording quantities only. The company multiplies the 20 pairs of Teva Sandals on hand by the cost of each pair to compute the ending inventory for the balance sheet, as follows:

Cost of inventory on hand	=	Quantity on hand	×	Unit cost
$600	=	20 pairs	×	$30

DETERMINING THE QUANTITY OF INVENTORY   Many businesses count their inventory on the last day of the fiscal year. If you have worked at a retail business, you will recall the process of "taking inventory." Some entities shut the business down to get a good inventory count.

A complication in counting inventory arises from consigned goods. In a **consignment** arrangement, the owner of the inventory (the *consignor*) transfers the goods to another business (the *consignee*). Then the consignee sells the inventory for the owner. The consignee does *not* own the consigned goods and therefore should not include them in its own inventory. Consignments are common in retailing. Suppose Deckers Outdoor is the consignee for a line of backpacks. Should Deckers include this consigned merchandise in its inventory? No, because Deckers does not own the goods. Instead, the backpack manufacturer—the consignor—includes the consigned goods in its inventory. *Include in inventory only what the business owns.*

CONSIGNMENT. Transfer of goods by the owner (consignor) to another business (consignee) that sells the inventory on the owner's behalf. The consignee does not take title to the consigned goods.

DETERMINING THE UNIT COST OF INVENTORY   As we've seen, *inventory cost* is the price the business pays to purchase the goods—not the selling price. Suppose Deckers Outdoor purchases a T-shirt for $10 and sells it for $15. Deckers would report the inventory at its cost of $10 per unit, not at its selling price of $15.

Inventory cost includes invoice price, less any purchase discount, plus sales tax, tariffs, transportation charges, insurance while in transit, and all other costs incurred to make the goods ready for sale. *Net purchases* means the net cost of inventory acquired for resale, after subtracting any purchase discounts and purchase returns and allowances. As we stated earlier, we use the terms *purchases* and *net purchases* interchangeably.

Periodic Inventory System

In the periodic inventory system, the business does not keep a running record of the inventory on hand. Instead, at the end of the period, the business counts the goods on hand and computes the cost of ending inventory. This inventory figure appears on the balance sheet and is used to compute cost of goods sold. The periodic system is also called the *physical system* because it relies on the actual physical count of inventory.

It's a Bird . . . It's a Plane . . . It's a Warehouse!
DHL Worldwide Express

Say "inventory" and you probably conjure up a warehouse filled with auto tires await-ing shipment. In the new world economy, however, inventory is likely to be zipping over-head via overnight air express. At 3:00 A.M. in Brussels, Belgium, you get a snapshot of just what lean inventory means: Workers at the **DHL Air Express** hub use forklifts to hoist **Dell Computers**, **Nokia** cell phones and **Ford** car parts onto planes bound for Finland, South Africa, and Argentina. And all these products just came off other planes: nothing sits in a warehouse.

The pressure to keep inventory levels low has fueled the profits of the air express industry. "You can't have any dead space in your supply chain," says Lynnette McIntire of **UPS**. McIntire says her customers no longer stock a month of inventory. Instead, they depend on today's deliveries for tomorrow's manufacturing.

DHL may play second fiddle to **FedEx** and **UPS** in the United States, but it rules the world of overseas business-to-business transactions. In fact, DHL invented the industry. International air shipments are growing at 18% a year, twice the rate of domestic. With over 40% of the international market, DHL Worldwide Express was named the "World's Most Global Company" by *Global Finance* magazine.

Source: Based on Andrew Tanzer, "Warehouses that fly," *Forbes*, October 18, 1999, pp. 120–124. Vanessa Drucker, "B2B boom," *Global Finance,* April 2000, pp. 46–48. Anonymous, "New offerings: DHL considers an IPO after buy-back of stake, "Daily Investing Report, *Atlanta Constitution*, December 14, 1999, p. F6. http://www.dhl-usa.com/press_display/press release dated 9/29/99.

In the periodic system (Exhibit 9-4, Panel A), the business uses a Purchases account to record the purchase of inventory. Purchases is an expense account. Throughout the period, the Inventory account carries the beginning balance left over from the end of the preceding period. Then at the end of the current period, the Inventory account is updated for the financial statements. The end-of-period entries can be made during the closing process. Exhibit 9-4 illustrates the accounting for inventory in the periodic sys-tem. Your professor may have you compare the perpetual and periodic inventory sys-tems. The appendix to this chapter provides a side-by-side comparison.

INVENTORY COSTING METHODS

Measuring the cost of inventory is easy when $50 cost per unit remains constant. But the unit cost often changes. For example, during inflation, prices rise. A pair of Teva sandals that cost **Deckers Outdoor** $50 in January may cost $52 in June and $55 in October. Suppose Deckers sells 10,000 pairs of Tevas in December. How many of the pairs cost $50? How many cost $52 or $55? To compute the cost of goods sold and ending inventory, the accountant must assign a cost to each item sold. The four costing methods GAAP allows are

1. Specific unit cost
2. Weighted-average cost
3. First-in, first-out (FIFO) cost
4. Last-in, first-out (LIFO) cost

| PANEL A—Recording in the Journal and Posting to the T-accounts—Periodic System | | | INVENTORY AND COST OF GOODS SOLD ACCOUNTS | |

PANEL A—Recording in the Journal and Posting to the T-accounts—Periodic System

1. Credit purchases of $560,000:

   Purchases 560,000

      Accounts Payable..............   560,000

2. Credit sales of $900,000:

   Accounts Receivable 900,000

      Sales Revenue...................   900,000

3. End-of-period entries to update Inventory and record Cost of Goods Sold:

   a. Transfer the cost of beginning inventory ($100,000) to Cost of Goods Sold:

        Cost of Goods Sold........... 100,000

          Inventory (beginning balance).......................   100,000

   b. Record the cost of ending inventory ($120,000) based on a count:

        Inventory (ending balance) 120,000

          Cost of Goods Sold.......   120,000

   c. Transfer the cost of purchases to Cost of Goods Sold:

        Cost of Goods Sold........... 560,000

          Purchases   560,000

INVENTORY AND COST OF GOODS SOLD ACCOUNTS

INVENTORY			COST OF GOODS SOLD	
100,000*	100,000		100,000	120,000
120,000			560,000	
			540,000	

* Beginning inventory was $100,000.

PANEL B—Reporting in the Financial Statements

Income Statement (partial)

Sales revenue............................		$900,000
Cost of goods sold:		
Beginning inventory	$100,000	
Purchases	560,000	
Cost of goods available	660,000	
Less: Ending inventory..........	(120,000)	
Cost of goods sold		540,000
Gross profit		$360,000

Balance Sheet (partial)

Current assets:		
Cash...	$	XXX
Short-term investments.............................		XXX
Accounts receivable...................................		XXX
Inventories...		120,000
Prepaid expenses...		XXX

DAILY EXERCISE 9-4

A company can use any of these methods. The computation of inventory cost is essentially the same under both the perpetual and the periodic systems.[1]

Specific Unit Cost

Some businesses deal in inventory items that differ from unit to unit, such as automobiles, jewels, and real estate. These businesses usually cost their inventory at the specific unit cost of the particular unit. For instance, a Chevrolet dealer may have two vehicles in the showroom—a "stripped-down" model that cost $14,000 and a "loaded" model that cost $17,000. If the dealer sells the loaded model for $19,700, cost of goods sold is $17,000, the cost of the specific unit. The gross margin on this sale is $2,700 ($19,700 − $17,000). If the stripped-down auto is the only unit left in inventory at the end of the period, ending inventory is $14,000, the dealer's cost of the specific unit on hand.

Objective 2

Apply the inventory costing methods: specific unit cost, weighted-average cost, FIFO, and LIFO

---

[1]Theoretically, there can be a difference between the last-in, first-out (LIFO) costs under the perpetual and the periodic systems. In actual practice, however, this difference does not exist. Complications with LIFO cause companies to wait until year end to compute ending inventory and cost of goods sold. Their computations for perpetual LIFO then parallel those for periodic LIFO. This topic is covered in later accounting courses.

Inventory cost method based on the specific cost of partic-ular units of inventory. Also called the **specific identifica-tion method.**

The **specific-unit-cost method** is also called the **specific identification method.** This method is not practical for inventory items that have common char-acteristics, such as bushels of wheat, gallons of paint, or boxes of laundry detergent.

The weighted-average cost, FIFO (first-in, first-out) cost, and LIFO (last-in, first-out) cost methods are fundamentally different from the specific-unit-cost method. These methods do not assign to inventory the specific cost of particular units. Instead, they assume different flows of costs into and out of inventory, as illustrated in Exhibit 9-5. Panel A gives the illustrative data for all three inventory cost methods.

EXHIBIT 9-5
Inventory and Cost of Goods Sold Under Three Costing Methods: *Weighted-Average (Panel B), FIFO (Panel C), LIFO (Panel D)*

⊙ DAILY EXERCISE 9-5

⊙ DAILY EXERCISE 9-6

⊙ DAILY EXERCISE 9-7

PANEL A—Illustrative Data

Beginning inventory (10 units @ $10 per unit)		$ 100
Purchases:		
No. 1 (25 units @ $14 per unit)	$ 350	
No. 2 (25 units @ $18 per unit)	450	
Total purchases...		800
Cost of goods available for sale (60 units)		900
Ending inventory (20 units @ $? per unit)		(?)
Cost of goods sold (40 units @ $? per unit)...................		$?

PANEL B—Ending Inventory and Cost of Goods Sold (Weighted-Average Cost Method)

Cost of goods available for sale—see Panel A (60 units @ average cost of $15* per unit)	$ 900
Ending inventory (20 units @ $15 per unit).................................	(300)
Cost of goods sold (40 units @ $15 per unit)................................	$ 600

$$\text{* } \frac{\text{Cost of goods available for sale, \$900}}{\text{Number of units available for sale, 60}} = \text{Average cost per unit, \$15}$$

PANEL C—Ending Inventory and Cost of Goods Sold (FIFO Cost Method)

Cost of goods available for sale (60 units—see Panel A)		$ 900
Ending inventory (cost of the *last* 20 units available):		
20 units @ $18 per unit (from purchase No. 2)............................		(360)
Cost of goods sold (cost of the *first* 40 units available):		
10 units @ $10 per unit (all of beginning inventory).................	$ 100	
25 units @ $14 per unit (all of purchase No. 1)	350	
5 units @ $18 per unit (from purchase No. 2)...........................	90	
Cost of goods sold...	$ 540	$ 540

PANEL D—Ending Inventory and Cost of Goods Sold (LIFO Cost Method)

Cost of goods available for sale (60 units—see Panel A)		$ 900
Ending inventory (cost of the *first* 20 units available):		
10 units @ $10 per unit (all of beginning inventory).................	$(100)	
10 units @ $14 per unit (from purchase No. 1)...........................	(140)	
Ending inventory		(240)
Cost of goods sold (cost of the *last* 40 units available):		
25 units @ $18 per unit (all of purchase No. 2)	$ 450	
15 units @ $14 per unit (from purchase No. 1)...........................	210	
Cost of goods sold...	$ 660	$ 660

WEIGHTED-AVERAGE COST METHOD. Inventory costing method based on the weighted-average cost of inventory during the period. Weighted-average cost is determined by dividing the cost of goods available for sale by the number of units available. Also called the **average-cost method.**

Weighted-Average Cost

The **weighted-average cost method,** often called the *average-cost method,* is based on the weighted-average cost of inventory during the period. Weighted-average cost is determined as follows:

- Determine the weighted-average cost by dividing the cost of goods available for sale (beginning inventory plus purchases) by the number of units available (beginning inventory plus purchases).
- Compute the ending inventory and cost of goods sold by multiplying the number of units by the weighted-average cost per unit.

To illustrate the costing methods, suppose the business has 60 units of inventory available for sale during the period.

- Ending inventory consists of 20 units.
- Cost of goods sold is based on 40 units.

Panel A of Exhibit 9-5 gives the data for computing ending inventory and cost of goods sold, and Panel B shows the weighted-average cost computations.

First-In, First-Out (FIFO) Cost

Under the **first-in, first-out (FIFO) method,** the company must keep a record of the cost of each inventory unit purchased. The unit costs for ending inventory may differ from the unit costs used to compute the cost of goods sold. Under FIFO,

- The first costs into inventory are the first costs out to cost of goods sold—hence the name *first-in, first-out.*
- Ending inventory is based on the costs of the most recent purchases.

In Exhibit 9-5, the FIFO cost of ending inventory is $360. Cost of goods sold is $540. Panel A gives the data, and Panel C shows the computations.

FIRST-IN, FIRST-OUT (FIFO) INVENTORY COSTING METHOD. Inventory costing method by which the first costs into inventory are the first costs out to cost of goods sold. Ending inventory is based on the costs of the most recent purchases.

Last-In, First-Out (LIFO) Cost

The **last-in, first-out (LIFO) method** also depends on the costs of particular inventory purchases. LIFO is the opposite of FIFO. Under LIFO,

- The last costs into inventory are the first costs out to cost of goods sold.
- Ending inventory is based on the oldest costs—those of beginning inventory and plus the earliest purchases of the period.

Exhibit 9-5 shows that the LIFO cost of ending inventory is $240. Cost of goods sold is $660. Again, Panel A gives the data, and Panel D shows the computations.

Remember that the terms *FIFO* and *LIFO* do not describe which goods are left in ending inventory, but rather which goods are sold. FIFO assumes that goods purchased first are sold first; therefore, the last goods purchased are left in ending inventory. LIFO assumes that the last goods in are sold first; therefore, the first goods purchased are left in ending inventory.

LAST-IN, FIRST-OUT (LIFO) INVENTORY COSTING METHOD. Inventory costing method by which the last costs into inventory are the first costs out to cost of goods sold. This method leaves the oldest costs—those of beginning inventory and the earliest purchases of the period—in ending inventory.

The Income Effects of FIFO, LIFO, and Weighted-Average Cost

In our example, the cost of inventory rose during the accounting period from $10 per unit to $14 and finally to $18 (Exhibit 9-5, Panel A). When inventory unit costs change, the different costing methods produce different cost of goods sold and ending inventory figures, as Exhibit 9-5 shows (Panels B, C, and D).

When inventory unit costs are *increasing,*

- FIFO ending inventory is *highest* because it is priced at the most recent (highest) costs.
- LIFO ending inventory is *lowest* because it is priced at the oldest (lowest) costs.

When inventory unit costs are *decreasing,*

- FIFO ending inventory is lowest.
- LIFO ending inventory is highest.

Exhibit 9-6 on page 356 summarizes the income effects of the three inventory methods, using the data from Exhibit 9-5. Study the exhibit carefully, focusing on ending inventory, cost of goods sold, and gross profit.

	FIFO		LIFO		Weighted-Average	
Sales revenue (assumed)........		$1,000		$1,000		$1,000
Cost of goods sold:						
Goods available for sale (from Exhibit 9-5)...........	$900		$900		$900	
Ending inventory................	(360)		(240)		(300)	
Cost of goods sold		540		660		600
Gross profit............................		$ 460		$ 340		$ 400

Summary of Income Effects—When inventory unit costs are *increasing*

FIFO:	Highest ending inventory	LIFO:	Lowest ending inventory	Weighted-average:	Results fall between the extremes of FIFO and LIFO
	Lowest cost of goods sold		Highest cost of goods sold		
	Highest gross profit		Lowest gross profit		

Summary of Income Effects—When inventory unit costs are *decreasing*

FIFO:	Lowest ending inventory	LIFO:	Highest ending inventory	Weighted-average:	Results fall between the extremes of FIFO and LIFO
	Highest cost of goods sold		Lowest cost of goods sold		
	Lowest gross profit		Highest gross profit		

 DAILY EXERCISE 9-8

 DAILY EXERCISE 9-9

Objective 3
Identify the income effects and the tax effects of the inventory costing methods

 DAILY EXERCISE 9-10

The Income Tax Advantage of LIFO

When prices are rising, the LIFO method results in the *lowest taxable income* and thus the *lowest income taxes*. Using the gross profit data of Exhibit 9-6, we have the following (using assumed data):

	FIFO	LIFO	Weighted-Average
Gross profit...	$460	$340	$400
Operating expenses (assumed)	260	260	260
Income before income tax....................	200	80	140
Income tax expense (40%)	$ 80	$ 32	$ 56

Income tax expense is lowest under LIFO ($32) and highest under FIFO ($80). The most attractive feature of LIFO is reduced income tax payments, which is why **Lands' End, PepsiCo,** and **Wal-Mart** use the LIFO method. These companies are willing to report lower profits in order to save on taxes.

Some periods are marked by high inflation, and companies change to LIFO for its tax advantage. Exhibit 9-7, based on an American Institute of Certified Public Accountants (AICPA) survey of 600 companies, indicates that FIFO and LIFO are the most popular inventory costing methods.

EXHIBIT 9-7
Use of the various Inventory Costing Methods

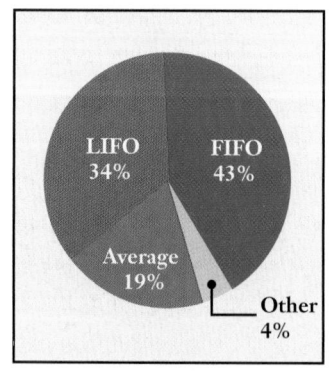

GAAP and Practical Considerations: A Comparison of Inventory Methods

To judge the three major inventory costing methods, ask three questions:

1. How well does each method measure net income on the income statement?
2. Which method reports the most up-to-date inventory amount on the balance sheet?
3. What effects do the methods have on income taxes?

MEASURING NET INCOME ON THE INCOME STATEMENT   LIFO best matches the current value of cost of goods sold with current revenue by assigning to this expense the most recent inventory costs. Therefore, LIFO produces the cost-of-goods-sold figure that is closest to what it would cost the company to replace the goods that were sold. In this sense, LIFO produces the best measure of net income. In contrast, FIFO matches the oldest inventory costs against the period's revenue—a poor match of current expense with current revenue.

CURRENT INVENTORY COST ON THE BALANCE SHEET FIFO reports the most current inventory costs on the balance sheet. LIFO can result in misleading inventory costs on the balance sheet because the oldest prices are left in ending inventory.

INCOME TAX LIFO results in the lowest income tax payments when prices are rising. Tax payments are highest under FIFO. When inventory prices are falling, tax payments are highest under LIFO and lowest under FIFO. The weighted-average cost method produces amounts between the extremes of LIFO and FIFO.

LIFO ALLOWS OWNERS TO MANAGE REPORTED INCOME—UP OR DOWN LIFO is often criticized because it allows managers to manipulate net income. When inventory prices are rising rapidly and a company wants to show less income for the year (in order to pay less taxes), managers can buy a large amount of inventory before the end of the year. Under LIFO, these high inventory costs immediately become expense—as cost of goods sold. As a result, the income statement reports a lower net income.

Conversely, if the business is having a bad year, the owner may wish to increase reported income. To do so, he or she can delay a large purchase of high-cost inventory until the next period. This high-cost inventory is not expensed as cost of goods sold in the current year. This avoids decreasing the current year's reported income. In the process, the company draws down inventory quantities below the level of the previous period, a practice known as **LIFO liquidation.**

LIFO LIQUIDATION. Situation when the LIFO inventory method is used and inventory quantities fall below the level of the previous period.

HIGHER INCOME OR LOWER TAXES? A company may want to report the highest income, and FIFO meets this need when prices are rising. But FIFO leads to the highest income taxes. When prices are falling, LIFO reports the highest income.

Which inventory method is better—LIFO or FIFO? There is no single answer to this question. Different companies have different motives for the inventory method they choose. **The Gap** uses FIFO, **Lands' End** uses LIFO, and **Pier 1 Imports** uses weighted-average cost. Still other companies use more than one method. **The Quaker Oats Company** uses all three methods.

INTERNATIONAL PERSPECTIVE Many companies manufacture their inventory in foreign countries. Companies that value inventory by the LIFO method often use another accounting method for inventories in foreign countries. Why? LIFO is allowed in the United States, but other countries are not bound by U.S. accounting practices. Australia and the United Kingdom, for example, do not permit the use of LIFO. Exhibit 9-8 lists a sampling of countries and whether or not they permit LIFO.

 DAILY EXERCISE 9-11

Country	LIFO Permitted?	Country	LIFO Permitted?
Australia	No	Netherlands	Yes
Canada	Yes	Singapore	No
France	Yes	Switzerland	No
Germany	Yes	United Kingdom	No
Japan	Yes	United States	Yes

EXHIBIT 9-8
LIFO Use by Country

MID-CHAPTER

SUMMARY PROBLEM

Suppose a division of **IBM Corporation** that handles computer components has these inventory records for January 20X6:

Date	Item	Quantity	Unit Cost	Sale Price
Jan. 1	Beginning inventory	100 units	$ 8	
6	Purchase	60 units	9	
13	Sale	70 units		$20
21	Purchase	150 units	9	
24	Sale	210 units		22
27	Purchase	90 units	10	
30	Sale	30 units		25

Company accounting records reveal that operating expense for January was $1,900.

Required

1. Prepare the January income statement, showing amounts for FIFO, LIFO, and weighted-average cost. Label the bottom line "Operating income." (Round the weighted-average cost per unit to three decimal places and all other figures to whole-dollar amounts.) Show your computations, and use the periodic inventory model in Exhibit 9-6 to compute cost of goods sold.
2. Suppose you are the financial vice president of IBM. Which inventory method will you use if your motive is to (state the reason for each answer)
   a. Minimize income taxes?
   b. Report the highest operating income?
   c. Report operating income between the extremes of FIFO and LIFO?
   d. Report inventory on the balance sheet at the most current cost?
   e. Attain the best measure of net income for the income statement?

Solution

Requirement 1

IBM CORPORATION
Income Statement for Component
Month Ended January 31, 20X6

	FIFO		LIFO		Weighted-Average	
Sales revenue		$6,770		$6,770		$6,770
Cost of goods sold:						
Beginning inventory	$ 800		$ 800		$ 800	
Net purchases	2,790		2,790		2,790	
Cost of goods available for sale	3,590		3,590		3,590	
Ending inventory	(900)		(720)		(808)	
Cost of goods sold		2,690		2,870		2,782
Gross profit		4,080		3,900		3,988
Operating expenses		1,900		1,900		1,900
Operating income		$2,180		$2,000		$2,088

Computations

Sales revenue:	$(70 \times \$20) + (210 \times \$22) + (30 \times \$25)$	= $6,770
Beginning inventory:	$100 \times \$8$	= $800
Purchases:	$(60 \times \$9) + (150 \times \$9) + (90 \times \$10)$	= $2,790
Ending inventory		
FIFO	$90^* \times \$10$	= $900
LIFO	$90 \times \$8$	= $720
Weighted-average:	$90 \times \$8.975^{**}$	= $808 (rounded from $807.75)

* Number of units in ending inventory = $100 + 60 - 70 + 150 - 210 + 90 - 30 = 90$
** $3,590/400 units† = $8.975 per unit
† Number of units available = $100 + 60 + 150 + 90 = 400$

Requirement 2

a. Use LIFO to minimize income taxes because operating income is lowest when inventory costs are rising, as in this situation.

b. Use FIFO to report the highest operating income. Income under FIFO is highest when inventory unit costs are increasing, as in this situation.

c. Use weighted-average cost to report an operating income amount between the FIFO and LIFO extremes. This is true both in this situation and in others when inventory unit costs are increasing or decreasing.

d. Use FIFO to report inventory on the balance sheet at the most current cost. This is always true.

e. Use LIFO to best measure net income. LIFO always produces the best matching of current expense with current revenue.

THE PERPETUAL SYSTEM AND INVENTORY COSTING METHODS

Many companies keep their perpetual inventory records in quantities only, as illustrated in Exhibit 9-2. Other companies keep perpetual records in both quantities and dollar costs. Here we show how the inventory costing methods are applied in a *perpetual* inventory system.

FIFO

Deckers Outdoor uses the FIFO inventory method. Exhibit 9-9 shows Deckers' perpetual inventory record for a particular style of Teva sandals in both quantities and dollar costs for the month of November.

EXHIBIT 9-9   Perpetual Inventory Record—FIFO Cost for Deckers Outdoor Corporation

Item: Teva Sandals

Date	Received Qty.	Received Unit Cost	Received Total	Sold Qty.	Sold Unit Cost	Sold Total	Balance on Hand Qty.	Balance on Hand Unit Cost	Balance on Hand Total
Nov. 1							10	$30	$300
5				6	$30	$ 180	4	30	120
7	25	$31	$ 775				4	30	120
							25	31	775
12				4	30	120			
				9	31	279	16	31	496
26	25	32	800				16	31	496
							25	32	800
30				16	31	496			
				5	32	160	20	32	640
Totals	50		$1,575	40		$1,235	20	$32	$640

To prepare financial statements at November 30, Deckers can take the ending inventory cost ($640) straight to the balance sheet. Cost of goods sold for the November income statement is $1,235. Here is Deckers' cost of goods sold for the sandals during November (data taken from Exhibit 9-9):

Cost of Goods Sold (Teva sandals)—November

Beginning inventory	$ 300
+ Purchases	1,575
= Cost of goods available for sale	1,875
− Ending inventory	(640)
= Cost of goods sold	$1,235

 DAILY EXERCISE 9-12

LIFO

Few companies keep perpetual inventory records at LIFO cost. The record-keeping is expensive, and LIFO liquidations can occur during the year. To avoid these problems, LIFO companies follow different strategies than FIFO and average-cost companies. LIFO companies can keep perpetual inventory records in terms of quantities only, as illustrated in Exhibit 9-2. For financial statements, they apply LIFO costs at the end of the period. Other LIFO companies maintain perpetual inventory records at FIFO cost and then convert the FIFO amounts to LIFO costs for the financial statements. These procedures arrive at ending inventory and cost-of-goods-sold figures that parallel those from the periodic inventory system.

Weighted-Average Cost

Perpetual inventory records can be kept at weighted-average cost. Most companies using this method compute the weighted-average cost for the entire period. They apply this cost to both ending inventory and cost of goods sold. These procedures parallel those used in the periodic inventory system (Exhibit 9-5).

WORK IT OUT

Examine Exhibit 9-9. What was Deckers' weighted-average unit cost during November? How much were ending inventory and cost of goods sold at weighted-average cost?

Answer

$$\text{Weighted-average unit cost} = \frac{\text{Cost of goods available for sale}}{\text{Units available for sale}}$$

$$= \frac{\text{Cost of beginning inventory} + \text{Cost of purchases}}{\text{Units of beginning inventory} + \text{Units purchased}}$$

$$= \frac{\$300 + \$1,575}{10 \text{ units} + 50 \text{ units}} = \frac{\$1,875}{60 \text{ units}} = \$31.25$$

Ending Inventory = 20 units × $31.25 = $ 625
Cost of goods sold = 40 units × $31.25 = $1,250

ACCOUNTING PRINCIPLES AND INVENTORIES

Several accounting principles have special relevance to inventories. Among them are consistency, disclosure, materiality, and accounting conservatism.

Consistency Principle

CONSISTENCY PRINCIPLE. A business should use the same accounting methods and procedures from period to period.

The **consistency principle** states that businesses should use the same accounting methods and procedures from period to period. Consistency helps investors compare a company's financial statements from one period to the next.

Suppose you are analyzing a company's net income pattern over a two-year period. The company switched from LIFO to FIFO during that time. Its net income increased dramatically but only as a result of the change in inventory method. If you did not know of the change, you might believe that the company's income increased because of improved operations.

The consistency principle does not require that all companies within an industry use the same accounting method. Nor does it mean that a company may *never* change its methods. However, a company making an accounting change must disclose the effect of the change on net income. **Sun Company, Inc.,** an oil company, disclosed the following in a note to its annual report:

EXCERPT FROM NOTE 6 OF SUN COMPANY STATEMENTS
. . . Sun changed its method of accounting for the cost of crude oil and refined product inventories . . . from . . . FIFO . . . to . . . LIFO . . . . Sun believes that the . . . LIFO method better matches current costs with current revenues . . . . The change decreased the 20X1 net loss . . . by $3 million. . . .

Disclosure Principle

The **disclosure principle** holds that a company's financial statements should report enough information for outsiders to make knowledgeable decisions about the company. In short, the company should report *relevant, reliable,* and *comparable* information about its economic affairs. With respect to inventories, the disclosure principle means disclosing the method being used to value inventories. Suppose a banker is comparing two companies—one using LIFO and the other FIFO. The FIFO company reports higher net income, but only because it uses the FIFO inventory method. Without knowledge of the accounting methods the companies are using, the banker could loan money to the wrong business.

DISCLOSURE PRINCIPLE. A business's financial statements must report enough information for outsiders to make knowledgeable decisions about the company.

Materiality Concept

The **materiality concept** states that a company must perform strictly proper accounting *only* for items that are significant for the business's financial statements. Information is significant—or, in accounting terminology, *material*—when its presentation in the financial statements would cause someone to change a decision because of that information. Immaterial items justify less-than-perfect accounting. Their inclusion and proper presentation would not affect a statement user's decision. The materiality concept frees accountants from having to report every last item in strict accordance with GAAP.

MATERIALITY CONCEPT. A company must perform strictly proper accounting only for items that are significant to the business's financial statements.

How does a business decide where to draw the line between the material and the immaterial? This decision depends on how large the business is. **Lucent Technologies,** the maker of cordless phones, for example, has over $38 billion in assets. Management would likely treat as immaterial a $1,000 loss of inventory due to spoilage. A loss of this amount may be immaterial to Lucent's total assets and net income, so company accountants may not report the loss separately. Will this accounting treatment affect banker's or investor's decision about Lucent? Probably not. So it doesn't matter whether the loss is reported separately or simply embedded in cost of goods sold.

Accounting Conservatism

Conservatism in accounting means reporting items in the financial statements at amounts that lead to the most cautious immediate results. What advantage does conservatism give a business? Managers must be optimistic to be good leaders. This optimism sometimes causes them to look on the bright side of operations, and they may overstate a company's income and asset values. Many accountants regard conservatism as a counterbalance to managers' optimistic tendencies. The goal is for financial statements to present realistic figures.

CONSERVATISM. Reporting the least favorable figures in the financial statements.

Conservatism appears in accounting guidelines such as

- "Anticipate no gains, but provide for all probable losses."
- "If in doubt, record an asset at the lowest reasonable amount and a liability at the highest reasonable amount."
- When there's a question, record an expense rather than an asset."

Conservatism directs accountants to decrease the accounting value of an asset if it appears unrealistically high. Assume that a company paid $35,000 for inventory that has become obsolete and whose current value is only $12,000. Conservatism dictates that the inventory be *written down* (that is, decreased) to $12,000.

Objective 4
Apply the lower-of-cost-or-market rule to inventory

Lower-of-Cost-or-Market Rule

The **lower-of-cost-or-market rule** (abbreviated as **LCM**) shows accounting conservatism in action. LCM requires that inventory be reported in the financial statements at whichever is lower—the inventory's historical cost or its market value. For inventories, *market value* generally means *current replacement cost* (that is, the cost to replace the inventory on hand). If the replacement cost of inventory falls below its historical cost, the business must write down the value of its goods. The business reports ending inventory at its LCM value on the balance sheet.

LOWER-OF-COST-OR-MARKET (LCM) RULE. Rule that an asset should be reported in the financial statements at whichever is lower—its historical cost or its market value.

Suppose a business paid $3,000 for inventory on September 26. By December 31, its value has fallen. The inventory can now be replaced for $2,200 and the decline in value appears permanent. Market value is below cost, and the December 31 balance sheet reports this inventory at its LCM value of $2,200.

Exhibit 9-10 shows the effects of LCM on the income statement and the balance sheet. The exhibit shows that the lower of (a) cost or (b) market value is the relevant amount for valuing inventory on the balance sheet. Now examine the income statement in Exhibit 9-10. What expense absorbs the impact of the $800 inventory write-down? The entry to write down the inventory to LCM debits Cost of Goods Sold:

Cost of Goods Sold (cost, $3,000 − market, $2,200) 800
    Inventory 800

EXHIBIT 9-10
Lower-of-Cost-or-Market (LCM) Effects

 DAILY EXERCISE 9-13

Balance Sheet

Current assets:
  Inventories, at market
    (which is lower than $3,000 cost) .... $ 2,200

Income Statement

Sales revenue..	$20,000
Cost of goods sold:	
Beginning inventory (LCM = Cost).......................	$ 2,800
Net purchases...	11,000
Cost of goods available for sale	13,800
Ending inventory—	
Cost = $3,000	
Replacement cost (market value) = $2,200	
LCM = Market	(2,200)
Cost of goods sold...	11,600
Gross profit	$ 8,400

Companies often disclose LCM in notes to their financial statements, as shown here for **Cisco Systems,** the worldwide leader in networking for the Internet.

NOTE 2: STATEMENT OF SIGNIFICANT ACCOUNTING POLICIES
Inventories. Inventories are stated at the *lower of cost or market.* [Emphasis added.]

Effects of Inventory Errors

Objective 5
Determine the effects of inventory errors on cost of goods sold and net income

Businesses count their inventories at the end of the period. As the period 1 segment of Exhibit 9-11 shows, an error in the ending inventory creates errors in cost of goods sold and gross profit. Compare period 1, when ending inventory is overstated and cost of goods sold is understated, each by $5,000, with period 3, which is correct. Period 1 should look exactly like period 3.

Recall that one period's ending inventory is the next period's beginning inventory. Thus, the error in ending inventory carries over into the next period; note the amounts highlighted in Exhibit 9-11.

Because ending inventory is *subtracted* in computing cost of goods sold in one period and the same amount is *added* as beginning inventory to compute next period's cost of goods sold, the error's effect cancels out at the end of the second period. The overstatement of cost of goods sold in period 2 counterbalances the understatement for period 1. Thus, the total gross profit for the two periods is correct. As a result, owner's equity at the end of period 2 is correct. These effects are summarized in Exhibit 9-12.

Inventory errors cannot be ignored simply because they counterbalance, however. Suppose you are analyzing trends in the business's operations. Exhibit 9-11 shows a drop in gross margin from period 1 to period 2, followed by an increase in period 3. But that picture of operations is untrue because of the accounting error.

 DAILY EXERCISE 9-14

 DAILY EXERCISE 9-15

EXHIBIT 9-11   Inventory Errors: An Example

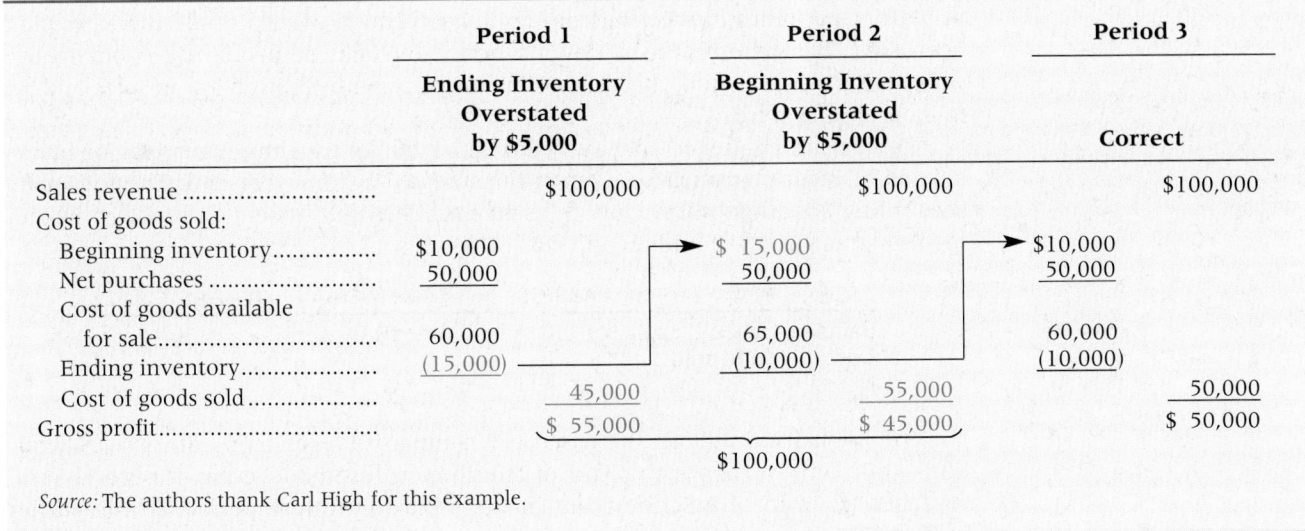

	Period 1		Period 2		Period 3	
	Ending Inventory Overstated by $5,000		Beginning Inventory Overstated by $5,000		Correct	
Sales revenue		$100,000		$100,000		$100,000
Cost of goods sold:						
Beginning inventory................	$10,000		$ 15,000		$10,000	
Net purchases	50,000		50,000		50,000	
Cost of goods available for sale.................................	60,000		65,000		60,000	
Ending inventory.....................	(15,000)		(10,000)		(10,000)	
Cost of goods sold		45,000		55,000		50,000
Gross profit.................................		$ 55,000		$ 45,000		$ 50,000

$100,000

Source: The authors thank Carl High for this example.

EXHIBIT 9-12   Effects of Inventory Errors

	Period 1			Period 2		
Inventory Error	Cost of Goods Sold	Gross Profit and Net Income	Ending Owner's Equity	Cost of Goods Sold	Gross Profit and Net Income	Ending Owner's Equity
Period 1 Ending inventory *overstated*	Understated	Overstated	Overstated	Overstated	Understated	Correct
Period 1 Ending inventory *understated*	Overstated	Understated	Understated	Understated	Overstated	Correct

The correct gross profit is $50,000 for each period. Providing accurate information for decision making requires that all inventory errors be corrected.

OTHER INVENTORY ISSUES

Ethical Issues

No area of accounting has a deeper ethical dimension than inventory. Owners and managers of companies whose profits are lagging are sometimes tempted to "cook the books" to increase reported income. The increase in income may lead investors and creditors to think the business is more successful than it really is.

There are two main schemes for cooking the books. The easiest, and the most obvious, is simply to overstate ending inventory. In Exhibit 9-12, we saw how an error in ending inventory affects net income. A company can intentionally overstate its ending inventory. Such an error understates cost of goods sold and overstates net income and owner's equity, as shown in the accounting equation. The upward-pointing arrows indicate an overstatement—reporting more assets and equity than are actually present:

$$\text{ASSETS} \ = \ \text{LIABILITIES} \ + \ \text{OWNERS' EQUITY}$$
$$\uparrow \ = \ 0 \ + \ \uparrow$$

 DAILY EXERCISE 9-16

The second way of using inventory to cook the books involves sales. Sales schemes are more complex than simple inventory overstatements. **Datapoint Corporation** and **MiniScribe,** both computer-related concerns, were charged with creating fictitious sales to boost reported profits.

Datapoint is alleged to have hired drivers to transport its inventory around San Antonio so that the goods could *not* be physically counted. Datapoint's logic seemed to be that excluding the goods from ending inventory would imply that they had been sold. The scheme broke down when the trucks returned the goods to the warehouse. What would you think of a company with $10 million in sales and $4 million of sales returns?

MiniScribe is alleged to have cooked its books by shipping boxes of bricks labeled as computer parts to its distributors right before year end. The following accounting equations show how the scheme affected MiniScribe's reported figures (assuming sales of $10 million and cost of goods sold of $6 million):

	ASSETS	=	LIABILITIES	+	OWNERS' EQUITY
Sales............................	10	=	0	+	10
Cost of goods sold......	−6	=	0	−	6
Net effect	4	=	0	+	4

The bogus transactions increased the company's assets and equity by $4 million—but only temporarily. The distributors refused to accept the goods and returned them to MiniScribe—but in the next accounting period. In the earlier period, MiniScribe recorded sales revenue and temporarily reported millions of dollars of sales and income that did not exist. The scheme boomeranged in the next period when MiniScribe had to record the sales returns. In virtually every area, accounting imposes a discipline that works to keep every business honest in its financial reporting.

Estimating Inventory

Objective 6

Estimate ending inventory by the gross profit method

Often a business must *estimate* the value of its inventory. Because of cost and inconvenience, few companies physically count inventories at the end of each month, yet they may need monthly financial statements. Suppose the company does not use the perpetual inventory system and thus cannot determine ending inventory by looking at the Inventory account. Fortunately, there is a way to estimate ending inventory for monthly or quarterly financial statements. Also, a fire may destroy inventory, and to file an insurance claim, the business must estimate the value of its loss.

GROSS PROFIT METHOD. A way to estimate inventory on the basis of the cost-of-goods-sold model: Beginning inventory + Net purchases = Cost of goods available for sale. Cost of goods available for sale − Cost of goods sold = Ending inventory. Also called the **gross margin method.**

The **gross profit method,** also known as the *gross margin method,* is a way of estimating inventory on the basis of the familiar cost-of-goods-sold model (amounts assumed for illustration):

Beginning inventory	**$10**
+ Purchases	**50**
= Cost of goods available for sale	**60**
− Ending inventory	**(20)**
= Cost of goods sold	**$40**

Rearranging *ending inventory* and *cost of goods sold* makes the model useful for estimating ending inventory and is illustrated in the following equation and in Exhibit 9-13 (amounts assumed for illustration):

Beginning inventory	**$10**
+ Purchases	**50**
= Cost of goods available for sale	**60**
− Cost of goods sold	**(40)**
= Ending inventory	**$20**

 DAILY EXERCISE 9-17

Suppose a fire destroys your inventory. To collect insurance, you must estimate the cost of the ending inventory. Using your normal *gross profit percent* (that is, gross profit divided by net sales revenue), you can estimate cost of goods sold. Then subtract cost of goods sold from goods available to estimate ending inventory. Exhibit 9-13 illustrates the gross profit method.

Beginning inventory		$14,000
Purchases		66,000
Cost of goods available for sale		80,000
Estimated cost of goods sold:		
Sales revenue..	$100,000	
Less: Estimated gross profit of 40%	(40,000)	
Estimated cost of goods sold.............................		(60,000)
Estimated cost of *ending inventory*.........................		$20,000

WORK IT OUT

Beginning inventory is $70,000, net purchases total $298,000, and net sales are $480,000. With a normal gross profit rate of 40% of sales, how much is ending inventory?

Answer

Beginning inventory		$ 70,000
Net purchases...		298,000
Cost of goods available for sale		368,000
Estimated cost of goods sold:		
Net sales revenue	$480,000	
Less: Estimated gross profit of 40%...........	(192,000)	
Estimated cost of goods sold......................		(288,000)
Estimated cost of ending inventory		$ 80,000

Internal Control

Internal control over inventory is important because inventory is such an important asset. Successful companies take great care to protect their inventory. Elements of good internal control include

1. Physically counting inventory at least once each year
2. Storing inventory to protect it against theft, damage, and decay
3. Giving access only to personnel who have *no* access to the accounting records
4. Not stockpiling too much inventory; this avoids tying up money in unneeded items

Computerized inventory systems allow companies to minimize the amount of inventory on hand (item 4). In a competitive environment, companies cannot afford to tie up cash in too much inventory. Many manufacturing companies use *just-in-time (JIT) inventory systems,* which require suppliers to deliver materials just in time to be used in the production process.

This chapter has discussed various aspects of controlling and accounting for inventory. The Decision Guidelines feature on page 366 summarizes some basic decision guidelines that are helpful in managing a business's inventory operations.

DECISION GUIDELINES

Guidelines for Inventory Management

DECISION	GUIDELINES	SYSTEM OR METHOD
Which inventory system to use?	• Expensive merchandise • Cannot control inventory by visual inspection	→ Perpetual system
	• Can control inventory by visual inspection	→ Periodic system
Which costing method to use?	• Unique inventory items	→ Specific unit cost
	• Most current cost of ending inventory • Maximizes reported income when costs are rising	→ FIFO
	• Most current measure of cost of goods sold and net income • Minimizes income tax when costs are rising	→ LIFO
	• Middle-of-the-road approach for income tax and reported income	→ Weighted-average
How to estimate the cost of ending inventory?	• The cost-of-goods-sold model provides the framework	→ Gross profit (gross margin) method

EXCEL APPLICATION PROBLEM

Goal: Create an Excel spreadsheet that compares gross profit, ending inventory, and cost of goods sold under the LIFO, FIFO, and weighted-average methods of inventory valuation.

Scenario: John Kalinich, Chief Operations Officer at Teva Sport Sandals in Flagstaff, Arizona, has a decision to make. He's in charge of Teva's on-line store, and is responsible for the inventory sold through the Web. John must decide which inventory method to use for the business.

Your task is to create a spreadsheet and embedded graph that compares gross profit, ending inventory, and cost of goods sold under three methods: weighted-average, FIFO, and LIFO. John has provided the following data from the most recent month of operations for your use in creating the spreadsheet:

July	1	Beginning inventory	2,000 units @ $30.00 cost per unit
	6	Purchase	600 units @ $31.25 cost per unit
	17	Purchase	400 units @ $33.50 cost per unit
	28	Purchase	200 units @ $34.75 cost per unit

Sales for July: 1,800 pairs of sandals sold @ $69.00 each

After you have prepared your spreadsheet, answer these questions:

1. Which method produces the lowest cost of goods sold? Why?
2. Which method produces the lowest ending inventory? Why?
3. If John Kalinich wants to maximize gross profit for Teva, which method should he choose? Does this method do a good job of matching inventory expense (cost of goods sold) to sales revenue?

Step-by-step:

1. Open a new Excel spreadsheet.
2. Create a heading for your spreadsheet that contains the following:
   a. Chapter 9 Decision Guidelines
   b. Inventory Management
   c. Teva Sport Sandals
   d. Today's date
3. At the top of your spreadsheet, create a "Data Section" for the July data provided by John Kalinich. Set up columns for Date, Activity (Beginning Inventory, Purchases, Goods Available for Sale, Sales, and Ending Inventory), Units, Unit Cost, and Total Cost. Compute goods available for sale and ending inventory.
4. Include the calculation for "average unit cost" on a separate row in this section.
5. Next, create a section titled "Inventory Method Comparison" in bold print and underlined. Include one column for each method (weighted-average, FIFO, and LIFO). Include rows for Ending Inventory, Cost of Goods Sold, and Gross Profit. Format as necessary. Be sure your calculations are based on the Data Section figures. Do not "hard-code" any amounts in this section.
6. When done, create an embedded bar chart underneath the Inventory Method Comparison section that compares Gross Profit, Ending Inventory, and Cost of Goods Sold for all three methods. (*Hint:* Use the Chart Wizard button on the Standard Excel toolbar.)
7. Save your spreadsheet, and print a copy for your files.

SUMMARY PROBLEM

Mesa Hardware Company began 20X4 with 60,000 units of inventory that cost $36,000. During 19X8, Mesa purchased merchandise on account for $352,500 as follows:

Purchase 1 (100,000 units costing)...............	$ 65,000
Purchase 2 (270,000 units costing)...............	175,500
Purchase 3 (160,000 units costing)...............	112,000

www.prenhall.com/horngren
End-of-Chapter Assessment

Cash payments on account for inventory totaled $326,000 during the year.

Mesa's sales during 20X4 consisted of 520,000 units of inventory for $660,000, all on account. The company uses the FIFO inventory method.

Cash collections from customers were $630,000. Operating expenses totaled $240,500, of which Mesa paid $211,000 in cash. Mesa credited Accrued Liabilities for the remainder.

Required

1. Make summary journal entries to record Mesa Hardware's transactions for the year, assuming the company uses a perpetual inventory system.
2. Determine the FIFO cost of Mesa's ending inventory at December 31, 20X4, two ways:
   a. Use a T-account.
   b. Multiply the number of units by the unit cost.
3. Use the cost-of-goods-sold model to show how Mesa would compute cost of goods sold for 20X4 under the periodic inventory system.
4. Prepare Mesa Hardware's income statement for 20X4. Show totals for the gross profit and net income.

Solution

Requirement 1

Inventory ($65,000 + $175,500 + $112,000)..........	352,500	
Accounts Payable...		352,500
Accounts Payable..	326,000	
Cash...		326,000
Accounts Receivable	660,000	
Sales Revenue...		660,000
Cost of Goods Sold..	339,500	
Inventory..		339,500
[$36,000 + $65,000 + $175,500 + $63,000;		
(90,000 units × $0.70)]($112,000 ÷ 160,000		
units = $0.70 per unit)		
Cash	630,000	
Accounts Receivable		630,000
Operating Expenses	240,500	
Cash...		211,000
Accrued Liabilities		29,500

Requirement 2

a.

INVENTORY	
36,000	339,500
352,500	
49,000	

b. Number of units in ending inventory

(60,000 + 100,000 + 270,000 + 160,000 − 520,000)......................	70,000
Unit cost of ending inventory at FIFO ($112,000 ÷ 160,000)	× $0.70
FIFO cost of ending inventory...........................	$49,000

Requirement 3

Cost of goods sold (periodic inventory system):	
Beginning inventory	$ 36,000
Purchases	352,500
Cost of goods available for sale	388,500
Less: Ending inventory	(49,000)
Cost of goods sold	$339,500

Requirement 4

MESA HARDWARE COMPANY
Income Statement
Year Ended December 31, 20X4

Sales revenue	$660,000
Cost of goods sold	339,500
Gross profit	320,500
Operating expenses	240,500
Net income	$ 80,000

LESSONS LEARNED

1. **Account for inventory by the perpetual and periodic systems.** Inventory is the heart of a merchandiser's business. *Cost of goods sold* is usually the largest expense on the income statement.

   Merchandisers can choose between two inventory systems. *A periodic system* does not keep a running record of the inventory on hand. Instead, at the end of the period, the business counts the inventory and then updates its records. In a *perpetual inventory system,* the business keeps a running record to show inventory on hand at all times. A physical count of inventory is needed in both systems.

2. **Apply the inventory costing methods: specific-unit-cost, weighted-average cost, FIFO, and LIFO.** Businesses multiply inventory quantity by unit cost to determine the cost of this asset. The four inventory costing methods are *specific-unit-cost; weighted-average cost; first-in, first-out (FIFO) cost;* and *last-in, first-out (LIFO) cost.* Businesses that sell unique items use the specific-unit-cost method. Most other companies use the other methods. FIFO reports ending inventory at the most current cost. LIFO reports cost of goods sold at the most current cost. Weighted-average cost falls in the middle.

3. **Identify the income effects and the tax effects of the inventory costing methods.** When prices are rising, LIFO produces the highest cost of goods sold and the lowest income, thus minimizing income taxes. FIFO results in the highest income. The weighted-average cost method falls between the extremes of FIFO and LIFO.

4. **Apply the lower-of-cost-or-market rule to inventory.** The *lower-of-cost-or-market (LCM) rule*—an example of accounting *conservatism*—requires that businesses report inventory on the balance sheet at the lower of its cost or current replacement value. Companies can disclose LCM in notes to their financial statements.

5. **Determine the effects of inventory errors on cost of goods sold and net income.** Inventory overstatements in one period are counterbalanced by understatements in the next period, and understatements are counterbalanced by overstatements.

6. **Estimate ending inventory by the gross profit method.** The *gross profit method* estimates the cost of inventory. It comes in handy for preparing interim financial statements and for estimating the cost of inventory destroyed by fire or other disasters.

ACCOUNTING VOCABULARY

average-cost method (p. 354)
conservatism (p. 361)
consignment (p. 351)
consistency principle (p. 360)
cost of goods available for sale (p. 350)
disclosure principle (p. 361)
first-in, first-out (FIFO) inventory costing method (p. 355)
gross margin (p. 347)

gross margin method (p. 364)
gross profit (p. 347)
gross profit method (p. 364)
last-in, first-out (LIFO) inventory costing method (p. 355)
LIFO liquidation (p. 357)
lower-of-cost-or-market (LCM) rule (p. 361)
materiality concept (p. 361)
merchandising company (p. 347)

periodic inventory system (p. 347)
perpetual inventory system (p. 348)
specific identification method (p. 354)
specific-unit-cost method (p. 354)
weighted-average cost method (p. 354)

QUESTIONS

1. Suppose your company deals in expensive jewelry. Which inventory system should you use to achieve good internal control over the inventory? If your business is a hardware store that sells low-cost goods, which inventory system would you be likely to use? Why would you choose this system?
2. Identify the accounts debited and credited in the standard purchase and sale entries under (a) the perpetual inventory system, and (b) the periodic inventory system.
3. If beginning inventory is $10,000, purchases total $85,000, and ending inventory is $12,700, how much is cost of goods sold?
4. If beginning inventory is $32,000, purchases total $119,000, and cost of goods sold is $127,000, how much is ending inventory?
5. Briefly describe the four generally accepted inventory cost methods. During a period of rising prices, which method produces the highest reported income? Which produces the lowest reported income?
6. Which inventory costing method produces the ending inventory valued at the most current cost? Which method produces the cost-of-goods-sold amount valued at the most current cost?
7. What is the most attractive feature of LIFO? Does LIFO have this advantage during periods of increasing prices or during periods of decreasing prices?
8. Identify the chief criticism of LIFO.
9. Briefly describe the influence that the concept of conservatism has on accounting for inventory.
10. Manley Company's inventory has a cost of $48,000 at the end of the year, and the current replacement cost of the inventory is $51,000. At which amount should the company report the inventory on its balance sheet? Suppose the current replacement cost of the inventory is $45,000 instead of $51,000. At which amount should Manley report the inventory? What rule governs your answers to these questions?
11. Gabriel Company accidentally overstated its ending inventory by $10,000 at the end of period 1. Is gross margin of period 1 overstated or understated? Is gross margin of period 2 overstated, understated, or unaffected by the period-1 error? Is total gross margin for the two periods overstated, understated, or correct? Give the reason for your answers.
12. Identify an important method of estimating inventory amounts. What familiar model underlies this estimation method?
13. True or false? A company that sells inventory of low unit cost needs no internal controls over the goods. Any inventory loss would probably be small.

ASSESS YOUR PROGRESS

DAILY EXERCISES

DE9-1 Beakman Ventures purchased 2,000 units of inventory for $60 each and marked up the goods by $40 per unit. It then sold 1,600 units. For these transactions, show what Beakman would report on its balance sheet at December 31, 20X0 and on its income statement for the year ended December 31, 20X0. Include a complete heading for each statement.

Basic concept of accounting for inventory (Obj. 1)

DE9-2 Study Exhibit 9-3, page 349, and answer these questions:

1. What was the cost of **Deckers'** inventory purchases during the year?
2. How much were Deckers' sales for the year? How much were cost of goods sold and the gross profit? What was the cost of ending inventory?
3. Study the journal entries in Panel A of the exhibit. How can you tell from the journal entries that Deckers is using the perpetual inventory system?

Using the inventory records (Obj. 1)

DE9-3 Rugged River Outfitters purchased inventory costing $85,000 and sold half the goods for $103,000, with all transactions on account.

Journalize these two transactions under the perpetual inventory system. How much gross profit did Rugged River earn on these sales? Which statement reports the gross profit?

Accounting for inventory in the perpetual system (Obj. 1)

DE9-4 Use the data in Daily Exercise 9-3 to record Rugged River Outfitters' purchase and sale transactions under the periodic inventory system. Why can't you measure Rugged River's gross profit under the periodic system? What additional information is needed to compute cost of goods sold and the gross profit?

Accounting for inventory in the periodic system (Obj. 1)

DE9-5 Study Exhibit 9-5, page 354, and answer these questions.

1. In Panel A, are the company's inventory costs stable, increasing, or decreasing during the period? Cite specific figures to support your answer.
2. Which inventory method results in the *lowest* amount for ending inventory (give this figure)? Explain why this method produces the lowest amount for ending inventory.
3. Does this method result in the highest, or the lowest, cost of goods sold? Explain.
4. Does this method result in the highest, or the lowest, gross profit? Explain your answer.

Applying the FIFO, LIFO, and weighted-average methods (Obj. 2)

DE9-6 Study Exhibit 9-5, page 354, and answer these questions.

1. In Panel A, are the company's inventory costs stable, increasing, or decreasing during the period? Cite specific figures to support your answer.
2. Which inventory method results in the *highest* amount for ending inventory (give this figure)? Explain why this method produces the highest amount for ending inventory.
3. Does this method result in the highest, or the lowest, cost of goods sold? Explain.
4. Does this method result in the highest, or the lowest, gross profit? Explain your answer.

Applying the weighted-average, FIFO, and LIFO methods
(Obj. 2)

DE9-7 Return to Exhibit 9-5, page 354, and assume that the business sold 50 units of inventory during the period (instead of 40 units as in the exhibit). Compute ending inventory and cost of goods sold for each of the following costing methods:

a. Weighted-average   **b.** FIFO   **c.** LIFO

Follow the computational format illustrated in the exhibit.

Applying the weighted-average, FIFO, and LIFO methods
(Obj. 2)

DE9-8 Jetlink Data Systems markets ink used in inkjet printers. Jetlink started the year with 100 containers of ink (weighted-average cost of $9.14 each; FIFO cost of $9 each, LIFO cost of $8 each). During the year, Jetlink purchased 800 containers of ink at $14 and sold 700 units for $22 each, with all transactions on account.

Journalize Jetlink's purchases, sales, and cost of goods sold transactions using the following format. Jetlink uses the perpetual inventory method to account for inkjet-printer ink.

	Debit/Credit Amounts		
Accounts	Weighted-Average*	FIFO	LIFO
* Round weighted-average unit cost to the nearest cent.			

Income effects of the inventory costing methods
(Obj. 3)

DE9-9 This exercise uses the data from Daily Exercise 9-8. It can follow Daily Exercise 9-8, or it can be solved independently. Operating expenses totaled $4,000.

Prepare Jetlink Data Systems' income statement for the current year ended December 31 under the weighted-average, FIFO, and LIFO inventory costing methods. Include a complete statement heading, and use a format similar to that illustrated for Daily Exercise 9-8 for the three inventory methods.

Income tax effects of the inventory costing methods
(Obj. 3)

DE9-10 This exercise should be used in conjunction with Daily Exercise 9-9.

Assume Jetlink Data Systems in Daily Exercise 9-9 is a corporation subject to a 40% income tax. Compute Jetlink's income tax expense under the weighted-average, FIFO, and LIFO inventory costing methods. Which method would you select to (a) maximize reported income, or (b) minimize income tax expense? Format your answer as shown on page 356.

Income and tax effects of LIFO
(Obj. 3)

DE9-11 Lands' End, the mail-order merchant, uses the LIFO method to account for inventory. Suppose Lands' End is having an unusually good year, with net income far above expectations. Assume Lands' End's inventory costs are rising rapidly. What can Lands' End managers do immediately before the end of the year to decrease reported profits and thereby save on income taxes? Explain how this action decreases reported income.

Income effects of the inventory methods; using a perpetual inventory record
(Obj. 3)

DE9-12 Examine the perpetual inventory record in Exhibit 9-9, page 359. Answer these questions about **Deckers Outdoor's** inventory of Teva sandals.

1. Which costing method does Deckers use? Prove your answer by citing cost data from the exhibit. Focus on the November 12 sale.
2. Deckers sold all the sandals in the exhibit for $50 each. How much did Deckers report for November sales revenue, cost of goods sold, and gross profit? On which financial statement did Deckers report these figures?

Applying the lower-of-cost-or-market rule to inventory
(Obj. 4)

DE9-13 Deckers Outdoor uses the perpetual inventory record for Teva sandals in Exhibit 9-9, page 359. At December 31, 1999, Scott Ash, chief financial officer of the company, applied the lower-of-cost-or-market rule to Deckers' inventories. Suppose Ash determined that the current replacement cost (current market value) of the sandals was $550. Show how Decker would report this inventory on the balance sheet and cost of goods sold on the income statement.

Measuring the effect of an inventory error—one year only
(Obj. 5)

DE9-14 Examine **Deckers Outdoor's** financial statements in Exhibit 9-1, on page 347. Suppose Deckers' reported cost of inventory at December 31 is overstated by $3 million. What are Deckers' correct amounts for (a) inventory, (b) cost of goods sold, (c) gross profit and (d) net income (net loss)? Ignore income tax.

DE9-15 Barbara Warren, staff accountant of Shimeido Fragrance Co., learned that Shimeido's $4 million cost of inventory at the end of last year was understated by $2 million. She notified the company president of the need to alert Shimeido's lenders that last year's reported net income was incorrect. Akiro Luhara, president of Shimeido, explained to Warren that there is no need to report the error to lenders because the error will counterbalance this year. This year's error will affect this year's net income in the opposite direction of last year's error. Even with no correction, Luhara reasons that net income for both years combined will be the same whether or not Shimeido corrects its error.

Measuring the effect of an inventory error on two years' statements (Obj. 5)

1. Was last year's reported net income of $6.3 million overstated, understated, or correct? What was the correct amount of net income last year?
2. Is this year's net income of $7 million overstated, understated, or correct? What is the correct amount of net income for the current year?
3. Whose perspective is better, Warren's or Luhara's? Give your reason. Consider the trend of reported net income both without the correction and with the correction.

DE9-16 Determine whether each of the following actions in buying, selling, and accounting for inventories is ethical or unethical. Give your reason for each answer.

Ethical implications of inventory actions (Obj. 3, 4, 5)

1. Lake Fork Motors consciously overstated purchases to produce a high figure for cost of goods sold (low amount of net income). The real reason was to decrease the company's income tax payments to the government.
2. In applying the lower-of-cost-or-market rule to inventories, Old World Restoration Co. recorded an excessively low market value for ending inventory. This allowed the company to keep from paying income tax for the year.
3. Lamplight Fixtures Ltd. purchased lots of inventory shortly before year end to increase the LIFO cost of goods sold and decrease reported income for the year.
4. T & M Beauty Products delayed the purchase of inventory until after December 31, 20X2, in order to keep 20X2's cost of goods sold from growing too large. The delay in purchasing inventory helped net income of 20X2 to reach the level of profit demanded by the company's investors.
5. Calais Ferry Supply deliberately overstated ending inventory in order to report higher profits (net income).

DE9-17 Answer the following questions.

Estimating ending inventory by the gross profit method (Obj. 6)

1. Asamax Insulation Company began the year with inventory of $350,000. Inventory purchases for the year totaled $1,600,000. Asamax managers estimate that cost of goods sold for the year will be $1,800,000. How much is Asamax's estimated cost of ending inventory? Use the gross profit method.
2. Cyrus Roofing, a related company, began the year with inventory of $350,000 and purchased $1,600,000 of goods during the year (the same as in requirement 1). Sales for the year are $3,000,000, and Cyrus's gross profit percentage is 40% of sales. Compute Cyrus's estimated cost of ending inventory by the gross profit method. Compare this answer to your answer in requirement 1; they should be the same. Focus on the computation of estimated cost of goods sold to explain why the two answers are the same.

EXERCISES

E9-1 Accounting records for Durall Luggage yield the following data for the year ended December 31, 20X5 (amounts in thousands):

Accounting for inventory in the perpetual system (Obj. 1)

Inventory, December 31, 20X4..	$ 370
Purchases of inventory (on account)	3,105
Sales of inventory—80% on account; 20% for cash (cost $2,821).........	4,395
Inventory, December 31, 20X5..	?

Required

1. Journalize Durall's inventory transactions in the perpetual system. Show all amounts in thousands. Use Exhibit 9-3 on page 349 as a guide.
2. Report ending inventory, sales, cost of goods sold, and gross profit on the appropriate financial statement (amounts in thousands).
3. Show the computation of cost of goods sold in the periodic system.

E9-2 Use the data in Exercise 9-1.

Accounting for inventory in the periodic system (Obj. 1)

Required

1. Journalize Durall's inventory transactions in the periodic system. Show all amounts in thousands, and use Exhibit 9-4, page 353, as a guide.

2. Report inventory, sales, cost of goods sold, and gross profit on the appropriate financial statement (amounts in thousands).

Budgeting inventory purchases
(Obj. 1)

E9-3 **Toys "Я" Us** is budgeting for the fiscal year ended January 31, 2000. During the preceding year ended January 31, 1999, cost of goods sold was $8,191 million. Inventory stood at $1,902 million at January 31, 1999.

During the upcoming 2000 year, suppose Toys "Я" Us expects sales and cost of goods sold to increase by 6%. The company budgets next year's ending inventory at $2,020 million.

Required

How much inventory should Toys "Я" Us purchase during the upcoming year in order to reach its budgeted figures? Round to the nearest $1 million.

Determining ending inventory
and cost of goods sold by four
methods
(Obj. 2)

E9-4 The inventory records of Flexon Prosthetics indicate the following at October 31:

Oct.	1	Beginning inventory	9 units @ $160
	8	Purchase	4 units @ 160
	15	Purchase	12 units @ 170
	26	Purchase	3 units @ 176

The physical count of inventory at October 31 indicates that eight units are on hand, and there are no consignment goods.

Required

Compute ending inventory and cost of goods sold, using each of the following methods. Follow the approach illustrated in Exhibit 9-5.

1. Specific unit cost, assuming four $170 units and four $160 units are on hand
2. Weighted-average cost (round weighted-average unit cost to three decimal places)
3. First-in, first-out   **4.** Last-in, first-out

Recording inventory
transactions—perpetual
system
(Obj. 1, 2)

E9-5 Use the data in Exercise 9-4 to journalize the following for the perpetual inventory system.

a. Total October purchases in one summary entry. All purchases were on credit.
b. Total October sales in a summary entry. The selling price was $300 per unit and all sales were on credit. Flexon Prosthetics uses FIFO.

Recording inventory
transactions—periodic
system
(Obj. 1, 2)

E9-6 Use the data in Exercise 9-4 to journalize the following for the periodic system:

a. Total October purchases in one summary entry. All purchases were on credit.
b. Total October sales in a summary entry. The selling price was $300 per unit and all sales were on credit. Flexon Prosthetics uses LIFO.
c. October 31 end-of-period entries for inventory in the periodic system. Flexon Prosthetics uses LIFO. Post to the Cost of Goods Sold T-account. Label each item in the account. What is the balance of cost of goods sold?

Computing the tax advantage
of LIFO over FIFO   (Obj. 3)

E9-7 Use the data in Exercise 9-4 to illustrate income tax advantage of LIFO over FIFO for Flexon Prosthetics. Sales revenue is $8,000, operating expenses are $1,100, and the income tax rate is 30%. How much in taxes would Flexon Prosthetics save by using the LIFO method?

Determining amounts for the
income statement: periodic
system   (Obj. 1)

E9-8 Supply the missing income statement amounts for each of the following companies:

Company	Net Sales	Beginning Inventory	Net Purchases	Ending Inventory	Cost of Goods Sold	Gross Profit
Maple	$101,800	$12,500	$62,700	$19,400	(a)	$37,000
Walnut	(b)	25,450	93,000	(c)	$94,100	43,200
Pine	94,700	(d)	54,900	22,600	62,500	(e)
Magnolia	84,300	10,700	(f)	8,200	(g)	47,100

Prepare the income statement for Magnolia Company, which uses the periodic inventory system. Include a complete heading. Magnolia's operating expenses for the year were $31,600.

E9-9 ← *Link Back to Chapter 5 (Gross Profit Percentage and Inventory Turnover).* Refer to the data in Exercise 9-8. Suppose you are a financial analyst, and a client has asked you to recommend an investment in one of these companies. Which company is likely to be the most profitable, based on its gross profit percentage and rate of inventory turnover? Write a memo outlining which company you recommend, and explain your reasoning. Use the following format for your memo:

Measuring profitability
(Obj. 3)

Date:	_____
To:	Investor
From:	_____
RE:	Investment recommendation

E9-10 Picker's Paradise carries a large inventory of guitars and other musical instruments. Because each item is expensive, Picker's uses a perpetual inventory system. Company records indicate the following for a particular line of Honeydew guitars:

Determining ending inventory and cost of goods sold in a perpetual system
(Obj. 1, 2)

Date	Item	Quantity	Unit Cost
May 1	Balance....................	5	$95
6	Sale.........................	3	
8	Purchase..................	11	83
17	Sale.........................	4	
30	Sale.........................	1	

Required

Determine the amounts that Picker's should report for ending inventory and cost of goods sold by the FIFO method. Prepare the perpetual inventory record for the guitars, using Exhibit 9-9 as a guide.

E9-11 Homestake Industries is considering a change from the LIFO inventory method to the FIFO method. Managers are concerned about the effect of this change on income tax expense and reported net income. If the change is made, it will become effective on March 1. Inventory on hand at February 28 is $63,000. During March, Homestake managers expect sales of $295,000, net purchases between $159,000 and $182,000, and operating expenses of $83,000. Inventories at March 31 are budgeted as follows: FIFO, $85,000; LIFO, $78,000.

Change from LIFO to FIFO
(Obj. 3)

Required

Create a spreadsheet to compute estimated net income four ways: Net purchases may be $159,000 or $182,000 for March under both FIFO and LIFO. Format your answer as follows:

	A	B	C	D	E
1		**HOMESTAKE INDUSTRIES**				
2		**Estimated Income under FIFO and LIFO**				
3		**March 20XX**				
4						
5		**FIFO**	**LIFO**	**FIFO**	**LIFO**
6					
7	Sales	$295,000	$295,000	$295,000	$295,000
8					
9	Cost of goods sold				
10	Beginning inventory	63,000	63,000	63,000	63,000
11	Net purchases	159,000	159,000	182,000	182,000
12					
13	Cost of goods available				
14	Ending inventory	85,000	78,000	85,000	78,000
15					
16	Cost of goods sold				
17					
18	Gross profit				
19	Operating expenses	83,000	83,000	83,000	83,000
20					
21	Net income	$	$	$	$

Managing income taxes under
the LIFO method
(Obj. 3)

E9-12 Willitz Paper Supply is nearing the end of its best year ever. With three weeks until year end, it appears that net income for the year will have increased by 70% over last year. Bruce Willitz, the principal stockholder and president, is pleased with the year's success but unhappy about the huge increase in income taxes that the business will have to pay.

He asks you, the financial vice president, to come up with a way to decrease the business's income tax. Inventory quantities are a little lower than normal because sales have been especially strong during the last few months. Willitz Paper Supply uses the LIFO inventory method, and inventory costs have risen dramatically late in the year.

Required

Write a memorandum to Bruce Willitz to explain how Willitz Paper Supply can decrease its income taxes for the current year. Willitz is a man of integrity, so your plan must be completely honest. Adapt the memo format given for Exercise 9-9.

Identifying income, tax, and other
effects of the inventory methods
(Obj. 3)

E9-13 This exercise tests your understanding of the four inventory methods. In the space provided, write the name of the inventory method that best fits the description. Assume that the cost of inventory is rising.

_____ a. Generally associated with saving income taxes.
_____ b. Results in a cost of ending inventory that is close to the current cost of replacing the inventory.
_____ c. Used to account for automobiles, jewelry, and art objects.
_____ d. Provides a middle-ground measure of ending inventory and cost of goods sold.
_____ e. Maximizes reported income.
_____ f. Enables a company to buy high-cost inventory at year end and thereby decrease reported income.
_____ g. Reported income and income taxes rise when the company liquidates older, low-cost, layers of inventory.
_____ h. Matches the most current cost of goods sold against sales revenue.
_____ i. Results in an old measure of the cost of ending inventory.

Applying the lower-of-cost-or-
market rule to inventories:
perpetual system
(Obj. 1, 4)

E9-14 Alcoa Enterprises, which uses a perpetual inventory system, has these account balances at December 31, 20X1, prior to releasing the financial statements for the year:

INVENTORY	COST OF GOODS SOLD	SALES REVENUE
Beg. bal. 12,489		
End bal. 18,028	Bal. 113,245	Bal. 225,000

A year ago, when Alcoa prepared its 20X0 financial statements, the replacement cost of ending inventory was $13,051. Alcoa has determined that the replacement cost (current market value) of the December 31, 20X1, ending inventory is $16,840.

Required

Prepare Alcoa Enterprises 20X1 income statement through gross profit to show how Alcoa would apply the lower-of-cost-or-market rule to its inventories. Include a complete heading for the statement.

Applying the lower-of-cost-or-
market rule to inventories:
periodic system
(Obj. 1, 4)

E9-15 Nash-Robin Food Wholesalers uses a periodic inventory system and reports inventory at the lower of FIFO cost or market. Prior to releasing its March 20X4 financial statements, Nash-Robin's preliminary income statement appears as follows:

NASH-ROBIN FOOD WHOLESALERS
Income Statement (partial)

Sales revenue...		$112,000
Cost of goods sold:		
Beginning inventory...	$17,200	
Net purchases..	51,700	
Cost of goods available for sale	68,900	
Ending inventory...	(23,800)	
Cost of goods sold		45,100
Gross profit..		$ 66,900

Nash-Robin has determined that the current replacement cost of ending inventory is $19,800.

Required

Adjust the preceding income statement to apply the lower-of-cost-or market rule to Nash-Robin's inventory. Also show the relevant portion of Nash-Robin's balance sheet. The replacement cost of Nash-Robin's beginning inventory was $18,600.

E9-16 Lazlo Power Tools reported the following comparative income statement for the years ended September 30, 20X2 and 20X1.

Correcting an inventory error—two years (Obj. 5)

LAZLO POWER TOOLS				
Income Statements				
Years Ended September 30, 20X2 and 20X1				
	20X2		**20X1**	
Sales revenue......................		$137,300		$121,700
Cost of goods sold:				
Beginning inventory.........	$14,000		$12,800	
Net purchases..................	72,000		66,000	
Cost of goods available.....	86,000		78,800	
Ending inventory.............	(16,600)		(14,000)	
Cost of goods sold............		69,400		64,800
Gross profit......................		67,900		56,900
Operating expenses...........		30,300		26,100
Net income......................		$ 37,600		$ 30,800

During 20X2, accountants for the company discovered that ending 20X1 inventory was overstated by $3,500. Prepare the corrected comparative income statement for the two-year period, complete with a heading for the statement. What was the effect of the error on net income for the two years combined? Explain your answer.

E9-17 Lakely Marineland began January with inventory of $47,500. The business made net purchases of $37,600 and had net sales of $60,000 before a fire destroyed the company's inventory. For the past several years, Lakely's gross profit on sales has been 40%. Use the gross profit method to estimate the cost of the inventory destroyed by the fire. Identify another purpose for which managers use the gross profit method to estimate inventory cost.

Estimating ending inventory by the gross profit method (Obj. 6)

Challenge Exercises

E9-18 For each of the following situations, identify the inventory method that you would use, or, given the use of a particular method, state the strategy that you would follow to accomplish your goal.

Inventory policy decisions (Obj. 2, 3)

a. Suppliers of your inventory are threatening a labor strike, and it may be difficult for your company to obtain inventory. This situation could increase your income taxes.

b. Inventory costs are decreasing, and your company's board of directors wants to minimize income taxes.

c. Inventory costs are increasing. Your company uses LIFO and is having a very good year. It is near year end, and you need to keep net income from increasing too much.

d. Inventory costs have been stable for several years, and you expect costs to remain stable for the indefinite future. (Give the reason for your choice of method.)

e. Company management, like those of **Polaroid** and **Hewlett-Packard,** prefers a middle-of-the-road inventory policy that avoids extremes.

f. Inventory costs are increasing, and the company prefers to report high income.

E9-19 ◄═ *Link Back to Chapter 5 (Income Statement and Balance Sheet).* **Campbell Soup Company** uses a perpetual inventory system and the LIFO method to determine the cost of its inventory. During the year ended July 31, 19X9, Campbell Soup reported the following items (adapted) in its financial statements (amounts in millions)

Reporting inventory transactions on the income statement and balance sheet (Obj. 1)

Cost of goods sold............	$3,050	Revenues, total...............	$6,424
Other expenses................	2,650	Total assets......................	5,522
Owners' equity................	?	Total liabilities.................	5,287

Required

1. Prepare Campbell Soup Company's summary income statement for the year ended July 31, 19X9, complete with a heading.
2. Prepare Campbell Soup Company's summary balance sheet at July 31, 19X9, complete with a heading.

(Group A) PROBLEMS

Accounting for inventory in a
perpetual system
(Obj. 1, 2)

P9-1A **Pier 1 Imports** operates more than 800 stores. Assume you are dealing with one department in a Pier 1 store in Dallas. The company's fiscal year ends each February 28. Also assume the department began fiscal year 20X0 with an inventory of 50 units that cost $2,135. During the year, the department purchased merchandise on account as follows:

March (60 units @ $32)	$1,920
August (40 units @ $34)	1,360
October (180 units @ $35)	6,300
Total purchases	$9,580

Cash payments on account during the year totaled $9,110.

During fiscal year 20X0, the department sold 300 units of merchandise for $13,400, of which $4,700 was for cash and the balance was on account. Pier 1 uses the weighted-average cost method for inventories.

Operating expenses for the year were $2,430. The department paid two-thirds in cash and accrued the rest.

Required

1. Make summary journal entries to record the department's transactions for the year ended February 28, 20X0. The company uses a perpetual inventory system.
2. Determine the weighted-average cost of the department's ending inventory at February 28, 20X0. Follow the computational approach illustrated in Exhibit 9-5.
3. Prepare the department's income statement for the year ended February 28, 20X0. Show totals for gross profit and net income.

Using the cost-of-goods-sold
model to budget operations
(Obj. 1)

P9-2A Condensed versions of a **Shell** convenience store's most recent income statement and balance sheet reported the following. The business is organized as a proprietorship, so it pays no income tax. It uses a periodic inventory system.

SHELL CONVENIENCE STORE Income Statement Year Ended December 31, 20X1	
(Thousands)	
Sales...	$900
Cost of sales	720
Gross profit	180
Operating expenses...................	90
Net income...............................	$ 90

SHELL CONVENIENCE STORE Balance Sheet December 31, 20X1			
(Thousands) **Assets**		**Liabilities and Capital**	
Cash	$ 40	Accounts payable	$ 30
Inventories	70	Note payable	190
Land and buildings, net.........	270	Total liabilities	220
		Owner, capital......................	160
Total assets...........................	$380	Total liabilities and capital.....	$380

The owner is budgeting for 20X2. He expects sales and cost of sales to increase by 9%. To meet customer demand for the increase in sales, ending inventory will need to be $80 thousand at December 31, 20X2. The owner can lower operating expenses by doing some of the work himself. He hopes to earn a net income of $110 thousand next year.

Required

1. A key variable the owner can control is the amount of inventory he purchases. Show how to determine the amount of purchases the owner should make in 20X2.
2. Prepare the store's budgeted income statement for 20X2 to reach the target net income of $110 thousand.

Using the perpetual and periodic
inventory systems
(Obj. 1, 2)

P9-3A Rambler Lawn Supply began March with 50 units of inventory that cost $17 each. The sale price of each unit was $36. During March, Rambler completed these inventory transactions:

	Units	Unit Cost	Unit Sale Price
March 2 Purchase.........	12	$20	$37
8 Sale......................	27	17	36
13 Sale......................	23	17	36
	1	20	37
17 Purchase..............	24	20	37
22 Sale......................	31	20	37
29 Purchase..............	24	21	39

Required

1. The preceding data are taken from Rambler's perpetual inventory records. Which cost method does Rambler use?
2. Determine Rambler's cost of goods sold for March under the

   a. Perpetual inventory system   b. Periodic inventory system

3. Compute gross profit for March.

P9-4A A Best Yet Electronic Center began December with 140 units of inventory that cost $75 each. During December, the store made the following purchases:

Computing inventory by three methods (Obj. 2, 3)

Dec. 3	217 @ $79
12	95 @ 82
18	210 @ 83
24	248 @ 87

The store uses the periodic inventory system, and the physical count at December 31 indicates that ending inventory consists of 229 units.

Required

1. Determine the ending inventory and cost-of-goods-sold amounts for the December financial statements under the weighted-average, FIFO, and LIFO cost methods. Round weighted-average cost per unit to the nearest cent and all other amounts to the nearest dollar.
2. How much income tax would Best Yet save during December for this one store by using LIFO versus FIFO? The income tax rate is 40%.

P9-5A Assume the records of **Drug Emporium** include the following accounts for one of its products at December 31 of the current year:

Preparing an income statement directly from the accounts (Obj. 2, 3)

INVENTORY

Jan. 1	Balance	300 units @ $3.00	1,215
		100 units @ 3.15	

PURCHASES

Feb. 6	800 units @ $3.15	2,520
May 19	600 units @ 3.35	2,010
Aug. 12	460 units @ 3.50	1,610
Oct. 4	800 units @ 3.95	3,160
Dec. 31—Balance		9,300

SALES REVENUE

Dec. 31	2,600 units	11,200

Required

1. Prepare a partial income statement through gross profit under the weighted-average, FIFO, and LIFO cost methods. Round weighted-average cost to the nearest cent and all other amounts to the nearest dollar. Assume **Drug Emporium** uses a periodic inventory system.
2. Which inventory method would you use to report the highest net income?

Applying the lower-of-cost-or-market rule to inventories
(Obj. 4)

P9-6A **Revco Drug** has been plagued with lackluster sales, and some of the company's merchandise is gathering dust. It is now December 31, 20X1. Assume the current replacement cost of a Revco store's ending inventory is $700,000 below what Revco paid for the goods, which was $3,900,000. Before any adjustments at the end of the period, assume the store's Cost of Goods Sold account has a balance of $22,400,000.

What action should Revco take in this situation, if any? Give any journal entry required. At what amount should Revco report Inventory on the balance sheet? At what amount should the company report Cost of Goods Sold on the income statement? Discuss the accounting principle or concept that is most relevant to this situation.

Correcting inventory errors over a three-year period
(Obj. 5)

P9-7A The accounting records of Treviño's Mexican Restaurant show these data (in thousands):

	20X3		20X2		20X1	
Net sales revenue......................		$210		$165		$170
Cost of goods sold:						
Beginning inventory	$ 15		$ 25		$ 40	
Net purchases........................	135		100		90	
Cost of goods available..........	150		125		130	
Less: Ending inventory.......	(30)		(15)		(25)	
Cost of goods sold..................		120		110		105
Gross profit		90		55		65
Operating expenses...................		74		38		46
Net income..............................		$ 16		$ 17		$ 19

In early 20X4, internal auditors discovered that the ending inventory for 20X1 had been understated by $8 thousand and that the ending inventory for 20X3 had been overstated by $5 thousand. The ending inventory at December 31, 20X2, was correct.

Required

1. Show corrected income statements for the three years.
2. State whether each year's net income as reported here and the related owner's equity amounts are understated or overstated. Ignore income tax because Treviño's is organized as a proprietorship. For each incorrect figure, indicate the amount of the understatement or overstatement.

Estimating ending inventory by the gross profit method; preparing the income statement
(Obj. 6)

P9-8A Padgitt Camera Store estimates its inventory by the gross profit method when preparing monthly financial statements. For the past two years, gross profit has averaged 32% of net sales. Assume further that the company's inventory records for stores in the northwestern region reveal the following data (amounts in thousands):

Inventory, March 1...............................	$ 292
Transactions during March:	
Purchases	6,585
Purchase discounts...........................	149
Purchase returns	8
Sales	8,657
Sales returns....................................	17

Required

1. Estimate the March 31 inventory using the gross profit method.
2. Prepare the March income statement through gross profit for the Padgitt Camera Store stores in the northwestern region.

Reporting inventory items on the income statement and balance sheet
(Obj. 1)

P9-9A ◄ *Link Back to Chapter 5 (Merchandiser's Income Statement and Balance Sheet).* **Gap Inc.,** uses a perpetual inventory system and the FIFO method to determine the cost of its inventory. During a recent year, Gap reported the following items (as adapted) in its financial statements (amounts in millions):

Cost of goods sold....................	$ 6,775	Owners' equity	$	?
Long-term liabilities	1,203	Property, plant, and		
Net sales revenue	11,635	equipment, net.....................		2,715
Other assets.............................	276	Total current assets		2,198
Other expenses........................	3,733	Total current liabilities		1,753

Required

1. Prepare Gap's single-step income statement for the year ended January 29, 20X0, complete with a heading.
2. Prepare Gap's balance sheet at January 29, 20X0, complete with a heading.

PROBLEMS

P9-1B **Toys "Я" Us** purchases inventory in crates of merchandise, so each unit of inventory is a crate of toys. Assume you are dealing with a single department in the Toys "Я" Us store in Santa Barbara, California. The fiscal year of Toys "Я" Us ends each January 31.

Accounting for inventory using the perpetual system (Obj. 1, 2)

Assume the department began fiscal year 20X5 with an inventory of 20 units that cost a total of $1,200. During the year, the department purchased merchandise on accounts as follows:

April (30 units @ $65)	$ 1,950
August (50 units @ $65)......................	3,250
November (110 units @ $70)...............	7,700
Total purchases	$12,900

Cash payments on account during the year totaled $11,390.

During fiscal year 20X5, the department sold 180 units of merchandise for $16,400, of which $5,300 was for cash and the balance was on account. Toys "Я" Us uses the LIFO method for inventories. Department operating expenses for the year were $3,630. The department paid two-thirds in cash and accrued the rest.

Required

1. Make summary journal entries to record the department's transactions for the year ended January 31, 20X5. Toys "Я" Us uses a perpetual inventory system.
2. Determine the LIFO cost of the store's ending inventory at January 31, 20X5. Use a T-account.
3. Prepare the department's income statement for the year ended January 31, 20X5. Include a complete heading, and show totals for gross profit and net income.

P9-2B Condensed versions of a **Chevron** convenience store's most recent income statement and balance sheet reported the following figures. The business uses a periodic inventory system.

Using the cost-of-goods-sold model to budget operations (Obj. 1)

CHEVRON CONVENIENCE STORE
Balance Sheet
December 31, 20X4

(Thousands)	Assets	Liabilities and Capital	
Cash.........................	$ 70	Accounts payable.............	$ 35
Inventories	35	Note payable	280
Land and buildings, net...	360	Total liabilities..................	315
		Owner, capital..................	150
Total assets......................	$465	Total liabilities and capital	$465

CHEVRON CONVENIENCE STORE
Income Statement
Year Ended December 31, 20X4

	(Thousands)
Sales..	$800
Cost of sales	660
Gross profit.................................	140
Operating expenses	80
Net income	$ 60

The owner is budgeting for 20X5. He expects sales and cost of sales to increase by 8%. To meet customer demand for the increase in sales, ending inventory will need to be $40 thousand at December 31, 20X5. The owner can lower operating expenses by doing some of the work himself. He hopes to earn a net income of $75 thousand next year.

Required

1. A key variable the owner can control is the amount of inventory he purchases. Show how to determine the amount of purchases he should make in 20X5 (amounts in thousands).
2. Prepare the store's budgeted income statement for 20X5 to reach the target net income of $75 thousand.

P9-3B A **Samsonite** outlet store began August 20X1 with 50 units of inventory that cost $40 each. The sale price of these units was $70. During August, the store completed these inventory transactions:

Using the perpetual and periodic inventory systems (Obj. 1, 2)

		Units	Unit Cost	Unit Sale Price
Aug. 3	Sale........................	16	$40	$70
8	Purchase................	80	41	72
11	Sale........................	34	40	70
19	Sale........................	9	41	72
24	Sale........................	35	41	72
30	Purchase................	18	42	73
31	Sale........................	11	41	72

Required

1. The preceding data are taken from the store's perpetual inventory records. Which cost method does the store use?
2. Determine the store's cost of goods sold for August under the

   a. Perpetual inventory system   b. Periodic inventory system

3. Compute gross profit for August.

Computing inventory by three methods (Obj. 2, 3)

P9-4B Lafferty Framing Co. began March with 73 units of inventory that cost $23 each. During the month, Lafferty made the following purchases:

March 4................................	113 @ $26
12................................	81 @ 30
19................................	167 @ 32
25................................	44 @ 35

The company uses the periodic inventory system, and the physical count at March 31 includes 51 units.

Required

1. Determine the ending inventory and cost-of-goods-sold amounts for the March financial statements under (a) weighted-average cost, (b) FIFO cost, and (c) LIFO cost. Round weighted-average cost per unit to the nearest cent and all other amounts to the nearest dollar.
2. How much income tax would Lafferty Framing save during the month by using LIFO versus FIFO? The income tax rate is 35%.

Preparing an income statement directly from the accounts (Obj. 2, 3)

P9-5B The records of Heavenly Confection Co. include the following accounts at December 31 of the current year:

INVENTORY

Jan.	1	Balance (700 units @ $6.45)	4,515	

PURCHASES

Jan.	6	300 units @ $7.05	2,115	
Mar.	19	1,100 units @ 7.35	8,085	
June	22	8,400 units @ 7.50	63,000	
Oct.	4	500 units @ 8.50	4,250	
Dec.	31	Balance	77,450	

SALES REVENUE

			Dec. 31	10,100 units	138,070

Required

1. Prepare a partial income statement through gross profit under the weighted-average, FIFO, and LIFO methods. Round weighted-average cost to the nearest cent and all other amounts to the nearest dollar. Heavenly Confection uses a periodic inventory system.
2. Which inventory method would you use to minimize income tax?

P9-6B The Army/Navy Surplus Store has experienced lackluster sales, and some of the company's merchandise is gathering dust. It is now December 31, 20X2, and the current replacement cost of the ending inventory is $650,000 below what Army/Navy actually paid for the goods, which was $4,900,000. Before any adjustments at the end of the period, the company's Cost of Goods Sold account has a balance of $29,600,000.

Applying the lower-of-cost-or-market rule to inventories (Obj. 4)

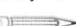

What action should The Army/Navy Surplus Store take in this situation, if any? Give any journal entry required. At what amount should Army/Navy report Inventory on the balance sheet? At what amount should the company report Cost of Goods Sold on the income statement? Discuss the accounting principle or concept that is most relevant to this situation.

P9-7B The Lamarque Copper Company books show the data (in thousands) on page 435. In early 20X3, internal auditors found that the ending inventory for 20X0 had been overstated by $8 thousand and that the ending inventory for 20X2 had been understated by $4 thousand. The ending inventory at December 31, 20X1, was correct.

Correcting inventory errors over a three-year period (Obj. 5)

(Thousands)	20X2	20X1	20X0
Net sales revenue	$360	$285	$244
Cost of goods sold:			
Beginning inventory...........	$ 65	$ 55	$ 70
Net purchases.....................	195	135	130
Cost of goods available	260	190	200
Less: Ending inventory.....	(70)	(65)	(55)
Cost of goods sold	190	125	145
Gross profit............................	170	160	99
Operating expenses................	113	109	76
Net income............................	$ 57	$ 51	$ 23

Required

1. Show corrected income statements for the three years.
2. State whether each year's net income and owner's equity amounts are understated or overstated. Ignore income tax because Lamarque is a proprietorship. For each incorrect figure, indicate the amount of the understatement or overstatement.

P9-8B Beaucock Publishing estimates its inventory by the gross profit method when preparing monthly financial statements. The gross profit has averaged 43% of net sales. The company's inventory records reveal the following data (amounts in thousands):

Estimating ending inventory by the gross profit method; preparing the income statement (Obj. 6)

Inventory, July 1.............................	$ 367
Transactions during July:	
Purchases	3,789
Purchase discounts....................	26
Purchase returns	12
Sales	6,430
Sales returns.............................	25

Required

1. Estimate the July 31 inventory, using the gross profit method.
2. Prepare the July income statement through gross profit for Beaucock Publishing.

P9-9B ◂ *Link Back to Chapter 5 (Merchandiser's Income Statement and Balance Sheet).* **Lands' End, Inc.,** uses a perpetual inventory system and the LIFO method to determine the cost of its inventory. During a recent year, Lands' End reported the following items (adapted) in its financial statements (amounts in millions):

Reporting inventory items on the income statement and balance sheet (Obj. 1)

Cost of goods sold......................	$ 727	Interest revenue	$ 1
Long-term liabilities	9	Owners' equity.............................	?
Net sales revenue	1,320	Property, plant, & equipment, net	166
Other assets...............................	1	Total current assets.......................	289
Other expenses...........................	546	Total current liabilities.................	151

Required

1. Prepare a single-step income statement for Lands' End for the year ended January 28, 2000, complete with a heading.
2. Prepare the Lands' End balance sheet at January 28, 2000, complete with a heading.

Apply Your Knowledge

Decision Cases

Measuring the impact of a year-end purchase of inventory (Obj. 2, 3)

Case 1. Lena's Shoes is nearing the end of its first year of operations. The company made inventory purchases of $745,000 during the year, as follows:

January..................	1,000 units @ $100.00 =		$100,000
July.......................	4,000	121.25	485,000
November.............	1,000	160.00	160,000
Totals....................	6,000		$745,000

Sales for the year will be 5,000 units for $1,200,000 revenue. Expenses other than cost of goods sold and income taxes will be $200,000. The president of the company is undecided about whether to adopt the FIFO method or the LIFO method for inventories.

The company has storage capacity for 5,000 additional units of inventory. Inventory prices are expected to stay at $160 per unit for the next few months. The president is considering purchasing 1,000 additional units of inventory at $160 each before the end of the year. He wishes to know how the purchase would affect net income under both FIFO and LIFO. The income tax rate is 42%.

Required

1. To aid the decision, prepare income statements under FIFO and under LIFO, both without and with the year-end purchase of 1,000 units of inventory at $160 per unit.
2. Compare net income under FIFO without and with the year-end purchase. Make the same comparison under LIFO. Under which method does the year-end purchase affect net income?

Assessing the impact of the inventory costing methods on the financial statements (Obj. 2, 3, 4)

Case 2. The inventory costing method a company chooses can affect the financial statements and thus the decisions of the people who use those statements.

Required

1. A leading accounting researcher stated that one inventory costing method reports the most recent costs in the income statement, while another reports the most recent costs in the balance sheet. What did the researcher mean? Name the methods.
2. Conservatism is an accepted accounting concept. Would you want the management of your company to be conservative in accounting for inventory? Give your reason.
3. TriArc Co. follows conservative accounting and writes the value of its inventory of bicycles down to market, which has declined below cost. The following year, an unexpected cycling craze results in a demand for bicycles that far exceeds supply, and the market price increases above the previous cost. What effect will conservatism have on the income of TriArc during each year?

Ethical Issue

During 20X2, Darden Furniture Company changed to the LIFO method of accounting for inventory. Suppose that during 20X3, Darden changes back to the FIFO method and the following year switches back to LIFO again.

Required

1. What would you think of a company's ethics if it changes accounting methods every year?

2. What accounting principle would changing methods every year violate?

3. Who can be harmed when a company changes its accounting methods too often? How?

FINANCIAL STATEMENT CASE

Analyzing inventories
(Obj. 2)

The notes are an important part of a company's financial statements, giving valuable details that would clutter the tabular data presented in the statements. This case will help you learn to use a company's inventory notes. Refer to the **Target** financial statements and related notes in Appendix A and answer the following questions:

Required

1. How much was the Target merchandise inventory at January 29, 2000? At January 30, 1999?

2. How does Target value its inventories? Which cost methods does the company use? Ignore the *retail method* that Target refers to.

3. By rearranging the cost-of-goods-sold formula, you can determine purchases, which are not disclosed in the Target statements. How much were the company's inventory purchases during the year ended January 29, 2000?

TEAM PROJECT

◀◀ *Link Back to Chapter 5 (Gross Profit Percentage and Inventory Turnover).* Obtain the annual reports of as many companies as you have team members—one company per team member. Most companies post their financial statements on their Web sites.

Required

1. Identify the inventory method used by each company.

2. Compute each company's gross profit percentage and rate of inventory turnover for the most recent two years.

3. For the industries of the companies you are analyzing, obtain the industry averages for gross profit percentage and inventory turnover from Robert Morris Associates, *Annual Statement Studies;* Dun and Bradstreet, *Industry Norms and Key Business Ratios;* or Leo Troy, *Almanac of Business and Industrial Financial Ratios.*

4. How well does each of your companies compare to the average for its industry? What insight about your companies can you glean from these ratios?

INTERNET EXERCISE

General Motors (GM) remains the world's Number 1 maker of cars and trucks, including the Buick, Cadillac, Chevrolet, GMC, Oldsmobile, Pontiac, and Saturn brands.

1. In the past, General Motors has also been ranked Number 1 in the Fortune 500 listing. Go to **http://www.Fortune.com** and under "Lists" click on *Fortune 500.* What is GM's Fortune 500 ranking this year?

2. Click on *General Motors* and then click on the URL for GM, **www.gm.com,** and go to GM's Web site. Click on *The Company* followed by *Investor Information.* Select the *most recent annual report* and watch the video show. Use the information in the annual report to answer the following questions.

   a. Read the "Letter to Stockholders." Did GM have a good year? Give the basis for your evaluation.

   b. Refer to the "Consolidated Statements of Income for General Motors Corporation and Subsidiaries." For the two most recent years, list the amounts reported for "Total net sales and revenues" and "Cost of sales and other operating expenses." For each year, calculate gross profit. Comment on the trend of gross profit, what the trend indicates, and whether the trend is favorable or unfavorable.

   c. Refer to the "Consolidated Balance Sheets for General Motors Corporation and Subsidiaries." For the two most recent years, list the amounts reported for "Inventories." For the most recent year, calculate the rate of inventory turnover. On average, how many days does GM hold inventory before selling it?

General Motors

[m̲ B̲ accounting]
MASTERING
BUSINESS

Go to the "Depreciation Methods and Inventory Cost Flow Assumptions" episode on the *Mastering Accounting* CD-Rom for an interactive, video-enhanced exercise focused on the different methods for depreciation and inventory. CanGo staff must prepare reports that present potential investors with the best possible financial outlook for the company.

APPENDIX TO CHAPTER 9

COMPARING THE PERPETUAL AND PERIODIC INVENTORY SYSTEMS

DAILY EXERCISE 9-4

Exhibit 9A-1 provides a side-by-side comparison of the two inventory accounting systems. It combines the material from Exhibits 9-3 and 9-4. Both systems report the same amounts for inventory, cost of goods sold, and everything else.

 THINK IT OVER

Answer the following questions about various features of the perpetual inventory system and the periodic inventory system.

1. Do the perpetual and periodic inventory systems result in the same or different dollar amounts for Inventory and Cost of Goods Sold? Explain.

2. a. Which inventory system records the cost of inventory purchased as an asset and the cost of inventory sold as expense?

   b. Which inventory system records the cost of inventory purchased as an expense (name the expense account) and then sets up the cost of ending inventory as an asset?

3. Suppose your company produces microchips for use in making computer circuit boards. Technology is advancing rapidly, and you need monthly financial statements to remain competitive. Which inventory system should you use?

PANEL A—Recording in the Journal and Posting to the T-accounts

Perpetual System	Periodic System

1. Credit purchases of $560,000:
Inventory.................................... 560,000
    Accounts Payable.............. 560,000
	1. Credit purchases of $560,000:
	Purchases..................................... 560,000
	    Accounts Payable.............. 560,000

2. Credit sales of $900,000 (cost $540,000):
Accounts Receivable................... 900,000
    Sales Revenue......................... 900,000
Cost of Goods Sold 540,000
    Inventory........................ 540,000
	2. Credit sales of $900,000:
	Accounts Receivable................... 900,000
	    Sales Revenue................... 900,000

3. End-of-period entries:
 	
No entries required. Both Inventory and Cost of Goods Sold are up-to-date.
	3. End-of-period entries to update Inventory and record Cost of Goods Sold:
	a. Transfer the cost of beginning inventory ($100,000) to Cost of Goods Sold:
	Cost of Goods Sold 100,000
	    Inventory (beginning balance) 100,000
	
	b. Record the cost of ending inventory ($120,000) based on a physical count:
	Inventory (ending balance)........ 120,000
	    Cost of Goods Sold............ 120,000
	
	c. Transfer the cost of purchases to Cost of Goods Sold:
	Cost of Goods Sold 560,000
	    Purchases......................... 560,000

INVENTORY AND COST OF GOODS SOLD ACCOUNTS (Perpetual)

INVENTORY		COST OF GOODS SOLD	
100,000*	540,000	540,000	
560,000			
120,000			

*Beginning inventory was $100,000

INVENTORY AND COST OF GOODS SOLD ACCOUNTS (Periodic)

INVENTORY		COST OF GOODS SOLD	
100,000**	100,000	100,000	120,000
120,000		560,000	
		540,000	

**Beginning inventory was $100,000

PANEL B—Reporting in the Financial Statements

Perpetual System	Periodic System

Income Statement (partial)

Perpetual System		Periodic System		
Sales revenue	$900,000	Sales revenue		$900,000
Cost of goods sold	540,000	Cost of goods sold:		
Gross profit.............................	$360,000	Beginning inventory......................	$100,000	
		Purchases.....................................	560,000	
		Cost of goods available for sale......	660,000	
		Less: Ending inventory	(120,000)	
		Cost of goods sold		540,000
		Gross profit.......................................		$360,000

Balance Sheet (partial)

Perpetual System		Periodic System	
Current assets:		Current assets:	
Cash	$ XXX	Cash...	$ XXX
Accounts receivable	XXX	Accounts receivable........................	XXX
Inventories.........................	120,000	Inventories	120,000

10

Plant Assets and Intangible Assets

LEARNING OBJECTIVES

*After studying this chapter,
you should be able to*

1. Measure the cost of a plant asset

2. Account for depreciation

3. Select the best depreciation method for income tax purposes

4. Account for the disposal of a plant asset

5. Account for natural resource assets and depletion

6. Account for intangible assets and amortization

The Home Depot is the world's largest home improvement dealer and ranks among the largest retailers in the United States. The company has experienced major growth, and it plans to keep expanding. The Home Depot's business strategy is twofold: (1) offer high-quality merchandise at "Day-In, Day-Out" warehouse prices and (2) provide exceptional customer service.

Fiscal 1999 (the year ended January 30, 2000) marked the 13th straight year of record profits. Assets topped $17 billion. Over $10 billion of these assets are property, plant, and equipment, the subject of this chapter.

Source: The Home Depot® *1999 Annual Report.*

ow did **The Home Depot** grow so rapidly? By opening new stores at a fast pace. The Home Depot's balance sheet (Exhibit 10-2) shows the effect of the company's growth. During the most recent year, total assets grew to $17.1 billion (line 13). Much of the growth shows up in Property and equipment (lines 2–10), collectively labeled *plant assets,* which we examine in this chapter. ➡

This chapter also covers *intangibles,* those assets without physical form, such as Cost in excess of the fair value of net assets acquired—better known as *goodwill.* This is the next-to-last asset reported on Home Depot's balance sheet (line 11). Finally, we discuss natural resources (such as oil, gas, timber, and gravel). The expenses that relate to plant assets, natural resources, and intangible assets are *depreciation, depletion,* and *amortization.*

Chapter 10 concludes our coverage of assets, except for investments (Chapter 16). After completing this chapter, you should understand the various assets of a business and how to account for them.

◄ We introduced plant assets in Chapter 3, page 90.

MEASURING THE COST OF PLANT ASSETS

Plant assets, or **fixed assets,** are long-lived tangible assets—for instance, land, buildings, and equipment—used to operate a business and not held for sale. Their physical form provides their usefulness. The expense associated with plant assets is called *depreciation.* ➡ Of the plant assets, land is unique. Its cost is *not* depreciated—expensed over time—because its usefulness does not decrease. Most companies report plant assets under the heading Property, plant, and equipment on the balance sheet.

Intangible assets do not have a physical form. We cannot see or touch them. They are useful only because of the special rights they carry. Patents, copyrights, and trademarks are intangible assets, and their accounting is similar to that for plant assets. Accounting for intangibles has its own terminology. Exhibit 10-1 shows that we refer to the using up of intangibles as *amortization,* which is the same concept as depreciation.

To begin our study, let's take a tour of **The Home Depot** balance sheet in Exhibit 10-2. The company holds land, buildings, and other plant assets (lines 2–8). Total cost is $11.9 billion (line 8). Home Depot has used up (depreciated) $1.7 billion of its plant assets (line 9). This is what accumulated depreciation on the balance sheet means—the used-up portion of the plant asset. The book value of these assets (cost less accumulated depreciation) is $10.2 billion (line 10). Home Depot's goodwill has a book value of $311 million (line 11).

The *cost principle* directs a business to carry an asset on the balance sheet at its cost—the amount paid for the asset. The general rule for measuring cost (repeated from Chapter 9, page 350) is

PLANT ASSETS. Long-lived tangible assets, such as land, buildings, and equipment, used to operate a business. Also called **fixed assets.**

◄ We introduced the concept of depreciation in Chapter 3, page 90.

INTANGIBLE ASSETS. Assets with no physical form. Valuable because of the special rights they carry. Examples are patents and copyrights.

Objective 1
Measure the cost of a plant asset

$$\text{The cost of an asset} = \frac{\text{The sum of all the costs incurred to bring the asset}}{\text{to its intended purpose, net of all discounts}}$$

The *cost of a plant asset* is its purchase price plus applicable taxes, purchase commissions, and all other amounts paid to acquire the asset and make it ready for its intended use. In Chapter 9, we applied this principle to inventory. The types of costs differ for the various plant assets, so we discuss each asset individually.

Asset Account on the Balance Sheet	Related Expense Account on the Income Statement
Plant Assets	
Land..	None
Buildings, Machinery, and Equipment, Furniture and Fixtures, and Land Improvements..	Depreciation
Natural Resources..	Depletion
Intangibles...	Amortization

EXHIBIT 10-2
The Home Depot Balance Sheet
(partial, adapted)

THE HOME DEPOT, INC.
Balance Sheet (Adapted, Assets Only)
Amounts in Millions
January 30, 2000

Assets

	Current Assets:	
1	Total Current Assets	$6,390
	Property and Equipment, at cost:	
2	Land	3,248
3	Buildings	4,834
4	Furniture, fixtures, and equipment	2,279
5	Leasehold improvements	493
6	Construction in progress	791
7	Capital leases	245
8	Total cost of plant assets	11,890
9	Less Accumulated depreciation	(1,663)
10	Net property and equipment	10,227
11	Cost in excess of the fair value of net assets acquired, net of accumulated amortization of $33	311
12	Other assets	153
13	Total Assets	$17,081

Plant assets = lines 2–7. *Intangibles* = lines 11–12.

DAILY EXERCISE 10-1

Land and Land Improvements

The cost of land includes its purchase price, brokerage commission, survey and legal fees, and any back property taxes that the purchaser pays. Land cost also includes the cost of clearing the land and removing any unwanted buildings. The cost of land is not depreciated.

The cost of land does *not* include fencing, paving, sprinkler systems, and lighting. These separate plant assets—called *land improvements*—are subject to depreciation.

Suppose The Home Depot signs a $500,000 note payable to purchase land for a store site. Home Depot also pays $40,000 in back property tax, $8,000 in transfer taxes, $5,000 to remove an old building, a $1,000 survey fee, and $260,000 to pave the parking lot, all in cash. What is the cost of this land? The cost of paving the lot, $260,000, is *not* included in the Land account. The pavement is a land improvement.

Purchase price of land..............		$500,000
Add related costs:		
Back property taxes..............	$40,000	
Transfer taxes	8,000	
Removal of building.............	5,000	
Survey fee	1,000	
Total related costs................		54,000
Total cost of land.....................		$554,000

Home Depot's entries to record purchase of the land and pavement of the parking lot are as follows:

Land	554,000	
Note Payable		500,000
Cash		54,000

We would say that The Home Depot *capitalized* the cost of the land at $554,000. This means that the company debited an asset account (Land) for $554,000.

Land Improvements	260,000	
Cash		260,000

Land and Land Improvements are two entirely separate asset accounts. Land improvements include lighting, signs, fences, paving, sprinkler systems, and landscaping. These costs are debited to the Land Improvements account and then depreciated over their useful life.

Buildings

 DAILY EXERCISE 10-2

The cost of constructing a building includes architectural fees, building permits, contractors' charges, and payments for material, labor, and overhead. The time to complete a building can be months, even years. If the company constructs its own assets, the cost of the building may include the cost of interest on borrowed money. (We discuss this topic in the next section of the chapter.) When an existing building is purchased, its cost includes all the usual items, plus the cost to repair and renovate the building.

Machinery and Equipment

The cost of machinery and equipment includes its purchase price (less any discounts), plus transportation charges, insurance while in transit, sales and other taxes, purchase commission, installation costs, and the cost of testing the asset before it is used. After the asset is up and running, we cease capitalizing these costs to the Equipment account. Thereafter, insurance, taxes, and maintenance costs are recorded as expenses.

Leasehold Improvements

Leasehold improvements are similar to land improvements. Leasehold improvements are alterations to assets the company is leasing. For example, The Home Depot leases store buildings, warehouses, and vehicles. The company customizes leased assets by painting its logo on trucks and buildings.

These improvements are assets of The Home Depot even though the company does not own the truck or building. Leasehold improvements appear on the company's balance sheet (see line 5 of Home Depot's balance sheet on page 388). Leasehold improvements should be amortized (depreciated) over the term of the lease.

Construction in Progress and Capital Leases

The Home Depot's balance sheet includes two additional categories of plant assets: Construction in progress (line 6) and Capital leases (line 7).

CONSTRUCTION IN PROGRESS *Construction in progress* is an asset, such as a warehouse, that the company is constructing for its own use. The construction is incomplete and the warehouse is not ready for use. However, the construction costs are assets because the warehouse, when completed, will render future benefits for the company.

CAPITAL LEASES A *capital lease* is a lease arrangement similar to the installment purchase of an asset. Companies report assets leased through capital leases as assets even though they do not own them. After all, their lease payments secure the use of the asset over the term of the lease. For example, The Home Depot has long-term capital leases on some of its store buildings. The Home Depot reports the cost of these plant assets under Capital leases on the balance sheet.

DAILY EXERCISE 10-3

A capital lease is different from an *operating lease,* which is an ordinary rental agreement, such as your dorm room or apartment lease or the rental of a **Hertz** automobile. The renter records rent expense for each payment under an operating lease.

Capitalizing the Cost of Interest

CAPITALIZE A COST. To record a cost as part of an asset's cost, rather than as an expense.

The Home Depot constructs some of its plant assets and finances the construction with borrowed money. The Home Depot pays interest that it includes as part of the cost of a self-constructed asset. Including interest in the asset's total cost is called *capitalizing interest.* To **capitalize a cost** means to debit an asset (versus an expense) account.

Suppose on July 2, 20X2, The Home Depot borrows $1,000,000 on a two-year, 10% note payable to build a warehouse. The interest cost for 20X2 on this note payable is $50,000 ($1,000,000 × .10 × 6/12). Assume all of this interest cost should be capitalized as part of the cost of the building. The Home Depot's entry for the construction cost is

20X2			
July–Dec.	Building..	1,000,000	
	Cash		1,000,000
	Incurred construction cost.		

The Home Depot's entry to capitalize the interest paid at year end is as follows:

DAILY EXERCISE 10-4

20X2			
Dec. 31	Building..	50,000	
	Cash		50,000
	Paid interest on construction loan.		

A Lump-Sum (Basket) Purchase of Assets

Businesses often purchase several assets as a group, or in a "basket," for a single amount. For example, a company may pay one price for land and an office building. For accounting purposes the company must identify the cost of each asset. The total cost is divided among the assets according to their relative sales (or market) values. This allocation technique is called the *relative-sales-value method.*

Suppose **Xerox Corporation** purchases land and a building in Kansas City for a midwestern sales office. The combined purchase price of land and building is $2,800,000. An appraisal indicates that the land's market (sales) value is $300,000 and that the building's market (sales) value is $2,700,000.

First, figure the ratio of each asset's market value to the total market value of both assets combined. Suppose the total appraised value is $2,700,000 + $300,000 = $3,000,000. Thus, the land, valued at $300,000, is 10% of the total market value. The building's appraised value is 90% of the total. The cost of each asset is determined as follows:

Asset	Market (Sales) Value	Percentage of Total Value		Total Purchase Price	Cost of Each Asset
Land	$ 300,000	$300,000/$3,000,000 =	10% ×	$2,800,000 =	$ 280,000
Building	2,700,000	$2,700,000/$3,000,000 =	90% ×	2,800,000 =	2,520,000
Total	$3,000,000		100%		$2,800,000

If Xerox pays cash, the entry to record the purchase of the land and building is

Land..	280,000	
Building	2,520,000	
Cash		2,800,000

WORK IT OUT

How would a business divide a $120,000 lump-sum purchase price for land, building, and equipment with estimated market values of $40,000, $95,000, and $15,000, respectively? Round decimals to three places.

Answer

Asset	Market (Sales) Value	Percentage of Total Value			Total Purchase Price		Cost of Each Asset
Land..............	$ 40,000	$40,000/$150,000	=	26.7% ×	$120,000	=	$ 32,040
Building	95,000	$95,000/$150,000	=	63.3% ×	120,000	=	75,960
Equipment...	15,000	$15,000/$150,000	=	10.0% ×	120,000	=	12,000
Total	$150,000			100.0%			$120,000

 DAILY EXERCISE 10-5

Capital Expenditures

When a company makes a plant asset expenditure, it must decide whether to debit an asset account or an expense account. In this context, *expenditure* refers to a cash or a credit purchase of goods or services related to the asset. Examples of such expenditures range from **General Motors'** purchase of robots for an assembly plant to a motorist's replacing the windshield on a Chevrolet.

Expenditures that increase the asset's capacity or efficiency or extend its useful life are called **capital expenditures.** For example, the cost of a major overhaul that extends a taxi's useful life is a capital expenditure. Repair work that generates a capital expenditure is called a **major repair,** or an **extraordinary repair.** The amount of the capital expenditure, said to be capitalized, is debited to an asset account. For an extraordinary repair on a taxi, we would debit the asset account Automobiles.

Other expenditures that do not extend the asset's capacity, which merely maintain the asset or restore it to working order, are called *expenses.* These costs are matched against revenue. Examples include the costs of repainting a taxi, repairing a dented fender, and replacing tires. These costs are debited to an expense account. For the **ordinary repairs** on the taxi, we would debit Repair Expense.

The distinction between capital and maintenance expenditures is often a matter of opinion. Does the cost extend the life of the asset (a capital expenditure), or does it only maintain the asset in good order (an expense)? When in doubt, companies tend to debit an expense, for two reasons. First, many expenditures are minor and most companies have a policy of debiting expense for all expenditures below a specific minimum, such as $1,000. Second, the income tax motive favors debiting all borderline expenditures to expense in order to create an immediate tax deduction. Exhibit 10-3 illustrates the distinction between capital expenditures and expenses for several delivery-truck expenditures.

CAPITAL EXPENDITURE. Expenditure that increases the capacity or efficiency of an asset or extends its useful life. Capital expenditures are debited to an asset account.

MAJOR REPAIR OR EXTRAORDINARY REPAIR. Repair work that generates a capital expenditure.

ORDINARY REPAIR. Repair work that is debited to an expense account.

DEBIT AN ASSET ACCOUNT FOR CAPITAL EXPENDITURES	DEBIT REPAIR AND MAINTENANCE EXPENSE FOR AN EXPENSE
Extraordinary repairs:	*Ordinary repairs:*
Major engine overhaul	Repair of transmission or engine
Modification of truck body for new use	Oil change, lubrication, and so on
Addition to storage capacity of truck	Replacement tires or windshield
	Paint job

EXHIBIT 10-3
Delivery-Truck Expenditures— Capital Expenditure or Expense

Treating a capital expenditure as an expense, or vice versa, creates errors in the financial statements. Suppose a company makes a capital expenditure and erroneously expenses this cost. A capital expenditure should have been debited to an asset account. This accounting error overstates expenses and understates net income on the income statement. On the balance sheet, the Equipment account is understated, and so is owner's equity, as follows:

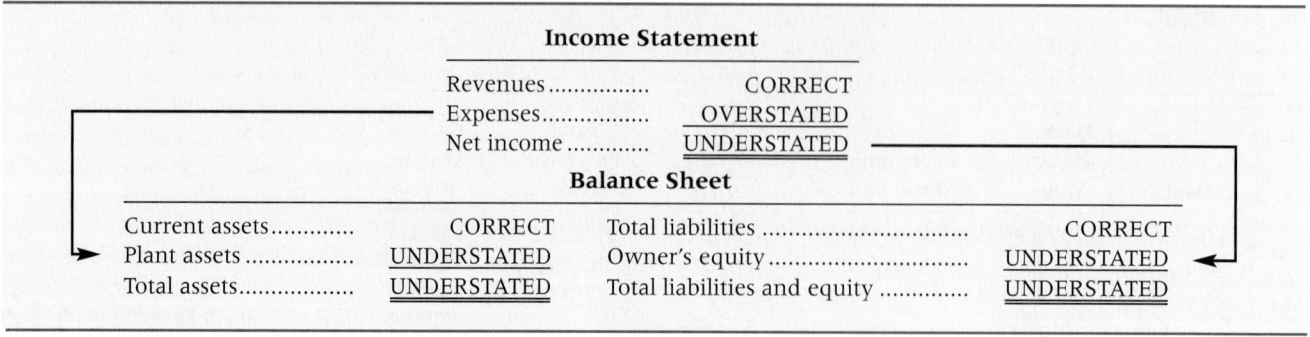

Income Statement

Revenues................	CORRECT
Expenses................	OVERSTATED
Net income	UNDERSTATED

Balance Sheet

Current assets.............	CORRECT	Total liabilities	CORRECT
Plant assets	UNDERSTATED	Owner's equity	UNDERSTATED
Total assets..................	UNDERSTATED	Total liabilities and equity	UNDERSTATED

⊙ DAILY EXERCISE 10-6

Capitalizing the cost of an ordinary repair creates the opposite error. Expenses are then understated, and net income is overstated. The balance sheet overstates assets and owner's equity.

MEASURING PLANT ASSET DEPRECIATION

➔ See Chapter 3, page 86, for a discussion of the matching principle.

The allocation of a plant asset's cost to expense over the asset's useful life is called *depreciation*. Depreciation accounting matches the asset's cost (expense) against the revenue earned by the asset, as the matching principle directs. ◂ Exhibit 10-4 shows depreciation for the purchase of a Boeing 737 jet by **United Airlines**.

EXHIBIT 10-4
Depreciation and the Matching of Expense with Revenue

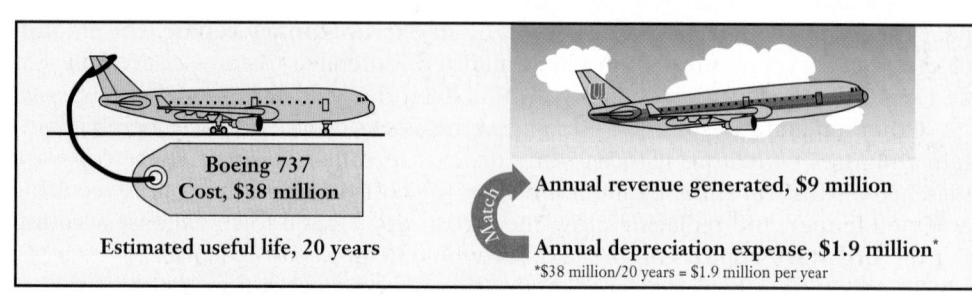

Boeing 737
Cost, $38 million

Estimated useful life, 20 years

Match

Annual revenue generated, $9 million

Annual depreciation expense, $1.9 million*
*$38 million/20 years = $1.9 million per year

Suppose **The Home Depot** buys a computer for use in its accounting system. Home Depot believes it will get four years of service from the computer, and it will then be worthless. Using the straight-line depreciation method, The Home Depot expenses one-quarter of the asset's cost in each of its four years of use.

Let's contrast what depreciation accounting is with what it is *not*.

1. *Depreciation is not a process of valuation.* Businesses do not record depreciation based on the market (sales) value of their plant assets at the end of each year. Instead, businesses allocate an asset's cost to expense during the period of its use.

2. *Depreciation does not mean that the business sets aside cash to replace an asset when it is used up.* Establishing a cash fund is entirely separate from depreciation, and depreciation does not represent cash.

Causes of Depreciation

All assets but land wear out. For some plant assets, physical *wear and tear* and the elements cause depreciation. For example, physical deterioration wears out the trucks that move Home Depot merchandise from warehouses to company stores. The store fixtures used to display merchandise are also subject to physical wear and tear.

Assets such as computers, software, and airplanes may be *obsolete* before they deteriorate. An asset is obsolete when another asset can do the job better or more efficiently. Thus, an asset's useful life may be much shorter than its physical life.

Accountants usually depreciate computers over a short period—perhaps two to four years—even though the computers will continue working much longer. Whether wear and tear or obsolescence causes depreciation, the asset's cost is depreciated over its expected useful life.

Measuring Depreciation

Depreciation of a plant asset is based upon the asset's

1. Cost   **2.** Estimated useful life   **3.** Estimated residual value

Cost is a known amount. The other two factors must be estimated.

Estimated useful life is the length of the service period expected from the asset. Useful life may be expressed in years, units of output, miles, or another measure. For example, the useful life of a building is stated in years. The useful life of a bookbinding machine is the number of books the machine can bind—that is, its expected units of output. A delivery truck's useful life can be measured in miles. Companies make such estimates from past experience, industry information, and government publications.

Estimated residual value—also called **scrap value** or **salvage value**—is the expected cash value of an asset at the end of its useful life. For example, a machine's useful life may be seven years. After seven years, the company expects to sell the machine as scrap metal. The cash the business thinks it can sell the machine for is its estimated residual value. Estimated residual value is *not* depreciated because the business expects to receive this amount from disposing of the asset. If there's no residual value, then it depreciates the full cost of the asset. Cost minus residual value is called the **depreciable cost** of the asset.

ESTIMATED USEFUL LIFE. Length of the service period expected from an asset. May be expressed in years, units of output, miles, or another measure.

ESTIMATED RESIDUAL VALUE. Expected cash value of an asset at the end of its useful life. Also called **scrap value**, or **salvage value**.

DEPRECIABLE COST. The cost of a plant asset minus its estimated residual value.

Depreciation Methods

Three major methods exist for computing depreciation:

- straight-line
- units-of-production
- declining-balance

These methods allocate different amounts of depreciation to each period. However, they all result in the same total amount of depreciation over the life of the asset. Exhibit 10-5 gives the data we will use to illustrate the depreciation computations for a Home Depot truck. We cover the three most widely used methods. We omit the sum-of-years'-digits method because only around 1% of all companies use it.

Objective 2
Account for depreciation

Data Item	Amount
Cost of truck	$41,000
Less: Estimated residual value	(1,000)
Depreciable cost......................................	$40,000
Estimated useful life:	
Years..	5 years
Units of production............................	100,000 units [miles]

EXHIBIT 10-5
Data for Depreciation Computations for a Home Depot Truck

STRAIGHT-LINE METHOD   In the **straight-line (SL) method,** an equal amount of depreciation is assigned to each year of asset use. Depreciable cost is divided by useful life in years to determine the annual amount of depreciation. The equation for SL depreciation, applied to the Home Depot truck data from Exhibit 10-5, is

STRAIGHT-LINE (SL) DEPRECIATION METHOD. Depreciation method in which an equal amount of depreciation expense is assigned to each year of asset use.

$$\text{Straight-line depreciation per year} = \frac{\text{Cost} - \text{Residual value}}{\text{Useful life, in years}}$$

$$= \frac{\$41,000 - \$1,000}{5}$$

$$= \$8,000$$

The entry to record one year's depreciation is

Depreciation Expense	8,000	
Accumulated Depreciation		8,000

This truck was purchased on January 1, 20X1, and let's assume The Home Depot's fiscal year ends on December 31. A *straight-line depreciation schedule* is given in Exhibit 10-6. The final column in the exhibit shows the asset's *book value,* which is its cost less accumulated depreciation. Book value is also called *carrying amount* or *carrying value.* ◄

➤ We introduced book value in Chapter 3, page 91.

As an asset is used, accumulated depreciation increases, and the book value decreases. Compare the Accumulated Depreciation and the Book Value columns of Exhibit 10-6. An asset's final book value is its *residual value* ($1,000 in Exhibit 10-6). At the end of its useful life, the asset is said to be *fully depreciated.*

EXHIBIT 10-6
Straight-Line Depreciation Schedule for a Home Depot Truck

Date	Asset Cost	Depreciation for the Year				Accumulated Depreciation	Asset Book Value
		Depreciation Rate		Depreciable Cost	Depreciation Expense		
1-1-20X1	$41,000						$41,000
12-31-20X1		0.20*	×	$40,000	=	$8,000	$ 8,000	33,000
12-31-20X2		0.20	×	40,000	=	8,000	16,000	25,000
12-31-20X3		0.20	×	40,000	=	8,000	24,000	17,000
12-31-20X4		0.20	×	40,000	=	8,000	32,000	9,000
12-31-20X5		0.20	×	40,000	=	8,000	40,000	1,000

*1/5 year = 0.20 per year

WORK IT OUT An asset with cost of $10,000, useful life of five years, and residual value of $2,000 was purchased on January 1. What is the SL depreciation for the first year? For the second year? For the fifth year?

Answer:

$$\frac{\text{SL depreciation}}{\text{per year}} = \frac{\text{Cost} - \text{Residual value}}{\text{Useful life, in years}}$$

$$= \frac{\$10,000 - \$2,000}{5} = \frac{\$1,600 \text{ per year}}{\text{every year}}$$

UNITS-OF-PRODUCTION (UOP) METHOD In the **units-of-production (UOP) method,** a fixed amount of depreciation goes with each *unit of output* produced by the asset. Depreciable cost is divided by useful life, in units of production. This per-unit expense is then multiplied by the number of units produced each period to compute depreciation for that period. The UOP depreciation equation for the Home Depot truck data in Exhibit 10-5 is

UNITS-OF-PRODUCTION (UOP) DEPRECIATION METHOD. Depreciation method by which a fixed amount of depreciation is assigned to each unit of output produced by an asset.

$$\frac{\text{Units-of-production depreciation}}{\text{per unit of output}} = \frac{\text{Cost} - \text{Residual value}}{\text{Useful life, in units of production}}$$

$$= \frac{\$41,000 - \$1,000}{100,000 \text{ miles}}$$

$$= \$0.40 \text{ per mile}$$

This the truck is expected to be driven 20,000 miles during the first year, 30,000 during the second, 25,000 during the third, 15,000 during the fourth, and 10,000 during the fifth. The amount of UOP depreciation each period varies with the number of units the asset produces. The UOP schedule for this asset is shown in Exhibit 10-7.

Date	Asset Cost	Depreciation for the Year			Accumulated Depreciation	Asset Book Value
		Depreciation Per Unit	Number of Units	Depreciation Expense		
1-1-20X1	$41,000					$41,000
12-31-20X1		$0.40 ×	20,000 =	$ 8,000	$ 8,000	33,000
12-31-20X2		0.40 ×	30,000 =	12,000	20,000	21,000
12-31-20X3		0.40 ×	25,000 =	10,000	30,000	11,000
12-31-20X4		0.40 ×	15,000 =	6,000	36,000	5,000
12-31-20X5		0.40 ×	10,000 =	4,000	40,000	1,000

WORK IT OUT

The asset in the preceding Work It Out produced 3,000 units in the first year, 4,000 in the second, 4,500 in the third, 2,500 in the fourth, and 2,000 units in the last year. Its total estimated useful life is 16,000 miles. What is UOP depreciation for each year?

Answer

$$\frac{\text{Depreciation}}{\text{per unit}} = \frac{\text{Cost} - \text{Residual value}}{\text{Useful life, in units of production}} = \frac{\$10,000 - \$2,000}{16,000 \text{ miles}} = \$0.50 \text{ per mile}$$

Yr. 1: $1,500 (3,000 × $0.50)   Yr. 4: $1,250 (2,500 × $0.50)
Yr. 2: $2,000 (4,000 × $0.50)   Yr. 5: $1,000 (2,000 × $0.50)
Yr. 3: $2,250 (4,500 × $0.50)

DOUBLE-DECLINING BALANCE METHOD An **accelerated depreciation method** writes off more of the asset's cost near the start of its useful life than the straight-line method does. The main accelerated depreciation method, **double-declining-balance (DDB),** multiplies the asset's decreasing book value by a constant percentage that is 2 times the straight-line depreciation rate. DDB amounts can be computed in four steps:

1. Compute the straight-line depreciation rate per year. A five-year truck has a straight-line depreciation rate of 1/5, or 20% per year. A ten-year asset has a straight-line rate of 1/10, or 10% per year, and so on.
2. Compute the DDB rate: Multiply the straight-line rate by 2. The DDB rate for a ten-year asset is 20% per year (10% × 2 = 20%). For a five-year asset, such as the Home Depot truck, the DDB rate is 40% (20% × 2 = 40%).
3. Compute DDB depreciation for each year. Multiply the asset's book value (cost less accumulated depreciation) at the beginning of each year by the DDB rate. You should ignore the asset's residual value in computing depreciation, except for the last year. The first-year depreciation for the truck in Exhibit 10-5 is

DDB depreciation for the first year	=	Asset book value at the begining of the year	× DDB rate
$16,400	=	$41,000	× 0.40

The same approach is used to compute DDB depreciation for all later years, except for the final year, as follows.

4. Determine the final year's depreciation, the amount needed to reduce the asset's carrying amount to its residual value. In the DDB depreciation schedule in Exhibit 10-8 (on page 396), the last year's depreciation is $4,314—book value of $5,314 less the $1,000 residual value.

ACCELERATED DEPRECIATION METHOD. A depreciation method that writes off more of the asset's cost near the start of its useful life than the straight-line method does.

DOUBLE-DECLINING-BALANCE (DDB) DEPRECIATION METHOD. An accelerated depreciation method that computes annual depreciation by multiplying the asset's decreasing book value by a constant percent that is 2 times the straight-line rate.

		Depreciation for the Year				
Date	Asset Cost	DDB Rate	Asset Book Value	Depreciation Expense	Accumulated Depreciation	Asset Book Value
1-1-20X1	$41,000					$41,000
12-31-20X1		0.40 ×	$41,000 =	$16,400	$16,400	24,600
12-31-20X2		0.40 ×	24,600 =	9,840	26,240	14,760
12-31-20X3		0.40 ×	14,760 =	5,904	32,144	8,856
12-31-20X4		0.40 ×	8,856 =	3,542	35,686	5,314
12-31-20X5				4,314*	40,000	1,000

*Last-year depreciation is the amount needed to reduce asset book value to the residual value ($5,314 − $1,000 = $4,314).

The DDB method differs from the other methods in two ways:

- The asset's residual value is ignored at the start. In the first year, depreciation is computed on the asset's full cost.
- The final year's depreciation is the amount needed to bring the asset's carrying amount to residual value. The final-year depreciation amount is like a "plug" figure.

Many companies change to the straight-line method during the next-to-last year of the asset's life. Under this plan, annual depreciation for 20X4 and 20X5 is $3,928. Look at Exhibit 10-8. Depreciable cost at the end of 20X3 is $7,856 (book value of $8,856 less residual value of $1,000). Depreciable cost can be spread evenly over the last two years of the asset's life ($7,856 ÷ 2 remaining years = $3,928 per year).

WORK IT OUT

What is DDB depreciation for each year for the asset in the Work It Out on page 394?

Answer: DDB rate = 1/5 × 2 = 40%

Yr. 1: $4,000 ($10,000 × 40%)
Yr. 2: $2,400 [($10,000 − $4,000 = $6,000) × 40%]
Yr. 3: $1,440 [($6,000 − $2,400 = $3,600) × 40%]
Yr. 4: $160 ($3,600 − $1,440 − $2,000*)

*An asset's cost is not depreciated below its residual value.

Comparing Depreciation Methods

Let's compare the depreciation methods we've just discussed. Annual depreciation varies by method, but the total is the same for all methods—$40,000.

			Amount of Depreciation Per Year		
				Accelerated Method	
	Year	Straight-Line	Units-of-Production	Double-Declining-Balance	
	1	$ 8,000	$ 8,000	$16,400	
	2	8,000	12,000	9,840	
	3	8,000	10,000	5,904	
	4	8,000	6,000	3,542	
	5	8,000	4,000	4,314	
	Total	$40,000	$40,000	$40,000	

DAILY EXERCISE 10-7

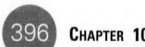
DAILY EXERCISE 10-8

STRAIGHT-LINE A business should match an asset's expense against the revenue that asset produces. For an asset that generates revenue evenly over time, the straight-line method follows the matching principle. Each period the asset is used, an equal amount of depreciation is recorded.

UNITS-OF-PRODUCTION The units-of-production method best fits an asset that wears out because of physical use rather than obsolescence. Depreciation is expensed only when the asset is used, and more asset use causes greater depreciation.

DOUBLE-DECLINING-BALANCE The accelerated method (DDB) works best for assets that produce more revenue in their early years. The greater expense in the earlier periods is matched against those periods' greater revenue. This is the mark of an accelerated depreciation method.

COMPARISONS Exhibit 10-9 graphs annual depreciation for the three methods.

- The graph of *straight-line* depreciation is flat because annual depreciation is the same in all periods.
- Units-of-production depreciation follows no pattern because annual depreciation varies depending on the use of the asset. The greater the use, the greater the amount of depreciation.
- Accelerated depreciation is greatest in the asset's first year and less in the later years.

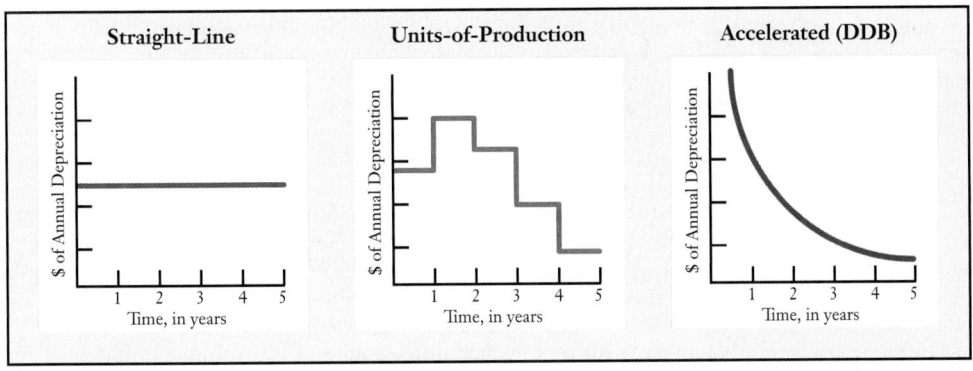

EXHIBIT 10-9
Depreciation Patterns Through Time

A recent survey of 600 companies, conducted by the American Institute of CPAs, indicated that the straight-line method is most popular. Exhibit 10-10 shows the percentages of companies that use each depreciation method.

EXHIBIT 10-10
Use of Depreciation Methods

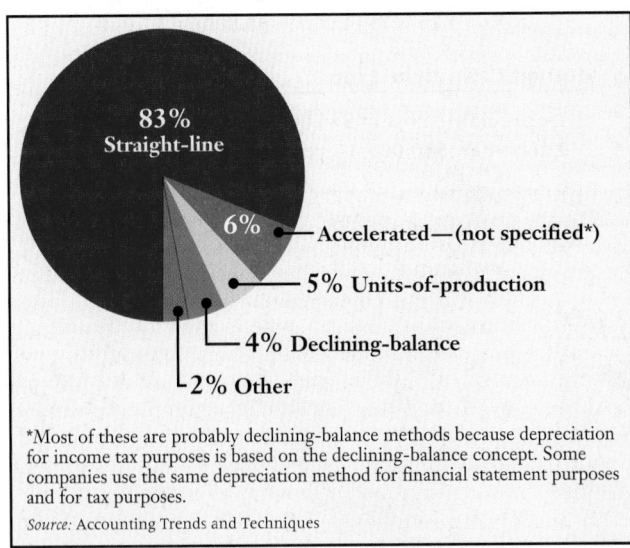

*Most of these are probably declining-balance methods because depreciation for income tax purposes is based on the declining-balance concept. Some companies use the same depreciation method for financial statement purposes and for tax purposes.
Source: Accounting Trends and Techniques

SUMMARY PROBLEM

Not Just Copies purchased equipment on January 1, 20X5, for $44,000. Its expected useful life is ten years or 100,000 units of production, and its residual value is $4,000. Under three depreciation methods, the annual depreciation and the balance of accumulated depreciation at the end of 20X5 and 20X6 are as follows:

Year	Method A		Method B		Method C	
	Annual Depreciation Expense	Accumulated Depreciation	Annual Depreciation Expense	Accumulated Depreciation	Annual Depreciation Expense	Accumulated Depreciation
20X5	$1,200	$1,200	$8,800	$ 8,800	$4,000	$4,000
20X6	5,600	6,800	7,040	15,840	4,000	8,000

Required

1. Identify the depreciation method used in each instance, and show the equation and computation for each. (Round amounts to the nearest dollar.)
2. Assume continued use of the same method through year 20X7. Determine the annual depreciation expense, accumulated depreciation, and book value of the equipment for 20X5 through 20X7 under each method, assuming 12,000 units of production in 20X7.

Solution

Requirement 1

Method A: Units-of-Production

$$\text{Depreciation per unit} = \frac{\$44,000 - \$4,000}{100,000 \text{ units}} = \$0.40$$

20X5: $0.40 × 3,000 units = $1,200
20X6: $0.40 × 14,000 units = $5,600

Method B: Double-Declining-Balance

$$\text{Rate} = \frac{1}{10 \text{ years}} \times 2 = 10\% \times 2 = 20\%$$

20X5: 0.20 × $44,000 = $8,800
20X6: 0.20 × ($44,000 − $8,800) = $7,040

Method C: Straight-Line

Depreciable cost = $44,000 − $4,000 = $40,000
Each year: $40,000/10 years = $4,000

Method A: Units-of-Production

Year	Annual Depreciation Expense	Accumulated Depreciation	Book Value
Start			$44,000
20X5	$1,200	$ 1,200	42,800
20X6	5,600	6,800	37,200
20X7	4,800	11,600	32,400

Method B: Double-Declining-Balance

Year	Annual Depreciation Expense	Accumulated Depreciation	Book Value
Start			$44,000
20X5	$8,800	$ 8,800	35,200
20X6	7,040	15,840	28,160
20X7	5,632	21,472	22,528

Method C: Straight-Line

Year	Annual Depreciation Expense	Accumulated Depreciation	Book Value
Start			$44,000
20X5	$4,000	$ 4,000	40,000
20X6	4,000	8,000	36,000
20X7	4,000	12,000	32,000

Computations for 20X7:

Units-of-production	$0.40 \times 12,000$ units = $4,800
Double-declining-balance	$0.20 \times \$28,160 = \$5,632$
Straight-line	$40,000/10$ years = $4,000

OTHER ISSUES IN ACCOUNTING FOR PLANT ASSETS

Plant assets are complex because of their long lives. Depreciation affects income taxes, and companies may have gains or losses when they sell their plant assets. This section covers these topics.

Depreciation and Income Taxes

Most companies use the straight-line depreciation method for their financial statements. But they keep separate depreciation records for income taxes. For tax purposes, most companies use an accelerated method.

Objective 3
Select the best depreciation method for income tax purposes

Suppose you manage a **Home Depot** store. The IRS allows the DDB depreciation method, and most managers prefer that to straight-line depreciation. Why? Because it provides the most depreciation expense as quickly as possible. The accelerated depreciation method decreases immediate tax payments. You can then invest the cash you save to earn more income. This is a common strategy.

To understand the relationships between cash flow (cash provided by operations), depreciation, and income tax, recall our earlier depreciation of the Home Depot truck: First-year depreciation is $8,000 under straight-line and $16,400 under double-declining-balance. Now let's assume that DDB is permitted for income tax reporting, and let's apply DDB to the Home Depot truck as before. This store has $400,000 in cash sales and $300,000 in cash operating expenses during the truck's first year and an income tax rate of 30%. The cash-flow analysis appears in Exhibit 10-11 on page 400.

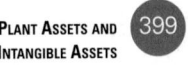

● DAILY EXERCISE 10-9

		Income Tax Rate (30%)	
		SL	Accelerated
(1)	Cash revenues	$400,000	$400,000
(2)	*Cash* operating expenses	300,000	300,000
(3)	Cash provided by operations before income tax	100,000	100,000
(4)	Depreciation expense (a noncash expense)	8,000	16,400
(5)	Income before income tax.....................................	92,000	83,600
(6)	Income tax expense (30%)	27,600	25,080
(7)	Net income	$ 64,400	$ 58,520
	Cash-flow analysis:		
(8)	Cash provided by operations before income tax.....	$100,000	$100,000
(9)	Income tax expense	27,600	25,080
(10)	Cash provided by operations	$ 72,400	$ 74,920
(11)	Extra cash available for investment if DDB is used ($74,920 − $72,400)		$ 2,520

Exhibit 10-11 reveals some important relationships. Compare the amount of cash provided by operations before income tax (line 3). Both columns show $100,000. If there were no income taxes, the cash provided by operations would be the same for all depreciation methods. Depreciation is a noncash expense (it requires no outlay of cash) and thus does not affect cash from operations.

But depreciation is a tax-deductible expense. The higher the depreciation (line 4), the lower the income and the lower the tax payment. Therefore, accelerated depreciation helps conserve cash for use in the business. Exhibit 10-11 indicates that the business will have $2,520 more cash to invest at the end of the first year if it uses accelerated depreciation (line 11). The additional investment will earn a return and increase the company's net income.

A special depreciation method called the *modified accelerated cost recovery system (MACRS)* is used only for income tax purpose. Under MACRS, assets are segmented into classes by asset life, as shown in Exhibit 10-12. Depreciation for the first three classes is computed by the double-declining-balance method. Depreciation for 20-year assets is computed by the 150%-declining-balance method. Under 150% DB, the annual depreciation rate is computed by multiplying the straight-line rate by 1.50 (rather than by 2, as for DDB). For a 20-year asset, the straight-line rate is 0.05 × (1/20 = 0.05), so the annual MACRS depreciation rate is 0.075 (0.05 × 1.50 = 0.075). Finally, as the exhibit shows, most real estate is depreciated by the straight-line method.

Class Identified by Asset Life (years)	Representative Assets	Depreciation Method
3	Race horses	DDB
5	Automobiles, light trucks	DDB
10	Equipment	DDB
20	Certain real estate	150% DB
27 1/2	Residential rental property	SL
39	Nonresidential rental property	SL

Depreciation for Partial Years

Companies purchase plant assets whenever they need them. They don't wait until the beginning of a period. Therefore, companies must develop policies to compute depreciation for partial years. Suppose **Towels 'n Things** in St. Louis purchases a building on April 1 for $500,000. The building's estimated life is 20 years, and its estimated residual value is $80,000. How does Towels 'n Things compute depreciation for the year ended December 31?

Many companies compute partial-year depreciation by first computing a full year's depreciation. They then multiply the full-year amount by the fraction of the year that they held the asset. Assuming the straight-line method, the year's depreciation for the Towels 'n Things building is $15,750, computed as follows:

$$\text{Full year depreciation:} \quad \frac{\$500,000 - \$80,000}{20 \text{ years}} = \$21,000$$

$$\text{Partial-year depreciation:} \quad \$21,000 \times 9/12 = \$15,750$$

What if the company bought the asset on April 18? One widely used policy is to record no depreciation on assets purchased after the 15th of the month and to record a full month's depreciation on an asset bought on or before the 15th. In that case, the year's depreciation would be $14,000 for eight months ($21,000 \times 8/12 = $14,000$).

How is partial-year depreciation computed under the other depreciation methods? Suppose Towels 'n Things acquired the building on October 4 and uses the double-declining-balance method. For a 20-year asset, the DDB rate is 10% (1/20 = 5%; 5% $\times$ 2 = 10%). The annual depreciation computations for 20X1, 20X2, and 20X3 are shown in Exhibit 10-13.

EXHIBIT 10-13 Annual DDB Depreciation for Partial Years

			Depreciation for the Year					
Date	Asset Cost	DDB Rate	Asset Book Value, Beginning	Fraction of the Year		Depreciation Expense	Accumulated Depreciation	Asset Book Value, Ending
10- 4-20X1	$500,000							$500,000
12-31-20X1		1/20 × 2 = 0.10 ×	$500,000 ×	3/12	=	$12,500	$ 12,500	487,500
12-31-20X2		0.10 ×	487,500 ×	12/12	=	48,750	61,250	438,750
12-31-20X3		0.10 ×	438,750 ×	12/12	=	43,875	105,125	394,875

Most companies use computerized systems to account for fixed assets. The system will automatically calculate the depreciation expense for each period.

 DAILY EXERCISE 10-10

Changing the Useful Life of a Depreciable Asset

Estimating the useful life of each plant asset poses an accounting challenge. As the asset is being used, the business may refine its estimate on the basis of experience and new information. The **Walt Disney Company** made such a change, called a *change in accounting estimate*. Disney refigured depreciation for the revised useful lives of several theme-park assets. The following note in Disney's financial statements reports this change in accounting estimate:

> **Note 5**
> . . . [T]he Company extended the estimated useful lives of certain theme park . . . assets based upon . . . engineering studies. The effect of this change was to decrease depreciation by approximately $8 million (an increase in net income of approximately $4.2 million. . .).

Accounting changes like these are common because no one has perfect foresight. Generally accepted accounting principles require the business to report the nature, reason, and effect of the accounting change on net income, as the Disney example shows. For a change in accounting estimate, the remaining book value of the asset is spread over its remaining useful life. The new useful life may be longer or shorter than the original useful life.

Assume that a Disney World hot dog stand cost $40,000 and that the company originally believed the asset had an eight-year life with no residual value. Using the straight-line method, the company would record depreciation of $5,000 each year ($40,000/8 years = $5,000).

Suppose Disney used the asset for two years. Accumulated depreciation reached $10,000, leaving a remaining depreciable book value (cost *less* accumulated depreciation *less* residual value) of $30,000 ($40,000 − $10,000). Suppose Disney management believes the hot dog stand will remain useful for an additional ten years. The company would revise the annual depreciation amount as follows:

Asset's remaining depreciable book value	÷	(New) Estimated useful life remaining	=	(New) Annual depreciation
$30,000	÷	10 years	=	$3,000

The yearly depreciation entry based on the new useful life is

DAILY EXERCISE 10-11

Depreciation Expense—Hot Dog Stand..............................	3,000	
Accumulated Depreciation—Hot Dog Stand		3,000

The equation for revised straight-line depreciation is

$$\text{Revised SL depreciation} = \frac{\text{Cost} - \text{Accumulated depreciation} - \text{New residual value}}{\text{Estimated remaining useful life in years}}$$

Using Fully Depreciated Assets

A *fully depreciated asset* is an asset that has reached the end of its *estimated* useful life. No more depreciation is recorded for the asset. If the asset is no longer suitable for its purpose, it is disposed of. However, the company may be unable to replace the asset. Or the asset may remain useful. In any event, companies sometimes continue using fully depreciated assets. The asset account and its accumulated depreciation remain on the books, even though no additional depreciation is recorded.

> **THINK IT OVER**
>
> A fully depreciated asset has a cost of $80,000 and zero residual value. What is the asset's accumulated depreciation?
>
> *Answer:* $80,000 (same as the asset's cost).
>
> Now suppose the asset's residual value is $10,000. How much is accumulated depreciation?
>
> *Answer:* $70,000 ($80,000 − $10,000).

Disposing of Plant Assets

Objective 4
Account for the disposal of a plant asset

Eventually, an asset ceases to serve its purpose. The asset may have become worn out or obsolete. In general, a company disposes of a plant asset by selling it or exchanging it. If the asset cannot be sold or exchanged, then it is junked. Whatever the method of disposal, the business should bring depreciation up-to-date to measure the asset's final book value properly.

To record the disposal, credit the asset account and debit its accumulated depreciation to remove these accounts from the books. Suppose the final year's depreciation expense has just been recorded for a machine that cost $6,000 with no residual value. The machine's accumulated depreciation thus totals $6,000. This asset cannot be sold or exchanged, so it is junked. The entry to record its disposal is

Accumulated Depreciation—Machinery	6,000	
Machinery...		6,000

To dispose of fully depreciated machine.

MACHINERY	
6,000	6,000

ACCUMULATED DEPRECIATION—MACHINERY	
6,000	6,000

Now both accounts have a zero balance, as shown in the T-accounts at the right.

If assets are junked before being fully depreciated, the company records a loss equal to the asset's book value. Suppose Home Depot fixtures that cost $4,000 are junked at a loss. Accumulated depreciation is $3,000, and book value is therefore $1,000. Disposal of these store fixtures generates a loss equal to the book value of the asset, as follows:

Accumulated Depreciation—Store Fixtures	3,000	
Loss on Disposal of Store Fixtures	1,000	
Store Fixtures		4,000
To dispose of store fixtures.		

All losses, including this Loss on Disposal of Store Fixtures, decrease net income. Along with expenses, losses are reported on the income statement.

SELLING A PLANT ASSET   Suppose Clarkson Eyecare sells furniture (a plant asset) on September 30, 20X4, for $5,000 cash. The furniture cost $10,000 when purchased on January 1, 20X1, and has been depreciated on a straight-line basis. Clarkson estimated a ten-year useful life and no residual value. Prior to recording the sale of the furniture, accountants must update its depreciation. Because Clarkson uses the calendar year as its accounting period, partial-year depreciation must be recorded for the asset's expense from January 1, 20X4, to the sale date on September 30. The straight-line depreciation entry at September 30, 20X4, is

Sep. 30	Depreciation Expense ($10,000/10 years × 9/12)	750	
	Accumulated Depreciation—Furniture		750
	To update depreciation.		

After this entry is posted, the Furniture account and the Accumulated Depreciation—Furniture account appear as follows. The furniture book value is $6,250 ($10,000 − $3,750).

FURNITURE		ACCUMULATED DEPRECIATION—FURNITURE	
Jan. 1, 20X1 10,000		Dec. 31, 20X1	1,000
		Dec. 31, 20X2	1,000
		Dec. 31, 20X3	1,000
		Sep. 30, 20X4	750
		Balance	3,750

Book Value = $6,250

Suppose Clarkson sells the furniture for $5,000 cash. The loss on the sale is $1,250, determined as follows:

Cash received from sale of the asset		$5,000
Book value of asset sold:		
Cost	$10,000	
Less: Accumulated depreciation up to date of sale	(3,750)	6,250
Gain (loss) on sale of the asset		($1,250)

Clarkson's entry to record sale of the furniture for $5,000 cash is

Sep. 30	Cash	5,000	
	Accumulated Depreciation—Furniture	3,750	
	Loss on Sale of Furniture	1,250	
	Furniture		10,000
	To sell furniture.		

When recording the sale of a plant asset, the business must remove the balances in the asset account (Furniture, in this case) and its accumulated depreciation account and also record a gain or a loss if the amount of cash received differs from the asset's book value. In our example, cash of $5,000 is less than the book value of the furniture, $6,250. The result is a loss of $1,250.

If the sale price had been $7,000, Clarkson Eyecare would have had a gain of $750 (Cash, $7,000—asset book value, $6,250). The entry to record this transaction would be

Sep. 30	Cash	7,000	
	Accumulated Depreciation—Furniture	3,750	
	Furniture..		10,000
	Gain on Sale of Furniture		750
	To sell furniture.		

⊙ DAILY EXERCISE 10-12

A gain is recorded when an asset is sold for a price (sale proceeds) greater than the asset's book value. A loss is recorded when the sale price is less than book value.

> • **Gain = Sale proceeds > Book value**
> • **Loss = Sale proceeds < Book value**

Gains increase net income, and losses decrease net income. All gains and losses are reported on the income statement.

EXCHANGING PLANT ASSETS Businesses often exchange (trade in) their old plant assets for newer, more efficient assets. For example, **Domino's Pizza** may trade in a five-year-old delivery car for a newer model. To record the exchange, Domino's must remove from the books the balances for the old asset and its accumulated depreciation exactly as we did for the disposal of furniture in the preceding section.

In many cases, the business simply carries forward the book value of the old asset plus any cash payment as the cost of the new asset. For example, assume Domino's old delivery car cost $9,000 and has accumulated depreciation of $8,000. The car's book value is $1,000. Domino's trades in the old auto and pays cash of $10,000. Domino's should first record depreciation on its old auto up to the date of the exchange. This updates the asset's book value. Then the business records the exchange transaction with this journal entry:

Delivery Auto (new)..	11,000	
Accumulated Depreciation (old).........................	8,000	
Delivery Auto (old)		9,000
Cash...		10,000
Traded in old delivery car for new auto.		

Domino's cost of the new car is $11,000 (cash paid $10,000, plus the book value of the old auto, $1,000).

ACCOUNTING FOR NATURAL RESOURCES

Objective 5
Account for natural resource assets and depletion

Natural resources such as iron ore, petroleum (oil), natural gas, and timber are plant assets of a special type. Natural resources are like inventories in the ground (oil) or on top of the ground (timber). Natural resource assets are expensed through *depletion*. **Depletion expense** is that portion of the cost of natural resources used up in a particular period. Depletion expense is computed in the same way as units-of-production depreciation:

DEPLETION EXPENSE. The portion of a natural resource's cost used up in a particular period. Depletion expense is computed in the same way as units-of-production depreciation.

$$\frac{\text{Depletion}}{\text{per unit}} = \frac{\text{Cost} - \text{Residual value}}{\text{Estimated total units of natural resource}}$$

An oil well may cost $100,000 and contain an estimated 10,000 barrels of oil. The well has no residual value. The depletion rate would thus be $10 per barrel ($100,000/10,000 barrels). If 3,000 barrels are extracted during the year, depletion expense is $30,000 (3,000 barrels × $10 per barrel). The depletion entry for the year is

Depletion Expense (3,000 barrels × $10)...............	30,000	
Accumulated Depletion—Oil		30,000

If 4,500 barrels are removed the next year, that period's depletion is $45,000 (4,500 barrels × $10 per barrel). Accumulated Depletion is a contra account similar to Accumulated Depreciation.

Natural resource assets can be reported on the balance sheet as follows:

Property, Plant, and Equipment:		
Land...		$120,000
Buildings..	$800,000	
Equipment	160,000	
	960,000	
Less: Accumulated depreciation	(410,000)	550,000
Oil...	$380,000	
Less: Accumulated depletion......................	(80,000)	300,000
Property, plant, and equipment, net		$970,000

 DAILY EXERCISE 10-13

WORK IT OUT

Ladue Paper Products pays $500,000 for land that contains an estimated 500,000 board feet of lumber. The land can be sold for $100,000 after the timber has been cut. If Ladue Paper harvests 200,000 board feet in the year of purchase, how much depletion should be recorded?

Answer: **(Cost − Residual) ÷ Total = Depletion rate × Production = Depletion**
($500,000 − $100,00) ÷ 500,000 = $0.80 per foot ×   200,000 = $160,000

ACCOUNTING FOR INTANGIBLE ASSETS

Objective 6
Account for intangible assets and amortization

As we saw earlier in the chapter, *intangible assets* are long-lived and have no physical form. Instead, these assets are special rights from patents, copyrights, trademarks, and so on.

In today's technology-driven economy, intangibles are surpassing tangible assets in value. The electronic economy rewards brand and customer loyalty. Consider online auction pioneer **eBay.** The company has no physical products or equipment, but it helps people buy and sell everything from Batman toys to bathroom tiles. In 1999, eBay served 10 million customers and earned $225 billion in revenues with fewer than 150 employees.

Alas, accountants typically deal with historical costs rather than future value. A company's intellectual capital is difficult to measure. But when one company buys another, we get a glimpse of the value of the acquired company's intellectual capital. For example, **America Online** announced it would acquire **Time Warner.** AOL said it would exchange $146 billion worth of stock and agree to pay $38 billion of future liabilities for Time Warner's net tangible assets of only $9 billion. Why? Because Time Warner's intangible assets were worth $190 billion. Intangibles can account for as much as 85% of a company's perceived value, so companies must find ways to account for intangibles just as they do for their inventory and equipment.

The acquisition cost of a patent is debited to Patents, an asset account. The intangible is expensed through **amortization,** the systematic reduction of the asset's carrying value on the books. Amortization applies to intangible assets exactly as depreciation applies to plant assets and depletion applies to natural resources. Depreciation, depletion, and amortization are conceptually the same.

Amortization is generally computed on a straight-line basis over the asset's estimated useful life—up to a maximum of 40 years, according to generally accepted accounting principles. But obsolescence often shortens an intangible's useful life. Amortization expense for an intangible asset can be written off directly against the asset account rather than held in an accumulated amortization account. The residual value of most intangible assets is zero.

Assume that **Sealy Mattress Company** purchases a patent on a special manufacturing process. Legally, the patent may run for 20 years. Sealy realizes, however, that new technologies will limit the process's life to 4 years. If the patent cost $80,000, each year's amortization expense is $20,000 ($80,000/4). Sealy's balance sheet reports the patent at its acquisition cost less accumulated amortization to date. After 1 year, the patent has a $60,000 balance ($80,000 − $20,000), after 2 years a $40,000 balance ($80,000 − $40,000), and so on.

AMORTIZATION. The systematic reduction of the asset's carrying value on the books. Expense that applies to intangibles in the same way depreciation applies to plant assets and depletion applies to natural resources.

Specific Intangibles

PATENTS   **Patents** are federal government grants giving the holder the exclusive 20-year right to produce and sell an invention. The invention may be a product or a process—for example, **Sony** compact disc players and the **Dolby** noise-reduction process. Like any other asset, a patent may be purchased. Suppose **General Electric Company (GE)** pays $170,000 to acquire a patent on January 1, and GE believes its expected useful life is only five years. Amortization expense is $34,000 per year ($170,000/5 years). Acquisition and amortization entries for this patent are

Jan. 1	Patents	170,000	
	Cash		170,000
	To acquire a patent.		
Dec. 31	Amortization Expense—Patents ($170,000/5)	34,000	
	Patents...		34,000
	To amortize the cost of a patent.		

COPYRIGHTS   **Copyrights** are exclusive rights to reproduce and sell a book, musical composition, film, or other work of art. Copyrights also protect computer software programs, such as **Microsoft** Windows® and the Excel spreadsheet. Issued by the federal government, copyrights extend 50 years beyond the author's (composer's, artist's, or programmer's) life.

The cost of obtaining a copyright from the government is low, but a company may pay a large sum to purchase an existing copyright. For example, **Simon & Schuster,** the publisher, may pay the author of a popular novel $1 million for the book's copyright. The useful life of a copyright is usually no longer than two or three years, so most copyrights have short lives.

TRADEMARKS, BRAND NAMES   **Trademarks** and **trade names** (or **brand names**) are assets that represent distinctive identifications of products or services. The "eye" symbol is the trademark of the **CBS** television network. You are probably also familiar with **NBC's** peacock. Seven-Up, Pepsi, and Egg McMuffin are everyday trade names. Advertising slogans that are legally protected include **United Airlines'** "Fly the friendly skies" and **Avis Rent A Car's** "We try harder."

The cost of a trademark or trade name is amortized over its useful life, not to exceed 40 years. The cost of advertising and promotion is not a part of the asset's cost, but rather an advertising expense.

FRANCHISES, LICENSES   **Franchises** and **licenses** are privileges granted by a private business or a government to sell a product or service under specified conditions. The **Green Bay Packers** football organization is a franchise granted by the National Football League. **McDonald's** restaurants and **Holiday Inns** are popular business franchises. The acquisition costs of a franchise or license is amortized over its useful life, subject to the 40-year maximum.

GOODWILL   The term *goodwill* in accounting has a very different meaning from the everyday term, "goodwill among men." In accounting, **goodwill** is the excess of the cost to purchase another company over the market value of the other company's net assets (assets minus liabilities). **Wal-Mart** has now expanded into Mexico. Suppose Wal-Mart acquired Mexana Company at a cost of $10 million. The sum of the market values of Mexana's assets was $9 million and its liabilities totaled $1 million, so Mexana's net assets totaled $8 million. In this case, Wal-Mart paid $2 million for goodwill, computed as follows:

Purchase price paid for Mexana Company		$10 million
The market value of Mexana Company's assets................	$9 million	
Less: Mexana Company's liabilities	(1 million)	
Market value of Mexana Company's net assets		8 million
Excess is called *goodwill*		$ 2 million

Wal-Mart's entry to record the purchase of Mexana Company, including the goodwill that Wal-Mart purchases would be

Assets (Cash, Receivables, Inventories, Plant Assets, all at market value)	9,000,000	
Goodwill	2,000,000	
Liabilities		1,000,000
Cash		10,000,000
Purchased Mexana Company.		

Note that Wal-Mart acquired all of Mexana's assets *and* all of Mexana's liabilities.
  Goodwill has some special features:

1. Goodwill is recorded only when it is purchased in the acquisition of another company. A company's favorable location, superior product, or outstanding reputation may create goodwill for a company, but that entity never records goodwill for its own business. Instead, goodwill is recorded *only* by the acquiring entity when it buys another company.
2. According to generally accepted accounting principles (GAAP), goodwill is amortized over a period not to exceed 40 years. In reality, the goodwill of many entities actually increases in value. Nevertheless, GAAP requires that the cost of all intangible assets be amortized as expense.

 DAILY EXERCISE 10-14

DAILY EXERCISE 10-15

 e-Accounting

Singapore International Airlines: Ratcheting Up the Value of Tangibles and Intangibles

During the Asian recession of 1997–1998, **Singapore International Airlines (SIA)** was able to keep its profitability high. The secret to the airline's success has always been the impeccable quality of its assets, tangible and intangible: its fleet of 90 planes and its service. It recently spent $300 million for first-class seats that recline 180% and personal TV screens in all seats.

    An airline's ground service is as important as its planes. You might be surprised to know that **American Airlines'** reservation system—Sabre—was valued at 60% of the company's assets, far more than American's fleet of planes. And **Singapore Airlines Terminal Services Group (SATS)** is so profitable that the company is taking it public. The company credits SATS for its success in reducing the adverse effects of the Asian economic downturn. "Ongoing investment in staff training continues to be a decisive, motivating factor in our success," says CEO Karmit Singh. The company's YES! campaign trains everyone—from baggage handlers to security personnel—to act like frontline staff. No wonder business travelers have chosen Singapore International Airlines as the "best airline" for eleven years running.

Source: Based on Leonard Hill, "Two for the money," *Air Transport World,* May 2000, pp. 59–63. Perry Flint, "SIA's global tilt," *Air Transport World,* May 2000, pp. 50–55. Anonymous, "Business travelers select Singapore Airlines No. 1," *Houston Chronicle,* January 23, 2000, p. 5. Ben Dolven, "Profitable romance," *Far Eastern Economic Review,* December 30, 1999–January 6, 2000, pp. 78–79. Staff Reports, Companies may be unwittingly ignoring the bulk of their asset value," *Investor Relations Business,* December 13, 1999, p. 4.

Special Issues

INTERNATIONAL ACCOUNTING FOR GOODWILL   Companies in The Netherlands (such as **Royal Dutch Shell** and **Phillips**), in Great Britain (such as **British Petroleum** and **British Airways**), and in other European nations do not have to record goodwill when they purchase another business. Instead, they may record the cost of goodwill as a decrease in owner's equity. These companies never have to amortize the cost of goodwill, so their net income is higher than a U.S. company's net income would be. As a result, U.S. companies often cry "foul" when bidding against a European firm to acquire another business. Americans claim the Europeans can pay higher prices because their income never takes a hit for amortization expense.

THINK IT OVER

How could companies around the world be placed on the same accounting basis?

Answer: If all companies worldwide followed the same accounting rules, they would be reporting income and other amounts computed similarly. But this is not the case. A company must follow the accounting rules of its own nation, and there are differences, as the goodwill situation illustrates.

⊙ DAILY EXERCISE 10-16

RESEARCH AND DEVELOPMENT COSTS   Accounting for research and development (R&D) costs is one of the toughest issues the accounting profession has faced. R&D is the lifeblood of companies such as **Procter & Gamble, General Electric, Intel,** and **Boeing** because it is vital to the development of new products and processes. The cost of R&D activities is one of these companies' most valuable (intangible) assets. But, in general, they do not report R&D assets on their balance sheets.

GAAP requires companies to expense R&D costs as they incur those costs. Only in certain circumstances may the company capitalize an R&D asset. Consider a company that incurs R&D costs under a contract guaranteeing it will recover the costs from the customer. In this case, the company records R&D cost as an asset. But this is the exception. Otherwise, the Financial Accounting Standards Board (FASB) requires that R&D cost be expensed as incurred.

ETHICAL ISSUES: PLANT ASSETS AND INTANGIBLES

The main ethical issue in accounting for plant assets and intangibles is whether to capitalize or to expense a particular cost. In this area, companies have split personalities. On the one hand, they all want to save on taxes. This motivates them to expense all costs in order to decrease their taxable income. On the other hand, most companies also want their financial statements to look as good as possible, with high net income and high reported amounts for assets.

In most cases, a cost that is capitalized or expensed for tax purposes must be treated the same way for reporting to stockholders and creditors in the financial statements. What, then, is the ethical path? Accountants should follow the general guidelines for capitalizing a cost: Capitalize all costs that provide a future benefit for the business, and expense all other costs, as outlined in the Decision Guidelines box that follows.

➥ We discussed accounting conservatism in Chapter 9, page 361.

Many companies have gotten into trouble by capitalizing costs they should have expensed. They made their financial statements look better than the facts warranted. But there are very few cases of companies getting into trouble by following the general guidelines, or even by erring on the side of expensing questionable costs. This is another example of accounting conservatism in action. It works. ◀

DECISION GUIDELINES

Accounting for Plant Assets and Related Expenses

DECISION	GUIDELINES
Capitalize or expense a cost?	General rule: Capitalize all costs that provide *future benefit* for the business.
	Expense all costs that provide *no future benefit.*
Capitalize or expense:	
• Cost associated with a new asset?	Capitalize all costs that bring the asset to its intended use.
• Cost associated with an existing asset?	Capitalize only those costs that add to the asset's usefulness or its useful life.
	Expense all other costs as maintenance or repairs.
• Interest cost incurred to finance the asset's acquisition?	Capitalize interest cost only on assets constructed by the business for its own use. Expense all other interest cost.
Which depreciation method to use:	
• For financial reporting?	Use the method that best matches depreciation expense against the revenues produced by the asset.
• For income tax?	Use the method that produces the fastest tax deductions (MACRS). A company can use different depreciation methods for financial reporting and for income tax purposes. In the United States, this practice is considered both legal and ethical.

REVIEW PLANT ASSETS

SUMMARY PROBLEM

The following figures appear in the Answers to the Mid-Chapter Summary Problem, requirement 2, on page 339.

	Method B: Double-Declining-Balance			Method C: Straight-Line		
Year	Annual Depreciation Expense	Accumulated Depreciation	Book Value	Annual Depreciation Expense	Accumulated Depreciation	Book Value
Start			$44,000			$44,000
20X5	$8,800	$ 8,800	35,200	$4,000	$ 4,000	40,000
20X6	7,040	15,840	28,160	4,000	8,000	36,000
20X7	5,632	21,472	22,528	4,000	12,000	32,000

Not Just Copies purchased equipment on January 1, 20X5. Management has depreciated the equipment by using the double-declining-balance method. On July 1, 20X7, the company sold the equipment for $27,000 cash.

Required

1. Suppose the income tax authorities permit a choice between the two depreciation methods shown. Which method would you select for income tax purposes? Why?
2. Record Not Just Copies' depreciation for 20X7 and the sale of the equipment on July 1, 20X7.

www.prenhall.com/horngren

End-of-Chapter Assessment

Solution

Requirement 1

For tax purposes, most companies select the accelerated method because it results in the most depreciation in the earliest years of the equipment's life. Accelerated depreciation minimizes taxable income and income tax payments in the early years of the asset's life, thereby maximizing the business's cash at the earliest possible time.

Requirement 2

To record depreciation to date of sale and sale of Not Just Copies' equipment:

20X7

July 1	Depreciation Expense—Equipment ($5,632 × 1/2 year)		2,816	
	Accumulated Depreciation—Equipment			2,816
	To update depreciation.			
July 1	Cash		27,000	
	Accumulated Depreciation—Equipment ($15,840 + $2,816)........		18,656	
	Equipment			44,000
	Gain on Sale of Equipment..			1,656
	To record sale of equipment.			

LESSONS LEARNED

1. *Measure the cost of a plant asset.* Plant assets are long-lived tangible assets, such as land, buildings, and equipment, used in the operation of a business. The cost of a plant asset is the purchase price plus all taxes, purchase commissions, and all other amounts paid to acquire the asset and to prepare it for its intended use.

2. *Account for depreciation.* Businesses may account for depreciation (the allocation of a plant asset's cost to expense over its useful life) by four methods: *straight-line, units-of-production, double-declining-balance,* or *sum-of-the-years'-digits.* The SYD method is not used much.

3. *Select the best depreciation method for income tax purposes.* Most companies use an accelerated depreciation method for income tax purposes. Accelerated depreciation results in higher expenses, lower taxable income, and lower tax payments early in the asset's life.

4. *Account for the disposal of a plant asset.* Before disposing of a plant asset, the company must update the asset's depreciation. Disposal is then recorded by removing the book balances from both the asset and its accumulated depreciation account. Sales often result in a gain or loss, which is reported on the income statement.

5. *Account for natural resource assets and depletion.* The cost of natural resources, a special category of long-lived assets, is expensed through *depletion.* Depletion is computed on a units-of-production basis.

6. *Account for intangible assets and amortization. Intangible assets* have no physical form. They give their owners special rights. The major types of intangible assets are patents, copyrights, trademarks, franchises and licenses, leaseholds, and goodwill. The cost of intangibles is expensed through *amortization,* which is the same as depreciation.

ACCOUNTING VOCABULARY

accelerated depreciation method (p. 395)
amortization (p. 405)
brand names (p. 407)
capital expenditure (p. 391)
capitalize a cost (p. 390)
copyright (p. 406)
depletion expense (p. 404)
depreciable cost (p. 393)
double-declining-balance (DDB) depreciation method (p. 395)

estimated residual value (p. 393)
estimated useful life (p. 393)
extraordinary repair (p. 391)
fixed assets (p. 387)
franchises (p. 407)
goodwill (p. 407)
intangible asset (p. 387)
licenses (p. 407)
major repair (p. 391)
ordinary repair (p. 391)
patent (p. 406)

plant assets (p. 387)
salvage value (p. 393)
scrap value (p. 393)
straight-line (SL) depreciation method (p. 393)
trademark (p. 407)
trade name (p. 407)
units-of-production (UOP) depreciation method (p. 394)

QUESTIONS

1. To what types of long-lived assets do the following expenses apply: depreciation, depletion, and amortization?
2. Describe how to measure the cost of a plant asset. Would an ordinary cost of repairing the asset after it is placed in service be included in the asset's cost?
3. When assets are purchased as a group for a single price and no individual asset cost is given, how is each asset's cost determined?
4. Distinguish a capital expenditure from an expense.
5. Define depreciation. Present the common misconceptions about depreciation.
6. Explain the concept of accelerated depreciation. Which of the depreciation methods results in the most depreciation in the first year of the asset's life?

7. The level of business activity fluctuates widely for Harwood Delivery Service, reaching its peak around Christmas each year. At other times, business is slow. Which depreciation method is most appropriate for Harwood's fleet of minivans? Explain your answer.
8. Which type of depreciation method is best from an income tax standpoint? Why?
9. Describe how to compute depreciation for less than a full year and how to account for depreciation for less than a full month.
10. Describe how to determine whether a company experiences a gain or a loss when it sells an old plant asset.
11. What expense applies to natural resources? By which depreciation method is this expense computed?

12. How do intangible assets differ from most other assets? Why are they assets at all? What expense applies to intangible assets?
13. Your company has just purchased another company for $400,000. The market value of the other company's net assets is $325,000. What is the $75,000 excess called? What type of asset is it? What is the maximum period over which its cost is amortized under generally accepted accounting principles?
14. Oracle Corporation is a world leader in the development of software. The company's past success has created vast amounts of business goodwill. Would you expect to see this goodwill reported on Oracle's financial statements? Why or why not?

Assess Your Progress

DAILY EXERCISES

DE10-1 Examine the balance sheet of **The Home Depot** in Exhibit 10-2 at the beginning of this chapter. Answer these questions about the company:

Cost and book value of a company's plant assets (Obj. 1)

1. When does The Home Depot's fiscal year end? Why does the company's fiscal year end on this date?
2. What is The Home Depot's largest category of assets—current assets, property and equipment, or other category?
3. What was The Home Depot's cost of property and equipment at January 30, 2000? What was the book value of property and equipment on this date?

DE10-2 Page 388 of this chapter lists the costs included for the acquisition of land. First is the purchase price of the land, which is obviously included in the cost of the land. The reasons for including the related costs are not so obvious. For example, the removal of a building looks more like an expense. State why the costs listed are included as part of the cost of the land. After the land is ready for use, will these costs be capitalized or expensed?

Measuring the cost of a plant asset (Obj. 1)

DE10-3 A lessee (who is renting an asset such as a building) makes periodic lease payments to the lessor (who owns the building). The lessee does not have a legal title to the building. Nevertheless, under certain conditions the lessee may account for the building as though the lessee owned an asset. How can a capital lease be fundamentally like an asset to the lessee?

Understanding leases (Obj. 1)

DE10-4 Suppose Florida Power, the utility company, is constructing power-generating equipment for use in its operations. To finance construction, Florida Power borrows $800,000 on notes payable on January 2, 20X3. During 20X3, Florida Power incurs interest cost equal to 9% of its construction loan. All of the company's interest cost should be capitalized to the Equipment account.

Capitalizing interest cost (Obj. 1)

1. Make the journal entry to pay Florida Power's interest cost at December 31, 20X3.
2. At December 31, 20X3, what is the balance in the Equipment account? Prepare a T-account for Equipment to answer this question.

DE10-5 Return to the Work It Out feature on page 391. Suppose at the time of your acquisition, the land has a current market value of $80,000, the building's market value is $60,000, and the equipment's market value is $20,000. Journalize the lump-sum purchase of the three assets for a total cost of $100,000. You sign a note payable for this amount.

Lump-sum purchase of assets (Obj. 1)

DE10-6 Vantas Airways repaired one of its Boeing 767 aircraft at a cost of $750,000, which Vantas paid in cash. Vantas erroneously capitalized this cost as part of the cost of the plane.

Capitalizing versus expensing plant asset costs (Obj. 1)

1. Journalize both the incorrect entry the accountant made to record this transaction and the correct entry that the accountant should have made.
2. Show the effects of the accounting error on Vantas Airways' income statement and balance sheet, using the format illustrated on page 392.

DE10-7 At the beginning of the year, Vantas Airways purchased a used Boeing MD-11 aircraft at a cost of $36,000,000. Vantas expects the plane to remain useful for five years (5 million miles) and to have a residual value of $6,000,000. Vantas expects the plane to be flown 750,000 miles the first year and 1,250,000 miles the last year.

Computing depreciation by three methods—first year only (Obj. 2)

1. Compute Vantas' first-year depreciation on the plane using the following methods:
   a. Straight-line **b.** Units-of-production **c.** Double-declining-balance
2. Show the airplane's book value at the end of the first year under each depreciation method.

DE10-8 At the beginning of 20X1, Vantas Airways purchased a used Boeing MD-11 aircraft at a cost of $36,000,000. Vantas expects the plane to remain useful for five years (5 million miles) and to have a residual value of $6,000,000. Vantas expects the plane to be flown 750,000 miles the first year and 1,250,000 miles the fifth year. Compute Vantas's fifth-year depreciation on the plane using the following methods:

Computing depreciation by three methods—final year only (Obj. 2)

a. Straight-line
b. Units-of-production
c. Double-declining-balance (you must compute depreciation for all five years)

DE10-9 This exercise uses the Vantas Airways' data from Daily Exercise 10-7. Assume Vantas Airways is trying to decide which depreciation method to use for income tax purposes.

Selecting the best depreciation method for income tax purposes
(Obj. 3)

1. Which depreciation method offers the tax advantage for the first year? Describe the nature of the tax advantage.
2. How much income tax will Vantas save for the first year of the airplane's use as compared to using the straight-line depreciation method? Vantas' income tax rate is 40%.

Partial-year depreciation
(Obj. 2)

DE10-10 On March 31, 20X2, Vantas Airways purchased a used Boeing MD-11 aircraft at a cost of $36,000,000. Vantas expects the plane to remain useful for five years (5,000,000 miles) and to have a residual value of $6,000,000. Vantas expects the plane to be flown 800,000 miles during the remainder of the first year ended December 31, 20X2. Compute Vantas' depreciation on the plane for the year ended December 31, 20X2, using the following methods:

    a. Straight-line   **b.** Units-of-production   **c.** Double-declining-balance

Computing and recording depreciation after a change in useful life of the asset
(Obj. 2)

DE10-11 Return to the example of the **Disney World** hot dog stand on pages 401–402. Suppose that after using the hot dog stand for four years, the company determines that the asset will remain useful for only two more years. Record Disney's depreciation on the hot dog stand for year 5 by the straight-line method.

Recording a gain or loss on disposal under two depreciation methods
(Obj. 4)

DE10-12 Return to the **Home Depot** delivery-truck depreciation example in Exhibits 10-6 and 10-8. Suppose The Home Depot sold the truck on December 31, 20X2, for $23,000 cash, after using the truck for two full years. Depreciation for 20X2 has already been recorded.

1. Make a separate journal entry to record The Home Depot's sale of the truck under
   a. Straight-line depreciation (Exhibit 10-6)
   b. Double-declining-balance depreciation (Exhibit 10-8)
2. Why is there such a big difference between the gain or loss on disposal under the two depreciation methods?

Accounting for the depletion of a company's natural resources
(Obj. 5)

DE10-13 **Chevron,** the giant oil company, holds huge reserves of oil and gas assets. At the end of 20X0, Chevron's cost of mineral assets totaled approximately $18 billion, representing 2.4 billion barrels of oil and gas reserves in the ground.

1. Which depreciation method do Chevron and other oil companies use to compute their annual depletion expense for the minerals removed from the ground?
2. Suppose Chevron removed 0.6 billion barrels of oil during 20X1. Record Chevron's depletion expense for 20X1.
3. At December 31, 20X0, Chevron's Accumulated Depletion account stood at $11.5 billion. If Chevron did not add any new oil and gas reserves during 20X1, what would be the book value of the company's oil and gas reserves after recording depletion at December 31, 20X1?

Accounting for goodwill
(Obj. 6)

DE10-14 Media-related companies have little in the way of tangible plant assets. Instead, their main asset is goodwill. When one media company buys another, goodwill is often the most costly asset acquired. Flannahan Newsprint paid $700,000 to acquire *The Thrifty Nickel,* an advertising paper headquartered in Texas. At the time of Flannahan's acquisition, *The Thrifty Nickel's* balance sheet reported total assets of $1,150,000 and liabilities of $600,000. The fair market value of *The Thrifty Nickel's* assets was $990,000.

1. How much goodwill did Flannahan purchase as part of the acquisition of *The Thrifty Nickel?*
2. Make Flannahan's summary journal entry to record the acquisition of *The Thrifty Nickel.*
3. What is the maximum useful life of the goodwill under GAAP? If Flannahan amortizes the goodwill over the maximum useful life, how much amortization expense will Flannahan record each year?

Analyzing a company's goodwill
(Obj. 6)

DE10-15 Examine the balance sheet of **The Home Depot** in Exhibit 10-2 at the beginning of this chapter. Answer these questions about the company:

1. What account title does The Home Depot use for goodwill?
2. What was the book value of The Home Depot's goodwill at January 30, 2000? What was the amount of accumulated amortization on the goodwill? What was The Home Depot's cost of its goodwill on this date?
3. One year earlier, on January 30, 1999, The Home Depot had Goodwill at a cost of $329 million, less Accumulated Amortization of $21 million, for a book value of $308 million. During the year ended January 30, 2000, The Home Depot sold no companies and thus sold none of its goodwill. Use your answer to requirement 2 to compute the cost of the goodwill The Home Depot purchased during the year ended January 30, 2000.

Accounting for patents and research and development cost
(Obj. 6)

DE10-16 This exercise summarizes the accounting for patents, which like copyrights and trademarks, provide the owner with a special right. It also covers research and development.

    Questor Applications paid $875,000 to research and develop a new software program. Questor also paid $300,000 to acquire a patent on the new software. After readying the software for production, Questor's sales revenue for the first year totaled $1,500,000. Cost of goods sold was $200,000 and selling expenses were $400,000. All these transactions occurred during 20X3. Questor expects the patent to have a useful life of three years.

1. Prepare Questor Applications' income statement for the year ended December 31, 20X3, complete with a heading.
2. Considering the makeup of Questor's expenses, what should the company's outlook for future profits be on the new software program?

EXERCISES

E10-1 Delmar Mining Company purchased land, paying $77,000 cash as a down payment and signing a $120,000 note payable for the balance. In addition, Delmar paid delinquent property tax of $2,000, title insurance costing $2,500, and a $5,400 charge for leveling the land and removing an unwanted building. The company constructed an office building on the land at a cost of $799,000. It also paid $51,000 for a fence around the boundary of the property, $10,400 for the company sign near the entrance to the property, and $6,000 for special lighting of the grounds. Determine the cost of the company's land, land improvements, and building. Which of the assets will Delmar depreciate?

Determining the cost of plant assets (Obj. 1)

E10-2 Weidman Belts, Inc. manufactures conveyor belts in St. Louis, Missouri. Early in January 20X3, Weidman constructed its own factory building with borrowed money. The 9% loan was for $600,000. During the year, Weidman spent the loan amount on construction of the building. At year end, Weidman paid the interest for one year.

Measuring the cost of an asset; capitalizing interest (Obj. 1)

Required

1. How much should Weidman record as the cost of the building in 20X3?
2. Record all of Weidman's transactions during 20X3.

E10-3 The Williamsburg Equestrian Center bought three valuable saddles in a $10,000 lump-sum purchase. An independent appraiser valued the saddles as follows:

Allocating cost to assets acquired in a lump-sum purchase (Obj. 1)

Saddle	Appraised Value
1	$3,350
2	5,400
3	4,250

Williamsburg paid half in cash and signed a note payable for the remainder. Record the purchase in the journal, identifying each saddle's individual cost in a separate Saddle account. Round decimals to three places.

E10-4 Classify each of the following expenditures as a capital expenditure or an expense related to machinery: (a) major overhaul to extend useful life by three years; (b) ordinary recurring repairs to keep the machinery in good working order; (c) lubrication of the machinery before it is placed in service; (d) periodic lubrication after the machinery is placed in service; (e) purchase price; (f) sales tax paid on the purchase price; (g) transportation and insurance while machinery is in transit from seller to buyer; (h) installation; (i) training of personnel for initial operation of the machinery; (j) special reinforcement to the machinery platform; and (k) income tax paid on income earned from the sale of products manufactured by the machinery.

Distinguishing capital expenditures from expenses (Obj. 1)

E10-5 Leslie Peres has just slept through the class in which Professor Dobbins explained the concept of depreciation. Because the next test is scheduled for Wednesday, Peres telephones Kim Barnes to get her notes from the lecture. Barnes's notes are concise: "Depreciation— Sounds like Greek to me." Peres next tries Tim Lake, who says he thinks depreciation is what happens when an asset wears out. Lee McPherson is confident that depreciation is the process of building up a cash fund to replace an asset at the end of its useful life. Explain the concept of depreciation for Peres. Evaluate the explanations of Lake and McPherson. Be specific.

Explaining the concept of depreciation (Obj. 2)

E10-6 De Plain International bought a delivery truck on January 2, 20X1, for $15,000. The truck was expected to remain in service four years and to last 100,000 miles. At the end of its useful life, De Plain officials estimated that the truck's residual value would be $3,000. The truck traveled 34,000 miles the first year, 28,000 the second year, 18,000 the third year, and 20,000 the fourth year. Prepare a schedule of *depreciation expense* per year for the truck under the three depreciation methods. After two years under the double-declining-balance method, the company switched to the straight-line method. Show your computations.

Which method tracks the wear and tear on the truck most closely? Which method would De Plain prefer to use for income tax purposes? Explain in detail why De Plain prefers this method.

Determining depreciation amounts by three methods (Obj. 2, 3)

E10-7 Taylor Marshall Co. paid $165,000 for equipment that is expected to have a seven-year life. The residual value of equipment is approximately 10% of the asset's cost.

Select the appropriate MACRS depreciation method for income tax purposes. Then determine the extra amount of cash that Marshall Co. can invest by using MACRS depreciation, versus straight-line, during the first two years of the equipment's life. Ignore any interest Marshall can earn by investing the extra cash.

E10-8 Relax-the-Back Mattress Store purchased a building for $775,000 and depreciated it on a straight-line basis over a 40-year period. The estimated residual value was $100,000. After using the building for 15 years, Relax-the-Back realized that wear and tear on the building would force the company to replace it before 40 years. Starting with the 16th year, Relax-the-Back began depreciating the building over a revised total life of 30 years and increased the estimated residual value to $200,000. Record depreciation expense on the building for years 15 and 16.

E10-9 On January 2, 20X3, Kloss Furniture Warehouse purchased showroom fixtures for $9,500 cash, expecting the fixtures to remain in service five years. Kloss has depreciated the fixtures on a double-declining-balance basis, with a $1,000 estimated residual value. On September 30, 20X4, Kloss sold the fixtures for $4,950 cash. Record both the depreciation expense on the fixtures for 20X4 and the sale of the fixtures on September 30, 20X4.

E10-10 Lasseter Transportation, based in Natchez, Mississippi, is a large trucking company that operates throughout the southern United States. Lasseter uses the units-of-production (UOP) method to depreciate its trucks because UOP depreciation best measures wear and tear. Lasseter trades in used trucks often to keep driver morale high and to maximize fuel efficiency. Consider these facts about one Mack truck in the company's fleet.

When acquired in 20X1, the tractor/trailer rig cost $385,000 and was expected to remain in service for ten years or 1,000,000 miles. Estimated residual value was $100,000. The truck was driven 75,000 miles in 20X1, 120,000 miles in 20X2, and 210,000 miles in 20X3. After 40,000 miles in 20X4, the company traded in the Mack truck for a less-expensive Freightliner. Lasseter paid cash of $80,000. Determine Lasseter's cost of the new truck. Journal entries are not required.

E10-11 El Dorado Drilling paid $298,500 for the right to extract ore from a 200,000-ton mineral deposit. In addition to the purchase price, El Dorado also paid a $500 filing fee, a $1,000 license fee to the state of Wyoming, and $60,000 for a geological survey of the property. Because the company purchased the rights to the minerals only, the company expected the asset to have zero residual value when fully depleted. During the first year, El Dorado removed 42,000 tons of ore. Make journal entries to record (a) purchase of the minerals (debit Mineral Asset), (b) payment of fees and other costs, and (c) depletion for the first year.

E10-12 *Part 1.* Westmark Printing Co., which manufactures high-speed printers, has recently paid $1.37 million for a patent on a new laser printer. Although it gives legal protection for 20 years, the patent is expected to provide Westmark with a competitive advantage for only 8 years. Assuming the straight-line method of amortization, make journal entries to record (a) the purchase of the patent, and (b) amortization for year 1.

Part 2. After using the patent for 4 years, Westmark learns at an industry trade show that another company is designing a more efficient printer. On the basis of this new information, Westmark decides, starting with year 5, to amortize the remaining cost of the patent over 2 remaining years, giving the patent a total useful life of 6 years. Record amortization for year 5.

E10-13 Campbell Soup Company's 19X9 statement of cash flows includes the following (adapted):

	Millions
	19X9
Cash Flows from Investing Activities:	
Payments to acquire other businesses..............	$105

Campbell's Note 16 to the balance sheet includes the following for Intangible Assets:

	Millions	
	19X9	**19X8**
Purchase price in excess of net assets of businesses acquired......................................	$1,697	$1,655
Less: Accumulated amortization	(219)	(179)

Required

1. What title does Campbell Soup Company use to describe its goodwill? How well does Campbell's title agree with the text definition of goodwill?
2. How much did Campbell Soup Company pay to acquire other businesses during 19X9? How much of the purchase price was for goodwill? How much did Campbell pay for the other assets of the businesses it acquired, such as receivables, inventory, property, and equipment?

E10-14 **PepsiCo, Inc.,** has aggressively acquired other companies, such as **Frito-Lay,** famous for its snack foods. Assume that PepsiCo purchased Adelaide Bakeries for $12 million cash. The market value of Adelaide's assets is $15 million, and it has liabilities of $10 million.

Measuring and recording goodwill (Obj. 6)

Required

1. Compute the cost of the goodwill purchased by PepsiCo.
2. Record the purchase of Adelaide Bakeries by PepsiCo.
3. Record PepsiCo's amortization of goodwill for year 1, assuming the straight-line method and a useful life of ten years.

CHALLENGE EXERCISES

E10-15 Papillon Knits is a catalog merchant in France similar to **L. L. Bean** and **Lands' End** in the United States. The company's assets consist mainly of inventory, a warehouse, and automated shipping equipment. Assume that early in year 1, Papillon purchased equipment at a cost of $4.5 million francs (F4.5 million). Management expects the equipment to remain in service five years. Because the equipment is so specialized, estimated residual value is negligible. Papillon uses the straight-line depreciation method. Through an accounting error, Papillon accidentally expensed the entire cost of the equipment at the time of purchase. The company is family-owned and operated as a partnership, so it pays no income tax.

Capitalizing versus expensing; measuring the effect of an error (Obj. 1)

Required

Prepare a schedule to show the overstatement or understatement in the following items at the end of each year over the five-year life of the equipment.

   1. Total current assets   2. Equipment, net   3. Net income

E10-16 **General Motors Corporation's** comparative balance sheet reported these amounts (in millions of dollars):

Reconstructing transactions from the financial statements (Obj. 2, 4)

	December 31,	
	19X9	**19X8**
Property:		
Land, plant, and equipment...............	$ 59,777	$ 59,565
Less accumulated depreciation..............	(34,363)	(34,641)
Net land, plant, and equipment..............	25,414	24,924
Unamortized special tools...........................	7,365	7,298
Net property..	$ 32,779	$ 32,222

GM's income statement for 19X9 reported the following expenses (in millions):

Depreciation	$4,155
Amortization of special tools	2,492

Unamortized special tools refers to the remaining asset balance after amortization expense has been subtracted. GM does not use an accumulated amortization account for special tools.

Required

1. There were no disposals of special tools during 19X9. Compute the cost of new acquisitions of special tools. Use a T-account for Special Tools.
2. Assume that during 19X9, GM sold land, plant, and equipment for $215 million and that this transaction produced a gain of $15 million. What was the book value of the assets sold?

PROBLEMS

(Group A)

P10-1A Metropolitan Glass Company incurred the following costs in acquiring land and a garage, making land improvements, and constructing and furnishing an office building:

Identifying the elements of a plant asset's cost (Obj. 1, 2)

a. Purchase price of 3 1/2 acres of land, including a building that will be used as a garage for company vehicles (land market value is $700,000; building market value is $100,000)... $640,000
b. Delinquent real estate taxes on the land to be paid by Metropolitan 3,700
c. Landscaping (additional dirt and earth moving) 5,175
d. Title insurance on the land acquisition 1,000
e. Fence around the boundary of the land.. 44,100
f. Building permit for the office building... 200
g. Architect's fee for the design of the office building 32,000
h. Company signs near the approaches to the company property 20,950
i. Renovation of the garage 27,500
j. Concrete, wood, and materials used to construct the office building 814,000
k. Masonry, carpentry, roofing, and other labor to construct the office building... 734,000
l. Interest cost on construction loan for the office building............................ 3,400
m. Parking lots and concrete walks on the property 17,450
n. Lights for the parking lot, walkways, and company signs........................... 8,900
o. Salary of construction supervisor (90% to office building; 6% to fencing, parking lot, and concrete walks; and 4% to garage renovation) 55,000
p. Furniture for the office building... 123,500
q. Transportation of furniture from seller to the office building 1,100
r. Landscaping (trees and shrubs) 9,100

Metropolitan Glass depreciates buildings over 40 years, land improvements over 20 years, and furniture over 8 years, all on a straight-line basis with zero residual value.

Required

1. Set up columns for Land, Land Improvements, Office Building, Garage, and Furniture. Show how to account for each of Metropolitan's costs by listing the cost under the correct account. Determine the total cost of each asset.
2. All construction was complete and the assets were placed in service on March 29. Record depreciation for the year ended December 31. Round to the nearest dollar.

Recording plant asset transactions, exchange, and disposal (Obj, 1, 2, 4)

P10-2A Lee & Smythe surveys American television-viewing trends. The company's balance sheet reports the following assets under Property and Equipment: Land, Buildings, Office Equipment, Communication Equipment, and Televideo Equipment, with a separate accumulated depreciation account for each depreciable asset. During 20X2, Lee & Smythe completed the following transactions:

May 3   Purchased communication and televideo equipment from the Gallup polling organization. Total cost was $80,000 paid in cash. An independent appraisal valued the communication equipment at $90,000 and the televideo equipment at $10,000.

July 30   Traded in old office equipment with book value of $11,000 (cost of $96,000) for new equipment with a cash cost of $88,000. The seller gave Lee & Smythe a trade-in allowance of $20,000 on the old equipment, and Lee & Smythe paid the remainder in cash.

Sep. 1   Sold a building that had cost $475,000 (accumulated depreciation of $353,500 through December 31 of the preceding year. Depreciation is computed on a straight-line basis. The building has a 30-year useful life and a residual value of $47,500. Lee & Smythe received $150,000 cash and a $450,000 note receivable.

Dec. 31   Recorded depreciation as follows:
Communication equipment and televideo equipment are depreciated by the double-declining-balance method over a five-year life with zero residual value. Office equipment is depreciated straight-line over seven years with $9,000 residual value. Record depreciation on the equipment acquired on May 3 and on July 30 separately.

Required

Record the transactions in the journal of Lee & Smythe.

Explaining the concept of depreciation (Obj. 2)

P10-3A The board of directors of Ameritech Satellite Technology is having its regular quarterly meeting. Accounting policies are on the agenda, and depreciation is being discussed. A new board member, an attorney, has some strong opinions about two aspects of depreciation policy. Clay Fitzhugh argues that depreciation must be coupled with a fund to replace company assets. Otherwise, there is no substance to depreciation, he argues. Fitzhugh also challenges the three-year depreciable life of company computers. He states that the computers will last much longer and should be depreciated over at least five years.

Required

Write a memo to explain the concept of depreciation to Fitzhugh and to answer his arguments. Format your memo as follows:

P10-4A On January 2, 20X1, Machinery Unlimited purchased a used trailer at a cost of $63,000. Before placing the trailer in service, the company spent $2,200 painting it, $800 replacing tires, and $4,000 overhauling the chassis. Machinery Unlimited management estimates that the trailer will remain in service for six years and have a residual value of $14,200. The trailer's annual mileage is expected to be 18,000 miles in each of the first four years and 14,000 miles in each of the next two years. In deciding which depreciation method to use, Brett Vivecek, the general manager, requests a depreciation schedule for each of the depreciation methods (straight-line, units-of-production, and double-declining-balance).

Computing depreciation by three methods and the cash-flow advantage of accelerated depreciation for tax purposes (Obj. 2, 3)

Required

1. Prepare a depreciation schedule for each depreciation method, showing asset cost, depreciation expense, accumulated depreciation, and asset book value. For the units-of-production method, round depreciation per mile to three decimal places.
2. Machinery Unlimited reports to creditors in the financial statements using the depreciation method that maximizes reported income in the early years of asset use. For income tax purposes, however, the company uses the depreciation method that minimizes income tax payments in those early years. Consider the first year that Machinery Unlimited uses the trailer. Identify the depreciation methods that meet the general manager's objectives, assuming the income tax authorities permit the use of any of the methods.
3. Cash provided by operations before income tax is $150,000 for the trailer's first year. The combined federal and state income tax rate is 40%. For the two depreciation methods identified in requirement 2, compare the net income and cash provided by operations (cash flow). Show which method gives the net-income advantage and which method gives the cash-flow advantage.

P10-5A *Note:* This problem uses the statement of cash flows, but all items are self-explanatory. **Curtiss-Wright Corporation** is a medium-sized manufacturer of high-tech parts used in commercial and military aircraft. The following excerpts come from Curtiss-Wright's 19X9 financial statements:

Analyzing plant asset transactions from a company's financial statements (Obj. 2, 4)

CURTISS-WRIGHT CORPORATION
Balance Sheet (Adapted)

(In thousands) Assets	December 31, 19X9	December 31, 19X8
Current assets:		
Cash and cash equivalents	$ 9,547	$ 5,809
Short-term investments	25,560	66,444
Receivables, net...	70,729	60,912
Inventories	60,584	54,048
Other current assets	13,950	11,360
Total current assets..	180,370	198,573
Property, plant, and equipment, at cost.............	242,000	237,215
Less: Accumulated depreciation.......................	(147,422)	(162,704)
Property, plant, and equipment, net................	94,578	74,511
Other assets..	112,178	79,656
Total assets	$387,126	$352,740

CURTISS-WRIGHT CORPORATION
Statements of Cash Flows (Excerpts, Adapted)

(In thousands) Cash Flows from Investing Activities	For the Years Ended December 31, 19X9	For the Years Ended December 31, 19X8
Cash receipts from sales of plant assets	$ 2,586	$ 950
Payments for property, plant, and equipment...............	(19,883)	(10,642)

Required

Answer these questions about Curtiss-Wright's plant assets.

1. At December 31, 19X9, what was Curtiss-Wright's cost of its plant assets? What was the amount of accumulated depreciation? What was the book value of the plant assets? Does book value measure how much Curtiss-Wright could sell the assets for? Explain.
2. Curtiss-Wright's depreciation expense for 19X9 was $12,864 thousand. Why is the amount of depreciation expense so different from accumulated depreciation at December 31, 19X9?
3. How much did Curtiss-Wright pay to purchase plant assets during 19X9? Prepare a T-account showing the 19X8 and 19X9 balances of Property, Plant, and Equipment cost. Post to the T-account the cost of plant assets purchased during 19X9. Then compute the cost of plant assets *sold* during 19X9. Finally, determine whether Curtiss-Wright bought or sold more plant assets during the year.

Accounting for intangibles, natural resources, and the related expenses (Obj. 5, 6)

P10-6A *Part 1.* **United Telecommunications, Inc.** (United Telecom) provides communication services in Florida, North Carolina, New Jersey, Texas, and other states. The company's balance sheet reports the asset Cost of Acquisitions in Excess of the Fair Market Value of the Net Assets of Subsidiaries. Assume that United Telecom purchased this asset as part of the acquisition of another company, which had these figures:

Book value of assets	$575,000
Market value of assets	906,000
Liabilities	405,000

Required

1. What is another title for the asset Cost of Acquisitions in Excess of the Fair Market Value of the Net Assets of Subsidiaries?
2. Make the journal entry recording United Telecom's purchase of the other company for $1,650,000 cash. Use the account titled Goodwill.
3. Assume United Telecom amortizes Cost of Acquisitions in Excess of the Fair Market Value of the Net Assets of Subsidiaries over 20 years. Record straight-line amortization for one year. Use the account titled Goodwill.

Part 2. **Continental Pipeline Company** operates a pipeline that provides natural gas to Atlanta, Washington, D.C., Philadelphia, and New York City. The company's balance sheet includes the asset Oil and Gas Properties.

Suppose Continental paid $7 million cash for oil and gas reserves with an estimated 500,000 barrels of oil. Assume the company paid $350,000 for additional geological tests of the property and $110,000 to prepare the surface for drilling. Prior to production, the company signed a $65,000 note payable to have a building constructed on the property. The building will be abandoned when the oil is depleted, so its cost is debited to the Oil Properties account and included in depletion charges. During the first year of production, Continental removed 77,000 barrels of oil, which it sold on credit for $19 per barrel. Operating expenses related to this project totaled $185,000 for the first year, all paid in cash.

Required

1. Record all of Continental's transactions, including depletion, for the year.
2. Prepare the company's income statement for this oil and gas project for the first year. Evaluate the profitability of the project.

Reporting plant asset transactions in the financial statements—a review (Obj. 1, 2, 4)

P10-7A At the end of 1998, **Sprint Corporation,** the telecommunications company, had total assets of $33.3 billion and total liabilities of $20.9 billion. Included among the assets were property, plant, and equipment with a cost of $32.1 billion and accumulated depreciation of $13.1 billion.

Assume that Sprint completed the following selected transactions during 1999: The company earned total revenues of $19.9 billion and incurred total expenses of $20.8 billion, which included depreciation of $3.7 billion. During the year, Sprint paid $6.1 billion for new property, plant, and equipment, and sold old plant assets for $0.2 billion. The cost of the assets sold was $1.1 billion, and their accumulated depreciation was also $1.1 billion.

Required

1. Show how Sprint Corporation would report property, plant, and equipment on the balance sheet at December 31, 1999.
2. How much of the plant assets that Sprint sold during 1999 had been depreciated? Did Sprint have a gain or a loss on the sale of plant assets? What was the amount of the gain or loss?
3. How much was Sprint's owner's equity at December 31, 1998?
4. Did Sprint report net income or net loss on its 1999 income statement? Compute the amount.

PROBLEMS

P10-1B Bobby Jones Golf Company incurred the following costs in acquiring land, making land improvements, and constructing and furnishing its own sales building.

Identifying the elements of a plant asset's cost
(Obj. 1, 2)

a.	Purchase price of four acres of land, including a building that will be used for a garage (land market value is $280,000; building market value is $40,000)	$300,000
b.	Landscaping (additional dirt and earth moving)......................................	8,100
c.	Fence around the boundary of the land	17,650
d.	Attorney fee for title search on the land...	770
e.	Delinquent real estate taxes on the land to be paid by Bobby Jones..........	5,900
f.	Company signs at front of the company property	4,475
g.	Building permit for the sales building..	350
h.	Architect's fee for the design of the sales building	22,500
i.	Masonry, carpentry, roofing, and labor to construct the sales building	709,000
j.	Concrete, wood, and other materials used to construct the sales building..	214,000
k.	Renovation of the garage building..	36,900
l.	Interest cost on construction loan for sales building.................................	9,000
m.	Landscaping (trees and shrubs)..	6,400
n.	Parking lot and concrete walks on the property	29,750
o.	Lights for the parking lot, walkways, and company signs	7,300
p.	Salary of construction supervisor (85% to sales building; 9% to fencing, parking lot, and concrete walks; and 6% to garage building).....................	40,000
q.	Furniture for the sales building..	107,100
r.	Transportation and installation of furniture...	2,270

Bobby Jones depreciates buildings over 40 years, land improvements over 20 years, and furniture over 8 years, all on a straight-line basis with zero residual value.

Required

1. Set up columns for Land, Land Improvements, Sales Building, Garage Building, and Furniture. Show how to account for each of Bobby Jones's costs by listing the cost under the correct account. Determine the total cost of each asset.
2. All construction was complete and the assets were placed in service on May 2. Record depreciation for the year ended December 31. Round to the nearest dollar.

P10-2B Westway Freight Co. provides local freight service in Lincoln, Nebraska. The company's balance sheet includes the following assets under Property, Plant, and Equipment: Land, Buildings, and Motor-Carrier Equipment. Westway has a separate accumulated depreciation account for each of these assets except land. Assume that Westway Freight Co. completed the following transactions:

Recording plant asset transactions, exchange, and disposal
(Obj. 1, 2, 4)

Jan. 2   Traded in motor-carrier equipment with book value of $47,000 (cost of $130,000) for similar new equipment with a cash cost of $176,000. Westway received a trade-in allowance of $70,000 on the old equipment and paid the remainder in cash.

July 1   Sold a building that cost $550,000 and that had accumulated depreciation of $247,500 through December 31 of the preceding year. Depreciation is computed on a straight-line basis. The building has a 30-year useful life and a residual value of $55,000. Westway received $100,000 cash and a $600,000 note receivable.

Oct. 26   Purchased land and a building for a single price of $300,000. An independent appraisal valued the land at $115,000 and the building at $230,000.

Dec. 31   Recorded depreciation as follows:
      Motor-carrier equipment has an expected useful life of six years and an estimated residual value of 5% of cost. Depreciation is double-declining-balance.
      Depreciation on buildings is straight-line. The new building has a 40-year useful life and a residual value equal to 12% of its cost.

Required

Record the transactions in Westway Freight's journal.

P10-3B The board of directors of Wentzville Corporation is reviewing the 20X1 annual report. A new board member—a professor—questions the company accountant about the depreciation amounts. The professor wonders why depreciation expense has decreased from $200,000 in 19X9 to $184,000 in 20X0 to $172,000 in 20X1. He states that he could understand the decreasing annual amounts if the company had been selling properties each year, but that has not occurred. Further, growth in the city is increasing the values of property. Why is the company recording depreciation when property values are increasing?

Explaining the concept of depreciation
(Obj. 2)

Required

Write a paragraph or two to explain the concept of depreciation and answer the professor's questions. Which depreciation method does Wentzville appear to be using?

P10-4B On January 3, 20X1, Dobb Automotive Company paid $224,000 for equipment used in manufacturing automotive supplies. In addition to the basic purchase price, the company paid $700 transportation charges, $100 insurance for the equipment while in transit, $12,100 sales tax, and $3,100 for a special platform on which to place the equipment in the plant. Dobb management estimates that the equipment will remain in service five years and have a residual value of $17,000. The equipment will produce 50,000 units the first year, with annual production decreasing by 5,000 units during each of the next four years (that is, 45,000 units in year 2; 40,000 units in year 3; and so on). In trying to decide which depreciation method to use, Jacqueline Dobb has requested a depreciation schedule for each of three depreciation methods (straight-line, units-of-production, and double-declining-balance).

Required

1. For each depreciation method, prepare a depreciation schedule showing asset cost, depreciation expense, accumulated depreciation, and asset book value. For the units-of-production method, round depreciation per unit to three decimal places.
2. Dobb reports to stockholders and creditors in the financial statements using the depreciation method that maximizes reported income in the early years of asset use. For income tax purposes, the company uses the depreciation method that minimizes income tax payments in those early years. Consider the first year Dobb uses the equipment. Identify the depreciation methods that meet Dobb's objectives, assuming the income tax authorities permit the use of any of the methods.
3. Assume that cash provided by operations before income tax is $180,000 for the equipment's first year. The combined federal and state income tax rate is 40%. For the two depreciation methods identified in requirement 2, compare the net income and cash provided by operations (cash flow). Show which method gives the net-income advantage and which method gives the cash-flow advantage.

P10-5B *Note:* This problem uses the statement of cash flows, but all items are self-explanatory. **IBM** is the world's largest computer company. After a few lean years, Big Blue, as the company is called, has rebounded strongly with some new products and improving profits. The following excerpts come from IBM's 19X9 financial statements:

INTERNATIONAL BUSINESS MACHINES CORPORATION
Balance Sheet (Adapted)

(Dollars in Millions) At December 31:	19X9	19X8
Assets		
Current assets:		
Cash and cash equivalents	$ 5,043	$ 5,375
Marketable securities	788	393
Notes and accounts receivable—trade, net of allowances	20,039	18,958
Sales-type leases receivable	6,220	6,510
Other accounts receivable	1,359	1,313
Inventories	4,868	5,200
Prepaid expenses and other current assets	4,838	4,611
Total current assets	43,155	42,360
Plant, machines, and other property, at cost	39,616	44,870
Less: Accumulated depreciation	(22,026)	(25,239)
Plant, machines, and other property—net	17,590	19,631
Software	663	599
Investments and sundry assets	26,087	23,510
Total assets	$87,495	$86,100

INTERNATIONAL BUSINESS MACHINES CORPORATION
Statement of Cash Flows (Excerpts)

(Dollars in Millions) For the year ended December 31:	19X9	19X8
Cash flows from investing activities:		
Payments for plant, machines, and other property	$(5,959)	$(6,520)
Cash received from the sale of plant, rental machines, and other property	1,207	905

Required

1. At December 31, 19X9, what was IBM's cost of its plant assets? What was the amount of accumulated depreciation? What percent of the cost has been used up?
2. IBM's depreciation expense for 19X9 was $6,159 million. Why is the amount of depreciation expense so different from accumulated depreciation at December 31, 19X9?
3. How much did IBM pay to purchase plant assets during 19X9? Prepare a T-account showing the 19X8 and 19X9 balances of total Plant Assets at cost. Post the cost of plant asset purchases during 19X9. Then compute the cost of plant assets *sold* during 19X9. Finally, determine whether IBM bought or sold more plant assets during the year.
4. IBM's balance sheet reports Software. What category of asset is software?

P10-6B *Part 1.* **Collins Foods International Inc.** is the majority owner of Sizzler Restaurants. The company's balance sheet reports the asset Cost in Excess of Net Assets of Purchased Businesses. Assume that Collins purchased this asset as part of the acquisition of another company, which carried these figures:

Accounting for intangibles, natural resources, and the related expenses (Obj. 5, 6)

Book value of assets	$2.4 million
Market value of assets	2.8 million
Liabilities	2.2 million

Required

1. What is another title for the asset Cost in Excess of Net Assets of Purchased Businesses?
2. Make the journal entry to record Collins's purchase of the other company for $2.7 million cash. Use the account titled Goodwill.
3. Assume Collins amortizes Cost in Excess of Net Assets of Purchased Businesses over 20 years. Record the straight-line amortization for one year. Use the account titled Goodwill.

Part 2. **Georgia-Pacific Corporation** is one of the world's largest forest products companies. The company's balance sheet includes the assets Natural Gas, Oil, and Coal.

Suppose Georgia-Pacific paid $2.8 million cash for the right to work a mine with an estimated 100,000 tons of coal. Assume the company paid $60,000 to remove unwanted buildings from the land and $45,000 to prepare the surface for mining. Further, assume that Georgia-Pacific signed a $30,000 note payable to a company that will return the land surface to its original condition after the lease ends. During the first year, Georgia-Pacific removed 35,000 tons of coal, which it sold on account for $37 per ton. Operating expenses for the first year totaled $252,000, all paid in cash.

Required

1. Record all of Georgia-Pacific's transactions, including depletion, for the year.
2. Prepare the company's income statement for its coal operations for the first year. Evaluate the profitability of the coal operations.

P10-7B At the end of 19X8, **The Coca-Cola Company** had total assets of $19.1 billion and total liabilities of $10.7 billion. Included among the assets were property, plant, and equipment with a cost of $5.7 billion and accumulated depreciation of $2.0 billion.

Reporting plant asset transactions in the financial statements—a review (Obj. 1, 2, 4)

Coca-Cola completed the following selected transactions during 19X9: The company earned total revenues of $19.8 billion and incurred total expenses of $17.3 billion, which included depreciation of $0.8 billion. During the year, Coca-Cola paid $1.1 billion for new property, plant, and equipment and sold old plant assets, receiving cash of $0.2 billion. The cost of the assets sold was $0.1 billion; their accumulated depreciation was also $0.1 billion.

Required

1. Show how Coca-Cola would report property, plant, and equipment on the balance sheet at December 31, 19X9. What was the book value of property, plant, and equipment on that date?
2. How much of the assets that Coca-Cola sold during 19X9 had been depreciated? Did Coca-Cola have a gain or loss on the sale of plant assets during 19X9? What was the amount of the gain or loss?
3. How much was Coca-Cola's owners' equity at December 31, 19X8?
4. Did Coca-Cola report net income or net loss on its 19X9 income statement? Compute the amount.

DECISION CASES

Measuring profitability based on different inventory and depreciation methods (Obj. 2, 3)

Case 1. ◄ *Link Back to Chapter 9 (Inventory Methods).* Suppose you are considering investing in two businesses, Astoria Enterprises and Hilton Systems. The two companies are virtually identical, and both began operations at the beginning of the current year. During the year, each company purchased inventory as follows:

Jan.	4	10,000 units at $4 =	$ 40,000
Apr.	6	5,000 units at 5 =	25,000
Aug.	9	7,000 units at 6 =	42,000
Nov.	27	10,000 units at 7 =	70,000
Totals		32,000	$177,000

During the first year, both companies sold 25,000 units of inventory.

In early January, both companies purchased equipment costing $143,000 (ten-year estimated useful life and a $20,000 residual value). Astoria uses the inventory and depreciation methods that maximize reported income (FIFO and straight-line). By contrast, Hilton uses the inventory and depreciation methods that minimize income tax payments (LIFO and double-declining-balance). Both companies' trial balances at December 31 included the following:

Sales revenue.........................	$370,000
Operating expenses	80,000

Required

1. Prepare both companies' income statements.
2. Write an investment newsletter to address the following questions for your clients: Which company appears to be more profitable? Which company has more cash to invest in promising projects? If prices continue rising in both companies' industries over the long-term, which company would you prefer to invest in? Why?

Plant assets and intangible assets (Obj. 1, 6)

Case 2. The following questions are unrelated except that they all apply to fixed assets and intangible assets:

a. The manager of Clarkson Corporation regularly debits the cost of repairs and maintenance of plant assets to Plant and Equipment. Why would she do that, since she knows she is violating generally accepted accounting principles (GAAP)?
b. It has been suggested that, because many intangible assets have no value except to the company that owns them, they should be valued at $1.00 or zero on the balance sheet. Many accountants disagree with this view. Which view do you support? Why?
c. The manager of Ladue Company regularly buys plant assets and debits the cost to Repairs and Maintenance Expense. Why would he do that, since this action violates GAAP?

ETHICAL ISSUE

Reflection Cove Apartments purchased land and a building for the lump sum of $4.1 million. To get the maximum tax deduction, Reflection Cove managers allocated 90% of the purchase price to the building and only 10% to the land. A more realistic allocation would have been 70% to the building and 30% to the land.

Required

1. Explain the tax advantage of allocating too much to the building and too little to the land.
2. Was Reflection Cove's allocation ethical? If so, state why. If not, why not? Identify who was harmed.

FINANCIAL STATEMENT CASE

Plant assets and intangible assets (Obj. 2, 3, 4, 6)

Refer to the **Target Corporation** financial statements in Appendix A, and answer the following questions.

Required

1. Which depreciation method does Target use for reporting in the financial statements? What type of depreciation method does the company probably use for income tax purposes? Why is this method preferable for tax purposes?
2. Depreciation and amortization expense is embedded in the selling, general, and administrative expense amounts listed on the income statement. The statement of cash flows gives the amount of depreciation and amortization expense. What was the amount of depreciation and amortization for fiscal year 1999? Record Target's depreciation and amortization expense for 1999.
3. The statement of cash flows reports the purchases of plant assets and the proceeds (sale prices) received on disposal of plant assets. How much were Target's plant asset acquisitions during 1999? Journalize the company's acquisition of plant assets.
4. How much cash did Target receive on the sale of plant assets during 1999? Assume the plant assets that were sold had a cost of $988 million and accumulated depreciation of $697 million. Record the sale of these plant assets. How much was the gain or loss on the sale of plant assets during the year?

TEAM PROJECT

Required

Visit a local business.

1. List all its plant assets.
2. If possible, interview the manager. Gain as much information as you can about the business's plant assets. For example, try to determine the assets' costs, the depreciation method the company is using, and the estimated useful life of each asset category. If an interview is impossible, then develop your own estimates of the assets' costs, useful lives, and book values, assuming an appropriate depreciation method.
3. Determine whether the business has any intangible assets. If so, list them and gain as much information as possible about their nature, cost, and estimated useful lives.
4. Write a detailed report of your findings and be prepared to present it to the class.

INTERNET EXERCISE

On Saturday, July 8, 2000, **FedEx** teamed up with **Amazon.com** to deliver 250,000 copies of the book *Harry Potter and the Goblet of Fire*. To deliver this unprecedented number of books, 100 regularly scheduled FedEx flights, 9,000 FedEx delivery personnel, and vehicles from 700 stations were mobilized from Amazon.com distribution centers to distribute approximately 675,000 pounds (more than 300 tons) of the book.

1. Go to **http://www.fedex.com** and in the left-hand column click on *Investor Relations*. Select the *on-line* version of the most recent annual report. Within the Annual Report menu, click on *Financial Information*. (Note: There are two links titled *Financial Information*. Use the link classified under Annual Report.) Use this information to answer the following questions.
    a. At the most recent year-end, examine *Property and Equipment, at cost*. List the four types of property and equipment reported by FedEx Corporation. What is the total cost of these assets? What is the book value? What amount of cost has already been expensed through depreciation? What is the expensed portion called?
    b. Which financial statement reports depreciation expense? For the most recent year identify the amount reported for *Depreciation and amortization expense*.
2. Refer to Note 2: Summary of Significant Accounting Policies to answer the following.
    a. Which method of depreciation does FedEx use for financial reporting purposes? For tax reporting purposes? Explain why a company uses different depreciation methods for tax reporting and for financial statement purposes. Is this ethical? Is it legal? Does this comply with the Consistency Principle?
    b. What is the range of useful lives FedEx uses for flight equipment? For computer and electronic equipment? Do these useful lives make sense?
    c. What amount of residual value does FedEx use for aircraft frames and engines? For all other property and equipment?

FedEx Corporation

Go to the "Depreciation Methods and Inventory Cost Flow Assumptions" episode on the *Mastering Accounting* CD-ROM for an interactive, video-enhanced exercise that shows how CanGo staff must choose when and how to depreciate fixed assets, such as a new warehouse the company needs.

11

Current Liabilities and Payroll

ACCOUNTING

LEARNING OBJECTIVES

After studying this chapter, you should be able to

1. Account for current liabilities of known amount

2. Account for current liabilities that must be estimated

3. Compute payroll amounts

4. Record basic payroll transactions

5. Use a payroll system

6. Report current liabilities on the balance sheet

www.prenhall.com/horngren
Readiness Assessment

Advantage®, Mileage Plus®, and SkyMiles®—these are the frequent-flier plans of **American Airlines, United,** and **Delta.** American was the first to capitalize on this mode of creating loyal customers. Boy, does it work!

When Ron and Lisa Schmidt fly on American Airlines, they get a mile of frequent-flier credit for every mile they fly. They also get mileage credit when they pay their VISA bill, whether it's for gas at the pump or carpet in their home. Had Ron and Lisa been able to fly American on a recent trip to Florida, they would have gotten VIP treatment. But flying on Delta landed them back in ordinary no-frills coach. Of course, it works both ways. Delta's frequent fliers don't automatically get kid-glove treatment when they fly American or United.

The mileage credit granted to frequent fliers adds up to quite an accounting challenge for the airlines. It's both promotion expense and a major liability. For each mile of credit granted to the Schmidts, American Airlines books a liability for their free travel in the future. How do the airlines estimate this payable—called Air Traffic Liability? The answer is "Very carefully, because they must report this liability on their balance sheets."

In this chapter, we explain how to account for all types of current liabilities. The first half of the chapter concentrates on current liabilities, and the second half on payrolls, which generate some specific current liabilities. Exhibit 11-1 shows how **AMR Corporation,** the parent company of American Airlines, reported its current liabilities at March 31, 2000. Recall that *current liabilities* are obligations due within one year or within the company's normal operating cycle if it is longer than one year. Obligations due beyond that period are classified as *long-term liabilities*. ➡

◄ We discussed current liabilities and long-term liabilities in Chapter 4, p. 139.

CURRENT LIABILITIES OF KNOWN AMOUNT

Current liabilities fall into two categories: liabilities of a known amount and liabilities that must be estimated. We look first at current liabilities of known amount.

Objective 1
Account for current liabilities of known amount

Accounts Payable

Amounts owed to suppliers for products or services purchased on open account are *accounts payable.* We have seen many accounts payable illustrations in preceding chapters. For example, most businesses purchase inventory and office supplies on account. **AMR Corporation** reported Accounts payable of $1,231 million at March 31, 2000 (see line 1 of Exhibit 11-1).

Let's see how AMR's accounts payable get onto the company's balance sheet. One of AMR's common transactions is the credit purchase of its inventory of food to be served on flights. AMR's accounts payable and inventory systems are integrated. When the food inventory dips below a certain level, the computer automatically prepares a purchase request for more food. The order is placed and the goods are received. AMR makes the following journal entry to buy the inventory of account (amount assumed):

Inventory	600	
Accounts Payable		600
Purchase on account.		

The computer thus increases Inventory and Accounts Payable. Then for payments, the computer debits Accounts Payable and credits Cash, as follows:

Accounts Payable	400	
Cash		400
Paid on account.		

EXHIBIT 11-1
How AMR Reports Its Current
Liabilities

AMR CORPORATION (PARENT COMPANY OF AMERICAN AIRLINES) Balance Sheet (partial; adapted) March 31, 2000		
	Liabilities	**(In Millions)**
	Current Liabilities	
1	Accounts payable..	$1,231
2	Accrued liabilities payable	1,818
3	Air traffic liability...	2,758
4	Current maturities of long-term debt	241
5	Current obligations under capital leases.............	231
6	Total current liabilities.......................................	$6,279

After AMR Corporation buys inventory and pays the account payable in the two preceding transactions, how much does AMR owe the other company? Stated differently, how much is AMR's account payable to the supplier?

Answer: $200 ($600 − $400)

AMR Corporation completes thousands of transactions such as these. AMR's $1,231 million balance of Accounts Payable (Exhibit 11-1) is the sum of all the amounts AMR still owes on account.

Short-Term Notes Payable

SHORT-TERM NOTE PAYABLE.
Promissory note payable due within one year, a common form of financing.

Short-term notes payable are a common form of financing. They are promissory notes that must be paid within one year. Companies often issue short-term notes payable to borrow cash or to purchase inventory. The following entries are typical for a short-term note payable:

20X1			
Sep. 30	Inventory...	8,000	
	Note Payable, Short-Term.............................		8,000
	Purchased inventory on a one-year, 10% note.		
20X1			
Dec. 31	Interest Expense ($8,000 × 0.10 × 3/12)	200	
	Interest Payable..		200
	Accrued interest expense at year end.		

The balance sheet at December 31, 20X1, will report the Note Payable of $8,000 and Interest Payable of $200 as current liabilities. The 20X1 income statement will report interest expense of $200, as illustrated.

Balance Sheet December 31, 20X1		Income Statement Year Ended December 31, 20X1	
Liabilities		**Expenses**	
Current liabilities:....................		Interest expense..........................	$200
Note payable, short-term	$8,000		
Interest payable....................	200		

The following entry records payment of the note at maturity:

DAILY EXERCISE 11-1

DAILY EXERCISE 11-2

DAILY EXERCISE 11-3

20X2
Sep. 30   Note Payable, Short-Term   8,000
           Interest Payable   200
           Interest Expense ($8,000 × 0.10 × 9/12).............   600
                 Cash [$8,000 + ($8,000 × 0.10)]   8,800
           Paid a note and interest at maturity.

The cash payment entry must separate the total interest on the note ($800) between

- the interest expense of 20X1 ($200), and
- the interest expense of 20X2 ($600).

This way, each year's financial statements report the correct amounts for *that* year.

Short-Term Notes Payable Issued at a Discount

There is another way to set up a borrowing arrangement. It is called **discounting a note payable.** The lender subtracts the interest amount from the note's face value, and the borrower receives the net amount. At maturity, the borrower pays back the full face value, which includes all the interest.

Suppose **Procter & Gamble** discounts a $100,000, 60-day note payable to its bank at 12%. P&G will receive $98,000—that is, the $100,000 face value less interest of $2,000 ($100,000 × 0.12 × 60/360). Assume that this transaction occurs on November 25, 20X1. Procter & Gamble's entry to record discounting the note follows.[1]

DISCOUNTING A NOTE PAYABLE. A borrowing arrangement in which the bank subtracts the interest amount from a note's face value. The borrower receives the net amount.

20X1
Nov. 25   Cash ($100,000 − $2,000*)   98,000
                 Note Payable, Short-Term...........................   98,000
           Discounted a $100,000, 60-day, 12% note payable.
           *Discount = $100,000 × 0.12 × 60/360 = $2,000.

THINK IT OVER

How much did Procter & Gamble actually borrow from the bank—$98,000 or $100,000? How much will P&G pay back? How much interest expense will P&G record for the borrowing arrangement?

Answers: Procter & Gamble borrowed $98,000, the amount of cash the company received. P&G will pay back $100,000 at maturity. P&G's interest expense will be $2,000 ($100,000 paid back − $98,000 borrowed).

Procter & Gamble must record accrued interest at year end as it would for any note payable. P&G's adjusting entry at December 31 records interest for 36 days, as follows:

20X1
Dec. 31   Interest Expense ($100,000 × 0.12 × 36/360)   1,200
                 Note Payable   1,200
           Accrued interest expense at year end.

After the year-end adjustment, the Note Payable account carries its current balance of $99,200.

	NOTE PAYABLE	
	Nov. 25	98,000
	Dec. 31	1,200
	Bal.	99,200

---

[1] Another set of journal entries can be used to record the discounting of a note payable. The alternate method uses a separate Discount on Note Payable account and obscures the true nature of the borrowing arrangement.

At maturity, the business records the final amount of interest expense on the note:

20X2
Jan. 24 Interest Expense ($100,000 × 0.12 × 24/360) 800
                  Note Payable   800
             To record interest expense.

On the note's maturity date, the Note Payable account holds the maturity value of $100,000.

NOTE PAYABLE		
	Nov. 25, 20X1	98,000
	Dec. 31, 20X1	1,200
	Jan. 24, 20X2	800
	Bal.	100,000

DAILY EXERCISE 11-4

The final entry pays off the note at maturity.

20X2
Jan. 24 Note Payable, Short-Term 100,000
                  Cash...   100,000
             To pay note at maturity.

Sales Tax Payable

Most states levy a sales tax on retail sales. Only Delaware, Montana, New Hampshire, and Oregon do not have a sales tax. Retailers collect the sales tax in addition to the price of the item sold. The retailers owe the state the sales tax, so, the account Sales Tax Payable is a current liability. For example, **ShowBiz Pizza Time, Inc.** (operator of family restaurants and entertainment centers, such as Chuck E. Cheese), reported sales tax payable of $737,712 as a current liability.

Suppose one Saturday's sales at a ShowBiz Pizza Time totaled $10,000. The business collected an additional 5% in sales tax, which would equal $500 ($10,000 × 0.05). The business would record that day's sales as follows:

Cash ($10,000 × 1.05) 10,500
         Sales Revenue..   10,000
         Sales Tax Payable ($10,000 × 0.05)   500
To record cash sales and the related sales tax.

CASH	SALES TAX PAYABLE	SALES REVENUE
10,500	500	10,000

Companies forward the collected sales tax to the taxing authority at regular intervals. Then they debit Sales Tax Payable and credit Cash.

Many companies do not credit Sales Tax Payable for each sale. Instead, they record sales revenue and sales tax together. Then, prior to paying the tax, they make an adjusting entry to bring Sales Revenue and Sales Tax Payable to their correct balances.

Suppose a **Kinko** store earned service revenue of $100,000 during July, subject to sales tax of 6%. Kinko's summary entry to record the month's revenue could be as follows:

July 31 Cash ($100,000 × 1.06) 106,000
                  Service Revenue...   106,000
             Revenue for the month.

The entry to adjust Service Revenue and Sales Tax Payable to their correct balances would then be

July 31 Service Revenue [$106,000 − ($106,000 ÷ 1.06)]..... 6,000
                  Sales Tax Payable   6,000
             To record sales tax.

Now both accounts are ready for the financial statements:

SERVICE REVENUE			SALES TAX PAYABLE	
6,000	106,000			6,000
	100,000			

A Taxing Dilemma: Sales Tax Liability and the Internet

e-Commerce offers two big pluses: shopping from home in your pajamas and no sales tax. Say you live in New York City and purchase a CD from a music store. You pay the

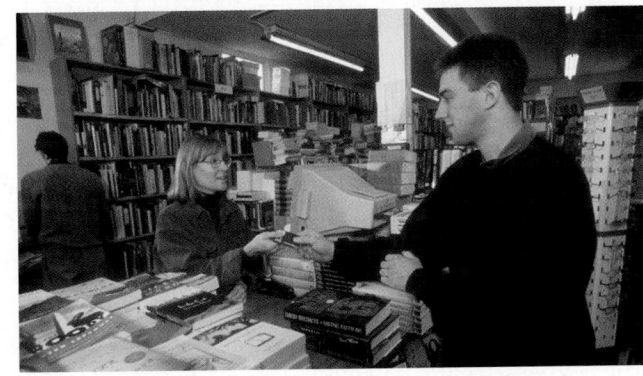

retail price of $15.99, plus sales tax of 8.25%. The sales tax is a current liability, payable to the State of New York. A purchase of the same CD from **Amazon.com** will be $1.32 cheaper. Fortunately for on-line (and mail-order) consumers, the Supreme Court ruled that only the U.S. Congress can require retailers who don't have a physical location in the state to charge sales taxes.

We consumers are always happy to pay less for a product, but we may be wise to consider the long-term effects of the e-commerce sales tax loophole. By 2003 state and local governments may lose $20 billion in tax revenues if Internet sales are exempted. The sales tax you pay builds roads and pays your governor, the mayor, and other state and local employees, such as firefighters and teachers. In addition, if e-commerce takes over, there may be no downtowns left in San Antonio or Tacoma—just boarded up businesses and empty strip malls.

If you are civic-minded, you can voluntarily pay your "use tax," which is imposed in the state in which you use the goods that you purchase. Most consumers don't pay this tax, but states may start collecting it if Congress continues to exempt dot.coms from sales tax. Expect to hear more on this issue. And if you're starting your own dot.com, see **EcommerceTax.com** for up-to-the-minute news. How sales tax is treated may influence how you set up your business.

Source: Based on Peter Schrag, "loophole.com," *The Nation,* May 15, 2000, pp. 6–7. Anonymous, "United States: Offline," *The Economist,* March 25, 2000, p. 35. http://www.ecommercetax.com/doc/043000.htm.

Current Portion of Long-Term Debt

Some long-term notes payable and bonds payable are paid in installments. The **current portion of long-term debt,** or **current maturity,** is the amount of the principal payable within one year. At the end of each year, a company reclassifies (from long-term debt to a current liability) the amount that must be paid during the upcoming year.

AMR's balance sheet (Exhibit 11-1) reports Current maturities of long-term debt, the next-to-last current liability (line 4). On its full balance sheet, AMR reports Long-term debt immediately after total current liabilities. *Long-term debt* refers to notes payable that are payable later than one year beyond the balance sheet date.

The liability for the current portion of long-term debt (line 4) does *not* include any accrued interest payable. The account, Current Maturities of Long-Term Debt, represents only the *principal amount owed.* Interest Payable is a separate account for a

CURRENT PORTION OF LONG-TERM DEBT. Amount of the principal that is payable within one year. Also called **current maturity.**

different liability. AMR includes interest payable under the current liability caption Accrued liabilities payable (line 2).

AMR Corporation reports Current obligations under capital leases as its last current liability (line 5). This liability is similar to current maturities of long-term debt because it is next year's lease payment on leases that AMR has capitalized as an asset.

WORK IT OUT Suppose AMR Corporation owes $600 million on long-term notes payable at December 31, 20X5. The borrowing agreement requires AMR to pay $241 million of this debt on September 30, 20X6. Show how AMR will report both current and long-term liabilities on its balance sheet at December 31, 20X5.

Answer

	(Millions)
Current liabilities:	
Current maturities of long-term debt	$241
Long-term liabilities:	
Long-term debt ($600 − $241)........................	359

Accrued Expenses (Accrued Liabilities)

ACCRUED EXPENSE. An expense that the business has not yet paid. Also called **accrued liability.**

An **accrued expense** is an expense that the business has not yet paid. Therefore, an accrued expense is also a liability. This explains why accrued expenses are also called **accrued liabilities.** Accrued expenses typically occur with the passage of time, such as interest payable on long-term debt. By contrast, an account payable results from the purchase of a good or a service. ◄◄

➡ We introduced accrued expenses in Chapter 3, p. 92.

Like most other companies, AMR Corporation reports accrued liabilities on its balance sheet (line 2 in Exhibit 11-1). The total of $1,818 million includes salaries and wages payable. This caption also includes other payroll-related liabilities, such as taxes withheld from employee paychecks, plus current liabilities for interest payable and income tax payable. AMR Corporation's Air traffic liability, discussed in the chapter opening story, is another example of an accrued liability. See line 3 of Exhibit 11-1.

We illustrate accounting for interest payable under the heading Short-Term Notes Payable on page 426. The next section, plus the second half of this chapter, covers accounting for accrued salaries, wages, and other payroll liabilities.

Payroll Liabilities

PAYROLL. A major expense. Also called **employee compensation.**

Payroll, also called **employee compensation,** is a major expense. For service organizations—such as CPA firms, physicians, and travel agents—payroll is *the* major expense. Service organizations sell their personnel's services, so employee compensation is their primary cost of doing business, just as cost of goods sold is the largest expense for a merchandising company.

Employee compensation takes different forms:

- *Salary* is pay expressed in a yearly, monthly, or weekly rate.
- *Wages* are employee pay amounts stated at an hourly figure.
- *Commissions* are compensation computed as a percentage of the sales the employee made.
- *Bonus* is an amount over and above regular compensation.

Journalizing all these forms of compensation follows the same pattern, as illustrated in Exhibit 11-2 (using assumed figures).

EXHIBIT 11-2
Accounting for Payroll Expenses and Liabilities

Salary Expense (or Wage Expense or Commission Expense)..............	10,000	
Employee Income Tax Payable...		1,200
FICA Tax Payable...		800
Employee Union Dues Payable		140
Salary Payable to Employees [take-home pay].........................		7,860
To record salary expense.		

Salary (or other payroll) expense represents employees' *gross pay* (pay before subtractions for taxes and other deductions). Salary expense creates several liabilities.

- Salary payable to employees is their net (take-home) pay.
- *Employee Income Tax Payable* is income tax that has been withheld from employee paychecks.
- *FICA Tax Payable* is the employees' Social Security tax, which also is withheld from paychecks. (FICA stands for the Federal Insurance Contributions Act, which created the Social Security tax.) The company owes these liabilities to the U.S. government.
- In Exhibit 11-2, employees authorize the company to withhold union dues. These amounts are payable to the union.

In addition to salaries and wages, companies also pay some payroll taxes and other expenses for employee fringe benefits. Accounting for these expenses is similar to the illustration in Exhibit 11-2 and is covered in more detail in the second half of this chapter.

Unearned Revenues

Unearned revenues are also called *deferred revenues, revenues collected in advance,* and *customer prepayments.* ➥ All these account titles indicate that the business has received cash from its customers before earning the revenue. For unearned revenue, the company has an obligation to provide goods or services to the customer. Let's consider an example.

➥ As we saw in Chapter 3, p. 94, an unearned revenue is a liability because it represents an obligation to provide a good or service.

The **Dun & Bradstreet (D&B) Corporation** provides credit reports for subscribers. Finance companies pay D&B in advance to have D&B investigate the credit histories of potential customers. By receiving cash before earning the revenue, D&B incurs a liability for future service. The liability account is called Unearned Subscription Revenue (or Unearned Subscription *Income*).

Assume that D&B charges $600 for a three-year subscription. D&B's cash-receipt entry would be

20X1			
Jan. 1	Cash	600	
	Unearned Subscription Revenue..............		600
	Received cash in advance.		

After receiving the cash on January 1, 20X1, D&B owes its professional service to customers over three years. D&B's liability is

UNEARNED SUBSCRIPTION REVENUE

	600

During 20X1, D&B performs one-third of the total service and earns $200 ($600 × 1/3) of the revenue. At December 31, 20X1, D&B makes the following adjusting entry to decrease Unearned Subscription Revenue, the liability account, and to increase Subscription Revenue:

20X1			
Dec. 31	Unearned Subscription Revenue	200	
	Subscription Revenue ($600 × 1/3)		200
	Earned revenue that was collected in advance.		

After posting, the two accounts are

UNEARNED SUBSCRIPTION REVENUE				SUBSCRIPTION REVENUE		
Dec. 31	200	Jan. 1	600		Dec. 31	200
		Bal.	400			

At December 31, 20X1, D&B has earned $200 of the revenue. D&B still owes its customer $400 in total liabilities:

- $200 for the service D&B will perform during 20X2. This is a current liability.
- $200 for the service D&B will perform during 20X3. This is a long-term liability.

D&B's financial statements would report the following at the end of the first year:

◉ DAILY EXERCISE 11-5

Balance Sheet at December 31, 20X1		Income Statement for the Year Ended December 31, 20X1	
Current liabilities:		Revenues:	
Unearned subscription revenue..............................	$200	Subscription revenue	$200
Long-term liabilities:			
Unearned subscription revenue..............................	$200		

CURRENT LIABILITIES THAT MUST BE ESTIMATED

Objective 2
Account for current liabilities that must be estimated

A business may know that a liability exists but not know the exact amount. It cannot simply ignore the liability. The unknown amount must be estimated, recorded in the accounts, and reported on the balance sheet.

Estimated current liabilities vary among companies. As a first example, let's look at Estimated Warranty Payable, a common liability for merchandisers.

Estimated Warranty Payable

Many companies guarantee their products against defects under *warranty* agreements. Ninety-day warranties and one-year warranties are common. The automobile companies—**Toyota, Ford,** and **BMW,** for example—accrue liabilities for their five-year, 50,000-mile warranties.

➤ For a review of the matching principle, see Chapter 3, p. 86.

The matching principle demands that the company record the *warranty expense* in the same period that the business recognizes sales revenue, regardless of when the company pays warranty claims. ◄ Offering the warranty—and incurring warranty expense—is a cost of making sales. At the time of the sale, the company does not know the exact amount of warranty expense. But the business must estimate its warranty expense and the related liability.

Assume that **Whirlpool Corporation,** which manufactures appliances for **Sears** and other companies, made sales of $200,000, subject to product warranties. Assume that in the past between 2% and 4% of the products proved defective. Whirlpool management could estimate that 3% of the products it sells this year will require warranty payments. The company would record the sales of $200,000 and the warranty expense of $6,000 ($200,000 × 0.03) in the same period as follows:

Accounts Receivable....................................	200,000	
Sales Revenue....................................		200,000
Sales on account.		
Warranty Expense	6,000	
Estimated Warranty Payable..............		6,000
To accrue warranty expense.		

Assume that Whirlpool's warranty payments total $5,800. If Whirlpool repairs the defective appliances, Whirlpool makes this journal entry:

Estimated Warranty Payable...	5,800	
Cash		5,800

To *repair* defective products sold under warranty.

If Whirlpool gives customers replacement appliances for their warranty claims, Whirlpool would instead make this entry:

Estimated Warranty Payable...	5,800	
Inventory		5,800

To *replace* defective products sold under warranty.

Whirlpool's expense on the income statement is $6,000 in all cases. The amount of the cash payment or the cost of the replacement inventory has no bearing on the amount of warranty expense for the period. After paying these warranty claims, Whirlpool's Estimated Warranty Payable account appears as follows:

ESTIMATED WARRANTY PAYABLE

5,800	6,000	
	Bal.	200

The balance sheet reports a current liability for Estimated Warranty Payable of $200.

 DAILY EXERCISE 11-6

 DAILY EXERCISE 11-7

 WORK IT OUT

Maxim Company made sales of $400,000 and estimated warranty repairs at 5% of the sales. Maxim's actual warranty outlays were $19,000. Record the sales (ignore cost of goods sold), the warranty expense, and the warranty payments. The beginning balance of Estimated Warranty Payable was zero. How much is Maxim's estimated warranty payable at the end of the period?

Answer

Accounts Receivable	400,000	
Sales Revenue		400,000
Warranty Expense ($400,000 × 0.05)..............	20,000	
Estimated Warranty Payable		20,000
Estimated Warranty Payable............................	19,000	
Cash		19,000

ESTIMATED WARRANTY PAYABLE

19,000	20,000	
	Bal.	1,000

Estimated Vacation Pay Liability

Most companies grant paid vacations to their employees. The employees receive this benefit when they take their vacation, but they earn the benefit by working the remainder of the year. Two-week vacations are common. To match expense with revenue, the company accrues the vacation pay expense and liability over the course of the year. Then, the company records payment during the two-week vacation period. Companies must estimate their vacation pay liability.

Suppose a company's January payroll is $100,000 and vacation pay adds 4%, or $4,000. Experience indicates that only 90% of the available vacations will be taken, so the January vacation pay estimate is $3,600 ($4,000 × 0.90). In January, the company records vacation pay as follows:

Jan. 31	Vacation Pay Expense	3,600	
	Estimated Vacation Pay Liability		3,600

Each month thereafter, the company makes a similar entry.

If an employee takes a two-week vacation during August, his or her $2,000 salary is recorded as follows:

Aug. 31	Estimated Vacation Pay Liability..............	2,000		
	Cash...		2,000	

Income Tax Payable (for a Corporation)

Corporations pay income tax in the same way that individuals do. Corporations file their tax returns after the end of the year, so they must estimate their income tax payable for the balance sheet. During the year, corporations make quarterly tax payments to the government. A corporation would record the payment of $100,000 of income tax expense for the third quarter as follows:

Sept. 30	Income Tax Expense	100,000	
	Cash...		100,000
	To pay quarterly income tax.		

The corporation's entry to accrue $40,000 of income tax expense and payable at year end is

Dec. 31	Income Tax Expense	40,000	
	Income Tax Payable.......................		40,000
	To accrue income tax at year end.		

The corporation will pay off this tax liability early in the next year, so Income Tax Payable is a current liability.

Contingent Liabilities

➤ We introduced contingent liabilities in the Appendix to Chapter 8, p. 344.

A *contingent liability* is not an actual liability. Instead, it is a potential liability that depends on a *future* event. ◄ For example, suppose **AMR Corporation,** the parent company of **American Airlines,** faces a possible loss if its pilots walk off the job in a threatened labor strike. The future event is the negotiation between the airline and the pilots' labor union. The airline thus faces a contingent liability, which may or may not become an actual liability.

It would be unethical for the airline to withhold knowledge of the labor negotiations from anyone considering investing in the business. Another contingent liability arises when one company *cosigns a note payable* for another company. Suppose Company A guarantees that Company B will pay a note payable owed to another party. This practice obligates Company A to pay the note and interest if Company B fails to pay. Thus, Company A has a contingent liability until the note becomes due. If Company B pays off the note, the contingent liability ceases to exist. If not, Company A's liability becomes actual.

The most important source of contingent liabilities is a lawsuit in which the company is being sued. Until the case is settled, the defendant has a contingent liability. One of the most famous lawsuits occurred when **Microsoft Corporation** was sued for matters related to the Java programming language technology. Until the court reached its decision, Microsoft reported the contingency in the notes to its financial statements. In its 1999 annual report, Microsoft included the following (excerpt):

> **Sun Microsystems, Inc. brought suit against Microsoft in the U.S. District Court for [. . .] California. Sun's complaint alleges several claims against Microsoft, all related to the [. . .] Java programming language technology.**

SHORT PRESENTATION. A way to report contingent liabilities in the body of the balance sheet, after total liabilities but with no amount given. An explanatory note accompanies the presentation.

Contingent liabilities may be reported in two ways. In what is called a **short presentation,** the contingent liability appears in the body of the balance sheet, after total liabilities, but with no amounts given. In general, an explanatory note accompanies a short presentation. The Microsoft note is typical for a contingent liability arising from a lawsuit.

 DAILY EXERCISE 11-8

ETHICAL ISSUES IN REPORTING LIABILITIES

Accounting for current liabilities poses ethical and legal challenges. Business owners and managers want their company to look as successful as possible. They like to report high levels of net income on the income statement. High net income makes

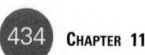

the company look profitable and helps the company raise money from investors. And high net income leads to large bonuses for managers. Owners want their balance sheet to report high asset values and low liability amounts, which make the company look safe to lenders and help the company borrow money at low interest rates.

- Low expenses   ————————→   High net income
- Low liabilities   ————————→   High owner's equity

Owners and managers may be tempted to overlook some accrued expenses at the end of the accounting period. For example, a company can fail to accrue warranty expense. This failure will cause total expenses to be understated and net income to be overstated on the income statement.

Contingent liabilities also pose an ethical challenge. Because contingencies are not real liabilities, they are easy to overlook. But a contingent liability can be very important. The **Microsoft** contingency is an example. Ethical business owners and managers do not play games with their accounting. Falsifying financial statements can ruin one's reputation. It can also land a person in a federal or state prison.

At this half-way point in the chapter, review what you have learned by studying the following Decision Guidelines.

DECISION GUIDELINES

Accounting for Current and Contingent Liabilities, Including Payroll

DECISION	GUIDELINES
What are the two main issues in accounting for current liabilities?	• *Recording* the liability and the asset acquired or the expense incurred • *Reporting* the liability on the balance sheet

What are the two basic categories of current liabilities?	• Current liabilities of *known amount:*
	  Accounts payable Accrued expenses
	  Short-term notes payable (accrued liabilities)
	  Sales tax payable Payroll liabilities
	  Current portion of long- Salary, wages, commission,
	    term debt and bonus payable
	  Unearned revenues
	• Current liabilities that *must be estimated:*
	  Estimated warranty payable
	  Estimated vacation pay liability
	  Income tax payable (for a corporation)

How to account for contingent (potential) liabilities?	Report contingent liabilities either • *Short* (with no dollar amount) on the balance sheet, along with an explanatory note, or • With *only* the explanatory note
What is the ethical and legal challenge in accounting for current and contingent liabilities?	To ensure that the balance sheet (and the related notes) reports the *full amount of all* the business's current and contingent liabilities

SUMMARY PROBLEM

This problem consists of three independent parts.

Required

1. A **Wendy's** hamburger restaurant made cash sales of $4,000 subject to a 5% sales tax. Record the sales and the related sales tax. Also record Wendy's payment of the tax to the state government.
2. Assume that at April 30, 20X2, **H. J. Heinz Company** reported its 6% long-term debt as follows:

Current Liabilities (in part)

Portion of long-term debt due within one year	$ 14,000,000
Interest payable ($200,000,000 × 0.06 × 5/12)	5,000,000

Long-Term Debt and Other Liabilities (in part)

Long-term debt..	$186,000,000

The company pays interest on its long-term debt on November 30 each year.

Show how Heinz Company would report its liabilities on the year-end balance sheet one year later—April 30, 20X3. Assume that the current maturity of its long-term debt is $16 million.

3. What distinguishes a contingent liability from an actual liability?

Solution

1.

Cash ($4,000 × 1.05)	4,200	
Sales Revenue		4,000
Sales Tax Payable ($4,000 × 0.05)		200
To record cash sales and related sales tax.		
Sales Tax Payable..	200	
Cash		200
To pay sales tax to the state government.		

2. H. J. Heinz Company balance sheet at April 30, 20X3:

Current Liabilities (in part)

Portion of long-term debt due within one year	$ 16,000,000
Interest payable ($186,000,000 × 0.06 × 5/12)	4,650,000

Long-Term Debt and Other Liabilities (in part)

Long-term debt..	$170,000,000

3. A contingent liability is a *potential* liability, which may or may not become an actual liability.

Objective 3

Compute payroll amounts

ACCOUNTING FOR PAYROLL

Payroll costs are so important to most businesses that they adopt special systems to account for their labor costs. This section covers the basics of accounting for payroll.

Businesses often pay employees at a base rate for a set number of hours—called *straight time*. For working any additional hours—called *overtime*—the employee receives a higher rate.

Lucy Childres is an accountant for Bobby Jones Golf Company. Lucy earns $600 per week straight time. The company work week runs 40 hours, so Lucy's hourly straight-time pay is $15 ($600/40). Her company pays her *time and a half* for overtime. That rate is 150% (1.5 times) the straight-time rate. Thus, Lucy earns $22.50 for each hour of overtime she works ($15.00 × 1.5 = $22.50). For working 42 hours during a week, she earns $645, computed as follows:

Straight-time pay for 40 hours..	$600
Overtime pay for 2 overtime hours: 2 × $22.50..............	45
Total pay...	$645

Gross Pay and Net Pay

Before withholding taxes were introduced in 1943, employees brought home all they earned. Back in 1940, Lucy Childres would have taken home the full $645 that she made. Those days are long past.

The federal government, most state governments, and even some city governments require employers to act as collection agents for employee taxes. Employers then deduct the taxes from employee checks. Insurance companies, labor unions, and other organizations may also receive pieces of employees' pay. Amounts withheld from an employee's check are called *deductions.*

Gross pay is the total amount of salary, wages, commissions, or any other employee compensation before taxes and other deductions. **Net pay**—or "take-home pay"—equals gross pay minus all deductions. As Exhibit 11-3 shows, net pay is the amount the employee actually takes home.

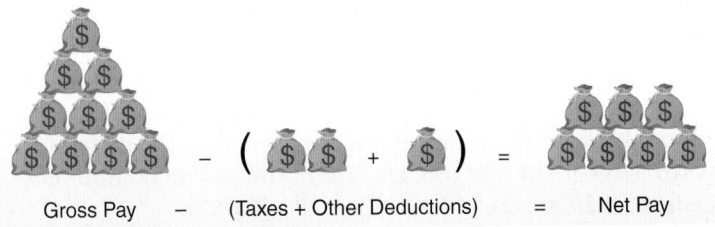

Gross Pay   −   (Taxes + Other Deductions)   =   Net Pay

EXHIBIT 11-3
Gross Pay and Net Pay

Many companies also pay employee *benefits,* another form of employee compensation. Examples include health and life insurance. Other examples include retirement pay and health insurance during the retirement years. Payroll accounting has become quite complex.

Payroll Deductions

Payroll deductions withheld from employees' pay fall into two categories: (1) *required deductions,* such as employee income tax and social security tax; and (2) *optional deductions* for union dues, insurance premiums, charitable contributions, and other amounts withheld at the employee's request. After their withholding, payroll deductions become the liability of the employer, who then must pay the outside party. For example, the employer pays the government the employee income tax withheld and pays the union the union dues withheld.

 DAILY EXERCISE 11-9

REQUIRED PAYROLL DEDUCTIONS: EMPLOYEE INCOME TAX In the United States, the law requires most employers to withhold income tax from employees' pay. Income tax is the largest sources of national tax revenues. Employee income tax generates approximately 36% of tax receipts in the United States, 38% in Sweden, and 41% in Canada.

The amount of income tax deducted from gross pay is called **withheld income tax.** The amount withheld depends on the employee's gross pay and on the number of *withholding allowances* the employee claims.

All employees file a Form W-4 with their employer to indicate the number of allowances claimed for withholding purposes. Each allowance lowers the tax withheld from the employee's paycheck. An unmarried taxpayer can claim only one allowance; a childless married couple, up to two allowances; a married couple with one child, up to three allowances; and so on. Exhibit 11-4 shows a W-4 for R. C. Dean, who claims four allowances (line 5).

EXHIBIT 11-4   Form W-4

Form **W-4**	**Employee's Withholding Allowance Certificate**		OMB No. 1545-0010
Department of the Treasury Internal Revenue Service	► **For Privacy Act and Paperwork Reduction Act Notice, see page 2.**		**2000**

1 Type or print your first name and middle initial	Last name	2 Your social security number
R. C.	Dean	344 ¦ 86 ¦ 4529

Home address (number and street or rural route)	3 ☐ Single ☒ Married ☐ Married, but withhold at higher Single rate.
4376 Palm Drive	Note: If married, but legally separated, or spouse is a nonresident alien, check the Single box.

City or town, state, and ZIP code	4 If your last name differs from that on your social security card, check
Fort Lauderdale, FL 33317	here. **You must call 1-800-772-1213 for a new card** . . . ► ☐

5	Total number of allowances you are claiming (from line **H** above **OR** from the applicable worksheet on page 2)	5	4
6	Additional amount, if any, you want withheld from each paycheck	6	$
7	I claim exemption from withholding for 2000, and I certify that I meet **BOTH** of the following conditions for exemption:		
	• Last year I had a right to a refund of **ALL** Federal income tax withheld because I had **NO** tax liability **AND**		
	• This year I expect a refund of **ALL** Federal income tax withheld because I expect to have **NO** tax liability.		
	If you meet both conditions, write "EXEMPT" here . . . . ►	7	

Under penalties of perjury, I certify that I am entitled to the number of withholding allowances claimed on this certificate, or I am entitled to claim exempt status.

Employee's signature (Form is not valid unless you sign it) ► *R. C. Dean*	**Date ►**	7-22,1997

8	Employer's name and address (Employer: Complete lines 8 and 10 only if sending to the IRS.) Blumenthal's Crescent Square Shopping Center Fort Lauderdale, FL 33310	9 Office code (optional) 14	10 Employer identification number 83 ¦ 19475

Cat. No. 10220Q

REQUIRED PAYROLL DEDUCTIONS: EMPLOYEE SOCIAL SECURITY (FICA) TAX   The *Federal Insurance Contributions Act (FICA),* also known as the Social Security Act, created the Social Security Tax. The Social Security program provides retirement, disability, and medical benefits. The law requires employers to withhold **Social Security (FICA) tax** from employees' pay. The FICA tax has two components:

SOCIAL SECURITY TAX. Federal Insurance Contributions Act (FICA) tax, which is withheld from employees' pay. Also called **FICA tax.**

1. Old age, survivors', and disability insurance (OASDI)
2. Health insurance (Medicare)

The amount of tax withheld from employees' pay varies from year to year. As of 2000, the OASDI portion of the tax applies to the first $76,200 of employee earnings in a year. The taxable amount of earnings is adjusted annually depending on the rate of inflation. The OASDI tax rate is 6.2%. Therefore, the maximum OASDI tax that an employee paid in 2000 was $4,724 ($76,200 × 0.062).

The Medicare portion of the FICA tax applies to all employee earnings. This tax rate is 1.45%. An employee thus pays a combined FICA tax rate of 7.65% (6.2% + 1.45%) of the first $76,200 of annual earnings, plus 1.45% of earnings above $76,200.

To ease the computational burden and focus on the concepts, we assume that the FICA tax is 8% of the first $75,000 of employee earnings each year. (Use these numbers when you complete this chapter's assignment material, unless instructed otherwise.) For each employee who earns $75,000 or more, the employer withholds $6,000 ($75,000 × 0.08) and sends that amount to the federal government. The employer records this employee tax in the account FICA Tax Payable.

Assume that Rex Jennings, an employee, earned $73,500 prior to December. Jennings' salary for December is $7,000. How much FICA tax will be withheld from his December paycheck? The computation is as follows:

Employee earnings subject to the tax in one year	$75,000
Employee earnings prior to the current pay period	−73,500
Current pay subject to FICA tax..	$ 1,500
FICA tax rate	×0.08
FICA tax to be withheld from current pay...........................	$ 120

OPTIONAL PAYROLL DEDUCTIONS   As a convenience to employees, many companies make payroll deductions and disburse cash according to employee instructions. Union dues, insurance payments, payroll savings plans, and gifts to charities such as **United Way** and **Habitat for Humanity** are examples.

Many employers offer *cafeteria plans* that allow workers to select from a menu of insurance coverage. Suppose **Ford Motor Company** provides each employee with $450 of insurance coverage each month. One employee may use the monthly allowance to purchase only life insurance. Another employee may select only disability coverage. A third worker may choose a combination of life insurance and disability coverage.

Employer Payroll Taxes

Employers must bear the expense of at least three payroll taxes:

1. Employer Social Security (FICA) tax
2. State **unemployment compensation tax**
3. Federal **unemployment compensation tax.**

EMPLOYER **FICA** TAX   In addition to collecting the employee's Social Security tax, the employer also must pay into the program. The employer's Social Security tax is the same as the amount withheld from employee pay. Thus, the Social Security system is funded by equal contributions from employees and employers. Using our 8% and $75,000 annual pay figures, the maximum annual employer tax on each employee is $6,000 ($75,000 × 0.08). The employer records this payroll tax in the same FICA Tax Payable account that is used for the withholding from employee paychecks.

STATE AND FEDERAL UNEMPLOYMENT COMPENSATION TAXES   State and federal unemployment taxes are products of the Federal Unemployment Tax Act (FUTA). These taxes finance workmen's compensation for people who have been laid off from work. *In recent years, employers have paid a combined tax of 6.2% on the first $7,000 of each employee's annual earnings.* The proportion paid to the state is 5.4%, and 0.8% is paid to the federal government. The employer uses the accounts Federal Unemployment Tax Payable and State Unemployment Tax Payable. Exhibit 11-5 shows a typical disbursement of payroll costs by an employer company.

UNEMPLOYMENT COMPENSATION TAX. Payroll tax paid by employers to the government, which uses the money to pay unemployment benefits to people who are out of work.

 DAILY EXERCISE 11-10

 DAILY EXERCISE 11-11

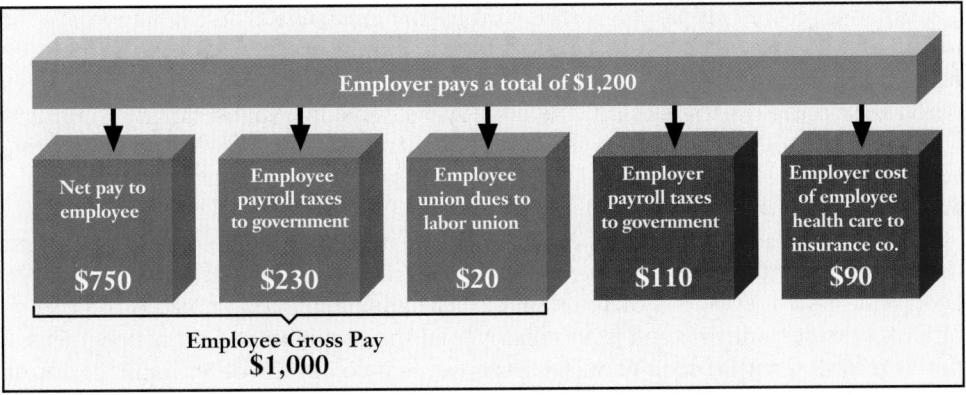

EXHIBIT 11-5
Typical Breakdown of Payroll Costs for One Employee

Payroll Entries

Exhibit 11-6 summarizes an employer's entries to record a monthly payroll of $10,000. All amounts are assumed for illustration only.

Entry A in Exhibit 11-6 records the employer's *salary expense*. The *gross salary* of all employees, $10,000, is their monthly pay before any deductions. The federal government imposes the income tax and the FICA tax. Most states and some cities also levy income taxes, which are accounted for in the same way. The union dues are optional. Employees' take-home (net) pay is $7,860. One important point about this payroll transaction is that the employees pay their own income and FICA taxes and union dues. The employer serves merely as collecting agent and sends these amounts to the government and the union.

Entry B records the employer's *payroll tax expense*. In addition to the employee's FICA tax ($800 in entry A), the employer also pays the $800 FICA tax

Objective 4
Record basic payroll transactions

 DAILY EXERCISE 11-12

Exhibit 11-6   **Payroll Accounting by the Employer**

A. Salary Expense

Salary Expense (or Wage Expense or Commission Expense)	10,000	
Employee Income Tax Payable		1,200
FICA Tax Payable ($10,000 × 0.08)		800
Employee Union Dues Payable..		140
Salary Payable to Employees [take-home pay]		7,860

To record *salary expense.*

B. Payroll Tax Expense

Payroll Tax Expense	1,420	
FICA Tax Payable ($10,000 × 0.08)		800
State Unemployment Tax Payable ($10,000 × 0.054)..................		540
Federal Unemployment Tax Payable ($10,000 × 0.008)..............		80

To record employer's *payroll taxes.*

C. Benefits Expense

Health Insurance Expense for Employees.....................................	800	
Life Insurance Expense for Employees	200	
Pension Expense	500	
Employee Benefits Payable...		1,500

To record employee benefits payable by employer.

Total Payroll Expense ($12,920) = Salary Expense ($10,000) + Payroll Tax Expense ($1,420)
+ Benefits Expense ($1,500)

in entry B. The other two employer payroll taxes are for state and federal unemployment. Employees do not pay the unemployment taxes. Only the employer pays them.

Entry C records employee *benefits* paid by the employer. The company pays for health and life insurance on its employees, a common practice. Also, the employer funds pensions (that is, pays cash into a pension plan) for the benefit of employees when they retire. In the exhibit, the employer's pension expense for the month is $500, and the total employer expense for benefits is $1,500. *The total payroll expense of the employer in Exhibit 11-6 is $12,920 (salary expense of $10,000 + payroll tax expense of $1,420 + benefits expense of $1,500).*

A company's payments to people who are not employees—outsiders called independent contractors—are *not* company payroll expenses. Consider two CPAs, Lyon and Franco. Lyon is a corporation's chief financial officer. Franco is the corporation's outside auditor. Lyon is an employee of the corporation, and his compensation is recorded with a debit to Salary Expense. Franco, on the other hand, performs consulting services for many clients, and the corporation debits Consulting Expense when it pays her. *Any payment for services performed by a person outside the company is a debit to an expense account other than payroll.*

⊙ Daily Exercise 11-13

⊙ Daily Exercise 11-14

WORK IT OUT

Record the payroll and payroll taxes for the following information:

Gross salary (subject to all taxes)	$190,000
Employees' federal income tax withheld	35,800
Life insurance withheld from employees..............	2,000
FICA tax rate	8%
State unemployment tax rate................................	5.4%
Federal unemployment tax rate	0.8%

Answer

Payroll Entry:

Salary Expense	190,000	
FICA Tax Payable ($190,000 × 0.08)		15,200
Life Insurance Premium Payable		2,000
Employee Income Tax Payable		35,800
Salary Payable		137,000

Payroll Tax Entry:

Payroll Tax Expense	26,980	
FICA Tax Payable		15,200
State Unemployment Tax Payable ($190,000 × 0.054)		10,260
Federal Unemployment Tax Payable ($190,000 × 0.008)		1,520

THE PAYROLL SYSTEM

Objective 5
Use a payroll system

Good business means paying employees accurately and on time. Companies must handle both employees' and their own payroll taxes, as we have seen. Thus, companies process lots of payroll data. For accurate and timely payrolls, accountants have developed the *payroll system.*

The components of the payroll system are

- A payroll record
- A special payroll bank account
- Payroll checks
- An earnings record for each employee

Payroll Record

Each pay period the company organizes the payroll data in a special journal called the *payroll record* or *payroll journal.* This record lists each employee and the figures the business needs to record payroll amounts. The payroll record, which resembles the cash payments journal, also serves as a check register by providing a place to record each payroll check. ➤➤

A payroll record similar to that for **Blumenthal's** in Exhibit 11-7 is used by companies such as **Marriott Corp.,** the hotel chain. The *Gross Pay* section has columns for straight-time pay, overtime pay, and total gross pay for each employee. The *Deductions* columns vary from company to company, but every employer must deduct federal income tax and FICA tax. (State income tax is left out for convenience.) Additional column headings depend on the optional deductions the business handles. In Exhibit 11-7, the employer deducts employee payroll taxes, union dues, and gifts to **United Way,** and then sends the amounts to the proper parties. The *Net Pay* section lists each employee's net (take-home) pay and the number of the check issued to him or her. The last two columns indicate the *Account Debited* for the employee's gross pay. (The company has both office workers and salespeople.)

The payroll record in Exhibit 11-7 gives the employer the information needed to record salary expense for the pay period. Using the total amounts for columns (d) through (l), the employer records total salary expense as follows:

◄◄ We introduced the cash payments journal in Chapter 6, p. 242.

Dec. 31	Office Salary Expense	4,464.00	
	Sales Salary Expense	9,190.00	
	Employee Income Tax Payable		3,167.76
	FICA Tax Payable		861.94
	Employee Union Dues Payable		85.00
	Employee United Way Payable		155.00
	Salary Payable to Employees		9,384.30

 DAILY EXERCISE 11-15

Payroll Bank Account

After journalizing the payroll, the company books show a credit balance in Salary Payable to Employees for net pay of $9,384.30. (See column (i) in Exhibit 11-7.) How the business pays this liability depends on its payroll system. Many companies

EXHIBIT 11-7 Blumenthal's Payroll Record

Week ended December 31, 2000

		a	b	c	d	e	f	g	b	i	j	k	l
		Gross Pay	Gross Pay				Deductions	Deductions		Net Pay	Net Pay	Account Debited	Account Debited
Employee Name	Hours	Straight-Time	Overtime	Total	Federal Income Tax	FICA Tax	Union Dues	United Way Charities	Total	(c − h) Amount	Check No.	Office Salary Expense	Sales Salary Expense
Chen, W. L.*	40	500.00		500.00	71.05	40.00	5.00	2.50	118.55	381.45	1621	500.00	
Dean, R. C.	46	400.00	90.00	490.00	59.94	39.20		2.00	101.14	388.86	1622		490.00
Ellis, M.	41	560.00	21.00	581.00	86.14	46.48	5.00		137.62	443.38	1623	581.00	
Trimble, E. A.†	40	1,360.00		1,360.00	463.22			15.00	478.22	881.78	1641		1,360.00
Total		12,940.00	714.00	13,654.00	3,167.76	861.94	85.00	155.00	4,269.70	9,384.30		4,464.00	9,190.00

*W. L. Chen earned gross pay of $500. His net pay was $381.45, paid with check number 1621. Chen is an office worker, so his salary is debited to Office Salary Expense.

†The business deducted no FICA tax from E. A. Trimble. She has already earned more than $75,000. Any employee whose earnings exceed this annual maximum pays no additional FICA tax during that year.

Note: For simplicity we ignore the additional tax for Medicare benefits.

pay employees from a special *payroll bank account.* The employer transfers the net pay ($9,384.30 in our illustration) from its regular bank account into the special payroll bank account. Then the company writes paychecks to employees from the payroll account. When the paychecks clear the bank, the payroll account has a zero balance. Writing paychecks from a separate bank account isolates payroll amounts for analysis and control, as we discuss later in the chapter.

Payroll Checks

Most companies pay employees by check or by electronic fund transfer (EFT). A *paycheck* is like any other check except that its attachment details the employee's payroll amounts. These figures come from the payroll record in Exhibit 11-7. Exhibit 11-8 shows payroll check number 1622, issued to R. C. Dean for net pay of $388.86 earned during the week ended December 31, 2000. To enhance your ability to use payroll data, trace all amounts on the check attachment to the payroll record in Exhibit 11-7.

EXHIBIT 11-8 Payroll Check

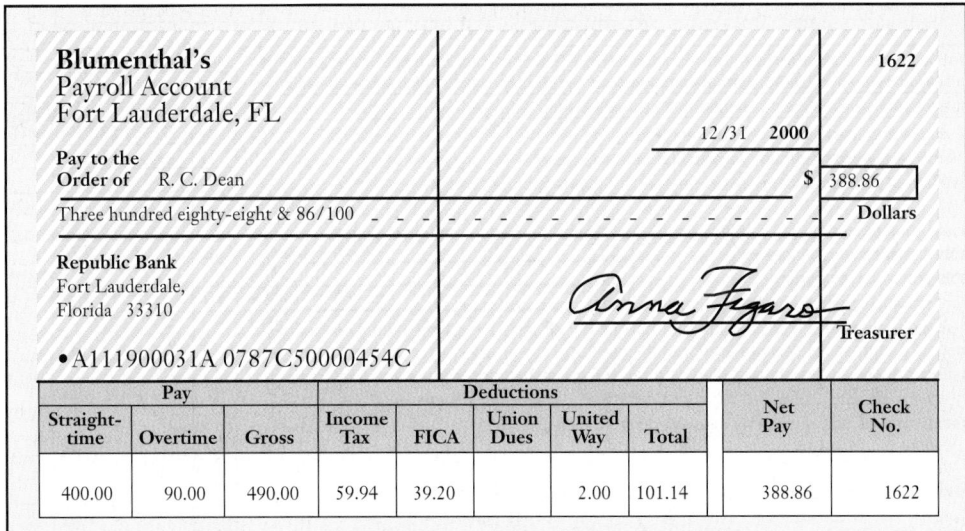

Increasingly, companies are paying employees by electronic funds transfer. The employee can authorize the company to make all deposits directly to his or her bank. With no check to deliver to the employee, the company saves time and money. As evidence of the deposit, most companies, including **American Airlines,** issue a voided check to employees. The employee doesn't have to receive, endorse, and deposit the paycheck.

Earnings Record

The employer must file payroll tax returns with the federal and state governments. Exhibit 11-9 (on page 444) is the Form 941 that Blumenthal's filed with the Internal Revenue Service for the quarter ended December 31, 2000. These forms must be filed no later than one month after the end of a quarter.

Line 13 of the exhibit shows that Blumenthal's payroll taxes for the quarter totaled $35,200. Line 14 indicates that during the quarter Blumenthal's paid the full tax bill, so the balance due on line 15 was zero. (There are heavy penalties for paying these taxes late.)

The employer must also provide the employee with a wage and tax statement, Form W-2, at the end of the year. Therefore, employers maintain an *earnings record* for each employee. Exhibit 11-10 (on page 445) is a five-week excerpt from the earnings record of employee R. C. Dean.

The employee earnings record is not a journal or a ledger, and it is not required by law. It is an accounting tool—like the work sheet—that the employer uses to prepare payroll tax reports to the Internal Revenue Service.

Exhibit 11-11 (on page 445) is the Wage and Tax Statement, Form W-2, for employee R. C. Dean. The employer prepares this statement and gives copies to the employee and to the Internal Revenue Service (IRS). Dean uses the W-2 to prepare

Exhibit 11-9 Payroll Tax Return

Form 941
(Rev. January 2000)
Department of the Treasury
Internal Revenue Service

Employer's Quarterly Federal Tax Return

► See separate instructions for information on completing this return.

Please type or print.

OMB No. 1545-0029

T	
FF	
FD	
FP	
I	
T	

Enter state code for state in which deposits were made ONLY if different from state in address to the right ► `F L` (see page 2 of instructions).

Name (as distinguished from trade name)

Date quarter ended

Trade name, if any
Blumenthal's

Employer identification number

Address (number and street)
Crescent Square Shopping Center
Fort Lauderdale, FL 33310-1234

City, state, and ZIP code

If address is different from prior return, check here ►

IRS Use

1 1 1 1 1 1 1 1 1	2	3 3 3 3 3 3 3	4 4 4	5 5 5
6 7 8 8 8 8 8 8 8		9 9 9 9 9	10 10 10 10 10 10 10 10 10	

If you do not have to file returns in the future, check here ► ☐ and enter date final wages paid ►

If you are a seasonal employer, see **Seasonal employers** on page 1 of the instructions and check here ►

1	Number of employees in the pay period that includes March 12th ►	1	19
2	Total wages and tips, plus other compensation	2	113,654
3	Total income tax withheld from wages, tips, and sick pay	3	18,168
4	Adjustment of withheld income tax for preceding quarters of calendar year	4	—
5	Adjusted total of income tax withheld (line 3 as adjusted by line 4—see instructions) . . .	5	18,168

6	Taxable social security wages	6a	110,774	× 12.4% (.124) =	6b	13,736
	Taxable social security tips	6c		× 12.4% (.124) =	6d	
7	Taxable Medicare wages and tips . . .	7a	113,654	× 2.9% (.029) =	7b	3,296

8	Total social security and Medicare taxes (add lines 6b, 6d, and 7b). Check here if wages are not subject to social security and/or Medicare tax . . . . ► ☐	8	17,032
9	Adjustment of social security and Medicare taxes (see instructions for required explanation) Sick Pay $_____ ± Fractions of Cents $_____ ± Other $_____ =	9	—
10	Adjusted total of social security and Medicare taxes (line 8 as adjusted by line 9—see instructions)	10	17,032
11	**Total taxes** (add lines 5 and 10)	11	35,200
12	Advance earned income credit (EIC) payments made to employees	12	—
13	Net taxes (subtract line 12 from line 11). If $1,000 or more, this must equal line 17, column (d) below (or line D of Schedule B (Form 941))	13	35,200
14	Total deposits for quarter, including overpayment applied from a prior quarter	14	35,200
15	**Balance due** (subtract line 14 from line 13). See instructions	15	–0–
16	**Overpayment.** If line 14 is more than line 13, enter excess here ► $_____ and check if to be: ☐ Applied to next return **OR** ☐ Refunded.		

● **All filers:** If line 13 is less than $1,000, you need not complete line 17 or Schedule B (Form 941).
● **Semiweekly schedule depositors:** Complete Schedule B (Form 941) and check here . . . . ► ☐
● **Monthly schedule depositors:** Complete line 17, columns (a) through (d), and check here . . . . ► ☐

17   Monthly Summary of Federal Tax Liability. Do not complete if you were a semiweekly schedule depositor.

(a) First month liability	(b) Second month liability	(c) Third month liability	(d) Total liability for quarter
35,017	35,336	34,967	35,200

Sign Here

Under penalties of perjury, I declare that I have examined this return, including accompanying schedules and statements, and to the best of my knowledge and belief, it is true, correct, and complete.

Signature ► *Anna Figaro*   Print Your Name and Title ► Anna Figaro, Treasurer   Date ► 1/30/00

For Privacy Act and Paperwork Reduction Act Notice, see back of Payment Voucher.   Cat. No. 17001Z   Form **941** (Rev. 1-2000)

his income tax return. To ensure that Dean is paying income tax on all his income from that job, the IRS matches Dean's income as reported on his tax return with his earnings as reported on the W-2.

Paying the Payroll

Up to this point, we have talked about the recording of payroll expenses. We now turn to the *payment* of these liabilities. Most employers must record at least three cash payments for payrolls:

- net pay to employees
- payroll taxes to the government and other payroll deductions
- employee benefits

EXHIBIT 11-10 Employee Earnings Record for 2000

EMPLOYEE NAME AND ADDRESS:	SOCIAL SECURITY NO.: 344-86-4529
	MARITAL STATUS: MARRIED
DEAN, R. C.	WITHHOLDING EXEMPTIONS: 4
4376 PALM DRIVE	PAY RATE: $400 PER WEEK
FORT LAUDERDALE, FL 33317	JOB TITLE: SALESPERSON

		Gross Pay				Deductions					Net Pay	
Week Ended	Hrs.	Straight-Time	Over-time	Total	To Date	Federal Income Tax	FICA Tax	Union Dues	United Way Charity	Total	Amount	Check No.
Dec. 3	40	400.00		400.00	21,340.00	42.19	32.00		2.00	76.19	323.81	1525
Dec. 10	40	400.00		400.00	21,740.00	42.19	32.00		2.00	76.19	323.81	1548
Dec. 17	44	400.00	60.00	460.00	22,200.00	54.76	36.80		2.00	93.56	366.44	1574
Dec. 24	48	400.00	120.00	520.00	22,720.00	66.75	41.60		2.00	110.35	409.65	1598
Dec. 31	46	400.00	90.00	490.00	23,210.00	59.94	39.20		2.00	101.14	388.86	1622
Total		20,800.00	2,410.00	23,210.00		1,946.72	1,856.80		104.00	3,907.52	19,302.48	

EXHIBIT 11-11
Employee Wage and Tax
Statement, Form W-2

a Control number 22222 Void ☐	For Official Use Only ▶ OMB No. 1545-0008	
b Employer identification number 83-19475	1 Wages, tips, other compensation 23,210.00	2 Federal income tax withheld 1,946.72
c Employer's name, address, and ZIP code Blumenthal's Crescent Square Shopping Center Fort Lauderdale, FL 33310-1234	3 Social security wages 23,210.00	4 Social security tax withheld 1,439.02
	5 Medicare wages and tips 23,210.00	6 Medicare tax withheld 417.78
	7 Social security tips	8 Allocated tips
d Employee's social security number 344-86-4529	9 Advance EIC payment	10 Dependent care benefits
e Employee's name (first, middle initial, last) R. C. Dean	11 Nonqualified plans	12 Benefits included in box 1
4376 Palm Drive Fort Lauderdale, FL 33317	13 See instrs. for box 13	14 Other
	15 Statutory employee ☐ Deceased ☐ Pension plan ☐ Legal rep. ☐ Deferred compensation ☐	
f Employee's address and ZIP code		

16 State Employer's state I.D. no.	17 State wages, tips, etc.	18 State income tax	19 Locality name	20 Local wages, tips, etc.	21 Local income tax

Form **W-2** Wage and Tax Statement **2000**

Copy A For Social Security Administration—Send this entire page with Form W-3 to the Social Security Administration; photocopies are **not** acceptable.

Cat. No. 10134D

Department of the Treasury—Internal Revenue Service
For Privacy Act and Paperwork Reduction Act Notice, see separate instructions.

NET PAY TO EMPLOYEES   When the company pays employees, it debits Salary Payable to Employees and credits Cash. Using the data in Exhibit 11-7, the company would make the following entry to record the cash payment (column (i)) for the December 31 weekly payroll:

Dec. 31	Salary Payable to Employees	9,384.30	
	Cash		9,384.30

PAYROLL TAXES TO THE GOVERNMENT AND OTHER PAYROLL DEDUCTIONS   The employer must send the government two sets of payroll taxes: those withheld from employees' pay and those paid by the employer. In Exhibit 11-7, columns (d) through (g), the business would record a series of cash payment entries that can be summarized as follows (the unemployment tax amounts are assumed):

	Dec. 31	Employee Income Tax Payable	3,167.76	
		FICA Tax Payable ($861.94 × 2)	1,723.88	
		Employee Union Dues Payable........................	85.00	
		Employee United Way Payable........................	155.00	
		State Unemployment Tax Payable	104.62	
		Federal Unemployment Tax Payable	15.50	
		Cash		5,251.76

DAILY EXERCISE 11-16

BENEFITS   The employer might pay for employees' insurance coverage and their pension plan. If the total cash payment for these benefits is $1,927.14, the entry is

	Dec. 31	Employee Benefits Payable	1,927.14	
		Cash..		1,927.14

Many companies provide *postretirement benefits* such as medical insurance for retired workers. The companies accrue this liability during the employees' working years and then pay it off during their retirement.

Internal Control over Payroll

The internal controls over cash payments discussed in Chapter 7 apply to payroll. The large number of transactions and the complex arrangements increase the risk of a control failure. There are two main types of special controls for payroll: controls for efficiency and controls for safeguarding payroll disbursements.

CONTROLS FOR EFFICIENCY   Reconciling the bank account can be time-consuming because of the large number of paychecks. For example, a March 30 paycheck would probably clear the bank before a March 31 bank statement. This check and others would be outstanding. A large number of outstanding checks for the bank reconciliation increases accounting expense. To limit the number of outstanding paychecks, many companies use two payroll bank accounts. They pay the payroll from one bank account one month and from the other payroll account the next month. This way they can reconcile each account every other month. In this system, a March 30 paycheck has until April 30 to clear the bank before the account is reconciled. Outstanding checks are almost eliminated, the bank reconciliation is streamlined, and accounting expense decreases.

Payroll transactions are ideal for computer processing. Employee payroll data are stored in a file. Each pay period, keyboarders enter the number of hours worked by each employee. The computer makes all calculations, prints the payroll record and the paychecks, and updates employee earnings records. The program also computes payroll taxes and prepares the quarterly tax reports.

CONTROLS FOR SAFEGUARDING PAYROLL DISBURSEMENTS   Owners and managers of small businesses can monitor their payrolls by personal contact with employees. Large corporations cannot. These businesses must establish controls to ensure that paychecks go only to legitimate employees and for the correct amounts. A particular danger is that a paycheck may be written to a fictitious employee and cashed by a dishonest employee. To guard against this and other crimes, large businesses adopt strict internal control policies.

The duties of hiring and firing employees should be separated from the duties of payroll accounting and passing out paychecks. Requiring a photo ID also helps internal control. Issuing paychecks only to employees with badges ensures that only actual employees receive pay.

A formal timekeeping system helps ensure that employees actually worked the number of hours claimed. Having employees punch time cards at the start and end of the workday proves their attendance.

DAILY EXERCISE 11-17

As we saw in Chapter 7, the key to good internal control is separation of duties. The responsibilities of the personnel department, the payroll department, the accounting department, time-card management, and paycheck distribution should be separate.

THINK IT OVER

Centurion Homes of Omaha, Nebraska, builds houses with four construction crews. The foremen hire—and fire—workers and keep their hourly records. Each Friday morning, the foremen telephone their workers' hours to the home office, where accountants prepare the weekly paychecks. Around noon, the foremen pick up the paychecks. They return to the construction site and pay the workers at day's end. What is the internal control weakness in this situation? Propose a way to improve the internal controls.

Answer: Construction workers often have limited contact with the home office. The foremen control most of the payroll information, so they can forge the payroll records of fictitious employees and pocket their pay. To improve internal control, Centurion could hire and fire all workers through the home office. This practice would establish the identity of all workers listed in the payroll records. Another way to improve the internal controls would be to have a home-office employee distribute paychecks on a surprise basis. Any unclaimed checks would arouse suspicion. This system would probably prevent foremen from cheating the company.

REPORTING PAYROLL EXPENSE AND LIABILITIES

Objective 6
Report current liabilities on the balance sheet

On the balance sheet, **IBM** and other companies report the amount of *payroll liability* owed to all parties—employees, governments, unions, and so on. Payroll liability is *not* the payroll expense for the year. The liability at year end is the amount of the expense that is still unpaid. Payroll expense appears on the income statement payroll liability on the balance sheet. On a recent balance sheet, IBM reported compensation and benefits payable of $3,840 million as a current liability as shown in Exhibit 11-12. The exhibit also presents the other current liabilities we have discussed.

Current Liabilities	Millions
Taxes payable	$ 4,792
Short-term debt	14,230
Accounts payable	6,400
Compensation and benefits payable	3,840
Unearned revenue	4,529
Other accrued expenses and liabilities	5,787
Total current liabilities	**$39,578**

EXHIBIT 11-12
IBM Balance Sheet (partial, adapted) December 31, 1999

DAILY EXERCISE 11-18

DAILY EXERCISE 11-19

The following Decision Guidelines feature summarizes some of the more important payroll decisions that a business must consider.

DECISION GUIDELINES

Accounting for Payroll

DECISION	GUIDELINES
What are the key elements of a payroll accounting system?	• Employee's Withholding Allowance Certificate, Form W-4 • Payroll register • Payroll bank account and payroll checks • Employer's quarterly tax returns, such as Form 941 • Employee earnings record • Employee wage and tax statement, Form W-2
What are the key terms in the payroll area?	Gross pay (Total amount earned by the employee) – *Payroll deductions* **a.** Withheld income tax **b.** FICA (Social Security) tax—equal amount also payable by employer **c.** Optional deductions (insurance, savings, charitable contributions, union dues) = *Net (take-home) pay*
What is the employer's total payroll expense?	Gross pay + *Employer's payroll taxes* **a.** FICA (Social Security) tax—equal amount also payable by employee **b.** State and federal unemployment taxes + *Benefits for employees* **a.** Insurance (health, life, and disability) **b.** Pension (and other retirement) benefits **c.** Club memberships and other = *Employer's total payroll costs*
Where to report payroll costs?	• Payroll expenses on the income statement • Payroll liabilities on the balance sheet

REVIEW CURRENT LIABILITIES

www.prenhall.com/horngren
End-of-Chapter Assessment

SUMMARY PROBLEM

Beth Denius, Limited, a clothing store, employs one salesperson, Alan Kingsley. His straight-time salary is $360 per week. He earns time and a half for hours worked in excess of 40 per week. The owner, Beth Denius, withholds income tax (11.0%) and FICA tax (8.0%) from Kingsley's pay. She pays the following employer payroll taxes: FICA (8.0%) and state and federal unemployment (5.4% and 0.8%, respectively). In addition, Denius contributes to a pension plan an amount equal to 10% of Kingsley's gross pay.

During the week ended December 26, 20X4, Kingsley worked 48 hours. Prior to this week, Kingsley had earned $5,470.

Required

1. Compute Kingsley's gross pay and net pay for the week.
2. Record the following payroll entries that Denius would make:
   a. Expense for Kingsley's salary, including overtime pay
   b. Employer payroll taxes
   c. Expense for employee benefits
   d. Payment of cash to Kingsley
   e. Payment of all payroll taxes
   f. Payment for employee benefits
3. How much total payroll expense did Denius incur for the week? How much cash did the business spend on its payroll?

Solutions

Requirement 1

Gross pay:	Straight-time pay for 40 hours		$360.00
	Overtime pay:		
	Rate per hour ($360/40 × 1.5)	$13.50	
	Hours (48 − 40)	8	108.00
	Total gross pay		$468.00
Net pay:	Gross pay		$468.00
	Less: Withheld income tax ($468 × 0.11)	$51.48	
	Withheld FICA tax ($468 × 0.08)	37.44	88.92
	Net pay...		$379.08

Requirement 2

a.	Sales Salary Expense	468.00	
	Employee Income Tax Payable		51.48
	FICA Tax Payable		37.44
	Salary Payable to Employee		379.08
b.	Payroll Tax Expense	66.45	
	FICA Tax Payable ($468 × 0.08)		37.44
	State Unemployment Tax Payable ($468 × 0.054)		25.27
	Federal Unemployment Tax Payable (468 × 0.008)		3.74
c.	Pension Expense ($468 × 0.10)	46.80	
	Employee Benefits Payable		46.80
d.	Salary Payable to Employee	379.08	
	Cash		379.08
e.	Employee Income Tax Payable...	51.48	
	FICA Tax Payable ($37.44 × 2)	74.88	
	State Unemployment Tax Payable	25.27	
	Federal Unemployment Tax Payable.....................................	3.74	
	Cash		155.37
f.	Employee Benefits Payable	46.80	
	Cash		46.80

Requirement 3

- Denius incurred *total payroll expense* of $581.25 (gross salary of $468.00 + payroll taxes of $66.45 + benefits of $46.80). See entries (a) through (c).
- Denius *paid cash* of $581.25 on payroll (Kingsley's net pay of $379.08 + payroll taxes of $155.37 + benefits of $46.80). See entries (d) through (f).

L ESSONS L EARNED

1. *Account for current liabilities of known amount.* Trade accounts payable, short-term notes payable, interest payable, sales tax payable, payrolls, and unearned revenues are current liabilities of known amount.

2. *Account for current liabilities that must be estimated.* Current liabilities that must be estimated include warranties payable, vacation pay, and corporations' income tax payable. *Contingent liabilities* are potential liabilities that may arise in the future.

3. *Compute payroll amounts.* *Payroll* accounting handles the expenses and liabilities arising from compensating employees. Employers must withhold income and FICA taxes from employees' pay and send these tax amounts to the government. In addition, many employers allow employees to pay for insurance and union dues and to make gifts to charities through payroll deductions. An employee's net pay is the gross pay less all payroll taxes and optional deductions.

4. *Record basic payroll transactions.* An *employer's* payroll expenses include FICA and unemployment taxes, which are separate from the payroll taxes borne by the employees. Also, most employers provide employees with benefits such as insurance coverage and pensions.

5. *Use a payroll system.* A *payroll system* consists of a payroll record, a payroll bank account, payroll checks, and an earnings record for each employee. Good *internal controls* over payrolls help the business to achieve efficiency and to safeguard the company's cash.

6. *Report current liabilities on the balance sheet.* The company reports on the balance sheet all current liabilities that it owes: current liabilities of known amount, including payroll liabilities, and current liabilities that must be estimated.

ACCOUNTING VOCABULARY

accrued expense (p. 430)	employee compensation (p. 430)	Social Security tax (p. 438)
accrued liability (p. 430)	FICA tax (p. 438)	unemployment compensation tax
current portion of long-term debt	gross pay (p. 437)	(p. 439)
(p. 429)	net pay (p. 437)	withheld income tax (p. 437)
current maturity (p. 429)	payroll (p. 430)	
discounting a note payable	short presentation (p. 434)	
(p. 427)	short-term note payable (p. 426)	

QUESTIONS

1. What distinguishes a current liability from a long-term liability? What distinguishes a contingent liability from an actual liability?
2. A company purchases a machine by signing a $21,000, one-year, 10% note payable on July 31. Interest is to be paid at maturity. What two current liabilities related to this purchase does the company report on its December 31 balance sheet? What is the amount of each current liability?
3. Explain why sales tax that is paid by consumers is a liability of the store that sold the merchandise.
4. What is meant by the term *current portion of long-term debt*, and how is this item reported in the financial statements?
5. At the beginning of the school term, what type of account is the tuition that your college or university collects from students? What type of account is the tuition at the end of the school term?
6. Patton Company warrants its products against defects for three years from date of sale. During the current year, the company made sales of $300,000. Store management estimated that warranty costs on those sales would total 6% of sales over the three-year warranty period. Ultimately, the company paid $22,000 cash on warranties. What was the company's warranty expense for the year? What accounting principle governs this answer?

7. Why is payroll expense more important to a service business such as a CPA firm than it is to a merchandising company such as **Target?**
8. Two persons are studying Allen Company's manufacturing process. One person is Allen's factory supervisor, and the other is an outside consultant who is an expert in the industry. Which person's salary is the payroll expense of Allen Company? Identify the expense account that Allen would debit to record the pay of each person.
9. What are two elements of an employer's payroll expense in addition to salaries, wages, commissions, and overtime pay?
10. What are FICA taxes? Who pays them? What are the funds used for?
11. Identify two required deductions and four optional deductions from employee paychecks.
12. Who pays state and federal unemployment taxes? What are these funds used for?
13. How much Social Security tax is withheld from the pay of an employee who earns $70,000 during the current year? How much Social Security tax is withheld if the employee earns $77,000?
14. Identify three internal controls designed to safeguard payroll cash.

ASSESS YOUR PROGRESS

DAILY EXERCISES

Accounts payable and notes payable (Obj. 1)

DE11-1 Describe the similarities and the differences between an account payable and a short-term note payable. If necessary, review notes receivable in Chapter 8.

Accounting for a note payable (Obj. 1)

DE11-2 Return to the $8,000 purchase of inventory on a short-term note payable that begins on page 426. Assume that the purchase of inventory occurred on June 30, 20X1, instead of September 30, 20X1. Journalize the company's (a) purchase of inventory, (b) accrual of interest expense on December 31, 20X1, and (c) payment of the note plus interest on June 30, 20X2.

Reporting a short-term note payable and the related interest in the financial statements (Obj. 1)

DE11-3 This exercise should be done in conjunction with Daily Exercise 11-2.

1. Refer to the data in Daily Exercise 11-2. Show what the company would report for the note payable on its balance sheet at December 31, 20X1, and on its income statement for the year ended on that date.
2. What one item will the financial statements for the year ended December 31, 20X2, report? Identify the financial statement, the item, and its amount.

Accounting for a discounted note payable (Obj. 1)

DE11-4 Accounting for a discounted note payable is illustrated for a $100,000 note at the top of page 427.

1. Why did **Procter & Gamble (P&G)** sign the note payable? What did P&G receive?
2. Suppose P&G signed the note payable on November 16, 20X1, instead of November 25, 20X1. Make P&G's adjusting entry to accrue interest expense at December 31, 20X1.
3. Show how P&G would report the note payable on its balance sheet at December 31, 20X1.
4. Journalize P&G's interest expense and payment of the note payable at maturity. Give the date.

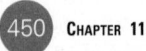

DE11-5 The chapter opening story describes the airlines' frequent-flier programs. Suppose passengers fly 1,000,000 miles on **American Airlines** and the AAdvantage® frequent-flier program costs American $.0015 per mile. During the next six months, AAdvantage® customers use 200,000 of the miles for free trips on American Airlines.

Accounting for unearned revenue (Obj. 1)

1. Using American Airlines' actual account titles (see Exhibit 11-1), journalize American's (a) accrual of Promotion Expense and Air Traffic Liability and (b) the provision of free transportation for the AAdvantage® customers (credit Cash). Explanations are not required.
2. Post to the Air Traffic Liability T-account. How much does American Airlines owe the AAdvantage® customers after the preceding transactions?

DE11-6 **Ford,** the automaker, guarantees its automobiles for three years or 36,000 miles, whichever comes first. Suppose Ford's experience indicates that the company can expect warranty costs during the three-year period to add up to 5% of sales.

Accounting for warranty expense and estimated warranty payable (Obj. 2)

Assume that Five Points Ford in Cincinnati made sales of Ford Escorts totaling $600,000 during 20X7, its first year of operations. The company received cash for 30% of the sales and notes receivable for the remainder. Payments to satisfy customer warranty claims totaled $22,000 during 20X7.

1. Record the sales, warranty expense, and warranty payments for Five Points Ford.
2. Post to the Estimated Warranty Payable T-account. At the end of 20X7, how much in estimated warranty payable does Five Points Ford owe its customers? Why must the warranty payable amount be estimated?

DE11-7 Refer to the data given in Daily Exercise 11-6.

Applying GAAP; reporting warranties in the financial statements (Obj. 2)

What amount of warranty expense will Five Points Ford report during 20X7? Which accounting principle addresses this situation? Does the warranty expense for the year equal the year's cash payments for warranties? Explain how the accounting principle works for measuring warranty expense.

DE11-8 **Harley-Davidson, Inc.,** the motorcycle manufacturer, included the following note (adapted) in its annual report:

Interpreting a company's contingent liabilities (Obj. 2)

NOTES TO CONSOLIDATED FINANCIAL STATEMENTS

7 (In Part): Commitments and Contingencies

The Company self-insures its product liability losses in the United States up to $3 million (catastrophic coverage is maintained for individual claims in excess of $3 million up to $25 million). Outside the United States, the Company is insured for product liability up to $25 million per individual claim and in the aggregate.

---

1. Why are these *contingent* (versus real) liabilities?
2. In the United States, how can the contingent liability become a real liability for Harley-Davidson? What are the limits to the company's product liabilities in the United States? Explain how these limits work.
3. How can a contingency outside the United States become a real liability for the company? How does Harley-Davidson's potential liability differ for claims outside the United States?

DE11-9 Consider the operations of a **Wendy's** restaurant, **Toyota Motor Corporation,** and a large accounting firm. Rank these businesses in terms of the percentage of labor cost to the company's total expenses—from most important to least important. Give the reason for your ranking.

Assessing the importance of payroll expenses (Obj. 3)

Daily Exercise 11-10 begins a sequence of exercises that ends with Daily Exercise 11-12.
DE11-10 Examine the payroll situation of Lucy Childres on page 437.

Computing an employee's total pay (Obj. 3)

1. Compute Childres's total pay for working 50 hours during the first week of February.
2. Childres is single, and her income tax withholding is 9% of total pay. Her only payroll deductions are payroll taxes. Compute Childres's net pay for the week. (Use an 8% FICA tax rate.)

DE11-11 Return to the Lucy Childres payroll situation in Daily Exercise 11-10. Childres's employer, Bobby Jones Golf Company, pays all the standard payroll taxes plus benefits for employee pensions (6% of total pay), health insurance ($60 per employee per month), and disability insurance ($8 per employee per month).

Computing total payroll expense of an employer (Obj. 3)

Compute Bobby Jones's total expense of employing Lucy Childres for the 50 hours that she worked during the first week of February. Carry amounts to the nearest cent.

DE11-12 After solving Daily Exercises 11-10 and 11-11, journalize for Bobby Jones Golf Company the following expenses related to the employment of Lucy Childres:

Making payroll entries (Obj. 4)

a. Salary expense   b. Employer payroll taxes   c. Benefits

Use Exhibit 11-6 (p. 440) to format your journal entries. Carry all amounts to the nearest cent.

Computing payroll amounts late
in the year
(Obj. 3)

DE11-13 Suppose you have worked for an accounting firm all year and you earn a monthly salary of $8,000. Your withheld income taxes consume 15% of your gross pay. In addition to payroll taxes, which are required, you elect to contribute 5% monthly to your pension plan. Your employer also deducts $200 monthly for your co-pay of the health insurance premium.

Compute your net pay for October. Use an 8% FICA tax rate on the first $75,000 of income.

DE11-14 Exhibit 11-5, page 439, shows the breakdown of an employer's total payroll cost of $1,180 for one employee. Journalize the employer's (a) salary expense (use a single Payroll Tax Payable account), (b) payroll taxes (use a single Payroll Tax Payable account), and (c) cost of health insurance. Follow the pattern of the entries in Exhibit 11-6, page 440.

DE11-15 Refer to the payroll record in Exhibit 11-7, page 442.

1. How much cash did the employees take home for their work this week?
2. How much was the company's total salary expense for the week? What accounts were debited? How much was debited to each account?
3. How much did *employees* pay this week for
   a. Withheld federal income tax?
   b. Withheld FICA tax?
4. How much expense did the *employer* have this week for
   a. Employee federal income tax?
   b. FICA tax?
5. Which employees earned less than $75,000, and which employees earned more than $75,000 this year? How can you tell?

Using a payroll system to compute total payroll expense
(Obj. 5)

DE11-16 Study the Employee Earnings Record for R. C. Dean in Exhibit 11-10, page 445. In addition to the amounts shown in the exhibit, the employer also paid all payroll taxes plus (a) an amount equal to 7% of gross pay into Dean's pension retirement account, and (b) health insurance for Dean at a cost of $140 per month.

Compute the employer's total payroll expense for employee R. C. Dean during 2000. Carry all amounts to the nearest cent.

DE11-17 ← *Link Back to Chapter 7 (Internal Controls)*

1. What are some of the important elements of good internal control to safeguard payroll disbursements?
2. Explain how the use of two payroll bank accounts (one account the first month, the other account the next month) makes accounting for the payroll of a large company more efficient. Identify another control for efficiency in the payroll area.

DE11-18 Study the payroll record of **Blumenthal's** in Exhibit 11-7, page 442. Assume Blumenthal's will pay this payroll on January 2, 2001. In addition to the payroll liabilities shown in the exhibit, Blumenthal's has the following liabilities at December 31, 2000:

Accounts payable...................	$44,140	Current portion of	
Employer FICA tax payable....	862	long-term debt	$20,000
Long-term debt.......................	80,000	Interest payable	1,116
Unearned revenue.................	4,430	Contingent liabilities..............	—

Prepare the current liabilities section of Blumenthal's balance sheet at December 31, 2000. List current liabilities in descending order starting with the largest first. Also list each of the payroll liabilities from Exhibit 11-7, rounded to the nearest dollar. Show the total of current liabilities.

Interpreting the current liabilities
of a company
(Obj. 6)

DE11-19 Refer to **IBM Corporation's** current liabilities in Exhibit 11-12, page 447.

1. Explain in your own words each of the company's current liabilities.
2. When will IBM pay these liabilities? When is the latest date that IBM will pay the liabilities? How can you tell?

E X E R C I S E S

E11-1 Make general journal entries to record the following transactions of Club Lanai Vacation Co. for a two-month period. Explanations are not required.

March 31   Recorded cash sales of $200,000 for the month, plus sales tax of 5% collected on behalf of the state of Arizona. Recorded sales tax in a separate account.

April   6   Sent March sales tax to the state.

Required

Journalize these transactions a second time. Record the sales tax initially in the Sales Revenue account.

E11-2 **Pier 1 Imports, Inc.,** reported the following current liabilities (adapted, all amounts in thousands):

	February 28,	
	20X2	**20X1**
Accrued payroll liabilities..............	$27,194	$25,068
Gift certificates outstanding	11,276	8,242

Required

1. The purpose of this requirement is to show how Pier 1's ending balance of accrued payroll liabilities arose from the company's transactions during the year ended February 28, 20X2. Create a T-account for accrued Payroll Liabilities. Insert the balance at February 28, 20X1 as the beginning balance. Assume that during the year ended February 28, 20X2, Pier 1 accrued payroll expense of $265,000 and paid $262,874 of this total. Post both amounts directly into the Accrued Payroll Liabilities T-account and compute its ending balance. Compare your result to Pier 1's actual ending balance. The two amounts should be the same.
2. Explain the nature of Pier 1's Gift certificates outstanding. What is another name for this account?

E11-3 Assume **The Dallas Morning News** publishing company completed the following transactions during 20X1:

Nov. 1 Sold a six-month subscription, collecting cash of $120, plus sales tax of 5%.
Dec. 15 Remitted (paid) the sales tax to the state of Texas.
     31 Made the necessary adjustment at year end to record the amount of subscription revenue earned during the year.

Required

Journalize these transactions (explanations are not required). Then report the liability on the company's balance sheet at December 31, 20X1.

E11-4 The accounting records of Blaze Electronics included the following balances at the end of the period:

ESTIMATES WARRANTY PAYABLE	SALES REVENUE	WARRANTY EXPENSE
Beg. bal. 3,100	161,000	

In the past, Blaze's warranty expense has been 7% of sales. During the current period, the business paid $10,400 to satisfy the warranty claims of customers.

Required

1. Journalize Blaze's warranty expense for the period and the company's cash payments during the period to satisfy warranty claims. Explanations are not required.
2. What ending balance of Estimated Warranty Payable will Blaze report on its balance sheet?

E11-5 Record the following note payable transactions of Carnegie Publishing, Inc., in the company's general journal. Explanations are not required.

20X2
Apr. 1 Purchased equipment costing $15,000 by issuing a one-year, 8% note payable.
Dec. 31 Accrued interest on the note payable.

20X3
Apr. 1 Paid the note payable at maturity.

E11-6 On September 1, 20X4, Tic-Toc Watch Repair discounted a six-month, $12,000 note payable to the bank at 8%.

Required

1. Prepare general journal entries to record (a) issuance of the note, (b) accrual of interest at December 31, and (c) payment of the note at maturity in 20X5. Explanations are not required.
2. Show how Tic-Toc would report the note on the December 31, 20X4, balance sheet.

E11-7 Vanguard Security Systems is a defendant in lawsuits brought against the marketing and distribution of its products. Damages of $9.1 million are claimed against Vanguard, but the company denies the charges and is vigorously defending itself. In a recent press conference, the president of the company said management does not believe that any actual liabilities resulting from the lawsuits will significantly affect the company's financial position.

Required

Write Note X to describe the contingency.

Reporting current liabilities (Obj. 6)

E11-8   ◄◄ *Link Back to Chapter 4 (Current Ratio).* The owner of Ciliotta Pharmacy examines the company accounting records at December 29, immediately before the end of the year:

Total current assets...................	$ 490,000
Noncurrent assets.....................	730,000
	$1,220,000
Total current liabilities..............	$ 260,000
Noncurrent liabilities................	300,000
Owner's equity	660,000
	$1,220,000

Ciliotta's borrowing agreements with creditors require the company to keep a current ratio of 2.0 or better. How much in current liabilities should Ciliotta pay off within the next two days in order to comply with its borrowing agreements?

Computing net pay (Obj. 3)

E11-9 Ken Shermac is manager of the men's department of Parisian Department Store in Birmingham. He earns a base monthly salary of $750 plus a 10% commission on his personal sales. Through payroll deductions, Shermac donates $25 per month to a charitable organization, and he authorizes Parisian to deduct $22.50 monthly for his family's health insurance. Tax rates on Shermac's earnings are 10% for income tax and 8% of the first $75,000 for FICA. During the first 11 months of the year, he earned $72,140.

Required

Compute Shermac's gross pay and net pay for December, assuming his sales for the month are $80,000.

Computing and recording gross pay and net pay (Obj. 3, 4)

E11-10 Ruby Degrate works for a Steak 'n Shake diner for straight-time earnings of $6 per hour, with time-and-a-half compensation for hours in excess of 40 per week. Degrate's payroll deductions include withheld income tax of 7% of total earnings, FICA tax of 8% of total earnings, and a weekly deduction of $5 for a charitable contribution to United Fund.

Required

Assuming she worked 50 hours during the week, (a) compute her gross pay and net pay for the week, and (b) make a general journal entry to record the store's wage expense for Degrate's work, including her payroll deductions. Explanations are not required. Round all amounts to the nearest cent.

Recording a payroll (Obj. 3, 4)

E11-11 Clarkson Eyecare incurred salary expense of $92,000 for December. The store's payroll expense includes employer FICA tax of 8% in addition to state unemployment tax of 5.4% and federal unemployment tax of 0.8%. Of the total salaries, $88,400 is subject to FICA tax, and $9,100 is subject to unemployment tax. Also, the store provides the following benefits for employees: health insurance (cost to the store, $2,062.15), life insurance (cost to the store, $351.07), and pension benefits (cost to the store, 8% of salary expense).

Required

Record Clarkson's payroll taxes and its expenses for employee benefits. Explanations are not required.

Reporting payroll expense and liabilities (Obj. 6)

E11-12 Norwest Bank has annual salary expense of $900,000. In addition, the bank incurs payroll tax expense equal to 9% of the total payroll. At December 31, the end of the bank's accounting year, Norwest owes salaries of $4,000 and FICA and other payroll tax of $1,000. The bank will pay these amounts early next year.

Required

Show what Norwest Bank will report for these facts on its income statement and year-end balance sheet.

Reporting current and long-term liabilities (Obj. 6)

E11-13 Suppose Unity Medical Group borrowed $5,000,000 on January 2, 20X1, by issuing 9% long-term debt that must be paid in five equal annual installments plus interest each January 2.

Required

Insert the appropriate amounts to show how Unity Medical Group would report its long-term debt.

	December 31,				
	20X1	20X2	20X3	20X4	20X5
Current liabilities:					
Current portion of long-term debt	$____	$____	$____	$____	$____
Interest payable	____	____	____	____	____
Long-term liabilities:					
Long-term debt......................................	____	____	____	____	____

E11-14 Assume that **Wilson Sporting Goods** completed these selected transactions during December 20X1:

Reporting current and long-term liabilities
(Obj. 6)

a. Sales of $1,000,000 are subject to estimated warranty cost of 3.4%.
b. On December 1, Wilson signed a $200,000 note payable that requires annual payments of $20,000 plus 9% interest on the unpaid balance each December 1.
c. Champs, a chain of sporting goods stores, ordered $9,000 of tennis and golf equipment. With its order, Champs sent a check for $9,000 in advance. Wilson will ship the goods on January 3, 20X2.
d. The December payroll of $195,000 is subject to employee withheld income tax of 9%, FICA tax of 8% (employee and employer), state unemployment tax of 5.4%, and federal unemployment tax of 0.8%. On December 31, Wilson pays employees but accrues all tax amounts.

Required

Classify each liability as current or long-term, and report the amount that would appear for each item on Wilson's balance sheet at December 31, 20X1. Show total current liabilities.

Challenge Exercises

E11-15 ← *Link Back to Chapter 4 (Current Ratio).* The balance sheets of **PepsiCo, Inc.,** for two years reported these figures:

Analyzing current liabilities
(Obj. 1, 6)

	Billions	
	20X2	20X1
Total current assets...................	$ 4.6	$ 4.1
Noncurrent assets......................	14.2	13.0
	$18.8	$17.1
Total current liabilities	$ 3.7	$ 4.8
Noncurrent liabilities	9.5	7.4
Stockholders' equity	5.6	4.9
	$18.8	$17.1

Assume that during 20X2, PepsiCo reclassified $2.1 billion of current liabilities as long-term.

Required

1. Compute PepsiCo's current ratio as reported at the end of each year. Describe the trend you observe.
2. Assume that PepsiCo had not reclassified $2.1 billion of current liabilities as long-term during 20X2. Recompute the current ratio at the end of 20X2. Why do you think PepsiCo reclassified the liabilities as long-term?

E11-16 **PepsiCo, Inc.,** reported short-term debt payable and salary payable (adapted, in millions), as follows:

Analyzing current liabilities
(Obj. 1, 6)

	December 31,	
	20X2	20X1
Current liabilities (partial):		
Short-term debt payable..............	$707	$228
Salary payable............................	327	334

Assume that during 20X2, PepsiCo borrowed $1,106 million on short-term debt. Also assume that PepsiCo paid $3,200 million for salaries during 20X2.

Required

1. Compute PepsiCo's payment of short-term debt during 20X2.
2. Compute PepsiCo's salary expense during 20X2.

(Group A) PROBLEMS

Journalizing liability-related transactions
(Obj. 1, 2)

P11-1A The following transactions of Leland Communications occurred during 20X4 and 20X5:

20X4

Jan. 9   Purchased equipment at a cost of $20,000, signing a six-month, 8% note payable for that amount.

     29   Recorded the week's sales of $40,200, three-fourths on credit, and one-fourth for cash. Sales amounts are subject to an additional 6% state sales tax.

Feb. 5   Sent the last week's sales tax to the state.

     28   Borrowed $200,000 on a four-year, 9% note payable that calls for annual installment payments of $50,000 principal plus interest.

July 9   Paid the six-month, 8% note at maturity.

Oct. 22   Discounted a $10,000, 90-day, 8% note payable to the bank, receiving cash for the net amount after interest was deducted from the note's maturity value.

Nov. 30   Purchased inventory for $3,100, signing a six-month, 10% note payable.

Dec. 31   Accrued warranty expense, which is estimated at 3% of sales of $650,000.

     31   Accrued interest on all outstanding notes payable. Made a separate interest accrual entry for each note payable.

20X5

Jan. 20   Paid off the 8% discounted note payable. Made a separate entry for the interest.

Feb. 28   Paid the first installment and interest for one year on the long-term note payable.

May 31   Paid off the 10% note plus interest on maturity.

Required

Record the transactions in the company's general journal. Explanations are not required.

Identifying contingent liabilities
(Obj. 2)

P11-2A Rountree Acura is one of the largest **Acura** dealers in the Midwest. The dealership sells new and used cars and operates a body shop and a service department. Mitch McGee, the general manager, is considering changing insurance companies because of a disagreement with Hank Callendar, agent for the **Travelers Insurance Company**. Travelers is doubling Rountree's liability insurance cost for the next year. In discussing insurance coverage with you, a trusted business associate, McGee brings up the subject of contingent liabilities.

Required

Write a memorandum to inform Rountree Acura of specific contingent liabilities arising from the business. In your discussion, define a contingent liability.

Computing and recording payroll amounts
(Obj. 3, 4)

P11-3A The partial monthly records of Allstar Cycle Co. show the following figures:

Employee Earnings	
(a) Straight-time earnings	$16,431
(b) Overtime pay	?
(c) Total employee earnings	?

Deductions and Net Pay	
(d) Withheld income tax	$ 2,403
(e) FICA tax	?
(f) Charitable contributions	340
(g) Medical insurance	668
(h) Total deductions	5,409
(i) Net pay	18,540

Accounts Debited	
(j) Salary Expense	$?
(k) Wage Expense	8,573
(l) Sales Commission Expense	2,077

Required

1. Determine the missing amounts on lines (b), (c), (e), and (j).
2. Prepare the general journal entry to record Allstar's payroll for the month. Credit Payrolls Payable for net pay. No explanation is required.

P11-4A Virginia Nadair is a vice president of Palm City Bank's leasing operations in Pensacola, Florida. During 20X2, she worked for the company all year at a $5,625 monthly salary. She also earned a year-end bonus equal to 12% of her salary.

Computing and recording payroll amounts
(Obj. 3, 4)

Nadair's federal income tax withheld during 20X2 was $737 per month. Also, there was a one-time federal withholding tax of $1,007 on her bonus check. State income tax withheld came to $43 per month, and there was a one-time state withholding tax of $27 on the bonus. The FICA tax withheld was 8.0% of the first $75,000 in annual earnings. Nadair authorized the following payroll deductions: United Fund contribution of 1% of total earnings and life insurance of $19 per month.

Palm City Bank incurred payroll tax expense on Nadair for FICA tax of 8% of the first $75,000 in annual earnings. The bank also paid state unemployment tax of 5.4% and federal unemployment tax of 0.8% on the first $7,000 in annual earnings. In addition, the bank provides Nadair with health insurance at a cost of $35 per month and pension benefits. During 20X2, Palm City Bank paid $7,178 into Nadair's pension program.

Required

1. Compute Nadair's gross pay, payroll deductions, and net pay for the full year 20X2. Round all amounts to the nearest dollar.
2. Compute Palm City Bank's total 20X2 payroll cost for Nadair.
3. Prepare Palm City Bank's summary general journal entries to record its expense for the following:
   a. Nadair's total earnings for the year, her payroll deductions, and her net pay. Debit Salary Expense and Executive Bonus Compensation as appropriate. Credit liability accounts for the payroll deductions and Cash for net pay.
   b. Employer payroll taxes on Nadair. Credit liability accounts.
   c. Benefits provided to Nadair. Credit a liability account. Explanations are not required.

P11-5A The general ledger of Red Mountain Investments at June 30, 20X3, the end of the company's fiscal year, includes the following account balances before adjusting entries.

Journalizing, posting, and reporting liabilities
(Obj. 1, 2, 3, 4, 5, 6)

Accounts Payable	$105,520
Current Portion of Long-Term Debt	_____
Interest Payable	_____
Salary Payable	_____
Employee Payroll Taxes Payable	_____
Employer Payroll Taxes Payable	_____
Estimated Vacation Pay Liability	7,620
Unearned Rent Revenue	6,000
Long-Term Debt	200,000

The additional data needed to develop the adjusting entries at June 30 are as follows:

a. The long-term debt is payable in annual installments of $40,000 with the next installment due on July 31. On that date, Red Mountain will also pay one year's interest at 9%. Interest was last paid on July 31 of the preceding year. (Make the adjusting entry to shift the current installment of the long-term debt to a current liability.)
b. Gross salaries for the last payroll of the fiscal year were $5,044. Of this amount, employee payroll taxes payable were $1,088, and salary payable was $3,956.
c. Employer payroll taxes payable were $876.
d. Red Mountain estimates that vacation pay expense is 5% of gross salaries.
e. On February 1, the company collected one year's rent of $6,000 in advance.
f. At June 30, Red Mountain is the defendant in a $300,000 lawsuit, which the company expects to win. However, the outcome is uncertain. Write the note to report this contingent liability in the financial statements.

Required

1. Open the listed accounts, inserting their unadjusted June 30 balances.
2. Journalize and post the June 30 adjusting entries to the accounts opened. Key adjusting entries by letter.
3. Prepare the liability section of the balance sheet at June 30.

P11-6A Assume that the payroll records of a district sales office of **Spalding Sporting Goods** provided the following information for the weekly pay period ended December 21, 20X3.

Using a payroll record; recording a payroll
(Obj. 5)

Employee	Hours Worked	Hourly Earnings Rate	Federal Income Tax	Union Dues	United Way Contributions	Earnings Through Previous Week
Larry Fisher...............	42	$28	$278	$6	$35	$77,474
Felicia Jones..............	47	8	87	4	4	23,154
Sara Opper	40	11	64	—	4	4,880
Brian Tate..................	41	22	188	6	8	74,600

Fisher and Tate are salesmen. Jones and Opper work in the office. All employees are paid time and a half for hours worked in excess of 40 per week. Round all amounts to the nearest dollar. Show your computations. Explanations are not required for journal entries.

Required

1. Enter the appropriate information in a payroll record similar to Exhibit 11-7, page 442. In addition to the deductions listed, the employer also takes out FICA tax: 8% of the first $75,000 of each employee's annual earnings.
2. Record the payroll information in the general journal.
3. Assume that the first payroll check is number 319, paid to Larry Fisher. Record the check numbers in the payroll record. Also, prepare the general journal entry to record payment of net pay to the employees
4. The employer's payroll taxes include FICA tax of 8% of the first $75,000 of each employee's earnings. The employer also pays unemployment taxes of 6.2% (5.4% for the state and 0.8% for the federal government on the first $7,000 of each employee's annual earnings). Record the employer's payroll taxes in the general journal.

Reporting current liabilities (Obj. 6)

P11-7A Following are pertinent facts about events during the current year at Innovech, Inc.:

a. On November 30, Innovech received rent of $6,600 in advance for a lease on a building. This rent will be earned evenly over three months.
b. December sales totaled $113,000, and Innovech collected an additional state sales tax of 7%. This amount will be sent to the State of Tennessee early in January.
c. Innovech owes $100,000 on a long-term note payable. At December 31, 6% interest since July 31 and $20,000 of this principal are payable within one year.
d. Sales of $430,000 were covered by Innovech's product warranty. At January 1, estimated warranty payable was $8,100. During the year, Innovech recorded warranty expense of $22,300 and paid warranty claims of $24,900.
e. On September 30, Innovech signed a six-month, 9% note payable to purchase equipment costing $30,000. The note requires payment of principal and interest at maturity.

Required

For each item, indicate the account and the related amount to be reported as a current liability on Innovech's December 31 balance sheet.

(Group B) PROBLEMS

Journalizing liability-related transactions (Obj. 1, 2)

P11-1B The following transactions of **Bethlehem Steel** occurred during 20X2 and 20X3.

20X2
Feb. 3 Purchased equipment for $10,200, signing a six-month, 9% note payable.
28 Recorded the week's sales of $51,000, one-third for cash, and two-thirds on credit. All sales amounts are subject to a 5% state sales tax.
Mar. 7 Sent the last week's sales tax to the state.
Apr. 30 Borrowed $100,000 on a four-year, 9% note payable that calls for annual installment payments of $25,000 principal plus interest.
Aug. 3 Paid the six-month, 9% note at maturity.
Sep. 14 Discounted a $6,000, 60-day, 7% note payable to the bank, receiving cash for the net amount after interest was deducted from the note's maturity value.
Nov. 13 Recorded interest on the 7% discounted note and paid off the note at maturity.
30 Purchased inventory at a cost of $7,200, signing a three-month, 9% note payable for that amount.
Dec. 31 Accrued warranty expense, which is estimated at 3% of sales of $260,000.
31 Accrued interest on all outstanding notes payable. Made a separate interest accrual entry for each note payable.

20X3
Feb. 28 Paid off the 9% inventory note, plus interest, at maturity.
Apr. 30 Paid the first installment and interest for one year on the long-term note payable.

Required

Record the transactions in the company's general journal. Explanations are not required.

P11-2B Briarwood Stables provides riding lessons for girls ages 8–15. Most students are beginners, and none of the girls owns her own horse. Sally Arnold, the owner of the stable, uses horses stabled at her farm and owned by the O'Malleys. Most of the horses are for sale, but the economy has been bad for several years and sales have been slow. The O'Malleys are happy that Arnold uses their horses in exchange for boarding them. Because of a recent financial setback, Arnold cannot afford liability insurance. She seeks your advice about her business's exposure to liabilities.

Identifying contingent liabilities
(Obj. 2)

Required

Write a memorandum to inform Arnold of specific contingent liabilities arising from the business. It will be necessary to define a contingent liability because she is a professional horse trainer, not a businessperson. Propose a way for Arnold to limit her risk due to these liabilities.

P11-3B The partial monthly records of Aramark Food Service show the following figures:

Computing and recording payroll amounts
(Obj. 3, 4)

Employee Earnings

(a) Straight-time earnings	$?
(b) Overtime pay	5,109
(c) Total employee earnings	?

Deductions and Net Pay

(d) Withheld income tax	$ 9,293
(e) FICA tax	6,052
(f) Charitable contributions	?
(g) Medical insurance	1,373
(h) Total deductions	18,880
(i) Net pay	64,813

Accounts Debited

(j) Salary Expense	$31,278
(k) Wage Expense	?
(l) Sales Commission Expense	27,931

Required

1. Determine the missing amounts on lines (a), (c), (f), and (k).
2. Prepare the general journal entry to record Aramark's payroll for the month. Credit Payrolls Payable for net pay. No explanation is required.

P11-4B Jan Summers is a commercial lender at Harbor State Bank in Boston. During 20X2, she worked for the bank all year at a $5,195 monthly salary. She also earned a year-end bonus equal to 10% of her annual salary.

Computing and recording payroll amounts
(Obj. 3, 4)

Summers' federal income tax withheld during 20X2 was $822 per month. Also, there was a one-time withholding of $2,487 on her bonus check. State income tax withheld came to $61 per month, and the city of Boston withheld income tax of $21 per month. In addition, Summers paid one-time withholdings of $64 (state) and $19 (city) on the bonus. The FICA tax withheld was 8% of the first $75,000 in annual earnings. Summers authorized the following payroll deductions: United Fund contribution of 1% of total earnings and life insurance of $17 per month.

Harbor State Bank incurred payroll tax expense on Summers for FICA tax of 8% of the first $75,000 in total annual earnings. The bank also paid state unemployment tax of 5.4% and federal unemployment tax of 0.8% on the first $7,000 in annual earnings. The bank provided Summers with the following benefits: health insurance at a cost of $48 per month, and pension benefits to be paid to Summers during her retirement. During 20X2, the bank's cost of Summers' pension program was $4,083.

Required

1. Compute Summers' gross pay, payroll deductions, and net pay during 20X2. Round all amounts to the nearest dollar.
2. Compute Harbor State Bank's total 20X2 payroll cost for Summers.
3. Prepare the bank's summary general journal entries to record its expense for the following:
   a. Summers' total earnings for the year, her payroll deductions, and her net pay. Debit Salary Expense and Executive Bonus Compensation as appropriate. Credit liability accounts for the payroll deductions and Cash for net pay.
   b. Employer payroll taxes for Summers. Credit liability accounts.
   c. Benefits provided to Summers. Credit a liability account.

Explanations are not required.

P11-5B The St. Charles Consulting general ledger at September 30, 20X2, the end of the company's fiscal year, includes the following account balances before adjusting entries. Parentheses indicate a debit balance.

Accounts Payable	$ 88,240
Current Portion of Long-Term Debt	
Interest Payable	
Salary Payable	
Employee Payroll Taxes Payable	
Employer Payroll Taxes Payable	
Estimated Vacation Pay Liability	2,105
Unearned Rent Revenue	3,900
Long-Term Debt	100,000

The additional data needed to develop the adjusting entries at September 30 are as follows:

a. The long-term debt is payable in annual installments of $50,000, with the next installment due on January 31, 20X3. On that date, St. Charles Consulting will also pay one year's interest at 6.6%. Interest was last paid on January 31. (Make the adjusting entry to shift the current installment of the long-term debt to a current liability.)
b. Gross salaries for the last payroll of the fiscal year were $4,319. Of this amount, employee payroll taxes payable were $958, and salary payable was $3,361.
c. Employer payroll taxes payable were $890.
d. St. Charles estimates that vacation pay is 4% of gross salaries.
e. On August 1, the company collected six months' rent of $3,900 in advance.
f. At September 30, St. Charles is the defendant in a $500,000 lawsuit, which the company expects to win. However, the outcome is uncertain. Write the note to report this contingent liability in the financial statements.

Required

1. Open the listed accounts, inserting their unadjusted September 30 balances.
2. Journalize and post the September 30 adjusting entries to the accounts opened. Key adjusting entries by letter.
3. Prepare the liability section of St. Charles Consulting's balance sheet at September 30. Show total current liabilities.

P11-6B Assume that payroll records of a district sales office of Audi Motor Systems provided the following information for the weekly pay period ended December 26, 20X3:

Employee	Hours Worked	Weekly Earnings Rate	Federal Income Tax	Health Insurance	United Way Contributions	Earnings Through Previous Week
Clay Cooper	43	$ 400	$ 74	$ 9	$ 7	$17,060
Tim LeMann	46	480	90	5	5	22,365
Lena Marx	47	1,200	319	16	30	74,247
Karen York	40	240	32	4	2	3,413

Cooper and York work in the office, and LeMann and Marx work in sales. All employees are paid time and a half for hours worked in excess of 40 per week.

Required

For convenience, round all amounts to the nearest dollar. Show your computations. Explanations are not required for journal entries.

1. Enter the appropriate information in a payroll record similar to Exhibit 11-7. In addition to the deductions listed, the employer also takes out FICA tax: 8% of the first $75,000 of each employee's annual earnings.
2. Record the payroll information in the general journal.
3. Assume that the first payroll check is number 178, paid to Cooper. Record the check numbers in the payroll record. Also, prepare the general journal entry to record payment of net pay to the employees.
4. The employer's payroll taxes include FICA of 8% of the first $75,000 of each employee's annual earnings. The employer also pays unemployment taxes of 6.2% (5.4% for the state and 0.8% for the federal government) on the first $7,000 of each employee's annual earnings. Record the employer's payroll taxes in the general journal.

P11-7B Following are pertinent facts about events during the current year at Nevis Marine Company:

Reporting current liabilities (Obj. 6)

a. December sales totaled $404,000 and Nevis collected sales tax of 9%. The sales tax will be sent to the state of Washington early in January.

b. Nevis owes $75,000 on a long-term note payable. At December 31, 6% interest for the year plus $25,000 of this principal are payable within one year.

c. On August 31, Nevis signed a six-month, 6% note payable to purchase a machine costing $80,000. The note requires payment of principal and interest at maturity.

d. Sales of $909,000 were covered by Nevis' product warranty. At January 1, estimated warranty payable was $11,300. During the year, Nevis recorded warranty expense of $27,900 and paid warranty claims of $30,100.

e. On October 31, Nevis received rent of $2,400 in advance for a lease on a building. This rent will be earned evenly over four months.

Required

For each item, indicate the account and the related amount to be reported as a current liability on Nevis's December 31 balance sheet.

APPLY YOUR KNOWLEDGE

DECISION CASES

Case 1. SureBuilt Homes is a construction company in Fond du Lac, Wisconsin. The owner and manager, Art Waverly, oversees all company operations. He employs 15 work crews, each made up of six to ten members. Construction supervisors, who report directly to Waverly, lead the crews. Most supervisors are longtime employees, so Waverly trusts them. Waverly's office staff consists of an accountant and an office manager.

Identifying internal control weaknesses and their solution (Obj. 5)

Because employee turnover is high in the construction industry, supervisors hire and fire their own crew members. Supervisors notify the office of all personnel changes. Also, supervisors forward to the office the employee W-4 forms, which the crew members fill out. Each Thursday, the supervisors submit weekly time sheets for their crews, and the accountant prepares the payroll. At noon on Friday, the supervisors come to the office to get paychecks for distribution to the workers at 5 p.m.

SureBuilt's accountant prepares the payroll, including the payroll checks, which are written on a single payroll bank account. Waverly signs all payroll checks after matching the employee name to the time sheets submitted by the foremen. Often the workers wait several days to cash their paychecks. To verify that each construction worker is a bona fide employee, the accountant matches the employee's endorsement signature on the back of the canceled payroll check with the signature on that employee's W-4 form.

Required

1. Identify one *efficiency* weakness in SureBuilt's payroll accounting system. How can the business correct this weakness?
2. Identify one way that a supervisor can defraud SureBuilt Homes under the present system.
3. Discuss a control feature that SureBuilt Homes can use to *safeguard* against the frauds you identified in requirement 2.

Case 2. The Boeing Company, manufacturer of jet aircraft, is the defendant in numerous lawsuits claiming unfair trade practices. Boeing has strong incentives not to disclose these contingent liabilities. However, GAAP requires that companies report their contingent liabilities.

Unearned revenues, warranties, and contingent liabilities (Obj. 1, 2)

Required

1. Why would a company prefer *not* to disclose its contingent liabilities.
2. Describe how a bank could be harmed if a company seeking a loan did not disclose its contingent liabilities.
3. What ethical tightrope must companies walk when they report contingent liabilities?

ETHICAL ISSUE

LTV, manufacturer of aircraft and aircraft-related electronic devices, has at times borrowed heavily to finance operations. Often LTV is able to earn operating income much higher than its interest expense and is therefore quite profitable. However, when the business cycle turns down, LTV's debt burden has pushed the company to the brink of bankruptcy. Operating income is sometimes less than interest expense.

Required

Is it unethical for managers to saddle a company with a high level of debt? Or is it just risky? Who can get hurt when a company takes on too much debt? Discuss.

FINANCIAL STATEMENT CASE

Current and contingent liabilities (Obj. 1, 2)

Details about a company's current and contingent liabilities appear in a number of places in the annual report. Use **Target's** financial statements to answer the following questions.

Required

1. Give the breakdown of Target's current liabilities at January 29, 2000. Give the February 2000 entry to record the payment of accounts payable that Target owed at January 29, 2000.
2. How much was Target's long-term debt at January 29, 2000? Of this amount, how much was due within one year? How much was payable beyond one year in the future?
3. The balance sheet lists a $318 million liability for "Income Taxes Payable." Was income tax expense for the year, as reported on the income statement, equal to, less than, or greater than this amount? Why is one amount greater than the other?
4. Locate Target's report of its contingent liabilities. What event caused Target's contingent liabilities?

TEAM PROJECTS

Project 1. In recent years, the airline industry has dominated headlines. Consumers are shopping **Priceline.com** and other Internet sites for the lowest rates. The airlines have also lured customers with frequent-flyer programs, which award free flights to passengers who accumulate specified miles of travel. Unredeemed frequent-flyer mileage represents a liability that airlines must report on their balance sheets, usually as Air Traffic Liability.

Southwest Airlines, a profitable, no-frills carrier based in Dallas, has been rated near the top of the industry. Southwest controls costs by flying to smaller, less expensive airports; using only one model of aircraft; serving no meals; increasing staff efficiency; and having a shorter turnaround time on the ground between flights. The fact that most of the cities served by Southwest have predictable weather maximizes its on-time arrival record.

Required

With a partner or group, lead your class in a discussion of the following questions, or write a report as directed by your instructor.

1. Frequent-flyer programs have grown into significant obligations for airlines. Why should a liability be recorded for those programs? Discuss how you might calculate the amount of this liability. Can you think of other industries that offer similar incentives that create a liability?
2. One of Southwest Airlines' strategies for success is shortening stops at airport gates between flights. The company's chairman has stated, "What [you] produce is lower fares for the customers because you generate more revenue from the same fixed cost in that airplane." Look up *fixed cost* in the index of this book. What are some of the "fixed costs" of an airline? How can better utilization of assets improve a company's profits?

Project 2. Consider three different businesses:

   a. A bank   **b.** A magazine publisher   **c.** A department store

Required

For each business, list all of its liabilities—both current and long-term. If necessary, study Chapter 15 on long-term liabilities. Then compare your lists to identify what liabilities the three businesses have in common. Also identify the liabilities that are unique to each type of business.

INTERNET EXERCISE

Amazon.com

In 1995, **Amazon.com** opened its virtual doors and now serves over 17 million customers in over 150 different countries.

1. Go to **http://www.hoovers.com** and use the "Search" scroll bar to select *Company*, in the next box type <u>AMZN,</u> and then click on *Go.* For Amazon.com, Inc., click on *Capsule.* Scan the paragraph description of the company. What products does Amazon.com offer online?
2. Go to the top of the page and click on the *Financials* tab. Under "Free Financial Information" click on *Annual Financials.*

a. For the two most recent years, list the amounts reported for "Total Current Assets" and "Total Current Liabilities." Calculate the current ratio. Does Amazon.com have the ability to pay its current liabilities? Which year reports a stronger ratio?

b. For the two most recent years, list the amounts reported for "Total Liabilities" and "Total Assets." Calculate the debt ratio. How is Amazon.com financing its asset growth? Founder Jeff Bezos and family own about 34% of the company. Why do you think Mr. Bezos has chosen this method to finance asset growth?

c. Of approximately 100 Internet stocks, most showed staggering increases in revenue but only five showed net income in 1999. Is Amazon.com a typical Internet stock? Why or why not?

ACCOUNTING

12 Partnerships

LEARNING OBJECTIVES

*After studying this chapter,
you should be able to*

1. Identify the characteristics of a partnership
2. Account for the partners' investments in a partnership
3. Allocate profits and losses to the partners
4. Account for the admission of a partner to the business
5. Account for a partner's withdrawal from the firm
6. Account for the liquidation of a partnership
7. Prepare partnership financial statements

Once upon a time **Arthur Andersen LLP** was a stodgy accounting firm. No longer. Arthur Andersen—or "Arthur" as insiders call it—has shed its old image. For starters, the firm now earns much of its income from consulting, not accounting.

The firm is a profit-making machine, and it doesn't have to share its income with millions of stockholders the way corporations do. Arthur Andersen LLP is a partnership. That means the people who own the firm, around 2,000 of them—are all partners. Each partner's profit from the firm averages well over a half million dollars a year.

The most interesting thing about Arthur Andersen is the divorce the partners worked out. The consulting partners formed **Andersen Consulting,** a different firm. But they wanted to continue using the Andersen name, and that's where the rub came. The partners of Arthur Andersen, the original firm, demanded billions from Andersen Consulting because the consulting firm was launched from contacts with the firm's audit clients. As a compromise, the consulting firm took the name of **!Accenture.**

Is all this confusing? You bet it is. That's why the Andersen divorce was so difficult. It is a classic case for showing the fragile nature of a partnership. So, if you ever consider going into business with anyone besides your mother, choose your partners carefully. And don't forget to get the partnership agreement in writing.

The partnership form of business introduces some complexities that a proprietorship avoids. How much cash should a new partner contribute to the business? How should the partners divide profits and losses? This seems to be the most difficult issue for the partners. How should a partner who leaves the firm be compensated for his or her share of the business? This issue seems paramount to the partners of **Arthur Andersen LLP.**

A **partnership** is an association of two or more persons who co-own a business for profit. This definition comes from the Uniform Partnership Act, which nearly every state in the United States has adopted to regulate partnership practice.

Forming a partnership is easy. It requires no permission from the government and no legal procedures. When two persons decide to go into business together, a partnership is automatically formed.

A partnership brings together the assets and the experience of the partners. Business opportunities closed to an individual may open up to a partnership. Perhaps none of the Arthur Andersen partners has enough money individually to operate a large firm. But they are able to afford it together in a partnership. They pool their talents and know-how. Their partnership thus offers clients a fuller range of services than any one person can offer alone.

Partnerships come in all sizes. Many partnerships have fewer than ten partners. Some medical and law firms have 20 or more partners. The largest accounting/consulting firms have over 2,000 partners. Exhibit 12-1 lists the eight largest accounting/consulting firms in the United States, the number of partners in each firm, and their revenues in 1999.

CHARACTERISTICS OF A PARTNERSHIP

Starting a partnership is voluntary. A person cannot be forced to join a partnership, and partners cannot be forced to accept another person as a partner. Although the partnership agreement may be oral, a written agreement between the partners reduces the chance of a misunderstanding. The following characteristics distinguish partnerships from sole proprietorships and corporations.

The Written Agreement

A business partnership is like a marriage. To be successful, the partners must cooperate. But business partners do not vow to remain together for life. To make certain that each partner fully understands how the partnership operates and to lower the chances that any partner might misunderstand how the business is run, partners may draw up a **partnership agreement,** also called the **articles of**

PARTNERSHIP. An association of two or more persons who co-own a business for profit.

Objective 1
Identify the characteristics of a partnership

PARTNERSHIP AGREEMENT. The contract between partners that specifies such items as the name, location, and nature of the business; the name, capital investment, and duties of each partner; and the method of sharing profits and losses among the partners. Also called **articles of partnership.**

Revenue Rank (1999)	Firm Location	Partners	Revenue Per Partner (in millions)
1	Arthur Andersen, New York	2,117	$3.7
2	PricewaterhouseCoopers, New York	2,938	$2.3
3	Ernst & Young, New York	2,546	$2.5
4	Deloitte & Touche, Wilton, Connecticut	1,913	$2.8
5	KPMG, New York	1,800	$2.6
6	RSM McGladrey, Bloomington, Minnesota	369	$1.1
7	Grant Thornton, Chicago	274	$1.5
8	BDO Seidman, Chicago	335	$0.9

Source: Adapted from *Accounting Today* (March 13–April 2, 2000), Special Supplement, and the *Wall Street Journal,* August 8, 2000, page A3.

partnership. This agreement is a contract between the partners, so transactions involving the agreement are governed by contract law. The articles of partnership should make the following points clear:

1. Name, location, and nature of the business
2. Name, capital investment, and duties of each partner
3. Method of sharing profits and losses among the partners
4. Withdrawals of assets allowed to the partners
5. Procedures for settling disputes between the partners
6. Procedures for admitting new partners
7. Procedures for settling up with a partner who withdraws from the business
8. Procedures for liquidating the partnership—selling the assets, paying the liabilities, and disbursing any remaining cash to the partners

Limited Life

DISSOLUTION. Ending of a partnership.

A partnership has a life limited by the length of time that all partners continue to own the business. If one or more **Arthur Andersen** partners withdraws from the business, the old partnership will cease to exist. A new partnership may emerge to continue the same business, but the old partnership will have been dissolved. **Dissolution** is the ending of a partnership. The addition of a new partner dissolves the old partnership and creates a new partnership. Large partnerships such as Arthur Andersen retain the firm name even after partners resign from the firm.

Mutual Agency

MUTUAL AGENCY. Every partner can bind the business to a contract within the scope of the partnership's regular business operations.

Mutual agency in a partnership means that every partner can bind the business to a contract within the scope of the partnership's regular business operations. If Jana Jones, a partner in the firm of Willis and Jones, enters into a contract with a business to provide accounting service, then the firm of Willis & Jones—not just Jones—is bound to provide that service. If Jones signs a contract to purchase lawn services for her home, however, the partnership will not be bound to pay because the lawn service is a personal matter for Jones. It is not a regular business operation of the partnership.

Unlimited Liability

UNLIMITED PERSONAL LIABILITY. When a partnership (or a proprietorship) cannot pay its debts with business assets, the partners (or the proprietor) must use personal assets to meet the debt.

Each partner has an **unlimited personal liability** for the debts of the partnership. When a partnership cannot pay its debts with business assets, the partners must use their personal assets to meet the debt. Proprietors also have unlimited personal liability for the debts of their business.

Suppose the Willis & Jones firm has had an unsuccessful year and the partnership's liabilities exceed its assets by $20,000. Willis and Jones must pay this amount with their personal assets. Because each partner has unlimited liability, if a partner is unable to pay his or her part of the debt, the other partner (or partners) must pay. If Jones can pay only $5,000 of the liability, Willis must pay $15,000.

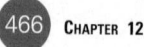

Unlimited liability and mutual agency are closely related. A dishonest partner or a partner with poor judgment may commit the partnership to a contract under which the business loses money. In turn, creditors may force *all* the partners to pay the debt from personal assets.

Partners can avoid unlimited personal liability for partnership obligations by forming a *limited partnership*. **Arthur Andersen LLP** is a limited liability partnership, as are the other large accounting and consulting firms in Exhibit 12-1. In this form of business organization, the partners have limited liability similar to the limited liability enjoyed by the stockholders of a corporation.

Co-Ownership of Property

Any asset—cash, inventory, machinery, and so on—that a partner invests in the partnership becomes the joint property of all the partners. Also, each partner has a claim to his or her share of the business's profits.

No Partnership Income Taxes

A partnership pays no income tax on its business income. Instead, the net income of the partnership is divided and becomes the taxable income of the partners. Suppose Willis & Jones, Certified Public Accountants, earned net income of $200,000, shared equally by the partners. The firm would pay no income tax *as a business entity*. Willis and Jones, however, would each pay income tax as individuals on their $100,000 shares of partnership income.

Partners' Owner's Equity Accounts

 DAILY EXERCISE 12-1

Accounting for a partnership is much like accounting for a proprietorship. We record buying and selling goods and services and collecting and paying cash for a partnership just as we do for a proprietorship. But because a partnership has more than one owner, the partnership must have more than one owner's equity account.

Every partner in the business—whether the firm has 2 or 2,000 partners—has an individual owner's equity account. Often these accounts carry the name of the particular partner and the word *capital*. For example, the owner's equity account for Blake Willis would read "Willis, Capital." Similarly, each partner has a withdrawal account. If the number of partners is large, the general ledger may contain the single account Partners' Capital, or Owners' Equity. A subsidiary ledger can be used for individual partner accounts.

Exhibit 12-2 lists the advantages and disadvantages of partnerships (compared with proprietorships and corporations). A partnership is really a "multiple proprietorship." Most features of a proprietorship also apply to a partnership—in particular, limited life and unlimited liability.

DAILY EXERCISE 12-2

EXHIBIT 12-2
Advantages and Disadvantages of Partnerships

Partnership Advantages	Partnership Disadvantages
Versus Proprietorships: 1. Can raise more capital. 2. Brings together the expertise of more than one person. 3. 1 + 1 > 2 in a good partnership. If the partners work well together, they can add more value than by working alone. *Versus Corporations:* 4. Less expensive to organize than a corporation, which requires a charter from the state. 5. No taxation of business income, which is taxed to the partners as individuals.	1. Partnership agreement may be difficult to formulate. Each time a new partner is admitted or a partner withdraws, the business needs a new partnership agreement. 2. Relationships among partners may be fragile. 3. Mutual agency and unlimited personal liability create personal obligations for each partner.

TYPES OF PARTNERSHIPS

There are two basic types of partnerships: general and limited.

General Partnerships

GENERAL PARTNERSHIP. A form of partnership in which each partner is an owner of the business, with all the privileges and risks of ownership.

A **general partnership** is the basic form of partnership organization. Each partner is an owner of the business with all the privileges and risks of ownership. The general partners share the profits, losses, and the risks of the business. The partnership *reports* its income to governmental tax authorities (the Internal Revenue Service in the United States), but the partnership itself pays *no* income tax. The profits and losses of the partnership pass through the business to the partners, who then pay personal income tax on their income.

Limited Partnerships

LIMITED PARTNERSHIP. A partnership with at least two classes of partners: a general partner and limited partners.

A **limited partnership** has at least two classes of partners. There must be at least one *general partner,* who takes primary responsibility for the management of the business. The general partner also takes the bulk of the risk of failure in the event the partnership goes bankrupt (liabilities exceed assets). In real-estate limited partnerships, the general partner often invests little cash in the business. Instead, the general partner's contribution is his or her skill in managing the organization. Usually, the general partner is the last owner to receive a share of partnership profits and losses. But the general partner may earn all excess profits after satisfying the limited partners' demands for income.

The *limited partners* are so named because their personal obligation for the partnership's liabilities is limited to the amount they have invested in the business. Usually, the limited partners have invested the bulk of the partnership's assets and capital. They therefore usually have first claim to partnership profits and losses, but only up to a specified limit. In exchange for their limited liability, their potential for profits usually has a limit as well.

LIMITED LIABILITY PARTNERSHIP. A form of partnership in which each partner's personal liability for the business's debts is limited to a certain amount. Also called **LLPs.**

Most of the large accounting firms are organized as **limited liability partnerships,** or **LLPs,** which means that each partner's personal liability for the business's debts is limited to a certain amount. The LLP must carry a large insurance policy to protect the public in case the partnership is found guilty of malpractice. Medical, legal, and other firms of professionals can also be organized as LLPs.

S Corporations

S CORPORATION. A corporation taxed in the same way as a partnership.

An **S Corporation** is a corporation that is taxed in the same way that a partnership is taxed. Therefore, S corporations are often discussed in conjunction with partnerships. This form of business organization derives its name from Subchapter S of the U.S. Internal Revenue Code.

An S corporation offers its owners the benefits of a corporation—no personal liability for business debts—and of a partnership—no double taxation. An ordinary (Subchapter C) corporation is subject to double taxation. First, the corporation pays corporate income tax on its income. Then, when the corporation pays dividends to the stockholders, they pay personal income tax on their dividend income. An S corporation pays no corporate income tax. Instead, the corporation's income flows through directly to the stockholders (the owners), who pay personal income tax on their share of the S corporation's income. The one-time taxation of an S corporation's income is an important advantage over an ordinary corporation. From a tax standpoint, an S corporation operates like a partnership.

To qualify as an S corporation, a company can have no more than 75 stockholders, all of whom must be citizens or residents of the United States. Accounting for an S corporation resembles that of accounting for a partnership because the allocation of corporate income follows the same procedure used by partnerships.

The popularity of S corporations rises and falls with the passage of new legislation. When individual income tax rates exceed corporate tax rates, S corporations increase in number. When corporate tax rates fall, there is less incentive to form an S corporation. Also, new entities called limited-liability companies have formed. **Arthur Andersen Limited Liability Partnership (LLP)** is an example. An LLP offers its owners the same limited liability as a corporation, and an LLP avoids some of the restrictions that S corporations face. Currently, LLPs are more popular than S corporations.

THE PARTNERSHIP START-UP

Let's examine the start-up of a partnership. We will see how to account for the owner's equity accounts of the partners. We will also learn how they appear on the balance sheet.

Objective 2
Account for the partners' investments in a partnership

Partners in a new partnership may invest assets and liabilities in the business. These contributions are entered in the books in the same way that a proprietor's

e-Accounting

The Limited but Lively Life of a Dot.Com Partnership

Founding partners say that starting up a business is *the life*. Sleep is scant and cash is low, but hopes and energy run high. Some Internet businesses have started with nothing more than enthusiastic partners and a winning idea.

- The story of **Yahoo!** founders Jerry Yang and David Filo is now legend. In 1994, the two Stanford graduate students came up with a way to categorize Web sites. Their guide, named Yahoo!, was the first place for Web browsers to find sites easily. Now Yahoo! is a global Internet communications, commerce, and media company with over 2,000 employees. Yahoo! has a global Web network of 21 properties and offices in Europe, Asia, Latin America, Canada, and the United States.
- Founded in 1999 by 19-year-old Shawn Fanning and 20-year-old Sean Parker, **Napster** created software that lets people trade music files on the Internet for free. In almost no time, the company was turning the music industry upside down. Twenty million users downloaded the free software in just seven months, and *Fortune* magazine commended the company for pioneering one of the hottest business concepts of our time: peer-to-peer information sharing. Napster is so successful at stealing copyrighted music that the music industry threatens to put the organization out of business.
- In 1994, Todd Krizelman and Stephan Paternot, both 25 and at Cornell, came up with an on-line community where participants go to find news, discussion forums, and products—**TheGlobe.com**. Krizelman and Paternot recruited employees in the student lounge, paid them with Domino pizza, drained their own bank accounts, and lived off credit cards. Four years later, TheGlobe.com brought in $27 million in an initial public offering, and the former dorm buddies are now joint CEOs.

Sources: Based on [Yahoo!] Information from http://join.yahoo.com/chief.html and http://join.yahoo.com/overview.html. [Napster] Chuck Philips, "Company town; THE BIZ Q & A; Humming a hopeful tune at napster," *The Los Angeles Times*, July 19, 2000, p. 1. Amy Kover, "Napster: The hot idea of the year," *Fortune*, June 26, 2000, pp. 128–136. [TheGlobe.com] Stephanie Armour, "Tech grads loving life: Pizza, jeans, happy hour," June 21, 1999, *USA Today*, p. 01B assets and liabilities are recorded. Subtraction of each partner's liabilities from his or her assets yields the amount to be credited to that partner's capital account. Often, the partners hire an independent firm to appraise their assets and liabilities at current market value at the time a partnership is formed. This outside evaluation assures an objective accounting for what each partner brings into the business.

Assume that Dave Benz and Joan Hanna form a partnership to manufacture and sell computer software. The partners agree on the following values based on an independent appraisal:

Benz's Contributions

- Cash, $10,000; inventory, $70,000; and accounts payable, $85,000 (The appraiser believes that the current market values for these items equal Benz's values.)
- Accounts receivable, $30,000, less allowance for doubtful accounts of $5,000
- Computer equipment—cost, $800,000; accumulated depreciation, $200,000; current market value, $450,000

Hanna's Contributions

- Cash, $5,000
- Computer software: cost, $18,000; market value, $100,000

The partnership records receipt of the partners' initial investments at the current market values of the assets and liabilities because, in effect, the partnership is buying the assets and assuming the liabilities at their current market values. The partnership entries are as follows:

Benz's Investment

June 1	Cash..	10,000	
	Accounts Receivable.......................................	30,000	
	Inventory...	70,000	
	Computer Equipment.......................................	450,000	
	Allowance for Doubtful Accounts..........................		5,000
	Accounts Payable		85,000
	Benz, Capital ($560,000 − $90,000)		470,000
	To record Benz's investment in the partnership.		

Hanna's Investment

June 1	Cash..		5,000
	Computer Software	100,000	
	Hanna, Capital		105,000
	To record Hanna's investment in the partnership.		

DAILY EXERCISE 12-3

DAILY EXERCISE 12-4

The initial partnership balance sheet reports the amounts shown in Exhibit 12-3. Note that the asset and liability sections on the balance sheet are the same for a proprietorship and a partnership.

SHARING PROFITS AND LOSSES, AND DRAWINGS

Objective 3
Allocate profits and losses to the partners

Allocating profits and losses among partners is one of the most challenging aspects of managing a partnership. If the partners have not drawn up an agreement or if the agreement does not state how the partners will divide profits and losses, then by law, the partners must share profits and losses equally. If the agreement specifies a method for sharing profits but not losses, then losses are shared in the same proportion as profits. For example, a partner who was allocated 75% of the profits would likewise absorb 75% of any losses. Partners may agree to any profit-and-loss-sharing method they desire.

EXHIBIT 12-3
Partnership Balance Sheet

BENZ AND HANNA
Balance Sheet
June 1, 20X5

Assets			Liabilities		
Cash.............................		$ 15,000	Accounts payable		$ 85,000
Accounts receivable......	$30,000				
Less Allowance					
for doubtful					
accounts	(5,000)	25,000	**Capital**		
Inventory.....................		70,000	Benz, capital..............		470,000
Computer equipment...		450,000	Hanna, capital		105,000
Computer software.......		100,000	Total liabilities		
Total assets...................		$660,000	and capital		$660,000

In some cases, an equal division is not fair. One partner may perform more work for the business than the other partner, or one partner may make a larger capital contribution. In the preceding example, Joan Hanna might agree to work longer hours for the partnership than Dave Benz to earn a greater share of profits. Benz could argue that he should share in more of the profits because he contributed more net assets ($470,000) than Hanna did ($105,000). Hanna might contend that her computer software program is the partnership's most important asset and that her share of the profits should be greater than Benz's share. Agreeing on a fair sharing of profits and losses in a partnership may be difficult.

Sharing Based on a Stated Fraction

Partners may state a particular fraction of the total profits and losses each individual partner will share. Suppose the partnership agreement of Lou Cagle and Justin Dean allocates two-thirds of the business profits and losses to Cagle and one-third to Dean. If net income for the year is $90,000 and all revenue and expense accounts have been closed, the Income Summary account has a credit balance of $90,000:

INCOME SUMMARY	
	Bal. 90,000

DAILY EXERCISE 12-5

The entry to close this account and allocate the profit to the partners' capital accounts is

Dec. 31	Income Summary	90,000	
	Cagle, Capital ($90,000 × 2/3)...........		60,000
	Dean, Capital ($90,000 × 1/3)		30,000
	To allocate net income to partners.		

Consider the effect of this entry. Does Cagle get cash of $60,000 and Dean cash of $30,000? No. The increase in the partners' capital accounts cannot be linked to any particular asset, including cash. Instead, the entry indicates that Cagle's ownership in *all* the assets of the business increased by $60,000 and Dean's by $30,000.

If the year's operations resulted in a net loss of $66,000, the Income Summary account would have a debit balance of $66,000. In that case, the closing entry to allocate the loss to the partners' capital accounts would be

Dec. 31	Cagle, Capital ($66,000 × 2/3).....................	44,000	
	Dean, Capital ($66,000 × 1/3)	22,000	
	Income Summary		66,000
	To allocate net loss to partners.		

DAILY EXERCISE 12-6

Just as a profit of $90,000 did not mean that the partners received cash of $60,000 and $30,000, so the loss of $66,000 does not mean that the partners must contribute cash of $44,000 and $22,000. A profit or loss will increase or decrease each partner's capital account, but cash may not change hands.

Sharing Based on Capital Contributions

Profits and losses are often allocated in proportion to capital contributions in the business. Suppose that Jenny Aycock, Erika Barber, and Sue Cordoba are partners in ABC Company. Their capital accounts have the following balances at the end of the year, before the closing entries:

Aycock, Capital......................	$ 40,000
Barber, Capital.......................	60,000
Cordoba, Capital....................	50,000
Total capital balances..............	$150,000

Assume that the partnership earned a profit of $120,000 for the year. To allocate this amount on the basis of capital contributions, compute each partner's percentage share of the partnership's total capital balance by dividing each partner's contribution by the total capital amount. These figures, multiplied by the $120,000 profit amount, yield each partner's share of the year's profits:

Aycock:	($40,000/$150,000) × $120,000 =	$ 32,000
Barber:	($60,000/$150,000) × $120,000 =	48,000
Cordoba:	($50,000/$150,000) × $120,000 =	40,000
	Net income allocated to partners =	$120,000

The closing entry to allocate the profit to the partners' capital accounts is

Dec. 31	Income Summary	120,000	
	Aycock, Capital...................................		32,000
	Barber, Capital....................................		48,000
	Cordoba, Capital.................................		40,000
	To allocate net income to partners.		

After this closing entry, the partners' capital balances are

Aycock, Capital ($40,000 + $32,000).....................................	$ 72,000
Barber, Capital ($60,000 + $48,000).....................................	108,000
Cordoba, Capital ($50,000 + $40,000)..................................	90,000
Total capital balances after allocation of net income	$270,000

Sharing Based on Capital Contributions and on Service

One partner, regardless of capital contribution, may put more work into the business than the other partners do. Even among partners who log equal service time, one person's superior experience and knowledge may command a greater share of income. To reward the harder-working or more valuable person, the profit-and-loss-sharing method may be based on a combination of contributed capital *and* service to the business. The Chicago-based law firm **Baker & McKenzie,** for example, which has nearly 500 partners, takes seniority into account in determining partner compensation.

Assume that Debbie Randolph and Nancy Scott formed a partnership in which Randolph invested $60,000 and Scott invested $40,000, a total of $100,000. Scott devotes more time to the partnership and earns the larger salary. Accordingly, the two partners have agreed to share profits as follows:

1. The first $50,000 of partnership profits is to be allocated on the basis of partners' capital contributions to the business.
2. The next $60,000 of profits is to be allocated on the basis of service, with Randolph receiving $24,000 and Scott receiving $36,000.
3. Any remaining amount is to be allocated equally.

If net income for the first year is $125,000, the partners' shares of this profit are computed as follows:

	Randolph	Scott	Total
Total net income			$125,000
Sharing of first $50,000 of net income, based on capital contributions:			
Randolph ($60,000/$100,000 × $50,000) ..	$30,000		
Scott ($40,000/$100,000 × $50,000)		$20,000	
Total...			50,000
Net income remaining for allocation..............			75,000
Sharing of next $60,000, based on service:			
Randolph	24,000		
Scott		36,000	
Total...			60,000
Net income remaining for allocation..............			15,000
Remainder shared equally:			
Randolph ($15,000 × 1/2)	7,500		
Scott ($15,000 × 1/2)		7,500	
Total...			15,000
Net income remaining for allocation..............			$ 0
Net income allocated to the partners..............	$61,500	$63,500	$125,000

On the basis of this allocation, the closing entry is

Dec. 31	Income Summary..	125,000	
	Randolph, Capital...............................		61,500
	Scott, Capital		63,500
	To allocate net income to partners.		

 DAILY EXERCISE 12-7

Sharing Based on Salaries and on Interest

Partners may be rewarded for service and capital contributions in other ways. In one sharing plan, the partners are allocated salaries plus interest on their capital balances. Assume that Randy Lewis and Gerald Clark form an oil-exploration partnership. At the beginning of the year, their capital balances are $80,000 and $100,000, respectively. The partnership agreement allocates annual salaries of $43,000 to Lewis and $35,000 to Clark. After salaries are allocated, each partner earns 8% interest on his beginning capital balance. Any remaining net income is divided equally. Partnership profit of $96,000 will be allocated as follows:

	Lewis	Clark	Total
Total net income			$96,000
First, salaries:			
Lewis	$43,000		
Clark..		$35,000	
Total...			78,000
Net income remaining for allocation			18,000
Second, interest on beginning capital balances:			
Lewis ($80,000 × 0.08)....................................	6,400		
Clark ($100,000 × 0.08)		8,000	
Total...			14,400
Net income remaining for allocation			3,600
Third, remainder shared equally:			
Lewis ($3,600 × 1/2)	1,800		
Cleark ($3,600 × 1/2)		1,800	
Total...			3,600
Net income remaining for allocation			$ 0
Net income allocated to the partners...................	$51,200	$44,800	$96,000

DAILY EXERCISE 12-8

In the preceding illustration, net income exceeded the sum of salary and interest. If the partnership profit is less than the allocated sum of salary and interest, a negative remainder will occur at some stage in the allocation process. Even so, the partners use the same method for allocation purposes. For example, assume that Lewis and Clark Partnership earned only $82,000:

	Lewis	Clark	Total
Total net income			$82,000
First, salaries:			
Lewis	$43,000		
Clark...		$35,000	
Total			78,000
Net income remaining for allocation			4,000
Second, interest on beginning capital balances:			
Lewis ($80,000 × 0.08)..................................	6,400		
Clark ($100,000 × 0.08)		8,000	
Total			14,400
Net income remaining for allocation			10,400
Third, remainder shared equally:			
Lewis ($10,400 × 1/2)	(5,200)		
Clark ($10,400 × 1/2).....................................		(5,200)	
Total			(10,400)
Net income remaining for allocation			$ 0
Net income allocated to the partners.................	$44,200	$37,800	$82,000

A net loss would be allocated to Lewis and Clark in the same manner outlined for net income. The sharing procedure would begin with the net loss and then allocate salary, interest, and any other specified amounts to the partners.

THINK IT OVER
Are these salaries and interest amounts business expenses in the usual sense? Explain your answer.

Answer: No, partners do not work for their own business to earn a salary, as an employee does. They do not loan money to their own business to earn interest. Their goal is for the partnership to earn a profit. Therefore, salaries and interest in partnership agreements are simply ways of expressing the allocation of profits and losses to the partners. For example, the salary component of partner income rewards service to the partnership. The interest component rewards a partner's investment of cash or other assets in the business. But the partners' salary and interest amounts are *not* salary expense and interest expense in the partnership's accounting or tax records.

Partner Drawings of Cash and Other Assets

Like anyone else, partners need cash for personal living expenses. Partnership agreements usually allow partners to withdraw cash or other assets from the business. Drawings from a partnership are recorded exactly as for a proprietorship. Assume that both Randy Lewis and Gerald Clark are allowed a monthly withdrawal of $3,500. The partnership records the March withdrawals with this entry:

Mar. 31	Lewis, Drawing	3,500	
	Clark, Drawing..	3,500	
	Cash..		7,000
	Monthly partner withdrawals of cash.		

During the year, each partner's drawing account accumulates 12 such amounts, a total of $42,000 ($3,500 × 12) per partner. At the end of the period, the general ledger shows the following account balances immediately after net income has been closed to the partners' capital accounts. Assume these beginning balances for Lewis and Clark at the start of the year and that $82,000 of profit has been allocated on the basis of the preceding illustration.

LEWIS, CAPITAL			CLARK, CAPITAL	
	Jan. 1 Bal. 80,000			Jan. 1 Bal. 100,000
	Dec. 31 Net. inc. 44,200			Dec. 31 Net. inc. 37,800

LEWIS, DRAWING			CLARK, DRAWING	
Dec. 31 Bal. 42,000			Dec. 31 Bal. 42,000	

The drawing accounts must be closed at the end of the period, exactly as for a proprietorship: The closing entry credits each partner's drawing account and debits each capital account. ➡

◄ We covered this closing entry in Chapter 4, page 137.

ADMISSION OF A PARTNER

The addition of a new member or the withdrawal of an existing member dissolves the partnership. We turn now to a discussion of how partnerships dissolve—and how new partnerships arise.

Objective 4
Account for the admission of a new partner to the business

Often, a new partnership is formed to carry on the former partnership's business. In fact, the new partnership may retain the dissolved partnership's name. **PricewaterhouseCoopers LLP,** for example, is an accounting/consulting firm that retires and hires partners during the year. Thus, the former partnership dissolves and a new partnership begins many times. But the business retains its name and continues operations. Other partnerships may dissolve and then re-form under a new name. Let's look at the ways a new member may gain admission into an existing partnership.

Admission by Purchasing a Partner's Interest

A person may become a member of a partnership by gaining the approval of the other partner (or partners) for entrance into the firm *and* by purchasing a present partner's interest in the business. Let's assume that Roberta Fisher and Benitez Garcia have a partnership that carries these figures:

Cash	$ 40,000	Total liabilities	$120,000
Other assets	360,000	Fisher, capital	110,000
		Garcia, capital	170,000
Total assets	$400,000	Total liabilities and capital	$400,000

Business is going so well that Fisher receives an offer from Barry Dynak, an outside party, to buy her $110,000 interest in the business for $150,000. Fisher agrees to sell out to Dynak, and Garcia approves Dynak as a new partner. The firm records the transfer of capital interest in the business with this entry:

Apr. 16	Fisher, Capital	110,000	
	Dynak, Capital		110,000
	To transfer Fisher's equity in the business to Dynak.		

The debit side of the entry closes Fisher's capital account because she is no longer a partner in the firm. The credit side opens Dynak's capital account because Fisher's equity has been transferred to Dynak. The entry amount is Fisher's capital balance ($110,000) and not the $150,000 Dynak paid Fisher to buy into the business. The full $150,000 goes to Fisher, including the $40,000 difference between her capital balance and the price received from Dynak. In this example, the partnership receives no cash because the transaction was between Dynak and Fisher, not between Dynak and the partnership. Suppose Dynak pays Fisher less than Fisher's capital balance. The entry on the partnership books is not affected. Fisher's equity is transferred to Dynak at book value ($110,000).

The old partnership has dissolved. Garcia and Dynak draw up a new partnership agreement with a new profit-and-loss-sharing ratio and continue business operations. If Garcia does not accept Dynak as a partner, Dynak gets no voice in management of the firm. However, under the Uniform Partnership Act, the purchaser shares in the profits and losses of the firm and in its assets at liquidation.

Admission by Investing in the Partnership

A person may be admitted as a partner by investing directly in the partnership rather than by purchasing an existing partner's interest. The new partner contributes assets—for example, cash, inventory, or equipment—to the business. Assume that the partnership of Robin Ingel and Michael Jay has the following assets, liabilities, and capital:

Cash	$ 20,000	Total liabilities......................	$ 60,000
Other assets........................	200,000	Ingel, capital	70,000
		Jay, capital	90,000
Total assets	$220,000	Total liabilities and capital	$220,000

Laura Kahn offers to invest equipment and land (Other Assets) with a market value of $80,000 to persuade the existing partners to take her into the business. Ingel and Jay agree to dissolve the existing partnership and to start up a new business, giving Kahn one-third interest—[$80,000/($70,000 + $90,000 + $80,000) = 1/3]—in exchange for the contributed assets. Notice that Kahn is buying into the partnership at book value because her one-third investment ($80,000) equals one-third of the new partnership's total capital ($240,000). The entry to record Kahn's investment is

July 18	Other Assets	80,000	
	Kahn, Capital...		80,000
	To admit L. Kahn as a partner with a one-third interest in the business.		

After this entry, the partnership books show

Cash	$ 20,000	Total liabilities......................	$ 60,000
Other assets........................		Ingel, capital	70,000
($200,000 + $80,000)......	280,000	Jay, capital	90,000
		Kahn, capital	80,000
Total assets	$300,000	Total liabilities and capital	$300,000

DAILY EXERCISE 12-9

DAILY EXERCISE 12-10

Kahn's one-third interest in the partnership does not necessarily entitle her to one-third of the profits. The sharing of profits and losses is a separate element in the partnership agreement.

ADMISSION BY INVESTING IN THE PARTNERSHIP—BONUS TO THE OLD PARTNERS The more successful a partnership, the higher the payment the partners may demand from a person entering the business. Partners in a business that is doing quite well might require an incoming person to pay them a bonus. The bonus increases the current partners' capital accounts.

Suppose that Hiro Nagasawa and Ralph Osburn's partnership has earned above-average profits for ten years. The two partners share profits and losses equally. The partnership balance sheet carries these figures:

Cash	$ 40,000	Total liabilities......................	$100,000
Other assets........................	210,000	Nagasawa, capital	70,000
		Osburn, capital	80,000
Total assets	$250,000	Total liabilities and capital	$250,000

The partners agree to admit Glen Parker to a one-fourth interest with his cash investment of $90,000. Parker's capital balance on the partnership books is only $60,000, computed as follows:

Partnership capital before Parker is admitted ($70,000 + $80,000)	$150,000
Parker's investment in the partnership...	90,000
Partnership capital after Parker is admitted...	$240,000
Parker's capital in the partnership ($240,000 × 1/4)	$ 60,000
Bonus to the old partners ($90,000 − $60,000)	$ 30,000

 DAILY EXERCISE 12-11

In effect, Parker had to buy into the partnership at a price ($90,000) above the book value of his one-fourth interest ($60,000). Parker's investment of an extra $30,000 creates a *bonus* for the existing partners. The entry on the partnership books to record Parker's investment is

Mar. 1	Cash	90,000	
	Parker, Capital		60,000
	Nagasawa, Capital ($30,000 × 1/2)............................		15,000
	Osburn, Capital ($30,000 × 1/2)................................		15,000
	To admit G. Parker as a partner with a one-fourth interest in the business.		

Parker's capital account is credited for his one-fourth interest in the partnership. The *bonus* is allocated to the partners on the basis of their profit-and-loss ratio.

The new partnership's balance sheet reports these amounts:

Cash ($40,000 + $90,000)...	$130,000	Total liabilities.......................	$100,000
Other assets..........................	210,000	Nagasawa, capital	
		($70,000 + $15,000)	85,000
		Osburn, capital	
		($80,000 + $15,000)	95,000
		Parker, capital......................	60,000
Total assets	$340,000	Total liabilities and capital	$340,000

 DAILY EXERCISE 12-12

Mia and Susan are partners with capital balances of $25,000 and $75,000, respectively. They share profits and losses in a 30:70 ratio. Mia and Susan admit Tab to a 10% interest in a new partnership when Tab invests $20,000 in the business.

1. Journalize the partnership's receipt of cash from Tab.
2. What is each partner's capital in the new partnership?

Answers

1.	Cash	20,000	
	Tab, Capital		12,000
	Mia, Capital ($8,000 × 0.30)		2,400
	Susan, Capital ($8,000 × 0.70).................................		5,600
	To admit Tab with a 10% interest in the business.		

Partnership capital before Tab is admitted ($25,000 + $75,000)............	$100,000
Tab's investment in the partnership...	20,000
Partnership capital after Tab is admitted...	$120,000
Tab's capital in the partnership ($120,000 × 1/10)	$ 12,000
Bonus to the old partners ($20,000 − $12,000)	$ 8,000

2. Partners' capital balances:

Mia, capital ($25,000 + $2,400).................	$ 27,400
Susan, capital ($75,000 + $5,600)	80,600
Tab, capital	12,000
Total partnership capital.............................	$120,000

ADMISSION BY INVESTING IN THE PARTNERSHIP—BONUS TO THE NEW PARTNER   A potential new partner may be so important that the existing partners offer him or her a partnership share that includes a bonus. A law firm may strongly desire a former governor or other official as a partner because of the person's reputation and connections. A restaurant owner may want to go into partnership with a famous sports personality, movie star, or model. The popular chain **Planet Hollywood,** for example, opened its first restaurant in New York City with the help of celebrity partners Sylvester Stallone, Arnold Schwarzenegger, Bruce Willis, and Don Johnson.

Suppose that Allan Page and Olivia Franco have a law partnership. The firm's balance sheet appears as follows:

◉ DAILY EXERCISE 12-13

Cash	$140,000	Total liabilities	$120,000
Other assets	360,000	Page, capital	230,000
		Franco, capital	150,000
Total assets	$500,000	Total liabilities and capital	$500,000

Page and Franco admit Martin Schiller, a former attorney general, as a partner with a one-third interest in exchange for his cash investment of $100,000. At the time of Schiller's admission, the firm's capital is $380,000 (Page, $230,000, plus Franco, $150,000). Page and Franco share profits and losses in the ratio of two-thirds to Page and one-third to Franco. The computation of Schiller's equity in the partnership is

Partnership capital before Schiller is admitted ($230,000 + $150,000)	$380,000
Schiller's investment in the partnership	100,000
Partnership capital after Schiller is admitted	$480,000
Schiller's capital in the partnership ($480,000 × 1/3)	$160,000
Bonus to the new partner ($160,000 − $100,000)	$ 60,000

In this case, Schiller bought into the partnership at a price ($100,000) below the book value of his interest ($160,000). The bonus of $60,000 went to Schiller from the other partners. The capital accounts of Page and Franco are debited for the $60,000 difference between the new partner's equity ($160,000) and his investment ($100,000). The existing partners share this decrease in capital as though it were a loss, on the basis of their profit-and-loss ratio. The entry to record Schiller's investment is

Aug. 24	Cash	100,000	
	Page, Capital ($60,000 × 2/3)	40,000	
	Franco, Capital ($60,000 × 1/3)	20,000	
	Schiller, Capital		160,000
	To admit M. Schiller as a partner with a one-third interest in the business.		

The new partnership's balance sheet reports these amounts:

Cash		Total liabilities	$120,000
($140,000 + $100,000)	$240,000	Page, capital	
Other assets	360,000	($230,000 − $40,000)	190,000
		Franco, capital	
		($150,000 − $20,000)	130,000
		Schiller, capital	160,000
Total assets	$600,000	Total liabilities and capital	$600,000

WORK IT OUT

John and Ron are partners with capital balances of $30,000 and $40,000, respectively. They share profits and losses in a 25:75 ratio. John and Ron admit Lou to a 20% interest in a new partnership when Lou invests $10,000 in the business.

1. Journalize the partnership's receipt of cash from Lou.
2. What is each partner's capital in the new partnership?

Answers

1. Cash 10,000

  John, Capital ($6,000 × 0.25) 1,500

  Ron, Capital ($6,000 × 0.75) 4,500

      Lou, Capital 16,000

  To admit Lou with a 20% interest in the business.

Partnership capital before Lou is admitted ($30,000 + $40,000)	$70,000
Lou's investment in the partnership	10,000
Partnership capital after Lou is admitted	$80,000
Lou's capital in the partnership ($80,000 × 0.20)	$16,000
Bonus to the new partner ($16,000 − $10,000)	$ 6,000

2. Partners' capital balances:

John, capital ($30,000 − $1,500)	$28,500
Ron, capital ($40,000 − $4,500)	35,500
Lou, capital...	16,000
Total partnership capital...........................	$80,000

WITHDRAWAL (RESIGNATION OR DEATH) OF A PARTNER

Objective 5
Account for a partner's withdrawal (resignation) from the firm

A partner may withdraw from the business for many reasons, including retirement or a dispute with the other partners. The resignation of a partner dissolves the old partnership. The partnership agreement should contain a provision to govern how to settle with a withdrawing partner. In the simplest case, illustrated on page 476, a partner may resign and sell his or her interest to another partner in a personal transaction.

The only entry needed to record this transfer of equity debits the withdrawing partner's capital account and credits the purchaser's capital account. The dollar amount of the entry is the capital balance of the withdrawing partner, regardless of the price paid by the purchaser. The accounting when one current partner buys a second partner's interest is the same as when an outside party buys a current partner's interest.

If the partner resigns in the middle of an accounting period, the partnership books should be updated to determine each partner's capital balance. The business must measure net income or net loss for the fraction of the year up to the resignation date and allocate profit or loss according to the existing ratio. After the books have been closed, the business accounts for the change in partnership capital.

The withdrawing partner may receive his or her share of the business in partnership assets other than cash. Then the question is what value to assign the partnership assets—book value or current market value? The settlement procedure may specify an independent appraisal to determine current market value. If market values have changed, the appraisal will result in revaluing the partnership assets. The partners share in any market value changes that their efforts caused.

Suppose that Keith Isaac is retiring in midyear from the partnership of Green, Henry, and Isaac. After the books have been adjusted for partial-period income but before the asset appraisal, revaluation, and closing entries, the balance sheet reports the following:

Cash.............................		$ 39,000	Total liabilities	$ 80,000
Inventory....................		44,000	Green, capital	54,000
Land		55,000	Henry, capital	43,000
Building......................	$95,000		Isaac, capital	21,000
Less Accum. depr. ...	(35,000)	60,000	Total liabilities and	
Total assets.................		$198,000	capital	$198,000

An independent appraiser revalues the inventory at $38,000 (down from $44,000) and the land at $101,000 (up from $55,000). The partners share the differences between these assets' market values and their prior book values on the basis of their profit-and-loss ratio.

The partnership agreement has allocated one-fourth of the profits to Susan Green, one-half to Charles Henry, and one-fourth to Keith Isaac. (This ratio may be written 1 : 2 : 1 for one part to Green, two parts to Henry, and one part to Isaac.) For each share that Green or Isaac has, Henry has two. The entries to record the revaluation of the inventory and land are

July 31	Green, Capital ($6,000 × 1/4)	1,500		
	Henry, Capital ($6,000 × 1/2)	3,000		
	Isaac, Capital ($6,000 × 1/4)	1,500		
	Inventory ($44,000 − $38,000)		6,000	
	To revalue the inventory and allocate the loss to the partners.			
31	Land ($101,000 − $55,000)	46,000		
	Green, Capital ($46,000 × 1/4)		11,500	
	Henry, Capital ($46,000 × 1/2)		23,000	
	Isaac, Capital ($46,000 × 1/4)		11,500	
	To revalue the land and allocate the gain to the partners.			

After the revaluations, the partnership balance sheet reports the following:

Cash		$ 39,000	Total liabilities...	$80,000
Inventory		38,000	Green, capital ($54,000 − $1,500 + $11,500)	64,000
Land..............................		101,000	Henry, capital ($43,000 − $3,000 + $23,000)	63,000
Building	$95,000		Isaac, capital ($21,000 − $1,500 + $11,500).............	31,000
Less Accum. depr.	(35,000)	60,000		
Total assets		$238,000	Total liabilities and capital	$238,000

The books now carry the assets at current market value, which becomes the new book value, and the capital accounts have been adjusted accordingly. As the balance sheet shows, Isaac has a claim to $31,000 in partnership assets. How is his withdrawal from the business accounted for?

Withdrawal at Book Value

If Keith Isaac withdraws by receiving cash equal to the book value of his owner's equity, the entry will be

July 31	Isaac, Capital..	31,000	
	Cash..		31,000
	To record withdrawal of K. Isaac from the business.		

 DAILY EXERCISE 12-14

This entry records the payment of partnership cash to Isaac and the closing of his capital account upon his withdrawal from the business.

Withdrawal at Less than Book Value

The withdrawing partner may be so eager to leave the business that he or she is willing to take less than his or her equity. Assume that Keith Isaac withdraws from the business and agrees to receive partnership cash of $10,000 and the new partnership's note for $15,000. This $25,000 settlement is $6,000 less than Isaac's $31,000 equity in the business. The remaining partners share this $6,000 difference—which is a bonus to them—according to their profit-and-loss ratio.

Because Isaac has withdrawn from the partnership, a new agreement—and a new profit-and-loss ratio—must be drawn up. In forming a new partnership, Henry and Green may decide on any ratio that they see fit. Let's assume they agree that Henry will earn two-thirds of partnership profits and losses and Green one-third. The entry to record Isaac's withdrawal at less than book value is

July 31	Isaac, Capital	31,000	
	Cash		10,000
	Note Payable to K. Isaac		15,000
	Green, Capital ($6,000 × 1/3)		2,000
	Henry, Capital ($6,000 × 2/3)		4,000
	To record withdrawal of K. Isaac from the business.		

Isaac's account is closed, and Henry and Green may or may not continue the business as a new partnership.

 DAILY EXERCISE 12-15

Withdrawal at More than Book Value

The settlement with a withdrawing partner may allow him or her to take assets of greater value than the book value of that partner's capital. Also, the remaining partners may be so eager for the withdrawing partner to leave the firm that they pay him or her a bonus to withdraw from the business. In either case, the partner's withdrawal causes a decrease in the book equity of the remaining partners. This decrease is allocated to the partners on the basis of their profit-and-loss ratio.

The accounting for this situation follows the pattern illustrated for withdrawal at less than book value—with one exception. The remaining partners' capital accounts are debited because the withdrawing partner receives more than his or her book equity.

 DAILY EXERCISE 12-16

WORK IT OUT

Matt is withdrawing from the partnership of Matt, Lee, and Karla. The partners share profits and losses in a 1:2:3 ratio for Matt, Lee, and Karla, respectively. After the revaluation of assets, Matt's capital balance is $50,000, and the other partners agree to pay her $60,000. Journalize the payment to Matt and his withdrawal from the partnership.

Answer

Matt, Capital	50,000	
Lee, Capital [($60,000 − $50,000) × 2/5]	4,000	
Karla, Capital [($60,000 − $50,000) × 3/5]	6,000	
Cash		60,000
To record withdrawal of Matt from the business.		

Death of a Partner

Like any other form of partnership withdrawal, the death of a partner dissolves a partnership. The partnership accounts are adjusted to measure net income or loss for the fraction of the year up to the date of death, then closed to determine the partners' capital balances on that date. Settlement with the deceased partner's estate is based on the partnership agreement. The estate commonly receives partnership assets equal to the partner's capital balance. The partnership closes the deceased partner's capital account with a debit. This entry credits a payable to the estate.

Suppose Susan Green (of the partnership on page 480) dies after all accounts have been adjusted to current market value. Green's capital balance is $64,000. Green's estate may request cash for her final share of the partnership's assets. At this time the business has only $39,000 of cash, so it must borrow. Let's assume the partnership borrows $50,000 and then pays Green's estate for her capital balance. The partnership's journal entries are

Objective 6
Account for the liquidation of a partnership

Aug. 1	Cash	50,000	
	Note Payable		50,000
	To borrow money		
Aug. 1	Green, Capital	64,000	
	Cash		64,000
	To record withdrawal of Green from the business.		

Alternatively, a remaining partner may purchase the deceased partner's equity. The deceased partner's equity is debited, and the purchaser's equity is credited. The journal entry to record this transaction follows the pattern given on page 475 for the transfer of Fisher's equity over to Dynak. The amount of this entry is the ending credit balance in the deceased partner's capital account.

LIQUIDATION OF A PARTNERSHIP

LIQUIDATION. The process of going out of business by selling the entity's assets and paying its liabilities. The final step in liquidation is the distribution of any remaining cash to the owner(s).

Admission of a new partner or withdrawal or death of an existing partner dissolves the partnership. However, the business may continue operating with no apparent change to outsiders such as customers and creditors. In contrast, business **liquidation** is the process of going out of business by selling the entity's assets and paying its liabilities. The final step in liquidation is the *distribution of the remaining cash to the owners.* Before the business is liquidated, its books should be adjusted and closed. After closing, only asset, liability, and partners' capital accounts remain open.

Liquidation of a partnership includes three basic steps:

1. Sell the assets. Allocate the gain or loss to the partners' capital accounts on the basis of the profit-and-loss ratio.
2. Pay the partnership liabilities.
3. Disburse the remaining cash to the partners on the basis of their capital balances.

In practice, the liquidation of a business can stretch over weeks or months. Selling every asset and paying every liability of the entity takes time. After the partners of **Shea & Gould,** one of New York's best-known law firms, voted to dissolve their partnership, the firm remained open for an extra year to collect bills and pay off liabilities.

To avoid excessive detail in our illustrations, we include only two asset categories—Cash and Noncash Assets—and a single liability category—Liabilities. Our examples assume that the business sells the noncash assets in a single transaction and pays the liabilities in a single transaction.

Assume that Jane Avignon, Elaine Bloch, and Mark Crane have shared profits and losses in the ratio of 3:1:1. (This ratio is equal to 3/5, 1/5, 1/5, or a 60%, 20%, 20% sharing ratio.) They decide to liquidate their partnership. After the books are adjusted and closed, the general ledger contains the following balances:

Cash	$ 10,000	Liabilities	$ 30,000
Noncash assets	90,000	Avignon, capital.....................	40,000
		Bloch, capital.........................	20,000
		Crane, capital	10,000
Total assets	$100,000	Total liabilities and capital	$100,000

Sale of Noncash Assets at a Gain

Assume that the Avignon, Bloch, and Crane partnership sells its noncash assets (shown on the balance sheet as $90,000) for cash of $150,000. The partnership realizes a gain of $60,000, which is allocated to the partners on the basis of their profit-and-loss-sharing ratio. The entry to record this sale and allocation of the gain is

Oct. 31	Cash	150,000	
	Noncash Assets...		90,000
	Avignon, Capital ($60,000 × 0.60)		36,000
	Bloch, Capital ($60,000 × 0.20)		12,000
	Crane, Capital ($60,000 × 0.20)....................		12,000
	To sell noncash assets at a gain.		

The partnership must next pay off its liabilities:

Oct. 31	Liabilities..	30,000	
	Cash..		30,000
	To pay liabilities.		

In the final liquidation transaction, the remaining cash is disbursed to the partners. *The partners share in the cash according to their capital balances.* (*Gains and losses* on the sale of assets are shared by the partners on the basis of their profit-and-loss-sharing ratio.) The amount of cash left in the partnership is $130,000—the $10,000 beginning balance plus the $150,000 cash sale of assets minus the $30,000 cash payment of liabilities. The partners divide the remaining cash according to their capital balances:

Oct. 31	Avignon, Capital ($40,000 + $36,000)..............	76,000	
	Bloch, Capital ($20,000 + $12,000).................	32,000	
	Crane, Capital ($10,000 + $12,000).................	22,000	
	Cash..		130,000
	To pay cash in liquidation.		

A convenient way to summarize the transactions in a partnership liquidation is given in Exhibit 12-4. Remember: Upon liquidation, gains on the sale of assets are divided according to the *profit-and-loss ratio*. The final cash payment to the partners is based on *capital balances*.

 DAILY EXERCISE 12-17

DAILY EXERCISE 12-18

EXHIBIT 12-4 **Partnership Liquidation—Sale of Assets at a Gain**

					Capital		
	Cash	+	Noncash Assets	= Liabilities +	Avignon (60%) +	Bloch (20%) +	Crane (20%)
Balance before sale of assets	$ 10,000		$90,000	$30,000	$40,000	$20,000	$10,000
Sale of assets and sharing of gain ...	150,000		(90,000)		36,000	12,000	12,000
Balances...	160,000		0	30,000	76,000	32,000	22,000
Payment of liabilities......................	(30,000)			(30,000)			
Balances...	130,000		0	0	76,000	32,000	22,000
Payment of cash to partners	(130,000)				(76,000)	(32,000)	(22,000)
Balances...	$ 0		$ 0	$ 0	$ 0	$ 0	$ 0

After the payment of cash to the partners, the business has no assets, liabilities, or owners' equity. All the balances are zero. By the accounting equation, partnership assets *must* equal partnership liabilities plus partnership capital.

Sale of Noncash Assets at a Loss

Liquidation of a business often includes the sale of noncash assets at a loss. When this occurs, the partners' capital accounts are debited as they share the loss in their profit-and-loss-sharing ratio. Otherwise, the accounting follows the pattern illustrated for the sale of noncash assets at a gain.

THINK IT OVER

The liquidation of the Dirk & Cross partnership included the sale of assets at a $150,000 loss. Lorraine Dirk's capital balance of $45,000 was less than her $60,000 share of the loss. Allocation of losses to the partners created a $15,000 deficit (debit balance) in Dirk's capital account. Identify ways that the partnership could deal with the negative balance (a capital deficiency) in Dirk's capital account.

Answer: Two possibilities are

1. Dirk could contribute assets to the partnership in an amount equal to her capital deficiency.
2. Joseph Cross could absorb Dirk's capital deficiency by decreasing his own capital balance.

PARTNERSHIP FINANCIAL STATEMENTS

EXHIBIT 12-5 Financial Statements of a Partnership and a Proprietorship

Partnership financial statements are much like those of a proprietorship. However, a partnership income statement includes a section showing the division of net income to the partners. For example, the partnership of Leslie Gray and Wayne Hayward might report its statements for the year ended December 31, 20X3, as shown in Panel A of Exhibit 12-5. A proprietorship's statements are presented in Panel B for comparison.

PANEL A—Partnership

GRAY & HAYWARD CONSULTING
Income Statement
Year Ended December 31, 20X3

		Thousands
Revenues		$460
Expenses		(270)
Net income		$190
Allocation of net income:		
To Gray	$114	
To Hayward	76	$190

GRAY & HAYWARD CONSULTING
Statement of Owners' Equity
Year Ended December 31, 20X3

	Thousands	
	Gray	Hayward
Capital, December 31, 20X2	$ 50	$ 40
Additional investments	10	—
Net income	114	76
Subtotal	174	116
Drawings	(72)	(48)
Capital, December 31, 20X3	$102	$ 68

GRAY & HAYWARD CONSULTING
Balance Sheet
December 31, 20X3

Assets	Thousands
Cash and other assets	$170
Owners' Equity	
Gray, capital	$102
Hayward, capital	68
Total capital	$170

PANEL B—Proprietorship

GRAY CONSULTING
Income Statement
Year Ended December 31, 20X3

	Thousands
Revenues	$460
Expenses	(270)
Net income	$190

GRAY CONSULTING
Statement of Owners' Equity
Year Ended December 31, 20X3

	Thousands
Capital, December 31, 20X2	$ 90
Additional investment	10
Net income	190
Subtotal	290
Drawings	(120)
Capital, December 31, 20X3	$170

GRAY CONSULTING
Balance Sheet
December 31, 20X3

Assets	Thousands
Cash and other assets	$170
Owner's Equity	
Gray, capital	$170

EXHIBIT 12-6 Reporting Net Income for a Large Partnership

DAILY EXERCISE 12-19

DAILY EXERCISE 12-20

MAIN PRICE & ANDERS
Statements of Earnings
Year Ended August 31, 20X4

	Thousands
Fees for professional services	$2,507,690
Earnings for the year	$ 832,340
Allocation of Earnings:	
To partners active during the year—	
Resigned, retired, and deceased partners	$ 109,901
Partners active at year end	627,730
To retired and deceased partners—retirement and death benefits	18,310
Not allocated to partners—retained for specific partnership purposes	76,399
	$ 832,340
Average earnings per partner active at year end (1,340 partners)	$ 621

Large partnerships may not find it feasible to report the net income of every partner. Instead, the firm may report the allocation of net income to active and retired partners and average earnings per partner. Exhibit 12-6 shows how the accounting/consulting firm Main Price & Anders reported its earnings.

The following Decision Guidelines feature summarizes the main points of accounting for partnerships.

DECISION GUIDELINES

Accounting for Partnerships

DECISION	GUIDELINES
How to organize the business?	A partnership offers both advantages and disadvantages in comparison with proprietorships and corporations. (See Exhibit 12-2).
On what matters should the partners agree?	See the list on page 466, under the heading "The Written Partnership Agreement."
At what value does the partnership record assets and liabilities?	Current market value on the date of acquisition, because, in effect, the partnership is buying its assets at their current market value.

How are partnership profits and losses shared among the partners?	• Equally if there is no profit-and-loss-sharing agreement.
	• As provided in the partnership agreement. Can be based on the partners'
	  a. Stated fractions
	  b. Capital contributions
	  c. Service to the partnership
	  d. Salaries and interest on their capital contributions

What happens when a partner withdraws from the partnership?	The old partnership ceases to exist. The remaining partners may or may not form a new partnership.
How are new partners admitted to the partnership?	• *Purchase a partner's interest.* The old partnership is dissolved. The remaining partners may admit the new partner to the partnership. If not, the new partner gets no voice in the management of the firm but shares in the profits and losses. Close the withdrawing partner's Capital account, and open a Capital account for the new partner. Carry over the old partner's Capital balance to the Capital account of the new partner. • *Invest in the partnership.* Buying in at book value creates no bonus to any partner. Buying in at a price above book value creates a bonus to the old partners. Buying in at a price below book value creates a bonus for the new partner.

How to account for the withdrawal of a partner from the business?	• First, adjust and close the books up to the date of the partner's withdrawal from the business.
	• Second, appraise the assets and the liabilities at their current market value.
	• Third, account for the partner's withdrawal
	  a. At book value (no change in remaining partners' Capital balances)
	  b. At less than book value (increase the remaining partners' Capital balances)
	  c. At more than book value (decrease the remaining partners' Capital balances)

What happens if the partnership goes out of business?	Liquidate the partnership, as follows:
	  a. Adjust and close the partnership books up to the date of liquidation.
	  b. Sell the partnership's assets. Allocate gain or loss to the partner's Capital accounts based on their profit-and-loss ratio.
	  c. Pay the partnership liabilities.
	  d. Pay any remaining cash to the partners based on their Capital balances.

How do partnership financial statements differ from those of a proprietorship?	• The partnership income statement reports the allocation of net income or net loss to the partners. • The partnership balance sheet (or a separate schedule) reports the Capital balance of each partner. • The statement of cash flows is the same for a partnership as for a proprietorship.

www.prenhall.com/horngren

End-of-Chapter Assessment

SUMMARY PROBLEM

The partnership of Taylor & Uvalde is considering admitting Steven Vaughn as a partner on January 1, 20X5. The partnership general ledger includes the following balances on that date:

Cash......................................	$ 9,000	Total liabilities	$ 50,000
Other assets	110,000	Taylor, capital	45,000
		Uvalde, capital.........................	24,000
Total assets............................	$119,000	Total liabilities and capital.......	$119,000

Ross Taylor's share of profits and losses is 60%, and Thomas Uvalde's share is 40%.

Required (Items 1 and 2 Are Independent)

1. Suppose that Vaughn pays Uvalde $31,000 to acquire Uvalde's interest in the business. Taylor approves Vaughn as a partner.
   a. Record the transfer of owner's equity on the partnership books.
   b. Prepare the partnership balance sheet immediately after Vaughn is admitted as a partner.
2. Suppose that Vaughn becomes a partner by investing $31,000 cash to acquire a one-fourth interest in the business.
   a. Compute Vaughn's capital balance, and record his investment in the business.
   b. Prepare the partnership balance sheet immediately after Vaughn is admitted as a partner. Include the heading.
3. Which way of admitting Vaughn to the partnership increases its total assets? Give your reason.

Solution

Requirement 1

a. Jan. 1   Uvalde, Capital... 24,000

            Vaughn, Capital............................... 24,000

            To transfer Uvalde's equity in the partnership to Vaughn.

b. The balance sheet for the partnership of Taylor and Vaughn is identical to the balance sheet given for Taylor and Uvalde in the problem, except that Vaughn's name replaces Uvalde's name in the title and in the listing of Capital accounts.

Requirement 2

a. Computations of Vaughn's capital balance:

Partnership capital before Vaughn is admitted ($45,000 + $24,000)...	$ 69,000
Vaughn's investment in the partnership..................................	31,000
Partnership capital after Vaughn is admitted..........................	$100,000
Vaughn's capital in the partnership ($100,000 × 1/4)	$ 25,000

Jan. 1   Cash 31,000

            Vaughn, Capital 25,000

            Taylor, Capital [($31,000 − $25,000) × 0.60]......... 3,600

            Uvalde, Capital [($31,000 − $25,000) × 0.40] 2,400

            To admit Vaughn as a partner with a one-fourth interest in the business.

b.

TAYLOR, UVALDE, & VAUGHN
Balance Sheet
January 1, 20X5

Cash ($9,000 + $31,000)	$ 40,000	Total liabilities	$ 50,000
Other assets	110,000	Taylor, capital	
		($45,000 + $3,600)	48,600
		Uvalde, capital	
		($24,000 + $2,400)	26,400
		Vaughn, capital	25,000
Total assets	$150,000	Total liabilities and capital......	$150,000

Vaughn's investment in the partnership increases its total assets by the amount of his contribution. Total assets of the business are $150,000 after his investment, compared with $119,000 before. In contrast, Vaughn's purchase of Uvalde's interest in the business is a personal transaction between the two individuals. It does not affect the assets of the partnership regardless of the amount Vaughn pays Uvalde.

LESSONS LEARNED

1. *Identify the characteristics of a partnership.* A *partnership* is a business co-owned by two or more persons for profit. The characteristics of this form of business organization are its *ease of formation, limited life, mutual agency, unlimited liability,* and *no partnership income taxes.* A written *partnership agreement* establishes procedures for admission of a new partner, withdrawal of a partner, and the sharing of profits and losses among the partners.

2. *Account for the partners' investments in a partnership.* Accounting for a partnership is similar to accounting for a proprietorship. Each partner has an individual capital account and a withdrawal account.

3. *Allocate profits and losses to the partners.* Partners share net income or loss in any manner they choose. Common sharing agreements base the *profit-and-loss ratio* on a stated fraction, partners' capital contributions, and/or their service to the partnership.

4. *Account for the admission of a partner to the business.* An outside person may become a partner by purchasing a current partner's interest or by investing in the partner-

ship. The new partner may pay the current partners a bonus to join. Or the new partner may receive a bonus to join.

5. *Account for a partner's withdrawal (resignation) from the firm.* When a partner withdraws, partnership assets may be reappraised. Partners share any gain or loss on the asset revaluation on the basis of their profit-and-loss ratio. The withdrawing partner may receive payment equal to, greater than, or less than his or her capital book value, depending on the agreement with the other partners.

6. *Account for the liquidation of a partnership.* In *liquidation,* a partnership goes out of business by selling the assets, paying the liabilities, and disbursing any remaining cash to the partners.

7. *Prepare partnership financial statements.* Partnership *financial statements* are similar to those of a proprietorship. The partnership income statement commonly allocates net income to the partners, and the balance sheet has a Capital account for each partner.

ACCOUNTING VOCABULARY

articles of partnership   (p. 465)
dissolution   (p. 466)
general partnership   (p. 468)
limited liability partnership
   (p. 468)

limited partnership   (p. 468)
liquidation   (p. 482)
LLPs   (p. 468)
mutual agency   (p. 466)
partnership   (p. 465)

partnership agreement   (p. 465)
S Corporation   (p. 468)
unlimited personal liability
   (p. 466)

QUESTIONS

1. What is another name for a partnership agreement? List eight items that the agreement should specify.
2. Ron Montgomery, who is a partner in M&N Associates, commits the firm to a contract for a job within the scope of its regular business operations. What term describes Montgomery's ability to obligate the partnership?
3. If a partnership cannot pay a debt, who must make the payment? What term describes this obligation of the partners?
4. How is the income of a partnership taxed?
5. Identify the advantages and disadvantages of the partnership form of business organization.
6. Rex Randall and Ken Smith's partnership agreement states that Randall gets 60% of profits and Smith gets 40%. If the agreement does not discuss the treatment of losses, how are losses shared? How do the partners share profits and losses if the agreement specifies no profit-and-loss-sharing ratio?

7. Do partner withdrawals of cash for personal use affect the sharing of profits and losses by the partner? If so, explain how. If not, explain why not.
8. Name two events that can cause the dissolution of a partnership.
9. When a partner resigns from the partnership and receives assets greater than his or her capital balance, how is the excess shared by the other partners?
10. Name the three steps in liquidating a partnership.
11. The partnership of Cope and Hope is in the process of liquidation. How do the partners share (a) gains and losses on the sale of noncash assets, and (b) the final cash distribution?
12. Summarize the situations in which partnership allocations are based on (a) the profit-and-loss-sharing ratio, and (b) the partners' capital balances.

DAILY EXERCISES

Partnership characteristics
(Obj. 1)

DE12-1 After studying the characteristics of a partnership, write two short paragraphs, as follows:

1. Explain the *advantages* of a partnership over a proprietorship and a corporation.
2. Explain the *disadvantages* of a partnership over a proprietorship and a corporation.

Partnership characteristics
(Obj. 1)

DE12-2 Timothy Lane and Sam Medford are forming a business to imprint T-shirts. Lane suggests that they organize as a partnership in order to avoid the unlimited personal liability of a proprietorship. According to Lane, partnerships are not very risky.

Lane explains to Medford that if the business does not succeed, each partner can withdraw from the business, taking the same assets that he or she invested at its beginning. Lane states that the main disadvantage of the partnership form of organization is double taxation: First, the partnership pays a business income tax; second, each partner also pays personal income tax on his or her share of the business's profits.

Correct the errors in Lane's explanation.

A partner's investment in a partnership
(Obj. 2)

DE12-3 Dean Hahn invests a building in a partnership with Margo Klem. Hahn purchased the building in 20X1 for $300,000. Accumulated depreciation to the date of forming the partnership is $80,000. A real estate appraiser states that the building is now worth $285,000. Hahn wants $400,000 capital in the new partnership, but Klem objects. Klem believes that capital contribution into the partnership should be measured by the book value of his building.

Klem and Hahn seek your advice. Which value of the building is appropriate for measuring Hahn's capital, book value or current market value? State the reason for your answer. Give the partnership's journal entry to record Hahn's investment in the business.

Investments by partners
(Obj. 2)

DE12-4 Seth Green and Nate Smith are forming the partnership Sun Florida Development to develop a theme park near Panama City. Green contributes cash of $4 million and land valued at $17 million. When Green purchased the land in 20X1, its cost was $8 million. The partnership will assume Green's $3 million note payable on the land. Smith invests cash of $10 million and construction equipment that he purchased for $7 million (accumulated depreciation to date, $3 million). The equipment's market value is equal to its book value.

1. Before recording any journal entries, compute the partnership's total assets, total liabilities, and total owners' equity immediately after organizing.
2. Journalize the partnership's receipt of assets and liabilities from Green and from Smith. Record each asset at its current market value with no entry to accumulated depreciation.
3. Use your journal entries to prove the correctness of total owners' equity from requirement 1.

Partners' profits, losses, and capital balances
(Obj. 3)

DE12-5 Examine the Benz and Hanna balance sheet in Exhibit 12-3, page 471. Note that Benz invested far more in the partnership than Hanna. Suppose the two partners fail to agree upon a profit-and-loss-sharing ratio. For the first month (June 20X5), the partnership lost $15,000.

1. How much of this loss goes to Benz? How much goes to Hanna?
2. Assume the partners withdrew no cash or other assets during June. What is each partner's capital balance at June 30? Prepare a T-account for each partner's capital to answer this question.

Partners' profits, drawings, and capital balances; closing entries
(Obj. 3)

DE12-6 ← *Link Back to Chapter 4 (Closing Entries).* Return to the Benz and Hanna balance sheet in Exhibit 12-3, page 471. The partnership earned $115,000 during the year ended May 31, 20X6, its first year of operation. The partners share profits and losses based on their capital balances at the beginning of the year. During the first year, Benz withdrew $70,000 cash from the business and Hanna's drawings totaled $50,000.

1. Journalize the entries for (a) partner withdrawals of cash, (b) closing the business's profits into the partner's capital accounts at May 31, 20X6, and (c) closing the partners' drawing accounts.
2. Post to the partners' capital accounts after inserting their beginning amounts. What is the amount of total partnership capital at May 31, 20X6?

Allocating partnership profits based on capital contributions and service
(Obj. 3)

DE12-7 Lawson, Martinez, and Edwards have capital balances of $20,000, $30,000, and $50,000, respectively. The partners share profits and losses as follows:

a. The first $40,000 is divided based on the partners' capital balances.
b. The next $40,000 is based on service, equally shared by Lawson and Edwards.
c. The remainder is divided equally.

Compute each partner's share of the business's $140,000 net income for the year.

DE12-8 Lucy Fung and Ako Kiawa have capital balances of $30,000 and $40,000, respectively. The partners share profits and losses as follows:

Allocating partnership profits based on salaries and interest (Obj. 3)

a. Fung receives a salary of $15,000 and Kiawa a salary of $10,000.
b. The partners earn 7% interest on their capital balances.
c. The remainder is shared equally.

Compute each partner's share of the year's net income of $50,000.

DE12-9 Study the Ingel and Jay partnership balance sheet near the top of page 476. Claire Reynoldo pays $110,000 to purchase Michael Jay's interest in the partnership.

Admitting a partner who purchases an existing partner's interest (Obj. 4)

1. Journalize the partnership's transaction to admit Reynoldo to the partnership. What happens to the $20,000 difference between Reynoldo's payment and Jay's capital balance?
2. Must Robin Ingel accept Claire Reynoldo as a full partner? What right does Reynoldo have after purchasing Jay's interest in the partnership?

DE12-10 Return to the partnership balance sheet of Ingel and Jay near the top of page 476. Larry Welsh invests cash of $80,000 to acquire a one-third interest in the partnership.

Admitting a partner who invests in the business (Obj. 4)

1. Does Welsh's investment provide a bonus to the partners? Show calculations to support your answer.
2. Journalize the partnership's receipt of the $80,000 from Welsh.

Admitting a new partner; bonus to the existing partners (Obj. 4)

DE12-11 Study the partnership balance sheet of Nagasawa and Osburn on page 476. Suppose Christine Kliptel invests $50,000 to purchase a one-fifth interest in the new partnership of Nagasawa, Osburn, and Kliptel (NOK Partners).
Journalize the partnership's receipt of cash from Kliptel.

Preparing a partnership balance sheet (Obj. 7)

DE12-12 This exercise uses the data given in Daily Exercise 12-11. After recording the partnership's receipt of cash from Kliptel in Daily Exercise 12-11, prepare the balance sheet of the new partnership of NOK Partners at June 30, 20X2. Include a complete heading.

Admitting a new partner; bonus to the new partner (Obj. 4)

DE12-13 Refer to the partnership balance sheet of Page and Franco near the top of page 478 and the paragraph immediately following the balance sheet. Assume Everett invests $140,000 to acquire a 30% interest in the new partnership of Page, Franco, and Everett.
Journalize the partnership's receipt of cash from Everett.

DE12-14 Examine the Green, Henry, and Isaac balance sheet at the top of page 480.

Withdrawal of a partner (Obj. 5)

1. The partners share profits and losses as follows: 25% to Green, 50% to Henry, and 25% to Isaac. Suppose Susan Green is withdrawing from the business, and the partners agree that no appraisal of assets is needed. How much in assets can Green take from the partnership? Give the reason for your answer, including an explanation of why the profit-and-loss-sharing ratio is not used for this determination.
2. Henry and Isaac plan to form a new partnership to continue the business. If Green demands cash for her full settlement upon withdrawing from the business, how can Henry and Isaac come up with the cash to pay Green? Identify two ways.

Withdrawal of a partner at more than book value; asset revaluation (Obj. 5)

DE12-15 Return to the Green, Henry, and Isaac partnership balance sheet near the middle of page 480. Suppose Henry is retiring from the business and the partners agree to revalue the assets at their current market value. A real-estate appraiser issues his professional opinion that the current market value of the land is $150,000. The book values of all other assets approximate their current market value.
Journalize (a) the revaluation of the land, (b) borrowing $90,500 on a note payable in order to pay Henry, and (c) payment of $90,500 to Henry upon his retirement from the business on July 31.

Withdrawal of a partner at less than book value (Obj. 5)

DE12-16 This exercise uses the data given in Daily Exercise 12-15 with one modification. Assume Henry is retiring from the partnership and agrees to take cash of $60,500.
Journalize the payment of $60,500 to Henry upon his withdrawal from the partnership.

Liquidation of a partnership at a loss (Obj. 6)

DE12-17 Use the data in Exhibit 12-4, page 483. Suppose the partnership of Avignon, Bloch, and Crane liquidates by selling all noncash assets for $75,000.
Complete the liquidation schedule as shown in Exhibit 12-4.

DE12-18 This exercise builds on the solution to Daily Exercise 12-17. After completing the liquidation schedule in Daily Exercise 12-17, journalize the partnership's (a) sale of noncash assets for $75,000 (use a single account for Noncash Assets), (b) payment of liabilities, and (c) payment of cash to the partners. Include an explanation with each entry.

Liquidation of a partnership (Obj. 6)

DE12-19 This exercise uses the Green, Henry, and Isaac balance sheet, after revaluation of inventory and land, given in the middle of page 480. Furthermore, assume Isaac has withdrawn from the partnership at less than his book value, as recorded at the top of page 481.
Prepare the balance sheet of the new partnership of Green and Henry on July 31.

Partnership balance sheet (Obj. 7)

Partnership income statement
(Obj. 7)

DE12-20 The partnership of Frost and Martin had these balances at September 30, 20X4:

Cash	$20,000	Service revenue	$140,000
Liabilities	40,000	Frost, capital	30,000
Martin, capital	10,000	Total expenses	35,000
Other assets	60,000		

Frost gets two-thirds of profits and losses, and Martin one-third.

Prepare the partnership's income statement for the year ended September 30, 20X4.

EXERCISES

Organizing a partnership
(Obj. 1)

E12-1 Suzanne Drake, a friend from college, approaches you about forming a partnership to export software. Since graduating, Drake has worked for the International Trade Bank, developing important contacts among government officials and business leaders in Eastern Europe. Drake believes she is in a unique position to capitalize on the growing market in Eastern Europe for American computers. With expertise in finance, you would have responsibility for accounting and finance in the partnership.

Required

Discuss the advantages and disadvantages of organizing the export business as a partnership rather than a proprietorship. Comment on how partnership income is taxed and how your taxes would change if you organized as an S corporation.

Recording a partner's investment
(Obj. 2)

E12-2 Mason Flute has been operating an apartment-locater service as a proprietorship. He and Barrett Schraeder have decided to reorganize the business as a partnership. Flute's investment in the partnership consists of cash, $16,300; accounts receivable, $10,600, less allowance for uncollectibles, $800; office furniture, $2,700, less accumulated depreciation, $1,100; a small building, $55,000, less accumulated depreciation, $27,500; accounts payable, $3,300; and a note payable to the bank, $10,000.

To determine Flute's equity in the partnership, he and Schraeder hire an independent appraiser. This outside party provides the following market values of the assets and liabilities that Flute is contributing to the business: cash, accounts receivable, office furniture, accounts payable, and note payable—the same as Flute's book value; allowance for uncollectible accounts, $2,900; building, $71,000; and accrued expenses payable (including interest on the note payable), $1,200.

Required

Make the entry on the partnership books to record Flute's investment.

Computing partners' shares of
net income and net loss
(Obj. 3)

E12-3 Adam Meppen and Bailey Quaid form a partnership, investing $40,000 and $70,000, respectively. Determine their shares of net income or net loss for each of the following situations:

  a. Net loss is $52,000 and the partners have no written partnership agreement.

  b. Net income is $77,000, and the partnership agreement states that the partners share profits and losses on the basis of their capital contributions.

  c. Net loss is $33,000, and the partnership agreement states that the partners share profits on the basis of their capital contributions.

  d. Net income is $98,000. The first $60,000 is shared on the basis of partner capital contributions. The next $30,000 is based on partner service, with Meppen receiving 30% and Quaid receiving 70%. The remainder is shared equally.

Computing partners' capital
balances
(Obj. 3)

E12-4 Adam Meppen withdrew cash of $47,000 for personal use, and Bailey Quaid withdrew cash of $53,000 during the year. Using the data from situation (d) in Exercise 12-3, journalize the entries to close (a) the income summary account, and (b) the partners' drawing accounts. Explanations are not required. What was the overall effect on partnership capital?

Admitting a new partner
(Obj. 4)

E12-5 Trey Falco is admitted to a partnership. Prior to his admission, the partnership books show Sean Graham's capital balance at $100,000 and Kelly Ott's capital balance at $50,000. Compute each partner's equity on the books of the new partnership under the following plans:

  a. Falco pays $92,000 for Ott's equity. Falco's payment is not an investment in the partnership, but instead goes directly to Ott.

  b. Falco invests $75,000 to acquire a one-third interest in the partnership.

  c. Falco invests $60,000 to acquire a one-fourth interest in the partnership.

E12-6 Make the partnership journal entry to record the admission of Falco under plans (a), (b), and (c) in Exercise 12-5. Explanations are not required.

Admitting a new partner   (Obj. 4)

E12-7 After the books are closed, Echols & Schaeffer's partnership balance sheet reports capital of $60,000 for Echols and $80,000 for Schaeffer. Echols is withdrawing from the firm. The partners agree to write down partnership assets by $45,000. They have shared profits and losses in the ratio of one-third to Echols and two-thirds to Schaeffer. The partnership agreement states that a withdrawing partner will receive assets equal to the book value of his owner's equity.

Withdrawal of a partner (Obj. 5)

1. How much will Echols receive? Schaeffer will continue to operate the business as a proprietorship.
2. What is Schaeffer's beginning capital on the proprietorship books?

E12-8 Eve Bermuda is retiring from the partnership of Bermuda, Rye, and Augustine on May 31. The partner capital balances are Bermuda, $36,000; Rye, $51,000; and Augustine, $22,000. The partners agree to have the partnership assets revalued to current market values. The independent appraiser reports that the book value of the inventory should be decreased by $12,000, and the book value of the land should be increased by $32,000. The partners agree to these revaluations. The profit-and-loss ratio has been 5:3:2 for Bermuda, Rye, and Augustine, respectively. In retiring from the firm, Bermuda receives $25,000 cash and a $25,000 note from the partnership.

Withdrawal of a partner (Obj. 5)

Required

Journalize (a) the asset revaluations, and (b) Bermuda's withdrawal from the firm.

E12-9 Barry, McCall, and Flaten are liquidating their partnership. Before selling the noncash assets and paying the liabilities, the capital balances are Barry, $23,000; McCall, $20,000; and Flaten, $11,000. The partnership agreement divides profits and losses equally.

Liquidation of a partnership (Obj. 6)

Required

1. After selling the noncash assets and paying the liabilities, the partnership has cash of $54,000. How much cash will each partner receive in final liquidation?
2. After selling the noncash assets and paying the liabilities, the partnership has cash of $45,000. How much cash will each partner receive in final liquidation?

E12-10 Prior to liquidation, the accounting records of Deluth, Liu, and Bush included the following balances and profit-and-loss-sharing percentages:

Liquidation of a partnership (Obj. 6)

					Capital		
	Cash	+	Noncash Assets	= Liabilities +	Deluth (40%) +	Liu (30%) +	Bush (30%)
Balances before sale of assets............	$ 8,000		$57,000	$19,000	$20,000	$15,000	$11,000

The partnership sold the noncash assets for $69,000, paid the liabilities, and disbursed the remaining cash to the partners. Complete the summary of transactions in the liquidation of the partnership. Use the format illustrated in Exhibit 12-4.

E12-11 The partnership of Valahu, Leman, and Sucre is dissolving. Business assets, liabilities, and partners' capital balances prior to dissolution follow. The partners share profits and losses as follows: Marie Valahu, 25%; Pierre Leman, 45%; and Anna Sucre, 30%.

Liquidation of a partnership (Obj. 6)

Required

Create a spreadsheet or solve manually (see the top of page 492)—as directed by your instructor—to show the ending balances in all accounts after the noncash assets are sold for $136,000 and for $90,000. Determine the unknown amounts. Identify two ways the partners can deal with the negative ending balance in Sucre's capital account.

Challenge Exercise

E12-12 On October 31, 20X2, Steve Klatt and Russell Stover agree to combine their proprietorships as a partnership. Their balance sheets on October 31 are shown on page 492.

Partnership balance sheet (Obj. 7)

Required

Prepare the partnership balance sheet at October 31, 20X2.

	A	B	C	D	E	F
1			VALAHU, LEMAN, AND SUCRE			
2			Sale of Noncash Assets			
3			(For $136,000)			
4						
5		Noncash		Valahu	Leman	Sucre
6	Cash	Assets	Liabilities	Capital	Capital	Capital
7	$ 6,000	$126,000	$77,000	$12,000	$37,000	$6,000
8	136,000	(126,000)		?	?	?
9						
10	$142,000	$ 0	$77,000	$?	$?	$?
11						
12				($A8–$B7) * .25		
13						
14						
15			(For $90,000)			
16		Noncash		Valahu	Leman	Sucre
17	Cash	Assets	Liabilities	Capital	Capital	Capital
18	$ 6,000	$126,000	$77,000	$12,000	$37,000	$6,000
19	90,000	(126,000)		?	?	?
20						
21	$96,000	$ 0	$77,000	$?	$?	$?
22						
23				($A19–$B18) * .25		
24						

EXERCISE 12-12
Klatt and Stover

	Klatt's Business		Stover's Business	
	Book Value	Current Market Value	Book Value	Current Market Value
Assets				
Cash	$ 3,700	$ 3,700	$ 4,000	$ 4,000
Accounts receivable (net)	22,000	20,200	8,000	6,300
Inventory	51,000	46,000	34,000	35,100
Plant assets (net)	121,800	103,500	53,500	57,400
Total assets	$198,500	$173,400	$99,500	$102,800
Liabilities and Capital				
Accounts payable	$ 25,500	$ 25,500	$ 8,300	$ 8,300
Accrued expenses payable	2,200	2,200	1,400	1,400
Notes payable	55,000	55,000		
Klatt, capital	115,800	?		
Stover, capital			89,800	?
Total liabilities and capital	$198,500	$173,400	$99,500	$102,800

(Group A) PROBLEMS

Writing a partnership agreement
(Obj. 1)

P12-1A Levita Nuñez and Rosa Lupe Gaitan are discussing the formation of a partnership to import dresses from Guatemala. Nuñez is especially artistic, so she will travel to Central America to buy merchandise. Gaitan is a super salesperson and has already lined up several large stores to which she can sell the dresses.

Required

Write a partnership agreement to cover all elements essential for the business to operate smoothly. Make up names, amounts, profit-and-loss-sharing percentages, and so on as needed.

Investments by partners
(Obj. 2, 7)

P12-2A Beth Saran and Jake Gentry formed a partnership on March 15. The partners agreed to invest equal amounts of capital. Gentry invested his proprietorship's assets and liabilities (credit balances in parentheses). See the table at the top of the next page.

	Gentry's Book Value	Current Market Value
Accounts receivable............................	$12,000	$12,000
Allowance for doubtful accounts.......	(740)	(1,360)
Inventory...	43,850	31,220
Prepaid expenses	3,700	3,700
Store equipment..................................	36,700	26,600
Accumulated depreciation.................	(9,200)	(–0–)
Accounts payable................................	(22,300)	(22,300)

On March 15, Saran invested cash in an amount equal to the current market value of Gentry's partnership capital. The partners decided that Gentry would earn 70% of partnership profits because he would manage the business. Saran agreed to accept 30% of profits. During the period ended December 31, the partnership earned net income of $70,000. Saran's drawings were $27,000, and Gentry's drawings were $41,000.

Required

1. Journalize the partners' initial investments.
2. Prepare the partnership balance sheet immediately after its formation on March 15.
3. Journalize the December 31 entries to close the Income Summary account and the partners' drawing accounts.

P12-3A Lost Pines Escape is a partnership, and its owners are considering admitting Victor Lampe as a new partner. On July 31 of the current year, the capital accounts of the three existing partners and their shares of profits and losses are as follows:

Admitting a new partner (Obj. 4)

	Capital	Profit-and-Loss Ratio
Eric Runyan................	$48,000	1/6
Sara Braden................	64,000	1/3
Ken Maness................	88,000	1/2

Required

Journalize the admission of Lampe as a partner on July 31 for each of the following independent situations:

1. Lampe pays Maness $114,000 cash to purchase Maness's interest.
2. Lampe invests $50,000 in the partnership, acquiring a one-fifth interest in the business.
3. Lampe invests $50,000 in the partnership, acquiring a one-eighth interest in the business.
4. Lampe invests $30,000 in the partnership, acquiring an 18% interest in the business.

P12-4A Rudy Trump, Monica Rivers, and Courtney Jetta have formed a partnership. Trump invested $20,000; Rivers, $40,000; and Jetta, $60,000. Trump will manage the store, Rivers will work in the store three-quarters of the time, and Jetta will not work.

Computing partners' shares of net income and net loss (Obj. 3, 7)

Required

1. Compute the partners' shares of profits and losses under each of the following plans:
   a. Net income is $87,000, and the articles of partnership do not specify how profits and losses are shared.
   b. Net loss is $47,000, and the partnership agreement allocates 45% of profits to Trump, 35% to Rivers, and 20% to Jetta. The agreement does not discuss the sharing of losses.
   c. Net income is $104,000. The first $50,000 is allocated on the basis of salaries of $34,000 for Trump and $16,000 for Rivers. The remainder is allocated on the basis of partner capital contributions.
   d. Net income for the year ended September 30, 20X4, is $86,000. The first $30,000 is allocated on the basis of partner capital contributions. The next $30,000 is based on service, with $20,000 going to Trump and $10,000 going to Rivers. Any remainder is shared equally.
2. Revenues for the year ended September 30, 20X4, were $572,000, and expenses were $486,000. Under plan (d), prepare the partnership income statement for the year.

P12-5A Custom Homes is a partnership owned by three individuals. The partners share profits and losses in the ratio of 30% to Pam Tracy, 40% to Bill Mertz, and 30% to Cameron Brucks. At December 31, 20X3, the firm has the balance sheet shown at the top of page 494. Tracy withdraws from the partnership on this date.

Withdrawal of a partner (Obj. 4, 5)

Required

Record Tracy's withdrawal from the partnership under the following plans:

Cash		$ 25,000	Total liabilities	$103,000
Accounts receivable	$ 16,000			
Less allowance for				
uncollectibles	(1,000)	15,000		
Inventory		92,000	Tracy, capital	38,000
Equipment	130,000		Mertz, capital	49,000
Less accumulated			Brucks, capital	42,000
depreciation	(30,000)	100,000	Total liabilities and	
Total assets		$232,000	capital	$232,000

1. Tracy gives her interest in the business to Sally Schuster, her cousin.
2. In personal transactions, Tracy sells her equity in the partnership to Walt Fair and Beverly Holtz, who each pay Tracy $35,000 for half her interest. Mertz and Brucks agree to accept Fair and Holtz as partners.
3. The partnership pays Tracy cash of $9,000 and gives her a note payable for the remainder of her book equity in settlement of her partnership interest.
4. Tracy receives cash of $6,000 and a note payable for $34,000 from the partnership.
5. The partners agree that the equipment is worth $160,000 and that accumulated depreciation should remain at $30,000. After the revaluation, the partnership settles with Tracy by giving her cash of $15,000 and inventory for the remainder of her book equity.

Liquidation of a partnership
(Obj. 6)

P12-6A The partnership of Jackson, Pierce, & Fenner has experienced operating losses for three consecutive years. The partners—who have shared profits and losses in the ratio of Leigh Jackson, 15%; Trent Pierce, 60%; and Bruce Fenner, 25%—are considering the liquidation of the business. They ask you to analyze the effects of liquidation under various possibilities regarding the sale of the noncash assets. They present the following condensed partnership balance sheet at December 31, end of the current year:

Cash	$ 7,000	Liabilities	$ 63,000
Noncash assets	163,000	Jackson, capital	24,000
		Pierce, capital	66,000
		Fenner, capital	17,000
		Total liabilities and	
Total assets	$170,000	capital	$170,000

Required

1. Prepare a summary of liquidation transactions (as illustrated in Exhibit 12-4) for each of the following situations:
   a. The noncash assets are sold for $183,000.
   b. The noncash assets are sold for $141,000.
2. Make the journal entries to record the liquidation transactions in requirement 1(b).

Liquidation of a partnership
(Obj. 6)

P12-7A ◄ *Link Back to Chapter 4 (Closing Entries).* ABS & Company is a partnership owned by Alberts, Beech, and Sumner, who share profits and losses in the ratio of 1:3:4. The adjusted trial balance of the partnership (in condensed form) at June 30, end of the current fiscal year, follows.

ABS & COMPANY		
Adjusted Trial Balance		
June 30, 20XX		
Cash	$ 24,000	
Noncash assets	116,000	
Liabilities		$100,000
Alberts, capital		22,000
Beech, capital		41,000
Sumner, capital		62,000
Alberts, drawing	14,000	
Beech, drawing	35,000	
Sumner, drawing	54,000	
Revenues		108,000
Expenses	90,000	
Totals	$333,000	$333,000

Required

1. Prepare the June 30 entries to close the revenue, expense, income summary, and drawing accounts.
2. Insert the opening capital balances in the partners' capital accounts, post the closing entries to the capital accounts, and determine each partner's ending capital balance.
3. The partnership liquidates on June 30 by selling the noncash assets for $105,000. Using the ending balances of the partners' capital accounts computed in requirement 2, prepare a summary of liquidation transactions (as illustrated in Exhibit 12-4).

PROBLEMS

(Group B)

P12-1B Anne Avonlee and Gus Teamley are discussing the formation of a partnership to install payroll accounting systems. Avonlee is skilled in systems design, and she is convinced that her designs will draw large sales volumes. Teamley is a super salesperson and has already lined up several clients.

Writing a partnership agreement (Obj. 1)

Required

Write a partnership agreement to cover all elements essential for the business to operate smoothly. Make up names, amounts, profit-and-loss-sharing percentages, and so on as needed.

P12-2B On June 30, Lou Busby and Marshall Box formed a partnership. The partners agreed to invest equal amounts of capital. Busby invested his proprietorship's assets and liabilities (credit balances in parentheses).

Investments by partners (Obj. 2, 7)

	Busby Book Value	Current Market Value
Accounts receivable	$ 7,200	$ 7,200
Allowance for doubtful accounts	(–0–)	(1,050)
Inventory	22,340	24,100
Prepaid expenses	1,700	1,700
Office equipment	45,900	27,600
Accumulated depreciation	(15,300)	–0–
Accounts payable	(19,100)	(19,100)

On June 30, Box invested cash in an amount equal to the current market value of Busby's partnership capital. The partners decided that Busby would earn two-thirds of partnership profits because he would manage the business. Box agreed to accept one-third of the profits. During the remainder of the year, the partnership earned net income of $75,000. Busby's drawings were $39,100, and Box's drawings were $31,000.

Required

1. Journalize the partners' initial investments.
2. Prepare the partnership balance sheet immediately after its formation on June 30.
3. Journalize the December 31 entries to close the Income Summary account and the partners' drawing accounts.

P12-3B Cedarlake Solutions is a partnership, and its owners are considering admitting Emily Conyers as a new partner. On March 31 of the current year, the capital accounts of the three existing partners and their shares of profits and losses are as follows:

Admitting a new partner (Obj. 4)

	Capital	Profit-and-Loss Share
Nick Nelson	$ 40,000	15%
Luke Bright	100,000	30
Lela Clapton	160,000	55

Required

Journalize the admission of Conyers as a partner on March 31 for each of the following independent situations:

1. Conyers pays Clapton $219,000 cash to purchase Clapton's interest in the partnership.
2. Conyers invests $60,000 in the partnership, acquiring a one-sixth interest in the business.
3. Conyers invests $80,000 in the partnership, acquiring a one-fourth interest in the business.
4. Conyers invests $50,000 in the partnership, acquiring a 12% interest in the business.

Computing partners' shares of
net income and net loss
(Obj. 3, 7)

P12-4B Charles Lake, Liz Wood, and Hal Parks have formed a partnership. Lake invested $15,000, Wood $18,000, and Parks $27,000. Lake will manage the store, Wood will work in the store half-time, and Parks will not work in the business.

Required

1. Compute the partners' shares of profits and losses under each of the following plans:
   a. Net loss is $42,900, and the articles of partnership do not specify how profits and losses are shared.
   b. Net loss is $60,000, and the partnership agreement allocates 40% of profits to Lake, 25% to Wood, and 35% to Parks. The agreement does not discuss the sharing of losses.
   c. Net income is $92,000. The first $40,000 is allocated on the basis of salaries, with Lake receiving $28,000 and Wood receiving $12,000. The remainder is allocated on the basis of partner capital contributions.
   d. Net income for the year ended January 31, 20X4, is $210,000. The first $75,000 is allocated on the basis of partner capital contributions, and the next $36,000 is based on service, with Lake receiving $28,000 and Wood receiving $8,000. Any remainder is shared equally.
2. Revenues for the year ended January 31, 20X4, were $870,000, and expenses were $660,000. Under plan (d), prepare the partnership income statement for the year.

P12-5B Priority Accounting Firm is a partnership owned by three individuals. The partners share profits and losses in the ratio of 28% to Cary Blesh, 38% to Dick McNut, and 34% to Jen Tate. At December 31, 20X2, the firm has the following balance sheet:

Cash		$ 12,000	Total liabilities	$ 75,000
Accounts receivable	$ 22,000			
Less allowance for				
uncollectibles	(4,000)	18,000		
Building	$310,000		Blesh, capital..............	83,000
Less accumulated			McNut, capital............	50,000
depreciation	(70,000)	240,000	Tate, capital	62,000
			Total liabilities and	
Total assets		$270,000	capital......................	$270,000

McNut withdraws from the partnership on December 31, 20X2, to establish his own consulting practice.

Required

Record McNut's withdrawal from the partnership under the following plans:

1. McNut gives his interest in the business to Rich Blynn, his nephew.
2. In personal transactions, McNut sells his equity in the partnership to Ashley Napper and Jim Lucks, who each pay McNut $40,000 for half his interest. Blesh and Tate agree to accept Napper and Lucks as partners.
3. The partnership pays McNut cash of $15,000 and gives him a note payable for the remainder of his book equity in settlement of his partnership interest.
4. McNut receives cash of $10,000 and a note for $70,000 from the partnership.
5. The partners agree that the building is worth only $250,000 and that its accumulated depreciation should remain at $70,000. After the revaluation, the partnership settles with McNut by giving him cash of $14,100 and a note payable for the remainder of his book equity.

P12-6B The partnership of Parr, Johnston, & Rake has experienced operating losses for three consecutive years. The partners—who have shared profits and losses in the ratio of Sharon Parr 10%; Alicia Johnston, 30%; and Chet Rake, 60%—are considering the liquidation of the business. They ask you to analyze the effects of liquidation under various possibilities regarding the sale of the noncash assets. They present the following condensed partnership balance sheet at December 31, end of the current year:

Cash	$ 27,000	Liabilities	$131,000
Noncash assets...................	202,000	Parr, capital.........................	21,000
		Johnston, capital	39,000
		Rake, capital	38,000
Total assets........................	$229,000	Total liabilities and capital ...	$229,000

Required

1. Prepare a summary of liquidation transactions (as illustrated in Exhibit 12-4) for each of the following situations:
   a. The noncash assets are sold for $208,000.
   b. The noncash assets are sold for $189,000.
2. Make the journal entries to record the liquidation transactions in requirement 1(b).

Liquidation of a partnership (Obj. 6)

P12-7B ◄ *Link Back to Chapter 4 (Closing Entries)*. VT&P is a partnership owned by Vela, Thomas, and Prago, who share profits and losses in the ratio of 5:3:2. The adjusted trial balance of the partnership (in condensed form) at September 30, end of the current fiscal year, follows.

VT&P Adjusted Trial Balance September 30, 20XX		
Cash	$ 10,000	
Noncash assets	177,000	
Liabilities...........................		$135,000
Vela, capital.......................		57,000
Thomas, capital		44,000
Prago, capital.....................		21,000
Vela, drawing	45,000	
Thomas, drawing	37,000	
Prago, drawing.................	18,000	
Revenues...........................		211,000
Expenses	181,000	
Totals................................	$468,000	$468,000

Required

1. Prepare the September 30 entries to close the revenue, expense, income summary, and drawing accounts.
2. Insert the opening capital balances in the partner capital accounts, post the closing entries to the capital accounts, and determine each partner's ending capital balance.
3. The partnership liquidates on September 30 by selling the noncash assets for $147,000. Using the ending balances of the partner capital accounts computed in requirement 2, prepare a summary of liquidation transactions (as illustrated in Exhibit 12-4).

APPLY YOUR KNOWLEDGE

DECISION CASES

Settling disagreements among partners (Obj. 3)

Case 1. Kimberly Gardner invested $20,000 and Leah Johanssen invested $10,000 in a public relations firm that has operated for ten years. Neither partner has made an additional investment. Gardner and Johanssen have shared profits and losses in the ratio of 2:1, which is the ratio of their investments in the business. Gardner manages the office, supervises the 16 employees, and does the accounting. Johanssen, the moderator of a television talk show, is responsible for marketing. Her high profile generates important revenue for the business. During the year ended December 20X4, the partnership earned net income of $87,000, shared in the 2:1 ratio. On December 31, 20X4, Gardner's capital balance was $150,000, and Johanssen's capital balance was $100,000.

Required

Respond to each of the following situations.

1. What explains the difference between the ratio of partner capital balances at December 31, 20X4, and the 2:1 ratio of partner investments and profit sharing?
2. Johanssen believes that the profit-and-loss-sharing ratio is unfair. She proposes a change, but Gardner insists on keeping the 2:1 ratio. What two factors may underlie Johanssen's unhappiness?
3. During January 20X5, Gardner learned that revenues of $18,000 were omitted from the reported 20X4 income. She brings this omission to Johanssen's attention, pointing out that Gardner's share of this added income is two-thirds, or $12,000, and Johanssen's share is one-third, or $6,000. Johanssen believes that they should share this added income on the basis of their capital balances—60%, or $10,800, to Gardner and 40%, or $7,200, to herself. Which partner is correct? Why?

4. Assume that the 20X4 $18,000 omission was an account payable for an operating expense. On what basis would the partners share this amount?

Case 2. The following questions relate to issues faced by partnerships.

1. The text suggests that a written partnership agreement should be drawn up between the partners in a partnership. One benefit of an agreement is that it provides a mechanism for resolving disputes between the partners. List five areas of dispute that might be resolved by a partnership agreement.
2. The statement has been made that "if you must take on a partner, make sure the partner is richer than you are." Why is this statement valid?
3. Corwin & Corwin is a law partnership. Natalie Corwin is planning to retire from the partnership and move to Israel. What options are available to Corwin to enable her to convert her share of the partnership assets to cash?

ETHICAL ISSUE

Tracy Wynn and Lee Spitz operate New England Engraving in Portsmouth, New Hampshire. The partners split profits and losses equally, and each takes an annual salary of $80,000. To even out the workload, Spitz does the buying and Wynn serves as the accountant. From time to time, they use small amounts of store merchandise for personal use. In preparing for her daughter's wedding, Wynn took engraved invitations and other goods that cost $2,700. She recorded the transaction as follows:

Cost of Goods Sold	2,700
Inventory	2,700

1. How should Wynn have recorded this transaction?
2. Discuss the ethical dimensions of Wynn's action.

FINANCIAL STATEMENT CASE

KPMG is an international accounting firm. Summary data from the partnership's *19X7 Annual Report* follow:

(Dollars in millions except where indicated)	19X7	19X6	Years Ended June 30 19X5	19X4	19X3
Revenues					
Assurance	$1,234	$1,122	$1,064	$1,093	$1,070
Consulting	1,007	775	658	473	349
Tax	743	628	567	515	557
Total Revenues	$2,984	$2,525	$2,289	$2,081	$1,976
Operating Summary					
Revenues	$2,984	$2,525	$2,289	$2,081	$1,976
Personnel Costs	1,215	1,004	887	805	726
Other Costs	1,212	1,030	967	898	829
Income to Partners	$ 557	$ 491	$ 435	$ 378	$ 421
Statistical Data					
Average Number of Partners	1,494	1,428	1,413	1,449	1,453

Required

1. What percentages of total revenues did KPMG earn by performing assurance services (similar to audit), consulting services, and tax services during 19X3? What were the percentages in 19X7? Which type of services grew the most from 19X3 to 19X7?
2. Compute the average revenue per partner in 19X7.
3. How much net income did each KPMG partner earn, on average, in 19X7?

TEAM PROJECT

Visit a business partnership in your area, and interview one or more of the partners. Obtain answers to the following questions and ask your instructor for directions. As directed by your instructor, either (a) prepare a written report of your findings, or (b) make a presentation to your class.

Required

1. Why did you organize the business as a partnership? What advantages does the partnership form of organization offer the business? What are the disadvantages of the partnership form of organization?
2. Is the business a general partnership, or is it a limited partnership?
3. Do the partners have a written partnership agreement? What does the agreement cover? Obtain a copy if possible.
4. Who manages the business? Do all partners participate in day-to-day management, or is management the responsibility of only certain partners?
5. If there is no written agreement, what is the mechanism for making key decisions?
6. Have you ever admitted a new partner? If so, when? What are the partnership's procedures for admitting a new partner?
7. Has a partner ever withdrawn from the business? If so, when? What are the partnership's procedures for settling up with a withdrawing partner?
8. If possible, learn how the partnership divides profits and losses among the partners.
9. Ask for any additional insights the partner you interview can provide about the business.

INTERNET EXERCISE

Arthur Andersen LLP is a limited liability partnership and one of the most respected accounting/consulting firms in the world. Since 1913, Arthur Andersen has offered accounting and business solutions and helped companies view change as an opportunity to learn, think, see, and leap ahead.

Arthur Andersen LLP

1. Go to **http://www.arthurandersen.com** and watch the video. Click on *About Us*. What does Arthur Andersen LLP do to stay ahead of its competitors?
2. Under "Our Scorecard" click on *facts*. For the most recent years, Arthur Andersen LLP reported how much in revenue? Information is available on the revenues of the company, but the entire set of financial statements is not publicly available. Why not? Does Arthur Andersen LLP pay income tax? Are the partners of a limited liability partnership personally liable for the debts of the partnership?
3. Click on *Careers*. Arthur Andersen LLP provides services in how many different countries?
4. Arthur Andersen, the founder of the company, was a university professor and recruited the brightest students into his classes. He helped his students understand how to improve financial performance. Click on "start your career *here*." What characteristics is Arthur Andersen LLP currently looking for in an employee?
5. Click on *Words of Wisdom*. What words of wisdom does Arthur Andersen LLP offer?

13

Corporations: Paid-in Capital and the Balance Sheet

LEARNING OBJECTIVES

After studying this chapter, you should be able to

1. Identify the characteristics of a corporation

2. Record the issuance of stock

3. Prepare the stockholders' equity section of a corporation's balance sheet

4. Account for cash dividends

5. Use different stock values in decision making

6. Evaluate a company's return on assets and return on stockholders' equity

7. Account for the income tax of a corporation

www.prenhall.com/horngren

Readiness Assessment

Initial public offerings of stock, or IPOs as they are called, reached new highs during the late 1990s. Consider what happened to this well-known company.

IHOP Corporation operates International House of Pancakes restaurants throughout the United States and in several foreign countries. IHOP serves pancakes, sandwiches, and other casual food along the interstate highway system. The restaurant chain caters to college students and families, with late hours and reasonable prices.

IHOP began as a small company in Glendale, California. To spur growth, IHOP *went public*. This means that IHOP offered its stock to anyone who would buy it. The initial public offering of IHOP's stock was fairly successful. The company offered to sell 6.2 million shares of its stock for $10 per share. As it turned out, investors bought only 3.2 million shares. IHOP thus received $32 million (3.2 million $\times$ $10), which the company then invested to open new restaurants and upgrade old ones.

This chapter covers the issuance of stock by large corporations such as IHOP. Any company—large or small—can sell (issue) its stock to investors. All companies issue their stock for the same reasons: to raise money (cash), to obtain assets such as land and buildings, or to pay off debt. Now let's explore how corporations differ from the proprietorships and partnerships we have been studying.

CORPORATIONS: AN OVERVIEW

Objective 1
Identify the characteristics of a corporation

The corporation is the dominant form of business organization in the United States. **IHOP** is one example. Proprietorships and partnerships are more numerous, but corporations transact more business and are larger in terms of total assets and sales revenue. Most well-known companies, such as **Target** and **Intel,** are corporations. Their full names include *Corporation* or *Incorporated* (abbreviated *Corp.* and *Inc.*) to show that they are corporations—for example, Target Corporation and **Nike, Inc.**

Characteristics of a Corporation

What makes the corporate form of organization so attractive? We now examine how corporations differ from proprietorships and partnerships and the advantages and disadvantages of corporations.

SEPARATE LEGAL ENTITY   A corporation is a business entity formed under state law. The state grants a **charter,** a document that gives a business the state's permission to form a corporation. Neither a proprietorship nor a partnership requires a charter, because in the eyes of the law the business is the same as the owner(s).

CHARTER. Document that gives the state's permission to form a corporation.

From a legal perspective, a corporation is a totally separate entity from its owners, who are called **stockholders** or **shareholders.** The corporation has many of the rights that a person has. For example, a corporation may buy, own, and sell property. The assets and liabilities of IHOP belong to the corporation rather than to its owners. The corporation may enter into contracts, sue, and be sued. If IHOP accidentally serves contaminated food and customers get sick, they may sue IHOP.

STOCKHOLDER. A person who owns the stock of a corporation. Also called **shareholder.**

CONTINUOUS LIFE AND TRANSFERABILITY OF OWNERSHIP   The owners' equity of a corporation is divided into shares of **stock.** Most corporations have *continuous lives* regardless of changes in the ownership of their stock. The stockholders of IHOP or any corporation may sell or trade the stock to another person, give it away, or bequeath it in a will. The transfer of the stock does not affect the continuity of the corporation. In contrast, proprietorships and partnerships terminate when their ownership changes.

STOCK. Shares into which the owners' equity of a corporation is divided.

NO MUTUAL AGENCY   *Mutual agency* means that all owners act as agents of the business. A contract signed by one owner is binding for the whole company.

➤➤ We introduced the idea of mutual agency for partnerships in Chapter 12, page 466.

LIMITED LIABILITY. No personal obligation of a stockholder for corporation debts. A stockholder can lose no more on an investment in a corporation's stock than the cost of the investment.

DOUBLE TAXATION. Corporations pay their own income taxes on corporate income. Then, the stockholders pay personal income tax on the cash dividends they receive from corporations.

⊙ DAILY EXERCISE 13-1

EXHIBIT 13-1
Advantages and Disadvantages of a Corporation

AUTHORIZATION OF STOCK. Provision in a corporate charter that gives the state's permission for the corporation to issue—that is, to sell—a certain number of shares of stock.

Mutual agency operates in partnerships but *not* in corporations. ◄◄ A stockholder of IHOP Corp. cannot commit the corporation to a contract (unless he or she is also an officer in the business).

LIMITED STOCKHOLDER LIABILITY   Stockholders have **limited liability** for corporation debts. That means they have no personal obligation for corporation liabilities. The most that a stockholder can lose on an investment in a corporation is the amount invested. In contrast, proprietors and partners are personally liable for all the debts of their businesses.

The combination of limited liability and no mutual agency means that persons can invest in a corporation without fear of losing all their personal wealth if the business fails. This feature enables a corporation to raise more money from a wider group of investors than proprietorships and partnerships can.

SEPARATION OF OWNERSHIP AND MANAGEMENT   Stockholders own the business, but a *board of directors*—elected by the stockholders—appoints the officers to manage the business. Stockholders may invest $1,000 or $1 million in the corporation without having to manage the business or disrupt their personal affairs.

Management's goal is to maximize the firm's value for the benefit of the stockholders. However, the separation between the owners—stockholders—and management can create problems. Corporate officers may decide to run the business for their own benefit and not for the stockholders. The distance between the stockholders and management may make it difficult for stockholders to protest bad management. How else can stockholders protest? They can sell their stock in that corporation.

CORPORATE TAXATION   Corporations are separate taxable entities. They pay several taxes not borne by proprietorships or partnerships, including an annual franchise tax levied by the state. The franchise tax keeps the corporate charter in force and enables the corporation to continue in business. Corporations also pay federal and state income taxes just as individuals do.

Corporate earnings are subject to **double taxation.** First, corporations pay income taxes on corporate income. Then, stockholders pay personal income tax on the cash dividends they receive from corporations. Proprietorships and partnerships pay no business income tax. Instead, the tax falls solely on the owners.

GOVERNMENT REGULATION   As we have seen, stockholders have only limited liability for corporation debts. Outsiders can look no further than the corporation for any claims that may arise against the business. To protect persons who do business with the corporation, both federal agencies and the states monitor corporations. This *government regulation* consists mainly of ensuring that corporations disclose adequate information for investors and creditors.

Exhibit 13-1 summarizes the advantages and disadvantages of the corporate form of business organization.

Advantages	Disadvantages
1. Can raise more money than a proprietorship or partnership	1. Separation of ownership and management
2. Continuous life	2. Corporate taxation
3. Easy transfer of ownership	3. Government regulation
4. No mutual agency of the stockholders	
5. Limited liability of the stockholders	

Organizing a Corporation

The process of creating a corporation begins when its organizers, called the *incorporators*, obtain a charter from the state. The charter includes the **authorization** for the corporation to issue a certain number of shares of stock for the ownership in the corporation. The incorporators pay fees, sign the charter, and file documents with the state. The corporation then becomes a legal entity. The stockholders agree to a set of **bylaws,** which act as the constitution for the corporation.

Ultimate control of the corporation rests with the stockholders. The stockholders elect the **board of directors,** which sets policy and appoints the officers. The board elects a **chairperson,** who is the most powerful person in the corporation. The board also designates the **president,** who is in charge of day-to-day operations. Most corporations also have vice presidents of sales, manufacturing, accounting and finance, and other key areas. The president and one or more vice presidents are usually elected to the board of directors. Exhibit 13-2 shows the authority structure in a corporation.

BYLAWS. Constitution for governing a corporation.

BOARD OF DIRECTORS. Group elected by the stockholders to set policy and to appoint the officers.

CHAIRPERSON. Elected by a corporation's board of directors, the most powerful person in the corporation.

EXHIBIT 13-2 **Authority Structure in a Corporation**

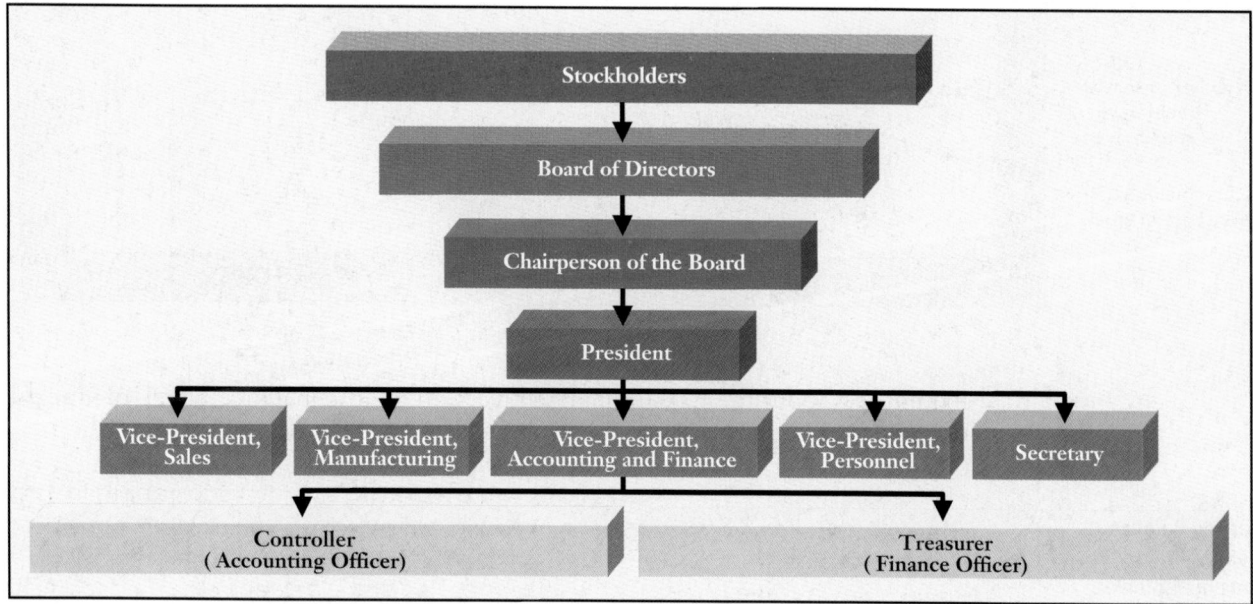

Capital Stock

A corporation issues *stock certificates* to its owners when they invest in the business. The stock represents the corporation's capital, so it is called *capital stock.* The basic unit of stock is a *share.* A corporation may issue a stock certificate for any number of shares—1, 100, or any other number—but the total number of *authorized* shares is limited by charter. Exhibit 13-3, at the top of the next page, depicts an actual stock certificate for 288 shares of **Central Jersey Bancorp** common stock. The certificate shows the company's name, the stockholder's name, the number of shares, and the par value of the stock (discussed later in this chapter).

Stock that is held by a stockholder is said to be **outstanding.** The total shares of stock outstanding represent 100% ownership of the corporation.

STOCKHOLDERS' EQUITY: THE BASICS

The balance sheet of a corporation reports assets and liabilities in the same way as a proprietorship or a partnership. However, the owners' equity of a corporation—called **stockholders' equity**—is reported differently. State laws require corporations to report the sources of their capital. The two basic sources of capital are

- **Paid-in capital** (also called **contributed capital**) represents stockholder investments in the corporation.
- **Retained earnings** is capital that the corporation has earned through profitable operations.

PRESIDENT. Chief operating officer in charge of managing the day-to-day operations of a corporation.

 DAILY EXERCISE 13-2

OUTSTANDING STOCK. Stock in the hands of of stockholders.

STOCKHOLDERS' EQUITY. Owners' equity of a corporation.

PAID-IN CAPITAL. A corporation's capital from investments by the stockholders. Also called **contributed capital.**

RETAINED EARNINGS. A corporation's capital that is earned through profitable operation of the business.

Exhibit 13-3   Stock Certificate

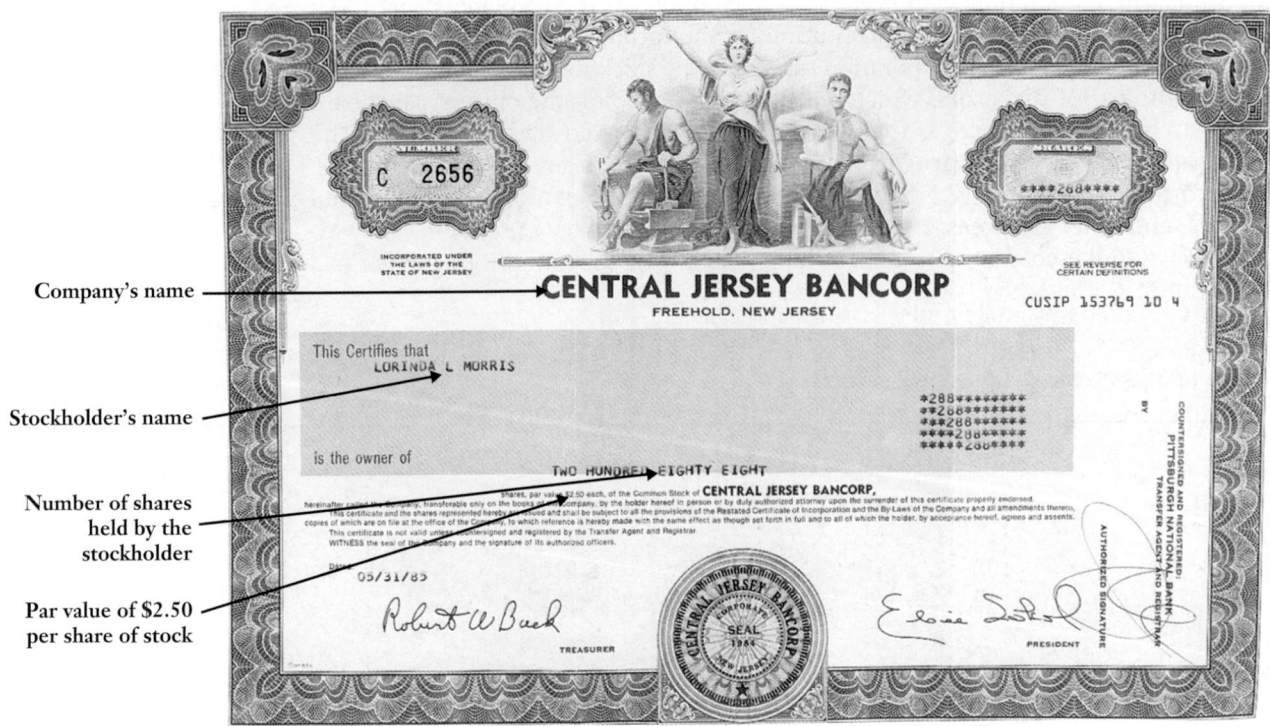

Company's name

Stockholder's name

Number of shares held by the stockholder

Par value of $2.50 per share of stock

Exhibit 13-4 outlines a summarized version of the balance sheet of **Target Corporation** to show how to report these categories of stockholders' equity.

EXHIBIT **13-4**
Summarized Balance Sheet of Target Corporation (Amounts in Millions)

 DAILY EXERCISE **13-3**

Assets	$17,143	Liabilities	$11,281
		Stockholders' Equity	
		Paid-in capital:	
		Common stock	806
		Retained earnings	5,056
		Total stockholders' equity...	5,862
		Total liabilities and	
Total assets	$17,143	stockholders' equity	$17,143

Paid-in Capital Is Received from the Stockholders

COMMON STOCK. The basic form of capital stock. In a corporation, the common stockholders are the owners of the business.

Common stock is paid-in capital because it comes from the stockholders. Target's entry to record the receipt of $20,000 cash and the issuance of Target stock is

Oct. 20	Cash		20,000	
	Common Stock			20,000
	Issued stock.			

This entry illustrates the fact that the issuance of stock increases both the assets and the stockholders' equity of the corporation.

Retained Earnings Are Earned from the Customers

Profitable operations generate income for the corporation, and income increases stockholders' equity through a separate account called Retained Earnings. At the end of the year, the balance of the Income Summary account (a net income or a net loss) is closed to Retained Earnings. For example, if Target's net income is $1,200 million, Income Summary will have a $1,200 million credit balance (see the T-account on p. 505). Target's closing entry will debit Income Summary to close that account. The credit side of the closing entry transfers net income to Retained

Earnings as follows (in millions of dollars):

Jan. 31   Income Summary   1,200
          Retained Earnings   1,200
          To close *net income* to Retained Earnings.

INCOME SUMMARY				RETAINED EARNINGS		
Closing	1,200	Net income	1,200		Closing	1,200
		Balance	-0-			

The T-accounts show that net income winds up in the Retained Earnings account.

If operations produce a net *loss* rather than net income, the Income Summary account will have a debit balance. To close a $60,000 loss, the closing entry credits Income Summary and debits Retained Earnings as follows:

Dec. 31   Retained Earnings   60,000
          Income Summary   60,000
          To close *net loss* to Retained Earnings.

WORK IT OUT

Prepare a T-account for Income Summary to show its debit balance of $60,000. Also prepare a T-account for Retained Earnings (no balance yet). Then post the $60,000 closing entry and take the balance for Income Summary and Retained Earnings. Where does the net loss of $60,000 end up?

Answer:

INCOME SUMMARY				RETAINED EARNINGS		
Net loss	60,000	Closing	60,000	Closing	60,000	
Balance	-0-					

A large loss may cause a debit balance in the Retained Earnings account. This condition—called a Retained Earnings **deficit**—is reported on the balance sheet as a negative amount in stockholders' equity. **HAL, Inc.,** which owns Hawaiian Airlines, Inc., reported this deficit:

DEFICIT. Debit balance in the Retained Earnings account.

Stockholders' Equity	(In Millions)
Paid-in capital: Common stock	$ 50
Deficit	(193)
Total stockholders' equity	$(143)

HAL's deficit was so large that it produced a negative amount of stockholders' equity. This situation is unusual for a going concern.

Corporations May Pay Dividends to the Stockholders

If the corporation has been profitable and has sufficient cash, it may distribute cash to the stockholders. Such distributions—called **dividends**—are similar to a proprietor's withdrawal of cash from a business or by a partner from a partnership. Dividends decrease both the assets and the retained earnings of the business. Most states prohibit using paid-in capital for dividends. Accountants use the term **legal capital** to refer to the portion of stockholders' equity that *cannot* be used for dividends.

DIVIDENDS. Distributions by a corporation to its stockholders.

LEGAL CAPITAL. The portion of stockholders' equity that cannot be used for dividends.

Some people think of Retained Earnings as a fund of cash. It is not, because Retained Earnings is an element of stockholders' equity. *Remember that cash dividends are paid out of assets, not out of retained earnings.*

Stockholders' Rights

The ownership of stock entitles stockholders to four basic rights, unless specific rights are withheld by agreement with the stockholders:

1. *Vote.* Stockholders participate in management by voting on matters that come before them. This is a stockholder's sole right to manage the corporation. Each share of stock carries one vote.
2. *Dividends.* Stockholders receive a proportionate part of any dividend. Each share of stock receives an equal dividend with every other share of the same class.
3. *Liquidation.* Stockholders receive their proportionate share of any assets remaining after the corporation pays its liabilities in liquidation (goes out of business).
4. *Preemption.* Stockholders can maintain their proportionate ownership in the corporation. Suppose you own 5% of a corporation's stock. If the corporation issues 100,000 new shares of stock, it must offer you the opportunity to buy 5% (5,000) of the new shares. This right, called the *preemptive right,* is usually withheld from the stockholders.

Classes of Stock

Corporations issue different types of stock. The stock of a corporation may be either common or preferred and either par or no-par.

COMMON AND PREFERRED STOCK   Every corporation issues *common stock,* the basic form of capital stock. Unless designated otherwise, the word *stock* is understood to mean "common stock." Common stockholders have the four basic rights of stock ownership, unless a right is specifically withheld. For example, some companies issue Class A common stock, which carries the right to vote. They may also issue Class B common stock, which may be nonvoting. (Classes of common stock may also be designated Series A, Series B, and so on.) There is a separate account for each class of stock.

Investors who buy common stock take the ultimate risk with a corporation. The corporation makes no promises to pay them. If the corporation succeeds, it will pay dividends to its stockholders, but if net income and cash are too low, stockholders may receive no dividends. The stock of successful corporations increases in value, and investors may sell the stock at a gain. But stock prices can decrease, leaving the investors holding worthless stock. Because common stockholders take a risk, they demand increases in stock prices, high dividends, or both. If the corporation does not deliver, the stockholders sell the stock.

Preferred stock gives its owners certain advantages over common stockholders. These benefits include the right to receive dividends before the common stockholders and the right to receive assets before the common stockholders if the corporation liquidates. Corporations pay a fixed amount of dividends on preferred stock. Investors usually buy preferred stock to earn those fixed dividends.

Owners of preferred stock also have the four basic stockholder rights, unless a right is specifically denied. The right to vote may be withheld from preferred stockholders. Companies may issue different classes of preferred stock (Class A and Class B or Series A and Series B, for example). Each class of stock is recorded in a separate account. Preferred stock is rarer than you might think. A recent survey of 600 corporations revealed that only 99 of them (16.5%) had some preferred stock outstanding (Exhibit 13-5).

All corporations have common stock. Exhibit 13-6 summarizes the similarities and differences among common stock, preferred stock, and long-term debt.

PREFERRED STOCK. Stock that gives its owners certain advantages over common stockholders, such as the right to receive dividends before the common stockholders and the right to receive assets before the common stockholders if the corporation liquidates.

EXHIBIT 13-5
Preferred Stock

EXHIBIT 13-6
Comparison of Common Stock, Preferred Stock, and Long-Term Debt

	Common Stock	Preferred Stock	Long-Term Debt
Investment risk	High	Medium	Low
Corporate obligation to repay principal	No	No	Yes
Dividends/Interest	Dividends	Dividends	Interest

PAR VALUE, STATED VALUE, AND NO-PAR STOCK   Stock may be par-value stock or no-par stock. **Par value** is an arbitrary amount assigned by a company to a share of its stock. Most companies set the par value of their common stock quite low to avoid legal difficulties from issuing their stock below par. Most states require companies to maintain a minimum amount of stockholders' equity for the protection of creditors, and this minimum represents the corporation's legal capital. For corporations with par-value stock, *legal capital* is usually the par value of the shares issued.

The common stock par value of **Oracle Corporation,** the software giant, is $0.01 (1 cent) per share. **Pier 1 Imports'** common carries a par value of $1 per share. Par value of preferred stock is often higher; some preferred stocks have par values of $25 and $100. Par value is used to compute dividends on preferred stock, as we shall see.

No-par stock does not have par value. **Kimberly Clark** has 20 million shares of preferred stock authorized with no par value. But some no-par stock has a **stated value,** which makes it similar to par-value stock. The stated value is an arbitrary amount that accountants treat as though it were par value.

PAR VALUE. Arbitrary amount assigned to a share of stock.

 DAILY EXERCISE 13-4

STATED VALUE. An arbitrary amount that accountants treat as though it were par value.

ISSUING STOCK

Objective 2
Record the issuance of stock

Large corporations such as **Hewlett-Packard, Coca-Cola,** and **British Petroleum Amoco** need huge quantities of money to operate. They cannot finance all their operations through borrowing. They need capital that they raise by issuing stock. Corporations may sell the stock directly to stockholders or use the services of an *underwriter,* such as the brokerage firms **Merrill Lynch** and **Morgan Stanley, Dean Witter.** An underwriter agrees to buy all the stock it cannot sell to its clients.

The price that the corporation receives from issuance of its stock is called the *issue price.* Often, the issue price far exceeds the stock's par value because the par value is intentionally set quite low. The company's profits, financial position, and future prospects determine the issue price. Investors will pay no more than market value for the stock. In the following sections, we show how to account for the issuance of stock.

Issuing Common Stock

Companies advertise their stock to attract investors. The *Wall Street Journal* is the most popular medium for the advertisements. They are called *tombstones.* Exhibit 13-7 at the top of page 508 is a reproduction of IHOP's tombstone, which appeared in the *Wall Street Journal.*

The lead underwriter of **IHOP's** public offering was **The First Boston Corporation.** Other brokerage firms and investment bankers also sold IHOP's stock to their clients. IHOP's tombstone shows that IHOP hoped to raise approximately $62 million of capital. But in the final analysis, IHOP issued only 3.2 million of the shares and received cash of approximately $32 million.

COMMON STOCK AT PAR   Suppose IHOP's common stock carried a par value of $10 per share. The stock issuance entry of 3.2 million shares would be

Jan. 31	Cash (3,200,000 × $10)	32,000,000	
	Common Stock.........................		32,000,000
	Issued common stock at par.		

COMMON STOCK AT A PREMIUM   Most corporations set par value low and issue common stock for a price above par value. The amount above par is called a *premium.* IHOP's common stock has an actual par value of $0.01 (1 cent) per share. The $9.99 difference between issue price ($10) and par value ($0.01) is a premium. This sale of stock increases the corporation's paid-in capital by the full $10, the total issue price of the stock.

A premium on the sale of stock is not gain, income, or profit to the corporation, because the entity is dealing with its own stockholders. This situation illustrates one of the fundamentals of accounting: *A company neither earns a profit nor incurs a loss when it sells its stock to, or buys its stock from, its own stockholders.*

Exhibit 13-7   Announcement of Public Offering of IHOP Stock (Partial)

Number of shares offered to the public

This announcement is neither an offer to sell nor a solicitation of offers to buy any of these securities. The offering is made only by the Prospectus, copies of which may be obtained in any State in which this announcement is circulated only from such of the undersigned as may legally offer these securities in such State.

6,200,000 Shares

Company issuing the stock

INTERNATIONAL HOUSE *P MARKS* RESTAURANT

IHOP CORP.

Class of stock

Common Stock
($.01 par value)

Par value per share

Issue price—the amount per share that IHOP received for the stock

Price $10 Per Share

These securities are being offered in the United States and internationally.

United States Offering
4,960,000 Shares

Lead U.S. underwriter

The First Boston Corporation

Alex. Brown & Sons Incorporated	Donaldson, Lufkin & Jenrette Securities Corporation	A. G. Edwards & Sons, Inc.
Goldman, Sachs & Co.	Lehman Brothers	Montgomery Securities
PaineWebber Incorporated		Prudential Securities Incorporated

International Offering
1,240,000 Shares

Lead foreign underwriter

Credit Suisse First Boston Limited

WORK IT OUT

Prepare IHOP's classified balance sheet immediately after this issuance of stock. Assume zero balances prior to the transaction.

Answer

IHOP CORPORATION
Balance Sheet
January 31, 20XX

Assets		Liabilities	
Current:			
Cash	$32,000,000	No liabilities	0
		Stockholders' Equity	
		Common stock	$32,000,000
		Total liabilities and	
Total assets	$32,000,000	stockholders' equity	$32,000,000

With a par value of $0.01, IHOP's entry to record the issuance of the stock is

July 31	Cash (3,200,000 × $10)	32,000,000	
	Common Stock (3,200,000 × $0.01)		32,000
	Paid-in Capital in Excess of Par—		
	Common (3,200,000 × $9.99)		31,968,000
	Issued common stock at a premium.		

● DAILY EXERCISE 13-5

Account titles that could be used in place of Paid-in Capital in Excess of Par—Common are *Additional Paid-in Capital—Common* and *Premium on Common Stock*. Since both par value and premium amounts increase the corporation's capital, they appear in the stockholders' equity section of the balance sheet.

At the end of the year, IHOP Corp. would report stockholders' equity on its balance sheet as follows, assuming that the corporate charter authorizes 40,000,000 shares of common stock and the balance of retained earnings is $26,000,000.

Stockholders' Equity

Paid-in capital:	
Common stock, $0.01 par, 40 million shares	
authorized, 3.2 million shares issued	$ 32,000
Paid-in capital in excess of par	31,968,000
Total paid-in capital	32,000,000
Retained earnings	26,000,000
Total stockholders' equity	$58,000,000

● DAILY EXERCISE 13-6

● DAILY EXERCISE 13-7

We determine the dollar amount reported for common stock by multiplying the total number of shares *issued* (3.2 million) by the par value per share ($0.01). The *authorization* reports the maximum number of shares of stock the company may issue under its charter.

All transactions recorded in this section include a receipt of cash by the corporation as it issues new stock to stockholders. These transactions are different from

e-Accounting

UPS Delivers the Dough at Record-Breaking IPO

If you want stock in a company that operates in the global electronic marketplace, what comes to mind? Pioneering dot.coms like **Amazon.com** or **eBay?** Think again. There's a 97-year-old business whose workers drive old-fashioned brown trucks and run parcels up to your door. **United Parcel Service (UPS)** is a business as traditional as apple pie. UPS raised a record-breaking $5.5 billion at its IPO (initial public offering) when it went public. All this money came from investors who saw UPS as a sign of the new economy.

Why would UPS sell its stock to the public? To build a cross-border, USA/European infrastructure, UPS figured it would need to acquire and merge with foreign firms. That required a lot of money. During the first hours of trading in UPS stock, the company's share price soared 40%. By the end of a week, the UPS workforce included 10,000 new millionaires.

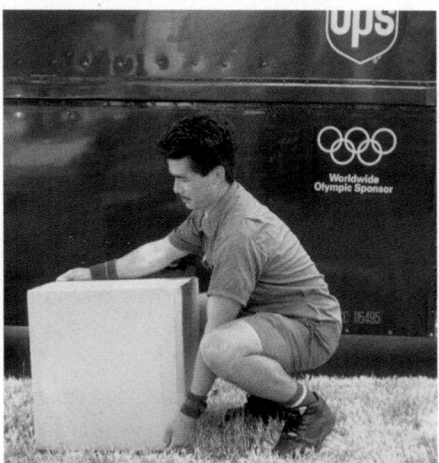

Source: Based on Avital Louria Hahn, "Men in brown: A growth story—UPS recasts itself for IPO," *The Investment Dealers' Digest: IDD,* December 13, 1999, p. 35. Elise Ackerman, "UPS delivers as IPO investors give the world's no. 1 package-delivery company full dot-com treatment," *U.S. News & World Report,* November 22, 1999, p. 53. Jenny Anderson, "Up, UPS and away," *Institutional Investor,* January 2000, pp. 96–98.

the vast majority of stock transactions reported each day in the financial press. In those transactions, one stockholder sells his or her stock to another investor, and the corporation makes no formal journal entry because its paid-in capital is unchanged.

NO-PAR COMMON STOCK   When a company issues stock that has no par value, there can be no premium. A recent survey of 600 companies revealed 59 issues of no-par stock.

When a company issues no-par stock, it debits the asset received and credits the stock account. Glenwood Corporation, which manufactures ski equipment, issues 4,000 shares of no-par common stock for $20 per share. The stock issuance entry is

Aug. 14	Cash (4,000 × $20)..............................	80,000	
	Common Stock...........................		80,000
	Issued no-par common stock.		

Regardless of the stock's price, Cash is debited and Common Stock is credited for the cash received. There is no Paid-in Capital in Excess of Par for no-par stock.

Glenwood Corporation's charter authorizes Glenwood to issue 10,000 shares of no-par stock, and the company has $151,000 in retained earnings. The corporation reports stockholders' equity on the balance sheet as follows:

Stockholders' Equity

Paid-in capital:	
Common stock, no par, 10,000 shares	
authorized, 4,000 shares issued.....................	$ 80,000
Retained earnings	151,000
Total stockholders' equity	$231,000

⊙ DAILY EXERCISE 13-8 NO-PAR COMMON STOCK WITH A STATED VALUE   Accounting for no-par stock with a stated value is identical to accounting for par-value stock. The premium account for no-par common stock with a stated value is Paid-in Capital in Excess of *Stated Value*—Common.

COMMON STOCK FOR ASSETS OTHER THAN CASH   When a corporation issues stock and receives assets other than cash, it records the assets received at their current market value and credits the capital accounts accordingly. The assets' prior book value is irrelevant because the stockholder will demand stock equal to the market value of the asset given. Kahn Corporation issued 15,000 shares of its $1 par common stock for equipment worth $4,000 and a building worth $120,000. Kahn's entry is

Nov. 30	Equipment	4,000	
	Building..	120,000	
	Common Stock (15,000 × $1)		15,000
	Paid-in Capital in Excess of Par—		
	Common ($124,000 − $15,000)		109,000
	Issued common stock in exchange for equipment and a building.		

WORK IT OUT

Prepare the stockholders' equity section of Kahn's balance sheet immediately after this transaction. Before this issuance of stock, Kahn already had outstanding 10,000 shares of common stock that the company had issued for $8 per share. Kahn's corporate charter authorizes the issuance of 100,000 shares of common stock. Retained earnings is $519,000 and liabilities total $622,000.

Stockholders' Equity

Paid-in capital:	
Common stock, $1 par, 100,000 shares authorized,	
25,000 (10,000 + 15,000) shares issued	$ 25,000
Paid-in capital in excess of par ($70,000* + $109,000)..............	179,000
Total paid-in capital	204,000
Retained earnings	519,000
Total stockholders' equity	$723,000

*10,000 shares × ($8 − $1 par) = $70,000

Issuing Preferred Stock

Accounting for preferred stock follows the pattern illustrated for common stock. **Chiquita Brands International, Inc.,** famous for its bananas, has some preferred stock outstanding. Assume Chiquita issued 110,887 shares of preferred stock at par value of $1 per share. The issuance entry is

July 31	Cash	110,887	
	Preferred Stock (110,887 shares × $1)		110,887
	Issued preferred stock at par.		

If Chiquita had issued the preferred stock at a premium, the entry would have credited Paid-in Capital in Excess of Par—Preferred for the excess over par value. A corporation lists separate accounts for Paid-in Capital in Excess of Par on Preferred Stock and on Common Stock to differentiate the two classes of equity. The balance sheet then lists preferred stock, common stock, and retained earnings, in that order.

Ethical Considerations in Accounting for the Issuance of Stock

Issuance of stock for *cash* poses no ethical challenge. The company receives cash and issues stock, giving the stockholders certificates as evidence of their ownership.

Issuing stock for assets other than cash can pose an ethical challenge. The company issuing the stock often wishes to record a large amount for the asset received (such as land or a building) and for the stock being issued. Why? Because large asset and equity amounts make the business look prosperous and creditworthy. The motivation to look good can inject a subtle bias into the amount recorded for the assets received and the stock issued.

A company is supposed to record an asset received at its current market value. But one person's evaluation of a building can differ from another person's valuation. One person may appraise the building at a market value of $4 million. Another may honestly believe it is worth only $3 million. A company receiving the building in exchange for its stock must decide whether to record the building received and the stock issued at $3 million, $4 million, or some other amount.

The ethical course of action is to record the asset at its current fair market value, as determined by a good-faith estimate of market value from independent appraisers. It is rare for a public corporation to be found guilty of *understating* the asset values on its balance sheet, but companies have been embarrassed by *overstating* their asset values. Investors who rely on the financial statements may be able to prove that an overstatement of asset values caused them to pay too much for the company's stock. In that case, a court of law may render a judgment against the company. So companies tend to value assets conservatively (that is, on the low side) in order to avoid an overstatement of their book value.

Review of Accounting for Paid-in Capital

Let's review the first half of this chapter by showing the stockholders' equity section of MedTech.com Corporation's balance sheet in Exhibit 13-8 on page 512.

Objective 3
Prepare the stockholders' equity section of a corporation's balance sheet

511

EXHIBIT 13-8
Part of MedTech.com
Corporation's Balance Sheet

DAILY EXERCISE 13-10

DAILY EXERCISE 13-11

DAILY EXERCISE 13-12

Stockholders' Equity	
Paid-in capital:	
Preferred stock, 5%, $100 par, 5,000 shares authorized, 400 shares issued	$ 40,000
Paid-in capital in excess of par—preferred	14,000
Common stock, $10 par, 20,000 shares authorized, 4,500 shares issued	45,000
Paid-in capital in excess of par—common	72,000
Total paid-in capital	171,000
Retained earnings	85,000
Total stockholders' equity	$256,000

Note the two sections of stockholders' equity: paid-in capital and retained earnings. Also observe the order of the equity accounts:

- Preferred stock at par value
- Paid-in capital in excess of par—preferred
- Common stock at par value
- Paid-in capital in excess of par—common
- Retained earnings (after the paid-in capital accounts)

ADDITIONAL PAID-IN CAPITAL. The paid-in capital in excess of par—common plus other accounts combined for reporting on the balance sheet.

Many companies combine several accounts, including Paid-in Capital in Excess of Par—Common, and report the sum as **Additional Paid-in Capital** on the balance sheet. However, they are careful not to include Paid-in Capital in Excess of Par—Preferred because that paid-in capital belongs to the preferred stockholders.

THINK IT OVER

Examine MedTech.com Corporation's stockholders' equity in Exhibit 13-8, and answer these questions.

1. How much did MedTech.com's preferred stockholders pay into the corporation?
2. How much did the common stockholders pay into MedTech.com?
3. What did the stockholders get for their payments into the company?

Answers

1. $54,000 ($40,000 + $14,000)
2. $117,000 ($45,000 + $72,000)

3. The stockholders received stock, which represents their ownership in the assets of the corporation.

Now review the Decision Guidelines feature to solidify your understanding of stockholders' equity as it is reported on the balance sheet.

DECISION GUIDELINES

Reporting Stockholders' Equity on the Balance Sheet

DECISION	GUIDELINES
What are the two main segments of stockholders' equity?	• Paid-in capital • Retained earnings
Which is more permanent, paid-in capital or retained earnings?	Paid-in capital is more permanent because corporations use their retained earnings for declaring dividends.

How are paid-in capital and retained earnings
• Similar?
 	
• Different?
	• Both represent the stockholders' equity (ownership) in the assets of the corporation.
	• Paid-in capital and retained earnings come from different sources:
	  a. *Paid-in capital* comes from the corporation's stockholders, who invested in the company.
	  b. *Retained earnings* comes from the corporation's customers. It was earned by profitable operations.

What are the main categories of paid-in capital?	• Preferred stock, plus paid-in-capital in excess of par • Common stock, plus paid-in-capital in excess of par

SUMMARY PROBLEM

www.prenhall.com/horngren

Mid-Chapter Assessment

1. Test your understanding of the first half of this chapter: Is each of the following statements true or false?
   a. Issuance of 1,000 shares of $5 par-value stock at $12 increases contributed capital by $7,000.
   b. The issuance of no-par stock with a stated value is fundamentally different from issuing par-value stock.
   c. A corporation issues its preferred stock in exchange for land and a building with a combined market value of $200,000. This transaction increases the corporation's owners' equity by $200,000 regardless of the assets' prior book value.
   d. A stockholder may bind the corporation to a contract.
   e. The policy-making body in a corporation is called the board of directors.
   f. The owner of 100 shares of preferred stock has greater voting rights than the owner of 100 shares of common stock.
   g. Par-value stock is worth more than no-par stock.
2. The brewery **Adolph Coors Company** has two classes of common stock. Only the Class A common stockholders are entitled to vote. The company's balance sheet included the following presentation:

Stockholders' Equity

Capital stock	
Class A common stock, voting, $1 par value,	
authorized and issued 1,260,000 shares	$ 1,260,000
Class B common stock, nonvoting, no par value,	
authorized and issued 46,200,000 shares	11,000,000
	12,260,000
Additional paid-in capital	2,011,000
Retained earnings	872,403,000
	$886,674,000

Required

1. Record the issuance of the Class A common stock. The additional paid-in capital is related to the Class A common stock. Use the Coors account titles.
2. Record the issuance of the Class B common stock. Use the Coors account titles.
3. Rearrange the Coors stockholders' equity section to correspond to the following format:

Stockholders' Equity

Paid-in capital:	
Class A common stock..	$
Paid-in capital in excess of par—Class A common stock...............	
Class B common stock..	
Total paid-in capital..	
Retained earnings	
Total stockholders' equity	$

4. What is the total paid-in capital of the company?
5. How did Coors withhold the voting privilege from the Class B common stockholders?

Solutions

1. Answers to true/false statements:
   a. False   c. True   e. True   g. False
   b. False   d. False   f. False

(1) Cash	3,271,000	
Class A Common Stock		1,260,000
Additional Paid-in Capital		2,011,000
To record issuance of Class A common stock at a premium.		
(2) Cash	11,000,000	
Class B Common Stock		11,000,000
To record issuance of Class B common stock.		

(3) **Shareholders' Equity**
Paid-in capital:

Class A common stock, voting, $1 par value,		
authorized and issued 1,260,000 shares	$	1,260,000
Paid-in capital in excess of par—Class A common stock		2,011,000
Class B common stock, nonvoting, no par value,		
authorized and issued 46,200,000 shares		11,000,000
Total paid-in capital		14,271,000
Retained earnings		872,403,000
Total shareholders' equity		$886,674,000

(4) Total paid-in capital is $14,271,000.
(5) The voting privilege was withheld by specific agreement with the stockholders.

ACCOUNTING FOR CASH DIVIDENDS

Corporations share the company's wealth with their stockholders through dividends. Corporations declare dividends from retained earnings and pay the dividends with cash. The corporation must have enough *retained earnings* to declare the dividend and enough *cash* to pay the dividend.

Dividend Dates

A corporation must declare a dividend before paying it. The board of directors alone has the authority to declare a dividend. The corporation has no obligation to pay a dividend until the board declares one, but once declared, the dividend becomes a legal liability of the corporation. Three relevant dates for dividends are

1. *Declaration date.* On the declaration date, the board of directors announces the intention to pay the dividend. The declaration creates a liability for the corporation. Declaration is recorded by debiting Retained Earnings and crediting Dividends Payable.

2. *Date of record.* At declaration, the corporation also announces the record date, which follows the declaration date by a few weeks. Those stockholders who own the stock on the date of record will receive the dividend when it is paid. The corporation makes no journal entry on the date of record because no transaction occurs. But much work takes place behind the scenes to identify stockholders of record on this date.

3. *Payment date.* Payment of the dividend usually follows the record date by two to three weeks. Payment is recorded by debiting Dividends Payable and crediting Cash.

Dividends on Preferred and Common Stock

Declaration of a cash dividend is recorded by debiting Retained Earnings and crediting Dividends Payable as follows:[1]

June 19	Retained Earnings	XXX	
	Dividends Payable		XXX
	Declared a cash dividend.		

[1] In Chapters 1–4, we debited the Dividends account, which is closed to Retained Earnings. Many businesses debit Retained Earnings directly, as shown here.

Payment of the dividend, which usually follows declaration by a few weeks, is recorded by debiting Dividends Payable and crediting Cash:

◉ DAILY EXERCISE 13-13

July 2   Dividends Payable........................   XXX
           Cash....................................   XXX
         Paid the cash dividend.

Dividends Payable is a current liability. When a company has issued both preferred stock and common stock, the preferred stockholders receive their dividends first. The common stockholders receive dividends only if the total declared dividend is large enough to pay the preferred stockholders first.

In addition to its common stock, Pine Industries, Inc., has 9,000 shares of preferred stock outstanding. Preferred dividends are paid at the annual rate of $1.75 per share. Exhibit 13-9 shows the division between preferred and common for three amounts of the total annual dividend declared by Pine Industries.

Case A: Total dividend of $150,000
     Preferred dividend (9,000 shares × $1.75 per share) .... $ 15,750
     Common dividend ($150,000 − $15,750)   134,250
     Total dividend.. $150,000
Case B: Total dividend of $20,000
     Preferred dividend (9,000 shares × $1.75 per share) .... $ 15,750
     Common dividend ($20,000 − $15,750)   4,250
     Total dividend.. $ 20,000
Case C: Total dividend of $8,000
     Preferred dividend (the full $8,000 goes to preferred
         because the annual preferred dividend is $15,750) .... $ 8,000
     Common dividend (none because the total dividend
         did not cover the preferred dividend for the year).............   0
     Total dividend .... $ 8,000

EXHIBIT 13-9
Division of a Dividend Between Preferred Stock and Common Stock

If Pine Industries' annual dividend is large enough to cover the preferred dividend for the year (Cases A and B), the preferred stockholders receive their regular dividend, and the common stockholders receive the remainder. But if the year's dividend falls below the amount of the annual preferred dividend (Case C), the preferred stockholders receive the entire dividend, and the common stockholders receive nothing that year.

This example illustrates an important relationship between preferred stock and common stock. To an investor, the preferred stock is safer because it receives dividends first. However, the earnings potential from an investment in common stock is much greater. Preferred stockholders usually receive only the specified dividend, but there is no upper limit on the amount of common dividends.

When a company has more than one class of preferred stock or common stock, the division of dividends among the various classes of stock follows this same pattern: The most senior preferred stock gets the first dividends, and so on.

We noted that preferred stockholders enjoy the advantage of priority over common stockholders in receiving dividends. The dividend preference is stated as a percentage rate or a dollar amount. For example, preferred stock may be "6% preferred," which means that owners of the preferred stock receive an annual dividend of 6% of the par value of the stock. If par value is $100 per share, preferred stockholders receive an annual cash dividend of $6 per share (6% of $100). The preferred stock may be "$3 preferred," which means that stockholders receive an annual dividend of $3 per share regardless of the preferred stock's par value. The dividend rate on no-par preferred stock is stated in a dollar amount per share.

◉ DAILY EXERCISE 13-14

Dividends on Cumulative and Noncumulative Preferred Stock

The allocation of dividends may be complex if the preferred stock is *cumulative*. Corporations sometimes fail to pay a dividend to their preferred stockholders. This is called *passing the dividend,* and the passed dividends are said to be *in arrears.* The owners of **cumulative preferred stock** must receive all dividends in arrears plus the current year's dividend before the corporation pays dividends to the common stockholders.

The preferred stock of Pine Industries is cumulative. Suppose the company passed the 20X4 preferred dividend of $15,750. Before paying dividends to its common stockholders in 20X5, the company must first pay preferred dividends of $15,750 for both 20X4 and 20X5, a total of $31,500. *Preferred stock is cumulative in the eyes of the law unless it is labeled as noncumulative.* Most preferred stock is cumulative.

Assume that Pine Industries passes its 20X4 preferred dividend. In 20X5, the company declares a $50,000 dividend. The entry to record the declaration of this dividend is

Sep. 6	Retained Earnings	50,000	
	Dividends Payable, Preferred ($15,750 × 2)............		31,500
	Dividends Payable, Common		
	($50,000 − $31,500)...		18,500
	Declared a cash dividend.		

If the preferred stock is *noncumulative,* the corporation is not obligated to pay dividends in arrears. Suppose the Pine Industries preferred stock was noncumulative and the company passed the 20X4 preferred dividend of $15,750. The preferred stockholders would lose the 20X4 dividend forever. Of course, the common stockholders would not receive a 20X4 dividend either. Before paying any common dividends in 20X5, the company would have to pay the 20X5 preferred dividend of $15,750.

Having dividends in arrears on cumulative preferred stock is *not* a liability for the corporation. (A liability for dividends arises only after the board of directors declares the dividend.) Nevertheless, a corporation must report cumulative preferred dividends in arrears. This information alerts common stockholders as to how much in preferred dividends must be paid before the common stockholders will receive any dividends.

Dividends in arrears are often disclosed in notes, as follows (all dates and amounts assumed). Observe the two references to Note 3 in this section of the balance sheet. The "6%" after "Preferred stock" is the annual dividend rate.

Preferred stock, 6%, $50 par, 2,000 shares issued (Note 3)	$100,000
Retained earnings (Note 3)..	414,000

Note 3—Cumulative preferred dividends in arrears. At December 31, 20X2, dividends on the preferred stock were in arrears for 20X1 and 20X2, in the amount of $12,000 (6% × $100,000 × 2 years).

DIFFERENT VALUES OF STOCK

There are several different *stock values* in addition to par value. Market value, liquidation value, and book value are used for various investor decisions.

Market Value

A stock's **market value,** or *market price,* is the price for which a person could buy or sell a share of the stock. The issuing corporation's net income, financial position, and future prospects and general economic conditions determine market value. The Internet and most newspapers report the market price of many stocks. Log onto any company's Web site to track its stock price. *In almost all cases, stockholders are more concerned about the market value of a stock than about any other value.* In the chapter-opening story, **IHOP's** stock had a market price of $10 when it was issued. Shortly thereafter, the stock shot up to a market price of $36, which means that the stock could be sold for, or bought for, $36 per share. The purchase of 100 shares of IHOP stock at $36 would cost $3,600 ($36 × 100), plus a commission. If you were selling 100 shares of IHOP stock, you would receive cash of $3,600 less a commission. The commission is the fee an investor pays to a stockbroker for buying or selling the stock. The price of a share of IHOP stock has fluctuated from $10 at issuance to a recent high of $25.

If you buy IHOP stock from another investor, IHOP gets no cash. The transaction is a sale between you and the other investor. IHOP records only the change in stockholder name.

Liquidation Value

Some preferred stocks have a liquidation value. The *liquidation value* is the amount the corporation agrees to pay the preferred stockholder per share if the company liquidates. Dividends in arrears are added to liquidation value in determining the payment to the preferred stockholders if the company liquidates.

DAILY EXERCISE 13-15

Some companies report their preferred stock at its liquidation value on the balance sheet. Consider **BF Goodrich Company,** which makes chemicals and aerospace components and sells tires under the Michelin label. BF Goodrich has 2.2 million shares of convertible preferred stock that is stated at "a liquidation value of $50 per share." The balance in BF Goodrich's preferred stock account is thus $110 million (2.2 million shares × $50).

Book Value

The **book value** of a stock is the amount of owners' equity on the company's books for each share of its stock. Corporations often report this amount in their annual reports. If the company has only common stock outstanding, its book value is computed by dividing total stockholders' equity by the number of shares *outstanding*. A company with stockholders' equity of $180,000 and 5,000 shares of common stock outstanding has a book value of $36 per share ($180,000/5,000 shares).

BOOK VALUE. Amount of owners' equity on the company's books for each share of its stock.

If the company has both preferred stock and common stock outstanding, the preferred stockholders have the first claim to owners' equity. Ordinarily, preferred stock has a specified liquidation value. The book value of preferred stock is its liquidation value plus any cumulative dividends in arrears on the stock. Its book value *per share* equals the sum of liquidation value and any cumulative dividends in arrears divided by the number of preferred shares *outstanding*. After the corporation figures the book value of the preferred shares, it computes the book value per share of the common. The corporation divides the common equity (total stockholders' equity minus preferred equity) by the number of common shares outstanding.

Lille Corporation's balance sheet reports the following amounts:

Stockholders' Equity	
Paid-in capital:	
Preferred stock, 6%, $10 par, 5,000 shares authorized,	
5,000 shares issued (liquidation value $13 per share)	$ 50,000
Paid-in capital in excess of par—preferred	14,000
Common stock, $1 par, 20,000 shares authorized,	
15,000 shares issued	15,000
Paid-in capital in excess of par—common	172,000
Total paid-in capital	251,000
Retained earnings	422,000
Total stockholders' equity	$673,000

Suppose that four years' (including the current year) cumulative preferred dividends are in arrears. The book-value-per-share computations are as follows:

Preferred	
Liquidation value (5,000 shares × $13)	$ 65,000
Cumulative dividends ($50,000 × 0.06 × 4)	12,000
Stockholders' equity allocated to preferred	$ 77,000
Book value per share ($77,000/5,000 shares)	$ 15.40
Common	
Total stockholders' equity	$673,000
Less stockholders' equity allocated to preferred	(77,000)
Stockholders' equity allocated to common	$596,000
Book value per share ($596,000/15,000 shares)	$39.73

DAILY EXERCISE 13-16

If the preferred stock has no specified liquidation value, then we would use the sum of par value plus paid-in capital in excess of par-preferred, $64,000, plus cumulative dividends to compute the book value of the preferred stock.

BOOK VALUE AND DECISION MAKING How is book value used in decision making? Book value may figure into the negotiated purchase price of a corporation whose stock is not publicly traded. Also, a corporation may buy out a retiring executive or other stockholder by agreeing to pay the book value of the person's stock in the company.

Some investors have traditionally compared the book value of a share of a company's stock with the stock's market value. The idea was that a stock selling below its book value was underpriced and thus a good buy. The relationship between book value and market value is far from clear. Some investors believe that a company whose stock sells at a price below book value must be experiencing financial difficulty. Exhibit 13-10 contrasts the book values and ranges of market values for the common stocks of three well-known companies. For all three companies, the market value of the stock exceeds its book value—a mark of success. The market price of **Dell Computer's** stock far exceeds its book value per share.

⊙ DAILY EXERCISE 13-17

EXHIBIT 13-10
Book Value and Market Value
for Three Well-Known
Companies

	Book Value Per Share	July 6, 2000 Stock Price
IHOP Corp.*........................	$11.28	$17.13
MCI WORLDCOM*	18.02	$46.44
Dell Computer**..................	2.06	$47.75

* December 31, 1999.
** January 28, 2000.

EVALUATING OPERATIONS

Objective 6
Evaluate a company's return on assets and return on stockholders' equity

Investors and creditors are constantly evaluating companies' profits. Investors search for companies whose stocks are likely to increase in value. The decision often requires a comparison of companies. But **IHOP's** net income may not be comparable with the net income of a new company. IHOP's profits may run into the millions of dollars, which far exceed a new company's net income. To compare companies of different size, investors use standard profitability measures. Two of the most widely used are the rate of return on total assets and rate of return on stockholders' equity.

Rate of Return on Total Assets

RATE OF RETURN ON TOTAL ASSETS. The sum of net income plus interest expense divided by average total assets. This ratio measures the success a company has in using its assets to earn income for the persons who finance the business. Also called return on assets.

The **rate of return on total assets,** or simply **return on assets,** measures a company's success in using its assets to earn income for those who are financing the business.

- Creditors have loaned money to the corporation and thus earn interest.
- Stockholders have invested in the corporation's stock and therefore own the company's net income.

The sum of interest expense and net income is the return to the two groups that have financed the corporation's assets, and this is the numerator of the return-on-assets ratio. The denominator is average total assets. Return on assets is computed as follows, using data from the 1999 annual report of IHOP Corp. (dollar amounts in thousands):

$$\begin{array}{c} \text{Rate of return} \\ \text{on total} \\ \text{assets} \end{array} = \frac{\text{Net income} + \text{Interest expense}}{\text{Average total assets}}$$

$$= \frac{\$32,125 + \$19,391}{(\$443,032 + \$520,402)/2} = \frac{\$51,516}{\$481,717} = 0.107$$

Net income and interest expense are taken from the income statement. Average total assets is computed from the beginning and ending balance sheets.

What is a good rate of return on total assets? There is no single answer to this question because rates of return vary widely by industry. For example, high technology companies such as **Intel** and **Hewlett-Packard** earn higher returns than utility companies and manufacturers of consumer goods such as toothpaste. In most industries a return on assets of 10% is considered good.

Rate of Return on Common Stockholders' Equity

RATE OF RETURN ON COMMON STOCKHOLDERS' EQUITY. Net income minus preferred dividends, divided by average common stockholders' equity. A measure of profitability. Also called **return on equity.**

DAILY EXERCISE 13-18

DAILY EXERCISE 13-19

Rate of return on common stockholders' equity, often called **return on equity,** shows the relationship between net income and average common stockholders' equity. The numerator is net income minus preferred dividends. Preferred dividends are subtracted because the preferred stockholders have the first claim to dividends from the company's net income. The denominator is average *common stockholders' equity*—total stockholders' equity minus preferred equity. IHOP's rate of return on common stockholders' equity for 1999 is computed as follows (dollar amounts in thousands):

$$\text{Rate of return on common stockholders' equity} = \frac{\text{Net income} - \text{Preferred dividends}}{\text{Average common stockholders' equity}}$$

$$= \frac{\$32,125 - \$0}{(\$187,868 + \$226,480)/2} = \frac{\$32,125}{\$207,174} = 0.155$$

IHOP Corp. has no preferred stock, so preferred dividends are zero. With no preferred stock outstanding, average *common* stockholders' equity is the same as average *total* equity—the average of the beginning and ending amounts.

IHOP's return on equity (15.5%) is higher than its return on assets (10.7%). This indicates a financially healthy company because IHOP is earning more for its stockholders than it is paying for interest expense. Companies such as IHOP borrow at one rate (say, 7%) and invest the funds to earn a higher rate (almost 16%). Borrowing at a lower rate than the return on investments is called *using leverage.*

If return on assets is higher than return on equity, the company is in trouble because its interest expense is greater than its return on equity. Interest expense should always be lower than the amount the company earns on its investments. Investors and creditors use return on common stockholders' equity in much the same way they use return on total assets—to compare companies. The higher the rate of return, the more successful the company. IHOP's 15.5% return on common stockholders' equity would be considered good in most industries.

ACCOUNTING FOR INCOME TAXES BY CORPORATIONS

Objective 7
Account for the income tax of a corporation

Corporations pay income tax just as individuals do, but not at the same rates. At this writing, the federal tax rate on most corporate income is 35%. Most states also levy a corporate income tax, so most corporations have a combined federal and state income tax rate of approximately 40%.

To account for income tax, the corporation measures

- Income tax expense, an expense on the income statement
- Income tax payable, a liability on the balance sheet

Accounting for income tax by a corporation follows the general principles that govern accounting for all other transactions. Let's return to **IHOP Corp.** In 20X0, suppose IHOP reported income before tax (also called pretax accounting income) of approximately $50 million on its income statement. IHOP's combined income tax rate is 40%. Assume IHOP's income tax expense and income tax payable are the same. Then IHOP would record income tax for the year as follows (amounts in millions):

20X0			
Dec. 31	Income Tax Expense ($50 × 0.40)	20	
	Income Tax Payable		20
	Recorded income tax for the year.		

IHOP's 20X0 financial statements would report these figures (adapted, in millions):

Income Statement		Balance Sheet	
Income before income tax	$ 50	Current liabilities:	
Income tax expense	(20)	Income tax payable	$20
Net income	$ 30		

Early in 20X1, IHOP would pay its income tax payable when the company files its 20X0 income tax return with the Internal Revenue Service. Now, let's move to 20X1 with a more realistic income tax example. In general, income tax expense and income tax payable can be computed as follows:[2]

Income tax expense	=	Income before income tax (from the income statement)	×	Income tax rate		Income tax payable	=	Taxable income (from the income tax return filed with the IRS)	×	Income tax rate

For most companies, income tax expense and income tax payable differ. The most important difference between income tax expense and income tax payable occurs when a corporation uses the straight-line depreciation method for the financial statements and an accelerated depreciation method for the tax return. The tax depreciation method is called the *modified accelerated cost recovery system,* abbreviated as MACRS. For any one year, MACRS depreciation may differ from accounting depreciation on the income statement.

➤ We learned in Chapter 10, page 400, that the MACRS depreciation method is similar to the double-declining-balance method.

Continuing with the IHOP illustration, suppose for 20X1 that IHOP Corp. has

- Income before income tax of $60 million on the income statement
- Taxable income of $55 million on the company's income tax return

IHOP will record income tax for 20X1 as follows (dollar amounts in millions and an income tax rate of 40%):

```
20X1
Dec. 31    Income Tax Expense ($60 × 0.40) ....................   24
               Income Tax Payable ($55 × 0.40)............        22
               Deferred Tax Liability................................         2
           Recorded income tax for the year.
```

IHOP will pay the $22 million of Income Tax Payable, a current liability, within a few months. The Deferred Tax Liability account is long-term, so IHOP will pay this debt over a number of years. IHOP's 20X1 financial statements would report these figures (adapted, in millions):

DAILY EXERCISE 13-20

Income Statement		Balance Sheet	
Income before income tax............	$60	Current liabilities:	
Income tax expense......................	(24)	Income tax payable	$22
Net income	$36	Long-term liabilities:	
		Deferred tax liability................	2*

* Assumes the beginning balance of Deferred tax liability was zero.

The Decision Guidelines feature provides an overview of the second half of the chapter.

[2] The authors thank Jean Marie Hudson for suggesting this presentation.

DECISION GUIDELINES

Dividends, Stock Values, Evaluating Operations, & Accounting for Income Tax

DECISION	GUIDELINES
Dividends	
Whether to declare a cash dividend?	• Must have enough retained earnings to declare the dividend. • Must have enough cash to pay the dividend.
What happens with a dividend?	• The corporation's board of directors declares the dividend. Then the dividend becomes a liability of the corporation. • The date of record fixes who will receive the dividend. • Payment of the dividend occurs later.
Who receives the dividend?	• Preferred stockholders first receive their dividends at a specified rate. • Common stockholders receive the remainder.
Stock Values	
How much to pay for a stock?	Its market value.
What unique value applies to preferred stock?	• Liquidation value—the amount the corporation agrees to pay if the company liquidates
What is book value's role in decision making?	Sometimes used to help determine the market value of a stock that is not traded on a stock exchange.
Evaluating Operations	
How to evaluate the operations of a corporation?	Two measures that relate earnings to the amount stockholders have invested include • Rate of return on assets • Rate of return on common stockholders' equity For a healthy company, return on stockholders' equity should exceed return on assets.
Accounting for Income Tax	
What are the three main accounts?	• Income tax expense • Income tax payable, a current liability • Deferred tax liability, usually a long-term liability
How to measure	
• Income tax expense?	Income before income tax × Income tax rate (from the income statement)
• Income tax payable?	Taxable income × Income tax rate (from the income tax return filed with the Internal Revenue Service)
• Deferred tax liability?	Difference between income tax expense and income tax payable for any one year

EXCEL APPLICATION PROBLEM

Goal: Create an Excel spreadsheet that compares financial performance of several publicly traded stocks.

Scenario: Your task is to create an Excel spreadsheet that compares the historical performance of **The Gap** and **Abercrombie & Fitch** on three key financial measures. Embedded graphs of each financial dimension also must be created. All data used in your spreadsheet will come from Morningstar's Web site.

When done, answer these questions:

1. Which company has earned a consistently higher return on equity?
2. Which company has earned a consistently higher return on assets?
3. Increasing cash flow from operations is a good sign for investing. Which company has experienced increasing cash flows over the past five years?
4. Based on these very limited data, would you invest in either of these companies? Why or why not?

521

Step-by-step:
1. Locate **www.morningstar.com** on the Web.
2. Under the "Quotes & Reports" section, enter the ticker symbol for each company. Then, look under "Company Performance" and "Historical Overview." You should see a five-year summary of fiscal-year-end financial performance. Print out the Historical Overview for each company.
3. Open a new Excel spreadsheet.
4. Create a boldfaced heading for your spreadsheet that contains the following:
   a. Chapter 13 Decision Guidelines
   b. Investing in Stock
   c. Stock Performance Analysis
   d. Today's date
5. Under the heading, create a boldfaced, underlined section titled "Return on Equity %." Move down one row.

Create one column each for the last five years (for example, "1999," "1998," and so on). Create one row each for The Gap and Abercrombie & Fitch.
6. Enter the return on equity data for the past five years found on the Morningstar Historical Overview for each company.
7. Repeat steps 5 and 6 for "Return on Assets %" and "Operating Cash Flow (in millions)."
8. Using the Excel Chart Wizard, create separate graphs for Return on Equity %, Return on Assets %, and Operating Cash Flow. Resize and position each graph to the right of the data so that everything appears on one page when you print.
9. Save your work, and print your spreadsheet in landscape mode (with graphs) for your files.

REVIEW CORPORATIONS: PAID-IN CAPITAL AND THE BALANCE SHEET

SUMMARY PROBLEM

www.prenhall.com/horngren

End-of-Chapter Assessment

1. Use the following accounts and related balances to prepare the classified balance sheet of Whitehall, Inc., at September 30, 20X4. Use the account format of the balance sheet.

Common stock, $1 par, 50,000 shares authorized, 20,000 shares issued	$ 20,000	Long-term note payable	$ 73,000
		Inventory	85,000
Dividends payable	4,000	Property, plant, and equipment, net	225,000
Cash	9,000	Accounts receivable, net	23,000
Accounts payable	28,000	Preferred stock, $3.75, no-par, 10,000 shares authorized,	
Retained earnings	75,000		
Paid-in capital in excess of par—common	115,000	2,000 shares issued	24,000
		Accrued liabilities	3,000

2. The balance sheet of Trendline Corporation reported the following at March 31, 20X6, the end of its fiscal year. Note that Trendline reports paid-in capital in excess of par or stated value after the stock accounts.

Stockholders' Equity	
Preferred stock, 4%, $10 par, 10,000 shares authorized (liquidation value $110,000)	$100,000
Common stock, no-par, $5 stated value, 100,000 shares authorized	250,000
Paid-in capital in excess of par: Common stock	231,500
Retained earnings	395,000
Total stockholders' equity	$976,500

Required

1. Is the preferred stock cumulative or noncumulative? How can you tell?
2. What is the total amount of the annual preferred dividend?
3. How many shares of preferred and common stock has the company issued?

4. Compute the book value per share of the preferred and the common stock. No prior year preferred dividends are in arrears, but Trendline has not declared the current-year dividend.

Solution

WHITEHALL, INC.
Balance Sheet
September 30, 20X4

Assets		**Liabilities**	
Current:		Current:	
Cash	$ 9,000	Accounts payable....................	$ 28,000
Accounts receivable, net	23,000	Dividends payable..................	4,000
Inventory	85,000	Accrued liabilities	3,000
Total current assets....................................	117,000	Total current liabilities........	35,000
Property, plant and equipment, net..............	225,000	Long-term note payable	73,000
		Total liabilities.........................	108,000
		Stockholders' Equity	
		Paid-in capital:	
		Preferred stock, $3.75, no-par,	
		10,000 shares authorized,	
		2,000 shares issued	$ 24,000
		Common stock, $1 par, 50,000	
		shares authorized, 20,000	
		shares issued	20,000
		Paid-in capital in excess of	
		par—common	115,000
		Total paid-in capital	159,000
		Retained earnings.......................	75,000
		Total stockholders' equity.......	234,000
		Total liabilities and	
Total assets	$342,000	stockholders' equity................	$342,000

Required

1. The preferred stock is cumulative because it is not specifically labeled otherwise.
2. Total annual preferred dividend: $4,000 ($100,000 × 0.04).
3. Preferred stock issued: 10,000 shares ($100,000/$10 par value).
   Common stock issued: 50,000 shares ($250,000/$5 stated value).
4. Book values per share of preferred and common stock:

Preferred:	
Liquidation value	$110,000
Cumulative dividend for current year ($100,000 × 0.04)	4,000
Stockholders' equity allocated to preferred............................	$114,000
Book value per share ($114,000/10,000 shares)	$11.40
Common:	
Total stockholders' equity...	$976,500
Less stockholders' equity allocated to preferred....................	(114,000)
Stockholders' equity allocated to common	$862,500
Book value per share ($862,500/50,000 shares)	$17.25

LESSONS LEARNED

1. *Identify the characteristics of a corporation.* A corporation is a separate legal and business entity. *Continuous life,* the *ease of raising large amounts of capital and transferring ownership,* and *limited liability* are among the advantages of the corporate form of organization. An important disadvantage is *double taxation.* Corporations pay *income taxes,* and stockholders pay tax on dividends. *Stockholders* are the owners of the corporations. They elect a *board of directors,* which elects a chairperson and appoints the officers to manage the business.

2. *Record the issuance of stock.* Corporations may issue different classes of stock: *par value, no-par value, common,* and *preferred.* Stock is usually issued at a *premium*—an amount above par value.

3. *Prepare the stockholders' equity section of a corporation's balance sheet.* The balance sheet carries the capital raised through stock issuance under the heading Paid-in Capital or Contributed Capital in the stockholders' equity section.

4. Account for cash dividends. Only when the board of directors declares a *dividend* does the corporation incur the liability to pay dividends. Preferred stock has priority over common stock as to dividends, which may be stated as a percent of par value or as a dollar amount per share. In addition, preferred stock has a claim to dividends in arrears if it is *cumulative*.

5. Use different stock values in decision making. A stock's *market value* is the price for which a share may be bought or sold. *Liquidation value* and *book value*—the amount of owners' equity per share of company stock—are other values that may apply to stock.

6. Evaluate a company's return on assets and return on stockholders' equity. *Return on assets* and *return on stockholders' equity* are two standard measures of profitability. A healthy company's return on equity will exceed its return on assets.

7. Account for the income tax of a corporation. Corporations pay income tax and must account for the income tax expense and income tax payable. A difference between the expense and the payable creates another account, Deferred Tax Liability.

Accounting Vocabulary

additional paid-in capital (p. 512)
authorization of stock (p. 502)
board of directors (p. 503)
book value (p. 517)
bylaws (p. 503)
chairperson (p. 503)
charter (p. 501)
common stock (p. 504)
contributed capital (p. 503)
cumulative preferred stock (p. 516)
deficit (p. 505)

dividends (p. 505)
double taxation (p. 502)
legal capital (p. 505)
limited liability (p. 502)
market value (p. 516)
outstanding stock (p. 503)
paid-in capital (p. 503)
par value (p. 507)
preferred stock (p. 506)
president (p. 503)
rate of return on common stockholders' equity (p. 519)

rate of return on total assets (p. 518)
retained earnings (p. 503)
return on assets (p. 518)
return on equity (p. 519)
shareholder (p. 501)
stated value (p. 507)
stock (p. 501)
stockholder (p. 501)
stockholders' equity (p. 503)

Questions

1. Identify the characteristics of a corporation.
2. Explain why corporations face a tax disadvantage.
3. How are the structures of a partnership and a corporation similar, and how are they different?
4. Dividends on preferred stock may be stated as a percent or a dollar amount. What is the annual dividend on these preferred stocks: 4%, $100 par; $3.50, $20 par; and 6%, no-par with $50 stated value?
5. Which event increases the assets of the corporation: authorization of stock or issuance of stock? Explain.
6. Suppose H. J. Heinz Company issued 1,000 shares of its 3.65%, $100 par preferred stock for $120. How much would this transaction increase the company's paid-in capital? How much would it increase Heinz's retained earnings? How much would it increase Heinz's annual cash dividend payments?
7. Give two alternative account titles for Paid-in Capital in Excess of Par—Common Stock.
8. How does issuance of 1,000 shares of no-par stock for

land and a building, together worth $150,000, affect paid-in capital? Total stockholders' equity?
9. Rank the following accounts in the order they would appear on the balance sheet: Common Stock, Preferred Stock, Retained Earnings, Dividends Payable. Also, give each account's balance sheet classification.
10. As a preferred stockholder, would you rather own cumulative or noncumulative preferred? If all other factors are the same, would the corporation rather the preferred stock be cumulative or noncumulative? Give your reason.
11. Distinguish between the market value of stock and the book value of stock. Which is more important to investors?
12. How is book value per share of common stock computed when the company has both preferred stock and common stock outstanding?
13. Why should a healthy company's rate of return on stockholders' equity exceed its rate of return on total assets?
14. Explain the difference between the income tax expense and the income tax payable of a corporation.

Assess Your Progress

Daily Exercises

Characteristics of a corporation
(Obj. 1)

DE13-1 Suppose you are forming Spuds, Inc., which will feature 20 different toppings for baked potatoes. You need some outside money from other investors, and you have decided to organize the business as a corporation that will issue stock to raise the needed funds. Briefly discuss your most important reason for organizing Spuds as a corporation rather than as a partnership. If you had organized as a partnership, what would be your most important reason for not organizing as a corporation?

Authority structure in a corporation
(Obj. 1)

DE13-2 Consider the authority structure in a corporation, as diagrammed in Exhibit 13-2.
1. Who is in charge of day-to-day operations?
2. Who manages the accounting?

3. Who has primary responsibility for the corporation's cash?

4. What group holds the ultimate power in a corporation?

5. Who is the most powerful person in the corporation?

DE13-3 Examine the summarized balance sheet of **Target Corporation** in Exhibit 13-4 page 504. Suppose Target were a proprietorship owned by Lee Target. How would the Target proprietorship balance sheet differ from the one given in Exhibit 13-4? How would the proprietorship balance sheet be similar to the one given in Exhibit 13-4?

Similarities and differences between the balance sheets of a corporation and a proprietorship (Obj. 1)

DE13-4 Answer the following questions about the characteristics of a corporation's stock.

Characteristics of preferred and common stock (Obj. 1)

1. What privileges do preferred stockholders enjoy that common stockholders do not have?

2. Which class of stockholders would expect to reap greater benefits from a highly profitable corporation? Why?

3. Which stockholders are the real owners of a corporation?

4. Which right clearly distinguishes a stockholder from a creditor (who has lent money to the corporation)?

DE13-5 Study **IHOP's** July 31 stock issuance entry given on page 507, and answer these questions about the nature of the IHOP transaction.

Effect of a stock issuance on net income (Obj. 2)

1. IHOP received $32,000,000 for the issuance of its stock. The par value of the IHOP stock was only $32,000. Was the excess amount of $31,968,000 a profit to IHOP? If not, what was it?

2. Suppose the par value of the IHOP stock had been $1 per share, $5 per share, or $10 per share. Would a change in the par value of the company's stock affect IHOP's net income? Give the reason for your answer.

DE13-6 **The Coca-Cola Company** reported the following on its balance sheet at December 31, 1999 (adapted, amounts in millions, except for par value):

Issuing stock and interpreting stockholders' equity (Obj. 2)

Common stock, $0.25 par value	
Authorized: 5,600 shares	
Issued: 3,466 shares	$ 867
Paid-in capital in excess of par..............	2,584
Retained earnings	20,773

1. Assume Coca-Cola issued all of its stock during 1999. Journalize the company's issuance of the stock for cash.

2. Was Coca-Cola's main source of stockholders' equity paid-in capital or profitable operations? How can you tell?

DE13-7 At December 31, 1999, **The Coca-Cola Company** reported the following on its comparative balance sheet, which included 1998 amounts for comparison (adapted, with all amounts except par value in millions):

Issuing stock and analyzing retained earnings (Obj. 2)

	December 31,	
	1999	**1998**
Common stock $0.25 par value		
Authorized: 5,600 shares		
Issued: 3,466 shares in 1999	$ 867	
3,460 shares in 1998		$ 865
Paid-in capital in excess of par...............	2,584	2,158
Retained earnings	20,773	19,922

1. How much did Coca-Cola's total paid-in capital increase during 1999? What caused total paid-in capital to increase? How can you tell?

2. Journalize Coca-Cola's issuance of stock for cash during 1999.

3. Did Coca-Cola have a profit or a loss for 1999? How can you tell?

DE13-8 Brunnheimer Corporation has three classes of stock: Common, $1 par; Preferred Class A, $10 par; and Preferred Class B, no-par.

Issuing stock (Obj. 2)

Journalize Brunnheimer's issuance of

a. 1,000 shares of common stock for $30 per share

b. 1,000 shares of Class A preferred stock for a total of $32,000

c. 1,000 shares of Class B preferred stock for $14 per share

Explanations are not required.

Issuing stock to finance the
purchase of assets
(Obj. 2)

DE13-9 This exercise shows the similarity and the difference between two ways to acquire plant assets.

Case A—Issue stock and buy the assets in separate transactions:

Avisa Machines, Inc., issued 10,000 shares of its $10 par common stock for cash of $700,000. In a separate transaction, Avisa Machines purchased a warehouse building for $480,000 and equipment for $220,000. Journalize the two transactions.

Case B—Issue stock to acquire the assets:

Avisa Machines issued 10,000 shares of its $10 par common stock to acquire a warehouse building valued at $480,000 and equipment worth $220,000. Journalize this transaction.

Compare the balances in all accounts after making both sets of entries. Are the account balances similar or different?

Preparing the stockholders'
equity section of a balance sheet
(Obj. 3)

DE13-10 The financial statements of Arthur Binding, Inc., reported the following accounts (adapted, in millions except for par value):

Paid-in capital in excess of par......	$ 17.3	Net sales	$1,081.5
Cost of goods sold..........................	588.0	Accounts payable	62.4
Common stock $0.01 par,		Retained earnings.......................	166.2
40.2 shares issued	0.4	Other current liabilities..............	52.3
Cash..	24.0	Operating expenses....................	412.9
Long-term debt.............................	7.6	Total assets.................................	?

Prepare the stockholders' equity section of the Arthur Binding balance sheet. Net income has already been closed to Retained Earnings.

DE13-11 ◄ *Link Back to Chapter 1 (Accounting Equation, Income Statement).* Use the Arthur Binding data in Daily Exercise 13-10 to compute Arthur's

  a. Net income   **b.** Total liabilities   **c.** Total assets

Reporting stockholders' equity on
the balance sheet
(Obj. 3)

DE13-12 Varlux Corporation began operations in 20X3 with a charter that authorized the company to issue 10,000 shares of 5%, $8 par preferred stock and 100,000 shares of no-par common stock. During 20X3 through 20X8, Varlux issued 3,000 shares of the preferred stock for $25 per share and 50,000 shares of its common stock for $5 per share. At December 31, 20X8, Varlux had retained earnings of $110,000. During 20X9, Varlux earned net income of $70,000 and declared cash dividends of $15,000.

    Show how Varlux Corporation reported stockholders' equity on its balance sheet at December 31, 20X9.

DE13-13 Colombia Coffee Company earned net income of $85,000 during the year ended December 31, 20X3. On December 15, Colombia declared the annual cash dividend on its 6% preferred stock (10,000 shares with total par value of $100,000) and a $0.50 per share cash dividend on its common stock (50,000 shares with total par value of $250,000). Colombia then paid the dividends on January 4, 20X4.

    Journalize for Colombia Company
  a. Declaring the cash dividends on December 15
  b. Closing net income to Retained Earnings on December 31, 20X3
  c. Paying the cash dividends on January 4, 20X4

Did Retained Earnings increase or decrease during 20X3? By how much?

Dividing cash dividends between
preferred and common stock
(Obj. 4)

DE13-14 Refer to the stockholders' equity of MedTech.com Corporation in Exhibit 13-8, page 512. Answer these questions about MedTech.com's dividends.

  1. How much in dividends must MedTech.com declare each year before the common stockholders receive cash dividends for the year?
  2. Suppose MedTech.com declares cash dividends of $20,000 for 20X1. How much of the dividends goes to preferred? How much goes to common?
  3. Is MedTech.com's preferred stock cumulative or noncumulative? How can you tell?
  4. Suppose MedTech.com passed the preferred dividend in 20X2 and 20X3. In 20X4, the company declares cash dividends of $9,000. How much of the dividends goes to preferred? How much goes to common?

Similarities and differences
between preferred stock and
common stock
(Obj. 5)

DE13-15 Indicate whether each of the following characteristics applies to preferred stock, common stock, or both.
  a. Cumulative   **d.** Stated dividend
  b. Callable   **e.** Voting rights
  c. Liquidation value   **f.** Priority to receive assets in the event of liquidation

DE13-16 Refer to the stockholders' equity of MedTech.com Corporation in Exhibit 13-8, page 512. MedTech.com's preferred stock has a liquidation value of $125 per share, and MedTech.com has not declared preferred dividends for three years (including the current year). Compute the book value of MedTech.com's (a) preferred stock and (b) common stock.

Book value per share of preferred and common stock
(Obj. 5)

DE13-17 Answer the following questions about various stock values.

1. Suppose you are an investor considering the purchase of **Intel** common stock as an investment. You have called your stockbroker to inquire about the stock. Which stock value are you most concerned about and why?
2. How is the book value of a stock used in decision making?
3. Suppose you are the general manager of a small company that is considering going public, as **IHOP Corp.** did in the chapter-opening story. Which stock value are you most concerned about and why?

Explaining the use of different stock values for decision making
(Obj. 5)

DE13-18 Answer these questions about two rates of return.

1. Give the formula for computing (a) rate of return on common stockholders' equity and (b) rate of return on total assets.
2. Why are preferred dividends subtracted from net income to compute return on common stockholders' equity?
3. Why is interest expense added to net income to compute return on assets?

Computing and explaining return on assets and return on equity
(Obj. 6)

DE13-19 **The Coca-Cola Company** has earned solid rates of return on its assets and its stockholders' equity in recent years. Coca-Cola's 1999 financial statements reported the following items—with 1998 figures given for comparison (adapted, in millions):

Computing return on assets and return on equity for a leading company
(Obj. 6)

	1999	1998
Balance sheet		
Total current assets	$ 6,480	$ 6,380
Total long-term assets	15,143	12,765
Total assets	$21,623	$19,145
Total liabilities	$12,110	$10,742
Total stockholders' equity (all common)	9,513	8,403
Total liabilities and equity	$21,623	$19,145
Income statement		
Net sales	$19,805	
Cost of goods sold	6,009	
Gross profit	13,796	
Selling, administrative, and general expenses	9,814	
Interest expense	337	
All other expenses, net	1,214	
Net income	$ 2,431	

Compute Coca-Cola's rate of return on total assets and rate of return on common stockholders' equity for 1999. Do these rates of return look high or low?

DE13-20 Harry's Hot Dogs had income before income tax of $120,000 and taxable income of $90,000 for 20X1, the company's first year of operations. The income tax rate is 40%.

Accounting for a corporation's income tax
(Obj. 7)

1. Make the entry to record Harry's income taxes for 20X1.
2. Show what Harry's Hot Dogs will report on its 20X1 income statement starting with income before income tax. Also show what Harry will report for current and long-term liabilities on its December 31, 20X1, balance sheet.

EXERCISES

E13-1 Dena Kelly and Tiffany Lewis are opening a limousine service to be named D & T Limo. They need outside capital, so they plan to organize the business as a corporation. They come to you for advice. Write a memorandum informing them of the steps in forming a corporation. Identify specific documents used in this process, and name the different parties involved in the ownership and management of a corporation.

Organizing a corporation
(Obj. 1)

E13-2 New England Systems completed the following stock issuance transactions:

April 19   Issued 1,000 shares of $1.50 par common stock for cash of $10.50 per share.
May   3   Sold 300 shares of $4.50, no-par Class A preferred stock for $12,000 cash.
      11   Received inventory valued at $23,000 and equipment with market value of $11,000. Issued 3,300 shares of the $1.50 par common stock.
      15   Issued 1,000 shares of 5%, no-par Class B preferred stock with stated value of $50 per share. The issue price was cash of $62 per share.

Required

1. Journalize the transactions. Explanations are not required.
2. How much paid-in capital did these transactions generate for New England Systems?

E13-3 The charter for Sartis Rugs, Inc., authorizes the company to issue 100,000 shares of $3, no-par preferred stock and 500,000 shares of common stock with $1 par value. During its start-up phase, Sartis completed the following transactions:

Aug.   6   Issued 500 shares of common stock to the promoters who organized the corporation, receiving cash of $15,000.
      12   Issued 300 shares of preferred stock for cash of $18,000.
      14   Issued 1,000 shares of common stock in exchange for land valued at $26,000.
      31   Earned a small profit for August and closed the $13,000 net income into Retained Earnings.

Required

1. Record the transactions in the general journal.
2. Prepare the stockholders' equity section of the Sartis balance sheet at August 31.

E13-4 The balance sheet of Levitz Corporation, as adapted, reported the following stockholders' equity. Levitz has two separate classes of preferred stock, labeled Series A and Series B.

Stockholders' Equity	$ Thousands
Preferred stock, $2 par, authorized 4,000,000 shares (Note 7)	
Series A	$ 100
Series B	740
Common stock, $0.10 par, authorized 20,000,000,	
issued 9,000,000 shares	900
Capital in excess of par (sum of preferred and common)	74,580

Note 7. Preferred Stock:

Shares Issued	
Series A	50,000
Series B	370,000

Required

The Series A preferred stock was issued for $5 cash per share, the Series B preferred was issued for $10 cash per share, and the common was issued for cash of $72,370 thousand. Make the summary journal entries to record issuance of all the Levitz stock. Explanations are not required. After you record these entries, what is the total balance of Capital in Excess of Par?

E13-5 Modern Furniture Co., located in Boston, Massachusetts, imports European furniture and Oriental rugs. The corporation issued 5,000 shares of no-par common stock for $8 per share. Record issuance of the stock if the stock (a) is true no-par stock and (b) has stated value of $2 per share.

E13-6 The charter of Laurelake Corporation authorizes the issuance of 5,000 shares of Class A preferred stock, 1,000 shares of Class B preferred stock, and 10,000 shares of common stock. During a two-month period, Laurelake completed these stock-issuance transactions:

Nov. 23   Issued 2,000 shares of $1 par common stock for cash of $12.50 per share.

Dec. 2   Sold 300 shares of $4.50, no-par Class A preferred stock for $20,000 cash.

     12   Received inventory valued at $25,000 and equipment with market value of $16,000 for 3,300 shares of the $1 par common stock.

     17   Issued 1,000 shares of 5%, no-par Class B preferred stock with stated value of $50 per share. The issue price was cash of $60 per share.

Required

Prepare the stockholders' equity section of the Laurelake balance sheet for the transactions given in this exercise. Retained Earnings has a balance of $46,000.

E13-7 ReadyTech Co. recently organized. The company issued common stock to an attorney in exchange for his patent with a market value of $40,000. In addition, ReadyTech received cash both for 2,000 shares of its $50 par preferred stock at $80 per share and for 26,000 shares of its no-par common stock at $11 per share. Retained Earnings at the end of the first year was $70,000. Without making journal entries, determine the total paid-in capital created by these transactions.

Paid-in capital for a corporation (Obj. 2)

E13-8 Gene Shattler, Inc., has the following selected account balances at June 30, 20X2. Prepare the stockholders' equity section of the company's balance sheet.

Stockholders' equity section of a balance sheet (Obj. 3)

Common stock, no par with $1 stated value, 100,000 shares authorized and issued	$100,000	Inventory	$112,000
		Machinery and equipment	109,000
		Preferred stock, 5%, $20 par, 20,000 shares authorized, 5,000 shares issued	100,000
Accumulated depreciation—machinery and equipment	62,000	Paid-in capital in excess of par—preferred stock	88,000
Retained earnings	119,000		
Cost of goods sold	81,000		

E13-9 Qualcomm Communications has the following stockholders' equity:

Dividing dividends between preferred and common stock (Obj. 4)

Preferred stock, 8%, $10 par, 100,000 shares authorized, 20,000 shares issued	$ 200,000
Common stock, $0.50 par, 500,000 shares authorized, 300,000 shares issued	150,000
Paid-in capital in excess of par—common	600,000
Total paid-in capital	$ 950,000
Retained earnings	150,000
Total stockholders' equity	$1,100,000

First, determine whether preferred stock is cumulative or noncumulative. Then compute the amount of dividends to preferred and to common for 20X1 and 20X2 if total dividends are $10,000 in 20X1 and $60,000 in 20X2.

E13-10 The following elements of stockholders' equity are adapted from the balance sheet of Levitz Corporation.

Computing dividends on preferred and common stock (Obj. 4)

Stockholders' Equity	$ Thousands
Preferred stock, cumulative, $2 par (Note 7)	
Series A, 50,000 shares issued	$100
Series B, 370,000 shares issued	740
Common stock, $0.10 par, 9,000,000 shares issued	900

Note 7. Preferred Stock:

Designated Annual Cash Dividend per Share	
Series A	$0.40
Series B	1.30

The Series A preferred has preference over the Series B preferred, and the company has paid all preferred dividends through 20X3.

Required

Compute the dividends to both series of preferred stock and to common for 20X4 and 20X5 if total dividends are $0 in 20X4 and $1,100,000 in 20X5.

Book value per share of preferred and common stock
(Obj. 5)

E13-11 The balance sheet of Iota Corporation reported the following:

Preferred stock; 100 shares issued and outstanding, liquidation value $6,000	$ 4,800
Common stockholders' equity, 10,000 shares issued and outstanding	222,000
Total stockholders' equity	$226,800

Assume that Iota has paid preferred dividends for the current year and all prior years (no dividends in arrears). Compute the book value per share of the preferred stock and the common stock.

Book value per share of preferred and common stock; preferred dividends in arrears *(Obj. 5)*

E13-12 Refer to Exercise 13-11. Compute the book value per share of the preferred stock and the common stock if three years' preferred dividends (including dividends for the current year) are in arrears. The preferred stock dividend rate is 6%. Round book value to the nearest cent.

Evaluating profitability
(Obj. 6)

E13-13 Weimeyer Furniture, Inc., reported these figures for 20X3 and 20X2:

	20X3	20X2
Income statement:		
Interest expense...................................	$ 17,400,000	$ 7,100,000
Net income	12,000,000	18,700,000
Balance sheet:		
Total assets...	326,000,000	317,000,000
Preferred stock, $1.30, no-par,		
100,000 shares issued and		
outstanding	2,500,000	2,500,000
Common stockholders' equity	164,000,000	157,000,000
Total stockholders' equity......................	166,500,000	159,500,000

Compute rate of return on total assets and rate of return on common stockholders' equity for 20X3. Do these rates of return suggest strength or weakness? Give your reason.

Accounting for income tax by a corporation
(Obj. 7)

E13-14 The income statement of **Pier 1 Imports, Inc.,** reported income before income tax of $130 million during a recent year. Assume Pier 1's taxable income for the year was $100 million. The company's income tax rate was 40%.

1. Journalize Pier 1's entry to record income tax for the year.
2. Show how Pier 1 would report income tax on its income statement and on its balance sheet. Complete the income statement, starting with income before tax. For the balance sheet, assume all beginning balances were zero.

Challenge Exercise

Accounting for stockholders' equity transactions
(Obj. 2, 4)

E13-15 **Wal-Mart Stores, Inc.,** reported these comparative stockholders' equity data (adapted, with amounts in millions except par value):

	January 31,	
	20X0	19X9
Common stock ($0.10 par value).............	$ 446	$ 445
Capital in excess of par value	714	435
Retained earnings.....................................	25,129	20,741

During 20X0, Wal-Mart completed these transactions:

a. Net income, $5,377
b. Cash dividends declared and paid, $989
c. Issuance of stock for cash, $280

Required

1. Journalize these 20X0 transactions.
2. For each stockholders' equity account, start with the January 31, 19X9, balance and work toward the balance at January 31, 20X0 to show how your journal entries accounted for the changes in the Wal-Mart accounts.

PROBLEMS

(Group A)

P13-1A Joy Shields and Lin Liu are opening a **Cracker Barrel Restaurant** in Denver, Colorado. There are no competing family restaurants in the immediate vicinity. Their fundamental decision is how to organize the business, which will manage the restaurant and country store. Shields thinks the partnership form is best for their business. Liu favors the corporate form of organization. They seek your advice.

Organizing a corporation (Obj. 1)

Required

Write a memo to Shields and Liu to make them aware of the advantages and the disadvantages of organizing the business as a corporation. Use the following format:

Date:	_____
To:	Joy Shields and Lin Liu
From:	Student Name
Subject:	Advantages and disadvantages of the corporate form of business organization

P13-2A The partnership of Duran & Nueces needed additional capital to expand into new markets, so the business incorporated as Ventura, Inc. The charter from the state of Arizona authorizes Ventura to issue 50,000 shares of 6%, $100-par preferred stock and 100,000 shares of no-par common stock. To start, Ventura completed the following transactions:

Journalizing corporation transactions and preparing the stockholders' equity section of the balance sheet (Obj. 2, 3)

Dec. 2 Issued 9,000 shares of common stock to Duran and 12,000 shares to Nueces, both for cash of $5 per share.

10 Issued 400 shares of preferred stock to acquire a patent with a market value of $50,000.

27 Issued 12,000 shares of common stock to other investors for cash of $96,000.

Required

1. Record the transactions in the general journal.
2. Prepare the stockholders' equity section of the Ventura, Inc., balance sheet at December 31. The ending balance of Retained Earnings is $57,100.

P13-3A Hudson Corporation was organized in 20X1. At December 31, 20X1, Hudson's balance sheet reported the following stockholders' equity:

Issuing stock and preparing the stockholders' equity section of the balance sheet (Obj. 2, 3)

Preferred stock, 6%, $50 par, 100,000 shares authorized, none issued	$ —
Common stock, $1 par, 500,000 shares authorized, 60,000 shares issued...	60,000
Paid-in capital in excess of par—common	40,000
Retained earnings	25,000
Total stockholders' equity..	$125,000

Required

Answer the following questions, making journal entries as needed.

1. What does the 6% mean for the preferred stock? After Hudson issues preferred stock, how much in annual cash dividends will Hudson expect to pay on 1,000 shares?
2. At what price per share did Hudson issue the common stock during 20X1?

3. Were first-year operations profitable? Give your reason.

4. During 20X2, the company completed the following selected transactions. Journalize each transaction. Explanations are not required.

   a. Issued for cash 1,000 shares of preferred stock at par value.

   b. Issued for cash 2,000 shares of common stock at a price of $3 per share.

   c. Issued 50,000 shares of common stock to acquire a building valued at $150,000.

   d. Net income for the year was $82,000, and the company declared no dividends. Make the closing entry for net income.

5. Prepare the stockholders' equity section of the Hudson Corporation balance sheet at December 31, 20X2.

Stockholders' equity section of the balance sheet
(Obj. 3)

P13-4A The following summaries for Yurman Jewelry, Inc., and Northern Lights Insurance Company provide the information needed to prepare the stockholders' equity section of each company's balance sheet. The two companies are independent.

- *Yurman Jewelry, Inc.* Yurman Jewelry is authorized to issue 40,000 shares of $1 par common stock. All the stock was issued at $12 per share. The company incurred net losses of $50,000 in 20X1 and $14,000 in 20X2. It earned net income of $23,000 in 20X3 and $71,000 in 20X4. The company declared no dividends during the four-year period.
- *Northern Lights Insurance Company.* Northern Lights Insurance Company's charter authorizes the company to issue 50,000 shares of 7%, $10 par preferred stock and 500,000 shares of no-par common stock. Northern Lights Insurance issued 1,000 shares of the preferred stock at $15 per share. It issued 100,000 shares of the common stock for $400,000. The company's retained earnings balance at the beginning of 20X4 was $120,000. Net income for 20X4 was $90,000, and the company declared the specified preferred dividend for 20X4. Preferred dividends for 20X3 were in arrears.

Required

For each company, prepare the stockholders' equity section of its balance sheet at December 31, 20X4. Show the computation of all amounts. Entries are not required.

Analyzing the stockholders' equity of an actual corporation
(Obj. 3, 4)

P13-5A **The Procter & Gamble Company** reported the following stockholders' equity, as adapted, on its balance sheet at June 30, 19X9:

Stockholders' Equity	$ Millions
Preferred stock, 6.125%—	
Authorized 600,000,000 shares; issued 1,781,000 shares	$ 1,781
Common stock—$1 stated value—	
Authorized 5,000,000,000 shares; issued 1,320,000,000	1,320
Additional paid-in capital, common..	1,337
Retained earnings..	10,778
Other	(3,158)
Total...	$12,058

Required

1. Identify the different issues of stock Procter & Gamble has outstanding.

2. Make two summary journal entries to record issuance of all the Procter & Gamble stock. Assume all the stock was issued for cash. Explanations are not required.

3. Assume preferred dividends are in arrears for fiscal year 19X9. Journalize the declaration of a $1,626 million dividend at June 30, 20X0. Use separate Dividends Payable accounts for Preferred and Common. Round to the nearest $1 million. An explanation is not required.

Preparing a corporation balance sheet; measuring profitability
(Obj. 3, 6)

P13-6A ◄ *Link Back to Chapter 1 (Accounting Equation).* The following accounts and related balances of Omaha Mutual, Inc., are arranged in no particular order.

Common stock, $5 par,		Retained earnings........................	$?
100,000 shares authorized,		Inventory......................................	181,000
22,000 shares issued..............	$110,000	Property, plant, and	
Dividends payable	3,000	equipment, net	278,000
Total assets,		Prepaid expenses	13,000
November 30, 20X1...............	581,000	Goodwill, net..............................	37,000
Net income..............................	47,200	Accrued liabilities	17,000
Common stockholders' equity,		Long-term note payable	104,000
November 30, 20X1..............	383,000	Accounts receivable, net.............	102,000
Interest expense	12,800	Preferred stock, 4%, $10 par,	
Additional paid-in capital—		25,000 shares authorized,	
common...............................	140,000	3,700 shares issued	37,000
Accounts payable	31,000	Cash...	43,000

Required

1. Prepare the company's classified balance sheet in the account format at November 30, 20X2. Use the accounting equation to compute Retained Earnings.
2. Compute rate of return on total assets and rate of return on common stockholders' equity for the year ended November 30, 20X2.
3. Do these rates of return suggest strength or weakness? Give your reason.

P13-7A Eastern Seaboard Airline Corporation has 5,000 shares of 5%, $10 par value preferred stock and 100,000 shares of $1.50 par common stock outstanding. During a three-year period, Eastern Seaboard declared and paid cash dividends as follows: 20X1, $1,500; 20X2, $15,000; and 20X3, $23,000.

Computing dividends on preferred and common stock (Obj. 4)

Required

1. Compute the total dividends to preferred stock and to common stock for each of the three years if
   a. Preferred is noncumulative
   b. Preferred is cumulative
2. For case (1b), record the declaration of the 20X3 dividends on December 22, 20X3, and the payment of the dividends on January 14, 20X4. Use separate Dividends Payable accounts for Preferred and Common.

P13-8A The balance sheet of Hardwood Furniture, Inc., reported the following:

Analyzing the stockholders' equity of an actual corporation (Obj. 4, 5)

Stockholders' Investment [same as Stockholders' Equity]	($ Thousands)
Cumulative preferred stock...	$ 45
Common stock, $1 par, authorized 40,000,000 shares; issued 16,000,000 shares	16,000
Additional paid-in capital..	217,000
Retained earnings (Deficit)...	(77,165)
Total stockholders' investment..	$155,880

Notes to the financial statements indicate that 9,000 shares of $1.45 preferred stock with a stated value of $5 per share were issued and outstanding. The preferred stock has a liquidation value of $25 per share, and preferred dividends are in arrears for two years, including the current year. The additional paid-in capital belongs to common. On the balance sheet date, the market value of the Hardwood Furniture common stock was $9.50 per share.

Required

1. Is the preferred stock cumulative or noncumulative? How can you tell?
2. What is the amount of the annual preferred dividend?
3. What is the total paid-in capital of the company?
4. What was the total market value of the common stock?
5. Compute the book value per share of the preferred stock and the common stock.

P13-9A The accounting (not the income tax) records of Solarex Energy Corporation provide the income statement for 20X4.

Computing and recording a corporation's income tax (Obj. 7)

Total revenue......................................	$930,000
Expenses:	
Cost of goods sold	$430,000
Operating expenses........................	270,000
Total expenses before tax..............	700,000
Income before income tax...............	$230,000

The operating expenses include depreciation of $50,000 computed on the straight-line method. In calculating taxable income on the tax return, Solarex uses the modified accelerated cost recovery system (MACRS). MACRS depreciation was $80,000 for 20X4. The corporate income tax rate is 35%.

Required

1. Compute taxable income for the year.
2. Journalize the corporation's income tax for 20X4.
3. Prepare the corporation's single-step income statement for 20X4.

(Group B) PROBLEMS

Organizing a corporation
(Obj. 1)

P13-1B Ted Andrews and Ron Durham are opening a **Pier 1 Imports** store in a shopping center in Taos, New Mexico. The area is growing, and no competitors are located nearby. Their basic decision is how to organize the business. Andrews thinks the partnership form is best. Durham favors the corporate form of organization. They seek your advice.

Required

Write a memo to Andrews and Durham to make them aware of the advantages and the disadvantages of organizing the business as a corporate. Use the following format for your memo:

Date:	_____
To:	Ted Andrews and Ron Durham
From:	Student Name
Subject:	Advantages and disadvantages of the corporate form of business organization

Journalizing corporation transactions and preparing the stockholders' equity section of the balance sheet
(Obj. 2, 3)

P13-2B The partners who own Craven & Thames wished to avoid the unlimited personal liability of the partnership form of business, so they incorporated the partnership as C & T Services, Inc. The charter from the state of Louisiana authorizes the corporation to issue 10,000 shares of 6%, $100 par preferred stock and 250,000 shares of no-par common stock. In its first month, C & T Services completed the following transactions:

Jan. 3   Issued 6,300 shares of common stock to Craven and 3,800 shares to Thames, both for cash of $10 per share.
  12   Issued 1,000 shares of preferred stock to acquire a patent with a market value of $110,000.
  22   Issued 1,500 shares of common stock to other investors for $15 cash per share.

Required

1. Record the transactions in the general journal.
2. Prepare the stockholders' equity section of the C & T Services, Inc., balance sheet at January 31. The ending balance of Retained Earnings is $40,300.

Issuing stock and preparing the stockholders' equity section of the balance sheet
(Obj. 2, 3)

P13-3B Zaponata Corporation was organized in 20X1. At December 31, 20X1, Zaponata's balance sheet reported the following stockholders' equity:

Preferred stock, 5%, $10 par, 50,000 shares authorized, none issued	$ —
Common stock, $2 par, 100,000 shares authorized, 10,000 shares issued	20,000
Paid-in capital in excess of par—common..............................	30,000
Retained earnings (Deficit)..	(5,000)
Total stockholders' equity..	$45,000

Required

Answer the following questions, making journal entries as needed.

1. What does the 5% mean for the preferred stock? After Zaponata issues preferred stock, how much in annual cash dividends will Zaponata expect to pay on 1,000 shares?
2. At what price per share did Zaponata issue the common stock during 20X1?
3. Were first-year operations profitable? Give your reason.
4. During 20X2, the company completed the following selected transactions. Journalize each transaction. Explanations are not required.
   a. Issued for cash 5,000 shares of preferred stock at par value.
   b. Issued for cash 1,000 shares of common stock at a price of $7 per share.
   c. Issued 20,000 shares of common stock to acquire a building valued at $120,000.
   d. Net income for the year was $50,000, and the company declared no dividends. Make the closing entry for net income.
5. Prepare the stockholders' equity section of the Zaponata Corporation balance sheet at December 31, 20X2.

P13-4B Stockholders' equity information for two independent companies, Granada Enterprises, Inc., and Traigon Corp. is as follows:

Stockholders' equity section of the balance sheet (Obj. 3)

- *Granada Enterprises, Inc.* Granada is authorized to issue 60,000 shares of $5 par common stock. All the stock was issued at $12 per share. The company incurred a net loss of $41,000 in 20X1. It earned net income of $60,000 in 20X2 and $90,000 in 20X3. The company declared no dividends during the three-year period.
- *Traigon Corp.* Traigon's charter authorizes the company to issue 10,000 shares of $2.50 preferred stock with par value of $50 and 120,000 shares of no-par common stock. Traigon issued 1,000 shares of the preferred stock at $54 per share. It issued 40,000 shares of the common stock for a total of $220,000. The company's Retained Earnings balance at the beginning of 20X3 was $64,000, and net income for the year was $90,000. During 20X3, the company declared the specified dividend on preferred and a $0.50 per share dividend on common. Preferred dividends for 20X2 were in arrears.

Required

For each company, prepare the stockholders' equity section of its balance sheet at December 31, 20X3. Show the computation of all amounts. Entries are not required.

P13-5B **Tandy Corporation,** which operates Radio Shack stores, included the following stockholders' equity on its year-end balance sheet at December 31, 19X8, with all dollar amounts, except par value per share, in millions:

Analyzing the stockholders' equity of an actual corporation (Obj. 3, 4)

Stockholders' Equity	($ Millions)
Preferred stock, 6% cumulative	$ 100
Common stock—par value $1 per share; 250,000,000 shares authorized, 139,000,000 shares issued	139
Paid-in capital in excess of par—common............................	110
Retained earnings..	1,693
	$2,042

Required

1. Identify the different issues of stock Tandy has outstanding.
2. Give two summary entries to record issuance of all the Tandy stock. Assume that all the stock was issued for cash. Explanations are not required.
3. Assume that preferred dividends are in arrears for 19X7 and 19X8. Record the declaration of a $50 million cash dividend on December 30, 19X9. Use separate Dividends Payable accounts for Preferred and Common. An explanation is not required.

P13-6B ◄ *Link Back to Chapter 1 (Accounting Equation).* The following accounts and related balances of Witt, Inc., are arranged in no particular order:

Preparing a corporation balance sheet; measuring profitability (Obj. 3, 6)

Interest expense	$ 6,100	Accounts receivable, net	$ 46,000
Property, plant, and equipment, net	261,000	Paid-in capital in excess of par—common.......................	19,000
Common stock, $1 par, 500,000 shares authorized, 236,000 shares issued	236,000	Accrued liabilities	26,000
		Long-term note payable............	42,000
		Inventory....................................	81,000
Dividends payable	9,000	Prepaid expenses	10,000
Retained earnings.....................	?	Common stockholders' equity, June 30, 20X1.............	222,000
Accounts payable......................	31,000		
Trademark, net	9,000	Net income	51,000
Preferred stock, $0.10, no-par, 10,000 shares authorized and issued	25,000	Total assets, June 30, 20X1........	404,000
		Cash...	10,000

Required

1. Prepare the company's classified balance sheet in the account format at June 30, 20X2. Use the accounting equation to compute Retained Earnings.
2. Compute rate of return on total assets and rate of return on common stockholders' equity for the year ended June 30, 20X2.
3. Do these rates of return suggest strength or weakness? Give your reason.

Computing dividends on
preferred and common stock
(Obj. 4)

P13-7B OnPoint Consulting, Inc., has 10,000 shares of $4.50, no-par preferred stock and 50,000 shares of no-par common stock outstanding. OnPoint declared and paid the following dividends during a three-year period: 20X1, $20,000; 20X2, $100,000; and 20X3, $215,000.

Required

1. Compute the total dividends to preferred stock and to common stock for each of the three years if
   a. Preferred is noncumulative   **b.** Preferred is cumulative
2. For case (1b), record the declaration of the 20X3 dividends on December 28, 20X3, and the payment of the dividends on January 17, 20X4. Use separate Dividends Payable accounts for Preferred and Common.

Analyzing the stockholders'
equity of an actual corporation
(Obj. 4, 5)

P13-8B The balance sheet of The Gonzalez Group reported the following:

Stockholders' Investment [same as stockholders' equity]	
Nonvoting preferred stock, no-par (liquidation value, $358,000)	$320,000
Common stock, $1.50 par value, authorized 75,000 shares; issued 36,000 shares	54,000
[Additional] paid-in capital	231,000
Retained earnings	141,000
Total stockholders' investment	$746,000

Notes to the financial statements indicate that 8,000 shares of $3.40 preferred stock with a stated value of $40 per share were issued and outstanding. Preferred dividends are in arrears for three years, including the current year. The additional paid-in capital belongs to common. On the balance sheet date, the market value of the Gonzalez common stock was $10 per share.

Required

1. Is the preferred stock cumulative or noncumulative? How can you tell?
2. What is the amount of the annual preferred dividend?
3. Which class of stockholders controls the company? Give your reason.
4. What is the total paid-in capital of the company?
5. What was the total market value of the common stock?
6. Compute the book value per share of the preferred stock and the common stock.

Computing and recording a
corporation's income tax
(Obj. 7)

P13-9B The accounting (not the income tax) records of Fox Security Systems, Inc., provide the income statement for 20X3.

Total revenue	$680,000
Expenses:	
Cost of goods sold..........................	$290,000
Operating expenses.......................	180,000
Total expenses before tax	470,000
Income before income tax	$210,000

The operating expenses include depreciation of $40,000 computed under the straight-line method. In calculating taxable income on the tax return, Fox uses the modified accelerated cost recovery system (MACRS). MACRS depreciation was $50,000 for 20X3. The corporate income tax rate is 40%.

Required

1. Compute taxable income for the year.
2. Journalize the corporation's income tax for 20X3.
3. Prepare the corporation's single-step income statement for 20X3.

APPLY YOUR KNOWLEDGE

DECISION CASES

Case 1. Terry Caine and Nicole Jacks have written a spreadsheet program that they believe will rival Excel and Lotus. They need additional capital to market the product, and they plan to incorporate the business. They are considering alternative capital structures for the corporation. Their primary goal is to raise as much capital as possible without giving up control of the business. The partners plan to invest the software program and receive 110,000 shares of the corporation's common stock. The partners have been offered $110,000 for the rights to the software program.

Evaluating alternative ways to raise capital (Obj. 2, 3)

The corporation's plans for a charter include an authorization to issue 5,000 shares of preferred stock and 500,000 shares of $1 par common stock. Caine and Jacks are uncertain about the most desirable features for the preferred stock. Prior to incorporating, the partners are discussing their plans with two investment groups. The corporation can obtain capital from outside investors under either of the following plans:

- *Plan 1.* Group 1 will invest $105,000 to acquire 1,000 shares of $5, no-par preferred stock and $70,000 to acquire 70,000 shares of common stock. Each preferred share receives 50 votes on matters that come before the stockholders.
- *Plan 2.* Group 2 will invest $160,000 to acquire 1,400 shares of 6%, $100 par nonvoting, noncumulative preferred stock.

Required

Assume that the corporation is chartered.

1. Journalize the issuance of common stock to Caine and Jacks. Explanations are not required.
2. Journalize the issuance of stock to the outsiders under both plans. Explanations are not required.
3. Assume that net income for the first year is $180,000 and total dividends are $30,000. Prepare the stockholders' equity section of the corporation's balance sheet under both plans.
4. Recommend one of the plans to Caine and Jacks. Give your reasons.

Case 2. Answering the following questions will enhance your understanding of the capital stock of corporations. Consider each question independently of the others.

Characteristics of corporations' capital stock (Obj. 2, 5)

1. Why are capital stock and retained earnings shown separately in the shareholders' equity section?
2. Chiu Wang, major shareholder of C-W, Inc., proposes to sell some land she owns to the company for common shares in C-W. What problem does C-W, Inc., face in recording the transaction?
3. Preferred shares have advantages with respect to dividends and corporate liquidation. Why would investors buy common stock when preferred stock is available?
4. What does it mean if the liquidation value of a company's preferred stock is greater than its market value?
5. If you owned 100 shares of stock in **Dell Computer Corporation** and someone offered to buy the stock for its book value, would you accept the offer? Why or why not?

ETHICAL ISSUE

Note: This case is based on an actual situation.

Jeremy Copeland paid $50,000 for a franchise that entitled him to market Success Associates software programs in the countries of the European Common Market. Copeland intended to sell individual franchises for the major language groups of western Europe—German, French, English, Spanish, and Italian. Naturally, investors considering buying a franchise from Copeland asked to see the financial statements of his business.

Believing the value of the franchise to be greater than $50,000, Copeland sought to capitalize his own franchise at $500,000. The law firm of St. Charles & LaDue helped Copeland form a corporation chartered to issue 500,000 shares of common stock with par value of $1 per share. Attorneys suggested the following chain of transactions:

- a. A third party borrows $500,000 and purchases the franchise from Copeland.
- b. Copeland pays the corporation $500,000 to acquire all its stock.
- c. The corporation buys the franchise from the third party, who repays the loan.

In the final analysis, the third party is debt-free and out of the picture. Copeland owns all the corporation's stock, and the corporation owns the franchise. The corporation's balance sheet lists a franchise acquired at a cost of $500,000. This balance sheet is Copeland's most valuable marketing tool.

Required

1. What is unethical about this situation?
2. Who can be harmed? How can they be harmed? What role does accounting play?

FINANCIAL STATEMENT CASE

Analyzing stockholders' equity (Obj. 2, 3)

The **Target Corporation** financial statements appear in Appendix A. Answer the following questions about Target's stock.

Required

1. How much of Target's preferred stock was outstanding at January 29, 2000? How can you tell? The statement of shareholders' investment (stockholders' equity) reports what happened to Target's preferred stock during the fiscal year ended January 29, 2000. What was it?
2. Examine Target's balance sheet. Which stockholders' equity account increased the most during the year ended January 29, 2000 (fiscal year 2000)? Did this increase occur because of new paid-in capital that Target received from stockholders during this year? If not, explain where the additional paid-in capital came from.
3. Give Target's journal entries during fiscal year 2000 to record (a) closing net income to Retained Earnings and (b) declaring cash dividends. The statement of shareholders' investment gives the details for these transactions.

TEAM PROJECT

Competitive pressures are the norm in business. **Lexus** automobiles (made in Japan) have cut into the sales of **Mercedes Benz** (a German company), **Jaguar Motors** (a British company), **General Motors'** Cadillac Division, and **Ford's** Lincoln Division (both U.S. companies). **Dell, Gateway,** and **Compaq** computers have siphoned business away from **IBM.** Foreign steelmakers have reduced the once-massive U.S. steel industry to a fraction of its former size.

Indeed, corporate downsizing has occurred on a massive scale. During the past few years, each company or industry mentioned here has pared down plant and equipment, laid off employees, or restructured operations.

Required

1. Identify all the stakeholders of a corporation and the stake each group has in the company. A *stakeholder* is a person or a group who has an interest (that is, a stake) in the success of the organization.
2. Identify several measures by which a corporation may be considered deficient and which may indicate the need for downsizing. How can downsizing help to solve this problem? Discuss how each measure can indicate the need for downsizing.
3. Debate the downsizing issue. One group of students takes the perspective of the company and its stockholders, and another group of students takes the perspective of other stakeholders of the company.

INTERNET EXERCISE

Yahoo! Inc.

Go to the "Dividends and Treasury Stock" episode on the *Mastering Accounting* CD-ROM for an interactive, video-enhanced exercise on how CanGo can boost investor confidence after poor quarterly performance reports. The episode focuses on the difference between cash and stock dividends.

1. Go to **http://finance.yahoo.com** and type in the stock symbol <u>YHOO</u>. Using the pull-down menu, select *Basic,* and then click on *Get Quotes.* In the chart under "Last Trade," identify how much investors were willing to pay for a share of stock on the last trade.
2. In the chart under "More Info" click on *Profile.*
   a. Review the "Business Summary." How many users does **Yahoo!** serve each month?
   b. Scroll down to review "Statistics at a Glance." What is Yahoo!'s book value per share? Compare the book value to the market value of the last trade. Which is greater?
   c. What is Yahoo!'s return on assets and return on equity? Explain what both of these ratios indicate for Yahoo! Which ratio is greater? What does this indicate?
   d. How much is Yahoo's annual dividend?
3. Go to **http://www.forbes.com** and under "Stocks" type <u>YHOO</u>, and then click on *Go.* In the left-hand column click on "Financials" to find the answers to the following questions.

a. As of the most recent balance sheet date, how much have shareholders paid in total for Yahoo! stock? During the most recent year, how much capital did Yahoo! raise through the issuance of stock? Yahoo! does not pay dividends. Why would shareholders be interested in purchasing stock in this company?

b. As of the most recent balance sheet date, what is Yahoo!'s reported retained earnings balance? Is this balance positive or negative? How does a company get a retained earnings deficit? Does Yahoo! have enough retained earnings to declare dividends?

c. What is the primary source of financing for Yahoo!'s assets?

14

Retained Earnings, Treasury Stock, and the Income Statement

LEARNING OBJECTIVES

After studying this chapter, you should be able to

1. Account for stock dividends

2. Distinguish stock splits from stock dividends

3. Account for treasury stock

4. Report restrictions on retained earnings

5. Identify the elements of a complex income statement

6. Prepare a statement of stockholders' equity

America Online (AOL), the world leader in Internet technology, and **Time Warner,** the world's largest media and entertainment company, have merged. AOL's e-commerce capability, plus Time Warner's empire—CNN and HBO, *Time* and *Sports Illustrated*, and Warner Bros., has created a powerhouse.

Wall Street is sorting out the effects on investors. Which company will dominate the new organization? Will it be AOL, or will Time Warner take the lead? How do the companies' finances figure into the plan? These questions arise as investors decide whether to buy or sell AOL and Time Warner stock. It is critical for companies to report accurate accounting information so that investors have a fair chance to make an informed decision.

AOL turned a profit for the first time in 1999 after years of losses. Time Warner's profits have been up and down. Top executives of the two companies obviously think the combined company—AOL Time Warner—can earn a healthy net income for years to come. Boot up and stay tuned to see if the profits do in fact roll in.

Exhibit 14-1 (page 542) shows an adapted version of the income statement that **AOL Time Warner Inc.** sent out to show how the *combined* company would have performed in 1999. "Pro Forma" (as if) in the title means that the income statement depicts results *as if* the two companies had merged in 1999. Overall, the result would have been a loss of $2.5 billion. Included in the net loss is a gain on the sale of cable systems.

Special gains and losses such as this often appear on a corporation's income statement. Discontinued operations and extraordinary gains and losses can also make the income statement quite complex. This chapter explains the full range of items that can appear on an income statement in the real world of accounting and finance.

The chapter also covers several stockholders' equity topics to round out your understanding of a corporation's balance sheet. Let's begin with Retained Earnings, the element of stockholders' equity that results from profitable operations. Over time, AOL Time Warner must build up a large balance of Retained Earnings. If not, the company will not survive.

RETAINED EARNINGS, STOCK DIVIDENDS, AND STOCK SPLITS

We have seen that the equity section on a corporate balance sheet is called *stockholders' equity* or *shareholders' equity*. The paid-in capital accounts and retained earnings make up the stockholders' equity section.

Retained Earnings

Retained Earnings carries the balance of the business's net income less all net losses and less any dividends accumulated over the corporation's lifetime. *Retained* means "held onto." Retained Earnings is the shareholders' stake in total assets that come from profits. A debit balance in Retained Earnings is called a *deficit*. In a recent survey, 68 of 600 companies (11%) had a retained earnings deficit (see Exhibit 14-2 on page 542).

 WORK IT OUT

Assume that the beginning balance of Retained Earnings was $720,000. The net loss for the year was $810,000. What will the Retained Earnings balance be after this net income?

Answer

RETAINED EARNINGS			
Dec. 31, 20X1 Net loss	810,000	Jan. 1, 20X1 Bal.	720,000
Dec. 31, 20X1 Bal. (Deficit)	90,000		

EXHIBIT 14-1
AOL Time Warner
Income Statement
(Pro Forma, adapted)

AOL TIME WARNER, INC. Pro Forma Income Statement, adapted (as if the two companies were already merged) Year Ended December 31, 1999	
	Millions
Revenues	$33,051
Gain on sale of cable systems and other gains............................	2,355
Cost of revenues	17,998
Selling, general, and administrative expenses............................	9,085
Amortization expense of goodwill and other intangibles..............	8,393
Interest expense and other expenses..	1,825
Income (loss) before income tax	(1,895)
Income tax expense	(627)
Net income (net loss)..	$ (2,522)

Source: AOL Time Warner Merger, *Joint Proxy Statement-Prospectus.*

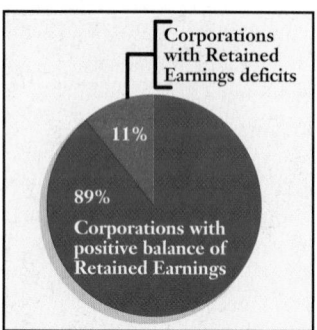

When you see a balance sheet, remember these facts about Retained Earnings:

1. *Credits to the Retained Earnings account arise only from net income.* To learn how much net income a corporation has earned and retained in the business, see Retained Earnings. Its balance is the cumulative, life-time earnings of the company minus all net losses and all dividends.

2. *The Retained Earnings account is not a reservoir of cash waiting for the board of directors to pay out in dividends.* Instead, Retained Earnings is simply one of several owners' equity accounts. Retained Earnings represents no asset in particular. In fact, the corporation may have a large balance in Retained Earnings but not have enough cash to pay a dividend. To *declare* a dividend, the company must have an adequate balance in Retained Earnings. To *pay* the dividend, it must have the cash.

Cash and Retained Earnings are two separate accounts with no particular relationship. Retained Earnings is *not* a bank account. A $5,000 balance in Retained Earnings means that $5,000 of capital has been created by profits that the corporation has reinvested in the business.

Stock Dividends

Objective 1
Account for stock dividends

STOCK DIVIDEND. A distribution by a corporation of its own stock to its stockholders.

A **stock dividend** is a distribution by a corporation of its own stock to its stockholders. Stock dividends are fundamentally different from cash dividends because stock dividends do not give any assets to the stockholders. Stock dividends

- Affect *only* stockholders' equity accounts (Retained Earnings and Common Stock).
- Have *no* effect on total stockholders' equity.

A stock dividend decreases Retained Earnings and increases Common Stock. Both accounts are elements of stockholders' equity, so total equity is unchanged. There is merely a transfer from Retained Earnings to Common Stock. No asset or liability is affected by a stock dividend.

The corporation distributes stock dividends to stockholders in proportion to the number of shares they already own. Suppose you own 300 shares of **AOL Time Warner** common stock. If AOL distributes a 10% common stock dividend, you would receive 30 (300 × 0.10) additional shares. You would now own 330 shares of the stock. All other AOL stockholders would receive additional shares equal to 10% of their prior holdings. Both you and all other AOL stockholders would be in the same relative position after the dividend as before.

REASONS FOR STOCK DIVIDENDS   Why do companies issue stock dividends? There are several reasons:

1. *To continue dividends but conserve cash*. A company may want to keep cash in the business in order to expand, pay off debts, and so on. Yet the company may wish to continue dividends in some form. Stockholders pay tax on cash dividends but not on stock dividends.

2. *To reduce the market price of its stock*. Distribution of a stock dividend may cause the market price of the company's stock to fall because of the increased supply of the stock. Suppose the market price of a share of AOL stock is $60. Doubling the number of shares of stock outstanding by issuing a stock dividend would drop the stock's market price by approximately half, to $30 per share. The objective is to make the stock less expensive and thus more attractive to a wider range of investors.

RECORDING STOCK DIVIDENDS   The board of directors announces stock dividends on the declaration date. The date of record and the distribution date then follow. (This is the same sequence of dates used for a cash dividend.) The declaration of a stock dividend does *not* create a liability because the corporation is not obligated to pay assets. (Recall that a liability is a claim on *assets*.) Instead, the corporation has declared its intention to distribute its stock. Assume that Georgia Lumber Corporation has the following stockholders' equity prior to a stock dividend:

Georgia Lumber Corporation
Stockholders' Equity

Paid-in capital:	
Common stock, $10 par, 50,000 shares authorized,	
20,000 shares issued	$200,000
Paid-in capital in excess of par—common	70,000
Total paid-in capital	270,000
Retained earnings	85,000
Total stockholders' equity	$355,000

The entry to record a stock dividend depends on its size. Generally accepted accounting principles distinguish between

- a *large* stock dividend (25% or more of issued stock), and
- a *small* stock dividend (less than 20–25% of issued stock).

Stock dividends between 20% and 25% are rare.

Large Stock Dividends—25% or More. A *large* stock dividend significantly increases the number of shares available in the market and usually lowers the stock price. A common practice is to transfer the par value of the dividend shares from Retained Earnings to Common Stock, as shown in Exhibit 14-3 on page 544.

Small Stock Dividends—Less Than 20–25%. A *small* stock dividend is less likely to affect the price of the company's stock significantly. For this reason, generally accepted accounting principles (GAAP) requires small stock dividends to be accounted for at their market value. Retained Earnings is decreased for the market value of the dividend shares, Common Stock is credited for the stock's par value, and Paid-in Capital in Excess of Par is credited for the remainder.

Assume Georgia Lumber Corporation distributes a stock dividend when the market value of the company's common stock is $16 per share. Exhibit 14-3 illustrates the accounting if the dividend is large (a 50% dividend) or small (a 10% dividend).[1]

---

[1] A stock dividend can be recorded with two journal entries for (1) the declaration and (2) the stock distribution. Most companies record stock dividends with a single entry on the date of distribution, as we illustrate here.

EXHIBIT 14-3 Accounting for Stock Dividends—Georgia Lumber Corporation

Large Stock Dividend—for example, 50% (Accounted for at *par* value)		Small Stock Dividend—for example, 10% (Accounted for at *market* value)	
Retained Earnings	100,000	Retained Earnings (20,000 ×	
Common Stock		0.10 × $16 market value)	32,000
(20,000 shares × 0.50 ×		Common Stock	
$10 par)	100,000	(20,000 × 0.10 × $10 par)	20,000
		Paid-in Capital in Excess of Par ..	12,000

Neither a large nor a small stock dividend affects assets, liabilities, or total stockholders' equity. A stock dividend merely rearranges the stockholders' equity accounts, leaving total equity unchanged.

DAILY EXERCISE 14-1

DAILY EXERCISE 14-2

DAILY EXERCISE 14-3

THINK IT OVER

Suppose Georgia Lumber Corporation issues 1,000 shares of its $15 par common as a stock dividend when the stock's market price is $25 per share. Assume that the 1,000 shares issued are (1) 10% of the outstanding shares and (2) 100% of the outstanding shares. Which stock dividend decreases total stockholders' equity?

Answer: Neither a large stock dividend nor a small stock dividend affects total stockholders' equity.

Stock Splits

STOCK SPLIT. An increase in the number of outstanding shares of stock coupled with a proportionate reduction in the par value of the stock.

A **stock split** is an increase in the number of authorized, issued, and outstanding shares of stock, coupled with a proportionate reduction in the stock's par value. For example, if the company splits its stock 2 for 1, the number of outstanding shares is doubled and each share's par value is cut in half. A stock split, like a large stock dividend, decreases the market price of the stock—with the intention of making the stock more affordable for investors. Most leading companies in the United States—**General Electric, IBM,** and many others—have split their stock.

The market price of a share of IBM common stock has been approximately $100. Assume that the company wishes to decrease the market price to approximately $25. That is, IBM decides to split the common stock 2 for 1 to reduce the stock's market price from $100 to $50. A 2-for-1 stock split means that the company would have twice as many shares of stock outstanding after the split as it had before and that each share's par value would be cut in half. Assume that IBM had 1,875 million shares of $0.20 (20 cents) par common stock before the split:

IBM Stockholders' Equity (Adapted) Before 2-for-1 Stock Split	(In Millions)	After 2-for-1 Stock Split	(In Millions)
Common stock, $0.20 par, 5,000 million shares authorized, 1,875 million shares issued	$ 375	Common stock, $0.10 par, 10,000 million shares authorized, 3,750 million shares issued	$ 375
Capital in excess of par	11,387	Capital in excess of par.............................	11,387
Retained earnings	16,878	Retained earnings	16,878
Other...	(8,376)	Other...	(8,376)
Total stockholders' equity	$20,264	Total stockholders' equity	$20,264

After the 2-for-1 stock split, IBM would have 10,000 million shares authorized and 3,750 million shares (1,875 million shares × 2) of $0.10 (10 cents) par ($0.20/2) common stock outstanding. Total stockholders' equity would be exactly as before. Indeed, the balance in the Common Stock account does not even change. Only the par value of the stock and the number of shares change. Compare the figures in color in the preceding stockholders' equity presentations for IBM.

Because the stock split affects no account balances, no formal journal entry is necessary. Instead, the split is recorded in a *memorandum entry* such as the following:

Aug. 19	Split the common stock 2 for 1. Called in the $0.20 par common stock and distributed two shares of $0.10 par common stock for each old share previously outstanding.

A company may engage in a reverse split to decrease the number of shares of stock outstanding. For example, IBM could split its stock 1 for 2. After the split, par value would be $0.40 (40 cents, that is, $0.20 × 2); shares authorized would be 2,500 million (5,000 million/2); and shares issued and outstanding would be 937.5 million (1,875 million/2). Reverse splits are unusual.

⊙ DAILY EXERCISE 14-4

⊙ DAILY EXERCISE 14-5

Similarities and Differences Between Stock Dividends and Stock Splits

Objective 2
Distinguish stock splits from stock dividends

Both stock dividends and stock splits increase the number of shares of stock owned by each stockholder. Neither stock dividends nor stock splits change investors' cost of the stock they own.

SIMILARITIES   Consider **Avon Products, Inc.,** whose beauty products are sold in countries around the world. Assume you paid $3,000 to acquire 150 shares of Avon common stock.

- If Avon distributes a 100% stock dividend, your 150 shares increase to 300, but your total cost is still $3,000.
- If Avon distributes a 2-for-1 stock split, your shares increase to 300, but your total cost is unchanged.
- Neither a stock dividend nor a stock split creates taxable income for the investor.

DIFFERENCES   Stock dividends and stock splits differ in that

- A stock *dividend* shifts an amount from retained earnings to the stock account, leaving the par value per share unchanged.
- A stock *split* affects no account balances. A stock split changes the par value of the stock. It also increases the number of shares of stock authorized, issued, and outstanding.

⊙ DAILY EXERCISE 14-6

Exhibit 14-4 summarizes the effects of dividends and stock splits on total stockholders' equity.

Event	Effect on Total Stockholders' Equity
Declaration of *cash* dividend	Decrease
Payment of *cash* dividend	No effect
Distribution of *stock* dividend	No effect
Stock split	No effect

Source: Adapted from material provided by Beverly Terry.

EXHIBIT 14-4
Effects of Dividends and Stock Splits on Total Stockholders' Equity

TREASURY STOCK

Objective 3
Account for treasury stock

A company's own stock that it has issued and later reacquired is called **treasury stock.**[2] In effect, the corporation holds the stock in its treasury. Corporations may purchase their own stock for several reasons:

TREASURY STOCK. A corporation's own stock that it has issued and later reacquired.

1. The company has issued all its authorized stock and needs the stock for distributions to employees under stock purchase plans.

---

[2]In this text, we illustrate the *cost* method of accounting for treasury stock because it is used most widely. Other methods are presented in intermediate accounting courses.

2. The purchase helps support the stock's market price by decreasing the supply of stock available.
3. The business is trying to increase net assets by buying its shares low and hoping to sell them for a higher price later.
4. Management wants to avoid a takeover by an outside party.

When **AOL Time Warner, General Motors,** or **Eastman Kodak** buys its own stock as treasury stock, the company gives up cash and becomes a smaller entity as a result. Now let's see how companies actually account for their treasury stock.

Purchase of Treasury Stock

We record the purchase of treasury stock by debiting Treasury Stock and crediting the asset given in exchange—usually Cash. Suppose that Jupiter Drilling Company had the following stockholders' equity before purchasing treasury stock:

JUPITER DRILLING COMPANY	
Stockholders' Equity [*Before* Purchase of Treasury Stock]	
Common stock, $1 par, 10,000 shares authorized,	
8,000 shares issued	$ 8,000
Paid-in capital in excess of par—common	12,000
Retained earnings	14,600
Total stockholders' equity	$34,600

On November 22, Jupiter purchases 1,000 shares of its $1 par common as treasury stock, paying cash of $7.50 per share. Jupiter records the purchase of treasury stock as follows:

TREASURY STOCK—COMMON

7,500 |

Nov. 22	Treasury Stock—Common (1,000 × $7.50)	7,500	
	Cash		7,500
	Purchased 1,000 shares of treasury stock at $7.50 per share.		

The Treasury Stock account has a debit balance, which is the opposite of the other owners' equity accounts. Therefore, *Treasury Stock is a contra stockholders' equity account.* Treasury stock is recorded at cost, without reference to par value. The Treasury Stock account is often reported beneath Retained Earnings on the balance sheet. Treasury Stock's balance is subtracted from the sum of total paid-in capital and retained earnings, as follows:

◉ DAILY EXERCISE 14-7

JUPITER DRILLING COMPANY	
Stockholders' Equity [*After* Purchase of Treasury Stock]	
Common stock, $1 par, 10,000 shares authorized,	
8,000 shares issued, 7,000 shares outstanding	$ 8,000
Paid-in capital in excess of par—common	12,000
Retained earnings	14,600
Subtotal	34,600
Less: Treasury stock, 1,000 shares at cost	(7,500)
Total stockholders' equity	$27,100

Total stockholders' equity decreases by the cost of the treasury stock. Also, shares of stock *outstanding* decrease. The number of *outstanding* shares is computed as follows:

Number of shares of stock *issued*	8,000
Less: Number of shares of treasury stock held	(1,000)
Number of shares of stock *outstanding*	7,000

Although the number of *outstanding shares* is not required to be reported on the balance sheet, this figure is important. Only outstanding shares have voting rights, receive cash dividends, and share in assets if the corporation liquidates.

THINK IT OVER

Ethical Issue: Treasury stock transactions have a serious ethical and legal dimension. A company such as **PENTAX** buying its own shares as treasury stock must be careful that its disclosures of information are complete and accurate. What would happen if PENTAX purchases treasury stock at $17 per share and one day later announces a technological breakthrough that will generate millions of dollars in new business?

Answer: PENTAX's stock price would likely rise in response to the new information. If it could be proved that PENTAX management withheld the information, a shareholder selling stock back to PENTAX could file a lawsuit against PENTAX. The stockholder would claim that with knowledge of the technological advance, he or she would have been able to sell the PENTAX stock at a higher price.

Sale of Treasury Stock

A company may sell its treasury stock at any price agreeable to the corporation and the purchaser: at cost, above cost, or below cost.

SALE AT COST If the stock is sold for the same price the corporation paid to reacquire it, the entry is a debit to Cash and a credit to Treasury Stock for the same amount.

SALE ABOVE COST If the sale price of treasury stock is greater than its reacquisition cost, the difference is credited to the account Paid-in Capital from Treasury Stock Transactions because the excess came from the company's stockholders. Suppose Jupiter Drilling Company resold 200 of its treasury shares for $9 per share (cost was $7.50 per share). The entry is

Dec. 7	Cash (200 × $9)...	1,800	
	Treasury Stock—Common (200 × $7.50 cost)...................		1,500
	Paid-in Capital from Treasury Stock Transactions................		300
	Sold treasury stock at $9 per share.		

TREASURY STOCK—COMMON	
7,500	1,500
6,000	

Paid-in Capital from Treasury Stock Transactions is reported with the other paid-in capital accounts on the balance sheet, beneath the Common Stock and Paid-in Capital in Excess of Par accounts as shown here:

JUPITER DRILLING COMPANY
Stockholders' Equity [*After* Purchase and Sale of Treasury Stock]

Paid-in capital:	
Common stock, $1 par, 10,000 shares authorized,	
8,000 shares issued, 7,200 shares outstanding	$ 8,000
Paid-in capital in excess of par—common..	12,000
Paid-in capital from treasury stock transactions...............................	300
Retained earnings	14,600
Subtotal...	34,900
Less treasury stock, 800 shares at cost (of $7.50 per share)...............	(6,000)
Total stockholders' equity	$28,900

DAILY EXERCISE 14-8

DAILY EXERCISE 14-9

Compare Jupiter Drilling's total equity after the sale of the treasury stock ($28,900) to equity before the sale ($27,100). Notice that total equity increased by the full amount received from the sale of treasury stock ($1,800). Jupiter Drilling is now a larger company because of the increase in assets and stockholders' equity.

Paid-in Capital from Treasury Stock Transactions can be combined as part of Additional Paid-in Capital, as shown in the Real-World Format (Exhibit 14-6, page 551).

SALE BELOW COST   At times, the resale price of treasury stock is less than cost. The difference between these two amounts is debited to Paid-in Capital from Treasury Stock Transactions if this account has a credit balance, as in our example. If this account's balance is too small, then the company debits Retained Earnings for the remaining amount.

Treasury Stock Transactions: A Summary

Neither the purchase nor the sale of treasury stock creates a gain or a loss for the income statement, and thus treasury stock transactions have no effect on net income. Exhibit 14-5 on page 549 illustrates a sequence of assumed treasury stock transactions for Eastman Kodak Company.

e-Accounting

"Aktienrueckkauf," "Rachat des actions," "Recompra de acciones": Stock Buybacks Catch On in Europe

Stock repurchase plans—called stock buybacks—are common in the United States, but are new to Europe. Until a few years ago, European companies were either prohibited from buying back their own stock or slapped with harsh tax penalties. These companies normally invest their spare cash conservatively or plow it into the acquisition of other companies. The Europeans may turn out to be smarter than their American counterparts, who have rushed to buy back company stock. In Europe, 1999 saw only an estimated $50 billion in buybacks, whereas American companies bought back that much in the first two months of 2000.

Do buybacks really prop up the price of a stock? In one view, a buyback sends a message that a company's top managers think its stock is undervalued. After all, who knows the most about the company's backlog of sales and future prospects? But the stock prices of **Anheuser Busch, Carnival Corp.,** and Germany's **Siemens**—all of which announced big buybacks in 2000—barely budged. Analysts say that a buyback announcement may now stigmatize a company as too "old economy." It may show that a company doesn't have any new tricks up its sleeve, no interesting new investment projects on the horizon.

Source: Based on Robert O'Brien, "Deals & deal makers: Stock buybacks gain popularity, but price pops aren't guaranteed," *Wall Street Journal,* March 6, 2000, C17. David Nicklaus, "Stock buybacks have lost their magic for the area's 'Old Economy' companies." *St. Louis Post-Dispatch,* March 18, 2000, p. Biz. 1. Joan Warner, "Buyback fever hits europe," *Business Week,* May 11, 1998, p. 46. Suzanne McGee, "Buybacks catch on in Europe with mixed results," *Wall Street Journal,* January 25, 1999, p. C14. Caspar Busse and Angela Cullen, "Germany's Siemens posts surge in profit; stock buyback, U.S. spinoff are planned," *Wall Street Journal,* April 28, 2000, p. A17.

REPORTING ISSUES

Companies may retire their stock, restrict retained earnings, and vary the way they report stockholders' equity. This section covers these reporting issues.

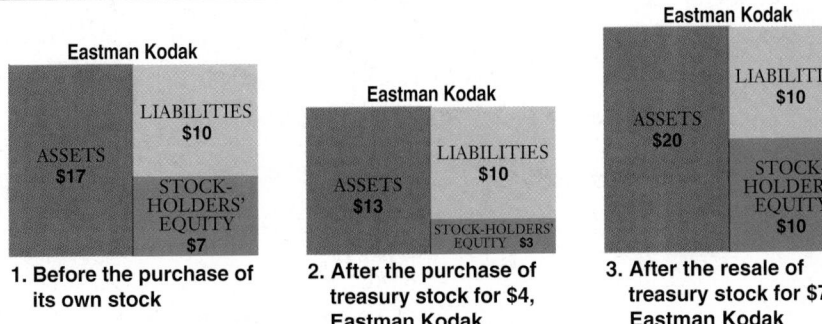

1. Before the purchase of its own stock

2. After the purchase of treasury stock for $4, Eastman Kodak is smaller by $4.

3. After the resale of treasury stock for $7, Eastman Kodak is larger by $7.

Retirement of Stock

A corporation may purchase its own stock and *retire* it by canceling the stock certificates. Retirements of preferred stock occur more often than retirements of common stock, as companies seek to avoid having to pay dividends on the preferred stock. The retired stock cannot be reissued.

Retiring stock, like purchasing treasury stock, decreases the corporation's outstanding stock. Retirement also decreases the number of shares issued. In retiring stock, the corporation removes the balances from all stock and paid-in capital accounts related to the retired shares, such as Preferred Stock and Capital in Excess of Par.

⊙ DAILY EXERCISE 14-10

Review the first half of the chapter by studying the following Decision Guidelines feature.

DECISION GUIDELINES

Accounting for Retained Earnings, Dividends, and Treasury Stock

DECISION	GUIDELINES		
How to record:			
• Distribution of a small stock dividend? (20–25%)	Retained Earnings	Market value	
	Common Stock.................................		Par value
	Paid-in Capital in Excess of Par.........		Excess
• Distribution of a large stock dividend? (25% or more)	Retained Earnings	Par value	
	Common Stock.......................................		Par value
• Stock split?	Memorandum only: Split the common stock 2 for 1. Called in the outstanding $10 par common stock and distributed two shares of $5 par for each old share outstanding (amounts assumed).		

| | Effects of Stock | |
What are the effects of stock dividends and stock splits on:	Dividend	Split
• Number of shares of stock authorized?	No effect	Increase
• Shares issued?	Increase	Increase
• Shares outstanding?	Increase	Increase
• Par value per share?	No effect	Decrease
• Total assets and total liabilities?	No effect	No effect
• Total stockholders' equity?	No effect	No effect
• Common Stock account?	Increase	No effect
• Retained Earnings account?	Decrease	No effect

Accounting for Retained Earnings, Dividends, and Treasury Stock

DECISION	GUIDELINES

How to record:
- Purchase of treasury stock?
- Sale of treasury stock?

Treasury Stock	Cost	
Cash..		Cost

At cost?

Cash	Amt received	
Treasury Stock		Cost

Above cost?

Cash	Amt received	
Treasury Stock		Cost
Paid-in Capital from Treasury		
Stock Transactions		Excess

Below cost?

Cash	Amt received	
Paid-in Capital from Treasury		
Stock Transactions	Amt up to prior bal.	
Retained Earnings	Excess	
Treasury Stock		Cost
or Cash	Amt received	
Retained Earnings	Excess	
Treasury Stock		Cost

What are the effects of the purchase and sale of treasury stock on:

	Effects of	
	Purchase	**Sale**
• Total assets?	Decrease by full amount of payment	Increase by full amount of cash receipt
• Total stockholders' equity?	Decrease by full amount of payment	Increase by full amount of cash receipt

Restrictions on Retained Earnings

Dividends, purchases of treasury stock, and retirements of stock require payments by the corporation to its stockholders. These outlays decrease the corporation's assets, so fewer assets are available to pay liabilities. A bank may agree to loan $500,000 only if the borrowing corporation limits dividend payments and the purchase of treasury stock.

LIMITS ON DIVIDENDS AND TREASURY STOCK PURCHASES   To ensure that corporations maintain a minimum level of stockholders' equity for the protection of creditors, state laws restrict the amount of treasury stock a corporation may purchase. Restrictions on dividends and treasury stock purchases often focus on the balance of retained earnings.

Companies usually report their retained earnings restrictions in notes to the financial statements. The following disclosure by RTE Corporation, a manufacturer of electronic transformers, is typical:

> **NOTES TO CONSOLIDATED FINANCIAL STATEMENTS**
>
> **NOTE F—LONG-TERM DEBT**
>
> The . . . Company's loan agreements . . . restrict cash dividends and similar payments to shareholders. Under the most restrictive of these provisions, retained earnings of $4,300,000 were unrestricted as of December 31, 20X0.

With this restriction, the maximum dividend that RTE Corporation can pay its stockholders is $4,300,000.

APPROPRIATIONS OF RETAINED EARNINGS **Appropriations** are restrictions on Retained Earnings that are recorded by formal journal entries. A corporation may *appropriate*—segregate in a separate account—a portion of Retained Earnings for a specific use. For example, the board of directors may appropriate part of Retained Earnings for expansion or to pay future liabilities. A debit to Retained Earnings and a credit to a separate account—Retained Earnings Appropriated for Plant Expansion—records the appropriation. Appropriated Retained Earnings appears directly above the regular Retained Earnings account on the balance sheet as shown near the bottom of Exhibit 14-6.

> **APPROPRIATION OF RETAINED EARNINGS.** Restriction of retained earnings that is recorded by a formal journal entry.

Retained earnings appropriations are rare. Most companies report any retained earnings restrictions in the notes to the financial statements, as illustrated for RTE Corporation above.

 DAILY EXERCISE 14-11

Variations in Reporting Stockholders' Equity

Accountants sometimes use formats for reporting stockholders' equity that differ from our examples. We use a detailed format to help you learn the components of stockholders' equity. Companies assume that readers of their statements already understand the details.

One of the most important skills you will learn in this course is the ability to understand the financial statements of real companies. In Exhibit 14-6, we present a side-by-side comparison of our general teaching format and the format that you are likely to encounter in real-world balance sheets. Note the following points in the real-world format:

1. The heading Paid-in Capital does not appear. It is commonly understood that Preferred Stock, Common Stock, and Additional Paid-in Capital are elements of paid-in capital.
2. Preferred stock is often reported in a single amount that combines its par value and premium.

EXHIBIT 14-6 Formats for Reporting Stockholders' Equity

General Teaching Format		Real-World Format	
Stockholders' equity		**Stockholders' equity**	
Paid-in capital:			
Preferred stock, 8%, $10 par,		Preferred stock, 8%, $10 par,	
30,000 shares authorized and issued..................	$ 300,000	30,000 shares authorized	
Paid-in capital in excess of par—preferred.............	10,000	and issued......................................	$ 310,000
Common stock, $1 par, 100,000 shares		Common stock, $1 par,	
authorized, 60,000 shares issued.........................	60,000	100,000 shares authorized,	
Paid-in capital in excess of par—common.............	2,140,000	60,000 shares issued......................	60,000
Paid-in capital from treasury stock		Additional paid-in capital..................	2,160,000
transactions, common	9,000	Retained earnings (Note 7)................	1,565,000
Paid-in capital from retirement of		Less: Treasury stock, common	
preferred stock..	4,000	(1,400 shares at cost)......................	(42,000)
Donated capital...	7,000		$4,053,000
Total paid-in capital	2,530,000		
Retained earnings appropriated for		*Note 7—Restriction on retained earnings.*	
contingencies	400,000	At December 31, 20XX, $400,000 of retained	
Retained earnings—unappropriated	1,165,000	earnings is restricted by the company's board	
Total retained earnings	1,565,000	of directors to absorb the effect of any	
Subtotal..	4,095,000	contingencies that may arise. Accordingly,	
Less: Treasury stock, common		any dividend declarations are restricted to a	
(1,400 shares at cost)...	(42,000)	maximum of $1,165,000 ($1,565,000 −	
Total stockholders' equity.......................................	$4,053,000	$400,000).	

3. For presentation in the financial statements, all additional paid-in capital—from capital in excess of par on common stock, treasury stock transactions, and stock retirement—appears as a single amount labeled Additional Paid-in Capital. Additional Paid-in Capital belongs to the common stockholders, and so it follows Common Stock in the real-world format.

4. Often, total stockholders' equity ($4,053,000 in Exhibit 14-6) is not specifically labeled.

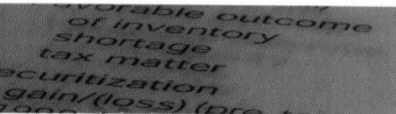

MID-CHAPTER

SUMMARY PROBLEM

www.prenhall.com/horngren

Mid-Chapter Assessment

Simplicity Pattern Co., Inc., the maker of sewing patterns, reported shareholder's equity:

Shareholders' Equity	($ Thousands)
Preferred stock, $1.00 par value	
Authorized—10,000,000 shares; Issued—None	$ —
Common Stock, 8 1/3 cents par value	
Authorized, 30,000,000 shares; Issued 13,733,229 shares	1,144
Capital in excess of par value	48,122
Earnings retained in business	89,320
	138,586
Less: Treasury stock, at cost (1,919,000 common shares)	(14,742)
	$123,844

Required

1. What was the average issue price per share of the common stock?
2. Journalize the issuance of 1,200 shares of common stock at $4 per share. Use Simplicity's account titles.
3. How many shares of Simplicity's common stock are outstanding?
4. How many shares of common stock would be outstanding after Simplicity split its common stock 3 for 1?
5. Using Simplicity account titles, journalize the distribution of a stock dividend when the market price of Simplicity common stock is $3 per share. Consider each of the following stock dividends independently:
   a. Simplicity distributes a 10% common stock dividend on the shares outstanding, computed in requirement 3.
   b. Simplicity distributes a 100% common stock dividend on the shares outstanding, computed in requirement 3.
6. Journalize the following treasury stock transactions, assuming they occur in the order given:
   a. Simplicity purchases 500 shares of treasury stock at $8 per share.
   b. Simplicity sells 100 shares of treasury stock for $9 per share.

Solution

1. Average issue price of common stock was $3.59 per share
   [($1,144,000 + $48,122,000)/13,733,229 shares = $3.59].
2. Cash (1,200 × $4) 4,800
       Common Stock (1,200 × $0.08 1/3) 100
       Capital in Excess of Par Value 4,700
     Issued common stock at a premium.
3. Shares outstanding = 11,814,229 (13,733,229 shares issued minus 1,919,000 shares of treasury stock).
4. Shares outstanding after a 3-for-1 stock split = 35,442,687 (11,814,229 shares outstanding × 3).

5a. Earnings Retained in Business (11,814,229 × 0.10 × \$3)	3,544,269		
Common Stock (11,814,229 × 0.10 × \$0.08 1/3)			98,452
Capital in Excess of Par Value...			3,445,817
Distributed a 10% common stock dividend.			
b. Earnings Retained in Business (11,814,229 × \$0.08 1/3)............	984,519		
Common Stock..			984,519
Distributed a 100% common stock dividend.			
6a. Treasury Stock (500 × \$8)..	4,000		
Cash..			4,000
Purchased 500 shares of treasury stock at \$8 per share.			
b. Cash (100 × \$9)	900		
Treasury Stock (100 × \$8)			800
Paid-in Capital from Treasury Stock Transactions..............			100
Sold 100 shares of treasury stock at \$9 per share.			

The Corporate Income Statement:
Analyzing the Quality of Earnings

Objective 5
Identify the elements of a complex income statement

Now that we have covered stockholders' equity in detail, we turn to the corporate income statement. A corporation's net income (revenues plus gains minus expenses and losses) receives more attention than any other item in the financial statements. In fact, net income is probably the most important piece of information about a company. Net income measures the business's ability to earn a profit and indicates how successfully the company has operated.

Suppose you are considering investing in the stock of **AOL Time Warner, Inc.** You would examine the company's income statement. Of particular interest is the amount of net income (or net loss) that AOL Time Warner can expect to earn year after year. To understand net income, let's examine Exhibit 14-7 on page 554. It is the income statement of Allied Electronics Corporation, a small manufacturer of precision instruments.

Continuing Operations

Income from a business's continuing operations helps investors make predictions about future earnings. In Exhibit 14-7, the topmost section reports income from continuing operations. This part of the business is expected to continue from period to period. We may use this information to predict that Allied Electronics Corporation will earn income of approximately \$54,000 next year.

The continuing operations section of Allied Electronics' statement includes three items needing explanation. *First,* during 20X5, the company had a \$10,000 loss on restructuring operations. Restructuring costs include severance pay to laid-off workers, moving expenses for employees transferred to other locations, and environmental cleanup expenses. The restructuring loss is part of continuing operations because Allied Electronics is remaining in the same line of business. But the loss is highlighted as an "Other" item (unusual) on the income statement because its cause—restructuring—falls outside Allied's main business, which is selling electronics products.

Second, Allied had a gain on the sale of machinery, which is also outside the company's core business activity. This explains why the gain is reported separately from Allied's sales revenue, cost of goods sold, and gross profit.

Third, income tax expense has been deducted in arriving at income from continuing operations. We use a tax rate of 40% in our illustrations (\$90,000 × 0.40 = \$36,000).

⊙ DAILY EXERCISE 14-12

⊙ DAILY EXERCISE 14-13

Special Items

An income statement may include three categories of special gains and losses:

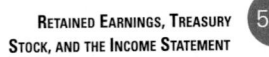

EXHIBIT 14-7 Allied Electronics Corporation's Income Statement

ALLIED ELECTRONICS CORPORATION
Income Statement
Year Ended December 31, 20X5

Net sales revenue	$500,000
Cost of goods sold	240,000
Gross profit	260,000
Operating expenses (detailed)	181,000
Operating income	79,000
Other gains (losses):	
Loss on restructuring operations	(10,000)
Gain on sale of machinery	21,000
Income from continuing operations before income tax	90,000
Income tax expense	36,000
Income from continuing operations	54,000
Discontinued operations, income of $35,000, less income tax of $14,000	21,000
Income before extraordinary item and cumulative effect of change in depreciation method	75,000
Extraordinary flood loss, $20,000, less income tax saving of $8,000	(12,000)
Cumulative effect of change in depreciation method, $10,000, less income tax of $4,000	6,000
Net income	$ 69,000
Earnings per share of common stock (20,000 shares outstanding):	
Income from continuing operations	$2.70
Income from discontinued operations	1.05
Income before extraordinary item and cumulative effect of change in depreciation method	3.75
Extraordinary loss	(0.60)
Cumulative effect of change in depreciation method	0.30
Net income	$3.45

Continuing operations brace encompasses Net sales revenue through Income from continuing operations.
Special items brace encompasses Discontinued operations through Net income.
Earnings per share brace encompasses the Earnings per share section.

- Discontinued operations
- Extraordinary gains and losses
- Cumulative effect of a change in accounting principle

DISCONTINUED OPERATIONS Most large corporations engage in several lines of business. For example, **Sears, Roebuck & Co.** best known for its retail stores, has a real-estate development company **(Homart)** and an insurance company **(Allstate).** We call each identifiable division of a company a **segment of the business.** Allstate is the insurance segment of Sears.

SEGMENT OF THE BUSINESS. One of various separate divisions of a company.

A company may sell a segment of its business. For example, **May Department Stores,** the chain that operates **Lord & Taylor, Foley's,** and **Robinsons-May** stores, sold **Payless,** its chain of shoe stores. Such a sale is not a regular source of income because the sale of a business segment is viewed as a one-time transaction. Financial analysts typically do not include income or loss on discontinued operations to predict a company's future income. The discontinued segments will generate no income in the future.

The income statement carries information on the segment that has been disposed of under the heading Discontinued operations. Income from the discontinued operation ($35,000) is taxed at the 40% rate and reported by Allied Electronics Corporation, as shown in Exhibit 14-7. A loss on discontinued operations is reported similarly, with a subtraction for the income tax *savings* on the loss.

In the normal course of business, companies dispose of old plant and equipment. Gains and losses on these asset dispositions are *not* reported as discontinued operations. Gains and losses on normal asset dispositions can be reported along with operating revenues and expenses or highlighted as "Other gains (losses)" on the income statement.

EXTRAORDINARY GAINS AND LOSSES (EXTRAORDINARY ITEMS) **Extraordinary gains and losses,** also called **extraordinary items,** are both unusual for the company and infrequent. Losses from natural disasters (floods, earthquakes, and tornadoes) and the taking of company assets by a foreign government (expropriation) are extraordinary. Gains and losses on the early retirement of debt are also extraordinary items.

Extraordinary items are reported along with their income tax effect. During 20X5, Allied Electronics Corporation lost $20,000 of inventory in a flood. This flood loss, which reduced income, also reduced Allied's income tax. The tax effect of the loss is computed by multiplying the amount of the loss by the tax rate. The tax effect decreases the net amount of the loss in the same way that the income tax reduces the amount of net income. An extraordinary loss can be reported along with its tax effect on the income statement as follows:

> **EXTRAORDINARY GAINS AND LOSSES.** A gain or loss that is both unusual for the company and infrequent. Also called **extraordinary items.**

Extraordinary flood loss	$(20,000)
Less: Income tax saving..........................	8,000
Extraordinary flood loss, net of tax	(12,000)

Trace this item to the income statement in Exhibit 14-7. An extraordinary gain is reported in the same way as a loss, net of the income tax on the gain.

Gains and losses due to employee strikes, lawsuits, discontinued operations, and the sale of plant assets are *not* extraordinary items. They are considered normal business events. However, they are outside the business's central operations, so they are reported on the income statement as other gains and losses. Examples include the gain on sale of machinery and the restructuring loss in the Other gains (losses) section of Exhibit 14-7.

Cumulative Effect of a Change in Accounting Principle

Companies sometimes change accounting methods, such as from double-declining-balance (DDB) to straight-line depreciation, or from first-in, first-out (FIFO) to weighted-average cost for inventory. ➡ An accounting change makes it difficult to compare one period's financial statements with the statements of preceding periods.

> ◀ For a review of depreciation methods, see Chapter 10. For a review of inventory methods, see Chapter 9.

Without detailed information, investors and creditors can be misled into thinking that the current year is better than the preceding year when in fact the only difference is a change in accounting. Investors must separate the effects of business operations from effects created by accounting. This leads companies to report the effect of the accounting change in a special section of the income statement. This section usually appears after extraordinary items.

Suppose Allied Electronics Corporation changes from DDB to straight-line depreciation at the beginning of 20X5. If the company had been using straight-line depreciation every year, depreciation expense would have been less in prior years, and net income would have been higher. Exhibit 14-7 reports the $6,000 cumulative effect of this accounting change. A change from straight-line to double-declining-balance usually produces a negative cumulative effect.

WORK IT OUT

Examine all the income tax amounts in Exhibit 14-7. How much was Allied Electronics' *total* income tax expense during 19X5?

Answer: **46,000 = $36,000 + $14,000 − $8,000 + $4,000**

Note that $36,000 is the company's income tax expense from continuing operations; $46,000 is *total* income tax expense.

Earnings Per Share

The final segment of a corporate income statement presents the company's earnings per share, abbreviated as EPS. EPS is the most widely used of all accounting statistics. **Earnings per share (EPS)** is the amount of a company's net income for each share of its *outstanding common stock*. It is a key measure of a business's success:

EARNINGS PER SHARE (EPS).
Amount of a company's net income per share of its outstanding common stock.

$$\text{Earnings per share} = \frac{\text{Net income} - \text{Preferred dividends}}{\substack{\text{Weighted-average number of}\\\text{common shares outstanding}}}$$

Just as the corporation lists its different sources of income separately—from continuing operations, discontinued operations, and so on—it also lists a separate EPS figure for each element of income. Allied Electronics Corporation's EPS calculations are as follows:

Earnings per share of common stock (20,000 shares outstanding):	
Income from continuing operations ($54,000/20,000)......................................	$2.70
Income from discontinued operations ($21,000/20,000)	1.05
Income before extraordinary item and cumulative effect of change	
in depreciation method ($75,000/20,000)	3.75
Extraordinary loss ($12,000/20,000)	(0.60)
Cumulative effect of change in depreciation method ($6,000/20,000)	0.30
Net income ($69,000/20,000)	$3.45

The final section of Exhibit 14-7 reports the EPS figures for Allied Electronics.

WEIGHTED-AVERAGE NUMBER OF COMMON SHARES OUTSTANDING   Computing EPS is straightforward if the number of common shares outstanding does not change during the accounting period. For many corporations, however, this figure varies as the company issues new stock and purchases treasury stock during the year. Suppose **Qualcomm Corporation** had 100,000 shares outstanding from January through May, then purchased 40,000 shares as treasury stock. Qualcomm's EPS would be misleadingly high if computed using 60,000 (100,000 − 40,000) shares. To make EPS as meaningful as possible, corporations use the weighted average of the number of common shares outstanding during the period.

Let's assume that Qualcomm Corporation had these shares of common stock outstanding for the following periods:

- January through June—100,000 shares
- July through August—60,000 shares (after buying 40,000 treasury shares)
- September through December—90,000 shares (after issuing 30,000 new shares)

We compute the weighted-average number of common shares outstanding by considering the outstanding shares per month as a fraction of the year:

Number of Common Shares Outstanding	×	Fraction of Year	Period During the Year	=	Weighted-Average Number of Common Shares Outstanding
100,000	×	6/12	January through June	=	50,000
60,000	×	2/12	July through August	=	10,000
90,000	×	4/12	September through December	=	30,000
			Weighted-average number of common shares outstanding during the year	=	90,000

The weighted-average number (90,000) of common shares outstanding would then be used to compute Qualcomm's EPS.

EFFECT OF PREFERRED DIVIDENDS ON EARNINGS PER SHARE   Preferred dividends also affect EPS. Recall that EPS is earnings per share of *common* stock. Recall also that dividends on preferred stock are paid first.   ➡ Therefore, preferred dividends must be subtracted from income to compute EPS. If Allied Electronics Corporation had 10,000 shares of preferred stock outstanding, each with a $1.00 dividend, the annual preferred dividend would be $10,000 (10,000 × $1.00). The $10,000 would be subtracted from each of the income subtotals (lines 1, 3, and 6), resulting in the following EPS computations for the company:

◄◄ Chapter 13, p. 506, provides detailed information on preferred stock.

	Earnings per share of common stock (20,000 shares outstanding):	
1	Income from continuing operations ($54,000 − $10,000)/20,000................	$2.20
2	Income from discontinued operations ($21,000/20,000)	1.05
3	Income before extraordinary item and cumulative effect of change in depreciation method ($75,000 − $10,000)/20,000....................................	3.25
4	Extraordinary loss ($12,000/20,000)	(0.60)
5	Cumulative effect of change in depreciation method ($6,000/20,000)	0.30
6	Net income ($69,000 − $10,000)/20,000	$2.95

● DAILY EXERCISE 14-14

● DAILY EXERCISE 14-15

BASIC AND DILUTED EARNINGS PER SHARE   Some corporations must report two sets of EPS figures as follows.

- EPS based on outstanding common shares (*basic* EPS).
- EPS based on outstanding common shares plus the number of additional common shares that would arise from conversion of the preferred stock into common stock (*diluted* EPS). Diluted EPS is always lower than basic EPS.

THINK IT OVER   What makes earnings per share so useful as a business statistic?

Answer: Earnings per share is useful because it relates a company's income to one share of stock. Stock prices are quoted at an amount per share, and investors usually consider how much they must pay for a certain number of shares. Earnings per share is used to help determine the value of a share of stock.

● DAILY EXERCISE 14-16

● DAILY EXERCISE 14-17

Combined Statement of Income and Retained Earnings

Some companies report income and retained earnings on a single statement. Exhibit 14-8 illustrates how Allied Electronics would combine its income statement and its statement of retained earnings.

EXHIBIT 14-8
Combined Statement of Income and Retained Earnings

ALLIED ELECTRONICS CORPORATION	
Statement of Income and Retained Earnings	
Year Ended December 31, 20X5	
Sales revenue	$500,000
Cost of goods sold	240,000
Gross profit...	260,000
Expenses (listed individually)	191,000
Net income for 20X5...	$ 69,000
Retained earnings, December 31, 20X4..............	130,000
	199,000
Dividends for 20X5	(21,000)
Retained earnings, December 31, 20X5..............	$178,000

(Left bracket labels: Income statement for first five rows; Statement of retained earnings for last four rows.)

Reporting Comprehensive Income

As we have seen throughout this book, all companies report net income or net loss on the income statement. Companies with certain gains and losses must also report another income figure. **Comprehensive income** is the company's change in total stockholders' equity from all sources other than from the owners. Comprehensive income includes net income plus some specific gains and losses. FASB Statement

COMPREHENSIVE INCOME. Company's change in total stockholders' equity from all sources other than from the owners.

130 includes these components of comprehensive income (Chapter 16 explains these items):

- Unrealized gains or losses on certain investments
- Foreign-currency translation adjustments

These items do not enter into the determination of net income but instead are reported as other comprehensive income, as shown in Exhibit 14-9. Assumed figures are used for all items.

NATIONAL EXPRESS COMPANY
Income Statement
Year Ended December 31, 20X2

Revenues..	$10,000
Expenses (summarized)	6,000
Net income...	4,000
Other comprehensive income:	
Unrealized gain on investments..............	1,000
Comprehensive income	$ 5,000

DAILY EXERCISE 14-18

Earnings per share applies only to net income and its components, as discussed earlier. Earnings per share is not reported for other comprehensive income.

The Decision Guidelines feature summarizes a corporate income statement.

DECISION GUIDELINES

Analyzing a Corporate Income Statement

DECISION	GUIDELINES	
What are the main sections of the income statement? See Exhibit 14-7 for an example.	**Continuing operations**	• Continuing operations, including other gains and losses and less income tax expense
	Special items	• Discontinued operations—gain or loss—less the income tax effect
		• Extraordinary gain or loss, less the income tax effect
		• Cumulative effect of change in accounting principle, less the income tax effect
		• Net income (or net loss)
		• Other comprehensive income (Exhibit 14-9)
What earnings per share (EPS) figures must a corporation report?		• Earnings per share—applies only to net income (or net loss) and its components, not to other comprehensive income
		Separate EPS figures for
	Earnings per share	• Income from continuing operations
		• Discontinued operations
		• Income before extraordinary item and cumulative effect of accounting change
		• Extraordinary gain or loss
		• Cumulative effect of accounting change
		• Net income (or net loss)

How to compute EPS for net income?

$$EPS = \frac{\text{Net income} - \text{Preferred dividends}}{\text{Weighted-average number of common shares outstanding}}$$

Prior-Period Adjustments

A company may make an error in recording revenues or expenses. After the revenue and expense accounts are closed, the Retained Earnings account holds the error. The balance of Retained Earnings is wrong until corrected. Corrections to Retained Earnings for errors of an earlier period are called **prior-period adjustments.** The prior-period adjustment (correction) either increases or decreases the beginning balance of Retained Earnings and appears on the statement of retained earnings.

PRIOR-PERIOD ADJUSTMENT. A correction to retained earnings for an error of an earlier period.

Assume De Graff Corporation recorded $30,000 of income tax expense for 20X4. The correct amount was $40,000. This error

- Understated expenses by $10,000
- Overstated net income by $10,000

In 20X5, the government required De Graff to pay the additional $10,000 in taxes for the prior year. De Graff's prior-period adjustment will decrease retained earnings as follows.

DE GRAFF CORPORATION Statement of Retained Earnings Year Ended December 31, 20X5	
Retained earnings, December 31, 20X4, as originally reported	$390,000
Prior-period adjustment—To correct error in the income tax of 20X4	(10,000)
Retained earnings, December 31, 20X4, as adjusted	380,000
Net income for 20X5	114,000
	494,000
Dividends for 20X5	(41,000)
Retained earnings, December 31, 20X5	$453,000

◉ DAILY EXERCISE 14-19

Statement of Stockholders' Equity

Most companies report a statement of stockholders' equity, which is more comprehensive than a statement of retained earnings. The statement of stockholders' equity is formatted exactly as a statement of retained earnings but with columns for each element of equity. The **statement of stockholders' equity** reports the changes in all categories of equity during the period:

- Common stock
- Treasury stock
- Additional paid-in capital
- Total stockholders' equity
- Retained earnings

Objective 6
Prepare a statement of stockholders' equity

STATEMENT OF STOCKHOLDERS' EQUITY. Reports the changes in all categories of stockholders' equity during the period.

Exhibit 14-10 uses assumed figures for Allied Electronics Corporation to illustrate the statement of stockholders' equity. Negative amounts—debits—appear in parentheses. If the company has preferred stock, the statement needs a column for Preferred Stock.

◉ DAILY EXERCISE 14-20

EXHIBIT 14-10 Statement of Stockholders' Equity

ALLIED ELECTRONICS CORPORATION Statement of Stockholders' Equity Year Ended December 31, 20X5					
	Common Stock	Additional Paid-in Capital	Retained Earnings	Treasury Stock	Total
Balance, December 31, 20X4	$ 80,000	$160,000	$130,000	$(25,000)	$345,000
Issuance of stock	20,000	65,000			85,000
Net income			69,000		69,000
Cash dividends			(21,000)		(21,000)
Stock dividends—8%	8,000	26,000	(34,000)		–0–
Purchase of treasury stock				(9,000)	(9,000)
Sale of treasury stock		13,000		4,000	17,000
Balance, December 31, 20X5	$108,000	$264,000	$144,000	$(30,000)	$486,000

559

SUMMARY PROBLEM

www.prenhall.com/horngren
End-of-Chapter Assessment

The following information was taken from the ledger of **Kraft Corporation:**

Common stock, no-par, 45,000 shares issued............	$180,000		Discontinued operations, income..................................	$ 20,000
Sales revenue..........................	620,000		Prior-period adjustments— credit to Retained Earnings	5,000
Extraordinary gain.................	26,000		Gain on sale of plant assets.....	21,000
Loss due to lawsuit	11,000		Cost of goods sold	380,000
General expenses....................	62,000		Income tax expense (saving):	
Preferred stock, 8%, $100 par, 500 shares issued................	50,000		Continuing operations.........	32,000
			Discontinued operations......	8,000
Retained earnings, beginning, as originally reported	103,000		Extraordinary gain	10,000
Cumulative effect of change in inventory method (debit)	(10,000)		Cumulative effect of change in inventory method........	(4,000)
Dividends...............................	16,000		Treasury stock, common (5,000 shares at cost)...........	25,000
Selling expenses.....................	108,000			

Required

Prepare a single-step income statement and a statement of retained earnings for Kraft Corporation for the current year ended December 31. Include the EPS presentation and show your computations. Kraft had no changes in its stock accounts during the year.

Solution

KRAFT CORPORATION
Income Statement
Year Ended December 31, 20XX

Revenue and gains:		
Sales revenue...		$620,000
Gain on sale of plant assets..		21,000
Total revenues and gains..		641,000
Expenses and losses:		
Cost of goods sold	$380,000	
Selling expenses...	108,000	
General expenses...	62,000	
Loss due to lawsuit...	11,000	
Income tax expense	32,000	
Total expenses and losses		593,000
Income from continuing operations...		48,000
Discontinued operations, income of $20,000, less income tax of $8,000		12,000
Income before extraordinary item and cumulative effect of change in inventory method		60,000
Extraordinary gain, $26,000, less income tax, $10,000		16,000
Cumulative effect of change in inventory method, $10,000, less income tax saving, $4,000		(6,000)
Net income		$ 70,000
Earnings per share:		
Income from continuing operations [($48,000 − $4,000)/40,000 shares]		$1.10
Income from discontinued operations ($12,000/40,000 shares).....................................		0.30
Income before extraordinary item and cumulative effect of change in inventory method [($60,000 − $4,000)/40,000 shares]		1.40
Extraordinary gain ($16,000/40,000 shares)..		0.40
Cumulative effect of change in inventory method ($6,000/40,000)................................		(0.15)
Net income [($70,000 − $4,000)/40,000 shares]		$1.65

Computations:

$$EPS = \frac{Income - Preferred\ dividends}{Common\ shares\ outstanding}$$

Preferred dividends: $50,000 × 0.08 = $4,000
Common shares outstanding
45,000 shares issued − 5,000 treasury shares = 40,000 shares outstanding

KRAFT CORPORATION
Statement of Retained Earnings
Year Ended December 31, 20XX

Retained earnings balance, beginning, as originally reported	$103,000
Prior-period adjustment—credit	5,000
Retained earnings balance, beginning, as adjusted	108,000
Net income for current year	70,000
	178,000
Dividends for current year	(16,000)
Retained earnings balance, ending	$162,000

LESSONS LEARNED

1. **Account for stock dividends.** *Retained Earnings* carries the balance of cumulative net income, less all dividends and net losses. *Cash dividends* are distributions of corporate assets. *Stock dividends* are distributions of the corporation's own stock to its stockholders.

2. **Distinguish stock splits from stock dividends.** Stock dividends shift amounts from retained earnings to paid-in capital. *Stock splits* do not change any account balance. Both increase the number of shares outstanding and lower the market price per share of stock.

3. **Account for treasury stock.** *Treasury stock* is the corporation's own stock that has been issued and reacquired, and the company is currently holding. The corporation may sell treasury stock for cost or for more or less than cost.

4. **Report restrictions on retained earnings.** Retained earnings may be *restricted* by law or contract or by the corporation itself.

5. **Identify the elements of a complex income statement.** The corporate *income statement* lists the various sources of income—*continuing operations; discontinued operations;* and *extraordinary gains and losses.* The bottom line of the income statement reports *net income* or *net loss* for the period. *Earnings-per-share* (EPS) figures also appear on the income statement, likewise divided into the different categories of income.

6. **Prepare a statement of stockholders' equity.** A statement of stockholders' equity reports the change in each stockholders' equity account.

ACCOUNTING VOCABULARY

appropriation of retained earnings (p. 551)

comprehensive income (p. 557)

earnings per share (EPS) (p. 556)

extraordinary gains and losses (p. 555)

extraordinary item (p. 555)

prior-period adjustment (p. 559)

segment of the business (p. 554)

statement of stockholders' equity (p. 559)

stock dividend (p. 542)

stock split (p. 544)

treasury stock (p. 545)

QUESTIONS

1. Identify the two main parts of stockholders' equity.
2. A friend receives a stock dividend on an investment. He believes that stock dividends are the same as cash dividends. Explain why the two are not the same.
3. What percentage distinguishes a small stock dividend from a large stock dividend? What is the main difference in accounting for small and large stock dividends?
4. To an investor, a stock split and a stock dividend have essentially the same effect. Explain the similarity and difference to the corporation between a 100% stock dividend and a 2-for-1 stock split.
5. Give four reasons why a corporation might purchase treasury stock.
6. What effect does the purchase of treasury stock have on the (a) assets, (b) issued stock, and (c) outstanding stock of the corporation?
7. What is the normal balance of the Treasury Stock account? What type of account is Treasury Stock? Where is Treasury Stock reported on the balance sheet?

8. What are two ways to report a retained earnings restriction? Which way is more common?
9. Identify four items on the income statement that generate income tax expense. What is an income tax saving, and how does it arise?
10. Why is it important for a corporation to report income from continuing operations separately from discontinued operations and extraordinary items?
11. Give two examples of extraordinary gains and losses and four examples of gains and losses that are *not* extraordinary.
12. What is the most widely used of all accounting statistics?
13. What is the earnings per share of a company with net income of $5,500, issued common stock of 12,000 shares, and treasury common stock of 1,000 shares?
14. What account is affected by all prior-period adjustments? On what financial statement are prior-period adjustments reported?

DAILY EXERCISES

Recording a small stock dividend
(Obj. 1)

DE14-1 Vartec Telecom Company has 200,000 shares of $2.50 par common stock outstanding. Vartec distributes a 5% stock dividend when the market value of its stock is $13 per share.

1. Journalize Vartec's distribution of the stock dividend on March 19. An explanation is not required.
2. What is the overall effect of the stock dividend on Vartec Telecom's total assets? On total stockholders' equity?

Recording a large stock dividend and reporting stockholders' equity
(Obj. 1)

DE14-2 Strongarm Steel Works has 30,000 shares of $1 par common stock outstanding. Strongarm issued this stock at a price of $10 per share. Strongarm declares and distributes a 50% stock dividend when the market value of its common stock is $62.50 per share.

1. Journalize Strongarm's distribution of the stock dividend on July 15. An explanation is not required.
2. Prepare the stockholders' equity section of Strongarm's balance sheet after distribution of the stock dividend. Retained Earnings had a balance of $60,000 before the dividend, and Strongarm's corporate charter authorizes the company to issue 100,000 shares of common stock.

Comparing and contrasting cash dividends and stock dividends
(Obj. 1)

DE14-3 ◄ *Link Back to Chapter 13 (Cash Dividends).* Compare and contrast the accounting for cash dividends and stock dividends. In the space provided, insert either "Cash dividends," "Stock dividends," or "Both cash dividends and stock dividends" to complete each of the following statements:

1. _____ decrease Retained Earnings.
2. _____ have no effect on a liability.
3. _____ increase paid-in capital by the same amount that they decrease Retained Earnings.
4. _____ decrease both total assets and total stockholders' equity, resulting in a decrease in the size of the company.
5. _____ rearrange the account balances within stockholders' equity but have no effect on total stockholders' equity.

Accounting for a stock split
(Obj. 2)

DE14-4 Examine Georgia Lumber's stockholders' equity on page 543. Suppose Georgia Lumber split its common stock 2-for-1 in order to decrease the market price of its stock. The company's stock was trading at $15 immediately before the split.

1. Prepare the stockholders' equity section of Georgia Lumber's balance sheet after the stock split.
2. Which account balances changed after the stock split? Which account balances were unchanged?

Accounting for a reverse stock split
(Obj. 2)

DE14-5 Examine Georgia Lumber's stockholders' equity on page 543. Suppose Georgia Lumber split its common stock 1 for 2 (a reverse stock split) in order to increase the market price of its stock. The company's stock was trading at $15 immediately before the split.

1. Prepare the stockholders' equity section of Georgia Lumber's balance sheet after the stock split.
2. Which account balances changed after the stock split? Which account balances were unchanged?

Using a stock split or a stock dividend to decrease the market price of a stock *(Obj. 2)*

DE14-6 Wearall Rubber Products has prospered during the past ten years, and the company's stock price shot up to $59 recently. Wearall management wishes to decrease its stock price to around $30, which will be attractive to more investors. Should Wearall issue a 100% stock dividend or split the stock? If you propose a stock split, state the split ratio that will accomplish the company's objective. Show your computations.

Accounting for the purchase of treasury stock
(Obj. 3)

DE14-7 Jupiter Drilling Company's stockholders' equity (before the purchase of treasury stock) appears on page 546. Suppose Jupiter later purchases 600 shares of its common stock as treasury stock, paying cash of $5 per share.

1. Journalize the purchase of treasury stock.
2. Prepare the stockholders' equity section of Jupiter's balance sheet immediately after the purchase of treasury stock.
3. What effect does the purchase of treasury stock always have on total stockholders' equity? How did Jupiter's purchase of treasury stock affect the company's total stockholders' equity? Give the amount.

Accounting for the sale of treasury stock
(Obj. 3)

DE14-8 Return to the Jupiter Drilling Company situation in Daily Exercise 14-7. After purchasing the 600 shares of treasury stock for $5 per share, Jupiter later sold 400 of the treasury shares for $12 per share.

1. Journalize the sale of treasury stock.
2. Prepare the stockholders' equity section of Jupiter's balance sheet immediately after the sale of treasury stock.
3. What effect does the sale of treasury stock always have on total stockholders' equity? How did Jupiter's sale of treasury stock affect the company's total stockholders' equity? Give the amount.

DE14-9 Biscoff Productions, Inc., began operations in 20X0. After issuing its common stock to the public, Biscoff completed the following treasury stock transactions during the year:

Accounting for the purchase and sale of treasury stock (above cost) (Obj. 3)

a. Purchased 2,000 shares of the company's $1 par common stock as treasury stock, paying cash of $6 per share.
b. Sold 1,000 shares of the treasury stock for cash of $8 per share.

Journalize these transactions. Explanations are not required. Show how Biscoff will report treasury stock on its December 31, 20X0, balance sheet after completing the two transactions. In reporting the treasury stock, focus solely on the Treasury Stock account. You may ignore all other accounts.

DE14-10 Study Exhibit 14-6 on page 551. Suppose the corporation retired its preferred stock. What will be the amount of the company's total stockholders' equity if the cost to retire the preferred stock is $353,000? Is the company larger or smaller after the stock retirement? Give your reason.

Accounting for the retirement of preferred stock (Obj. 3)

DE14-11 Study Exhibit 14-6, page 551. The company's board of directors is preparing to declare a cash dividend.

Interpreting a restriction of retained earnings (Obj. 4)

1. The company has plenty of cash. What is the maximum amount of cash dividends the board of directors can declare? Explain how you arrived at your answer.
2. What is the nature of the retained earnings restriction in the exhibit? Why did the company restrict (appropriate) its retained earnings? Explain.

DE14-12 List the major parts of a complex corporate income statement for Ninja Motor Corporation for the year ended December 31, 20X1. Include all the major parts of the income statement, starting with net sales revenue and ending with net income (net loss). You may ignore dollar amounts and earnings per share. Use Exhibit 14-7, page 554, as a guide.

Preparing a complex corporate income statement (Obj. 5)

DE14-13 Study the income statement of Allied Electronics Corporation in Exhibit 14-7, page 554. Answer these questions about the company's operations:

Explaining the items on a complex corporate income statement (Obj. 5)

1. How much total gross profit did Allied earn on the sale of its products—before deducting any operating expenses? Name this item and give its amount.
2. Why are the loss on restructuring and the gain on sale of machinery reported as Other gains (losses)?
3. What dollar amount of net income would most sophisticated investors predict for Allied Electronics to earn during 20X6 and beyond? Name this item, give its amount, and state your reason.

DE14-14 **MCI WorldCom, Inc.,** reported a net loss for 19X8. The net loss included a $58 million expense from the cumulative effect of an accounting change, less income tax saving of $22 million, and an extraordinary loss of $207 million, less income tax saving of $78 million. The company's loss before the cumulative effect of the accounting change and before the extraordinary loss was $2,560 million.

Computing net loss after the effects of an accounting change and an extraordinary loss (Obj. 5)

1. Compute MCI WorldCom's net loss for 19X8.
2. Compute EPS for the final amount of the net loss. MCI WorldCom had 1,906 million shares of common stock outstanding during the year.

DE14-15 ETransmission Corporation accounting records include the following items, listed in no particular order, at December 31, 20X3.

Preparing a complex corporate income statement (Obj. 5)

Extraordinary gain	$ 5,000	Other gains (losses)	$ (2,000)
Cost of goods sold	71,000	Net sales revenue	182,000
Operating expenses	64,000	Loss on discontinued	
Accounts receivable	19,000	operations	(15,000)

Income tax of 35% applies to all items.

Prepare ETransmission Corporation's income statement for the year ended December 31, 20X3. Use Exhibit 14-7, page 554, as a guide. Omit earnings per share.

DE14-16 Return to the ETransmission Corporation data in Daily Exercise 14-15. ETransmission had 8,000 shares of common stock outstanding at December 31, 20X2. The company issued an additional 6,000 shares of common stock on August 31, 20X3. ETransmission declared and paid preferred dividends of $3,000 during 20X3.

Reporting earnings per share (Obj. 5)

Show how ETransmission Corporation reported earnings-per-share data on its 20X3 income statement.

Interpreting earnings-per-share data
(Obj. 5)

DE14-17 The **Procter & Gamble Company** has preferred stock outstanding, and the corporation issued additional common stock during the year.

1. Give the basic equation to compute earnings per share of common stock for net income.
2. List all the income items for which Procter & Gamble must report earnings-per-share data.
3. What makes earnings per share so useful as a business statistic?

Reporting comprehensive income
(Obj. 5)

DE14-18 Use the ETransmission Corporation data in Daily Exercise 14-15. In addition, ETransmission had unrealized losses of $4,000 on investments and a $2,000 foreign-currency translation adjustment (a gain) during 20X3. Start with ETransmission Corporation's net income from Daily Exercise 14-15 and show how the company could report other comprehensive income on its 20X3 income statement.

Should ETransmission Corporation report earnings-per-share data for other comprehensive income?

Reporting a prior-period adjustment *(Obj. 6)*

DE14-19 Examine De Graff Corporation's statement of retained earnings on page 559. Suppose instead that De Graff had overpaid 20X4 income tax expense by $10,000. Show how De Graff would report this prior-period adjustment on the statement of retained earnings for 20X5.

Using the statement of stockholders' equity
(Obj. 6)

DE14-20 ← *Link Back to Chapter 1 (Accounting Equation)*. Use the statement of stockholders' equity in Exhibit 14-10, page 559, to answer the following questions about Allied Electronics Corporation.

1. Make a single journal entry to record Allied's declaration and payment of cash dividends during 20X5.
2. How much cash did the issuance of common stock bring in during 20X5?
3. Was the stock dividend that Allied declared and distributed during 20X5 "large" or "small"? How can you tell?
4. What was the cost of the treasury stock that Allied purchased during 20X5? What was Allied's cost of the treasury stock that Allied sold during the year? For how much did Allied sell the treasury stock during 20X5?

EXERCISES

Journalizing cash and stock dividends and reporting stockholders' equity
(Obj. 1)

E14-1 Ogden Aviation Services, Inc., is authorized to issue 500,000 shares of $1 par common stock. The company issued 80,000 shares at $4 per share, and all 80,000 shares are outstanding. When the retained earnings balance was $150,000, Ogden distributed a 50% stock dividend. Later, Ogden declared and paid a $0.30 per share cash dividend.

Required

1. Journalize the distribution of the stock dividend.
2. Journalize both the declaration and the payment of the cash dividend.
3. Prepare the stockholders' equity section of the balance sheet after both dividends.

Journalizing a small stock dividend and reporting stockholders' equity
(Obj. 1)

E14-2 The stockholders' equity for Jaworski, Inc., on September 30, 20X4—end of the company's fiscal year—follows:

Stockholders' Equity	
Common stock, $8 par, 100,000 shares authorized,	
50,000 shares issued..	$400,000
Paid-in capital in excess of par—common	50,000
Retained earnings	140,000
Total stockholders' equity	$590,000

On May 26, the market price of Jaworski's common stock was $16 per share and the company distributed a 10% stock dividend.

Required

1. Journalize the distribution of the stock dividend.
2. Prepare the stockholders' equity section of the balance sheet after the stock dividend.

Reporting stockholders' equity after a stock split *(Obj. 2)*

E14-3 Redwood Construction, Inc., had the following stockholders' equity at May 31:

Common stock, $4 par, 200,000 shares authorized,	
50,000 shares issued	$200,000
Paid-in capital in excess of par	100,000
Retained earnings	210,000
Total stockholders' equity	$510,000

On November 6, Redwood split its $4 par common stock 4 for 1. Make the necessary entry to record the stock split, and prepare the stockholders' equity section of the balance sheet immediately after the split.

E14-4 Identify the effects of the following transactions on total stockholders' equity. Each transaction is independent.

Effects of stock issuance, dividends, and treasury stock transactions (Obj. 1, 2, 3)

  a. Purchase of 1,500 shares of treasury stock (par value $0.50) at $5 per share.
  b. A 50% stock dividend. Before the dividend, 5,000,000 shares of $1 par common stock were outstanding; market value was $13.75 at the time of the dividend.
  c. A 10% stock dividend. Before the dividend, 500,000 shares of $1 par common stock were outstanding; market value was $7.625 at the time of the dividend.
  d. Sale of 600 shares of $5 par treasury stock for $7.00 per share. Cost of the treasury stock was $2.00 per share.
  e. A 3-for-1 stock split. Prior to the split, 60,000 shares of $4.50 par common were outstanding.
  f. Issuance of 50,000 shares of $10 par common at $16.50.

E14-5 Journalize the following transactions of **Foot Locker,** a chain of sports stores:

Journalizing treasury stock transactions (Obj. 3)

Feb. 4   Issued 20,000 shares of no-par common stock at $15 per share.
Apr. 22   Purchased 1,000 shares of treasury stock at $14 per share.
Aug. 22   Sold 600 shares of treasury stock at $16 per share.

E14-6 Lordstrom's, Inc., had the following stockholders' equity on November 30:

Journalizing treasury stock transactions and reporting stockholders' equity (Obj. 3)

Stockholders' Equity

Common stock, $5 par, 500,000 shares authorized,	
50,000 shares issued	$250,000
Paid-in capital in excess of par	150,000
Retained earnings	520,000
Total stockholders' equity	$920,000

On November 27, the company purchased 25,000 shares of treasury stock at $6 per share. Journalize the purchase of the treasury stock, and prepare the stockholders' equity section of the balance sheet at December 31.

E14-7 The agreement under which Tadashi, Inc., issued its long-term debt requires the restriction of $100,000 of the company's retained earnings balance. Total retained earnings is $250,000, and total paid-in capital is $220,000.

Reporting a retained earnings restriction (Obj. 4)

Required

Show how to report stockholders' equity on Tadashi's balance sheet, assuming the following:

  a. Tadashi discloses the restriction in a note. Write the note.
  b. Tadashi appropriates retained earnings in the amount of the restriction and includes no note in its statements.
  c. Tadashi's cash balance is $185,000. What is the maximum amount of dividends Tadashi can declare?

E14-8 Beauvette Corporation's accounting records include the following for 20X3:

Sales revenue	$410,000	Income tax expense—	
Operating expenses		extraordinary gain	$ 6,000
(including income tax)	106,000	Income tax saving—change	
Cumulative effect of change in		in depreciation method	3,000
depreciation method (debit)	(7,000)	Income tax saving—loss	
Cost of goods sold	245,000	on discontinued operations	20,000
Loss on discontinued operations	50,000	Extraordinary gain	15,000

Preparing a multi-step income statement
(Obj. 5)

Computing earnings per share
(Obj. 5)

Computing earnings per share
(Obj. 5)

Preparing a statement of retained earnings with a prior-period adjustment
(Obj. 6)

Preparing a combined statement of income and retained earnings
(Obj. 5, 6)

Computing comprehensive income
(Obj. 5)

Preparing a statement of stockholders' equity *(Obj. 6)*

Required

Prepare a multi-step income statement for 20X3. Omit earnings per share. Was 20X3 a good year, a fair year, or a bad year for Beauvette Corporation? Explain your answer in terms of the outlook for 20X4.

E14-9 Kilgore Corporation earned net income of $71,000 for the second quarter of 20X6. The ledger reveals the following figures:

Preferred stock, $5.00 per year, no-par, 1,600 shares issued and outstanding	$ 70,000
Common stock, $10 par, 52,000 shares issued	520,000
Treasury stock, common, 2,000 shares at cost........................	36,000

Required

Compute Kilgore's EPS for the quarter. Kilgore Corporation had no changes in its stock accounts during the quarter.

E14-10 Bastrop, Inc., had 40,000 shares of common stock and 10,000 shares of 5%, $10 par preferred stock outstanding on December 31, 20X1. On April 30, 20X2, the company issued 9,000 additional common shares and ended 20X2 with 49,000 shares of common stock outstanding. Income from continuing operations of 20X2 was $115,400, and loss on discontinued operations (net of income tax saving) was $8,280. The company had an extraordinary gain (net of tax) of $59,400.

Required

Compute Bastrop's EPS amounts for 20X2, starting with income from continuing operations.

E14-11 Light Crust, Inc., a bakery, reported a prior-period adjustment in 20X3. An accounting error caused net income of prior years to be overstated by $3.8 million. Retained earnings at December 31, 20X2, as previously reported, stood at $395.3 million. Net income for 20X3 was $111.9 million, and dividends totaled $39.8 million.

Required

Prepare the company's statement of retained earnings for the year ended December 31, 20X3.

E14-12 The Parisian Hotel Company, a large hotel chain, had retained earnings of $413 million at the beginning of 20X7. The company showed these figures at December 31, 20X7:

	($ Millions)
Net income	$141
Cash dividends—preferred	2
common	85
Decrease in retained earnings due to retirement of preferred stock	11

Required

Beginning with net income, prepare a combined statement of income and retained earnings for The Parisian Hotel Company for 20X7.

E14-13 During 20X3, The Belleville Group earned income from continuing operations of $95,000. The company also sold its land development segment (discontinued operations) at a loss of $30,000 and had an extraordinary gain of $8,000 on an insurance settlement. Late in the year, Belleville sold treasury stock for $9,000 that the company had purchased for $4,000 two years earlier. At year end, Belleville had a foreign-currency translation adjustment (a loss) of $3,000.

1. Compute Belleville's net income and comprehensive income for 20X3. All amounts are net of income taxes.
2. What would be the final earnings-per-share figure that Belleville would report for 20X3? During the year, Belleville had 20,000 shares of common stock (and no preferred stock) outstanding.

E14-14 At December 31, 20X1, NEWSTATE Corp. reported the following stockholders' equity on page 567.

During 20X2, NEWSTATE completed these transactions and events (listed in chronological order):

Common stock, $5 par, 200,000 shares authorized,		
120,000 shares issued..		$ 600,000
Additional paid-in capital		1,100,000
Retained earnings		1,700,000
Treasury stock, 2,500 shares at cost...................................		(78,000)
		$3,322,000

a. Declared and issued a 50% stock dividend. At the time, NEWSTATE's stock was quoted at a market price of $31 per share.

b. Sold 1,000 shares of treasury stock for $36 per share (cost of these shares was $31 per share).

c. Issued 500 shares of common stock to employees at $28 per share.

d. Net income for the year was $275,000.

e. Declared and paid cash dividends of $180,000.

Required

Prepare NEWSTATE's statement of stockholders' equity for 20X2.

Challenge Exercise

E14-15 Omni Communications, Inc., began 20X5 with 3 million shares of $1 par common stock issued and outstanding. Beginning paid-in capital in excess of par was $6 million, and retained earnings was $7 million. In February 20X5, Omni issued 100,000 shares of stock at $11 per share. In September, when the stock's market price was $12 per share, the board of directors distributed a 10% stock dividend.

Recording a small stock dividend and preparing a statement of stockholders' equity
(Obj. 1, 6)

Required

1. Make the journal entries for the issuance of stock for cash and for the distribution of the 10% stock dividend.

2. Prepare the company's statement of stockholders' equity for the year ended December 31, 20X5.

PROBLEMS

(Group A)

P14-1A Driemann Corp. completed the following transactions during the current year:

Journalizing stockholders' equity transactions
(Obj. 1, 3)

April 18	Declared a cash dividend on the 5%, $100 par preferred stock (1,000 shares outstanding). Declared a $0.20 per share dividend on the 100,000 shares of common stock outstanding. The date of record is May 2, and the payment date is May 23.
May 23	Paid the cash dividends.
June 10	Split common stock 2 for 1 by calling in the 100,000 shares of $10 par common and issuing new stock in its place.
July 30	Distributed a 10% stock dividend on the common stock. The market value of the common stock was $15 per share.
Oct. 26	Purchased 2,500 shares of the company's own common stock at $14 per share.
Nov. 8	Sold 950 shares of treasury common stock for $17 per share.

Required

Record the transactions in Driemann's general journal.

P14-2A The balance sheet of Kugel, Inc., at December 31, 20X6, reported 100,000 shares of no-par common stock authorized, with 30,000 shares issued and a Common Stock balance of $180,000. Retained Earnings had a balance of $141,500. During 20X7, the company completed the following selected transactions:

Journalizing dividend and treasury stock transactions and reporting stockholders' equity
(Obj. 1, 2, 3)

Mar. 15	Purchased 4,000 shares of the company's own common stock for the treasury at $5 per share.
Apr. 30	Distributed a 20% stock dividend on the 26,000 shares of *outstanding* common stock. The market value of Kugel common stock was $10 per share.
Oct. 8	Sold 2,800 shares of treasury common stock for $12 per share.
Dec. 19	Split the no-par common stock 2 for 1 by issuing two new no-par shares for each old no-par share previously issued. Prior to the split, the corporation had issued 35,200 shares. Stock splits affect all authorized and issued stock, including treasury stock as well as stock that is outstanding.
31	Earned net income of $117,000 during the year. Closed net income to Retained Earnings.

Required

1. Record the transactions in the general journal. Explanations are not required.
2. Prepare the stockholders' equity section of Kugel's balance sheet at December 31, 20X7.

Increasing dividends to fight off a takeover of the corporation
(Obj. 1)

P14-3A Ecker Enterprises is ideally positioned in the clothing business. Located in Lansing, Michigan, Ecker is the only company with a distribution network for its imported goods. The company does a brisk business with specialty stores such as **Neiman Marcus, Saks Fifth Avenue,** and **Nordstrom.** Ecker's recent success has made the company a prime target for a takeover. Against the wishes of Ecker's board of directors, an investment group from Detroit is attempting to buy 51% of Ecker's outstanding stock. Board members are convinced that the Detroit investors would sell off the most desirable pieces of the business and leave little of value.

At the most recent board meeting, several suggestions were advanced to fight off the hostile takeover bid. One suggestion is to increase the stock outstanding by distributing a 100% stock dividend.

Required

As a significant stockholder of Ecker Corporation, write a short memo to explain to the board whether distributing the stock dividend would make it more difficult for the investor group to take over Ecker Corporation. Include in your memo a discussion of the effect that the stock dividend would have on assets, liabilities, and total stockholders' equity—that is, the dividend's effect on the size of the corporation.

Journalizing dividend and treasury stock transactions; reporting retained earnings and stockholders' equity
(Obj. 1, 3)

P14-4A The balance sheet of Beech Bros. Design Co. at December 31, 20X6, reported the following stockholders' equity:

Paid-in capital:	
Common stock, $10 par, 100,000 shares authorized,	
20,000 shares issued	$200,000
Paid-in capital in excess of par-common	300,000
Total paid-in capital	500,000
Retained earnings	177,000
Total stockholders' equity	$677,000

During 20X7, Beech Bros. completed the following selected transactions:

Feb.	6	Distributed a 10% stock dividend on the common stock. The market value of Beech Bros.' common stock was $24 per share.
July	29	Purchased 2,000 shares of the company's own common stock at $21 per share.
Nov.	13	Sold 400 shares of treasury common stock for $22 per share.
	27	Declared a $0.30 per share dividend on the common stock outstanding. The date of record is December 17, and the payment date is January 7, 20X8.
Dec.	31	Closed the $62,000 net income to Retained Earnings.

Required

1. Record the transactions in the general journal.
2. Prepare a retained earnings statement at December 31, 20X7.
3. Prepare the stockholders' equity section of the balance sheet at December 31, 20X7.

Preparing a detailed income statement   (Obj. 5)

P14-5A The following information was taken from the records of Beaulac Excursions, Inc., at September 30, 20X1.

Interest expense	$ 11,000	General expenses	$113,000
Cost of goods sold	424,000	Preferred stock, $2, no-par,	
Cumulative effect of change in		10,000 shares authorized,	
depreciation method (expense)	(3,000)	5,000 shares issued	200,000
Loss on sale of plant assets	20,000	Retained earnings, beginning	88,000
Income from discontinued		Selling expenses	121,000
operations	8,000	Common stock, $10 par, 25,000	
Income tax expense (tax saving):		shares authorized and issued	250,000
Continuing operations	72,000	Net sales revenue	833,000
Income from discontinued		Treasury stock, common	
operations	2,000	(1,000 shares)	11,000
Extraordinary loss (tax saving)	(12,000)	Interest revenue	4,000
Cumulative effect of change in		Extraordinary loss	30,000
depreciation method (tax saving)	(1,000)		

Required

Prepare a single-step income statement, including earnings per share, for Beaulac Excursions, Inc., for the fiscal year ended September 30, 20X1. Evaluate income for the year ended September 30, 20X1, in terms of the outlook for 20X2. Assume that 20X1 was a typical year and that Beaulac managers hoped to earn income from continuing operations equal to 10% of net sales. The number of shares of common stock outstanding was unchanged during fiscal year 20X1.

P14-6A Luke Capps, accountant for Mabry Furniture Company, was injured in a boating accident. Another employee prepared the accompanying income statement for the year ended December 31, 20X3.

Preparing a corrected combined statement of income and retained earnings
(Obj. 5)

The individual *amounts* listed on the income statement are correct. However, some accounts are reported incorrectly, and others do not belong on the income statement at all. Also, income tax has not been applied to all appropriate figures. The income tax rate on discontinued operations and on the extraordinary loss, was 40%. Mabry Furniture Company issued 52,000 shares of common stock in 20X1 and held 2,000 shares as treasury stock during 20X3. Retained earnings, as originally reported at December 31, 20X2, was $361,000.

MABRY FURNITURE COMPANY
Income Statement
Year Ended December 31, 20X3

Revenue and gains:		
Sales		$362,000
Gain on retirement of preferred stock		
(issued for $81,000; purchased for $71,000)		10,000
Paid-in capital in excess of par—common		80,000
Total revenues and gains		452,000
Expenses and losses:		
Cost of goods sold	$105,000	
Selling expenses	67,000	
General expenses	61,000	
Sales returns	11,000	
Dividends	7,000	
Sales discounts	6,000	
Income tax expense	20,000	
Total expenses and losses		277,000
Income from operations		175,000
Other gains and losses:		
Loss on discontinued operations	$ (3,000)	
Extraordinary flood loss	(20,000)	
Prior-period adjustment—understated		
income tax for 20X2	(14,000)	
Total other losses		(37,000)
Net income		$138,000
Earnings per share		$2.76

Required

Prepare a corrected combined statement of income and retained earnings for 20X3; include earnings per share. Prepare the income statement in single-step format.

P14-7A The capital structure of Midori Flooring, Inc., at December 31, 20X6, included 20,000 shares of $1.25 preferred stock and 44,000 shares of common stock. Common shares outstanding during 20X7 were 44,000 January through May, 50,000 June through August, and 60,500 September through December. Income from continuing operations during 20X7 was $94,100. The company discontinued a segment of the business at a gain of $6,630, and also had an extraordinary gain of $33,660. Midori's board of directors restricts $100,000 of retained earnings for contingencies.

Computing earnings per share and reporting a retained earnings restriction
(Obj. 4, 5)

Required

1. Compute Midori's earnings per share. Start with income from continuing operations. Income and loss amounts are net of income tax.
2. Show two ways of reporting Midori's retained earnings restriction. Retained earnings at December 31, 20X6, was $107,000, and Midori declared cash dividends of $29,000 during 20X7.

P14-8A Boulder Technology, Inc., reported the following statement of stockholders' equity for the year ended October 31, 20X4:

(Dollar Amounts in Millions)	Common Stock	Additional Paid-in Capital	Retained Earnings	Treasury Stock	Total
Balance, Nov. 1, 20X3	$427	$1,622	$904	$(117)	$2,836
Net income			336		336
Cash dividends			(194)		(194)
Issuance of stock (61,500,000 shares)..............	123	260			383
Stock dividend..	22	48	(70)		–0–
Sale of treasury stock		9		19	28
Balance, Oct. 31, 20X4......................................	$572	$1,939	$976	$ (98)	$3,389

BOULDER TECHNOLOGY, INC.
Statement of Stockholders' Equity
Year Ended October 31, 20X4

Using a statement of stockholders' equity (Obj. 6)

Required

Answer these questions about Boulder Technology's stockholders' equity transactions.

1. What is the par value of the company's common stock?
2. At what price per share did Boulder Technology issue its common stock during the year?
3. What was the cost of treasury stock sold during the year? What was the selling price of the treasury stock sold? What was the increase in total stockholders' equity?
4. Boulder Technology's statement lists the stock transactions in the order they occurred. What was the percentage of the stock dividend? Round to the nearest percentage.

(Group B) PROBLEMS

Journalizing stockholders' equity transactions (Obj. 1, 3)

P14-1B Taylor Tennis, Inc., completed the following selected transactions during 20X6:

Feb. 6	Declared a cash dividend on the 10,000 shares of $2.25, no-par preferred stock. Declared a $0.20 per share dividend on the 10,000 shares of common stock outstanding. The date of record is February 17, and the payment date is February 20.
Feb. 20	Paid the cash dividends.
Mar. 21	Split common stock 3 for 1 by calling in the 10,000 shares of $15 par common and issuing new stock in its place.
Apr. 18	Distributed a 50% stock dividend on the common stock. The market value of the common stock was $27 per share.
June 18	Purchased 2,400 shares of the company's own common stock at $12 per share.
Dec. 22	Sold 700 shares of treasury common stock for $16 per share.

Required

Record the transactions in the general journal.

Journalizing dividend and treasury stock transactions and reporting stockholders' equity (Obj. 1, 2, 3)

P14-2B The balance sheet of Jade, Inc., at December 31, 20X1, reported 500,000 shares of $1 par common stock authorized with 100,000 shares issued. Paid-in Capital in Excess of Par—Common had a balance of $300,000. Retained Earnings had a balance of $57,000. During 20X2, the company completed the following selected transactions:

Feb. 15	Purchased 5,000 shares of the company's own common stock for the treasury at $4 per share.
Mar. 8	Sold 2,000 shares of treasury common stock for $7 per share.
Sep. 28	Distributed a 10% stock dividend on the *outstanding* common stock. The market value of Jade's common stock was $5 per share.
Nov. 5	Split the common stock 2 for 1 by calling in the 109,700 shares of old $1 par common stock and issuing twice as many shares of $0.50 par common. (Stock splits affect all authorized and issued stock, including treasury stock and stock that is outstanding.)
Dec. 31	Earned net income of $73,000 during the year. Closed net income to Retained Earnings.

Required

1. Record the transactions in the general journal. Explanations are not required.
2. Prepare the stockholders' equity section of the balance sheet at December 31, 20X2.

P14-3B Stouse Import Corporation is positioned ideally in its business. Located in Tucson, Arizona, Stouse is the only company between Texas and California with reliable sources for its imported gifts. The company does a brisk business with specialty stores such as **Pier 1 Imports.** Stouse's recent success has made the company a prime target for a takeover. An investment group from Hong Kong is attempting to buy 51% of Stouse's outstanding stock against the wishes of Stouse's board of directors. Board members are convinced that the Hong Kong investors would sell the most desirable pieces of the business and leave little of value.

Purchasing treasury stock to fight off a takeover of the corporation (Obj. 3)

At the most recent board meeting, several suggestions were advanced to fight off the hostile takeover bid. The suggestion with the most promise is to purchase a huge quantity of treasury stock. Stouse has the cash to carry out this plan.

Required

1. As a significant stockholder of Stouse Corporation, write a memorandum to explain to the board how the purchase of treasury stock would make it difficult for the Hong Kong group to take over Stouse. Include a discussion of the effect that purchasing treasury stock would have on stock outstanding and on the size of the corporation.
2. Suppose Stouse management is successful in fighting off the takeover bid and later sells the treasury stock at prices greater than the purchase price. Explain what effect these sales will have on assets, stockholders' equity, and net income.

P14-4B The balance sheet of Bradley Laser Corporation at December 31, 20X3, presented the following stockholders' equity:

Journalizing dividend and treasury stock transactions; reporting retained earnings and stockholders' equity (Obj. 1, 3)

Paid-in capital:	
Common stock, $1 par, 250,000 shares authorized,	
50,000 shares issued	$ 50,000
Paid-in capital in excess of par—common	350,000
Total paid-in capital	400,000
Retained earnings...	99,000
Total stockholders' equity..	$499,000

During 20X4, Bradley completed the following selected transactions:

Mar. 29	Distributed a 50% stock dividend on the common stock. The market value of Bradley common stock was $5 per share.
July 13	Purchased 2,000 shares of the company's own common stock at $6 per share.
Oct. 4	Sold 1,600 shares of treasury common stock for $8 per share.
Dec. 27	Declared a $0.20 per share dividend on the common stock outstanding. The date of record is January 17, 20X5, and the payment date is January 31.
31	Closed the $71,000 net income to Retained Earnings.

Required

1. Record the transactions in the general journal.
2. Prepare the retained earnings statement at December 31, 20X4.
3. Prepare the stockholders' equity section of the balance sheet at December 31, 20X4.

P14-5B The following information was taken from the records of Escobedo Corporation at June 30, 20X5:

Preparing a detailed income statement (Obj. 5)

Common stock, no-par, 22,000		Selling expenses	$ 87,000
shares authorized and issued	$350,000	General expenses...	71,000
Preferred stock, 6%, $25 par,		Income from discontinued operations.......	1,000
20,000 shares authorized,		Cost of goods sold.....................................	279,000
4,000 shares issued	100,000	Interest expense...	23,000
Cumulative effect of change in		Dividend revenue	19,000
depreciation method (income)	7,000	Treasury stock, common (2,000 shares)....	28,000
Income tax expense (tax saving):		Extraordinary loss......................................	27,000
Continuing operations	28,000	Loss on sale of plant assets	10,000
Gain on discontinued operations....	400	Net sales revenue.......................................	567,000
Extraordinary loss (tax saving)	(10,800)	Retained earnings, beginning...................	63,000
Cumulative effect of change in			
depreciation method	3,000		

Required

Prepare a single-step income statement, including earnings per share, for Escobedo Corporation for the fiscal year ended June 30, 20X5. Evaluate income for the year ended June 30, 20X5, in terms of the outlook for 20X6. Note that 20X5 was a typical year, and Escobedo managers hoped to earn income from continuing operations equal to 10% of net sales.

Preparing a corrected combined statement of income and retained earnings (Obj. 5)

P14-6B Felicia Barrow, accountant for Lackland Aviation, Inc., was injured in a bicycle accident. Another employee prepared the following income statement for the fiscal year ended June 30, 20X4:

LACKLAND AVIATION
Income Statement
June 30, 20X4

Revenues and gains:		
Sales		$733,000
Gain on retirement of preferred stock (issued for $70,000; purchased for $59,000)		11,000
Paid-in capital in excess of par—common		100,000
Total revenues and gains		844,000
Expenses and losses:		
Cost of goods sold	$383,000	
Selling expenses	103,000	
General expenses	91,000	
Sales returns	22,000	
Prior-period adjustment—understated income tax for fiscal year 20X3	4,000	
Dividends	15,000	
Sales discounts	10,000	
Income tax expense—continuing operations	32,000	
Total expenses and losses		660,000
Income from operations		184,000
Other gains and losses:		
Extraordinary gain	$ 30,000	
Loss on discontinued operations	(15,000)	
Total other gains		15,000
Net income		$199,000
Earnings per share		$9.95

The individual *amounts* listed on the income statement are correct. However, some accounts are reported incorrectly, and others do not belong on the income statement at all. Also, income tax has not been applied to all appropriate figures. The income tax rate on discontinued operations and on the extraordinary gain, is 40%. Lackland issued 24,000 shares of common stock in 20X1 and held 4,000 shares as treasury stock during the fiscal year 20X4. The retained earnings balance, as originally reported at June 30, 20X3, was $209,000.

Required

Prepare a corrected combined statement of income and retained earnings for fiscal year 20X4; include earnings per share. Prepare the income statement in single-step format.

Computing earnings per share and reporting a retained earnings restriction (Obj. 4, 5)

P14-7B The capital structure of The Martin Rehabilitation Group at December 31, 20X2, included 5,000 shares of $2.50 preferred stock and 130,000 shares of common stock. Common shares outstanding during 20X3 were 130,000 January through February; 119,000 during March; 121,000 April through October; and 128,000 during November and December. Income from continuing operations during 20X3 was $353,360. The company discontinued a segment of the business at a gain of $69,160, and also had an extraordinary loss of $49,510. The board of directors of The Martin Rehabilitation Group has restricted $300,000 of retained earnings for expansion of the company's office facilities.

Required

1. Compute Martin's earnings per share for 20X3. Start with income from continuing operations. Income and loss amounts are net of income tax.
2. Show two ways of reporting Martin's retained earnings restriction. Retained earnings at December 31, 20X2, was $127,800, and Martin declared cash dividends of $109,000 during 20X3.

P14-8B Pacer Communications, Inc., reported the following statement of stockholders' equity for the year ended September 30, 20X1:

PACER COMMUNICATIONS, INC.
Statement of Stockholders' Equity
Year Ended September 30, 20X1

(Dollar Amounts in Millions)	Common Stock	Additional Paid-in Capital	Retained Earnings	Treasury Stock	Total
Balance, October 1, 20X0	$173	$2,118	$1,706	$(18)	$3,979
Net income...			520		520
Cash dividends...			(117)		(117)
Issuance of stock (5,000,000 shares)	9	46			55
Stock dividend	18	92	(110)		–0–
Sale of treasury stock...................................		5		11	16
Balance, September 30, 20X1.......................	$200	$2,261	$1,999	$ (7)	$4,453

Using a statement of stockholders' equity
(Obj. 6)

Required

1. What is the par value of Pacer's common stock?
2. At what price per share did Pacer issue its common stock during the year?
3. What was the cost of treasury stock sold during the year? What was the selling price of the treasury stock sold? What was the increase in total stockholders' equity from selling the treasury stock?
4. Pacer's statement of stockholders' equity lists the stock transactions in the order in which they occurred. What was the percentage of the stock dividend? Round to the nearest percentage.

APPLY YOUR KNOWLEDGE

DECISION CASES

Case 1. Ganache Industries had the following stockholders' equity amounts on June 30, 20X2:

Analyzing cash dividends and stock dividends
(Obj. 1)

Common stock, no-par, 100,000 shares issued	$ 750,000
Retained earnings...	790,000
Total stockholders' equity..	$1,540,000

In the past, Ganache has paid an annual cash dividend of $1.50 per share. Despite the large retained earnings balance, the board of directors wished to conserve cash for expansion. The board delayed the payment of cash dividends and in July distributed a 10% stock dividend. During August, the company's cash position improved. The board declared and paid a cash dividend of $1.364 per share in September.

Suppose you owned 10,000 shares of Ganache common stock, acquired three years ago, prior to the 10% stock dividend. The market price of the stock was $30 per share before any of these dividends.

Required

1. What amount of cash dividends did you receive last year—before the stock dividend? What amount of cash dividends will you receive after the dividend action?
2. How does the stock dividend affect your proportionate ownership in Ganache Industries? Explain.
3. Immediately after the stock dividend was distributed, the market value of Ganache stock decreased from $30 per share to $27.273 per share. Does this decrease represent a loss to you? Explain.

Case 2. The following accounting issues have arisen at Cooltouch Cotton, Inc.:

Reporting special items
(Obj. 3, 5)

1. Corporations sometimes purchase their own stock. When asked why they do so, Cooltouch management responds that the stock is undervalued. What advantage would Cooltouch gain by buying and selling its own undervalued stock?
2. The treasurer of Cooltouch wants to report a large loss as an extraordinary item because Cooltouch produced too much product and cannot sell it. Why do you think the treasurer wants to report the loss as extraordinary? Would that be acceptable?

3. Cooltouch earned a significant profit in the year ended November 30, 20X2, because land that it held was purchased by the State of North Carolina for a new highway. The company proposes to treat the sale of land as operating revenue. Why do you think Cooltouch is proposing this plan? Is this disclosure appropriate?

ETHICAL ISSUE

◄◄ *Link Back to Chapter 9 (Accounting Principles).* Gladewater Petroleum Company is an independent oil producer in Gladewater, Texas. In February, company geologists discovered a pool of oil that tripled the company's proven reserves. Prior to disclosing the new oil to the public, top managers of the company quietly bought most of Gladewater's stock as treasury stock. After the discovery was announced, Gladewater's stock price rose from $7 to $52.

Required

1. Did Gladewater managers behave ethically? Explain your answer.
2. Identify the accounting principle relevant to this situation. Review Chapter 9 if necessary.
3. Who was helped and who was harmed by management's action?

FINANCIAL STATEMENT CASE

Complex income statement, earnings per share, and dividends (Obj. 1, 5)

Use the **Target Corporation** financial statements in Appendix A to answer the following questions.

Required

1. Study Target's income statement, which the company labels "consolidated results of operations." *Consolidated* means that Target owns other companies. Target reported one "special" item of income on its income statement. What was it, and what was its amount for 1999? Was this special item a gain or a loss? How can you tell?
2. Target's preferred dividends during 1999 were $19 million. Show how Target computed Basic earnings per share of $2.55.
3. The statement of stockholders' equity, which Target labels "consolidated statement of shareholders' investment," gives details of transactions that affected stockholders' equity. Use Target's statement of shareholders' investment to answer these questions:
   a. Journalize Target's closing entry for net income of 1999.
   b. Journalize Target's declaration of dividends during 1999.
   c. How much did Target pay to repurchase its stock during 1999?
   d. During 1999, Target issued common stock to its Employee Stock Option Plan (ESOP). Assume Target received cash for the stock it issued. How much cash did Target receive?

TEAM PROJECT

Required

Obtain the annual reports (or annual report data) of five well-known companies. You can get the reports either from your college library or by mailing a request directly to the company (allow two weeks for delivery). Or you can visit the Web site for this book (http://www.prenhall.com/harrison/) or the SEC EDGAR database, which includes the financial reports of most well-known companies.

1. After selecting five companies, examine their income statements to search for the following items:
   a. Income from continuing operations
   b. Discontinued operations
   c. Extraordinary gains and losses
   d. Cumulative effects of accounting changes
   e. Net income or net loss
   f. Earnings-per-share data
2. Study the companies' balance sheets to see
   a. What classes of stock each company has issued.
   b. Which item carries a larger balance—the Common Stock account, or Paid-in Capital in Excess of Par (also labeled Additional Paid-in Capital)?
   c. What percentage of each company's total stockholders' equity is made up of retained earnings?
   d. Whether the company has treasury stock. If so, how many shares and how much is the cost?
3. Examine each company's statement of stockholders' equity for evidence of
   a. Cash dividends
   b. Stock dividends (Some companies use the term *stock split* to refer to a large stock dividend.)
   c. Treasury stock purchases and sales

4. As directed by your instructor, either write a report or present your findings to your class. You may be unable to understand *everything* you find, but neither can the Wall Street analysts! You will be amazed at how much you have learned.

INTERNET EXERCISE

In 1993, **International Business Machines (IBM)** reported a record loss of $8,101,000,000 and also stopped paying cash dividends. Today IBM is thriving as the largest provider of computer hardware in the world. It produces PCs, notebooks, mainframes, servers, and peripherals, along with software, where it is second only to **Microsoft.**

1. Go to **http://www.ibm.com** and in the left-hand column, click on *Investors*. What is the current market price of IBM stock?
2. In the left-hand column, click on *Financials* and then *Stock split information*. Describe the most recent stock split and note the date of the payment (distribution) of the split shares. What effect would this stock split have on the par value per share? on total stockholders' equity?
3. In the left-hand column, click on *Annual reports* and select the *most recent annual report*. Click on *Financial Report,* and then under "Consolidated Financial Statements (Audited)," click on *Earnings*. Does IBM report any special items on the income statement? If so, what are they and what are their amounts? For the most recent year, show how IBM computed basic earnings per share of common stock.
4. At the bottom of the screen, click on *next page* to display the "Consolidated Statement of Financial Position."
   a. How many types of stock has IBM issued? List them. What is the par value per share of the common shares? As of the most recent balance sheet date, how many common shares has IBM issued? How many shares of common stock would receive a cash dividend? (*Note:* Treat the shares in the Employee Benefits Trust the same as Treasury Stock shares. Both of these accounts contain only common shares.)
   b. As of the most recent balance sheet date, how much have shareholders paid in total for the common shares issued? What was the average issue price per common share? How much has IBM paid in total to repurchase treasury stock? What was the average price paid per treasury share? Compare the average issue price, average price paid for treasury stock, and the current market price. What conclusions can you draw about when IBM purchased the treasury stock?

IBM

Go to the "Dividends and Treasury Stock" episode on the *Mastering Accounting* CD-ROM for an interactive, video-enhanced exercise on how CanGo can boost investor confidence after poor quarterly performance reports. The episode focuses on the difference between cash and stock dividends.

15

Long-Term Liabilities

LEARNING OBJECTIVES

After studying this chapter, you should be able to

1. Account for basic bonds payable transactions by the straight-line amortization method

2. Measure interest expense by the effective-interest method

3. Account for retirement of bonds payable

4. Account for conversion of bonds payable

5. Show the advantages and disadvantages of borrowing

6. Account for lease liabilities and pension liabilities

www.prenhall.com/horngren

Readiness Assessment

What's the best way to finance an Internet startup—issue stock or borrow the money? When the stock market declines, companies find it hard to sell their stock. That may be why **International Rectifier** of El Segundo, California, and Houston-based **Quanta Services, Inc.,** looked to the bond market for cash to expand. Both are high-tech support companies: International Rectifier provides enabling technology for power management; Quanta specializes in transmission infrastructure for telecommunications and electric power.

Even **Amazon.com** resorted to borrowing by issuing convertible notes payable. Convertible bonds offer advantages for companies that need to borrow and for individuals with money to invest. By issuing convertibles, companies can borrow at lower interest rates than if they issued straight bonds. Then, if the company's stock goes up, investors can swap the bonds for stock. Convertibility gives companies a low interest rate and investors the opportunity to benefit from a strong stock market.

Accessing bond information has never been easier. Investors can log onto www.convertbond.com for data on 800 convertible bond issues plus chat rooms and search functions. Or they can go to www.investinginbonds.com for the definitions of bond terms and to explore topics such as What Are Bonds? All these newly available data may make it easier for companies to borrow.

Sources: *Forbes,* May 22, 2000, "Best of the Web," p. 86; Jennifer Ablan, "Volume of convertible bond offerings continues to rise with big deals by technology concerns," *Wall Street Journal,* July 13, 2000, p. C25.

Chapters 13 and 14 covered two ways to finance operations: contributed capital (the stock accounts and additional paid-in capital) and profitable operations (retained earnings). This chapter discusses the third way to finance a company—borrowing money on long-term liabilities. The chapter appendix provides background on the valuation of long-term liabilities.

Before launching into accounting for bonds payable, let's compare stocks and bonds.

STOCKS

1. Stock represents the *ownership* (equity) of the corporation.
2. Each shareholder is an *owner* of the corporation.
3. The corporation *may or may not* pay dividends.
4. Dividends are *not* an expense of the corporation.
5. Corporation is *not* obligated to repay stock amounts to the shareholders.

BONDS

1. Bonds represent a *liability* of the corporation.
2. Each bondholder is a *creditor* of the corporation.
3. The corporation *must* pay interest.
4. Interest is a *tax-deductible* expense of the corporation.
5. Corporation *must* repay the bonds payable at maturity.

BONDS: AN INTRODUCTION

Well-known companies such as **Amazon.com, Inc.,** and **eBay** cannot borrow billions from a single lender because no lender will risk that much money on a single company. Even smaller companies such as **Quanta Services** may find it impossible to borrow all they need from a bank. Banks and other lenders diversify their risk by making loans to numerous customers. That way if a borrower cannot repay, the bank is not devastated.

How then do corporations borrow the huge amounts they need to expand? They issue bonds payable to the public. **Bonds payable** are groups of notes payable issued to multiple lenders, called bondholders. Amazon can borrow large amounts from thousands of individual investors, each of whom buys a modest amount of Amazon bonds.

Purchasers of the bonds receive a bond certificate, which carries the issuing company's name. The certificate states the *principal,* which is the amount the

BONDS PAYABLE. Groups of notes payable (bonds) issued to multiple lenders called bondholders.

company has borrowed from the bondholder. This figure, typically stated in units of $1,000, is also called the bond's face value, maturity value, or par value. The bond obligates the issuing company to pay the holder the principal amount at a specific future date, called the maturity date, which appears on the certificate.

Bondholders lend their money to earn interest. The bond certificate states the interest rate the issuer will pay the bondholder and the dates the interest payments are due (generally twice a year). Some bond certificates name the bondholder (the investor). Exhibit 15-1 shows an actual bond certificate.

EXHIBIT 15-1 Bond (Note) Certificate

Issuing Corporation →

Annual Contract (stated) Interest Rate →

Semiannual Interest Payments on January 1 and July 1 of each year →

Maturity Date July 1, 2010

Principal Amount

Issuing bonds usually requires the services of a securities firm, such as **Merrill Lynch,** to act as the *underwriter* of the bond issue. The **underwriter** purchases the bonds from the issuing company and resells them to its clients. Alternatively, the underwriter may sell the bonds for a commission, and agree to buy all unsold bonds.

Types of Bonds

All the bonds in a particular issue may mature at a specified time **(term bonds),** or they may mature in installments over a period of time **(serial bonds).** Serial bonds are like installment notes payable.

Secured, or mortgage, bonds give the bondholder the right to take specified assets of the issuer (called collateral) if the company defaults—that is, fails to pay interest or principal. Unsecured bonds, called **debentures,** are backed only by the good faith of the borrower.

Bond Prices

A bond issued at a price above its maturity (par) value is said to be issued at a **premium,** and a bond issued at a price below maturity (par) value has a **discount.** As a bond nears maturity, its market price moves toward par value. On the maturity date, the market value of a bond exactly equals its par value because the company that issued the bond pays that amount to retire the bond.

After a bond is issued, investors may buy and sell it through the bond market just as they buy and sell stocks through the stock market. The most famous bond market is the **New York Exchange,** which lists several thousand bonds. Bond prices are quoted at a percentage of their maturity value. For example, a $1,000 bond quoted at 100 is bought or sold for $1,000, which is 100% of its par value. The same bond quoted at 101 1/2 has a market price of $1,015 (101.5% of par value, or $1,000 × 1.015). Prices are quoted to one-eighth of 1%. A $1,000 bond quoted at 88 3/8 is priced at $883.75 ($1,000 × 0.88375).

Exhibit 15-2 contains price information for the bonds of **Ohio Edison Company,** taken from *The Wall Street Journal.* On this particular day, 12 of Ohio Edison's 9 1/2%, $1,000 par-value bonds maturing in the year 2006 (indicated by 06) were traded. The bonds' highest price on this day was $795 ($1,000 × 0.795). The lowest price of the day was $785 ($1,000 × 0.785). The closing price (last sale of the day) was $795. This price was 2% higher than the closing price of the preceding day. What was the bonds' closing price the preceding day? It was 77 1/2 (79 1/2 − 2).

Bonds	Volume	High	Low	Close	Net Change
OhEd 9 1/2 06	12	79 1/2	78 1/2	79 1/2	+2

EXHIBIT 15-2
Bond Price Information for Ohio Edison Company (OhEd)

Present Value[1]

A dollar received today (present value) is worth more than a dollar received in the future (future value). Why? Because you can invest today's dollar and earn income from it. Money earns income over time, a fact called the *time value of money.* Let's examine how the time value of money affects the pricing of bonds.

Assume that a bond with a face value of $1,000 reaches maturity three years from today and carries no interest. As an investor, would you pay $1,000 to purchase the bond? No, because the payment of $1,000 today to receive the same amount in the future provides you with no income on the investment. How much would you pay today in order to receive $1,000 at the end of three years? The answer is some amount *less* than $1,000. Let's suppose that $750 is a fair price. By investing $750 now to receive $1,000 later, you will earn $250 interest revenue over the three years. The issuing company sees the transaction this way: It pays you $250 interest for the use of your $750 for three years.

The amount that a person would invest *at the present time* to receive a greater amount at a future date is called the **present value.** In our example, $750 is the present value, and the $1,000 to be received three years later is the future amount.

The difference between present value and future value is interest. Present value is always less than future value. We discuss the method of computing present value in the appendix that follows this chapter. Keep the present-value concept in mind in the discussion of bond prices that follows. If your instructor so directs you, study the appendix now.

Bond Interest Rates

Bonds are sold at market price, which is the maximum investors will pay at a given time. Market price is the bond's present value, which is the sum of the present value of the principal payment plus the present value of the cash interest payments (semi-annual, annual, or quarterly).

[1]The chapter appendix covers present value in more detail.

CONTRACT INTEREST RATE.
Interest rate that determines the amount of cash interest the borrower pays and the investor receives each year. Also called the **stated interest rate.**

MARKET INTEREST RATE. Interest rate that investors demand in order to loan their money. Also called the **effective interest rate.**

 DAILY EXERCISE 15-2

Two interest rates work to set the price of a bond:

- The **contract interest rate,** or **stated interest rate,** is the interest rate that determines the amount of cash interest the borrower pays—and the investors receive—each year. The contract interest rate is set by the bond contract and *does not change* during the life of the bonds. For example, Amazon.com's 10% notes payable have a contract interest rate of 10%. Thus, Amazon pays $10,000 of interest annually on each $100,000 bond. Each semiannual interest payment is $5,000 ($100,000 × 0.10 × 1/2).

- The **market interest rate,** or **effective interest rate,** is the rate that investors demand for loaning their money. The market interest rate *varies,* sometimes daily. A company may issue bonds with a contract interest rate that differs from the prevailing market interest rate. Amazon.com may issue its 10% notes when the market rate has risen to 11%. Will the Amazon bonds attract investors in this market? No, because investors can earn 11% on other bonds and notes of similar risk. Therefore, investors will purchase Amazon notes only at a price less than par value. The difference between the lower price and the notes' face value is a *discount*.

Conversely, if the market interest rate is 8%, Amazon's 10% notes will be so attractive that investors will pay more than face value for them. The difference between the higher price and face value is a *premium*. Exhibit 15-3 shows how the contract (stated) interest rate and the market interest rate interact to determine the issuance price of a bond payable.

EXHIBIT 15-3
Interaction of the Contract Interest Rate and the Market Interest Rate to Determine the Price of a Bond Payable

 DAILY EXERCISE 15-3

 DAILY EXERCISE 15-4

(Example: Bond with a Contract Interest Rate of 9%)

Bond's Contract Interest Rate*		Market Interest Rate**		Issuance Price of Bonds Payable
9%	=	9%	⇒	Par (face, or maturity) value
9%	<	11%	⇒	Discount (price below par)
9%	>	7%	⇒	Premium (price above par)

* Determines the amount of interest of each cash interest payment.
** Used to set the bond's market price.

ISSUING BONDS PAYABLE TO BORROW MONEY

Suppose **Amazon.com, Inc.,** has $50 million of 9% bonds that mature in five years. Assume that Amazon issues these bonds at par on January 1, 2002. The issuance entry is

```
2002
Jan. 1   Cash.................................................   50,000,000
             Bonds Payable................................                50,000,000
         Issued bonds payable.
```

Amazon, the borrower, makes a one-time entry similar to this to record the receipt of cash and the issuance of bonds. Interest payments occur each January 1 and July 1. Amazon's entry to record the first semiannual interest payment is

```
2002
July 1   Interest Expense ($50,000,000 × 0.09 × 6/12) .....   2,250,000
             Cash .........................................                2,250,000
         Paid semiannual interest.
```

At maturity, Amazon.com will record payment of the bonds as follows:

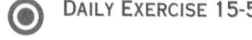 DAILY EXERCISE 15-5

```
2007
Jan. 1   Bonds Payable .....................................   50,000,000
             Cash .........................................                50,000,000
         Paid off bonds payable at maturity.
```

Issuing Bonds and Notes Payable Between Interest Dates

These entries to record Amazon.com's bond transactions are straightforward because the company issued the bonds on an interest payment date (January 1). However, corporations often issue bonds between interest dates.

Suppose Amazon.com issued these bonds on March 1, 2002, rather than on January 1. The bonds were dated January 1, so interest on the bonds started accruing on January 1. On the first interest date, July 1, 2002, Amazon will pay six months' interest to whoever owns the bonds on that date. The price of this Amazon.com bond would thus be expressed as "100 plus accrued interest."

- *100* means that the price of the bond is 100% of par, or face, value, that is, $50 million. Amazon will receive $50 million from issuance of the bonds, plus
- *Accrued interest* means that to buy an Amazon.com bond, investors must also pay accrued interest from the last interest date (January 1) up to the date of issuance (March 1). Amazon will thus receive two months of accrued interest when it issues the bonds.

As we saw earlier, issuing the bonds when they were dated—on January 1, 2002—brings Amazon exactly $50 million of cash. But issuing the bonds on March 1 brings in $50 million plus accrued interest. Amazon.com's issuance entry on March 1 is

```
2002
Mar. 1   Cash ................................................   50,750,000
              Bonds Payable .............................                50,000,000
              Interest Payable
                ($50,000,000 × 0.09 × 2/12) .................               750,000
         Issued bonds at par, two months after the date
         of the bonds.
```

Amazon.com has collected two months of interest in advance. Then, on July 1, Amazon pays semiannual interest and makes this entry:

```
2002
July 1   Interest Expense ($50,000,000 × 0.09 × 4/12)....   1,500,000
         Interest Payable ($50,000,000 × 0.09 × 2/12,
              from Mar. 1) .....................................     750,000
              Cash ($50,000,000 × 0.09 × 6/12) .............                2,250,000
         Paid semiannual interest.
```

Amazon's T-accounts for Interest Payable and Interest Expense appear as follows after the July 1 transaction:

INTEREST PAYABLE			INTEREST EXPENSE	
July 1 750,000	Mar. 1 750,000		July 1 1,500,000	

Interest Payable has a zero balance because Amazon paid the interest that it collected in advance on March 1. Interest Expense shows a $1,500,000 balance for Amazon.com's interest expense for the four months that the bonds have been outstanding (March, April, May, and June).

From the forgoing sequence of transactions, what would Amazon.com, Inc., report if it prepared financial statements immediately after July 1?

Answer

Balance sheet: Nothing to report because Interest payable is $0

Income statement: Interest expense $1,500,000

 DAILY EXERCISE 15-6

Borrowers Online: Click Here to Lend Us $6 Billion

Original art, Uncle Lester's gold fillings, and vintage Barbie dolls are being sold on-line. Then why not bonds? Companies in need of cash are stepping into e-commerce and borrowing money on-line.

Y2K fears evaporated on January 1, 2000. A few days later, bonds made their debut in cyber-space. The U.S. government went on-line first: On January 5, its mort-gage agency, **Freddie Mac**, kicked off a $6 billion bond issue. **Ford Motor** took the lead among corpo-rate borrowers: Five days later Ford announced a three-year bond issue to borrow $1 billion.

Online bond trading offers some real advantages, such as a wider array of lenders. And online trading lets issuers see their orders filling in real time.

For all these reasons, there has been a frenzy of activity in online borrowing. But borrowers and lenders beware: The ease of selling debt online can be its undoing. Companies just *might* be seduced into borrowing more money than they can pay back.

Source: Based on Chris Wright, "Cutting through the hype of Internet bond issuance," *Corporate Finance,* April 2000, pp. 5–6. Fiona Haddock, "The seduction of on-line debt," *Global Finance,* April 2000, pp. 30–33. Antony Currie, "Bonding on the Internet," *Euromoney,* February 2000, pp. 43–50.

Issuing Bonds Payable at a Discount

Unlike stocks, bonds are often issued at a discount. We know that market conditions may force the issuing corporation to accept a discount price for its bonds. Suppose Amazon.com, Inc., issues $100,000 of its 9%, five-year bonds when the market interest rate is 9 1/2%. The market price of the bonds drops to 98, which means 98% of par value. Amazon receives $98,000 ($100,000 × 0.98) at issuance and makes the following journal entry:

```
2002
Jan. 1   Cash ($100,000 × 0.98) .................   98,000
         Discount on Bonds Payable..............   2,000
                Bonds Payable .......................          100,000
         Issued bonds payable at a discount.
```

After posting, the bond accounts have the following balances:

BONDS PAYABLE	DISCOUNT ON BONDS PAYABLE
100,000	2,000

Amazon's balance sheet reports the following immediately after issuance of the bonds:

Long-term liabilities:
Bonds payable, 9%, due 2007 .... $100,000
Less: Discount on bonds payable............. (2,000) $98,000

Discount on Bonds Payable is a contra account to Bonds Payable. Subtracting the discount from Bonds Payable yields the carrying amount of the bonds. The relationship between Bonds Payable and the Discount account is similar to the relationship between Equipment and Accumulated Depreciation. Thus, Amazon.com's liability is $98,000, which is the amount the company borrowed. If Amazon were to pay off the bonds immediately, the company would pay only $98,000 because the market price of the bonds is $98,000.

INTEREST EXPENSE ON BONDS PAYABLE ISSUED AT A DISCOUNT   We earlier discussed the difference between the contract interest rate and the market interest rate. Suppose the market rate is 9 1/2% when Amazon.com issues its 9% bonds. The 1/2% interest-rate difference creates the $2,000 discount on the bonds. Investors are willing to pay only $98,000 for a $100,000, 9% bond when they can purchase similar bonds and earn 9 1/2% on the investment. Amazon borrows $98,000 cash but must pay $100,000 cash when the bonds mature five years later.

   What happens to the $2,000 balance of the discount account over the life of the bond issue? The $2,000 discount is additional interest expense to Amazon. The $2,000 is a cost—beyond the stated 9% interest—that the business pays for borrowing money. The discount has the effect of raising the interest expense on the bonds to the market interest rate of 9 1/2%. For each accounting period over the life of the bonds, the discount is accounted for as interest expense through a process called amortization.

STRAIGHT-LINE AMORTIZATION OF BOND DISCOUNT   We amortize a bond discount by dividing it into equal amounts for each interest period. This method is called *straight-line amortization*. In our example, the initial discount is $2,000, and there are ten semiannual interest periods during the bonds' five-year life. Therefore, 1/10 of the $2,000 ($200) of bond discount is amortized each interest period. Amazon.com's semiannual interest entry on July 1, 2002 is recorded as follows:[2]

2002			
July 1	Interest Expense..	4,700	
	Cash ($100,000 × 0.09 × 6/12)		4,500
	Discount on Bonds Payable ($2,000/10)		200
	Paid semiannual interest and amortized discount		
	on bonds payable.		

Interest expense of $4,700 for the six-month period is the sum of

- the contract interest ($4,500, which is paid in cash), plus
- the amortization of discount ($200).

   Discount on Bonds Payable is credited to amortize (reduce) its debit balance. Because Discount on Bonds Payable is a contra account, each reduction in its balance increases the carrying amount of the bonds payable. Ten amortization entries will decrease the discount balance to zero, and the carrying amount of bonds payable will have increased to the bonds' face value of $100,000. The entry to pay off the bonds at maturity is

 DAILY EXERCISE 15-7

2007			
Jan. 1	Bonds Payable	100,000	
	Cash..		100,000
	Paid off bonds payable at maturity.		

---

[2]Some accountants record the payment of interest and the amortization of the discount in two separate entries, as follows:

2002			
July 1	Interest Expense...	4,500	
	Cash ($100,000 × 0.09 × 6/12)............................		4,500
	Paid semiannual interest.		
July 1	Interest Expense...	200	
	Discount on Bonds Payable ($2,000/10)		200
	Amortized discount on bonds payable.		

Issuing Bonds Payable at a Premium

The issuance of bonds at a premium is rare because to do so companies must commit to a contract interest rate that is higher than the market rate. To illustrate, let's change the Amazon example. Assume that the market interest rate is 8% when the company issues its 9%, five-year bonds. Because 9% bonds are attractive in this market, investors pay a premium price to acquire them. If the bonds are priced at 104 (104% of par value), Amazon receives $104,000 cash upon issuance. The entry is

```
2002
Jan. 1   Cash ($100,000 × 1.04) .............................   104,000
              Bonds Payable ...................................              100,000
              Premium on Bonds Payable ...............               4,000
         Issued bonds payable at a premium.
```

After posting, the bond accounts have the following balances:

BONDS PAYABLE	PREMIUM ON BONDS PAYABLE
100,000	4,000

Amazon.com's balance sheet reports the following immediately after issuance of bonds:

Long-term liabilities:		
Bonds payable, 9%, due 2004..................	$100,000	
Premium on bonds payable.....................	4,000	$104,000

Premium on Bonds Payable is added to Bonds Payable to show the book value, or carrying amount, of the bonds. Amazon's liability is $104,000, which is the amount that the company borrowed. Immediate payment of the bonds would cost $104,000 because that is the market price of the bonds.

INTEREST EXPENSE ON BONDS PAYABLE ISSUED AT A PREMIUM   The 1% difference between the 9% contract interest rate on the bonds and the 8% market rate creates the $4,000 premium. Amazon borrows $104,000 cash but must pay only $100,000 at maturity. The premium is like a savings of interest expense to Amazon. The premium cuts Amazon's cost of borrowing and reduces the company's interest expense to an effective interest rate of 8%, the market rate. We account for the premium much as we handled the discount. But we amortize the bond premium as a decrease in interest expense over the life of the bonds.

STRAIGHT-LINE AMORTIZATION OF BOND PREMIUM   In our example, the beginning premium is $4,000, and there are ten semiannual interest periods during the bonds' five-year life. Therefore, 1/10 of the $4,000 ($400) of bond premium is amortized each interest period. Amazon.com's semiannual interest entry on July 1, 2002, is[3]

```
2002
July 1   Interest Expense...........................................    4,100
             Premium on Bonds Payable ($4,000/10) .....      400
                 Cash ($100,000 × 0.09 × 6/12) .........               4,500
         Paid semiannual interest and amortized premium
         on bonds payable.
```

DAILY EXERCISE 15-8

Interest expense of $4,100 is the contract interest paid ($4,500) less the amount of premium amortized ($400).

---

[3]The payment of interest and the amortization of bond premium can be recorded in separate entries as follows:

```
2002
July 1   Interest Expense ...............................................    4,500
             Cash ($100,000 × 0.09 × 6/12) ............................              4,500
         Paid semiannual interest.

July 1   Premium on Bonds Payable ($4,000/10) .........................      400
             Interest Expense ........................................              400
         Amortized premium on bonds payable.
```

Consider bonds issued at a discount. Which will be greater, the cash interest paid per period or the amount of interest expense? Answer the same question for bonds issued at a premium.

Answer: For bonds issued at a *discount,* interest expense will be greater than cash interest paid, by the amount of the discount amortized each period. Remember that the company received less than face value when it issued the bonds. But at maturity the company must pay the full face value back to the bondholders. This discount increases the company's interest expense above the amount of cash interest paid each period.

For bonds issued at a *premium,* interest expense will be less than the amount of cash interest paid, by the amount of the premium amortized for the period. This is because the premium amount received at issuance decreases the interest expense below the amount of cash interest paid each period.

Reporting Bonds Payable

Bonds payable are reported on the balance sheet at their maturity amount plus any unamortized premium or minus any unamortized discount. For example, in the preceding example at December 31, Amazon.com has amortized Premium on Bonds Payable for two semiannual periods ($400 × 2 = $800). The Amazon balance sheet would show these bonds payable as follows:

Long-term liabilities:		
Bonds payable, 9%, due 2004...	$100,000	
Premium on bonds payable [$4,000 − ($2 × $400)]...........	3,200	$103,200

Over the life of the bonds, ten amortization entries will decrease the premium balance to zero. The payment at maturity will debit Bonds Payable and credit cash for $100,000.

Adjusting Entries for Interest Expense

Companies issue bonds when they need cash. The interest payments seldom occur on December 31 (or the end of the fiscal year). Nevertheless, interest expense must be accrued at the end of the period to measure income accurately. ➥ The accrual entry may often be complicated by the need to amortize a discount or a premium for a partial interest period.

Xenon Corporation issued $100,000 of its 8%, ten-year bonds at a $2,000 discount on October 1, 2002. The interest payments occur on March 31 and September 30 each year. On December 31, Xenon records interest for the three-month period (October, November, and December) as follows:

◄ The adjusting entry for bond interest expense follows the pattern for the adjusting entries for other accrued liabilities, as in Chapters 3 (p. 95) and 11 (p. 447), except for the addition of the amortization of the premium or discount.

2002			
Dec. 31	Interest Expense...	2,050	
	Interest Payable ($100,000 × 0.08 × 3/12)......................		2,000
	Discount on Bonds Payable ($2,000/10 × 3/12)..............		50
	Accrued three months' interest and amortized discount		
	on bonds payable.		

Interest Payable is credited for the three months of cash interest that have accrued since September 30. Discount on Bonds Payable is credited for three months of amortization.

Xenon's balance sheet at December 31, 2002, reports Interest Payable of $2,000 as a current liability. Bonds Payable appears as a long-term liability, presented as follows:

Long-term liabilities:		
Bonds payable, 8%, due 2009	$100,000	
Less: Discount on bonds payable ($2,000 − $50)	(1,950)	$98,050

Observe that the balance of Discount on Bonds Payable decreases by $50. The bonds' carrying amount therefore increases by $50. The bonds' carrying amount continues to increase over its ten-year life, reaching $100,000 at maturity, when the discount will be fully amortized.

The next semiannual interest payment occurs on March 31, 2003:

DAILY EXERCISE 15-9

DAILY EXERCISE 15-10

2003			
Mar. 31	Interest Expense	2,050	
	Interest Payable	2,000	
	Cash ($100,000 × 0.08 × 6/12)		4,000
	Discount on Bonds Payable ($2,000/10 × 3/12)		50
	Paid semiannual interest, part of which was accrued, and amortized three months' discount on bonds payable.		

Amortization of a premium over a partial interest period is similar except that Premium on Bonds Payable is debited.

Take a few moments and review the first half of the chapter by studying the Decision Guidelines feature.

DECISION GUIDELINES

Accounting for Long-Term Liabilities—Part A

DECISION	GUIDELINES
Need to pay back principal amount of bonds • All at maturity? • In installments?	Type of bond to issue: • Term bonds • Serial bonds
Are the bonds secured? • Yes • No	Then they are • Mortgage, or secured, bonds • Debenture, or unsecured, bonds
How are bond prices • Quoted?	• As a percentage of maturity value (Example: A $500,000 bond priced at $510,000 would be quoted at 102 ($510,000 ÷ $500,000 = 1.02.)
• Determined?	• Present value of the future principal amount to pay plus present value of the future interest payments (see chapter appendix)
What are the two interest rates used for bonds?	• *Contract (stated) interest rate* determines the amount of cash interest the borrower pays. This interest rate is set by contract and does not change during the life of the bonds. • *Market (effective) interest rate* is the rate that investors demand for loaning their money. The market interest rate determines the borrower's true rate of interest expense. This rate varies, sometimes daily.
What causes a bond to be priced at • Par (face, or maturity) value?	When the bonds are issued, • Contract interest rate on the bond *equals* the Market interest rate
• A premium?	• Contract interest rate on the bond is *greater than* the Market interest rate
• A discount?	• Contract interest rate on the bond is *less than* the Market interest rate
What is the relationship between interest expense and interest payments when bonds are issued at • Par (face, or maturity) value? • A premium? • A discount?	• Interest expense *equals* Interest payment • Interest expense is *less than* Interest payment • Interest expense is *greater than* Interest payment
How to report bonds payable on the balance sheet?	Par (face or maturity amount) { + Premium on bonds payable or − Discount on bonds payable

SUMMARY PROBLEM

Assume that Alabama Power Company has outstanding an issue of 9% bonds that mature on May 1, 2022. The bonds are dated May 1, 2002, and Alabama Power pays interest each April 30 and October 31.

www.prenhall.com/horngren
Mid-Chapter Assessment

Required

1. Will the bonds be issued at par, at a premium, or at a discount if the market interest rate is 8% at date of issuance? If the market interest rate is 10%?
2. Assume that Alabama Power issued $1,000,000 of the bonds at 104 on May 1, 2002.
   a. Record issuance of the bonds.
   b. Record the interest payment and amortization of premium or discount on October 31, 2002.
   c. Accrue interest and amortize premium or discount on December 31, 2002.
   d. Show how the company would report the bonds on the balance sheet at December 31, 2002.
   e. Record the interest payment on April 30, 2003.

Solution

Requirement 1

If the market interest rate is 8%, 9% bonds will be issued at a *premium*. If the market rate is 10%, the 9% bonds will be issued at a *discount*.

Requirement 2

2002			
a. May 1	Cash ($1,000,000 × 1.04)..	$1,040,000	
	Bonds Payable...		1,000,000
	Premium on Bonds Payable.............................		40,000
	Issued 9%, 20-year bonds at a premium.		
b. Oct. 31	Interest Expense..	44,000	
	Premium on Bonds Payable ($40,000/40).................	1,000	
	Cash ($1,000,000 × 0.09 × 6/12)		45,000
	Paid semiannual interest and amortized premium on bonds payable.		
c. Dec. 31	Interest Expense..	14,667	
	Premium on Bonds Payable		
	($40,000/40 × 2/6)	333	
	Interest Payable		
	($1,000,000 × 0.09 × 2/12)...........................		15,000
	Accrued interest and amortized bond premium for two months.		

d. Long-term liabilities:

Bonds payable, 9%, due 2022	$1,000,000	
Premium on bonds payable		
($40,000 − $1,000 − $333)	38,667	$1,038,667

2003			
e. Apr. 30	Interest Expense..	29,333	
	Interest Payable..	15,000	
	Premium on Bonds Payable ($40,000/40 × 4/6)........	667	
	Cash ($1,000,000 × 0.09 × 6/12)		45,000
	Paid semiannual interest, part of which was accrued, and amortized four months' premium on bonds payable.		

Supplement to Solution

Bond problems include many details. You may find it helpful to check your work. We verify the answers to the summary problem in the following supplement.

On April 30, 2003, the bonds have been outstanding for one year. After the entries have been recorded, the account balances should show the results of one year's cash interest payments and one year's bond premium amortization.

Fact 1: Cash interest payments should be $90,000 ($1,000,000 × 0.09).

Accuracy check: Two credits to Cash of $45,000 each = $90,000. Cash payments are correct.

Fact 2: Premium amortization should be $2,000 ($40,000/40 semiannual periods × 2 semiannual periods in 1 year).

Accuracy check: Three debits to Premium on Bonds Payable ($1,000 + $333 + $667) = $2,000. Premium amortization is correct.

Fact 3: We can also check the accuracy of interest expense recorded during the year ended December 31, 2002.

The bonds in this problem will be outstanding for a total of 20 years, or 240 (that is, 20 × 12) months. During 2002, the bonds are outstanding for eight months (May through December).

Interest expense for eight months *equals* payment of cash interest for eight months minus premium amortization for eight months. Interest expense should therefore be ($1,000,000 × 0.09 × 8/12 = $60,000) minus [($40,000/240) × 8 = $1,333], or ($60,000 − $1,333 = $58,667).

Accuracy check: Two debits to Interest Expense ($44,000 + $14,667) = $58,667. Interest expense for 2002 is correct.

Objective 2
Measure interest expense by the effective-interest method

EFFECTIVE-INTEREST METHOD OF AMORTIZATION

We presented the straight-line amortization method first to introduce the concept of amortizing bond discount and premium. However, that method has a theoretical weakness. Each period's amortization amount for a premium or discount is the same dollar amount over the life of the bonds. Over that time, however, the bonds' carrying amount continues to increase (with a discount) or decrease (with a premium). Thus, the fixed dollar amount of interest expense as a percentage of the bonds' carrying amount, making it appear that the bond issuer's interest rate changes over time. But in reality, the issuer locked in a fixed interest rate when the bonds were issued. The interest *rate* on the bonds does not change.

Generally accepted accounting principles require that interest expense be measured using the *effective-interest method* unless the difference between the straight-line method and the effective-interest method is immaterial. In that case, either method is permitted. We will see how the effective-interest method keeps interest expense at the same percentage over the bonds' life. The total amount of interest expense over the life of the bonds is the same under both methods.

Effective-Interest Method of Measuring Interest Expense — Bond Discount

Assume that **eBay Inc.** issues $100,000 of 9% bonds at a time when the market rate of interest is 10%. Assume also that these bonds mature in five years and pay interest semiannually, so there are ten semiannual interest payments. The issue price of the bonds is $96,149.[4] The discount on these bonds is $3,851 ($100,000 − $96,149). Exhibit 15-4 shows how to measure interest expense by the effective-interest method.

The *accounts* debited and credited under the effective-interest method and the straight-line method are the same. Only the *amounts* differ. We may take the amortization *amounts* directly from the table in Exhibit 15-4. We assume that the first interest payment occurs on July 1 and so we use the appropriate amounts from Exhibit 15-4, reading across the line for the first interest payment date:

 DAILY EXERCISE 15-11

 DAILY EXERCISE 15-12

July 1	Interest Expense (column B) 4,807	
	Discount on Bonds Payable (column C).............	307
	Cash (column A)	4,500
	To pay semiannual interest and amortize discount on bonds payable.	

[4]We compute this present value in the chapter appendix.

PANEL A—Bond Data

Maturity value—$100,000

Contract interest rate—9%

Interest paid—4 1/2% semiannually, $4,500 ($100,000 × 0.045)

Market interest rate at time of issue—10% annually, 5% semiannually

Issue price—$96,149

PANEL B—Amortization Table

End of Semiannual Interest Period	A Interest *Payment* (4 1/2% of Maturity Value)	B Interest *Expense* (5% of Preceding Bond Carrying Amount)	C Discount Amortization (B − A)	D Discount Balance (D − C)	E Bond Carrying Amount ($100,000 − D)
Issue Date				$3,851	$ 96,149
1	$4,500	$4,807	$307	3,544	96,456
2	4,500	4,823	323	3,221	96,779
3	4,500	4,839	339	2,882	97,118
4	4,500	4,856	356	2,526	97,474
5	4,500	4,874	374	2,152	97,848
6	4,500	4,892	392	1,760	98,240
7	4,500	4,912	412	1,348	98,652
8	4,500	4,933	433	915	99,085
9	4,500	4,954	454	461	99,539
10	4,500	4,961*	461	−0−	100,000

* Adjusted for effect of rounding.

Notes

- *Column A* The semiannual interest payments are constant—fixed by the contract interest rate and the bonds' maturity value.
- *Column B* The interest expense each period is computed by multiplying the preceding bond carrying amount by the market interest rate. This *effective interest rate* determines the interest expense each period. The amount of interest each period increases as the effective interest rate, a constant, is applied to the increasing bond carrying amount (E).
- *Column C* The excess of each interest expense amount (B) over each interest payment amount (A) is the discount amortization for the period.
- *Column D* The discount balance decreases by the amount of amortization for the period (C), from $3,851 at the issue date to zero at maturity. Balance of discount + Bonds' carrying amount = Bonds' maturity value ($100,000).
- *Column E* The bonds' carrying amount increases from $96,149 at issuance to $100,000 at maturity.

Exhibit 15-5, on page 590, Panel A, diagrams the interest expense over the life of bonds payable issued at a discount. Panel B shows how the carrying amount of the bonds rises to the maturity date. All amounts are taken from Exhibit 15-4. Focus on the highlighted items to understand the main points of the exhibit.

THINK IT OVER

Over the life of a bond issued at a *discount,* will the periodic amount of interest expense increase or decrease under the effective-interest amortization method?

Answer: The periodic amount of interest expense *increases* because the carrying amount of the bond *increases* toward maturity value. To see this, refer to columns B and E of Exhibit 15-4. The upward-sloping line in Exhibit 15-5, Panel A, illustrates the increasing amount of interest expense.

EXHIBIT 15-5

Interest Expense and the Bond
Carrying Amount Both Increase
for Bonds Payable Issued
at a Discount

PANEL A—Interest Expense on Bonds Payable Issued at a Discount

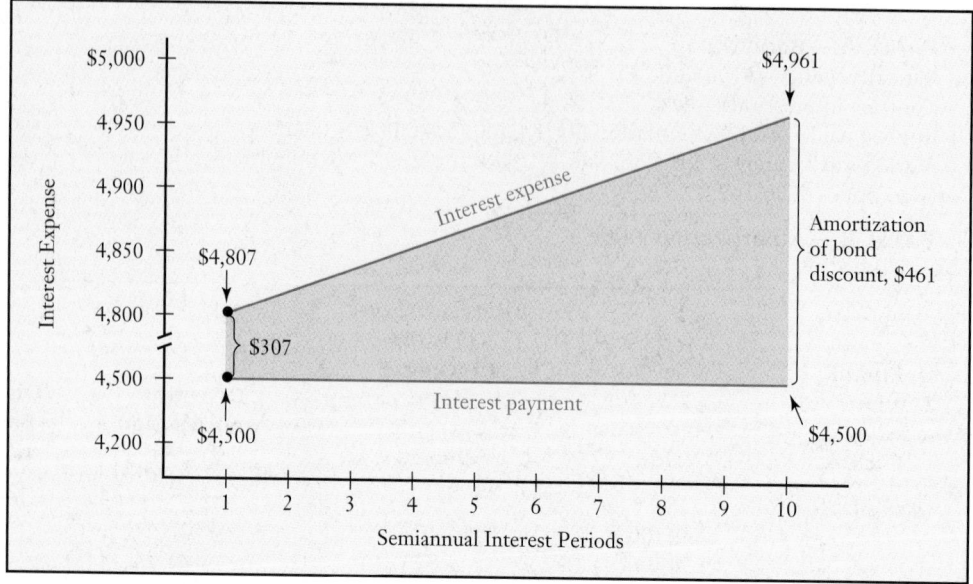

PANEL B—Carrying Amount of Bonds Payable Issued at a Discount

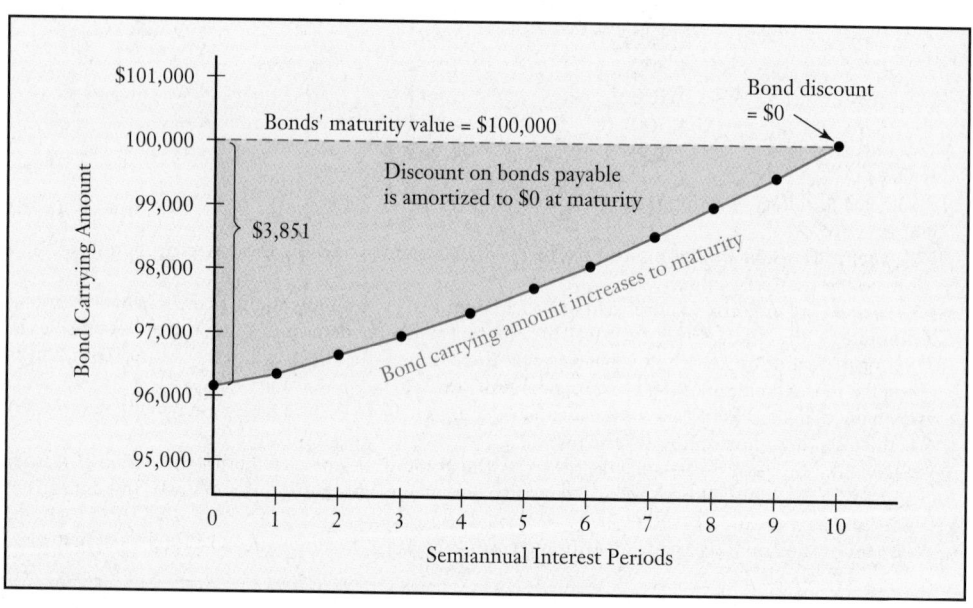

Effective-Interest Method of Measuring Interest Expense— Bond Premium

Let's modify the **eBay** bonds payable example to illustrate the interest method of measuring interest expense for a bond premium situation. Assume that **eBay** issues $100,000 of five-year, 9% bonds that pay interest semiannually. If the bonds are issued when the market interest rate is 8%, their issue price is $104,100.[5] The premium on these bonds is $4,100, and Exhibit 15-6 shows how to measure interest expense by the effective-interest method.

Assuming that the first interest payment occurs on October 31, we read across the line in Exhibit 15-6 for the first payment date and get the appropriate amounts:

Oct. 31	Interest Expense (column B)..................................... 4,164	
	Premium on Bonds Payable (column C) 336	
	Cash (column A)...	4,500
	To pay semiannual interest and amortize premium	
	on bonds payable.	

[5]Again, we compute the present value of the bonds in this chapter's appendix

PANEL A—Bond Data

Maturity value—$100,000
Contract interest rate—9%
Interest paid—4 1/2% semiannually, $4,500 ($100,000 × 0.045)
Market interest rate at time of issue—8% annually, 4% semiannually
Issue price—$104,100

PANEL B—Amortization Table

End of Semiannual Interest Period	A Interest Payment (4 1/2% of Maturity Value)	B Interest *Expense* (4% of Preceding Bond Carrying Amount)	C Premium Amortization (A − B)	D Premium Balance (D − C)	E Bond Carrying Amount ($100,000 + D)
Issue Date				$4,100	$104,100
1	$4,500	$4,164	$336	3,764	103,764
2	4,500	4,151	349	3,415	103,415
3	4,500	4,137	363	3,052	103,052
4	4,500	4,122	378	2,674	102,674
5	4,500	4,107	393	2,281	102,281
6	4,500	4,091	409	1,872	101,872
7	4,500	4,075	425	1,447	101,447
8	4,500	4,058	442	1,005	101,005
9	4,500	4,040	460	545	100,545
10	4,500	3,955*	545	–0–	100,000

* Adjusted for effect of rounding.

Notes
- *Column A* The semiannual interest payments are constant—fixed by the contract interest rate and the bonds' maturity value.
- *Column B* The interest expense each period is computed by multiplying the preceding bond carrying amount by the effective interest rate. The amount of interest decreases each period as the bond carrying amount decreases.
- *Column C* The excess of each interest payment (A) over the period's interest expense (B) is the premium amortization for the period.
- *Column D* The premium balance decreases by the amount of amortization for the period (C) from $4,100 at issuance to zero at maturity. Bonds' carrying amount − Premium balance = Bonds' maturity value ($100,000).
- *Column E* The bonds' carrying amount decreases from $104,100 at issuance to $100,000 at maturity.

THINK IT OVER

How does the method of amortizing bond premium or discount affect the amount of cash interest paid on a bond?

Answer: The amortization method has *no effect* on the amount of cash interest paid on a bond. The amount of cash interest depends on the contract interest rate stated on the bond. That interest rate, and the amount of cash interest paid, remain constant over the life of the bond. To see this, examine column A of Exhibits 15-4 and 15-6.

At year end, it is necessary to make an adjusting entry to accrue interest and amortize the bond premium for a partial period. In our example, the last interest payment occurred on October 31. The adjustment for November and December covers two months, or one-third of a semiannual period. The entry, with amounts drawn from Exhibit 15-6, line 2, is as follows:

Dec. 31	Interest Expense ($4,151 × 1/3).........................	1,384	
	Premium on Bonds Payable ($349 × 1/3)...........	116	
	Interest Payable ($4,500 × 1/3)................		1,500
	To accrue two months' interest and amortize premium on bonds payable for two months.		

The second interest payment occurs on April 30 of the following year. The payment of $4,500 includes

- Interest expense for four months (January through April)
- The interest payable at December 31
- Premium amortization for four months

The payment entry is as follows:

Apr. 30	Interest Expense ($4,151 × 2/3)	2,767	
	Interest Payable	1,500	
	Premium on Bonds Payable ($349 × 2/3)	233	
	Cash		4,500
	To pay semiannual interest, some of which was accrued, and amortize premium on bonds payable for four months.		

If these bonds had been issued at a discount, procedures for these interest entries would be the same, except that Discount on Bonds Payable would be credited.

Exhibit 15-7, Panel A, diagrams the interest expense over the life of bonds issued at a premium. Panel B shows how the carrying amount of the bonds falls to maturity. All amounts are taken from Exhibit 15-6. Focus on the highlighted items.

 DAILY EXERCISE 15-13

 THINK IT OVER

For a bond issued at a *premium*, will the periodic amount of interest expense increase or decrease? Use the effective-interest method.

Answer: The periodic amount of interest expense *decreases* because the carrying amount of the bond *decreases* toward maturity value. To see this, study columns B and E of Exhibit 15-6. The downward-sloping line in Exhibit 15-7, Panel A, illustrates the decreasing amount of interest expense.

Objective 3
Account for retirement of bonds payable

ADDITIONAL BOND TOPICS

Companies that issue bonds payable face additional issues, such as how to account for the retirement of bonds and convertible bonds. Two other important long-term liabilities are leases and pensions.

Retirement of Bonds Payable

Normally, companies wait until maturity to pay off, or retire, their bonds payable. All bond discount or premium has been amortized. The retirement entry debits Bonds Payable and credits Cash for the bonds' maturity value. But companies sometimes retire their bonds payable prior to maturity. The main reason for retiring bonds early is to relieve the pressure of making interest payments. Interest rates fluctuate. The company may be able to borrow at a lower interest rate and use the proceeds from new bonds to pay off the old bonds, which bear a higher interest rate.

CALLABLE BONDS. Bonds that the issuer may call or pay off at a specified price whenever the issuer wants.

Some bonds are **callable,** which means that the bonds' issuer may *call,* or pay off, those bonds at a specified price whenever the issuer so chooses. The call price is usually 100 or a few percentage points above the par value, perhaps 101 or 102. Callable bonds give the issuer the benefit of being able to take advantage of low interest rates by paying off the bonds whenever it is favorable to do so. An alternative to calling the bonds is to purchase them in the open market at their current market price. Whether the bonds are called or purchased in the open market, the journal entry is the same.

ETrade Associates has $70 million of debentures outstanding with a discount of $350,000. Lower interest rates in the market may convince management to pay off these bonds now. Assume that the bonds are callable at 103. If the market price of the bonds is 99 1/4, will ETrade call the bonds or purchase them in the open market? The market price is lower than the call price, so market price is the better choice. Retiring the bonds at 99 1/4 results in an extraordinary gain of $175,000, computed as follows:

EXHIBIT 15-7
Interest Expense and the Bond
Carrying Amount Both Decrease
for Bonds Payable Issued
at a Premium

PANEL A—Interest Expense on Bonds Payable Issued at a Premium

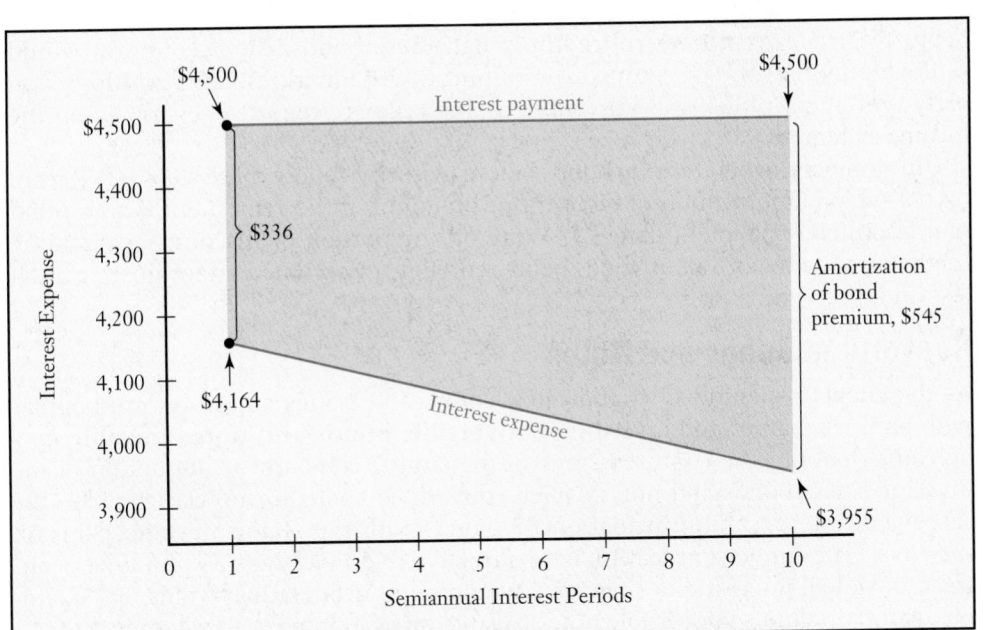

PANEL B—Carrying Amount of Bonds Payable Issued at a Premium

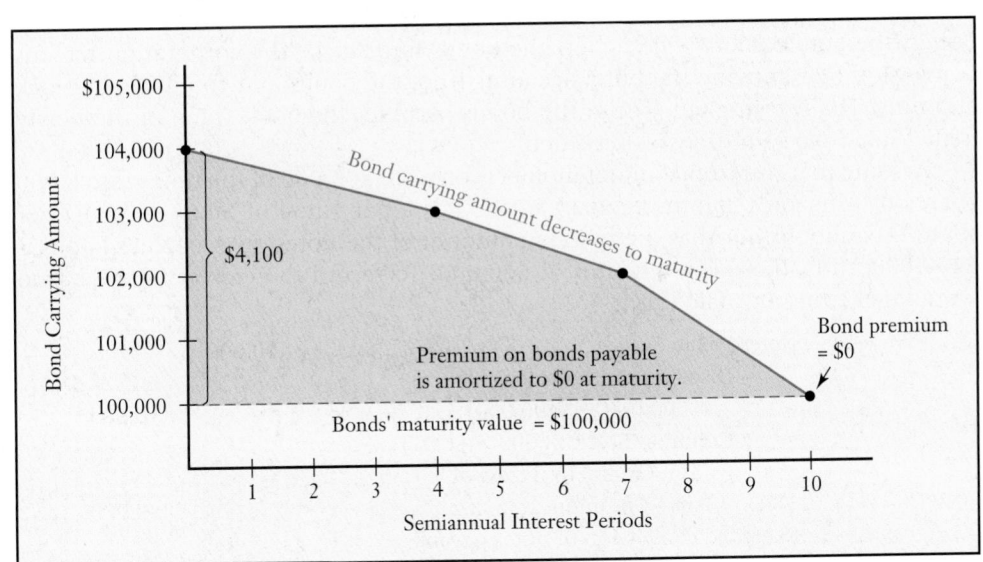

Par value of bonds being retired	$70,000,000
Less: Discount on bonds payable	(350,000)
Carrying amount of bonds payable...	69,650,000
Market price ($70,000,000 × 0.9925)	69,475,000
Extraordinary gain on retirement of bonds payable..............	$ 175,000

The following entry records retirement of the bonds, immediately after an interest date:

June 30	Bonds Payable	70,000,000	
	Discount on Bonds Payable		350,000
	Cash ($70,000,000 × 0.9925)		69,475,000
	Extraordinary Gain on Retirement		
	of Bonds Payable.............................		175,000
	Retired bonds payable.		

The entry removes the bonds payable and the related discount from the accounts and records a gain on retirement. Any existing premium would be removed with a debit. If ETrade Associates retired only half these bonds, the accountant would remove only half the discount or premium. GAAP identifies gains and losses on early retirement of debts as *extraordinary,* and they are reported separately on the income statement.

In summary, when retiring bonds before maturity, follow these steps: (1) Record partial-period amortization of discount or premium, if the retirement date is other than an interest payment date. (2) Write off the portion of Discount or Premium that relates to the portion of bonds being retired. (3) Compute extraordinary gain or loss on retirement.

Objective 4
Account for conversion of bonds payable

CONVERTIBLE BONDS. Bonds (or notes payable) that may be converted into the common stock of the issuing company at the option of the investor.

Convertible Bonds and Notes

As the chapter-opening story indicates, convertible bonds and notes are popular with both companies and investors. **Convertible bonds and notes payable** may be converted into the common stock of the issuing company at the option of the investor. These bonds and notes, called convertible bonds (or notes), combine the receipts of interest and principal on the bonds with the opportunity for gains on the stock. The conversion feature is so attractive that investors accept a lower contract, or stated, interest rate than they would on nonconvertible bonds. For example, **Amazon.com's** convertible notes payable carry an interest rate of only 4 3/4%. The low cash interest payments benefit Amazon.com. The issuance of convertible bonds payable is recorded like any other debt.

If the market price of Amazon.com's stock gets above the market value of the bonds, the bondholders will convert the bonds into stock. The corporation records conversion by removing the bond accounts from the books and crediting the stock accounts. The carrying amount of the bonds becomes the book value of the newly issued stock. No gain or loss is recorded.

Assume that Amazon.com noteholders convert $500,000 of the notes into 8,000 shares of Amazon's common stock, which has a par value of $0.01 (1 cent) per share. Assume further that the carrying amount of the notes on Amazon's books is $490,000; thus, there is a discount of $10,000. To record the conversion, Amazon would make this journal entry:

May 14	Notes Payable	500,000	
	Discount on Notes Payable		
	($500,000 − $490,000)		10,000
	Common Stock (8,000 × $0.01)		80
	Paid-in Capital in Excess of		
	Par—Common		489,920
	Recorded conversion of notes payable.		

The entry closes the notes (or bonds) payable account and its related discount. The carrying amount of the notes ($490,000) becomes the amount of new stockholders' equity ($489,920 + $80).

Current Portion of Long-Term Debt

Serial bonds and serial notes are payable in serials, or installments. The portion payable within one year is a current liability, and the remaining debt is long-term. At January 29, 2000, Toys "Я" Us, Inc., had $1,251 million of long-term debt maturing in various amounts in future years. Assume that the portion payable in the next year was $21 million. Therefore, $21 million was a current liability at January 29, 2000, and $1,230 million was a long-term liability. Toys "Я" Us could report the following among its liabilities at January 29, 2000:

	$ Millions
Current liabilities:	
Current maturities of long-term debt.............	$ 21
Long-term debt less current maturities..............	1,230

Mortgage Notes Payable

You have probably heard of mortgage payments. Many notes payable are mortgage notes, which actually contain two agreements:

- The *note* is the borrower's promise to pay the lender the amount of the debt.
- The **mortgage**—a security agreement related to the note—is the borrower's promise to transfer to the lender the legal title to certain assets if the debt is not paid on schedule.

MORTGAGE. Borrower's promise to transfer the legal title to certain assets to the lender if the debt is not paid on schedule.

The borrower is pledging these assets as security for the note. Often the asset pledged was acquired with the borrowed money. For example, most homeowners sign mortgage notes to purchase their residences, pledging that property as security for the loan. Businesses sign mortgage notes to acquire buildings, equipment, and other long-term assets. Mortgage notes are usually serial notes that require monthly or quarterly payments.

Advantage of Issuing Bonds Versus Stock

Objective 5
Show the advantages and disadvantages of borrowing

Businesses have different ways to acquire assets. The money to pay for the asset may be financed by the business's retained earnings, by a stock issue, or by borrowing. Each financing strategy has its advantages, as follows:

Advantages of Financing Operations by	
Issuing Stock	Borrowing
Creates no liabilities or interest expense. Less risky to the issuing corporation.	Does not dilute control of the corporation. Usually results in higher earnings per share because interest expense is tax-deductible.

Exhibit 15-8 shows the earnings-per-share (EPS) advantage of borrowing. Suppose that Vista.com, an Internet startup, has net income of $300,000 and 100,000 shares of common stock outstanding. Vista needs $500,000 for expansion and company management is considering two plans to finance the expansion:

Earnings per share (EPS) is a company's net income per share of outstanding common stock (Chapter 14, p. 556). EPS may be the most important figure on the income statement.

- Plan 1 is to borrow $500,000 at 10% (issue $500,000 of 10% bonds payable).
- Plan 2 is to issue 50,000 shares of common stock for $500,000.

Vista management believes the new cash can be invested in operations to earn income of $200,000 before interest and taxes.

EXHIBIT 15-8   Earnings-Per-Share Advantage of Borrowing Versus Issuing Stock

	Plan 1 Borrow $500,000 at 10%		Plan 2 Issue $500,000 of Common Stock	
Net income before expansion		$300,000		$300,000
Expected income on the new project before interest and income tax expenses	$200,000		$200,000	
Less: Interest expense ($500,000 × 0.10)	(50,000)		–0–	
Project income before income tax........................	150,000		200,000	
Less: Income tax expense (40%)	(60,000)		(80,000)	
Project net income		90,000		120,000
Total company net income...................................		$390,000		$420,000
Earnings per share after expansion:				
Plan 1 ($390,000/100,000 shares)		$3.90		
Plan 2 ($420,000/150,000 shares)				$2.80

The EPS figure is higher if Vista.com borrows. If all goes well, Vista can earn more on the investment ($90,000) than the interest it pays on the bonds ($50,000).

DAILY EXERCISE 15-16

DAILY EXERCISE 15-17

LEVERAGE. Earning more income on borrowed money than the related interest expense, thereby increasing the earnings for the owners of the business.

Objective 6
Account for lease and pension liabilities

LEASE. Rental agreement in which the tenant (lessee) agrees to make rent payments to the property owner (lessor) to obtain the use of the asset.

LESSEE. Tenant in a lease agreement.

LESSOR. Property owner in a lease agreement.

OPERATING LEASE. Usually a short-term or cancelable rental agreement.

CAPITAL LEASE. Lease agreement that meets any one of four criteria: (1) The lease transfers title of the leased asset to the lessee. (2) The lease contains a bargain purchase option. (3) The lease term is 75% or more of the estimated useful life of the leased asset. (4) The present value of the lease payments is 90% or more of the market value of the leased asset.

Earning more income on borrowed money than the related interest expense increases the earnings for common stockholders and is called using **leverage.** It is widely used in business to increase earnings per share of common stock.

Borrowing has its disadvantages. Interest expense may be high enough to eliminate net income and lead to a cash crisis or even bankruptcy. This has happened to lots of Internet startups. Also, borrowing creates liabilities that accrue during bad years as well as good years.

Lease Liabilities

A **lease** is a rental agreement in which the tenant **(lessee)** obtains the use of an asset and agrees to make rent payments to the property owner **(lessor).** Leasing avoids having to make the large initial cash down payment that a purchase requires. Accountants divide leases into two types: operating leases and capital leases.

OPERATING LEASES **Operating leases** may be short-term or cancelable. Many apartment leases and car-rental agreements are for a year or less. These operating leases give the lessee the right to use the asset but provide the lessee with no continuing rights to the asset. The lessor retains the usual risks and rewards of owning the leased asset. To account for an operating lease, the lessee debits Rent Expense (or Lease Expense) and credits Cash for the amount of the lease payment. The lessee's books report no leased asset and no lease liability. This is why lessees prefer operating leases over capital leases.

CAPITAL LEASES A capital lease requires the lessee to record both an asset and a lease liability. Capital leases are long-term and noncancelable. How can we distinguish a capital lease from an operating lease? A **capital lease** meets any *one* of the following criteria:

1. The lease transfers title of the leased asset to the lessee at the end of the lease term. Thus, the lessee becomes the legal owner of the leased asset.
2. The lease contains a *bargain purchase option.* The lessee can be expected to purchase the leased asset and become its legal owner.
3. The lease term is 75% or more of the estimated useful life of the leased asset. The lessee uses up most of the leased asset's service potential.
4. The present value of the lease payments is 90% or more of the market value of the leased asset. In effect, the lease payments operate as installment payments for the leased asset.

Only those leases that fail to meet all these criteria are treated as operating leases.

ACCOUNTING FOR A CAPITAL LEASE Accounting for a capital lease is like accounting for a purchase. The lessee records an asset and also records a lease liability at the beginning of the lease term. The lessee capitalizes the asset in its own financial statements, even though the lessee may never actually own the property.

Safeway, the grocery chain, operates stores in buildings that it leases from other companies. Suppose Safeway leases a store building and agrees to pay annual rentals for a 20-year period. This arrangement is similar to purchasing the building on an installment plan.

Suppose Safeway's liability under this capital lease totals $1,000,000 at the beginning of the lease term. The lease liability determines Safeway's cost of the building. If Safeway makes the first annual lease payment of $100,000 up front, Safeway makes this entry as the lease begins:

2000			
Jan. 1	Building	1,000,000	
	Lease Liability		900,000
	Cash		100,000
	Acquired building under a capital lease.		

Each year end Safeway will record depreciation expense on the building as though Safeway owned the building. The life of the building is the lease term (20 years in this example), and residual value is zero. At December 31, 2000, Safeway will report its lease liabilities on the balance sheet as follows:

Liabilities	
Current:	
Current obligation under capital lease (next year's lease payment)	$100,000
Long-term:	
Lease liability ($900,000 − $100,000)	800,000

 DAILY EXERCISE 15-18

Pension and Postretirement Benefit Liabilities

Most companies have a pension plan for their employees. A **pension** is employee compensation paid during retirement. Employees earn pensions by their service, so the company records pension expense while employees work for the company. Companies also provide postretirement benefits, mainly health insurance for retirees.

PENSION. Employee compensation that will be received during retirement.

To record the company's payment into a retirement plan, the company debits Pension Expense and credits Cash. The assets of the pension plan grow. The obligation for future pension payments to employees also accumulates. At the end of each period, the company compares the fair market value of the pension plan assets with the accumulated benefit obligation of the pension plan. The *accumulated benefit obligation* is the amount of promised future pension payments to retirees.

If the plan assets exceed the accumulated benefit obligation, the plan is said to be *overfunded*. For an overfunded pension plan, the asset and obligation amounts are reported only in the notes to the financial statements. But if the accumulated benefit obligation exceeds the pension plan's assets, the plan is *underfunded*. For an underfunded plan, the company must report the excess liability amount on the balance sheet. Underfunded plans have been rare in recent years.

The pension plan of Mainstream Sales, Inc., has assets with a fair market value of $3 million on December 31, 20X3, and the accumulated pension obligation is $4 million. At December 31, 20X3, Mainstream Sales makes the following comparison:

	Millions
Accumulated pension benefit obligation	$4
Pension plan assets	3
Pension liability to report on the balance sheet	$1

DAILY EXERCISE 15-19

The Decision Guidelines feature provides a summary of the major points of the chapter's second half.

DECISION GUIDELINES

Accounting for Long-Term Liabilities—Part B

DECISION	GUIDELINES
What happens to the bonds' carrying amount when bonds payable are issued at • Par? • A premium? • A discount?	• Carrying amount *stays* at par (face, or maturity) value during the life of the bonds. • Carrying amount *falls* gradually to the bonds' maturity value on their maturity date. • Carrying amount *rises* gradually to the bonds' maturity value on their maturity date.

How to account for the retirement of bonds payable?

At maturity date:

Bonds Payable .... Maturity value
    Cash .... Maturity value

Before maturity date (assume a discount on the bonds and a gain on retirement):

Bonds Payable .... Maturity value
    Discount on Bonds
        Payable .... Balance
    Cash .... Amount Paid
    Extraordinary Gain on
        Retirement of
        Bonds Payable .... Excess

How to account for the conversion of convertible bonds payable into common stock?

Remove all the bonds payable (and related premium or discount) accounts and credit Common Stock at par, plus any excess to Paid-in Capital in Excess of Par.

What are the advantages of financing operations with
• Stock?

• Bonds (or notes) payable?

• Creates no liability or interest expense. Less risky to the issuing corporation.
• Does not dilute stock ownership or control of the corporation.
    Results in higher earnings per share—under normal conditions.

How to account for
• An operating lease?
• A capital lease?

• Debit lease (or rent) expense for each lease payment.
• At the beginning of the lease period, record
  a. Asset (as though it were purchased).
  b. Lease liability—present value of future lease payments.

EXCEL APPLICATION PROBLEM

Goal: Set up an Excel spreadsheet to compare earnings per share under two financing plans: borrowing and issuing stock.

Scenario: Target is thinking about building a new distribution warehouse to serve its growing Web-based retail operations. In order to finance the warehouse, managers must recommend whether to borrow the funds for construction or issue stock. Construction costs are estimated at $5 million. If borrowing is chosen, long-term bonds payable will be issued at 8% to raise the $5 million. If stock is chosen, 80,000 shares will be issued to cover the $5 million cost. Managers expect on-line sales to increase by $700,000 in the first year. Income tax expense is 40%. Assume net income before construction is $4 million, and shares outstanding before construction total 500,000.

Your task is to create a spreadsheet that compares earnings per share under the two plans described above. After completing the spreadsheet, answer these questions:

1. Which plan generates the higher earnings per share? Why?
2. Under what circumstances would Target consider using debt to finance its new warehouse?
3. Under what circumstances would Target consider the use of equity to finance its new warehouse?
4. Which option do you recommend for Target? Why? Does your recommendation change if the interest rate on the bonds is 10% rather than 8%?

EXCEL APPLICATION PROBLEM (CONT.)

Step-by-step:

1. Open a new Excel spreadsheet.
2. Create a heading for your spreadsheet that contains the following:
   a. Chapter 15 Decision Guidelines
   b. Financing with Debt or Stock
   c. Target Corporation
   d. Today's date
3. Use Exhibit 15-8 in your textbook as a model for the layout of your spreadsheet. Label the long-term bonds as

"Plan 1," and the issuance of common stock as "Plan 2." Be sure to set up the spreadsheet so that you can change variables, such as the interest rate on the bonds, without re-typing any formulas in the body of the spreadsheet.

4. When finished, your spreadsheet should show earnings per share under both plans, and be capable of re-computing earnings per share simply by changing the interest rate on the bonds.
5. Save your work and print a copy of the worksheet (in landscape mode) for your files.

REVIEW LONG-TERM LIABILITIES

SUMMARY PROBLEM

Trademark, Inc., has outstanding an issue of 8% convertible bonds payable that mature in 2020. Suppose the bonds were dated October 1, 2000, and pay interest each April 1 and October 1.

Required

1. Complete the following effective-interest amortization table through October 1, 2002:

BOND DATA:

- Maturity value—$100,000
- Contract interest rate—8%
- Interest paid—4% semiannually, $4,000 ($100,000 × 0.04)

- Market interest rate—9% annually, 4 1/2% semiannually
- Issue price—90 3/4

www.prenhall.com/horngren

End-of-Chapter Assessment

AMORTIZATION TABLE:

	A	B	C	D	E
Semiannual Interest Date	Interest Payment (4% of Maturity Amount)	Interest Expense (4 1/2% of Preceding Bond Carrying Amount)	Discount Amortization (B − A)	Discount Balance (D − C)	Bond Carrying Amount ($100,000 − D)
10-1-00					
4-1-01					
10-1-01					
4-1-02					
10-1-02					

2. Using the amortization table, record the following transactions:
   a. Issuance of the bonds on October 1, 2000.
   b. Accrual of interest and amortization of discount on December 31, 2000.
   c. Payment of interest and amortization of discount on April 1, 2001.
   d. Conversion of one-third of the bonds payable into no-par common stock on October 2, 2002.
   e. Retirement of two-thirds of the bonds payable on October 2, 2002. Purchase price of the bonds was 102.

Solution

Requirement 1

Semiannual Interest Date	A Interest Payment (4% of Maturity Amount)	B Interest Expense (4 1/2% of Preceding Bond Carrying Amount)	C Discount Amortization (B − A)	D Discount Balance (D − C)	E Bond Carrying Amount ($100,000 − D)
10-1-00				$9,250	$90,750
4-1-01	$4,000	$4,084	$84	9,166	90,834
10-1-01	4,000	4,088	88	9,078	90,922
4-1-02	4,000	4,091	91	8,987	91,013
10-1-02	4,000	4,096	96	8,891	91,109

Requirement 2

2000

a. Oct. 1

Cash ($100,000 × 0.9075)	90,750	
Discount on Bonds Payable	9,250	
Bonds Payable		100,000
To issue 8%, 20-year bonds at a discount.		

b. Dec. 31

Interest Expense ($4,084 × 3/6)	2,042	
Discount on Bonds Payable ($84 × 3/6)		42
Interest Payable ($4,000 × 3/6)		2,000
To accrue interest and amortize bond discount for three months.		

2001

c. Apr. 1

Interest Expense	2,042	
Interest Payable	2,000	
Discount on Bonds Payable ($84 × 3/6)		42
Cash		4,000
To pay semiannual interest, part of which was accrued, and amortize three months' discount on bonds payable.		

2002

d. Oct. 2

Bonds Payable ($100,000 × 1/3)	33,333	
Discount on Bonds Payable ($8,891 × 1/3)		2,964
Common Stock ($91,109 × 1/3)		30,369
To record conversion of bonds payable.		

e. Oct. 2

Bonds Payable ($100,000 × 2/3)	66,667	
Extraordinary Loss on Retirement Bonds	7,260	
Discount on Bonds Payable ($8,891 × 2/3)		5,927
Cash ($100,000 × 2/3 × 1.02)		68,000
To retire bonds payable before maturity.		

LESSONS LEARNED

1. *Account for basic bonds payable transactions by the straight-line amortization method.* A corporation may borrow money by issuing long-term notes and *bonds payable*. Bonds may be secured (*mortgage* bonds) or unsecured (*debenture* bonds).

   Bonds are typically divided into $1,000 units. Their prices are quoted at a percentage of face value. *Market interest rates* fluctuate and may differ from the contract rate on a bond. If a bond's contract rate exceeds the market rate, the bond sells at a *premium*. A contract rate below the market rate creates a bond *discount*. An investor will pay a price for a bond equal to the present value of the bond principal plus the present value of the bond interest.

   Straight-line amortization allocates an equal amount of premium or discount to each interest period.

2. *Measure interest expense by the effective-interest method.* In the *effective-interest method* of amortization, the market interest rate at the time of issuance is multiplied by the bonds' carrying amount to determine the interest expense each period.

3. *Account for retirement of bonds payable.* Companies may retire their bonds payable before maturity. Any gain or loss on early extinguishment of debt is classified as *extraordinary*.

4. Account for conversion of bonds payable. *Convertible bonds* and notes give the investor the privilege of trading the bonds in for the stock of the issuing corporation. The carrying amount of the bonds becomes the book value of the newly issued stock.

5. Show the advantages and disadvantages of borrowing. A key advantage of borrowing (versus issuing stock) is that interest expense on debt is tax-deductible. Thus, borrowing is less costly than issuing stock. Borrowing's disadvantage results from the fact that the company *must* repay the loan and its interest.

6. Account for lease and pension liabilities. A *lease* is a rental agreement between the *lessee* and the *lessor*. In an *operating lease*, the lessee debits Rent Expense and credits Cash for each lease payment. A *capital lease* is long-term, noncancelable, and similar to an installment purchase of the leased asset. In a capital lease, the lessee capitalizes the leased asset and reports a lease liability.

Companies also report a *pension liability* on the balance sheet if the pension plan's accumulated benefit obligation exceeds the market value of the pension plan assets.

ACCOUNTING VOCABULARY

bond discount   (p. 579)
bond premium   (p. 579)
bonds payable   (p. 577)
callable bonds   (p. 592)
capital lease   (p. 596)
contract interest rate   (p. 580)
convertible bonds   (p. 594)
debentures   (p. 579)
discount (on a bond)   (p. 579)

effective interest rate   (p. 580)
lease   (p. 596)
lessee   (p. 596)
lessor   (p. 596)
leverage   (p. 596)
market interest rate   (p. 580)
mortgage   (p. 595)
notes payable   (p. 594)
operating lease   (p. 596)

pension   (p. 597)
premium   (p. 579)
present value   (p. 579)
serial bonds   (p. 579)
stated interest rate   (p. 580)
term bonds   (p. 578)
underwriter   (p. 578)

QUESTIONS

1. Compute the price to the nearest dollar for the following bonds with a face value of $10,000:
   a. 93
   b. 88 3/4
   c. 101 3/8
   d. 122 1/2
   e. 100
2. In which of the following situations will bonds sell at par? At a premium? At a discount?
   a. 9% bonds sold when the market rate is 9%
   b. 9% bonds sold when the market rate is 10%
   c. 9% bonds sold when the market rate is 8%
3. Identify the accounts to debit and credit for transactions
   a. to issue bonds at *par*
   b. to pay interest
   c. to accrue interest at year end
   d. to pay off bonds at maturity.
4. Identify the accounts to debit and credit for transactions
   a. to issue bonds at a *discount*
   b. to pay interest
   c. to accrue interest at year end
   d. to pay off bonds at maturity
5. Identify the accounts to debit and credit for transactions
   a. to issue bonds at a *premium*
   b. to pay interest
   c. to accrue interest at year end
   d. to pay off bonds at maturity
6. Why are bonds sold for a price "plus accrued interest"? What happens to accrued interest when the bonds are sold by an individual?

7. How does the straight-line method of amortizing bond discount (or premium) differ from the effective-interest method?
8. A company retires ten-year bonds payable of $100,000 after five years. The business issued the bonds at 104 and called them at 103. Compute the amount of gain or loss on retirement. How is this gain or loss reported on the income statement?
9. Bonds payable with a maturity value of $100,000 are callable at 102 1/2. Their market price is 101 1/4. If you are the issuer of these bonds, how much will you pay to retire them before maturity?
10. Why are convertible bonds attractive to investors? Why are they popular with borrowers?
11. What characteristics distinguish a capital lease from an operating lease?
12. A business signs a capital lease for the use of a building, with the first lease payment due immediately. What accounts are debited and credited to begin the lease term?
13. Show how a lessee reports on the balance sheet the lease liability under a capital lease.
14. Distinguish an overfunded pension plan from an underfunded plan. Which situation requires the company to report a pension liability on the balance sheet? How is this liability computed?

ASSESS YOUR PROGRESS

DAILY EXERCISES

DE15-1 Compute the price of the following bonds:

   a. $100,000 quoted at 94 1/2
   b. $600,000 quoted at 102 5/8
   c. $2,000,000 quoted at 77 3/4
   d. $300,000 quoted at 110 3/8

Pricing bonds   (Obj. 1)

DE15-2 Washington Public Power Supply System **(WPSS)** borrowed money by issuing the bond payable in Exhibit 15-1 (page 578). Assume the issue price was 93 1/2.

1. How much cash did WPPSS receive when it issued the bond payable?
2. How much must WPPSS pay back at maturity? When is the maturity date?
3. How much cash interest will WPPSS pay each six months? Carry the interest amount to the nearest cent.

DE15-3 Assume the **WPSS** bond in Exhibit 15-1 was issued at a price of 93 1/2. Was the market interest rate at the date of issuance 6 1/2%, above 6 1/2%, or below 6 1/2%? How can you tell?

DE15-4 Determine whether the following bonds payable will be issued at par value, at a premium, or at a discount:

a. The market interest rate is 9%. Sicily, Inc., issues bonds payable with a stated rate of 8 1/2%.
b. Galatia Corp. issued 7 1/2% bonds payable when the market rate was 7 1/2%.
c. Cyprus Corporation issued 8% bonds when the market interest rate was 6 7/8%.
d. Tyre Company issued bonds payable that pay cash interest at the contract rate of 7%. At the date of issuance, the market interest rate was 8 1/4%.

DE15-5 Suppose **WPPSS** issued the ten-year bond in Exhibit 15-1 when the market interest rate was 6 1/2%. Assume that the fiscal year of WPPSS ends on June 30. Journalize the following transactions for WPPSS. Include an explanation for each entry.

a. Issuance of the bond payable at par on July 1, 2000.
b. Payment of cash interest on January 1, 2001. (Round to the nearest dollar.)
c. Payment of the bonds payable at maturity. (Give the date.)

DE15-6 Assume **WPPSS** issued the ten-year bond in Exhibit 15-1 at par value on November 1, 2000, four months after the bond's original issue date of July 1, 2000. Assume that the fiscal year of WPPSS ends on June 30. Journalize the following transactions for WPPSS. Include an explanation for each entry.

a. Issuance of the bonds payable on November 1, 2000. (Carry amounts to the nearest cent.)
b. Payment of the first semiannual interest amount on January 1, 2001. (Carry amounts to the nearest cent.)

DE15-7 Assume **WPPSS** issued the ten-year bond in Exhibit 15-1 at a price of 86 on July 1, 2000. Also assume that WPPSS's fiscal year ends on June 30. Journalize the following transactions for WPPSS. Include an explanation for each entry.

a. Issuance of the bond payable on July 1, 2000.
b. Payment of interest and amortization of bond discount on January 1, 2001. (Use the straight-line method to amortize the discount. Round interest to the nearest dollar.)

DE15-8 Assume **WPPSS** issued the bond payable in Exhibit 15-1 at a price of 104 on July 1, 2000. Also assume that WPPSS's fiscal year ends on June 30. Journalize the following transactions for WPPSS. Include an explanation for each entry.

a. Issuance of the bond payable on July 1, 2000.
b. Payment of interest and amortization of bond premium on January 1, 2001. (Use the straight-line method to amortize the premium. Round interest to the nearest dollar.)

DE15-9 Return to the **WPPSS** bond in Exhibit 15-1. Assume that WPPSS issued the bond payable on July 1, 2000, at a price of 92. Also assume that WPPSS's accounting year ends on December 31. Journalize the following transactions for WPPSS. Include an explanation for each entry.

a. Issuance of the bonds on July 1, 2000.
b. Accrual of interest expense and amortization of bond discount on December 31, 2000. (Use the straight-line amortization method, and round the interest amount to the nearest dollar.)
c. Payment of the first semiannual interest amount on January 1, 2001.

DE15-10 Use the situation in Daily Exercise 15-9, and show how **WPPSS** would report interest payable and the bond payable on its balance sheet at December 31, 2000.

DE15-11 Braemar Drilling, Inc., issued $650,000 of 7%, ten-year bonds payable at a price of 87 on March 31, 20X3. The market interest rate at the date of issuance was 9%, and the Braemar bonds pay interest semiannually.

1. How much cash did Braemar receive upon issuance of the bonds payable?

2. Prepare an effective-interest amortization table for the bond discount, through the first three interest payments. Use Exhibit 15-4 (page 589) as a guide, and round amounts to the nearest dollar.
3. Record Braemar's issuance of the bonds on March 31, 20X3, and on September 30, 20X3, payment of the first semiannual interest amount and amortization of the bond discount. Explanations are not required.

DE15-12 ACE Furniture, Inc., issued $400,000 of 6%, five-year bonds payable to partially finance a warehouse. At the time of issuance, the market interest rate was 8%, so ACE received cash of $368,058. ACE pays interest annually.

Preparing a complete bond amortization table and using the table for relevant information (Obj. 2)

1. Prepare ACE's effective-interest amortization table for the bonds. Use Exhibit 15-4 (page 589) as a guide, and round amounts to the nearest dollar.
2. Use the amortization table to answer these questions about ACE's bonds payable and related interest expense:
   a. At what amount will ACE report the bonds payable at the end of Year 1? At the end of Year 3?
   b. How much cash interest will ACE pay for Year 1? Year 3? Year 5?
   c. How much interest expense will ACE record for Year 1? Year 5?

DE15-13 Unix, Inc., issued $200,000 of 8%, ten-year bonds payable at at price of 110 on May 31, 20X2. The market interest rate at the date of issuance was 6%, and the Unix bonds pay interest semiannually.

Issuing bonds payable and measuring interest expense by the effective-interest method (Obj. 2)

1. How much cash did Unix receive upon issuance of the bonds payable?
2. Prepare an effective-interest amortization table for the bond premium, through the first three interest payments. Use Exhibit 15-6 (page 591) as a guide, and round amounts to the nearest dollar.
3. Record Unix's issuance of the bonds on May 31, 20X2, and, on November 30, 20X2, payment of the first semiannual interest amount and amortization of the bond premium. Explanations are not required.

DE15-14 Assume that Tradinghouse, Inc., issued the bonds payable in Exhibit 15-6 (page 591). Tradinghouse has extra cash and wishes to retire the bonds payable immediately after making the fifth semiannual interest payment. The bonds are quoted in the market at a price of 95.

Accounting for the retirement of bonds payable (Obj. 3)

1. What is Tradinghouse's carrying amount of the bonds payable on the retirement date?
2. How much cash must Tradinghouse pay to retire the bonds payable?
3. Compute Tradinghouse's gain or loss on the retirement of the bonds payable. What type of gain or loss is this?
4. Journalize Tradinghouse's transaction to retire the bonds payable.

DE15-15 ← *Link Back to Chapter 4 (Debt Ratio).* Blade Automotive Corp. has $1,000,000 of convertible bonds payable outstanding, with a bond premium of $60,000 also on the books. The bondholders have notified Blade that they wish to convert the bonds into stock. Specifically, the bonds may be converted into 200,000 shares of Blade's $1 par common stock.

Accounting for the conversion of bonds payable (Obj. 4)

1. What is Blade's carrying amount of its convertible bonds payable prior to the conversion?
2. Journalize, on Blade's books, the conversion of the bonds payable into common stock. No explanation is required.
3. How will the conversion affect Blade's debt ratio?

DE15-16 Northern Accounting Services of Madison, Wisconsin, needs to raise $1 million to expand company operations into Minnesota. Northern's president is considering the issuance of either

Earnings-per-share effects of financing with bonds versus stock (Obj. 5)

- Plan A: $1,000,000 of 8% bonds payable to borrow the money
- Plan B: 100,000 shares of common stock at $10 per share

Before any new financing, Northern expects to earn net income of $350,000, and the company already has 200,000 shares of common stock outstanding. Northern believes the expansion will increase income before interest and income tax by $200,000. Northern's income tax rate is 35%.

Prepare an analysis similar to Exhibit 15-8 (page 595) to determine which plan is likely to result in the higher earnings per share. Which financing plan would you recommend for Northern?

DE15-17 Return to the financing situation of Northern Accounting Services in Daily Exercise 15-16. What other factors, besides the effect on earnings per share, should Northern consider in deciding how to raise the $1 million? Give the advantages of issuing (a) stock and (b) bonds.

Advantages and disadvantages of financing with bonds versus stock (Obj. 5)

DE15-18 Horchow, Inc., includes the following selected accounts in its general ledger at December 31, 20X3:

Notes payable, long-term.......	$100,000
Bonds payable......................	350,000
Equipment under capital lease	114,000
Interest payable (due March 1, 20X4)	7,000
Current portion of bonds payable...................	65,000

Current obligation under capital lease	$ 8,000
Accounts payable	19,000
Long-term capital lease liability................................	42,000
Discount on bonds payable (all long-term)........	6,000

Prepare the liabilities section of Horchow's balance sheet at December 31, 20X3, to show how Horchow would report these items. Report a total for current liabilities.

Reporting liabilities, including capital lease obligations (Obj. 6)

Reporting pension liabilities (Obj. 6)

DE15-19 NM Aviation Fuel has a pension plan for its employees. NM's pension plan has an accumulated benefit obligation of $3,000,000. This means that NM would have to pay $3,000,000 now if the company had to settle the plan's pension liability today. To offset this, NM has invested in a pension fund that holds investments in stocks, bonds, and real estate.

a. The market value of the investments held by NM's pension fund is $2,400,000. Is the pension plan overfunded or underfunded? How much pension liability should NM report on its balance sheet?

b. Assume instead that the market value of the investments in NM's pension fund is $3,500,000. Is the pension plan overfunded or underfunded? How much pension liability should NM report on its balance sheet?

EXERCISES

Issuing bonds payable, paying and accruing interest, and amortizing discount by the straight-line method (Obj. 1)

E15-1 On February 1, The Oasis Corp. issues 8%, 20-year bonds payable with a face value of $100,000. The bonds sell at 98 and pay interest on January 31 and July 31. The Oasis Corp. amortizes bond discount by the straight-line method. Record (a) issuance of the bonds on February 1, (b) the semiannual interest payment on July 31, and (c) the interest accrual on December 31.

Issuing bonds payable, paying and accruing interest, and amortizing premium by the straight-line method (Obj. 1)

E15-2 Saturn Photo Corporation issues 8%, 20-year bonds payable with a face value of $1,000,000 on March 31. The bonds sell at 103 1/2 and pay interest on March 31 and September 30. Assume that Saturn amortizes bond premium by the straight-line method. Record (a) issuance of the bonds on March 31, (b) payment of interest on September 30, and (c) accrual of interest on December 31.

Issuing bonds between interest dates (Obj. 1)

E15-3 Refer to the data for Saturn Photo Corporation in Exercise 15-2. If Saturn issued the bonds payable on June 30, how much cash would Saturn receive upon issuance of the bonds?

Issuing bonds and paying interest (Obj. 1)

E15-4 Newton, Inc., issues $400,000 of 7%, 20-year bonds payable that are dated April 30. Record (a) issuance of bonds at par on May 31, and (b) the next semiannual interest payment on October 31.

Preparing an effective-interest amortization table; recording interest payments and interest expense (Obj. 2)

E15-5 Assume Network Navigator Corp. is authorized to issue $500,000 of 7%, ten-year bonds payable. On January 2, when the market interest rate is 8%, the company issues $300,000 of the bonds and receives cash of $279,615. Network Navigator measures interest expense by the effective-interest method.

Required

1. Prepare an amortization table for the first four semiannual interest periods. Follow the format of Exhibit 15-4, Panel B (page 589).
2. Record the first semiannual interest payment on June 30 and the second payment on December 31.

Preparing an effective-interest amortization table; recording interest accrual and payment and the related interest expense (Obj. 2)

E15-6 On September 30, 20X2, the market interest rate is 7%. Lemmon-Blake Software, Inc., issues $200,000 of 8%, 20-year bonds payable at 110 5/8. The bonds pay interest on March 31 and September 30. Lemmon-Blake Software measures interest expense by the effective-interest method.

Required

1. Prepare an amortization table for the first four semiannual interest periods. Follow the format of Exhibit 15-6, Panel B (page 591).
2. Record issuance of the bonds on September 30, 20X2, the accrual of interest at December 31, 20X2, and the semiannual interest payment on March 31, 20X3.

Debt payment and discount amortization schedule (Obj. 2)

E15-7 Fairfield Circuitry, Inc., issued $500,000 of 8 3/8% (0.08375), five-year bonds payable when the market interest rate was 9 1/2% (0.095). Fairfield pays interest annually at year end. The issue price of the bonds was $478,402.

604

Required

Create a spreadsheet model to prepare a schedule to measure interest expense on these bonds. Use the effective-interest method of amortization. Round to the nearest dollar, and format your answer as follows:

1	A	B	C	D	E	F
2						**Bond**
3		**Interest**	**Interest**	**Discount**	**Discount**	**Carrying**
4	**Date**	**Payment**	**Expense**	**Amortization**	**Balance**	**Amount**
5	1-1-X1				$ ⬚	$478,402
6	12-31-X1	$ ⬚	$ ⬚	$ ⬚		⬚
7	12-31-X2					
8	12-31-X3					
9	12-31-X4					
10	12-31-X5					
		500000*.08375	+F5*.095	+C6−B6	500000−F5	+F5+D6

E15-8 Brenham Communications issued $600,000 of 8% bonds payable at 97 on October 1, 20X0. These bonds mature on October 1, 20X8, and are callable at 101. Brenham pays interest each April 1 and October 1. On October 1, 20X5, when the bonds' market price is 104, Brenham retires the bonds in the most economical way available.

Recording retirement of bonds payable (Obj. 3)

Required

Record the payment of the interest and amortization of bond discount at October 1, 20X5, and the retirement of the bonds on that date. Brenham uses the straight-line amortization method.

E15-9 Computer Diagnostics Company issued $700,000 of 8 1/2% bonds payable on July 31, 20X3, at a price of 98 1/2. After five years, the bonds may be converted into the company's common stock. Each $1,000 face amount of bonds is convertible into 40 shares of $20 par stock. The bonds' term to maturity is 15 years. On July 31, 20X9, bondholders exercised their right to convert the bonds into common stock.

Recording conversion of bonds payable (Obj. 4)

Required

1. What would cause the bondholders to convert their bonds into common stock?
2. Without making journal entries, compute the carrying amount of the bonds payable at July 31, 20X9. Computer Diagnostics uses the straight-line method to amortize bond premium and discount.
3. All amortization has been recorded properly. Journalize the conversion transaction at July 31, 20X9.

E15-10 Viewpoint Industries reported the following at September 30:

Recording early retirement and conversion of bonds payable (Obj. 3, 4)

Long-term liabilities:		
Convertible bonds payable, 9%, eight years to maturity	$400,000	
Less: Discount on bonds payable	(12,000)	$388,000

Required

1. Record retirement of half of the bonds on October 1 at the call price of 102.
2. Record conversion of the remainder of the bonds into 4,000 shares of Viewpoint's $5 par common stock on October 1. What would cause the bondholders to convert their bonds into stock?

E15-11 Talbot Electronics is considering two plans for raising $1,000,000 to expand operations. Plan A is to borrow at 9%, and plan B is to issue 100,000 shares of common stock. Before any new financing, Talbot has net income of $600,000 and 100,000 shares of common stock outstanding. Management believes the company can use the new funds to earn additional income of $420,000 before interest and taxes. The income tax rate is 35%.

Analyzing alternative plans for raising money (Obj. 5)

Required

Analyze Talbot's situation to determine which plan will result in higher earnings per share. Use Exhibit 15-8 (page 595) as a guide.

E15-12 The chief accounting officer of Royal Textile, Inc., is considering how to report long-term notes payable and pension liabilities.

Reporting long-term debt and pension liability on the balance sheet (Obj. 6)

Required

1. Royal's bookkeeper has assembled the following for long-term notes payable:

Long-Term Notes Payable	
Total	$537,000
Less: Current portion	(33,000)
Discount on notes payable	(1,000)
	$503,000

None of the discount is related to the current portion of long-term notes payable. Show how Royal's balance sheet should report these liabilities.

2. Royal's pension plan has assets with a market value of $800,000. The plan's accumulated benefit obligation is $865,000. What amount of long-term pension liability, if any, will Royal report on its balance sheet?

Journalizing capital lease and operating lease transactions (Obj. 6)

E15-13 A capital lease agreement for equipment requires Motorama Automotive Company to make ten annual payments of $7,000, with the first payment due on January 2, 20X5. Motorama's liability under the lease is $40,313.

Required

1. Journalize the following transactions of Motorama Automotive:

20X5

Jan. 2 Beginning of lease term and the first annual payment.
Dec. 31 Depreciation of equipment.

At December 31, how much lease liability will Motorama report under a capital lease?

2. Journalize the January 2, 20X5, lease payment if this is an operating lease.
At December 31, how much lease liability will Motorama report under an operating lease?

Challenge Exercises

Analyzing bond transactions (Obj. 1, 2)

E15-14 This (partial and adapted) advertisement appeared in the *Wall Street Journal*.

BEAR STEARNS

This announcement is neither an offer to sell nor a solicitation of an offer to buy any of these securities. The offering is made only by the Prospectus.

New Issue

$300,000,000

MARK IV INDUSTRIES INC.

13⅜% Subordinated Debentures due March 31, 2010

Interest payable March 31 and September 30

Price 98.50%   **March 31, 2000**

A *subordinated* debenture gives rights to the bondholder that are more restricted than the rights of other bondholders.

Required

Answer these questions about **Mark IV Industries'** debenture bonds payable:

1. Suppose Mark IV Industries issued these bonds payable at their offering price on March 31, 2000. Describe the transaction in detail, indicating who received cash, who paid cash, and how much.

2. Why is the contract interest rate on these bonds so high?
3. Compute Mark IV Industries' annual cash interest payment on the bonds.
4. Compute Mark IV Industries' annual interest expense under the straight-line amortization method.
5. Prepare an effective-interest amortization table for Mark IV Industries' first two interest payments on September 30, 2000, and March 31, 2001. Use Exhibit 15-4 (page 589) as a guide and show all amounts in thousands. The market rate of interest on the bonds is 13.65% per year.
6. Compute Mark IV Industries interest expense for the first full year ended March 31, 2001, under the effective-interest method. Use the amortization table you prepared for requirement 5.

E15-15 Refer to the bond situation of **Mark IV Industries** in Exercise 15-14. Assume Mark IV Industries issued the bonds at the advertised price and that the company uses the effective-interest amortization method and reports financial statements on a calendar-year basis.

Analyzing bond transactions (Obj. 1,2)

Required

1. Journalize the following bond transactions of Mark IV Industries. Show all amounts in thousands of dollars. Explanations are not required.

2000
Mar. 31   Issuance of the bonds.
Sep. 30   Payment of interest expense and amortization of discount on bonds payable.
Dec. 31   Accrual of interest expense and amortization of discount on bonds payable.

2. What is Mark IV Industries' carrying amount of the bonds payable at

   a. September 30, 2000?
   b. December 31, 2000?
   c. March 31, 2001?

PROBLEMS

(Group A)

P15-1A Zefer.com issued $500,000 of ten-year, 8% bonds payable at par on May 1, 20X5. The bonds pay interest each April 30 and October 31, and the company ends its accounting year on December 31.

Analyzing bonds, recording bond transactions at par, and reporting on the financial statements (Obj. 1)

Required

1. Fill in the blanks to complete these statements:
   a. Zefer.com's bonds are priced at (express the price as a percentage) _____.
   b. When Zefer.com issued its bonds, the market interest rate was _____%.
   c. The amount of bond discount or premium for Zefer.com to account for is $_____ because the bonds were issued at _____.
2. Journalize for Zefer.com
   a. Issuance of the bonds payable on May 1, 20X5.
   b. Payment of interest on October 31, 20X5.
   c. Accrual of interest at December 31, 20X5.
   d. Payment of interest on April 30, 20X6.
3. Show what Zefer.com will report on its income statement for 20X5 and on its balance sheet at December 31, 20X5.

P15-2A The board of directors of Galaxy Production Company authorizes the issue of $8 million of 7%, ten-year bonds payable. The semiannual interest dates are May 31 and November 30. The bonds are issued on June 30, 20X5, at par plus accrued interest.

Journalizing bond transactions (at par) and reporting bonds payable on the balance sheet— bond issued between interest dates (Obj. 1)

Required

1. Journalize the following transactions:
   a. Issuance of the bonds on June 30, 20X5.
   b. Payment of interest on November 30, 20X5.
   c. Accrual of interest on December 31, 20X5.
   d. Payment of interest on May 31, 20X6.
2. Check your recorded interest expense for 20X5, using as a model the supplement to the summary problem on page 588.
3. Report interest payable and bonds payable as they would appear on the Galaxy balance sheet at December 31, 20X5.

P15-3A On March 1, 20X4, Haupstrasse Corp. issues 8 1/4%, 20-year bonds payable with a face value of $400,000. The bonds pay interest on February 28 and August 31. Haupstrasse amortizes premium and discount by the straight-line method.

Issuing bonds, amortizing by the straight-line method, and reporting on the balance sheet (Obj. 1, 2)

Required

1. If the market interest rate is 7 3/8% when Haupstrasse issues its bonds, will the bonds be priced at par, at a premium, or at a discount? Explain.

2. If the market interest rate is 8 7/8% when Haupstrasse issues its bonds, will the bonds be priced at par, at a premium, or at a discount? Explain.
3. Assume that the issue price of the bonds is 96. Journalize the following bond transactions:
   a. Issuance of the bonds on March 1, 20X4.
   b. Payment of interest and amortization of discount on August 31, 20X4.
   c. Accrual of interest and amortization of discount on December 31, 20X4.
   d. Payment of interest and amortization of discount on February 28, 20X5.
4. Check your recorded interest expense for the year ended February 28, 20X5, using as a model the supplement to the summary problem on page 588.

Analyzing a company's long-term debt and journalizing its transactions
(Obj. 2)

P15-4A Metrovan Rental Company's balance sheet reported the following data on September 30, Year 1, end of the fiscal year (amounts rounded):

Long-Term Debt:
6.00% debenture bonds payable due Year 20 with an
    effective interest rate of 8.00%, net of discount of $39,200............... $164,800

Metrovan measures interest expense by the effective-interest method.

Required

1. Answer the following questions about Metrovan's long-term debt.
   a. What is the maturity value of the 6.00% debenture bonds?
   b. What is the carrying amount of the 6.00% debenture bonds at September 30, Year 1?
   c. What is Metrovan's annual cash interest payment on the 6.00% debenture bonds?
2. Prepare an amortization table through September 30, Year 3, for the 6.00% debenture bonds. Metrovan pays interest annually on September 30.
3. Record the September 30, Year 3 interest payment and amortization of the discount on the 6.00% debenture bonds.
4. What is Metrovan's carrying amount of the 6% debenture bonds at September 30, Year 3, immediately after the interest payment?

Issuing convertible bonds at a premium, measuring interest expense by the effective-interest method, retiring bonds early, and reporting on the balance sheet
(Obj. 2, 3, 4)

P15-5A On December 31, 20X1, Diplomat Linens, Inc., issues 9%, ten-year convertible bonds with a maturity value of $500,000. The semiannual interest dates are June 30 and December 31. The market interest rate is 8%, and the issue price of the bonds is 106.8. Diplomat measures interest expense by the effective-interest method.

Required

1. Prepare an effective-interest method amortization table for the first four semiannual interest periods.
2. Journalize the following transactions:
   a. Issuance of the bonds on December 31, 20X1. Credit Convertible Bonds Payable.
   b. Payment of interest on June 30, 20X2.
   c. Payment of interest on December 31, 20X2.
   d. Retirement of bonds with face value of $100,000 on December 31, 20X3. Diplomat pays the call price of 102.
3. Prepare the balance sheet presentation of the bonds payable that are outstanding at December 31, 20X3.

Journalizing bonds payable and capital lease transactions
(Obj. 1, 6)

P15-6A Journalize the following transactions of Berkshire Properties, Inc.:

20X1
Jan. 1 Issued $400,000 of 9%, ten-year bonds payable at 97.
        1 Signed a five-year capital lease on equipment. The agreement requires annual lease payments of $20,000, with the first payment due immediately. The liability for the four remaining lease payments is $60,750.
July 1 Paid semiannual interest and amortized discount by the straight-line method on 9% bonds payable.
Dec. 31 Accrued semiannual interest expense, and amortized discount by the straight-line method on 9% bonds payable.
Dec. 31 Recorded depreciation on leased equipment.

Financing operations with debt or with stock
(Obj. 5)

P15-7A Two businesses are considering how to raise $10 million.
    Franklin Corporation is in the midst of its most successful period since it began operations in 1972. For each of the past ten years, net income and earnings per share have increased by at least 15%. The outlook for the future is equally bright, with new markets opening up and competitors unable to manufacture products of Franklin's quality. Franklin Corporation is planning a large-scale expansion.

Westchase Company has fallen on hard times. Net income has remained flat for five of the last six years, with this year falling by 10% from last year's level of profits. Top management has experienced unusual turnover, and the company lacks strong leadership. To become competitive again, Westchase Company desperately needs $10 million for expansion.

Required

1. Propose a plan for each company to raise the needed cash. Which company should borrow? Which company should issue stock? Consider the advantages and the disadvantages of raising money by borrowing and by issuing stock, and discuss them in your answer. Use the following memorandum headings to report your plans for the two companies:
   - Plan for Franklin Corporation to raise $10 million
   - Plan for Westchase Company to raise $10 million
2. How will what you learned in this problem help you manage a business?

P15-8A The accounting records of Global Hardwood, Inc., include the following items:

Reporting liabilities on the balance sheet (Obj. 6)

Capital lease liability, long-term	$ 73,000	Mortgage note payable, long-term...........................	$116,000
Accumulated pension benefit obligation...........................	207,000	Capital lease liability, current.............................	11,000
Bonds payable, long-term......	160,000	Pension plan assets (market value).................................	190,000
Premium on bonds payable (all long-term)....................	13,000	Bonds payable, current portion..............................	20,000
Interest payable.....................	14,200		

Required

Report these liabilities on Global's balance sheet, including headings and totals for current liabilities and long-term liabilities.

PROBLEMS

(Group B)

P15-1B Focalpoint.com issued $600,000 of 20-year, 9% bonds payable at par on February 1, 20X3. The bonds pay interest each January 31 and July 31, and the company ends its accounting year on December 31.

Analyzing bonds, recording bond transactions at par, and reporting on the financial statements (Obj. 1)

1. Fill in the blanks to complete these statements:
   a. Focalpoint.com's bonds are priced at (express the price as a percentage) _____.
   b. When Focalpoint.com issued its bonds, the market interest rate was _____%.
   c. The amount of bond discount or premium for Focalpoint.com to account for is $_____ because the bonds were issued at _____.
2. Journalize for Focalpoint.com
   a. Issuance of the bonds payable on February 1, 20X3.
   b. Payment of interest on July 31, 20X3.
   c. Accrual of interest at December 31, 20X3.
   d. Payment of interest on January 31, 20X4.
3. Show what Focalpoint.com will report on its income statement for 20X3 and on its balance sheet at December 31, 20X3.

P15-2B The board of directors of Tucker Communications authorizes the issue of $3 million of 9%, 20-year bonds payable. The semiannual interest dates are March 31 and September 30. The bonds are issued on April 30, 20X4, at par.

Journalizing bond transactions (at par) and reporting bonds payable on the balance sheet—bonds issued between interest dates (Obj. 1)

Required

1. Journalize the following transactions:
   a. Issuance of the bonds on April 30, 20X4.
   b. Payment of interest on Sept. 30, 20X4.
   c. Accrual of interest on December 31, 20X4.
   d. Payment of interest on March 31, 20X5.
2. Check your recorded interest expense for 20X4, using as a model the supplement to the summary problem on pages 587–588.
3. Report interest payable and bonds payable as they would appear on the Tucker balance sheet at December 31, 20X4.

P15-3B Assume that on March 31, 20X6, **Goretex Corp.** issues 8%, ten-year notes payable with a face value of $400,000. The notes pay interest on March 31 and September 30, and Goretex amortizes premium and discount by the straight-line method.

Required

1. If the market interest rate is 8 1/2% when Goretex issues its notes, will the notes be priced at par, at a premium, or at a discount? Explain.
2. If the market interest rate is 7% when Goretex issues its notes, will the notes be priced at par, at a premium, or at a discount? Explain.
3. Assume that the issue price of the notes is 101. Journalize the following note payable transactions:
   a. Issuance of the notes on April 1, 20X6.
   b. Payment of interest and amortization of premium on September 30, 20X6.
   c. Accrual of interest and amortization of premium on December 31, 20X6.
   d. Payment of interest and amortization of premium on March 31, 20X7.
4. Check your recorded interest expense for the year ended March 31, 20X7, using as a model the supplement to the summary problem on pages 587–588.

P15-4B CoStar Temp Employment, Inc.'s balance sheet reported the following data on September 30, Year 1, end of the fiscal year (amounts rounded):

Long-Term Debt
5% debenture bonds payable due Year 14, net
    of discount of $45,200 (effective interest rate of 8%) $124,800

CoStar measures interest expense by the effective-interest method.

Required

1. Answer the following questions about CoStar's long-term debt:
   a. What is the maturity value of the 5% debenture bonds?
   b. What is the carrying amount of the 5% debenture bonds at September 30, Year 1?
   c. What is CoStar's annual cash interest payment on the 5% debenture bonds?
2. Prepare an amortization table through September 30, Year 3, for the 5% debenture bonds. CoStar pays interest annually on September 30.
3. Record the September 30, Year 3, interest payment and amortization of the discount on the 5% debenture bonds.
4. What is CoStar's carrying amount of the 5% debenture bonds at September 30, Year 3, immediately after the interest payment?

P15-5B On December 31, 20X1, Sportif Corp. issues 8%, ten-year convertible bonds with a maturity value of $700,000. The semiannual interest dates are June 30 and December 31. The market interest rate is 9%, and the issue price of the bonds is 94. Sportif amortizes bond premium and discount by the effective-interest method.

Required

1. Prepare an effective-interest method amortization table for the first four semiannual interest periods.
2. Journalize the following transactions:
   a. Issuance of the bonds on December 31, 20X1. Credit Convertible Bonds Payable.
   b. Payment of interest on June 30, 20X2.
   c. Payment of interest on December 31, 20X2.
   d. Retirement of bonds with face value of $100,000 December 31, 20X3. Sportif purchases the bonds at 96 in the open market.
3. Prepare a balance sheet presentation of the bonds payable that are outstanding at December 31, 20X3.

P15-6B Journalize the following transactions of Sephora Cosmetics, Inc.:

20X1
Jan. 1   Issued $1,000,000 of 7%, ten-year bonds payable at 97.
       1   Signed a five-year capital lease on machinery. The agreement requires annual lease payments of $16,000, with the first payment due immediately. The liability for the remaining lease payments is $48,590.
July 1   Paid semiannual interest and amortized discount by the straight-line method on 7% bonds payable.
Dec. 31   Accrued semiannual interest expense and amortized discount by the straight-line method on 7% bonds payable.
      31   Recorded depreciation on leased machinery.

P15-7B Research indicates that consumers prefer upscale restaurants. To capitalize on this trend, Palomino Eurobistros, Inc., is embarking on a massive expansion. Plans call for opening 20 new restaurants within the next two years. Each restaurant is scheduled to be 30% larger than the company's existing locations and feature upgraded menus. Management estimates that company operations will provide $3 million of the cash needed for expansion. Palomino must raise the remaining $1.5 million from outsiders. The board of directors is considering obtaining the $1.5 million either through borrowing or by issuing common stock.

Financing operations with debt or with stock
(Obj. 5)

Required

1. Write a memo to company management. Discuss the advantages and disadvantages of borrowing and of issuing common stock to raise the needed cash. Use the following format for your memo:

Date:	_____
To:	Management of Palomino Eurobistros, Inc.
From:	Student Name
Subject:	Advantages and disadvantages of borrowing versus issuing stock to raise $1.5 million for expansion
Advantages and disadvantages of borrowing:	
Advantages and disadvantages of issuing stock:	

2. How will what you learned in this problem help you manage a business?

P15-8B The accounting records of LeBeau Fashions, Inc., include the following items:

Reporting liabilities on the balance sheet
(Obj. 6)

Bonds payable, long-term......	$300,000	Accumulated pension benefit obligation...........................	$419,000
Pension plan assets (market value)...................	382,000	Mortgage note payable, long-term...........................	93,000
Bonds payable, current portion.............................	75,000	Capital lease liability, current...............................	18,000
Capital lease liability, long-term	81,000	Mortgage note payable, current...............................	23,000
Discount on bonds payable (all long-term)...................	7,000	Interest payable....................	11,000

Required

Report these liabilities on LeBeau's balance sheet, including headings and totals for current liabilities and long-term liabilities.

Apply Your Knowledge

Decision Cases

Case 1. Business is going well for DFW Designs. The board of directors of this family-owned company believes that DFW could earn an additional $1,500,000 income before interest and taxes by expanding into new markets. However, the $5 million the business needs for growth cannot be raised within the family. The directors, who strongly wish to retain family control of the company, must issue securities to outsiders. They are considering three financing plans.

Analyzing alternative ways of raising $5 million
(Obj. 5)

Plan A is to borrow at 8%. Plan B is to issue 100,000 shares of common stock. Plan C is to issue 100,000 shares of nonvoting, $3.75 preferred stock ($3.75 is the annual cash dividend paid on each share of preferred stock). DFW presently has net income of $6,000,000 and 1,000,000 shares of common stock outstanding. The company's income tax rate is 35%.

Required

1. Prepare an analysis similar to Exhibit 15-8 (page 595) to determine which plan will result in the highest earnings per share of common stock.
2. Recommend one plan to the board of directors. Give your reasons.

Case 2. ◄ *Link Back to Chapter 4 (Debt Ratio).* The following questions are not related.

1. **IMAX Corporation** likes to borrow for longer periods when interest rates are low and for shorter periods when interest rates are high. Why is this a good business strategy?

Questions about long-term debt
(Obj. 6 and Appendix to Chapter 15)

2. IMAX needs to borrow $2 million to open new theaters. IMAX can borrow $2 million by issuing 8%, 20-year bonds at a price of 96. How much will IMAX actually be borrowing under this arrangement? How much must IMAX pay back at maturity? How will IMAX account for the difference between the amount borrowed and the amount paid back?

ETHICAL ISSUE

Python.com owes $6 million on notes payable that will come due for payment in $1.5 million installments over a four-year period. The company has used its cash to advertise heavily in the competitive dotcom business environment. The result is that cash is scarce, and Python.com's management doesn't know where next year's note payment will come from. Python.com has prepared its balance sheet at December 31, 20X4, and reports the following:

Liabilities	
Current:	
Accounts payable..	$1,900,000
Salary payable and other accrued liabilites	300,000
Unearned revenue collected in advance	500,000
Income tax payable	200,000
Total current liabilities..	2,900,000
Long-term:	
Notes payable	6,000,000

What is wrong with the way Python.com reported its liabilities? Why did Python.com report its liabilities this way? What is unethical about this way of reporting *these* liabilities? Who can be harmed as a result?

FINANCIAL STATEMENT CASE

Analyzing long-term debt (Obj. 1)

The **Target Corporation** income statement, balance sheet, and statement of cash flows in Appendix A provide details about the company's long-term debt. Use those data to answer the following questions.

Required

1. How much did Target owe on long-term debt at January 29, 2000? How much was payable in the coming year?
2. Examine the statement of cash flows for 1999. Journalize the two transactions that affected long-term debt during the year. Ignore the notes payable transaction.
3. Journalize in a single entry Target's interest expense for 1999. Target paid cash of $405 million for interest, including $12 million capitalized to the Building account.

TEAM PROJECT

Note: This project uses the chapter appendix.

Bermuda Corporation leases the equipment that it uses in operations. Bermuda prefers operating leases (versus capital leases) in order to keep the lease liability off its balance sheet and maintain a low debt ratio.

Bermuda is negotiating a ten-year lease on equipment with an expected useful life of 15 years. The lease requires Bermuda to make ten annual lease payments of $20,000 each, due at the end of the period, plus a down payment that is due at the beginning of the lease term. The interest rate in the lease agreement is 10%. The leased asset has a market value of $160,000. The lease agreement specifies no transfer to title to the lessee and includes no bargain purchase option.

Write a report for Bermuda's management to explain how Bermuda should account for this lease—as an operating lease or as a capital lease. Use the following format for your report:

Date:	_____
To:	Bermuda Management
From:	Student Names
Subject:	Accounting for the company's equipment lease

INTERNET EXERCISE

1. Our nation has amassed a huge public debt. Just how huge? Go to **http://www.pub-licdebt.treas.gov/sec/sec.htm.** In the left-hand column under "The Public Debt," click on *Debt Figure*. How much is the current public debt to the penny? Is the amount of the public debt in millions, billions, or trillions of dollars?
2. Go to **http://www.investinginbonds.com.** In the left-hand column under "Bond Prices," click on *Corporate Bonds*. In the right-hand column under "Please show me bonds traded yesterday for:" use the pull-down menu to select *All Market Sectors*. Select to sort by *Price* and then click on *Search*. "Coupon" refers to the contract interest rate and "Yield" refers to the market interest rate.
   a. Refer to the bond at the *top* of the list to answer these questions. Is this bond selling at a premium, at par, or at a discount? How can you tell? Assume this entity issues a bond with a face value of $10,000. The issuing entity will receive how much cash at issuance? What is the amount of the annual interest payment? When does this bond mature? How much will the issuing entity pay at maturity?
   b. Refer to bond at the *bottom* of the list to answer these questions. Is this bond selling at a premium, at par, or at a discount? Why is this bond selling at the current price? What rate are investors demanding to loan money to this entity? What is the true rate of interest expense for the issuing entity?
3. Bonds are issued by different entities. In the left-hand column under "Investor's Guides," click on *Municipal Bonds*. Read the information displayed. Who issues municipal bonds? What do the funds raised help pay for?
4. In the left-hand column under "Bond Prices," click on *Municipal Bonds*. In the right-hand column under "Please show me bonds traded yesterday for:" use the pull-down menu to find bonds issued in your state. Select to sort by *Coupon* and then click on *Search*. What is the greatest contract (coupon) interest rate offered? What entity issued this bond?

APPENDIX TO CHAPTER 15

TIME VALUE OF MONEY: FUTURE VALUE AND PRESENT VALUE

This discussion of future value lays the foundation for present value but is not essential. For the valuation of long-term liabilities, some instructors may wish to begin at the bottom of page 616.

The term *time value of money* refers to the fact that money earns interest over time. Interest is the cost of using money. To borrowers, interest is the expense of renting money. To lenders, interest is the revenue earned from lending. We must recognize the interest. Otherwise we overlook an important part of the transaction.

Suppose you invest $4,545 in corporate bonds that pay 10% interest each year. After one year, the value of your investment has grown to $5,000. The difference between your original investment ($4,545) and the future value of the investment ($5,000) is the amount of interest revenue you will earn during the year ($455). If you ignore the interest, you would not account for the interest revenue you have earned. Interest becomes more important as the time period lengthens because the amount of interest depends on the span of time the money is invested.

Let's consider a second example, but from the borrower's perspective. Suppose you purchase a machine for your business. The cash price of the machine is $8,000, but you cannot pay cash now. To finance the purchase, you sign an $8,000 note payable. The note requires you to pay the $8,000 plus 10% interest one year from date of purchase. Is your cost of the machine $8,000, or is it $8,800 [$8,000 plus interest of $800 ($8,000 × 0.10)]? The cost is $8,000. The additional $800 is interest expense.

FUTURE VALUE

The main application of future value is the accumulated balance of an investment at a future date. In our first example, the investment earned 10% per year. After one year, $4,545 grew to $5,000, as shown in Exhibit 15A-1. If the money were invested for five years, you would have to perform five such calculations. You would also have to consider the compound interest that your investment is earning. *Compound interest* is the interest you earn not only on your principal amount, but also on the interest to date. Most business applications include compound interest. The following table shows the interest revenue earned each year at 10%:

End of Year	Interest	Future Value
0	—	$4,545
1	$4,545 × 0.10 = $455	5,000
2	5,000 × 0.10 = 500	5,500
3	5,500 × 0.10 = 550	6,050
4	6,050 × 0.10 = 605	6,655
5	6,655 × 0.10 = 666	7,321

Earning 10%, a $4,545 investment grows to $5,000 at the end of one year, to $5,500 at the end of two years, and so on. (Throughout this discussion, we round off to the nearest dollar.)

Future-Value Tables

The process of computing a future value is called *accumulating* because the future value is *more* than the present value. Mathematical tables ease the computational burden. Exhibit 15A-2, Future Value of $1, gives the future value for a single sum (a

EXHIBIT 15A-2 **Future Value of $1**

	Future Value of $1									
Period	4%	5%	6%	7%	8%	9%	10%	12%	14%	16%
1	1.040	1.050	1.060	1.070	1.080	1.090	1.100	1.120	1.140	1.160
2	1.082	1.103	1.124	1.145	1.166	1.188	1.210	1.254	1.300	1.346
3	1.125	1.158	1.191	1.225	1.260	1.295	1.331	1.405	1.482	1.561
4	1.170	1.216	1.262	1.311	1.360	1.412	1.464	1.574	1.689	1.811
5	1.217	1.276	1.338	1.403	1.469	1.539	1.611	1.762	1.925	2.100
6	1.265	1.340	1.419	1.501	1.587	1.677	1.772	1.974	2.195	2.436
7	1.316	1.407	1.504	1.606	1.714	1.828	1.949	2.211	2.502	2.826
8	1.369	1.477	1.594	1.718	1.851	1.993	2.144	2.476	2.853	3.278
9	1.423	1.551	1.689	1.838	1.999	2.172	2.358	2.773	3.252	3.803
10	1.480	1.629	1.791	1.967	2.159	2.367	2.594	3.106	3.707	4.411
11	1.539	1.710	1.898	2.105	2.332	2.580	2.853	3.479	4.226	5.117
12	1.601	1.796	2.012	2.252	2.518	2.813	3.138	3.896	4.818	5.936
13	1.665	1.886	2.133	2.410	2.720	3.066	3.452	4.363	5.492	6.886
14	1.732	1.980	2.261	2.579	2.937	3.342	3.797	4.887	6.261	7.988
15	1.801	2.079	2.397	2.759	3.172	3.642	4.177	5.474	7.138	9.266
16	1.873	2.183	2.540	2.952	3.426	3.970	4.595	6.130	8.137	10.748
17	1.948	2.292	2.693	3.159	3.700	4.328	5.054	6.866	9.276	12.468
18	2.026	2.407	2.854	3.380	3.996	4.717	5.560	7.690	10.575	14.463
19	2.107	2.527	3.026	3.617	4.316	5.142	6.116	8.613	12.056	16.777
20	2.191	2.653	3.207	3.870	4.661	5.604	6.727	9.646	13.743	19.461

present value), $1, invested to earn a particular interest rate for a specific number of periods. Future value depends on three factors: (1) the amount of the investment, (2) the length of time between investment and future accumulation, and (3) the interest rate.

The heading in Exhibit 15A-2 states $1. Future-value and present-value tables are based on $1 because unity (the value 1) is so easy to work with. Look at the Period column and the interest-rate columns 4–16%. In business applications, interest rates are always stated for the annual period of one year unless specified otherwise. In fact, an interest rate can be stated for any period, such as 3% per quarter or 5% for a six-month period. The length of the period is arbitrary.

For example, an investment may promise a return (income) of 3% per quarter for six months (two quarters). In that case, you would be working with 3% interest for two periods. It would be incorrect to use 6% for one period because the interest is 3% compounded quarterly, and that amount differs somewhat from 6% compounded semiannually. Take care in studying future-value and present-value problems to align the interest rate with the appropriate number of periods.

Let's use Exhibit 15A-2. The future value of $1.00 invested at 8% for one year is $1.08 ($1.00 × 1.080, which appears at the junction under the 8% column and across from 1 in the Period column). The figure 1.080 includes both the principal (1.000) and the compound interest for one period (0.080).

Suppose you deposit $5,000 in a savings account that pays annual interest of 8%. The account balance at the end of one year will be $5,400. To compute the future value of $5,000 at 8% for one year, multiply $5,000 by 1.080 to get $5,400. Now suppose you invest in a ten-year, 8% certificate of deposit (CD). What will be the future value of the CD at maturity? To compute the future value of $5,000 at 8% for ten periods, multiply $5,000 by 2.159 (from Exhibit 15A-2) to get $10,795. This future value of $10,795 indicates that $5,000 earning 8% interest compounded annually grows to $10,795 at the end of ten years. You can find any present amount's future value at a particular future date.

Future Value of an Annuity

In the preceding example, we made an investment of a single amount. Other investments, called annuities, include multiple investments of an equal periodic amount at fixed intervals over the duration of the investment. Consider a family investing for a child's education. The Dietrichs can invest $4,000 annually to accumulate a college fund for 15-year-old Helen. The investment can earn 7% annually until Helen turns 18—a three-year investment. How much will be available for Helen on the date of the last investment? Exhibit 15A-3 shows the accumulation—a total future value of $12,860.

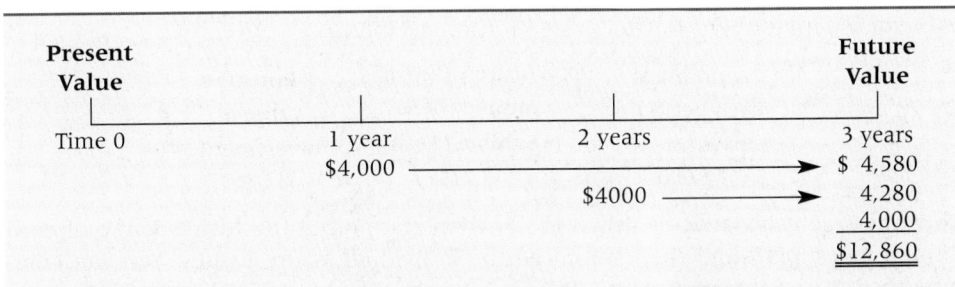

The first $4,000 invested by the Dietrichs grows to $4,580 over the investment period. The second amount grows to $4,280, and the third amount stays at $4,000 because it has no time to earn interest. The sum of the three future values ($4,580 + $4,280 + $4,000) is the future value of the annuity ($12,860), which can be computed as follows:

End of Year	Annual Investment	+	Interest	=	Increase for the Year	Future Value of Annuity
0	—		—		—	0
1	$4,000		—		$4,000	$ 4,000
2	4,000	+	($4,000 × 0.07 = $280)	=	4,280	8,280
3	4,000	+	($8,280 × 0.07 = $580)	=	4,580	12,860

As with the Future Value of $1 table (a lump sum), mathematical tables ease the strain of calculating annuities. Exhibit 15A-4, Future Value of Annuity of $1, gives the future value of a series of investments, each of equal amount, at regular intervals.

EXHIBIT 15A-4   Future Value of Annuity of $1

	Future Value of Annuity of $1									
Period	4%	5%	6%	7%	8%	9%	10%	12%	14%	16%
1	1.000	1.000	1.000	1.000	1.000	1.000	1.000	1.000	1.000	1.000
2	2.040	2.050	2.060	2.070	2.080	2.090	2.100	2.120	2.140	2.160
3	3.122	3.153	3.184	3.215	3.246	3.278	3.310	3.374	3.440	3.506
4	4.246	4.310	4.375	4.440	4.506	4.573	4.641	4.779	4.921	5.066
5	5.416	5.526	5.637	5.751	5.867	5.985	6.105	6.353	6.610	6.877
6	6.633	6.802	6.975	7.153	7.336	7.523	7.716	8.115	8.536	8.977
7	7.898	8.142	8.394	8.654	8.923	9.200	9.487	10.089	10.730	11.414
8	9.214	9.549	9.897	10.260	10.637	11.028	11.436	12.300	13.233	14.240
9	10.583	11.027	11.491	11.978	12.488	13.021	13.579	14.776	16.085	17.519
10	12.006	12.578	13.181	13.816	14.487	15.193	15.937	17.549	19.337	21.321
11	13.486	14.207	14.972	15.784	16.645	17.560	18.531	20.655	23.045	25.733
12	15.026	15.917	16.870	17.888	18.977	20.141	21.384	24.133	27.271	30.850
13	16.627	17.713	18.882	20.141	21.495	22.953	24.523	28.029	32.089	36.786
14	18.292	19.599	21.015	22.550	24.215	26.019	27.975	32.393	37.581	43.672
15	20.024	21.579	23.276	25.129	27.152	29.361	31.772	37.280	43.842	51.660
16	21.825	23.657	25.673	27.888	30.324	33.003	35.950	42.753	50.980	60.925
17	23.698	25.840	28.213	30.840	33.750	36.974	40.545	48.884	59.118	71.673
18	25.645	28.132	30.906	33.999	37.450	41.301	45.599	55.750	68.394	84.141
19	27.671	30.539	33.760	37.379	41.446	46.018	51.159	63.440	78.969	98.603
20	29.778	33.066	36.786	40.995	45.762	51.160	57.275	72.052	91.025	115.380

What is the future value of an annuity of three investments of $1 each that earn 7%? The answer 3.215 can be found in the 7% column and across from 3 in the Period column of Exhibit 15A-4. This amount can be used to compute the future value of the investment for Helen's education, as follows:

Amount of each periodic investment	×	Future value of annuity of $1 (Exhibit 15A-4)	=	Future value of investment
$4,000	×	3.215	=	$12,860

This one-step calculation is much easier than computing the future value of each annual investment and then summing the individual future values. You can compute the future value of any investment consisting of equal periodic amounts at regular intervals. Businesses make periodic investments to accumulate funds for plant expansion and other uses—an application of the future value of an annuity.

PRESENT VALUE

Often a person knows a future amount and needs to know the related present value. Recall Exhibit 15A-1, in which present value and future value are on opposite ends of the same time line. Suppose an investment promises to pay you $5,000 at the *end* of one year. How much would you pay *now* to acquire this investment? You would be willing to pay the present value of the $5,000 future amount.

Present value also depends on three factors: (1) the amount of payment (or receipt), (2) the length of time between investment and future receipt (or payment), and (3) the interest rate. The process of computing a present value is called *discounting* because the present value is *less* than the future value.

In our example, the future receipt is $5,000. The investment period is one year. Assume that you demand an annual interest rate of 10% on your investment. With all three factors specified, you can compute the present value of $5,000 at 10% for one year:

$$\frac{\text{Future value}}{(1 + \text{Interest rate})} = \frac{\$5,000}{1.10} = \$4,545$$

By turning the data around into a future-value problem, we verify the present-value computation:

Amount invested (present value)...	$4,545
Expected earnings ($4,545 × 0.10)	455
Amount to be received one year from now (future value).............	$5,000

This example illustrates that present value and future value are based on the same equation:

$$\text{Present value} \times (1 + \text{Interest rate}) = \text{Future value}$$

$$\frac{\text{Future value}}{(1 + \text{Interest rate})} = \text{Present value}$$

If the $5,000 is to be received two years from now, you will pay only $4,132 for the investment, as shown in Exhibit 15A-5.

EXHIBIT 15A-5
Two-Year Investment

By turning the data around, we verify that $4,132 accumulates to $5,000 at 10% for two years:

Amount invested (present value)...	$4,132
Expected earnings for first year ($4,132 × 0.10)	413
Value of investment after one year	4,545
Expected earnings for second year ($4,545 × 0.10)	455
Amount to be received two years from now (future value)	$5,000

You would pay $4,132—the present value of $5,000—to receive the $5,000 future amount at the end of two years at 10% per year. The $868 difference between the amount invested ($4,132) and the amount to be received ($5,000) is the return on the investment, the sum of the two interest receipts: $413 + $455 = $868.

Present-Value Tables

We have shown the simple formula for computing present value. However, figuring present value "by hand" for investments spanning many years is burdensome. Present-value tables ease our work. Let's reexamine our examples of present value by using Exhibit 15A-6, Present Value of $1.

EXHIBIT 15A-6   Present Value of $1

| | | | | Present Value of $1 | | | | | |
Period	4%	5%	6%	7%	8%	10%	12%	14%	16%
1	0.962	0.952	0.943	0.935	0.926	0.909	0.893	0.877	0.862
2	0.925	0.907	0.890	0.873	0.857	0.826	0.797	0.769	0.743
3	0.889	0.864	0.840	0.816	0.794	0.751	0.712	0.675	0.641
4	0.855	0.823	0.792	0.763	0.735	0.683	0.636	0.592	0.552
5	0.822	0.784	0.747	0.713	0.681	0.621	0.567	0.519	0.476
6	0.790	0.746	0.705	0.666	0.630	0.564	0.507	0.456	0.410
7	0.760	0.711	0.665	0.623	0.583	0.513	0.452	0.400	0.354
8	0.731	0.677	0.627	0.582	0.540	0.467	0.404	0.351	0.305
9	0.703	0.645	0.592	0.544	0.500	0.424	0.361	0.308	0.263
10	0.676	0.614	0.558	0.508	0.463	0.386	0.322	0.270	0.227
11	0.650	0.585	0.527	0.475	0.429	0.350	0.287	0.237	0.195
12	0.625	0.557	0.497	0.444	0.397	0.319	0.257	0.208	0.168
13	0.601	0.530	0.469	0.415	0.368	0.290	0.229	0.182	0.145
14	0.577	0.505	0.442	0.388	0.340	0.263	0.205	0.160	0.125
15	0.555	0.481	0.417	0.362	0.315	0.239	0.183	0.140	0.108
16	0.534	0.458	0.394	0.339	0.292	0.218	0.163	0.123	0.093
17	0.513	0.436	0.371	0.317	0.270	0.198	0.146	0.108	0.080
18	0.494	0.416	0.350	0.296	0.250	0.180	0.130	0.095	0.069
19	0.475	0.396	0.331	0.277	0.232	0.164	0.116	0.083	0.060
20	0.456	0.377	0.312	0.258	0.215	0.149	0.104	0.073	0.051

For the 10% investment for one year, we find the junction in the 10% column and across from 1 in the Period column. The figure 0.909 is computed as follows: 1/1.10 = 0.909. This work has been done for us, and only the present values are given in the table. The heading in Exhibit 15A-6 states $1. To figure present value for $5,000, we multiply $5,000 by 0.909. The result is $4,545, which matches the result we obtained by hand.

For the two-year investment, we read down the 10% column and across the Period 2 row. We multiply 0.826 (computed as 0.909/1.10 = 0.826) by $5,000 and get $4,130, which confirms our earlier computation of $4,132 (the difference is due to rounding in the present-value table). Using the table, we can compute the present value of any single future amount.

Present Value of an Annuity

Let's return to the investment example that provided the investor with only a single future receipt ($5,000 at the end of two years). Annuity investments provide multiple receipts of an equal amount at fixed intervals over the investment's duration.

Consider an investment that promises *annual* cash receipts of $10,000 to be received at the end of each of three years. Assume that you demand a 12% return on your investment. What is the investment's present value? What would you pay today to acquire the investment? The investment spans three periods, and you would pay the sum of three present values. The computation appears at the top of page 619.

The present value of this annuity is $24,020. By paying this amount today, you will receive $10,000 at the end of each of the three years while earning 12% on your investment.

Year	Annual Cash Receipt	×	Present of $1 at 12% (Exhibit 15A-6)	=	Present Value of Annual Cash Receipt
1	$10,000	×	0.893	=	$ 8,930
2	10,000	×	0.797	=	7,970
3	10,000	×	0.712	=	7,120
			Total present value of investment	=	$24,020

The example illustrates repetitive computations of the three future amounts, a time-consuming process. One way to ease the computational burden is to add the three present values of $1 (0.893 + 0.797 + 0.712) and multiply their sum (2.402) by the annual cash receipt ($10,000) to obtain the present value of the annuity ($10,000 × 2.402 = $24,020).

An easier approach is to use a present value of an annuity table. Exhibit 15A-7 shows the present value of $1 to be received at the end of each period for a given number of periods. The present value of a three-period annuity at 12% is 2.402 (the junction of the Period 3 row and the 12% column). Thus, $10,000 received annually at the end of each of three years, discounted at 12%, is $24,020 ($10,000 × 2.402), which is the present value.

EXHIBIT 15A-7   Present Value of Annuity of $1

	Present Value of Annuity of $1								
Period	4%	5%	6%	7%	8%	10%	12%	14%	16%
1	0.962	0.952	0.943	0.935	0.926	0.909	0.893	0.877	0.862
2	1.886	1.859	1.833	1.808	1.783	1.736	1.690	1.647	1.605
3	2.775	2.723	2.673	2.624	2.577	2.487	2.402	2.322	2.246
4	3.630	3.546	3.465	3.387	3.312	3.170	3.037	2.914	2.798
5	4.452	4.329	4.212	4.100	3.993	3.791	3.605	3.433	3.274
6	5.242	5.076	4.917	4.767	4.623	4.355	4.111	3.889	3.685
7	6.002	5.786	5.582	5.389	5.206	4.868	4.564	4.288	4.039
8	6.733	6.463	6.210	5.971	5.747	5.335	4.968	4.639	4.344
9	7.435	7.108	6.802	6.515	6.247	5.759	5.328	4.946	4.607
10	8.111	7.722	7.360	7.024	6.710	6.145	5.650	5.216	4.833
11	8.760	8.306	7.887	7.499	7.139	6.495	5.938	5.453	5.029
12	9.385	8.863	8.384	7.943	7.536	6.814	6.194	5.660	5.197
13	9.986	9.394	8.853	8.358	7.904	7.103	6.424	5.842	5.342
14	10.563	9.899	9.295	8.745	8.244	7.367	6.628	6.002	5.468
15	11.118	10.380	9.712	9.108	8.559	7.606	6.811	6.142	5.575
16	11.652	10.838	10.106	9.447	8.851	7.824	6.974	6.265	5.669
17	12.166	11.274	10.477	9.763	9.122	8.022	7.120	6.373	5.749
18	12.659	11.690	10.828	10.059	9.372	8.201	7.250	6.467	5.818
19	13.134	12.085	11.158	10.336	9.604	8.365	7.366	6.550	5.877
20	13.590	12.462	11.470	10.594	9.818	8.514	7.469	6.623	5.929

Present Value of Bonds Payable

The present value of a bond—its market price—is the present value of the future principal amount at maturity plus the present value of the future contract interest payments. The principal is a single amount to be paid at maturity. The interest is an annuity because it occurs periodically.

Let's compute the present value of the 9%, five-year bonds of **eBay Inc.** The face value of the bonds is $100,000, and they pay 4 1/2% contract (cash) interest semiannually. At issuance, the market interest rate is expressed as 10%, but it is computed at 5% semiannually. Therefore, the effective interest rate for each of the ten semiannual periods is 5%. We use 5% in computing the present value (PV) of the maturity and of the interest. The market price of these bonds is $96,149, as follows:

	Effective annual interest rate ÷ 2	Number of semiannual interest payments	
PV of principal:			
$100,000 × PV of single amount at 5%		for 10 periods	
($100,000 × 0.614—Exhibit 15A-6)			$61,400
PV of interest:			
($100,000 × 0.045) × PV of annuity at 5%		for 10 periods	
($4,500 × 7.722—Exhibit 15A-7)			34,749
PV (market price) of bonds			$96,149

The market price of the eBay bonds show a discount because the contract interest rate on the bonds (9%) is less than the market interest rate (10%). We discuss these bonds in more detail on pages 588–590.

Let's consider a premium price for the eBay bonds. Assume that the market interest rate is 8% at issuance. The effective rate is 4% for each of the ten semiannual periods:

	Effective annual interest rate ÷ 2	Number of semiannual interest periods	
PV of principal:			
$100,000 × PV of single amount at 4%		for 10 periods	
($100,000 × 0.676—Exhibit 15A-6)			$ 67,600
PV of interest:			
($100,000 × 0.045) × PV of annuity at 4%		for 10 periods	
($4,500 × 8.111—Exhibit 15A-7)			36,500
PV (market price) of bonds			$104,100

We discuss accounting for these bonds on pages 590–592.

Capital Leases

How does a lessee compute the cost of an asset acquired through a capital lease? Consider that the lessee gets the use of the asset but does *not* pay for the leased asset in full at the beginning of the lease. A capital lease is therefore similar to an installment purchase of the leased asset. The lessee must record the leased asset at the present value of the lease liability. The time value of money must be weighed.

The cost of the asset to the lessee is the sum of any payment made at the beginning of the lease period plus the present value of the future lease payments. The lease payments are equal amounts occurring at regular intervals—that is, they are annuity payments.

Consider the 20-year building lease of **Safeway.** The lease starts on January 1, 20X4, and requires 20 annual payments of $10,000 each, with the first payment due immediately. The interest rate in the lease is 10%, and the present value of the 19 future payments at the end of each period is $83,650 ($10,000 × PV of annuity at 10% for 19 periods, or 8.365 from Exhibit 15A-7). Safeway's cost is $93,650 (the sum of the initial payment, $10,000, plus the present value of the future payments, $83,650). The entries for this capital lease are

```
20X4
Jan. 1   Building.........................................................   93,650
              Cash........................................................          10,000
              Lease Liability (PV of the 19 lease payments) .........        83,650
         Acquired building under capital lease and made the
         first lease payment.

Dec. 31  Depreciation Expense ($93,650/20 years) ......................    4,683
              Accumulated Depreciation—Building....................              4,683
         Recorded depreciation on leased building.
```

APPENDIX PROBLEMS

P15A-1 Jerry Dyer is considering two plans for building an education fund for his children.

Computing future values of investments

Plan A—Invest $10,000 now, to earn 8% annually for six years.
Plan B—Invest $2,000 each year to earn 10% annually for six years.

Which plan provides the larger amount at the end of six years? At the outset, which plan would you expect to provide the larger future amount?

P15A-2 Magnuson, Inc., needs new manufacturing equipment. Two companies can provide similar equipment but under different payment plans:

Computing present-value amounts

a. **General Electric (GE)** offers to let Magnuson pay $50,000 each year for five years. The payments include interest at 12% per year. What is the present value of the payments?
b. **Westinghouse** will let Magnuson make a single payment of $300,000 at the end of five years. This payment includes both principal and interest at 12%. What is the present value of this payment?
c. Magnuson will purchase the equipment that costs the least, as measured by present value. Which equipment should Magnuson select? Why?

P15-A3 The purpose of this problem is to show the relationship between the future value of 1 and the present value of 1.

Relating future-value and present-value amounts

1. Jan Schmidt will need $10,000 at the end of ten years in order to cover a business expense due at that time. To meet this future expense, Schmidt can invest a sum today. His investment will earn 6% each year over the ten-year period. How much must Schmidt invest today (present value)?
2. Now, let's turn this present-value situation around and view it in terms of a future value: Schmidt has $5,580 to invest today. He can earn 6% each year over a ten-year period. How much will his investment be worth at the end of ten years (future value)?

P15A-4 For each situation, compute the required amount.

Computing the future value of an investment

1. Pentateuch Enterprises is budgeting for the acquisition of land over the next several years. Pentateuch can invest $700,000 today at 9%. How much cash will Pentateuch have for land acquisitions at the end of five years? At the end of six years?
2. Hassell Associates is planning to invest $6,000 each year for five years. The company's investment adviser believes that Hassell can earn 6% interest without taking on too much risk. What will be the value of Hassell's investment on the date of the last deposit if Hassell can earn 6%? If Hassell can earn 8%?

P15A-5 Determine the present value of the following notes and bonds:

Computing the present values of various notes and bonds

a. Ten-year bonds payable with maturity value of $88,000 and contract interest rate of 12%, paid semiannually. The market rate of interest is 10% at issuance.
b. Same bonds payable as in a, but the market interest rate is 8%.
c. Same bonds payable as in a, but the market interest rate is 12%.

P15A-6 On December 31, 20X1, when the market interest rate is 8%, Willis Realty Co. issues $400,000 of 7.25%, ten-year bonds payable. The bonds pay interest semiannually.

Computing a bond's present value, recording its issuance at a discount and interest payments

Required

1. Determine the present value of the bonds at issuance.
2. Assume that the bonds are issued at the price computed in requirement 1. Prepare an effective-interest method amortization table for the first two semiannual interest periods.
3. Using the amortization table prepared in requirement 2, journalize issuance of the bonds and the first two interest payments.

P15A-7 Osaka Children's Choir needs a fleet of vans to transport the children to singing engagements throughout Japan. **Toyota** offers the vehicles for a single payment of 7,200,000 yen due at the end of four years. **Nissan** prices a similar fleet of vans for four annual payments of 1,700,000 yen each. The children's home could borrow the funds at 6%, so this is the appropriate interest rate. Which company should get the business, Toyota or Nissan? Base your decision on present value, and give your reason.

Deciding between two payment plans

P15A-8 Escort, Inc., acquired equipment under a capital lease that requires six annual lease payments of $12,000. The first payment is due when the lease begins, on January 1, 20X6. Future payments are due on January 1 of each year of the lease term. The interest rate in the lease is 16%.

Computing the cost of equipment acquired under a capital lease and recording the lease transactions

Required

1. Compute Escort's cost of the equipment.
2. Journalize the (a) acquisition of the equipment and (b) depreciation for 20X6.

16

Investments and International Operations

LEARNING OBJECTIVES

After studying this chapter, you should be able to

1. Account for trading investments
2. Account for available-for-sale investments
3. Use the equity method for investments
4. Understand consolidated financial statements
5. Account for long-term investments in bonds
6. Account for transactions stated in a foreign currency

Move over, croissants and fine wine. Here come the Golden Arches. In 1999 McDonald's invaded Disneyland-Paris and also entered Azerbaijan and Gibraltar. With restaurants in 118 countries, **McDonald's Corporation** is one of the world's best-known companies.

McDonald's 1999 Annual Report features a Chinese boy eating French fries. Can you guess where McDonald's bought those potatoes? It was in China, because the company prefers to buy raw materials close to its restaurants. The produce is fresh, and McDonald's demonstrates its commitment to the local economy. But buying potatoes in China adds a new twist to doing business. McDonald's must pay in yuan, the Chinese currency unit, rather than dollars. In Russia, McDonald's pays for potatoes in rubles, and in France, you guessed it—in francs. Where does McDonald's get yuan, rubles, and francs? That brings up accounting for international operations, one of the topics of this chapter.

Recently McDonald's split its stock and increased its cash dividend. Investors like rising stock prices and dividend increases. These topics bring up accounting for investments, the other topic of this chapter.

Throughout this course, you have become increasingly familiar with the financial statements of companies such as **Intel, Target,** and **IHOP.** This chapter continues our discussion of the real world of accounting by discussing long-term investments and international operations. We begin with investments.

Investments extend from a few shares of stock to the acquisition of an entire company. In earlier chapters, we discussed the stocks and bonds that IHOP and **Amazon.com** issued. Here we examine stocks and bonds from the perspective of the investor who bought them. Different accounting methods apply to different types of investments. We begin with stock investments and then move to bonds and notes.

STOCK INVESTMENTS: AN OVERVIEW

Some Basics

STOCK PRICES   A broker may "quote a stock price," which means to state the current market price per share. The financial community quotes stock prices in dollars and cents. Big-city newspapers carry daily information on the stocks of thousands of corporations.

Exhibit 16-1 presents information for the common stock of **McDonald's Corporation** as it appeared in the newspaper. During the previous 52 weeks, McDonald's common stock reached a high price of $49.56 and a low price of $29.81 per share. The annual cash dividend is $0.20 (20 cents) per share. During the previous day, 206,767,000 (2067670 × 100) shares of McDonald's common stock were traded. The stock price ranged from a high of $30.38 to a low of $29.63 per share. The day's closing price of $29.88 was $0.25 lower than the closing price of the preceding day.

The person or company that owns stock in a corporation is the *investor*. The corporation that issued the stock is the *investee*. If you own shares of McDonald's common stock, you are an investor and McDonald's is the investee.

CLASSIFYING INVESTMENTS   Investments are assets to the investor. The investments may be short-term or long-term. **Short-term investments**—sometimes called **marketable securities**—are current assets. To be listed on the balance sheet as short-term, investments must be liquid (readily convertible to cash). Also, the investor must intend to convert the investments to cash within one year or use them to pay a current liability.

Investments that are not short-term are classified as **long-term investments** on the balance sheet. Long-term investments include stocks and bonds

 DAILY EXERCISE 16-1

SHORT-TERM INVESTMENT. A current asset; an investment that is readily convertible to cash and that the investor intends either to convert to cash within one year or use to pay a current liability. Also called a **marketable security.**

LONG-TERM INVESTMENT. A noncurrent asset, a separate asset category reported on the balance sheet between current assets and plant assets.

Exhibit 16-1 Stock Price Information for McDonald's Corporation

52 weeks								
High	**Low**	**Stock Symbol**	**Dividend**	**Volume 100s**	**High**	**Low**	**Close**	**Net Change**
49^{56}	29^{81}	MCD	.20	2067670	30^{38}	29^{63}	29^{88}	-0^{25}

that the investor expects to hold longer than one year or that are not readily marketable—for instance, real estate held for sale. Exhibit 16-2 shows the positions of short-term and long-term investments on the balance sheet.

Exhibit 16-2
Reporting Investments on the Balance Sheet

```
ASSETS
Current Assets
  Cash.......................................................................................   $X
  Short-term investments..........................................................    X
  Accounts receivable ..............................................................    X
  Inventories.............................................................................    X
  Prepaid expenses ..................................................................    X
     Total current assets...........................................................        $X
Long-term investments [or simply Investments]..............    X
Property, plant, and equipment ..........................................    X
Intangible assets ....................................................................    X
Other assets............................................................................    X
```

TRADING INVESTMENTS. Investments that are to be sold in the very near future with the intent of generating profits on price changes.

AVAILABLE-FOR-SALE INVESTMENTS. Stock investments other than trading securities in which the investor cannot exercise significant influence over the investee.

⊙ **DAILY EXERCISE 16-2**

⊙ **DAILY EXERCISE 16-3**

Objective 1
Account for trading investments

MARKET-VALUE METHOD. Used to account for all trading investments. These investments are reported at their current market value.

We report assets in the order of their liquidity, starting with cash. Long-term investments are less liquid than current assets but more liquid than property, plant, and equipment. Nevertheless, many companies report their long-term investments after property, plant, and equipment.

TRADING AND AVAILABLE-FOR-SALE INVESTMENTS   We begin our discussion of stock investments with situations in which the investor holds less than a 20% interest in the investee company. These investments in stock are classified as trading investments or as available-for-sale securities. **Trading investments** are investments that are to be sold in the very near future—days, weeks, or only a few months—with the intent of generating profits on price changes. Trading investments are therefore recorded as short-term investments and reported on the balance sheet under *current assets*, as shown in Exhibit 16-2.

Available-for-sale investments are all investments other than trading investments in which the investor cannot exercise significant influence over the investee. Available-for-sale investments are classified as current assets if the business expects to sell them within the next year or within the business's normal operating cycle if longer than a year. All other available-for-sale investments are classified as long-term (Exhibit 16-2).

The investor accounts for the two categories separately. We begin by illustrating the accounting for a trading investment. Then we show how to account for a long-term available-for-sale investment.

Accounting for Trading Investments

The **market-value method** is used to account for all trading investments because they will be sold in the near future at their current market value. Cost is used only as the initial amount to record trading investments. Assume **Intel Corporation** has excess cash for short-term investing. Suppose Intel buys 500 shares of **Ford Motor Company** stock for $50 per share on October 23, 20X5. Assume further that Intel's management hopes to sell this stock within three months. It is a trading investment. Intel's entry to record the purchase is

20X5

Oct. 23	Short-Term Investment (500 × $50)......................	25,000	
	Cash		25,000
	Purchased investment.		

Ford stock pays a cash dividend of $2 per share, so Intel would receive a dividend on the investment. Intel's entry to record receipt of a cash dividend is

20X5

Nov. 14	Cash (500 × $2.00)	1,000	
	Dividend Revenue		1,000
	Received cash dividend		

REPORTING TRADING INVESTMENTS ON THE BALANCE SHEET Trading investments are reported on the balance sheet at current market value, not at cost. This rule requires a year-end adjustment of the trading investment from its last carrying amount to current market value. Assume that the Ford stock has decreased in value, and at December 31, 20X5, Intel's investment in Ford stock is worth $20,000 ($5,000 less than the purchase price). At year end, Intel would make the following adjustment:

20X5

Dec. 31	Loss on Trading Investment		
	($25,000 − $20,000)	5,000	
	Short-Term Investment......................................		5,000
	Adjusted trading investment to market value.		

SHORT-TERM INVESTMENT

25,000	5,000
20,000	

The T-account shows the $20,000 ($25,000 − $5,000) balance of Short-Term Investment. Intel would report its trading investment on the balance sheet at December 31, 20X5, and the loss on trading investment on the 20X5 income statement, as follows:

◉ DAILY EXERCISE 16-4

Balance Sheet (partial):	**Income Statement (partial):**
ASSETS	Other gains and losses:
Current assets:	Gain (loss) on trading investment.............. $(5,000)
Short-term investments, at market value............. $20,000	

If the investment's market value had risen above $25,000, Intel would have debited Short-Term Investment and credited Gain on Trading Investment.

SELLING A TRADING INVESTMENT When a company sells a trading investment, the gain or loss on the sale is the difference between the sale proceeds and the last carrying amount of the investment. Suppose Intel sells the Ford stock for $18,000 on January 19, 20X6. Intel would record the sale as follows:

20X6

Jan. 19	Cash..	18,000	
	Loss on Sale of Investment..	2,000	
	Short-Term Investment......................................		20,000
	Sold investment.		

SHORT-TERM INVESTMENT

25,000	5,000
20,000	20,000

For reporting on the income statement, Intel could combine all gains and losses ($5,000 + $2,000) on short-term investments and report a single net amount under "Other gains (losses). . . . $(7,000).

◉ DAILY EXERCISE 16-5

◉ DAILY EXERCISE 16-6

◉ DAILY EXERCISE 16-7

Accounting for Long-Term Available-for-Sale Investments

The *market-value method* is used to account for all available-for-sale investments in stock because the company expects to resell the stock at its market value. Available-for-sale investments are therefore reported on the balance sheet at their *current market value,* just as for trading investments.

Objective 2
Account for available-for-sale investments

625

Suppose **Dell Corporation** purchases 1,000 shares of **Hewlett-Packard Company** common stock at the market price of $35.75. Dell intends to hold this investment for longer than a year and classifies it as a long-term available-for-sale investment. Dell's entry to record the investment is

20X1			
Feb. 23	Long-Term Available-for-Sale Investment		
	(1,000 × $35.75)...	35,750	
	Cash..		35,750
	Purchased investment.		

Dell receives a $0.64 per share cash dividend on the Hewlett-Packard stock. Dell's entry to record receipt of the dividend is

20X1			
July 14	Cash (1,000 × $0.64)..	640	
	Dividend Revenue..		640
	Received cash dividend.		

➤ For a review of stock dividends, see Chapter 14, page 542.

STOCK DIVIDEND VERSUS A CASH DIVIDEND Receipt of a *stock* dividend is different from receipt of a cash dividend. ◄ For a stock dividend, the investor records no dividend revenue. Instead, the investor makes a memorandum entry in the accounting records to show the new number of shares of stock now held. The number of investment shares has increased, so the investor's cost per share decreases. For example, suppose Dell Corporation receives a 5% stock dividend from Hewlett-Packard. Dell would receive 50 shares (5% of 1,000 shares previously held) and make this memorandum entry in its accounting records:

◉ DAILY EXERCISE 16-8

> MEMORANDUM—Receipt of stock dividend: Received 50 shares of Hewlett-Packard common stock in 5% stock dividend. New cost per share is $34.05 (cost of $35,750 ÷ 1,050 shares). For all future Hewlett-Packard investment transactions, Dell will use the new cost per share of $34.05.

REPORTING AVAILABLE-FOR-SALE INVESTMENTS ON THE BALANCE SHEET Available-for-sale investments are reported on the balance sheet at their market value. This reporting requires an adjustment of the investment from its last carrying amount to current market value. Assume that the market value of Dell's investment in Hewlett-Packard common stock is $36,400 on December 31, 20X1. In this case, Dell makes the following adjustment:

20X1			
Dec. 31	Allowance to Adjust Investment to Market		
	($36,400 − $35,750)..	650	
	Unrealized Gain on		
	Available-for-Sale Investment		650
	Adjusted investment to market value.		

Allowance to Adjust Investment to Market is a companion account that is used with the Long-Term Investment account to bring the investment's carrying amount to current market value. Here the investment's cost ($35,750) plus the Allowance ($650) equals the investment carrying amount ($36,400).

LONG-TERM AVAILABLE-FOR-SALE INVESTMENT	ALLOWANCE TO ADJUST INVESTMENT TO MARKET
35,750		650	

Investment carrying amount = Market value of $36,400 ($35,750 − $650)

In this case, the Allowance has a debit balance because the investment value (an asset) increased. If the investment's value declines, the Allowance is credited, and the investment carrying amount is cost *minus* the Allowance. When the Allowance has a credit balance, it becomes a contra account. ➤

➤ Other contra accounts are Accumulated Depreciation (Chapter 3) and Allowance for Uncollectible Accounts (Chapter 8).

The other side of the December 31 adjustment entry is a credit to Unrealized Gain on Available-for-Sale Investment. If the investment's market value declines, the company debits an Unrealized Loss. *Unrealized* means that the gain or loss resulted from a change in the investment's market value, not from the sale of the investment. A gain or loss on the sale of an investment is said to be *realized* because the company received cash from the sale. It is *cash* that turns the gain or loss into a realized gain or loss.[1] For available-for-sale investments, the Unrealized Gain (or the Unrealized Loss) account is reported on the balance sheet as part of stockholders' equity, as shown here.

Balance Sheet (partial)			
ASSETS		**STOCKHOLDERS' EQUITY**	
Total current assets	$ XXX	Common stock	$XXX
Long-term available-for-sale		Retained earnings	XXX
investments—at market value		Unrealized gain on available-for-sale	
($35,750 + $650).......................	36,400	investments	650
Property, plant, and equipment, net..............	XXX		

The Unrealized Gain (or Loss) account is reported on the balance sheet (not on the income statement) because it may take a year or longer for the company to sell this investment. When the investment is sold, the gain or loss will be realized in cash.

SELLING AN AVAILABLE-FOR-SALE INVESTMENT   The sale of an available-for-sale investment can result in a *realized* gain or loss, which we call a Gain (or Loss) on Sale of Investment to indicate that a sale transaction has occurred. For available-for-sale investments, realized gains and losses measure the difference between the amount received from the sale of the investment and the cost of the investment.

Suppose Dell Corporation sells its investment in Hewlett-Packard stock for $34,000 during 20X2. Dell would record the sale as follows:

```
20X2
May 19   Cash ........................................      34,000
           Loss on Sale of Investment ..........       1,750
              Long-Term Available-for-Sale
                Investment (cost)...............                    35,750
           Sold investment.
```

DAILY EXERCISE 16-9

Dell would report the Loss on Sale of Investment as an "Other gain or loss" on the income statement.[2]

DAILY EXERCISE 16-10

Accounting for Equity-Method Investments

Objective 3
Use the equity method for investments

An investor with a stock holding between 20% and 50% of the investee's voting stock may *significantly influence* decisions on dividends, product lines, and other important matters.

For this reason, investments in the range of 20–50% of another company's stock are common. For example, **General Motors** owns nearly 40% of **Isuzu Motors Overseas Distribution Corporation,** and **Dow Jones & Company,** publisher of the *Wall Street Journal,* owns 50% of **Smart Money,** the magazine com-

---

[1]In accounting, the term *realized* usually means "made real" by a cash transaction. Suppose **Bank of America** (BOA) paid $6,000 for an investment in **General Electric** (GE) stock. If BOA sells the stock for $10,000, the bank has a realized gain of $4,000. Selling the stock for $5,000 results in a realized loss of $1,000. Whether a gain or loss is realized or unrealized is important for available-for-sale investments, but not for trading investments. It is also important for income taxes, because only realized gains are taxed.

[2]We omit the complex journal entry to adjust the Allowance account at year end. That topic is covered in intermediate accounting courses.

WORK IT OUT

Suppose Xenon Corporation holds the following available-for-sale securities as long-term investments at December 31, 20X3:

Stock	Cost	Current Market Value
The Coca-Cola Company	$ 85,000	$ 71,000
Eastman Kodak Company	16,000	12,000
Scott Paper Company	122,000	136,000
	$223,000	$219,000

Show how Xenon Corporation will report long-term investments and the unrealized loss on its December 31, 20X3, balance sheet.

Answer

ASSETS
Long-term available-for-sale investments, at market value............... $219,000

STOCKHOLDERS' EQUITY
Unrealized loss on available-for-sale investments
($223,000 − $219,000) .... $ (4,000)

pany. With a 20–50% investment, the investor has a voice in shaping the investee's operations.

We use the **equity method** to account for investments in which the investor owns 20–50% of the investee's stock and can significantly influence the decisions of the investee. A recent survey of 600 companies by *Accounting Trends & Techniques* indicated that 279 (46%) of the companies held investments that they accounted for by the equity method. These investee companies are often called *affiliates* or *affiliated companies*.

RECORDING THE INITIAL INVESTMENT   Investments accounted for by the equity method are recorded initially at cost. Suppose **Phillips Petroleum Company** pays $400,000 for 30% of the common stock of White Rock Corporation. Phillips may refer to White Rock Corporation as an *affiliated company*. Phillips's entry to record the purchase of this investment is as follows:

20X1			
Jan. 6	Long-Term Equity-Method Investment..............	400,000	
	Cash..		400,000
	Purchased equity-method investment.		

ADJUSTING THE INVESTMENT ACCOUNT FOR INVESTEE NET INCOME   Under the equity method, Phillips, as the investor, applies its percentage of ownership (30%) to record its share of the investee's net income and dividends. White Rock reported net income of $250,000 for the year, and Phillips records 30% of this amount as an increase in the investment account and as equity-method investment revenue, as follows:

Dec. 31	Long-Term Equity-Method Investment		
	($250,000 × 0.30)	75,000	
	Equity-Method Investment Revenue.......		75,000
	Recorded investment revenue.		

The Investment Revenue account carries the Equity-Method label to identify its source. This labeling is similar to distinguishing Sales Revenue from Service Revenue.

EQUITY METHOD. The method used to account for investments in which the investor has 20–50% of the investee's voting stock and can significantly influence the decisions of the investee.

The investor increases the Investment account and records Investment Revenue when the investee reports income because of the close relationship between the two companies. As the investee's owners' equity increases, so does the Investment account on the investor's books.

RECEIVING DIVIDENDS ON AN EQUITY-METHOD INVESTMENT Phillips records its proportionate part of cash dividends received from White Rock. White Rock declares and pays a cash dividend of $100,000. Phillips receives 30% of this dividend and makes this journal entry:

20X2
Jan. 17   Cash ($100,000 × 0.30) 30,000
                Long-Term Equity-Method Investment......................   30,000
          Received cash dividend on equity-method investment.

The Investment account is credited for the receipt of a dividend on an equity-method investment. Why? Because the dividend decreases both the investee's owners' equity and the investor's investment. The investor received cash for this portion of the investment and that reduced the investor's claim against the investee.

After the preceding entries are posted, Phillips's Investment account reflects its equity in the net assets of White Rock:

LONG-TERM EQUITY-METHOD INVESTMENT

20X1			20X2		
Jan. 6	Purchase	400,000	Jan. 17	Dividends received	30,000
Dec. 31	Net income	75,000			
20X2					
Jan. 17	Balance	445,000			

◉ DAILY EXERCISE 16-11

Phillips can report the long-term investment on the balance sheet and the equity-method investment revenue on the income statement as follows:

Balance sheet (partial):		Income statement (partial):	
ASSETS		Income from operations....................	$ XXX
Total current assets....................................	$ XXX	Other revenue:	
Long-term equity-method		Equity-method investment	
investments..	445,000	revenue...	75,000
Property, plant, and equipment, net	XXX	Net income	$ XXX

SELLING AN EQUITY-METHOD INVESTMENT There may be a gain or loss on the sale of an equity-method investment. The gain or loss is measured as the difference between the sale proceeds and the carrying amount of the investment. Suppose Phillips sells one-tenth of the White Rock common stock for $41,000. The sale is recorded as follows:

Feb. 13   Cash... 41,000
          Loss on Sale of Investment...   3,500
                Long-Term Equity-Method Investment
                ($445,000 × 1/10)   44,500
          Sold one-tenth of investment.

◉ DAILY EXERCISE 16-12

In summary, this T-account illustrates how to account for equity-method investments:

LONG-TERM EQUITY-METHOD INVESTMENT

Cost	Share of losses
Share of income	Share of dividend received

JOINT VENTURES ARE ACCOUNTED FOR BY THE EQUITY METHOD A *joint venture* is a separate entity owned by a small group of businesses. Joint ventures are common in risky endeavors such as oil exploration in the petroleum industry and also in the construction of nuclear power plants. **Aramco,** which stands for Arabian American Oil Company, is a joint venture half owned by Saudi Arabia. Several multinational oil companies (**Exxon, Chevron,** and others) own the remaining 50%.

A participant in a joint venture accounts for its investment by the equity method even when the investor owns less than 20% of the venture. Joint ventures are common in international business. Companies such as **British Telecom, Total** (of France) and **Toyota** partner with companies in other countries.

Accounting for Consolidated Subsidiaries

Objective 4
Understand consolidated financial statements

Most large corporations own controlling interests in other companies. A **controlling** (or **majority**) **interest** is the ownership of more than 50% of the investee's voting stock. Such an investment enables the investor to elect a majority of the investee's board of directors and thereby control the investee. The corporation that controls the other company is called the **parent company,** and the company that is controlled by another corporation is called the **subsidiary.** A well-known example is **Saturn Corporation,** which is a subsidiary of **General Motors,** the parent company. Because GM owns Saturn Corporation, the stockholders of GM control Saturn, as diagrammed in Exhibit 16-3.

EXHIBIT 16-3
Ownership Structure of General Motors Corporation and Saturn Corporation

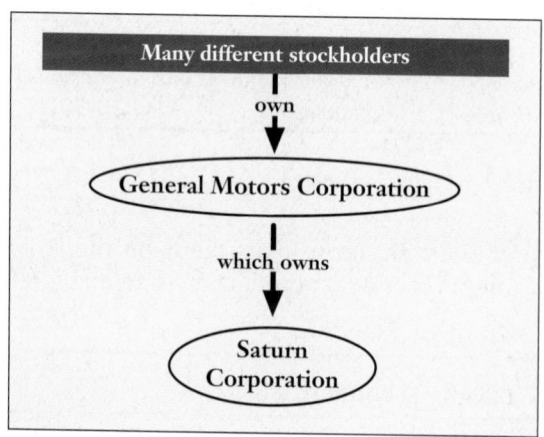

CONTROLLING INTEREST. Ownership of more than 50% of an investee company's voting stock. Also called **majority interest.**

PARENT COMPANY. An investor company that owns more than 50% of the voting stock of a subsidiary company.

SUBSIDIARY COMPANY. A company in which a parent company owns more than 50% of the voting stock.

Why have subsidiaries? Why not have the corporation take the form of a single legal entity? Subsidiaries may enable the parent to save on income taxes, limit the parent's liabilities in a risky venture, and ease expansion into foreign countries. For example, **McDonald's Corporation** finds it more feasible to operate in France through a French-based subsidiary company than through the U.S. parent company. Exhibit 16-4 shows some of the subsidiaries of three large automakers.

EXHIBIT 16-4
Selected Subsidiaries of Three Large Automobile Manufacturers

Parent Company	Selected Subsidiaries
General Motors Corporation Total assets: $275 billion	Saturn Corporation Hughes Aircraft Company
Ford Motor Company Total assets: $276 billion	Ford Aerospace Corporation Jaguar, Ltd.
DaimlerChrysler Corporation Total assets: $176 billion	Jeep/Eagle Corporation DaimlerChrysler Rail Systems

MAJORITY-OWNED SUBSIDIARIES *Consolidation accounting* is a method of combining the financial statements of two or more companies controlled by the same owners. This method implements the entity concept of accounting by reporting a single set of financial statements for the consolidated entity.

Most published financial reports include consolidated statements. To understand real financial statements, you need to know the basic concepts underlying consolidation accounting. **Consolidated statements** combine the balance sheets, income statements, and cash-flow statements of the parent company plus those of its majority-owned subsidiaries. The final outcome of the consolidation process is a single set of statements as if the parent and its subsidiaries were a single entity.

In consolidation accounting, the assets, liabilities, revenues, and expenses of each subsidiary are added to the parent's accounts. The consolidated financial statements report the combined account balances. For example, the balance in the Cash account of Saturn Corporation is added to the cash balance of General Motors, and the sum of the two amounts is reported on GM's balance sheet as a single amount. The consolidated financial statements bear the name of the parent company only, in this case General Motors Corporation.

Exhibit 16-5 illustrates which accounting method should be used for each stock investment according to the percentage of ownership by the investor.

 DAILY EXERCISE 16-13

GOODWILL AND MINORITY INTEREST *Goodwill* is an intangible asset that is measured in the consolidation process. Goodwill is reported among the intangible assets on the consolidated balance sheet of the parent company. As we saw in Chapter 10, *goodwill* is the excess of the cost to acquire another company over the sum of the market value of its net assets.

A parent company may purchase less than 100% of the stock of a subsidiary company. For example, **Nokia,** the cellular telephone company, owns less than 100% of several other companies. The portions of those companies owned by outsiders is called the minority interest. **Minority interest** is the portion (less than 50%) of a subsidiary's stock that is owned by stockholders other than the parent company. Nokia Corporation, the parent company, therefore reports on its consolidated balance sheet an account titled Minority Interest. Most companies list Minority Interest among their liabilities.

Preparing consolidated financial statements is illustrated in the chapter appendix. Advanced accounting courses cover consolidation accounting in more detail.

 DAILY EXERCISE 16-14

THE INCOME OF A CONSOLIDATED ENTITY The income of a consolidated entity is the net income of the parent plus the parent's proportion of the subsidiaries' net income. Suppose Parent Company owns all the stock of Subsidiary S-1 and 60% of the stock of Subsidiary S-2. During 20X8, Parent earned net income of $330,000, S-1 earned $150,000, and S-2 had a net loss of $100,000. Parent Company would report consolidated net income of $420,000, computed as follows:

	Net Income (Net Loss)	×	Parent Stockholders' Ownership	=	Parent's Consolidated Net Income (Net Loss)
Parent Company....................	$ 330,000	×	100%	=	$330,000
Subsidiary S-1	150,000	×	100%	=	150,000
Subsidiary S-2	(100,000)	×	60%	=	(60,000)
Consolidated net income.............					$420,000

THINK IT OVER

Answer these questions about consolidated financial statements:

1. Whose name appears on the consolidated statements—the parent company, the subsidiary company, or both?
2. Company A owns 90% of Company B. What is the remaining 10% of Company B's stock called, and where does it appear in Company A's financial statements?
3. Company C paid $1 million to acquire Company D, whose stockholders' equity (same as net assets) totaled $700,000. What is the $300,000 excess called? Which company reports the excess? Where in the financial statements is the excess reported?

Answers

1. Parent Company only.
2. Minority Interest—reported on (Parent) Company A's balance sheet among the liabilities.
3. Goodwill—reported on (Parent) Company C's balance sheet as an intangible asset.

Objective 5
Account for long-term investments in bonds

LONG-TERM INVESTMENTS IN BONDS AND NOTES

Most companies invest far more in stocks than they do in bonds. The major investors in bonds are banks, pension plans, mutual funds, and insurance companies. The relationship between the issuing corporation and bondholders may be diagrammed as follows:

ISSUING CORPORATION HAS		BONDHOLDER HAS
Bonds payable	⟷	Investment in bonds
Interest expense	⟷	Interest revenue

➤ See Chapter 15, pages 583–585 for discussion of bonds payable

The dollar amount of a bond transaction is the same for both the issuer and the bondholder because money passes from one to the other. However, the accounts debited and credited differ. For example, the corporation has bonds payable. To the bondholder, the bonds are an investment. The corporation's interest expense is the bondholder's interest revenue. Chapter 15 covered bonds payable ◄.

An investment in bonds is classified as short-term (a current asset) or as long-term. *Short-term investments in bonds are rare.* We focus on long-term investments in bonds that the investor intends to hold until the bonds mature. These are called **held-to-maturity investments.**

HELD-TO-MATURITY INVESTMENTS. Investment in bonds, notes, and other debt securities that the investor expects to hold until their maturity date.

Accounting for Held-to-Maturity Investments— The Amortized-Cost Method

Bond investments are recorded at cost. Then at maturity, the investor will receive the bonds' full face value. We must amortize any discount or premium to account for interest revenue over the period the bonds will be held. The amortization of discount or premium on a bond investment follows the same pattern as for bonds payable, as in Chapter 15. Held-to-maturity investments in bonds are reported at their *amortized cost.*

Suppose an investor purchases $10,000 of 6% **CBS** bonds at a price of 95.2 (95.2% of maturity value) on April 1, 20X2. The investor intends to hold the bonds as a long-term investment until their maturity. Interest dates are April 1 and October 1. These bonds mature on April 1, 20X6, so they will be outstanding for 48 months. Let us amortize the discount by the straight-line method ◄. The following are the bondholder's entries for this long-term investment:

➤ Straight-line amortization of premium or discount on a bond investment is calculated the same way as it is calculated for bonds payable (see Chapter 15, page 583).

Apr. 1	Long-Term Investment in Bonds ($10,000 × 0.952)	9,520	
	Cash..		9,520
	Purchased bond investment.		
Oct. 1	Cash ($10,000 × 0.06 × 6/12)	300	
	Interest Revenue		300
	Received semiannual interest.		

Oct. 1 Long-Term Investment in Bonds
[($10,000 − $9,520)/48] × 6 60

Interest Revenue 60

Amortized discount on bond investment.

At December 31, the year-end adjustments are

Dec. 31 Interest Receivable ($10,000 × 0.06 × 3/12) 150

Interest Revenue 150

Accrued interest revenue.

◉ DAILY EXERCISE 16-15

Dec. 31 Long-Term Investment in Bonds
[($10,000 − $9,520)/48] × 3 30

Interest Revenue 30

Amortized discount on bond investment.

◉ DAILY EXERCISE 16-16

Each amortization entry (October 1 and December 31) has two effects:

1. It increases the Long-Term Investment account on its march toward maturity value.
2. It records the interest revenue earned because of the increase in the carrying amount of the investment.

The financial statements at December 31, 20X2, report the following for this investment in bonds:

Balance sheet at December 31, 20X2:

Current assets:

Interest receivable.. $ 150

Total current assets .... X,XXX

Long-term investments in bonds ($9,520 + $60 + $30)—Note 6 9,610

Property, plant, and equipment .... X,XXX

Income statement for 19X2:

Other revenues:

Interest revenue ($300 + $60 + $150 + $30) .... $ 540

◉ DAILY EXERCISE 16-17

This chapter has illustrated how to account for various types of investments. The Decision Guidelines feature summarizes the accounting by showing which method applies to each type of investment.

DECISION GUIDELINES

Accounting Method to Use for Each Type of Investment

DECISION	GUIDELINES
Investment Type	**Accounting Method**
Short-Term Investment	
Trading investment	Market value—report all gains (losses) on the income statement.
Long-Term Investment	
Investor owns less than 20% of investee stock (available-for-sale investment)	Market value—report *unrealized* gains (losses) on the balance sheet.
	—report *realized* gains (losses) from sale of the investment on the income statement.
Investor owns between 20 and 50% of investee stock	Equity
Investment in a joint venture	Equity
Investor owns more than 50% of investee stock	Consolidation
Long-term investment in bonds (held-to-maturity investment)	Amortized cost

SUMMARY PROBLEM

1. Identify the appropriate accounting method for each of the following situations:
   a. Investment in 25% of investee company's stock.
   b. Available-for-sale investment in stock.
   c. Investment in more than 50% of investee company's stock.
2. At what amount should the following available-for-sale investment portfolio be reported on the December 31 balance sheet? All the investments are less than 5% of the investee's stock.

Stock	Investment Cost	Current Market Value
Amazon.com	$ 5,000	$ 5,500
Intelysis	61,200	53,000
Procter & Gamble	3,680	6,230

Journalize any adjusting entry required by these data.

3. Investor paid $67,900 to acquire a 40% equity-method investment in the common stock of Investee. At the end of the first year, Investee's net income was $80,000, and Investee declared and paid cash dividends of $55,000. Journalize Investor's (a) purchase of the investment, (b) share of Investee's net income, (c) receipt of dividends from Investee, and (d) sale of Investee stock for $80,100.

Solution

1. (a) Equity.   (b) Market value.   (c) Consolidation
2. Report the investments at market value, $64,730, as follows:

Stock	Investment Cost	Current Market Value
Amazon.com	$ 5,000	$ 5,500
Intelysis	61,200	53,000
Procter & Gamble	3,680	6,230
Totals	$69,880	$64,730

Adjusting entry:

Unrealized Loss on Investments ($69,880 − $64,730)	5,150	
Allowance to Adjust Investment to Market		5,150
To adjust investments to current market value.		

3. a.

Long-Term Equity-Method Investment	67,900	
Cash		67,900
Purchased equity-method investment.		

b.

Long-Term Equity-Method Investment ($80,000 × 0.40)	32,000	
Equity-Method Investment Revenue		32,000
Recorded investment revenue.		

c.

Cash ($55,000 × 0.40)	22,000	
Long-Term Equity-Method Investment		22,000
Recorded receipt of cash dividend on equity-method investment.		

d.

Cash	80,100	
Long-Term Equity-Method Investment		
($67,900 + $32,000 − $22,000)		77,900
Gain on Sale of Investment		2,200
Sold investment.		

ACCOUNTING FOR INTERNATIONAL OPERATIONS

Accounting for business activities across national boundaries makes up the field of *international accounting.*

Did you know that **Coca-Cola, IBM,** and **Bank of America** earn most of their revenue outside the United States? It is common for U.S. companies to do a large part of their business abroad. **McDonald's, Toys "Я" Us,** and **Procter & Gamble** are also very active in other countries. Exhibit 16-6 shows the percentages of international sales for these companies. *International* often means outside North America.

EXHIBIT 16-6
Extent of International Business

Company	Percent of International Sales
McDonald's	62%
Toys "Я" Us	27
Procter & Gamble	49

The economic environment varies from country to country. The United States may be booming while the Pacific Rim is depressed economically. International accounting must deal with such differences.

Foreign Currencies and Foreign-Currency Exchange Rates

Each country uses its own national currency. If **Boeing,** a U.S.-owned company, sells a 747 jet to **Air France,** will Boeing receive U.S. dollars or French francs? If the transaction takes place in dollars, Air France must buy dollars to pay Boeing in U.S. currency. If the transaction takes place in francs, Boeing will receive francs, which it exchanges for dollars. In either case, a step has been added to the transaction: One company must convert domestic currency into foreign currency, or vice versa.

The price of one nation's currency can be stated in terms of another country's monetary unit. The price of a foreign currency is called the **foreign-currency exchange rate.** In Exhibit 16-7, the U.S. dollar value of a French franc is $0.14. This means that one French franc can be bought for 14 cents. Other currencies, such as the pound and the yen (also listed in Exhibit 16-7), are similarly bought and sold.

FOREIGN-CURRENCY EXCHANGE RATE. The measure of one currency against another currency.

EXHIBIT 16-7   Foreign-Currency Exchange Rates

Country	Monetary Unit	U.S. Dollar Value	Country	Monetary Unit	U.S. Dollar Value
Canada	Dollar	$0.68	Great Britain	Pound	$1.51
European Common Market	European currency unit	0.93	Italy	Lira	0.0004
France	Franc	0.14	Japan	Yen	0.009
Germany	Mark	0.48	Mexico	Peso	0.107

Source: The Wall Street Journal, July 21, 2000, p. C13.

We use the exchange rate to convert the price of an item stated in one currency to its price in a second currency. We call this conversion a *translation.* Suppose an item costs 200 French francs. To compute its cost in dollars, we multiply the amount in francs by the conversion rate: 200 French francs × $0.14 = $28.

Currencies are often described as "strong" or "weak." The exchange rate of a **strong currency** is rising relative to other nations' currencies. The exchange rate of a **weak currency** is falling relative to other currencies.

STRONG CURRENCY. A currency that is rising relative to other nations' currencies.

WEAK CURRENCY. A currency that is falling relative to other nations' currencies.

Foreign-Currency Transactions

As international transactions become common, more companies manage cash transactions conducted in foreign currencies. **D. E. Shipp Belting,** a family-owned company in Waco, Texas, provides an example. Shipp makes conveyor belts for several industries, including dot.coms that sell their goods on-line. **M&M Mars** which makes Snickers candy bars in Waco, is an important customer of Shipp Belting. Farmers along the Texas-Mexico border use Shipp conveyor belts to process vegetables. Some of these customers are on the Mexican side of the border, so Shipp Belting conducts some of its business in pesos, the Mexican monetary unit.

COLLECTING CASH IN A FOREIGN CURRENCY   Consider Shipp Belting's sale of conveyor belts to Artes de Mexico, a vegetable grower in Matamoros, Mexico. The sale can be conducted in dollars or pesos. If Artes de Mexico agrees to pay in dollars, Shipp avoids the foreign currency complication, and the transaction is the same as selling to M&M Mars across town. But suppose that Artes de Mexico orders conveyor belts valued at 1 million pesos (approximately $107,000). Further suppose that Artes demands to pay in pesos and that Shipp agrees to receive pesos instead of dollars.

Shipp will need to convert the pesos to dollars, so the transaction creates a new risk. What if the peso weakens (loses value) before Shipp collects from Artes? In this case, Shipp will not earn as much as expected on the sale. Let's see how to account for this transaction.

Shipp Belting sells goods to Artes de Mexico for a price of 1 million pesos on June 2. On that date, a peso was worth $0.107. One month later, on July 2, the peso has weakened against the dollar and a peso is worth only $0.102. Shipp still receives 1 million pesos from Artes because that was the price agreed upon. But the dollar value of Shipp's cash receipt is $5,000 less than the original amount, so Shipp ends up earning $5,000 less than expected. The following journal entries show how Shipp Belting would account for these transactions:

June 2	Accounts Receivable—Artes		
	(1,000,000 pesos × $0.107)	107,000	
	Sales Revenue		107,000
	Sale on account.		

DAILY EXERCISE 16-18

July 2	Cash (1,000,000 pesos × $0.102)	102,000	
	Foreign-Currency Loss	5,000	
	Accounts Receivable—Artes		107,000
	Collection on account.		

If Shipp had required Artes to pay at the time of the sale, Shipp would have received pesos worth $107,000. But during the 30-day collection period, Shipp was exposed to *foreign-currency exchange risk,* the risk of loss in an international transaction. In this case, Shipp experienced a $5,000 foreign-currency loss and received $5,000 less than expected, as shown in the collection entry on July 2.

PAYING CASH IN A FOREIGN CURRENCY   Purchasing from a foreign company can also expose a company to foreign-currency exchange risk. Shipp Belting buys inventory from Gesellschaft Ltd., a Swiss company. The two companies decide on a price of 20,000 Swiss francs. On August 10, when Shipp receives the goods, the Swiss franc is priced at $0.800. When Shipp pays two weeks later, on August 24, the Swiss franc has weakened against the dollar, and is now worth only $0.78. This works to Shipp's advantage. Shipp would record the purchase and payment as follows:

Aug. 10	Inventory (20,000 Swiss francs × $0.80)	16,000	
	Accounts Payable—Gesellschaft Ltd.		16,000
	Purchase on account.		

DAILY EXERCISE 16-19

Aug. 24	Accounts Payable—Gesellschaft Ltd.	16,000	
	Foreign-Currency Gain		400
	Cash (20,000 Swiss francs × $0.78)		15,600
	Payment on account.		

In this case, the Swiss franc weakened against the dollar, which gave Shipp a foreign-currency gain. A company with a payable stated in a foreign currency hopes that the dollar gets stronger. The company can then use fewer dollars to pay the debt and have a foreign-currency gain on the transaction.

REPORTING FOREIGN-CURRENCY GAINS AND LOSSES ON THE INCOME STATEMENT   The Foreign-Currency Gain account reports gains on transactions in a currency other than the dollar. The Foreign-Currency Loss account shows losses on foreign-currency transactions. The company reports the *net amount* of these two accounts on the income statement as Other gains (losses). For example, Shipp Belting would combine the $5,000 foreign-currency loss and the $400 gain and report the net loss of $4,600 on the income statement, as follows:

Other gains (losses):	
Foreign-currency gain (loss), net ($5,000 − $400)	$(4,600)

These gains and losses fall into the "Other" category because they arise from outside activities. Buying and selling foreign currencies are not Shipp Belting's main business.

Managers examine these gains and losses to see how well the company is doing in foreign-currency transactions. The gains and losses may offset each other, and the net result may be small. But if losses exceed gains and grow large, managers will take action to shield themselves against further loss. One possible action is hedging.

HEDGING TO AVOID FOREIGN-CURRENCY LOSSES   U.S. companies can avoid foreign-currency losses by insisting that international transactions be settled in dollars. But that strategy may alienate customers. Another way for a company to protect itself is by hedging.

Hedging means to protect oneself from losing money by engaging in a counterbalancing transaction. Suppose **Lucent Technologies** is selling goods to be collected in Japanese yen. Lucent will receive a fixed number of yen in the future. If yen are losing value, they will be worth fewer dollars than the amount of Lucent's receivable. Lucent can expect a loss in this situation.

Keep in mind that Lucent Technologies has a receivable stated in Japanese yen. In other international transactions, Lucent may have accumulated payables stated in another foreign currency, say Mexican pesos. Losses on the receipt of yen may be offset by gains on the payment of pesos to the Mexican company. This is a natural foreign-currency hedge. It is inexpensive because Lucent has to take no new action to protect against foreign-currency loss.

Most companies do not have equal amounts of receivables and payables in foreign currency, so offsetting receivables and payables is imprecise. To obtain a more precise hedge, companies buy *futures contracts,* which are agreements for foreign currencies to be received in the future. Futures contracts can create a payable to exactly offset a receivable, and vice versa. Most companies that do business internationally use hedging to avoid losses.

HEDGING. Protecting oneself from losing money in one transaction by engaging in a counterbalancing transaction.

Consolidation of Foreign Subsidiaries

McDonald's Corporation forms foreign subsidiaries to do business in the various foreign countries. McDonald's can establish a French subsidiary to operate in France, a Russian company to do business in that country, and so on. A U.S. company with foreign subsidiaries consolidates all subsidiaries' financial statements into its own for reporting to the public. The consolidation of a foreign subsidiary poses two accounting challenges.

1. Many countries outside the United States specify accounting treatments that differ from American accounting principles. To report to the American public, accountants must first bring the subsidiary's statements into conformity with American generally accepted accounting principles (GAAP).

2. Subsidiary statements are expressed in a foreign currency. A preliminary step in the consolidation process is to translate the subsidiary statements into dollars. Then the dollar-value statements of the subsidiary can be combined with the parent's statements in the usual manner.

e-Accounting

Avon Products Inc.:
Staying Up When the Currency Goes Down

Cosmetics giant **Avon Products** is regularly exposed to foreign-currency crises because 66% of the company's sales occur outside the United States. As a result, the company has developed strategies for minimizing financial risk overseas.

To protect against volatile currencies, Avon tries to buy raw materials and make its products close to markets where they are sold. For instance, Avon replaced a European vendor with a local company for the lace it uses to make lingerie in Thailand.

Another key strategy is to sacrifice profit for market share. Avon is willing to trade short-term losses for long-term gains. Tactics for carrying out this strategy vary from market to market. In Russia, Avon quotes prices in "currency units" tied to the U.S. dollar. When the ruble drops, prices soar. Avon may leave prices alone but give customers a hefty discount on the conversion rate of rubles for dollars, thus giving customers the incentive to buy Avon products. In Mexico, Avon slows price increases for brands aimed at the poor and middle class. To keep margins intact, the company raises prices faster on premium brands that compete with expensive imports.

Source: Based on David Whitford, "A currency drowns—Can you stay afloat?" *Fortune,* March 1, 1999, pp. 229–235. Mel Mandell, "Asia: converting crisis to opportunity," *World Trade,* April 1998, pp. 36–39. Fred R. Bleakley, "How U.S. firm copes with Asia crisis—Avon moves to protect against volatile currencies," *Wall Street Journal,* December 26, 1997, p. A2.

International Accounting Standards

In this text, we focus on accounting principles that are generally accepted in the United States. Most accounting methods are consistent throughout the world. Double-entry, the accrual system, and the basic financial statements (balance sheet, income statement, and so on) are used worldwide. But some differences exist among countries, as shown in Exhibit 16-8.

Exhibit 16-8   **Some International Accounting Differences**

Country	Inventories	Goodwill	Research and Development Costs
United States	Specific unit cost, FIFO, LIFO, weighted-average.	Amortized over period not to exceed 40 years.	Expensed as incurred.
Germany	LIFO is unacceptable for tax purposes and is not widely used.	Amortized over 5 years.	Expensed as incurred.
Japan	Similar to U.S.	Amortized over 5 years.	May be capitalized and amortized over 5 years.
United Kingdom (Great Britain)	LIFO is unacceptable for tax purposes and is not widely used.	Amortized over useful life or not amortized if life is indefinite.*	Expense research costs. Some development costs may be capitalized.

638   * Proposal being considered.

In the United States, the depreciation method used for tax purposes can differ from the method used for reporting to shareholders. By contrast, in many countries tax reporting and shareholder reporting are identical. For example, France has a "Plan Compatible," which specifies that the same chart of accounts must be used for both tax returns and reporting to shareholders. German accounting is also influenced by tax laws. Despite the common heritage of the United States and the United Kingdom, U.S. and British accounting practices vary widely. For example, LIFO is not widely used in Great Britain.

A company that sells its stock on a stock exchange must follow the accounting principles of that country. For example, **British Petroleum-Amoco (BP)** stock is traded on the New York Stock Exchange, so BP follows American GAAP for financial statements issued in the United States. **Infosys Technology** is an Indian company that sells its stock in the United States. Infosys therefore prepares U.S.-type financial statements, as does **Nokia,** which is based in Finland.

Several organizations seek worldwide harmony of accounting standards. The International Accounting Standards Committee (IASC) is headquartered in London and operates much as the Financial Accounting Standards Board in the United States. It has the support of the accounting professions in the United States, most of the British Commonwealth countries, Japan, France, Germany, the Netherlands, and Mexico. However, the IASC has no authority to require compliance and must rely on cooperation by the various national accounting professions.

 DAILY EXERCISE 16-20

Reporting Comprehensive Income

We introduced comprehensive income in Chapter 14 as required by *FASB Statement 130.* ➡ The coverage of accounting for available-for-sale investments and international operations in this chapter completes the discussion of comprehensive income. Recall that *other comprehensive income* can be reported below net income on the income statement. One of the elements of other comprehensive income is the unrealized gain or loss on available-for-sale investments. Exhibit 16-9 illustrates how to report other comprehensive income, using assumed amounts for the first year of the company.

◄ See Chapter 14, page 558, for reporting comprehensive income.

EXHIBIT 16-9
Comprehensive Income

PANEL A—Reporting Comprehensive Income

NATIONAL EXPRESS COMPANY
Income Statement
Year Ended December 31, 20X1

Revenues	$10,000
Expenses (summarized)	6,000
Net income	4,000
Other comprehensive income: Unrealized gain on available-for-sale investments	1,000
Comprehensive income	$ 5,000

PANEL B—Reporting Unrealized Gains (Losses) on Available-for-Sale Investments on the Balance Sheet

NATIONAL EXPRESS COMPANY
Balance Sheet (partial)
December 31, 20X1

Stockholders' Equity

Common stock	$ 3,000
Retained earnings	7,000
Accumulated other comprehensive income:	
Unrealized gain on available-for-sale investments	1,000
Total stockholders' equity	$11,000

DECISION GUIDELINES

Foreign-Currency, Comprehensive Income, and Statement of Cash Flows

DECISION	GUIDELINES
When to record a • Foreign-currency gain?	• When you receive foreign currency worth *more* in U.S. dollars than the amount of the receivable recorded earlier. • When you pay foreign currency that costs *less* in U.S. dollars than the amount of the payable recorded earlier.
• Foreign-currency loss?	• When you receive foreign currency worth *less* in U.S. dollars than the amount of the receivable recorded earlier. • When you pay foreign currency that costs *more* in U.S. dollars than the amount of the payable recorded earlier.
What are the elements of comprehensive income?	• Net income, plus other comprehensive income: Unrealized gains and losses on available-for-sale investments

REVIEW INVESTMENTS AND INTERNATIONAL OPERATIONS

www.prenhall.com/horngren

End-of-Chapter Assessment

SUMMARY PROBLEM

1. Journalize the following transactions of American Corp. Explanations are not required.

20X5
Nov. 16   Purchased equipment on account for 40,000 Swiss francs when the exchange rate was $0.63 per Swiss franc.
     27   Sold merchandise on account to a Belgian company for 700,000 Belgian francs. Each franc is worth $0.0305.
Dec. 22   Paid the Swiss company when the franc's exchange rate was $0.625.
     31   Adjusted for the change in the exchange rate of the Belgian franc. Its current exchange rate is $0.0301.

20X6
Jan.   4   Collected from the Belgian company. The exchange rate is $0.0307.

2. In the 20X5 transactions, identify each of the following currencies as strong or weak:
a. Swiss franc   **b.** Belgian franc   **c.** U.S. dollar
Which currency strengthened during 20X6? Which currency weakened during 20X6?

Solution

1. Entries for transactions stated in foreign currencies:

20X5				
Nov. 16	Equipment (40,000 × $0.63)	25,200	
	Accounts Payable		25,200
27	Accounts Receivable (700,000 × $0.0305)	21,350	
	Sales Revenue		21,350
Dec. 22	Accounts Payable	25,200	
	Cash (40,000 × $0.625)...............................		25,000
	Foreign-Currency Gain		200
31	Foreign-Currency Loss		
	[700,000 × ($0.0305 − $0.0301)]	280	
	Accounts Receivable		280

LESSONS LEARNED

1. *Account for trading investments. Trading investments* are those the investor expects to sell within a few months. Therefore, trading investments are reported at current market value among current assets.

2. *Account for available-for-sale investments. Available-for-sale investments* are all stock investments other than trading securities. Most are classified as long-term investments and reported at current *market value.*

3. *Use the equity method for investments.* The *equity method* is used for 20–50% stock investments. To measure investment revenue, the investor applies its percentage of ownership to the investee's net income. Equity-method investment revenue is reported as Other revenues on the income statement.

4. *Understand consolidated financial statements.* Ownership of more than 50% of a company's voting stock creates a *parent-subsidiary* relationship, and the parent company uses the *consolidation method* to account for subsidiaries.

The subsidiary's financial statements are included in the parent's consolidated financial statements.

5. *Account for long-term investments in bonds. Held-to-maturity investments* are bonds the investor intends to hold until maturity. The *amortized-cost method* is used to account for held-to-maturity investments. Interest receivable is accrued and bond discount or premium is amortized. Long-term bond investments appear on the balance sheet after current assets; interest revenue from the investments appears on the income statement.

6. *Account for transactions stated in a foreign currency.* When foreign currency is involved in a transaction, there may be a gain or loss on the foreign currency. These gains and losses are reported on the income statement as Other gains (losses). To protect against foreign-currency losses, companies engage in *hedging*—they protect themselves from losing money by engaging in a counterbalancing transaction.

ACCOUNTING VOCABULARY

available-for-sale investments (p. 624)
consolidated statements (p. 631)
controlling interest (p. 630)
equity method for investments (p. 628)
foreign-currency exchange rate (p. 635)

hedging (p. 637)
held-to-maturity investments (p. 632)
long-term investment (p. 623)
majority interest (p. 630)
marketable security (p. 623)
market-value method for investments (p. 686)
minority interest (p. 631)

parent company (p. 630)
short-term investment (p. 623)
strong currency (p. 635)
subsidiary company (p. 630)
trading investments (p. 624)
weak currency (p. 635)

QUESTIONS

1. How are stock prices quoted in the securities market? What is the investor's cost of 1,000 shares of Ford Motor Company stock at 55.75?

2. Outline the accounting methods for the different types of investments.

3. How does an investor record the receipt of a cash dividend on an available-for-sale investment? How does this investor record receipt of a stock dividend?

4. An investor paid $11,000 for 1,000 shares of stock—a trading investment—and later received a 10% stock dividend. At December 31, the investment's market value is $11,800. Compute the gain or loss on the investment.

5. When is an investment accounted for by the equity method? Outline how to apply the equity method to purchase of the investment, the investor's proportion of the investee's net income, and receipt of a cash dividend from the investee.

6. Name the account that expresses the excess of the cost of an investment over the market value of the subsidiary's

owners' equity. What type of account is this, and where in the financial statements is it reported?

7. When a parent company buys more than 50% but less than 100% of a subsidiary's stock, a new item appears on the balance sheet. What is this category called, and under what heading do most companies report it?

8. An investor purchases Texaco bonds as a long-term investment. Suppose the face amount of the bonds is $100,000 and the purchase price is 101.3. The bonds pay interest at the stated annual rate of 8%. How much did the investor pay for the bonds? How much principal will the investor collect at maturity?

9. Buying and selling transactions stated in a foreign currency create a new complexity. What is this complexity, and what new risk does it carry?

10. What is a foreign-currency hedge? Why do companies hedge their foreign-currency transactions? State how a company with both foreign-currency receivables and payables can create a foreign-currency hedge.

11. McVey, Inc., purchased inventory from a French company, agreeing to pay 100,000 francs. On the purchase date, the franc was quoted at $0.17. When McVey paid the debt, the price of a franc was $0.18. What account does McVey debit for the $1,000 difference between the cost of the inventory and the amount of cash paid?

12. Which country does not allow the use of the LIFO method for inventories?

ASSESS YOUR PROGRESS

DAILY EXERCISES

Computing the cost of a stock investment
(Obj. 1, 2)

DE16-1 Compute the cost of each investment. Carry final figures to the nearest cent.

   a. 200 shares of **Nokia** stock at 85.38.
   b. 450 shares of **IBM** stock at 99.81. IBM pays a cash dividend of $0.52 per year.
   c. 8,000 shares of **Nike** stock at 46.50.
   d. 70 shares of **Target** stock at 52.75.

Classifying investments as current or long-term
(Obj. 1, 2)

DE16-2 ◄ *Link Back to Chapter 4 (Current Assets).* Answer these questions about the investments held by **AOL Time Warner Corporation.**

   1. Why is a trading investment always a current asset? Explain.
   2. Is an available-for-sale investment a current asset or a long-term asset? What is the deciding factor?

Classifying investments as trading or available-for-sale
(Obj. 1, 2)

DE16-3 Marquette Corp. reports its annual financial statements on June 30 each year. Marquette purchased 100 shares of stock in each of three companies:

   a. Investment in **Dell Computer** to be sold within the next 9–12 months.
   b. Investment in **AT&T** to be sold within the next 90 days.
   c. Investment in **eBay** to be sold within the next two years.

Classify each investment as (1) a current asset or a long-term asset, and (2) a trading investment or an available-for-sale investment.

Accounting for a trading investment
(Obj. 1)

DE16-4 Return to page 625, the example of **Intel Corporation's** short-term trading investment in **Ford Motor Company** stock.

   1. How much did Intel pay for the short-term investment in Ford stock? Stated differently, what was Intel's cost of the Ford stock?
   2. At December 31, 20X5, what was the current market value of Intel's short-term investment in Ford stock?
   3. Suppose the Ford stock had increased in value to $30,000 on December 31, 20X5. Give Intel's adjusting entry at December 31, and show how Intel would report the short-term investment on its balance sheet.

Accounting for a trading investment loss
(Obj. 1)

DE16-5 Dierberg Bank completed the following transactions during 20X1 and 20X2:

20X1
Dec. 6   Purchased 1,000 shares of **Toyota** stock at a price of $92.25 per share, intending to sell the investment next month.
     23   Received a cash dividend of $1.12 per share on the Toyota stock.
     31   Adjusted the investment to its market value of $91 per share.
20X2
Jan. 27   Sold the Toyota stock for $88.38 per share.

   1. Classify Dierberg's investment as trading or available-for-sale.
   2. Journalize Dierberg's investment transactions. Explanations are not required.

Accounting for a trading investment gain
(Obj. 1)

DE16-6 Vincent Marketing Associates completed the following investment transactions during 20X6 and 20X7:

20X6
Dec. 12   Purchased 500 shares of **MCI WorldCom** stock at a price of $41.13 per share, intending to sell the investment next month.
     21   Received a cash dividend of $0.23 per share on the MCI WorldCom stock.
     31   Adjusted the investment to its market value of $43.13 per share.
20X7
Jan. 16   Sold the MCI WorldCom stock for $44.50 per share.

   1. Classify Vincent's investment as trading or available-for-sale.
   2. Journalize Vincent's investment transactions. Explanations are not required.

DE16-7 Trilogy Corp. holds a significant portfolio of short-term investments. On November 19, 20X6, Trilogy purchased a trading investment for $85,000. At December 31, 20X6, the market value of the trading investment was $83,000. Trilogy sold the investment for $90,000 on January 6, 20X7.

Compute Trilogy's gains and losses for 20X6 and 20X7.

Measuring gains and losses on a trading investment (Obj. 1)

DE16-8 **BankOne** buys 500 shares of **Chevron** stock, paying $64 per share. Suppose Chevron distributes a 10% stock dividend. Later, BankOne sells the Chevron stock for $58 per share.

1. Compute BankOne's new cost per share after receiving the stock dividend.
2. Compute BankOne's gain or loss on the sale of this available-for-sale investment.

Measuring gain or loss on the sale of an investment after receiving a stock dividend (Obj. 2)

DE16-9 BLT Financial, Inc., completed these long-term available-for-sale investment transactions during 20X7:

20X7
Jan. 14   Purchased 300 shares of **PepsiCo** stock, paying $19.75 per share. BLT intends to hold the investment for the indefinite future.
Aug. 22   Received a cash dividend of $1.25 per share on the PepsiCo stock.
Dec. 31   Adjusted the PepsiCo investment to its current market value of $5,514.

1. Journalize BLT's investment transactions. Explanations are not required.
2. Show how to report the investment and any unrealized gain or loss on BLT's balance sheet at December 31, 20X7.

Accounting for an available-for-sale investment; unrealized loss (Obj. 2)

DE16-10 Use the data given in Daily Exercise 16-9. On August 4, 20X8, BLT Financial, Inc., sold its investment in **PepsiCo** stock for $20.75 per share.

1. Journalize the sale. No explanation is required.
2. How does the gain or loss that you recorded differ from the gain or loss that was recorded at December 31, 20X7?

Accounting for the sale of an available-for-sale investment (Obj. 2)

DE16-11 Suppose on January 6, 20X2, **General Motors** paid $100 million for its 40% investment in **Isuzu**. Assume Isuzu earned net income of $15 million and paid cash dividends of $10 million during 20X2.

1. What method should General Motors use to account for the investment in Isuzu? Give your reason.
2. Journalize these three transactions on the books of General Motors. Show all amounts in millions of dollars and include an explanation for each entry.
3. Post to the Long-Term Equity-Method Investment T-account. What is its balance after all the transactions are posted?

Accounting for a 40% investment in another company (Obj. 3)

DE16-12 Use the data given in Daily Exercise 16-11. Assume that early in January 20X3, General Motors sold half its investment in Isuzu to **Toyota Motor Corporation.** The sale price was $59 million. Compute General Motors' gain or loss on the sale.

Accounting for the sale of an equity-method investment (Obj. 3)

DE16-13 Answer these questions about consolidation accounting:

1. Define a parent company. Define a subsidiary company.
2. Which company's name appears on the consolidated financial statements? How much of the subsidiary's stock must the parent own before reporting consolidated statements?
3. How do consolidated financial statements differ from the financial statements of a single company?

Understanding consolidated financial statements (Obj. 4)

DE16-14 Two accounts that arise from consolidation accounting are minority interest and goodwill.

1. What is minority interest, and which company reports it, the parent or the subsidiary? Where is minority interest reported?
2. What is goodwill, and how does it arise? Which company reports goodwill, the parent or the subsidiary? Where is goodwill reported?

Understanding goodwill and minority interest (Obj. 4)

DE16-15 **Edward Jones & Co.** owns vast amounts of corporate bonds. Suppose Edward Jones buys $1,500,000 of **MCI WorldCom** bonds at a price of 96. The MCI WorldCom bonds pay cash interest at the annual rate of 7% and mature within five years.

1. How much did Edward Jones pay to purchase the bond investment? How much will Edward Jones collect when the bond investment matures?
2. How much cash interest will Edward Jones receive each year from MCI WorldCom?
3. Will Edward Jones' annual interest revenue on the bond investment be more or less than the amount of cash interest received each year? Give your reason.
4. Compute Edward Jones' annual interest revenue on this bond investment. Use the straight-line method to amortize the discount on the investment.

Working with a bond investment (Obj. 5)

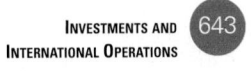

DE16-16 Return to Daily Exercise 16-15, the Edward Jones investment in **MCI WorldCom** bonds. Journalize on Edward Jones' books:

a. Purchase of the bond investment on January 2, 20X1. Edward Jones expects to hold the investment to maturity.
b. Receipt of annual cash interest on December 31, 20X1.
c. Amortization of discount on December 31, 20X1.
d. Collection of the investment's face value at the maturity date on January 2, 20X6. (Assume the receipt of 20X5 interest and amortization of discount for 20X5 have already been recorded, so you may ignore these entries.)

Recording bond investment transactions
(Obj. 5)

DE16-17 Return to the bond investment situation on page 632. Assume the investor purchased the **CBS** bond investment on June 1, 20X2, and intends to hold the bonds until maturity on June 1, 20X6. For this Daily Exercise, assume that CBS pays cash interest on June 1 and December 1 each year, rather than on April 1 and October 1 (as on page 632).

The investor made all entries as needed on December 1. Now journalize the investor's accrual of cash interest and amortization of discount on the investment at December 31, 20X2. Use the straight-line amortization method.

Recording interest revenue on a bond investment
(Obj. 5)

DE16-18 Suppose **Nike Incorporated** sells athletic shoes to a Russian company on March 14. Nike agrees to accept 2,000,000 Russian rubles. On the date of sale, the ruble is quoted at $0.036. Nike collects half the receivable on April 19, when the ruble is worth $0.034. Then, on May 10, when the price of the ruble is $0.037, Nike collects the final amount.

Journalize these three transactions for Nike. Overall, how well did Nike come out in terms of a net foreign-currency gain or loss?

Accounting for transactions stated in a foreign currency
(Obj. 6)

DE16-19 Page 636 includes a sequence of **Shipp Belting** journal entries for transactions denominated in Mexican pesos. Suppose the foreign-exchange rate for a peso is $0.118 on July 2. Record Shipp Belting's collection of cash on July 2.

On page 636, Shipp Belting buys inventory for which Shipp must pay Swiss francs. Suppose a Swiss franc costs $0.82 on August 24. Record Shipp Belting's payment of cash on August 24.

Accounting for transactions stated in a foreign currency
(Obj. 6)

DE16-20 Exhibit 16-8, page 638, outlines some differences between accounting in the United States and accounting in other countries. American companies transact more business with British companies than with any other. Contrary to what you might expect, there are several important differences between American and British accounting. In your own words, describe those differences for inventories, goodwill, and research and development.

International accounting differences
(Obj. 6)

EXERCISES

E16-1 **Nations Bank,** headquartered in Charlotte, North Carolina, holds huge portfolios of investments. Suppose Nations Bank completed the following investment transactions:

Accounting for a trading investment
(Obj. 1)

20X1
Dec. 6 Purchased 1,000 shares of **Goodyear Tire & Rubber Co.** stock for $70,000. Nations Bank plans to sell the stock at a profit next month.
    30 Received a quarterly cash dividend of $0.85 per share on the Goodyear stock.
    31 Adjusted the investment in Goodyear stock. Current market value is $67,000, and Nations Bank plans to sell the stock early in 20X2.
20X2
Jan. 14 Sold the Goodyear stock for $71,000.

Required

1. Journalize the Nations Bank investment transactions. Explanations are not required.
2. Show how Nations Bank would report its investment in the Goodyear stock on the balance sheet at December 31, 20X1.

E16-2 Journalize the following long-term available-for-sale investment transactions of Abbey-Simms Inc. Explanations are not required.

Journalizing transactions for an available-for-sale investment
(Obj. 2)

a. Purchased 400 shares (8%) of Marcor Corporation common stock at $38 per share, with the intent of holding the stock for the indefinite future.
b. Received cash dividend of $1 per share on the Marcor investment.
c. At year end, adjusted the investment account to current market value of $45 per share.
d. Sold the Marcor stock for the market price of $42 per share.

E16-3 Journalize the following investment transactions of Vemcor Manufacturing, Inc.:

Journalizing transactions for an available-for-sale investment
(Obj. 2)

Aug. 1 Purchased 500 shares (2%) of Vardaman Corporation common stock as a long-term available-for-sale investment, paying $44 per share.
Sep. 12 Received cash dividend of $1 per share on the Vardaman investment.
Nov. 23 Received 250 shares of Vardaman common stock in a 50% stock dividend. Round new cost per share to three decimal places.
Dec. 4 Unexpectedly sold the Vardaman stock for $29 per share.

E16-4 Late in the current year, Travel Consumer Corporation bought 3,000 shares of **National Geographic** common stock at $81.88, 600 shares of **AT&T Corp.** stock at $46.75, and 1,400 shares of **Hitachi** stock at $79—all as available-for-sale investments. At December 31, the *Wall Street Journal* reports National Geographic stock at $80.38, AT&T at $48.50, and Hitachi at $68.25.

Accounting for long-term investment transactions (Obj. 2)

Required

1. Determine the cost and the market value of the long-term investment portfolio at December 31.
2. Record any adjusting entry needed at December 31.
3. What two items would Travel Consumer Corporation report on its balance sheet for the information given? Make the necessary disclosures.

E16-5 Suppose **Dillard's, Inc.,** owns equity-method investments in several other department-store companies. Suppose Dillard's paid $2 million to acquire a 25% investment in Italian Imports Company. Assume that Italian Imports Company reported net income of $780,000 for the first year and declared and paid cash dividends of $500,000. Record the following in Dillard's journal: (a) purchase of the investment, (b) its proportion of Italian Imports' net income, and (c) receipt of the cash dividends.

Accounting for transactions under the equity method (Obj. 3)

E16-6 Without making journal entries, record the transactions of Exercise 16-5 directly in the **Dillard's** account, Long-Term Equity-Method Investment in Italian Imports. Assume that after all the noted transactions took place, Dillard's sold its entire investment in Italian Imports for cash of $2,600,000. How much is Dillard's gain or loss on the sale of the investment?

Measuring gain or loss on the sale of an equity-method investment (Obj. 3)

E16-7 Precision Automotive Parts paid $145,000 for a 40% investment in the common stock of Auto Chief, Inc. For the first year, Auto Chief reported net income of $84,000 and at year end declared and paid cash dividends of $16,000. On the balance sheet date, the market value of Precision's investment in Auto Chief stock was $134,000.

Applying the appropriate accounting method for investments (Obj. 3)

Required

1. Which method is appropriate for Precision Automotive to use in accounting for its investment in Auto Chief? Why?
2. Show everything that Precision would report for the investment and any investment revenue in its year-end financial statements.
3. What role does the market value of the investment play in this situation?

E16-8 On March 31, 20X3, Remke Corporation paid 92 1/4 for 7% bonds of **Dean Witter Financial Services** as a long-term held-to-maturity investment. The maturity value of the bonds will be $30,000 on September 30, 20X7. The bonds pay interest on March 31 and September 30. At December 31, the bonds' market value is 93.

Recording bond investment transactions (Obj. 5)

Required

1. What method should Remke Corporation use to account for its investment in the Dean Witter bonds?
2. Using the straight-line method of amortizing the discount, journalize all of Remke Corporation's transactions on the bonds for 20X3.
3. Show how Remke would report the bond investment on its balance sheet at December 31, 20X3.

E16-9 Journalize the following foreign-currency transactions. Explanations are not required.

Managing and accounting for foreign-currency transactions (Obj. 6)

Nov. 17 Purchased inventory on account from a Japanese company. The price was 200,000 yen, and the exchange rate of the yen was $0.0088.

Dec. 16 Paid the Japanese supplier when the exchange rate was $0.0091.

   19 Sold merchandise on account to a French company at a price of 60,000 French francs. The exchange rate of the franc was $0.15.

   30 Collected from the French company when the exchange rate was $0.17.

On November 18, immediately after your purchase, and on December 20, immediately after your sale, which currencies did you want to strengthen? Which currencies did in fact strengthen? Explain your reasoning in detail.

Challenge Exercises

E16-10 **AMP Incorporated,** a world leader in the manufacture of electronic connection devices, reported the stockholders' equity on its balance sheet on page 646, as adapted, at December 31.

Analyzing available-for-sale investments (Obj. 2)

Required

1. AMP's balance sheet also reports available-for-sale investments at $288 million. What was AMP's cost of the investments? What was the market value of the investments on December 31, 19X9?
2. Suppose AMP sold its available-for-sale investments in 20X0 for $259 million. Determine the gain or loss on sale of the investments.

AMP INCORPORATED Balance Sheet (partial, adapted)	
Millions	**19X9**
Shareholders' Equity:	
Common stock	$ 12
Other capital..	214
Unrealized gains on available-for-sale investments	22
Retained earnings...	2,330
Treasury stock, at cost	(243)
Total shareholders' equity	$2,335

*Analyzing equity-method
investments
(Obj. 3)*

E16-11 **Whirlpool Corporation** is a leading manufacturer of household appliances. In Brazil and Mexico, Whirlpool operates through affiliated companies, whose stock Whirlpool owns in various percentages between 20% and 50%. Whirlpool's financial statements reported these items (adapted):

	Millions	
	19X9	**19X8**
Balance Sheet (adapted)		
Equity-method investments...	$296	$286
Income Statement		
Equity-method investments revenue (losses)	(13)	4

Whirlpool's financial statements reported no sales of equity-method investments during 19X9 or 19X8. During 19X9, Whirlpool paid $42 million to purchase equity-method investments.

Required

Prepare a T-account for Equity-Method Investments to determine the amount of dividends Whirlpool Corporation received from investee companies during 19X9. Show your work.

(Group A) PROBLEMS

*Accounting for trading
investments
(Obj. 1)*

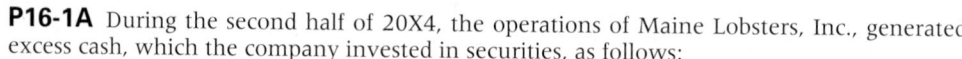

P16-1A During the second half of 20X4, the operations of Maine Lobsters, Inc., generated excess cash, which the company invested in securities, as follows:

July 2	Purchased 3,500 shares of common stock as a trading investment, paying $12.75 per share.
Aug. 21	Received semiannual cash dividend of $0.45 per share on the trading investment.
Sep. 16	Sold the trading investment for $13.50 per share.
Oct. 8	Purchased trading investments in stock for $136,000.
Dec. 31	Adjusted the trading securities to their market value of $130,000.

Required

1. Record the transactions in the journal of Maine Lobsters, Inc. Explanations are not required.
2. Post to the Short-Term Investments account, and show how to report the short-term investments on Maine Lobster's balance sheet at December 31.

*Accounting for available-for-sale
and equity-method investments
(Obj. 2, 3)*

P16-2A The beginning balance sheet of Quill.com, Inc., included the following:

Long-Term Equity-Method Investments.................. $657,000

During the year the company completed the following investment transactions:

Mar. 3	Purchased 5,000 shares of LBO Software common stock as a long-term available-for-sale investment, paying $9.25 per share.
4	Purchased new long-term equity-method investment at cost of $408,000.
May 14	Received cash dividend of $0.82 per share on the LBO investment.
June 15	Received cash dividend of $27,000 from equity-method investment.
Oct. 24	Purchased long-term available-for-sale investment in Eastern Communication stock for $226,000.
Dec. 15	Received cash dividend of $31,000 from equity-method investment.
31	Received annual reports from equity-method investee companies. Their total net income for the year was $620,000. Of this amount, Quill.com's proportion is 25%.
31	Adjusted the available-for-sale investments to market value. The market values of Quill.com's investments are LBO, $49,100; Eastern, $221,000.

Required

1. Record the transactions in the journal of Quill.com, Inc.
2. Post entries to the Long-Term Equity-Method Investments T-account, and determine its balance at December 31. Do likewise for the Long-Term Available-for-Sale Investments T-account and the Allowance to Adjust Investments to Market T-account.
3. Show how to report the Long-Term Available-for-Sale Investments and the Long-Term Equity-Method Investments on Quill.com's balance sheet at December 31.

P16-3A Orly Chemical Company owns stock in numerous other companies. During 20X4, Orly completed the following long-term investment transactions:

Reporting investments on the balance sheet and the related revenue on the income statement
(Obj. 2, 3)

20X4

May 1	Purchased 8,000 shares, which exceeds 20%, of the common stock of DeGaulle Company at total cost of $720,000.
July 1	Purchased 2,000 additional shares of DeGaulle common stock at cost of $140,000.
Sep. 15	Received semiannual cash dividend of $4.40 per share on the DeGaulle investment.
Oct. 12	Purchased 1,000 shares of TEC Corporation common stock as an available-for-sale investment paying $22.50 per share.
Dec. 14	Received semiannual cash dividend of $0.75 per share on the TEC investment.
Dec. 31	Received annual report from DeGaulle Company. Net income for the year was $360,000. Of this amount, Orly's proportion is one third.

The current market value of the TEC stock is $19,400. The market value of the DeGaulle stock is $965,000.

Required

1. For which investment is current market value used in the accounting? Why is market value used for one investment and not the other?
2. Show what Orly Chemical Company would report on its year-end balance sheet for these investments. (It is helpful to use a T-account for the investment in DeGaulle stock.)

P16-4A Financial institutions hold large quantities of bond investments. Suppose **Goldman Sachs** purchases $800,000 of 8% bonds of **Xerox Corporation** for 92 on January 31, 20X0. These bonds pay interest on January 31 and July 31 each year. They mature on July 31, 20X8.

Accounting for a bond investment; amortizing discount by the straight-line method
(Obj. 5)

Required

1. Journalize Goldman Sachs' purchase of the bonds as a long-term investment on January 31, 20X0 (to be held to maturity), receipt of cash interest and amortization of discount on July 31, 20X0, and accrual of interest revenue and amortization of discount at December 31, 20X0. The straight-line method is appropriate for amortizing discount.
2. Show how to report this long-term bond investment on Goldman Sachs' balance sheet at December 31, 20X0.

P16-5A ◄ *Link Back to Chapter 15 (Effective-Interest Amortization of Discount)*. On December 31, 20X1, when the market interest rate is 10%, an investor purchases $400,000 of Yuma Inc., 9.5%, ten-year bonds at issuance. The cost of this bond investment was $387,578 and the investor expects to hold the investment to maturity.

Accounting for a bond investment; amortizing discount by the effective-interest method
(Obj. 5)

Required

Journalize the purchase on December 31, 20X1, the first semiannual interest receipt on June 30, 20X2, and the year-end interest receipt on December 31, 20X2. The investor uses the effective-interest amortization method. Prepare a schedule for amortizing the discount on the bond investment through December 31, 20X2. Use Exhibit 15-4, as a guide.

P16-6A Suppose **Gap, Inc.,** completed the following transactions:

Recording foreign-currency transactions and reporting the transaction gain or loss
(Obj. 6)

May 4	Sold clothing on account to a Mexican department store for $71,000. The exchange rate of the Mexican peso is $0.141, and the customer agrees to pay in dollars.
13	Purchased inventory on account from a Canadian company at a price of Canadian $65,000. The exchange rate of the Canadian dollar is $0.75, and payment will be in Canadian dollars.
20	Sold goods on account to an English firm for 89,000 British pounds. Payment will be in pounds, and the exchange rate of the pound is $1.50.
27	Collected from the Mexican company.
June 21	Paid the Canadian company. The exchange rate of the Canadian dollar is $0.72.
July 17	Collected from the English firm. The exchange rate of the British pound is $1.47.

Required

1. Record these transactions in Gap's journal, and show how to report the net foreign-currency gain or loss on the income statement. Explanations are not required.
2. How will what you learned in this problem help you structure international transactions?

Accounting for trading investments (Obj. 1)

P16-1B During the second half of 20X2, the operations of Regency Systems generated excess cash, which the company invested in securities, as follows:

July 3	Purchased 3,000 shares of common stock as a trading investment, paying $9.25 per share.
Aug. 14	Received semiannual cash dividend of $0.32 per share on the trading investment.
Sep. 15	Sold the trading investment for $10.50 per share.
Nov. 24	Purchased trading investments for $226,000.
Dec. 31	Adjusted the trading securities to their market value of $221,000.

Required

1. Record the transactions in the journal of Regency Systems. Explanations are not required.
2. Post to the Short-Term Investment account. Then show how to report the short-term investment on the Regency Systems balance sheet at December 31.

Accounting for available-for-sale and equity-method investments (Obj. 2, 3)

P16-2B The beginning balance sheet of TalkNET On-line Incorporated included the following:

Long-Term Equity-Method Investments.............. $344,000

During the year, the company completed the following investment transactions:

Mar. 2	Purchased 2,000 shares of DLV Inc., common stock as a long-term available-for-sale investment, paying $12.25 per share.
5	Purchased new long-term equity-method investment at cost of $540,000.
Apr. 21	Received cash dividend of $0.75 per share on the DLV investment.
May 17	Received cash dividend of $47,000 from the equity-method investment.
Oct. 8	Purchased long-term available-for-sale investment in Blinn Corp. stock for $136,000.
17	Received cash dividend of $49,000 from the equity-method investment.
Dec. 31	Received annual reports from the equity-method investee companies. Their total net income for the year was $550,000. Of this amount, TalkNET On-line's proportion is 33%.
31	Adjusted the available-for-sale investments to market value. The market values of TalkNET On-line's investments are DLV, $26,800; Blinn, $134,400.

Required

1. Record the transactions in the journal of TalkNET On-line Incorporated.
2. Post entries to the Long-Term Equity-Method Investments T-account, and determine its balance at December 31. Do likewise for the Long-Term Available-for-Sale Investments T-account and the Allowance to Adjust Investments to Market T-account.
3. Show how to report the Long-Term Available-for-Sale Investments and the Long-Term Equity-Method Investments accounts on TalkNET On-line's balance sheet at December 31.

Reporting investments on the balance sheet and the related revenue on the income statement (Obj. 2, 3)

P16-3B Steinway Company owns numerous investments in the stock of other companies. Assume that Steinway completed the following long-term investment transactions:

20X2

Feb. 12	Purchased 20,000 shares, which exceeds 20%, of the common stock of Growtech, Inc., at total cost of $715,000.
July 1	Purchased 8,000 additional shares of Growtech common stock at cost of $300,000.
Aug. 9	Received annual cash dividend of $0.90 per share on the Growtech investment.
Oct. 16	Purchased 950 shares of Varnix Company common stock as an available-for-sale investment, paying $41.50 per share.
Nov. 30	Received semiannual cash dividend of $0.60 per share on the Varnix investment.
Dec. 31	Received annual report from Growtech, Inc. Net income for the year was $510,000. Of this amount, Steinway's proportion is 30%.

The current market value of the Varnix stock is $41,100. The market value of the Growtech stock is $967,000.

Required

1. For which investment is current market value used in the accounting? Why is market value used for one investment and not the other?
2. Show what Steinway Company would report on its year-end balance sheet for these investments. It is helpful to use a T-account for the investment in Growtech stock.

P16-4B Financial institutions such as insurance companies hold large quantities of bond investments. Suppose Bastrop Insurance Co. purchases $400,000 of 9% bonds of Inwood Corporation for 103 on March 1, 20X1. These bonds pay interest on March 1 and September 1 each year. They mature on March 1, 20X8.

Accounting for a bond investment; straight-line amortization of premium
(Obj. 5)

Required

1. Journalize Bastrop's purchase of the bonds as a long-term investment on March 1, 20X1 (to be held to maturity). Then record Bastrop's receipt of cash interest and amortization of premium at September 1, 20X1, and the amortization of premium and accrual of interest revenue at December 31, 20X1. The straight-line method is appropriate for amortizing premium.
2. Show how to report this long-term bond investment on Bastrop Insurance Co.'s balance sheet at December 31, 20X1.

P16-5B ← *Link Back to Chapter 15 (Effective-Interest Amortization of Discount).* On December 31, 20X1, when the market interest is 8%, ChaseBank purchases $500,000 of **Michelin Corp.**, 7.4%, six-year bonds at issuance. The cost of this long-term bond investment is $486,123, and ChaseBank expects to hold the investment to maturity.

Accounting for a bond investment; effective-interest amortization of discount
(Obj. 5)

Required

Journalize the purchase on December 31, 20X1, the first semiannual interest receipt on June 30, 20X2, and the year-end interest receipt on December 31, 20X2. ChaseBank uses the effective-interest amortization method. Prepare a schedule for amortizing the discount on bond investment through December 31, 20X2. Use Exhibit 15-4 as a guide.

P16-6B Manifesto Publishing Company completed the following transactions:

Recording foreign-currency transactions and reporting the transaction gain or loss
(Obj. 6)

May 1	Sold inventory on account to Marconi Telegraph, an Italian public utility, for $19,000. The exchange rate of the Italian lira is $0.0007, and Marconi agrees to pay in dollars.
10	Purchased supplies on account from a Canadian company at a price of Canadian $38,000. The exchange rate of the Canadian dollar is $0.80, and payment will be in Canadian dollars.
17	Sold inventory on account to an English firm for 112,000 British pounds. Payment will be in pounds, and the exchange rate of the pound is $1.50.
22	Collected from Marconi Telegraph.
June 18	Paid the Canadian company. The exchange rate of the Canadian dollar is $0.77.
24	Collected from the English firm. The exchange rate of the British pound is $1.47.

Required

1. Record these transactions in Manifesto Publishing's journal, and show how to report the net foreign-currency gain or loss on the income statement. Explanations are not required.
2. How will what you learned in this problem help you structure international transactions?

APPLY YOUR KNOWLEDGE

DECISION CASES

Case 1. Carla Allman is the manager of Stagg Corp., whose year end is December 31. The company made two investments during the first week of January 20X2. Both investments are to be held for the indefinite future. Information about the investments follows:

Explaining the market value and equity methods of accounting for investments
(Obj. 1, 2)

a. Stagg purchased 30% of the common stock of Frontenac Mfg. Co. for its book value of $250,000. During the year ended December 31, 20X2, Frontenac earned $146,000 and paid dividends totaling $53,000. At year end, the market value of the Frontenac investment is $261,000.
b. One thousand shares of the common stock of St. John Medical Corporation were purchased as an available-for-sale investment for $95,000. During the year ended December 31, 20X2, St. John paid Stagg a dividend of $3,000. St. John earned a profit of $317,000 for that period, and at year end, the market value of Stagg's investment in St. John stock was $92,000.

Allman has come to you to ask how to account for the investments. Stagg has never had such investments before. Explain the proper accounting to her by indicating that different accounting methods apply to different situations.

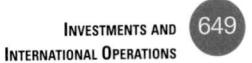

Help Allman understand by writing a memo to

1. Describe the methods of accounting applicable to these investments.
2. Identify which method should be used to account for the investments in Frontenac Mfg. Co. and St. John Medical Corporation. Also indicate the dollar amount to report for each investment on the year-end balance sheet.

Understanding the consolidation method for investments (Obj. 4)

Case 2. Caesar Saled inherited some investments, and he has received the annual reports of the companies. The financial statements of the companies are puzzling to Saled, and he asks you the following questions:

1. The companies label their financial statements as *consolidated* balance sheet, *consolidated* income statement, and so on. What are consolidated financial statements?
2. The consolidated balance sheet lists the asset Goodwill. What is goodwill? Does the presence of goodwill mean that the company's stock has increased in value?

Write a memo to answer each of Saled's questions.

ETHICAL ISSUE

Blaze Utilities owns 18% of the voting stock of Southwest Electric Power Company. The remainder of the Southwest stock is held by numerous investors with small holdings. Dee Falco, president of Blaze Utilities and a member of Southwest's board of directors, heavily influences Southwest Electric Power Company's policies.

Under the market-value method of accounting for investments, Blaze's net income increases as it receives dividend revenue from Southwest Power. Blaze Utilities pays President Falco a bonus computed as a percentage of Blaze's net income. Therefore, Falco can control her personal bonus to a certain extent by influencing Southwest's dividends.

A recession occurs in 20X0 and Blaze Utilities' income is low. Falco uses her power as a board member to have Southwest pay a large cash dividend. The action requires Southwest to borrow in order to pay the dividend.

Required

1. In getting Southwest to pay the large cash dividend, is Falco acting within her authority as a member of the Southwest board of directors? Are Falco's actions ethical? Whom can her actions harm?
2. Discuss how using the equity method of accounting for investments would decrease Falco's potential for manipulating her bonus.

FINANCIAL STATEMENT CASE

Investments in stock (Obj. 3, 4)

Obtain the annual report of a company of your choosing. Answer the following questions about the company. Concentrate on the current year in the annual report you select.

Required

1. Many companies refer to other companies in which they own equity-method investments as *affiliated companies*. This signifies the close relationship between the two entities even though the investor does not own a controlling interest.

   Does the company have equity-method investments? Cite the evidence. If present, what were the balances in the investment account at the beginning and the end of the current year? If the company has no equity-method investments, continue searching until you find a company with equity-method investments.

2. Scan the income statement. If equity-method investments are present, what amount of revenue (or income) did the company earn on the investments during the current year?

TEAM PROJECT

Pick a stock from the *Wall Street Journal* or other database or publication. Assume that your group purchases 1,000 shares of the stock as a short-term trading investment. Research the stock in *Value Line, Moody's Investor Record,* or other source to determine whether the company pays cash dividends and, if so, how much and at what intervals.

1. Track the stock for a period assigned by your professor. Over the specified period, keep a daily record of the price of the stock to see how well your investment has performed. Each day, search the Corporate Dividend News in the *Wall Street Journal* to keep a record of any dividends you've received. End the period of your analysis with a month end, such as September 30 or December 31.

2. Journalize all transactions that you have experienced, including the investment purchase, dividends received (both cash dividends and stock dividends), any year-end adjustment required by the accounting method that is appropriate for your investment; and the sale of your investment two ways: at a gain; and at a loss. Assume you will prepare financial statements on the ending date of your study.

3. Show what you will report on your company's balance sheet, income statement, and statement of cash flows as a result of your investment transactions.

INTERNET EXERCISE

The Coca-Cola Company is the world's largest producer of soft-drink concentrates, syrups, and juices. Its soft-drink brands include Coke, Diet Coke, Cherry Coke, Sprite, and Nestea.

The Coca-Cola Company

1. Go to **http://www.cocacola.com** and click on *Investor Relations* followed by the *most recent annual report*. Click on *operations review* and use the pull-down menu to select *Worldwide Case Volume*. What percent of Coca-Cola's worldwide case volume is from outside of North America?

2. Click on *financials* and then use the pull-down menu to select the *Consolidated Financial Statements* or the *Notes to Consolidated Financial Statements* to answer the following questions:

   a. Refer to the "Consolidated Balance Sheets." How many accounts report amounts for marketable securities? Why? For the most recent year, what amount is reported for current marketable securities? Refer to Note 8: Financial Instruments. Of the amount reported for current marketable securities, how much is held in trading securities? Available-for-sale securities? Held-to-maturity securities?

   b. The equity method is used to account for how many different investments of The Coca-Cola Company? Refer to Note 2: Bottling Investments. The Coca-Cola Company owns approximately what percent of the outstanding common shares of Coca-Cola Enterprises Inc.? What type of business is Coca-Cola Enterprises Inc.?

   c. In 1999, did Coca-Cola report equity-method income or an equity-method loss? How much? What does the equity-method income or loss represent?

3. Refer to Note 1: Organization and Summary of Significant Accounting Policies. The Coca-Cola Company operates in how many countries worldwide? What companies are included in the consolidated financial statements? Which companies are accounted for using the equity method?

APPENDIX TO CHAPTER 16

PREPARING CONSOLIDATED FINANCIAL STATEMENTS

The preparation of consolidated financial statements includes summing the statement amounts (cash, receivables, inventory, and so on) of the parent company and its majority-owned subsidiaries. This appendix shows how the consolidation method works for the balance sheet. We illustrate two cases:

- Parent Company owns all of Subsidiary's Stock (called a wholly-owned subsidiary).
- Parent Company owns less than 100% of Subsidiary's Stock.

CONSOLIDATED BALANCE SHEET — PARENT CORPORATION OWNS ALL OF SUBSIDIARY'S STOCK

Suppose Parent Corporation has purchased all the outstanding common stock of Subsidiary Corporation at its book value of $150,000. In addition, Parent Corporation loaned Subsidiary Corporation $80,000. To record these transactions, Parent Corporation and Subsidiary Corporation would make the following entries:

Parent Corporation Books[1]		Subsidiary Corporation Books	
Investment in Subsidiary			
Corporation 150,000		No entry	
Cash................................	150,000		
Note Receivable from		Cash 80,000	
Subsidiary................................. 80,000		Note Payable to Parent ...	80,000
Cash................................	80,000		

Each legal entity keeps its own set of books. The consolidated entity does not maintain consolidated accounts. Instead, a work sheet is used to prepare the consolidated statements. (We will see two of these work sheets here.) A major concern in consolidation accounting is this: Do not double-count—that is, do not count the same item twice in a set of consolidated financial statements.

EXPLANATION OF ELIMINATION ENTRY (A)   Exhibit 16-A1 shows the work sheet for consolidating the balance sheet. Consider the elimination entry for the parent-subsidiary ownership accounts. Entry (a) credits the parent Investment account to eliminate its debit balance. It also eliminates the subsidiary stockholder's equity accounts by debiting Common Stock for $100,000 and Retained Earnings for $50,000. Because these accounts represent the same thing—Subsidiary's equity—they must be eliminated from the consolidated totals. If they are not, the same item would be counted twice.

The resulting consolidated balance sheet reports no Investment in Subsidiary account, and the consolidated totals for Common Stock and Retained Earnings are those of Parent Corporation only. The consolidated amounts appear in the final column of the consolidation work sheet.

EXPLANATION OF ELIMINATION ENTRY (B)   Parent Corporation loaned $80,000 to Subsidiary Corporation, and Subsidiary signed a note payable to Parent. Therefore, Parent's balance sheet includes an $80,000 note receivable, and Subsidiary's balance sheet reports a note payable for the same amount. The parent's receivable and the subsidiary's payable represent the same resources (all entirely within the consolidated entity) and so must be eliminated. Entry (b) accomplishes this. After this work sheet entry, the consolidated amount for notes receivable is zero. The $190,000 balance of Notes Payable is the amount that the Consolidated entity owes outsiders.

EXHIBIT 16-A1   Work Sheet for Consolidated Balance Sheet—Parent Corporation Owns All of Subsidiary's Stock

	Parent Corporation	Subsidiary Corporation	Eliminations		Consolidated Amounts
			Debit	Credit	
Assets					
Cash	12,000	18,000			30,000
Note receivable from Subsidiary...............	80,000	—		(b) 80,000	—
Inventory...	104,000	91,000			195,000
Investment in Subsidiary..........................	150,000	—		(a) 150,000	—
Other assets...	218,000	138,000			356,000
Total	564,000	247,000			581,000
Liabilities and Stockholders' Equity					
Accounts payable.....................................	43,000	17,000			60,000
Notes payable..	190,000	80,000	(b) 80,000		190,000
Common stock..	176,000	100,000	(a) 100,000		176,000
Retained earnings	155,000	50,000	(a) 50,000		155,000
Total	564,000	247,000	230,000	230,000	581,000

[1]The parent company may use either the cost method or the equity method for entries to the Investment account. Regardless of the method used, the consolidated statements are the same. Advanced accounting courses deal with this topic.

In summary, the elimination entries that we illustrate require, at most, four steps:

1. Eliminate intercompany receivables and payables.
2. Eliminate the stockholders' equity accounts of the subsidiary.
3. Eliminate the Investment in Subsidiary account.

APPENDIX PROBLEMS

P16-A1 ◄ *Link Back to Chapter 4 (Debt Ratio).* This problem demonstrates the dramatic effect that consolidation accounting can have on a company's ratios. **Ford Motor Company** (Ford) owns 100% of **Ford Motor Credit Corporation** (FMCC), its financing subsidiary. Ford's main operations consist of manufacturing automotive products. FMCC mainly helps people finance the purchase of automobiles from Ford and its dealers. The two companies' individual balance sheets are adapted and summarized as follows (amounts in billions):

Analyzing consolidated financial statements
(Obj. 3)

	Ford (Parent)	FMCC (Subsidiary)
Total assets	$89.6	$170.5
Total liabilities	$65.1	$156.9
Total stockholders' equity	24.5	13.6
Total liabilities and equity..............	$89.6	$170.5

Assume that FMCC's liabilities include $8.1 billion owed to Ford, the parent company.

Required

1. Compute the debt ratio of Ford Motor Company considered alone.
2. Determine the consolidated total assets, total liabilities, and stockholders' equity of Ford Motor Company after consolidating the financial statements of FMCC into the totals of Ford, the parent company. Remember to eliminate the subsidiary's stockholders' equity.
3. Recompute the debt ratio of the consolidated entity. Explain why it took an FASB statement to get companies to consolidate their financing subsidiaries into their own financial statements.

P16-A2 Darnell Air Corp. paid $289,000 to acquire all the common stock of Royal Dutch, Inc., and Royal Dutch owes Darnell Air $81,000 on a note payable. Immediately after the purchase on June 30, 20X3, the two companies' balance sheets were as follows:

Consolidating a wholly-owned subsidiary

	Darnell Air Corp.	Royal Dutch, Inc.
Assets		
Cash	$ 24,000	$ 20,000
Accounts receivable, net.............................	91,000	65,000
Note receivable from Royal Dutch..............	81,000	—
Inventory	145,000	214,000
Investment in Royal Dutch........................	289,000	—
Plant assets, net..	178,000	219,000
Total	$808,000	$518,000
Liabilities and Stockholders' Equity		
Accounts payable..	$ 57,000	$ 49,000
Notes payable..	177,000	149,000
Other liabilities...	129,000	31,000
Common stock...	297,000	173,000
Retained earnings	148,000	116,000
Total	$808,000	$518,000

Required

Prepare the consolidated balance sheet for Darnell Air Corp. (It is sufficient to complete a consolidation work sheet.)

17

The Statement of Cash Flows

DRKOOP.COM, INC.
Statement of Cash Flows (Adapted)
Year Ended December 31, 1999

	Thousands
Cash flows from *operating* activities:	
1 Cash receipts from customers	$13,356
2 Cash receipts from interest revenue	1,344
3 Cash payments to suppliers and employees	(72,871)
4 Other, net	5,497
5 Net cash inflow (outflow) from operating activities	(52,674)
Cash flows from *investing* activities:	
6 Purchase of property and equipment	$(9,726)
7 Net cash inflow (outflow) from investing activities	(9,726)
Cash flows from *financing* activities:	
8 New borrowing—issuing notes payable	$ 5,775
9 Issuance of common stock	88,831
10 Issuance of preferred stock	3,500
11 Net cash inflow (outflow) from financing activities	98,106
12 Increase (decrease) in cash	$35,706
13 Cash balance, beginning of year	—
14 Cash balance, end of year	$35,706

LEARNING OBJECTIVES

After studying this chapter, you should be able to

1. Identify the purposes of the statement of cash flows

2. Report cash flows from operating, investing, and financing activities

3. Prepare a statement of cash flows by the direct method

4. Compute the cash effects of a wide variety of business transactions

5. Prepare a statement of cash flows by the indirect method

What do **drkoop.com, Inc., MotherNature.com, Inc.,** and many other dot.coms have in common? They hold the promise of revolutionizing business in the new millennium.

drkoop.com, Inc., named for former U.S. Surgeon General C. Everett Koop, operates an Internet-based health network. The company offers an interactive Web site that provides comprehensive health information and services. A year and a half after its formation, the company's Web site had attracted over 18 million users.

MotherNature.com, Inc., is an on-line retail store offering vitamins, other health products, information and powerful search capabilities. Customers can buy more than 14,000 products with the click of a mouse—24 hours a day, 7 days a week. In addition, MotherNature.com offers incentives in conjunction with physicians, HMOs, and health clubs.

Are you ready to invest in these new companies? If so, you need to take a close look at their financial statements. Neither company has ever turned a profit, and, more important, neither company is generating cash flow from operations. The cash crunch is so severe at drkoop.com that the auditors say the financial statements are okay only if the company can continue as a going concern. That *if* depends largely on the company's cash flows, which are the topic of this chapter.

T he statement of cash flows, a required financial statement, reports where cash came from and how the company spent it. ➤ Like the income statement and the balance sheet, the cash-flow statement provides important information about an organization. For **drkoop.com, Inc.,** the picture is bleak because operations are generating *negative* cash flow (see line 5 of the statement on the facing page). This is a danger signal about any company because operations should be the main source of cash. Time will tell whether drkoop.com, Inc., survives.

◄ We learned in Chapter 1 (Exhibit 1-8) that the statement of cash flows is a required financial statement.

THE STATEMENT OF CASH FLOWS: BASIC CONCEPTS

The balance sheet reports **drkoop.com's** cash balance at the end of the period. By comparing the beginning and ending balance sheets, you can tell that the company's cash increased during 1999. But the balance sheet does not indicate *why* the cash balance changed. The income statement reports revenues, expenses and net income (or net loss)—clues about the sources and uses of cash. But neither does the income statement tell *why* cash increased or decreased.

The **statement of cash flows** (page 654) reports drkoop.com's **cash flows** (cash receipts and cash payments) during the period. It shows the *causes* of the change in cash. drkoop.com's cash is coming from investors and lenders—from borrowing and issuing stock (page 654, lines 8–10). This cannot go on forever. Soon investors will require drkoop.com to earn a profit and generate cash from operations (line 5). At some point, they will demand a return on their investment.

Examine the heading of drkoop.com's statement of cash flows (page 654). The statement covers a span of time and is dated "Year Ended December 31, 1999." Exhibit 17-1 on the following page shows the timing of the various financial statements.

Purpose of the Statement of Cash Flows

The statement of cash flows is designed to:

1. *Predict future cash flows.* It takes cash to pay the bills. Past cash receipts and cash payments are good predictors of future cash flows.
2. *Evaluate management decisions.* Wise decisions lead to profits and strong cash flows. Bad decisions bring bankruptcy. The statement of cash flows reports on the investments a company is making.
3. *Determine the company's ability to pay dividends to stockholders and principal and interest to creditors.* Stockholders are interested in receiving dividends on

STATEMENT OF CASH FLOWS. Reports cash receipts and cash payments classified according to the entity's major activities: operating, investing, and financing.

CASH FLOWS. Cash receipts and cash payments (disbursements).

Objective 1
Identify the purposes of the statement of cash flows

EXHIBIT 17-1
Timing of the Financial
Statements

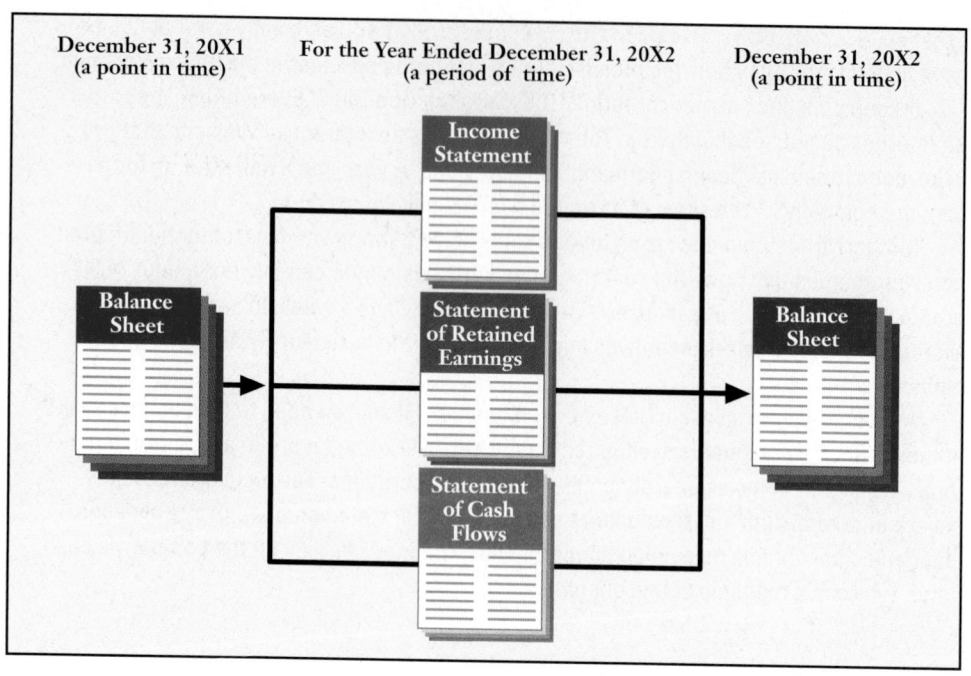

Their investments. Creditors want their principal and interest amounts on time. The statement of cash flows reports where the business's cash comes from and how it is being spent. Thus far, all of drkoop.com's cash is coming from investors and creditors—not from profitable operations. The outlook for dividends is not very promising.

 DAILY EXERCISE 17-1

4. *Show the relationship of net income to cash flow.* Usually, cash and net income move together. High profits lead to increases in cash, and vice versa. In 1999, drkoop.com had a net loss and cash flows from operating activities were negative, as one would expect.

Cash and Cash Equivalents

CASH EQUIVALENTS. Liquid short-term investments that can be converted into cash at will.

 DAILY EXERCISE 17-2

On financial statements, *Cash* has a broader meaning than just cash on hand and cash in the bank. It includes **cash equivalents,** which are liquid short-term investments that can be converted into cash at will. Examples are money-market investments and investments in U.S. Government Treasury bills. Businesses invest extra cash rather than let it sit idle. Here, *cash* refers to cash and cash equivalents.

Objective 2
Report cash flows from operating, investing, and financing activities

Operating, Investing, and Financing Activities

A business engages in three basic categories of business activities:

- operating activities
- investing activities
- financing activities

Operations are the most important activity. Investing activities are generally more important than financing activities because *what* a company invests in is more important than *how* the company finances the acquisition.

The statement of cash flows in Exhibit 17-2 shows how cash receipts and payments are divided into operating activities, investing activities, and financing activities for Anchor Corporation, a small manufacturer of glass products. Exhibit 17-2 shows that each set of activities includes both cash inflows (receipts) and cash outflows (payments). Outflows have parentheses to indicate that payments are subtracted. Each section of the statement reports a net cash inflow (net cash receipt) or a net cash outflow (net cash payment).

ANCHOR CORPORATION
Statement of Cash Flows
Year Ended December 31, 20X2

	Thousands	
Cash flows from operating activities:		
Receipts:		
Collections from customers	$ 271	
Interest received on notes receivable	10	
Dividends received on investments in stock	9	
Total cash receipts		$290
Payments:		
To suppliers	$(133)	
To employees	(58)	
For interest	(16)	
For income tax	(15)	
Total cash payments		(222)
Net cash inflow from operating activities		68
Cash flows from investing activities:		
Acquisition of plant assets	$(306)	
Loan to another company	(11)	
Proceeds from sale of plant assets	62	
Net cash outflow from operating activities		(255)
Cash flows from financing activities:		
Proceeds from issuance of common stock	$ 101	
Proceeds from issuance of long-term notes payable	94	
Payment of long-term notes payable	(11)	
Payment of dividends	(17)	
Net cash inflow from financing activities		167
Increase (decrease) in cash		$(20)
Cash balance, December 31, 20X1		42
Cash balance, December 31, 20X2		$ 22

Operating activities create revenues and expenses. The statement of cash flows reports the cash impacts of the revenues and expenses. The largest cash inflow from operations is the collection of cash from customers. Smaller inflows are receipts of interest and dividends. The operating outflows include cash payments to suppliers and employees and cash payments for interest and taxes. Exhibit 17-2 shows that Anchor's net cash inflow from operating activities is $68,000. A large positive cash flow from operations is a good sign. *In the long run, operations must be the main source of a business's cash.* Dot.com investors and lenders are well aware of this business truth.

Operating activities are related to the transactions that make up net income.[1]

Cash flows from operating activities require analysis of each revenue and expense on the income statement, along with the related current asset or current liability from the balance sheet.

Investing activities are the buying and selling of the long-term assets the business uses. A purchase or sale of land, a building, or equipment is an investing activity, as is the purchase or sale of a stock or bond investment. Making a loan is an investing activity because the loan creates a receivable for the lender. Collecting on the loan is also reported as an investing activity. The acquisition of plant assets

OPERATING ACTIVITY. Activity that creates revenue or expense in the entity's major line of business; a section of the statement of cash flows. Operating activities affect the income statement.

INVESTING ACTIVITY. Activity that increases and decreases the long-term assets available to the business; a section of the statement of cash flows.

[1]The authors thank Alfonso Oddo for suggesting this display.

dominates Anchor Corporation's investing activities, which produce a net cash outflow of $255,000.

Investing activities relate to the long-term asset accounts.

Investments in plant assets lay the foundation for future operations. A company that invests in plant and equipment appears stronger than one that is selling off its plant assets. Why? The latter company may be selling income-producing assets to pay the bills. Most companies need long-term assets to operate.

Financing activities obtain the cash needed to launch and sustain the business. Financing activities include issuing stock, buying or selling treasury stock, borrowing money, and paying dividends to the stockholders.

Payments to creditors include *principal* payments only. The payment of *interest* is an operating activity. Financing activities of Anchor Corporation brought in net cash receipts of $167,000. One thing to watch in financing activities is whether the business is borrowing heavily. Excessive borrowing has been the downfall of many companies.

Financing activities relate to the long-term liability accounts and the owners' equity accounts.

Overall, Anchor's cash decreased by $20,000 during 20X2. The company began the year with cash of $42,000 and ended with $22,000. Each category of activities includes both cash receipts and cash payments, as shown in Exhibit 17-3 on the facing page. The exhibit lists the more common cash receipts and payments that appear on the statement of cash flows.

Examine drkoop.com's statement of cash flows on page 654, and reread the chapter-opening story. Which of the following statements explains why drkoop.com's cash outflow from operations occurred? Give your reason.

a. The company invested too heavily in new properties.
b. Payments to suppliers and employees exceeded cash receipts from customers.
c. drkoop.com did not borrow enough money to finance operations during the year.

Answer: The statement of cash flows reports that cash payments to suppliers and employees exceeded cash receipts from customers, so the answer is b.

Interest and Dividends as Operating Activities

You may be puzzled by the listing of cash receipts of interest and dividends as operating activities. After all, these cash receipts result from investing activities. Interest comes from investments in loans, and dividends come from investments in stock.

Equally puzzling is listing the payment of interest as part of operations. Interest expense results from borrowing money—a financing activity. After much debate, the FASB decided to include all these items—cash receipts of interest and dividends and the payment of interest—as part of operations. Why? Because they affect net income. Interest revenue and dividend revenue increase net income, and interest expense decreases income. Therefore, cash receipts of interest and dividends and cash payments of interest are reported as operating activities on the cash-flow statement.

In contrast, dividend payments are not operating activities. Why? Because they do not enter the computation of income. Dividend payments are financing activities on the cash-flow statement because they go to the entity's stockholders who finance the business. See the first financing activity in Exhibit 17-3.

FINANCING ACTIVITY. Activity that obtains the funds from investors and creditors needed to launch and sustain the business; a section of the statement of cash flows.

⊙ DAILY EXERCISE 17-3

⊙ DAILY EXERCISE 17-4

⊙ DAILY EXERCISE 17-5

⊙ DAILY EXERCISE 17-6

Format of the Statement of Cash Flows

The FASB approves two formats for reporting cash flows from operating activities. The **direct method,** illustrated in Exhibit 17-2, lists cash receipts from specific operating activities and cash payments for each major operating activity. The FASB has a clear preference for the direct method because it reports where cash came from and how it was spent on operating activities. The direct method is required for some insurance companies. Most governmental entities also use it.

    Companies' accounting systems are designed for accrual accounting, and that makes it easy to compute cash flows from operating activities by a shortcut method. The **indirect method** starts with net income and reconciles to cash flows from operating activities. Exhibit 17-4 gives an overview of the process of converting from accrual-basis income to the cash basis for the statement of cash flows.

    The direct method is easier to understand, it provides better information for decisions, and the FASB prefers it. By learning how to compute the cash-flow amounts for the direct method, you will be learning something far more important: how to determine the cash effects of business transactions. Then, after you have a firm foundation in cash-flow analysis, it is easier to learn the indirect method. If your instructor chooses to focus solely on the indirect method, you can study that

DIRECT METHOD. Format of the operating activities section of the statement of cash flows that lists the major categories of operating cash receipts (collections from customers and receipts of interest and dividends) and cash payments (payments to suppliers, to employees, for interest and income taxes).

INDIRECT METHOD. Format of the operating activities section of the statement of cash flows that starts with net income and shows the reconciliation from net income to operating cash flows. Also called the **reconciliation method.**

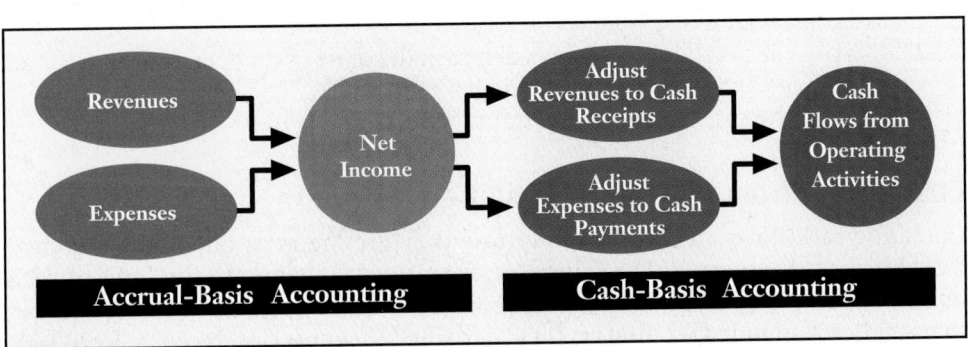

EXHIBIT 17-4
Converting from the Accrual Basis to the Cash Basis for the Statement of Cash Flows (Indirect Method)

method, which begins on page 674, with a minimum of references to earlier sections of this chapter.

The two basic ways of presenting the statement of cash flows—direct and indirect—arrive at all the same subtotals and at the same change in cash for the period. They differ only in the manner of reporting *operating activities*.

Objective 3
Prepare a statement of cash flows by the direct method

STATEMENT OF CASH FLOWS: THE DIRECT METHOD

Let's see how to prepare the statement of cash flows (direct method) illustrated in Exhibit 17-2. Suppose Anchor Corporation has assembled the summary of 20X2 transactions in Exhibit 17-5. These transactions give data for both the income statement and the statement of cash flows. Some transactions affect one statement, some the other. Sales, for example, are reported on the income statement, but cash collections appear on the cash-flow statement. Other transactions, such as the cash receipt of dividend revenue, affect both. *The statement of cash flows reports only those transactions with cash effects* (those with an asterisk in Exhibit 17-5).

EXHIBIT 17-5

Summary of Anchor Corporation's Transactions for 20X2

Operating Activities:
 1. Sales on credit, $284,000
*2. Collections from customers, $271,000
 3. Interest revenue on notes receivable, $12,000
*4. Collection of interest receivable, $10,000
*5. Cash receipt of dividend revenue on investments in stock, $9,000
 6. Cost of goods sold, $150,000
 7. Purchases of inventory on credit, $147,000
*8. Payments to suppliers, $133,000
 9. Salary expense, $56,000
*10. Payments of salaries, $58,000
 11. Depreciation expenses, $18,000
 12. Other operating expense, $17,000
*13. Interest expense and payments, $16,000
*14. Income tax expense and payments, $15,000

Investing Activities:
*15. Cash payments to acquire plant assets, $306,000
*16. Loan to another company, $11,000
*17. Proceeds from sale of plant assets, $62,000, including $8,000 gain

Financing Activities:
*18. Proceeds from issuance of common stock, $101,000
*19. Proceeds from issuance of long-term note payable, $94,000
*20. Payment of long-term note payable, $11,000
*21. Declaration and payment of cash dividends, $17,000

* Indicates a cash-flow transaction to be reported on the statement of cash flows.

To prepare the statement of cash flows, follow three steps:

1. Identify the activities that increased or decreased cash—those items with asterisks in Exhibit 17-5.
2. Classify each cash increase and each cash decrease as an operating activity, an investing activity, or a financing activity.
3. Identify the cash effect of each transaction.

Cash Flows from Operating Activities

Operating cash flows are listed first because they are the most important source of cash for most businesses. The failure of operations to generate the bulk of cash inflows for an extended period will signal trouble for a company. Exhibit 17-2 shows that Anchor is sound; operating activities provided the most cash receipts, $290,000.

CASH COLLECTIONS FROM CUSTOMERS Cash sales bring in cash immediately, credit sales later when cash is collected. "Collections from customers" in Exhibit 17-2 include both cash sales and collections on account, $271,000.

CASH RECEIPTS OF INTEREST Interest revenue is earned on notes receivable. As the clock ticks, interest revenue accrues, but cash interest is received only on specific dates. Only the cash receipts of interest appear on the statement of cash flows— $10,000 in Exhibit 17-2.

CASH RECEIPTS OF DIVIDENDS Dividends are earned on stock investments. Dividend revenue is reported on the income statement, and this cash receipt is reported on the statement of cash flows—$9,000 in Exhibit 17-2. (Dividends *received* are part of operating activities, but dividends *paid* are a financing activity.)

PAYMENTS TO SUPPLIERS Payments to suppliers include all cash payments for inventory and most operating expenses, but not for interest, income taxes, and employee compensation expenses. *Suppliers* are entities that provide the business with inventory and essential services. For example, a clothing store's payments to **Levi, Strauss, Liz Claiborne,** and **Reebok** are payments to suppliers. A grocery store's suppliers include **Nabisco, Campbell Soup,** and **Coca-Cola.** Other suppliers provide advertising, utility, and other services. Payments to suppliers *exclude* payments to employees, payments for interest, and payments for income taxes because these are separate categories of operating cash payments. In Exhibit 17-2, Anchor Corporation's payments to suppliers are $133,000.

PAYMENTS TO EMPLOYEES Salaries, wages, commissions, and other forms of compensation require payments to employees. The statement of cash flows in Exhibit 17-2 reports cash payments of $58,000.

PAYMENTS FOR INTEREST EXPENSE AND INCOME TAX EXPENSE These cash payments are reported separately from the other expenses. In the Anchor Corporation example, interest and income tax expenses equal the cash payments. In practice, the expense and cash payment amounts may differ. The cash-flow statement reports the cash payments for interest ($16,000) and income tax ($15,000).

 DAILY EXERCISE 17-7

DEPRECIATION, DEPLETION, AND AMORTIZATION EXPENSE These expenses are *not* listed on the statement of cash flows in Exhibit 17-2 because they do not affect cash. Depreciation is recorded by debiting the expense and crediting Accumulated Depreciation. There is no debit or credit to the Cash account.

Cash Flows from Investing Activities

Investing activities are important because a company's investments determine its future. Purchases of plant assets signal expansion, which is a good sign. Low levels of investing activities indicate that the business is not replenishing its assets.

CASH PAYMENTS FOR PLANT ASSETS, INVESTMENTS, AND LOANS TO OTHER COMPANIES All these cash payments acquire a long-term asset. The first investing activity reported by Anchor Corporation on its statement of cash flows in Exhibit 17-2 is the purchase of plant assets, such as land, buildings, and equipment ($306,000). The second transaction is an $11,000 loan; Anchor obtains a note receivable. These are investing activities because the company is investing in assets for business use rather than for resale. Another transaction in this category—not shown in Exhibit 17-2— is a purchase of a stock or bond investment.

PROCEEDS FROM THE SALE OF PLANT ASSETS, INVESTMENTS, AND THE COLLECTIONS OF LOANS These transactions are the opposites of acquisitions of plant assets and investments, and making loans. They are cash receipts from investment transactions.

The sale of the plant assets needs explanation. The statement of cash flows in Exhibit 17-2 reports that Anchor Corporation received $62,000 cash on the sale of plant assets. The income statement shows an $8,000 gain on this transaction. What is the appropriate amount to show on the cash-flow statement? It is $62,000, the cash proceeds from the sale. If we assume that Anchor sold equipment that cost $64,000 and had accumulated depreciation of $10,000, the following journal entry would record the sale:

Cash	62,000	
Accumulated Depreciation	10,000	
Equipment...		64,000
Gain on Sale of Plant Assets		
(from income statement)		8,000

The analysis indicates that the book value of the equipment was $54,000 ($64,000 − $10,000). However, the book value of the asset sold is not reported on the statement of cash flows. Only the cash proceeds of $62,000 are reported on the statement. For the income statement, only the gain is reported.

Because a gain occurred, you may wonder why this cash receipt is not reported as part of operations. Operations consist of buying and selling *merchandise* or rendering services to earn revenue. Investing activities are the acquisition and disposition of assets used in operations. Therefore, the sale of plant assets and the sale of investments are cash inflows from investing activities.

WORK IT OUT Suppose **Scott Paper Company** sold timber land at a $35 million gain. The land cost Scott Paper $9 million when it was purchased in 1979. What amount will Scott Paper Company report as an investing activity on the statement of cash flows?

Answer: Cash receipt of $44 million (cost of $9 million plus the gain of $35 million).

DAILY EXERCISE 17-8

Investors and creditors are often critical of a company that sells large amounts of its plant assets. Such sales may signal an urgent need for cash. In other situations, selling off fixed assets may be good news if the company is getting rid of an unprofitable division. Whether sales of plant assets are good news or bad news should be evaluated in light of a company's net income (or net loss), financial position, and other cash flows.

Cash Flows from Financing Activities

Cash flows from financing activities include several specific items. All are related to obtaining money from investors and lenders and paying them back. Readers of financial statements want to know how the entity obtains its financing.

PROCEEDS FROM ISSUANCE OF STOCK AND NOTES PAYABLE   Issuing stock (preferred and common) and notes payable are two common ways to finance operations. In Exhibit 17-2, Anchor Corporation reports that it issued common stock for cash of $101,000 and long-term notes payable for $94,000. The proceeds from issuance of notes payable can also be labeled as "Borrowing . . . $94,000."

PAYMENT OF NOTES PAYABLE AND PURCHASES OF THE COMPANY'S OWN STOCK   The payment of notes payable decreases Cash, which is the opposite effect of borrowing money. Anchor Corporation paid $11,000 on its long-term notes payable. Other transactions in this category are purchases of treasury stock and payments to retire the company's stock.

PAYMENT OF CASH DIVIDENDS   The payment of cash dividends decreases Cash and is therefore reported as a cash payment. Anchor's $17,000 payment in Exhibit 17-2 is an example. A dividend in another form—such as a stock dividend—has no effect on Cash and is *not* reported on the cash-flow statement.

Cash Crunch Turns CDNOW into CDNOW Bertelsmann

CDNOW is one of the top 5 Web sites and the leading online music destination, with over 700,000 visitors a day and 4 million customers. Yet like its e-retailer cousins, CDNOW had been having trouble turning customers into cash. CDNOW's Web site didn't feature the sound of coins rattling in a near-empty piggybank. Yet, that sound made investors flee the cash-poor dot.com in the Spring of 2000, slashing CDNOW's stock price 80% to $4 a share. Its accounting firm, **Arthur Andersen,** expressed "substantial doubt" about the company's survival.

So what's an e-retailer to do? Unlike traditional companies, dot.coms don't issue bonds or hit up the bank for a loan. Instead, they issue stocks to get their cash. The best hope for CDNOW was to merge with or be bought by another company. That hope was realized in September 2000, when publishing giant **Bertelsmann AG,** one of the world's leading media, e-commerce, and interactive companies, completed its puchase of CDNOW. Said former CDNOW President and co-founder Jason Olim: ". . . We believe our combination with Bertelsmann is the best outcome for our shareholders, employees and customers . . . This transaction allows CDNOW to fulfill its vision of providing music fans with the ultimate music experience by being part of the Bertelsmann family . . . ." And it gives CDNOW the backing of a huge empire with no cash flow problems.

Source: Based on Charles Piller, "CDNow shares plummet on survival 'doubt'; e-Commerce: Accountants cite cash crunch at one of Web's most visited sites. Observers see signal of impending shakeout," *Los Angeles Times,* March 30, 2000, p. C1. Matt Krantz, "e-Retailers run low on fuel. Exclusive analysis: Turn profit soon or else," *USA Today,* April 26, 2000, p. 01B. Press release, Bertelsmann AG and CDNOW, Inc., July 20, 2000; September 1, 2000.

Computerized Statements

Computerized accounting systems are programmed to generate the statement of cash flows as easily as they do the balance sheet and the income statement. The amounts for the operating section can be obtained by copying cash inflows and outflows from the posted accounts. For example, the cash receipts posted to Accounts Receivable provide the information for Cash Collections from Customers. All other cash flows for operating activities, financing activities, and investing activities are handled similarly.

◉ DAILY EXERCISE 17-9

◉ DAILY EXERCISE 17-10

◉ DAILY EXERCISE 17-11

MID-CHAPTER

SUMMARY PROBLEM

Drexel Corporation's accounting records include the following information for the year ended June 30, 20X3:

a. Salary expense, $104,000.
b. Interest revenue, $8,000
c. Proceeds from issuance of common stock, $31,000.
d. Declaration and payment of cash dividends, $22,000.
e. Collection of interest receivable, $7,000.
f. Payments of salaries, $110,000.
g. Credit sales, $358,000.
h. Loan to another company, $42,000.
i. Proceeds from sale of plant assets, $18,000, including $1,000 loss.
j. Collections from customers, $369,000.
k. Cash receipt of dividend revenue on stock investments, $3,000.
l. Payments to suppliers, $319,000.
m. Cash sales, $92,000.
n. Depreciation expense, $32,000.

o. Proceeds from issuance of short-term notes payable, $38,000.
p. Payments of long-term notes payable, $57,000.
q. Interest expense and payments, $11,000.
r. Loan collections, $51,000.
s. Proceeds from sale of investments, $22,000, including $13,000 gain.
t. Amortization expense, $5,000.
u. Purchases of inventory on credit, $297,000.
v. Income tax expense and payments, $16,000.
w. Cash payments to acquire plant assets, $83,000.
x. Cost of goods sold, $284,000.
y. Cash balance: June 30, 20X2—$83,000
June 30, 20X3—$?

www.prenhall.com/horngren

Mid-Chapter Assessment

Required

Prepare Drexel Corporation's income statement and statement of cash flows for the year ended June 30, 20X3. Follow the cash-flow statement format of Exhibit 17-2 and the single-step format for the income statement (grouping all revenues together and all expenses together, as shown in Exhibit 17-6, page 665).

Solution

DREXEL CORPORATION
Income Statement
Year Ended June 30, 20X3

(Ref. Letter)		Thousands	
	Revenue and gains:		
(g, m)	Sales revenue ($358 + $92).............	$450	
(s)	Gain on sale of investments.............	13	
(b)	Interest revenue..............................	8	
(k)	Dividend revenue............................	3	
	Total revenues and gains..............		$474
	Expenses and losses:		
(x)	Cost of goods sold............................	$284	
(a)	Salary expense.................................	104	
(n)	Depreciation expense.......................	32	
(v)	Income tax expense..........................	16	
(q)	Interest expense...............................	11	
(t)	Amortization expense......................	5	
(i)	Loss on sale of plant assets..............	1	
	Total expenses...............................		453
	Net income..		$ 21

DREXEL CORPORATION
Statement of Cash Flows
Year Ended June 30, 20X3

(Ref. Letter)		Thousands	
	Cash flows from operating activities:		
	Receipts:		
(j, m)	Collections from customers ($369 + $92).............	$ 461	
(e)	Interest received on notes receivable...................	7	
(k)	Dividends received on investments in stock..........	3	
	Total cash receipts...		$ 471
	Payments:		
(l)	To suppliers...	$(319)	
(f)	To employees...	(110)	
(q)	For interest..	(11)	
(v)	For income tax...	(16)	
	Total cash payments..		(456)
	Net cash inflow from operating activities...........		15
	Cash flows from investing activities:		
(w)	Acquisition of plant assets....................................	$ (83)	
(h)	Loan to another company......................................	(42)	
(s)	Proceeds from sale of investments........................	22	
(i)	Proceeds from sale of plant assets........................	18	
(r)	Collection of loans..	51	
	Net cash outflow from investing activities.........		(34)
	Cash flows from financing activities:		
(o)	Proceeds from issuance of short-term notes payable	$ 38	
(c)	Proceeds from issuance of common stock.............	31	
(p)	Payments of long-term notes payable...................	(57)	
(d)	Dividends paid..	(22)	
	Net cash outflow from financing activities.........		(10)
	Increase (decrease) in cash....................................		$ (29)
(y)	Cash balance, June 30, 20X2....................................		83
(y)	Cash balance, June 30, 20X3....................................		$ 54

Objective 4
Compute the cash effects of a wide
variety of business transactions

How do we compute the amounts for the statement of cash flows? We use the income statement and *changes* in the related balance sheet accounts. For the *operating* cash-flow amounts, the adjustment process follows this basic approach:

Revenue or expense from the income statement	±	Adjusted for the change in the related balance sheet account(s)	=	Amount for the statement of cash flows

This is called the T-account approach. Learning to analyze T-accounts is one of the most useful accounting skills you will acquire. It enables you to measure the cash effects of a wide variety of transactions.

The following discussions use Anchor Corporation's income statement in Exhibit 17-6, comparative balance sheet in Exhibit 17-7, and cash-flow statement in Exhibit 17-2. First, trace the ending and beginning cash balances of $22,000 and $42,000, respectively, from the balance sheet in Exhibit 17-7 to the bottom part of the cash-flow statement in Exhibit 17-2. As you see, the beginning and ending cash amounts come from the balance sheet. Now let's compute the cash flows from operating activities.

EXHIBIT 17-6
Income Statement

ANCHOR CORPORATION
Income Statement
Year Ended December 31, 20X2

	Thousands
Revenues and gains:	
Sales revenue	$284
Interest revenue	12
Dividend revenue	9
Gain on sale of plant assets	8
Total revenues and gains	$313
Expenses:	
Cost of goods sold	$150
Salary expense	56
Depreciation expense	18
Other operating expense	17
Interest expense	16
Income tax expense	15
Total expenses	272
Net income	$ 41

Computing the Cash Amounts of Operating Activities

CASH COLLECTIONS FROM CUSTOMERS Collections can be computed by converting sales revenue (an accrual-basis amount) to the cash basis. Anchor Corporation's income statement (Exhibit 17-6) reports sales of $284,000. Exhibit 17-7 shows that Accounts Receivable increased from $80,000 at the beginning of the year to $93,000 at year end, a $13,000 increase. Based on those amounts, Cash Collections equal $271,000, as shown in the Accounts Receivable T-account:

ACCOUNTS RECEIVABLE			
Beg. bal.	80,000		
Sales	284,000	Collections	271,000
End. bal.	93,000		

Another explanation: Accounts Receivable increased by $13,000, so Anchor Corporation must have received $13,000 less cash than sales revenue for the

EXHIBIT 17-7 Comparative Balance Sheet

ANCHOR CORPORATION
Comparative Balance Sheet
December 31, 20X2 and 20X1

Thousands	20X2	20X1	Increase (Decrease)	
Assets				
Current:				
Cash..	$ 22	$ 42	$(20)	
Accounts receivable............................	93	80	13	
Interest receivable	3	1	2	
Inventory...	135	138	(3)	Changes in current assets—**Operating**
Prepaid expenses	8	7	1	
Long-term receivable from				
another company	11	—	11	Changes in noncurrent assets—**Investing**
Plant assets, net of depreciation.............	453	219	234	
Total...	$725	$487	$238	
Liabilities				
Current:				
Accounts payable...............................	$ 91	$ 57	$ 34	
Salary payable	4	6	(2)	Changes in current liabilities—**Operating**
Accrued liabilities	1	3	(2)	
Long-term notes payable	160	77	83	Changes in long-term liabilities and paid-in capital—**Financing**
Stockholders' Equity				
Common stock...................................	359	258	101	Changes due to net income—**Operating,** and to dividends—**Financing**
Retained earnings	110	86	24	
Total...	$725	$487	$238	

period. The following equation shows another way to compute collections from customers.

Accounts Receivable				
Beginning balance	+ Sales	− Collections	= Ending balance	
$80,000	+ $284,000 −	X	= $93,000	
		−X	= $93,000 − $80,000 − $284,000	
		X	= $271,000	

A decrease in Accounts Receivable would mean that the company received more cash than the amount of sales revenue. This computation is the first item summarized in Exhibit 17-8.

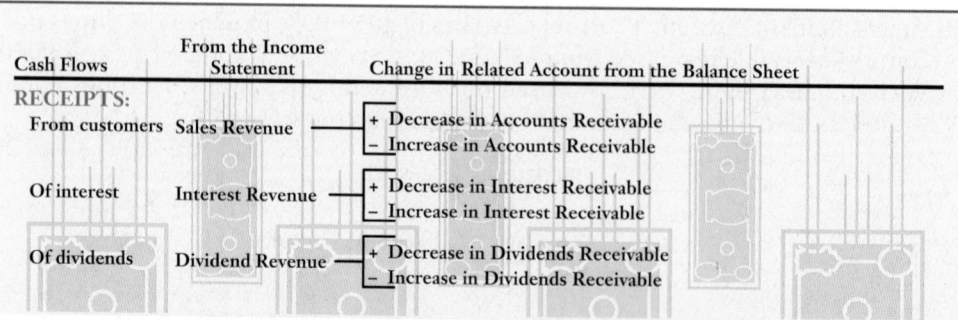

Source: We thank Barbara Gerrity for suggesting this exhibit.

All collections of receivables are computed the same way. In our example, Anchor Corporation's income statement, Exhibit 17-6, reports interest revenue of $12,000. Interest Receivable's balance in Exhibit 17-7 increased $2,000. Cash receipts of interest must be $10,000 (Interest Revenue of $12,000 minus the $2,000 increase in Interest Receivable). Exhibit 17-8 summarizes the computation of cash receipts of interest.

PAYMENTS TO SUPPLIERS   This computation includes two parts, payments for inventory (related to Cost of Goods Sold) and payments for operating expenses.

Payments for inventory are computed by converting cost of goods sold to the cash basis. To do this, we analyze the Inventory and Accounts Payable accounts. To "analyze" an account means to explain each amount in the account. For companies that purchase inventory on short-term notes payable, we must also analyze Short-Term Notes Payable in the same manner as Accounts Payable. To compute Anchor Corporation's cash payments for inventory, we analyze the T-accounts (again, we are using Exhibits 17-6 and 17-7 for our numbers):

INVENTORY				ACCOUNTS PAYABLE		
Beg. inventory	138,000	Cost of goods sold	150,000	Payments for		Beg. bal.	57,000
Purchases	147,000			inventory	113,000	Purchases	147,000 ◄
End. inventory	135,000					End. bal.	91,000

The first equation details the activity in the Inventory account to compute purchases, as follows:

Inventory

Beginning inventory	+ Purchases	−	Cost of goods sold	=	Ending inventory
$138,000	+ X	−	$150,000	=	$135,000
	X				$135,000 − $138,000 + $150,000
	X				= $147,000

Now we insert the Purchases figure into Accounts Payable to compute the amount of cash paid for inventory, as follows:

Accounts Payable

Beginning balance	+ Purchases	−	Payments for inventory	=	Ending balance
$57,000	+ $147,000	−	X	=	$91,000
			−X	=	$91,000 − $57,000 − $147,000
			X	=	$113,000

Beginning and ending inventory amounts come from the balance sheet, and Cost of Goods Sold from the income statement. Exhibit 17-9 shows the general approach to compute Payments to suppliers of inventory (first item).

Payments to suppliers ($133,000 in Exhibit 17-2) equal the sum of payments for inventory ($113,000) plus payments for operating expenses ($20,000), as explained next.

◉ DAILY EXERCISE 17-12

PAYMENTS FOR OPERATING EXPENSES   Payments for operating expenses other than interest and income tax can be computed as "plug" figures by analyzing Prepaid Expenses and Accrued Liabilities (again, all amounts come from Exhibits 17-6 and 17-7).

EXHIBIT 17-9
**Direct Method of Computing
Cash Payments for Operating
Activities**

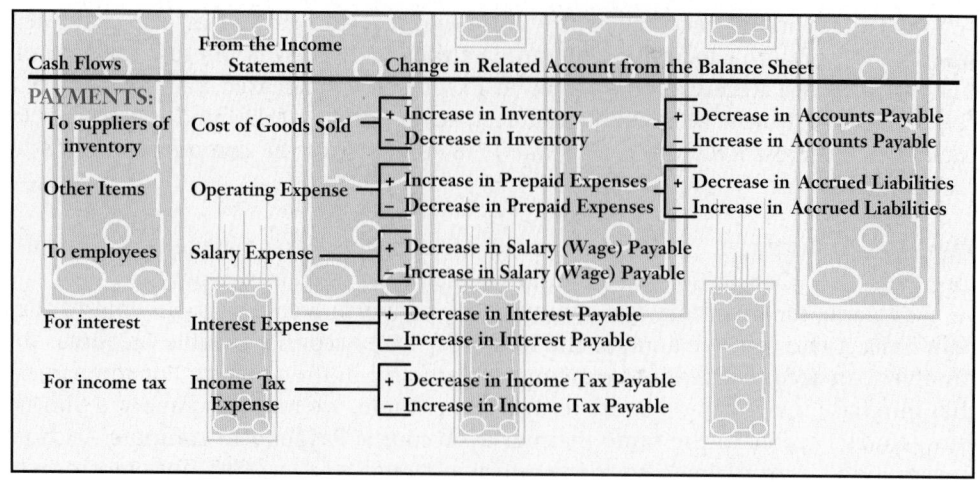

Source: We thank Barbara Gerrity for suggesting this exhibit.

T-ACCOUNTS:

PREPAID EXPENSES			
Beg. bal.	7,000	Expiration	
		of prepaid	
Payments	8,000	expense	7,000
End. bal.	8,000		

ACCRUED LIABILITIES			
Payments	3,000	Beg. bal.	3,000
		Accrual of	
		expense at	
		year end	1,000
		End. bal.	1,000

OPERATING EXPENSES (OTHER THAN SALARIES, WAGES, AND DEPRECIATION)			
Accrual of			
expense at			
year end	1,000		
Expiration			
of prepaid			
expense	7,000		
Payments	9,000		
End. bal.	17,000		

Total payments for operating expenses = $20,000
$8,000 + $3,000 + $9,000 = $20,000

EQUATIONS:

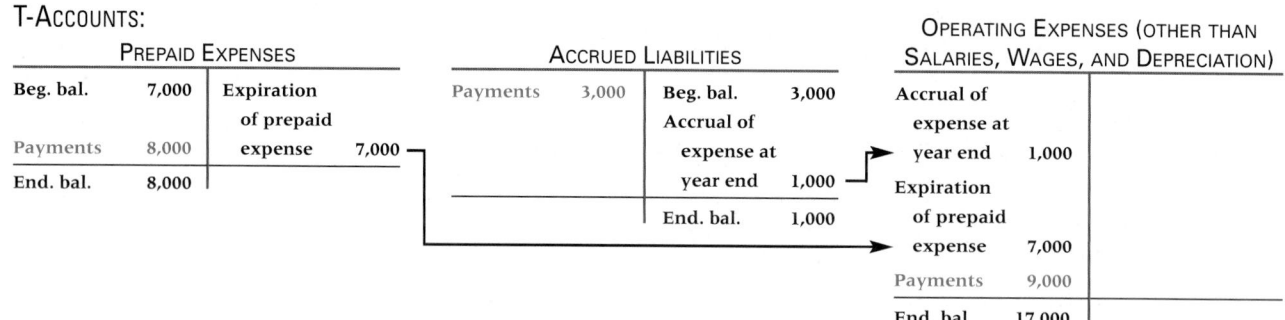

Prepaid Expenses

Beginning balance	+	Payments	−	Expiration of prepaid expense	=	Ending balance
$7,000	+	X	−	$7,000	=	$8,000
		X			=	$8,000 − $7,000 + $7,000
		X			=	$8,000

Accrued Liabilities

Beginning balance	+	Accrual of expense at year end	−	Payments	=	Ending balance
$3,000	+	$1,000	−	X	=	$1,000
				−X	=	$1,000 − $3,000 − $1,000
				X	=	$3,000

Operating Expenses

Accrual of expense at year end	+	Expiration of prepaid expense	+	Payments	=	Ending balance
$1,000	+	7,000	+	X	=	$17,000
				X	=	$17,000 − $1,000 − $7,000
				X	=	$9,000

PAYMENTS TO EMPLOYEES Companies keep separate accounts for salaries, wages, and other forms of employee compensation. It is convenient to combine all compensation amounts into one account. Anchor's calculation adjusts Salary Expense for the change in Salary Payable, as shown in the following T-account:

SALARY PAYABLE

		Beg. bal.	6,000
Payments to employees	58,000	Salary expense	56,000
		End. bal.	4,000

Salary Payable

Beginning balance	+	Salary expense	−	Payments	=	Ending balance
$6,000	+	$56,000	−	X	=	$4,000
				−X	=	$4,000 − $6,000 − $56,000
				X	=	$58,000

Exhibit 17-9 summarizes this computation under Payments to employees.

 DAILY EXERCISE 17-13

PAYMENTS OF INTEREST AND INCOME TAX In our example, the expense and payment amount is the same for interest and for income tax. Therefore, no analysis is required to determine the payment amount. But if the expense and the payment differ, the payment can be computed by analyzing the related liability account. Exhibit 17-9 summarizes the procedure for interest and income tax.

Computing the Cash Amounts of Investing Activities

Investing activities affect asset accounts, such as Plant Assets, Investments, and Notes Receivable. Cash flows from investing activities can be computed by analyzing those accounts. The income statement and the beginning and ending balance sheets provide the data.

ACQUISITIONS AND SALES OF PLANT ASSETS Companies keep separate accounts for Land, Buildings, Equipment, and other plant assets. It is helpful to combine all these accounts into a single summary. Also, we subtract accumulated depreciation from the assets' cost and get a net figure for plant assets. This approach allows us to work with a single total for plant assets.

To illustrate, observe that Anchor Corporation's balance sheet (Exhibit 17-7) reports beginning plant assets, net of depreciation, of $219,000 and an ending net amount of $453,000. The income statement (Exhibit 17-6) shows depreciation expense of $18,000 and an $8,000 gain on sale of plant assets. Further, the acquisitions of plant assets total $306,000 (see Exhibit 17-2). How much are the proceeds from the sale of plant assets? First, we compute the book value of plant assets sold, as follows:

PLANT ASSETS, NET

Beg. bal.	219,000	Depreciation	18,000
Acquisitions	306,000	Book value of assets sold	54,000
End. bal.	453,000		

Plant Assets, Net

Beginning balance	+	Acquisitions	−	Depreciation	−	Book value of assets sold	=	Ending balance
$219,000	+	$306,000	−	$18,000	−	X	=	$453,000
						−X	=	$453,000 − $219,000 − $306,000 + $18,000
						X	=	$54,000

Now we can compute the proceeds from the sale of plant assets, as follows:

Book value of assets sold	+	Gain	−	Loss	=	Sale proceeds
$54,000	+	$8,000	−	$0	=	$62,000

Trace the sale proceeds ($62,000) to the statement of cash flows in Exhibit 17-2. If the sale resulted in a loss of $3,000, the sale proceeds would be $51,000

($54,000 − $3,000), and the statement would report $51,000 as a cash receipt from this investing activity. Remember:

	Balance Sheet		Income Statement		Cash-Flow Statement
	Book value	+	Gain	=	Proceeds
	Book value	−	Loss	=	Proceeds

ACQUISITIONS AND SALES OF INVESTMENTS, AND LOANS AND LOAN COLLECTIONS The cash amounts of investment and loan transactions can be computed in the manner illustrated for plant assets. Investments are easier to analyze because there is no depreciation, as shown in the following T-account:

INVESTMENTS			
Beg. bal.*	XXX		
Purchases**	XXX	Book value of assets sold	XXX
End. bal.*	XXX		

*From the balance sheet.   **From the statement of cash flows.

Investments (amounts assumed for illustration only)

Beginning balance	+	Purchases	−	Book value of investments sold	=	Ending balance
$100,000	+	$50,000	−	X	=	$140,000
				−X	=	$140,000 − $100,000 − $50,000
				X	=	$10,000

Loan transactions follow the pattern described on page 665 for collections from customers. New loans increase the receivable and decrease cash. Collections decrease the receivable and increase cash, as follows:

LOANS AND NOTES RECEIVABLE			
Beg. bal.*	XXX		
New loans made**	XXX	Collections	XXX
End. bal.*	XXX		

*From the balance sheet.   **From the statement of cash flows.

Loans and Notes Receivable (amounts assumed for illustration only)

Beginning balance	+	New loans made	−	Collections	=	Ending balance
$90,000	+	$10,000	−	X	=	$30,000
				−X	=	$30,000 − $90,000 − $10,000
				X	=	$70,000

Exhibit 17-10 summarizes the computation of cash flows from investing activities. We must solve for the dollar amount of each item highlighted in color. Use this exhibit as a guide when you solve the assignment material at the end of the chapter.

Computing the Cash Amounts of Financing Activities

Financing activities affect the liability and stockholders' equity accounts, such as Notes Payable, Bonds Payable, Long-Term Debt, Common Stock, Paid-in Capital in Excess of Par, and Retained Earnings. To compute the cash-flow amounts, analyze these accounts.

ISSUANCES AND PAYMENTS OF LONG-TERM NOTES PAYABLE (BORROWING) The Notes Payable, Bonds Payable, and Long-Term Debt accounts are related to borrowing, a financing activ-

DAILY EXERCISE 17-14

EXHIBIT 17-10   Cash Flows from Investing Activities

Cash Receipts from Investing Activities

From sale of plant assets	Beginning plant assets (net)	+	Acquisition cost	−	Depreciation	−	Book value of assets sold	=	Ending plant assets (net)
	Cash received from sale of assets	=	Book value of assets sold	+	Gain on sale, or − Loss on sale				
From sale of investments	Beginning investments	+	Purchase cost of investments	−	Book value of investments sold	=	Ending investments		
	Cash received from sale of investments	=	Book value of investments sold	+	Gain on sale, or − Loss on sale				
From collection of loans and notes receivable	Beginning loans or notes receivable	+	New loans made	−	Collections	=	Ending loans or notes receivable		

Cash Payments for Investing Activities

For acquisition of plant assets	Beginning plant assets (net)	+	Acquisition cost	−	Depreciation	−	Book value of assets sold	=	Ending plant assets (net)
For purchase of investments	Beginning investments	+	Purchase cost of investments	−	Book value of investments sold	=	Ending investments		
For new loans made	Beginning loans or notes receivable	+	New loans made	−	Collections	=	Ending loans or notes receivable		

ity. Their balances come from the balance sheet. If either the amount of new issuances or the amount of payments is known, the other can be computed. New issuances of notes payable total $94,000 (see Exhibit 17-2). Payments of notes payable are computed from the Long-Term Notes Payable T-account, as follows (amounts from Exhibit 17-7):

LONG-TERM NOTES PAYABLE

		Beg. bal.	77,000
Payments	11,000	Issuance of new debt	94,000
		End. bal.	160,000

Long-Term Notes Payable

Beginning balance	+	Issuance of new debt	−	Payments of debt	=	Ending balance
$77,000	+	$94,000	−	X	=	$160,000
				−X	=	$160,000 − $77,000 − $94,000
				X	=	$11,000

ISSUANCES AND RETIREMENTS OF STOCK, AND PURCHASES AND SALES OF TREASURY STOCK
These financing activities are computed from the various stock accounts. Combine Common Stock and Capital in Excess of Par into a single total as we do for plant assets. Using data from Exhibits 17-2 and 17-7, we have

COMMON STOCK

		Beg. bal.	258,000
Retirements of stock	0	Issuance of new stock	101,000
		End. bal.	359,000

Common Stock

Beginning balance	+	Issuance of new stock	−	Retirements of stock	=	Ending balance
$258,000	+	$101,000	−	X	=	$359,000
				−X	=	$359,000 − $258,000 − $101,000
				X	=	0

Cash flows affecting Treasury Stock can be analyzed by using the T-account. Recall that Treasury Stock is a contra equity account, so it has a debit balance.

TREASURY STOCK

Beg. bal.	XXX		
Purchases of treasury stock	XXX	Cost of treasury stock sold	XXX
End. bal.	XXX		

Treasury Stock (amounts assumed for illustration only)

Beginning balance	+	Purchase of treasury stock	−	Cost of treasury stock sold	=	Ending balance
$16,000	+	$3,000	−	X	=	$5,000
				−X	=	$5,000 − $16,000 − $3,000
				X	=	$14,000

If either the cost of treasury stock purchased or sold is known, the other amount can be computed. For a sale of treasury stock, the amount to report on the cash-flow statement is the amount of cash received from the sale. Suppose a sale brought in $2,000 less cash than the $14,000 cost of the treasury stock. The statement of cash flows would report a cash receipt of $12,000 ($14,000 − $2,000).

DIVIDEND PAYMENTS If the amount of the dividends is not given elsewhere (for example, in a statement of retained earnings), it can be computed as follows:

RETAINED EARNINGS

Dividend declarations	17,000	Beg. bal.	86,000
		Net income	41,000
		End. bal.	110,000

DIVIDENDS PAYABLE

		Beg. bal. (assumed)	0
Dividend payments	17,000	Dividend declarations	17,000
		End. bal. (assumed)	0

DAILY EXERCISE 17-15

First, we compute dividend declarations by analyzing Retained Earnings. Then we solve for dividend payments with the Dividends Payable account. Anchor Corporation has no Dividends Payable account, so dividend payments are the same as declarations. The following computations show how to compute Anchor Corporation's dividend payments.

Retained Earnings

Beginning balance	+	Net income	−	Dividend declarations	=	Ending balance
$86,000	+	$41,000	−	X	=	$110,000
				−X	=	$110,000 − $86,000 − $41,000
				X	=	$17,000

Dividends Payable

Beginning balance	+	Dividend declarations	−	Dividend payments	=	Ending balance
$0	+	$17,000	−	X	=	$0
				−X	=	$0 − $17,000 − $0
				X	=	$17,000

Exhibit 17-11 summarizes the computation of cash flows from financing activities. The color highlights show amounts that must be computed. This exhibit will come in handy as you solve the assignments at the end of the chapter.

Exhibit 17-11   Cash Flows from Financing Activities

Cash Receipts from Financing Activities

From issuance of long-term debt (notes payable)	Beginning long-term notes payable	+	Cash received from issuance of long-term notes payable	−	Payment of notes payable	=	Ending long-term notes payable
From issuance of stock	Beginning stock	+	Cash received from issuance of new stock	−	Payments to retire stock	=	Ending stock
From sale of treasury stock	Beginning treasury stock	+	Purchase cost of treasury stock	−	Cost of treasury stock sold	=	Ending treasury stock
	Cash received from sale of treasury stock	=	Cost of treasury stock sold	+	Extra amount of sale above cost, or— amount of cost above sale amount		

Cash Payments for Financing Activities

Of long-term debt (notes payable)	Beginning long-term notes payable	+	Cash received from issuance of long-term notes payable	−	Payment of notes payable	=	Ending long-term notes payable
To retire stock	Beginning stock	+	Cash received from issuance of new stock	−	Payments to retire stock	=	Ending stock
To purchase treasury stock	Beginning treasury stock	+	Purchase cost of treasury stock	−	Cost of treasury stock sold	=	Ending treasury stock
For dividends	Beginning retained earnings	+	Net income	−	Dividend declarations	=	Ending retained earnings
	Beginning dividends payable	+	Dividend declarations	−	Dividend payments	=	Ending dividends payable

Noncash Investing and Financing Activities

Companies make investments that do not require cash. For example, they may issue a note payable to buy land, or they may pay off a note by issuing stock. Our examples thus far have included none of these transactions. Suppose that Anchor Corporation issued $320,000 of common stock to acquire a warehouse. Anchor would make this journal entry:

Warehouse Building	320,000	
Common Stock...............		320,000

This transaction would not appear on the cash-flow statement because Anchor paid no cash. But the importance of the warehouse and the issuance of stock requires that the transaction be reported. This is a noncash investing (buying a building) and financing (issuance of stock) transaction. Exhibit 17-12 illustrates how to report noncash investing and financing activities (all amounts are assumed). This information can be reported in a schedule that follows the cash-flow statement.

	Thousands
Acquisition of building by issuing common stock	$320
Acquisition of land by issuing note payable	72
Payment of long-term debt by giving investments to the creditor...............	104
Acquisition of equipment by issuing short-term note payable	37
Total noncash investing and financing activities	$533

Exhibit 17-12
Noncash Investing and Financing Activities (All Amounts Assumed)

 DAILY EXERCISE 17-16

Reconciling Net Income to Net Cash Flow from Operating Activities

The FASB requires companies that format operating activities by the direct method to report a separate reconciliation from net income to net cash flow from operating activities. The reconciliation shows how the company's net income is related to cash flow from operating activities. Exhibit 17-13 shows the reconciliation for Anchor Corporation.

ANCHOR CORPORATION
Reconciliation of Net Income to Net Cash Inflow from Operating Activities

	Thousands	
Net income		$41
Add (subtract) items that affect net income and cash flows differently:		
Depreciation	$18	
Gain on sale of plant assets.................................	(8)	
Increase in accounts receivable	(13)	
Increase in interest receivable	(2)	
Decrease in inventory..	3	
Increase in prepaid expenses................................	(1)	
Increase in accounts payable	34	
Decrease in salary payable....................................	(2)	
Decrease in accrued liabilities..............................	(2)	27
Net cash inflow from operating activities		$68

The end result—net cash inflow from operating activities of $68,000—is the same as for the *direct* method (see Exhibit 17-2). *The reconciliation also shows the indirect method of computing operating cash flows.*

Objective 5
Prepare a statement of cash flows
by the indirect method

RECONCILIATION METHOD.
Another name for the indirect
method.

STATEMENT OF CASH FLOWS: THE INDIRECT METHOD

An alternative to the direct method of computing cash flows from *operating* activities is the *indirect method,* or the **reconciliation method,** as we just saw in Exhibit 17-13. This method starts with net income from the income statement and reconciles to operating cash flows. For example, the cash-flow statement of **Hewlett-Packard** Company starts with "Net earnings," followed by "Adjustments to reconcile net earnings to net cash provided by operating activities."

The indirect method shows the link between net income and cash flow from operations better than the direct method. In fact, the vast majority of companies use the indirect method even though the FASB recommends the direct method. The main drawback of the indirect method is that it does not report the detailed operating cash flows—collections from customers and payments to suppliers, employees, and for interest and taxes.

These two methods (direct and indirect) of preparing the cash-flow statement affect only the operating activities section of the statement. No difference exists for investing or financing activities.

Exhibit 17-14 is Anchor Corporation's cash-flow statement prepared by the indirect method. Only the operating section of the statement differs from the direct method format (Exhibit 17-2). The new items Ⓐ, Ⓑ, and Ⓒ are keyed to their explanations, which are discussed in the following section. For ease of reference, we repeat Anchor Corporation's income statement and balance sheet here as Exhibits 17-15 and 17-16.

Logic Behind the Indirect Method

The indirect-method cash-flow statement begins with net income from the income statement. Additions and substractions follow. These are labeled "Add (subtract) items that affect net income and cash flows differently." The first adjustment is for depreciation.

DEPRECIATION, DEPLETION, AND AMORTIZATION EXPENSES Ⓐ These expenses are added back to net income to compute cash flow from operations. Let's see why.

Depreciation is recorded as follows:

Depreciation Expense	18,000	
Accumulated Depreciation..............		18,000

(continued at bottom of page 675)

ANCHOR CORPORATION
Statement of Cash Flows
Year Ended December 31, 20X2

	Thousands	
Cash flows from operating activities:		
Net income		$ 41
Add (subtract) items that affect net income and cash flows differently:		
(A) Depreciation	$18	
(B) Gain on sale of plant assets	(8)	
(C) Increase in accounts receivable	(13)	
Increase in interest receivable	(2)	
Decrease in inventory	3	
Increase in prepaid expenses	(1)	
Increase in accounts payable	34	
Decrease in salary payable	(2)	
Decrease in accrued liabilities	(2)	27
Net cash inflow from operating activities		$ 68
F **Cash flows from investing activities:**		
r Acquisition of plant assets	$(306)	
o Loan to another company	(11)	
m Proceeds from sale of plant assets	62	
Net cash outflow from investing activities		(255)
E **Cash flows from financing activities:**		
x Proceeds from issuance of common stock	$101	
h Proceeds from issuance of long-term notes payable	94	
i Payment of long-term notes payable	(11)	
b Payment of dividends	(17)	
i Net cash inflow from financing activities		167
t **Increase (decrease) in cash**		**$ (20)**
Cash balance, December 31, 20X1		42
17-2 Cash balance, December 31, 20X2		$ 22

DAILY EXERCISE 17-17

EXHIBIT 17-15
Income Statement
(Repeated from Exhibit 17-6)

ANCHOR CORPORATION
Income Statement
Year Ended December 31, 20X2

	Thousands	
Revenues and gains:		
Sales revenue	$284	
Interest revenue	12	
Dividend revenue	9	
Gain on sale of plant assets	8	
Total revenues and gains		$313
Expenses:		
Cost of goods sold	$150	
Salary expense	56	
Depreciation expense	18	
Other operating expense	17	
Interest expense	16	
Income tax expense	15	
Total expenses		272
Net income		$ 41

This entry neither debits nor credits Cash because depreciation has no cash effect. But depreciation expense is deducted from revenues to compute net income. Therefore, in going from net income to cash flow, we add depreciation back to net income. The addback cancels the earlier deduction.

EXHIBIT 17-16
Comparative Balance Sheet
Repeated from Exhibit 17-7)

ANCHOR CORPORATION
Comparative Balance Sheet
December 31, 20X2 and 20X1

Thousands	20X2	20X1	Increase (Decrease)
Assets			
Current:			
Cash	$ 22	$ 42	$(20)
Accounts receivable	93	80	13
Interest receivable	3	1	2
Inventory	135	138	(3)
Prepaid expenses......................................	8	7	1
Long-term receivable from another company...	11	—	11
Plant assets, net of depreciation......................	453	219	234
Total..	$725	$487	$238
Liabilities			
Current:			
Accounts payable	$ 91	$ 57	$ 34
Salary payable	4	6	(2)
Accrued liabilities.....................................	1	3	(2)
Long-term notes payable	160	77	83
Stockholders' Equity			
Common stock..	359	258	101
Retained earnings	110	86	24
Total..	$725	$487	$238

The following example should help. Suppose a company had only two transactions, a $1,000 cash sale and depreciation expense of $300. Net income is $700 ($1,000 − $300). But cash flow from operations is $1,000. To go from net income ($700) to cash flow ($1,000), we must add back the depreciation amount ($300).

> **All expenses with no cash effects are added back to net income on the cash-flow statement.**

Depreciation, depletion, and amortization are added back.

> **Likewise, revenues that do not provide cash are subtracted from net income.**

➡ We saw equity-method investment revenue in Chapter 16, p. 628.

An example is equity-method investment revenue. ⬅

GAINS AND LOSSES ON THE SALES OF ASSETS Ⓑ Sales of plant assets are investing activities on the cash-flow statement. Recall that Anchor sold equipment for $62,000, producing a gain of $8,000. The $8,000 gain is reported on the income statement and included in net income.

The cash receipt from the sale is $62,000, and that is what we report on the cash-flow statement. The $62,000 of cash received also includes the $8,000 gain on the sale. To avoid counting the gain twice, we need to remove the gain from income and report the cash receipt of $62,000 in the investing activities section of the statement. Starting with net income, we subtract the gain. This deduction removes the gain's earlier effect on income. The sale of plant assets is reported as a $62,000 cash receipt from an investing activity, as shown in Exhibit 17-14.

A loss on the sale of plant assets is also an adjustment to net income on the statement of cash flows. A loss is *added back* to income to compute cash flow from operations. The proceeds from selling the plant assets are then reported under investing activities.

CHANGES IN THE CURRENT ASSET AND CURRENT LIABILITY ACCOUNTS ⓒ Most current assets and current liabilities result from operating activities. Changes in the current accounts are reported as adjustments to net income on the cash-flow statement. The following rules apply:

1. **An *increase* in a current asset other than cash is subtracted from net income to compute cash flow from operations.** Suppose Anchor Corporation makes a sale on account. Income is increased by the sale amount. Accounts Receivable increases, but Anchor receives no cash. Exhibit 17-16 reports that Anchor Corporation's Accounts Receivable increased by $13,000 during 20X2. To compute the impact of revenue on Anchor's cash flows, we must subtract the $13,000 increase in Accounts Receivable from net income (see Exhibit 17-13). The reason is this: We have *not* collected this $13,000 in cash. The same logic applies to the other current assets. If they increase during the period, subtract the increase from net income.

Remember this:[2]

> **Current asset other than Cash** ↑ **and Cash** ↓
> **(Receivables, Inventory, Supplies)**

2. **A *decrease* in a current asset other than cash is added to net income.** Suppose Anchor's Accounts Receivable balance decreased by $4,000. Anchor's Accounts Receivable decreased and Cash increased, so decreases in Accounts Receivable and the other current assets are *added* to net income.

Symbolically,

> **Current asset other than Cash** ↓ **and Cash** ↑
> **(Receivables, Inventory, Supplies)**

3. **A *decrease* in a current liability is subtracted from net income.** The payment of a current liability decreases both cash and the current liability, so subtract the decrease from net income. In Exhibit 17-14, the $2,000 decrease in Accrued Liabilities is *subtracted* from net income to compute net cash inflow from operating activities. This summary will help you remember that

> **Current liability (Accounts Payable, Salary Payable, Accrued Liabilities, Unearned Revenue)** ↓ **and Cash** ↑

4. **An *increase* in a current liability is added to net income.** Anchor's Accounts Payable increased during the year. This increase can occur only if cash is not spent to pay this liability. Therefore, cash payments are less than the related expense. As a result, we have more cash. Increases in current liabilities are *added* to net income.

> **Current liability (Accounts Payable, Salary Payable, Accrued Liabilities, Unearned Revenue)** ↑ **and Cash** ↓

Exhibit 17-17 summarizes the adjustments needed to convert net income to net cash flow from operating activities by the indirect method.

If you are studying *only* the indirect method for operating cash flows, please turn back to page 669 for investing and financing activities.

DAILY EXERCISE 17-18

DAILY EXERCISE 17-19

---

[2]The authors thank Mari S. duToit for suggesting these displays.

Net Income
+ Depreciation, depletion, and amortization
+ Loss on disposal of a long-term asset or early
   extinguishment of note (bond) payable
− Gain on disposal of a long-term asset or early
   extinguishment of note (bond) payable

Add (subtract) items
that affect net income
and cash flow differently

+ Decrease in current asset other than cash
− Increase in current asset other than cash
+ Increase in current liability*
− Decrease in current liability*

Net cash inflow (or outflow) from operating activities

* Short-term notes payable for general borrowing, and current portion of long-term notes payable,
are related to *financing* activities, not to operating activities.
Source: We thank Barbara Gerrity and Jean Marie Hudson for suggesting this exhibit.

THINK IT OVER

Examine Anchor Corporation's statement of cash flows, Exhibit 17-14, and answer these questions:

1. Does Anchor Corporation appear to be growing or shrinking? How can you tell?
2. Where did most of Anchor's cash for expansion come from?
3. Suppose Accounts Receivable decreased by $40,000 (instead of increasing by $13,000) during the current year. What then would be Anchor's cash flow from operating activities?

Answers

1. Anchor appears to be growing. The company acquired more plant assets ($306,000) than it sold during the year.
2. Most of the cash for expansion came from issuing common stock ($101,000) and from borrowing ($94,000).
3. Accounts Receivable ↓ and Cash ↑ Therefore, net cash inflow from operating activities is $121,000 ($68,000 + $40,000 + $13,000).

USING CASH-FLOW INFORMATION IN INVESTMENT AND CREDIT ANALYSIS

The chapter-opening story about **drkoop.com** and **MotherNature.com** makes it clear that cash flows are important to a company's survival. A cash shortage is usually the most pressing problem of a struggling organization. Abundant cash allows a company to expand, invest in research and development, and hire the best employees. How, then, do investors and creditors use cash-flow information for decision making?

Neither cash-flow, net income, nor balance sheet data tell investors all they need to know about a company. Decision making is much more complex than plugging a few numbers into a formula. Investors analyze **Hewlett-Packard's** financial statements, articles in the financial press, and data about the industry, to decide whether to invest in Hewlett-Packard stock. To evaluate a large loan request by **MCI WorldCom,** a bank loan officer may interview the company's top management to decide whether they are trustworthy. Both investors and creditors are mainly interested in where a company is headed. They want to make predictions about net income and future cash flows.

It has been said that cash-flow data help spot losers better than they help spot winners. This is often true. When a company's business is booming, profits are high, and cash flows are usually improving. In almost all cases, a negative cash flow from operations warrants investigation. A cash downturn in a single year is not necessarily a danger signal. But negative cash flows for two consecutive years may throw a company into bankruptcy. Without cash flow from operations, a business simply cannot survive.

You may ask, "Can't the business raise money by issuing stock or by borrowing?" The answer is no, because if operations cannot generate enough cash, then stockholders will not buy the company's stock. Bankers will not lend it money. Over the long run, if a company cannot generate cash from operations, it is doomed.

The Decision Guidelines feature provides investors and creditors with a few suggestions on how to use cash-flow information for decision making.

 DAILY EXERCISE 17-20

DECISION GUIDELINES

Investors' and Creditors' Use of Cash-Flow and Related Information

Question	Financial Statement	What to Look For
INVESTORS		
Where is most of the company's cash coming from?	Statement of cash flows	Operating activities → Good sign Investing activities → Bad sign Financing activities → Okay sign
Do high sales and profits translate into more cash?	Statement of cash flows	Usually, but cash flows from *operating* activities must be the main source of cash for long-term success.
If sales and profits are low, how is the company generating cash?	Statement of cash flows	If *investing* activities are generating the cash, the business may be in trouble because it is selling off its long-term assets. If *financing* activities are generating the cash, that cannot go on forever. Sooner or later, investors will demand cash flow from operating activities.
Is the cash balance large enough to provide for expansion?	Balance sheet	The cash balance should be growing over time. If not, the company may be in trouble.
CREDITORS		
Can the business pay its debts?	Income statement	Increasing trend of net income.
	Statement of cash flows	Cash flows from operating activities should be the main source of cash.
	Balance sheet	Current ratio, debt ratio.

REVIEW THE STATEMENT OF CASH FLOWS

SUMMARY PROBLEM

Prepare the 20X3 statement of cash flows for Robins Corporation, using the indirect method to report cash flows from operating activities. In a separate schedule, report Robin's noncash investing and financing activities.

	December 31,	
	20X3	20X2
Current assets:		
Cash and cash equivalents	$19,000	$ 3,000
Accounts receivable..	22,000	23,000
Inventories	34,000	31,000
Prepaid expenses	1,000	3,000
Current liabilities:		
Notes payable (for inventory purchases)	$11,000	$ 7,000
Accounts payable	24,000	19,000
Accrued liabilities	7,000	9,000
Income tax payable	10,000	10,000

Transaction data for 20X3:

Depreciation expense	$ 7,000	Purchase of equipment....................	$98,000
Issuance of long-term note		Payment of cash dividends..............	18,000
payable to borrow cash................	7,000	Net income	26,000
Issuance of common stock		Issuance of common stock to	
for cash	19,000	retire bonds payable....................	13,000
Sale of building...............................	74,000	Purchase of long-term	
Amortization expense	3,000	investment	8,000
Purchase of treasury stock...............	5,000	Issuance of long-term note	
Loss on sale of building	2,000	payable to purchase patent	37,000

Solution

ROBINS CORPORATION
Statement of Cash Flows
Year Ended December 31, 20X3

Cash flows from operating activities:		
Net income		$26,000
Add (subtract) items that affect net income		
and cash flows differently:		
Depreciation..	$ 7,000	
Amortization	3,000	
Loss on sale of building...	2,000	
Decrease in accounts receivable.................................	1,000	
Increase in inventories...	(3,000)	
Decrease in prepaid expenses	2,000	
Increase in notes payable, short-term..........................	4,000	
Increase in accounts payable......................................	5,000	
Decrease in accrued liabilities	(2,000)	19,000
Net cash inflow from opeating activities		45,000
Cash flows from investing activities:		
Purchase of equipment..	$(98,000)	
Sale of building...	74,000	
Purchase of long-term investment	(8,000)	
Net cash outflow from investing activities		(32,000)
Cash flows from financing activities:		
Issuance of common stock..	$ 19,000	
Payment of cash dividends	(18,000)	
Issuance of long-term note payable......................................	7,000	
Purchase of treasury stock...	(5,000)	
Net cash inflow from financing activities		3,000
Increase in cash and cash equivalents...................................		$16,000
Cash balance, December 31, 20X2		3,000
Cash balance, December 31, 20X3		$19,000
Noncash investing and financing activities:		
Issuance of long-term note payable to purchase patent.........		$37,000
Issuance of common stock to retire bond payable		13,000
Total noncash investing and financing activities................		$50,000

Lessons Learned

1. **Identify the purposes of the statement of cash flows.** The *statement of cash flows* reports a business's cash receipts, payments, and change in cash for the period. It shows *why* cash increased or decreased during the period. The cash-flow statement aids prediction of future cash flows and evaluation of management decisions. Cash also includes *cash equivalents* such as liquid short-term investments.

2. **Report cash flows from operating, investing, and financing activities.** The cash-flow statement reports *operating activities, investing activities,* and *financing activities.* Operating activities create revenues and expenses in the entity's major line of business. Investing activities affect the long-term assets. Financing activities obtain the cash needed to launch and sustain the business. Each section of the statement includes cash receipts and cash payments and concludes with a net cash increase or decrease. In addition, *noncash investing and financing activities* are reported in an accompanying schedule.

3. **Prepare a statement of cash flows by the direct method.** Two formats can be used to report *operating* activities—the direct method and the indirect method. The *direct method* reports collections from customers and receipts of interest and dividends minus cash payments to suppliers, employees, and for interest and income taxes. Investing cash flows and financing cash flows are unaffected by the method used to report operating activities.

4. **Compute the cash effects of a wide variety of business transactions.** The analysis of T-accounts aids the computation of the cash effects of business transactions. The information comes from the balance sheet, the income statement, and the related accounts.

5. **Prepare a statement of cash flows by the indirect method.** The *indirect method* starts with net income and reconciles to cash flow from operations. Although the FASB permits both the indirect and the direct methods, it prefers the direct method. However, the indirect method is more widely used.

Accounting Vocabulary

cash equivalents (p. 656)
cash flows (p. 655)
direct method (p. 659)

financing activity (p. 658)
indirect method (p. 659)
investing activity (p. 657)

operating activity (p. 657)
reconciliation method (p. 659)
statement of cash flows (p. 655)

Questions

1. Identify four purposes of the statement of cash flows.
2. Identify and briefly describe the three types of activities that are reported on the statement of cash flows.
3. What is the check figure for the statement of cash flows? (In other words, which figure do you check to make sure you've done your work correctly?) Where is it obtained, and how is it used?
4. What is the most important source of cash for most successful companies?
5. How can cash decrease during a year when income is high? How can cash increase during a year when income is low? How can investors and creditors learn these facts about the company?
6. Why are depreciation, depletion, and amortization expenses *not* reported on a cash-flow statement prepared by the direct method? Why and how are these expenses reported on a statement prepared by the indirect method?
7. Taco Grande Restaurants collected cash of $92,000 from customers and $6,000 interest on notes receivable. Cash payments included $24,000 to employees, $13,000 to suppliers, $6,000 as dividends to stockholders, and $5,000 as a loan to another company. How much was Taco Grande's net cash inflow from operating activities?
8. How should issuance of a note payable to purchase land be reported in the financial statements? Identify three other transactions that fall in this same category.
9. Which format of the cash-flow statement gives a clearer description of the individual cash flows from *operating* activities? Which format better shows the relationship between net income and *operating* cash flow?
10. An investment that cost $65,000 was sold for $80,000, resulting in a $15,000 gain. Show how to report this transaction on a statement of cash flows prepared by the indirect method.
11. Identify the cash effects of increases and decreases in current assets other than cash. What are the cash effects of increases and decreases in current liabilities?
12. Milano Corporation earned net income of $38,000 and had depreciation expense of $22,000. Also, noncash current assets decreased $13,000, and current liabilities decreased $9,000. What was Milano's net cash flow from operating activities?

Assess Your Progress

Daily Exercises

DE17-1 For 19X9, 19X8, and 19X7, two well-known companies reported the following (in millions):

Using income and cash-flow data
to evaluate dividends
(Obj. 1)

	19X9	19X8	19X7
Safeway, Inc., the grocery chain:			
Net income...	$ 971	$ 807	$ 557
Net cash flow from operating activities..............	1,488	1,253	1,222
U.S. Airways Group, Inc.:			
Net income...	197	538	1,025
Net cash flow from operating activities..............	603	1,251	870

Which company quit paying dividends during this period? How can you tell?

DE17-2 **Pepsi Co, General Electric, Qualcomm,** and most other companies report the following on their balance sheets:

CURRENT ASSETS
    Cash and cash equivalents........... $XXX

What is a cash equivalent (give an example), and why is it combined with cash on the balance sheet?

Distinguishing operating, investing, and financing activities
(Obj. 2)

DE17-3 Describe operating activities, investing activities, and financing activities. For each category, give an example of (a) a cash receipt and (b) a cash payment.

Journal entries for operating,
investing, and financing activities
(Obj. 2)

DE17-4 ← *Link Back to Chapter 2 (Journal Entries).* Return to Daily Exercise 17-3. For each cash receipt and each cash payment that you identified, give the journal entry, using made-up figures.

Identifying operating, investing,
and financing cash flows
(Obj. 2)

DE17-5 Storage Technology Corporation prepares its statement of cash flows by the *direct* method for operating activities. Identify the section of Storage Technology's statement of cash flows where each of the following transactions will appear. If the transaction does not appear on the cash-flow statement, give the reason.

a. Cash 14,000
        Note Payable, Long-Term 14,000
b. Salary Expense............................. 7,300
        Cash...................................... 7,300
c. Cash 28,400
        Sales Revenue 28,400

d. Amortization Expense................... 6,500
        Goodwill 6,500
e. Accounts Payable 1,400
        Cash...................................... 1,400
f. Land 90,000
        Cash...................................... 90,000

DE17-6 Examine the statement of cash flows of **drkoop.com, Inc.,** on page 654. What is the main danger signal about the company's cash flows?

DE17-7 (Daily Exercise 17-10 is an alternative exercise.) eFax.com, Inc., accountants have assembled the following data for the year ended December 31, 20X2:

Cost of goods sold	$100,000	Payment of dividends	$ 6,000
Payments to suppliers	80,000	Proceeds from issuance	
Purchase of equipment	90,000	of common stock...........................	58,000
Payments to employees	70,000	Sales revenue	210,000
Payment of note payable	30,000	Collections from customers	170,000
Proceeds from sale of land	60,000	Payment of income tax......................	10,000
Depreciation expense.......................	15,000	Purchase of treasury stock................	5,000

Prepare the *operating* activities section of eFax.com's statement of cash flows for the year ended December 31, 20X2. eFax uses the direct method for operating cash flows.

DE17-8 (Daily Exercise 17-10 is an alternative exercise.) Use the data in Daily Exercise 17-7 to prepare the *investing* activities section of eFax.com's statement of cash flows for the year ended December 31, 20X2.

DE17-9 (Daily Exercise 17-10 is an alternative exercise.) Use the data in Daily Exercise 17-7 to prepare the *financing* activities section of eFax.com's statement of cash flows for the year ended December 31, 20X2.

Identifying financing cash flows (Obj. 2, 3)

DE17-10 eFax.com, Inc., accountants have assembled the following data for the year ended December 31, 20X2.

Preparing a statement of cash flows—direct method (Obj. 3)

Cost of goods sold	$100,000	Payment of dividends	$ 6,000
Payments to suppliers	80,000	Proceeds from issuance	
Purchase of equipment	90,000	of common stock	58,000
Payments to employees	70,000	Sales revenue	210,000
Payment of note payable	30,000	Collections from customers	170,000
Proceeds from sale of land	60,000	Payment of income tax	10,000
Depreciation expense	15,000	Purchase of treasury stock	5,000

Prepare eFax.com, Inc.'s statement of cash flows for the year ended December 31, 20X2. eFax uses the *direct* method for operating activities. Use Exhibit 17-2 (page 657) as a guide.

DE17-11 Inatome Processing began 20X1 with cash of $104,000. During the year, Inatome earned service revenue of $800,000 and collected $720,000 from customers. Expenses for the year totaled $670,000, of which Inatome paid $610,000 in cash to suppliers and employees. Inatome also paid $140,000 to purchase equipment and a cash dividend of $50,000 to its stockholders during 20X1.

Preparing a statement of cash flows—direct method (Obj. 3)

1. Compute net income for the year.
2. Determine the cash balance at the end of the year.
3. Prepare the company's statement of cash flows for the year. Format operating activities by the direct method, and show the beginning and ending balances of cash.

DE17-12 Exterra Communications reported the following financial statements for 20X3:

Computing cash-flow amounts (Obj. 4)

EXTERRA COMMUNICATIONS
Income Statement
Year Ended June 30, 20X3

	Thousands
Sales revenue	$660
Cost of goods sold	$340
Depreciation expense	40
Salary expense	50
Other expense	150
Total expenses	580
Net income	$ 80

EXTERRA COMMUNICATIONS
Comparative Balance Sheet
June 30, 20X3 and 20X2

Thousands	20X3	20X2		20X3	20X2
Assets			**Liabilities**		
Current:			Current:		
Cash	$ 39	$ 16	Accounts payable	$ 53	$ 42
Accounts receivable	54	48	Salary payable	25	21
Inventory	80	84	Accrued liabilities	6	11
Prepaid expenses	3	2	Long-term notes payable	63	68
Long-term investments	85	90			
Plant assets, net	215	185	**Stockholders' Equity**		
			Common stock	40	37
			Retained earnings	289	246
Total	$476	$425	Total	$476	$425

683

Compute the following operating cash flows:

a. Collections from customers.   **b.** Payments for inventory.

Computing cash-flow amounts
(Obj. 4)

DE17-13 Use the Exterra Communications data in Daily Exercise 17-12 to compute

a. Payments of other expenses. (Use the computational approach for Operating Expense outlined in Exhibit 17-9.)

b. Payments to employees.

Computing investing cash flows
(Obj. 4)

DE17-14 Use the Exterra Communications data in Daily Exercise 17-12 to compute

a. Proceeds from the sale of long-term investments. (Study Exterra's income statement to see whether there was a gain or loss on the sale. Exterra purchased no investments during the year.)

b. Acquisitions of plant assets (all acquisitions were for cash). Exterra sold no plant assets during the year.

Computing financing cash flows
(Obj. 4)

DE17-15 Use the Exterra Communications data in Daily Exercise 17-12 to compute

a. New borrowing or payment of long-term notes payable. Exterra had only one long-term note payable transaction during the year.

b. Issuance of common stock or retirement of common stock. Exterra had only one common stock transaction during the year.

c. Payment of cash dividends (same as amount of dividends declared).

Noncash investing and financing
transactions
(Obj. 4)

DE17-16 Return to the Anchor Corporation income statement (Exhibit 17-6, page 665) and comparative balance sheet (Exhibit 17-7, page 666). Assume that Anchor sold no plant assets during 20X2.

1. Compute the cost of Anchor's plant asset acquisition during the year.

2. Anchor financed the plant asset by signing a long-term note payable for $83,000 and paying the remainder in cash. Journalize this transaction.

3. Show how to report Anchor's acquisition of the plant assets on the statement of cash flows and the accompanying schedule of noncash investing and financing activities.

Identifying items for reporting
cash flows from operations—
indirect method
(Obj. 5)

DE17-17 Laclede Shipping, Inc., is preparing its statement of cash flows for the year ended September 30, 20X2. Laclede reports cash flows from operating activities by the *indirect* method. The company's head bookkeeper has provided the following list of items for you to consider in preparing the statement of cash flows. Identify each item as an operating activity—addition to net income (O+) or subtraction from net income (O−); an investing activity (I); a financing activity (F); or an activity that is not used to prepare the cash-flow statement by the indirect method (N). Answer by placing the appropriate symbol in the blank space.

___ **a.** Decrease in accounts receivable	___ **h.** Decrease in prepaid expense
___ **b.** Purchase of equipment	___ **i.** Issuance of common stock
___ **c.** Collection of cash from customers	___ **j.** Gain on sale of building
___ **d.** Increase in accounts payable	___ **k.** Retained earnings
___ **e.** Loss on sale of land	___ **l.** Sales revenue
___ **f.** Depreciation expense	___ **m.** Payment of dividends
___ **g.** Increase in inventory	___ **n.** Decrease in accrued liabilities

Reporting cash flows from
operating activities, indirect
method   (Obj. 5)

DE17-18 The Tribune Herald Publishing Company began 20X2 with accounts receivable, inventory, and prepaid expenses totaling $65,000. At the end of the year, the company had a total of $78,000 for these current assets. At the beginning of 20X2, The Tribune Herald owed current liabilities of $42,000, and at year end current liabilities totaled $40,000.

Net income for the year was $55,000, after including all revenues and gains and after subtracting all expenses and losses. Included in the computation of net income were a $4,000 gain on the sale of land and depreciation expense of $9,000.

Show how The Tribune Herald should report cash flows from operating activities for 20X2. The company uses the *indirect* method. Use Exhibit 17-14 (page 675) as a guide.

Preparing a statement of cash
flows, indirect method
(Obj. 5)

DE17-19 Exterra Communications reported the following financial statements for 20X3:

EXTERRA COMMUNICATIONS
Income Statement
Year Ended June 30, 20X3

	Thousands
Sales revenue	$660
Cost of goods sold	$340
Depreciation expense	40
Salary expense	50
Other expenses, including income taxes	150
Total expenses	580
Net income	$ 80

EXTERRA COMMUNICATIONS
Comparative Balance Sheet
June 30, 20X3 and 20X2

Thousands	20X3	20X2		20X3	20X2
Assets			**Liabilities**		
Current:			Current:		
Cash..	$ 39	$ 16	Accounts payable	$ 53	$ 42
Accounts receivable...........	54	48	Salary payable	25	21
Inventory............................	80	84	Accrued liabilities.....................	6	11
Prepaid expenses	3	2	Long-term notes payable	63	68
Long-term investments.........	85	90			
Plant assets, net....................	215	185	**Stockholders' Equity**		
			Common stock............................	40	37
			Retained earnings........................	289	246
Total	$476	$425	Total	$476	$425

Additional data during 20X3:

a. Exterra purchased no investments.
b. Exterra sold no plant assets.
c. Exterra had only one long-term note payable transaction.
d. Exterra had only one common stock transaction.

Prepare Exterra Communications' statement of cash flows for the year ended June 30, 20X3. Exterra uses the *indirect* method for operating activities. Use Exhibit 17-14 (page 675) as a guide.

DE17-20 ← *Link Back to Chapter-Opening Story.* A friend is a stockholder in MotherNature.com and has received the company's statement of cash flows, which follows, as adapted. Answer the following questions to help your friend understand this financial statement and its purpose.

Using an actual company's statement of cash flows (Obj. 5)

MOTHERNATURE.COM, INC.
Statement of Cash Flows (adapted)
Year Ended December 31, 1999

	Thousands
Operating Activities:	
Net loss...	$(159)
Adjustments to reconcile net loss to net cash used in operating activities	79
Net cash used in operating activities........................	(80)
Investing Activities:	
Purchases of property and equipment	(28)
Financing Activities:	
Borrowing	89
Issuance of common stock	25
Payments of debt..	(3)
Net cash provided by financing activities	111
Increase in cash and cash equivalents.......................	$ 3
Cash and cash equivalents, beginning	1
Cash and cash equivalents, ending	$ 4

1. What does the statement of cash flows reveal that you cannot learn from the income statement and the balance sheet?
2. MotherNature.com's statement indicates that the company uses the indirect method to report cash flows from operating activities. When you see other cash-flow statements, how can you tell that the company uses the indirect method?
3. Do MotherNature.com's cash flows for 1999 look strong or weak? Give your reason. What is the main thing you should look for in evaluating a company's cash flows?

EXERCISES

E17-1 Morningstar Foods, a bakery partnership in South Carolina, has experienced an unbroken string of ten years of growth in net income. Nevertheless, the business is facing bankruptcy! Creditors are calling all of Morningstar's outstanding loans for immediate payment, and the cash is simply not available. Attempts to explain where Morningstar Foods went wrong make it clear that managers placed undue emphasis on net income and gave too little attention to cash flows.

Required

Write a brief memo, in your own words, to explain to the managers of Morningstar Foods the purposes of the statement of cash flows.

E17-2 Identify each of the following transactions as an operating activity (O), an investing activity (I), a financing activity (F), a noncash investing and financing activity (NIF), or a transaction that is not reported on the statement of cash flows (N). Assume that the direct method is used to report cash flows from operating activities.

___	**a.** Payment of account payable	___	**k.** Payment of wages to employees
___	**b.** Issuance of preferred stock for cash	___	**l.** Collection of cash interest
___	**c.** Payment of cash dividend	___	**m.** Cash sale of land
___	**d.** Sale of long-term investment	___	**n.** Distribution of stock dividend
___	**e.** Amortization of bond discount	___	**o.** Acquisition of equipment by
___	**f.** Collection of account receivable		issuance of note payable
___	**g.** Issuance of long-term note payable	___	**p.** Payment of long-term debt
	to borrow cash	___	**q.** Acquisition of building by
___	**h.** Depreciation of equipment		issuance of common stock
___	**i.** Purchase of treasury stock	___	**r.** Accrual of salary expense
___	**j.** Purchase of long-term investment	___	**s.** Issuance of common stock for cash

E17-3 Indicate where, if at all, each of the following transactions would be reported on a statement of cash flows prepared by the *direct* method and the accompanying schedule of noncash investing and financing activities.

a. Salary Expense	4,300	
Cash		4,300
b. Equipment	18,000	
Cash		18,000
c. Cash	7,200	
Long-Term Investment		7,200
d. Bonds Payable	45,000	
Cash		45,000
e. Building	164,000	
Note Payable, Long-Term		164,000
f. Cash	1,400	
Accounts Receivable		1,400
g. Accounts Payable	8,300	
Cash		8,300
h. Cash	81,000	
Common Stock		12,000
Paid-in Capital in Excess of Par		69,000
i. Treasury Stock	13,000	
Cash		13,000
j. Retained Earnings	36,000	
Common Stock		36,000
k. Cash	2,000	
Interest Revenue		2,000
l. Land	87,700	
Cash		87,700
m. Dividends Payable	16,500	
Cash		16,500
n. Equipment	22,100	
Note Payable, Short-Term		22,100

E17-4 Analysis of the accounting records of Meister Corporation reveals the following:

Collection of accounts receivable.............	$128,000	Increase in current assets other than cash.............	$17,000
Payment of salaries and wages.................	34,000	Payment of dividends..	7,000
Depreciation...	12,000	Cash sales...	15,000
Decrease in current liabilities..................	23,000	Loss on sale of land..	5,000
Collection of dividend revenue...............	1,000	Acquisition of land	37,000
Payment of interest...............................	16,000	Payment of accounts payable	48,000
Net income...	21,000	Payment of income tax...	13,000

Computing cash flows from operating activities—direct method (Obj. 3)

Required

Compute cash flows from operating activities by the direct method. Use the format of the operating section of Exhibit 17-2 (page 657). Evaluate the operating cash flow of Meister Corporation. Give the reason for your evaluation.

E17-5 Selected accounts of ASP, Inc., show the following:

Identifying items for the statement of cash flows—direct method (Obj. 3)

LONG-TERM DEBT

Payments	69,000	Beg. bal.	161,000
		Issuance of debt for cash	90,000
		End. bal.	182,000

ACCOUNTS RECEIVABLE

Beg. bal.	30,000	Cash receipts from customers	139,000
Sales revenue	120,000		
End. bal.	11,000		

INVESTMENT IN LAND

Beg. bal.	90,000	Cost of investments sold	109,000
Acquisitions	127,000		
End. bal.	108,000		

Required

For each account, identify the item or items that should appear on a statement of cash flows prepared by the direct method. State where to report the item.

E17-6 The income statement and additional data of Gillette Satellite Network, Inc., follow.

Preparing the statement of cash flows—direct method (Obj. 3)

GILLETTE SATELLITE NETWORK, INC.
Income Statement
Year Ended September 30, 20X2

Revenues:		
Sales revenue.........................		$252,000
Expenses:		
Cost of goods sold..................	$115,000	
Salary expense.......................	45,000	
Depreciation expense	29,000	
Rent expense	11,000	
Interest expense.....................	2,000	
Income tax expense...............	9,000	211,000
Net income...........................		$ 41,000

Additional data during fiscal year 20X2:

a. Collections from customers were $7,000 more than sales.
b. Payments to suppliers were $5,000 less than the sum of cost of goods sold plus rent expense.
c. Payments to employees were $1,000 more than salary expense.
d. Interest expense and income tax expense equal their cash amounts.
e. Acquisition of equipment was $135,000. Of this amount, $100,000 was paid in cash and the remainder by signing a long-term note payable. Gillette sold no equipment during fiscal year 20X2.

f. Proceeds from sale of land, $14,000.
g. Proceeds from issuance of common stock, $35,000.
h. Payment of long-term note payable, $20,000.
i. Payment of dividends, $10,000.
j. No change in cash balance. The balance at September 30, 20X1, was $18,000.

Required

1. Prepare Gillette Satellite Network's statement of cash flows and accompanying schedule of noncash investing and financing activities. Report operating activities by the *direct* method.
2. Evaluate Gillette Satellite Network's cash flows for the year. Mention all three categories of cash flows, and give the reason for your evaluation.

Computing amounts for the statement of cash flows (Obj. 3, 4)

E17-7 Compute the following items for the statement of cash flows of Pep.com:

a. Beginning and ending Accounts Receivable are $24,000 and $19,000, respectively. Credit sales for the period total $81,000. How much are cash collections?
b. Cost of goods sold is $84,000. Beginning Inventory balance is $29,000, and ending Inventory balance is $21,000. Beginning and ending Accounts Payable are $11,000 and $8,000, respectively. How much are cash payments for inventory?

Computing investing and financing amounts for the statement of cash flows (Obj. 4)

E17-8 Compute the following items for the statement of cash flows of Steelcase Furniture:

a. Beginning and ending Plant Assets, net, are $103,000 and $112,000, respectively. Depreciation for the period is $16,000, and acquisitions of new plant assets are $27,000. Plant assets were sold at a $1,000 gain. What were the cash proceeds of the sale?
b. Beginning and ending Retained Earnings are $45,000 and $69,000, respectively. Net income for the period is $62,000, and stock dividends are $22,000. How much are cash dividend payments?

E17-9 The accounting records of Vintage Motor Corporation reveal the following:

Cash sales	$ 9,000	Payment of accounts payable	$48,000
Loss on sale of land	5,000	Net income	33,000
Acquisition of land	37,000	Payment of income tax	13,000
Collection of dividend revenue	7,000	Collection of accounts receivable	93,000
Payment of interest	16,000	Payment of salaries and wages	34,000
Increase in current assets other than cash	17,000	Depreciation	12,000
Payment of dividends	7,000	Decrease in current liabilities	29,000

Computing cash flows from operating activities—indirect method (Obj. 5)

Required

Compute cash flows from operating activities by the indirect method. Use the format of the operating section of Exhibit 17-14 (page 675). Then evaluate Vintage Motor's operating cash flows as strong or weak.

Classifying transactions for the statement of cash flows (Obj. 3, 5)

E17-10 Two transactions of Transworld Express, Inc., are recorded as follows:

a. Land 290,000
     Cash 130,000
     Note Payable 160,000
b. Cash 22,000
     Accumulated Depreciation 83,000
     Equipment 92,000
     Gain on Sale of Equipment 13,000

Required

1. Indicate where, how, and in what amount to report these transactions on the statement of cash flows and accompanying schedule of noncash investing and financing activities. Transworld reports cash flows from operating activities by the *direct* method.
2. Repeat requirement 1, assuming that Transworld reports cash flows from operating activities by the *indirect* method.

Preparing the statement of cash flows by the indirect method (Obj. 5)

E17-11 Use the income statement of Gillette Satellite Network, Inc., in Exercise 17-6, plus these additional data during fiscal year 20X2:

a. Acquisition of equipment was $135,000. Of this amount, $100,000 was paid in cash and the remainder by signing a long-term note payable. Gillette sold no equipment during fiscal year 20X2.
b. Proceeds from sale of land, $14,000.
c. Proceeds from issuance of common stock, $35,000.
d. Payment of long-term note payable, $20,000.

e. Payment of dividends, $10,000.

f. Change in cash balance, $? The balance at September 30, 20X1, was $18,000.

g. The comparative balance sheet:

GILLETTE SATELLITE NETWORK, INC.
Comparative Balance Sheet
September 30, 20X2 and 20X1

	20X2		20X1
Current assets:			
Cash		$ 18,000	$ 18,000
Accounts receivable		65,000	72,000
Inventory		59,000	53,000
Prepaid expenses...		6,000	5,000
Total current assets		148,000	148,000
Property, plant and equipment:			
Land		–0–	14,000
Equipment	$226,000		$91,000
Less: Accumulated depreciation......................	(70,000)	156,000	(41,000) 50,000
Total assets..		$304,000	$212,000
Current liabilities:			
Accounts payable		$ 41,000	$ 28,000
Accrued liabilities..		19,000	21,000
Total current liabilities..................................		60,000	49,000
Long-term notes payable		105,000	90,000
Stockholders' equity:			
Common stock, no-par		71,000	36,000
Retained earnings		68,000	37,000
Total liabilities and stockholders' equity.............		$304,000	$212,000

Required

1. Prepare Gillette Satellite Network's statement of cash flows for the year ended September 30, 20X2, using the indirect method.

2. Evaluate Gillette Satellite Network's cash flows for the year. In your evaluation, mention all three categories of cash flows, and give the reason for your evaluation.

Computing cash flows from operating activities—indirect method (Obj. 5)

E17-12 The accounting records of Digitex Security Systems include these selected accounts:

CASH			
Mar. 1	5,000		
Receipts	451,000	Payments	448,000
Mar. 31	8,000		

ACCOUNTS RECEIVABLE			
Mar. 1	18,000		
Sales	443,000	Collections	447,000
Mar. 31	14,000		

INVENTORY			
Mar. 1	19,000		
Purchases	337,000	Cost of sales	335,000
Mar. 31	21,000		

EQUIPMENT			
Mar. 1	93,000		
Acquisition	6,000		
Mar. 31	99,000		

ACCUMULATED DEPRECIATION—EQUIPMENT			
		Mar. 1	52,000
		Depreciation	6,000
		Mar. 31	58,000

ACCOUNTS PAYABLE			
		Mar. 1	14,000
Payments	332,000	Purchases	337,000
		Mar. 31	19,000

ACCRUED LIABILITIES			
		Mar. 1	9,000
Payments	14,000	Expenses	11,000
		Mar. 31	6,000

RETAINED EARNINGS			
		Mar. 1	64,000
Quarterly dividend	18,000	Net income	23,000
		Mar. 31	69,000

Compute Digitex's net cash inflow or outflow from operating activities during March. Use the indirect method. Does Digitex have trouble collecting receivables or selling inventory? How can you tell?

E17-13 Consider three independent cash-flow situations for Calico Textile Company:

	Case 1	Case 2	Case 3
Cash flows from operating activities:			
Net income	$ 30,000	$ 30,000	$ 30,000
Depreciation and amortization	11,000	11,000	11,000
Increase in current assets	(19,000)	(7,000)	(1,000)
Decrease in current liabilities	(6,000)	(8,000)	–0–
	$ 16,000	$ 26,000	$ 40,000
Cash flows from investing activities:			
Acquisition of plant assets	$(91,000)	$(91,000)	$(91,000)
Sale of plant assets	97,000	4,000	8,000
	$ 6,000	$(87,000)	$ (83,000)
Cash flows from financing activities:			
Net borrowing	$ 16,000	$104,000	$ 50,000
Payment of debt	(21,000)	(29,000)	(9,000)
	$ (5,000)	$ 75,000	$ 41,000
Increase (decrease) in cash	$ 17,000	$ 14,000	$ (2,000)

For each case, use the cash-flow statement to identify how Calico Textile Company generated the cash to acquire new plant assets.

Challenge Exercise

E17-14 **PepsiCo's** statements of cash flows (adapted) for 1999 and 1998, are reproduced on page 691.

Required

1. Which format does PepsiCo use for reporting cash flows from operating activities? How can you tell?
2. What was PepsiCo's largest source of cash during 1999? During 1998? Give each amount.
3. What was PepsiCo's largest use of cash during 1999? During 1998? Give each amount.
4. The operating activities section of the 1999 statement lists (in millions):

Accounts and notes receivable	$(149)
Accounts payable and other current liabilities	$ 636

Did these accounts' balances increase or decrease during 1999? How can you tell?
5. At December 31, 1998, PepsiCo's balance sheet (not reproduced here) reported long-term debt (similar to notes payable) of $4,028 million. Journalize PepsiCo's long-term debt transactions during 1999. Then post to the Long-Term Debt T-account to see how much long-term debt PepsiCo would owe after these transactions.

PEPSICO, INC.
Statement of Cash Flows (Adapted)
Years Ended December 31, 1999 and 1998

Millions	1999	1998
Cash Flows—Continuing Operations:		
Net income	$2,050	$1,993
Adjustments to reconcile net income to net cash provided by operations:		
Gain on sale of bottling operations	(1,000)	—
Depreciation and amortization	1,032	1,234
Other noncash charges and credits, net	847	382
Changes in:		
Accounts and notes receivable	(149)	(104)
Inventories	(186)	29
Prepaid expenses	(203)	(12)
Accounts payable and other current liabilities	636	(311)
Net Cash Provided by Continuing Operations	3,027	3,211
Cash Flows—Investing Activities:		
Investments in other companies	(430)	(4,537)
Purchases of property, plant, and equipment	(1,118)	(1,405)
Proceeds from sale of property, plant, and equipment	625	151
Other, net	(149)	772
Net Cash Used for Investing Activities	(1,072)	(5,019)
Cash Flows—Financing Activities:		
Borrowing on long-term debt	3,480	990
Payment of long-term debt	(1,123)	(2,277)
Payment of short-term debt	(1,906)	—
Borrowing on short-term debt	—	4,049
Cash dividends paid	(778)	(757)
Other, net	(975)	(1,814)
Net Cash Provided by (Used for) Financing Activities	(1,302)	191
Increase (Decrease) in Cash and Cash Equivalents	653	(1,617)
Cash and Cash Equivalents—Beginning of Year	311	1,928
Cash and Cash Equivalents—End of Year	$ 964	$ 311

PROBLEMS

(Group A)

Using cash-flow information to evaluate performance (Obj. 1)

P17-1A Top managers of Crédit Lyonnais Group are reviewing company performance for 20X4. The income statement reports a 15% increase in net income, the fifth consecutive year with an income increase above 10%. The income statement includes a nonrecurring loss without which net income would have increased by 16%. The balance sheet shows modest increases in assets, liabilities, and stockholders' equity. The assets posting the largest increases are plant and equipment because the company is halfway through a five-year expansion program. No other assets and no liabilities are increasing dramatically. A summarized version of the cash-flow statement reports the following:

Net cash inflow from operating activities	$ 310,000
Net cash outflow from investing activities	(290,000)
Net cash inflow from financing activities	$ 70,000
Increase in cash during 20X4	$ 90,000

Required

Write a memo giving top managers of Crédit Lyonnais Group your assessment of 20X4 and your outlook for the future. Focus on the information content of the cash-flow data.

Preparing the statement of cash flows—direct method (Obj. 2, 3)

P17-2A Fordham Clothing Corporation accountants have developed the following data from the company's accounting records for the year ended July 31, 20X1:

a. Loan to another company, $35,000.
b. Income tax expense and payments, $56,400.
c. Depreciation expense, $27,700.
d. Collections on accounts receivable, $673,100.
e. Loan collections, $74,400.
f. Proceeds from sale of investments, $34,700, including a $3,800 loss.
g. Payment of long-term debt by issuing preferred stock, $107,300.
h. Amortization expense, $23,900.
i. Cash sales, $146,000.
j. Proceeds from issuance of common stock, $116,900.
k. Payment of cash dividends, $50,500.
l. Cash balance: July 31, 20X0—$53,800
                 July 31, 20X1—$?
m. Salary expense, $105,300.
n. Cash payments to purchase plant assets, $181,000.
o. Proceeds from issuance of short-term debt, $44,100.
p. Payments of long-term debt, $18,800.
q. Proceeds from sale of plant assets, $59,700, including a $10,600 gain.
r. Interest revenue, $12,100.
s. Cash receipt of dividend revenue on stock investments, $2,700.
t. Payments to suppliers, $673,300.
u. Interest expense and payments, $37,800.
v. Cost of goods sold, $481,100.
w. Collection of interest revenue, $3,700.
x. Acquisition of equipment by issuing short-term note payable, $35,500.
y. Payments of salaries, $104,000.
z. Credit sales, $608,100.

Required

1. Prepare Fordham's statement of cash flows for the year ended July 31, 20X1. Follow the format of Exhibit 17-2 (page 657), but do *not* show amounts in thousands. Include an accompanying schedule of noncash investing and financing activities.
2. Evaluate 20X1 in terms of cash flow. Give your reasons.

Preparing the statement of cash flows—direct method (Obj. 2, 3, 4)

P17-3A The 20X3 income statement and comparative balance sheet of Zurich Telecom, Inc., are given below.

ZURICH TELECOM, INC.		
Income Statement for 20X3		
Revenues:		
Sales revenue		$427,000
Interest revenue		11,700
Total revenues		438,700
Expenses:		
Cost of goods sold........................	$205,200	
Salary expense	76,400	
Depreciation expense...................	15,300	
Other operating expense..............	49,700	
Interest expense	24,600	
Income tax expense	16,900	
Total expenses............................		388,100
Net income		$ 50,600

Zurich Telecom had no noncash investing and financing transactions during 20X3. During the year, there were no sales of land or equipment, no issuances of notes payable, no retirements of stock, and no treasury stock transactions.

Required

1. Prepare the 20X3 statement of cash flows, formatting operating activities by the direct method. See the company balance sheet at the top of the next page.
2. How will what you learned in this problem help you evaluate an investment?

Preparing the statement of cash flows—indirect method (Obj. 2, 3, 5)

P17-4A Use the Zurich Telecom data from Problem 17-3A.

Required

1. Prepare the 20X3 statement of cash flows by the indirect method. If your instructor also assigned Problem 17-3A, prepare only the operating activities section.
2. How will what you learned in this problem help you evaluate an investment?

ZURICH TELECOM, INC.
Comparative Balance Sheet

	December 31, 20X3	December 31, 20X2	Increase (Decrease)
Current assets:			
Cash and cash equivalents	$ 8,700	$ 15,600	$ (6,900)
Accounts receivable	35,500	43,100	(7,600)
Interest receivable..	600	900	(300)
Inventories..	94,300	89,900	4,400
Prepaid expenses...	1,700	2,200	(500)
Plant assets:			
Land	35,100	10,000	25,100
Equipment, net	100,900	93,700	7,200
Total assets..	$276,800	$255,400	$21,400
Current liabilities:			
Accounts payable	$ 16,400	$ 17,900	$ (1,500)
Interest payable..	6,300	6,700	(400)
Salary payable	2,100	1,400	700
Other accrued liabilities	18,100	18,700	(600)
Income tax payable.......................................	6,300	3,800	2,500
Long-term liabilities:			
Notes payable...	55,000	65,000	(10,000)
Stockholders' equity:			
Common stock, no-par	131,100	122,300	8,800
Retained earnings	41,500	19,600	21,900
Total liabilities and stockholders' equity...........	$276,800	$255,400	$21,400

P17-5A Accountants for Ross Retail Company have assembled the following data for the year ended December 31, 20X4:

Preparing the statement of cash flows—indirect method (Obj. 2, 5)

Current Accounts (All Result from Operations)	December 31, 20X4	20X3
Current assets:		
Cash and cash equivalents......................................	$49,600	$34,800
Accounts receivable	70,100	73,700
Inventories...	90,600	96,500
Prepaid expenses..	3,200	2,100
Current liabilities:		
Notes payable (for inventory purchases)	$36,300	$36,800
Accounts payable..	72,100	67,500
Income tax payable...	5,900	6,800
Accrued liabilities..	28,300	23,200

Transaction data for 20X4:

Stock dividends...	$ 12,600	Payment of cash dividends	$48,300
Collection of loan..	10,300	Issuance of long-term debt	
Depreciation expense.....................................	19,200	to borrow cash	71,000
Acquisition of equipment	69,000	Net income	61,500
Payment of long-term debt by		Issuance of preferred stock	
issuing common stock	89,400	for cash..	36,200
Acquisition of long-term.............................		Sale of long-term investment	12,200
investment...	44,800	Amortization expense.....................................	1,100
Acquisition of building by issuing		Payment of long-term debt.............................	47,800
long-term note payable	118,000	Gain on sale of investment.............................	3,500

Required

Prepare Ross Retail Company's statement of cash flows, using the *indirect* method for operating activities. Include a schedule of noncash investing and financing activities.

Preparing the statement of cash flows—indirect method (Obj. 2, 5)

P17-6A The comparative balance sheet of Fortis Software Co. at December 31, 20X5, reported the following:

	December 31, 20X5	December 31, 20X4
Current assets:		
Cash and cash equivalents	$10,600	$15,500
Accounts receivable	28,600	29,300
Inventories	51,600	53,000
Prepaid expenses	4,200	3,700
Current liabilities:		
Notes payable (for inventory purchases)	$ 9,200	$ -0-
Accounts payable	21,900	28,000
Accrued liabilities	11,000	16,800

Fortis's transactions during 20X5 included the following:

Amortization expense	$ 5,000	Cash acquisition of building	$124,000
Payment of cash dividends	17,000	Net income	28,600
Cash acquisition of equipment	55,000	Insurance of common stock	
Issuance of long-term note		for cash	105,600
payable to borrow cash	32,000	Stock dividend	13,000
Retirement of bonds payable by		Sale of long-term investment	6,000
issuing common stock	55,000	Depreciation expense	15,000

Required

1. Prepare the statement of cash flows of Fortis Software for the year ended December 31, 20X5. Use the *indirect* method to report cash flows from operating activities. Report non-cash investing and financing activities in an accompanying schedule.
2. Evaluate Fortis Software's cash flows for the year. Mention all three categories of cash flows, and give the reason for your evaluation.

Preparing the statement of cash flows—direct and indirect methods (Obj. 3, 5)

P17-7A To prepare the statement of cash flows, accountants for Shell City Oil Corp. have summarized 20X2 activity in two accounts as follows:

CASH

Beg. bal.	87,100	Payments of operating expenses	67,800
Issuance of common stock	34,600	Payment of long-term debt	78,900
Receipts of dividends	14,100	Payment of income tax	12,600
Sale of investments	9,900	Payments on accounts payable	101,600
Collections from customers	315,100	Payment of dividends	1,800
		Payment of salaries	67,500
		Purchase of equipment	79,900
End. bal.	50,700		

COMMON STOCK

	Beg. bal.	103,500
	Issuance for cash	34,600
	Issuance to acquire land	62,100
	End. bal.	200,200

Required

1. Prepare Shell City's statement of cash flows for the year ended December 31, 20X2, using the *direct* method to report operating activities. Also prepare the accompanying schedule

of noncash investing and financing activities. Shell City's 20X2 income statement and selected balance sheet data follow.

2. Use these data to prepare a supplementary schedule showing cash flows from operating activities by the *indirect* method. All activity in the current accounts results from operations.

SHELL CITY OIL CORP.
Income Statement
Year Ended December 31, 20X2

Revenues and gains:		
Sales revenue.....................................		$281,800
Dividend revenue		14,100
Total revenues and gains...............		295,900
Expenses:		
Cost of goods sold............................	$103,600	
Salary expense...................................	66,800	
Depreciation expense	10,900	
Other operating expense	64,500	
Income tax expense..........................	12,600	
Total expenses...............................		258,400
Net income..		$ 37,500

SHELL CITY OIL CORP.
Balance Sheet Data

	20X2 Increase (Decrease)
Current assets:	
Cash and cash equivalents................	$?
Accounts receivable.	(33,300)
Inventories...	5,700
Investments.	(9,900)
Equipment, net....................................	69,000
Land	62,100
Current liabilities:	
Accounts payable.............................	$ 7,700
Salary payable...................................	(700)
Other accrued liabilities	(3,300)
Long-term debt.................................	(78,900)
Common stock	96,700
Retained earnings..............................	35,700

P17-8A Unico, Inc.'s comparative balance sheet at September 30, 20X4, included the following balances as shown at the top of the next page.

Preparing the statement of cash flows—indirect method (Obj. 4, 5)

Transaction data for the year ended September 30, 20X4:

a. Net income, 85,900.
b. Depreciation expense, $8,500.
c. Acquired long-term investments, $37,300.
d. Sold land for $38,100, including a $10,900 gain.
e. Acquired equipment by issuing long-term note payable, $26,300.
f. Paid long-term note payable, $24,700.
g. Received cash of $51,900 for issuance of common stock.
h. Paid cash dividends, $64,300.
i. Acquired equipment by issuing short-term note payable, $22,000.

Required

Prepare Unico's statement of cash flows for the year ended September 30, 20X4, using the *indirect* method to report operating activities. Also prepare the accompanying schedule of noncash investing and financing activities. All current accounts except short-term notes payable result from operating transactions.

UNICO, INC.
Balance Sheet
September 30, 20X4 and 20X3

	20X4	20X3	Increase (Decrease)
Current assets:			
Cash	$ 40,700	$ 17,600	$23,100
Accounts receivable	46,000	46,800	(800)
Inventories	121,700	116,900	4,800
Prepaid expenses	8,600	9,300	(700)
Long-term investments	51,100	13,800	37,300
Equipment, net	131,900	92,100	39,800
Land	47,100	74,300	(27,200)
	$447,100	$370,800	$76,300
Current liabilities:			
Notes payable, short-term	$ 22,000	$ -0-	$22,000
Accounts payable	61,800	70,300	(8,500)
Income tax payable	21,800	24,600	(2,800)
Accrued liabilities	23,900	33,400	(9,500)
Long-term note payable	123,000	121,400	1,600
Common stock	113,900	62,000	51,900
Retained earnings	80,700	59,100	21,600
	$447,100	$370,800	$76,300

(Group B) PROBLEMS

Using cash-flow information to evaluate performance (Obj. 1)

P17-1B Top managers of Crane Furniture, Inc., are reviewing company performance for 20X2. The income statement reports a 20% increase in net income over 20X1. However, most of the increase resulted from an extraordinary gain on insurance proceeds from storm damage to a building. The balance sheet shows a large increase in receivables. The cash-flow statement, in summarized form, reports the following:

Net cash outflow from operating activities	$(80,000)
Net cash inflow from investing activities	40,000
Net cash inflow from financing activities	50,000
Increase in cash during 20X2	$ 10,000

Required

Write a memo giving Crane managers your assessment of 20X2 operations and your outlook for the future. Focus on the information content of the cash-flow data.

Preparing the statement of cash flows—direct method (Obj. 2, 3)

P17-2B Accountants for Westpac Pharmaceuticals, Inc., have developed the following data from the company's accounting records for the year ended April 30, 20X5:

a. Credit sales, $583,900.
b. Loan to another company, $12,500.
c. Cash payments to acquire plant assets, $59,400.
d. Cost of goods sold, $382,600.
e. Proceeds from issuance of common stock, $8,000.
f. Payment of cash dividends, $48,400.
g. Collection of interest, $4,400.
h. Acquisition of equipment by issuing common stock, $41,000.
i. Payments of salaries, $93,600.
j. Proceeds from sale of plant assets, $22,400, including a $6,800 loss.
k. Collections on accounts receivable, $462,600.
l. Interest revenue, $3,800.
m. Cash receipt of dividend revenue on stock investments, $4,100.
n. Payments to suppliers, $368,500.
o. Cash sales, $180,900.
p. Depreciation expense, $59,900.
q. Proceeds from issuance of short-term debt, $19,600.
r. Payments of long-term debt, $50,000.
s. Interest expense and payments, $13,300.
t. Salary expense, $95,300.

u. Loan collections, $12,800.

v. Proceeds from sale of investments, $9,100, including a $2,000 gain.

w. Payment of short-term note payable by issuing long-term note payable, $63,000.

x. Amortization expense, $2,900.

y. Income tax expense and payments, $37,900.

z. Cash balance: April 30, 20X4—$39,300
                      April 30, 20X5—$?

Required

1. Prepare Westpac's statement of cash flows for the year ended April 30, 20X5. Follow the format of Exhibit 17-2, but do *not* show amounts in thousands. Include an accompanying schedule of noncash investing and financing activities.

2. Evaluate 20X5 from a cash-flow standpoint. Give your reasons.

P17-3B The 20X5 comparative balance sheet and income statement of Dayrunner Corp. follow.

Preparing the statement of cash flows—direct method
(Obj. 2, 3, 4)

DAYRUNNER CORP.
Comparative Balance Sheet

	December 31, 20X5	December 31, 20X4	Increase (Decrease)
Current assets:			
Cash and cash equivalents...............	$ 14,200	$ 5,300	$ 8,900
Accounts receivable	28,600	26,900	1,700
Interest receivable............................	1,900	700	1,200
Inventories......................................	83,600	87,200	(3,600)
Prepaid expenses	2,500	1,900	600
Plant assets:			
Land..	89,000	60,000	29,000
Equipment, net................................	53,500	49,400	4,100
Total assets......................................	$273,300	$231,400	$41,900
Current liabilities:			
Accounts payable.............................	$ 31,400	$ 28,800	$ 2,600
Interest payable	4,400	4,900	(500)
Salary payable..................................	3,100	6,600	(3,500)
Other accrued liabilities	13,700	16,000	(2,300)
Income tax payable..........................	8,900	7,700	1,200
Long-term liabilities:			
Notes payable..................................	75,000	100,000	(25,000)
Stockholders' equity:			
Common stock, no-par.....................	88,300	64,700	23,600
Retained earnings	48,500	2,700	45,800
Total liabilities and stockholders' equity...................................	$273,300	$231,400	$41,900

DAYRUNNER CORP.
Income Statement for 20X5

Revenues:		
Sales revenue.................................		$220,000
Interest revenue		8,600
Total revenues............................		228,600
Expenses:		
Cost of goods sold..........................	$70,600	
Salary expense................................	27,800	
Depreciation expense	4,000	
Other operating expense	10,500	
Interest expense.............................	11,600	
Income tax expense.......................	29,100	
Total expenses		153,600
Net income		$ 75,000

Dayrunner had no noncash investing and financing transactions during 20X5. During the year, there were no sales of land or equipment, no issuances of notes payable, no retirements of stock, and no treasury stock transactions.

Required
1. Prepare the 20X5 statement of cash flows, formatting operating activities by the direct method.
2. How will what you learned in this problem help you evaluate an investment?

Preparing the statement of cash flows—indirect method (Obj. 2, 3, 5)

P17-4B Use the Dayrunner Corp. data from Problem 17-3B.

Required
1. Prepare the 20X5 statement of cash flows by the indirect method. If your instructor also assigned Problem 17-3B, prepare only the operating activities section of the statement.
2. How will what you learned in this problem help you evaluate an investment?

Preparing the statement of cash flows—indirect method (Obj. 2, 5)

P17-5B Flanagan Corporation accountants have assembled the following data for the year ended December 31, 20X3:

Current Accounts (All Result from Operations)	December 31, 20X3	20X2
Current Assets:		
Cash and cash equivalents	$67,700	$22,700
Accounts receivable	69,700	64,200
Inventories	88,600	83,000
Prepaid expenses	5,300	4,100
Current Liabilities:		
Notes payable (for inventory purchases)	$22,600	$18,300
Accounts payable	52,900	55,800
Income tax payable	18,600	16,700
Accrued liabilities	15,500	27,200

Transaction data for 20X3:

Acquisition of land by issuing long-term note payable	$107,000	Purchase of treasury stock	$14,300
Stock dividends	31,800	Loss on sale of equipment	11,700
Collection of loan	8,700	Payment of cash dividends	18,300
Depreciation expense	26,800	Issuance of long-term note payable to borrow cash	34,400
Acquisition of building	125,300	Net income	69,100
Retirement of bonds payable by issuing common stock	65,000	Issuance of common stock for cash	41,200
Acquisition of long-term investment	31,600	Sale of equipment	58,000
		Amortization expense	5,300

Required
Prepare Flanagan Corporation's statement of cash flows, using the *indirect* method for operating activities. Include a schedule of noncash investing and financing activities.

Preparing the statement of cash flows—indirect method (Obj. 2, 5)

P17-6B The comparative balance sheet of Kekst & Co. at March 31, 20X4, reported the following:

	March 31, 20X4	20X3
Current Assets:		
Cash and cash equivalents	$20,600	$ 4,000
Accounts receivable	14,900	21,700
Inventories	63,200	60,600
Prepaid expenses	1,900	1,700
Current Liabilities:		
Notes payable (for inventory purchases)	$ 4,000	$ 4,000
Accounts payable	30,300	27,600
Accrued liabilities	10,700	11,100
Income tax payable	8,000	4,700

Kekst & Co.'s transactions during the year ended March 31, 20X4, included the following:

Acquisition of land by issuing note payable	$76,000	Sale of long-term investment	$13,700
Amortization expense	2,000	Depreciation expense	9,000
Payment of cash dividend	30,000	Cash acquisition of building	47,000
Cash acquisition of equipment	78,700	Net income	77,000
Issuance of long-term note payable to borrow cash	50,000	Issuance of common stock for cash	11,000
		Stock dividend	18,000

Required

1. Prepare Kekst & Co.'s statement of cash flows for the year ended March 31, 20X4, using the *indirect* method to report cash flows from operating activities. Report noncash investing and financing activities in an accompanying schedule.
2. Evaluate Kekst & Co.'s cash flows for the year. Mention all three categories of cash flows, and give the reason for your evaluation.

P17-7B To prepare the statement of cash flows, accountants for Agilera.com, Inc., have summarized 20X3 activity in two accounts as follows:

Preparing the statement of cash flows—direct and indirect methods
(Obj. 3, 5)

CASH

Beg. bal.	53,600	Payments on accounts payable	399,100
Sale of investment	21,200	Payment of dividends	27,200
Collections from customers	669,700	Payment of salaries	143,800
Issuance of common stock	47,300	Purchase of equipment	31,400
Receipts of dividends	17,100	Payment of other operating expenses	63,600
		Payment of long-term debt	41,300
		Payment of income tax	18,900
End. bal.	83,600		

COMMON STOCK

Beg. bal.	84,400
Issuance for cash	47,300
Issuance to acquire land	99,100
End. bal.	230,800

Required

1. Prepare the statement of cash flows of Agilera.com, Inc., for the year ended December 31, 20X3, using the *direct* method to report operating activities. Also prepare the accompanying schedule of noncash investing and financing activities.
2. Use the following data from Agilera.com's 20X3 income statement and (selected) balance sheet to prepare a supplementary schedule showing cash flows from operating activities by the *indirect* method. All activity in the current accounts results from operations.

AGILERA.COM, INC.
Income Statement
Year Ended December 31, 20X3

Revenues:		
Sales revenue		$706,300
Dividend revenue		17,100
Total revenues		723,400
Expenses and losses:		
Cost of goods sold	$402,600	
Salary expense	158,500	
Depreciation expense	24,300	
Other operating expense	63,600	
Income tax expense	18,900	
Total expense		667,900
Net income		$ 55,500

AGILERA.COM, INC.
Balance Sheet Data

	20X3 Increase (Decrease)
Current assets:	
Cash and cash equivalents...............	$?
Accounts receivable	36,600
Inventories.......................................	(11,800)
Long-term investments	(21,200)
Equipment, net....................................	7,100
Land..	99,100
Current liabilities:	
Accounts payable	$ (8,300)
Salary payable.................................	14,700
Long-term debt................................	(41,300)
Common stock, no-par........................	146,400
Retained earnings..............................	28,300

Preparing the statement of cash flows — indirect method (Obj. 4, 5)

P17-8B The comparative balance sheet of Shin-Etsu Chemical Company at June 30, 20X2, included the following balances:

SHIN-ETSU CHEMICAL COMPANY
Balance Sheet
June 30, 20X2 and 20X1

	20X2	20X1	Increase (Decrease)
Current assets:			
Cash	$ 31,500	$ 8,600	$ 22,900
Accounts receivable	48,800	51,900	(3,100)
Inventories.....................................	68,600	60,200	8,400
Prepaid expenses............................	3,700	2,800	900
Long-term investment......................	10,100	5,200	4,900
Equipment, net................................	82,500	73,600	8,900
Land..	42,400	96,000	(53,600)
	$287,600	$298,300	$(10,700)
Current liabilities:			
Notes payable, short-term			
(for general borrowing).............	$ 13,400	$ 18,100	$ (4,700)
Accounts payable	42,400	40,300	2,100
Income tax payable........................	13,800	14,500	(700)
Accrued liabilities..........................	12,800	15,200	(2,400)
Long-term notes payable..................	47,400	94,100	(46,700)
Common stock	59,800	51,200	8,600
Retained earnings............................	98,000	64,900	33,100
	$287,600	$298,300	$(10,700)

Transaction data for the year ended June 30, 20X2:

 a. Net income, $71,200.
 b. Depreciation expense, $5,400.
 c. Purchased long-term investment, $4,900.
 d. Sold land for $46,900, including a $6,700 loss.
 e. Acquired equipment by issuing long-term note payable, $14,300.
 f. Paid long-term note payable, $61,000.
 g. Received cash for issuance of common stock, $3,900.
 h. Paid cash dividends, $38,100.
 i. Paid short-term note payable by issuing common stock, $4,700.

Required

Prepare the statement of cash flows of Shin-Etsu Chemical Company for the year ended June 30, 20X2, using the *indirect* method to report operating activities. Also prepare the accompanying schedule of noncash investing and financing activities. All current accounts except short-term notes payable result from operating transactions.

APPLY YOUR KNOWLEDGE

DECISION CASES

Case 1. The 20X2 comparative income statement and the 20X2 comparative balance sheet of Dexia Enterprises have just been distributed at a meeting of the company's board of directors. The members of the board of directors raise a fundamental question: Why is the cash balance so low? This question is especially troublesome because 20X2 showed record profits. As the controller of the company, you must answer the question.

Preparing and using the statement of cash flows to evaluate operations (Obj. 4, 5)

Required

1. Prepare a statement of cash flows for 20X2 in the format that best shows the relationship between net income and operating cash flow. The company sold no plant assets or long-

DEXIA ENTERPRISES
Comparative Income Statement
Years Ended December 31, 20X2 and 20X1

Thousands	20X2	20X1
Revenues and gains:		
Sales revenue	$452	$310
Gain on sale of equipment (sale price, $33)		18
Total revenues and gains	$452	$328
Expenses and losses:		
Cost of goods sold	$221	$162
Salary expense	48	28
Depreciation expense	46	22
Interest expense	13	20
Amortization expense on patent	11	11
Loss on sale of land (sale price, $61)		35
Total expenses and losses	339	278
Net income	$113	$ 50

DEXIA ENTERPRISES
Comparative Balance Statement
December 31, 20X2 and 20X1

Thousands	20X2	20X1
Assets		
Cash	$ 41	$ 63
Accounts receivable, net	72	61
Inventories	194	181
Long-term investments	31	–0–
Property, plant, and equipment	361	259
Accumulated depreciation	(244)	(198)
Patents	177	188
Totals	$632	$554
Liabilities and Owners' Equity		
Notes payable, short-term		
(for general borrowing)	$ 32	$101
Accounts payable	63	56
Accrued liabilities	12	17
Notes payable, long-term	147	163
Common stock, no-par	149	61
Retained earnings	229	156
Totals	$632	$554

term investments and issued no notes payable during 20X2. The changes in all current accounts except short-term notes payable arose from operations. There were *no* noncash investing and financing transactions during the year. Show all amounts in thousands.

2. Answer the board members' question: Why is the cash balance so low? In explaining the business's cash flows, identify two significant cash receipts that occurred during 20X1 but not in 20X2. Also point out the two largest cash payments during 20X2.

3. Considering net income and the company's cash flows during 20X2, was it a good year or a bad year? Give your reasons.

Using cash-flow data to evaluate an investment

(Obj. 1, 2)

Case 2. SPAR Corp. and Babcock, Inc., are asking you to recommend their stock to your clients. SPAR and Babcock earn about the same net income and have similar financial positions, so your decision depends on their cash flows, summarized as follows:

	SPAR Corp.		Babcock, Inc.	
Net cash inflows from operating activities		$90,000		$10,000
Net cash inflows (outflows) from investing activities:				
Purchase of plant assets	$(100,000)		$(20,000)	
Sale of plant assets..	10,000	(90,000)	80,000	60,000
Net cash inflows (outflows) from financing activities:				
Issuance of common stock...		30,000		—
Paying off long-term debt...				(40,000)
Net increase in cash..		$30,000		$30,000

Based on their cash flows, which company looks better? Give your reasons.

ETHICAL ISSUE

Absolute Entertainment (ET) Agency is having a bad year. Net income is only $50,000. Also, two important clients are falling behind in their payments to Absolute, and the agency's accounts receivable are ballooning. The company desperately needs a loan. The Absolute ET board of directors is considering ways to put the best face on the company's financial statements. The agency's bank closely examines cash flow from operations. Rachel McPherson, Absolute ET's controller, suggests reclassifying as *long-term* the receivables from the slow-paying clients. She explains that removing the $70,000 rise in accounts receivable will increase cash flow from operations. This may help Absolute ET get the loan.

Required

1. Using only the amounts given, compute net cash inflow from operations both with and without the reclassification of the receivables. Which way makes Absolute ET look better?

2. Under what condition would the reclassification of the receivables be ethical? Unethical?

FINANCIAL STATEMENT CASE

Using the statement of cash flows

(Obj. 2, 4)

Use the **Target Corporation** statement of cash flows along with the company's other financial statements, all in Appendix A, to answer the following questions.

Required

1. Which method does Target use to report net cash flows from *operating* activities? How can you tell?

2. Suppose Target reported net cash flows from operating activities by the direct method. Compute these amounts for the year ended January 29, 2000 (Target labels the year as "1999").

   a. Collections from customers (*Retained securitized receivables* means accounts receivable).
   b. Payments for inventory.
   c. Payments for operating expenses. (Use Selling General and Administrative Expense; Other Current Assets, which are Prepaid Expenses; and Accrued Liabilities.

3. Evaluate 1999 in terms of net income, cash flows, balance sheet position, and overall results. Be specific.

TEAM PROJECTS

Project 1. Select a company and obtain its annual report, including all the financial statements. Focus on the statement of cash flows and the cash flows from operating activities in particular. Identify whether the company uses the direct method or the indirect method to report operating cash flows. Use the other financial statements (income statement, balance sheet, and statement of stockholders' equity) and the notes, if necessary, to prepare the company's cash flows from operating activities by the *other* method.

Project 2. Each member of the group should obtain the annual report of a different company. Select companies in different industries. Evaluate each company's trend of cash flows for the most recent two years. In your evaluation of the companies' cash flows, you may use any other information that is publicly available—for example, the other financial statements (income statement, balance sheet, statement of stockholders' equity, and the related notes) and news stories from magazines and newspapers. Rank the companies' cash flows from best to worst, and write a two-page report on your findings.

INTERNET EXERCISE

Royal Caribbean Cruises Ltd. operates the Royal Caribbean International and Celebrity Cruises brands, with 18 modern ships and a passenger capacity of 34,900.

Go to **http://www.rclinvestor.com** and click on *Annual Reports,* and then the HTML version of the *most recent annual report.* Continue until you can click on the *financial table of contents* followed by the *Consolidated Statements of Cash Flows.* Use this statement to answer the following questions.

1. Does Royal Caribbean Cruises use the direct or the indirect method to prepare the statement of cash flows? How can you tell? Which activity section is affected by this choice of method?
2. For the most recent year, list the amount of net cash inflow or outflow for each of the three major types of activities reported on the Statement of Cash Flows. Which type of activity is providing the most cash? Is this considered favorable or unfavorable?
3. For the most recent year, what amount is reported for *Net Income/(Loss)* and *Net Cash provided by Operating Activities?* Are these amounts the same? Explain why or why not.
4. For the most recent year, did Royal Caribbean Cruises purchase or sell more property and equipment? Is this considered favorable or unfavorable? What was the net amount purchased/sold? Which activity section reports this information?
5. For the most recent year, did Royal Caribbean Cruises issue or pay back more debt? What was the net amount issued/repaid? For the most recent year, did Royal Caribbean Cruises issue or purchase more common stock? What was the net amount issued/purchased? For the most recent year, what amount of cash dividends did Royal Caribbean Cruises pay out? Which activity section reports this information?
6. Does this statement of cash flows indicate a strong or weak cash position? Explain.

Royal Caribbean Cruises

Go to the "Statement of Cash Flows" episode on the *Mastering Accounting* CD-ROM for an interactive, video-enhanced exercise focused on helping CanGo managers understand the difference between direct and indirect methods and the quality of earnings when comparing net income (on paper) to actual cash flow. The difference between cash on hand and what is owed to the company on paper can affect investor confidence.

APPENDIX TO CHAPTER 17

THE WORK SHEET APPROACH TO PREPARING THE STATEMENT OF CASH FLOWS

The body of this chapter discusses the uses of the statement of cash flows in decision making and shows how to prepare the statement using T-accounts. The T-account approach works well as a learning device. In practice, however, most companies face complex situations. In these cases, a work sheet can help accountants prepare the statement of cash flows. This appendix shows how to prepare that statement using a specially designed work sheet.

The work sheet starts with the beginning balance sheet and concludes with the ending balance sheet. Two middle columns—one for debit amounts and the other for credit amounts—complete the work sheet. These columns, labeled Transaction Analysis, contain the data for the statement of cash flows. Exhibit 17A-1 presents the work sheet. Accountants can prepare the statement directly from the lower part of the work sheet (Panel B in Exhibit 17A-1). All the exhibits in this appendix are based on the Anchor Corporation data presented in the chapter.

PREPARING THE WORK SHEET—DIRECT METHOD FOR OPERATING ACTIVITIES

The direct method separates operating activities into cash receipts and cash payments. The work sheet can be prepared by following these steps:

Step 1: Panel A gives the beginning and ending balances for Cash and all other balance sheet accounts through Retained Earnings. The amounts are taken directly from the beginning and ending balance sheets in Exhibit 17-7 (page 666).

Step 2: Panel B lays out the framework of the statement of cash flows—that is, the headings for cash flows from operating, investing, and financing activities. Exhibit 17A-1 is based on the direct method and splits operating activities into Receipts and Payments.

Step 3: The bottom of the work sheet shows Net Increase in Cash or Net Decrease in Cash, as the case may be. This final amount is the difference between ending cash and beginning cash, from the balance sheet. The statement of cash flows explains why this change in cash occurred during the period.

Step 4: Analyze the period's transactions in the middle columns of the work sheet.

Step 5: Prepare the statement of cash flows directly from Panel B of the work sheet.

Transaction Analysis on the Work Sheet—Direct Method

For your convenience, we repeat the Anchor Corporation transaction data from Exhibit 17-5. These data are given below.

The transaction analysis on the work sheet appears in the form of journal entries. Only balance sheet accounts appear on the work sheet. There are no income statement accounts. Therefore, revenue transactions are entered on the work sheet as credits to Retained Earnings. For example, in transaction (a), sales on account are entered on the work sheet by debiting Accounts Receivable and crediting Retained Earnings. Cash is neither debited nor credited because credit sales do not affect cash. But all transactions should be entered on the work sheet to identify all the cash effects of the period's transactions. In transaction (c), the earning of interest revenue is entered by debiting Interest Receivable and crediting Retained Earnings. The revenue transactions that generate cash are also recorded by crediting Retained Earnings.

Operating Activities:
1. Sales on credit, $284,000
*2. Collections from customets, $271,000
3. Interest revenue on notes receivable, $12,000
*4. Collection of interest receivable, $10,000
*5. Cash receipt of dividend revenue on investments in stock, $9,000
6. Cost of goods sold, $150,000
7. Purchase of inventory on credit, $147,000

*8. Payments to suppliers, $133,000
9. Salary expense, $56,000
*10. Payments of salaries, $58,000
11. Depreciation expense, $18,000
12. Other operating expense, $17,000
*13. Interest expense and payments, $16,000
*14. Income tax expense and payments, $15,000

Investing Activities:
*15. Cash payments to acquire plant assets, $306,000
*16. Loan to another company, $11,000

*17. Proceeds from sale of plant assets, $62,000, including $8,000 gain

Financing Activities:
*18. Proceeds from issuance of common stock, $101,000
*19. Proceeds from issuance of long-term note payable, $94,000

*20. Payment of long-term note payable, $11,000
*21. Declaration and payment of cash dividends, $17,000

* Indicates a cash-flow transaction to be reported on the statement of cash flows.

ANCHOR CORPORATION
Work Sheet for Statement of Cash Flows (Direct Method)
Year Ended December 31, 20X2

(In thousands)

	Balances Dec. 31, 20X1	Transaction Analysis Debit	Transaction Analysis Credit	Balances Dec. 31, 20X2
PANEL A—Account Titles				
Cash	42		(v) 20	22
Accounts receivable	80	(a) 284	(b) 271	93
Interest receivable	1	(c) 12	(d) 10	3
Inventory	138	(g) 147	(f) 150	135
Prepaid expenses	7	(h3) 1		8
Long-term receivable from another company	—	(p) 11		11
Plant assets, net	219	(o) 306	(k) 18	
			(q) 54	453
Totals	487			725
Accounts payable	57	(h1) 113	(g) 147	91
Salary and wage payable	6	(j) 58	(i) 56	4
Accrued liabilities	3	(h2) 19	(l) 17	1
Long-term notes payable	77	(t) 11	(s) 94	160
Common stock	258		(r) 101	359
Retained earnings	86	(f) 150	(a) 284	110
		(l) 17	(c) 12	
		(i) 56	(e) 9	
		(k) 18	(q) 8	
		(m) 16		
		(n) 15		
		(u) 17		
Totals	487	1,251	1,251	725
PANEL B—Statement of Cash Flows				
Cash flows from operating activities:				
Receipts:				
Collections from customers		(b) 271		
Interest received		(d) 10		
Dividends received		(e) 9		
Payments:				
To suppliers			(h1) 113	
			(h2) 19	
			(h3) 1	
To employees			(j) 58	
For interest			(m) 16	
For income tax			(n) 15	
Cash flows from investing activities:				
Acquisition of plant assets			(o) 306	
Proceeds from sale of plant		(q) 62		
Loan to another company			(p) 11	
Cash flows from financing activities:				
Proceeds from issuance of common stock		(r) 101		
Proceeds from issuance of long-term note payable		(s) 94		
Payment of long-term note payable			(t) 11	
Payment of dividends			(u) 17	
		547	567	
Increase (decrease) in cash		(v) 20		
Totals		567	567	

Expense transactions are entered on the work sheet as debits to Retained Earnings. In transaction (f), cost of goods sold is entered by debiting Retained Earnings and crediting Inventory. Transaction (m) is a cash payment of interest expense. The work sheet entry debits Retained Earnings and credits Payments for Interest under operating activities. The remaining expense transactions follow a similar pattern.

NET INCREASE (DECREASE) IN CASH The net increase or net decrease in cash for the period is the balancing amount needed to equate the total debits and total credits ($567,000) on the statement of cash flows. In Exhibit 17A-1, Anchor Corporation experienced a $20,000 decrease in cash. This amount is entered as a credit to Cash, transaction (v), at the top of the work sheet and a debit to Net Decrease in Cash at the bottom. Totaling the columns completes the work sheet.

Preparing the Statement of Cash Flows from the Work Sheet

To prepare the statement of cash flows, Exhibit 17-2 (page 657) in the text, rewrite Panel B of the work sheet and add subtotals for the three categories of activities.

PREPARING THE WORK SHEET—INDIRECT METHOD FOR OPERATING ACTIVITIES

The indirect method shows the reconciliation from net income to net cash inflow (or net cash outflow) from operating activities. Exhibit 17A-2 is the work sheet for preparing the statement of cash flows by the indirect method.

The steps for completing the work sheet by the indirect method are the same as those used in the direct method. The analysis of investing activities and financing activities uses the information presented in Exhibit 17-5 (page 660) and repeated at the bottom of page 704. As mentioned previously, there is no difference for investing activities or financing activities between the direct- and indirect-method work sheets. Therefore, the analysis that follows focuses on cash flows from operating activities. The Anchor Corporation data come from the income statement (Exhibit 17-6, page 665) and the comparative balance sheet (Exhibit 17-7, page 666).

Transaction Analysis on the Work Sheet—Indirect Method

Net income, transaction (a), is the first operating cash inflow.* Net income is entered on the work sheet as a debit to Net Income under cash flows from operating activities and a credit to Retained Earnings. Next come the additions to, and subtractions from, net income, starting with depreciation—transaction (b)—which is debited to Depreciation on the work sheet and credited to Plant Assets, Net. Transaction (c) is the sale of plant assets. The $8,000 gain on the sale is entered as a credit to Gain on Sale of Plant Assets under operating cash flows—a subtraction from net income. This credit removes the $8,000 gain in cash flow from operations because the cash proceeds from the sale were not $8,000. The cash proceeds were $62,000, so this amount is entered on the work sheet as a debit under investing activities. Entry (c) is completed by crediting the plant assets' book value of $54,000 ($62,000 − $8,000) to the Plant Assets, Net account.

Entries (d) through (j) reconcile net income to cash flows from operations for increases and decreases in the current assets other than Cash and for increases and decreases in the current liabilities. Entry (d) debits Accounts Receivable for its $13,000 increase during the year. This decrease in cash flows is credited to Increase in Accounts Receivable under operating cash flows. Entries (e) and (g) are similar for Interest Receivable and Prepaid Expenses.

The final item in Exhibit 17A-2 is the Net Increase (Decrease) in Cash—transaction (q) on the work sheet—a credit to Cash and a debit to Net Decrease in Cash, exactly as in Exhibit 17A-1. To prepare the statement of cash flows, the accountant merely rewrites Panel B of the work sheet, adding subtotals for the three categories of activities.

*Note that we are now using the *indirect* method. The transactions we analyze here are *not* the same as those listed on pages 704–706.

ANCHOR CORPORATION
Work Sheet for Statement of Cash Flows (Indirect Method)
Year Ended December 31, 20X2

	Balances	Transaction Analysis		Balances
	Dec. 31, 20X1	Debit	Credit	Dec. 31, 20X2
PANEL A—Account Titles				
Cash	42		(q) 20	22
Accounts receivable	80	(d) 13		93
Interest receivable	1	(e) 2		3
Inventory	138		(f) 3	135
Prepaid expenses	7	(g) 1		8
Long-term receivable from another company		(l) 11		11
Plant assets, net	219	(k) 306	(b) 18	
			(c) 54	453
Totals	487			725
Accounts payable	57		(h) 34	91
Salary and wage payable	6	(i) 2		4
Accrued liabilities	3	(j) 2		1
Long-term notes payable	77	(o) 11	(n) 94	160
Common stock	258		(m) 101	359
Retained earnings	86	(p) 17	(a) 41	110
Totals	487	365	365	725
PANEL B—Statement of Cash Flows				
Cash flows from operating activities:				
Net income		(a) 41		
Add (subtract) items that affect net income and cash flow differently:				
Depreciation		(b) 18		
Gain on sale of plant assets			(c) 8	
Increase in accounts receivable			(d) 13	
Increase in interest receivable			(e) 2	
Decrease in inventory		(f) 3		
Increase in prepaid expenses			(g) 1	
Increase in accounts payable		(h) 34		
Decrease in salary and wage payable			(i) 2	
Decrease in accrued liabilities			(j) 2	
Cash flows from investing activities:				
Acquisition of plant assets			(k) 306	
Proceeds from sale of plant assets		(c) 62		
Loan to another company			(l) 11	
Cash flows from financing activities:				
Proceeds from issuance of common stock		(m) 101		
Proceeds from issuance of long-term note payable		(n) 94		
Payment of long-term note payable			(o) 11	
Payment of dividends			(p) 17	
		353	373	
Increase (decrease) in cash		(q) 20		
Totals		373	373	

NONCASH INVESTING AND FINANCING ACTIVITIES ON THE WORK SHEET   Noncash investing and financing activities can also be analyzed on the work sheet. Because these types of transactions include both an investing activity and a financing activity, they require two work sheet entries. Suppose Anchor Corporation purchased a building by issuing common stock of $320,000. Exhibit 17A-3 illustrates the transaction analysis of this noncash investing and financing activity. Cash is unaffected.

Work sheet entry (t1) records the purchase of the building, and entry (t2) records the issuance of the stock. The order of these entries is unimportant.

EXHIBIT 17A-3 Noncash Investing and Financing Activities on the Work Sheet

	Balances Dec. 31, 20X1	Transaction Analysis		Balances Dec. 31, 20X2
		Debit	Credit	
ANCHOR CORPORATION Work Sheet for Statement of Cash Flows Year Ended December 31, 20X2				
PANEL A—Account Titles				
Cash				
Building	650,000	(t1) 320,000		970,000
Common stock...	890,000		(t2) 320,000	1,210,000
PANEL B—Statement of Cash Flows				
Noncash investing and financing transactions:				
Purchase of building by issuing common stock		(t2) 320,000	(t1) 320,000	

APPENDIX PROBLEMS

Preparing the work sheet for the statement of cash flows—direct method

P17A-1 The 20X3 comparative balance sheet and income statement of Alden Group, Inc., follow. Alden had no noncash investing and financing transactions during 20X3.

ALDEN GROUP, INC.
Comparative Balance Sheet

	December 31		Increase (Decrease)
	20X3	**20X2**	
Current assets:			
Cash and cash equivalents	$ 13,700	$ 15,600	$ (1,900)
Accounts receivable	41,500	43,100	(1,600)
Interest receivable	600	900	(300)
Inventories	94,300	89,900	4,400
Prepaid expenses...................................	1,700	2,200	(500)
Plant assets:			
Land	35,100	10,000	25,100
Equipment, net	100,900	93,700	7,200
Total assets	$287,800	$255,400	$32,400
Current liabilities:			
Accounts payable	$ 16,400	$ 17,900	$ (1,500)
Interest payable....................................	6,300	6,700	(400)
Salary payable	2,100	1,400	700
Other accrued liabilities	18,100	18,700	(600)
Income tax payable	6,300	3,800	2,500
Long-term liabilities:			
Notes payable	55,000	65,000	(10,000)
Stockholder' equity:			
Common stock, no-par	131,100	122,300	8,800
Retained earnings	52,500	19,600	32,900
Total liabilities and stockholders' equity	$287,800	$255,400	$32,400

ALDEN GROUP, INC.		
Income Statement for 20X3		
Revenues:		
Sales revenue		$438,000
Interest revenue		11,700
Total revenues..........................		449,700
Expenses:		
Cost of goods sold........................	$205,200	
Salary expense.............................	76,400	
Depreciation expense	15,300	
Other operating expense.............	49,700	
Interest expense	24,600	
Income tax expense	16,900	
Total expenses..........................		388,100
Net income.....................................		$ 61,600

Required

Prepare the work sheet for the 20X3 statement of cash flows. Format cash flows from operating activities by the *direct* method.

P17A-2 Using the Alden Group, Inc., data from Problem 17A-1, prepare the work sheet for Alden's 20X3 statement of cash flows. Format cash flows from operating activities by the *indirect* method.

Preparing the work sheet for the statement of cash flows— indirect method

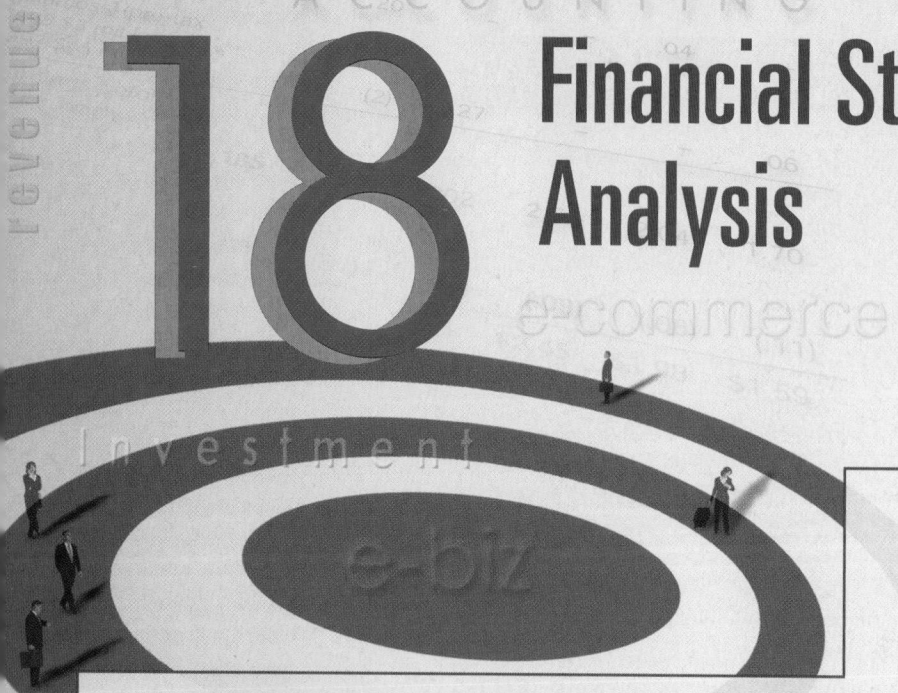

18 Financial Statement Analysis

LEARNING OBJECTIVES

After studying this chapter, you should be able to

1. Perform a horizontal analysis of financial statements
2. Perform a vertical analysis of financial statements
3. Prepare common-size financial statements
4. Compute the standard financial ratios
5. Use ratios in decision making
6. Measure economic value added

LUCENT TECHNOLOGIES, INC.
Consolidated Statement of Income (Adapted)
Year Ended September 30, 1999

	Millions
Revenues	$38,303
Cost [of sales]	19,688
Gross profit	18,615
Operating expenses:	
Selling, general, and administrative	8,417
Research and development	4,792
Operating income	5,406
Other income (expense)	2,187
Income before income taxes	7,593
Income tax expense	2,827
Net income	$ 4,766

MCI WORLDCOM, INC.
Consolidated Statement of Operations (Adapted)
Year Ended December 31, 1999

	Millions
Revenues	$37,120
Line costs (similar to cost of sales)	15,951
Gross margin	21,169
Operating expenses:	
Selling, general, and administrative	13,281
Operating income	7,888
Other income (expense)	(910)
Income before income taxes	6,978
Income tax expense	2,965
Net income	$ 4,013

Analysts at the investment banking firm of **Marquardt Pennile** have identified telecommunications as a growth area and will recommend telecom stocks to their clients. Clint Herzog heads a team of analysts who are focusing on two companies: **Lucent Technologies** and **MCI WorldCom.** Lucent Technologies is best known for cordless telephones. MCI WorldCom describes itself as the preeminent Internet and data company in the world.

Herzog and his team wish to compare the performance of Lucent and MCI WorldCom. As the two companies' income statements (on the facing page) show, Lucent is more profitable than MCI WorldCom. MCI WorldCom, on the other hand, doubled revenues during 1999 and turned a loss into a nice profit. How can Herzog and his fellow analysts compare these two companies?

The way to compare companies is to use *standard* measures. Throughout this book, we have discussed financial ratios, such as the current ratio, inventory turnover, and return on equity. These ratios enable investors to compare companies that operate in different industries. Managers use the ratios to help make decisions. In this chapter, we discuss most of the basic ratios and related measures that managers use to run a company. Investors and lenders use the same tools to search for good investments and loan prospects.

THE OBJECTIVES OF FINANCIAL STATEMENT ANALYSIS

The analysis of financial statements applies some specific techniques to the data contained in the annual report. In addition to the financial statements, annual reports usually contain

1. Notes to the financial statements, including a summary of the accounting methods used
2. Management's discussion and analysis of the financial results
3. The auditor's report
4. Comparative financial data for 5–10 years

Management's discussion and analysis (MD&A) of financial results is especially important because top managers are in the best position to know how well or how poorly their company is performing. The SEC requires the MD&A from public corporations. For example, the 1999 annual report of **Lucent Technologies** includes 12 pages of MD&A. As the following excerpt shows, Lucent is acquiring companies all over the world.

Lucent Technologies, Inc.
Management's Discussion and Analysis
of Results of Operations and Financial Condition

January 1999—Acquisition of the remaining 80% interest in WaveAccess, a developer of high-speed systems for wireless data communications

September 1998—Acquisition of JNA, an Australian telecom equipment manufacturer

August 1998—Acquisition of LANNET, an Israel-based supplier of Ethernet and asynchronous transfer mode ("ATM") switching solutions

---

Consider Lucent Technologies' January 1999 acquisition of the "remaining 80% interest in WaveAccess. . ." Then answer these questions.

1. Chapter 16 covered investments such as Lucent's acquisition of **WaveAccess**. What percentage of WaveAccess's stock does Lucent now own?
2. In the relationship between Lucent and WaveAccess, we refer to Lucent as the _____ company and to WaveAccess as the _____ company.
3. After purchasing WaveAccess, Lucent's financial statements now also include the statements of WaveAccess. Refer to Lucent's income statement (page 713) to see the word used to describe Lucent's financial statements.

Answers: 1. Lucent now owns 100% of WaveAccess.
2. Lucent = parent company; WaveAccess = subsidiary company.
3. *Consolidated* financial statements.

The Objectives of Financial Statement Analysis

Investors who purchase a company's stock expect to receive dividends and hope the stock's value will increase. Creditors make loans to receive cash for the interest and principal. They use financial statement analysis to (1) predict the amount of expected returns, and (2) assess the risks associated with those returns.

The tools and techniques the business community uses in evaluating financial statement information can be divided into three broad categories: horizontal analysis, vertical analysis, and ratio analysis.

HORIZONTAL ANALYSIS

Many managerial decisions hinge on whether the dollar amounts—of sales, income, expenses, and so on—are increasing or decreasing over time. Have sales risen from last year? From two years ago? By how much? Sales may have risen by $200,000. This fact may be interesting, but considered alone it is not very useful. The *percentage change* in the net sales over time offers a more useful perspective. It is better to know that sales have increased by 20% than to know that sales rose by $200,000.

The study of percentage changes in comparative statements is called **horizontal analysis.** Computing a percentage change in comparative statements requires two steps:

1. Compute the dollar amount of the change from the base (earlier) period to the later period.
2. Divide the dollar amount of change by the base-period amount.

Horizontal analysis is illustrated for **Lucent Technologies** as follows (dollar amounts in millions):

	1999	1998	Increase (Decrease) Amount	Increase (Decrease) Percent
Revenues...............	$38,303	$31,806	$6,497	20.4%
Net income.............	4,766	1,035	3,731	360.5%

The percentage change in Lucent Technologies' net income during 1999 is computed as follows:

Step 1. Compute the dollar amount of change in sales from 1998 to 1999:

1999	1998	Increase
$4,766 − $1,035 =		$3,731

Step 2. Divide the dollar amount of change by the base-period amount to compute the percentage change during the later period:

$$\text{Percentage change} = \frac{\textbf{Dollar amount of change}}{\textbf{Base-year amount}}$$

$$= \frac{\$3,731}{\$1,035} = 360.5\%$$

A 360.5% increase means that net income of 1999 was 3.6 times as high as the net income of 1998. That's why technology stocks have been so popular.

Detailed horizontal analyses of comparative income statements and comparative balance sheets are shown in the two right-hand columns of Exhibits 18-1 and 18-2, the financial statements of Lucent Technologies, Inc. The income statements (statements of earnings) reveal that revenues increased by 20.4% during 1999. Expenses grew less. As a result, net income increased by a whopping 360%.

EXHIBIT 18-1
Comparative Income
Statement—Horizontal Analysis

DAILY EXERCISE 18-1

LUCENT TECHNOLOGIES, INC. Consolidated Statement of Income (Adapted) Years Ended September 30, 1999 and 1998				
			Increase (Decrease)	
Dollar Amounts in Millions	1999	1998	Amount	Percent
Revenues	$38,303	$31,806	$6,497	20.4%
Cost [of sales]	19,688	16,715	2,973	17.8
Gross profit	18,615	15,091	3,524	23.4
Operating expenses:				
Selling, general, administrative	8,417	6,867	1,550	22.6
Research and development	4,792	5,586	(794)	(14.2)
Operating income	5,406	2,638	2,768	104.9
Other income (expense)	2,187	(126)	2,313	1,835.7
Income before income taxes	7,593	2,512	5,081	202.3
Income tax expense	2,827	1,477	1,350	91.4
Net income	$ 4,766	$ 1,035	$3,731	360.5%

THINK IT OVER Identify the item on Lucent Technologies' 1999 income statement that experienced the largest percentage *increase* from 1998. Considering all other changes on the 1999 income statement, is this item of great importance? Give your reason.

Answer: Other income increased by 1,835.7%. This is relatively unimportant because (a) other income is outside the company's main operations, (b) the dollar amounts are small in comparison to revenues, and (c) other income may not repeat from year to year.

Trend Percentages

Trend percentages are a form of horizontal analysis. Trends show the direction a business is heading. How have sales changed over a five-year period? What is the trend of the company's gross profit? These questions can be answered by analyzing trend percentages over a recent period, such as the most recent five or ten years.

Trend percentages use a base year whose amounts are set equal to 100%. The amounts of each following year are expressed as a percentage of the base amount. To compute trend percentages, divide each item for following years by the corresponding amount during the base year:

$$\text{Trend \%} = \frac{\textbf{Any year \$}}{\textbf{Base year \$}}$$

continued in the middle of page 714

EXHIBIT 18-2
Comparative Balance Sheet—
Horizontal Analysis

LUCENT TECHNOLOGIES, INC.
Consolidated Balance Sheet (Adapted)
September 30, 1999 and 1998

DAILY EXERCISE 18-2

Dollar Amounts in Millions	1999	1998	Increase (Decrease) Amount	Increase (Decrease) Percent
Assets				
Cash and cash equivalents.............	$ 1,816	$ 1,154	$ 662	57.4%
Receivables, net	10,438	7,405	3,033	41.0
Inventories......................................	6,151	4,538	1,613	35.5
Prepaid expenses	3,526	2,687	839	31.2
Total current assets....................	21,931	15,784	6,147	38.9
Property, plant, and				
equipment, net..........................	6,847	5,693	1,154	20.3
Prepaid pension costs	6,175	3,754	2,421	64.5
Other assets	3,822	4,132	(310)	(7.5)
Total assets....................................	$38,775	$29,363	$9,412	32.1%
Liabilities				
Accounts payable...........................	$ 2,878	$ 2,157	$ 721	33.4%
Salary and other				
compensation payable	2,437	2,779	(342)	(12.3)
Debt due within one year..............	2,864	2,231	633	28.4
Other current liabilities	3,599	3,718	(119)	(3.2)
Total current liabilities	11,778	10,885	893	8.2
Long-term debt..............................	4,162	2,409	1,753	72.8
Other long-term liabilities	9,251	8,360	891	10.7
Total liabilities..............................	25,191	21,654	3,537	16.3
Shareowners' Equity				
Common stock, including				
additional paid-in capital	7,729	6,570	1,159	17.6
Retained earnings..........................	6,099	1,422	4,677	328.9
Other equity	(244)	(283)	39	13.8
Total shareowners' equity	13,584	7,709	5,875	76.2
Total liabilities and equity.............	$38,775	$29,363	$9,412	32.1%

Lucent Technologies showed sales, cost of goods sold, and gross profit for the past five years as follows:

(In Millions)	1999	1998	1997	1996	1995
Revenues.....................	$38,303	$31,806	$27,611	$24,215	$21,718
Cost [of sales]..............	19,688	16,715	15,318	14,709	13,049
Gross profit.................	18,615	15,091	12,293	9,506	8,669

We want trend percentages for a four-year period starting with 1996. The base year is 1995. Trend percentages for revenues are computed by dividing each revenues amount by the 1995 amount of $21,718 million. Trend percentages for Cost of sales are calculated by dividing each Cost of sales amount by $13,049 (the base-year amount), and trend percentages for Gross profit are calculated by dividing each gross profit amount by $8,669 (the base-year amount). The resulting trend percentages are as follows (1995, the base year = 100%):

	1999	1998	1997	1996	1995
Revenues.....................	176%	146%	127%	111%	100%
Cost [of sales]..............	151	128	117	113	100
Gross profit.................	215	174	142	110	100

Lucent Technologies' revenues and cost of goods sold have trended upward. Gross profit has increased steadily, with the most dramatic growth during 1998 and 1999. This trend is good news for Lucent stockholders.

DAILY EXERCISE 18-3

VERTICAL ANALYSIS

Objective 2
Perform a vertical analysis of financial statements

The horizontal analysis that we have just seen highlights changes in an item *over time*. **Vertical analysis** of a financial statement reveals the relationship of each statement item to a specified base, which is the 100% figure. Every item on the financial statement is then reported as a percentage of that base.

VERTICAL ANALYSIS. Analysis of a financial statement that reveals the relationship of each statement item to the total, which is 100%.

For an income statement, revenues (or net sales) is usually the base. Suppose under normal conditions a company's gross profit is 70% of revenues. A drop in gross profit to 60% may throw the company into a net loss on the income statement. A large decline in gross profit creates alarm. Exhibit 18-3 shows the vertical analysis of **Lucent Technologies'** income statement as a percentage of revenues. In this case,

$$\text{Vertical analysis } \% = \frac{\text{Each income statement item}}{\text{Net sales (Revenues)}}$$

So, for example, the vertical analysis percentage for Cost of sales for 1999 equals 51.4% ($19,688/$38,303 = 0.514). Exhibit 18-4 shows the vertical analysis of the balance sheet amounts as a percentage of total assets.

LUCENT TECHNOLOGIES, INC. Consolidated Statement of Income (Adapted) Years Ended September 30, 1999 and 1998				
	1999		**1998**	
Dollar Amounts in Millions	**Amount**	**Percent**	**Amount**	**Percent**
Revenues...	$38,303	100.0%	$31,806	100.0%
Cost [of sales].................................	19,688	51.4	16,715	52.6
Gross profit......................................	18,615	48.6	15,091	47.4
Operating expenses:				
Selling, general, administrative ..	8,417	22.0	6,867	21.6
Research and development	4,792	12.5	5,586	17.5
Operating income	5,406	14.1	2,638	8.3
Other income (expense)	2,187	5.7	(126)	(0.4)
Income before income taxes	7,593	19.8	2,512	7.9
Income tax expense	2,827	7.4	1,477	4.6
Net income......................................	$ 4,766	12.4%	$ 1,035	3.3%

EXHIBIT 18-3
Comparative Income Statement—Vertical Analysis

DAILY EXERCISE 18-4

The vertical analysis of Lucent Technologies' income statement (Exhibit 18-3) shows no unusual relationships. The gross profit percentage was up a bit from 1998. Net income's percentage of sales increased in 1999 because Lucent controlled operating expenses and also because of the other income.

The vertical analysis of Lucent's balance sheet (Exhibit 18-4) also yields few surprises. Current assets' percentage of total assets increased a little in 1999, while current liabilities' percentage decreased. The best news on the balance sheet is the increase in stockholders' (shareowners') equity.

Lucent's financial position is strong. For example, the current ratio is 1.86 ($21,931 million/$11,778 million), and the company has little long-term debt.

EXHIBIT 18-4
Comparative Balance Sheet—
Vertical Analysis

LUCENT TECHNOLOGIES, INC.
Consolidated Balance Sheet (Adapted)
September 30, 1999 and 1998

Dollar Amounts in Millions	1999 Amount	1999 Percent	1998 Amount	1998 Percent
Assets				
Cash and cash equivalents.............	$ 1,816	4.7%	$ 1,154	3.9%
Receivables, net	10,438	26.9	7,405	25.2
Inventories......................................	6,151	15.9	4,538	15.5
Prepaid expenses............................	3,526	9.1	2,687	9.2
Total current assets.....................	21,931	56.6	15,784	53.8
Property, plant, and equipment, net........................	6,847	17.7	5,693	19.4
Prepaid pension costs.....................	6,175	15.9	3,754	12.8
Other assets....................................	3,822	9.8	4,132	14.0
Total assets	$38,775	100.0%	$29,363	100.0%
Liabilities				
Accounts payable	$ 2,878	7.4%	$ 2,157	7.3%
Salary and other compensation payable...............	2,437	6.3	2,779	9.5
Debt due within one year...............	2,864	7.4	2,231	7.6
Other current liabilities.................	3,599	9.3	3,718	12.7
Total current liabilities...............	11,778	30.4	10,885	37.1
Long-term debt	4,162	10.7	2,409	8.2
Other long-term liabilities..............	9,251	23.9	8,360	28.4
Total liabilities	25,191	65.0	21,654	73.7
Shareowner's Equity				
Common stock, including additional paid-in capital............	7,729	19.9	6,570	22.4
Retained earnings	6,099	15.7	1,422	4.8
Other equity...................................	(244)	(0.6)	(283)	(0.9)
Total shareowners' equity..............	13,584	35.0	7,709	26.3
Total liabilities and equity..............	$38,775	100.0%	$29,363	100.0%

 DAILY EXERCISE 18-5

 DAILY EXERCISE 18-6

Objective 3
Prepare common-size financial statements

COMMON-SIZE STATEMENT. A financial statement that reports only percentages (no dollar amounts); a type of vertical analysis.

COMMON-SIZE STATEMENTS

The percentages in Exhibits 18-3 and 18-4 can be presented as a separate statement that reports only percentages (no dollar amounts). Such a statement is called a **common-size statement.**

A common-size income statement reports each item as a percentage of the net sales (revenues) amount. Net sales is the *common size* for reporting amounts. In the balance sheet, the common size is total assets. A common-size statement eases the comparison of different companies because all amounts are stated in percentages.

Common-size statements may identify the need for a closer look at manager decisions. Exhibit 18-5 is the common-size income statement of **Lucent Technologies,** taken from Exhibit 18-3. Exhibit 18-5 shows research and development expense as 17.5% of revenues for 1998. The percentage drops in 1999. The result is higher net income for 1999. However, research and development (R&D) are essential for a high-tech company such as Lucent. If the company cuts back too far on R&D, that could hurt profits for years to come.

EXHIBIT 18-5
Common-Size Income Statement
of Lucent Technologies

LUCENT TECHNOLOGIES, INC.
Common-Size Statement of Income (Adapted)
Years Ended September 30, 1999 and 1998

	1999	1998
Revenues...	100.0%	100.0%
Cost [of sales]...	51.4	52.6
Gross profit..	48.6	47.4
Operating expenses:		
Selling, general, administrative..............	22.0	21.6
Research and development....................	12.5	17.5
Operating income	14.1	8.3
Other income (expense)	5.7	(0.4)
Income before income taxes	19.8	7.9
Income tax expense	7.4	4.6
Net income..	12.4%	3.3%

Percent of Revenues

Note: Other income does not appear for 1999 because it is an income amount.
As a result, the percentages do not total to 100%.

WORK IT OUT

Calculate common-size percentages for the income statement below:

Net sales.................................	$150,000
Cost of goods sold.................	60,000
Gross profit	90,000
Operating expense.................	40,000
Operating income	50,000
Income tax expense.............	15,000
Net income	$ 35,000

Answer:

Net sales	100%	(= $150,000 ÷ $150,000)
Cost of goods sold	40	(= $ 60,000 ÷ $150,000)
Gross margin	60	(= $ 90,000 ÷ $150,000)
Operating expense	27	(= $ 40,000 ÷ $150,000)
Operating income	33	(= $ 50,000 ÷ $150,000)
Income tax expense	10	(= $ 15,000 ÷ $150,000)
Net income...........................	23%	(= $ 35,000 ÷ $150,000)

BENCHMARKING. The practice of comparing a company to a standard set by other companies, with a view toward improvement.

BENCHMARKING

Benchmarking is the practice of comparing a company to a standard set by other companies, with a view toward improvement.

Benchmarking Against the Industry Average

A company's financial statements show past results and help investors predict future performance. Still, that knowledge is limited to that one company. We may learn that research and development (R&D) decreased and that net income increased last year. This information is helpful, but it does not consider how businesses in the same industry have fared over the same time period. Have other companies in the same line of business also decreased R&D? Is there an industry-wide increase in net income? Managers, investors, creditors, and other interested parties need to know how one company compares with other companies in the same line of business.

Exhibit 18-6 compares the common-size income statement of **Lucent Technologies** with the average for the communications industry. This analysis compares Lucent with all other companies in its line of business. The industry averages were adapted from Robert Morris Associates' *Annual Statement Studies.* Analysts at **Merrill Lynch, Edward Jones,** and other companies specialize in a particular industry and make such comparisons in deciding which companies' stocks to buy or sell.

Exhibit 18-6
Common-Size Income Statement of Lucent Technologies Compared with the Industry Average

LUCENT TECHNOLOGIES, INC.
Common-Size Income Statement for Comparison with Industry Average
Year Ended September 30, 1999

	Lucent Technologies	Industry Average
Revenues..	100.0%	100.0%
Cost of goods sold	51.4	63.9
Gross profit	48.6	36.1
Operating expenses, other income or expense	28.8	32.8
Operating income before income tax	19.8	3.3
Income tax expense	7.4	3.5
Net income (net loss)	12.4%	(0.2)%

Percent of Revenues

Lucent Technologies — Cost of goods sold 51.4%; Operating expenses 28.8%; Net income 12.4%; Income tax 7.4%

Industry Average* — Cost of goods sold 63.9%; Operating expenses 32.8%; Income tax 3.5%; Net loss (0.2%)

* Percentages total to greater than 100% because of the net loss.

Exhibit 18-6 shows that Lucent Technologies is much more profitable than competing companies in its industry. Its gross profit percentage is much higher, and its percentage of revenues siphoned off by operating expenses is lower, than the industry average. The company does a good job of controlling total expenses, and as a result, its net income percentage is significantly above the industry average.

Benchmarking Against Another Company

Common-size statements are also used to compare individual companies. Suppose you are a member of Clint Herzog's team at Marquardt Pennile. You are considering an investment in the stock of either **Lucent Technologies** or **MCI**

(text continues on page 720)

LUCENT TECHNOLOGIES AND MCI WORLDCOM
Common-Size Income Statement (Adapted)
Fiscal Year 1999

	Lucent Technologies	MCI WorldCom
Revenues	100.0%	100.0%
Cost of goods (or services)	51.4	43.0
Gross profit	48.6	57.0
Operating expenses	28.8	38.2
Operating income, before income tax	19.8	18.8
Income tax expense	7.4	8.0
Net income	12.4%	10.8%

Percent of Revenues

Lucent Technologies — Cost of goods sold 51.4%; Operating expenses 28.8%; Net income 12.4%; Income tax 7.4%

MCI WorldCom — Cost of goods sold 43.0%; Operating expenses 38.2%; Net income 10.8%; Income tax 8.0%

e-Accounting

Peer Performance: Benchmarking on the Web

The Internet makes many accounting functions that were once time-consuming and tedious incredibly quick and easy. The Internet also helps with benchmarking, the practice of sys-tematically comparing your company with a leader. In April 2000, **Fourth Shift Corp.** and **Grant Thornton LLP** announced the creation of a free financial bench-marking service on the Web. The site lets manu-facturers and service providers evaluate such variables as days' sales in receivables, inventory turnover, and other ratios. **BenchmarkReport. com** lists three reasons to use benchmark ratios: (1) to set goals and action programs,

(2) to monitor performance, and (3) to share the results with others. Current and future stakeholders of the company can objectively compare a company's condition against a key competitor. Finance professionals can also use them to benchmark data.

Source: Based on Anonymous, "Online benchmarking service launched," *Electronic Buyers' News,* April 17, 2000, p. 70. Christine A. Gattenio, "Beyond lean & mean," *Electric Perspectives,* May/June 2000, pp. 40–52. And informa-tion from www.BenchmarkReport.com.

WorldCom. To compare the companies, you can convert their income statements to common size.

Exhibit 18-7 on page 719 presents the common-size income statements of Lucent Technologies and MCI WorldCom. MCI WorldCom serves as an excellent benchmark because it also operates in the communications industry. In this comparison, Lucent Technologies has the higher percentage of net income. Otherwise, the two companies are quite similar.

MID-CHAPTER

www.prenhall.com/horngren

Mid-Chapter Assessment

SUMMARY PROBLEM

Perform a horizontal analysis and a vertical analysis of the comparative income statement of TRE Corporation, which makes metal detectors. State whether 20X3 was a good year or a bad year, and give your reasons.

TRE CORPORATION
Comparative Income Statement
Months Ended December 31, 20X3 and 20X2

	20X3	20X2
Total revenues	$275,000	$225,000
Expenses:		
Cost of products sold	$194,000	$165,000
Engineering, selling, and administrative expenses	54,000	48,000
Interest expense	5,000	5,000
Income tax expense	9,000	3,000
Other expense (income)	1,000	(1,000)
Total expenses	263,000	220,000
Net earnings	$ 12,000	$ 5,000

Solution

TRE CORPORATION
Horizontal Analysis of Comparative Income Statement
Months Ended December 31, 20X3 and 20X2

	20X3	20X2	Increase (Decrease) Amount	Increase (Decrease) Percent
Total revenues	$275,000	$225,000	$50,000	22.2%
Expenses:				
Cost of products sold	$194,000	$165,000	$29,000	17.6
Engineering, selling, and administrative expenses	54,000	48,000	6,000	12.5
Interest expense	5,000	5,000	—	—
Income tax expense	9,000	3,000	6,000	200.0
Other expense (income)	1,000	(1,000)	2,000	—*
Total expenses	263,000	220,000	43,000	19.5
Net earnings	$ 12,000	$ 5,000	$ 7,000	140.0%

* Percentage changes are typically not computed for shifts from a negative amount to a positive amount, and vice versa.

The horizontal analysis shows that total revenues increased 22.2%. This increase was greater than the 19.5% increase in total expenses, resulting in a 140% increase in net earnings.

The vertical analysis shows that cost of products sold decreased from 73.3% to 70.5% of revenues, and engineering, selling, and administrative expenses decreased from 21.3% to 19.6%. These two items are TRE's largest expenses, so their decreases are important. The reduction in these expenses raised December 20X3 net earnings to 4.4% of sales, compared with 2.2% the preceding December. Overall, December 20X3 was much better than December 20X2.

TRE CORPORATION				
Vertical Analysis of Comparative Income Statement				
Months Ended December 31, 20X3 and 20X2				
	20X3		**20X2**	
	Amount	**Percent**	**Amount**	**Percent**
Total revenues.................................	$275,000	100.0 %	$225,000	100.0 %
Expenses:				
Cost of products sold..................	$194,000	70.5	$165,000	73.3
Engineering, selling, and				
administrative expenses	54,000	19.6	48,000	21.3
Interest expense	5,000	1.8	5,000	2.2
Income tax expense	9,000	3.3	3,000	1.4*
Other expense (income)	1,000	0.4	(1,000)	(0.4)
Total expenses.........................	263,000	95.6	220,000	97.8
Net earnings.................................	$ 12,000	4.4 %	$ 5,000	2.2 %

* Number rounded up.

USING RATIOS TO MAKE BUSINESS DECISIONS

Objective 4
Compute the standard financial ratios

Ratios play an important part in financial analysis. A ratio is a useful way to show the relationship of one number to another number. For example, if the balance sheet shows current assets of $100,000 and current liabilities of $50,000, the ratio of current assets to current liabilities is $100,000 to $50,000. We simplify this numerical expression to 2 to 1, which may also be written 2:1 and 2/1. Other acceptable ways of expressing this ratio include (1) "current assets are 200% of current liabilities," (2) "the business has two dollars in current assets for every one dollar in current liabilities," or simply, (3) "the current ratio is 2.0."

We often reduce the ratio fraction by writing the ratio as one figure over the other—for example, 2/1—and then dividing the numerator by the denominator. In this way, the ratio 2/1 may be expressed simply as 2. The 1 that represents the denominator of the fraction is understood, not written. Consider the ratio $175,000:$165,000. After dividing the first figure by the second, we come to 1.06:1, which we state as 1.06. The second part of the ratio, the 1, is understood.

A manager, lender, or financial analyst may use any ratio that is relevant to a particular decision. Many companies include ratios in a special section of their annual reports. **Rubbermaid, Inc.**—the manufacturer of plastic products for home, office, and industry—displays ratio data in the financial summary section of its annual report. Exhibit 18-8 shows an excerpt from that summary section.

EXHIBIT 18-8 Financial Summary of Rubbermaid, Inc. (Dollar Amounts in Thousands Except Per-Share Amounts)

Years Ended December 31,	20X1	20X0	19X9	19X8
Operating Results				
Net earnings	$211,413	$164,095	$162,650	$143,520
Earnings per common share	$1.32	$1.02	$1.02	$0.90
Percent of sales..	10.8%	9.1%	9.8%	9.4%
Return on average shareholders' equity	20.0%	17.5%	19.7%	20.2%
Financial Position				
Current assets..	$829,744	$699,650	$663,999	$602,697
Current liabilities.......................................	$259,314	$223,246	$245,500	$235,300
Current ratio...	3.20	3.13	2.70	2.56

Investment services—**Moody's, Standard & Poor's, Robert Morris Associates,** and others—report these ratios for companies and industries.

The Decision Guidelines feature on page 733 summarizes the ratios we discuss in this chapter. The ratios may be classified as follows:

1. Ratios that measure the company's ability to pay current liabilities
2. Ratios that measure the company's ability to sell inventory and collect receivables
3. Ratios that measure the company's ability to pay short-term and long-term debt
4. Ratios that measure the company's profitability
5. Ratios used to analyze the company's stock as an investment

How much can a computer help in analyzing financial statements for investment purposes? Time yourself as you perform one of the financial-ratio problems in this chapter. Multiply your efforts by, say, 100 companies that you are comparing by means of this ratio. Now consider ranking these 100 companies on the basis of four or five additional ratios.

On-line financial databases, such as **Lexis/Nexis** and the **Dow Jones NewsRetrieval Service,** offer quarterly financial figures for thousands of corporations going back as far as ten years. Assume you want to compare companies' recent earnings histories. You might have the computer compare hundreds of companies on the basis of their price/earnings ratio and rate of return on stockholders' equity. The computer could then give you the names of the 20 (or however many) companies that appear most favorable in terms of these ratios.

Measuring Ability to Pay Current Liabilities

WORKING CAPITAL. Current assets minus current liabilities; measures a business's ability to meet its short-term obligations with its current assets.

Working capital is defined as follows:

$$\text{Working capital} = \text{Current assets} - \text{Current Liabilities}$$

Working capital is widely used to measure ability to pay current liabilities with current assets. In general, the larger the working capital, the better able the business is to pay its debt. Recall that capital (owners' equity) is total assets minus total liabilities. Working capital is like a "current" version of total capital. The working-capital amount considered alone does not give a complete picture of the entity's working-capital position, however. Consider two companies with equal working capital:

	Company A	Company B
Current assets	$100,000	$200,000
Less: Current liabilities..............	(50,000)	(150,000)
Working capital........................	$ 50,000	$ 50,000

Both companies have working capital of $50,000, but Company A's working capital is as large as its current liabilities. Company B's working capital is only one-third as large as its current liabilities. Which business has the better working-capital position? Company A, because its working capital is a higher percentage of current assets and current liabilities. Two decision-making tools based on working-capital data are the *current ratio* and the *acid-test ratio*.

CURRENT RATIO. Total current assets divided by total current liabilities. Measures the ability to pay current liabilities from current assets.

CURRENT RATIO The most common ratio using current-asset and current-liability data is the **current ratio,** which is total current assets divided by total current liabilities. ← Recall the makeup of current assets and current liabilities. Current assets consist of cash, short-term investments, net receivables, inventory, and prepaid expenses. Current liabilities include accounts payable, short-term notes payable, unearned revenues, and all types of accrued liabilities. The current ratio measures the company's ability to pay current liabilities with current assets.

➤ We introduced the current ratio in Chapter 4 (p. 141).

Exhibits 18-9 and 18-10 give the comparative income statement and balance sheet of Palisades Furniture, Inc., respectively. The current ratios of Palisades Furniture at December 31, 20X2 and 20X1, follow, along with the average for the retail furniture industry, a benchmark for evaluating Palisades Furniture's ratios.

| Formula | Palisades' Current Ratio | | Industry Average |
	20X2	20X1	
Current ratio = $\dfrac{\text{Total current assets}}{\text{Total current liabilities}}$	$\dfrac{\$262,000}{\$142,000} = 1.85$	$\dfrac{\$236,000}{\$126,000} = 1.87$	1.80

EXHIBIT 18-9
Comparative Income Statement

PALISADES FURNITURE, INC.
Comparative Income Statement
Years Ended September 30, 20X2 and 20X1

	20X2	20X1
Net sales	$858,000	$803,000
Cost of goods sold	513,000	509,000
Gross profit	345,000	294,000
Operating expenses:		
Selling expenses	126,000	114,000
General expenses	118,000	123,000
Total operating expenses	244,000	237,000
Income from operations	101,000	57,000
Interest revenue	4,000	—
Interest expense	(24,000)	(14,000)
Income before income taxes	81,000	43,000
Income tax expense	33,000	17,000
Net income	$ 48,000	$ 26,000

EXHIBIT 18-10
Comparative Balance Sheet

PALISADES FURNITURE, INC.
Comparative Balance Sheet
September 30, 20X2 and 20X1

	20X2	20X1
Assets		
Current assets:		
Cash	$ 29,000	$ 32,000
Accounts receivable, net	114,000	85,000
Inventories	113,000	111,000
Prepaid expenses	6,000	8,000
Total current assets	262,000	236,000
Long-term investments	18,000	9,000
Property, plant, and equipment, net	507,000	399,000
Total assets	$787,000	$644,000
Liabilities		
Current liabilities:		
Notes payable	$ 42,000	$ 27,000
Accounts payable	73,000	68,000
Accrued liabilities	27,000	31,000
Total current liabilities	142,000	126,000
Long-term debt	289,000	198,000
Total liabilities	431,000	324,000
Stockholders' Equity		
Common stock, no par	186,000	186,000
Retained earnings	170,000	134,000
Total stockholders' equity	356,000	320,000
Total liabilities and stockholders' equity	$787,000	$644,000

 DAILY EXERCISE 18-9

The current ratio decreased slightly during 20X2. In general, a higher current ratio indicates a stronger financial position. A igher current ratio suggests that the business has sufficient liquid assets to maintain normal business operations. Compare Palisades Furniture's current ratio of 1.85 with the industry average of 1.80 and with the current ratios of some well-known companies:

Company	Current Ratio
Lucent Technologies..............	1.86
Wal-Mart Stores	1.26
MCI WorldCom......................	0.60

What is an acceptable current ratio? The answer depends on the nature of the industry. **Lucent Technologies'** current ratio of 1.86 is similar to that of Palisades Furniture, even though the two companies operate in different industries, **MCI WorldCom** has a very low current ratio. Apparently this is okay because MCI collects cash monthly from millions of long-distance customers. The norm for companies in most industries is between 1.40 and 1.70. A current ratio of 2.0 is considered very strong.

Acid-Test Ratio. Ratio of the sum of cash plus short-term investments plus net current receivables to current liabilities. Tells whether the entity could pay all its current liabilities if they came due immediately. Also called the quick ratio.

➟ We saw in Chapter 8 (pp. 326–327) that the higher the acid-test ratio, the better able the business is to pay its current liabilities

Acid-Test Ratio The **acid-test** (or **quick**) **ratio** tells us whether the entity could pay all its current liabilities if they came due immediately. ◄ That is, could the company pass this *acid test*? To do so, the company would have to convert its most liquid assets to cash.

To compute the acid-test ratio, we add cash, short-term investments, and net current receivables (accounts and notes receivable, net of allowances) and divide by total current liabilities. Inventory and prepaid expenses are *not* included because a business cannot convert these assets to cash immediately to pay current liabilities.

Palisades Furniture's acid-test ratios for 20X2 and 20X1 are as follows:

Formula	Palisades' Current Ratio		Industry Average
	20X2	**20X1**	
Acid-test ratio = $\dfrac{\text{Cash + Short-term investments + Net current receivables}}{\text{Total current liabilities}}$	$\dfrac{\$29,000 + \$0 + \$114,000}{\$142,000} = 1.01$	$\dfrac{\$32,000 + \$0 + \$85,000}{\$126,000} = 0.93$	0.60

The company's acid-test ratio improved considerably during 20X2 and is significantly better than the industry average. Compare Palisades' 1.01 acid-test ratio with those of three well-known companies:

◉ Daily Exercise 18-10

Company	Acid-Test Ratio
Lucent Technologies..............	1.04
Wal-Mart Stores	0.18
MCI WorldCom......................	0.39

How can leading companies such as **Wal-Mart** and **MCI WorldCom** function with such low acid-test ratios? Wal-Mart has almost no receivables. Its inventory is priced low to turn over very quickly. MCI WorldCom holds no inventory and collects cash monthly from millions of customers. The norm for the acid-test ratio ranges from 0.20 for high-tech companies to 1.00 for manufacturers of paperboard containers and certain other equipment. An acid-test ratio of 0.90 to 1.00 is safe in most industries.

THINK IT OVER Palisades Furniture's 20X2 current ratio is 1.85, which looks strong, and its acid-test ratio is 1.01, also strong. Suppose Palisades' acid-test ratio is low, say 0.48. What would be the most likely reason for the difference between a strong current ratio and a weak acid-test ratio?

Answer: It would appear that the company is having trouble selling its inventory. The level of inventory must be relatively high, and the inventory is propping up the current ratio. The rate of inventory turnover may be low.

Measuring Ability to Sell Inventory and Collect Receivables

The ability to sell inventory and collect receivables is fundamental to business success. Recall the operating cycle of a merchandiser: cash to inventory to receivables and back to cash. In this section, we discuss three ratios that measure the company's ability to sell inventory and collect receivables.

INVENTORY TURNOVER **Inventory turnover** is a measure of the number of times a company sells its average level of inventory during a year. ⇒ In general, companies prefer a high rate of inventory turnover. An inventory turnover of 6 means that the company sells its average level of inventory six times during the year. This is generally better than a turnover of 3 or 4. But a high value can mean the business is not keeping enough inventory on hand, and that can result in lost sales if the company cannot meet a customer's need. Therefore, a business strives for the *most profitable* rate of inventory turnover, not necessarily the *highest* rate.

To compute the inventory turnover ratio, we divide cost of goods sold by the average inventory for the period. We use the cost of goods sold—not sales—in the computation because both cost of goods sold and inventory are stated *at cost*. Sales is stated at the sales value of inventory and therefore is not comparable with inventory cost.

Palisades Furniture's inventory turnover for 20X2 is

⇐ We introduced inventory turnover in Chapter 5, pp. 186–188. Average inventory is computed as follows: (Beginning inventory + Ending inventory)/2.

INVENTORY TURNOVER. Ratio of cost of goods sold to average inventory. Measures the number of times a company sells its average level of inventory during a year.

Formula	Palisades' Inventory Turnover	Industry Average
Inventory turnover = $\dfrac{\text{Cost of goods sold}}{\text{Average inventory}}$	$\dfrac{\$513,000}{\$112,000} = 4.58$	2.70

Cost of goods sold appears in the income statement (Exhibit 18-9). Average inventory is figured by averaging the beginning inventory ($111,000) and ending inventory ($113,000). (See the balance sheet, Exhibit 18-10.)

Inventory turnover varies widely with the nature of the business. For example, companies that remove natural gas from the ground hold their inventory for a very short period of time and have an average turnover of 30. Palisades Furniture's turnover of 4.58 times a year is high for the retail furniture industry, which has an average turnover of 2.70. Palisades' high turnover results from its policy of keeping little inventory. The company takes customer orders and has its suppliers ship directly to customers.

Inventory turnover rates can vary greatly within a company. At **Toys "Я" Us,** diapers and formula turn over more than 12 times a year, while seasonal toys turn over less than 3 times a year. The entire Toys "Я" Us inventory turns over an average of 4 times a year.

To evaluate a company's inventory turnover, we must compare the ratio over time. A sudden sharp decline or a steady decline over a long period suggests the need for corrective action.

ACCOUNTS RECEIVABLE TURNOVER **Accounts receivable turnover** measures a company's ability to collect cash from customers. In general, the higher the ratio, the more successfully the business collects cash. To compute the accounts receivable turnover, we divide net credit sales by average net accounts receivable. The resulting ratio indicates how many times during the year the average level of receivables was turned into cash.

ACCOUNTS RECEIVABLE TURNOVER. Ratio of net credit sales to average net accounts receivable. Measures ability to collect cash from customers.

Palisades Furniture's accounts receivable turnover ratio for 20X2 is computed as follows:

Formula	Palisades' Accounts Receivable Turnover	Industry Average
Accounts receivable turnover $= \dfrac{\text{Net credit sales}}{\text{Average net accounts receivable}}$	$\dfrac{\$858,000}{\$99,500} = 8.62$ times	22.2 times

The net credit sales figure comes from the income statement. Average net accounts receivable is figured by adding the beginning accounts receivable balance ($85,000) and the ending balance ($114,000), then dividing by 2.

Palisades' receivable turnover of 8.62 is much lower than the industry average. The explanation is this: Palisades is a home-town store that sells to local people who tend to pay their bills over a long period of time. Many larger furniture stores have tighter credit policies and collect their receivables faster.

DAYS' SALES IN RECEIVABLES Businesses must convert accounts receivable to cash. All else equal, the lower the Accounts Receivable balance, the more successful the business has been in converting receivables into cash, and the better off the business is.

The **days'-sales-in-receivables** ratio tells us how many days' sales remain in Accounts Receivable. To compute the ratio, we follow a two-step process. First, divide net sales by 365 days to figure the average sales amount for one day. Second, divide this average day's sales amount into the average net accounts receivable.

The data to compute this ratio for Palisades Furniture, Inc., for 20X2 are taken from the income statement and the balance sheet (Exhibits 18-9 and 18-10):

DAYS' SALES IN RECEIVABLES. Ratio of average net accounts receivable to one day's sales. Tells how many days' sales remain in Accounts Receivable awaiting collection.

Formula	Palisades' Days' Sales in Accounts Receivables	Industry Average
Days' Sales in Accounts Receivable:		
1. One day's sales $= \dfrac{\text{Net sales}}{365 \text{ days}}$	$\dfrac{\$858,000}{365 \text{ days}} = \$2,351$	
2. Days' sales in accounts receivable $= \dfrac{\text{Average net accounts receivable}}{\text{One day's sales}}$	$\dfrac{\$99,500}{\$2,351} = 42$ days	16 days

DAILY EXERCISE 18-11

Days' sales in receivables can also be computed in a single step: $99,500/($858,000/365 days) = 42 days.

Palisades' ratio tells us that 42 days' sales remained in average accounts receivable during the year. The company will increase its cash flow if it can decrease this ratio.

Measuring Ability to Pay Short-Term and Long-Term Debt

The ratios discussed so far give us insight into current assets and current liabilities. Most businesses also have long-term liabilities. Two measures of a business's ability to pay both short-term and long-term liabilities are the *debt ratio* and the *times-interest-earned ratio*.

DEBT RATIO. Ratio of total liabilities to total assets. Tells the proportion of a company's assets financed with debt.

DEBT RATIO The ratio of total liabilities to total assets—called the **debt ratio**—tells us the proportion of the company's assets financed with debt. If the debt ratio is 1, then debt has been used to finance all the assets. A debt ratio of 0.50 means that the company has financed half its assets with debt and half with owners' equity. The higher the debt ratio, the higher the strain of paying interest each year and the principal amount at maturity. The lower the ratio, the lower the business's future obligations.

Creditors view a high debt ratio with caution. If a business trying to borrow already has large liabilities, then additional debt payments may be too much for it to handle. Creditors generally charge higher interest rates on new borrowing to companies with an already high debt ratio.

Palisades Furniture's debt ratios at the end of 20X2 and 20X1 are as follows:

	Formula	Palisades' Debt Ratio		Industry Average
		20X2	20X1	
Debt ratio =	$\dfrac{\text{Total liabilities}}{\text{Total assets}}$	$\dfrac{\$431,000}{\$787,000} = 0.55$	$\dfrac{\$324,000}{\$644,000} = 0.50$	0.61

Palisades Furniture expanded operations during 20X2 by financing the purchase of property, plant, and equipment through borrowing, which is common. This expansion explains the firm's increased debt ratio. Even after the increase in 20X2, the company's debt is not very high. Robert Morris Associates reports that the average debt ratio for most companies ranges around 0.57–0.67. Palisades' 0.55 debt ratio indicates a fairly low-risk debt position.

TIMES-INTEREST-EARNED RATIO   The debt ratio measures the effect of debt on the company's *financial position* (balance sheet). However, the debt ratio says nothing about the ability to pay interest expense. Analysts use a second ratio—the **times-interest-earned ratio**—to relate income to interest expense. To compute this ratio, we divide income from operations by interest expense. This ratio measures the number of times that operating income can *cover* interest expense. For this reason, the ratio is also called the **interest-coverage ratio.** A high times-interest-earned ratio indicates ease in paying interest expense; a low value suggests difficulty.

> **TIMES-INTEREST-EARNED RATIO.** Ratio of income from operations to interest expense. Measures the number of times operating income can cover interest expense. Also called the **interest-coverage ratio.**

Palisades' times-interest-earned ratio follows:

	Formula	Palisades' Times-Interest-Earned Ratio		Industry Average
		20X2	20X1	
Times-interest-earned ratio =	$\dfrac{\text{Income from operations*}}{\text{Interest expense}}$	$\dfrac{\$101,000}{\$24,000} = 4.21$ times	$\dfrac{\$57,000}{\$14,000} = 4.07$ times	2.00 times

* A company's income statement may not report income from operations. To estimate income from operations, you can add interest expense to income before income tax.

The company's times-interest-earned ratio increased in 20X2. This is a favorable sign, especially since liabilities rose substantially during the year. Palisades Furniture's new plant assets, we conclude, have earned more income than they have cost the business in interest expense. The company's times-interest-earned ratio of around 4.00 is much better than the 2.00 average for furniture retailers. The norm for U.S. business, as reported by Robert Morris Associates, falls in the range of 2.0–3.0 for most companies.

⊙ DAILY EXERCISE 18-12

On the basis of its debt ratio and its times-interest-earned ratio, Palisades Furniture appears to have little difficulty *servicing its debt*—that is, paying its liabilities.

Measuring Profitability

The fundamental goal of business is to earn a profit. Ratios that measure profitability play a large role in decision making. These ratios are reported in the business press, by investment services, and in companies' annual financial reports.

RATE OF RETURN ON NET SALES   In business, the term *return* is used broadly and loosely as an evaluation of profitability. Consider a ratio called the **rate of return on net sales,** or simply **return on sales.** (The word *net* is usually omitted for convenience, even though the net sales figure is used to compute the ratio.) This ratio shows the percentage of each sales dollar earned as net income. The rate-of-return-on-sales ratios for Palisades Furniture are calculated as follows:

> **RATE OF RETURN ON NET SALES.** Ratio of net income to net sales. A measure of profitability. Also called **return on sales.**

	Formula	Palisades' Rate of Return on Sales		
		20X2	20X1	Industry Average
Rate of return on sales =	$\dfrac{\text{Net income}}{\text{Net sales}}$	$\dfrac{\$48,000}{\$858,000} = 0.056$	$\dfrac{\$26,000}{\$803,000} = 0.032$	0.008

Companies strive for a high rate of return. The higher the rate of return, the more that sales are providing income to the business and the less of sales that are absorbed by expenses. The increase in Palisades Furniture's return on sales is significant and identifies the company as more successful than the average furniture store. Compare Palisades' rate of return on sales to the rates of some other companies:

Company	Rate of Return on Sales
Lucent Technologies..............	0.124
General Motors	0.039
Wal-Mart Stores	0.032

As these numbers indicate, the rate of return on sales varies widely from industry to industry.

A return measure can be computed on any revenue and sales amount. Return on net sales, as we have seen, is net income divided by net sales. *Return on total revenues* is net income divided by total revenues. A company can compute a return on other specific portions of revenue as its information needs dictate.

RATE OF RETURN ON TOTAL ASSETS. The sum of net income plus interest expense divided by average total assets. This ratio measures the success a company has in using its assets to earn income for the persons who finance the business. Also called **return on assets.**

➡ We first discussed the rate of return on total assets in Chapter 13, p. 518.

RATE OF RETURN ON TOTAL ASSETS   The **rate of return on total assets,** or **return on assets (ROA),** measures a company's success in using its assets to earn a profit. ◄ Creditors have loaned money to the company, and the *interest* they receive is the return on their investment. Shareholders have invested in the company's stock, and *net income* is their return. The sum of interest expense and net income is thus the return to the two groups that have financed the company's operations, and this amount is the numerator of the return-on-assets ratio. Average total assets is the denominator. Palisades Furniture's return on total assets is computed as follows:

	Formula	Palisades' 20X2 Rate of Return on Total Assets	Industry Average
Rate of return on assets =	$\dfrac{\text{Net income} + \text{Interest expense}}{\text{Average total assets}}$	$\dfrac{\$48,000 + \$24,000}{\$715,500} = 0.101$	0.049

Net income and interest expense are taken from the income statement (Exhibit 18-9). To compute average total assets, we take the average of beginning and ending total assets from the comparative balance sheet (Exhibit 18-10). Compare Palisades Furniture's rate of return on assets to the rates of some other companies:

Company	Rate of Return on Assets
Gap, Inc.	0.170
Lucent Technologies..............	0.140
Wal-Mart Stores	0.110

RATE OF RETURN ON COMMON STOCKHOLDERS' EQUITY. Net income minus preferred dividends, divided by average common stockholders' equity. A measure of profitability. Also called **return on stockholders' equity** or **return on equity (ROE).**

As you can see, the rate of return on assets varies from industry to industry.

RATE OF RETURN ON COMMON STOCKHOLDERS' EQUITY   Perhaps the most widely used measure of profitability is **rate of return on common stockholders' equity,** which is often shortened to **return on stockholders' equity,** or simply **return on equity (ROE).**

→ This ratio shows the relationship between net income and common stockholders' investment in the company—how much income is earned for every $1 invested by the common shareholders. To compute this ratio, we first subtract preferred dividends from net income. This remainder is net income available to the common stockholders. We then divide net income available to common stockholders by the average stockholders' equity during the year. The 20X2 rate of return on common stockholders' equity for Palisades Furniture is calculated as follows:

← We examined this ratio in detail in Chapter 13. For a review, see p. 518.

Formula		Palisades' 20X2 Rate of Return on Common Stockholders' Equity	Industry Average
Rate of return on common stockholders' equity	$= \dfrac{\text{Net income} - \text{Preferred dividends}}{\text{Average common stockholders' equity}}$	$\dfrac{\$48,000 - \$0}{\$338,000} = 0.142$	0.093

We compute average equity by adding the beginning and ending balances, and then dividing by 2 [($356,000 + $320,000)/2 = $338,000]. Common stockholders' equity is total equity minus preferred equity.

Observe that Palisades' return on equity (14.2%) is higher than its return on assets (10.1%). This difference results from borrowing at one rate—say, 8%—and investing the funds to earn a higher rate, such as the firm's 14.2% return on stockholders' equity. This practice is called **trading on the equity,** or using **leverage.**

It is critical that a company's return on equity exceed its return on assets—for two reasons:

- The stockholders take more risk and therefore demand a higher return on equity than the company's lenders, who take less risk.
- If return on assets exceeds return on equity, that means the company's lenders are getting a better return than the company's stockholders are getting. If this continues, the stockholders will stop financing the company.

TRADING ON THE EQUITY. Earning more income on borrowed money than the related expense, thereby increasing the earnings for the owners of the business. Also called **leverage.**

 DAILY EXERCISE 18-13

Fortunately, Palisades Furniture's return on equity (14.2%) exceeds its return on assets (10.1%). Let's compare Palisades Furniture's rate of return on equity with the rates of some leading companies:

Company	Rate of Return on Common Equity
Lucent Technologies	0.45
Wal-Mart Stores.....................	0.22
General Motors.....................	0.34

Palisades Furniture is not as profitable as these leading companies. Lucent Technologies' high rate of return on equity explains why high-tech companies are so popular with investors.

EARNINGS PER SHARE OF COMMON STOCK *Earnings per share of common stock,* or simply **earnings per share (EPS),** is perhaps the most widely quoted of all financial statistics. → EPS is the only ratio that must appear on the face of the income statement. EPS is the amount of income earned for each share of the company's outstanding *common* stock.

Earnings per share is computed by dividing net income available to common stockholders by the number of common shares outstanding during the year. Preferred dividends are subtracted from net income because the preferred stockholders have a prior claim to their dividends. Palisades Furniture, Inc., has no preferred stock outstanding and thus has no preferred dividends. Computation of the firm's EPS for 20X2 and 20X1 follows (the company had 10,000 shares of common stock outstanding throughout 20X1 and 20X2):

EARNINGS PER SHARE (EPS). Amount of a company's income earned for each share of its outstanding common stock.

← Recall from Chapter 14, pp. 556–557, that GAAP requires corporations to report EPS on the income statement.

		Palisades' Earnings Per Share	
	Formula	20X2	20X1
Earnings per share of common stock	$= \dfrac{\text{Net income} - \text{Preferred dividends}}{\substack{\text{Number of shares of} \\ \text{common stock outstanding}}}$	$\dfrac{\$48,000 - \$0}{10,000} = \$4.80$	$\dfrac{\$26,000 - \$0}{10,000} = \$2.60$

Palisades Furniture's EPS increased 85%. Its stockholders should not expect such a large boost in EPS every year. Most companies strive to increase EPS by 10–15% annually, and strong companies do so. But even the most successful companies have an occasional bad year.

Analyzing a Company's Stock as an Investment

Investors purchase stock to earn a return on their investment. This return consists of two parts: (1) gains (or losses) from selling the stock at a price that differs from the investors' purchase price, and (2) dividends, the periodic distributions to stockholders. The ratios we examine in this section help analysts evaluate stock in terms of market price or dividend payments.

PRICE/EARNINGS RATIO   The **price/earnings (P/E) ratio** relates the market price of a share of common stock to the company's earnings per share. This ratio appears in the *Wall Street Journal* stock listings. P/E ratios play an important part in decisions to buy, hold, and sell stocks. They indicate the market price of $1 of earnings.

Calculations for the P/E ratios of Palisades Furniture, Inc., follow. The market price of its common stock was $58 at the end of 20X2 and $35 at the end of 20X1. These prices can be obtained from a financial publication, a stockbroker, or some other source outside the accounting records.

PRICE/EARNINGS RATIO. Ratio relates the market price of a share of common stock to the company's earnings per share. Measures the value the stock market places on $1 of a company's earnings.

		Palisades' Price/Earnings Ratio	
	Formula	20X2	20X1
P/E Ratio	$= \dfrac{\substack{\text{Market price per share of} \\ \text{common stock}}}{\text{Earnings per share}}$	$\dfrac{\$58.00}{\$4.80} = 12.1$	$\dfrac{\$35.00}{\$2.60} = 13.5$

⊙ DAILY EXERCISE 18-14

⊙ DAILY EXERCISE 18-15

A P/E ratio of 12.1 means that Palisades Furniture's stock is selling at 12.1 times earnings. Like most other ratios, P/E ratios vary from industry to industry. P/E ratios range from 8 to 10 for electric utilities (**Pennsylvania Power & Light,** for example) to 40 or more for "glamor stocks" such as **Lucent Technologies** and **Oracle Corporation,** the software company.

DIVIDEND YIELD. Ratio of dividends per share of stock to the stock's market price. Measures the percentage of the stock's market value that the company pays to stockholders as dividends.

DIVIDEND YIELD   **Dividend yield** is the ratio of dividends per share of stock to the stock's market price. This ratio measures the percentage of the stock's market value that is returned annually as dividends. *Preferred* stockholders, who invest primarily to receive dividends, pay special attention to dividend yield.

Palisades Furniture paid annual cash dividends of $1.20 per share of common stock in 20X2 and $1.00 in 20X1, and market prices of the company's common stock were $58 in 20X2 and $35 in 20X1. Calculation of the firm's dividend yields on common stock is at the top of the next page.

An investor who buys Palisades Furniture common stock for $58 can expect to receive almost 2.1% of the investment annually in the form of cash dividends. Dividend yields vary widely, from 5% to 8% for older, established firms (such as **Procter & Gamble** and **General Motors**) down to the range of 0–3% for young, growth-oriented companies. **MCI WorldCom,** for example, pays no dividends. Palisades Furniture's dividend yield places the company in the second group.

BOOK VALUE PER SHARE OF COMMON STOCK. Common equity divided by the number of shares of common stock outstanding.

BOOK VALUE PER SHARE OF COMMON STOCK   **Book value per share of common stock** is common equity divided by the number of shares of common stock

		Dividend Yield on Palisades' Common Stock	
	Formula	20X2	20X1
Dividend yield on common stock*	$= \dfrac{\text{Dividend per share of common stock}}{\text{Market price per share of common stock}}$	$\dfrac{\$1.20}{\$58.00} = 0.021$	$\dfrac{\$1.00}{\$35.00} = \$0.029$

*Dividend yields may also be calculated for preferred stock.

outstanding. Common equity equals total stockholders' equity less preferred equity. Palisades Furniture has no preferred stock outstanding. Calculations of its book value follows. Recall that 10,000 shares of common stock were outstanding at the end of years 20X2 and 20X1.

		Book Value Per Share of Palisades' Common Stock	
	Formula	20X2	20X1
Book value per share of common stock	$= \dfrac{\text{Total stockholders' equity} - \text{Preferred equity}}{\text{Number of shares of common stock outstanding}}$	$\dfrac{\$356,000 - \$0}{10,000} = \$35.60$	$\dfrac{\$320,000 - \$0}{10,000} = \$32.00$

Many experts argue that book value is not useful for investment analysis. It bears no relationship to *market value*. But some investors still base their decisions on book value. For example, some analysts rank stocks on the basis of the ratio of market price to book value. By this reasoning, the lower the ratio, the more attractive the stock.

LIMITATIONS OF FINANCIAL ANALYSIS

Business decisions are made in a world of uncertainty. As useful as ratios are, they have limitations. We can liken their use in decision making to a physician's use of a thermometer. A reading of 101.6°F indicates that something is wrong with the patient, but the temperature alone does not indicate what the problem is or how to cure it.

In financial analysis, a sudden drop in a company's current ratio signals that *something* is wrong, but this change does not identify the problem or show how to correct it. The business manager must analyze the figures that go into the ratio to determine whether current assets have decreased, current liabilities have increased, or both. If current assets have dropped, is the problem a cash shortage? Are accounts receivable down? Are inventories too low?

Only by analyzing the individual items that make up the ratio can the manager determine how to solve the problem. The manager must evaluate data on all ratios in light of other information about the company and about its particular line of business, such as increased competition or a slowdown in the economy.

Legislation, international affairs, competition, scandals, and many other factors can turn profits into losses, and vice versa. To be most useful, ratios should be analyzed over a period of years to take into account a representative group of these factors. Any one year, or even any two years, may not be representative of the company's performance over the long term.

Economic Value Added (EVA®)— A New Measure of Performance

The top managers of **Coca-Cola, Quaker Oats,** and other leading companies use **economic value added (EVA®)** to evaluate a company's operating performance. EVA® combines accounting and finance to measure whether the company's operations have increased stockholder wealth. EVA® can be computed as follows:

$$\text{EVA}^® = \text{Net income} + \text{Interest expense} - \text{Capital charge}$$

 DAILY EXERCISE 18-16

 DAILY EXERCISE 18-17

DAILY EXERCISE 18-18

Objective 5
Use ratios in decision making

Objective 6
Measure economic value added

ECONOMIC VALUE ADDED (EVA®).
Combines accounting income and finance to measure whether the company's operations have increased stockholder wealth.

where

$$\text{Capital charge} = \left(\begin{array}{c} \text{Short-term} \\ \text{debt} \end{array} + \begin{array}{c} \text{Long-term} \\ \text{debt} \end{array} + \begin{array}{c} \text{Stockholders'} \\ \text{equity} \end{array} \right) \times \begin{array}{c} \text{Cost of} \\ \text{capital} \end{array}$$

COST OF CAPITAL. A weighted average of the returns demanded by a company's stockholders and lenders.

All amounts for the EVA® computation, except the cost of capital, are taken from the financial statements. The **cost of capital** is a weighted average of the returns demanded by the company's stockholders and lenders. The cost of capital varies with the company's level of risk. For example, stockholders would demand a higher return from a start-up computer software company than from **AT&T.** Lenders would also charge the new company a higher interest rate because of this greater risk. Thus, the new company has a higher cost of capital than AT&T. In the following discussions, we assume a value for the cost of capital (such as 10%, 12%, or 15%) to illustrate the computation of EVA®.

The idea behind EVA® is that the returns to the company's stockholders (net income) and to its creditors (interest expense) should exceed the company's capital charge. The **capital charge** is the amount that stockholders and lenders *charge* a company for the use of their money. A positive EVA® amount indicates an increase in stockholder wealth, and the company's stock price should rise. If the EVA® measure is negative, the stockholders will probably be unhappy with the company's progress and sell its stock.

CAPITAL CHARGE. The amount that stockholders and lenders charge a company for the use of their money.

Let's apply EVA® to **Lucent Technologies.** Lucent's EVA® for 1999 can be computed as follows, assuming a 12% cost of capital for the company (dollar amounts in millions):

$$\text{Lucent's EVA}^® = \begin{array}{c} \text{Net} \\ \text{income} \end{array} + \begin{array}{c} \text{Interest} \\ \text{expense} \end{array} - \left[\left(\begin{array}{c} \text{Short-term} \\ \text{debt} \end{array} + \begin{array}{c} \text{Long-term} \\ \text{debt} \end{array} + \begin{array}{c} \text{Stockholders'} \\ \text{equity} \end{array} \right) \times \begin{array}{c} \text{Cost of} \\ \text{capital} \end{array} \right]$$

$$= \$4,766 + \$406^* - [(\$2,864 + \$4,162 + \$13,584) \times 0.12]$$

$$= \$5,172 - \$20,610 \times 0.12$$

$$= \$5,172 - \$2,473$$

$$= \$2,699$$

*Included as part of Other income (expense) on the company's income statement (as adapted) in this chapter.

DAILY EXERCISE 18-19

By this measure, Lucent Technologies' operations during 1999 added $2.7 billion ($2,699 million) of value to its stockholders' wealth after meeting the company's capital charge. This performance is outstanding. Lucent's positive EVA® explains why the company's stock is popular with investors.

Efficient Markets, Management Action, and Investor Decisions

EFFICIENT CAPITAL MARKET. A capital market in which market prices reflect the impact of all information available to the public.

An **efficient capital market** is one in which market prices reflect the impact of all information available to the public. Market efficiency means that managers cannot fool the market with accounting gimmicks. If the information is available, the market as a whole can translate accounting data into a "fair" price for the company's stock.

Suppose you are the president of Anacomp Company. Reported earnings per share are $4, and the stock price is $40—so the P/E ratio is 10. You believe the corporation's stock is underpriced in comparison with other companies in your industry. To correct this situation, you are considering changing from accelerated to straight-line depreciation. The accounting change will increase earnings per share to $5. Will the stock price then rise to $50? Probably not. The stock price will probably remain at $40 because the market can understand the change in depreciation method, not improved operations, caused earnings to increase.

In an efficient market, the search for "underpriced" stock is fruitless unless the investor has private information. But it is unlawful to invest on the basis of *inside* information. For outside investors, an appropriate strategy seeks to manage risk, diversify investments so that you don't lose everything if one stock goes bad, and minimize transaction costs. The role of financial statement analysis is mainly to help measure the risks of various stocks. The goal is to manage the risk of the overall investment portfolio.

Managers, owners, investors, and creditors all use financial ratios to measure an entity's progress. The Decision Guidelines feature summarizes the ratios covered in this chapter. Memorize each ratio's computation and the information it provides because you will be using these ratios for the rest of your life.

DECISION GUIDELINES

Using Ratios in Financial Statement Analysis

RATIO	COMPUTATION	INFORMATION PROVIDED
Measuring the company's ability to pay current liabilities:		
1. Current ratio	$$\dfrac{\text{Total current assets}}{\text{Total current liabilities}}$$	Measures ability to pay current liabilities with current assets.
2. Acid-test (quick) ratio	$$\dfrac{\text{Cash} + \dfrac{\text{Short-term}}{\text{investments}} + \dfrac{\text{Net current}}{\text{receivables}}}{\text{Total current liabilities}}$$	Shows ability to pay all current liabilities if they come due immediately.
Measuring the company's ability to sell inventory and collect receivables:		
3. Inventory turnover	$$\dfrac{\text{Cost of goods sold}}{\text{Average inventory}}$$	Indicates saleability of inventory—the number of times a company sells its average inventory level during a year.
4. Accounts receivable turnover	$$\dfrac{\text{Net credit sales}}{\text{Average net accounts receivable}}$$	Measures ability to collect cash from credit customers.
5. Days' sales in receivables	$$\dfrac{\text{Average net accounts receivable}}{\text{One day's sales}}$$	Shows how many days' sales remain in Accounts Receivable—how many days it takes to collect the average level of receivables.
Measuring the company's ability to pay short-term and long-term debt:		
6. Debt ratio	$$\dfrac{\text{Total liabilities}}{\text{Total assets}}$$	Indicates percentage of assets financed with debt.
7. Times-interest-earned ratio	$$\dfrac{\text{Income from operations}}{\text{Interest expense}}$$	Measures the number of times operating income can cover interest expense.
Measuring the company's profitability:		
8. Rate of return on net sales	$$\dfrac{\text{Net income}}{\text{Net sales}}$$	Shows the percentage of each sales dollar earned as net income.
9. Rate of return on total assets	$$\dfrac{\text{Net income} + \text{Interest expense}}{\text{Average total assets}}$$	Measures how profitably a company uses its assets.
10. Rate of return on common stockholders' equity	$$\dfrac{\text{Net income} - \text{Preferred dividends}}{\text{Average common stockholders' equity}}$$	Gauges how much income is earned with the money invested by common shareholders.
11. Earnings per share of common stock	$$\dfrac{\text{Net income} - \text{Preferred dividends}}{\text{Number of shares of common stock outstanding}}$$	Gives the amount of net income earned for each share of the company's common stock.
Analyzing the company's stock as an investment:		
12. Price/earnings ratio	$$\dfrac{\text{Market price per share of common stock}}{\text{Earnings per share}}$$	Indicates the market price of $1 of earnings.
13. Dividend yield	$$\dfrac{\text{Dividends per share of common (or preferred) stock}}{\text{Market price per share of common (or preferred) stock}}$$	Shows the percentage of a stock's market value returned to stockholders as dividends each period.
14. Book value per share of common stock	$$\dfrac{\text{Total stockholders' equity} - \text{Preferred equity}}{\text{Number of shares of common stock outstanding}}$$	Indicates the recorded accounting amount for each share of common stock outstanding.

EXCEL APPLICATION PROBLEM

Goal: Create an Excel spreadsheet that calculates financial ratios to compare **Gap Inc.,** and **Lands' End.** Then use the results to determine which company has the stronger financial performance.

Scenario: You've recently received a $1,000 bonus from your employer, Gap Inc. You've been thinking about investing the bonus in the stock of your employer, but your parents think that Lands' End is the better investment.

Before making your purchase, your task is to create an Excel spreadsheet to compare the following ratios for Gap and Lands' End:

1. Acid-test (quick) ratio
2. Inventory turnover
3. Times-interest-earned ratio
4. Return on net sales

When done with the spreadsheet, answer the following questions:

1. Which company is in a better position to pay all current liabilities if they come due immediately?
2. Which company moves its inventory faster?
3. Which company can cover its interest expense better?
4. Which company earned more profit, as a percentage, on each sales dollar?

Step-by-step:

1. Locate the data required for each ratio in the annual reports of Gap and Lands' End. These reports may be accessed via the Web.
2. Open a new Excel spreadsheet.
3. Create a boldfaced heading for your spreadsheet that contains the following:
   a. Chapter 18 Decision Guidelines
   b. Using Ratios in Financial Statement Analysis
   c. Gap and Lands' End Comparison
   d. Today's date
4. In the first column, enter the names of all four ratios. Skip a row between each ratio name.
5. Create boldfaced, underlined column headings for Gap and Lands' End.
6. Enter the data located in step 1, using the correct ratio formulas found in the Decision Guidelines. Format all cells as necessary.
7. Save your work, and print a copy for your files.

REVIEW FINANCIAL STATEMENT ANALYSIS

SUMMARY PROBLEM

The following financial data are adapted from the annual report of **Gap Inc.,** which operates Gap, Banana Republic, and Old Navy clothing stores.

GAP INC. Five-Year Selected Financial Data					
Operating Results (in millions)	**19X9**	**19X8**	**19X7**	**19X6**	**19X5**
Net sales	$2,960	$2,519	$1,934	$1,587	$1,252
Cost of goods sold and occupancy expenses, excluding depreciation and amortization.................	1,856	1,496	1,188	1,007	814
Interest expense (net)...	4	4	1	3	3
Income from operations	340	371	237	163	126
Income taxes..	129	141	92	65	52
Net earnings..	211	230	145	98	74
Cash dividends..	44	41	30	23	18
Financial Position					
Merchandise inventory...	366	314	247	243	193
Total assets	1,379	1,147	777	579	481
Working capital...	355	236	579	129	434
Stockholders' equity	888	678	466	338	276
Current ratio...	2.06:1	1.71:1	1.39:1	1.69:1	1.70:1
Average number of shares of common stock outstanding (in thousands)	144	142	142	141	145

www.prenhall.com/horngren

End-of-Chapter Assessment

Required

Compute the following ratios for 19X9–19X6, and evaluate Gap's operating results. Are operating results strong or weak? Did they improve or deteriorate during the four-year period?

a. Gross profit percentage

b. Net income as a percentage of sales

c. Earnings per share

d. Inventory turnover

e. Times-interest-earned ratio

f. Rate of return on stockholders' equity

Solution

Requirement	19X9	19X8	19X7	19X6
a. Gross profit percentage	$\dfrac{\$2,960 - \$1,856}{\$2,960}$ $= 37.3\%$	$\dfrac{\$2,519 - \$1,496}{\$2,519}$ $= 40.6\%$	$\dfrac{\$1,934 - \$1,188}{\$1,934}$ $= 38.6\%$	$\dfrac{\$1,587 - \$1,007}{\$1,587}$ $= 36.5\%$
b. Net income as a percentage of sales	$\dfrac{\$211}{\$2,960} = 7.1\%$	$\dfrac{\$230}{\$2,519} = 9.1\%$	$\dfrac{\$145}{\$1,934} = 7.5\%$	$\dfrac{\$98}{\$1,587} = 6.2\%$
c. Earnings per share	$\dfrac{\$211}{144} = \$1.47$	$\dfrac{\$230}{142} = \$1.62$	$\dfrac{\$145}{142} = \$1.02$	$\dfrac{\$98}{141} = \$0.70$
d. Inventory turnover	$\dfrac{\$1,856}{(\$366 + \$314)/2}$ $= 5.5$ times	$\dfrac{\$1,496}{(\$314 + \$247)/2}$ $= 5.3$ times	$\dfrac{\$1,188}{(\$247 + \$243)/2}$ $= 4.8$ times	$\dfrac{\$1,007}{(\$243 + \$193)/2}$ $= 4.6$ times
e. Times-interest-earned ratio	$\dfrac{\$340}{\$4} = 85$ times	$\dfrac{\$371}{\$4} = 93$ times	$\dfrac{\$237}{\$1} = 237$ times	$\dfrac{\$163}{\$3} = 54$ times
f. Rate of return on stockholders' equity	$\dfrac{\$211}{(\$888 + \$678)/2}$ $= 26.9\%$	$\dfrac{\$230}{(\$678 + \$466)/2}$ $= 40.2\%$	$\dfrac{\$145}{(\$466 + \$338)/2}$ $= 36.1\%$	$\dfrac{\$98}{(\$338 + \$276)/2}$ $= 31.9\%$

Evaluation: During this four-year period, Gap's operating results were outstanding. Operating results improved, with all ratio values but return on stockholders' equity higher in 19X9 than in 19X6. Moreover, all the performance measures indicate high levels of income and return to investors.

LESSONS LEARNED

1. **Perform a horizontal analysis of financial statements.** *Horizontal analysis* is the study of percentage changes in financial statement items from one period to the next. *Trend percentages* are a form of horizontal analysis.

2. **Perform a vertical analysis of financial statements.** *Vertical analysis* of a financial statement reveals the relationship of each statement item to a specified base, which is the 100% figure. In an income statement, net sales is the base. On a balance sheet, total assets is the 100% figure.

3. **Prepare common-size financial statements.** *Common-size statements* report only percentages, no dollar amounts. They ease the comparison of different companies and may signal the need for corrective action. *Benchmarking* is the practice of comparing a company to a standard set by other companies.

4. **Compute the standard financial ratios.** An important part of financial analysis is the use of ratios. A ratio expresses the relationship of one item to another. The most important ratios measure a company's ability to pay current liabilities, ability to sell inventory and collect receivables, ability to pay long-term debt, its profitability, and its value as an investment.

5. **Use ratios in decision making.** Analysis of financial ratios over time helps track a company's progress. A change in the ratios over time may signal a problem. The company's managers must then find the source of this problem and correct it.

6. **Measure economic value added.** *Economic value added (EVA®)* measures whether a company's operations have increased its stockholders' wealth. EVA® is defined as the excess of net income and interest expense over the company's capital charge (the amount the company's stockholders and lenders charge for the use of their money).

ACCOUNTING VOCABULARY

horizontal analysis (p. 712)
interest-coverage ratio (p. 727)
inventory turnover (p. 725)
leverage (p. 729)
price/earnings (P/E) ratio (p. 730)
quick ratio (p. 724)
rate of return on common
  stockholders' equity (p. 728)

rate of return on net
  sales (p. 727)
rate of return on total
  assets (p. 728)
return on assets (ROA) (p. 728)
return on equity (ROE) (p. 728)
return on stockholders'
  equity (p. 728)

return on sales (p. 727)
times-interest-earned
  ratio (p. 727)
trading on the equity (p. 729)
vertical analysis (p. 715)
working capital (p. 722)

Q UESTIONS

1. Name the three broad categories of analytical tools that are based on accounting information.
2. Briefly describe horizontal analysis. How do decision makers use this analytical tool?
3. What is vertical analysis, and what is its purpose? What is the purpose of common-size statements?
4. Identify two ratios used to measure a company's ability to pay current liabilities. Show how the ratios are computed.
5. Why is the acid-test ratio given that name?
6. What does the inventory turnover ratio measure?
7. Suppose the days'-sales-in-receivables ratio of Klaras Corp. increased from 36 at January 1 to 43 at December 31. Is this a good sign or a bad sign? What might Klaras management do in response to this change?
8. Snap Tool Company's debt ratio has increased from 0.50 to 0.70. Identify a decision maker to whom this increase is important, and state how the increase affects this party's decisions about the company.
9. Company A is a chain of grocery stores, and Company B is a construction company. Which company is likely to

have the higher (a) current ratio, (b) inventory turnover, and (c) rate of return on sales? Give your reasons.
10. The price/earnings ratio of **Ford Motor Company** was 8, and the price/earnings ratio of **Lucent Technologies** was 40. Which company did the stock market favor? Explain.
11. Hold all other factors constant and indicate whether each of the following situations generally signals good or bad news about a company:
    a. Increase in return on sales
    b. Decrease in earnings per share
    c. Increase in price/earnings ratio
    d. Increase in book value per share
    e. Increase in current ratio
    f. Decrease in inventory turnover
    g. Increase in debt ratio
    h. Decrease in interest-coverage ratio
12. What is EVA®, how is it computed, and how is it used in financial analysis?

ASSESS YOUR PROGRESS

D AILY E XERCISES

Horizontal analysis of revenues and gross profit
(Obj. 1)

DE18-1 **Phillips Electronics** reported the following amounts on its 1999 comparative income statement:

(In millions)	1999	1998	1997
Revenues	$78,596	$74,391	$72,055
Cost of sales	29,561	26,820	15,941

Perform a horizontal analysis of revenues and gross profit—both in dollar amounts and in percentages—for 1999 and 1998.

Using horizontal analysis for decision making
(Obj. 1)

DE18-2 Study Exhibit 18-2, the horizontal analysis of **Lucent Technologies'** balance sheet at September 30, 1999. Focus on the 41.0% increase in receivables and the 35.5% increase in inventories during 1999. Assume that Lucent's income statement reported a decrease in sales during 1999.
    Would the large percentage increases in receivables and inventories convey good news or bad news about the company? Explain your reasoning.

Trend analysis of revenues and net income
(Obj. 1)

DE18-3 **Pier 1 Imports,** reported the following revenues and net income amounts:

(In millions)	1999	1998	1997	1996	1995
Net sales	$1,139	$1,075	$947	$811	$712
Net income	80	78	48	10	22

1. Show Pier 1 Imports' trend percentages for revenues and net income. Start with 1995, and use 1995 as the base year.
2. Which trend looks better—net sales or net income?

DE18-4 Bernstein Bros. Scuba Shop has recently introduced a new ultra-light wet suit for diving. Demand for the product has been high, and Bernstein is shipping goods to many new diving shops. Bernstein's comparative income statement reports these figures for 20X2 and 20X1:

Vertical analysis of the income statement
(Obj. 2)

	20X2	20X1
Net sales	$204,000	$171,000
Cost of goods sold..............	61,000	50,000
Selling expenses	45,000	36,000
General expenses	18,000	17,000
Net income........................	$ 80,000	$ 68,000

Perform a vertical analysis of Bernstein's income statements for 20X2 and 20X1. Does the analysis reflect favorably or poorly on the company? Cite specifics in your answer.

DE18-5 Bernstein Bros. Scuba Shop reported the following amounts on its balance sheets at December 31, 20X2, 20X1, and 20X0:

Vertical analysis to correct a cash shortage
(Obj. 2)

	20X2	20X1	20X0
Cash	$ 4,000	$ 8,000	$ 9,000
Receivables, net	46,000	32,000	20,000
Inventory..	42,000	36,000	33,000
Prepaid expenses	2,000	2,000	1,000
Property, plant, and equipment, net.........	96,000	88,000	87,000
Total assets	$190,000	$166,000	$150,000

1. Sales and profits are high. Nevertheless, the company is experiencing a cash shortage. Perform a vertical analysis of Bernstein's assets at the end of each year 20X2, 20X1, and 20X0. Use the analysis to explain the reason for the cash shortage.
2. Suggest a way for Bernstein to generate more cash.

DE18-6 Return to Exhibit 18-4, the vertical analysis of **Lucent Technologies'** balance sheets at December 31, 1999 and 1998. Consider that Lucent's revenues and profits reached all-time highs during 1999. Focus on receivables and inventories.

Using vertical analysis for decision making
(Obj. 2)

1. Did receivables and inventories make up more or less of total assets in 1999 than in 1998? Give the percentages for each year.
2. Do the increases in receivables and inventories worry you? Explain your reasoning.

DE18-7 **Nike, Inc.,** and **The Home Depot** are leaders in their respective industries. Compare the two companies by converting their income statements (adapted) to common size.

Common-size income statements of two leading companies
(Obj. 3)

(In millions)	Nike	Home Depot
Net sales..	$8,777	$38,434
Cost of goods sold	5,494	27,023
Selling and administrative expenses.............	2,427	7,579
Interest expense	44	28
Other expense	66	—
Income tax expense.................................	295	1,484
Net income	$ 451	$ 2,320

Which company earns more net income? Which company's net income is a higher percentage of net sales? Which company is more profitable? Explain your answer.

DE18-8 Prepare a common-size analysis to compare **Nike, Inc.,** and **The Home Depot** on the makeup of their assets (amounts in millions).

Assets	Nike	Home Depot
Current assets:		
Cash and equivalents	$ 198	$ 168
Short-term investments	—	2
Accounts receivable, net	1,540	587
Inventories	1,199	5,489
Other current assets	328	144
Total current assets	3,265	6,390
Property, plant, and equipment, net............	1,266	10,227
Goodwill and other intangibles	427	311
Other assets..	290	153
Total assets	$5,248	$17,081

To which company are *current assets* more important? Which company places more emphasis on its *plant assets*?

Evaluating the trend in a
company's current ratio
(Obj. 4, 5)

DE18-9 Examine the actual financial data of **Rubbermaid, Inc.,** in Exhibit 18-8 (page 721). Show how to compute Rubbermaid's current ratio for each year 19X8–20X1. Is the company's ability to pay its current liabilities improving or deteriorating?

DE18-10 Use the **Lucent Technologies** balance sheet data in Exhibit 18-2 (page 714).

1. Compute the company's acid-test ratio at September 30, 1999 and 1998.
2. Compare Lucent's ratio values to those of **MCI WorldCom** and **Wal-Mart** on page 724. Is Lucent's acid-test ratio strong or weak? Explain.

Computing inventory turnover
and days' sales in receivables
(Obj. 4)

DE18-11 Use the **Lucent Technologies** 1999 income statement (page 713) and year-end balance sheet (page 714) to compute

a. Inventory turnover for 1999. (Round turnover to one decimal place.)
b. Days' sales in receivables during 1999. All revenues are earned on account. (Round dollar amounts to one decimal place.)

DE18-12 Use the actual financial statements of **Lucent Technologies** (pages 715 and 716).

1. Compute the company's debt ratio at September 30, 1999.
2. Compute the company's times-interest-earned ratio for 1999. Interest expense for 1999 was $406 million.
3. Is Lucent Technologies' ability to pay its liabilities and interest expense strong or weak? Comment on the value of each ratio computed for requirements 1 and 2.

DE18-13 Use the financial statements of **Lucent Technologies** (pages 715 and 716) to determine or, if necessary, to compute these profitability measures for 1999:

a. Rate of return on net sales.
b. Rate of return on total assets. Interest expense for 1999 was $406 million.
c. Rate of return on common stockholders' equity.

Are these rates of return strong or weak? Explain.

Computing EPS and the
price/earnings ratio
(Obj. 4)

DE18-14 The annual report of **The Home Depot** for the year ended January 31, 2000, included the following items:

Market price per share of common stock..........................	$55.63
Preferred stock outstanding................................	$0
Net earnings (net income).................................	$2,320,000,000
Number of shares of common stock outstanding	2,244,000,000

1. Compute earnings per share (EPS) and the price/earnings ratio for The Home Depot's stock. Round to the nearest cent.
2. How much does the stock market say that $1 of The Home Depot's net income is worth?

DE18-15 During 1999, **Lucent Technologies** had earnings per share of common stock (EPS) of $1.52. The company had no preferred stock outstanding, so there were no preferred dividends. Use the income statement (Exhibit 18-3, page 715), and the formula for EPS (page 730) to compute the number of shares of common stock that Lucent had outstanding during 1999. Keep in mind that net income is in millions of dollars. Therefore, you will need to multiply the reported net income figures by 1,000,000.

Working with earnings per share (Obj. 4)

DE18-16 Use **Lucent Technologies'** balance sheet (Exhibit 18-2, page 714) to compute the book value per share of the company's common stock at September 30, 1999 and at September 30, 1998. At September 30, 1999, Lucent had 3,072 million shares of common stock outstanding. At September 30, 1998, shares outstanding were 3,022 million. Is the trend of book value per share positive or negative?

Computing book value per share of common stock (Obj. 4)

DE18-17 A skeleton of **Campbell Soup Company's** income statement (as adapted) for the year ended August 1, 19X9, appears as follows (amounts in millions):

Using ratio data to reconstruct an income statement (Obj. 4)

Income Statement

Net sales	$6,424
Cost of goods sold	(a)
Selling expenses	1,634
Administrative expenses	304
Interest expense	(b)
Other expenses	166
Income before taxes	1,097
Income tax expense	(c)
Net income	$ (d)

Use the following ratio data to complete Campbell Soup's income statement.

a. Inventory turnover is 5.174 (beginning inventory is $564; ending inventory was $615).

b. Rate of return on sales is 0.1127.

DE18-18 A skeleton of **Campbell Soup Company's** balance sheet at August 1, 19X9 (as adapted) appears as follows (amounts in millions):

Using ratio data to reconstruct a balance sheet (Obj. 4)

Balance Sheet

Cash	$ 6	Total current liabilities	$ 3,146
Receivables	(a)	Long-term debt	(e)
Inventories	615	Other long-term liabilities	811
Prepaid expenses	(b)		
Total current assets	(c)	Common stock	402
Plant assets, net	(d)	Retained earnings	4,041
Other assets	2,502	Other stockholders' equity	(4,208)
Total assets	$5,522	Total liabilities and equity	$ (f)

Use the following ratio data to complete Campbell Soup's balance sheet:

a. Debt ratio is 0.9574.   **b.** Current ratio is 0.4113.   **c.** Acid-test ratio is 0.1739.

DE18-19 Use the 1999 income statement of **MCI WorldCom,** page 710, and the following data for MCI: interest expense, $966 million; short-term and long-term debt, $21,205 million; stockholders' equity, $45,241 million.

Computing economic value added (Obj. 6)

1. Compute economic value added (EVA®) by MCI's operations during 1999. Assume the company's cost of capital is 12%. Round all amounts to the nearest million dollars.
2. Should the company's stockholders be happy with the EVA® for 1999? How did the company's stock perform?

EXERCISES

E18-1 What were the amount of change and the percentage change in Berkshire Property Management's working capital during 20X2 and 20X3? Is this trend favorable or unfavorable?

Computing year-to-year changes in working capital (Obj. 1)

	20X3	20X2	20X1
Total current assets	$408,000	$399,000	$385,000
Total current liabilities	250,000	211,000	232,000

Horizontal analysis of an income statement
(Obj. 1)

E18-2 Prepare a horizontal analysis of the following comparative income statement of Saladin Publishing. Round percentage changes to the nearest one-tenth percent (three decimal places):

SALADIN PUBLISHING
Comparative Income Statement
Years Ended December 31, 20X4 and 20X3

	20X4	20X3
Total revenue	$460,000	$373,000
Expenses:		
Cost of goods sold	$202,000	$188,000
Selling and general expenses	98,000	93,000
Interest expense	7,000	4,000
Income tax expense	52,000	37,000
Total expenses	359,000	322,000
Net income	$101,000	$ 51,000

Why did net income increase by a higher percentage than total revenues during 20X4?

Computing trend percentages
(Obj. 1)

E18-3 Compute trend percentages for Traigon Corporation's net sales and net income for the following five-year period, using year 1 as the base year. Round to the nearest full percent.

(In thousands)	Year 5	Year 4	Year 3	Year 2	Year 1
Net sales	$1,310	$1,147	$1,065	$1,104	$1,043
Net income	120	114	74	81	85

Which grew faster during the period, net sales or net income?

Vertical analysis of a balance sheet
(Obj. 2)

E18-4 Artisan International has requested that you perform a vertical analysis of its balance sheet to determine the component percentages of its assets, liabilities, and stockholders' equity.

ARTISAN INTERNATIONAL
Balance Sheet
December 31, 20X3

Assets

Total current assets	$ 99,000
Long-term investments	35,000
Property, plant, and equipment, net	217,000
Total assets	351,000

Liabilities

Total current liabilities	$ 58,000
Long-term debt	118,000
Total liabilities	176,000

Stockholders' Equity

Total stockholders' equity	175,000
Total liabilities and stockholders' equity	$351,000

Preparing a common-size income statement *(Obj. 3)*

E18-5 Prepare a comparative common-size income statement for Saladin Publishing, using the 20X4 and 20X3 data of Exercise 18-2 and rounding percentages to one-tenth percent (three decimal places).

E18-6 The financial statements of Lambert Enterprises, Inc., include the following items:

Computing five ratios
(Obj. 4)

	Current Year	Preceding Year
Balance Sheet Data		
Cash..	$ 29,000	$ 22,000
Short-term investments	11,000	26,000
Net receivables	64,000	73,000
Inventory......................................	87,000	71,000
Prepaid expenses.........................	6,000	8,000
Total current assets.....................	197,000	200,000
Total current liabilities.................	121,000	91,000
Income Statement Data		
Net credit sales	$480,000	
Cost of goods sold........................	260,000	

Required

Compute the following ratios for the current year: (a) current ratio, (b) acid-test ratio, (c) inventory turnover, (d) accounts receivable turnover, and (e) days' sales in average receivables.

E18-7 Cincinnati Light Company has asked you to determine whether the company's ability to pay its current liabilities and long-term debts has improved or deteriorated during 20X2. To answer this question, compute the following ratios for 20X2 and 20X1: (a) current ratio, (b) acid-test ratio, (c) debt ratio, and (d) times-interest-earned ratio. Summarize the results of your analysis in a written report.

Analyzing the ability to pay current liabilities
(Obj. 4, 5)

	20X2	20X1
Cash	$ 21,000	$ 47,000
Short-term investments	28,000	—
Net receivables	102,000	116,000
Inventory	226,000	263,000
Prepaid expenses.........................	11,000	9,000
Total assets	511,000	493,000
Total current liabilities	232,000	301,000
Total liabilities	261,000	273,000
Income from operations..............	174,000	160,000
Interest expense..........................	36,000	39,000

E18-8 Compute four ratios that measure ability of Legend Data Systems, Inc., to earn profits. The company's comparative income statement follows.

Analyzing profitability
(Obj. 4, 5)

LEGEND DATA SYSTEMS, INC.
Comparative Income Statement
Years Ended December 31, 20X3 and 20X2

	20X3	20X2
Net sales.......................................	$178,000	$163,000
Cost of goods sold........................	93,000	86,000
Gross profit	85,000	77,000
Selling and general expenses............	48,000	41,000
Income from operations	37,000	36,000
Interest expense.............................	21,000	10,000
Income before income tax..............	16,000	26,000
Income tax expense..........................	4,000	8,000
Net income	$ 12,000	$ 18,000

Additional data:

	20X3	20X2
Average total assets...	$204,000	$191,000
Average common stockholders' equity..............	$96,000	$89,000
Preferred dividends..	$3,000	$3,000
Shares of common stock outstanding................	20,000	20,000

Did the company's operating performance improve or deteriorate during 20X3?

Evaluating a stock as an investment
(Obj. 4, 5)

E18-9 Evaluate the common stock of LeaseNet.com as an investment. Specifically, use the three stock ratios to determine whether the stock has increased or decreased in attractiveness during the past year.

	20X4	20X3
Net income..	$ 58,000	$ 55,000
Dividends (half on preferred stock)	28,000	28,000
Common stockholders' equity at year end (80,000 shares)	630,000	600,000
Preferred stockholders' equity at year end	200,000	200,000
Market price per share of common stock at year end..............	15.12	10.88

Using economic value added to measure corporate performance
(Obj. 6)

E18-10 Two companies with very different economic-value-added (EVA®) profiles are **IHOP,** the restaurant chain, and **Texaco,** the giant oil company. Adapted versions of the two companies' 1999 financial statements are presented here (in millions):

	IHOP	Texaco
Balance Sheet Data		
Total assets	$520	$28,972
Interest-bearing debt	$ 41	$ 5,503
All other liabilities..........................	253	14,022
Stockholders' equity	226	9,447
Total liabilities and equity..............	$520	$28,972
Income Statement Data		
Total revenue	$273	$34,975
Interest expense..............................	19	504
All other expenses	222	33,294
Net income......................................	$ 32	$ 1,177

Required

1. Before performing any calculations, which company do you think would represent the better investment? Give your reason.
2. Compute the EVA® for each company, and then decide which company's stock you would rather hold as an investment. Assume each company's cost of capital is 12%, and round to the nearest million dollars.

Challenge Exercises

Using ratio data to reconstruct a company's income statement
(Obj. 2, 3, 4)

E18-11 The following data (dollar amounts in millions) are from the financial statements of **McDonald's Corporation,** the restaurant chain.

Average stockholders' equity	$9,639
Interest expense...	$436
Preferred stock	–0–
Operating income as a percent of sales..............	25.04%
Rate of return on sales.......................................	14.692%
Rate of return on stockholders' equity	20.21%
Income tax rate..	32.45%

Required

Complete the following condensed income statement. Report amounts to the nearest million dollars.

Sales	$?
Operating expenses...............	?
Operating income	?
Interest expense	?
Income before tax	?
Income tax expense	?
Net income............................	?

E18-12 The following data (dollar amounts in millions) are from the financial statements of **Wal-Mart Stores, Inc.,** the largest retailer in the world:

Using ratio data to reconstruct a company's balance sheet (Obj. 2, 3, 4)

Total liabilities.....................................	$44,515
Preferred stock......................................	–0–
Total current assets	$24,356
Accumulated depreciation................	$8,224
Debt ratio...	63.277%
Current ratio..	0.94392

Required

Complete the following condensed balance sheet. Report amounts to the nearest million dollars.

Current assets		$?
Property, plant, and equipment	$?	
Less: Accumulated depreciation	?	?
Total assets		$?
Current liabilities		$?
Long-term liabilities...		?
Stockholders' equity		?
Total liabilities and stockholders' equity		$?

PROBLEMS

(Group A)

P18-1A Net sales, net income, and common stockholders' equity for Keel Furniture Company for a four-year period follow.

Trend percentages, return on common equity, and comparison with the industry (Obj. 1, 4, 5)

(In thousands)	20X2	20X1	20X0	19X9
Net sales..	$782	$714	$622	$634
Net income	75	50	32	40
Ending common stockholders' equity..............	391	370	305	252

Required

1. Compute trend percentages for each item for 20X0–20X2. Use 19X9 as the base year. Round to the nearest percent.
2. Compute the rate of return on average common stockholders' equity for 20X0–20X2, rounding to three decimal places. In this industry, rates of 13% are average, rates above 16% are good, and rates above 20% are outstanding.
3. How does Keel's return on common stockholders' equity compare with the industry? Is the trend promising or not?

P18-2A CJ Home Appliance Center has asked your help in comparing the company's profit performance and financial position with the average for the home appliance industry. The general manager has given you the company's income statement and balance sheet and also the industry average data for home appliance companies.

CJ HOME APPLIANCE CENTER
Income Statement
Compared with Industry Average
Year Ended December 31, 20X1

	CJ	Industry Average
Net sales	$781,000	100.0%
Cost of goods sold	497,000	65.8
Gross profit	284,000	34.2
Operating expenses	159,000	19.7
Operating income	125,000	14.5
Other expenses	5,000	0.4
Net income	$120,000	14.1%

CJ HOME APPLIANCE CENTER
Balance Sheet
Compared with Industry Average
December 31, 20X1

	CJ	Industry Average
Current assets	$350,000	70.9%
Plant assets, net	84,000	23.6
Intangible assets, net	6,000	0.8
Other assets	20,000	4.7
Total	$460,000	100.0 %
Current liabilities	$207,000	48.1%
Long-term liabilities	72,000	16.6
Stockholders' equity	181,000	35.3
Total	$460,000	100.0 %

Required

1. Prepare a two-column common-size income statement and balance sheet for CJ. The first column of each statement should present CJ's common-size statement, and the second column should show the industry averages.
2. For the profitability analysis, compute CJ's (a) ratio of gross profit to net sales, (b) ratio of operating income to net sales, and (c) ratio of net income to net sales. Compare these figures with the industry averages. Is CJ's profit performance better or worse than the industry average?
3. For the analysis of financial position, compute CJ's (a) ratio of current assets to total assets, and (b) ratio of stockholders' equity to total assets. Compare these ratios with the industry averages. Is CJ's financial position better or worse than the industry averages?

P18-3A Financial statement data of Willsboro Farms, Inc., include the following items:

Cash	$ 22,000	Accounts payable	$ 94,000
Short-term investments	19,000	Accrued liabilities	38,000
Accounts receivable, net	97,000	Long-term notes payable	160,000
Inventories	141,000	Other long-term liabilities	31,000
Prepaid expenses	8,000	Net income	71,000
Total assets	657,000	Number of common shares	
Short-term notes payable	49,000	outstanding	23,000

Required

1. Compute Willsboro's current ratio, debt ratio, and earnings per share.
2. Compute the three ratios after evaluating the effect of each transaction that follows. Consider each transaction *separately.*

a. Purchased merchandise costing $26,000 on account, debiting Inventory.

b. Paid off long-term liabilities, $31,000.

c. Declared, but did not pay, a $22,000 cash dividend on common stock.

d. Borrowed $85,000 on a long-term note payable.

e. Sold short-term investments for $18,000 (cost, $11,000); assume no income tax on the gain.

Use the following format for your answer:

Requirement 1:	**Current Ratio**	**Debt Ratio**	**Earnings Per Share**
	Transaction			
Requirement 2:	**(letter)**	**Current Ratio**	**Debt Ratio**	**Earnings Per Share**

P18-4A Comparative financial statement data of Swanner Resources, Inc., follow.

Using ratios to evaluate a stock investment

(Obj. 4, 5)

SWANNER RESOURCES, INC.
Comparative Income Statement
Years Ended December 31, 20X4 and 20X3

	20X4	20X3
Net sales	$462,000	$427,000
Cost of goods sold	289,000	278,000
Gross profit	173,000	149,000
Operating expenses	81,000	78,000
Income from operations	92,000	71,000
Interest expense	11,000	12,000
Income before income tax	81,000	59,000
Income tax expense	30,000	27,000
Net income	$ 51,000	$ 32,000

SWANNER RESOURCES, INC.
Comparative Balance Sheet
December 31, 20X4 and 20X3
(selected 20X2 amounts given for computation of ratios)

	20X4	20X3	20X2
Current assets:			
Cash	$116,000	$ 97,000	
Current receivables, net	112,000	116,000	$103,000
Inventories	104,000	122,000	101,000
Prepaid expenses	64,000	47,000	
Total current assets	396,000	382,000	
Property, plant, and equipment, net	189,000	178,000	
Total assets	$585,000	$560,000	598,000
Total current liabilities	$206,000	$223,000	
Long-term liabilities	119,000	117,000	
Total liabilities	325,000	340,000	
Preferred stockholders' equity, 6%, $100 par	100,000	100,000	
Common stockholders' equity, no par	160,000	120,000	90,000
Total liabilities and stockholders' equity	$585,000	$560,000	

Other information:

a. Market price of Swanner's common stock: $53 at December 31, 20X4, and $31.50 at December 31, 20X3.

b. Common shares outstanding: 10,000 during 20X4 and 9,000 during 20X3.

Required

1. Compute the following ratios for 20X4 and 20X3:
   a. Current ratio
   b. Inventory turnover
   c. Accounts receivable turnover
   d. Times-interest-earned ratio
   e. Return on assets
   f. Return on common stockholders' equity
   g. Earnings per share of common stock

2. Decide (a) whether Swanner's financial position improved or deteriorated during 20X4, and (b) whether the investment attractiveness of its common stock appears to have increased or decreased.

3. How will what you learned in this problem help you evaluate an investment?

Using ratio data to complete a set of financial statements (Obj. 4)

P18-5A ← *Link Back to Chapter 17 (Statement of Cash Flows).* Summarized and adapted versions of the financial statements of **Pepsi Co, Inc.,** follow (amounts in *millions*).

Income Statement
Year Ended May 31, 19X9

Net sales	$20,367
Cost of goods sold	(a)
Gross profit...	(b)
Selling and general expenses	9,103
Other expense (income)	(590)
Income before income tax	(c)
Income tax expense (43.93%)....................	(d)
Net income...	$ (e)

Balance Sheet
May 31, 19X9 and 19X8

Assets	19X9	19X8
Current:		
Cash	$ (f)	$ 311
Short-term investments	92	83
Receivables, net....................................	1,704	2,453
Inventories	899	1,016
Prepaid expenses.................................	(g)	499
Total current assets.............................	(h)	4,362
Long-term assets.................................	13,378	18,298
Total assets	$ (i)	$22,660
Liabilities		
Current liabilities	$ 3,788	$ 7,914
Long-term liabilities...............................	(j)	8,345
Total liabilities	(k)	16,259
Stockholders' Equity		
Common stockholders' equity...............	(l)	6,401
Total liabilities and equity.....................	$ (m)	$22,660

Ratio data:

a. Current ratio at May 31, 19X9 is 1.1016.

b. Inventory turnover for 19X9 was 8.562.

c. Debt ratio at May 31, 19X9 is 0.60794.

d. Increase in cash during 19X9, $653.

Required

Complete the financial statements. Start with the income statement and then complete the balance sheet last.

Using ratios to decide between two stock investments; measuring economic value added (Obj. 4, 5, 6)

P18-6A Assume that you are purchasing an investment and have decided to invest in a company in the automotive supply business. You have narrowed the choice to Bowie, Inc., and Drane Corp. and have assembled the following data.

Selected income statement data for current year:

	Bowie, Inc.	Drane Corp.
Net sales (all on credit)	$497,000	$371,000
Cost of goods sold	258,000	209,000
Income from operations	138,000	79,000
Interest expense............................	19,000	—
Net income....................................	72,000	48,000

746 CHAPTER 18

Selected balance sheet and market price data at end of current year:

	Bowie, Inc.	Drane Corp.
Current assets:		
Cash	$ 19,000	$ 22,000
Short-term investments.......................................	18,000	20,000
Current receivables, net......................................	46,000	42,000
Inventories..	100,000	87,000
Prepaid expenses	3,000	2,000
Total current assets	186,000	173,000
Total assets...	328,000	265,000
Total current liabilities...	98,000	108,000
Total liabilities..	131,000*	108,000*
Preferred stock: 5%, $100 par..............................	20,000	—
Common stock, $1 par (10,000 shares)		10,000
$2 par (6,000 shares)	12,000	
Total stockholders' equity.......................................	197,000	157,000
Market price per share of common stock..............	$81.50	$45

* Notes payable: Bowie, $86,000
  Drane, $ 1,000

Selected balance sheet data at beginning of current year:

	Bowie, Inc.	Drane Corp.
Current receivables, net	$ 48,000	$ 40,000
Inventories	88,000	93,000
Total assets...	270,000	259,000
Preferred stock, 5%, $100 par............................	20,000	—
Common stock, $1 par (10,000 shares)		10,000
$2 par (6,000 shares)	12,000	
Total stockholders' equity...................................	126,000	118,000

Your investment strategy is to purchase the stocks of companies that have low price/earnings ratios but appear to be in good shape financially. Assume that you have analyzed all other factors and your decision depends on the results of the ratio analysis to be performed.

Required

1. Compute the following ratios for both companies for the current year, and decide which company's stock better fits your investment strategy.
   a. Current ratio
   b. Acid-test ratio
   c. Inventory turnover
   d. Times-interest-earned ratio
   e. Return on common stockholders' equity
   f. Earnings per share of common stock
   g. Book value per share of common stock
   h. Price/earnings ratio

2. Compute each company's economic-value-added (EVA®) measure, and determine whether their EVA®s confirm or alter your investment decision. Each company's cost of capital is 13.5%. Round all amounts to the nearest $1,000.

PROBLEMS

(Group B)

P18-1B Net sales, net income, and total assets for Oaklea Corporation for a four-year period follow:

Trend percentages, return on sales, and comparison with the industry
(Obj. 1, 4, 5)

(In thousands)	20X2	20X1	20X0	19X9
Net sales	$360	$313	$266	$241
Net income..........	27	21	11	13
Total assets...........	296	254	212	166

Required

1. Compute trend percentages for each item for 20X0–20X2. Use 19X9 as the base year. Round to the nearest percent.
2. Compute the rate of return on net sales for 20X0–20X2, rounding to three decimal places. In this industry, rates above 5% are considered good, and rates above 7% are outstanding.
3. How does Oaklea's return on net sales compare with that of the industry?

Common-size statements, analysis of profitability, and comparison with the industry (Obj. 2, 3, 4, 5)

P18-2B Top managers of Geolab Exploration, Inc. have asked your help in comparing the company's profit performance and financial position with the average for the geological engineering industry. The accountant has given you the company's income statement and balance sheet and also the following data for the geological engineering industry.

GEOLAB EXPLORATION, INC.
Income Statement
Compared with Industry Average
Year Ended December 31, 20X3

	Geolab	Industry Average
Net sales	$988,000	100.0%
Cost of goods sold...............	653,000	65.9
Gross profit.........................	335,000	34.1
Operating expenses.............	257,000	28.1
Operating income...............	78,000	6.0
Other expenses...................	2,000	0.4
Net income.........................	$ 76,000	5.6%

GEOLAB EXPLORATION, INC.
Balance Sheet
Compared with Industry Average
December 31, 20X3

	Geolab	Industry Average
Current assets.....................	$501,000	74.4%
Plant assets, net	127,000	20.0
Intangible assets, net	42,000	0.6
Other assets	13,000	5.0
Total...................................	$683,000	100.0%
Current liabilities...............	$246,000	35.6%
Long-term liabilities	144,000	19.0
Stockholders' equity...........	293,000	45.4
Total...................................	$683,000	100.0%

Required

1. Prepare a two-column common-size income statement and balance sheet for Geolab. The first column of each statement should present Geolab's common-size statement, and the second column should show the industry averages.
2. For the profitability analysis, compute Geolab's (a) ratio of gross profit to net sales, (b) ratio of operating income (loss) to net sales, and (c) ratio of net income (loss) to net sales. Compare these figures with the industry averages. Is Geolab's profit performance better or worse than the average for the industry?
3. For the analysis of financial position, compute Geolab's (a) ratio of current assets to total assets, and (b) ratio of stockholders' equity to total assets. Compare these ratios with the industry averages. Is Geolab's financial position better or worse than average for the industry?

Effects of business transactions on selected ratios (Obj. 4, 5)

P18-3B Financial statement data on Braum's Food Co. include the following items:

Cash	$ 47,000	Accounts payable...........................	$ 96,000
Short-term investments..................	21,000	Accrued liabilities	42,000
Accounts receivable, net.................	102,000	Long-term notes payable...............	146,000
Inventories.......................................	274,000	Other long-term liabilities	78,000
Prepaid expenses	15,000	Net income	119,000
Total assets	952,000	Number of common	
Short-term notes payable	72,000	shares outstanding.....................	26,000

Required

1. Compute Braum's Food Co.'s current ratio, debt ratio, and earnings per share.
2. Compute the three ratios after evaluating the effect of each transaction that follows. Consider each transaction *separately*.
   a. Borrowed $76,000 on a long-term note payable.
   b. Sold short-term investments for $44,000 (cost, $66,000); assume no tax effect of the loss.
   c. Issued 14,000 shares of common stock, receiving cash of $168,000.
   d. Received cash on account, $6,000.
   e. Paid short-term notes payable, $51,000.

Use the following format for your answer:

Requirement 1:   **Current Ratio**   **Debt Ratio**   **Earnings Per Share**

Requirement 2: **Transaction (letter)**   **Current Ratio**   **Debt Ratio**   **Earnings Per Share**

P18-4B Comparative financial statement data of Adolphus, Inc., follow.

Using ratios to evaluate a stock investment (Obj. 4, 5)

ADOLPHUS, INC.
Comparative Income Statement
Years Ended December 31, 20X3 and 20X2

	20X3	20X2
Net sales	$667,000	$599,000
Cost of goods sold	358,000	283,000
Gross profit	309,000	316,000
Operating expenses	149,000	147,000
Income from operations	160,000	169,000
Interest expense	57,000	41,000
Income before income tax	103,000	128,000
Income tax expense	34,000	53,000
Net income	$ 69,000	$ 75,000

ADOLPHUS, INC.
Comparative Balance Sheet
December 31, 20X3 and 20X2
(selected 20X1 amounts given for computations of ratios)

	20X3	20X2	20X1
Current assets:			
Cash	$ 37,000	$ 60,000	
Current receivables, net	208,000	151,000	$138,000
Inventories	340,000	286,000	184,000
Prepaid expenses	5,000	20,000	
Total current assets	590,000	517,000	
Property, plant, and equipment, net	287,000	256,000	
Total assets	$877,000	$773,000	707,000
Total current liabilities	$286,000	$267,000	
Long-term liabilities	245,000	235,000	
Total liabilities	531,000	502,000	
Preferred stockholders' equity, 4%, $20 par	50,000	50,000	
Common stockholders' equity, no-par	296,000	221,000	148,000
Total liabilities and stockholders' equity	$877,000	$773,000	

Other information:

a. Market price of Adolphus's common stock: $24.50 at December 31, 20X3, and $36.25 at December 31, 20X2.

b. Common shares outstanding: 15,000 during 20X3 and 14,000 during 20X2.

Required

1. Compute the following ratios for 20X3 and 20X2:
   a. Current ratio
   b. Inventory turnover
   c. Accounts receivable turnover
   d. Times-interest-earned ratio
   e. Return on assets
   f. Return on common stockholders' equity
   g. Earnings per share of common stock

2. Decide whether (a) Adolphus' financial position improved or deteriorated during 20X3, and (b) the investment attractiveness of its common stock appears to have increased or decreased.

3. How will what you learned in this problem help you evaluate an investment?

Using ratio data to complete a set of financial statements (Obj. 4)

P18-5B Summarized and adapted versions of the financial statements of **The Coca-Cola Company** follow at the top of the next page (amounts in millions).

INCOME STATEMENT
Year Ended December 31, 19X9

Net sales	$19,805
Cost of goods sold	(a)
Gross profit	(b)
Selling and general expenses	9,814
Other expense (income)	163
Income before income tax	(c)
Income tax expense (36.34%)	(d)
Net income	$ (e)

Balance Sheet
December 31, 19X9 and 19X8

	19X9	19X8
Assets		
Current:		
Cash	$ (f)	$ 1,648
Short-term investments	201	159
Receivables, net	1,798	1,666
Inventories	1,076	890
Prepaid expenses	(g)	2,017
Total current assets	(h)	6,380
Long-term assets	15,143	12,765
Total assets	$ (i)	$19,145
Liabilities		
Current liabilities	$ 9,856	$ 8,640
Long-term liabilities	(j)	2,102
Total liabilities	(k)	10,742
Stockholders' Equity		
Common stockholders' equity	(l)	8,403
Total liabilities and equity	$ (m)	$19,145

Ratio data:

   a. Current ratio at December 31, 19X9 is 0.6575.
   b. Inventory turnover for 19X9 was 6.113.
   c. Debt ratio at December 31, 19X9 is 0.56005.
   d. Decrease in cash during 19X9, $37.

Required

Complete the financial statements. Start with the income statement. Then complete the balance sheet.

Using ratios to decide between two stock investments; measuring economic value added (Obj. 4, 5, 6)

P18-6B Assume that you are considering purchasing stock in a company in the pharmaceutical industry. You have narrowed the choice to Eckert, Inc., and Biomed, Inc., and have assembled the following data.

Selected income statement data for current year:

	Eckert, Inc.	Biomed, Inc.
Net sales (all on credit)	$519,000	$603,000
Cost of goods sold	387,000	454,000
Income from operations	72,000	93,000
Interest expense	8,000	—
Net income	32,000	56,000

Selected balance sheet and market price data at end of current year:

	Eckert, Inc.	Biomed, Inc.
Current assets:		
Cash..	$ 39,000	$ 25,000
Short-term investments.......................................	13,000	6,000
Current receivables, net	164,000	189,000
Inventories..	183,000	211,000
Prepaid expenses	15,000	19,000
Total current assets	414,000	450,000
Total assets...	938,000	974,000
Total current liabilities..	338,000	366,000
Total liabilities	691,000*	667,000*
Preferred stock, 4%, $100 par.............................	25,000	
Common stock, $1 par (150,000 shares)		150,000
$5 par (20,000 shares)	100,000	
Total stockholders' equity	247,000	307,000
Market price per share of common stock..............	$55.50	$9.75

* Notes and bonds payable: Eckert, Inc., $303,000
Biomed, Inc., $4,000

Selected balance sheet data at beginning of current year:

	Eckert, Inc.	Biomed, Inc.
Current receivables, net	$193,000	$142,000
Inventories	197,000	209,000
Total assets..	909,000	842,000
Preferred stock, 4%, $100 par.............................	25,000	
Common stock, $1 par (150,000 shares)		150,000
$5 par (20,000 shares)	100,000	
Total stockholders' equity......................................	215,000	263,000

Your investment strategy is to purchase the stocks of companies that have low price/earnings ratios but appear to be in good shape financially. Assume that you have analyzed all other factors, and your decision depends on the results of the ratio analysis to be performed.

Required

1. Compute the following ratios for both companies for the current year and decide which company's stock better fits your investment strategy.
   - **a.** Current ratio
   - **b.** Acid-test ratio
   - **c.** Inventory turnover
   - **d.** Times-interest-earned ratio
   - **e.** Return on common stockholders' equity
   - **f.** Earnings per share of common stock
   - **g.** Book value per share of common stock
   - **h.** Price/earnings ratio
2. Compute each company's economic-value-added (EVA®) measure, and determine whether their EVA®s confirm or alter your investment decision. Each company's cost of capital is 12%. Round all amounts to the nearest $1,000.

APPLY YOUR KNOWLEDGE

DECISION CASES

Case 1. Suppose you manage Lancer.com, an e-commerce startup that lost money during the past year. Before you can set the business on a successful course, you must analyze the company and industry data for the current year to learn what is wrong. The company's data follow at the top of the next page.

Identifying action to cut losses and establish profitability (Obj. 2, 4, 5)

Required

On the basis of your analysis of these figures, suggest three courses of action Lancer.com might take to reduce its losses and establish profitable operations. Give your reasons for each suggestion.

Lancer.com Balance Sheet Data

	Lancer.com	Industry Average
Cash and short-term investments	3.0%	6.8%
Inventory	79.4	71.5
Prepaid expenses	1.0	0.0
Total current assets	83.4	78.3
Plant assets, net	12.6	15.2
Other assets	4.0	6.5
Total assets	100.0%	100.0%
Notes payable, short-term, 12%	26.2%	14.0%
Accounts payable	12.0	25.1
Accrued liabilities	7.8	7.9
Total current liabilities	46.0	47.0
Long-term debt, 11%	24.8	16.4
Total liabilities	70.8	63.4
Common stockholders' equity	29.2	36.6
Total liabilities and stockholders' equity	100.0%	100.0%

Lancer.com Income Statement Data

	Lancer.com	Industry Average
Net sales	100.0%	100.0%
Cost of sales	(74.2)	(64.8)
Gross profit	25.8	35.2
Operating expense	(35.1)	(32.3)
Operating income (loss)	(9.3)	2.9
Interest expense	(8.5)	(1.3)
Other revenue	1.1	0.3
Income (loss) before income tax	(16.7)	1.9
Income tax (expense) saving	4.4	(0.8)
Net income (loss)	(12.3)%	1.1%

Taking unethical action to improve the ratios (Obj. 4)

Case 2. Amanda Catlin is the controller of Success Marketing, whose year end is December 31. Catlin prepares checks for suppliers in December and posts them to the appropriate accounts in that month. However, she holds on to the checks and mails them to the suppliers in January. What financial ratio(s) are most affected by the action? What is Catlin's purpose in undertaking the activity?

ETHICAL ISSUE

Lindsey Contractors' borrowing agreements make certain demands on the business. Lindsey's Long-Term Debt may not exceed Stockholders' Equity, and the current ratio may not fall below 1.50. If Lindsey fails to meet this requirement, the company's lenders can take over management of the corporation.

Current liabilities have mounted faster than current assets, causing the current ratio to fall to 1.47. Before releasing financial statements, Lindsey management is scrambling to improve the current ratio. The controller points out that an investment can be classified as either long-term or short-term, depending on management's intention. By deciding to convert an investment to cash within one year, Lindsey can classify the investment as short-term—a current asset. On the controller's recommendation, Lindsey's board of directors votes to reclassify long-term investments as short-term.

Required

1. What effect will reclassifying the investments have on the current ratio? Is Lindsey's real financial position stronger as a result of reclassifying the investments?
2. Shortly after the financial statements are released, sales improve and so then does the current ratio. As a result, Lindsey management decides not to sell the investments it had reclassified as short-term. Accordingly, Lindsey reclassifies the investments as long-term. Has management behaved unethically? Give your reason.

FINANCIAL STATEMENT CASE

Use the Summary Financial and Operating Data (Unaudited) that appears at the end of the **Target Corporation** financial statements (Appendix A) to answer the following questions.

Measuring profitability and analyzing stock as an investment (Obj. 1)

Required

1. From the Summary Financial Data, perform a five-year trend analysis of
   a. Revenues   **b.** Net earnings
   Start with 1995, and end with 1999. Use 1994 as the base year.
2. Evaluate Target's revenues and profitability trends during this five-year period.

TEAM PROJECTS

Project 1. Select an industry that interests you, and use the leading company in that industry as the benchmark. Then select two other companies in the same industry. For each category of ratios in the Decision Guidelines feature on page 731, compute at least two ratios for all three companies. Write a two-page report that compares the two companies with the benchmark company.

Project 2. Select a company and obtain its financial statements. Convert the income statement and the balance sheet to common-size, and compare the company you selected to the industry average. Robert Morris Associates' *Annual Statement Studies*, Dun & Bradstreet's *Industry Norms & Key Business Ratios*, and Prentice Hall's *Almanac of Business and Industrial Financial Ratios*, by Leo Troy, all publish common-size statements for most industries.

INTERNET EXERCISE

Home Depot serves both the do-it-yourself and the professional construction markets by stocking over 40,000 items, including lumber, floor and wall coverings, plumbing and gardening supplies, tools, and paint.

Home Depot

Computing ratios for two well-known companies (Obj. 4)

Go to the "Generally Accepted Accounting Principles and Audited Financial Statements" and the "Managerial Accounting and Cost Analysis" episodes on the *Mastering Accounting* CD-ROM for interactive, video-enhanced exercises that focus on CanGo's need for standardized accounting reports to prepare for an IPO and to attract investors to fund new business projects. In these episodes, CanGo managers learn the value of properly prepared financial reports.

1. Go to **http://www.fortune.com** and in the left-hand column under "Lists," click on *Fortune 500*. What is Home Depot's current Fortune 500 ranking?
2. Click on *Home Depot*. Review the information displayed. Does Home Depot appear financially strong or weak? Why?
3. Click on the Industry: *Specialty Retailers*. Review the Industry Snapshot to answer the following questions.
   a. **Lowe's** is a primary competitor of Home Depot. Examine the information reported for both companies. Which company is more profitable? Why?
   b. Among all the Specialty Retailers, identify the company with the greatest "profits as % of revenues" ratio and the "profits as % of stockholders' equity" ratio. For the companies identified, what do these ratios indicate? The text refers to these ratios by what titles?
4. In the left-hand column in the "Stock/Fund Quotes:" box, type in *HD*, the stock symbol for Home Depot, and click on *Go*. At the bottom of the screen under "Financials," click on *Annual Income Statement*. For the most current years available, compute the trend percentages for "Net sales" and "Cost of Merchandise" using the earliest of the four years as the base year. Net sales have increased by what percent since the base year? Which account, Net sales or Cost of merchandise (sold) increased at a greater rate? Is this favorable or unfavorable?
5. Go to **http://www.homedepot.com** and click on Home Depot stores *opening soon*. How many Home Depot stores will be opening within the next month? Do you think future revenues for Home Depot will be increasing? Why or why not?

19 Introduction to Management Accounting

LEARNING OBJECTIVES

After studying this chapter, you should be able to

1. Distinguish between financial accounting and management accounting

2. Describe the value chain and classify costs by value-chain function

3. Distinguish direct costs from indirect costs

4. Distinguish among full product costs, inventoriable product costs, and period costs

5. Prepare the financial statements of a manufacturing company

6. Identify major trends in the business environment, and use cost-benefit analysis to make business decisions

7. Use reasonable standards to make ethical judgments

Dell Computer Corporation—the direct-order computer-assembly firm—saw its net income for the year ending in January 2000 surge to nearly $1.9 billion, double its earnings only two years earlier. This phenomenal growth helped Dell pass **IBM** and become the second largest U.S. PC seller. But Dell's outlook hasn't always been so rosy. Just a few years earlier, the company posted its first-ever net loss—$36 million—after a major product recall and a shareholder lawsuit.

How did Michael Dell turn his company around? What information helped him make wise choices?

Dell knew that cost control should drive his business, because most customers prefer a good price over a specific brand name. Dell executives also had to decide how to market and distribute the computers. Should the company sell via the Internet or telephone and eliminate the middleman? Or should it sell computers through discount chains like **Sam's Club** and **Best Buy**? Should Dell focus on the U.S. market, or expand in Latin America, Europe, or the Pacific? Decisions, decisions, decisions!

Accounting information helps executives like Michael Dell make these and many other decisions. For example, the accounting system provides managers with cost and profit information broken down by

1. Type of product, such as desktop and laptop models
2. Marketing strategy, such as Internet sales versus direct-telephone sales versus sales to retailers like Best Buy
3. Geographic regions, such as U.S., Latin American, European, or Pacific operations

This kind of information helped Michael Dell steer Dell Computer in the right direction. The result? Soaring income and stock price. A $1,000 investment in Dell at the end of 1993 was worth $143,000 by January 2000.

Source: Based on Gary McWilliams, "Dell's New Push: Cheaper Laptops Built to Order," *Wall Street Journal,* June 19, 1999, p. B1; Louise Lee, "Dell Computer Profit Soars, Tops Forecasts," *Wall Street Journal,* May 21, 1997, p. A3; Toni Mack, "Michael Dell's New Religion," *Forbes,* June 6, 1994, pp. 45–46.

So far, we have focused on reporting accounting information for decision makers *outside* the organization: investors, creditors, and government authorities. We analyzed *financial accounting* reports—the income statement, the balance sheet, and the statement of cash flows. These statements report the company's *past* performance and financial position.

We now shift our focus to how accounting information helps shape the company's *future*. We will examine accounting through the eyes of the people who run the business. Decision makers *inside* a company are its managers, and accounting designed to meet their information needs is called *management accounting.* ➤

◄ We introduced the distinction between financial and management accounting in Chapter 1, p. 6.

THE FUNCTIONS OF MANAGEMENT

Managers perform two broad functions: planning and controlling (Exhibit 19-1). **Planning** means choosing goals and deciding how to achieve them. For example, one of **Dell Computer's** goals is to increase operating income. The company's managers could

1. Raise sale prices
2. Increase advertising to stimulate sales
3. Redesign the computers for faster production and servicing

PLANNING. Choosing goals and deciding how to achieve them.

Suppose Dell's managers choose alternative 3. Dell's engineers, purchasing officer, and production, marketing, and service managers work together to redesign the laptop computer to speed assembly and servicing while still meeting customer needs. Managers use the new design to budget the cost of the laptops, considering both the cost per laptop and the number of laptops they expect to

BUDGET. Quantitative expression of a plan that helps managers coordinate and implement the plan.

CONTROLLING. Evaluating the results of business operations by comparing the actual results to the plan.

sell. The **budget** is a quantitative expression of a plan that helps managers coordinate and implement the plan.

Dell's purchasing officer uses the new design and the number of laptops they expect to sell to decide how many component parts to order, and the production manager alerts the plant workers to the design changes before they begin assembling the laptops. After they implement the plan, controlling begins. **Controlling** means evaluating the results of business operations by comparing the actual results to the plan. Dell's accounting system records the number of laptops produced. The system also records the purchase prices and number of components used to assemble the laptops.

After completing the day's production, managers can compare the actual costs with the budgeted costs to evaluate the performance of the laptop operation and its employees. If actual costs fall below budgeted costs, that is good news. But if actual costs exceed budgeted amounts, managers may need to take corrective action. The operating costs provide feedback that helps managers decide whether their decision to redesign the laptop was a good decision that increased profits or a bad decision that decreased profits.

EXHIBIT 19-1 **The Functions of Management**

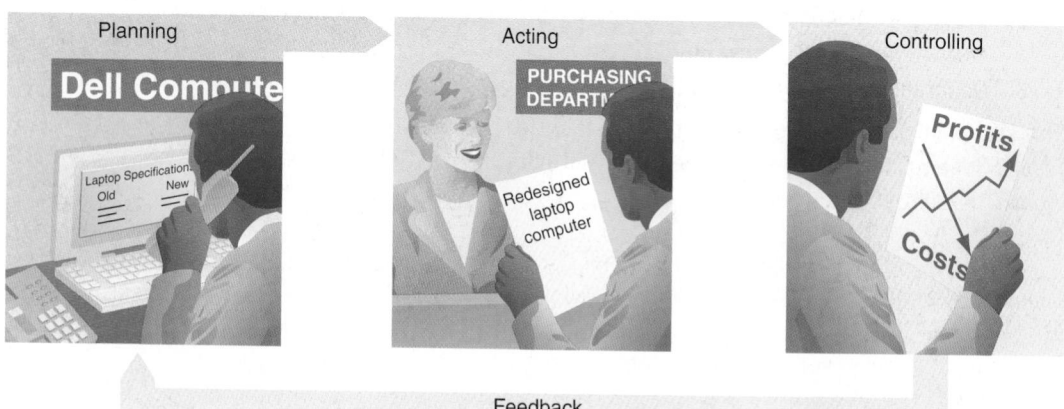

Managers make both shorter-term and longer-term planning and controlling decisions. In the shorter term, Dell must decide whether Internet sales will increase market share and reduce marketing costs, which will in turn increase profits. Dell's executives must also plan far into the future when they decide whether to expand in Latin America. Building a new plant in Brazil will tie up cash for years to come.

Objective 1
Distinguish between financial accounting and management accounting

HOW IS MANAGEMENT ACCOUNTING DIFFERENT FROM FINANCIAL ACCOUNTING?

Financial and management accounting both use the accrual basis, and both reflect the same underlying economic transactions. However, their focus differs. As you learned in Chapters 1–18, financial accounting focuses on preparing financial statements that allow stockholders and creditors to make informed investment decisions. These highly summarized reports, which are constrained by GAAP, focus on the company's past financial performance. In contrast, company managers need more detailed and timely information to decide how to run the company efficiently and effectively in the future.

Exhibit 19-2 summarizes the distinctions between management accounting and financial accounting. Consider points 1, 2, and 3 of the exhibit. Deciding whether to build a new production plant in Brazil relates to **Dell's** future, and the decision makers are Dell managers. Dell will budget (predict) the plant's future income and cash flows. Managers will then compare the benefits and costs of operating the plant with the benefits and costs of other investments. For example, Dell could use the money required for the Brazilian plant to develop a new workstation model. Management

EXHIBIT 19-2
Management Accounting Versus
Financial Accounting

	Management Accounting	Financial Accounting
1. Primary users	Internal—the company's managers	External—investors, creditors, and government authorities such as the IRS and SEC
2. Purpose of information	Help managers plan and control business operations	Help investors, creditors, and others make investment, credit, and other decisions
3. Focus and time dimension	Relevance and focus on the future—example: 2004 budget prepared in 2003	Reliability, objectivity, and focus on the past—example: 2001 actual performance reported in 2002
4. Type of report	Internal reports not restricted by GAAP—determined by cost-benefit analysis	Financial statements restricted by GAAP
5. Verification	No independent audit	Annual independent audit by certified public accountant
6. Scope of information	Detailed reports on parts of the company (products, departments, territories) often on a daily, weekly, or monthly basis	Summary reports primarily on the company as a whole, usually on a quarterly or annual basis
7. Behavioral implications	Concern about how reports will affect employee behavior	Concern about adequacy of disclosure; behavioral implications are secondary

accounting helps Dell executives choose the investment with the greatest expected net benefit to the company.

Now consider point 4 of Exhibit 19-2—the types of accounting reports decision makers use. There are no GAAP-type standards for preparing the information that managers use to plan and control a company's operations. Managers are thus free to tailor the company's management accounting system to provide information that will help them make better decisions. Managers weigh

- The *benefits* of the system—helping managers make better decisions that increase profit, against
- The *cost* of the system—including costs of training managers, as well as the cost to develop and run the system

Weighing costs against benefits to help make decisions is called **cost-benefit analysis.** The costs and benefits of any particular management accounting system differ from one company to the next, so different companies create different systems. For example, companies vary in the way they figure the manufacturing cost of a product, as we shall see in Chapters 20 and 21. For external reporting, though, all businesses follow GAAP and use the accrual basis of accounting. Also, externally reported financial statements are audited each year by independent certified public accountants. Internal management accounting reports are not audited, as shown in point 5 of Exhibit 19-2.

Point 6 of Exhibit 19-2 highlights another difference between management accounting and financial accounting—the scope of the information provided. Management accounting generates more detailed reports on parts of the company (products, departments, or territories) on a daily, weekly, or monthly basis. Managers need this more detailed and timely information to run the company. For example, detailed, timely information helps managers (a) identify ways to cut costs, (b) set prices that will be competitive yet yield a profit, (c) identify the most profitable products and customers so that the company can focus on key strategic profit-makers, and (d) evaluate managers' job performance. Information technology, from Web-based company Intranet systems to hand-held computers, lets managers access this information with the touch of a button or the click of a mouse.

DAILY EXERCISE 19-1

COST-BENEFIT ANALYSIS. Weighing costs against benefits to help make decisions.

e-Accounting

Refining Dining with Data Mining

As the chefs in the kitchen slice and dice meat and veggies, the managers back at head-quarters are asking the accountants to "slice and dice" the data. Using the latest in data mining technology from **Digital Equipment Corp.** and **Informix,** large restaurant operators now analyze a dizzying amount of data that extend well beyond sales, cash management, and inventory.

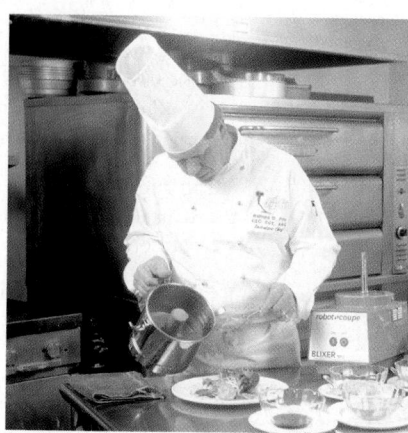

- **AFC,** operator and franchiser of more than 3,300 Church's, Popeye's Chicken & Biscuits, Seattle Coffee Company, and Torrefazione Italia outlets worldwide, collects customer-purchase data by item, item combination, day, and location. Information is stored in a data warehouse. Then sophisticated data mining software ferrets out patterns, trends, and even challenges and problems. Managers get information on how factors such as location affect the profitability of sales promotions and which patrons respond to which offers.

- **Red Robin International,** a 135-unit casual-dining chain based in Englewood, Colorado, relies on patterns revealed by its data warehouse to hone menus. "We do a lot of menu changes, with new items and specials," explains Howard Jenkins, Red Robin's Vice President of Information Systems. "With data mining in place, we can ask ourselves, 'If we put the items with the high margin in the middle of the menu, do we sell more versus putting [them] at the top or bottom . . . ?"

- **Pizzeria Uno** uses a more economical decision-support system to define and analyze data in response to specific queries, such as take-out versus eat-in pizza sales. A nifty tool called "80/20" identifies the 20% of customers who contribute 80% of sales, so management can adjust menus and promos to suit top patrons' preferences.

Source: Based on Anonymous, "Mining the data of dining," *Nation's Restaurant News,* May 22, 2000, pp. S22–S24.

Point 7 of Exhibit 19-2 highlights the behavioral implications of management accounting reports. Managers' actions depend on how their performance is measured, and the accounting system measures performance. For example, the manager of a **Baskin Robbins** store will care about cleanliness and cheerful service if her performance evaluation depends on the store's profit. Excellent customer service leads to higher sales, which increase profit. In contrast, if the manager is evaluated only on her ability to control costs, she will be less concerned about customer service and she may save money by cleaning the store less often. Top executives create performance evaluation plans very carefully because they understand that "you get what you measure."

SERVICE, MERCHANDISING, AND MANUFACTURING COMPANIES

SERVICE COMPANY. A company that provides intangible services, rather than tangible products.

MERCHANDISING COMPANY. A company that resells products previously bought from suppliers.

Previous chapters focused on service and merchandising firms. Now we add manufacturing companies to the mix. **Service companies** do not sell tangible products. Rather, they provide intangible services such as Web site development, hair styling, and legal advice. Labor is typically their most significant cost—often as high as 70% of total costs. Well-known service businesses include **H&R Block** (tax return preparation), **Randstad** (temporary personnel services), and **eBay** (on-line auction).

In contrast, merchandisers and manufacturers sell tangible products. **Merchandising companies** resell products previously bought from suppliers. **Amazon.com, Wal-Mart,** and **Footlocker** are merchandising companies. Consider Footlocker, which sells athletic shoes. Like other merchandisers,

Footlocker buys ready-made inventory for resale to customers. Determining Footlocker's cost of inventory is relatively easy. Cost is the price Footlocker pays for the shoes plus freight-in costs. ➡ Because merchandise inventory consists only of goods ready for sale, a merchandiser's balance sheet typically reports a single category of inventory.

◄ See Chapter 5, pages 170–177, for a review of inventory in merchandising firms.

Manufacturing companies use labor, plant, and equipment to convert raw materials into new finished products. For example, companies that supply athletic shoes to stores such as Footlocker—**New Balance** and **NIKE**—begin their manufacturing processes with raw materials (cloth, rubber, plastics). These materials are cut, glued, stitched, and formed into athletic shoes. Converting raw materials into finished products makes it more difficult to measure New Balance's inventory cost than to measure Footlocker's.

MANUFACTURING COMPANY. A company that uses labor, plant, and equipment to convert raw materials into new finished products.

Manufacturers have three kinds of inventory:

1. **Materials inventory:** *raw materials for use in manufacturing.* For example, a shoe manufacturer's materials include leather, glue, plastic, cloth, and thread. Raw materials for Bethlehem Steel include iron ore, coal, and chemicals.

MATERIALS INVENTORY. Raw materials for use in manufacturing.

2. **Work in process inventory:** *goods that are partway through the manufacturing process, but not yet complete.* At **Dell Computer,** partially completed computers make up work in process inventory. At **Texaco,** work in process inventory is half-processed crude oil that is being refined into gasoline.

WORK IN PROCESS INVENTORY. Goods that are partway through the manufacturing process, but not yet complete.

3. **Finished goods inventory:** *completed goods that have not yet been sold.* Finished goods are what the manufacturer sells to a merchandising business. For example, **Proctor & Gamble** (P&G) manufacturers Tide laundry soap and Crest toothpaste, which are finished goods that P&G sells to **Safeway** and **Kmart.** P&G's finished goods inventory then becomes the inventory of Safeway and Kmart.

FINISHED GOODS INVENTORY. Completed goods that have not yet been sold.

Exhibit 19-3 summarizes the differences among service, merchandising, and manufacturing companies.

EXHIBIT 19-3   Service, Merchandising, and Manufacturing Companies

	Service Companies	Merchandising Companies	Manufacturing Companies
Examples	Advertising agencies eBay H&R Block Law firms Merrill Lynch	Amazon.com Kroger The Gap Wal-Mart Wholesalers	Bethlehem Steel Cisco Systems DaimlerChrysler Dell Computer General Mills
Primary Output	Intangible services (for example, auctions, entertainment, or advice)	Tangible products purchased from suppliers	New tangible products made as workers and equipment convert raw materials (purchased from suppliers) into new finished products
Type(s) of Inventory	None	Inventory	Materials inventory Work in process inventory Finished goods inventory

THE VALUE CHAIN

Objective 2
Describe the value chain and classify costs by value-chain function

Many people describe **Dell** (or **IBM** or **Hewlett-Packard**) as a manufacturing company. Dell is perhaps more accurately described as a company that does manufacturing. Why? Because manufacturing or production is only one of its major business functions.

Companies that do manufacturing also do many other things. For example, Dell also conducts research and development to determine what kinds of new computers to introduce. It uses that information to design new computers, which it then

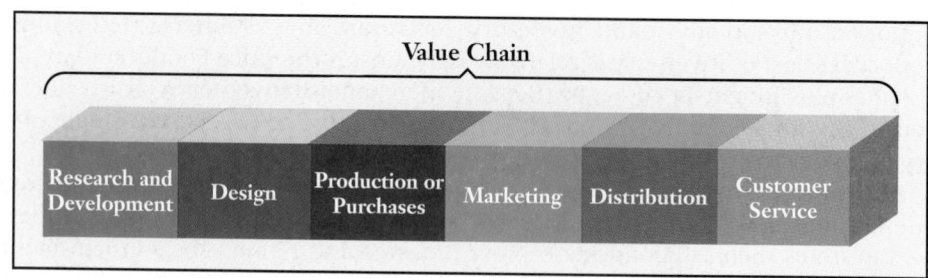

Value Chain

| Research and Development | Design | Production or Purchases | Marketing | Distribution | Customer Service |

VALUE CHAIN. Sequence of activities that adds value to a firm's products or services. Includes R&D, design, production or purchases, marketing, distribution, and customer service.

RESEARCH AND DEVELOPMENT (R&D). The process of researching and developing new or improved products or services, or the processes for producing them.

DESIGN. Detailed engineering of products and services, or processes for producing them.

PRODUCTION OR PURCHASES. Resources used to produce a product or service, or to purchase finished merchandise.

MARKETING. Promotion of products or services.

DISTRIBUTION. Delivery of products or services to customers.

CUSTOMER SERVICE. Support provided for customers after the sale.

produces, markets, and distributes. These business functions collectively are called the **value chain**—the sequence of activities that adds value to a firm's products or services (Exhibit 19-4).

- **Research and development (R&D)**—the process of researching and developing new or improved products or services, or the processes for producing them. Examples: (1) identifying a need for a lighter laptop computer through market research, and (2) developing a breakthrough technology that drastically reduces the size or weight of the motherboard.
- **Design**—detailed engineering of products and services, or the processes for producing them. Example: redesigning the laptop's case and reengineering the manufacturing process to accommodate the new case.
- **Production or purchases**—Resources used to produce a product or service, or to purchase finished merchandise. Examples: (1) For a manufacturer such as Dell, the actual production of products—such as the materials, labor, and equipment used to assemble the new laptop; or (2) for a merchandiser such as **Best Buy,** the purchase of merchandise inventory (such as laptop computers) to resell to customers.
- **Marketing**—promotion of products or services. Example: an ad campaign for the new laptop.
- **Distribution**—delivery of products or services to customers. Example: delivery of the new laptop via truck to customers.
- **Customer service**—support provided for customers after the sale. Example: a hotline for owners of the new laptop.

Managers do not proceed step by step in this exact order through the value chain. Indeed, managers may form a laptop project team to work on R&D, design, production, marketing, and customer service simultaneously.

The value chain applies equally to service, merchandising, and manufacturing firms. For example, an advertising agency such as **Saatchi & Saatchi** incurs

- *Marketing* costs to obtain a new client
- *Research and development* and *design* costs to develop the new client's ad campaign
- *Customer service* costs to address the new client's concerns
- *Distribution* costs to get the ads to the media

Managers are concerned about the value chain as a whole. They must control the total costs of the entire chain. For example, Dell recently decided to spend more in product design to make its laptop easier to service and thereby reduce the costs of honoring product warranties. Even though design costs increase, the total cost of the computer—as measured by the entire value chain—is lower.

Objective 3
Distinguish direct costs from indirect costs

COST OBJECTS, DIRECT COSTS, AND INDIRECT COSTS

COST OBJECT. Anything for which managers want a separate measurement of costs.

A **cost object** is anything for which managers want a separate measurement of costs. For example, **Dell Computer's** cost objects may include

- Individual products (laptop computers or desktop models)
- Alternative marketing strategies (direct-telephone sales versus Internet sales)
- Geographic segments of the business (United States, European, or Pacific)
- Departments (personnel, accounting, or information systems)

Costs that can be specifically traced to the cost object are **direct costs.** Costs that cannot be specifically traced to the cost object are **indirect costs.**

The manager of a Dell Computer plant wants to know the cost of assembling a specific laptop. The cost of the chip in the laptop is a *direct* cost of that computer because the chip can be specifically traced to the particular laptop. In contrast, the plant manager's salary cannot be specifically traced to any one computer, so the plant manager's salary is an *indirect* cost of the laptop.

Consider another example. Suppose Dell headquarters asks for the costs incurred by a production plant. The plant now becomes the cost object. The plant manager's salary becomes a direct cost because it can be specifically traced to the plant.

Now let's focus on the most common cost object: products.

PRODUCT COSTS

Accountants use the term *product costs* for the costs of producing (or purchasing) tangible products intended for sale. We distinguish between two types of product costs: full product costs and inventoriable product costs. Managers use full product costs for certain decisions, like setting long-term sale prices for the goods and services their companies sell. However, GAAP requires accountants to use inventoriable costs for external reporting (Inventory on the balance sheet and Cost of Goods Sold on the income statement). Let's see how the two types of product costs differ.

Full Product Costs

Full product costs are the costs of all resources used throughout the value chain for a product. For **New Balance,** the full product cost of a particular shoe model is the total cost incurred to research, design, manufacture, market, and distribute the model, as well as to service the customers who buy it. Before launching a new model, managers must predict the full product costs of the shoe to set a long-run average sale price that will cover all the shoe's costs, from R&D to customer service, plus return a profit. New Balance can also compare each model's sale price to its full cost to determine which models are the most profitable. Marketing can then focus on selling the more profitable models.

External Reporting: Inventoriable Product Costs or Period Costs?

Inventoriable product costs are product costs that are initially regarded as an asset for external financial reporting and are not expensed until the product is sold. GAAP requires a very specific definition of inventoriable product costs that includes only a *portion* of full product costs. Thus, inventoriable costs do not include costs from all elements of the value chain.

THINK IT OVER

Why do managers need to know the difference between full product costs and inventoriable product costs?

Answer: 1. Only inventoriable product costs are used to determine Inventory and Cost of Goods Sold amounts for the balance sheet and income statement.

2. Inventoriable product costs do not include all the costs the company must cover to earn a profit. Therefore, managers need to know the full costs of producing a product to set a long-run sale price that will cover total costs plus return a profit, and to determine which products, services, and customers are the most profitable.

Which costs are inventoriable under GAAP? The answer depends on whether the company is a merchandiser or a manufacturer.

Merchandising Companies' Inventoriable Product Costs

As we saw in Chapter 5, merchandising companies' inventoriable costs include *only* the cost of purchasing the inventory from suppliers (for example, the price

Footlocker pays **New Balance** for shoes), plus freight-in. (These are the costs in the third element of the value chain in Exhibit 19-4.) Footlocker's inventoriable cost (purchase price plus freight-in) of shoes is an asset—Inventory—in Footlocker's accounting records. This inventoriable cost remains an asset (Inventory) until the shoes are *sold*. Then it becomes an expense—Cost of Goods Sold.

In contrast, costs incurred in other elements of the value chain—such as Footlocker's employees' salaries, commissions paid to its sales staff, and distribution costs—are not inventoriable product costs. Instead, these are **period costs,** operating costs that are always expensed in the period in which they are incurred. Period costs are never part of the Inventory asset account. This contrasts with inventoriable product costs that are first considered inventory (an asset) and are not expensed (as cost of goods sold) until later when the products are sold.

Full Product Costs	
Inventoriable Product Costs (Production or Purchases)	**Period Costs (R&D, Design, Marketing, Distribution, Customer Service)**

What would be the inventoriable costs for a service firm such as **H&R Block?**

Answer: Service firms like H&R Block have no tangible inventory of products intended for sale. Services cannot be produced today and stored up to sell later. Because service firms have no inventory, they have no inventoriable costs. Instead, they have only period costs that are expensed as incurred.

Manufacturing Companies' Inventoriable Product Costs

DAILY EXERCISE 19-5

Manufacturing firms' product costs are more complex than those for merchandising firms. Manufacturers' inventoriable costs include raw materials plus all other costs incurred in the manufacturing/production process. Let's take a closer look.

Exhibit 19-5 illustrates the major categories of inventoriable product costs for a manufacturer such as New Balance:

EXHIBIT 19-5 **Inventoriable Product Costs for a Manufacturer**

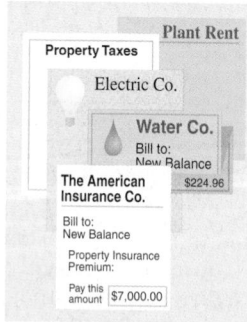

Direct Materials	Direct Labor	Indirect Materials	Indirect Labor	Other

Manufacturing Overhead

762

- **Direct materials** (1) must become a physical part of the finished product, and (2) their costs (invoice cost plus freight-in) must be separately and conveniently traceable to the finished product. Consider New Balance shoes—the leather uppers, the rubber and plastic soles, and the shoelaces are direct materials. They become part of the finished shoe, and we can trace the costs directly to the shoe as it moves through the production process.

- **Direct labor** is the compensation of employees who physically convert materials into the company's products. For New Balance, direct labor includes the wages of machine operators and persons who assemble the shoes. Their effort can be traced *directly* to the finished products.
- **Manufacturing overhead** includes all manufacturing costs other than direct materials and direct labor. Examples include indirect materials, indirect labor, plant utilities, plant repairs, plant maintenance, plant rent, insurance on the plant, plant property taxes, and depreciation on plant buildings and equipment. Manufacturing overhead also is called **factory overhead** or **indirect manufacturing cost.**

The key point is that manufacturing overhead includes only indirect manufacturing costs—that is, indirect costs related to the manufacturing plant. Depreciation on the plant's building and equipment is an indirect manufacturing cost, so it is part of manufacturing overhead. Likewise, insurance on the plant's building and equipment is part of manufacturing overhead. In contrast, depreciation on delivery trucks is not a manufacturing cost. Delivery is part of the distribution element of the value chain, not the production (or manufacturing) element (see Exhibit 19-4). Depreciation on delivery trucks is therefore part of distribution expense (a period expense), not part of manufacturing overhead. Similarly, auto insurance for the sales force is part of the marketing element of the value chain, not the production element. Insurance related to the sales force is part of marketing expense (a period expense), not part of manufacturing overhead.

Let's take a closer look at two major components of manufacturing overhead: indirect materials and indirect labor. First consider indirect materials. The glue and thread used in athletic shoes become physical parts of the finished product. But, compared with the cost of the leather uppers and rubber soles, the costs of glue and thread are minor. It is hard to measure the costs of those low-priced materials for a single pair of shoes. How would a supervisor figure the cost of a brushful of glue? How useful would such detailed information be? These kinds of materials, whose costs cannot conveniently be directly traced to particular finished products, are called **indirect materials.** Indirect materials are part of manufacturing overhead.

Some manufacturing labor costs are classified as **indirect labor.** Like indirect materials, indirect labor is difficult to trace to specific products. Examples include the pay of forklift operators, janitors, and plant managers. Indirect labor, like indirect materials, is part of manufacturing overhead.

To summarize, a manufacturing company computes inventoriable product costs as follows:

> Direct materials
> + **Direct labor**
> + **Manufacturing overhead**
> = **Inventoriable product costs**

New Balance's balance sheet will report the inventoriable cost of the finished shoes on hand at the end of the period (direct materials, direct labor, and manufacturing overhead) as an asset—Finished Goods Inventory. New Balance's income statement will report as Cost of Goods Sold the inventoriable costs of the shoes the company sold.

Remember that New Balance's inventoriable product costs include *only* the manufacturing costs—that is, only *costs incurred in the third element of the value chain in Exhibit 19-4.* Costs in other elements of the value chain—such as New Balance's cost to research and develop a new style of shoe, and to advertise and deliver shoes to customers—are *not* inventoriable product costs for external reporting. Instead, these are period costs that are expensed in the income statement in the period incurred. Period costs are never part of the Inventory asset account.

Exhibit 19-6 summarizes the differences between inventoriable and period costs for service, merchandising, and manufacturing companies. Study this exhibit carefully. When are costs like depreciation, insurance, utilities, and property taxes treated as inventoriable product costs? *Only* when those costs are related to the manufacturing plant. When those costs are related to nonmanufacturing activities like R&D or marketing, they are treated as period costs. Service companies and

DIRECT LABOR. The compensation of employees who physically convert materials into the company's products; labor costs that are directly traceable to finished products.

MANUFACTURING OVERHEAD. All manufacturing costs other than direct materials and direct labor. Also called **factory overhead** or **indirect manufacturing cost.**

 DAILY EXERCISE 19-6

INDIRECT MATERIALS. Materials whose costs cannot conveniently be directly traced to particular finished products.

INDIRECT LABOR. Labor costs that are difficult to trace to specific products.

 DAILY EXERCISE 19-7

Type of Company	Inventoriable Product Costs (Initially an asset (Inventory), and not expensed (Cost of Goods Sold) until inventory is sold)	Period Costs (Expensed in period incurred; never considered an asset)
Service companies	None	Salaries, depreciation expense, utilities, insurance, property taxes, advertising
Merchandising companies	Purchases plus freight-in	Salaries, depreciation expense, utilities, insurance, property taxes, advertising, freight-out
Manufacturing companies	Direct materials, plus direct labor, plus manufacturing overhead (including indirect materials; indirect labor; depreciation on plant and equipment; plant insurance, plant utilities, and property taxes on plant)	R&D; freight-out; depreciation expense, utilities, insurance, and property taxes on executive headquarters (separate from plant); advertising; CEO's salary

DAILY EXERCISE 19-8

merchandisers do no manufacturing, so they always treat depreciation, insurance, utilities, and property taxes as period costs.

The difference between inventoriable product costs and period costs is important because these two kinds of cost are treated differently in the financial statements. The next section takes a closer look at how the financial statements of service companies, merchandisers, and manufacturers differ.

Objective 5
Prepare the financial statements of a manufacturing company

PRODUCT AND PERIOD COSTS IN FINANCIAL STATEMENTS

How do inventoriable product costs and period costs affect financial statements? We begin with a short review to help you see how a manufacturer's financial statements differ from those of service and merchandising companies.

Service Companies

➡ Chapter 1, p. 17, introduced income statements for service companies.

Service companies have the simplest accounting. Exhibit 19-7 shows the income statement of eNow!, a group of e-commerce consultants. ◄ The firm has no inventory and thus no inventoriable costs, so eNow!'s income statement has no Cost of Goods Sold. The statement groups all expenses (period costs) together. As for most service companies, eNow!'s largest expense is for the salaries of employees who perform the services.

EXHIBIT 19-7
Service Company Income Statement

ENOW! Income Statement Month Ended December 31, 20X2		
Revenues		$160,000
Expenses:		
Salary expense	$104,000	
Office rent expense	18,000	
Depreciation expense—furniture and equipment	3,500	
Marketing expense	2,500	
Training expense	2,000	(130,000)
Operating income		$ 30,000

Merchandising Companies

Exhibit 19-8 presents a bird's-eye view of how inventoriable costs and period costs affect the financial statements of merchandising companies.

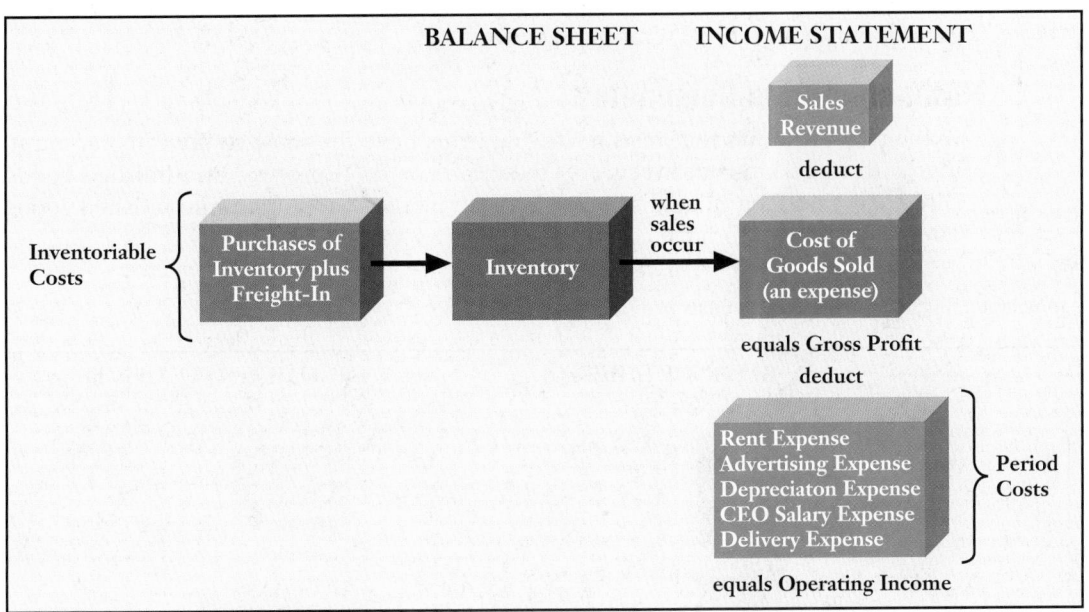

Apex Showrooms, a merchandiser of lighting fixtures, buys chandeliers and track lights ready for resale. Apex's *only* inventoriable costs are for the purchase of these goods, plus freight-in. Exhibit 19-9 shows Apex's income statement.[1]

APEX SHOWROOMS		
Income Statement		
Month Ended December 31, 20X2		
Sales revenue...		$150,000
Cost of goods sold:		
Beginning inventory	$ 9,500	
Purchases and freight-in	110,000	
Cost of goods available for sale	119,500	
Ending inventory	(13,000)	
Cost of goods sold		106,500
Gross profit		43,500
Operating expenses:................................		
Showroom rent expense	5,000	
Sales salary expense	2,500	
Administrative expense........................	1,500	9,000
Operating income		$ 34,500

EXHIBIT 19-9
Merchandising Company Income Statement

⊚ DAILY EXERCISE 19-9

⊚ DAILY EXERCISE 19-10

In contrast to the service company (Exhibit 19-7), the merchandiser's income statement features Cost of Goods Sold as the major expense. Merchandisers like Apex compute Cost of Goods Sold as follows:

Beginning inventory	$ 9,500	What Apex had at the beginning of the period
+ Purchases and freight-in	110,000	What Apex bought during the period
= Cost of goods available for sale	119,500	Total available for sale during the period
− Ending inventory	13,000	What Apex had left at the end of the period
= Cost of goods sold	$106,500	What Apex sold

[1]To highlight the roles of beginning inventory, purchases, freight-in, and ending inventory, we assume that Apex uses a periodic inventory system. However, the concepts in this chapter apply equally to companies that use perpetual inventory systems.

➤ Panel B of Exhibit 9-3, p. 349, shows a merchandiser's cost-of-goods-sold computation.

On the income statement, Cost of Goods Sold is deducted from Sales Revenue to obtain Gross profit. ◄ Apex's operating expenses (period costs) are deducted from gross profit to measure operating income.

Manufacturing Companies

Exhibit 19-10 shows that manufacturing firms have the most complicated accounting, with three kinds of inventory: materials, work in process, and finished goods. Direct labor and manufacturing overhead convert raw materials into finished goods. These are all inventoriable costs.

EXHIBIT 19-10   Manufacturing Company: Inventoriable Costs and Period Costs

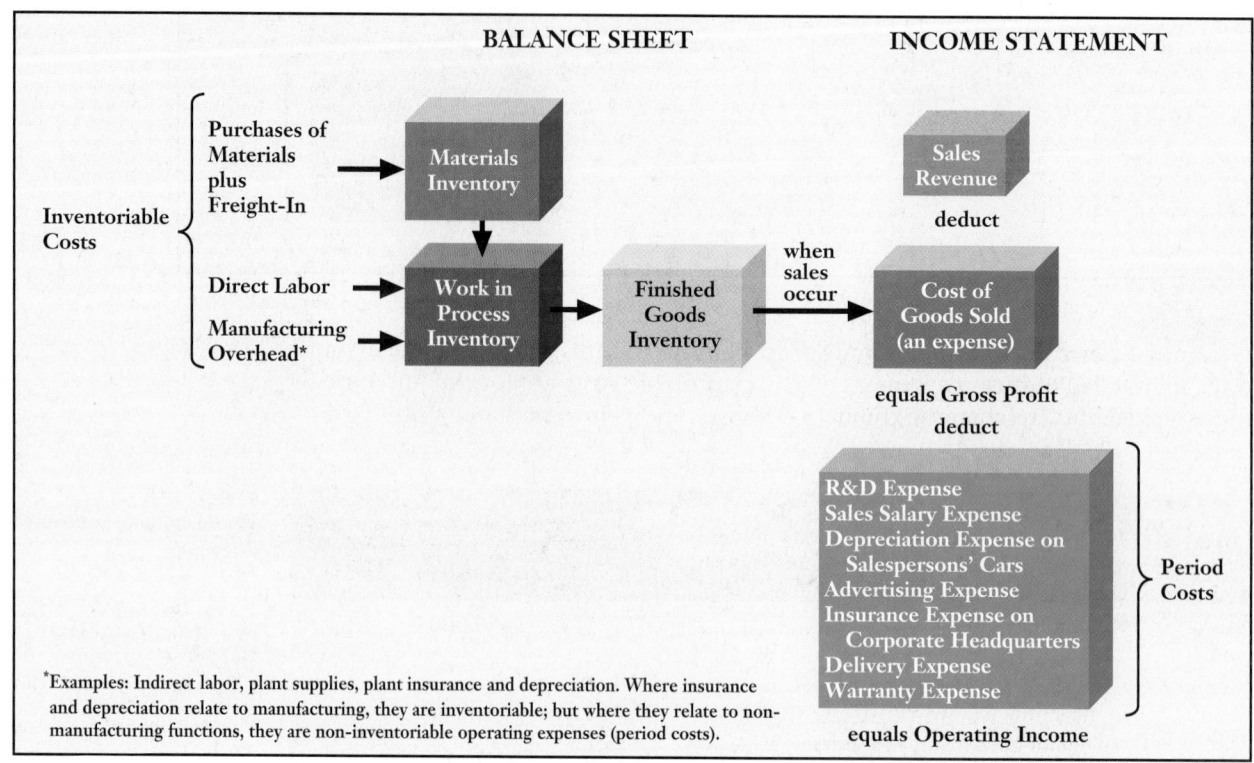

Consider Top-Flight, a manufacturer of golf equipment and athletic shoes. Compare its income statement in Exhibit 19-11 with the merchandiser's income statement in Exhibit 19-9. Both Apex and Top-Flight subtract cost of goods sold from

EXHIBIT 19-11
Manufacturing Company Income Statement

TOP-FLIGHT Income Statement Year Ended December 31, 20X2		
Sales revenue		$65,000
Cost of goods sold:		
Beginning finished goods inventory	$ 6,000	
Cost of goods manufactured*	42,000	
Cost of goods available for sale	48,000	
Ending finished goods inventory	(8,000)	
Cost of goods sold		40,000
Gross profit		25,000
Operating expenses:		
Sales salary expense	3,000	
Delivery expense	5,000	
Administrative expense	2,000	10,000
Operating income		$15,000

* From the Schedule of Cost of Goods Manufactured in Exhibit 19-12.

 DAILY EXERCISE 19-11

sales revenue to obtain gross profit. Both companies subtract operating expenses from gross profit to get operating income. The only difference between the two statements is that the merchandiser (Apex) uses *purchases* in computing cost of goods sold, while the manufacturer (Top-Flight) uses the *cost of goods manufactured* in computing cost of goods sold. Otherwise, the format of a manufacturer's income statement is identical to the format of a merchandiser's income statement.

COST OF GOODS MANUFACTURED. The (manufacturing) cost of the goods that were *finished*—that is, the plant-related cost of the units that completed the production process this period.

CALCULATING COST OF GOODS MANUFACTURED   Now let's see how to compute cost of goods manufactured. The **cost of goods manufactured** is the (manufacturing) cost of the goods that were *finished*—that is, the plant-related cost of the units that completed the production process this period. This is the manufacturer's counterpart to the merchandiser's purchases because it is the cost of new completed goods ready for sale that is added to beginning inventory of finished goods.

The cost of goods manufactured computation is more complex than the merchandiser's simple tally of purchases. Exhibit 19-12 shows how Top-Flight computes cost of goods manufactured during 20X2.

- DAILY EXERCISE 19-12
- DAILY EXERCISE 19-13
- DAILY EXERCISE 19-14
- DAILY EXERCISE 19-15

EXHIBIT **19-12**   Schedule of Cost of Goods Manufactured

TOP-FLIGHT Schedule of Cost of Goods Manufactured Year Ended December 31, 20X2			
Beginning work in process inventory			$ 2,000
Add: Direct materials used			
Beginning materials inventory	$ 9,000		
Purchases of direct materials plus freight-in	27,000		
Available for use	36,000		
Ending materials inventory	(22,000)		
Direct materials used		$14,000	
Direct labor		19,000	
Manufacturing overhead:			
Indirect materials	$ 1,500		
Indirect labor	3,500		
Depreciation—plant building and equipment	3,000		
Plant utilities and insurance	3,500		
Property taxes on plant and equipment	500	12,000	
Total manufacturing costs incurred during year			45,000
Total manufacturing costs to account for			47,000
Less: Ending work in process inventory			(5,000)
Costs of goods manufactured			$42,000

The computation begins with the Work in Process Inventory balance at the beginning of the year ($2,000). To this amount, we add the three manufacturing costs incurred during the year: direct materials used ($14,000), direct labor ($19,000), and manufacturing overhead ($12,000). Adding the sum of these costs ($45,000) to the beginning Work in Process Inventory balance of $2,000 gives the total cost assigned to goods worked on during the year—$47,000. Some of these goods were completed and sent to Finished Goods Inventory during the year; others are still in process at the end of the year. Thus, we subtract the cost of goods in process at the end of the year on December 31 ($5,000) to arrive at the cost of the completed goods—that is, the cost of goods manufactured—$42,000.

Exhibit 19-13 diagrams the flow of costs through a manufacturer's inventory accounts. It reveals a similar computational format at all three stages—direct materials, work in process, and finished goods. The final amount at each stage flows into the next stage. This flow of costs through the inventory accounts can be seen in the income statement in Exhibit 19-11 and the schedule of cost of goods manufactured shown in Exhibit 19-12.

EXHIBIT 19-13
Flow of Costs Through a
Manufacturer's Inventory
Accounts

Direct Materials Inventory	Work in Process Inventory	Finished Goods Inventory

Beginning inventory
+ Purchases and
  freight-in
	Beginning inventory
	+ Direct materials used
	+ Direct labor
	+ Manufacturing
	  overhead
		Beginning inventory
		+ Cost of goods
		  manufactured

= Direct materials
  available for use
− Ending inventory
	= Total manufacturing
	  costs to account for
	− Ending inventory
		= Cost of goods
		  available for sale
		− Ending inventory

= Direct materials used	= Cost of goods manu- factured	= Cost of goods sold

Source: The authors are indebted to Judith Cassidy for this presentation.

Keep in mind that cost of goods manufactured is not the same as manufacturing costs:

MANUFACTURING COSTS:	COST OF GOODS MANUFACTURED:
Direct materials used + **Direct labor** + **Manufacturing overhead** = **Manufacturing costs**	**Beginning work in process inventory** + **Manufacturing costs** − **Ending work in process inventory** = **Cost of goods manufactured**

Effects on the Balance Sheet

The only difference in the balance sheets of service, merchandising, and manufacturing companies relates to inventories. Exhibit 19-14 shows how the current asset sections of eNOW! (service company), Apex Showrooms (merchandising company), and Top-Flight (manufacturing company) might differ at the end of 20X2. eNOW! has no inventory at all, Apex has a single category of inventory, and Top-Flight has three categories of inventory (materials, work in process, and finished goods).

 DAILY EXERCISE 19-16

EXHIBIT 19-14   Current Asset Sections of Balance Sheets

eNOW! (Service Company)		Apex Showrooms (Merchandising Company)		Top-Flight (Manufacturing Company)		
Cash............................	$ 4,000	Cash............................	$ 4,000	Cash....................................		$ 4,000
Accounts receivable...	5,000	Accounts receivable...	5,000	Accounts receivable..........		5,000
		Inventory		Materials inventory		
		(Exhibit 19-9)	13,000	(Exhibit 19-12)	$22,000	
				Work in process inventory		
				(Exhibit 19-12)	5,000	
				Finished goods inventory		
				(Exhibit 19-11)	8,000	35,000
Prepaid expenses	1,000	Prepaid expenses	1,000	Prepaid expenses..............		1,000
Total current assets	$10,000	Total current assets	$23,000	Total current assets..........		$45,000

It is important that you take time now to review the following Decision Guidelines. Make sure you have a solid understanding of all these concepts before you read further.

Decision Guidelines

Building Blocks of Management Accounting

DECISION	GUIDELINES
What information should management accountants provide? What is the primary focus of management accounting?	Management accounting provides information that helps managers make better decisions; it has a • *Future* orientation • Focus on *relevance* to business decisions
How do you decide on a company's management accounting system, which is not restricted by GAAP?	Cost-benefit analysis: Design management accounting system so that benefits (from helping managers make wiser decisions) outweigh the costs of the system.

How do you distinguish among service, merchandising, and manufacturing companies? How do their balance sheets differ?	*Service companies:*
	• Provide customers with intangible services
	• Have no inventories on the balance sheet
	
	Merchandising companies:
	• Resell tangible products they purchased ready-made from suppliers
	• Have only one category of inventory on the balance sheet
	
	Manufacturing companies:
	• Apply labor, plant, and equipment to transform raw materials into new finished products
	• Have three categories of inventory on the balance sheet:
	    Materials inventory
	    Work in process inventory
	    Finished goods inventory

How do you compute cost of goods sold?	• *Service companies:* No cost of goods sold, because they don't sell tangible goods • *Merchandising companies:*

      Beginning inventory

+ Purchases and freight-in

<u>− Ending inventory</u>

= Cost of goods sold

• *Manufacturing companies:*

      Beginning finished goods inventory

+ Cost of goods manufactured

<u>− Ending finished goods inventory</u>

= Cost of goods sold

How do you compute the cost of goods manufactured for a manufacturer?	Beginning work in process inventory + Current period manufacturing costs (Direct materials used + direct labor + manufacturing overhead) <u>− Ending work in process inventory</u> = Cost of goods manufactured
Which costs are initially treated as assets for external reporting? When are these costs expensed? What costs are inventoriable under GAAP?	*Inventoriable product costs* are initially treated as assets (Inventory); these costs are not expensed (as Cost of Goods Sold) until the products are sold. • *Service companies:* No inventoriable product costs because they do not sell tangible products • *Merchandising companies:* Purchases and freight-in • *Manufacturing companies:* Direct materials used, direct labor, and manufacturing overhead

MID-CHAPTER

SUMMARY PROBLEM

1. Show how to compute cost of goods manufactured. Use the following amounts: direct materials used ($24,000); direct labor ($9,000); manufacturing overhead ($17,000); beginning work in process inventory; ($5,000) and ending work in process inventory ($4,000).
2. For a manufacturing company, identify the following as either an inventoriable product cost or a period cost:
   a. Depreciation on plant equipment
   b. Depreciation on salespersons' automobiles
   c. Insurance on plant building
   d. Marketing manager's salary

www.prenhall.com/horngren
Mid-Chapter Assessment

Solution

Requirement 1

Cost of goods manufactured:

Beginning work in process inventory		$ 5,000
Add: Direct materials used	$24,000	
Direct labor	9,000	
Manufacturing overhead	17,000	
Total manufacturing costs incurred during the period		50,000
Total manufacturing costs to account for		55,000
Less: Ending work in process inventory		(4,000)
Cost of goods manufactured		$51,000

Requirement 2

(a) Inventoriable product cost; (b) Period cost; (c) Inventoriable product cost; (d) Period cost

---

Objective 6
Identify major trends in the business environment and use cost-benefit analysis to make business decisions

THE MODERN BUSINESS ENVIRONMENT

The rest of this textbook describes management accounting tools and techniques designed to help managers make wise business decisions that lead to profits. Before we turn to these specific accounting tools, let's first consider recent trends in business that affect managers' decisions and the management accounting systems that support these decisions. These trends include the shift toward a service economy; the rise of the global marketplace; time-based competition (including electronic commerce and the just-in-time management philosophy); and total quality management.

Shift toward a Service Economy

Service companies provide health care, communication, transportation, banking, and other important benefits to society. The last century has seen our economy shift from manufacturing to service. Service companies now make up the largest sector of the U.S. economy, and employ 55% of the work force. The U.S. Bureau of the Census expects this number to increase to 60% by 2005. Even companies that do manufacturing, such as **General Electric** (GE), are shifting their focus toward selling services. It's easy to see why. In GE's jet engine business, services contribute only 30% of the revenues, but generate two-thirds of the profit.

Managers of service companies need information to make decisions. For example, banks must include the cost of servicing checking and savings accounts in the fees they charge customers. Hospitals need to know the cost of performing appendectomies to justify reimbursement from insurance companies and from Medicare.

Competing in the Global Marketplace

The costs of international trade have plummeted over the last decade, largely due to

- The Internet and the explosion of electronic commerce (e-commerce)
- Improved telecommunications, including video conferencing and e-mail
- Improved worldwide transportation, such as **UPS's** and **DHL's** worldwide overnight delivery services
- Reduced barriers to free trade, including the European Union free-trade zone (which includes more than a dozen European countries) and the North American Free Trade Agreement trading bloc (the United States, Canada, and Mexico)

These changes enable foreign companies to compete with local firms. Firms that are not world-class competitors will not survive in the global marketplace. For example, **RCA** stereos have largely been replaced by **Yamaha, Sony,** and **JVC** models. However, global markets do provide competitive companies with tremendous potential. For instance, GE's revenue is growing twice as fast in foreign countries as in the United States. Foreign operations account for over 30% of GE's revenues and nearly 40% of **Dell's** revenues. **McDonald's** has expanded in Russia and China, two countries with billions of consumers.

Manufacturers often move operations to other countries to be closer to new markets and less expensive labor. For example, **Thomson SA,** maker of GE television sets, closed the world's largest TV factory in Bloomington, Indiana, and moved the work to Mexico to save an estimated $75 million a year in labor costs. **Ford, General Motors,** and **DaimlerChrysler** are building assembly plants in Brazil to churn out cars for Brazil's car-hungry emerging middle class. Dell Computer is also considering opening a plant in Brazil. Dell's managers will go ahead with the plant if the benefits (proximity to a large untapped market and less expensive labor) outweigh the costs of building the new plant.

Globalization has several implications for management accounting:

1. Stiffer competition means managers need more accurate information to make wise decisions. For example, if **Nokia** overestimates the cost of its new cell phone, it may set prices too high and lose business to competitors.
2. Companies must decide whether to expand sales and/or production into foreign countries. To make these decisions, managers need estimates of the costs and benefits of international expansion.
3. Globalization fosters the transfer of management philosophy across international borders. For example, many U.S. companies now follow the just-in-time philosophy developed in Japan.

Time-Based Competition

Question: When did you need that order?
Response: Yesterday, of course!

The Internet, electronic commerce (e-commerce), e-mail, and express delivery services speed the pace of business in the new millennium. Customers who surf the Web and use e-mail to correspond in real time with people all over the world will not wait four weeks to receive their purchases. Companies that do not satisfy customers' demands quickly will not survive. Time is the latest competitive turf for world-class business.

Dell Computer commits to delivering your desktop computer within a week of receiving your order. Even automakers are getting in on the act: **Toyota** says it can now make a car within five days of receiving a custom order. Tom Meredith, Dell's chief financial officer, recently addressed an automakers' conference on the "Dell way" (high-quality custom-built products delivered shortly after the customer places an order). U.S. automakers, who have often kept customers waiting 30–60 days for custom orders, were all ears. To compete with Toyota, General Motors plans to cut its order-to-delivery time from 8 weeks in 1999 to no more than 11 days by 2003. How can GM do it? e-Commerce and the just-in-time management philosophy are two ways managers speed up responses to customers.

E-COMMERCE How does Dell assemble and deliver your computer within a week after you order it? e-Commerce helps. In e-commerce, everyday business practices such as budgeting, planning, purchasing, and selling are conducted over the Internet. e-Commerce is changing the way companies do business. Companies have embraced e-commerce to survive in an increasingly competitive globally wired economy. Imagine a sales clerk who can sell to thousands of customers at once. This sales clerk instantly provides every product, option, and price the company offers. It works 24 hours a day, 365 day a year, and never takes a break or vacation. This sales clerk is an e-commerce Web site!

Business-to-business e-commerce takes this speed and efficiency to new levels. Imagine that you are sitting in your office, anywhere in the world. You enter Dell's Web site and customize your own computer. The site shows computer systems and prices your employer has pre-negotiated with Dell. After you fill your virtual shopping cart, the entire process of ordering, approval, and delivery is automated through your employer's business-to-business software.

Electronic purchases below specified dollar limits are often untouched by human hands, generate little if any paper, and avoid the time and cost of processing this paperwork. General Motors indicates that moving such purchases on-line will slash the roughly $100 it now costs to process each of the hundreds of thousands of purchase orders it issues each year.

Firms also use the Internet to tap into other companies' business processes. Companies that supply component computer parts to Dell can use the Internet to look into Dell's production process through the virtual window Dell provides each supplier. Through this customized window, each supplier sees the current demand for, and inventory levels of, the parts it supplies Dell. In addition to automating the size of the next day's order, the virtual window provides current information that helps the supplier plan, or budget, Dell's demand for their products. Access to real-time information that lets suppliers forecast Dell's demand for their products is key to Dell's ability to cut order-to-delivery times and to control costs.

In addition to reducing their own processing costs, firms that purchase on-line can often cut the prices they pay for goods and services. Competition is stiff because buyers can ask vendors throughout the world for price quotes. Firms in some industries, such as the auto industry, are cooperating to establish virtual marketplaces that link manufacturers and suppliers. A small low-cost supplier in Asia that has never before had timely information to make competitive bids needs only a password and an Internet browser to enter the on-line market and bid against every other potential supplier in the world. By joining Ford and General Motors in establishing virtual markets for their purchases, DaimlerChrysler's chairman estimates a cost saving of nearly $1,000 per vehicle. How? The big automakers expect price concessions from their suppliers not only on their own purchases, but also on purchases their suppliers make from each other. By reducing costs throughout the value chain, the automakers expect to reap substantial cost reductions.

We have seen how e-commerce provides suppliers with virtual windows into their customers' business operations, and how Internet marketplaces cut the prices businesses pay for the goods and services they purchase. e-Commerce is thus an important means of **supply-chain management,** where companies exchange information with suppliers and customers to reduce costs, improve quality, and speed delivery of goods and services from suppliers, through the company itself, and on to customers.

e-Commerce increases firms' ability (and need) to move toward a just-in-time management philosophy.

SUPPLY-CHAIN MANAGEMENT. Companies exchange information with suppliers and customers to reduce costs, improve quality, and speed delivery of goods and services from suppliers, through the company itself, and on to customers.

THE JUST-IN-TIME MANAGEMENT PHILOSOPHY Traditionally, companies held a lot of inventory to ensure they would have enough raw materials for production and enough finished goods to fill customer orders. However, money tied up in inventory cannot be used for other purposes. Inventory held too long becomes obsolete. Storing the inventory takes space. The costs of holding inventory can easily add up to 25% of the inventory's value. The just-in-time philosophy helps managers cut these costs and speed the transformation of raw materials into new finished products by reducing the need to hold inventory. Let's see how.

Toyota generally gets credit for pioneering the **just-in-time (JIT)** management philosophy. As the name suggests, the JIT philosophy means producing *just in time* to satisfy needs. Materials are purchased and finished goods are completed only as needed to satisfy customer orders. Ideally, suppliers deliver materials for today's production in (small) batches of exactly the right quantities *just in time* to begin production, and finished units are completed *just in time* for delivery to customers.

Firms adopting JIT report sharp reductions in inventory. Reducing inventory and speeding the production process reduce **throughput time,** the time between buying raw materials and selling the finished products. For example, Dell Computer recently cut its throughput time from 31 to 17 days. Why is this important? The *Wall Street Journal* estimates that the onslaught of new technologies reduces the value of a completed PC by 1% *per week.*[2] Moving inventory quickly gives Dell pricing and manufacturing advantages over its competitors. For example, Dell can cut its prices immediately when component part costs decline. Less inventory also means that Dell can quickly incorporate new technologies.

Manufacturers adopting just-in-time depend on their suppliers to make on-time deliveries of perfect-quality raw materials. Thus, JIT requires close communications with suppliers. As we noted earlier, Dell has even designed special Web pages for its major suppliers that give them a "virtual window" into the Dell operations they supply. Suppliers use these windows to decide when and how much raw material to deliver to Dell.

Companies that adopt JIT must strive for perfect quality. Defects stop production lines. To avoid disrupting production, defects must be rare.

Managers considering JIT must weigh its costs against its benefits. Suppose New-Tell, a computer chip manufacturer, is considering JIT. If New-Tell adopts JIT, the company will incur costs, including employee training, searching for the most reliable suppliers, and lost sales due to initial slowing of production as it makes the transition. New-Tell estimates that these costs will total $2 million. The benefits of adopting JIT include savings on inventory and storage space, reduction in inventory obsolescence, and higher sales because of better-quality products. New-Tell estimates that these benefits will save an average of $650,000 a year for ten years.

To make this decision, New-Tell must compare the eventual benefits of adopting JIT with the immediate $2 million cost. The cost of adopting JIT comes immediately, but the benefits accrue over time. New-Tell must determine the present value today of the future benefits of adopting JIT. This is called *discounting* the future amounts to their *present values.* ➤ Let's assume that New-Tell's benefits of adopting JIT have a present value of $3,141,450.[3]

The costs of adopting JIT occur now, so the cost data are already stated at their present values. Stating all amounts at present values allows us to accurately compare the costs and benefits of adopting a JIT system. New-Tell's decision follows this rule:

- Present value of JIT's benefits exceed the cost of adopting JIT → Adopt JIT
- Cost of adopting JIT exceeds the present value of JIT's benefits → Do not adopt JIT

The analysis is as follows:

Present value of benefits	$3,141,450
Present value of costs	(2,000,000)
Excess of benefits over costs	$1,141,450

Decision: Invest in JIT system

[2]"Compaq Stumbles as PCs Weather New Blow," *Wall Street Journal,* March 9, 1998, page B1.
[3]JIT will reduce New-Tell's costs by $650,000 per year for ten years. Using a 16% discount rate, the present value of $650,000 per year for ten years is $3,141,450 ($650,000 × 4.833 from Exhibit 15A-7 on page 619 of the appendix to Chapter 15).

JUST-IN-TIME (JIT). A system in which a company produces just in time to satisfy needs. Materials are purchased and finished goods are completed only as needed to satisfy customer orders.

THROUGHPUT TIME. The time between buying raw materials and selling the finished products.

 DAILY EXERCISE 19-18

◄ The Appendix to Chapter 15 discusses present-value computations, and we will cover this subject in more detail in Chapter 26.

Total Quality Management

TOTAL QUALITY MANAGEMENT (TQM). A philosophy of delighting customers by providing them with superior products and services. Involves improving quality and eliminating defects and waste throughout the value chain.

Today companies must deliver high-quality goods and services to remain competitive. **Hewlett-Packard** and **Ford** in the United States, **British Telecom** in the United Kingdom, and **Toyota** in Japan view **total quality management (TQM)** as key to succeeding in the global economy. The goal of total quality management is to delight customers by providing them with superior products and services. Companies achieve this goal by improving quality and by eliminating defects and waste throughout the value chain. Each business function examines its own activities and works to improve by setting higher and higher goals.

TQM emphasizes educating, training, and cross-training employees to do multiple tasks. **Motorola's** purchasing department is an example. Motorola wanted to reduce the time required to issue a purchase order. Before starting the project, a departmental team took a two-day company course called High-Commitment, High-Performance Team Training. Team members then reduced the number of steps in handling a purchase order from 17 to 6, slashing average processing time from 30 minutes to 3. The department now processes 45% more purchase orders with no added employees. Service organizations also strive to improve quality. For example, the American Institute of Certified Public Accountants is the first professional membership organization in the United States to earn the ISO 9001 international certification for quality management and assurance.

Like JIT, quality improvement programs cost money today, but the benefits usually accrue over time. Because no one can foresee the future, the exact amount of the future benefits is not known. Accountants often adjust for this uncertainty.

Consider GE. The company recently started nearly 3,000 quality-related projects at a cost of more than $200 million. The first-year cost savings from these projects totaled only $170 million. Does this mean that GE made a bad decision? Not necessarily. GE expects these projects to continue yielding benefits in the future.

Suppose GE managers predict these projects will be either moderately successful or extremely successful. Assume that if the projects are moderately successful, they will yield additional benefits (cost savings) with a present value of $20 million. If the projects are extremely successful, they will yield extra benefits with a present value of $100 million. GE managers think the projects are more likely to be extremely successful, but they do not know for sure. Suppose they estimate a 60% chance that the projects will be extremely successful, and a 40% chance that they will be moderately successful.

In an uncertain environment such as GE's, managers make decisions based on expected values. We compute expected values by multiplying the dollar value of each possible outcome by the probability of that outcome, and then adding the results:

Outcome	Benefit	×	Probability	=	Expected Value (of Additional Benefit)
Extremely successful	$100 million	×	60% chance	=	$60 million
Moderately successful	20 million	×	40% chance	=	8 million
Total expected value of benefits					$68 million

What does this $68 million mean? If GE faced this exact situation ten times, it would expect to get $100 million in extra benefits six times, and only $20 million of additional benefits four times. The *average* extra benefits across the ten situations is $68 million, calculated as [(6 × $100) + (4 × $20)]/10 = $68. In effect, GE's best guess of the additional benefit is the expected value of $68 million.

The following summary shows that the total benefits expected from GE's quality projects ($238 million) exceed the $200 million cost of the projects, suggesting that GE's quality project was worthwhile:

DAILY EXERCISE 19-19

	Total Benefits	Total Costs
Initial benefits and costs	$170 million	$200 million
Additional expected benefits	68 million	
Total	$238 million	$200 million

Even after adopting quality programs, companies cannot rest on their laurels. TQM requires that companies (and individual employees) continually look for ways to improve performance. Jack Welch, CEO of General Electric, says: "The human mind is always able to find a better way to do things." This is the **continuous improvement** philosophy.

How do companies improve? Many businesses find that investments in higher quality earlier in the value chain (R&D and design) generate savings in later stages (production, marketing, and customer service). Successful companies design and build quality into the product or service rather than depending on finding and fixing defects later. Carefully designed products and better employee training reduce costs of inspections, rework, and warranty claims, all of which eat into profits.

CONTINUOUS IMPROVEMENT. A philosophy requiring employees to continually look for ways to improve performance.

PROFESSIONAL ETHICS FOR MANAGEMENT ACCOUNTANTS

Objective 7 Use reasonable standards to make ethical judgments

A key indicator of quality is ethical behavior. As we've seen throughout this text, ethical behavior is necessary for the orderly functioning of society and business. How would you feel if parents, teachers, employers, friends, and co-workers constantly lied to you? Relationships necessary for everyday life would break down. Business would be much more difficult to conduct, and the range and quality of goods and services would decline. Because ethical behavior is so important, society enacts laws that require social responsibility. For example, it is illegal for companies to sell products that are clearly defective, such as automobiles that do not meet government safety standards.

Unfortunately, the ethical path is not always clear. You may want to act ethically and do the right thing, but the consequences can make it difficult to decide what to do. Consider the following examples:

- Sarah Baker is examining the expense reports of her staff of management accountants, who counted inventory at Top-Flight's warehouses in Arizona. She discovers that Mike Flinders has claimed but not included hotel receipts for over $1,000 of accommodation expenses. The other staff members, who also claimed $1,000, did attach hotel receipts. When asked about the receipt, Mike admits that he stayed with an old friend, not in the hotel. His wife is expecting their first child, and he believes he deserves the money he saved. After all, the company would have paid his hotel bill.
- As the accountant of Entreé Computer Co., you are aware of your company's weak financial condition. Entreé is close to signing a lucrative contract that should ensure its future. To do so, the controller states that the company *must* report a profit this year (ending December 31). He suggests: "Two customers have placed orders that are really not supposed to be shipped until early January. Ask production to fill and ship those orders on December 31, so we can record them in this year's sales."

The Institute of Management Accountants (IMA) has developed standards to help management accountants deal with these kinds of situations. An excerpt from the *Standards of Ethical Conduct for Management Accountants* appears in Exhibit 19-15. These standards require management accountants to

- Maintain their professional competence
- Preserve the confidentiality of the information they handle
- Act with integrity and objectivity

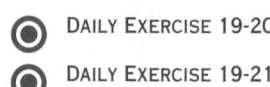
DAILY EXERCISE 19-20

DAILY EXERCISE 19-21

Management accountants have an obligation to the organizations they serve, their profession, the public, and themselves to maintain the highest standards of ethical conduct. These standards include

Competence

- Maintain an appropriate level of professional competence by ongoing development of their knowledge and skills.
- Perform their professional duties in accordance with relevant laws, regulations, and technical standards.

Confidentiality

- Refrain from disclosing confidential information acquired in the course of their work except when authorized, unless legally obligated to do so.

Integrity

- Avoid actual or apparent conflicts of interest and advise all appropriate parties of any potential conflict.
- Refuse any gift, favor, or hospitality that would influence or would appear to influence their actions.
- Communicate unfavorable as well as favorable information and professional judgments or opinions.

Objectivity

- Communicate information fairly and objectively.

Source: Adapted from Institute of Management Accountants, *Standards of Ethical Conduct for Management Accountants* (Montvale, N.J.).

To resolve ethical dilemmas, the IMA also suggests discussing ethical situations with your immediate supervisor, or with an objective adviser.

There are fairly clear-cut solutions to many situations, but not to true ethical dilemmas. The IMA's *Standards of Ethical Conduct* serve as a reminder that society expects professional accountants to uphold the highest level of ethical behavior.

Let's return to the two ethical dilemmas. By asking to be reimbursed for hotel expenses he did not incur, Mike Flinders clearly violated the IMA's integrity standards (conflict of interest in which he tried to enrich himself at company expense). Because Sarah Baker discovered the inflated expense report, she would not be fulfilling her ethical responsibilities (integrity and objectivity) if she allowed the reimbursement and did not take disciplinary action.

The second dilemma, in which the controller asked you to accelerate the shipments, is less clear-cut. You should discuss the available alternatives and their consequences with others. Many people believe that following the controller's suggestion to manipulate the company's income would violate the standards of competence, integrity, and objectivity. Others would argue that because Entreé Computer already has the customer order, shipping the goods and recording the sale in December is still ethical behavior. If you refused to ship the goods in December and you simply resign without attempting to find an alternative solution, you might only hurt yourself and your family.

You have now seen cost-benefit analysis applied to several different business decisions. The general approach of weighing costs against benefits to make the best decision comes up again and again in management accounting. Study the Cost-Benefit Analysis Decision Guidelines to make sure you understand this important concept.

DECISION GUIDELINES

Cost-Benefit Analysis

DECISION	GUIDELINES
How to compete in a globally wired economy?	Embrace e-commerce and use supply chain management to compete more effectively.
How to decide whether to undertake new projects like international expansion, JIT, and TQM?	Cost-benefit analysis: Compute the benefits of the project, and compare with the costs. Undertake the project if benefits exceed costs. Abandon the project if costs exceed benefits.
How to adjust the cost-benefit analysis if the exact amount of the benefit (or cost) is not known?	Compute the *expected value* of the benefits (or costs) of each outcome as follows:

$$\begin{array}{ccc} \text{Estimated} \\ \text{amount} \end{array} \times \begin{array}{c} \text{Probability of} \\ \text{occurrence} \end{array} = \begin{array}{c} \text{Expected} \\ \text{value} \end{array}$$

Then add the expected values across all possible outcomes.

How to resolve an ethical dilemma?

Weigh the costs and benefits of alternative courses of action. Consult the IMA's *Standards of Ethical Conduct for Management Accountants* (Exhibit 19-15). Also consult the Framework for Ethical Judgments in Chapter 7.

EXCEL APPLICATION PROBLEM

Goal: Create an Excel spreadsheet to assess the costs and benefits of a new project, and use the results to answer questions about the decision.

Scenario: Dennis Popper of EZ-Rider Motorcycles has asked you to prepare an Excel spreadsheet that calculates the net benefits (expected value of benefits—total costs) of expansion into Germany. The background data for EZ-Rider's expansion project appears in the Summary Problem. When your spreadsheet is finished, you will be able to answer these questions:

1. What is the expected value of the benefits of the expansion project? What are the total costs? Does the expected value of the benefits exceed total costs? If so, what is the expected value of the net benefits?
2. What is the minimum probability of a gas price increase that would justify the expansion? What is the expected value of the net benefits at this point?

Step-by-step:

1. Open a new Excel spreadsheet.
2. Create a boldfaced heading for your spreadsheet that contains the following:
   a. Chapter 19 Decision Guidelines
   b. Cost-Benefit Analysis
   c. EZ-Rider Motorcycles
   d. Today's date
3. Move down two rows, and enter the heading "Cost Data" in Column A. Under the heading, enter the data (with descriptions) needed to calculate total costs. Compute total costs.

4. Move down two rows. In the first column, enter the boldfaced and underlined heading "PV if Stable Gas Price."
5. Under this heading, enter the present value of the project if gas prices remain stable. Copy the cell contents down 10 more rows.
6. In the next column, enter the boldfaced and underlined heading "Probability of Stable Gas Price." Spread the heading over two rows.
7. Under this heading, enter a probability of 100%. In the next 10 rows, decrement 100% by 10% each row, so that the probability is zero at the bottom.
8. In the next column, enter the boldfaced and underlined heading "PV If Gas Price Increases."
9. Under this heading, enter the present value of the project if gas prices increase. Copy the cell contents down 10 more rows.
10. In the next column, enter the boldfaced and underlined heading "Probability of Gas Price Increase." Spread the heading over two rows.
11. Under this heading, enter a probability of 0%. In the next 10 rows, increment the percentage by 10% each row, so that the probability is 100% at the bottom.
12. In the next column, enter the boldfaced and underlined heading "Expected Value of Benefits." Spread the heading over two rows. Compute the expected value for all combinations of percentages for each row.
13. In the last column, enter the boldfaced and underlined heading "Expected Value of Net Benefits." Spread the heading over two rows. Compute the next benefits for all rows.
14. Save your file to disk and print a copy for your files.

SUMMARY PROBLEM

Cost-benefit analysis applies to many decisions. This chapter showed how managers use cost-benefit analysis to decide whether to adopt JIT or TQM. Managers also use cost-benefit analysis for more specific decisions. This summary review problem shows how you can apply cost-benefit analysis to a more specific decision about international expansion.

EZ-Rider Motorcycles is considering whether to expand into Germany, where reunification has increased market size. Public concern over air pollution may cause the government to raise gasoline taxes. If gas prices increase, EZ-Rider expects more interest in fuel-efficient transportation such as motorcycles. Thus, EZ-Rider is considering setting up a motorcycle-assembly plant on the outskirts of Berlin.

EZ-Rider estimates it will cost $850,000 to convert an existing building to motorcycle production. The workers will need training for specific jobs, at a total cost to the company of $65,000. The CEO of EZ-Rider, Dennis Popper, would have to spend a month in Berlin to organize the business and to establish relationships. He estimates the cost of this travel at $43,000. All these costs would be incurred in the next six months.

Popper sees a 60% chance that the price of gasoline in Germany will increase significantly. If this increase occurs, he believes EZ-Rider can sell enough motorcycles over the next eight years to earn profits (before considering the costs in the preceding paragraph) with a present value of $1,624,000. However, if gas prices remain stable, Popper expects to earn profits of only about $812,000. He believes there is a 40% chance that gas prices will remain stable.

Required

1. What are the total costs of EZ-Rider's proposed expansion into Germany?
2. Compute the *expected value* of the benefits Dennis Popper expects EZ-Rider to receive if EZ-Rider expands into Germany.
3. Do the benefits outweigh the costs of expanding into Germany?

Solution

Requirement 1

The total costs are as follows:

Conversion of manufacturing plant...................	$850,000
Work force training..	65,000
Popper's trip to Berlin	43,000
Total costs...	$958,000

Requirement 2

Expected value of the benefits is computed as follows:

Benefit	×	Probability	=	Expected Value
$1,624,000	×	0.60	=	$ 974,400
812,000	×	0.40	=	324,800
				$1,299,200

The *expected value* of the benefits, or profits, is $1,299,200. This means that should EZ-Rider find itself in this exact situation many times, its average benefits in the form of profits across all the situations would be $1,299,200.

Requirement 3

Yes, the total expected benefits outweigh the costs of the expansion:

Total expected benefits of expansion (from requirement 2)....	$1,299,200
Total costs of expansion (from requirement 1)........................	958,000
Net benefits of expansion...	$ 341,200

LESSONS LEARNED

1. **Distinguish between financial accounting and management accounting.** Financial accounting information is used primarily by external groups such as investors, creditors, and government authorities; it focuses on past performance of the company as a whole; it is restricted by GAAP; and it is subject to annual independent audit. Management accounting information is used primarily by internal managers to help plan and control business operations. It focuses on the future, is restricted only by the cost of generating the information versus the benefits, often reports on parts of the company, and may be produced on a daily, weekly, or monthly basis.

2. **Describe the value chain and classify costs by value-chain function.** The *value chain* is the sequence of activities that adds value to a firm's products or services. Value-chain functions are research and development, design, production or purchases, marketing, distribution, and customer service. Managers want to control total costs throughout the value chain as a whole.

3. **Distinguish direct costs from indirect costs.** Managers need cost data on many aspects of a business to make wise decisions. *A cost object* is anything for which managers want a separate measurement of costs. Costs that can be specifically traced to the cost object are *direct costs*. Costs that cannot be specifically traced to the cost object are *indirect costs*.

4. **Distinguish among full product costs, inventoriable product costs, and period costs.** *Product costs* are costs of producing (or purchasing) tangible products intended for sale. *Full product costs* include the costs of all resources used throughout the value chain. These costs are used for internal decisions such as setting prices and do not conform to GAAP. *Inventoriable product costs* include only costs

of the *production or purchases* element of the value chain, and must conform to GAAP because they are used for external financial reporting. These costs are first considered inventory (an asset), and are not expensed (as cost of goods sold) until the products are sold. *Period costs* are operating costs that are always expensed in the period in which they are incurred, and are never part of the Inventory asset account.

5. **Prepare the financial statements of a manufacturing company.** Manufacturers use three inventory accounts: *Materials Inventory, Work in Process Inventory,* and *Finished Goods Inventory.* Manufacturers compute cost of goods sold by adding the *cost of goods manufactured* to beginning finished goods inventory, and subtracting ending finished goods inventory.

6. **Identify major trends in the business environment, and use cost-benefit analysis to make business decisions.** Major trends in the business environment influencing management accounting are the shift toward a service economy, the rise of the global marketplace, time-based competition, including e-commerce and the just-in-time management philosophy, and total quality management. In making business decisions, managers compare the present value of expected future costs and benefits of alternative courses of action.

7. **Use reasonable standards to make ethical judgments.** Ethical behavior is necessary for the orderly functioning of society and business. The Institute of Management Accountants (IMA) standards require management accountants to maintain their professional competence, preserve the confidentiality of the information they handle, and act with integrity and objectivity.

ACCOUNTING VOCABULARY

budget (p. 756)
continuous improvement (p. 775)
controlling (p. 756)
cost-benefit analysis (p. 757)
cost object (p. 760)
cost of goods manufactured (p. 767)
customer service (p. 760)
design (p. 760)
direct cost (p. 761)
direct labor (p. 763)
direct materials (p. 762)
distribution (p. 760)
factory overhead (p. 761)

finished goods inventory (p. 759)
full product costs (p. 761)
indirect cost (p. 761)
indirect labor (p. 763)
indirect manufacturing cost (p. 761)
indirect materials (p. 763)
inventoriable product costs (p. 761)
just-in-time (JIT) (p. 773)
manufacturing company (p. 759)
manufacturing overhead (p. 763)
marketing (p. 760)
materials inventory (p. 759)

merchandising company (p. 758)
period costs (p. 762)
planning (p. 755)
production or purchases (p. 760)
research and development (R&D) (p. 760)
service company (p. 758)
supply-chain management (p. 772)
throughput time (p. 773)
total quality management (TQM) (p. 774)
value chain (p. 760)
work in process inventory (p. 759)

QUESTIONS

1. Explain four distinctions between management accounting and financial accounting.
2. How do manufacturing companies differ from service firms and merchandisers? What inventory accounts does each type of company use?
3. Identify the six business functions in the value chain of a manufacturing company. To which function(s) is management accounting relevant?
4. What is the manufacturer's counterpart to the merchandiser's purchases?
5. Give examples of direct materials and indirect materials for a home builder.

6. Identify at least six examples of manufacturing overhead costs.
7. Distinguish between inventoriable product costs and period costs. Which is initially an asset, and which is never an asset, only an expense?
8. What costs should managers consider in deciding on the long-term sale price of a product: inventoriable product costs or full product costs? Give your reason.
9. What is the main difference between a service company's income statement and the income statements of merchandising and manufacturing companies?

10. What is the primary difference between a merchandiser's and a manufacturer's income statement?

11. Summarize the computation of cost of goods manufactured. Use any dollar amounts.

12. List and briefly explain four recent changes in the business environment.

13. Explain two ways globalization affects management accounting.

14. Describe two ways managers respond to time-based competition.

15. Once a company decides to adopt a just-in-time philosophy, what kinds of costs and benefits should it expect?

16. The Institute of Management Accountants' *Standards of Ethical Conduct for Management Accountants* lists four broad requirements. In your own words, list and briefly explain three.

ASSESS YOUR PROGRESS

DAILY EXERCISES

Distinguishing financial from management accounting (Obj. 1)

DE19-1 Your roommate, who plans to specialize in international business, is considering whether to enroll in the second principles of accounting course. She says, "I don't want to be an accountant, so why do I need a second accounting course? I just spent a whole term on financial accounting. Most of this second course focuses on management accounting, but how can that be so different from what I already learned in financial accounting?" Respond.

Classifying costs by value-chain function (Obj. 2)

DE19-2 List the six business functions in the value chain (Exhibit 19-4, page 760). Give an example of costs that **Honda** might incur in each function for a new gas-electric hybrid car.

Classifying costs by value-chain function (Obj. 2)

DE19-3 Give an example of costs that **E*TRADE** (an online brokerage firm) might incur in each of the six business functions in the value chain. Provide another example that shows how E*TRADE might deliberately decide to spend more money on one of the six business functions in order to reduce the costs in other business functions.

Classifying costs by value-chain function (Obj. 2)

DE19-4 Classify each of **Hewlett-Packard's** costs as one of the six business functions in the value chain.

a. Depreciation on Roseville, California, plant.
b. Costs of a customer support center Web site.
c. Transportation costs to deliver laser printers to retailers, like **Best Buy.**
d. Depreciation on research lab.
e. Cost of a prime-time TV ad featuring the new Hewlett-Packard logo.
f. Salary of scientists at Hewlett-Packard Laboratories who are developing new printer technologies.
g. Purchase of plastic used in printer casings.
h. Salary of engineers who are redesigning the printer's on-off switch.
i. Depreciation on delivery vehicles.
j. Plant manager's salary.

Distinguishing between direct and indirect costs (Obj. 3)

DE19-5 Consider **Marvin Windows'** manufacturing plant. Give two examples of

a. Direct materials
b. Direct labor
c. Indirect materials
d. Indirect labor
e. Other manufacturing overhead

Inventoriable vs. period costs (Obj. 4)

DE19-6 Classify each of **Georgia-Pacific's** costs as either inventoriable or period costs:

a. Depreciation on the gypsum board plant.
b. Purchase of lumber to be cut into boards.
c. Life insurance on CEO.
d. Salaries of scientists studying ways to speed forest growth.
e. Cost of a new software package to track inventory.
f. Cost of electricity at one of Georgia-Pacific's paper mills.
g. Salaries of Georgia-Pacific's top executives.
h. Cost of mold inhibitor applied to treated lumber.
i. Cost of TV ads promoting environmental awareness.

Direct versus indirect, full versus inventoriable costs (Obj. 3, 4)

DE19-7 Listed on the following page are several terms relating to various cost definitions. Complete the following statements with one of these terms. You may use a term more than once, and some terms may not be used at all.

Cost object	Direct labor	Inventoriable product cost
Direct cost	Full product cost	Manufacturing overhead
Direct materials	Indirect cost	Period cost

a. ___ is expensed in the period incurred.
b. The product cost used for external reporting is called ___.
c. ___ includes all the elements of the value chain and is used for internal decisions such as setting long-run average selling prices.
d. ___ is initially considered an asset, and is not expensed until the related products are sold.
e. The sum of direct materials, direct labor, and manufacturing overhead is ___ for a manufacturing company.
f. ___ is all costs incurred in the plant other than direct materials and direct labor.

DE19-8 Consider **Toyota, United Parcel Service,** and **Home Depot.** For each company, answer the following questions.

1. Is this a service company, a merchandiser, or a manufacturer?
2. What is the primary output the company sells to customers?
3. What inventory accounts would this company have on its balance sheet?
4. Does this company have any inventoriable product costs? If so, how would you compute these costs?

Inventoriable costs; balance sheets of service, merchandising, and manufacturing companies (Obj. 4, 5)

DE19-9 ◄ *Link Back to Chapter 5.* Refer to Exhibit 19-9 on page 765. What would be Apex's beginning inventory if revenues, purchases and freight-in, and ending inventory are all the same as in Exhibit 19-9, but gross profit is $45,000 rather than $43,500?

Preparing the cost-of-goods-sold section of a merchandiser's income statement (Obj. 5)

DE19-10 ◄ *Link Back to Chapter 5.* Given the following information for Gemz, a fashion jewelry e-tailer, compute the cost of goods sold.

Prepare the cost-of-goods-sold section of a merchandiser's income statement (Obj. 5)

Web site maintenance.....	$1,000	Delivery expenses..........	$	500
Freight-in........................	2,500	Purchases.......................		30,000
Ending inventory............	5,500	Revenues.......................		60,000
Marketing expenses........	6,000	Beginning inventory		3,000

DE19-11 Look at Exhibit 19-11 (page 766). What would be Top-Flight's cost of goods sold and operating income if the cost of goods manufactured were $35,000 rather than $42,000? (Other costs and revenues remain the same as in Exhibit 19-11.)

Income statement for a manufacturing company (Obj. 5)

DE19-12 Turn to Exhibit 19-12 (page 767). If direct material purchases were $35,000 rather than $27,000, what would be the cost of direct materials used and the cost of goods manufactured? (Other costs remain the same as in Exhibit 19-12.)

Computing the cost of goods manufactured (Obj. 5)

DE19-13 Jell's manufactures women's plastic sandals. Suppose the company's March records include the following items. What is Jell's total manufacturing overhead cost in March?

Computing manufacturing overhead (Obj. 5)

Ink for printing shoe boxes.....	$ 100	Company president's salary....	$15,000
Depreciation expense on		Plant foreman's salary	2,000
company cars used by		Plant janitor's salary	1,000
sales force	3,000	Oil for manufacturing	
Plant depreciation expense	10,000	equipment	25
Interest expense.....................	1,500	Plastic for shoes	50,000

DE19-14 You are a new accounting intern at Mountain Gear, Inc. Your boss gives you the following information and asks you to compute direct materials used.

Computing direct materials used (Obj. 5)

Purchases of direct materials	$25,000
Freight-in...	200
Freight-out	1,000
Ending inventory of direct materials....................	1,500
Beginning inventory of direct materials..............	4,000

DE19-15 Use Exhibit 19-12 (page 767) to explain the differences between *manufacturing costs* and the *cost of goods manufactured.* How much are the *manufacturing costs?* How much is the *cost of goods manufactured?* Explain the difference between these two amounts.

Explaining the cost-of-goods-manufactured schedule (Obj. 5)

Differences among service, merchandising, and manufacturing
companies' balance sheets
(Obj. 5)

DE19-16 The current asset sections of the balance sheets of three companies follow. Which company is a service company? Which is a merchandiser? Which is a manufacturer? How can you tell?

X-Treme		Y-Not?		Zesto	
Cash.............................	$ 2,500	Cash	$3,000	Cash.................................	$ 2,000
Accounts receivable........	5,500	Accounts receivable	6,000	Accounts receivable..........	5,000
Inventory........................	8,000	Prepaid expenses...............	500	Materials inventory..........	1,000
Prepaid expenses............	300	Total.................................	$9,500	Work in process inventory	800
Total..............................	$16,300			Finished goods inventory .	4,000
				Total.................................	$12,800

DE19-17 You work for X-Rays, a company that produces and markets upscale sunglasses. One of your competitors, SunStop, has just hired eNow! Consultants to establish an on-line sales system that will enable customers to place orders via the Internet. How could this affect X-Rays, which still takes sales orders in person or over the phone? Be specific.

DE19-18 Is JIT more appropriate for **Amazon.com,** a book, music, and electronics e-tailer, or **Mouton-Rothschild,** a French winemaker specializing in fine red wines? Explain.

Expected value of the benefits of
a quality program
(Obj. 6)

DE19-19 Consider the cost-benefit analysis for the **GE** quality program discussed on page 774. Suppose GE's managers now estimate a 90% chance that the projects will yield an extra $20 million in benefits, and a 10% chance that the projects will yield an extra $80 million. What is the expected value of the additional benefits *now?* Assuming total costs remain $200 million, does this change your mind about whether the quality program was a worthwhile investment?

DE19-20 Explain why each of the four broad ethical standards in the Institute of Management Accountants' *Standards of Ethical Conduct for Management Accountants* (Exhibit 19-15, page 776) is necessary.

DE19-21 The Institute of Management Accountants' *Standards of Ethical Conduct for Management Accountants* (Exhibit 19-15, page 776) require management accountants to meet standards regarding

- Competence   • Confidentiality   • Integrity   • Objectivity

Consider the following situations. Which guidelines are violated in each situation?

a. You tell your brother that your company will report earnings significantly above financial analysts' estimates.
b. You see that others take home office supplies for personal use. As an intern, you do the same thing, assuming that this is a "perk."
c. At a conference on e-commerce, you skip the afternoon session and go sightseeing.
d. You failed to read the detailed specifications of a new general ledger package that you asked your company to purchase. After it is installed, you are surprised that it is incompatible with some of your company's older accounting software.
e. You do not provide top management with the detailed job descriptions they requested, because you fear they may use this information to cut a position from your department.

EXERCISES

Management vs. financial
accounting and managers' use of
information
(Obj. 1)

E19-1 Listed below are several terms relating to the functions of managers and the differences between financial and management accounting. Complete the following statements with one of these terms. You may use a term more than once, and some terms may not be used at all.

Budget	Creditors	Managers	Planning
Controlling	Financial accounting	Management accounting	Shareholders

a. Financial accounting develops reports for external parties, such as ___ and ___.
b. When managers evaluate the company's performance compared to the plan, they are performing the ___ role of management.
c. Companies must follow GAAP in their ___ systems.
d. ___ are decision makers inside a company.
e. ___ provides information on a company's past performance.
f. ___ systems are not restricted by GAAP, but are chosen by comparing the costs versus the benefits of the system.
g. Choosing goals and the means to achieve them is the _____ function of management.

E19-2 Suppose the computer manufacturer Gateway, Inc., provides the following information for its costs last month (in hundreds of thousands):

Value chain, direct and indirect costs, inventoriable costs (Obj. 2, 3, 4)

Salaries of telephone salespeople ..	$ 4	Hard drives	$50
Depreciation on manufacturing plant and equipment..................	52	Rearrange production process to accommodate new robot	2
Exterior case for computer	6	Assembly-line workers' wages	10
Salaries of scientists who developed new lightweight laptop model	12	Technical support hotline for customer support after purchase...	3
Delivery expense via Airborne Express......................................	7	1-800 (toll-free) line for customer orders	1

Required

1. Use the following format to classify each cost according to its place in the value chain. (*Hint:* You should have at least one cost in each value-chain function.)

	Design of Products, Services, or Processes	Production					
R&D		Direct Materials	Direct Labor	Manufacturing Overhead	Marketing	Distribution	Customer Service

2. Compute the total costs for each value-chain category.
3. How much are the total inventoriable product costs?

E19-3 Suppose **Target** incurred the following costs at its Charleston, South Carolina, store.

Value chain, inventoriable costs (Obj. 2, 4)

Research to determine whether store should add a travel agency service.........	$ 400	Payment to consultant for advice on location of new store	$2,500
Purchases of merchandise.......	50,000	Freight-in.................................	3,000
Rearranging store layout.........	1,500	Salespersons' salaries...............	8,000
Newspaper advertisements	10,000	Customer complaint department...........................	
Depreciation expense on delivery trucks.....................	2,000		800

Required

1. Use the following format to classify each cost according to its place in the value chain.

	Design of Products, Services, or Processes	Purchases of Merchandise Inventory	Marketing	Distribution	Customer Service
R&D					

2. Compute the total costs for each value-chain category.
3. How much are the total inventoriable product costs?

E19-4 Listed below are several terms relating to service, merchandising, and manufacturing firms and their inventories. Complete the following statements with one of these terms. You may use a term more than once, and some terms may not be used at all.

Service, merchandising, and manufacturing companies and their inventories (Obj. 5)

Finished goods inventory	Inventory (merchandise)	Service companies
Manufacturing companies	Merchandising companies	Work in process inventory
Materials inventory		

a. _____ do not have tangible products intended for sale.

b. _____ resell products they previously purchased ready-made from suppliers.

c. _____ produce their own inventory.

d. _____ typically have a single category of inventory.

e. _____ use their work force and equipment to transform raw materials into new finished products.

f. Swaim, a company based in North Carolina, makes furniture. Partially completed sofas are _____. Completed sofas that remain unsold in the warehouse are _____. Fabric and wood are _____.

g. For **Kellogg's,** corn, cardboard boxes, and waxed paper liners are classified as _____.

Reporting current assets (Obj. 5)

E19-5 Consider the following selected amounts and account balances of Boyds:

Cost of goods sold	$96,000	Prepaid expenses	$ 6,000
Direct labor	47,000	Marketing expense	39,000
Direct materials	25,000	Work in process inventory	42,000
Accounts receivable	75,000	Manufacturing overhead	26,000
Cash	19,000	Finished goods inventory	72,000
Cost of goods manufactured	94,000	Materials inventory	10,000

Show how Boyds reports current assets on the balance sheet. Not all data are used. Is Boyds a service company, a merchandiser, or a manufacturer? How do you know?

Computing CGM and CGS (Obj. 4, 5)

E19-6 Compute the 20X5 cost of goods manufactured and cost of goods sold for Strike Marine Company using the following amounts:

	Beginning of Year	End of Year		End of Year
Materials inventory	$22,000	$28,000	Insurance on plant	9,000
Work in process inventory	42,000	30,000	Depreciation—plant building and equipment	$16,000
Finished goods inventory	18,000	25,000	Repairs and maintenance—plant	4,000
Purchases of raw materials		78,000	Marketing expenses	77,000
Direct labor		82,000	General and administrative expenses	29,000
Indirect labor		15,000	Income tax expense	30,000

Preparing a manufacturer's I/S (Obj. 5)

E19-7 Prepare the 20X5 income statement for the Strike Marine Company in Exercise 19-6. Assume that it sold 28,000 units of its product at a price of $14 during 20X5.

Computing GP for a manufacturer (Obj. 5)

E19-8 Supply the missing amounts from the following computation of gross profit for Alon Plastics.

Sales revenue				$473,000
Cost of goods sold:				
Beginning finished goods inventory			$ 91,000	
Cost of goods manufactured:				
Beginning work in process inventory		$ 52,000		
Direct materials used	$64,000			
Direct labor	X			
Manufacturing overhead	51,000			
Total manufacturing costs incurred during the period		226,000		
Total manufacturing costs to account for		X		
Ending work in process inventory		(40,000)		
Costs of goods manufactured			X	
Cost of goods available for sale			X	
Ending finished goods inventory			(107,000)	
Cost of goods sold				X
Gross profit				$ X

E19-9 Listed below are several terms relating to the modern business environment. Complete the following statements with one of these terms. You may use a term more than once, and some terms may not be used at all.

E-commerce	JIT	Present value
Expected value	North American Free Trade	Shift to service economy
Future	Agreement (NAFTA)	Throughput time
Future value	Present	TQM

a. To account for uncertainty in the amounts of future costs and benefits, we compute the _____ by multiplying the probability of each outcome by the dollar value of that outcome.
b. To make a cost-benefit decision today, we must find the _____ of the costs and benefits that are incurred in the future.
c. The goal of _____ is to delight customers by providing them with superior products and services by eliminating defects and waste throughout the value chain.
d. Most of the costs of adopting JIT, expanding into a foreign market, or improving quality are incurred in the _____, but most of the benefits occur in the _____.
e. _____ is the time between buying raw materials and selling the finished products.
f. The main purpose of _____ is to loosen trade restrictions and promote trade among the United States, Canada, and Mexico.
g. Firms adopt _____ to conduct business on the Internet.

E19-10 Cool Cuts manufactures casual menswear. Eric Haynes, the CEO, is trying to decide whether to adopt just-in-time (JIT). He expects that in present-value terms, adopting JIT would save $113,000 in warehousing expenses and $67,800 in spoilage costs.

Adopting JIT will require several one-time up-front expenditures: (1) $27,000 for an employee training program, (2) $49,500 to streamline the plant's production process, and (3) $8,000 to identify suppliers that will guarantee zero defects and on-time delivery.

Required

1. What are the total costs of adopting JIT?
2. What are the total benefits of adopting JIT?
3. Should Cool Cuts adopt JIT? Why or why not?

E19-11 Mary Gonzales is the controller at Automax, a car dealership. Cory Loftus has recently been hired as bookkeeper. Cory wanted to attend a class on Excel spreadsheets, so Mary temporarily took over Cory's duties, including overseeing a fund for topping up a car's gas before a test drive. Mary found a shortage in this fund and confronted Cory when he returned to work. Cory admitted that he occasionally takes advantage of his access to this fund to pay for his own gas when his finances are low. Mary estimated that the amount involved is close to $300.

Required

1. What should Mary Gonzales do?
2. Would you change your answer to the previous question if Mary Gonzales was the one recently hired as controller, while Cory Loftus was a well-liked longtime employee, and he indicated that he always eventually repaid the fund?

CHALLENGE EXERCISE

E19-12 CoverUp manufactures and sells a new line of sun-protection clothing. Unfortunately, CoverUp suffered serious hurricane damage at its home office in Miami, Florida, As a result, the accounting records for October were partially destroyed—and completely jumbled. CoverUp has hired you to help figure out the missing pieces of the accounting puzzle.

Work in process inventory, October 31	$ 1,000	Accounts payable, October 1	$3,000
Finished goods inventory, October 1	4,000	Direct materials used in October	8,000
Direct labor in October	3,000	Accounts payable, October 31	4,800
Purchases of direct materials in October	9,000	Accounts receivable, October 31	6,000
Work in process inventory, October 1	0	Direct materials inventory, October 31	2,000
Revenues in October	27,000	Manufacturing overhead in October	7,000
Accounts receivable, October 1	2,000		
Gross profit in October	10,100		

(continued)

Required

Find the following amounts:

a. Cost of goods sold in October
b. Beginning direct materials inventory
c. Ending finished goods inventory

(*Hint:* You may find Exhibit 19-13 helpful.)

(Group A) PROBLEMS

Value chain, direct vs. indirect costs, inventoriable costs (Obj. 2, 3, 4)

P19-1A Suppose Dell Computer reported the following costs last month. (All costs are in millions.)

Payment to UPS for delivering PCs to customers	$ 250
Cost of hard drives used	3,300
Cost of Internet banner ads	400
Plant janitors' wages	10
Wages of workers who assemble the PCs	1,000
Cost of customer hotline for troubleshooting problems	30
Wages of forklift drivers moving parts and completed computers around the plant floor	20
Plant utilities	35
Cost of software loaded on computers	25
Depreciation on plant and equipment	250
Salaries of scientists working on next generation laptops	30
Insurance and taxes on plant property	40
Cost of oil used for conveyor belt and other plant equipment	5
Payment to engineers redesigning the exterior case	15
Wages of sales associates taking phone orders	50
Cost of circuit boards used	4,000
Total	$9,460

Required

1. Use the following format to classify each of these costs according to its place in the value chain. (*Hint:* You should have at least one cost in each value-chain function.)

	Design of Products or Processes	Production					
R&D		Direct Materials	Direct Labor	Manufacturing Overhead	Marketing	Distribution	Customer Service

2. Compute the total costs for each category.
3. How much are the total inventoriable product costs?
4. Suppose the managers of the R&D and design functions receive year-end bonuses based on meeting their own unit's target cost reductions. What are they likely to do? How might this affect costs incurred in other elements of the value chain?

Preparing financial statements for merchandising and manufacturing companies (Obj. 4, 5)

P19-2A *Part One:* On January 1, 2000, Matt Berrigan opened Boards of Paradise, a small retail store dedicated to selling snowboards, wakeboards, and skateboards. On December 31, 2000, his accounting records show the following:

Store rent	$ 6,500		Sales revenue	$87,000
Sales salaries	3,500		Store utilities	1,950
Freight-in	750		Purchases of merchandise	42,000
Inventory on December 31, 2000	8,750		Inventory on January 1, 2000	12,700
			Advertising expense	2,300

Required

Prepare an income statement for Boards of Paradise, a merchandiser.

Part Two: Boards of Paradise succeeded so well that Matt Berrigan decided to manufacture his own special brand of snowboards, to be called Paradise. At the end of December 20X3, his accounting records show the following:

Finished goods inventory, December 31, 20X3	$ 4,000	Rent on manufacturing plant	$ 11,000
Work in process inventory, December 31, 20X3	1,750	Finished goods inventory, December 31, 20X2	0
Direct materials inventory, December 31, 20X3	7,750	Depreciation expense on delivery truck	2,500
R&D for graphic designs	3,700	Depreciation expense on manufacturing	
Sales commissions	6,500	equipment	4,700
Utilities for plant	2,900	Work in process inventory, December 31, 20X2	0
Plant janitorial services	1,750	Sales revenue	126,450
Direct labor	23,500	Customer warranty refunds	1,500
Direct material purchases	37,000	Direct materials inventory, December 31, 20X2	15,000

Required

1. Prepare a schedule of cost of goods manufactured for Paradise Manufacturing.
2. Prepare an income statement for Paradise Manufacturing.
3. How does the format of the income statement for Paradise Manufacturing differ from the income statement of Boards of Paradise?

Part Three: Show the ending inventories that would appear on these balance sheets:

1. Boards of Paradise at December 31, 2000.
2. Paradise Manufacturing at December 31, 20X3.

P19-3A Certain item descriptions and amounts are missing from the monthly schedule of cost of goods manufactured and income statement of Southern Manufacturing Company. Fill in the missing items.

Preparing financial statements for a manufacturer (Obj. 5)

MANUFACTURING COMPANY
April 30, 20X4

_____ work in process inventory		$ 17,000
Direct materials used:		
_____ materials _____	$ X	
_____ of materials	62,000	
_____	75,000	
_____ materials _____	(23,000)	
Direct _____		$ X
Direct _____		68,000
Manufacturing overhead		X
Total _____ costs _____		X
Total _____ costs _____		175,000
_____ work in process inventory		X
_____		$148,000

MANUFACTURING COMPANY
April 30, 20X4

_____ revenue		$445,000
_____:		
Beginning _____	$ X	
_____	X	
Cost of goods _____	X	
Ending _____	(67,000)	
Cost of goods sold		X
_____		243,000
_____ expenses:		
Marketing expenses	X	
Administrative expenses	$ 64,000	X
_____		$ 76,000

P19-4A Quantx, Inc., manufactures computer disk drives. It sells these disk drives to other manufacturers, which use them in assembling computers. Quantx is having trouble with its new DVD drive. If the parts are not engineered to exact specifications, the drive does not function. About half the time, Quantx employees find these defects while the disk drive is still on the production line. These drives are immediately reworked in the plant. Otherwise, Quantx's customers do not identify the problem until they install the disk drives they've purchased from Quantx. Customers return defective drives for replacement under warranty, and they have also complained that after they install the disk drive, the drive's connector (which plugs into the computer system board) often shakes loose while the computer is being assembled. The customer must then reassemble the computer after fixing the loose connection.

Quantx CEO Jay Batson has just returned from a seminar on total quality management (TQM). He forms a team to address these quality problems. The team includes the plant engineer, the production foreman, a customer service representative, the marketing director, and the management accountant.

Three months later, the team proposes a major project to *prevent* these quality problems. Quantx's accountant Anna Hamm reports that implementing the team's proposal will require Quantx to incur the following costs over the next three months:

- $180,500 for Quantx research scientists to develop a completely new disk drive that works even with small deviations from specified part sizes.
- $70,000 for company engineers to redesign the connector so that it better tolerates rough treatment.

The project team is unsure whether this investment will pay off. If the effort fixes the problem, Hamm expects that

- A reputation for higher quality will increase sales, which in turn will increase the present value of profits by $200,042.
- Fewer disk drives will fail. The present value of the savings from fewer warranty repairs is $163,998.
- The plant will have fewer defective disk drives to rework. The present value of this savings is $100,221.

However, if this project is not successful, there will be no cost savings and no additional sales. The team predicts a 70% chance that the project will succeed, and a 30% chance that it will fail.

Required

1. If the quality improvement project succeeds, what is the dollar amount of the benefits?
2. Should Quantx undertake this project? Why or why not? Show supporting calculations.

P19-5A Problem 19-4A provided both quantitative and qualitative information about Quantx's quality project, and asked you to perform a *quantitative* analysis to help Quantx's managers decide whether to embark on the project. Now consider some *qualitative* factors in Quantx's quality improvement project.

Required

1. Why did Jay Batson create a team to address this quality problem, rather than assigning the task to one person? Consider each piece of cost/benefit information reported by management accountant Anna Hamm. Which person on the team is most likely to have contributed each item? (*Hint:* Which team member is likely to have the most information about each cost or benefit?)
2. Classify the following amounts into one of the six value-chain business functions.
   a. $180,500 cost to develop the new disk drive.
   b. $70,000 cost to redesign the connector.
   c. $163,998 for warranty repairs on disk drives.
   d. $100,221 to rework disk drives identified as defective while still in the factory.
3. This problem illustrates how Quantx can make trade-offs across business functions in the value chain. Which of the six value-chain functions are involved in the trade-offs proposed by the quality improvement team? What specific trade-offs do they propose?

P19-6A West Bank is a regional bank in California that also processes checks for smaller banks and insurance companies. This results in mounds of paperwork, because West Bank tracks which checks have been deposited and which accounts have been debited or credited. When a customer complains that a check was not deposited to its account, a West Bank clerk takes the complaint over the phone and fills out a paper form. The complaint form triggers a long search through piles of canceled checks in a warehouse to find the check in question. West Bank then compares this check to its computer and paper records.

West Bank is considering moving this process to the Web. When a customer has a question, its employee simply uses a Web browser and a password to access West Bank's databases. The customer's employee pulls up a computerized image of the check in question to verify the amount and then queries West Bank's databases to locate the mistake. If required, a credit to the customer's account can be issued immediately.

The Web-based system will require the bank to invest $74,000 in a new server and check-scanning equipment. eNow! consultants will charge $110,000 for the software and consulting fees to get the system running. The system will also require increasing the bank's Internet capacity. The present value of this cost is $20,000.

West Bank has identified two benefits of this project. First, several bank clerks freed from searching through stacks of canceled checks will be reassigned to other more responsible and interesting tasks, which will lead to cost savings with a present value of $156,000. Second, the new system's additional capacity will enable West Bank to accept more check-processing business, which should lead to additional profits with a present value of $39,600.

Required

Does a cost-benefit analysis justify the Web-based system? Explain why, showing supporting calculations.

P19-7A Consider the West Bank project described in Problem 19-6A. West Bank has revised its estimates of additional profits the bank is likely to earn. There is a 50% chance that the bank will earn $39,600 in extra profits, but also a 50% chance the bank will earn $75,000.

e-Commerce, cost-benefit analysis, expected value (Obj. 6)

Required

1. Compute the expected value of the benefits from the additional business.
2. Would you recommend that West Bank accept the proposal? Give your reason, showing supporting calculations.
3. Are there other potential benefits not listed in Problems 19-6A or 19-7A that may make the proposal more attractive to West Bank?

P19-8A Jan Hobbs is the new controller for Kromeware, a designer and manufacturer of outdoor wear. Shortly before the December 31 fiscal year end, Lashea Hare (the company president) asks Jan how things look for the year-end numbers. Lashea is not happy to learn that earnings growth may be below 10% for the first time in the company's five-year history. Lashea explains that financial analysts have again predicted a 20% earnings growth for the company and that she does not intend to disappoint them. She suggests that Jan talk to the assistant controller, who can explain how the previous controller dealt with this situation. The assistant controller suggests the following strategies:

Ethics (Obj. 7)

a. Do not record sales returns and allowances on the basis that they are individually immaterial.
b. Persuade retail customers to accelerate January orders to December.
c. Reduce the allowance for bad debts, given the company's continued strong performance.
d. Kromeware has very limited warehouse space. It regularly ships finished goods to public warehouses across the country for temporary storage, until Kromeware receives firm orders from customers. As Kromeware receives orders, it directs the warehouse to ship the goods to the nearby customer. The assistant controller suggests recording goods sent to the public warehouses as sales.
e. Postpone planned advertising expenditures from December to January.

Which of these suggested strategies are inconsistent with IMA standards? What should Jan Hobbs do if Lashea Hare insists that she follow all of these suggestions?

PROBLEMS

(Group B)

P19-1B Healthy Foods produces canned chicken á la king—chicken, mushrooms, and bell peppers in a cream sauce. The production process starts with raw chicken that workers debone. Cream sauce is prepared, the chicken is cooked, and the two are combined with the vegetables. Because chickens naturally vary in salt content, the amount of salt added varies from batch to batch.

Healthy Foods incurs the following costs (in thousands):

Value chain, direct and indirect costs, inventoriable costs (Obj. 2, 3, 4)

Plant utilities	$ 900	Production costs of "cents-off"	
Depreciation on plant and		store coupons for customers	$ 600
equipment	2,500	Delivery truck drivers' wages	250
Payment to chef for developing		Cream	1,300
new low-fat recipe	1,200	Sales commissions	400
Salt	20	Plant janitors' wages	1,000
Replace products with expired		Wages of workers who	
dates upon customer		debone chicken	10,000
complaint	50	Customer hotline for recipes	
Rearranging plant layout to		and problems	200
smooth production flow	1,100	Depreciation on delivery	
Chicken	18,000	truck	150
Mushrooms and peppers	1,000	Freight-in	1,500
		Total	$40,170

789 INTRODUCTION TO MANAGEMENT ACCOUNTING

Required

1. Use the following format to classify each of these costs according to its place in the value chain. (*Hint:* You should have at least one cost in each value-chain function.)

R&D	Design of Products or Processes	Production			Marketing	Distribution	Customer Service
		Direct Materials	Direct Labor	Manufacturing Overhead			

2. Compute the total costs for each value-chain category.
3. How much are the total inventoriable product costs?
4. Suppose the managers of the R&D and design functions receive year-end bonuses based on meeting their own unit's target cost reductions. What are they likely to do? How might this affect costs incurred in other elements of the value chain?

Preparing financial statements for merchandising and manufacturing companies
(Obj. 4, 5)

P19-2B *Part One:* In 20X3, Kelly Williams opened Kelly's Boutique, a small retail boutique selling makeup. On December 31, 20X4, her accounting records show the following:

Inventory on December 31, 20X4	$ 9,850
Inventory on January 1, 20X4	10,700
Sales revenue	46,000
Utilities for boutique	2,450
Rent for boutique	4,000
Sales commissions	1,500
Purchases of merchandise	27,000

Required

Prepare an income statement for Kelly's Boutique, a merchandiser.

Part Two: Kelly's Boutique succeeded so well that Kelly Williams decided to manufacture her own brand of sun-protection makeup—CoverUp. At the end of December 20X5, her accounting records show the following:

Work in process inventory, December 31, 20X5.	$ 640	Plant janitorial services	$ 1,250
Finished goods inventory, December 31, 20X4 ..	0	Direct labor	17,500
Finished goods inventory, December 31, 20X5 ..	5,700	Direct material purchases	30,000
Sales revenue	97,450	Rent on manufacturing plant	9,000
Customer service hotline	1,000	Direct materials inventory, December 31, 20X4 .	12,000
Utilities for plant	3,400	Direct materials inventory, December 31, 20X5 .	8,750
Delivery expense	1,500	Work in process inventory, December 31, 20X4.	0
Sales salaries	4,500		

Required

1. Prepare a schedule of cost of goods manufactured for CoverUp Manufacturing.
2. Prepare an income statement for CoverUp Manufacturing.
3. How does the format of the income statement for CoverUp Manufacturing differ from the income statement of Kelly's Boutique?

Part Three: Show the ending inventories that would appear on these balance sheets:

1. Kelly's Boutique at December 31, 20X4.
2. CoverUp Manufacturing at December 31, 20X5.

Preparing financial statements for a manufacturer (Obj. 5)

P19-3B Certain item descriptions and amounts are missing from the monthly schedule of cost of goods manufactured and the income statement of Henriquez Manufacturing Company shown on the facing page. Fill in the missing items.

_____ MANUFACTURING COMPANY

_____ JUNE 30, 20X4

Beginning _____			$ 21,000
Direct _____:			
Beginning materials inventory	$ X		
Purchases of materials..............................	51,000		
_____	82,000		
Ending materials inventory	(23,000)		
Direct _____		$ X	
Direct _____		X	
Manufacturing overhead...........................		40,000	
Total _____ costs _____			166,000
Total _____ costs _____			X
Ending _____			(30,000)
_____			$ X

_____ MANUFACTURING COMPANY

_____ June 30, 20X4

Sales revenue		$ X
Cost of goods sold:		
Beginning _____	$101,000	
_____	X	
Cost of goods _____	X	
Ending _____	X	
Cost of goods sold		201,000
Gross profit..		245,000
_____ expenses:		
Marketing expense	99,000	
Administrative expense......................................	X	154,000
_____ income		$ X

P19-4B Pameon manufactures fine watches. The company is having trouble with one of its watches. If the parts are not machined to exact specifications, the watch will not operate. Even a speck of dust under the crystal causes the watch to stop. About half the time, Pameon employees find the defect while the watch is still on the production line. These watches are immediately reworked in the plant. When a defect escapes detection until the customer complains, Pameon repairs the watch.

TQM, cost-benefit analysis, expected value (Obj. 6)

    Pameon CEO Jon Vaucluse has just returned from a seminar on total quality management (TQM). He forms a team to address this quality problem. The team includes the plant engineer, the production foreman, the plant's watch repair specialist, the marketing director, and the management accountant.

    Three months later, the team proposes a major project to *prevent* these quality problems. Pameon accountant Lily Peugot reports that implementing the team's proposal will require Pameon to incur the following costs over the next six months:

a. $52,500 to redesign the watch so it operates even with small deviations from specified part sizes.

b. $80,000 for Pameon scientists to develop a completely new watch mechanism that tolerates dust particles

    The project team is unsure whether this investment will pay off. If these efforts fix the problem, Peugot expects the following to occur:

a. The plant will have no defective watches to rework. The present value of this savings is $47,450.

b. Fewer watches will fail. The present value of the savings from fewer warranty repairs is $101,440.

c. A reputation for higher quality will increase sales, which in turn will increase the present value of profits by $126,800.

However, if this project is not successful, there will be no cost savings and no additional sales. The team predicts that there is a 60% chance that the project will succeed, and a 40% chance that it will fail.

Required

1. If the quality improvement project succeeds, what is the dollar amount of the benefits?
2. Should Pameon undertake this project? Why or why not? Show supporting calculations.

Value chain, TQM
(Obj. 2, 6)

P19-5B Problem 19-4B provided both quantitative and qualitative information about Pameon's quality project, and asked you to perform a *quantitative* analysis to help Pameon's managers decide whether to embark on the quality project. Now consider some *qualitative* factors in Pameon's quality improvement project.

Required

1. Why did Jon Vaucluse create a team to address this quality problem, rather than assigning the task to one person? Consider each piece of cost/benefit information reported by management accountant Lily Peugot. Which person on the team is most likely to have contributed each item? (*Hint:* Which team member is likely to have the most information about each cost or benefit?)
2. Classify the following costs into one of the six value-chain business functions:
   a. $52,500 cost to redesign the watch.
   b. $80,000 cost to develop a completely new watch mechanism.
   c. $47,450 to rework watches identified as defective while still in the factory.
   d. $101,440 to make warranty repairs on watches returned by customers.
3. The Pameon problem illustrates how managers make trade-offs across different business functions in the value chain. Which of the six value-chain functions are involved in the trade-offs proposed by the quality improvement team? What specific trade-offs do they propose?

---

e-Commerce, cost-benefit
analysis
(Obj. 6)

P19-6B Discount Gas Corporation wants to move its sales-order system to the Web. Under the proposed system, gas stations and other merchants will use a Web browser and, after typing in a password for the Discount Gas Web page, will be able to check the availability and current price of various products and place an order. The system processes the order electronically through links with the firm's traditional mainframe-based ordering system, without human intervention. Currently, customer service representatives take dealers' orders over the phone; they first record the information on a paper order form, then manually enter it into the firm's computer system.

CFO Steve Pronai believes that dealers will not adopt the new Web system unless Discount Gas provides financial assistance to help them purchase or upgrade their PCs. Pronai estimates this one-time cost at $800,000. Discount Gas will also have to invest $150,000 in upgrading its own computer hardware. Consultants tell Pronai that together the cost of the software and the consulting fee for installing the system will be $230,000. The Web system will enable Discount Gas to eliminate 25 clerical positions. Pronai estimates that the benefits of the new system's lower labor costs will have a present value of $1,400,000.

Required

Use a cost-benefit analysis to recommend to Steve Pronai whether or not Discount Gas should proceed with the Web-based ordering system. Give your reasons, showing supporting calculations.

---

e-Commerce, cost-benefit analysis, expected value
(Obj. 6)

P19-7B Consider the Discount Gas proposed entry into e-commerce in Problem 19-6B. Steve Pronai revises his estimates of the benefits from the new system's lower labor costs. He now thinks there is a 40% chance of receiving the $1,400,000 in benefits and a 60% chance the benefits will only be $920,000.

Required

1. Compute the expected benefits of the Web-based ordering system.
2. Would you recommend Discount Gas accept the proposal?
3. Before Steve Pronai makes a final decision, what other factors should he consider?

Ethics
(Obj. 7)

P19-8B Renee Abby is the new controller for Gate Software, Inc., which develops and sells educational software. Shortly before the December 31 fiscal year end, Matt Berrigan, the company president, asks Abby how things look for the year-end numbers. He is not happy to learn that earnings growth may be below 30% for the first time in the company's five-year history. Berrigan explains that financial analysts have again predicted a 30% earnings growth for the company and that he does not intend to disappoint them. He suggests that Abby talk to the assistant controller, who can explain how the previous controller dealt with this situation. The assistant controller suggests the following strategies:

a. Record as sales certain software awaiting sale that is held in a public warehouse.

b. Delay the year-end closing a few days into January of the next year, so that some of next year's sales are included as this year's sales.

c. Reduce the allowance for bad debts (and bad debts expense), given the company's continued strong performance.

d. Persuade suppliers to postpone billing until January 1.

e. Postpone routine monthly maintenance expenditures from December to January.

Which of these suggested strategies are inconsistent with IMA standards? What should Abby do if Berrigan insists that she follow all of these suggestions?

APPLY YOUR KNOWLEDGE

DECISION CASES

Case 1. Digiteck, Inc., designs and manufactures switches used in telecommunications. Digiteck's main facility is in California's Silicon Valley. Its second facility in North Carolina's Research Triangle Park services the Park's concentration of telecommunications firms. The serious flooding caused by Hurricane Floyd throughout North Carolina also affected Digiteck's facilities. Inventory was completely ruined, and the company's computer system, including all accounting records, was destroyed.

Flow of costs through manufacturing companies (Obj. 5)

Before the disaster recovery specialists clean the buildings, Annette Couch, the company controller, is anxious to salvage whatever records she can to support an insurance claim for the destroyed inventory. She is standing in what is left of the accounting department with Jay Boros, the cost accountant.

"I didn't know mud could smell so bad." Jay says, "What should I be looking for?"

"Don't worry about beginning inventory numbers," responds Annette, "we'll get them from last year's annual report. We need first-quarter cost data."

"I was working on the first-quarter results just before the hurricane hit," Jay says. "Look, my report's still in my desk drawer. But all I can make out is that for the first quarter, material purchases were $434,000 and that direct labor, manufacturing overhead, and total manufacturing costs to account for were $430,000, $245,000, and $1,300,000, respectively. Wait, and cost of goods available for sale was $1,280,000."

"Great," says Annette, "I remember that sales for the period were approximately $1.5 million. Given our gross profit of 30%, that's all you should need."

Jay is not sure about that, but decides to see what he can do with this information. The beginning inventory numbers are

- Direct materials, $109,000
- Work in process, $215,000
- Finished goods, $145,000

He remembers a schedule he learned in college that may help him get started.

Required

1. Exhibit 19-13 resembles the schedule Jay has in mind. Use it to determine the ending inventories of direct materials, work in process, and finished goods.

2. Draft an insurance claim letter for the controller, seeking reimbursement for the flood damage to inventory. Digiteck's insurance representative is Don Snowball, at Industrial Insurance Co., 1122 Main Street, Hartford, CT 06268. The policy number is #3454340-23. Digiteck's address is 5 Research Triangle Way, Raleigh, NC 27698.

Case 2. To help management accountants meet obligations to their profession, employer, the public, and themselves, the IMA has issued *Standards of Ethical Conduct for Management Accountants*. In defining ethical behavior, these standards can be applied to more than just management accounting. They are also relevant to college students. Explain at least one situation that shows how each IMA standard in Exhibit 19-15 is relevant to your experiences as a student. For example, the ethical standard of competence would suggest not cutting classes!

Ethics (Obj. 7)

ETHICAL ISSUE

◄ *Link Back to Chapter 7.* ComDigital, Inc., designs and manufactures chips used in digital cell phones. ComDigital is currently developing the next generation of computer chips that will allow users to receive e-mail and surf the Net using voice commands over a cell phone. Because of competition to be the first to perfect the new chip, ComDigital is investing heavily in development. Work is going slowly, and revenue growth from older chips is starting to drop. With year-end approaching, ComDigital's CEO, Jim Mann, calls a meeting with Joan

Ethics (Obj. 7)

Peters, Vice-President of Marketing, Tammy Myers, Vice-President of Finance, and Larry Case, Controller. Larry Case asks that as assistant controller, you also attend the meeting.

The CEO starts the meeting by expressing concern that with the slowdown in revenue growth and the heavy investment in new chip development, ComDigital may not meet financial analysts' earnings predictions this year. The conversation eventually turns to the new chip. Mann says the company cannot slow its R&D efforts but, since the new chip will be so profitable when it goes into production, some of the costs should be capitalized now, and then expensed later when the chip is generating revenue. VP of Finance Tammy Myers then suggests capitalizing some of these costs and charging them against revenues of chips currently being produced and sold. She argues that the new chip's R&D efforts must be providing some insights for improving the production process for existing chips. You are surprised by Controller Larry Case's silence during this discussion, as you believe these are R&D costs that GAAP requires to be expensed as incurred. The meeting ends without resolution.

Later, you learn that the CEO has told your boss to capitalize a large amount of this year's development costs for the new chip. Before talking to anyone, you decide to work through this ethical dilemma, using the following framework from Chapter 7.

1. List the facts.
2. Identify the ethical issues.
3. Specify the alternatives.
4. Identify the people involved.
5. Assess the possible consequences.
6. Make a decision.

Complete the framework.

FINANCIAL STATEMENT CASE

Identifying type of company and its cost objects, and analyzing its response to time-based competition
(Obj. 4, 6)

To help determine whether current profits will continue and grow in the future, investors need information on management's plans. Investors are especially interested in how management plans to compete in the modern business environment. Let's use **Target Corporation's** annual report to consider the company's operations and management's plans. To answer the following questions, you will need to refer to the description of Target Corporation, the chairman's letter to shareholders in the company's annual report, and the financial statements.

Required

1. Is Target Corporation a service company, a merchandiser, or a manufacturer? What financial statement information supports your answer? What information outside the financial statements supports your answer?
2. What costs would Target classify as inventoriable?
3. Use Management's Discussion and Analysis in the annual report to identify some of the company's cost objects.
4. Does Target's management see time-based competition as critical to the company's success? What specific steps is it taking to meet this challenge?

TEAM PROJECT

Management accounting and e-commerce in the real world
(Obj. 1, 6)

Search the Internet for a nearby company that also has a Web page. Arrange an interview with a management accountant, a controller, or other accounting/finance officer of the company. Before you conduct the interview, answer the following questions:

1. Is this a service, merchandising, or manufacturing company? What is its primary product or service?
2. Is the primary purpose of the company's Web site to provide information about the company and its products, to sell on-line, or to provide financial information for investors?
3. Are parts of the company's Web site restricted so that you need password authorization to enter? What appears to be the purpose of limiting access?
4. Does the Web site provide an e-mail link for contacting the company?

At the interview, begin by clarifying your answers to questions 1–4, and ask the following additional questions:

5. If the company sells over the Web, what benefits has the company derived? Did the company perform a cost-benefit analysis before deciding to begin Web sales?

   Or

   If the company does not sell over the Web, why not? Has the company performed a cost-benefit analysis and decided not to sell over the Web?

6. What is the biggest cost of operating the Web site?
7. Does the company make any purchases over the Internet? What percentage?

8. How has e-commerce affected the company's management accounting system? Have the management accountant's responsibilities become more or less complex? More or less interesting?
9. Does the company use Web-based accounting applications, such as accounts receivable or accounts payable?

Prepare a report describing the results of your interview.

INTERNET EXERCISE

1. Go to **http://www.forbes.com.** Under "Quotes & Research" type <u>TOY,</u> the stock symbol for **Toys "Я" Us, Inc.,** and click on *Go.* In the left-hand column click on *Company Info* and scan the information provided.
   a. Is this primarily a service, merchandising, or manufacturing company? What is the company's major product or service?
   b. Is this a global company? If so, in what countries does it operate?
2. In the left-hand column click on *Financials* and use the financial statements to answer the following questions.
   a. Review the annual balance sheet. Does this company report amounts for inventory? If so, for the most recent year what amount is reported? What major categories of cost are included in this account?
   b. Review the annual income statement. How many operating expense accounts does this company report? Of these accounts, how many contain inventoriable product costs? Period costs?
   c. Does this company report costs of goods sold? If so, for the most recent year what amount is reported? What title does the company use for this account?
3. At the top of the page in the "Quotes & Research" box type <u>HRB,</u> the stock symbol for **H&R Block, Inc.,** and click on *Go.* Follow the instructions above to answer the questions in items 1 and 2 for H&R Block, Inc.

Toys "Я" Us and H&R Block

Go to the "Managerial Accounting and Cost Analysis" episode on the *Mastering Accounting* CD-ROM for an interactive, video-enhanced exercise that focuses on CanGo's need for standardized accounting reports as it prepares for an IPO.

20

Job Costing

LEARNING OBJECTIVES

*After studying this chapter,
you should be able to*

1. Distinguish between job costing
   and process costing

2. Account for materials and labor
   in a manufacturer's job costing
   system

3. Account for manufacturing
   overhead in a manufacturer's
   job costing system

4. Account for noninventoriable
   costs in job costing

How did Michael Dell turn **Dell Computer** around from losses in 1993 to record profits of $1.9 *billion* for the fiscal year ending January 2000? Most companies can increase gross profit either by increasing selling prices or by reducing costs. But computer prices were falling throughout the industry, so Dell could not increase selling prices. He had no choice—Dell had to reduce manufacturing costs.

Recent estimates indicate that Dell now enjoys a 10–15% cost advantage over its competitors in the personal computer market. How did it develop this advantage? Management accounting information helped Dell and his managers decide which costs could be cut. The first step was to figure out how much it cost the company to assemble a computer.

To determine the manufacturing cost of its products, Dell uses a *job costing* system. Each computer is built to a specific customer order, called a *job*. Dell's job costing system traces direct materials (such as CD-ROMs and hard drives) and direct labor (such as assembly-line labor) to each job. Then Dell allocates indirect manufacturing overhead costs (such as depreciation on the plant) to each job. The sum of the job's direct materials, direct labor, and manufacturing overhead is its total cost.

Dell needs to know how much a product—for example, a particular computer model—costs for two main reasons:

1. *To help managers plan and control business operations, so they can:*
   - Control costs
   - Identify the most profitable products
   - Develop financial plans
   - Set selling prices for products
2. *To help managers gather information for external reporting:*
   - Cost of goods manufactured and cost of goods sold for the income statement
   - Inventory for the balance sheet

Source: McWilliams, G. "Mimicking Dell, Compaq to sell its PCs directly," *Wall Street Journal*, November 11, 1998, Page B1.

In this chapter, we will explain how **Dell Computer** and other companies use a job cost system to measure the cost of producing a product or a service. But before we get started on the details, let's pause to see where job costing fits in the big picture of cost determination for management decisions and external reporting.

In Chapter 19, you learned that managers make certain business decisions based on *full product costs* from all elements of the value chain: R&D, design, production, marketing, distribution, and customer service. Managers need to know full product costs because they must, for example, set the long-run average sale price of the products higher than the full product costs, to make a profit.

Recall that full product costs have two components: inventoriable product costs and period costs (also called noninventoriable costs). Inventoriable product costs are from the third element of the value chain in Exhibit 19-4: production for manufacturers and purchases for merchandisers. They are called inventoriable costs because in addition to serving as building blocks for computing full product costs, these are the costs GAAP requires companies to use in computing inventory and cost of goods sold for the balance sheet and income statement. Most of Chapter 20 focuses on how companies determine these inventoriable product costs. The chapter concludes with a discussion of assigning noninventoriable costs (period costs) to products and services. By adding noninventoriable costs to the inventoriable costs, managers can build up full product costs to guide internal decisions.

As you read this chapter, keep in mind that *products* are not the only cost objects. ➡ For example, managers use costs of *manufacturing processes* to identify inefficiencies and to cut costs. Knowing the costs of serving different *customers* allows managers to identify their most profitable (valuable) customers. Knowing the costs of doing business in different *geographic regions* can help managers decide which regions are more profitable and thus better candidates for expansion.

◄ For a review of cost objects, see Chapter 19, p. 760.

This chapter focuses on assigning costs to products and services because (1) products and services are the most common cost objects, and (2) managers use the costs of individual products and services to build costs of customers, geographic regions, and other cost objects.

TWO APPROACHES TO PRODUCT COSTING

Objective 1
Distinguish between job costing and process costing

➡ We discussed direct and indirect costs in Chapter 19, p. 761.

 DAILY EXERCISE 20-1

It is hard for companies like **Dell** to figure out how much it costs to manufacture a particular computer. Dell can trace the cost of direct materials like hard drives to the individual computers in which they are installed. But indirect costs such as depreciation on the manufacturing plant cannot be traced directly to an individual computer because Dell cannot determine exactly how much depreciation a particular computer "caused." ◄ Also, Dell makes many different computer models, and each requires different resources. How can Dell accurately measure product costs?

Unfortunately, it is impossible to determine the precise costs of producing a specific individual product. Instead, companies use product costing systems that *average* costs across products. There are two broad types of systems:

- Process costing
- Job costing

Process costing systems accumulate costs for each production process. *Job costing* systems accumulate costs for each individual job. Process costing and job costing also differ in the extent to which they average costs.

Process Costing

PROCESS COSTING. System for assigning costs to large numbers of identical units that usually proceed in a continuous fashion through a series of uniform production steps or processes.

Process costing is used by companies that produce large numbers of identical units in a continuous fashion through a series of uniform production steps or processes. Consider **Pace Foods,** producer of picante sauce. Picante sauce requires two major processes: (1) chopping vegetables, and (2) mixing and bottling the sauce. Pace separately accumulates the costs for each of the two production processes. Next, the company averages the costs of the chopping process over all units passing through the process. Then it averages the costs of the mixing and bottling process over all units passing through that process. For example, if Pace spent $50,000 to mix and bottle 100,000 one-pound bottles of picante sauce, the mixing and bottling cost per bottle would be

$$\text{Cost per bottle of mixing and bottling picante sauce} = \frac{\$50,000}{100,000 \text{ bottles}} = \$0.50$$

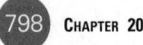 DAILY EXERCISE 20-2
DAILY EXERCISE 20-3

To get the total cost of a bottle of picante sauce, Pace would add the $0.50 per bottle of mixing and bottling cost to the cost per bottle of vegetables and the chopping process. Each bottle of picante sauce is identical to every other bottle, so each bears the same average cost of the mixing and bottling process. In process costing, the cost assigned to each unit (bottle) is a broad average, because the costs are spread evenly over the thousands of units (bottles) passing through the production process.

Some other examples of companies that use process costing:

- Oil refining—**Texaco** produces billions of gallons of unleaded gasoline.
- Food and beverage—**Kellogg's** produces thousands of pounds of cornflakes.
- Pharmaceuticals—**Bayer** produces millions of aspirin tablets.

Exhibit 20-1 shows that process costing is not limited to manufacturers. Service companies like banks use it to determine the cost of processing customer transactions. Merchandisers, such as granaries, use process costing to determine the storage cost for each bushel of grain. We consider process costing in detail in Chapter 21.

Job Costing

JOB COSTING. System for assigning costs to a specific unit or to a small batch of products or services that (1) pass through production steps as a distinct identifiable job lot, and (2) can vary considerably in terms of materials, labor, and overhead costs.

This chapter focuses on **job costing,** which assigns costs to a specific unit or to a small batch of products or services that pass through production steps as a distinct identifiable job lot. Different jobs can vary considerably in terms of materials, labor, and overhead costs, so job costing accumulates costs separately for each individual

	Service	Merchandising	Manufacturing
Job Costing	Law firms (cases)	e-tailers such as	Commercial build-
	Health care	Amazon.com and	ing construction
	(diagnoses, proce-	Drugstore.com	Custom furniture
	dures, or patients)	Mail-order catalog	
	Public relations	companies such as	
	(campaigns)	L.L. Bean	
Process Costing	Banks and other	Granaries (distribute	Paper mills
	financial institu-	tons of identical	Mining operations
	tions (processing	grains)	Textile mills
	customer deposit		
	transactions)		

job. The job may be a customer order for a mail-order catalog company like **L.L. Bean,** a production order for specialized machinery for a metal fabricator, or a project such as the construction of the Olympic Stadium in Sydney, Australia. Job costing is common in industries that produce goods to customer specifications, such as

- Aircraft—in Seattle, **Boeing** produces five new 767 airplanes to complete an order from **Delta.**
- Furniture—in High Point, North Carolina, **Swaim Furniture** produces eight dining room chairs for a customer in Baltimore.
- Construction—in Atlanta, **John Wieland Homes** constructs a new home for a linebacker on the **Atlanta Falcons** football team.

Boeing, Swaim Furniture, and John Wieland Homes produce individual products or small batches of products. Dell Computer also assembles computers to specific customer orders. In each company, different jobs can vary widely in the resources and time required, and in the complexity of the production process. Because the jobs are so different, they are not assigned equal costs.

To assign job costs accurately, accountants try to determine the *drivers* of the costs. A **cost driver** is the primary factor that causes costs. When a cost driver changes, the job's total cost changes. For example, direct labor *hours* drive direct labor *costs.* If Dell Computer uses an extra half hour of direct labor to complete an order of three computers, Dell's total direct labor cost of the three computers also increases. Because Dell is in a competitive industry where selling prices are declining, cost control is the key to earning a profit on each job.

COST DRIVER. The primary factor that causes costs.

A job may consist of one unit, like the custom home built by John Wieland. Or a job may consist of a group similar units in a distinct batch, like the eight dining room chairs ordered by Swaim's customer. When a single job includes more than one unit, the manufacturer determines the average cost of each unit in that job. Suppose Swaim's total cost for the eight chairs is $800. Then Swaim's average cost per chair is

$$\text{Average cost per chair} = \frac{\$800}{8 \text{ chairs}} = \$100$$

The cost per individual unit (chair) in job costing may require averaging, just as in process costing. However, the number of units over which costs are averaged is typically much smaller in job costing. And because each job is distinct, there is less averaging of costs *across* jobs. Exhibit 20-2 summarizes key differences between job costing and process costing.

Job costing is becoming more common in manufacturing industries like electronics. Dell Computer's made-to-order assembly process is one example. Another example is contract manufacturing, where manufacturing plants (often in Mexico and Asia) produce electronic goods for a variety of customers, including **Cisco Systems, Hewlett-Packard,** and **Sony.** Most contract manufacturers make goods for several well-known companies. For example, the **Flextronics** plant in Guadalajara, Mexico, makes **Sony** Web TV set-top boxes, **PalmPilots, Hewlett-**

EXHIBIT 20-2
Differences Between Job and
Process Costing

	Job Costing	Process Costing
Cost object	Job	Process
Outputs	Single units or small batches, with large differences between jobs	Large quantities of identical units
Extent of averaging	Less averaging—costs are averaged over the small number of units in a batch (often 1 unit)	More averaging—costs are averaged over the many identical units in the large batch

Packard printers, and **Johnson & Johnson** blood glucose monitors. Clearly, the plant must carefully track the costs of each of these separate jobs.

Job costing is not confined to manufacturers. Exhibit 20-1 shows that service organizations such as hospitals and physicians also use job costing. A hospital might consider each medical procedure a different job, while a doctor considers each individual patient a job. Professional service providers such as architects, accountants, and attorneys use job costing to determine the costs of jobs for individual clients. Merchandisers like **Amazon.com** can use job costing to determine the cost of meeting each customer order.

Job costing is most complex for manufacturers, so this chapter focuses on job costing in a manufacturing setting. The last section of the chapter applies the same principles to nonmanufacturing companies.

JOB COST RECORD Let's consider how a manufacturer, E-Z-Boy Furniture Company, could use job costing. For E-Z-Boy, each individual customer order can be treated as a different job. **Job cost records** are documents used to accumulate the costs of individual jobs. Exhibit 20-3 shows a completed job cost record for the **Macy's** New York City order of ten recliner chairs from E-Z-Boy, Job 293. The job cost record has separate sections for the costs of direct materials, direct labor, and manufacturing overhead allocated to Job 293. The total cost of the job is $1,220. The average cost of each of the ten recliners is $122 ($1,220 ÷ 10).

JOB COST RECORD. Document used to accumulate the costs of an individual job.

EXHIBIT 20-3
Job Cost Record

Job Cost Record — E-Z-Boy

Job No. 293
Customer Name and Address: Macy's New York City
Job Description: 10 recliner chairs

Date Promised	7-31	Date Started	7-24	Date Completed	7-29

Date	Direct Materials		Direct Labor		Manufacturing Overhead Allocated		
	Requisition Numbers	Amount	Labor Time Record Numbers	Amount	Date	Rate	Amount
20X5 7-24	334	$ 90	236, 251, 258	$150	7-29	80% of direct labor cost	$320
25	338	180	264, 269, 273, 291	200			
28	347	230	305	50			

Overall Cost Summary

Direct materials .... $ 500
Direct labor 400
Manufacturing Overhead Allocated 320

Totals		$500		$400	Total Job Cost $1,220

Managers use job cost data like E-Z-Boy's job cost record in Exhibit 20-3 to plan and control manufacturing operations. Suppose managers planned to spend $450 on direct materials for Job 293. The $500 actual cost exceeds the plan by more than 10%. Managers can investigate this cost overrun to help reduce costs in the future.

The company starts a job cost record like Exhibit 20-3 when it begins working on a job. Records of jobs in process (started but not yet completed) form a subsidiary ledger for the general ledger account Work in Process Inventory. ➡ As costs are incurred for a particular job, they are added to the job cost record in the subsidiary ledger and the Work in Process Inventory in the general ledger. When the job is completed, its costs are totaled and transferred out of Work in Process Inventory into Finished Goods Inventory. When the job's output is sold, its costs are moved out of Finished Goods Inventory into Cost of Goods Sold. Exhibit 20-4 summarizes this process.

● DAILY EXERCISE 20-4

◄ For a review of ledgers and subsidiary ledgers, see Chapter 6, p. 240.

EXHIBIT 20-4   Job Costing—Flow of Costs Through the Accounts

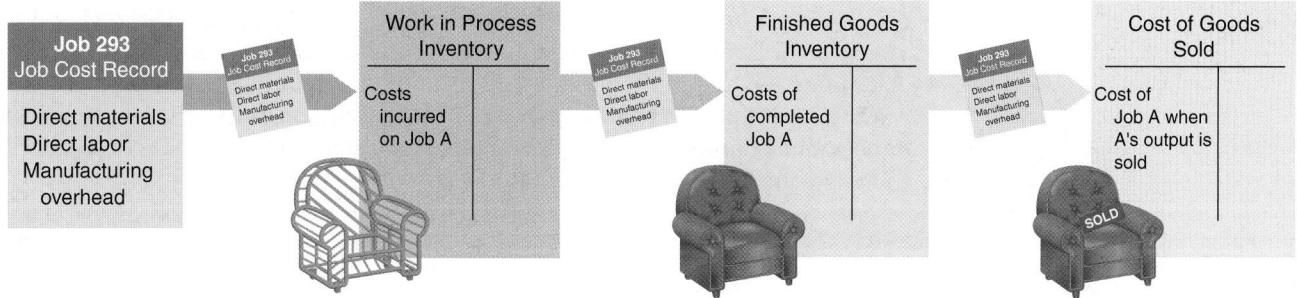

JOB COSTING ILLUSTRATED

We next illustrate accounting in a job costing system. You will see how E-Z-Boy:

1. *Accumulates* total direct material costs, direct labor costs, and manufacturing overhead costs incurred during the period for all jobs,
2. *Assigns* appropriate amounts of these costs to individual jobs such as Job 293.

On December 31, 20X4, E-Z-Boy reports the following inventories:

Materials inventory (many kinds)	$20,000
Work in process inventory (5 jobs)	29,000
Finished goods inventory (unsold recliners from 2 completed jobs)	12,000

The following data summarize transactions for the year 20X5. We will explain the accounting for these transactions, step by step.

1. Materials purchased on account	$320,000
2. Direct materials used for manufacturing	285,000
Indirect materials used for manufacturing	40,000
3. Manufacturing wages incurred	335,000
4. Direct labor on jobs	250,000
Indirect labor to support manufacturing	85,000
5. Depreciation on plant and equipment	50,000
6. Plant utilities	20,000
7. Plant insurance	5,000
8. Property taxes—plant	10,000
9. Manufacturing overhead allocated to jobs	200,000
10. Cost of goods manufactured	740,000
11. Sales on account	996,000
Cost of goods sold	734,000

Accounting for Materials in a Job Costing System

ACCOUNTING FOR PURCHASES   To offer an overview of the big picture of job costing, we use summary entries for the entire year 20X5. In practice, however, companies update their general ledgers more frequently.

Recall that the goals of our accounting process are to *accumulate* the total costs, and then *assign* the appropriate costs to each individual job. We begin by making the entry to *accumulate* the costs. Thus, our first entry is for purchases of materials—in this case, lumber (data from page 801):

(1) Materials Inventory........................   320,000
            Accounts Payable..................   320,000

E-Z-Boy receives the lumber and stores it. Control over materials is established with a subsidiary *materials ledger.* This ledger holds perpetual inventory records that list the quantity and cost of all manufacturing materials on hand. Exhibit 20-5 shows a subsidiary materials ledger record for the lumber that goes into the recliner chairs.

E-Z-Boy's materials are logged in by receiving report number (abbreviated as *Rec. Report No.* in Exhibit 20-5). E-Z-Boy received 20 units of lumber, at $9 each, on July 23. Materials used in the product are recorded by materials requisition number (*Mat. Req. No.*). Exhibit 20-5 shows that E-Z-Boy used ten units of lumber on July 24. Management can use these records to trace materials into the production process and thereby control the amount of materials used in various jobs.

EXHIBIT 20-5
Materials Ledger Record

◉ DAILY EXERCISE 20-5

MATERIALS LEDGER RECORD

E-Z-Boy

ITEM No. B-220   DESCRIPTION   LUMBER/RECLINER CHAIRS

	RECEIVED				USED				BALANCE		
DATE	REC. REPORT No.	UNITS	COST	TOTAL COST	MAT. REQ. No.	UNITS	COST	TOTAL COST	UNITS	COST	TOTAL COST
20X5 7-20									30	$9.00	$270
7-23	678	20	$9.00	$180					50	9.00	450
7-24					334	10	$9.00	$90	40	9.00	360

The general ledger has a Materials Inventory account. This account is supported by the materials subsidiary ledger that includes a separate record for each type of raw material. Exhibit 20-6 illustrates the Materials Inventory general ledger account and the subsidiary ledger for the materials E-Z-Boy uses. The balance of Materials Inventory in the general ledger ($1,170) equals the sum of the balances in the subsidiary materials ledger.

After materials are purchased, the manufacturing process begins with a document called a **materials requisition.** This is a request for materials, prepared by manufacturing personnel. In effect, they ask that the lumber be moved from storage to the manufacturing plant so work can begin. Exhibit 20-7 illustrates a materials requisition for the lumber needed to manufacture the ten recliner chairs in E-Z-Boy's Job 293.

The "Direct Materials" section in the job cost record (Exhibit 20-3) shows how the details of the materials requisitions are posted to the individual job cost records. Follow the $90 cost of the lumber from materials requisition 334 (Exhibit 20-7) to the materials ledger record (Exhibit 20-5) to the job cost record (Exhibit 20-3). Note that all the dollar amounts in Exhibits 20-3 through 20-13 show E-Z-Boy's *costs*— not the prices at which E-Z-Boy *sells* its products.

Technology simplifies the collection of data, including direct material costs. Companies such as **Dell Computer** use electronic bar codes to track material costs,

MATERIALS REQUISITION.
Request for materials, prepared by manufacturing personnel.

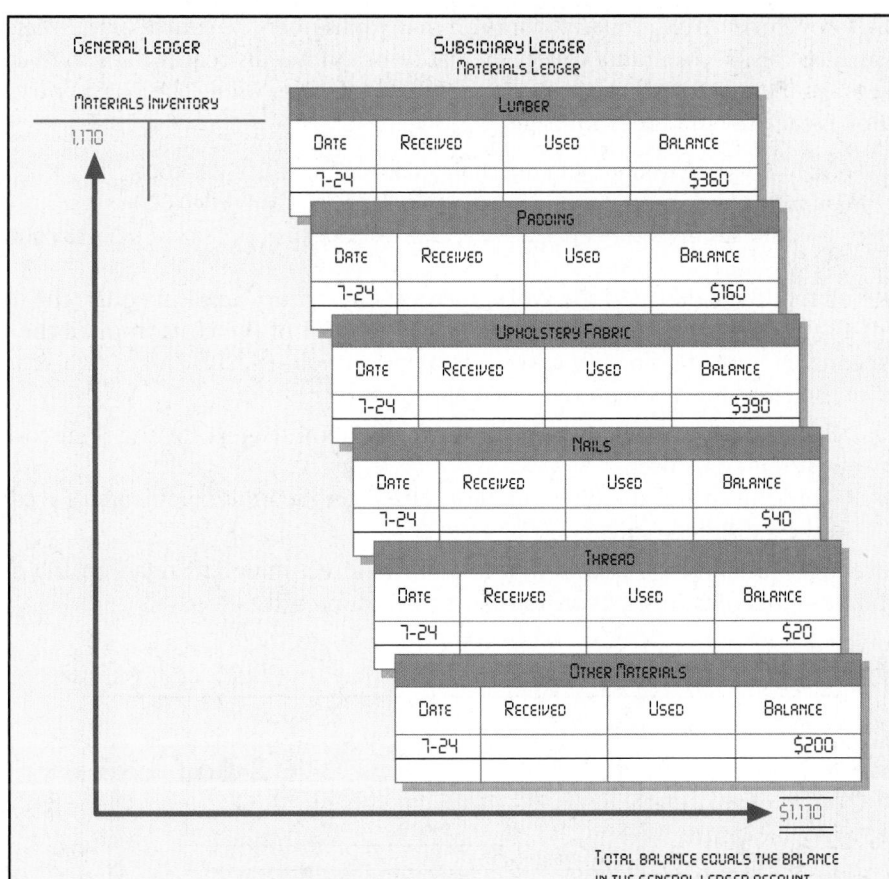

EXHIBIT 20-6
Materials Inventory Accounts

⊙ DAILY EXERCISE 20-6

tracing materials to individual computers by scanning bar codes on the component parts as they are installed.

DIRECT AND INDIRECT MATERIALS   Materials Inventory is debited for the costs of all materials purchased—both direct materials and indirect materials. Note that the Materials Inventory account in Exhibit 20-6 includes the costs of both direct materials (lumber, padding, and upholstery fabric) and indirect materials (nails, thread, and other materials).

When either direct or indirect materials are requisitioned from storage, Materials Inventory and the accompanying account in the subsidiary materials ledger are credited. What account is debited? The answer depends on the type of materials requisitioned. For direct materials, the debit is made directly to Work in Process Inventory. When indirect materials are used, the debit is made to a separate account called Manufacturing Overhead. ➵

Keep this distinction in mind: *Indirect manufacturing costs, such as indirect materials used, are not debited directly to Work in Process Inventory. Instead, they are accumulated in the (separate) Manufacturing Overhead account.*

◄ Recall from Chapter 19, p. 763, that manufacturing overhead includes all manufacturing costs other than direct materials and direct labor.

EXHIBIT 20-7
Materials Requisition

MATERIALS REQUISITION No.	334			
			E-Z-Boy	
DATE	7-24-X5		JOB No.	293
ITEM No.	ITEM	QUANTITY	UNIT COST	AMOUNT
8-220	LUMBER/RECLINER CHAIRS	10	$9.00	$90

E-Z-Boy Furniture Company works on many jobs over the course of the year. At regular intervals, accountants collect the data from materials requisitions to make a single journal entry for all the materials that E-Z-Boy has used. The 20X5 entry for E-Z-Boy is (again, data are from page 801):

(2) Work in Process Inventory (for direct materials) 285,000
        Manufacturing Overhead (for indirect materials) 40,000
            Materials Inventory... 325,000

Recall that the balance of the Work in Process Inventory account equals the total cost of all the jobs currently in process. This is the sum of the costs from all the job cost records of jobs that are still in process. For each job, E-Z-Boy takes two actions to *assign* the cost of direct materials used appropriately:

1. Debit Work in Process Inventory (in the general ledger) for the total cost of direct materials used.
2. Record the cost of the direct materials used on the individual job cost records (in the subsidiary ledger).

For example, Exhibit 20-7 shows that $90 of the direct materials relate to Job 293. Exhibit 20-8 includes this $90 on Job 293's job cost record.

EXHIBIT 20-8
Direct Materials Entry on Job Cost Record

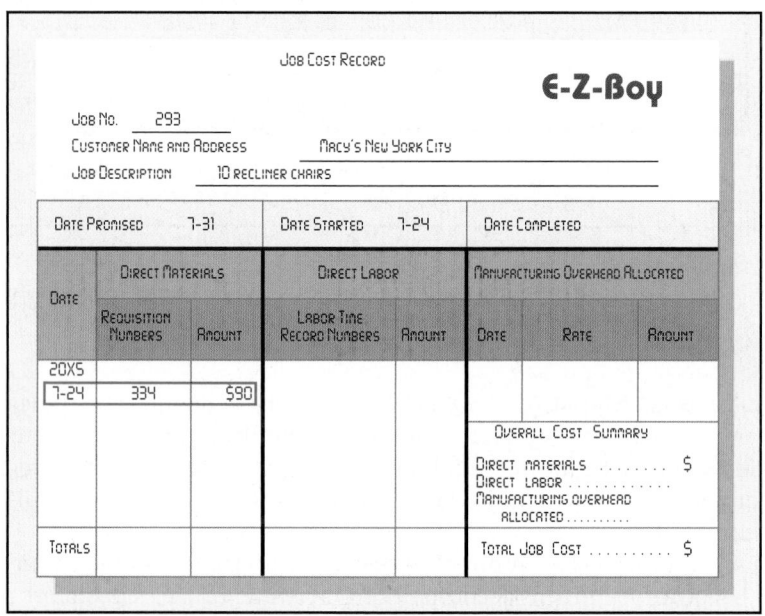

By definition, the costs of indirect materials like nails and thread cannot be traced directly to individual jobs. (If they could be traced to individual jobs, they would be *direct* materials.) Thus, indirect material costs *cannot* be entered in the job cost records of specific jobs. Indirect costs are simply debited to the Manufacturing Overhead account in the general ledger.

The flow of materials costs through the T-accounts is as follows:

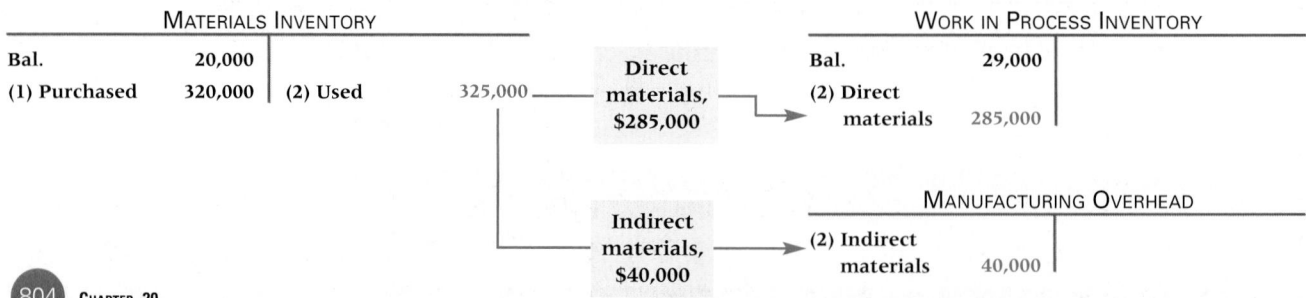

Accounting for Labor in a Job Costing System

Control over labor costs in a job costing system is established through payroll registers and time records. ➥ A **labor time record** identifies the employee, the amount of time spent on a particular job, and the labor cost charged to the job. Time records are accumulated for each job to determine its total direct labor cost. Exhibit 20-9 shows a labor time record used in a job costing system like E-Z-Boy's.

◄◄ Chapter 11, defined the payroll register as a special journal that lists each employee and the data to record payroll amounts.

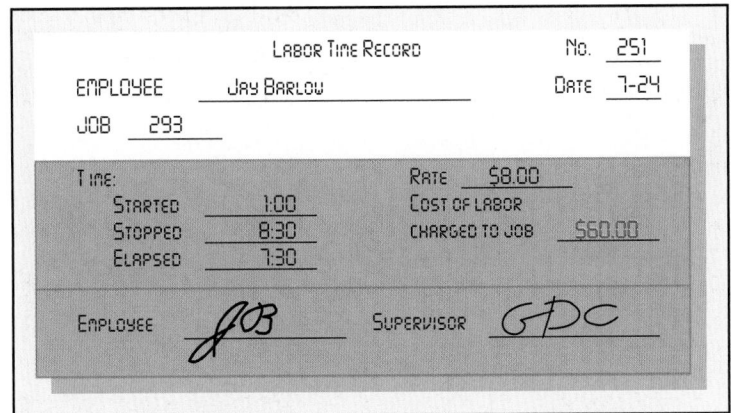

EXHIBIT 20-9
Labor Time Record

LABOR TIME RECORD. Identifies the employee, the amount of time spent on a particular job, and the labor cost charged to the job; a record that manufacturing firms commonly use to trace direct labor time to specific job cost records.

Technology can simplify collection of direct labor costs. Companies can set up computer terminals on the production floor. At various stages in the manufacturing process of **Saturn** automobiles, for example, employees insert their identification cards into the terminals. This system captures direct labor time and cost without detailed labor documents.

E-Z-Boy's entry for 20X5 *accumulates* and records the actual labor costs E-Z-Boy incurred for all jobs (data from page 801):

(3) Manufacturing Wages... 335,000	
Wages Payable	335,000

DIRECT AND INDIRECT LABOR   Similar to the distinction between direct and indirect materials costs, direct and indirect labor costs are *assigned* separately. Direct labor is debited directly to Work in Process Inventory. Indirect labor cannot be traced to a specific job so it is added to the Manufacturing Overhead account. This assignment of labor cost credits Manufacturing Wages (data from page 801):

⊙ **DAILY EXERCISE 20-9**

(4) Work in Process Inventory (for direct labor) 250,000	
Manufacturing Overhead (for indirect labor) 85,000	
Manufacturing Wages	335,000

This entry brings the balance in Manufacturing Wages to zero, its transferred balance now divided between Work in Process Inventory (direct labor) and Manufacturing Overhead (indirect labor) as shown in the following T-accounts:

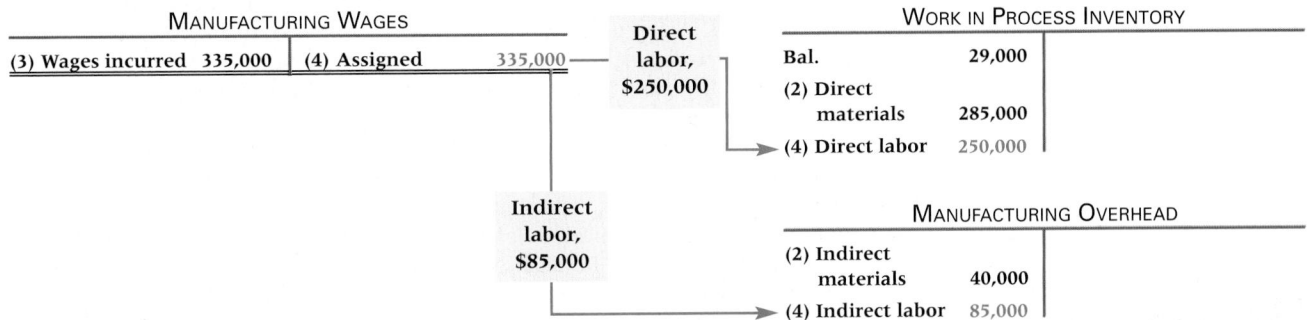

Assume that $150 of one day's direct labor cost is for Job 293. E-Z-Boy Furniture enters Job 293's direct labor on the job cost record. The $150 amount in the Direct Labor section of Exhibit 20-10 includes Jay Barlow's wages of $60 (from labor time record 251, Exhibit 20-9) and the labor costs entered on labor time records 236 and 258 (not shown).

EXHIBIT 20-10   Direct Labor Entry on Job Cost Record

JOB COST RECORD

E-Z-Boy

Job No. ___293___
Customer Name and Address   Macy's New York City
Job Description   10 recliner chairs

Date Promised	7-31	Date Started	7-24	Date Completed		
Date	Direct Materials		Direct Labor		Manufacturing Overhead Allocated		
	Requisition Numbers	Amount	Labor Time Record Numbers	Amount	Date	Rate	Amount
20X5 7-24	334	$90	236, 251, 258	$150			

Overall Cost Summary

Direct materials .... $
Direct labor ....
Manufacturing overhead
    allocated ....

| Totals | | | | | Total Job Cost .... $ | | |

The Work in Process Inventory account now contains the costs of direct materials and direct labor charged to Job 293—and the costs of many other jobs as well. Work in Process Inventory serves as a control account, with the job cost records giving the supporting details for each job.

To see why, keep in mind that the total direct labor debits to Work in Process Inventory equal the total direct labor costs assigned to all the individual jobs worked on during the period (and recorded on the individual job cost records). Similarly, the total direct material debits to Work in Process Inventory equal the total costs of direct materials used on all the jobs worked on during the period (and recorded on their job cost records). The job cost records thus serve as a subsidiary ledger for the general ledger balance in Work in Process Inventory.

THINK IT OVER   How can the materials inventory subsidiary ledger (Exhibit 20-6), labor time records (Exhibit 20-9), and job cost records (Exhibits 20-8 and 20-10) help managers run the company more effectively and efficiently?

Answer: Managers can look at the materials inventory subsidiary ledger to see when inventories of individual materials like lumber, padding, upholstery fabric, nails, and thread are running low, so they can decide when to reorder.

Managers can use the labor time records in two ways: (1) to control employees, and (2) to control labor costs incurred on individual jobs. First, suppose an employee is paid for 7 1/2 hours of work per day. Adding across all her labor time records for each job she worked on during the day should yield a total of 7 1/2 hours worked. If not, the manager needs to find out how the employee spent any time unaccounted for. Second, managers can use labor time records to track how much time employees spend on a particular job. Managers need to ensure that employees work efficiently—if they spend longer than expected on a job, the job may not yield a profit.

The job cost record tallies materials, labor, and manufacturing overhead as they are assigned to the job. If costs exceed budget, managers must do a better job of controlling costs in the future, or else they may need to raise the sale price on similar jobs to ensure that the company remains profitable.

How Has Information Technology Changed Job Costing?

The flow of costs through the T-accounts and the journal entries applies to systems ranging from simple manual costing to sophisticated automated database systems. The main difference is in the source of data underlying the costs. In traditional systems, the sources of data include source documents such as material requisitions, labor time records, and job cost records like those we have described. These documents can be paper-based or automated.

Highly automated systems may have no physical source documents. Employees use bar codes to record materials used and scan their identification cards to record their labor time. The software immediately tracks these material and labor costs to the specific job, and updates the general ledger accounts (for example, Materials Inventory, Work in Process Inventory, Manufacturing Wages, and Manufacturing Overhead). Automated database systems may not store data in the form of separate job cost records. But when employees enter the job number, the system quickly tallies costs assigned to the job so far.

Advances in information technology may

1. Eliminate physical source documents
2. Hasten the speed with which
   a. Materials and labor costs are linked to specific jobs
   b. The general ledger accounts are updated

However, the cost flows and journal entries are identical to those we have described for E-Z-Boy.

e-Accounting

Radio-Frequency Identification System: Smart Tags for Tracking Parts and Products

How do manufacturers trace direct materials to products? The standard way to identify and follow a product through the factory and down the supply chain is the familiar bar code. Bar codes have been used for 25 years on everything from cans of beans to car bodies. Each of its stripes stands for a coded number. But the stripes are unique, like a thumbprint. If the contents or the destination of the part or product change, someone must print and attach a new bar code level.

So bar codes require a lot of labor: As many as 60% of workers in warehouses spend time checking bar codes. And they must line up each item individually for scanning, even in automated identification systems.

Now there is a better method, called radio-frequency identification, or RFID, which uses electromagnetic waves. An RFID system uses a plastic tag, sometimes as small as two matches laid side by side. The tag's digital memory chip is the size of a pinhead, and it contains far more information than a bar code. And because radio is used, tagged products don't have to be aligned carefully for scanning.

In its more sophisticated "read-write" version, RFID has a stunning advantage. Without touching or removing the tag, users can alter the information on it. Workers can change the itinerary of a component on the factory floor, for example, or the destination of a shipment. The read-write tag is really a small data base that can be synchronized with a company's other data bases—and, eventually, with customers who have RFID technology.

Source: Adapted from Gene Bylinsky, "Hot new technologies for American factories," *Fortune,* June 26, 2000, pp. 288A–288K.

SUMMARY PROBLEM

www.prenhall.com/horngren

Mid-Chapter Assessment

Ecosphere Associates, Ltd. in Tucson, Arizona, produces ecospheres—self-sustaining enclosed glass spheres that include water, algae, tiny shrimp, and snails. Suppose Ecosphere has the following transactions:

a. Purchased raw materials on account, $35,000.

b. Materials costing $30,000 were requisitioned for production. Of this total, $3,000 were indirect materials.

c. Labor time records for the month show direct labor of $22,000, and indirect labor of $4,000.

Required

Prepare journal entries for each transaction.

Solution

a. Materials Inventory............................ 35,000
      Accounts Payable   35,000

When materials are purchased on account:

- Debit (increase) the Materials Inventory asset for the *cost* of the materials, and
- Credit (increase) Accounts Payable to record the liability for the cost of the materials.

b. Work in Process Inventory.................. 27,000
    Manufacturing Overhead.................... 3,000
      Materials Inventory   30,000

When materials are requisitioned (used) in production, we record the movement of materials out of materials inventory and into production:

- Debit (increase) Work in Process Inventory for the cost of the *direct* materials (in this case, $27,000—the $30,000 total materials requisitioned less the $3,000 indirect materials)
- Debit (increase) Manufacturing Overhead for the cost of the *indirect* materials
- Credit (decrease) Materials Inventory for the cost of both direct and indirect materials moved out of the materials storage area and into production

c. Manufacturing Wages 26,000
      Wages Payable...........................   26,000

To record total labor costs actually incurred ($22,000 + 4,000):

- Debit (increase) Manufacturing Wages
- Credit (increase) Wages Payable to record the liability for wages incurred, but not paid

    Work in Process Inventory.................. 22,000
    Manufacturing Overhead.................... 4,000
      Manufacturing Wages   26,000

To assign the labor costs:

- Debit (increase) Work in Process Inventory for the cost of the *direct* labor
- Debit (increase) Manufacturing Overhead for the cost of the *indirect* labor
- Credit (decrease) Manufacturing Wages for the cost of both direct and indirect labor

Objective 3
Account for manufacturing overhead in a manufacturer's job costing system

ACCOUNTING FOR MANUFACTURING OVERHEAD IN A JOB COSTING SYSTEM

All manufacturing overhead costs are *accumulated* as debits to a single general ledger account—Manufacturing Overhead. We have already recorded the indirect materials (entry 2) and indirect labor (entry 4) manufacturing overhead costs. Entries 5–8 record the other manufacturing overhead costs E-Z-Boy Furniture actually incurred, as given on page 801. The account titles in parentheses indicate the specific records debited in the overhead subsidiary ledger.

(5)	Manufacturing Overhead (Depreciation—Plant and Equipment) ...	50,000	
	Accumulated Depreciation—Plant and Equipment................		50,000
(6)	Manufacturing Overhead (Plant Utilities)...	20,000	
	Cash..		20,000
(7)	Manufacturing Overhead (Plant Insurance)	5,000	
	Prepaid Insurance—Plant		5,000
(8)	Manufacturing Overhead (Property Taxes—Plant).........................	10,000	
	Property Taxes Payable		10,000

The actual manufacturing overhead costs (such as indirect materials, indirect labor, and depreciation, utilities, insurance and property taxes related to the plant) are debited to the Manufacturing Overhead account as they occur throughout the year. By the end of the year, the Manufacturing Overhead account has accumulated all the actual overhead costs as debits:

MANUFACTURING OVERHEAD

(2) Indirect materials	40,000	
(4) Indirect labor	85,000	
(5) Depreciation—plant and equipment	50,000	
(6) Plant utilities	20,000	
(7) Plant insurance	5,000	
(8) Property taxes—plant	10,000	
Total overhead cost	210,000	

THINK IT OVER

How can managers use the manufacturing overhead subsidiary ledger to control overhead costs?

Answer: Managers plan the expected amount of each individual manufacturing overhead cost, such as plant-related depreciation, utilities, and insurance. Then they investigate why actual costs differ from planned costs. For example, if plant utilities are higher than expected, managers will want to know why. Did utility rates increase? Did workers waste electricity or water? Was there a delay in installing more energy-efficient machinery? Answers to these questions can help managers control (reduce) utility costs and develop more accurate estimates of future utility costs.

Now you have seen how the overhead costs are *accumulated* in the accounting records. But how are overhead costs *assigned* to individual jobs? Materials requisitions and labor time records make it easy to trace direct materials and direct labor costs to specific jobs. But as you can see from the manufacturing overhead T-account, overhead includes a variety of costs that cannot be traced to individual jobs. For example, it is impossible to say that a specific amount of the cost incurred to cool the plant is related to Job 293. Yet manufacturing overhead costs are as essential as direct materials and direct labor in producing goods, so we must find some way to assign these costs to specific jobs.

Allocating Overhead Costs to Jobs

Managers want to know the costs incurred in each job, including both direct and indirect costs. Accountants use **cost tracing** to assign direct costs (such as direct materials and direct labor) to cost objects such as jobs. They use **cost allocation** to assign manufacturing overhead and other indirect costs to cost objects. The general term **cost assignment** refers to tracing direct costs and allocating indirect costs to cost objects (jobs, in a job costing system).

COST TRACING. Assigning direct costs (such as direct materials and direct labor) to cost objects (such as jobs or production processes).

COST ALLOCATION. Assigning indirect costs (such as manufacturing overhead) to cost objects (such as jobs or production processes).

COST ASSIGNMENT. Tracing direct costs to cost objects and allocating indirect costs to cost objects.

```
                  ┌─  Direct Costs          Cost Tracing
                  │   (Direct materials and direct labor)  ───────────►    Cost
Cost Assignment ──┤                                                        Object
                  │   Indirect Costs        Cost Allocation                (Job)
                  └─  (Manufacturing overhead)   ···············►
```

Direct material and direct labor costs are traced directly to each job, as we've seen. But managers also want to know the *total* manufacturing costs incurred on each job, including manufacturing overhead costs. Somehow, the company must allocate to each individual job its share of the wide variety of indirect manufacturing costs like depreciation and insurance on the plant and equipment, indirect materials, and indirect labor.

CHOOSING AN ALLOCATION BASE The key to assigning indirect manufacturing costs to jobs is to identify a manufacturing overhead allocation base. The **allocation base** is a common denominator that links indirect manufacturing overhead costs to the cost objects. Ideally, the allocation base is the primary cost driver of manufacturing overhead costs. For example, in many companies, manufacturing overhead costs rise and fall with direct labor costs. In this case, accountants can use either direct labor costs or direct labor hours as the manufacturing overhead allocation base. The more direct labor a job uses, the more manufacturing overhead cost the job is allocated. This is a wise choice if direct labor is a driver of manufacturing overhead costs.

But direct labor is not always the best allocation base. Labor is less important in companies that have highly automated production processes, like **Saturn.** Saturn's manufacturing overhead costs are primarily machine-related. Plant depreciation, maintenance, and utilities are likely to fluctuate with the number of machine hours used. Companies with automated operations often use machine hours as the manufacturing overhead allocation base. The important point is that the cost allocation base should be the primary driver of the manufacturing overhead costs.

For simplicity, we'll assume the company uses only one allocation base to assign manufacturing overhead costs to jobs. Chapter 25 relaxes this assumption. There, we'll see how many companies use a method called *activity-based costing* to identify several different allocation bases that more accurately link indirect costs with the jobs that caused those costs. Because activity-based costing is a straightforward extension of the single allocation base method, it is important to begin by developing a solid understanding of the simpler system we describe here.

DEVELOPING A PREDETERMINED MANUFACTURING OVERHEAD RATE The most accurate allocation cannot be made until the total amount of the manufacturing overhead cost is known, at the end of the year. But that would be much too late. Managers making decisions today cannot wait until the end of the year for product cost information. To solve this timing problem, accountants develop an estimated manufacturing overhead allocation rate at the beginning of the year. This **predetermined manufacturing overhead rate** (sometimes called the **budgeted manufacturing overhead rate**) is computed as follows:

$$\text{Predetermined manufacturing overhead rate} = \frac{\text{Total estimated manufacturing overhead costs}}{\text{Total estimated quantity of the manufacturing overhead allocation base}}$$

Both the numerator and the denominator of the predetermined manufacturing overhead rate are based on *estimated* amounts. These are estimated *before* the year begins. They cannot be actual amounts because actual overhead costs and the actual quantity of the allocation base are not known until after the end of the period. Companies use this predetermined manufacturing overhead rate to allocate overhead to individual jobs.

Six Steps in Allocating Manufacturing Overhead Cost to Jobs

Companies follow six steps in allocating manufacturing overhead cost to jobs:

1. Estimate the total overhead cost for the planning period, which is usually a year. Late in 20X4, E-Z-Boy predicted overhead costs for 20X5 of $220,000.
2. Identify the manufacturing overhead (cost) allocation base. As the Manufacturing Overhead section of Exhibit 20-3 shows, E-Z-Boy selected direct labor cost.

ALLOCATION BASE. A common denominator that links indirect costs to cost objects. Ideally, the allocation base is the primary cost driver that causes the indirect cost to be incurred.

PREDETERMINED MANUFACTURING OVERHEAD RATE. Estimated manufacturing overhead rate computed at the beginning of the year, calculated as the total estimated manufacturing overhead costs divided by the total estimated quantity of the manufacturing overhead allocation base. Also called the budgeted manufacturing overhead rate.

DAILY EXERCISE 20-11

3. Estimate the total quantity of the overhead allocation base. E-Z-Boy production managers expect to incur $275,000 of direct labor cost during 20X5.

4. Compute the predetermined manufacturing overhead rate as follows:

$$\text{Predetermined manufacturing overhead rate} = \frac{\text{Total estimated manufacturing overhead costs}}{\text{Total estimated quantity of the manufacturing overhead allocation base}}$$

$$= \frac{\text{Total estimated manufacturing overhead costs}}{\text{Total estimated direct labor costs}}$$

$$= \frac{\$220,000}{\$275,000} = 0.80 \text{ or } 80\%$$

Thus, the predetermined manufacturing overhead rate is computed as the total *estimated* manufacturing overhead cost (estimated *before* the year starts, as in step 1) divided by the total *estimated* quantity of the allocation base (also estimated *before* the year starts, as in step 3). Because the numerator and the denominator are both based on amounts that are *estimated before* the year starts, this overhead rate is *predetermined.*

5. Obtain *actual* quantities of the overhead allocation base used by individual jobs, as the year unfolds. The total actual direct labor cost of Job 293 is $400, as Exhibits 20-3 and 20-11 show.

6. Allocate manufacturing overhead cost to jobs by multiplying the *predetermined* manufacturing overhead rate (computed in step 4) by the *actual* quantity of the allocation base used by each job (from step 5). The same predetermined rate (80% of direct labor cost) is used to allocate manufacturing overhead to all jobs worked on throughout the year. Because the total direct labor cost for Job 293 is $400, and the predetermined overhead allocation rate is 80% of direct labor cost, the manufacturing overhead allocated to Job 293 is $320 ($400 × 0.80).

The complete job cost record for Job 293 in Exhibit 20-11 provides details supporting the $1,220 total cost and the $122 ($1,220 ÷ 10) unit cost of the **Macy's** order.

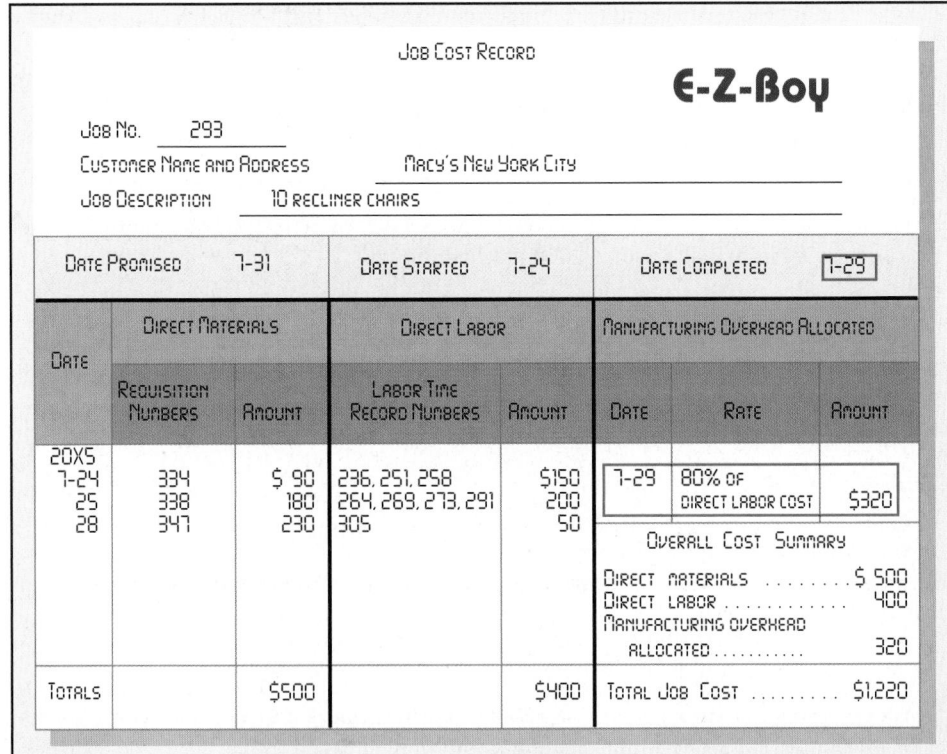

EXHIBIT 20-11
Manufacturing Overhead Entry on Job Cost Record

⊙ DAILY EXERCISE 20-11

⊙ DAILY EXERCISE 20-12

⊙ DAILY EXERCISE 20-13

Of course, E-Z-Boy has made similar allocations of manufacturing overhead for each of the other jobs worked on during 20X5. The total overhead allocated to all jobs is 80% of the total $250,000 direct labor cost, or $200,000 (data from page 801). The journal entry to allocate manufacturing overhead costs to Work in Process Inventory is

| (9) | Work in Process Inventory .... | 200,000 | |
| | Manufacturing Overhead.................... | | 200,000 |

E-Z-Boy's allocation of manufacturing overhead flows through the T-accounts as follows:

MANUFACTURING OVERHEAD			
(2) Indirect materials	40,000	(9) Allocated	200,000
(4) Indirect labor	85,000		
(5) Depreciation—plant and equipment	50,000		
(6) Plant utilities	20,000		
(7) Plant insurance	5,000		
(8) Property taxes—plant	10,000		
Actual overhead cost	210,000		
Bal.	10,000		

WORK IN PROCESS INVENTORY		
Bal.	29,000	
(2) Direct materials	285,000	
(4) Direct labor	250,000	
(9) Manufacturing overhead allocated	200,000	

Note that after allocation, there is still a $10,000 debit balance in the Manufacturing Overhead account. This means that E-Z-Boy's actual overhead costs exceed the amount of overhead allocated to Work in Process Inventory. We say that E-Z-Boy's Manufacturing Overhead is *underallocated*. We'll discuss how accountants correct this problem on page 814.

WORK IT OUT

The Jarvis Company allocates manufacturing overhead cost based on machine hours. The company records the following actual costs for the year:

Indirect labor	$40,000	Rent on plant	$16,000
Plant supplies...................	20,000	Plant utilities	10,000
Machinery repair.............	14,000	Sales commissions.............	30,000
Advertising	6,000	Direct labor........................	70,000

Jarvis had budgeted 60,000 machine hours and $90,000 of manufacturing overhead costs for the year. Jarvis actually used 64,000 machine hours.

Questions

1. Compute the predetermined manufacturing overhead rate.
2. How much is actual manufacturing overhead?
3. Compute the allocated manufacturing overhead.
4. What is the ending balance in the Manufacturing Overhead account?

Answers

1. Predetermined manufacturing overhead rate based on budgeted machine hours = $90,000 ÷ 60,000 machine hours = $1.50 per machine hour.
2. Actual manufacturing overhead = $100,000 ($40,000 + $20,000 + $14,000 + $16,000 + $10,000).
3. Allocated manufacturing overhead equals the *actual* quantity of the allocation base (machine hours) multiplied by the *predetermined* overhead rate:

Allocated manufacturing overhead = 64,000 machine hours × $1.50 per machine hour = $96,000

4.

MANUFACTURING OVERHEAD			
Actual costs (from Question 2)	100,000	Allocated costs (from Question 3)	96,000
Bal.	4,000		

There is a $4,000 debit balance in the Manufacturing Overhead account. Jarvis's Manufacturing Overhead is *underallocated* because the actual costs exceed the allocated costs by $4,000.

ACCOUNTING FOR FINISHED GOODS, SALES, AND COST OF GOODS SOLD

As each job is completed, its total cost moves out of Work in Process Inventory into Finished Goods Inventory. Sales of finished goods are recorded as they occur.

The $740,000 cost of goods manufactured (from the data on page 801) is the cost of the jobs that E-Z-Boy finished this year. E-Z-Boy credits Work in Process Inventory as the jobs leave the plant floor. The debit is to Finished Goods Inventory because the completed products move into the finished goods storage area. A summary entry for E-Z-Boy's goods completed in 20X5 is as follows:

(10) Finished Goods Inventory 740,000
        Work in Process Inventory   740,000

In turn, E-Z-Boy makes the usual entries for sales and cost of goods sold (data from page 801):

(11) Accounts Receivable 996,000
        Sales Revenue   996,000
      Cost of Goods Sold 734,000
        Finished Goods Inventory   734,000

The key T-accounts for E-Z-Boy's manufacturing costs now show

WORK IN PROCESS INVENTORY					FINISHED GOODS INVENTORY					COST OF GOODS SOLD	
Bal.	29,000	(10)	740,000 →	Cost of goods manufactured (completed this period)	Bal.	12,000	(11)	734,000 →	Cost of goods sold this period	→ (11)	734,000
(2)	285,000			→ (10)	740,000						
(4)	250,000			Bal.	18,000						
(9)	200,000										
Bal.	24,000										

The Work in Process Inventory T-account summarizes what happens on the manufacturing plant floor. We start the period with beginning inventory of jobs that were started but not finished last period ($29,000). During the current period, the plant uses direct materials ($285,000) and direct labor ($250,000), and manufacturing overhead is allocated to the jobs passing through the plant floor ($200,000). Some jobs are completed, and their costs are transferred out to Finished Goods Inventory ($740,000). We end the period with other jobs started but not finished during this period ($24,000).

Notice also that the Work in Process T-account summarizes the Schedule of Cost of Goods Manufactured. For E-Z-Boy, the Work in Process T-account shows

● DAILY EXERCISE 20-14

● DAILY EXERCISE 20-15

● DAILY EXERCISE 20-16

Beginning Work in Process Inventory..................		$ 29,000
Current manufacturing costs:		
Direct materials used	$285,000	
Direct labor	250,000	
Manufacturing overhead allocated....................	200,000	735,000
Total manufacturing costs to account for		764,000
Ending Work in Process Inventory.......................		24,000
Cost of Goods Manufactured................................		$740,000

DISPOSING OF UNDERALLOCATED OR OVERALLOCATED MANUFACTURING OVERHEAD

UNDERALLOCATED (MANUFACTURING) OVERHEAD. The amount of manufacturing overhead allocated to Work in Process Inventory is *less* than the amount of manufacturing overhead costs actually incurred.

OVERALLOCATED (MANUFACTURING) OVERHEAD. The amount of manufacturing overhead allocated to Work in Process Inventory is *more* than the amount of manufacturing overhead costs actually incurred.

During the year, E-Z-Boy's accountants debit Manufacturing Overhead for the overhead costs the company actually incurred, and credit Manufacturing Overhead for amounts allocated to Work in Process Inventory. The total debits rarely equal the total credits. Why? Because overhead is allocated to jobs using a *predetermined* allocation rate that represents the *expected* relation between overhead costs and the allocation base. In our example, the $10,000 debit balance of Manufacturing Overhead shown on page 812 is called **underallocated manufacturing overhead** (or simply **underallocated overhead**) because the amount of manufacturing overhead allocated to Work in Process Inventory is *less* than the amount actually incurred. (**Overallocated manufacturing overhead** is just the opposite.)

Accountants dispose of underallocated and overallocated overhead at year end, when the Manufacturing Overhead account is closed. When overhead is underallocated, as in our example, a credit to Manufacturing Overhead brings the account balance to zero. What account is debited?

To see the answer, you need to understand why $10,000 of manufacturing overhead was underallocated. In our example, E-Z-Boy's accountants expected to incur 20X5 manufacturing overhead at the predetermined rate of

$$\frac{\$220,000 \ \textit{expected } \textbf{manufacturing overhead costs}}{\$275,000 \ \textit{expected } \textbf{direct labor cost}} = 80\%$$

The accountants computed this 80% manufacturing overhead rate before they knew the *actual* manufacturing overhead cost and the *actual* quantity of the allocation base (direct labor cost, in this example).

Without a crystal ball to foretell the future, it would be surprising indeed if *actual* manufacturing overhead costs and *actual* quantities of the allocation base—which are not known until the end of the year—exactly match the expected amounts. At the end of 20X5, E-Z-Boy's actual manufacturing overhead rate turns out to be

$$\frac{\$210,000 \ \textit{actual } \textbf{manufacturing overhead costs}}{\$250,000 \ \textit{actual } \textbf{direct labor cost}} = 84\%$$

If E-Z-Boy's accountants had a crystal ball at the beginning of the year, they would have predicted a manufacturing overhead rate of 84%. But they did not. They *underestimated* the manufacturing overhead rate, expecting it to be only 80%.

Because the predetermined manufacturing overhead rate that E-Z-Boy used to allocate overhead to each job was *less* than the actual manufacturing overhead rate, the company allocated too *little* manufacturing overhead to every job. In other words, every job worked on in 20X5 was *undercosted*. To correct this error, the cost of these jobs should be *increased*.

Ideally, E-Z-Boy would go back and increase the cost of each individual job. Many companies use software that automatically corrects each job at the end of the year. In companies without such software, accountants usually close the balance in the Manufacturing Overhead account to Cost of Goods Sold, because most of the jobs have been sold (especially in a company that follows a just-in-time philosophy).

In this case, the jobs E-Z-Boy worked on during the year are undercosted. Because the jobs in Cost of Goods Sold are *undercosted,* the correction should increase (debit) Cost of Goods Sold, as shown in the following journal entry:

(12)   Cost of Goods Sold   10,000
            Manufacturing Overhead   10,000

◉ DAILY EXERCISE 20-17

◉ DAILY EXERCISE 20-18

The T-accounts show that the Manufacturing Overhead balance is now zero:

MANUFACTURING OVERHEAD				COST OF GOODS SOLD	
Actual	210,000	Allocated	200,000	734,000	
		Closed	10,000 →	10,000	

Exhibit 20-12 summarizes the accounting for manufacturing overhead:

- Before the period
- During the period
- At the end of the period

EXHIBIT 20-12
Summary of Accounting for Manufacturing Overhead

Before the Period

$$\text{Compute predetermined manufacturing overhead rate} = \frac{\text{Total estimated manufacturing overhead cost}}{\text{Total estimated quantity of allocation base}}$$

During the Period

$$\text{Allocate the overhead} = \begin{array}{c}\text{Actual quantity of the manufacturing overhead allocation base}\end{array} \times \begin{array}{c}\text{Predetermined manufacturing overhead rate}\end{array}$$

At the End of the Period

Close the Manufacturing Overhead account:

Jobs are *undercosted*   If actual > allocated → *Underallocated* manufacturing overhead
                                Need to *increase* Cost of Goods Sold

                                Cost of Goods Sold   xxx
                                   Manufacturing Overhead   xxx

Jobs are *overcosted*   If actual < allocated → *Overallocated* manufacturing overhead
                                Need to *reduce* Cost of Goods Sold

                                Manufacturing Overhead   xxx
                                   Cost of Goods Sold..................   xxx

---

WORK IT OUT

Suppose E-Z-Boy's actual manufacturing overhead costs were $180,000 rather than $210,000.

Questions

1. What would the actual overhead rate have been?
2. Would manufacturing overhead have been underallocated or overallocated?
3. What journal entry would you make to close the Manufacturing Overhead account?

Answers

1. The actual manufacturing overhead rate would have been

$$\frac{\$180,000 \text{ } actual \text{ manufacturing overhead costs}}{\$250,000 \text{ } actual \text{ direct labor cost}} = 72\%$$

2. The predetermined manufacturing overhead rate (80%) is *higher* than the actual manufacturing overhead rate (72%). In this case, each job would be *overcosted*. And

(*continued*)

Manufacturing Overhead would be *overallocated* by $20,000, as shown in this T-account:

MANUFACTURING OVERHEAD		
Actual	180,000	Allocated $200,000

3. The jobs E-Z-Boy worked on during the year were allocated too much manufacturing overhead. Accordingly, jobs in Cost of Goods Sold were *overcosted*, so the correction should decrease (credit) Cost of Goods Sold, as shown in the following journal entry:

Manufacturing Overhead.............. 20,000
    Cost of Goods Sold..............   20,000

OVERVIEW OF JOB COSTING IN A MANUFACTURING COMPANY

Exhibit 20-13 provides an overview of the E-Z-Boy Furniture Company's job costing illustration. Each entry is keyed to one of the 12 transactions described on pages 801–815 (amounts in thousands). Take the time to study this exhibit carefully.

EXHIBIT 20-13 E-Z-Boy Furniture Company Job Costing Illustration—Flow of Costs Through Accounts (amounts in thousands)

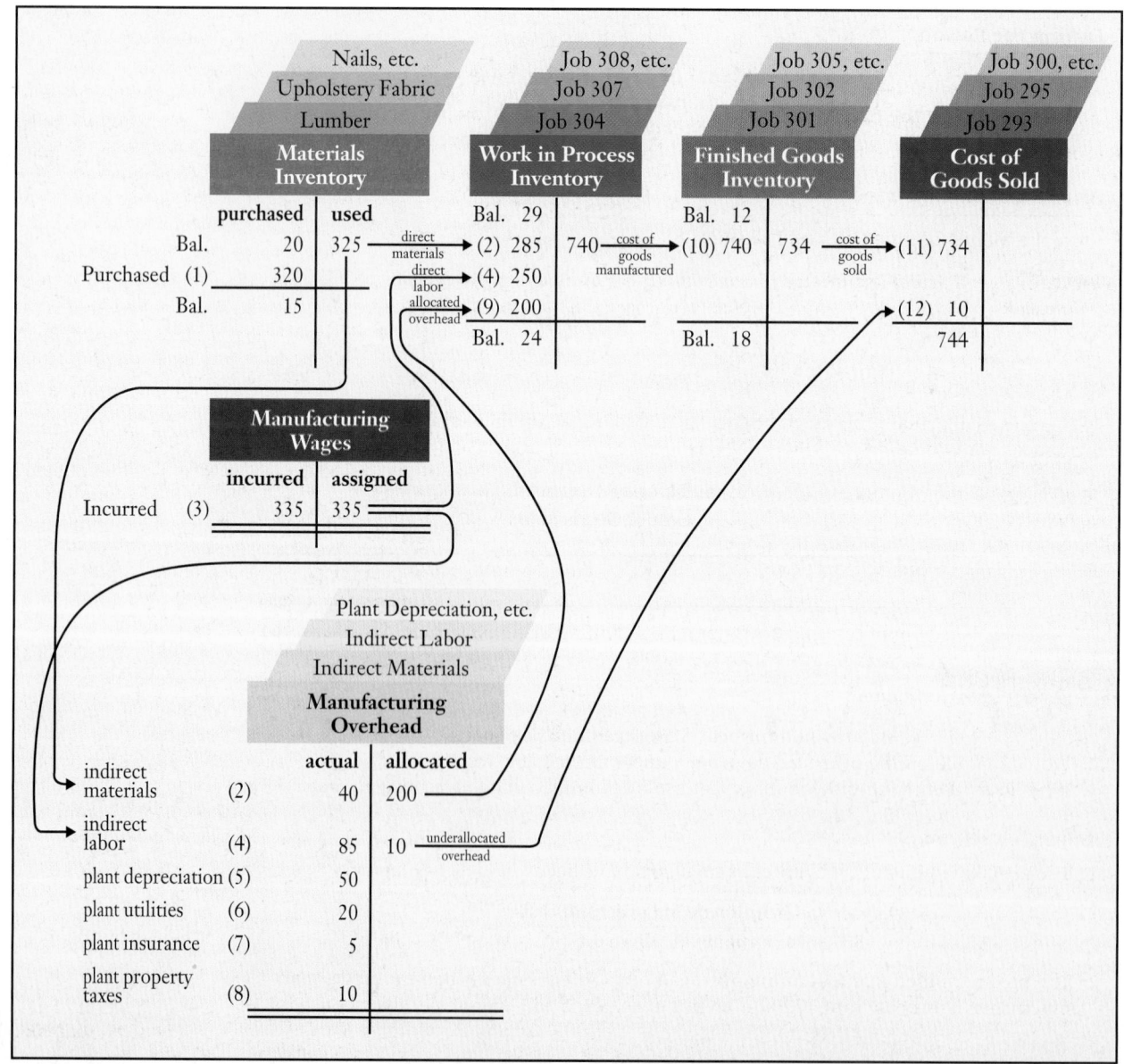

Review the flow of costs through the general ledger accounts:

- Material and labor costs are split between directs costs (traced directly to specific jobs in Work in Process Inventory) and indirect costs (added to Manufacturing Overhead).
- The Work in Process Inventory account summarizes the transactions that occurred on the floor of the manufacturing plant.
- The $740,000 credit to Work in Process (debit to Finished Goods) is the cost of goods manufactured—the manufacturer's counterpart to merchandise purchases.

Study the Manufacturing Overhead account. Actual overhead items are recorded as debits as they occur throughout the period. Credits to the Manufacturing Overhead account represent allocated overhead. E-Z-Boy also closed the $10,000 underallocated Manufacturing Overhead to Cost of Goods Sold.

The T-accounts shown in Exhibit 20-13 are general ledger control accounts. Behind the general ledger accounts appear three examples of subsidiary accounts that would underlie the general ledger control account.

◄ We discussed control accounts in Chapter 6, p. 237

INVENTORIABLE COSTS, NONINVENTORIABLE COSTS, AND JOB COSTING

Objective 4
Account for noninventoriable costs in job costing

Job costing can be complex for manufacturers, because manufacturers have

1. The most complex business operations—they use labor and overhead to transform raw materials into different finished goods
2. Three different kinds of inventory—materials, work in process, and finished goods

Job costing in manufacturing companies has traditionally focused on assigning *manufacturing* costs (*inventoriable* costs) to jobs. This is why our E-Z-Boy illustration focuses on assigning only manufacturing costs to jobs. We have not considered costs incurred in other elements of the value chain, such as R&D or marketing.

The focus on manufacturing costs stems from external reporting requirements. Generally accepted accounting principles require that the accounting records treat only inventoriable costs (manufacturing costs, for a manufacturer) as assets. Costs incurred in other elements of the value chain are treated as expenses (or period costs) for financial accounting. For this reason, the general ledger entries in this chapter have been limited to manufacturing costs.

As we noted in Chapter 19, managers often want to know the full (total) cost of a product or a job, not just the inventoriable cost. The same principles of tracing direct costs and allocating indirect costs (using predetermined allocation rates) apply to noninventoriable period costs incurred in other elements of the value chain: R&D, design, marketing, distribution, and customer service. Managers can add these noninventoriable (period) costs to inventoriable costs to build the full cost of the product or job to guide internal decisions, such as setting long-run average sale prices. However, these noninventoriable costs are assigned to products (or jobs) *only for internal decision making.* No journal entries assign noninventoriable costs to individual jobs, because noninventoriable costs are not assigned to products for external reporting.

JOB COSTING IN A NONMANUFACTURING COMPANY

Management accounting is increasingly important to service firms. Recall that a service firm has no inventoriable costs because it has no inventory. Service firms incur only noninventoriable costs. But managers of service companies still need to know the (noninventoriable) costs of different jobs to make decisions. Thus, we now illustrate the assignment of noninventoriable costs to jobs in a service firm. (A manufacturer such as E-Z-Boy or a merchandiser such as **L.L. Bean** could use the same approach to assign noninventoriable costs to individual jobs.)

Barnett Legal Associates specializes in employment law. Each client is considered a separate job. Barnett's most significant cost is direct labor—attorney time spent on clients' cases. How do service firms trace direct labor to individual jobs?

For automated services like Web site design, information technology consulting, and external auditing, employees simply enter the client number to start on the client's job. Software records the time elapsed until the employee signs off that job. When the service is not automated, employees typically fill out a computerized weekly **time record.** The software tallies the weekly total time spent on each job. Attorney Teresa Fox's time record appears in Exhibit 20-14. Fox's time record shows that she devoted 14 hours to client 367 during the week of June 10, 20X5.

EXHIBIT 20-14
Employee Time Record

BARNETT LEGAL ASSOCIATES
EMPLOYEE TIME RECORD

NAME ___TERESA FOX___
WEEK OF ___6/10/X5___

	M	T	W	TH	F
8:00–8:30	367	520	415	367	415
8:30–9:00					
9:00–9:30					
9:30–10:00					
10:00–10:30			367		
10:30–11:00					
11:00–11:30	520				
11:30–12:00	520				
12:00–12:30					
12:30–1:00					
1:00–1:30	520	367	367	520	415
1:30–2:00			367		
2:00–2:30			415		
2:30–3:00					
3:00–3:30					
3:30–4:00					
4:00–4:30					
4:30–5:00					

WEEKLY SUMMARY:	CLIENT #	TOTAL HOURS
	367	14
	415	13
	520	13

Fox's salary and benefits total $100,000 per year. Assuming a 40-hour workweek and 50 workweeks in each year, Fox has 2,000 available work hours per year (50 weeks × 40 hours per week). Barnett Legal Associates' hourly (cost) rate of employing Teresa Fox is

$$\text{Hourly cost rate to the employer} = \frac{\$100{,}000 \text{ per year}}{2{,}000 \text{ hours per year}} = \$50 \text{ per hour}$$

Fox is the only attorney who served client 367, so the direct labor cost traced to the client is 14 hours × $50 per hour = $700.

Founding partner John Barnett wants to know the total costs of serving clients, not just the direct labor cost. Barnett Legal Associates also allocates indirect costs to individual jobs (clients). The law firm develops a predetermined indirect cost allocation rate, following the same six-step approach that E-Z-Boy (page 810–811) used to develop its indirect manufacturing (overhead) cost rate:

1. *Estimate the total indirect costs.*

   In December 20X4, Barnett estimates that the following indirect costs will be incurred in 20X5:

Office rent..	$200,000
Office support staff	70,000
Maintaining and updating law library for case research	25,000
Advertisements in the yellow pages...	3,000
Sponsorship of the symphony..	2,000
Total indirect costs	$300,000

2. *Identify a cost allocation base.*

Barnett uses direct labor hours as the allocation base, because the number of hours that attorneys work on clients' cases is the main driver of indirect costs.

3. *Estimate the total quantity of the indirect cost allocation base.*

Barnett estimates that its attorneys will work 10,000 direct labor hours in 20X5.

4. *Compute the predetermined indirect cost allocation rate. (Divide step 1 by step 3.)*

$$\text{Predetermined indirect cost allocation rate} = \frac{\$300,000 \text{ expected indirect costs}}{10,000 \text{ expected direct labor hours}}$$

$$= \$30 \text{ per direct labor hour}$$

5. *Obtain the actual quantity of the indirect cost allocation base used by individual jobs, as the year unfolds.*

Exhibit 20-14 shows that client 367 required 14 direct labor hours.

6. *Allocate indirect costs to jobs by multiplying the predetermined indirect cost rate (step 4) by the actual quantity of the allocation base used by each job (step 5).*

Client 367 is allocated indirect costs as follows:

14 direct labor hours × $30/hour = $420

To summarize, the total costs assigned to client 367 are

Direct labor: 14 hours × $50/hour...	$ 700
Indirect costs: 14 hours × $30/hour...	420
Total costs..	$1,120

THINK IT OVER

Would John Barnett want to know the total cost of each job for each of the following purposes? Why or why not?

a. Inventory valuation

b. External financial reporting

c. To determine fees charged to clients

Answers

a. No. Service firms like Barnett Legal Associates have no inventories.

b. No. Costs need not be assigned to individual clients to prepare financial statements.

c. Yes. Fees charged to clients must be high enough to cover indirect costs (and profits) as well as direct labor costs.

In summary: Noninventoriable costs are assigned to jobs only for internal decision making, not for external financial reporting.

You have now learned how to use a job cost system to assign costs to jobs. Review the Job Costing Decision Guidelines to solidify your understanding.

DECISION GUIDELINES

Job Costing

DECISION	GUIDELINES
Should I use job costing or process costing?	• *Job costing* for unique products produced in small batches • *Process costing* for identical products produced in large batches, often in a continuous flow

How to record:
• Purchase and use of materials?

Purchase:

Materials Inventory	XX	
Accounts Payable (or Cash)		XX

Use:

Work in Process (direct materials)	XX	
Manufacturing Overhead (indirect materials)	XX	
Materials Inventory		XX

• Incurrence and assignment of labor?

Incurred:

Manufacturing Wages	XX	
Wages Payable (or Cash)		XX

Assigned:

Work in Process (direct labor)	XX	
Manufacturing Overhead (indirect labor)	XX	
Manufacturing Wages		XX

How to determine whether utilities, insurance, property taxes, depreciation, and so on are
• Manufacturing overhead?

Utilities, insurance, property taxes, and depreciation expense are part of manufacturing overhead *only* if they are incurred in the manufacturing plant.

• Operating expenses?

If not related to manufacturing, such expenses are operating expenses. For example, if related to a sales office or store, such expenses are marketing expenses. If related to executive headquarters, they are administrative expenses. If related to delivery vehicles or distribution centers, they are distribution expenses. These are all operating expenses, not manufacturing overhead.

How to record *actual* manufacturing overhead costs?

Manufacturing Overhead	XXX	
Accumulated Depreciation— Plant and Equipment		XX
Prepaid Insurance—Plant and Equipment		XX
Utilities Payable (or Cash)		XX
and so on		XX

How to compute a predetermined manufacturing overhead rate?

$$\frac{\textbf{Total estimated manufacturing overhead cost}}{\textbf{Total estimated quantity of allocation base}}$$

How to record allocation of manufacturing overhead?

Work in Process Inventory	XX	
Manufacturing Overhead		XX

What is the *amount* of the allocated manufacturing overhead?

$$\begin{array}{c}\textbf{Actual quantity}\\\textbf{of the manufacturing}\\\textbf{overhead allocation base}\end{array} \times \begin{array}{c}\textbf{Predetermined}\\\textbf{manufacturing}\\\textbf{overhead rate}\end{array}$$

How to close Manufacturing Overhead at the end of the period?

Close directly to Cost of Goods Sold.

Which T-account summarizes the schedule of cost of goods manufactured?

Work in Process Inventory

How do service companies trace employees' direct labor to individual jobs?

Automated software directly captures time employee spends on a client's job, or employee fills out a (usually computerized) time record.

Why do companies allocate noninventoriable costs to jobs?

Because they need total product costs for internal decisions (such as setting selling prices). For external reporting, companies assign only inventoriable costs to jobs.

REVIEW JOB COSTING

SUMMARY PROBLEM

Hillis Incorporated had the following inventories at the end of 20X4:

Materials Inventory	$20,000
Work in Process Inventory	17,000
Finished Goods Inventory	11,000

www.prenhall.com/horngren

End-of-Chapter Assessment

During January 20X5, Hillis actually used 300 machine hours and recorded the following transactions:
a. Purchased materials on account, $31,000.
b. Requisitioned (placed into production) direct materials, $39,000.
c. Manufacturing labor cost incurred was $40,000.
d. Manufacturing labor was: 90% direct labor; 10% indirect labor.
e. Requisitioned indirect materials, $3,000.
f. Incurred other manufacturing overhead, $13,000 (credit Accounts Payable).
g. Allocated manufacturing overhead to production at $60 per machine hour.
h. Completed production, $99,000.
i. Sold goods on account, $172,000, cost of goods sold, $91,400.

Required

1. Record the transactions in the general journal.
2. Post the transactions and inventory balances to the following accounts:

MATERIALS INVENTORY	WORK IN PROCESS INVENTORY	FINISHED GOODS INVENTORY	COST OF GOODS SOLD

MANUFACTURING WAGES	MANUFACTURING OVERHEAD

3. Record the journal entry to close the ending balance of Manufacturing Overhead. Post your entry to the T-accounts.
4. What are the ending balances in the three inventory accounts and Cost of Goods Sold?

Solution

Requirement 1
Journal entries:

a.	Materials Inventory	31,000	
	Accounts Payable		31,000
b.	Work in Process Inventory	39,000	
	Materials Inventory		39,000
c.	Manufacturing Wages	40,000	
	Wages Payable		40,000
d.	Work in Process Inventory ($40,000 × 0.90)	36,000	
	Manufacturing Overhead ($40,000 × 0.10)	4,000	
	Manufacturing Wages		40,000
e.	Manufacturing Overhead	3,000	
	Materials Inventory		3,000
f.	Manufacturing Overhead	13,000	
	Accounts Payable		13,000
g.	Work in Process Inventory (300 × $60)	18,000	
	Manufacturing Overhead		18,000
h.	Finished Goods Inventory	99,000	
	Work in Process Inventory		99,000
i.	Accounts Receivable	172,000	
	Sales Revenue		172,000
	Cost of Goods Sold	91,400	
	Finished Goods Inventory		91,400

Requirement 2

Post the transactions:

MATERIALS INVENTORY			
Bal.	20,000	(b)	39,000
(a)	31,000	(e)	3,000
Bal.	9,000		

WORK IN PROCESS INVENTORY			
Bal.	17,000	(h)	99,000
(b)	39,000		
(d)	36,000		
(g)	18,000		
Bal.	11,000		

FINISHED GOODS INVENTORY			
Bal.	11,000	(i)	91,400
(h)	99,000		
Bal.	18,600		

COST OF GOODS SOLD	
(i)	91,400

MANUFACTURING WAGES			
(c)	40,000	(d)	40,000

MANUFACTURING OVERHEAD			
(d)	4,000	(g)	18,000
(e)	3,000		
(f)	13,000		
Bal.	2,000		

Requirement 3

Close Manufacturing Overhead:

Cost of Goods Sold.................................... 2,000

        Manufacturing Overhead   2,000

MANUFACTURING OVERHEAD			
(d)	4,000	(g)	18,000
(e)	3,000		2,000
(f)	13,000		

COST OF GOODS SOLD			
(i)	91,400		
	2,000		
Bal.	93,400		

Requirement 4

Ending Balances:

Materials Inventory (from requirement 2)	$ 9,000
Work in Process Inventory (from requirement 2)	11,000
Finished Goods Inventory (from requirement 2)	18,600
Cost of Goods Sold (from requirement 3)..........................	93,400

LESSONS LEARNED

1. **Distinguish between job costing and process costing.** Companies that use job costing usually produce individual products or small batches of products that pass through production steps as a distinct, identifiable job lot. Jobs can differ greatly in terms of materials, labor, and overhead. Costs are accumulated for each individual job. The *job cost record* includes direct materials, direct labor, and manufacturing overhead costs of producing the job.

   Companies that produce large numbers of identical products use process costing. Costs are accumulated for each production process, and then averaged over the many (identical) units passing through that process.

2. **Account for materials and labor in a manufacturer's job costing system.** *Direct materials* costs are traced to individual jobs and added (debited) to Work in Process Inventory. *Indirect materials* cannot be easily traced to specific jobs, so their costs are added (debited) to the Manufacturing Overhead account. *Direct labor* costs are traced to jobs and added (debited) to Work in Process Inventory. *Indirect labor* cost, such as maintenance and janitorial, is difficult to trace to individual jobs. Indirect labor costs are added (debited) to Manufacturing Overhead.

   In highly automated systems, employees use bar codes to record materials used and scan their identification cards to record their labor. The software immediately tracks these material and labor costs to the specific job and updates the general ledger accounts.

3. **Account for manufacturing overhead in a manufacturer's job costing system.** *Manufacturing overhead* is all manufacturing costs except direct materials and direct labor. Actual manufacturing overhead costs are accumulated as debits in the Manufacturing Overhead account. Manufacturing Overhead is allocated to jobs using a predetermined rate per unit of a *cost allocation* base. Ideally, the allocation base is the driver of the manufacturing overhead costs. Allocating manufacturing overhead requires a debit to Work in Process and a credit to Manufacturing Overhead. At the end of the period, software may automatically adjust each job for any underallocated or overallocated manufacturing overhead, or else the balance is closed to Cost of Goods Sold.

4. **Account for noninventoriable costs in job costing.** Service companies trace direct labor to individual jobs (clients) using software or time records. Service, merchandising, or manufacturing firms can allocate indirect costs such as marketing, office rent, and support staff salaries to jobs using predetermined indirect cost allocation rates.

ACCOUNTING VOCABULARY

allocation base (p. 810)
budgeted manufacturing
   overhead rate (p. 810)
cost allocation (p. 809)
cost assignment (p. 809)
cost driver (p. 799)
cost tracing (p. 809)

job cost record (p. 800)
job costing (p. 798)
labor time record (p. 805)
materials requisition (p. 802)
overallocated (manufacturing)
   overhead (p. 814)

predetermined manufacturing
   overhead rate (p. 810)
process costing (p. 798)
time record (p. 818)
underallocated (manufacturing)
   overhead (p. 814)

QUESTIONS

1. Explain the basic difference between job costing and process costing.
2. Give three examples of companies that would use job costing rather than process costing, and explain why.
3. Distinguish direct materials from indirect materials and direct labor from indirect labor. Direct materials and direct labor are debited to what account when placed in production? To what account are indirect materials and indirect labor debited?
4. Give examples of direct materials and indirect materials for a caterer.
5. How can information technology simplify tracing direct materials and direct labor to specific jobs?
6. Is Manufacturing Overhead a temporary or permanent account? Explain how the account operates. What do the debits represent? What do the credits represent?
7. Is manufacturing overhead cost allocated to jobs by precisely identifying the overhead cost of each job or by an estimation? Explain.
8. Would a heavily automated manufacturing plant be more likely to use machine hours or direct labor hours as the manufacturing overhead allocation base? Explain.
9. Why do companies use predetermined rather than actual manufacturing overhead rates?
10. Transactions in what account summarize the cost of goods manufactured? Show the T-account and label the transactions.
11. Which of the following accounts have their balances brought to zero at the end of the period, and which keep their ending balances to start the next period? Materials Inventory, Manufacturing Overhead, Finished Goods Inventory, Manufacturing Wages.
12. Cost of goods sold is just one line-item in the Income Statement. What kinds of costs are included in cost of goods sold?
13. Why would an international professional services firm like **PricewaterhouseCoopers** use job costing?
14. How do professional service firms such as law firms and management consulting firms trace direct labor to individual jobs?

ASSESS YOUR PROGRESS

DAILY EXERCISES

DE20-1 Job costing and process costing differ in (a) the cost object, and (b) the number of units over which costs are averaged. Explain these two differences.

Distinguishing between job and process costing (Obj. 1)

DE20-2 Would the following companies use job costing or process costing?

a. A manufacturer of plywood.
b. A manufacturer of wakeboards.
c. A manufacturer of luxury yachts.
d. A professional services firm.
e. A landscape garden contractor.

Distinguishing between job and process costing (Obj. 1)

DE20-3 Suppose **Olympic Paints** incurs $560,000 to produce 250,000 gallons of deck stain. What is the cost per gallon? Would Olympic Paints use job or process costing? Why?

Distinguishing between job and process costing (Obj. 1)

DE20-4 For a manufacturer that uses job costing, diagram the flow of costs through the accounts. Label each transaction. Include the following accounts in your diagram: Finished Goods Inventory, Manufacturing Wages, Cost of Goods Sold, Work in Process Inventory, Materials Inventory, Manufacturing Overhead.

Flow of costs in job costing (Obj. 2, 3)

DE20-5 ◄ *Link Back to Chapter 9 (Inventory).* Refer to E-Z-Boy's Material Ledger Record in Exhibit 20-5. Suppose material requisition #334 indicated that on July 24, 20 units of lumber (rather than ten), were used in Job 293. What is the ending balance of item B-220—Lumber/Recliner Chairs?

Accounting for materials (Obj. 2)

DE20-6 Turn to E-Z-Boy's Materials subsidiary ledger in Exhibit 20-6. Suppose that on July 24, the balance of the Upholstery Fabric account was $300 rather than $390. What is the total Materials Inventory balance?

Accounting for materials (Obj. 2)

DE20-7 Walkabout manufactures backpacks. Its plant records the following materials-related transactions:

Purchases of canvas (on account)	$70,000
Purchases of thread (on account).............	700
Material requisitions:	
Canvas..	63,000
Thread...	280

What journal entries record these transactions? Post these transactions to the Material Inventory account. If the company had $28,560 of Materials Inventory at the beginning of the period, what is the ending balance of Materials Inventory?

DE20-8 Use the following T-accounts to determine direct materials used and indirect materials used.

MATERIALS INVENTORY			
Bal.	16		
Purchases	320	X	
Bal.	24		

WORK IN PROCESS INVENTORY			
Bal.	32		
Direct materials	Y	Cost of goods	
Direct labor	240	manufactured	744
Manufacturing overhead	200		
Bal.	8		

DE20-9 Art Glass reports the following labor-related transactions at its plant in Seattle, Washington.

Plant janitor's wages......................	600
Furnace operator's wages..............	900
Glass blowers' wages.....................	76,000

Record the journal entries for the incurrence and assignment of these wages.

DE20-10 Touch Enterprises produces LCD touch screen products. The company reports the following information at December 31, 20X4. Touch began operations on January 30, 20X4.

WORK IN PROCESS INVENTORY		MANUFACTURING WAGES		MANUFACTURING OVERHEAD		FINISHED GOODS INVENTORY		MATERIALS INVENTORY	
40,000	136,000	70,000	70,000	4,000	48,000	136,000	122,000	52,000	44,000
60,000				10,000					
48,000				37,000					

1. What is the cost of direct materials used? The cost of indirect materials used?
2. What is the cost of direct labor? The cost of indirect labor?
3. What is the cost of goods manufactured?
4. What is cost of goods sold (before adjusting for any under- or overallocated manufacturing overhead)?

DE20-11 Refer to Daily Exercise 20-10.

1. What is the actual manufacturing overhead? Allocated manufacturing overhead?
2. What is the predetermined manufacturing overhead rate, as a percentage of direct labor cost?
3. Is manufacturing overhead underallocated or overallocated? By how much?

DE20-12 All-Wood Outdoor furniture reports the following costs for June 20X4. What is the balance in the Manufacturing Overhead account?

Wood	$120,000
Nails and glue	15,000
Wood preserving stain	8,000
Depreciation on saws.............................	3,000
Depreciation on delivery truck..............	2,200
Assembly-line workers' wages	56,000
Salesman's auto lease	1,400
Indirect manufacturing labor	23,000

DE20-13 Arctic-Tex produces fleece textiles woven from recycled plastic bottles. The company uses a predetermined manufacturing overhead rate to allocate overhead based on the machine hours each job requires. Arctic-Tex reports the following data for 20X5:

Computing a predetermined manufacturing overhead rate (Obj. 3)

	Expected	Actual
Manufacturing overhead..............	$715,000	$600,000
Direct labor hours........................	11,000	11,375
Direct labor costs	100,000	103,125
Machine hours	13,000	10,000

Compute Arctic-Tex's predetermined manufacturing overhead rate.

DE20-14 Refer to Daily Exercise 20-13. Arctic-Tex's Job 744 required

Accounting for overhead (Obj. 3)

a. 20 direct labor hours, at a total cost of $4,096
b. $2,140 of direct materials
c. 15 machine hours

1. Record the journal entry to allocate the manufacturing overhead to Job 744.
2. Compute the total cost of Job 744.

DE20-15 In the E-Z-Boy job cost record (Exhibit 20-11), how much manufacturing overhead cost would be allocated to Job 293 if the predetermined manufacturing overhead allocation rate is 90% of direct labor cost rather than 80%? What would be the total cost assigned to Job 293?

Accounting for overhead (Obj. 3)

DE20-16 Turn to the E-Z-Boy illustration on pages 801–814. Suppose direct material requisitions totaled $300,000 rather than $285,000. (Indirect materials used and cost of goods manufactured remain the same.) Use T-accounts to show the new ending balances of Materials Inventory and Work in Process Inventory.

Accounting for materials, labor, and work in process inventory (Obj. 2, 3)

DE20-17 In the E-Z-Boy illustration on pages 814–815, actual manufacturing overhead was $210,000. Suppose instead that the actual manufacturing overhead was $175,000.

Under/overallocated overhead (Obj. 3)

1. What would be the actual manufacturing overhead rate?
2. Is manufacturing overhead underallocated or overallocated? By how much?
3. Is Cost of Goods Sold too high or too low?

DE20-18 Refer to Daily Exercise 20-17. Make the journal entry to close out E-Z-Boy's Manufacturing Overhead account if the balance is closed to Cost of Goods Sold.

Close out under/overallocated overhead (Obj. 3)

DE20-19 In the Barnett Legal Associates example on page 818, suppose Teresa Fox's annual salary is $120,000 rather than $100,000.

Job costing in a service company (Obj. 4)

1. What would be the hourly (cost) rate to Barnett Legal Associates of employing Fox?
2. What direct labor cost would be traced to client 367?

DE20-20 Return to the original data in the Barnett Legal Associates example on pages 818–819. Suppose the Barnett attorneys expected to work a total of 8,000 direct labor hours rather than 10,000 direct labor hours.

Job costing in a service company (Obj. 4)

1. What is the indirect cost allocation rate?
2. What indirect costs will be allocated to client 367?

EXERCISES

E20-1 Listed below are several terms. Complete the following statements with one of these terms. You may use a term more than once, and some terms may not be used at all.

Distinguishing job and process costing (Obj. 1)

Cost allocation	Cost driver	Job costing	Process costing
Cost tracing	Job cost record	Materials requisition	

a. ___ is used by companies that produce small quantities of many different products.
b. A ___ is any factor that affects costs.
c. **Boise Cascade** pulverizes wood into pulp to manufacture cardboard. The company would use a ___ system.
d. To record costs of maintaining thousands of identical mortgage files, financial institutions like **Fleet Mortgage** would use a ___ system.
e. ___ is assigning direct costs to cost objects.
f. A ___ accumulates the costs of an individual job.
g. Companies that produce large numbers of identical products use ___ systems for product costing.

JOB COSTING 825

(continued)

h. The computer repair service that visits your home and repairs your computer would use a ___ system.

i. A ___ is manufacturing personnel's request that materials be moved to the production floor.

j. ___ is assigning indirect costs to cost objects.

Accounting for job costs (Obj. 2, 3)

E20-2 Horn's Printing job cost records yielded the following information:

Job No.	Date Started		Date Finished		Date Sold		Total Cost of Job at March 31
1	February	21	March	16	March	17	$ 2,800
2	February	29	March	21	March	26	17,000
3	March	3	April	11	April	13	5,900
4	March	7	March	29	April	1	6,200
5	March	9	March	30	April	2	5,600
6	March	22	April	11	April	13	1,300
7	March	23	March	27	March	29	5,400

Required

Compute Horn's cost of (a) work in process inventory at March 31, (b) finished goods inventory at March 31, and (c) cost of goods sold for March.

Job costing journal entries (Obj. 2, 3)

E20-3 Record the following transactions in Systems Engineering's general journal.

a. Incurred and paid Web site expenses, $6,500.

b. Incurred and paid manufacturing wages, $16,000.

c. Purchased materials on account, $13,500.

d. Used in production: direct materials, $9,000; indirect materials, $2,000.

e. Assigned $16,000 of manufacturing labor to jobs, 70% of which was direct labor and 30% of which was indirect labor.

f. Recorded manufacturing overhead: depreciation on plant, $13,000; plant insurance, $1,700; plant property tax, $4,200 (credit Property Tax Payable).

g. Allocated manufacturing overhead to jobs, 200% of direct labor cost.

h. Completed production, $27,000.

i. Sold inventory on account, $22,000; cost of goods sold, $14,000.

Identifying job costing journal entries (Obj. 2, 3)

E20-4 Describe the lettered transactions in the following manufacturing accounts:

MANUFACTURING WAGES		MANUFACTURING OVERHEAD		COST OF GOODS SOLD	
(a)	(b)	(b)	(e)	(g)	
		(c)	(f)	(f)	
		(d)			

MATERIALS INVENTORY		WORK IN PROCESS INVENTORY		FINISHED GOODS INVENTORY	
(h)	(i)	(i)	(j)	(j)	(g)
	(c)	(b)			
		(e)			

Using the Work in Process Inventory account (Obj. 2, 3)

E20-5 September production generated the following activity in Digital Connection's Work in Process Inventory:

WORK IN PROCESS INVENTORY	
September 1 Bal.	14,000
Direct materials used	28,000
Direct labor assigned to jobs	30,000
Manufacturing overhead allocated to jobs	11,000

Completed production, not yet recorded, consists of Jobs B-78, G-65, and Y-11, with total costs of $17,000, $26,000, and $34,000, respectively.

Required

1. Compute the cost of work in process at September 30.

2. Prepare the journal entry for production completed in September.

3. Prepare the journal entry to record the sale (on credit) of Job G-65 for $38,000. Also make the cost-of-goods-sold entry.

4. What is the gross profit on Job G-65? What other costs must this gross profit cover?

E20-6 Selected cost data for All-Flooring Co. are as follows:

Expected manufacturing overhead cost for the year..................	$119,600
Expected direct labor cost for the year	46,000
Actual manufacturing overhead cost for the year......................	104,600
Actual direct labor cost for the year...	40,500

Required

1. Compute the predetermined manufacturing overhead rate per direct labor dollar.
2. Prepare the journal entry to allocate overhead cost for the year.
3. Use a T-account to determine the amount of overallocated or underallocated manufacturing overhead.
4. Prepare the journal entry to close the balance of the manufacturing overhead account.

E20-7 Isle Awning Company in Charleston, South Carolina, uses a predetermined manufacturing overhead rate to allocate overhead to individual jobs, based on the direct labor hours required. At the beginning of 20X4, the company expected to incur the following:

Manufacturing overhead costs.....................................	$500,000
Direct labor cost	$1,000,000
Machine hours	60,000 hours
Direct labor hours	100,000 hours

At the end of 20X4, the company had actually incurred:

Direct labor cost...	$1,210,000
Depreciation on manufacturing property, plant, and equipment...	480,000
Property taxes on plant	20,000
Sales salaries	25,000
Delivery drivers' wages..	15,000
Plant janitors' wages..	10,000
Machine hours	55,000 hours
Direct labor hours...	110,000 hours

Required

1. Compute Isle Awning's predetermined manufacturing overhead rate.
2. Record the summary journal entry for *allocating* manufacturing overhead.
3. Post the manufacturing overhead transactions to the Manufacturing Overhead T-account. Is manufacturing overhead underallocated or overallocated? By how much?
4. Close the Manufacturing Overhead account to Cost of Goods Sold. Does your entry increase or decrease cost of goods sold?

E20-8 Refer to the data in Exercise 20-7. Isle Awning's accountant found an error in her 20X4 expense records. Depreciation on manufacturing property, plant, and equipment was actually $600,000, not the $480,000 she had originally reported. Unadjusted balances at the end of 20X4 include

Finished Goods Inventory	130,000
Cost of Goods Sold..	600,000

Required

1. Use a T-account to determine whether manufacturing overhead is underallocated or overallocated, and by how much.
2. Record the entry to close out the underallocated or overallocated manufacturing overhead.
3. What is the adjusted ending balance of Cost of Goods Sold?

E20-9 Terra Nova, an environmental consulting firm, specializes in advising electric utilities on compliance with recent environmental regulations. Terra Nova uses a job cost system with a predetermined indirect cost allocation rate, computed as a percentage of expected direct labor costs.

At the beginning of 20X5, managing partner Jim Bladen prepared the following plan, or budget, for 20X5:

Direct labor hours (professionals)	16,000 hours
Direct labor costs (professionals)...............	$2,240,000
Office rent	350,000
Support staff salaries	860,000
Utilities	246,000

Northern Electric is inviting several consultants to bid for work. Jim Bladen estimates that this job will require about 220 direct labor hours.

Required

1. Compute Terra Nova's (a) hourly direct labor cost rate, and (b) indirect cost allocation rate.
2. Compute the predicted cost of the Northern Electric job.
3. If Bladen wants to earn a profit that equals 20% of the job's cost, how much should he bid for the Northern Electric job?

Challenge Exercise

Accounting for manufacturing overhead
(Obj. 3)

E20-10 At the end of the 20X4 fiscal year, SeaPro's manufacturing records show the following unadjusted ending account balances:

	Work in Process Inventory	Finished Goods Inventory	Cost of Goods Sold
Direct materials...................	$100,000	$170,000	$360,000
Direct labor	80,000	250,000	600,000
Manufacturing overhead....	70,000	310,000	460,000
Total...................................	$250,000	$730,000	$1,420,000

SeaPro's accountants allocated overhead during the year using a predetermined rate of $48 per machine hour. At year end, they computed the actual rate of $52 per machine hour. The beginning balances of both Work in Process Inventory and Finished Goods Inventory were zero.

Required

1. How many machine hours did SeaPro use in 20X4?
2. Was manufacturing overhead over- or underallocated for the year? By how much?
3. Record the entry to close out the over- or underallocated overhead.

(Group A) PROBLEMS

Analyzing job cost data
(Obj. 2, 3)

P20-1A Highcountry Manufacturing builds storage systems for office and home use. Its job cost records yield the following information. The company uses a perpetual inventory system.

Job No.	Date Started	Date Finished	Sold	Total Cost of Job at November 30	Total Manufacturing Costs Added in December
1	10/26	11/7	11/9	$1,700	
2	11/3	11/12	11/13	1,400	
3	11/3	11/30	12/1	1,900	
4	11/17	12/24	12/27	300	$ 700
5	11/29	12/29	1/3	500	1,600
6	12/8	12/12	12/14		750
7	12/23	1/6	1/9		500
8	12/30	1/22	1/26		1,900

Required

1. Compute Highcountry's cost of (a) work in process inventory at November 30 and December 31, (b) finished goods inventory at November 30 and December 31, and (c) cost of goods sold for November and December.
2. Record summary journal entries for the transfer of completed units from work in process to finished goods for November and December.
3. Record the sale of Job 4 for $1,200.
4. What is the gross profit for Job 4? What other costs must this gross profit cover?

P20-2A Plantation Construction, Inc., is a home builder in the Southeast. Plantation uses a perpetual inventory system and a job cost system in which each house is a job. Because it constructs houses, the company uses accounts titled Construction Wages, Construction Overhead, and Supervisory Salaries (for indirect labor). The following events occurred during August:

Accounting for manufacturing transactions (Obj. 2, 3)

a. Purchased materials on account, $375,600.
b. Incurred construction wages of $189,200. Requisitioned direct materials and used direct labor in construction:

	Direct Materials	Direct Labor
House 302	$38,600	$25,300
House 303	49,100	17,400
House 304	47,400	32,000
House 305	63,900	33,700

c. Depreciation of construction equipment, $5,800.
d. Other overhead costs incurred on houses 302–305:

Indirect labor	$89,000
Equipment rentals paid in cash	17,300
Liability insurance expired	5,100

e. Allocated overhead to jobs at the predetermined overhead rate of 40% of direct labor cost.
f. Houses completed: 302, 304.
g. House sold: 304 for $152,500.

Required

1. Record the events in the general journal.
2. Open T-accounts for Work in Process Inventory and Finished Goods Inventory. Post the appropriate entries to these accounts, identifying each entry by letter. Determine the ending account balances, assuming that the beginning balances were zero.
3. Add the costs of unfinished houses, and show that this total amount equals the ending balance in the Work in Process Inventory account.
4. Add the costs of completed houses that have not yet been sold, and show that this total amount equals the ending balance in the Finished Goods Inventory account.
5. Compute the gross profit on each house that was sold. What costs must the gross profit cover for Plantation Construction?

P20-3A Digital Reproductions manufactures CDs and DVDs for computer software and entertainment companies. Digital Reproductions uses job costing and has a perpetual inventory system.

Preparing and using a job cost record (Obj. 2, 3)

On November 2, Digital Reproductions began production of 5,000 DVDs, Job 378, for Hollywood Pictures for $1.20 each. The company incurred the following costs:

Date	Time Record No.	Description	Amount
11-2	556	12 hours @ $20	$240
11-3	557	25 hours @ $18	450

Date	Materials Requisition No.	Description	Amount
11-2	36	31 lb. polycarbonate plastic @ $12	$372
11-2	37	25 lb. acrylic plastic @ $28	700
11-3	42	3 lb. refined aluminum @ $48	144

Digital Reproductions allocates overhead to jobs based on the relation between expected overhead ($537,600) and expected direct labor ($448,000). Job 378 was completed and shipped on November 3.

Required

1. Prepare a job cost record similar to Exhibit 20-3 for Job 378.
2. Journalize in summary form the requisition of direct materials and the assignment of direct labor and manufacturing overhead to Job 378.
3. Journalize completion of the job and the sale of the 5,000 DVDs.

Accounting for manufacturing overhead (Obj. 3)

P20-4A Intercraft/Burns manufactures picture frames. The primary materials (wood, plastic, and glass) and direct labor are traced directly to the products. Manufacturing costs are allocated based on machine hours. Data for the year 20X4 follow:

	Budget	Actual
Machine hours	25,000 hours	29,600 hours
Direct labor hours	42,000 hours	40,000 hours
Wood	$150,000	$148,000
Maintenance labor (repairs to equipment)	5,000	16,500
Plant supervisor's wages	30,000	32,000
Screws, nails, and glue	15,500	32,000
Plant utilities	25,000	49,575
Plastic	75,000	70,500
Glass	125,000	126,275
Freight out	35,000	44,500
Direct labor	65,000	63,000
Depreciation on plant and equipment	62,000	62,000
Advertising expenses	40,000	55,000

Required

1. Compute the predetermined manufacturing overhead rate.
2. Post actual and allocated manufacturing overhead to the Manufacturing Overhead T-account.
3. Close the under- or overallocated overhead to cost of goods sold.
4. The predetermined manufacturing overhead rate usually turns out to be inaccurate. Why don't accountants just use the actual manufacturing overhead rate?

Comprehensive accounting for manufacturing transactions (Obj. 2, 3)

P20-5A ← *Link Back to Chapters 2 and 19.* Citronix Systems produces components for digital network routers. Initially the company manufactured the parts for its own routers, but it gradually began selling them to other companies as well.

April 1 balances in the subsidiary ledgers were

- Materials ledger: circuit boards, $1,580; electronic parts, $1,960; indirect materials, $430.
- Work in process ledger: Job 145, $35,880.
- Finished goods ledger: relays, $5,310; switches, $8,870.

Citronix's trial balance on April 1 follows on page 383.

April transactions are summarized as follows:

a. Collections on account, $137,470.
b. Marketing and general expenses incurred and paid, $27,470.
c. Payments on account, $36,040.
d. Materials purchased on credit: circuit boards, $6,540; electronic parts, $15,830; indirect materials, $3,590.

CITRONIX SYSTEMS		
Trial Balance		
April 1, 20XX		
Cash	$ 19,160	
Accounts receivable	74,290	
Inventories:		
Materials...	3,970	
Work in process..................................	35,880	
Finished goods...................................	14,180	
Plant assets	244,570	
Accumulated depreciation		$ 98,900
Accounts payable		23,960
Wages payable..		3,670
Common stock		120,000
Retained earnings		145,520
Sales revenues..		—
Cost of goods sold....................................	—	
Manufacturing wages................................	—	
Manufacturing overhead	—	
Marketing and general expenses	—	
	$392,050	$392,050

e. Materials used in production (requisitioned):

- Job 145: circuit boards, $340.
- Job 146: circuit boards, $3,570; electronic parts, $5,980.
- Job 147: circuit boards, $1,970; electronic parts, $4,730.
- Indirect materials, $1,580.

f. Manufacturing wages incurred during April, $32,430, of which $30,520 was paid. Wages payable at March 31 were paid during April, $3,670.

g. Labor time records for the month: Job 145, $3,500; Job 146, $11,050; Job 147, $9,940; indirect labor, $7,940.

h. Other actual miscellaneous manufacturing overhead costs incurred on account, $4,630.

i. Depreciation on plant and equipment (not included in item h above), $3,450.

j. Manufacturing overhead was allocated at the predetermined rate of 70% of direct labor cost.

k. Jobs completed during the month: Job 145, 400 relays at total cost of $42,170; Job 146, 200 switches at total cost of $28,335.

l. Credit sales on account: all of Job 145 for $97,640 (cost $42,170); Job 146, 120 switches for $35,100 (cost, $17,001).

m. Closed the Manufacturing Overhead account to Cost of Goods Sold.

Required

1. Open T-accounts for the general ledger, the materials ledger, the work in process ledger, and the finished goods ledger. Insert each account balance as given, and use the reference *Bal.*
2. Record the April transactions directly in the accounts, using the letters as references. Citronix uses a perpetual inventory system.
3. Prepare a trial balance at April 30.
4. Use the work in process T-account to prepare a schedule of cost of goods manufactured for the month of April.
5. Prepare an income statement for the month of April. (*Hint:* In transaction *m* you closed any under/overallocated manufacturing overhead to Cost of Goods Sold. In the income statement, show this correction as an adjustment to Cost of Goods Sold. If manufacturing overhead is underallocated, the adjustment will increase Cost of Goods Sold. If overhead is overallocated, the adjustment will reduce Cost of Goods Sold.)

P20-6A OneClick is a Web site design and consulting firm. The firm uses a job cost system, where each client is a different "job." OneClick traces direct labor, licensing costs, and travel costs directly to each job (client). It allocates indirect costs to jobs based on a predetermined indirect cost allocation rate, computed as a percentage of direct labor costs.

Job costing in a service company (Obj. 4)

At the beginning of 20X4, managing partner Lauren Pearle prepared the following budget:

Direct labor hours (professional)	6,000 hours
Direct labor costs (professional)	$600,000
Support staff salaries	70,000
Computer leases	34,000
Office supplies	11,000
Office rent	35,000

In November 20X4, OneClick served several clients. Records for two clients appear here:

	Planet Foods	Deception Fragrances
Direct labor hours	675 hours	20 Hours
Licensing costs	$ 1,325	$125
Travel costs	$10,500	—

Required

1. Compute OneClick's predetermined indirect cost allocation rate for 20X4.
2. Compute the total cost of each job.
3. If Pearle wants to earn profits equal to 30% of sales revenue, how much (what total fee) should she charge each of these two clients?
4. Why does OneClick assign costs to jobs?

(Group B) PROBLEMS

Analyzing job cost data
(Obj. 2, 3)

P20-1B Office Solutions refurbishes photocopy machines and sells them on the Web. Its job cost records yield the following information. Office Solutions uses a perpetual inventory system.

Job No.	Date Started	Date Finished	Sold	Total Cost of Job at March 31	Total Manufacturing Cost Added in April
1	2/26	3/7	3/9	$1,400	
2	2/3	3/12	3/13	1,600	
3	3/29	3/31	4/3	1,300	
4	3/31	4/1	4/1	500	$ 400
5	3/17	4/24	4/27	500	1,500
6	4/8	4/12	4/14		700
7	4/23	5/6	5/9		1,200
8	4/30	5/22	5/26		600

Required

1. Compute Office Solutions' cost of (a) work in process inventory at March 31 and April 30, (b) finished goods inventory at March 31 and April 30, and (c) cost of goods sold for March and April.
2. Make summary journal entries to record the transfer of completed units from work in process to finished goods for March and April.
3. Record the sale of Job 5 for $3,800.
4. Compute the gross profit for Job 5. What costs must the gross profit cover?

Accounting for manufacturing
transactions
(Obj. 2, 3)

P20-2B Mountain Homes builds prefabricated log houses in Montana. The company uses a perpetual inventory system and a job cost system in which each house is a job. The following events occurred during May.

a. Purchased materials on account, $315,000.
b. Incurred manufacturing wages of $142,800. Requisitioned direct materials and used direct labor in manufacturing:

	Direct Materials	Direct Labor
House 13	$36,100	$12,300
House 14	41,700	22,500
House 15	51,000	15,000
House 16	54,000	23,800

c. Depreciation of manufacturing equipment used on different houses, $16,000.
d. Other overhead costs incurred on houses 13–16:

Indirect labor	$21,600
Equipment rentals paid in cash	8,000
Liability insurance expired	3,900

e. Allocated overhead to jobs at the predetermined rate of 30% of direct labor cost.
f. Houses completed: 13, 15, 16.
g. Houses sold: 13 for $79,000; 16 for $113,900.

Required

1. Record the preceding events in the general journal.
2. Open T-accounts for Work in Process Inventory and Finished Goods Inventory. Post the appropriate entries to these accounts, identifying each entry by letter. Determine the ending account balances, assuming that the beginning balances were zero.
3. Add the costs of unfinished houses, and show that this total amount equals the ending balance in the Work in Process Inventory account.
4. Add the costs of completed houses that have not yet been sold, and show that this total amount equals the ending balance in the Finished Goods Inventory account.
5. Compute the gross profit on each house that was sold. What costs must the gross profit cover for Mountain Homes?

P20-3B Alliance Rubber produces transmission belts that other companies use in their manufacturing processes. Alliance Rubber uses job costing and has a perpetual inventory system.

Preparing and using a job cost record
(Obj. 2, 3)

On September 22, Alliance Rubber received an order for 50 industrial-grade belts from Hoyt Corporation at a price of $110 each. The job, assigned number 449, was promised for October 10. After purchasing the materials, Alliance Rubber began production on September 30 and incurred the following costs in completing the order:

Date	Time Ticket No.	Description	Amount
9/30	1754	10 hours @ $19	$190
10/3	1805	40 hours @ $18	720

Date	Materials Requisition No.	Description	Amount
9/30	593	20 lb. rubber @ $15	$300
10/2	598	30 meters polyester fabric @ $9	270
10/3	622	12 meters steel cord @ $12	144

Alliance Rubber allocates manufacturing overhead to jobs on the basis of the relation between expected overhead ($375,000) and direct labor ($250,000). Job 449 was completed on October 3 and shipped to Hoyt on October 5.

Required

1. Prepare a job cost record similar to Exhibit 20-3 for Job 449.
2. Journalize in summary form the requisition of direct materials and the assignment of direct labor and manufacturing overhead to Job 449.
3. Journalize completion of the job and sale of the goods.

Accounting for manufacturing overhead
(Obj. 3)

P20-4B Super-Tex produces specialized textiles. The company allocates manufacturing overhead based on the machine hours each job uses. Super-Tex reports the following cost data for 20X5:

	Budget	Actual
Direct labor hours	6,000 hours	5,000 hours
Machine hours	6,900 hours	6,000 hours
Depreciation on salespersons' autos	$20,000	$20,000
Indirect materials	40,000	42,000
Depreciation on trucks used to deliver textiles to customers	12,000	11,000
Depreciation on plant and equipment	50,000	55,000
Indirect manufacturing labor	35,000	38,000
Customer service hotline	17,000	20,000
Plant utilities	13,000	15,000
Direct labor cost	60,000	80,000

Required

1. Compute the predetermined manufacturing overhead rate.
2. Post actual and allocated manufacturing overhead to the Manufacturing Overhead T-account.
3. Close the under- or overallocated overhead to cost of goods sold.
4. How can managers use accounting information to help control manufacturing overhead costs?

Comprehensive accounting for manufacturing transactions
(Obj. 2, 3)

P20-5B ← *Link Back to Chapters 2 and 19.* Coalton Electric manufacturers specialized parts used in power generation. Initially, the company manufactured the parts for its own use, but it gradually began selling them to public utilities as well. The trial balance of Coalton Electric's manufacturing operation on January 1 is as follows:

COALTON ELECTRIC—MANUFACTURING OPERATIONS
Trial Balance
January 1, 20XX

Cash	$ 54,000	
Accounts receivable	65,860	
Inventories:		
Materials	14,180	
Work in process	43,350	
Finished goods	56,640	
Plant assets	342,860	
Accumulated depreciation		$145,050
Accounts payable		83,920
Wages payable		5,700
Common stock		200,000
Retained earnings		142,220
Sales revenues		—
Cost of goods sold	—	
Manufacturing wages	—	
Manufacturing overhead	—	
Marketing and general expenses	—	
	$576,890	$576,890

January 1 balances in the subsidiary ledgers were

- Materials ledger: petrochemicals, $5,280; electronic parts, $7,800; indirect materials, $1,100.
- Work in process ledger: Job 86, $43,350.
- Finished goods ledger: transformers, $35,770; switches, $20,870.

January transactions are summarized as follows.

a. Payments on account, $79,330.
b. Marketing and general expenses incurred and paid, $21,660.
c. Collections on account, $187,880.
d. Materials purchased on credit: petrochemicals, $19,570; electronic parts, $28,360; indirect materials, $6,130.
e. Materials used in production (requisitioned):

- Job 86: petrochemicals, $3,800.
- Job 87: petrochemicals, $9,870; electronic parts, $5,690.
- Job 88: petrochemicals, $7,680; electronic parts, $29,920.
- Indirect materials, $6,760.

f. Manufacturing wages incurred during January, $52,080, of which $49,560 was paid. Wages payable at December 31 were paid during January, $5,700.
g. Labor time records for the month: Job 86, $4,000; Job 87, $20,880; Job 88, $16,560; indirect labor, $10,640.
h. Other actual miscellaneous manufacturing overhead costs incurred on account, $27,660.
i. Depreciation on manufacturing plant and equipment (not included in item h above), $6,710.
j. Manufacturing overhead was allocated at the predetermined rate of 120% of direct labor cost.
k. Jobs completed during the month: Job 86, one transformer at total cost of $55,950; Job 87, 400 switches at total cost of $61,496.
l. Credit sales on account: All of Job 86 for $96,490 (cost $55,950); Job 87, 300 switches for $88,030 (cost, $46,122).
m. Close Manufacturing Overhead account to Cost of Goods Sold.

Required

1. Open T-accounts for the general ledger, the materials ledger, the work in process ledger, and the finished goods ledger. Insert each account balance as given, and use the reference *Bal.*
2. Record the January transactions directly in the accounts, using the letters as references. Coalton Electric uses a perpetual inventory system.
3. Prepare a trial balance at January 31.
4. Use the work in process T-account to prepare a schedule of cost of goods manufactured for the month of January.
5. Prepare an income statement for the month of January. To calculate cost of goods sold, you may want to review Exhibit 19-11. (*Hint:* In transaction *m* you closed any under/overallocated manufacturing overhead to Cost of Goods Sold. In the income statement, show this correction as an adjustment to Cost of Goods Sold. If manufacturing overhead is underallocated, the adjustment will increase Cost of Goods Sold. If overhead is overallocated, the adjustment will reduce Cost of Goods Sold.)

P20-6B Banner.com is an Internet advertising agency. The firm uses a job cost system in which each client is a different "job." Banner.com traces direct labor, software licensing costs, and travel costs directly to each job (client). The company allocates indirect costs to jobs based on a predetermined indirect cost allocation rate, computed as a percentage of direct labor costs.

Job costing in a service company (Obj. 4)

At the beginning of 20X3, managing partner Michael Egan prepared the following budget:

Direct labor hours (professional)	20,000 hours
Direct labor costs (professional)	$1,500,000
Support staff salaries	365,000
Rent and utilities	124,000
Supplies	16,000
Leased computer hardware	320,000

In January 20X3, Banner.com served several clients. Records for two clients appear here:

	Renolds Tennis and Golf Resort	Malaysia Cuisine
Direct labor hours	320 hours	24 hours
Software licensing costs	$1,250	$150
Travel costs..	6,000	—

Required

1. Compute Banner.com's predetermined indirect cost allocation rate for 20X3.
2. Compute the total cost of each job.
3. If Banner.com wants to earn profits equal to 20% of sales revenue, how much (what total fee) should it charge each of these two clients?
4. Why does Banner.com assign costs to jobs?

APPLY YOUR KNOWLEDGE

DECISION CASES

Costing and pricing identical products
(Obj. 2, 3)

Case 1. Coffee Central prepares gift baskets of its own blends of coffee, espresso, and coffee candies for sale to corporate clients. Each customer selects items from Coffee Central's Web site, and Coffee Central prints the customer's corporate logo on the packages. Coffee Central uses a job cost system and allocates manufacturing overhead based on direct labor cost.

One of Coffee Central's largest customers is the consulting firm Howell and Bunn. This firm sends baskets to its clients each Christmas, and also gives baskets to employees at the firm's annual holiday party. The consulting firm's managing partner, Paul Bunn, placed the client gift order in September for 650 baskets. Bunn forgot to place the December staff-party order until the beginning of December. This staff-party order was for an additional 150 baskets identical to the ones sent to clients.

Coffee Central budgeted the cost per basket for the original 650-basket order as follows:

Coffees, wrappers, basket...	$28.00
Employee time to produce items and fill the baskets (15 min.)	5.00
Manufacturing overhead	2.00
Total manufacturing cost...	$35.00

Andy Tavolo, president of Coffee Central, priced the order at $40 per basket.

In the past few months, Coffee Central has experienced price increases for both unroasted coffee and direct labor. *All other costs have remained the same.* The cost per basket for the second order was budgeted as

Coffees, wrappers, basket...	$30.00
Employee time to produce items and fill the baskets (15 min.)	6.00
Manufacturing overhead	2.40
Total manufacturing cost...	$38.40

Required

1. Do you agree with the cost analysis for the second order? Explain your answer.
2. Should the two orders be accounted for as one job or two in Coffee Central's system?
3. What sale price per basket should Tavolo set for the second order? What are the advantages and disadvantages of this price?

Case 2. Wild Berries manufactures organic fruit preserves sold primarily through health food stores and on the Web. The company closes for two weeks each December to allow employees to spend time with their families over the holiday season. Wild Berries' manufacturing overhead is mostly straight-line depreciation on its plant and air-conditioning costs for keeping the berries cool during the summer months. The company uses direct labor hours as the allocation base. President Kelly Appling has just approved new accounting software and is telling Controller Melissa Powers about her decision.

*Accounting for manufacturing overhead
(Obj. 3)*

"I think this new software will be great," Appling says. "It will save you time in preparing all those reports."

"Yes, and having so much more information just a click away will help us make better decisions and help control costs," replies Powers. "We need to consider how we can use the new system to improve our business practices."

"And I know just where to start," says Appling. "You complain each year about having to predict the weather months in advance for estimating air-conditioning costs, and direct labor hours for the denominator of the predetermined manufacturing overhead rate, when professional meteorologists can't even get tomorrow's forecast right! I think we should calculate the predetermined overhead rate on a monthly basis."

Controller Melissa Powers is not so sure this is a good idea.

Required

1. What are the advantages and disadvantages of Appling's proposal?
2. Should Wild Berries compute its predetermined manufacturing overhead rate on an annual basis or monthly basis? Explain.

ETHICAL ISSUE

←= *Link back to Chapter 19.* Wave Electronics is a contract manufacturer that produces customized computer components for several well-known computer-assembly companies. Wave's latest contract with CompNow.com calls for Wave to deliver sound cards that simulate surround sound from two speakers. Wave Electronics spent several hundred thousand dollars to design the sound card to meet CompNow.com's specifications.

*Ethics
(Obj. 4)*

Wave Electronic's president Angie Harrison has stipulated a pricing policy that requires bids (selling prices) for new contracts to be based on Wave's estimated full product cost from all elements of the value chain, plus a profit margin. Upon reviewing the contract figures, Wave's controller Lilian Gomez was startled to find that the cost estimates developed by Wave's cost accountant Anthony Haywood for the CompNow.com bid were based on only the *inventoriable* costs. Gomez is upset with Haywood. She is not sure what to do next.

Required

1. How did using inventoriable cost rather than full product cost affect the amount of Wave's bid for the CompNow.com job?
2. Identify the parties involved in Lilian Gomez's ethical dilemma. What are her alternatives? How would each party be affected by each alternative? What should Gomez do next?

TEAM PROJECT

GourmetGifts prepares cheese, bread, and fruit gift baskets for sale from the company's Web site. The company obtains these products from several vendors. Customers select items for their customized gift baskets on GourmetGifts' Web site, and then GourmetGifts assembles and decorates the baskets to order. Workers earn $21 per hour, and they prepare an average of 3 baskets per hour. For pricing, GourmetGifts determines the full "product cost" of each basket and then adds a profit margin that equals 20% of the full product cost. Indirect costs, including supervisors' and quality inspectors' wages, spoilage, Web site support, rent, and utilities, are allocated to baskets based on direct food costs.

*Job costing in merchandising
(Obj. 3, 4)*

GourmetGifts president Jennifer Wildt wants to grow the company by targeting corporate customers who would place large orders for many identical baskets. But she believes the company does not have the resources to finance such expansion. She is discussing the issue with controller Jay Boros and cost accountant Ling Chen, who has just returned from an e-commerce seminar. Chen suggests that GourmetGifts use an e-commerce software provider and use the Web to connect electronically with its main vendors. GourmetGifts could then order food items as needed for next-day delivery, avoiding the cost of holding a larger inventory and the associated spoilage. Wildt likes Chen's suggestion. Wildt also expects that filling many baskets with the same items should cut the direct labor time per basket in half. Boros and Chen calculate the following cost estimates, assuming that in addition to the 10,000 baskets currently sold to individuals, the company would sell 6,000 baskets to corporate clients.

		16,000 Baskets
Direct materials		$480,000
Direct labor		91,000
Indirect costs:		
Supervisors' and quality inspectors' wages	$64,000	
Spoilage	27,500	
Web site support	17,000	
Rent and utilities	28,000	
Total indirect costs		136,500
Total costs		$707,500

When Chen calculates the average cost per basket, all are surprised that the cost savings for the corporate sales are not as large as expected. At the estimated cost of approximately $42.03, GourmetGifts might not be able to attract corporate customers. Controller Jay Boros suggests changing the indirect cost allocation base from direct materials cost to direct labor cost. Wildt is skeptical because the firm has always used direct materials cost as the allocation base, and the last thing she wants is to have individual sales subsidize corporate sales.

Required

Form groups of three students for a role-play.

- The first person assumes the role of GourmetGifts president Jennifer Wildt. Before the meeting, prepare a written report that costs baskets sold to individuals using (a) direct materials cost, and (b) direct labor cost as the indirect cost allocation base. Also, estimate the selling price under each allocation base. Carry computations of the indirect cost allocation rate to four decimal places. Prepare arguments supporting direct materials cost as the cost allocation base.
- The second person assumes the role of cost accountant Ling Chen. Before the meeting, prepare a written report that costs baskets sold to corporate customers using (a) direct materials cost, and (b) direct labor cost as the indirect cost allocation base. Estimate the selling price under each allocation base. Carry computations of the indirect cost allocation rate to four decimal places. Prepare arguments supporting direct labor cost as the cost allocation base.
- The third person assumes the role of controller Jay Boros. Before the meeting, prepare a written report on the factors GourmetGifts should consider in identifying a cost allocation base.

During the meeting, the three team members decide which cost allocation base is best for GourmetGifts and what additional information, if any, would help in making this decision.

INTERNET EXERCISE

Dell Computer

Dell Computer Corporation entered the twenty-first century with an enviable record as the most successful company in the global computer systems industry. In terms of market share, it is the number one company in the United States, and number two in the world. One bold concept—direct customer contact—has made Dell one of the world's most successful companies.

1. Go to **http://www.dell.com/** and in the navigation bar at the top of the screen click on *About Dell* followed by *Investor Relations*. In the left-hand column, click on *Annual Reports* and then the HTML version of the most recent *Year in Review*.
   a. In the left-hand column, click on the *Five-Year Statistical Review*. Most of Dell's net revenues are generated from which region? From which product line?
   b. How can this information help managers?
2. At the top of the page, click on the *Annual Report on Form 10-K*. Scroll down until you reach the table of contents. Click on *Item: Financial Statements and Supplementary Data*. Scroll down to review the *Consolidated Statement of Income*.
   a. Which expense account(s) contain inventoriable costs? Noninventoriable costs?
   b. For what reason are noninventoriable costs assigned to products?

3. Scroll down and find *Note 13—Supplemental Consolidated Financial Information.* Refer to the information regarding inventories. (Note: In the 2000 annual report it was on page 46.)
   a. For the most recent year-end, what amount was reported for Production materials inventory? Work-in-process and finished goods inventory? Which type of inventory has the greatest dollar value? What might explain this?
   b. Which of these types of inventory includes direct material costs? Direct labor costs? Depreciation on the manufacturing plant?

Go to the "Alternative Income Statement Formats and Extraordinary Items" episode on the Mastering Accounting CD-ROM for an interactive, video-enhanced exercise on CanGo managers' need to consider the different income statement formats and their effect on investors.

21 Process Costing

LEARNING OBJECTIVES

After studying this chapter, you should be able to

1. Distinguish between the flow of costs in process costing and job costing

2. Record process costing transactions

3. Compute equivalent units

4. Assign costs to units completed and to units in ending work in process inventory

5. Account for a second processing department by the FIFO method

6. Account for a second processing department by the weighted-average method

www.prenhall.com/horngren

Readiness Assessment

Pace Foods, a division of **Campbell Soup Co.,** leads the market in the dynamic "Mexican sauces" food category, which has surpassed ketchup in supermarket sales in the United States. The San Antonio, Texas, company mass-produces several-ton batches of mild, medium, and hot sauces in both regular and thick-and-chunky styles. Pace Foods can produce more than 150 million pounds of picante sauce and salsa a year.

Pace picante sauce is made in two processes. In the first, jalapeño peppers, onions, and other fresh vegetables are received from suppliers and then chopped into small pieces. In the second process, workers mix the vegetables with tomato products and spices. Then the picante sauce is cooked, bottled, and boxed for shipping. Inspectors test each batch to ensure purity and consistent texture and flavor.

Pace has invested in state-of-the-art manufacturing processes as well as in continuous improvement programs targeted at reducing costs and increasing the quality of the sauce. The result? Despite intense competition from major international food companies, Pace Foods has achieved steady double-digit growth.

How much does it cost **Pace Foods** to make a batch of hot picante sauce? How efficient was the cooking and bottling process last week? What is the value of the inventory of fresh vegetables in the chopping process? Like their counterparts in other manufacturing companies, managers at Pace use accounting information to answer these questions.

PROCESS COSTING: AN OVERVIEW

The two basic types of product costing systems are *job costing* and *process costing*. We saw in Chapter 20 that companies like **Dell Computer, Boeing,** and **PricewaterhouseCoopers** use job costing to determine the cost to produce custom goods and services. Job cost records accumulate the cost of each individual job.

In contrast, companies like **Pace Foods, Shell Oil,** and **Sony** use process costing to assign costs to goods that are mass-produced in a continuous sequence of steps called processes. Process industries produce large numbers of identical units (CDs, electronics like Sony Playstations or PalmPilots, and packaged foods like Hershey Kisses or Pace picante sauce). Many companies in the petroleum, food and beverage, pharmaceutical, and electronics industries use process costing.

In process industries, the flow of goods through the processes or departments is continuous and repetitive. For example, to produce picante sauce, Pace Foods has one department for chopping the vegetables and a second department for mixing and bottling. The company does not use job cost records. Instead, it accumulates costs in each department for each production period. Unit cost is computed by dividing the cost incurred in a department by the number of units produced in that department. For example, if the Chopping Department incurs $350,000 of costs to chop 1,000,000 pounds of vegetables, the unit cost of the Chopping Department is $0.35 ($350,000/1,000,000). If the Mixing & Bottling Department then incurs $500,000 to mix and bottle 1,000,000 pounds of picante sauce, the Mixing & Bottling Department's unit cost is $0.50 ($500,000/1,000,000). The *total* cost for a 1-pound bottle of chopped, mixed, and bottled picante sauce is then $0.85 ($0.35 + $0.50).

Exhibit 21-1 compares the flow of costs in

- A job costing system for Blue Ridge Fabrication, a manufacturer of custom-built machinery
- A process costing system for Pace Foods

Panel A shows that in Blue Ridge Fabrication's job costing system, there is a single Work in Process Inventory control account, supported by individual subsidiary job cost records for each job in process. Blue Ridge assigns direct materials, direct labor, and manufacturing overhead to individual jobs, as explained in Chapter 20. When the job is finished, its costs flow directly into Finished Goods Inventory, *not* from one Work in Process Inventory account into another.

EXHIBIT 21-1
Comparison of Job Costing and Process Costing

 DAILY EXERCISE 21-1

Objective 1
Distinguish between the flow of costs in process costing and job costing

Panel A: Job Costing
Blue Ridge Fabrication, custom-built machinery

[Diagram: Direct Materials, Direct Labor, Manufacturing Overhead flow into Job 100, Job 101, and Job 102, which flow into Finished Goods, then Cost of Goods Sold.]

[T-accounts: Materials Inventory (xx), Manufacturing Wages (xx), Manufacturing Overhead (xx) flow into Work in Process Inventory (xx, xx, xx) then (xx) to Finished Goods Inventory (xx, xx) then (xx) to Cost of Goods Sold (xx).]

Panel B: Process Costing
Pace Picante Sauce

[Diagram: Direct Materials, Direct Labor, Manufacturing Overhead flow into Chopping Process, then Mixing & Bottling Process, then Finished Goods, then Cost of Goods Sold.]

[T-accounts: Materials Inventory (xx, xx), Manufacturing Wages (xx, xx, xx), Manufacturing Overhead (xx, xx) flow into Work in Process Inventory—Chopping (xx, xx, xx) then (xxx) to Work in Process Inventory—Mixing & Bottling (xx, xxx, xx, xx) then (xxx) to Finished Goods Inventory (xxx, xxx) then (xxx) to Cost of Goods Sold (xxx).]

In contrast to Blue Ridge Fabrication's individual jobs, Pace Foods uses a series of *manufacturing processes* to produce large quantities of picante sauce. Pace has two manufacturing departments: (1) Chopping, and (2) Mixing & Bottling. Exhibit 21-2 illustrates the Pace manufacturing process. In the chopping process, Pace uses labor and equipment to chop the vegetables. In the mixing and bottling process, Pace uses labor and equipment first to add tomato products, and then to mix and bottle the sauce. Companies like Pace that use a series of manufacturing processes to produce large quantities of similar products typically use process costing systems.

EXHIBIT 21-2
Flow of Costs in Production of
Picante Sauce

Chopping Process

Direct Materials — (jalapeño peppers, onions)
Direct Labor — (workers operating chopping equipment)
Manufacturing Overhead — (depreciation on chopping equipment)
Chopped vegetables

DAILY EXERCISE 21-2

Mixing and Bottling Process

Direct Materials — (tomato products, bottles, caps)
Direct Labor — (workers operating bottling equipment)
Manufacturing Overhead — (depreciation on bottling equipment)
Finished Picante sauce

Notice four aspects of the process costing system in Panel B of Exhibit 21-1:

1. Each manufacturing process (chopping; mixing and bottling) has its own separate Work in Process Inventory account.
2. Direct materials, direct labor, and manufacturing overhead are assigned to each manufacturing process. For example:

	Work in Process Inventory—Chopping	Work in Process Inventory—Mixing & Bottling
Direct materials	Peppers, onions	Tomato products, bottles, caps
Direct labor	Wages of workers operating chopping equipment	Wages of workers operating bottling equipment
Manufacturing overhead	Depreciation on chopping equipment	Depreciation on bottling equipment

3. When the chopping process is complete, the chopped vegetables move out of the chopping process and into the mixing and bottling process. The cost of the vegetables is likewise transferred out of Work in Process Inventory—Chopping, and into Work in Process Inventory—Mixing & Bottling.
4. When the mixing and bottling process is complete, the finished picante sauce goes to finished goods storage. The costs (including costs from the Chopping Department as well as the Mixing & Bottling Department) flow into Finished Goods Inventory. Costs flow into Finished Goods Inventory only from the Work in Process Inventory of the *last* manufacturing process.

Exhibit 21-3 on page 844 summarizes the flow of costs through this process costing system (all amounts are in thousands and are assumed).

DAILY EXERCISE 21-3

RECORDING COSTS

Process costing journal entries are similar to those for job costing. Accountants first *accumulate* the costs of materials purchased, and labor and actual manufacturing overhead incurred during the period (for all processes). These journal entries are identical to those made in job costing. For example, to record the purchase of materials ($11,000), and the cost of manufacturing labor ($4,000) and actual manufacturing overhead ($10,000), **Pace** would make the following journal entries (amounts in thousands):

Objective 2
Record process costing transactions

Materials Inventory	11	
Accounts Payable		11
Manufacturing Wages	4	
Wages Payable		4
Manufacturing Overhead	10	
Accumulated Depreciation—Plant		2
Property Tax Payable—Plant		2
Accounts Payable, and so on		6

To purchase materials and incur direct labor and actual manufacturing overhead.

EXHIBIT 21-3

Flow of Costs Through a Process Costing System (Amounts in Thousands)

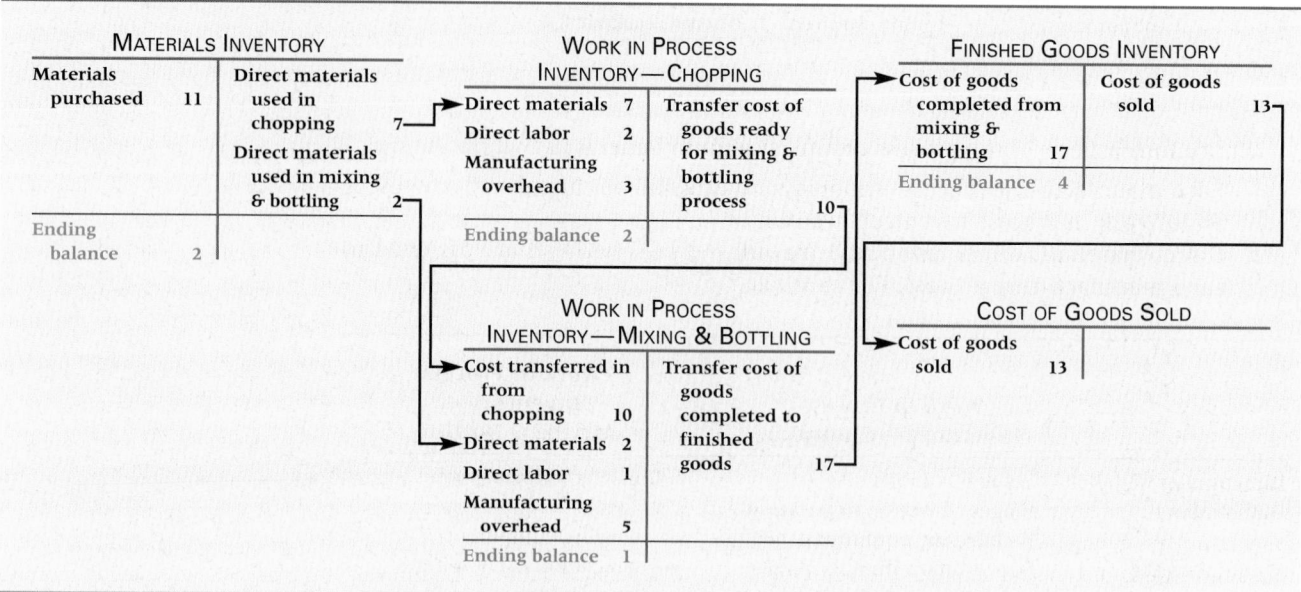

The main difference between job costing and process costing is in *assigning* the costs of direct materials, direct labor, and manufacturing overhead. Job costing assigns costs to individual *jobs* that are transferred from Work in Process Inventory directly to Finished Goods Inventory. Process costing assigns costs to *processes*. There is a separate Work in Process Inventory account for each process. As products move from one process to the next, their costs flow from one Work in Process Inventory account to the next.

➤ Chapter 20, p. 801, distinguishes between *accumulating* actual costs and *assigning* costs to jobs and processes.

The following entries detail the flow of costs through the process costing system in Exhibit 21-3.

DAILY EXERCISE 21-4

Work in Process Inventory—Chopping	12	
Materials Inventory		7
Manufacturing Wages		2
Manufacturing Overhead		3

To requisition direct materials, assign direct labor cost, and allocate manufacturing overhead to the Chopping Department.

Work in Process Inventory—Mixing & Bottling	10	
Work in Process Inventory—Chopping		10

To transfer cost out of the Chopping Department and into the Mixing & Bottling Department.

Work in Process Inventory—Mixing & Bottling............................	8	
Materials Inventory...		2
Manufacturing Wages..		1
Manufacturing Overhead		5
To record the additional direct materials, direct labor, and		
overhead allocated to the Mixing & Bottling Department.		
Finished Goods Inventory..	17	
Work in Process Inventory—Mixing & Bottling............................		17
To transfer the cost of goods completed out of the Mixing		
& Bottling Department and into Finished Goods Inventory.		
Cost of Goods Sold	13	
Finished Goods Inventory		13
To account for the cost of goods sold.		

Notice that in process costing

- Direct materials, direct labor, and manufacturing overhead costs are assigned to separate Work in Process Inventory accounts *for each process.*
- Costs are transferred, along with the units, from one Work in Process Inventory account to the next. Costs are not transferred to Finished Goods Inventory *until the last process is completed.*

 DAILY EXERCISE 21-5

 DAILY EXERCISE 21-6

BUILDING BLOCKS OF PROCESS COSTING

Exhibit 21-3 shows that the total cost of the first process, chopping, was $12,000 ($7,000 direct materials + $2,000 direct labor + $3,000 manufacturing overhead). Where did this $12,000 in costs go? The exhibit shows that $10,000 was transferred out of Work in Process—Chopping and into Work in Process—Mixing & Bottling, leaving a $2,000 ending balance in Work in Process—Chopping. How do we know how much of the $12,000 to assign to the chopped vegetables transferred out versus those still in ending inventory? Before we can answer this key question, we must first learn about two building blocks of process costing:

- Conversion costs
- Equivalent units

Conversion Costs

Chapter 19 introduced three kinds of manufacturing costs: direct materials, direct labor, and manufacturing overhead. Companies like **Hewlett-Packard** and **Harley-Davidson** that use automated production processes often find that direct labor costs are only a small part of total manufacturing costs. Such companies often use only two categories:

- Direct materials
- **Conversion costs** (direct labor plus manufacturing overhead)

CONVERSION COSTS. Direct labor plus manufacturing overhead.

Collapsing direct labor and manufacturing overhead into a single category simplifies the accounting. We call this category *conversion costs* because it is the cost (direct labor plus manufacturing overhead) to *convert* raw materials into new finished products.

Equivalent Units

Objective 3
Compute equivalent units

Equivalent units measure the amount of work done during a period, expressed in terms of fully complete units of output. Assume **Calloway's** golf ball production plant has 5,000 balls in ending work in process inventory. Each ball is 80% of the way through the production process. If conversion costs are incurred evenly throughout the process, then getting 5,000 balls each 80% of the way through the process takes about the same amount of work as getting 4,000 balls (5,000 × 80%)

EQUIVALENT UNITS. A measure of the amount of work done during a period, expressed in terms of fully complete units of output.

all the way through. Thus, ending work in process inventory has 4,000 equivalent units. For costs that are incurred evenly throughout the production process:

○ DAILY EXERCISE 21-7

Number of partially complete units	×	Percentage of process completed	=	Number of equivalent units
5,000	×	80%	=	4,000

This formula holds only for costs that are incurred evenly throughout the production process. This is usually true for conversion costs (direct labor and manufacturing overhead). However, direct materials are often added at a particular point in the production process. Rubber is added at the very beginning of the production process and packaging materials are not added until the very end. How many equivalent units of rubber and packaging materials are in the ending inventory of 5,000 balls?

You can answer this question by looking at the time line in Exhibit 21-4:

EXHIBIT 21-4   Calloway Production Plant Time Line

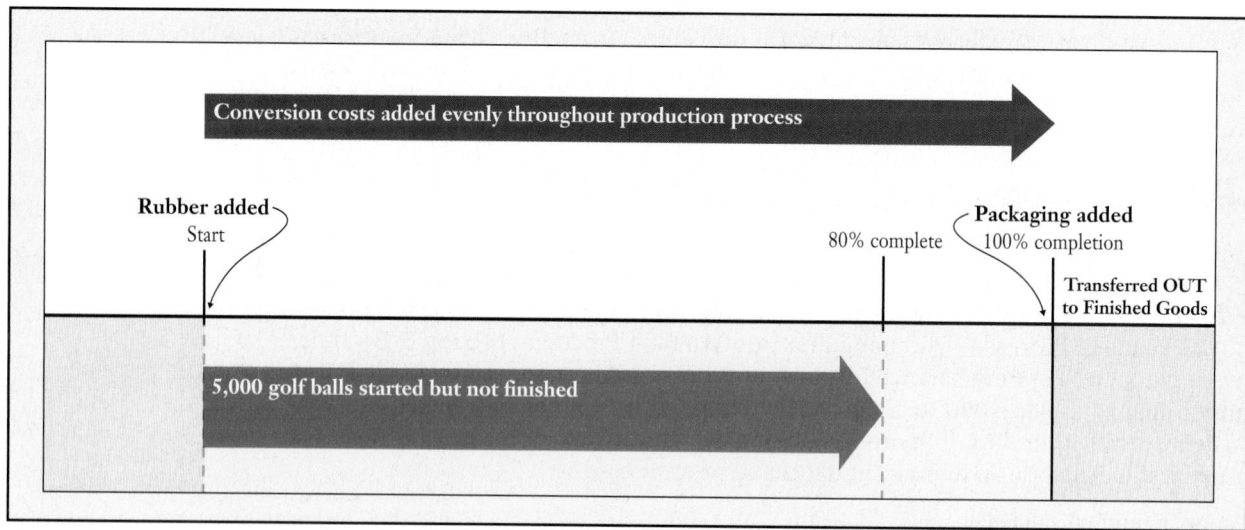

All 5,000 balls are 80% complete, so they have all passed the point where rubber is added. Thus, each ball has its full share of rubber, so the balls have 5,000 equivalent units of rubber. In contrast, the time line shows that *none* of the 5,000 balls has made it to the end of the process, where the packaging materials are added. The ending inventory therefore has *zero* equivalent units of packaging materials.

To summarize, the 5,000 balls in ending work in process inventory have

- 5,000 equivalent units of rubber
- 0 equivalent units of packaging materials
- 4,000 equivalent units of conversion costs

The point is that inputs added at different points in the process can have different equivalent units. In this case, the 5,000 physical balls have different equivalent units of rubber, packaging materials, and conversion costs.

Be careful to distinguish the *end of the production process* from the *end of the accounting period*. Goods at the end of the production process are transferred to the next process or to finished goods. For example, Calloway's completed golf balls proceed to the finished goods warehouse. By contrast, at the end of the accounting period, goods that are only partway through the production process are the ending work in process inventory. Calloway's ending work in process inventory includes 5,000 golf balls that have their rubber cores but no packaging.

PROCESS COSTING: AN ILLUSTRATION

Let's examine SeaView, a sporting goods company that manufactures swim masks. The Shaping Department shapes the body of the swim masks. The process begins with direct materials (including plastic) that labor and equipment transform into shaped masks. The direct materials are added at the beginning of the process, but conversion costs are incurred evenly throughout the shaping process. After shaping, the partially completed masks move to the Finishing Department, where the mask bodies are finished and the clear faceplates are inserted and sealed in place.

During October, the Shaping Department incurs the following costs in processing 50,000 masks:

Direct materials...............................		$140,000
Conversion costs:		
Direct labor..................................	$21,250	
Manufacturing overhead..............	46,750	68,000
Costs to account for		$208,000

If the shaping process is complete for all 50,000 masks, the costs transferred to Work in Process Inventory—Finishing are the full $208,000. The unit cost is $4.16 ($208,000/50,000 masks).

But what if only 40,000 masks are completely through the shaping process? At October 31, the Shaping Department still has 10,000 masks that are only one-quarter of the way through. How do we split the $208,000 between

- 40,000 completely shaped masks transferred to the Finishing Department
- 10,000 partially shaped masks remaining in the Shaping Department's ending work in process inventory

The answer lies in a five-step process costing procedure. We begin with the Shaping Department.

Step 1: Summarize the Flow of Physical Units

Exhibit 21-5 tracks the movement of swim masks into and out of the Shaping Department. We assume for simplicity that work began October 1, so the Work in

 DAILY EXERCISE 21-8

 DAILY EXERCISE 21-9

EXHIBIT 21-5
Step 1: Summarize the Flow of Physical Units; Step 2: Compute Output in Terms of Equivalent Units

		Step 2 Equivalent Units	
	Step 1		
Flow of Production	**Flow of Physical Units**	**Direct Materials**	**Conversion Costs**
Units to account for:			
Beginning work in process, September 30	—		
Started in production during October	50,000		
Total physical units to account for......................................	50,000		
Units accounted for:			
Completed and transferred out during October	40,000	40,000	40,000
Ending work in process, October 31	10,000	10,000	2,500*
Total physical units accounted for	50,000		
Equivalent units...		50,000	42,500

SEAVIEW
SHAPING DEPARTMENT
Month of October 31, 20XX

*10,000 units each 25% complete = 2,500 equivalent units

847

Process Inventory account had a zero balance at September 30. Of the 50,000 masks started in October, 40,000 were completely shaped and transferred out to the Finishing Department during the month. The remaining 10,000 partially shaped masks are the Shaping Department's ending work in process inventory on October 31.

Step 2: Compute Output in Terms of Equivalent Units

We compute equivalent units separately for direct materials and conversion costs because work progresses differently for materials and for conversion. The Shaping Department time line in Exhibit 21-6 shows that all direct materials are added at the beginning of the process. In contrast, conversion costs are incurred evenly throughout the process. As Exhibit 21-6 shows, 40,000 masks are complete as to both materials and conversion costs. These completed masks have incurred 40,000 equivalent units of direct materials, and 40,000 equivalent units of conversion costs.

EXHIBIT 21-6 SeaView's Shaping Department Time Line

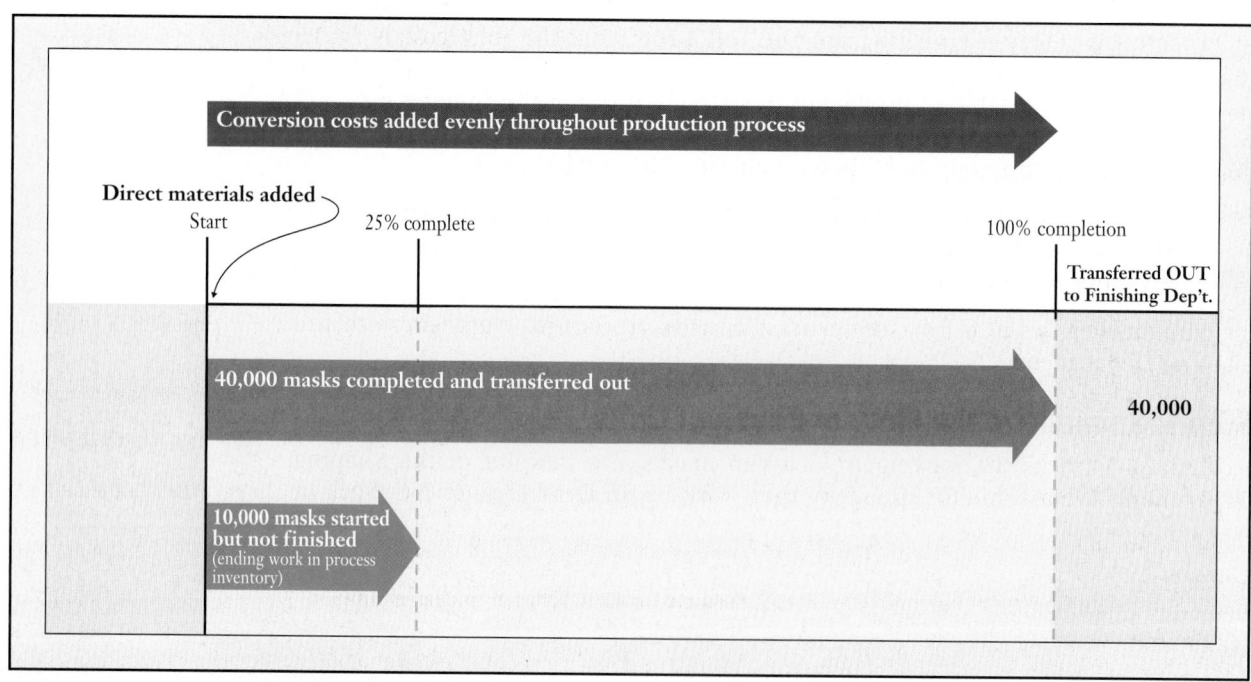

The Shaping Department has another 10,000 masks that are only 25% of the way through the process on October 31. Direct materials are added at the beginning of the process, so the time line shows that all the direct materials have been added to these 10,000 masks, even though the masks are only 25% of the way through the shaping process. The total equivalent units of direct materials include the 40,000 finished masks plus the 10,000 masks in ending (work in process) inventory that are complete as to direct materials, as shown in step 2 of Exhibit 21-5.

Shaping Department conversion costs are incurred evenly throughout the process. The time line shows that for each of the 10,000 partially completed masks, 25% of the conversion costs have been incurred by October 31. The equivalent units of conversion costs are

10,000 × 25% = 2,500 equivalent units

DAILY EXERCISE 21-10

The total equivalent units of conversion costs include the 40,000 finished masks plus the 2,500 equivalent units of conversion costs from the masks in ending work in process inventory that are only partially completed on October 31, as shown in step 2 of Exhibit 21-5.

WORK IT OUT

Suppose that direct materials were added at the *end* of SeaView's shaping process rather than at the beginning.

1. Draw a new time line similar to Exhibit 21-6.
2. Use the time line to determine the number of equivalent units of direct materials in the Shaping Department.

Answers

1. Conversion costs added evenly throughout production process

2. The time line shows that direct materials are not added until the *end* of the process, and the 10,000 masks in ending work in process inventory have not made it to the end of the shaping process. Since *no* direct materials have been added to the ending work in process inventory, materials have been added *only* to the 40,000 masks completed and transferred out. Thus, there are 40,000 equivalent units of direct materials.

Step 3: Summarize Total Costs to Account For

Exhibit 21-7 summarizes the total costs to account for in the Shaping Department (cost data are from page 847). These costs are the total debits in Work in Process Inventory—Shaping, including any beginning balance.

EXHIBIT 21-7
Step 3: Summarize Total Costs to Account For

SEAVIEW SHAPING DEPARTMENT
Month Ended October 31, 20XX

WORK IN PROCESS INVENTORY—SHAPING

	Physical Units	Dollars		Physical Units	Dollars
Beginning inventory September 30	-0-	$ -0-	Transferred out	40,000	$?
Production started:	50,000				
Direct materials		140,000			
Conversion costs:					
Direct labor		21,250			
Manufacturing overhead		46,750			
Total to account for	50,000	$208,000			
Ending inventory, October 31	10,000	$?			

The Shaping Department has 50,000 physical units and $208,000 of costs to account for. Our next task is to split these costs between the 40,000 shaped masks transferred out to the Finishing Department, and the 10,000 masks that remain in the Shaping Department's ending work in process inventory.

Step 4: Compute the Cost per Equivalent Unit

In step 2, we computed the total number of equivalent units for direct materials (50,000) and conversion costs (42,500). Because the equivalent units differ, we must compute a separate cost per unit for each category. Exhibit 21-7 shows that the direct materials cost is $140,000. Conversion cost is $68,000, which is the sum of direct labor ($21,250) and manufacturing overhead ($46,750).

To compute the direct material cost per equivalent unit, remember that the word *per* means "divided by." So the direct material cost *per* equivalent unit is the direct material cost *divided by* the number of direct material equivalent units:

$$\frac{\$140{,}000 \text{ total direct material cost}}{50{,}000 \text{ total direct material equivalent units}} = \substack{\$2.80 \text{ direct material cost per} \\ \text{equivalent unit}}$$

We compute the conversion cost per equivalent unit similarly:

 DAILY EXERCISE 21-11

 DAILY EXERCISE 21-12

$$\frac{\$68{,}000 \text{ total conversion cost}}{42{,}500 \text{ total conversion cost equivalent units}} = \substack{\$1.60 \text{ conversion cost per} \\ \text{equivalent unit}}$$

Exhibit 21-8 summarizes the computation of equivalent-unit costs.

EXHIBIT 21-8
Step 4: Compute the Cost per Equivalent Unit

SEAVIEW SHAPING DEPARTMENT Month Ended October 31, 20XX		
	Direct Materials	**Conversion Costs**
Beginning work in process, September 30......................	$ 0	$ 0
Costs added during October (from Exhibit 21-7)...........	$140,000	$68,000
Divide by equivalent units (from Exhibit 21-5).............	÷ 50,000	÷ 42,500
Cost per equivalent unit...	$2.80	$1.60

In addition to using the cost per equivalent unit in the five-step process costing procedure, managers also use this information to determine how well they have controlled costs. If the cost per equivalent unit of conversion (or direct materials) meets or beats the budgeted target cost per equivalent unit, the manager has successfully controlled the conversion (or direct materials) costs.

Objective 4
Assign costs to units completed and to units in ending work in process inventory

 DAILY EXERCISE 21-13

Step 5: Assign Costs to Units Completed and to Units in Ending Work in Process Inventory

Exhibit 21-9 shows how the equivalent units computed in step 2 (Exhibit 21-5) are costed at the cost per equivalent unit computed in step 4 (Exhibit 21-8). The goal of Exhibit 21-9 is to determine how much of the $208,000 total costs incurred by the Shaping Department should be assigned to (1) the 40,000 completely shaped masks that have been transferred out to the Finishing Department, and (2) the 10,000 partially shaped masks remaining in Shaping's ending work in process inventory.

EXHIBIT 21-9
Step 5: Assign Costs to Units Completed and to Units in Ending Work in Process Inventory

SEAVIEW SHAPING DEPARTMENT Month Ended October 31, 20XX			
	Direct Materials	**Conversion Costs**	**Total**
Completed and transferred out (40,000)...................................	[40,000 × ($2.80 + $1.60)]		= $176,000
Ending work in process inventory (10,000):			
Direct materials..	[10,000 × $2.80]		= $ 28,000
Conversion costs		[2,500 × $1.60]	= 4,000
Total cost of ending work in process inventory			$ 32,000
Total cost accounted for...			$208,000

First consider the 40,000 masks completed and transferred out. Exhibit 21-5 reveals 40,000 equivalent units of work for both direct materials and conversion costs. Thus, the total cost of these completed masks is (40,000 × $2.80) + (40,000 × $1.60), or simply 40,000 × $4.40 = $176,000, as shown in Exhibit 21-9.

Next consider the 10,000 masks still being shaped at the end of the month. These masks have 10,000 equivalent units of direct materials (at $2.80 per unit), so the direct material cost is 10,000 × $2.80 = $28,000. The 2,500 equivalent units of conversion work in the ending inventory at $1.60 per equivalent unit yields conversion costs of $4,000 (2,500 × $1.60). As Exhibit 21-9 shows, the total cost of the 10,000 partially completed masks in Shaping's ending (work in process) inventory is the sum of these direct material and conversion costs: $28,000 + $4,000 = $32,000.

Exhibit 21-9 has accomplished our goal of splitting the $208,000 total cost identified in step 3 (Exhibit 21-7) between

The 40,000 masks completed and transferred out to the Finishing Department..	$176,000
The 10,000 masks remaining in the Shaping Department's ending work in process inventory on October 31	32,000
Total costs of the Shaping Department	$208,000

RECORDING THE COSTS   Journal entries to record October production in the Shaping Department follow (data from Exhibit 21-7):

Work in Process Inventory—Shaping	208,000	
Materials Inventory..		140,000
Manufacturing Wages		21,250
Manufacturing Overhead..		46,750
To requisition materials and assign labor and overhead cost to the Shaping Department.		

The entry to transfer the cost of the 40,000 completed masks out of the Shaping Department and into the Finishing Department is as follows (data from Exhibit 21-9):

Work in Process Inventory—Finishing	176,000	
Work in Process Inventory—Shaping......................		176,000

After these entries are posted, the Work in Process Inventory—Shaping account appears as follows:

WORK IN PROCESS INVENTORY—SHAPING

Balance, September 30	—	**Transferred to Finishing**	176,000
Direct materials	140,000		
Direct labor	21,250		
Manufacturing overhead	46,750		
Balance, October 31	32,000		

 DAILY EXERCISE 21-14

 WORK IT OUT   What is the shaping cost per mask for each of the 40,000 masks completed and transferred out of the Shaping Department and into the Finishing Department? Why would SeaView's managers be interested in this information?

Answer: Shaping's cost per mask is $4.40—the $176,000 total Shaping Department cost assigned to the masks completed and transferred out (from Exhibit 21-9), divided by the total number of masks completed and transferred out of Shaping and into Finishing (40,000).

SeaView's managers would compare the cost per mask of the shaping process in October against the planned cost per mask to evaluate the efficiency of the Shaping Department's October operations. Also, the costs of the shaped masks will flow into the Finishing Department, and will become part of the total cost of the completed masks. Management can use the total cost of the masks to set selling prices and to determine which products are most profitable.

Before continuing, review the Process Costing Decision Guidelines to make sure you understand equivalent units and the flow of costs in process costing.

DECISION GUIDELINES

Process Costing—First Process (No Beginning Inventory)

DECISION	GUIDELINES
How do costs flow from Work in Process Inventory to Finished Goods Inventory?	Job costing → Costs flow from Work in Process Inventory directly to Finished Goods Inventory.
	Process costing → Costs flow from one Work in Process Inventory account to the next, until the last process. Costs flow from Work in Process Inventory of the last process into Finished Goods Inventory.
How many Work in Process Inventory accounts in a process costing system?	There is one Work In Process Inventory account for each separate manufacturing process.
How to account for partially complete goods?	Use equivalent units.

If cost is incurred evenly throughout the production process:

$$\text{Equivalent units} = \text{Number of partially complete units} \times \text{Percentage of process completed}$$

If cost is added at a specific point in the production process:
- If physical units have passed the point where cost is added → units are complete with respect to that cost, so equivalent units of that cost = physical units
- If physical units have *not* passed the point where cost is added → units have not incurred any of that cost, so equivalent units of that cost = 0

DECISION	GUIDELINES
Which costs require separate equivalent-unit computations?	Perform separate equivalent-unit computations for each input added at a different point in the production process. Often this requires separate computations for (1) direct materials, and (2) conversion costs.
How to compute the cost per equivalent unit?	Divide the cost by the number of equivalent units
How to split the costs of a process between • Units completed and transferred out?	Multiply the cost per equivalent unit by • Number of equivalent units of work in the physical units completed and transferred out
• Units in ending work in process inventory?	• Number of equivalent units of work in the ending work in process inventory
How to evaluate whether a manager controlled his department's costs?	If direct material and conversion cost per equivalent unit meets or beats target unit costs, the manager has controlled costs

MID-CHAPTER

SUMMARY PROBLEM

Use the five steps of process costing to identify the missing amounts X and Y in the following report prepared by Florida Tile Industries for May.

TILE-FORMING DEPARTMENT
Production Cost Report
Month Ended May 31, 20XX

	Physical Units	Total Costs
Beginning work in process, April 30	—	$ —
Started in production during May	20,000	43,200*
Total to account for	20,000	$43,200
Completed and transferred to Finishing Department during May	16,000	$ X
Ending work in process, May 31 (25% complete as to direct materials, 55% complete as to conversion cost)	4,000	Y
Total accounted for	20,000	$43,200

*Includes direct materials of $6,800 and conversion costs of $36,400

Solution

Step 1: Summarize the flow of physical units.

Step 2: Compute output in terms of equivalent units.

TILE-FORMING DEPARTMENT
Month Ended May 31, 20XX

	Step 1	Step 2 Equivalent Units	
Flow of Production	**Flow of Physical Units**	**Direct Materials**	**Conversion Costs**
Units to account for:			
Beginning work in process, April 30	—		
Started in production during May	20,000		
Total physical units to account for	20,000		
Units accounted for:			
Completed and transferred out in May	16,000	16,000	16,000
Ending work in process, May 31	4,000	1,000*	2,200*
Total physical units accounted for	20,000		
Equivalent units		17,000	18,200

*Direct materials: 4,000 units each 25% complete = 1,000 equivalent units
Conversion costs: 4,000 units each 55% complete = 2,200 equivalent units

Step 3: Summarize total costs to account for.

TILE-FORMING DEPARTMENT
Month Ended May 31, 20XX

	Direct Materials	Conversion Costs	Total
Beginning work in process, April 30	$ 0	$ 0	$ 0
Costs added during May*	6,800	36,400	43,200
Total cost to account for	$6,800	$36,400	$43,200

*From information in the Production Cost Report above.

Step 4: Compute the cost per equivalent unit.

TILE-FORMING DEPARTMENT
Month Ended May 31, 20XX

	Direct Materials	Conversion Costs
Beginning work in process, April 30	$ 0	$ 0
Costs added during May	$ 6,800	$36,400
Divide by equivalent units...	÷17,000	÷18,200
Cost per equivalent unit	$0.40	$2.00

Step 5: Assign costs to units completed and to units in ending work in process inventory.

TILE-FORMING DEPARTMENT
Month Ended May 31, 20XX

	Direct Materials	Conversion Costs	Total
X: Units completed and transferred out (16,000)	[16,000 × ($0.40 + $2.00)]		= $38,400
Units in ending work in process inventory (4,000):			
Direct materials	[1,000 × $0.40]		= 400
Conversion costs...........................		[2,200 × $2.00] =	4,400
Y: Total cost of ending work in process inventory..............................			4,800
Total cost accounted for			$43,200

PROCESS COSTING FOR A SECOND DEPARTMENT

Most products require a series of processing steps. In this section, we introduce a second department—SeaView's Finishing Department—to complete the picture of process costing.

The Finishing Department receives the shaped masks, then smoothes and polishes them before inserting the faceplates at the end of the process. Thus,

- Shaped masks are transferred in from Shaping at the beginning of Finishing's process.
- Finishing's conversion costs are added evenly throughout the process.
- Finishing's direct materials (faceplates) are not added until the end of the finishing process.

Keep in mind that the label *direct materials* in the Finishing Department refers to the faceplates added *in that department* and not to the materials (the plastic) added in the Shaping Department. Likewise, *conversion cost* in the Finishing Department refers to all manufacturing costs (other than direct materials) incurred only in Finishing.

Don't confuse the Finishing Department with finished goods inventory. The Finishing Department is SeaView's second process. The masks do not become part of finished goods inventory until they have *completed* SeaView's second process, which in this case happens to be the Finishing Department.

As in many areas of accounting, there are alternative methods of accounting for process costs. We discuss two: the first-in, first-out (FIFO) method and the weighted-average method. *The FIFO and weighted-average methods differ only in their treatment of beginning work in process inventory.*

Because SeaView's Shaping Department (discussed in the first half of the chapter) had no beginning work in process inventory, we did not need to specify whether that department used the FIFO or weighted-average method. By contrast, SeaView's Finishing Department does have beginning work in process inventory. We now use the Finishing Department to illustrate the FIFO method. (The following section covers the weighted-average method.) Although the details of the FIFO and weighted average methods differ, both use the same basic five-step process costing procedure we used earlier in the chapter.

THE FIFO METHOD

The **first-in, first-out (FIFO) method** of process costing assigns to each period's equivalent units of production that period's costs per equivalent unit. ➤ Consider a batch of swim masks that were transferred out of the Shaping Department and into the Finishing Department at the end of September. These masks did not make it completely through the Finishing Department during September, so the masks are in the Finishing Department's ending (work in process) inventory at the end of September. The masks are not completed until October. Under the FIFO method, when these masks are completed in October, the total Finishing Department cost of these masks is the sum of

- September's equivalent units of Finishing's work on these masks, costed at September's cost per equivalent unit, *plus*
- October's equivalent units of Finishing's work on these masks, costed at October's cost per equivalent unit

Steps 1 and 2: Summarize the Flow of Physical Units and Compute Output in Terms of Equivalent Units

Exhibit 21-10 lists October information for SeaView's Finishing Department. Exhibit 21-11 diagrams these data on a time line to help you see what equivalent units of work the Finishing Department performed *during October*. This is important because under FIFO, the focus is on the current period—October in this example. The FIFO method determines October equivalent units of work and costs those units with October unit costs. The advantage of the FIFO method is that managers can use

Objective 5
Account for a second processing department by the FIFO method

◄ In Chapter 9, we saw that in the FIFO method of inventory costing, the first costs into Inventory are the first costs out to Cost of Goods Sold.

FIRST-IN, FIRST-OUT (FIFO) PROCESS COSTING METHOD. A process costing method that assigns to each period's equivalent units of production that period's costs per equivalent unit.

 DAILY EXERCISE 21-15

EXHIBIT 21-10
SeaView's Finishing Department Data for October

Units:		
Beginning work in process, September 30		
(0% complete as to direct materials,		
60% complete as to conversion work)		5,000 units
Transferred in from Shaping Department		
during October		40,000 units
Completed and transferred out to Finished Goods		
Inventory during October		38,000 units
Ending work in process, October 31 (0% complete as		
to direct materials, 30% complete as to		
conversion work)		7,000 units
Costs:		
Beginning work in process, September 30		
(transferred-in costs, $22,900;		
conversion costs, $1,100)		$ 24,000
Transferred in from Shaping Department		
during October (from Exhibit 21-9)		176,000
Direct materials added during October in		
Finishing Department		19,000
Conversion costs added during October in		
Finishing Department:		
Direct labor	$ 3,710	
Manufacturing overhead	11,130	14,840

these current costs per unit to measure the efficiency of production during the month of October.

Exhibits 21-11 and 21-12 summarize the flow of physical units (step 1). The Finishing Department time line in Exhibit 21-11 is more complex than Shaping's time line in Exhibit 21-6. Why? Finishing has beginning work in process inventory (left over from the end of September), while Shaping does not. The 38,000 total masks that were completed and transferred out of the Finishing Department and into Finished Goods Inventory include

- 5,000 masks that were the Finishing Department's beginning work in process inventory. These masks were *completed* (but not started) in October.
- 33,000 masks that Finishing both *started* and *completed* during October. This number is computed as

38,000	masks completed and transferred out of the Finishing Department in October
(5,000)	masks completed from Finishing's beginning inventory
33,000	masks *started and completed during October*

The time line also shows that the 40,000 masks *transferred into* Finishing from Shaping during October (see Exhibits 21-5 and 21-6) also fall into two categories:

- 33,000 masks *started and completed* in the Finishing Department during October, plus
- 7,000 masks *started* in Finishing but not completed in October

Exhibit 21-12 uses the flow of physical units from step 1 and the time line diagram in Exhibit 21-11 to perform step 2—tabulating the Finishing Department's equivalent units of work performed in October. The Finishing Department has three categories of equivalent units. In addition to equivalent units for direct materials (faceplates) and conversion costs added in the Finishing Department, SeaView's

EXHIBIT 21-11   SeaView's Finishing Department Time Line (FIFO)

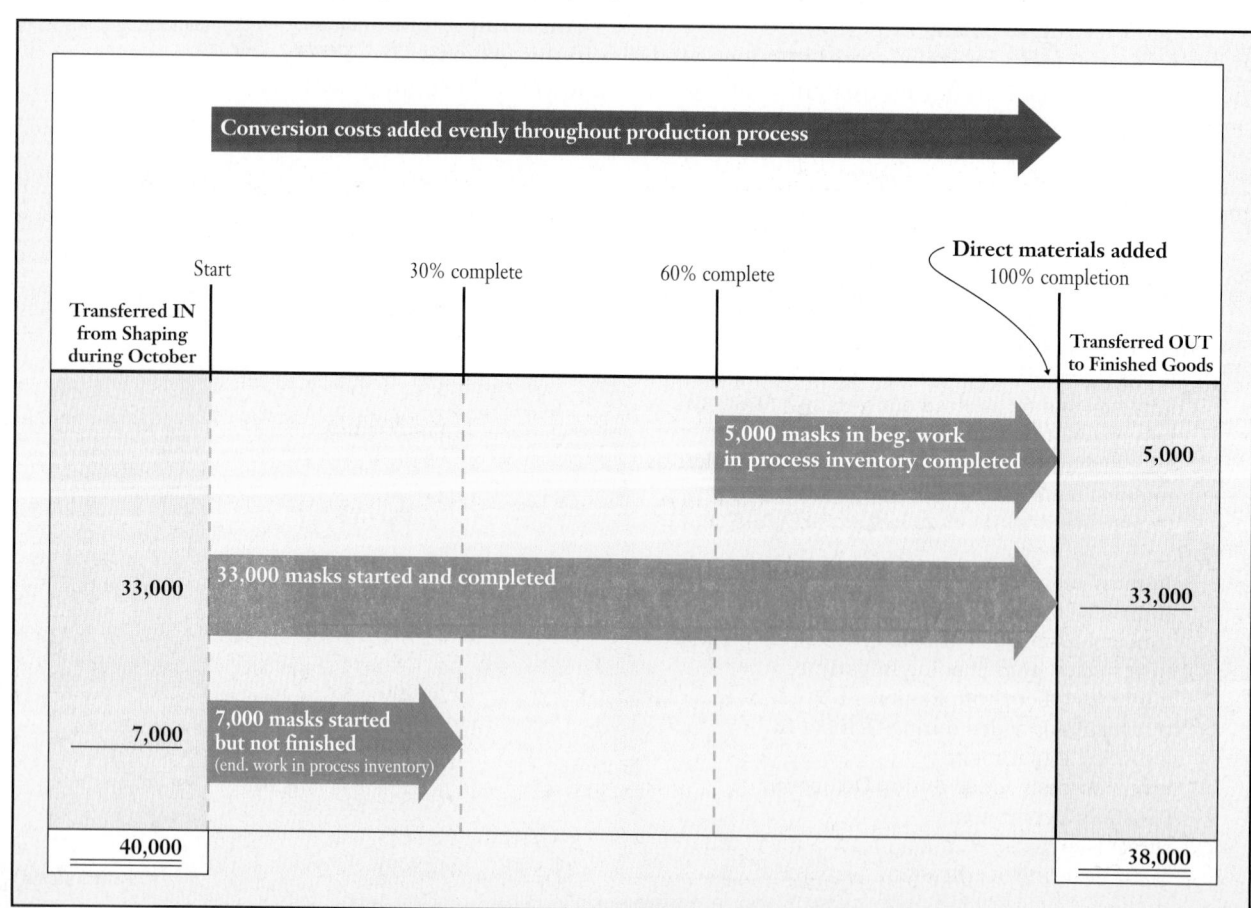

accountant must also compute equivalent units for the shaped swim masks that are *transferred in* from Shaping Department. All second and later departments in a production sequence have units (and costs) transferred in from preceding departments.

SeaView must figure out how many equivalent units of work the Finishing Department performed *during October*. SeaView's accountant looks at Exhibit 21-11 and adds the number of equivalent units of work performed to

- *Complete* the 5,000 masks in beginning inventory that were started in September,
- *Start and complete* an additional 33,000 masks, and
- *Start* (but not complete) the 7,000 masks that make up the department's work in process inventory at the end of October.

The accountant repeats these computations for each of the three categories of costs.

◉ DAILY EXERCISE 21-16

EQUIVALENT UNITS TRANSFERRED-IN   Let's begin with the Transferred In column of Exhibit 21-12. Keep in mind that our goal is to figure the number of equivalent units of work performed *during October*.

After the Shaping Department completes its work on the masks and transfers them out, the Finishing Department receives those units (and their accumulated costs) for final processing. Thus, transferred-in costs (from Shaping) act like costs that are added at the very beginning of the Finishing process. The time line in Exhibit 21-11 shows that the 5,000 units in Finishing's beginning inventory were *not* transferred in from Shaping *this* month. (Instead, these 5,000 units were transferred in from Shaping last month.) Consequently, beginning inventory has no transferred-in equivalent units *during October*.

Look at the time line again—it shows that the 33,000 masks the Finishing Department started and completed during October, and the 7,000 masks in Finishing's ending inventory, *were* transferred in during October. Exhibit 21-12 summarizes this equivalent-unit tabulation, showing that the total transferred-in equivalent units during October is 40,000 (33,000 + 7,000).

EXHIBIT 21-12   FIFO, Step 1: Summarize the Flow of Physical Units; Step 2: Compute Output in Terms of Equivalent Units

SEAVIEW FINISHING DEPARTMENT Month Ended October 31, 20XX				
	Step 1	Step 2: Equivalent Units		
Flow of Production	Flow of Physical Units	Transferred In	Direct Materials	Conversion Costs
Units to account for:				
Beginning work in process, September 30............	5,000			
Transferred in during October................................	40,000			
Total physical units to account for	45,000			
Units accounted for:				
Completed and transferred out during October:				
From beginning work in process inventory	5,000	—	5,000*	2,000*
Started and completed during October (38,000 − 5,000)	33,000	33,000	33,000	33,000
Ending work in process, October 31	7,000	7,000	—†	2,100†
Total physical units accounted for.........................	45,000			
Equivalent units		40,000	38,000	37,100

During October in the Finishing Department:
* Finish beginning inventory
    Direct materials: 5,000 units each 100% completed = 5,000 equivalent units
    Conversion costs: 5,000 units each 40% completed = 2,000 equivalent units
† Start ending inventory
    Direct materials: 7,000 units each 0% completed = 0 equivalent units
    Conversion costs: 7,000 units each 30% completed = 2,100 equivalent units

EQUIVALENT UNITS OF DIRECT MATERIALS Now let's turn to the direct materials added in the Finishing Department (faceplates). Direct materials are not added until the end of the finishing process, as shown in Exhibit 21-11. Exhibit 21-11 shows that during October, the 5,000 units in beginning inventory were completed, so they reached the end of the production process where the faceplates are added. The 33,000 units started and completed also reached the end of the process. However, the time line shows that the ending inventory does not yet have faceplates, so it has not incurred Finishing Department direct materials during October. Thus, Finishing added 5,000 + 33,000 = 38,000 equivalent units of materials (faceplates) during October, as shown in Exhibit 21-12.

EQUIVALENT UNITS OF CONVERSION COSTS Finally, consider conversion costs. According to the time line, beginning inventory was 60% complete at the beginning of October. This means that during October, these 5,000 masks from the Finishing Department's beginning inventory went through the final 40% of the Finishing Department's process. This yields 5,000 × 0.40 = 2,000 equivalent units of conversion work during October. The 33,000 masks started and completed during October went through the entire Finishing Department process during October, so these units incurred 33,000 units of conversion work. Finally, the time line shows that the 7,000 masks in ending inventory that were *started* in Finishing during October made it 30% of the way through the process by October 31. The Finishing Department performed 7,000 × 0.30 = 2,100 equivalent units of conversion work on this ending inventory during October. Thus, the total conversion work performed in Finishing during October includes

2,000	units to *complete* the beginning inventory
33,000	units from masks started *and* completed during October
2,100	units to *start* the ending inventory
37,100	total equivalent units of conversion costs during October

The conversion costs column of step 2 in Exhibit 21-12 summarizes this calculation.

Steps 3 and 4: Summarize Total Costs to Account for and Compute the Cost per Equivalent Unit

Exhibit 21-13 accumulates the Finishing Department's October costs. The exhibit shows how to compute the cost per equivalent unit. The $24,000 beginning balance of work in process is kept separate from the costs incurred during the current period. That is, the $24,000 is not included in computing the cost per equivalent unit for

EXHIBIT 21-13   FIFO, Steps 3 and 4: Summarize Total Costs to Account for and Compute the Cost per Equivalent Unit

SEAVIEW FINISHING DEPARTMENT Month Ended October 31, 20XX				
	Transferred In	Direct Materials	Conversion Costs	Total
Beginning work in process, September 30 (from Exhibit 21-10)..				$ 24,000
Costs added during October (from Exhibit 21-10)	$176,000	$ 19,000	$ 14,840	209,840
Divide by equivalent units (from Exhibit 21-12)	÷ 40,000	÷ 38,000	÷ 37,100	
Cost per equivalent unit	$4.40	$0.50	$0.40	
Total cost to account for...				$233,840

work done in October because this $24,000 was incurred in *September* to start the 5,000 physical units still in process on October 1. Under FIFO, each *October* cost per equivalent unit is computed by dividing October costs by the number of equivalent units of work performed in October.

⊙ DAILY EXERCISE 21-17

Exhibit 21-13 shows that the Finishing Department has transferred-in costs as well as direct material costs and conversion costs. **Transferred-in costs** are incurred in a previous process (the Shaping Department, in the SeaView example), and are carried forward as part of the product's cost when it moves to the next process. All second (and later) processes have transferred in costs from previous processes.

TRANSFERRED-IN COSTS. Costs incurred in a previous process that are carried forward as part of the product's cost when it moves to the next process.

Step 5: Assign Costs to Units Completed and to Units in Ending Work in Process Inventory

Exhibit 21-14 shows how SeaView assigns the Finishing Department costs to

⊙ DAILY EXERCISE 21-18

- Units completed and transferred out to Finished Goods Inventory
- Units still in process in the Finishing Department's ending work in process inventory

The method illustrated in Exhibit 21-14 is identical to the approach used for the Shaping Department in Exhibit 21-9: Multiply the number of equivalent units from step 2 (Exhibit 21-12) by the cost per equivalent unit from step 4 (Exhibit 21-13).

Exhibit 21-14 shows that when computing the cost of masks completed and transferred out of Finishing, we must remember to include the costs of the beginning inventory:

- $24,000 of Finishing Department beginning inventory costs (incurred in September)
- $3,300 of costs to complete that beginning inventory in October [(5,000 equivalent units of materials added × $0.50) + (2,000 equivalent units of conversion costs added × $0.40)]

EXHIBIT 21-14   FIFO, Step 5: Assign Costs to Units Completed and to Units in Ending Work in Process Inventory

SEAVIEW FINISHING DEPARTMENT Month Ended October 31, 20XX				
	Transferred In	Direct Materials	Conversion Costs	Total
Units completed and transferred out to Finished Goods Inventory:				
From beginning work in process, September 30				$ 24,000
Costs added during October:				
Direct materials		[5,000 × $0.50]		2,500
Conversion costs			[2,000 × $0.40]	800
Total completed from beginning inventory				27,300
Units started and completed during October	[33,000 × ($4.40 + $0.50 + $0.40)]			174,900
Total cost transferred out				202,200
Ending work in process, October 31:				
Transferred-in costs	[7,000 × $4.40]			30,800
Direct materials		—		—
Conversion costs			[2,100 × $0.40]	840
Total ending work in process, October 31				31,640
Total cost accounted for				$233,840

The Finishing Department's journal entries are similar to those for the Shaping Department. First, recall the entry previously made to transfer the cost of shaped swim masks into the Finishing Department (page 850):

Work in Process Inventory—Finishing	176,000	
Work in Process Inventory—Shaping		176,000

The following entries record other Finishing Department activity during October (data from Exhibit 21-10):

Work in Process Inventory—Finishing	33,840	
Materials Inventory		19,000
Manufacturing Wages		3,710
Manufacturing Overhead		11,130

To requisition materials and assign conversion costs to the Finishing Department.

The entry to transfer the cost of completed units out of the Finishing Department and into Finished Goods Inventory is based on the dollar amount in Exhibit 21-14:

Finished Goods Inventory	202,200	
Work in Process Inventory—Finishing		202,200

DAILY EXERCISE 21-19

After posting, the key accounts appear as follows:

WORK IN PROCESS INVENTORY—SHAPING

(Exhibit 21-7)		(Exhibit 21-9)	
Balance, September 30	—	Transferred to Finishing	176,000
Direct materials	140,000		
Direct labor	21,250		
Manufacturing overhead	46,750		
Balance, October 31	32,000		

WORK IN PROCESS INVENTORY—FINISHING

(Exhibit 21-10)		(Exhibit 21-14)	
Balance, September 30	24,000	Transfered to Finished Goods Inventory	202,200
Transferred in from Shaping	176,000		
Direct materials	19,000		
Direct labor	3,710		
Manufacturing overhead	11,130		
Balance, October 31	31,640		

FINISHED GOODS INVENTORY

Balance, September 30	—	
Transferred in from Finishing	202,000	

WORK IT OUT

1. What is the average total cost per mask completed and transferred out of the Finishing Department into Finished Goods Inventory?
2. For what decisions would SeaView's managers use this cost per mask information?

Answers

1. The total costs of the masks completed and transferred out to Finished Goods Inventory is $202,200 (from Exhibit 21-14). Exhibit 21-11 shows that 38,000 masks were completed and transferred out. Thus, the average total cost per mask completed and

transferred out to Finished Goods Inventory is

$$\frac{\text{Total cost}}{\text{per mask}} = \frac{\$202,200}{38,000 \text{ masks}}$$

$$= \$5.3211 \text{ (rounded)}$$

2. SeaView's managers would use the $5.3211 cost per mask in
   - Setting the masks' sale price
   - Profitability analysis aimed at deciding which products to emphasize
   - Controlling costs and evaluating the efficiency of the production process
   - Assigning costs to Finished Goods Inventory for financial reporting

Production Cost Report

A **production cost report** summarizes a processing department's operations for the period. Exhibit 21-15 is a FIFO production cost report for SeaView's Finishing Department for October. The report combines Exhibits 21-13 and 21-14. It shows the beginning inventory, the cost transferred in during the month, and the costs added in the Finishing Department during the month. The report also shows the costs transferred out of the department, and the ending work in process inventory.

PRODUCTION COST REPORT. Summarizes a processing department's operations for a period.

How do managers use the production cost report? SeaView managers compare actual direct materials and conversion costs—particularly the equivalent unit costs in Exhibit 21-15—with expected amounts. If actual unit costs are too high, managers will investigate, with the goal of finding a way to reduce the costs. If costs are less than expected, employees may receive praise or even a bonus.

EXHIBIT 21-15 FIFO Production Cost Report

	Transferred In	Direct Materials	Conversion Costs	Total
SEAVIEW FINISHING DEPARTMENT Production Cost Report (FIFO Method) Month Ended October 31, 20XX				
Beginning work in process, September 30				$ 24,000
Costs added during October.............................	$176,000	$19,000	$14,840	209,840
Total cost to account for...................................				$233,840
Equivalent units..	÷40,000	÷38,000	÷37,100	
Cost per equivalent unit	$4.40	$0.50	$0.40	
Assignment of total costs:				
Units completed during October:				
From beginning work in process, September 30...				$ 24,000
Costs added during October	—	[5,000 × $0.50] = $2,500	[2,000 × $0.40] = $800	3,300
Total completed from beginning inventory...				27,300
Units started and completed during October	[33,000 × ($4.40 + $0.50 + $0.40)]			174,900
Total completed and transferred out				202,200
Ending work in process, October 31:				
Transferred-in costs.......................................	[7,000 × $4.40]			30,800
Direct materials		—		—
Conversion costs			[2,100 × $0.40]	840
Total ending work in process, October 31.....				31,640
Total cost accounted for..................................				$233,840

Using Overseas Labor to Cut Process Costs

• At the Tsai family plant in Dongguan, China, the production lines stretch longer than a football field. Workers from China, Indonesia, and Vietnam cut, glue, stitch, and mold Air Jordans and other sneakers, then pack them into boxes ready for store shelves. The Dongguan plants are home to more than 70,000 workers responsible for 14% of the world's footwear production.

• At **IBM's** massive plant in Guadalajara, Mexico, white-coated workers produce 60% of the world's Thinkpads. At **Solectron's** Guadalajara plant, half-assembled printers whiz by on conveyer belts as rows of factory workers clip on parts.

In the past two decades, more and more American companies have relocated manufacturing overseas to take advantage of cheaper labor and raw materials. Assembly-line workers in Tijuana and Guadalajara earn only 25% of the wages their U.S. counterparts take home. In Vietnam, a **Nike** factory worker earns about $65 a month—less than a U.S. factory worker might earn in a day. Lower manufacturing wages in the process costing equation shave unit costs and increase profit margins.

Nike, Timberland, and other shoe companies discovered years ago that it pays to let somebody else do the manufacturing while you concentrate on research, marketing, and distribution. A few years ago, Timberland produced 80% of its shoes in its own plants. Today, it produces just 18%.

Fierce competition and free-falling prices have forced America's tech companies to combine capital-intensive production with low-cost labor. **IBM** keeps the lab, headquarters, service providers, and logistics in the United States and subcontracts almost everything else overseas. Yet, even these jobs will not remain the province of U.S. workers: Developing countries are adopting sophisticated manufacturing techniques, computer programming, and other high-tech processes—and charging less to do them.

Source: Based on: Jon E. Hilsenrath, "Overseas suppliers to U.S. brands thrive: Taiwan maker of Nikes outdoes customer," *Wall Street Journal,* March 10, 2000, p. A11. Michael Riley, "High-tech industries meet low-cost labor/Mexican plants defy image of sweatshops." *Houston Chronicle,* February 12, 2000, p. C1.

Objective 6
Account for a second processing department by the weighted-average method

➡ Chapter 9, introduced the weighted-average method of inventory costing.

WEIGHTED-AVERAGE PROCESS COSTING METHOD. A process costing method that costs all equivalent units of work with a weighted average of that period's and the previous period's costs per equivalent unit.

THE WEIGHTED-AVERAGE METHOD

We now rework SeaView's Finishing Department example to demonstrate the second process costing method, weighted-average. ◄

The FIFO method separately computes the cost per equivalent unit for each different month. The work performed in a particular month is then costed by that specific month's cost per equivalent unit. In contrast, the **weighted-average method** costs all equivalent units of work with a weighted average of that period's and the previous period's costs per equivalent unit. Exhibits 21-16 through 21-20 are the weighted-average equivalents of Exhibits 21-11 through 21-15. We apply the weighted-average method using the same five steps we used with FIFO.

Steps 1 and 2: Summarize the Flow of Physical Units and Compute Output in Terms of Equivalent Units

The weighted-average method is simpler than the FIFO method because it does not require us to separate the work and costs for beginning inventory versus units started and completed this period. Instead, all the units completed and transferred out—whether from beginning inventory or units started and completed this period—are treated identically. Each unit is assigned the same average cost per equivalent unit, using

- All costs incurred for the physical units in process this period, whether those costs were incurred this period or last
- All work performed on the physical units in process this period, whether that work was performed this period or last

Exhibit 21-16 shows the time line for SeaView's Finishing Department, using the weighted-average method. The weighted-average time line is simpler than the FIFO time line. The weighted-average method combines all 38,000 units completed

EXHIBIT 21-16   SeaView's Finishing Department Time Line (Weighted-Average)

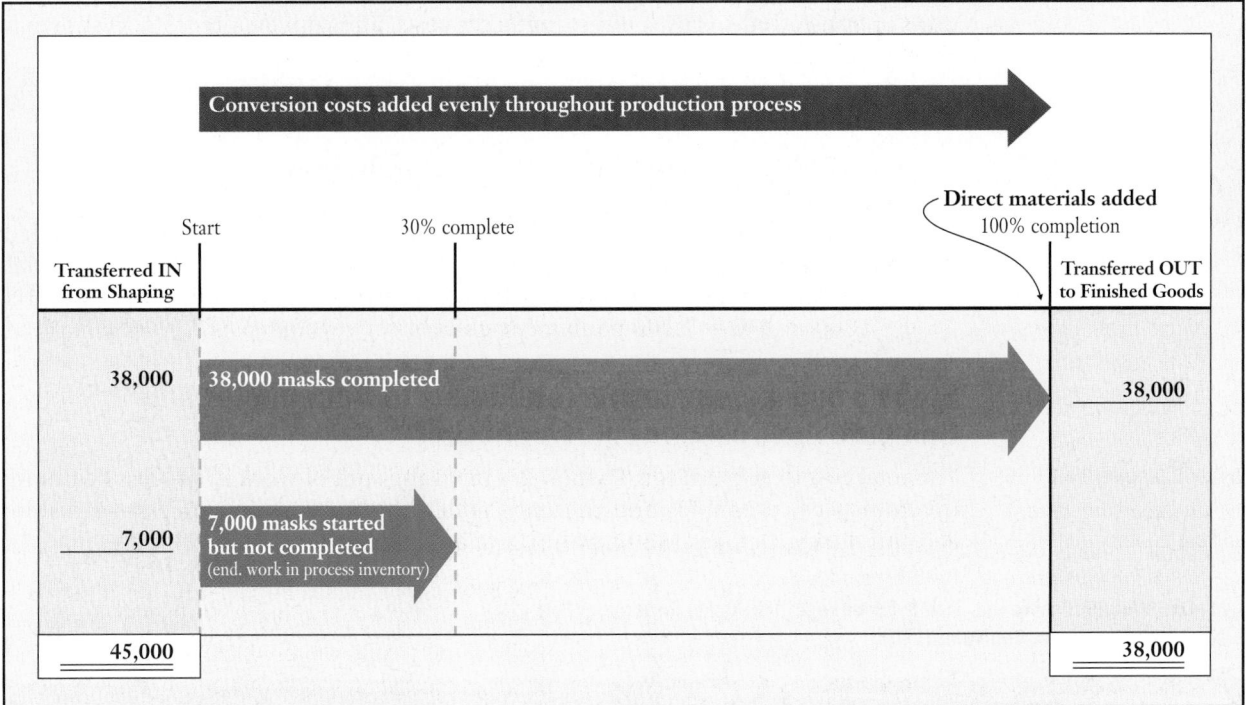

during October—whether those units are from the beginning work in process inventory, or are both started and completed in October.

Exhibits 21-10, 21-16, and 21-17 show that 38,000 masks were completed and transferred out of the Finishing Department in October (5,000 masks from beginning inventory were completed, and 33,000 masks were started and completed). The weighted-average method computes the equivalent units of all the work ever done on these units completed and transferred out—not just the work done this period. Because these 38,000 masks have been transferred to Finished Goods

⊙ DAILY EXERCISE 21-20

EXHIBIT 21-17   Weighted-Average, Step 1: Summarize the Flow of Physical Units;
Step 2: Compute Output in Terms of Equivalent Units

	Step 1	Step 2: Equivalent Units		
SEAVIEW FINISHING DEPARTMENT Month Ended October 31, 20XX				
Flow of Production	**Flow of Physical Units**	**Transferred In**	**Direct Materials**	**Conversion Costs**
Units to account for:				
Beginning work in process, September 30	5,000			
Transferred in during October	40,000			
Total physical units to account for	45,000			
Units accounted for:				
Completed and transferred out during October.......	38,000	38,000	38,000*	38,000*
Ending work in process, October 31	7,000	7,000	— †	2,100†
Total physical units accounted for...........................	45,000			
Equivalent units		45,000	38,000	40,100

In the Finishing Department:
* Units completed and transferred out
    Direct materials: 38,000 units each 100% completed = 38,000 equivalent units
    Conversion costs: 38,000 units each 100% completed = 38,000 equivalent units
† Start ending inventory
    Direct materials: 7,000 units each 0% completed   = 0 equivalent units
    Conversion costs: 7,000 units each 30% completed = 2,100 equivalent units

Inventory, they are complete with respect to transferred-in costs, direct materials, and conversion costs. Consequently, the masks have incurred 38,000 equivalent units of transferred-in costs, direct materials costs, and conversion costs, as shown in Exhibit 21-17.

The equivalent units for ending work in process inventory are the same under the weighted-average method as with FIFO. These 7,000 units

- have been transferred in from Shaping, so they have incurred 7,000 equivalent units of transferred-in costs
- have not reached the end of Finishing's process where faceplates are inserted; thus, they have no equivalent units of Finishing Department direct materials
- are 30% of the way through Finishing's process, so they have incurred 7,000 × 0.30 = 2,100 equivalent units of conversion costs

Steps 3 and 4: Summarize Total Costs to Account for and Compute the Cost per Equivalent Unit

 DAILY EXERCISE 21-21

The total cost to account for (Exhibit 21-18) is the sum of work in process beginning inventory cost ($24,000) and the costs added to the Work in Process—Finishing account during October ($209,840). (Data are taken from Exhibit 21-10.)

EXHIBIT 21-18   Weighted-Average, Step 3: Summarize Total Costs to Account For;
Step 4: Compute the Cost per Equivalent Unit

SEAVIEW FINISHING DEPARTMENT Month Ended October 31, 20XX				
	Transferred In	Direct Materials	Conversion Costs	Total
Beginning work in process, September 30 (from Exhibit 21-10)	$ 22,900	$ —	$ 1,100	$ 24,000
Costs added during October (from Exhibit 21-10)	176,000	19,000	14,840	209,840
Total cost	$198,900	$19,000	$15,940	
Divide by equivalent units (from Exhibit 21-17)	÷ 45,000	÷38,000	÷40,100	
Cost per equivalent unit	$4.42	$0.50	$0.3975	
Total cost to account for				$233,840

In the weighted-average method, step 2 computes the equivalent units of all the work ever done on the units in process this period, including work done last period to start the beginning inventory. To find the weighted-average cost per equivalent unit, we match these units with all the costs ever incurred for the units in process this period. This includes costs incurred last period to start the beginning work in process inventory, as well as costs incurred in the current period (October).

Exhibit 21-18 shows the weighted-average cost per equivalent unit for SeaView's Finishing Department. Consider conversion costs first. The Finishing Department incurred $1,100 of conversion costs in September to get the 5,000 masks in beginning inventory 60% of the way through the production process by the end of September. This $1,100 is added to the $14,840 total Finishing Department conversion cost incurred in October. We divide the sum, $15,940, by the total number of (weighted-average) equivalent units, 40,100, to obtain a weighted-average conversion cost per equivalent unit of $0.3975 (rounded). The transferred-in cost per equivalent unit and the direct materials cost per equivalent unit are computed in the same way.

 DAILY EXERCISE 21-22

 DAILY EXERCISE 21-23

Step 5: Assign Total Cost to Units Completed and to Units in Ending Work in Process Inventory

With the weighted-average method, the 38,000 physical units completed and transferred out of SeaView's Finishing Department are costed in one step. The 38,000 equivalent units are multiplied by the full equivalent-unit cost of $5.3175 ($4.42 +

$0.50 + $0.3975). The result is $202,065 (Exhibit 21-19). Equivalent units in the ending work in process inventory are also costed at the appropriate unit amounts.

EXHIBIT 21-19 Weighted Average, Step 5: Assign Total Cost to Units Completed and to Units in Ending Work in Process Inventory

SEAVIEW FINISHING DEPARTMENT Month Ended October 31, 20XX				
	Transferred In	Direct Materials	Conversion Costs	Total
Units completed and transferred out to Finished Goods Inventory..................................	[38,000 × ($4.42 + $0.50 + $0.3975)]			202,065
Ending work in process, October 31:				
Transferred in costs	[7,000 × $4.42]			30,940
Direct materials..		—		—
Conversion costs			[2,100 × $0.3975]	835*
Total ending work in process, October 31..........				31,775
Total cost accounted for...				$233,840

*Rounded.

The weighted-average production cost report in Exhibit 21-20 is similar to its FIFO counterpart, Exhibit 21-15. The weighted-average report may signal the need for action if actual unit costs or production quantities differ materially from planned amounts. But weighted-average costs per equivalent unit are not as useful for evaluating the efficiency of October production because they are affected by costs incurred in September. Even so, managers may use the weighted-average method because (1) the computations are simpler than those of the FIFO method, and (2) the difference between FIFO and weighted-average results is often insignificant.

⊙ DAILY EXERCISE 21-24

EXHIBIT 21-20 Weighted Average, Production Cost Report

SEAVIEW FINISHING DEPARTMENT Production Cost Report (Weighted Average Method) Month Ended October 31, 20XX				
	Transferred In	Direct Materials	Conversion Costs	Total
Beginning work in process, September 30	$ 22,900	$ —	$ 1,100	$ 24,000
Costs added during October	176,000	19,000	14,840	209,840
Total cost to account for	$198,900	$ 19,000	$15,940	$233,840
Equivalent units	÷ 45,000	÷38,000	÷40,100	
Cost per equivalent unit..	$4.42	$0.50	$0.3975	
Assignment of total costs:				
Units completed during October	[38,000 × ($4.42 + $0.50 + $0.3975)]			$202,065
Ending work in process, October 31:				
Transferred-in costs..	[7,000 × $4.42]			30,940
Direct materials..		—		—
Conversion costs			[2,100 × $0.3975]	835*
Total ending work in process, October 31..........				31,775
Total cost accounted for...				$233,840

*Rounded.

When will FIFO and weighted average give different results?

Answer: FIFO and weighted average give different results when

- There is beginning inventory. If there is no beginning inventory, FIFO and weighted average yield identical results. This is why we did not need to specify whether SeaView's Shaping Department used FIFO or weighted average—shaping had no beginning inventory.
- The cost per unit changes from one period to the next. If the cost per unit in the current period is the same as in the prior period, then FIFO and weighted average yield identical results.

FIFO and weighted average yield significantly different results only when there are large beginning inventories *and* costs change dramatically from one period to the next. This could happen, for example, in the wine-making industry, where there are significant work in process inventories, and where the cost of grapes fluctuates depending on weather and other crop conditions.

The following Decision Guidelines review key issues arising in process costing systems with multiple processes and beginning work in process inventories.

DECISION GUIDELINES

Process Costing—Second Process (with Beginning Inventory)

DECISION	GUIDELINES
At what point in a second process are transferred-in costs incurred?	Transferred in costs are typically incurred at the *beginning* of the second (or subsequent) process.
When do FIFO and weighted-average methods of process costing yield different results?	When there is beginning work in process inventory and cost per unit changes from one period to the next.
Which periods' costs are included in the cost per equivalent unit computation?	• *FIFO* → Only costs incurred in current period • *Weighted average* → Cost of work done in prior period to start the beginning inventory, plus all costs incurred in the current period
How to compute equivalent units using • FIFO method?	*FIFO* equivalent units of work done in current period equals work done to • *Complete* beginning inventory, plus • *Start* and *complete* additional units, plus • *Start* ending inventory
• Weighted-average method?	*Weighted-average* equivalent units of all work done on units in process equals • All work ever done on units completed and transferred out this period (whether work was done this period or last period), plus • Work done to *start* the ending inventory

REVIEW PROCESS COSTING

SUMMARY PROBLEM

This problem extends the Mid-Chapter Summary problem to a second department. During May, Florida Tile Industries reports the following in its Finishing Department:

Finishing Department Data for May	
Units:	
Beginning work in process, April 30 (20% complete as to direct materials, 70% complete as to conversion work)	4,000 units
Transferred in from Tile-Forming Department during May	16,000 units
Completed and transferred out to Finished Goods Inventory during May	15,000 units
Ending work in process, May 31 (36% complete as to direct materials, 80% complete as to conversion work)	5,000 units
Costs:	
Work in process, April 30 (transferred-in costs, $11,982; direct materials costs, $488; conversion costs, $5,530)	$18,000
Transferred in from Tile-Forming Department during May (from page 854)	38,400
Direct materials added during May	6,400
Conversion costs added during May	24,300

Required

Assign total cost to units completed and to units in ending work in process inventory for the Finishing Department in May, using
1. The FIFO method
2. The weighted-average method

Solution

Requirement 1

Steps 1 and 2: Summarize the flow of physical units; compute output in terms of equivalent units.

FINISHING DEPARTMENT (FIFO)
Month Ended May 31, 20XX

	Step 1	Step 2: Equivalent Units		
Flow of Production	**Flow of Physical Units**	**Transferred In**	**Direct Materials**	**Conversion Costs**
Units to account for:				
Beginning work in process, April 30	4,000			
Transferred in from Tile-Forming during May	16,000			
Total physical units to account for	20,000			
Units accounted for:				
Completed and transferred out during May:				
From beginning inventory	4,000	—	3,200*	1,200*
Started and completed during May (15,000 − 4,000)	11,000	11,000	11,000	11,000
Ending work in process, May 31	5,000	5,000	1,800†	4,000†
Total physical units accounted for	20,000			
Equivalent units		16,000	16,000	16,200

During May in the Finishing Department:

* Finish beginning inventory

        Direct materials: 4,000 units each 80% completed in May = 3,200 equivalent units.

        Conversion costs: 4,000 units each 30% completed in May = 1,200 equivalent units.

† Start ending inventory

        Direct materials: 5,000 units each 36% completed in May = 1,800 equivalent units.

        Conversion costs: 5,000 units each 80% completed in May = 4,000 equivalent units.

Steps 3 and 4: Summarize total costs to account for; compute the cost per equivalent unit.

FINISHING DEPARTMENT (FIFO)
Month Ended May 31, 20XX

	Transferred In	Direct Materials	Conversion Costs	Total
Beginning work in process, April 30				$18,000
Costs added during May	$ 38,400	$ 6,400	$ 24,300	69,100
Divide by equivalent units....................................	÷16,000	÷16,000	÷ 16,200	
Cost per equivalent unit	$2.40	$0.40	$1.50	
Total cost to account for..				$87,100

Step 5: Assign costs to units completed and to units in ending work in process inventory.

FINISHING DEPARTMENT (FIFO)
Month Ended May 31, 20XX

	Transferred In	Direct Materials	Conversion Costs	Total
Units completed and transferred out to Finished Goods Inventory:				
From beginning work in process, April 30.........				$18,000
Costs added during May:				
Direct materials...		[3,200 × $0.40]		1,280
Conversion costs...			[1,200 × $1.50]	1,800
Total completed from beginning inventory........				21,080
Units started and completed during May	[11,000 × ($2.40 + $0.40 + $1.50)]			47,300
Total cost transferred out				68,380
Ending work in process, May 31:				
Transferred-in costs...	[5,000 × $2.40]			12,000
Direct materials...		[1,800 × $0.40]		720
Conversion costs..			[4,000 × $1.50]	6,000
Total ending work in process, May 31				18,720
Total cost accounted for..				$87,100

Requirement 2

Steps 1 and 2: Summarize the flow of physical units; compute output in terms of equivalent units.

FINISHING DEPARTMENT (Weighted Average)
Month Ended May 31, 20XX

Flow of Production	Step 1 Flow of Physical Units	Step 2: Equivalent Units		
		Transferred In	Direct Materials	Conversion Costs
Units to account for:				
Beginning work in process, April 30	4,000			
Transferred in from Tile-Forming during May	16,000			
Total physical units to account for............................	20,000			
Units accounted for:				
Completed and transferred out during May..............	15,000	15,000	15,000	15,000
Ending work in process, May 31	5,000	5,000	1,800*	4,000*
Total physical units accounted for............................	20,000			
Equivalent units...		20,000	16,800	19,000

* Finish beginning inventory
  Direct materials: 5,000 units each 36% completed = 1,800 equivalent units
  Conversion costs: 5,000 units each 80% completed = 4,000 equivalent units

Steps 3 and 4: Summarize total costs to account for; compute the cost per equivalent unit.

FINISHING DEPARTMENT (Weighted Average)
Month Ended May 31, 20XX

	Transferred In	Direct Materials	Conversion Costs	Total
Beginning work in process, April 30	$11,982	$ 488	$ 5,530	$18,000
Costs added during May	38,400	6,400	24,300	69,100
Total cost	$50,382	$ 6,888	$29,830	
Divide by equivalent units...	÷20,000	÷16,800	÷19,000	
Cost per equivalent unit	$2.5191	$0.41	$1.57	
Total cost to account for...				$87,100

Step 5: Assign costs to units completed and to units in ending work in process inventory.

FINISHING DEPARTMENT (Weighted Average)
Month Ended May 31, 20XX

	Transferred In	Direct Materials	Conversion Costs	Total
Units completed and transferred out to Finished Goods Inventory:..............................	[15,000 × ($2.5191 + $0.41 + $1.57)]			$67,486*
Ending work in process, May 31:				
Transferred-in costs...	[5,000 × $2.5191]			12,596*
Direct materials...		[1,800 × $0.41]		738
Conversion costs			[4,000 × $1.57]	6,280
Total ending work in process, May 31				19,614
Total cost accounted for..				$87,100

* Rounded.

LESSONS LEARNED

1. **Distinguish between the flow of costs in process costing and job costing.** In process costing systems, costs are accumulated by processing departments and flow from one department to the next until the product is completed. In contrast, job cost systems accumulate costs for each individual job using job cost records, and the cost of a completed job flows directly to finished goods inventory.

2. **Record process costing transactions.** Journal entries in a process costing system are like those in a job cost system, with one key exception: A job cost system typically uses one Work in Process Inventory account, but a process costing system uses a separate account for each processing department. As goods move from one department to the next, the Work in Process Inventory account of the receiving department is debited and the account of the transferring department is credited. After processing is completed, the cost of the goods moves with them into Finished Goods Inventory.

3. **Compute equivalent units.** Because goods in process may be in various stages of completion, we compute *equivalent units*—the amount of work expressed in terms of fully completed units of output. Equivalent units are computed for each input that is added at a different point in the production process.

4. **Assign costs to units completed and to units in ending work**

in process inventory. Accounting for a department's costs is a five-step procedure. First, the flow of physical (output) units is determined. Second, we compute equivalent units. Third, the total cost to account for is determined. Fourth, costs per equivalent unit are computed for each input that is added at a different point in the production process. Fifth, physical units are costed by multiplying equivalent units from step 2 by equivalent-unit costs from step 4.

5. **Account for a second processing department by the FIFO method.** FIFO matches equivalent units of work done in the current period with costs incurred in the current period. Equivalent units of work performed in the current month are costed at current-month unit costs. Managers compare the actual costs with planned costs to evaluate the efficiency of production.

6. **Account for a second processing department by the weighted-average method.** The *weighted-average method* costs all work to account for each month—work in process at the beginning of the month and the current month's work—with unit costs that are a weighted average of current- and prior-month costs. In contrast to FIFO, the weighted-average method computes the equivalent units of all work ever performed on units in process—whether this work was done in the current or the prior period—to obtain a weighted-average cost per equivalent unit.

ACCOUNTING VOCABULARY

conversion costs (p. 845)
equivalent units (p. 845)
first-in, first-out (FIFO) process
  costing method (p. 855)

production cost report (p. 861)
transferred-in costs (p. 859)

weighted-average process costing
  method (p. 862)

QUESTIONS

1. Distinguish a process costing system from a job cost system.
2. Give the type of costing system—job or process—that is better suited to account for the following products: (a) chemicals, (b) textbooks, (c) lumber, (d) specialty machinery, (e) custom lampshades.
3. Why does a process costing system use multiple Work in Process Inventory accounts but a job costing system uses only one such account?
4. Give the entries (accounts only) to record the following: (a) purchase of materials on account; (b) incurrence of labor; (c) incurrence of manufacturing overhead cost; (d) requisition of materials and assignment of labor and overhead to Work in Process Inventory—Department 1 (combine in one entry); (e) transfer of cost of work in process inventory from Department 1 to Department 2; (f) transfer of cost of completed units to finished goods; (g) cost of goods sold.
5. What is an equivalent unit? Give an example of equivalent units.
6. **Georgia-Pacific** completed and transferred 35,000 units of its product to a second department during the period. At the end of the period, another 10,000 units were in the first department's work in process inventory, 20%

complete. How many equivalent units did the first department produce during the period?
7. How are equivalent units used in Exhibits 21-8 and 21-9?
8. Why might a company have different numbers of equivalent units for direct materials and conversion costs?
9. What information does a production cost report give?
10. Using the FIFO method, compute the equivalent units for Department 2 during July:

Work in process, June 30	
(10% complete as to direct materials,	
40% complete as to conversion costs) ..	1,000 units
Transferred in from Department 1	
during July	25,000 units
Completed during July	22,000 units
Work in process, July 31	
(20% complete as to direct materials,	
70% complete as to conversion costs)...	4,000 units

11. Repeat Question 10, using the weighted-average method.
12. Under what conditions are FIFO equivalent-unit costs equal to weighted-average equivalent-unit costs?
13. "Unit costs in process costing are averages, but this is not true in job costing." Do you agree or disagree? Explain.

ASSESS YOUR PROGRESS

DAILY EXERCISES

Distinguishing between the flow of costs in job costing and process costing   (Obj. 1)

DE21-1 Use Exhibit 21-1 to help you describe, in your own words, the major difference in the flow of costs between a job costing system and a process costing system.

Flow of costs in process costing (Obj. 1)

DE21-2 Consider the SeaView example on pages 847–866. Diagram the flow of costs for the Shaping and Finishing Departments' production of swim masks, similar to Exhibit 21-2.

Flow of costs in process costing (Obj. 1)

DE21-3 In Exhibit 21-3 (page 844), suppose direct materials added in the chopping process are $20 rather than $7 (keep all amounts in thousands as in the exhibit). Assume that direct labor and manufacturing overhead amounts remain the same, as do each of the ending inventory balances.

1. Show the revised flow of costs through the Work in Process Inventory—Chopping; Work in Process Inventory—Mixing & Bottling; Finished Goods Inventory; and Cost of Goods Sold T-accounts.
2. How much are the following?
   a. Cost of goods completed and transferred out of the Chopping Department and into the Mixing & Bottling Department.
   b. Cost of goods completed and transferred out of the Mixing & Bottling Department and into Finished Goods Inventory.
   c. Cost of goods sold.

Process costing journal entries (Obj. 2)

DE21-4 Refer to your answer to Daily Exercise 21-3. Record the journal entries for the following:

1. The use of $20 rather than $7 of direct materials in the chopping process.
2. Cost of goods completed and transferred out of the Chopping Department and into the Mixing & Bottling Department.

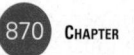

3. Cost of goods completed and transferred out of the Mixing & Bottling Department and into Finished Goods Inventory.

4. Cost of goods sold.

DE21-5 Polar Spring produces premium bottled water. Polar Spring purchases artesian water, stores the water in large tanks, and then runs the water through two processes:

Flow of costs in process costing, cost per equivalent unit
(Obj. 1, 3)

- Filtration, where workers microfilter and ozonate the water
- Bottling, where workers bottle and package the filtered water

During February, the filtration process incurs the following costs in processing 100,000 liters:

Wages of workers operating the filtration equipment	$ 5,550
Manufacturing overhead allocated to filtration	12,025
Water..	50,000
Wages of workers operating ozonation equipment	6,425

Polar Spring has no beginning inventories.

1. Compute the February conversion costs in the Filtration Department.
2. If the Filtration Department completely processed 100,000 liters, what is the *total* filtration cost per liter?
3. Now assume that 80,000 liters are completely filtered and ozonated, while the remaining 20,000 are only part way through the process at the end of February. Is the cost per completely filtered and ozonated liter higher, lower, or the same as in requirement 2? Why?

DE21-6 Record the journal entries for the *use* of direct materials and direct labor, and for the allocation of manufacturing overhead to Polar Spring's filtration process, described in Daily Exercise 21-5.

Process costing journal entries
(Obj. 2)

DE21-7 Colleges and universities use the equivalent-unit concept to describe the number of faculty as well as the number of students. The **University of Georgia** has about 2,000 full-time faculty and 400 part-time faculty. Assume the following:

Computing equivalent units
(Obj. 3)

- A full-time faculty member teaches six courses per year
- 100 part-time faculty teach three courses per year
- 300 part-time faculty teach two courses per year

What is the "full-time equivalent" faculty—the number of equivalent units of faculty?

DE21-8 Refer to Daily Exercise 21-5. At Polar Spring, water is added at the beginning of the filtration process. Conversion costs are added evenly throughout the process, and in February 80,000 liters have been completed and transferred out of the Filtration Department, and into the Bottling Department. The 20,000 units remaining in Filtration's ending work in process inventory are 80% of the way through the filtration process. Recall that Polar Spring has no beginning inventories.

Drawing a time line, computing equivalent units
(Obj. 3)

1. Draw a time line for the filtration process, similar to the one in Exhibit 21-6.
2. Compute the equivalent units of direct materials and conversion costs for the Filtration Department. (Refer to Exhibit 21-5 if necessary.)

DE21-9 Look at SeaView Shaping Department's equivalent-unit computation in Exhibit 21-5. Suppose the ending work in process inventory is 40% of the way through the shaping process, rather than 25% of the way through. Compute the equivalent units of direct materials and conversion costs.

Computing equivalent units
(Obj. 3)

DE21-10 Consider the original SeaView Shaping Department equivalent-unit computations in Exhibit 21-5. Suppose plastic and chemicals are added at the beginning of the shaping process, and another direct material—a hardening agent—is added 75% of the way through the shaping process. SeaView needs to compute the equivalent units separately for each input that is added at a different point in the production process. This means that SeaView needs a separate computation of equivalent units for the hardening agent.

Drawing a time line, computing equivalent units
(Obj. 3)

1. Draw a time line of the Shaping Department process showing where the different materials are added, similar to the one in Exhibit 21-6.
2. How many equivalent units of the hardening agent are incurred in the Shaping Department during October?

DE21-11 Return to the original SeaView example. Suppose direct labor is $38,250 rather than $21,250. Now what is the conversion cost per equivalent unit? (Use Exhibit 21-8 to format your answer.)

DE21-12 Return to Polar Spring's Filtration Department described in Daily Exercises 21-5 and 21-8. Using your answers to those exercises, compute the cost per equivalent unit for direct materials and for conversion costs in the Filtration Department. (Recall that there were no beginning inventories.)

DE21-13 Return to Polar Spring's Filtration Department. Use the information in Daily Exercises 21-5, 21-8, and 21-12 to fulfill the following requirements:

1. What is the cost of the 80,000 liters completed and transferred out of Polar Spring's Filtration Department?
2. What is the cost of the 20,000 liters remaining in Filtration's ending work in process inventory?

DE21-14 Use the information in Daily Exercises 21-5 and 21-13 to

1. Record the journal entry to transfer the cost of the 80,000 liters completed and transferred out of Filtration and into the Bottling Department.
2. Record all the transactions in the Work in Process Inventory—Filtration T-account. (*Hint:* Use SeaView's Work in Process Inventory—Shaping T-account on page 851 as a guide.)

DE21-15 Polar Spring produces premium bottled water. Preceding daily exercises considered Polar Spring's first process—filtration. We now consider Polar Spring's second process—bottling. In the Bottling Department, workers bottle the filtered water and pack the bottles into boxes. Conversion costs are incurred evenly throughout the bottling process, but packaging materials are not added until the end of the process.

February data from the Bottling Department follow:

Beginning work in process inventory	
(40% of the way through the process)	4,000 liters
Transferred in from Filtration*	80,000 liters
Completed and transferred out to Finished Goods	
Inventory in February	77,000 liters
Ending work in process inventory	
(70% of the way through the bottling process)	7,000 liters

Costs in beginning work in process inventory:		Costs added during February:	
Transferred in	$480	Transferred in*	$ 60,000
Direct materials	0	Direct materials	15,400
Direct labor	250	Direct labor	16,863
Manufacturing overhead	150	Manufacturing overhead	11,242
Total beginning work in process		Total costs added	
inventory as of February 1	$880	during February	$103,505

* Daily Exercise 21-13 showed that Polar Spring's Filtration Department completed and transferred out 80,000 liters at a total cost of $60,000.

Draw a time line for Polar Spring's Bottling Department, similar to the one in Exhibit 21-11, assuming that Polar Spring uses FIFO.

DE21-16 Use the time line you developed in Daily Exercise 21-15 to help you compute the Bottling Department's equivalent units, using the FIFO method.

DE21-17 Consider Polar Spring's Bottling Department, as described in Daily Exercise 21-15. Compute the cost per equivalent unit, using FIFO.

DE21-18 Use the information about Polar Spring's Bottling Department in Daily Exercises 21-15 through 21-17 to assign the costs to units completed and transferred out, and to ending inventory, under FIFO.

DE21-19 Refer to Polar Spring's Bottling Department and the computations you made in Daily Exercises 21-15 through 21-18.

Journal entry; T-account; second department; FIFO (Obj. 1, 2, 5)

1. Prepare the journal entry to record the cost of units completed and transferred out, using FIFO.
2. Post all transactions from Daily Exercises 21-15 through 21-18 to the Work in Process Inventory—Bottling Department T-account. What is the ending balance?

DE21-20 Using the data from Polar Spring's Bottling Department from Daily Exercise 21-15:

Drawing a time line; computing equivalent units; second department; weighted-average method (Obj. 1, 6)

1. Draw a time line similar to the one in Exhibit 21-16, using the weighted-average method.
2. Use the time line to help you compute the Bottling Department equivalent units, using the weighted-average method.

DE21-21 Using data from Polar Spring's Bottling Department in Daily Exercise 21-15 and the equivalent units computed in Daily Exercise 21-20, compute the cost per equivalent unit, using the weighted-average method.

Cost per equivalent unit; second department; weighted-average (Obj. 6)

DE21-22 Use the information on Polar Spring's Bottling Department in Daily Exercise 21-15, and the equivalent units and cost per equivalent unit you computed in Daily Exercises 21-20 and 21-21, to assign the costs to units completed and transferred out, and to ending inventory, using the weighted-average method. (*Hint:* The conversion cost per unit does not work out to an even number. Carry your computation to at least three decimal places. Should you have a "rounding error" of less than $10 in your "Total costs accounted for," assign the rounding error to the cost of units completed and transferred out.)

Assigning costs to units completed and ending inventory; second department; weighted-average method (Obj. 6)

DE21-23 Using data from Polar Spring's Bottling Department in Daily Exercise 21-15 and the cost assignments in Daily Exercise 21-22:

Journal entry, T-account; second department; weighted-average method (Obj. 1, 2, 6)

1. Prepare the journal entry to record the cost of units completed and transferred out under the weighted-average method.
2. Post all transactions from Daily Exercises 21-15 and 21-22 to the Work in Process Inventory—Bottling Department T-account. What is the ending balance?

DE21-24 ← *Link Back to Chapter 9 (Difference Between FIFO and Weighted Average).* For Polar Spring's Bottling Department, use your answers to Daily Exercise 21-18 and Daily Exercise 21-22 to compare the cost of the units completed and transferred out under FIFO to that under weighted-average. Compare the cost of the Bottling Department's ending work in process inventory under FIFO to that under weighted average. Did the Bottling Department cost per unit increase or decrease in February? How do you know?

Comparing FIFO and weighted-average results; second department (Obj. 5, 6)

EXERCISES

E21-1 Chesnut Furniture produces oak furniture in a three-stage process that includes milling, assembling, and finishing, in that order. Direct materials are added in the Milling and Finishing Departments. Direct labor and overhead are incurred in all three departments. The company's general ledger includes the following accounts:

Diagramming flows through a process costing system (Obj. 1)

Cost of Goods Sold	Work in Process Inventory—Finishing
Manufacturing Wages	Materials Inventory
Work in Process Inventory—Milling	Finished Goods Inventory
Work in Process Inventory—Assembling	Manufacturing Overhead

Outline the flow of costs through the company's accounts. Include a T-account for each account title given.

E21-2 Record the following process costing transactions in the general journal:

Journalizing process costing transactions (Obj. 2)

a. Purchase of raw materials on account, $8,400
b. Requisition of direct materials to
   Assembly Department, $3,800
   Finishing Department, $2,000
c. Incurrence and payment of manufacturing labor, $10,800.
d. Incurrence of manufacturing overhead costs:
   Property taxes—plant, $1,900
   Utilities—plant, $4,500
   Insurance—plant, $1,100
   Depreciation—plant, $3,400
e. Assignment of conversion costs to the Assembly Department:
   Direct labor, $4,700
   Manufacturing overhead, $2,900

f. Assignment of conversion costs to the Finishing Department:
Direct labor, $4,400
Manufacturing overhead, $6,200

g. Cost of goods completed and transferred out of Assembly and into Finishing, $10,250.

h. Cost of goods completed and transferred out of the Finishing Department into Finished Goods Inventory, $15,600.

Drawing a time line; computing equivalent units and assigning cost to completed units and ending work in process; no beginning inventory or cost transferred in (Obj. 3, 4)

E21-3 Apple Acres prepares and packages fruit juice products. Apple Acres has two departments: (1) Blending and (2) Packaging. Direct materials are added at the beginning of the blending process (raw fruit juice) and at the end of the packaging process (cartons). Conversion costs are added evenly throughout each process. Data from the month of May for the Blending Department are as follows:

Gallons:	
Beginning work in process inventory..............................	0
Started production	6,000 gallons
Completed and transferred out to Packaging in May	4,500 gallons
Ending work in process inventory (30% of the way through the blending process)	1,500 gallons
Costs:	
Beginning work in process inventory..............................	$ 0
Costs added during May:	
Direct materials (raw fruit juice).................................	3,600
Direct labor..	500
Manufacturing overhead...	985
Total costs added during May	$5,085

Required

1. Draw a time line for the Blending Department, similar to Exhibit 21-6.
2. Use the time line to help you compute the equivalent units for direct materials and for conversion costs.
3. Compute the total costs of the units (gallons)
   a. Completed and transferred out to the Packaging Department
   b. In the Blending Department ending work in process inventory

Journal entries, work in process T-account (Obj. 1, 2, 4)

E21-4 Return to the Blending Department for Apple Acres in Exercise 21-3.

Required

1. Present the journal entries to record the use of direct materials and direct labor, and the allocation of manufacturing overhead to the Blending Department. Also, give the journal entry to record the costs of the gallons completed and transferred out to the Packaging Department.
2. Post the journal entries to the Work in Process Inventory—Blending T-account. What is the ending balance?
3. What is the average cost per gallon transferred out of Blending and into Packaging? Why would Apple Acres' managers want to know this cost?

Computing equivalent units; assigning costs to goods completed and ending work in process inventory; first department, no beginning inventory (Obj. 2, 3, 4)

E21-5 The Assembly Department of Bentley Surge Protectors began September with no work in process inventory. During the month, production that cost $38,850 (direct materials, $8,550, and conversion costs, $30,300) was started on 21,000 units. Bentley completed and transferred to the Testing Department a total of 17,000 units. The ending work in process inventory was 50% complete as to direct materials and 80% complete as to conversion work.

Required

1. Compute the equivalent units for direct materials and conversion costs.
2. Compute the cost per equivalent unit.
3. Assign the costs to units completed and transferred out and ending work in process inventory.
4. Record the journal entry for the costs transferred out of Assembly and into Testing.
5. Post all the transactions in the Work in Process Inventory—Assembly Department T-account. What is the ending balance?

E21-6 Goodtimes is a microbrewery in Centreville, Virginia. Goodtimes has two departments—Fermenting and Packaging. Direct materials are added at the beginning of the fermenting process (barley, malt, hops) and at the end of the packaging process (bottles). Conversion costs are added evenly throughout each process. Data from the month of March for the Fermenting Department are as follows:

Drawing a time line; computing equivalent units; assigning cost to completed units and ending work in process; no beginning inventory or cost transferred in (Obj. 3, 4)

Gallons:	
Beginning work in process inventory	0
Started production	8,000 gallons
Completed and transferred out to Packaging in March	6,550 gallons
Ending work in process inventory (70% of the way through the fermenting process)	1,450 gallons
Costs:	
Beginning work in process inventory	$ 0
Costs added during March:	
Direct materials	10,000
Direct labor...	1,540
Manufacturing overhead..	4,512
Total costs added during May...	$16,052

Required

1. Draw a time line for the Fermenting Department, similar to Exhibit 21-6.
2. Use the time line to help you compute the equivalent units for direct materials and for conversion costs.
3. Compute the total costs of the units (gallons)
   a. Completed and transferred out to the Packaging Department
   b. In the Fermenting Department ending work in process inventory

E21-7 Return to the Fermenting Department for Goodtimes in Exercise 21-6.

Journal entries, work in process T-account (Obj. 1, 2, 4)

Required

1. Present the journal entries to record the use of direct materials and direct labor, and the allocation of manufacturing overhead to the Fermenting Department. Also give the journal entry to record the costs of the gallons completed and transferred out to the Packaging Department.
2. Post the journal entries to the Work in Process Inventory—Fermenting T-account. What is the ending balance?
3. What is the average cost per gallon transferred out of Fermenting and into Packaging? Why would Goodtimes' managers want to know this cost?

E21-8 The following information was taken from the ledger of Newport Glass. Ending inventory is 50% complete as to direct materials but 30% complete as to conversion work.

Computing equivalent units; assigning cost to goods completed and ending work in process inventory; first department, no beginning inventory (Obj. 2, 3, 4)

WORK IN PROCESS—FORMING

	Physical Units	Dollars		Physical Units	Dollars
Beginning inventory, September 30	-0-	$ -0-	Transferred to Finishing	72,000	$?
Production started:	80,000				
Direct materials		247,000			
Conversion costs		238,080			
Ending inventory	8,000	?			

Required

Journalize the transfer of cost to the Finishing Department. (*Hint:* First compute the number of equivalent units and the cost per equivalent unit.)

E21-9 Assume that **Edy's Grand Ice Cream Co.** reports the following data from its FIFO process costing system. Insert the missing values.

Computing equivalent units in a single department that has beginning inventory, FIFO (Obj. 5)

Flow of Production	Flow of Physical Units	Equivalent Units Direct Materials	Equivalent Units Conversion Costs
Units to account for:			
Beginning work in process, March 31.............................	14,000		
Started in production during April.................................	X		
Total physical units to account for.................................	67,000		
Units accounted for:			
Completed and transferred out during April			
From beginning work in process inventory...............	14,000	X*	X*
Started and completed during April	47,000	X	X
Ending work in process, April 30..................................	X	X†	X†
Total physical units accounted for.................................	67,000		
Equivalent units..		X	X

* Finished beginning inventory
    Direct materials: 40% completed during April
    Conversion costs: 60% completed during April
† Started ending inventory
    Direct materials: 20% completed during April
    Conversion costs: 50% completed during April

Computing equivalent units, 2 departments, FIFO method (Obj. 5)

E21-10 Selected production and cost data of Clarke Chemical Co. follow for May 20X3.

Flow of Production	Flow of Physical Units Mixing Department	Flow of Physical Units Heating Department
Units to account for:		
Beginning work in process, April 30......................	20,000	6,000
Transferred in during May	70,000	80,000
Total physical units to account for	90,000	86,000
Units accounted for:		
Completed and transferred out during May		
From beginning work in process inventory	20,000	6,000
Started and completed during May....................	60,000	70,000
Ending work in process, May 31............................	10,000	10,000
Total physical units accounted for	90,000	86,000

Clarke uses FIFO process costing.

Required

1. Fill in the blanks:
   a. On April 30, the Mixing Department beginning work in process inventory was 70% complete as to materials and 85% complete as to conversion costs. This means that for the beginning inventory _____% of the materials and _____% of the conversion costs were added during May.
   b. On May 31, the Mixing Department ending work in process inventory was 60% complete as to materials and 40% complete as to conversion costs. This means that for the ending inventory _____% of the materials and _____% of the conversion costs were added during May.
   c. On April 30, the Heating Department beginning work in process inventory was 40% complete as to materials and 70% complete as to conversion costs. This means that for the beginning inventory _____% of the materials and _____% of the conversion costs were added during May.
   d. On May 31, the Heating Department ending work in process inventory was 70% complete as to materials and 60% complete as to conversion costs. This means that for the ending inventory _____% of the materials and _____% of the conversion costs were added during May.

2. Use the information in the Flow of Production table and the information in Requirement 1 to compute the equivalent units for transferred-in costs, direct materials, and conversion costs for both the Mixing and the Heating Departments.

E21-11 Repeat Requirement 2 of Exercise 21-10 for Clarke Chemical's Heating Department, using the weighted-average method.

EU in a second department, WA method   (Obj. 6)

E21-12 Silicon Semiconductors, Inc., experienced the following activity in its Photolithography Department during December. Materials are added at the beginning of the photolithography process.

*Computing equivalent units and assigning costs to completed units and to ending work in process inventory; second department, FIFO
(Obj. 5)*

Units:	
Work in process, November 30	
(80% of the way through the process)...	8,000 units
Transferred in from the Polishing and Cutting Department	
during December	27,000 units
Completed during December	26,000 units
Work in process, December 31	
(70% of the way through the process)	9,000 units
Costs:	
Work in process, November 30	$60,116
Transferred in from the Polishing and Cutting Department	
during December	97,200
Direct materials added during December..	74,250
Conversion costs added during December	90,650

Required

1. Draw a time line for the Photolithography Department using the FIFO method. (See Exhibit 21-11.)
2. Use the time line to help you compute the number of equivalent units of work performed by the Photolithography Department during December. Use the FIFO method.
3. Compute the costs per equivalent unit, and assign total cost to (a) units completed and transferred to Finished Goods Inventory, and (b) units in December 31 work in process inventory.

E21-13 Repeat Exercise 21-12, using the weighted-average method. (See Exhibit 21-16 for a weighted-average time line.) The November 30 balance of Work in Process Inventory—Photolithography Department ($60,116) is composed of the following amounts: transferred-in costs, $20,050; direct materials costs, $20,250; and conversion costs, $19,816.

*Computing equivalent units and assigning costs to completed units and to ending work in process inventory; second department, weighted average
(Obj. 6)*

Challenge Exercise

E21-14 The following data pertain to the Packaging Department of Nature's Way Supplements, for the month of July 20X3:

Using equivalent units to determine the physical flow of production   (Obj. 5, 6)

	Equivalent Units		
Method	Transferred In	Direct Materials	Conversion Costs
FIFO	200,000	210,000	206,250
Weighted-average	210,000	210,000	208,750

Direct materials are added when the units are halfway through the packaging process. During July, 205,000 physical units were completed and transferred out.

Required

1. How many physical units were transferred in to the Packaging Department in July?
2. How many physical units were in the beginning work in process inventory?
3. How many physical units were both transferred in (started) and completed in July?
4. How many physical units were in the ending work in process inventory?
5. What percentage of the total required conversion work was done on the beginning work in process inventory during June? That is, at what percentage of completion were the beginning inventory units on July 1?

P21-1A Find-it, Inc., engraves and prints address books. Production occurs in three processes: engraving, printing, and binding. The Engraving Department had no work in process on May 31. In mid-June, Find-it started production on 80,000 books. Of this number, 67,600 books were engraved during June. Direct materials are added at the beginning of the engraving process. Conversion costs are incurred evenly throughout the process. The June 30 work in process in the Engraving Department was 60% of the way through the engraving process. Direct materials costing $212,000 were placed in production in Engraving during June, and direct labor of $97,720 and manufacturing overhead of $74,872 were assigned to that department.

Required

1. Draw a time line for the Engraving Department, similar to Exhibit 21-6.
2. Use the time line to help you compute the number of equivalent units and the cost per equivalent unit in the Engraving Department for June.
3. Assign total cost in the Engraving Department to (a) units completed and transferred to Printing during June, and (b) units still in process at June 30.
4. Prepare a T-account for Work in Process Inventory—Engraving to show its activity during June, including the June 30 balance.

P21-2A Premium Paper produces the paper used by wallpaper manufacturers (**Imperial, Norwall**). Premium Paper's four-stage process includes mixing, cooking, rolling, and cutting. In the Mixing Department, wood pulp and chemicals are blended. The resulting mix is heated in the Cooking Department in much the same way food is prepared. Then the cooked mix is rolled to produce sheets. The final process, cutting, divides the sheets into large rolled units. The Mixing Department incurred the following costs during August:

WORK IN PROCESS INVENTORY—MIXING	
Aug. 1 balance	0
Direct materials	25,872
Direct labor	6,250
Manufacturing overhead	17,246

During August, the Mixing Department started and completed mixing for 2,500 rolls of paper. The department started but did not finish the mixing for an additional 700 rolls, which were 20% complete with respect to both direct materials and conversion work at the end of August.

Required

1. Draw a time line for the Mixing Department, similar to Exhibit 21-6.
2. Use the time line to help you compute the number of equivalent units and the cost per equivalent unit in the Mixing Department for August.
3. Show that the sum of (a) cost of goods transferred out of the Mixing Department, and (b) ending Work in Process Inventory—Mixing equals the total cost accumulated in the department during August.
4. Journalize all transactions affecting the company's mixing process during August, including those already posted.

P21-3A Greenply produces exterior siding for homes. The Preparation Department begins with wood, which is chopped into small bits. At the end of the process, an adhesive is added. Then the wood/adhesive mixture goes on to the Compression Department, where the wood is compressed into sheets. Assume conversion costs are added evenly throughout the preparation process. Suppose that April data for the Preparation Department are as follows (in millions):

Sheets		Costs		
Beginning work in process inventory	0 sheets	Beginning work in process inventory	$	0
Started production.......................................	1,500 sheets	Costs added during April:		
Completed and transferred out to		Wood...		1,650
Compression in April.............................	950 sheets	Adhesives		380
Ending work in process inventory		Direct labor...		205
(40% of the way through the		Manufacturing overhead		497
preparation process)	550 sheets	Total costs..		$2,732

Required

1. Draw a time line for the Preparation Department, similar to Exhibit 21-6.
2. Use the time line to help you compute the equivalent units for direct materials and for conversion costs. (*Hint:* Each direct material added at a different point in the production process requires its own equivalent-unit computation.)
3. Compute the total costs of the units (sheets)
    a. Completed and transferred out to the Compression Department
    b. In the Preparation Department's ending work in process inventory
4. Prepare the journal entry to record the cost of the sheets completed and transferred out to the Compression Department.
5. Post the journal entries to the Work in Process Inventory—Preparation T-account. What is the ending balance?

P21-4A Cox Carpeting manufactures broadloom carpet in seven processes: spinning, dyeing, plying, spooling, tufting, latexing, and shearing. First, fluff nylon purchased from a company such as **DuPont** or **Monsanto** is spun into yarn that is dyed the desired color. Then threads of the yarn are joined together, or plied, for added strength. The plied yarn is spooled for carpet making. Tufting is the process by which yarn is added to burlap backing. After the backing is latexed to hold it together and make it skid-resistant, the carpet is sheared to give it an even appearance and feel.

Computing equivalent units for a second department with beginning inventory; assigning cost to completed units and ending work in process; FIFO method (Obj. 3, 4, 5)

At March 31, before recording the transfer of costs out of the Dyeing Department, the Cox Carpeting general ledger included the following account for one of its lines of carpet:

WORK IN PROCESS INVENTORY—DYEING

Feb. 28 Balance	9,500
Transferred in from Spinning	23,520
Direct materials	11,760
Direct labor	8,445
Manufacturing overhead	42,900

In the Dyeing Department, direct materials (dye) are added at the beginning of the process. Conversion costs are incurred evenly throughout the process. Work in process inventory of the Dyeing Department on February 28 consisted of 75 rolls that were 50% of the way through the production process. During March, 560 rolls were transferred in from the Spinning Department. The Dyeing Department completed and transferred 500 rolls to the Plying Department in March, and 135 rolls were still in process on March 31. The ending inventory was 80% of the way through the dyeing process. Cox Carpeting uses FIFO process costing.

Required

1. Prepare a time line for the Dyeing Department, similar to Exhibit 21-11.
2. Use the time line to help you compute the equivalent units, cost per equivalent unit, and total costs to account for in the Dyeing Department for March.
3. Assign total Dyeing Department cost to (a) goods transferred from Dyeing to Plying, and (b) Work in Process Inventory—Dyeing on March 31.

P21-5A Refer to Problem 21-4A.

Required

1. Prepare the March production cost report for Cox's Dyeing Department.
2. Journalize all transactions affecting the Dyeing Department during March, including the entries that have already been posted.

Preparing a production cost report and recording transactions on the basis of the report's information (Obj. 3, 4, 5)

P21-6A EZ Lift uses three processes to manufacture lifts for personal watercraft: forming the lift's parts from galvanized steel, assembling the lift, and testing the completed lifts. The lifts are transferred to finished goods before shipment to marinas across the country.

EZ Lift's Testing Department requires no direct materials. Other process costing information follows:

Computing equivalent units for a second department with beginning inventory; assigning cost to completed units and ending work in process; FIFO method (Obj. 3, 4, 5)

Units:	
Beginning work in process (60% complete as to conversion work)...	2,000 units
Transferred in from the Assembling Department during the period...	7,000 units
Completed during the period...	4,000 units
Ending work in process (40% complete as to conversion work)........	5,000 units
Costs:	
Beginning work in process...	$111,000
Transferred in from the Assembling Department during the period...	672,000
Conversion costs added during the period.............................	48,000

The cost transferred into Finished Goods Inventory is the cost of the lifts transferred out of the Testing Department. EZ Lift uses FIFO process costing.

Required

1. Draw a time line for the Testing Department, similar to the one in Exhibit 21-11.
2. Use the time line to compute the number of equivalent units of work performed by the Testing Department during the period, the cost per equivalent unit, and total costs to account for.
3. Assign total cost to (a) units completed and transferred out of Testing, and (b) units in Testing's ending work in process inventory.
4. Compute the cost per unit for lifts completed and transferred out to Finished Goods Inventory. Why would management be interested in this cost?

EU for a second department with beginning inventory; assigning cost to completed units and ending WIP; WA method (Obj. 3, 4, 6)

P21-7A Repeat Problem 21-6A, using the weighted-average method. The $111,000 beginning balance of Work in Process—Testing includes $93,000 of transferred-in cost and $18,000 of conversion cost. (For requirement 1, use the time line in Exhibit 21-16 as a guide.)

(Group B) PROBLEMS

Computing equivalent units and assigning cost to completed units and ending work in process; no beginning inventory or cost transferred in
(Obj. 1, 3, 4)

P21-1B Quickcomm, Inc., produces components for the telecommunications industry. One part, a laser diode is manufactured in a single processing department. No laser diodes were in process on May 31, and Quickcomm started production on 10,600 units during June. Direct materials are added at the beginning of the process, but conversion costs are incurred evenly throughout the process. Completed production for June totaled 8,500 units. The June 30 work in process was 40% of the way through the production process. Direct materials costing $6,360 were placed in production during June, and direct labor of $4,900 and manufacturing overhead of $2,105 were assigned to the process.

Required

1. Draw a time line for Quickcomm, similar to Exhibit 21-6.
2. Use the time line to help you compute the number of equivalent units and the cost per equivalent unit for June.
3. Assign total cost to (a) units completed and transferred to finished goods, and (b) units still in process at June 30.
4. Prepare a T-account for Work in Process Inventory to show activity during June, including the June 30 balance.

Computing equivalent units; assigning cost to completed units and ending work in process; journalizing transactions; no beginning inventory or cost transferred in
(Obj. 2, 3, 4)

P21-2B The Southern Cotton Company produces cotton fabric in a three-stage process: cleaning, spinning, and weaving. Costs incurred in the Cleaning Department during September are summarized as follows:

WORK IN PROCESS INVENTORY—CLEANING	
Sep. 1 balance	0
Direct materials	66,500
Direct labor	4,458
Manufacturing overhead	6,950

Direct materials (raw cotton) are added at the beginning of the cleaning process, while conversion costs are incurred evenly throughout the process. September activity in the Cleaning Department included cleansing of 17,000 pounds of cotton, which were transferred to the Spinning Department. Also, work began on 2,000 pounds of cotton, which on September 30 were 70% of the way through the cleaning process.

Required

1. Draw a time line for the Cleaning Department, similar to Exhibit 21-6.
2. Use the time line to help you compute the number of equivalent units and the cost per equivalent unit in the Cleaning Department for September.
3. Show that the sum of (a) cost of goods transferred out of the Cleaning Department, and (b) ending Work in Process Inventory—Cleaning equals the total cost accumulated in the department during September.
4. Journalize all transactions affecting the company's cleaning process during September, including those already posted.

EU and assigning costs to completed units and ending WIP; materials added at different points in the production process; no beginning inventory or costs transferred in (Obj. 1, 2, 3, 4)

P21-3B Royal Chicken produces canned chicken à la king. The chicken à la king passes through three departments—(1) Mixing, (2) Retort (sterilization), and (3) Packing. In the Mixing Department, chicken and cream are added at the beginning of the process, the mixture is partly cooked, and then chopped green peppers and mushrooms are added at the end of the mixing process. Conversion costs are added evenly throughout the mixing process. November data from the Mixing Department are as follows:

Gallons		Costs	
Beginning work in process inventory	0 gallons	Beginning work in process inventory.............	$ 0
Started production	10,000 gallons	Costs added during November:	
Completed and transferred out to		Chicken	12,500
Retort in November...........................	8,700 gallons	Cream...	4,500
		Green peppers and mushrooms	6,090
Ending work in process inventory		Direct labor...	8,002
(60% of the way through the		Manufacturing overhead	2,900
mixing process)	1,300 gallons	Total costs...	$33,992

Required

1. Draw a time line for the Mixing Department, similar to Exhibit 21-6.
2. Use the time line to help you compute the equivalent units. (*Hint:* Each direct material added at a different point in the production process requires its own equivalent-unit computation.)
3. Compute the total costs of the units (gallons)
   a. Completed and transferred out to the Retort Department
   b. In the Mixing Department's ending work in process inventory
4. Prepare the journal entry to record the cost of the gallons completed and transferred out to the Retort Department.
5. Post the transactions to the Work in Process Inventory—Mixing T-account. What is the ending balance?
6. What is the primary purpose of the work required in steps 1–3?

P21-4B Rule, Inc., manufacturers auto roof racks in a two-stage process that includes shaping and plating. Steel alloy is the basic raw material of the shaping process. The steel is molded according to the design specifications of automobile manufacturers (**Ford** and **General Motors**). The Plating Department then adds an anodized finish.

At March 31, before recording the transfer of cost from the Plating Department to Finished Goods Inventory, the Rule general ledger included the following account:

Computing equivalent units for a second department with beginning inventory; assigning cost to completed units and ending work in process; FIFO method (Obj. 3, 4, 5)

WORK IN PROCESS INVENTORY—PLATING

Feb. 28 balance	30,200
Transferred in from Shaping	36,000
Direct materials	24,200
Direct labor	21,732
Manufacturing overhead	35,388

The direct materials (rubber pads) are added at the end of the plating process. Conversion costs are incurred evenly throughout the process. Work in process of the Plating Department on February 28 consisted of 600 racks that were 30% of the way through the production process. During March, 3,000 racks were transferred in from the Shaping Department. The Plating Department transferred 2,200 racks to Finished Goods Inventory in March, and 1,400 were still in process on March 31. This ending inventory was 50% of the way through the plating process. Rule uses FIFO process costing.

Required

1. Draw a time line for the Plating Department, similar to Exhibit 21-11.
2. Use the time line to help you compute the equivalent units, cost per equivalent unit, and total costs to account for in the Plating Department for March.
3. Assign total Plating Department cost to (a) goods transferred out of the Plating Department, and (b) Work in Process Inventory—Plating on March 31.

P21-5B Refer to Problem 21-4B.

Preparing a production cost report and recording transactions based on the report (Obj. 3, 4, 5)

Required

1. Prepare the March production cost report for the Plating Department.
2. Journalize all transactions affecting the Plating Department during March, including the entries that have already been posted.

P21-6B ToolTime uses three departments to produce screwdrivers with plastic handles. Forming the handles requires mixing the raw materials, molding, and drying.

ToolTime's Drying Department requires no direct materials. Other process costing information follows:

EU for a second department with BI; assigning cost to completed units and ending WIP; FIFO (Obj. 3, 4, 5)

Units:	
Beginning work in process (30% complete as to conversion work).....	7,000 units
Transferred in from the Molding Department during the period..........	28,000 units
Completed during the period..	16,000 units
Ending work in process (20% complete as to conversion work)..........	19,000 units
Costs:	
Beginning work in process..	$ 371
Transferred in from the Moldling Department during the period.........	4,760
Conversion costs added during the period..	1,947

After the drying process, the screwdrivers are completed by assembling the handles and shanks and packaging for shipment to retail outlets. The cost transferred in to the assembling phase is the cost of the plastic handles transferred out of the Drying Department. ToolTime uses FIFO process costing.

Required

1. Draw a time line of the Drying Department's process, similar to the one in Exhibit 21-11.
2. Use the time line to compute the number of equivalent units of work performed by the Drying Department during the period, the cost per equivalent unit, and the total costs to account for.
3. Assign total cost to (a) units completed and transferred to the assembly operation, and (b) units in the Drying Department's ending work in process inventory.

EU for a second department with BI; assigning cost to completed units and ending WIP; WA method (Obj. 3, 4, 6)

P21-7B Repeat Problem 21-6B, using the weighted-average method. The $371 beginning balance of Work in Process—Drying includes $140 of transferred-in cost and $231 of conversion cost. For requirement 1, use the time line in Exhibit 21-16 as a guide. From management's perspective, what are the advantages of the weighted-average method versus the FIFO method of process costing?

APPLY YOUR KNOWLEDGE

DECISION CASES

Using FIFO process cost information to evaluate production performance (Obj. 5)

Case 1. Bobby Jones operates Bobby's Cricket Farm in Baton Rouge, Louisiana. Bobby's raises about 18 million crickets a month. Most are sold to pet stores at $13 for a box of 1,000 crickets. Pet stores sell the crickets for 5–10 cents each as live feed for reptiles.

Raising crickets requires a two-step process: incubation and brooding. In the first process, incubation employees place cricket eggs on mounds of peat moss to hatch. In the second process, employees move the newly hatched crickets into large boxes filled with cardboard dividers. Depending on the desired size, the crickets spend approximately two weeks in Brooding before shipment to pet stores. In the brooding process, Bobby's crickets consume about 16 tons of food and produce 12 tons of manure.

Jones has invested $400,000 in the cricket farm and he had hoped to earn a 24% annual rate of return, which works out to a 2% monthly return on his investment. After looking at the farm's bank balance, Jones fears he is not achieving this return. To get more accurate information on the farm's performance, Jones bought new accounting software that provides process cost information. After Jones input data, the software provided the reports on the next page. However, Jones needs help interpreting these reports.

Jones does know that a unit of production is a box of 1,000 crickets. For example, in June's production cost report, the 7,000 physical units of beginning work in process inventory are 7,000 boxes (each one of the 7,000 boxes contains 1,000 immature crickets). The finished goods inventory is zero as the crickets ship out as soon as they reach the required size. Monthly operating expenses total $1,000.

Required

Bobby Jones has the following questions about the farm's performance during June.

1. What is the cost per box of crickets sold? (*Hint:* This is the cost of the boxes completed and shipped out of brooding.)
2. What is the gross profit per box?
3. How much operating income did Bobby's Cricket Farm make in June?
4. What is the return on Jones' investment of $400,000 for the month of June? (Compute this as June's operating income divided by Jones' $400,000 investment, expressed as a percentage.)
5. What monthly operating income would provide a 2% monthly rate of return? What price per box would Bobby's Cricket Farm have had to charge in June to achieve a 2% monthly rate of return?

BOBBY'S CRICKET FARM
Brooding Department
Month Ended June 30, 20XX

		Equivalent Units		
Flow of Production	Flow of Physical Units	Transferred In	Direct Materials	Conversion Costs
Units to account for:				
Beginning work in process inventory	7,000			
Transferred in during June	21,000			
Total units to account for............................	28,000			
Units accounted for:				
Completed and shipped out during June:				
From beginning inventory......................	7,000	—	1,400	4,200
Started and completed during June.........	12,000	12,000	12,000	12,000
Ending work in process, June 30	9,000	9,000	7,200	3,600
Total physical units accounted for	28,000			
Equivalent units...		21,000	20,600	19,800

BOBBY'S CRICKET FARM
Brooding Department
Production Cost Report (FIFO Method)
Month Ended June 30, 20XX

	Transferred In	Direct Materials	Conversion Costs	Total
Unit costs:				
Beginning work in process, May 31				$ 74,740
Costs added during June	$46,200	$156,560	$51,480	254,240
Divide by equivalent units	÷21,000	÷20,600	÷19,800	
Cost per equivalent unit...................................	$2.20	$7.60	$2.60	
Total cost to account for				$328,980
Assignment of total cost:				
Units completed and shipped out:				
From beginning work in process, May 31				$ 74,740
Costs added during June:				
Direct materials.......................................		[1,400 × $7.60]		10,640
Conversion costs......................................			[4,200 × $2.60]	10,920
Total completed from beginning inventory				96,300
Units transferred in from Incubation				
and completed during June		[12,000 × ($2.20 + $7.60 + $2.60)]		148,800
Total cost shipped out				245,100
Ending work in process, June 30:				
Transferred-in costs......................................	[9,000 × $2.20]			19,800
Direct materials...		[7,200 × $7.60]		54,720
Conversion costs..			[3,600 × $2.60]	9,360
Total ending work in process, June 30				83,880
Total cost accounted for...................................				$328,980

Case 2. Refer to Case 1. During June, Bobby Jones made a big effort to control the farm's costs. He expects the level of costs incurred during June to continue in the future.

Using FIFO process cost information to assess profitability and make business decisions (Obj. 5)

Required

1. What is the cost per box for June production only? (*Hint:* Do not include beginning Work in Process Inventory costs.)
2. Using the June production cost per unit, what is the gross profit per box?

3. If the farm sells 18,000 boxes of crickets a month and keeps costs at the June level, will Jones earn his desired return on investment? What is the monthly return on investment using only the June data?

ETHICAL ISSUE

Effect of percentage completion of ending inventory on financial results

(Obj. 1, 3, 4)

Jay Stolz and Ben Moyer are the plant managers for Southern Lumber's particle board division. Southern Lumber has adopted a just-in-time management philosophy. Each plant combines wood chips with chemical adhesives to produce particle board to order, and all production is sold as soon as it is completed. Laura Dagosta is Southern Lumber's regional controller. All of Southern Lumber's plants and divisions send Dagosta their production and cost information. While reviewing the numbers of the two particle board plants, she is surprised that both plants estimate their ending work in process inventories at 80% complete, which is higher than usual. Dagosta calls Moyer, whom she has known for some time. He admits that to ensure their division met its profit goal and both he and Stolz made their bonus (which is based on division profit), he and Stolz agreed to inflate the percentage completion. Moyer explains, "Determining the percent complete always requires judgment. Whatever the percent complete, we'll finish the work in process inventory first thing next year."

Required

1. How would inflating the percentage completion of ending Work in Process inventory help Stolz and Moyer get their bonus?
2. The particle board division is the largest of Southern Lumber's divisions. If Dagosta does not correct the percentage completion of this year's ending work in process inventory, how will the misstatement affect Southern Lumber's financial statements?
3. Evaluate Moyer's justification, including the effect, if any, on next year's financial statements.
4. ← *Link Back to Chapter 7.* Apply the ethical framework from Chapter 7 (page 290) in considering what Dagosta should do.

TEAM PROJECT

Computing allowable cost per unit; computing cost per equivalent unit; second process; FIFO

(Obj. 3, 5)

Hermiston Food Processors in Hermiston, Oregon, processes potatoes into french fries. Production requires two processes: cutting and cooking. The cutting process begins as scalding steam explodes the potatoes' brown skins. Workers using paring knives gouge out black spots before high pressure water blasts potatoes through a pipe and into blades arranged in a quarter-inch grid. In the cooking process, the raw shoestring fries are cooked in a bleacher, dried, partially fried at 380°F and immediately flash frozen at minus 75°F before being dropped into 5-pound bags. Direct materials are added at the beginning of the cutting process (potatoes) and at the end of the cooking process (bags). Conversion costs are incurred evenly throughout each process. Hermiston uses the FIFO method of process costing.

Assume that **McDonald's** offers Hermiston $2 per 5-pound bag to supply restaurants in the Far East. If Hermiston accepts McDonald's offer, the extra cost per equivalent unit that Hermiston will incur to fill the McDonald's order equals the April cost per equivalent unit. J. R. Simlott, manager of the cooking process, must prepare a report explaining whether Hermiston should accept the offer. Simlott gathers the following information from April's cooking operations:

HERMISTON FOOD PROCESSORS	
Cooking Department	
April 20XX Activity and Costs	
Beginning work in process inventory (40% of way through process)	12,000 pounds
Raw shoestring fries started in April	129,000 pounds
French fries completed and transferred out	130,000 pounds
Ending work in process inventory (30% of way through process)	11,000 pounds
Costs to start the 12,000 pounds of beginning work in process inventory in March	$ 640
Costs added during April:	
Direct materials	6,500
Conversion costs	15,420

Lola Mendez manages the cutting process. She reports the following data for her department's April operations.

HERMISTON FOOD PROCESSORS	
Cutting Department	
April 20XX Activity and Costs	
Beginning work in process inventory (40% of way through process)	21,000 pounds
Potatoes started in April	121,000 pounds
Raw shoestring fries completed and transferred out	129,000 pounds
Ending work in process inventory (60% of way through process)	13,000 pounds
Costs to start the 21,000 pounds of beginning work in process inventory in March	$ 2,310
Costs added during April:	
Direct materials	9,680
Conversion costs	12,840

Split your team into two groups. Each group should meet separately before a meeting of the entire team.

Required

1. The first group takes the role of J. R. Simlott, manager of the cooking production process. Before meeting with the entire team, determine the maximum transferred-in cost per pound of raw shoestring fries the Cooking Department can incur from the Cutting Department if Hermiston is to make a profit on the McDonald's order. (*Hint:* You may find it helpful to prepare a time line and to use Exhibits 21-11 through 21-14 as a guide to your analysis.)
2. The second group takes the role of Lola Mendez, manager of the cutting process. Before meeting with the entire team, determine the April cost per pound of raw shoestring fries in the cutting process. (*Hint:* You may find it helpful to prepare a time line and to use Exhibits 21-11 through 21-14 as a guide to your analysis.)
3. After each group meets, the entire team should meet to decide whether Hermiston should accept or reject McDonald's offer.

INTERNET EXERCISE

Hershey Foods Corporation is the market leader in the candy business, making the well-known chocolate and candy brands Hershey's Kisses, Reese's peanut butter cups, and Kit Kat.

Hershey Foods Corporation

Required

1. Go to **http://www.hersheys.com** and, in the left-hand column, click on *Plant Tour* and then *From Bean to Bar*. Hershey identifies how many steps for making a candy bar? Review the steps. During what step are milk and sugar added? When are the nuts added? Do the nuts or the chocolate go into the mold first? Should Hershey Foods use job costing or process costing? Why?
2. How many raw material inventory accounts should Hershey maintain for its candy-bar ingredients? When are the milk and sugar ingredient costs transferred to a Work in Process Inventory account? To the Finished Goods account? To Cost of Goods Sold?
3. Assume that the processing steps each incur equal amounts of conversion costs. Assume the ingredients for 100,000 candy bars have completed step 5: blending. At this point, how many equivalents units have been added of: Milk and sugar? Nuts? Conversion costs?
4. Go to **http://www.hersheys.com/annualreport/** and read the information displayed. Did Hershey Foods have a good year financially? At the bottom of the page, use the pull-down menu to select *Assuring an Adequate Cocoa Supply*. Read the information displayed. Is Hershey concerned about maintaining an adequate supply of cocoa beans? What is the CMA?

22

ACCOUNTING

Cost-Volume-Profit Analysis

e-commerce

Investment

e-biz

LEARNING OBJECTIVES

After studying this chapter, you should be able to

1. Identify different cost behavior patterns

2. Use a contribution margin income statement to make business decisions

3. Compute breakeven sales and perform sensitivity analyses

4. Compute the sales level needed to earn a target operating income

5. Graph a set of cost-volume-profit relationships

6. Compute a margin of safety

7. Use the sales mix in CVP analysis

8. Compute income using variable costing and absorption costing

www.prenhall.com/horngren
Readiness Assessment

"All aboard!" shouts the conductor of the **Grand Canyon Railway** as the train departs from the Williams, Arizona, depot. The restored turn-of-the-century train features musicians in period costumes. Passengers have breakfast on the morning trip to the canyon and nibble appetizers on the afternoon trip back to Williams. The railway offers three classes of service: (1) Coach, in restored 1923 cars; (2) Club, with a mahogany bar; and (3) Chief, with an open-air rear platform.

Few of the railway's costs vary with the number of passengers because most costs are *fixed*. Track maintenance, insurance, the costs to operate the depot's railway museum, and depreciation on the locomotive and cars stay the same whether 1 or 1,000 passengers travel the scenic 65-mile route. But food and beverage costs are *variable*. They rise and fall with the number of passengers on board.

The railway's managers have to find a delicate balance. They must set ticket prices high enough to cover costs and earn a profit, but low enough to fill seats. Most costs are fixed, so the extra costs to serve each additional passenger are low. Once fixed costs are covered, most of the revenue from extra guests goes toward profits.

ow do the railway's managers ensure that revenues cover costs and provide profits? How do they decide how many seats to offer in each class? How many seats must the railway fill to cover costs? **Grand Canyon's** managers perform cost-volume-profit analysis to answer these questions.

Cost-volume-profit (CVP) analysis expresses the relationships among costs, volume, and profit or loss. We begin our study by explaining how to compute *profit* in a way that is tailor-made for CVP analysis. To do this, we first need to discuss the different types of *costs*.

COST-VOLUME-PROFIT (CVP) ANALYSIS. Expresses the relationships among costs, volume, and profit or loss.

VARIABLE, FIXED, AND MIXED COSTS

Chapter 20 defined a *cost driver* as any factor that affects costs. *Volume* is a common cost driver; it is often expressed as physical units produced or sold, or as sales dollars. For example, the more T-shirts **Hanes** produces, the more costs the company incurs. Nonvolume factors can also drive costs. For example, weight drives freight costs. In this chapter, we focus on volume as the cost driver. **Cost behavior** describes how costs change—if they change at all—as the cost driver changes. We examine three basic types of costs: variable, fixed, and mixed.

Objective 1
Identify different cost behavior patterns

COST BEHAVIOR. Describes how costs change as a cost driver changes.

Variable Costs

Variable costs change in total in direct proportion to changes in the volume of activity. In the **Grand Canyon Railway** story, variable costs include food and beverages. On the morning trip from Williams, Arizona, to Grand Canyon National Park, passengers enjoy a continental breakfast of pastries, orange juice, and coffee. Let's assume this breakfast costs the railway $3 per person. On the afternoon return trip, passengers enjoy appetizers, champagne, and soft drinks. We'll say this afternoon snack costs Grand Canyon Railway $10 per person. If Grand Canyon carries 20% more passengers this month, its total food and beverage costs will increase by 20%. If the railway carries 10% fewer passengers, the total food and beverage costs will fall by 10%. But while the total amount of the food and beverage costs fluctuates with the number of passengers, the per-person costs remain constant. That is, Grand Canyon incurs $3 in breakfast costs and $10 in afternoon snack costs for each passenger, no matter how many passengers the railway carries. The key point is that *total variable costs fluctuate with the volume of activity, but the variable cost per unit remains constant.*

Exhibit 22-1 graphs Grand Canyon's $3 per-person breakfast cost and the $10 per-person afternoon snack cost. The vertical axis shows the total variable costs, while the horizontal axis plots total volume (thousands of passengers, in this case).

VARIABLE COSTS. Costs that change in total in direct proportion to changes in volume of activity.

EXHIBIT 22-1   Variable Costs

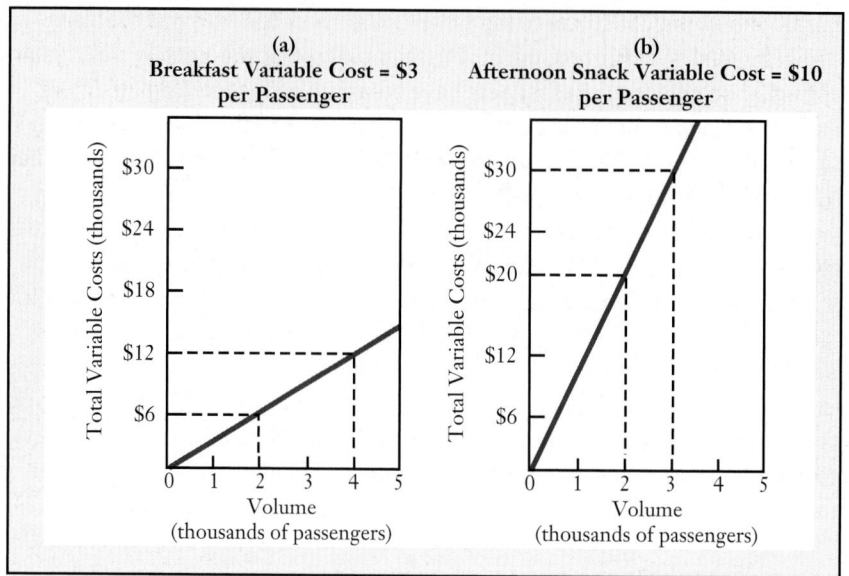

(a)
Breakfast Variable Cost = $3
per Passenger

(b)
Afternoon Snack Variable Cost = $10
per Passenger

Look at the total variable breakfast costs in Exhibit 22-1(a). If there are no passengers, Grand Canyon incurs no breakfast costs. The total variable cost line begins at the bottom left corner. This point is called the *origin*, and represents zero volume and zero cost. The *slope* of the total variable cost line is the change in total variable cost (on the vertical axis) divided by the change in the total volume (on the horizontal axis). This equals the variable cost per unit. In Exhibit 22-1(a), the slope of Grand Canyon Railway's breakfast service total variable cost line is the $3 variable cost per passenger. This means that the railway spends an additional $3 on breakfast for each additional passenger. If the railroad carries 2,000 passengers, it will spend a total of $6,000 (2,000 passengers × $3 each) for breakfast service. Follow this total variable cost line to the right to see that doubling the number of passengers to 4,000 likewise doubles the total variable cost for breakfast service to $12,000 (4,000 × $3 = $12,000).

Exhibit 22-1(b) shows total variable costs for afternoon snacks and beverages. The slope of the total variable cost line for the afternoon snack service is the $10 cost of providing the refreshments for each passenger. This is much steeper than the line for breakfast service, which costs only $3 per person. So the rule is

> **The higher the variable cost per unit, the steeper the slope of the total variable cost line.**

Study Exhibit 22-1(b) to confirm that the total cost of afternoon snacks for 2,000 passengers is $20,000 (2,000 × $10). This is much higher than the breakfast cost for 2,000 passengers ($6,000), so the slope of the afternoon snack's total variable cost line is much steeper than that for breakfast. If the number of passengers increases to 3,000 (a 50% increase), then the total variable cost of providing snack service also increases by 50%—from $20,000 to $30,000 (3,000 × $10).

 DAILY EXERCISE 22-1

Fixed Costs

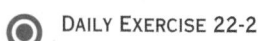 DAILY EXERCISE 22-2

FIXED COST. Cost that does not change in total despite wide changes in volume.

A **fixed cost** does not change in total despite wide changes in volume. Most of Grand Canyon Railway's costs are fixed. The train makes one round-trip each day, regardless of the number of passengers. Grand Canyon's fixed costs include

- Depreciation and maintenance on the track, the locomotive, and the museum
- Entertainment costs (salaries of the strolling musicians)
- Administrative expenses (salaries of managers and accountants)

Suppose Grand Canyon has $200,000 of fixed costs per month, as shown in Exhibit 22-2. Like all graphs of fixed costs, Exhibit 22-2 shows a flat line that intersects the cost axis at the total fixed cost. This graph shows that the $200,000 monthly total fixed cost is the same for any volume of passengers. However, the *fixed cost per*

passenger depends on the number of passengers. If the railway carries 2,000 passengers, the fixed cost per passenger is $100 ($200,000 ÷ 2,000 passengers). If the number of passengers doubles to 4,000, the fixed cost per passenger is cut in half to $50 ($200,000 ÷ 4,000 passengers). Thus, the fixed cost per passenger is *inversely* proportional to the number of passengers. The key point is that *total fixed costs remain constant, but fixed cost per unit is inversely proportional to the volume of activity.*

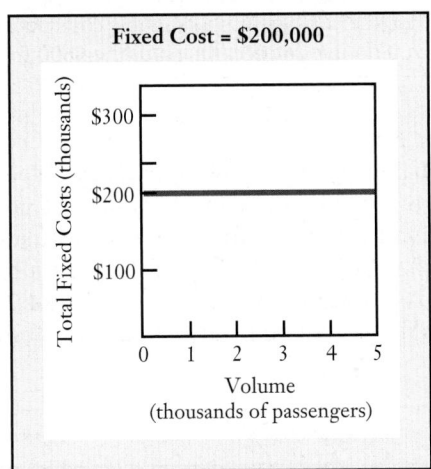

EXHIBIT 22-2
Fixed Costs

Mixed Costs

A **mixed cost** is part variable and part fixed. Suppose you start a business finding information on the Internet. Assume that **WorldCom** offers you a high-speed Internet access plan that costs $50 per month for several password accounts plus $0.05 per minute for connect time. In this plan you will pay a fixed cost of $600 per year ($50 per month × 12 months), plus $3 per hour ($0.05 per minute × 60 minutes) for connect time. Exhibit 22-3 shows the *total* (variable plus fixed) yearly costs at different volume (connect-time) levels.

MIXED COST. Cost that is part variable and part fixed.

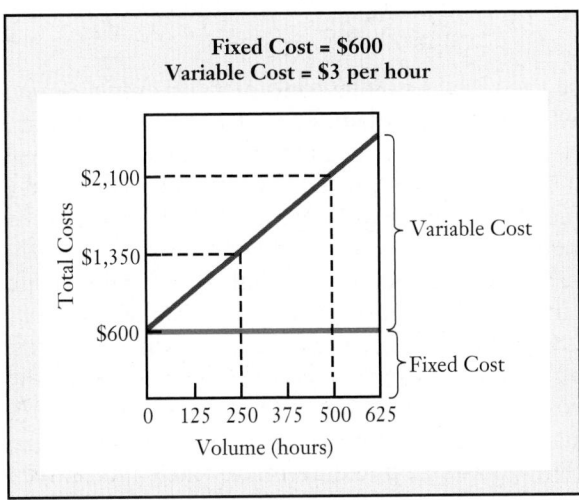

EXHIBIT 22-3
Mixed Costs

Total cost is the sum of the fixed cost plus the variable cost. If you use 250 hours of connect time, your total annual cost is $1,350 [fixed cost of $600 plus variable cost of $750 (250 hours × $3 per hour)]. If you double connect time to 500 hours, you will pay $2,100 [fixed cost of $600 plus variable cost of $1,500 (500 hours × $3 per hour)]. Even if you use no connect time, you will still pay the $600 fixed cost. Graphs of total mixed costs start at total fixed costs—not at zero as with variable costs. The slope of the total mixed cost line is the variable cost per unit.

Accountants frequently treat the fixed and variable components of mixed costs as two separate costs. They add the fixed component to other fixed costs to

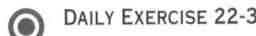
DAILY EXERCISE 22-3

determine the total cost that does not vary with the volume of goods and services produced or sold. They combine the variable component with other variable costs to compute the costs that increase in direct proportion to volume.

WORK IT OUT

In the Internet mixed cost example (Exhibit 22-3), if you double connect time from 250 to 500 hours, does your cost double? Explain.

Answer: No, total cost increases, but by less than double [(($2,100 − $1,350) ÷ $1,350 = 55.6% increase]. Variable costs double (from $750 to $1,500) when you double connect time, but the $600 fixed cost does not change.

Relevant Range

A **relevant range** is a band of volume within which a specific relationship exists between cost and volume. Outside the relevant range, the cost changes. A fixed cost is fixed only within a given relevant range of volume (usually large) and a given time span (often a month or a year). Exhibit 22-4 shows a fixed cost of $40,000 for the volume range of 0–10,000 units. Between 10,000 and 20,000 units, fixed costs increase to $80,000, and they increase to $120,000 for volumes above 20,000 units.

EXHIBIT 22-4   Relevant Range

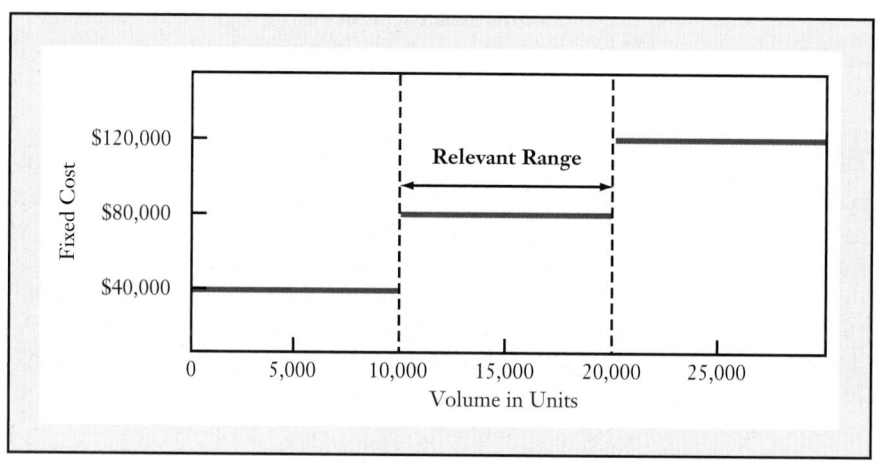

Companies use the relevant range concept in planning. Suppose a **Footlocker** store expects to sell 12,000 pairs of shoes next year. The relevant range is between 10,000 and 20,000 pairs of shoes, so managers budget fixed expenses of $80,000 (see Exhibit 22-4). If actual sales exceed 20,000 pairs, Footlocker will expand the store, which will increase rent expense. Exhibit 22-4 shows how fixed costs increase as the relevant range shifts to a higher band of volume.

Conversely, if Footlocker expects to sell only 8,000 pairs of shoes next year, the store will budget fixed costs of only $40,000. Its managers may have to cut back operating hours, lay off employees, or take other actions to cut costs.

Accountants and managers analyze cost behavior to predict how business decisions will affect costs and profits. Grand Canyon Railway managers may decide between (1) setting a higher ticket price and selling fewer seats, and (2) setting a lower price and selling more seats. To determine which alternative is likely to lead to higher profits, managers predict total costs at both volume levels. Variable costs throughout the value chain will be higher at the higher volume level. Fixed costs may or may not be higher, depending on the relevant ranges. Managers must understand how costs change with volume to predict profits from the two actions.

Objective 2
Use a contribution margin income statement to make business decisions

THE CONTRIBUTION MARGIN INCOME STATEMENT

➤ Recall from Chapter 19 that managers are concerned with the costs of the entire value chain, from R&D through manufacturing, distribution, and customer service.

The conventional income statement, illustrated for Kast-A-Ways Swimwear in Panel A of Exhibit 22-5, classifies expenses by value-chain function. ➤ Manufacturing costs of swimsuits sold are expensed as cost of goods sold. Sales revenue minus cost of goods sold equals gross profit. Most other costs (for example, marketing and

EXHIBIT 22-5   Alternative Income Statement Formats

PANEL A—Conventional Format

KAST-A-WAYS SWIMWEAR
Conventional Income Statement
Year Ended December 31, 20X5

Sales revenue......................		$2,100,000
Cost of goods sold...............		1,320,000
Gross profit.........................		780,000
Operating expenses:		
Marketing expense..........	$310,000	
Distribution expense	290,000	600,000
Operating income		$ 180,000

 DAILY EXERCISE 22-6

DAILY EXERCISE 22-7

PANEL B—Contribution Margin Format

KAST-A-WAYS SWIMWEAR
Contribution Margin Income Statement
Year Ended December 31, 20X5

Sales revenue		$2,100,000
Variable expenses:		
Variable manufacturing		
cost of goods sold	$840,000	
Variable marketing expense	150,000	
Variable distribution expense	210,000	1,200,000
Contribution margin		900,000
Fixed expenses:		
Fixed manufacturing expense	480,000	
Fixed marketing expense ..	160,000	
Fixed distribution expense	80,000	720,000
Operating income..................		$ 180,000

distribution costs) are grouped as "operating expenses." As explained in Chaper 5, gross profit minus operating expenses equals operating income. ➡

A conventional income statement's cost of goods sold includes both variable and fixed manufacturing costs. Variable costs include direct materials, direct labor, and variable overhead like electricity. Fixed manufacturing costs include depreciation, factory rent, and property taxes. As Panel A shows, conventional income statements do not distinguish between variable and fixed expenses.

◄ See Chapter 5 for a discussion of operating income.

Companies use conventional income statements for external reporting. For decision making, many managers prefer a different format. To see why, suppose CEO Linda Kast wants to predict operating income if sales increase by 10%. The conventional income statement does not help Kast predict how the change in volume will affect income because it does not separate variable costs from fixed costs. The **contribution margin income statement** in Panel B of Exhibit 22-5 groups variable and fixed expenses separately. It highlights the **contribution margin,** which is sales revenue minus all variable expenses.

CONTRIBUTION MARGIN INCOME STATEMENT. Income statement that groups variable and fixed expenses separately, and highlights the contribution margin.

The contribution margin—the excess of revenues over variable expenses—contributes to "covering" fixed expenses and to providing operating income. Think about fixed expenses. Many fixed costs are incurred before production or sales can take place. For instance, Kast-A-Ways must buy plant and equipment to produce the swimwear. The cost of the plant and machines becomes depreciation expense. As the company produces and sells swimwear, the contribution margin grows and covers this depreciation expense. After all fixed costs are recovered by the contribution margin, the contribution from additional sales provides operating income.

CONTRIBUTION MARGIN. Sales revenue minus all variable expenses.

Compare the conventional income statement in Exhibit 22-5, Panel A, with the contribution margin income statement in Panel B. The conventional income statement subtracts cost of goods sold (including both variable and fixed manufacturing costs) from sales to obtain *gross profit.* In contrast, the contribution margin income statement subtracts all variable costs (both manufacturing and nonmanufacturing) to obtain *contribution margin.* The following chart highlights the differences between gross profit and contribution margin:

 DAILY EXERCISE 22-4

 DAILY EXERCISE 22-5

CONVENTIONAL INCOME STATEMENT	CONTRIBUTION MARGIN INCOME STATEMENT
Sales revenue	**Sales revenue**
deduct Cost of Goods Sold:	**deduct Variable Expenses:**
Variable manufacturing cost of goods sold	**Variable manufacturing cost of goods sold**
Fixed manufacturing cost of goods sold	Other (nonmanufacturing) variable expenses
= Gross profit	**= Contribution margin**

The two major differences are

- Fixed manufacturing cost of goods sold is subtracted from sales to compute gross profit, but not to compute contribution margin.
- Variable nonmanufacturing expenses are subtracted from sales to calculate contribution margin, but not to compute gross profit.

Let's see how Linda Kast uses the contribution margin income statement to predict the company's operating income. If sales volume increases by 10%, variable costs (expenses) should also increase by 10%. Fixed costs (expenses), however, should remain the same, assuming Kast-A-Ways stays in the same relevant range:

⊙ DAILY EXERCISE 22-8

Increase in sales (10% × $2,100,000)	$210,000
Increase in variable expenses (10% × $1,200,000)	(120,000)
Increase in contribution margin	90,000
Increase in fixed expenses	0
Increase in operating income	$ 90,000

MID-CHAPTER

SUMMARY PROBLEM

www.prenhall.com/horngren

Mid-Chapter Assessment

The 20X5 contribution margin income statement of RainGear follows. RainGear's Goretex jackets sell for $45.

RAINGEAR
Contribution Margin Income Statement
Year Ended December 31, 20X5

Sales revenue		$900,000
Variable expenses:		
Variable manufacturing cost of goods sold	$280,000	
Variable operating expenses	120,000	400,000
Contribution margin		500,000
Fixed expenses:		
Fixed manufacturing expenses	225,000	
Fixed operating expenses	75,000	300,000
Operating income		$200,000

Required

1. How many jackets did RainGear sell in 20X5?
2. What operating income will the company earn in 20X6 if sales volume increases by 20% and all sale prices, unit variable costs, and total fixed costs do not change? There are no beginning or ending inventories.
3. Recast the 20X5 income statement in the conventional format.

Solution

Requirement 1

RainGear sold 20,000 jackets in 20X5:

$$\text{Sales revenue} = \left(\begin{array}{c}\text{Sales price} \\ \text{per jacket}\end{array}\right) \times \left(\begin{array}{c}\text{Number of} \\ \text{jackets sold}\end{array}\right)$$

$$\$900,000 = \$45 \times (\text{Number of jackets sold})$$

$$\frac{\$900,000}{\$45} = \text{Number of jackets sold}$$

$$20,000 = \text{Number of jackets sold}$$

Requirement 2

Increase in sales revenue (20% × $900,000)	$180,000
Increase in variable expenses (20% × 400,000)	80,000
Increase in contribution margin	100,000
Increase in fixed expenses	0
Increase in operating income	100,000
20X5 operating income	200,000
20X6 operating income	$300,000

Requirement 3

RAINGEAR
Conventional Income Statement
Year Ended December 31, 20X5

Sales revenue	$900,000
Cost of goods sold ($280,000 + $225,000)	505,000
Gross profit	395,000
Operating expenses ($120,000 + $75,000)	195,000
Operating income	$200,000

BASIC COST-VOLUME-PROFIT (CVP) ANALYSIS

The Kast-A-Ways Swimwear example illustrates how changes in volume affect costs and profits. This is one type of cost-volume-profit (CVP) analysis. Before proceeding further, let's take a moment to consider the assumptions underlying CVP analysis.

Assumptions Underlying CVP Analysis

Cost-volume-profit analysis assumes that

1. Expenses are either variable or fixed.
2. Cost-volume-profit relationships are linear over a wide range of production and sales. Linear relationships appear on graphs as straight lines (as in Exhibits 22-1 and 22-2).
3. Sale prices, unit variable costs, and total fixed expenses will not change during the period.
4. Volume is the only cost driver. Other possible cost drivers (such as weight or size) are held constant or are insignificant.
5. The relevant range of volume is specified.
6. Inventory levels will not change.
7. The sales mix of products will not change during the period. **Sales mix** is the combination of products that make up total sales. For example, Furniture Warehouse may sell 70% household furniture and 30% office furniture.

SALES MIX. Combination of products that make up total sales.

When these conditions are met, CVP analysis is accurate. But most business conditions do not perfectly correspond to these assumptions. That is why managers regard CVP analysis as approximate rather than exact.

Basic CVP Analysis—The Breakeven Point

Objective 3
Compute breakeven sales and perform sensitivity analyses

Kay Pak is considering starting an e-tail business to sell art posters on the Internet. Pak plans to use business-to-business software that will enable her to purchase only those posters needed to satisfy her customers' demand. The posters will cost Pak $21 each, and she plans to sell them for $35 apiece. Monthly fixed costs for server leasing and maintenance, high-speed Internet access, and office rental total $7,000. We'll use this information to answer several questions about Pak's business.

QUESTION 1. What Is Pak's Breakeven Sales Level?

The **breakeven point** is the sales level at which operating income is zero: Total

BREAKEVEN POINT. The sales level at which operating income is zero: Total revenues equal total expenses.

revenues equal total expenses. Sales below the breakeven point result in a loss. Sales above breakeven provide a profit.

Breakeven analysis is only one type of CVP analysis. The breakeven point is often only incidental to managers of ongoing operations who focus on the sales level needed to earn a target profit. However, when demand for an old product is declining, the breakeven point is important. It is also a useful place to start the analysis of a new product's potential.

Let's use two different methods to determine the breakeven point.

THE INCOME STATEMENT EQUATION APPROACH We start by separating total expenses into variable expenses and fixed expenses. Kay Pak's variable cost is her cost to purchase the posters. Her total variable expense equals the number of posters sold multiplied by the $21 cost per poster. Her $7,000 fixed costs include server leasing and maintenance, Internet access, and office rental.

Our next step expresses income in equation form:

Sales revenue − Variable expenses − Fixed expenses = Operating income

At the breakeven point, operating income is zero, so sales revenue equals expenses. Sales revenue equals the unit sale price multiplied by the number of units sold. Variable expenses equals variable cost per unit times the number of units sold. We substitute these terms into the equation and enter the dollar amounts:

Sales revenue	−	Variable expenses	− Fixed expenses = Operating income
$\left(\dfrac{\text{Sale price}}{\text{per unit}} \times \text{Units sold}\right)$ −		$\left(\dfrac{\text{Variable cost}}{\text{per unit}} \times \text{Units sold}\right)$	− Fixed expenses = Operating income
($35 × Units sold) −		($21 × Units sold) −	$7,000 = $0
($35 −		$21) × Units sold −	$7,000 = $0
		$14 × Units sold	= $7,000
		Units sold	= $7,000/$14
		Breakeven sales in units	= 500 posters

Kay Pak must sell 500 posters to break even. Her breakeven sales level in dollars is $17,500 (500 units × $35).

It is wise to check your calculations by "proving" the breakeven point with a contribution margin income statement:

Sales revenue (500 × $35).....................................		$17,500
Less: Variable expenses (500 × $21)	$10,500	
Fixed expenses	7,000	(17,500)
Operating income...		$ 0

THE CONTRIBUTION MARGIN CVP FORMULA: A SHORTCUT METHOD There is a shortcut method for CVP analysis. To use the shortcut, we must first understand more about Pak's contribution margin. Each unit sold has a **contribution margin per unit,** which equals sales revenue per unit (sale price) minus variable expense per unit.

CONTRIBUTION MARGIN PER UNIT. Sales revenue per unit (sale price) minus variable expense per unit.

Contribution margin per unit = Sales revenue per unit − Variable expense per unit

Contribution margin can be expressed on a per-unit basis or as a ratio computed as a percentage of sales revenue. For Kay Pak's business:

	Per Unit	Percent	Ratio
Sales revenue..	$35	100	1.00
Deduct: Variable expense............................	(21)	(60)	(0.60)
Contribution margin.....................................	$14	40	0.40

CONTRIBUTION MARGIN RATIO. The ratio of contribution margin to sales revenue.

Contribution margin ratio is the ratio of contribution margin to sales revenue:

$$\text{Contribution margin ratio} = \frac{\text{Contribution margin}}{\text{Sales revenue}}$$

For Kay Pak's poster business, the contribution margin ratio is 40% ($14/$35). The contribution margin ratio tells how much a dollar of sales revenue contributes to contribution margin. Kay Pak's 40% contribution margin ratio means that each dollar of sales revenue contributes $0.40 toward fixed costs and profit, as shown in Exhibit 22-6.

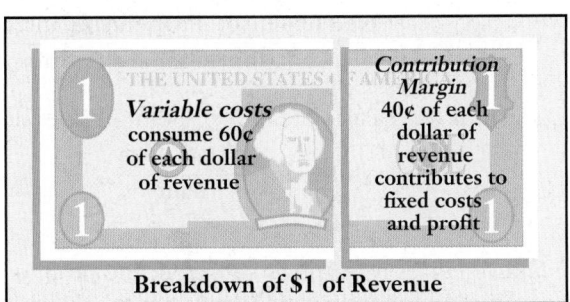

Breakdown of $1 of Revenue

EXHIBIT 22-6
Breakdown of $1 of Revenue into Variable Costs and Contribution Margin

Computing the Breakeven Point in Number of Units Sold. Now let's rearrange the income statement equation and use the contribution margin to develop a shortcut method for finding the number of posters Pak must sell to break even. We solve the equation for the number of units sold:

Sales revenue − Variable expenses − Fixed expenses = Operating income

$$\left(\frac{\text{Sale price}}{\text{per unit}} \times \text{Units sold}\right) - \left(\frac{\text{Variable cost}}{\text{per unit}} \times \text{Units sold}\right) - \text{Fixed expenses} = \text{Operating income}$$

$$\underbrace{\left(\frac{\text{Sale price}}{\text{per unit}} - \frac{\text{Variable cost}}{\text{per unit}}\right)}_{\text{Contribution margin per unit}} \times \text{Units sold} = \frac{\text{Fixed}}{\text{expenses}} + \frac{\text{Operating}}{\text{income}}$$

The sale price per unit minus the variable cost per unit equals the contribution margin per unit, so

⊙ DAILY EXERCISE 22-9

Contribution margin per unit × Units sold = Fixed expenses + Operating income

Dividing both sides of the equation by contribution margin per unit yields

$$\text{Units sold} = \frac{\text{Fixed expenses} + \text{Operating income}}{\text{Contribution margin per unit}}$$

Kay Pak can use this contribution margin CVP formula to find her breakeven point. Her fixed expenses total $7,000. Operating income is zero at the breakeven point. The contribution margin per poster is $14 ($35 sale price − $21 variable cost). Pak's breakeven computation is

$$= \frac{\$7,000 + \$0}{\$14}$$

$$= 500 \text{ posters}$$

The contribution margin CVP formula is derived from the income statement equation, so the two approaches are mathematically equivalent. Both approaches give the same answer (500 posters, in Pak's case).

Why does this shortcut method work? The formula shows that each poster Pak sells provides $14 of contribution margin. To break even, Pak must generate enough contribution margin to cover $7,000 of fixed expenses. At the rate of $14 per poster, Pak must sell 500 posters ($7,000/$14) to cover her $7,000 of fixed expenses.

Computing the Breakeven Point in Sales Dollars Using the Contribution Margin Ratio. It's easy to compute the breakeven point for a simple business, like Kay Pak's, that has only one product. The sale price per poster and the variable cost per poster are readily available. But what about companies that have hundreds of products, like **Sony** and **Procter & Gamble?**

Large companies often use the contribution margin ratio to compute breakeven points in terms of *sales dollars,* without detailed information on individual products. The contribution margin ratio approach differs from the contribution margin CVP formula we've just seen in only one way—fixed expenses plus operating income are divided by the contribution margin *ratio* to yield sales in *dollars:*

⊙ DAILY EXERCISE 22-10

$$\text{Sales in dollars} = \frac{\text{Fixed expenses} + \text{Operating income}}{\text{Contribution margin ratio}}$$

Using this ratio formula, Kay Pak's breakeven point in sales dollars is

$$\text{Sales in dollars} = \frac{\$7,000 + \$0}{0.40}$$

$$= \$17,500$$

This is the same breakeven sales revenue as shown in the proof on page 894.

Why does the contribution margin ratio formula work? Each dollar of Kay Pak's sales contributes $0.40 to fixed expenses and profit. To break even, she must generate enough contribution margin at the rate of $0.40 per sales dollar to cover the $7,000 fixed expenses ($7,000 ÷ 0.40 = $17,500).

Large companies find it easier to compute breakeven points in sales dollars using the contribution margin ratio approach because it does not require detailed information on individual products. The only information required is total fixed expenses and the contribution margin ratio. If Sony's total fixed expenses are $10 billion and its contribution margin ratio is 40%, the breakeven point in sales dollars would be

$$\text{Breakeven sales in dollars} = \frac{\$10 \text{ billion}}{0.40}$$

$$= \$25 \text{ billion}$$

CVP Sensitivity Analysis

SENSITIVITY ANALYSIS. A "what if" technique that asks what a result will be if a predicted amount is not achieved or if an underlying assumption changes.

Sensitivity analysis is a "what if" technique that asks what a result will be if a predicted amount is not achieved or if an underlying assumption changes. Let's use sensitivity analysis to see how changes in the sale price, variable costs, and fixed costs affect CVP analysis and the breakeven point.

QUESTION 2. If the Sale Price per Unit Is Changed, What Will the New Breakeven Sales Be?

Suppose the sale price per poster is $38.50 rather than $35. Variable expense per poster remains at $21, and fixed expenses stay at $7,000. What is the revised breakeven point? The per-unit contribution margin becomes $17.50 ($38.50 − $21.00), and the new contribution margin ratio is 0.4545 ($17.50 ÷ $38.50).

Using the contribution margin CVP formula:

$$\text{Sales in units} = \frac{\text{Fixed expenses} + \text{Operating income}}{\text{Contribution margin per unit}}$$

$$= \frac{\$7,000 + \$0}{\$17.50}$$

$$= 400 \text{ posters}$$

The higher sale price per unit increases the contribution margin per unit. As a result, Pak does not have to sell as many posters to break even.

Proof:

Sales revenue (400 × $38.50).....................................		$15,400
Less: Variable expenses (400 × $21)	$8,400	
Fixed expenses..	7,000	(15,400)
Operating income..		$ 0

The proof shows that Pak needs sales revenue of $15,400 to break even with a $38.50 sales price. We could also directly compute the breakeven sales in dollars using the contribution margin ratio form of the CVP formula:

$$\text{Sales in dollars} = \frac{\text{Fixed expenses} + \text{Operating income}}{\text{Contribution margin ratio}}$$

$$= \frac{\$7,000 + \$0}{0.4545}$$

$$= \$15,400 \text{ (rounded)}$$

This example shows that increasing the sale price reduces breakeven sales, both in units and in dollars. With a higher sale price, each poster contributes more toward fixed expenses, so Pak breaks even with fewer sales. Conversely, cutting the sale price would decrease the contribution margin. Then Kay Pak would have to sell more posters just to break even.

WORK IT OUT

Kay Pak believes she could dominate the e-commerce art poster business if she cut the sale price to $20. Is this a good idea?

Answer: No. The variable cost per poster is $21. If Pak sells posters for $20 each, she loses $1 on each poster. There can be no profit if the sale price does not even cover variable expenses.

QUESTION 3. If Variable Costs Change, What Will Breakeven Sales Be?

◉ DAILY EXERCISE 22-11

Suppose Pak's variable expense per poster is $23.80 instead of $21. The sale price per poster remains $35, and fixed expenses stay at $7,000. What is the breakeven point in units and in dollars?

The new contribution margin per unit drops to $11.20 ($35.00 − $23.80), and the new contribution margin ratio falls to 0.32 ($11.20/$35.00). Breakeven sales are

$$\text{Sales in units} = \frac{\text{Fixed expenses} + \text{Operating income}}{\text{Contribution margin per unit}}$$

$$= \frac{\$7,000 + \$0}{\$11.20}$$

$$= 625 \text{ posters}$$

$$\text{Sales in dollars} = \frac{\text{Fixed expenses} + \text{Operating income}}{\text{Contribution margin ratio}}$$

$$= \frac{\$7,000 + \$0}{0.32}$$

$$= \$21,875$$

As these numbers make clear, higher variable expenses per unit reduce the contribution margin. As a result, Pak must sell more posters to break even. Conversely, a decrease in variable cost per unit would lower the breakeven point.

QUESTION 4. If Fixed Costs Change, What Will Breakeven Sales Be?

◉ DAILY EXERCISE 22-12

Suppose the fixed costs total $10,500 instead of the original $7,000. Variable expense per poster remains at $21, and sale price stays at $35. What is Kay Pak's breakeven point in units and in dollars?

Using the contribution margin CVP formula:

$$\text{Sales in units} = \frac{\text{Fixed expenses} + \text{Operating income}}{\text{Contribution margin per unit}}$$

$$= \frac{\$10,500 + \$0}{\$14}$$

$$= 750 \text{ posters}$$

$$\text{Sales in dollars} = \frac{\text{Fixed expenses} + \text{Operating income}}{\text{Contribution margin ratio}}$$

$$= \frac{\$10,500 + \$0}{0.40}$$

$$= \$26,250$$

The $10,500 in fixed expenses is an increase of $3,500, or 50%, over the original fixed cost of $7,000. Note that fixed expenses increase by 50%, and breakeven sales also increase by 50% [(750 − 500) ÷ 500]. Pak must sell more posters to cover the higher fixed costs. However, if fixed expenses had declined, she could have sold fewer posters and still covered these (lower) costs.

Managers usually prefer a lower breakeven point to a higher one. But don't overemphasize this one aspect of CVP analysis. Managers are more interested in profits than in breakeven sales levels. Kay Pak may be willing to pay an extra $3,500 ($10,500 − $7,000) for Web banner ads if she expects the ads to stimulate enough extra sales volume to provide contribution margin to cover the extra advertising expense and to provide extra operating income.

Using CVP Analysis to Plan Profits

Managers of ongoing operations with established products and services are more interested in the sales level needed to earn a target profit than in the breakeven point. Now let's look at how managers use CVP analysis to plan profits.

Objective 4
Compute the sales level needed to earn a target operating income

 DAILY EXERCISE 22-13

QUESTION 5. How Many Units Must Be Sold to Earn a Target Operating Income?

Suppose Pak hopes to earn operating income of $4,900. Assuming fixed expenses of $7,000, variable expenses of $21 per poster, and a $35 per-poster sale price, how many posters must she sell to earn a profit of $4,900?

Until now, we have concentrated on the point at which operating income is zero. How should we consider a target operating income greater than zero? The contribution margin must be high enough to cover the fixed expenses *and* return a profit. We can still use the contribution margin CVP formula. The only difference is that target operating income is $4,900, compared to zero when we computed breakeven sales.

With a $14 ($35 − $21) contribution margin per unit:

$$\text{Sales in units} = \frac{\text{Fixed expenses + Operating income}}{\text{Contribution margin per unit}}$$

$$= \frac{\$7,000 + \$4,900}{\$14}$$

$$= \frac{\$11,900}{\$14}$$

$$= 850 \text{ posters}$$

Proof:

Sales revenue (850 × $35).....................................		$29,750
Less: Variable expenses (850 × $21)	$17,850	
Fixed expenses	7,000	(24,850)
Target operating income...		$ 4,900

This proof shows that Pak needs sales revenues of $29,750 to earn profit of $4,900. Alternatively, we can compute the dollar sales necessary to earn a $4,900 profit directly, using the contribution margin ratio form of the CVP formula:

$$\text{Sales in dollars} = \frac{\text{Fixed expenses + Operating income}}{\text{Contribution margin ratio}}$$

$$= \frac{\$7,000 + \$4,900}{0.40}$$

$$= \frac{\$11,900}{0.40}$$

$$= \$29,750$$

QUESTION 6. What Operating Income Is Expected at Various Sales Levels?

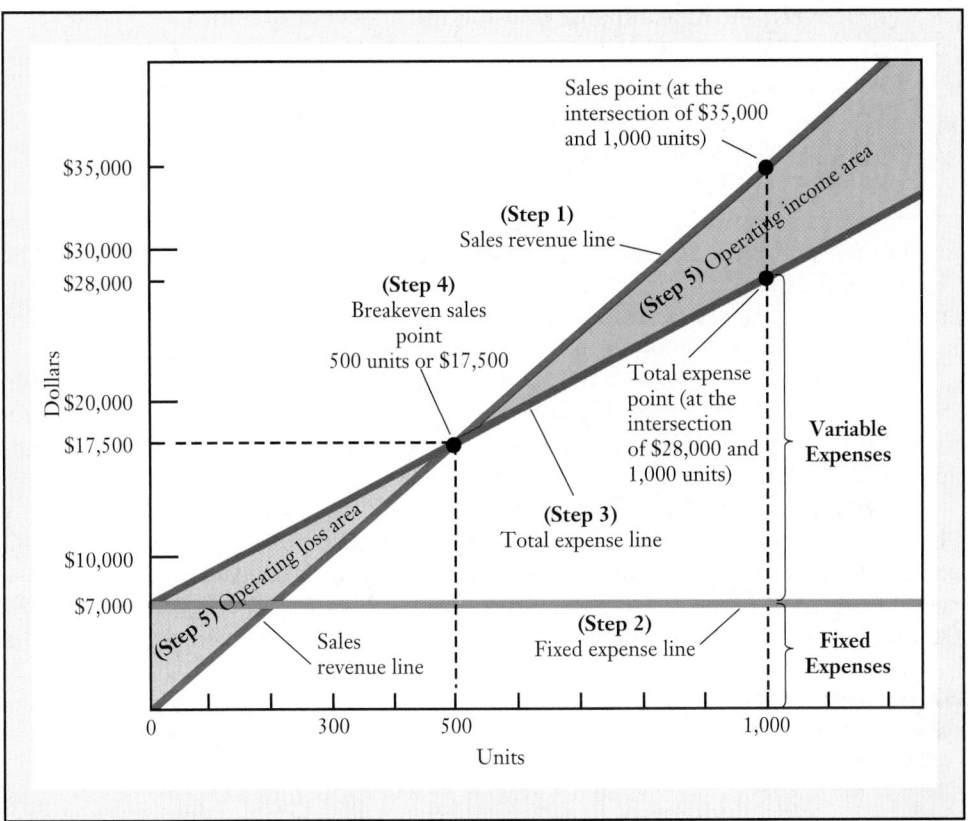

The cost-volume-profit graph in Exhibit 22-7 provides a convenient way to determine expected operating income at various sales levels. As in the cost behavior graphs earlier in this chapter (Exhibits 22-1 through 22-4), we place units on the horizontal axis and dollars on the vertical axis. We use Kay Pak's data (as originally given on page 893) and follow five steps:

Step 1. Choose a sales volume, such as 1,000 units. Plot the point for total sales revenue at that volume: 1,000 units × $35 per unit = sales of $35,000. Draw the *sales revenue line* from the origin (0) through the $35,000 point. Why does the sales revenue line start at the origin? If no posters are sold, there is no sales revenue.

Step 2. Draw the *fixed expense line,* a horizontal line that intersects the dollars axis at $7,000. Why is the fixed expense line flat? Because fixed expenses are the same ($7,000) no matter how many posters Pak sells.

Step 3. Draw the *total expense line.* Total expense is the sum of variable expense plus fixed expense. Compute variable expense at the chosen sales volume: 1,000 units × $21 per unit = variable expense of $21,000. Add variable expense to fixed expense: $21,000 + $7,000 = $28,000. Plot the total expense point ($28,000) for 1,000 units. Then draw a line through this point from the $7,000 fixed expense intercept on the dollars axis. This is the *total expense line.* Why does the total expense line start at the fixed expense line? If Pak sells no posters, she still incurs the $7,000 fixed cost for the server leasing, Internet access, and office rental, but she incurs no variable costs.

Step 4. Identify the *breakeven point.* The breakeven point is the point where the sales revenue line intersects the total expense line. This is the point where sales revenue exactly equals total expenses. The formulas we used earlier told us that Pak's breakeven point is 500 units, or $17,500 in sales. The graph shows us this information visually.

Step 5. Mark the *operating income* and the *operating loss* areas on the graph. To the left of the breakeven point, the total expense line lies above the sales revenue line. Expenses exceed sales revenue, leading to an operating loss. For example, Exhibit 22-7 shows that if Pak sells only 300 posters, she incurs an operating loss. The amount of the loss is the vertical distance between the total expense line and the sales revenue line:

Sales revenue (300 × $35)......................................			$10,500
Deduct: Variable expenses (300 × $21)		$6,300	
Fixed expenses		7,000	(13,300)
Operating income..			$ (2,800)

To the right of the breakeven point in Exhibit 22-7, the business earns a profit. The vertical distance between the sales revenue line and the total expense line equals income. The graph shows that if Pak sells 1,000 posters, she earns operating income of $7,000 ($35,000 sales revenue − $28,000 total expenses).

Why bother with a graph? Why not just use the equation approach or the contribution margin CVP formula? Graphs like Exhibit 22-7 help managers quickly estimate the profit or loss earned at different levels of sales. The equation or formula approaches only indicate income or loss for a single sales amount.

Sophisticated enterprise resource planning software like SAP, Oracle, and Peoplesoft provides detailed data that managers can use in CVP analysis. For example, after **Sears** stores lock their doors at 9:00 P.M., records for each individual transaction flow into a massive database. From a Diehard battery sold in Texas to a Trader Bay polo shirt sold in New Hampshire, the system compiles an average of 1.5 million

e-Accounting

Kozmo.com and Urbanfetch.com: Can They Continue to Deliver the Goods for Free?

It's a service made to order for couch potatoes and hectic, housebound moms. Dot.com "delivery boys" **Kozmo.com** and **Urbanfetch.com** will deliver anything from video rentals and Doritos to diapers and extra-strength Tylenol directly to your door in an hour or less. And delivery is free. Kozmo.com's friendly, spandex-suited "Kozmonauts" even tuck in a little bundle of jellybeans with your order.

Kozmo.com and Urbanfetch.com have won over both consumers and investors. Founded in 1997, Kozmo is located in five cities and plans to expand to 30 markets by the end of 2000. How can these companies make a profit, much less survive? The more people use their service, the higher their delivery costs—*variable costs*. Unlike **Amazon.com** and other e-tailers, they can't recover those costs by charging customers.

Both companies are trying various strategies to beef up revenue and keep delivery costs from sucking them dry.

- **Minimum order.** Kozmo will no longer deliver a 99¢ box of Junior Mints to the door for free; it now requires a minimum order. And Urbanfetch now requires customers to spend at least $10.
- **High-margin items.** Urbanfetch has begun stocking high-ticket items like $250 air-conditioners and PalmPilots. Its average order is $40.
- **Corporate clients.** Kozmo has a deal to deliver books, music, and toys to Amazon.com customers, and Amazon pays for the service. Urbanfetch delivers packages for **Sony Corp.** and a prominent New York law firm.

Source: Based on Andrea Petersen, "Web delivery firms adapt to turn profit," *Wall Street Journal*, June 22, 2000, p. B13. Erik Sherman, "Web delivery—in an hour," *Computerworld*, March 6, 2000, pp. 54–56. Lyle Harris, "Service while you sit, Kozmo.com fills orders fast, but selection limited." Digital Living: REPORTS FROM THE E-WORLD Buyer's Edge: YOUR THURSDAY GUIDE TO SAVING TIME and MONEY, *The Atlanta Constitution*, April 13, 2000, p. D1.

transactions a day. With the click of a mouse, managers access sale price, variable cost, and sales volume for individual products to conduct breakeven or profit planning analyses. And they can call up summary sales revenue, variable cost, and fixed cost data to perform similar analyses by individual stores or by regions.

Companies without sophisticated software systems use simple spreadsheets to answer "what if" questions such as: What will variable expenses be if sales rise by $1,000? By 200 units? If we cut fixed expenses by $20,000, how many units must we sell to earn a profit of $100,000? Spreadsheets allow managers to analyze the results of one change or several changes in the business's operations. Most software also displays CVP graphs similar to Exhibit 22-7.

OTHER CVP APPLICATIONS

Objective 6
Compute a margin of safety

Margin of Safety

The **margin of safety** is the excess of expected sales over breakeven sales. This is the drop in sales the company can absorb before incurring an operating loss. A low margin of safety is a warning. Managers use the margin of safety to evaluate current operations or to measure the risk of a new business plan.

Pak's breakeven point in our original data is 500 posters. Suppose she expects to sell 950 posters. Her margin of safety is

MARGIN OF SAFETY. Excess of expected sales over breakeven sales. Drop in sales a company can absorb before incurring an operating loss.

Margin of safety in units = Expected sales in units − Breakeven sales in units

⊙ DAILY EXERCISE 22-15

$$= 950 \text{ posters} \quad - \quad 500 \text{ posters}$$
$$= 450 \text{ posters}$$

Margin of safety in dollars = Margin of safety in units × Sale price per unit

⊙ DAILY EXERCISE 22-17

$$= 450 \text{ posters} \quad \times \$35$$
$$= \$15,750$$

Sales can drop by 450 posters, or $15,750, before Pak incurs a loss.

Managers can also compute the margin of safety as a percentage for any level of sales. Simply divide the margin of safety by sales. We obtain the same percentage whether we use units or dollars.

In units:

$$\text{Margin of safety as a percentage} = \frac{\text{Margin of safety in units}}{\text{Expected sales in units}}$$

$$= \frac{450 \text{ posters}}{950 \text{ posters}}$$

$$= 47.4\% \text{ (rounded)}$$

In dollars:

$$\text{Margin of safety as a percentage} = \frac{\text{Margin of safety in dollars}}{\text{Expected sales in dollars}}$$

$$= \frac{450 \text{ units} \times \$35}{950 \text{ units} \times \$35}$$

$$= \frac{\$15,750}{\$33,250}$$

$$= 47.4\% \text{ (rounded)}$$

Sales Mix

Objective 7
Use the sales mix in CVP analysis

Our CVP example has focused on a business with a single product, art posters. Companies that sell more than one product must consider *sales mix* in figuring CVP relationships. Sales mix has an important effect on profits. A company earns more income by selling high-margin products than by selling an equal number of low-margin items.

For example, **Continental Airlines** has focused on attracting more businesspeople. Business travelers generally pay more for the same flight than leisure travelers. By increasing the proportion of higher-paying business fliers, Continental recently boosted its sales revenue per available seat-mile (available seats × miles flown) from $0.074 to $0.09. Improving sales mix by selling more high-margin tickets reduced Continental's breakeven point. Before the change, Continental had to fill 63% of its seats to break even. By attracting more business travelers, Continental only has to fill 61%.

In contrast to Continental's more favorable sales mix, **Deere and Company,** manufacturer of John Deere farm equipment, indicates that profits have decreased because of "a less favorable mix of products sold." What is a *less favorable mix* of products? It is a mix with a higher percentage of items that have below-average contribution margins.

We can use the same CVP formulas we used for a company with a single product to perform CVP analysis for a company that sells more than one product. But first, we must compute the *weighted-average contribution margin* of all products. The sales mix provides the weights.

→ We saw another weighted-average procedure—for inventory costing—in Chapter 9 and for process costing in Chapter 21. ←

Suppose Kay Pak plans to sell two types of posters. Recall that the regular poster costs $21 and sells for $35. Its contribution margin is $14 ($35 − $21). The second, larger poster costs $40, and sells for $70. Its contribution margin is $30 ($70 − $40).

An established business estimates its sales mix based on experience. But Pak is starting a new venture. Suppose she expects to sell 500 regular posters and 300 large posters. This is a 5 : 3 sales mix. For every 5 regular posters, Pak expects to sell 3 large posters, so she expects 5/8 of the sales to be regular posters and 3/8 to be large posters. To compute breakeven sales in units, Pak arranges the data as follows:

DAILY EXERCISE 22-18

DAILY EXERCISE 22-20

	Regular Posters	Large Posters	Total
Sale price per unit	$35	$70	
Deduct: Variable expense per unit	(21)	(40)	
Contribution margin per unit	$14	$30	
Sales mix in units	5	3	8
Contribution margin	$70	$90	$160
Weighted-average contribution margin per unit ($160/8)			$ 20

$$\text{Sales in total units} = \frac{\text{Fixed expenses} + \text{Operating income}}{\text{Weighted-average contribution margin per unit}}$$

$$= \frac{\$7,000 + \$0}{\$20}$$

$$= 350 \text{ posters}$$

Breakeven sales of regular posters (350 × 5/8)	218.75 regular posters
Breakeven sales of large posters (350 × 3/8)	131.25 large posters

DAILY EXERCISE 22-19

DAILY EXERCISE 22-21

As is often the case in real situations, these computations don't yield round numbers. Since Pak cannot sell partial posters, she must sell 219 regular posters and 132 large posters to avoid a loss. Using these rounded numbers would lead to a small rounding error in our check figures, however, so the rest of our computations will use the exact results: 218.75 regular posters and 131.25 large posters.

The overall breakeven point in sales dollars is $16,844 (amounts rounded to the nearest dollar):

218.75 regular posters at $35 each	$ 7,656
131.25 large posters at $70 each	9,188
Total revenues	$16,844

We can check these amounts by preparing a contribution margin income statement (amounts rounded to the nearest dollar):

	Regular	Large	Total
Sales revenue:			
Regular (218.75 × $35)	$7,656		
Large (131.25 × $70)		$9,188	$16,844
Variable expenses:			
Regular (218.75 × $21)	4,594		
Large (131.25 × $40)		5,250	9,844
Contribution margin	$3,062	$3,938	$ 7,000
Fixed expenses			(7,000)
Operating income			$ 0

Let's review our approach:

- Compute the weighted-average contribution margin per unit. This figure expresses both types of posters in terms of a single hypothetical product that has a contribution margin of $20. From here on, the contribution margin approach follows the usual pattern.
- Divide fixed expenses (plus operating income) by the weighted-average contribution margin per unit to determine the required sales in total units.
- Separate total units (350) into regular posters (218.75) and large posters (131.25).

The breakeven proof shows that Pak's breakeven sales are $16,844. Pak could also use the contribution margin ratio formula to estimate breakeven sales in dollars. But first, she must estimate her contribution margin ratio:

Total expected contribution margin:		
Regular posters (500 × $14)	$ 7,000	
Large posters (300 × $30)	9,000	$ 16,000
Divided by total expected sales:		
Regular posters (500 × $35)	$17,500	
Large posters (300 × $70)	21,000	÷38,500
Contribution margin ratio		41.558%

Then, Pak uses the contribution margin ratio form of the CVP formula to estimate breakeven sales in dollars:

$$\text{Sales in dollars} = \frac{\textbf{Fixed expenses + Operating income}}{\textbf{Contribution margin ratio}}$$

$$= \frac{\$7,000 + \$0}{0.41558}$$

$$= \underline{\$16,844} \quad \text{(rounded)}$$

If Pak's actual sales mix is not 5 regular posters to 3 large posters, her actual operating income will differ from the planned amount, even if she sells exactly 800 total posters. For each total number of posters sold, there are as many different operating incomes as there are sales mixes. Similarly, there are as many different breakeven points—in total units and in sales dollars—as there are sales mixes. The sales-mix factor greatly complicates planning.

 THINK IT OVER Suppose Kay Pak plans to sell 800 total posters in the 5:3 sales mix (5 regular posters sold for every 3 large posters). She *actually* sells 800 posters—375 regular and 425 large. The unit sale prices and variable expenses are exactly as predicted, and the fixed expense is the budgeted $7,000. Can you tell, without computations, whether Pak's actual operating income is greater than, less than, or equal to her expected income?

Answer: Pak sold more of the higher-margin large posters. This favorable change in the sales mix increased her operating income.

Companies use CVP analysis to motivate their sales forces. Salespeople who know the contribution margin of each product they sell can generate more profit by emphasizing high-margin products. Many companies base sales commissions on the contribution margins produced by sales rather than on sales revenue alone.

The next section uses the building blocks of CVP analysis (contribution margin, the distinction between variable and fixed costs) to explain a costing approach that many managers use for internal decisions. Before continuing, review the CVP Analysis Decision Guidelines to make sure you understand these basic concepts.

DECISION GUIDELINES

Cost-Volume-Profit Analysis

DECISION	GUIDELINES
How do changes in the number of units affect • total costs?	Total variable costs → Change in proportion to changes in volume Total fixed costs → No change
• cost per unit?	Variable cost per unit → No change Fixed cost per unit: 　Increases when volume drops (Fixed costs are spread over fewer units) 　Decreases when volume rises (Fixed costs are spread over more units)
What is the difference between gross profit and contribution margin?	Gross profit = Sales − Cost of goods sold Contribution margin = Sales − Total variable expenses
How to compute sales needed to break even or earn a target operating income • in units?	$$\frac{\text{Fixed expense + Operating income}}{\text{Contribution margin per unit}}$$
• in dollars?	$$\frac{\text{Fixed expense + Operating income}}{\text{Contribution margin ratio}}$$
How to use CVP analysis to measure risk?	Margin of safety = Expected sales − Breakeven sales

EXCEL APPLICATION PROBLEM

Goal: Create an Excel spreadsheet and graph to show the relationship between costs, volume, and profit, and discover the breakeven point.

Scenario: Phonetronix, Inc., is a small manufacturer of telephone and communications devices. Recently, company management decided to investigate the profitability of cellular phone production. Their proposed new phone would sell for $99.00. Variable cost per unit is $55.00, and total fixed costs are $110,000.

1. Using the data in the spreadsheet, at what volume does Phonetronix break even on production? On the graph embedded in the spreadsheet, point the cursor at the breakeven point. Does the "pop-up" value for Total Costs match Total Revenue?
2. What is the breakeven point if Phonetronix raises the price per unit to $129? Note the changes in the graph. Which direction did the breakeven point move?
3. What is the breakeven point if the price per unit is $99, but Phonetronix slashes the variable costs per phone down to $49? Note the changes in the graph. Which direction did the breakeven point move?

Step-by-Step:
1. Open a new Excel spreadsheet.
2. Create a boldfaced heading for your spreadsheet that contains the following:
   a. Chapter 22 Decision Guidelines
   b. CVP Analysis
   c. Phonetronix, Inc.
   d. Today's date
3. Move down two rows and enter the boldfaced and underlined heading "Data Section" in Column A.
4. Move down one row. Starting in Column A, enter three rows of data, with these descriptions: price, variable cost per unit, and total fixed costs. Format cells as needed as you work.
5. Move down two rows. Enter the following boldfaced and underlined column headings, in order:
   a. # Units Sold
   b. Total Revenue
   c. Total Variable Costs
   d. Total Fixed Costs
   e. Total Costs
   f. Total Profit

6. Enter # Units Sold, in 200 unit increments, starting at 100 units, and going up to 3,500 units. (*Hint:* use a formula for this.)
7. Enter the formulas for the remaining five columns.
8. Create your graph by selecting one row of titles and all data except the "Total Profit" column. Then, click on the Chart Wizard. Select the basic line graph without data values or 3D effects.
9. Title your graph "CVP Analysis," label the X-axis

"# Units Sold" and Y-axis "Dollars." Click to finish the graph. (Your X-axis values will range from "1" to "17", not the actual unit values. To see the actual values, position your cursor over the X-axis to see a pop-up box containing the values.)
10. Position the graph at the bottom of your data in the spreadsheet, and size to fit if necessary.
11. Save your file to disk, and print a copy (in color, if possible) for your files after each change.

VARIABLE COSTING AND ABSORPTION COSTING

Objective 8
Compute income using variable costing and absorption costing

Thus far, we have assigned both variable and fixed manufacturing costs to products. This approach is called **absorption costing** because products absorb fixed manufacturing costs as well as variable manufacturing costs. Supporters of absorption costing argue that companies cannot produce products without fixed manufacturing costs, so these costs are an important part of product costs.

ABSORPTION COSTING. The costing method that assigns both variable and fixed manufacturing costs to products.

For planning and decision making, many managers prefer a different approach. **Variable costing** assigns only variable manufacturing costs to products. Under variable costing, fixed manufacturing costs are considered period costs, and are expensed in the period when they are incurred. Supporters of variable costing argue that fixed manufacturing costs (such as depreciation on the plant) provide the capacity to produce during a period. Because the company incurs these fixed expenses whether or not it produces any products or services, they are period costs, not product costs.

VARIABLE COSTING. The costing method that assigns only variable manufacturing costs to products.

While variable costing often provides a more useful basis for management decisions, companies can use variable costing only for internal reports. GAAP requires that inventory be costed at the full cost to manufacture (or purchase) the goods. Consequently, published financial statements are based on absorption costing. Exhibit 22-8 clarifies the difference between variable and absorption costing.

> The only difference between absorption costing and variable costing is that absorption costing considers fixed manufacturing costs as inventoriable product costs, while variable costing considers fixed manufacturing costs as period costs (expenses).

EXHIBIT 22-8
Differences Between Absorption Costing and Variable Costing

	Absorption Costing	Variable Costing
Product Costs (Capitalized as Inventory until expensed as Cost of Goods Sold)	Direct materials Direct labor Variable manufacturing overhead Fixed manufacturing overhead	Direct materials Direct labor Variable manufacturing overhead
Period Costs (Expensed in period incurred)	Variable nonmanufacturing costs Fixed nonmanufacturing costs	Fixed manufacturing overhead Variable nonmanufacturing costs Fixed nonmanufacturing costs
Focus	External reporting— required by GAAP	Internal reporting only
Typical Income Statement Format	Conventional income statement as in Chapters 1–19	Contribution margin statement

All other costs are treated the same way under both absorption and variable costing:

- Variable manufacturing costs are inventoriable products costs.
- All nonmanufacturing costs are period costs.

Illustrating Variable Versus Absorption Costing: Sportade

To see how absorption costing and variable costing differ, let's consider the following example. Sportade manufactures a sports beverage in both liquid and powdered form. Sportade incurs the following costs for its powdered mix in March 20X5.

Direct material cost per case...	$ 6.00
Direct labor cost per case..	3.00
Variable manufacturing overhead cost per case....................	2.00
Sales commission per case..	2.50
Total fixed manufacturing overhead expenses......................	50,000
Total fixed marketing and administrative expenses..............	25,000

Sportade produced 10,000 cases of powdered mix as planned, but sold only 8,000 cases, at a price of $30 per case. There were no beginning inventories, so Sportade has 2,000 cases of powdered mix in ending finished goods inventory (10,000 cases produced − 8,000 cases sold).

What is Sportade's inventoriable product cost per case under absorption costing and variable costing?

	Absorption Costing	Variable Costing
Direct materials...	$ 6.00	$ 6.00
Direct labor	3.00	3.00
Variable manufacturing overhead..............	2.00	2.00
Fixed manufacturing overhead..................	5.00*	
Total cost per case	$16.00	$11.00

$$* \frac{\$50{,}000 \text{ fixed manufacturing overhead}}{10{,}000 \text{ cases}} = \$5 \text{ per case}$$

The only difference between absorption and variable costing is that fixed manufacturing overhead is a product cost under absorption costing, but a period cost under variable costing. This is why the cost per case is $5 higher under absorption costing (total cost of $16) than under variable costing ($11).

Exhibit 22-9 shows that absorption costing income statements typically use the conventional format from Chapters 1–19: Sales minus cost of goods sold equals gross profit. Chapter 19 showed that manufacturers compute cost of goods sold by starting with beginning finished goods inventory (zero, in Sportade's case). They then add the cost of goods *manufactured,* computed by multiplying the number of units *produced* (10,000 cases) by the absorption costing product cost per unit ($16/case). They then subtract the ending finished goods inventory—the number of

EXHIBIT 22-9
Absorption Costing Income Statement

DAILY EXERCISE 22-21

SPORTADE Income Statement (Absorption Costing) Month Ended March 31, 20X5		
Sales revenue (8,000 × $30)		$240,000
Deduct: Cost of goods sold:		
Beginning finished goods inventory	$ 0	
Cost of goods manufactured (10,000 × $16)..................	160,000	
Cost of goods available for sale	160,000	
Ending finished goods inventory (2,000 × $16)..............	(32,000)	
Cost of goods sold..		(128,000)
Gross profit		112,000
Deduct: Operating expenses		
[(8,000 × $2.50) + $25,000]		(45,000)
Operating income		$ 67,000

units multiplied by the absorption cost per unit (2,000 cases $\times$ $16 per case in our example)—to obtain the cost of goods sold. From gross profit we subtract operating expenses (nonmanufacturing expenses) to find absorption costing operating income. The data on page 906 indicate that Sportade paid a $2.50 per-case sales commission for each case *sold,* so the total sales commission is $20,000 (8,000 cases sold $\times$ $2.50 per case). Fixed marketing and administrative costs are $25,000, somarketing and administrative expenses total $45,000 ($20,000 + $25,000).

◉ DAILY EXERCISE 22-22

◉ DAILY EXERCISE 22-23

Notice that the total cost of goods manufactured is the number of cases *produced,* multiplied by the total manufacturing cost per case. In contrast, total variable marketing expenses (for example, sales commissions) equal the variable cost per case multiplied by the number of cases *sold.*

Exhibit 22-10 shows that variable costing income statements use the contribution margin income statement format illustrated earlier in Exhibit 22-5 (Panel B). All the variable expenses are deducted from sales to get contribution margin. First, notice that the details of the (variable) cost of goods sold computation parallel those in the absorption costing income statement, *except we use the $11 variable costing product cost per case rather than the $16 absorption cost per case.*

**EXHIBIT 22-10
Variable Costing Income Statement**

SPORTADE Income Statement (Variable Costing) Month Ended March 31, 20X5		
Sales revenue (8,000 $\times$ $30)		$240,000
Deduct: Variable expenses:		
Variable cost of goods sold:		
Beginning finished goods inventory.............................	$ 0	
Variable cost of goods manufactured (10,000 $\times$ $11) ..	110,000	
Variable cost of goods available for sale.......................	110,000	
Ending finished goods inventory (2,000 $\times$ $11)	(22,000)	
Variable cost of goods sold...	88,000	
Sales commission expense (8,000 $\times$ $2.50)....................	20,000	(108,000)
Contribution margin...		132,000
Deduct: Fixed expenses:		
Fixed manufacturing overhead.......................................	50,000	
Fixed marketing and administrative expenses.................	25,000	(75,000)
Operating income		$ 57,000

To get the contribution margin, we subtract from sales both the variable cost of goods sold [$88,000 = (10,000 $\times$ $11) − (2,000 $\times$ $11)] and variable operating expenses like the sales commission (8,000 cases sold $\times$ $2.50 sales commission per case). Finally, to obtain variable costing operating income, we subtract from contribution margin all the fixed expenses ($50,000 fixed manufacturing overhead + $25,000 fixed marketing and administrative expenses).

Reconciling the Difference Between Absorption and Variable Costing Incomes

Exhibit 22-9 shows that Sportade's absorption costing operating income is $67,000. However, Exhibit 22-10 shows that variable costing yields only $57,000 of operating income. Why is operating income $10,000 lower under variable costing? To answer this question, we need to understand what happened to the $160,000 ($110,000 variable + $50,000 fixed) total manufacturing costs under each costing method.

The total manufacturing costs incurred in March are either

- Expensed in March, or
- Held back in inventory (an asset).

Exhibit 22-11 shows that of the $160,000 manufacturing costs incurred during March, absorption costing holds back $32,000 (2,000 $\times$ $16) as inventory. This $32,000 assigned to inventory is not expensed until next month, when the units are sold. Thus, only $160,000 − $32,000 = $128,000 of the manufacturing costs are expensed as cost of goods sold during March.

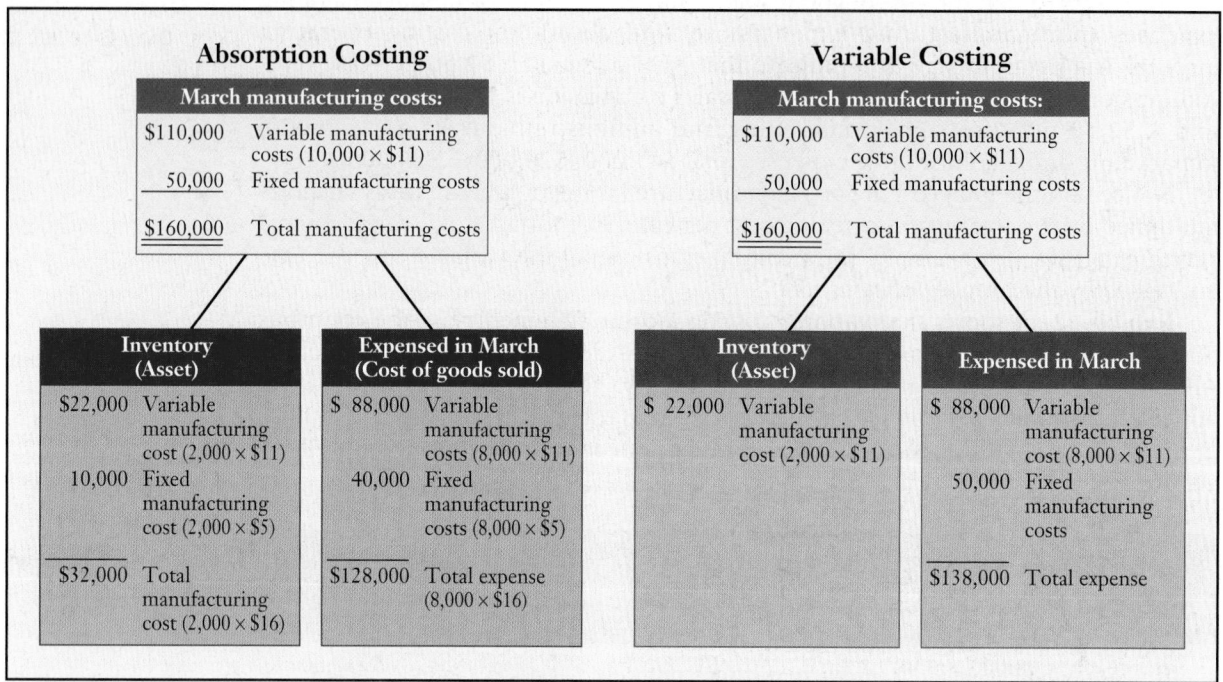

Variable costing holds back in ending inventory only $22,000 (2,000 × $11) of the total manufacturing costs. This is $10,000 ($22,000 − $32,000) *less* than absorption costing holds back in inventory. The difference arises because absorption costing assigns the $5 per case fixed manufacturing overhead costs to the 2,000 cases in ending inventory, while variable costing does not—it expenses all the fixed manufacturing overhead in the current month.

Costs that are not held back in inventory are expensed in the current period, so variable costing expenses $138,000 ($160,000 − $22,000) of manufacturing costs in March. (This $138,000 also equals the $88,000 variable cost of goods sold plus the $50,000 fixed manufacturing overhead.) This is $10,000 *more* than the $128,000 absorption costing expenses during March. *Variable costing has $10,000 more expense in March, so its income is $10,000 lower than absorption costing income.*

THINK IT OVER

Suppose Sportade has no inventory at the end of the next month, April. Will absorption costing report higher or lower operating income than variable costing for the month of April?

Answer: Absorption costing will report lower income than variable costing during April. Ending inventory in March becomes the beginning inventory of April. Absorption costing assigns a higher value to beginning inventory in April. When that beginning inventory is sold, the higher beginning inventory costs increase cost of goods sold for April, which in turn reduces income.

DAILY EXERCISE 22-24

Absorption Costing and Managers' Incentives

The general rule is this: When inventories increase (more units are produced than sold), absorption costing income is higher than variable costing income. When inventories decline (when fewer units are produced than sold), absorption costing income is lower than variable costing income. Suppose the Sportade manager receives a bonus based on absorption costing income. Will the manager want to increase or decrease production?

The manager knows that absorption costing assigns each case of Sportade $5 of fixed manufacturing overhead.

- For every case that is produced but not sold, absorption costing "hides" $5 of fixed overhead in ending inventory (an asset).

- The more cases added to inventory, the more fixed overhead is "hidden" in ending inventory at the end of the month.
- The more fixed overhead in ending inventory, the smaller the cost of goods sold, and the higher the operating income.

To maximize the bonus under absorption costing, the manager may try to increase production to build up inventory.

This incentive directly conflicts with the just-in-time philosophy, which emphasizes minimal inventory levels. ➡ Companies that have adopted just-in-time should either (1) evaluate their managers based on variable costing income, or (2) implement strict controls to prevent inventory build-up.

◀ Chapter 19 introduced the just-in-time philosophy.

Before continuing, take time to study the Absorption and Variable Costing Decision Guidelines to make sure you understand the differences between these two costing methods.

DECISION GUIDELINES

Absorption and Variable Costing

DECISION	GUIDELINE
When to use absorption costing? Variable costing?	Absorption costing must be used for external reporting. Variable costing is used only for internal reporting.
What is the difference between absorption and variable costing?	Fixed manufacturing costs are treated as • inventoriable product costs under absorption costing • period costs under variable costing

Absorption Costing	Variable Costing
Direct materials	Direct materials
+ Direct labor	+ Direct labor
+ Variable overhead	+ Variable overhead
+ Fixed overhead	—
= Product cost	= Product cost

DECISION	GUIDELINE
How to compute product costs under absorption costing and variable costing?	*(see table above)*
How to determine whether absorption costing income is higher, lower, or the same as variable costing income?	If units produced > units sold: Absorption costing income > Variable costing income If units produced < units sold: Absorption costing income < Variable costing income If units produced = units sold: Absorption costing income = Variable costing income

REVIEW CVP ANALYSIS

SUMMARY PROBLEM

Problem 1

Fleet Foot buys hiking socks for $6 a pair and sells them for $10. Management budgets monthly fixed costs of $10,000 for sales volumes between 0 and 12,000 pairs.

Required

1. Use both the income statement equation approach and the shortcut contribution margin CVP formula to compute the company's monthly breakeven sales in units.
2. Use the contribution margin ratio approach to compute the breakeven point in sales dollars.
3. Compute the monthly sales level (in units) required to earn a target operating income of $14,000. Use either the income statement equation approach or the contribution margin approach.

www.prenhall.com/horngren

End-of-Chapter Assessment

4. Prepare a graph of Fleet Foot's CVP relationships, similar to Exhibit 22-7. Draw the sales revenue line, the fixed expense line, and the total expense line. Label the axes, the breakeven point, the operating income area, and the operating loss area.

Problem 2

Suppose Fleet Foot sells a second product—heavy-duty shoelaces. Each pair costs $7 and sells for $15. Fixed costs remain $10,000 a month.

Required

1. If Fleet Foot sells 2 pairs of hiking socks for every 3 pairs of shoelaces, what is the company's breakeven sales in units? (Use the contribution margin approach.)
2. If expected sales total 11,000 units, what is Fleet Foot's margin of safety in units?

Solutions

Problem 1

Requirement 1

Income statement equation approach:

$$\text{Sales} - \text{Variable expenses} - \text{Fixed expenses} = \text{Operating income}$$

$$\left(\begin{array}{c}\text{Sale price} \\ \text{per unit}\end{array} \times \begin{array}{c}\text{Sales in} \\ \text{units}\end{array}\right) - \left(\begin{array}{c}\text{Variable} \\ \text{cost per unit}\end{array} \times \begin{array}{c}\text{Sales in} \\ \text{units}\end{array}\right) - \begin{array}{c}\text{Fixed} \\ \text{expenses}\end{array} = \begin{array}{c}\text{Operating} \\ \text{income}\end{array}$$

($10 × Sales in units) −	($6 × Sales in units)	− $10,000 = $0
($10 −	$6) × Sales in units	= $10,000
	$4 × Sales in units	= $10,000
	Sales in units	= $10,000 ÷ $4
	Breakeven sales in units	= 2,500 units

Contribution margin approach:

$$\text{Sales in units} = \frac{\text{Fixed expenses} + \text{Operating income}}{\text{Contribution margin per unit}}$$

$$\text{Breakeven sales in units} = \frac{\$10,000 + \$0}{\$10 - \$6}$$

$$= \frac{\$10,000}{\$4}$$

$$= 2,500 \text{ units}$$

Requirement 2

$$\text{Breakeven sales in dollars} = \frac{\text{Fixed expenses} + \text{Operating income}}{\text{Contribution margin ratio}}$$

$$= \frac{\$10,000 + \$0}{0.40*}$$

$$= \$25,000$$

*Contribution margin ratio = $\dfrac{\text{Contribution margin per unit}}{\text{Sale price per unit}} = \dfrac{\$4}{\$10} = 0.40$

Requirement 3

Income statement equation approach:

$$\text{Sales} - \text{Variable expenses} - \text{Fixed expenses} = \text{Operating income}$$

$$\left(\begin{array}{c}\text{Sale price} \\ \text{per unit}\end{array} \times \begin{array}{c}\text{Sales in} \\ \text{units}\end{array}\right) - \left(\begin{array}{c}\text{Variable} \\ \text{cost per unit}\end{array} \times \begin{array}{c}\text{Sales in} \\ \text{units}\end{array}\right) - \begin{array}{c}\text{Fixed} \\ \text{expenses}\end{array} = \begin{array}{c}\text{Operating} \\ \text{income}\end{array}$$

($10 × Sales in units) −	($6 × Sales in units)	− $10,000 = $14,000
($10 −	$6) × Sales in units	= $10,000 + $14,000
	$4 × Sales in units	= $24,000
	Sales in units	= $24,000 ÷ $4
	Sales in units	= 6,000 units

Contribution margin approach:

$$\text{Sales in units} = \frac{\text{Fixed expenses} + \text{Operating income}}{\text{Contribution margin per unit}}$$

$$= \frac{\$10,000 + \$14,000}{(\$10 - \$6)}$$

$$= \frac{\$24,000}{\$4}$$

$$= 6,000 \text{ units}$$

Requirement 4

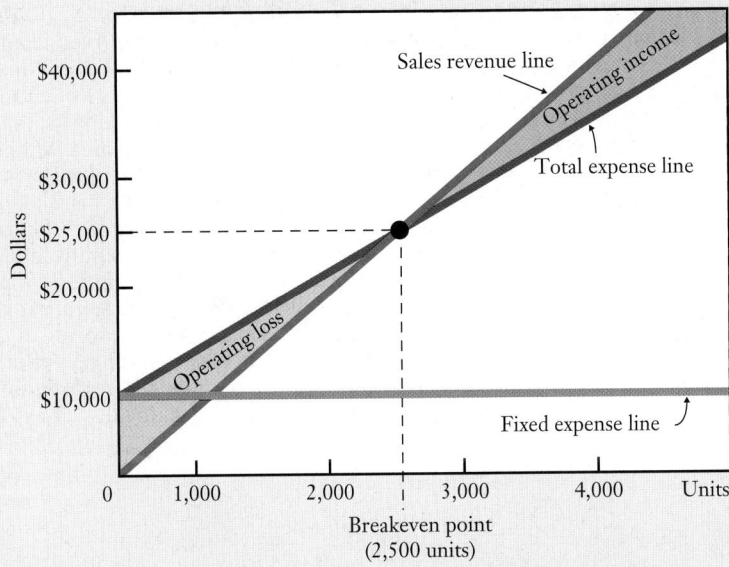

Breakeven point
(2,500 units)

Problem 2

Requirement 1

	Hiking Socks	Shoelaces	Total
Sale price per unit	$10	$15	
Deduct: Variable expense per unit	6	7	
Contribution margin per unit	$ 4	$ 8	
Sales mix in units...	× 2	× 3	5
Contribution margin	$ 8	$24	$ 32
Weighted-average contribution margin per unit ($32 ÷ 5 units)			$6.40

$$\text{Breakeven sales in units} = \frac{\text{Fixed expenses} + \text{Operating income}}{\text{Weighted-average contribution margin per unit}}$$

$$= \frac{\$10,000 + \$0}{\$6.40}$$

$$= 1,563 \text{ units (rounded)}$$

Breakeven sales of hiking socks (1,563 × 2/5) ....   625 pairs of hiking socks
Breakeven sales of shoelaces (1,563 × 3/5)...................   938 pairs of shoelaces

Requirement 2

Margin of safety in units = Expected sales in units − Breakeven sales
$$= 11,000 - 1,563$$
$$= 9,437 \text{ units}$$

LESSONS LEARNED

1. **Identify different cost behavior patterns.** *Cost-volume-profit (CVP) analysis* expresses the relationships among costs, volume of activity, and profit. These relationships depend on *cost behavior*. We classify costs as *variable, fixed,* or *mixed*.

2. **Use a contribution margin income statement to make business decisions.** *A contribution margin income statement* reports variable expenses and fixed expenses separately. It features the total *contribution margin,* the excess of sales revenues over variable expenses. This format helps managers predict the operating income that will result from various decisions.

3. **Compute breakeven sales and perform sensitivity analyses.** We use an equation or formula derived from the contribution margin income statement to compute a company's *breakeven point*—the sales level at which operating income is zero. We also perform sensitivity analyses to determine how changes in sale price, variable costs, or fixed costs affect the breakeven point.

4. **Compute the sales level needed to earn a target operating income.** CVP analysis also can show how many units the company must sell to earn a target operating income. The target operating income is added to the total fixed expense to determine the total contribution margin required. That amount is divided by the per-unit contribution margin to give the number of units that must be sold.

5. **Graph a set of cost-volume-profit relationships.** CVP graphs show the breakeven point and the ranges of sales volume that yield operating incomes and operating losses.

6. **Compute a margin of safety.** *The margin of safety* is the excess of expected sales over breakeven sales. The larger the margin, the lower the risk.

7. **Use the sales mix in CVP analysis.** *Sales mix* is the combination of products that make up total sales. There is a unique breakeven point for each different sales mix—the greater the proportion of higher margin items, the lower the breakeven point. Companies with multiple products use the weighted-average contribution margin per unit in computing the breakeven point.

8. **Compute income using variable costing and absorption costing.** Variable costing considers fixed manufacturing costs as period costs that are expensed in the period incurred. Absorption costing considers fixed manufacturing costs as inventoriable product costs. Variable and absorption costing yield different income figures when the number of units in inventory changes. Absorption costing assigns some of the current period's fixed manufacturing costs to ending inventory, so this portion of current period fixed manufacturing cost is not expensed until future periods when the units are sold. In contrast, variable costing always expenses all fixed manufacturing costs in the current period. **GAAP** requires absorption costing for external reporting, but many managers prefer variable costing for internal use because the separation of variable and fixed costs is helpful in making decisions.

ACCOUNTING VOCABULARY

absorption costing (p. 905)
breakeven point (p. 893)
contribution margin (p. 891)
contribution margin income statement (p. 891)
contribution margin per unit (p. 894)

contribution margin ratio (p. 894)
cost behavior (p. 887)
cost-volume-profit (CVP) analysis (p. 887)
fixed cost (p. 888)
margin of safety (p. 901)
mixed cost (p. 889)

relevant range (p. 890)
sales mix (p. 893)
sensitivity analysis (p. 896)
variable costs (p. 887)
variable costing (p. 905)

QUESTIONS

1. How do managers use cost-volume-profit analysis in planning?
2. Define the three types of cost behavior patterns.
3. Draw graphs of the three types of costs.
4. What are three questions cost-volume-profit analysis can answer?
5. How does a contribution margin income statement differ from a conventional income statement? Which is more useful for predicting how a change in sales will affect income? Why?
6. Why is the relevant range important in cost-volume-profit analysis?
7. What is the breakeven point? What is its significance to a business?
8. How does an increase in fixed expenses affect the breakeven point? How does a decrease in fixed expenses affect breakeven sales? Give the reason for each answer.

9. How does an increase in variable expenses affect the breakeven point? How does a decrease in variable expenses affect breakeven sales? Give the reason for each answer.
10. How does an increase in sale price affect the breakeven point? How does a decrease in sale price affect breakeven sales? Give the reason for each answer.
11. Briefly outline two ways to compute the sales in dollars needed to earn a target operating income.
12. What advantages does a CVP graph have over the income statement equation approach and the contribution margin approach?
13. How does the margin of safety serve as a measure of risk?
14. Briefly describe how to perform CVP analysis when a company sells more than one product.
15. How is fixed manufacturing overhead cost expensed under absorption costing? Under variable costing?

ASSESS YOUR PROGRESS

DAILY EXERCISES

DE22-1 Vandersteen builds innovative loudspeakers for music and home theater. Identify the following costs as variable or fixed:

Variable and fixed costs
(Obj. 1)

a. Depreciation on routers used to cut wood enclosures
b. Wood for speaker enclosures
c. Patents on crossover relays
d. Crossover relays
e. Grill cloth
f. Glue
g. Quality inspector's salary

DE22-2 Fill in the blanks using one of the following:

Variable and fixed costs
(Obj. 1)

- Stays the same
- Decreases
- Increases

a. As the number of units increases, the variable cost per unit _____.
b. As the number of units decreases, the variable cost per unit _____.
c. As the number of units increases, the fixed cost per unit _____.
d. As the number of units decreases, the fixed cost per unit _____.
e. As the number of units increases, the total variable cost _____.
f. As the number of units decreases, the total variable cost _____.
g. As the number of units increases, the total fixed cost _____.
h. As the number of units decreases, the total fixed cost _____.

DE22-3 Suppose World-Link offers an international calling plan that charges $3.00 per month plus $0.45 per minute for calls to China.

Mixed costs
(Obj. 1)

1. Under this plan, what is your monthly international long-distance cost if you call China for
   a. 20 minutes?   b. 40 minutes?   c. 80 minutes?

2. Draw a graph illustrating your total cost under this plan. Label the axes, and show your costs at 20, 40, and 80 minutes.

DE22-4 Suppose you were recently hired as an accounting intern at Optical Cable Corporation. Your boss, Bob Knechel, hands you the following information from November's operations and asks you to compute gross profit and contribution margin.

Gross profit and contribution margin
(Obj. 2)

Sales revenue	$120,000
Sales commissions	2,500
Variable manufacturing cost of goods sold	50,000
Fixed marketing expense	12,000
Research and development (fixed)	3,000
Fixed manufacturing cost of goods sold	20,000
Delivery expense (variable)	5,000

DE22-5 Your boss at Optical Cable (Daily Exercise 22-4) is puzzled by the difference between gross profit and contribution margin. Write a short memo explaining the primary difference between gross profit and contribution margin, using the following format:

Gross profit and contribution margin
(Obj. 2)

Date:	_____
To:	_____
From:	_____
Subject:	_____

DE22-6 Consider the Kast-A-Ways Swimwear income statements in Exhibit 22-5, page 891. How much of the total cost of goods sold consists of fixed manufacturing costs?

Cost of goods sold
(Obj. 2)

DE22-7 Blue Sky, Inc., produces climbing rope. The company incurs $100,000 of fixed expenses per month. It sells the rope for $23 per yard, and it incurs variable expenses at the rate of $9 per yard. Prepare a contribution margin income statement, assuming that Blue Sky sells 15,000 yards of rope in July.

Preparing a contribution margin income statement *(Obj. 2)*

Using a contribution margin
income statement to make a
decision (Obj. 2)

DE22-8 CEO John Hand thinks Blue Sky could increase its sales to 25,000 yards of rope in August if the company paid its sales force a commission of $1 per yard. What would be Blue Sky's operating income if it adopted the sales commission plan? Should Blue Sky adopt the sales commission plan? Why or why not?

DE22-9 Consider the **Grand Canyon Railway** example from the chapter opening story. Suppose the railway decides to offer only one class of service, Coach class, at an all-inclusive round-trip ticket price of $55 per passenger. Assume variable expenses of $15 per passenger. If Grand Canyon has $250,000 of fixed expenses per month, compute the number of round-trip tickets it must sell to break even:

a. Using the income statement equation approach
b. Using the shortcut contribution margin CVP formula

Perform a numerical proof to ensure that your answer is correct.

DE22-10 Refer to the information given in Daily Exercise 22-9.

1. Compute **Grand Canyon Railway's** contribution margin ratio. Carry your computation to five decimal places.
2. Use the contribution margin ratio CVP formula to determine the sales revenue Grand Canyon needs to break even.

Sensitivity analysis of changing
sale price and variable expense
on breakeven point
(Obj. 3)

DE22-11 Refer to the information given in Daily Exercise 22-9.

1. Suppose **Grand Canyon Railway** cuts its round-trip ticket price from $55 to $50 in order to increase the number of passengers. Compute the new breakeven point in units (passenger round-trips) and in sales dollars.
2. Return to the original information in Daily Exercise 22-9. Grand Canyon Railway could reduce its variable costs by eliminating champagne from the afternoon beverages. Suppose this reduces the variable expense from $15 to $12 per passenger. Compute the new breakeven point in units (passenger round-trips) and in dollars.

Sensitivity analysis of changing
fixed cost on breakeven point
(Obj. 3)

DE22-12 Consider the original **Grand Canyon Railway** information in Daily Exercise 22-9. Suppose Grand Canyon embarks on a cost reduction drive, and slashes fixed expenses from $250,000 per month to $200,000 per month.

1. Compute the new breakeven point in units (passenger round-trips) and in sales dollars.
2. Is the breakeven point higher or lower than in Daily Exercise 22-9? Explain.

DE22-13 If **Grand Canyon Railway** has a target operating income of $30,000 per month, how many round-trip tickets must the company sell? Use the original data given in Daily Exercise 22-9.

DE22-14 Using the original information in Daily Exercise 22-9, draw a graph of **Grand Canyon Railway's** cost-volume-profit relationships. Include the sales revenue line, the fixed expense line, and the total expense line. Label the axes, the breakeven point, the income area, and the loss area.

DE22-15 Consider the original **Grand Canyon Railway** information in Daily Exercise 22-9. If Grand Canyon expects to sell 7,000 round-trip tickets, compute the margin of safety.

a. In units (round-trip tickets) **b.** In sales dollars **c.** As a percentage of expected sales

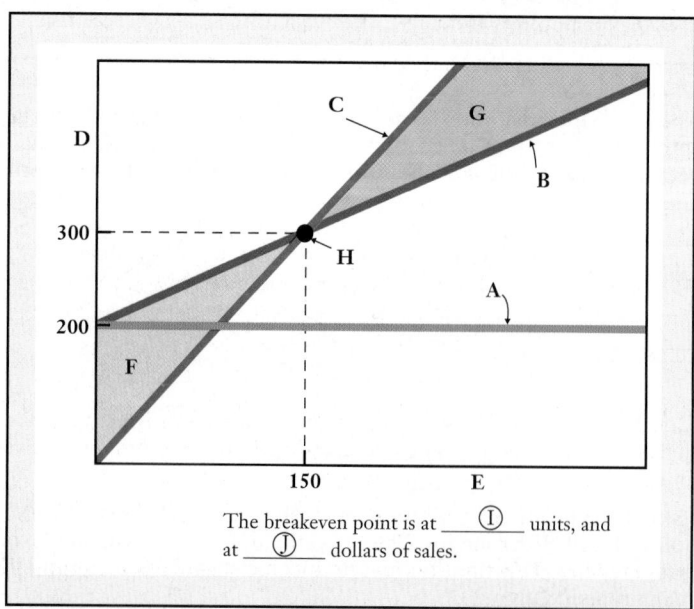

The breakeven point is at _____Ⓘ_____ units, and at _____Ⓘ_____ dollars of sales.

DE22-16 Describe what each letter stands for in the cost-volume-profit graph.

Interpreting a CVP graph
(Obj. 5)

DE22-17 Consider Kay Pak's e-tail poster business. Suppose Pak expects to sell 900 posters. Use the original data on pages 894–896 to compute her margin of safety:

Computing margin of safety
(Obj. 6)

a. In units (posters)   b. In sales dollars   c. As a percentage of expected sales

DE22-18 Kay Pak's e-tail poster business incurs $7,000 of fixed expenses and has the following sales and variable expenses per poster:

Sales mix and weighted-average contribution margin (Obj. 7)

	Regular Posters	**Large Posters**
Sale price per unit...........................	$35	$70
Variable expense per unit	21	40

Suppose Pak estimates she will sell 10 regular posters for every 2 large posters. Compute the weighted-average contribution margin per unit. Carry your computations to five decimal places.

DE22-19 Refer to the data in Daily Exercise 22-18 and your answer. Compute

Breakeven point and sales mix
(Obj. 7)

a. The total number of posters Pak must sell to break even.
b. The number of regular posters and the number of large posters she must sell to break even.
c. Compare your answer to the breakeven point calculated on page 902–903. Does the 10:2 sales mix increase or decrease the breakeven point? Why?

DE22-20 Consider the **Grand Canyon Railway** example from the chapter opening story. Suppose Grand Canyon decides to offer two classes of service: Coach class and Chief class. Assume Grand Canyon incurs $250,000 of fixed expenses per month and that it has the following ticket prices and variable expenses:

Sales mix and weighted-average contribution margin
(Obj. 7)

	Coach Class	**Chief Class**
Sale price per ticket	$55.00	$124.00
Variable expense per passenger..............	15.00	24.00

If Grand Canyon Railway expects to sell five tickets in Coach class for every three tickets in Chief class, compute the weighted-average contribution margin per unit (round-trip ticket).

DE22-21 Refer to the **Grand Canyon Railway** data in Daily Exercise 22-20 and your answer. Compute

Breakeven point and sales mix
(Obj. 7)

a. The total number of tickets Grand Canyon must sell to break even.
b. The number of Coach class tickets and the number of Chief class tickets the company must sell to break even.

DE22-22 Consider the Sportade example on pages 906–909. Suppose that during April, the company produces 10,000 cases of powdered drink mix, and sells 12,000 cases. Sale price, variable cost per case, and total fixed expenses remain the same as in March. Prepare the April income statement using variable costing.

Computing variable costing income
(Obj. 8)

DE22-23 Refer to the Sportade example on pages 906–909, and the data and your answer to Daily Exercise 22-22.

Comparing variable and absorption costing income (Obj. 8)

1. Prepare the April income statement under absorption costing.
2. Is absorption costing income higher or lower than variable costing income? Explain why.

DE22-24 For a service company like **Grand Canyon Railway,** will absorption and variable costing give different operating income figures? Explain.

Absorption and variable costing
(Obj. 8)

Graphing cost behavior
(Obj. 1)

E22-1 Graph the following cost behavior patterns over a relevant range of 0–10,000 units:

a. Variable expenses of $8 per unit
b. Mixed expenses made up of fixed costs of $20,000 and variable costs of $3 per unit
c. Fixed expenses of $15,000

Preparing a contribution margin
income statement
(Obj. 2)

E22-2 Riley Watches' April income statement follows:

RILEY WATCHES Income Statement For the Month of April 20XX		
Sales revenue		$720,000
Cost of goods sold		448,000
Gross profit		272,000
Operating expenses:		
Marketing expense	$92,000	
General and administrative expense	42,000	134,000
Operating income		$138,000

Riley's cost of goods sold is a variable expense. Marketing expense is 30% fixed and 70% variable. General and administrative expense is 60% fixed and 40% variable.

Required

1. Prepare Riley's contribution margin income statement for April.
2. Compute the expected increase in operating income to the nearest $1,000 if sales increase by $50,000.

Using a contribution margin
income statement and comput-
ing breakeven sales
(Obj. 2, 3)

E22-3 For its top managers, Blue Sea Travel formats its income statement as follows:

BLUE SEA TRAVEL Contribution Margin Income Statement Three Months Ended March 31, 20XX	
Sales revenue	$ 320,000
Variable expenses	96,000
Contribution margin	224,000
Fixed expenses	210,000
Operating income	$ 14,000

Blue Sea's relevant range is between sales of $250,000 and $360,000. Prepare contribution margin income statements at those volume levels. Also, compute breakeven sales in dollars.

Computing breakeven sales by
the contribution margin approach
(Obj. 3)

E22-4 Baker Breakfast Co. produces frozen bagels. The company has fixed expenses of $63,000, and variable expenses of $1.10 per package. Each package sells for $2.00.

Required

1. Compute the contribution margin per package and the contribution margin ratio.
2. Determine the breakeven point in units and in dollars, using the contribution margin approach.

Computing a change in
breakeven sales
(Obj. 3)

E22-5 Noodles Now fast-food restaurant has been doing such great business that owner May Chen is considering franchising her restaurant concept. She believes that customers across the country will happily pay $6 for a large bowl of noodles, veggies, and meat. Variable costs are $2.10 a bowl. Chen estimates that monthly fixed cost for franchisees would be $7,150.

Required

1. Use the contribution margin ratio approach to compute a franchisee's breakeven sales in dollars.
2. Is franchising a good idea for Chen if franchisees will want a minimum monthly operating income of $7,800, but Chen does not believe most locations could generate more than $25,000 in monthly sales?

Computing breakeven sales and
operating income or loss under
different conditions (Obj. 3, 4)

E22-6 West Coast Motor Freight delivers freight throughout California, Oregon, and Washington. The company has monthly fixed expenses of $490,000 and a contribution margin of 70% of revenues.

Required

1. Compute West Coast's monthly breakeven sales in dollars. Use the contribution margin ratio approach.
2. Compute West Coast's monthly operating income or operating loss if revenues are $500,000 and if they are $800,000.

E22-7 William Calhoun is considering starting a Web-based educational business, e-Prep MBA. He plans to offer a short-course review of mathematics for students entering MBA programs. The materials would be available on a password-protected Web site and students would complete the course through self-study. Calhoun would have to grade the course assignments, but most of the work is in developing the course materials, setting up the site, and marketing. Unfortunately, Calhoun's hard drive crashed before he finished his financial analysis. However, he did recover the following partial CVP chart:

Analyzing a cost-volume-profit graph
(Obj. 5)

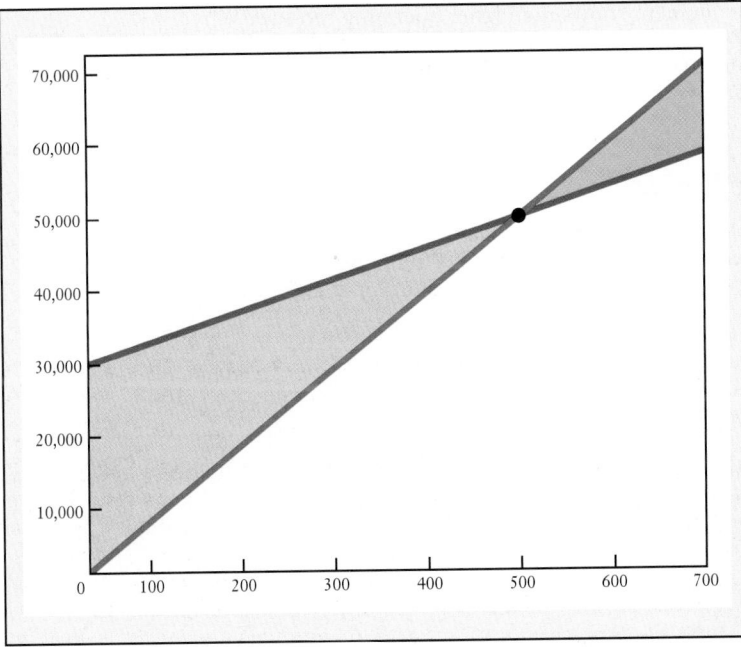

Required

1. Label each axis, sales revenue, total expenses, fixed expenses, operating income, and operating loss.
2. If Calhoun is certain he can attract 340 students to take the course, will the venture be profitable?
3. What are the breakeven sales in students and dollars?

E22-8 Suppose that Coors Field, the home of the Colorado Rockets, earns total revenue that averages $18 for every ticket sold. Assume that annual fixed expenses are $24 million, and variable expenses are $2 per ticket.

Graphing cost-volume-profit relationships
(Obj. 5)

Required

1. Prepare the ballpark's CVP graph under these assumptions. Label the axes, sales revenue line, fixed expense line, total expense line, the operating loss area, and the operating income area on the graph.
2. Show the breakeven point in dollars and in tickets.

E22-9 Waldron's drug store has a monthly target operating income of $11,000. Variable expenses are 60% of sales, and monthly fixed expenses are $9,000.

Computing breakeven and a margin of safety *(Obj. 3, 6)*

Required

1. Compute the monthly margin of safety in dollars if the store achieves its income goal.
2. Express Waldron's margin of safety as a percentage of target sales.

E22-10 Three college friends open an off-campus shop named Campus Sweats. They plan to sell a standard sweatshirt for $18 and a fancier version for $22. The $18 sweatshirt costs them $10, and the $22 sweatshirt costs them $12. The friends expect to sell two fancy sweatshirts for every three standard sweatshirts. Their monthly fixed expenses are $9,680. How many of each type of sweatshirt must they sell monthly to break even? To earn $6,600?

CVP analysis with a sales mix
(Obj. 7)

Preparing absorption costing and
variable costing income statements; business decision
(Obj. 2, 8)

E22-11 The 20X4 data that follow pertain to Oakley, a manufacturer of solid oak coffee tables. (Oakley has no beginning inventories in January 20X4.)

Sale price	$350	Fixed manufacturing	
Variable manufacturing		overhead	$2,000,000
expense per table	275	Fixed operating expense	250,000
Sales commission		Number of tables produced	100,000
expense per table	40	Number of tables sold	85,000

Required

1. Prepare both conventional (absorption costing) and contribution margin (variable costing) income statements for Oakley.
2. Which statement shows the higher operating income? Why?
3. Oakley's marketing vice president believes a new sales promotion that costs $150,000 would increase sales to 100,000 tables. Should the company go ahead with the promotion? Give your reason.

Challenge Exercise

Computing contribution margin
for one of two products
(Obj. 7)

E22-12 Solo, Inc., manufactures two styles of climbing shoe—the Mountaineer and the Pro Mountaineer. The following data pertain to the Mountaineer:

Variable manufacturing cost	$ 70
Variable operating cost	20
Sale price	160

Solo's monthly fixed expenses total $140,000. When Mountaineers and Pro Mountaineers are sold in the mix of 7:3, respectively, the sale of 2,000 total pairs results in an operating income of $60,000. Compute the contribution margin per pair for the Pro Mountaineers.

(Group A) PROBLEMS

Explaining the effects of different
cost behavior patterns
(Obj. 1)

P22-1A Lelaine Johnson is in charge of the Los Angeles Regional Head Start program. Legislators have just cut the program's funding by 15%. Johnson cannot cut total fixed costs like the rent for the program's offices or salaries of the administrative staff. The other main costs are salaries for teachers ($30,000/yr) and teachers' aides ($12,000/yr). Johnson cannot cut the salary paid per teacher or teacher's aid.

What alternatives does Johnson have to meet the budget? Will the 15% funding cut reduce services provided by more than 15%, less than 15%, or close to 15%? Explain your reasoning.

Computing contribution margins
and breakeven points
(Obj. 2, 3)

P22-2A The budgets of four companies yield the following information:

	Company			
	E	**F**	**G**	**H**
Target sales	$340,000	$ _____	$550,000	$ _____
Variable expenses	_____	100,000	280,000	104,000
Fixed expenses	_____	82,000	138,000	
Operating income (loss)	$ 60,000	$ _____	$ _____	$ 35,000
Units sold	93,500	5,000		
Contribution margin per unit	$2		$100	$12
Contribution margin ratio		0.20		0.60

Fill in the blanks for each company. Which company has the lowest breakeven point in sales dollars? What causes the low breakeven point?

P22-3A The Royal Blue schooner sails in the U.S. Virgin Islands during the winter. The average cruise has 45 tourists on board, and each person pays $75 for a day's sail. The ship sails 80 days each year. The Royal Blue also has a crew of fifteen, each earning an average of $95 per cruise. The crew is paid only when the ship sails. The other variable expense is for refreshments, which average $14 per passenger per cruise. Annual fixed expenses total $66,000.

Required

1. Compute revenue and variable expenses for each cruise.
2. Use the income statement equation approach to compute the number of cruises the Royal Blue must make each year to break even.
3. Use the contribution margin approach to compute the number of cruises needed each year to earn $85,800. Is this profit goal realistic? Give your reason.
4. Prepare the Royal Blue contribution margin income statement for 80 cruises for the year. Report only two categories of expenses: variable and fixed.

P22-4A Studio Signatures imprints T-shirts with company logos. Studio has fixed expenses of $585,000 per year plus variable expenses of $4.20 per T-shirt. Each T-shirt sells for $12.00.

Analyzing CVP relationships (Obj. 2, 3, 4)

Required

1. Use the income statement equation approach to compute the number of T-shirts Studio must sell each year to break even.
2. Use the contribution margin ratio CVP formula to compute the dollar sales Studio needs to earn $32,500 in operating income.
3. Prepare Studio's contribution margin income statement for 20X4 for sales of 70,000 T-shirts. Cost of goods sold is 80% of variable expenses. Operating expenses make up the rest of variable expenses and all of fixed expenses.
4. The company is considering an expansion that will increase fixed expenses by 20% and variable expenses by 30 cents per T-shirt. Compute the new breakeven point in units and in dollars. Use either the income statement equation approach or the contribution margin approach.
5. Should Studio undertake the expansion? Give your reason.

P22-5A Pacific Paradise Travel is opening an office in Seattle. Fixed monthly expenses are office rent ($3,700), depreciation on office furniture ($300), utilities ($210), a special telephone line ($650), a connection with the airlines' computerized reservation service ($480), and the salary of a travel agent ($2,500). Variable expenses include commissions for the travel agent (7% of sales), advertising (8% of sales), supplies and postage (2% of sales), and usage fees for the telephone line and computerized reservation service (3% of sales).

Computing breakeven sales and sales needed to earn a target operating income; graphing CVP relationships (Obj. 1, 3, 4, 5)

Required

1. Use the contribution margin ratio CVP formula to compute Pacific Paradise's breakeven sales in dollars. If the average sale is a $700 plane ticket, how many tickets must be sold to break even?
2. Use the income statement equation approach to compute the dollar sales needed to earn a target monthly operating income of $4,160.
3. Graph the travel agency's CVP relationships. Assume that an average sale is a $700 plane ticket. Show the breakeven point, sales revenue line, fixed expense line, total expense line, operating loss area, operating income area, and the sales in units (tickets) and dollars when monthly operating income of $4,160 is earned. The graph should range from 0 to 25 units (plane tickets).
4. Assume that the average sale price decreases to $490 per ticket. Use the contribution margin approach to compute the new breakeven point in tickets sold. How does the lower sale price affect the breakeven point?

P22-6A The contribution margin income statement of Brick Oven Pizza for February 20XX follows:

Using a contribution margin income statement for breakeven analysis; sales mix, margin of safety, and changes in CVP relationships (Obj. 2, 3, 6, 7)

BRICK OVEN PIZZA		
Contribution Margin Income Statement		
For the Month of February 20XX		
Sales revenue		$185,000
Variable expenses:		
Cost of goods sold...............................	$32,000	
Marketing expense................................	25,000	
General and administrative expense..............	3,000	60,000
Contribution margin...................................		125,000
Fixed expenses:		
Marketing expense................................	17,000	
General and administrative expense..............	10,500	27,500
Operating income		$ 97,500

Brick Oven sells three small pizzas for every large pizza. A small pizza sells for $8, with a variable expense of $3.75. A large pizza sells for $16, with a variable expense of $6.75.

Required

1. Determine Brick Oven's monthly breakeven point in the numbers of small pizzas and large pizzas. Prove your answer by preparing a summary contribution margin income statement at the breakeven level of sales. Show only two categories of expenses: variable and fixed.
2. Compute Brick Oven's margin of safety in dollars.
3. If Brick Oven can increase monthly sales volume by 15%, what will operating income be?

Preparing absorption and variable costing income statements and explaining the difference in income
(Obj. 8)

P22-7A ↞ *Link Back to Chapter 19 (Manufacturing Company Income Statement) and Chapter 20 (Manufacturing Overhead).* Magical Melodies manufactures music boxes, which it sells for $45 each. The company uses the FIFO inventory costing method, and it computes a new monthly fixed manufacturing overhead rate based on the actual number of music boxes produced that month. All costs and production levels are exactly as planned. The following data are from Magical Melodies' first two months in business during 20X4:

	October	November
Sales	2,000 units	2,200 units
Production	2,500 units	2,000 units
Variable manufacturing expense per music box	$15	$15
Sales commission per music box	$8	$8
Total fixed manufacturing overhead	$10,000	$10,000
Total fixed marketing and administrative expenses	$9,000	$9,000

Required

1. Compute the product cost per music box produced under absorption costing and under variable costing. Do this first for October and then for November.
2. Prepare separate monthly income statements for October and for November, using
   a. Absorption costing
   b. Variable costing
3. Is operating income higher under absorption costing or variable costing in October? In November? Explain the pattern of differences in operating income based on absorption costing versus variable costing.

(Group B) PROBLEMS

Explaining the effects of different cost behavior patterns on the breakeven point and on likely profits
(Obj. 1)

P22-1B Techman Computer Parts is opening early next year. India Landrum, the owner, is considering two plans for obtaining the plant assets and the sales force needed for operations. Plan 1 calls for purchasing all equipment and paying the sales force straight salaries. Under plan 2, Techman would lease equipment month by month and pay the sales force low salaries but give them a big part of their pay in commissions. Discuss the effects of the two plans on variable expenses, fixed expenses, breakeven sales, and likely profits for a new business in the start-up stage. Indicate which plan you favor for Techman.

Computing contribution margins and breakeven points
(Obj. 2, 3)

P22-2B The budgets of four companies yield the following information:

	Company			
	P	**Q**	**R**	**S**
Target sales	$360,000	$600,000	$190,000	$ ___
Variable expenses	108,000			130,000
Fixed expenses		312,000	100,000	
Operating income (loss)	$ 15,000	$ ___	$ ___	$160,000
Units sold	___	112,000	12,000	8,000
Contribution margin per unit	$6	___	9.50	$40
Contribution margin ratio	___	0.30	___	___

Fill in the blanks for each company. Which company has the lowest breakeven point in sales dollars? What causes the low breakeven point?

BE sales and sales to earn a target Op. Inc.; CM IS   (Obj. 2, 3, 4)

P22-3B Bahama Sunset sails a schooner from Nassau, Bahamas. The average cruise has 80 tourists on board. Each person pays $85 for a day's sail in the Atlantic. The ship sails 100 days each year.

The schooner has a crew of 12. Each crew member earns an average of $105 per cruise. The crew is paid only when the ship sails. Other variable expenses are for refreshments, which average $18 per passenger per cruise. Annual fixed expenses total $184,500.

Required

1. Compute revenue and variable expenses for each cruise.
2. Use the income statement equation approach to compute the number of cruises needed annually to break even.
3. Use the contribution margin approach to compute the number of cruises needed annually to earn $196,800. Is this profit goal realistic? Give your reason.
4. Prepare Bahama's contribution margin income statement for 100 cruises each year. Report only two categories of expenses: variable and fixed.

P22-4B Colorworks imprints calendars with company names. The company has fixed expenses of $415,000 each month plus variable expenses of $2.49 per carton of calendars. Colorworks sells each carton of calendars for $4.15.

Analyzing CVP relationships (Obj. 2, 3, 4)

Required

1. Use the income statement equation approach to compute the number of cartons of calendars Colorworks must sell each month to break even.
2. Use the contribution margin ratio CVP formula to compute the dollar amount of monthly sales Colorworks needs to earn $35,000 in operating income.
3. Prepare Colorworks' contribution margin income statement for June for sales of 450,000 cartons of calendars. Cost of goods sold is 70% of variable expenses. Operating expenses make up the rest of the variable expenses and all of the fixed expenses.
4. The company is considering an expansion that will increase fixed expenses by 40% and variable expenses by one-third. Compute the new breakeven point in units and in dollars. Use either the income statement equation approach or the contribution margin approach.
5. How would this expansion affect Colorworks' risk?

P22-5B Small World Travel is opening an office in Chicago. Fixed monthly expenses are office rent ($3,700), depreciation of office furniture ($190), utilities ($160), a special telephone line ($390), a connection with the airlines' computerized reservation service ($480), and the salary of a travel agent ($1,800). Variable expenses include commissions for the travel agent (12% of sales), advertising (9% of sales), supplies and postage (2% of sales), and usage fees for the telephone line and computerized reservation service (7% of sales).

Computing breakeven sales and sales needed to earn a target operating income; graphing CVP relationships (Obj. 1, 3, 4, 5)

Required

1. Use the contribution margin ratio CVP formula to compute the travel agency's breakeven sales in dollars. If the average sale is an $800 plane ticket, how many tickets must be sold to break even?
2. Use the income statement equation approach to compute dollar sales needed to earn monthly operating income of $3,430.
3. Graph the travel agency's CVP relationships. Assume that an average sale is an $800 plane ticket. Show the breakeven point, sales revenue line, fixed expense line, total expense line, operating loss area, operating income area, and the sales in units (tickets) and dollars when monthly operating income of $3,430 is earned. The graph should range from 0 to 20 units (plane tickets).
4. Assume that the average sale price decreases to $640 per ticket. Use the contribution margin approach to compute the new breakeven point in units (tickets). How does the lower sale price affect the breakeven point?

P22-6B The November 20X4 contribution margin income statement of Fazzio Fashion accessories store follows:

Using a contribution margin income statement for breakeven analysis; sales mix, margin of safety, and changes in CVP relationships (Obj. 2, 3, 6, 7)

FAZZIO FASHION
Contribution Margin Income Statement
For the Month of November 20X4

Sales revenue		$60,000
Variable expenses:		
Cost of goods sold	$22,000	
Marketing expenses	13,000	
General and administrative expenses	7,000	42,000
Contribution margin		18,000
Fixed expenses:		
Marketing expenses	11,000	
General and administrative expenses	3,850	14,850
Operating income		$ 3,150

Fazzio Fashion sells two hats for every purse. The hats sell for $18, with a variable expense of $7 each. The purses sell for $45, with a variable cost of $22 each.

Required

1. Determine Fazzio Fashion's monthly breakeven point in the numbers of hats and purses. Prove your answer by preparing a summary contribution margin income statement at the breakeven level of sales. Show only two categories of expenses: variable and fixed.
2. Compute Fazzio Fashion's margin of safety in dollars.
3. Suppose Fazzio Fashion increases monthly sales volume by 20%. Compute operating income.

Preparing absorption and variable costing income statements and explaining the difference in income
(Obj. 8)

P22-7B ← *Link Back to Chapter 19 (Manufacturing Company Income Statement) and Chapter 20 (Manufacturing Overhead).* Spacesaver Corporation manufactures plastic storage bins, which it sells for $8 each. The company uses the FIFO inventory costing method, and it computes a new monthly fixed manufacturing overhead rate based on the actual number of bins produced that month. All costs and production levels are exactly as planned. The following data are from Spacesaver's first two months in business:

	January 20X4	February 20X4
Sales	1,000 bins	1,200 bins
Production	1,400 bins	1,000 bins
Variable manufacturing expense per bin	$4	$4
Sales commission expense per bin	$1	$1
Total fixed manufacturing overhead	$700	$700
Total fixed marketing and administrative expenses	$600	$600

Required

1. Compute the product cost per bin produced under absorption costing and under variable costing. Do this first for January and then for February.
2. Prepare separate monthly income statements for January and for February, using
   a. Absorption costing
   b. Variable costing
3. Is operating income higher under absorption costing or variable costing in January? In February? Explain the pattern of differences in operating income based on absorption costing versus variable costing.

APPLY YOUR KNOWLEDGE

DECISION CASES

Effect of changing the sales mix in CVP analysis
(Obj. 7)

Case 1. Companies like **Compaq** and **Proctor & Gamble** have recently added a new employee benefit—on-site dinner-to-go. Employees can order reheatable pre-packaged dinners during the day, and have these meals delivered to their offices at 5:00 P.M. Similar to a company cafeteria, employees pay less for these meals than they would for similar items at a for-profit take-out. Garland Enterprises, a software development company, is considering starting a similar program. The company plans to offer pre-packaged: (1) children's meals, and (2) adult dinners. Data relating to the two types of meals follows:

	Children's	Adults'
Sale price	$2.00	$5.00
Cost of food	1.00	2.75
Cost of labor to prepare food	0.50	1.25
Cost of plastic containers	0.10	0.10
Delivery expense	0.15	0.15

Other (annual) costs of offering this new service are

Chef's salary...	$20,000
Utilities expense...	5,000
Marketing the new service to the employees..............	750

Required

1. If employees purchase on average *two children's dinners for every adult dinner,* how many adult dinners and how many children's dinners must employees purchase each year for Garland to break even on the new service? (Carry your computations to five decimal places.)
2. If employees purchase on average *two adult meals for every children's dinner,* how many adult dinners and how many children's dinners must employees purchase each year for Garland to break even on the new service? (Carry your computations to five decimal places.)
3. Explain why your answers to requirements 1 and 2 differ.
4. In light of your analysis, should Garland focus on promoting the availability of adult meals or children's meals? Why?
5. Why might Garland be satisfied with breaking even on the dinner-to-go service (rather than requiring the service to earn a profit)?

Case 2. ← *Link Back to Chapter 19 (Just-in-Time Philosophy).* Suppose you serve on the board of directors of American Faucet, a manufacturer of bathroom fixtures that recently adopted just-in-time production. Part of your responsibility is to develop a compensation contract for Toni Moen, the Vice President of Manufacturing. To give her the incentive to make decisions that will increase the company's profits, the Board decides to give Moen a year-end bonus if American Faucet meets a target operating income.

Absorption and variable cost incentives
(Obj. 8)

Write a memo to the Chairman of the Board, Herbert Kohler, explaining whether the bonus contract should be based on absorption costing or variable costing. Use the memo format outlined in Daily Exercise 22-5.

ETHICAL ISSUE

SpringSong is a medium-sized manufacturer of squirrel-proof bird feeders. Your father, the plant manager, helped you get a summer internship working for SpringSong's CFO. Your father has told you that the company is struggling and that he is worried about his job. With a breakeven point at 80% of capacity, the company has barely been breaking even.

Assumptions of CVP analysis
(Obj. 1, 2)

As the CFO's assistant, you are attending a meeting with President Gail Ayala, Vice-President of Marketing Warren Thrasher, and CFO Shane Corwin.

"I've decided to go forward with selling on our Web site," the president announces excitedly. "We can manage the cost of setting up the Web site."

"Great," responds Thrasher. "Web sales will give us a national market. Even at our current sale price, I'm sure we can increase our sales threefold."

Corwin shows a CVP chart he has prepared and points to the operating income area. "Given our contribution margin ratio, these higher sales will mean no more sweating our quarterly income figures. The sky's the limit!"

Looking at the CVP chart, you recall studying CVP analysis and the importance of its assumptions. If SpringSong is operating at about 80% of capacity, you cannot see how a threefold increase in production can be in the relevant range. You wonder if you should raise the issue now or check your accounting textbook and make sure of the facts first. You are also reluctant to dampen the group's enthusiasm and good spirits.

Required

1. Should you raise the question of CVP analysis' assumptions during the meeting, afterward with the CFO when you have had time to do some research, or not at all? Explain.
2. The CFO asks you to draft a report explaining the role of the relevant range in CVP analysis. Address the report to President Gail Ayala, and use the memo format outlined in Daily Exercise 22-5.

FINANCIAL STATEMENT CASE

Refer to **Target Corporation's** Consolidated Results of Operations, included in the financial statements in Appendix A. Ignoring interest expense and taxes, answer the following questions:

Identifying cost behavior patterns, computing breakeven sales and margin of safety, effect of changing sales mix
(Obj. 1, 3, 6, 7)

1. Is Target Corporation's cost of sales a fixed cost or a variable cost? Is depreciation and amortization a fixed cost or a variable cost? Explain.

2. Assume that 40% of Target's selling, general, and administrative expenses are fixed costs. What is the contribution margin? (*Hint:* Use sales revenues rather than total revenues in your calculations.)

3. What is the contribution margin ratio? (Carry your computation to 5 decimal places.)

4. What is the breakeven sales in dollars?

5. Calculate the margin of safety in dollars as sales revenue less breakeven sales in dollars. What is the margin of safety as a percentage?

6. Target division's sales are growing faster than sales in either the Mervyn's or the Department Stores divisions. Since Target stores are the lowest margin division, how will this change in sales mix affect the corporation's breakeven point?

TEAM PROJECT

Variable and absorption costing, bonus contract incentives, using contribution margin statements to make decisions
(Obj. 2, 8)

Paktape Manufacturing produces filament packaging tape. In 20X4, Paktape produced and sold 15 million rolls of tape. The company has recently expanded its capacity, so it can now produce up to 30 million rolls per year. Paktape's accounting records show the following results from 20X4:

Sale price per roll	$2.00
Variable manufacturing expenses per roll..................................	$1.00
Variable marketing and administrative expenses per roll	$0.50
Total fixed manufacturing overhead costs..................................	$8,400,000
Total fixed marketing and administrative expenses	$600,000
Sales	15 million rolls
Production...	15 million rolls

There were no beginning or ending inventories in 20X4.

In January 20X5, Paktape hired a new president, Kevin McDaniel. McDaniel has a one-year contract that specifies he will be paid 10% of Paktape's 20X5 absorption costing operating income, instead of a salary. In 20X5, McDaniel must make two major decisions:

- Should Paktape undertake a major advertising campaign? This campaign would raise sales to 25 million rolls. This is the maximum level of sales Paktape can expect to make in the near future. The ad campaign would add an additional $3.5 million in marketing and administrative costs. Without the campaign, sales will be 15 million rolls.
- How many rolls of tape will Paktape produce?

At the end of the year, Paktape Manufacturing's Board of Directors will evaluate McDaniel's performance, and decide whether to offer him a contract for the following year.

Required

Within your group, form two subgroups. The first subgroup assumes the role of Kevin McDaniel, Paktape Manufacturing's new president. The second subgroup assumes the role of Paktape Manufacturing's Board of Directors. McDaniel will meet with the Board of Directors shortly after the end of 20X5 to decide whether he will remain at Paktape. Most of your effort should be devoted to advance preparation for this meeting. Each subgroup should meet separately to prepare for the meeting between the Board and McDaniel.

Kevin McDaniel should:

1. Compute Paktape Manufacturing's 20X4 operating income.

2. Decide whether to adopt the advertising campaign. Prepare a memo to the Board of Directors explaining this decision. Use the memo format outlined in Daily Exercise 22-5. Give this memo to the Board of Directors as soon as possible (before the joint meeting).

3. Assume Paktape adopts the advertising campaign. Decide how many rolls of tape to produce in 20X5.

4. Prepare an absorption costing income statement for 20X5, ending with operating income before bonus. Then compute your bonus separately. The variable cost per unit and the total fixed expenses (with the exception of the advertising campaign) remain the same as in 20X4. Give this income statement and your bonus computation to the Board of Directors as soon as possible (before your meeting with the Board).

5. Decide whether you wish to remain at Paktape for another year. You currently have an offer from another company. The contract with the other company is identical to the one you currently have with Paktape—you will be paid 10% of absorption costing operating income instead of a salary.

The Board of Directors should:

1. Compute Paktape's 20X4 operating income.

2. Determine whether Paktape should adopt the advertising campaign.

3. Determine how many rolls of tape Paktape should produce in 20X5.

4. Evaluate McDaniel's performance, based on his decisions and the information he provided the Board. (*Hint:* You may want to prepare a variable costing income statement.)
5. Evaluate the contract's bonus provision. Are you satisfied with this provision? If so, explain why. If not, recommend how it should be changed.

After McDaniel has given the Board his memo and income statement, and after the Board has had a chance to evaluate McDaniel's performance, McDaniel and the Board should meet. The purpose of the meeting is to decide whether it is in their mutual interest for McDaniel to remain with Paktape, and if so, the terms of the contract Paktape will offer McDaniel.

INTERNET EXERCISE

Rainforest Café, Inc., is a restaurant that recreates the atmosphere of a tropical rainforest and includes a retail facility that offers an assortment of creative, signature items. Approximately 40 Rainforest Cafés are located in the United States, United Kingdom, Canada, France, Mexico, Singapore, and Hong Kong.

1. Go to **http://www.rainforestcafe.com.** Click on *Invest* and scan the information displayed. What special effects create the ambience of a tropical rainforest?
2. At the top of the screen click on *SEC Filings,* followed by *Click here to continue on to view SEC Filings,* select the *most recent annual report* (Form type 10-K), and under Item 8: Financial Statements select the *Consolidated Statements of Operations. Only* use amounts included in the computation of "Income from unit operations & licensing," to answer the following questions. Assume all assumptions underlying CVP analysis hold true. (*Note:* For easier viewing you may want to select font size 1 = smallest and click on enter.)
   a. Identify the cost behavior pattern of each account listed under "Costs and Expenses:" as fixed, mixed, or variable. Assume the primary cost driver is number of customers.
   b. Recast the income statement in the contribution margin format using amounts from the most recent year. For this computation assume 40% of the restaurant operating expenses and retail operating expenses are fixed.
   c. Compute the contribution margin ratio (rounding to the nearest whole percent). Calculate the breakeven point in sales dollars. Assume the company has set a target of $500,000 for "Income from unit operations & licensing" for next year. To reach this target how much in total revenues must Rainforest Café earn?
   d. Calculate the contribution margin and the contribution margin ratio for both restaurant sales and retail sales for the most recent year. If restaurant sales increase by $10,000 company profits will increase by what amount? After customers finish a meal the "safari guide" can suggest either dessert or a trip to the retail store. Assuming the same amount of dollars will be spent, which suggestion would generate more operating profit? Explain why.

Rainforest Café

Go to the "Cost-Volume-Profit Analysis" episode on the *Mastering Accounting* CD-ROM for an interactive, video-enhanced exercise showing CanGo managers' use of reports that predict outcomes based on estimates of cost and revenue to help make a new venture decision.

23

The Master Budget and Responsibility Accounting

LEARNING OBJECTIVES

After studying this chapter, you should be able to

1. Identify the benefits of budgeting
2. Prepare an operating budget
3. Prepare the components of a financial budget
4. Use sensitivity analysis in budgeting
5. Distinguish among different types of responsibility centers
6. Prepare a performance report for management by exception
7. Allocate indirect costs to departments

The home of the:

SALAS FAMILY

In partnership with:

HABITAT WORLD

ΥΤΥ *Habitat for Humanity*

Everyone in the world should have a simple, decent, affordable place to live. That's the mission of **Habitat for Humanity International,** a worldwide nonprofit organization with nearly 2,000 local affiliates that oversee construction of homes in their own communities. Habitat International and its affiliates solicit donations of building materials, and families who will become the homeowners invest "sweat equity" alongside volunteers. The total now is more than 90,000 homes built in over 60 countries across the globe, from Australia and Bangladesh to Uganda, the United States, and Zimbabwe.

Habitat plans to build 100,000 new houses over the next five years—a tall order since it took 24 years to build the first 100,000. Founder and President Millard Fuller must plan carefully to meet this lofty goal:

- How much will it cost to support construction of 100,000 houses over the next five years?
- How can Habitat raise enough revenue to pay these expenses?
- Can Habitat raise contributions in time to fund these expenses, or will it have to borrow to finance a cash shortfall?

Fuller and his management team use *budgets* to help answer these questions. The budget is Habitat's financial roadmap: It spells out how it will obtain and spend its resources. To develop the expense budget, managers predict the funds that headquarters will transfer to affiliates for house-building and the money to be spent on educational programs. The revenue budget predicts the contributions individuals, corporations, and government grants will offer Habitat. After developing the revenue budget, Habitat's managers realized that they would not have enough money to fund the ambitious house-building goal. So Habitat is embarking on a 5-year fund-raising campaign, and is using its Web site to encourage additional on-line donations.

Habitat also uses budgets to control revenues and costs. Simply preparing the expense budget helps managers identify cost-cutting opportunities. And the budget is a benchmark for comparing actual results. Reports compare

- actual revenues to budgeted revenues for each type of donor (individuals, corporations, governments)
- actual expenses to budgeted expenses for each type of expense (funds transferred to affiliates for house-building, technology upgrades)

Managers investigate differences between actual and budgeted figures. For example, if actual revenues from individuals fall short of the budget, managers may redouble efforts to solicit funds from individuals, or they may decide to focus elsewhere, perhaps on obtaining larger donations from corporations.

WHY MANAGERS USE BUDGETS

Managers of for-profit companies as well as nonprofits like **Habitat for Humanity** play several key roles. First, they develop strategies—overall business goals like Habitat's goal to build 100,000 houses over the next five years. Next, they plan and take specific actions to achieve those goals. Finally, managers control operations by comparing actual results with plans or budgets. This performance evaluation provides valuable feedback. For example, if Habitat's expenses are higher than budgeted, managers must either cut costs or increase revenues, and these decisions will affect their future strategies and plans.

Exhibit 23-1 shows that managers develop budgets to implement the organization's strategy, and then use these budgets to plan, act, and control business operations. The process is continuous: Determine strategy, develop plans and budgets to implement the strategy, act to implement the strategy, control by comparing actual results to the budget or plan, and then use feedback from the control step to start the process again.

DAILY EXERCISE 23-1

EXHIBIT 23-1
Budgets, Performance
Evaluation, and the
Management Cycle

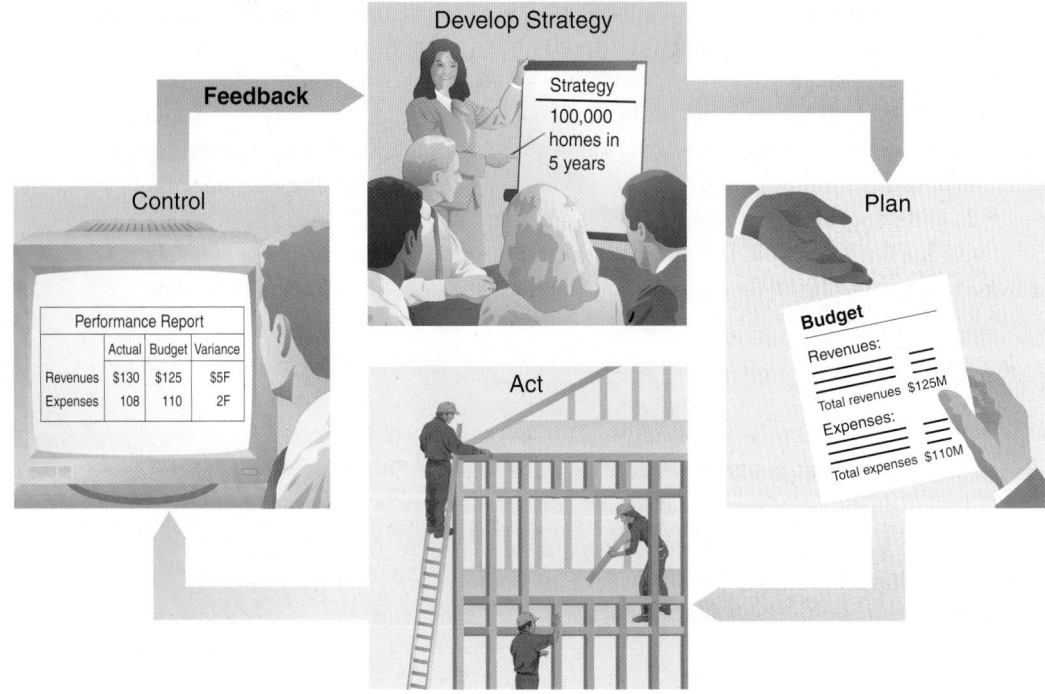

Budget Time Frames

In Chapter 19, we defined a *budget* as a quantitative expression of a plan that helps managers coordinate and implement the plan. Budgets can focus on the short-term or the long-term. Habitat developed a long-term budget to predict the costs required to reach its goal of building 100,000 houses over the next five years. **Boeing's** long-term budgets forecast demand for its planes for the next twenty years!

Other budgets have a short-term focus. Many companies budget their cash flows monthly, weekly, and daily to ensure that they have enough cash to meet their needs. They also budget revenues and expenses—and thus operating income—for months, quarters, and years. This chapter focuses on shorter-term budgets of a year or less. Chapter 26 focuses on budgets for large capital expenditures (property, plant, and equipment, for example) that naturally have a longer-term focus.

Budgeting for a Small Service Company

Let's begin by considering a budget for a small service company. Ram Dharan started a small business—an on-line service that provides travel itineraries for leisure travelers. Dharan wants to earn $275 per month to help cover his college expenses. He develops a budget to determine whether he can expect to meet this goal.

Dharan expects to sell 100 itineraries per month at a price of $3 each. Over the last six months, he paid his Internet service provider an average of $18 per month, and he spent an additional $20 per month on travel-related reference materials. He expects these monthly costs to remain about the same. Finally, he spends 5% of his sales revenues for banner ads on various other travel and leisure Web sites.

To prepare the budget, Dharan computes his total budgeted revenues and subtracts his total budgeted expenses:

RAM DHARAN TRAVEL ITINERARIES		
Budget for May 20X9		
Budgeted sales revenue (100 × $3)		$300
Less budgeted expenses:		
Internet access expense..............................	$18	
Reference materials expense......................	20	
Advertising expense (5% × $300).............	15	53
Budgeted operating income............................		$247

The budget shows that if business goes according to plan, Ram Dharan will not meet his $275 per month operating income goal. He will have to increase revenue (by using word-of-mouth advertising) or cut expenses (by finding a less expensive Internet access provider) to meet his goal.

Ram Dharan is the sole proprietor of a simple business, so his budget covers the entire company's operations. While managers of large companies also prepare budgets for the organization as a whole, individual subunits prepare their own budgets, as well. For example, each of Habitat's Regional Support Centers across the United States and Area Offices in Costa Rica, Thailand, and South Africa prepare budgets. Headquarters in Americus, Georgia, uses the individual budgets to prepare the organizationwide budget.

THE BUDGET AS A MANAGEMENT TOOL

Objective 1
Identify the benefits of budgeting

Budgets are key management tools that help large organizations like **Habitat for Humanity, Boeing,** and **Sunoco** just as much as sole proprietors like Ram Dharan. Exhibit 23-2 summarizes budgeting's benefits.

EXHIBIT 23-2   **Benefits of Budgeting**

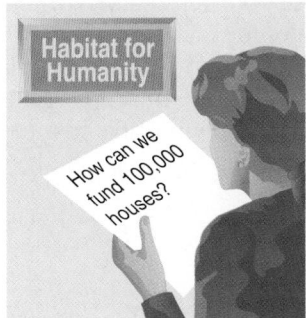

Budgets require managers to plan.

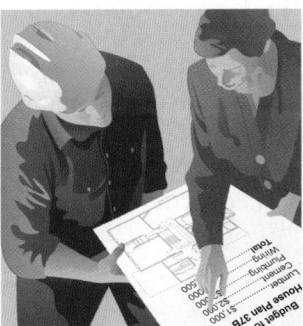

Budgets promote coordination and communication.

Budgets provide a benchmark that helps managers evaluate performance.

Budgets motivate employees to help achieve organization goals.

⊙ **DAILY EXERCISE 23-2**

Benefits of Budgeting

BUDGETING REQUIRES PLANNING Ram Dharan discovered that his expected income fell short of his target. The sooner he learns of the expected shortfall, the more time he has to plan how to increase revenues or cut expenses. The better his plan and the more time he has to execute the plan, the more likely he will meet his income target. In the chapter opening story, Habitat for Humanity's budget prompted managers to immediately initiate a major fund-raising campaign.

BUDGETING PROMOTES COORDINATION AND COMMUNICATION The master budget coordinates the company's activities. It forces managers to consider relationships among operations across the entire value chain. Consider **Cincinnati Milacron, Inc.,** a manufacturer of machine tools and accessories. Sales managers at Cincinnati Milacron are evaluated on the basis of volume, so they prefer to accept all special orders. But some special orders cost the company more than the customer is willing to pay. The budget promotes coordination by encouraging managers to accept orders only for machines Cincinnati Milacron can manufacture at a profit.

Coordination requires effective communication. Budgets can communicate a consistent set of plans throughout the company. Suppose **Mazda's** engineers plan to redesign the Miata's brake system. By participating in the budgeting process alongside the engineers, the manufacturing vice president can see how to change the production process. He explains the plan to plant managers so they can make the changes in an orderly way.

BUDGETS PROVIDE A BENCHMARK THAT HELPS MANAGERS EVALUATE PERFORMANCE

Managers can evaluate a department or activity by comparing actual results with either the budget or past performance. The budget is usually a better benchmark because the company's operations or its markets may have changed since last year.

Suppose that **Coldwell Banker's** real-estate agents sell 10% more houses in the third quarter of 2002 than in the third quarter of 2001. Is this good performance? Not necessarily. If nationwide sales are up 20% for the quarter, Coldwell Banker's results may be disappointing. But if the overall market has declined, the 10% increase may be excellent.

Another problem with past results is that they may represent inefficient performance. Suppose that difficulties obtaining donations of material or land drove Habitat For Humanity's cost per house in Mexico to $3,500. An average cost of $3,200 the following year is better, but may still fall short of expectations if the budgeted cost is $3,000 per house.

A BUDGET MOTIVATES EMPLOYEES Budgets motivate employees to achieve the business's goals, especially when employees believe the budget is fair. For this reason, companies often ask employees to help prepare the budgets that will be used to judge their performance.

Unrealistic budgets can hurt employee morale. Suppose Coldwell Banker's management imposed a budgeted increase of 15% in house sales for each territory. That budget may be acceptable to agents in areas with strong economies. They may work hard to achieve the increase. Agents in depressed areas may believe it is impossible to meet the budget. They may simply give up if they believe it is not possible to meet the budget. Management should allow agents in each territory a voice in the budget so budgets will be tailored to local conditions.

The Performance Report

We have seen how budgets can help managers plan. However, budgets are just as useful for controlling. To control operations, managers prepare performance reports that compare actual results to the budget. These reports help managers

- Evaluate operations
- Decide how to fix problems
- Prepare next period's budget

Suppose that Cincinnati Milacron has the performance report in Exhibit 23-3.

EXHIBIT 23-3
**Summary Income Statement
Performance Report**

	Actual	Budget	Variance (Actual–Budget)
Sales revenue	$550,000	$600,000	$(50,000)
Total expenses	510,000	520,000	10,000
Net income	$ 40,000	$ 80,000	$(40,000)

Actual sales in Exhibit 23-3 are $550,000, which is $50,000 less than budgeted sales. The actual net income is half the budgeted amount. The vice president of sales will have to explain why sales revenue was so far below the budgeted amount. The vice president, in turn, will meet with the sales staff to learn why they failed to meet the budget. There are three possible explanations:

- The budget was unrealistic.
- The sales force did a poor job of selling during the period.
- Uncontrollable factors (such as a sluggish economy) reduced sales.

Of course, all three factors may have contributed to the poor results.

Managers use performance reports like the one in Exhibit 23-3 to decide how to fix problems. If the sales department did not perform well, perhaps their compensation should be tied to sales revenue so they will be more motivated to sell. Or the company may need a new advertising campaign. Managers must decide whether to reduce budgeted sales for the next period—a decision that directly affects next period's budgeted net income.

THINK IT OVER

The performance report in Exhibit 23-3 shows that actual sales revenue is 8.33% less than budgeted sales revenue ($50,000 ÷ $600,000). However, actual expenses are only 1.9% less than budgeted expenses ($10,000 ÷ $520,000). Why is the percentage shortfall in expenses so much lower than the percentage shortfall in revenue?

Answer: One reason why expenses did not fall as far short of the budget is that some expenses do not increase or decrease with revenue (sales volume). For example, the vice president of sales may receive a salary of $90,000 regardless of sales revenue. Expenses such as depreciation, rent, and insurance are *fixed*. When revenue and variable expenses decline, fixed expenses remain the same. Thus, total expense does not decline as rapidly as revenue.

PREPARING THE MASTER BUDGET

The **master budget** is the set of budgeted financial statements and supporting schedules for the entire organization. This comprehensive budget includes (1) the operating budget, (2) the capital expenditures budget, and (3) the financial budget. The **operating budget** sets the expected revenues and expenses—and thus operating income—for the period. The **capital expenditures budget** presents the company's plan for purchases of property, plant, equipment, and other long-term assets. The **financial budget** projects cash inflows and outflows, the period-ending balance sheet, and the statement of cash flows. This chapter focuses on the operating budget and the financial budget. You learned about the cash budget in Chapter 7; here we will show more details behind the figures in the cash budget. Chapter 26 covers budgeting for capital expenditures.

The components of the master budget include:

1. Operating budget
   a. Sales budget
   b. Inventory budget and purchases and cost of goods sold budget
   c. Operating expenses budget
   d. Budgeted income statement
2. Capital expenditures budget
3. Financial budget
   a. Cash budget: statement of budgeted cash receipts and payments
   b. Budgeted balance sheet
   c. Budgeted statement of cash flows

The end result of the *operating* budget is the budgeted income statement, which shows expected revenues, expenses, and operating income for the period. The *financial* budget results in the budgeted statement of cash flows, which shows budgeted cash flows for operating, investing, and financing activities. The budgeted financial statements look exactly like ordinary statements. The only difference is that they list budgeted rather than actual figures. Exhibit 23-4 on the next page diagrams the master budget for a merchandising company such as **Safeway** or **J.C. Penney**.

The sales budget is the cornerstone of the master budget, because sales affect most of the other components of the master budget. After projecting sales and expenses, management can prepare the budgeted income statement. The income statement, the capital expenditures budget, and plans for raising cash and paying debts provide information for the cash budget, which feeds into the budgeted balance sheet. The budgeted statement of cash flows is usually the last step in the process.

The best way to learn about budgeting is to prepare a master budget.

MASTER BUDGET. The set of budgeted financial statements and supporting schedules for the entire organization. This comprehensive budget includes the operating budget, the capital expenditures budget, and the financial budget.

OPERATING BUDGET. Sets the expected revenues and expenses—and thus operating income—for the period.

CAPITAL EXPENDITURES BUDGET. A company's plan for purchases of property, plant, equipment, and other long-term assets.

FINANCIAL BUDGET. Projects cash inflows and outflows, the period-ending balance sheet, and the statement of cash flows.

 DAILY EXERCISE 23-3

EXHIBIT 23-4
Master Budget for a
Merchandising Company

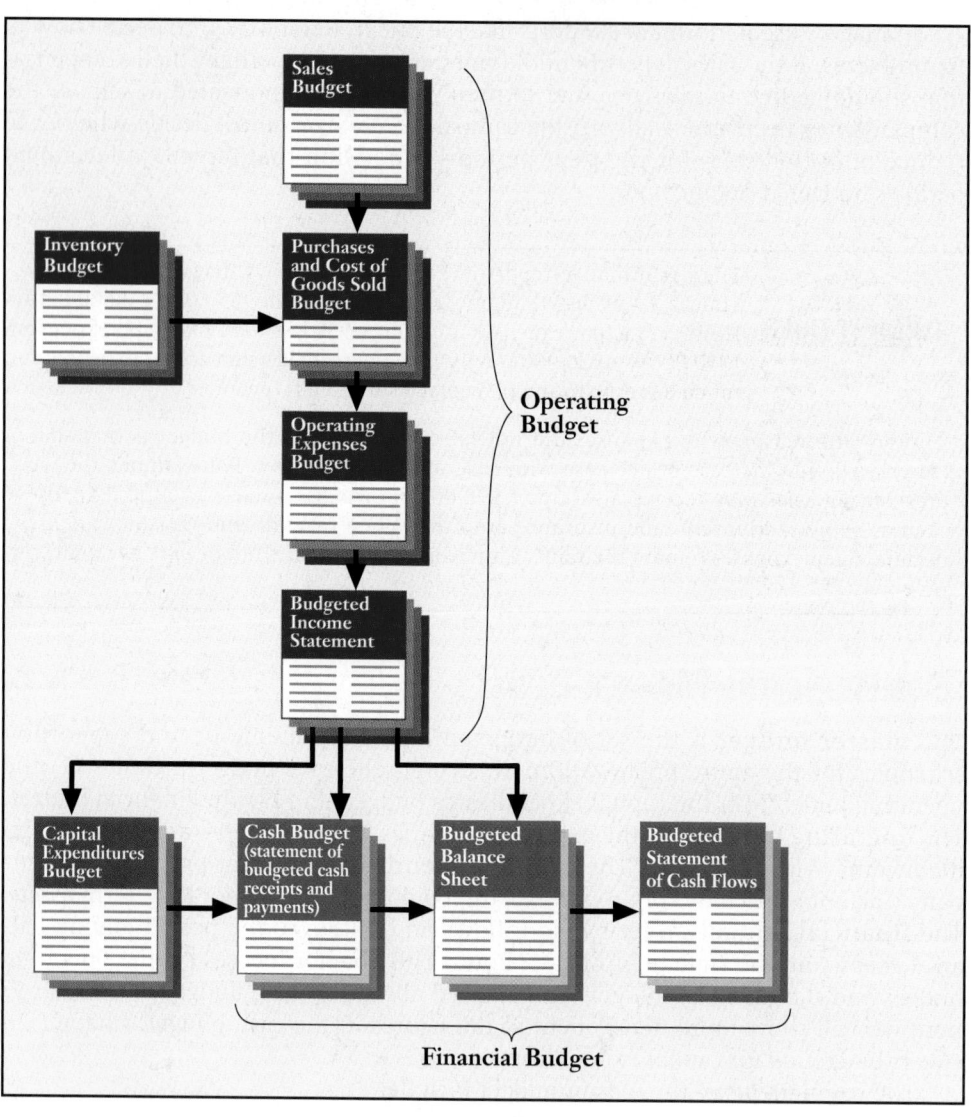

Whitewater Sporting Goods Master Budget

1. *You manage Whitewater Sporting Goods Store No. 18, which carries a complete line of outdoor recreation gear.* You are to prepare the store's master budget for April, May, June, and July, the main selling season. The division manager and the assistant controller (head of the Accounting Department) will arrive from headquarters next week to review the budget with you.

2. *Cash collections follow sales because the company sells on account.* When the company needs extra cash, it borrows on six-month installment notes payable.

3. *Your store's balance sheet at March 31, 20X6, the beginning of the budget period, appears in Exhibit 23-5 on the next page.* ◄◄

►► We examined the balance sheet in Chapter 5, pages 180–182.

4. *Sales in March were $40,000.* The sales force predicts these future monthly sales:

April...............	$50,000
May	80,000
June...............	60,000
July...............	50,000

Sales are 60% cash and 40% on credit. Whitewater collects all credit sales the month after the sale. The $16,000 of accounts receivable at March 31 arose from credit sales in March (40% of $40,000). Uncollectible accounts are insignificant.

5. *Whitewater maintains inventory equal to $20,000 plus 80% of the budgeted cost of goods sold for the following month.* Target ending inventory on July 31 is

Exhibit 23-5
Balance Sheet

WHITEWATER SPORTING GOODS STORE NO. 18				
Balance Sheet				
March 31, 20X6				

Assets			**Liabilities**	
Current assets:			Current liabilities:	
Cash	$ 15,000		Accounts payable	$ 16,800
Accounts receivable	16,000		Salary and commissions	
Inventory	48,000		payable	4,250
Prepaid insurance	1,800		Total liabilities	21,050
Total current assets	80,800			
Plant assets:			**Owner's Equity**	
Equipment and fixtures	32,000		Owners' equity	78,950
Accumulated depreciation	(12,800)			
Total plant assets	19,200		Total liabilities	
Total assets	$100,000		and owners' equity	$100,000

$42,400. Cost of goods sold averages 70% of sales. (These percentages are based on past experience.) Inventory on March 31 is $48,000:

$$\text{March 31 inventory} = \$20,000 + 0.80 \times (0.70 \times \text{April sales of } \$50,000)$$
$$= \$20,000 + (0.80 \times \$35,000)$$
$$= \$20,000 + \$28,000 = \$48,000$$

Whitewater pays for inventory as follows: 50% during the month of purchase and 50% during the next month. Accounts payable consists of inventory purchases only. March purchases were $33,600, so accounts payable at the end of March total $16,800 ($33,600 × 0.50).

6. *Monthly payroll has two parts: a salary of $2,500 plus sales commissions equal to 15% of sales.* The company pays half this amount during the month and half early in the following month. Therefore, at the end of each month Whitewater reports salary and commissions payable equal to half the month's payroll. The $4,250 liability on the March 31 balance sheet is half the March payroll of $8,500:

$$\text{March payroll} = \text{Salary of } \$2,500$$
$$+ \text{Sales commissions of } \$6,000 \ (0.15 \times \$40,000)$$
$$= \$8,500$$
$$\text{March 31 salary and commissions payable} = 0.50 \times \$8,500 = \$4,250$$

7. *Other monthly expenses are as follows:*

Rent expense	$2,000, paid as incurred
Depreciation expense, including truck	500
Insurance expense	200 expiration of prepaid amount
Miscellaneous expenses	5% of sales, paid as incurred

8. *Whitewater plans to purchase a used delivery truck in April for $3,000 cash.*
9. *Whitewater requires each store to maintain a minimum cash balance of $10,000 at the end of each month.* The store can borrow money on 6-month notes payable of $1,000 each at an annual interest rate of 12%. Management borrows no more than the amount needed to maintain the $10,000 minimum. Notes payable require six equal monthly payments of principal, plus monthly interest on the entire unpaid principal. Borrowing and all principal and interest payments occur at the end of the month.
10. *Income taxes are the responsibility of corporate headquarters, so you can ignore tax for budgeting purposes.*

Preparing the Operating Budget

As you prepare the master budget, remember that you are developing the store's operating and financial plan for the next four months. The steps in this process may seem mechanical, but managers must think carefully about pricing, product lines, job assignments, needs for additional equipment, and negotiations with banks. Successful managers use this opportunity to make decisions that affect the future

Objective 2
Prepare an operating budget

course of business. The operating budget—the sales budget; the inventory, purchases, and cost of goods sold budgets; and the operating expenses budget—leads to the budgeted income statement.

PREPARING THE BUDGETED INCOME STATEMENT There are four steps to preparing the budgeted income statement shown in Exhibit 23-6.

EXHIBIT 23-6   Budgeted Income Statement

WHITEWATER SPORTING GOODS STORE NO. 18
Budgeted Income Statement
Four Months Ending July 31, 20X6

		Amount	Source
Sales revenue		$240,000	Sales Budget (Exhibit 23-7)
Cost of goods sold		168,000	Inventory, Purchases, and Cost of Goods Sold
Gross profit		72,000	Budget (Exhibit 23-8)
Operating expenses:			
Salary and commissions	$46,000		Operating Expenses Budget (Exhibit 23-9)
Rent expense	8,000		Operating Expenses Budget (Exhibit 23-9)
Depreciation expense	2,000		Operating Expenses Budget (Exhibit 23-9)
Insurance expense	800		Operating Expenses Budget (Exhibit 23-9)
Miscellaneous expenses	12,000	68,800	Operating Expenses Budget (Exhibit 23-9)
Operating income		3,200	
Interest expense		225*	Cash Budget (Exhibit 23-13)
Net income		$ 2,975	

* $90 + $75 + $60

Step 1. The sales budget. Sales is the key business activity. Budgeted total sales for each product is the sale price multiplied by the expected number of units sold. The overall sales budget in Exhibit 23-7 is the sum of the budgets for the individual products. Trace the April through July total sales ($240,000) to the budgeted income statement in Exhibit 23-6.

DAILY EXERCISE 23-4

DAILY EXERCISE 23-6

EXHIBIT 23-7   Sales Budget

WHITEWATER SPORTING GOODS STORE NO. 18
Sales Budget

	April	May	June	July	April–July Total
Cash sales, 60%	$30,000	$48,000	$36,000	$30,000	
Credit sales, 40%	20,000	32,000	24,000	20,000	
Total sales, 100%	$50,000	$80,000	$60,000	$50,000	$240,000

Step 2. Inventory, purchases, and cost of goods sold budget. This schedule determines cost of goods sold for the budgeted income statement, ending inventory for the budgeted balance sheet, and purchases for the cash budget. The familiar cost-of-goods-sold computation specifies the relation among these items:

$$\text{Beginning inventory} + \text{Purchases} - \text{Ending inventory} = \text{Cost of goods sold}$$

Beginning inventory is known from last month's balance sheet, budgeted cost of goods sold is a fixed percentage of sales, and budgeted ending inventory is a computed amount. You must solve for the budgeted purchases figure. To do this, take the cost-of-goods-sold computation and then move beginning inventory and ending inventory to the right side of the equation, isolating purchases on the left side:

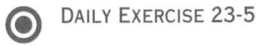

DAILY EXERCISE 23-5

DAILY EXERCISE 23-7

$$\text{Beginning inventory} + \text{Purchases} - \text{Ending inventory} = \text{Cost of goods sold}$$

$$\text{Purchases} = \text{Cost of goods sold} + \text{Ending inventory} - \text{Beginning inventory}$$

This second equation makes sense. How much does Whitewater have to purchase? Enough to cover sales and desired ending inventory, less the amount of beginning inventory already on hand at the start of the period. Exhibit 23-8 shows Whitewater's inventory, purchases, and cost of goods sold budget.

EXHIBIT 23-8   Inventory, Purchases, and Cost of Goods Sold Budget

| | | WHITEWATER SPORTING GOODS STORE NO. 18 | | | |
| | | Inventory, Purchases, and Cost of Goods Sold Budget | | | |
	April	May	June	July	April–July Total
Cost of goods sold (0.70 × sales, from Sales Budget in Exhibit 23-7)	$35,000	$ 56,000	$42,000	$35,000	$168,000
+ Desired ending inventory ($20,000 + 0.80 × Cost of goods sold for the next month)	64,800 *	53,600	48,000	42,400 ‡	
= Total inventory required	99,800	109,600	90,000	77,400	
− Beginning inventory	(48,000)†	(64,800)	(53,600)	(48,000)	
= Purchases	$51,800	$ 44,800	$36,400	$29,400	

* $20,000 + (0.80 × $56,000) = $64,800.
† Balance at March 31 (Exhibit 23-5).
‡ Given in item 5 on page 933.

Trace the total budgeted cost of goods sold from Exhibit 23-8 ($168,000) to the budgeted income statement in Exhibit 23-6. We will use the budgeted inventory and purchases amounts later.

Step 3. Operating expenses budget. Budgeted operating expenses such as sales commissions fluctuate with sales. Other expenses, such as rent and insurance, are the same each month (fixed).

Trace the April through July totals from the operating expenses budget in Exhibit 23-9 (salary and commissions of $46,000, rent expense of $8,000, and so on) to the budgeted income statement in Exhibit 23-6.

EXHIBIT 23-9   Operating Expenses Budget

| | | WHITEWATER SPORTING GOODS STORE NO. 18 | | | |
| | | Operating Expenses Budget | | | |
	April	May	June	July	April–July Total
Salary, fixed amount (item 6, page 933)	$ 2,500	$ 2,500	$ 2,500	$ 2,500	
Commission, 15% of sales from Sales Budget (item 6, page 933 and Exhibit 23-7	7,500	12,000	9,000	7,500	
Total salary and commissions	10,000	14,500	11,500	10,000	$46,000
Rent expense, fixed amount (item 7, page 933)	2,000	2,000	2,000	2,000	8,000
Depreciation expense, fixed amount (item 7, page 933)	500	500	500	500	2,000
Insurance expense, fixed amount (item 7, page 933)	200	200	200	200	800
Miscellaneous expenses, 5% of sales from Sales Budget (item 7, page 933 and Exhibit 23-7)	2,500	4,000	3,000	2,500	12,000
Total operating expenses	$15,200	$21,200	$17,200	$15,200	$68,800

Step 4. Budgeted income statement. Use steps 1 through 3 to prepare the budgeted income statement in Exhibit 23-6. We explain the computation of interest expense as part of the cash budget in the next section.

Preparing the Financial Budget

Objective 3
Prepare the components of a financial budget

The second major section of the master budget that we will discuss is the financial budget. This includes the cash budget, the budgeted balance sheet, and the budgeted statement of cash flows. The **cash budget,** or **statement of budgeted cash receipts and payments,** details how the business expects to go from the beginning cash balance to the desired ending balance. ➡ We introduced the cash budget in Chapter 7, page 286. ◄ Cash receipts and payments depend on revenues and expenses, which appear in the budgeted income statement. This is why the cash budget is not prepared until after the budgeted income statement.

CASH BUDGET. Details how the business expects to go from the beginning cash balance to the desired ending balance. Also called the **statement of budgeted cash receipts and payments.**

⊙ DAILY EXERCISE 23-8

⊙ DAILY EXERCISE 23-10

PREPARING THE CASH BUDGET   The cash budget has four major parts:

- Cash collections from customers (Exhibit 23-10)
- Cash payments for purchases (Exhibit 23-11)
- Cash payments for operating expenses (Exhibit 23-12)
- Capital expenditures (for example, the $3,000 capital expenditure to acquire the delivery truck)

Exhibit 23-10 shows how to compute budgeted cash collections. April's cash collections consist of two parts: (1) April's cash sales from the sales budget in Exhibit 23-7 ($30,000), plus (2) March's credit sales ($16,000 from the March 31 balance sheet, Exhibit 23-5). Trace April's $46,000 ($30,000 + $16,000) total cash collections to the cash budget in Exhibit 23-13.

EXHIBIT 23-10   **Budgeted Cash Collections**

WHITEWATER SPORTING GOODS STORE NO. 18
Budgeted Cash Collections from Customers

	April	May	June	July	April–July Total
Cash sales from Sales Budget (Exhibit 23-7)	$30,000	$48,000	$36,000	$30,000	
Collections of last month's credit sales, from Sales Budget (Exhibit 23-7).....................................	16,000 *	20,000	32,000	24,000	
Total collections..	$46,000	$68,000	$68,000	$54,000	$236,000

* March 31 accounts receivable, Exhibit 23-5.

⊙ DAILY EXERCISE 23-9

Exhibit 23-11 uses the inventory, purchases, and cost of goods sold budget from Exhibit 23-8 and payment information from item 5 to compute budgeted cash

EXHIBIT 23-11   **Budgeted Cash Payments for Purchases**

WHITEWATER SPORTING GOODS STORE NO. 18
Budgeted Cash Payments for Purchases

	April	May	June	July	April–July Total
50% of last month's purchases from Inventory, Purchases, and Cost of Goods Sold Budget (Exhibit 23-8).....................................	$16,800*	$25,900	$22,400	$18,200	
50% of this month's purchases from Inventory, Purchases, and Cost of Goods Sold Budget (Exhibit 23-8).....................................	25,900	22,400	18,200	14,700	
Total payments for purchases...................................	$42,700	$48,300	$40,600	$32,900	$164,500

* March 31 accounts payable, Exhibit 23-5.

payments for purchases of inventory. April's cash payments for purchases consists of two parts: (1) payment of 50% of March's purchases ($16,800 accounts payable balance from the March 31 balance sheet, Exhibit 23-5), plus (2) payment for 50% of April's purchases ($25,900 = 50% × $51,800 from Exhibit 23-8). Trace April's $42,700 ($16,800 + $25,900) cash outlay for purchases to the cash budget in Exhibit 23-13.

Exhibit 23-12 uses items 6 and 7 and the operating expenses budget (Exhibit 23-9) to compute cash payments for operating expenses. April's cash payments for operating expenses consists of four items:

Payment of 50% of March's salary and commissions (from March 31 balance sheet, Exhibit 23-5)	$ 4,250
Payment of 50% of April's salary and commissions (50% × $10,000, Exhibit 23-9)	5,000
Payment of rent expense (Exhibit 23-9)	2,000
Payment of miscellaneous expenses (Exhibit 23-9)	2,500
Total April cash payments for operating expenses...............................	$13,750

Follow April's $13,750 cash payments for operating expenses from Exhibit 23-12 to the cash budget in Exhibit 23-13.

EXHIBIT 23-12 Budgeted Cash Payments for Operating Expenses

WHITEWATER SPORTING GOODS STORE NO. 18 Budgeted Cash Payments for Operating Expenses					
	April	May	June	July	April–July Total
Salary and commissions:					
50% of last month's expenses, from Operating Expenses Budget (Exhibit 23-9).........	$ 4,250*	$ 5,000	$ 7,250	$ 5,750	
50% of this month's expenses, from Operating Expenses Budget (Exhibit 23-9).........	5,000	7,250	5,750	5,000	
Total salary and commissions.................................	9,250	12,250	13,000	10,750	
Rent expense, from Operating Expenses Budget (Exhibit 23-9)	2,000	2,000	2,000	2,000	
Miscellaneous expenses, from Operating Expenses Budget (Exhibit 23-9)	2,500	4,000	3,000	2,500	
Total payments for operating expenses	$13,750	$18,250	$18,000	$15,250	$65,250

* March 31 salary and commissions payable, Exhibit 23-5.

THINK IT OVER Why are depreciation expense and insurance expense from the operating expenses budget (Exhibit 23-9) *excluded* from the budgeted cash payments for operating expenses in Exhibit 23-12?

Answer: These expenses do not require cash outlays in the current period. Depreciation is the periodic write-off of the cost of the equipment and fixtures that Whitewater acquired previously. Insurance expense is the expiration of prepaid insurance.

To prepare the cash budget in Exhibit 23-13, start with the beginning cash balance and add the budgeted cash collections from Exhibit 23-10 to determine the cash available. Then subtract cash payments for purchases (Exhibit 23-11), operating expenses (Exhibit 23-12), and any capital expenditures. This yields the ending cash balance before financing.

Item 9 states that Whitewater requires a minimum cash balance of $10,000. The $1,550 budgeted cash balance before financing falls $8,450 short of the minimum required ($10,000 − $1,550). Because Whitewater borrows in $1,000 notes, the company will have to borrow $9,000 to cover April's expected shortfall. The

DAILY EXERCISE 23-11

EXHIBIT 23-13 Cash Budget

WHITEWATER SPORTING GOODS STORE NO. 18
Cash Budget
Four Months Ending July 31, 20X6

	April	May	June	July
Beginning cash balance..	$15,000*	$10,550	$10,410	$18,235
Cash collections (Exhibit 23-10)	46,000	68,000	68,000	54,000
Cash available	$61,000	$78,550	$78,410	$72,235
Cash payments:				
Purchases of inventory (Exhibit 23-11)	$42,700	$48,300	$40,600	$32,900
Operating expenses (Exhibit 23-12).........................	13,750	18,250	18,000	15,250
Purchase of delivery truck (item 8, page 933)	3,000	—	—	—
Total cash payments..	59,450	66,550	58,600	48,150
(1) Ending cash balance before financing....................	1,550	12,000	19,810	24,085
Minimum cash balance desired..............................	10,000	10,000	10,000	10,000
Cash excess (deficiency)	$ (8,450)	$ 2,000	$ 9,810	$14,085
Financing of cash deficiency (see notes a–c):				
Borrowing (at end of month)	$ 9,000			
Principal payments (at end of month)		$(1,500)	$ (1,500)	$(1,500)
Interest expense (at 12% annually)......................		(90)	(75)	(60)
(2) Total effects of financing..	9,000	(1,590)	(1,575)	(1,560)
Ending cash balance (1) + (2)................................	$10,550	$10,410	$18,235	$22,525

* March 31 cash balance, Exhibit 23-5.

Notes

a. Borrowing occurs in multiples of $1,000 and only for the amount needed to maintain a minimum cash balance of $10,000.
b. Monthly principal payments: $9,000 ÷ 6 = $1,500.
c. Interest expense:
  May: $9,000 × (0.12 × 1/12) = $90
  June: ($9,000 − $1,500) × (0.12 × 1/12) = $75
  July: ($9,000 − $1,500 − $1,500) × (0.12 × 1/12) = $60

DAILY EXERCISE 23-12

budgeted ending cash balance equals the "ending cash balance before financing," adjusted for the total effects of the financing (a $9,000 inflow in April). Exhibit 23-13 shows that Whitewater expects to end April with $10,550 of cash ($1,550 + $9,000). The exhibit also shows the cash balance at the end of May, June, and July.

Item 9 states that Whitewater must repay the notes in six equal installments. Thus, May through July show principal repayments of $1,500 ($9,000 ÷ 6) per month. Whitewater also pays interest expense on the outstanding notes payable, at 12% per year. The June interest expense is $75 [($9,000 principal − $1,500 repayment at the end of May) × 12% × 1/12]. Interest expense for the four months totals $225 ($90 + $75 + $60). This interest expense appears on the budgeted income statement in Exhibit 23-6.

Notice that the cash balance at the end of July is $22,525. This becomes the cash balance in the July 31 budgeted balance sheet in Exhibit 23-14.

PREPARING THE BUDGETED BALANCE SHEET The next step in preparing the master budget is to complete the balance sheet. Project each asset, liability, and owners' equity account based on the plans outlined in the previous exhibits.

Study the budgeted balance sheet in Exhibit 23-14 to make certain you understand the computation of each figure. For example, on the budgeted balance sheet as of July 31, 20X6, budgeted cash equals the ending cash balance from the cash budget in Exhibit 23-13 ($22,525). Accounts receivable as of July 31 equal July's credit sales of $20,000, shown in the sales budget (Exhibit 23-7). July 31 inventory of $42,400 is July's desired ending inventory in the inventory, purchases, and cost of goods sold budget in Exhibit 23-8. Detailed computations for each of the other accounts appear in Exhibit 23-14.

EXHIBIT 23-14   **Budgeted Balance Sheet**

WHITEWATER SPORTING GOODS STORE NO. 18
Budgeted Balance Sheet
July 31, 20X6

Assets

Current assets:

Cash (Exhibit 23-13)	$22,525	
Accounts receivable (Sales Budget, Exhibit 23-7)	20,000	
Inventory (Inventory, Purchases, and Cost of Goods Sold Budget, Exhibit 23-8)	42,400	
Prepaid insurance (beginning balance of $1,800 − $800 for four months' expiration; Operating Expenses Budget, Exhibit 23-9)	1,000	
Total current assets		$ 85,925

Plant assets:

Equipment and fixtures (beginning balance of $32,000 + $3,000 truck acquisition; item 8, page 933)	$35,000	
Accumulated depreciation (beginning balance of $12,800 + $2,000 for four months' depreciation; Operating Expenses Budget, Exhibit 23-9)	(14,800)	
Total plant assets		20,200
Total assets..		$106,125

Liabilities

Current liabilities:

Accounts payable (0.50 × July purchases of $29,400; Inventory, Purchases, and Cost of Goods Sold Budget, Exhibit 23-8)................	$14,700	
Short-term note payable ($9,000 − $4,500 paid back; Exhibit 23-13)	4,500	
Salary and commissions payable (0.50 × July expenses of $10,000; Operating Expenses Budget, Exhibit 23-9)	5,000	
Total liabilities..		$ 24,200

Owners' Equity

Owners' equity (beginning balance of $78,950 + $2,975 net income; Exhibit 23-6)...		81,925
Total liabilities and owners' equity.......................................		$106,125

PREPARING THE BUDGETED STATEMENT OF CASH FLOWS   The final step in preparing the master budget is completing the budgeted statement of cash flows. Use the information from the schedules of cash collections and payments, the cash budget, and the beginning balance of cash to project cash flows from operating, investing, and financing activities. Take time to study Exhibit 23-15, and make sure you understand the origin of each figure.

Now the *master budget* is complete. It consists of the budgeted financial statements and all supporting schedules.

THINK IT OVER

Many companies allow the manager of each department to participate in setting the budget for his or her own department. Participation can help employees accept the budget and motivate them to achieve the budget. What is the *disadvantage* of allowing managers to set budgets for their own departments? (*Hint:* Superiors often use the budget as a benchmark against which to compare actual performance.)

Answer: Managers who are evaluated by comparing their department's actual results to the budget have incentives to build *slack* into their budgets. For example, the manager might budget less sales than she really expects, and budget purchases costs higher than she expects. This increases the chance that her department's actual performance will be better than the budget, and that she will receive a good evaluation. Consequently, higher-level managers usually negotiate with lower-level managers to remove at least part of the slack lower-level managers add to the budget.

EXHIBIT 23-15
Budgeted Statement
of Cash Flows

WHITEWATER SPORTING GOODS STORE NO. 18
Budgeted Statement of Cash Flows
Four Months Ending July 31, 20X6

Cash flows from operating activities:
Receipts:		
Collections from customers (Exhibit 23-10)....................	$ 236,000	
Total cash receipts..		$236,000
Payments:		
Purchases of inventory (Exhibit 23-11)..........................	$(164,500)	
Operating expenses, excluding interest expense (Exhibit 23-12)..	(65,250)	
Payment of interest expense (Exhibits 23-13 and 23-6) .	(225)	
Total cash payments...		(229,975)
Net cash inflow from operating activities..........................		6,025
Cash flows from investing activities:		
Acquisition of delivery truck (item 8, page 933).................	$ (3,000)	
Net cash outflow from investing activities		(3,000)
Cash flows from financing activities:		
Proceeds from issuance of notes payable (Exhibit 23-13)...	$ 9,000	
Payment of notes payable (Exhibit 23-13).........................	(4,500)	
Net cash inflow from financing activities		4,500
Net increase in cash		$ 7,525
Cash balance, April 1, 20X6 (Exhibit 23-5)		15,000
Cash balance, July 31, 20X6 (Exhibits 23-13 and 23-14).......		$ 22,525

Objective 4
Use sensitivity analysis in
budgeting

DAILY EXERCISE 23-13

BUDGETING, SENSITIVITY ANALYSIS, AND INFORMATION TECHNOLOGY

The master budget models the organization's *planned* activities. The most important budget documents are the budgeted income statement (Exhibit 23-6), the cash budget (Exhibit 23-13), and the budgeted balance sheet (Exhibit 23-14). Top management analyzes these statements to ensure that all the budgeted figures are consistent with the company's goals or strategies.

Sensitivity Analysis

➤ Sensitivity analysis is
introduced in Chapter 22, page
896.

Actual results often differ from plans, so managers conduct sensitivity analyses to plan for various possibilities. Recall that Chapter 22 defined *sensitivity analysis* as a *what-if* technique that asks *what* a result will be *if* a predicted amount is not achieved or *if* an underlying assumption changes. ◄ *What if* the stock market crashes? How will this affect contributions to Habitat for Humanity? Will it have to postpone the planned expansion in Eastern Europe? *What* will be Whitewater Store No. 18's cash balance on July 31 *if* the period's sales are 45% cash, not 60% cash? Will Whitewater have to borrow more cash?

Many companies use computer spreadsheet programs to prepare master budget schedules and statements. In fact, one of the earliest spreadsheet programs was developed by graduate business students specifically to perform master budget sensitivity analyses. The students realized that computers could take the drudgery out of hand-computed master budget sensitivity analyses. Managers and accountants could answer what-if questions simply by changing a number. At the press of a key, the spreadsheet prepares a revised budget that includes all the effects of the change.

Budget Management Software

Suppose the manager of Whitewater Store No. 18 uses a spreadsheet to develop the store's master budget. Then Whitewater's headquarters must "roll up" the budget data from Store No. 18, along with budgets for each of the other individual stores, to prepare the companywide master budget. This roll-up can be difficult for companies with far-flung operations, whose units may use different spreadsheets. Companies like **Sunoco** are beginning to use budget management software. Often designed to work with the company's Web-based Intranet and data warehouse (or ERP database), this software provides a companywide system that helps managers develop and analyze budgets.

Across the globe, managers can sit at their desks, log into the company's budget system, and enter their numbers. The software allows them to conduct sensitivity analyses on their own unit's data—for example, how a change in oil prices would affect the unit's budget. When the manager is satisfied with her budget, she can enter it in the companywide budget with the click of a mouse, and her unit's budget automatically "rolls up" with budgets from all other units around the world. Whether at headquarters or on the road, top executives can log into the budget system and conduct their own sensitivity analyses on individual units' budgets, or on the companywide budget. The new technology allows managers to spend less time compiling and summarizing data and more time analyzing it to ensure that the budget leads the company to achieve the goals identified at the beginning of the budget process.

e-Accounting

ERP: Enterprise Resource Planning or Enterprise Ruins Plans?

Most accountants know—though few will admit—that at least three-quarters of the best-laid budgets and corporate plans gather dust. Now some pioneering Fortune 1000 companies are reengineering their budgeting processes. To make it all happen, they're shelving their Excel spreadsheets in favor of Enterprise Resource Planning (ERP) software.

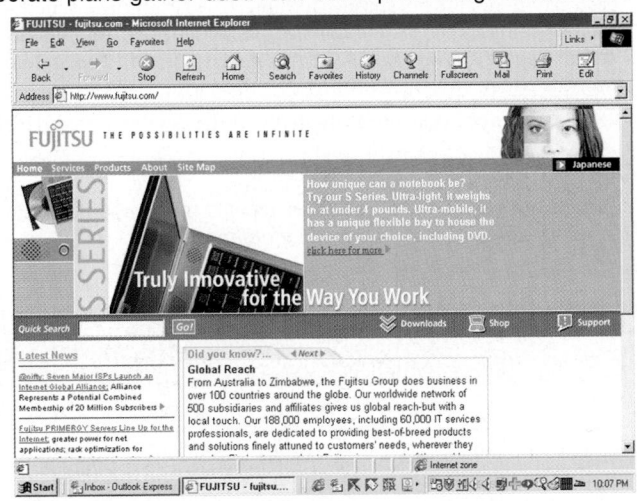

ERP software links corporate data across the entire enterprise. At **Fujitsu Computer Products of America**, an Oracle ERP program tracks the entire supply chain, including data on shipments of materials and supplies, purchases, inventory, accounts receivable, and accounts payable. An enterprise application system (EAS) program links to the ERP and allows managers to set up what-if scenarios.

Reengineering the budget via ERP is not cheap. Fujitsu invested $40 million. **Allstate Insurance** invested $60 million. But, implemented correctly, the savings can be enormous. Allstate has saved roughly $100 million in processing costs in just 18 months.

Yet well-publicized ERP fiascoes have kept many companies from taking the plunge. In 1999 **Hershey Foods Corp.** installed an ERP system, squeezing what was originally supposed to be a 4-year project into just 30 months. Hershey rolled out its new ERP system just when retailers began ordering large amounts of candy for back-to-school; Halloween profits fell 19% due to disrupted delivery of its kisses and candies, and Hershey is still trying to regain market share. Consultants caution that implementation alone takes at least one to two years. And the reengineering process must start well before the technology is in place, with clear business goals for the ERP system.

Source: Based on Russ Banham, "Better Budgets," *Journal of Accountancy,* February 2000, pp. 37–40. J. W. Dysart, "Planning for real-time information," *Banking Strategies,* May/June 2000, pp. 6–10. Louisa Wah, "Give ERP a chance," *Management Review,* March 2000, pp. 20–24. Craig Stedman, "Failed ERP gamble haunts Hershey," *Computerworld,* November 1, 1999, pp. 1, 89.

Consider two budget situations: (1) Whitewater Sporting Goods' marketing analysts produce a near-certain forecast for four-month sales of $4,500,000 for the company's 20 stores. (2) Much uncertainty exists about the period's sales. The most likely amount is $4,500,000, but marketing considers any amount between $3,900,000 and $5,100,000 to be possible. How will the budgeting process differ in these two circumstances?

Answer: Whitewater will prepare a master budget for the expected sales level of $4,500,000 in either case. Because of the uncertainty about sales in situation 2, executives will want a set of budgets covering the entire range of volume rather than a single level. Whitewater's managers may prepare budgets based on sales of, say, $3,900,000, $4,200,000, $4,500,000, $4,800,000, and $5,100,000. These budgets will help managers plan for sales levels throughout the forecasted range.

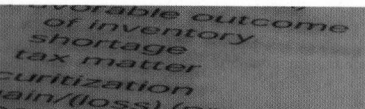

MID-CHAPTER

SUMMARY PROBLEM

www.prenhall.com/horngren
Mid-Chapter Assessment

Review the Whitewater Sporting Goods example in this chapter. You now think July sales might be $40,000 instead of the projected $50,000 in Exhibit 23-7. You want to perform a sensitivity analysis to see how this change in sales affects the budget.

Required

1. Revise the sales budget (Exhibit 23-7), the inventory, purchases, and cost of goods sold budget (Exhibit 23-8), and the operating expenses budget (Exhibit 23-9). Prepare a revised budgeted income statement for the four months ended July 31, 20X6.
2. Revise the schedule of budgeted cash collections (Exhibit 23-10), the schedule of budgeted cash payments for purchases (Exhibit 23-11), and the schedule of budgeted cash payments for operating expenses (Exhibit 23-12). Prepare a revised cash budget, a revised budgeted balance sheet at July 31, 20X6, and a revised budgeted statement of cash flows for the four months ended July 31, 20X6.

   Note: You need not repeat the parts of the revised schedules that do not change.

Solution

Although not required, this solution repeats the budgeted amounts for April, May, and June. Revised figures appear in boldface for emphasis.

Requirement 1

WHITEWATER SPORTING GOODS STORE NO. 18 REVISED—Sales Budget					
	April	**May**	**June**	**July**	**Total**
Cash sales, 60%	$30,000	$48,000	$36,000	**$24,000**	
Credit sales, 40%	20,000	32,000	24,000	**16,000**	
Total sales, 100%	$50,000	$80,000	$60,000	**$40,000**	$230,000

WHITEWATER SPORTING GOODS STORE NO. 18 REVISED—Inventory, Purchases, and Cost of Goods Sold Budget					
	April	**May**	**June**	**July**	**Total**
Cost of goods sold (0.70 × sales, from Revised Sales Budget)	$35,000	$56,000	$42,000	**$28,000**	$161,000
+ Desired ending inventory ($20,000 + 0.80 × cost of goods sold for next month)	64,800	53,600	**42,400**	42,400†	
= Total inventory required	99,800	109,600	**84,400**	70,400	
− Beginning inventory	(48,000)*	(64,800)	(53,600)	**(42,400)**	
= Purchases.......................................	$51,800	$44,800	**$30,800**	**$28,000**	

* Balance at March 31, Exhibit 23-5.
† Given in item 5 on page 933.

WHITEWATER SPORTING GOODS STORE NO. 18
REVISED — Operating Expenses Budget

	April	May	June	July	Total
Salary, fixed amount	$ 2,500	$ 2,500	$ 2,500	$ 2,500	
Commission, 15% of sales from Revised Sales Budget	7,500	12,000	9,000	6,000	
Total salary and commissions	10,000	14,500	11,500	8,500	$44,500
Rent expense, fixed amount	2,000	2,000	2,000	2,000	8,000
Depreciation expense, fixed amount	500	500	500	500	2,000
Insurance expense, fixed amount	200	200	200	200	800
Miscellaneous expenses, 5% of sales from Revised Sales Budget	2,500	4,000	3,000	2,000	11,500
Total operating expenses	$15,200	$21,200	$17,200	$13,200	$66,800

WHITEWATER SPORTING GOODS STORE NO. 18
Revised Budgeted Income Statement
Four Months Ending July 31, 20X6

	Amount		Source
Sales revenue		$230,000	Revised Sales Budget
Cost of goods sold		161,000	Revised Inventory, Purchases, and Cost of Goods Sold
Gross profit		69,000	Budget
Operating expenses:			
Salary and commissions	$44,500		Revised Operating Expenses Budget
Rent expense	8,000		Revised Operating Expenses Budget
Depreciation expense	2,000		Revised Operating Expenses Budget
Insurance expense	800		Revised Operating Expenses Budget
Miscellaneous expenses	11,500	66,800	Revised Operating Expenses Budget
Operating income		2,200	
Interest expense		225	Revised Cash Budget
Net income		$ 1,975	

Requirement 2

WHITEWATER SPORTING GOODS STORE NO. 18
REVISED — Budgeted Cash Collections

	April	May	June	July	Total
Cash sales, from Revised Sales Budget	$30,000	$48,000	$36,000	$24,000	
Collections of last month's credit sales, from Revised Sales Budget	16,000*	20,000	32,000	24,000	
Total collections	$46,000	$68,000	$68,000	$48,000	$230,000

* March 31 accounts receivable, Exhibit 23-5.

WHITEWATER SPORTING GOODS STORE NO. 18
REVISED — Budgeted Cash Payments for Purchases

	April	May	June	July	Total
50% of last month's purchases, from Revised Inventory, Purchases, and Cost of Goods Sold Budget	$16,800*	$25,900	$22,400	$15,400	
50% of this month's purchases, from Revised Inventory, Purchases, and Cost of Goods Sold Budget	25,900	22,400	15,400	14,000	
Total payments for purchases	$42,700	$48,300	$37,800	$29,400	$158,200

* March 31 accounts payable, Exhibit 23-5.

WHITEWATER SPORTING GOODS STORE NO. 18
REVISED — Budgeted Cash Payments for Operating Expenses

	April	May	June	July	Total
Salary and commissions:					
50% of last month's expenses, from Revised Operating Expenses Budget	$ 4,250*	$ 5,000	$ 7,250	$ 5,750	
50% of this month's expenses, from Revised Operating Expenses Budget	5,000	7,250	5,750	4,250	
Total salary and commissions	9,250	12,250	13,000	10,000	
Rent expense, from Revised Operating Expenses Budget	2,000	2,000	2,000	2,000	
Miscellaneous expenses, from Revised Operating Expenses Budget	2,500	4,000	3,000	2,000	
Total payments for operating expenses	$13,750	$18,250	$18,000	$14,000	$64,000

* March 31 salary and commissions payable, Exhibit 23-5.

WHITEWATER SPORTING GOODS STORE NO. 18
Revised Cash Budget
Four Months Ending July 31, 20X6

	April	May	June	July
Beginning cash balance	$15,000*	$10,550	$10,410	$21,035
Cash collections (Revised Budgeted Cash Collections)	46,000	68,000	68,000	48,000
Cash available	$61,000	$78,550	$78,410	$69,035
Cash payments:				
Purchases of inventory (Revised Budgeted Cash Payments for Purchases)	$42,700	$48,300	$37,800	$29,400
Operating expenses (Revised Budgeted Cash Payments for Operating Expenses)	13,750	18,250	18,000	14,000
Purchase of delivery truck (item 8, page 933)	3,000	—	—	—
Total cash payments	59,450	66,550	55,800	43,400
(1) Ending cash balance before financing	1,550	12,000	22,610	25,635
Minimum cash balance desired	10,000	10,000	10,000	10,000
Cash excess (deficiency)	$(8,450)	$ 2,000	$12,610	$15,635
Financing of cash deficiency (see notes a–c):				
Borrowing (at end of month)	$ 9,000			
Principal payments (at end of month)		$(1,500)	$(1,500)	$(1,500)
Interest expense (at 12% annually)		(90)	(75)	(60)
(2) Total effects of financing	9,000	(1,590)	(1,575)	(1,560)
Ending cash balance (1) + (2)	$10,550	$10,410	$21,035	$24,075

* March 31 cash balance, Exhibit 23-5.

Notes

a. Borrowing occurs in multiples of $1,000 and only for the amount needed to maintain a minimum cash balance of $10,000.

b. Monthly principal payments: $9,000 ÷ 6 = $1,500.

c. Interest expense:

May: $9,000 × (0.12 × 1/12) = $90

June: ($9,000 − $1,500) × (0.12 × 1/12) = $75

July: ($9,000 − $1,500 − $1,500) × (0.12 × 1/12) = $60

WHITEWATER SPORTING GOODS STORE NO. 18
Revised Budgeted Balance Sheet
July 31, 20X6

Assets

Current assets:

Cash (Revised Cash budget)	**$24,075**	
Accounts receivable (Revised Sales Budget)	**16,000**	
Inventory	42,400	
Prepaid insurance	1,000	
Total current assets		$ 83,475

Plant assets:

Equipment and fixtures	$35,000	
Accumulated depreciation	(14,800)	
Total plant assets		20,200
Total assets		$103,675

Liabilities

Current liabilities:

Accounts payable (0.50 × July purchases of **$28,000;** Revised Inventory, Purchases, and Cost of Goods Sold Budget)	**$14,000**	
Short-term note payable	4,500	
Salary and commissions payable (0.50 × July expenses of **$8,500;** Revised Operating Expenses Budget)	**4,250**	
Total liabilities		$ 22,750

Owners' Equity

Owners' equity (beginning balance of $78,950 + **$1,975** net income, Revised Budgeted Income Statement)		80,925
Total liabilities and owners' equity		$103,675

WHITEWATER SPORTING GOODS STORE NO. 18
Revised Budgeted Statement of Cash Flows
Four Months Ending July 31, 20X6

Cash flows from operating activities:

Receipts:		
Collections (Revised Budgeted Cash Collections)	**$230,000**	
Total cash receipts		$230,000
Payments:		
Purchases of inventory (Revised Budgeted Cash Payments for Purchases)	**(158,200)**	
Operating expenses, excluding interest expense (Revised Budgeted Cash Payments for Operating Expenses)	**(64,000)**	
Payment of interest expense	(225)	
Total cash payments		**(222,425)**
Net cash inflow from operating activities		**7,575**
Cash flows from investing activities:		
Acquisition of delivery truck	$ (3,000)	
Net cash outflow from investing activities		(3,000)
Cash flows from financing activities:		
Proceeds from issuance of notes payable	$ 9,000	
Payment of notes payable	(4,500)	
Net cash inflow from financing activities		4,500
Net increase in cash		$ 9,075
Cash balance, April 1, 20X6 (Exhibit 23-5)		15,000
Cash balance, July 31, 20X6 (Revised Cash Budget)		$ 24,075

RESPONSIBILITY CENTER. A part or subunit of an organization whose manager is accountable for specific activities.

RESPONSIBILITY ACCOUNTING

You've now seen how managers set strategic goals, and then develop plans and budget resources for activities that will help reach those goals. Each manager is responsible for planning and controlling some part of the firm's activities. A **responsibility center** is a part or subunit of the organization whose manager is accountable for specific activities. Lower-level managers are often responsible for budgeting and controlling costs of a single value-chain function. For example, one manager is responsible for planning and controlling the *production* of **Pace** picante sauce at the plant, while another is responsible for planning and controlling the *distribution* of the picante sauce to customers. Lower-level managers report to higher-level managers who have broader responsibilities. For example, managers in charge of production and distribution report to senior managers responsible for profits (revenues minus costs) earned by the entire product line.

Types of Responsibility Centers

RESPONSIBILITY ACCOUNTING. A system for evaluating the performance of each responsibility center and its manager.

Responsibility accounting is a system for evaluating the performance of each responsibility center and its manager. Responsibility accounting reports compare plans (budgets) with actions (actual results) for each responsibility center. Superiors then evaluate how well each manager: (1) used the budgeted resources to achieve the responsibility center's goals, and thereby (2) controlled the operations for which he or she is responsible. Exhibit 23-16 illustrates four types of responsibility centers: cost centers, revenue centers, profit centers, and investment centers.

EXHIBIT 23-16
Four Types of Responsibility Centers

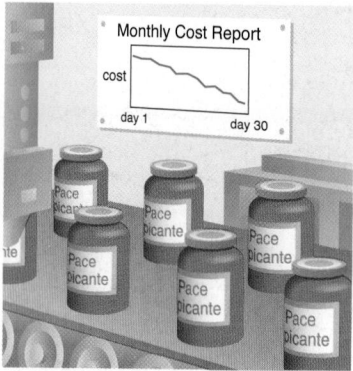

(a) A **cost center**, such as a production line for Pace picante sauce—where managers are responsible for costs

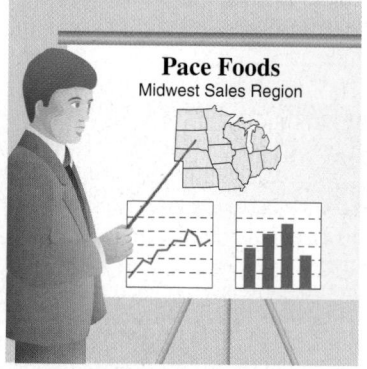

(b) A **revenue center**, such as the Midwest sales region—where managers are responsible for generating sales revenue

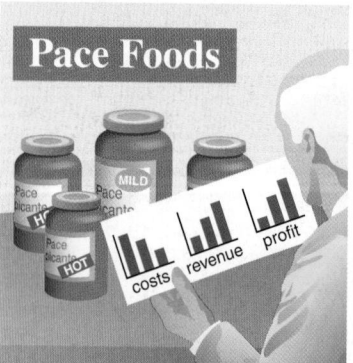

(c) A **profit center**, such as the Pace picante sauce line of products—where managers are responsible for generating income

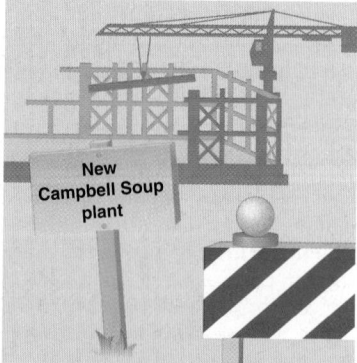

(d) An **investment center**, such as Campbell Soups' soups and sauces division—where managers are responsible for income and invested capital

 DAILY EXERCISE 23-14

1. *Cost center: A responsibility center where managers are accountable for costs (expenses) only.* Manufacturing operations like the Pace picante sauce production lines are cost centers. The line foreman controls costs by ensuring that employees

work efficiently with minimal waste of ingredients. The foreman is *not* responsible for generating revenues, because he is not involved in selling the picante sauce. The plant manager evaluates the foreman on his ability to control *costs* by comparing actual costs to budgeted costs. All else being equal (for example, holding quality constant), the manager is likely to receive a more favorable performance evaluation if actual costs are less than budgeted costs.

2. *Revenue center: A responsibility center where managers are primarily accountable for revenues.* Examples include the Midwest and Southeast sales regions of businesses like **Pace Foods** and **Reebok.** Managers of revenue centers are primarily responsible for generating sales revenue, although they may also be responsible for the costs of their own sales operations. Revenue center performance reports compare actual with budgeted revenues and may also include the costs incurred by the revenue center itself. All else being equal, the manager is likely to receive a more favorable performance evaluation if actual revenues exceed the budget.

3. *Profit center: A responsibility center where managers are accountable for revenues and costs (expenses), and therefore profits.* The (higher-level) manager responsible for the entire Pace product line would be accountable for increasing sales revenue *and* controlling costs to achieve the profit goals. Other examples of profit centers include an **Outback Steakhouse** restaurant and the housewares department of a **Target** store. Profit center reports include both revenues and expenses to show the profit center's income. Superiors evaluate the manager's performance by comparing actual revenues, expenses, and profits to the budget. All else being equal, the manager is likely to receive a more favorable performance evaluation if actual profits exceed the budget.

4. *Investment center: A responsibility center where managers are accountable for investments, revenues, and costs (expenses).* Examples include the **Nutrasweet Company,** which is owned by **J.W. Childs Equity Partners,** the Saturn division of **General Motors,** and the Soups and Sauces Division (which includes Pace Foods) of **Campbell Soup.** Managers of investment centers are responsible for: (1) generating sales, (2) controlling expenses, and (3) managing the amount of investment required to earn the income (revenues minus expenses).

Top management often evaluates investment center managers based on return on investment. ➡ Chapter 18 introduced a common return on investment measure—the rate of return on total assets:

← See Chapter 18, p. 728, for discussion of rate of return on total assets.

$$\frac{\text{Net income plus interest expense}}{\text{Average total assets}}$$

When evaluating a division rather than the entire company, however, the return on investment is often computed as:

$$\frac{\text{Division's operating income}}{\text{Division's average total assets}}$$

All else being equal, the manager will receive a more favorable performance evaluation if the division's actual return on investment exceeds the budgeted return on investment.

Responsibility Accounting: An Example

The simplified organization chart in Exhibit 23-17 shows how a company may assign responsibility in the fast-food industry. At the top level of O'Toole Restaurant Corporation, the Northern California district manager oversees the branch managers, who supervise the managers of the individual restaurants (called stores).

Store managers make operating decisions. They may decide the quantities of food to order, the number of employees and their schedules, and store hours.

EXHIBIT 23-17
O'Toole Restaurant Corporation
Partial Organization Chart

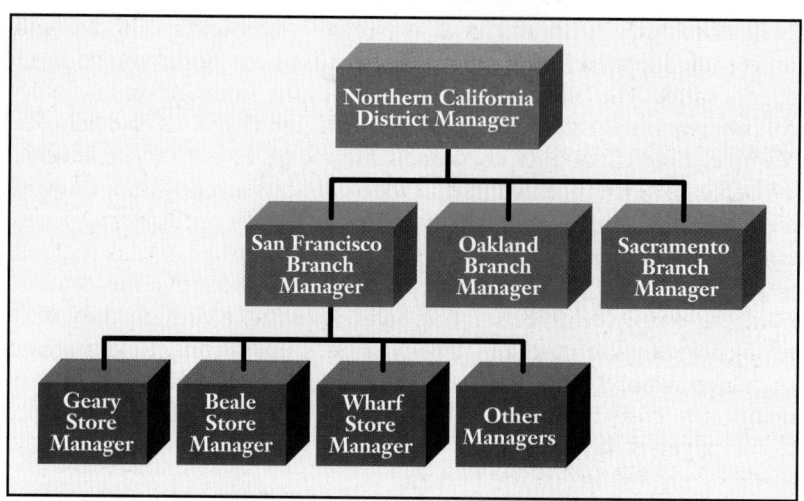

Branch managers oversee several stores, evaluate store managers' performance, and set store managers' compensation. District managers oversee several branches, evaluate branch managers' performance and compensation, set food prices, and approve sales promotions. District managers are accountable to regional managers, who answer to home-office vice presidents.

THINK IT OVER

O'Toole's store managers do not have authority to set sale prices or control advertising. Both factors affect store revenues. But the corporation nevertheless evaluates each store as a profit center instead of as a cost center. Why?

Answer: If each store were a cost center, then store managers would be motivated to cut costs to keep actual costs below the budget. Excessive cost cutting can hurt quality and service. By evaluating each store as a profit center, executives give store managers the incentive to keep stores clean and to ensure that employees provide fast and friendly service. Store managers thus are more likely to work hard to increase customer satisfaction, the foundation of long-run profitability.

○ DAILY EXERCISE 23-15

Exhibit 23-18 provides a more detailed view of how managers use responsibility accounting performance reports to evaluate profit centers. At each level, the reports compare actual results with the budget. Examine the lowest level and move to the top. Follow how the reports are related through the three levels of responsibility.

Trace the $54,000 budgeted operating income from the Beale store manager's report to the San Francisco branch manager's report. The branch manager's report summarizes the results of all the stores he supervises. This report also includes charges the branch manager's office incurs.

Now trace the $465,000 total budgeted operating income from the San Francisco branch manager's report to the Northern California district manager's report. The district manager's report includes costs from her own district office plus a summary of each branch's operating performance.

Objective 6
Prepare a performance report for management by exception

Management by Exception

MANAGEMENT BY EXCEPTION. Directs management's attention to important differences between actual and budgeted amounts.

Exhibit 23-18 presents variances from budget. This reporting format aids **management by exception,** which directs executives' attention to important differences between actual and budgeted amounts. Look at the district manager's report, and consider the San Francisco branch. Its actual operating income of $460,000 is very close to its budget for the current month ($465,000). Under management by exception, the district manager will not waste time investigating such a small variance. In contrast, the Oakland branch earned substantially more profit than budgeted. The district manager will want to find out why. Suppose the Oakland manager believes that a local sales promotion was especially effective. That promotion may be repeated and may also be used in other cities.

EXHIBIT 23-18 Responsibility Accounting Performance Report

O'TOOLE RESTAURANT CORPORATION
Responsibility Accounting at Various Levels
(In Thousands of Dollars)

NORTHERN CALIFORNIA DISTRICT MANAGER— Monthly Responsibility Report

Operating Income of Branches and District Manager Office Expense	Budget This Month	Budget Year to Date	Actual This Month	Actual Year to Date	Variance Favorable/(Unfavorable) This Month	Variance Favorable/(Unfavorable) Year to Date
District manager office expense	$ (150)	$ (600)	$ (154)	$ (620)	$(4)	$(20)
San Francisco branch	465	1,730	460	1,780	(5)	50
Oakland branch	390	1,540	475	1,855	85	315
Sacramento branch	520	2,240	468	2,061	(52)	(179)
Operating income	$1,225	$4,910	$1,249	$5,076	$24	$166

SAN FRANCISCO BRANCH MANAGER— Monthly Responsibility Report

Operating Income of Stores and Branch Manager Office Expense	Budget This Month	Budget Year to Date	Actual This Month	Actual Year to Date	Variance Favorable/(Unfavorable) This Month	Variance Favorable/(Unfavorable) Year to Date
Branch manager office expense	$(20)	$ (306)	$ (25)	$ (302)	$(5)	$ 4
Geary store	48	148	40	136	(8)	(12)
Beale store	54	228	61	244	7	16
Wharf store	38	160	42	170	4	10
Others	345	1,500	342	1,532	(3)	32
Operating income	$465	$1,730	$460	$1,780	$(5)	$50

BEALE STORE MANAGER— Monthly Responsibility Report

Revenues and Expenses	Budget This Month	Budget Year to Date	Actual This Month	Actual Year to Date	Variance Favorable/(Unfavorable) This Month	Variance Favorable/(Unfavorable) Year to Date
Revenues	$170	$690	$178	$702	$8	$12
Food expense	67	262	61	251	6	11
Paper expense	15	62	18	64	(3)	(2)
Wages expense	24	98	28	103	(4)	(5)
Depreciation expense	10	40	10	40	—	—
Total expenses	116	462	117	458	(1)	4
Operating income	$ 54	$228	$ 61	$244	$7	$16

Managers investigate large favorable variances as well as large unfavorable variances. A large favorable variance could reflect good performance. But a large favorable variance for costs such as food or wages could indicate that the store manager is skimping on the food or service.

The Northern California district manager will concentrate on improving the Sacramento branch. Its actual income of $468,000 is 10% ($52,000 ÷ $520,000) lower than its budget. The district manager may ask to see the branch manager's monthly responsibility report. That report reveals whether the income shortfall is due

DAILY EXERCISE 23-16

DAILY EXERCISE 23-17

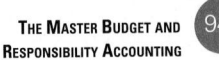

to excessive branch office expenses, below-budget operating income from individual stores, or both. The two managers will work together to identify and correct problems.

Exhibit 23-18 also shows that summarized data may hide problems. Although the San Francisco branch as a whole performed well, the Geary store did not. Its actual income of $40,000 is 16.7% ($8,000 ÷ $48,000) below budget. This shortfall is offset by excellent performances by the Beale and Wharf stores. If the district manager receives only the condensed report at the top of the exhibit, she must rely on branch managers to spot and correct problems with individual stores. Some upper-level executives prefer the more detailed middle-level reports so they can keep tighter control over their responsibility centers.

Not a Question of Blame

Responsibility accounting helps top executives delegate decisions. Responsibility accounting assigns lower-level managers responsibility for their unit's actions and provides a way to evaluate the manager's and unit's performance. By allowing top managers to delegate decisions, responsibility accounting and management by exception free them to concentrate on strategic issues that affect the entire business.

Managers should not misuse responsibility accounting systems to find fault or to place blame. The question is not, Who should be blamed for an unfavorable variance? Instead, the question is, Who can best explain why a specific variance occurred? Consider again the Sacramento branch in Exhibit 23-18. Suppose that a month of unusually bad weather resulted in a 15% drop in restaurant volume. It may be that only efficient operations by the branch's stores kept the income variance as low as $52,000 (only 10% below the budget). Therefore, the Sacramento branch manager may have done a good job despite the unfavorable variance.

Objective 7
Allocate indirect costs to departments

DEPARTMENTAL ACCOUNTING

Responsibility centers are often called *departments*. Consider a retailer such as **Macy's, Lazarus,** or **Nordstrom.** Top managers of a department store want more information than just the net income of the store as a whole. They want to know each department's gross profit (sales minus cost of goods sold). They also usually want to know each department's operating income. These data can help identify the most profitable departments, so managers can decide whether to expand some departments and phase out others.

It is easy to measure gross profit for each department because the department records sales and cost of goods sold. However, it is more difficult to measure a department's operating income (gross profit minus operating expenses). Why? Many operating expenses are indirect costs that are not directly traced to the department.

➡ Chapter 19, pp. 760–761, explains how direct costs are traced.

As we noted in Chapter 19, *direct costs* are traceable to a particular department or product. ◄ Consider Macy's Shoe Department. Clerks' wages, the cost of ads for shoes, and depreciation on display racks are all directly traceable to the Shoe Department. *Indirect costs*—all expenses other than direct costs—are not traceable to a single department. For example, Macy's Receiving Department and Stockroom serve all departments. How should Macy's allocate the cost of its Receiving Department and its Stockroom?

Allocation of Indirect Costs

➡ See Chapters 20 and 21, pp. 810–812 and 843–845, for a discussion of allocating indirect costs.

Chapters 20 and 21 explained how indirect costs are allocated to *products*. ◄ Indirect costs are allocated to *departments* or responsibility centers using a similar process.

- Choose an allocation base for the indirect cost
- Compute an indirect cost allocation rate:

$$\frac{\text{Total indirect costs}}{\text{Total quantity of allocation base}}$$

- Allocate the indirect cost:

$$\text{Quantity of allocation} \atop \text{base used by department} \quad \times \quad \text{Indirect cost} \atop \text{allocation rate}$$

As we noted in Chapter 20, the ideal cost allocation base is also a cost driver. Because different costs have different cost drivers, companies use several different allocation bases to allocate different indirect costs to various departments. Exhibit 23-19 lists common allocation bases for different indirect costs. Managers use their experience and judgment to choose these bases, but there is no single "correct" allocation base for each indirect cost.

EXHIBIT 23-19
Bases for Allocating Costs to Departments

 DAILY EXERCISE 23-18

Cost or Expense	Base for Allocating Cost
Direct materials	Separately traced
Merchandise inventory purchases	Separately traced
Direct labor	Separately traced
Other labor	Time spent in each department
Supervision	Time spent, or number of employees, in each department
Equipment depreciation	Separately traced, or hours used by each department
Building depreciation, property taxes	Square feet of space
Heat, light, and air conditioning	Square feet or cubic feet of space
Janitorial services	Square feet of space
Advertising	Separately traced if possible; otherwise, in proportion to sales
Materials Handling Department	Number or weight of items handled for each department
Payroll Department	Number of employees in each department
Personnel Department	Number of employees in each department
Purchasing Department	Number of purchase orders placed for each department

Consider Macy's receiving costs. Suppose Macy's decides that these costs are driven by the number of orders placed to purchase inventory. If 15% of the orders are for the Shoe Department and 20% are for the Menswear Department, then Macy's will allocate 15% of the Receiving Department costs to the Shoe Department and 20% to the Menswear Department. (The remaining Receiving Department costs will be allocated to other departments in proportion to the number of orders each issued.)

Allocating Indirect Costs to Departments: An Example

Exhibit 23-20 on the following page shows a departmental income statement for WorldPC, a retail computer store. We focus on allocating indirect operating expenses to the store's two departments: Hardware and Software.

SALARIES AND WAGES WorldPC traces salespersons' salaries and department managers' salaries directly to each department.

◉ DAILY EXERCISE 23-19

RENT WorldPC allocates the $600,000 rent expense based on the square feet each department occupies. The Hardware and Software Departments occupy 20,000 square feet and 5,000 square feet, respectively, so WorldPC allocates rent as follows:

Rent for entire store	$600,000
Total square feet (20,000 + 5,000)	÷ 25,000
Rent per square foot	$ 24

Hardware Department: 20,000 square feet × $24 per square foot = $480,000
Software Department: 5,000 square feet × $24 per square foot = 120,000
Total rent expense = $600,000

EXHIBIT 23-20
Departmental Income Statement

WORLDPC
Departmental Income Statement
Year Ended December 31, 20X9
(In Thousands)

	Total	Department Hardware	Software
Sales revenue..	$10,000	$7,000	$3,000
Cost of goods sold.....................................	6,500	4,500	2,000
Gross profit...	3,500	2,500	1,000
Operating expenses:			
Salaries and wages expense	1,400	660	740
Rent expense	600	480	120
Purchasing department expense.............	48	36	12
Total operating expenses	2,048	1,176	872
Operating income......................................	$ 1,452	$1,324	$ 128

PURCHASING DEPARTMENT WorldPC found that it takes just as long to complete a purchase order for inexpensive modems as for expensive "loaded" notebook computers. Consequently, the company allocates the $48,000 costs of the Purchasing Department based on the number of purchase orders processed. Hardware had 300 purchase orders, Software had 100 purchase orders.

Purchasing Department costs...	$48,000
Total number of purchase orders (300 + 100)......................................	÷ 400
Cost per purchase order	$ 120

Hardware Department: 300 purchase orders × $120 per purchase order = $36,000
Software Department: 100 purchase orders × $120 per purchase order = 12,000
                              Total Purchase Department cost = $48,000

WorldPC's top executives can use the departmental income statements in Exhibit 23-20 to evaluate how well each department and its manager performed in 20X9. The Hardware Department was more profitable than the Software Department. Hardware's profit margin (income divided by sales) was $1,324 ÷ $7,000 = 18.9%, while Software's profit margin was only $128 ÷ $3,000 = 4.3%. However, it is usually better to compare a department's actual results to its budget rather than to another department's results. For example, if WorldPC has just added the Software Department, performance may have exceeded expectations.

The following Decision Guidelines review budgets and how they are used in responsibility accounting. Take a moment to study these guidelines before working the summary review problem.

DECISION GUIDELINES

The Master Budget and Responsibility Accounting

DECISION	GUIDELINES
Why should a company develop a budget?	• Requires managers to plan • Promotes organization and communication • Provides a benchmark that helps managers evaluate performance • Motivates employees
In what order should you prepare the components of the master budget?	Begin with the *operating budget*. • Start with the *sales budget,* which feeds into all other budgets. • The sales and *ending inventory budgets* determine the *purchases and cost of goods sold budget*. • The sales, cost of goods sold, and *operating expense budgets* determine the *budgeted income statement*. Next, prepare the *capital expenditures budget*. Finally, prepare the *financial budget*. • Start with the *cash budget*. • The cash budget provides the ending cash balance for the *budgeted balance sheet* and the details for the *budgeted statement of cash flows*.
What if the sales forecast is uncertain?	Prepare a *sensitivity analysis* and project budgeted results at different sales levels.
How to compute budgeted purchases?	$$\text{Beginning inventory} + \text{Purchases} - \text{Ending inventory} = \text{Cost of goods sold}$$ so $$\text{Purchases} = \text{Cost of goods sold} + \text{Ending inventory} - \text{Beginning inventory}$$
What kind of a responsibility center does a given manager supervise?	Cost center: Manager is responsible for costs. Revenue center: Manager is responsible for revenues. Profit center: Manager is responsible for both revenues and costs, and therefore profits. Investment center: Manager is responsible for revenues, costs, and the amount of the investment required to earn the income.
How to evaluate managers?	Compare actual performance with the budget for the manager's responsibility center. *Management by exception* focuses only on large differences between budgeted and actual results.
How to identify the most profitable departments or product lines?	Departmental or product line income statements
How to allocate indirect costs to departments or product lines?	1. Choose an allocation base for each indirect cost. 2. Compute an indirect cost allocation rate: $$\frac{\text{Total indirect cost (\$)}}{\text{Total quantity of allocation base}}$$ 3. Allocate the indirect cost: $$\text{Quantity of allocation base used by department} \times \text{Indirect cost allocation rate}$$

SUMMARY PROBLEM

www.prenhall.com/horngren

End-of-Chapter Assessment

The Ritz-Carlton Club, an exclusive "hotel within a hotel," provides an even more luxurious atmosphere than the hotel's regular accommodations. Access is limited to guests residing on the hotel's top floors. The Club's private lounge serves complimentary continental breakfast, afternoon snacks, and evening cocktails and chocolates. The Club has its own concierge staff that provides personal service to Club guests. Guests staying in regular accommodations do not receive complimentary snacks and beverages, nor do they have a private concierge.

Ritz-Carlton Club floors are considered one department, and regular accommodations are considered a separate department.

Suppose the general manager of the new Ritz-Carlton hotel in St. Thomas, an island in the Caribbean, wants to know the costs of her hotel's Club Accommodations Department and Regular Accommodations Department. Housekeeping costs are allocated based on the number of occupied room-nights, utilities are allocated based on the number of cubic feet, and building depreciation is allocated based on the number of square feet. Assume each department reports the following information for March:

	Club Accommodations	Regular Accommodations
Number of occupied room-nights	540	7,560
Cubic feet	192,000	1,440,000
Square feet	16,000	144,000

Required

1. Given the following (assumed) total costs, what are the costs assigned to the Club Accommodations and the Regular Accommodations Departments?

Food and beverage expense	$ 12,000
Housekeeping expense..........................	194,400
Utilities expense	97,920
Building depreciation expense	480,000
Concierage staff salaries	15,000
Total..	$799,320

 DAILY EXERCISE 23-20

2. What is the cost per occupied room in Club Accommodations? In Regular Accommodations?

Solution

	Club Accommodations	Regular Accommodations	Total
Food and beverage expense[a]	$12,000	$ —	$ 12,000
Housekeeping expense[b]	12,960	181,440	194,400
Utilities expense[c]	11,520	86,400	97,920
Building depreciation expense[d]	48,000	432,000	480,000
Concierage staff salaries[a]	15,000	—	15,000
Total	$99,480	$699,840	$799,320

[a] Food and beverage expenses and concierge staff salaries are directly traced to the Club Accommodations Department.

[b] Housekeeping expense:

$$\text{Cost per occupied room} = \frac{\$194,400}{540 + 7,560}$$

$$= \$24/\text{room}$$

Club Accommodations: 540 rooms $\times$ \$24/room = $ 12,960
Regular Accommodations: 7,560 rooms $\times$ \$24/room = 181,440
  Total housekeeping expense .... = $194,400

[c] Utilities expense:

$$\text{Cost per cubic foot} = \frac{\$97,920}{192,000 + 1,440,000}$$

$$= \$0.06/\text{cubic foot}$$

Club Accommodations: 192,000 cu. ft. $\times$ \$0.06/cu. ft. = \$11,520
Regular Accommodations:
  1,440,000 cu. ft. $\times$ \$0.06/cu. ft. = 86,400
  Total utilities expense .... = $97,920

[d] Building depreciation expense:

$$\text{Cost per square foot} = \frac{\$480,000}{16,000 + 144,000}$$

$$= \$3/\text{square foot}$$

Club Accommodations: 16,000 sq. ft. $\times$ \$3/sq. ft. = $ 48,000
Regular Accommodations: 144,000 sq. ft. $\times$ \$3/sq. ft. = 432,000
  Total building depreciation expense .... = $480,000

	Club Accommodations	Regular Accommodations
Total costs	$99,480	$699,840
÷ Occupied rooms............................	÷ 540	÷ 7,560
= Cost per occupied room	$184.22	$ 92.57

LESSONS LEARNED

1. **Identify the benefits of budgeting.** A budget is a quantitative expression of a plan of action that helps managers coordinate and implement the plan. Budgets require managers to plan, coordinate activities, and communicate plans throughout the company. Budgets also help managers evaluate performance and motivate employees to achieve goals.

2. **Prepare an operating budget.** The *operating budget* sets the target revenues and expenses—and thus operating income—for the period. To budget income, accountants must budget sales, inventory, purchases, cost of goods sold, and operating expenses. Sales revenue is budgeted first because other income statement elements depend on sales volume.

3. **Prepare the components of a financial budget.** A capital expenditures budget presents plans for purchasing long-term capital assets. This budget and the budgeted income statement provide data for the cash budget. Accountants use all three to prepare the budgeted balance sheet and the budgeted statement of cash flows.

4. **Use sensitivity analysis in budgeting.** Managers should make contingency plans in case actual results differ from predictions. *Sensitivity analysis* asks *what* a result will be *if* a predicted amount is not achieved or *if* an underlying assumption changes. Managers use spreadsheets or special Web-based software to study a broad range of budget possibilities.

5. **Distinguish among different types of responsibility centers.** Most companies divide operations into *responsibility centers* to establish authority for planning and controlling business operations. Four types of responsibility centers are cost centers, revenue centers, profit centers, and investment centers.

6. **Prepare a performance report for management by exception.** Performance reports show differences between budgeted and actual amounts. By focusing on important variances, managers can direct attention to areas that need improvement. This is called *management by exception.*

7. **Allocate indirect costs to departments.** First, choose an allocation base, which ideally should be a cost driver. Second, calculate an indirect cost allocation rate: Divide the indirect cost by the total quantity of the allocation base. Third, use this indirect cost allocation rate to allocate indirect costs to departments: Multiply the quantity of the allocation base used by the department times the indirect cost allocation rate.

ACCOUNTING VOCABULARY

capital expenditures budget (p. 931)

cash budget (p. 936)

financial budget (p. 931)

management by exception (p. 948)

master budget (p. 931)

operating budget (p. 931)

responsibility accounting (p. 946)

responsibility center (p. 946)

statement of budgeted cash receipts and payments (p. 936)

QUESTIONS

1. What are four benefits of budgeting?
2. List the components of a master budget.
3. Taft Corporation installs a budgeting system in which the president sets all the goals for the company. The vice president checks up on all 90 employees to ensure that they are meeting the president's budget goals. What is the weakness in this budgeting system? How can the system be improved?
4. Why should the capital expenditures budget be prepared before the cash budget, the budgeted balance sheet, and the budgeted statement of cash flows?
5. How does a company budget inventory purchases? In your answer, show the relationships among purchases, cost of goods sold, and inventory.
6. Outline the four steps in preparing an operating budget.
7. Is sales forecasting important only to a profit-seeking business, or is it used by nonprofit organizations such as colleges and hospitals? Give your reason.
8. Why are computer spreadsheets and budget management software well suited for budgeting?
9. Which manager will control expenses better: Grant, whose performance is measured by his department's sales, or Bruns, whose performance is gauged by her department's income? Why?
10. Identify four types of responsibility centers, and give examples of each. State the information they report.
11. A company owns 50 **Burger King** restaurants in Philadelphia, Pittsburgh, and Harrisburg. In each city, a local manager oversees operations. Starting at the individual store level, describe the likely flow of information in a responsibility accounting system. What data are reported?
12. What is the objective of management by exception?
13. Identify a reasonable allocation base for the following indirect expenses: heating expense, depreciation of manufacturing equipment used by three departments, and advertising expense.
14. Why do companies allocate indirect costs to departments?

ASSESS YOUR PROGRESS

DAILY EXERCISES

Managers' use of budgets (Obj. 1)

DE23-1 What are the key roles managers play in running their business operations? How do budgets help managers with each role?

Identifying benefits of budgeting (Obj. 1)

DE23-2 Consider Ram Dharan's budget for his travel itinerary business (page 928). Explain how Dharan benefits from preparing the budget.

Ordering components of the master budget (Obj. 2, 3)

DE23-3 In what order should you prepare the following components of the master budget?

Budgeted income statement	Operating expense budget	Cash budget
Budgeted statement of cash flows	Purchases and cost of goods sold budget	Capital expenditures budget
Budgeted balance sheet	Sales budget	Inventory budget

Which are components of the operating budget? Which are components of the financial budget?

Preparing a sales budget (Obj. 2)

DE23-4 In a series of Daily Exercises, we are going to prepare parts of the master budget for Shādz, a major East Coast retailer of high-end sunglasses. We will concentrate on Shādz's budget for January and February.

Shādz expects to sell 3,000 pairs of glasses for $235 each in January, and 4,500 pairs of glasses for $240 each in February. All sales are cash only. Prepare the sales budget for January and February.

Preparing a purchases, cost of goods sold, and inventory budget (Obj. 2)

DE23-5 In Daily Exercise 23-4, Shādz expects cost of goods sold to average 65% of sales revenue, and the company expects to sell 4,300 pairs of sunglasses in March for $240 each. Shādz's target ending inventory is $10,000 plus 50% of the next month's cost of goods sold. Use this information and the sales budget from Daily Exercise 23-4 to prepare Shādz's purchases, cost of goods sold, and inventory budget for January and February.

DE23-6 Turn to the Whitewater Sporting Goods example on pages 932–940. Suppose June sales are expected to be $84,000 rather than $60,000. Revise Whitewater's sales budget.

What other components of Whitewater's master budget would be affected by this change in the sales budget?

Preparing a sales budget (Obj. 2, 4)

DE23-7 Refer to the original Whitewater Sporting Goods example on pages 932–940. Suppose cost of goods sold averages 65% of sales rather than 70%. Revise Whitewater's purchases, cost of goods sold, and inventory budget for April and May.

What other components of Whitewater's master budget would be affected by the change in the budgeted cost of goods sold?

Preparing a purchases, cost of goods sold, and inventory budget (Obj. 2, 4)

DE23-8 Turn to the original Whitewater Sporting Goods example on pages 932–940. Suppose 30% of sales are cash and 70% are credit. Revise Whitewater's sales budget and budgeted cash collections from customers for April and May.

Preparing a sales budget and cash collections budget (Obj. 2, 3, 4)

DE23-9 Refer to the original Whitewater Sporting Goods example on pages 932–940. Suppose Whitewater pays for 40% of inventory purchases in the month of the purchase and 60% during the next month. Revise Whitewater's budgeted cash payments for purchases of inventory for April and May. (*Hint:* Assume these new percentages also apply to March purchases of $33,600 given in item 5 on page 933).

Preparing a cash payments for purchases budget (Obj. 3, 4)

DE23-10 You prepared Shādz's sales budget in Daily Exercise 23-4. Now assume that Shādz's sales are 25% cash and 75% on credit. Shādz's collection history indicates that credit sales are collected as follows:

- 30% in the month of the sale
- 60% in the month after the sale
- 6% two months after the sale
- 4% are never collected

November sales totaled $391,500 and December sales were $398,250. Prepare a schedule for the budgeted cash collections for January and February.

Budgeting cash collections (Obj. 3)

DE23-11 Refer to Daily Exercise 23-10. Shādz's has $8,300 cash on hand on January 1. The company requires a minimum cash balance of $7,500. January cash collections are $531,705 (as you calculated in Daily Exercise 23-10). Total cash payments for January are $583,200. Prepare a cash budget for January. Will Shādz's need to borrow cash by the end of January?

Preparing a cash budget (Obj. 3)

DE23-12 Return to the original Whitewater Sporting Goods example on pages 932–940. Suppose Whitewater can borrow only in notes payable of $2,000 each, at an annual interest rate of 15%. The notes payable require ten equal monthly payments of the principal. Whitewater must also pay interest on the unpaid principal. Borrowing and all principal and interest payments occur at the end of the month. Answer the following questions.

Financing (Obj. 3)

1. How much will Whitewater have to borrow in April?
2. How much principal will Whitewater repay each month?
3. How much interest expense will Whitewater pay in May, June, and July?

DE23-13 How has information technology affected sensitivity analysis in budgeting?

Sensitivity analysis (Obj. 4)

DE23-14 Fill in the blanks with the phrase that best completes the sentence.

Distinguishing among different types of responsibility centers (Obj. 5)

- A cost center
- An investment center
- A profit center
- A responsibility center
- A revenue center
- Higher
- Lower

a. The Maintenance Department at the **San Diego Zoo** is _____.
b. The concession stand at the San Diego Zoo is _____.
c. The Menswear Department at **Bloomingdale's,** which is responsible for buying and selling merchandise, is _____.
d. A production line at a **Palm Pilot** plant is _____.
e. _____ is any segment of the business whose manager is accountable for specific activities.
f. Gatorade, a division of **Quaker Oats** is _____.
g. The sales manager in charge of **NIKE's** northwest sales territory oversees _____.
h. Managers of cost and revenue centers are at _____ levels of the organization than are managers of profit and investment centers.

DE23-15 In Exhibit 23-18, the first line of the district manager's report and the first line of the branch manager's report consist entirely of expenses. Describe the kinds of expenses that would be included in these categories. Explain why the store manager's report at the bottom of Exhibit 23-18 does not have a similar expense line item.

Distinguishing among responsibility centers, analyzing a performance report (Obj. 5, 6)

DE23-16 Examine the performance report in Exhibit 23-18. On which variances should the Beale store manager focus his efforts next month, according to the management by exception principle? For these variances, compute the variance as a percent of the budgeted amount, and suggest some questions that the Beale store manager may want to investigate.

Analyzing a performance report, management by exception (Obj. 6)

DE23-17 Exhibit 23-18 shows that the Beale store had a favorable food expense variance. Does this favorable variance necessarily mean that the Beale store manager is doing a good job? Explain.

DE23-18 Listed below are several cost drivers.

Number of loads of materials moved	Number of customer complaints	Number of pages
Number of purchase orders	Number of inches	Number of square feet
Number of shipments received	Number of machine hours	Number of employees

Which of these is most likely the driver for the following costs?

a. Photocopying Department costs   **f.** Material handling costs
b. Maintenance Department costs   **g.** Personnel Department costs
c. Receiving Department costs   **h.** Building rent and utilities
d. Customer Service Department costs   **i.** Newspaper advertising costs
e. Purchasing Department costs

DE23-19 Consider the WorldPC example on page 952. Suppose the Hardware Department occupies 15,000 square feet and the Software Department occupies 5,000 square feet. How would the $600,000 rent expense be allocated?

DE23-20 ← *Link Back to Chapter 20 (uses of product cost information).* Study the summary review problem on pages 954–955. Why might the general manager of the new **Ritz-Carlton** hotel in St. Thomas want to know the cost per occupied room for the Club Accommodations and the Regular Accommodations?

EXERCISES

E23-1 John Smith owns a store that sells athletic shoes. Last year, his sales staff sold 10,000 pairs of shoes at an average sale price of $65. Variable expenses were 80% of sales revenue, and the total fixed expense was $100,000. This year the store sold more expensive product lines. Sales were 8,000 pairs at an average price of $90. The variable expense percentage and the total fixed expense were the same both years. Smith evaluates the store manager by comparing this year's income with last year's income.

Prepare a performance report for this year, similar to Exhibit 23-3. How would you improve Smith's performance evaluation system to better analyze this year's results?

Budgeting purchases, cost of
goods sold, and inventory
(Obj. 2)

E23-2 i-Tote is an e-tailer of womens' accessories. Their sales budget for the nine months ended September 30 follows:

	Quarter Ended			
	March 31	June 30	Sep. 30	Nine-Month Total
Cash sales, 30%..................	$ 30,000	$ 45,000	$ 37,500	$112,500
Credit sales, 70%................	70,000	105,000	87,500	262,500
Total sales, 100%................	$100,000	$150,000	$125,000	$375,000

In the past, cost of goods sold has been 70% of total sales. The director of marketing and the financial vice president agree that each quarter's ending inventory should not be below $20,000 plus 10% of cost of goods sold for the following quarter. Thomas expects sales of $110,000 during the fourth quarter. The January 1 inventory was $22,000.

Prepare a purchases, cost of goods sold, and inventory budget for each of the first three quarters of the year. Compute cost of goods sold for the entire nine-month period. (Use Exhibit 23-8 as a model.)

Budgeting quarterly income
for a year
(Obj. 2)

E23-3 Suresale is a real-estate firm. Suppose that its San Francisco office projects that 20X4 quarterly sales will increase by 4% in quarter 1, by 3% in quarter 2, by 5% in quarter 3, and by 6% in quarter 4. Management expects operating expenses to be 85% of revenues during each of the first two quarters, 79% of revenues during the third quarter, and 81% during the fourth. The office manager expects to borrow $100,000 on July 1, with quarterly principal payments of $10,000 beginning on September 30 and interest paid at an annual rate of 17%. Assume that fourth-quarter 20X3 sales were $3,000,000.

Prepare a budgeted income statement for each of the four quarters of 20X4 and for the entire year. Present the 20X4 budget as follows:

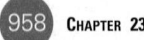

E23-4 Scents Unlimited is a distributor of fragrances. For each of items a through c, compute the amount of cash receipts or payments Scents will budget for September. The solution to one item may depend on the answer to an earlier item.

Computing cash receipts and payments
(Obj. 3)

a. Management expects to sell equipment that cost $12,000 at a gain of $2,000. Accumulated depreciation on this equipment is $7,000.

b. Management expects to sell 7,500 bottles in August and 8,400 in September. Each bottle sells for $16. Cash sales average 30% of total sales, and credit sales make up the rest. Three-fourths of credit sales are collected in the month of sale, with the balance collected the following month.

c. The company pays rent and property taxes of $3,500 each month. Commissions and other selling expenses average 25% of sales. Scents pays two-thirds of commissions and other selling expenses in the month incurred, with the balance paid in the following month.

E23-5 Harrison Woods, a family-owned gardening store, began October with $7,500 cash. Management forecasts that collections from credit customers will be $9,500 in October and $13,000 in November. The store is scheduled to receive $6,000 cash on a business note receivable in October. Projected cash payments include inventory purchases ($11,000 in October and $14,100 in November) and operating expenses ($3,000 each month).

Preparing a cash budget; sensitivity analysis
(Obj. 3, 4)

Harrison's bank requires a $6,500 minimum balance in the store's checking account. At the end of any month when the account balance dips below $6,500, the bank automatically extends credit to the store in multiples of $1,000. Harrison's borrows as little as possible and pays back these loans in quarterly installments of $2,000, plus 4.5% interest on the entire unpaid principal. The first payment occurs three months after the loan.

Required

1. Prepare the store's cash budget for October and November.
2. How much cash will Harrison's borrow in November if collections from customers that month total $9,300 instead of $13,000?

E23-6 Use the following information to prepare a budgeted balance sheet for Cinderella's Closet at March 31, 20X2. Show computations for the cash and owners' equity amounts.

Preparing a budgeted balance sheet
(Obj. 3)

a. March 31 inventory balance, $14,000
b. March payments for inventory, $5,900
c. March payments of accounts payable and accrued liabilities, $8,200
d. March 31 accounts payable balance, $4,900
e. February 28 furniture and fixtures balance, $34,800; accumulated depreciation balance, $26,400
f. February 28 owner's equity, $25,100

g. March depreciation expense, $600
h. Cost of goods sold, 50% of sales
i. Other March expenses, including income tax, total $5,000; paid in cash
j. February 28 cash balance, $10,300
k. March budgeted sales, $11,600
l. March 31 accounts receivable balance, one-fourth of March sales
m. March cash receipts, $14,300

E23-7 Identify each responsibility center as a cost center, a revenue center, a profit center, or an investment center.

Identifying different types of responsibility centers
(Obj. 5)

a. The bakery department of a **Kroger** supermarket reports income for the current year.
b. **Netscape Communication** is a subsidiary of **America Online, Inc.**
c. A personnel department of **State Farm Insurance Companies** prepares its budget and subsequent performance report on the basis of its expected expenses for the year.
d. The shopping section of **Garden.com** reports both revenues and expenses.
e. **Garden.com's** investor relations Web site provides operating and financial information to investors and other interested parties.
f. The manager of a **BP** service station is evaluated based on the station's revenues and expenses.
g. A charter airline records revenues and expenses for each airplane each month. The airplane's performance report shows its ratio of operating income to average book value.
h. The manager of the southwest sales territory is evaluated based on a comparison of current period sales against budgeted sales.

E23-8 D*Books.com is a New York company that sells discount books on the Web. D*Books.com has assistant managers for its adult-fiction and adult-nonfiction operations. These assistant managers report to the manager of adult books, who with the manager of children's books reports to the manager for all book sales, Beth Beverly. Beverly received the following data for November operations:

Using responsibility accounting to evaluate profit centers
(Obj. 6)

	Adult		
	Nonfiction	Fiction	Children's
Revenues, budget..............	$102,000	$600,000	$1,200,000
Expenses, budget	74,000	390,000	775,000
Revenues, actual...............	107,000	630,000	1,000,000
Expenses, actual...............	65,000	400,000	690,000

Arrange the data in a performance report similar to Exhibit 23-18. Show November results, in thousands of dollars, for adult-nonfiction, adult, and books as a whole. Should Beverly investigate the performance of adult-nonfiction operations?

Allocating indirect expenses to departments
(Obj. 7)

E23-9 Johnston Fabricating incurred the following indirect costs in April:

Indirect labor expense...............................	$16,000
Equipment depreciation expense..............	22,500
Marketing expense....................................	24,000

Data for cost allocations:

	Department		
	Priming	Welding	Custom Orders
Sales revenue.........................	$70,000	$50,000	$80,000
Indirect labor hours	400	500	100
Machine hours.......................	300	450	150
Building square feet..............	9,000	3,000	1,500
Marketing expense—allocated to departments in proportion to sales.			

Required

1. Allocate Johnston Fabricating's April indirect expenses to the three departments.
2. Compute total indirect expenses for each department.

Preparing a departmental income
statement
(Obj. 7)

E23-10 Hold-It.com is an e-tailer of cedar and plastic storage containers. It has two divisions: Cedar and Plastic. The company's income statement for 20X3 appears as follows:

Sales revenue......................................	$325,000
Cost of goods sold.............................	116,000
Gross profit	209,000
Operating expenses:	
Salaries expense............................	$ 78,000
Depreciation expense....................	20,000
Advertising expense......................	4,000
Other expenses	10,000
Total operating expenses..............	112,000
Operating income	$ 97,000

Hold-It.com sales are $136,000 of cedar storage containers and $189,000 of plastic containers. Cost of goods sold is distributed $42,000 to Cedar and $74,000 to Plastic. Salaries are traced directly to departments: Cedar $36,000, and Plastic $42,000. The Cedar Department accounts for 80% of advertising. Depreciation is allocated based on the warehouse square footage occupied by each department: Cedar has 20,000 square feet and Plastic has 30,000 square feet. Other expenses are allocated based on the number of employees. Each department currently employs an equal number of employees.

Required

1. Prepare departmental income statements that show revenues, expenses, and operating income for each of the two departments.
2. Which of the expenses in the departmental performance report are the most important for evaluating Hold-It.com department managers? Give your reason.

Challenge Exercise

E23-11 You recently began a job as an accounting intern at Trailblazers Ltd. Your first task was to help prepare the cash budget for February and March. Unfortunately, the computer with the budget file crashed, and you did not have a backup or even a hard copy. You ran a program to salvage bits of data from the budget file. After entering the following data in the budget, you may have just enough information to reconstruct the budget.

Preparing a cash budget (Obj. 3)

Trailblazers eliminates any cash deficiency by borrowing the exact amount needed from Second State Bank, where the current interest rate is 12%. Trailblazers repays all borrowed amounts at the end of the month, as cash becomes available.

Complete the following cash budget:

TRAILBLAZERS LTD.
Cash Budget
February and March

	February	March
Beginning cash balance	$10,900	$?
Cash collections	?	74,800
Cash from sale of plant assets	0	1,800
Cash available	90,900	?
Cash payments:		
Purchase of inventory	$?	$41,000
Operating expenses	31,900	?
Total payments	82,500	?
(1) Ending cash balance before financing	?	19,500
Minimum cash balance desired	15,000	15,000
Cash excess (deficiency)	$?	$?
Financing of cash deficiency:		
Borrowing (at end of month)	$?	$?
Principal repayments (at end of month)	?	?
Interest expense	?	?
(2) Total effects of financing	?	?
Ending cash balance (1) + (2)	$?	$?

PROBLEMS

(Group A)

P23-1A Representatives of the various departments of Software Direct have assembled the following data. As the business manager, you must prepare the budgeted income statements for August and September 20X3.

Budgeting income for two months (Obj. 2)

a. Sales in July were $184,000. You forecast that monthly sales will increase 2% in August and 2% in September.

b. Software Direct tries to maintain inventory of $50,000 plus 20% of sales budgeted for the following month. Monthly purchases average 60% of sales. Actual inventory on July 31 is $80,000. Sales budgeted for October are $198,000.

c. Monthly salaries amount to $15,000. Sales commissions equal 6% of sales. Combine salaries and commissions into a single figure.

d. Other monthly expenses are

Rent expense	$14,000, paid as incurred
Depreciation expense	$ 3,000
Insurance expense	$ 1,000, expiration of prepaid amount
Income tax	30% of operating income

Prepare Software Direct's budgeted income statements for August and September. Show cost-of-goods sold computations. Round *all* amounts to the nearest $1,000. For example, budgeted August sales are $188,000 ($184,000 × 1.02) and September sales are $192,000 ($188,000 × 1.02).

THE MASTER BUDGET AND
RESPONSIBILITY ACCOUNTING
961

P23-2A Refer to Problem 23-1A. Software Direct's sales are 50% cash and 50% credit. Credit sales are collected in the month after sale. Inventory purchases are paid 70% in the month of purchase and 30% the following month. Salaries and sales commissions are paid three-fourths in the month earned and one-fourth the next month. Income tax is paid at the end of the year.

The July 31, 20X3 balance sheet showed the following balances:

Cash	$20,000
Accounts payable	48,000
Salaries and commissions payable	13,500

Required

1. Prepare schedules of (a) budgeted cash collections from customers, (b) budgeted cash payments for purchases, and (c) budgeted cash payments for operating expenses. Show amounts for each month and totals for August and September. Carry your computations to the *nearest dollar*.
2. Prepare a cash budget similar to Exhibit 23-13. If no financing activity took place, what is the budgeted cash balance on September 30, 20X3?

P23-3A The Book Closet has applied for a loan. Westside Bank has requested a budgeted balance sheet at June 30, 20X5, and a budgeted statement of cash flows for June. As the controller (chief accounting officer) of The Book Closet, you have assembled the following information:

a. May 31 equipment balance, $60,600; accumulated depreciation, $11,700.
b. June capital expenditures of $15,800 budgeted for cash purchase of equipment.
c. June depreciation expense, $400.
d. Cost of goods sold, 50% of sales.
e. Other June operating expenses, including income tax, total $46,000, 75% of which will be paid in cash and the remainder accrued at June 30.
f. May 31 owners' equity, $104,800.
g. May 31 cash balance, $40,900.
h. June budgeted sales, $85,000, 30% of which is for cash. Of the remaining 70%, half will be collected in June and half in July.
i. June cash collections on May sales, $15,300.
j. June cash payments of liabilities for May inventory purchases on credit, $10,700.
k. May 31 inventory balance, $10,400.
l. June purchases of inventory, $11,000 for cash and $30,600 on credit. Half the credit purchases will be paid in June and half in July.

Required

1. Prepare the budgeted balance sheet for The Book Closet at June 30, 20X5. Show separate computations for cash, inventory, and owners' equity balances.
2. Prepare the budgeted statement of cash flows for June.
3. On the basis of this data, if you were a Westside Bank loan officer, would you grant The Book Closet a loan? Give your reason.

P23-4A Refer to Problem 23-3A. Before granting a loan to The Book Closet, Westside Bank asks for a sensitivity analysis assuming that June sales are only $65,000 rather than the $85,000 originally budgeted. (While cost of goods sold will change, assume that purchases, depreciation, and the other operating expenses will remain the same as in Problem 23-3A.)

Required

1. Prepare a revised budgeted balance sheet for The Book Closet, showing separate computations for cash, inventory, and owners' equity balances.
2. Suppose The Book Closet has a minimum desired cash balance of $15,000. Will the company borrow cash in June?
3. How would this sensitivity analysis affect Westside's loan decision?

P23-5A Is each of the following most likely a cost center, a revenue center, a profit center, or an investment center?

a. Personnel Department of **E* Trade**, the on-line broker
b. Quality Control Department of **Mayfield Dairies**
c. European subsidiary of **Coca-Cola**
d. Payroll Department of the **University of Wisconsin**
e. Lighting Department in a **Sears** store
f. Children's nursery in a church or synagogue
g. Purchasing Department of **Milliken**, a textile manufacturer
h. **Bluefly.com,** an e-tailer of womenswear

i. Service Department of an automobile dealership
j. Customer Service Department of **Procter & Gamble Co.**
k. Proposed new office of **Deutsche Bank**
l. Southwest region of **Pizza Inns, Inc.**
m. **Delta Air Lines, Inc.**
n. Order-Taking Department at **Lands' End** mail order company
o. Editorial Department of the **Wall Street Journal**

p. A **Ford Motor Company** production plant
q. Police Department of Boston
r. **Century 21 Real Estate Co.**
s. A small pet grooming business
t. Northeast sales territory for **Boise-Cascade**
u. Different product lines of **Broyhill,** a furniture manufacturer
v. **McDonald's** restaurants under the supervision of a regional manager
w. Job superintendents of a home builder

P23-6A Audio and Video is a chain of home electronics stores. Each store has a manager who answers to a city manager, who in turn reports to a statewide manager. The actual income statements of Store No. 13, all stores in the Topeka area (including Store No. 13), and all stores in the state of Kansas (including all Topeka stores) are summarized as follows for April:

Preparing a profit-center performance report for management by exception; benefits of budgeting (Obj. 1, 6)

	Store No. 13	Topeka	State of Kansas
Sales revenue	$39,800	$486,000	$3,264,500
Expenses:			
City/state manager's office expenses	$ —	$ 16,000	$ 44,000
Cost of goods sold	13,000	171,300	1,256,800
Salary expense	5,000	37,500	409,700
Depreciation expense	3,000	26,100	320,000
Utilities expense	2,700	19,300	245,600
Rent expense	1,600	16,400	186,000
Total expenses	25,300	286,600	2,462,100
Operating income	$14,500	$199,400	$ 802,400

Budgeted amounts for April were as follows:

	Store No. 13	Topeka	State of Kansas
Sales revenue	$42,000	$470,000	$3,145,000
Expenses:			
City/state manager's office expenses	$ —	$ 17,000	$ 43,000
Cost of goods sold	14,200	172,800	1,209,000
Salary expense	5,600	37,900	412,000
Depreciation expense	3,500	25,400	320,000
Utilities expense	2,100	17,000	240,000
Rent expense	1,600	15,700	181,000
Total expenses	27,000	285,800	2,405,000
Operating income	$15,000	$184,200	$ 740,000

Required

1. Prepare a report for April that shows the performance of Store No. 13, all the stores in the Topeka area, and all the stores in the state of Kansas. Follow the format of Exhibit 23-18.
2. As the city manager of Topeka, would you investigate Store No. 13 on the basis of this report? Why or why not?
3. Briefly discuss the benefits of budgeting. Base your discussion on Audio and Video's performance report.

P23-7A The Printed Page has both a Printing and a Copy Services Department. At May 31, the end of the fiscal year, the bookkeeper prepared the adjusted trial balance on page 964.

The Printed Page owns its printing equipment and leases a high-speed copier from **Xerox.** The Printed Page performs print jobs on a credit basis for established customers, but copy services are cash only. The store manager spends 60% of her time on Printing Services and 40% on Copy Services. The bookkeeper spends approximately two-thirds of

Allocating indirect costs; departmental income statements (Obj. 7)

Cash	$ 2,400	
Accounts receivable	3,300	
Prepaid expenses	1,100	
Building and office furniture	84,900	
Accumulated depreciation—building and furniture		$ 26,300
Other assets	4,700	
Accounts payable		3,200
Unearned service revenue		2,200
Owners' equity		24,800
Printing service revenue		68,750
Copy service revenue		56,250
Salary expense—machine operators	23,600	
Salary expense—store manager	22,900	
Salary expense—bookkeeper	18,300	
Lease expense—copy equipment	12,000	
Property tax expense	2,800	
Depreciation expense—building	2,000	
Depreciation expense—printing equipment	1,300	
Insurance expense	1,600	
Bad debt expense	600	
	$181,500	$181,500

his time on accounts receivable and other Printing Department transactions, and the remainder on Copy Services transactions. Insurance expense is evenly divided between the two departments. The company allocates all other expenses based on relative service revenue.

Required

1. Prepare departmental income statements.
2. Which department is more profitable? What factor contributes most to the profit differences between the two departments?

(Group B) PROBLEMS

Budgeting income for two months
(Obj. 2)

P23-1B The budget committee of Morton Restaurant Supply Co. has assembled the following data. As the business manager, you must prepare the budgeted income statements for May and June 20X2.

a. Sales in April were $31,300. You forecast that monthly sales will increase 2.4% in May and 2.4% in June.
b. Morton maintains inventory of $9,000 plus 25% of sales budgeted for the following month. Monthly purchases average 55% of sales. Actual inventory on April 30 is $14,000. Sales budgeted for July are $42,400.
c. Monthly salaries amount to $4,000. Sales commissions equal 4% of sales. Combine salaries and commissions into a single figure.
d. Other monthly expenses are

Rent expense	$3,200, paid as incurred
Depreciation expense	$ 500
Insurance expense	$ 200, expiration of prepaid amount
Income tax	20% of operating income

Prepare Morton's budgeted income statements for May and June. Show cost-of-goods-sold computations. Round *all* amounts to the nearest $100. For example, budgeted May sales are $32,100 ($31,300 × 1.024), and June sales are $32,900 ($32,100 × 1.024).

Budgeting cash receipts and payments (Obj. 3)

P23-2B Refer to Problem 23-1B. Morton's sales are 70% cash and 30% credit. Credit sales are collected in the month after sale. Inventory purchases are paid 60% in the month of purchase and 40% the following month. Salaries and sales commissions are paid half in the month earned and half the next month. Income tax is paid at the end of the year.
The April 30, 20X2 balance sheet showed the following balances:

Cash	$10,000
Accounts payable	6,200
Salary and commissions payable..............	2,800

Required

1. Prepare schedules of (a) budgeted cash collections, (b) budgeted cash payments for purchases, and (c) budgeted cash payments for operating expenses. Show amounts for each month and totals for May and June. Carry your computations to the nearest dollar.
2. Prepare a cash budget similar to Exhibit 23-13. If no financing activity took place, what is the budgeted cash balance on June 30, 20X2?

P23-3B Frank's Used Cars of Asheville, North Carolina, has applied for a loan. Bank of America has requested a budgeted balance sheet at April 30, 20X4, and a budgeted statement of cash flows for April. As the controller (chief accounting officer) of Frank's Used Cars, you have assembled the following information:

Preparing a budgeted balance sheet and budgeted statement of cash flows
(Obj. 3)

a. March 31 equipment balance, $42,500; accumulated depreciation, $31,400.
b. April capital expenditures of $41,700 budgeted for cash purchase of equipment.
c. April depreciation expense, $900.
d. Cost of goods sold, 60% of sales.
e. Other April operating expenses, including income tax, total $13,200, 25% of which will be paid in cash and the remainder accrued at April 30.
f. March 31 owners' equity, $87,000.
g. March 31 cash balance, $36,200.
h. April budgeted sales, $90,000, 60% of

which is for cash. Of the remaining 40%, half will be collected in April and half in May.
i. April cash collections on March sales, $29,700.
j. April cash payments of March 31 liabilities incurred for March purchases of inventory, $17,300.
k. March 31 inventory balance, $27,300.
l. April purchases of inventory, $9,000 for cash and $36,800 on credit. Half of the credit purchases will be paid in April and half in May.

Required

1. Prepare the budgeted balance sheet for Frank's Used Cars at April 30, 20X4. Show separate computations for cash, inventory, and owners' equity balances.
2. Prepare the budgeted statement of cash flows for April.
3. Suppose that Frank's Used Cars has become aware of more efficient (and more expensive) equipment than it budgeted for purchase in April. What is the total amount of cash available for equipment purchases in April, before financing, if the minimum desired ending cash balance is $21,000? (For this requirement, disregard the $41,700 initially budgeted for equipment purchases.)

P23-4B Refer to Problem 23-3B. Before granting a loan to Frank's Used Cars, Bank of America asks for a sensitivity analysis assuming April sales are only $60,000 rather than the $90,000 originally budgeted. (While the cost of goods sold will change, assume that purchases, depreciation, and the other operating expenses will remain the same as in Problem 23-3B.)

Preparing a budgeted balance sheet; sensitivity analysis
(Obj. 3, 4)

Required

1. Prepare a revised budgeted balance sheet for Frank's Used Cars, showing separate computations for cash, inventory, and owners' equity balances.
2. Suppose Frank's has a minimum desired cash balance of $23,000. Will the company need to borrow cash in April?
3. In this sensitivity analysis, sales declined by $33\frac{1}{3}\%$ ($30,000 ÷ $90,000). Is the decline in expenses and income more or less than $33\frac{1}{3}\%$? Explain why.

P23-5B Is each of the following most likely a cost center, a revenue center, a profit center, or an investment center?

Identifying different types of responsibility centers
(Obj. 5)

a. Shipping department of **Amazon.com**
b. Eastern district of a salesperson's territory
c. Music director of a church or synagogue
d. Catering operation of Sonny's BBQ restaurant
e. Executive director of a **United Way** agency
f. Accounts payable section of the Accounting Department at **Home Depot**
g. Proposed new office of **Coldwell Banker,** a real-estate firm
h. **Disneyland**
i. The Empire State Building in New York City
j. Branch warehouse of **Dalton Carpets**
k. Information systems director for **Habitat for Humanity**
l. Service Department of Audio Forest stereo shop
m. Investments Department of **Citibank**
n. Assembly-line supervisors at **Dell Computer**
o. American subsidiary of a Japanese manufacturer

p. Surgery unit of a privately owned hospital
q. Research and Development Department of **Cisco Systems**
r. Childrenswear department at a **Target** store
s. Typesetting Department of Northend Press, a printing company
t. Prescription Filling Department of **Drugstore.com**
u. Order-Taking Department at **L.L. Bean**
v. Personnel Department of **Goodyear Tire and Rubber Company**
w. Grounds crew at Augusta National golf course

Preparing a profit-center performance report for management by exception; benefits of budgeting (Obj. 1, 6)

P23-6B Home-Aid is a charitable organization, recently established in the Midwest, that builds low-income housing. The manager of each city's Home-Aid office reports to the state's director, who in turn reports to headquarters in Milwaukee, Wisconsin. The *actual* income statements for the Cincinnati office, the Ohio region (including the Cincinnati office) and the organization as a whole (including the Ohio region) for July 20X3 are

	Cincinnati	Ohio	Organizationwide
Revenue	$148,900	$1,647,000	$4,200,000
Expenses:			
State director/			
headquarters office	$ —	$ 60,000	$ 116,000
Cost of materials	81,100	871,900	1,807,000
Salary expense	38,100	415,500	1,119,000
Depreciation expense	7,200	91,000	435,000
Utilities expense	4,200	46,200	260,000
Rent expense	2,400	34,700	178,000
Total expenses	133,000	1,519,300	3,915,000
Operating income	$ 15,900	$ 127,700	$ 285,000

Budgeted amounts for July were as follows:

	Cincinnati	Ohio	Organizationwide
Revenue	$162,400	$1,769,700	$4,450,000
Expenses:			
State director/			
headquarters office	$ —	$ 65,600	$ 118,000
Cost of materials	85,500	963,400	1,972,000
Salary expense	38,800	442,000	1,095,000
Depreciation expense	7,200	87,800	449,000
Utilities expense	4,700	54,400	271,000
Rent expense	2,800	32,300	174,000
Total expenses	139,000	1,645,500	4,079,000
Operating income	$ 23,400	$ 124,200	$ 371,000

Required

1. Prepare a report for July 20X3 that shows the performance of the Cincinnati office, the Ohio region, and the organization as a whole. Follow the format of Exhibit 23-18.
2. As the director of the Ohio region manager, would you investigate the Cincinnati office on the basis of this report? Why or why not?
3. Briefly discuss the benefits of budgeting. Base your discussion on Home-Aid's performance report.

Allocating indirect costs; departmental income statements (Obj. 7)

P23-7B World Travel.com is an Internet-based travel agency. The company has a Custom Travel Department and a Group Discount Travel Department. At August 31, the end of World-Travel's fiscal year, the bookkeeper prepared the adjusted trial balance at the top of the next page.

Last September, World Travel hired a specialist in group discount travel at an annual salary of $27,000. Remaining agent salaries of $12,500 are for part-time agents who handle custom travel plans. The office manager spends 70% of her time on group discount plans and 30% on custom travel planning. The bookkeeper spends approximately two-thirds of his time on accounting for custom travel and the remainder on group discount plans. About 80% of the time spent developing and maintaining the Web site is for custom travel, and the remaining 20% is for group discount packages. Insurance expense is evenly divided between the two departments. The company allocates commissions and all other expenses based on relative service revenue.

Cash	$ 2,400	
Receivables	29,700	
Prepaid expenses	1,700	
Building and office furniture	115,600	
Accumulated depreciation—building and furniture		$ 28,200
Other assets	5,300	
Accounts payable		11,400
Accrued liabilities		6,900
Unearned service revenue		5,800
Owners' equity		19,200
Custom travel service revenue		88,000
Group discount travel service revenue		132,000
Salary expense—travel agents	39,500	
Commission expense—travel agents	30,800	
Salary expense—office manager	25,000	
Salary expense—bookkeeper	16,800	
Web site maintenance expense	15,000	
Property tax expense	2,200	
Depreciation expense—building and furniture	4,600	
Insurance expense	1,700	
Web advertising expense	1,200	
	$291,500	$291,500

Required

1. Prepare departmental income statements.
2. Which department is more profitable? Was the decision to hire the group specialist wise? Give your reason.

APPLY YOUR KNOWLEDGE

DECISION CASES

Case 1. Liquid Sky designs, manufactures, and sells wakeboards through water-sports specialty stores and sports superstores. In 20X5, Liquid Sky incurred the following costs that are directly traceable to its Blowout product line:

Allocating indirect costs (Obj. 7)

Production—Molding (direct materials and direct labor)	$288,000
Production—Graphics (direct materials and direct labor)	430,000
Advertising for Blowout	100,000

In addition to these direct costs, Liquid Sky also incurred other costs that cannot be traced directly to individual product lines. These indirect costs are allocated to the different product lines. For 20X5, Liquid Sky reports the following information about its indirect costs:

	Total Indirect Costs	Allocation Base for Indirect Costs	Total Quantity of Allocation Base
Product design	$ 180,000	New designs	3 new designs
Production— Molding	1,200,000	Machine hours	6,000 machine hours
Production— Graphics	1,800,000	Labor hours	18,000 labor hours
Distribution	300,000	Shipments	1,000 shipments

(continued)

During 20X5, the whole Blowout product line required a total of one new product design, 1,000 machine hours, 3,500 labor hours, and 140 shipments. There were no beginning inventories of any kind.

Required

➡ To review *inventoriable product costs*, see Chapter 19, page 761.

1. Compute an indirect cost allocation rate for each of the four indirect costs.
2. Use the indirect cost allocation rates from requirement 1 to compute the *total costs* for the Blowout wakeboard product line, including all direct and indirect costs. Assuming Liquid Sky produced 7,000 Blowout wakeboards, what is the total cost per wakeboard?
3. ◀ At the end of 20X5, Liquid Sky's ending inventory consists solely of 600 Blowout wakeboards. What inventory value would appear on Liquid Sky's December 31, 20X5 balance sheet? (*Hint:* Round your inventoriable cost per unit to the nearest penny.)
4. A snow ski manufacturer has asked Liquid Sky to produce snowboards, which the ski manufacturer would sell under its own name. Suppose Liquid Sky decides to produce the snowboards for the snow ski manufacturer on a cost-plus-fixed-fee basis. (That is, the sale price is Liquid Sky's cost to make the snowboards plus a fixed fee of $50,000.) The rest of Liquid Sky's business is at fixed sale prices—for example, $300 for Blowout wakeboards. What cost allocation incentives would this give Liquid Sky's managers? When there are difficult allocation decisions, will Liquid Sky be tempted to allocate a bigger or smaller share of indirect costs to the snowboards? Why?
5. Liquid Sky's top management knows that the sale price of Blowout wakeboards may change over the product's life. But management wishes to identify a target sale price Liquid Sky should receive on average over the life of the product. Which of Liquid Sky's costs are relevant in setting the long-run average sale price for Blowout wakeboards? Give your reason.

Using a budgeted income statement (Obj. 1)

Case 2. Renee Willis has recently accepted the position of assistant manager at Jack and Jill, a children's clothing store in St. Louis. She has just finished her accounting courses. Jack and Jill's manager and owner, Kristy Simms, asks Renee to prepare a budgeted income statement for 20X6 based on the information she has collected. Willis' budget follows:

JACK AND JILL
Budgeted Income Statement
For the Year Ending July 31, 20X6

Sales revenue		$240,000
Cost of goods sold		172,000
Gross profit		68,000
Operating expenses:		
Salary and commission expense	$46,000	
Rent expense	8,000	
Depreciation expense	2,000	
Insurance expense	800	
Miscellaneous expenses	12,000	68,800
Operating loss		(800)
Interest expense		225
Net loss		$ (1,025)

Required

Willis does not want to give Simms this budget without making constructive suggestions for steps Simms could take to improve expected performance. Write a memo to Simms outlining your suggestions. Your memo should take the following form:

Date:	_____
To:	**Ms. Kristy Simms, Manager**
	Jack and Jill
From:	**Renee Willis**
Subject:	**Jack and Jill's 20X6 budgeted income statement**

ETHICAL ISSUE

← Link Back to Chapter 7, p. 290, for Ethics, Decision Guidelines box. Guest Suites operates a regional motel chain. Each motel is operated by a manager and an assistant manager/controller. Many of the staff who run the front desk, clean the rooms, and prepare the breakfast buffet work part-time or have a second job, so turnover is high.

Assistant manager/controller Carrie Pronai asked the new bookkeeper to help prepare the motel's master budget. The master budget is prepared once a year and submitted to company headquarters for approval. Once approved, the master budget is used to evaluate the motel's performance. These performance evaluations affect motel managers' bonuses and they also affect company decisions on which motels deserve extra funds for capital improvements.

When the budget was almost complete, Pronai asked the bookkeeper to increase amounts budgeted for labor and supplies by 15%. When asked why, Pronai responded that motel manager Clay Murry told her to do this when she began working at the motel. Murry explained that this budgetary cushion gave him flexibility in running the motel. For example, since company headquarters tightly controls capital improvement funds, Murry can use the extra money budgeted for labor and supplies to replace broken televisions or pay "bonuses" to keep valued employees. Pronai initially accepted this explanation because she had observed similar behavior at the motel where she worked previously.

Put yourself in Pronai's position. Use the ethical judgment decision guidelines in Chapter 7 (page 290) to decide how Pronai should deal with the situation.

Budget slack
(Obj. 2, 6)

FINANCIAL STATEMENT CASE

Budgets are an important management tool in a large company like **Target.** Refer to Target's annual report to answer the following questions:

1. When preparing the master budget, would Target budget approximately the same sales and profit amounts for each quarter? Explain. (*Hint:* Quarterly results appear on page 35 of the annual report.)
2. Target Corporation distinguishes among three segments: (1) Target, (2) Mervyn's, and (3) Department Stores. Are these segments cost centers, revenue centers, profit centers, or investment centers? Explain.
3. Calculate return on assets for the Target, Mervyn's, and Department Stores segments for 1999, 1998, and 1997. Use pretax segment profit in the numerator of the return on assets computation and average segment assets in the denominator. Carry your computations to four decimal places. (*Hint:* Business segment data are presented on page 37).
4. Target changed its name from Dayton Hudson Corporation to Target Corporation in 2000. Explain why the name change makes sense in terms of requirement 3's analysis.

Budgeting by quarter and segment, types of responsibility centers, performance evaluation
(Obj. 3, 5, 6)

TEAM PROJECT

Nova Solutions provides e-commerce software for the pharmaceuticals industry. Nova is organized into several divisions. A companywide planning committee sets general strategy and goals for the company and its divisions, but each division develops its own budget.

Rick Watson is the new division manager of Business-to-Business software. His division has two departments: Development and Sales. Patti McKeown manages the 20 or so programmers and systems specialists typically employed in Development to create and update the division's software applications. Liz Smith manages the sales department.

Nova considers the divisions to be investment centers. To earn his bonus next year, Watson must achieve a 30% return on the $3 million invested in his division. Within the Business-to-Business Division, Development is a cost center, while Sales is a revenue center.

Budgeting is in progress. Patti McKeown met with her staff and is now struggling with two sets of numbers. Alternative A is her best estimate of next year's costs. However,

Responsibility accounting, return on assets
(Obj. 5, 6)

NOVA SOLUTIONS Business-to-Business Division Development Budget 20XX	Alternative A	Alternative B
Salaries expense (including overtime and part-time)	$2,300,000	$2,530,000
Software expense..	120,000	132,000
Travel expense	65,000	71,500
Depreciation expense......................................	255,000	255,000
Miscellaneous expense	100,000	110,000
Total expense	$2,840,000	$3,098,500

unexpected problems can arise when writing software, and finding competent programmers is an ongoing challenge. She knows that Watson was a programmer before he earned an MBA, so he should be sensitive to this uncertainty. Consequently, she is thinking of adding another 10% to her budgeted costs (Alternative B). Her department's bonuses largely depend on whether the department meets its budgeted costs.

Liz Smith is also struggling with her sales budget. Companies have made their initial investments in business-to-business software, so it is harder to win new customers. If things go well, she believes her sales team can maintain the level of growth achieved over the last few years. This is Alternative A in the Sales Budget. However, if Smith is too optimistic, sales may fall short of the budget. If this happens, her team will not receive bonuses. Smith is therefore considering reducing the sales numbers and submitting Alternative B.

NOVA SOLUTIONS Business-to-Business Division Sales Budget 20XX		
	Alternative A	**Alternative B**
Sales revenue...................	$5,000,000	$4,500,000
Salaries expense	360,000	360,000
Travel expense.................	340,000	320,500

Split your team into three groups. Each group should meet separately before the entire team meets.

Required

1. The first group plays the role of development manager Patti McKeown. Before meeting with the entire team, determine which set of budget numbers you are going to present to Rick Watson. Write a memo supporting your decision. Use the format shown in Decision Case 2. Give this memo to the third group before the team meeting.
2. The second group plays the role of sales manager Liz Smith. Before meeting with the entire team, determine which set of budget numbers you are going to present to Rick Watson. Write a memo supporting your decision. Use the format shown in Decision Case 2. Give this memo to the third group before the team meeting.
3. The third group plays the role of division manager Rick Watson. Before meeting with the entire team, prepare a division budget based on the sales and development budgets submitted to you by McKeown and Smith. Your divisional overhead costs are approximately $390,000. Determine whether the Business-to-Business Division can meet its targeted 30% return on assets given the budgeted alternatives submitted by your department managers.

During the meeting of the entire team, the group playing Watson presents the division budget and considers its implications. Each group should take turns discussing its concerns with the proposed budget. The team as a whole should consider whether the division budget must be revised. The team should prepare a report that includes the division budget and a summary of the issues covered in the team meeting.

INTERNET EXERCISE

Starbucks

Starbucks Corporation is the number 1 specialty coffee retailer, operating more than 2,800 shops. The company also sells coffee beans to restaurants, businesses, airlines, and hotels, and offers mail order and on-line shopping.

1. Go to **http://www.Forbes.com** and under "Stocks" type SBUX, the stock symbol for Starbucks Corporation. Click on *Go*. In the left-hand column, click on *Company Info*, and scan the information provided. What one-year sales growth was reported?
2. In the left-hand column, click on *Financials*. For the most recent year identify or compute the amounts reported for total revenue, cost of goods sold, and operating expenses. Calculate operating income.
3. Is Cost of Sales a variable or fixed expense? Add the operating expenses (Store Operating Expenses, Other Operating Expenses, Depreciation, and General/Administrative Expenses) and assume that 40% of the total is fixed. Compute total variable operating expenses and total fixed operating expenses for the most recent year.

4. Consider each of the following *independent* situations regarding next year:

   a. Suppose Starbucks is anticipating a 9% increase in the number of transactions per store next year. Prepare the sales budget, cost of goods sold budget, and operating expense budget, and calculate budgeted operating income.

   b. Assume Starbucks is considering raising the price of beverages by 7 cents per cup because of a 10% increase in fixed operating costs. If the increase of 7 cents per cup increases revenues by 3%, will the increase in revenue cover the increase in costs?

   c. Suppose that due to opening new stores, Starbucks expects operating revenues to increase at the same rate as the one-year sales growth of last year. Prepare only the sales budget. Will fixed costs increase? Why or why not?

5. A Starbucks store is what type of responsibility center?

Go to the "Employee Performance Evaluation and Responsibility" episode on the *Mastering Accounting* CD-ROM for an interactive, video-enhanced exercise focused on how CanGo managers use income statements showing revenues for the whole organization and for individual subunits to assess the performance of individual product divisions.

24

Flexible Budgets and Standard Costs

LEARNING OBJECTIVES

After studying this chapter, you should be able to

1. Prepare a flexible budget for the income statement

2. Prepare an income statement performance report

3. Identify the benefits of standard costs

4. Compute standard cost variances for direct materials and direct labor

5. Analyze manufacturing overhead in a standard cost system

6. Record transactions at standard cost

7. Prepare a standard cost income statement for management

How does **McDonald's** ensure that its 26,000 restaurants deliver quality, service, cleanliness, and value to over 43 million customers worldwide each day? How do McDonald's managers use management accounting to earn a profit?

The answers are budgets, standards, and variances. McDonald's managers budget sales for each hour. The manager schedules just enough workers to handle the budgeted level of sales. During the day, the manager computes variances for sales (for example, actual sales minus budgeted sales) and for direct labor. These variances are computed *hourly*. If actual sales fall short of the budget, the manager quickly sees an unfavorable sales variance. If sales are less than budgeted, the manager can send employees home early. This helps control direct labor cost.

McDonald's also sets budgets and standards for direct materials. From Beijing to Miami, the standards for a regular McDonald's hamburger are the same: 1 bun, 1 hamburger patty, 1 pickle slice, 1/8 teaspoon dehydrated onion, 1/8 teaspoon mustard, and 1/3 ounce of ketchup. To control direct materials costs, the manager compares the number of, say, hamburger patties actually used with the number of patties that should have been used.

McDonald's uses budgets, standards, and variances to control costs so prices remain low enough that customers believe McDonald's provides good *value*. McDonald's also uses standards and variances to motivate employees to focus on *quality, service,* and *cleanliness:*

- Quality—sandwiches unsold within 10 minutes are thrown away.
- Service—customers should receive food within 90 seconds of beginning to order.
- Cleanliness—visiting inspectors score restaurants on cleanliness.

I n Chapter 23, we saw how managers use budgets to quantify their plans. Executives compare actual revenues and expenses with budgeted amounts to evaluate the performance of responsibility centers and managers. This chapter explores budgeting in greater depth. The first half of the chapter shows how flexible budgets and variances help managers learn *why* actual results differed from the plan. The second half of the chapter discusses standard costs, which companies like McDonald's use to build flexible budgets.

STATIC VERSUS FLEXIBLE BUDGETS

The master budget in Chapter 23 is a **static budget**—it is prepared for one level of sales volume. The static budget does not change after it is developed, regardless of changes in volume, sale prices, or costs.

Consider Kool-Time Pools, a company that installs residential swimming pools. Kool-Time buys direct materials—gunite (a concrete derivative). It then uses labor and equipment to convert the gunite into finished outputs—installed pools. Kool-Time's static master budget forecasts that the company will install eight pools in June. However, due to an early heat wave, Kool-Time actually installed ten pools.

The comparison of June's actual results with the static budget in Exhibit 24-1 shows that Kool-Time's actual operating income is $3,000 higher than originally expected. This is a $3,000 favorable difference, or variance, in Kool-Time's June operating income. A **variance** is the difference between an actual amount and the budget. The variances in the third column of Exhibit 24-1 are favorable (F) if a higher actual amount increases operating income and unfavorable (U) if a higher actual amount decreases operating income. The variance for the number of pools installed is favorable because higher volume (ten rather than eight pools) tends to increase income.

The report in Exhibit 24-1 is hard to analyze because the static budget is based on eight pools, but actual results are for ten pools. Why did the $21,000

Objective 1
Prepare a flexible budget for the income statement

STATIC BUDGET. The budget prepared for only one level of sales volume. Also called the **master budget.**

VARIANCE. The difference between an actual amount and the budget. A variance is labeled as favorable if it increases operating income and unfavorable if it decreases operating income.

EXHIBIT 24-1   Actual Results versus Static Budget

KOOL-TIME POOLS
Comparison of Actual Results with Static Budget
Month Ended June 30, 20X5

	Actual Results	Static Budget	Variance
Output units (pools installed)......	10	8	2 F
Sales revenue...............................	$120,000	$96,000	$24,000 F
Expenses	(105,000)	(84,000)	21,000 U
Operating income	$ 15,000	$12,000	$ 3,000 F

FLEXIBLE BUDGET. A summarized budget that can easily be computed for several different volume levels. Flexible budgets separate variable costs from fixed costs; it is the variable costs that put the "flex" in the flexible budget.

➡ Chapter 23, pp. 932–940, discusses the White-water budget process.

unfavorable expense variance occur? Did workers waste materials? Did the cost of gunite suddenly increase? How much of the additional expense arose because Kool-Time built ten rather than eight pools? Exhibit 24-1's simple comparison of actual results with the static budget does not give managers enough information to answer these questions.

Flexible budgets do help managers answer such questions. Exhibit 24-2 illustrates the difference between static and flexible budgets. Companies develop a static master budget—like the Whitewater Sporting Goods Store budget developed in Chapter 23—for a single level of sales volume. ◄ In contrast, **flexible budgets** are summarized budgets that can easily be computed for several different volume levels.

EXHIBIT 24-2   Static versus Flexible Budgets

Exhibit 24-3 uses flexible budgets to show how Kool-Time's revenues and expenses should vary as sales increase from five pools to eight pools to eleven pools. The budgeted sale price per pool is $12,000. The condensed flexible budget shows

EXHIBIT 24-3   Flexible Budget

   DAILY EXERCISE 24-2

KOOL-TIME POOLS
Flexible Budget
Month Ended June 30, 20X5

	Flexible Budget per Output Unit	Output Units (Pools Installed)		
		5	8	11
Sales revenue....................	$12,000	$60,000	$96,000	$132,000
Variable expenses..............	8,000	40,000	64,000	88,000
Fixed expenses*................		20,000	20,000	20,000
Total expenses...................		60,000	84,000	108,000
Operating income		$ 0	$12,000	$ 24,000

* Fixed expenses are given as a total amount rather than as a cost per unit.

two costs or expenses: variable and fixed. ➡ The *flexible budget formula for total cost* is:

See Chapter 22, page 887, to review the distinction between variable costs and fixed costs.

$$\text{Flexible budget total cost} = \left(\begin{array}{c} \text{Number of} \\ \text{output units} \end{array} \times \begin{array}{c} \text{Variable cost} \\ \text{per output unit} \end{array} \right) + \text{Total fixed cost}$$

Budgeted total variable costs (such as the cost of gunite and labor) increase at the rate of $8,000 per pool installed. It is these variable costs that put the "flex" in the flexible budget, because budgeted total monthly fixed costs (such as administrative salaries and depreciation on equipment) remain constant at $20,000 throughout the range of five to eleven pools. For example, Kool-Time's flexible budget cost for installing 11 pools is $108,000:

DAILY EXERCISE 24-1

$$
\begin{aligned}
\text{Flexible budget total cost} &= \left(\begin{array}{c} \text{Number of} \\ \text{output units} \end{array} \times \begin{array}{c} \text{Variable cost} \\ \text{per output unit} \end{array} \right) + \text{Total fixed cost} \\
&= \;\; (11 \text{ pools} \;\; \times \;\; \$8,000 \text{ per pool}) \;+\; \$20,000 \\
&= \;\; \$ \; 88,000 \qquad\qquad\qquad\qquad\qquad +\; \$20,000 \\
&= \;\; \$108,000
\end{aligned}
$$

Kool-Time's managers could prepare a more detailed flexible budget that lists individual variable and fixed costs separately. Each of the variable costs would increase with the number of pools installed, like the total variable costs in Exhibit 24-3, and each of the fixed costs would remain constant over the relevant range.

Managers develop flexible budgets like Exhibit 24-3 for any number of outputs, using a simple spreadsheet or more sophisticated Web-based budget management software. Kool-Time's flexible budget could include additional columns for seven, nine, or any other number of pools for which management wants to know budgeted sales revenues, costs, and profits.

However, managers must be wary: *The flexible budget total cost formula applies only to a specific relevant range.* Why? Because total monthly fixed costs and the variable cost per pool change outside this range. Kool-Time's relevant range is 0–11 pools. If the company installs 12 pools, it will have to rent additional equipment, so fixed costs will exceed $20,000. Kool-Time will also have to pay workers an overtime premium, so the variable cost per pool will be more than $8,000.

Managers prepare flexible budgets like those in Exhibit 24-3

- *Before* the period, or   • At the *end* of the period

Flexible budgets prepared *before* the period help managers *plan*. They can estimate revenues, costs, and profits, and plan for alternative levels of sales. Flexible budgets prepared at the *end* of the period help managers *control* operations. They can compare actual costs to the costs that *should have been* incurred for that level of output. For example, Kool-Time can compare the actual costs to install 10 pools with the budgeted costs (the costs that should have been incurred) to install 10 pools.

Graphing the Flexible Budget

Managers use flexible budget graphs to budget total costs at various output levels for both planning and control. Exhibit 24-4 shows budgeted total costs for the entire relevant range of 0–11 pools. The flexible budget total cost line in Exhibit 24-4 intersects the vertical axis at the amount of the total fixed cost ($20,000) Kool-Time will incur whether it installs 0 pools or 11 pools. ➡ The flexible budget's total cost line slopes upward at the rate of $8,000 per pool, which is Kool-Time's variable cost per pool. For example, the cost for one pool is $28,000 [(1 pool × $8,000 variable cost per pool) + $20,000 fixed cost]. But the *extra* cost of installing a second pool is only the additional $8,000 variable cost. The cost to install two pools is therefore $36,000 [(2 pools × $8,000 variable cost per pool) + $20,000 fixed cost].

Kool-Time's managers initially expected to install eight pools per month ($84,000). The graph also shows the flexible budget costs for 5 pools ($60,000) and

The flexible budget cost line in Exhibit 24-4 follows the same principles as the cost-volume-profit graph's total cost line in Exhibit 22-7, page 899.

EXHIBIT 24-4 Kool-Time Pools
Monthly Flexible Budget Graph

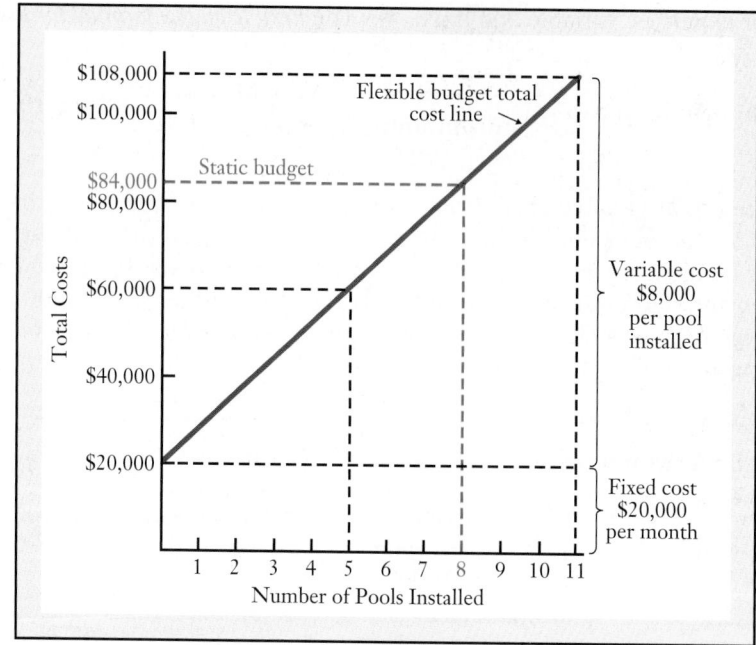

EXHIBIT 24-5 Kool-Time Pools
Graph of Actual and Budgeted
Monthly Costs

DAILY EXERCISE 24-3

DAILY EXERCISE 24-4

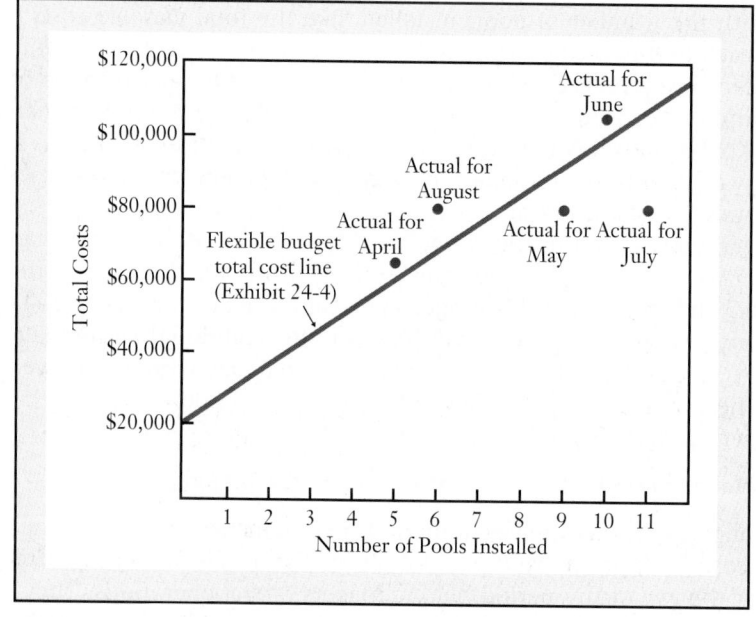

11 pools ($108,000). Managers can use the flexible budget graph in Exhibit 24-4 to plan costs for anywhere from 0 to 11 pools.

At the end of the period, managers can also use the flexible budget to help control costs. They plot actual costs on the graph, as shown in Exhibit 24-5. Consider June, when Kool-Time actually installed ten pools. The flexible budget graphs in Exhibits 24-4 and 24-5 show that *budgeted* total costs for ten pools are

Variable costs (10 × $8,000)	$ 80,000
Fixed costs	20,000
Total costs	$100,000

June's *actual* costs, or expenses, were $105,000 (Exhibit 24-1). Consequently, Exhibit 24-5 shows that June's actual costs for ten pools ($105,000) exceed the budget for ten pools ($100,000). Managers use graphs of actual versus budgeted costs to see at a glance whether actual costs are

- Higher than budgeted for the actual level of output, as in April, June, and August, or
- Lower than budgeted for the actual level of output, as in May and July

WORK IT OUT

Use the graph in Exhibit 24-5 and Kool-Time's flexible budget formula (page 975) to answer the following questions:
1. How many pools did Kool-Time install in July?
2. What were Kool-Time's actual costs in July?
3. Using Kool-Time's flexible budget formula, what is the flexible budget total cost for the month of July?
4. Is Kool-Time's variance for total costs favorable or unfavorable in July?

Answers

1. Exhibit 24-5 shows that Kool-Time installed 11 pools in July.
2. Exhibit 24-5 shows that Kool-Time's actual costs in July were about $80,000.
3. Using Kool-Time's flexible budget total cost formula:

Variable costs (11 × $8,000)..............	$ 88,000
Fixed costs	20,000
Total costs	$108,000

4. Kool-Time's July variance for total costs is $28,000 ($80,000 − $108,000) favorable, since actual costs are less than the budget.

The Flexible Budget and Variance Analysis

Objective 2
Prepare an income statement performance report

Managers also use flexible budgets at the *end* of the period to help explain why actual results differ from budgeted results.

Let's step back for a moment and consider managers' major planning and controlling activities:

1. Quantify the company's goals in a static master budget.
2. Take action to achieve the goals.
3. Analyze the variance between actual results and static budget amounts (the static budget variance).
4. Change actions (or plans) so that future results conform to the plan.

The flexible budget is an important tool in step 3. To analyze the variance (step 3), managers begin by asking

- How many units did we actually sell?
- How much sales revenue *should* we have received from selling this number of outputs?
- How much *should* this number of output units have cost us?

The *flexible budget for the number of units that were actually sold* helps answer the second and third questions. Of course, the number of units actually sold is not known until the end of the period. Why calculate a budget for a period that is already over? Because *the flexible budget for the number of units actually sold shows how much the company should have spent to obtain that level of output.*

Exhibit 24-6 shows how managers use this flexible budget for the number of units actually sold to divide the static budget variance into two broad categories:

- **Sales volume variance**—arises only because the number of units actually sold differs from the static budget sales.
- **Flexible budget variance**—arises because the company actually earned more or less revenue, or incurred more or less cost, than expected for the actual level of output.

Exhibit 24-6 shows that the sales volume variance is the difference between

1. The *static* (master) budget—for the number of units *expected* to be sold (8 pools, for Kool-Time), and
2. The *flexible* budget—for the number of units *actually* sold (10 pools in June)

SALES VOLUME VARIANCE. The difference arising only because the number of units actually sold differs from the static budget sales. This is computed as the difference between a static budget amount and a flexible budget amount.

FLEXIBLE BUDGET VARIANCE. The difference arising because the company actually earned more or less revenue, or incurred more or less cost, than expected for the actual level of output. This is computed as the difference between the actual amount and a flexible budget amount.

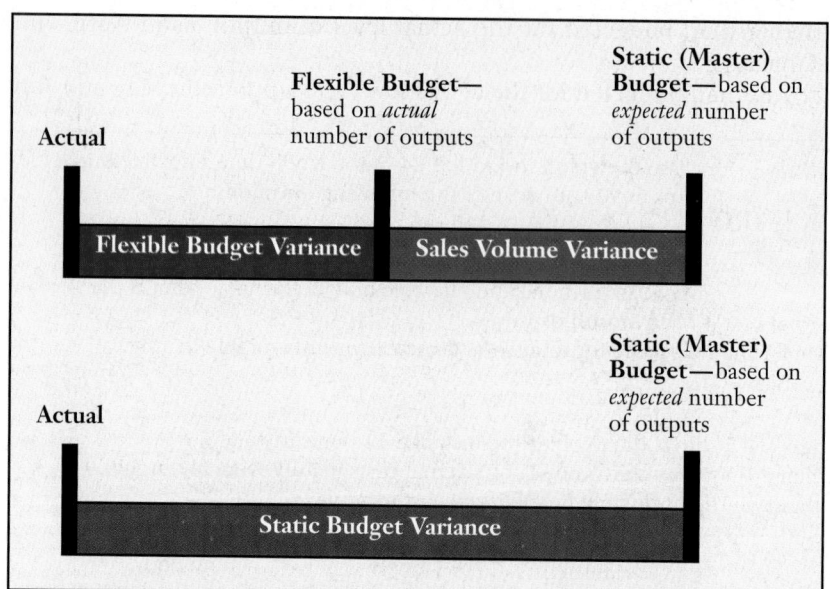

Consider Kool-Time Pool's performance report in Exhibit 24-7. The static budget amounts in column 5 are based on the static budget sales forecast developed at the *beginning* of the period—the eight pools Kool-Time *expected* to install. For these eight pools, Kool-Time's

DAILY EXERCISE 24-5

* Budgeted sales revenue is $96,000 (8 × $12,000).
* Budgeted variable expenses (costs) are $64,000 (8 × $8,000).
* Budgeted fixed expenses (costs) are $20,000.

DAILY EXERCISE 24-6

DAILY EXERCISE 24-7

In contrast to the static budget, which is developed *before* the period, the flexible budget used in the performance report is not developed until the *end* of the period. Why? Because *flexible budgets used in performance reports are based on the actual number of outputs, which is not known until the end of the period.* For Kool-Time, the flexible

EXHIBIT 24-7   Income Statement Performance Report

	(1) Actual Results at Actual Prices	(2) (1) − (3) Flexible Budget Variance	(3) Flexible Budget for Actual Number of Output Units*	(4) (3) − (5) Sales Volume Variance	(5) Static (Master) Budget*
Output units (pools installed)	10	−0−	10	2 F	8
Sales revenue	$120,000	$ −0−	$120,000	$24,000 F	$96,000
Variable expenses	83,000	3,000 U	80,000	16,000 U	64,000
Fixed expenses	22,000	2,000 U	20,000	−0−	20,000
Total expenses	105,000	5,000 U	100,000	16,000 U	84,000
Operating income	$ 15,000	$5,000 U	$ 20,000	$ 8,000 F	$12,000

KOOL-TIME POOLS
Income Statement Performance Report
Month Ended June 30, 20X5

Flexible budget variance,
$5,000 U

Sales volume variance,
$8,000 F

Static budget variance,
$3,000 F

* Budgeted sale price is $12,000 per pool, budgeted variable expense is $8,000 per pool, and budgeted total monthly fixed expenses are $20,000.

budget used in the performance report (column 3 of Exhibit 24-7) is based on the ten pools actually installed:

- Budgeted sales revenue is $120,000 (10 × $12,000).
- Budgeted variable expenses are $80,000 (10 × $8,000).
- Budgeted fixed expenses are $20,000.

The only difference between the static budget and the flexible budget used in the performance report is the number of outputs on which the budget is based (eight pools versus ten pools in the Kool-Time example). Both budgets use the same

- Budgeted sale price per unit ($12,000 per pool)
- Budgeted variable cost per unit ($8,000 per pool)
- Budgeted total fixed costs ($20,000 per month)

Holding selling price per unit, variable cost per unit, and total fixed costs constant at their budgeted amounts highlights the effects of differences in sales volume—the variance in column 4. This variance is typically the responsibility of the marketing staff. Exhibit 24-7 shows that by installing two more pools than initially expected, Kool-Time's

- Sales revenue should increase from $96,000 (8 × $12,000) to $120,000 (10 × $12,000)—a $24,000 favorable sales volume variance.
- Variable costs should increase from $64,000 (8 × $8,000) to $80,000 (10 × $8,000)—a $16,000 unfavorable sales volume variance.

Budgeted total fixed expenses are unaffected because eight pools and ten pools are within the relevant range where fixed expenses total $20,000 (0–11 pools). Consequently, installing two more pools should increase operating income by $8,000 ($24,000 F − $16,000 U).

THINK IT OVER

When is there a sales volume variance for fixed expenses?

Answer: Only when the number of units actually sold falls within a different relevant range than the static budget sales volume. When actual and expected number of units sold fall in the same relevant range, there is no sales volume variance for fixed expenses.

 DAILY EXERCISE 24-8

 DAILY EXERCISE 24-9

Exhibits 24-6 and 24-7 show that the second piece of the static budget variance is the flexible budget variance—the difference between

- Actual amounts (column 1 in Exhibit 24-7) and
- Flexible budget amounts that should have been incurred *for the actual number of output units* (column 3 in Exhibit 24-7).

Kool-Time actually incurred $83,000 of variable costs to install the ten pools. This is $3,000 more than the $80,000 (10 pools × $8,000 per pool) budgeted variable cost for ten pools. The company also spent $2,000 more than budgeted on fixed expenses ($22,000 − $20,000). Consequently, the flexible budget variance for total expenses is $5,000 unfavorable ($3,000 U + $2,000 U). The $5,000 unfavorable flexible budget variance offsets much of the $8,000 favorable sales volume variance, resulting in a $3,000 favorable static budget variance (Exhibits 24-1 and 24-7).

THINK IT OVER

When is there a flexible budget variance for sales revenue?

Answer: When the actual sale price differs from the budgeted sale price, the difference is a flexible budget variance for sales revenue. Suppose Kool-Time's actual sale price was $13,000 rather than $12,000 per pool. Actual sales revenue would have been $130,000 (10 × $13,000) and there would have been a $10,000 favorable flexible budget variance for sales revenue ($130,000 − $120,000).

We have now shown why simply comparing the static budget with actual results (like Exhibit 24-1) does not explain much. This is because the *actual* number of units sold may differ from the *expected* sales used to prepare the static budget. The flexible budget provides part of the information managers need to understand why actual revenues, expenses, and income differ from the budget.

 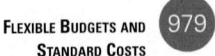

Exhibit 24-7 shows how the flexible budget splits the static budget variance into the sales volume variance and the flexible budget variance. How would Kool-Time's managers use these variances? Managers use variances to help decide which business operations deserve praise or need improvement. The favorable sales volume variance reveals that strong sales caused actual income to exceed the budget by $8,000. Kool-Time may therefore reward the sales staff. On the other hand, Exhibit 24-7 shows a $5,000 unfavorable flexible budget variance for expenses. Management will want to find out why expenses were too high.

Kool-Time's higher-than-expected expenses might be due to an uncontrollable increase in the cost of gunite. Or higher costs might have resulted from more controllable factors such as employees wasting materials or working inefficiently. If so, managers can take action to reduce waste or inefficiency. The second half of this chapter explains how Kool-Time's managers probe flexible budget variances to identify the reason for the cost overrun.

Before proceeding, take some time to test your understanding of the flexible budget, static budget, and variances by reviewing the Decision Guidelines and then working the mid-chapter review problem.

DECISION GUIDELINES

Flexible Budgets

DECISION	GUIDELINES
How to estimate sales revenues, costs, and profits over the range of likely output levels?	Prepare a set of flexible budgets for different output levels.
How to prepare a flexible budget for total costs?	$$\text{Flexible budget total cost} = \left(\begin{array}{c} \text{Number} \\ \text{of output} \\ \text{units} \end{array} \times \begin{array}{c} \text{Variable} \\ \text{cost per} \\ \text{output unit} \end{array} \right) + \begin{array}{c} \text{Fixed} \\ \text{cost} \end{array}$$
How to use budgets to help control costs?	• Graph actual costs versus flexible budget costs, as in Exhibit 24-5. • Prepare an income statement performance report, as in Exhibit 24-7.
On which output level is the budget based?	Static (master) budget—*expected* number of outputs, estimated before the period Flexible budget (made at the end of the period)—*actual* number of outputs, not known until the end of the period
Why does actual income differ from budgeted income?	Prepare income statement performance report comparing actual results, flexible budget for actual number of outputs, and static (master) budget.

How much of the difference occurs because the actual number of output units sold does not equal budgeted sales?	Compute the sales volume variance (SVV) by comparing the flexible budget with the static budget.
	 • Favorable SVV—Income effect if
	   Flexible budget sales revenue > Static budget sales revenue
	   Flexible budget expenses < Static budget expenses
	 • Unfavorable SVV—Income effect if
	   Flexible budget sales revenue < Static budget sales revenue
	   Flexible budget expenses > Static budget expenses

How much of the difference occurs because actual revenues and costs are not what they should have been for the actual number of outputs?	Compute the flexible budget variance (FBV) by comparing actual results with the flexible budget.
	 • Favorable FBV—Income effect if
	   Actual sales revenue > Flexible budget sales revenue
	   Actual expenses < Flexible budget expenses
	 • Unfavorable FBV—Income effect if
	   Actual sales revenue < Flexible budget sales revenue
	   Actual expenses > Flexible budget expenses

MID-CHAPTER

SUMMARY PROBLEM

Exhibit 24-7 indicates that Kool-Time Pools installed ten swimming pools during June. Now assume that Kool-Time installed seven pools (instead of ten) and that the actual sale price averaged $12,500 per pool instead of $12,000. Actual variable expenses were $57,400, and actual fixed expenses were $19,000.

www.prenhall.com/horngren
Mid-Chapter Assessment

Required

1. Prepare a revised income statement performance report using Exhibit 24-7 as a guide.
2. Show that the sum of the flexible budget variance and the sales volume variance for operating income equals the static budget variance for operating income.
3. As the company owner, which employees would you praise or criticize after you analyze this performance report?

Solution

Requirements 1 and 2

KOOL-TIME POOLS
Income Statement Performance Report—Revised
Month Ended June 30, 20X5

	(1) Actual Results at Actual Prices	(2) (1) − (3) Flexible Budget Variance	(3) Flexible Budget for Actual Number of Output Units	(4) (3) − (5) Sales Volume Variance	(5) Static (Master) Budget
Output units	7	–0–	7	1 U	8
Sales revenue	$87,500	$3,500 F	$84,000	$12,000 U	$96,000
Variable expenses	57,400	1,400 U	56,000	8,000 F	64,000
Fixed expenses	19,000	1,000 F	20,000	—	20,000
Total expenses	76,400	400 U	76,000	8,000 F	84,000
Operating income	$11,100	$3,100 F	$ 8,000	$ 4,000 U	$12,000

Flexible budget variance, $3,100 F   Sales volume variance, $4,000 U

Static budget variance, $900 U

Requirement 3

As the company owner, you should determine the *causes* of the variances before deciding who deserves praise or criticism. It is especially important to determine who is responsible for the variance and whether the variance is due to factors the manager can control. For example, the unfavorable sales volume variance could be due to an ineffective sales staff. Or it could be due to an uncontrollable long period of heavy rain that brought work to a standstill. Similarly, the $1,000 favorable flexible budget variance for fixed expenses could be due to an employee finding a lower-cost source of rented equipment. Or the savings may have come from delaying a needed overhaul of equipment that could increase the company's costs in the long run. Smart managers use variances to raise questions and direct attention, not to fix blame.

STANDARD COSTING

Many companies—especially those that routinely produce similar or identical products—use standard costs for budgeting and control. A **standard cost** is a carefully predetermined cost that usually is expressed on a per-unit basis. In contrast, the term *budgeted cost* usually refers to a total amount. To budget a variable cost, accountants multiply a number of output units by a standard or budgeted cost per unit. Continuing

STANDARD COST. A carefully predetermined cost that usually is expressed on a per-unit basis.

our Kool-Time Pools example, the $8,000 budgeted variable cost of an installed pool is made up of *inputs*, including direct materials, direct labor, and variable overhead costs. Suppose the variable costs in Exhibit 24-3 include direct materials costs as follows:

	Flexible Budget per Output Unit (Standard Cost)	Output Units (Pools Installed)		
		5	8	11
Direct materials	$2,000	$10,000	$16,000	$22,000

The standard cost of direct materials is $2,000 *per pool*. Budgeted cost is the expected total cost of all pools sold during the month. As volume increases from five to eleven pools, the budgeted direct materials cost increases from $10,000 to $22,000. But the standard direct materials cost is $2,000 per pool at all three flexible budget output levels. Think of a standard cost as *a budget for a single unit of output*.

In a standard cost system, each input has both a quantity standard and a price standard. **McDonald's** has a standard for the amount of beef per hamburger and for the price paid per pound of beef. Kool-Time Pools has a standard for cubic feet of gunite per pool and for price per cubic foot of gunite.

Setting Standards

Accountants help managers set price standards. For direct labor, they take into account payroll taxes and fringe benefits as well as hourly wage rates. For overhead, accountants help identify the overhead allocation bases and then compute the overhead allocation rates.

➤ We discuss continuous improvement in Chapter 19, page 775.

In setting direct materials price standards, accountants consider early-payment discounts, freight-in, and receiving costs, in addition to base purchase price. World-class businesses set continuous improvement standards ◄ for direct material prices. Companies work with suppliers to cut direct material costs. For example, **Toyota** sent its own engineers to one of its bumper suppliers' plants to help the supplier cut costs. Toyota expected the supplier to pass on much of the savings in lower prices for the bumpers. E-commerce also helps managers continuously lower direct material price standards. Purchasing managers use the Internet to solicit price quotes from suppliers throughout the world. Major U.S. automakers are collaborating on an electronic market linking the automakers with their suppliers. The automakers expect price concessions from suppliers not only on their own purchases but also on purchases the suppliers make from each other through the electronic marketplace. Automakers expect these cost-cutting efforts throughout the supply chain to yield substantially lower direct material price standards.

Engineers and production managers usually set direct material and direct labor quantity standards, often following the continuous improvement philosophy. For example, groups of managers and workers in **Westinghouse Air Brake's** Chicago plant analyzed every moment in the production of the brakes. The goal was to (1) eliminate unnecessary work, (2) reduce the time and effort required for necessary work, and (3) set a time standard for the work. To eliminate unnecessary work, the company rearranged machines in tight U-shaped cells so production wasn't spread over a vast expanse of the factory floor. Workers no longer had to move parts all over the plant. The team conducted time-and-motion studies to streamline and reduce the physical demands of various tasks. For example, the plant installed a conveyer at waist height to minimize bending and lifting. The result? By 2000, workers had slashed the standard time to produce the slack adjustor component by 90%.

 WORK IT OUT **General Motors (GM)** had cut average labor time per vehicle to 45.6 hours by 2000. But this far exceeds **Toyota's** average of 30.4 labor hours per vehicle. If GM workers earn an average of $45 per hour, how much cost does this extra labor add to each GM car?

Answer: $684. On average, GM workers put in an extra 15.2 hours (45.6 − 30.4) per car at an average rate of $45 per hour.

Many companies set currently attainable standards that allow normal amounts of waste and spoilage. This represents very good performance that can be achieved, but with difficulty. However, more and more companies, from **Ritz-Carlton** to **Federal Express,** are using standards based on "best practice." This is often called **benchmarking.**

Best practice may be an internal benchmark from inside the company or an external benchmark from other companies. Internal benchmarks are easy to obtain. Companies can purchase external benchmark data from consulting firms. Consider a consulting firm that develops reports comparing the costs of treating specific diagnoses (say an appendectomy) across hospitals. **Riverside Hospital** in Columbus, Ohio, can compare its cost of an appendectomy with the "best practice" cost from the report.

BENCHMARKING. Using standards based on "best practice." Best practice may be an internal benchmark from inside the company or an external benchmark from other companies.

e–Accounting

"It's 10:00, Do You Know What Your Suppliers Are Doing?"

These days it's not enough for companies to simply have their own house in order with regard to continuous improvement standards. Shrinking product cycles and increased 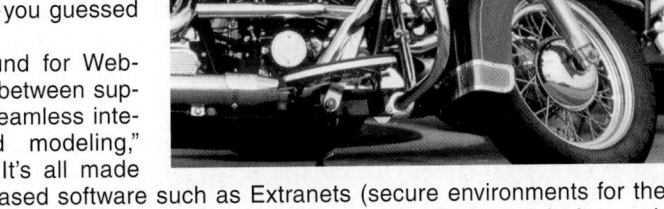 pressure to reduce overhead have made it imperative for vendors to collaborate with suppliers to cut costs while maintaining or improving product quality. Companies are transferring the responsibility for crafting more of their product to suppliers or outside contractors. What enables vendors to keep close tabs on their suppliers is—you guessed it, the Internet.

Buzzwords abound for Web-enabled collaboration between suppliers and vendors: "seamless integration," "Web-based modeling," "electronic *keiretsu.*" It's all made possible by Internet-based software such as Extranets (secure environments for the interchange of critical data with approved business partners) or Web-based design, project management, and data-management tools.

Companies must meld product design and development all along the supply chain. The Milwaukee-based motorcycle company **Harley-Davidson, Inc.,** manages interaction with its supply base through a Supplier Advisory Council (SAC). Sixteen top suppliers sit on the council, and each member communicates with about ten other top-level suppliers, giving Harley-Davidson access to some 200 suppliers. In 1999, one of the key issues SAC addressed was understanding the cost drivers of the suppliers' production. Suppliers bidding on jobs give Harley the details behind cost breakdowns, such as process flow, run times, yield, and overhead. Says Greg Smith, a Harley-Davidson purchasing director, "We want to understand their cost drivers because they can have a huge [effect] on how we design our products."

Source: Based on Tim Stevens, "Designs in sync," http://www.iwvaluechain.com, June 12, 2000. Alorie Gilbert, "Online collaboration tools help simplify product design," *Informationweek*, April 24, 2000, pp. 130–136. Richard Vlosky and Renee J. Fontenot, "Learning to love extranets," *Marketing Management*, Fall 1999, pp. 33–55. Richard W. Oliver, "Killer KEIRETSU," *Management Review*, September 1999, pp. 10–11.

Benefits of Standard Costs

Carefully set standard costs yield several benefits (Exhibit 24-8 on the next page):

1. They help managers plan by providing the unit amounts—the building blocks—for budgeting.
2. They help managers control business operations by setting target levels of operating performance. *Management by exception* suggests that managers focus attention where actual results differ significantly from standards. ➤

Objective 3
Identify the benefits of standard costs

◄ Chapter 23, page 948, introduced management-by-exception.

EXHIBIT 24-8 **The Benefits of Standard Costs**

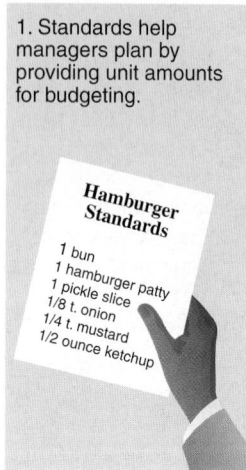

1. Standards help managers plan by providing unit amounts for budgeting.

Hamburger Standards

1 bun
1 hamburger patty
1 pickle slice
1/8 t. onion
1/4 t. mustard
1/2 ounce ketchup

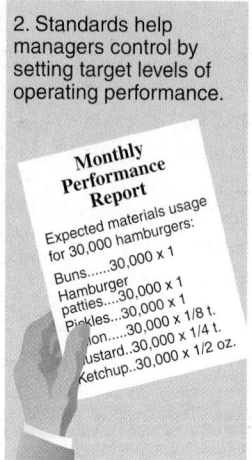

2. Standards help managers control by setting target levels of operating performance.

Monthly Performance Report

Expected materials usage for 30,000 hamburgers:

Buns......30,000 x 1
Hamburger patties....30,000 x 1
Pickles...30,000 x 1/8 t.
onion.....30,000 x 1/8 t.
mustard..30,000 x 1/4 t.
Ketchup..30,000 x 1/2 oz.

3. Standards motivate employees by serving as benchmarks for measuring performance.

Employee Award
Speediest Worker of the Month

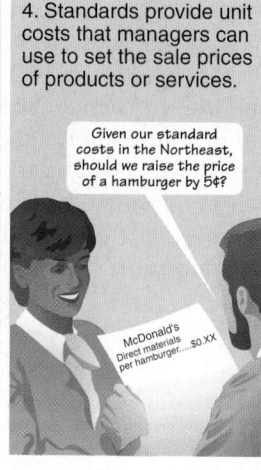

4. Standards provide unit costs that managers can use to set the sale prices of products or services.

Given our standard costs in the Northeast, should we raise the price of a hamburger by 5¢?

McDonald's
Direct materials per hamburger......$0.XX

5. Standards simplify record keeping, reducing clerical costs.

Branch Office

Standard cost...

3. They help motivate employees by serving as benchmarks for measuring performance.

4. They provide unit costs managers can use to set sale prices of products or services.

5. They help simplify record keeping and so reduce clerical costs.

 DAILY EXERCISE 24-10

Standard cost systems might appear to be expensive. Indeed, the company must invest in developing the standards. But standards can save data-processing costs. It is easier to value all inventories at standard costs rather than at actual costs. With standard costs, accountants avoid the expense of tracking actual unit costs and of making LIFO, FIFO, or average-cost computations.

Given these benefits, it is not surprising that companies around the globe use standard costing. U.S. surveys have shown that over 80% of responding companies use standard costing. International surveys suggest that over half the responding companies in Ireland, the United Kingdom, Sweden, and Japan use standard costing, primarily because it helps managers control costs.

Objective 4
Compute standard cost variances for direct materials and direct labor

AN EXAMPLE OF STANDARD COSTING

Let's return to our Kool-Time Pools example. To focus on the main aspects of standard costing, we assume that Kool-Time's standard costing system covers direct materials (gunite), direct labor, and manufacturing overhead but not design, marketing, or administrative expenses. We assume also that the quantity of direct materials purchased equals the quantity used.

 DAILY EXERCISE 24-11

Recall that Kool-Time installed ten swimming pools during June. Exhibit 24-9 provides cost data for this actual level of output. Exhibit 24-9 also shows Kool-Time's flexible budget variances for direct materials ($3,100 U) and direct labor ($200 F). Accountants separate these variances into two components: a price variance and an efficiency variance.

Price and Efficiency Variances

PRICE VARIANCE. Measures how well the business keeps unit prices of material and labor inputs within standards. This is computed as the difference in prices (actual price per unit minus standard price per unit) of an input, multiplied by the actual quantity of the input.

A **price variance** measures how well the business keeps unit prices of material and labor inputs within standards. As the name suggests, the price variance is the *difference in prices* (actual price per unit − standard price per unit) of an input, multiplied by the *actual quantity* of the input:

$$\text{Price variance} = \left(\begin{array}{c} \text{Difference between} \\ \text{actual and standard} \\ \text{prices per input unit} \end{array} \right) \times \left(\begin{array}{c} \text{Actual quantity} \\ \text{of input} \end{array} \right)$$

$$\text{Price variance} = \left(\begin{array}{c} \text{Actual} \\ \text{price per} \\ \text{input unit} \end{array} - \begin{array}{c} \text{Standard} \\ \text{price per} \\ \text{input unit} \end{array} \right) \times \left(\begin{array}{c} \text{Actual quantity} \\ \text{of input} \end{array} \right)$$

EXHIBIT 24-9 Data for Standard Costing Example

KOOL-TIME POOLS
Data for Standard Costing Example
Month of June 20X5

PANEL A—Comparison of Actual Results with Flexible Budget for 10 Swimming Pools

	Actual Results at Actual Prices	Flexible Budget for 10 Pools	Flexible Budget Variance
Variable expenses:			
Direct materials	$ 23,100*	$ 20,000†	$3,100 U
Direct labor	41,800*	42,000†	200 F
Variable overhead	9,000	8,000†	1,000 U
Marketing and administrative expenses	9,100	10,000	900 F
Total variable expenses	83,000	80,000	3,000 U
Fixed expenses:			
Fixed overhead	12,300	12,000‡	300 U
Marketing and administrative expenses	9,700	8,000	1,700 U
Total fixed expenses	22,000	20,000	2,000 U
Total expenses	$105,000	$100,000	$5,000 U

* See Panel C
† See Panel B
‡ Fixed overhead was budgeted at $12,000 per month.

PANEL B—Computation of Flexible Budget for Direct Materials, Direct Labor, and Variable Overhead for 10 Swimming Pools

	(1) Standard Quantity of Inputs Allowed for 10 Pools	(2) Standard Price per Unit of Input	(1) × (2) Flexible Budget for 10 Pools
Direct materials	1,000 cubic feet per pool × 10 pools = 10,000 cubic feet	$ 2.00	$20,000
Direct labor	400 hours per pool × 10 pools = 4,000 hours	10.50	42,000
Variable overhead	400 hours per pool × 10 pools = 4,000 hours	2.00	8,000

PANEL C—Computation of Actual Costs for Direct Materials and Direct Labor for 10 Swimming Pools

	(1) Actual Quantity of Inputs Used for 10 Pools	(2) Actual Price per Unit of Input	(1) × (2) Actual Cost for 10 Pools
Direct materials	11,969 cubic feet actually used	$1.93 actual cost/cubic foot	$23,100
Direct labor	3,800 hours actually used	$11.00 actual cost/hour	41,800

The standard price per unit of input is the *price that should have been paid per unit* of the input (per cubic foot of gunite or per direct labor hour). If the company actually pays less, the price variance is favorable. If the company actually pays more than the standard price, the price variance is unfavorable. The manager who purchases the input is responsible for the price variance. For example, the Kool-Time employee who buys the gunite is responsible for the difference between the actual and standard price for all the gunite he purchased, so the difference in price is multiplied by the *actual quantity* purchased.

EFFICIENCY VARIANCE. Measures whether the quantity of materials or labor used to make the actual number of outputs is within the standard allowed for that number of outputs. This is computed as the difference in quantities (actual quantity of input used minus standard quantity of input allowed for the actual number of outputs), multiplied by the standard price per unit of the input.

An **efficiency variance** measures whether the quantity of materials or labor actually used to make the *actual number of outputs* is within the standard allowed for that number of outputs. The efficiency variance is the *difference in quantities* (actual quantity of input used − standard quantity of input allowed for the actual number of outputs), multiplied by the *standard price per unit* of the input.

$$\text{Efficiency variance} = \left(\begin{array}{c}\text{Difference between actual quantity of}\\\text{inputs used and the standard quantity}\\\text{of inputs that should have been used}\\\text{for the actual number of outputs}\end{array}\right) \times \left(\begin{array}{c}\text{Standard price}\\\text{per input unit}\end{array}\right)$$

$$\text{Efficiency variance} = \left(\begin{array}{c}\text{Actual}\\\text{quantity}\\\text{of input}\end{array} - \begin{array}{c}\text{Standard}\\\text{quantity}\\\text{of input}\end{array}\right) \times \left(\begin{array}{c}\text{Standard price}\\\text{per input unit}\end{array}\right)$$

The standard quantity of inputs is the *quantity that should have been used,* or the standard quantity of inputs *allowed,* for the actual output. If the company actually uses less than the standard quantity of inputs allowed to produce the output, the efficiency variance is favorable. If the company uses more than the standard quantity, the efficiency variance is unfavorable.

Price variances show how changes in prices of raw materials and labor affect the company's profit. But price variances that reflect changes in the market prices of materials and labor are largely beyond the company's control. Because managers generally have limited control over changes in prices, *efficiency* variances are computed by multiplying the difference in quantity by the *standard* price per unit of the input. Efficiency variances thus capture the controllable aspect of how the company's *use* of materials and labor affects profits.

We can now compute Kool-Time Pool's standard cost variances for direct materials and direct labor.

Direct Materials Variances

We begin our analysis of direct materials variances by compiling the relevant data from Exhibit 24-9, as follows:

DAILY EXERCISE 24-12

DAILY EXERCISE 24-13

Direct Materials	Actual	Flexible Budget	Flexible Budget Variance
Cubic feet...............	11,969	10,000	
Unit price...............	×$1.93	×$2.00	
Total.......................	$23,100	$20,000	$3,100 U

We use these data to compute the price and efficiency variances:

$$\text{Price variance} = \left(\begin{array}{c}\text{Actual}\\\text{price per}\\\text{input unit}\end{array} - \begin{array}{c}\text{Standard}\\\text{price per}\\\text{input unit}\end{array}\right) \times \begin{array}{c}\text{Actual}\\\text{quantity}\\\text{of input}\end{array}$$

$$= \left(\begin{array}{c}\$1.93\text{ per}\\\text{cubic foot}\end{array} - \begin{array}{c}\$2.00\text{ per}\\\text{cubic foot}\end{array}\right) \times 11,969\text{ cubic feet} = \$838\text{ F}$$

$$\text{Efficiency variance} = \left(\begin{array}{c}\text{Actual}\\\text{quantity}\\\text{of input}\end{array} - \begin{array}{c}\text{Standard}\\\text{quantity}\\\text{of input}\end{array}\right) \times \begin{array}{c}\text{Standard}\\\text{price per}\\\text{input unit}\end{array}$$

$$= \left(\begin{array}{c}11,969\\\text{cubic feet}\end{array} - \begin{array}{c}10,000\\\text{cubic feet}\end{array}\right) \times \begin{array}{c}\$2.00\text{ per}\\\text{cubic foot}\end{array} = \$3,938\text{ U}$$

The price variance indicates that Kool-Time's operating income will be $838 higher because the company paid less than the standard price for gunite in June. The efficiency variance indicates that Kool-Time's operating income will be $3,938 lower because workers used more gunite than the standard allowed for ten pools.

Exhibit 24-10 summarizes the direct materials variance computations. Variance analysis begins with a total variance to be explained—in this example, the $3,100 unfavorable flexible budget variance for direct materials. This variance is the sum of the price and efficiency variances:

Direct materials price variance.............................	$ 838 F
Direct materials efficiency variance	3,938 U
Direct materials flexible budget variance...............	$3,100 U

EXHIBIT 24-10   Kool-Time Pools Direct Materials Variances

Splitting the $3,100 unfavorable direct materials flexible budget variance into price and efficiency variances explains why Kool-Time actually spent $3,100 more than it should have for gunite:

- A good price for the gunite increased profits by $838, but
- Inefficient use of the gunite reduced profits by $3,938.

Who is most likely responsible for the direct materials price variance? For the direct materials efficiency variance?

- Purchasing personnel are typically responsible for the direct materials price variance because they should know why the actual price differs from the standard price. Purchasing personnel may have negotiated a good price for gunite, thus obtaining the favorable variance. Should the gunite supplier raise prices, purchasing personnel will know why an unfavorable price variance occurred.
- Production personnel are generally responsible for the direct materials efficiency variance. Perhaps their equipment malfunctioned, causing them to use more than the standard quantity of gunite.

Common Pitfalls: Price and Efficiency Variances

Make sure you avoid three common pitfalls in computing price and efficiency variances:

1. *Static budgets like column 5 of Exhibit 24-7 play no role in computing the flexible budget variance or how it is split into the price and efficiency variances.* Exhibit 24-11 shows that the static budget is used *only* in computing the sales volume

variance—never in computing the flexible budget variance (or its component price and efficiency variances).

As Exhibit 24-11 shows, the price variance and the efficiency variance are components of the flexible budget variance—the difference between actual amounts and flexible budget amounts. The $838 F + $3,938 U = $3,100 U direct materials flexible budget variance is part of the $3,000 U flexible budget variance for variable expenses shown in column 2 of Exhibit 24-7. (The rest of the variable cost flexible budget variance is composed of flexible budget variances for other variable expenses, as shown in Panel A of Exhibit 24-9.)

EXHIBIT 24-11
Price, Efficiency, Flexible Budget, Sales Volume, and Static Budget Variances

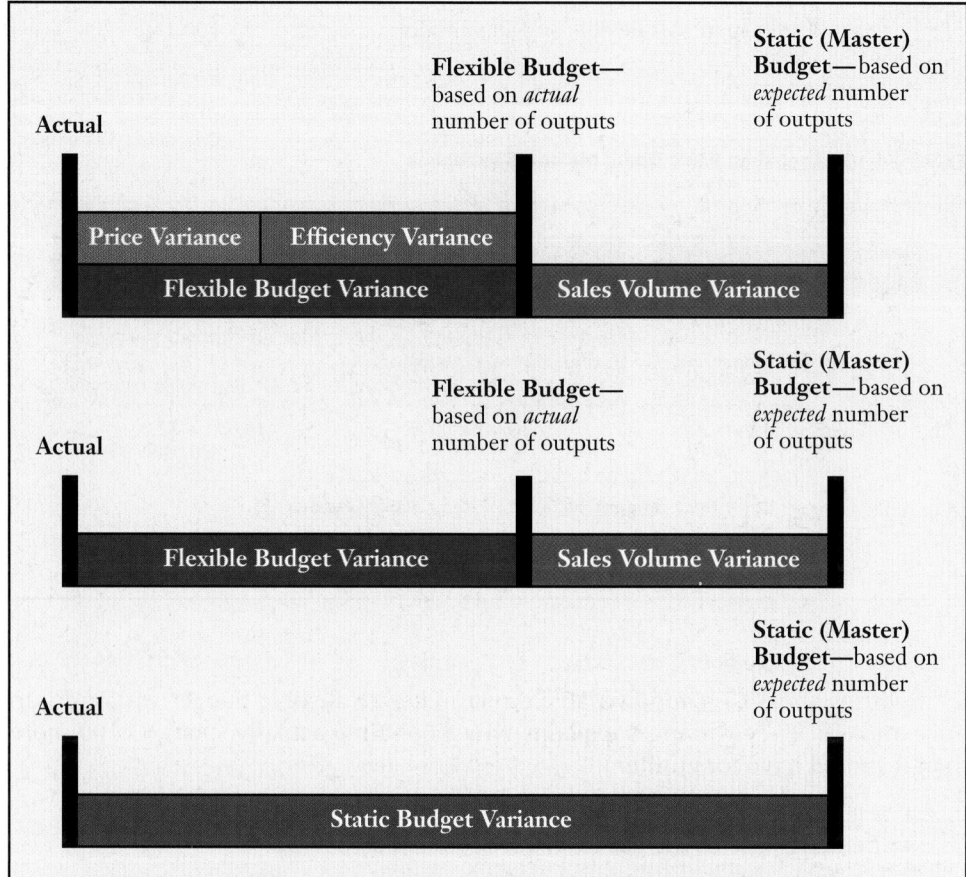

2. In the efficiency variance, the standard quantity is the *standard quantity of inputs allowed for the actual number of outputs*—the basis for the flexible budget. To compute the standard quantity of inputs allowed, first determine the actual number of outputs. For Kool-Time Pools, the actual number of outputs is ten pools. Next, compute how many inputs should have been used to produce the actual number of outputs (10 pools). Each pool should use 1,000 cubic feet of gunite, so the standard quantity of gunite allowed for ten pools is $10 \times 1,000$ cubic feet = 10,000 cubic feet.

Notice that the standard quantity of inputs is *not* based on the budgeted number of outputs (8 pools). That number is the basis for the static budget, which is not used to compute price and efficiency variances.

3. In the direct materials price variance, the difference in prices is multiplied by the *actual quantity* of materials. In the direct materials efficiency variance, the difference in quantities is multiplied by the *standard price* of the materials. The following explanation can help you remember this difference.
   • The materials price variance is usually the responsibility of purchasing personnel; they purchase the actual quantity used, not just the amount of

materials that should have been used (the standard quantity). So the price variance is the difference in prices multiplied by the *actual quantity* of materials they purchased.

- The materials efficiency variance is usually the responsibility of production personnel; they have no influence over the actual price paid. So the efficiency variance is computed as the difference in quantities multiplied by the *standard* price (the price that should have been paid).

Direct Labor Variances

We begin our analysis of direct labor variances by compiling the relevant data from Exhibit 24-9, as follows:

Direct Labor	Actual	Flexible Budget	Flexible Budget Variance
Hours............................	3,800	4,000	
Hourly rate.................	× $11.00	× $10.50	
Total.............................	$41,800	$42,000	$200 F

We then use these data to compute the direct labor price and efficiency variances in the same way we computed the direct materials variances:

DAILY EXERCISE 24-14

$$
\text{Price variance} = \left(\begin{array}{c} \text{Actual} \\ \text{price per} \\ \text{input unit} \end{array} - \begin{array}{c} \text{Standard} \\ \text{price per} \\ \text{input unit} \end{array} \right) \times \begin{array}{c} \text{Actual quantity} \\ \text{of input} \end{array}
$$

$$
= \left(\begin{array}{c} \$11.00 \text{ per} \\ \text{hour} \end{array} - \begin{array}{c} \$10.50 \text{ per} \\ \text{hour} \end{array} \right) \times 3{,}800 \text{ hours} = \$1{,}900 \text{ U}
$$

$$
\text{Efficiency variance} = \left(\begin{array}{c} \text{Actual} \\ \text{quantity} \\ \text{of input} \end{array} - \begin{array}{c} \text{Standard} \\ \text{quantity} \\ \text{of input} \end{array} \right) \times \begin{array}{c} \text{Standard} \\ \text{price per} \\ \text{input unit} \end{array}
$$

$$
= (3{,}800 \text{ hours} - 4{,}000 \text{ hours}) \times 10.50/\text{hour} = \$2{,}100 \text{ F}
$$

Had they looked only at the $200 favorable direct labor flexible budget variance, Kool-Time's managers may have concluded that direct labor costs were close to expectations. But this illustrates the danger in ending the analysis after computing only the flexible budget variance. "Peeling the onion" to examine the price and efficiency variances yields more insight:

- The unfavorable direct labor price variance means that Kool-Time's operating income is $1,900 lower than expected, because the company paid its employees an average of $11.00 per hour in June instead of the standard rate of $10.50. But this unfavorable variance was more than offset by
- The favorable direct labor efficiency variance. Kool-Time's operating income is $2,100 higher than expected because workers installed ten pools in 3,800 hours instead of the budgeted 4,000 hours.

As with direct materials, the direct labor price and efficiency variances sum to the flexible budget variance.

Direct labor price variance	$1,900 U
Direct labor efficiency variance........................	2,100 F
Direct labor flexible budget variance	$ 200 F

Exhibit 24-12 (next page) summarizes the direct labor variance computations.

EXHIBIT 24-12
Kool-Time Pools Direct Labor
Variances

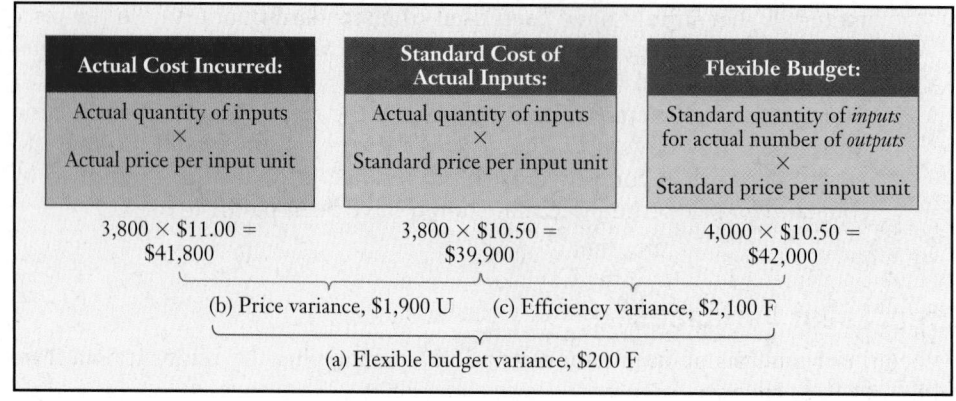

Actual Cost Incurred:	Standard Cost of Actual Inputs:	Flexible Budget:
Actual quantity of inputs × Actual price per input unit	Actual quantity of inputs × Standard price per input unit	Standard quantity of *inputs* for actual number of *outputs* × Standard price per input unit
3,800 × $11.00 = $41,800	3,800 × $10.50 = $39,900	4,000 × $10.50 = $42,000

(b) Price variance, $1,900 U   (c) Efficiency variance, $2,100 F

(a) Flexible budget variance, $200 F

THINK IT OVER

Why might an auto assembly plant experience a favorable direct labor efficiency variance? Should managers investigate favorable as well as unfavorable efficiency variances? Why?

Answer

1. The plant may have redesigned the manufacturing process to avoid wasted motion. For example, a **Dodge** van plant in Canada significantly reduced direct labor by reorganizing production so employees reach for raw materials as needed rather than carry armloads of materials across the plant floor.
2. Employees may have worked harder or more intensely than budgeted.
3. Employees may have rushed through the work and skimped on quality.

There are two reasons why managers should investigate favorable efficiency variances. First, managers want to maximize improvements that increase profits. For example, can managers capitalize on 1 and 2 to further improve labor efficiency at this or other plants? Second, managers want to prevent employees from achieving favorable variances at the expense of long-run profits through strategies like 3, which hurt the company in the long run.

DAILY EXERCISE 24-15

Using Variances

How often should companies compute variances? Many firms monitor sales, materials quantities, and direct labor hours on a day-to-day or even hour-to-hour basis. For example, **McDonald's** restaurants compute variances for sales and direct labor each hour. Material efficiencies are computed for each shift. The Brass Products Division of **Parker Hannafin** computes variances for each job the day after workers finish the job. This allows managers to ask questions about any large variances while the job is still fresh in workers' minds. The division also prepares weekly reports showing variances by product line. The resulting database allows managers to examine variances by product (part number), by job, or by the dollar amount of the variance, with just a few keystrokes. Technology like bar coding and computerized data entry allows companies like McDonald's and Parker Hannafin to quickly compute efficiency variances. In contrast to efficiency variances, monthly computations of material and labor price variances may be sufficient if long-term contracts with suppliers or labor unions make large price variances unlikely.

Variances by themselves do not identify problems or opportunities. But large variances raise questions that deserve attention. When is a variance "large" or "significant"? The answer depends on the manager's judgment. Many managers use rules of thumb such as "investigate all variances over $10,000 or 8%, whichever is greater." For example, Parker Hannafin's Brass Products Division requires managers to investigate all variances over 5% of sales revenue and to develop a plan of action to correct any problems.

Returning to our Kool-Time Pools example, in June Kool-Time bought gunite for $1.93 per cubic foot (less than the standard price of $2.00). Kool-Time's 3.5% [($1.93 − $2.00)/$2.00] favorable direct materials price variance could arise because the purchasing officer did a good job negotiating prices with suppliers. Or perhaps the officer purchased lower-quality gunite. This is why smart managers interpret variances carefully—even a "favorable" variance can hurt long-run profits.

Kool-Time's 19.7% [(11,969 − 10,000)/10,000] unfavorable direct materials efficiency variance may indicate that the gunite was of low quality. Poor-quality materials spoil, break, or crack more often, requiring replacement. Or perhaps an uncontrollable event led to excess usage. For example, earth tremors may have cracked several pools after the gunite had hardened but before all work was completed. Workers may have used some of the extra gunite to repair the damage.

Now consider Kool-Time's direct labor flexible budget variance. Although this variance is only $200, as indicated earlier, splitting it into its two components is revealing. The 4.8% [($11.00 − $10.50)/$10.50] unfavorable price variance indicates that the company used more expensive labor than was budgeted. But those workers were more efficient. The average number of hours worked per pool (3,800 hours ÷ 10 pools = 380) was 5% less than the standard of 400 hours per pool. Kool-Time's managers may have decided to hire more experienced workers and trade off an unfavorable price variance for a favorable efficiency variance. If so, the strategy was successful—the overall effect of the decision was favorable.

These examples lead to two conclusions:

1. *Executives should be careful in using standard cost variances to evaluate performance*. First, some variances are caused by factors managers cannot control. Second, managers often make tradeoffs among variances. **Chrysler** intentionally accepted a large order for customized Dodge vans because it expected the favorable sales volume variance to more than offset the unfavorable direct labor price variance from the overtime premium and the unfavorable sales revenue price variance from extra rebates offered to the customer. Similarly, managers often trade off price variances against efficiency variances. Purchasing personnel may decide to buy higher-quality (but more-expensive) direct materials to reduce waste and spoilage. The unfavorable price variance may be more than offset by a favorable efficiency variance.

2. *Executives should consider using several measures to evaluate managers' performance*. Evaluations based on only one variance sometimes inadvertently encourage managers to take actions that make the variance look good, but hurt the company in the long run. For example, Kool-Time's managers could

   - Purchase low-quality gunite or hire less-experienced labor to get favorable price variances
   - Use less gunite or less labor (resulting in lower-quality installed pools) to get favorable efficiency variances

How can upper management discourage such actions? One approach is to base performance evaluation on *nonfinancial* measures as well, such as quality indicators like variances in the grade of gunite or labor used, or customer satisfaction measures. For example, McDonald's discourages skimping on labor by evaluating nonfinancial measures such as the difference between actual and standard time to serve drive-through customers. If the McDonald's shift manager does not have enough workers, drive-through customers may have to wait too long to get their French fries. They may take their business to **Wendy's** or **Burger King.**

MANUFACTURING OVERHEAD VARIANCES

Objective 5
Analyze manufacturing overhead in a standard cost system

Ideally, manufacturing overhead cost variances should be computed and monitored for individual overhead costs like plant-related property taxes, utilities, and insurance. However, many companies compute variances on total overhead costs. These companies often split the variances on total manufacturing overhead cost into two parts: a *flexible budget variance* and a *production volume variance*.

The *flexible budget variance* for manufacturing overhead shows whether managers are keeping the period's total overhead cost within the budget for the actual number of outputs. The *production volume variance* arises when the actual number of outputs differs from the expected number of outputs used in the static (master) budget. The two variances combine to explain the difference between actual overhead cost and the standard overhead cost that has been allocated to production (under- or overallocated overhead). Before discussing how companies compute overhead variances, let's see how they allocate manufacturing overhead.

◉ DAILY EXERCISE 24-16

Allocating Manufacturing Overhead in a Standard Costing System

In a standard costing system, the amount of the manufacturing overhead allocated to production is

$$\text{Manufacturing overhead allocated to production} = \text{Standard predetermined manufacturing overhead rate} \times \text{Standard quantity of the allocation base allowed for the } \textit{actual} \text{ number of outputs}$$

Let's begin by computing the first term on the right-hand side, the standard predetermined manufacturing overhead rate. Kool-Time allocates manufacturing overhead based on direct labor hours. As explained in Chapter 20, the predetermined overhead rate is the budgeted manufacturing overhead cost, divided by the budgeted quantity of the allocation base. ◄

➥ To review the computation of the predetermined overhead rate, see Chapter 20, page 810.

But which budget? Exhibit 24-13 shows Kool-Time's budgeted overhead costs and direct labor hours for

- The flexible budget for actual output, which is based on actual output of 10 pools (not known until the end of the period)
- The static budget, which is based on expected output of 8 pools (known at the beginning of the period)

Notice that the $12,000 budgeted *fixed* manufacturing overhead is the same in both the static budget for 8 pools and the flexible budget for 10 pools. Why? Because fixed costs do not change throughout the relevant range of 0–11 pools. In contrast, the budgeted *variable* manufacturing overhead is higher in the flexible budget for 10 pools than in the static budget for 8 pools. Why? Because variable costs vary (in total) with the number of outputs, so Kool-Time expects to use more variable overhead items (indirect materials, indirect labor) for 10 pools than for 8 pools.

EXHIBIT 24-13
Budgeted Manufacturing Overhead Costs and Allocation Rates

KOOL-TIME POOLS Budget Data for the Month Ended June 30, 20X5		
	Flexible Budget for Actual Output	**Static Budget for Expected Output**
Output units (pools installed)............................	10	8
Standard direct labor hours (400 hours per pool).....................................	4,000	3,200
Budgeted manufacturing overhead cost:		
Variable	$ 8,000	$ 6,400
Fixed	12,000	12,000
Total	$20,000	$18,400
Standard variable manufacturing overhead rate per direct labor hour.............................		$ 6,400 ÷ 3,200 = $2.00
Standard fixed manufacturing overhead rate per direct labor hour.............................		$12,000 ÷ 3,200 = $3.75
Standard total manufacturing overhead rate per direct labor hour.............................		$18,400 ÷ 3,200 = $5.75

Keep in mind that managers use predetermined overhead rates because they cannot wait until the end of the year to figure the overhead costs of products. Thus, *predetermined* overhead rates use data that are available at the *beginning* of the year. Most companies base their predetermined overhead rates on amounts from the static (master) budget, which is known at the beginning of the year. (The predetermined manufacturing overhead rate cannot be based on the flexible budget for actual production because the actual number of outputs is not known until the end of the year.)

Exhibit 24-13 shows that Kool-Time's standard manufacturing overhead rates are

- Variable—$2.00 per direct labor hour ($6,400 static budget variable manufacturing overhead divided by 3,200 static budget standard direct labor hours),
- Fixed—$3.75 per direct labor hour ($12,000 static budget fixed manufacturing overhead divided by 3,200 static budget standard direct labor hours),
- Total—$5.75 per direct labor hour ($2.00 + $3.75). This is the standard predetermined manufacturing overhead rate Kool-Time uses to allocate manufacturing overhead to products.

Now that we have computed the standard predetermined manufacturing overhead rate, the next step is to identify the standard quantity of the allocation base allowed for the *actual* number of outputs. Kool-Time allocates manufacturing overhead based on direct labor hours. Kool-Time actually installed ten pools during June. Thus, the standard quantity of the allocation base (direct labor hours) allowed for the actual number of outputs (10 pools) is 4,000 direct labor hours (400 direct labor hours per pool × 10 pools actually installed). Notice that 4,000 direct labor hours is the standard number of direct labor hours for the flexible budget at the actual output level of 10 pools in Exhibit 24-13, and for the direct labor efficiency variance (Exhibit 24-12).

Thus, Kool-Time allocates manufacturing overhead as follows:

Manufacturing overhead allocated to production	=	Standard predetermined manufacturing overhead rate	×	Standard quantity of the allocation base allowed for the *actual* number of outputs
	=	$5.75 per hour	×	4,000 hours
	=	$23,000		

The total manufacturing overhead variance is the amount of under- or overallocated manufacturing overhead. This is the difference between actual and allocated manufacturing overhead, as explained in Chapter 20. ➟ Exhibit 24-14 shows that actual manufacturing overhead is $21,300.

Given $21,300 of actual manufacturing overhead and $23,000 of allocated manufacturing overhead, Kool-Time has *overallocated* overhead of $1,700. Overallocated overhead is considered a favorable variance because actual overhead costs are less than allocated costs. We now will see how Kool-Time splits this total $1,700 variance into the overhead flexible budget variance and the production volume variance.

◄ To review under- and overallocated overhead, see Chapter 20, pages 814–816.

Overhead Flexible Budget Variance

The **overhead flexible budget variance** is the difference between the actual overhead cost and the flexible budget overhead for the actual number of outputs. Kool-Time's overhead flexible budget variance for June is computed as follows (data from Exhibit 24-14):

Actual overhead cost	$21,300
Flexible budget overhead for actual outputs (10 pools)	20,000
Overhead flexible budget variance	$ 1,300 U

OVERHEAD FLEXIBLE BUDGET VARIANCE. The difference between the actual overhead cost and the flexible budget overhead for the actual number of outputs.

EXHIBIT 24-14   Data for Computing Manufacturing Overhead Variances

KOOL-TIME POOLS
Data for Computing Manufacturing Overhead Variances

	Actual Overhead Cost (Exhibit 24-9)	Flexible Budget Overhead for Actual Number of Outputs (Exhibits 24-9 and 24-13)	Standard Overhead Allocated to Production (Rates from Exhibit 24-13)
Variable overhead........	$ 9,000	$ 8,000	$2.00 × 4,000 direct labor hours = $ 8,000
Fixed overhead............	12,300	12,000	$3.75 × 4,000 direct labor hours = 15,000
Total overhead.............	$21,300	$20,000	$5.75 × 4,000 direct labor hours = $23,000

Overhead flexible budget variance, $1,300 U

Production volume variance, $3,000 F

Total manufacturing overhead variance, $1,700 F

 DAILY EXERCISE 24-17

Kool-Time actually spent $21,300 on manufacturing overhead, when the flexible budget indicated that installing 10 pools should have required only $20,000 of overhead. The unfavorable variance raises questions regarding managers' control of overhead costs.

Production Volume Variance

PRODUCTION VOLUME VARIANCE. The difference between (1) the manufacturing overhead cost in the flexible budget for actual outputs, and (2) the standard overhead allocated to production.

The **production volume variance** is the difference between (1) the manufacturing overhead cost in the flexible budget for actual outputs, and (2) the standard overhead allocated to production. Kool-Time computes its production volume variance using data from Exhibit 24-14:

Flexible budget overhead for actual outputs (10 pools)	$20,000
Standard overhead allocated to (actual) production	23,000
Production volume variance..	$ 3,000 F

The production volume variance is favorable whenever actual output (ten pools, for Kool-Time) exceeds expected output—(eight pools, Exhibit 24-13). By installing ten pools instead of eight, Kool-Time used its production capacity more fully than originally planned. If Kool-Time had installed seven or fewer pools, the production volume variance would have been unfavorable because the company would have used less production capacity than expected.

Exhibit 24-14 reveals that the *variable* overhead cost in the flexible budget for actual outputs is always the same as the standard variable overhead allocated (standard predetermined variable overhead rate × the standard quantity of the allocation base allowed for the actual number of outputs). Thus, the production volume variance is due only to fixed overhead.

 WORK IT OUT

How did the increase in Kool-Time's "production volume," from 8 pools (the expected static budget amount) to 10 pools (actually installed), affect June's profit? Is this amount equal to the production volume variance?

Answer: To see how the increase from 8 to 10 pools affected Kool-Time's June profits, use the contribution margin income statement approach from Chapter 22:

Increase in sales revenue (2 × $12,000).....................	$24,000
Increase in variable expenses (2 × $8,000)	16,000
Increase in contribution margin	8,000
Increase in fixed expenses	–0–
Increase in operating income.......................................	$ 8,000

Installing two more pools than initially expected increased Kool-Time's profits by $8,000, not by the $3,000 favorable "production volume variance." Thus, the production volume variance does *not* reveal how changes in production volume affect profits. The production volume variance only captures the difference between the flexible budget manufacturing overhead and the allocated manufacturing overhead. Companies use the term *production volume variance* because this variance arises only when actual production differs from expected (static budget) production.

ACCOUNTING FOR STANDARD COSTS
Standard Costing Journal Entries

Objective 6
Record transactions at standard cost

Recall that manufacturing companies have three inventory accounts: Materials Inventory, Work in Process Inventory, and Finished Goods Inventory. Most companies with standard cost accounting systems record variances in separate accounts.

We use Kool-Time Pools' June transactions to demonstrate standard costing in a job costing context. Our entries are based on an important assumption: Kool-Time recognizes variances from standards as soon as possible. This means that Kool-Time records direct materials price variances when materials are purchased. It also means that Work in Process Inventory is debited (swimming pools are costed) at standard input quantities and standard prices. June's entries follow:

 DAILY EXERCISE 24-18

1. Materials Inventory (11,969 × $2.00) 23,938
   Direct Materials Price Variance..................... 838
   Accounts Payable (11,969 × $1.93) 23,100
   To record purchases of direct materials.

The credit to Accounts Payable is for the *actual quantity* of gunite purchased (11,969 cubic feet) costed at the *actual price* ($1.93 per cubic foot). In contrast, the debit to Materials Inventory is for the *actual quantity* purchased (11,969 cubic feet) costed at the *standard price* ($2 per cubic foot). Maintaining Materials Inventory at the *standard price* ($2.00) allows Kool-Time's accountants to record the direct materials price variance at time of purchase. Recall that Kool-Time's direct materials price variance was $838 favorable (page 986). A favorable variance has a credit balance in the accounts and is a contra expense, or a reduction in expense. Consequently, the $838 favorable direct materials price variance is a contra expense that increases Kool-Time's June profits.

2. Work in Process Inventory (10,000 × $2.00) 20,000
   Direct Materials Efficiency Variance....................... 3,938
   Materials Inventory (11,969 × $2.00) 23,938
   To record use of direct materials.

Kool-Time's direct materials efficiency variance was $3,938 unfavorable (page 986). An unfavorable variance has a debit balance, which increases expense. Kool-Time's $3,938 unfavorable direct materials efficiency variance is an expense that decreases June profits. Kool-Time debits Work in Process for the *standard price × standard quantity* of direct materials that should have been used for the actual output of ten pools. This maintains Work in Process Inventory at standard cost. Of course, Materials Inventory is credited for the *actual quantity* of material put into production (11,969 cubic feet) costed at the *standard price* at which journal entry 1 entered them into the Materials Inventory account.

 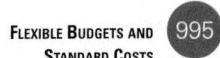

3. Manufacturing Wages (3,800 × $10.50)................. 39,900
    Direct Labor Price Variance 1,900
        Wages Payable (3,800 × $11.00).................. 41,800
    To record direct labor costs incurred.

By maintaining Manufacturing Wages at the *standard* price for direct labor ($10.50), Kool-Time records the direct labor price variance at the time work is performed. Of course, Wages Payable is credited for the *actual* hours worked at the *actual* wage rate.

4. Work in Process Inventory (4,000 × $10.50) 42,000
        Direct Labor Efficiency Variance................... 2,100
        Manufacturing Wages (3,800 × $10.50) 39,900
    To assign direct labor costs.

Kool-Time debits Work in Process for the standard price × standard quantity of direct labor that should have been used for ten pools, similar to the (earlier) direct materials entry #2. This maintains Work in Process Inventory at standard cost.

5. Manufacturing Overhead...................................... 21,300
        Accounts Payable, Accumulated
        Depreciation, and so on............................... 21,300
    To record actual overhead costs incurred.
    (See Exhibit 24-14.)

6. Work in Process Inventory (4,000 × $5.75) 23,000
        Manufacturing Overhead 23,000
    To allocate overhead. (See Exhibit 24-14.)

In standard costing, the overhead allocated to Work in Process Inventory is computed as the standard predetermined overhead rate × standard quantity of the allocation base that should have been used for the actual output (ten pools, in this case).

7. Finished Goods Inventory...................................... 85,000
        Work in Process Inventory 85,000
    To record completion of 10 pools ($20,000 of materials +
    $42,000 of labor + $23,000 of manufacturing overhead).

8. Cost of Goods Sold 85,000
        Finished Goods Inventory 85,000
    To record the cost of sales of 10 pools.

⦿ DAILY EXERCISE 24-19

⦿ DAILY EXERCISE 24-20

9. Manufacturing Overhead...................................... 1,700
    Overhead Flexible Budget Variance 1,300
        Production Volume Variance 3,000
    To record overhead variances and close the
    Manufacturing Overhead account. (See Exhibit 24-14.)

Entry 9 closes Manufacturing Overhead. Many companies wait until the end of the fiscal year to close this account.

Exhibit 24-15 shows selected Kool-Time accounts, after posting the preceding journal entries.

Objective 7
Prepare a standard cost income statement for management

Standard Cost Income Statement for Management

Exhibit 24-16 shows Kool Time's standard cost income statement. After sales revenue, the statement shows the cost of goods sold at standard cost. Then the statement separately lists each variance, followed by the cost of goods sold at actual cost. (Recall that since Kool-Time had no raw materials, work in process, or finished goods inventories, all the variances relate to June's sales.) At the end of the period, all the variance accounts are closed to zero-out their balances. The net amount is closed to Income Summary.

The income statement shows that the net effect of this adjustment is $1,200 unfavorable. Thus, June's operating income is $1,200 lower than it would have been if all actual costs had been equal to standard amounts. Management can prepare statements with similar detail for research and development, design, marketing, distribution, and customer service costs, if they are subject to standard cost analysis.

EXHIBIT 24-15   Kool-Time Pools Flow of Costs in Standard Costing System

EXHIBIT 24-16
Standard Cost Income Statement

DAILY EXERCISE 24-21

KOOL-TIME POOLS
Standard Cost Income Statement
Month Ended June 30, 20X5

Sales revenue (10 × $12,000).................................		$120,000
Cost of goods sold at standard cost.........................		85,000
Manufacturing cost variances:		
Direct materials price variance	$ (838)	
Direct materials efficiency variance....................	3,938	
Direct labor price variance.................................	1,900	
Direct labor efficiency variance	(2,100)	
Manufacturing overhead flexible		
budget variance...	1,300	
Production volume variance	(3,000)	
Total manufacturing variances		1,200
Cost of goods sold at actual cost...........................		86,200
Gross profit..		33,800
Marketing and administrative expenses*..............		18,800
Operating income..		$15,000

*$9,100 + $9,700 from Exhibit 24-9.

Take a moment to review standard costing by studying the Decision Guidelines on the following page. Then work the summary problem.

DECISION GUIDELINES

Standard Costs

DECISION	GUIDELINES
How to set standards?	Historical performance data Engineering analysis/time-and-motion studies Continuous improvement standards Benchmarking
How to compute a price variance for materials or labor?	$$\text{Price variance} = \left(\begin{array}{c} \text{Actual price} \\ \text{per input unit} \end{array} - \begin{array}{c} \text{Standard price} \\ \text{per input unit} \end{array} \right) \times \begin{array}{c} \text{Actual} \\ \text{quantity of} \\ \text{input} \end{array}$$
How to compute an efficiency variance for materials or labor?	$$\text{Efficiency variance} = \left(\begin{array}{c} \text{Actual} \\ \text{quantity of} \\ \text{input} \end{array} - \begin{array}{c} \text{Standard quantity} \\ \text{of input for actual} \\ \text{number of outputs} \end{array} \right) \times \begin{array}{c} \text{Standard} \\ \text{price per} \\ \text{input unit} \end{array}$$
Who is most likely responsible for: 　Sales volume variance? 　Sales revenue flexible budget variance? 　Direct material price variance? 　Direct material efficiency variance? 　Direct labor price variance? 　Direct labor efficiency variance?	 Marketing Department Marketing Department Purchasing Department Production Department Personnel Department or Production Department Production Department
How to allocate manufacturing overhead in a standard costing system?	$$\begin{array}{c} \text{Manufacturing} \\ \text{overhead} \\ \text{allocated} \end{array} = \left(\begin{array}{c} \text{Standard} \\ \text{predetermined} \\ \text{manufacturing} \\ \text{overhead rate} \end{array} \right) \times \left(\begin{array}{c} \text{Standard quantity of} \\ \text{allocation base allowed} \\ \text{for actual outputs} \end{array} \right)$$
How to analyze over- or underallocated manufacturing overhead?	Split over- or underallocated overhead into $$\text{Flexible budget variance} = \begin{array}{c} \text{Actual} \\ \text{overhead} \end{array} - \begin{array}{c} \text{Flexible budget} \\ \text{overhead} \end{array}$$ $$\text{Production volume variance} = \begin{array}{c} \text{Flexible budget} \\ \text{overhead} \end{array} - \begin{array}{c} \text{Standard overhead} \\ \text{allocated to} \\ \text{actual outputs} \end{array}$$
How to record standard costs in the accounts?	Materials Inventory: Actual quantity at standard price Work in Process Inventory (and Finished Goods Inventory and Cost of Goods Sold): Standard quantity of inputs allowed for actual outputs, at standard price of inputs

REVIEW FLEXIBLE BUDGETS AND STANDARD COSTING

www.prenhall.com/horngren

End-of-Chapter Assessment

SUMMARY PROBLEM

Exhibit 24-9 indicates that Kool-Time Pools installed ten swimming pools in June. Suppose Kool-Time had installed seven pools instead of ten and that actual expenses were

Direct materials (gunite)............	7,400 cubic feet @ $2.00 per cubic foot
Direct labor.................................	2,740 hours @ $10.00 per hour
Variable overhead......................	$5,400
Fixed overhead..........................	$11,900

Required

1. Given these new data, prepare two exhibits similar to Exhibits 24-9 and 24-13. Ignore marketing and administrative expenses in your first exhibit.
2. Compute price and efficiency variances for direct materials and direct labor.
3. Compute the total variance, the flexible budget variance, and the production volume variance for manufacturing overhead.
4. Prepare a June income statement through operating income for the president of Kool-Time Pools. Report all standard cost variances; assume that actual marketing and administrative expenses for the month totaled $17,700.

Solution

Requirement 1

KOOL-TIME POOLS
Revised Data for Standard Costing Example
Month of June, 20X5

PANEL A — Comparison of Actual Results with Flexible Budget for 7 Swimming Pools

	Actual Results at Actual Prices	Flexible Budget for 7 Pools	Flexible Budget Variance
Variable expenses:			
Direct materials	$14,800*	$14,000†	$ 800 U
Direct labor	27,400*	29,400†	2,000 F
Variable overhead	5,400	5,600†	200 F
Total variable expenses	47,600	49,000	1,400 F
Fixed expenses:			
Fixed overhead	11,900	12,000 ‡	100 F
Total expenses	$59,500	$61,000	$1,500 F

* See Panel C
† See Panel B
‡ Fixed overhead was budgeted at $12,000 per month.

PANEL B — Computation of Flexible Budget for Direct Materials, Direct Labor, and Variable Overhead for 7 Swimming Pools

	(1) Standard Quantity of Inputs Allowed for 7 Pools	(2) Standard Price per Unit of Input	(1) × (2) Flexible Budget for 7 Pools
Direct materials	1,000 cubic feet per pool × 7 pools = 7,000 cubic feet	$ 2.00	$14,000
Direct labor	400 hours per pool × 7 pools = 2,800 hours	10.50	29,400
Variable overhead	400 hours per pool × 7 pools = 2,800 hours	2.00	5,600

KOOL-TIME POOLS (continued)
Revised Data for Standard Costing Example
Month of June, 20X5

PANEL C—Computation of Actual Costs for Direct Materials and Direct Labor for 7 Swimming Pools

	(1) Actual Quantity of Inputs Used for 7 Pools	(2) Actual Price per Unit of Input	(1) × (2) Actual Cost for 7 Pools
Direct materials..................	7,400 cubic feet actually used	$ 2.00 actual cost/cubic foot	$14,800
Direct labor........................	2,740 hours actually used	$10.00 actual cost/hour	27,400

KOOL-TIME POOLS
Revised Budget Data for the Month Ended June 30, 20X5

	Flexible Budget for Actual Output	Static Budget for Expected Output
Output units (pools installed)......................	7	8
Standard direct labor hours (400 hours per pool)................................	2,800	3,200
Budgeted manufacturing overhead cost:		
Variable...	$ 5,600*	$ 6,400
Fixed...	12,000†	12,000
Total..	$17,600	$18,400
Standard variable manufacturing overhead rate per direct labor hour.........		$ 6,400 ÷ 3,200 = $2.00
Standard fixed manufacturing overhead rate per direct labor hour.........		$12,000 ÷ 3,200 = $3.75
Standard total manufacturing overhead rate per direct labor hour.........		$18,400 ÷ 3,200 = $5.75

* Flexible budget variable overhead is computed as the standard quantity of the allocation base allowed for actual outputs (2,800 direct labor hours = 7 pools × 400 direct labor hours per pool) multiplied by the $2.00 standard variable manufacturing overhead rate per direct labor hour: 2,800 hours × $2.00 per hour = $5,600.
† Budgeted fixed overhead is *fixed* within the relevant range, so flexible budget fixed overhead is $12,000, the same as static budget fixed overhead.

Requirement 2

$$\text{Price variance} = \left(\begin{array}{c} \text{Actual price} \\ \text{per input unit} \end{array} - \begin{array}{c} \text{Standard price} \\ \text{per input unit} \end{array} \right) \times \begin{array}{c} \text{Actual} \\ \text{quantity of} \\ \text{input} \end{array}$$

Direct materials:

Price variance = ($2.00 − $2.00) × 7,400 cubic feet = $-0-

Direct labor:

Price variance = ($10.00 − $10.50) × 2,740 hours = $1,370 F

$$\text{Efficiency variance} = \left(\begin{array}{c} \text{Actual} \\ \text{quantity} \\ \text{of input} \end{array} - \begin{array}{c} \text{Standard} \\ \text{quantity of} \\ \text{input} \end{array} \right) \times \begin{array}{c} \text{Standard} \\ \text{price per} \\ \text{input unit} \end{array}$$

Direct materials:

$$\text{Efficiency variance} = \left(\begin{array}{c} 7,400 \\ \text{cubic feet} \end{array} - \begin{array}{c} 7,000 \\ \text{cubic feet} \end{array} \right) \times \begin{array}{c} \$2.00 \text{ per} \\ \text{cubic foot} \end{array} = \$800 \text{ U}$$

Direct labor:

$$\text{Efficiency variance} = \left(\begin{array}{c} 2,740 \\ \text{hours} \end{array} - \begin{array}{c} 2,800 \\ \text{hours} \end{array} \right) \times \begin{array}{c} \$10.50 \text{ per} \\ \text{hour} \end{array} = \$630 \text{ F}$$

Total overhead variance:

Actual overhead cost ($5,400 variable + $11,900 fixed).........................	$17,300
Standard overhead allocated to production	
(2,800 standard direct labor hours × $5.75)	16,100
Total overhead variance	$ 1,200 U

Overhead flexible budget variance:

Actual overhead cost ($5,400 + $11,900)	$17,300
Flexible budget overhead for actual outputs ($5,600 + $12,000)	17,600
Overhead flexible budget variance..	$ 300 F

Production volume variance:

Flexible budget overhead for actual outputs ($5,600 + $12,000)	$17,600
Standard overhead allocated to (actual) production	
(2,800 standard direct labor hours × $5.75)	16,100
Production volume variance	$ 1,500 U

Requirement 4

KOOL-TIME POOLS
Revised Standard Cost Income Statement
Month Ended June 30, 20X5

Sales revenue (7 × $12,000).................................		$84,000
Cost of goods sold at standard cost*......................		59,500
Manufacturing cost variances:		
Direct materials price variance	$ 0	
Direct materials efficiency variance....................	800	
Direct labor price variance..................................	(1,370)	
Direct labor efficiency variance	(630)	
Overhead flexible budget variance	(300)	
Production volume variance	1,500	
Total manufacturing variances		0
Cost of goods sold at actual cost............................		59,500
Gross profit..		24,500
Marketing and administrative expenses		17,700
Operating income...		$ 6,800

*Cost of goods sold at standard cost:

Direct materials (7,000 cubic feet × $2.00 per cubic foot)	$14,000
Direct labor (2,800 direct labor hours × $10.50 per direct labor hour).........	29,400
Standard overhead allocated (2,800 direct labor hours ×	
$5.75 per direct labor hour)	$16,100
Cost of goods sold at standard cost..	$59,500

LESSONS LEARNED

1. **Prepare a flexible budget for the income statement.** A *flexible budget* is a summarized budget that can easily be computed for different volume levels. Flexible budgets separate variable costs from fixed costs. These budgets show how revenues and costs vary—if at all—as the number of outputs varies within the budget range.

2. **Prepare an income statement performance report.** Static budget variances are differences between actual amounts and corresponding amounts (revenues and expenses) in the static budget. At the end of the period, accountants prepare an after-the-fact flexible budget for the actual number of outputs. Accountants use this flexible budget to divide static budget variances into two broad categories: *sales volume variances* and *flexible budget variances*.

3. **Identify the benefits of standard costs.** *Standard costs* are carefully predetermined costs that usually are expressed

on a per-unit basis. Standards help managers plan and control, motivate employees, provide unit costs, and simplify record keeping.

4. **Compute standard cost variances for direct materials and direct labor.** Companies divide flexible budget variances for direct materials and direct labor into price and efficiency (quantity) variances. A *price variance* reveals the effect on total cost—and thus the effect on operating income—of paying more or less for an input than the standard allows. An *efficiency variance* reveals the effect on total cost of using more or less input than allowed by the flexible budget for the actual number of outputs.

5. **Analyze manufacturing overhead in a standard cost system.** The total variance between actual manufacturing overhead cost incurred and standard overhead cost allocated has two components: the *overhead flexible budget*

variance and the *production volume variance*. Overhead flexible budget variance is the difference between actual overhead and flexible budget overhead that should have been incurred given the actual number of outputs. Production volume variance is the difference between flexible budget overhead for actual outputs and standard overhead allocated to production.

6. **Record transactions at standard cost.** Many companies record standard costs in inventory and expense accounts.

They also record standard cost variances. At year's end, all variance accounts are closed out.

7. **Prepare a standard cost income statement for management.** The statement shows cost of goods sold at standard cost, lists all variances, and then shows the adjusted cost of goods sold—at actual cost. Operating expenses are treated similarly if they are part of the company's standard cost system.

ACCOUNTING VOCABULARY

benchmarking (p. 983)
efficiency variance (p. 986)
flexible budget (p. 974)
flexible budget variance (p. 977)
master budget (p. 973)

overhead flexible budget
 variance (p. 993)
price variance (p. 984)
production volume
 variance (p. 994)

sales volume variance (p. 977)
standard cost (p. 981)
static budget (p. 973)
variance (p. 973)

QUESTIONS

1. How does a static budget differ from a flexible budget?
2. What is the relevant range, and why must it be considered in preparing a flexible budget?
3. McLaren, Inc., prepared its static (master) budget for a sales level of 35,000 for the month. Actual sales totaled 46,000. Describe the problem of using the static budget to evaluate company performance for the month. Propose a better way to evaluate McLaren's performance.
4. What advantage does a flexible budget graph offer over a columnar flexible budget with four levels of volume?
5. What do the sales volume variance and the flexible budget variance for operating income measure?
6. Describe the benefits of a standard cost system.
7. What does a price variance measure? How is it computed?
8. What does an efficiency variance measure? How is it computed?

9. How are the price variance and the efficiency variance related to the flexible budget variance for direct materials and direct labor?
10. Describe how managers can trade off direct materials price and efficiency variances.
11. When should a cost variance be investigated?
12. What causes an overhead flexible budget variance? What information does this variance provide?
13. Scott & White, Inc., uses standard costing. The actual quantity of direct materials used to manufacture inventory, costed at standard prices, was $21,600. The direct materials efficiency variance was $1,400 favorable. Make the journal entry to record the use of materials in production.
14. How does a standard cost income statement for management differ from an income statement reported to the public?

ASSESS YOUR PROGRESS

DAILY EXERCISES

Preparing flexible budgets
(Obj. 1)

DE24-1 In a series of Daily Exercises, we are going to prepare budgets and variance analyses for Digital Systems, Inc., a firm that installs household wiring for high-speed Internet connections and high-definition audio and video. For each installation, Digital Systems has budgeted direct materials costs of $500 and direct labor costs of $800. The company has budgeted fixed expenses at $8,000 per month, for 0–50 installations per month. Digital Systems' budgeted sale price is $2,500 per installation.

1. Write out Digital Systems' flexible budget total cost formula.
2. Using Exhibit 24-3 (page 974) as a guide, prepare flexible budgets for Digital Systems for
   a. 20 installations per month
   b. 30 installations per month

Preparing and using flexible budgets (Obj. 1)

DE24-2 Turn to the Kool-Time Pools example on page 974.

1. Using the data from Exhibit 24-3 (page 974), develop flexible budgets for three- and ten-pool levels of output.
2. Would Kool-Time's managers use the flexible budgets you developed in requirement 1 for planning or for controlling? What specific insights can Kool-Time's managers gain from the flexible budgets you prepared in requirement 1?

Preparing a flexible budget graph
(Obj. 1)

DE24-3 ➡ *Link Back to Chapter 22, Exhibit 22-7 (page 899).* Refer to Daily Exercise 24-1. Digital Systems reports the following actual results for January and February:

	January	February
Expected number of installations, per the static budget..................................	20	30
Actual number of installations	25	20
Actual sale price per installation...................................	$2,500	$2,800
Actual direct materials cost per installation.................	$ 450	$ 560
Actual direct labor cost per installation	$ 760	$ 800
Actual fixed monthly expenses	$7,000	$9,000

1. Prepare a graph of Digital Systems' monthly flexible budget total cost formula, using data from Daily Exercise 24-1. Use Exhibit 24-4 on page 976 as a guide.
2. Plot January's and February's actual costs on the flexible budget graph from requirement 1.

DE24-4 Look at Kool-Time Pools' graph of actual and budgeted monthly costs in Exhibit 24-5 on page 976.

Interpreting flexible budget graph and formula (Obj. 1)

1. How many pools did Kool-Time install in May?
2. How much were Kool-Time's actual expenses in May?
3. Using Kool-Time's flexible budget formula, what is the flexible budget total cost for the month of May?
4. What is Kool-Time's flexible budget variance for total costs? Is the variance favorable or unfavorable in May?

DE24-5 Refer to the Digital Systems data in Daily Exercises 24-1 and 24-3. Compute January and February flexible budget variances for total costs. Has Digital Systems done a better-than-expected job or a worse-than-expected job of controlling total costs in January? In February? Explain.

Computing flexible budget variances (Obj. 1)

DE24-6 Use your results from Daily Exercise 24-4 to prepare an income statement performance report for Kool-Time Pools for May. Use Exhibit 24-7 (page 978) as a guide. Assume that the actual sale price per pool remains $12,000, actual variable expenses total $59,000, and actual fixed expenses are $21,000 in May. The static budget number of pools remains eight.

Explain to Kool-Time's management why May's operating income differs from the static budget operating income.

Preparing and interpreting an income statement performance report (Obj. 2)

DE24-7 Use the data in Daily Exercises 24-1, 24-3, and 24-5 to prepare an income statement performance report for Digital Systems for January. Use Exhibit 24-7 (page 978) as a guide. Interpret the variances for Digital Systems' management.

Income statement performance report (Obj. 2)

DE24-8 Consider the Kool-Time Pools example on pages 973–980.

Role of fixed costs (Obj. 1, 2)

1. What is the relevant range for the flexible budget total cost formula?
2. Explain whether Kool-Time would have a sales volume variance for fixed expenses in Exhibit 24-7 (page 978) if
   a. Kool-Time installs 14 pools per month.
   b. Kool-Time installs 8 pools per month.

DE24-9 Fill in the blank with the phrase that best completes the sentence.

Static budgets and flexible budgets (Obj. 2)

Actual number of outputs	Beginning of the period	Static budget variance
Expected number of outputs	End of the period	
Sales volume variance	Flexible budget variance	

a. The static budget is developed at the _____.
b. The flexible budget used in a performance report is based on the _____.
c. The master budget is based on the _____.
d. The flexible budget used in a performance report is developed at the _____.
e. The difference between actual costs and the costs that should have been incurred for the actual number of outputs is the _____.

DE24-10 Lladró is a Spanish manufacturer of porcelain art objects. Raw materials are mixed to form clay, which is shaped into figurines. The pieces are then glazed and fired at high temperatures.

Benefits of standard costs (Obj. 3)

Explain how the five benefits of standard costs (pages 983–984) apply to Lladró. Be as specific as possible.

DE24-11 As explained in the chapter opening story, each **McDonald's** uses historical data to budget sales for each hour, and the restaurant computes hourly sales variances. If actual sales are less than budgeted, the manager can send employees home.

Sales and labor variances (Obj. 2, 4)

1. What variance does McDonald's control by sending employees home early if actual sales volume falls short of the budget? Explain.
2. What sales variance does McDonald's compute hourly?

Computing materials variances (Obj. 4)

DE24-12 In a series of Daily Exercises, we will compute variances and record journal entries for TimTam Pottery, a manufacturer of ceramic cookie jars. The company has the following standards:

Direct materials (clay)	1 pound per jar, at a cost of $0.50 per pound
Direct labor	1/5 hour per jar, at a cost of $13 per hour
Static budget variable overhead	$60,000
Static budget fixed overhead	$20,000
Static budget direct labor hours	10,000 hours
Static budget number of cookie jars	50,000

TimTam allocates manufacturing overhead to production based on standard direct labor hours. Last month, TimTam reported the following actual results for the production of 60,000 jars:

Direct materials	1.1 pound per jar, at a cost of $0.60 per pound
Direct labor	1/4 hour per jar, at a cost of $12 per hour
Actual variable overhead	$84,000
Actual fixed overhead	$18,000

Compute TimTam's variances for materials.

Computing materials efficiency variances (Obj. 4)

DE24-13 As explained in the chapter opening story, the standard direct materials for a regular **McDonald's** hamburger are

1 bun	1 pickle slice	1/4 teaspoon mustard
1 hamburger patty	1/8 teaspoon dehydrated onion	1/2 ounce ketchup

Assume that a San Diego, California, McDonald's sold 500 hamburgers yesterday and actually used the following materials:

510 buns	490 pickle slices	120 teaspoons mustard
520 hamburger patties	70 teaspoons dehydrated onion	300 ounces ketchup

Compute the direct materials efficiency variances for each material, using the following standard materials prices (all amounts assumed):

Buns	$0.10 each	Dehydrated onion	$0.04 per teaspoon
Hamburger patties	0.15 each	Mustard	0.02 per teaspoon
Pickle slices	0.01 per slice	Ketchup	0.04 per ounce

Computing direct labor variances (Obj. 4)

DE24-14 Refer to the TimTam data in Daily Exercise 24-12. Compute the direct labor variances.

Interpreting materials and labor variances (Obj. 4)

DE24-15 Refer to Daily Exercises 24-12 and 24-14. For each variance, who in TimTam's organization is most likely responsible? Interpret the direct materials and direct labor variances for TimTam's management.

Standard overhead rates (Obj. 5)

DE24-16 Use the TimTam data in Daily Exercise 24-12 to compute the standard predetermined variable manufacturing overhead rate and the standard predetermined fixed manufacturing overhead rate.

Computing overhead variances (Obj. 5)

DE24-17 Refer to the TimTam data in Daily Exercises 24-12 and 24-16.

1. Compute the overhead variances. (Use Exhibit 24-14 as a guide.)
2. Is manufacturing overhead under- or overallocated? By how much?

Materials and labor journal entries (Obj. 6)

DE24-18 Refer to the information in Daily Exercises 24-12 and 24-14. Record TimTam's direct materials and direct labor journal entries.

Overhead journal entries (Obj. 6)

DE24-19 Refer to the information in Daily Exercises 24-12 and 24-17. Record TimTam's journal entries for Manufacturing Overhead, including the entry that records the overhead variances and closes the Manufacturing Overhead account.

DE24-20 Refer to the information in Daily Exercises 24-12, 24-14, and 24-17 through 24-19. TimTam sold on account each of the 60,000 jars at a sale price of $8.00 each. There were no beginning or ending inventories of any kind.

Record the journal entries for the completion and sale of the 60,000 jars.

Journal entries for goods completed and sold (Obj. 6)

DE24-21 Use the information from Daily Exercises 24-12, 24-14, and 24-17 through 24-20 to prepare a standard cost income statement for TimTam's management, using Exhibit 24-16 as a guide. Actual marketing and administrative expenses were $88,500.

Standard cost income statement (Obj. 7)

EXERCISES

E24-1 CompuGear sells its main product, ergonomic mouse pads, for $10 each. Its variable cost is $4 per pad. Fixed expenses are $200,000 per month for volumes up to 60,000 pads. Above 60,000 pads, monthly fixed expenses are $300,000.

Prepare a monthly flexible budget for the product, showing sales, variable expenses, fixed expenses, and operating income or loss for volume levels of 40,000, 50,000, and 70,000 pads.

Preparing a flexible budget for the income statement (Obj. 1)

E24-2 ➡ *Link Back to Chapter 22, Exhibit 22-7 (page 899).* Graph the flexible budget total cost line for CompuGear in Exercise 24-1. Show total costs for volume levels of 40,000, 50,000, and 70,000 pads.

Graphing cost behavior (Obj. 1)

E24-3 Beach Blanket Company managers received the following incomplete performance report:

Completing a performance report (Obj. 2)

BEACH BLANKET COMPANY
Income Statement Performance Report
Year Ended July 31, 20X3

	Actual Results at Actual Prices	Flexible Budget Variance	Flexible Budget for Actual Number of Output Units	Sales Volume Variance	Static (Master) Budget
Output units..........................	24,000	‾‾‾	24,000	4,000 F	‾‾‾
Sales Revenue	$192,000	‾‾‾	$192,000	$32,000 F	‾‾‾
Variable expenses	85,000	‾‾‾	80,000	20,000 U	‾‾‾
Fixed expenses	104,000	‾‾‾	100,000	–0–	‾‾‾
Total expenses	189,000	‾‾‾	180,000	20,000 U	‾‾‾
Operating income..................	$ 3,000	‾‾‾	$ 12,000	$12,000 F	‾‾‾

Complete the performance report. Identify the employee group that may deserve praise and the group that may be subject to criticism. Give your reasons.

E24-4 Top managers of Wang Industries predicted 20X4 sales of 145,000 units of its product at a unit price of $7. Actual sales for the year were 140,000 units at $8.50 each. Variable expenses were budgeted at $2.20 per unit, and actual variable expenses were $2.25 per unit. Actual fixed expenses of $420,000 exceeded budgeted fixed expenses by $10,000. Prepare Wang's income statement performance report in a format similar to Exercise 24-3. What variance contributed most to the year's favorable results? What caused this variance?

Preparing an income statement performance report (Obj. 2)

E24-5 The following direct materials variance computations are incomplete:

$$\text{Price variance} = (\$? - \$12) \times 14{,}500 \text{ pounds} = \$5{,}800 \text{ U}$$
$$\text{Efficiency variance} = (? - 14{,}700 \text{ pounds}) \times \$12 = ? \text{ F}$$
$$\text{Flexible budget variance} = \$?$$

Fill in the missing values, and identify the flexible budget variance as favorable or unfavorable.

Computing price and efficiency variances for direct materials (Obj. 4)

E24-6 Forever Frames, which uses a standard cost accounting system, manufactured 400,000 picture frames during the year, using 1,350,000 board feet of lumber purchased at $1.55 per foot. Production required 9,500 direct labor hours that cost $12.00 per hour. The materials standard was 3 board feet of lumber per frame, at a standard cost of $1.70 per foot. The labor standard was 0.025 direct labor hour per frame, at a standard cost of $11.50 per hour. Compute the price and efficiency variances for direct materials and direct labor. Does the pattern of variances suggest Forever Frames' managers have been making tradeoffs? Explain.

Price and efficiency variances for materials and labor (Obj. 4)

E24-7 Make the journal entries to record the purchase and use of direct materials and direct labor in Exercise 24-6.

Journal entries (Obj. 6)

E24-8 The managers of Diaz Co., a contract manufacturer of disk drives, are seeking explanations for the variances in the following report. Explain the meaning of each of Diaz's materials, labor, and overhead variances.

DIAZ CO.
Standard Costing Income Statement
Year Ended December 31, 20X4

Sales revenue		$1,200,000
Cost of goods sold at standard cost		700,000
Manufacturing cost variances:		
Direct materials price variance	$ 8,000 F	
Direct materials efficiency variance	32,000 U	
Direct labor price variance	24,000 F	
Direct labor efficiency variance	10,000 U	
Manufacturing overhead flexible budget variance	28,000 U	
Production volume variance	8,000 F	
Total manufacturing variances		30,000
Cost of goods sold at actual cost		730,000
Gross profit		470,000
Marketing and administrative expenses		418,000
Operating income		$ 52,000

E24-9 Polystar manufactures carpeting. The company charges the following standard unit costs to production on the basis of static budget volume of 30,000 linear feet of carpet per month:

Direct materials	$2.50
Direct labor	2.00
Manufacturing overhead	1.50
Standard unit cost	$6.00

Polystar uses the following monthly flexible budget overhead:

	Number of Outputs (linear feet)		
	27,000	**30,000**	**33,000**
Standard machine hours	2,700	3,000	3,300
Budgeted manufacturing overhead cost:			
Variable	$13,500	$15,000	$16,500
Fixed	30,000	30,000	30,000

Polystar actually produced 33,000 linear feet of carpet, using 3,100 machine hours. Actual variable overhead was $16,200, and fixed overhead was $30,500. Compute the total overhead variance, the overhead flexible budget variance, and the production volume variance.

Preparing a standard cost income
statement for management
(Obj. 7)

E24-10 European Cuisine, Inc., revenue and expense information for the month of April follows.

Sales revenue	$440,000
Cost of good sold (standard)	242,000
Direct materials price variance	2,000 F
Direct materials efficiency variance	4,000 F
Direct labor price variance	3,000 U
Direct labor efficiency variance	2,000 F
Overhead flexible budget variance	2,500 U
Production volume variance	6,000 F

Prepare a standard cost income statement for management through gross profit. Report all standard cost variances for management's use. Has management done a good or poor job of controlling costs? Explain.

Challenge Exercise

Overhead variances
(Obj. 5)

E24-11 Laptop Solutions repairs and upgrades laptop computers. The company measures "production output" in terms of the number of laptops serviced. The company allocates overhead at the rate of $80 per laptop serviced.

	Overhead Rate per Unit
Variable	$30
Fixed	50

In June, 20X6, Laptop Solutions "produced" 5,200 serviced laptops. Its production volume variance was $10,000 favorable. Compute Laptop Solutions' budgeted fixed overhead cost per month. What monthly capacity level did Laptop Solutions use to compute the fixed overhead rate of $50 per unit?

PROBLEMS

(Group A)

Preparing a flexible budget income statement and graphing cost behavior
(Obj. 1)

P24-1A ➡ *Link Back to Chapter 22, Exhibit 22-7 (page 899).* Cellular Technologies manufactures capacitors for cellular base stations and other communications applications. The company's static budget income statement for October 20X4 follows. It is based on expected sales volume of 9,000 units.

Cellular Technologies' plant capacity is 9,500 units. If actual volume exceeds 9,500 units, Cellular Technologies must rent additional space. In that case, salaries will increase by 15%, rent will double, and insurance expense will increase by $1,000. Depreciation will be unaffected.

CELLULAR TECHNOLOGIES
Static Budget Income Statement
October 20X4

Sales revenue................................	$189,000
Variable expenses:	
Cost of goods sold....................	72,000
Sales commissions....................	9,450
Shipping expense	4,500
Fixed expenses:	
Salary expense	27,500
Depreciation expense.............	13,250
Rent expense............................	11,250
Insurance expense....................	2,750
Total expenses............................	140,700
Operating income	$ 48,300

Required

1. Prepare flexible budget income statements for 7,500, 9,000, and 11,000 units.
2. Graph the behavior of the company's total costs.
3. Why might Cellular Technologies' managers want to see the graph you prepared in requirement 2 as well as the columnar format analysis in requirement 1? What is the disadvantage of the graphic approach in requirement 2?

Preparing an income statement performance report *(Obj. 2)*

P24-2A Refer to Cellular Technologies, Problem 24-1A. The company sold 11,000 units during October 20X4, and its actual operating income was as follows:

CELLULAR TECHNOLOGIES
Income Statement
October 20X4

Sales revenue	$235,000
Variable expenses:	
Cost of goods sold	90,250
Sales commissions	11,250
Shipping expense	6,750
Fixed expenses:	
Salary expense	33,200
Depreciation expense	13,250
Rent expense	22,000
Insurance expense	3,700
Total expenses	180,400
Operating income	$ 54,600

Required

1. Prepare an income statement performance report for October.
2. What was the effect on Cellular Technologies' operating income of selling 2,000 units more than the static budget level of sales?
3. What is Cellular Technologies' static budget variance? Explain why the income statement performance report provides more useful information to Cellular Technologies' managers than the simple static budget variance. What insights can Cellular Technologies' managers draw from this performance report?

Preparing a flexible budget and computing standard cost variances
(Obj. 1, 3, 4, 5)

P24-3A Bronx Co. manufactures insulated hunting jackets and uses flexible budgeting and a standard cost system. Bronx allocates overhead based on yards of direct materials. The company's performance report includes the following selected data:

	Static Budget (1,000 jackets)	Actual Results (975 jackets)
Sales (1,000 jackets × $200)	$200,000	
(975 jackets × $192)		$187,200
Variable manufacturing expenses:		
Direct materials (4,000 yd × $7.90)	31,600	
(4,100 yd × $7.65)		31,365
Direct labor (5,000 hr × $6.00)	30,000	
(4,800 hr × $6.05)		29,040
Variable overhead (4,000 yd × $5.00)	20,000	
(4,100 yd × $6.40)		26,240
Fixed manufacturing expenses:		
Fixed overhead	27,000	28,500
Total cost of goods sold	108,600	115,145
Gross profit	$ 91,400	$ 72,055

Required

1. Prepare a flexible budget based on the actual number of jackets sold.
2. Compute the price variance and the efficiency variance for direct materials and for direct labor. For manufacturing overhead, compute the total variance, the flexible budget variance, and the production volume variance.
3. What is the total flexible budget variance for Bronx's manufacturing costs? Show how the total flexible budget variance is divided into materials, labor, and overhead variances.
4. Have Bronx's managers done a good job or a poor job controlling material and labor costs? Why?
5. Describe how Bronx's managers can benefit from the standard costing system.

Using incomplete cost and variance information to determine the direct labor hours *(Obj. 4)*

P24-4A The State of Ohio has a shop that manufactures road signs used throughout the state. The manager of the shop uses standard costs to judge performance. Recently, a clerk mistakenly threw away some of the records, and the manager has only partial data for March. The manager knows that the direct labor flexible budget variance for the month was $350 U and that the standard labor price was $8 per hour. The shop experienced an unfavorable labor price variance of $0.40 per hour. The standard direct labor hours for actual March output were 3,500.

Required

1. Find the actual number of direct labor hours worked during March. First, find the actual direct labor price per hour. Then, determine the actual direct labor hours by setting up the computation of the direct labor flexible budget variance of $350 U.
2. Compute the direct labor price and efficiency variances. Do these variances suggest the manager may have made any tradeoffs? Explain.

P24-5A SportsTime manufactures T-shirts that it sells to other companies for customizing with their own logos. SportsTime prepares flexible budgets and uses a standard cost system to control manufacturing costs. The standard unit cost of a basic white T-shirt is based on static budget volume of 40,000 T-shirts per month. The unit cost is computed as follows:

Computing and journalizing, standard cost variances (Obj. 4, 5, 6)

Direct materials (2 sq. yd @ $0.25 per sq. yd)..............		$0.50
Direct labor (3 minutes @ $0.12 per minute)		0.36
Manufacturing overhead:		
Variable (3 minutes @ $0.06 per minute)	$0.18	
Fixed (3 minutes @ $0.14 per minute)	0.42	0.60
Total cost per T-shirt...		$1.46

Transactions during May of the current year included the following:

a. Actual production and sales were 42,700 T-shirts.
b. Actual direct materials usage was 1.80 square yards per T-shirt at an actual cost of $0.20 per square yard.
c. Actual direct labor usage of 130,000 minutes cost $18,850.
d. Actual overhead cost was $28,200.

Required

1. Compute the price and efficiency variances for direct materials and direct labor.
2. Journalize the usage of direct materials and the assignment of direct labor, including the related variances.
3. For manufacturing overhead, compute the total variance, the flexible budget variance, and the production volume variance.
4. SportsTime intentionally hired more skilled workers during May. How did this decision affect the cost variances? Overall, was the decision wise?

P24-6A School Tools manufactures ring binders. During August, the company produced and sold 104,000 binders and recorded the following cost data:

Computing standard cost variances and reporting to management (Obj. 4, 5, 7)

		Standard Unit Cost	Actual Total Cost
Direct materials:			
Standard (2 parts @ $0.12 per part)		$0.24	
Actual (209,500 parts @ $0.16 per part)			$33,520
Direct labor:			
Standard (0.02 hr @ $6.00 per hr)		0.12	
Actual (1,560 hr @ $6.20 per hr)			9,672
Manufacturing overhead:			
Standard:			
Variable (0.02 machine hr @ $6.00 per hr)	$0.12		
Fixed ($24,000 for static budget volume of			
100,000 units and 3,000 machine hours).........	0.24	0.36	
Actual			45,500
Total manufacturing costs...		$0.72	$88,692

Required

1. Compute the price and efficiency variances for direct materials and direct labor.
2. For manufacturing overhead, compute the total variance, the flexible budget variance, and the production volume variance.
3. Prepare a standard cost income statement through gross profit to report all variances to management. Sale price of the binders to college bookstores was $1.25 each.
4. School Tools' management used more experienced workers during August. Discuss the tradeoff between the two direct labor variances.

Preparing a flexible budget
income statement and graphing
cost behavior
(Obj. 1)

P24-1B ➤ *Link Back to Chapter 22, Exhibit 22-7 (page 899).* Medix Inc., produces and sells prepackaged first-aid kits. The company's static budget income statement for August 20X3 follows. It is based on expected sales volume of 55,000 kits.

MEDIX, INC. Static Budget Income Statement August 20X3	
Sales revenue..................................	$220,000
Variable expenses:	
Cost of goods sold....................	60,500
Sales commissions...................	16,500
Utilities expense	5,500
Fixed expenses:	
Salary expense	36,500
Depreciation expense..............	24,000
Rent expense............................	11,500
Utilities expense	6,200
Total expenses............................	160,700
Operating income	$ 59,300

Medix's plant capacity is 62,500 kits. If actual volume exceeds 62,500 kits, the company must expand the plant. In that case, salaries will increase by 10%, depreciation by 15%, and rent by $6,000. Fixed utilities will be unchanged by any volume increase.

Required

1. Prepare flexible budget income statements for the company, showing output levels of 55,000, 60,000, and 65,000 kits.
2. Graph the behavior of the company's total costs.
3. Why might Medix's managers want to see the graph you prepared in requirement 2 as well as the columnar format analysis in requirement 1? What is the disadvantage of the graphic approach?

P24-2B Refer to Medix, Inc., of Problem 24-1B. The company sold 60,000 kits during August 20X3, and its actual operating income was as follows:

MEDIX, INC. Income Statement August 20X3	
Sales revenue	$245,000
Variable expenses:	
Cost of goods sold....................	$ 66,500
Sales commissions	21,000
Utilities expense	6,000
Fixed expenses:	
Salary expense..........................	38,000
Depreciation expense	24,000
Rent expense	10,500
Utilities expense	6,200
Total expenses.............................	172,200
Operating income.........................	$ 72,800

Required

1. Prepare an income statement performance report for August 20X3.
2. What accounts for most of the difference between actual operating income and static budget operating income?
3. What is Medix's static budget variance? Explain why the income statement performance report provides Medix's managers with more useful information than the simple static budget variance. What insights can Medix's managers draw from this performance report?

P24-3B Multicast Co. assembles TVs and uses flexible budgeting and a standard cost system. Multicast allocates overhead based on the number of direct materials parts. The company's performance report includes the following selected data:

Preparing a flexible budget and computing standard cost variances (Obj. 1, 3, 4, 5)

	Static Budget (20,000 TVs)	Actual Results (22,000 TVs)
Sales (20,000 TVs × $200)	$4,000,000	
(22,000 TVs × $210)		$4,620,000
Variable manufacturing expenses:		
Direct materials (200,000 parts @ $8.00)	1,600,000	
(214,200 parts @ $7.85)		1,681,470
Direct labor (40,000 hr @ $10.00)	400,000	
(42,500 hr @ $10.25)		435,625
Variable overhead (200,000 parts @ $2.00)...	400,000	
(214,200 parts @ $2.05)...		439,110
Fixed manufacturing expenses:		
Fixed overhead	600,000	610,000
Total cost of goods sold.....................................	3,000,000	3,166,205
Gross profit	$1,000,000	$1,453,795

Required

1. Prepare a flexible budget based on the actual number of TVs sold.
2. Compute the price variance and the efficiency variance for direct materials and for direct labor. For manufacturing overhead, compute the total variance, the flexible budget variance, and the production volume variance.
3. What is the total flexible budget variance for Multicast's manufacturing costs? Show how the total flexible budget variance is divided into materials, labor, and overhead variances.
4. Have Multicast's managers done a good job or a poor job controlling material and labor costs? Why?
5. Describe how Multicast's managers can benefit from the standard costing system.

P24-4B The City of Jackson has a shop that manufactures park benches. The manager of the shop uses standard costs to judge performance. Recently, a clerk mistakenly threw away some of the records, and the manager has only partial data for October. The manager knows that the direct labor flexible budget variance for the month was $404 F and that the standard labor price was $7.25 per hour. A recent pay cut caused a favorable labor price variance of $0.30 per hour. The standard direct labor hours for actual October output were 3,200.

Using incomplete cost and variance information to determine the number of direct labor hours worked (Obj. 4)

Required

1. Find the actual number of direct labor hours worked during October. First, find the actual direct labor price per hour. Then, determine the actual number of direct labor hours worked by setting up the computation of the direct labor flexible budget variance of $404 F.
2. Compute the direct labor price and efficiency variances. Do these variances suggest the manager may have made any tradeoffs? Explain.

P24-5B Pacific Products manufactures fishing waders. The company prepares flexible budgets and uses a standard cost system to control manufacturing costs. The following standard unit cost of a pair of waders is based on the static budget volume of 14,000 pairs per month:

Computing and journalizing standard cost variances (Obj. 4, 5, 6)

Direct materials (3.0 sq. ft @ $2.00 per sq. ft)		$ 6.00
Direct labor (2 hours @ $9.40 per hour)		18.90
Manufacturing overhead:		
Variable (2 hours @ $0.65 per hour)	$1.30	
Fixed (2 hours @ $2.20 per hour)	4.40	5.70
Total cost per pair		$30.60

Data for November of the current year include the following:

a. Actual production was 13,600 pair.
b. Actual direct materials usage was 2.70 square feet per pair of waders at an actual cost of $2.15 per square foot.
c. Actual direct labor usage of 24,480 hours cost $235,008.
d. Total actual overhead cost was $79,000.

 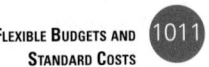

Required

1. Compute the price and efficiency variances for direct materials and direct labor.
2. Journalize the usage of direct materials and the assignment of direct labor, including the related variances.
3. For manufacturing overhead, compute the total variance, the flexible budget variance, and the production volume variance.
4. Pacific Products' management intentionally purchased superior materials for November production. How did this decision affect the other cost variances? Overall, was the decision wise?

Computing standard cost variances and reporting to management (Obj. 4, 5, 7)

P24-6B Tucker Industries produces industrial plastics. During May, the company produced and sold 42,000 sheets of plastic and recorded the following cost data:

	Standard Unit Cost	Actual Total Cost
Direct materials:		
Standard (3 lb @ $1.25 per lb)	$3.75	
Actual (134,400 lb @ $1.20 per lb)		$161,280
Direct labor:		
Standard (0.1 hr @ $6.90 per hr)	0.69	
Actual (4,400 hr @ $6.80 per hr)		29,920
Manufacturing overhead:		
Standard:		
Variable (0.2 machine hr @ $7.00 per hr)	$1.40	
Fixed ($64,000 for static budget volume of		
40,000 units and 8,000 machine hours)......	1.60	3.00
Actual...		118,900
Total manufacturing costs......................................	$7.44	$310,100

Required

1. Compute the price and efficiency variances for direct materials and direct labor.
2. For manufacturing overhead, compute the total variance, the flexible budget variance, and the production volume variance.
3. Prepare a standard cost income statement through gross profit to report all variances to management. Sale price of the plastic was $10.50 per sheet.
4. Tucker intentionally purchased cheaper materials during May. Was the decision wise? Discuss the tradeoff between the two materials variances.

APPLY YOUR KNOWLEDGE

DECISION CASES

Preparing a performance report and using it to evaluate performance (Obj. 1, 2)

Case 1. Source, Inc., distributes computer games to software retailers, including dot.coms. Source's top management meets monthly to evaluate the company's performance. Controller Jennifer Lee prepared the performance report on page 1013 for the meeting.

Lee also revealed that the actual sale price of $30 per game was equal to the budgeted sale price and that there were no changes in inventories for the month.

Management is disappointed by the operating income results. CEO Mark Baker exclaims, "How can actual operating income be roughly half the static budget amount when there are so many favorable variances?"

Required

1. Prepare a more informative performance report. Be sure to include a flexible budget for the actual number of computer games bought and sold.
2. As a member of Source's management team, which variances would you want investigated? Why?
3. Baker believes that many consumers are postponing purchases of new games until after the introduction of **Microsoft's** Xbox game machine. In light of this information, how would you rate the company's performance?

Efficiency variances and setting standards (Obj. 4)

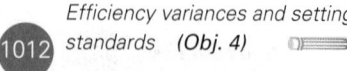

Case 2. Assume you manage your local **McDonald's** restaurant. Your restaurant is chosen to test the company's "Made-for-You" kitchen system. The system eliminates batch

	Actual Result	Static Budget	Variance
Sales revenue	$2,010,000	$2,490,000	$480,000 U
Variable expenses:			
Cost of goods sold	891,750	1,162,000	270,250 F
Sales commissions	87,675	124,500	36,825 F
Shipping expense.....................	48,000	62,250	14,250 F
Fixed expenses:			
Salary expense.........................	331,200	320,250	10,950 U
Depreciation expense	229,500	234,750	5,250 F
Rent expense	128,250	128,250	−0−
Advertising expense.................	95,100	82,500	12,600 U
Total expenses	1,811,475	2,114,500	303,025 F
Operating income.........................	$ 198,525	$ 375,500	$176,975 U

production and the use of holding bins, and allows patrons to customize their orders. You think the new system is a good idea given increasing competition in the fast-food market.

Customers like the new system, and your staff appears to be adapting, but you wonder whether the new system is as efficient as the old one. Efficiency is a special concern because your performance is evaluated in part on the restaurant's efficient use of materials and labor. Assume that your superiors consider efficiency variances greater than 5% unacceptable.

You decide to look at your restaurant's hamburger sales for a typical day. You find that the restaurant used 491 lbs. of hamburger patties and 72 hours of direct labor to produce and sell 2,000 hamburgers. Assume for simplicity that the standard quantity allowed for a hamburger is a quarter pound of meat and 0.03 hours (1.8 minutes) of direct labor. Further, assume that standard costs are $2 per pound for hamburger and $9 an hour for labor.

Required

1. Compute the efficiency variances for direct labor and direct materials.
2. Provide likely explanations for the variances. Do you have reason to be concerned about your performance evaluation? Explain.
3. Write a memo to McDonald's national office explaining your concern and suggesting a remedy. Your memo should take the following form:

Date:	_____
To:	McDonald's National Office
From:	_____
Subject:	"Made-for-you" kitchen system

ETHICAL ISSUE

Terry Tubbs is a bottling machine operator for Harmony, Inc., which produces dietary supplements and homeopathic medicines. Harmony uses standard costing.

Costs and benefits of standard cost systems
(Obj. 3, 4)

Tubbs enters the beginning and ending times for each job on a computer touch screen. This provides the actual direct labor hours and machine hours used to compute labor and manufacturing overhead efficiency variances. When the machine is idle due to product changeover or production-line delays, Tubbs' labor cost is recorded as indirect labor.

Tubbs has become frustrated with the maintenance department's slow response to machinery problems. Now when his machinery is not running efficiently, he clocks off the job before it is actually finished so that his efficiency does not look bad. Tubbs believes that his performance evaluation should not suffer because of the maintenance department's slow response.

1. Explain the consequences of Tubbs' behavior.
2. Is Tubbs acting ethically? Explain. What should he do?
3. In computerized information systems, including enterprise resource planning (ERP) systems, production employees directly enter data into the system. What are the implications for accountants when the data are then used in the employee's evaluation, as with Terry Tubbs?

Cabletronix is a contract manufacturer of electronic components, including Cisco equipment cables. Cabletronix has a number of network installers who are regular customers for the company's cables. To grow its business, Cabletronix has joined a business-to-business trading community.

Sales manager Jenny Wang informs CEO Elizabeth Pronai of a potentially promising order for 1,000 Cisco-equivalent cables on the trading community's Web site. This is a large order, and Pronai recognizes that meeting the job's three-week deadline will require a coordinated effort by the cable division and may disrupt completion of some existing orders. Still, Pronai believes the company must move in this direction to be successful.

Pronai checks with Cabletronix purchasing manager Steve Hunt, who tells her that the company has the necessary supply of wire in stock, but the connectors must be rush-ordered. Production manager Tony Alvarez suggests that he could manage the production schedule by hiring a temporary worker and using overtime. Finally, Pronai asks Wang for a sale price that would give Cabletronix a good chance of landing the order. Based on the information these managers provided, Pronai sends the following e-mail:

Subject:	Special Web Cable Order
Date:	May 15, 2005
From:	Elizabeth <EPronai@Cabletronix.com>
To:	Tony <TAlvarez@Cabletronix.com>
	Steve <SHunt@Cabletronix.com>
	Jenny <JWang@Cabletronix.com>

Thanks for your quick response to my request for information on the feasibility of meeting the special order. I have summarized our expected "actual" quantities and costs. Please consider this information and let me know whether you think we should proceed with the bid. I need a response this afternoon. We may need to meet first thing in the morning to make a final decision.

Direct materials:	
Wire (3,200 feet @ $5 a foot)	$16,000
Connectors (2,400 @ $8.50 each)	$20,400
Direct labor (350 hours @ $26 per hour)	$9,100
Variable manufacturing overhead (350 hours @ $24 per hour) ($24 per hour is the standard variable overhead rate)	$8,400
Fixed manufacturing overhead	No change
Sale price	$60 per cable

Required

Each member of your team should play the role of one of the four members of Cabletronix's management. Team members must exchange e-mails and decide when they will meet as a group, leaving enough time for each team member to perform his or her own analysis and provide the result to CEO Elizabeth Pronai before the meeting.

Jenny Wang: Unit sales volume and the sales revenue flexible budget variance are primary determinants of your own performance evaluation as sales manager. The standard sale price is $65 a cable. Before meeting with the entire team, determine whether bidding on the order is (1) in the company's interest and (2) in your own interest. As a starting point, prepare a contribution margin income statement for the order. ←

Send an e-mail presenting your recommendation (and the analysis on which the recommendation is based) to CEO Elizabeth Pronai before the team meeting.

Steve Hunt: Before meeting with the entire team, determine whether bidding on the order is (1) in the company's interest and (2) in your own interest. As a starting point, prepare a contribution margin income statement for the order.

The direct materials price variances are primary determinants of your own performance evaluation as purchasing manager. Standard prices for the materials are: wire $5 a foot, connectors $7 each. Send an e-mail presenting your recommendation (and the analysis on which the recommendation is based) to CEO Elizabeth Pronai before the team meeting.

Tony Alvarez: Before meeting with the entire team, determine whether bidding on the order is (1) in the company's interest and (2) in your own interest. As a starting point, prepare a contribution margin income statement for the order.

The direct materials efficiency variances and the direct labor variances are important determinants of your own performance evaluation as production manager. Standard quantities for the materials are 3 feet of wire and 2 connectors per cable. The direct labor standards

➡ Chapter 22, p. 890, discusses the contribution margin income statement.

are 0.3 hours a cable at $21 an hour. Send an e-mail presenting your recommendation (and the analysis on which the recommendation is based) to CEO Elizabeth Pronai before the team meeting.

Elizabeth Pronai: Before meeting with the entire team, determine whether bidding on the order is in the company's interest. As a starting point, prepare a contribution margin income statement for the order.

Based on the e-mail received from your managers, lead the team meeting to (1) reach a consensus on whether accepting the order is in the best interests of the company, (2) recognize any concerns the managers may have, and (3) lead the team discussion in how Cabletronix can address their concerns. After the team meeting, prepare an e-mail for distribution to managers that summarizes the team's final decision and supporting discussion.

INTERNET EXERCISE

Vail Resorts, Inc., is a holding company operating in two business segments, mountain resorts and real-estate development. For the mountain resort segment, revenues and expenses can vary widely depending on the amount of snow and other weather conditions. Assume that to plan for these differences, each year Vail Resorts prepares a flexible budget with three levels of operating activity. Use *only* operating revenues and operating expenses to answer the following questions:

1. Go to **http://www.Forbes.com** and under "Stocks," type **MTN,** the stock symbol for Vail Resorts, Inc., and click on *Go*. In the left-hand column, click on *Financials*. Assume the average mountain resort guest pays $1,000 for lodging, meals, entertainment, and lift tickets and that 30% of resort expenses are fixed costs. For the most recent year, how many guests were served? What is the variable cost per resort guest (rounded to the nearest whole dollar)?

2. Corporate expense and depreciation and amortization are fixed costs. Assume real-estate revenue and expense is not expected to change next year. Prepare a flexible budget income statement for 375,000 guests; 450,000 guests; and 525,000 guests.

3. The company understands its competition is not only other mountain resorts but also alternative leisure activities. In the left-hand column, click on *Competitors*. Identify other types of companies competing for the leisure and recreational dollar.

4. In an effort to stay competitive in the leisure and recreation industry, Vail Resorts compares its financial statistics with industry averages. In the left-hand column under "Company Info," click on *Profile*. Does Vail Resorts compare favorably or unfavorably with the industry average for net profit margin (return on sales), return on equity, current ratio, and three-year revenue growth?

Vail Resorts

Go to the "Flexible Budgeting and Variances" episode on the *Mastering Accounting* CD-ROM for an interactive, video-enhanced exercise that presents CanGo's managers with a problem. The company uses flexible budgeting and variances to determine actual costs for wages and raw materials. When managers want to know why a certain division is performing poorly, they discover that the conclusions they reach from the reports depend on who reviews the report and how data for the budget variances are analyzed.

25

Activity-Based Costing and Other Cost Management Tools

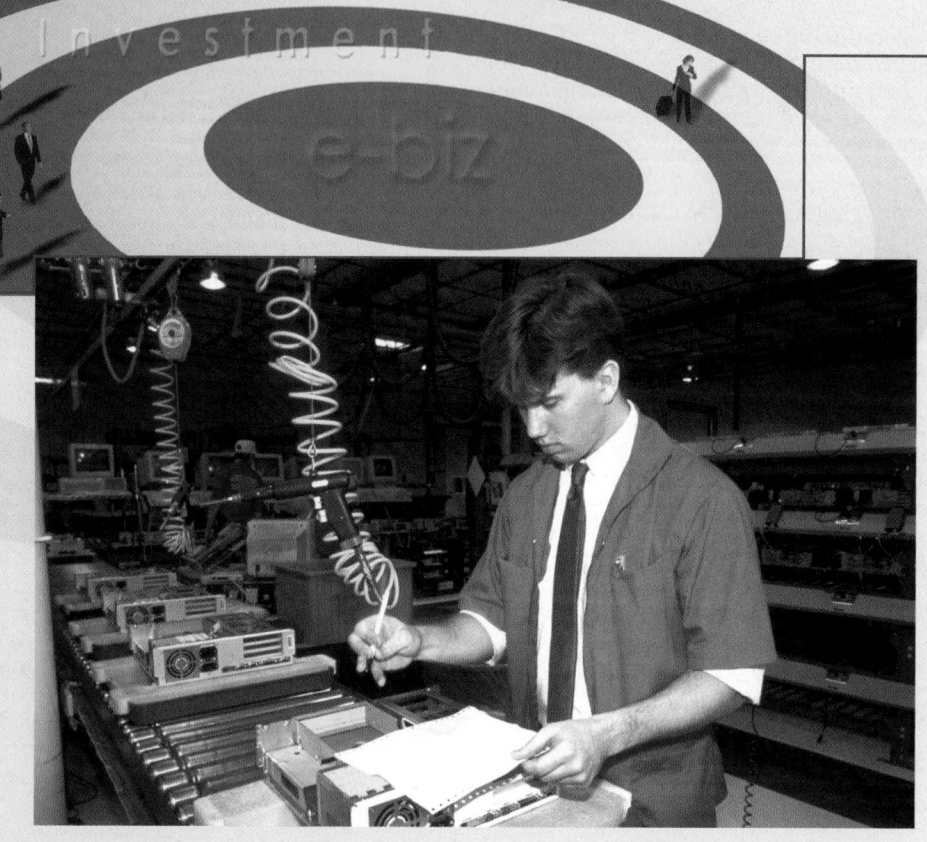

LEARNING OBJECTIVES

After studying this chapter, you should be able to

1. Describe and develop activity-based costs (ABC)

2. Use ABC data and activity-based management (ABM) to make business decisions

3. Use ABM and value engineering to achieve target costs for target pricing

4. Decide when ABC is most likely to pass the cost-benefit test

5. Compare a traditional production system to a just-in-time (JIT) production system

6. Record manufacturing costs for a just-in-time costing system

7. Contrast the four types of quality costs and use these costs to make decisions

Dell Computer pioneered custom-building computers for individual orders on a just-in-time basis. But when the company reported its first-ever quarterly loss several years ago, CEO Michael Dell had to act quickly to turn the company around.

Dell decided to focus on the company's most profitable products. But which products were they? The accounting system traced direct materials and direct labor to individual product lines, but did not do a good job matching indirect costs with the specific products that caused those costs.

Dell needed a more finely tuned cost accounting system. The answer was *activity-based costing (ABC)*. Employee teams identified the ten most important indirect activities from all elements of the value chain—for example, purchases of raw materials, indirect assembly labor, and warranty service. Then, *for each activity*, the teams developed a separate indirect cost allocation rate.

The goal was to assign the cost of each activity to the product lines that caused that activity's cost. For example:

- Purchasing costs are assigned based on the number of different "part numbers" in a product.
- Indirect assembly labor is assigned based on the number of times the product is "touched."
- Warranty costs are assigned based on the number of service calls (failure rate) for the product line.

ABC costing is more accurate than simpler cost systems that combine the indirect costs of many activities into a single cost pool and then allocate these costs using a single allocation base, often direct labor or machine hours. Such a crude assignment of indirect costs can lead to a hit-or-miss pricing structure.

Has ABC worked for Dell? In 2000, Dell was earning record profits. The Controller of Dell Americas Operations says: "Activity-based costing has really allowed Dell to go to the next level of understanding of its profitability for each of the products it sells."

Given the rapidly changing costs in the computer industry, Dell uses ABC costs for pricing its computers every day. Each month, Dell reanalyzes the profitability of each product line. ABC also helps Dell's managers find ways to cut costs, especially by highlighting non-value-added activities such as inventory storage.

To thrive in a globally competitive market, **Dell Computer** must provide customers with goods or services at an attractive price, while managing costs so the company still earns a profit. This is called delivering value to the customer. This chapter will show you several methods managers use to deliver value to the customer at a profit:

- Activity-based costing
- Activity-based management and target costing
- Just-in-time systems
- Costs of quality

These methods, largely unheard of 15 years ago, are now routinely used by companies like **Dell, General Motors,** and **Toyota.** Before discussing activity-based costing and activity-based management, we first consider why companies need more detailed and accurate cost systems.

REFINING COST SYSTEMS

The Need for Refined Cost Systems

To allocate indirect costs to cost objects like departments or products, companies use average allocation rates. The broader the indirect cost pool used in the numerator of the allocation rate, and the broader the allocation base used in the denominator, the less accurate the resulting cost allocation. Similarly, the narrower the cost pools and cost allocation bases, the more refined the average rates and the more accurate the cost allocation. A simple example shows that organizations from **Dell Computer,** to **Carolina Power and Light,** to the **IRS** and the **U.S. Postal Service,** are developing more refined costing systems like ABC. Why? Because simple systems that do not match costs with the consumption of resources can assign costs inaccurately and inequitably.

David Larimer, Matt Sewell, and Marc Bryan are three college friends who decide to room together during their sophomore year. They agree to share on an equal basis the following monthly costs:

Rent and utilities	$570
Cable TV	50
High-speed Internet access	40
Groceries	240
Total monthly costs	$900

Each roommate's share is $300 ($900/3).

Things go smoothly for the first few months. But then David calls a meeting. "Since I started having dinner at Amy's each night, I shouldn't have to chip in for the groceries." Matt then pipes in: "I'm so busy studying and surfing the Net that I never have time to watch TV. I don't want to pay for the cable TV anymore." And, he continues, "Marc, since your friend Jennifer eats here most evenings, you should pay a double share of the grocery bill." Marc retorts, "If that's the way you feel, Matt, then you should pay for the Internet access, since you're the only one around here who uses it!"

What happened? The friends originally agreed to share the costs equally. But they soon discover that they are not participating equally in three costly activities: watching cable TV, surfing the Net, and eating. Equal assignment of the costs is therefore not equitable.

The roommates could use a refined approach that better matches the costs with the people who participate in each activity. This means splitting the cable TV costs between David and Marc, assigning the Internet access cost to Matt, and allocating the grocery bill 1/3 to Matt and 2/3 to Marc. Exhibit 25-1 compares the results of this refined system with the original system.

EXHIBIT 25-1   More Refined Versus Less Refined Cost Allocation System

	David Larimer	Matt Sewell	Marc Bryan	Total
More refined cost allocation system:				
Rent and utilities	$190	$190	$190	$570
Cable TV	25	—	25	50
High-speed Internet access	—	40	—	40
Groceries	—	80	160	240
Total costs allocated	$215	$310	$375	$900
Less refined original cost allocation system	$300	$300	$300	$900
Difference	$ (85)	$ 10	$ 75	$ 0

No wonder David called a meeting! The original system allocated him $300 a month, but the refined system shows that a more equitable share would be only $215. On the other hand, the new system allocates Marc $375 a month instead of $300. David was paying for resources he did not consume (Internet access and groceries), while Marc was not paying for all the resources (groceries) he and his guest consumed. We could say that David was "overcosted" and Marc was "undercosted."

Notice, however, that the total monthly costs are the same ($900) under both systems. The only difference is how that $900 is allocated among the three roommates. The amount by which David is "overcosted" ($85) must exactly equal the amounts by which Matt and Marc are "undercosted" ($10 + $75).

In a highly competitive, globally wired marketplace, companies from **Coca-Cola** to **Dell Computer** need to know how much it costs to bring each product to market. Dell needs to know what it costs to assemble and deliver a customized laptop to a client in Eugene, Oregon. Why? So Dell can set a price that covers the costs of all the resources required to assemble and deliver that specific laptop (and provide some profit), yet remain competitive with prices charged by **Gateway** and **Compaq**.

Sharpening the Focus: From Business Functions, to Departments, to Activities

Refining the cost system requires drilling down from the six broad business functions that compose the value chain, to individual departments in each function, to specific activities in those departments.

Panel A of Exhibit 25-2 lists these six broad value-chain functions for a manufacturer: R&D, design, production, marketing, distribution, customer service. In Chapter 19, we showed that companies need to know the full costs (from all elements of the value chain) to set sale prices that cover all these costs, and to determine the profitability of different products. ➡ However, remember that under GAAP, only costs incurred in the production element of the value chain are inventoriable for financial reporting. Since most companies begin refining their cost systems in the production/manufacturing function, our discussion and examples focus on this function. But managers in companies like **Dell** and **Dow Chemical** can apply the same principles to costs incurred in other elements of the value chain.

◄ For full value-chain costs discussion, see Chapter 19, pp. 759–760.

EXHIBIT 25-2
Overview of Business Functions, Departments, and Activities

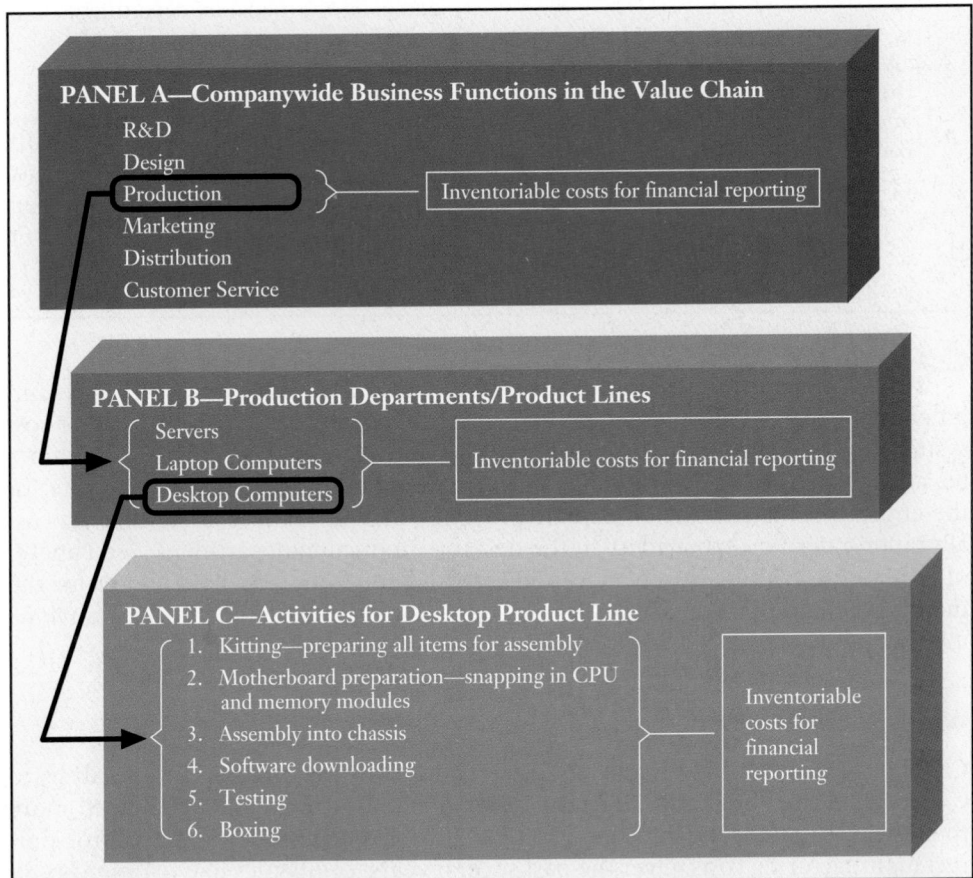

PANEL A—Companywide Business Functions in the Value Chain
R&D
Design
Production → Inventoriable costs for financial reporting
Marketing
Distribution
Customer Service

PANEL B—Production Departments/Product Lines
Servers
Laptop Computers → Inventoriable costs for financial reporting
Desktop Computers

PANEL C—Activities for Desktop Product Line
1. Kitting—preparing all items for assembly
2. Motherboard preparation—snapping in CPU and memory modules
3. Assembly into chassis → Inventoriable costs for financial reporting
4. Software downloading
5. Testing
6. Boxing

Panel B of Exhibit 25-2 shows that the production function is divided into departments (servers, laptop computers, and desktop computers). Panel C then zeroes in on the desktop computer production department, and lists six common activities in assembling desktop computers. Managers need to know the costs of cost objects at each level:

- Business functions—such as Dell Computer's production function
- Departments—such as Dell's desktop production line
- Activities—such as Dell's assembly or software downloading activities in the desktop production department

Exhibit 25-3 shows that when managers limited their focus to broad business functions, simple cost systems that allocated indirect costs using broad-based averages were often good enough to meet their needs. As increasing competition forced managers to drill down to individual departments within a function, companies often developed separate indirect cost allocation rates for each individual department. Rather than using a plantwide manufacturing overhead rate, for example, the company could develop one overhead rate for the server production department and another rate for the desktop production department.

EXHIBIT 25-3
Sharpening the Business Focus

Managers Focus on:	Indirect Cost Allocation System:
Broad business functions, such as production	Single functionwide indirect cost allocation rate—for example, a plantwide manufacturing overhead rate
↓	↓
Departments within a function, such as the server, laptop, and desktop computer production departments	Separate indirect cost allocation rates for each different department—for example, separate manufacturing overhead rates for the server, laptop, and desktop production departments
↓	↓
Activities within a department, such as the kitting, motherboard preparation, and assembly activities in the desktop computer production department	Specific indirect cost allocation rates for each activity within a department—for example, one indirect cost allocation rate for kitting, a separate rate for motherboard preparation, and so on. The indirect cost allocation rate for each activity uses a different cost driver.

Now managers are drilling down farther to focus on specific activities within individual departments. Exhibit 25-3 shows that companies further refine their cost systems to develop separate indirect cost allocation rates for each activity within a department. For example, rather than using one manufacturing overhead rate for the entire desktop production department, they may develop separate indirect cost allocation rates for each activity in the desktop production department. See Panel C of Exhibit 25-2: There is one allocation rate for the kitting activity, another for the motherboard preparation activity, and so on. Such a refined system is called an *activity-based costing system*.

Objective 1
Describe and develop activity-based costs (ABC)

➤ Controlling direct material and direct labor costs, see Chapter 24, pp. 984–991.

ACTIVITY-BASED COSTING (ABC).
A system that focuses on activities as the fundamental cost objects. The costs of those activities become building blocks for compiling costs as ABC links costs to the activities that cause those costs.

ACTIVITY-BASED COSTING

Chapter 24 showed how managers use standard costing and variance analysis to control direct material and direct labor costs. ◄ But most managers need more than the aggregate manufacturing overhead flexible budget variance to control indirect manufacturing costs. Over the past several years, companies like **Allied Signal, Coca-Cola,** and **Carrier Corporation** have developed refined systems like ABC to help control indirect costs.

Activity-based costing (ABC) focuses on *activities* as the fundamental cost objects. The costs of those activities become building blocks for compiling costs, as ABC links costs to the activities that cause those costs. Activity-based costing can be used with job costing or process costing. Financial institutions like **American Express** and hospitals also use ABC.

ABC systems trace direct materials and direct labor to cost objects, as described in Chapter 20. ➡ The only difference is that ABC systems make more effort to allocate *indirect costs*—such as manufacturing overhead—to the products that caused these costs.

◀ See Chapter 20, pp. 802–806, to review how direct materials and direct labor are traced to cost objects.

Many companies start out using a simple system that combines all the indirect costs into a single cost pool, and then allocates those costs using a single allocation base. This may not work if

⊙ DAILY EXERCISE 25-1

1. *The allocation base is not a cost driver.* Recall that a *cost driver* is any factor whose change causes a change in a related total cost. For example, in a highly automated production process, most overhead costs are not related to direct labor, so direct labor is not the main driver of overhead costs.
2. *One allocation base is insufficient.* In most companies, no *single* factor drives all indirect costs.

In either case, allocation bases that are not cost drivers lead to inaccurate product costs.

Activity-based costing reduces these problems by separately estimating the indirect costs of each activity, and then allocating those costs based on what caused the costs. Each activity's indirect cost has its own (usually unique) cost allocation base, or cost driver. For example, **Dell's** ABC system allocates indirect assembly labor costs based on the number of times workers touch a computer as it moves through assembly. A computer that requires more touches is allocated more of the indirect assembly labor activity cost than a model that requires fewer touches. Exhibit 25-4 lists common activities and related cost drivers.

EXHIBIT 25-4
Activities and Cost Drivers

Activity	Cost Driver
Materials purchasing	Number of purchase orders
Materials handling	Number of parts
Production scheduling	Number of batches
Quality inspections	Number of inspections
Photocopying	Number of pages copied
Warranty services	Number of service calls
Shipping	Number of pounds

Accountants have long known that product costs would be more accurate if companies allocated indirect costs using several cost drivers. Until recently, however, it was too expensive to develop multiple-cost-driver cost systems. However, "data warehouses" and other information technology have made ABC feasible. Optical scanning and bar coding reduce the cost of collecting activity costs and cost driver information. Powerful enterprise resource planning (ERP) systems like SAP, Oracle, and Peoplesoft now contain ABC applications. Or companies can buy specialized ABC software or develop their own. Dell began its ABC system using Excel spreadsheets.

Dell builds the manufacturing cost of each computer from the direct costs plus the indirect costs of the specific activities required to produce it. This buildup of *manufacturing costs* determines the inventoriable product cost used for *financial reporting*. However, for internal decisions such as pricing and product profitability analysis, Dell also assigns the costs of nonmanufacturing activities to products. For example, Dell assigns the costs of the warranty service activity to product lines based on the number of service calls.

Developing an Activity-Based Costing System

The main difference between ABC and traditional systems is that ABC systems have separate indirect cost allocation rates for each activity. ABC requires seven steps:

⊙ DAILY EXERCISE 25-2

1. Identify the activities.
2. Estimate the total indirect costs of each activity.
3. Identify the allocation base for each activity's indirect costs—this is the primary cost driver.

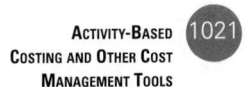

4. Estimate the total quantity of each allocation base.
5. Compute the cost allocation rate for each activity:

$$\text{Cost allocation rate for activity} = \frac{\text{Estimated total indirect costs of activity}}{\text{Estimated total quantity of cost allocation base}}$$

6. Obtain the actual quantity of each allocation base used by the cost object (for example, the quantity used by a particular product).
7. Allocate the costs to the cost object:

$$\text{Allocated activity cost} = \text{Cost allocation rate for activity} \times \text{Actual quantity of cost allocation base used by the cost object}$$

The first step in developing an activity-based costing system is identifying the activities. Analyzing all the activities required to make a product forces managers to think about how each activity might be improved—or whether the activity is necessary at all. Steps 2–7 are the same approach used to allocate manufacturing overhead, as explained in Chapter 20. The only difference is that ABC systems repeat steps 2–7 for each activity.

Traditional Versus Activity-Based Costing Systems: Chemtech

We use a streamlined example to emphasize the distinctions between ABC systems and traditional costing systems. Our example necessarily simplifies the process that would occur in a real company, which might identify more than 50 different activities.

Chemtech's Chemical Manufacturing Department produces hundreds of different chemicals. The company has focused on producing mass quantities of "commodity" chemicals for many large customers. It also manufactures small quantities of specialty chemicals for individual customers.

Last updated in 1990, the Chemical Manufacturing Department's cost system uses a single indirect cost pool and allocates manufacturing overhead at 200% of direct labor cost. Chemtech's controller, Martha Wise, gathered data for two of the department's many products:

- Aldehyde—a commodity chemical used in producing plastics
- Phenylephrine hydrochloride (PH)—a specialty chemical (A single customer uses PH in blood-pressure medications.)

	Aldehyde	Phenylephrine Hydrochloride (PH)
Number of pounds per year	7,000 lb	5 lb
Direct materials cost per pound	$5	$20
Direct labor cost per pound	$1	$10
Sale price per pound	$10	$70

Wise used this information to compute each product's gross profit, as shown in Exhibit 25-5.

EXHIBIT 25-5
Chemtech's Traditional Cost System—Product Cost and Gross Profit

DAILY EXERCISE 25-4

DAILY EXERCISE 25-10

	Aldehyde	PH
Sale price per pound	$10.00	$70.00
Less: Manufacturing cost per pound:		
Direct materials	5.00	20.00
Direct labor	1.00	10.00
Manufacturing overhead (at 200% of direct labor cost)	2.00	20.00
Total manufacturing cost per pound	8.00	50.00
Gross profit per pound	$ 2.00	$20.00

The gross profit for the PH (phenylephrine hydrochloride) specialty chemical is $20 per pound—ten times as high as the gross profit for the aldehyde commodity chemical ($2). Chemtech CEO Randy Smith is surprised that PH appears so much more profitable (per pound) than aldehyde. He asks Wise to check 50 of the department's other products. Wise confirms that the gross profit per pound is ten times as high for specialty chemicals as it is for commodity chemicals. As a result, Smith wonders whether Chemtech should switch its focus to specialty chemicals.

WORK IT OUT

1. What is the *total* direct labor cost assigned to
   a. Aldehyde?
   b. PH (phenylephrine hydrochloride)?
2. What is the *total* manufacturing overhead allocated to
   a. Aldehyde?
   b. PH?

Answers

1. Total direct labor cost assigned to aldehyde is 7,000 pounds × $1 per pound = $7,000. Total direct labor cost assigned to PH is 5 pounds × $10 per pound = $50. Thus, Chemtech assigns to aldehyde 140 times as much total direct labor cost as it does to PH ($7,000 ÷ $50 = 140).
2. **Key Point:** Because Chemtech uses direct labor cost as its single allocation base, Chemtech also allocates 140 times as much total overhead to aldehyde as to PH. Total overhead allocated to aldehyde is 7,000 pounds × $2 per pound = $14,000. Total overhead allocated to PH is 5 pounds × $20 per pound = $100. Thus, the direct labor single-allocation-base system allocates 140 times as much total overhead to aldehyde as to PH ($14,000 ÷ $100). This traditional costing procedure is accurate only if aldehyde really does cause 140 times as much overhead as PH. That is, the existing system assumes that direct labor really is the primary overhead cost driver.

CEO Smith calls a meeting with the department foreman Steve Pronai and controller Wise. Smith is perplexed that the accounting numbers show specialty chemicals are more profitable (on a per-pound basis) than commodity chemicals. He expected the department would be more efficient producing a few commodity chemicals (in a few very large batches) than producing a wide variety of specialty chemicals (in many small batches). Foreman Pronai echoes Smith's concern. Pronai says it takes just as long to mix a small batch of specialty chemicals as a large batch of commodity chemicals. Finally, Smith is puzzled because Chemtech's competitors seem to be earning good profits, even though they usually undercut Chemtech's prices on commodity chemicals.

Wise fears that the problem could be Chemtech's cost accounting system. For years she had tried to get Smith to update the costing system, but Smith chose to invest in new equipment and in marketing. Now Wise has Smith's attention. Wise suggests that foreman Pronai and the plant engineer work with her to develop a pilot ABC system for part of the Chemical Manufacturing Department's operations. Exhibit 25-6 on the following page compares the original direct labor single-allocation-base system (Panel A) with the new ABC system (Panel B).

In developing their new system, Chemtech's ABC team followed the seven steps:

Step 1. Identify the activities.

Wise and her team identify three activities in the Chemical Manufacturing Department: mixing, processing, and testing. See Exhibit 25-7, page 1025, column 1.

Step 2. Estimate the total indirect costs of each activity.

Pronai estimates that total mixing costs for all products will be $600,000. Estimated costs for each activity appear in Exhibit 25-7, column 2.

Step 3. Identify the allocation base for each activity's indirect costs—the primary cost driver.

Workers mix ingredients separately for each batch of chemicals, so the number of batches drives mixing costs. Exhibit 25-7, column 3, lists the allocation base (cost driver) for each activity.

Step 1: Identify activities

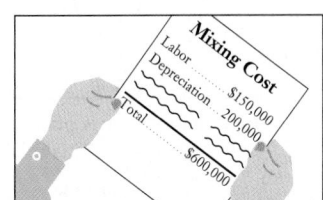

Step 2: Estimate indirect cost of each activity

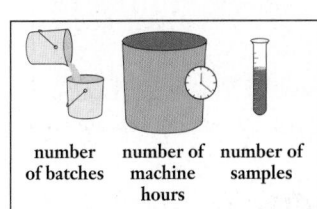

Step 3: Identify allocation bases

1023

EXHIBIT 25-6
Chemtech's Traditional and ABC
Systems

PANEL A—Traditional System

| Departmental Indirect Cost Pool | Chemical Manufacturing Department Overhead |

Cost Allocation Base — Direct Labor Cost

Product Cost Objects — Chemical A, Chemical B, Chemical C

PANEL B—ABC System

Departmental Indirect Cost Pool — Chemical Manufacturing Department Overhead

Activity Indirect Cost Pool — Mixing, Processing, Testing

Cost Allocation Base — Number of Batches, Number of Machine Hours, Number of Samples Taken

Product Cost Objects — Chemical A, Chemical B, Chemical C

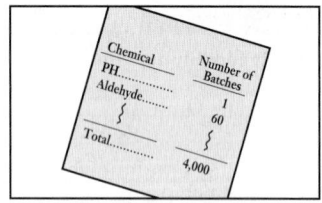

Chemical	Number of Batches
PH.........	
Aldehyde.......	1
§	60
§	§
Total............	4,000

Step 4: Estimate quantity of each allocation base

Step 4. Estimate the total quantity of each allocation base.

Wise and Pronai estimate that the department will produce a total of 4,000 batches of chemicals. Estimated quantities of the cost driver allocation bases appear in column 4 of Exhibit 25-7.

Step 5. Compute the cost allocation rate for each activity.

Wise computes the allocation rate for mixing, as follows:

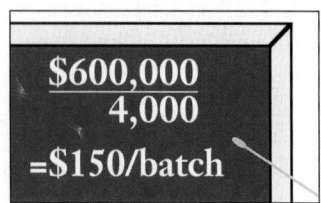

$$\dfrac{\$600,000}{4,000} = \$150/\text{batch}$$

Step 5: Compute allocation rates

$$\text{Cost allocation rate for mixing} = \dfrac{\$600,000}{4,000 \text{ batches}} = \$150 \text{ per batch}$$

Column 5 of Exhibit 25-7 shows the cost allocation rate for each activity.

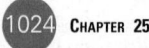

EXHIBIT 25-7 Chemtech's Activity-Based Costing System

(1) Activity	(2) Estimated Costs	(3) Cost Allocation Base	(4) Estimated Quantity of Cost Allocation Base	(5) Cost Allocation Rate	(6) Actual Quantity of Cost Allocation Base Used by:		(7) Allocated Activity Cost	
					Aldehyde	PH	Aldehyde	PH
Mixing	$600,000	# Batches	4,000 batches	$\frac{\$600,000}{4,000} = \$150/\text{batch}$	60 batches	1 batch	$150 \times 60 = \$9,000$	$150 \times 1 = \$150$
Processing	$3,000,000	# Machine hours (MH)	50,000 MH	$\frac{\$3,000,000}{50,000} = \$60/\text{MH}$	30 1/2 MH	2 MH	$60 \times 30\ 1/2 = \$1,830$	$60 \times 2 = \$120$
Testing	$600,000	# Samples	3,000 samples	$\frac{\$600,000}{3,000} = \$200/\text{sample}$	14 samples	1 sample	$200 \times 14 = \$2,800$	$200 \times 1 = \$200$

Step 6. Obtain the actual quantity of each allocation base used by each product.

During the year, Chemtech produces 60 batches of aldehyde and 1 batch of PH. (This total of 61 batches is only a small fraction of the 4,000 total batches Chemtech produces. The remaining batches consist of Chemtech's other chemicals.) Exhibit 25-7, column 6, shows the actual quantities of each activity's allocation base used by aldehyde and PH.

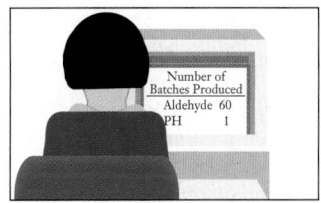

Step 6: Obtain actual quantities of each allocation base

Step 7. Allocate the costs to each product.

Wise allocates mixing costs as follows:

$$\text{Aldehyde:} \quad 60 \text{ batches} \times \$150 \text{ per batch} = \$9,000$$
$$\text{PH:} \quad 1 \text{ batch} \times \$150 \text{ per batch} = \$\ \ 150$$

Column 7 of Exhibit 25-7 shows the cost allocation for all three activities.

Wise then recomputes manufacturing overhead costs (Panel A) and gross profit (Panel B), as shown in Exhibit 25-8. For each product, Wise adds the total costs of the three activities to obtain the total manufacturing overhead allocated to each product. Panel A shows that total ABC overhead is $13,630 for aldehyde and $470 for PH. As in the original direct labor single-allocation-base system, this multiple-allocation-base ABC system allocates more *total* overhead to aldehyde, because

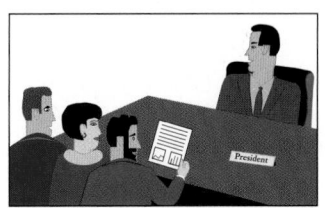

Step 7: Allocate costs

PANEL A—Manufacturing Overhead Per Pound

	Aldehyde	PH
Mixing (from Exhibit 25-7)	$ 9,000	$150
Processing (from Exhibit 25-7)	1,830	120
Testing (from Exhibit 25-7)	2,800	200
Total manufacturing overhead	$13,630	$470
Divide by number of pounds	÷ 7,000 lb	÷ 5 lb
Manufacturing overhead per pound	$1.95 /lb*	$94 /lb

* Rounded

PANEL B—Gross Profit Per Pound

	Aldehyde	PH
Sale price	$10.00	$ 70.00
Less: Manufacturing costs:		
Direct materials	$ 5.00	$ 20.00
Direct labor	1.00	10.00
Manufacturing overhead (from Panel A)	1.95	94.00
Total manufacturing cost	7.95	124.00
Gross profit (Loss)	$ 2.05	$(54.00)

EXHIBIT 25-8
Chemtech's Activity-Based Costing System

⊙ DAILY EXERCISE 25-6

⊙ DAILY EXERCISE 25-7

⊙ DAILY EXERCISE 25-13

⊙ DAILY EXERCISE 25-14

Chemtech produces much more aldehyde than PH. However, there is a big difference in the *ratio* of overhead allocated to aldehyde versus PH. The ABC system allocates only 29 times as much overhead to aldehyde as to PH ($13,630 ÷ $470 = 29). This is much less than in the original direct-labor-based system, which allocated 140 times as much overhead to aldehyde as to PH (see Work It Out on page 1023).

DAILY EXERCISE 25-5

After totaling the manufacturing overhead costs for each product, Wise computes the overhead cost per pound, as shown in Exhibit 25-8, Panel A. For aldehyde, Wise divides the $13,630 total manufacturing overhead by the 7,000 pounds of aldehyde produced, to get an overhead cost per pound of $1.95 (rounded). For PH, the ABC overhead cost per pound is $94.00 ($470 ÷ 5 pounds).

Compare the overhead cost per pound under the original direct-labor-based system with the ABC costs:

	Overhead Cost Per Pound	
	Traditional Direct Labor System (Exhibit 25-5)	ABC System (Exhibit 25-8)
Aldehyde..............	$ 2.00	$ 1.95
PH.........................	20.00	94.00

Which approach is more accurate? *ABC costs are more accurate because ABC takes into account the resources (mixing costs, machine time, and testing) each product actually uses.* The old direct labor single-allocation-base system allocated too much overhead to the product that uses more total direct labor (aldehyde) and too little overhead to the product that uses less total direct labor (PH). The simpler system *overcosted* aldehyde and *undercosted* PH.

DAILY EXERCISE 25-15

With more precise allocations, ABC shifts costs out of aldehyde and into PH where the costs belong. Why? Exhibit 25-7 shows that aldehyde uses more of each activity's resources than PH, but *not* 140 times as much. Column 6 shows that aldehyde uses 60 times as much mixing, about 15 times as many machine hours (processing costs), and 14 times as much testing as PH.

Although Chemtech made only 5 pounds of PH, this product still required

- Workers to mix a batch, at a mixing cost of $150
- 2 machine hours at $60 per hour
- One sample tested at a cost of $200

Spreading these costs over the 5 pounds of PH yields an overhead cost of $94 per pound, as shown in Exhibit 25-8, Panel A.

Allocating overhead based on actual *usage* of the resources increases the costs of low-volume products like PH that are produced in small batches. Why? Because costs like mixing and testing a batch are spread over the small number of units in that batch. On the other hand, mixing and testing costs are spread over the larger number of pounds for high-volume products that are produced in large batches, like aldehyde.

Controller Martha Wise is now ready to recompute product costs and gross profit using the ABC data. Exhibit 25-8, Panel B, shows that the cost per pound of aldehyde is $7.95 under the ABC system. Contrast this with the $8.00 cost per pound under Chemtech's original system (Exhibit 25-5). More important, the ABC data in Exhibit 25-8 show that specialty chemical PH costs $124 per pound, rather than the $50 per pound as indicated by the old system (Exhibit 25-5). Exhibit 25-8, Panel B shows that by selling PH for $70 per pound, Chemtech has been losing $54 on each pound—and this is *before* considering nonmanufacturing costs such as R&D, marketing, and distribution. Wise finds that most of Chemtech's other specialty chemicals show similar increases in cost under the ABC system.

The Chemtech example shows how dramatically ABC can affect product costs. In many cases, ABC systems show that companies lose money on low-volume products like Chemtech's specialty chemicals. One business consultant says: "20% of a company's products usually produce 80% of its profits." ABC spurs many companies to cut money-losing products.

ACTIVITY-BASED MANAGEMENT: USING ABC FOR DECISION MAKING

Activity-based management (ABM) refers to using activity-based cost information to make decisions that increase profits while satisfying customers' needs. We consider how Chemtech can use ABC information in three kinds of decisions: (1) pricing and product mix, (2) cost reduction, and (3) routine planning and control.

Pricing and Product Mix Decisions

Exhibit 25-9 compares key cost and gross profit information for aldehyde and PH, based on Chemtech's original cost system and then on the new ABC system. ABC shows that PH costs Chemtech $124 rather than the $50 reported by the old cost system. Chemtech is losing $54 on every pound of PH—*before* considering nonmanufacturing costs!

Objective 2
Use ABC data, and activity-based management (ABM) to make business decisions

ACTIVITY-BASED MANAGEMENT. Using activity-based cost information to make decisions that increase profits while satisfying customers' needs.

 DAILY EXERCISE 25-3

 DAILY EXERCISE 25-16

	Aldehyde	PH
Original cost system (from Exhibit 25-5):		
Sale price per pound	$10.00	$ 70.00
Less: Manufacturing cost per pound	8.00	50.00
Gross profit per pound	$ 2.00	$ 20.00
Activity-based cost system (from Exhibit 25-8):		
Sale price per pound	$10.00	$ 70.00
Less: Manufacturing cost per pound	7.95	124.00
Gross profit per pound	$ 2.05	$(54.00)

EXHIBIT 25-9
Comparison of Chemtech's Product Costs Under Original Versus ABC Systems

Chemtech may be able to use the ABC analysis to find ways to cut costs. If it cannot cut costs enough to earn a profit on PH, then it will have to consider raising the sale price. If customers will not pay a higher price, Chemtech should consider dropping PH. More generally, if the ABC system shows that commodity chemicals are more profitable than Chemtech thought, and specialty chemicals are less profitable, Chemtech may shift its product mix away from specialty chemicals toward commodity chemicals. This is the exact opposite of the strategy suggested by cost data from the original system.

Cost Reduction Decisions

Most companies adopt ABC to get more accurate product costs for pricing and product mix decisions. But managers often find that they reap even greater benefits by using ABM to pinpoint opportunities to cut costs.

VALUE ENGINEERING With an ABC system in place, organizations can use value engineering to reduce costs. **Value engineering** means systematically evaluating activities in an effort to reduce costs while satisfying customer needs. Companies conduct value engineering using cross-functional teams: marketers identify customer needs, engineers and production personnel design more efficient processes and products, and accountants estimate how proposed changes will affect costs.

Carrier Corporation, the world's largest manufacturer of air conditioning and heating products, assembled a cross-functional team that used ABM in a value engineering drive to minimize complexity or variety in products, component parts, and manufacturing processes. The goal is to cut by half the 280 different circuit breakers and 580 different fasteners used in its products. Slashing the number of different component parts will significantly cut Carrier's ordering costs, since ABC often estimates that purchase orders cost up to $100–$200 each. It will also cut receiving,

VALUE ENGINEERING. Systematically evaluating activities in an effort to reduce costs while satisfying customer needs.

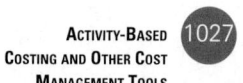

inspection, and materials-handling costs. Carrier may benefit from quantity discounts on larger orders of the remaining parts. Since experts estimate that 75–90% of a product's costs are locked in when the design is set, design changes usually present the greatest opportunities to slash costs. Even the U.S. government is getting in on the ABM act. The Internal Revenue Service recently used ABM to simplify its processes, improve the quality of its services, and cut costs.

e-Accounting

Point, Click, Buy, Sell: Businesses Cut Costs by Buying and Selling Online

The cost of processing a single purchase order for direct or indirect materials is about $175. Make that same purchase online, however, and the cost drops to as little

as $10. With the electronic connection of buyers and suppliers, all authorized users in the buying organization can initiate purchases from their desktops. Companies can automate processes and access critical information across continents, business units, divisions, and departments. This incredible potential for wringing excess costs from supply chains is making business-to-business (B2B) e-commerce "the next big killer app" of the World Wide Web. Analysts estimate the B2B e-commerce market will soar to $6.4 trillion in 2004.

The Big Three automakers (**Ford, General Motors,** and **Daimler-Chrysler**), recently announced they will move all business—more than $250 billion and 60,000 suppliers—to the Internet. This change will replace a bloated procurement system built on phone calls and faxes. General Motors alone issues over 100,000 purchase orders a year. Suppliers field huge sales staffs to fly on the company's dime to meet with prospects.

So moving B2B commerce to the Internet makes buying and selling more cost-efficient. Buyers and sellers get exposure to a worldwide market at the click of a mouse. Buyers conduct real-time trading to get the parts they need. Sellers auction off excess inventory. And now corporate accountants and financial managers can use their time to focus on strategic activities, such as finding the most profitable B2B relationships.

Source: Based on Russ Banham, "The B-to-B virtual bazaar," *Journal of Accountancy,* July 2000, pp. 26–30. Don Tapscot, "Manager's journal: Virtual webs will revolutionize business," *Wall Street Journal,* April 24, 2000, P. A38. Kevin P. O'Brien, "Value-chain report: Should your firm be using e-procurement?" June 12, 2000, http://www.iwvaluechain.com.

Let's return to our illustration. Chemtech assembles a cross-functional value engineering team that includes marketing manager Liz Smith, plant engineer Edward Michaels, and production foreman Steve Pronai, along with controller Martha Wise. The team analyzes each of Chemtech's three production activities: mixing, processing, and testing. For each activity, the team considers (1) how to cut costs given current production processes, and (2) how to redesign the production process to further cut costs. The team presents the following proposals to the CEO:

Mixing activity

- Group raw materials that are frequently used together, to reduce time required to assemble raw materials when mixing each batch.

- Automate the mixing process so workers can use a few mouseclicks to instruct the automated system to pipe chemicals into the mixing vat.

Processing activity

- Schedule preventive maintenance at nights and weekends to reduce emergency repairs and spoilage from breakdowns while a batch of chemicals is in-process.
- Purchase new equipment that cuts processing time in half.

Testing activity

- Improve quality control to reduce the need for testing.
- Fully automate testing.

USING ABM AND VALUE ENGINEERING TO ACHIEVE TARGET COSTS FOR TARGET PRICING Companies like **Carrier Corporation, General Motors,** and **Compaq** are following Japanese automakers like **Toyota** and **Nissan,** and setting sale prices based on **target prices**—what customers are willing to pay for the product or service. Instead of starting with the full product cost from all elements of the value chain (as discussed in Chapter 19) and then adding a profit to determine the sale price, Exhibit 25-10 shows that target pricing does just the opposite. Target pricing starts with the price customers are willing to pay, and then subtracts the company's desired profit to determine the **target** (or allowable) **cost** to develop, produce, and deliver the product or service. Target costs are usually less than the (current) full product cost of the product or service. The target cost is really a goal the company must shoot for.

Objective 3
Use ABM and value engineering to achieve target costs for target pricing

TARGET PRICE. What customers are willing to pay for the product or service.

TARGET COST. Allowable cost to develop, produce, and deliver the product or service.

Target Pricing	Traditional Cost-Based Pricing
Target sale price (based on market research)	Full product cost (from entire value chain)
Less desired profit	Plus desired profit
Target cost	Sale price

EXHIBIT 25-10
Target Pricing Versus Traditional Cost-Based Pricing

DAILY EXERCISE 25-9

Returning to Chemtech's ABC analysis, CEO Randy Smith decides to focus on commodity chemicals. The marketing department informs him that the market price of aldehyde is likely to fall to $9.50 per pound. Smith wants to earn a target profit equal to 20% of the sale price. In addition to the manufacturing costs in Exhibit 25-8, Chemtech incurs a total of $0.50 per pound in nonmanufacturing costs (R&D, design, marketing, distribution, and customer service).

WORK IT OUT

What is Chemtech's target cost per pound of aldehyde? Do Chemtech's current costs meet this target?

Answer

Target sale price per pound of aldehyde..............	$9.50
Desired profit ($9.50 × 20%)...............................	(1.90)
Target cost per pound of aldehyde	$7.60

Chemtech's current costs do not meet the target cost.

Current total manufacturing cost (from Exhibit 25-8)..............	$7.95
Nonmanufacturing costs..	0.50
Current full product cost per pound of aldehyde	$8.45

Chemtech's current full product costs ($8.45) exceed the target cost of $7.60.

Smith decides to implement three of the cost reduction strategies Chemtech's value engineering team proposed earlier (pages 1028–1029):

- Group raw materials that are frequently used together. Total estimated savings is $150,000, and the plant's total number of batches remains unchanged at 4,000.
- Purchase equipment that cuts processing time by half. This will increase total processing costs by $1,000,000. Total machine hours will remain 50,000, but each product will require only half as many machine hours (Chemtech will use the extra machine hours to produce other profitable products).
- Improve quality control to reduce the need to test samples of each product. This action will cut total testing costs by $375,000, and cut the total number of samples tested throughout the plant by half (from 3,000 to only 1,500). Chemtech will now test only 7 (rather than 14) samples of aldehyde.

Will these changes allow Chemtech to reach the target cost? Exhibit 25-11 shows how Controller Wise starts with the original data summarized in Exhibit 25-7 and adjusts these data for the value engineering changes. Wise first recomputes the cost allocation rates for each activity: She incorporates changes in both the numerator (estimated indirect costs of the activity) and the denominator (estimated total quantity of the activity's allocation base). She then uses these new allocation rates to assign the costs of each activity to aldehyde, based on how much of each allocation base aldehyde uses after the value engineering changes.

Exhibit 25-11   Recomputing Activity Costs for Aldehyde after Value Engineering Changes

	Mixing	Processing	Testing
Estimated total indirect costs of activity:			
Mixing ($600,000 − $150,000)	$450,000		
Processing ($3,000,000 + $1,000,000)		$4,000,000	
Testing ($600,000 − $375,000)			$225,000
Estimated total quantity of each allocation base	4,000 batches	50,000 MH	1,500 samples
Compute the cost allocation rate for each activity:			
(Divide estimated indirect cost by	$450,000	$4,000,000	$225,000
estimated quantity of the allocation base)	÷ 4,000 batches	÷ 50,000 MH	÷ 1,500 samples
Cost allocation rate for each activity	= $112.50/batch	= $80/MH	= $150/sample
Actual quantity of each allocation base used			
by aldehyde:			
Mixing	60 batches		
Processing (30 1/2 × 50%)		15 1/4 MH	
Testing			7 samples
Allocate the costs to aldehyde:			
Mixing (60 batches × $112.50)	$6,750		
Processing (15 1/4 MH × $80)		$1,220	
Testing (7 samples × $150)			$1,050

DAILY EXERCISE 25-8

Exhibit 25-11 shows that value engineering cuts the total manufacturing overhead costs assigned to aldehyde to $9,020 ($6,750 + $1,220 + $1,050), from $13,630 (in Exhibit 25-8). Spread over 7,000 pounds of aldehyde, this is $1.29 per pound ($9,020 ÷ 7,000, rounded). Now Wise totals the revised cost estimates for aldehyde:

Direct materials (from Exhibit 25-8)	$5.00
Direct labor (from Exhibit 25-8)	1.00
Manufacturing overhead	1.29
Total manufacturing costs	7.29
Nonmanufacturing costs	0.50
Full product cost of aldehyde	$7.79

These changes are quite an improvement from the prior full product cost of $8.45 per pound. But they are *not* enough to meet the $7.60 target cost. Chemtech must conduct more value engineering (or accept less profit) to meet the target sale price.

Routine Planning and Control Decisions

In addition to pricing, product mix, and cost reduction decisions, Chemtech can also use ABC in routine planning and control. Companies using ABC can do activity-based budgeting, where managers budget costs of individual activities to build up the indirect cost schedules in the master budget (discussed in Chapter 23). ➡ Chemtech can also analyze manufacturing overhead variances (presented in Chapter 24) ➡ in more detail by computing variances for each of the three individual indirect activities (mixing, processing, and testing). Finally, Chemtech's managers can use ABC information to evaluate workers. For example, foreman Steve Pronai may receive a bonus if he can cut:

◄ For the master budget, see Chapter 23, pp. 931–940.

◄ Analyzing manufacturing overhead variances: see Chapter 24, pp. 941–994.

- the cost per sample tested (that is, cut the cost allocation rate for the testing activity) or
- the number of samples tested (that is, cut the consumption of the activity) *while maintaining product quality.*

ACTIVITY-BASED COSTING AND THE COST-BENEFIT TEST

Objective 4
Decide when ABC is most likely to pass the cost-benefit test

The ABC concept is deceptively simple: Products cause activities, and activities consume resources. However, it is not easy for a company to develop an ABC/ABM system. In the Chemtech example in Exhibit 25-6, ABC triples the number of allocation bases—from the single allocation base (direct labor) in the original system, to three allocation bases (for mixing, processing, and testing) under ABC. ABC systems are even more complex in real-world companies that have many more activities and cost drivers.

The Cost-Benefit Test

 DAILY EXERCISE 25-12

Like all other management tools, ABC must pass the cost-benefit test. The system should be refined enough to provide accurate product costs, but simple enough for managers to understand. ABC requires the wholehearted support of top management and operating managers, not just accountants. Dell's ABC team included representatives of all areas affected by ABC—from product engineering, to manufacturing, to customer service. Cross-functional teams increase the chance that ABC will succeed. The system will be more accurate because it incorporates a wider variety of perspectives, and managers of different functions are more likely to understand and believe costs from a system they helped build.

Activity-based costing and activity-based management pass the cost-benefit test when the benefits of adopting ABC/ABM exceed the costs. Benefits of adopting ABC/ABM are higher for companies in competitive markets because

- Accurate product cost information is essential for setting competitive sale prices that still allow the company to earn a profit.
- ABM can pinpoint opportunities for cost savings, which increase the company's profit, or are passed on to customers in lower sale prices.

ABC's benefits are higher when ABC gives managers new insights by reporting different product costs than the old system. This is likely to happen when

- The company produces many different products that use different amounts of resources. (If all products use similar amounts of resources, then a simple single-allocation-base system works fine.)
- The company has high indirect costs. (If indirect costs are immaterial, it does not matter how they are allocated.)
- The company produces high volumes of some products, and low volumes of other products. (Traditional single-allocation-base systems tend to overcost high-volume products and undercost low-volume products.)

The costs of adopting ABC are lower when the company has

- Accounting and information system expertise to develop the system.
- Information technology like bar coding, optical scanning, or "data warehouse" systems to record and compile cost driver data.

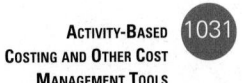

Contrast **General Motors** with **Burrito Brothers** (a fast-food take-out store in Gainesville, Florida).

General Motors	Burrito Brothers
Wide variety of different automotive products	Limited variety of similar burritos
High indirect costs	Low indirect costs
Employs experts in accounting and information systems	No accounting or information systems experts
Advanced information technology	Limited information technology

These differences help explain why General Motors was an early adopter of ABC, while Burrito Brothers has not adopted ABC.

Are real-world companies glad they adopted ABC? Usually, but not always. A recent survey has shown that 89% of the companies using ABC data say it was worth the cost.[1] Adoption is on the rise among financial companies like **American Express,** utilities like **Indianapolis Power and Light,** and nonprofits like the **U.S. Postal Service.** Organizations adopting ABC and ABM have more diverse product lines and processes, higher overhead costs, and more sophisticated information technology than nonadopters. But ABC is not a cure-all. As the controller for one Midwest manufacturer said, "ABC will not reduce cost, it will only help you understand costs better to know what to correct."

Signs That the Cost System May Be Broken

Broken cars or computers simply stop running. But unlike cars and computers, even broken or outdated product cost systems continue to report "product costs." Without flashing lights or ringing bells, how can you tell whether a cost system needs repair?

DAILY EXERCISE 25-11

Management accounting expert Robin Cooper and others suggest that a company's product cost system may need repair when

Managers don't understand costs and profits:

- In bidding for jobs, managers lose bids they expected to win, and win bids they expected to lose.
- Competitors with products similar to our high-volume products price their products below our costs, but still earn good profits.
- Employees do not believe the cost numbers reported by the accounting system.

The cost system is outdated:

- The company uses a single-allocation-base system developed long ago.
- The company has reengineered its production process, but has not changed its accounting system.

THINK IT OVER

Review the Chemtech example on pages 1022–1027. List the symptoms that Chemtech's original cost system may be broken.

Answer

1. The Chemical Manufacturing Department uses a single allocation base (direct labor cost) in a cost system developed over ten years ago.
2. Competitors that focused on high-volume commodity chemicals earned good profits, despite undercutting Chemtech's sale prices. This was puzzling because Chemtech should be especially efficient at producing large batches of commodity chemicals.
3. Cost numbers reported by the accounting system were inconsistent with employees' intuition.

To make sure you understand activity-based costing, take a few minutes to study the Decision Guidelines before working the Mid-Chapter Summary Problem.

---

[1]K. Krumwiede, "ABC: Why it's tried and how it succeeds," *Management Accounting* (April 1998), pp. 32–38.

DECISION GUIDELINES

Activity-Based Costing

DECISION	GUIDELINES
How to develop an ABC system?	**1.** Identify the activities. **2.** Estimate total indirect costs of each activity. **3.** Identify the allocation base (primary cost driver) for each activity's indirect costs. **4.** Estimate the total quantity of each allocation base. **5.** Compute the cost allocation rate for each activity. **6.** Obtain the actual quantity of each allocation base used by cost object. **7.** Allocate costs to cost object.
How to compute a cost allocation rate for an activity?	$$\dfrac{\text{Estimated total indirect cost of activity}}{\text{Estimated total quantity of allocation base}}$$
How to allocate an activity's cost to the cost object?	$$\begin{matrix}\text{Cost allocation} \\ \text{rate for} \\ \text{activity}\end{matrix} \times \begin{matrix}\text{Actual quantity of} \\ \text{allocation base used by} \\ \text{cost object}\end{matrix}$$
For what kinds of decisions do managers use ABC?	Managers use ABC data in ABM to make decisions on • Pricing and product mix • Cost reduction • Routine planning and control
How to set target costs?	Target sale price (based on market research) <u>– less desired profit</u> = Target cost
How to achieve target costs?	Cross-functional teams use value engineering to cut costs by improving product design or production processes
What are the main benefits of ABC?	• More accurate product cost information. • More detailed information on costs of activities and drivers of those costs helps managers control costs.
When is ABC most likely to pass the cost-benefit test?	• Company is in competitive environment and needs accurate product costs. • Company makes different products that use different amounts of resources. • Company has high indirect costs. • Company produces high volumes of some products and lower volumes of other products. • Company has accounting and information technology expertise to implement system. • Old cost system appears "broken."
How to tell when a cost system needs revision?	• Managers lose bids they expected to win and win bids they expected to lose. • Competitors earn profits despite pricing high-volume products below our costs. • Employees do not believe cost numbers. • Company uses a single-allocation-base system developed long ago. • Company has reengineered the production process but not the accounting system.

SUMMARY PROBLEM

Indianapolis Auto Parts (IAP) has a Seat Manufacturing Department that uses activity-based costing. IAP's system has the following features:

Activity	Allocation Base	Cost Allocation Rate
Purchasing	Number of purchase orders	$60.00 per purchase order
Assembling	Number of parts	0.50 per part
Packaging	Number of finished seats	0.90 per finished seat

Each seat has 20 parts; direct materials cost per seat is $11. Suppose **Ford** has asked for a bid on 50,000 built-in baby seats that would be installed as an option on some Ford SUVs. IAP will use a total of 200 purchase orders if Ford accepts IAP's bid.

Required

1. Compute the total cost IAP will incur to purchase the needed materials and then assemble and package 50,000 baby seats. Also compute the average cost per seat.
2. For bidding, IAP adds a 30% markup to total cost. What price will the company bid for the Ford order?
3. Suppose that instead of an ABC system, IAP has a traditional product costing system that allocates all costs other than direct materials at the rate of $65 per direct labor hour. The baby-seat order will require 10,000 direct labor hours. What price will IAP bid using this system's total cost?
4. Use your answers to requirements 2 and 3 to explain how ABC can help IAP make a better decision about the bid price it will offer Ford.

Solution

Requirement 1

Total Cost of Order and Average Cost Per Seat:

Direct materials, 50,000 × $11.00	$ 550,000
Activity costs:	
Purchasing, 200 × $60.00	12,000
Assembling, 50,000 × 20 × $0.50	500,000
Packaging, 50,000 × $0.90	45,000
Total cost of order	$1,107,000
Divide by number of seats	÷ 50,000
Average cost per seat	$ 22.14

Requirement 2

Bid Price (ABC System):

Bid price ($1,107,000 × 130%)	$1,439,100

Requirement 3

Bid Price (Traditional System):

Direct materials, 50,000 × $11.00	$ 550,000
Other product costs, 10,000 × $65	650,000
Total cost of order	$1,200,000
Bid price ($1,200,000 × 130%)	$1,560,000

Requirement 4

IAP's bid would be $120,900 higher using the direct labor single-allocation-base system than using ABC ($1,560,000 − $1,439,100). Assuming the ABC system more accurately captures the costs caused by the order, the traditional direct labor system overcosts the order. This leads to a higher bid price that reduces IAP's chance of winning the bid. The ABC system shows that IAP can increase its chance of winning the bid by bidding a lower price and still make a profit.

TRADITIONAL VERSUS JUST-IN-TIME PRODUCTION SYSTEMS

Objective 5
Compare a traditional production system to a just-in-time (JIT) production system

ABC and ABM often reveal the high costs of (1) buying, storing, and moving inventories, and (2) poor quality products and services. So it is not surprising that a recent study of "best practices" companies revealed most had linked their ABC/ABM systems to just-in-time (JIT) or quality initiatives. For example, **Carrier Corporation's** ABC/ABM system's evidence that materials handling was a major cost driver prompted Carrier to adopt JIT. The rest of this chapter expands on Chapter 19's introduction to JIT and quality. ➡

◄ Chapter 19, p. 773, introduced JIT.

We begin by contrasting just-in-time production systems with traditional systems.

Traditional Systems

Traditional businesses keep large inventories of raw materials, work in process, and finished goods. Why? First, to protect against poor quality. Poor quality raw materials leads companies to buy more than they need. Also, machine breakdowns and production problems *within* departments prompt managers to keep extra work in process *between* departments. Exhibit 25-12 describes the production of drill bits from bar stock (the raw material). Work in process inventory between the grinding and smoothing operations allows smoothing work to continue even if grinding machines break down.

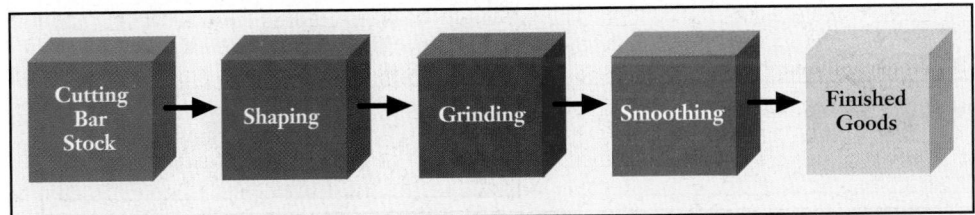

EXHIBIT 25-12
Sequence of Operations for
Drill-Bit Production

A second reason for large inventories is long setup times on production equipment. Manufacturing operations can require setup times ranging from a few minutes to several hours, with correspondingly high setup costs. Companies with long setup times often make products in large batches to spread setup costs over many units. A third reason for stocking large inventories is uncertainty in deliveries from suppliers and orders from customers. Large raw material inventories protect against delayed deliveries. Large inventories of finished goods protect against lost sales if customer demand is higher than expected.

Why are large inventories a problem? First, inventories tie up cash. Companies incur interest expense or forgo interest revenue on that cash. Second, inventories often hide quality problems, production bottlenecks, and obsolescence.

Just-in-Time Systems

As the name suggests, companies with JIT systems buy materials and complete finished goods *just in time* for delivery to customers. This reduces waste. Many managers regard JIT as a *general philosophy of waste elimination* rather than a particular type of manufacturing system.

Companies that follow JIT have several common characteristics:

1. *Arrangement of production activities.* Companies following JIT arrange their equipment differently than traditional manufacturers. A traditional drill-bit manufacturer would group all the shaping machines in one area, all the grinding machines in another area, and all the smoothing machines in a third area, as illustrated in Exhibit 25-13 on the next page. After switching to JIT, the company would group the machines in self-contained production cells, or production lines, as in Panel B of Exhibit 25-13. Machines performing sequential steps may even be physically joined. The goal is continuous production without interruptions or work in process inventories.

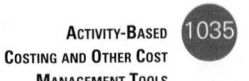

EXHIBIT 25-13   Arrangement of Equipment in JIT and Traditional Production Systems

PANEL A—Traditional Production System
Each type of machine is grouped together in one area of the plant.

Building A
- Cutting Department
- Shaping Department
- work-in-process

Building B
- Grinding Department
- Smoothing Department
- work-in-process
- finished drill bits
- finished ratchets

PANEL B—Just-in-Time Production System
Several *different* kinds of machines necessary to manufacture the product are arranged in a self-contained production cell.

Building A
- Drill Bit Production Line 1
  - cutting machine → shaping machine → grinding machine → smoothing machine → finished drill bits
- Drill Bit Production Line 2
  - cutting machine → shaping machine → grinding machine → smoothing machine → finished drill bits

Building B
- Ratchet Production Line 1
  - cutting machine → shaping machine → grinding machine → smoothing machine → finished ratchets
- Ratchet Production Line 2
  - cutting machine → shaping machine → grinding machine → smoothing machine → finished ratchets

Arranging machines in sequential production cells slashes production time. For example, within six years after adopting JIT, **Harley-Davidson** reduced the time to produce a motorcycle by 77%.

2. *Setup times.* JIT companies reduce setup times on machines used for more than one product. Employee training and technology helped **Toyota** cut setup times from several hours to a few minutes. This increases flexibility in scheduling production to meet customer orders, which in turn increases customer satisfaction and company profits.

3. *Employee roles.* Employees in JIT systems do more than operate a single machine. They also conduct maintenance, perform setups, inspect their own work, and operate other machines. This cross-training boosts morale and lowers costs.

4. *Production scheduling.* JIT businesses schedule production in small batches *just in time* to satisfy needs. A customer order triggers manufacturing. The final operation in the production sequence (smoothing, in our drill-bit example) "pulls" parts from the preceding operation (grinding). The grinding-machine operator pulls shaped parts from shaping, and so on. This "demand-pull" system extends back to suppliers of materials. Suppliers make frequent deliveries of defect-free materials *just in time* for production.

   Purchasing and producing only what customers demand reduces inventory. As inventory declines, hidden problems are exposed. Correcting these problems before the company produces a large number of defective units saves rework and scrap costs. Also, less inventory frees floor space for more productive use. When **Hewlett-Packard** adopted JIT, the company cut its work-in-process inventory by 82%, and its production floor space by 40%.

5. *Supply chain management.* Because there are no inventory buffers, JIT requires close coordination with suppliers who will guarantee on-time delivery of defect-free materials. ➥ Chapter 19 defined *supply-chain management* as exchanging information with suppliers and customers to reduce costs, improve quality, and speed delivery of goods and services from the company's suppliers, through the company itself, and on to the company's end customers. Consider the following examples.[2]

◄ See Chapter 19, pp. 772–773, for a discussion of the JIT management philosophy.

Chrysler's Brazilian plant, which makes Dakota pickup trucks, buys a partially completed chassis from supplier **Dana Corporation's** plant 2 miles down the road. Dana assembles 320 parts onto the truck's frame, including axles, brakes, and wheels, within 108 minutes of receiving an electronic order from the Chrysler plant. Dana then delivers each partially complete chassis to the Chrysler production line, in the sequence that Chrysler specifies, so Chrysler can add the engines, transmissions, and body to complete each truck.

Wal-Mart shares its sales data to help suppliers match their production to Wal-Mart's needs. When **Procter & Gamble** delivers Crest toothpaste on a just-in-time basis to Wal-Mart's distribution center, Wal-Mart immediately unloads the toothpaste directly onto trucks headed for Wal-Mart stores. On average, the toothpaste is on the Wal-Mart shelf within 4 hours, and sold within 24 hours. "It is our objective to sell the merchandise before we pay for it" says a Wal-Mart senior vice president.

Cisco Systems, the Internet hardware maker, is working with **Federal Express** to manage Cisco's supply chain so Cisco can replace its parts warehouses with the distribution link in its value chain. A single customer order for Cisco's products may require component parts that Cisco buys from companies across the globe. Cisco currently holds these parts at a warehouse near its factory so it can ship the whole order at once. Federal Express is working with Cisco to design a system that will merge all the component parts for each individual order *en route to the customer.* The result? All parts necessary to fill a specific order should arrive from the various suppliers at the customer's door within a few hours of each other, ready for assembly at the customer's location.

Often credited for developing JIT, **Toyota** is not standing still. Toyota recently shocked competitors—who often keep customers waiting 30–60 days for custom-ordered cars—by announcing plans to custom-make vehicles within 5 days of receiving an order. How can Toyota meet this goal? By further streamlining and standardizing its production process, and by rolling out its "next generation just-in-time logistics system." Suppliers deliver parts to the assembly lines up to 24 times a day. These changes cut storage requirements by 37% and freed more space for manufacturing. In addition to saving on inventory, warehousing, and production costs, faster make-to-order times mean that Toyota dealers can cut their retail inventories, savings thousands in inventory carrying costs.

While companies like **Toyota, Carrier,** and **Dell** credit JIT for saving them millions of dollars, JIT is not without problems. With no inventory buffers, JIT adopters are vulnerable when problems strike suppliers or distributors. The Teamsters' walk-out against **UPS** in the 1990s left manufacturing plants across the country starved for raw materials. More recently, **Ford** cut production of its SUVs in response to the tire shortage resulting from the **Firestone** tire recall. The electronics industry has also suffered from shortages of components. As we write this chapter, assemblers who normally obtain capacitors (parts that control the flow of electricity in telecommunications equipment) in 4 weeks are now waiting up to 40 weeks. Companies like Dell that have limited supplies of these components are hurting because their raw materials are scarce. This shortage has led one electronics executive to exclaim that just-in-time has become "just-in-trouble."

---

[2]*Sources:* "Chrysler makes manufacturing inroads at plant in Brazil," Gregory L. White, *Wall Street Journal* 8/3/98. "Wal-Mart sets supply plan as net tops forecasts," Emily Nelson, *Wall Street Journal* 11/10/99, B12. "Overnight, everything changed for FedEx; Can it reinvent itself?" Douglas A. Blackmon, *Wall Street Journal* 11/4/99, A1. "Toyota develops a way to make a car within five days of a custom order," Robert L. Simison, *Wall Street Journal* 8/6/99, A4. "Parts shortages hamper electronics makers," John E. Hillsenrath, *Wall Street Journal* 7/7/00, B5.

EXHIBIT 25-14 **Traditional Versus JIT Production Systems**

Traditional Production Systems	Just-in-Time Production Systems
Arrange machines by function.	Arrange machines in sequence of operations.
Long machine setup times.	Short machine setup times.
Production workers operate a single machine.	Cross-trained workers perform many tasks.
Produce large batches.	Produce small batches.
Many suppliers.	Fewer, well-coordinated suppliers.

⊙ DAILY EXERCISE 25-17

Exhibit 25-14 compares traditional production systems with JIT production systems. Now let's see how JIT can simplify cost accounting.

Just-in-Time Costing

Objective 6
Record manufacturing costs for a just-in-time costing system

After adopting JIT, many companies simplify their cost accounting systems. **Just-in-time costing,** sometimes called **backflush costing,** is a standard costing system that starts with output completed and then assigns manufacturing costs to units sold and to inventories. There are three major differences between JIT costing and the traditional standard costing system we described in Chapter 24:

JUST-IN-TIME (JIT) COSTING. A standard costing system that starts with output completed and then assigns manufacturing costs to units sold and to inventories. Also called **backflush costing.**

1. JIT systems do not track the cost of products from raw materials inventory, to work in process inventory, to finished goods inventory, like traditional standard costing systems do. Instead, JIT costing systems wait until the units are completed to record the cost of production.

2. Because JIT systems do not track costs attached to units in the production process, JIT systems do not need a separate Work in Process Inventory account. They combine raw materials and work in process inventories into a single account called Raw and In Process Inventory.

3. Under the JIT philosophy, workers perform many tasks. Since little labor is directly traceable to individual finished products, most companies using JIT costing do not track direct labor separately. They combine labor and manufacturing overhead costs into an account called Conversion Costs (as we saw in Chapter 21 on process costing). ◄ The Conversion Cost account is a temporary account that works just like the Manufacturing Overhead account described in Chapter 20. Actual conversion costs accumulate as debits in the Conversion Cost account, and the account is credited when conversion costs are allocated to completed units. Accountants close any under- or overallocated conversion costs to Cost of Goods Sold at the end of the year, just like under- or overallocated manufacturing overhead in Chapter 20.

➡ Chapter 21, p. 845, introduced conversion costs.

Just-in-Time Costing: An Example

To illustrate JIT costing, consider Mintel Company, which converts silicon wafers into integrated circuits for computers.

Mintel has only one direct manufacturing product cost: silicon wafers, which are labeled "raw." All other manufacturing costs, including labor and various chemicals, are indirect costs of converting the "raw" silicon wafers into the finished integrated circuits. These indirect costs are collected in the "Conversion Costs" account.

Mintel does not use a separate Work in Process Inventory account. Instead, it uses the following two inventory accounts:

- Raw and In Process Inventory, which combines direct materials with work in process
- Finished Goods Inventory, which is the usual Finished Goods account

Mintel has $100,000 of Raw and In Process Inventory and $900,000 of Finished Goods Inventory at July 31. In August, Mintel purchases $3,020,000 of direct materials (silicon wafers), and spends $18,540,000 on labor and overhead to produce

3,000,000 integrated circuits. The standard cost of the circuit is $7 ($1 direct materials and $6 conversion cost). Mintel sells 2,930,000 circuits in August.

Mintel uses JIT costing to record the August transactions.

DAILY EXERCISE 25-18

DAILY EXERCISE 25-19

1. Mintel purchases $3,020,000 of direct materials (silicon wafers) on account. These costs are debited (added) to Raw and In Process Inventory.

Raw and In Process Inventory..	3,020,000	
Accounts Payable		3,020,000

2. Record the $18,540,000 actual conversion costs incurred. Mintel debits the Conversion Cost account. It works just like the Manufacturing Overhead account, except conversion costs also include all manufacturing labor costs.

Conversion Costs...	18,540,000	
Various Accounts (such as wages payable and accumulated depreciation on property, plant, and equipment.)............................		18,540,000

3. Record the standard cost of goods completed. Since Mintel completed 3,000,000 circuits at a cost of $7 each, the debit (increase) to finished goods is $21,000,000 (3,000,000 completed circuits × $7). What accounts are credited? There is no work in process inventory in JIT costing, so Mintel credits

- Raw and In Process Inventory, $3,000,000 (3,000,000 completed circuits × $1 standard raw material cost per circuit) for the silicon wafers, and
- Conversion Costs, $18,000,000 (3,000,000 completed circuits × $6 standard conversion cost per completed circuit) for the labor and other indirect costs allocated to the finished circuits. This credit is similar to the way traditional systems allocate manufacturing overhead to products.

Finished Goods Inventory	21,000,000	
Raw and In Process Inventory (3,000,000 × $1)..		3,000,000
Conversion Costs (3,000,000 × $6)........................		18,000,000

This is the essence of JIT costing. The system does not track costs as the circuits move through manufacturing operations. Instead, *completion* of the circuits triggers the accounting system to go back and pull costs from Raw and In Process Inventory and to allocate conversion costs to the finished products.

4. Record cost of goods sold in the usual manner. Mintel sold 2,930,000 circuits (2,930,000 circuits × $7 per circuit = $20,510,000).

Cost of Goods Sold..	20,510,000	
Finished Goods Inventory...		20,510,000

The August 31 inventory balances are

Raw and In Process Inventory ($100,000 beginning inventory + $3,020,000 purchased − $3,000,000 used in complete circuits)	$ 120,000
Finished Goods Inventory ($900,000 beginning inventory + $21,000,000 completed − $20,510,000 sold)	1,390,000
Total inventory...	$1,510,000

Exhibit 25-15 shows Mintel's major accounts. Combining the raw materials inventory with work in process inventory to form the single Raw and In Process Inventory account eliminates detail. Although Mintel tracks the number of physical units in process, the company does not use material requisitions or time records to

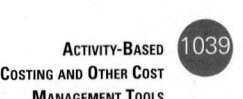

EXHIBIT 25-15 Mintel's Major JIT Costing Accounts

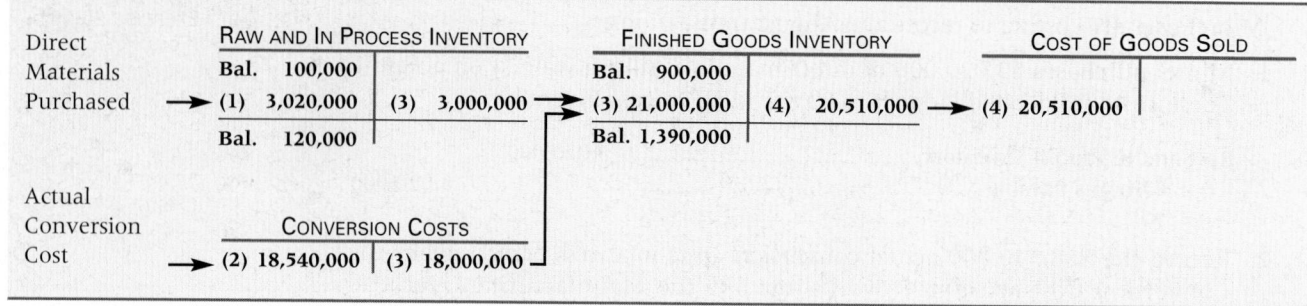

Direct Materials Purchased	RAW AND IN PROCESS INVENTORY				FINISHED GOODS INVENTORY				COST OF GOODS SOLD	
	Bal. 100,000				Bal. 900,000					
→	(1) 3,020,000	(3) 3,000,000 →		→	(3) 21,000,000	(4) 20,510,000 →		→	(4) 20,510,000	
	Bal. 120,000				Bal. 1,390,000					

Actual Conversion Cost	CONVERSION COSTS	
→	(2) 18,540,000	(3) 18,000,000 ┘

assign *costs* to circuits as they flow through the production process. Mintel does not assign costs to physical products until the goods are completed.

Exhibit 25-15 shows that conversion costs are underallocated by $540,000 ($18,540,000 − $18,000,000). Under- and overallocated conversion costs are treated just like under- and overallocated manufacturing overhead, and closed to Cost of Goods Sold. ◄

➤ See Chapter 20, p. 814, for a review of under- and overallocated manufacturing overhead.

Cost of Goods Sold	540,000	
Conversion Costs		540,000

THINK IT OVER Activity-based costing is a more detailed and complex costing method that provides more accurate product costs. Just-in-time costing is simplified and does not track costs through the sequence of manufacturing operations. Are these two costing systems incompatible? Or can they be used together?

Answer: ABC and JIT costing can be compatible. Mintel's $6 standard conversion cost per circuit used in JIT costing could be provided by an ABC system.

Objective 7
Contrast the four types of quality costs and use these costs to make decisions

CONTINUOUS IMPROVEMENT AND THE MANAGEMENT OF QUALITY

Companies using JIT strive for high-quality production. Because goods are produced only as needed, there are no inventories to hide inefficiencies. Poor-quality materials or defective manufacturing processes just shut down production.

Today managers know that if they fail to satisfy customers' demand for high-quality goods, their competitors will not. As we explained in Chapter 19, many companies adopt *total quality management (TQM)* to meet this challenge. ◄ The goal of TQM is to provide customers with superior products and services. Companies achieve this goal by improving quality and by eliminating defects and waste. Each business function in the value chain examines its own activities and sets higher and higher goals.

➤ See TQM discussion in Chapter 19, pp. 774–775.

Many managers invest in the front end of the value chain (R&D and design) to generate savings in the back end (production, marketing, and customer service). They strive to *design* and *build* quality into the product rather than having to *inspect* and *repair* it later. Carefully designed products reduce manufacturing time, inspections, rework, and warranty claims. The theme of total quality management is that superior work benefits the whole organization.

Types of Quality Costs

PREVENTION COSTS. Costs incurred to *avoid* poor-quality goods or services.

Business analysts have identified four types of quality-related costs: prevention costs, appraisal costs, internal failure costs, and external failure costs.

1. **Prevention costs** are incurred to *avoid* poor-quality goods or services. For example, **Deloitte & Touche** and other accounting firms invest heavily to

train personnel in auditing and consulting procedures. Highly trained accountants are more likely to follow company policies and to make fewer errors. Production workers assigned to quality teams at **General Motors** carry beepers so line workers can page when they spot a problem. The quality team then identifies and corrects the cause of the defect (for example, a misaligned robot) right away. The plant does not waste time and materials churning out defective cars.

2. **Appraisal costs** are incurred to *detect* poor-quality goods or services. For example, **Intel**, a manufacturer of integrated circuits, incurs appraisal costs when it tests its products. One procedure, called burn-in, heats circuits to a high temperature. A circuit that fails the burn-in test is also likely to fail when in customer use.

3. **Internal failure costs** occur when the company detects and corrects poor-quality goods or services *before* delivery to customers. An example is the labor of a **BMW** mechanic who reworks a faulty brake job after inspection by a supervisor.

4. **External failure costs** occur when the company does not detect poor-quality goods or services until *after* delivery to customers. If an auto-repair shop does faulty work, the customer will discover the flawed brakes. Then the shop may have to repair the body of the car as well as the brakes. External failures can ruin a company's reputation.

APPRAISAL COSTS. Costs incurred to *detect* poor-quality goods or services.

INTERNAL FAILURE COSTS. Costs incurred when the company detects and corrects poor-quality goods or services *before* delivery to customers.

EXTERNAL FAILURE COSTS. Costs incurred when the company does not detect poor-quality goods or services until *after* delivery to customers.

⊙ DAILY EXERCISE 25-20

Exhibit 25-16 lists some examples of the four types of quality costs. Study these examples closely and you will see that most prevention costs occur in the R&D and design stages of the value chain. In contrast, most appraisal and internal failure costs occur in the production element of the value chain. External failure costs occur in the customer-service stage, or are opportunity costs of lost sales. Companies make trade-offs among these costs. Many prevention costs are incurred only periodically, while internal and external failure costs are ongoing. One expert estimates that 8¢ spent on prevention saves most manufacturers $1 in failure costs.

EXHIBIT 25-16
Examples of Quality Costs

Prevention Costs	Appraisal Costs
Training personnel	Inspection of incoming materials
Evaluating potential suppliers	Inspection at various stages of production
Improved materials	Inspection of final products or services
Preventive maintenance	Product testing
Improved equipment and processes	

Internal Failure Costs	External Failure Costs
Production loss caused by downtime	Lost profits from lost customers
Rework	Warranty costs
Scrap	Service costs at customer sites
Rejected product units	Sales returns and allowances due to quality
Disposal of rejected units	problems
	Product liability claims

Let's revisit Chemtech, the chemical processing company. Chemtech is considering spending the following amounts on a new quality program:

Inspect raw materials	$100,000
Reengineer the production process to improve product quality	750,000
Inspect finished goods	150,000
Supplier screening and certification	25,000
Preventive maintenance of plant and equipment	75,000

Chemtech expects this quality program to reduce the following costs:

Lost profits from lost sales due to disappointed customers	$800,000
Fewer sales returns to be processed	50,000
Lost profits from lost production time due to rework	250,000
Reduced warranty costs	125,000

Chemtech's CEO Randy Smith asks controller Martha Wise to

1. Classify each of these costs into one of the four categories (prevention, appraisal, internal failure, external failure) and total the estimated costs in each category.
2. Recommend whether Chemtech should undertake the quality program.

DAILY EXERCISE 25-21

Exhibit 25-17 classifies each cost and totals the estimated costs in each of the four categories. Wise uses these results to analyze Chemtech's two alternatives:

- Incur the prevention and appraisal costs to undertake the quality program.
- Do not undertake the quality program and incur the internal and external failure costs.

EXHIBIT 25-17   **Analysis of Chemtech's Quality Program**

Undertake the Quality Program		Do Not Undertake the Quality Program	
Prevention		**Internal Failure**	
Reengineer the production process to improve product quality	$ 750,000	Lost profits from lost production time due to rework	$ 250,000
Supplier screening and certification	25,000	Total internal failure costs	$ 250,000
Preventive maintenance of plant and equipment	75,000	**External Failure**	
Total prevention costs	$ 850,000	Lost profits from lost sales due to disappointed customers	$ 800,000
Appraisal		Sales return processing	50,000
Inspect raw materials	$ 100,000	Warranty costs	125,000
Inspect finished goods	150,000	Total external failure costs	$ 975,000
Total appraisal costs	$ 250,000		
Total costs of undertaking the quality program	$1,100,000	**Total costs of not undertaking the quality program**	$1,225,000
Decision: Undertake the Quality Program			

These estimates suggest that Chemtech would save $125,000 ($1,225,000 − $1,100,000) by undertaking the quality program.

Quality costs can be hard to measure. For example, design engineers may spend only part of their time on quality. Allocating their salaries to various activities is subjective. It is especially hard to measure external failure costs. The biggest external failure cost—profits lost because unhappy customers never return ($800,000)—does not even appear in the accounting records! Consequently, total quality management programs also emphasize nonfinancial measures such as number of customer complaints.

The Decision Guidelines feature summarizes key points about just-in-time and quality costs. Study these guidelines before working through the summary review problem.

DECISION GUIDELINES

Just-in-Time and Quality Costs

DECISION	GUIDELINES	
	JIT	**Traditional**
How to distinguish between just-in-time and traditional production systems?	Production cells	Like machines grouped together
	Short setup times	Longer setup times
	Smaller batches	Larger batches
	Lower inventories	Higher inventories
	An individual does wider range of tasks	An individual does fewer tasks
	Fewer, but well-coordinated suppliers	Many suppliers

How does JIT costing differ from traditional costing?

In JIT costing,
1. Summary journal entries are not made until units are completed—costs are not separately tracked as units move through production.
2. Raw materials and work in process are combined into a single Raw and In Process Inventory account.
3. Labor and overhead are combined into a Conversion Cost account.

What are the four types of quality costs?

Prevention costs
Appraisal costs
Internal failure costs
External failure costs

How to make trade-offs among the four types of quality costs?

Investment in prevention costs and appraisal costs reduces later internal and external failure costs.

REVIEW ACTIVITY-BASED COSTING AND OTHER COST MANAGEMENT TOOLS

SUMMARY PROBLEM

The Flores Company manufactures cellular telephones. Flores uses a JIT costing system. The standard unit cost is $37: $24 direct materials and $13 conversion costs. Direct materials purchased on account during June totaled $2,540,000. Actual conversion costs totaled $1,295,000. Flores completed 102,000 telephones in June, and sold 98,000.

Required

1. Prepare the June journal entries for these transactions.
2. Make the entry to close the under- or overallocated conversion costs to Cost of Goods Sold.

www.prenhall.com/horngren

End-of-Chapter Assessment

Solutions

Requirement 1

Raw and In Process Inventory	2,540,000	
Accounts Payable		2,540,000
Conversion Costs	1,295,000	
Various accounts (such as payables and accumulated depreciation)		1,295,000
Finished Goods Inventory	3,774,000	
Raw and In Process Inventory (102,000 × $24)		2,448,000
Conversion Costs (102,000 × $13)		1,326,000
Cost of Goods Sold (98,000 × $37)	3,626,000	
Finished Goods Inventory		3,626,000

(Continued)

Requirement 2		
Conversion Costs...	31,000	
Cost of Goods Sold		31,000

LESSONS LEARNED

1. **Describe and develop activity-based costs (ABC).** *Activity-based costing* focuses on activities as the fundamental cost objects. It uses the costs of activities as building blocks for compiling the costs of products and other cost objects. ABC uses multiple cost allocation bases to allocate activity costs.

2. **Use ABC data and ABM to make business decisions.** In ABM, managers use ABC data to make decisions that increase profits while satisfying customers' needs. Managers use ABC information to make pricing, product mix, cost reduction, and routine planning and control decisions.

3. **Use ABM and value engineering to achieve target costs for target pricing.** Target price is what customers are willing to pay for the product or service. Managers subtract desired profit from target price to obtain target cost. Target cost usually exceeds the current cost to produce the product or service, so managers use value engineering to improve design or production processes to cut costs to the target.

4. **Decide when ABC is most likely to pass the cost-benefit test.** ABC passes the cost-benefit test when the benefits (more accurate product cost information, better information for cost control) outweigh the costs of implementing the system. Companies (1) in competitive markets with (2) high indirect costs that (3) produce a wide variety of different products that make different demands on resources, and that (4) have accounting and information technology to implement the system are most likely to pass the cost-benefit test. This is especially true if the company produces (5) high volumes of some products but low volumes of other products.

5. **Compare a traditional production system to a just-in-time (JIT) production system.** Traditional production systems have functionally arranged clusters of machines, large inventories, long setup times, and relatively inflexible employees. *Just-in-time production systems* have sequentially arranged production activities, "demand-pull" production scheduling, minimal inventories, quick setup times, cross-trained employees, and fewer but better-coordinated suppliers.

6. **Record manufacturing costs for a just-in-time costing system.** *Just-in-time costing* is a standard costing system that begins with output completed and then assigns manufacturing cost to units sold and to inventories. This differs from traditional sequential tracking standard costing that moves forward, step by step, from materials inventory, to work in process inventory, to finished goods inventory, to cost of goods sold. JIT costing is simpler because it uses a single Raw and In Process Inventory rather than separate accounts for raw materials and work in process.

7. **Contrast the four types of quality costs and use these costs to make decisions.** Four types of quality costs are *prevention, appraisal, internal failure,* and *external failure.* Managers make trade-offs among these costs, often investing more in prevention and appraisal to reduce internal and external failure costs.

ACCOUNTING VOCABULARY

activity-based costing (ABC) (p. 1020)
activity-based management (ABM) (p. 1027)
appraisal costs (p. 1041)
backflush costing (p. 1038)

external failure costs (p. 1041)
internal failure costs (p. 1041)
just-in-time (JIT) costing (p. 1038)

prevention costs (p. 1040)
target cost (p. 1029)
target price (p. 1029)
value engineering (p. 1027)

QUESTIONS

1. List three management accounting techniques that managers use to achieve their strategic goal of delivering value to customers.
2. Give two reasons why allocating manufacturing overhead based on direct labor can yield inaccurate product costs.
3. Managers often use standards and variance analysis to control direct material and direct labor costs. What accounting tool can they use to help control manufacturing overhead cost?
4. Give three examples of technology that have made gathering ABC data less expensive.
5. What kinds of decisions do managers make using ABC data?
6. What is target pricing and how does it affect cost management?

7. "Activity-based costing systems provide more accurate information than traditional systems that use a single allocation rate. Every company should adopt ABC." Do you agree? Why or why not?
8. Contrast the traditional and JIT approaches to managing machine setups.
9. Describe "demand-pull" production scheduling.
10. Do companies that implement JIT usually increase or decrease the number of suppliers they use? Why?
11. List three differences between JIT costing and traditional standard costing.
12. The just-in-time costing account Raw and In Process Inventory represents two accounts in a sequential-tracking system. What are they?
13. "Prevention costs are the most important quality costs." Explain.

ASSESS YOUR PROGRESS

DAILY EXERCISES

DE25-1 Fill in each blank with a term. You may use a term more than once. Some terms may not be used at all.

activity-based costing	direct labor	overcost
a cost allocation base	direct material	target costing
a cost driver	indirect	undercost
correctly cost	job costing	

a. ABC systems differ from traditional cost systems in the treatment of _____ costs.
b. Traditional costing systems that use a single overhead allocation base usually _____ high-volume products that are produced in large batches.
c. _____ uses the costs of activities as building blocks for compiling product costs.
d. _____ is any factor whose change causes a change in the related total cost.
e. Traditional cost systems that allocate manufacturing overhead based on direct labor hours or direct labor costs usually _____ direct-labor-intensive products.

DE25-2 List the seven steps in developing an ABC system. For each step, decide whether primary responsibility for the step should be assigned to

- The company accountant
- Production personnel (for example, the production foreman)
- Shared equally between the accountant and production personnel

(*Hint:* Think about who would likely have the most information about each step.)

DE25-3 The vice president of marketing storms into your office, exclaiming:

> **Activity-based costing is worse than useless. It's endangering the future of our company! Because of your ABC cost "information," the CEO is pressuring us to (1) charge customers higher prices for customized products, (2) shift customers from customized products to standard products, and (3) require customers to accept larger deliveries than they would prefer. This completely violates our motto of "delighting the customer." Worse yet, we are being pressured to drop some of the customers we have spent a great deal of effort cultivating. This stupid ABC system will ruin us all!**

Reply to your colleague.

DE25-4 Consider Chemtech's original cost system on pages 1022–1023. Suppose Chemtech allocates manufacturing overhead at 225% of direct labor cost, instead of 200% of direct labor cost.

1. Compute the gross profit per pound for aldehyde and for PH.
2. Compute the *total overhead* assigned to all the aldehyde and to all the PH.
3. Did the new manufacturing overhead rate change the ratio of total overhead allocated to aldehyde versus PH?

DE25-5 Suppose Chemtech's activity-based costing team identifies a fourth activity—machine setup. The foreman estimates that the total setup cost will be $270,000, and that production will require 3,000 setups. (This is less than the 4,000 total batches in Exhibit 25-7. Chemtech often eliminates a setup by running two batches of the same chemical in a row.) Aldehyde will require 35 setups, and PH will require 1 setup.

1. Compute the cost allocation rate for machine setups.
2. Compute the total machine setup costs allocated to aldehyde and to PH.
3. Did Chemtech's original allocation base (200% of direct labor cost) allocate setup costs appropriately? Give your reason.

DE25-6 Consider the Chemtech example on pages 1022–1027 and your analysis in Daily Exercise 25-5.

1. Compute the machine setup cost per pound for aldehyde and for PH.
2. Use your answer to requirement 1 to explain why switching from a traditional single-allocation-base system to an ABC system usually shifts costs away from high-volume products, toward low-volume products.

DE25-7 Use the results of Daily Exercise 25-5 and the information in Exhibit 25-8 to revise the

1. Manufacturing overhead cost per pound for aldehyde and for PH
2. Gross profit per pound for aldehyde and for PH

DE25-8 Chemtech's value engineering team determines that new software for managing the mixing process will reduce mixing costs from $450,000 to $362,000. Given the other information in Exhibit 25-11, compute the new mixing activity cost allocation rate. Will this cost saving allow Chemtech to reach the target cost of $7.60 per pound?

DE25-9 Arnold Business Stationery produces engraved business stationery, which it sells for $360 per ream. The stationery currently costs Arnold's $280 per ream. A competitor has just cut the sale price of its comparable stationery to $300 per ream. Marketing believes that Arnold must cut its sale price to $300 per ream to remain competitive. Arnold currently sells 100,000 reams of engraved stationery each year. If the target profit is 25% of sales revenue, what is the target cost of a ream of stationery?

DE25-10 Daily Exercises 25-10 through 25-16 center on Soliloquy Softworks, Inc., a technology consulting firm and Microsoft Solutions Provider focused on Web site development and integration of Internet business applications. President Mary Nelson's ear is ringing after an unpleasant call from client Barry Wilner. Wilner was irate after opening his bill for Soliloquy's redesign of his company's Web site. Wilner said that Nelson's major competitor, Delta Applications, charged much more reasonable fees to another company for which Wilner serves on the board of directors.

Nelson is puzzled for two reasons. First, she is confident that her firm knows Web site design and support as well as any of Soliloquy's competitors. Nelson cannot understand how Delta Applications can undercut Soliloquy's rates and still make a profit. But Delta Applications is reputed to be very profitable. Second, just yesterday Nelson received a call from client Bob Lee. Lee was happy with the excellent service and reasonable fees Nelson charged him for adding a database-driven job posting feature to his company's Web site. Nelson was surprised by Lee's compliments because this was an unusual job for Soliloquy that required development of complex database management and control applications, and she had felt a little uneasy accepting it.

Like most consulting firms, Soliloquy traces direct labor to individual engagements (jobs). Soliloquy allocated indirect costs to engagements using a budgeted rate based on direct labor hours. Nelson is happy with this system, which she has used since she established Soliloquy in 1995.

Nelson expects to incur $180,000 of indirect costs this year, and she expects her firm to work 3,000 direct labor hours. Nelson and the other systems consultants earn $200 per hour. Clients are billed at 150% of direct labor cost. Last month Soliloquy's consultants spent 90 hours on Wilner's engagement. They also spent 90 hours on Lee's engagement.

1. Compute Soliloquy's indirect cost allocation rate.
2. Compute the total costs assigned to the Wilner and Lee engagements.
3. Compute the operating income from the Wilner and Lee engagements.

DE25-11 Review Soliloquy Softworks' situation in Daily Exercise 25-10. List all the signals or clues that indicate Soliloquy's cost system may be "broken."

Deciding whether ABC will pass
cost-benefit test
(Obj. 3, 4)

DE25-12 Mary Nelson has employed your management consulting firm to help her decide whether to develop an activity-based costing system. After reviewing the information in Daily Exercises 25-10 and 25-11, draft a memo to Nelson. Make a recommendation whether her firm should develop an ABC system. Be sure to include an explanation of the costs and benefits Nelson could expect from adopting ABC. Use the following format for your memo.

Date:	_____
To:	Ms. Mary Nelson, President, Soliloquy Softworks, Inc.
From:	Student name
Subject:	Cost system recommendation

DE25-13 Mary Nelson from Daily Exercise 25-10 suspects that her allocation of indirect costs could be giving misleading results, so she decides to develop an ABC system. She identifies three activities: documentation preparation, information technology support, and training. Nelson figures that documentation costs are driven by the number of pages, information technology support costs are driven by the number of software applications used, and training costs are most closely associated with the number of direct labor hours worked. Estimates of the costs and quantities of the allocation bases follow:

Activity	Estimated Cost	Allocation Base	Estimated Quantity of Cost Driver
Documentation preparation............	$100,000	Pages	3,125 pages
Information technology support	56,000	Applications used	140 applications
Training	24,000	Direct labor hours	3,000 hours
Total indirect costs...........................	$180,000		

Compute the cost allocation rate for each activity.

Using ABC to allocate costs and compute profit (Obj. 1)

DE25-14 Refer to the Soliloquy Softworks example in Daily Exercises 25-10 and 25-13. The Wilner and Lee engagements used the following resources last month:

Cost Driver	Wilner	Lee
Direct labor hours...............	90	90
Pages....................................	50	300
Applications used	1	7

1. Compute the cost assigned to the Wilner engagement and to the Lee engagement, using the ABC system.
2. Compute the operating income from the Wilner engagement and from the Lee engagement.

Explaining results of ABC analysis (Obj. 2)

DE25-15 Write a memo to Mary Nelson comparing the costs of the Wilner and Lee jobs using the original direct labor single-allocation-base system (Daily Exercise 25-10) and the ABC system (Daily Exercise 25-14). Be sure to explain

- How have the costs changed under the ABC system?
- Why have the costs changed in the direction they changed, rather than in the opposite direction?
- Do the ABC results solve Nelson's puzzle from Daily Exercise 25-10?

Your memo should follow the format outlined in Daily Exercise 25-12.

Using ABC information to make decisions (Obj. 2)

DE25-16 Write a memo to Mary Nelson (Daily Exercises 25-10 through 25-15) explaining how she can use the ABC information to make decisions about her consulting firm. Consider how she could use ABC information in

- Setting fees (prices)
- Responding to client concerns about fees
- Controlling costs

Your memo should follow the format outlined in Daily Exercise 25-12.

Comparing JIT and traditional production systems (Obj. 5)

DE25-17 Indicate whether each of the following is characteristic of a JIT production system or a traditional production system.

- a. Management works with suppliers to ensure defect-free materials.
- b. Products produced in large batches.
- c. Large stocks of finished goods protect against lost sales if customer demand is higher than expected.
- d. Suppliers make frequent deliveries of small quantities of raw materials.
- e. Long setup times.
- f. Employees do a variety of jobs, including maintenance and setups as well as operating machines.
- g. Machines are grouped into self-contained production cells or production lines.
- h. Machines are grouped according to function. For example, all cutting machines are located in one area.
- i. Suppliers can access the company's intranet.
- j. The final operation in the production sequence "pulls" parts from the preceding operation.
- k. Each employee is responsible for inspecting his or her own work.

Recording JIT costing journal entries (Obj. 6)

DE25-18 Look at the Mintel Company example on pages 1038–1040. Suppose Mintel's standard cost per circuit is $1.05 for materials and $6.20 for conversion costs, and that Mintel sold 2,950,000 circuits. How would this change Mintel's journal entries, including the entry to close the Conversion Cost account? Prepare new journal entries as necessary.

Recording JIT costing journal entries
(Obj. 6)

DE25-19 Hamilton Products uses a JIT system to manufacture trading pins for the 2002 Olympic Games in Salt Lake City. The standard cost per pin is $2 for raw materials and $3 for conversion costs. Last month Hamilton recorded the following data:

Number of pins completed..	4,000 pins	Raw material purchases..........	$ 8,800
Number of pins sold............	3,500 pins	Conversion costs....................	$12,660

Use JIT costing to prepare journal entries for the month, including the entry to close the Conversion Cost account.

Giving examples of four types of quality costs
(Obj. 7)

DE25-20 Bombardier, Inc., manufactures SeaDoo personal watercraft (jet-skis). Give examples of costs Bombardier might incur in each of the four categories of quality costs:

- Prevention costs
- Appraisal costs
- Internal failure costs
- External failure costs

Be as specific as possible.

Classifying and using quality costs in decision making
(Obj. 7)

DE25-21 Porsche manufactures expensive, high-quality sports cars including the 911 and Boxster. Suppose Porsche is considering spending the following amounts on a new quality program for the 911:

Additional 20 minutes of testing for each car	$ 500,000
Negotiating with and training suppliers to obtain higher quality materials and on-time delivery	200,000
Redesigning the 911 model to make it easier to manufacture...................	1,200,000

Porsche expects this quality program to save costs, as follows:

Reduced warranty repair costs	$150,000
Avoid inspection of raw materials	400,000
Rework avoided because of fewer defective units..............	550,000

It also expects this program to avoid lost profits from

Lost sales due to disappointed customers............................	$800,000
Lost production time due to rework....................................	250,000

1. Classify each of these costs into one of the four categories of quality costs (prevention, appraisal, internal failure, external failure).
2. Should Porsche implement the quality program? Give your reasons.

EXERCISES

Product costing in an activity-based costing system
(Obj. 1)

E25-1 Wheels, Inc., uses activity-based costing to account for its chrome wheel manufacturing process. Company managers have identified four manufacturing activities: materials handling, machine setup, insertion of parts, and finishing. The budgeted activity costs for 20X3 and their allocation bases are as follows:

Activity	Total Budgeted Cost	Allocation Base
Materials handling	$ 18,000	Number of parts
Machine setup	2,800	Number of setups
Insertion of parts	24,000	Number of parts
Finishing	60,000	Finishing direct labor hours
Total	$104,800	

Wheels, Inc., expects to produce 2,000 chrome wheels during the year. The wheels are expected to use 12,000 parts, require 8 setups, and consume 1,000 hours of finishing time.

Required

1. Compute the cost allocation rate for each activity.
2. Compute the indirect manufacturing cost of each wheel.

E25-2 Several years after reengineering its production process, Spokes, Inc., hired a new controller, Lindsay Bays. She developed an ABC system very similar to the one used by Spokes' chief rival, Wheels, Inc., of Exercise 25-1. Part of the reason Bays developed the ABC system was that Spokes' profits had been declining, even though the company had shifted its product mix toward the product that had appeared most profitable under the old system. Before adopting the new ABC system, Spokes had used a direct labor hour single-allocation-base system that was developed 20 years ago.

Product costing in ABC and traditional systems (Obj. 1)

For 20X3, Spokes' budgeted ABC allocation rates are

Activity	Allocation Base	Cost Allocation Rate
Materials handling	Number of parts	$ 1.75 per part
Machine setup	Number of setups	300.00 per setup
Insertion of parts	Number of parts	4.00 per part
Finishing	Finishing direct labor hours	70.00 per hour

The number of parts is now a feasible allocation base because Spokes recently purchased bar coding technology. Spokes produces two wheel models: standard and deluxe. Budgeted data for 20X3 are as follows:

	Standard	Deluxe
Parts per wheel...	5.0	7.0
Setups per 1,000 wheels.....................................	3.0	3.0
Finishing direct labor hours per wheel	0.2	1.0
Total direct labor hours per wheel	2.0	3.0

The company's managers expect to produce 1,000 units of each model during the year.

Required

1. Compute the total budgeted indirect manufacturing cost for 20X3.
2. Compute the ABC indirect manufacturing cost per unit of each model.
3. Using Spokes' old direct labor hour single-allocation-base system, compute the (single) allocation rate based on direct labor hours. Use this rate to determine the indirect manufacturing cost per wheel for each model under the old single-allocation-base method.

E25-3 Refer to Exercise 25-2. For 20X4, Spokes' managers have decided to use the same indirect manufacturing costs per wheel that they computed in 20X3. In addition to the unit indirect manufacturing costs, the following data are budgeted for the company's standard and deluxe models for 20X4:

Using activity-based costing to make decisions (Obj. 2)

	Standard	Deluxe
Sale price	$155.00	$215.00
Direct materials	15.00	25.00
Direct labor.....................	30.00	45.00

Because of limited machine hour capacity, Spokes can produce either 2,000 standard wheels or 2,000 deluxe wheels.

Required

1. If the managers rely on the ABC unit cost data computed in Exercise 25-2, which model will they produce? (All nonmanufacturing costs are the same for both models.)
2. If the managers rely on the single-allocation-base cost data, which model will they produce?
3. Which course of action will yield more income for Spokes?

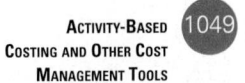

E25-4 Refer to Exercise 25-2. Controller Lindsay Bays is surprised by the increase in cost of the deluxe model under ABC. Market research shows that to remain a viable product while still providing a reasonable profit, Spokes will have to meet a target cost of $165 for the deluxe wheel. A value engineering study by Spokes' employees suggests that modifications to the finishing process could cut finishing cost from $70 to $60 per hour and reduce the finishing direct labor hours per deluxe wheel from 1 hour to 0.8 hour per wheel. Direct materials would remain unchanged at $25 per wheel, as would direct labor at $45 per wheel. The materials handling, machine setups, and insertion of parts activity costs would remain the same as in Exercise 25-2. Would implementing the value engineering recommendation allow Spokes to achieve its target ABC-based cost for the deluxe wheel?

E25-5 Refer to Exercise 25-2. Why might controller Lindsay Bays have expected ABC to pass the cost-benefit test? Were there any warning signs that Spokes' old direct-labor-based allocation system was "broken"?

Recording manufacturing costs in
a JIT costing system
(Obj. 6)

E25-6 Circuit Creations produces circuit boards. Circuit Creations uses a JIT costing system. One of the company's products has a standard direct materials cost of $6 per unit and a standard conversion cost of $20 per unit.

During 20X5, Circuit Creations produced 500,000 units and sold 480,000. It purchased $3,300,000 of direct materials and incurred actual conversion costs totaling $9,550,000.

Required

1. Prepare summary journal entries for 20X5.
2. The January 1, 20X5, balance of the Raw and In Process Inventory account was $80,000. Use a T-account to find the December 31, 20X5 balance.
3. Use a T-account to determine whether conversion cost is over- or underallocated for the year. By how much? Give the journal entry to close the Conversion Cost account.

Recording manufacturing costs in
a JIT costing system
(Obj. 6)

E25-7 E-Voice produces cellular phones. Suppose that E-Voice's standard cost per phone is $22 for materials and $30 for conversion costs. The following data apply to July production:

Materials purchased	$5,300,000
Conversion costs incurred	$6,120,000
Number of phones completed	200,000 phones
Number of phones sold	196,000 phones

E-Voice uses JIT costing.

Required

1. Prepare summary journal entries for July, including the entry to close the Conversion Costs account.
2. The beginning balance of Finished Goods Inventory was $100,000. Use a T-account to find the ending balance of Finished Goods Inventory.

E25-8 JIT costing is typically used by businesses that (1) assign standard costs to each product, and (2) have low inventories. Explain why each of these conditions makes JIT costing more feasible.

E25-9 Abraham & Co. makes electronic components. Evan Abraham, the president, recently instructed vice president Steve Givens to develop a total quality control program. "If we don't at least match the quality improvements our competitors are making," he told Givens, "we'll soon be out of business."

Givens began by listing various "costs of quality" that Abraham incurs. The first six items that came to mind were

a. Costs incurred by Abraham customer representatives traveling to customer sites to repair defective products.
b. Lost profits from lost sales due to reputation for less than perfect quality products.
c. Costs of inspecting components in one of Abraham's production processes.
d. Salaries of engineers who are designing components to withstand electrical overloads.
e. Costs of electronic components returned by customers.
f. Costs of reworking defective components after discovery by company inspectors.

Required

Classify each item as a prevention cost, an appraisal cost, an internal failure cost, or an external failure cost.

E25-10 RPP manufactures radiation shielding glass panels. Suppose RPP is considering spending the following amounts on a new total quality management (TQM) program:

Classifying quality costs and using these costs to make decisions
(Obj. 7)

Strength-testing one item from each batch of panels...................	$50,000
Training employees in TQM	25,000
Training suppliers in TQM	35,000
Identifying preferred suppliers who commit to on-time delivery of perfect quality materials...	60,000

RPP expects the new program would save costs through the following:

Avoid lost profits from lost sales due to disappointed customers...........	$75,000
Avoid rework and spoilage..	50,000
Avoid inspection of raw materials...	40,000
Avoid warranty costs...	15,000

Required

1. Classify each item as a prevention cost, an appraisal cost, an internal failure cost, or an external failure cost.
2. Should RPP implement the new quality program? Give your reason.

Challenge Exercise

E25-11 Baxter Fabricators, Inc., completed two jobs in June 20X4. Baxter recorded the following costs assigned to the jobs by the company's activity-based costing system:

Using activity-based costing
(Obj. 1, 2)

		Allocated Cost	
Activity	Allocation Base	Job 204	Job 609
Materials handling	Number of parts	$ 400	$ 1,200
Lathe work	Number of turns	4,000	12,000
Milling	Number of machine hours	3,000	21,000
Grinding	Number of parts	300	1,200
Testing	Number of output units	150	3,000

Job 609 required 3,000 parts; 60,000 lathe turns; and 1,050 machine hours. All 300 of the job's output units were tested, and all units of the Job 204 were tested.

Required

1. How do you know that at least one of the costs recorded for the two jobs is inaccurate?
2. Disregard materials-handling costs. How many parts were used for Job 204? How many lathe turns did Job 204 require? How many machine hours? How many units were produced in Job 204?
3. A nearby company has offered to test all product units for $13 each. On the basis of ABC data, should Baxter accept or reject the offer? Give your reason.

P R O B L E M S

(Group A)

P25-1A The Electronics Manufacturing Department of Digital Sound, Inc., in Dallas, Texas, assembles and tests electronic components used in digital music equipment. Consider the following data regarding component Q42:

Product costing in an ABC system
(Obj. 1)

Direct materials cost	$71.00
Activity costs allocated	?
Manufacturing product cost	$?

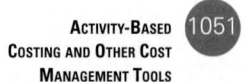

The activities required to build the component follow.

Activity	Allocation Base	Cost Allocated to Each Unit
Start station	Number of raw component chasses	1 × $1.30 = $ 1.30
Dip insertion	Number of dip insertions	? × $0.60 = 12.00
Manual insertion	Number of manual insertions	13 × $0.80 = ?
Wave solder	Number of components soldered	1 × $1.50 = 1.50
Backload	Number of backload insertions	6 × $? = 4.20
Test	Standard time each component is in test activity	0.30 × $90.00 = ?
Defect analysis	Standard time for defect analysis and repair	0.10 × $? = 5.00
Total		$?

Required

1. Fill in the blanks in both the opening schedule and the list of activities.
2. How is labor cost assigned to products under this product costing system?
3. Why might managers favor this ABC system instead of the older system, which allocated all conversion costs on the basis of direct labor?

Product costing in an ABC system
(Obj. 1, 2)

P25-2A MacArthur, Inc., manufactures CD racks and uses an activity-based costing system. MacArthur's activity areas and related data follow.

Activity	Budgeted Cost of Activity	Allocation Base	Cost Allocation Rate
Materials handling	$ 200,000	Number of parts	$ 0.30
Assembling	3,000,000	Direct labor hours	18.00
Finishing	160,000	Number of finished units	5.00

MacArthur produced two styles of CD racks in April—the standard rack and an unfinished rack, which has fewer parts per rack and requires no finishing. The totals for quantities, direct materials costs, and other data follow.

Product	Total Units Produced	Total Direct Materials Costs	Total Number of Parts	Total Assembling Direct Labor Hours
Standard CD rack	2,500	$24,000	30,000	3,000
Unfinished CD rack	3,500	27,000	36,000	2,800

Required

1. Compute the manufacturing product cost per unit of each type of CD rack.
2. Suppose that premanufacturing activities, such as product design, were assigned to the standard CD racks at $4 each and to the unfinished racks at $3 each. Similar analyses were conducted of postmanufacturing activities such as distribution, marketing, and customer service. The postmanufacturing costs were $18 per standard rack and $13 per unfinished rack. Compute the full product costs per unit.
3. Which product costs are reported in the external financial statements? Which costs are used for management decision making? Explain the difference.
4. What price should MacArthur's managers set for unfinished racks to earn a unit profit of $15?

Comparing costs from ABC versus single-rate systems; clues that ABC passes cost-benefit test
(Obj. 1, 4)

P25-3A Camden Pharmaceuticals manufactures an over-the-counter allergy medication called Breathe. Camden is trying to win market share from Sudafed and Tylenol. Camden has developed several different Breathe products tailored to specific markets. For example, the company sells large commercial containers of 1,000 capsules to health-care facilities and travel packs of 15 capsules to shops in airports, train stations, and hotels.

Camden's controller Sandra Whitney has just returned from a conference on activity-based costing. She asks Keith Miller, foreman of the Breathe product line, to help her develop an activity-based costing system. Whitney and Miller identify the following activities, related costs, and cost allocation bases:

Activity	Estimated Indirect Activity Costs	Allocation Base	Estimated Quantity of Allocation Base
Materials handling..............	$180,000	Kilos............................	18,000 kilos
Packaging...........................	300,000	Machine hours..............	2,000 hours
Quality assurance	112,500	Samples........................	2,250 samples
Total indirect costs	$592,500		

The commercial-container Breathe product line had a total weight of 6,000 kilos, used 1,000 machine hours, and required 200 samples. The travel-pack line had a total weight of 4,000 kilos, used 200 machine hours, and required 300 samples. Camden produced 2,500 commercial containers of Breathe and 50,000 travel packs.

Required

1. Compute the cost allocation rate for each activity.
2. Use the activity-based cost allocation rates to compute the activity costs of the commercial containers and the travel packs. (*Hint:* First compute the total activity costs allocated to each product line, and then compute the cost per unit.)
3. Camden's original single-allocation-base cost system allocated indirect costs to products at $300 per machine hour. Compute the total indirect costs allocated to the commercial containers and to the travel packs under the original system. Then compute the indirect cost per unit for each product.
4. Compare the activity-based costs per unit to the costs from the original system. How have the unit costs changed? Explain why the costs changed as they did.
5. What clues indicate that Camden's ABC system is likely to pass the cost-benefit test?

P25-4A Continuing Problem 25-3A, Camden controller Sandra Whitney is surprised that ABC reports such a higher indirect production cost per travel pack. She wonders whether Camden is making the desired profit of $1.25 per unit on this product. The current sale price is $5.75 per travel pack, direct production costs are $2.15 per pack, marketing and distribution costs are $0.90 per pack, and the indirect production costs are $1.70 per pack (from Problem 25-3A). Whitney believes that to reach estimated sales of 50,000 units, the sale price cannot exceed $5.75. If the travel pack is not providing the desired profit of $1.25 per unit, Whitney decides that the next step should be to establish a cross-functional value engineering team to identify opportunities for cost savings. If this does not provide the desired profit, Whitney doubts it will be possible to increase market share to sales of 50,000 travel packs.

Activity-based management, target cost, and value engineering (Obj. 2, 3)

Required

1. Determine the sale price that yields a profit of $1.25 per travel pack. Does this meet the $5.75 target price?
2. Whitney establishes a value engineering team. The value engineering team finds that improved supply-chain management can cut the travel pack's direct production costs from $2.15 per pack to $2.03 per pack. Further, the team believes it can cut materials-handling costs from $180,000 to $171,000. Changes in the packaging department will save $76,000 in packaging costs and 400 in machine hours. Improvements to quality assurance should reduce costs to $107,500 based on 2,150 samples. Marketing and distribution costs will remain unchanged.

   Given these cost savings, compute the indirect activity cost allocation rates for materials handling, packaging, and quality assurance?
3. If the value engineering team's suggestions are implemented, the travel pack line would require 4,000 kilos, use 180 machine hours, and require 256 samples. Compute the new indirect production cost per travel pack (including all three activities).
4. With these changes, can Camden set a sale price of $5.75 and still earn a profit of $1.25 per travel pack?

P25-5A Rugged Ways produces backpacks. The company uses JIT costing for its JIT production system.

Rugged Ways has two inventory accounts: Raw and In Process Inventory and Finished Goods Inventory. On October 1, 20X4, the account balances were Raw and In Process Inventory, $3,000; Finished Goods Inventory, $5,000.

The standard cost of a backpack is $40—$10 direct materials plus $30 conversion costs. Data for October's activity follow.

Recording manufacturing costs for a JIT costing system (Obj. 4, 6)

Number of backpacks completed............	15,000 backpacks	Direct materials purchased.........................	$156,000
Number of backpacks sold......................	14,800 backpacks	Conversion costs incurred..........................	467,000

Required

1. What are the major features of a JIT production system such as Rugged Ways?
2. Prepare summary journal entries for October. Under- or overallocated conversion costs are closed to Cost of Goods Sold monthly.
3. Use a T-account to determine the October 31, 20X4, balance of Raw and In Process Inventory.

Analyzing costs of quality
(Obj. 7)

P25-6A Pedals, Inc., is using a costs-of-quality approach to evaluate design engineering efforts for a new bicycle helmet. Pedal's senior managers expect the engineering work to reduce appraisal, internal failure, and external failure activities. The predicted reductions in activities over the 2-year life of the bicycle helmets follow. Also shown are the cost allocation rates for each activity.

Activity	Predicted Reduction in Activity Units	Activity Cost Allocation Rate Per Unit
Inspection of incoming materials	300	$ 40
Inspection of work in process...........................	300	20
Number of defective units discovered in-house..	1,000	50
Number of defective units discovered by customers...	400	70
Lost sales to dissatisfied customers..................	200	110

Required

1. Calculate the predicted quality cost savings from the design engineering work.
2. Pedals spent $110,000 on design engineering for the new bicycle helmet. What is the net benefit of this "preventive" quality activity?
3. What major difficulty would Pedal's managers have in implementing this costs-of-quality approach? What alternative approach could they use to measure quality improvement?

(Group B) PROBLEMS

Product costing in an ABC system
(Obj. 1)

P25-1B Nouveau Technology's Desktop PC Department, which assembles and tests printed circuit (PC) boards, reports the following data regarding PC Board XR1:

Direct materials cost	$45.00
Activity costs allocated	?
Manufacturing product cost	$?

The activities required to build the PC boards are as follows:

Activity	Allocation Base	Cost Allocated to Each Board
Start station	Number of raw PC boards	1 × $ 0.90 = $0.90
Dip insertion	Number of dip insertions	20 × $ 0.15 = ?
Manual insertion	Number of manual insertions	6 × $? = 2.40
Wave solder	Number of boards soldered	1 × $ 3.50 = 3.50
Backload	Number of backload insertions	? × $ 0.70 = 2.80
Test	Standard time each board is in test activity (hr)	0.25 × $80.00 = ?
Defect analysis	Standard time for defect analysis and repair (hr)	0.16 × $? = 8.00
Total		$?

Required

1. Fill in the blanks in both the opening schedule and the list of activities.
2. How is labor cost assigned to products under this product costing system?
3. Why might managers favor this ABC system instead of the older system that allocated all conversion costs on the basis of direct labor?

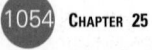

P25-2B Canyon Creek's Shelf Department manufactures bookshelves in its Santa Clarita, California, plant. The company uses activity-based costing. Its activities and related data follow.

Product costing in an ABC system
(Obj. 1, 2)

Activity	Budgeted Cost of Activity	Allocation Base	Cost Allocation Rate
Materials handling	$ 300,000	Number of parts	$ 0.50
Assembling	3,000,000	Direct labor hours	15.00
Painting	170,000	Number of painted bookshelves	6.00

Canyon Creek produced two styles of bookshelves in March—the standard bookshelf and an unpainted bookshelf, which has fewer parts and requires no painting. The totals for quantities, direct materials costs, and other data are as follows:

Product	Total Units Produced	Total Direct Materials Costs	Total Number of Parts	Total Assembling Direct Labor Hours
Standard bookshelf	5,000	$90,000	100,000	5,000
Unpainted bookshelf	1,000	15,000	15,000	900

Required

1. Compute the per-unit manufacturing product cost of standard bookshelves and unpainted bookshelves.
2. Premanufacturing activities, such as product design, were assigned to the standard bookshelves at $5 each and to the unpainted bookshelves at $3 each. Similar analyses were conducted of postmanufacturing activities such as distribution, marketing, and customer service. The post-manufacturing costs were $21 per standard bookshelf and $18 per unpainted bookshelf. Compute the full product costs per bookshelf.
3. Which product costs are reported in the external financial statements? Which costs are used for management decision making? Explain the difference.
4. What price should Canyon Creek's managers set for standard bookshelves to earn a $34.00 profit per bookshelf?

P25-3B The Software Department of Innovations, Inc., develops software for Internet applications. The market is very competitive, and Innovations' competitors continue to introduce new products at low prices. Innovations offers a wide variety of different software—from simple programs that enable new users to create personal Web pages, to complex commercial search engines. Like most software companies, Innovations' raw material costs are insignificant.

Comparing costs from ABC versus single-rate systems; clues that ABC passes cost-benefit test
(Obj. 1, 4)

Innovations has just hired Lou Zeller, a recent graduate of State University's accounting program. Zeller asks Software Department manager Ken Guess to join him in a pilot activity-based costing study. Zeller and Guess identify the following activities, related costs, and cost allocation bases.

Activity	Estimated Indirect Activity Costs	Allocation Base	Estimated Quantity of Allocation Base
Applications development	$3,000,000	New applications	6 new applications
Content production	4,800,000	Lines of code	15 million lines
Testing	315,000	Testing hours	2,100 testing hours
Total indirect costs	$8,115,000		

Innovations is planning to develop two new applications:

- MyPage—for developing personal Web pages
- Bullseye!—a commercial search engine

MyPage requires 500,000 lines of code and 100 hours of testing, while Bullseye! requires 7.5 million lines of code and 600 hours of testing. Innovations expects to produce and sell 30,000 units of MyPage and 10 units of Bullseye!

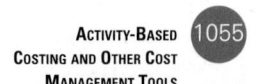

Required

1. Compute the cost allocation rate for each activity.
2. Use the activity-based cost allocation rates to compute the activity costs of MyPage and Bullseye! (*Hint:* First compute the total activity costs allocated to each product line, and then compute the cost per unit.)
3. Innovations' original single-allocation-base cost system allocated indirect costs to products at $100 per programmer hour. MyPage requires 10,000 programmer hours, while Bullseye! requires 20,000 programmer hours. Compute the total indirect costs allocated to MyPage and Bullseye! under the original system. Then compute the indirect cost per unit for each product.
4. Compare the activity-based costs per unit to the costs from the simpler original system. How have the unit costs changed? Explain why the costs changed as they did.
5. What are the clues that Innovations' ABC system is likely to pass the cost-benefit test?

Activity-based management, target cost, and value engineering (Obj. 3)

P25-4B Even though Problem 25-3B shows that MyPage's ABC costs are lower than under the simpler original cost system, Innovations' CEO Tony Millano is still concerned that the software's profitability may be less than expected. Millano asks Zeller to recommend a sale price that will yield a profit of $12 per unit, after direct production costs of $3 per unit, marketing and distribution costs of $5 per unit, and the indirect production costs of $22.50 per unit (from Problem 25-3B). Millano believes that the sale price must be $39 or less to reach estimated sales of 30,000 units. If Zeller's "cost-plus-based" recommended sale price exceeds $39, Millano authorizes him to establish a cross-functional value engineering team to squeeze out cost savings.

Required

1. Determine the sale price that yields a profit of $12 per unit. Will this meet Millano's target price?
2. Zeller establishes a value engineering team that finds new software writing routines can cut application development costs for the six new applications from $3 million to $2.7 million. This would also save $600,000 in content production and require 14 million instead of 15 million lines of code. Testing would be unaffected. The value engineering team also finds that improved supply-chain management can cut MyPage's direct production costs from $3 per unit to $2 per unit. However, marketing and distribution costs for MyPage are unchanged.

   Given these cost savings, what are the indirect activity cost allocation rates for application development, content production, and testing?
3. If the value engineering team's suggestions are implemented, MyPage would require 480,000 lines of code and the same 100 hours of testing. What is the new indirect activity (production) cost per unit (including all three activities) for MyPage?
4. With these changes, can Innovations set a sale price of $39 and still earn a profit of $12 per unit?

Recording manufacturing costs for a JIT costing system (Obj. 4, 5)

P25-5B Connection produces cellular phones. The company has a JIT production system and uses JIT costing.

Connection has two inventory accounts, Raw and In Process Inventory and Finished Goods Inventory. On August 1, 20X5, the account balances were Raw and In Process Inventory, $1,500; Finished Goods Inventory, $2,500.

Connection's standard cost per phone is $45: $30 direct materials plus $15 conversion costs. The following data pertain to August manufacturing and sales:

Number of phones completed	10,000 phones	Raw material purchased	$301,000
Number of phones sold	9,600 phones	Conversion costs incurred	$139,000

Required

1. What are the major features of a JIT production system such as Connection's?
2. Prepare summary journal entries for August. Under- and overallocated conversion costs are closed to Cost of Goods Sold at the end of each month.
3. Use a T-account to determine the August 31, 20X5, balance of Raw and In Process Inventory.

Analyzing costs of quality (Obj. 6)

P25-6B KoffeeKup is using a costs-of-quality approach to evaluate design engineering efforts for a new electric coffeemaker. The company's senior managers expect the engineering work to reduce appraisal, internal failure, and external failure activities. The predicted reductions in activities over the 2-year life of the coffeemaker follow. Also shown are the cost allocation rates for each activity.

Activity	Predicted Reduction in Activity Units	Activity Cost Allocation Rate Per Unit
Inspection of incoming materials	200	$20
Inspection of finished goods	200	30
Number of defective units discovered in-house	3,000	15
Number of defective units discovered by customers	800	35
Lost sales to dissatisfied customers	300	55

Required

1. Calculate the predicted quality cost savings from the design engineering work.
2. KoffeeKup spent $55,000 on design engineering for the new coffeemaker. What is the net benefit of this "preventive" quality activity?
3. What major difficulty would KoffeeKup's managers have had in implementing this costs-of-quality approach? What alternative approach could they use to measure quality improvement?

APPLY YOUR KNOWLEDGE

DECISION CASES

Case 1. SunSystems specializes in servers for workgroup, e-commerce, and ERP applications. The company's original job cost system has two direct cost categories—direct materials and direct labor. Overhead is allocated to jobs at the single rate of $23 per direct labor hour.

Comparing costs from ABC versus single-rate systems; using these costs to make decisions (Obj. 1, 2)

A task force headed by SunSystem's CFO recently designed an ABC system with four activities. The ABC system retains the current system's two direct cost categories. Thus, it budgets only overhead costs for each activity. Pertinent data follow.

Activity	Allocation Base	Cost Allocation Rate
Materials handling	Number of parts	$ 0.75
Machine setup	Number of setups	500.00
Assembling	Assembling hours	80.00
Shipping	Number of shipments	1,500.00

SunSystems has been awarded two new contracts, which will be produced as Job A and Job B. Budget data relating to the contracts follow.

	Job A	Job B
Number of parts..................................	15,000	2,000
Number of setups................................	6	4
Number of assembling hours..............	1,500	200
Number of shipments	1	1
Total direct labor hours......................	8,000	600
Number of output units......................	100	10
Direct materials cost...........................	$210,000	$30,000
Direct labor cost.................................	$160,000	$12,000

Required

1. Compute the product cost per unit for each job, using the original costing system (with two direct cost categories and a single overhead allocation rate).
2. Suppose SunSystems adopts the ABC system. Compute the product cost per unit for each job using ABC.

3. Which costing system more accurately assigns to jobs the costs of the resources consumed to produce them? Explain.
4. A dependable company has offered to produce both jobs for SunSystems for $5,500 per output unit. SunSystems may outsource (buy from the outside company) either Job A only, Job B only, or both jobs. Which course of action will SunSystems' managers take if they base their decision on (a) the original system? (b) ABC system costs? Which course of action will yield more income? Explain.

Activity-based management, target cost, and value engineering (Obj. 1, 2, 3)

Case 2. To remain competitive, SunSystems' management believes the company must produce Job B-type servers (from Decision Case 1) at a target cost of $5,400. SunSystems has just joined a B2B e-market site that management believes will enable the firm to cut direct material costs by 10%. SunSystems' management also believes that a value engineering team can reduce assembly time.

Compute the assembly cost saving per Job B-type server required to meet the $5,400 target cost. (*Hint:* Begin by calculating the direct material, direct labor, and allocated activity cost per server.)

ETHICAL ISSUE

ABC and ethical decisions (Obj. 1, 2)

Grace Luft is assistant controller at Allpax Packaging, Inc., a manufacturer of cardboard boxes and other packaging materials. Luft has just returned from a packaging industry conference on activity-based costing. She realizes that ABC may help Allpax meet its goal of reducing costs by 5% over each of the next three years.

Allpax Packaging's Order Department is a likely candidate for ABC. While orders are entered into a computer that updates the accounting records, clerks manually check customers' credit history and hand-deliver orders to shipping. This process occurs whether the sales order is for a dozen specialty boxes worth $60, or 10,000 basic boxes worth $8,500.

Luft believes that identifying the cost of processing a sales order would justify (1) further computerization of the order process, and (2) changing the way the company processes small orders. However, the significant cost savings would arise from elimination of two positions in the Order Department. The company's sales order clerks have been with the company many years. Luft is uncomfortable with the prospect of proposing a change that will likely result in terminating these employees.

Required

Use the IMA's ethical standards (Exhibit 19-15) to consider Luft's responsibility when cost savings come at the expense of employees' jobs.

TEAM PROJECTS

Project 1

Activity-based costing in the service sector; target costing (Obj. 1, 2, 4)

Quick Trades, Inc., began operations in 1988 as a regional discount brokerage firm. The company grew quickly because of its low trading fees. In the late 1990s, Quick Trades began offering on-line trading. Quick Trades established two types of accounts: a standard service account that provides restricted access to investment advice, and an extended service account for more active customers who maintain a minimum investment balance. Quick Trades charges customers an annual flat service fee plus a per-trade fee.

Quick Trades' CEO Mary Pownall is not happy with the company's recent profits and growth. As on-line trading has become more and more competitive, Pownall tried to increase the extended service accounts. Unfortunately, this has not helped profits. To remain competitive, she now believes that the basic per-trade fee for standard service accounts must be cut to $10. Other firms are starting to lower their per-trade charges to $10 per trade, but Pownall just does not understand how they can charge so little. Controller Joan Lipe wonders whether Quick Trades' cost accounting system may be part of the problem.

While Quick Trades has invested significantly in the latest Internet trading software, the company still uses its original accounting software. The accounting software does not trace any costs directly to customers. The company simply assigns total indirect costs to customer lines (standard service accounts and extended service accounts) based on the total number of trades processed. Lipe thinks that activity-based costing may be helpful, but Pownall wants to see how an ABC system could be helpful before investing in new accounting software.

Lipe assembles an ABC team that includes her assistant, a broker, and the information technology manager. The team begins by identifying three of Quick Trades' critical activities:

- Processing trades
- Personalized broker investment advice
- Answering customer account inquiries

The ABC team then analyzes the company's total indirect cost of $10,500,000. Classifying the components of this total indirect cost into the appropriate activity cost pools leads to the following estimates:

Assignment of Indirect Costs to Activity Cost Pools

Indirect Cost	Activity Cost Pool to Which Indirect Cost Is Assigned	Estimated Total Costs
Salaries of trade processing personnel	Trades processed	$ 1,120,000
Information technology	Trades processed	3,430,000
Brokers' salaries	Broker support	3,100,000
Investment research support	Broker support	2,300,000
Customer support staff department	Customer account inquiry	550,000
Total indirect costs		$10,500,000

The team identifies the following cost drivers for each activity pool:

Activity Cost Pool	Activity Cost Driver
Trades processed	Number of trades processed
Broker support	Number of broker contacts
Customer account inquiry	Number of account inquiry calls

The ABC team estimates that the total number of standard and extended service customers will require the following *total* resources:

Activity Cost Drivers by Customer Line

Activity Cost Driver	Total Number of Units of Activity Cost Driver Used by Standard Service Customers	Total Number of Units of Activity Cost Driver Used by Extended Service Customers	Total
Trades processed	450,000 trades	425,000 trades	875,000 trades
Broker contacts	10,000 contacts	90,000 contacts	100,000 contacts
Account inquiry calls	50,000 calls	200,000 calls	250,000 calls

Quick Trades currently has 15,000 standard service customers who average 30 trades a year, and 8,500 extended service customers who average 50 trades a year.

Split your team into two groups. Each group should meet separately before the entire team meets.

Required

Group 1: Use the original, less-refined cost system that assigns indirect costs based on the total number of trades processed and

1. Compute the indirect cost allocation rate.
2. Use the indirect cost allocation rate to determine the total indirect cost allocated to (a) the standard service customer line, and (b) the extended service customer line.
3. Compute the indirect cost per (a) standard service customer, and (b) extended service customer.
4. Based on this analysis, can CEO Mary Pownall cut the basic per-trade fee to $10 per trade (not per customer) for the standard service customer line?
5. What warning signs indicate that Quick Trades' cost accounting system may be broken? Do you believe that Lipe is correct to question the original cost system? Explain.

Group 2: Use the proposed activity-based cost (ABC) system to compute

1. The indirect activity cost allocation rates for each of the three activities.
2. The total indirect activity costs allocated to (a) the standard service customer line, and (b) the extended service customer line. (*Hint:* This is the sum of the indirect activity costs allocated to each customer line for all three activities.)

3. Compute the indirect cost per (a) standard service customer, and (b) extended service customer.

4. Can CEO Mary Pownall cut the basic per-trade fee to $10 per trade (not per customer) for the standard service customer line? Why or why not?

Team meeting: After each group has completed its individual assignments, the team as a whole should meet to compare results. The team should prepare a memo to CEO Mary Pownall that (1) explains why the costs are so different under the two cost systems, and (2) provides a recommendation along with a justification for which system Quick Trades should use for pricing decisions. Use the following format for the memo:

Memo	
Date:	_____
To:	CEO Mary Pownall
From:	ABC Team
Re:	Differences between Quick Trades' present cost system and an ABC cost system

Project 2

Interviewing a company about its ABC system (Obj. 1, 2, 4)

Form groups of four to six students. Identify a local company that has developed an activity-based costing system, and interview the accounting staff. Before the interview, learn

- The name of your company contact
- What the company produces
- Who are the company's major customers

As part of your advance preparation, decide who will ask which questions during the interview.

Required

The purpose of your interview is to learn how the company developed its ABC system. Be sure to cover the following questions. By listening carefully in the interview, you will likely think of other questions to add to this list.

1. How did the company perform each of the seven steps in developing an ABC system (see pages 1021–1022)? Who was involved in each step? Which step was most difficult? Why?

2. How many separate activities, indirect activity cost pools, and allocation bases does the company's ABC system use? Are there plans to increase or decrease the number of activities, cost pools, and allocation bases in the future?

3. Are the ABC product costs used in the general ledger, or is ABC a separate stand-alone system used primarily for management decisions? If the latter, are there plans to integrate ABC into the general ledger?

4. What spurred the company to develop an ABC system?

5. What benefits has ABC provided? Has management used the ABC data in activity-based management? If so, in what kinds of decisions has the company used ABC information? Has the ABC system lived up to expectations?

6. What problems arose in developing the ABC system? How did the company solve these problems?

7. Have the benefits of the ABC system outweighed its costs?

As directed by your instructor, report the results of your interview in

- A 3- to 5-page typed paper, or
- A 5- to 8-minute oral class presentation

Start with the background information (name of the company, contact person, company's major products and customers). Then discuss the company's ABC system, using the seven questions as a guide. If you don't have space in the paper (or time in the oral report) to cover everything, focus on the insights you found most interesting. (*Hint:* Make sure everyone in your group has a chance to critique the report. Use their suggestions to improve the report before you turn in the written report or make the oral presentation.)

INTERNET EXERCISE

K2 Inc.

K2, Inc., is a leading designer, manufacturer, and marketer of brand name sporting goods, other recreational products, and selected industrial products. The sporting goods and recreational products markets are highly competitive, with competition centering on product innovation, performance, and price. In 1999, sporting goods represented 75% of company sales.

1. Go to **http://www.k2sports.com** to watch the introduction and then click on *Go*. Pass the cursor over each colored button. What are K2's four major product lines?
2. Click on the K2 Snowboards button and watch the introduction. Review the nature of the products listed and consider the four types of quality costs. Would you expect K2 to spend more on prevention and appraisal costs to reduce external failure costs? Why or why not?
3. Go to **http://www.Forbes.com** and under "Stocks" type *KTO*, the stock symbol for K2, Inc., and click on *Go*. In the left-hand column, click on *Financials*. Of the first four operating expense accounts listed, which contain manufacturing costs? Which are used for pricing and profitability analysis? Which contain indirect costs?
4. Assume "Cost of Products" includes indirect costs for materials purchasing, materials handling, indirect assembly labor, and quality inspections for the four major product lines. Identify the primary cost drivers for each of these activities. How would K2 allocate these costs to the four major product lines?
5. Would K2 benefit from using an activity-based costing system? Why or why not? Would ABC likely pass the cost/benefit test for K2? Why or why not?

26

Special Business Decisions and Capital Budgeting

LEARNING OBJECTIVES

After studying this chapter, you should be able to

1. Identify the relevant information for a special business decision

2. Make five types of short-term special business decisions

3. Explain the difference between correct and incorrect analysis of a particular business decision

4. Use opportunity costs in decision making

5. Use four capital budgeting models to make longer-term investment decisions

6. Compare and contrast popular capital budgeting methods

www.prenhall.com/horngren

Readiness Assessment

On the slopes of **Deer Valley Ski Resort** in Park Valley, Utah—site of the 2002 Winter Olympics slalom competition—management accounting seems a world away. But the counter where you rent your skis, the chairlift that whisks you up the mountain, and the restaurant that serves you dinner are all part of the resort's recent expansion. How did Deer Valley's developers decide to spend $13 million to expand the Snow Park Lodge?

Director of Finance Jim Madsen explains that the answer is *capital budgeting*. Deer Valley has a long-term strategic expansion plan. When the resort reaches a target number of skiers per day and target level of profit, the owners expand.

Each expansion project must meet two requirements. First, the project must be profitable. Second, Deer Valley must expect to get its money back on the investment in a relatively short time. To figure out which projects meet these requirements, Deer Valley's managers compare

- The amount of the investment needed to expand the resort with
- The additional revenues expected from expansion.

How do managers make this comparison? They use two management accounting techniques:

- Net present value—to predict whether the investment will be profitable
- Payback period—to predict how long it will take to "get the money back"

In this chapter, we'll see how companies like **Deer Valley** use net present value, payback period, and other capital budgeting techniques to decide which long-term capital investments to make. Deer Valley's capital expansion project is a *long-term* special decision because it will tie up the company's resources for years to come. We'll tackle these long-term special decisions in the second half of this chapter. But first we need to consider *shorter-term* special decisions.

USING RELEVANT INFORMATION

Business managers develop and implement strategies. A **strategy** is a set of business goals and the tactics to achieve them. The main financial goals in business are to earn profits and to build a strong financial position. But managers must make many decisions about how to achieve those goals.

Decision making means choosing among alternative courses of action. Exhibit 26-1 on page 1064 illustrates the process.

Managers often choose the action that maximizes expected operating income. To do this, they analyze relevant information. **Relevant information** has two distinguishing characteristics. It is

- expected *future data* that also
- *differ among alternatives*

Suppose you are buying your first car. You are deciding whether to buy a **Toyota** or a **Saturn**. The cost of the car you want to buy, the insurance premium on this car, and the cost to maintain the car are all relevant because these costs

- will be incurred in the *future* (after you decide to buy the car), and
- will *differ between alternatives* (each car has a different cost, and the maintenance and insurance costs will also differ)

The cost of the car, the insurance, and the maintenance are *relevant* because they can affect your decision of which car to purchase.

Costs that were incurred in the past and costs that do not differ between alternatives are *irrelevant* because they do not affect your decision. For example, a campus parking sticker will cost the same whether you buy the Toyota or the Saturn, so that cost is irrelevant to your decision.

The same distinction applies to all situations—*only relevant data affect decisions*. Let's consider another application of this general principle.

Objective 1
Identify the relevant information for a special business decision

STRATEGY. A set of business goals and the tactics to achieve them.

RELEVANT INFORMATION. Expected future data that differ among alternative courses of action.

 DAILY EXERCISE 26-1

EXHIBIT 26-1   How Businesses Make Special Decisions

Define strategies, business goals, and tactics to achieve them		Identify alternative courses of action		Gather relevant information		Analyze relevant information to compare alternatives		Choose best alternative to achieve goals
	→		→		→		→	

Suppose **Pendleton Woolen Mills** is deciding whether to use pure wool or a wool blend in a new line of sweaters. Assume Pendleton predicts the following costs under the two alternatives:

	Expected Materials and Labor Cost Per Sweater		
	Wool	Wool Blend	Cost Difference
Direct materials	$10	$6	$4
Direct labor	2	2	0
Total cost of direct materials and direct labor	$12	$8	$4

The cost of direct materials is relevant because this cost differs between alternatives (the wool costs $4 more than the wool blend). The labor cost is irrelevant because that cost is the same for both alternatives.

The point is worth emphasizing:

Relevant information is expected *future* data that differ among alternative courses of action.

Managers should base their decisions on expected future data rather than on historical data. Historical data supplied by the accounting system are useful guides for predictions. However, historical data by themselves are irrelevant for making decisions about the future.

THINK IT OVER   You are considering replacing your Pentium III computer with the latest model. Is the $1,500 you spent (in 2000) on the Pentium relevant to your decision about buying the new model?

Answer: The $1,500 cost of your Pentium is irrelevant. The $1,500 is a *past* (sunk) cost that has already been incurred, so it is the same whether or not you buy the new computer.

SHORT-TERM SPECIAL DECISIONS

Our approach to making decisions is called the *relevant information approach,* or the *incremental analysis approach*. This approach applies to a wide variety of special business decisions. We now consider five short-term special decisions:

- Special sales orders
- Dropping products, departments, and territories
- Product mix
- Outsourcing (make or buy)
- Selling as is or processing further

As you study these decisions, keep in mind that two keys in analyzing short-term special business decisions are

KEYS TO ANALYZING SHORT-TERM SPECIAL DECISIONS

Focus on *relevant* revenues, costs, and profits.

Use a *contribution margin approach* that separates variable costs from fixed costs.

◄ Chapter 22, page 891, explains that contribution margin equals revenues minus all variable expenses.

Special Sales Order

Objective 2
Make five types of short-term special business decisions

Suppose that **ACDelco,** a manufacturer of automobile parts, sells oil filters for $3.20 each. Assume that a mail-order company has offered ACDelco $35,000 for 20,000 oil filters, or $1.75 per filter ($35,000 ÷ 20,000 = $1.75). This sale will not affect regular business. Further, the special sales order

- Will not change fixed costs
- Will not require any additional variable nonmanufacturing expenses
- Will use manufacturing capacity that would otherwise be idle

To set the stage for the analysis, examine ACDelco's income statement in Exhibit 26-2. Suppose ACDelco made and sold 250,000 oil filters before considering the special order. Using the conventional (absorption costing) income statement on the left-hand side of Exhibit 26-2, the manufacturing cost per unit is $2 ($500,000 ÷ 250,000). This suggests that ACDelco should *not* accept the special order at a sale price of $1.75, because each oil filter costs $2 to manufacture. But appearances can be deceiving!

EXHIBIT 26-2 **Conventional (Absorption Costing) Format and Contribution Margin Format Income Statements**

INCOME STATEMENT				
Year Ended December 31, 20X5				
Conventional (Absorption Costing) Format		**Contribution Margin Format**		
Sales revenue	$800,000	Sales revenue		$800,000
Less manufacturing cost of goods sold	500,000	Less variable expenses: Manufacturing	$300,000	
Gross profit	300,000	Marketing and administrative	75,000	375,000
Less marketing and administrative expenses	200,000	Contribution margin		425,000
		Less fixed expenses: Manufacturing	$200,000	
		Marketing and administrative	125,000	325,000
Operating income	$100,000	Operating income		$100,000

The right-hand-side of Exhibit 26-2 shows the more helpful contribution margin income statement. Recall from Chapter 22 that contribution margin income statements separate variable expenses from fixed expenses. ➡ Managers find this contribution margin format more useful for decision making because it shows how sales volume affects costs and income. The contribution margin income statement shows that the *variable* manufacturing cost per unit is only $1.20 ($300,000 ÷ 250,000). Now let's reconsider the key question facing ACDelco: How would the special sale affect the company's operating income?

◄ Chapter 22 compares conventional and contribution margin income statements.

CORRECT ANALYSIS: CONTRIBUTION MARGIN APPROACH   The correct analysis shown in Exhibit 26-3 (page 1066) is an incremental approach that follows the two key guidelines for special business decisions:

1. Focus on relevant revenues, costs, and profits, and
2. Use a contribution margin approach.

 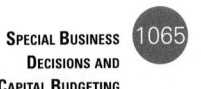

Exhibit 26-3
Incremental Analysis
of Special Sales Order

Expected increase in revenues—	
sale of 20,000 oil filters × $1.75 each	$35,000
Expected increase in expenses—variable manufacturing costs:	
20,000 oil filters × $1.20 each	(24,000)
Expected increase in operating income	$11,000

Exhibit 26-3 shows that this special sale increases revenues by $35,000 (20,000 × $1.75). The only cost that will differ between the alternatives is the variable manufacturing cost, which is expected to increase by $24,000 (20,000 × $1.20). The other costs are irrelevant. Variable marketing and administrative expenses will be the same whether ACDelco accepts the special order or not, because no special efforts were made to get this sale. Fixed expenses are unchanged because ACDelco has enough idle capacity to produce 20,000 extra oil filters without requiring additional facilities.

 DAILY EXERCISE 26-2

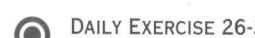 DAILY EXERCISE 26-3

To decide whether to accept the special order, ACDelco compares the additional (incremental) revenues with the additional (incremental) expenses. As long as the increase in revenues exceeds the increase in expenses, the sale contributes to profits. Management predicts that the order will increase operating income by $11,000, as shown in Exhibit 26-3, so they should accept the special order.

Thus, the guiding principle in special order decisions is

Special orders increase income if the revenue from the order exceeds the *extra* variable and fixed costs incurred to fill the order.

Exhibit 26-4 gives the contribution margin income statements both without the special sales order (column 1) and with it (column 2). Column 3 shows the differences from accepting the special order, an $11,000 increase in operating income.

EXHIBIT 26-4 Total Analysis of Special Sales Order—Income Statements without and with the Special Order

INCOME STATEMENT Year Ended December 31, 20X5				
	(1) Without Special Order (250,000 units)	(2) With Special Order (270,000 units)	(3) Difference (20,000 units) Total	(3) Difference (20,000 units) Per Unit
Sales revenue	$800,000	$835,000	$35,000	$1.75
Variable expenses:				
Manufacturing.....................................	$300,000	$324,000	$24,000	$1.20
Marketing and administrative	75,000	75,000	—	—
Total variable expenses........................	375,000	399,000	24,000	1.20
Contribution margin	425,000	436,000	11,000	0.55
Fixed expenses:				
Manufacturing.....................................	200,000	200,000	—	—
Marketing and administrative	125,000	125,000	—	—
Total fixed expenses............................	325,000	325,000	—	—
Operating income	$100,000	$111,000	$11,000	$0.55

We have shown two correct ways of deciding whether to accept or reject a special sales order at a sale price less than the total cost per unit:

- An incremental analysis that quickly summarizes the differences (Exhibit 26-3)
- An analysis of total revenues, expenses, and operating income under both courses of action (Exhibit 26-4)

Which should you use? The answer depends on your question. The *incremental* analysis answers the question: What will be the *difference* in revenues, expenses, and operating income if the business accepts the special order? The *total* analysis shows the summary of differences and answers an additional question: What will be the *total* revenues, expenses, and operating income under each course of action? Managers can use either analysis to decide whether to accept or reject a special sales order.

INCORRECT ANALYSIS: IGNORING THE NATURE OF FIXED COSTS Now consider an incorrect analysis of the special sales order decision. The conventional approach, using only the left-hand side of Exhibit 26-2, leads to an incorrect prediction of the change in expenses resulting from the sale.

Objective 3
Explain the difference between correct and incorrect analysis of a particular business decision

Total manufacturing costs..	$500,000
Units produced	÷ 250,000
Manufacturing product cost per unit ($500,000 ÷ 250,000)	$2.00

 DAILY EXERCISE 26-5

A manager who follows this incorrect approach reasons that it costs $2 to make an oil filter, so it is unprofitable to sell the product for less than $2. *The flaw in this analysis arises from treating a fixed cost as though it changes in total like a variable cost does.* Manufacturing one extra oil filter will only cost $1.20—the variable manufacturing cost. *Fixed expenses are irrelevant to the decision because ACDelco will incur the fixed expenses whether or not the company accepts the special sales order.* Producing 20,000 more oil filters will not increase *total* fixed expenses. As volume increases, manufacturing costs increase at the rate of $1.20 per unit, not $2.00 per unit. In the correct (contribution margin) analysis, the variable expenses are relevant, and the fixed expenses are irrelevant.

SHORT-TERM VERSUS LONG-TERM: OTHER FACTORS TO CONSIDER Our special sales order analysis focused on the short-term expected effect on operating income. We must also consider long-term factors. How will the special order affect ACDelco's regular customers? Will acceptance of the order at $1.75 per unit hurt ACDelco's ability to sell the oil filter at the regular price of $3.20? Will regular customers find out about the special price and balk at paying more? How will competitors react? Will this sale start a price war?

 DAILY EXERCISE 26-4

Accepting the order increases operating income by $11,000. Will potential disadvantages offset this income? The sales manager may think so and reject the order. In turning away the business, the manager would say that the company is better off passing up $11,000 now to protect its long-term market position and customer relations. Rejecting the special sales order may be an $11,000 "investment" in the company's long-term future.

To make special sales order decisions, we analyzed changes in revenues and costs among the different alternatives. We will use this same approach of analyzing differences in revenues and costs for the remaining short-term special decisions.

Dropping Products, Departments, Territories

To decide whether a company should drop a product line, a department, or a territory, let's modify our ACDelco example. We will assume that ACDelco already is operating at the 270,000-unit level, as shown in column 2 of Exhibit 26-4. Suppose the company is now considering *dropping* the air cleaner product line with $35,000 (20,000 units) in sales and total variable costs per unit of $1.50. A contribution margin income statement by product line follows:

 DAILY EXERCISE 26-6

 DAILY EXERCISE 26-7

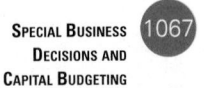

	Product Line		
	Total (270,000 units)	Oil Filters (250,000 units)	Air Cleaners (20,000 units)
Sales revenue	$835,000	$800,000	$ 35,000
Variable expenses	405,000	375,000	30,000
Contribution margin	430,000	425,000	5,000
Fixed expenses:			
Manufacturing	200,000	185,185*	14,815*
Marketing and administrative	125,000	115,741†	9,259 †
Total fixed expenses	325,000	300,926	24,074
Operating income (loss)	$105,000	$124,074	$(19,074)

* $200,000 ÷ 270,000 units = $0.74074 per unit; 250,000 units × $0.74074 = $185,185; 20,000 units × $0.74074 = $14,815

† $125,000 ÷ 270,000 units = $0.462963 per unit; 250,000 units × $0.462963 = $115,741; 20,000 units × $0.462963 = $9,259

Suppose that to measure product-line operating income, ACDelco allocates fixed expenses in proportion to the number of units sold. Dividing the fixed manufacturing expense of $200,000 by 270,000 total units yields a fixed manufacturing cost of $0.74074 per unit. Allocating this unit cost to the 250,000 units of the oil filter product line results in a fixed manufacturing cost of $185,185 for this product. The same procedure allocates $14,815 to air cleaners. Fixed marketing and administrative expenses are allocated in the same manner.

The result is an operating loss of $19,074 for air cleaners. Should ACDelco drop the air cleaner product line? The answer depends on whether or not fixed costs change.

FIXED COSTS REMAIN UNCHANGED   As in the special sales order example, we follow the two key guidelines for special business decisions: (1) focus on relevant data items, and (2) use a contribution margin approach. The relevant items are still the changes in revenues and expenses, but now we are considering a decrease in volume rather than an increase. If fixed costs will in fact remain the same whether or not the air cleaner product line is dropped, the fixed costs are not relevant to the decision. Only the revenues and variable expenses are relevant.

The preceding table shows that the air cleaner product line has a positive contribution margin of $5,000. If this product line is dropped, the company will forego this $5,000 contribution. Exhibit 26-5 verifies this amount—expected revenue decreases by $35,000, and expected variable expenses decrease by $30,000, a net $5,000 decrease in operating income (since fixed costs are unaffected). This analysis suggests that management should *not* drop air cleaners.

EXHIBIT 26-5
Dropping a Product—Fixed Costs Unchanged

Expected decrease in revenues:	
Sale of air cleaners (20,000 × $1.75)	$35,000
Expected decrease in expenses:	
Variable manufacturing expenses (20,000 × $1.50)	30,000
Expected decrease in operating income	$ 5,000

FIXED COSTS CHANGE   Don't jump to the conclusion that fixed costs never change and are always irrelevant. Suppose ACDelco had employed a foreman to oversee the air cleaner product line. The foreman's $28,000 salary can be avoided if the company stops producing air cleaners. Exhibit 26-6 shows how this additional savings affects the analysis.

DAILY EXERCISE 26-8

In this situation, operating income will increase by $23,000 if ACDelco drops air cleaners. Here, a "fixed" cost *is* relevant, so managers must consider the change in the cost. Special decisions should take into account all costs affected by the choice of action. Managers must ask: What costs—variable *and* fixed—will change?

EXHIBIT 26-6
Dropping a Product—Fixed
Costs Change

Expected decrease in revenues:		
Sale of air cleaners (20,000 × $1.75)		$35,000
Expected decrease in expenses:		
Variable manufacturing expenses (20,000 × $1.50)	$30,000	
Fixed expenses—foreman's salary	28,000	
Expected decrease in total expenses.....................................		58,000
Expected increase in operating income.................................		$23,000

As Exhibit 26-5 and 26-6 show, the key to deciding whether to drop products, departments, or territories is to compare the lost revenue against the costs that can be saved from dropping. The decision rule is

If the lost revenues from dropping a product, department, or territory exceed the cost savings from dropping → Do not drop.

If the cost savings exceed the lost revenues from dropping a product, department, or territory → Drop.

Product Mix—Which Product to Emphasize?

Companies do not have unlimited resources. They must decide which products to emphasize and which to deemphasize to maximize profits.

DAILY EXERCISE 26-9

Consider Chazz, a manufacturer of shirts and slacks. The following data suggest that shirts are more profitable than slacks:

	Per Unit	
	Shirts	**Slacks**
Sale price	$30	$60
Variable expenses	12	48
Contribution margin	$18	$12
Contribution margin ratio:		
Shirts—$18 ÷ $30	60%	
Slacks—$12 ÷ $60......................		20%

However, an important piece of information is missing—the time it takes to manufacture each product. This factor, called the **constraint,** restricts production or sale of a product. In some companies, the constraint is production capacity. The factory or labor force may be unable to produce more than a certain number of units.

CONSTRAINT. A factor that restricts production or sale of a product.

Constraints vary from company to company. The constraint that limits how much the company can produce may be labor hours, machine hours, materials, or square feet of shelf space. For example, storage may be limited to 50,000 square feet of space in a warehouse. Some companies are constrained by sales. Competition may be stiff, and the business may be able to sell only so many units.

Chazz can produce either 20 pairs of slacks *or* 10 shirts per machine hour. The company can sell all the shirts and slacks it produces. The company has 2,000 machine hours of capacity. Which product should it emphasize?

To answer this question, follow the guiding principle:

To maximize profits, produce the product with the highest contribution margin *per unit of the constraint.*

In our example, Chazz can sell all the slacks and shirts it makes, so production (machine hours) is the constraint. Thus, Chazz should produce the product with the highest contribution margin per machine hour.

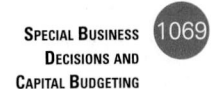

SPECIAL BUSINESS
DECISIONS AND
CAPITAL BUDGETING

1069

Exhibit 26-7 first determines the contribution margin per machine hour for each product. Slacks have a higher contribution margin per machine hour ($240 = 20 pairs of slacks × $12 per pair) than shirts ($180 = 10 shirts × $18 per shirt). Chazz will earn more profit by producing slacks. Exhibit 26-7 proves this by multiplying the contribution margin per machine hour by the available number of machine hours. Chazz can earn $480,000 of contribution margin by producing slacks, but only $360,000 by producing shirts.

EXHIBIT 26-7
Product Mix—Which Product to Emphasize

	Shirts	Slacks
(1) Units that can be produced each hour	10	20
(2) Contribution margin per unit	× $18	× $12
Contribution margin per hour (1) × (2)	$180	$240
Capacity—number of hours	× 2,000	× 2,000
Total contribution margin at full capacity	$360,000	$480,000

Exhibit 26-7 shows that Chazz should *not* produce the product with the highest contribution margin *per unit* (shirts). The key point is that Chazz will earn more profit if it produces the product with the highest contribution margin per unit of the (machine hours) constraint—slacks.

Notice that the analysis in Exhibit 26-7 has once again followed the two guidelines for special business decisions: (1) focus on relevant data (contribution margin in this example, because only sales revenue and variable costs are relevant), and (2) use a contribution margin approach.

THINK IT OVER

Why are Chazz's fixed expenses irrelevant in the decision to produce slacks or shirts?

Answer: Chazz will use the same property, plant, and equipment to make either slacks or shirts. The fixed expenses will be the same whether the company makes slacks or shirts, so the fixed expenses are irrelevant.

Outsourcing

Manufactured goods include specialized parts. Overhead garage doors, for example, have electronic controls. **Genie,** the garage-door manufacturer, must decide whether to make the control device itself or buy from a supplier. **Swaim Furniture** may ask: Should we stain and lacquer the furniture we make or hire another company to do the finish work? These make-or-buy decisions are often called **outsourcing** decisions, because managers must decide whether to buy a component product or service, or to produce it in-house. Assuming that quality is unaffected, the heart of these decisions is *how best to use available facilities.*

Let's see how managers make outsourcing decisions. DefTone, a manufacturer of music CDs, is deciding whether to make the paper liners for the CD jewel boxes in-house, or whether to outsource them to Mūz-Art, a company that specializes in producing these paper liners. DefTone's cost to produce 250,000 liners is

OUTSOURCING. A make-or-buy decision, where managers must decide whether to buy a component product or service or to produce it in-house.

	Total Cost (250,000 liners)
Direct materials	$ 40,000
Direct labor	20,000
Variable overhead	15,000
Fixed overhead	50,000
Total manufacturing cost	$125,000
Cost per liner ($125,000 ÷ 250,000)	$0.50

Mūz-Art offers to sell DefTone the liners for $0.37 each. Should DefTone make the liners or buy them from Mūz-Art? DefTone's $0.50 cost per unit to make the liner is $0.13 higher than the cost of buying it from Mūz-Art. It appears that DefTone should outsource the liners. But the correct answer is not so simple. To make the best decision, you must compare the difference in expected future costs between the alternatives. Which costs will differ depending on whether DefTone makes or buys the liners?

By purchasing the liner, DefTone can avoid all variable manufacturing costs and reduce its fixed overhead cost by $10,000. (Fixed overhead will decrease to $40,000.) Exhibit 26-8 shows the differences in costs between the make and buy alternatives.

EXHIBIT 26-8
Outsourcing Decision

◉ DAILY EXERCISE 26-10

◉ DAILY EXERCISE 26-11

◉ DAILY EXERCISE 26-12

Liner Costs	Make Liners	Buy Liners	Difference
Direct materials.....................................	$ 40,000	—	$40,000
Direct labor	20,000	—	20,000
Variable overhead	15,000	—	15,000
Fixed overhead	50,000	$ 40,000	10,000
Purchase cost from Mūz-Art			
(250,000 × $0.37).........................	—	92,500	(92,500)
Total cost of liners................................	$125,000	$132,500	$(7,500)
Cost per unit—250,000 liners..............	$0.50	$0.53	$(0.03)

The decision: It would cost less to make the liners than to buy them from Mūz-Art. The net savings from making 250,000 liners is $7,500, which works out to $0.03 each.

This example shows that *fixed costs are relevant to a special decision when those fixed costs differ between alternatives.* Exhibit 26-8 also shows that outsourcing decisions follow our two guidelines for special business decisions: (1) focus on relevant data (variable and fixed manufacturing costs in this case), and (2) use a contribution margin approach that separates variable costs from fixed costs. These guidelines help managers answer the fundamental question: What difference does the proposed change make?

◉ DAILY EXERCISE 26-13

BEST USE OF FACILITIES   Suppose that buying the liners from Mūz-Art will release factory facilities that DefTone can use to make more CDs at an expected annual profit of $18,000. DefTone's managers must decide among three alternatives:

1. Use the facilities to make the liners.
2. Buy the liners and leave facilities idle.
3. Buy the liners and use facilities to make more CDs.

The alternative with the lowest *net* cost is the best use of DefTone's facilities. Exhibit 26-9 compares net cost under the three alternatives.

EXHIBIT 26-9   Best Use of Facilities

		Buy Liners	
	Make Liners	Facilities Idle	Make Additional CDs
Expected cost of obtaining 250,000 liners (from Exhibit 26-8)	$125,000	$132,500	$132,500
Expected profit from additional CDs............................	—	—	(18,000)
Expected net cost of obtaining 250,000 liners	$125,000	$132,500	$114,500

This analysis of net cost indicates that DefTone should buy the liners from Mūz-Art and use the vacated facilities to make more CDs. If the facilities remain idle, DefTone will forgo the opportunity to earn $18,000.

Managers making special decisions must often consider qualitative factors—that is, factors that are difficult to quantify. For example, DefTone managers may believe they can better control quality by making the liners themselves. This argues for making the liners. But Mūz-Art may be located very close to DefTone's plant. Mūz-Art may be able to achieve a higher on-time delivery rate than DefTone's own plant. This would favor buying from Mūz-Art. DefTone's managers should consider these qualitative factors as well as revenue and cost differences in making their final decision.

Outsourcing decisions are increasingly important in today's globally wired economy. In the past, make-or-buy decisions often ended up as "make," because coordination, information exchange, and paperwork problems made buying from suppliers too inconvenient. The Internet has largely eliminated these problems. Business-to-business applications allow companies to tap into suppliers' and customers' information systems and business processes, even if those suppliers and customers are located halfway around the world. Paperwork vanishes, and information required to satisfy the most stringent just-in-time delivery schedule is available in real time. As a result, companies are focusing on their core competencies and outsourcing more and more other functions.

Like **Cisco Systems, Dell,** and **Nike,** many world-class competitors have discovered that their core competency lies not in manufacturing but in research and

e-Accounting

We Brand it, You Make It: The Outsourcing Trend

Your cell phone may sport the **Motorola, Inc.,** logo, but there's a good chance it was actually made by a little-known company based in Singapore, **Flextronics International Ltd.** In May 2000, Motorola announced that it expects to outsource over $30 billion of consumer electronics production. It was the largest outsourcing agreement to date between a name-brand electronics company and a contract manufacturer. In 1998, contract manufacturing was a $60 billion industry. By 2003 it will grow to nearly $150 billion.

According to a *Purchasing* magazine survey, 81% of electronics buyers cited cost as their reason for outsourcing everything from motherboards and set-top boxes to entire products. How do contract manufacturers like Flextronics and Militpas, CA,-based **Solectron** do the job more cheaply than original equipment manufacturers (OEMs)? "We leverage our overhead," says Solectron's CFO Susan Wang. In other words, orders from multiple clients keep contract manufacturers' plants busy around the clock and cover overhead costs.

OEMs are also rushing to outsource manufacturing so they can concentrate on the activities that add value. Product development, marketing, and customer support are all areas in which OEMs can gain a competitive edge. The manufacturing process is increasingly viewed as a commodity. "OEM is an oddity as an acronym," says Pamela Gordon of Technology Forecasters, a consulting firm: "What it really means is a company whose brand name goes on the product."

Because of the importance of distinguishing their brand name, OEMs must ensure that far-flung contract manufacturers in Brazil, Mexico, or Hungary deliver quality products. Most OEMs with multi-million or -billion-dollar contract manufacturer contracts maintain a team of their own people to oversee quality control. For Motorola, the Internet will play a major role in keeping close tabs on contract manufacturers around the globe. After announcing the Flextronics deal, both companies said they plan to use Internet technology to tie themselves more closely together and streamline Motorola's supply chain.

Sources: based on Scott Thurm, "Motorola plans to outsource production to Flextronics in $30 billion agreement," *Wall Street Journal,* May 31, 2000, p. A3. Paul Gibson, "The asset paradox," *Electronic Business,* April 2000, pp. 120–126. James Carbone, "What buyers look for in contract manufacturers," *Purchasing,* March 23, 2000, pp. 32–38. John Teresko, "E-collaboration," *Industry Week,* June 12, 2000, pp. 31–36.

development and in brand marketing. Such companies outsource much of their manufacturing to contract manufacturers like **Flextronics** and **Yue Yuen Industrial Holdings,** which operate huge plants in countries where labor is less expensive, such as Mexico and Taiwan.

Cisco currently operates three plants that make its most sophisticated components, but outside suppliers directly fill 55% of Cisco's customers' orders. **Hewlett-Packard** is a leader in laser printers, but it outsources production of the laser mechanisms to **Canon.** Outsourcing doesn't stop at production. **Eastman Kodak** decided to outsource its cafeteria and security operations, and **BP Amoco** is considering outsourcing its accounting function.

Many outsourcing decisions are short-term in nature, but Cisco's decision to subcontract most of its manufacturing is a long-term one. When making decisions with long-term consequences, managers identify and analyze the relevant costs and benefits of different alternatives, as DefTone did in Exhibits 26-8 and 26-9. The only difference is that these cost and benefit calculations may extend many years into the future. In this case, managers discount these costs and benefits to their *present values,* as we explain in the second half of the chapter.

Sell As Is or Process Further?

Should a product be sold as it is, or should the product be processed further into another item? For example, suppose that the **Chevron** oil company spent $48,000 to produce 50,000 gallons of regular gasoline, as shown in Exhibit 26-10. Assume Chevron can sell this regular gasoline for $1.20 per gallon, for a total of $60,000 (50,000 × $1.20). Alternatively, Chevron could further process this regular gasoline into premium-grade gas. Suppose the additional cost to process the gas further is $0.11 per gallon, for an additional cost of $5,500 (50,000 gallons × $0.11). Assume the sale price of premium gasoline is $1.40 per gallon, for a total of $70,000 (50,000 × $1.40).

 DAILY EXERCISE 26-14

($48,000) Sunk Cost of Producing Regular Gasoline

($5,500) Cost of Further Processing

Sell As Is

Regular Gasoline: $60,000 Sales Revenue

Premium Gasoline: $70,000 Sales Revenue

EXHIBIT 26-10
Sell As Is or Process Further Decision

As in other special business decisions, managers need to know which items are relevant. The $48,000 cost of producing the 50,000 gallons of regular gasoline is *not* relevant to Chevron's sell or process further decision. Why? Because the $48,000 is a **sunk cost**—a past cost that cannot be changed regardless of which future action is taken. Exhibit 26-10 shows that the $48,000 has been incurred whether Chevron sells the regular gasoline as is or processes it further into premium gasoline.

Exhibits 26-10 and 26-11 show that the relevant items that differ between Chevron's (1) sell as is and (2) process further alternatives are

- Expected revenues   • Expected costs of processing further

The analysis indicates that Chevron should process the gasoline into the premium grade, because the $10,000 extra revenue ($70,000 − $60,000) outweighs the $5,500 cost of the extra processing.

SUNK COST. A past cost that cannot be changed regardless of which future action is taken.

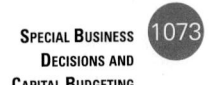

EXHIBIT 26-11 Sell As Is or Process Further Decision

	Sell As Is	Process Further	Difference
Expected revenue from selling 50,000 gallons of regular gasoline at $1.20 per gallon	$60,000		
Expected revenue from selling 50,000 gallons of premium gasoline at $1.40 per gallon		$70,000	$10,000
Additional costs of $0.11 per gallon to convert 50,000 gallons of regular gasoline into premium gasoline		(5,500)	(5,500)
Total net revenue..	$60,000	$64,500	
Difference in net revenue..			$ 4,500

Thus, the key guideline for sell as is or process further decisions is

Process further only if the extra sales revenue (from processing further) exceeds the extra costs of additional processing.

THINK IT OVER Some companies have obsolete inventories that cannot be sold at regular prices. How should managers decide whether to sell the units as is or to incur additional manufacturing costs to rework them?

Answer: This is a sell or process further decision. Managers should predict the additional costs of reworking the inventory. Then they should forecast the additional revenues after rework. If reworking will lead to additional revenues that exceed the additional costs, they should process further. If not, sell the units as is.

Objective 4
Use opportunity costs in decision making

OPPORTUNITY COST. The benefit that can be obtained from the next-best course of action.

OPPORTUNITY COST

We have illustrated five types of special business decisions. For each of these decisions, managers decided on one course of action—and thereby rejected the opportunity to take other actions. When the managers rejected alternatives, their companies incurred an opportunity cost. An **opportunity cost** is the benefit that can be obtained from the next-best course of action. Opportunity cost is *not* an outlay cost that is recorded in accounting. An outlay cost requires a cash payment sooner or later, but an opportunity cost does not.

An example of an opportunity cost is the salary forgone by an engineer who may quit his job with IBM to start his own business. Suppose the engineer analyzes his job opportunities as follows:

DAILY EXERCISE 26-15

DAILY EXERCISE 26-16

Expected Future Event	Open an Independent Business	Remain with IBM
Salary from IBM.............................		$60,000
Sales revenue	$200,000	
Expenses..	120,000	
Net income	$ 80,000	$60,000

The opportunity cost of staying with IBM is the forgone $80,000 of net income from the independent business. The opportunity cost of starting a new business is the $60,000 salary from IBM.

How do managers use opportunity costs in decision making? Consider two examples.

1. *Suppose the IBM engineer has a third job opportunity—employment by* **Microsoft.** To determine the best alternative, the engineer can compare Microsoft's offer with the $80,000 opportunity cost of not opening an independent business. If the engineer's goal is to maximize his personal income, he will accept Microsoft's

offer only if it exceeds his $80,000 opportunity cost. (The IBM salary is irrelevant because opportunity cost is the benefit from the next-best course of action.)

2. *Refer to Exhibit 26-11.* Suppose **Chevron** is approached by a customer who needs 50,000 gallons of regular gasoline. The customer is willing to pay more than $1.20 per gallon. Chevron's managers can use the $64,500 ($70,000 − $5,500) opportunity cost of not further processing the gas to determine the sale price that will provide an equivalent income ($64,500 ÷ 50,000 = $1.29). If the customer offers more than Chevron's opportunity cost of $1.29 per gallon, Chevron will be better off selling the regular gasoline. If the customer offers less than $1.29, Chevron will be better off further processing the gas.

The special decisions we reviewed here usually pertain to relatively short periods of time, such as a year. In this time frame:

- Many costs are fixed and do not vary with the volume of goods or services produced. This is why short-term special business decisions use the contribution margin approach that distinguishes variable from fixed costs.
- There is no need to worry about the time value of money. Managers do not bother computing present values of revenues and expenses for short-term decisions.

In the next half of the chapter, we turn to longer-term special decisions, like **Deer Valley's** decision to build a major expansion of Snow Park Lodge. For long-term decisions:

- Few if any costs are fixed.
- Managers often take into account the time value of money.

The approach to long-term decisions will reflect these differences.

But before moving on to long-term special decisions, stop for a moment to review the Decision Guidelines that summarize key points from our discussion of short-term decisions. Then work the mid-chapter summary problems.

DECISION GUIDELINES

Short-Term Special Business Decisions

DECISION	GUIDELINE
What information is relevant to a short-term special business decision?	Relevant data: 1. are expected *future* data that 2. *differ* between alternatives.
What are two key guidelines in making short-term special business decisions?	Key guidelines: 1. focus on *relevant* data. 2. use a *contribution margin* approach that separates variable costs from fixed costs.
When will accepting a special sales order increase income?	If the revenue from the order exceeds the extra variable and fixed costs incurred to fill the order, then operating income will increase.
When will dropping a product, department, or territory increase income?	If the cost savings exceed the lost revenues from dropping a product, department, or territory, then dropping will increase operating income.
To maximize profit, which product to emphasize when there is a constraining factor?	Emphasize the product with the highest contribution margin per unit of the constraint.
How to decide whether to sell a product as is or process further?	Process further only if the extra sales revenue (from processing further) exceeds the extra costs of additional processing.
How to determine the opportunity cost of a decision?	The opportunity cost of a decision is the benefit forgone by not choosing the next-best course of action.

SUMMARY PROBLEMS

Problem 1.

Aziz, Inc., produces two styles of sunglasses, a standard model and a deluxe model, with the following data:

	Per Pair	
	Standard	Deluxe
Sale price............................	$20	$30
Variable expenses...............	16	21

The company has 15,000 machine hours of capacity available. Seventy pairs of the standard model can be produced in an hour, compared with 30 pairs of the deluxe model. Which style should the company emphasize?

Problem 2.

Just Do It! has the following manufacturing costs for 20,000 pair of its high-tech hiking socks:

Direct materials	$ 20,000
Direct labor..	80,000
Variable overhead..	40,000
Fixed overhead..	80,000
Total manufacturing cost..............................	$220,000
Cost per pair ($220,000 ÷ 20,000)...............	$11

Another manufacturer has offered to sell Just Do It! similar socks for $10, a total purchase cost of $200,000. By outsourcing, Just Do It! can save $50,000 of fixed overhead cost. The company can use the released facilities to make other products that will contribute $60,000 to profits. Identify and analyze the alternatives. What is the best course of action?

Solutions:
Problem 1

	Style of Sunglasses			
	Standard		Deluxe	
Sale price per pair	$	20	$	30
Variable expense per pair..		(16)		(21)
Contribution margin per pair..	$	4	$	9
Units that can be produced each machine hour..............		× 70		× 30
Contribution margin per machine hour	$	280	$	270
Capacity—number of hours...		× 15,000		× 15,000
Total contribution margin at full capacity........................	$4,200,000		$4,050,000	

Decision: Emphasize the standard model because it has the higher contribution margin per unit of the constraint—machine hours.

Problem 2

	Make Socks	Buy Socks	
		Facilities Idle	Make Other Products
Relevant costs:			
Direct materials	$ 20,000	—	
Direct labor	80,000	—	
Variable overhead....................	40,000	—	
Fixed overhead........................	80,000	$ 30,000	$ 30,000
Purchase cost from outsider			
(20,000 × $10)	—	200,000	200,000
Total cost of obtaining socks........	220,000	230,000	230,000
Profit from other products	—	—	(60,000)
Net cost of obtaining 20,000			
pairs of socks..........................	$220,000	$230,000	$170,000

Decision: Just Do It! should buy the socks from the outside supplier and use the released facilities to make other products.

CAPITAL BUDGETING: PAYBACK AND ACCOUNTING RATE OF RETURN

We have seen how managers make short-term special business decisions. Now let's turn to decisions that have long-term effects on business operations.

Think back to the chapter opening story. The **Deer Valley** owners' decision to spend $13 million to expand Snow Park Lodge will tie up resources for years to come. How did the owners decide that the expansion would be a good investment? The Snow Park Lodge expansion met two conditions:

- First, the investment was part of the company's long-term plan. Deer Valley's long-term plan called for expansion when the resort served a target number of skiers per day and achieved a target level of profits.
- Second, Deer Valley's owners used capital budgeting techniques to analyze the expected financial effects of the investment.

Capital budgeting is a formal means of analyzing long-term investment decisions. The term describes budgeting for the acquisition of *capital assets*—assets used for a long period of time. Examples of capital budgeting decisions include expanding the Deer Valley resort, building a new plant, or developing a major commercial Web site for an expansion into e-commerce.

Before proceeding, you need to understand this: Capital budgeting is not an exact science. No matter how precise your calculations, they are based on predictions about an uncertain future. Because capital budgeting decisions have effects far into the future, your predictions must consider many unknown factors, such as changing consumer preferences, competition, and government regulations. The farther into the future the decision extends, the more likely that actual results will differ from predictions. Long-term decisions are thus riskier than short-term decisions.

We now discuss four popular capital budgeting decision models: payback, accounting rate of return, net present value, and internal rate of return. Three of these models compare the *net cash inflows from operations* each alternative generates. ⇒ Generally accepted accounting principles are based on accrual accounting, but capital budgeting focuses on cash flows. The desirability of a capital asset depends on its ability to generate net cash inflows—that is, inflows in excess of outflows—over the asset's useful life.

CAPITAL BUDGETING. A formal means of analyzing long-term investment decisions. Describes budgeting for the acquisition of capital assets.

◄ We discussed cash flows from operating activities, often the primary source of cash, in Chapter 17, page 657.

PAYBACK. The length of time it will take to recover, in net cash inflows from operations, the dollars of a capital outlay.

⊙ DAILY EXERCISE 26-17

⊙ DAILY EXERCISE 26-18

⊙ DAILY EXERCISE 26-19

Payback Period

Payback is the length of time it will take to recover, in net cash inflows from operations, the dollars of a capital outlay. The payback model measures how quickly managers expect to recover their investment dollars. The shorter the payback period, the more attractive the asset, all else being equal. Computing the payback period depends on whether cash flows are equal each year, or whether they differ over time. We consider each in turn.

PAYBACK WITH EQUAL CASH FLOWS Tierra Firma, a manufacturer of high-quality camping gear, is considering investing $240,000 in information technology (hardware and software) to develop a portal, or interface, with a business-to-business (B2B) electronic market. The portal will enable employees throughout the company to enter the electronic market of certified suppliers, to purchase goods and services appropriate to their jobs. Accountants will be able to buy office supplies, and maintenance workers will be able to buy parts. The portal will incorporate controls on the kinds of goods and services each employee can buy, as well as preset spending limits. Tierra Firma expects the portal to save $60,000 a year for the six years of its useful life. The savings will arise from reducing the number of purchasing personnel the company employs and through lower prices on the goods and services purchased.

When net cash inflows are equal each year, managers compute the payback period as follows:

$$\text{Payback Period} = \frac{\text{Amount invested}}{\text{Expected annual net cash inflow}}$$

In general, net cash inflows can arise from an increase in revenues, a decrease in expenses, or both. In Tierra's case, the net cash inflows result from lower expenses. Tierra computes the investment's payback as follows:

$$\text{Payback period for B2B portal} = \frac{\$240,000}{\$60,000} = 4 \text{ years}$$

Exhibit 26-12 verifies that Tierra expects to recoup the $240,000 investment in the B2B portal by the end of year 4, when the accumulated cash inflows (savings) total $240,000.

Tierra Firma is also considering investing $240,000 to develop a Web site to sell its camping gear. The company expects the Web site to generate $80,000 in cash inflows each year of its three-year life. The payback period is computed as follows:

$$\text{Payback period for Web site development} = \frac{\$240,000}{\$80,000} = 3 \text{ years}$$

Exhibit 26-12 verifies that Tierra Firma will recoup the $240,000 investment for Web site development by the end of year 3, when the accumulated net cash inflows

EXHIBIT 26-12
Payback—Equal Annual Net Cash Inflows

| | | Net Cash Inflows | | | | |
| | | B2B Portal | | Web site Development | | |
Year	Amount Invested	Annual	Accumulated	Annual	Accumulated
0	$240,000	—	—	—	
1	—	$60,000	$ 60,000	$80,000	$ 80,000
2	—	60,000	120,000	80,000	160,000
3	—	60,000	180,000	80,000	240,000
4	—	60,000	240,000		
5	—	60,000	300,000		
6	—	60,000	360,000		

total $240,000. Thus, the payback criterion favors Web site development because it recovers the investment more quickly.

A major criticism of the payback model is that it does not consider profitability. The payback technique can lead managers to make unwise decisions. For example, consider the two projects' useful lives. The Web site's useful life is the same as its payback period—three years. Exhibit 26-12 shows that the Web site will merely cover its cost and provide no profits. But the B2B portal has a useful life of six years. It will continue to generate net cash inflows for two years after its payback period. This will give the company an additional net cash inflow of $120,000 ($60,000 × 2 years). Unlike the Web site, the B2B portal will be profitable. After considering the assets' useful lives, the B2B portal appears to be the better investment.

PAYBACK WITH UNEQUAL ANNUAL CASH FLOWS   The payback equation only works when net cash inflows are the same for each period. When periodic cash flows are unequal, you must accumulate net cash inflows until the amount invested is recovered. Suppose Tierra Firma's B2B portal will generate net cash inflows of $100,000 in Year 1, $80,000 in Year 2, $50,000 each year in Years 3–5, and $30,000 in Year 6. Exhibit 26-13 shows the payback schedule for these unequal annual cash flows.

EXHIBIT 26-13
Payback—Unequal Annual Net Cash Inflows

Year	Amount Invested	Net Cash Inflow Each Year	Net Cash Inflow Accumulated
0	$240,000	—	—
1	—	$100,000	$100,000
2	—	80,000	180,000
3	—	50,000	230,000
3.2	—	10,000	240,000
4		40,000	280,000
5		50,000	330,000
6		30,000	360,000

By the end of Year 3, we have recovered $230,000. Recovery of the amount invested ($240,000) occurs during Year 4. Payback occurs in 3.2 years:

$$\text{Payback} = 3 \text{ years} + \frac{\$10,000 \text{ needed to complete recovery in Year 4}}{\$50,000 \text{ net cash inflow in year 4}} \times 1 \text{ year}$$

$$= 3 \text{ years} + 0.2 \text{ year} = 3.2 \text{ years}$$

Managers compare the payback period with the asset's useful life. The asset's payback period must be shorter than its useful life. If an asset like information technology has a payback period of five years and a useful life of three years, the company will never earn a profit from the asset.

How much shorter than the useful life the payback period must be is a business decision that varies by industry and business conditions. When the business is deciding between two or more assets, the asset with the shortest payback period is better *only if all other factors are the same*. This leads to the following decision rule:

Invest only if payback is *shorter* than the asset's useful life. Investments with shorter payback periods are more desirable, *all else being equal.*

The payback method highlights cash flows, a key factor in business decisions. And payback is easy to understand. Managers like those at Deer Valley Resort often use the payback method to eliminate proposals that are too risky (projects with long payback periods). However, a major weakness of payback is that it ignores profitability.

➨ Recall from Chapter 10, page 393, that straight-line depreciation assigns an equal amount of depreciation expense to each year of an asset's life. ◄

EXHIBIT 26-14
Accounting Rate of Return

Accounting Rate of Return

Companies are in business to earn profits. One measure of profitability is the rate of return on investment. The **accounting rate of return** on an asset is computed as follows:

$$\text{Accounting rate of return} = \frac{\text{Average annual operating income from asset}}{\text{Average amount invested in asset}}$$

The accounting rate of return focuses on the operating income an asset generates. Operating income from an asset can be computed as net cash inflow from the asset minus depreciation on the asset. Exhibit 26-14 computes the accounting rate of return for Tierra Firma's B2B portal in the original payback example. Recall that Tierra expects the portal to generate annual net cash inflows of $60,000. The portal's development costs $240,000, and it has a useful life of six years with no residual value. Annual straight-line depreciation is $40,000 ($240,000 ÷ 6 years). ◄ Exhibit 26-14 shows that Tierra expects the portal to generate average annual operating income of $20,000 ($60,000 − $40,000).

$$\text{Accounting rate of return} = \frac{\text{Average annual operating income from asset*}}{\text{Average amount invested in asset}}$$

$$= \frac{\text{Annual net cash inflow from asset} - \text{Annual depreciation on asset}}{(\text{Amount invested in asset} + \text{Residual value})/2}$$

$$= \frac{\$60,000 - \$40,000^\dagger}{(\$240,000 + \$0)/2}$$

$$= \frac{\$20,000}{\$120,000} = 0.167 = 16.7\%$$

* Operating income can also be computed as revenues minus operating expenses.

$\dagger \$40,000 = \dfrac{\$240,000}{6 \text{ years}}$

The accounting rate of return is an *average*. It measures the average rate of return from using the asset over its entire life. First, consider the average annual operating income in the computation. If operating income varies by year (as in the second payback example), compute the *total* operating income over the asset's life. Then divide the total by the number of years of life to find the *average* annual operating income from the asset.

Second, consider the average amount invested. The book value of the asset decreases as it is used and depreciated. Thus, the company's investment in the asset declines over time. If the asset's residual value is zero, the average investment is half the asset's cost. Exhibit 26-14 shows that the average amount invested in Tierra's B2B portal from the original payback example is $120,000 ($240,000 ÷ 2).

If the asset's residual value is not zero, the average amount invested is greater than half the asset's cost. For example, assume the residual value of the portal's technology is $30,000. Then annual depreciation declines to $35,000 [($240,000 − $30,000)/6]. The accounting rate of return is

$$\text{Accounting rate of return} = \frac{\$60,000 - \$35,000}{(\$240,000 + \$30,000)/2} = \frac{\$25,000}{\$135,000} = 0.185 = 18.5\%$$

Companies that use the accounting rate of return model set a minimum required rate of return. They invest only in assets with accounting rates of return equal to or greater than the minimum required rate. Suppose Tierra Firma requires a rate of return of at least 20 percent. Would its managers approve an investment in the B2B portal technology in Exhibit 26-14? No, because the average annual return is less than the company's minimum required rate (20%). Thus, the decision rule is:

> **Invest in assets whose expected accounting rate of return exceeds the company's required accounting rate of return.**

CAPITAL BUDGETING: DISCOUNTED CASH-FLOW MODELS

Chapter 15 introduced the concept of present value. ➡ A dollar received today is worth more than a dollar to be received in the future. Why? Because you can invest today's dollar and earn extra income. Suppose you can choose between receiving a dollar today and a dollar one year from today. If you receive $1 today and deposit it in a bank that pays 6% interest, a year from today you will have $1.06 (the original $1 plus $0.06 interest). Presumably, you would rather receive the $1 now, which will grow to $1.06 a year from today, rather than simply receive $1 a year from today. The fact that money can be invested to earn income over time is called the **time value of money,** and this explains why businesses as well as individuals would rather receive cash sooner than later.

◄ Recall from Chapter 15, page 579, that present value is the amount a person would invest now to receive a greater amount in the future.

TIME VALUE OF MONEY. The fact that money can be invested to earn income over time.

The time value of money ➡ means that the timing of capital investments' net cash flows is important. Consider two $10,000 investments that both promise future cash inflows of $11,000. Investment 1 will bring in cash of $5,500 at the end of each of the next two years. Investment 2 will return the full $11,000 at the end of the second year. Which investment is better? Investment 1, because it brings in cash sooner. Its $5,500 net cash inflow at the end of the first year can be reinvested right away to earn additional returns.

◄ The time value of money is discussed in the Chapter 15 appendix, page 613.

Neither the payback period nor the accounting rate of return recognizes the time value of money. That is, these models fail to consider the *timing* of the net cash flows an asset generates. *Discounted cash-flow models*—the net present value and the internal rate of return—overcome this weakness. Over 85% of large industrial firms in the United States use discounted cash flow methods to make capital budgeting decisions. Companies that provide services, like Deer Valley Resort, also use these models.

Net Present Value

Allegra is considering producing two products, CD players and VCRs. The products require different specialized machines that each cost $1 million. Each machine has a five-year life and zero residual value. The two products have different patterns of predicted net cash inflows:

	Annual Net Cash Inflows	
Year	CD Players	VCRs
1	$ 305,450	$ 500,000
2	305,450	350,000
3	305,450	300,000
4	305,450	250,000
5	305,450	40,000
Total	$1,527,250	$1,440,000

Total net cash inflows are greater if Allegra invests in the CD-player project. However, the VCR project brings in cash sooner. To decide which investment is better, we use **net present value (NPV)** to bring cash inflows and outflows back to a common time period. We *discount* these expected future cash flows to their present value, using Allegra's minimum desired rate of return. We then compare the discounted cash inflows with the discounted cash outflows to decide which, if any, projects to undertake.

NET PRESENT VALUE (NPV). The decision model that brings cash inflows and outflows back to a common time period by discounting these expected future cash flows to their present value, using a minimum desired rate of return.

DISCOUNT RATE. Management's minimum desired rate of return on an investment. Also called the **hurdle rate, required rate of return,** and **cost of capital.**

ANNUITY. A stream of equal periodic cash flows.

Management's minimum desired rate of return on an investment is called the **discount rate.** Synonyms are **hurdle rate, required rate of return,** and **cost of capital.** The discount rate depends on the riskiness of investments. The higher the risk, the higher the discount rate. Allegra's discount rate for these investments is 14%.

NET PRESENT VALUE WITH EQUAL PERIODIC CASH FLOWS (ANNUITY)   Allegra expects the CD players to generate $305,450 of new cash inflow each year. This kind of stream of equal periodic cash flows is an **annuity.** The present value of an annuity is computed by multiplying the periodic cash flow ($305,450 in this case) by the present value of an annuity of $1, obtained from the present value of an annuity table in Exhibit 26-15. The table indicates that the present value of an annuity of $1 received each year for five years, discounted at 14% per year, is $3.433. That is, the value today of receiving $1 at the end of each year for the next five years, discounted at 14%, is $3.433. Another way to think about this is that if Allegra invested $3.433 today at a 14% annual interest rate, there would be just enough money to pay out $1 at the end of each year for the next five years.

EXHIBIT 26-15   Present Value of Annuity of $1

				Present Value of Annuity of $1					
Period	**4%**	**5%**	**6%**	**7%**	**8%**	**10%**	**12%**	**14%**	**16%**
1	0.962	0.952	0.943	0.935	0.926	0.909	0.893	0.877	0.862
2	1.886	1.859	1.833	1.808	1.783	1.736	1.690	1.647	1.605
3	2.775	2.723	2.673	2.624	2.577	2.487	2.402	2.322	2.246
4	3.630	3.546	3.465	3.387	3.312	3.170	3.037	2.914	2.798
5	4.452	4.329	4.212	4.100	3.993	3.791	3.605	3.433	3.274
6	5.242	5.076	4.917	4.767	4.623	4.355	4.111	3.889	3.685
7	6.002	5.786	5.582	5.389	5.206	4.868	4.564	4.288	4.039
8	6.733	6.463	6.210	5.971	5.747	5.335	4.968	4.639	4.344
9	7.435	7.108	6.802	6.515	6.247	5.759	5.328	4.946	4.607
10	8.111	7.722	7.360	7.024	6.710	6.145	5.650	5.216	4.833
11	8.760	8.306	7.887	7.499	7.139	6.495	5.938	5.453	5.029
12	9.385	8.863	8.384	7.943	7.536	6.814	6.194	5.660	5.197
13	9.986	9.394	8.853	8.358	7.904	7.103	6.424	5.842	5.342
14	10.563	9.899	9.295	8.745	8.244	7.367	6.628	6.002	5.468
15	11.118	10.380	9.712	9.108	8.559	7.606	6.811	6.142	5.575
16	11.652	10.838	10.106	9.447	8.851	7.824	6.974	6.265	5.669
17	12.166	11.274	10.477	9.763	9.122	8.022	7.120	6.373	5.749
18	12.659	11.690	10.828	10.059	9.372	8.201	7.250	6.467	5.818
19	13.134	12.085	11.158	10.336	9.604	8.365	7.366	6.550	5.877
20	13.590	12.462	11.470	10.594	9.818	8.514	7.469	6.623	5.929

Appendix C-2 provides a more comprehensive table for the present value of an annuity of $1.

Panel A of Exhibit 26-16 uses this present value of an annuity factor (3.433) to compute the present value of the CD-player project's net cash flows. Allegra's managers multiply the $305,450 to be received each year by the present value factor for a five-year annuity of $1 discounted at 14% (3.433) to obtain the present value of the net cash inflows, $1,048,610. After subtracting the $1,000,000 investment, the net present value of the CD-player project is $48,610.

A positive net present value means that the project earns more than the target rate of return. A negative net present value means that the project fails to earn the target rate of return. This leads to the following decision rule:

Invest in projects with a positive net present value.

In Allegra's case, the CD-player project is an attractive investment. The $48,610 positive net present value means that the CD-player project earns more than Allegra's 14% target rate of return.

EXHIBIT 26-16   Net Present Value

	Present Value at 14%		Net Cash Inflow		Total Present Value
PANEL A—Net Present Value with Equal Cash Flows					
CD-Player Project					
Present value of annuity of equal annual net cash inflows for 5 years at 14%	3.433*	×	$305,450 per year	=	$1,048,610
Investment...					(1,000,000)
Net present value of the CD-player project					$ 48,610
PANEL B—Net Present Value with Unequal Cash Flows					
VCR Project					
Present value of each year's net cash inflows discounted at 14%:					
Year 1..	0.877†	×	$500,000	=	$ 438,500
Year 2..	0.769	×	350,000	=	269,150
Year 3..	0.675	×	300,000	=	202,500
Year 4..	0.592	×	250,000	=	148,000
Year 5..	0.519	×	40,000	=	20,760
Total present value of net cash inflows....................					1,078,910
Investment...					(1,000,000)
Net present value of the VCR project					$ 78,910

* Present value of annuity of $1 for 5 years at 14%, Exhibit 26-15.
† Present value of $1 in 1 year, 2 years, 3 years, and so on, at 14%, Exhibit 26-17.

Another way managers can use present value analysis is to *start* the capital budgeting process by computing the total present value of the net cash inflows from the project to determine the maximum the company can invest in the project and still earn the target rate of return. For Allegra, the present value of the net cash inflows is $1,048,610. This means that Allegra can invest a maximum of $1,048,610 in the CD-player project and still earn the 14% target rate of return. Since Allegra's managers believe they can undertake the project for $1,000,000, the project is an attractive investment.

NET PRESENT VALUE WITH UNEQUAL PERIODIC CASH FLOWS In contrast to the CD-player project, the net cash inflows of the VCR project are unequal—$500,000 in Year 1, $350,000 in Year 2, and so on. Because these amounts vary by year, Allegra's managers must compute the present value of each amount separately:

Year	Present Value of $1 from Exhibit 26-17, 14% Column	Net Cash Inflow	Present Value of Net Cash Inflow
1	0.877	× $500,000 =	$438,500
2	0.769	× 350,000 =	269,150

Panel B of Exhibit 26-16 includes these present-value computations, along with similar computations for Years 3–5. The exhibit indicates that the total present value of the VCR project's net cash inflows is $1,078,910. After subtracting the $1,000,000 investment, Panel B shows that the VCR project has a total net present value of $78,910. This positive net present value means that Allegra expects the VCR project to earn more than the 14% target rate of return. Thus, the VCR project is an attractive investment.

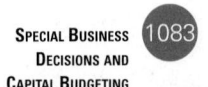

EXHIBIT 26-17   Present Value of $1

Present Value of $1

Period	4%	5%	6%	7%	8%	10%	12%	14%	16%
1	0.962	0.952	0.943	0.935	0.926	0.909	0.893	0.877	0.862
2	0.925	0.907	0.890	0.873	0.857	0.826	0.797	0.769	0.743
3	0.889	0.864	0.840	0.816	0.794	0.751	0.712	0.675	0.641
4	0.855	0.823	0.792	0.763	0.735	0.683	0.636	0.592	0.552
5	0.822	0.784	0.747	0.713	0.681	0.621	0.567	0.519	0.476
6	0.790	0.746	0.705	0.666	0.630	0.564	0.507	0.456	0.410
7	0.760	0.711	0.665	0.623	0.583	0.513	0.452	0.400	0.354
8	0.731	0.677	0.627	0.582	0.540	0.467	0.404	0.351	0.305
9	0.703	0.645	0.592	0.544	0.500	0.424	0.361	0.308	0.263
10	0.676	0.614	0.558	0.508	0.463	0.386	0.322	0.270	0.227
11	0.650	0.585	0.527	0.475	0.429	0.350	0.287	0.237	0.195
12	0.625	0.557	0.497	0.444	0.397	0.319	0.257	0.208	0.168
13	0.601	0.530	0.469	0.415	0.368	0.290	0.229	0.182	0.145
14	0.577	0.505	0.442	0.388	0.340	0.263	0.205	0.160	0.125
15	0.555	0.481	0.417	0.362	0.315	0.239	0.183	0.140	0.108
16	0.534	0.458	0.394	0.339	0.292	0.218	0.163	0.123	0.093
17	0.513	0.436	0.371	0.317	0.270	0.198	0.146	0.108	0.080
18	0.494	0.416	0.350	0.296	0.250	0.180	0.130	0.095	0.069
19	0.475	0.396	0.331	0.277	0.232	0.164	0.116	0.083	0.060
20	0.456	0.377	0.312	0.258	0.215	0.149	0.104	0.073	0.051

Appendix C-1 provides a more comprehensive table for the present value of $1.

WORK IT OUT

Use the present value of $1 table in Exhibit 26-17 to find the present value of an *annuity* of $1 for five years, discounted at 14%. Compare the result to the present value of an annuity of $1 factor from the table in Exhibit 26-15.

Answer: Exhibit 26-17 shows that at a 14% discount rate, the present value of $1 received:

In one year is	$0.877
In two years is	0.769
In three years is	0.675
In four years is	0.592
In five years is	0.519
Total present value of $1 received at the end of each year for five years, discounted at 14% is	$3.432

Except for a slight rounding error, this sum ($3.432) equals the present value of an annuity of $1 for five years discounted at 14%, shown in Exhibit 26-15 ($3.433). This shows how entries in the present value of an annuity table (Exhibit 26-15) are the sums of the present value of $1 factors from Exhibit 26-17.

Exhibit 26-16 shows that both the CD-player and the VCR projects have positive net present values. Therefore, both are attractive investments. If Allegra wants to pursue only one of the two projects, the net present value analysis in Exhibit 26-16 favors the VCR project. The VCR project should earn an additional $78,910 beyond the 14% required rate of return, while the CD-player project returns only an additional $48,610 beyond the required rate of return.

This example illustrates an important point about present-value analysis. The CD-player project promises more *total* net cash inflows. But the *timing* of the VCR cash flows—loaded near the beginning of the project—gives the VCR investment a higher net present value. The VCR project is more attractive because of the time value of money. Its dollars, which are received sooner, are worth more now than the more-distant dollars of the CD-player project.

NET PRESENT VALUE OF A PROJECT WITH RESIDUAL VALUE   Many assets yield cash inflows at the end of their useful lives. The present-value analysis must consider this residual value, discounting it to its present value when determining the total present value of the project's net cash inflows. The residual value is discounted as a single amount—not as an annuity—because it will be received only once, when the asset is sold.

 DAILY EXERCISE 26-21

Suppose Allegra expects the equipment to manufacture CD players will be worth $100,000 at the end of its five-year life. To determine the CD-player project's net present value, we discount $100,000 for five years at 14%—using the present value of $1 factor from Exhibit 26-17—and add its present value ($51,900), as shown in Exhibit 26-18.

EXHIBIT 26-18   Net Present Value of a Project with Residual Value

CD-Player Project	Present Value at 14%	Net Cash Inflow	Total Present Value
Present value of annuity of equal annual net cash inflows for 5 years at 14%	3.433* ×	$305,450 per year =	$1,048,610
Present value of residual value	0.519† ×	$100,000 =	51,900
Total present value of net cash inflows.....................			1,100,510
Investment..			(1,000,000)
Net present value of CD-player project			$ 100,510

* Present value of an annuity of $1 for 5 years at 14%, Exhibit 26-15.
† Present value of $1 in 5 years at 14%, Exhibit 26-17.

Compare Exhibits 26-16 and 26-18. The discounted residual value in Exhibit 26-18 raises the CD-player project's net present value to $100,510, which is higher than the VCR project. If Allegra expects the VCR equipment to have zero disposal value, then the CD-player project is now more attractive.

SENSITIVITY ANALYSIS   Great uncertainty surrounds capital budgeting decisions that affect cash flows far into the future. Allegra's managers might want to know whether their decision would be affected by

- Changing the discount rate from 14% to 12% or to 16%
- Changing the net cash flows by 10%
- Changing the residual value of the equipment

After entering the basic information for net present value analysis into spreadsheet software, managers perform sensitivity analyses with just a few keystrokes. The computer quickly displays the results.

 WORK IT OUT

Suppose Allegra uses a 6% discount rate rather than the 14% rate from Exhibit 26-16. Would the net present value of the CD-player project (assuming zero residual value) be higher or lower using the 6% rate than the original 14% rate? Why?

Answer: The smaller the discount rate, the higher the present value (today) of dollars to be received in the future. Thus, discounting the cash flows at 6% rather than 14% *increases* the net present value of the CD-player project, as follows:

(Continued)

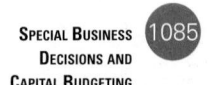

CD-Player Project	Present Value at 6%	Net Cash Inflow	Total Present Value
Present value of annuity of equal annual net cash inflows for 5 years......	4.212*	× $305,450 =	$1,286,555
Investment....................................			(1,000,000)
Net present value at 6%			286,555
Net present value at 14% (from Ex. 26-16)			(48,610)
Difference.....................................			$ 237,945

* Present value of an annuity of $1 for 5 years at 6%, Exhibit 26-15.

Internal Rate of Return

INTERNAL RATE OF RETURN (IRR). The rate of return (based on discounted cash flows) that a company can expect to earn by investing in the project. The discount rate that makes the net present value of the project's cash flows equal to zero.

DAILY EXERCISE 26-22

Another discounted cash-flow model for capital budgeting is the internal rate of return. The **internal rate of return (IRR)** is the rate of return (based on discounted cash flows) a company can expect to earn by investing in the project. The higher the IRR, the more desirable the project. The lower the IRR, the less desirable. The internal rate of return is the discount rate that makes the net present value of the project's cash flows equal to zero.

Exhibit 26-19 shows that Allegra's CD-player project's IRR is 16%. The 16% rate produces a net present value of zero. To see why, we follow three steps:

1. Identify the expected net cash inflows ($305,450 each year for five years) exactly as in calculating the net present value.

2. Find the discount rate that makes the total present value of the cash inflows equal to the present value of the cash outflows. This is easy when the investment consists of a single immediate cash outflow followed by a series of equal cash inflows (an annuity). Work backward to find the discount rate that makes the present value of the annuity of cash inflows equal to the amount of the investment, by solving the following equation for the annuity present-value (PV) factor:

$$\text{Investment} = \text{Expected annual net cash flow} \times \text{Annuity PV factor}$$

$$\text{Annuity PV factor} = \frac{\text{Investment}}{\text{Expected annual net cash flow}}$$

$$= \frac{\$1,000,000}{\$305,450}$$

$$= 3.274$$

3. Turn to the table presenting the present value of an annuity of $1 (Exhibit 26-15). Scan the row corresponding to the project's expected life—period 5, in our example. Choose the column with the number closest to the annuity PV factor that was calculated. The 3.274 annuity factor is in the 16% column. Therefore, the IRR of the CD-player project is 16%. Allegra expects the project to earn an annual rate of return of 16% over its life.

To decide whether the project is acceptable, compare the IRR with the minimum desired rate of return. If the IRR is equal to or greater than that minimum rate, the project is acceptable. Otherwise, it is not. That is, the decision rule is

Invest in projects whose internal rate of return exceeds the required rate of return.

If CD players were the only investment under consideration, Allegra would invest in CD players because their 16% IRR exceeds the 14% discount rate. But recall that the VCR project has a higher net present value than the CD-player project. The VCR investment also has a higher IRR. Because the VCR project has

ExHIBIT 26-19   Internal Rate of Return, CD-Player Project

	Present Value at 16%	Net Cash Inflow	Total Present Value
Present value of annuity of equal annual net cash inflows for 5 years at 16%	3.274*	× $305,450 =	$1,000,000†
Investment...			(1,000,000)
Net present value of the CD-player project			$0‡

* Present value of annuity of $1 for 5 years at 16%, Exhibit 26-15.
† Slight rounding error.
‡ The zero difference proves that the IRR is 16%.

unequal cash inflows, however, computation of the VCR's IRR requires a trial-and-error procedure that is covered in more advanced courses. (Spreadsheet software and even calculators can perform these necessary computations.)

COMPARING CAPITAL BUDGETING METHODS

Payback period, net present value, and internal rate of return are all based on *cash inflows and outflows*. Only the accounting rate of return is based on accrual accounting *revenues and expenses*. Payback is the simplest to compute, but it ignores profitability and the time value of money. The accounting rate of return considers profitability, but it also ignores the time value of money. Only net present value and internal rate of return consider the time value of money.

How do the net present value and IRR approaches compare? Net present value indicates the amount of the excess (or deficiency) of a project's present value of net cash inflows over (or under) its cost—at a specified discount rate. But net present value does not show the project's unique rate of return. The internal rate of return shows the project's rate but does not indicate the dollar difference between the project's present value and its investment cost. In many cases, the two discounted cash flow methods lead to the same investment decision.

The discounted cash-flow methods are superior because they consider both the time value of money and profitability. The time value of money enters the analysis through the discounting of future dollars to present value. Profitability is built into the discounted cash-flow methods because they consider all cash inflows and outflows over the project's life. The payback model considers only the cash flows necessary to recover the initial cash invested.

Exhibit 26-20 summarizes the strengths and weaknesses of payback, accounting rate of return, and the discounted cash-flow methods. Managers often use more than one method to gain different perspectives on risks and returns. For example, **Deer Valley's** owners could decide to pursue capital projects with positive net present values, provided that those projects have a payback of four years or less.

Objective 6
Compare and contrast popular capital budgeting methods

⊙ DAILY EXERCISE 26-23

ExHIBIT 26-20
Capital Budgeting Methods

Method	Strengths	Weaknesses
Payback	Easy to understand Based on cash flows Highlights risks	Ignores profitability and the time value of money
Accounting rate of return	Based on profitability	Ignores the time value of money
Discounted cash flow: Net present value Internal rate of return	Based on cash flows, profitability, and the time value of money	Difficult to determine discount rate

Deer Valley's use of both payback and net present value methods is typical of U.S. companies. Surveys have shown that companies headquartered in the United States often use both payback and discounted cash-flow methods. The payback method is most popular in Japan. Discounted cash-flow methods are more popular in Canada, Ireland, and South Korea.

THINK IT OVER

A pharmaceutical company is considering two research projects. Project A has a net present value of $232,000 and a 3-year payback period. Project B has a net present value of $237,000 and a payback period of 4.5 years. Which project do you think the managers will choose?

Answer: Many managers would choose project A. Net present value is a better guide to decision making than payback period. But managers would consider the 2.2% [($237,000 − $232,000)/$232,000] difference between the net present values to be insignificant. In contrast, the 50% [(4.5 years − 3.0 years)/3.0 years] difference between payback periods *is* significant. The uncertainty of receiving operating cash flows increases with each passing year. Managers often forgo small differences in expected cash inflows to decrease the risk of investments.

Take a moment to review the different capital budgeting methods by studying the Decision Guidelines. This will help solidify your understanding of capital budgeting before you work the summary review problem.

DECISION GUIDELINES

Capital Budgeting

DECISION	GUIDELINE

How to decide whether a long-term investment is worthwhile?	Investments may be worthwhile if:
	• Payback period is shorter than asset's useful life.
	• Expected accounting rate of return on asset exceeds required accounting rate of return.
	• Discounted cash flow methods:
	  Net present value (NPV) is positive.
	  Internal rate of return (IRR) exceeds required rate of return.

How to compute the payback period with
• Equal annual cash flows?

$$\text{Payback period} = \frac{\text{Amount invested}}{\text{Expected annual net cash inflow}}$$

• Unequal annual cash flows?

Accumulate cash flows until amount invested is recovered.

How to compute the accounting rate of return?

$$\frac{\text{Accounting}}{\text{rate of return}} = \frac{\text{Average annual operating income from asset}}{\text{Average amount invested in asset}}$$

$$= \frac{\text{Average annual net cash} - \text{Annual}}{\text{inflow from asset} \quad \text{depreciation on asset}}{(\text{Amount invested in asset} + \text{Residual value})/2}$$

How to compute net present value with
• Equal annual cash flows?

$$\begin{matrix}\text{Present value of} \\ \textit{annuity} \text{ of }\$1 \\ (\text{Exhibit 26-15})\end{matrix} \times \begin{matrix}\text{Annual net cash} \\ \text{inflow or outflow}\end{matrix}$$

• Unequal annual cash flows?

Compute the present value of each year's net cash inflow or outflow (present value of $1 from Exhibit 26-17 × net cash inflow or outflow) and add up yearly present values.

How to compute internal rate of return with
• Equal annual cash flows?

$$\begin{matrix}\text{Annuity PV factor} \\ (\text{Use Exhibit 26-15})\end{matrix} = \frac{\text{Investment}}{\text{Expected annual net cash inflow}}$$

• Unequal annual cash flows?

Trial and error, spreadsheet software, or calculator

Which capital budgeting methods are best?

Discounted cash-flow methods (net present value and IRR) are best because they incorporate both profitability and the time value of money.

EXCEL APPLICATION PROBLEM

Goal: Create an Excel spreadsheet to compute payback period, accounting rate of return, and net present value of a machine.

Scenario: Tar-jay Corporation is considering the purchase of a new bar-coding machine for one of its warehouses. You are asked to prepare a simple analysis to determine whether the machine should be purchased. The summary problem for review at the end of the chapter provides a good outline for completing your analysis.

The bar-code machine costs $60,000. Its estimated residual value is $10,000, and it has a five-year useful life. The estimated annual net cash flow from the machine is $16,000. Tar-jay's required rate of return is 16%.
1. Compute the machine's payback period.
2. Compute the machine's accounting rate of return.
3. Compute the machine's net present value (NPV).
4. Should Tar-jay purchase the machine? Why or why not?

Step-by-step:

1. Open a new Excel spreadsheet.
2. Create a boldfaced heading for your spreadsheet that contains the following:
   a. Chapter 26 Decision Guidelines
   b. Capital Budgeting Decision
   c. Tar-jay Corporation
   d. Today's Date
3. Move down two rows and create a boldfaced and under-lined "Data Section" heading. Enter the data and descriptions provided in the problem under this heading in your spreadsheet.
4. At the end of the Data Section, add a row for "Annual Depreciation on Asset." Use the "SLN" financial function to compute depreciation.
5. Move down two rows. In column A, enter the description "Payback Period (years)." Compute the payback period in column B.
6. Move down one row. In column A, enter the description "Accounting Rate of Return." Compute the accounting rate of return in column B.
7. Move down two rows, and enter "Net Present Value" as a boldfaced and underlined heading.
8. Underneath the heading, use the textbook's Summary Problem format (listed as requirement 3 on page 1090) to compute net present value. Use the "PV" financial function for the present value of an annuity. Use the "NPV" function to calculate the present value of the residual value. (Put zeroes in the first four values and the residual value cell reference in the fifth value to calculate the PV of the lump-sum residual value.)
9. Save your file to disk, and print a copy for your files.

REVIEW SPECIAL BUSINESS DECISIONS AND CAPITAL BUDGETING

SUMMARY PROBLEM

Zetamax is considering buying a new bar-coding machine for its Austin, Texas, plant. The data for the machine follow:

Cost of machine	$48,000
Estimated residual value	$ 6,000
Estimated annual net cash inflow	$13,000
Estimated useful life	5 years
Required rate of return	16%

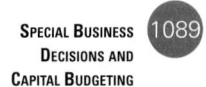

www.prenhall.com/horngren
End-of-Chapter Assessment

Required

1. Compute the bar-coding machine's payback period.
2. Compute the bar-coding machine's accounting rate of return.
3. Compute the bar-coding machine's net present value.
4. Would you decide to buy the bar-coding machine? Give your reason.

Solution

Requirement 1

$$\text{Payback period} = \frac{\text{Amount invested}}{\text{Expected annual net cash inflow}} = \frac{\$48,000}{\$13,000} = 3.7 \text{ years}$$

Requirement 2

$$\text{Accounting rate of return} = \frac{\text{Average annual operating income from asset}}{\text{Average amount invested in asset}}$$

$$= \frac{\substack{\text{Average annual net cash} \\ \text{inflow from asset}} - \substack{\text{Annual} \\ \text{depreciation on asset}}}{(\text{Amount invested in asset} + \text{Residual value})/2}$$

$$= \frac{\$13{,}000 - \$8{,}400^*}{(\$48{,}000 + \$6{,}000)/2}$$

$$= \frac{\$4{,}600}{\$27{,}000}$$

$$= 0.170$$

$$= 17\%$$

$$^*\frac{\$48{,}000 - \$6{,}000}{5 \text{ years}} = \$8{,}400$$

Requirement 3

Present value of annuity of equal annual net cash inflows at 16% ($13,000 × 3.274†)	$42,562
Present value of residual value ($6,000 × 0.476‡)	2,856
Total present value of net cash inflows..	45,418
Investment...	(48,000)
Net present value...	$(2,582)

† Present value of annuity of $1 for 5 years at 16%, Exhibit 26-15.
‡ Present value of $1 in 5 years at 16%, Exhibit 26-17.

Requirement 4

Decision: Do not buy the bar-coding machine because it has a negative net present value. The net present value model considers profitability and the time value of money. The other models ignore at least one of those factors.

LESSONS LEARNED

1. *Identify the relevant information for a special business decision. Relevant information* is expected future data that differ among alternative courses of action. Historical data are irrelevant per se, but they often help managers make predictions about the future.

2. *Make five types of short-term special business decisions.* Two keys to making short-term special business decisions are (1) focusing on relevant revenues and relevant costs, and (2) using a contribution margin approach that separates variable costs from fixed costs. Managers use these techniques when deciding whether to accept or reject a special sales order; whether to drop a product, department, or territory; which product to emphasize when a constraint is present; outsourcing; and whether to sell a product as is or to process it further. Managers often select the course of action that is expected to produce the most operating income.

3. *Explain the difference between correct and incorrect analysis of a particular business decision.* Correct analysis of a business decision focuses on differences in revenues and expenses. The conventional absorption costing approach may mislead managers into treating a fixed cost as a variable cost. The contribution margin approach is more useful because it highlights how sales volume affects expenses and income.

4. *Use opportunity costs in decision making. Opportunity cost* is the benefit that can be obtained from the next-best course of action. Opportunity cost is not an outlay cost, so it is not recorded in the accounting records.

5. *Use four capital budgeting methods to make longer-term investment decisions. Capital budgeting* is a formal means of analyzing long-term investment decisions. Four popular capital budgeting methods are payback, accounting rate of return, net present value, and internal rate of return. *Payback* is the length of time it will take to recover the dollars invested. The *accounting rate of return* is the average annual operating income from an asset divided by the average amount invested in that asset. *Net present value (NPV)* discounts the project's expected future cash flows by the minimum desired rate of return. The project's *internal rate of return (IRR)* is the discount rate that makes the net present value of the project's cash flows equal to zero.

6. *Compare and contrast popular capital budgeting methods.* The discounted cash-flow methods—net present value and internal rate of return—are conceptually superior to payback and accounting rate of return. Payback ignores profitability and the time value of money. Accounting rate of return ignores the time value of money. Net present value and IRR consider both profitability and the time value of money.

ACCOUNTING VOCABULARY

accounting rate of return   (p. 1080)
annuity   (p. 1082)
capital budgeting   (p. 1077)
constraint   (p. 1069)
cost of capital   (p. 1082)
discount rate   (p. 1082)

hurdle rate   (p. 1082)
internal rate of return
   (IRR)   (p. 1086)
net present value (NPV)   (p. 1081)
opportunity cost   (p. 1074)
outsourcing   (p. 1070)

payback   (p. 1078)
relevant information   (p. 1063)
required rate of return   (p. 1082)
strategy   (p. 1063)
sunk cost   (p. 1073)
time value of money   (p. 1081)

QUESTIONS

1. Discuss the roles of expected future data and historical data in decision analysis. On which data are special decisions based?
2. Name two key guidelines for making short-term special decisions.
3. Identify two income statement formats. Which is more useful for deciding whether to accept a special sales order? Why?
4. Identify two long-term factors managers should consider in deciding whether to accept a special sales order.
5. What is the similarity between a special sales order decision and a decision to drop a product? The difference?
6. Which cost is more likely to change in a short-term decision situation, a fixed or a variable cost? Can both costs change?
7. Outline how to decide which product to emphasize when there is a constraining factor. Give four examples of constraining factors.
8. What is an opportunity cost? How does it differ from an ordinary accounting cost?

9. Name three capital budgeting decision methods. State the strengths and the weaknesses of each method. Which method is best? Why?
10. Which capital budgeting method is (a) based on operating income, (b) based on cash flows without regard for their timing or profitability, (c) based on the time value of money.
11. How is the payback period computed for assets that generate equal annual cash inflows? How does the estimated useful life of the asset affect the payback computation?
12. How is the accounting rate of return computed when the annual amounts of operating income vary?
13. Explain why a positive net present value indicates an attractive investment project and a negative net present value indicates an unattractive project.
14. Which capital budgeting strategy is better? (a) Pick the best capital budgeting method and use it exclusively. (b) Use multiple capital budgeting methods. Explain your answer.

ASSESS YOUR PROGRESS

DAILY EXERCISES

DE26-1 You are trying to decide whether to trade in your inkjet printer for a more recent model. Your usage pattern will remain unchanged, but the old and new printers use different ink cartridges. Are the following items relevant or irrelevant to your decision?

Identifying relevant data
(Obj. 1)

  a. The price of the new printer
  b. The price you paid for the old printer
  c. The trade-in value of the old printer

  d. Paper costs
  e. The difference between ink cartridges' costs

DE26-2 Consider the **ACDelco** special sales order example on pages 1065–1067. Suppose that

Accepting or rejecting a special sales order
(Obj. 2)

  a. ACDelco's variable manufacturing cost is $1.45 per oil filter (instead of $1.20).
  b. ACDelco would have to buy a special stamping machine that costs $9,000 to mark the customer's logo on the special-order oil filters. The machine would be scrapped when the special order is complete.

Use the incremental analysis approach from Exhibit 26-3 to determine whether you would recommend that ACDelco accept the special order under these conditions.

DE26-3 Maui Jane sunglasses sell for about $120 per pair. Suppose that the company incurs the following average costs per pair:

Deciding on a special sales order
(Obj. 2)

Direct materials	$40
Direct labor	12
Variable manufacturing overhead	8
Variable marketing expenses	4
Fixed manufacturing overhead	20*
Total costs	$84

$$* \quad \frac{\$2{,}000{,}000 \text{ total fixed manufacturing overhead}}{100{,}000 \text{ pairs of sunglasses}}$$

Maui Jane has enough idle capacity to accept a one-time-only special order from Lenscrafters for 20,000 pairs of sunglasses at $76 per pair. Maui Jane will not incur any additional variable marketing expenses for the order.
    How would accepting the special order affect Maui Jane's operating income?

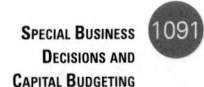

Deciding on a special sales order
(Obj. 2)

DE26-4 Consider the Maui Jane company in Daily Exercise 26-3. In addition to the special order's effect on profits, what other (longer-term qualitative) factors should Maui Jane's managers consider in deciding whether to accept Lenscrafters' special order?

Explaining the difference
between correct and incorrect
analysis for a special sales order
(Obj. 2, 3)

DE26-5 Refer to Daily Exercises 26-3 and 26-4. Maui Jane's marketing manager, Janet Sky, argues that Maui Jane should not accept Lenscrafters' special sales order because Lenscrafters' $76 offer price is less than Maui Jane's $84 cost to make the sunglasses. Sky asks you, one of Maui Jane's staff accountants, to write a memo explaining whether her analysis is correct. Use the following format:

Date:	_____
To:	Ms. Janet Sky, Marketing manager
From:	_____
Subject:	Lenscrafters' special order

Dropping a department
(Obj. 2)

DE26-6 Sam's Video in Philadelphia operates three departments: Video, Music, and Accessories. Sam's Video allocates fixed expenses (building depreciation and utilities) based on the square feet occupied by each department. Departmental operating income data for the third quarter of 20X3 are as follows:

	Department			
	Video	Music	Accessories	Total
Sales revenue......................	$105,000	$54,000	$100,000	$259,000
Variable expenses	60,000	35,000	75,000	170,000
Fixed expenses	25,000	15,000	30,000	70,000
Total expenses....................	85,000	50,000	105,000	240,000
Operating income (loss)	$ 20,000	$ 4,000	$ (5,000)	$ 19,000

Should Sam's Video drop any of the departments? Give your reason. (The store will remain in the same building regardless of the decision.)

Dropping a department; explaining the difference between correct and incorrect analysis
(Obj. 2, 3)

DE26-7 Betsy Lanier is the wife of Sam Lanier, the owner of Sam's Video in Daily Exercise 26-6. Betsy is concerned. "Look at the Accessories Department's results. That department is costing us $5,000 a quarter. We would have had $10,000 more in our retirement fund if you had gotten rid of the Accessories Department like I suggested six months ago!"

Help Sam reply to Betsy. Your response should include an analysis of how dropping the Accessories Department would affect Sam's Video's operating income.

Dropping a department
(Obj. 2)

DE26-8 Consider Sam's Video from Daily Exercise 26-6. Assume that the fixed expenses assigned to each department include only

- Salaries of the department's manager
- Cost of advertising directly related to that department

Sam's Video will not incur these fixed expenses if the department is dropped. Under these circumstances, should Sam's Video drop any of the departments? Give your reason.

Determining product mix
(Obj. 1, 2)

DE26-9 Runmaster, Inc., produces two types of exercise treadmills: Regular and Deluxe.

The exercise craze is such that Runmaster could use all its available machine hours producing either model. The two models are processed through the same production departments.

Which model should Runmaster produce? If both models should be produced, compute the mix that will maximize operating income.

	Per Unit	
	Deluxe	Regular
Sale price	$1,300	$750
Costs:		
Direct materials..	$ 330	$140
Direct labor	150	250
Variable manufacturing overhead*............	375	125
Fixed manufacturing overhead*.................	150	50
Variable operating expenses......................	140	100
Total cost	1,145	665
Operating income...	$ 155	$ 85

* Allocated on the basis of machine hours.

DE26-10 U.S. Surgical Corporation in Norwalk, Connecticut, manufactures and markets surgical equipment. Lilian Gonzalez manages the company's fleet of 550 automobiles. Gonzalez has been charged with "reengineering" the fleet management function. She has an important decision to make.

Outsourcing decision for services (Obj. 1, 2)

- Should she continue to manage the fleet in-house with the five employees reporting to her? To do so, she will have to acquire new fleet management software to streamline U.S. Surgical's fleet management process.
- Should she outsource the fleet management function to Fleet Management Services, a company that specializes in managing fleets of automobiles for other companies? Fleet Management Services would take over the maintenance, repair, and scheduling of U.S. Surgical's fleet (but U.S. Surgical would retain ownership of its fleet). This alternative would require Gonzalez to lay off her five employees. However, her own job would be secure as she would be U.S. Surgical's liaison with Fleet Management Services.

Assume that Gonzalez's records show the following data concerning U.S. Surgical's fleet:

Book value of U.S. Surgical's autos, with an estimated 5-year life	$7,750,000
Annual leasing fee for new fleet management software	10,000
Annual maintenance of autos	295,500
Fleet supervisor Gonzalez's annual salary	80,000
Total annual salaries of U.S. Surgical's five other fleet management employees	175,000

Suppose that Fleet Management Services offers to manage U.S. Surgical's fleet for an annual fee of $460,000.
Which alternative will maximize U.S. Surgical's short-term operating income?

DE26-11 Refer to U.S. Surgical Corporation in Daily Exercise 26-10. What qualitative factors should Gonzalez consider before making a final decision?

Outsourcing decision for services (Obj. 2)

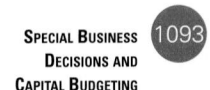

DE26-12 Etron Contract Manufacturing has been purchasing digital filters for $3 each. Etron believes it can make these filters using its excess capacity. No extra equipment or other fixed costs would be required. Etron estimates that it will need 50,000 filters and that the cost per filter would include the following:

Outsourcing decision (Obj. 1, 2)

Direct materials	$1.30
Direct labor	0.80
Variable manufacturing overhead	0.40
Fixed manufacturing overhead (allocated based on machine hours)	0.75
Total average cost per filter.............................	$3.25

Should Etron make or buy the filter?

DE26-13 Refer to Etron Contract Manufacturing in Daily Exercise 26-12. Suppose that

Outsourcing; best use of facilities (Obj. 1, 2)

- Making the filters will require Etron to hire a new part-time supervisor at a cost of $8,000.
- If Etron buys the filters, it could rent its idle facilities to another company, Alon Products, for $20,000.

Should Etron make or buy the filters?

DE26-14 Auto Components, Inc., has an inventory of 1,000 obsolete remote entry keys that are carried in inventory at a manufacturing cost of $160,000. Production supervisor Tony Ray must decide whether to

Deciding whether to sell as is or process further (Obj. 1, 2)

- Process the inventory further at a cost of $40,000, with the expectation of selling it for $65,000, or
- Scrap the inventory for a sale price of $16,000

What should Ray do? Present figures to support your decision.

DE26-15 Auto Components, Inc., from Daily Exercise 26-14 is approached by a customer who wants to buy the 1,000 obsolete keys. The customer is willing to pay more than $16,000 for the 1,000 keys.

Using opportunity costs to make decisions (Obj. 4)

1. What is Auto Components' opportunity cost of *not* processing the inventory further?
2. How can Ray use this opportunity cost to set a minimum sale price for the customer? What should be Auto Components' minimum sale price per key?

DE26-16 The concept of opportunity cost applies to all business decisions for which there are alternative courses of action. For example, in Exhibit 26-3, page 1066, the opportunity cost of rejecting the special sales order is the $11,000 of operating income that **ACDelco** would forgo if it rejects the special order.

1. Now consider the Chazz example. In Exhibit 26-7, page 1070,
   a. What is the opportunity cost of manufacturing the shirts?
   b. What is the opportunity cost of manufacturing the slacks?

DE26-17 Sound Insurance Company of America, a property/casualty insurer based in Branchville, New Jersey, is deciding whether to purchase new accounting software. Assistant vice president Tom Selling calculated that the payback period for the $30,000 software package would be 8 years.

What are the expected annual cash savings from the new software? Would you recommend that Sound Insurance purchase this software? Give your reason.

DE26-18 Daily Exercises 26-18 through 26-23 consider how **Deer Valley Resort** (from the chapter opening story) could use capital budgeting methods to decide whether the $13 million Snow Park Lodge expansion would be a good investment.

Assume that Deer Valley's managers developed the following estimates concerning the expansion (all numbers assumed):

Number of additional skiers per day	100
Average number of days per year that weather conditions allow skiing at Deer Valley	150
Useful life of expansion (in years)	15
Average cash spent by each skier per day	$245
Average variable cost of serving each skier per day	$85
Cost of expansion	$13,000,000
Discount rate	12%

Assume that Deer Valley uses the straight-line depreciation method and expects the lodge expansion to have a residual value of $1 million at the end of its 15-year life.

Compute the average annual net cash inflow from the expansion.

DE26-19 Refer to the Deer Valley Snow Park Lodge expansion project in Daily Exercise 26-18. Compute the payback period for the expansion project.

DE26-20 Refer to the Deer Valley Snow Park Lodge expansion project in Daily Exercise 26-18. What is the accounting rate of return?

DE26-21 ← *Link Back to Chapter 15 (Present-Value Concepts).* Refer to Daily Exercise 26-18. What is the project's net present value?

DE26-22 Refer to Daily Exercise 26-18. *Assume the expansion has zero residual value.* What is the project's internal rate of return?

DE26-23 Use your results from Daily Exercises 26-18 through 26-22 to write a memo to Deer Valley director of finance Jim Madsen. The purpose of your memo is to recommend whether Deer Valley should undertake the expansion. You should cover the strengths and weaknesses of each capital budgeting method cited in your memo. Follow the memo format outlined in Daily Exercise 26-5.

EXERCISES

E26-1 Suppose the **Baseball Hall of Fame** in Cooperstown, New York, has approached Sports-Cardz, Inc., with a special order. The Hall of Fame wishes to purchase 100,000 baseball card packs for a special promotional campaign and offers $0.95 per pack, a total of $95,000. Sports-Cardz total production cost is $1.25 per pack, as follows:

Variable costs:	
Direct materials	$0.20
Direct labor	0.14
Variable overhead	0.41
Fixed overhead	0.50
Total cost	$1.25

Sports-Cardz has enough excess capacity to handle the special order.

Required

1. Prepare an incremental analysis to determine whether Sports-Cardz should accept the special sales order.
2. Now assume that the Hall of Fame wants special hologram baseball cards. Sports-Cardz will spend $35,000 to develop this hologram, which will be useless after the special order is completed. Should Sports-Cardz accept the special order under these circumstances?

E26-2 Top managers of New Rock Records are alarmed about their operating losses. They are considering dropping the cassette-tape product line. Company accountants have prepared the following analysis to help make this decision:

Keeping or dropping a product line (fixed costs unchanged) (Obj. 1, 2, 3)

	Total	Compact Discs	Cassette Tapes
Sales revenue	$480,000	$290,000	$190,000
Variable expenses	240,000	140,000	100,000
Contribution margin	240,000	150,000	90,000
Fixed expenses:			
Manufacturing	165,000	70,000	95,000
Marketing and administrative	85,000	55,000	30,000
Total fixed expenses	250,000	125,000	125,000
Operating income (loss)	$(10,000)	$25,000	$(35,000)

Total fixed costs will not change if the company stops selling cassette tapes.

Prepare an incremental analysis to show whether New Rock should drop the cassette-tape product line. Will dropping cassette tapes add $35,000 to operating income? Explain.

E26-3 Refer to Exercise 26-2. Assume that New Rock Records can avoid $65,000 of fixed expenses by dropping the cassette-tape product line. Prepare an incremental analysis to show whether New Rock should stop selling cassette tapes.

Keeping or dropping a product line (fixed costs change) (Obj. 1, 2)

E26-4 Modern Styles sells both designer and moderately priced fashion accessories. Top management is deciding which product line to emphasize. Accountants have provided the following data:

Determining product mix (Obj. 1, 2)

	Per Item	
	Designer	Moderately Priced
Average sale price	$200	$80
Average variable expenses	85	24
Average contribution margin	115	56
Average fixed expenses (allocated)	20	10
Average operating income	$95	$46

The Modern Styles store in Reno, Nevada, has 10,000 square feet of floor space. If it emphasizes moderately priced goods, 650 items can be displayed in the store. If it emphasizes designer wear, only 300 designer items can be displayed. These numbers are also the average monthly sales in units.

Prepare an analysis to show which product to emphasize.

E26-5 Millenia Systems manufactures an electronic control that it uses in its final product. The electronic control has the following manufacturing costs per unit:

Outsourcing decision (Obj. 1, 2, 3)

Direct materials	$ 7.00
Direct labor	1.00
Variable overhead	1.50
Fixed overhead	5.50
Manufacturing product cost	$15.00

Another company has offered to sell Millenia the electronic control for $11 per unit. If Millenia buys the control from the outside supplier, the manufacturing facilities that will be idled cannot be used for any other purpose. Should Millenia make or buy the electronic controls? Explain the difference between correct analysis and incorrect analysis of this decision.

Determining best use of facilities (Obj. 1, 2)

E26-6 Refer to Exercise 26-5. Millenia needs 90,000 electronic controls. By outsourcing them, Millenia can use its idle facilities to manufacture another product that will contribute $150,000 to operating income. Identify the *incremental* costs that Millenia will incur to acquire 90,000 electronic controls under three alternative plans. Which plan makes the best use of Millenia's facilities? Support your answer.

Sell or process further; identifying opportunity costs (Obj. 1, 3, 4)

E26-7 Norris Creations has damaged some custom cabinets, which cost the company $10,000 to manufacture. Owner Fay Norris is considering two options for disposing of this inventory. One plan is to sell the cabinets as damaged inventory for $1,400. The alternative is to spend an additional $450 to repair the damage and expect to sell the cabinets for $2,200. What should Norris do? Support your answer with an analysis that shows expected net revenue under each alternative. Identify the opportunity cost of each alternative.

Computing payback with equal cash flows (Obj. 5)

E26-8 Adkins Co. is considering acquiring a manufacturing plant. The purchase price is $1,457,100. The owners believe the plant will generate net cash inflows of $485,700 annually. It will have to be replaced in seven years. Use the payback method to determine whether Adkins should purchase this plant.

Computing payback with unequal cash flows (Obj. 5)

E26-9 Sikes Hardware is adding a new product line that will require an investment of $1,454,000. Managers estimate that this investment will generate net cash inflows of $310,000 the first year, $280,000 the second year, and $240,000 each year thereafter. Compute the payback period of the investment.

Determining accounting rate of return (Obj. 5)

E26-10 Barker Mills is shopping for new equipment. Managers are considering two investments. Equipment manufactured by Li, Inc., costs $400,000 and will last for five years, with no residual value. The Li equipment is expected to generate annual operating income of $48,000. Equipment manufactured by Veras Products is priced at $500,000 and will remain useful for six years. It promises annual operating income of $92,750, and its expected residual value is $30,000.

Which equipment offers the higher accounting rate of return?

Computing net present value (Obj. 5)

E26-11 ◄◄ *Link Back to Chapter 15 (Present-Value Concepts).* Use the net present value method to determine whether Pine Products should invest in the following projects:

- *Project A:* Costs $295,000 and offers eight annual net cash inflows of $65,000. Pine Products requires an annual return of 14% on projects like A.
- *Project B:* Costs $435,000 and offers nine annual net cash inflows of $80,000. Pine Products demands an annual return of 12% on investments of this nature.

What is the net present value of each project? What is the maximum acceptable price to pay for each project?

Computing internal rate of return (Obj. 5)

E26-12 Refer to Exercise 26-11. Compute the internal rate of return of each project, and use this information to identify the better investment.

Challenge Exercise

Determining product mix (Obj. 2)

E26-13 Each morning, Ken Gaver stocks the drink case at Ken's Beach Hut in Sanibel Island, Florida. Ken's has 100 linear feet of refrigerated display space for cold drinks. Each linear foot can hold either six 12-ounce cans or four 20-ounce plastic or glass bottles. Ken's sells three types of cold drinks:

- Coca-Cola in 12-oz cans, for $1.25 per can
- Coca-Cola in 20-oz plastic bottles, for $1.50 per bottle
- SoBe in 20-oz glass bottles, for $2.00 per bottle

Ken's pays its suppliers:

- $0.25 per 12-oz can of Coca-Cola
- $0.30 per 20-oz bottle of Coca-Cola
- $0.70 per 20-oz bottle of SoBe

Ken's monthly fixed expenses include

Hut rental............................	$ 250
Refrigerator rental	50
Gaver's salary......................	1,000
Total fixed expenses.............	$1,300

Ken's can sell all the drinks stocked in the display case each morning.

1. What is Ken's constraining factor? What should Gaver stock in order to maximize profits?
2. Suppose Ken's refuses to devote more than 60 linear feet to any individual product. Under this condition, how many linear feet of each drink should Gaver stock? How many units of each product will be available for sale each day?

PROBLEMS

P26-1A Price United Co.'s contribution margin income statement for the most recent month reports the following:

Accepting or rejecting a special sales order
(Obj. 1, 2)

Sales in units	760,000
Sales revenue	$190,000
Variable expenses:	
Manufacturing	$ 60,800
Marketing and administrative	31,200
Total variable expenses	92,000
Contribution margin	98,000
Fixed expenses:	
Manufacturing	58,000
Marketing and administrative	16,000
Total fixed expenses	74,000
Operating income	$ 24,000

Victoria Vineyards wants to buy 10,000 labels from Price. Acceptance of the order will not increase any of Price's marketing and administrative expenses. Price's plant has unused capacity to manufacture the additional labels. Victoria Vineyards has offered $0.18 per label, which is considerably below the normal sale price of $0.25.

Required

1. Prepare an incremental analysis to determine whether Price should accept this special sales order.
2. Prepare a total analysis to show Price's operating income with and without the special sales order.
3. Identify long-term factors that Price should consider in deciding whether to accept the special sales order.

P26-2A The following operating income data of Sea Cuisine highlights the losses of the fresh seafood product line:

Keeping or dropping a product line *(Obj. 1, 2, 3)*

		Product Line	
		Fresh	**Frozen**
	Total	**Seafood**	**Seafood**
Sales revenue	$857,500	$227,500	$630,000
Cost of goods sold:			
Variable	$164,000	$ 64,000	$100,000
Fixed	131,000	41,000	90,000
Total cost of goods sold	295,000	105,000	190,000
Gross profit	562,500	122,500	440,000
Marketing and administrative expenses:			
Variable	378,000	108,000	270,000
Fixed	129,500	49,500	80,000
Total marketing and administrative expenses	507,500	157,500	350,000
Operating income (loss)	$ 55,000	$ (35,000)	$ 90,000

Sea Cuisine is considering discontinuing the fresh seafood product line. The company's accountants estimate that dropping the fresh seafood line will decrease fixed cost of goods sold by $32,000 and decrease fixed marketing and administrative expenses by $15,000.

Required

1. Prepare an incremental analysis to show whether Sea Cuisine should drop the fresh seafood product line.

2. Prepare a total analysis to show Sea Cuisine's operating income with and without the fresh seafood product line. Prepare the income statement in contribution-margin format.
3. Explain the difference between correct analysis and incorrect analysis of the decision to keep or drop the fresh seafood product line.

Determining product mix (Obj. 1, 2)

P26-3A Green's Outdoors of Harrisburg, Virginia, specializes in outdoor furniture and barbecues. Owner Linda Green is expanding the store. She is deciding which product line to emphasize. To make this decision, she assembles the following data:

| | Per Unit | |
	Patio Sets	Barbecues
Sale price..	$500	$300
Variable expenses.............................	240	162
Contribution margin	$260	$138
Contribution margin ratio...............	52 %	46 %

After renovation, the store will have 8,000 square feet of floor space. By devoting the new floor space to barbecues, Green's Outdoors can display 60 barbecues. Alternatively, Green's could display 30 patio sets. Green expects monthly sales to equal the maximum number of units displayed.

Required

1. Identify the constraining factor for Green's Outdoors.
2. Prepare an analysis to show which product line to emphasize.

Outsourcing; best use of facilities (Obj. 1, 2)

P26-4A Afloat, Inc., manufactures swim fins. Cost data for producing 2,000 pairs of fins each year are as follows:

Direct materials.............................	$21,000
Direct labor	15,000
Variable overhead	5,600
Fixed overhead	38,400
Total manufacturing costs............	$80,000

Suppose SwimTime will sell Afloat the fins for $35 per pair. Afloat would pay $1.80 per pair to transport the fins to its warehouse.

Required

1. Afloat's accountants predict that purchasing the fins from SwimTime will enable the company to avoid $12,000 of fixed overhead. Prepare an analysis to show whether Afloat should make or buy the fins.
2. Assume that the Afloat facilities freed up by the purchase of the fins from SwimTime can be used to manufacture swim masks. The masks will contribute $35,000 to profit. Total fixed costs will be the same as if Afloat used the plant to make fins. Prepare an analysis to show which alternative makes the best use of Afloat's facilities: (a) make fins, (b) buy fins and leave facilities idle, or (c) buy fins and make masks.

Deciding whether to sell as is or process further; identifying opportunity costs (Obj. 1, 2, 4)

P26-5A Long Petroleum Company produces a variety of petroleum products. Assume that Long has spent $300,000 to refine 60,000 gallons of petroleum distillate. Suppose Long can sell the distillate for $5.50 a gallon. Alternatively, it can process the distillate further and produce cleaner for tape heads. Assume that the additional processing will cost another $1.25 a gallon and that the cleaner can be sold for $7.50 a gallon. To make this sale, Long must pay a sales commission of $0.10 a gallon and a transportation charge of $0.15 a gallon.

Required

1. Prepare a diagram of Long's alternatives, using Exhibit 26-10, page 1073, as a guide.
2. Identify the sunk cost. Is the sunk cost relevant to Long's decision?
3. Prepare an analysis to indicate whether Long should sell the distillate or process it into tape-head cleaner. Show the expected net revenue difference between the two alternatives.
4. Identify the opportunity cost of each option. Explain how managers can use opportunity cost to make this decision.

Capital budgeting (Obj. 5, 6)

P26-6A Waters Investments, Inc., operates a resort near Door County in the Great Lakes region of Wisconsin. The company is considering an expansion. The architectural plan calls for a construction cost of $5,200,000. Top managers of Waters believe the expansion will generate annual net cash inflows of $675,000 for ten years. Architects and engineers estimate that the new facilities will remain useful for ten years and have a residual value of $1,900,000. The company uses straight-line depreciation, and its stockholders demand an annual return of 12% on investments of this nature.

Required

1. Compute the payback period, the accounting rate of return, and the net present value of this investment.
2. Make a recommendation to Waters management as to whether the company should invest in this project.

P26-7A Crystal's Candle Shop is considering two possible expansion plans. Plan A is to open 8 candle shops at a cost of $3,220,000. Expected annual net cash inflows are $690,000, with residual value of $350,000 at the end of seven years. Under plan B, Crystal's would open 12 candle shops at a cost of $4,200,000. This investment is expected to generate net cash inflows of $1,050,000 each year for seven years, which is the estimated useful life of the properties. Estimated residual value of the plan B candle shops is zero. Crystal's uses straight-line depreciation and requires an annual return of 14%.

Capital budgeting
(Obj. 5, 6)

Required

1. Compute the payback period, the accounting rate of return, and the net present value of each plan. What are the strengths and weaknesses of these capital budgeting models?
2. Which expansion plan should Crystal's adopt? Why?
3. Estimate the internal rate of return (IRR) for plan B. How does plan B's IRR compare with Crystal's required rate of return?

PROBLEMS

(Group B)

P26-1B Play Day Corporation manufactures toys in Tampa, Florida. Play Day's contribution-margin income statement for the most recent month contains the following data:

Accepting or rejecting a special sales order
(Obj. 1, 2)

Sales in units	42,000
Sales revenue	$420,000
Variable expenses:	
Manufacturing	$ 84,000
Marketing and administrative	100,000
Total variable expenses	184,000
Contribution margin	236,000
Fixed expenses:	
Manufacturing	116,000
Marketing and administrative	85,000
Total fixed expenses	201,000
Operating income	$ 35,000

Sienna Studios, Inc., wishes to buy 4,000 toys from Play Day. Acceptance of the order will not increase any of Play Day's marketing and administrative expenses. The Play Day plant has unused capacity to manufacture the additional toys. Sienna has offered $8.00 per toy, which is below the normal sale price of $10.

Required

1. Prepare an incremental analysis to determine whether Play Day should accept this special sales order.
2. Prepare a total analysis to show Play Day's operating income with and without the special sales order.
3. Identify long-term factors Play Day should consider in deciding whether to accept the special sales order.

P26-2B Members of the board of directors of Energy Saver Electric, Inc., have received the following operating income data for the year just ended, shown at the top of the next page.

Members of the board are surprised that the industrial-systems product line is losing money. They commission a study to determine whether the company should drop the industrial-systems line. Company accountants estimate that dropping industrial systems will decrease fixed cost of goods sold by $95,000 and decrease fixed marketing and administrative expenses by $15,000.

Keeping or dropping a product line
(Obj. 1, 2, 3)

Required

1. Prepare an incremental analysis to show whether Energy Saver should drop the industrial-systems product line.
2. Prepare a total analysis to show Energy Saver's operating income with and without industrial systems. Prepare the income statement in contribution-margin format.
3. Explain the difference between correct analysis and incorrect analysis of the decision to keep or drop the industrial-systems product line.

	Product Line		
	Industrial Systems	Household Systems	Total
Sales revenue	$405,000	$421,000	$826,000
Cost of goods sold:			
Variable	$ 50,000	$ 55,000	$105,000
Fixed..	241,000	86,000	327,000
Total cost of goods sold	291,000	141,000	432,000
Gross profit..	114,000	280,000	394,000
Marketing and administrative expenses:			
Variable	86,000	92,000	178,000
Fixed..	58,000	31,000	89,000
Total marketing and administrative expenses...	144,000	123,000	267,000
Operating income (loss)	$ (30,000)	$157,000	$127,000

Determining product mix
(Obj. 1, 2)

P26-3B Oral-E Corp., located in Detroit, Michigan, produces two lines of electric toothbrushes: deluxe and standard models. Because Oral-E can sell all the toothbrushes it can produce, the owners are expanding the plant, and they are deciding which product line to emphasize. To make this decision, they assemble the following data.

	Per Unit	
	Deluxe Toothbrush	Standard Toothbrush
Sale price	$50	$30
Variable expenses..........................	15	12
Contribution margin......................	$35	$18
Contribution margin ratio	70%	60%

After expansion, the factory will have a production capacity of 2,200 machine hours per month. The plant can manufacture either 50 standard electric toothbrushes or 20 deluxe electric toothbrushes per machine hour.

Required

1. Identify the constraining factor for Oral-E Corp.
2. Prepare an analysis to show which product line to emphasize.

Outsourcing; best use of facilities
(Obj. 1, 2)

P26-4B Smooth Sailing manufactures sailboats. Assume that Smooth Sailing's cost of making 1,200 seat covers is

Direct materials	$ 7,260
Direct labor...	1,440
Variable overhead..	960
Fixed overhead..	2,400
Total manufacturing costs for 1,200 seat covers	$12,060

Suppose Sof-Seatz will sell seat covers to Smooth Sailing for $8 each. Smooth Sailing would pay $0.90 per unit to transport the seat covers to its manufacturing plant, where it would add its own Smooth Sailing logo at a cost of $0.12 per seat cover.

Required

1. Smooth Sailing's accountants predict that purchasing the seat covers from Sof-Seatz will enable the company to avoid $900 of fixed overhead. Prepare an analysis to show whether Smooth Sailing should make or buy the seat covers.
2. Assume that the Smooth Sailing facilities freed up by the purchase of seat covers from Sof-Seatz can be used to manufacture another product that will contribute $2,300 to profit. Total fixed costs will be the same as if Smooth Sailing had produced the seat covers. Prepare an analysis to show which alternative makes the best use of Smooth Sailing's facilities: (a) make seat covers, (b) buy seat covers and leave facilities idle, or (c) buy seat covers and make another product.

P26-5B Cisco Chemical Corporation has spent $320,000 to refine 84,000 gallons of acetone, which can be sold for $3.32 a gallon. Alternatively, Cisco can process the acetone further and produce 77,000 gallons of lacquer thinner that can be sold for $4.80 a gallon. The additional processing will cost $0.89 per gallon of lacquer thinner. To sell the lacquer thinner, Cisco must pay a transportation charge of $0.34 a gallon and administrative expenses of $0.16 a gallon.

Deciding whether to sell as is or process further; identifying opportunity costs (Obj. 1, 2, 4)

Required

1. Prepare a diagram of Cisco's decision, using Exhibit 26-10 (page 1073) as a guide.
2. Identify the sunk cost. Is the sunk cost relevant to Cisco's decision?
3. Prepare an analysis to indicate whether Cisco should sell the acetone or process it into lacquer thinner. Show the expected net revenue difference between the two alternatives.
4. Identify the opportunity cost of each alternative. Explain how managers use the notion of opportunity cost in making their decision.

P26-6B Rising Sun Developers, west of Roswell, New Mexico, is considering purchasing a water park for $1,850,000. Top managers of Rising Sun believe the new facility will generate annual net cash inflows of $420,000 for eight years. Architects and engineers estimate that the facility will remain useful for eight years and have a residual value of $300,000. The company uses straight-line depreciation, and its stockholders demand an annual return of 16% on investments of this nature.

Capital budgeting (Obj. 5, 6)

Required

1. Compute the payback period, the accounting rate of return, and the net present value of this investment.
2. Make a recommendation to Rising Sun management as to whether the company should invest in this project.

P26-7B TechNo operates a chain of electronics stores. The company is considering two possible expansion plans. Plan A would open eight smaller stores at a cost of $6,450,000. Expected annual net cash inflows are $860,000, with zero residual value at the end of 20 years. Under plan B, TechNo would open three larger stores at a cost of $6,420,000. This plan is expected to generate net cash inflows of $600,000 per year for 20 years, the estimated life of the store properties. Estimated residual value is $3,000,000. TechNo uses straight-line depreciation and requires an annual return of 8%.

Capital budgeting (Obj. 5, 6)

Required

1. Compute the payback period, the accounting rate of return, and the net present value of these two plans. What are the strengths and weaknesses of these capital budgeting models?
2. Which expansion plan should TechNo choose? Why?
3. Estimate plan A's internal rate of return (IRR). How does the IRR compare with the company's required rate of return?

APPLY YOUR KNOWLEDGE

DECISION CASES

Case 1. BKFin.com provides banks access to sophisticated financial information and analysis systems over the Web. The company combines these tools with benchmarking data access, including e-mail and wireless communications, so that banks can instantly evaluate individual loan applications and entire loan portfolios.

Outsourcing e-mail (Obj. 1, 2)

BKFin.com's CEO Aamer Sheikh is very happy with the company's strong growth. To better focus on client service, Sheikh is considering outsourcing some functions. CFO Isabelle Wang suggests that the company's e-mail may be the place to start. She recently attended a conference and learned that companies like **Continental Airlines, DellNet, GTE,** and **NBC** were outsourcing their e-mail function. Sheikh asks Wang to identify costs related to BKFin.com's inhouse **Microsoft** Exchange mail application, which has 2,300 mailboxes. This information follows:

Variable costs:	
E-mail license	$6 per mailbox per month
Virus protection license	$1 per mailbox per month
Other variable costs	$7 per mailbox per month
Fixed costs:	
Computer hardware costs......................................	$85,100 per month
$6,900 monthly salary for two information technology staff members who work only on e-mail......................	$13,800 per month

SPECIAL BUSINESS 1101
DECISIONS AND
CAPITAL BUDGETING

1. Compute the *total cost* per mailbox per month of BKFin.com's current e-mail function.
2. Suppose **Mail.com,** a leading provider of Internet messaging outsourcing services, offers to host BKFin.com's e-mail function for $8 per mailbox per month. If BKFin.com outsources its e-mail to Mail.com, BKFin.com will still need the virus protection software, its computer hardware, and one information technology staff member, who would be responsible for maintaining virus protection, quarantining suspicious e-mail, and managing content (e.g., screening e-mail for objectionable content). Should CEO Sheikh accept Mail.com's offer?
3. Suppose for an additional $5 per mailbox per month, Mail.com will also provide virus protection, quarantine, and content-management services. Outsourcing these additional functions would mean that BKFin.com would not need either an e-mail information technology staff member or the separate virus protection license. Should CEO Sheikh outsource these extra services to Mail.com?

Deciding whether to purchase a new machine
(Obj. 1, 5, 6)

Case 2. Suppose that **Intel** is considering a new computer-controlled machine for etching trenches in the surfaces of silicon wafers. The company processes these wafers into semiconductor chips. The etching machine costs $900,000, and an additional $250,000 would be required for installation. Thus $1,150,000 is the required cash outlay for the investment.

Assume the new etching machine would replace an existing machine that was purchased five years ago for $715,000. That machine has five years of useful life remaining. Intel must either keep the old machine or replace it with the new machine. The expected useful life of the new machine is five years. Suppose Intel managers believe that the new machine would save $355,000 per year in cash operating costs. However, annual maintenance cost would be $40,000 higher with the new machine than with the old.

Disposal values of the machines are as follows:

	Old Machine	New Machine
Now	$-0-	—
In five years	-0-	$150,000

Assume Intel has a minimum desired rate of return of 14% on similar investments.

Required

1. Is the $715,000 cost of the old machine relevant to the decision of whether to keep or replace the old machine? Why or why not? (*Hint:* What are the requirements for a cost to be relevant?)
2. Which of the four capital budgeting methods is best suited for making this decision? Use that method to decide which course of action is better for Intel. (*Hint:* Identify the relevant items.)

ETHICAL ISSUE/FINANCIAL STATEMENT CASE

Dropping a product line
(Obj. 2)

◄ *Link Back to the EPS Calculation in Chapter 14 and the IMA Ethical Guidelines in Chapter 19.* In 1996 **Target** was the third-largest retailer in the United States, with over 750 stores in 38 states. So it was big news when the company decided to stop selling cigarettes in its stores. Cigarettes often have markups of 20 to 30%. Analysts estimate that Target's decision to eliminate this product line may have cost the company up to $64 million in lost revenues and $18 million in earnings.

If Target had continued selling cigarettes and if cigarette sales had grown at the same rate as Target's other sales, Target's earnings could have been $23 million higher in 1999.

Required

1. Use Target Corporation's 1999 Annual Report to determine the company's earnings per share (EPS) before extraordinary items for 1999. (*Hint:* Look at the basic EPS calculation in the EPS footnote to the financial statements.) Estimate what EPS would have been in 1999 if Target had continued selling cigarettes.
2. As the CFO of Target, justify to the company's stockholders how the company could make a decision that reduced earnings. How do ethical considerations enter this decision? Would the IMA's Ethical Guidelines help if you had been asked to make the initial recommendation to drop this product line?

Identify relevant data, outsourcing, capital budgeting
(Obj. 1, 2, 5)

TEAM PROJECT

John Menard is the founder and sole owner of **Menard, Inc.** Analysts have estimated that his chain of home improvement stores scattered around nine midwestern states generate about $3 billion in annual sales. But how can Menard compete with giant **Home Depot?**

Suppose Menard is trying to decide whether to invest $45 million in a state-of-the-art manufacturing plant in Eau Claire, Wisconsin. Menard expects the plant would operate for 15 years, after which the plant would have no residual value. The plant would produce Menard's own line of Formica countertops, cabinets, and picnic tables.

Suppose Menard would incur the following unit costs in producing its own product lines:

	Per Unit		
	Countertops	Cabinets	Picnic Tables
Direct materials	$15	$10	$30
Direct labor..	10	5	20
Variable manufacturing overhead......	5	2	7

Rather than making these products, assume Menard could buy them from outside suppliers. Suppliers would charge Menard $40 per countertop, $25 per cabinet, and $75 per picnic table.

Whether Menard makes or buys these products, assume that he expects the following annual sales:

- Countertops—487,200 at $130 each
- Cabinets—150,000 at $75 each
- Picnic tables—100,000 at $225 each

If "making" is sufficiently more profitable than outsourcing these products, then Menard will build the new plant. John Menard has asked your consulting group for a recommendation. Menard uses a 14% discount rate and the straight-line depreciation method.

Required

1. Are the following items relevant or irrelevant in Menard's decision to build a new plant that will manufacture his own products?
   a. The unit sale prices of the countertops, cabinets, and picnic tables (the sale prices that Menard charges its customers)
   b. The prices outside suppliers would charge Menard for the three products, if Menard decides to outsource the products rather than make them
   c. The $45 million to build the new plant
   d. The direct materials, direct labor, and variable overhead Menard would incur to manufacture the three product lines
   e. Menard's salary

2. Determine whether Menard should make or outsource the countertops, cabinets, and picnic tables, *assuming that the company had already built the plant and therefore has the manufacturing capacity to produce these products.* In other words, what is the annual difference in cash flows if Menard decides to make rather than outsource each of these three products?

3. In requirement 2, you computed the annual difference in cash flows if Menard decides to make rather than buy the three products. To analyze the investment in the plant relative to the alternative of outsourcing the products, use this *difference* in annual cash flows to compute the following for the investment in the new plant:
   a. Payback period
   b. Accounting rate of return
   c. Net present value
   d. Internal rate of return

   (*Hint:* Base the benefit side of your computations on the *difference* in annual cash flows you computed in requirement 2, *not* the total expected cash flows from building the plant.)

4. Write a memo giving your recommendation to John Menard. The memo should clearly state your recommendation, along with a brief summary of the reasons for your recommendation. Use the memo format outlined in Daily Exercise 26-5.

INTERNET EXERCISE

Papa John's International Inc. has surpassed **Little Caesars** to become the number 3 pizza chain, behind **Pizza Hut** and **Domino's,** with more than 2,300 restaurants scattered across the United States and five other countries. Most restaurants offer delivery or take-out only.

1. Go to **http://www.papajohns.com** and click on *Papa John's Story.* In what year did the first Papa John's restaurant open? Click on *Our Pizza Story.* What is the focus of Papa John's?

2. In the left-hand column, click on *Investor Relationships* followed by *SEC Filings* in the right-hand column. Choose the most recent annual report by clicking on Form Type *10-K.* Under Part I select *Item 1: Business.* Scan the first three pages. (Note: For easier viewing you may want to select font size 1 = smallest and click on enter.)
   a. For a company-owned restaurant, over the past fiscal year Papa John's reported how much in average sales? Average cash flow? Average operating income? What is the expected cash investment per company-owned restaurant opening next year?

Papa John's International

Go to the "Special Decisions/Make-or-Buy" episode on the *Mastering Accounting* CD-ROM for an interactive, video-enhanced exercise that focuses on the need for CanGo's managers to understand the benefits and costs directly related to a project so that they can plan correctly for the holiday season rush.

b. Why is Papa John's expansion strategy to cluster restaurants in targeted markets?

3. Assume the value of the investment decreases to zero over a ten-year period of time. Use the information from 2(a) for the following computations. For one company-owned Papa John's restaurant, compute the

a. payback period

b. accounting rate of return

c. net present value assuming a 16% required rate of return

d. internal rate of return (Appendix B contains present-value tables.)

4. Does a Papa John's company-owned restaurant appear to be a good investment? Why or why not?

5. Continue to scroll down the document. How much does a franchisee pay for the right to operate a Papa John's restaurant in the United States? (Note: In the 1999 Annual Report this information was around page 7.)

6. Should a new franchisee expect to achieve the same rate of return as a company-owned Papa John's restaurant? Why or why not?

APPENDIX A

Target Corporation Annual Report

We are Target Corporation.

Annual Report 1999

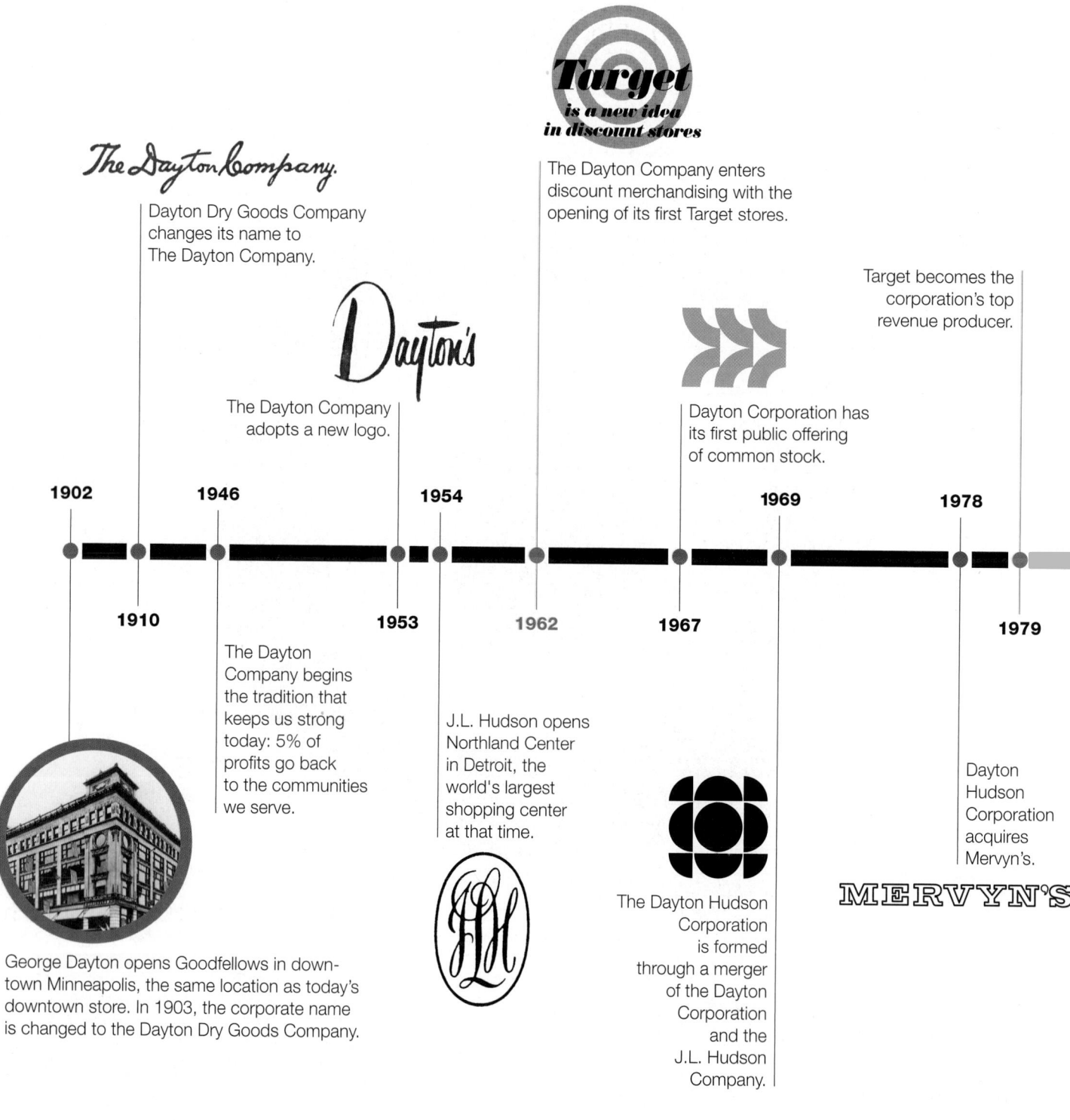

The Dayton Company.

Dayton Dry Goods Company
changes its name to
The Dayton Company.

Dayton's

The Dayton Company
adopts a new logo.

Target *is a new idea in discount stores*

The Dayton Company enters
discount merchandising with the
opening of its first Target stores.

Target becomes the
corporation's top
revenue producer.

Dayton Corporation has
its first public offering
of common stock.

1902   **1946**   **1954**   **1969**   **1978**

1910   **1953**   **1962**   **1967**   **1979**

The Dayton
Company begins
the tradition that
keeps us strong
today: 5% of
profits go back
to the communities
we serve.

J.L. Hudson opens
Northland Center
in Detroit, the
world's largest
shopping center
at that time.

The Dayton Hudson
Corporation
is formed
through a merger
of the Dayton
Corporation
and the
J.L. Hudson
Company.

Dayton
Hudson
Corporation
acquires
Mervyn's.

MERVYN'S

George Dayton opens Goodfellows in downtown Minneapolis, the same location as today's
downtown store. In 1903, the corporate name
is changed to the Dayton Dry Goods Company.

Dayton Hudson
Corporation acquires
Rivertown Trading
Company and
The Associated
Merchandising
Corporation.

Marshall Field's

Mervyn's changes
its name to
Mervyn's California.

Target launches
the industry's first
discount store credit
card, the Target
Guest Card.

First SuperTarget
stores open.

1984 **1990**

1999

Dayton Hudson
Corporation acquires
Marshall Field's.

1995

1998

2000

Dayton Hudson
Corporation launches its
e-commerce capability
with new store brand
web sites.

Dayton Hudson
Corporation
celebrates its
name change to
Target Corporation.

Dayton's and
Hudson's combine
to form Dayton
Hudson Department
Store Company.

TARGET CORPORATION
◎

DAYTON'S
HUDSON'S

TARGET CORPORATION

———————⊙———————

Our mission is to be the retailer of choice in

the discount, middle market and department store

retail segments. By focusing on trend leadership, excellent

guest service, exciting team member opportunities, and

community outreach, we create long-term

shareholder value.

Revenues

(millions)

Pre-tax Segment Profit

(millions)

Net Earnings

(millions)

Diluted Earnings per Share

Operating Results ($ millions)	1999	1998	Change
Revenues	$33,702	$30,662	10%
Pre-tax segment profit	$ 2,523	$ 2,097	20%
Net earnings*	$ 1,144	$ 935	22%

Per Share Data			
Diluted earnings*	$ 2.45	$ 1.98	24%
Cash dividends declared	$ .40	$ .36	11%

At Year-End			
Common shares outstanding	455,841,388	441,809,806	
Retail square feet	138,640,000	130,172,000	
Number of stores	1,243	1,182	

*Includes unusual items, resulting in net after-tax charges of $44 million ($.09 per share) in 1999, $35 million ($.08 per share) in 1998, $24 million ($.05 per share) in 1997, and $92 million ($.20 per share) in 1996.

Acknowledging the strength of the **Target brand and the future growth** opportunities of our largest retail division, we recently changed our name to Target Corporation. Our new name recognizes that the Target division, today, comprises more than 75 percent of the company's sales and profits, and that this contribution will continue to increase over time as we further expand our store base. Our new name also reflects our continuing commitment to leverage our resources for the benefit of the total corporation, and as a result, to improve our overall financial results and create substantial value for our shareholders.

Our performance in 1999 was driven by superior results at our Target division. Revenues for the segment increased 13 percent to $26 billion and pre-tax profit grew 28 percent to over $2 billion, establishing a new milestone in Target's history. In addition, Target's pre-tax profit as a percent of revenues equaled the reported profit margin at Wal*Mart's domestic discount/supercenter division for the year, eliminating a significant differential that existed in prior years. These outstanding results at Target in 1999, combined with record sales and profits at our Department Stores, produced our fourth consecutive year of earnings per share growth in excess of 20 percent.

We are very pleased with our performance in the past year and we are excited about the opportunities for profitable growth in 2000 and beyond. As we look forward, we remain confident that Target Corporation can continue to deliver average annual earnings per share growth of 15 percent or more over time.

New Store Growth With less than 1,000 stores in the U.S. today, Target's opportunities for domestic new store growth remain plentiful. During 1999, Target added a total of 74 new stores, increasing square footage by 9 percent. We continued to focus our efforts on markets in the Northeast and Mid-Atlantic, devoting nearly 40 percent of our new store openings to this region.

Importantly, by becoming more flexible in our site selection and store design without compromising the Target brand, we continue to have success in penetrating these markets despite difficult real estate challenges. In 1999, we entered two new markets, Boston and Pittsburgh, and in 2000, we will enter two new states, Connecticut and West Virginia, bringing the number of states in which we operate to 46.

Bob Ulrich,
Chairman and
Chief Executive Officer

Our store expansion in 2000 will also include a significant acceleration of SuperTarget store openings, reflecting our increased confidence in the sales and profit potential of this concept. We will essentially double our number of SuperTarget stores during the year, adding 15 new locations, primarily in the Midwest and South. About half of these stores will be relocations of existing discount stores, giving us the ability to capture greater market share in key metropolitan areas. With plans for at least 200 SuperTarget locations within the next ten years, we believe this strategy will generate profitable growth for many years to come.

Other Growth Opportunities At the core of Target's future growth and financial success is our differentiated merchandise strategy — with an emphasis on quality and original design, unique product, impactful presentation and value pricing. During the past year, we strengthened our merchandise assort-ment with the addition of new brands such as Calphalon, Stiffel, Discovery Channel toys and designs by Michael Graves and Robert Abbey. In 2000, we will continue to create excitement for our guests with new initiatives. Examples include an expanded offering of Michael Graves housewares and a new assort-ment of electronics; the introduction of Martex bed and bath collections; exclusive new lines of sporting goods equipment and accessories; and the expansion of our Archer Farms brand of premier food. Each of these efforts reinforces and enhances Target's brand image in the marketplace and contributes to our financial strength.

Credit is also an important contributor to our overall earnings growth. During the past five years, contribution from credit has increased at a compound annual rate of 17 percent, and both return on investment and EVA have risen sharply. While we continue to invest in credit programs at all three of our segments, the Target Guest Card is the primary driver of growth for this business. In 2000, we will continue to increase our card penetration, enhance our guest loyalty programs and leverage our credit operation to sustain our profitable growth.

In 1999, Target Corporation devoted greater resources to developing web-based strategies, reflecting our belief that the Internet and e-commerce are vital to our future. In our view, the Internet provides an important tool for communicating with our guests as well as a new distribution channel for our merchandise. Through our new business unit called target.direct, we are focused on leveraging our strengths as a well-known and trusted retailer to increase guest service and generate profitable sales. We believe our powerful marketing, our differentiated merchandise and more than 1,200 convenient store locations give us a competitive advantage in the on-line world. In 2000, we will continue to make the necessary investments in this business to attract experienced and talented team members, to improve our technology and fulfillment capability, and to provide our guests with appropriate services and merchandise selection.

Though our name has changed to reflect the growth and importance of Target, we remain committed to Dayton's, Marshall Field's, Hudson's and Mervyn's. During the past five years, Target Corporation has averaged a total return to shareholders on an annualized basis of 43 percent. During this same period, both Mervyn's and our Department Stores were key contributors to our overall strategy and financial performance. In 1999 alone, their combined net pre-tax cash flow again exceeded a half billion dollars. We believe that these two segments will continue to create value for Target Corporation in the years ahead.

We are excited about the future for Target Corporation and believe that we are well-positioned to build on our past performance. As we look forward, we remain confident that we will continue to deliver strong growth in sales and earnings and achieve our objective of generating at least 15 percent average annual earnings per share growth over time.

March 24, 2000

Bob Ulrich

Bob Ulrich, Chairman and Chief Executive Officer

We are now

Target Corporation, a name that reflects

the powerful recognition of our largest retail brand.

Today, Target Stores makes up more than 75 percent of our

sales and profits, a percentage that will continue to grow as we

open new Target stores across the country. The Target name best

reflects our business and our company, today and in the future.

We remain a company that is committed to growth

and delivering superior returns to our

shareholders.

Target Corporation's goal is to deliver average annual earnings per share growth of 15 percent or more over time.

To deliver on that pledge to shareholders we will continue to grow the Target store base; innovate to grow sales at existing stores; pursue new retail strategies; and enhance our credit programs. Our continued success depends on clearly defined brand strategies at each of our stores, great execution every day for our guests, a commitment to constant innovation and reinvention, and support of our communities.

New Store Growth Our primary growth comes from new store expansion. Target continues to open stores in new U.S. markets and increase store density in existing markets, growing retail square footage by 8 to 10 percent annually. In 2000, Target will open approximately 80 total new stores, including 15 new SuperTarget stores, essentially doubling the number of SuperTarget locations we operated at year end. Target will add locations in two new states — West Virginia and Connecticut — and expand our presence in key markets like Pittsburgh, Boston and Dallas/Fort Worth. As Target's brand becomes stronger, it allows us to add more stores in existing metropolitan markets. To provide guests with added value and convenience, all new Target stores and remodels will feature pharmacies, optical shops, one-hour photo labs and portrait studios. Our newest stores will feature an updated look with an arched entrance with more glass for a brighter, more inviting feel. We will also continue to invest in store remodels to ensure that all Target stores continue to represent the Target brand.

Our goal at SuperTarget is to bring "fashion to food."

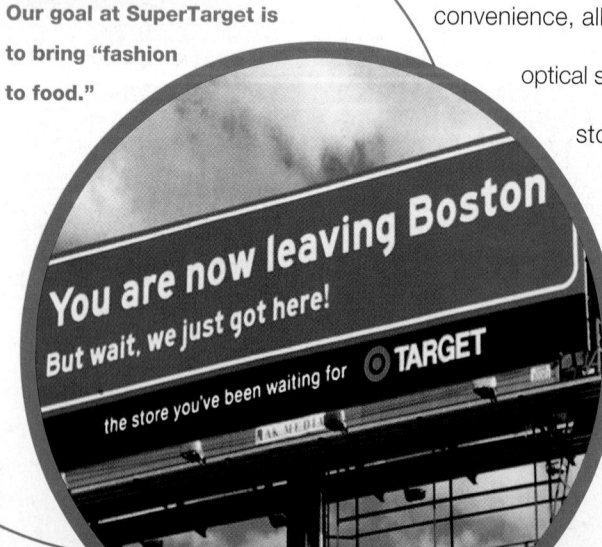

Target entered the Boston market in July 1999 with five stores, under the advertising theme, "the store you've been waiting for." Northeast and Mid-Atlantic markets are key areas for Target's expansion.

Differentiated Merchandise and Presentation Target's core merchandising strategy centers on consistent delivery of differentiation and value. We know we have to deliver excitement and value in dramatic new ways every time our guests visit our stores. The primary way we do this is by offering well-designed, trend-right merchandise at great prices, with powerful presentations in attractive stores. We are adding more exclusive product to our stores, with a greater emphasis on design and a greater depth of trend-right product.

For example, in 1999 Target completely reinvented the toy area. While we still carry traditional toy categories, we increased our offering of toys characterized by quality, craftsmanship, exclusivity and value. We carry great brand names such as Playmobil and Sanrio — and toys from the Discovery Channel. We also completely redesigned our in-store presentation of toys with new, vibrant signing and displays.

In addition, our home department is evolving to become a shopping destination similar to a specialty store. In the past year we have added brands like Calphalon and Stiffel, and designs by Michael Graves and Robert Abbey. Most recently, Target introduced exclusive bedding and bath products from Martex, featuring 250-thread-count cotton sheets, duvets and plush towels. These assortments enhance Target's powerful brand image among our guests and are the heart of our strategy to offer compelling, differentiated merchandise.

The Target "Sign of the Times" advertising campaign leverages the acceptance of the Target bullseye logo. The campaign was launched in New York City with posters, images on New York metro water towers and postings on construction sites.

Target's new toy offerings and the toy area's new signing reflect the company's commitment to constant innovation and reinvention in all merchandise areas. Target continues to add more exclusive products to its stores, with offerings like Sonia Kashuk Professional Makeup.

Better Guest Service In addition to our merchandise, we are working to differentiate Target's service as well. We know that guests want ultra-fast service with a respectful tone. That means getting in and out of the store quickly, finding merchandise in-stock, and obtaining rapid and knowledgeable answers to questions. We want to inject speed in every service area that affects the guest. Guests at Target tell us

Target is investing in technology and training to deliver faster, more knowledgeable service for our guests.

service is more important to them than any other aspect of their store experience, and therefore service is our highest priority.

In addition to speed of service, ensuring that merchandise is available and in-stock is essential to delivering great guest service. To improve Target's in-stocks we have made supply chain performance a top priority.

SuperTarget Expansion SuperTarget provides us with tremendous opportunities for future growth. SuperTarget combines general merchandise with high-quality grocery items to offer a convenient one-stop shopping experience for guests. Our SuperTarget strategy is exactly the same as our general merchandise strategy: "Expect More. Pay Less." Our goal is to leverage Target's brand heritage and differentiate ourselves from other supercenters. Expanding the Archer Farms brand for the grocery side of the business — including an extensive line of Archer Farms private label grocery products that are of higher quality than most national brands — is key to this differentiation.

Target is including pharmacies in all new and remodeled Target stores, adding more than 100 pharmacies in 2000 alone. Pharmacy was one of the top performing areas at Target in 1999, producing double-digit comparable-store sales results.

In 1999, SuperTarget improved its gross margin performance, the quality of its perishable foods offering and its expense structure. As a result of these merchandising and operational improvements, we are accelerating the growth of SuperTarget, adding 15 stores in 2000. In the next ten years, we expect to open at least 200 SuperTarget stores that will generate $15 billion or more in sales. Relocations of existing Target stores provide significant opportunity for SuperTarget growth, allowing us to update our store base as it ages, and replace older stores with our newest and biggest stores. This will help fuel many years of growth for Target.

E-Commerce In early 2000, Target formed a new business unit called target.direct, which is responsible for the company's electronic retailing and direct marketing efforts. The Internet and e-commerce are a vital part of Target Corporation; target.direct will help us leverage the power of all our store brands and catalogs.

We see the Internet not only as a channel for selling merchandise, but as an important communications tool to reach guests and drive increased guest service. In 1999, we devoted more resources to building the merchandising, marketing, fulfillment and technology processes required to support this new channel. Today we operate ten websites — eight of which are full-service selling sites. The largest is target.com, an exciting site that is consistent with the Target brand, offering thousands of unique and highly differentiated items that are also available in Target Stores. In addition to buying merchandise, guests can apply for a Target Guest Card, access information on programs like Take Charge of Education, find out what's new in our stores, get a map to a specific store location, or even apply for a job.

SuperTarget offers the best in high-quality groceries and general merchandise. We plan to open more than 200 SuperTarget locations in the next ten years.

We are excited about the possibilities of this medium to drive profitable sales, increase guest service and enhance the brand equity of our stores. We believe our competitive advantage in the electronic world will come from leveraging our existing strengths as a retailer, including our trusted brand names, marketing power, store presence and differentiated merchandise. We will continue investing in this area in 2000, expanding our on-line merchandise assortments and guest services.

Multiple Retail Segments Target Corporation also competes in the middle-market and traditional department store segments of the retail marketplace through Mervyn's California and Dayton's, Marshall Field's and Hudson's. Mervyn's and the Department Stores are key contributors to our overall strategy.

At our Department Stores, we remain focused on our commitment to be "The Best Store in Town" in our core Midwest markets as we strive to deliver fashion leadership and superior guest service. In 2000, we are working to enhance the shopping experience at our stores in several ways: by building stronger relationships with our guests through more personalized selling and enhanced guest loyalty programs; through a stronger commitment to newness and fashion product in our assortments; and with the creation of a more captivating store environment, with visual drama and ease of shopping. One way we are reinventing the shopping experience is through events like the Paris Flea Market and our popular "Fash Bash" fashion shows. Marketing initiatives for our department stores will continue to reinforce the strong brand heritage of our stores.

At Dayton's, Marshall Field's and Hudson's, we are committed to being "The Best Store in Town."

At Mervyn's, we are working to differentiate ourselves in the middle-market with our national and owned brands. Over the last three years, Mervyn's has added more than 125 national and market brands to the sales floor. In 1999, we made a more concerted effort to let our guests know about our brands by reinforcing our "Big Brands. Small Prices." promise in all of our marketing vehicles. We also updated our in-store presentations with more national brand shops and stronger in-store brand identification. We have introduced into our assortment more exclusive merchandise designed by individuals with national

Mervyn's California offers a strong assortment of national brands and high-quality owned brands for the middle market.

or international reputations, like craft artist Debbie Mumm and Australian painter and designer Ken Done. We also continue to upgrade and improve the quality and fashion content of our core owned brands, like Hillard & Hanson. In addition to better merchandise content, in 2000 Mervyn's will focus on improving in-stocks, guest service and merchandise presentation.

Credit Programs We offer proprietary credit in each of our business segments. Our credit portfolio is the second largest among retailers that issue their own cards and currently includes more than 30 million cards held by our guests. The growth of the Target Guest Card continues to drive increases in profit contribution from credit. Guest loyalty programs at each of our stores help us build stronger relationships with our guests and increase patronage of our stores. At Target, more than 4 million guests are enrolled in our Take Charge of Education program, where 1 percent of purchases made on the Target Guest Card are donated to a K-12 school of the guest's choice. We plan to grow credit's contribution to our results in the future by opening new accounts, enhancing guest loyalty programs and managing the business with financial discipline.

Credit programs contribute to earnings growth by driving sales at our stores and through credit's contribution to profits. The Target Guest card is now carried by more than 15 million Americans.

A Community Partner Our commitment to be an active member of the communities where we operate is also essential to our success. In 1999, we gave more than $67 million to nonprofit organizations across the country. We support the United Way with a $3 million corporate contribution — and our team members donated another $9 million to their local United Ways. In 2000, our grantmaking will exceed $80 million.

One of our greatest and most heartfelt contributions is called Target House. Dedicated in May 1999, Target House is a home-away-from-home for patients and their families undergoing treatment at St. Jude Children's Research Hospital in Memphis. Our guests help support Target House and the families it serves whenever they make pharmacy, and health and beauty product purchases at Target. In March, Target announced its intention to build a Target House annex, with an additional 44 suites, to serve even more families.

At Target House, which opened in May 1999, children who are undergoing long-term treatment at St. Jude Children's Research Hospital have a home-away-from-home for themselves and their families.

Education is important to our guests and to our company. Target has donated more than $18 million to schools across the country since our Take Charge of Education program began in 1997. More than 100,000 schools across the country participate in the program.

The Target Foundation was created in early 2000, with a continued emphasis on funding arts and social action initiatives in Minnesota. A key focus area for giving is to support immediate community needs for food, clothing and shelter. To that end, the Foundation awarded a $1 million grant to Sharing & Caring Hands, the Minneapolis nonprofit organization that serves the needs of inner city residents.

Mervyn's award-winning Community Closet program toured 15 cities in 10 states in 1999. In partnership with 82 nonprofit agencies, the Community Closet clothed 1,000 women making the transition from welfare to work. In addition, Mervyn's helped send more than 15,000 economically disadvantaged kids back to school in new clothes in 1999 through our ChildSpree program.

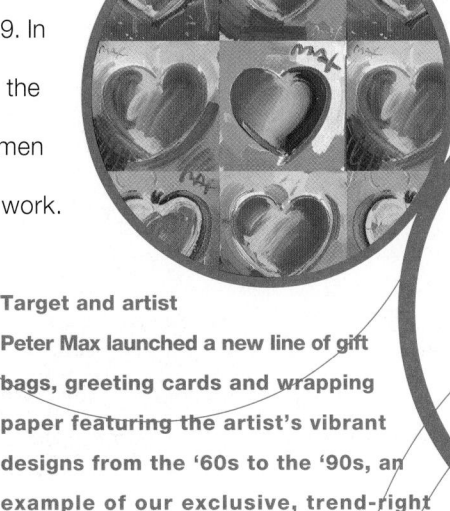

Target and artist Peter Max launched a new line of gift bags, greeting cards and wrapping paper featuring the artist's vibrant designs from the '60s to the '90s, an example of our exclusive, trend-right products.

Dayton's, Marshall Field's and Hudson's have always placed a special emphasis on supporting arts and cultural institutions. The Department Stores' "Project Imagine" showcases the arts in our communities, putting the promotional power of our stores behind arts organizations to help them achieve new levels of public awareness. Project Imagine has made possible events ranging from "Free Tuesdays" at Chicago's Museum of Contemporary Art to MacBeth at the Minnesota Opera. In recognition of the positive influence of the arts in young people's lives, the Project Imagine Scholarship was launched, awarding two scholarships per store to high school seniors.

We continue to look for innovative ways to partner with nonprofit agencies to build stronger communities across the country.

Target now offers 12 new high-style chairs from a number of designers, including Philippe Starck. Fresh design and differentiated merchandise are key to Target's merchandising strategy.

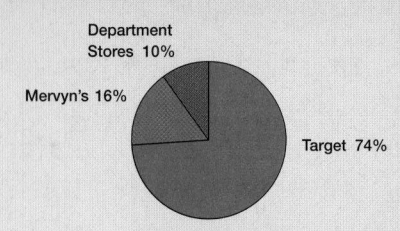

Revenues
(percent of total)

Pre-tax Segment Profit
(percent of total)

Retail Square Feet
(percent of total)

Target

(dollars in millions)	1999	1998	1997
Revenues	$26,080	$23,014	$20,298
Pre-tax Segment Profit	$ 2,022	$ 1,578	$ 1,287
Stores	912	851	796
Retail Square Feet*	102,945	94,553	87,158

* In thousands, reflects total square feet less office, warehouse and vacant space.

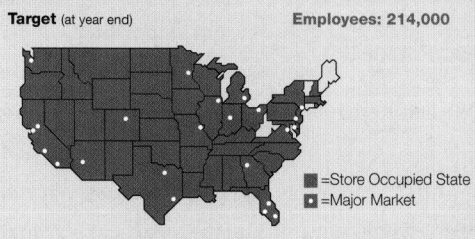

Target (at year end)   **Employees: 214,000**

■ =Store Occupied State
◻ =Major Market

	Retail Sq. Ft. (in thousands)	No. of Stores		Retail Sq. Ft. (in thousands)	No. of Stores		Retail Sq. Ft. (in thousands)	No. of Stores		Retail Sq. Ft. (in thousands)	No. of Stores
Alabama	117	1	Kansas	1,290	10	New Hampshire	392	3	South Dakota	391	4
Arizona	2,982	27	Kentucky	1,274	12	New Jersey	1,625	13	Tennessee	2,001	19
Arkansas	229	2	Louisiana	203	2	New Mexico	870	8	Texas	9,297	85
California	16,355	145	Maryland	2,158	18	New York	2,288	18	Utah	1,178	7
Colorado	2,533	23	Massachusetts	522	4	North Carolina	2,668	24	Virginia	2,769	23
Delaware	146	1	Michigan	4,908	46	North Dakota	437	4	Washington	2,557	24
Florida	7,442	66	Minnesota	6,024	51	Ohio	3,571	31	Wisconsin	2,599	24
Georgia	3,445	30	Mississippi	239	2	Oklahoma	817	8	Wyoming	182	2
Idaho	406	4	Missouri	1,885	17	Oregon	1,194	11			
Illinois	6,050	52	Montana	423	4	Pennsylvania	1,600	13			
Indiana	2,876	30	Nebraska	1,074	9	Rhode Island	128	1			
Iowa	1,868	17	Nevada	1,267	11	South Carolina	665	6	**Total**	**102,945**	**912**

Major Markets	No. of Stores
Greater Los Angeles	71
Chicago	38
Minneapolis/St. Paul	34
San Francisco Bay Area	28
Dallas/Ft. Worth	24
Atlanta	24
Detroit	23
Houston	21
Greater Miami	20
Phoenix	18
Denver/Boulder	15
Greater New York City	15
San Diego	14
Washington DC	14
Seattle/Tacoma	13
St. Louis	13
Tampa/St. Petersburg	12
Greater Philadelphia	12
Greater Cleveland	11
Indianapolis	11
Orlando	10
Sacramento	10
Baltimore	10

Mervyn's

(dollars in millions)	1999	1998	1997
Revenues	$4,099	$4,150	$4,219
Pre-tax Segment Profit	$ 205	$ 240	$ 280
Stores	267	268	269
Retail Square Feet*	21,635	21,729	21,810

* In thousands, reflects total square feet less office, warehouse and vacant space.

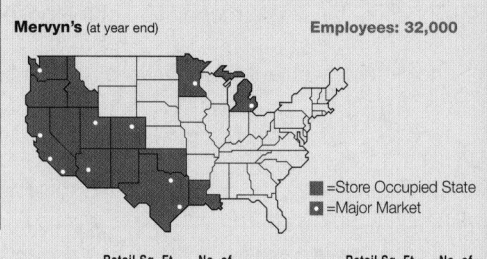

Mervyn's (at year end)   **Employees: 32,000**

■ =Store Occupied State
◻ =Major Market

	Retail Sq. Ft. (in thousands)	No. of Stores		Retail Sq. Ft. (in thousands)	No. of Stores		Retail Sq. Ft. (in thousands)	No. of Stores		Retail Sq. Ft. (in thousands)	No. of Stores
Arizona	1,202	15	Louisiana	449	6	New Mexico	267	3	Utah	753	8
California	9,607	124	Michigan	1,162	15	Oklahoma	269	3	Washington	1,440	16
Colorado	853	11	Minnesota	1,157	9	Oregon	559	7			
Idaho	82	1	Nevada	491	7	Texas	3,344	42	**Total**	**21,635**	**267**

Major Markets	No. of Stores
Greater Los Angeles	48
San Francisco Bay Area	29
Dallas/Ft. Worth	12
San Diego	12
Phoenix	11
Detroit	9
Houston	9
Minneapolis/St. Paul	9
Seattle/Tacoma	9
Greater Salt Lake City	8
Denver/Boulder	6

Department Stores

(dollars in millions)	1999	1998	1997
Revenues	$3,074	$3,064	$2,970
Pre-tax Segment Profit	$ 296	$ 279	$ 240
Stores	64	63	65
Retail Square Feet*	14,060	13,890	14,090

* In thousands, reflects total square feet less office, warehouse and vacant space.

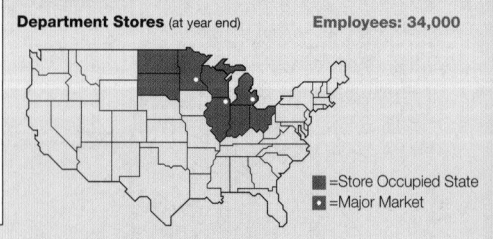

Department Stores (at year end)   **Employees: 34,000**

■ =Store Occupied State
◻ =Major Market

	Retail Sq. Ft. (in thousands)	No. of Stores		Retail Sq. Ft. (in thousands)	No. of Stores		Retail Sq. Ft. (in thousands)	No. of Stores
Dayton's			**Hudson's**			**Marshall Field's**		
Minnesota	3,040	12	Michigan	4,784	21	Illinois	4,173	17
North Dakota	297	3				Indiana	246	2
South Dakota	102	1				Ohio	618	3
Wisconsin	373	3				Wisconsin	427	2
						Total	**14,060**	**64**

Major Markets	No. of Stores
Chicago	16
Detroit	11
Minneapolis/St.Paul	10

Analysis of Operations

Our 1999 results mark the fourth consecutive year of earnings per share growth in excess of 20 percent. This exceptional growth in earnings per share was driven by substantial expansion in Target's gross margin rate.

Diluted Earnings per Share

● / ● as reported

● before unusual items

Earnings

Our net earnings were $1,144 million in 1999, compared with $935 million in 1998 and $751 million in 1997. Earnings per share were $2.45 in 1999, $1.98 in 1998 and $1.59 in 1997. References to earnings per share refer to diluted earnings per share. Earnings per share, dividends per share and common shares outstanding reflect our 1998 two-for-one share split and our 1996 three-for-one share split.

Management's discussion and analysis is based on our reclassified Consolidated Results of Operations as shown and discussed on page 24.

Revenues and Comparable-Store Sales

In 1999, our total revenues increased 9.9 percent and comparable-store sales increased 5.1 percent. Total revenues include retail sales and net credit revenues. Comparable-store sales are sales from stores open longer than one year. Revenue growth in 1999 and 1998 reflected Target's strong comparable-store sales growth and new store expansion. The impact of inflation was minimal and, as a result, the overall comparable-store sales increase closely approximated real growth.

Revenues

(millions)

Earnings Analysis
(millions, except per share data)

	Earnings			Diluted Earnings per Share		
	1999	1998	1997	**1999**	1998	1997
Net earnings before unusual items	**$1,188**	$970	$775	**$2.54**	$2.06	$1.64
Mainframe outsourcing (pre-tax 1999 $5 mil, 1998 $42 mil)	**(3)**	(26)	–	**(.01)**	(.06)	–
Favorable outcome of inventory shortage tax matter	–	20	–	–	.04	–
Securitization gain/(loss) (pre-tax 1998 $3 mil loss, 1997 $45 mil gain)	–	(2)	27	–	–	.06
Net earnings before extraordinary charges	**1,185**	962	802	**2.54**	2.04	1.70
Extraordinary charges — debt repurchase	**(41)**	(27)	(51)	**(.09)**	(.06)	(.11)
Net earnings	**$1,144**	$935	$751	**$2.45**	$1.98	$1.59

Management uses net earnings before unusual items, among other standards, to measure operating performance. It supplements, and is not intended to represent a measure of performance in accordance with, disclosures required by generally accepted accounting principles. Each per share amount is calculated independently.

Revenues and Comparable-Store Sales Growth

	1999		1998	
	Revenues	**Comparable-Store Sales**	Revenues	Comparable-Store Sales
Target	**13.3%**	**6.7%**	13.4%	6.1%
Mervyn's	**(1.2)**	**(0.7)**	(1.6)	0.9
Department Stores	**0.3**	**0.8**	3.2	4.5
Total	**9.9%**	**5.1%**	11.6%	5.2%

Revenues per Square Foot

	1999	1998	1997
Target	**$264**	$253	$243
Mervyn's	**189**	191	187
Department Stores	**220**	219	211

Thirteen-month average retail square feet.

Gross Margin Rate

The gross margin rate represents gross margin as a percent of sales. In 1999, our gross margin rate increased primarily due to rate expansion at Target and the Department Stores, resulting from improved markup and markdowns at Target and improved markup at the Department Stores. This increase was partially offset by the mix impact of strong growth at Target, our lowest gross margin rate division. In 1998, our overall gross margin rate increased modestly from the prior year, primarily due to lower markdowns at Target.

The LIFO provision, included in cost of sales, is calculated based on inventory levels, markup rates and internally generated retail price indices. In 1999, the LIFO provision was a $7 million credit ($.01 per share), compared with an $18 million credit ($.02 per share) in 1998 and a $6 million charge ($.01 per share) in 1997. The 1999 LIFO credit resulted primarily from higher markup. The 1998 LIFO credit resulted primarily from higher markup and higher inventory levels.

Operating Expense Rate

Operating expense rate represents selling, general and administrative expense (including buying and occupancy, advertising, start-up and other expense) as a percent of revenues. Our operating expense rate was essentially even with the prior year, benefiting from the overall growth of Target, our lowest expense rate division, and lower bad debt expense. These factors were offset by the lack of sales leverage in 1999 at Mervyn's and the Department Stores. The operating expense rate in 1998 was essentially even with 1997.

Pre-tax Segment Profit
(millions)

Pre-tax Segment Profit

Pre-tax segment profit increased 20 percent in 1999 to $2,523 million, compared with $2,097 million in 1998 and $1,807 million in 1997. Pre-tax segment profit is earnings before LIFO, securitization effects, interest, other expense and unusual items. Target provided substantially all of our pre-tax profit growth in 1999 with a 28 percent pre-tax profit increase. Target's full-year profit margin rate increased to 7.8 percent of revenues in 1999 from 6.9 percent in 1998.

Pre-tax Segment Profit and Percent Change from Prior Year (millions)	1999		1998	
Target	$2,022	28%	$1,578	23%
Mervyn's	205	(14)	240	(14)
Department Stores	296	6	279	16
Total	$2,523	20%	$2,097	16%

Pre-tax Segment Profit as a Percent of Revenues	1999	1998
Target	7.8%	6.9%
Mervyn's	5.0%	5.8%
Department Stores	9.6%	9.1%

EBITDA

EBITDA is pre-tax segment profit before depreciation and amortization.

EBITDA and Percent Change from Prior Year (millions)	1999		1998	
Target	$2,589	25%	$2,074	20%
Mervyn's	343	(9)	378	(7)
Department Stores	429	4	414	12
Total	$3,361	17%	$2,866	15%

EBITDA as a Percent of Revenues	1999	1998
Target	9.9%	9.0%
Mervyn's	8.4%	9.1%
Department Stores	14.0%	13.5%

Management uses pre-tax segment profit and EBITDA, among other standards, to measure operating performance. Pre-tax segment profit and EBITDA supplement, and are not intended to represent measures of performance in accordance with, disclosures required by generally accepted accounting principles.

Interest Expense

We consider payments to holders of our sold securitized receivables as "interest equivalent." In 1999, the total of interest expense and interest equivalent was $442 million, $4 million lower than 1998. The average portfolio interest rate in 1999 was 7.5 percent. In 1998, the total of interest expense and interest equivalent was $3 million lower than 1997. The average portfolio interest rate in 1998 was 7.8 percent. In both years, the reduction in interest expense and interest equivalent was due to a lower average portfolio interest rate, partially offset by higher average funded balances.

During 1999, we repurchased $381 million of debt for $444 million, resulting in an after-tax extraordinary charge of $41 million ($.09 per share). The debt repurchased had a weighted-average interest rate of 9.3 percent and an average remaining life of 18 years. The replacement of this debt with lower interest rate financing will have a favorable impact on interest expense going forward. In 1998 and 1997, we repurchased $127 million and $503 million of long-term debt, resulting in after-tax extraordinary charges of $27 million ($.06 per share) and $51 million ($.11 per share), respectively.

Income Tax Rate

The effective income tax rate was 38.8 percent in 1999, and 38.2 percent and 39.5 percent in 1998 and 1997, respectively. The 1998 effective tax rate reflected the beneficial effect of $20 million ($.04 per share), resulting from the favorable outcome of our inventory shortage tax matter.

Securitized Receivables

In 1998, Target Receivables Corporation (TRC), a special-purpose subsidiary, sold to the public $400 million of securitized receivables. This issue of asset-backed securities had an expected maturity of five years and a stated rate of 5.90 percent. Proceeds from the sale were used for general corporate purposes, including funding the growth of receivables. The 1998 sale transaction and the maturity of our 1995 securitization resulted in a net pre-tax loss of $3 million (less than $.01 per share), which reduced 1998 finance charge revenues and pre-tax earnings.

In 1997, TRC sold to the public $400 million of securitized receivables, with an expected maturity of five years and a stated rate of 6.25 percent. This transaction, combined with the impact of the application of SFAS No. 125 to our 1995 securitization, resulted in a $45 million ($.06 per share) increase in finance charge revenues and pre-tax earnings.

Our Consolidated Results of Operations also include reductions of finance charge revenues and bad debt expense related to sold securitized receivables. The amounts that represent payments to holders of our sold securitized receivables are included in our pre-tax earnings reconciliation on page 37 as interest equivalent. Interest equivalent was $49 million in 1999, $48 million in 1998 and $33 million in 1997.

Mainframe Outsourcing

In 1998, we announced our plan to outsource our mainframe computer data center functions and expensed $42 million ($.06 per share) of related charges. During 1999, we completed the transition and expensed an additional $5 million ($.01 per share) related to the outsourcing. These expenses are included in selling, general and administrative expense.

Year 2000 Readiness Disclosure

We began mitigating the risks associated with the year 2000 date conversion in 1993. In 1997, we established a corporate-wide, comprehensive plan of action designed to achieve an uninterrupted transition into the year 2000. This project included three major elements: 1) information technology (IT) systems, 2) non-IT, or embedded technology, systems and 3) relationships with our key business partners. The project was divided into five phases: awareness, assessment, renovation, validation and implementation. During 1999, we completed all phases for the three elements, using both internal and external resources to implement our plan.

For our IT systems, we assessed both existing and newly implemented hardware, application software and operating systems. We also assessed non-IT systems, or embedded technology/infrastructure, risks at our stores, distribution centers and headquarters facilities. We identified our key business partners and worked closely with them to assess their readiness and mitigate the risk to us if they were not prepared for the year 2000. We installed the year 2000 ready version of Electronic Data Interchange (EDI) software and tested the software with our key vendors.

To date, we have not experienced any significant issues associated with the date rollover. We have experienced no systems failures, no unusually high levels of returned merchandise, no interruptions of data transmission using EDI software and no major disruptions in the supply of product from our vendors. We continue to test and monitor our systems and applications for such issues in order to address them promptly, should any arise.

In 1999, we expensed $16 million related to year 2000 readiness. Prior to 1999, we expensed $32 million related to year 2000 readiness. In addition, this program accelerated the timing of $15 million of planned capital expenditures. All expenditures related to our year 2000 readiness initiative were within our estimates, were funded by cash flow from operations and did not materially impact our other operating or investment plans.

Fourth Quarter Results

Due to the seasonal nature of the retail industry, fourth quarter operating results typically represent a substantially larger share of total year revenues and earnings due to the inclusion of the holiday shopping season.

Fourth quarter 1999 net earnings were $494 million, compared with $423 million in 1998. Earnings per share were $1.06 for the quarter, compared with $.90 in 1998. Total revenues increased 8.7 percent and comparable-store sales increased 3.5 percent. Our pre-tax profit increased 16 percent to $1,000 million, driven by Target's strong results.

Fourth Quarter Pre-tax Segment Profit and Percent Change from Prior Year

(millions)	1999		1998	
Target	$ 811	26%	$646	26%
Mervyn's	69	(34)	104	–
Department Stores	120	5	115	12
Total	$1,000	16%	$865	20%

Analysis of Financial Condition

Our financial condition remains strong. Cash flow from operations was $2,252 million, driven by earnings growth, strong inventory control and accounts payable leveraging. Internally generated funds continue to be the most important component of our capital resources and, along with our ability to access a variety of financial markets, provide funding for our expansion plans. We continue to fund the growth in our business through a combination of internally generated funds, debt and sold securitized receivables.

During 1999, our average total receivables serviced (which includes both retained and sold securitized receivables)

increased 5 percent, or $124 million, due to growth of the Target Guest Card. Year-end total receivables serviced increased 7 percent from last year. In 1999, the number of Target Guest Card holders grew to over 15 million accounts at year end, compared with 12 million in 1998.

Inventory levels increased $323 million in 1999. This growth was more than fully funded by the $364 million increase in accounts payable over the same period.

Cash Flow from Operations
(millions)

Capital expenditures were $1,918 million in 1999, compared with $1,657 million in 1998. Investment in Target accounted for 87 percent of 1999 capital expenditures and included the purchase of real estate assets of a membership-based, general merchandise retailer for approximately $125 million. Net property and equipment increased $930 million. During 1999, Target opened 61 net new stores.

Capital Expenditures
(millions)

Approximately 69 percent of total expenditures was for new stores, expansions and remodels. Other capital investments were for information systems, distribution and other infrastructure to support store growth, primarily at Target. Over the past five years, Target's retail square footage has grown at a compound annual rate of approximately 10 percent.

Our financing strategy is to ensure liquidity and access to capital markets, to manage the amount of floating-rate debt and to maintain a balanced spectrum of debt maturities. Within these parameters, we seek to minimize our cost of borrowing.

In January 1999, our Board of Directors authorized the repurchase of $1 billion of our common stock. We repurchased 9.4 million shares of stock during 1999 at a total cost of $588 million ($62.58 per share), net of the premium from exercised and expired put options. In March 2000, our Board of Directors authorized the repurchase of an additional $1 billion of our common stock.

Repurchases are made primarily in open market transactions, subject to market conditions. Our program also includes the sale of put options that entitle the holder to sell shares of our common stock to us, at a specified price, if the holder exercises the option. During 2000, we expect to continue to repurchase shares at a pace similar to that of 1999.

A key to our access to liquidity and capital markets is maintaining strong investment-grade debt ratings. During the year, our debt ratings were upgraded by Duff & Phelps. Subsequent to year-end, as reflected in the table below, our debt ratings were also upgraded by Moody's. Further liquidity is provided by $1.6 billion of committed lines of credit obtained through a group of 31 banks.

Credit Ratings

	Moody's	Standard and Poor's	Duff & Phelps
Long-term debt	A2	A-	A
Commercial paper	P-1	A-2	D-1
Sold securitized receivables	Aaa	AAA	N/A

Performance Objectives

Market Price per Share
(year-end close)

Shareholder Return

Our primary objective is to maximize shareholder value over time through a combination of share price appreciation and dividend income while maintaining a prudent and flexible capital structure. Our total return to shareholders over the last five years averaged 43 percent annually, returning about $618 for each $100 invested in our stock at the beginning of this period.

Measuring Value Creation

We measure value creation internally using a form of Economic Value Added (EVA), which we define as after-tax segment profit less a capital charge for all investment employed. The capital charge is an estimate of our after-tax cost of capital adjusted for the age of our stores, recognizing that mature stores inherently have higher returns than newly opened stores. We estimate the after-tax cost of capital for our retail business is approximately 9 percent, while our credit operations' after-tax cost of capital is approximately 5 percent as a result of its ability to support higher debt levels. We expect to generate returns in excess of these costs of capital, thereby producing EVA.

EVA is used to evaluate our performance and to guide capital investment decisions. A significant portion of executive incentive compensation is tied to the achievement of targeted levels of annual EVA improvement.

Financial Objectives

We believe that managing our business with a focus on EVA helps achieve our objective of average annual earnings per share growth of 15 percent or more over time. Our financial strategy is to produce these results with strong interest coverage and prudent levels of debt, which will allow efficient capital market access to fund our growth. Earnings per share before unusual items has grown at a compound annual rate of 23 percent over the last five years.

Reflecting our strong cash flow, we ended 1999 with a retail debt ratio of 40 percent. In evaluating our debt level, we separate retail operations from credit operations due to their inherently different financial characteristics. We view the appropriate capitalization of our credit operations to be 88 percent debt and 12 percent equity, similar to ratios of comparable credit card businesses.

Debt Ratios and Interest Coverage

	1999	1998	1997
Retail	40%	41%	45%
Credit	88%	88%	88%
Total debt ratio	49%	50%	54%
Interest coverage	4.6x	4.0x	3.4x

Debt ratios and interest coverage include the impact of sold securitized receivables and off-balance sheet operating leases as if they were debt. Interest coverage represents the ratio of pre-tax earnings before unusual items and fixed charges to fixed charges (interest expense, interest equivalent and the interest portion of rent expense).

Retail Capitalization
(millions)
● debt ● total

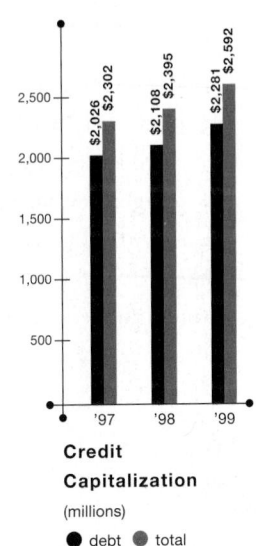

Credit Capitalization
(millions)
● debt ● total

Credit Operations

We offer proprietary credit in each of our business segments. These credit programs strategically support our core retail operations and are an integral component of each business segment. The programs contribute to our earnings growth by driving sales at our stores and through growth in credit contribution. Therefore, credit contribution, shown below, is reflected in each business segment's pre-tax profit on a receivables serviced basis. Because we service both the retained and sold securitized receivables, we manage our portfolio on a serviced basis. In contrast, our consolidated financial statements reflect only our retained securitized receivables.

In 1999, pre-tax contribution from credit increased 16 percent over the prior year, compared with a 5 percent growth in average receivables serviced. The improved credit performance reflects continued growth of the Target Guest Card, improved delinquency experience and a decrease in write-offs as a percent of receivables. In 1998 and 1997, the bad debt provision exceeded net write-offs during the year. In 1999, the bad debt provision was equal to net write-offs.

Average Receivables Serviced

(millions)	1999	1998	1997
Target	$ 974	$ 803	$ 644
Mervyn's	718	764	812
Department Stores	719	720	707
Total average receivables serviced	$2,411	$2,287	$2,163
Total year-end receivables serviced	$2,681	$2,496	$2,424

Allowance for Doubtful Accounts

(millions)	1999	1998	1997
Allowance at beginning of year	$203	$168	$119
Bad debt provision	147	180	190
Net write-offs	(147)	(145)	(141)
Allowance at end of year	$203	$203	$168
As a percent of year-end receivables serviced	7.6%	8.1%	6.9%
As a multiple of current year net write-offs	1.4x	1.4x	1.2x

Credit Contribution

(millions)	1999	1998	1997
Revenues:			
Finance charges, late fees and other revenues	$609	$588	$510
Merchant fees	90	81	77
Total revenues	699	669	587
Expenses:			
Bad debt	147	180	190
Operations and marketing	182	169	125
Total expenses	329	349	315
Pre-tax credit contribution	**$370**	**$320**	**$272**

Merchant fees are intercompany fees charged to our retail operations on a basis similar to fees charged by third-party credit card issuers. These fees, which include deferred billing fees charged for carrying non-revenue-earning revolving balances, are eliminated in consolidation. Operations and marketing expenses include costs associated with the opening, retention and servicing of accounts.

Credit Contribution

(millions)

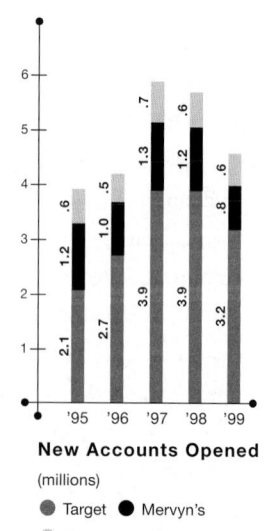

New Accounts Opened

(millions)

● Target ● Mervyn's
● Department Stores

Fiscal Year 2000

As we look forward into 2000, we believe that we will deliver another year of strong growth in revenues and earnings, driven primarily by increases in comparable-store sales and new store growth at Target. Our gross margin rate is expected to be essentially even with 1999. Our operating expense rate is expected to benefit modestly from the leveraging of fixed costs. Our credit operations are also expected to contribute to our growth in earnings as we continue to open new accounts, especially at Target, and leverage operating expenses.

In 2000, we expect to reinvest $2.5 to $3 billion in our business, through a combination of capital investment and repurchase of our shares. In the upcoming year, Target plans to open approximately 80 total new stores, including locations in two new states, West Virginia and Connecticut. Once again, our opening plans will focus on markets in the Mid-Atlantic and Northeast, and we will essentially double our number of SuperTarget locations from the 16 we operated at year-end. We expect Target's retail square footage to expand in the range of 8 to 10 percent annually for the foreseeable future. Our planned capital expenditures also include ongoing remodeling programs at all three operating segments and other capital support. Funding sources for the growth of our business include internally generated funds, debt and sold securitized receivables.

The total of interest expense and interest equivalent is expected to be moderately higher than 1999 due to higher average funded balances, partially offset by a lower average portfolio interest rate. Our $800 million of sold securitized receivables will result in approximately $50 million of interest equivalent for the year.

The effective income tax rate is expected to approximate 38.5 percent.

Forward-Looking Statements

This Annual Report, including the preceding management's discussion and analysis, contains forward-looking statements regarding our performance, liquidity and the adequacy of our capital resources. Those statements are based on our current assumptions and expectations and are subject to certain risks and uncertainties that could cause actual results to differ materially from those projected. We caution that the forward-looking statements are qualified by the risks and challenges posed by increased competition, shifting consumer demand, changing consumer credit markets, changing capital markets and general economic conditions, hiring and retaining effective team members, sourcing merchandise from domestic and international vendors, investing in new business strategies, achieving our growth objectives, and other risks and uncertainties. As a result, while we believe that there is a reasonable basis for the forward-looking statements, you should not place undue reliance on those statements. You are encouraged to review Exhibit (99)C attached to our Form 10-K Report for the year ended January 29, 2000, which contains additional important factors that may cause actual results to differ materially from those predicted in the forward-looking statements.

> As we look forward into 2000, we believe that we will deliver another year of strong growth in revenues and earnings.

(millions, except per share data)	1999	1998	1997
Sales	$33,212	$30,203	$27,019
Net credit revenues	490	459	468
Total revenues	33,702	30,662	27,487
Cost of sales	23,029	21,085	18,944
Selling, general and administrative expense	7,490	6,843	6,108
Depreciation and amortization	854	780	693
Interest expense	393	398	416
Earnings before income taxes and extraordinary charges	1,936	1,556	1,326
Provision for income taxes	751	594	524
Net earnings before extraordinary charges	1,185	962	802
Extraordinary charges from purchase and redemption of debt, net of tax	41	27	51
Net earnings	$ 1,144	$ 935	$ 751
Earnings before extraordinary charges	$ 2.64	$ 2.14	$ 1.80
Extraordinary charges	(.09)	(.06)	(.12)
Basic earnings per share	$ 2.55	$ 2.08	$ 1.68
Earnings before extraordinary charges	$ 2.54	$ 2.04	$ 1.70
Extraordinary charges	(.09)	(.06)	(.11)
Diluted earnings per share	$ 2.45	$ 1.98	$ 1.59
Weighted average common shares outstanding:			
Basic	441.3	440.0	436.1
Diluted	465.7	467.3	463.7

See Notes to Consolidated Financial Statements throughout pages 24-37.

Summary of Accounting Policies

Organization Effective beginning of fiscal year 2000, Dayton Hudson Corporation changed its name to Target Corporation. We are a general merchandise retailer, comprised of three operating segments: Target; Mervyn's; and Dayton's, Marshall Field's, Hudson's (the Department Stores). Target, an upscale discount chain located in 44 states at year-end, contributed 78 percent of our 1999 total revenues. Mervyn's, a middle-market promotional department store located in 14 states in the West, South and Midwest, contributed 12 percent of total revenues. The Department Stores, traditional department stores located in eight states in the upper Midwest, contributed 9 percent of total revenues.

Consolidation The financial statements include the balances of the Corporation and its subsidiaries after elimination of material intercompany balances and transactions. All material subsidiaries are wholly owned.

Use of Estimates The preparation of our financial statements, in conformity with generally accepted accounting principles, requires management to make estimates and assumptions that affect the reported amounts in the financial statements and accompanying notes. Actual results may differ from those estimates.

Fiscal Year Our fiscal year ends on the Saturday nearest January 31. Unless otherwise stated, references to years in this report relate to fiscal years rather than to calendar years. Fiscal years 1999, 1998 and 1997 consisted of 52 weeks.

Reclassifications Within the Consolidated Results of Operations, certain reclassifications have been made to prior years' income and expense amounts to conform to the 1999 presentation. None of the reclassifications impacted our net earnings or earnings per share in any period. The reclassifications include the separate presentation of sales and net credit revenues; the application of the provisions of Staff Accounting Bulletin No. 101, "Revenue Recognition in Financial Statements"; the classification of buying and occupancy expenses in selling, general and administrative expense rather than cost of sales; and the classification of taxes other than income taxes in selling, general and administrative expense.

Revenues

Revenue from retail sales is recognized at the time of sale. Leased department sales, net of related cost of sales, are included within sales and were $31 million in 1999, $29 million in 1998, and $25 million in 1997. Net credit revenues include finance charges and late fees on internal credit sales, net of the effect of sold securitized receivables. Internal credit sales were $5.0 billion, $4.5 billion and $4.2 billion in 1999, 1998 and 1997, respectively.

Advertising Costs

Advertising costs, included in selling, general and administrative expense, are expensed as incurred and were $791 million, $745 million and $679 million for 1999, 1998 and 1997, respectively.

Impact of Year 2000

Year 2000 related costs, included in selling, general and administrative expense, were expensed as incurred. In 1999, we expensed $16 million related to year 2000 readiness. Prior to 1999, we expensed $32 million. In addition, we accelerated the timing of $15 million of planned capital expenditures, which are recorded in property and equipment at cost less accumulated depreciation.

Mainframe Outsourcing

In 1998, we announced our plan to outsource our mainframe computer data center functions and expensed $42 million ($.06 per share) of related charges. During 1999, we completed the transition and expensed an additional $5 million ($.01 per share) related to the outsourcing. These expenses are included in selling, general and administrative expense.

Start-up Expense

In first quarter 1999, we adopted SOP 98-5, "Reporting on the Costs of Start-Up Activities." The adoption did not impact total year start-up expense, which is included in selling, general and administrative expense.

Earnings per Share

Basic EPS is net earnings, less dividend requirements on the Employee Stock Ownership Plan (ESOP) preferred shares prior to their conversion to common shares, divided by the average number of common shares outstanding during the period. In January 2000, each outstanding ESOP preferred share was converted into 60 shares of our common stock. These shares are now included within weighted average common shares outstanding.

Diluted EPS assumed conversion of the ESOP preferred shares into common shares and replacement of the ESOP preferred dividends with common stock dividends, prior to the conversion of all preferred shares in January 2000. In addition, net earnings were adjusted for expense required to fund the ESOP debt service, prior to repayment of the loan in 1998. References herein to earnings per share refer to Diluted EPS.

All earnings per share, dividends per share and common shares outstanding reflect our 1998 two-for-one share split.

(millions, except per share data)	Basic EPS			Diluted EPS		
	1999	1998	1997	**1999**	1998	1997
Net earnings*	**$1,185**	$ 962	$ 802	**$1,185**	$ 962	$ 802
Less: ESOP net earnings adjustment	**(18)**	(20)	(20)	**(4)**	(8)	(13)
Adjusted net earnings*	**$1,167**	$ 942	$ 782	**$1,181**	$ 954	$ 789
Weighted average common shares outstanding	**441.3**	440.0	436.1	**441.3**	440.0	436.1
Performance shares	**–**	–	–	**.1**	.8	1.3
Stock options	**–**	–	–	**5.8**	5.5	3.9
Assumed conversion of ESOP preferred shares	**–**	–	–	**18.5**	21.0	22.4
Total common equivalent shares outstanding	**441.3**	440.0	436.1	**465.7**	467.3	463.7
Earnings per share*	**$ 2.64**	$2.14	$1.80	**$ 2.54**	$2.04	$1.70

*Before extraordinary charges

(millions)	January 29, 2000	January 30, 1999
Assets		
Cash and cash equivalents	$ 220	$ 255
Retained securitized receivables	1,837	1,656
Inventory	3,798	3,475
Other	628	619
Total current assets	6,483	6,005
Property and equipment		
Land	2,069	1,868
Buildings and improvements	7,807	7,217
Fixtures and equipment	3,422	3,274
Construction-in-progress	526	378
Accumulated depreciation	(3,925)	(3,768)
Property and equipment, net	9,899	8,969
Other	761	692
Total assets	**$17,143**	**$15,666**
Liabilities and shareholders' investment		
Accounts payable	$ 3,514	$ 3,150
Accrued liabilities	1,520	1,444
Income taxes payable	318	207
Current portion of long-term debt and notes payable	498	256
Total current liabilities	5,850	5,057
Long-term debt	4,521	4,452
Deferred income taxes and other	910	822
Convertible preferred stock, net	–	24
Shareholders' investment		
Convertible preferred stock	–	268
Common stock	76	74
Additional paid-in-capital	730	286
Retained earnings	5,056	4,683
Total shareholders' investment	5,862	5,311
Total liabilities and shareholders' investment	**$17,143**	**$15,666**

See Notes to Consolidated Financial Statements throughout pages 24-37.

Cash Equivalents

Cash equivalents represent short-term investments with a maturity of three months or less from the time of purchase.

Retained Securitized Receivables

Through our special purpose subsidiary, Target Receivables Corporation (TRC), we transfer, on an ongoing basis, substantially all of our receivables to a trust in return for certificates representing undivided interests in the trust's assets. TRC owns the undivided interest in the trust's assets, other than the sold securitized receivables and the 2 percent of trust assets held by Retailers National Bank (RNB), a wholly owned subsidiary of the Corporation that also services the receivables. Prior to June 1998, RNB held 5 percent of trust assets. The undivided interests held by TRC and RNB, as well as related income and expenses, are reflected in each operating segment's assets and operating results based on the origin of the credit sale giving rise to the receivable.

In 1998, TRC sold to the public $400 million of securitized receivables. This issue of asset-backed securities had an expected maturity of five years and a stated rate of 5.90 percent. Proceeds from the sale were used for general corporate purposes, including funding the growth of receivables. The 1998 sale transaction and the maturity of our 1995 securitization resulted in a net loss of $3 million (less than $.01 per share), which reduced 1998 finance charge revenues and pre-tax earnings.

In 1997, TRC sold to the public $400 million of securitized receivables, with an expected maturity of five years and a stated rate of 6.25 percent. This transaction, combined with the impact of the application of SFAS No. 125 to our 1995 securitization, resulted in a $45 million ($.06 per share) increase in finance charge revenues and pre-tax earnings.

At year-end 1999, $800 million of securitized receivables had been sold to investors and TRC had borrowed $100 million through the issuance of notes payable secured by receivables.

The fair value of the retained securitized receivables, classified as available for sale, was $1,837 million and $1,656 million at year-end 1999 and 1998, respectively. The fair value of the retained securitized receivables was lower than the aggregate receivables value by $157 million and $156 million at year-end 1999 and 1998, respectively, due to our estimates of ultimate collectibility. Write-downs have been included in selling, general and administrative expense.

Inventory

Inventory and the related cost of sales are accounted for by the retail inventory accounting method using the last-in, first-out (LIFO) basis and are stated at the lower of LIFO cost or market. The cumulative LIFO provision was $53 million and $60 million at year-end 1999 and 1998, respectively.

Property and Long-lived Assets

Property and long-lived assets are recorded at cost less accumulated depreciation or amortization. Depreciation and amortization are computed using the straight-line method over estimated useful lives. Accelerated depreciation methods are generally used for income tax purposes.

Estimated useful lives by major asset category are as follows:

Asset	Life (in years)
Buildings and improvements	8 – 50
Fixtures and equipment	5 – 8
Computer hardware and software	4
Intangible assets and goodwill	3 – 20

On an ongoing basis, we evaluate our long-lived assets for impairment using undiscounted cash flow analysis.

Accounts Payable

Outstanding drafts included in accounts payable were $599 million and $519 million at year-end 1999 and 1998, respectively.

consolidated statements of cash flows

(millions)	1999	1998	1997
Operating activities			
Net earnings before extraordinary charges	$ 1,185	$ 962	$ 802
Reconciliation to cash flow:			
Depreciation and amortization	854	780	693
Deferred tax provision	75	(11)	(63)
Other noncash items affecting earnings	163	70	43
Changes in operating accounts providing/(requiring) cash:			
Retained securitized receivables	(181)	(56)	(235)
Sold securitized receivables	–	400	400
Maturity of sold securitized receivables	–	(400)	–
Inventory	(323)	(198)	(220)
Other current assets	(57)	(46)	(35)
Other assets	(65)	(65)	(33)
Accounts payable	364	336	199
Accrued liabilities	100	75	182
Income taxes payable	137	15	62
Cash flow provided by operations	2,252	1,862	1,795
Investing activities			
Expenditures for property and equipment	(1,918)	(1,657)	(1,354)
Proceeds from disposals of property and equipment	126	107	123
Acquisition of subsidiaries, net of cash received	–	(100)	–
Other	(15)	(5)	–
Cash flow required for investing activities	(1,807)	(1,655)	(1,231)
Net financing sources	445	207	564
Financing activities			
Increase/(decrease) in notes payable, net	564	(305)	(127)
Additions to long-term debt	285	600	375
Reductions of long-term debt	(600)	(343)	(690)
Principal payments received on loan to ESOP	–	8	22
Dividends paid	(195)	(178)	(165)
Repurchase of stock	(581)	–	–
Other	47	55	31
Cash flow used for financing activities	(480)	(163)	(554)
Net (decrease)/increase in cash and cash equivalents	(35)	44	10
Cash and cash equivalents at beginning of year	255	211	201
Cash and cash equivalents at end of year	$ 220	$ 255	$ 211

Amounts presented herein are on a cash basis and therefore may differ from those shown in other sections of this Annual Report. Cash paid for income taxes was $575 million, $564 million and $454 million during 1999, 1998 and 1997, respectively. Cash paid for interest (including interest capitalized) was $405 million, $393 million and $485 million during 1999, 1998 and 1997, respectively.

See Notes to Consolidated Financial Statements throughout pages 24-37.

Lines of Credit

At January 29, 2000, two committed credit agreements totaling $1.6 billion were in place through a group of 31 banks at specified rates. There were no balances outstanding at any time during 1999 or 1998 under these agreements.

Long-term Debt and Notes Payable

At January 29, 2000, $664 million of notes payable were outstanding, $564 million of which were classified as long-term debt as they were supported by our $800 million committed credit agreement that expires in 2002. The remaining $100 million of notes payable is financing secured by the Target Credit Card Master Trust Series 1996-1 Class A variable funding certificate. This certificate is debt of TRC and is classified in the current portion of long-term debt and notes payable. The average amount of secured and unsecured notes payable outstanding during 1999 was $775 million at a weighted-average interest rate of 5.5 percent.

In 1999, we issued $285 million of floating-rate notes bearing interest at initial rates between 5.32 and 5.52 percent, maturing in July through September 2001. The proceeds were used for general corporate purposes. Also during 1999, we repurchased $381 million of long-term debt with an average remaining life of 18 years and a weighted-average interest rate of 9.3 percent, resulting in an after-tax extraordinary charge of $41 million ($.09 per share).

In 1998, we issued $200 million of long-term debt at 6.65 percent, maturing in 2028 and $200 million at 5.88 percent, maturing in 2008. We also issued $200 million of long-term debt maturing in 2010, which is puttable in 2000, and we sold to a third party the right to call and remarket these securities in 2000 to their final maturity. Also during 1998, we repurchased $127 million of long-term debt, resulting in an after-tax extraordinary charge of $27 million ($.06 per share).

At year end our debt portfolio was as follows:

Long-term Debt and Notes Payable

(millions)	January 29, 2000 Rate*	January 29, 2000 Balance	January 30, 1999 Rate*	January 30, 1999 Balance
Notes payable	5.8%	$ 664	5.2%	$ 100
Notes and debentures:				
Due 1999-2003	7.8	1,682	8.1	1,544
Due 2004-2008	7.5	699	7.6	701
Due 2009-2013	7.9	472	8.1	564
Due 2014-2018	9.5	34	9.6	70
Due 2019-2023	8.5	759	8.7	1,009
Due 2024-2028	6.6	474	6.6	475
Due 2029-2037	5.9	100	5.9	100
Total notes payable, notes and debentures**	7.5%	$4,884	7.9%	$4,563
Capital lease obligations		135		145
Less: current portion		(498)		(256)
Long-term debt and notes payable		$4,521		$4,452

*Reflects the weighted-average stated interest rate as of year end.
**The estimated fair value of total notes payable and notes and debentures, using a discounted cash flow analysis based on our incremental interest rates for similar types of financial instruments, was $4,893 million at January 29, 2000 and $5,123 million at January 30, 1999.

Required principal payments on long-term debt and notes payable over the next five years, excluding capital lease obligations, are $488 million in 2000, $638 million in 2001, $756 million in 2002, $464 million in 2003 and $105 million in 2004.

Subsequent to year-end 1999, we issued $500 million of additional long-term debt bearing interest at 7.50 percent, maturing in February 2005.

Derivatives

From time to time we use interest rate swaps to hedge our exposure to interest rate risk. The fair value of the swaps is not reflected in the financial statements and any gain or loss recognized upon early termination is amortized over the life of the related debt obligation. The fair value of existing swaps is immaterial.

In 1998, the Financial Accounting Standards Board issued SFAS No. 133, "Accounting for Derivative Instruments and Hedging Activities," which is required to be adopted for fiscal years beginning after June 15, 2000. We have analyzed the impact of SFAS No. 133 on our existing and currently anticipated activities and do not believe the adoption of this new statement will have a material effect on our earnings or financial position.

(millions, except share data)	Convertible Preferred Stock	Common Stock	Additional Paid-in Capital	Retained Earnings	Loan to ESOP	Total
February 1, 1997	$271	$72	$146	$3,348	$(47)	$3,790
Consolidated net earnings	–	–	–	751	–	751
Dividends declared	–	–	–	(169)	–	(169)
Tax benefit on unallocated preferred stock dividends and options	–	–	17	–	–	17
Conversion of preferred stock and other	9	–	18	–	–	27
Net reduction in loan to ESOP	–	–	–	–	28	28
Stock option activity	–	1	15	–	–	16
January 31, 1998	280	73	196	3,930	(19)	4,460
Consolidated net earnings	–	–	–	935	–	935
Dividends declared	–	–	–	(182)	–	(182)
Tax benefit on unallocated preferred stock dividends and options	–	–	25	–	–	25
Conversion of preferred stock and other	(12)	–	37	–	–	25
Net reduction in loan to ESOP	–	–	–	–	19	19
Stock option activity	–	1	28	–	–	29
January 30, 1999	268	74	286	4,683	–	5,311
Consolidated net earnings	–	–	–	1,144	–	1,144
Dividends declared	–	–	–	(191)	–	(191)
Repurchase of stock	–	(1)	–	(580)	–	(581)
Issuance of stock for ESOP	–	–	81	–	–	81
Tax benefit on unallocated preferred stock dividends and options	–	–	29	–	–	29
Conversion of preferred stock	(268)	3	289	–	–	24
Stock option activity	–	–	45	–	–	45
January 29, 2000	$ –	$76	$730	$5,056	$ –	$5,862

Common Stock Authorized 3,000,000,000 shares, $.1667 par value; 455,841,388 shares issued and outstanding at January 29, 2000; 441,809,806 shares issued and outstanding at January 30, 1999.

In January 1999, our Board of Directors authorized the repurchase of $1 billion of our common stock. We repurchased 9.4 million shares of stock during 1999 at a total cost of $588 million ($62.58 per share), net of the premium from exercised and expired put options. In March 2000, our Board of Directors authorized the repurchase of an additional $1 billion of our common stock. Repurchases are made primarily in open market transactions, subject to market conditions. Our program also includes the sale of put options that entitle the holder to sell shares of our common stock to us, at a specified price, if the holder exercises the option.

We sold put options on 4.7 million shares in 1999. Options on 1.4 million shares outstanding at the end of 1999 entitled their holders to sell shares of our common stock to us at prices ranging from $63 to $74 per share on specific dates during February through June 2000. Premiums received from the sale of put options during the year were recorded in retained earnings and totaled $23 million, $7 million of which represents premiums received on put options outstanding at year end.

Preferred Stock Authorized 5,000,000 shares; no shares of Series B ESOP Convertible Preferred Stock, $.01 par value, were issued and outstanding at January 29, 2000 and 338,492 shares were issued and outstanding at January 30, 1999. In January 2000, each share of Series B ESOP Convertible Preferred Stock was converted into 60 shares of our common stock. Prior to conversion, these shares had voting rights equal to the equivalent number of common shares and were entitled to cumulative annual dividends of $56.20.

Junior Preferred Stock Rights In 1996, we declared a distribution of shares of preferred share purchase rights. Terms of the plan provide for a distribution of one preferred share purchase right for each outstanding share of our common stock. Each right will entitle shareholders to buy one six-hundredth of a share of a new series of junior participating preferred stock at an exercise price of $50.00, subject to adjustment. The rights will be exercisable only if a person or group acquires ownership of 20 percent or more of our common stock or announces a tender offer to acquire 30 percent or more of our common stock.

See Notes to Consolidated Financial Statements throughout pages 24-37.

Stock Option Plan

We have a stock option plan for key employees. Options include incentive stock options, non-qualified stock options or a combination of the two. A majority of the options vest annually in equal amounts over a four-year period. These options are cumulatively exercisable and expire no later than ten years after the date of the grant. The non-employee members of our Board of Directors also participate in our stock option plan. Their options become exercisable after one year and have a ten-year term. The typical frequency of stock option grants is once each fiscal year.

We also have a performance share and restricted share plan for key employees. The last grant was made in 1995, and all shares relating to outstanding grants were issued in 1999 pursuant to the plan. Performance shares were issued to the extent certain financial goals were met over the four-year period from the date of grant. Restricted shares were issued four years from the date of grant. Once issued, performance shares and restricted shares generally vest only upon retirement.

Options, Performance Shares and Restricted Shares Outstanding

| | Options | | | | | |
| | Total Outstanding | | Currently Exercisable | | | |
(shares in thousands)	Number of Shares	Weighted Average Exercise Price	Number of Shares	Weighted Average Exercise Price	Perform- ance Shares	Restricted Shares
February 1, 1997	14,610	$13.48	4,782	$10.88	1,264	311
Granted	2,653	33.63				
Canceled	(346)	15.02				
Exercised	(2,450)	10.27				
January 31, 1998	14,467	$17.69	4,860	$13.15	794	212
Granted	3,309	48.16				
Canceled	(173)	23.77				
Exercised	(2,023)	12.27				
January 30, 1999	15,580	$24.79	5,685	$16.49	519*	123*
Granted	1,906	67.63				
Canceled	(176)	34.91				
Exercised	(1,279)	14.03				
January 29, 2000	**16,031**	**$30.63**	**7,858**	**$20.46**	**–**	**–**

*All shares were issued in 1999 pursuant to the plan.

Options Outstanding

(shares in thousands)	Shares Outstanding at January 29, 2000	Range of Exercise Price
	5,209	$ 9.97 - $15.00
	3,424	$15.00 - $25.00
	2,246	$25.00 - $35.00
	1,211	$35.00 - $45.00
	2,032	$45.00 - $55.00
	1,909	$55.00 - $68.69
Total	16,031	$ 9.97 - $68.69

As of January 29, 2000, outstanding options had a weighted-average remaining contractual life of 7.2 years. The number of unissued common shares reserved for future grants under the stock option plans was 24,489,897 at January 29, 2000, and 4,136,969 at January 30, 1999.

We apply APB No. 25, "Accounting for Stock Issued to Employees," to account for our stock option and performance share plans. Because the exercise price of our employee stock options equals the market price of the underlying stock on the grant date, no compensation expense related to options is recognized. Performance share compensation expense was recognized based on the fair value of the shares at the end of each reporting period. If we had elected to recognize compensation cost based on the fair value of the options and performance shares at grant date as prescribed by SFAS No. 123, "Accounting for Stock-Based Compensation," net earnings would have been the pro forma amounts shown below. EPS calculated under SFAS No. 123 would be $.03 lower than reported EPS in 1999 and unchanged from reported EPS in 1998 and 1997.

Pro Forma Earnings

(millions)	1999	1998	1997
Net earnings — as reported	$1,144	$935	$751
Net earnings — pro forma	$1,132	$934	$751

The Black-Scholes method was used to estimate the fair value of the options at grant date based on the following factors:

	1999	1998	1997
Dividend yield	.6%	.7%	1.0%
Volatility	30%	30%	25%
Risk free interest rate	6.6%	4.6%	5.4%
Expected life in years	5.6	5.6	5.6
Weighted average fair value at grant date	$25.81	$16.24	$10.52

Pension and Postretirement Health Care Benefits

We have defined benefit pension plans that cover all employees who meet certain age, length of service and hours worked per year requirements. Benefits are provided based upon years of service and the employee's compensation. Retired employees also become eligible for certain health care benefits if they meet minimum age and service requirements and agree to contribute a portion of the cost.

In 1999, we adopted a change in the measurement date of our pension and postretirement health care benefits plans from December 31 to October 31. Prior periods have not been restated, as the impact of the change is not material.

Change in Benefit Obligation

(millions)	Pension Benefits		Postretirement Health Care Benefits	
	1999	1998	1999	1998
Benefit obligation at beginning of measurement period	$729	$610	$ 85	$ 81
Service cost	44	35	2	1
Interest cost	53	45	6	6
Actuarial loss	76	65	9	5
Acquisitions	–	26	–	–
Benefits paid	(40)	(52)	(8)	(8)
Benefit obligation at end of measurement period	$862	$729	$ 94	$ 85

Change in Plan Assets

	Pension Benefits		Postretirement Health Care Benefits	
Fair value of plan assets at beginning of measurement period	$859	$718	$ –	$ –
Actual return on plan assets	62	106	–	–
Employer contribution	100	59	8	8
Acquisitions	–	25	–	–
Benefits paid	(39)	(49)	(8)	(8)
Fair value of plan assets at end of measurement period	$982	$859	$ –	$ –

Reconciliation of Prepaid/(Accrued) Cost

	Pension Benefits		Postretirement Health Care Benefits	
Funded status	$120	$130	$(94)	$ (85)
Unrecognized actuarial loss/(gain)	51	(16)	(7)	(18)
Unrecognized prior service cost	8	2	2	3
Net prepaid/(accrued) cost	$179	$116	$(99)	$(100)

The benefit obligation and fair value of plan assets, for the pension plans with benefit obligations in excess of plan assets, were $49 and $0 as of October 31, 1999, and $34 and $0 as of December 31, 1998.

Net Pension and Postretirement Health Care Benefits Expense

(millions)	Pension Benefits			Postretirement Health Care Benefits		
	1999	1998	1997	1999	1998	1997
Service cost benefits earned during the period	$44	$35	$27	$2	$1	$1
Interest cost on projected benefit obligation	53	45	39	6	6	6
Expected return on assets	(72)	(58)	(48)	–	–	–
Recognized gains and losses	9	3	–	–	(1)	(2)
Recognized prior service cost	1	–	1	–	–	1
Total	$35	$25	$19	$8	$6	$6

The amortization of any prior service cost is determined using a straight-line amortization of the cost over the average remaining service period of employees expected to receive benefits under the plan.

Actuarial Assumptions

	Pension Benefits			Postretirement Health Care Benefits		
	1999	1998	1997	1999	1998	1997
Discount rate	7½%	7%	7¼%	7½%	7%	7¼%
Expected long-term rate of return on plans' assets	9	9	9	n/a	n/a	n/a
Average assumed rate of compensation increase	4½	4	4¼	n/a	n/a	n/a

An increase in the cost of covered health care benefits of 6 percent is assumed for 2000. The rate is assumed to remain at 6 percent in the future. The health care cost trend rate assumption has a significant effect on the amounts reported. A 1 percent change in assumed health care cost trend rates would have the following effects:

	1% Increase	1% Decrease
Effect on total of service and interest cost components of net periodic postretirement health care benefit cost	$–	$ –
Effect on the health care component of the postretirement benefit obligation	$5	$(4)

Employee Stock Ownership Plan

We sponsor a defined contribution employee benefit plan. Employees who meet certain eligibility requirements can participate by investing up to 20 percent of their compensation. We match 100 percent of each employee's contribution up to 5 percent of respective total compensation. Our contribution to the plan is invested in the ESOP. Through December 1998, ESOP preferred shares (401(k) preferred shares) were allocated to participants. In January 1999, we began providing new common shares to the ESOP to fund the employer match.

In 1989, we loaned $379 million to the ESOP at a 9 percent interest rate. Proceeds from the loan were then used by the ESOP to purchase 438,353 shares of 401(k) preferred shares. The original issue value of the 401(k) preferred shares of $864.60 per share was guaranteed by the Corporation. The loan was paid off during 1998 using dividends paid on all 401(k) preferred shares held by the ESOP. In January 2000, each 401(k) preferred share was converted into 60 shares of common stock.

Prior to the conversion of all 401(k) preferred shares to common stock, we were required to exchange at fair value each 401(k) preferred share for 60 shares of common stock and cash, if any, upon a participant's termination. The 401(k) preferred shares were classified as shareholders' investment to the extent the preferred shares were permanent equity.

Dividends earned on 401(k) preferred shares held by the ESOP were $19 million in both 1999 and 1998 and $21 million in 1997. The dividends on allocated 401(k) preferred shares were paid to participants' accounts in additional 401(k) preferred shares until June 1998. Dividends are now paid to participants in cash. Benefits expense was $78 million in 1999, $29 million in 1998 and $17 million in 1997.

Leases

Assets held under capital leases are included in property and equipment and are charged to depreciation and interest over the life of the lease. Operating leases are not capitalized and lease rentals are expensed. Rent expense on buildings, classified in selling, general and administrative expense, includes percentage rents that are based on a percentage of retail sales over stated levels. Total rent expense was $168 million, $150 million and $143 million in 1999, 1998 and 1997, respectively. Most of the long-term leases include options to renew, with terms varying from five to 30 years. Certain leases also include options to purchase the property.

Future minimum lease payments required under non-cancelable lease agreements existing at January 29, 2000, were:

Future Minimum Lease Payments

(millions)	Operating Leases	Capital Leases
2000	$ 113	$ 22
2001	105	21
2002	96	21
2003	80	19
2004	70	18
After 2004	634	124
Total future minimum lease payments	$1,098	$225
Less: interest*	(302)	(90)
Present value of minimum lease payments	$ 796	$135**

*Calculated using the interest rate at inception for each lease (the weighted average interest rate was 8.8 percent).

**Includes current portion of $10 million.

Owned and Leased Store Locations

At year end, owned, leased and "combined" (combination owned/leased) store locations by operating segment were as follows:

	Owned	Leased	Combined	Total
Target	705	92	115	912
Mervyn's	160	68	39	267
Department Stores	51	12	1	64
Total	916	172	155	1,243

Income Taxes

Reconciliation of tax rates is as follows:

Percent of Earnings Before Income Taxes

	1999	1998	1997
Federal statutory rate	35.0%	35.0%	35.0%
State income taxes, net of federal tax benefit	3.9	4.5	4.5
Dividends on ESOP stock	(.4)	(.5)	(.5)
Work opportunity tax credits	(.2)	(.2)	(.1)
Inventory shortage tax matter	–	(1.3)	–
Other	.5	.7	.6
Effective tax rate	38.8%	38.2%	39.5%

The components of the provision for income taxes were:

Income Tax Provision: Expense/(Benefit)

(millions)	1999	1998	1997
Current:			
Federal	$570	$497	$488
State	106	110	99
	676	607	587
Deferred:			
Federal	63	(10)	(55)
State	12	(3)	(8)
	75	(13)	(63)
Total	$751	$594	$524

The components of the net deferred tax asset/(liability) were:

Net Deferred Tax Asset/(Liability)

(millions)	January 29, 2000	January 30, 1999
Gross deferred tax assets:		
Self-insured benefits	$ 146	$ 132
Deferred compensation	130	128
Inventory	84	72
Valuation allowance	63	64
Postretirement health care obligation	41	42
Other	106	132
	570	570
Gross deferred tax liabilities:		
Property and equipment	(408)	(374)
Other	(104)	(63)
	(512)	(437)
Total	$ 58	$ 133

Inventory Shortage Tax Matter

In 1998, we received a favorable ruling from the United States Court of Appeals on a 1983 case related to the deductibility of accrued inventory shortage expense. The beneficial effect resulting from the outcome of the case was $20 million ($.04 per share) and was reflected as a reduction in the 1998 effective income tax rate. This issue has been settled for all years.

Acquisitions

In 1998, we acquired The Associated Merchandising Corporation, an international sourcing company that provides services to our operating divisions and other retailers, and we also acquired Rivertown Trading Company, a direct marketing firm. Both subsidiaries are included in the consolidated financial statements. Their revenues and operating results are included in "other" in revenues and in our pre-tax earnings reconciliation on page 37 and were immaterial in 1999 and 1998.

Commitments and Contingencies

Commitments for the purchase, construction, lease or remodeling of real estate, facilities and equipment were approximately $534 million at year-end 1999. We are exposed to claims and litigation arising out of the ordinary course of business. Management, after consulting with legal counsel, believes the currently identified claims and litigation will not have a material adverse effect on our results of operations or our financial condition taken as a whole.

Quarterly Results (Unaudited)

The same accounting policies are followed in preparing quarterly financial data as are followed in preparing annual data. The table below summarizes results by quarter for 1999 and 1998:

(millions, except per share data)	First Quarter		Second Quarter		Third Quarter		Fourth Quarter		Total Year	
	1999	1998	**1999**	1998	**1999**	1998	**1999**	1998	**1999**	1998
Total revenues	$7,158	6,402	$7,687	6,987	$7,927	7,218	$10,930	10,055	$33,702	30,662
Gross margin (a)	$2,182	1,924	$2,376	2,097	$2,441	2,172	$ 3,184	2,925	$10,183	9,118
Net earnings before extraordinary charges (c) (d)	$ 194	160	$ 228	172	$ 241	183	$ 522	447	$ 1,185	962
Net earnings (b) (c) (d)	$ 194	158	$ 224	172	$ 232	182	$ 494	423	$ 1,144	935
Basic earnings per share (b) (c) (d) (e)	$ .43	.35	$ .50	.38	$ .52	.40	$ 1.11	.95	$ 2.55	2.08
Diluted earnings per share (b) (c) (d) (e)	$ .41	.33	$ .48	.36	$ .50	.39	$ 1.06	.90	$ 2.45	1.98
Dividends declared per share (e)	$ .10	.09	$ .10	.09	$ .10	.09	$ .10	.09	$ .40	.36
Common stock price (f)										
High	$75.75	44.81	$72.44	52.63	$69.50	48.25	$ 75.00	63.75	$ 75.75	63.75
Low	$58.75	36.25	$57.94	42.50	$55.25	33.75	$ 60.75	42.69	$ 55.25	33.75

(a) Gross margin is sales less cost of sales. The LIFO provision, included in gross margin, is analyzed each quarter for estimated changes in year-end inventory levels, markup rates and internally generated retail price indices. A final adjustment is recorded in the fourth quarter for the difference between the prior quarters' estimates and the actual total year LIFO provision.

(b) In 1999, second, third and fourth quarter net earnings include extraordinary charges, net of tax, related to the purchase and redemption of debt of $4 million, $9 million and $28 million ($.01, $.02 and $.06 per basic and diluted share), respectively. In 1998, first, third and fourth quarter net earnings include extraordinary charges, net of tax of $2 million, $1 million and $24 million ($.01, $.00 and $.05 per basic and diluted share), respectively.

(c) Third quarter and total year 1999 net earnings before extraordinary charges, net earnings and earnings per share include a mainframe outsourcing pre-tax charge of $5 million ($.01 per share). Fourth quarter and total year 1998 net earnings before extraordinary charges, net earnings and earnings per share include a mainframe outsourcing pre-tax charge of $42 million ($.06 per basic and diluted share) and the beneficial effect of $20 million ($.04 per basic and diluted share) of the favorable outcome of our inventory shortage tax matter.

(d) Third quarter 1998 net earnings include a $3 million securitization pre-tax net loss (less than $.01 per basic and diluted share).

(e) Per share amounts are computed independently for each of the quarters presented. The sum of the quarters may not equal the total year amount due to the impact of changes in average quarterly shares outstanding and/or rounding caused by the 1998 two-for-one common share split.

(f) Our common stock is listed on the New York Stock Exchange and Pacific Exchange. At March 17, 2000, there were 13,883 shareholders of record and the common stock price was $69.50 per share.

(dollars in millions, except per share data)	1999	1998	1997	1996	1995(a)	1994
Results of operations						
Total revenues	$33,702	30,662	27,487	25,092	23,234	21,093
Net earnings (c) (d) (e)	$ 1,144	935	751	463	311	434
Financial position data						
Total assets	$17,143	15,666	14,191	13,389	12,570	11,697
Long-term debt	$ 4,521	4,452	4,425	4,808	4,959	4,488
Per common share data (b)						
Diluted earnings per share (c) (d) (e)	$ 2.45	1.98	1.59	.97	.65	.92
Cash dividend declared	$ .40	.36	.33	.32	.30	.28
Other data						
Weighted average common shares outstanding (b)	441.3	440.0	436.1	433.3	431.0	429.6
Diluted average common shares outstanding (b)	465.7	467.3	463.7	460.9	458.3	457.4
Capital expenditures	$ 1,918	1,657	1,354	1,301	1,522	1,095
Number of stores: Target	912	851	796	736	670	611
Mervyn's	267	268	269	300	295	286
Department Stores	64	63	65	65	64	63
Total stores	1,243	1,182	1,130	1,101	1,029	960
Total retail square footage (thousands)	138,640	130,172	123,058	117,989	109,091	101,163
Number of employees	281,000	256,000	230,000	218,000	214,000	194,000

(a) Consisted of 53 weeks.

(b) Earnings per share, dividends per share and common shares outstanding reflect our 1998 two-for-one common share split and our 1996 three-for-one common share split.

(c) Extraordinary charges, net of tax, related to the purchase and redemption of debt were $41 million ($.09 per share) in 1999, $27 million ($.06 per share) in 1998, $51 million ($.11 per share) in 1997 and $11 million ($.02 per share) in 1996.

(d) 1999 includes a mainframe outsourcing pre-tax charge of $5 million ($.01 per share). 1998 included a mainframe outsourcing pre-tax charge of $42 million ($.06 per share) and the beneficial effect of $20 million ($.04 per share) of the favorable outcome of our inventory shortage tax matter. 1996 included a real estate repositioning pre-tax charge of $134 million ($.18 per share).

(e) 1998 included a $3 million pre-tax net loss (less than $.01 per share) related to securitization maturity and sale transactions. 1997 included a $45 million pre-tax gain ($.06 per share) related to securitization sale transactions.

The Summary Financial and Operating Data should be read in conjunction with the Notes to Consolidated Financial Statements throughout pages 24-37.

Business Segment Comparisons
(millions)

	1999	1998	1997	1996	1995*	1994
Revenues						
Target	$26,080	$23,014	$20,298	$17,810	$15,752	$13,574
Mervyn's	4,099	4,150	4,219	4,350	4,491	4,565
Department Stores	3,074	3,064	2,970	2,932	2,991	2,954
Other	449	434	–	–	–	–
Total revenues	$33,702	$30,662	$27,487	$25,092	$23,234	$21,093
Pre-tax segment profit and earnings reconciliation						
Target	$ 2,022	$ 1,578	$ 1,287	$ 1,048	$ 721	$ 732
Mervyn's	205	240	280	272	117	198
Department Stores	296	279	240	151	192	259
Total pre-tax segment profit	$ 2,523	$ 2,097	$ 1,807	$ 1,471	$ 1,030	$ 1,189
LIFO provision credit/(expense)	7	18	(6)	(9)	(17)	19
Securitization adjustments:						
Gain/(loss)	–	(3)	45	–	–	–
Interest equivalent	(49)	(48)	(33)	(25)	(10)	–
Interest expense	(393)	(398)	(416)	(442)	(442)	(426)
Mainframe outsourcing	(5)	(42)	–	–	–	–
Real estate repositioning	–	–	–	(134)	–	–
Other	(147)	(68)	(71)	(78)	(60)	(68)
Earnings before income taxes and extraordinary charges	$ 1,936	$ 1,556	$ 1,326	$ 783	$ 501	$ 714
Assets						
Target	$12,048	$10,475	$ 9,487	$ 8,257	$ 7,330	$ 6,247
Mervyn's	2,248	2,339	2,281	2,658	2,776	2,917
Department Stores	2,149	2,123	2,188	2,296	2,309	2,392
Other	698	729	235	178	155	141
Total assets	$17,143	$15,666	$14,191	$13,389	$12,570	$11,697
Depreciation and amortization						
Target	$ 567	$ 496	$ 437	$ 377	$ 328	$ 294
Mervyn's	138	138	126	151	150	145
Department Stores	133	135	128	119	113	108
Other	16	11	2	3	3	1
Total depreciation and amortization	$ 854	$ 780	$ 693	$ 650	$ 594	$ 548
Capital expenditures						
Target	$ 1,665	$ 1,352	$ 1,155	$ 1,048	$ 1,067	$ 842
Mervyn's	108	169	72	79	273	146
Department Stores	124	127	124	173	161	96
Other	21	9	3	1	21	11
Total capital expenditures	$ 1,918	$ 1,657	$ 1,354	$ 1,301	$ 1,522	$ 1,095
Segment EBITDA						
Target	$ 2,589	$ 2,074	$ 1,724	$ 1,425	$ 1,049	$ 1,026
Mervyn's	343	378	406	423	267	343
Department Stores	429	414	368	270	305	367
Total segment EBITDA	$ 3,361	$ 2,866	$ 2,498	$ 2,118	$ 1,621	$ 1,736
Net assets**						
Target	$ 8,413	$ 7,302	$ 6,602	$ 5,711	$ 5,109	$ 4,269
Mervyn's	1,908	2,017	2,019	2,268	2,484	2,363
Department Stores	1,795	1,785	1,896	1,879	1,940	1,812
Other	428	514	169	53	96	72
Total net assets	$12,544	$11,618	$10,686	$ 9,911	$ 9,629	$ 8,516

Each operating segment's assets and operating results include the retained securitized receivables held by Target Receivables Corporation and Retailers National Bank, as well as related income and expense.

*Consisted of 53 weeks

** Net assets represent total assets (including sold securitized receivables) less non-interest bearing current liabilities.

Report of Independent Auditors

Board of Directors and Shareholders

Target Corporation

We have audited the accompanying consolidated statements of financial position of Target Corporation and subsidiaries as of January 29, 2000 and January 30, 1999 and the related consolidated results of operations, cash flows and shareholders' investment for each of the three years in the period ended January 29, 2000. These financial statements are the responsibility of the Corporation's management. Our responsibility is to express an opinion on these financial statements based on our audits.

We conducted our audits in accordance with auditing standards generally accepted in the United States. Those standards require that we plan and perform the audit to obtain reasonable assurance about whether the financial statements are free of material misstatement. An audit includes examining, on a test basis, evidence supporting the amounts and disclosures in the financial statements. An audit also includes assessing the accounting principles used and significant estimates made by management, as well as evaluating the overall financial statement presentation. We believe that our audits provide a reasonable basis for our opinion.

In our opinion, the financial statements referred to above present fairly, in all material respects, the consolidated financial position of Target Corporation and subsidiaries at January 29, 2000 and January 30, 1999 and the consolidated results of their operations and their cash flows for each of the three years in the period ended January 29, 2000 in conformity with accounting principles generally accepted in the United States.

Minneapolis, Minnesota

February 28, 2000

Ernst & Young LLP

Report of Management

Management is responsible for the consistency, integrity and presentation of the information in the Annual Report. The consolidated financial statements and other information presented in this Annual Report have been prepared in accordance with accounting principles generally accepted in the United States and include necessary judgments and estimates by management.

To fulfill our responsibility, we maintain comprehensive systems of internal control designed to provide reasonable assurance that assets are safeguarded and transactions are executed in accordance with established procedures. The concept of reasonable assurance is based upon a recognition that the cost of the controls should not exceed the benefit derived. We believe our systems of internal control provide this reasonable assurance.

The Board of Directors exercises its oversight role with respect to the Corporation's systems of internal control primarily through its Audit Committee, which is comprised of five independent directors. The Committee oversees the Corporation's systems of internal control, accounting practices, financial reporting and audits to assess whether their quality, integrity and objectivity are sufficient to protect shareholders' investments. The Committee's report appears on this page.

In addition, our consolidated financial statements have been audited by Ernst & Young LLP, independent auditors, whose report also appears on this page. As a part of its audit, Ernst & Young LLP develops and maintains an understanding of the Corporation's internal accounting controls and conducts such tests and employs such procedures as it considers necessary to render its opinion on the consolidated financial statements. Their report expresses an opinion as to the fair presentation, in all material respects, of the consolidated financial statements and is based on independent audits made in accordance with auditing standards generally accepted in the United States.

Robert J. Ulrich
Chairman of the Board and
Chief Executive Officer
February 28, 2000

Douglas A. Scovanner
Executive Vice President and
Chief Financial Officer

Report of Audit Committee

The Audit Committee met two times during fiscal 1999 to review the overall audit scope, plans for internal and independent audits, the Corporation's systems of internal control, emerging accounting issues, officer and director expenses, audit fees and retirement plans. The Committee also met individually with the independent auditors, without management present, to discuss the results of their audits. The Committee encourages the internal and independent auditors to communicate closely with the Committee.

Audit Committee results were reported to the full Board of Directors and the Corporation's annual financial statements were reviewed and approved by the Board of Directors before issuance. The Audit Committee also recommended to the Board of Directors that the independent auditors be reappointed for fiscal 2000, subject to the approval of the shareholders at the annual meeting.

February 28, 2000

Directors

Livio D. DeSimone
Chairman and
Chief Executive Officer,
3M
(diversified manufacturer)
(1) (5) (6)

Roger A. Enrico
Chairman and
Chief Executive Officer,
PepsiCo, Inc.
(domestic and international
beverage and food company)
(1) (2) (3)

William W. George
Chairman and
Chief Executive Officer,
Medtronic, Inc.
(therapeutic medical device
company) (1) (2) (4)

Michele J. Hooper
President and
Chief Executive Officer,
Voyager Expanded Learning
(educational development
company) (1) (2) (6)

James A. Johnson
Chairman and
Chief Executive Officer,
Johnson Capital Partners
(private investment
company) (1) (3) (4) (5)

Richard M. Kovacevich
President and
Chief Executive Officer,
Wells Fargo & Company
(banking and financial
services company) (1) (2) (6)

Susan A. McLaughlin
President, Consumer
Services, BellSouth
Telecommunications, Inc.
(communications services
company) (1) (2) (4)

Anne M. Mulcahy
Executive Vice President and
President,
General Markets Operations,
Xerox Corporation
(document management
company) (1) (4) (5)

Stephen W. Sanger
Chairman and
Chief Executive Officer,
General Mills, Inc.
(consumer food products
company) (1) (3) (5) (6)

George W. Tamke
Former Vice Chairman and
Co-Chief Executive Officer,
Emerson Electric Co.
(industrial manufacturer) (1)

Solomon D. Trujillo
Chairman, President and
Chief Executive Officer,
US WEST, Inc.
(telecommunications
company) (1) (3) (4) (5)

Robert J. Ulrich
Chairman and
Chief Executive Officer,
Target Corporation and
Target Stores (1)

(1) *Executive Committee*
(2) *Audit Committee*
(3) *Compensation Committee*
(4) *Corporate Responsibility
Committee*
(5) *Finance Committee*
(6) *Nominating Committee*

Officers

Robert J. Ulrich*
Chairman and
Chief Executive Officer,
Target Corporation and
Target Stores

Kenneth B. Woodrow*
Vice Chairman,
Target Corporation

Linda L. Ahlers*
President, Dayton's
Marshall Field's and Hudson's

Bart Butzer*
President, Mervyn's

Gregg W. Steinhafel*
President, Target Stores

Gerald L. Storch*
President, Financial Services
and New Businesses,
Target Corporation

Larry V. Gilpin*
Executive Vice President,
Team, Guest and
Community Relations,
Target Corporation and
Target Stores

James T. Hale*
Executive Vice President,
General Counsel and
Corporate Secretary,
Target Corporation

John E. Pellegrene*
Executive Vice President,
Marketing,
Target Corporation and
Target Stores

Douglas A. Scovanner*
Executive Vice President,
Finance and
Chief Financial Officer,
Target Corporation and
Target Stores

Ertugrul Tuzcu*
Executive Vice President,
Store Operations,
Dayton's Marshall Field's and
Hudson's

Todd V. Blackwell*
Senior Vice President, Stores,
Mervyn's

John D. Griffith*
Senior Vice President,
Property Development,
Target Corporation

Maureen W. Kyer*
Senior Vice President,
Merchandising, Mervyn's

Paul L. Singer*
Senior Vice President,
Technology Services and
Chief Information Officer,
Target Corporation

Gail J. Dorn
Vice President,
Communications and
Community Relations,
Target Corporation

Nate K. Garvis
Vice President,
Government Affairs,
Target Corporation

Susan D. Kahn
Vice President,
Investor Relations,
Target Corporation

Stephen C. Kowalke
Vice President and Treasurer,
Target Corporation

Jane P. Windmeier
Vice President, Finance,
Target Corporation and
Target Stores

Richard J. Kuzmich
President and
Chief Executive Officer,
Associated Merchandising Corp.

Dale Nitschke
President, target.direct

Erica C. Street
President, Target Brands, Inc.

Jack N. Reif
Assistant Treasurer,
Target Corporation

Sara J. Ross
Assistant Treasurer,
Target Corporation

*Executive Officer and Corporate
Operating Committee Member*

A-41

Annual Meeting

The Annual Meeting of Shareholders is scheduled for May 17, 2000, at 9:30 a.m. CDT at The Children's Theatre, 2400 Third Avenue South, Minneapolis, Minnesota.

Shareholder Information

Quarterly and annual shareholder information, including the Form 10-Q and Form 10-K Annual Report, which are filed with the Securities and Exchange Commission, is available at no charge to shareholders. To obtain copies of these materials, you may call 612-370-6736, send an email to InvestorRelations@target.com, or write to:

Vice President, Investor Relations

Target Corporation

777 Nicollet Mall

Minneapolis, MN 55402

Our quarterly earnings release conference calls are webcast on the Internet through our website www.targetcorp.com. For additional information call investor relations at 612-370-6736.

Other information about Target Corporation is available at the same website.

Sales Information

Comments regarding the company's sales results are provided periodically throughout the year on a recorded telephone message. You may access this message by calling 612-370-6500.

Direct Stock Purchase/Dividend Reinvestment Plan

First Chicago Trust Company of New York administers a direct service investment plan that allows interested investors to purchase Target Corporation stock directly, rather than through a broker, and become a registered shareholder of the Company. The program offers many features including dividend reinvestment. For detailed information regarding this program, call First Chicago Trust toll free at 888-268-0203, or write to:

The DirectSERVICE Investment Program

c/o First Chicago Trust Company

P.O. Box 2598

Jersey City, NJ 07303-2598

Transfer Agent, Registrar and Dividend Disbursing Agent

First Chicago Trust Company of New York, a division of Equiserve

Trustee, Employee Savings 401(k) and Pension Plans

State Street Bank and Trust Company

Stock Exchange Listings

Trading symbol TGT

New York Stock Exchange and Pacific Exchange

Shareholder Assistance

For assistance regarding individual stock records, lost certificates, name or address changes, dividend or tax questions, call First Chicago Trust at 800-317-4445, or write to:

First Chicago Trust Company of New York

P.O. Box 2500

Jersey City, NJ 07303-2500.

Taking big steps, growing in size, moving forward.

Typical Charts of Accounts for Different Types of Businesses

(FOR BUSINESSES DISCUSSED IN CHAPTERS 1–12)

Service Proprietorship

Assets	**Liabilities**	**Owner's Equity**
Cash	Accounts Payable	Owner, Capital
Accounts Receivable	Notes Payable, Short-Term	Owner, Withdrawals
Allowance for Uncollectible Accounts	Salary Payable	**Revenues and Gains**
Notes Receivable, Short-Term	Wage Payable	Service Revenue
Interest Receivable	Employee Income Tax Payable	Interest Revenue
Supplies	FICA Tax Payable	Gain on Sale of Land (or Furniture, Equipment, or Building)
Prepaid Rent	State Unemployment Tax Payable	
Prepaid Insurance	Federal Unemployment Tax Payable	**Expenses and Losses**
Notes Receivable, Long-Term	Employee Benefits Payable	Salary Expense
Land	Interest Payable	Payroll Tax Expense
Furniture	Unearned Service Revenue	Insurance Expense for Employees
Accumulated Depreciation—Furniture	Notes Payable, Long-Term	Rent Expense
Equipment		Insurance Expense
Accumulated Depreciation—Equipment		Supplies Expense
Building		Uncollectible Account Expense
Accumulated Depreciation—Building		Depreciation Expense—Furniture
		Depreciation Expense—Equipment
		Depreciation Expense—Building
		Property Tax Expense
		Interest Expense
		Miscellaneous Expense
		Loss on Sale (or Exchange) of Land (Furniture, Equipment, or Building)

Service Partnership

Same as Service Proprietorship, except for Owners' Equity:

Owners' Equity

Partner 1, Capital
Partner 2, Capital
Partner N, Capital

Partner 1, Drawing
Partner 2, Drawing
Partner N, Drawing

Merchandising Corporation

Assets	Liabilities	Stockholders' Equity
Cash	Accounts Payable	Preferred Stock
Short-Term Investments (Trading Securities)	Notes Payable, Short-Term	Paid-in Capital in Excess of Par—Preferred
Accounts Receivable	Current Portion of Bonds Payable	Common Stock
Allowance for Uncollectible Accounts	Salary Payable	Paid-in Capital in Excess of Par—Common
Notes Receivable, Short-Term	Wage Payable	Paid-in Capital from Treasury Stock Transactions
Interest Receivable	Employee Income Tax Payable	Paid-in Capital from Retirement of Stock
Inventory	FICA Tax Payable	Retained Earnings
Supplies	State Unemployment Tax Payable	Foreign Currency Translation Adjustment
Prepaid Rent	Federal Unemployment Tax Payable	Treasury Stock
Prepaid Insurance	Employee Benefits Payable	
Notes Receivable, Long-Term	Interest Payable	
Investments in Subsidiaries	Income Tax Payable	
Investments in Stock (Available-for-Sale Securities)	Unearned Sales Revenue	
Investments in Bonds (Held-to-Maturity Securities)	Notes Payable, Long-Term	
Other Receivables, Long-Term	Bonds Payable	
Land	Lease Liability	
Land Improvements	Minority Interest	
Furniture and Fixtures		
Accumulated Depreciation—Furniture and Fixtures		
Equipment		
Accumulated Depreciation—Equipment		
Buildings		
Accumulated Depreciation—Buildings		
Organization Cost		
Franchises		
Patents		
Leaseholds		
Goodwill		

Expenses and Losses

Cost of Goods Sold
Salary Expense
Wage Expense
Commission Expense
Payroll Tax Expense
Insurance Expense for Employees
Rent Expense
Insurance Expense
Supplies Expense
Uncollectible Account Expense
Depreciation Expense—Land Improvements
Depreciation Expense—Furniture and Fixtures
Depreciation Expense—Equipment
Depreciation Expense—Buildings
Organization Expense
Amortization Expense—Franchises
Amortization Expense—Leaseholds
Amortization Expense—Goodwill
Income Tax Expense
Unrealized Holding Loss on Trading Investments
Loss on Sale of Investments
Loss on Sale (or Exchange) of Land (Furniture and Fixtures, Equipment, or Buildings)
Discontinued Operations—Loss
Extraordinary Losses

Revenues and Gains

Sales Revenue
Interest Revenue
Dividend Revenue
Equity-Method Investment Revenue
Unrealized Holding Gain on Trading Investments
Gain on Sale of Investments
Gain on Sale of Land (Furniture and Fixtures, Equipment, or Buildings)
Discontinued Operations—Gain
Extraordinary Gains

Manufacturing Corporation

Same as Merchandising Corporation, except for
Assets and Expenses:

Assets	Expenses (Contra Expenses If Credit Balance)
Inventories:	Direct Materials Price Variance
Materials Inventory	Direct Materials Efficiency Variance
Work in Process Inventory	Direct Labor Price Variance
Finished Goods Inventory	Direct Labor Efficiency Variance
	Manufacturing Overhead Flexible Budget Variance
	Manufacturing Overhead Production Volume Variance

APPENDIX C

Present-Value Tables and Future-Value Tables

This appendix provides present value tables and future-value tables (more complete than those in the Chapter 15 appendix and in Chapter 26).

EXHIBIT C-1

Present Value of $1

					Present Value						
Periods	1%	2%	3%	4%	5%	6%	7%	8%	9%	10%	12%
1	0.990	0.980	0.971	0.962	0.952	0.943	0.935	0.926	0.917	0.909	0.893
2	0.980	0.961	0.943	0.925	0.907	0.890	0.873	0.857	0.842	0.826	0.797
3	0.971	0.942	0.915	0.889	0.864	0.840	0.816	0.794	0.772	0.751	0.712
4	0.961	0.924	0.888	0.855	0.823	0.792	0.763	0.735	0.708	0.683	0.636
5	0.951	0.906	0.883	0.822	0.784	0.747	0.713	0.681	0.650	0.621	0.567
6	0.942	0.888	0.837	0.790	0.746	0.705	0.666	0.630	0.596	0.564	0.507
7	0.933	0.871	0.813	0.760	0.711	0.665	0.623	0.583	0.547	0.513	0.452
8	0.923	0.853	0.789	0.731	0.677	0.627	0.582	0.540	0.502	0.467	0.404
9	0.914	0.837	0.766	0.703	0.645	0.592	0.544	0.500	0.460	0.424	0.361
10	0.905	0.820	0.744	0.676	0.614	0.558	0.508	0.463	0.422	0.386	0.322
11	0.896	0.804	0.722	0.650	0.585	0.527	0.475	0.429	0.388	0.350	0.287
12	0.887	0.788	0.701	0.625	0.557	0.497	0.444	0.397	0.356	0.319	0.257
13	0.879	0.773	0.681	0.601	0.530	0.469	0.415	0.368	0.326	0.290	0.229
14	0.870	0.758	0.661	0.577	0.505	0.442	0.388	0.340	0.299	0.263	0.205
15	0.861	0.743	0.642	0.555	0.481	0.417	0.362	0.315	0.275	0.239	0.183
16	0.853	0.728	0.623	0.534	0.458	0.394	0.339	0.292	0.252	0.218	0.163
17	0.844	0.714	0.605	0.513	0.436	0.371	0.317	0.270	0.231	0.198	0.146
18	0.836	0.700	0.587	0.494	0.416	0.350	0.296	0.250	0.212	0.180	0.130
19	0.828	0.686	0.570	0.475	0.396	0.331	0.277	0.232	0.194	0.164	0.116
20	0.820	0.673	0.554	0.456	0.377	0.312	0.258	0.215	0.178	0.149	0.104
21	0.811	0.660	0.538	0.439	0.359	0.294	0.242	0.199	0.164	0.135	0.093
22	0.803	0.647	0.522	0.422	0.342	0.278	0.226	0.184	0.150	0.123	0.083
23	0.795	0.634	0.507	0.406	0.326	0.262	0.211	0.170	0.138	0.112	0.074
24	0.788	0.622	0.492	0.390	0.310	0.247	0.197	0.158	0.126	0.102	0.066
25	0.780	0.610	0.478	0.375	0.295	0.233	0.184	0.146	0.116	0.092	0.059
26	0.772	0.598	0.464	0.361	0.281	0.220	0.172	0.135	0.106	0.084	0.053
27	0.764	0.586	0.450	0.347	0.268	0.207	0.161	0.125	0.098	0.076	0.047
28	0.757	0.574	0.437	0.333	0.255	0.196	0.150	0.116	0.090	0.069	0.042
29	0.749	0.563	0.424	0.321	0.243	0.185	0.141	0.107	0.082	0.063	0.037
30	0.742	0.552	0.412	0.308	0.231	0.174	0.131	0.099	0.075	0.057	0.033
40	0.672	0.453	0.307	0.208	0.142	0.097	0.067	0.046	0.032	0.022	0.011
50	0.608	0.372	0.228	0.141	0.087	0.054	0.034	0.021	0.013	0.009	0.003

EXHIBIT C-1
(cont'd)

Present Value

14%	15%	16%	18%	20%	25%	30%	35%	40%	45%	50%	Periods
0.877	0.870	0.862	0.847	0.833	0.800	0.769	0.741	0.714	0.690	0.667	1
0.769	0.756	0.743	0.718	0.694	0.640	0.592	0.549	0.510	0.476	0.444	2
0.675	0.658	0.641	0.609	0.579	0.512	0.455	0.406	0.364	0.328	0.296	3
0.592	0.572	0.552	0.516	0.482	0.410	0.350	0.301	0.260	0.226	0.198	4
0.519	0.497	0.476	0.437	0.402	0.328	0.269	0.223	0.186	0.156	0.132	5
0.456	0.432	0.410	0.370	0.335	0.262	0.207	0.165	0.133	0.108	0.088	6
0.400	0.376	0.354	0.314	0.279	0.210	0.159	0.122	0.095	0.074	0.059	7
0.351	0.327	0.305	0.266	0.233	0.168	0.123	0.091	0.068	0.051	0.039	8
0.308	0.284	0.263	0.225	0.194	0.134	0.094	0.067	0.048	0.035	0.026	9
0.270	0.247	0.227	0.191	0.162	0.107	0.073	0.050	0.035	0.024	0.017	10
0.237	0.215	0.195	0.162	0.135	0.086	0.056	0.037	0.025	0.017	0.012	11
0.208	0.187	0.168	0.137	0.112	0.069	0.043	0.027	0.018	0.012	0.008	12
0.182	0.163	0.145	0.116	0.093	0.055	0.033	0.020	0.013	0.008	0.005	13
0.160	0.141	0.125	0.099	0.078	0.044	0.025	0.015	0.009	0.006	0.003	14
0.140	0.123	0.108	0.084	0.065	0.035	0.020	0.011	0.006	0.004	0.002	15
0.123	0.107	0.093	0.071	0.054	0.028	0.015	0.008	0.005	0.003	0.002	16
0.108	0.093	0.080	0.060	0.045	0.023	0.012	0.006	0.003	0.002	0.001	17
0.095	0.081	0.069	0.051	0.038	0.018	0.009	0.005	0.002	0.001	0.001	18
0.083	0.070	0.060	0.043	0.031	0.014	0.007	0.003	0.002	0.001		19
0.073	0.061	0.051	0.037	0.026	0.012	0.005	0.002	0.001	0.001		20
0.064	0.053	0.044	0.031	0.022	0.009	0.004	0.002	0.001			21
0.056	0.046	0.038	0.026	0.018	0.007	0.003	0.001	0.001			22
0.049	0.040	0.033	0.022	0.015	0.006	0.002	0.001				23
0.043	0.035	0.028	0.019	0.013	0.005	0.002	0.001				24
0.038	0.030	0.024	0.016	0.010	0.004	0.001	0.001				25
0.033	0.026	0.021	0.014	0.009	0.003	0.001					26
0.029	0.023	0.018	0.011	0.007	0.002	0.001					27
0.026	0.020	0.016	0.010	0.006	0.002	0.001					28
0.022	0.017	0.014	0.008	0.005	0.002						29
0.020	0.015	0.012	0.007	0.004	0.001						30
0.005	0.004	0.003	0.001	0.001							40
0.001	0.001	0.001									50

EXHIBIT C-2
Present Value of Annuity of $1

Present Value

Periods	1%	2%	3%	4%	5%	6%	7%	8%	9%	10%	12%
1	0.990	0.980	0.971	0.962	0.952	0.943	0.935	0.926	0.917	0.909	0.893
2	1.970	1.942	1.913	1.886	1.859	1.833	1.808	1.783	1.759	1.736	1.690
3	2.941	2.884	2.829	2.775	2.723	2.673	2.624	2.577	2.531	2.487	2.402
4	3.902	3.808	3.717	3.630	3.546	3.465	3.387	3.312	3.240	3.170	3.037
5	4.853	4.713	4.580	4.452	4.329	4.212	4.100	3.993	3.890	3.791	3.605
6	5.795	5.601	5.417	5.242	5.076	4.917	4.767	4.623	4.486	4.355	4.111
7	6.728	6.472	6.230	6.002	5.786	5.582	5.389	5.206	5.033	4.868	4.564
8	7.652	7.325	7.020	6.733	6.463	6.210	5.971	5.747	5.535	5.335	4.968
9	8.566	8.162	7.786	7.435	7.108	6.802	6.515	6.247	5.995	5.759	5.328
10	9.471	8.983	8.530	8.111	7.722	7.360	7.024	6.710	6.418	6.145	5.650
11	10.368	9.787	9.253	8.760	8.306	7.887	7.499	7.139	6.805	6.495	5.938
12	11.255	10.575	9.954	9.385	8.863	8.384	7.943	7.536	7.161	6.814	6.194
13	12.134	11.348	10.635	9.986	9.394	8.853	8.358	7.904	7.487	7.103	6.424
14	13.004	12.106	11.296	10.563	9.899	9.295	8.745	8.244	7.786	7.367	6.628
15	13.865	12.849	11.938	11.118	10.380	9.712	9.108	8.559	8.061	7.606	6.811
16	14.718	13.578	12.561	11.652	10.838	10.106	9.447	8.851	8.313	7.824	6.974
17	15.562	14.292	13.166	12.166	11.274	10.477	9.763	9.122	8.544	8.022	7.120
18	16.398	14.992	13.754	12.659	11.690	10.828	10.059	9.372	8.756	8.201	7.250
19	17.226	15.678	14.324	13.134	12.085	11.158	10.336	9.604	8.950	8.365	7.366
20	18.046	16.351	14.878	13.590	12.462	11.470	10.594	9.818	9.129	8.514	7.469
21	18.857	17.011	15.415	14.029	12.821	11.764	10.836	10.017	9.292	8.649	7.562
22	19.660	17.658	15.937	14.451	13.163	12.042	11.061	10.201	9.442	8.772	7.645
23	20.456	18.292	16.444	14.857	13.489	12.303	11.272	10.371	9.580	8.883	7.718
24	21.243	18.914	16.936	15.247	13.799	12.550	11.469	10.529	9.707	8.985	7.784
25	22.023	19.523	17.413	15.622	14.094	12.783	11.654	10.675	9.823	9.077	7.843
26	22.795	20.121	17.877	15.983	14.375	13.003	11.826	10.810	9.929	9.161	7.896
27	23.560	20.707	18.327	16.330	14.643	13.211	11.987	10.935	10.027	9.237	7.943
28	24.316	21.281	18.764	16.663	14.898	13.406	12.137	11.051	10.116	9.307	7.984
29	25.066	21.844	19.189	16.984	15.141	13.591	12.278	11.158	10.198	9.370	8.022
30	25.808	22.396	19.600	17.292	15.373	13.765	12.409	11.258	10.274	9.427	8.055
40	32.835	27.355	23.115	19.793	17.159	15.046	13.332	11.925	10.757	9.779	8.244
50	39.196	31.424	25.730	21.482	18.256	15.762	13.801	12.234	10.962	9.915	8.305

EXHIBIT C-2
(cont'd)

Present Value

14%	15%	16%	18%	20%	25%	30%	35%	40%	45%	50%	Periods
0.877	0.870	0.862	0.847	0.833	0.800	0.769	0.741	0.714	0.690	0.667	1
1.647	1.626	1.605	1.566	1.528	1.440	1.361	1.289	1.224	1.165	1.111	2
2.322	2.283	2.246	2.174	2.106	1.952	1.816	1.696	1.589	1.493	1.407	3
2.914	2.855	2.798	2.690	2.589	2.362	2.166	1.997	1.849	1.720	1.605	4
3.433	3.352	3.274	3.127	2.991	2.689	2.436	2.220	2.035	1.876	1.737	5
3.889	3.784	3.685	3.498	3.326	2.951	2.643	2.385	2.168	1.983	1.824	6
4.288	4.160	4.039	3.812	3.605	3.161	2.802	2.508	2.263	2.057	1.883	7
4.639	4.487	4.344	4.078	3.837	3.329	2.925	2.598	2.331	2.109	1.922	8
4.946	4.772	4.607	4.303	4.031	3.463	3.019	2.665	2.379	2.144	1.948	9
5.216	5.019	4.833	4.494	4.192	3.571	3.092	2.715	2.414	2.168	1.965	10
5.553	5.234	5.029	4.656	4.327	3.656	3.147	2.752	2.438	2.185	1.977	11
5.660	5.421	5.197	4.793	4.439	3.725	3.190	2.779	2.456	2.197	1.985	12
5.842	5.583	5.342	4.910	4.533	3.780	3.223	2.799	2.469	2.204	1.990	13
6.002	5.724	5.468	5.008	4.611	3.824	3.249	2.814	2.478	2.210	1.993	14
6.142	5.847	5.575	5.092	4.675	3.859	3.268	2.825	2.484	2.214	1.995	15
6.265	5.954	5.669	5.162	4.730	3.887	3.283	2.834	2.489	2.216	1.997	16
6.373	6.047	5.749	5.222	4.775	3.910	3.295	2.840	2.492	2.218	1.998	17
6.467	6.128	5.818	5.273	4.812	3.928	3.304	2.844	2.494	2.219	1.999	18
6.550	6.198	5.877	5.316	4.844	3.942	3.311	2.848	2.496	2.220	1.999	19
6.623	6.259	5.929	5.353	4.870	3.954	3.316	2.850	2.497	2.221	1.999	20
6.687	6.312	5.973	5.384	4.891	3.963	3.320	2.852	2.498	2.221	2.000	21
6.743	6.359	6.011	5.410	4.909	3.970	3.323	2.853	2.498	2.222	2.000	22
6.792	6.399	6.044	5.432	4.925	3.976	3.325	2.854	2.499	2.222	2.000	23
6.835	6.434	6.073	5.451	4.937	3.981	3.327	2.855	2.499	2.222	2.000	24
6.873	6.464	6.097	5.467	4.948	3.985	3.329	2.856	2.499	2.222	2.000	25
6.906	6.491	6.118	5.480	4.956	3.988	3.330	2.856	2.500	2.222	2.000	26
6.935	6.514	6.136	5.492	4.964	3.990	3.331	2.856	2.500	2.222	2.000	27
6.961	6.534	6.152	5.502	4.970	3.992	3.331	2.857	2.500	2.222	2.000	28
6.983	6.551	6.166	5.510	4.975	3.994	3.332	2.857	2.500	2.222	2.000	29
7.003	6.566	6.177	5.517	4.979	3.995	3.332	2.857	2.500	2.222	2.000	30
7.105	6.642	6.234	5.548	4.997	3.999	3.333	2.857	2.500	2.222	2.000	40
7.133	6.661	6.246	5.554	4.999	4.000	3.333	2.857	2.500	2.222	2.000	50

EXHIBIT C-3
Future Value of $1

Future Value

Periods	1%	2%	3%	4%	5%	6%	7%	8%	9%	10%	12%	14%	15%
1	1.010	1.020	1.030	1.040	1.050	1.060	1.070	1.080	1.090	1.100	1.120	1.140	1.150
2	1.020	1.040	1.061	1.082	1.103	1.124	1.145	1.166	1.188	1.210	1.254	1.300	1.323
3	1.030	1.061	1.093	1.125	1.158	1.191	1.225	1.260	1.295	1.331	1.405	1.482	1.521
4	1.041	1.082	1.126	1.170	1.216	1.262	1.311	1.360	1.412	1.464	1.574	1.689	1.749
5	1.051	1.104	1.159	1.217	1.276	1.338	1.403	1.469	1.539	1.611	1.762	1.925	2.011
6	1.062	1.126	1.194	1.265	1.340	1.419	1.501	1.587	1.677	1.772	1.974	2.195	2.313
7	1.072	1.149	1.230	1.316	1.407	1.504	1.606	1.714	1.828	1.949	2.211	2.502	2.660
8	1.083	1.172	1.267	1.369	1.477	1.594	1.718	1.851	1.993	2.144	2.476	2.853	3.059
9	1.094	1.195	1.305	1.423	1.551	1.689	1.838	1.999	2.172	2.358	2.773	3.252	3.518
10	1.105	1.219	1.344	1.480	1.629	1.791	1.967	2.159	2.367	2.594	3.106	3.707	4.046
11	1.116	1.243	1.384	1.539	1.710	1.898	2.105	2.332	2.580	2.853	3.479	4.226	4.652
12	1.127	1.268	1.426	1.601	1.796	2.012	2.252	2.518	2.813	3.138	3.896	4.818	5.350
13	1.138	1.294	1.469	1.665	1.886	2.133	2.410	2.720	3.066	3.452	4.363	5.492	6.153
14	1.149	1.319	1.513	1.732	1.980	2.261	2.579	2.937	3.342	3.798	4.887	6.261	7.076
15	1.161	1.346	1.558	1.801	2.079	2.397	2.759	3.172	3.642	4.177	5.474	7.138	8.137
16	1.173	1.373	1.605	1.873	2.183	2.540	2.952	3.426	3.970	4.595	6.130	8.137	9.358
17	1.184	1.400	1.653	1.948	2.292	2.693	3.159	3.700	4.328	5.054	6.866	9.276	10.76
18	1.196	1.428	1.702	2.026	2.407	2.854	3.380	3.996	4.717	5.560	7.690	10.58	12.38
19	1.208	1.457	1.754	2.107	2.527	3.026	3.617	4.316	5.142	6.116	8.613	12.06	14.23
20	1.220	1.486	1.806	2.191	2.653	3.207	3.870	4.661	5.604	6.728	9.646	13.74	16.37
21	1.232	1.516	1.860	2.279	2.786	3.400	4.141	5.034	6.109	7.400	10.80	15.67	18.82
22	1.245	1.546	1.916	2.370	2.925	3.604	4.430	5.437	6.659	8.140	12.10	17.86	21.64
23	1.257	1.577	1.974	2.465	3.072	3.820	4.741	5.871	7.258	8.954	13.55	20.36	24.89
24	1.270	1.608	2.033	2.563	3.225	4.049	5.072	6.341	7.911	9.850	15.18	23.21	28.63
25	1.282	1.641	2.094	2.666	3.386	4.292	5.427	6.848	8.623	10.83	17.00	26.46	32.92
26	1.295	1.673	2.157	2.772	3.556	4.549	5.807	7.396	9.399	11.92	19.04	30.17	37.86
27	1.308	1.707	2.221	2.883	3.733	4.822	6.214	7.988	10.25	13.11	21.32	34.39	43.54
28	1.321	1.741	2.288	2.999	3.920	5.112	6.649	8.627	11.17	14.42	23.88	39.20	50.07
29	1.335	1.776	2.357	3.119	4.116	5.418	7.114	9.317	12.17	15.86	26.75	44.69	57.58
30	1.348	1.811	2.427	3.243	4.322	5.743	7.612	10.06	13.27	17.45	29.96	50.95	66.21
40	1.489	2.208	3.262	4.801	7.040	10.29	14.97	21.72	31.41	45.26	93.05	188.9	267.9
50	1.645	2.692	4.384	7.107	11.47	18.42	29.46	46.90	74.36	117.4	289.0	700.2	1,084

EXHIBIT C-4
Future Value of Annuity $1

Future Value

Periods	1%	2%	3%	4%	5%	6%	7%	8%	9%	10%	12%	14%	15%
1	1.000	1.000	1.000	1.000	1.000	1.000	1.000	1.000	1.000	1.000	1.000	1.000	1.000
2	2.010	2.020	2.030	2.040	2.050	2.060	2.070	2.080	2.090	2.100	2.120	2.140	2.150
3	3.030	3.060	3.091	3.122	3.153	3.184	3.215	3.246	3.278	3.310	3.374	3.440	3.473
4	4.060	4.122	4.184	4.246	4.310	4.375	4.440	4.506	4.573	4.641	4.779	4.921	4.993
5	5.101	5.204	5.309	5.416	5.526	5.637	5.751	5.867	5.985	6.105	6.353	6.610	6.742
6	6.152	6.308	6.468	6.633	6.802	6.975	7.153	7.336	7.523	7.716	8.115	8.536	8.754
7	7.214	7.434	7.662	7.898	8.142	8.394	8.654	8.923	9.200	9.487	10.09	10.73	11.07
8	8.286	8.583	8.892	9.214	9.549	9.897	10.26	10.64	11.03	11.44	12.30	13.23	13.73
9	9.369	9.755	10.16	10.58	11.03	11.49	11.98	12.49	13.02	13.58	14.78	16.09	16.79
10	10.46	10.95	11.46	12.01	12.58	13.18	13.82	14.49	15.19	15.94	17.55	19.34	20.30
11	11.57	12.17	12.81	13.49	14.21	14.97	15.78	16.65	17.56	18.53	20.65	23.04	24.35
12	12.68	13.41	14.19	15.03	15.92	16.87	17.89	18.98	20.14	21.38	24.13	27.27	29.00
13	13.81	14.68	15.62	16.63	17.71	18.88	20.14	21.50	22.95	24.52	28.03	32.09	34.35
14	14.95	15.97	17.09	18.29	19.60	21.02	22.55	24.21	26.02	27.98	32.39	37.58	40.50
15	16.10	17.29	18.60	20.02	21.58	23.28	25.13	27.15	29.36	31.77	37.28	43.84	47.58
16	17.26	18.64	20.16	21.82	23.66	25.67	27.89	30.32	33.00	35.95	42.75	50.98	55.72
17	18.43	20.01	21.76	23.70	25.84	28.21	30.84	33.75	36.97	40.54	48.88	59.12	65.08
18	19.61	21.41	23.41	25.65	28.13	30.91	34.00	37.45	41.30	45.60	55.75	68.39	75.84
19	20.81	22.84	25.12	27.67	30.54	33.76	37.38	41.45	46.02	51.16	63.44	78.97	88.21
20	22.02	24.30	26.87	29.78	33.07	36.79	41.00	45.76	51.16	57.28	72.05	91.02	102.4
21	23.24	25.78	28.68	31.97	35.72	39.99	44.87	50.42	56.76	64.00	81.70	104.8	118.8
22	24.47	27.30	30.54	34.25	38.51	43.39	49.01	55.46	62.87	71.40	92.50	120.4	137.6
23	25.72	28.85	32.45	36.62	41.43	47.00	53.44	60.89	69.53	79.54	104.6	138.3	159.3
24	26.97	30.42	34.43	39.08	44.50	50.82	58.18	66.76	76.79	88.50	118.2	158.7	184.2
25	28.24	32.03	36.46	41.65	47.73	54.86	63.25	73.11	84.70	98.35	133.3	181.9	212.8
26	29.53	33.67	38.55	44.31	51.11	59.16	68.68	79.95	93.32	109.2	150.3	208.3	245.7
27	30.82	35.34	40.71	47.08	54.67	63.71	74.48	87.35	102.7	121.1	169.4	238.5	283.6
28	32.13	37.05	42.93	49.97	58.40	68.53	80.70	95.34	113.0	134.2	190.7	272.9	327.1
29	33.45	38.79	45.22	52.97	62.32	73.64	87.35	104.0	124.1	148.6	214.6	312.1	377.2
30	34.78	40.57	47.58	56.08	66.44	79.06	94.46	113.3	136.3	164.5	241.3	356.8	434.7
40	48.89	60.40	75.40	95.03	120.8	154.8	199.6	259.1	337.9	442.6	767.1	1,342	1,779
50	64.46	84.58	112.8	152.7	209.3	290.3	406.5	573.8	815.1	1,164	2,400	4,995	7,218

APPENDIX D

Check Figures

Check Figures—Chapter 1

DE1-1	No check figure
DE1-2	No check figure
DE1-3	No check figure
DE1-4	Capital $2,000
DE1-5	Capital $10,000
DE1-6	No check figure
DE1-7	Capital $33,500
DE1-8	No check figure
DE1-9	Capital $30,000
DE1-10	Net inc. $5,400
	Capital $35,400
DE1-11	No check figure
DE1-12	No check figure
DE1-13	1. Net inc. $4,100
	2. Capital $32,000
DE1-14	No check figure
DE1-15	Net inc. $50,000
DE1-16	Capital, 12/31/X3 $27,000
DE1-17	Total assets $35,000
DE1-18	No check figure
E1-1	No check figure
E1-2	No check figure
E1-3	No check figure
E1-4	C: $1,900
E1-5	OE increased by $737 mil.
E1-6	1. Net inc. $18,000
	3. Net loss $12,000
E1-7	No check figure
E1-8	Total assets $94,800
E1-9	2. Net inc. $5,400
1-10	2. Capital $14,200
E1-11	1. Net inc. $76,200
	2. Capital $27,100
E1-12	1. Net loss for 19X9 $132 mil.
E1-13	Cash bal., end of year $21 mil.
E1-14	Circle $25,000
	Triangle $185,000
	Square $170,000
P1-1A	Total assets $90,000
P1-2A	Total assets $68,000
P1-3A	Total assets $160,000
P1-4A	No check figure
P1-5A	1. Net inc. $64,000
	3. Total assets $279,000
P1-6A	2. Net inc. $2,100
	4. Total assets $30,750
P1-1B	Total assets $105,100
P1-2B	Total assets $61,000
P1-3B	Total assets $95,000
P1-4B	No check figure
P1-5B	1. Net inc. $47,000
	3. Total assets $102,000
P1-6B	2. Net inc. $4,240
	4. Total assets $40,920
Case 1	No check figure
Case 2	No check figure
Financial Statement Case	3. Stockholders' equity $5,862 mil.
	4. Rev. increased by $3,040 mil.

Check Figures—Chapter 2

DE2-1	1. $3,000
DE2-2	No check figure
DE2-3	No check figure
DE2-4	No check figure
DE2-5	No check figure
DE2-6	No check figure
DE2-7	No check figure
DE2-8	No check figure
DE2-9	No check figure
DE2-10	3. $1,500
DE2-11	3. a. $5,000
	b. $5,000
DE2-12	Trial bal. total $40,000
DE2-13	Trial bal. total $66 bil.
DE2-14	Incorrect trial bal. total assets $24,200
DE2-15	No check figure
DE2-16	Total debits $145,000
E2-1	No check figure
E2-2	2. Net inc. $2 bil.
E2-3	No check figure
E2-4	Total debits $183,600
E2-5	No check figure
E2-6	Trial bal. total $59,700
E2-7	Trial bal. total $37,850
E2-8	No check figure
E2-9	Trial bal. total $69,400
E2-10	Trial bal. total $124,100
E2-11	Trial bal. total $76,100
E2-12	Cash bal. $1,700
E2-13	Trial bal. total $19,700
E2-14	Total debits $78,000
E2-15	4. Trial bal. total $20,400
E2-16	b. $66,000
	c. $74,000
	d. $2,500
E2-17	No check figure
P2-1A	No check figure
P2-2A	No check figure
P2-3A	3. Trial bal. total $50,300
P2-4A	3. Trial bal. total $41,600
P2-5A	1. Trial bal. total $70,500
	2. Net inc. $6,370
P2-6A	3. Trial bal. total $103,600
P2-7A	1. Net inc. $2,800
	3. Total assets $92,200
P2-1B	No check figure
P2-2B	No check figure
P2-3B	3. Trial bal. total $55,500
P2-4B	3. Trial bal. total $53,500
P2-5B	1. Trial bal. total $65,100
	2. Net inc. $10,140
P2-6B	3. Trial bal. total $66,200
P2-7B	1. Net inc. $400
	3. Total assets $59,900
Case 1	No check figure
Case 2	3. Trial bal. total $22,800
	4. Net inc. $5,550
Financial Statement Case	No check figure

Check Figures—Chapter 3

DE3-1	No check figure
DE3-2	No check figure
DE3-3	Revenue $750,000
DE3-4	Expense $280,000
DE3-5	1. $55 mil.
DE3-6	1. Salary Expense for 2000 $9 mil.
DE3-7	1. Prepaid Rent $2,750
	Rent Expense $250
DE3-8	3. $34,500
DE3-9	3. Interest Payable Nov. 30 $200
DE3-10	3. Interest Receivable Nov. 30 $200
DE3-11	No check figure
DE3-12	No check figure
DE3-13	No check figure
DE3-14	No check figure
DE3-15	1. Assets $47,250
	Liabilities $13,550
DE3-16	1. Net inc. $5,650
E3-1	No check figure
E3-2	No check figure
E3-3	No check figure
E3-4	A: Insur. Exp. $1,600
E3-5	No check figure
E3-6	Net income overstated by $4,300
E3-7	No check figure
E3-8	Service Rev. $5,550
E3-9	Adj. trial bal. total $55,090
E3-10	No check figure
E3-11	Net inc. $7,150
	Total assets $29,100
E3-12	Net inc. $74,500
E3-13	1. End. capital $191,000
E3-14	7. net inc. $1,690
	Total assets $18,790
E3-15	Revenue $8,500
E3-16	Cash collected $4,400
P3-1A	2. Net inc. $750
P3-2A	No check figure
P3-3A	c. Art Supplies Exp. $6,360
	f. Insurance Exp. $2,700
P3-4A	No check figure
P3-5A	3. Adj. trial bal. total $62,500
P3-6A	1. Net inc. $78,470
	Total assets $129,030
P3-7A	2. Net inc. $6,950
	Total assets $44,550
P3-1B	2. Net inc. $683
P3-2B	No check figure
P3-3B	a. Rent Exp. $2,400
	d. Supplies Exp. $6,710
P3-4B	No check figure
P3-5B	3. Adj. trial bal. total $50,080
P3-6B	1. Net inc. $42,030
	Total assets $58,810

P3-7B	2. Net inc. $7,500
	Total assets $46,200
Case 1	Your highest price $127,000
Case 2	No check figure
Financial Statement Case	No check figure
E3A-1	Supplies $860
E3A-2	Unearned Service Rev. $3,700
P3A-1	Prepaid Rent $2,250
	Unearned Service Rev. $2,400

Check Figures—Chapter 4

DE4-1	No check figure
DE4-2	No check figure
DE4-3	No check figure
DE4-4	No check figure
DE4-5	No check figure
DE4-6	1. d. Close $3,525
	3. a. $31,575
DE4-7	1. $31,575
DE4-8	No check figure
DE4-9	No check figure
DE4-10	Trial bal. total $7,260 mil.
DE4-11	No check figure
DE4-12	c. $5,266 mil.
	d. $13,378 mil.
	e. $6,882 mil.
DE4-13	1. $1.79
	2. 49%
	3. 51%
DE4-14	1. Current ratio 2.07
	Debt ratio 0.31
E4-1	Net inc. $2,330
E4-2	No check figure
E4-3	End. bal. Gail Pfeiffer, Capital $36,360
E4-4	Trial bal. total $42,340
E4-5	No check figure
E4-6	Liu Hyundai, Capital $50,900
E4-7	2. Felix Rohr, Capital $175,700
E4-8	Matthew Knowles, Capital Dec. 31, 20X2 $465,000
E4-9	2. Net inc. $12,400
E4-10	1. Total assets $52,700
E4-11	2. Total assets $18,790
	Amos Faraday, Capital $14,090
E4-12	Net inc. $53,100
P4-1A	Net inc. $16,300
P4-2A	2. Net inc. $87,630
	Total assets $240,680
P4-3A	2. Net inc. $90,000
	Total assets $131,000
P4-4A	Trial bal. total $153,000
P4-5A	3. Net inc. $26,000
	Total assets $104,320
	5. Trial bal. total $146,220
P4-6A	1. Total assets $114,600
	2. Debt ratio 0.41
P4-7A	c. Overall, net inc. understated by $1,060
P4-1B	Net inc. $15,000
P4-2B	2. Net inc. $30,000
	Total assets $175,860
P4-3B	2. Net inc. $87,000
	Total assets $134,000
P4-4B	2. Trial bal. total $151,000
P4-5B	3. Net inc. $12,090

	Total assets $101,080
	5. Trial bal. total $117,410
P4-6B	1. Total assets $108,200
	2. Debt ratio 0.40
P4-7B	c. Overall, net inc. understated by $2,520
Case 1	1. Net inc. $55,440
	2. Total assets $58,390
Case 2	No check figure
Financial Statement Case	3. Debt ratio at 2/29/00 0.66
	5. Cost of plant assets $13,824 mil.
Team Project	Net inc. $1,500
	Total assets $1,640
P4A-1	No check figure

Check Figures—Chapter 5

DE5-1	No check figure
DE5-2	No check figure
DE5-3	No check figure
DE5-4	No check figure
DE5-5	a. $130,000
	b. $126,100
DE5-6	c. Credit cash for $126,100
DE5-7	Net cost $137,200
DE5-8	Gross profit $55,200
DE5-9	c. Debit Cash for $36,260
DE5-10	b. $321,240
DE5-11	No check figure
DE5-12	No check figure
DE5-13	Net inc. $1,666 mil.
DE5-14	Total assets $11,471 mil.
DE5-15	C. Ernest, Capital bal. $25,650
DE5-16	No check figure
DE5-17	Gross profit % 20.7%
	Invy. turnover 56.4 times
DE5-18	b. Excess of collections over payments $641 mil.
DE5-19	COGS $23,029 mil.
DE5-20	3. F150,000
DE5-21	Purchases $7,181 mil.
E5-1	2. Gross profit for 2000 $3,541 mil.
E5-2	Sept. 23 Debit Cash for $2,254
E5-3	May 22 Credit Cash for $469.54
E5-4	June 14 Credit Cash for $7,054
E5-5	May 14 Debit Cash for $6,984
E5-6	Owner Capital bal. at 12/31/00 $10,805
E5-7	Net inc. $74,860
E5-8	Net inc. $74,860
E5-9	20X2 Gross profit % 51%; Invy. turnover 3.72 times
E5-10	1. Net inc. $31,300
E5-11	Net inc. $31,300
E5-12	Excess of collections over payments $29 bil.
E5-13	COGS $99,300
E5-14	(e) $16,200 (f) $37,400
	(i) $112,100
E5-15	$180 mil.
E5-16	3. Net inc. $4,900
P5-1A	No check figure
P5-2A	No check figure
P5-3A	No check figure
P5-4A	Net inc. $49,890
P5-5A	2. $66,260
P5-6A	1. Net inc. $55,600
	2. Total assets $200,100

P5-7A	1. Net inc. $55,600
	2. Total assets $200,100
P5-8A	1. Net inc. $58,710
	2. 20X4 Gross profit % 60%
	Invy. turnover 2.03 times
P5-9A	2. Gross profit % 32%
	3. Invy. turnover 3.2 times
P5-1B	No check figure
P5-2B	No check figure
P5-3B	No check figure
P5-4B	Net inc. $31,370
P5-5B	2. $58,190
P5-6B	1. Net inc. $7,900
	2. Total assets $371,700
P5-7B	1. Net inc. $7,900
	2. Total assets $371,700
P5-8B	1. Net inc. $38,760
	2. 2000 Gross profit % 56%
	Invy. turnover 8.9 times
P5-9B	2. Gross profit % 48%
	3. Invy. turnover 3.63 times
Case 1	2. Net inc. $78,380
	Total assets $104,590
Case 2	No check figure
Financial Statement Case	
	2. $1,144 mil. closed to R/E
	3. Gross profit % 30.7%
	Invy. turnover 6.3 times
E5A-1	June 23 Debit Cash for $2,352
E5A-2	May 22 Credit Cash for $469.54
E5A-3	June 14 Credit Cash for $7,054
E5A-4	May 14 Debit Cash for $6,984
P5A-1	Hillcrest: Nov. 27 Credit Cash for $2,600
P5A-2	No check figure
P5A-3	No check figure
P5A-4	1. Net inc. $88,850
	2. Total assets $218,110
	4. Ben Latham, Capital bal. $195,590

Check Figures—Chapter 6

DE6-1	No check figure
DE6-2	No check figure
DE6-3	No check figure
DE6-4	No check figure
DE6-5	No check figure
DE6-6	No check figure
DE6-7	No check figure
DE6-8	No check figure
DE6-9	4. Decrease in Accts. Rec. $1,235
DE6-10	2. $2,876
	3. Payments $798
DE6-11	2. Net Purchases $3,885
DE6-12	4. Net sales revenue $7,456
E6-1	No check figure
E6-2	No check figure
E6-3	No check figure
E6-4	No check figure
E6-5	Total Debit to cash $5,987.60
E6-6	No check figure
E6-7	No check figure
E6-8	Purchases journal: Total credit to Accts. Pay. $21,216
E6-9	3. Total Accts.Pay. $3,042
E6-10	3. Total credit to Cash $14,897
E6-11	No check figure
E6-12	1. Gross profit $3,935
P6-1A	No check figure

P6-2A	1. Cash receipts journal: Total debit to Cash $36,619	
P6-3A	No check figure	
P6-4A	2. Cash pay. journal: Total credit to Cash $17,237	
P6-5A	6. Total Accts. Rec. $496 Total Accts. Pay. $2,692	
P6-1B	No check figure	
P6-2B	1. Cash recpts. journal: Total debit to Cash $58,650	
P6-3B	No check figure	
P6-4B	2. Cash pay. journal: Total credit to Cash $15,571	
P6-5B	6. Total Accts. Rec. $567 Total Accts. Pay. $2,925	
Case 1	No check figure	
Case 2	Sales journal: Total $16,198 Cash recpts. journal: Total debit to Cash $7,774	

Check Figures—Chapter 7

DE7-1	No check figure
DE7-2	No check figure
DE7-3	No check figure
DE7-4	No check figure
DE7-5	No check figure
DE7-6	No check figure
DE7-7	No check figure
DE7-8	No check figure
DE7-9	No check figure
DE7-10	Adj. bal. $2,570
DE7-11	No check figure
DE7-12	No check figure
DE7-13	Employee stole $980
DE7-14	No check figure
DE7-15	No check figure
DE7-16	No check figure
DE7-17	No check figure
DE7-18	3. $400
DE7-19	1. New financing needed $165 mil.
DE7-20	New financing needed $10 mil.
DE7-21	No check figure
E7-1	No check figure
E7-2	No check figure
E7-3	No check figure
E7-4	No check figure
E7-5	No check figure
E7-6	No check figure
E7-7	Adj. bal. $1,891
E7-8	Adj. bal. $4,071
E7-9	No check figure
E7-10	No check figure
E7-11	No check figure
E7-12	Apr. 10 Credit Cash for $181
E7-13	1. Credit Cash for $211.13
E7-14	New financing needed $19 mil.
E7-15	No check figure
E7-16	1. New financing needed $433 mil. 2. Current ratio after borrowing 1.30
P7-1A	No check figure 1. Adj. bal. $10,670
P7-2A	No check figure
P7-3A	1. Adj. bal. $10,670
P7-4A	1. Adj. bal. $20.948.77
P7-5A	No check figure
P7-6A	Apr. 30 Credit Cash in Bank for $382.64

P7-7A	New financing needed $1,300
P7-8A	1. Cash available for additional investments $727 mil.
P7-9A	No check figure
P7-1B	No check figure
P7-2B	No check figure
P7-3B	1. Adj. bal. $6,657
P7-4B	1. Adj. bal. $3,635.33
P7-5B	No check figure
P7-6B	June 30 Credit Cash in Bank for $307.63
P7-7B	New financing needed $3,300
P7-8B	1. New financing needed $76 mil.
P7-9B	No check figure
Case 1	Cashier stole $900
Case 2	No check figure
Financial Statement Case	5. Cash decreased by $35 mil.

Check Figures—Chapter 8

DE8-1	No check figure
DE8-2	No check figure
DE8-3	No check figure
DE8-4	No check figure
DE8-5	A/R, net $78,000
DE8-6	4. Uncollect. Acct. Exp. $14,400
DE8-7	3. A/R, net $173,600
DE8-8	Allowance for U/A end. bal. $4,000
DE8-9	Debit Uncollect. Acct. Exp. $4,900
DE8-10	No check figure
DE8-11	A/R bal., June 30 $5,500
DE8-12	Debit Cash $7,840
DE8-13	5. Pay at maturity $1,090
DE8-14	Note 1 $150 Note 4 $375
DE8-15	a. Credit Cash $400,000 b. Debit Cash $408,000
DE8-16	c. Debit Cash $1,090
DE8-17	a. Note rec. $1,000 Interest rec. $22.50 d. Interest rev. $67.50
DE8-18	Net realizable value: Intel $3,700 mil. Oracle $2,238 mil.
DE8-19	1. Net inc. $1,184 mil. 2. A/R, net $2,464 mil.
DE8-20	a. 1.17 b. 48 days
DE8-21	1. 1.73 c. 0.59 d. 3.20
E8-1	No check figure
E8-2	No check figure
E8-3	2&3. A/R, net $53,000
E8-4	2. A/R $55,930
E8-5	2. A/R, net $288,004
E8-6	Debit Uncollect. Acct.Exp.: a. $2,250; B. $4,300
E8-7	1. Interest for: 20X7 $60,000 20X8 $90,000 20X9 $30,000
E8-8	Dec. 31 Debit Interest Rec. $719
E8-9	Apr. 1, 20X4 Debit Cash $8,960
E8-10	Dec. 31 Debit Cash $5,490
E8-11	1. 20X3 0.80 2. 37 days
E8-12	1. 2 days
E8-13	Net inc.: Without bankcards

	$75,000; With bankcards $93,960
P8-1A	No check figure
P8-2A	Uncollected. Acct. Exp.: 1. $3,500 2. $8,900
P8-3A	3. A/R, net: 20X4 $247,017 20X3 $263,160
P8-4A	3. A/R, net $160,301
P8-5A	1. Note 1 $11,330 Note 2 $15,250 Note 3 $13,080
P8-6A	No check figure
P8-7A	Dec. 31, 20X1 Uncollect. Acct. Exp. $9,700
P8-8A	1. Ratios for 20X3: a. 1.71; b. 0.60; c. 20 days
P8-1B	No check figure
P8-2B	Uncollect. Acct. Exp. 1. $8,900 2. $12,800
P8-3B	3. A/R, net: 20X1 $132,684 20X0 $115,300
P8-4B	3. A/R, net $135,865
P8-5B	1. Note 1 $12,720 Note 2 $9,075 Note 3 $14,170
P8-6B	No check figure
P8-7B	Dec. 31, 20X1 Uncollect. Acct. Exp. $7,500
P8-8B	1. Ratios for 20X3: a. 1.85; b. 0.95; c. 18 days
Case 1	1. Net inc.: 20X3 $106,600 20X2 $85,550
Case 2	A/R bal. $90,000 Note Rec. bal. $5,000
Financial Statement Case 3.	Acid-test ratio 0.35
DE8A-1	Proceeds $498,200
E8A-1A	June 30 Debit Cash $498,200
E8A-2A	Dec. 1 Debit Interest Exp. $300
P8A-1	2. Note 1 $9,994; Note 2 $6,023; Note 3 $8,007
P8A-2	2. Note 1 $6,111; Note 2 $8,965; Note 3 $8,129

Check Figures—Chapter 9

DE9-1	Inventory $24,000 Gross profit $64,000
DE9-2	2. Gross profit $360,000
DE9-3	Gross profit $60,500
DE9-4	No check figure
DE9-5	No check figure
DE9-6	No check figure
DE9-7	COGS: wtd-avg. $750 LIFO $800
DE9-8	COGS: wtd-avg. $9,422 LIFO $9,800
DE9-9	Net inc.: wtd-avg. $1,978; LIFO $1,600
DE9-10	Inc. tax Exp.: wtd-avg. $791; LIFO $640
DE9-11	No check figure
DE9-12	2. Gross profit $765
DE9-13	Inventory $550 COGS $1,325

DE9-14	b. COGS $67.5 mil. d. Net loss $(0.1) mil.	P9-8B	1. Est. cost of end. invy. $467 thou.	P10-5A	3. Cost of assets sold $15,098,000
DE9-15	3. Correct net inc. Last yr. $8.3 mil.; This yr. $5 mil.	P9-9B	1. Net inc. $48 mil. 2. Total assets $456 mil.	P10-6A	Part 1. 3. Amortiz. of goodwill $57,450; Part 2. 2 Net inc. $119,150
DE9-16	No check figure	Case 1	Net inc.: FIFO with and without purchase $240,700; LIFO without purchase $205,900; with purchase $183,425	P10-7A	1. Book value $21.4 bil. 2. Gain on sale $0.2 bil. 3. Owners' equity $12.4 bil. 4. Net loss $0.9 bil.
DE9-17	1. & 2. End. invy. $150,000				
E9-1	2. Gross profit $1,574 thou.				
E9-2	2. Gross profit $1,574 thou.				
E9-3	Purchase $8,800 mil.				
E9-4	COGS: wtd-avg. $3,320 LIFO $3,368	Case 2	No check figure	P10-1B	2. Depr.-Land improve. $2,306; Sales bldg. $16,481; Garage $1,280; Furniture $9,114
E9-5	b. COGS $3,270	Financial Statement Case	Purchases $23,352 mil.		
E9-6	c. COGS $3,368			P10-2B	Dec. 31 Depr.-Motor-Carrier Equip. $51,000; Buildings $733
E9-7	LIFO tax saving $29				
E9-8	a. $64,800; d. $30,200 f. $34,700			P10-3B	No check figure
E9-9	Magnolia gross profit % 55.9%; Invy. T/O 3.9 times			P10-4B	3. Net inc. advantage of SL $30,840; Cash flow advantage of DDB $20,560

Check Figures—Chapter 10

E9-10	COGS $724; End. invy. $664	DE10-1	3. Book value $10,227 mil.
E9-11	Net inc. for cell B21 $75,000; cell C21 $68,000	DE10-2	No check figure
		DE10-3	No check figure
E9-12	No check figure	DE10-4	2. Bal. $872,000
E9-13	No check figure	DE10-5	Land $50,000; Building $37,500 Equipment $12,500
E9-14	Gross profit $110,567		
E9-15	Gross profit $62,900 Inventory $19,800	DE10-6	No check figure
		DE10-7	2. Book value—SL $30,000,000; DDB $21,600,000
E9-16	Net inc.: 20X2 $41,100 20X1 $27,300	DE10-8	b. Depr. $7,500,000 c. Depr. $-0-
E9-17	Est. cost of invy. destroyed $49,100	DE10-9	2. Tax saved $3,360,000
E9-18	No check figure	DE10-10	b. Depr. $4,800,000 c. Depr. $10,800,000
E9-19	1. Net inc. $724 mil. 2. Total assets $5,522 mil.	DE10-11	Depr. $10,000
P9-1A	3. Net inc. $320	DE10-12	1. a. Loss on Sale $2,000 b. Gain on Sale $8,240
P9-2A	2. Net inc. $110 thou.		
P9-3A	3. Gross profit $1,494	DE10-13	2. Depletion $4.5 bil. 3. Book value $2.0 bil.
P9-4A	1. COGS: wtd-avg. $55,707 FIFO $54,516 LIFO $56,908	DE10-14	1. Goodwill $310,000 3. Amort. exp. $7,750
P9-5A	1. Gross profit: wtd-avg. $2,267 FIFO $2,502 LIFO $2,089	DE10-15	2. Book value $311 mil. 3. Goodwill purchased $15 mil.
		DE10-16	1. Net loss $75,000
		E10-1	Land $206,900 Land improve. $67,400
P9-6A	No check figure	E10-2	1. Cost $654,000
P9-7A	1. Correct net inc.: 20X3 $11 thou. 20X2 $9 thou. 20X1 $27 thou.	E10-3	Saddle 1 $2,580 Saddle 2 $4,150 Saddle 3 $3,270
		E10-4	No check figure
		E10-5	No check figure
P9-8A	1. Est. cost of end. invy. $845 thou.	E10-6	20X4 Depr.: SL $3,000; UOP $2,400; DDB $375
P9-9A	1. Net inc. $1,127 mil. 2. Total assets $5,189 mil.	E10-7	Extra cash to invest with DDB $38,388
P9-1B	3. Net inc. $520	E10-8	Depr. Yr. 16 $21,458
P9-2B	2. Net inc. $75 thou.	E10-9	Gain on Sale $960
P9-3B	3. Gross profit $3,205	E10-10	Cost of new truck $338,175
P9-4B	1. COGS: wtd-avg. $12,445 FIFO $12,167 LIFO $12,758	E10-11	Depletion $75,600
		E10-12	Part 2. Amortiz. $342,500
		E10-13	Payment for other assets $63 mil.
P9-5B	1. Gross profit: wtd-avg. $62,810 FIFO $63,355 LIFO $62,030	E10-14	3. Amortiz. of goodwill $700,000
		E10-15	Yr. 5 equip., net Correct Net inc. 0.9 over
P9-6B	No check figure	E10-16	1. Acquisitions $2,559 mil.
P9-7B	1. Correct net inc.: 20X2 $61 thou. 20X1 $59 thou. 20X0 $15 thou.	P10-1A	2. Depr.-Land improve. $3,893; Office bldg. $30,621; Garage $2,057; Furniture $11,681
		P10-2A	Dec. 31 Depr.-Commun. Equip. $19,200; Televideo Equip. $2,133; Office Equip. $10,000
		P10-3A	No check figure
		P10-4A	3. Net inc. advantage of SL $8,420; Cash flow advantage of DDB $5,613

P10-5B	3. Cost of assets sold $11,213 mil.
P10-6B	Part 1. 3. Amortiz. of goodwill $105,000; Part 2. 2. Net inc. $15,750
P10-7B	1. Book value $4.0 bil. 2. Gain on sale $0.2 bil. 3. Owners' Equity $8.4 bil. 4. Net inc. $2.5 bil.
Case 1	1. Net inc.-Astoria $149,700; Hilton $112,400
Case 2	No check figure
Financial Statement Case	4. Loss on Sale $165 mil.

Check Figures—Chapter 11

DE11-1	No check figure
DE11-2	c. Credit Cash $8,800
DE11-3	2. Interest Exp. $400
DE11-4	3. Note pay. $99,500
DE11-5	2. Air Traffic Liab. $1,200
DE11-6	2. Est. Warranty Pay. $8,000
DE11-7	No check figure
DE11-8	No check figure
DE11-9	No check figure
DE11-10	2. Net pay $684.75
DE11-11	Total exp. $1,008.65
DE11-12	No check figure
DE11-13	Net pay $5,960
DE11-14	No check figure
DE11-15	No check figure
DE11-16	Total payroll exp. $28,805.50
DE11-17	No check figure
DE11-18	Total current liab. $84,202
DE11-19	No check figure
E11-1	No check figure
E11-2	1. Accrued Payroll Liab. $27,194
E11-3	Unearned subscription rev. $80
E11-4	2. Est. Warranty Pay. $3,970
E11-5	Apr. 1, 20X3 Credit Cash $16,200
E11-6	2. Note pay., short-term $11,840
E11-7	No check figure
E11-8	Pay off $30,000
E11-9	Net pay $7,598.70
E11-10	a. Net pay $275.50
E11-11	Payroll Tax Exp. $7,636.20
E11-12	Salary Exp. $900,000 Salary pay. $4,000
E11-13	20X1: Current portion of LT debt $1,000,000; Interest pay. $450,000
E11-14	Total current liab. $125,340

E11-15	1. Current ratio 0.85		E12-1	No check figure	DE13-3	No check figure
	2. Current ratio 0.79		E12-2	Credit Flute, Cap. $82,100	DE13-4	No check figure

E11-15　1. Current ratio 0.85
　　　　2. Current ratio 0.79
E11-16　1. Payments $627 mil.
　　　　2. Salary exp. $3,193 mil.
P11-1A　No check figure
P11-2A　No check figure
P11-3A　1. b. $7,518
　　　　c. $23,949
　　　　e. $1,998
　　　　j. $13,299
P11-4A　1. Net pay $58,222
　　　　2. Total cost $89,632
P11-5A　3. Total liab. $339,312
P11-6A　3. Credit Cash $2,178
　　　　4. Debit Payroll Tax Exp. $127
P11-7A　No check figure
P11-1B　No check figure
P11-2B　No check figure
P11-3B　1. a. $78,584
　　　　c. $83,693
　　　　f. $2,162
　　　　k. $24,484
P11-4B　1. Net pay $48,780
　　　　2. Total cost $79,153
P11-5B　3. Total liab. $202,727
P11-6B　3. Credit Cash $2,033
　　　　4. Debit Payroll Tax Exp. $177
P11-7B　No check figure
Case 1　No check figure
Case 2　No check figure
Financial Statement Case　No check figure

Check Figures—Chapter 12

DE12-1　No check figure
DE12-2　No check figure
DE12-3　Debit Building $285,000
DE12-4　3. Total equity $32 mil.
DE12-5　2. Benz, Cap. $462,500
　　　　Hanna, Cap. $97,500
DE12-6　2. Benz, Cap. $494,000
　　　　Hanna, Cap. $76,000
DE12-7　Lawson $48,000; Martinez
　　　　$32,000; Edwards $60,000
DE12-8　Fung $27,150
　　　　Kiawa $22,850
DE12-9　No check figure
DE12-10　No check figure
DE12-11　Credit Kliptel, Cap. $40,000;
　　　　Nagasawa, Cap. $5,000; Osburn,
　　　　Cap. $5,000
DE12-12　Nagasawa, Cap. $75,000
　　　　Osburn, Cap. $85,000
　　　　Kliptel, Cap. $40,000
DE12-13　Debit Page, Cap. $10,667;
　　　　Franco, Cap. $5,333; Credit
　　　　Everett, Cap. $156,000
DE12-14　No check figure
DE12-15　a. Credit Green, Cap. $23,750;
　　　　Henry, Cap. $47,500; Isaac, Cap.
　　　　$23,750
DE12-16　Debit Henry, Cap. $90,500;
　　　　Credit Green, Cap. $15,000;
　　　　Isaac, Cap. $15,000
DE12-17　Pay Avignon $31,000; Bloch
　　　　$17,000; Crane $7,000
DE12-18　No check figure
DE12-19　Green, Cap. $66,000
　　　　Henry, Cap. $67,000
DE12-20　Net inc.: Frost $70,000; Martin
　　　　$35,000

E12-1　No check figure
E12-2　Credit Flute, Cap. $82,100
E12-3　d. Net inc.: Meppen $34,818;
　　　Quaid $63,182
E12-4　Partnership capital decreased
　　　$2,000
E12-5　c. Falco, Cap. $52,500; Graham,
　　　Cap. $103,750
　　　Ott, Cap. $53,750
E12-6　c. Credit Falco, Cap. $52,500;
　　　Graham, Cap. $3,750; Ott, Cap.
　　　$3,750
E12-7　1. Echols receives $45,000;
　　　2. Schaeffer's equity $50,000
E12-8　b. Debit Bermuda, Cap. $46,000
E12-9　2. Barry gets $20,000; McCall
　　　gets $17,000; Flaten gets $8,000
E12-10　Pay Deluth $24,800;
　　　　Liu $18,600; Bush $14,600
E12-11　Selling for $90,000—Valahu,
　　　　Cap. $3,000; Leman, Cap.
　　　　$20,800; Sucre, Cap. $(4,800)
E12-12　Total assets $276,200
　　　　Klatt, Cap. $90,700
　　　　Stover, Cap. $93,100
P12-1A　No check figure
P12-2A　2. Total assets $122,020
　　　　Saran, Cap. $49,860
　　　　Gentry, Cap. $49,860
P12-3A　Lampe's Cap.:
　　　　2. $50,000
　　　　3. $31,250
　　　　4. $41,400
P12-4A　1. d. Net inc. to:
　　　　Trump $33,667
　　　　Rivers $28,667
　　　　Jetta $23,666
P12-5A　No check figure
P12-6A　1. b. Pay: Jackson $20,700;
　　　　Pierce $52,800; Fenner $11,500
P12-7A　3. Pay: Alberts $8,875; Beech
　　　　$8,625; Sumner $11,500
P12-8A　No check figure
P12-9A　2. Total assets $100,000
　　　　Busby, Cap. $40,450
　　　　Box, Cap. $40,450
P12-3B　Conyers' Cap.:
　　　　2. $60,000
　　　　3. $95,000
　　　　4. $42,000
P12-4B　1. d. Net inc. to:
　　　　Lake $79,750
　　　　Wood $63,500
　　　　Parks $66,750
P12-5B　No check figure
P12-6B　1. b. Pay: Parr $19,700;
　　　　Johnston $35,100; Rake
　　　　$30,200
P12-7B　3. Pay: Vela $12,000;
　　　　Thomas $7,000; Prago $3,000
Case 1　No check figure
Case 2　No check figure
Financial Statement Case
　　　　2. $1,997,323;
　　　　3. Avg. net inc. per Partner
　　　　$372,825

Check Figures—Chapter 13

DE13-1　No check figure
DE13-2　No check figure

DE13-3　No check figure
DE13-4　No check figure
DE13-5　No check figure
DE13-6　No check figure
DE13-7　1. Incr. in paid-in cap. $428 mil.
DE13-8　No check figure
DE13-9　Bldg. $480,000; Equip $220,000;
　　　　Common Stock $100,000; PIC in
　　　　Excess $600,000
DE13-10　Total S/E $183.9 mil.
DE13-11　a. Net inc. $80.6 mil.
　　　　b. Total liab. $122.3 mil.
　　　　c. Total assets $306.2 mil
DE13-12　Total S/E $490,000
DE13-13　R/E incr. $54,000
DE13-14　4. Pfd. gets $6,000
　　　　Com. gets $3,000
DE13-15　No check figure
DE13-16　a. Book value-Pfd.$140;
　　　　b. Book value-Com. $44.44
DE13-17　No check figure
DE13-18　No check figure
DE13-19　ROA 13.6%
　　　　ROE 27.1%
DE13-20　2. Net inc. $72,000
　　　　Inc. tax pay $36,000
　　　　Deferred tax liab. $12,000
E13-1　No check figure
E13-2　2. Total PIC $118,500
E13-3　2. Total S/E $72,000
E13-4　Cap. in Excess of Par $74,850
E13-5　No check figure
E13-6　Total S/E $192,000
E13-7　Total S/E $486,000
E13-8　Total S/E $407,000
E13-9　Pfd. gets $22,000;
　　　Com. gets $38,000
E13-10　Pfd. A gets $40,000;
　　　　Pfd. B gets $962,000;
　　　　Com. gets $98,000
E13-11　Book value-Pdf. $60;
　　　　Com. $22.08
E13-12　Book value-Pfd. $66.84;
　　　　Com. $21.99
E13-13　ROA .091
　　　　ROE .074
E13-14　2. Net inc. $78 mil.
　　　　Inc. tax pay. $40 mil.
　　　　Deferred tax liab. $12 mil.
E13-15　2. Bal. at Jan. 31, 20X0; Com.
　　　　stk. $446 mil.; Cap. in Excess
　　　　$714 mil.; R/E $25, 129 mil.
P13-1A　No check figure
P13-2A　2. Total S/E $308,100
P13-3A　5. Total S/E $413,000
P13-4A　Total S/E: Yurman $510,000;
　　　　No. Lights $623,000
P13-5A　3. Div. Pay., Pfg. $218 mil.; Div.
　　　　Pay., Com $1,408 mil.
P13-6A　1. Total assets $654,000; Total
　　　　S/E $499,000
P13-7A　1. b. 20X2 Pfd. gets $3,500;
　　　　Com. gets $11,500.
P13-8A　5. Book value-Pfd. $27.90; Com.
　　　　$9.73
P13-9A　3. Net inc. $149,500
P13-1B　No check figure
P13-2B　2. Total S/E $273,800

P13-3B	5. Total S/E $272,000
P13-4B	Total S/E; Granada $829,000; Traigon $403,000
P13-5B	3. Div. Pay., Pfd. $18 mil.; Div. Pay., Com. $32 mil.
P13-6B	1. Total assets $417,000 Total S/E $309,000
P13-7B	1. b. 20X2 Pfd. gets $70,000; Com. gets $30,000
P13-8B	6. Book value-Pfd. $54.95; Com. $8.51
P13-9B	3. Net inc. $126,000
Case 1.	3. Total S/E: Plan 1 $435,000; Plan 2 $420,000
Case 2.	No check figure
Financial Statement Case	No check figure

Check Figures—Chapter 14

DE14-1	No check figure
DE14-2	2. Total S/E $360,00
DE14-3	No check figure
DE14-4	1. Total S/E $355,000
DE14-5	1. Total S/E $355,000
DE14-6	No check figure
DE14-7	2. Total S/E $31,600
DE14-8	2. total S/E $36,400
DE14-9	Bal. sheet reports Treasury stk ($6,000)
DE14-10	Total S/E $3,700,000
DE14-11	No check figure
DE14-12	No check figure
DE14-13	No check figure
DE14-14	2. EPS = $(1.43)
DE14-15	Net inc. $22,750
DE14-16	EPS for net inc. $1.98
DE14-17	No check figure
DE14-18	Comprehensive inc. $20,750
DE14-19	R/E Dec. 31, 20X5 $473,000
DE14-20	2. $85,000 4. Sold T/S for $17,000
E14-1	3. Total S/E $434,000
E14-2	2. Total S/E $590,000
E14-3	Total S/E $510,000
E14-4	d. Increase S/E $4,200
E14-5	No check figure
E14-6	Total S/E $770,000
E14-7	b. Total S/E $470,000
E14-8	Net inc. $34,000
E14-9	EPS = $1.38
E14-10	EPS for net inc. $3.51
E14-11	R/E Dec. 31, 20X3 $463.6 mil.
E14-12	R/E Dec. 31, 20X7 $456 mil.
E14-13	Comprehensive inc. $70,000
E14-14	Total S/E, Dec. 31, 20X2 $3,467,000
E14-15	2. Total S/E, Dec. 31, 20X5 $17,100,000
P14-1A	No check figure
P14-2A	2. Total S/E $452,100
P14-3A	No check figure
P14-4A	3. Total S/E $699,680
P14-5A	Net inc. $62,000; EPS for net inc. $2.17
P14-6A	Net inc. $78,200 R/E, Dec. 31, 20X3 $418,200 EPS for net inc. $1.56
P14-7A	1. EPS for net inc. $2.14

P14-8A	1. Par value = $2 2. Price per share = $6.23 4. Stk. Div. % = 4%
P14-1B	No check figure
P14-2B	2. Total S/E $524,000
P14-3B	No check figure
P14-4B	3. Total S/E $555,880
P14-5B	Net inc. $76,400 EPS for net inc. $3.52
P14-6B	Net inc. $101,000 R/E June 30, 20X4 $291,000 EPS for net inc. $5.05
P14-7B	1. EPS for net inc. $2.92
P14-8B	1. Par value = $1.80 2. Price per share - $11 3. Stk. div. % = 9.9%
Case 1.	No check figure
Case 2.	No check figure
Financial Statement Case	No check figure

Check Figures—Chapter 15

DE15-1	b. $615,750 c. $331,125
DE15-2	a. $4,675
DE15-3	No check figure
DE15-4	No check figure
DE15-5	No check figure
DE15-6	Jan 1, 2001 Interest Exp. $54.17
DE15-7	Jan. 1, 2001 Interest Exp. $198
DE15-8	Jan 1, 2001 Interest Exp. $153
DE15-9	Dec. 31, 2000 Interest Exp. $183
DE15-10	LT liab.: Bonds Payable, net $4,620
DE15-11	2. Bond carrying amt., Ending $573,963
DE15-12	2. a. Bonds pay., End of yr. 3 $385,734
DE15-13	2. Bond carrying amt., Ending $215,673
DE15-14	3. EO gain $7,281
DE15-15	2. PIC in Excess of Par $860,000
DE15-16	EPS; Plan A $2.14; Plan B $1.60
DE15-17	No check figure
DE15-18	Total current liab. $99,000
DE15-19	No check figure
E15-1	c. Dec. 31 Interest Exp. $3,375
E15-2	c. Dec. 31 Interest Exp. $19,562
E15-3	Total cash received $1,055,000
E15-4	b. Oct. 31, Interest Exp. $11,667
E15-5	1. Bond carrying amt., Ending $282,522
E15-6	1. Bond carrying amt., Ending $220,171
E15-7	Dec. 31, 20X5 Bond carrying amt. $500,000
E15-8	Oct. 1, 20X5 EO Loss $12,750
E15-9	2. July 21, 20X9 Bond carrying amt. $693,700
E15-10	2. Oct. 1 PIC in Excess of Par $174,000
E15-11	EPS: Plan A $8.15; Plan B $4.37
E15-12	1. LT Notes pay., net $503,000
E15-13	1. Dec. 31 Depreciation Exp. $4,731
E15-14	5. Mar. 31, 2001 Bond carrying amt. $295,717

E15-15	2. a. $295,605; b. $295,661; c. $295,717
P15-1A	2. Apr. 30, 20X5 Interest Exp. $13,333
P15-2A	1. d. May 31, 20X6 Interest Exp. $233,333 2. Interest Exp. For 20X5 $280,000
P15-3A	3. d. Feb. 28, 20X5 Interest Exp. $5,633 4. Interest Exp. for year ended Feb. 28, 20X5 $33,800
P15-4A	2. Sep. 30, Yr 3 Bond carrying amt $166,764
P15-5A	3. Convertible bonds pay., net $423,327
P15-6A	Dec. 31, 20X1 Depreciation Exp. $16,150
P15-7A	No check figure
P15-8A	Total current liab. $45,200 Total LT liab. $379,000
P15-1B	2. Jan. 31, 20X4 Interest Exp. $4,500
P15-2B	1. d. Mar. 31, 20X5 Interest Exp. $67,500 2. Interest exp. for 20X4 $180,000
P15-3B	3. d. Mar. 31, 20X7 Interest Exp. $7,900 4. Interest exp. for year ended Mar. 31, 20X7 $31,600
P15-4B	2. Sep. 30, yr. 3 bond carrying amt. $127,887
P15-5B	3. Convertible bonds pay., net $569,903
P15-6B	Dec. 31, 20X1 Depreciation Exp. $12,918
P15-7B	No check figure
P15-8B	Total current liab. $127,000 Total LT liab. $504,000
Case 1.	EPS: Plan A $6.72; Plan B $6.34; Plan C $6.60
Case 2.	No check figure
Financial Statement Case	No check figure

Check Figures—Chapter 16

DE16-1	a. $17,076 b. $44,914.50
DE16-2	No check figure
DE16-3	No check figure
DE16-4	3. Short-term investment $30,000
DE16-5	2. Jan 27, 20X2 Loss on Sale of Investments $2,260
DE16-6	2. Jan. 16, 20X7 Gain on Sale of Investments $685
DE16-7	20X7 Gain on sale $7,000
DE16-8	2. Loss on sale $100
DE16-9	2. Unrealized loss $411
DE16-10	1. Gain on Sale of Investment $300
DE16-11	3. Long-Term Equity-Method Investment Bal. $102 mil.
DE16-12	Gain on sale $8 mil.
DE16-13	No check figure
DE16-14	No check figure
DE16-15	4. Annual interest rev. $117,000
DE16-16	b. Interest Rev. $105,000; c. Interest Rev. $12,000

DE16-17	Interest Rev. $50 + 10
DE16-18	Overall foreign-currency Loss $1,000
DE16-19	Aug. 24 Foreign-currency Loss $400
DE16-20	No check figure
E16-1	2. Short-term investment $87,000
E16-2	d. Gain or Sale of Investment $1,600
E16-3	Dec. 4 Loss on Sale of Investment $250
E16-4	3. LT avail.-for-sale invest. $365,790; Unrealized loss $18,500
E16-5	No check figure
E16-6	Gain on sale $530,000
E16-7	2. LT Equity-Method Investment Bal. $172,200
E16-8	3. LT invest. In bonds $28,062
E16-9	Dec. 16 FC Loss $60 Dec. 30 FC Gain $1,200
E16-10	1. Cost $266 mil. 2. Loss on sale $7 mil.
E16-11	Dividends received $19 mil.
P16-1A	2. ST investment $130,000
P16-2A	3. LT avail.-for-sale invest. $270,100; LT Equity-method invest. $1,162,000
P16-3A	2. LT Equity-method invest. $936,000; Unrealized loss $3,100
P16-4A	2. LT invest. in bonds $742,902
P16-5A	Investment carrying amt. Dec. 31, 20X2 $388,355
P16-6A	FC loss, net $720
P16-1B	2. ST investment $221,000
P16-2B	3. LT avail.-for-sale invest. $161,200; LT Equity-method invest. $969,500
P16-3B	2. LT Equity-method invest. $1,142,800; Unrealized gain $1,675
P16-4B	2. LT invest. in bonds $410,572
P16-5B	Investment carrying amt. Dec. 31, 20X2 $488,051
P16-6B	FC loss, net $2,220
Case 1.	No check figure
Case 2.	No check figure
Financial Statement Case	No check figure

Check Figures—Chapter 17

DE17-1	No check figure
DE17-2	No check figure
DE17-3	No check figure
DE17-4	No check figure
DE17-5	No check figure
DE17-6	No check figure
DE17-7	Net cash inflow, oper. $10,000
DE17-8	Net cash outflow, invest $(30,000)
DE17-9	Net cash inflow, finan. $17,000
DE17-10	Net decrease in cash $(3,000)
DE17-11	2. Ending cash $24,000
DE17-12	a. $654,000; b. $325,000
DE17-13	a. $156,000; b. $46,000

DE17-14	a. $5,000; b. $70,000
DE17-15	a. $5,000; b. $3,000; c. $37,000
DE17-16	1. $252,000
DE17-17	No check figure
DE17-18	Net cash inflow, oper. $45,000
DE17-19	Net cash inflow, oper. $127 thou.
DE17-20	No check figure
E17-1	No check figure
E17-2	No check figure
E17-3	No check figure
E17-4	Net cash inflow, oper. $33,000
E17-5	No check figure
E17-6	1. Net cash inflow. oper. $81,000
E17-7	a. $86,000; b. $79,000
E17-8	a. $3,000; b. $16,000
E17-9	Net cash inflow, oper. $4,000
E17-10	No check figure
E17-11	1. Net cash inflow, oper. $81,000; No change in cash bal.
E17-12	Net cash inflow, oper. $33,000
E17-13	No check figure
E17-14	No check figure
P17-1A	No check figure
P17-2A	1. Net cash outflow, oper. $(46,000); July 31, 20X1 Cash bal. $52,300
P17-3A	1. Net cash inflow, oper. $70,600
P17-4A	1. Net cash inflow, oper. $70,600
P17-5A	Net cash inflow, oper. $95,000
P17-6A	1. Net cash inflow, oper. $47,500
P17-7A	1. Net cash inflow, oper. $79,700
P17-8A	1. Net cash inflow, oper. $59,400
P17-1B	No check figure
P17-2B	1. Net cash inflow, oper. $138,700; Apr. 30, 20X5 Cash bal. $79,600
P17-3B	1. Net cash inflow, oper. $76,600
P17-4B	1. Net cash inflow, oper. $76,600
P17-5B	Net cash inflow, oper. $92,200
P17-6B	1. Net cash inflow, oper. $97,600
P17-7B	1. Net cash inflow, oper. $61,400
P17-6B	1. Net cash inflow, oper. $76,100
Case 1.	1. Net cash inflow, oper. $148 thou.
Case 2.	No check figure
Financial Statement Case	2. a. $33,031 mil; b. $22,988 mil; c. $7,423 mil.
P17A-1	Transaction Totals: Panel A $1,510,200 Panel B $462,800
P17A-2	Transaction Totals: Panels A & B $93,200

Check Figures—Chapter 18

DE18-1	1999 Rev. increase 5.7%
DE18-2	No check figure
DE18-3	Trend %: Net sales 1999 160%
DE18-4	20X2 Net inc. 39.2% of sales
DE18-5	20X2 Cash 2.1% of total assets
DE18-6	No check figure
DE18-7	Nike net inc. 5.1% of Net sales
DE18-8	Nike Cash 3.8% of Total assets
DE18-9	20X1 Current ratio 3.20
DE18-10	1. Acid-test ratio 1999 1.04
DE18-11	a. 3.7 times b. 85 days

DE18-12	1. 0.65 2. 13.3 times
DE18-13	2. 0.152 3. 0.448
DE18-14	1. P/E ratio 54
DE18-15	3. 135,526,316 shares
DE18-16	Book value 1999 $4.42
DE18-17	a. $3,050 mil b. $724
DE18-18	a. $541 mil. b. $1,330 mil.
DE18-19	1.EVA® $(2,995) mil.
E18-1	20X3 Work. Cap. decreased 16%
E18-2	Total rev. increase 23.3%; Net inc. increase 98.0%
E18-3	Trend %: Year 5 Net sales 126%; Net inc. 141%
E18-4	Total current assets 28.2% of total assets
E18-5	Net inc. 13.7% of total rev.
E18-6	c. 3.29 times e. 52 days
E18-7	Ratios for 20X2; a. 1.67; d. 4.83 times
E18-8	Ratios for 20X3; b. 0.162; c. 0.094
E18-9	Ratios for 20X4: a. 27.5; b. 0.012
E18-10	EVA® for IHOP $19 mil.
E18-11	Sales $13,259 mil; Net inc. $1,948 mil.
E18-12	Total assets $70,349 mil.; Current liab. $25,803 mil.
P18-1A	1. Trend %: Net sales 20X2 123% 2. Ret. On equity 20X2 0.197
P18-2A	1. Net inc. 15.4% of Net sales Current assets 76.1% of total assets
P18-3A	2. a. Current ratio 1.51; Debt ratio 0.58
P18-4A	1. Ratios for 20X4 b. 2.56; d. 8.36; f. 0.321
P18-5A	a. $8,198 mil; e. $2,050 mil.; i. $17,551 mil.
P18-6A	1. Bowie ratios: b. 0.85; c. 2.74 times; e. 0.502; h. 6.9
P18-1B	1. Trend %: Net sales 20X2 149%; 2. Ret. on sales 20X2 0.075
P18-2B	1. Net inc. 7.7% of Net sales; Current assets 73.4% of total assets
P18-3B	2. a. Current ratio 2.55; Debt ratio 0.50
P18-4B	1. Ratios for 20X3: b. 1.14; d. 2.81; f. 0.259
P18-5B	a. $4,009 mil.; e. $2,431 mil; i. $21,623 mil.
P18-6B	1. Eckert ratios: b. 0.64; c. 2.04 times; e. 0.150; h. 35.8
Case 1.	No check figure
Case 2.	No check figure
Financial Statement Case	1. Trend %: Rev. 1999 160%

Check Figures—Chapter 19

DE19-1	No check figure
DE19-2	No check figure
DE19-3	No check figure

DE19-4	No check figure
DE19-5	No check figure
DE19-6	No check figure
DE19-7	No check figure
DE19-8	No check figure
DE19-9	Beg. inv. $8,000
DE19-10	CGS $30,000
DE19-11	Op. income $22,000
DE19-12	CGM $50,000
DE19-13	Total manufacturing overhead $13,125
DE19-14	Direct materials used $27,700
DE19-15	No check figure
DE19-16	No check figure
DE19-17	No check figure
DE19-18	No check figure
DE19-19	Expected value of *additional* benefits $26 million
DE19-20	No check figure
DE19-21	No check figure
E19-1	No check figure
E19-2	Total inventoriable porduct costs $118
E19-3	Total inventoriable product costs $53,000
E19-4	No check figure
E19-5	Total current assets $224,000
E19-6	CGM $210,000
E19-7	NI $53,000
E19-8	Gross profit $251,000
E19-9	No check figure
E19-10	Excess of benefits over costs $96,300
E19-11	No check figure
E19-12	Ending finished goods inventory $4,100
P19-1A	Total inventoriable product costs $8,685
P19-2A	Paradise Manufacturing cost of goods manufactured $86,350
P19-3A	Manufacturing overhead $38,000
P19-4A	Expected value of the benefits exceeds cost by $74,483
P19-5A	No check figure
P19-4A	Expected value of the benefits exceeds cost by $74,483
P19-5A	No check figure
P19-6A	Present value of costs exceeds present value of benefits by $8,400
P19-7A	Req. 1 Expected value of benefit from additional business is $57,300
P19-8A	No check figure
P19-1B	Total inventoriable product costs $36,220
P19-2B	CoverUp Manufacturing cost of goods manufactured $63,760
P19-3B	Beginning materials inventory $31,000
P19-4B	Expected value of the benefits exceeds cost by $32,914
P19-5B	No check figure
P19-6B	Present value of benefits exceed present value of costs by $220,000
P19-7B	Req. 1 expected value of benefits is $1,112,000

P19-8B	No check figure
Case 1.	Ending material inventory $133,000
Case 2.	No check figure
Ethical Issue	No check figure
Financial Statement Case	No check figure
Team Project	No check figure

Check Figures—Chapter 20

DE20-1	No check figure
DE20-2	No check figure
DE20-3	Cost per gallon, $2.24
DE20-4	No check figure
DE20-5	Ending bal., $270
DE20-6	Ending bal., $1,080
DE20-7	Ending bal., $35,980
DE20-8	Indirect materials, $32
DE20-9	No check figure
DE20-10	Indirect labor $10,000
DE20-11	3. $3,000 underallocated
DE20-12	Bal., $49,000
DE20-13	Predetermined MOH rate, $55
DE20-14	Total cost $7,061
DE20-15	MOH Allocated $360
DE20-16	Ending bal. Materials Inventory $0
DE20-17	1. 70%
DE20-18	No check fig.
DE20-19	1. $60 per hour
DE20-20	1. $37.50 per hour
E20-1	No check figure
E20-2	CGS $25,200
E20-3	No check figure
E20-4	No check figure
E20-5	1. Ending bal. $6,000
E20-6	3. MOH is $700 overallocated
E20-7	3. MOH is $40,000 overallocated
E20-8	3. Adjusted CGS $680,000
E20-9	2. Total predicted cost $50,820
E20-10	1. 17,500 machine hours
P20-1A	1. December FGI $2,100 4. GP for Job 4 $200
P20-2A	2. FGI $74,020 5. GP House 304, $60,300
P20-3A	1. Total job cost $2,734
P20-4A	3. $29,275 underallocated
P20-5A	2. FGI $25,514 4. CGM $70-505
P20-6A	2. Planet Foods $96,200 3. Deception Fragrances $3,750
P20-1B	1. March FGI $1,300 4. GP for Job 5 $1,800
P20-2B	2. FGI $70,500 5. GP House 13 $26,910
P20-3B	1. Total job cost $2,989
P20-4B	3. $30,000 underallocated
P20-5B	2. FGI $72,014 5. Operating income $58,746
P20-6B	3. Fee charged to Malaysia $3,675
Case 1.	No check figure
Case 2.	No check figure
Ethical Issue	No check figure
Team Project	No check figure

Check Figures—Chapter 21

DE21-1	No check figure
DE21-2	No check figure
DE21-3	2c. $26

DE21-4	No check figure
DE21-5	1. cc $24,000
DE21-6	No check figure
DE21-7	2,150 full-time equivalent faculty
DE21-8	2. CCEU 96,000
DE21-9	CCEU 44,000
DE21-10	2. 40,000
DE21-11	CC per EU $2
DE21-12	CC per EU $0.25
DE21-13	1. $60,000
DE21-14	No check figure
DE21-15	73,000 liters started and completed
DE21-16	CC EU 80,300
DE21-17	CC per EU $0.35
DE21-18	Total cost transferred out $97,420
DE21-19	2. Ending Bal. $6,965
DE21-20	2. CC EU 81,900
DE21-21	CC per EU $0.348
DE21-22	Ending WIP $6,745
DE21-23	2. Ending Bal. $6,745
DE21-24	No check figure
E21-1	No check figure
E21-2	No check figure
E21-3	3b. Ending WIP $1,035
E21-4	3. Average cost per gallon transferred out $0.90
E21-5	5. Ending WIP $5,700
E21-6	3b. Ending WIP $2,624.50
E21-7	3. Average cost per gallon transferred out $2.05
E21-8	Transferred to Finishing $464,400
E21-9	53,800 Equivalent units of direct materials
E21-10	2. 67,000 Equivalent units of conversion costs in Mixing
E21-11	83,000EU of DM
E21-12	3. Ending WIP $79,200
E21-14	4. Ending WIP 5,000 units
P21-1A	Ending WIP $49,972
P21-2A	Ending WIP $2,618
P21-3A	Ending WIP $737
P21-4A	Ending WIP $18,225
P21-5A	No check figure
P21-6A	Ending WIP $500,000
P21-7A	Ending WIP $447,000
P21-1B	Ending WIP $1,890
P21-2B	Ending WIP $7,868
P21-3B	Ending WIP $3,107
P21-4B	Ending WIP $31,500
P21-5B	No check figure
P21-6B	Ending WIP $3,648
P21-7B	Ending WIP $3,078
Case 1.	3. $900
Case 2.	2. $0.60
Ethical Issue	No check figure
Team Project	Equivalent units of conversion costs in: Cooking 128,500 Cutting 128,400

Check Figures—Chapter 22

DE22-1	No check figure
DE22-2	No check figure
DE22-3	b. $21
DE22-4	CM $62,500
DE22-5	No check figure

DE22-6	$480,000
DE22-7	CM $210,000
DE22-8	CM $325,000
DE22-9	Breakeven point 6,250 tickets
DE22-10	Breakeven sales revenue $343,751 (rounded)
DE22-11	1. Breakeven sales dollars $357,150 (rounded)
DE22-12	1. Breakeven sales dollars $275,000 (rounded)
DE22-13	Required ticket sales 7,000
DE22-14	No check figure
DE22-15	Margin of safety: a. 750 round trips
DE22-16	No check figure
DE22-17	Margin of safety: a. 400 posters
DE22-18	Weighted-average CM per unit $16.66667 (rounded)
DE22-19	a. Breakeven in total units 420 posters
DE22-20	Weighted-average contribution margin per unit $62.50
DE22-21	Breakeven point: 2,500 Coach tickets 1,500 Chief tickets
DE22-22	CM $198,000
DE22-23	GP $168,000
DE22-24	No check figure
E22-1	No check figure
E22-2	Operating income $138,000
E22-3	Breakeven sales $300,000
E22-4	2. Breakeven is 70,000 units
E22-5	1. Breakeven sales $11,000
E22-6	1. Breakeven sales $700,000
E22-7	3. Breakeven sales $50,000
E22-8	Breakeven point 1,500,000 tickets
E22-9	2. margin of safety 55%
E22-10	Breakeven point: 660 standard sweatshirts 440 fancy sweatshirts
E22-11	Absorption costing income $1,025,000 Variable costing income $725,000
E22-12	Weighted-average contribution margin per unit $100
P22-1A	No check figure
P22-2A	Contribution Margin Ratio: E: 0.550 G: 0.491
P22-3A	2. Breakeven point 50 cruises 4. Operating income $39,600
P22-4A	3. Operating loss ($39,000) 4. Breakeven point 93,600 T-shirts
P22-5A	2. Target sales $15,000 4. Breakeven point 20 tickets
P22-6A	2. Margin of Safety $135,000 3. Operating income after sales increase $116,250
P22-7A	November operating income: Absorption $28,900 Variable $29,400
P22-1B	No check figure
P22-2B	Contribution margin ratio: P: 0.70 R: 0.60
P22-3B	2. Breakeven point 45 cruises 4. Operating income $225,500
P22-4B	3. Operating income $332,000 4. Breakeven sales $2,905,000

P22-5B	2. Target Sales $14,500 4. Breakeven point 15 tickets
P22-6B	2. Margin of Safety $33,270 3. Operating income after sales increase $6,750
P22-7B	February operating income: Absorption $2.240 Variable $2,300
Case 1.	1. Breakeven for: Children's meals 41,200 Adults' meals 20,600
Case 2.	No check figure
Ethical Issue	No check figure
Financial Statement Case	2. Contribution margin $5,689 million
Team Project	Absorption costing operating income $1.4 million

Check Figures—Chapter 23

DE23-1	No check figure
DE23-2	No check figure
DE23-3	No check figure
DE23-4	January sales, $705,000
DE23-5	February purchases, $686,400
DE23-6	April-July total, $264,000
DE23-7	April purchases, $46,100
DE23-8	May cash collections, $59,000
DE23-9	April total cash payments for purchases, $40,800
DE23-10	February cash collections, $848,171.25
DE23-11	Cash deficiency, $50,695
DE23-12	June interest expense, $112.50
DE23-13	No check figure
DE23-14	No check figure
DE23-15	No check figure
DE23-16	No check figure
DE23-17	No check figure
DE23-18	No check figure
DE23-19	Software department, $150,000
DE23-20	No check figure
E23-1	Income is $14,000 higher this year.
E23-2	Third-Quarter purchases, $86,450
E23-3	Net income for the year, $2,330,144.
E23-4	a. Cash receipt from sale of equipment, $7,000
E23-5	2. Cash borrowed in November, $6,000
E23-6	Ending Owners' Equity Balance, $25,300
E23-7	No check figure
E23-8	Operating Income Variance for books, $81,000 U
E23-9	2. Welding Total Indirect expense, $25,250
E23-10	Plastic Operating Income, $55,200
E23-11	March Interest Expense, $66
P23-1A	August Net Income, $27,000
P23-2A	September ending cash balance, $66,750
P23-3A	Ending Cash Balance, $24,150
P23-4A	Ending cash balance before financing, $11,150
P23-5A	No check figure
P23-6A	Kansas Operating Income Variance, $62,400 F

P23-7A	Copy Services Operating Income, $15,410
P23-1B	June Net Income, $6,400
P23-2B	June ending cash balance, $22,610
P23-3B	3. Cash available for equipment purchases, $68,900
P23-4B	Ending cash balance, $24,200
P23-5B	No check figure
P23-6B	Cincinnati office operating income variance, $7,500 U
P23-7B	Group Travel Operating Income, $54,770
Case 1.	Total cost per wakeboard, $210
Case 2.	No check figure
Ethical Issue	No check figure
Financial Statement Case	3. Mervyn's 1998 return on assets, 0.1034
Team Project	No check figure

Check Figures—Chapter 24

DE24-1	29. 20-installation operating income, $16,000
DE24-2	1. 3-pool operating loss, $8,000
DE24-3	No check figure
DE24-4	3. May flexible budget total cost, $92,000
DE24-5	Jan. FBV, $3,250 F
DE24-6	Operating income sales volume variance, $4,000 F
DE24-7	Op Inc. SW, $6,000 F
DE24-8	No check figure
DE24-9	No check figure
DE24-10	No check figure
DE24-11	No check figure
DE24-12	Material price variance, $6,600 U
DE24-13	Total direct material efficiency variance, $6.10 U
DE24-14	DLEV, $39,000 U
DE24-15	No check figure
DE24-16	VMOHR, $6
DE24-17	PW, $4,000 F
DE24-18	No check figure
DE24-19	No check figure
DE24-20	No check figure
DE24-21	Op. inc. $69,900
E24-1	40,000-level op. inc. $40,000
E24-2	No check figure
E24-3	Op. inc. FBV, $9,000 U
E24-4	Op. inc. FBV, $193,000 F
E24-5	FBV, $3,400 U
E24-6	DMEV, $255,000 U
E24-7	No check figure
E24-8	No check figure
E24-9	Overhead flexible budget variance, $200 U
E24-10	Gross Pprofit, $206,500
E24-11	Capacity level, 5,000 units
P24-1A	11,000-unit operating income, $54,825
P24-2A	Total expenses flexible budget variance, $4,225 U
P24-3A	Production volume variance, $675 U
P24-4A	DEV, $1,000 F

P24-5A	1. Materials price variance $3,843 F
	3. Overhead flexible budget variance, $3,714 U
P24-6A	Labor price variance, $312 U
P24-1B	65,000-unit operating income, $71,050
P24-2B	Operating income flexible budget variance, $1,000 F
P24-3B	Total overhead variance, $50,890 F
P24-4B	Actual direct labor hours, 3,280
P24-5B	1. Materials price variance, $5,508 U
	3. Overhead flexible budget
P24-6B	2. MOH flexible budget variance, $3,900 F
	3. Gross profit, $130,900
Case 1.	Flexible budget variance, $43,025 F
Case 2.	Direct labor efficiency variance, $108 U
Ethical Issue	No check figure
Team Project	No check figure

Check Figures—Chapter 25

DE25-1	No check figure
DE25-2	No check figure
DE25-3	No check figure
DE25-4	Total PH overhead, $112.50
DE25-5	Total PH set-up costs, $90
DE25-6	Set-up costs per lb. of PH, $18
DE25-7	Aldehyde GP $1.60
DE25-8	Full Product cost, $7.60/lb.
DE25-9	Target cost, $225/ream
DE25-10	Lee operating income, $3,600
DE25-11	No check figure
DE25-12	No check figure
DE25-13	Information technology, $400/application
DE25-14	Wilner operating income, $6,280
DE25-15	No check figure
DE25-16	No check figure
DE25-17	No check figure
DE25-18	No check figure
DE25-19	No check figure
DE25-20	No check figure
DE25-21	Total cost of implementing program, $1,900,000
E25-1	Indirect cost per wheel, $52.40
E25-2	Deluxe model ABC Cost, $111.15
E25-3	No check figure
E25-4	Cost of deluxe wheel, $159.15
E25-5	No check figure

E25-6	Conversion cost is $450,000 overallocated
E25-7	Ending balance FG, $308,000
E25-8	No check figure
E25-9	No check figure
E25-10	Total Cost of implementing program, $170,000
E25-11	Job 204 used 750 parts
P25-1A	Manufacturing Product Cost, $132.40
P25-2A	4. Sale price, $56.20
P25-3A	2. Commercial container ABC unit cost, $88
P25-4A	3. Indirect cost, $1.52/unit
P25-5A	3. 10/31 Raw and In Process balance, $9,000
P25-6A	2. Net benefit, $8,000
P25-1B	Manufacturing Product Cost, $85.60
P25-2B	4. Sale price, $109
P25-3B	2. Bullseye! ABC unit cost $299,000
P25-4B	3. Indirect activity cost per unit, $20.30.
P25-5B	3. 8/31 Raw and In Process bal., $2,500
P25-6B	2. Net benefit, $44,500
Case 1.	Job A ABC cost per unit, $5,057.50
Case 2.	Required cost savings in assembling, $600
Ethical Issue	No check figure
Team Projects: Project 1.	Indirect cost per standard service customer: Original cost system, $360 ABC cost system, $199.33 (rounded)
Project 2.	No check figure

Check Figures—Chapter 26

DE26-1	No check figure
DE26-2	Decrease in income, $3,000
DE26-3	Increase in income, $320,000
DE26-4	No check figure
DE26-5	No check figure
DE26-6	No check figure
DE26-7	Decrease in income, $25,000
DE26-8	Increase in income, $5,000
DE26-9	Deluxe CM per unit, $305
DE26-10	Advantage to outsourcing, $20,500 per year
DE26-11	No check figure
DE26-12	Advantage to making filter, $25,000
DE26-13	Advantage to buying filters, $3,000

DE26-14	Advantage to processing further, $9,000
DE26-15	Minimum sales price, $25 per key
DE26-16	Opportunity cost of shirts, $480,000
DE26-17	Annual cash savings, $3,750
DE26-18	Annual net cash inflow, $2,400,000
DE26-19	Payback, 5.42 years
DE26-20	ARR, 22.9%
DE26-21	NPV, $3,529,400
DE26-22	IRR, 16%
DE26-23	No check figure
E26-1	2. Decrease in income, $15,000
E26-2	Decrease in income, $90,000
E26-3	Decrease in income, $25,000
E26-4	Total CM at capacity, Moderate, $36,400
E26-5	Advantage to making, $1.50/unit
E26-6	Advantage to buy and use facilities for other project, $15,000
E26-7	Advantage to further processing, $350
E26-8	Payback, 3 years
E26-9	Payback, 5.6 years
E26-10	Accounting rate of return, Veras Products, 35%
E26-11	NPV of project B, ($8.760)
E26-12	IRR of project A, 14-16%
E26-13	1. Coca-Cola in 12 oz. cans
P26-1A	1. Increase in income, $1,000
P26-2A	1. Decrease in income, $8,500
P26-3A	Total CM at capacity, patio sets, $7,800
P26-4A	1. Advantage to making, $20,000
P26-5A	3. Advantage to processing further, $30,000
P26-6A	NPV, ($774,450)
P26-7A	Plan A's NPV ($121,280)
P26-1B	1. Increase in income, $24,000
P26-2B	1. Decrease in income, $159,000
P26-3B	1. Total CM at capacity, Deluxe, $1,540,000
P26-4B	1. Advantage to making, $264
P26-5B	3. Advantage to selling as is, $16,310
P26-6B	NPV, $65,980
P26-7B	3.Plan A's IRR, about 12%
Case 1.	2. Advantage to outsourcing, $8 per mailbox
Case 2.	NPV, $9,245
Ethical Issue/Financial Statement Case	1.EPS, $2.70
Team Project	2. Annual cost savings from making, $7,872,000 3c. NPV, $3,349,824

Glossary

Absorption Costing. The costing method that assigns both variable and fixed manufacturing costs to products.

Accelerated Depreciation Method. A depreciation method that writes off more of the asset's cost near the start of its useful life than the straight-line method does.

Account. The detailed record of the changes that have occurred in a particular asset, liability, or owner's equity during a period. The basic summary device of accounting.

Account Payable. A liability backed by the general reputation and credit standing of the debtor.

Account Receivable. A promise to receive cash from customers to whom the business has sold goods or for whom the business has performed services.

Accounting. The information system that measures business activities, processes that information into reports, and communicates the results to decision makers.

Accounting Equation. The basic tool of accounting, presenting the resources of the business and the claims to those resources: Assets = Liabilities + Owner's Equity.

Accounting Information System. The combination of personnel, records, and procedures that a business uses to provide financial data.

Accounting Rate of Return. A measure of profitability computed by dividing the average annual operating income from an asset by the average amount invested in the asset.

Accounts Receivable Turnover. Ratio of net credit sales to average net accounts receivable. Measures ability to collect cash from customers.

Accrual-Basis Accounting. Accounting that records the impact of a business event as it occurs, regardless of whether the transaction affected cash.

Accrued Expense. An expense that the business has not yet paid. Also called accrued liability.

Accrued Revenue. A revenue that has been earned but not yet collected in cash.

Accumulated Depreciation. The cumulative sum of all depreciation expense recorded for an asset.

Acid-Test Ratio. Ratio of the sum of cash plus short-term investments plus net current receivables to total current liabilities. Tells whether the entity could pay all its current liabilities if they came due immediately. Also called the **quick ratio**.

Activity-Based Costing (ABC). A system that focuses on activities as the fundamental cost objects. The costs of those activities become building blocks for compiling costs as ABC links costs to the activities that cause those costs.

Activity-Based Management. Using activity-based cost information to make decisions that increase profits while satisfying customers' needs.

Additional Paid-in Capital. The paid-in capital in excess of par—common plus other accounts combined for reporting on the balance sheet.

Adjusted Trial Balance. A list of all the ledger accounts with their adjusted balances.

Adjusting Entry. Entry made at the end of the period to assign revenues to the period in which they are earned and expenses to the period in which they are incurred. Adjusting entries help measure the period's income and bring the related asset and liability accounts to correct balances for the financial statements.

Aging-of-Accounts Method. A way to estimate bad debts by analyzing individual accounts receivable according to the length of time they have been receivable from the customer. Also called the **balance-sheet approach**.

Allocation Base. A common denominator that links indirect costs to cost objects. Ideally, the allocation base is the primary cost driver that causes the indirect cost to be incurred.

Allowance for Uncollectible Accounts. A contra account, related to accounts receivable, that holds the estimated amount of collection losses. Also called **Allowance for Doubtful Accounts**.

Allowance Method. A method of recording collection losses on the basis of estimates, instead of waiting to see which customers the company will not collect from.

Amortization. The systematic reduction of the asset's carrying value on the books. Expense that applies to intangibles in the same way depreciation applies to plant assets and depletion applies to natural resources.

Annuity. A stream of equal periodic cash flows.

Appraisal Costs. Costs incurred to detect poor-quality goods or services.

Appropriation of Retained Earnings. Restriction of retained earnings that is recorded by a formal journal entry.

Asset. An economic resource that is expected to be of benefit in the future.

Audit. An examination of a company's financial statements and the accounting system.

Authorization of Stock. Provision in a corporate charter that gives the state's permission for the corporation to issue—that is, to sell—a certain number of shares of stock.

Available-for-Sale Investments. Stock investments other than trading securities in which the investor cannot exercise significant influence over the investee.

Balance Sheet. List of an entity's assets, liabilities, and owner's equity as of a specific date. Also called the **statement of financial position**.

Bank Collection. Collection of money by the bank on behalf of a depositor.

Bank Reconciliation. Document explaining the reasons for the difference between a depositor's cash records and the depositor's cash balance in its bank account.

Bank Statement. Document the bank uses to report what it did with the depositor's cash. Shows the bank account's beginning and ending balances and lists the month's cash transactions conducted through the bank.

Batch Processing. Computerized accounting for similar transactions in a group or batch.

Benchmarking. The practice of comparing a company to a standard set by other companies, with a view toward improvement.

Board of Directors. Group elected by the stockholders to set policy and to appoint the officers.

Bonds Payable. Groups of notes payable (bonds) issued to multiple lenders called bondholders.

Book Value. Amount of owners' equity on the company's books for each share of its stock.

Book Value (of a Plant Asset). The asset's cost minus accumulated depreciation.

Book Value Per Share of Common Stock. Common equity divided by the number of shares of common stock outstanding.

Breakeven Point. The sales level at which operating income is zero: Total revenues equal total expenses.

Budget. A quantitative expression of a plan that helps managers coordinate the entity's activities.

Bylaws. Constitution for governing a corporation.

Callable Bonds. Bonds that the issuer may call or pay off at a specified price whenever the issuer wants.

Capital Budgeting. A formal means of analyzing long-term investment decisions. Describes budgeting for the acquisition of capital assets.

Capital Charge. The amount that stockholders and lenders charge a company for the use of their money.

Capital Expenditure. Expenditure that increases the capacity or efficiency of an asset or extends its useful life. Capital expenditures are debited to an asset account.

Capital Expenditures Budget. A company's plan for purchases of property, plant, equipment, and other long-term assets.

Capital Lease. Lease agreement that meets any one of four criteria: (1) The lease transfers title of the leased asset to the lessee. (2) The lease contains a bargain purchase option. (3) The lease term is 75% or more of the estimated useful life of the leased asset. (4) The present value of the lease payments is 90% or more of the market value of the leased asset.

Capitalize a Cost. To record a cost as part of an asset's cost, rather than as an expense.

Cash-Basis Accounting. Accounting that records transactions only when cash is received or paid.

Cash Budget. Details how the business expects to go from the beginning cash balance to the desired ending balance. Also called the **statement of budgeted cash receipts and payments**.

Cash Equivalents. Liquid short-term investments that can be converted into cash at will.

Cash Flows. Cash receipts and cash payments (disbursements).

Cash Payments Journal. Special journal used to record cash payments by check. Also called the **check register** or **cash disbursements journal**.

Cash Receipts Journal. Special journal used to record cash receipts.

Certified Management Accountant (CMA). A licensed accountant who works for a single company.

Certified Public Accountant (CPA). A licensed accountant who serves the general public rather than one particular company.

Chairperson. Elected by a corporation's board of directors, the most powerful person in the corporation.

Chart of Accounts. List of all the accounts and their account numbers in the ledger.

Charter. Document that gives the state's permission to form a corporation.

Check. Document that instructs a bank to pay the designated person or business a specified amount of money.

Closing Entries. Entries that transfer the revenue, expense, and owner withdrawal balances from these respective accounts to the capital account.

Closing the Accounts. Step in the accounting cycle at the end of the period. Closing the accounts consists of journalizing and posting the closing entries to set the balances of the revenue, expense, and withdrawal accounts to zero for the next period.

Common-Size Statement. A financial statement that reports only percentages (no dollar amounts); a type of vertical analysis.

Common Stock. The basic form of capital stock. In a corporation, the common stockholders are the owners of the business.

Comprehensive Income. Company's change in total stockholders' equity from all sources other than from the owners.

Computer Virus. A malicious program that (a) reproduces itself, (b) gets included in program code without consent, and (c) performs actions that can be destructive.

Conservatism. Reporting the least favorable figures in the financial statements.

Consignment. Transfer of goods by the owner (consignor) to another business (consignee) that sells the inventory on the owner's behalf. The consignee does not take title to the consigned goods.

Consistency Principle. A business should use the same accounting methods and procedures from period to period.

Consolidated Statements. Financial statements of the parent company plus those of majority-owned subsidiaries as if the combination were a single legal entity.

Constraint. A factor that restricts production or sale of a product.

Contingent Liability. A potential liability that will become an actual liability only if a particular event does occur.

Continuous Improvement. A philosophy requiring employees to continually look for ways to improve performance.

Contra Account. An account that always has a companion account and whose normal balance is opposite that of the companion account.

Contract Interest Rate. Interest rate that determines the amount of cash interest the borrower pays and the investor receives each year. Also called the **stated interest rate**.

Contribution Margin Income Statement. Income statement that groups variable and fixed expenses separately, and highlights the contribution margin.

Contribution Margin per Unit. Excess of the sales revenue per unit (sale price) over the variable expense per unit.

Contribution Margin Ratio. The ratio of contribution margin to sales revenue.

Contribution Margin. Sales revenue minus all variable expenses. Also called **sales revenue per unit (sale price) minus variable expense per unit.**

Control Account. An account whose balance equals the sum of the balances in a group of related accounts in a subsidiary ledger.

Controller. The chief accounting officer of a company.

Controlling. Evaluating the results of business operations by comparing the actual results to the plan.

Controlling Interest. Ownership of more than 50% of an investee company's voting stock. Also called **majority interest**.

Conversion Costs. Direct labor plus manufacturing overhead.

Convertible Bonds. Bonds (or notes payable) that may be converted into the common stock of the issuing company at the option of the investor.

Copyright. Exclusive right to reproduce and sell a book, musical composition, film, other work of art, or computer program. Issued by the federal government, copyrights extend 50 years beyond the author's life.

Corporation. A business owned by stockholders; it begins when the state approves its articles of incorporation. A corporation is a legal entity, an "artificial person," in the eyes of the law.

Cost Allocation. Assigning indirect costs (such as manufacturing overhead) to cost objects (such as jobs or production processes).

Cost Assignment. Tracing direct costs to cost objects and allocating indirect costs to cost objects.

Cost Behavior. Describes how costs change as a cost driver changes.

Cost Driver. The primary factor that causes costs.

Cost Object. Anything for which managers want a separate measurement of costs.

Cost of Capital. A weighted average of the returns demanded by a company's stockholders and lenders.

Cost of Goods Available for Sale Beginning inventory plus purchases.

Cost of Goods Manufactured. The (manufacturing) cost of the goods that were finished—that is, the plant-related cost of the units that completed the production process this period.

Cost of Goods Sold. The cost of the inventory that the business has sold to customers. Also called **cost of sales**.

Cost Tracing. Assigning direct costs (such as direct materials and direct labor) to cost objects (such as jobs or production processes).

Cost-Benefit Analysis. Weighing costs against benefits to help make decisions.

Cost-Volume-Profit (CVP) Analysis. Expresses the relationships among costs, volume, and profit or loss.

Credit. The right side of an account.

Credit Memorandum or Credit Memo. A document issued by a seller to credit a customer account for returned merchandise.

Creditor. The party to a credit transaction who sells goods or a service and obtains a receivable.

Cumulative Preferred Stock. Preferred stock whose owners must receive all dividends in arrears before the corporation pays dividends to the common stockholders.

Current Asset. An asset that is expected to be converted to cash, sold, or consumed during

the next 12 months, or within the business's normal operating cycle.

Current Liability. A debt due to be paid with cash or with goods and services within one year or within the entity's operating cycle if the cycle is longer than a year.

Current Portion of Long-Term Debt. Amount of the principal that is payable within one year. Also called **current maturity**.

Current Ratio. Total current assets divided by total current liabilities. Measures the ability to pay current liabilities from current assets.

Customer Service. Support provided for customers after the sale.

Database. A computerized storehouse of information.

Days' Sales in Receivables. Ratio of average net accounts receivable to one day's sales. Tells how many days' sales it takes to collect the average level of receivables. Also called the **collection period**.

Debentures. Unsecured bonds backed only by the good faith of the borrower.

Debit. The left side of an account.

Debit Memorandum or Debit Memo. A document issued by a buyer when returning merchandise. The memo informs the seller that the buyer no longer owes the seller for the amount of the returned purchases.

Debt Ratio. Ratio of total liabilities to total assets. Tells the proportion of a company's assets that it has financed with debt.

Debtor. The party to a credit transaction who makes a purchase and has a payable.

Deficit. Debit balance in the Retained Earnings account.

Depletion Expense. The portion of a natural resource's cost used up in a particular period. Depletion expense is computed in the same way as units-of-production depreciation.

Deposit in Transit. A deposit recorded by the company but not yet by its bank.

Depreciable Cost. The cost of a plant asset minus its estimated residual value.

Depreciation. The allocation of a plant asset's cost to expense over its useful life.

Design. Detailed engineering of products and services, or processes for producing them.

Direct Cost. A cost that can be specifically traced to a cost object.

Direct Labor. The compensation of employees who physically convert materials into the company's products; labor costs that are directly traceable to finished products.

Direct Materials. Materials that become a physical part of a finished product and whose costs are separately and conveniently traceable to the finished product.

Direct Method. Format of the operating activities section of the statement of cash flows that lists the major categories of operating cash receipts (collections from customers and receipts of interest and dividends) and cash payments (payments to suppliers, to employees, for interest and income taxes).

Direct Write-off Method. A method of accounting for uncollectible receivables, in which the company waits until the credit department decides that a customer's account receivable is uncollectible, and then debits Uncollectible-Account Expense and credits the customer's Account Receivable.

Disclosure Principle. A business's financial statements must report enough information for outsiders to make knowledgeable decisions about the company.

Discount (on a Bond). Excess of a bond's maturity (par value) over its issue price. Also called a **bond discount.**

Discount Rate. Management's minimum desired rate of return on an investment. Also called the **hurdle rate, required rate of return,** and **cost of capital.**

Discounting a Note Payable. A borrowing arrangement in which the bank subtracts the interest amount from a note's face value. The borrower receives the net amount.

Discounting Note Receivable. Selling a note receivable before its maturity date.

Dishonor of a Note. Failure of a note's maker to pay a note receivable at maturity. Also called **default on a note.**

Dissolution. Ending of a partnership.

Distribution. Delivery of products or services to customers.

Dividend Yield. Ratio of dividends per share of stock to the stock's market price. Measures the percentage of the stock's market value that the company pays to stockholders as dividends.

Dividends. Distributions by a corporation to its stockholders.

Double Taxation. Corporations pay their own income taxes on cor-porate income. Then, the stock-holders pay personal income tax on the cash dividends they receive from corporations.

Double-Declining-Balance (DDB) Depreciation Method. An accelerated depreciation method that computes annual depreciation by multiplying the asset's decreasing book value by a constant percent that is 2 times the straight-line rate.

Earnings Per Share (EPS). Amount of a company's net income per share of its outstanding common stock.

Economic Value Added (EVA®). Combines accounting income and finance to measure whether the company's operations have increased stockholder wealth.

Efficiency Variance. Measures whether the quantity of materials or labor used to make the actual number of outputs is within the standard allowed for that number of outputs. This is computed as the difference in quantities (actual quantity of input used minus standard quantity of input allowed for the actual number of outputs), multiplied by the standard price per unit of the input.

Efficient Capital Market. A capital market in which market prices reflect the impact of all information available to the public.

Electronic Funds Transfer (EFT). System that transfers cash by electronic communication rather than by paper documents.

Encryption. Rearranging plain-text messages by a mathematical process; the primary method of achieving confidentiality in e-commerce.

Entity. An organization or a section of an organization that, for accounting purposes, stands apart from other organizations and individuals as a separate economic unit.

Equity Method. The method used to account for investments in which the investor has 20–50% of the investee's voting stock and can significantly influence the decisions of the investee.

Equivalent Units. A measure of the amount of work done during a period, expressed in terms of fully complete units of output.

Estimated Residual Value. Expected cash value of an asset at the end of its useful life. Also called **scrap value,** or **salvage value.**

Estimated Useful Life. Length of the service period expected from an asset. May be expressed in years, units of output, miles, or another measure.

Expense. Decrease in owner's equity that occurs from using assets or increasing liabilities in the

course of delivering goods or services to customers.

External Failure Costs. Costs incurred when the company does not detect poor-quality goods or services until after delivery to customers.

Extraordinary gains and losses. A gain or loss that is both unusual for the company and infrequent. Also called **extraordinary items.**

Financial Accounting. The branch of accounting that focuses on information for people outside the firm.

Financial Accounting Standards Board (FASB). The private organization that determines how accounting is practiced in the United States.

Financial Budget. Projects cash inflows and outflows, the period-ending balance sheet, and the statement of cash flows.

Financial Statements. Documents that report on a business in monetary amounts, providing information to help people make informed business decisions.

Financing Activity. Activity that obtains the funds from investors and creditors needed to launch and sustain the business; a section of the statement of cash flows.

Finished Goods Inventory. Com-pleted goods that have not yet been sold.

Firewalls. Devices that enable members of a local network to access the Internet but keep nonmembers out of the network.

First-In, First-Out (FIFO) Inventory Costing Method. Inventory costing method by which the first costs into inventory are the first costs out to cost of goods sold. Ending inventory is based on the costs of the most recent purchases.

First-In, First-Out (FIFO) Process Costing Method. A process costing method that assigns to each period's equivalent units of production that period's costs per equivalent unit.

Fixed Cost. Cost that does not change in total despite wide changes in volume.

Flexible Budget. A summarized budget that can easily be computed for several different volume levels. Flexible budgets separate variable costs from fixed costs; it is the variable costs that put the "flex" in the flexible budget.

Flexible Budget Variance. The difference arising because the company actually earned more or less revenue, or incurred more or less cost, than expected for the actual level of output. This is computed as the difference between the actual amount and a flexible budget amount.

Foreign-Currency Exchange Rate. The measure of one currency against another currency.

Franchises, Licenses. Privileges granted by a private business or a government to sell a product or service under specified conditions.

Full Product Costs. The costs of all resources used throughout the value chain for a product.

General Journal. Journal used to record all transactions that do not fit one of the special journals.

General Ledger. Ledger of accounts that are reported in the financial statements.

General Partnership. A form of partnership in which each partner is an owner of the business, with all the privileges and risks of ownership.

Generally Accepted Accounting Principles (GAAP). Accounting guidelines, formulated by the Financial Accounting Standards Board, that govern how accountants measure, process, and communicate financial information.

Goodwill. Excess of the cost of an acquired company over the sum of the market values of its net assets (assets minus liabilities).

Gross Pay. Total amount of salary, wages, commissions, or any other employee compensation before taxes and other deductions.

Gross Profit. Excess of net sales revenue over cost of goods sold. Also called **gross margin.**

Gross Profit Method. A way to estimate inventory on the basis of the cost-of-goods-sold model: Beginning inventory + Net purchases = Cost of goods available for sale. Cost of goods available for sale − Cost of goods sold = Ending inventory. Also called the **gross margin method.**

Gross Profit or Gross Margin. Excess of sales revenue over cost of goods sold.

Gross Profit Percentage. Gross profit divided by net sales revenue. A measure of profitability. Also called **gross margin percentage.**

Hardware. Electronic equipment that includes computers, disk drives, monitors, printers, and the network that connects them.

Hedging. Protecting oneself from losing money in one transaction by engaging in a counterbalancing transaction.

Held-to-Maturity Investments. Investment in bonds, notes, and other debt securities that the investor expects to hold until their maturity date.

Horizontal Analysis. Study of percentage changes in comparative financial statements.

Imprest System. A way to account for petty cash by maintaining a constant balance in the petty cash account, supported by the fund (cash plus payment tickets) totaling the same amount.

Income Statement. Summary of an entity's revenues, expenses, and net income or net loss for a specific period. Also called the **statement of earnings** or the **statement of operations.**

Income Summary. A temporary "holding tank" account into which revenues and expenses are transferred prior to their final transfer to the capital account.

Indirect Cost. A cost that cannot be specifically traced to a cost object.

Indirect Labor. Labor costs that are difficult to trace to specific products.

Indirect Materials. Materials whose costs cannot conveniently be directly traced to particular finished products.

Indirect Method. Format of the operating activities section of the statement of cash flows that starts with net income and shows the reconciliation from net income to operating cash flows. Also called the **reconciliation method.**

Intangible Assets. Assets with no physical form. Valuable because of the special rights they carry. Examples are patents and copyrights.

Internal Control. Organizational plan and all the related measures adopted by an entity to safeguard assets, encourage adherence to company policies, promote operational efficiency, and ensure accurate and reliable accounting records.

Internal Failure Costs. Costs incurred when the company detects and corrects poor-quality goods or services before delivery to customers.

Internal Rate of Return (IRR). The rate of return (based on discounted cash flows) that a company can expect to earn by investing in the project. The discount rate that makes the net present value of the project's cash flows equal to zero.

Inventoriable Product Costs. All costs of a product that are regarded as an asset for external financial reporting, and are not expensed until the product is sold. Must conform to GAAP.

Inventory Profit. Difference between gross profit figured on the FIFO basis and gross profit figured on the LIFO basis.

Inventory Turnover. Ratio of cost of goods sold to average inventory. Measures the number of times a company sells its average level of inventory during a year.

Inventory. All the goods that the company owns and expects to sell in the normal course of operations.

Investing Activity. Activity that increases and decreases the long-term assets available to the business; a section of the statement of cash flows.

Invoice. A seller's request for cash from the purchaser.

Job Cost Record. Document used to accumulate the costs of an individual job.

Job Costing. System for assigning costs to a specific unit or to a small batch of products or services that (1) pass through production steps as a distinct identifiable job lot, and (2) can vary considerably in terms of materials, labor, and overhead costs.

Journal. The chronological accounting record of an entity's transactions.

Just-In-Time (JIT) Costing. A standard costing system that starts with output completed and then assigns manufacturing costs to units sold and to inventories. Also called **backflush costing.**

Just-in-Time (JIT). A system in which a company produces just in time to satisfy needs. Materials are purchased and finished goods are completed only as needed to satisfy customer orders.

Labor Time Record. Identifies the employee, the amount of time spent on a particular job, and the labor cost charged to the job; a record that manufacturing firms commonly use to trace direct labor time to specific job cost records.

Last-In, First-Out (LIFO) Inventory Costing Method. Inventory costing method by which the last costs into inventory are the first costs out to cost of goods sold. This method leaves the oldest costs—those of beginning inventory and the earliest purchases of the period—in ending inventory.

Lease. Rental agreement in which the tenant (lessee) agrees to make rent payments to the property owner (lessor) to obtain the use of the asset.

Ledger. The book of accounts.

Legal Capital. The portion of stockholders' equity that cannot be used for dividends.

Lessee. Tenant in a lease agreement.

Lessor. Property owner in a lease agreement.

Leverage. Earning more income on borrowed money than the related interest expense, thereby increasing the earnings for the owners of the business.

Liability. An economic obligation (a debt) payable to an individual or an organization outside the business.

LIFO Liquidation. Situation when the LIFO inventory method is used and inventory quantities fall below the level of the previous period.

Limited Liability. No personal obligation of a stockholder for corporation debts. A stockholder can lose no more on an investment in a corporation's stock than the cost of the investment.

Limited Liability Partnership. A form of partnership in which each partner's personal liability for the business's debts is limited to a certain amount. Also called **LLPs.**

Limited Partnership. A partnership with at least two classes of partners: a general partner and limited partners.

Liquidation. The process of going out of business by selling the entity's assets and paying its liabilities. The final step in liquidation is the distribution of any remaining cash to the owner(s).

Liquidity. Measure of how quickly an item can be converted to cash.

Long-Term Asset. An asset other than a current asset.

Long-Term Investment. A non-current asset, a separate asset category reported on the balance sheet between current assets and plant assets.

Long-Term Liability. A liability other than a current liability.

Lower-of-Cost-or-Market (LCM) Rule. Rule that an asset should be reported in the financial statements at whichever is lower—its historical cost or its market value.

Major Repair or Extraordinary Repair. Repair work that generates a capital expenditure.

Maker of a Note. The person or business that signs the note and promises to pay the amount required by the note agreement; the debtor.

Management Accounting. The branch of accounting that focuses on information for internal decision makers of a business.

Management by Exception. Directs management's attention to important differences between actual and budgeted amounts.

Manufacturing Company. A company that uses labor, plant, and equipment to convert raw materials into new finished products.

Manufacturing Overhead. All manufacturing costs other than direct materials and direct labor. Also called **factory overhead** or **indirect manufacturing cost.**

Margin of Safety. Excess of expected sales over breakeven sales. Drop in sales a company can absorb before incurring an operating loss.

Market Interest Rate. Interest rate that investors demand in order to loan their money. Also called the **effective interest rate.**

Marketing. Promotion of products or services.

Market Value. Price for which a person could buy or sell a share of stock.

Market-Value Method. Used to account for all trading investments. These investments are reported at their current market value.

Master Budget. The set of budgeted financial statements and supporting schedules for the entire organization. This comprehensive budget includes the operating budget, the capital expenditures budget, and the financial budget.

Matching Principle. The basis for recording expenses. Directs accountants to identify all expenses incurred during the period, to measure the expenses, and to match them against the revenues earned during that same span of time.

Materiality Concept. A company must perform strictly proper accounting only for items that are significant to the business's financial statements.

Materials Inventory. Raw materials for use in manufacturing.

Materials Requisition. Request for materials, prepared by manufacturing personnel.

Menu. A list of options for choosing computer functions.

Merchandising Company. A company that resells products previously bought from suppliers.

Minority Interest. A subsidiary company's equity that is held by stockholders other than the parent company.

Mixed Cost. Cost that is part variable and part fixed.

Module. Separate compatible units of an accounting package that are integrated to function together.

Mortgage. Borrower's promise to transfer the legal title to certain assets to the lender if the debt is not paid on schedule.

Multi-step Income Statement. Format that contains subtotals to highlight significant relationships. In addition to net income, it presents gross profit and operating income.

Mutual Agency. Every partner can bind the business to a contract within the scope of the partnership's regular business operations.

Net Income. Excess of total revenues over total expenses. Also called **net earnings** or **net profit.**

Net Loss. Excess of total expenses over total revenues.

Net Pay. Gross pay minus all deductions. The amount of compensation that the employee actually takes home.

Net Present Value (NPV). The decision model that brings cash inflows and outflows back to a common time period by discounting these expected future cash flows to their present value, using a minimum desired rate of return.

Net Purchases. Purchases less purchase discounts and purchase returns and allowances.

Net Sales. Sales revenue less sales discounts and sales returns and allowances.

Network. The system of electronic linkages that allows different computers to share the same information.

Nonsufficient Funds (NSF) Check. A "hot" check, one for which the maker's bank account has insufficient money to pay the check.

Normal Balance. The account balance that appears on the side of the account—debit or credit—where we record increases.

Note Payable. A written promise of future payment.

Note Receivable. A written promise for future collection of cash.

On-line Processing. Computerized processing of related functions, such as the recording and posting of transactions, on a continuous basis.

Operating Activity. Activity that creates revenue or expense in the entity's major line of business; a section of the statement of cash flows. Operating activities affect the income statement.

Operating Budget. Sets the expected revenues and expenses—and thus operating income—for the period.

Operating Cycle. Time span during which cash is paid for goods and services, which are then sold to customers from whom the business collects cash.

Operating Expenses. Expenses, other than cost of goods sold, that are incurred in the entity's major line of business. Examples include rent, depreciation, salaries, wages, utilities, and supplies expense.

Operating Income. Gross profit minus operating expenses plus any other operating revenues. Also called **income from operations.**

Operating Lease. Usually a short-term or cancelable rental agreement.

Opportunity Cost. The benefit that can be obtained from the next-best course of action.

Ordinary Repair. Repair work that is debited to an expense account.

Other Expense. Expense that is outside the

main operations of a business, such as a loss on the sale of plant assets.

Other Revenue. Revenue that is outside the main operations of a business, such as a gain on the sale of plant assets.

Outsourcing. A make-or-buy decision, where managers must decide whether to buy a component product or service or to produce it in-house.

Outstanding Check. A check issued by the company and recorded on its books but not yet paid by its bank.

Outstanding Stock. Stock in the hands of of stockholders.

Overallocated (Manufacturing) Overhead. The amount of manufacturing overhead allocated to Work in Process Inventory is more than the amount of manufacturing overhead costs actually incurred.

Overhead Flexible Budget Variance. The difference between the actual overhead cost and the flexible budget overhead for the actual number of outputs.

Owner Withdrawals. Amounts removed from the business by an owner.

Owner's Equity. The claim of a business owner to the assets of the business. Also called **capital**.

Paid-in Capital. A corporation's capital from investments by the stockholders. Also called **contributed capital**.

Par Value. Arbitrary amount assigned to a share of stock.

Parent Company. An investor company that owns more than 50% of the voting stock of a subsidiary company.

Partnership Agreement. The contract between partners that specifies such items as the name, location, and nature of the business; the name, capital investment, and duties of each partner; and the method of sharing profits and losses among the partners. Also called **articles of partnership**.

Partnership. An association of two or more persons who co-own a business for profit.

Patent. A federal government grant giving the holder the exclusive right to produce and sell an invention for 20 years.

Payback. The length of time it will take to recover, in net cash inflows from operations, the dollars of a capital outlay.

Payee of a Note. The person or business to whom the maker of a note promises future payment; the creditor.

Payroll. A major expense. Also called **employee compensation**.

Pension. Employee compensation that will be received during retirement.

Percent-of-Sales Method. A method of estimating uncollectible receivables that calculates uncollectible-account expense. Also called the **income statement approach**.

Period Costs. Operating costs that are expensed in the period in which they are incurred.

Periodic Inventory System. An inventory accounting system in which the business does not keep a continuous record of the inventory on hand. Instead, at the end of the period, the business counts the inventory on hand and uses this information to prepare the financial statements.

Permanent Accounts. Accounts that are not closed at the end of the period—asset, liability, and capital accounts. Also called **real accounts**.

Perpetual Inventory System. The accounting inventory system in which the business keeps a running record of inventory and cost of goods sold.

Petty Cash. Fund containing a small amount of cash that is used to pay for minor expenditures.

Planning. Choosing goals and deciding how to achieve them.

Plant Assets. Long-lived tangible assets, such as land, buildings, and equipment, used to operate a business. Also called **fixed assets**.

Plant or Fixed Asset. Another name for property, plant, and equipment.

Postclosing Trial Balance. List of the accounts and their balances at the end of the period after journalizing and posting the closing entries. The last step of the accounting cycle, the postclosing trial balance ensures that the ledger is in balance to start the next accounting period.

Posting. Copying amounts from the journal to the ledger.

Predetermined Manufacturing Overhead Rate. Estimated manufacturing overhead rate computed at the beginning of the year, calculated as the total estimated manufacturing overhead costs divided by the total estimated quantity of the manufacturing overhead allocation base. Also called the **budgeted manufacturing overhead rate**.

Preferred Stock. Stock that gives its owners certain advantages over common stockholders, such as the right to receive dividends before the common stockholders and the right to receive assets before the common stockholders if the corporation liquidates.

Premium. Excess of a bond's issue price over its maturity (par) value. Also called **bond premium**.

Prepaid Expense. Advance payments of expenses. A category of current assets that typically expire or are used up in the near future. Examples include prepaid rent, prepaid insurance, and supplies.

Present Value. Amount a person would invest now to receive a greater amount at a future date.

President. Chief operating officer in charge of managing the day-to-day operations of a corporation.

Prevention Costs. Costs incurred to avoid poor-quality goods or services.

Price Variance. Measures how well the business keeps unit prices of material and labor inputs within standards. This is computed as the difference in prices (actual price per unit minus standard price per unit) of an input, multiplied by the actual quantity of the input.

Price/Earnings Ratio. Ratio relates the market price of a share of common stock to the company's earnings per share. Measures the value the stock market places on $1 of a company's earnings.

Prior-period Adjustment. A correction to retained earnings for an error of an earlier period.

Process Costing. System for assigning costs to large numbers of identical units that usually proceed in a continuous fashion through a series of uniform production steps or processes.

Production Cost Report. Summarizes a processing department's operations for a period.

Production or Purchases. Resources used to produce a product or service, or to purchase finished merchandise.

Production Volume Variance. The difference between (1) the manufacturing overhead cost in the flexible budget for actual outputs, and (2) the standard overhead allocated to production.

Proprietorship. A business with a single owner.

Purchases Journal. Special journal used to record all purchases of inventory, supplies, and other assets on account.

Rate of Return on Common Stockholders' Equity. Net income minus preferred dividends, divided by average common stockholders' equity. A measure of profitability. Also called **return on stockholders' equity**.

Rate of Return on Net Sales. Ratio of net income to net sales. A measure of profitability. Also called **return on sales**.

Rate of Return on Total Assets. The sum of net income plus interest expense divided by average total assets. This ratio measures the success a company has in using its assets to earn income for the persons who finance the business. Also called **return on assets**.

Receivables. Monetary claims against a business or individual.

Reconciliation Method. Another name for the indirect method.

Relevant Information. Expected future data that differ among alternative courses of action.

Relevant Range. A band of volume within which a specific relationship exists between cost and volume.

Research and Development (R&D). The process of researching and developing new or improved products or services, or the processes for producing them.

Responsibility Accounting. A system for evaluating the performance of each responsibility center and its manager.

Responsibility Center. A part or subunit of an organization whose manager is accountable for specific activities.

Retained Earnings. A corporation's capital that is earned through profitable operation of the business.

Revenue. Amounts earned by delivering goods or services to customers. Revenues increase owner's equity.

Revenue Principle. The basis for recording revenues; tells accountants when to record revenue and the amount of revenue to record.

Reversing Entry. An entry that switches the debit and the credit of a previous adjusting entry. The reversing entry is dated the first day of the period after the adjusting entry.

S Corporation. A corporation taxed in the same way as a partnership.

Sales Discount. Reduction in the amount receivable from a customer, offered by the seller as an incentive for the customer to pay promptly. A contra account to Sales Revenue.

Sales Journal. Special journal used to record credit sales.

Sales Mix. Combination of products that make up total sales.

Sales Returns and Allowances. Decreases in the seller's receivable from a customer's return of merchandise or from granting the customer an allowance from the amount owed to the seller. A contra account to Sales Revenue.

Sales Revenue. The amount that a merchandiser earns from selling its inventory. Also called **sales**.

Sales Volume Variance. The difference arising only because the number of units actually sold differs from the static budget sales. This is computed as the difference between a static budget amount and a flexible budget amount.

Segment of the Business. One of various separate divisions of a company.

Sensitivity Analysis. A "what if" technique that asks what a result will be if a predicted amount is not achieved or if an underlying assumption changes.

Serial Bonds. Bonds that mature in installments over a period of time.

Server. The main computer in a network, where the program and data are stored.

Service Company. A company that provides intangible services, rather than tangible products.

Short Presentation. A way to report contingent liabilities in the body of the balance sheet, after total liabilities but with no amount given. An explanatory note accompanies the presentation.

Short-Term Investment. A current asset; an investment that is readily convertible to cash and that the investor intends either to convert to cash within one year or use to pay a current liability. Also called a **marketable security**.

Short-Term Note Payable. Prom-issory note payable due within one year, a common form of financing.

Single-Step Income Statement. Format that groups all revenues together and then lists and deducts all expenses together without drawing any subtotals.

Social Security Tax. Federal Insurance Contributions Act (FICA) tax, which is withheld from employees' pay. Also called FICA tax.

Software. Set of programs or instructions that drive the computer to perform the work desired.

Special Journal. An accounting journal designed to record one specific type of transaction.

Specific-Unit-Cost Method. Inven-tory cost method based on the specific cost of particular units of inventory. Also called the **specific identification method**.

Spreadsheet. A computer program that links data by means of formulas and functions; an electronic work sheet.

Standard Cost. A carefully predetermined cost that usually is expressed on a per-unit basis.

Stated Value. An arbitrary amount that accountants treat as though it were par value.

Statement of Cash Flows. Reports cash receipts and cash payments classified according to the entity's major activities: operating, investing, and financing.

Statement of Owner's Equity. Summary of the changes in an entity's owner's equity during a specific period.

Statement of Stockholders' Equity. Reports the changes in all categories of stockholders' equity during the period.

Static Budget. The budget prepared for only one level of sales volume. Also called the **master budget**.

Stock. Shares into which the owners' equity of a corporation is divided.

Stock Dividend. A distribution by a corporation of its own stock to its stockholders.

Stock Split. An increase in the number of outstanding shares of stock coupled with a proportionate reduction in the par value of the stock.

Stockholder. A person who owns the stock of a corporation. Also called a **shareholder**.

Stockholders' Equity. Owners' equity of a corporation.

Straight-Line (SL) Depreciation Method. Depreciation method in which an equal amount of depreciation expense is assigned to each year of asset use.

Strategy. A set of business goals and the tactics to achieve them.

Strong Currency. A currency that is rising relative to other nations' currencies.

Subsidiary Company. A company in which a parent company owns more than 50% of the voting stock.

Subsidiary Ledger. Record of ac-counts that provides supporting details on individual balances, the total of which appears in a general ledger account.

Sunk Cost. A past cost that cannot be changed regardless of which future action is taken.

Supply-Chain Management. Companies exchange information with suppliers and customers to reduce costs, improve quality, and speed delivery of goods and services from suppliers, through the company itself, and on to customers.

Target Cost. Allowable cost to develop, produce, and deliver the product or service.

Target Price. What customers are willing to pay for the product or service.

Temporary Accounts. The revenue and expense accounts that relate to a particular accounting period and are closed at the end of the period. For a proprietorship, the owner withdrawal account is also temporary. Also called **nominal accounts**.

Term Bonds. Bonds that all mature at the same time for a particular issue.

Throughput Time. The time between buying raw materials and selling the finished products.

Time Record. Source document used primarily by employees in service activities, to trace direct labor to specific jobs.

Time Value of Money. The fact that money can be invested to earn income over time.

Time-Period Concept. Ensures that accounting information is reported at regular intervals.

Times-Interest-Earned Ratio. Ratio of income from operations to interest expense. Measures the number of times operating income can cover interest expense. Also called the **interest-coverage ratio**.

Total Quality Management (TQM). A philosophy of delighting customers by providing them with superior products and services. Involves improving quality and eliminating defects and waste throughout the value chain.

Trademarks, Trade Names, or Brand Names. Assets that represent distinctive identifications of a product or service.

Trading Investments. Investments that are to be sold in the very near future with the intent of generating profits on price changes.

Trading on the Equity. Earning more income on borrowed money than the related expense, thereby in-creasing the earnings for the owners of the business. Also called **leverage**.

Transaction. An event that affects the financial position of a particular entity and can be recorded reliably.

Transferred-in Costs. Costs incurred in a previous process that are carried forward as part of the product's cost when it moves to the next process.

Treasury Stock. A corporation's own stock that it has issued and later reacquired.

Trial Balance. A list of all the accounts with their balances.

Trojan Horse. A malicious program that works like a virus but does not reproduce.

Uncollectible-Account Expense. Cost to the seller of extending credit. Arises from the fail-

ure to collect from credit customers. Also called **doubtful-account expense**, or **bad-debt expense**.

Underallocated (Manufacturing) Overhead. The amount of manufacturing overhead allocated to Work in Process Inventory is less than the amount of manufacturing overhead costs actually incurred.

Underwriter. Organization that purchases the bonds from an issuing company and resells them to its clients or sells the bonds for a commission, agreeing to buy all unsold bonds.

Unearned Revenue. A liability created when a business collects cash from customers in advance of doing work. The obligation is to provide a product or a service in the future. Also called **deferred revenue**.

Unemployment Compensation Tax. Payroll tax paid by employers to the government, which uses the money to pay unemployment benefits to people who are out of work.

Units-of-Production (UOP) Depre-ciation Method. Depreciation method by which a fixed amount of depreciation is assigned to each unit of output produced by an asset.

Unlimited Personal Liability. When a partnership (or a proprietorship) cannot pay its debts with business assets, the partners (or the proprietor) must use personal assets to meet the debt.

Value Chain. Sequence of activities that adds value to a firm's products or services. Includes R&D, design, production or purchases, marketing, distribution, and customer service.

Value Engineering. Systematically evaluating activities in an effort to reduce costs while satisfying customer needs.

Variable Costing. The costing method that assigns only variable manufacturing costs to products.

Variable Costs. Costs that change in total in direct proportion to changes in volume of activity.

Variance. The difference between an actual amount and the budget. A variance is labeled as favorable if it increases operating income and unfavorable if it decreases operating income.

Vertical Analysis. Analysis of a fi-nancial statement that reveals the relationship of each statement item to the total, which is 100%.

Voucher. Instrument authorizing a cash payment.

Weak Currency. A currency that is falling relative to other nations' currencies.

Weighted-Average Cost Method. Inventory costing method based on the weighted-average cost of inventory during the period. Weighted-average cost is determined by dividing the cost of goods available for sale by the number of units available. Also called the **average-cost method**.

Weighted-Average Process Costing Method. A process costing method that costs all equivalent units of work with a weighted average of that period's and the previous period's costs per equivalent unit.

Withheld Income Tax. Income tax deducted from employees' gross pay.

Work in Process Inventory. Goods that are partway through the manufacturing process, but not yet complete.

Work Sheet. A columnar document designed to help move data from the trial balance to the financial statements.

Working Capital. Current assets minus current liabilities; measures a business's ability to meet its short-term obligations with its current assets.

Company Index

price variance, 984–86
production volume variance, 997
sales volume variance, 977, 978
static budget variance, 978
using, 990–91
Variance analysis, flexible budget and, 977–80
Vertical analysis, 715
Virtual consultants, 231
Voting, by stockholders, 506
Voucher, 308
Voucher system, 308–9

W

Wages, 430
Wang, Susan, 1072
Weak currency, 635
Web-based modeling, 983
Weighted-average contribution margin, 902

Weighted-average-cost method
about, 354–55
illustrated, 354
income effects of, 355–56
in perpetual inventory system, 360
Weighted-average number of common shares outstanding, 556
Weighted-average process costing method
about, 862
assigning costs, 864–66
computing cost per equivalent unit, 864
computing output in terms of equivalent units, 862–64
summarizing flow of physical units, 862–64
summarizing total costs to account for, 864

Welch, Jack, 775
Willis, Bruce, 478
Withdrawals, as owner's equity, 40
Withheld income tax, 437–38
Withholding allowances, 437–38
Working capital, 722
Work in process inventory, 759
Work in Process Inventory account, 801, 804, 805, 816, 850–51, 859–61, 864–66
Work sheet
about, 128–32
account title column, 180, 216
adjusted trial balance column, 129–31
adjustments column, 129–30, 181, 216
balance sheet column, 130–31, 181, 216

direct method for operating activities, 704–6
example of, 133
income statement column, 181, 216
indirect method for operating activities, 706–8
in periodic inventory system, 215–16
in perpetual inventory system, 180–82
preparing statement of cash flows, 703–8
trial balance column, 128–31, 180, 216
World Wide Web. *See* e-Commerce

Y

Yang, Jerry, 469